Picture
the Perfect
Blend of
Literature,
Language,
and Life.

McDOUGAL, LITTELL

Thematic units organize selections that are relevant to students' lives. ▼

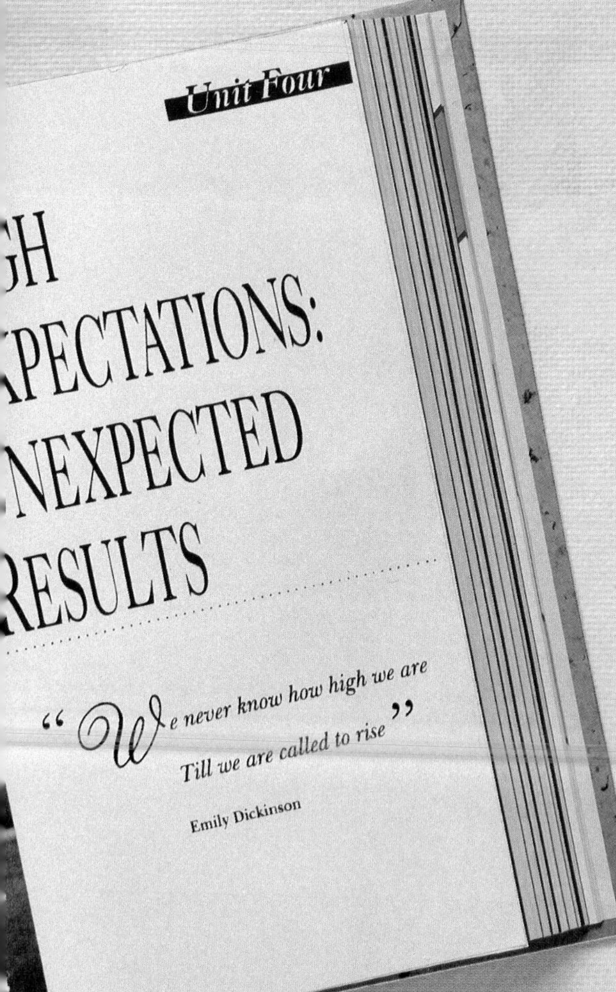

◄ **Subunits narrow the focus of the themes and integrate selections from different genres with guided workshop instruction in writing, language, and skills.**

Say It with Flowers

TOSHIO MORI

He was a queer one to come to the shop and ask Mr. Sasaki for a job, but at the time I kept my mouth shut. There was something about this young man's appearance which I could not altogether harmonize with a job as a clerk in a flower shop. I was a delivery boy for Mr. Sasaki then. I had seen clerks come and go, and although they were of various sorts of temperaments and conducts, all of them had the technique of waiting on the customers or acquired one eventually. You could never tell about a new one, however, and to be on the safe side I said nothing and watched our boss readily take on this young man. Anyhow, we were glad to have an extra hand.

Mr. Sasaki undoubtedly remembered last year's rush when Tommy, Mr Sasaki and I had to do everything and had our hands tied behind our backs for having so many things to do at one time. He wanted to be ready this time. "Another clerk and we'll be all set for any kind of business," he used to tell us. When Teruo came around looking for a job, he got it, and Morning Glory Flower Shop was all set for the year as far as our boss was concerned.

When Teruo reported for work the following morning, Mr. Sasaki left him in Tommy's hands. Tommy was our number one clerk for a long time.

"Tommy, teach him all you can," Mr. Sasaki said. "Teruo's going to be with us from now on."

"Sure," Tommy said.

"Tommy's a good florist. You watch and listen to him," the boss told the young man.

"All right, Mr. Sasaki," the young man said. He turned to us and said, "My name is Teruo." We shook hands.

We got to know one another pretty well after that. He was a quiet fellow with very little words for anybody, but his smile disarmed a person. We soon learned that he knew nothing about the florist business. He could identify a rose when he saw one, and gardenias and carnations too; but other flowers and materials were new to him.

"You fellows teach me something about this business, and I'll be grateful. I want to start from the bottom," Teruo said.

Tommy and I nodded. We were pretty sure by then he was all right. Tommy eagerly went about showing Teruo the florist game. Every morning for several days Tommy repeated the prices of the flowers

Words to Know and Use

harmonize (här' mə nīz') *v.* to bring into agreement
temperament (tem' pər ə mənt) *n.* a person's usual nature or disposition
disarm (dis ärm') *v.* to overcome the hostility of, especially by using charm

486

▲ **Unadapted classic and contemporary selections draw upon students' own experiences and serve as a starting point for integrated instruction in writing and language.**

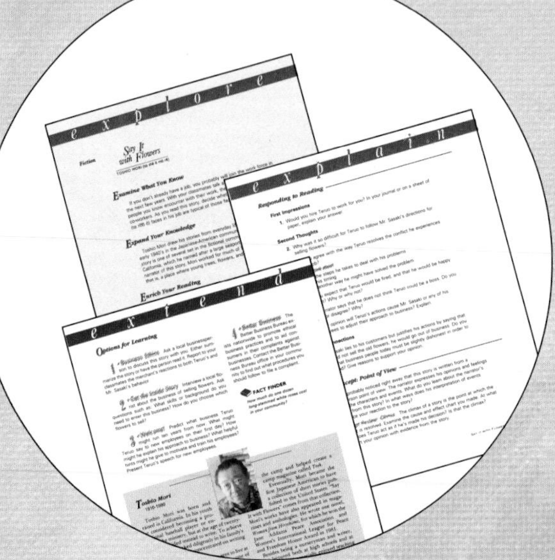

▲ **Reader response and learning styles strategies are implemented before, during, and after reading, making unadapted literature accessible to all students.**

A MASTERPIECE OF INTEGRATED INSTRUCTION– *IN A SINGLE BOOK!*

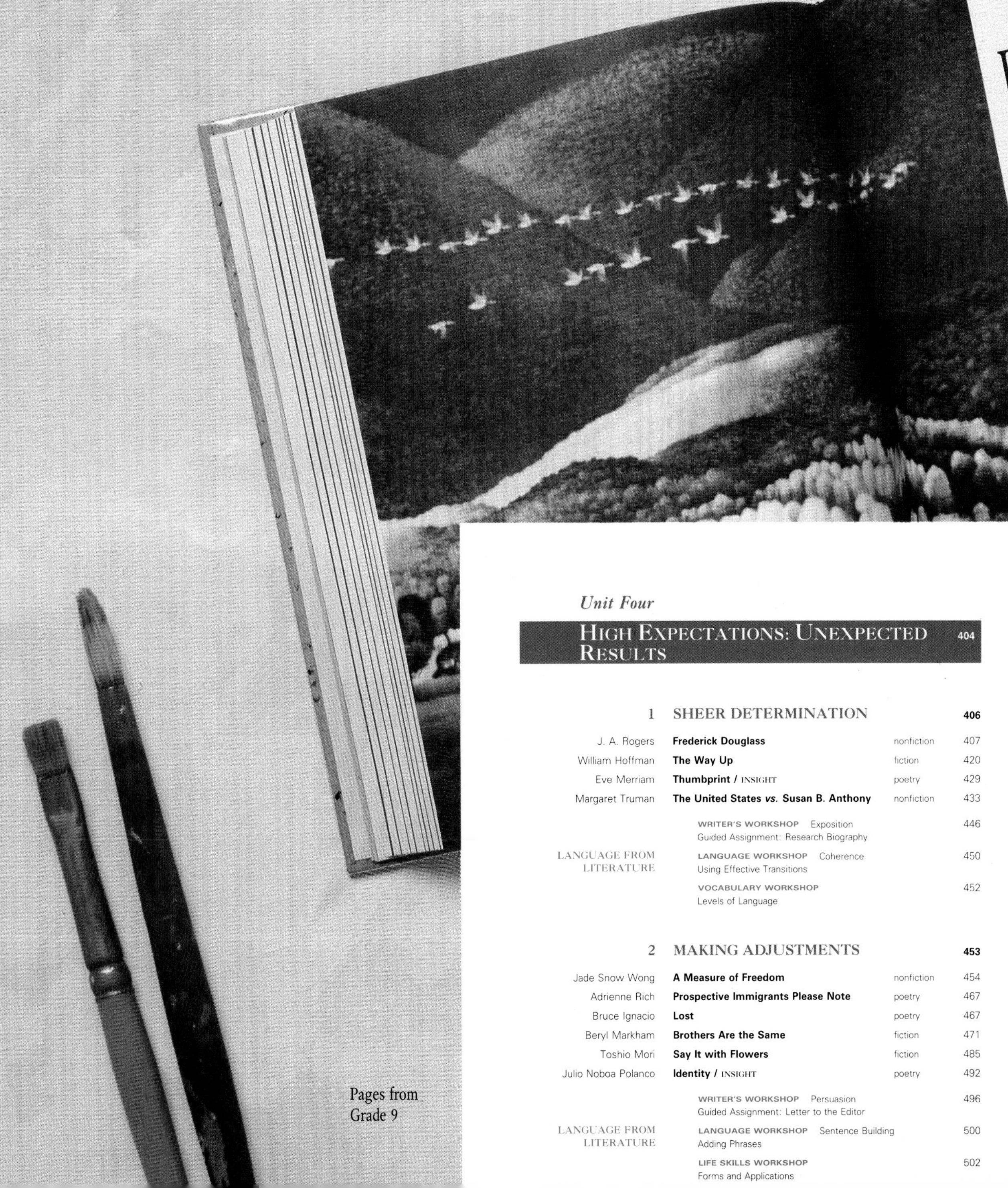

Unit Four

HIGH EXPECTATIONS: UNEXPECTED RESULTS 404

Pages from Grade 9

Plus...A Complete Language Handbook

A flexible *Language Handbook* in each text provides additional instruction and practice exercises in grammar and usage concepts that students need to apply in writing.

***Language Workshops* provide lessons that apply grammar, usage, and mechanics concepts to writing and help students look back at the literature to improve their style.** ▼

RITER'S
WORKSHOP

PERSUASION

Persuasive writing is used to influence the opinions of others. A writer who uses persuasion starts out with a strong opinion about an important issue that is controversial. The writer presents his or her opinion and then uses reasons and facts to convince others to agree with that opinion. Sometimes the writer urges readers to take action.

All of the selections in this subunit deal with making an adjustment of some kind. Several of the characters struggle with the problems of adjusting to new cultures and customs. For this assignment you will be asked to persuade others to agree with your opinion on the issue of how foreigners should adapt to American culture. You will respond to the following editorial.

Adapting to America

If America is to be "one nation under God," then its citizens must unite under one cultural banner. Although we must never lose sight of America's rich variety of ethnic groups, it's time to cast aside differences in color, language, and heritage in order to create a single American culture. We must not cater to the values, tastes, and languages of the many foreigners who move to our country. Instead, we must insist on a national language and a national culture. If immigrants choose to settle in our country, then they must also choose to adopt our cultural values and our language, which is an expression of those values. It is not our duty, nor is it in our national interest, to adjust our standards to satisfy all ethnic groups; for if we bend our standards to meet the needs of each nationality, then we weaken the national fabric that holds us together.

Here is your PASSkey to this assignment.

GUIDED ASSIGNMENT: LETTER TO THE EDITOR

Write a letter to the editor of a newspaper in response to the editorial, "Adapting to America." In the letter, persuade readers to adopt your opinion on the issue of how foreigners should adapt to American culture.

PURPOSE: To persuade opinion
AUDIENCE: The newspaper and its readers
SUBJECT: Adapting to American culture
STRUCTURE: Formal letter

496 UNIT FOUR MAKING ADJUSTMENTS

▲

Guided writing instruction tied to the ideas and themes of the literature is presented in a *Writer's Workshop* following each thematic grouping of selections.

ANGUAGE
WORKSHOP

ADDING PHRASES

One way to combine sentences is to take a descriptive phrase from one sentence and, without changing its form, simply add it to another sentence. When you use this method, place the phrase as near as possible to the person, thing, or action it describes. Notice that in the second set of examples, three sentences were combined.

The clerks were hard-working. *The clerks were* in the shop.
The clerks **in the shop** were hard-working.

The fresh flowers were hidden. *They were* in refrigerated cases. *The cases were* near the back of the shop.
The fresh flowers were hidden **in refrigerated cases near the back of the shop.**

Often you can add a phrase from one sentence that simply renames something in another sentence. A group of words that renames a noun is called an **appositive phrase.** Set off an appositive phrase with commas.

Mr. Sasaki hired a new clerk. *Mr. Sasaki was* the shop owner.
Mr. Sasaki, **the shop owner,** hired a new clerk.

Teruo quickly learned what to do. *Teruo was* the new clerk.
Teruo, **the new clerk,** quickly learned what to do.

IFE SKILLS
WORKSHOP

FORMS AND APPLICATIONS

What do these have in common: applying for a job, applying to college, applying for a driver's license? The answer is simple—forms! Sometimes it seems as if we're all drowning in a sea of forms and applications. Use the following guidelines to help you complete this task more efficiently.

1. **Read all directions.** Skim the entire form before you write anything and gather all the information you need—your social security number, your parents' birthdates, the names and addresses of all your previous employers, and so forth.
2. **Be neat.** Use a good pen with blue or black ink and your best handwriting or printing. When you are filling out a form at home, use a typewriter if possible. Do not use a pencil unless you are specifically told to do so.
3. **Fill out the form line by line.** Read the directions for each line before you fill it in. Sometimes there is very little space for the information, so plan ahead. If you make a mistake, carefully draw a line through the error and write the correction above the line.
4. **Be prepared to answer some basic questions.** For example, on an employment form you will often be asked for names of two or three references—people who know you well and would be willing to confirm your abilities. Teachers, coaches, or employers with whom you have a good relationship make good references. Be sure to get their permission, their complete addresses and daytime telephone numbers.
5. **Complete every line if you can.** If you find an item that does not apply to you, write, "Does not apply" in that space. When you are finished, check the entire form carefully for accuracy, spelling, and completeness.

Exercise As a homework assignment, find a blank form and bring it to class. Look for a form that requires extensive information such as an application for credit, an employment application, or a bank form. Exchange forms with a partner and fill out your partner's form. Then, discuss any problems you encountered. Report your findings to the class.

502 UNIT FOUR MAKING ADJUSTMENTS

A third workshop integrates vocabulary, speaking and listening, study and research, thinking, or life skills with the writing and language concepts presented in each subunit. ▶

LITERATURE THAT DRAWS ON LIFE FOR MOTIVATION

Experience-rich classic and contemporary selections are combined with high-interest pieces that have never appeared in literature anthologies. Each has been chosen to draw upon students' personal experiences, to motivate discussion, and to reflect a broad base of cultural backgrounds.

Fiction, nonfiction, poetry, and drama selections are combined within each thematic unit, helping students identify and respond to connections in literature.

In the American and English/World Literature texts, selections are organized by themes within a chronological framework, providing further opportunities for making literary connections.

Prereading instruction focuses on using prior knowledge, building background, and developing reading skills.

Opportunities abound for thinking and writing *before* reading.

Choices

NIKKI GIOVANNI

if i can't do
what i want to do
then my job is to not
do what i don't want
to do

it's not the same thing
but its the best i can
do

if i can't have
what i want   then
my job is to want
what i've got
and be satisfied
that at least there
is something more
to want

since i can't go
where i need
to go   then i must   go
where the signs point
though always understanding
parallel movement
isn't lateral

when i can't express
what i really feel
i practice feeling
what i can express
and none of it is equal
i know
but that's why mankind
alone among the mammals
learns to cry

PEARLBLOSSOM HWY., 11–18TH APRIL 1986 #2 (detail) 1986 David Hockney Photographic collage 78" × 111" © David Hockney, 1986.

CHOICES 51

Grade 10

from Beowulf

Translated by BURTON RAFFEL

The tale of Beowulf tells about the heroes of two clans, the Danes and the Geats (gā' ats), who lived in Scandinavia. The introduction explains that Hrothgar (roth' gar), king of the Danes, built a wonderful mead-hall which he called Herot (ha' a rot). In the passage you are about to read, Grendel, a fierce and powerful monster, invades the mead-hall.

Grendel

A powerful monster, living down
In the darkness, growled in pain, impatient
As day after day the music rang
Loud in that hall, the harp's rejoicing
Call and the poet's clear songs, sung
Of the ancient beginnings of us all, recalling
The Almighty making the earth, shaping
These beautiful plains marked off by oceans,
Then proudly setting the sun and moon
To glow across the land and light it;
The corners of the earth were made lovely with trees
And leaves, made quick with life, with each
Of the nations who now move on its face. And then
As now warriors sang of their pleasure:
So Hrothgar's men lived happy in his hall
Till the monster stirred, that demon, that fiend,
Grendel, who haunted the moors, the wild
Marshes, and made his home in a hell
Not hell but earth. He was spawned in that slime,
Conceived by a pair of those monsters born
Of Cain, murderous creatures banished

GUIDE FOR READING

1-14 Grendel broods in the darkness as the men of Herot fill the mead-hall with music and song. Predict how Grendel might react to such merriment.

17 *moors:* barren stretches of land.

19 *spawned:* produced.

21 *Cain:* a son of Adam and Eve; as told in the Bible (Genesis 4), he killed his younger brother Abel.

19-29 *Who are Grendel's earliest ancestors? How did he come to exist?*

Grade 12

On-page reading guides make classic selections accessible.

e x p l o r e

iction

Say It with Flowers

TOSHIO MORI (tō shē ō mō rē)

Examine What You Know

If you don't already have a job, you probably will join the the next few years. With your classmates talk about the pr people you know encounter with their work, their bosses, co-workers. As you read this story, decide whether the prc (te ro͞o ō) faces in his job are typical of those faced by emp

Expand Your Knowledge

Toshio Mori drew his stories from everyday life in the lat early 1940's in the Japanese-American community where h story is one of several set in the fictional community of Yo California, which he named after a large seaport in Japan. narrator of this story, Mori worked for much of his life in a that is, a place where young trees, flowers, and other plan

Enrich Your Reading

Relating Cause and Effect Often, events in a story c in a character's attitude toward himself or herself, toward character, or toward life. This change in attitude affects th actions. In this story you will find that as Teruo learns mor his feelings about himself and his job change. Create a cau chart like the one below to track the way each event affec attitude. The first event and its effect have been supplied. to predict how Teruo will resolve his conflict.

Cause	Eff
Teruo takes a job in a flower shop.	⟶ feels happy ar

biography of the uthor can be und on page 495.

SAY IT

Grade 9

e x p l a i n

Responding to Reading

First Impressions

1. Would you hire Teruo to work for you? In your journal or on a sheet of paper, explain your answer.

Second Thoughts

2. Why was it so difficult for Teruo to follow Mr. Sasaki's directions for selling flowers?
3. Do you agree with the way Teruo resolves the conflict he experiences in his job?

   Think about
   - the steps he takes to d
   - his timing
   - another way he might h
4. Did you expect that Teruo wo about it? Why or why not?
5. The narrator says that he doe agree or disagree? Why?
6. In your opinion will Teruo's ac employees to adjust their app

Broader Connections

7. Mr. Sasaki lies to his custome if he did not sell the old flowe think that business people toc succeed? Give reasons to sup

Literary Concept: Point of Vie

You probably noticed right a first-person point of view. The about the characters and ever values from this story? In wha influence your reaction to the

Concept Review: Climax T conflict is resolved. Examine t point does Teruo act as if he' Support your opinion with evi

Writing Options

1. Explain why Teruo would or would not agree with the speaker in "Identity." Which other characters you have read about might agree with the speaker? Give reasons for your answers.
2. This subunit is entitled "Making Adjustments." Write about a time when you had to adjust to accommodate another person's way of thinking or acting. Explain how successful you were at changing your ways.
3. Teruo has definite ideas about the business world. Considering his approach to business and ethics, in what occupations might Teruo find success? List them.
4. Imagine that one of Teruo's customers returns to the flower shop either to complain about flowers that did not last or to praise Teruo for his salesmanship. Write the conversation that might occur between the customer and Mr. Sasaki.

Vocabulary Practice

Exercise On your paper, write the word from the list that best completes each sentence.

1. Teruo could not ____ his ideas with those of his boss.
2. His quiet yet friendly behavior hinted at his mild ____.
3. With his cheerful smile, Teruo could ____ even the most unhappy customer.
4. Teruo's ____ nature caused him to ask many questions about the flower business.
5. The boys told Teruo to respond with a ____ when a customer asked about the freshness of the flowers.
6. Teruo acted with ____ when he carefully chose and arranged flowers on his last day of work.
7. When Teruo began his selling ____, he moved like a whirlwind through the shop.
8. The other clerks began to ____ at Teruo as he waited on three customers at once.
9. In one ____, Teruo discouraged a woman from buying orchids and sold her fresh gardenias instead.
10. In the ____ weeks after his firing, how do you think Teruo will feel?

Words to Know and Use

comeback
deliberation
disarm
ensuing
gape
harmonize
inquisitive
spree
temperament
transaction

Reader response-based questioning strategies developed by Arthur Applebee and Judith Langer from the *Center for the Learning and Teaching of Literature* motivate students to make a connection between the literature they read and the life they lead. Students are then guided to think critically about the selections.

Creative topics prompt written responses.

Literary concepts are studied in context.

A strong vocabulary program highlights and defines new words within the context of the selections. Students apply the words in practice activities following the selections.

e x t e n d

Options for Learning

1 • **Business Ethics** Ask a local businessperson to discuss this story with you. Either summarize the story or have the person read it. Report to your assmates the merchant's reactions to both Teruo's and Mr. Sasaki's behavior.

2 • **Get the Inside Story** Interview a local florist about the business of selling flowers. Ask uestions such as: What skills or background do you eed to enter this business? How do you choose which owers to sell?

3 • **Welcome!** Predict what business Teruo might run ten years from now. What might eruo say to new employees on their first day? How ight he explain his approach to business? What helpful nts might he give to motivate and train his employees? resent Teruo's speech for new employees.

4 • **Better Business** The Better Business Bureau exists nationwide to promote ethical business practices and to aid consumers in their complaints against businesses. Contact the Better Business Bureau office in your community to find out what procedures you should follow to file a complaint.

FACT FINDER

How much do one dozen long-stemmed white roses cost in your community?

Multi-modal activities allow students to express what they have learned through a variety of learning styles and offer opportunities for collaborative learning.

Toshio Mori
1910-1980

Toshio Mori was born and

the camp and helped create a camp magazine called *Trek*.

Eventually, Mori became the

WRITING THAT DRAWS ON LITERATURE FOR INSPIRATION

Varied, assignment-based writing workshops, linked to the ideas and themes of the selections, provide complete coverage of all writing modes.

LITERARY ANALYSIS

A literary analysis is an in-depth discussion of a literary work. The writer of the analysis studies the work and writes his or her interpretation for an audience who is familiar with the selection. The writer focuses on an important point and shows how the literature supports his or her idea.

High school and college literature courses frequently require you to write literary analyses. Usually the test or assignment provides a focus for your writing, but sometimes you will have to determine this on your own.

In this assignment you will write a literary analysis of *The Miracle Worker* that focuses on two characters. You will choose the characters and support a generalization about them by comparing and contrasting them, using evidence from the play as support for your interpretation.

GUIDED ASSIGNMENT: CHARACTERS IN CONTRAST

Write a composition that compares and contrasts two characters in *The Miracle Worker.*

Here is your PASSkey to this assignment.

PURPOSE: To inform
AUDIENCE: Other readers of *The Miracle Worker*
SUBJECT: Two characters from *The Miracle Worker*
STRUCTURE: A comparison/contrast composition

Guided assignments focus on audiences and purposes for writing.

Prewriting

Step 1 **Choose characters** Start with the character you find most interesting. As a second character, select one who is in conflict with your character. You might compare and contrast Helen and Annie, Captain Keller and Kate Keller, Captain Keller and James Keller, Annie and James, or another combination you find exciting.

Step 2 **Establish your point** What point do you want to make in your comparison? Work in pairs or in small groups to think of generalizations you can make about the characters. Consider what

706 UNIT FIVE AWAKENINGS

summary or quotation that illustrates your statement. Elaborate on how your evidence supports your generalizations. Then start a new paragraph about the next character, quality, or point.

Revising and Editing

Once you have completed your draft, ask a classmate to review your essay using the following checklist. Then revise your paper using those ideas that you feel will improve it.

Revision Checklist

1. Does the introduction mention the literary work being discussed?
2. Does the introduction include a clear statement of who is being compared and what generalization is being made?
3. Is the essay organized in a way that is clear and easy to follow?
4. ...ce in the form of quotations or summaries support the ...ns?
5. ...mparison and contrast support the writer's thesis

...ou have finished revising your analysis, proofread for spelling, clarity, and mechanics.

Notice the many collaborative writing and peer review activities.

Presenting

In a small group with others who wrote about different characters than you did, read your essay aloud. Notice how your classmates chose different approaches and have different insights about the characters.

Reflecting on Your Writing

Answer the following questions about this assignment. Place the answers and your paper in your writing portfolio.

1. What was the most difficult thing about writing this essay? Why?
2. Which part of your essay is the strongest? Why?
3. As you wrote this essay, did you develop new insights into the characters of the play? Explain.

The program facilitates the use of journals and portfolios.

WRITER'S WORKSHOP 709

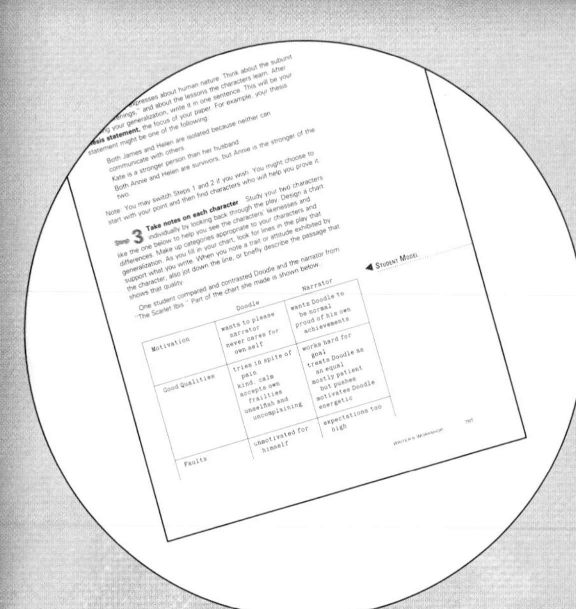

Grade 9

▲ ***Reflecting on Your Writing* involves students in self-evaluation and in setting personal goals for writing improvement.**

▲ **Student Models and flexible writing techniques guide students through each stage in the writing process.**

GRAMMAR THAT COMPLETES THE PICTURE

Language Workshops put coordinated instruction and application of grammar, usage, and mechanics concepts easily within reach as students revise writing activities in the *Writer's Workshops*. Additional help is provided in an extensive *Language Handbook*.

Lessons stress writing applications.

Grammar Reminders summarize key concepts.

ACHIEVING SENTENCE VARIETY

One way to add interest to your writing is to vary the structure of the sentences you use. In this workshop you will review three different kinds of sentence structure.

Simple Sentences

REMINDER

The **subject** of a sentence names the person or thing about which something is said. The **predicate** tells what the subject did or what happened. The **simple predicate** is the *verb*.

A **simple sentence** is a sentence that contains only one subject and one predicate. The subject or predicate of a simple sentence may be compound, but the parts are considered one unit. Each of the following sentences is a simple sentence with one compound part.

Compound Subject *Helen* and *Annie* had a violent fight at the dinner table.

Compound Predicate They *slapped each other* and *wrestled around on the floor.*

Compound Sentences

A **compound sentence** consists of two or more simple sentences joined together. The parts of a compound sentence may be joined by a coordinating conjunction *(and, or, but)* or by a semicolon *(;)*. In the following examples, the subject is underlined once; the verb is underlined twice.

Helen slapped Annie, **and** Annie slapped her back.
Helen wanted to eat with her hands, **but** Annie made her use a spoon.
Helen threw the napkin on the floor; Annie picked it up.

Complex Sentences

HELP!

Can you tell the difference between a **phrase** and a **clause**?
A clause has a subject and a verb. A phrase does not.
Phrase: at the movie
Clause: after the movie ended

A **complex sentence** contains one independent, or main, clause and one or more subordinate clauses.

Remember that a **clause** is a group of words that contains a verb and a subject. A simple sentence is a clause. A compound sentence has two clauses.

A clause that can stand as a sentence by itself is an **independent**

clause. All the clauses
because they can stan

A **subordinate** claus
because it begins with
at these examples:

Helen was born.
a verb and the m
when Helen was
and verb, but add
incomplete. The r
born?)

Now look at exampl

Subordinate Cla
When Helen was born, she was a perfect baby.

Independent Clause — Subordinate Clause
She became blind and deaf after she had brain fever.

The next time you write or revise, look for opportunities to vary the types of sentences you use.

Exercise 1 For each sentence, write *Simple, Compound,* or *Complex* to show what kind of structure it has.

1. "The Scarlet Ibis" is a hauntingly beautiful story.
2. The writer included vivid descriptions of nature and crafted a sensitive, powerful plot.
3. The main characters in the story are two brothers.
4. The brothers in this story love each other, but they spend a great deal of time fighting.
5. The younger brother was handicapped, but he went everywhere with his older brother.
6. Doodle had many successes in his life because he was so determined.
7. A scarlet ibis was rarely seen in the South; a storm must have carried the exotic bird there.
8. The red bird's death foreshadowed Doodle's tragic death.
9. Both the bird and Doodle lived in worlds where they could not survive.
10. The narrator was haunted by his brother's death because he felt responsible for it.

LANGUAGE HANDBOOK
For review and practice: clauses

Explanations, examples, and models provide relevant instruction.

Students are directed to the *Language Handbook* for extra help.

Varied exercises provide practice with grammar concepts and prompt students to look back at the literature to discover how other writers apply the concepts.

The Language Handbook helps students retouch their language skills!

The *Language Handbook* provides abundant practice, with special emphasis on common usage problems in students' writing.

Exercise 7 Illogical Comparisons Rewrite the following sentences, correcting the errors in comparison. If a sentence is already correct, write *Correct.*

Example Maria Elena likes books better than Christina.
Answer Maria Elena likes books better than Christina *does.*

1. My sister, Maria Elena, loves reading and writing poetry more than any person in my family.
2. Then again, she has a more sensitive nature than I have.
3. She enjoys Edna St. Vincent Millay more than my mother.
4. Word images appealed to her more than they did to any child.
5. Imagine having a sister who enjoys poetry more than her teachers!
6. Her English teacher calls on Maria Elena for examples of alliteration more than any student in the class.
7. My most recent poem was better than any poem I've written.
8. However, rhyme and rhythm don't come as easily to me as Maria Elena.
9. She just laughs and says that I can fix the engine of any car far better than she can.
10. Even though she is my sister, she makes me laugh more than any person I know.

Special Problems with Modifiers

Certain adjectives and adverbs are frequently used incorrectly. Study the following pages to avoid these errors.

Them and *Those*

***Them* is always a pronoun. It is never used as a modifier.**
***Those* is a pronoun when used alone; it is an adjective when followed by a noun.**

With *them* and *those,* the most common mistake is using *them* as an adjective. Remember that *them* is always a pronoun; use *those,* not *them,* as a modifier.

A RICH PALETTE OF TEACHING OPTIONS

Teacher's Edition

The *Teacher's Edition* offers a mosaic of choices you can use to design active, student-centered encounters with literature and language. Teaching strategies you'll have to support your lesson design include:

Prereading/Motivation

- **Prereading Discussion Prompts** to tap prior knowledge and build background
- **Topics for Journal Writing**

Teaching Strategies

- **Point-of-Use Suggestions** for teaching literary, reading, writing, language, and thinking skills
- **On-page tips** for integrating grammar and writing
- **Vocabulary Preview**
- **Support for Students** of Limited English Proficiency
- **Structured Reading** for Less Proficient Students
- **Check Tests**
- **Guidelines** for Observation Assessment

Enrichment

- **Collaborative Learning Activities**
- **Reteaching Exercises**
- **Data Bank** of information relevant to selection content
- **Cultural Connections** to shed light on the variety of multicultural backgrounds reflected in selections
- **Professional Notebook** that offers suggestions, advice, and refreshment
- **Critic's Corner** to offer professional, literary insights into selections
- PLUS… audiovisual resources, computer tips, and more!

Teacher's Resource File

The *Teacher's Resource File* provides a full spectrum of useful materials to make literature and language study enjoyable and accessible to all of your students.

The conveniently organized file contains **Unit Resource Books** for each unit. Each book includes:

- **Reader's Guidesheets**
- **Tests:** Selection and Vocabulary Checktests
  Selection Tests
  Subunit Tests
- **Writer's Workshop Copy Masters**
- **Vocabulary Worksheets**
- **Writer's Workshop Assessment Guidelines**
- **Peer and Self-Evaluation Guidelines**
- **Language Workshop Copy Masters**
- **Related Skills Copy Masters**

Plus … the *Teacher's Resource File* includes these additional materials for teaching and enrichment:

- Lesson Plans
- Student Revision Model Transparencies
- Revision, Proofreading, and Elaboration Worksheets
- Fine Art Writing Prompt Transparencies
- Thinking Skills Transparencies and Worksheets
- Standardized Test Practice
- Grammar and Usage: Practice, Reteaching, and Assessment
- Oral Communications Booklet
- Writing Prompts for Assessment

ALSO AVAILABLE:

- Software
- Audio Cassette Tapes

The *Literature and Language* series includes:

- Grade 9
- Grade 10
- American Literature
- English/World Literature

McDougal, Littell
Publishing for a new school of thought
P.O. Box 1667 Evanston, IL 60204

AR, OK, TX, NM Call 800-346-3570
AL, FL, GA, LA, MS, NC, SC, TN, VA, WV Call 800-258-9006
AK, AZ, ID, NV, OR, UT, WA Call 800-424-3077
California Call 800-845-6444
All other states & international 800-323-5435

#0235P

Table of Contents

⋆ Pages after **T32** are located at the back of the Teacher's Edition

The Design of the Program

Overview and Organization

***Literature and Language**, an entirely new kind of textbook, was developed with two major goals in mind. First, to motivate students -- helping them to see what most English teachers already know: that reading literature can be fun; that discussing literature can be stimulating, and that writing about what is read can be meaningful and satisfying. Second, using literature as a base, to integrate the language arts in a way that makes sense to both students and teachers.*

Goal 1

Motivating Students

Literature and Language was developed to give students a new and positive attitude toward literature, writing, and language study. Every aspect of the series was planned to engage the student and encourage him or her to become part of a community of readers and writers.

1. Selections
The tables of contents in the series represent a carefully chosen combination of old favorites and classics as well as fresh new fiction and nonfiction selections that have not previously appeared in high school anthologies. Such combinations bring new meaning and relevance to the classics and add depth and importance to the contemporary works. In addition, a broad range of authors reflects the cultural diversity of today's world.

2. Thematic Organization
An organization based on theme allows students to begin their study of literature with what they find most interesting--the meaning of the selection and how it relates to them. In addition, thematic groupings build broader contexts in which to consider what is read. Selections may be discussed in relation to larger issues as well as to other selections.

To gain insight from readers themselves, a student board of diverse ethnicity, geographic location, and ability was asked to read and comment on many of the selections. Their responses were both thoughtful and revealing. One surprising result indicated that the perceived difficulty level of a selection had little to do with whether or not students enjoyed it. When students found the material interesting and relevant, they worked through the selection and expressed enthusiasm for it regardless of their stated ability level.

3. Selection and Workshop Lesson Structure
The lesson design for literature selections is based on the reader-response approach developed by Senior Consultants Judith Langer and Arthur Applebee (see pages T18-T21). The design consists of three parts: *Explore* (prereading) and *Explain* and *Extend* (postreading). All of the activities and questions on these pages are designed to help students connect with the text in meaningful ways. Questions have no "right" answers and allow all students to build and share their personal responses to the text. For a detailed description of the lesson design, see pages T4 and T5 of this text.

Workshops in writing, language, and related skills spring naturally from the selections. Instruction is brief, clear, practical, and leads quickly to actual work. Students write instead of reading about writing, and they learn language skills that are necessary and useful as they write.

4. Visual Elements
The typography and layout of the series were designed with a fresh, contemporary look and color palette meant to invite readers into the text. Design elements such as call-out quotes, graphic organizers, expanded capital letters, and so on, help to break the monotony of long passages of dense text. The fine art illustrating the series was chosen for its direct relationship to the selections and for its appeal to students.

Goal 2

Integrating the Language Arts

Reading, writing, grammar, and vocabulary are all parts of the whole called language. In the past, however, each part has been taught as a discrete subject with separate texts and time periods — a semester of literature, six weeks of grammar, and so on. This fragmented curriculum has resulted in students who have also treated these subjects as discrete, generally failing to transfer information from one area of study to the next.

During the past few years, educational researchers have encouraged the integration of the language arts, and most teachers have been quick to recognize the logic of an integrated program. Indeed, many teachers have already tried to integrate their language arts curriculum. They have spent long hours attempting to coordinate lessons from separate texts. They have developed lesson plans, created and duplicated assignments and activities, and asked students to juggle a confusion of mismatched texts and materials. In the end, despite long hours and good intentions, the results have often been frustrating and unsuccessful.

In an effort to combat "integration through teacher exhaustion," textbooks were published that promised an integrated approach. However, since these programs seldom did more than insert new activities into existing texts, the outcome was disappointing.

In contrast, ***Literature and Language*** is an entirely new series with an innovative organization, intriguing tables of contents, and a dynamic lesson design based on the work of education's most respected researchers.

Teachers will discover that ***Literature and Language*** offers an entirely new framework for the study of language arts. It is a complete program in one book with all of the language arts strands woven together in a meaningful, relevant way. Students receive instruction (not merely activities) in writing, reading, grammar, vocabulary, and other related areas. Lessons occur when they are needed and when they fit logically into the instructional program, thus allowing students to understand why they are learning and how each part of language relates to the next.

Integration in *Literature and Language*

Each book in the ***Literature and Language*** series is arranged in thematic units of mixed-genre selections.

Since the unit themes are broad in scope, most units have been divided into three, more focused subunits which deal with specific aspects of the unit theme. At the end of each subunit, a series of three instructional workshops is presented: a Writer's Workshop, a Language Workshop, and a Related Skills Workshop. The workshops are integrated with each other and with the literature in the subunit. The graphic below provides a visual picture of this organization.

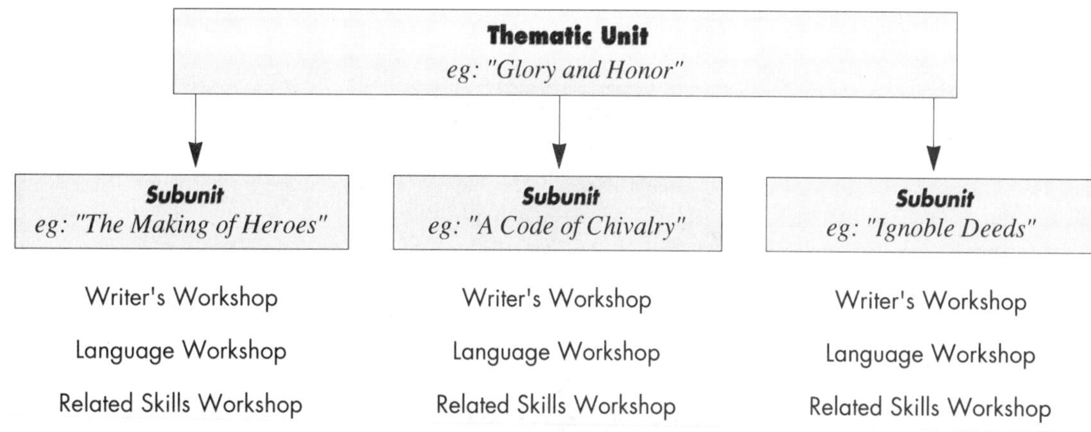

The Design of the Literature Lesson

A Three-Part Structure with a Variety of Options

*Selection lessons in **Literature and Language** are divided into a three-part design that surrounds the literature, as shown in the diagram on these two pages. Each part of the lesson offers a wide variety of activities. However, it is not expected that every activity will be used for every selection. Rather, it is assumed that each teacher will select those options most useful for his or her class.*

PART 1

Explore
Preparing Students to Read

*The gray-tinted **Explore** page provides three prereading activities designed to prepare students for the selection they are about to read. Research shows that such preparation improves reading comprehension and enhances reader response.*

Examine What You Know
Helps students activate what they already know about the events and ideas in the selection they are about to read

Expand Your Knowledge
Provides important background information relevant to the selection

Enrich Your Reading
Presents direct instruction in a reading skill designed to improve comprehension of the selection

Write Before You Read
Serves as an alternate to **Enrich Your Reading.** Allows students to explore selection-related ideas in writing before they read

Literature Selection

The literature selections include an exciting variety of unadapted pieces in all genre, chosen for their appeal to students and for their literary merit. Classic, contemporary, and multicultural authors are represented. The most challenging selections contain interlinear questions or sidenotes to enhance comprehension. Vocabulary enrichment is facilitated by on-page definitions.

Fear

GABRIELA MISTRAL

I do not want them to turn
my child into a swallow;
she might fly away into the sky
and never come down again to my doormat;
or nest in the eaves where my hands
could not comb her hair.
I do not want them to turn
my child into a swallow.

I do not want them to make
my child into a princess.
In tiny golden slippers how could
she play in the field?
And when night came, no longer
would she lie by my side.
I do not want them to make
my child into a princess.

And I would like even less
that one day they crown her queen.
They would raise her to a throne
where my feet could not climb.
I could not rock her to sleep
when nighttime came.
I do not want them to make
my child into a queen.

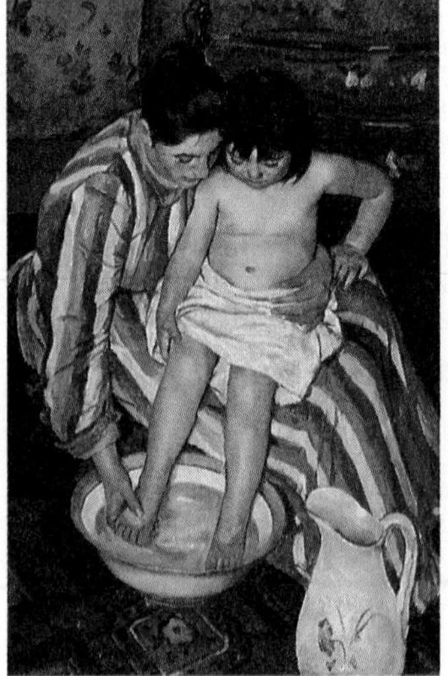

THE BATH 1891 Mary Cassatt The Art Institute of Chicago
Robert A. Waller Fund, 1910.2.

230 UNIT TWO ASPECTS OF LOVE

PART 2

Explain

Postreading Questions and Activities

Each selection is followed by an ***Explain*** *section which challenges students to investigate literature through their own personal responses in an atmosphere of shared exploration. These discussion questions, which are based on the conviction that all students have something of value to contribute, motivate students to develop personally meaningful interpretations and to build connections between the literature and the world around them. Finally, students are challenged to expand their reading experience to literary analysis, informal writing, and vocabulary enrichment.*

Responding to Reading
Provides a framework for meaningful class discussion

First Impressions Initiates discussion by encouraging each reader's personal response

Second Thoughts Encourages critical thinking as students develop more complex and sophisticated interpretations

Broader Connections Establishes relevance by making connections between the selection and the students' world

Literary Concept
Introduces a literary element found in the selection and often reviews previously taught elements

Writing Options
Presents a variety of informal, imaginative, "write-to-learn" assignments for further exploration of the selection

Vocabulary Practice
Reinforces the vocabulary words presented in the selection

PART 3

Extend

Postreading Activities

The activities on the ***Extend*** *page allow students to respond to the selection in a variety of modes and cross-curricular content areas.*

Options for Learning
Presents opportunities for students to express understanding of the selection in their preferred mode of expression and in various content areas

Fact Finder
Challenges students to research and answer questions in other subject areas

About the Author
Provides information about the author

A Special Note on Vocabulary

The vocabulary program is based on two research conclusions: first, that new words are best learned and remembered when taught in context; second, that readers need not know the meaning of every unfamiliar word in order to understand what they read.

Vocabulary words in *Literature and Language* were chosen based on the following criteria:

1. words that would be useful additions to a reader's vocabulary
2. words that add important meaning to the selection
3. words that are not easily inferred from context

These words are underlined in the text and defined in boxes at the bottom of the pages where they apear. Other unfamiliar words and terms are footnoted.

The Design of the Workshops

INTEGRATED LESSONS IN WRITING, LANGUAGE, AND RELATED SKILLS

The series of three workshops that follows each subunit in ***Literature and Language*** *is the foundation of the integrated program. The workshops are integrated with each other and with the literature in the subunit. However, each workshop may also be taught independently.*

The Writer's Workshops

Sixteen or more Writer's Workshops at each grade level provide an extensive range of writing opportunities. Each workshop presents a clearly-stated assignment and guides students through the writing process from prewriting to presentation. The concise, practical instruction and abundant models and strategies incorporated in each lesson allow all students to experience success with writing.

Although each assignment is based on the selections in the preceding subunit, it is not necessary to teach every selection in order to use the workshop. In addition, workshop instruction can easily be adapted to other student or teacher-selected writing topics.

The Writer's Workshops include the following features:

- clear, practical instruction
- emphasis on collaboration at all stages of the writing process
- a PASSkey feature that highlights the importance of purpose and audience
- extensive suggestions for using graphic organizers and other writing and thinking strategies
- clearly labeled student models
- peer evaluation guidelines
- self-evaluation questions
- portfolio use supported by the text

Workshops include guided assignments in the following modes. See the Table of Contents and the Index of Skills for the specific assignments included at this grade level.

Narration and Personal Writing

Description and Observation

Persuasion and Argumentation

Exposition

- process
- comparison-contrast
- cause-effect
- problem-solution
- definition
- evaluation
- analysis
- synthesis

Research Reports

Creative Expression

The Language Workshops

The Language Workshops support the Writer's Workshops by providing skill instruction that students can put to immediate use as they write. Workshop topics are usage-oriented and reflect both a relevance to the preceding writing task and a focus on the most common usage errors experienced by student writers. Language Workshops are part of the integrated workshop package and teachers may comfortably teach them before, during, or after the writing assignment. They may also be used at any other time such instruction is appropriate.

Language Workshop highlights include the following:

- a focus on the most common usage problems of student writers
- comfortable, informal instructional tone
- sidenotes with on-the-spot reminders, extension, and enrichment
- exercises that encourage collaborative work
- *Style* exercises that send students back to the literature to see how professional writers use language
- *Analyzing and Revising Your Writing* activities that allow students to put the skills they learn to immediate use
- Cross-references to additional practice in the Language Handbook

Language Workshops cover the following general categories. See the Table of Contents and the Index of Skills for a more detailed description of topics presented at this grade level.

Editing Skills

Work Choice

Clarity

Sentence Building

Sentence Skills

Coherence

Style

The Related Skills Workshops

This series of lessons covers a wide variety of topics integrated with either the Writer's Workshop assignment or other related content areas.

The lessons can be used as part of the integrated workshop program or at anytime during the year.

The general categories of Related Skills Workshops are listed below. The Table of Contents provides a more detailed description of the topics taught at this grade level.

Vocabulary

Speaking and Listening

Thinking Skills

Study Skills

Life Skills

INNOVATIVE RESOURCE MATERIALS ORGANIZED FOR CONVENIENCE

The Teacher's Resource File—a sturdy, durable container has all the resource material for ***Literature and Language****. The first part of the container consists of lesson-specific materials organized by order of use. The second part consists of supplementary materials. Every item in the file is thoughtfully designed to reflect the teaching philosophy of the text and the commitment to integrated language arts.*

Unit Resource Books:

Practical Help for Every Selection and Workshop

Each unit in *Literature and Language* has its own resource book. All support materials for the selections and workshops are grouped together by order of use, so that you will not have to hunt for what you need. Each Unit Resource Book contains the following items:

- **Reader's Guidesheets**
- **Vocabulary Worksheets**
- **Selection and Vocabulary Check Tests**
- **Selection Tests**
- **Subunit Tests**
- **Writer's Workshop: Worksheets**
- **Writer's Workshop: Assessment Guidelines**
- **Writer's Workshop: Peer and Self-Evaluation Guidelines**
- **Language Workshop: Worksheets**
- **Related Skills Workshop: Worksheets**

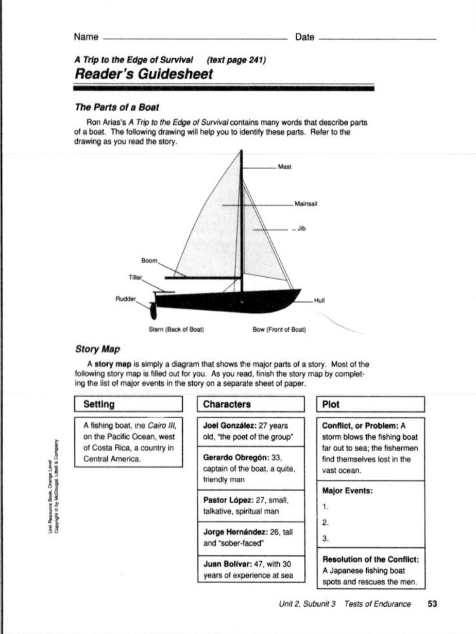

Name ________________ Date ________________

A Trip to the Edge of Survival ***(text page 241)***

Reader's Guidesheet

The Parts of a Boat

Ron Arias's *A Trip to the Edge of Survival* contains many words that describe parts of a boat. The following drawing will help you to identify these parts. Refer to the drawing as you read the story.

Story Map

A **story map** is simply a diagram that shows the major parts of a story. Most of the following story map is filled out for you. As you read, finish the story map by completing the list of major events in the story on a separate sheet of paper.

Setting	Characters	Plot
A fishing boat, the *Cairo III*, on the Pacific Ocean, west of Costa Rica, a country in Central America.	**Joel González:** 27 years old, "the poet of the group"	**Conflict, or Problem:** A storm blows the fishing boat far out to sea; the fishermen find themselves lost in the vast ocean.
	Gerardo Obregón: 33, captain of the boat, a quite, friendly man	**Major Events:** 1. 2. 3.
	Pastor López: 27, small, talkative, spiritual man	
	Jorge Hernández: 26, tall and "sober-faced"	
	Juan Bolívar: 47, with 30 years of experience at sea	**Resolution of the Conflict:** A Japanese fishing boat spots and rescues the men.

Unit 2, Subunit 3 Tests of Endurance 53

Reader's Guidesheets

A reader's guidesheet is provided for each selection. These guidesheets, which are meant to enhance reading comprehension, will be especially helpful for less proficient students. The guidesheets are structured to meet the unique challenges posed by each selection. The sheets may include maps, creative visuals, vocabulary help, and additional background information.

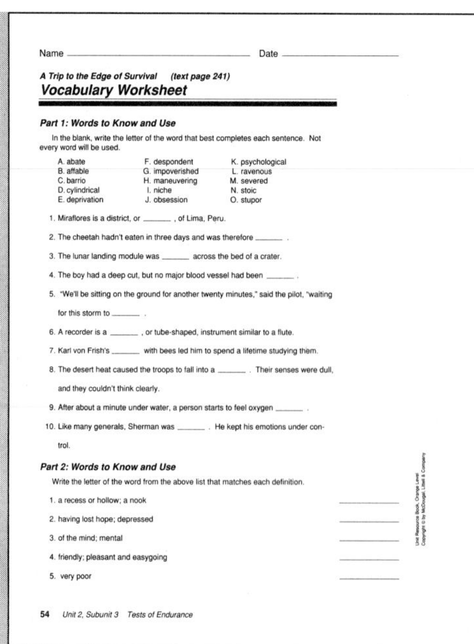

Name ________________ Date ________________

A Trip to the Edge of Survival ***(text page 241)***

Vocabulary Worksheet

Part 1: Words to Know and Use

In the blank, write the letter of the word that best completes each sentence. Not every word will be used.

A. abate	F. despondent	K. psychological
B. affable	G. impoverished	L. ravenous
C. barrio	H. maneuvering	M. severed
D. cylindrical	I. niche	N. stoic
E. deprivation	J. obsession	O. stupor

1. Miraflores is a district, or ______ , of Lima, Peru.
2. The cheetah hadn't eaten in three days and was therefore ______ .
3. The lunar landing module was ______ across the bed of a crater.
4. The boy had a deep cut, but no major blood vessel had been ______ .
5. "We'll be sitting on the ground for another twenty minutes," said the pilot, "waiting for this storm to ______ .
6. A recorder is a ______ , or tube-shaped, instrument similar to a flute.
7. Karl von Frish's ______ with bees led him to spend a lifetime studying them.
8. The desert heat caused the troops to fall into a ______ . Their senses were dull, and they couldn't think clearly.
9. After about a minute under water, a person starts to feel oxygen ______ .
10. Like many generals, Sherman was ______ . He kept his emotions under control.

Part 2: Words to Know and Use

Write the letter of the word from the above list that matches each definition.

1. a recess or hollow; a nook ________
2. having lost hope; depressed ________
3. of the mind; mental ________
4. friendly; pleasant and easygoing ________
5. very poor ________

54 Unit 2, Subunit 3 Tests of Endurance

Vocabulary Worksheets

Additional vocabulary exercises reinforce the practice exercises in the text. When a selection contains no Words to Know and Use, the worksheet is devoted to concentrated work on context clues and word analysis strategies. The creative range of activities includes crossword puzzles and word searches, as well as thematic paragraphs and poems that require students to use context clues to unlock word meaning.

Name ________________ Date ________________

A Trip to the Edge of Survival ***(text page 241)***

Selection and Vocabulary Check Tests

Part 1: Selection Check Test

Answer the questions in complete sentences.

1. What force of nature is the cause of the men's problems? ________________
2. Why does Joel write a letter to his wife? ________________
3. What doe the men eat during their ordeal? ________________
4. Who finally rescues the men on the *Cairo III*? ________________
5. What does Joel learn from this ordeal? ________________

Part 2: Vocabulary Check Test

In the blank, write the letter of the word that best completes each sentence. Not every word will be used.

A. abate	F. despondent	K. psychological
B. affable	G. impoverished	L. ravenous
C. barrio	H. maneuvering	M. severed
D. cylindrical	I. niche	N. stoic
E. deprivation	J. obsession	O. stupor

1. After several days with little to eat, the sailors on the Cairo III were ______ .
2. Joel wrote a letter to his wife, who lived in a ______ near Puntarenas.
3. The crew was ______ , or depressed. However, Pastor López gave the men a rousing talk to cheer them up again.
4. Jorge's finger was ______ by the tooth of a shark.
5. Gerardo Obregon, the skipper of the boat, was an ______ , or friendly, man.
6. Many of the people of Joel's hometown were ______ , or poor.
7. The most protected ______ on the ship was the icebox, where the men slept.

Selection and Vocabulary Check Tests

All selection check tests included in the Annotated Teacher's Edition are reproduced as copy masters. In addition, vocabulary check tests are provided for selections with vocabulary study.

Name ________________ Date ________________

The Feeling of Power ***(text page 644)***

Selection Test

Part 1: Broad Interpretation

A. Answer the following essay questions based on your understanding of the story. Write your answers on a separate sheet of paper.

1. Why do you think that multiplying nine times seven gives Programmer Shuman a feeling of power at the end of the story?
2. Why do you think Technician Aub's vision of the possibilities of graphics differs radically from that of his superiors?
3. Do you think the story presents a future society that could easily come about? Is it a society that you would like to be a part of? Explain your answers.

B. Think about the society that is presented in the story and what it would be like to be a part of it. Then, draw lines from the thinker in the middle of the box to the sentences that accurately describe that society.

Technology is an important part of everyday life.
Society's leaders are considered superior to ordinary citizens
New ideas are enthusiastically encouraged.
Many people feel alienated from the rest of society.
Everyone is considered equal
Little value is placed on human life.
Technological advances are rare.
People are free to choose their occupations.
People are often judged on the basis of their test scores.
International relations are mainly peaceful.

Part 2: Close Interpretation

A. Write **T** if the statement is true. Write **F** if it is false.

1. The main purpose of Project Number is to create the world's largest computer. ______
2. Aub's work on Project Number makes him feel guilty. ______
3. The leaders in the story are interested primarily in the military uses of graphics. ______

Selection Tests

Each selection is accompanied by a two-page test. The first part includes brief essay questions on topics such as theme and character as well as questions on central concepts. A graphic is often included here to make the testing process more accessible to students whose learning styles are not highly verbal. The second part of the test, which contains objective questions, focuses on more specific elements of the selection.

Name ________________ Date ________________

Strategies for Survival

Subunit Test

Part 1: Literature Review

Write the letter of the answer that best completes each sentence.

1. The setting of "The Most Dangerous Game," by Richard Connell, is
   A. ancient Egypt B. Memphis, Tennessee C. Ship-Trap Island D. an asteroid in deep space ______
2. The following line foreshadows the nature of Zaroff's "game":
   A. "My clothes will fit you, I think." B. "His smile showed red lips and pointed teeth." C. "We do our best to preserve the the amenities of civilization here." D. "Perhaps you were surprised that I recognized your name." ______
3. In "The Most Dangerous Game," Rainsford learns
   A. how to hunt tigers B. to understand how a hunted animal feels C. to use a bow and arrow D. how to reach India by sailing around the globe ______
4. Connell's description of the hunt creates in the reader a feeling of
   A. joy B. suspense C. thankfulness D. amusement ______
5. According to Robert Fulghum, one of the most important rules for living is
   A. study hard B. exercise regularly C. clean up your own mess D. vote in every election ______
6. A code for living is called a
   A. short story B. paraphrase C. credo D. biography ______
7. At the beginning of his story "The Street," Richard Wright personifies
   A. the boy's mother B. the father C. summertime D. hunger ______
8. In "The Street," the boy has to face his fear of
   A. the dark B. drowning C. dogs D. a gang of boys ______
9. In "The Street," the boy's story reaches its climax when
   A. he feels hungry B. his mother insists that he fight C. he leaves home to go to a grocery D. he gets a job ______
10. When the speaker in "Mother to Son" says, "Life for me ain't been no crystal stair." This line tells us that
   A. her building was destroyed B. she is very wealthy C. her son is grown up now D. her life has been hard ______

Subunit Tests

The two-page subunit tests cover the literature, literary terms, and language skills from one subunit. While objective questions are the mainstay of these tests, the questions evaluate a broad understanding rather than a superficial recall of details. Each test ends with a choice of synthesizing essay questions based on the subunit theme.

A Note on the Testing Program

The testing program for ***Literature and Language*** puts reader response theory into practice while providing a full complement of tests to serve classroom needs. Reflecting the research of Arthur Applebee and Judith Langer, the tests are primarily designed to stimulate critical thinking and to assess understanding of major issues in the selections, allowing students to formulate their own interpretations. Even the objective questions require students to think, to analyze, and to draw conclusions.

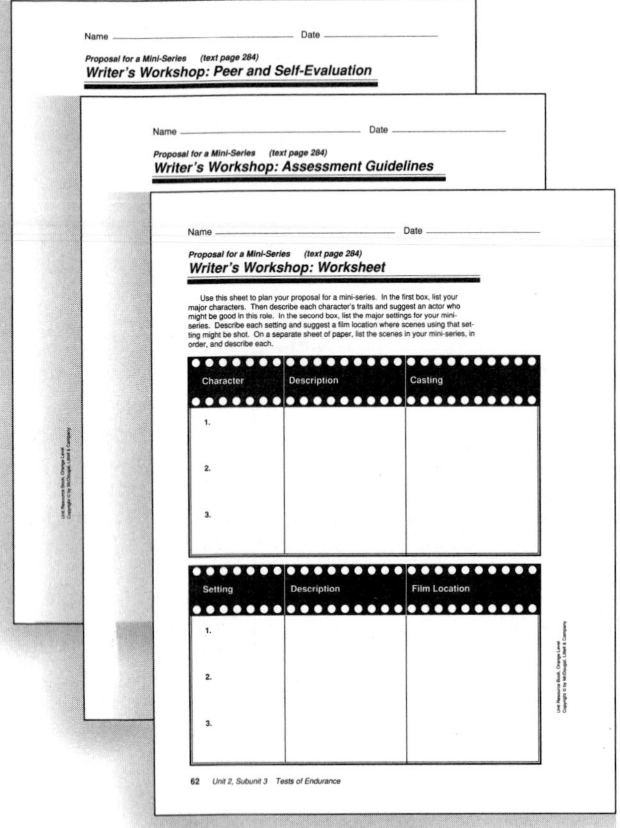

Name ____________ Date ____________

Proposal for a Mini-Series (text page 284)

Writer's Workshop: Peer and Self-Evaluation

Name ____________ Date ____________

Proposal for a Mini-Series (text page 284)

Writer's Workshop: Assessment Guidelines

Name ____________ Date ____________

Proposal for a Mini-Series (text page 284)

Writer's Workshop: Worksheet

Use this sheet to plan your proposal for a mini-series. In the first box, list your major characters. Then describe each character's traits and suggest an actor who might be good in this role. In the second box, list the major settings for your mini-series. Describe each setting and suggest a film location where scenes using that setting might be shot. On a separate sheet of paper, list the scenes in your mini-series, in order, and describe each.

Character	Description	Casting
1.		
2.		
3.		

Setting	Description	Film Location
1.		
2.		
3.		

62 *Unit 2, Subunit 3 Tests of Endurance*

Writer's Workshop: Peer and Self-Evaluation Guidelines

Clearly focused, specific guidelines provide students with the help they need to evaluate their own and their classmates' writing while reducing your paperload.

Writer's Workshop: Assessment Guidelines

To assist teachers with writing assessment, guidelines are provided for each Writer's Workshop assignment. Help for evaluating ongoing work and student progress as well as final product is included.

Writer's Workshop: Worksheets

Each Writer's Workshop is supported by an activity or activities designed to provide students with a specific prewriting or writing strategy.

Name ____________ Date ____________

Joining Sentences and Sentence Parts (text page 288)

Language Workshop: Worksheet

Part 1: Joining Sentences

Use the word in parentheses to combine each pair of sentences. Remember to use a comma before the conjunction. Write your answers in the spaces provided.

1. Several bands of warriors attacked Angie's cabin. She chased them away. (but) ____________
2. Three men cornered Ches Lane in a saloon. Ed Lowe died fighting on Ches's side. (and) ____________
3. Angie refused to join the Apache. Cochise brought her Ches as a gift. (so) ____________
4. Would Angie and Ches get married? Would they go their separate ways? (or) ____________
5. The reader ponders these questions. The story only hints at the answers (but) ____________

Part 2: Joining Sentence Parts

Use the word in parentheses to combine each pair of sentences. Eliminate the italicized words. Write your answers on a separate sheet of paper..

1. In "The Other Pioneers," Salazar speaks of the Hispanic men who came to the Americas as pioneers. *He also speaks of the* women. (and)
2. Many pioneers came to North America from Spain. *They also came* from Latin America. (and)
3. If you think about the names of cities in California and Texas, you will realize that many have Spanish names. *You will also notice this if you think about the names of* counties. (or)
4. Hispanics built much the American West. *They* are not given sufficient credit in many history textbooks. (but)
5. Salazar's poem describes the Hispanic contribution to our history. *It also* celebrates *this contribution.* (and)

Unit 2, Subunit 3 Tests of Endurance 63

Language Workshop: Worksheets

Additional practice exercises reinforce all language lessons. The thematically structured activities emphasize correct usage rather than identification.

Name ____________ Date ____________

Summarizing (text page 291)

Study Skills Workshop: Worksheet

Like a paraphrase, a **summary** (also called a **précis**) presents the basic meaning of a selection in simplified words. Unlike a paraphrase, however, a summary shortens the selection to about one-third of its original length. The purpose of the summary is to condense the original without sacrificing its basic meaning.

Use these steps to write a summary:

1. Locate the main idea and important points.
2. Reduce the information by eliminating unnecessary details, anecdotes, and repetitions.
3. Draft the summary, remembering to express the important points in the original order.
4. Revise the summary, making sure it is about one-third the original length.

Planning a Summary

Read the selection below. Then follow the directions to plan a summary of it.

> No species of lichen is, strictly speaking, a species at all. In every case what we call a lichen turns out to be a fungus—something like the mould on bread—and an alga—something like the green threadlike scum on a pond—living together in close, mutually beneficial association. When the time comes for reproduction, nature sees to it that the partners shall start life again together. In many cases what happens is that a bit of the fungus and a bit of the alga break off together. The wind blows the dry fragment away and then it comes to rest in some suitable place the two organisms begin again to grow in partnership.
>
> Many different species of fungi and of algae have been able to strike up this odd relationship and each different pair constitutes a different sort of lichen....Less than a hundred years ago botanists first came to understand the strange situation and for a while some remained skeptical about it. But they were convinced when an experimenter succeeded in actually synthesizing a lichen.
>
> Joseph Wood Krutch, *The Voice of the Desert*

1. State the main idea. ____________
2. List the important points. ____________
3. List unnecessary details, examples, anecdotes, and repetitions that could be reduced. ____________

64 *Unit 2, Subunit 3 Tests of Endurance*

Related Skills Workshop: Worksheets

Each Related Skills Workshop is also supported by additional exercises and activities. Topics include study skills, speaking and listening, thinking skills, vocabulary study, and life skills.

Enrichment Materials:

Practical Help, Creative Ideas, and Engaging Activities

In addition to the Unit Resource Books, the Teacher's Resource file includes a remarkable range of supplementary materials.

- **Thinking Skills Transparencies and Worksheets**
- **Fine Art Transparencies and Worksheets: Starting Points for Writing**
- **Writing Prompts for Assessment Copy Masters**
- **Student Revision Model Transparencies**
- **Elaboration, Revision, and Proofreading Worksheets**
- **Grammar and Usage: Practice, Reteaching and Assessment Copy Masters**
- **Standardized Test Practice Copy Masters**
- **Oral Communications Booklet**
- ***Literature and Language* Lesson Plans**

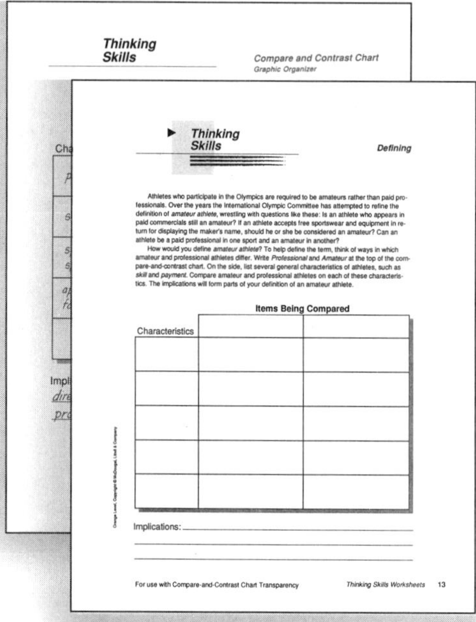

Thinking Skills — *Compare and Contrast Chart* — *Graphic Organizer*

Thinking Skills — *Defining*

Athletes who participate in the Olympics are required to be amateurs rather than paid professionals. Over the years the International Olympic Committee has attempted to refine the definition of *amateur athlete*, wrestling with questions like these: Is an athlete who appears in paid commercials still an amateur? If an athlete accepts free sportswear and equipment in return for displaying the maker's name, should he or she be considered an amateur? Can an athlete be a paid professional in one sport and an amateur in another?

How would you define *amateur athlete*? To help define the term, think of ways in which amateur and professional athletes differ. Write *Professional* and *Amateur* at the top of the compare-and-contrast chart. On the side, list several general characteristics of athletes, such as *skill* and *payment*. Compare amateur and professional athletes on each of these characteristics. The implications will form parts of your definition of an amateur athlete.

Items Being Compared

Characteristics		

Implications:

For use with Compare-and-Contrast Chart Transparency — *Thinking Skills Worksheets* 13

Thinking Skills Transparencies and Worksheets

A wide selection of transparencies with accompanying worksheets guides students in the development of sophisticated critical thinking skills. The activities utilize charts, diagrams, and other graphic organizers.

Starting Points for Writing — *Narration 1*

Starting Points for Writing — *Narration 1*

***Earth Knower**, L. Maynard Dixon, 1931, 1932, 1935*

L. Maynard Dixon (1875–1946) was a self-taught artist from California. Although the figures and objects in his works have a realistic quality, Dixon emphasized mood. He concentrated on presenting the most important details of a scene rather than rendering each detail in a realistic manner. As you look at this painting, think about the details that Dixon emphasized. What details do you think Dixon might have seen and eliminated?

For use with Narration Worksheet 1 — *Starting Points for Writing—Transparencies* 6

Fine Art Transparencies: Starting Points for Writing

Full-color fine art reproductions challenge students' observational skills and stimulate writing ideas.

Starting Points for Writing Worksheets

These thought-provoking worksheets help students to use the fine art transparencies as starting points for writing assignments.

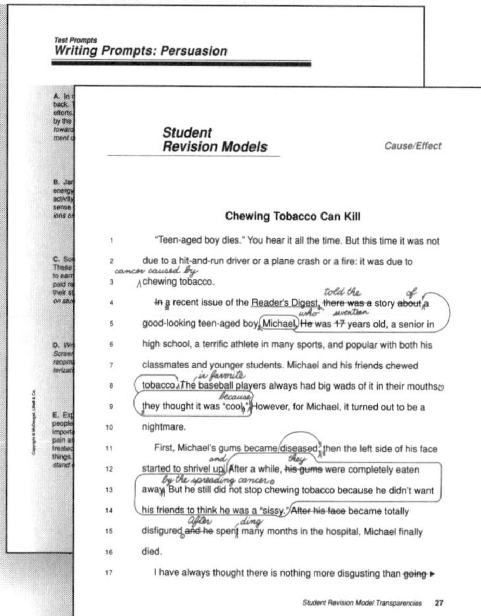

Test Prompts

Writing Prompts: Persuasion

Student Revision Models — *Cause/Effect*

Chewing Tobacco Can Kill

"Teen-aged boy dies." You hear it all the time. But this time it was not due to a hit-and-run driver or a plane crash or a fire: it was due to chewing tobacco.

In a recent issue of the Reader's Digest, there was a story about a good-looking teen-aged boy, Michael. He was 17 years old, a senior in high school, a terrific athlete in many sports, and popular with both his classmates and younger students. Michael and his friends chewed tobacco. The baseball players always had big wads of it in their mouths; they thought it was "cool." However, for Michael, it turned out to be a nightmare.

First, Michael's gums became diseased; then the left side of his face started to shrivel up. After a while, his gums were completely eaten away. But he still did not stop chewing tobacco because he didn't want his friends to think he was a "sissy." After his face became totally disfigured and he spent many months in the hospital, Michael finally died.

I have always thought there is nothing more disgusting than going ▸

Student Revision Model Transparencies 27

Writing Prompts for Assessment Copy Masters

Copy masters present writing topics in a variety of modes to help prepare students for timed writing assessments. Each writing prompt includes a purpose and audience for writing.

Student Revision Model Transparencies

An extensive collection of student models and revision overlays helps students visualize the process of effective revision.

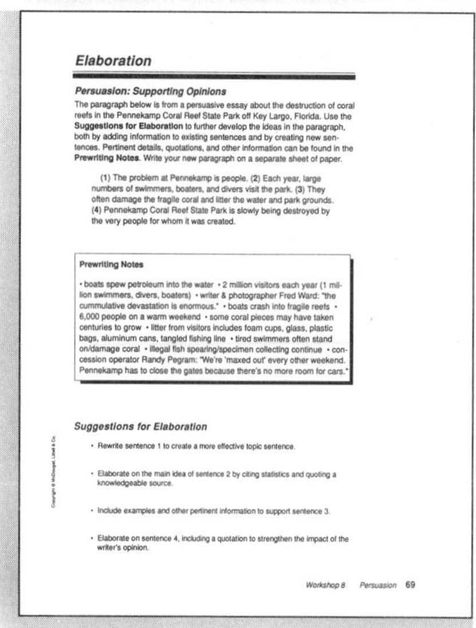

Elaboration

Persuasion: Supporting Opinions

The paragraph below is from a persuasive essay about the destruction of coral reefs in the Pennekamp Coral Reef State Park off Key Largo, Florida. Use the **Suggestions for Elaboration** to further develop the ideas in the paragraph, both by adding information to existing sentences and by creating new sentences. Pertinent details, quotations, and other information can be found in the **Prewriting Notes**. Write your new paragraph on a separate sheet of paper.

(1) The problem at Pennekamp is people. (2) Each year, large numbers of swimmers, boaters, and divers visit the park. (3) They often damage the fragile coral and litter the water and park grounds. (4) Pennekamp Coral Reef State Park is slowly being destroyed by the very people for whom it was created.

Prewriting Notes

• boats spew petroleum into the water • 2 million visitors each year (1 million swimmers, divers, boaters) • writer & photographer Fred Ward: "the cummulative devastation is enormous." • boats crash into fragile reefs • 6,000 people on a warm weekend • some coral pieces may have taken centuries to grow • litter from visitors includes foam cups, glass, plastic bags, aluminum cans, tangled fishing line • tired swimmers often stand on/damage coral • illegal fish spearing/specimen collecting continue • concession operator Randy Pegram: "We're 'maxed out' every other weekend. Pennekamp has to close the gates because there's no more room for cars."

Suggestions for Elaboration

- Rewrite sentence 1 to create a more effective topic sentence.
- Elaborate on the main idea of sentence 2 by citing statistics and quoting a knowledgeable source.
- Include examples and other pertinent information to support sentence 3.
- Elaborate on sentence 4, including a quotation to strengthen the impact of the writer's opinion.

Workshop 8 *Persuasion* 69

Elaboration, Revision, and Proofreading Worksheets

These practice sheets help students to add specific details to their writing and to refine their skills in revising and proofreading.

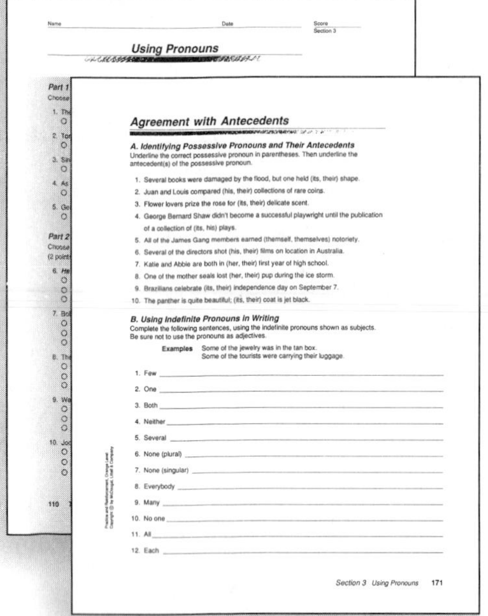

Name Date Score Section 3

Using Pronouns

Agreement with Antecedents

A. Identifying Possessive Pronouns and Their Antecedents
Underline the correct possessive pronoun in parentheses. Then underline the antecedent(s) of the possessive pronoun.

1. Several books were damaged by the flood, but one held (its, their) shape.
2. Juan and Louis compared (his, their) collections of rare coins.
3. Flower lovers prize the rose for (its, their) delicate scent.
4. George Bernard Shaw didn't become a successful playwright until the publication of a collection of (its, his) plays.
5. All of the James Gang members earned (themself, themselves) notoriety.
6. Several of the directors shot (his, their) films on location in Australia.
7. Katie and Abbie are both in (her, their) first year of high school.
8. One of the mother seals lost (her, their) pup during the ice storm.
9. Brazilians celebrate (its, their) independence day on September 7.
10. The panther is quite beautiful; (its, their) coat is jet black.

B. Using Indefinite Pronouns in Writing
Complete the following sentences, using the indefinite pronouns shown as subjects. Be sure not to use the pronouns as adjectives.

Examples Some of the jewelry was in the tan box.
Some of the tourists were carrying their luggage.

1. Few
2. One
3. Both
4. Neither
5. Several
6. None (plural)
7. None (singular)
8. Everybody
9. Many
10. No one
11. All
12. Each

Section 3 Using Pronouns 171

Grammar and Usage: Practice, Reteaching, and Assessment Copy Masters

Almost 200 pages of exercises and tests provide practice, reinforcement, and testing of all concepts taught in the Language Handbook. A challenge section of exercises is included for more advanced students.

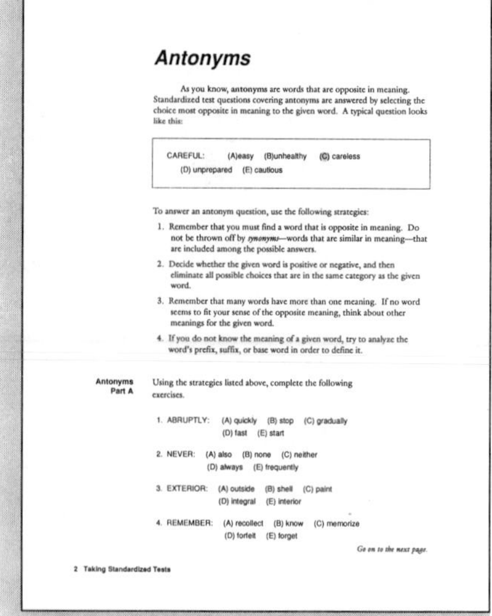

Antonyms

As you know, antonyms are words that are opposite in meaning. Standardized test questions covering antonyms are answered by selecting the choice most opposite in meaning to the given word. A typical question looks like this:

CAREFUL: (A) easy (B) unhealthy (C) careless (D) unprepared (E) cautious

To answer an antonym question, use the following strategies:

1. Remember that you must find a word that is opposite in meaning. Do not be thrown off by *synonyms*—words that are similar in meaning—that are included among the possible answers.
2. Decide whether the given word is positive or negative, and then eliminate all possible choices that are in the same category as the given word.
3. Remember that many words have more than one meaning. If no word seems to fit your sense of the opposite meaning, think about other meanings for the given word.
4. If you do not know the meaning of a given word, try to analyze the word's prefix, suffix, or base word in order to define it.

Antonyms Part A — Using the strategies listed above, complete the following exercises.

1. ABRUPTLY: (A) quickly (B) stop (C) gradually (D) fast (E) start
2. NEVER: (A) also (B) none (C) neither (D) always (E) frequently
3. EXTERIOR: (A) outside (B) shell (C) paint (D) integral (E) interior
4. REMEMBER: (A) recollect (B) know (C) memorize (D) forfeit (E) forget

Go on to the next page.

2 Taking Standardized Tests

Standardized Test Practice Copy Masters

The test booklet provides practice on antonyms, analogies, and sentence completion.

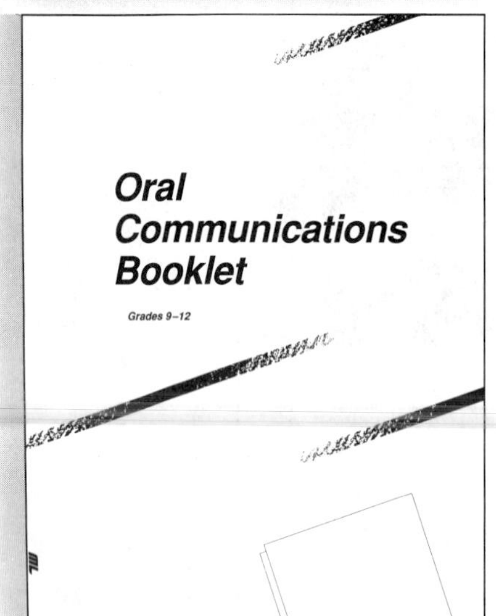

Oral Communications Booklet

Nearly 100 engaging activities and games to supplement and enrich oral communications lessons. The booklet includes speaking and listening activities for individuals and groups.

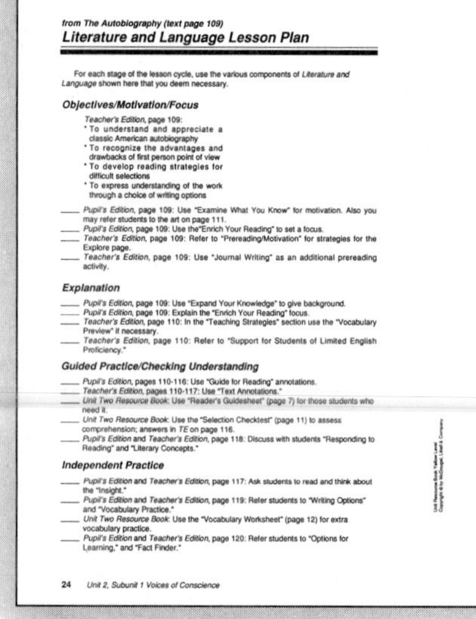

from The Autobiography (text page 109)

Literature and Language Lesson Plan

For each stage of the lesson cycle, use the various components of *Literature and Language* shown here that you deem necessary.

Objectives/Motivation/Focus

Teacher's Edition, page 109:
* To understand and appreciate a classic American autobiography
* To recognize the advantages and drawbacks of first person point of view
* To develop reading strategies for difficult selections
* To express understanding of the work through a choice of writing options

Explanation

Guided Practice/Checking Understanding

Independent Practice

24 Unit 2, Subunit 1 Voices of Conscience

Literature and Language Lesson Plans

Each plan shows the stages of a lesson cycle and the corresponding components of the *Literature and Language* program that can be used at each stage.

Also Available

Software

Writer's DataBank– includes sentence composing exercises, literary models, and questions for elaboration.

Electronic English Handbook– includes an on-screen writing reference that lets students browse rules and examples of usage, mechanics, and spelling as they draft and revise.

Audio Cassette Tapes

Two 60-minute tapes provide an enjoyable option for students—especially those with alternate learning styles—to listen to professional actors and actresses read many of the selections in each text.

The Design of the Teacher's Edition

Practical and Creative Ideas for Teaching Literature

The annotated teacher's edition of ***Literature and Language*** *is a professional sourcebook designed to promote effective and efficient teaching practices. Every unit and subunit opening page, every selection, and every workshop contain a wealth of useful teaching strategies as listed below.*

Unit Preparation and Preview

- unit objectives
- community resources
- multimedia materials
- purpose-setting discussion prompts

Subunit Preview

- motivational discussion prompts
- observation assessment suggestions
- challenge reading list

Before the Selection

- learning objectives
- discussion prompts
- additional background information
- journal writing topics
- lists of additional resources
- collaborative learning suggestions
- vocabulary previews
- support for students of limited English proficiency

Within the Selection

- annotations covering literary elements; reading skills; critical thinking skills; literary, historical, and cultural sidelights
- structured reading questions for less proficient students
- teaching tips
- suggestions for LEP students
- informative features: Data Bank, Real-Life Connections, Critic's Corner, Professional Notebook, Cultural Connections
- art notes

After the Selection

- answers to all questions and exercises in the student text
- suggestions and management tips for postreading activities
- check test on the selection
- independent reading bibliography
- journal update suggestions
- cross-curricular activities
- additional information about the author
- suggestions for achieving closure

Teaching the Workshops

The Language, Writer's, and Related Skills Workshops contain features similar to the literature lessons: objectives; teaching tips; answer keys; additional activities, exercises, and assignments; LEP tips; and suggestions for motivation and closure.

The *integrating* feature at the beginning of each workshop explains the carefully thought out integration of the workshops with the literature and with one another.

A Suggested Lesson Cycle

The lesson cycle presented below has been proven to be an effective teaching strategy. It can be adjusted or adapted to fit the needs of your classroom and the lessons you teach. ***Literature and Language*** *provides resources for each part of the cycle. A key identifying the location of these resources is provided on the opposite page.*

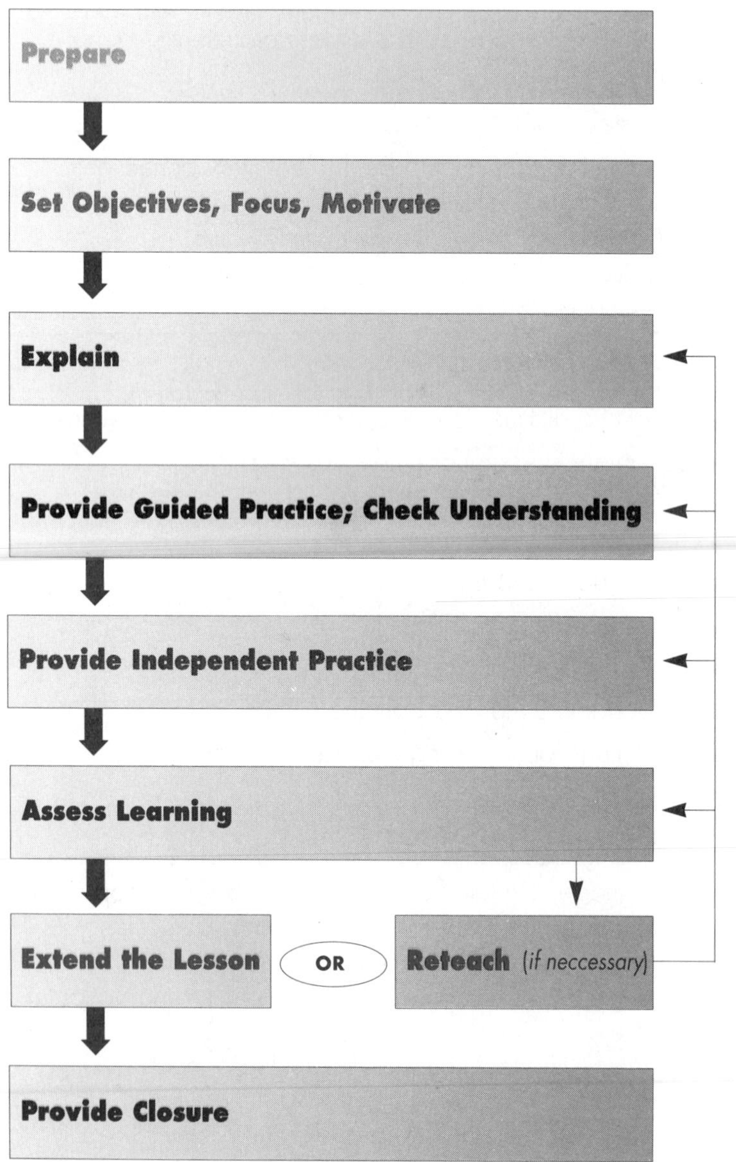

To Prepare, use

State and District Curricula

- ▲ Table of Contents to preview literary works, writing, language, and related skills lesson possibilities.
- ▲ Unit interleaf pages to preview unit objectives, selection difficulty level, and community/class room resources.
- ● *Literature and Language* Lesson Plans.
- ● Writing Assessment Prompts to identify writing weaknesses.
- ● Grammar and Usage: Practice, Reteaching, and Assessment to identify grammar needs.

To Set Objectives, Focus, and Motivate, use

- ▲ Unit interleaf page to preview all lessons and their objectives.
- ■▲ Unit and Subunit opening pages.
- ▲ Objectives for each individual selection and workshop.
- ■ *Explore* pages to activate prior knowledge and set a purpose for reading.
- ■▲ Fine art and About the Art notes.
- ▲ Prereading/Motivation for literature lessons; Integrating notes for workshops.
- ▲ Journal Writing
- ■ Author Biographies

To Explain, use

- ■ *Explore* pages for background information and explanation of reading skills.
- ■ *Explain* pages for discussion of literary elements.
- ▲ Vocabulary Preview, Teaching Strategies, Text Annotations, and Teaching Tips.

To Provide Guided Practice and Check Understanding, use

- ■ Interlinear or Guide for Reading questions when included in the selection.
- ▲ Teaching Strategies, Support for LEP Students, and Structured Reading for Less Proficient Students.
- ◆ Reader's Guidesheet for students who need extra comprehension help.
- ◆ Vocabulary worksheets and workshop copy masters.
- ▲◆ Check Tests.
- ■ Responding to Reading questions on *Explain* pages.
- ● Thinking Skills and Student Revision Model Transparencies.

To Provide Independent Practice, use

- ■ Writing Options and Vocabulary Practice on *Explain* pages; Options for Learning and Fact Finder on *Extend* pages.
- ■ Workshop exercises.
- ■ Insights.
- ◆ Peer and Self-Evaluation Guidelines.
- ■ The Language Handbook for practice in grammar skills.
- ▲ Encouraging Independent Reading and Journal Writing.

To Assess Learning, use

- ◆ Selection and Vocabulary Check Tests.
- ◆ Selection Tests.
- ◆ Subunit Tests.
- ◆● Writing Assessment Guidelines; Writing Prompts for Assessment.
- ● Grammar and Usage: Practice, Reteaching, and Assessment Copy Masters.

To Reteach, use

- ■ Reader's Handbook, Writer's Handbook, and Language Handbook.
- ▲ Reteaching activities for workshops.
- ● Grammar and Usage: Practice, Reteaching, and Assessment Copy Masters.
- ● Elaboration, Revision, and Proofreading Worksheets.

To Extend the Lesson, use

- ▲ Enrichment suggestions in Cross-Curricular Options, Data Bank, Critic's Corner, Real-Life Connections, Professional Notebook, Audio-visual Resources, Community Resources, Art Notes, Additional Writing and Research Topics.
- ▲ Additional Challenge and Encouraging Independent Reading lists.
- ● Audio Cassette tapes, Software, Standardized Test Practice, Oral Communications booklet, Fine Art Transparencies, and Student Revision Model Transparencies.

To Provide Closure, use

- ▲ Closure suggestions for summarizing or closing the lesson; Journal Update.

Key to Symbols

■ Pupil's Edition
▲ Annotated Teacher's Edition
◆ Unit Resource Books in Teacher's Resource File
● Enrichment Materials in Teacher's Resource File

The Logic of Integration: Putting It All Together

James Marshall, Senior Consultant

Why should we try to integrate the language arts in our English classrooms? Perhaps the best answer comes from the students themselves. Listen, for instance, to Jake, an 11th grader and a seasoned veteran of schools:

> In English class, they always give you that line about how they're preparing you for college. Whenever you ask teachers why you're doing what you're doing, that's the definitive answer. The teacher picks out the books that are on the list of classics, but I don't know what makes them a great work of art. I guess it has to be abstruse and have a lot of hidden meanings. You're not allowed to read it for pleasure. You have to think about the symbols. What does the fish mean? What does the merry-go-round mean? It doesn't mean anything to me. What teachers want is an opinion, and they have an opinion also, and they grade you against that opinion. And it really gets hard to write to please the teacher instead of writing what you're thinking. Sometimes I know what they want and I give it to them. Sometimes I know what they want and I refuse to give it to them because it's so absurd. And sometimes I have no idea what they want.

How would we answer Jake? What exactly do we want? In Jake's experience, the purpose driving the teacher of literature is to prepare students for something else—college perhaps, or maybe a job. The activity is not pleasurable, or even meaningful, in itself. It is a means to some other end. And the purpose is accomplished by taking apart the texts that Jake and his friends might read ("What does the fish mean? What does the merry-go-round mean?"), eliciting opinions about those texts, and then grading the students' opinions against the teacher's. The end result of such an approach, of course, is a profound alienation from the process of reading and understanding literature—an alienation that Jake articulates with a clear and discouraging force.

Jake's observations obviously do not apply to all English classrooms, but recent research on the teaching of literature suggests that they do apply to many. Arthur Applebee's study of schools with strong reputations in the teaching of English, for instance, found that literature instruction today looks largely the same as it did twenty-five years ago, even though many teachers had made significant changes in the way they teach writing. In other words, while students have been encouraged to value process, ownership, and small group work in learning to write, they have continued to search, in Jake's words, for those "abstruse" and "hidden" meanings when learning about literature. My own studies of classroom discussions of literature suggest how that search is usually carried out. In most discussions, regardless of grade or ability level, teachers talk three to five times more than their students; when students speak, they usually contribute one sentence or less. And that sentence is usually an abbreviated answer to the teacher's question.

Perhaps even more disturbing, both Applebee's research and my own suggest that it is the programs for non-academic students that are in the most trouble. It was those students, Applebee found, "the very students in most need of help," who received the least attention in curriculum planning and revision. And it was those students who expressed the most frustration about the patterns of classroom discussion that I have described. Given such findings, it is little wonder that both teachers and students have come to express increasing frustration with the models we have been using to guide our teaching in literature. Clearly it is time for a fresh approach.

What Integration Means

What alternatives do we have? One of the most promising is a model of teaching English that begins with the assumption that the basic components of language use—reading, writing, speaking and listening—cannot be learned well in isolation from one another. Rather, they are learned best when they are learned together within meaningful activities that call all of them into play. Young children, after all, first learn about language, not by studying it, but by using it. For them it is not an end in itself, but a tool to get things done. And because it is a useful tool—because controlling language empowers children to become increasingly competent in their world—they will practice the craft of language with an energy and a curiosity that seems long since lost by the time they enter secondary school.

What happens, of course, is that in school, reading and writing and speaking and listening are often treated as if they were isolated skills, and mastering those skills becomes an end in itself. Thus students are given reading assignments so that they will learn to read better and writing assignments so that they will learn to write better. We certainly want our students to grow in their ability to read and write, but the best way to accomplish that goal is to engage them in activities that call for extended practice in reading and writing—activities in which reading and writing become tools to get things done.

It is just such an approach that we have taken in *Literature and Language.* Here the skills of writing, language use, and vocabulary development have not been isolated from one another or from the study of literature. Instead, we have structured lessons and units so that the literature provides a context for practice in writing, language, and vocabulary. At the same time, the writing, language, and vocabulary exercises will provide students with a variety of tools for more deeply exploring the literature they read. We feel that when the language arts are integrated in this way, students will more clearly see the purposes driving the activities and thus will be more fully empowered to participate in the larger community of literate persons.

New Developments in the Study of Literature

Even teachers who are taking an integrated approach to the study of English, however, must still face questions about the kinds of literature they will ask their students to read and about the kinds of literary understanding that they will attempt to foster. On the one hand, it seems clear that at least part of our job is to introduce students to the great traditions of western literature. But on the other hand, recent scholarship and massive changes in our school population have awakened us to the necessity of teaching other traditions as well. There is the rich legacy of African-American, Native-American, Asian-American, and Hispanic literature that has for far too long gone unexplored in school. There is new and old literature written by women. There is an increasingly diverse range of contemporary fiction and non-fiction—some of the best of it directed specifically to adolescents. There is, in short, a whole new world of literature that our teaching cannot ignore.

At the same time, there is a whole new world of thought about what it means to understand a piece of literature—and this too we cannot ignore. The process of reading, it appears, is not a matter of extracting meanings from texts, but a matter of making meaning in interaction with texts. Readers bring a wide range of prior knowledge and personal history to bear on their reading, and what they bring helps to shape what they take away. What this means in practice, of course, is that students should be given wider opportunities to connect their reading in class to their lives outside of class, to use what they know to make sense of what they read. In addition to asking them what they think about a text, then, we can also ask them what the text makes them remember, what it makes them feel, what it helps them understand. Instead of reading to find answers about what texts mean, this new approach asks teachers and students to move together through a process of making meaning, drawing on both knowledge of the text and knowledge of themselves. The questions we ask will be different, the answers we seek will be different, and the end result may well be a richer and more deeply reasoned understanding of literature.

In *Literature and Language,* we directly address these new developments in the study of literature and again, the key word for our approach is integration. The great works of the western tradition are represented here, but they are connected within thematic units to great works from other traditions as well. Questions about the texts are here, but they are preceded and followed by questions about students' responses to those texts. We have attempted, in other words, to interrelate texts with one another and students with texts, to provide a structured occasion for students and teachers to explore the full range of opportunities that the study of literature affords.

Literature and Language can help teachers provide their students with a fresh point of departure in their study of literature, and in so doing, provide them with new reasons to continue reading and thinking about what they read. And that, after all, is probably what we want most for Jake and students like him.

Related Reading

- Applebee, A. N. (1989). "The Teaching of Literature in Programs with Reputations for Excellence in English." Technical Report. Center for the Learning and Teaching of Literature, State University at Albany, Albany, NY.
- Beach, R., & Marshall, J. (1991). *Teaching Literature in the Secondary School.* San Diego, CA: Harcourt, Brace, Jovanovich.
- Marshall, J. (1989). "Patterns of Discourse in Classroom Discussions of Literature." Technical Report. Center for the Learning and Teaching of Literature, State University at Albany, Albany, NY.
- Marshall, J. (1988). "Classroom Discourse and Literary Response." In Nelms, B. (Ed.). *Literature in the Classroom: Readers, Texts, Contexts.* Urbana, IL: National Council of Teachers of English.
- Rosenblatt, L. (1977). *The Reader, the Text, the Poem.* Carbondale, IL: Southern Illinois University Press
- Scholes, R. (1985). *Textual Power.* New Haven: Yale University Press.

A Reader-Based Approach to Literature

Judith A. Langer, Arthur N. Applebee, Senior Consultants

Literature instruction has long been at the center of the secondary curriculum of every state and school district, and literature continues to be the focus of instruction in most English classrooms.

The English Curriculum. Recent studies of the secondary school English curriculum have highlighted a number of problems in most programs: 1) Teachers' goals for the teaching of literature stress student response and understanding, but the questioning strategies in most programs treat literature as a source of "right answers." 2) In part as a result, the teaching of literature has remained a teacher-centered and text-centered activity, in contrast to an increasingly student-centered approach in composition. 3) The literature program is often completely separate from the writing program; writing is not treated as a context for enriching and extending student response to literature. 4) The selections chosen for study remain unnecessarily narrow; generally, they do not represent the many rich and diverse traditions that are part of the students' literary heritage. Even when a broader range of materials has been included in literature anthologies, teachers have avoided these materials because they are unfamiliar and often because the accompanying teaching support has been less than satisfactory.

Text-Based and Reader-Based Approaches. During the twentieth century, the major debates about the teaching of literature have centered on the relative contributions of the text and the reader's own understanding to "good" reading. New critical approaches, which dominated decades of instruction, involve close and careful textual analyses. They focus on the text as a source of knowledge, and by and large, emerge from a more generalized view that the text has a "message" that needs to be extracted by a reader following certain procedures. Recent studies indicate that the analytical procedure itself too often becomes the focus of instruction rather than a support for the reading process.

Another text-based approach to literature relies upon standard critical interpretations of works and urges teachers to rely on those interpretations as the focus of instruction. Rather than learning to develop their own responses, students are asked to learn the interpretations of others.

In contrast, approaches that focus on the reader—reader response theory, for example—consider meaning to reside in the reader or in the transaction between the reader and the text, with the reader's interpretations as evidence of good reading. Reader-based approaches are the views most consonant with current research on reading comprehension as an interactive and constructive process and with process-oriented research on reading, writing, and reasoning. Reader-based approaches also underlie the theoretical framework of the *Literature and Language* series, which builds upon current theories of writing, literature, and the teaching of literature. The series is designed to remedy the problems that have been identified in recent studies of the English curriculum.

Literature and Language: Conceptual Framework

For the past few years, Judith Langer has been developing a theory for the teaching of literature, which describes the process of coming to understand literature and the contribution that the teaching of literature can make to the intellectual and cultural development of the growing student. Langer's theory is based on research that has shown the following:

- The meaning-making processes used in reading literature are not necessarily the same as those used in other coursework.
- The special contribution of literary understanding to the developing intellect needs to be acknowledged.
- The teaching of critical thinking in literature—the kinds of questions asked and the kinds of responses sought—needs to differ from the teaching of critical thinking in other subjects focusing instead on helping students engage more successfully in the processes involved in literary understanding.
- Instructional focus in the process of understanding can help poorer as well as more successful readers engage in higher literacy and literature learning.

The Process of Reading Literature. A process view of reading suggests that making sense of a work of literature involves building envisionments, with understanding changing and growing over time. The term *envisionment* refers to a world of understanding a reader has about a text. When you read *Romeo and Juliet*, for instance, what you read in Scene 1 (when the two servants of the House of Capulet discuss their rivalry with the Montagues) provides you with only the scantest hints of what will unfold later in the play. The conversation is important at that time because it provides you with the necessary information to begin building an understanding of what will happen later. Thus the conversation is only of momentary importance, soon disappearing from your awareness, replaced with a deepening and ever-changing understanding of the lovers' plight and eventually of Juliet's decision to die.

Meaning-Making Through Envisionment-Building. An envisionment includes what a reader understands about a text, the questions the reader has, and the reader's hunches about how the piece will unfold. A reader has a different envisionment at each point in a reading; the envisionment changes as the reading progresses. As more is read, some details are dropped from the envisionment as no longer important (for example, the particular language the Capulet servants use to discuss their disdain for the Montagues), and new details are added. The effect is a continuing elaboration upon the reader's knowledge: for example, upon the reader's awareness of the depth of the enmity between the two families. Meaning gained from one portion of the reading is shaped by earlier interpretations and continues to change in light of interpretations developed later in the reading. This changing understanding is at the heart of the reader's response to literature, and needs to be at the heart of meaningful reader-based instruction.

Envisionment as Response.
Envisionment is the way in which a reader experiences a text—the reader's total understanding or response at any point in time. During the reading of a novel, story, play, or poem, a reader's envisionment changes as new information from the text and new inferences from the reader influence the reader's response. This evolving envisionment might be thought of as a series of envisionments, which leads to an envisionment at the end of a reading. This end point is not the sum total of all the other envisionments, but rather a result of all the changes and modifications in understanding that have occurred along the way.

The envisionment at the end of a reading—the text world of ideas, questions, and quandries that every reader comes away with after reading a work of literature—is a reader's starting point for contemplation and discussion. This envisionment can become fodder for further modification, as other readers offer alternative ways of making sense of a text.

The concept of envisionment as response is a critical one for instruction. The belief that when students read they continually modify their understandings demands questions that are not structured according to traditional hierarchies. There hierarchies, based on distinctions such as literal questions and inferential questions or on Bloom's taxonomy, are text-based and do not reflect the reader's process of sense-making. Words "on the page," for instance, are quite different from the ways in which those words are combined in a reader's mind at any given point in time. Talking about particular words from the text outside of the reader's text world disregards the response-building process the reader has engaged in. Rather than helping readers, discussions that begin by focusing on the "literal" meaning of the text rather than on what sense students have made of the text can actually get in the way of students' understanding. Similarly, retracing the plot line to check understanding ignores the envisionment-building process that led to the readers' response to the text as a whole. Rather than building on what students already understand, such activities force them to retreat from their understandings to focus on details out of context. Focusing on details may be helpful at a later point, however, as readers begin to sort out why their interpretations of the same text differ.

Readers naturally want to discuss their envisionments (or initial responses). Recall, for example, the experience of finishing a good book, a mystery perhaps. You probably ended up with ideas and questions you wanted to talk about with others who had read the same book. What you experienced was a desire to share your envisionment.

The best reader-based questions teachers can ask immediately after students have read a selection are questions that tap students' envisionments. These questions might be similar to the following: What were you thinking as you finished the story? Is there anything you'd like to talk about? What did the poem mean to you?

What Is Unique About Literary Understanding?

While readers use envisionment-building in both literary and informative contexts, the essential concerns are different for each type of reading. When engaged in informative reading (for example, to get information from social studies and science materials), readers early on establish a sense of the topic and of the author's slant, and they use this judgment as a point of reference to monitor new and growing understandings. Once a sense of direction is established, it takes a great deal of countervailing information to change a reader's notion of the whole.

In contrast, literary reading abounds with the exploration of possibilities. Readers continually open new possibilities for meaning, for alternative interpretations and changing points of view. The possibilities change over time, growing out of the readers' developing envisionments.

The reading of literature involves a great deal of critical thinking that is different from the kinds of thinking required by informative texts. For example, in social studies or science materials, students must focus on understanding an argument or on learning specific content. As with literary texts, the reader works with a sense of the whole. However, in informational reading the sense of the whole serves as a steady point of reference, while in literary reading it is a constantly changing horizon of possibilities.

Instruction that helps students become competent readers of literature needs to reflect on awareness of these distinctions. Teachers must encourage students to recognize ambiguities, to explore possibilities, and to seek ways of "filling out" meanings, using their knowledge of the text and of human experience to develop deeper insights. The goal is to support students in becoming mature, sophisticated readers, capable of dealing with complex texts in increasingly thoughtful ways.

Putting Theory into Practice

The ideal literature classroom is a literary community where students are active meaning-makers: where they have room to respond, interpret, think critically, and contrast their ideas with those of other readers. To move toward this ideal, the questions asked need to change dramatically, so that they support the process of understanding from the student's point of view. Rather than seeking right answers and predetermined interpretations, questions need to serve as "thought tappers." Students should respond to these open-ended questions individually, in small groups, or as a class, sharing their initial questions and understandings and then moving beyond into more fully developed interpretations.

The following are guidelines for supporting students through the rethinking process, after they have read a literary selection. The boldface heads correspond to those on the **Explain** pages of *Literature and Language.*

1. **First Impressions.** Begin with a question that encourages students to share their initial responses to the piece. For example: *What picture lingered in your mind after you read this story? How do you feel about what happened to Madame Loisel?*
2. **Second Thoughts.** Ask open-ended questions that operate as scaffolds, helping students to move beyond their initial understandings toward fuller and more carefully reasoned responses. Students might explore motivations, causes and effects, and implications, and might relate the parts to one another and to their understanding of the whole. Students might also consider how their ideas and feelings have changed as a result of their reading experience. The questions asked might be similar to the following: *Martha's grandfather refused to pay fifteen dollars for the scholarship jacket. Tell how you feel about his decision. Why do you think the principal finally awards Martha the jacket?*

   In addition, ask questions that help students explore the implications of current understandings or rethink either momentary or previous understandings, feelings, or questions. For example: *What might the story be like if it were told by Jerry instead of by the narrator in "A Mother in Mannville"? If Polyphemus had not brought the rams into the cave, how might Odysseus and his men have escaped? If Juliet had been too afraid to drink Friar Lawrence's potion, what other plan could the friar have devised?*
3. **Broader Connections.** After the students have worked through their understandings, ask them to make connections between the selection and the world around them. For example: *What conflicts in contemporary American society do you think are similar to the feud between the Montagues and the Capulets? Use specific details from the play to make the comparison.*

In addition to conducting discussions, it is important to involve students in collaborative activities and in writing both before and after reading. The following are guidelines for further analysis and for making writing an integral part of the meaning-making process.

Literary Concepts. After students have had a chance to develop their own interpretations, they can then turn their attention to the literacy elements that underlie the work. Students' appreciation of language and structure and of the effects these engender is enhanced when you assign groups of students to work collaboratively on literary analysis: for example, when pairs of students identify parts of the text that were particularly vivid for them and then analyze what created this effect, or when groups of students debate and defend their interpretation of the ending of a selection.

Writing Options. Writing offers a powerful context for thinking about literature, for clarifying understandings, and for sharing them with others. Writing before reading helps students connect the reading they will do with what they already know, thus providing a way into a new text or orienting the reader toward that text. Writing after reading provides students with opportunities to connect the reading they have done to other ideas and experiences.

This variety of questions and activities provide students with an array of vantage points from which to reflect upon a text. The guidelines for questions are not meant to imply that only one sequence of question types is effective or that each type of question and activity needs to be addressed during every lesson. However, one guideline is almost always applicable: Begin a discussion with an open-ended question that taps students' initial responses (not the teacher's understandings), thus inviting students to take an active role in building their own understandings of literature.

Effective Instruction: Underlying Principles

A teacher's techniques, and the activities within which they are embedded, are likely to be different in every classroom. The teacher alone has the professional knowledge to tailor instruction to the needs of a particular class. Across classrooms, however, the following principles underlie programs that effectively involve students in learning to develop rich, thoughtful interpretations of literature.

1. **Students are active makers of meaning.** Students are treated as thinkers, as if they can and will have interesting and cogent thoughts about a work of literature, which they will want to discuss.
2. **Literature reading generates questions.** Effective programs assume that after reading a work, students come away with initial responses and with questions that are part of their envisionments. Good instruction acknowledges that the process of understanding literature involves the raising of questions.
3. **Content questions tap student knowledge.** When teachers ask questions about content, they are tapping into student knowledge and understandings. Such questions have no predetermined right answers and are meant to prompt extended thought and sharing of ideas.
4. **Class meetings are a time to develop understandings.** Meaningful class discussions support the process of coming to understand. With the help of the teacher, students develop their envisionments. Thus, the cognitive behaviors students engage in during discussion are the same envisionment-building behaviors they engage in during reading.
5. **Instruction scaffolds the process of understanding.** All questions, activities, and assignments are designed to help students develop their own understandings, not memorize (or guess) the "right" interpretation of a text.
6. **Control is transferred from teacher to students.** Students work through their ideas alone, in small groups, and in class discussion. While students work, they are encouraged to interact collaboratively, to respond to and communicate with each other.

Literature and Language is a program designed to help the teacher put into practice these principles for effective instruction. The activities and questions in the program support envisionment-building, build confidence in dealing with literary texts, and encourage active participation in the classroom literary community.

Related Reading

■ Andrasick, Kathleen D. *Opening texts: Using writing to teach literature.* Portsmouth, NH: Heinemann. 1990.

■ Applebee, A. N. *The teaching of literature in programs with reputations for excellence in English.* Report Series 1.1, Center for the Learning and Teaching of Literature, State University of New York at Albany. 1989a.

■ Applebee, A. N. *Literature instruction in American schools.* Report Series 1.4, Center for the Learning and Teaching of Literature, State University of New York at Albany. 1989b.

■ Applebee, A. N., Langer, J. A., & Mullis, I. *Crossroads in American education.* Princeton, NJ: National Assessment of American Progress, Educational Testing Service. 1989.

■ Brody, P., DeMilo, C., & Purves, A. C. *The current state of assessment in literature.* Albany, NY: SUNY Albany, Center for the Learning and Teaching of Literature. 1989.

■ Diaz, P. and Hayhoe, M. *Developing response to poetry.* Philadelphia: Open University Press. 1988.

■ Langer, J. A. *The process of understanding literature,* Report Series 2.1, Center for the Learning and Teaching of Literature, State University of New York at Albany. 1989.

■ Langer, J. A. Understanding literature. *Language Arts,* December 1990.

■ Langer, J. A. and Applebee, A. N. *How writing shapes thinking: Studies of teaching and learning.* Urbana, IL: National Council of Teachers of English. 1987.

■ Langer, J. A., Bartolome, L., Vasquez, O., & Lucas, T. Meaning construction in school literacy tasks: A study of bilingual students. *American Educational Research Journal,* 1990.

■ Probst, R. E. *Response and analysis: Teaching literature in the junior and senior high school.* Portsmouth, NH: Boynton/Cook. 1988.

Cooperative Learning

Cooperative learning is not the traditional small group situation common in classrooms, in which students work in proximity toward individual goals. Nor is cooperative learning just a group of students working together in which one or two students do all of the work.

In cooperative learning:

- Students work interdependently to ensure that all of the group's members master the assigned material.
- Individuals are accountable, and each student's mastery is assessed.
- All members are held responsible for each other's learning.
- The membership of the group is heterogeneous in ability.
- All members participate actively in a group.
- The teacher monitors behavior and learning and gives feedback to groups on their effectiveness.
- Members of the group evaluate their own effectiveness.

Advocates of cooperative learning assert that it motivates students to learn, improves social skills, promotes self-esteem in students of all abilities, and lessens dependence on the teacher. Recent classroom research appears to validate claims about the effectiveness of the cooperative learning experience.

The Cooperative Learning Group

No more than three students in a group are recommended for the class that does not have much experience with cooperative learning. Six is probably the most members a group can have and still be effective.

The make-up of a cooperative learning group depends on its purpose. Grouping by interests and by a cross-section of ability are just two possibilities. Grouping might also be random: for example, students might count off to create groups in which no one has the same number. Then, when an assignment is made, the task may be divided into parts. All the students with the same number then become experts on one part and are held responsible for reporting on it. This technique is sometimes called *jigsawing.* All the pieces of the puzzle are put together so that everyone in a group sees the whole picture. Not only do members of the group pool their knowledge, but they also teach the others what they need to know.

While the groups are working, the teacher circulates and observes for appropriate behavior and also listens for any misunderstandings. Sometimes a teacher may intervene by asking a question that directs the students' thinking toward a solution. Even then, the emphasis should be on having the group, rather than the teacher, work through the problem. At other times, especially if more than one group is having difficulty, teachers may interrupt to discuss the point of confusion with the entire class.

Accountability and Assessment

When a group has completed an assignment, there remains the issue of accountability for both the group and the individuals in it. Some ways of assuring accountability are as follows:

1. Have the group produce a single report, paper, or other end result. Every member signs off on the final product to indicate agreement with its conclusions or answers. The teacher then chooses individual students at random to respond to additional questions: for example to explain the rationale behind an answer.
2. If members produce individual products, randomly choose one to evaluate as representative of the group, or have the group make the choice. You might also have one member demonstrate understanding of a concept.
3. Keep a progress chart on which the performance of each group and its individuals is charted, or have each group keep the chart. Hold students responsible for improving the performance of the group and its members.
4. Divide the tasks so that each member completes a different one. However, don't accept any work until all the group's members have completed their individual tasks and have compiled the results.

Grades, the most obvious rewards in most classrooms can be used to encourage cooperative learning. A teacher might average individual scores; give a group score for a product, which all members receive; randomly score one member's paper or exam; give individual scores plus bonus points for successful group performance; or give all members the lowest score.

In *Literature and Language . . .*

Opportunities for cooperative work appear throughout the text.

- Pre- and postreading activities and questions on the **Explore** and **Explain** pages are particularly well-suited to small group discussion.
- Multimodal activities on the **Extend** page include cooperative learning projects.
- **Writer's Workshop** assignments call for group work at all stages of the writing process.
- **Language Workshops** and **Related Skills Workshops** provide exercises and activities focused toward cooperative learning.

Multimodal Learning

We are all unique. We have different sets of characteristics, abilities, and needs. It should not be surprising, therefore, to learn that we have different learning styles as well. Yet it is only recently (the early 1980's) that this theory of learning gained acceptability, based largely on the initial research of Harvard psychologist Howard Gardner. Gardner recognizes seven types of intelligence: linguistic, logical-mathematical, spatial, bodily-kinesthetic, interpersonal, and intrapersonal. Everyone has all seven intelligences, but in different proportions.

Research indicates that the different kinds of intelligences are located in different parts of the brain. There seems to be a correlation between behavior and hemisphericity (the dominance of either the right or the left side of the brain). The various parts of the brain do cooperate with each other, which suggests that the seven types of intelligence interact as well.

Different environments favor and encourage the development of specific intelligences. From Chart A, which shows the characteristic strengths of each intelligence, you can infer how certain environments are likely to be more favorable to some intelligences than to others. As Gardner points out, when we address the notion of high intelligence in our society, we are usually talking about only two or three types: linguistic, logical-mathematical, and sometimes intrapersonal. Other researchers have suggested that because of their emphasis on formal testing, schools tend to favor students who are strong in linguistic and logical-mathematical intelligences and discriminate against those who are weak in those areas though strong in others.

The theory of multiple intelligences is the basis for recognizing that not only do all learners have different abilities but, because they do, they also have different styles of learning. Biological and developmental characteristics can determine how we learn, what we learn most easily, and what we have difficulty with. The same teaching method is not equally effective with all students. Student performance does improve markedly when learning styles are accommodated.

There are five elements to consider when accommodating various Learning Styles: environmental, emotional, sociological, physical, and psychological. Studies show that the individual needs of students are best met when classrooms are organized and teaching approaches are developed with learning styles in mind. As Chart B shows, these needs include the physical conditions of the classroom

Chart A

Linguistic	Is verbal; thinks in words; has highly developed auditory skills; likes to read and write
Logical-Mathematical	Thinks conceptually; capable of highly abstract thinking, logic, reasoning
Spatial	Thinks in visual images and pictures; enjoys drawing, designing, building, daydreaming, inventing
Musical	Is sensitive to music, nonverbal sounds, rhythm; enjoys listening to, singing, moving to, playing music
Bodily-Kinesthetic	Processes knowledge through bodily sensations; has fine-motor coordination; communicates through body language
Interpersonal	Understands other people; organizes, communicates, socializes
Intrapersonal	Prefers working alone; intuitive, independent, private, self-motivated

Chart B

Stimuli	Elements
Environmental	Sound, Light, Temperature, Design
Emotional	Motivation, Persistence, Responsibility, Structure
Sociological	Peers, Self, Pair, Team, Adult, Varied
Physical	Perceptual, Intake, Time, Mobility
Psychological	Analytic/Global, Hemispheric Preference, Impulsive/Reflective

[Rita Dunn and Kenneth Dunn. "Can Students Identify Their Own Learning Styles?" *Educational Leadership*, February 1983, p. 61.]

as well as interpersonal and pedagogical considerations.

Within every group a significant number of students has needs that are different enough from the standard to inhibit learning. Classroom design, for example, can affect students' achievement. Students tend to need more light as they grow older. The need for sound also tends to increase during adolescence. Yet often a class includes a minority of students who require less light and some who need complete silence—to the point of needing ear plugs—when they work. Temperature variations may also affect some students more than others. And while a majority of adolescents show a preference for sitting casually in soft chairs, some require the more formal support of a desk.

Schools tend to favor students who are strong in linguistic and logical-mathematical intelligences and discriminate against those who are weak in those areas.

To accommodate these varying physical needs, a classroom might include an informal area with cushions, couches, and carpeting; quiet areas for some; and an area where students can work while listening to music with a headset on. Loosening a bulb in one corner of the classroom creates an area for those who prefer low light.

The older students get, the less teacher motivated they become, preferring peer learning. By the ninth grade, there also is a greater need to learn and study alone. At all levels, though, some students have needs that are contrary to the general tendencies of the age group. Allowing for variation can accommodate the different styles. Thus students might set mutual objectives within a small group under teacher guidance, go off to study by themselves, and then return to share their findings with the group and the class.

Not all students learn verbally. If a student's modality is kinesthetic, for example, he or she will learn more if at least the initial instruction is presented through manipulatives. The students who require more mobility than others need to be able to move around the classroom. Instruction can be so organized that different learning takes place in different parts of the room, requiring students to move from one part to the other. Students with kinesthetic learning styles benefit from activities such as performing skits and observing the natural world. Students with a spatial orientation will enjoy building models and sketching illustrations. Students who have musical style will respond to activities such as composing ballads and choosing music to reflect the mood of a literary selection.

The majority of teachers teach analytically, reaching students with linguistic and logical-mathematical strengths. Teachers need to become aware of their own learning and teaching styles so that they can better meet student needs, and this will improve classroom performance. One goal should be for teachers to integrate the multimodal activities into their lessons. Another goal should be to help all students move from their single, favored modes to a mix of instructional modes from which they might benefit. (The essay "Assessment in the Literature Classroom," on page T29 provides strategies for evaluating students with various learning styles.)

In *Literature and Language* . . .

Addressing the variety of student learning styles is a primary focus of this text.

- Reader response questions on the **Explain** page allow all students to participate—not just those who can memorize "correct" answers.
- "Options for Learning" activities on the **Extend** page provide students with opportunities to express their knowledge using a wide variety of intelligences and learning modes.
- Innovative assessment options allow students to be evaluated on their particular strengths, not their weaknesses.
- **Writer's, Language,** and **Related Skills Workshops** are focused toward cooperative learning.

Related Reading

- Dunn, Kenneth, and Dunn, Rita. "Dispelling Outmoded Beliefs About Student Learning." *Educational Leadership.* March 1987.
- Dunn, Rita. "Can Students Identify Their Own Learning Styles?" *Educational Leadership.* February 1983.
- Dunn, Rita. *In Their Own Way: Discovering and Encouraging Your Child's Personal Learning Styles.* Los Angeles: Tarcher, 1987.
- Dunn, Rita; Beaudry, Jeffrey S; and Klavas, Angela. "Survey of Research on Learning Styles." *Educational Leadership.* March 1989.
- Gardner, Howard. *Frames of Mind, The Theory of Multiple Intelligences.* New York: Basic Books, Inc. 1983.
- Keefe, J.; M. Languis, C.; and R. Dunn. *Learning Style Profile.* Reston, Va.: National Association of Secondary School Principals. 1986.
- Wheeler, R. "An Alternative to Failure: Teaching Reading According to Students' Perceptual Strengths." *Kappa Delta Pi Record* 17, 2: 59-63. 1980.

LEP Students in the Literature Classroom

Andrea B. Bermúdez, Senior Consultant

The contemporary classroom reflects the diversity of language and cultures that live in the United States at the present time. The 1980 U.S. Census, for example, suggests that there are over sixteen million homes who communicate in a non-English language. The culturally and linguistically diverse students from these homes bring with them a wealth of potential and experiences that should be utilized by teachers to enrich the learning environment of all students. Transition to a mainstream classroom may not be dependent exclusively on the efforts of the students but on the degree of sensitivity of a teacher who can successfully mediate between the learner and instruction. Developing multicultural sensitivity is a fourfold process which involves: (a) acceptance of the student's circumstances, (b) a genuine search for information regarding the background and prior knowledge of the students, (c) an updated bank of teaching strategies, and (d) a desire to find the best options for the student.

A Profile of the LEP Learner

While many culturally and linguistically diverse students experience limited English proficiency (LEP), LEP students are not necessarily from homes whose first language is other than English. Many monolingual English speaking students, regardless of ethnic background, experience difficulty when dealing with text and written expression. These difficulties include problems in the following areas: (a) comprehending text (b) expressing ideas clearly (c) negotiating meaning regarding the context and symbolism expressed by words and/or phrases.

There are certain cultural and linguistic characteristics of learners that may set the LEP learner apart from the "standards" operating within a mainstream classroom. Teachers expect certain behaviors in response to the learning environment offered to students and often become frustrated when these behaviors do not occur. To avoid misunderstanding, it is critical that teachers disregard the assumption that all students have the same, or similar, frame of reference or perceptions about the world. The following is a partial list of behaviors that teachers commonly experience with LEP students.

- LEP students generally **focus attention on style**, not content. This is often a result of teachers who are very insistent on error-free products to the detriment of original ideas and creative expression.
- These students are often **unaware of learning strategies** that could facilitate comprehension such as brainstorming, mapping, and cooperative learning. These strategies must be taught directly to ensure their effectiveness.
- LEP students **may become disorderly** and disobedient as a result of frustration created by their inability to relate to the learning environment.
- LEP students often **do not make eye contact** when addressing others. Unlike mainstream U.S.A., many cultures consider eye contact a sign of disrespect to teachers or others of high status.
- LEP students may seem to **have difficulty meeting deadlines**. The concept of time varies across cultures. A teacher should not assume that students are familiar with the very precise chronology by which the mainstream classroom operates. Students need to be taught how to function within a deadline driven curriculum.
- LEPs **may not seem to understand classroom "rules."** Discipline is not a universally defined concept. Schools and homes need to establish common parameters of discipline to obtain positive results.
- LEPs generally **show a different speaking-listening style**. Not all cultures communicate in tandem. In some cultures, it is considered-acceptable to interrupt others while talking, finish their stories, or talk and listen simultaneously.
- LEPs may **organize thoughts in a pattern that does not correspond to the expected linear-sequential pattern** characteristic of English communication. For example, they may be redundant when trying to express ideas or explain a situation in a "roundabout" manner.
- LEPs may exhibit an **external locus of control**. Students sometimes seem dependent on teachers or peers for validation of their responses or for vital information related to the learning task. Self-dependence can be learned and should be taught, not expected.

Common Problem Areas

The following areas pose special challenges to LEP students in trying to comprehend literary selections.

- **Vocabulary difficulty.** If students do not have prior experience with the words appearing in the selection, the normal links between the concept and its label will not occur. Problems often arise when a selection contains low frequency words, idiomatic or dialectal expressions, and/or jargon.
- **Unfamiliar content.** The message in the literature may be misunder-

stood if students are not placed in the proper context of the selection. This often happens as a result of: (a) lack of prior experience with the context, (b) abstract nature of the ideas expressed (e.g., poetry), or (c) culture-specificity of ideas expressed.

- **Grammatical features of the selection.** Comprehension problems arise when students encounter: (a) dialectal forms, (b) out-dated grammatical forms, (c) unusual word order and/or (d) above average length of the selection.

Effective Teaching/Learning Strategies

The following instructional strategies have been shown to be successful with LEP learners.

Cognitive Mapping. Every individual has a unique history of experiences which plays a vital part in acquiring new knowledge. Many students, however, have poor strategies for organizing and categorizing this information. Instruction in cognitive mapping can enable students to integrate previous experience with new knowledge.

An Integrated Approach. The integrated approach to learning is particularly successful with LEP learners. Students learn about reading and writing while listening; they learn about writing from reading and gain insights into reading from writing. Any strategy or approach based on dissecting language into mutually exclusive components jeopardizes second language acquisition by not drawing on the prior knowledge and strengths of the learner.

Cooperative Learning. Cooperative learning is a generic term that refers to a variety of approaches to integrating students into group activities where each participant is responsible for contributing to group outcomes and products. Cooperative learning strategies significantly improve students' achievement and productivity for a wide range of subjects and grade levels. This approach also improves self-esteem and respect for others.

Lesson Format

Using **scientific inquiry** to present literature selections to LEP students maximizes learning. This format includes the following steps:

1. **Exploration Phase**
   Probe prior knowledge.
   - Use brainstorming, mapping, and discussion probes to assess how familiar the student is with the context of the selection, and to introduce new ideas.
2. **Instructional Phase**
   Provide familiarity with context.
   - Preteach any concepts for which students may not have a cultural reference. These may include historical references, mythological references, obscure terms, and dialect.
   - Define abstract concepts such as *opinion* or *evaluation* in concrete terms, giving specific examples.

   Teach new vocabulary in clusters.
   - When possible, present key vocabulary in clusters related by meaning or word family.

   Present in a variety of modes.
   - Present concepts in a variety of media, for example: pictures, signs, films, graphic organizers, videos, sketches, and so on.
   - Read some selections aloud as LEP students follow, or use commercially or student-produced audio tapes.
3. **Application Phase**
   Provide opportunities to relate groups of concepts/words.
   - Use webbing or mapping to help students establish relationships among concepts.
   - Have students write summaries of what they have read.
   - Develop (and encourage students to develop) cross-cultural analogies for concepts, characters, plots, and themes.

   Encourage alternate modes of expression.
   - Allow students to express themselves in various media.

Differing language backgrounds and prior cultural experiences will determine the degree of difficulty with the language and "culture" of the classroom. The teacher's ability to assess the strengths that students bring to the learning experience as well as a commitment made to continually search for better instructional alternatives will, to a great extent, determine the academic success of LEP students.

In *Literature and Language* . . .

LEP students are provided with the support they need to succeed.

- A rich variety of multicultural literature fosters self-esteem and cultural worth
- The integrated design of the series allows students to draw on prior knowledge while learning new material
- The reader-based approach to literature allows all students to develop meaningful interpretations
- Successful LEP learning strategies such as brainstorming, mapping, and cooperative learning are found throughout the series
- Special LEP support is provided in the Annotated Teacher's Edition and Unit Resource Books
- Options for Learning on **Extend** pages provide opportunities for alternate modes of expression

Never Too Late: Teaching Discouraged Learners

Jerry Conrath, Consultant

Teaching literature and language to discouraged learners can tax even the most patient and dedicated among us. We are not trained, either professionally or emotionally, to deal with the often hostile, unruly, or apathetic responses of such learners. But the rewards of reaching this audience, of tapping their hidden potential and rekindling their intellectual curiosity, are immense.

To help these students, we need to appreciate the evolution of their discouragement. Many students feel educationally defeated as early as the third grade when the instructional focus shifts from learning to read to reading to learn. This shift reflects a disproportionate emphasis on what Howard Gardner calls "linguistic intelligence," which rewards those who enjoy sitting quietly while engaged in the complex linguistic tasks of reading and writing.

Unfortunately, students whose intellectual strengths require alternative modes of learning are left behind. These students, not gifted with a quick linguistic facility, fall behind in reading, writing, spelling, and vocabulary and are stigmatized as "slow" or "reluctant." The labels unnaturally lower the ceiling of expectations both for the students and their teachers. In most cases, the cycle of defeat worsens as students progress through school, resulting in poor self-esteem and a conviction of intellectual inferiority.

We know, however, that most discouraged learners—a label more descriptive and humane than others —are not less intelligent than their peers. It is true that students who have developed at a slower pace may have problems requiring a precise linguistic focus, such as following verbal instructions or memorizing. But these students often possess a splendid ability to think creatively and to offer innovative solutions to problems. Their deficiencies, in sum, are linguistic, not intellectual. According to recent research, 74% of our discouraged learners are divergent, inventive, and utilitarian thinkers whose capabilities are barely tapped.

Most discouraged learners are not less intelligent than their peers.

English teachers who are most successful in dealing with discouraged learners do so by creating stimulating, interactive environments. They draw out every student's unique voice, building upon life experiences and prior knowledge. Instead of relying on rote learning, they encourage students to respond personally and to formulate their own opinions, whether discussing literature or writing.

To be effective with our low-achievers, we need to appeal to their intellectual strengths, not their weaknesses. Often, such learners are global thinkers who enjoy thinking about the whole but find analytic tasks involving details frustrating.

With literature, these students do best when allowed to focus on the "big picture." They should be encouraged to make predictions, draw inferences, explore alternate outcomes, examine practical consequences of decisions, and offer solutions to the problems faced by characters. Regrettably, many classrooms are unknowingly structured to emphasize the weaknesses of these students. For example, true/false and multiple choice tests often penalize them for not remembering details or sequences, which becomes another way of perpetuating failure.

When writing, discouraged learners experience similar difficulty in analytic tasks. Many simply cannot independently create an outline and then use it to structure their writing. They need to investigate topics through open discussions that allow them to explore divergent ideas. They need oral language activities that help them to walk through each stage of the writing process, to rehearse what they want to say before putting pen to paper, to interact with their peers in meaningful, task-driven work.

One thing these students do not need is "easy work." Discouraged learners need to be repeatedly challenged, to be called upon even when they don't raise their hands.

Sometimes, our insistence on excellence will create discomfort for our students, who have spent their academic life trying to escape failure by avoiding work. For those who see themselves as intellectually inaqeduate, who have badly damaged self-esteem, it makes sense to set minimal goals. For example, these students will insist on knowing the minimum page count for a writing assignment. However, we need to change their emphasis from quantity to quality, with comments such as, "I don't know how many words you should write. I want your best effort to describe what you think of that situation in the story." Or, "what do *you* think about the author's conclusion?" Though your students will protest the absence of quantitative guidelines, you need to let them know your priority is quality, which can only be produced by effort.

Perhaps the most serious obstacle to academic achievement can be found in what psychologists call an external locus of control. Discouraged learners do not attribute outcomes—test grades, completed assignments, a teacher's praise—to their own effort. Their excuses for failure, whether inventive or predictable, disguise an important problem: they do not see a relationship between cause and effect in their own lives. They view themselves as victims of chance, convinced that their own efforts have little or no influence on outcomes. In their perspective—a view of the world that requires patience and persistence to change—school achievements are the product of such uncontrollable factors as luck, innate talent, or the teacher's mood.

To be effective with our low-achievers, we need to appeal to their intellectual strengths.

To counteract this self-defeating cycle, teachers should reinforce the idea that the classroom is an arena of cause and effect, not chance. Students need to be told that grades are the result of sustained effort, that work, not ability, is the most important factor in achievement. When discouraged learners do something well, however marginally, we need to help them see the connection to their own effort. Whenever possible, we should point out that their knowledge and skills have increased as a direct result of their own labor. We must do whatever we can to undermine the myth of low achievers that any success they experience is merely the product of luck or an easy assignment. To achieve that goal, it is helpful to remind our students that our classes are structured to progressively increase the level of difficulty, which means that any success can only be attributed to hard work.

A student with an external locus of control needs plenty of instruction in cause-and-effect thinking. Teachers can accomplish a great deal by using literature as a means of addressing this. When talking about a story, ask students to identify the cause of a particular outcome or to explain how a character's actions contributed to the outcome. Ask them to think about the choices that a character faces and to discuss possible outcomes of those choices, both positive and negative. Ask them to evaluate the wisdom of a character's choices, comparing the desired outcome to what actually happens. These are not only questions that provoke intelligent thought; they are questions that students with an external locus of control must come to understand before they can apply them to their own lives.

Finally, we need to remember that a sense of accomplishment and self-esteem does not come from vague praise or rewards too easily learned. Self-esteem is derived from sustained effort in pursuit of meaningful goals; it can only happen when an individual feels personally responsible for the achievement of a desired outcome. Of course, praise is an important instrument for building self-esteem, but our words of praise should be clearly focused, a response to achievements great and small. However hard we try, we cannot give our students self-esteem—they must earn it for themselves.

As you will see, *Literature and Language* serves as an invaluable instructional tool to maximize involvement, to build self-esteem, and to encourage divergent thinking. It is the kind of text that many of us have been waiting for—a book that can make a difference in the lives of our students.

Related Reading

- Conrath, Jerry. *Our Other Youth.* Seattle, 1989. Available from the author.
- Gardner, Howard. *Frames of Mind: The Theory of Multiple Intelligences.* New York: Basic Books, 1985.
- Gould, Stephen Jay. *The Mismeasure of Man.* New York: Norton, 1981.
- Rose, Mike. *Lives on the Boundary: The Struggles and Achievements of America's Underprepared.* New York: Free Press, 1988.
- Sagor, Richard. "Teetering on the Edge of Failure." *Learning* April 1988.
- "Teaching Discouraged Learners." *Instructor* (Secondary Edition) Fall 1988.

In *Literature and Language* . . .

A variety of strategies for reaching discouraged learners are built into this text.

- Prereading activities on the **Explore** pages help students connect literature to their own lives.
- The literature selections are challenging and provocative, yet the open-ended questions will encourage all students to voice their opinions.
- Many questions about the selections are scaffolded, giving students guided help for thoughtful responses.
- "Options for Learning" activities on the **Extend** pages provide an alternative to paper-and-pencil assignments, allowing every student to showcase his or her strengths.
- Students are encouraged to explore divergent ideas and to work cooperatively in the literature lessons and in the **Language, Writer's,** and **Related Skills Workshops.**

Assessment in the Literature Classroom

Historically, the term *assessment* has been almost synonymous with testing and with pencil-and-paper testing in particular. Often, however, this form of evaluation does not ascertain how well students have learned the comprehension, thinking, and problem-solving skills they must be able to carry over to other learning situations.

In recent years, many attempts have been made to extend the concept of assessment to other strategies that may be more reliable in measuring both student growth and mastery of subject matter. They include self-assessment, interactive assessment, and multimodal assessment, as well as other strategies that go beyond the traditional pencil-and-paper methods. (Strategies for the assessment of writing are discussed in a separate essay, "Assessment and Response to Student Writing," on pages T30–T32 of this Teacher's Edition.)

Self-Assessment

One of the most popular, new self-assessment tools is the **portfolio**. Much like the portfolios of artists and writers, assessment portfolios are usually collections of the students' best work. While portfolios are most often used for student writing, the portfolio may also include drawings and illustrations, tape recordings or videotapes of group work, or readings and dramatic presentations. The significant factor is that students have a voice in what goes into the folder. For more about portfolios and developing a portfolio assessment plan see "Assessment and Response to Student Writing," pages T30–T32.

Observation Assessment

Unlike a written test, observation assessment goes beyond asking a question and getting a response; this method allows the questioners/evaluators to follow the students' thinking process. After hearing responses, they can ask students to clarify or justify what they have said, give reasons for their conclusions, or explain why they think as they do.

Through classroom observation, the evaluator can also follow the development of other skills such as the ability to work effectively in peer groups, the willingness to participate in class discussion, the level of preparedness, and the depth of involvement in the subject matter. For example, during classroom discussion teachers can observe how well students interact with their peers. Are they open-minded about accepting alternative answers? Do they raise important issues suggested by the questions? Do they stick to the main point of the discussion, indicating that they recognize what is relevant to it? Using an observation form such as the one included in each Unit Resource Book or a simple checklist that lists four to six criteria, allows the teacher to observe a number of students in one discussion period.

Journals and Logs

Journals and logs can be used in a directed manner as a place where students are asked to comment or report on particular issues. An example would be reader responses on assigned or elective reading. Student comments may be general or may be responses to specific questions.

The teacher would evaluate the responses on the basis of general qualities, such as critical thinking or open-mindedness, and of specific understandings of skills.

Another source of information is the teacher's own journal or log, in which entries may report examples that can be used to assess student growth.

Multimodal Assessment

Recognizing students' learning styles and allowing them the option of demonstrating knowledge through their preferred mode of learning and presentation offers other assessment options. Such students might choose to focus on drama, art, oral reports, dance, music, construction, or a variety of other forms to show their understanding of a work of literature. For further information see "Multimodal Learning," on pages T23–T24.

There is no doubt that teachers will continue to use more traditional testing devices to make their evaluations of students' skills. However, if teachers use these tools in conjunction with other, more innovative, evaluation techniques, they can form a more complete picture of students' skills and progress.

In *Literature and Language* . . .

Possibilities for alternative assessment can be found in all parts of the text.

- **Writer's Workshops** include "Reflecting on Your Writing" questions for self-assessment.
- Portfolio use and journal writing, which are encouraged and supported by the text, offer assessment alternatives.
- Specific guidelines for observation assessment are listed on the first page of each subunit.
- "Options for Learning" activities on **Extend** pages provide opportunities for multimodal assessment.

Assessment and Response to Student Writing

Arthur N. Applebee, Judith A. Langer, Senior Consultants

Traditionally, much of the work in the teaching of writing has occurred in the process of responding to and assessing what students write. Teachers have given students topics to write about, and then have spent a great deal of time marking the papers that result—giving grades, making suggestions for ways the writing could have been improved, and correcting errors.

Such an approach is exhausting for teachers—the paperload quickly becomes overwhelming—and discouraging for students—whose papers "bleed" with the teachers' red pencilling. Such an approach also works against what we know about the writing process. When students write about topics that have substance and depth, we can expect their work to be characterized by growth and change over time. They will try out and abandon ideas. They will reorganize sections. Beginnings and endings will drift out of alignment with the rest of the text and need to be redrafted. During the process of writing, grammar and usage often falter in the rush of new ideas—because the writer's immediate concerns are momentarily (and appropriately) focused more on the generation of ideas and on the growing clarity of the message than on the surface presentation of the paper. This is the "normal" state of affairs among the best of writers and characterizes the *process* of crafting a text. Rather than "errors" to be corrected and deplored, tentativeness and exploration of ideas and the accompanying imprecision of spelling and mechanics need to be accepted and encouraged, as a natural and productive part of the process of exploring new forms and new ideas.

Response vs. Evaluation

For students to engage in this kind of thoughtful exploration, evaluation—judgments about how well the work has been done—needs to be separated from response—reactions to the paper and ideas for further development that come from an interested reader. *Response* is the critical feature in writing instruction; it helps students know what works, what doesn't, and how to go about improving what they have written. The ideal writing environment invites students to engage in exploratory writing and offers response to work-in-process. However, for this to succeed, evaluation and grades must be postponed until later.

Although well-intentioned, evaluation that comes too early and that becomes too much a part of ongoing instruction is inhibiting to students—it shifts their focus from the development of ideas to the way things look. While writing instruction should encourage students to ponder ideas and try out new ways to present them, when they face early judgments, students learn instead not to take risks, not to try new forms, not to draft and redraft, but to concentrate on letter-perfect work that says little and goes nowhere.

Evaluation is, of course, necessary. Report cards demand grades and students want to know how they are doing. But there are a number of ways in which response and evaluation can be managed so they support rather than subvert teaching and learning.

1. *Limit the amount of writing to which you, the teacher, respond.*

   Writers need frequent responses from interested readers, but that does not mean that the teacher needs to read everything that is written. The workshops in the present series are structured to give students responses at many different points, when those responses can be helpful rather than evaluative. Thus students may be asked to share initial brainstorming about a topic, to reflect upon one another's notes and journals, to respond to early drafts, and to help polish a work for final publication. Such activities often work best in pairs or small groups, where everyone can receive some constructive response to their work quickly and directly. At other times the whole class may benefit from sharing ideas or discussing questions that have arisen as they work on their writing.

   Writers need frequent responses from interested readers, but that does not mean that the teacher needs to read everything that is written.

   These early writings, like students' journals or logs, have served their purpose once they have been discussed with an interested reader, or mined for the nuggets that will become parts of later drafts. There is no reason for the teacher to read them, too; indeed, the teacher can become a bottleneck.

2. *Respond to work in progress as a collaborator rather than an evaluator.*

Teachers can, of course, be very helpful while students are working on their drafts. They can show new ways to solve writing problems, suggest other issues to consider, and offer their own responses as readers about what parts are clear, what parts are interesting, and what parts fail to convince. These kinds of responses are instructional in the best sense: the teacher's suggestions about work in progress can become part of the developing writer's repertoire of strategies and models, available for use in other contexts.

It is important to avoid evaluations of work in progress, however. Students should not get the sense that their writing is "wrong" because it still needs work. They need, instead, to learn that it is normal to revise and rework what one has done, particularly when the topics being written about have substance and weight.

3. *Be clear and consistent about criteria for evaluation.*

Even when evaluation is separated from the process of writing, it is important to keep in mind what "counts." In this textbook, the workshops stress writing as a process for exploring ideas and sharing them with others. The conventions of writing are treated as part of this process rather than as the focus of instruction. It is easy, however, for evaluation to provide a different picture of what counts as important. If grading means primarily correcting errors and adding a summative comment about the need for more careful spelling and grammar, the student will quickly learn what "counts" in this classroom, and become more concerned with mechanics than with message.

If grading means primarily correcting errors and adding a summative comment about the need for more careful spelling and grammar, the student will quickly become more concerned with mechanics than with message.

Setting Criteria for Evaluation

In recent years, teachers have developed a number of different ways to formalize their evaluations of student writing. Most of these have been used in the context of large-group assessment, where the concern is with how well students are doing *relative to* one another or to some external criterion. Using such procedures (for example, general impression or holistic scoring, analytic scoring, or primary trait scoring) is generally inappropriate within a classroom when used in a formal sense, but can be extremely helpful when used informally to guide teachers' and students' mutual understandings of the goals of the writing task. While many teachers have begun to use such scoring systems to judge student papers, they are certain to look at many papers over an extended period of time before making overall judgments about students' writing abilities.

We know that evaluations of student performance will vary depending upon how important the evaluator considers each of the following to be: originality, correctness, amount of support provided, handwriting, spelling, word choice, and awareness of genre conventions. Because students are quick to concentrate on what "counts" in a particular classroom, it is important to have clear, consistent standards about what "writing well" will mean in your class. If "writing well" is to mean exploring ideas and experimenting with ways to share them effectively, then students who try to do this should be rewarded with higher grades—even if their experiments lead them to make mistakes. A new and difficult task, completed with some uncertainty, may reflect much more growth in writing achievement than a simple task completed with little thought and no "error."

Writing Portfolios

Writers vary in how well they write from topic to topic and day to day. Again this is normal and natural, but we often forget about it when judging how well a writer writes. To offer a well-grounded evaluation of a student's writing skills, we need to examine a broad sample of that student's work.

Portfolios of student work offer one of the best vehicles for classroom-based assessment, for two reasons: 1) They typically contain a variety of different samples of student work; and 2) they make it easy to separate evaluation from the process of instruction. Evaluation can be based on the diverse samples of work in the portfolio rather than on the day-to-day progress of an individual piece of classroom work.

Portfolios take almost as many forms as there are teachers, and can be tailored to virtually any classroom situation. The major options involve the form that portfolios take, what is included in them, and how they are evaluated.

Form. Portfolios are just a cumulative collection of the work students have done. The most popular forms include: 1) a traditional "writing folder" in which students keep their work, 2) a bound notebook with separate sections kept for work in progress and final drafts, 3) a loose-leaf notebook in which students keep their drafts and revision, 4) a large artist's portfolio, or 5) a published collection of carefully selected and hand-bound work.

Content. Portfolios provide an ideal way to illustrate how a student's work has developed over time, and will give students, parents, administrators, and other teachers a much richer sense of what a child can do than can be conveyed by any list of grades from a gradebook. Portfolios may contain 1) everything a student writes for a particular class, 2) a selection of "best work" representing the diverse kinds of writing that a student has done, 3) a cumulative collection of work that is passed on from grade to grade, 4) a diverse collection of a student's performance including drawings and illustrations, tape recordings or videotapes of group work, and readings or dramatic presentations of the student's writing, 5) drafts and revisions, or 6) a selection of finished work, chosen by the student, the teacher, or the student and teacher working together.

Portfolios will give students, parents, administrators, and other teachers a much richer sense of what a child can do than can be conveyed by any list of grades from a gradebook.

Evaluation. With portfolios, evaluation and grading can be planned to reflect the range of a student's writing skills, across topics and modes of writing. Just as teachers vary in the form and content of the portfolios they ask their students to build, they also vary in how they use portfolios to determine students' grades. Evaluation can be based on 1) everything a student has written, 2) selections chosen by the student or teacher to represent the best work during a grading period, 3) selections chosen to represent each of the types of writing the student has done during a grading period, 4) the student's and teacher's judgments about progress represented in accumulated drafts and revisions, or 5) "best and final" examples of the student's writing.

An approach that many teachers have found to be particularly effective is to base grading on a selection of work from the portfolio—chosen to reflect the range of types of writing that students have done during the grading period. Students can be asked to select the pieces to be graded, making the choice themselves or in conjunction with the teacher.

The ability to choose works to be graded—rather than being graded on everything—can be a powerful motivational device as well. Many teachers give their students the opportunity to work further on the selections they want to have graded. Returning to these writings at a later point, students often recognize for themselves ways to make their writing more effective.

Students can also be encouraged to reflect further upon their own progress as writers by providing an essay summarizing their work as they see it in the portfolio. Like the reflective activities included at the end of most workshops in this textbook, such reflection can help students become aware of and take control over their own growth as writers. Note that the final workshop in this text provides guidelines for a summarizing essay.

Changing to a Workshop Approach

Many teachers who are new to a workshop approach, postponing evaluation rather than interjecting it into the writing process, worry that students want quicker grades. One transitional device that works well in many classrooms is to give points when students have completed each separate part of the work. Everyone who completes a first draft, for example, might get a point, with another for doing a revision. And these points can be totaled across the marking period to become part of the final grade.

If evaluation is separated from instruction, if criteria for evaluation are kept consistent with those stressed during instruction, and if response becomes a responsibility shared with students as well as the teacher, assessment can become an effective complement to the process of learning to write.

In *Literature and Language . . .*

Writing response and assessment is supported in the following ways:

- **Writer's Workshops** encourage peer response during all stages of the writing process.
- Reflection questions at the end of most **Writer's Workshops** help students become aware of their progress and then progress as writers.
- The final **Writer's Workshop** in each text asks students to assess their year as writers and to set future writing goals.
- Portfolio use is encouraged and supported in the student text.
- The **Unit Resource Book** provides student Peer and Self-Evaluation Guidelines and teacher Writing Assessment Guidelines for each workshop.

ORANGE LEVEL

• BLUE LEVEL •

YELLOW LEVEL
American Literature

PURPLE LEVEL
English and World Literature

McDOUGAL, LITTELL LITERATURE AND LANGUAGE

Blue Level

Senior Consultants

Arthur N. Applebee
State University of New York at Albany

Andrea B. Bermudez
University of Houston—Clear Lake

Judith A. Langer
State University of New York at Albany

James Marshall
University of Iowa, Iowa City

Author

Robert S. Boone

McDOUGAL, LITTELL & COMPANY

Evanston, Illinois

New York · Dallas · Sacramento · Columbia, SC

Acknowledgments

Lynne Alvarez: "She Loved Him All Her Life" by Lynne Alvarez. By permission of the author.
American Council for Nationalities Service: "Chee's Daughter" by Juanita Platero and Siyowin Miller, from *Common Ground.* Used by permission of the American Council for Nationalities Service.
Arte Publico Press: "1910," first published in *Chants* by Pat Mora, 1984. "Like Mexicans," first published in *Small Faces* by Gary Soto, 1986. Houston: Arte Publico Press of the University of Houston.
Isaac Asimov: "The Feeling of Power" by Isaac Asimov. Copyright © 1957, Quinn Publishing Co. By permission of the author.
The Atlantic Monthly: "Gaston" by William Saroyan, as originally appeared in *The Atlantic Monthly,* February 1962. Used by permission of *The Atlantic Monthly.*
Brandt & Brandt Literary Agents, Inc.: "A Kind of Murder" by Hugh Pentecost, first published in *Ellery Queen Mystery Magazine.* Copyright © 1962 by Hugh Pentecost, copyright renewal © 1990 by Norma Phillips. "The Most Dangerous Game" by Richard Connell. Copyright 1924 by Richard Connell, copyright renewed 1952 by Louis Fox Connell. "Searching for Summer," from *The Green Flash* by Joan Aiken. Copyright © 1957, 1958, 1959, 1960, 1965, 1968, 1969, 1971 by Joan Aiken. Reprinted by permission of Brandt & Brandt Literary Agents, Inc.
The Helen Brann Agency, Inc.: "All Watched Over by Machines of Loving Grace," from *The Pill Versus the Springhill Mine Disaster* by Richard Brautigan. Copyright © 1968 by Richard Brautigan. Reprinted by permission of The Helen Brann Agency, Inc.
Joseph Bruchac: "Birdfoot's Grampa" by Joseph Bruchac. By permission of the author.
Don Congdon Associates, Inc.: Excerpt from *Dandelion Wine* by Ray Bradbury. Published in *Gourmet,* June 1953. Copyright © 1953, renewed 1981 by Ray Bradbury. Reprinted by permission of Don Congdon Associates, Inc.
Betty Dahlin: "Honor" by Betty Dahlin. Reprinted by permission of the author.
Doubleday & Company: "Red Eagle," from *The Whispering Wind* by Janet Campbell. Copyright © 1972 by The Institute of American Indian Arts. Used by permission of Doubleday, a division of Bantam, Doubleday, Dell Publishing Group, Inc. "The Euphio Question," from *Welcome to the Monkey House* by Kurt Vonnegut, Jr. Copyright 1951 by Kurt Vonnegut, Jr. Used by permission of Delacorte Press/Seymour Lawrence, a division of Bantam, Doubleday, Dell Publishing Group, Inc.
(continued on page 985)

Cover Art: *Midtown Sunset* Romare Bearden Estate of Romare Bearden.

Frontispiece: THRESHOLD 1986 Jeff Low ˊMaquette for an outdoor sculpture By permission of the artist.

ISBN TE : 0-8123-7105-4

Box 1667, Evanston, Illinois 60204

91 92 93 94 95 - VJM - 10 9 8 7 6 5 4 3 2 1

Senior Consultants

The senior consultants guided conceptual development for the *Literature and Language* series. They participated actively in shaping prototype materials for major components, and they reviewed completed units to ensure consistency with current research and the philosophy of the series.

Arthur N. Applebee
Professor of Education, State University of New York at Albany; Director, Center for the Learning and Teaching of Literature

Andrea B. Bermudez
Professor of Multicultural Education; Director, Research Center for Language and Culture; University of Houston—Clear Lake

Judith A. Langer
Professor of Education, State University of New York at Albany; Co-Director, Center for the Learning and Teaching of Literature

James Marshall
Associate Professor of English and Education, University of Iowa, Iowa City

Author

The author of this text participated in the conceptual development of the series and wrote lessons for the literary selections.

Robert S. Boone, Ph.D.
Director of the Glencoe Study Center, Glencoe, Illinois; formerly Teacher, Highland Park High School, Highland Park, Illinois

Consultants

The consultants worked with the senior consultants to establish the theoretical framework for the series. They reviewed completed units and made specific recommendations according to their areas of specialization.

Jerry Conrath
Educational consultant specializing in drop-out prevention and discouraged learners; Adjunct Instructor, Portland State University, Seattle Pacific University, University of Idaho; Director, Our Other Youth conferences

William Sweigart
Assistant Professor of English, Indiana University Southeast, New Albany; formerly Research Associate, Center for the Study of Writing, University of California at Berkeley

Special Contributors

Writer's Workshops

Stephen Kern
English and Humanities Teacher, New Trier Township High School, Winnetka, Illinois

Sherry Medwin
English Teacher, New Trier Township High School, Winnetka, Illinois; Adjunct Instructor, School of Education, Northwestern University, Evanston, Illinois

Design

Design 5
New York, New York

Manuscript Reviewers

The following educators reviewed prototype lessons and tables of contents during the development of the *Literature and Language* program.

Dr. Billy F. Birnie, Curriculum Consultant, University of Miami, Miami, Florida

Walter J. Cmielewski, English Department Chairperson (7–12), Mt. Olive High School, Flanders, New Jersey

Rose Marie Curley, Staff Development Specialist, Brooklyn High School Staff Development Site, Brooklyn, New York

Evelyn Baker Dandy, Ph.D., Professor of Education, Armstrong State College, Savannah, Georgia

Patricia Dose Garrison, English Teacher, Lake Highlands High School, Richardson Independent School District, Dallas, Texas

June Konno, English and Reading Teacher, South San Francisco High School, South San Francisco, California

Dr. Philip W. Loveall, English Chairperson, Maine South High School, Park Ridge, Illinois

Cathey A. Maples, Supervisor, Public Schools of Robeson County, Lumberton, North Carolina

Beth L. Torrison, Teacher, East High School, Madison Metropolitan School, Madison, Wisconsin

Sally J. Tupponce, English Department Chairman, Hackensack High School, Hackensack, New Jersey

Jacqueline Bryant Turner, Director, Language Arts, Dallas Independent School District, Dallas, Texas

John M. Walsh, Assistant Principal, B.N. Cardozo High School, New York City, New York

Roberta Young, Secondary Language Arts Coordinator, Spring Branch Independent School District, Houston, Texas

Field Test Reviewers

The following educators tested *Literature and Language* lessons in their classrooms for the purpose of assessing effectiveness and appropriateness for students and teachers.

Deborah E. Andrews, Southern High School, Durham, North Carolina **Sandra Beland,** North Shore High School, Houston, Texas **Mary G. Carr,** English High School, Jamaica Plain, Massachusetts **Rosanne Craemer,** English High School, Jamaica Plain, Massachusetts **Joseph DeCelles,** English High School, Jamaica Plain, Massachusetts **Elizabeth Dieckman,** Ball High School, Galveston, Texas **Malinda Frame,** Pearland High School, Pearland, Texas **Martin Friedman,** University City High School, Philadelphia, Pennsylvania **Terry Grantham,** Galena Park High School, Galena Park, Texas **Dale Halloran,** English High School, Jamaica Plain, Massachusetts **Helen Krumm,** Sacramento High School, Sacramento, California **Catherine Kurdt,** Lindenhurst Senior High School, Lindenhurst, New York **Ellen MacDonald,** Waltham Senior High School, Waltham, Massachusetts **Daphne Ritchie,** Livingston High School, Livingston, California **Edith Saltzberg,** University City High School, Philadelphia, Pennsylvania **Sharon Showalter,** Schlagle High School, Kansas City, Kansas **Dolores Wilson,** New Hyde Park Memorial High School, New Hyde Park, New York

Student Board

The student board members read and evaluated selections to assess their appeal for tenth-grade students.

Louis Haywood, West Philadelphia University City High School, Philadelphia, Pennsylvania **Tia Redo,** Stevenson High School, Prairie View, Illinois **Ivelisse Ruiz,** Clemente Community Academy High School, Chicago, Illinois **Mike Scioli,** Radnor High School, Radnor, Pennsylvania **Sarah Smith,** Lake Highlands High School, Dallas, Texas

Staff Credits

Julie A. Schumacher, Executive Editor
Diane Carlson, Senior Editor
William L. McBride, Ph.D., Editor

Barbara Dougan, Copy Editor
Sandra Linabury, Copy Editor
Linda Williams, Copy Editor

Robert C. St. Clair, Manager of Production
Gloria Muczynski, Production Editor

Craig Jobson, Art Director
Mary MacDonald, Senior Designer
Carmine Fantasia, Picture Editor

Contents

A The *Strategies for Reading* feature models a student's reading experience and increases student awareness of the reading process.

B Literary selections are organized in thematic units chosen for their relevancy to students' lives.

C Units are divided into subunits, each containing a variety of literary genre—fiction, nonfiction, poetry, and drama.

D The *Elements of Fiction, Nonfiction, Poetry,* and *Drama* provide an overview of the literary elements characteristic of each genre.

E Literary selections are preceded by an *Explore* page which activates prior knowledge, gives pertinent background information, and provides either instruction in a relevant reading skill or a journal writing idea.

F *Literature and Language* contains familiar stories as well as selections not previously anthologized, such as this absorbing tale of cultural misunderstanding in Equador.

G Writing, language, and related skills workshops are integrated with the preceding literary selections and provide step-by-step instruction in the writing process, grammar and language, and other important skills.

Unit Two

H Poems by Walt Whitman and Edna St. Vincent Millay add contrast and perspective to other, more contemporary selections.

I Each selection is followed by one or two *Explain* pages that challenge students to develop their personal and critical responses to the literature.

J The *Extend* page that follows most selections provides activities that allow students to demonstrate their understanding of a selection in a variety of learning styles and content areas.

K Because students especially enjoy drama, five complete plays are included. This assures thorough coverage of the dramatic mode and ample opportunities for speaking and listening activities.

3 BEATING THE ODDS 267

Unit Three

CHALLENGES: WINNERS AND LOSERS 324

L Gripping accounts, such as this autobiographical excerpt by Christy Brown, give students insight into the difficulties that people with major handicaps face.

M Most poems are studied in pairs. The study apparatus uses comparison and contrast to help students come to a deeper understanding of each poem.

N Many stories center on adolescent protagonists who are dealing with issues relevant to high school students such as competition, family interactions, and peer relationships.

O Familiar stories such as "The Most Dangerous Game" were chosen for the richness of their themes and the proven appeal of their characters and plots.

P *Insights,* short literary works that follow a main selection, reflect on and highlight the themes of a preceding selection.

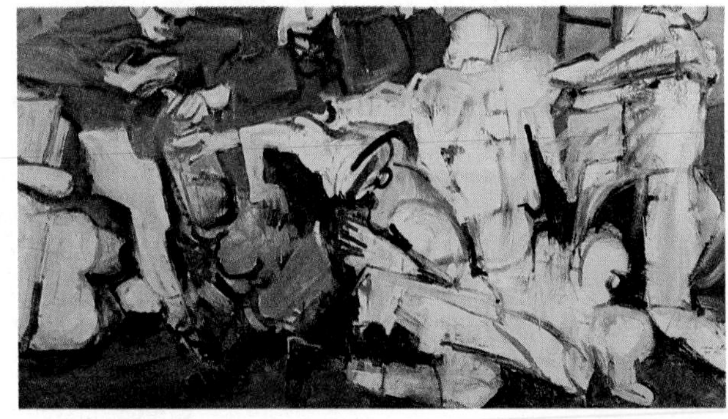

Unit Four

HUMAN RIGHTS: PAIN AND PRIDE 452

Q Selections about human rights include the experiences of people from many ethnic and social backgrounds.

R Autobiographies by such authors as Richard Wright and Yoshiko Uchida provide students with excellent writing models as well as inspiring stories of personal achievement.

S *Language Workshops* teach skills that directly relate to the *Writer's Workshop* assignment.

T The third workshops cover essential skills related to the other workshops. Subject matter includes speaking and listening, life skills, vocabulary, and study skills.

U *Unit Five*

THE FUTURE: HOPES AND FEARS 600

U The fine art found throughout the book and featured in Unit Openers exposes students to master artists. Students are led to explore possible connections between the subject matter of the art and the literary selections.

V Selections concerning the future of our environment provide students with timely issues for exploration and discussion.

W A special feature of this text is the inclusion of a selection written by a tenth-grade student, Andrew Holleman, describing his efforts to save the environment. Such a work provides an excellent student model for both academic and social achievement.

X Works by contemporary journalists such as Ellen Goodman and Dave Barry appeal to students' sense of humor while at the same time examining important social issues.

Unit Six

THE CLASSIC TRADITION 726

The unadapted, unabridged version here is the Folger Edition of Shakespeare's timeless story of power and ambition. Extensive sidenotes remove potential barriers to student understanding, enjoyment, and appreciation.

Handbook Section

AA An extensive, easy-to-use handbook section provides students with resources, reference, and practice.

Organization of Selections by Genre

FICTION

POETRY

NONFICTION

DRAMA

Literature and Language and You

Use this feature to acquaint students with their books. Since the philosophy and structure of the program are so appealing and nonthreatening, you may want to use it on the first day of class as a motivation tool.

Point out that this text is more a collaborative effort between the students and literature than a set of readings and assignments with right and wrong answers. Emphasize that students' personal experiences and their willingness to read good literature are the most important qualities they can bring to the selections as they begin this book.

Objectives

- To learn about oneself as a reader who brings unique and personal knowledge to the study of literature
- To become familiar with the content and structure of the text

Teaching Strategies

Introduction

Have students read the introduction. Then ask them to write a list of the qualities, likes, and dislikes that make each of them unique. Use examples from volunteers to write two or three short lists on the chalkboard. Next, discuss how the interests and strengths of each person will make his or her approach to the text different from everyone else's.

To illustrate the varied points of view that people bring to reading, ask students how they might react to the idea of reading a story about each of the following topics. Would they be curious, bored, interested, or pleased? Then ask them why they would feel that way. Have they already had experience with the topic? Does this make them more or less interested in reading?

- mystery and suspense
- prejudice
- sports
- getting along with family and friends
- romance

John Martin, Toronto, Canada.

LITERATURE AND LANGUAGE AND YOU

The book you are holding is unlike any textbook you have ever used. It is based on a unique philosophy—that what you bring to this book is just as important as what the book brings to you. This means that your own experiences become the basis for your involvement with the literature and activities. The special features in ***Literature and Language*** promote this relationship between you and the text.

Great Literature
Have students read this section on page 4 and find page vi in the front of the book that shows the *Student Board*. Explain that these students helped choose selections for the book. Then discuss their reading habits and preferences by asking the following questions:

1. What is the most recent book that you've read on your own and enjoyed?

2. Why did you choose it?

3. What kinds of books and magazines do you enjoy most?

4. What do you dislike most about reading?

5. What kind of help do you think a literature text should give you?

Important Themes
After students read this section, have them turn to the Table of Contents and page through it to note the themes around which their text is organized. Ask the following questions:

1. What units, themes, and/or subthemes can you relate to?

2. Which do you find most interesting? Why?

3. How is this book different from other literature texts that you have used?

4. Is there anything about the content of the book that surprises you?

Point out that each unit of *Literature and Language*, Grade 10, includes a mixture of genres and selections from several eras and countries.

Respect for Your Experiences
Have students turn to the *Explore* page for "Rules of the Game," page 366. Have students note the three subheads and skim the material under the first one, *Examine What You Know*. Ask the following questions:

1. What kinds of skills are usually needed in games?

2. What life principles other than planning or placing the good of the group before one's own might be helpful in games?

3. What life principles would be helpful in living one's life?

4. In general, why would it be important to recall what you already know about a subject before reading about it?

Information and Strategies for Learning

Have students skim the *Expand Your Knowledge* and *Enrich Your Reading* sections of the same *Explore* page. Have them read the title of the story and ask how the background information in *Expand Your Knowledge* might be useful. Point out that every selection will include background information on the *Explore* page. Then ask these questions about *Enrich Your Reading:*

1. How does the reading strategy presented here prepare you for the conflict that you will encounter in the story?

2. How might this strategy help you in other subjects that you study, such as science or mathematics?

Practical Vocabulary Study

Let students know that it is not necessary for them to know every word in the selection in order to understand the piece. However, expanding their vocabulary will make their reading more enjoyable as well as improve their writing and speaking skills. For this reason, certain words that will be useful for students to know and use in other situations have been chosen from the text. Since these are also words necessary for a deeper understanding of the selection, they have been boxed and defined on the page. Point out that the boxed words appear again in a practice exercise at the end of the lesson.

Obscure words and terms, allusions, and geographical and historical references have been footnoted. Again, use the footnotes on page 369 as an example. Be sure that students understand the difference in both format and purpose between the footnotes and the *Words to Know and Use.*

A Personal Response

Have students read the section silently. By now, the class should have some idea of the content and structure of a typical lesson. However, it is on the *Explain* pages that *Literature and Language* truly surpasses other literature texts.

Have students turn to the first *Explain* page for "Rules of the Game," page 377, and to read the subtitles. Then ask them these questions:

1. Is there a right or wrong answer for the first question?

2. Why do you think the first section is called *First Impressions?*

Great Literature The selections in this book represent some of the finest examples of unadapted traditional and contemporary literature. There are classics that have been read and enjoyed again and again, as well as exciting pieces that have never before appeared in a literature textbook. What you read will challenge your ways of thinking, illustrate the cultural and ethnic variety of your world, and relate to experiences in your own life. If you look at the acknowledgments in the front of the book, you will see that students just like you were involved in choosing these selections.

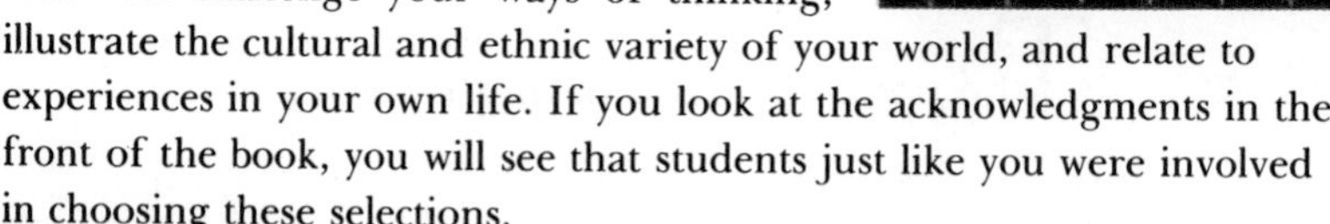

Important Themes ***Literature and Language*** is organized by unit themes chosen for their relevance to your life. Take a moment to preview the unit titles listed in the Contents. You will find six major themes on subjects such as decisions, escapes, challenges, human rights, the future, and judgments. To narrow the focus of these broad themes, the first five units are divided into three subunits. For example, the broad theme of **The Future: Hopes and Fears** is subdivided into **Saving the Environment, The Price of Technology,** and **In Whose Hands?** Because authors write about such topics in various genres, or forms, you will find a mix of fiction, nonfiction, poetry, and drama within these pages.

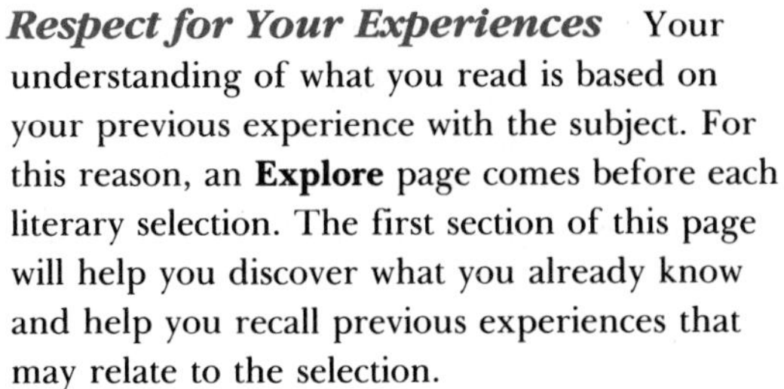

Respect for Your Experiences Your understanding of what you read is based on your previous experience with the subject. For this reason, an **Explore** page comes before each literary selection. The first section of this page will help you discover what you already know and help you recall previous experiences that may relate to the selection.

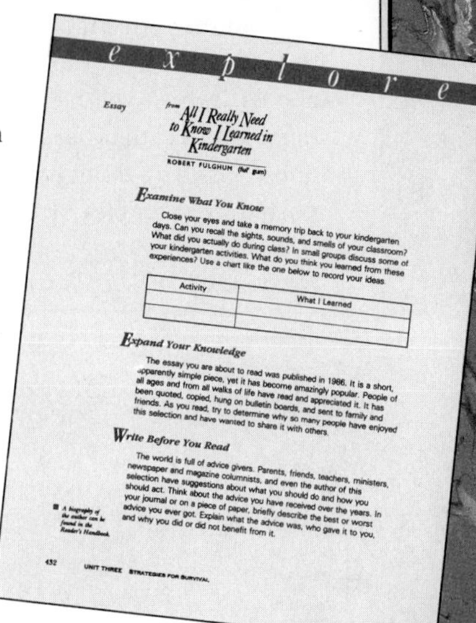

explore

Essay

from *All I Really Need to Know I Learned in Kindergarten*

ROBERT FULGHUM (fŭl' gəm)

Examine What You Know

Close your eyes and take a memory trip back to your kindergarten days. Can you recall the sights, sounds, and smells of your classroom? What did you actually do during class? In small groups discuss some of your kindergarten activities. What do you think you learned from these experiences? Use a chart like the one below to record your ideas.

Activity	What I Learned

Expand Your Knowledge

The essay you are about to read was published in 1986. It is a short, apparently simple piece, yet it has become amazingly popular. People of all ages and from all walks of life have read and appreciated it. It has been quoted, copied, hung on bulletin boards, and sent to family and friends. As you read, try to determine why so many people have enjoyed this selection and have wanted to share it with others.

Write Before You Read

The world is full of advice givers. Parents, friends, teachers, ministers, newspaper and magazine columnists, and even the author of this selection have suggestions about what you should do and how you should act. Think about the advice you have received over the years. In your journal or on a piece of paper, briefly describe the best or worst advice you ever got. Explain what the advice was, who gave it to you, and why you did or did not benefit from it.

A biography of the author can be found in the Reader's Handbook.

432 UNIT THREE STRATEGIES FOR SURVIVAL

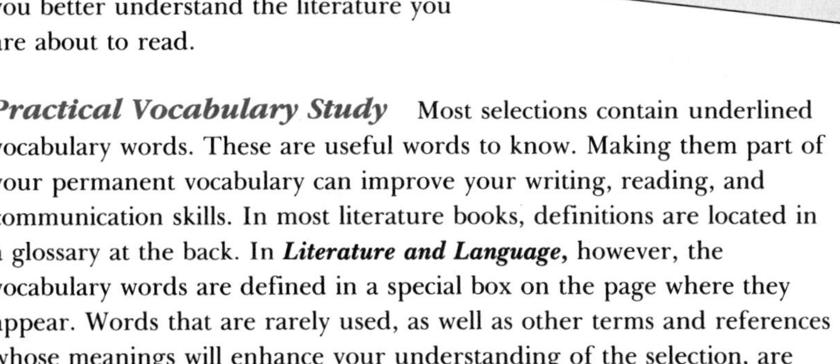

Information and Strategies for Learning The second section of the **Explore** page contains important background information about the literary selection. At the bottom of the page you will find a third section, which provides a specific reading or writing activity to help you better understand the literature you are about to read.

Practical Vocabulary Study Most selections contain underlined vocabulary words. These are useful words to know. Making them part of your permanent vocabulary can improve your writing, reading, and communication skills. In most literature books, definitions are located in a glossary at the back. In ***Literature and Language,*** however, the vocabulary words are defined in a special box on the page where they appear. Words that are rarely used, as well as other terms and references whose meanings will enhance your understanding of the selection, are footnoted and defined separately.

A Personal Response Unlike other literature texts that ask you unimportant questions about minor details in a piece of literature, ***Literature and Language*** focuses on your unique personal response to what you have read. An **Explain** page provides the framework for this response. The first question on the page always asks for your immediate impression after you finish reading. The remaining questions allow you

3. Why might the larger section be called *Second Thoughts*?

4. How is the section called *Broader Connections* different from each of the other sections?

Be sure students understand that the questions are meant to elicit *their* responses, based on the personal experiences *they* bring to the literature. There are no "right" and "wrong" answers, and no one, not even a teacher, can decide what a selection means to someone else. Assure the class that it is not a problem if they dislike a selection. All they must do is give their reasons based on the material in the text.

As students study the page, point out the *Think About*'s in Questions 2 and 3, and explain that such prompts are meant to help them focus their thoughts. As an example, have students read Question 2 and the *Think About* items that follow it. Ask how these points might aid them in arriving at an answer to the question. As an extra incentive, tell students that as they become accustomed to the kinds of focus points suggested in such *Think About*'s, they will subconsciously be learning how to structure their responses to questions in other subjects. Be sure students realize that the *Broader Connections* questions are formulated to connect the selection ideas and themes to real-life situations.

Respect for the Way You Learn

After students have read this section, ask them to think about their various styles of learning. Tell them that you will give them some survey statements to help them analyze the way they learn and the way in which they best express themselves. Students are to use their journals to record both the questions and their answers. Then dictate the following statements aloud, giving students time to write in between each one.

1. I usually read textbook pages (a) rather quickly, (b) slowly and carefully.

2. I usually find it (a) easy, (b) difficult to understand a paragraph after the first reading.

3. When I read a difficult passage, I usually (a) read the passage again, (b) take notes, (c) ask questions, (d) skip over it.

4. If the teacher makes a point I want to remember, I (a) take notes, (b) listen more carefully, (c) repeat it to myself, (d) discuss it.

5. I usually learn more from (a) a class discussion, (b) the textbook.

6. During a class discussion, I usually (a) speak freely, (b) keep my opinions to myself.

7. When I am asked for my opinion, I usually (a) find it difficult to express it, (b) make a suitable response.

8. Writing a clear and logical answer to a question is usually (a) difficult, (b) easy for me.

9. I prefer to express my reactions by (a) acting them out, (b) talking about them, (c) drawing something, (d) writing something.

10. I usually have (a) similar, (b) different ways of learning for each of my classes.

After the survey, have students turn to the *Extend* page for "Rules of the Game," page 379. Have them look over the activities listed in *Options for Learning* and ask volunteers which one they would probably choose. Then have students reread their survey statements to see whether their choice of activity is consistent with the responses that they gave.

Integration of Literature and Language

Tell students that the last part of each subunit includes a series of workshops designed to help them with their writing, language, and other related skills. As an example, have them turn to the Writer's Workshop for the subunit of which "Rules of the Game" is a part, page 401. Have them read the Guided Assignment then point out the PASSkey graphic, which spells out its purpose, audience, subject, and structure.

Have students recall that this subunit is entitled *Who Wins?*. Ask them how an essay analyzing the theme of a selection might be appropriate in a group of selections about winning and losing. *(It may make the connection between playing a game and playing out the game of one's life.)* Be sure they understand that there is always a connection between the themes and selections in the subunit and the workshops that follow it.

to build on your initial reactions and to explore the larger issues and themes covered in the selection. Some questions are supported by "think abouts," which will help you focus your answers. It is important to understand that there are never "right" or "wrong" answers to these questions. Any thoughtful response is acceptable as long as it can be supported by examples or evidence from the text.

Respect for the Way You Learn Each person has a "best" way of learning and of demonstrating what he or she has learned. Perhaps your strength is in reading and writing. Maybe you learn best by listening and discussing. Do you express yourself best by drawing, acting, building something, or giving an oral presentation? An **Extend** page, occurring at the end of many of the literature selections, will tap your unique learning and communicating styles. This page contains Options for Learning activities that offer a variety of exciting ways to show what you have learned.

Integration of Literature and Language The authors, editors, and educators who developed this textbook believe that the various parts of an English program should be related to each other, or **integrated.** Therefore, literature, writing, and grammar are combined in this one book. What you read is used as a basis for related writing and language activities. Each subunit is followed by a **Writer's Workshop,** a **Language Workshop,** and a third workshop that varies in content.

The **Writer's Workshop** presents a guided writing assignment that is linked to the ideas and themes of the literature in a particular subunit. This assignment stresses that you work with your classmates as a community of writers in developing writing ideas and revising your work. In addition, each assignment comes with a PASSkey that provides a framework for your writing.

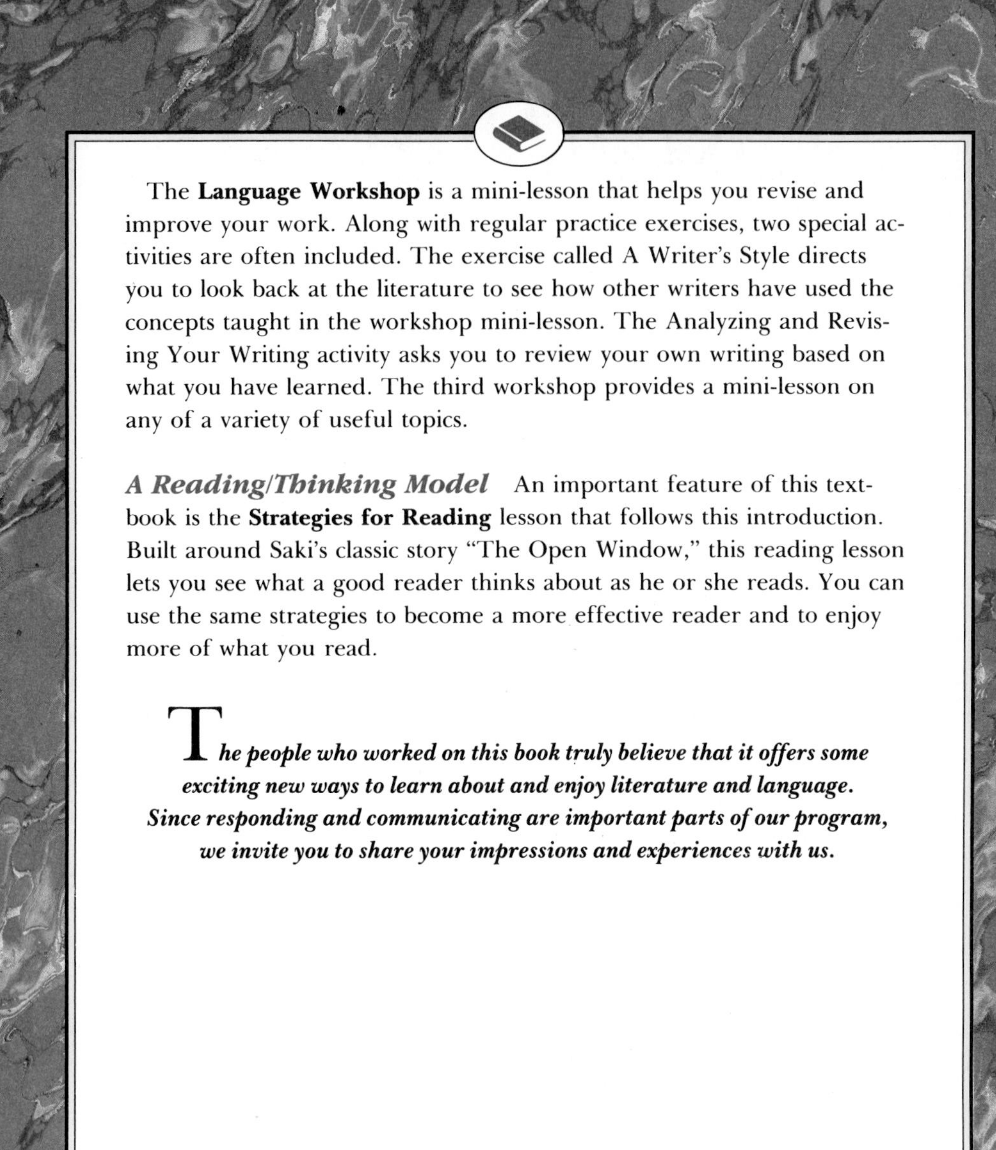

The **Language Workshop** is a mini-lesson that helps you revise and improve your work. Along with regular practice exercises, two special activities are often included. The exercise called A Writer's Style directs you to look back at the literature to see how other writers have used the concepts taught in the workshop mini-lesson. The Analyzing and Revising Your Writing activity asks you to review your own writing based on what you have learned. The third workshop provides a mini-lesson on any of a variety of useful topics.

A Reading/Thinking Model An important feature of this textbook is the **Strategies for Reading** lesson that follows this introduction. Built around Saki's classic story "The Open Window," this reading lesson lets you see what a good reader thinks about as he or she reads. You can use the same strategies to become a more effective reader and to enjoy more of what you read.

The people who worked on this book truly believe that it offers some exciting new ways to learn about and enjoy literature and language. Since responding and communicating are important parts of our program, we invite you to share your impressions and experiences with us.

To illustrate this point further, have the class turn to the **Language Workshop** for the subunit, page 405, and note its subject, *clarity derived from subject-verb agreement.* Point out that when writing about the theme of a selection, which is the genre selected for the **Writer's Workshop,** one's ideas must be clearly expressed or the reader might not understand how they relate to theme. Finally, have students note the topic of the **Vocabulary Workshop** on page 407. Help them to make the connection between the importance of critical listening and Waverly Jong's early lessons in chess.

You may also wish to point out the **Handbook** section at the back of the text and have students skim its parts. Point out that the information there will probably be useful as they work through their writing and language assignments.

A Reading/Thinking Model

Finally, have students turn to the model selection on page 9 of the text, Saki's "The Open Window." Explain that the student reader's responses to each part of the story may help them in shaping their own.

Writing to the Publisher

As the year progresses, encourage students to write to the publisher about their responses to the text. Typical responses may be in the following areas: (a) what they liked/didn't like about the text in general; (b) how they felt about one particular unit/subunit/selection/workshop; (c) responses to the artwork used throughout the text or in a particular selection; (d) changes that they think would make the program better; (e) how this program compares to others that they've used.

Whenever students write a letter of response, remind them to include the following information: their name, date, school, and grade level; the title and level of their text; and the page numbers of the selections to which they've referred.

Editors, Language Arts
McDougal, Littell & Company
Box 1667
Evanston, Illinois 60204

The writers and editors of *Literature and Language* wish you a happy and successful school year!

Strategies for Reading

Research has shown that effective reading is an active process. The strategies explained on this page will help guide students to become competent, involved readers.

Objectives

- To become accustomed to actively reading through questioning, connecting, predicting, clarifying, and evaluating
- To understand the link between thinking and reading
- To compare and contrast the model strategy to one's own methods of reading

Motivation

Ask students to brainstorm a list of the kinds of writing that they find difficult to read and those that they find easy. After students complete their lists, have volunteers read their lists. Then ask students to describe any strategies for getting through the difficult material. Write these on the chalkboard and have students copy them. Guide students to see that reading actively by using these strategies and others can make their reading experience more satisfying. As students read, have them check off on their lists the strategies that they are using.

Strategies for READING

Reading is like most things in life—the more you put into it, the more you get out of it. You may wonder, however, how one "puts" anything into reading. Readers get involved in their reading by performing certain mental tasks as they read. They don't just try to understand the words they see on the page; they also connect these words to their own experiences, question what doesn't seem to make sense, and predict what might come next. In these ways readers become actively involved in the reading process.

The following list of skills describes the thought processes of active readers. As you read this list, ask yourself how many of these thought processes you go through when reading.

- **Questioning:** When a word, statement, or action is unclear, question it. It may become clear later.
- **Connecting:** Make connections with people, places, and things you know.
- **Predicting:** Try to figure out what will happen.
- **Clarifying:** Watch for answers to questions you had earlier.
- **Evaluating:** Respond to what you have read. Draw your own conclusions about characters, actions, and the whole story.

The reader's notes with the story that begins on the next page provide a model of how these reading skills apply to a particular text. These notes will show you how one student got involved in the reading process. Though the connections this reader makes with the story are different from yours or anyone else's, they will help you see how a person's experiences also add to the understanding of what he or she reads.

The Open Window

SAKI

"My aunt will be down presently, Mr. Nuttel," said a very self-possessed young lady of fifteen; "in the meantime you must try and put up with me."

Framton Nuttel endeavored to say the correct something that should duly flatter the niece of the moment without unduly discounting the aunt that was to come. Privately he doubted more than ever whether these formal visits on a succession of total strangers would do much toward helping the nerve cure which he was supposed to be undergoing.

"I know how it will be," his sister had said when he was preparing to migrate to this rural retreat; "you will bury yourself down there and not speak to a living soul, and your nerves will be worse than ever from moping. I shall just give you letters of introduction to all the people I know there. Some of them, as far as I can remember, were quite nice."

Framton wondered whether Mrs. Sappleton, the lady to whom he was presenting one of the letters of introduction, came into the nice division.

"Do you know many of the people round here?" asked the niece, when she judged that they had had sufficient silent communion.

"Hardly a soul," said Framton. "My sister was staying here, at the rectory,[1] you know, some four years ago, and she gave me letters of introduction to some of the people here."

He made the last statement in a tone of distinct regret.

"Then you know practically nothing about my aunt?" pursued the self-possessed young lady.

"Only her name and address," admitted the caller. He was wondering whether Mrs. Sappleton was in the married or widowed state. An undefinable something about the room seemed to suggest masculine habitation.

1. **rectory** (rek′ tər ē): the house in which a priest or rector (pastor) of a parish lives.

➢ "The Open Window" Well, this story might be about a robbery, or maybe somebody catches a cold. ***(Predicting)***

➢ That's a strange name. It looks like a foreign name I've seen, or maybe it's a pen name like Mark Twain. ***(Connecting)***

➢ "endeavored" I'm not sure what that word means. It must mean "to try" since he wants to flatter her. ***(Clarifying)***

➢ Obviously this guy is not from around here, or he just moved here, since the niece is asking if he knows anyone. ***(Clarifying)***

➢ What's a "rectory"? Oh . . . there's a footnote. ***(Questioning)***

Teaching Strategies

1. To explain the active reading process introduced in "The Open Window," first discuss each of the terms on page 8.

2. Next, have students cover the selection annotations with a piece of paper and read the story through, writing in their own comments as they read. Emphasize that there is no "right" answer, for all readers have their own individual responses. Circulate around the classroom to make sure that students understand the process.

3. When students have finished reading and annotating, have them compare their comments, first to those of the reader modeled in the text, and then to those of other students. Students can also work together to compare comments. Use the variety of responses to emphasize the philosophy of active reading and that of this text—that students' own experiences become the basis of their involvement with literature.

4. Encourage students to continue using these strategies as they read further in the text. Tell them that even though active reading may seem awkward at first, it will soon become natural.

5. Point out that some selections, such as "A Kind of Murder," pages 37 to 43, have questions inserted in the text.

"Her great tragedy happened just three years ago," said the child; "that would be since your sister's time."

> ➢ Something bad has happened. Maybe a death in the family. ***(Predicting)***

"Her tragedy?" asked Framton; somehow in this restful country spot tragedies seemed out of place.

"You may wonder why we keep that window wide open on an October afternoon," said the niece, indicating a large French window[2] that opened on to a lawn.

> ➢ Well, there's where the title comes from. ***(Clarifying)***

"It is quite warm for the time of the year," said Framton; "but has that window got anything to do with the tragedy?"

"Out through that window, three years ago to a day, her husband and her two young brothers went off for their day's shooting. They never came back. In crossing the moor[3] to their favorite snipe-shooting ground they were all three engulfed by a treacherous piece of bog. It had been that dreadful wet summer, you know, and places that were safe in other years gave way suddenly without warning. Their bodies were never recovered. That was the dreadful part of it." Here the child's voice lost its self-possessed note and became falteringly human. "Poor aunt always thinks that they will come back some day, they and the little brown spaniel that was lost with them, and walk in that window just as they used to do. That is why the window is kept open every evening till it is quite dusk. Poor dear aunt, she has often told me how they went out, her husband with his white waterproof coat over his arm, and Ronnie, her youngest brother, singing 'Bertie, why do you bound?' as he always did to tease her, because she said it got on her nerves. Do you know, sometimes on still, quiet evenings like this, I almost get a creepy feeling that they will all walk in through that window—"

> ➢ Reminds me of my uncle who goes hunting. ***(Connecting)***
>
> ➢ "Their bodies were never recovered." I wonder if they'll find them now? ***(Questioning)*** Or maybe they never died. ***(Predicting)***
>
> ➢ Yep, the aunt wonders if they're going to be found too. ***(Clarifying)***
>
> ➢ These must be words to a song. ***(Clarifying)***
>
> ➢ She says she gets a creepy feeling. I bet something weird is going to happen. ***(Predicting)***

She broke off with a little shudder. It was a relief to Framton when the aunt bustled into the room with a whirl of apologies for being late in making her appearance.

"I hope Vera has been amusing you?" she said.

"She has been very interesting," said Framton.

---

2. **French window:** a tall window, usually extending to the floor, with hinges on the side.

3. **moor** (mo͝or): an open tract of land, often marshy or covered in heather.

FRENCH DOORS 1985 Harvey Gordon Fischbach Gallery, New York.

Art Note

Harvey Gordon (1941–) obtained a degree in fine arts from Cranbrook Academy of Art and a master's degree from the University of North Carolina, Greensboro. Since 1980, he has painted with acrylics on plexiglass. This method is called acrylic on acrylic. Gordon's still lifes and interior scenes sometimes contain one cryptic element. *What, if anything, do you find puzzling or odd in this picture?*

"I hope you don't mind the open window," said Mrs. Sappleton briskly; "my husband and brothers will be home directly from shooting, and they always come in this way. They've been out for snipe in the marshes to-day, so they'll make a fine mess over my poor carpets. So like you menfolk, isn't it?"

➢ Obviously the aunt can't accept that they are dead because she expects them to walk through the window. ***(Clarifying)***

She rattled on cheerfully about the shooting and the scarcity of birds, and the prospects for duck in the winter. To Framton it was all purely horrible. He made a desperate but only partially successful effort to turn the talk on to a less ghastly topic; he was conscious that his hostess was giving him only a fragment of her attention, and her eyes were constantly straying past him to the open window and the lawn beyond. It was certainly an unfortunate coincidence that he should have paid his visit on this tragic anniversary.

➢ That means she keeps looking out and hoping that they will come back. ***(Clarifying)***

➢ Maybe the aunt only does this on the anniversary of the tragedy? ***(Questioning)***

"The doctors agree in ordering me complete rest, an absence of mental excitement, and avoidance of anything in the nature of violent physical exercise," announced Framton, who labored under the tolerably widespread delusion that total strangers and chance acquaintances are hungry for the least detail of one's ailments and infirmities, their cause and cure. "On the matter of diet they are not so much in agreement," he continued.

"No?" said Mrs. Sappleton, in a voice which only replaced a yawn at the last moment. Then she suddenly brightened into alert attention—but not to what Framton was saying.

➢ I kind of like that statement, "No? . . . which only replaced a yawn . . ." She's like me, she yawns when she's bored. ***(Connecting)***

"Here they are at last!" she cried. "Just in time for tea, and don't they look as if they were muddy up to the eyes!"

➢ "Here they are at last!" What does she see? ***(Questioning)***

Framton shivered slightly, and turned toward the niece with a look intended to convey sympathetic comprehension. The child was staring out through the open window with dazed horror in her eyes. In a chill shock of nameless fear Framton swung round in his seat and looked in the same direction.

In the deepening twilight three figures were walking across the lawn toward the window; they all carried guns under their arms, and one of them was addi-

➢ It must be the three dead guys. ***(Predicting)***

tionally burdened with a white coat hung over his shoulders. A tired brown spaniel kept close at their heels. Noiselessly they neared the house, and then a hoarse young voice chanted out of the dusk:

"I said, Bertie, why do you bound?"

Framton grabbed wildly at his stick and hat; the hall door, the gravel drive, and the front gate were dimly noted stages in his headlong retreat. A cyclist coming along the road had to run into the hedge to avoid imminent collision.

"Here we are, my dear," said the bearer of the white mackintosh, coming in through the window; "fairly muddy, but most of it's dry. Who was that who bolted out as we came up?"

"A most extraordinary man, a Mr. Nuttle," said Mrs. Sappleton; "could only talk about his illnesses, and dashed off without a word of goodbye or apology when you arrived. One would think he had seen a ghost."

"I expect it was the spaniel," said the niece calmly; "he told me he had a horror of dogs. He was once hunted into a cemetery somewhere on the banks of the Ganges[4] by a pack of pariah dogs, and had to spend the night in a newly dug grave with the creatures snarling and grinning and foaming just above him. Enough to make anyone lose his nerve."

Romance at short notice was her specialty. ❧

4. **the Ganges** (gan′ jēz): a river in northern India.

➢ It is, cause they're singing that song. ***(Clarifying)***

➢ It says the cyclist almost runs into the three men. That doesn't seem to make sense. I need to reread that. Oh, I get it. Framton was in "headlong retreat," which means he's the one running. He's the one who almost runs into the cyclist. ***(Clarifying)***

➢ Wait a minute. He didn't say anything about dogs. ***(Questioning)***

➢ Ah, now I see. This last part is all a lie. The niece made the whole thing up. ***(Clarifying)***

➢ Boy, that girl is either mean or one of those compulsive liars. Frampton really fell for her story, but then he was already a mess when he got there. He was kind of an easy target. Good story. It even fooled me. ***(Evaluating)***

Unit One *Decisions: Action or Apathy*

Objectives

Students will develop skills in the following areas. An asterisk (*) indicates a workshop topic.

Reading and Thinking

contrasting *pp. 19, 130*
identifying cause and effect *p. 36*
visualizing *p. 63*
setting purposes for reading *p. 94*
understanding key words *p. 105*
predicting *pp. 122, 124, 126*
understanding dialect *p. 144*
*skimming and scanning *p. 171*

Vocabulary and Related Skills

*working in pairs and small groups *p. 61*
*analogies *p. 79*
synonyms *pp. 92, 128*
antonyms *pp. 92, 128*
using words in context *pp. 103, 162*
*levels of language *p. 120*

Literary Appreciation

elements of fiction *pp. 17–18*
elements of nonfiction *pp. 28–29*
point of view *p. 35*
characterization *p. 44*
elements of poetry *pp. 47–48*
rhyme scheme *p. 52*
suspense *p. 79*
mood *p. 91*
irony *p. 102*
autobiography *p. 111*
internal dialogue *p. 127*
external conflict *p. 139*
internal conflict *p. 139*
elements of drama *pp. 142–43*
foreshadowing *p. 161*

Writing

dialogue *pp. 27, 52, 92*
poem *p. 27*
newspaper column *p. 35*
diary entry *p. 45*
speech *pp. 45, 140*
newspaper article *p. 45*
*first-person narrative: memoir *pp. 54–57*
eulogy *p. 79*
letter *pp. 92, 128*
crime report *p. 103*
editorial *p. 112*
*first-person narrative: reflective essay *pp. 114–17*
*audience and purpose *pp. 118–19*
newspaper headline *p. 140*
*description: character portrait *pp. 164–67*

Language, Grammar, Usage, Mechanics

*common punctuation errors *pp. 58–60*
*using vivid modifiers *pp. 168–70*

Planning the Unit

You may find the following information and lists of resources helpful in preparing for the unit.

Difficulty Level of Selections

In determining the accessibility of the selections in this unit, many factors, including reading level and comprehension difficulty, have been taken into account. The ranking can be used as a general guide in determining how much preparation and assistance students will require in order to master the selection. No selection should be included or eliminated from the course based merely on difficulty level. Basic students will derive a great deal of confidence and self-esteem by working through a *challenge* selection; conversely, advanced students may find pleasure, relevance, and important themes in a selection that is rated *easy*.

The Fan Club *p. 19*	**easy**
Like Mexicans *p. 30*	**average**
A Kind of Murder *p. 36*	**average**
The Road Not Taken *p. 49*	**challenge**
Choices *p. 51*	**challenge**
Dandelion Wine *p. 63*	**average**
Marigolds *p. 81*	**challenge**
Honor *p. 94*	**average**
My Shirt Is for Church *p. 105*	**average**
Lather and Nothing Else *p. 122*	**average**
Tsali of the Cherokees *p. 130*	**average**
The Monkey's Paw *p. 144*	**average**

Classroom Resources

Videocassettes, Films, and Filmstrips

■ ***The Afterglow: A Tribute to Robert Frost***, 16mm film, video, Pyramid, 1989, (35 minutes). Burgess Meredith speaks the words of Frost as he visits the countryside surrounding Frost's cabin.

■ ***All Summer in a Day***, 16mm film, video, Learning Corp. of America, 1983, (25 minutes). The destructive nature of jealousy is revealed in this classic science fiction story by Ray Bradbury.

■ ***The Monkey's Paw***, 16mm film, video, Learning Corp. of America, 1983, (27 minutes). A dramatization of W.W. Jacob's short story classic.

■ ***The Open Window***, 16mm film, video, Pyramid, 1972, (11 minutes). Adaptation of Saki's classic "ghost" story.

Audiocassettes, Tapes, and Records

Cotton Candy on a Rainy Day, audiocassette, record, Folkways. Nikki Giovanni reads her poetry.

The Monkey's Paw and The Interruption, audiocassette, Caedmon. Presents a dramatic reading by Anthony Quayle of stories by W.W. Jacobs.

Ray Bradbury Library, 6 audiocassettes, Audio Book Company. Consists of Bradbury reading a group of his short stories.

Robert Frost Reading His Poetry, audiocassette, Caedmon, (60 minutes). Frost reads his poetry at the Kaufman Auditorium in 1953.

Community Resources

Involving the resources of your community in lesson preparation can add insight and relevance to the text. Consider the following possibilities as you plan.

■ For "The Fan Club" and/or "A Kind of Murder," invite a psychologist to discuss peer pressure.

■ For "Like Mexicans," have a panel of parents describe the characteristics and qualities they look for in potential mates for their sons and daughters.

■ For "A Kind of Murder," ask a prep school teacher, student, or graduate to discuss his or her experiences.

■ For "The Road Not Taken" and "Choices," invite people with unconventional careers to explain how they made their choices.

■ For "Dandelion Wine," invite a law enforcement officer to discuss strategies for avoiding attack.

■ For "Marigolds," invite senior citizens to join a symposium on building relationships between young and old people.

■ For "Honor," have a representative of a Latin-American Consulate discuss cultural attitudes often misunderstood.

■ For "My Shirt Is For Church," invite immigrants or Native Americans to talk about balancing acculturation with one's heritage.

■ For "Lather and Nothing Else," have students interview a judge or surgeon whose profession includes having the power of life or death over others.

■ For "Tsali of the Cherokees," contact the Bureau of Indian Affairs for information or a speaker on the status of Native American Indians in their state or community.

Unit Preview

In Unit 1, **Decisions: Action or Apathy,** students will explore how characters make decisions and face the consequences. The unit contains three subunits:

- Subunit 1: The Right Choice?
- Subunit 2: Paying the Price
- Subunit 3: A Matter of Life and Death

Art Note

Hughie Lee-Smith (1915–) has written that ". . . art . . . must express the needs and aspirations of the people . . ." His images of young black Americans who appear to have nowhere to go are emblems of all human beings whose lives are repressed by circumstances. In *Vista II* a young woman stands, as if on a stage, atop a cracked wall. Beneath her is darkness and behind her a landscape without life. *What might she say if she spoke her mind?*

About the Author

William James was an American philosopher and psychologist best known for his philosophy of pragmatism. James, born in 1842 to a wealthy New York family, was educated at private schools in America and abroad. While studying for his medical degree at Harvard, he went exploring in the Brazilian jungle with naturalist Louis Agassiz. After graduating from Harvard in 1869, he stayed on to teach medicine. The publication of his first book, *Principals of Psychology,* in 1890, established him as one of the most important thinkers of his day. His work on pragmatism solidified his standing. To James, "pragmatism" meant that the meaning of ideas is found only in terms of their possible consequences. This philosophy was further explored by philosopher John Dewey and others; Albert Einstein's later work in physics made James' theories appear prophetic. By the time of his death in 1910, James had earned worldwide fame.

VISTA II (detail) 1987
Hughie Lee Smith Courtesy of
June Kelly Gallery, New York.

Unit One

DECISIONS: ACTION OR APATHY

"When you have to make a choice and don't make it, that is in itself a choice."

William James

Discussion Questions

To help students probe connections among the fine art, quotation, and unit theme, have them consider the following questions:

1. Restate the quotation in your own words and explain its meaning *(Possible response: "Sometimes people think they can avoid making a choice by not selecting an option. But by not choosing, they are still making a choice." Students may say the quote means that you cannot avoid making choices in your life. Even if you try to get out of making a choice, you are in effect choosing.)*

2. Why do you think people avoid making choices? When might it be an *advantage* not to make a choice? When might it be a *disadvantage*? *(Possible response: Students might suggest people avoid choosing because they cannot make up their minds or because they procrastinate. Not choosing can be an advantage if it prevents a negative consequence arising from a rash action. Not choosing can be a disadvantage if it prevents something important from being accomplished.)*

3. Do you agree with the quotation? Explain your answer. *(Possible responses: Some students may agree that not making a choice is choosing, while others may argue that choosing involves a conscious act or decision.)*

4. How is the quotation related to the unit title? *(Possible response: Students may say that making a choice is action, not making a choice is apathy, as described in the quotation.)*

5. What connection do you see between the artwork and the quotation? *(Possible responses: Students might say that the woman in the picture seems to be pondering a choice.)*

Subunit Preview

Have students read the introduction to subunit 1, **The Right Choice?**. Then ask them to explore how fears about making the right choice relate to the larger unit theme. **Decisions: Action or Apathy.** Why might some people choose action when faced with making a decision? Why might others become apathetic instead? Is making the decision or facing the consequences more difficult? Have students explain their answer. You might also preview the subunit suggesting that students read the subunit Table of Contents and predict which selection they think will be the most interesting to read.

For Additional Challenge

The following selections offer extra challenge in the exploration of the subunit theme:

"The Piece of Yarn," a short story by Guy de Maupassant

"Ms. Found in a Bottle," a short story by E. A. Poe

Additional Resources

Subunit Test, pp. 26–27

THE RIGHT CHOICE?

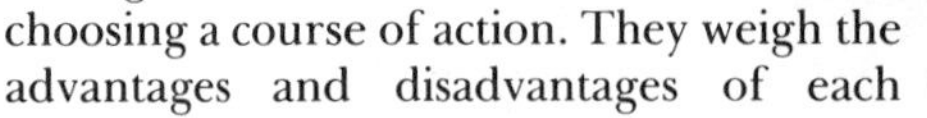

Everyone has probably worried about a decision he or she has made. People fear they might regret their choice later on. To avoid making a bad decision, many people learn to think through their alternatives before choosing a course of action. They weigh the advantages and disadvantages of each choice and consider every possible result of their actions.

The first subunit of Unit One includes selections in which the main characters make decisions and face the consequences. As you read these selections, think about the characters' alternatives and why they make the choices they do.

OBSERVATION ASSESSMENT

Observing how students respond to the text, to the classroom instruction, and to peers is an important part of an assessment program. The following suggestions and the form in each Unit Resource Book can be used to implement observation assessment.

- As students work through the subunit, assess how they use prereading strategies. Can they predict possible story lines and problems? What kinds of predictions did they make? Were their predictions logical? As they work through the subunit can you see growth in their use of prereading strategies?
- To evaluate how well students understand the illustrations or charts see if they look at them for help when they encounter difficulty with the text. Do they use the illustrations as a preceding strategy to help them formulate predictions? Can they relate on a personal level with the illustrations?
- As they work through the subunit, can you see growth in their use of postreading strategies?
- To evaluate how well students connect with a story, ask them to summarize the important idea(s) or event(s).

Elements of
FICTION

The word **fiction** means "anything made up or imagined." Although events in a work of fiction may be based on real experiences, the story itself is created in the imagination of the writer. The two major types of fiction are novels and short stories.

A **novel** is a long work of fiction. The events of a novel are normally quite complex and leave the reader with many impressions about the characters, the actions, and the places described. A **short story,** on the other hand, is a brief work of fiction that can usually be read in one sitting. Short stories generally focus on one or two main ideas. Despite these differences in length and complexity, short stories and novels share certain elements.

Understanding Fiction

Characters are the people who take part in the action of the story. You learn about characters through their actions, thoughts, and words, from how other people respond to them, and from how the writer describes them. The events of the story center on the most important characters, or **main characters.** Less important characters are known as **minor characters.**

The main idea that the author wishes to share with the reader is sometimes called the **theme.** A writer rarely states the theme directly; but after reading the selection, the reader should be able to infer the theme.

The events of a story occur in a particular time and place, or **setting.** The setting is very important to some stories but no more than background for others. A story can be set in a realistic or an imaginary place and can occur in the past, present, or future.

The **plot** is the chain of related events that make up a story. The plot centers on at least one major problem, or **conflict.** There are essentially five parts to a plot.

Exposition The opening of a short story or novel normally provides background information that the reader needs to know. This part of the story is called the **exposition.** The exposition introduces the characters, describes the setting, and may recap important events that occurred before the action of the story. The story's conflict is also introduced.

Rising Action As the story progresses, the chain of events becomes more complex. The actions and feelings of the characters intensify as their problems become more complicated. This part of the story, known as the **rising action,** creates a desire in the reader to find out what will happen next.

Climax When the intensity of the story reaches a peak, or **climax,** a turning point in the action occurs. The climax of a story usually involves an important event, decision, or discovery that affects the final outcome.

Falling Action Following the climax, the intensity of the story subsides. This part, known as the **falling action,** describes the results of the major events as the action winds down.

Elements of Fiction

This feature provides students with a common vocabulary to use in describing fiction. The terms on these pages are covered in depth in the selections that follow.

Objectives

- To understand and appreciate fiction
- To understand the elements of fiction
- To understand strategies for reading fiction
- To understand individual selections and apply story grammar as they read

Motivation

Have students create a story map to help them explore the elements of fiction. On the chalkboard, draw the following diagram and label it as follows:

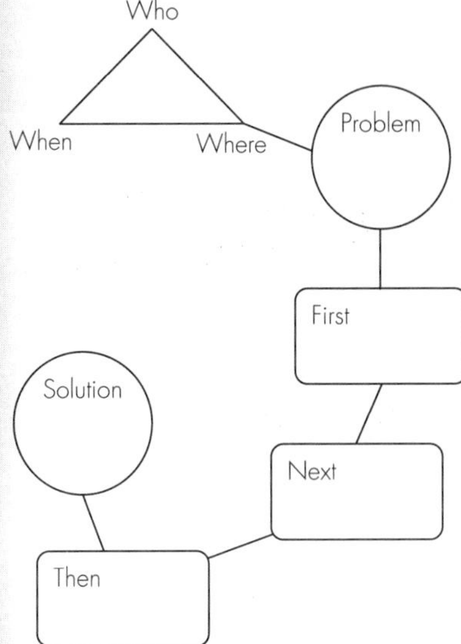

Then have students complete the story map by telling about a story that they have all already read in class. Guide students to be specific in their responses. Summarize the motivation by asking students the following questions: Based on this story map, what characteristics do you think all types of fiction share? Using the information on the story map you completed, how would you describe "fiction" to a classmate? What piece of fiction have you read recently that you found especially enjoyable and might like to share with a friend?

Teaching Strategies

1. To help students understand fiction, read the first two paragraphs on page 17 aloud while students follow along silently. Then have students paraphrase the paragraph.

Discussion Prompts: How do you think fiction writers might get ideas for their writing? If you have ever written a fictional story, where did you get ideas? What common elements might short stories and novels share?

2. Then discuss the different elements of fiction. You might also want to have students look through the text to find examples of each element.

3. Next, talk about each of the strategies for reading fiction on page 18. Ask whether students have used any of these strategies in their own reading of fiction.

Closure

Have students explain in their journals what fictional character they would like to be and why.

Resolution The final part of a story, or the **resolution,** tells how the story ends. In this part any loose ends are tied up and remaining questions resolved.

The diagram below shows the various elements of the plot in a short story or novel.

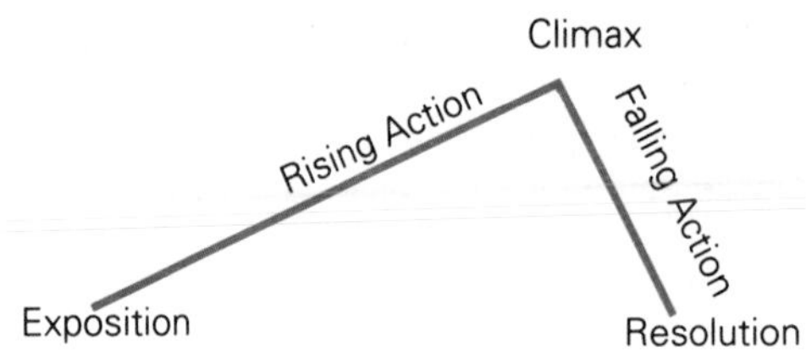

Strategies for Reading Fiction

1. Before you begin reading any literary work, **preview,** or look ahead, to see what the title, art, or any other noticeable features tell you about the selection.
2. As you read the exposition of the story, **visualize**—or picture in your mind—the characters and setting described. Look for specific adjectives that help you imagine how the opening scene looks.
3. Be an active reader by **making observations** and **asking questions** about the story. Note whether the person telling the story is a character within the story or someone watching the action from outside. Ask yourself what the central problem or conflict seems to be. Ask why the characters behave as they do.
4. The questions you ask yourself about the story can also help you **set purposes** for your reading. Rephrase each question as a purpose for reading. For example, you might say, "I will read to find out why this particular character left home."
5. Once you begin to understand the problems the characters face, **predict** what will happen next. Guess what the characters will do or say in a particular situation. Try to predict what will take place in the climax.
6. As you read, you will notice that the reasons for certain characters' actions become clear. As they do, your impressions about these characters may change. Continue to **clarify,** or refine, your understanding of the story. Reread particular sections of the text to fully understand what has happened or why.
7. Any reading experience leaves you with thoughts and feelings. When you finish reading, take a few minutes to **reflect** on, or think about, your impressions. Ask yourself how you feel about the story's events. What is your reaction to the main characters? What message about life does the story convey to you?
8. If you are confused about any of the events in a story, review them by answering the following **Story Grammar Questions.**

Story Grammar Questions

1. Where does the story take place?
2. Who are the main characters?
3. What problem, or conflict, do the main characters try to resolve?
4. How do they resolve this problem?
5. What happens in the end?

For an example of a reading model, see "The Open Window" on page 9.

Fiction

The Fan Club

RONA MAYNARD

Examine What You Know (Prior Knowledge)

The story you are about to read describes a group of teenagers who consider themselves to be the "in" group. In your journal or on a piece of paper, describe a time when you were not a member of an in group. Tell what the in group had that you didn't appear to have. Did you want to be a member of this group? Why or why not?

Expand Your Knowledge (Building Background)

Excluding others is a form of discrimination. To learn more about this word, fill out a word map like the one below. Then share your ideas with the class.

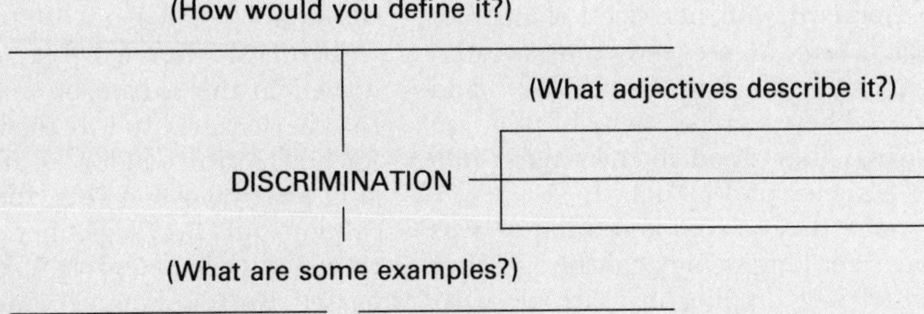

Enrich Your Reading (Reading Skill)

Contrast When you find differences between two things, you **contrast** them. Characters in fiction are often like real people in that what they say is different from what they feel or do. As you read, notice that what Laura says often contradicts what she is feeling or what she does. Use a chart like the one below to record your ideas.

What Laura Says	What Laura Does or Feels
1. Laura says she would be glad to accept Rachel's invitation to her house.	Laura is not really glad about visiting Rachel in her neighborhood.
2.	

Objectives

- To analyze a short story
- To recognize theme in a story
- To see the use of contrast in developing character
- To express understanding of the work through a choice of writing forms, including a list, description, narration, dialogue, and poetry

Prereading/Motivation

Examine What You Know

Discussion Prompts: What things might members of an "in" group believe they have that others do not? Does everyone at some time experience what it is like to be excluded from an "in" group? Explain. Should people try to change to be accepted by an "in" group?

Expand Your Knowledge

Discussion Prompts: What reasons do people give for discrimination? What do you think really causes it? Possible responses for the word map include:
definition: prejudiced act, favoritism
adjectives: biased, snobbish, exclusive
examples: male-only club, certain renting policies, certain employment policies.

Enrich Your Reading

Have students create a chart like the one in their books and complete it as they read. Possible answers are:

2. *Says:* Laura says she doesn't care about the "in" group because they are all clods. *Does:* Laura flushes painfully when she feels they are talking about her.

3. *Says:* Laura says "every American" must "respect the dignity of every other American." *Does:* Laura joins the "in" group in cruelly making fun of Rachel.

Thematic Link—The Right Choice?
In this story, the main character lets discrimination prevent her from making the right choice.

Journal Writing

Suggest these journal topics to students:

- Explain the usual purpose of a fan club and describe the activities of its members.
- Have you ever been a member of a fan club—or wanted to be? Describe the experience.
- Use your imagination to develop ideas and images about this sentence: "In the back row, she saw the 'in' group, laughing and joking and whispering."
- For other journal opportunities, refer students to Examine What You Know (above) and Annotation O.

Additional Resources

UNIT ONE RESOURCE BOOK
Reader's Guidesheet, p. 1
Vocabulary Worksheet, p. 2
Selection and Vocabulary Check Tests, p. 3
Selection Test, pp. 4–5

Collaborative Learning

Opportunities for collaborative learning appear throughout the lesson and include Annotation O and Real-Life Connections (p. T–27).

Teaching Strategies

Vocabulary Preview

These vocabulary words are defined at the bottom of the selection page on which they appear. You may wish to discuss them briefly before students begin reading.

cynical sneering
discrimination the act of showing bias
drone to talk monotonously
exclusive private
malicious hateful
mock false; imitation
stricken suffering from hurt

Support for Students of Limited English Proficiency

- Use the **Readers Guidesheet**, p. 1.
- Students with limited English proficiency might not be familiar with the allusions to different forms of discrimination contained in "The Fan Club." For example, the implications of Rachel's name change (to make herself seem more "American") may escape students who do not have experience with discrimination. Discuss the nuances of discrimination—how the same epithet might be considered a slur to one group, and trivial to another group. Encourage students to discuss their own experiences.
- Annotations C, L, and S focus on allusions.

Text Annotations

A. Reading Skill: CLARIFYING Ask students who "they" are and how "they" can be recognized. *("They" belong to a "tight little group" who sit together and dress alike; the "in" group.)*

B. Literary Sidelight Mohair sweaters, madras shirts, and pea-green raincoats are described as "all the same" here. The implication is that people who dress the same think the same, and are dull and unimaginative. Laura is torn by this idea in the story. She wants to belong, but does not want to be a thoughtless conformist.

C. LEP Allusions Some students may not realize the reason for Rachel's name change—to disguise her ethnic eastern European (Polish or Jewish) heritage. Discuss how people often (unfairly) judge others by their last name and how name-changing might make a person feel he or she "belongs."

The Fan Club

RONA MAYNARD

It was Monday again. It was Monday and the day was damp and cold. Rain splattered the cover of *Algebra I* as Laura heaved her books higher on her arm and sighed. School was such a bore.

School. It loomed before her now, massive and dark against the sky. In a few minutes, she would have to face them again—Diane Goddard with her sleek blond hair and Terri Pierce in her candy-pink sweater. A And Carol and Steve and Bill and Nancy . . . There were so many of them, so exclusive as they stood in their tight little groups laughing and joking.

Why were they so cold and unkind? Was it because her long stringy hair hung in her eyes instead of dipping in graceful curls? Was it because she wrote poetry in algebra class and got A's in Latin without really trying? Shivering, Laura remembered how they would sit at the back of English class, passing notes and whispering. She thought of their identical brown loafers, their plastic purses, their hostile stares as they passed her in the corridors. She didn't care. They SR-1 ▶ were clods, the whole lot of them.

She shoved her way through the door and there they were. They thronged the hall, streamed in and out of doors, clustered under red and yellow posters advertising the latest dance. Mohair sweaters, madras shirts, pea-green raincoats. They were all alike, all the same. And in the center of the B group, as usual, Diane Goddard was saying, "It'll be a riot! I just can't wait to see her face when she finds out."

Laura flushed painfully. Were they talking about her?

"What a scream! Can't wait to hear what she says!"

Silently she hurried past and submerged herself in the stream of students heading for the lockers. It was then that she saw Rachel Horton—alone as always, her too-long skirt billowing over the white, heavy columns of her legs, her freckled face ringed with shapeless black curls. She called herself Horton, but everyone knew her fa- C ther was Jacob Hortensky, the tailor. He ran that greasy little shop where you could always smell the cooked cabbage from the ◀ SR-2 back rooms where the family lived.

"Oh, Laura!" Rachel was calling her. Laura turned, startled.

"Hi, Rachel."

"Laura, did you watch *World of Nature* last night? On Channel 11?"

"No—no, I didn't," Laura hesitated. "I almost never watch that kind of program."

"Well, gee, you missed something—last night, I mean. It was a real good show.

Words to Know and Use

exclusive (eks klōō′ siv) *adj.* private; not admitting others

Structured Reading for Less Proficient Students

These questions can help to guide students through the reading. Ask each question at the point of the selection where the SR number appears in the margin.

SR–1. What is the discrimination that Laura feels? How does she react to it? *(She feels excluded from the "in" group's note passing and whispering; she reacts by claiming disinterest.)* **Clarifying**

SR–2. How would you describe Rachel? *(Her clothes are ill-fitting, her legs heavy, her face freckled, her hair a mass of shapeless black curls.)* **Literal recall**

SR–3. Predict whether or not Laura will accept Rachel's invitation. *(Some will predict that she will accept because Rachel is so eager to be friends and so nice to Laura; others, that she will not because Rachel is unattractive.)* **Predicting**

SR–4. What do Laura's feelings about Rachel's clothing reveal about Laura? *(Her objections reveal her superficial values and hypocrisy.)* **Analyzing**

Continued on page 21

D Laura, it showed this fly being born!" Rachel was smiling now; she waved her hands as she talked.

In the back row, she saw the "in" group, laughing and joking and whispering.

"First the feelers and then the wings. And they're sort of wet at first, the wings are. Gosh, it was a good show."

E "I bet it was." Laura tried to sound interested. She turned to go, but Rachel still stood there, her mouth half open, her pale, moonlike face strangely urgent. It was as if an invisible hand tugged at Laura's sleeve.

"And Laura," Rachel continued, "that was an awful good poem you read yesterday in English."

Laura remembered how Terri and Diane had laughed and whispered. "You really think so? Well, thanks, Rachel. I mean, not too many people care about poetry."

"Yours was real nice though. I wish I could write like you. I always like those things you write."

Laura blushed. "I'm glad you do."

"Laura, can you come over sometime after school? Tomorrow maybe? It's not very far and you can stay for dinner. I told
SR-3 ▶ my parents all about you!"

F Laura thought of the narrow, dirty street and the tattered awning in front of the tailor shop. An awful district, the kids said. But she couldn't let that matter. "Okay," she said. And then, faking enthusiasm, "I'd be glad to come."

She turned into the algebra room, sniffing at the smell of chalk and dusty erasers. In the back row, she saw the "in" group, laughing and joking and whispering.

"What a panic!"

"Here, you make the first one."

Diane and Terri had their heads together over a lot of little cards. You could see they were cooking up something.

Fumbling through the pages of her book, she tried to memorize the theorems she hadn't looked at the night before. The laughter at the back of the room rang in her ears. Also those smiles—those heartless smiles . . .

A bell buzzed in the corridors; students scrambled to their places. "We will now have the national anthem," said the voice on the loudspeaker. Laura shifted her weight from one foot to the other. It was so false, so pointless. How could they sing of the land of the free, when there was still discrimination. Smothered laughter behind her. Were they all looking at her?

And then it was over. Slumping in her seat, she shuffled through last week's half-finished homework papers and scribbled flowers in the margins.

"Now this one is just a direct application of the equation." The voice was hollow, distant, an echo beyond the sound of rustling papers and hushed whispers. Laura sketched a guitar on the cover of her notebook. Someday she would live in the Village,[1] and there would be no more algebra classes and people would accept her. G

1. **Village:** Greenwich Village, a neighborhood in New York City known for its tolerance of different lifestyles.

Words to Know and Use

discrimination (di skrim'i nā'shən) *n.* the act of showing favoritism or differential treatment; bias

21

D. Critical Thinking: ANALYZING Have students analyze the differences between Rachel and Laura based on their tastes in television shows. *(Rachel's delight in educational TV suggests she has more serious interests than Laura.)*

E. Literary Element: CHARACTERIZATION Ask students why Laura's friendship is so important to Rachel. *(Possible responses: Rachel admires Laura and needs her friendship for self-affirmation; Rachel is lonely.*

F. Critical Thinking: EVALUATING Ask students if they agree with Laura's decision to accept Rachel's invitation. *(Possible response: No, because she does not really want to go; yes, because she is being nice to Rachel and they may indeed become friends.)*

G. Literary Sidelight

Laura pits algebra class, to her the epitome of a place of stuffiness and useless rules, against Greenwich Village, the epitome of casual acceptance and no rules. By referring to it as the "Village" she implies intimate familiarity with Greenwich Village; it is somewhere that she belongs.

Structured Reading for Less Proficient Students

Continued from page 20

SR–5. Summarize Laura's speech. *(She argues that people must respect others' dignity, allow civil rights for all, and avoid irrational hatred for others.)* **Summarizing**

SR–6. Why does no one help Rachel? *(They dislike her and enjoy seeing her suffer; despite her speech, Laura wants to be accepted so much that she lets prejudice cloud her own humanity.)* **Inferring**

SR–7. What does the figure Laura sees on the cards represent? *(Rachel)* **Inferring**

SR–8. What happens at the end of the story? *(Laura pins the card to her sweater and joins in the clapping.)* **Literal recall**

H. Reading Skill: DRAWING CONCLUSIONS Ask students why Ellen criticizes Rachel's outfit to Laura. *(Possible response: Ellen considers Laura a part of the group; Ellen recognizes Laura is not friends with Rachel.)*

I. Critical Thinking: ANALYZING Ask students to analyze why Laura is so nervous. *(Possible response: because she is ill-prepared, fears social disgrace, wants to fit in.)*

J. Literary Sidelight Robert Frost (1874–1963) was among modern America's most visible and celebrated poets, winning the Pulitzer Prize four times. In his work he embraces the values of traditional New England individualism and self-reliance, an ironic counterpoint to this story's ending. His poem "The Road Not Taken" appears in this subunit.

K. LEP: Allusion Explain that in a strict sense "civil rights" are the rights mentioned in the U.S. Constitution which include freedom of speech, religion, assembly, right to vote, and so on. In common language, the term "civil rights" has come to mean the struggle of minorities to obtain the rights they are supposedly guaranteed in the Constitution. Laura uses this common association to underscore her point that even non-minorities like herself have to struggle to obtain their "civil rights."

L. Literary Element: CHARACTERIZATION Ask students why Laura might have selected this topic for her speech. *(Possible response: Since she perceives herself as a victim of discrimination by the "in" group, she may be trying to help herself or Rachel.)*

She turned toward the back row. Diane was passing around one of her cards. Terri leaned over, smiling. "Hey, can I do the next one?"

". . . by using the distributive law." Would the class never end? Math was so dull, so painfully dull. They made you multiply and cancel and factor, multiply, cancel, and factor. Just like a machine. The steel sound of the bell shattered the silence. Scraping chairs, cries of "Hey, wait!" The crowd moved into the hallway now, a thronging, jostling mass.

H Alone in the tide of faces, Laura felt someone nudge her. It was Ellen. "Hey, how's that for a smart outfit?" She pointed to the other side of the hall.

The gaudy flowers of Rachel Horton's blouse stood out among the fluffy sweaters and pleated skirts. What a lumpish, awkward creature Rachel was. Did she have to dress like that? Her socks had fallen untidily around her heavy ankles, and her slip showed a raggedy edge of lace. As she moved into the English room, shoelaces trailing, her books tumbled to the floor. SR-4 ▶

"Isn't that something?" Terri said. Little waves of mocking laughter swept through the crowd.

The bell rang; the laughter died away. As they hurried to their seats, Diane and Terri exchanged last-minute whispers. "Make one for Steve. He wants one too!"

Then Miss Merrill pushed aside the book she was holding, folded her hands, and beamed. "All right, people, that will be enough. Now, today we have our speeches. Laura, would you begin please?"

I So it was her turn. Her throat tightened as she thought of Diane and Carol and Steve grinning and waiting for her to stumble. Perhaps if she was careful, they'd never know she hadn't thought out everything beforehand. Careful, careful, she thought. Look confident.

"Let's try to be prompt." Miss Merrill tapped the cover of her book with her fountain pen.

Laura pushed her way to the front of the class. Before her, the room was large and still. Twenty-five round, blurred faces stared blankly. Was that Diane's laughter? She folded her hands and looked at the wall, strangely distant now, its brown paint cracked and peeling. A dusty portrait of Robert Frost, a card with the seven rules for better paragraphs, last year's calendar, and the steady, hollow ticking of the clock. J

Laura cleared her throat. "Well," she began, "my speech is on civil rights." A chorus of snickers rose from the back of the room. K

"Most people," Laura continued, "most people don't care enough about others. Here in New England, they think they're pretty far removed from discrimination and violence. Lots of people sit back and fold their hands and wait for somebody else to do the work. But I think we're all responsible for people that haven't had some of the advantages . . ."

Diane was giggling and gesturing at Steve Becker. All she ever thought about was parties and dates—and such dates! Always the president of the student council or the captain of the football team.

"A lot of people think that race prejudice is limited to the South. But most of us are prejudiced—whether we know it or not. It's not just that we don't give other people a chance; we don't give ourselves a chance either. We form narrow opinions, and then we don't see the truth. We keep right on believing that we're open-minded liberals when all we're doing is deceiving ourselves." L

How many of them cared about truth? Laura looked past the rows of blank, empty

PROFESSIONAL NOTEBOOK

Education, n. That which discloses to the wise and disguises from the foolish their lack of understanding.
Erudition, n. Dust shaken out of a book into an empty skull.
Learning, n. The kind of learning distinguishing the studious.
Lecturer, n. One with his hand in your pocket, his tongue in your ear and his faith in your patience.
AMBROSE BIERCE, *The Devil's Dictionary*

THREE SISTERS 1966 Moses Soyer Private collection.

faces, past the bored stares and cynical grins.

M "But I think we should try to forget our prejudices. We must realize now that we've done too little for too long. We must accept the fact that one person's misfortune is everyone's responsibility. We must defend the natural dignity of people—a dignity that thousands are denied."

None of them knew what it was like to be unwanted, unaccepted. Did Steve know? Did Diane?

"Most of us are proud to say that we live in a free country. But is this really true? Can we call the United States a free country when millions of people face prejudice and discrimination? As long as one person is forbidden to share the basic rights we take for granted, as long as we are still the victims of irrational hatreds, there can be no freedom. Only when every American learns to respect the dignity of every other American can we truly call our country free." ◀ SR-5

The class was silent. "Very nice, Laura." Things remained quiet as other students droned through their speeches. Then Miss Merrill looked briskly around the room. "Now, Rachel, I believe you're next."

There was a ripple of dry, humorless laughter—almost, Laura thought, like the N

Words to Know and Use

cynical (sin' i kəl) *adj.* possessing a negative attitude; sneering
drone (drōn) *v.* to talk in a monotonous, boring manner

Art Note
Three Sisters, by the Russian born American artist. Moses Soyer (1899–1975), is, like all his works, an intensely personal study. Although alike in physical resemblance, and placed close to one another, each young woman seems alone with her thoughts. The painting's muted colors deepen the atmosphere of quiet. *Explain how this picture might represent the various moods of a single character in The Fan Club.*

M. Literary Element THEME Ask volunteers to discuss whether Laura has in fact accepted her responsibility for Rachel's misfortune. *(Possible response: Yes, by accepting Rachel's invitation to dinner and by giving this speech; no, by not really offering her friendship to Rachel.)*

N. Reading Skill: PREDICTING Ask students to predict based on the details in this paragraph whether Rachel's speech will be a success. *(Students may point to the "dry, humorous laughter" and the way the others have treated Rachel as obstacles to the success of her speech. They may also mention Rachel's own clumsiness and insecurity.)*

O. Teaching Tip

Explore with students how Rachel's choice of speech topics only intensifies the prejudice against her. Ask them if a different topic might have helped win the class's admiration; have them provide examples. Can people make others like or admire them? Should they have to change themselves to do so?

P. LEP: Allusion Explain to students that Woolworth's is a variety store that sells reasonably-priced items. Make sure students understand that Rachel's classmate is using the store's name in a derogatory fashion to connote cheap trinkets and gimcracks.

Q. Critical Thinking: EVALUATING Point out Miss Merrill's cruelty to Rachel. Ask students to evaluate how her attitude might affect her students. *(Possible response: Miss Merrill's own prejudice sanctions her students' discrimination.)*

N sound of a rattlesnake. Rachel stood before the class now, her face red, her heavy arms piled with boxes.

Diane Goddard tossed back her head and winked at Steve.

"Well, well, don't we have lots of things to show," said Miss Merrill. "But aren't you going to put those boxes down, Rachel? No, no, not there!"

"Man, that kid's dumb," Steve muttered, and his voice could be clearly heard all through the room.

With a brisk rattle, Miss Merrill's pen tapped the desk for silence.

Rachel's slow smile twitched at the corners. She looked frightened. There was a crash and a clatter as the tower of boxes slid to the floor. Now everyone was giggling.

"Hurry and pick them up," said Miss Merrill sharply.

O Rachel crouched on her knees and began very clumsily to gather her scattered treasures. Papers and boxes lay all about, and some of the boxes had broken open, spilling their contents in wild confusion. No one went to help. At last she scrambled to her feet and began fumbling with her notes.

"My—my speech is on shells."

A cold and stony silence had settled upon the room.

"Lots of people collect shells, because they're kind of pretty—sort of, and you just find them on the beach."

"Well, whaddaya know!" It was Steve's voice, softer this time, but all mock amazement. Laura jabbed her notebook with her pencil. Why were they so cruel, so thoughtless? Why did they have to laugh?

"This one," Rachel was saying as she opened one of the boxes, "it's one of the best." Off came the layers of paper, and there, at last, smooth and pearly and shimmering, was the shell. Rachel turned it over lovingly in her hands. White, fluted sides, like the close-curled petals of a flower; a scrolled coral back. Laura held her breath. It was beautiful. At the back of the room, snickers had begun again.

"Bet she got it at Woolworth's," somebody whispered. P

"Or in a trash dump." That was Diane.

Rachel pretended not to hear, but her face was getting very red and Laura could see she was flustered.

"Here's another that's kind of pretty. I found it last summer at Ogunquit."[2] In her outstretched hand there was a small, drab, brownish object. A common snail shell. "It's called a . . . It's called . . ."

Rachel rustled through her notes. "I—I can't find it. But it was here. It was in here somewhere. I know it was." Her broad face had turned bright pink again. "Just can't find it . . ." Miss Merrill stood up and strode toward her. "Rachel," she said sharply, "we are supposed to be prepared when we make a speech. Now, I'm sure you remember those rules on page twenty-one. I expect you to know these things. Q Next time you must have your material organized." ◀SR-6

The bell sounded, ending the period. Miss Merrill collected her books.

Then, suddenly, chairs were shoved aside at the back of the room, and there was the sound of many voices whispering. They were standing now, whole rows of them, their faces grinning with delight. Choked giggles, shuffling feet—and then applause—wild, sarcastic, malicious applause. That was when Laura saw that they were all wearing little white cards with a fat, frizzy-

2. **Ogunquit:** a resort on the southern coast of Maine.

Words to Know and Use

mock (mäk) *adj.* false; imitation
malicious (mə lish′ əs) *adj.* hateful; intended to do harm

24

DATA BANK

People have long prized shells and amassed great shell collections. In the 17th and 18th centuries it became fashionable in Europe for cultivated people to assemble "cabinets" of rare, expensive shells. The cabinets assembled by these collectors formed the nucleus of today's great museum collections, including the ten million specimens at the Smithsonian in Washington, D.C.

Shell collectors search for specimens that are rare in nature, as well as difficult to obtain. The most sought-after shells are the cones, of the family *Conidae,* commonly known as Cowries. The Cowrie's shell is noted for its glossy finish and bright colors. Emperor Francis I of the Holy Roman Empire reportedly paid the equivalent of $20,000 in 1750 for a cone shell.

haired figure drawn on the front. What did it mean? She looked more closely. "HORTENSKY FAN CLUB," said the
SR-7 ▶ bright-red letters.

So that was what the whispering had been about all morning. She'd been wrong. They weren't out to get her after all. It was only Rachel.

Diane was nudging her and holding out a card. "Hey, Laura, here's one for you to wear."

For a moment Laura stared at the card. She looked from Rachel's red, frightened face to Diane's mocking smile, and she heard the pulsing, frenzied rhythm of the claps and the stamping, faster and faster. R Her hands trembled as she picked up the card and pinned it to her sweater. And as she turned, she saw Rachel's stricken look.

"She's a creep, isn't she?" Diane's voice was soft and intimate.

And Laura began to clap. ❧ S ◀ SR-8

NO HANDS Robert Vickrey Kennedy Galleries, New York.

Look at Me

PEG HODDINOTT

Look at me. Please, see me
Not my clothes or stubby nails
Or homely face.
Open your heart, so you can see mine.
I do not ask you to agree with
Or understand all you see
For I don't even do that.
Just look at what is really there
And allow it to be.

Words to Know and Use	**stricken** (strik' ən) *adj.* suffering from hurt or pain

R. Reading Skill: VISUALIZING Ask students how the sounds in this passage may influence Laura. *(Possible response: People can become caught up in loud, rhythmic sounds. The stamping and clapping may sway Laura to the group's side.)*

S. Literary Element: THEME Ask students what they think prevented Laura from making the right choice. *(Possible responses: her fear of discrimination; her own prejudice; her wish to be part of the "in" group.)*

Check Test

1. As the school day begins, what group of people does Laura dread facing? Why? *(Diane, Terri, and the rest of the "in" group because they are exclusive, cold, unkind, and a bunch of clods)*

2. What does Rachel look like? *(too-long skirt, heavy legs, freckled face, shapeless black curls)*

3. What is Laura's speech about? *(civil rights)*

4. What is written on the cards the students wear? *(Hortensky Fan Club)*

Encouraging Independent Reading

I Know Why the Caged Bird Sings, an autobiography by Maya Angelou
To Kill a Mockingbird, a novel by Harper Lee
The Chosen, a novel by Chaim Potok
"The Son from America," a short story by Isaac Bashevis Singer
"The Osage Orange Tree," a short story by William Stafford

Art Note

Bicycles are among the favorite subjects of artist Robert Vickrey (1926–), who paints with tempera, a mixture of color pigment and egg yolk. Here, his daughter Carri is shown in a precarious gesture, but at a distance. The larger, close-up bicycle forms and their cast shadows, like silhouettes, suggest both motion and pure pattern. *How might the figure on the bicycle relate to the speaker in the poem?*

Insight

This piece reflects on the ideas in the main selection and is suggested for students' independent reading. Optional discussion questions follow.

1. What does the speaker want people to do? *(look beyond her appearance to her true personality)*

2. What qualities might the speaker value? *(Possible responses: fairness, kindness, decency)*

3. What parallels can you draw between the speaker of this poem and Rachel in "The Fan Club"? *(Possible responses: Both have suffered prejudice because of their appearance; both reveal feelings of great pain and sensitivity.)*

Student Response

Responding to Reading

These questions are open-ended with no "right" or "wrong" answers. However, responses must be supported with information from the selection. Possible answers follow:

1. Any response is valid. Encourage students to voice their reactions to Laura's decision in specific terms.

2. Some students may say that Rachel becomes a victim because she is poorly dressed, comes from a family that seems "foreign," and is interested in such serious subjects as science and literature, not things important to the "in" group. Other students may say that Rachel becomes the victim because the fan club members are shallow and prejudiced.

3. Some may say that the two girls share a love of poetry and a sensitive nature but come from different backgrounds. Others may note that they are both outsiders but that Laura is far more desperate than Rachel to be accepted.

4. Some may say that Laura joins the clapping because she wants to be a member of the "in" group more than anything else; others may believe that she herself is prejudiced towards Rachel.

5. Some may believe that Laura hurts Rachel far more by betraying what Rachel takes as their friendship; others may claim that Diane's actions are far more injurious because they have been continuous and spark Rachel's final humiliation.

6. Some may now see the hidden as well as open manifestations of discrimination; others may still understand the word in the same way.

7. Opinions will vary. Some students may point out that in a real school a clique can set standards that most will want to imitate; others may cite actual instances of prejudice; others may believe this fictional situation is contrived. Possible prevention steps: Students may befriend those who are being left out; may act independently of the group; may form groups that act against discrimination.

Responding to Reading

First Impressions

1. What do you think about Laura's decision to join the fan club?

Second Thoughts

2. The members of the fan club pick on Rachel. Why does she become their victim?

   Think about
   - Rachel's general appearance, interests, and family background
   - the values of those in the fan club

3. Rachel tries to make friends with Laura at the beginning of the story. What do they have in common? How are they different?
4. Why does Laura decide to join in the clapping at the end of the story?
5. In your opinion, who hurt Rachel more, Laura or Diane?

   Think about
   - Laura and Rachel's conversations at the beginning of the story
   - Laura's speech about discrimination

6. Think about the word map you completed on *discrimination* before you read the story. Has your understanding of this word changed from reading the story? If so, how?

Broader Connections

7. Could this same situation occur in a real school? What could students do to prevent such discrimination against their classmates?

Literary Concept: Theme

Writers try to discuss an important idea about life or human nature in every literary work. This idea is called the **theme.** Reread Laura's speech about tolerance and acceptance of others. Notice how it contrasts with her actions at the end of the story. What idea about human nature do you think the writing is suggesting?

Literary Concept—Theme

Possible reponse: The writer suggests that people often deceive themselves by saying they believe one thing while doing just the opposite. By showing a character who speaks against prejudice and then joins a bigoted group in denigrating another person, the writer points out that people often don't live up to their ideals. The writer seems to urge readers to practice acceptance and tolerance of people who are different from themselves.

Writing Options

1. Laura is a hypocrite because she says she does not believe in discrimination but then acts otherwise. Look again at Laura's speech about civil rights and discrimination. Make a list of statements from the speech that point out the hypocrisy of Laura's behavior.

2. Sometimes people change as they grow older; sometimes they stay the same. What do you think might happen to Laura and Rachel ten years after this story ends? What might they be doing? Write a brief description of either Laura or Rachel when they are twenty-seven years old.

3. The writer might have chosen to end this story differently. For example, what if Laura had stood up for Rachel instead of pinning on the card? What do you think the characters would have said to each other? Rewrite the ending with this change.

4. Imagine that Laura and Rachel meet at their lockers the day after the clapping incident. What would they say to each other? Write an imaginary dialogue that might take place in the short time between classes.

5. If you have not already done so, read the poem "Look at Me" on page 25. Which character or characters in "The Fan Club" might have written this poem? Write a poem on adolescence from Diane's point of view.

Vocabulary Practice

Exercise Read each set of four words below. On a separate sheet of paper, write the letter of the word that is not related in meaning to the other words in the set.

1. (a) negative (b) sneering (c) cynical (d) hopeful
2. (a) imitation (b) mock (c) wishful (d) fake
3. (a) stricken (b) bored (c) hurt (d) injured
4. (a) bigotry (b) bias (c) equality (d) discrimination
5. (a) private (b) restricted (c) ugly (d) exclusive
6. (a) malicious (b) shy (c) hateful (d) vicious
7. (a) mock (b) phony (c) false (d) impossible
8. (a) sad (b) mean (c) malicious (d) hostile
9. (a) hum (b) drone (c) vibrate (d) change
10. (a) snobbish (b) open (c) selective (d) exclusive

Words to Know and Use

cynical
discrimination
drone
exclusive
malicious
mock
stricken

Writing Options

The Writing Options are designed to meet varied student interests and abilities. Have each student select one writing activity to complete. You may wish to guide some students to an option that requires less writing.

Journal Update Have students review their journal entries for "The Fan Club." What have they learned about "in" groups? What new reflections can be added to their earlier writing?

Vocabulary Practice

1. d
2. c
3. b
4. c
5. c
6. b
7. d
8. a
9. d
10. b

Real Life Connections

To help students understand the feelings of all the characters in the story, have them role-play ways to reduce discrimination. Suggest they consider varied forms of prejudice, such as ageism and sexism, as well. Have groups brainstorm their skits, then role-play them for the class. Class members can then offer comments and suggestions.

Elements of Nonfiction

This feature provides students with a common vocabulary to use in discussing different types of nonfiction. The terms on these pages are covered in depth in the selections that follow.

Objectives

- To understand and appreciate nonfiction
- To understand the different types of nonfiction
- To understand strategies for reading nonfiction
- To explore the link between form and content in nonfiction

Motivation

Have students create a Venn diagram to help them distinguish nonfiction from fiction and formulate a definition for nonfiction. On the chalkboard, draw two large intersecting circles. Write *Qualities of Fiction* under one independent portion and *Qualities of Nonfiction* under the other. Write *Shared Qualities* on the overlapping middle section. Then have students complete the diagram. Your diagram may look like this one:

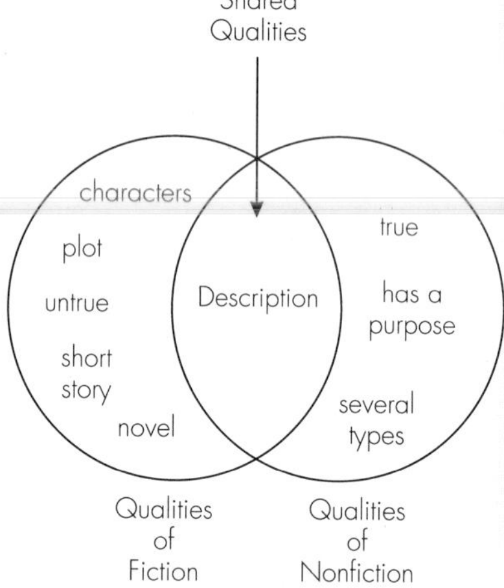

Summarize the motivation by asking students the following questions: Based on this diagram, how is nonfiction different from fiction? How would you define "nonfiction" according to the qualities that you listed on the chart?

Elements of *NONFICTION*

Writing that deals with real people, places, facts, and events is called **nonfiction.** The four main purposes for writing nonfiction are **to inform, to express an opinion, to persuade,** and **to entertain.** Often a writer has two or more purposes for writing, depending on the topic and the **audience,** the persons for whom he or she is writing.

Understanding Nonfiction

Autobiography An autobiography is the story of a person's life written by that person and almost always told in the first person, that is, by using the pronoun "I." In an autobiography, the writer focuses on the most significant events in his or her life. In this book, "My Shirt Is for Church" and "Wilma" are short excerpts taken from autobiographies.

An autobiography is usually book length because it covers the writer's entire lifetime, but there are shorter types of autobiographical narratives written in the first person. **Journals, diaries,** and **memoirs** are first-person narratives that relate brief incidents in the writer's life.

Biography A biography is the story of a person's life written by another person. The writer of a biography—a biographer—researches his or her subject in order to present accurate information. Biographers study personal letters, diaries, journals, interviews, and other available information about their subjects. If possible, they personally interview their subjects and people who know the subjects. A biographer then chooses which events to include in his or her book.

Essays An essay is a brief composition that offers an opinion on a particular subject. Essays are often written in the first person. A **formal essay** is written in a serious and highly organized manner. **Informal essays** are personal and less rigidly organized. They may include personal accounts and humor. Harold Krents's "Darkness at Noon" and Art Buchwald's "Diablo County" are examples of essays found in this book.

True-Life Adventures Accounts of actual heroic deeds or exciting adventures are another type of nonfiction writing. Such accounts are usually organized chronologically, or in the order in which the events took place. In this book, "Stowaway!" and "Survival in the Forty-Ninth" are true-life adventures.

Informative Articles Informative articles present factual information about a particular subject. Informative writing is found in newspapers, magazines, pamphlets, books, encyclopedias, and other publications. The information is generally organized around main ideas that are supported by details. "Don't Can Your Aluminum" is an example of an informative article in this book.

Strategies for Reading Nonfiction

Reading nonfiction requires some of the same strategies you use in reading other types of literature. Nonfiction, however, requires some additional reading strategies because of the large number of facts, opinions, and unfamiliar terms it may contain. Do not hesitate to read a work of nonfiction more slowly than a work of fiction. If you do not fully understand particular sections, reread them. The following tips will help you better comprehend nonfiction writing.

1. **Preview.** For clues as to what a nonfiction selection is about, look ahead at the title, at any subtitles, pictures, graphs, or charts, and at the general organization of the piece. If you are looking for specific information, previewing will help you decide if a particular piece addresses your concerns.
2. **Think about what you already know.** Once you know the topic of a selection, take a moment to recall what you already know about that topic. Activating your prior knowledge helps you understand what you read.
3. **Set purposes.** As you begin to read, focus your thinking by setting purposes to guide your reading. Ask yourself what information you want or expect to find.
4. **Identify the method of organization.** Writers of nonfiction organize their work according to their purpose for writing. In selections describing personal experiences, the information may be arranged chronologically. In selections meant to inform, the writer may organize the material around main ideas. Look for a **topic sentence,** which states the main idea of a paragraph. Sometimes the first sentence in a paragraph is a topic sentence. The other sentences in the paragraph provide details about the main idea. Some nonfiction writing has **subtitles,** or small titles in dark print, which state the topic of a section of the text.
5. **Separate facts from opinions.** Statements that can be proved are facts. In nonfiction, we expect the facts to be true. It is important to accurately judge the facts a writer presents. **Opinions** are unprovable statements that express a writer's beliefs. Sometimes, however, a writer presents an opinion as if it were a fact. Be sure to recognize which statements are facts and which are opinions.
6. **Consider the writer's tone.** The attitude a writer takes toward his or her subject is called the **tone.** A writer's tone may, for example, be critical, amused, cynical, or joyous. To identify a writer's tone, look closely at the writer's choice of words and the kinds of statements he or she makes.
7. **Summarize.** When you have finished reading a selection, take a few moments to summarize, or restate, the main points. Reread anything that is still unclear. If the selection has subtitles, use them as headings to review the text. You may wish to make some notes in the form of an outline. Summarizing shows you what you have learned and what you still might want to find out.

Teaching Strategies

1. To help students understand nonfiction, read the first paragraph on page 28 aloud while students follow along silently. Then have students paraphrase what they read.

Discussion Prompts: Which of these four purposes do you think authors might combine? What examples of nonfiction can you recall that had two or more purposes? What nonfiction selections have you read that you would recommend to your friends?

2. Then discuss in turn each of the different types of nonfiction. Students can look in the text for additional examples of each type.

3. Next, talk about each of the reading strategies on page 29. Ask which of these strategies might be most difficult for them and which might be the most useful in helping them improve their own reading of nonfiction pieces.

Closure

Have students briefly describe in their journals what makes nonfiction enjoyable to them.

Objectives

- To understand and analyze an autobiographical essay
- To explore the use of first-person point of view
- To express understanding of the work through a choice of writing forms, including a letter and exposition

Prereading/Motivation

Examine What You Know

Discussion Prompts: Who in your family would be most upset if you married out of your ethnic group or social class? What advantages and disadvantages might there be to following your family's wishes regarding your choice of a mate? What might be some of the results of marrying out of your class or ethnic group? Why do you think people feel so strongly about marrying "their own kind"?

Expand Your Knowledge

Discussion Prompts: Do people still categorize others as "Okies" or use other such derogatory terms?

Additional Background: Although we assume that people should be free to select their own mates, arranged marriages were the norm almost everywhere throughout history until recently. The most extreme version of the custom of arranged marriages occurred in prerevolutionary China, where a bride and groom often met for the first time on their wedding day.

Thematic Link—The Right Choice?
In this story, the narrator is forced to decide whether the right choice is marrying within his ethnic group or marrying the woman he loves.

Autobiography

Like Mexicans

GARY SOTO (sō' tō)

Examine What You Know (Prior Knowledge)

In this true story, the narrator faces pressure from his family and friends to marry someone of his own ethnic group and social class. How important do you think it is to marry someone from your own background? How important would your decision be to your parents or other relatives? Answer the questions below as *you* would answer them and then as you think your parents would answer them. Discuss your responses with your classmates. Then compare your responses with those made by Soto in the story.

1. How important is marrying someone of your own ethnic group?
2. How important is marrying someone of your own social class?

Expand Your Knowledge (Building Background)

In the selection you are about to read, Gary Soto's grandmother uses the term *Okie* to refer to anyone who is neither Mexican, Asian, not African-American. The word originally comes from the name *Oklahoma.* During the 1930's, Oklahoma and surrounding states were hit by violent wind and dust storms that destroyed farmland. Farmers who migrated west from any of these Dust Bowl states became known as Okies. Gary's grandmother, however, gives the term a wider meaning.

Write Before You Read (Journal Writing)

In this story, Gary Soto writes about his problems in choosing a person to marry. In your journal or on a piece of paper, write a description of the kind of person *you* would like to marry. Describe this person's personality, interests, and goals as well as his or her physical appearance and background. Entitle this profile "My Perfect Mate."

■ *A biography of the author can be found in the Reader's Handbook.*

Additional Journal Writing

Suggest these journal topics to students:

- Write your thoughts about this statement: "I was in love and there was no looking back."
- What advice would you give someone else about choosing a mate?
- How do you think your description of the ideal mate would compare to one your parents or guardians might draw up for you?

For other journal opportunities, refer students to First Impressions (p. 35) and annotation I.

Additional Resources

UNIT ONE RESOURCE BOOK
Reader's Guidesheet, p. 6
Vocabulary Worksheet, p. 7
Selection Checktest, p. 8
Selection Test, pp. 9–10

Collaborative Learning

Opportunities for collaborative learning appear throughout the lesson and include Cultural Connection (p. T-33) and Real Life Connections (p. T-34).

Like Mexicans

GARY SOTO

A My grandmother gave me bad advice and good advice when I was in my early teens. For the bad advice, she said that I should become a barber because they made good money and listened to the radio all day. "Honey, they don't work *como*[1] *burros,*" she would say every time I visited her. She made the sound of donkeys braying. "Like that, honey!" For the good advice, she said that I should marry a Mexican girl. "No Okies,[2] *hijo*"[3]—she would say—"Look my son. He marry one, and they fight every day about I don't know what and I don't know what." For her, everyone who wasn't Mexican, black, or Asian was an Okie. The French were Okies; the Italians in suits were Okies. When I asked about B Jews, whom I had read about, she asked for a picture. I rode home on my bicycle and returned with a calendar depicting the important races of the world. *"Pues si, son Okies tambien!"*[4] she said, nodding her head. She waved the calendar away, and we went to the living room where she lectured me on the virtues of the Mexican girl: first, she could cook, and second, she acted like a woman, not a man, in her husband's home. She said she would tell me about a third SR-1 ▶ when I got a little older.

I asked my mother about it—becoming a barber and marrying Mexican. She was in the kitchen. Steam curled from a pot of boiling beans; the radio was on, looking as squat as a loaf of bread. "Well, if you want to be a barber—they say they make good money." She slapped a round steak with a knife, her glasses slipping down with each strike. She stopped and looked up. "If you find a good Mexican girl, marry her of course." She returned to slapping the meat, and I went to the backyard, where my brother and David King were sitting on the lawn. . . .

I ignored them and climbed the back fence to see my best friend, Scott, a second-generation Okie. I called him, and his mother pointed to the side of the house where his bedroom was a small aluminum trailer, the kind you gawk at when they're flipped over on the freeway, wheels spinning in the air. I went around to find Scott C pitching horseshoes.

I picked up a set of rusty ones and joined him. While we played, we talked about school and friends and record albums. The

1. ***como*** (kô′ mô) *Spanish:* a term of comparison meaning "like" or "as."

2. **Okies:** farm workers who move from place to place to harvest seasonal crops; in this case, those forced to leave Oklahoma or other areas of the Great Plains as a result of drought or farm foreclosure in the late 1930's.

3. ***hijo*** (ē′ hô) *Spanish:* son.

4. ***"Pues si, son Okies tambien!"*** (pwes sē sôn ō′ kēs täm byen′): "Well yes, they are Okies also."

Teaching Strategies

Support for Students of Limited English Proficiency

■ Use the **Reader's Guidesheet,** p. 6.

■ Attitudes displayed by characters in "Like Mexicans" may be troubling to students with limited English proficiency. The way in which Gary's grandmother dismisses all ethnic whites as "Okies" is intended to be humorous but may strike some readers as offensive. Discuss the context and spirit in which these remarks and attitudes are made. Point out the irony in having a character who is a victim of prejudice mouthing her own somewhat bizarre prejudices. Terms that students may find unfamiliar include *braying, grounders, guys, patties, fiancée, pull-yourself-up-by-your-bootstraps,* and *U-turn.*

■ **Annotations C** and **E** address terms that may be troubling.

Text Annotations

A. Literary Element: POINT OF VIEW Explain that Soto is telling the story through his own eyes. Have students explore the advantages of this method of telling a story. *(Possible response: a sense of immediacy and identification; a feeling of intimacy)*

B. Critical Thinking: ANALYZING Ask students why Soto's grandmother finds it difficult to distinguish people of different races. *(Possible response: She has had very limited experience with people other than Mexicans; she may not even know about some races.)*

C. LEP: Setting Explain that "horseshoes" is a common rural game in which U-shaped metal pieces are tossed at a ring thirty to forty feet away.

Structured Reading for Less Proficient Students

These questions can help to guide students through the reading. Ask each question at the point of the selection where the SR number appears in the margin.

SR–1. What evidence does Soto's grandmother give as she tries to persuade him to marry a Mexican, not an Okie? *(Her son married an Okie, and he and his wife fight quite often.)* **Literal recall**

SR–2. How has Soto, as a seventh grader, reacted to his grandmother's advice? *(He has accepted it.)* **Synthesizing**

SR–3. Why is Soto thinking of marrying the Japanese woman? *(He loves her.)* **Literal recall**

SR–4. Why does Soto question whether he made the right choice? *(because he thinks about the advice of his mother, brother, and best friend, Scott.)* **Literal recall**

SR–5. What does Soto finally decide about his choice? *(Her people are like Mexicans, only different; he has made the right choice.)* **Literal recall**

Art Note

With the title *Sandía/Watermelon,* artist Carmen Lomas Garza (1948–) tells us that the family shown enjoying a popular hot-weather treat speaks both Spanish and English, *sandía* being the Spanish word for watermelon. *Judging by the house with its wide porch and surrounding shrubs, decide in what part of the United States a scene like this might be found.*

D. Reading Skill: COMPARING AND CONTRASTING Ask students to compare and contrast Gary and Scott. *(Possible response: Although each boy vows to marry only a woman of his ethnic background, they otherwise share the same "seventh-grade" goals: to marry, get jobs, buy cars, and buy a house if possible.)*

E. LEP: Setting Explain that J. C. Penney's is a well-known nationwide department store specializing in clothing, home furnishings, and catalog sales.

SANDIA/WATERMELON 1986 Carmen Lomas Garza By permission of the artist.

horseshoes scuffed up dirt, sometimes ringing the iron that threw out a meager shadow like a sundial. After three argued-over games, we pulled two oranges apiece from his tree and started down the alley, still talking school and friends and record albums. We pulled more oranges from the alley and talked about who we would marry. "No offense, Scott," I said with an orange slice in my mouth, "but I would never marry an Okie." We walked in step, almost D touching, with a sled of shadows dragging behind us. "No offense, Gary," Scott said, "but I would *never* marry a Mexican." I looked at him: a fang of orange slice showed from his munching mouth. I didn't think anything of it. He had his girl and I had mine. But our seventh-grade vision was D the same: to marry, get jobs, buy cars and ◀SR-2 maybe a house if we had money left over.

We talked about our future lives until, to our surprise, we were on the downtown mall, two miles from home. We bought a bag of popcorn at Penney's and sat on a E bench near the fountain watching Mexican and Okie girls pass. "That one's mine," I pointed with my chin when a girl with eyebrows arched into black rainbows ambled by. "She's cute," Scott said about a girl with yellow hair and a mouthful of gum. We

PROFESSIONAL NOTEBOOK

[In learning] we have to distinguish two points of view: [that of the adult teacher and the student]. [The teacher] knows the meaning and possesses the components of the structure. [The student] has no a priori *knowledge of what [the learning task] consists of, so long as he himself has not achieved it. . . . The temptation to provide feedback based on an adult understanding of the material is great, but it would disregard the appropriateness and validity of the student's own point of view. . . .*

The mistakes that the student perceives are dependent on his own cognitive level and not upon the level projected by the adult. . . . To say that the world of the student is qualitatively different from the adult is not merely a statement about style or an image; it reflects a reality.

GILBERT VOYAT, "THE DEVELOPMENT OF OPERATIONS: A THEORETICAL AND PRACTICAL MATTER," *Piaget in the Classroom* (ED. BY MILTON SCHWEBEL AND JANE RAPH)

dreamed aloud, our chins busy pointing out girls. We agreed that we couldn't wait to become men and lift them onto our laps.

F But the woman I married was not Mexican but Japanese. It was a surprise to me. For years, I went about wide-eyed in my search for the brown girl in a white dress at a dance. I searched the playground at the baseball diamond. When the girls raced for grounders, their hair bounced like something that couldn't be caught. When they sat together in the lunchroom, heads pressed together, I knew they were talking about us Mexican guys. I saw them and dreamed them. I threw my face into my pillow, making up sentences that were good as in the movies.

I was in love and there was no looking back.

But when I was twenty, I fell in love with this other girl who worried my mother, who had my grandmother asking once again to see the calendar of the important races of the world. I told her I had thrown it away years before. I took a much-glanced-at snapshot from my wallet. We looked at it together, in silence. Then grandma reclined in her chair, lit a cigarette, and said,

G "*Es*[5] pretty." She blew and asked with all her worry pushed up to her forehead: "Chinese?"

I was in love and there was no looking back. She was the one. I told my mother, who was slapping hamburger into patties, "Well, sure if you want to marry her," she said. But the more I talked, the more concerned she became. Later I began to worry. Was it all a mistake? "Marry a Mexican girl," I heard my mother say in my mind. I heard it at breakfast. I heard it over math problems, between Western civilization and cultural geography. But then one afternoon while I was hitchhiking home from school, it struck me like a baseball in the back: my H

mother wanted me to marry someone of my own social class—a poor girl. I considered my fiancée, Carolyn, and she didn't look poor, though I knew she came from a family of farm workers and pull-yourself-up-by-your-bootstraps ranchers. I asked my brother, who was marrying Mexican poor that fall, if I should marry a poor girl. He screamed, "Yeah," above his terrible guitar playing in his bedroom. I considered my sister who had married Mexican. Cousins I

were dating Mexican. Uncles were remarrying poor women. I asked Scott, who was still my best friend, and he said, "She's too good for you, so you better not." ◀SR-3 ◀SR-4

I worried about it until Carolyn took me home to meet her parents. We drove in her Plymouth until the houses gave way to farms and ranches and finally her house fifty feet from the highway. When we pulled into the drive, I panicked and begged Carolyn to make a U-turn and go back so we could talk about it over a soda. She pinched my cheek, calling me a "silly boy." I felt better, though, when I got out of the car and saw the house: the chipped paint, a cracked window, boards for a walk to the back door. There were rusting cars near the barn. A tractor J

with a net of spiderwebs under a mulberry. A field. A bale of barbed wire like children's scribbling leaning against an empty chicken coop. Carolyn took my hand and pulled me to my future mother-in-law, who was coming out to greet us.

5. *Es* (ës): she is.

F. Reading Skill: PREDICTING Ask students to predict why Soto would marry a Japanese woman when for years he had been looking to marry a Mexican woman. *(Possible responses: He fell in love with the Japanese woman; he wanted to go against what was expected of him.)*

G. Literary Element: CHARACTERIZATION Ask students to explain why Soto's grandmother says only, "*Es* pretty" and "Chinese?". *(Possible response: She wisely keeps her true opinions to herself; she has changed her mind and now values her grandson's happiness over all other considerations.)*

H. Reading Skill: UNDERSTANDING MAIN IDEA Ask what shared quality Soto concludes that his mother thinks is most crucial in a wife. *(social class)*

I. Teaching Tip

Point out to students that, despite his pose of certainty, Soto's survey of all his relatives and friends reveals his underlying doubt. Ask students to trace the process that they follow when they are faced with a key decision. What steps do they follow? Which people's opinions do they especially value, and why?

J. Literary Element: SETTING Ask students to explain what this setting reveals about the characters. *(Possible response: Soto's comfort at the sight reveals that his family is as poor as Carolyn's; her lack of shame reveals that she is proud of her parents' efforts to succeed despite adversity.)*

CULTURAL CONNECTION

To help students understand the tradition of grandparents living with their married children and commanding great respect within the home, ask students from other countries to discuss the definition of *family* in their cultures. You might want to compare and contrast their definitions. Relate this to young Soto's willingness to seek and then internalize his grandmother's advice.

K. Critical Thinking: EVALUATING Ask students if they agree that the differences between Soto's family and Carolyn's are erased by the shared bond of poverty. *(Possible response: Yes, because they are of the same social class; no, because they are still of different ethnic groups.)*

L. Critical Thinking: ANALYZING Have students analyze what message about class and race in America Soto is suggesting by having Carolyn's family and Gary share apple pie and coffee. *(Possible response: Sharing these "American" foods implies that, despite differences in class or ethnic background, we are united by a common culture.)*

Check Test

1. What two pieces of advice did Soto's grandmother give him during his early teens? *(become a barber and marry a Mexican girl)*

2. What was the ethnic group of the woman Soto finally married? *(Japanese)*

3. What did Soto's best friend, Scott, say of Soto's upcoming marriage to Carolyn? *("She's too good for you, so you better not.")*

4. What does Soto feel about Carolyn's family after he visits them? *(that they are "like Mexicans")*

Encouraging Independent Reading

"Modern Children," a short story by Sholom Aleichem

A Chicano in China, nonfiction by Rudolfo A. Anaya

"The Good Deed," a short story by Pearl S. Buck

"Gentlemen of Río en Medio," a short story by Juan A. A. Sedillo

Living up the Street, nonfiction by Gary Soto

We had lunch: sandwiches, potato chips, and iced tea. Carolyn and her mother talked mostly about neighbors and the congregation at the Japanese Methodist Church in West Fresno. Her father, who was in khaki work clothes, excused himself with a wave that was almost a salute and went outside. I heard a truck start, a dog bark, and then the truck rattle away.

Carolyn's mother offered another sandwich, but I declined with a shake of my head and a smile. I looked around when I could, when I was not saying over and over that I was a college student, hinting that I could take care of her daughter. I shifted my chair. I saw newspapers piled in corners, dusty cereal boxes and vinegar bottles in corners. The wallpaper was bubbled K from rain that had come in from a bad roof. Dust. Dust lay on lamp shades and window sills. These people are just like Mexicans, I thought. Poor people.

Carolyn's mother asked me through Carolyn if I would like a *sushi.*[6] A plate of black and white things was held in front of me. I took one, wide-eyed, and turned it over like a foreign coin. I was biting into one when I saw a kitten crawl up the window screen over the sink. I chewed, and the kitten opened its mouth of terror as she crawled higher, wanting in to paw the leftovers from our plates. I looked at Carolyn, who said that the cat was just showing off. I looked up in time to see it fall. It crawled up, then fell again.

We talked for an hour and had apple pie and coffee, slowly. Finally, we got up, with L Carolyn taking my hand. Slightly embarrassed, I tried to pull away, but her grip held me. I let her have her way as she led me down the hallway with her mother right behind me. When I opened the door, I was startled by a kitten clinging to the screen door, its mouth screaming "cat food, dog biscuits, *sushi* . . ." I opened the door, and the kitten, still holding on, whined in the language of hungry animals. When I got into Carolyn's car, I looked back: the cat was still clinging. I asked Carolyn if it was possibly hungry, but she said the cat was being silly. She started the car, waved to her mother, and bounced us over the rain-poked drive, patting my thigh for being her lover baby. Carolyn waved again. I looked back, waving, then gawking at a window screen where there were now three kittens clawing and screaming to get in. Like Mexicans, I thought. I remembered the Molinas and how the cats clung to their screens—cats they shot down with squirt guns. On the highway, I felt happy, pleased by it all. I patted Carolyn's thigh. Her people were like Mexicans, only different. ❧ ◀SR-5

6. ***sushi*** (sōō' shē): cold rice dressed with vinegar, formed into small cakes, topped with garnishes, and served with raw fish.

DATA BANK

Point out to students that Gary Soto comes to feel that, despite ethnic and cultural differences, he and Carolyn share a common socioeconomic background and will be happy together. Ask students what shared qualities they think are most important for ensuring a happy real-life marriage. Have them explain their answers.

Responding to Reading

First Impressions

1. Is the narrator's decision to marry Carolyn "the right choice"? Jot down your thoughts in your journal or on a piece of paper.

Second Thoughts

2. What do you think of the grandmother's advice that Soto should marry a Mexican girl?

   Think about
   - your decision on the importance of marrying in your social class
   - what you wrote in your profile of the perfect mate
   - what the grandmother says about people who marry Okies
   - how Soto reacts to her advice

3. Do you think any of the characters in this selection are prejudiced against other groups? Explain.

4. Why does Soto ask so many people for advice on whom to marry?

5. Why does Soto say that Carolyn's relatives are just "like Mexicans"?

   Think about
   - what he associates with being Mexican
   - what he expects to find at Carolyn's farm
   - what he actually finds

Literary Concept: Point of View

The way a writer tells a story is called the **point of view.** The narrator in "Like Mexicans" tells the story from the first-person point of view to show the narrator's thoughts and reactions. Could any other character have written about this experience as effectively as Soto has? Explain.

Writing Options

1. Soto asks a lot of people for advice before making his decision to marry Carolyn. Write a letter he might have sent to a newspaper advice columnist. Then write the columnist's advice to Soto.

2. What if Carolyn's house had been a mansion, complete with servants, immaculate and richly decorated rooms, and elegant and sophisticated parents. Would Soto have made the same decision? Explain your answer.

Student Response

Responding to Reading

These questions are open-ended with no "right" or "wrong" answers. However, reponses must be supported with information from the selection. Possible answers follow:

1. Any response is valid. Encourage students to express their opinions in specific terms.

2. Some students may say that the grandmother's advice is sound, given the wisdom that she has gathered through experience; others might claim that she discounts the power of love. Some might also feel that no one should give advice about selecting a mate, because this is a personal decision.

3. Some may feel that Gary's grandmother, for example, is prejudiced, as evident in her advice; others may say that since she sees other racial and ethnic groups as different but not inferior, her prejudice is harmless. Gary seems open-minded about other groups, yet in the end he confesses to being incapable of marrying someone who does not share his economic background. Scott exhibits prejudice when he says that he wouldn't marry a Mexican, but the fact that he is Gary's best friend tempers his remark. Only Carolyn and her family, who are briefly described, fail to exhibit any prejudice.

4. Some say that Soto seeks advice because he is unsure of himself; others may see his actions as wise because he is using the opinions of others to help clarify his own opinion about what is really important.

5. Some may believe that Soto's conclusion is based on their shared economic background; others may cite the warm hospitality extended to him.

Literary Concept—Point of View

There is no right or wrong answer to the question posed about point of view. Students should think about how other characters may have portrayed Gary's dilemma—his grandmother, his mother, his brother, Scott, and Carolyn.

Writing Options

The Writing Options are designed to meet varied student interests and abilities. Have each student select one writing activity to complete. You may wish to guide some students to an option that requires less writing.

Journal Update Have students review their journal entries for "Like Mexicans." Ask what they have learned about the problems of choosing a mate.

e x p l o r e

Objectives

- To understand and analyze a short story
- To analyze the use of characterization
- To understand cause and effect in a story
- To express understanding of the work through a choice of writing forms, including diary entries, a speech, a newspaper article, and a story ending

Prereading/Motivation

Examine What You Know

Discussion Prompts: What might be some positive effects of peer pressure? How can you lessen peer pressure?

Expand Your Knowledge

Discussion Prompts: What qualities might help a student fit in to life in a military academy? What might be some results of not fitting in there?

Enrich Your Reading

Have students copy the chart and complete it as they read. These are possible answers:
Cause 2: Students realize that Mr. Warren is deaf. **Effect 2:** They take advantage of him. **Cause 3:** Major Durand boxes with Mr. Warren. **Effect 3:** Mr. Warren is hit and gets a bloody nose. **Cause 4:** Mr. Warren saves Teddy. **Effect 4:** Mr. Warren is rehired. **Cause 5:** Pentecost helps Mr. Warren. **Effect 5:** The boys quiet down. **Cause 6:** Mr. Warren seeks help from Pentecost a second time. **Effect 6:** Pentecost looks away.

Thematic Link—The Right Choice?
In this story, the main character must choose between his conscience and peer pressure to make the right choice.

Fiction

A Kind of Murder

HUGH PENTECOST

Examine What You Know (Prior Knowledge)

The main character in the story you are about to read is influenced by peer pressure when making decisions. How much does peer pressure affect you and your classmates? To find out, discuss the following questions with your peers.

- How would you define peer pressure?
- What are some examples of peer pressure with which you are familiar?
- In what circumstances is peer pressure strongest?
- Why are some people apparently unaffected by peer pressure?

Expand Your Knowledge (Building Background)

The setting of "A Kind of Murder" is a private military academy. A military academy is run much like the armed forces. Discipline, order, and respect for authority are hallmarks of such schools. Students are given rank, wear uniforms, and adhere to strict rules. Students normally board, or eat and sleep, at these schools. Constant contact with one another and isolation from the outside often increase the peer pressures felt by the students and teachers.

Enrich Your Reading (Reading Skill)

Cause and Effect The events in a story are often connected by **cause and effect.** In other words, one event is the reason why another happens. The event that happens first is the **cause.** The **effect** is the event that follows. As you read "A Kind of Murder," you will be asked to note examples of cause and effect. When you reach these points, write your responses on a chart like the one below.

Cause	Effect
1. Mt. Etsweiler dies.	Mr. Warren is hired.
2.	

■ *A biography of the author can be found on page 46.*

Journal Writing

Suggest these journal topics to students:

- Think about literal meanings of the word *murder* in phrases such as *to murder the opposition* and *a murderous look.* Then write about what you think "A Kind of Murder" might be.
- Is it important to "fit in" and not be different from others? Explain.

For other journal opportunities, refer students to Real Life Connections (p. T-43).

Additional Resourses

UNIT ONE RESOURCE BOOK
Reader's Guidesheet, p. 11
Vocabulary Worksheet, p. 12
Selection and Vocabulary Check Tests, p. 13
Selection Test, pp. 14–15

Collaborative Learning

Opportunities for collaborative learning appear throughout the lesson and include Options for Learning (p. 46) and Cross-Curricular Options (p. T-46).

A Kind of Murder

HUGH PENTECOST

A You might say this is the story of a murder—although nobody was killed. I don't know what has become of Mr. Silas Warren, but I have lived for many years with the burden on my conscience of having been responsible for the existence of a walking dead man.

I was fifteen years old during the brief span of days that I knew Mr. Silas Warren. It was toward the end of the winter term at Morgan Military Academy. Mr. Etsweiler, the chemistry and physics teacher at Morgan, had died of a heart attack one afternoon while he was helping to coach the hockey team on the lake.

B **cause** Mr. Etsweiler dies. What is the effect?

Mr. Henry Huntingdon Hadley, the headmaster, had gone to New York to find a replacement. That replacement was Mr. Silas Warren.

I may have been one of the first people to see Mr. Warren at the Academy. I had been excused from afternoon study period because of a heavy cold, and allowed to take my books to my room to work there. I saw Mr. Warren come walking across the quadrangle toward Mr. Hadley's office, which was located on the ground floor under the hall where my room was.

Mr. Warren didn't look like a man who was coming to stay long. He carried one small, flimsy suitcase spattered with travel labels. Although it was a bitter March day he wore a thin, summer-weight topcoat. He stopped beside a kind of brown lump in the snow. That brown lump was Teddy, the school dog. ◀SR-1

Teddy was an ancient collie. They said that in the old days you could throw a stick for Teddy to retrieve until you, not he, dropped from exhaustion. Now the old, gray-muzzled dog was pretty much ignored by everyone except the chef, who fed him scraps from the dining room after the noon meal. Teddy would be at the kitchen door, promptly on time, and then find a comfortable spot to lie down. He'd stay there until someone forced him to move.

Mr. Warren stopped by Teddy, bent down, and scratched the dog's head. The old, burr-clotted tail thumped wearily in the snow. Mr. Warren straightened up and looked around. He had narrow, stooped shoulders. His eyes were pale blue, and they had a kind of frightened look in them. *He's scared,* I thought; *coming to a new place in the middle of a term, he's scared.* C

Words to Know and Use

quadrangle (kwä' draŋ' gəl) *n.* an area, at a school or college, that is surrounded on four sides by buildings

37

Teaching Strategies

Vocabulary Preview

These vocabulary words are defined at the bottom of the selection page where they appear. You may wish to discuss them briefly before students begin reading.

amiable appearing friendly
contempt a feeling of scorn
cordial warm, friendly
demise death
falsetto high-pitched
infirmary room where the sick are cared for
menace threat
pulverize crush
quadrangle an area surrounded by buildings on four sides
sadist a person who gets pleasure from hurting others
squeamish easily nauseated
tyranny harshness
valor bravery or courage

Support for Students of Limited English Proficiency

- Use Reader's Guidesheet, p. 11
- "A Kind of Murder" has words specific to a military academy, which is far removed from many students' experiences. Have them compare life in such a school to their own school experiences.
- Annotations D, H, M, Q, and W focus on vocabulary.

Text Annotations

A. Reading Skill: PREDICTING Ask students to explain how there could be a murder when no one was killed. *(Possible response: "Murder" can refer to an emotional rather than a physical death.)*

B. Reading Skill: CAUSE AND EFFECT *(Mr. Hadley, the headmaster, must find a replacement. He hires Mr. Warren.)*

C. Literary Element: CHARACTERIZATION Have students discuss Mr. Warren's traits and the details that reveal them. *(kindliness—he "scratched the dog's head"; defeated—with "narrow, stooped shoulders"; fearful—he has a "frightened look")*

Structured Reading for Less Proficient Students

These questions can help to guide students through the reading. Ask each question at the point of the selection where the SR number appears in the margin.

SR–1. What details suggest that Mr. Warren is not "coming to stay long"? *(His suitcase is small and covered with travel labels; his coat is thin.)* **Recognizing relevant details**

SR–2. Why might Mr. Warren be smiling? *(Possible responses: He wants to be liked. He is keeping up his spirits.)* Why might there be terror in his heart? *(Possible responses: He fears the boys or his ability to handle the job.)* **Inferring**

SR–3. How is the disturbance in the study hall settled? *(Old Beaver, the headmaster, appears and disciplines the boys.)* **Literal recall**

SR–4 How would you compare Mr. Warren and Major Durand? *(Possible response: They are opposites. Durand is aggressive, enjoys hurting others. Warren is a pacifist, eager to please.)* **Comparing**

Continued on page 38

D. LEP: Vocabulary Explain to students that a *cadet* is a student in a private military school and *major* is a rank. The *cadet major* is therefore a student leader. In this case, he is in charge of seeing that the other cadets enter the dining hall in an orderly manner.

E. Teaching Tip
Ask students to explain the different meanings *jump in the lake* can have. Guide them to see that it is most often used in a metaphorical sense (to get lost) but can also be taken literally. Tell students to keep Sammy's words in mind. The story hinges on the narrator's response to Mr. Warren's metaphorical and literal jumps into the lake.

F. Reading Skill: CAUSE AND EFFECT *(The students take advantage of him.)*

G. Literary Element: CHARACTERIZATION Have students contrast Old Beaver to Mr. Warren, explaining with specific references to the text how the two men are different. *(Old Beaver is clearly in command; Mr. Warren is terrified. Details include Old Beaver's "glittering" eyes and noiseless, sudden appearance; Mr. Warren crying "Boys!" as if in pain.)*

I guess most of the other fellows didn't see Mr. Warren until he turned up at supper time at the head of one of the tables in the dining room. D We marched into the dining room and stood behind our chairs waiting for the cadet major to give the order to be seated. The order was delayed. Mr. Henry Huntingdon Hadley, known as Old Beaver because of his snowy white beard, made an announcement.

"Mr. Warren has joined our teaching staff to fill the vacancy created by the unfortunate demise of Mr. Etsweiler." Old Beaver had false teeth and his *s*'s whistled musically. "I trust you will give him a cordial welcome."

"Be seated," the cadet major snapped.

We sat. Old Beaver said grace. Then we all began to talk. I was at Mr. Warren's right. He had a genial, want-to-be-liked smile.

"And your name is?" he asked me in a pleasant but flat voice.

"Pentecost, sir."

He leaned toward me. "How's that?" he asked.

"Pentecost, sir."

E Sammy Callahan sat across from me on Mr. Warren's left. Sammy was a fine athlete and a terrible practical joker. I saw a gleam of interest in his eyes. As Mr. Warren turned toward him Sammy spoke in an ordinary conversational tone. "Why don't you go take a jump in the lake, sir?"

Mr. Warren smiled. "Yes, I guess you're right," he said.

Sammy grinned at me. There was no doubt about it—Mr. Warren was quite deaf!

It was a strange kind of secret Sammy and I had. We didn't really know what to do with it, but we found out that night. Old Beaver was not a man to start anyone in gradually. It would have been Mr. Etsweiler's turn to take the night study hour, so that hour was passed on to Mr. Warren.

F The students realize Mr. Warren is deaf. What is the effect? **cause**

He sat on the little platform at the head of the study hall—smiling and smiling. I think there must have been terror in his heart then. I think he may even have been praying. ◀SR-2

Everyone seemed unusually busy studying, but we were all waiting for the test. The test always came for a new master the first time he had night study hour. There would be a minor disturbance and we'd find out promptly whether this man could maintain discipline, or not. It came after about five minutes—a loud, artificial belch.

Mr. Warren smiled and smiled. He hadn't heard it.

Belches sprang up all over the room. Then somebody threw a handful of torn paper in the air. Mr. Warren's smile froze.

"Now, now boys," he said.

More belches. More torn paper.

"Boys!" Mr. Warren cried out, like someone in pain.

G Then Old Beaver appeared, his eyes glittering behind rimless spectacles. There was something I never understood about Old Beaver. Ordinarily his shoes squeaked. You could hear him coming from quite a distance away—squeak-squeak, squeak-squeak. But somehow, when he chose, he could approach as noiselessly as a cat, without any squeak at all. And there he was.

Words to Know and Use

demise (dē mīz′) *n.* death
cordial (kôr′ jəl) *adj.* warm, friendly

38

STRUCTURED READING FOR LESS PROFICIENT STUDENTS

Continued from page 37

SR–5. Why is Mr. Warren leaving? *(Old Beaver may have fired him, or Mr. Warren may simply have given up.)* **Inferring**

SR–6. Why can't the boys save the old dog from drowning? *(Old Beaver forbids it.)* Why can't Old Beaver stop Mr. Warren? *(Mr. Warren no longer works for him.)* **Literal recall**

SR–7. What does the narrator believe is "the very last chance" that Mr. Warren will ever have? *(a second chance to teach at the academy)* **Literal recall**

SR–8. What happens the next time Mr. Warren has study hall? *(The boys act up again; Pentecost defends Mr. Warren and keeps the room quiet and orderly.)* **Summarizing**

SR–9. Why doesn't Pentecost answer Mr. Warren's wordless plea? *(Pentecost doesn't want to be snubbed and called a do-gooder. He thinks that Mr. Warren should be able to take care of himself and handle the high-spirited boys.)* **Literal recall**

The study hall was quiet as a tomb. But the silence was frighteningly loud, and the place was littered with paper.

"There will be ten demerit marks against every student in this room," Old Beaver said in his icy voice. "I want every scrap of paper picked up instantly."

Several of us scrambled down on our hands and knees. Mr. Warren smiled at the headmaster.

"Consider the lilies of the field," Mr. Warren said. "They toil not, neither do they spin. Yet I tell you that Solomon in all his glory—"[1]

There was an uncontrollable outburst of laughter.

"Silence!" Old Beaver hissed, with all the menace of a poised cobra. He turned to Mr. Warren. "I'll take the balance of this period, Mr. Warren. I suggest you go to your room and prepare yourself for tomorrow's curriculum."

I didn't have any classes with Mr. Warren the next day, but all you heard as you passed in the corridors from one class period to the next were tales of the jokes and disorders in the physics and chemistry courses. Somehow nobody thought it was wrong to take advantage of Mr. Warren.

The climax came very quickly. In the winter, if you weren't out for the hockey or winter sports teams, you had to exercise in the gym. There were the parallel bars, and the rings, and the tumbling mats. And there was boxing.

DAVID GRAVES, PEMBROKE STUDIOS, LONDON, TUESDAY 27TH APRIL 1982 1982 David Hockney Composite Polaroid 51¾" × 26¼" © David Hockney, 1982.

The boxing teacher was Major Durand, the military commandant. I know now that he was a sadist. Major Durand was filled

1. **"Consider the lilies of the field . . . glory":** a passage from the Bible (Matt. 6:28–29).

Words to Know and Use

menace (men′ əs) *n.* threat
sadist (sād′ ist) *n.* a person who gets pleasure from hurting others

39

H. LEP: Vocabulary Students may not understand what the "ten demerit" penalty means. Remind them of the system of rewards and punishments at a military academy.

I. Literary Sidelight Mr. Warren's allusion to the Bible (see footnote 1) continues "was not arrayed like one of these. . . . O ye of little faith?" It ends: "Take therefore no thought for the morrow: for the morrow shall take thought for the things of itself." The allusion implies that Mr. Warren believes that beauty is as valuable as physical prowess and that the future will take care of itself.

J. Critical Thinking: ANALYZING Ask students to discuss why the boys think that it is all right to take advantage of Mr. Warren. *(Possible responses: the effects of peer pressure; the fact that Mr. Warren seems inoffensive and powerless and that his appearance and bearing ill-fit a military academy.)*

Art Note

After British painter David Hockney (1937–) settled in Hollywood Hills in 1982, he suddenly saw that photography could be an art form. The grid placement of separate snapshots encourages the viewer to see and understand each object and part as distinct and vital in itself, yet necessary to the whole picture. *Who might this photocollage represent in "A Kind of Murder," and why?*

Professional Notebook

1. *Have students divide their tasks into small, clearly defined steps. Explain that instead of vowing to "finish all their work today," they should promise to spend half an hour reading or writing.*

2. *Suggest that students reward themselves as they complete their tasks, by calling a friend or playing a game of ball, for example.*

3. *Have them establish a series of small, realistic deadlines rather than a final date.*

4. *Finally, tell students to ask for support. Others may be able to tell them if their expectations are unrealistic.*

HINTS FOR PROCRASTINATORS FROM ERICA GOODE IN *U.S. NEWS & WORLD REPORT* (OCT. 1987)

K. Critical Thinking: EVALUATING Point out to students that Mr. Warren is baffled by the purpose of the demonstration. Ask students why they think Major Durand makes Mr. Warren box and if they think his actions are fair. *(Possible response: Major Durand is sadistic and insecure. Most students will find his actions reprehensible.)*

L. Reading Skill: CAUSE AND EFFECT *(Mr. Durand behaves like a bully and hits Mr. Warren.)*

M. LEP: Vocabulary Explain to students that a *payoff* can be the payment of a wager or salary, but it also refers to the moment of reckoning, as in retribution or reward. It is used in the latter sense here.

N. Reading Skill: COMPARE/CONTRAST Ask students to compare the narrator's opinion of Mr. Warren to the opinion held by the other students. Have them support their ideas with details from the story. *(Possible response: The narrator feels compassion for Mr. Warren; the others don't seem to. Details include "I felt a little squeamish about it," "He hadn't been given a chance." "Maybe he wasn't such a bad guy.")*

with contempt for everyone but Major Durand. I saw the look on his face when Mr. Warren appeared.

Mr. Warren had been assigned to help in the gym. He was something to see—just skin and bones. He had on a pair of ordinary black socks and, I suspect, the only pair of shoes he owned—black oxfords. He'd borrowed a pair of shorts that could have been wrapped twice around his skinny waist. Above that was a much mended short-sleeved undershirt. He looked around, hopeless, amiable.

K "Mr. Warren!" Major Durand said. "I'd like you to help me demonstrate. Put on these gloves if you will." He tossed a pair of boxing gloves at Mr. Warren, who stared at them stupidly. One of the boys helped him tie the laces.

"Now, Mr. Warren," Durand said. The Major danced and bobbed and weaved, and shot out his gloves in short vicious jabs at the air. "You will hold your gloves up to your face, sir. When you're ready you'll say 'Hit!'—and I shall hit you."

L

cause Major Durand boxes with Mr. Warren. What is the effect?

I'd seen Major Durand do this with a boy he didn't like. You held up the gloves and you covered your face and then, with your throat dry and aching, you said "Hit!"—and Major Durand's left or right would smash through your guard and pulverize your nose or mouth. It was sheer strength I know now, not skill.

Mr. Warren held up his gloves, and he looked like an actor in an old Mack Sennett[2] comedy—the absurd clothes, the sickly smile.

Durand danced in front of him. "Whenever you say, Mr. Warren. Now watch this, boys. The feint—and the jab."[3]

"Hit!" said Mr. Warren, his voice suddenly falsetto.

Pow! Major Durand's left jab smashed through the guard of Mr. Warren's nose. There was a sudden geyser of blood.

"Again, Mr. Warren!" the Major commanded, his eyes glittering.

"I think I'd better retire[4] to repair the damage," Mr. Warren said. His undershirt was spattered with blood and he had produced a soiled handkerchief which he held to his nose. He hurried out of the gym at a sort of shambling gallop. ◀ SR-5

M That night the payoff came in study hall. Mr. Warren was called on this time to substitute for Old Beaver, who had taken over for him the night before. Sammy Callahan staged it. Suddenly handkerchiefs were waved from all parts of the room—handkerchiefs stained red. Red ink, of course.

"Hit!" somebody shouted. "Hit, hit!" Nearly all the boys were bobbing, weaving, jabbing.

Mr. Warren, pale as a ghost, cotton visibly stuffed in one nostril, stared at us like a dead man.

Then there was Old Beaver again.

N Somehow the word was out at breakfast the next morning. Mr. Warren was leaving. He didn't show at the breakfast table. I felt a little squeamish about it. He hadn't been given a chance. Maybe he wasn't such a bad guy. ◀ SR-6

2. **Mack Sennett:** an early silent-film director famous for slapstick comedy.

3. **feint—and the jab:** boxing terms for faking and hitting.

4. **retire:** leave.

Words to Know and Use

contempt (kən tempt′) *n.* a feeling of scorn toward someone or something
amiable (ā′ mē ə bəl) *adj.* appearing friendly and pleasant
pulverize (pul′ vər īz′) *v.* to crush or destroy
falsetto (fôl set′ ō) *adj.* unusually high-pitched
squeamish (skwēm′ ish) *adj.* easily nauseated

40

PROFESSIONAL NOTEBOOK

Who [are discouraged learners]?

1. *They are low in self-confidence, have a deeply held sense of personal impotency, helplessness, and lack of self-worth.*

2. *They are avoiders. They avoid school because it is demanding and/or threatening [and] unresponsive to their needs. . . .*

3. *They are distrustful of adults and adult institutions. . . .*

4. *They have a limited notion of the future. . . .*

5. *They lack adequate . . . skills and have come to see themselves as "dumb" rather than unskilled.*

6. *. . . their parents often suffer similar characteristics. . . .*

7. *Because of . . . impatience . . . and low skills, [they are seen as] disruptive. . . .*

8. *[They] do not see a relationship between effort and achievement, but instead, see success as a matter of luck or ease of the task.*

JERRY CONRATH, *Our Other Youth*

POND PASS 1974
Neil Welliver Federal Reserve Bank of Boston.

It was during the morning classroom period that we heard it. It was a warm day for March and the ice was breaking up on the lake. The scream was piercing and terrified. Somebody went to the window. The scream came again.

"Somebody's fallen through the ice!"

The whole school—a hundred and fifty boys and masters—hurried down to the shore of the lake. The sun was so bright that all we could see was a dark shape flopping out there, pulling itself up on the ice and then disappearing under water as the ice broke. Each time the figure rose there was a wailing scream.

Then the identification. "It's Teddy!" someone shouted.

The school dog. He'd walked out there and the ice had caved in on him. The screams were growing weaker. A couple of us made for the edge of the ice. Old Beaver and Major Durand confronted us.

"I'm sorry, boys," Old Beaver said. "It's a tragic thing to have to stand here and watch the old dog drown. But no one—no one connected with the school—is to try to get to him. I'm responsible for your safety. That's an order." O

We stood there, sick with it. Old Teddy must have seen us because for a moment there seemed to be new hope in his strangled wailing.

Then I saw Mr. Warren. He was by the boathouse, his old suitcase in his hand. He

Art Note
Noted American landscape artist Neil Welliver (1929–) does most of his painting on the wooded acreage of his farm in Maine where, with his own crops and stock, he lives almost self-sufficiently. A patient observer of nature, he portrays its continually changing patterns and colors. *In this wintry scene, what are you reminded of when you look at the bright water reflecting treetops and sky?*

O. Critical Thinking: EVALUATING Point out that Old Beaver appears sincerely upset about the dog's plight but nonetheless forbids anyone to rescue the animal. Ask students if they agree with Old Beaver's decision. *(Possible responses: Some students may agree with Old Beaver that the boys' lives cannot be jeopardized; others may argue that there has to be a way to save the animal.)*

PROFESSIONAL NOTEBOOK

A school that devotes itself totally and unequivocally to salable skills, especially in a time of high unemployment, sending young men and women into the world armed with only a narrow range of skills, is also sending lambs into the lion's den. If these people gain nothing more from their studies than supposedly salable skills, and can't make the sale because of changes in the job market, they have been cheated. But if those skills were more than salable, if study made them better citizens and made them happier to be human beings, they have not been cheated. They will find some kind of job soon enough . . . . People who have learned how to learn can learn outside of school. That is where most of us have learned to do what we do, not in school. Learning to learn is one of the highest liberal skills.
ROBERT A. GOLDWIN, "IS IT ENOUGH TO ROLL WITH THE TIMES?"

P. Critical Thinking: ANALYZING Ask students to analyze the parallels between Teddy the dog and Mr. Warren. *(Possible response: The dog is literally sinking; Mr. Warren is figuratively drowning under the weight of his repeated failures.)*

Q. LEP: Vocabulary Explain that the phrase *old man* was sometimes used in the 1950's to refer in a friendly way to others. Ask volunteers for phrases that people commonly use today to refer to their friends. *(Possible responses: man, main man, bro, buddy)*

R. Literary Element CHARACTERIZATION Ask students to explain what Mr. Warren's actions in this paragraph reveal about his character. *(Possible responses: He is brave, courageous, strong; he shows humanity and decency.)*

S. Reading Skill: CAUSE AND EFFECT *(Everyone cheers him. He gets another chance at the school.)*

T. Reading Skill: CLARIFYING Ask students to explain why Sammy misbehaves in study hall and why the others giggle. *(Possible response: The students are testing Mr. Warren to see if he reacts differently now that he has bravely rescued Teddy. Their laughter indicates their delight in being able to continue their game.)*

looked out at the dog, and so help me there were tears in Mr. Warren's eyes. Then, very calmly, he put down his bag, took off his thin topcoat and suit jacket. He righted one of the overturned boats on the shore and pulled it to the edge of the lake. P

"Mr. Warren! You heard my order!" Old Beaver shouted at him.

Mr. Warren turned to the headmaster, smiling. "You seem to forget, sir, I am no longer connected with Morgan Military Academy, and therefore not subject to your orders." SR-7

"Stop him!" Major Durand ordered.

But before anyone could reach him, Mr. Warren had slid the flat-bottomed rowboat out onto the ice. He crept along on the ice himself, clinging to the boat, pushing it across the shiny surface toward Teddy. I heard Mr. Warren's thin, flat voice.

Q "Hold on, old man! I'm coming."

The ice gave way under him, but he clung to the boat and scrambled up—and on.

"Hold on, old man!"

R It seemed to take forever. Just before what must have been the last, despairing shriek from the half-frozen dog, Mr. Warren reached him. How he found the strength to lift the watersoaked collie into the boat, I don't know; but he managed, and then he came back toward us, creeping along the cracking ice, pushing the boat to shore.

The chef wrapped Teddy in blankets, put him behind the stove in the kitchen, and gave him a dose of warm milk and cooking brandy. Mr. Warren was hustled to the infirmary. Did I say that when he reached the shore with Teddy the whole school cheered him?

Old Beaver, for all his tyranny, must have been a pretty decent guy. He announced that night that Mr. Warren was not leaving after all. He trusted that, after Mr. Warren's display of valor, the boys would show him the respect he deserved.

Mr. Warren saves Teddy. What is the effect? **cause** S

I went to see Mr. Warren in the infirmary that first evening. He looked pretty done in, but he also looked happier than I'd ever seen him.

"What you did took an awful lot of courage," I told him. "Everybody thinks it was really a swell thing to do."

Mr. Warren smiled at me—a thoughtful kind of a smile. "Courage is a matter of definition," he said. "It doesn't take courage to stand up and let yourself get punched in the nose, boy. It takes courage to walk away. As for Teddy—somebody had to go after him. There wasn't anyone who could but me, so courage or not, I went. You'd have gone if Mr. Hadley hadn't issued orders." He sighed. "I'm glad to get a second chance here. Very glad."

Somehow I got the notion it was a last chance—the very last chance he'd ever have. SR-8

It was a week before Mr. Warren had the night study hall again. It was a kind of test. For perhaps fifteen minutes nothing happened and then I heard Sammy give his fine, artificial belch. I looked up at Mr. Warren. He was smiling happily. He hadn't heard. A delighted giggle ran around the room. T

I was on my feet. "If there's one more

Words to Know and Use

infirmary (in fur′ mə rē) *n.* a room or building where the sick or injured are cared for
tyranny (tir′ ə nē) *n.* harshness; cruel or unjust use of power
valor (val′ ər) *n.* bravery or courage

42

DATA BANK

It *is* remarkable that Mr. Warren was able to lift the water-soaked Teddy, because male collies weigh between 60 and 75 pounds dry and stand about 26 inches high at the shoulder. The collie has been one of the most popular dogs since the 1860's, when Queen Victoria of Great Britain became an enthusiastic sponsor of the breed. Collies are especially known as devoted family pets, very good as companions for children.

sound in this room I'm going after Old Beaver," I said. "And after that I'll personally take on every guy in this school if necessary, to knock sense into him!"

The room quieted. I was on the student council and I was also captain of the boxing team. The rest of the study period was continued in an orderly fashion. When it was over and we were headed for our rooms, SR-9 ▶ Mr. Warren flagged me down.

U

cause Pentecost stands up for Mr. Warren. What is the effect?

V "I don't know quite what was going on, Pentecost," he said, "but I gather you saved the day for me. Thank you. Thank you very much. Perhaps when the boys get to know me a little better they'll come to realize—" He made a helpless little gesture with his bony hands.

"I'm sure they will, sir," I said. "I'm sure of it."

"They're not cruel," Mr. Warren said. "It's just high spirits, I know."

Sammy Callahan was waiting for me in my room. "What are you, some kind of a do-gooder?" he said.

"Give the guy a chance," I said. "He proved he has guts when it's needed. But he's helpless there in the study hall."

Sammy gave me a sour grin. "You and he should get along fine," he said. "And you'll need to. The guys aren't going to be chummy with a do-gooder like you."

W It was a week before Mr. Warren's turn to run the study hour came around again. In that time I'd found that Sammy was right. I was being given the cold shoulder. Major Durand, who must have hated Mr. Warren for stealing the heroic spotlight from him, was giving me a hard time. One of the guys I knew well came to me.

"You're making a mistake," he told me. "He's a grown man and you're just a kid. If he can't take care of himself it's not your headache." X

I don't like telling the next part of it, but it happened. When Mr. Warren's night came again, the study hall was quiet enough for a while. Then came a belch. I looked up at Mr. Warren. He was smiling. Then someone waved one of those fake bloody handkerchiefs. Then, so help me, somebody let out a baying howl—like Teddy in the lake.

Mr. Warren knew what was happening now. He looked down at me, and there was an agonizing, wordless plea for help in his eyes. Y

Mr. Warren looks to Pentecost for help. What is the effect? **cause** Z

I—well, I looked away. I was fifteen. I didn't want to be called a do-gooder. I didn't want to be snubbed. Mr. Warren *was* a grown man and he should have been able to take care of himself. The boys weren't cruel: they were just high spirited—hadn't Mr. Warren himself said so? ◀ SR-10

I looked up from behind a book. Mr. Warren was standing, looking out over the room. His stooped, skinny shoulders were squared away. Two great tears ran down his pale cheeks. His last chance was played out. Then he turned and walked out of the study hall. AA

No one ever saw him again. He must have gone straight to his room, thrown his meager belongings into the battered old suitcase, and taken off on foot into the night.

You see what I mean when I say it was a kind of murder?

And I was the murderer. ❧

U. Reading Skill: CAUSE AND EFFECT *(The room quiets and orderly study resumes.)*

V. Critical Thinking: INFERRING Ask students to complete Mr. Warren's statement. *(Possible responses: that he is really a decent man; that he deserves their respect)*

W. LEP: Vocabulary Explain that the *cold shoulder* means to treat people with deliberate indifference.

X. Literary Element: THEME Ask students if they agree with the advice Pentecost is offered. *(Possible responses: All people are responsible for each other; kids should not have to be responsible for adults.)*

Y. Reading Skill: PREDICTING Ask students to predict Pentecost's response to Mr. Warren's plea. *(Possible responses: Pentecost will again intervene; Pentecost will do nothing.)*

Z. Reading Skill: CAUSE AND EFFECT *(Pentecost looks away.)*

AA. Literary Element: THEME Ask students if they feel that Mr. Warren made the "right choice" here. *(Possible responses: yes, because it took great courage; no, because he should have defended himself.)*

Check Test

1. Why is Mr. Warren coming to the school in the middle of a term? *(to replace Mr. Etsweiler, a teacher who has died)*

2. What disability does Mr. Warren have that the boys soon discover? *(He is deaf.)*

3. What caused Mr. Warren's bloody nose? *(a punch from Major Durand)*

4. Who does Mr. Warren save from the icy lake to win a second chance at the school? *(Teddy, the dog)*

Encouraging Independent Reading

"The Averted Strike," a short story by Charles W. Chesnutt

"Little Willie," a short story by Nadine Gordimer

Summer of My German Soldier, a novel by Bette Greene

"The Doll's House," a short story by Katherine Mansfield

"Fifteen," a poem by William Stafford

REAL LIFE CONNECTIONS

To help students understand the impulse to test a newcomer and the effects of peer pressure, have them discuss how baby sitters, substitute teachers, or new kids in school are sometimes tested. Ways of testing might include feigning illness, acting rudely, or playing tricks. Discuss the pangs of conscience people sometimes experience, perhaps years later, after they have misused someone in this manner.

To help students understand Pentecost's ability to protect Mr. Warren, ask them to describe what qualities make someone a leader. Then have them list the qualities that they admire in their peers. As a member of the student council and captain of the boxing team, Pentecost is a leader and an athlete. Are these attributes important to students? What other qualities earn respect?

Student Response

Responding to Reading

These questions are open-ended with no "right" or "wrong" answers. However, responses must be supported with information from the selection. Possible answers follow:

1. Almost any response to the end of the story is valid. Encourage students to voice their reactions in specific terms.

2. Some students may describe Mr. Warren as poor, frightened, deferential, and deaf; others may find him brave and sensitive.

3. Some may feel that Mr. Warren is such an easy target because he wants so much to be liked and appears unable to defend himself; others may say that simply being the newcomer with an obvious disability makes him a ready mark.

4. Some may say that the boys are cruel because Mr. Warren is obviously down on his luck and they are taking advantage of his handicap; others may cite peer pressure to argue that the boys are merely venting normal adolescent high spirits and testing a new teacher.

5. Some may agree with Mr. Warren's definition and admire his behavior; others may disagree, believing that his act is cowardly and that a person should not walk away from a confrontation.

6. Citing the effects of peer pressure, some may agree with Pentecost's decision not to defend Mr. Warren again; others may cite Pentecost's status to argue that he had a responsibility to help again.

7. Some may say that Pentecost uses the term *murder* to indicate his awareness that Mr. Warren is destroyed; others may say the term shows Pentecost's realization of his responsibility in hurting Mr. Warren.

8. Answers will vary. Possible responses: Students may say that they would base their decision on their closeness to the victim, the strength of their feelings about the issue, the degree of danger in the situation, their evaluation of the effect on themselves, and the neediness of the victim.

e x p l a i n

Responding to Reading

First Impressions

1. How did you feel about the ending of the story?

Second Thoughts

2. How would you describe Mr. Warren?

3. Why is Mr. Warren such an easy target for the students' pranks?

4. Mr. Warren says that the boys are not cruel, just high-spirited. What do you think? Why?

Think about
- the difference between cruelty and high spirits
- your earlier discussion about peer pressure
- the boys' antics in study hall

5. Read Mr. Warren's definition of courage on page 42. What do you think of this definition? Is Mr. Warren courageous? Why or why not?

6. Pentecost stands up for Mr. Warren in study hall once, but he does not defend him a second time. Do you agree with his decision?

Think about
- what might happen to Pentecost if he sided again with Mr. Warren
- your earlier discussion about your experiences with peer pressure

7. Why does Pentecost call what happened to Mr. Warren a murder, and is Pentecost responsible for Mr. Warren's death? Explain.

Broader Connections

8. How do you decide when to step in or speak out in someone's defense? When do you decide to keep silent?

Literary Concept: Characterization

The way a writer creates a character is called **characterization.** The reader learns about a character through the character's words and actions, through descriptions of the character, and through what other characters say about him or her. Look at page 37. What details about Mr. Warren does the writer give? From this description, what can you guess about Mr. Warren's past and future?

44 UNIT ONE THE RIGHT CHOICE?

Literary Concept—Characterization

(*Possible response:* *The writer gives details about Mr. Warren's appearance, clothing, luggage, and attitude. Mr. Warren has not been very successful in the past or stayed in one place very long. He is poor, oblivious to clothing, or perhaps has spent time in warm climates. Because of his unsuccessful past, he would not be expected to fare well at the academy.*)

Writing Options

1. Assume the character of Mr. Warren and write two brief diary entries for the night after the boxing incident and the night after the dog rescue.

2. You have been chosen by your classmates to head a committee to get Major Durand fired. As chairman, you must present Mr. Hadley with your case against Major Durand. Write a draft of the speech you will make.

3. As a reporter for the school newspaper, you are assigned to write a story about Mr. Warren's disappearance. Write an article that explains what happened, but be diplomatic to protect your friends.

4. What might have happened to Pentecost if he had stood up for Mr. Warren a second time? Rewrite the end of the story with the change.

Vocabulary Practice

Exercise Read the sentences below. On your paper write *True* if a sentence is true. Write *False* if it is false. Explain why each false statement is incorrect.

1. Mr. Etsweiler's **demise** created a vacancy in the faculty.
2. A **cordial** welcome would have made Mr. Warren feel defeated.
3. A **quadrangle** is an area usually enclosed on three sides.
4. An **amiable** teacher is one who is unfriendly and hostile.
5. **Tyranny** in the classroom helps students discuss issues freely.
6. Old Beaver asked the students to be pleasant and **cordial.**
7. A **sadist** like Durand is a very kind person.
8. The coach's friendly manner showed his **contempt** for others.
9. Mr. Warren sounded self-assured and confident when he shrieked "Hit" in a **falsetto** voice.
10. A direct hit from Major Durand could **pulverize** a student's nose or mouth.
11. Major Durand, a **sadist,** enjoyed hurting others.
12. Teddy, the gentle and lovable school mascot, was a **menace** to the students.
13. Mr. Warren showed great **valor** in saving Teddy.
14. Feeling sick, Mr. Warren ran to the **infirmary.**
15. Acting against his conscience left Pentecost with **squeamish** feelings.

Words to Know and Use

amiable
contempt
cordial
demise
falsetto
infirmary
menace
pulverize
quadrangle
sadist
squeamish
tyranny
valor

Writing Options

The Writing Options are designed to meet varied student interests and abilities. Have each student select one writing activity to complete. You may wish to guide some students to an option that requires less writing.

Journal Update: Have students review their journal entries for "A Kind of Murder." What have they learned about peer pressure?

Vocabulary Practice

1. **T**
2. **F** A cordial, or friendly, welcome would have made him feel good about coming to the school.
3. **F** A quadrangle is enclosed on four sides.
4. **F** An amiable teacher appears friendly.
5. **F** Tyranny, which means "unjust use of power," would discourage free discussion.
6. **T**
7. **F** Sadists, who like to hurt people, are not kind.
8. **F** A friendly manner would not show scorn.
9. **F** Generally, a high-pitched shriek would show fear, not confidence.
10. **T**
11. **T**
12. **F** A gentle mascot is not a threat.
13. **T**
14. **T**
15. **T**

Options for Learning

These activities suit a variety of learning styles and modes of expression. Allow students to review the options and then choose the one they wish to do. Many are excellent collaborative learning projects.

1. Design a Military Model Suggest that students use magazines or books to locate pictures of real military academies.

2. Writing a Classified Ad Suggest that students focus on finding newspaper ads for teachers in private and military schools.

3. Creating a Rap Students can listen to recordings of rap songs.

4. A "How-to" for Subs Students might interview substitute teachers.

Fact Finder

Students can locate this material in the dictionary or by calling a local recruiting station. A major is above a captain and below a lieutenant colonel.

Additional Information About the Author

Hugh Pentecost began writing professionally soon after his graduation from Columbia University in 1925 and published his first novel ten years later. His stories have appeared in many magazines, including *Cosmopolitan* and *Ellery Queen's Mystery Magazine.*

Closure

"A Kind of Murder" explores the difficulty of making the right choice. Young Pentecost feels guilty because he did not help Mr. Warren. Encourage students to become aware of their own reactions, and the reasons for them, when they are called on for help.

e x t e n d

Options for Learning

1 • Design a Military Model Draw or construct a model of Morgan Military Academy. Reread the story closely to figure out which buildings and features on the property to include. If possible, get some brochures of real academies from your school counselor to use as a guide.

2 • Writing a Classified Ad Morgan Military Academy needs a replacement for Mr. Warren; however, the administrators do not want to make another mistake by hiring someone who cannot do the job. It is your responsibility to write an announcement of this opening for the local paper. Be sure to include the qualifications you think are necessary to do the job. Look at classified advertisements in a newspaper to see how other job announcements are written.

3 • Creating a Rap Make up a rap or narrative poem that tells the story of Mr. Warren's short tenure at Morgan Military Academy. With a couple of your friends, perform your rap or poem for the class. If you wish, dress up like one of the popular rap groups.

4 • A "How-to" for Subs Your school has hired you to write a manual entitled *How to Succeed as a Substitute.* Based on your own experience and the experiences of Mr. Warren, write a brief set of recommendations for new substitute teachers.

FACT FINDER

In the United States military, between what two ranks does the rank of major fall?

Hugh Pentecost

1903–1989

While "A Kind of Murder" is not an actual murder mystery, Hugh Pentecost wrote many murder stories. Pentecost, whose real name was Judson Phillips, penned such novels as *Murder in Luxury, Murder as the Curtain Rises, Murder in High Places,* and *Past, Present, and Murder.* Pentecost also served as president of the Mystery Writers of America. In all, he wrote more than one hundred novels, as well as plays, movies, and radio and television scripts.

Cross-Curricular Options

Social Studies: Compile a list of presidents and vice-presidents who were educated at American military academies. Use an almanac or a book that contains presidential biographies to compile the list. Write the names and locations of the schools in which they were educated.

Social Studies: Compile a second list of other notable figures, such as artists, writers, scientists, inventors, and film makers. You might consult an almanac to find out about people to put on the list. Find out how many of these people attended military academies.

Math: Compare the percentages of people who attended military academies from each of the lists compiled above.

Art: Present the information about military academies in the form of a graph.

Critical Thinking: Discuss how important a military education is to the success of individuals later in life. Use your data to back up claims.

Elements of POETRY

Poetry is a special, exciting way of using language. Poets present ideas and feelings and even stories. They use sound and rhythm to emphasize their ideas. Poets also try to appeal to readers' emotions. That is why poetry is more than just words and meanings. Poetry—like other types of writing—creates experiences to be enjoyed and remembered.

Understanding Poetry

Form Poems usually look different from other types of writing. Poems are written in lines. The lines are grouped together in stanzas instead of paragraphs. Sometimes the poet uses the lengths of lines and the placement of words to create a shape on the page. The shape can add meaning or emphasis.

Sound More than other types of writing, poetry depends on the sounds as well as the meanings of words. The sound of a word can help create feeling and reinforce meaning. It can also give a musical quality to a work. Following are some techniques that poets use to create different sounds.

Alliteration is the repetition of a consonant sound at the beginnings of words.

Example: live and let live

Assonance is the repetition of a vowel sound within words.

Examples: rise and shine, down and out

Onomatopoeia is the use of words that imitate sounds.

Examples: whirr, creak, clunk, quack

Rhyme is the repetition of sounds at the ends of words as in *trod* and *plod.* Rhyming words usually come at the ends of lines of poetry.

Rhythm in a poem refers to the pattern of accented and unaccented syllables in a line. Some poems have a steady, regular rhythm or beat. The following lines of poetry are from "A Poison Tree" on page 642. In this example, the accented words are marked with (ʹ), while the unaccented, or light, syllables are marked with (˘).

I was angry with my friend:
I told my wrath, my wrath did end.
I was angry with my foe:
I told it not, my wrath did grow.

In other poems, the rhythm resembles the patterns of everyday speech. This type of rhythm, called **free verse,** is seen in this example from "Choices" on page 51.

if i can't do
what i want to do
then my job is to not
do what i don't want
to do

Imagery Poets choose words that help readers see, hear, feel, taste, and smell the things being described. This kind of sensory description is called **imagery.** Look at this example from "Birdfoot's Grampa" on page 627.

leathery hands full
of wet brown life,
knee deep in the summer
roadside grass.

Elements of Poetry

To help students verbalize their reactions to poetry, this feature offers them a common vocabulary that they can use to explore the poetry they will be reading. All the terms introduced here will be taught specifically in the selections that follow.

Objectives

- To understand and appreciate poetry
- To understand strategies for reading poetry
- To explore the link between form and content in poetry
- To understand ways of thinking about and interpreting a poem's message or theme

Motivation

Have students use the technique of cubing to explore the elements of poetry. On the chalkboard, draw three faces of a large cube. Write *Describe It* on one face, *Compare It* on another, and *Associate It* on the third. Then ask students to volunteer words and phrases to complete the cube. Your cube may look like this:

Complete the motivation by asking students to consider the following questions: How can you distinguish a poem from prose? What ways do poets have to help them convey exact meanings, feelings, and sounds to their readers? Why do you think people have come away with different meanings from the same poem? What poems have you read that you found meaningful?

Teaching Strategies

1. To help students understand poetry, read the first paragraph on page 47 aloud to students while they follow along silently. Then ask them to paraphrase what you read. Ask volunteers to share their paraphrases with the class.

Discussion Prompts: Why do you think poets try to appeal to their readers' emotions? If poetry is more than just words and meanings, what else is it? Why do you think some people like poetry very much and others do not?

2. Then talk about each of the terms, highlighting each example. For reinforcement, have students find additional examples from other poems in their text.

3. Next discuss each strategy on page 48. To make sure that students understand the strategies, select a poem from the text and show students how to use the reading strategies. "Choices" on page 51 works well. Read the poem aloud and demonstrate how to apply these strategies for reading poetry.

Closure

Have students explain in their journals how poets use language to present their thoughts and emotions. Encourage students to use in their explanations some of the terms that they just learned.

Figurative Language Language that describes things in a fresh new way is called **figurative language.** Poets often use figurative language to create word pictures. Types of figurative language include similes, metaphors, and personification.

A **simile** compares two dissimilar things using the words *like* or *as*. This line from "Ex-Basketball Player" on page 383 compares moving hands to birds.

His hands were like wild birds.

A **metaphor** is a direct comparison of unlike things. The words *like* or *as* are not used in the comparison. Here is an example from "Courage" on pages 354-355.

Your courage was a small coal that you kept swallowing.

Personification is another type of comparison. It gives human qualities to an object, animal, or idea. Notice how a basketball is given human qualities in this example from "Fast Break" on pages 381-382.

A hook shot kisses the rim, hangs there, helplessly, but doesn't drop.

Strategies for Reading Poetry

1. **Read** the poem aloud. **Listen** carefully in order to enjoy the sounds and rhythm of the words. Also pay attention to the punctuation. Read to a period, comma, or question mark rather than stopping at the end of each line.
2. Close your eyes and try to **visualize** any images in the poem.
3. **Imagine** the source of the voice you hear in the poem. Is the speaker a person, an animal, or an object? Is the speaker male or female, young or old, rich or poor? Does the speaker sound happy or sad, silly or serious?
4. **Think** about the words the poet has chosen. Do some have various meanings that might affect how you interpret the poem? Remember, in poetry every word is important; every word counts.
5. What is the **theme** of the poem? What important idea about life or human nature does the poem convey, or is the poem a lighthearted look at something?
6. **Paraphrase,** or put into your own words, the meaning or purpose of the poem. Also describe how the poem makes you feel.

e x p l o r e

Poetry

The Road Not Taken

ROBERT FROST

Choices

NIKKI GIOVANNI (jo vän' nē)

Examine What You Know (Prior Knowledge)

The two poems you are about to read deal with making choices. What do you think is the most important choice you have had to make in your life thus far? Fill out a chart like the one below to describe how you made this choice. Begin by describing your choice on the top line.

I decided to ______________________

People who influenced my decision	Reasons I chose to do this
______________	______________
______________	______________
______________	______________

Other options I had

______________ ______________

Expand Your Knowledge (Building Background)

In the poems you are about to read, the following words are used to describe directions you may choose to take. Read the definitions below. Then, as you read the next two poems, consider how these meanings affect your interpretation of the poems.

diverged—to branch off in different directions
parallel—extending in the same direction and always at the same distance apart
lateral—to or from the side, sideways

Write Before You Read (Journal Writing)

Making choices often means making compromises. Think about a choice you made recently when you also had to give up something in return. In your journal or on a piece of paper, write a brief description of this experience.

■ *Biographies of the authors can be found on page 53.*

Objectives

■ To understand and appreciate two poems

■ To understand rhyme scheme

■ To express understanding of the works through a choice of writing forms, including poetry and dialogue

Prereading/Motivation

Examine What You Know

Discussion Prompts: Why do you think this choice was so important? Do you think this choice will seem as important to you in five years? In ten years? What was the single most important factor in your eventual choice?

Expand Your Knowledge

Discussion Prompts: How would you use each of these three words in a sentence? Draw a picture that illustrates the positions or directions each word describes.

Thematic Link—The Right Choice?

In these poems, the speakers discuss ways of deciding upon "the right choice."

Additional Journal Writing

The speakers of "The Road Not Taken" and "Choices" are each faced with making *choices.* Suggest these additional journal topics to students:

■ What do you think are some of the most important choices you will have to make in your life?

■ How might having the freedom to choose be a drawback as well as an advantage?

■ Discuss a time when you wish you had chosen differently or followed a different direction.

For other journal opportunities, refer students to annotation C.

Additional Resources

UNIT ONE RESOURCE BOOK
Reader's Guidesheet, p. 16
Vocabulary Worksheet, p. 17
Selection Check Test, p. 18
Selection Test, pp. 19–20

Collaborative Learning

Opportunities for collaborative learning appear throughout the lesson and include Real Life Connection (p. T–53).

Teaching Strategies

Support for Students of Limited English Proficiency

■ Use the **Reader's Guidesheet,** p. 16.

■ "The Road Not Taken" has a formal style and contains dated terms and phrases and unusual syntax that students with limited English proficiency may find troubling. "Choices," while more conversational in style, contains non-standard punctuation and an elliptical structure that students may find confusing. Suggest that students treat each poem as a puzzle that can be solved with close reading. Point out that students might reverse the placement of subject and predicate for better understanding. Give assistance with terms like *yellow wood, trodden,* and *hence.*

Text Annotations

A. LEP: Paraphrasing Have students paraphrase these lines. (*Possible response: "This road attracted me more because the grass was overgrown."*)

B. Critical Thinking: ANALYZING Ask students why Frost called the poem "The Road *Not* Taken" rather than "The Road Taken." (*Possible response: In referring to the path he did not take he may be emphasizing the elements of uncertainty or sacrifice in any choice.*)

Student Response

Responding to Reading

These questions are open-ended with no "right" or "wrong" answers. However, responses must be supported with information from the selection. Possible answers follow:

1. Either choice is valid. Encourage students to explain their choice.

2. Some may say that one road "wanted wear"; others, that both roads were worn "really about the same." Some may say the road not taken had a bend.

3. Some may say that the speaker is drawn to both roads; others, that whatever the choice, the speaker regrets having to choose.

4. Some may say the roads symbolize choices about day-to-day decisions; others may cite career paths and other major life choices.

5. Some may say that this particular choice simply changed the speaker's life. Others may say the choice gave the speaker a more rewarding life.

The Road Not Taken

ROBERT FROST

Two roads diverged in a yellow wood,
And sorry I could not travel both
And be one traveler, long I stood
And looked down one as far as I could
SR-1 ▶ To where it bent in the undergrowth;

A | Then took the other, as just as fair,
And having perhaps the better claim,
Because it was grassy and wanted wear;
Though as for that, the passing there
Had worn them really about the same,

And both that morning equally lay
In leaves no step had trodden black.
Oh, I kept the first for another day!
Yet knowing how way leads on to way,
I doubted if I should ever come back.

I shall be telling this with a sigh
Somewhere ages and ages hence:
Two roads diverged in a wood, and I—
I took the one less traveled by, | B
And that has made all the difference. ◀ SR-2

Responding to Reading

First Impressions of "The Road Not Taken"

1. Which road would you have taken?

Second Thoughts on "The Road Not Taken"

2. Describe the physical differences in the two roads.

3. Why is choosing a road difficult for the speaker?

Think about
- the speaker's feelings about both roads
- your own experiences when making choices
- what the speaker says about returning to the other road at another time
- the speaker remembering his decision "with a sigh"

4. Is the speaker only talking about choosing between two roads? What else might he or she be describing?

5. The poem concludes by saying that taking the less traveled road "has made all the difference." What does this mean?

STRUCTURED READING FOR LESS PROFICIENT STUDENTS

These questions can help to guide students through the reading. Ask each question at the point of the selection where the SR number appears in the margin.

SR–1. Why is the speaker sorry? *(Two roads branch in different directions. The speaker would like to take both but must choose between them.)* **Clarifying**

SR–2. What choice does the speaker make? How does he feel about this decision? *(Possible response: He has chosen a less traveled road—a less common career—and this has given him a great deal of satisfaction.)* **Analyzing**

Continued on page 51

Choices

NIKKI GIOVANNI

if i can't do
what i want to do
then my job is to not
SR-3 ▶ do what i don't want
to do

it's not the same thing
but its the best i can
do

if i can't have
what i want then
my job is to want
C what i've got
and be satisfied
that at least there
is something more
SR-4 ▶ to want

since i can't go
where i need
to go then i must go
where the signs point
D though always understanding
parallel movement
isn't lateral

when i can't express
what i really feel
i practice feeling
what i can express
and none of it is equal
i know
but that's why mankind
E alone among the mammals
learns to cry

PEARBLOSSOM HWY., 11–18TH APRIL 1986 #2 (detail) 1986 David Hockney Photographic collage 78" × 111" © David Hockney, 1986.

Text Annotations

A. Critical Thinking: EVALUATING Ask students to explain how their view of the way people should live compares to the view Giovanni expresses in these lines. *(Possible response: Some will agree that such compromises can be smart and noble ways to live; others might disagree.)*

B. LEP: Paraphrasing Have students paraphrase these lines. *(Possible response: I must be flexible enough to go where life points me. I must understand that if I progress without moving up into a new level, I am not just wasting time moving sideways.)*

C. Literary Element: THEME Ask students why the speaker feels that people "alone among the mammals" learn to cry. *(Possible response: because humans learn they cannot always choose, and must compromise.)*

Check Test

1. Where are the roads in Frost's poem located? *(in a yellow wood)*

2. Which road does the speaker select? *(the one less traveled by)*

3. Where does the speaker in "Choices" feel she must go? *(where the signs point)*

4. What can people alone among mammals do? *(cry)*

Encouraging Independent Reading

"Regret," a short story by Kate Chopin
"If There Be Sorrow," a poem by Mari Evans
"Stopping by Woods on a Snowy Evening," a poem by Robert Frost
"The Choice," a poem by Dorothy Parker
"Parting Gift," and "Sanctuary," poems by Elinor Wylie

Art Note

In the five years David Hockney (1937–) spent with the camera, he produced nearly 400 photocollages on various subjects, including portrait narratives and landscapes. *Pearblossom Hwy. 11–18th April, 1986,* as the final large-scale piece, marked the end of his experiment. *How does this photocollage relate to the poem choices?*

STRUCTURED READING FOR LESS PROFICIENT STUDENTS

Continued from page 50

SR-3. What choice has the speaker made? *(not to do what she does not want to)* **Clarifying**

SR-4. What has the speaker decided to settle for if she can't have what she wants? *(what she's got)* What is the advantage in maintaining this attitude? *(Possible response: If she's satisfied with what she's got then she'll also be satisfied in knowing there is something that she still wants.)* **Understanding main idea/Clarifying**

Student Response

Responding to Reading

These questions are open-ended with no "right" or "wrong" answers. However, responses must be supported with information from the selection. Possible answers follow:

1. Any response is valid.

2. Some may say the speaker has learned that she cannot always have what she wants; others, that the speaker has learned to find satisfaction in knowing that there is something more to want.

3. Some may feel the speaker has lowered her goals to fit in with her restricted choices; others, that she has set realistic goals.

4. Some may say that the speaker does not see defeat in compromise; others may say that she does indeed feel defeated by the compromises she has made.

5. Those who take the last line of Frost's poem as positive might see that speaker as happier; those who see the speaker in "Choices" as defiant might claim she is more content.

6. Students might note the regular stanzas of "The Road Not Taken" and the irregular form of "Choices."

7. Discussion Prompts: Are you happy or unhappy with the choice you made? Do you feel that you made your choice freely or were you forced to compromise?

e x p l a i n

Responding to Reading

First Impressions of "Choices"

1. With what feeling does this poem leave you?

Second Thoughts on "Choices"

2. The speaker in this poem wants to do and have many things. What has the speaker learned about the things he or she wants?
3. Based on what the speaker has learned about choices, what kind of goals or expectations has he or she set?
4. Does the speaker feel that making a compromise is a defeat? Explain.

   Think about
   - the speaker's reaction to not getting what was wanted
   - the speaker's evaluation of what was obtained

Comparing the Poems

5. Reread "The Road Not Taken" and "Choices." Which of the speakers is happier about his or her choices in life?

   Think about
   - the choices each speaker makes
   - the ends of each poem

6. Look at the appearance of both poems on the page. How do they differ?

Broader Connections

7. Think back to your chart on the most important choice you made in your life. How has this choice "made all the difference" for you?

Literary Concept: Rhyme Scheme

In poetry, sounds are most often repeated at the ends of lines in a distinct pattern called **rhyme scheme.** Which lines rhyme in "The Road Not Taken"?

Writing Options

1. Use the chart you made about an important decision in your life as the basis for your own poem entitled either "Choices" or "The Road Not Taken."
2. Imagine that these two poets are having a debate over which one has more control over his or her choices. Write a dialogue of what each would say.

Literary Concept—Rhyme Scheme

Possible response: In each stanza of "The Road Not Taken," lines 1, 3, and 4 rhyme, and lines 2 and 5 rhyme.

Writing Options

The Writing Options are designed to meet varied student interests and abilities. Have each student choose one writing activity to complete. You may wish to guide some students to an option that requires less writing.

Journal Update Have students review their journal entries for this lesson. What have they learned about making choices? How might they revise their description after having read Giovanni's "Choices"?

e x t e n d

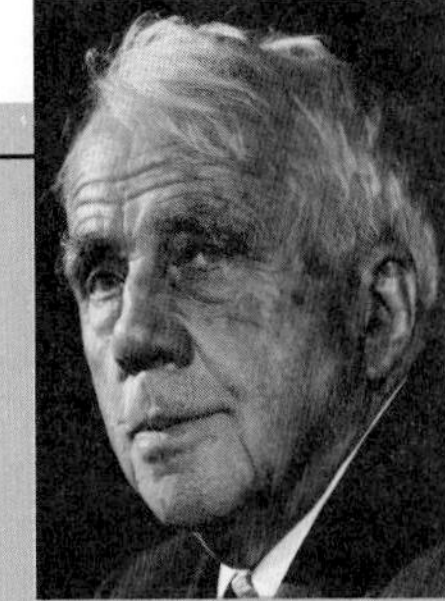

Robert Frost
1874–1963

Robert Frost was born in San Francisco, but at the age of ten his family moved to Massachusetts. As a young adult, Frost married and worked at many odd jobs—mill hand, shoe salesman, farmer—to support his family. When he was thirty-eight years old his farm failed, and Frost was faced with an important decision about which "road" to choose. He decided to move his family to England and concentrate on writing poetry. His work began to receive wide acclaim on both sides of the Atlantic, and he later returned to the United States. In 1960 he received a special congressional medal and is the only American poet to win four Pulitzer Prizes. In 1961 he was asked to read a newly composed poem at the inauguration of President John F. Kennedy.

Nikki Giovanni
1943–

Nikki Giovanni must have made many of the right choices to develop her considerable talents. Born Yolanda Cornelia Giovanni, Jr. in Knoxville, Tennessee, in 1943, and raised in Cincinnati, Ohio, Giovanni has become a celebrated American poet. Her poems for young readers are filled with joy, innocence, and imagination—mirrors of her happy childhood. Giovanni's essays and poems for adult audiences generally take a harder look at the world. She is known for her keen insights in such poetry collections as *Black Feeling, Black Talk,* and *Black Judgment.* Giovanni has also produced a record entitled "Truth Is on Its Way" which combines her poetry with gospel music. She presently lives in New York City.

Additional Information About the Authors

Robert Frost While Frost devoted the bulk of his energies to his poetry, he also taught and lectured at Amherst, Michigan, Harvard, and Dartmouth. His teaching was legendary, despite his generally conservative views about the world. Frost was a traditional man who valued simple things. With respect to the poetic innovation of free verse, Frost once said he would just as soon play tennis without a net as write poems without rhyme. Even so, Frost was considered an innovator with respect to meter and rhythm. His life's goal, he once said, "was to write a few poems it will be hard to get rid of." Most critics agree that Frost achieved his goal.

Nikki Giovanni One of the foremost contemporary black literary figures, Nikki Giovanni has become well-known as a lecturer as well as a writer. The success of her international speaking tours, for example, has earned her the title of "Princess of Black Poetry." Regardless of the way in which she chooses to express herself, however, Giovanni's concern with identity remains constant. As she herself has remarked: "I write out of my own experiences—which also happen to be the experiences of my people."

Closure

"The Road Not Taken" and "Choices" deal with making choices. The speakers in both poems explore how their choices have established the direction their lives have taken. Ask students to name people from public life who have made important, difficult, or highly publicized choices. Have students describe how the choices changed the lives of these public figures, and helped define who they were and what they were to accomplish.

Real Life Connections

Point out to students that the speaker in "Choices" feels that while she doesn't like compromise, it is better to accept compromise rather than fight it. Is this a good attitude to have in real life? Have the students discuss their attitudes toward compromise. Do they agree with the speaker? Have them illustrate their responses by discussing compromises they have made (or failed to make) in real life.

Writer's Workshop

Objectives

- To write a memoir about an important decision
- To use brainstorming to develop ideas and choose a topic
- To understand how to write a first-person narrative
- To draft, revise, edit, and share a memoir
- To revise for consistent past-tense verbs
- To reflect on the writing process

Integrating . . .

Literature and Writing Ask students if they have ever made a decision that they will remember as important when they look back on their lives. Tell students that when famous people write autobiographies, they often recount important decisions that they have made. Ask students who have read the autobiographies of any famous people to remember any important decisions that each person made. Ask them to consider why people like to read about other people's decisions and why people write about their decisions.

Writing and Language The Language Workshop in this subunit focuses on common punctuation errors. Explain to students that although punctuation rules sometimes seem complex, writers can eliminate many errors by learning to avoid a few common mistakes. Remind them that correct punctuation will help the reader understand the memoir they are about to write.

Writing and Study Skills The Study Skills Workshop in this subunit involves working in pairs and small groups. Point out to students the many advantages of working with others: access to different ideas, greater objectivity in judging one's own ideas, a chance to try out new ideas and writing techniques, and the opportunity to talk things through. Stress that working in pairs and small groups requires each student to listen carefully, to respond intelligently and tactfully to others, and to risk exposing his or her own ideas and writing.

FIRST-PERSON NARRATIVE

If you look at a list of best-selling books, you'll find many by Hollywood stars, sports figures, and even former U.S. Presidents, all eager to tell—and sell—their life stories, or **autobiographies.** Part of the attraction of these stories is that they are told from the subject's own point of view. In "Like Mexicans," for example, the author tells firsthand how other family members tried to influence his decision about whom he should marry.

When you tell a story from your own point of view, the account is called a **first-person narrative.** "First person" refers to the pronoun *I*, and "narrative" refers to a form of writing in which a narrator tells a story about actual or fictional experiences. For this workshop you will write a special kind of first-person narrative called a **memoir.** A memoir (related to the word *memory*) is a first-person recollection of some important experience or event.

GUIDED ASSIGNMENT: MEMOIR

The characters in the preceding selections were affected by decisions that they made or that were made by others. Write a memoir of a time when you or another person made a decision that had an important impact on your life.

Here is your PASSkey to this assignment.

PURPOSE: To narrate a personal memory
AUDIENCE: Your classmates
SUBJECT: A decision you made
STRUCTURE: Memoir

Prewriting

STEP 1 Brainstorm for ideas Think about the important decisions you have made in your life or about decisions made by others that had an impact on you. Jot down anything that comes to mind. You should end up with a list similar to the one on the following page created by a student.

Additional Resources

UNIT ONE RESOURCE BOOK
Writer's Workshop Copy Master, p. 21
Peer and Self-Evaluation Guidelines, p. 22
Writing Assessment Guidelines, p. 23

ENRICHMENT MATERIALS
Thinking Skills Transparency and Worksheet
Fine Art Transparency and Writing Prompts
Revision, Proofreading, and Elaboration Worksheet
Writing Prompts for Assessment

```
My fourth-grade teacher chose me for the lead in the play.
I decided to try out for track.
My parents decided to get divorced.
I decided to adopt my stepfather's last name.
```

◀ STUDENT MODEL

STEP 2 Choose your topic Which of the decisions that you listed in Step 1 stands out as the most important? Often, the importance of a decision can be determined by noting its consequences or outcome. The student who made the list, for example, selected the last item on her list. She chose to write about her decision to change her last name because of the far-reaching consequences of that decision.

STEP 3 Organize your ideas Now that you have chosen your topic, you'll need to build the before-and-after picture. What events led up to your decision? What were the outcomes of the decision? Map out the events surrounding your decision by constructing an arrow chart similar to the one below. This chart will serve as a rough outline of your memoir.

Before	Decision	After
• Parents divorced		• Felt like part of family
• My name different from my new family's	• Adopted my stepfather's name	• Had to adjust to new name
• Felt out of place		• Liked new name better

STEP 4 Ask a classmate Pair up with a classmate and share your arrow chart. Ask your classmate whether your chart is logical or whether more information should be added in order to clarify your ideas. Your classmate might also help you eliminate any information that does not suit your purpose.

Drafting

Write a rough draft of your memoir, using your arrow chart as a guide. Begin by describing the "before" picture—the circumstances leading up to your decision. Then tell about your decision and the reasons behind it. Finally, describe what happened after, or as a result of, your decision.

Teaching Strategies

Introduction Have students turn to the Writer's Workshop for this subunit on page 54. Discuss with them the meaning of first-person narrative.

Call students' attention to the Guided Assignment box on page 54 and be sure they understand that they will write a narrative, or story, in the first-person and that it should concern an important decision made by themselves or another person.

Teaching Tip

You may want to list some first-person pronouns on the chalkboard to remind students to keep to the first-person in narrating their memoirs. If LEP students choose to write about another person's decision rather than their own, you may wish to explain how they can use first-person pronouns to relate the experience *as if* it happened to them.

Prewriting Explain the arrow chart, pointing out that it is a kind of cause and effect chart similar to those used in the pupil edition to analyze short stories. Stress the importance of asking a classmate to give feedback on the chart so that students can clarify their ideas before they begin writing.

Drafting Suggest that students follow their arrow charts carefully in drafting their essays to ensure a logical structure for their memoirs.

Stress the importance of organizing a memoir in the following sequence: circumstances leading up to the decision; the decision and the reasons behind it; and the result of the decision.

Teaching Tip

Explain that although the chart and the sample memoir suggest that students will need only one paragraph for each major part of their memoir, some students may need more than one paragraph to explore the events leading up to their decision, the decision itself, or its result. Reassure students that they may have as many paragraphs as they need as long as they keep their paragraphs logical and sequential. Have LEP students number each of the vertical columns on their arrow charts in this manner: **Before,** 1, **Decision,** 2, and **After,** 3. Have them use each column, in numerical order, as the basis for three separate paragraphs in their memoir. Tell them that using the chart in this way will help them structure their memoirs in a logical way.

Revising and Editing To help students use the *Revision Checklist* on page 56, divide students into pairs or groups. Emphasize that the checklist offers specific help on specific aspects of their writing. Explain that students may choose to have others confine their comments to the specific questions on the checklist, or they may give their listeners permission to comment on other aspects of their work as well.

Emphasize that since their narratives take place in the past, students should be careful to be consistent in using past-tense verbs.

If students have difficulty with punctuation in the revising stage of their memoirs, you may want to conduct a mini-lesson or review the material in the **Language Workshop.**

Teaching Tip

Make sure students know that although most of the verbs used in their memoirs will be simple past-tense verbs, there may be instances in which they will need to use other tenses. Remind them to check all verbs not in the past tense, to be sure that the use of another tense is justified, rather than careless and inconsistent.

Revising and Editing

In pairs or small groups, share your draft with your peers. You may want to ask your classmates the following questions. Then revise your composition, taking into account your classmates' responses.

Revision Checklist

1. Do you understand the circumstances leading up to my decision?
2. Is it clear why I made that decision?
3. Do you understand the consequences of my decision?
4. Do the events seem to be ordered correctly?
5. Have I included any unnecessary information?

Special Tip

Because memoirs are accounts of past experiences or events, the verbs should be in the past tense. Also make sure that you have written in the first person throughout the memoir.

Editing After you have completed the major revisions, polish the mechanics: spelling, capitalization, and grammar.

Here is the final draft of the memoir based on the student's decision to adopt her stepfather's name.

STUDENT MODEL ▶

The Name Game

In sixth grade I made a decision that would change my life. My parents had been divorced for three years, and my mother had just remarried. Although my mom took my stepfather's last name, I kept my old one. In a sense, it was my only tie to my real father.

When my stepfather first moved in with his two sons, I clung to my old name. After a while, though, it started to bother me. I felt I didn't belong to any family anymore. I still saw my real father on weekends, but I was doing more and more things with my new family. I felt like a misfit. They were all Millers and I was a Johnson. Whenever they introduced me to someone, people looked at me like I was weird, since I had a different name.

The clincher came in May when we received an invitation to my cousin's wedding. The envelope was addressed to

"The Miller Family and Melissa Johnson." I felt like an outsider. Right then and there I decided to take my stepfather's last name, even if it meant changing all my ID cards. Although it took me a while to get used to my new name, it was the best decision I ever made. My teachers and friends occasionally forgot and called me "Johnson," but that was okay. My father was a bit disappointed that I gave up his name, but he understood why I did it. Three years later, I've grown into the new name and the new family.

Presenting

Read your memoir aloud in class. After all the memoirs have been read, discuss which ones might make suitable short stories similar to the ones you have read in this subunit.

Reflecting on Your Writing

Answer the following questions. Turn in your answers with your paper or place them in your writing portfolio.

1. Did you find it difficult to write about yourself? Why or why not?
2. How did sharing your draft with other students improve your writing?
3. What part of your memoir contains the best writing? Why?

Urge students to edit their memoirs for spelling, capitalization, and grammar.

Computer Tip
If students will be editing their memoirs on a computer, remind them to correct spelling errors by using the spell check function and to correct any errors in capitalization or grammar.

Presenting As an alternative to the *Presenting* suggestion in the pupil's edition, you might also consider these ideas:

- Have students recite or read their memoirs into a tape recorder and set up a listening corner in which recorded memoirs can be shared with others.
- Have students prepare a class book that includes everyone's memoir and make the book available for each student to read.

Reflecting on Your Writing When you review students' portfolios, remember to respond to their answers for the *Reflecting* questions. Students' answers to these questions will vary. If a majority of the class indicates by their answers to Question 1 that they are having difficulty understanding the *Reflecting* exercise, additional help may be appropriate.

Closure

Before beginning the next subunit, be sure that students have internalized these concepts:

- A first-person narrative is written from the point of view of the writer and uses the pronoun *I*.
- A memoir is a recollection of the author's personal experience.
- The events and meanings of a memoir should be developed and related in a logical, meaningful fashion so that others can understand the writer's experience.
- Most verbs in a memoir will be in the past tense.

Additional Writing and Research Topics

The following items provide additional writing practice based on the selection in this subunit.

Memoir

- Have you witnessed or participated in any practical jokes played on teachers or classmates? If so, write an account of what happened.
- Write a memoir from the point of view of one of the characters in "The Fan Club" or "A Kind of Murder." Assume that five years have passed since the story's incident took place and that the character is remembering the decision of five years ago.

Other Topics

Literary Analysis: Both Gary Soto in "Like Mexicans" and the speaker in Robert Frost's poem "The Road Not Taken" enter to some extent into unknown territory. Compare these two individuals by discussing the extent of the risks they take and the outcomes of their choices.

Language Workshop

Objectives

- To understand the use of commas, apostrophes, semicolons, colons, hyphens, and quotation marks
- To use punctuation correctly
- To proofread written material for punctuation errors

Integrating . . .

Grammar and Writing Ask students why they used punctuation when they wrote their memoirs in the Writer's Workshop. Explain that punctuation not only helps the reader make sense of what is read, but also helps the listener understand content. Write the following sentences on the board.

1. Jessica ordered asparagus salad and grilled salmon for dinner.

2. The waiter listened intently writing down her order.

Point out that without punctuation, neither sentence is clear. Ask students to identify Jessica's two possible orders: asparagus salad and grilled salmon; asparagus, salad, and grilled salmon.

Explain that in the first sentence, it is unclear whether asparagus salad is one item or two. In the second sentence, it is not clear whether the waiter listened intently or intently wrote the order. Mention that using punctuation incorrectly or not at all can be confusing to the reader. Point out that this Language Workbook focuses on ten important rules of punctuation.

Teaching Strategies

Read the introductory statement at the top of page 58 to students. Then have several volunteers attempt to read the capitalized passage that follows, and discuss the problems that occur due to the lack of punctuation.

Teaching Tip

Students who have difficulty in remembering rules of punctuation should be encouraged to use the punctuation section of the Language Handbook when writing until correct usage becomes automatic.

COMMON PUNCTUATION ERRORS

The ancient Romans used to write without any lowercase letters, punctuation, or spacing between words. In English, one of their inscriptions would have looked something like this:

> BUTWHATGOODISITTOTHEDEADTOBESHOWNFE
> ASTINGTHEYWOULDHAVEDONEBETTERTOHAV
> ELIVEDTHATWAY

Fortunately, people later invented word spacing, lowercase letters, and punctuation to make writing easier to read. By learning the rules that govern punctuation, you can save your readers a great deal of confusion. Following are ten of the most important punctuation rules for you to learn.

REMINDER The coordinating conjunctions are *and, or, nor, for, but, so,* and *yet.*

1. Use a comma before a coordinating conjunction that joins the two main clauses of a compound sentence.

Laura thought that school was a bore, but she might have enjoyed it if other students had been kinder.

Laura understood Rachel's pain, and she tried to accept Rachel's friendship.

EXCEPTION No comma is needed if the two clauses are very short: *We laughed and we cried.*

2. Use a comma after every item in a series except the last.

The students jammed the halls, streamed in and out of doors, and clustered under posters advertising the latest school dance.

Diane's friends were proud, successful at school, and cruel to people like Laura and Rachel.

HINT If you can put an *and* between the adjectives, then a comma is needed.

3. Use commas to separate adjectives of equal rank that modify the same noun. Do not place a comma between the last adjective and the noun.

Rachel wore unstylish, ragged clothes.

Rachel was a sweet, vulnerable, intelligent girl.

4. Use a comma to set off the explanatory words of a direct quotation.

"Most people," Laura continued, "don't care enough about others."

"No—I didn't," Laura hesitated. "I almost never watch that kind of program."

Additional Resources

UNIT ONE RESOURCE BOOK

Language Workshop Copy Master, p. 24

ENRICHMENT MATERIALS

Grammar and Usage Copy Masters

5. **Use a comma after two or more introductory prepositional phrases, after an introductory subordinate clause, or after an introductory word such as *finally* or *therefore.***

From the hall outside the classroom, one could hear the laughter of Diane and her friends.

Though she thought she was "in," Diane was really outside what most people consider to be the bounds of human decency.

Therefore, Laura had to make a decision.

6. **Use an apostrophe and an *-s* to form the possessive of a singular or plural noun. However, if a plural noun ends in *-s,* add only an apostrophe.**

What were Laura's feelings about the other children's behavior?

The other students' behavior bothered her a great deal.

7. **Use a semicolon to separate two sentences not joined by a comma and a conjunction. If the semicolon is followed by a transitional word such as *however* or *therefore,* use a comma after the transitional word.**

Everyone watched Rachel; she was fumbling with her things.

Rachel thought everyone was whispering about her; however, she did not give up.

8. **Use a colon to introduce a list of items.**

There were several members of the exclusive clique: Diane, Terri, Carol, Steve, Bill, and Nancy.

Laura stared at the items on the wall: a dusty portrait, a card with seven grammar rules, last year's calendar, and the clock.

9. **Use a hyphen between words that make up a compound adjective used before a noun and in numbers from twenty-one to ninety-nine.**

The fourteen-year-old girl had a lovely face.

Twenty-six students were in the class.

10. **Place quotation marks before and after a direct quotation and around the title of a short story or poem. No quotation marks are needed for long quotations that are set off from text and indented on either side.**

"Rachel," she said sharply, "we are supposed to be prepared when we make a speech."

In class we read Rona Maynard's story "The Fan Club."

REMINDER

A **prepositional phrase** consists of a preposition, such as *to, on, of, from,* or *at,* and a noun or a pronoun: *to the window, from her.*

A **subordinate clause** is a group of words containing a subject and verb that cannot stand on its own as a sentence: *After the class was over, When Laura came in.*

PUNCTUATION RULE

Commas and periods always appear within the quotation marks.

Direct students through the lesson, stopping before the exercises. Discuss each rule of punctuation and its application in each example. Also discuss the sidenotes that appear at point of use, asking volunteers to read and explain the examples. Help LEP students understand that the rules will help them use punctuation correctly when they write.

For Exercise 1, pair students, making sure LEP students are not paired with one another, and assign a sentence to each pair. Have each pair read their corrections aloud and identify the punctuation rule that applies. For additional practice have each pair draw a number from one to ten, signifying a numbered rule, and locate a sentence in any of the subunit selections to illustrate the correct usage. Have a member of each pair write the sentence on the board with the punctuation omitted. Call on volunteers to make the necessary corrections and cite the appropriate rule. When each sentence has been completed, have students draw a different number and repeat the exercise.

Teaching Tip

Point out that some writers omit the comma before the conjunction in a series, particularly in newspaper articles. It may be helpful to have students locate and discuss several examples of this convention and discuss whether the meaning is unclear as a result.

Have students form small groups. Be sure that LEP students are distributed evenly. Then assign Exercise 2 on page 60. Allow groups to discuss and agree upon the correct punctuation, as one member from each group records the passage with the correct punctuation. When all groups have finished, review correct responses.

Next assign Exercise 3 to students. As they work, circulate to offer help as needed. Encourage proper penmanship, pointing out that the purpose of this exercise is to produce a final copy of their work. You may wish to have students exchange papers before rewriting to check for errors in punctuation, or have several sample sentences written on transparencies and placed on an overhead projector to highlight correct usage.

Closure

Before beginning the next subunit, be sure students have internalized these concepts:

- Commas, apostrophes, semicolons, colons, hyphens, and quotation marks all have specific purposes in writing.
- The purpose of using correct punctuation is to make writing clearer.
- Proofreading your writing helps to locate errors in punctuation, which may then be corrected.

Answer Key
Exercise 1

1. My favorite poem is Robert Frost's "The Road Not Taken." He wrote beautifully about life's most important moments.
2. For twenty years Robert Frost submitted poetry to various magazines, but his poetry was rejected again and again.
3. To support his family, Frost worked as a mill hand, a shoemaker, a teacher, and a newspaper editor; however, it was years before he found a publisher for his poetry.
4. Frost wrote thoughtful poems about New England rural life.
5. Some of his favorite subjects were rural people, farm animals, storms, mountains, and wildflowers.
6. Some of Frost's poems were dialogues; the characters in these poems talk to one another in unrhymed verse.
7. One well-known poem by Frost tells how many of life's important decisions are made on a whim.
8. Frost showed great understanding of all his characters' lives.
9. Frost once said, "Happiness makes up in height for what it lacks in length."
10. At the age of seventy-two, Frost was still writing some of the best poetry of our century.

Exercise 2

After she finished reading Nikki Giovanni's poem "Choices," Mariana wrote in her journal about it. This is what she wrote:

From the age of sixteen to around the age of twenty-five or twenty-six, people make a lot of important choices. For example, I expect to be deciding whether to go to college, whether to get married, and whether to stay in this state or move to another. Doubtless, some of the decisions that I make will turn out well, but some may turn out badly. If a decision turns out badly, I will have to have the courage, wisdom, and intelligence to accept the consequences. That is what Nikki Giovanni's poem is about.

Exercise 3

Answers will vary; however, students should use the rules of punctuation on pages 58–59 to check and make corrections on their writing sample.

Exercise 1 Rewrite the following sentences, punctuating them correctly. Some sentences will require more than one correction.

1. My favorite poem is Robert Frosts The Road Not Taken. He wrote beautifully about lifes most important moments.
2. For twenty years Robert Frost submitted poetry to various magazines but his poetry was rejected again and again.
3. To support his family Frost worked as a mill hand a shoemaker a teacher and a newspaper editor however it was years before he found a publisher for his poetry.
4. Frost wrote interesting thoughtful poems about rural life.
5. Some of his favorite subjects were rural people farm animals storms mountains and wildflowers.
6. Some of Frosts poems were dialogues the characters in these poems talk to one another in unrhymed verse.
7. One well known poem by Frost tells how many of lifes important decisions are made on a whim.
8. Frost showed great understanding of all his characters lives.
9. Frost once said Happiness makes up in height for what it lacks in length.
10. At the age of seventy two Frost was still writing some of the best poetry of our century.

Exercise 2 Work with other students in a small group to punctuate the following passage correctly.

> After she finished reading Nikki Giovannis poem Choices Mariana wrote in her journal about it. This is what she wrote
>
> From the age of sixteen to around the age of twenty five or twenty six people make a lot of important choices. For example I expect to be deciding whether to go to college whether to get married and whether to stay in this state or move to another. Doubtless some of the decisions that I make will turn out well but some may turn out badly. If a decision turns out badly I will have to have the courage wisdom and intelligence to accept the consequences. That is what Nikki Giovannis poem is about.

LANGUAGE HANDBOOK

For review and practice, see Section 9, **Punctuation.**

Exercise 3 Analyzing and Revising Your Writing
Take a piece of writing from your writing portfolio and proofread it for errors in punctuation. Correct any errors that you find and make a clean, final copy.

ADDITIONAL PRACTICE

The following items provide additional practice for common punctuation errors.

Rewrite these sentences using the correct punctuation.

1. The pizza was cold but Jim enjoyed it anyway. *(cold, but)*

2. The topping choices included extra cheese mushrooms green pepper sausage and anchovies. *(cheese, mushrooms, . . . pepper, sausage)*

3. From the pizza shop on lower Main Street delicious odors wafted. *(Street, delicious)*

4. Most of Salvatores twenty three types of pizzas exclaimed Beth are absolutely delicious. *("Most . . . Salvatore's twenty-three . . . pizzas," . . . Beth, "are . . . delicious.")*

5. The Pizza Club consisted of five members Al Beth Cindy Dave and Earl. *(members: Al, Beth, Cindy, Dave)*

WORKING IN PAIRS AND IN SMALL GROUPS

In various assignments in this book, you will be asked to work in groups or pairs. The following guidelines will help you work better with your peers.

1. **Listen carefully.** Concentrate on what your partner or other group members are saying so that when your turn comes, you can make meaningful suggestions and contribute to the success of each person in the group. You will want others to listen attentively to you when it is your turn to speak or read from your writing.
2. **Participate.** A small group is successful only when each member contributes. Nothing creates more tension in a group than one or two members who don't participate.
3. **Treat each group member with respect.** Have concern for other's feelings and treat others the way you wish to be treated. Avoid sarcastic or destructive comments. Such statements, even said with humor, can hurt others deeply.
4. **Offer tactful suggestions.** There are many ways to be constructive when discussing a peer's work. Tell a peer what part of his or her work you like best before you point out the part you like least. Ask questions such as "Can you explain what you mean here?" instead of "Where did you get this ridiculous idea?"

Exercise Choose a partner and edit a piece of each other's writing for punctuation errors. Before you begin editing, create a checklist of punctuation errors that both of you will look for and eliminate. In compiling the list, concentrate on the most common errors you have noticed in your own writing. Then exchange papers with your partner and read each other's work carefully.

When you have finished editing, return the paper to your partner. Tactfully explain each of the corrections you have made on your partner's work. Discuss any sentences that confused you and decide together how correct punctuation could clarify the piece of writing. If there is any disagreement on the revisions, refer to the **Language Handbook** for punctuation rules.

When you and your partner are satisfied with the revisions on your papers, discuss your editing experiences with the other peer groups in the class. As a class, critique the revision process. Has having an editing partner improved your writing?

GROUP EVALUATION

◀ Name two things you and your partner did well and one thing you need to improve on.

Study Skills Workshop

Objective

- To use effective communication strategies when working in pairs and in groups

Integrating . . .

Literature, Writing and Study Skills Remind students that they were asked to do group work in both the *Writer's* and *Language Workshops* in this subunit. Emphasize that this workshop will provide guidelines for productive collaboration.

Teaching Strategies

Ask students to discuss why people sometimes work in groups. *(Possible responses: to share ideas; to achieve a common goal)* Ask them to identify some of the difficulties that can take place when people try to communicate within groups. *(Possible responses: some people may not listen to others; some may be too shy to speak.)*

Read through the material with students, asking them to provide examples (without naming people) of effective and ineffective use of each guideline.

Assign the exercise on page 61. Ask student partners to observe their team's strengths and problems to use in the Group Evaluation later.

Closure

Before beginning the next subunit, be sure students have internalized these concepts:

- Listening actively is important to the success of a group project.
- All members of a group are expected to contribute.
- It is important to respect each person's contribution.
- Sensitivity and courtesy are essential for maintaining group members' self-esteem.
- Tactful wording must be used as suggestions are made.

Additional Resources

UNIT ONE RESOURCE BOOK
Related Skills Copy, p. 25

ENRICHMENT MATERIALS
Standardized Test Practice Copy Masters

ADDITIONAL PRACTICE

Write these sentences, adding the necessary punctuation.

1. "Yes, the editor in chief is Ms. Chavez; however, she is busy now.
2. "Has anyone," asked Marla, "been to the new stadium yet?"
3. "No, John and Liz are not here; they are at the Williamses' house.
4. The mayor's aide said that ninety-five percent of her work was hard, but she enjoyed it.

Subunit Preview

Have students read the introduction to subunit 2, **Paying the Price.** Ask them to consider how a willingness to pay the price for a decision relates to the broader unit theme, **Decisions: Action or Apathy.** Why would someone take a risk when there's a safe alternative? Why would someone opt for doing something the hard way when there's an easy out? What kind of payoff might be worth personal risk? Invite students to look over the subunit Table of Contents and predict which selection that they expect to be most interesting.

For Additional Challenge

The following selections offer extra challenge in the exploration of the subunit theme:

"Daedalus and Icarus," a Greek myth retold by Robert Graves

"The Man Without a Country," a short story by Alan Paton

Additional Resources

Subunit Test, pp. 53–54

Paying the Price

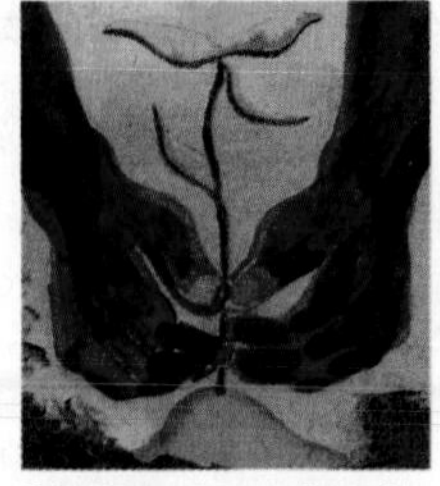

Every decision has its consequences. Over time, you learn to make decisions that, you hope, will bring you the best results. Still, any choice can have both advantages and disadvantages. A decision to join the school band, for example, may bring you a lot of enjoyment, new friends, and interesting experiences. Yet the time you spend practicing cuts into your time for other activities, such as homework, sports, or just relaxing. Part of decision making, then, is the process of weighing all the possible gains and losses.

In the selections in the next subunit, you will meet characters who pay a price for their decisions. What price does each person pay?

Observation Assessment

Observing how students respond to the text, to the classroom instruction, and to peers is an important part of an assessment program. The following suggestions and the form in each Unit Resource Book can be used to implement observation assessment.

- As students work through the subunit, assess their use of strategies for critical reading. Do they make judgments about a story and know how to support their views? Do they internalize the story and integrate it with their own experience?
- As they work through the subunit, can you see growth in their use of postreading strategies?
- To evaluate how well students connect with a story, ask them to summarize the important idea(s) or event(s) and explain its relevance to their own experience.

e x p l o r e

Fiction *from* *Dandelion Wine*

RAY BRADBURY

Examine What You Know (Prior Knowledge)

Sometimes people act tough even though they feel unsure or frightened. For example, if someone challenges you to do something dangerous, you might force yourself to go through with it even though you are afraid. In your journal or on a piece of paper, describe a time when you acted proud or in control even though you felt differently inside. Be sure to explain why you didn't express your real feelings. Compare your experience to the experience of the main character in the next story.

Expand Your Knowledge (Building Background)

The story you are about to read is based upon an actual series of crimes that took place in the 1920's in Waukegan, Illinois, thirty miles north of Chicago. Waukegan in the 1920's was like many small towns in that most people knew the town by heart and one another by name. Such towns offered little entertainment or excitement; consequently, a series of murders had an enormous impact on the community. As you read, ask yourself whether the peaceful atmosphere of Waukegan makes the crimes seem even more frightening.

WAUKEGAN READER

THE WAUKEGAN READER PRICE: THREE CENTS

MURDERER STRIKES AGAIN !!

Residents Live in Fear

Curfew in Effect

Jury Box

TAX DRIVE

Enrich Your Reading (Reading Skill)

Visualizing Writers often give important information about the setting, characters, and events of a story in the opening paragraphs. As you read this and other selections in this book, try to **visualize,** or picture in your mind, the images described by the writer. Visualizing helps you better understand and remember details about the selection. To help you get into the habit of visualizing, picture the images in your mind as you read the opening paragraphs of the next story. The description in these paragraphs is highly detailed. If necessary, stop after every few sentences in order to picture what you are reading.

■ *A biography of the author can be found on page 80.*

Objectives

- To understand and analyze a short work of fiction
- To recognize the use of suspense
- To use visualizing as a technique for constructing meaning
- To expand vocabulary by determining word meanings through analogies
- To express understanding of the work through a choice of writing forms, including narration and eulogy

Prereading/Motivation

Examine What You Know

Discussion Prompts: Why might someone act tough even though he or she is frightened? Would you call this kind of behavior brave or foolish? Why?

Expand Your Knowledge

Discussion Prompts: Why might the impact of a series of murders happening in a small town be greater than the impact of murders happening in a large city? What kinds of reactions to murder would you expect from people who live in a small town? In a place where everyone knows everyone else, who might be suspected of murder?

Enrich Your Reading

Have students reread small sections of the opening descriptions and ask themselves questions that focus on sensory details: What physical features are described? What sounds can be heard?

Thematic Link—Paying the Price

In this story, the main character chooses to ignore a real danger only to realize later that she may pay for her foolishness with her life.

Journal Writing

Suggest these journal topics to students:

- In your opinion, explain why you think so many people in our society feel a need to act tough around others.
- Write about a time in which you ignored someone's advice and took a risk. How did things turn out? Were you glad or sorry that you acted as you did?

For other journal opportunities, refer students to Examine What You Know (p. 63), Real-Life Connections (pp. T–65), and Broader Connections (p. 78).

Additional Resources

UNIT ONE RESOURCE BOOK

Reader's Guidesheet, p. 28

Vocabulary Worksheet, p. 29

Selection and Vocabulary Check Tests, p. 30

Selection Test, pp. 31–32

Collaborative Learning

Opportunities for collaborative learning appear throughout the lesson and include Teaching Tips (pp. T–66 and T–69), Options for Learning activities 1 and 4 (p. 80), and Cross-Curricular Options (p. T–80).

Teaching Strategies

Vocabulary Preview

These vocabulary words are defined at the bottom of the selection page on which they appear. You may wish to discuss them briefly before students begin reading.

dynamo a machine that generates electricity
overwrought overexcited
plummeting falling quickly
precariously in a risky way
ravine a deep ditch
scorched burned by heat
tremor a shaking motion
turbulent violently agitated
vapor visible moisture
veered turned away

LEP Students of Limited English Proficiency

- Use Reader's Guidesheet, p. 28.
- This excerpt from *Dandelion Wine* contains some difficult vocabulary and expressions. The small midwestern town setting and characters may be far removed from students' experience. Encourage them to visualize the setting and lifestyle of the townspeople as you read aloud the first ten paragraphs of the story. Be sure that students understand the slow, peaceful, easy atmosphere of the town and the friendly nature of the people. If students have experienced small-town life in other countries, have them describe the setting and lifestyles in those places.
- Annotations B, E, G, S, and Y focus on special help for LEP students.

A. Literary Element: SETTING Have students identify words and phrases that convey the setting of Waukegan, Illinois, in the 1920s. *(Possible responses: "warm summer twilight here in upper Illinois country"; "little town deep far away from everything else"; "moon rising in vanilla whiteness").*

B. LEP: Vocabulary The expression *see their tongues dance* may confuse students. Explain the meaning of this phrase as "gossip."

from Dandelion Wine

RAY BRADBURY

The courthouse clock chimed seven times. The echoes of the chimes faded.

Warm summer twilight here in upper Illinois country in this little town deep far away from everything, kept to itself by a river and a forest and a meadow and a lake. The sidewalks
A still scorched. The stores closing and the streets shadowed. And there were two moons; the clock moon with four faces in four night directions above the solemn black courthouse, and the real moon rising in vanilla whiteness from the dark east.

In the drugstore fans whispered in the high ceiling. In the rococo[1] shade of porches, a few invisible people sat. Cigars glowed pink, on occasion. Screen doors whined their springs and slammed. On the purple bricks of the summer-night streets, Douglas Spaulding ran; dogs and boys followed after.

"Hi, Miss Lavinia!"

The boys loped away. Waving after them quietly, Lavinia Nebbs sat all alone with a tall cool lemonade in her white fingers, tapping it to her lips, sipping, waiting.

"Here I am, Lavinia."

She turned and there was Francine, all in snow white, at the bottom steps of the porch, in the smell of zinnias and hibiscus.

Lavinia Nebbs locked her front door and, leaving her lemonade glass half empty on the porch, said, "It's a fine night for the movie."

They walked down the street.

"Where you going, girls?" cried Miss Fern and Miss Roberta from their porch over the way.

Lavinia called back through the soft ocean of darkness: "To the Elite Theater to see CHARLIE CHAPLIN!"[2]

"Won't catch us out on no night like this," wailed Miss Fern. "Not with the Lonely One strangling women. Lock ourselves up in our closet with a gun."

"Oh, bosh!" Lavinia heard the old women's door bang and lock, and she drifted on, feeling the warm breath of summer night shimmering off the oven-baked sidewalks. It was like walking on a hard crust of freshly warmed bread. The heat pulsed under your dress, along your legs, with a stealthy and not unpleasant sense of invasion.

"Lavinia, you don't believe all that about the Lonely One, do you?"

"Those women like to see their tongues dance." B

"Just the same, Hattie McDollis was killed two months ago, Roberta Ferry the month

1. **rococo:** elaborately ornamented.
2. **Charlie Chaplin:** a famous silent-movie comedian.

Words to Know and Use

scorched (skôrcht) *adj.* burned or parched by heat **scorch** *v.*

Structured Reading for Less Proficient Students

These questions can help to guide students through the reading. Ask each question at the point of the selection where the SR number sppears in the margin.

SR–1. Who are the two main characters in the story so far? *(Lavinia and Francine)* What have they found? *(the murdered remains of Elizabeth Ransell)* **Summarizing**

SR–2. What does Lavinia decide she and Francine should do after finding Elizabeth Ransell? How does she explain her decision? *(She decides they should go on to pick up Helen and go to the movies, so they can forget seeing their murdered friend.)* **Literal recall**

SR–3. How do most of the townspeople react to the murders? *(Possible responses: Most are afraid, nervous, upset; most avoid going out alone or at all, at night.)*

SR–4. What do the women decide to do immediately after the movie? *(They stop at a drugstore for ice-cream sodas.)* **Clarifying**

Continued on page 67

before, and now Elizabeth Ramsell's disappeared. . . ."

"Hattie McDollis was a silly girl, walked off with a traveling man, I bet."

"But the others, all of them, strangled, their tongues sticking out their mouths, they say."

They stood upon the edge of the ravine that cut the town half in two. Behind them were the lit houses and music, ahead was deepness, moistness, fireflies and dark.

"Maybe we shouldn't go to the show tonight," said Francine. "The Lonely One might follow and kill us. I don't like that ravine. Look at it, will you!"

C Lavinia looked and the ravine was a dynamo that never stopped running, night or day; there was a great moving hum, a bumbling and murmuring of creature, insect, or plant life. It smelled like a greenhouse, of secret vapors and ancient, washed shales and quicksands. And always the black dynamo humming, with sparkles like great electricity where fireflies moved on the air.

"It won't be *me* coming back through this old ravine tonight late, so darned late; it'll be you, Lavinia, you down the steps and over the bridge and maybe the Lonely One there."

D "Bosh!" said Lavinia Nebbs.

"It'll be you alone on the path, listening to your shoes, not me. You all alone on the way back to your house. Lavinia, don't you get lonely living in that house?"

"Old maids love to live alone." Lavinia pointed at the hot shadowy path leading down into the dark. "Let's take the short cut."

"I'm afraid!"

"It's early. Lonely One won't be out till late." Lavinia took the other's arm and led her down and down the crooked path into the cricket warmth and frog sound and mosquito-delicate silence. They brushed through summer-scorched grass, burs prickling at their bare ankles. D

"Let's run!" gasped Francine.

"No!"

They turned a curve in the path—and there it was.

In the singing deep night, in the shade of warm trees, as if she had laid herself out to enjoy the soft stars and the easy wind, her hands at either side of her like the oars of a delicate craft, lay Elizabeth Ramsell!

Francine screamed.

"Don't scream!" Lavinia put out her hands to hold onto Francine, who was whimpering and choking. "Don't! Don't!"

The woman lay as if she had floated there, her face moonlit, her eyes wide and like flint, her tongue sticking from her mouth. E

"She's dead!" said Francine. "Oh, she's dead, dead! She's dead!"

Lavinia stood in the middle of a thousand warm shadows with the crickets screaming and the frogs loud.

"We'd better get the police," she said at last.

"Hold me, Lavinia, hold me, I'm cold, oh, I've never been so cold in all my life!" ◀ SR-1

Lavinia held Francine and the policemen were brushing through the crackling grass, flashlights ducked about, voices mingled, and the night grew toward eight-thirty.

"It's like December. I need a sweater," said Francine, eyes shut, against Lavinia.

The policemen said, "I guess you can go now, ladies. You might drop by the station tomorrow for a little more questioning."

Lavinia and Francine walked away from

Words to Know and Use

ravine (rə vēn′) *n.* a deep ditch worn in the earth's surface by a stream
dynamo (dī′ nə mō) *n.* a machine that generates electricity
vapor (vā′ pər) *n.* any visible moisture or gas, such as mist, fog, smoke, or steam

65

C. Reading Skill: PREDICTING Ask students to recall the two major images to which the author compares the ravine. *(a dynamo and a greenhouse of "secret vapors" and "ancient" rock and quicksand)* Encourage students to speculate on the role the ravine might play in the story. *(Possible response: The ravine seems sinister and a likely place for a murder.)*

D. Literary Element: CHARACTERIZATION Ask students how the author reveals the thoughts and feelings of each woman. *(through dialogue)* Discuss Francine's and Lavinia's different reactions to the murders and what this conveys about each. *(Possible response: Francine seems weak, nervous, and upset; Lavinia seems strong, tough, and unafraid.)*

E. LEP: Vocabulary The word *flint* may be unknown to students. Explain that it refers to a hard kind of stone, usually black-gray in color. Suggest that the author uses this word to convey the cold, lifeless appearance of Elizabeth's eyes.

Real Life Connections

To help students understand the characters' fears, have them visualize themselves alone in a familiar park at night, when it is dark and deserted. Ask them to imagine how they might react to sounds or voices. Suggest that even though they know the park by day, they would feel uncomfortable there alone at night, especially knowing that a murderer might be prowling about.

F. Literary Element: IMAGERY Point out that early in the story the author had written of the "warm breath of summer night" and "oven-baked" sidewalks. Discuss how the sudden change to images of coldness evokes the characters' feelings. *(Possible response: The characters' experiencing coldness on a hot summer night helps to reveal their feelings of shock and fear.)*

G. LEP: Vocabulary Point out the references to *nuzzling* and *whispering* and *whispers and clicks.* Ask students to identify what these phrases refer to. *(Possible response: the movements and sounds of the police and photographers at the murder scene)*

H. Literary Sidelight In the original *Dandelion Wine* short story, Douglas Spaulding is a main character. The title refers to the wine Doug's grandfather makes from the dandelions so that the family can bring back the sweet taste of summer and memories of warmth all through the cold, long winter.

the police and the sheet over the delicate thing upon the ravine grass.

F Lavinia felt her heart going loudly in her and she was cold, too, with a February cold; there were bits of sudden snow all over her flesh, and the moon washed her brittle fingers whiter, and she remembered doing all the talking while Francine just sobbed against her.

A voice called from far off, "You want an escort, ladies?"

"No, we'll make it," said Lavinia to nobody, and they walked on. They walked

G through the nuzzling, whispering ravine, the ravine of whispers and clicks, the little world of investigation growing small behind them with its lights and voices.

"I've never seen a dead person before," said Francine.

Lavinia examined her watch as if it was a thousand miles away on an arm and wrist grown impossibly distant. "It's only eight-thirty. We'll pick up Helen and get on to the show."

"The show!" Francine jerked.

"It's what we need. We've got to forget this. It's not good to remember. If we went home now we'd remember. We'll go to the show as if nothing happened."

"Lavinia, you don't *mean* it!"

"I never meant anything more in my life. We need to laugh now and forget."

"But Elizabeth's back there—your friend, my friend—"

"We can't help her; we can only help our-

SR-2 ▶ selves. Come on."

H They started up the ravine side, on the stony path, in the dark. And suddenly there, barring their way, standing very still in one spot, not seeing them, but looking on down at the moving lights and the body and listening to the official voices, was Douglas Spaulding.

He stood there, white as a mushroom, with his hands at his sides, staring down into the ravine.

"Get home!" cried Francine.

He did not hear.

"You!" shrieked Francine. "Get home, get out of this place, you hear? Get home, get home, get *home!*"

Douglas jerked his head, stared at them as if they were not there. His mouth moved. He gave a bleating sound. Then, silently, he whirled about and ran. He ran silently up the distant hills into the warm darkness.

Francine sobbed and cried again and, doing this, walked on with Lavinia Nebbs.

"There you are! I thought you ladies'd never come!" Helen Greer stood tapping her foot atop her porch steps. "You're only an hour late, that's all. What happened?"

"We—" started Francine.

Lavinia clutched her arm tight. "There was a commotion. Somebody found Elizabeth Ramsell in the ravine."

"Dead? Was she—dead?"

Lavinia nodded. Helen gasped and put her hand to her throat. "Who found her?"

Lavinia held Francine's wrist firmly. "We don't know."

The three young women stood in the summer night looking at each other. "I've got a notion to go in the house and lock the doors," said Helen at last.

But finally she went to get a sweater, for though it was still warm, she, too, complained of the sudden winter night. While she was gone Francine whispered frantically, "Why didn't you *tell* her?"

"Why upset her?" said Lavinia. "Tomorrow. Tomorrow's plenty of time."

The three women moved along the street under the black trees, past suddenly locked houses. How soon the news had spread outward from the ravine, from house to house, porch to porch, telephone to telephone.

Teaching Tip

Students might better understand the emotions of the characters if they hear the dialogue spoken aloud. Once students have read the story silently, have volunteers role-play the characters and read portions of the dialogue aloud.

STREET LIGHT 1930 Constance Coleman Richardson © 1990 Indianapolis Museum of Art Gift of Mrs. W. Fesler.

Now, passing, the three women felt eyes looking out at them from curtained windows as locks rattled into place. How strange the popsicle, the vanilla night, the night of close-packed ice cream, of mosquito-lotioned wrists, the night of running children suddenly veered from their games and put away behind glass, behind wood, the popsicles in melting puddles of lime and strawberry where they fell when the children were scooped indoors. Strange the hot rooms with sweating people pressed tightly back into them behind the bronze knobs and knockers. Baseball bats and balls

Words to Know and Use

veered (vird) *adj.* turned away **veer** *v.*

67

Art Note

In this scene by Constance Coleman Richardson (1905–), the figures, the trees, and the neighborhood all are changed by the fall of light from the street lamp. *How does this painting remind you of the difference between day and night in the selection from* Dandelion Wine?

I. Reading Skill: **SENSORY DETAILS** Point out that an author can create a picture in readers' minds by appealing to their senses of sight, sound, smell, taste, and touch. Have students identify the senses to which the author appeals in the description of the night. *(Possible responses: sight, taste, touch)* Then have students explain what image is conveyed. *(Possible response: a happy, carefree, warm summer night)*

STRUCTURED READING FOR LESS PROFICIENT STUDENTS

Continued from page 64

SR–5. Where are the rest of the townspeople while Lavinia, Francine, and Helen walk home from the movies? *(at home, behind locked doors)* **Literal recall**

SR–6. What reasons does Lavinia give for not staying overnight with Helen but continuing on alone? *(She says that she is not afraid; she's curious; she's being logical, thinking that the presence of the police will deter the murderer; she's enjoying the risk.)* **Literal recall**

SR–7. What must Lavinia do to get through the ravine? *(go down 113 steps that lead down a steep hill, walk across a bridge, and then walk up the hill leading to Park Street* **Recognizing relevant details**

SR–8. Summarize what happens to Lavinia in the final moments of the story. *(Possible response: While Lavinia is going down the steps of the dark ravine, she hears echoes and begins to panic and run. When she gets home, she locks herself in and finally feels safe. It is then that someone inside her house clears his throat.)* **Summarizing**

J. Literary Element: SUSPENSE Have students tell what sights and sounds are used here to contribute to the suspense and tension. *(Possible responses: a shadow falling across the women's terrified faces; a figure looming behind a tree; the women screaming)*

K. Reading Skill: INFERRING Have students tell why they think Francine is crying so hard and why Lavinia puts off explaining the situation to Helen. *(Possible response: Francine and Lavinia have seen the horrible reality of death. Francine can't hide her feelings, and Lavinia probably doesn't want to scare Helen even more by explaining the sight of the body.)*

L. Reading Skill: PREDICTING Ask students to predict whether the stranger will prove to be a false scare, as Douglas Spaulding and Frank Dillon were, or a real danger. Have students give reasons for their predictions. *(Possible responses: The stranger will prove to be a real danger because he is not known in the town; he will prove to be a false scare because the author wants to build more tension and excitement.)*

lay upon the unfootprinted lawns. A half-drawn, white-chalk game of hopscotch lay on the broiled, steamed sidewalk. It was as if someone had predicted freezing weather a moment ago.

"We're crazy being out on a night like this," said Helen.

"Lonely One won't kill three ladies," said Lavinia. "There's safety in numbers. And besides, it's too soon. The killings always come a month separated."

SR-3 ▶

J

A shadow fell across their terrified faces. A figure loomed behind a tree. As if someone had struck an organ a terrible blow with his fist, the three women gave off a scream, in three different shrill notes.

"Got you!" roared a voice. The man plunged at them. He came into the light, laughing. He leaned against a tree, pointing at the ladies weakly, laughing again.

"Hey! I'm the Lonely One!" said Frank Dillon.

"Frank Dillon!"

"Frank!"

"Frank," said Lavinia, "if you ever do a childish thing like that again, may someone riddle you with bullets!"

"What a thing to do!"

Francine began to cry hysterically.

Frank Dillon stopped smiling. "Say, I'm sorry."

"Go away!" said Lavinia. "Haven't you heard about Elizabeth Ramsell—found dead in the ravine? You running around scaring women! Don't speak to us again!"

"Aw, now—"

They moved. He moved to follow.

"Stay right there, Mr. Lonely One, and scare yourself. Go take a look at Elizabeth Ramsell's face and see if it's funny. Good night!" Lavinia took the other two on along the street of trees and stars, Francine holding a kerchief to her face.

K

"Francine, it was only a joke." Helen turned to Lavinia. "Why's she crying so hard?"

"We'll tell you when we get downtown. We're going to the show no matter what! Enough's enough. Come on now, get your money ready, we're almost there!"

The drugstore was a small pool of sluggish air which the great wooden fans stirred in tides of arnica[3] and tonic and soda-smell out onto the brick streets.

"I need a nickel's worth of green peppermint chews," said Lavinia to the druggist.[4] His face was set and pale, like all the faces they had seen on the half-empty streets. "For eating in the show," said Lavinia as the druggist weighed out a nickel's worth of the green candy with a silver shovel.

"You sure look pretty tonight, ladies. You looked cool this afternoon, Miss Lavinia, when you was in for a chocolate soda. So cool and nice that someone asked after you."

"Oh?"

L

"Man sitting at the counter—watched you walk out. Said to me, 'Say, who's that?' Why, that's Lavinia Nebbs, prettiest maiden lady in town, I said. 'She's beautiful,' he said. 'Where does she live?'" Here the druggist paused uncomfortably.

"You didn't!" said Francine. "You didn't give him her address, I hope? You didn't!"

"I guess I didn't think. I said, 'Oh, over on Park Street, you know, near the ravine.' A casual remark. But now, tonight, them finding the body, I heard a minute ago, I thought, My God, what've I done!" He

3. **arnica:** a plant with yellow flowers.
4. **druggist:** a pharmacist.

CULTURAL CONNECTION

The town drugstore in this story serves as a combination pharmacy/soda shop/candy store/meeting place. Have students compare and contrast their neighborhood drugstore to the one in the story. Suggest students consider factors that contribute to the similarities or differences between the drugstores—the size of the town or city they live in, the availability of various kinds of stores, the lifestyle and habits of the neighborhood residents.

To help students have a better understanding of the drugstore aromas that the author describes, engage students in a discussion about the aromas in their neighborhood drugstore and the sources of these aromas. Since products and services may differ in various regions and countries, invite students who are from other countries to describe drugstores in their homelands in terms of what the stores look like, what kinds of products the stores sell, and what kinds of aromas they remember.

handed over the package, much too full.

"You fool!" cried Francine, and tears were in her eyes.

"I'm sorry. Course, maybe it was nothing."

Lavinia stood with the three people looking at her, staring at her. She felt nothing. Except, perhaps, the slightest prickle of excitement in her throat. She held out her money automatically.

"There's no charge on those peppermints," said the druggist, turning to shuffle some papers.

"Well, I know what I'm going to do right now!" Helen stalked out of the drugshop. "I'm calling a taxi to take us all home, I'll be no part of a hunting party for you, Lavinia. That man was up to no good. Asking about you. You want to be dead in the ravine next?"

M "It was just a man," said Lavinia, turning in a slow circle to look at the town.

"So is Frank Dillon a man, but maybe he's the Lonely One."

Francine hadn't come out with them, they noticed, and turning, they found her arriving. "I made him give me a description—the druggist. I made him tell what the man looked like. A stranger," she said, "in a dark suit. Sort of pale and thin."

N "We're all overwrought," said Lavinia. "I simply won't take a taxi if you get one. If I'm the next victim, let me *be* the next. There's all too little excitement in life, especially for a maiden lady thirty-three years old, so don't you mind if I enjoy it. Anyway, it's silly; I'm not beautiful."

"Oh, but you are, Lavinia; you're the loveliest lady in town, now that Elizabeth is—" Francine stopped. "You keep men off at a distance. If you'd only relax, you'd been married years ago!"

"Stop sniveling, Francine! Here's the theater box office, I'm paying forty-one cents to see Charlie Chaplin. If you two want a taxi, go on. I'll sit alone and go home alone."

"Lavinia, you're crazy; we can't let you do that—"

They entered the theater.

The first showing was over, intermission was on, and the dim auditorium was sparsely populated. The three ladies sat halfway down front, in the smell of ancient brass polish, and watched the manager step through the worn red velvet curtains to make an announcement.

"The police have asked us to close early tonight so everyone can be out at a decent hour. Therefore we are cutting our short subjects and running our feature again immediately. The show will be over at eleven. Everyone is advised to go straight home. Don't linger on the streets."

"That means us, Lavinia!" whispered Francine.

The lights went out. The screen leaped to life.

"Lavinia," whispered Helen.

"What?"

"As we came in, a man in a dark suit, across the street, crossed over. He just walked down the aisle and is sitting in the row behind us."

O "Oh, Helen!"

"Right behind us?"

One by one the three women turned to look.

They saw a white face there, flickering with unholy light from the silver screen. It

Words to Know and Use

overwrought (ō′ vər rôt′) *adj.* overexcited; upset; hysterical

M. Literary Sidelight In the introduction to his novel, Bradbury explains that there really was a Lonely One: "And he moved around at night in my home town when I was six years old and he frightened everyone and was never captured."

N. Critical Thinking: ANALYZING Have students discuss whether Lavinia's reasoning has any merit or is totally illogical, especially after she learns that a stranger knows where she lives. *(Possible response: Her reasoning is totally illogical because she is doing everything to put herself in danger just for the feeling of a little excitement.)*

O. Literary Element: SUSPENSE Ask students how they feel after reading this passage. *(Possible responses: edgy, nervous, tense, curious, excited)* Have them identify the lines that particularly evoke their feelings. *(Possible response: "They saw a white face there, flickering with unholy light from the silver screen.")*

Teaching Tip

To avoid the drudgery of traditional book reports, Criscuolo (1977) suggests creative alternatives. One alternative is as follows:

Computerized dating—Students attempt to have a date with a book. Volunteers complete a dating application that includes their name, age, hobbies, favorite TV program, last book they read, and types of books they enjoy. This information reveals personal characteristics, and it helps others be aware of potential books to recommend. The applications are posted so that classmates have opportunities to read them and to match the "right" book with the "right" friend.

"Creating the Lifetime Reading Habit in Social Studies," Criscuolo *Journal of Reading* *(March 1990)*

P. Reading Skill: CLARIFYING Ask students to clarify the reference to the theater manager's brother. *(He is the man with the white face sitting behind the women in the movie theater, the man who scared Helen so much that she screamed to stop the film.)*

Q. Literary Element: CHARACTER Point out to students that despite their fears and misgivings, both Francine and Helen accompany Lavinia to the movie and to the drugstore. Ask students what these actions reveal about them. *(Possible responses: They are followers rather than leaders; they are even more foolish than Lavinia because they recognize the danger but do not listen to their own and others' advice.)*

Art Note

Joseph Stella (1877–1946), known as America's outstanding Futurist (an artist who explores the dynamism of motion by recording its consecutive stages), also painted fantastic and surreal scenes. In *Nocturne*, the figurative shapes are nearly abstract, as is the crowded cityscape, while one realistic tower suggests another time. *What feeling do you get from this painting?*

NOCTURNE (detail) 1918 Joseph Stella The Toledo Museum of Art, Ohio.

seemed to be all men's faces hovering there in the dark.

"I'm going to get the manager!" Helen was gone up the aisle. "Stop the film! Lights!"

"Helen, come back!" cried Lavinia, rising.

They tapped their empty soda glasses down, each with a vanilla mustache on their upper lip, which they found with their tongues, laughing.

"You see how silly?" said Lavinia. "All that riot for nothing. How embarrassing."

"I'm sorry," said Helen faintly.

The clock said eleven-thirty now. They had come out of the dark theater, away from the fluttering rush of men and women hurrying everywhere, nowhere, on the street while laughing at Helen. Helen was trying to laugh at herself.

"Helen, when you ran up that aisle crying, 'Lights!' I thought I'd *die!* That *poor* man!"

"The theater manager's brother from Racine!" P

"I apologized," said Helen, looking up at the great fan still whirling, whirling the warm late night air, stirring, restirring the smells of vanilla, raspberry, peppermint and Lysol.

"We shouldn't have stopped for these sodas. The police warned—" Q

"Oh, bosh the police," laughed Lavinia, "I'm not afraid of anything. The Lonely One is a million miles away now. He won't be back for weeks and the police'll get him then, just wait. Wasn't the film wonderful?"

"Closing up, ladies." The druggist switched off the lights in the cool white-tiled silence. ◀SR-4

Outside, the streets were swept clean and empty of cars or trucks or people. Bright

Real Life Connections

Students are likely to be aware of crimes of murder, as such crimes exist in every part of society and every geographic area. Relating any personal experience may not be appropriate. However, some widely publicized crimes hold a fascination for many people. You might focus a discussion on stories that students have read about. Ask students to comment on Lavinia's attitude about the Lonely One as it relates to present-day situations.

lights still burned in the small store windows where the warm wax dummies lifted pink wax hands fired with blue-white diamond rings, or flourished orange wax legs to reveal hosiery. The hot blue-glass eyes of the mannequins watched as the ladies drifted down the empty river bottom street, their images shimmering in windows like blossoms seen under darkly moving waters.

"Do you suppose if we screamed they'd do anything?"

"Who?"

"The dummies, the window people."

"Oh, Francine."

"Well . . ."

There were a thousand people in the windows, stiff and silent, and three people on
R the street, the echoes following like gunshots from store fronts across the way when they tapped their heels on the baked pavement.

A red neon sign flickered dimly, buzzed like a dying insect, as they passed.

Baked and white, the long avenues lay ahead. Blowing and tall in a wind that touched only their leafy summits, the trees stood on either side of the three small women. Seen from
S the courthouse peak, they appeared like three thistles far away.

"First, we'll walk you home, Francine."

"No, I'll walk *you* home."

"Don't be silly. You live way out at Electric Park. If you walked me home you'd have to come back across the ravine alone, yourself. And if so much as a leaf fell on you, you'd drop dead."

Francine said, "I can stay the night at your house. You're the *pretty* one!"

And so they walked, they drifted like three prim clothes forms over a moonlit sea of lawn and concrete, Lavinia watching the black trees flit by each side of her, listening to the voices of her friends murmuring, trying to laugh; and the night seemed to quicken, they seemed to run while walking slowly, everything seemed fast and the color of hot snow.

"Let's sing," said Lavinia.

They sang, "Shine On, Shine On, Harvest Moon . . ."

They sang sweetly and quietly, arm in arm, not looking back. They felt the hot sidewalk cooling underfoot, moving, moving.

"Listen!" said Lavinia.

They listened to the summer night. The summernight crickets and the far-off tone of the courthouse clock making it eleven forty-five.

"Listen!"

Lavinia listened. A porch swing creaked in the dark and there was Mr. Terle, not saying anything to anybody, alone on his swing, having a last cigar. They saw the pink ash swinging gently to and fro.

Now the lights were going, going, gone. The little house lights and big house lights and yellow lights and green hurricane lights, the candles and oil lamps and porch lights, and everything felt locked up in brass and iron and steel, everything, thought Lavinia, is boxed and locked and wrapped and shaded. She imagined the people in their moonlit beds. And their T
breathing in the summer-night rooms, safe and together. And here we are, thought Lavinia, our footsteps on along the baked summer evening sidewalk. And above us the lonely street lights shining down, making a drunken shadow.

"Here's your house, Francine. Good night."

"Lavinia, Helen, stay here tonight. It's late, almost midnight now. You can sleep in

R. Literary Element: SIMILE Point out the simile "the echoes following like gunshots" and have students tell what this comparison is conveying. *(that the sound of the women's heels tapping on the pavement is like the sound of gunshots)* Have students locate other similes on the page. *(Students can find a simile in each descriptive paragraph in column 1 on page 71.)*

S. LEP: Vocabulary The word *thistle* may be troublesome for students. Explain that it refers to a prickly plant having showy purple flower heads. Ask students why the women might appear like thistles from far away. *(Possible response: They might be wearing floral-print clothing or perhaps wearing colorful hats, but at any rate they stand out on the empty street.)*

T. Reading Skill: PREDICTING Mention that once again the author is creating an atmosphere of uneasiness as the women begin to walk home. Have students speculate on what might happen. *(Answers will vary. Some students might think that one of the women will be murdered, because it seems likely that something will happen.)*

U. Critical Thinking: EVALUATING Ask students if they agree or disagree with Helen's statement, and why. *(Opinions will vary but should be supported with reasonable answers. Students might rule that Helen may be referring to Lavinia when she says "some people" since Lavinia's actions seem reckless to her.)*

V. Literary Sidelight The ravine and bridge exist in Waukegan, Illinois, as shown on page 77. Bradbury remembers ". . . nights when walking home late across town, after seeing Lon Chaney's . . . *The Phantom of the Opera,* my brother Skip would run ahead and hide under the ravine-creek bridge like the Lonely One and leap out and grab me, shrieking, so I ran, fell, and ran again, gibbering all the way home."

the parlor. I'll make hot chocolate—it'll be such fun!" Francine was holding them both now, close to her.

"No, thanks," said Lavinia.

And Francine began to cry.

"Oh, not again, Francine," said Lavinia.

"I don't want you dead," sobbed Francine, the tears running straight down her cheeks. "You're so fine and nice, I want you alive. Please, oh, please!"

"Francine, I didn't know how much this has done to you. I promise I'll phone when I get home."

"Oh, will you?"

"And tell you I'm safe, yes. And tomorrow we'll have a picnic lunch at Electric Park. With ham sandwiches I'll make myself, how's that? You'll see, I'll live forever!"

"You'll phone, then?"

"I promised, didn't I?"

"Good night, good night!" Rushing upstairs, Francine whisked behind a door, which slammed to be snap-bolted tight on the instant.

"Now," said Lavinia to Helen, "I'll walk *you* home."

The courthouse clock struck the hour. The sounds blew across a town that was empty, emptier than it had ever been. Over empty streets and empty lots and empty lawns the sound faded.

"Nine, ten, eleven, twelve," counted Lavinia, with Helen on her arm.

"Don't you feel funny?" asked Helen.

"How do you mean?"

"When you think of us being out here on the sidewalks, under the trees, and all those people safe behind locked doors, lying in their beds. We're practically the only walking people out in the open in a thousand miles, I bet." ◀SR-5

The sound of the deep warm dark ravine came near.

In a minute they stood before Helen's house, looking at each other for a long time. The wind blew the odor of cut grass between them. The moon was sinking in a sky that was beginning to cloud. "I don't suppose it's any use asking you to stay, Lavinia?"

"I'll be going on."

"Sometimes—"

"Sometimes what?"

"Sometimes I think people *want* to die. You've acted odd all evening." U

"I'm just not afraid," said Lavinia. "And I'm curious, I suppose. And I'm using my head. Logically, the Lonely One can't be around. The police and all."

"The police are home with their covers up over their ears."

"Let's just say I'm enjoying myself, precariously, but safely. If there was any real chance of anything happening to me, I'd stay here with you, you can be sure of that."

"Maybe part of you doesn't want to live anymore."

"You and Francine. Honestly!"

"I feel so guilty. I'll be drinking some hot cocoa just as you reach the ravine bottom and walk on the bridge." V

"Drink a cup for me. Good night."

Lavinia Nebbs walked alone down the midnight street, down the late summer-night silence. She saw houses with the dark windows and far away she heard a dog barking. In five minutes, she thought, I'll be safe at home. In five minutes I'll be phoning silly little Francine. I'll—" ◀SR-6

She heard the man's voice.

Words to Know and Use

precariously (prē ker′ ē əs lē) *adv.* in a risky or dangerous manner

A man's voice singing far away among the trees.

"Oh, give me a June night, the moonlight and you . . ."

She walked a little faster.

The voice sang, "In my arms . . . with all your charms . . ."

Down the street in the dim moonlight a man walked slowly and casually along.

I can run knock on one of these doors, thought Lavinia, if I must.

"Oh, give me a June night," sang the man, and he carried a long club in his hand. "The moonlight and you. Well, look who's *here!* What a time of night for you to be out, Miss Nebbs!"

"Officer Kennedy!"

And that's who it was, of course.

"I'd better see you home!"

"Thanks, I'll make it."

"But you live across the ravine. . . ."

W Yes, she thought, but I won't walk through the ravine with any man, not even an officer. How do I know who the Lonely One is? "No," she said, "I'll hurry."

"I'll wait right here," he said. "If you need any help, give a yell. Voices carry good here. I'll come running."

"Thank you."

She went on, leaving him under a light, humming to himself, alone.

Here I am, she thought.

The ravine.

She stood on the edge of the one hundred and thirteen steps that went down the steep hill and then across the bridge seventy yards and up the hills leading to Park Street. And only one lantern to see by. Three minutes from now, she thought, I'll be putting my key in my house door. Nothing can happen in just one hundred eighty seconds. SR-7 ▶

X She started down the long dark-green steps into the deep ravine.

"One, two, three, four, five, six, seven, eight, nine, ten steps," she counted in a whisper.

She felt she was running, but she was not running.

"Fifteen, sixteen, seventeen, eighteen, nineteen, twenty steps," she breathed.

"One fifth of the way!" she announced to herself.

The ravine was deep, black and black, black! And the world was gone behind, the world of safe people in bed, the locked doors, the town, the drugstore, the theater, the lights, everything was gone. Only the ravine existed and lived, black and huge, about her.

"Nothing's happened, has it? No one around, is there? Twenty-four, twenty-five steps. Remember that old ghost story you told each other when you were children?"

She listened to her shoes on the steps.

"The story about the dark man coming in your house and you upstairs in bed. And now he's at the first step coming up to your room. And now he's at the second step. And now he's at the third step and the fourth step and the fifth! Oh, how you used to laugh and scream at that story! And now the horrid dark man's at the twelfth step and now he's opening the door of your room and now he's standing by your bed. 'I GOT YOU!'"

She screamed. It was like nothing she'd ever heard, that scream. She had never screamed that loud in her life. She stopped, she froze, she clung to the wooden banister. Her heart exploded in her. The sound of the terrified beating filled the universe.

"There, *there!*" she screamed to herself. "At the bottom of the steps. A man, under the light! No, now he's gone! He was *waiting* there!"

W. Critical Thinking: ANALYZING Have students explain why Lavinia doesn't want to walk with any man in the ravine, even a familiar police officer. *(She feels safer alone because anyone could turn out to be the Lonely One.)* Ask what Lavinia's behavior shows about the actual effect the murders have had on her. *(Possible response: She can no longer depend on the security of a small town and can no longer trust people she knows.)*

X. Literary Element: RISING ACTION Explain that at this point in the story the action rises and Lavinia must confront her conflict alone. Suggest students notice how the author often uses short sentences and sentence fragments on this page and on page 75 to create a quick, staccato pace that draws readers into Lavinia's experience moment by moment.

Art Note

Nathan Oliveira (1928–) is best known for his paintings of single figures done during the late 1950s. From heavy layers of paint, the images appear to be emerging from their backgrounds, presenting a haunting, primitive aspect of humanity. *How might this be something like the image of the Lonely One as visualized by Francine? by Lavinia? by the others in* Dandelion Wine*?*

MAN WALKING 1958 Nathan Oliveira Hirshhorn Museum and Sculpture Garden, Smithsonian Institution, Washington, D.C.

She listened.

Silence.

The bridge was empty.

Nothing, she thought, holding her heart. Nothing. Fool! That story I told myself. How silly. What shall I do?

Her heartbeats faded.

Shall I call the officer—did he hear me scream?

She listened. Nothing. Nothing.

I'll go the rest of the way. That silly story.

She began again, counting the steps.

"Thirty-five, thirty-six, careful, don't fall. Oh, I am a fool. Thirty-seven steps, thirty-eight, nine and forty, and two makes forty-two—almost halfway."

She froze again.

Wait, she told herself.

She took a step. There was an echo.

She took another step.

Another echo. Another step, just a fraction of a moment later.

"Someone's following me," she whispered to the ravine, to the black crickets and dark-green hidden frogs and the black stream. "Someone's on the steps behind me. I don't dare turn around."

Another step, another echo.

"Every time I take a step, they take one."

A step and an echo.

Weakly she asked of the ravine, "Officer Kennedy, is that *you?*"

The crickets were still.

The crickets were *listening.* The night was listening to *her.* For a change, all of the far summer-night meadows and close summer-night trees were suspending motion; leaf, shrub, star, and meadow grass ceased their particular tremors and were listening to Lavinia Nebbs's heart. And perhaps a thousand miles away, across locomotive-lonely country, in an empty way station, a single traveler reading a dim newspaper under a solitary naked bulb, might raise up his head, listen, and think, What's that? and decide, Only a woodchuck, surely, beating on a hollow log. But it was Lavinia Nebbs, it was most surely the heart of Lavinia Nebbs. Y

Silence. A summer-night silence which lay for a thousand miles, which covered the earth like a white and shadowy sea.

Faster, faster! She went down the steps.

Run!

She heard music. In a mad way, in a silly way, she heard the great surge of music that pounded at her, and she realized as she ran, as she ran in panic and terror, that some part of her mind was dramatizing, borrowing from the turbulent musical score of some private drama, and the music was rushing and pushing her now, higher and higher, faster, faster, plummeting and scurrying, down, and down into the pit of the ravine. Z

Only a little way, she prayed. One hundred eight, nine, one hundred ten steps! The bottom! Now run! Across the bridge!

She told her legs what to do, her arms, her body, her terror; she advised all parts of herself in this white and terrible moment, over the roaring creek waters, on the hollow, thudding, swaying, almost alive, resilient bridge planks she ran, followed by the wild footsteps behind, behind, with the music following, too, the music shrieking and babbling.

He's following, don't turn, don't look, if you see him, you'll not be able to move, you'll be so frightened. Just run, run!

She ran across the bridge.

Oh, God, God, please, please let me get up the hill! Now up, the path, now

Words to Know and Use

tremor (trem′ ər) *n.* shaking or trembling motion
turbulent (tur′ byo͞o lənt) *adj.* violently agitated; stormy
plummeting (plum′ it iŋ) *adj.* falling or dropping very quickly **plummet** *v.*

Y. LEP: Vocabulary Students may not understand the reference to the *way station.* Explain that it refers to a stopping point along railroad tracks where people can board or get off a train. Bradbury uses the image of another lonely, solitary, silent place to point up the loudness of Lavinia's pounding heart.

Z. Literary Element: CHARACTERIZATION Have students explain how Lavinia's behavior has changed and what her actions reveal. *(Possible response: She is running instead of walking, and she is no longer acting coolly and logically. She is clearly afraid and panicked for her life.)*

AA. **Reading Skill: PREDICTING** Have students share their reactions and confirm or adjust predictions made earlier. Encourage new predictions about who is in Lavinia's house and what will happen to her. *(Possible responses: It is the murderer and she will be murdered; it is someone she knows and everything will turn out fine.)*

Literary Sidelight In the next chapter, readers find out that Lavinia has killed the intruder with a pair of scissors. Doug Spaulding and his friends don't want to believe that the Lonely One is actually dead. The chapter ends with them still wondering.

Check Test

1. Who discovers the body of Elizabeth Ransell? *(Lavinia and Francine)*

2. What name has been given to the murderer? *(the Lonely One)*

3. Where do the women go for food and entertainment? *(the drugstore and the movie theater)*

4. What terrain must Lavinia cover to reach her home? *(She must go down a steep hill, cross a ravine on a bridge, and go up a hill.)*

5. Does Lavinia seem to be safe at home at the end of the story? *(No, someone is in her house.)*

Encouraging Independent Reading

Dandelion Wine and *Something Wicked This Way Comes,* novels by Ray Bradbury
"The Wireless Tower," a short story by N. V. M. Gonzalez
The Body, a novella by Stephen King
"Through the Tunnel," a short story by Doris Lessing
"Circus at Dawn," a short story by Thomas Wolfe

between the hills, oh God, it's dark and everything so far away. If I screamed now it wouldn't help; I can't scream anyway. Here's the top of the path, here's the street, oh, God, please let me be safe, if I get home safe I'll never go out alone; I was a fool, let me admit it, I was a fool, I didn't know what terror was, but if you let me get home from this I'll never go without Helen or Francine again! Here's the street. Across the street!

She crossed the street and rushed up the sidewalk.

Oh God, the porch! My house! Oh God, please give me time to get inside and lock the door and I'll be safe!

And there—silly thing to notice—why did she notice, instantly, no time, no time—but there it was anyway, flashing by—there on the porch rail, the half-filled glass of lemonade she had abandoned a long time, a year, half an evening ago! The lemonade glass sitting calmly, imperturbably there on the rail . . . and . . .

She heard her clumsy feet on the porch and listened and felt her hands scrabbling and ripping at the lock with the key. She heard her heart. She heard her inner voice screaming.

The key fit.

Unlock the door, quick, quick!

The door opened.

Now, inside. Slam it!

She slammed the door.

"Now lock it, bar it, lock it!" she gasped wretchedly.

"Lock it, tight, *tight!*"

The door was locked and bolted tight.

The music stopped. She listened to her heart again and the sound of it diminishing into silence.

Home! Oh God, safe at home! Safe, safe and safe at home! She slumped against the door. Safe, safe. Listen. Not a sound. Safe, safe, oh thank God, safe at home. I'll never go out at night again. I'll stay home. I won't go over that ravine again ever. Safe, oh safe, safe home, so good, so good, safe! Safe inside, the door locked. Wait.

Look out the window.

She looked.

Why, there's no one there at all! Nobody. There was nobody following me at all. Nobody running after me. She got her breath and almost laughed at herself. It stands to *reason.* If a man *had* been following me, he'd have *caught* me! I'm not a fast runner. . . . There's no one on the porch or in the yard. How silly of me. I wasn't running from anything. That ravine's as safe as anyplace. Just the same, it's nice to be home. Home's the really good warm place, the only place to be.

She put her hand out to the light switch and stopped.

"What?" she asked. "What, *What?*" AA

Behind her in the living room, someone cleared his throat. ❧ ◀ SR-8

I N S I G H T

Author Ray Bradbury stands on the bridge over the ravine in his hometown of Waukegan, Illinois. Reprinted with permission, © 1990 *Chicago Sun-Times.*

Insight

This piece reflects on the ideas in the main selection and is suggested for students' independent reading. Optional discussion questions follow.

1. Have students read the caption and look at the photograph. Ask them what they think the photograph adds to the story. *(Possible response: a sense of realism and an understanding of the size and appearance of an important element in the setting of the story)*

2. Have students compare the impact of the ravine in the photograph with the impact of the descriptions of the ravine that the author presents in the story. *(Possible response: The description carries more impact because the author creates suspense and plays on the reader's imagination by describing the ravine in a scary way.)*

Literary Sidelight In 1974 Bradbury wrote that he had taken his daughters to the ravine a few years before, "fearful that the ravine might have gone shallow with time. I am relieved and happy to report that the ravine is deeper, darker, and more mysterious than ever."

Student Response

Responding to Reading

These questions are open-ended with no "right" or "wrong" answers. However, responses must be supported with information from the selection. Possible answers follow:

1. Any response based on the story is valid.

2. Some students may say that Lavinia is not frightened by the murders as everyone else is. She doesn't believe there is any real danger, so she takes no steps to protect herself; in contrast, most of the townspeople stay home behind locked doors. Other students may say that Lavinia, unlike other people, maintains a bold front, appearing to be unconcerned by the murders, but deep down she is very afraid.

3. Students may say that Lavinia is not logical because she ignores real evidence and chooses to believe in things that she cannot control, such as there being safety in numbers and the killings always coming a month apart. Other students may say she is logical since the murders follow a pattern of being one month apart.

4. Some may say that she doesn't want to die, but that she is looking for a little excitement and danger in her life and so is "tempting fate." This is shown by her panic when she is trying to escape the Lonely One. Others may feel that she does want to die because she is ignoring every reasonable precaution.

5. Students may say that when Lavinia is alone, in the darkness of the ravine, she hears noises and sees shadows, and her imagination gets the best of her. They may also say that she comes to the realization that she may be in real danger. Students may point out that her actions show that she is not the brave, fearless person she pretends to be when she is with others.

e x p l a i n

Responding to Reading

First Impressions

1. What emotion are you left with at the end of the story?

Second Thoughts

2. How is Lavinia's reaction to the killings different from the reactions of other people?

   Think about
   - how her friends, Francine and Helen, react
   - how the general population of Waukegan reacts

3. Lavinia takes pride in her cool logic and reasoning. How logical is she really?

   Think about
   - people whom you consider to be logical
   - Lavinia's reactions to the pattern of killings
   - what Lavinia says about her actions to her friends

4. Helen says to Lavinia, "Sometimes I think people *want* to die." Does Lavinia want to die? Why or why not?

   Think about
   - her actions on the way to the movie
   - her thoughts during her walk home
   - her reactions to Helen and others who offer her advice

5. Halfway through Lavinia's walk home from the movies, she becomes frightened and panics. Why does this happen? What does this reveal about Lavinia's character?

6. The ravine plays a significant part in this story. How does the writer make the ravine seem alive and threatening?

   Think about
   - the early description of the ravine, on page 65
   - the description of the ravine on Lavinia's walk home, on page 75

7. Why is the murderer called the Lonely One? Who do you think the Lonely One is? Could this phrase also refer to any other character in the story?

Broader Connections

8. What risks do people take in their own homes and communities? Think about such activities as going out alone to the store late at night or not locking doors. Why do you think people are more careless about their personal safety when they are in familiar settings?

6. Possible response: The writer first refers to the ravine as a living thing in terms of sound (bumbling and murmuring), sight (creature, insect, or plant life), and smell (secret vapors). He later describes the ravine's deepness and blackness, giving the imrpession of a giant monster closing in.

7. Students may say that the murderer is called the Lonely One because he attacks women in lonely, out-of-the-way places or because most townspeople could not conceive of a local friend being the murderer, so they think of him as a stranger, a lonely person. Opinions as to the identity of the Lonely One may include any character in the story or someone unknown. Some students may suggest that the phrase is also appropriate for Lavinia, who is a "maiden lady" and seems to be longing for some excitement in her life.

8. Students may note that people often leave their doors and windows unlocked or walk down dark streets alone. They may say that people are more careless about their personal safety in familiar settings because they feel that they know what to expect and feel comfortable. As a result, they don't watch carefully or think about measures to protect themselves.

Literary Concept: Suspense

The tension or excitement in a plot is called **suspense.** Ray Bradbury uses descriptions of sights and sounds to build excitement. For example, Bradbury has Lavinia count the steps across the ravine as she runs home. What other sights and sounds does the writer use to create suspense?

Writing Options

1. Ray Bradbury surprises the reader by having someone waiting for Lavinia in her house. Continue the story from this point. Be sure to identify who is in Lavinia's house and tell what happens to her. If possible, add another surprise to your new ending of the story.

2. A eulogy is a tribute, often spoken at funerals in praise of the person who has passed away. Imagine that Lavinia has been killed and Helen is asked to give a eulogy for Lavinia. What do you think she will say about her friend? Write Helen's eulogy.

Vocabulary Practice

Exercise In the pairs of words below, determine the relationship between each first pair of words. Then decide which vocabulary word best completes the second pair in order to express a similar relationship. Each word will be used only once. The double colon that follows the original pair means *as*. Thus, the first analogy can be expressed this way: *Sound* is to *ears* as *vapor* is to *nose*.

1. SOUND : EARS (We hear *sound* with our *ears.*) : : *vapor* : nose (We smell a *vapor* with our *nose.*)
2. CHASED : CAUGHT : : ____ : avoided.
3. ASCENDING : RISING : : ____ : falling
4. RUT : ROAD : : ____ : land
5. CALM : TRANQUIL : : ____ : stormy
6. WIND : STORM : : ____ : earthquake
7. FURNACE : HEAT : : ____ : electricity
8. CHILLED : COLD : : ____ : hot
9. ANGRY : GLAD : : ____ : calm
10. HARMLESSLY : SAFELY : : ____ : dangerously

Words to Know and Use

dynamo
overwrought
plummeting
precariously
ravine
scorched
tremor
turbulent
vapor
veered

Literary Concept—Suspense
Some examples of suspense follow: the description of the dead woman; the women's sudden sighting of Douglas Spaulding; the empty town with people behind locked doors; Frank Dillon's appearance; the dialogue with the druggist; the strange face in the movie theater; the sounds, like gunshots, of the women's heels; the clock striking at midnight over empty streets; the police officer's singing; Lavinia's hearing an echo to each step; the "summer night silence"; the sights and sounds Lavinia imagines; the man's clearing his throat at the end. Refer to annotations J, O, and X.

Writing Options
The Writing Options are designed to meet varied student interests and abilities. Have each student choose one writing activity to complete. You may wish to guide some students to an option that requires less writing.

Journal Update Have students review their journal entries for this excerpt from *Dandelion Wine.* What have they come to understand about people's reactions to possible danger? What new reflections can they add to their writing?

Vocabulary Practice
1. Vapor
2. veered
3. plummeting
4. ravine
5. turbulent
6. tremor
7. dynamo
8. scorched
9. overwrought
10. precariously

Options for Learning

These activities suit a variety of learning styles and modes of expression. Allow students to review the options and then choose the one they wish to do. Many are excellent collaborative learning projects.

1. Portrait of a Small Town Supply students with large sheets of drawing paper so they may include all the buildings. Tell them that they will need to reread the story closely to place all the landmarks.

2. What Happens Next? See the Literary Sidelight on page T–76 for information about the next chapter of *Dandelion Wine.*

3. Lavinia's Limerick Remind students that a limerick has five lines, with eight beats in each of the first, second, and fifth lines, five beats in the third line and the fourth line. The rhyme scheme is AABBA.

4. Ravine Research Students might make a model with modeling clay.

Fact Finder

Charlie Chaplin was an Englishman who became a great comedic star of silent movies. He portrayed many characters but is most famous for his tramp character with the little moustache, hat, and cane. This information can be found in an encyclopedia, a book about silent movies, or in a biography.

Additional Information About the Author

Ray Bradbury Bradbury claims that he never has a whole story in his mind when he sits down to write. He rummages in his mind for "words that could describe my personal nightmares, fears of night and time from my childhood, and shaped stories from these." The stories that appear a few hours later are a surprise to him.

Closure

The selection from *Dandelion Wine* explores the possibility of paying a very high price for taking risks in order to have excitement in life. Ask students to discuss what they think are good reasons for taking risks and also to indicate what are "part and parcel" of those risks.

e x t e n d

Options for Learning

1 • Portrait of a Small Town Using details from the story, draw the town described in this selection. Be sure to include and label such landmarks as the movie theater, the ravine, the drug store, the courthouse, and the homes of Lavinia, Helen, and Francine.

2 • What Happens Next? Find a copy of *Dandelion Wine* by Ray Bradbury at your school or local library. Read on to find out what happens to Lavinia and report your findings to the class.

3 • Lavinia's Limerick Create a limerick about Lavinia, beginning with the line "There once was a lady. . . ." If necessary, check out a book of limericks from the library to learn about the rhythm and rhyme of this type of poetry.

4 • Ravine Research Research the formation of ravines in a geology textbook or encyclopedia. Either draw a picture of this formation or, if possible, make a three-dimensional model. In an oral report, explain what ravines are and how they were formed. Use your picture or model to illustrate your talk.

FACT FINDER

Lavinia and her friends go to see a Charlie Chaplin movie at the Elite Theater. Who was Charlie Chaplin?

Ray Bradbury

1920–

Ray Bradbury was born in Waukegan, Illinois, the location of the actual "Lonely One" murders. Known today as one of America's most accomplished science fiction writers, Bradbury was writing stories by the age of twelve, pounding them out on his typewriter and illustrating them by hand. In high school he put out his own magazine. About his early writing Bradbury says, "I was in love with everything I did. I did not warm to a subject, I boiled over." Bradbury's enthusiasm for writing is evident in his writing schedule. He tries to write one thousand words each day and a story a week. So far he has published works in more than seven hundred anthologies. Bradbury lives in California. Though he writes about the future, in some ways he is a bit old-fashioned. For example, he has never learned to drive a car and has never flown in an airplane. His favorite way to get around is by bicycle. As one critic described him, Bradbury is "the grown-up child who still remembers, still believes."

Cross-Curricular Options

Journalism: Students might create a newspaper story about the murders. Have them focus on the *who, what, when, where, why,* and *how* questions that are the focus of a news story.

English: Students might attempt to write their own stories based on a modern crime. Suggest that they use the library to review old newspaper stories.

Health and Safety: Students might create posters about community safety and what people might do to protect themselves in their homes and towns.

e x p l o r e

Fiction *Marigolds*

EUGENIA COLLIER

Examine What You Know (Prior Knowledge)

Can you recall an incident or experience in your life that made you realize you were no longer a child? Perhaps you played a prank that backfired. Perhaps you felt self-conscious about or ashamed of some action that you suddenly realized was childish. In your journal or on a piece of paper, describe such an experience.

Expand Your Knowledge (Building Background)

The short story you are about to read takes place during the Great Depression. The Depression was a period in history beginning in 1929 and lasting through the 1930's. During the Depression industrial production and sales fell, causing a chain reaction in which businesses, industries, and banks were forced into bankruptcy. Countless people lost their jobs when banks closed. The poor were especially hard hit by the Depression, since it greatly lowered their chances of finding work or decent housing. In many towns and cities, the poor lived in shacks in groups called shantytowns and stood in bread lines to receive donated foods.

Write Before You Read (Journal Writing)

Why do people sometimes hurt someone who has never bothered them or done them harm? Are they acting out of ignorance? What might they be trying to gain by hurting someone else? In your journal or on a piece of paper, explain why you think people sometimes hurt others who have done nothing to them.

■ *A biography of the author can be found on page 93.*

Objectives

- To understand and analyze a short work of fiction
- To recognize the use of mood
- To expand vocabulary by determining word meanings through synonyms and antonyms
- To express understanding of the work through a choice of writing options, including dialogue, an explanatory paragraph, a letter of apology, and a paragraph of comparison

Prereading/Motivation

Examine What You Know

Discussion Prompts: What kinds of actions would you consider childish? What kinds of behavior would you consider grown up? If you were with a group of friends who wanted to play a prank or wanted to do something you knew was wrong, what would you do?

Expand Your Knowledge

Discussion Prompts: During the Great Depression, how do you think poor people felt about their lives and their hopes for the future? What do you picture in your mind about the way shantytowns looked? In today's world, what choices do people with little money have for coping with life?

Thematic Link—Paying the Price

In "Marigolds," the main character suffers great remorse for a senseless act of destruction and thus pays the price of the loss of her childhood innocence.

Additional Journal Writing

Suggest these additional journal topics to students:

- Write about marigolds—your impressions of the flowers and your associations with the name.
- What things about your hometown and life might you still remember in later years? Why?

For other journal opportunities, refer students to Examine What You Know (p. 81), Cultural Connections (p. T–83), Real Life Connections (pp. T–86, T–89), and Broader connections (p. 91).

Additional Resources

UNIT ONE RESOURCE BOOK

Reader's Guidesheet, p. 33
Vocabulary Worksheet, p. 34
Selection and Vocabulary Check Tests, p. 35
Selection Test, pp. 36–37

Collaborative Learning

Opportunities for collaborative learning appear throughout the lesson and include Cultural Connections (p. T–83), annotations H, Options for Learning activities 4 and 5 (p. 93), and Cross-Curricular Options (p. T–93).

Teaching Strategies

Vocabulary Preview

These vocabulary words are defined at the bottom of the selection page on which they appear. You may wish to discuss them briefly before students begin reading.

bravado pretense of courage
caricature picture that exaggerates
contrition a guilty feeling
eerie weird, scary
impotent powerless
impoverished poor
perverse improper or wicked
poignantly painfully
quest a search for something
retribution punishment
squalor filth; dirtiness
stoicism the act of not showing emotion
stupor dullness of mind

Support for Students of Limited English Proficiency

- Use Reader's Guidesheet, p. 33
- Students may find some of the figurative language and sentence structure difficult to understand. Explain that the purpose of the opening paragraphs is to establish setting and mood. Then read the first two paragraphs aloud.
- Annotations C, D, E, K, P, and X also focus on troublesome terms and ideas.

Text Annotations

A. Literary Concept: MOOD Ask students what feeling this passage evokes. *(Possible responses: a feeling of sadness, hopelessness, irritation, despair)* Ask students to point out phrases that create this feeling. *(Possible responses: "sterile dust"; "dirt roads"; "grassless yards")*

B. Literary Element: POINT OF VIEW Ask students to identify clues to the point of view of this selection and to the age of the narrator. *(I and my are clues to first-person point of view. The narrator is an adult looking back on her adolescence; clues: "as I recall . . . when I was . . . more woman than child."*

C. LEP: Support: Tell students that in the third paragraph the narrator describes her childhood. Read this and the next two paragraphs aloud. Ask students to listen for key words that describe the narrator's childhood. *(Possible responses: impoverished little community, black, rural Maryland, offering one's sweat for some meager share of bread, no radios, few newspapers, culturally deprived)*

Marigolds

EUGENIA COLLIER

When I think of the hometown of my youth, all I seem to remember is dust—the brown, crumbly dust of late summer—arid, sterile dust that gets into the eyes and makes them water, gets into the throat and between the toes of bare, brown feet. I don't know why I should remember only the dust. Surely there must have been lush green lawns and paved streets under leafy shade trees somewhere in town: but memory is an abstract painting—it does not present things as they are, but rather as they *feel.* And so, when I think of that time and that place, I remember only the dry September of the dirt roads and grassless yards of the shantytown[1] where I lived. And one other thing I remember, another incongruency of memory—a brilliant splash of sunny yellow against the dust—Miss Lottie's marigolds.

Whenever the memory of those marigolds flashes across my mind, a strange nostalgia comes with it and remains long after the picture has faded. I feel again the chaotic emotions of adolescence, illusive as smoke, yet as real as the potted geranium before me now. Joy and rage and wild animal gladness and shame become tangled together in the multicolored skein of fourteen-going-on-fifteen as I recall that devastating moment when I was suddenly more woman than child, years ago in Miss Lottie's yard. I think of those marigolds at the strangest times. I remember them vividly now as I desperately pass away the time waiting for you, who will not come.

I suppose that futile waiting was the sorrowful background music of our impoverished little community when I was young. The Depression that gripped the nation was no new thing to us, for the black workers of rural Maryland had always been depressed. I don't know what it was that we were waiting for; certainly not for the prosperity that was "just around the corner," for those were white folks' words, which we never believed. Nor did we wait for hard work and thrift to pay off, in shining success as the American Dream[2] promised, for we knew better than that, too. Perhaps we waited for a miracle, amorphous in concept but necessary if one were to have the grit to rise before dawn each day and labor in the white man's vineyard until after dark, or to wander about in the September dust offering one's sweat in return for some meager share of bread. But God was *chary*[3] with

1. **shantytown:** a poor section of town where people often live in small shacks.
2. **American Dream:** the belief that through hard work one will naturally have a comfortable and prosperous life.
3. **chary:** sparing or stingy.

Words to Know and Use	**impoverished** (im päv' ər isht) *adj.* poor

82

STRUCTURED READING FOR LESS PROFICIENT STUDENTS

These questions can help to guide students through the reading. Ask each question at the point of the selection where the SR number appears in the margin.

SR–1. What is the one bright thing the narrator remembers about her dull childhood? *(Miss Lottie's marigolds)* **Literal recall**

SR–2. Who is the narrator? *(Possible response: The narrator is a black woman who lived in rural Maryland as a child during the Depression. Her family was very poor.* **Summarizing**

SR–3. Who is Miss Lottie and with whom does she live? *(Miss Lottie is a poor neighbor who lives with her retarded son, John Burke.)* **Literal recall**

SR–4. Where do children go to have what they call "fun"? *(to Miss Lottie's house)* Why do you think they pick on Miss Lottie? *(Possible responses: She seems to be weak and defenseless, which makes her an easy target; they think she is crazy because she grows flowers.)* **Inferring**

Continued on page 84

miracles in those days, and so we waited—
SR-2 ▶ and waited.

We children, of course, were only vaguely aware of the extent of our poverty. Having no radios, few newspapers, and no magazines, we were somewhat unaware of the world outside our community. Nowadays we would be called "culturally deprived" and people would write books and hold conferences about us. In those days everybody we knew was just as hungry and ill-clad as we were. Poverty was the cage in which we all were trapped, and our hatred of it was still the vague, undirected restlessness of the zoo-bred flamingo who knows that nature created him to fly free. D

As I think of those days I feel most poignantly the tag end of summer, the bright, dry times when we began to have a sense of shortening days and the imminence of the cold.

By the time I was fourteen my brother Joey and I were the only children left at our house, the older ones having left home for early marriage or the lure of the city, and the two babies having been sent to relatives who might care for them better than we. Joey was three years younger than I, and a boy, and therefore vastly inferior. E Each morning our mother and father trudged wearily down the dirt road and around the bend, she to her domestic job, he to his daily unsuccessful quest for work. After our few chores around the tumble-down shanty, Joey and I were free to run wild in the sun with other children similarly situated.

For the most part, those days are ill-defined in my memory, running together and combining like a fresh watercolor painting left out in the rain. I remember squatting in the road, drawing a picture in the dust, a picture that Joey gleefully erased with one sweep of his dirty foot. I remember fishing for minnows in a muddy creek and watching sadly as they eluded my cupped hands, while Joey laughed uproariously. And I remember, that year, a strange restlessness of body and of spirit, a feeling that something old and familiar was ending, and something unknown and therefore terrifying was beginning. F

One day returns to me with special clarity for some reason, perhaps because it was the beginning of the experience that in some inexplicable way marked the end of innocence. I was loafing under the great oak tree in our yard, deep in some reverie that I have now forgotten except that it involved some secret thoughts of one of the Harris boys across the yard. Joey and a bunch of kids were bored now with the old tire suspended from an oak limb, which had kept them entertained for a while.

"Hey, Lizabeth," Joey yelled. He never talked when he could yell. "Hey, Lizabeth, let's us go somewhere." G

I came reluctantly from my private world. "Where at, Joey?"

The truth was that we were becoming tired of the formlessness of our summer days. The idleness whose prospect had seemed so beautiful during the busy days of spring now had degenerated to an almost desperate effort to fill up the empty midday hours.

"Let's go see can we find us some locusts on the hill," someone suggested.

Words to Know and Use	**poignantly** (poin′ yənt lē) *adv.* in a painful or sensitive manner **quest** (kwest) *n.* a search or hunt for something

83

D. LEP: Cultural Differences Discuss differences between the United States today, in which television is available to nearly all, and the United States at the time of the story. Then have students explain in their own words what it means for people to be "culturally deprived." *(Possible responses: to not have access to a good education or to such things as books, newspapers, magazines, art, music, and theater; to not have opportunities to gain the skills needed for a chance at a better life)*

E. LEP: Humor Students may take this reference literally. Point out that the narrator is making a joke that males, especially younger brothers, are inferior.

F. Literary Element: SIMILE Ask students to explain the comparison. *(Possible response: The memories of her childhood are all blurred and mixed just like watercolors mix and blur when they are wet.)*

G. Literary Element: PLOT Have students tell how the story changes at this point. *(It shifts in time from present to past, and characters and dialogue are added.)* Then have them identify Lizabeth. *(the woman telling the story)* Ask them what they expect to learn about as Lizabeth continues her story. *(Possible response: an experience that marked the end of her innocence)*

Cultural Connection

Although the story takes place during the Depression, the American Dream and the hope for a miracle have been universal experiences throughout the history of the United States.

Focus a discussion on the American Dream of yesterday and today. Discussion prompts: Has the American Dream changed in any way? Is it the same or different for different groups of people? If any of your students are immigrants, encourage them to share their experiences. What hopes and dreams do each of your students have for their own futures?

HER WORLD 1948 Philip Evergood Oil on canvas, 48″ × 35⅝″ The Metropolitan Museum of Art Arthur Hoppock Hearn Fund, 1950.

Joey was scornful. "Ain't no more locusts there. Y'all got 'em all while they was still green."

The argument that followed was brief and not really worth the effort. Hunting locust trees wasn't fun any more by now.

"Tell you what," said Joey finally, his eyes sparkling. "Let's us go over to Miss Lottie's."

The idea caught on at once, for annoying Miss Lottie was always fun. I was still child enough to scamper along with the group over rickety fences and through bushes that tore our already raggedy clothes, back to where Miss Lottie lived. I think now that we must have made a tragicomic spectacle, five or six kids of different ages, each of us clad in only one garment—the girls in faded dresses that were too long or too short, the boys in patchy pants, their sweaty brown chests gleaming in the hot sun. A little cloud of dust followed our thin legs and bare feet as we tramped over the barren land.

When Miss Lottie's house came into view we stopped, ostensibly to plan our strategy, but actually to reinforce our courage.

Miss Lottie's house was the most ramshackle of all our ramshackle homes. The sun and rain had long since faded its rickety

Art Note

Philip Evergood (1901–1973) was an American Social Realist painter. During the Depression, he was employed in the Federal Arts Project. In that work, as always, he expressed his concerns for social justice. In this pensive portrait, the young girl thoughtlessly rests one foot on a length of barbed wire. *Explain why her thoughts and feelings could be like those of the narrator in "Marigolds."*

H. Literary Element: DIALOGUE Have students explain what the dialogue adds to the story. *(Possible responses: The dialogue makes the characters seem real; makes the story more interesting; lets readers know how the children spoke.)* Students might enjoy role-playing the characters and reading the dialogue aloud wherever it appears in the story.

I. LEP: Vocabulary Students may have trouble understanding the meaning of *tragicomic spectacle.* Explain that it is a sight that is both sad and funny.

Structured Reading for Less Proficient Students

Continued from page 82

SR–5. What do the children do at Miss Lottie's? *(throw stones and then chant and dance around Miss Lottie, taunting her)* **Literal recall**

SR–6 How does the conversation Lizabeth overhears between her parents affect her? *(It makes her feel bewildered and afraid.)* **Literal recall**

SR–7 What does Lizabeth do after overhearing her parents' conversation? *(She goes to Miss Lottie's and destroys her marigolds.)* **Literal recall**

frame siding from white to a sullen gray. The boards themselves seemed to remain upright, not from being nailed together but rather from leaning together like a house that a child might have constructed from cards.

A brisk wind might have blown it down, and the fact that it was still standing implied a kind of enchantment that was stronger than the elements. There it stood, and as far as I know is standing yet—a gray, rotting thing with no porch, no shutters, no steps, set on a cramped lot with no grass, not even any weeds—a monument to decay.

In front of the house in a squeaky rocking chair sat Miss Lottie's son, John Burke, completing the impression of decay. John Burke was what was known as "queer-headed." Black and ageless, he sat, rocking day in and day out in a mindless stupor, lulled by the monotonous squeak-squawk of the chair. A battered hat atop his shaggy head shaded him from the sun. Usually John Burke was totally unaware of everything outside his quiet dream world. But if you disturbed him, if you intruded upon his fantasies, he would become enraged, strike out at you, and curse at you in some strange enchanted language which only he could understand. We children made a game of thinking of ways to disturb John Burke and then to elude his violent retribution.

But our real fun and our real fear lay in Miss Lottie herself. Miss Lottie seemed to be at least a hundred years old. Her big frame still held traces of the tall, powerful woman she must have been in youth, although it was now bent and drawn. Her smooth skin was a dark reddish-brown, and her face had Indian-like features and the stern stoicism that one associates with Indian faces. Miss Lottie didn't like intruders either, especially children. She never left her yard, and nobody ever visited her. We never knew how she managed those necessities that depend on human interaction—how she ate, for example, or even whether she ate. When we were tiny children, we thought Miss Lottie was a witch, and we made up tales, that we half believed ourselves, about her exploits. We were far too sophisticated now, of course, to believe the witch-nonsense. But old fears have a way of clinging like cobwebs, and so when we sighted the tumbledown shack, we had to stop to reinforce our nerves.

"Look, there she," I whispered, forgetting that Miss Lottie could not possibly have heard me from that distance. "She fooling with them crazy flowers."

"Yeh, look at 'er."

Miss Lottie's marigolds were perhaps the strangest part of the picture. Certainly they did not fit in with the crumbling decay of the rest of her yard. Beyond the dusty brown yard in front of the sorry gray house, rose suddenly and shockingly a dazzling strip of bright blossoms, clumped together in enormous mounds, warm and passionate and sun-golden. The old black witch-woman worked on them all summer; every summer, down on her creaky knees, weeding and cultivating and arranging, while the house crumbled and John Burke rocked. For some perverse reason, we children hated those marigolds. They interfered with the perfect ugliness of the place; they were too beautiful; they said too much that we could not understand; they did not

Words to Know and Use

stupor (sto͞o′ pər) *n.* a state in which one's mind is dulled or senseless
retribution (re′trə byo͞o′ shən) *n.* punishment for a wrongdoing
stoicism (stō′ i siz′ əm) *n.* the act of not showing emotion
perverse (pər vûrs′) *adj.* improper or wicked

J. Literary Element: IMAGERY Have students identify words or phrases that help them visualize Miss Lottie's house. *(Possible responses: "rickety frame"; "gray rotting thing with no porch, . . ."; "cramped lot"; "monument to decay")* Have students identify the senses to which the writer appeals. *(sight and smell)*

K. LEP: Vocabulary Students may be unfamiliar with the expression *queer-headed.* Use the context clues that follow this expression to help students understand that the term means "mentally retarded."

L. Reading Skill: DRAWING CONCLUSIONS Have students tell whether Lizabeth and the other children know and understand Miss Lottie as a real person or view her through their childish imaginations. Ask students to give evidence that supports their opinions. *(Possible response: The children view Miss Lottie primarily through their imaginations; they don't know why she lives as she does or how she manages; they remember thinking she was a witch; and they make up stories about her.)*

M. Literary Element: IMAGERY Have students identify the words used to create a picture in their minds of the marigolds. *(Possible responses: "dazzling strip of bright blossoms"; "enormous mounds"; "warm"; "passionate"; "sun-golden")*

N. Reading Skill: CLARIFYING Ask students to explain why Lizabeth and the others seem to hate the marigolds. *(They are too beautiful to be in such a dilapidated place and don't fit in with the ugliness. The children don't understand why they are there.)*

Professional Notebook

Expect success. Discouraged learners expect very little of themselves, and most adults expect little more. It is professionally irresponsible to put work in front of kids that we know they cannot do and is even, at their present skill level, out of their reach. When school work is requested that is responsible and success is carefully structured, let them know you expect success—for as the expert, you know it is possible—and effort, not luck, will bring it.

Jerry Conrath, *Our Other Youth*

O. Critical Thinking: ANALYZING Remind students of their earlier journal writing on why a person may hurt someone who has never done him or her harm and ask them to comment on Lizabeth's explanation about being destructive. Encourage students to offer their own ideas. *(Possible responses: People who are unhappy about themselves try to make themselves feel better by hurting others. The children in the story may have felt they themselves had no chance of growing beautiful, so they wanted to destroy the beauty of the flowers.)*

P. LEP: Setting Encourage students from urban areas to visualize the rural setting of dirt, broken-down shacks and farms, and distances between houses. Photographs of rural Maryland or other Mid-Atlantic states would be helpful.

Q. Literary Element: SIMILE Point out that the writer compares the children to swarming bees to help readers visualize the scene. Have students explain in their own words what is taking place. *(Possible response: The children are dancing around Miss Lottie and screaming at her while she curses them.)*

N make sense. There was something in the vigor with which the old woman destroyed the weeds that intimidated us. It should have been a comical sight—the old woman with the man's hat on her cropped white head, leaning over the bright mounds, her big backside in the air—but it wasn't comical; it was something we could not name. We had to annoy her by whizzing a pebble into her flowers or by veiling a dirty word, then dancing away from her rage, reveling in our youth and mocking her age. Actually, I think it was the flowers we wanted to destroy, but nobody had the nerve to try it, not even Joey, who was usually fool enough SR-4 ▶ to try anything.

"Y'all git some stones," commanded Joey now, and was met with instant giggling obedience as everyone except me began to gather pebbles from the dusty ground. "Come on, Lizabeth."

I just stood there peering through the bushes, torn between wanting to join the fun and feeling that it was all a bit silly.

"You scared, Lizabeth?"

I cursed and spat on the ground—my favorite gesture of phony bravado. "Y'all children get the stones, I'll show you how to use 'em."

O I said before that we children were not consciously aware of how thick were the bars of our cage. I wonder now, though, whether we were not more aware of it than I thought. Perhaps we had some dim notion of what we were, and how little chance we had of being anything else. Otherwise, why would we have been so preoccupied with destruction? Anyway, the pebbles were collected quickly, and everybody looked at me to begin the fun.

"Come on, y'all."

P We crept to the edge of the bushes that bordered the narrow road in front of Miss Lottie's place. She was working placidly, kneeling over the flowers. her dark hand plunged into the golden mound. Suddenly "zing"—an expertly aimed stone cut the head off one of the blossoms.

"Who out there?" Miss Lottie's backside came down and her head came up as her sharp eyes searched the bushes. "You better git!"

We had crouched down out of sight in the bushes, where we stifled the giggles that insisted on coming. Miss Lottie gazed wanly across the road for a moment, then cautiously returned to her weeding. "Zing"—Joey sent a pebble into the blooms, and another marigold was beheaded.

Miss Lottie was enraged now. She began struggling to her feet, leaning on a rickety cane and shouting. "Y'all get! Go on home!" Then the rest of the kids let loose with their pebbles, storming the flowers and laughing wildly and senselessly at Miss Lottie's impotent rage. She shook her stick at us and started shakily toward the road crying, "Git 'long! John Burke! John Burke, come help!"

Q Then I lost my head entirely, mad with the power of inciting such rage, and ran out of the bushes in the storm of pebbles, straight toward Miss Lottie chanting madly, "Old lady witch, fell in a ditch, picked up a penny and thought she was rich!" The children screamed with delight, dropped their pebbles and joined the crazy dance, swarming around Miss Lottie like bees and chanting, "Old lady witch!" while she screamed

Words to Know and Use	**bravado** (brə vä′ dō) *n.* a pretending to have courage when one really has little or none **impotent** (im′ pə tənt) *adj.* powerless or ineffective

Real Life Connections

Students may have read about or have known a character like Miss Lottie, a person who seemed as strange and frightening to them when they were children as Miss Lottie did to Lizabeth and the others.

If Miss Lottie reminds students of a real person from their past, encourage them to share memories. Did this person also seem strange and frightening? Was the person someone the student really knew or someone viewed from a distance? Did the student ever change his or her feelings about the person?

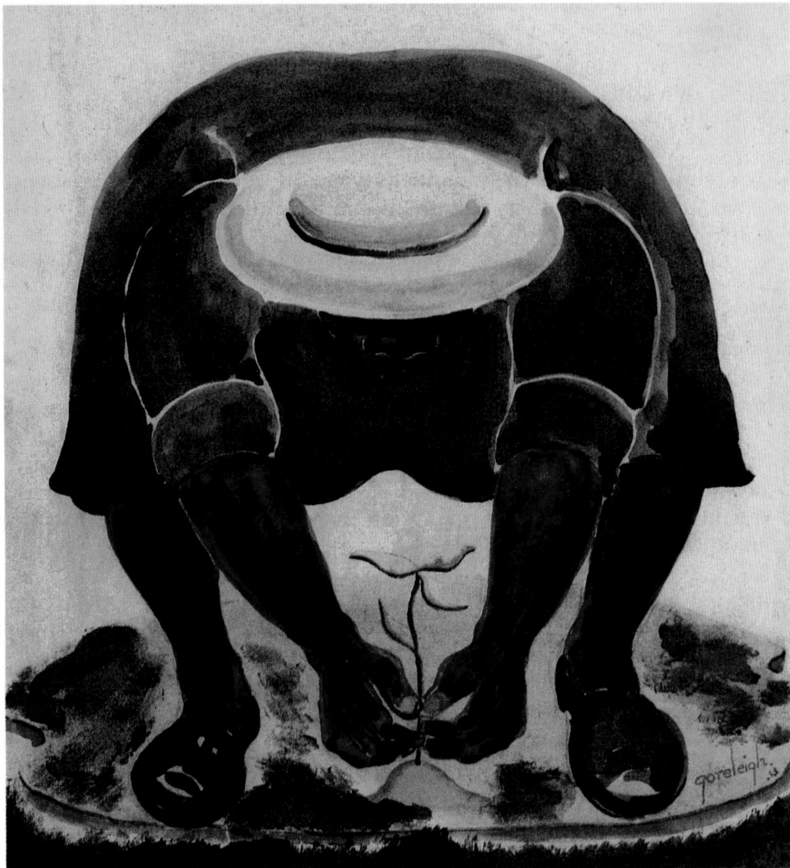

PLANTING 1943 Rex Gorleigh Smithsonian Institution, Washington, D.C.

Q curses at us. The madness lasted only a moment, for John Burke, startled at last, lurched out of his chair, and we dashed for the bushes just as Miss Lottie's cane went
SR-5 ▶ whizzing at my head.

I did not join the merriment when the kids gathered again under the oak in our bare yard. Suddenly I was ashamed, and I
R did not like being ashamed. The child in me sulked and said it was all in fun, but the woman in me flinched at the thought of the malicious attack that I had led. The mood lasted all afternoon. When we ate the beans R
and rice that was supper that night, I did not notice my father's silence, for he was always silent these days, nor did I notice my mother's absence, for she always worked S
until well into evening. Joey and I had a particularly bitter argument after supper; his exuberance got on my nerves. Finally I stretched out upon the pallet in the room we shared and fell into a fitful doze.

When I awoke, somewhere in the middle of the night, my mother had returned, and

Art Note
Rex Gorleigh (1902–1987) studied at the Art Students League in New York and with artist Andre Lhote in Paris. He later taught at a number of schools, including Chicago's Southside Community Center. In this powerful painting, the large figure of the woman bent over the tiny plant demonstrates an almost worshipful attitude. *How does the picture echo Miss Lottie's feelings about her marigolds?*

R. Literary Element: THEME Have students explain what Lizabeth's behavior and feelings reveal about the theme of growing up and the "end of innocence." *(Possible response: Her feeling ashamed shows that she is confused about acting as a thoughtless child while feeling the guilt of a young adult who realizes the consequences of her actions.)*

S. Critical Thinking: ANALYZING Ask students to explain how these details contribute to the reader's understanding of Lizabeth and her family situation. *(Possible response: Lizabeth's parents are not able to give her much attention and guidance, and Joey is still very much a child with no understanding of what Lizabeth is thinking and feeling.)*

T. Historical Sidelight It is not clear what kind of work Lizabeth's father did. However, it is possible that he had been a sharecropper—a tenant farmer—in the earlier part of the century because there were few other ways for black males living in rural areas to earn a living. Although the sharecropping system gave a family some source of income and food, it also kept the family in continual debt to the landowner. The family was required to pay a large part of their earnings back to the landowner for rent on housing and land.

U. Literary Element: MOOD Ask students to contrast the feeling of the man crying in the bedroom with the feeling of the laughing, singing man. *(Possible response: The feeling of sadness, pain, and helplessness contrasts with the feeling of lightness, joy, and strength.)*

V. Literary Element: SIMILE Have students identify the writer's comparison. *("Everything was suddenly out of tune, like a broken accordion.")* Then have them explain what Lizabeth is conveying about her life. *(Nothing in her life was going as it had been or should be, which left her feeling confused, upset, and fearful.)*

W. Reading Skill: INFERRING Ask students why they think Lizabeth could not admit her real feelings to Joey. *(Possible response: She is the older sister and the one who always leads and acts brave, so she doesn't want to admit her fear to Joey.)*

I vaguely listened to the conversation that was audible through the thin walls that separated our rooms. At first I heard no words, only voices. My mother's voice was like a cool, dark room in summer—peaceful, soothing, quiet. I loved to listen to it; it made things seem all right somehow. But my father's voice cut through hers, shattering the peace.

"Twenty-two years, Maybelle, twenty-two years," he was saying, "and I got nothing for you, nothing, nothing."

"It's all right, honey, you'll get something. Everybody out of work now, you know that."

"It ain't right. Ain't no man ought to eat his woman's food year in and year out, and see his children running wild. Ain't nothing right about that."

"Honey, you took good care of us when you had it. Ain't nobody got nothing nowadays."

"I ain't talking about nobody else, I'm talking about *me*. God knows I try." My mother said something I could not hear, and my father cried out louder. "What must a man do, tell me that?"

"Look, we ain't starving. I git paid every week, and Mrs. Ellis is real nice about giving me things. She gonna let me have Mr. Ellis's old coat for you this winter—"

"Forget Mr. Ellis's coat! And forget his money! You think I want white folks' leavings? Oh, Maybelle"—and suddenly he sobbed loudly and painfully, and cried helplessly and hopelessly in the dark night. I had never heard a man cry before. I did not know men ever cried. I covered my ears with my hands but could not cut off the sound of my father's harsh, painful, despairing sobs. My father was a strong man who would whisk a child upon his shoulders and go singing through the house. My father whittled toys for us and laughed so loud that the great oak seemed to laugh with him, and taught us how to fish and hunt rabbits. How could it be that my father was crying? But the sobs went on, unstifled, finally quieting until I could hear my mother's voice, deep and rich, humming softly as she used to hum to a frightened child.

The world had lost its boundary lines. My mother, who was small and soft, was now the strength of the family, my father, who was the rock on which the family had been built, was sobbing like the tiniest child. Everything was suddenly out of tune, like a broken accordion. Where did I fit into this crazy picture? I do not now remember my thoughts, only a feeling of great bewilderment and fear.

◀SR-6

Long after the sobbing and the humming had stopped, I lay on the pallet, still as stone with my hands over my ears, wishing that I could cry and be comforted. The night was silent now except for the sound of the crickets and of Joey's soft breathing. But the room was too crowded with fear to allow me to sleep, and finally, feeling the terrible aloneness of 4 A.M. I decided to awaken Joey.

"Ouch! What's the matter with you? What you want?" he demanded disagreeably when I had pinched and slapped him awake.

"Come on, wake up."

"What for? Go 'way."

I was lost for a reasonable reply. I could not say, "I'm scared, and I don't want to be alone," so I merely said, "I'm going out. If you want to come, come on."

The promise of adventure awoke him. "Going out now? Where at, Lizabeth? What you going to do?"

I was pulling my dress over my head. Until now I had not thought of going out. "Just come on," I replied tersely.

I was out the window and halfway down the road before Joey caught up with me.

"Wait, Lizabeth, where you going?"

I was running as if the Furies[4] were after me, as perhaps they were—running silently and furiously until I came to where I had half-known I was headed—to Miss Lottie's yard.

The half-dawn light was more eerie than complete darkness, and in it the old house was like the ruin that my world had become—foul and crumbling, a grotesque caricature. It looked haunted, but I was not afraid because I was haunted too.

"Lizabeth, you lost your mind?" panted Joey.

I had indeed lost my mind, for all the smoldering emotions of that summer swelled in me and burst—the great need for my mother who was never there, the hopelessness of our poverty and degradation, the bewilderment of being neither child nor woman and yet both at once, the fear unleashed by my father's tears. And these feelings combined in one great impulse toward destruction.

"Lizabeth!"

I leaped furiously into the mounds of marigolds and pulled madly, trampling and pulling and destroying the perfect yellow blooms. The fresh smell of early morning and of dew-soaked marigolds spurred me on as I went tearing and mangling and sobbing while Joey tugged my dress or my waist crying, "Lizabeth stop, please stop!"

And then I was sitting in the ruined little garden among the uprooted and ruined flowers, crying and crying, and it was too late to undo what I had done. Joey was sitting beside me, silent and frightened, not knowing what to say. Then, "Lizabeth, look."

◀SR-7

I opened my swollen eyes and saw in front of me a pair of large calloused feet; my gaze lifted to the swollen legs, the age-distorted body clad in a tight cotton night dress, and then the shadowed Indian face surrounded by stubby white hair. And there was no rage in the face now, now that the garden was destroyed and there was nothing any longer to be protected.

"M-miss Lottie!" I scrambled to my feet and just stood there and stared at her, and that was the moment when childhood faded and womanhood began. The violent, crazy act was the last act of childhood. For as I gazed at the immobile face with sad, weary eyes, I gazed upon a kind of reality that is hidden to childhood. The witch was no longer a witch but only a broken old woman who had dared to create beauty in the midst of ugliness and sterility. She had been born in squalor and had lived in it all her life.

4. **Furies:** the three goddesses in Greek mythology who take vengeance on unpunished criminals.

Words to Know and Use

eerie (ir′ ē) *adj.* weird, scary
caricature (kar′ i kə chər) *n.* a picture that exaggerates certain characteristics
squalor (skwäl′ ər) *n.* filth; dirtiness

X. LEP: Vocabulary Students may find the word *grotesque* troublesome in both pronunciation and meaning. Pronounce the word and explain that it means "ugly and unnaturally shaped."

Y. Literary Element: CLIMAX Remind students that the climax is the turning point of a story. Have students explain why this is the turning point. *(Possible response: This is the point at which Lizabeth gets out of control and does something to change her situation.)*

Z. Critical Thinking: ANALYZING Have students explain in their own words how Lizabeth has changed. *(Possible response: Lizabeth finally gets beyond her childish imagination and sees things as they really are.)*

Real Life Connections

Students may have experienced some feelings similar to Lizabeth's: the boredom of having too much time on their hands and little constructive help in dealing with it; the desire for more attention from parents; the feelings of uncertainty and bewilderment in changing from childhood to adolescence; the urge to lash out and hurt someone. Encourage students to write in their journals about feelings or experiences this story evokes.

AA. Literary Element: STATED THEME Point out that the writer here directly presents the main point, or message, of her story. Encourage students to state the author's message in their own words.

BB. Critical Thinking: ANALYZING Have students tell whether the narrator is Lizabeth the child or the older woman at the end of the story. *(older woman)* Then have them explain why Lizabeth feels that the memory will always be painful. *(Possible responses: It was a painful time in her childhood; she gained knowledge and compassion at the expense of hurting someone else; she feels that her life may be as barren as Miss Lottie's was and, like Miss Lottie, she has tried to nurture life and beauty.)*

Check Test

1. Who is telling the story? *(Lizabeth, a black woman)*

2. What time in her life is she telling about? *(her adolescence, when she was fourteen)*

3. Who is the person the children bait and what does she have that they hate? *(Miss Lottie; marigolds)*

4. How do Lizabeth's parents, in her eyes, reverse their roles? *(Her father, who has been the family's strength, cries like a baby; her mother, who had seemed soft, becomes strong, earning money and comforting the father.)*

5. What does Lizabeth do in the early morning? *(destroys Miss Lottie's marigolds)*

6. What did Lizabeth lose? *(her innocence)* What did she gain? *(compassion)*

Encouraging Independent Reading

Lord of the Flies, a novel by William Golding
"The Destructors," a short story by Graham Greene
A Separate Peace, a novel by John Knowles
"The Sand Castle," a short story by Mary Lavin
"A Visit of Charity," a short story by Eudora Welty

Now at the end of that life she had nothing except a falling-down hut, a wrecked body, and John Burke, the mindless son of her passion. Whatever verve there was left in her, whatever was of love and beauty and joy that had not been squeezed out by life, had been there in the marigolds she had so tenderly cared for.

Of course I could not express the things that I knew about Miss Lottie as I stood there awkward and ashamed. The years have put words to the things I knew in that moment, and as I look back upon it, I know that that moment marked the end of innocence. . . . Innocence involves an unseeing acceptance of things at face value, an ignorance of the area below the surface. In that
AA humiliating moment I looked beyond myself and into the depths of another person. This was the beginning of compassion, and one cannot have both compassion and innocence.

The years have taken me worlds away from that time and that place, from the dust and squalor of our lives and from the bright thing that I destroyed in a blind, childish striking out at God-knows-what. Miss Lottie died long ago and many years have passed since I last saw her hut, completely barren at last, for despite my wild contrition she never planted marigolds again. Yet, there are times when the image of those passionate yellow mounds returns with a painful
BB poignancy. For one does not have to be ignorant and poor to find that one's life is barren as the dusty yards of one's town. And I too have planted marigolds.

INSIGHT

Warning

JENNY JOSEPH

When I am an old woman I shall wear purple
With a red hat which doesn't go, and doesn't suit me,
And I shall spend my pension on brandy and summer gloves
And satin sandals, and say we've no money for butter.
I shall sit down on the pavement when I'm tired
And gobble up samples in shops and press alarm bells
And run my stick along the public railings
And make up for the sobriety of my youth.
I shall go out in my slippers in the rain
And pick the flowers in other people's gardens
And learn to spit.

Words to Know and Use	**contrition** (kən trish′ ən) *n.* a bad or guilty feeling from having done something wrong

90

Insight

This piece reflects on the ideas in the main selection and is suggested for students' independent reading. Optional discussion questions follow.

1. Who is the speaker of the poem? *(a girl or young woman)*

2. What clues do you have about her views of life? *(She seems determined to live life her own way and to find something to make her happy.)*

3. In what ways do you think this girl and Lizabeth are similar? *(Possible responses: Both Lizabeth and the girl in the poem are trying to learn and show the world who they are. Neither are afraid to strike out at the world if they think that might make them happy. They both want to pick someone else's flowers.* How are they different? *(Possible response: The girl in the poem is talking about her actions when she will be old. Lizabeth's actions and attitude occur when she is young.*

Responding to Reading

First Impressions

1. Briefly describe how the story made you feel.

Second Thoughts

2. Why does Miss Lottie grow marigolds?
3. What kind of people are Lizabeth's parents? Be sure to consider their occupations and family life.
4. Why does Lizabeth destroy Miss Lottie's marigolds?

   Think about
   - how much control Lizabeth feels she has over her life
   - how she feels about hearing her father cry
   - your earlier thoughts about leaving childhood
   - your earlier thoughts about why people hurt others
5. Miss Lottie and her marigolds are important to Lizabeth later in life because they represent a time when she learned something about herself. What does Lizabeth begin to understand about herself after she destroys the marigolds?
6. When Lizabeth says at the end of the story, "And I too have planted marigolds," what else might she mean besides that she has planted flowers?

Broader Connections

7. Lizabeth learns a painful lesson the hard way. Is there an easier way to learn the important lessons in life? Look back at what you wrote about an experience that made you realize you were no longer a child. What lessons have you learned through personal experience? Were these lessons easily learned, or was learning them painful?

Literary Concept: Mood

Mood is the feeling or attitude that the writer creates in the reader through carefully selected details and words. Writers often set a mood for a piece of writing in the opening paragraphs. For example, a writer may describe sounds of laughter at a picnic to create a mood of happiness. In "Marigolds," Collier emphasizes the "dust of late summer" and the "grassless yards of the shantytown where I lived." What mood does this set?

Literary Concept—Mood

The mood set in the first paragraph is one of sadness, depression, despair, irritation, and emptiness.

Student Response

Responding to Reading

These questions are open-ended with no "right" or "wrong" answers. However, responses must be supported with information from the selection. Possible answers follow:

1. Any descriptions of feelings based on the story are valid.

2. Some students may say that Miss Lottie grows marigolds to make her surroundings look prettier. Others may suggest that she grows marigolds because they give her a purpose in life, and it is one of the few things she can control in her poverty-stricken world.

3. Some students may say that Lizabeth's parents are good, caring, hardworking people who cannot provide their children with much attention because it is all they can do to eke out a living. Others may feel that Lizabeth's parents are weak and irresponsible because they let their children run wild in the neighborhood.

4. Some students may say that Lizabeth destroys the marigolds because she is so confused and angry about the poverty and despair in her life that she needs to strike out at something she can touch. Others may say that she destroys the marigolds because she feels they don't belong in such ugly surroundings. Still others may say that because she feels neglected by her parents, she resents seeing a woman so tenderly care for flowers.

5. Possible responses: Lizabeth begins to understand that she had been ignorant of many things, especially of not seeing how things really are for others; that by seeing things as they really are and having compassion for other people, she is starting to grow up and leave childhood.

6. Some students may say that she has found a way to bring beauty, joy, and love into a life that is not very happy. Others may say that she has found something to care for beyond herself—literally in marigolds or figuratively in other people.

7. Student answers will vary. Students may suggest that there are easier ways of learning a lesson, such as listening to someone else's advice and learning from others' experiences.

Writing Options

The Writing Options are designed to meet varied student interests and abilities. Have each student choose one writing activity to complete. You may wish to guide some students to an option that requires less writing.

Journal Update Have students review their journal entries for "Marigolds." Ask students what they have come to understand about why a person might hurt someone who has never bothered him or her. Also ask what they have discovered about the difference between being childish and being grown up.

Vocabulary Practice

1. Antonyms
2. Synonyms
3. Antonyms
4. Synonyms
5. Synonyms
6. Synonyms
7. Antonyms
8. Synonyms
9. Synonyms
10. Antonyms
11. Synonyms
12. Synonyms
13. Antonyms
14. Synonyms
15. Synonyms

Writing Options

1. Write a short dialogue that might have taken place between Miss Lottie and Lizabeth after the destruction of the marigolds.
2. The narrator says, "This was the beginning of compassion, and one cannot have both compassion and innocence." Using details from the story to support your opinion, explain briefly what you think she means.
3. What might Lizabeth have said to Miss Lottie if she had wanted to apologize later? Write a letter of apology from Lizabeth to Miss Lottie.
4. Explain in a paragraph how the lady described in "Warning" is like Miss Lottie. Then tell how she is different.

Vocabulary Practice

Exercise Read the pairs of words below. On your paper write *Synonyms* if the pair are synonyms. Write *Antonyms* if they are antonyms. Remember that synonyms are words with almost the same meaning. Antonyms have opposite meanings. Some words will appear more than once.

1. cleanliness—squalor
2. imitation—caricature
3. strong—impotent
4. daze—stupor
5. guilt—contrition
6. weak—impotent
7. emotionalism—stoicism
8. poor—impoverished
9. punishment—retribution
10. wealthy—impoverished
11. wicked—perverse
12. scary—eerie
13. cowardliness—bravado
14. painfully—poignantly
15. search—quest

Words to Know and Use

bravado
caricature
contrition
eerie
impotent
impoverished
perverse
poignantly
quest
retribution
squalor
stoicism
stupor

Options for Learning

1 • Realistic Art Realistic art depicts people or things in a recognizable manner. For example, a chair has four legs, and a face has eyes, a nose, and a mouth. Draw or paint a realistic scene from this story, such as:

- Miss Lottie's house and yard
- John Burke in his rocking chair
- Lizabeth tearing up the flowers
- the children teasing Miss Lottie

2 • Abstract Art Abstract art does not picture things as they actually are. Rather, it uses patterns, colors, lines, and shapes to express feelings or ideas. Eugenia Collier says, "Memory is an abstract painting—it does not present things as they are, but rather as they feel." Draw an abstract picture of the way this story makes you feel.

3 • To Rhyme or Not to Rhyme Write a poem entitled "Miss Lottie's Marigolds." The poem can be written from either Miss Lottie's or Lizabeth's point of view. Your poem does not have to rhyme.

4 • A Dramatic Moment Imagine that the children in Lizabeth's neighborhood have taken up a collection among themselves to replace Miss Lottie's marigolds. Act out the conversation between them and Miss Lottie as they bring her their money.

5 • Visual History Search in books, old magazines, and encyclopedias for pictures recording the depression. If possible, make photocopies of these pictures and create a display showing what life was like during this period. Be sure to write captions that explain your pictures to your audience.

FACT FINDER

What percentage of workers in the United States were unemployed during the height of the Great Depression?

Eugenia Collier
1928–

Regarded as one of America's foremost black writers, Eugenia Collier was born in Baltimore in 1928. She graduated *magna cum laude*, or with high honors, from Howard University in Washington, D.C. Mrs. Collier later earned her Master of Arts from Columbia University. She has contributed to many anthologies including *Modern Black Poets: A Collection of Critical Essays* and *A Bridge to Saying It Well.* Mrs. Collier has edited a collection of writing by Langston Hughes and published many stories. "Marigolds" won the Gwendolyn Brooks Award for fiction in 1969.

Cross-Curricular Options

Students might form groups to present segments of a "You Are There" show. Each group will focus on a different aspect of the Great Depression. The presentations may take the form of a dramatization, an interview, a radio program, a roundtable discussion, or a newspaper or magazine article. Suggestions follow:

Social Studies: Research information about the effects of the Great Depression on black Americans, including the use of boycotts, voting rights, and the emergence of black leaders. Research President Franklin D. Roosevelt's role during the period and the creation of the New Deal programs.

Literature: Research black writers of the 1930's, such as Zora Neale Hurston and Arna Bontemps.

Music/Art: Research photography, songs, slogans, and the entertainment culture of the period.

Math: Research the stock market crash of October 24, 1929, and the failure of the banks.

Science: Find out what inventions or technological breakthroughs were achieved between 1929 and 1939.

Options for Learning

These activities suit a variety of learning styles and modes of expression. Allow students to review the options and then choose the one they wish to do. Many are excellent collaborative learning projects.

1. Realistic Art Students may wish to look at drawings or photographs of marigolds or rural scenes to help create realism.

2. Abstract Art Show examples of abstract art as references.

3. To Rhyme or Not to Rhyme Poems can be read aloud or perhaps taped and played for a special "Poet's Day" or to be shared with other classes.

4. A Dramatic Moment Students might want to use props, such as play money and a small box or bag to hold the money, and a costume for Miss Lottie. Have students discuss how they think the children in the story would feel to help them get into character.

5. Visual History Students might enjoy making a photo album or art gallery exhibit of what they find.

Fact Finder

The percentage of workers unemployed at the height of the Depression (early 1930s) in the United States was about 25%, or somewhere between 13 and 15 million people. This information can be found in an encyclopedia.

Additional Information About the Author

Eugenia Collier The award-winning "Marigolds" was one of Collier's first writing efforts. She was a college teacher of literature, but she changed to writing as a result of her research into her culture and heritage.

Closure

Like other selections in this subunit, "Marigolds" focuses on a person "paying the price" for his or her actions. The price Lizabeth paid for her destruction of Miss Lottie's marigolds was the loss of her innocence and the pain she experienced for hurting another human being. Ask students what other characters in this unit have learned similar lessons. *(Students might suggest Laura in "The Fan Club" and the narrators of "Honor" and "A Kind of Murder.")*

Objectives

- To understand and analyze a short work of fiction
- To recognize the use of irony
- To understand the process of setting purposes for reading
- To express understanding of the work through a choice of writing options, including explanation, summary, expression of opinion, and comparison of characters

Prereading/Motivation

Examine What You Know

Discussion Prompts: What does it mean when someone says, "He or she acted in an honorable way"? Is acting in an honorable way an important quality? Explain your feelings. Is it sometimes difficult for people to act in an honorable way? Why?

Expand Your Knowledge

Discussion Prompts: What types of barriers may separate the whites and the Indians and keep them from understanding each other's lives? What misunderstandings may occur between people of different classes and ethnic backgrounds?

Additional Background: Although the Indians and mestizos (people of mixed Indian and European ancestry) make up 80 percent of the population of Ecuador, they have little wealth or power. They work mostly as laborers on large plantations owned by the whites but otherwise have little contact with those of white European ancestry.

Enrich Your Reading

These are possible answers: **Hotel Owner** must find and punish the thief to restore his pride and the reputation of his hotel; **Young Servant** must get money to bury his child.

Thematic Link—Paying the Price

In "Honor," a hotel servant chooses to pay the price of going to prison for stealing money so that he can bury his child.

e x p l o r e

Fiction *Honor*

BETTY DAHLIN

Examine What You Know (Prior Knowledge)

As you will discover in this story, *honor* means different things to different people. What does it mean to you? Make a list of five actions that you consider honorable. Share these ideas with your classmates.

Expand Your Knowledge (Building Background)

This story takes place in Quito, the capital of Ecuador. Ecuador is one of the smallest countries of South America, nestled between Colombia and Peru. Of the 10 million people in Ecuador, 80 percent are of Indian or mixed Indian heritage. Ten percent are black, and 10 percent are of white European ancestry. It is this small percentage of whites that makes up the wealthy and powerful upper class.

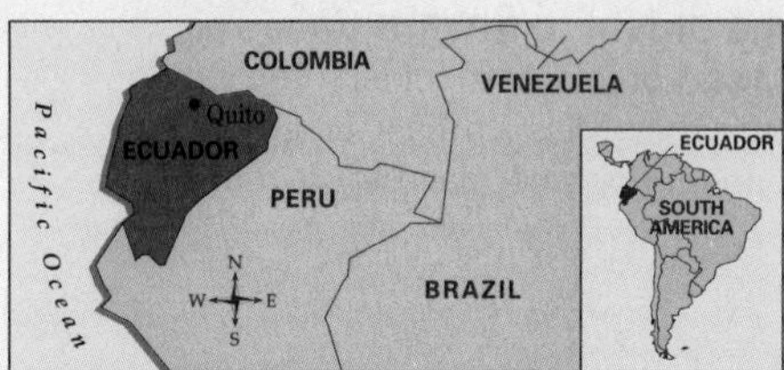

Enrich Your Reading (Reading Skill)

Setting Purposes for Reading You comprehend better when you set purposes for your reading. In the following story, the three main characters have very different problems. Read to find out what problems these characters have and how they solve them. As you read, keep a chart like the one below to note the different problems of the characters. One square has been filled in for you.

	Tourist (Narrator)	Hotel Owner	Young Servant
Problem	has money stolen from hotel room		

■ *A biography of the author can be found on page 104.*

Journal Writing

Suggest these journal topics to students:

- Have you ever been a tourist in another country and experienced difficulties with language or money? Describe your trip.
- Have you ever known someone who acted dishonorably? Describe the situation and your reaction.

For other journal opportunities, refer students to Examine What You Know (p. 94) and Broader Connections (p. 102).

Additional Resources

UNIT ONE RESOURCE BOOK

Reader's Guidesheet, p. 38
Vocabulary Worksheet, p. 39
Selection and Vocabulary Checktests, p. 40
Selection Test, pp. 41–42

Collaborative Learning

Opportunities for collaborative learning appear throughout the lesson and include annotations P, S, and V, Real Life Connections (p. T–98), Options for Learning activities 2 and 4 (p. 104), and Cross-Curricular Options (p. T–104).

Honor

BETTY DAHLIN

A We found the Hotel Crillón on our third day in Quito. Julie spotted its bright blue door and said it reminded her of the pensión[1] in Guatemala, which she considered the best spot we'd stayed in since we left the states four months ago. The owner greeted us himself. He had a European face with sagging yellow skin and wore a maroon sweater with a brown leather front. He showed us our room and assured us that we could have both hot and cold water 24 hours a day in his hotel.

Our room overlooked a patio. Two hundred years ago, when the house belonged to
B some minor Spanish bureaucrat, this space was open to the elements. Now it was covered over with corrugated green plastic. The rain clattered insistently on the plastic. Outside our window an antiquated window box held faded pink and red plastic flowers. They looked sad and, somehow, embarrassing. Below, the old stone floor of the patio was damp and cracked. Four potted plants stood in red pots like the corners of a checkerboard. The patio served as a dining room for the breakfast which was part of the hotel's daily room rate. Five or six tables with straight-backed wooden chairs were crowded into the square.

A young man watered one of the plants while the rain continued to clatter above. He was about 18, I think. He had soulful brown eyes and shiny black hair that seemed to grow down the back of his neck into his shirt collar. His shirt was white; it seemed whiter than most shirts. The skin on his cheeks was bright pink like nearly all the Indian people we had met in Quito. It seemed to glow in the brown of his skin. His eyes were fixed firmly on our room window. For a brief second our eyes locked. C
Then I turned back to the others.

Julie followed the usual pattern. She counted our cash on hand. She counted out enough for dinner and then found page 184 of "Gone with the Wind" and put the rest there. "We've got 985 sucres[2] to last us until Monday morning. That means we can only spend 265 for dinner tonight. Dad, you can't afford another *periódico*[3] on the way home from dinner." Neither of us was brave enough to argue with Julie about finances. She handed Cliff the money, and I D
extracted a pack of cigarettes from my cache in my suitcase. Cliff had to duck as we went out the 200-year-old door.

When we returned, it was still raining, and the room was cold and drear. Its one

1. **pensión** (pen sē ōn′): a small hotel.
2. **sucres** (so͞o′ krāz): units of money in Ecuador.
3. ***periódico*** (per ē ō′ dē kō): a newspaper.

Words to Know and Use	**corrugated** (kôr′ ə gāt′ id) *adj.* folded to form a wavy surface **antiquated** (an′ ti kwāt′ id) *adj.* old or obsolete **cache** (kash) *n.* a place where food or supplies are hidden

95

Teaching Strategies

Vocabulary Preview

These vocabulary words are defined at the bottom of the selection page on which they appear. You may wish to discuss them briefly before students begin reading.

antiquated old, obsolete
cache hiding place
corrugated folded
debris trash, litter
enunciation distinct pronunciation
haven a place of shelter
incongruous unsuitable
soprano the highest singing voice
stealthily secretively
urchin a small child

Support for Students of Limited English Proficiency

- Use **Reader's Guidesheet**, p. 38
- The foreign setting in Ecuador and the many Spanish terms may confuse some students. Encourage students from Spanish cultures to share their interpretations of the language and culture.
- "Honor" also contains some words and phrases that may be unfamiliar to many students.
- **Annotations B, H, J, P, S,** and **V** focus on support for LEP students.

Text Annotations

A. Literary Element: SETTING Ask students to identify the place and time of the story. *(The story is set in Quito, Ecuador, in the present.)*

B. LEP: Vocabulary The word *bureaucrat* may be unfamiliar to students. Explain that it refers to a government official whose job involves narrow, fixed routines and a large amount of paperwork.

C. Reading Skills: PREDICTING Ask students if they think that this young man is going to play an important role in the story and to explain why or why not. *(Possible responses: Yes, since the author describes him in some detail here; no, because the author may simply be describing the young man as representative of most Ecuadoreans.)*

D. Literary Element: POINT OF VIEW Have students explain how they know that a character in the story is the narrator. *(The use of* we, I, *and* us *indicates that the narrator is a character in the story.)*

Structured Reading for Less Proficient Students

These questions can help to guide students through the reading. Ask each question at the point of the selection where the SR number appears in the margin.

SR–1. On their second day at the hotel, what do the tourists discover? *(They discover that money has been stolen from them.)* **Literal recall**

SR–2. Summarize how the family members spend their weekend. *(They read and write in their room. At noon on Sunday, they walk to the festival where they see a man selling many baby coffins. They eat and remain in their room Sunday evening.)* **Summarizing**

SR–3. How does the hotel owner react after the woman tells him about the robbery? *(He is shocked and embarrassed and promises to find the thief. The owner, believing that his young servant is the thief, fills out papers to have the young man arrested and also beats him.)* **Literal recall**

Continued on page 96

E. Reading Skill: INFERRING Ask students what they think Julie is talking about here. *(Possible response: Julie can't find their money and thinks that her parents have spent it or put it in another place because they no longer want her to be in charge of the money.)* Ask students what could have happened. *(Possible response: They have been robbed.)*

F. Editorial Note Some original text that some may find offensive has been omitted, having to do with other articles not taken in the theft.

G. Critical Thinking: ANALYZING Ask students why they think the thief didn't take all of the cash. *(Possible responses: The person hoped that what was taken would not be noticed; the person is not a real criminal and just took what he needed.)*

H. LEP: Vocabulary Students may have trouble with this reference. Explain that a *den mother* is a woman who is in charge of a group of boys who belong to the Cub Scouts; although it is not an easy job, a den mother is usually thought of as being happy and cheerful, even when she is annoyed or angry. The narrator is trying to be cheerful when she really doesn't feel that way.

Cultural Connection Throughout the selection, the family members never relate how much money they have in terms of American dollars. Their original 985 sucres is equivalent to about $7.00. The 273 sucres they have left is equivalent to about $2.00, which means the theft amounted to about $5.00. Students should be aware of these amounts, as this knowledge will add impact to what later happens in the story.

lamp was forlorn. The rain pounded on the plastic outside our window. We slept.

Next morning Julie went to count out the day's allotment of money. She looked at us both with the accusing look that 15-year old girls get with their parents. "Okay, if you don't want me to handle the money, just say so. You don't have to be sneaky about it. That's just plain dumb." We cringed and pled innocence. Neither of us knew what she was talking about. E

"I can't deal with thievery on an empty stomach."

I dug into my suitcase for a pack of cigarettes and noted that the carton, which had been nearly full yesterday, now had only two packs. "Most of my cigarettes are gone." My voice sounded strangled when I said, "Well, at least the shutters are closed now." F

"So what do we do now?" This from Cliff.

"First we have breakfast. I can't deal with thievery on an empty stomach. Our breakfast is part of the room rent here, so we don't need any cash for that. Eat lots." SR-1

"Mom, it's Sunday. The banks are closed. We can't get any cash until Monday. We've got exactly 273 sucres to last until they open and we can begin the whole hassle with the manager on Monday. What do we do in the meantime?"

"We'll have a conference after breakfast. At least we know that whoever was in our room didn't know about the emeralds—and didn't even take ALL our cash. He left us 273 sucres. Maybe he thought we wouldn't even notice the difference. He didn't touch the tape player. Our clothes are all here, aren't they? We're not hurt. Now let's eat." G

Breakfast was silent. We eyed the 10-year-old serving boy. We could hear the señora in the kitchen shouting directions at him and slamming the pans. He and she seemed the same as yesterday. Were they? The solemn-eyed lad with the clean white shirt was nowhere in sight. From my seat at the table in the covered-over patio I glanced up at the shuttered windows of our room. How much could I see if they were open?

Once fed, back in our room, we conferred. "Obviously we can't move today. We can't even pay for our room," Julie pointed out.

"We need lunch, dinner today and bus fare to the bank tomorrow. How much will that cost about, Julie?"

"We can go to the market and buy stuff and eat here in our room. Make it like a rainy-day picnic." My voice reminded me of the grim cheerfulness of a den mother. Julie glared; Cliff grinned. H

"Let's wait until the rain stops anyway." Cliff hated getting wet.

The room seemed smaller and more depressing than it had been. I retreated to Montaigne.[4] Julie suffered with Melanie and Rhett and Scarlett.[5] Cliff wrote the letter he'd been planning to write to his brother ever since leaving the States. He did not mention our current problem. The quiet was piercing.

At noon we went outside. It had stopped raining. The sun came brilliant and strong, and the mountains loomed white and powerful against the blue sky. We walked the four blocks to the *feria*.[6] We bought a pineapple and some crackers, then wan-

4. **Montaigne:** Michel Eyquem de Montaigne (1533–1592), a French essay writer.

5. **Melanie and Rhett and Scarlett:** three characters from *Gone with the Wind*, Margaret Mitchell's Pulitzer Prize-winning novel.

6. ***feria*** (fer' ē ə): festival.

STRUCTURED READING FOR LESS PROFICIENT STUDENTS

Continued from page 95

SR–4. What does the woman discover about the servant and the reason for the theft? *(The servant took the money because he needed to buy a coffin for his child.)* **Clarifying**

SR–5. How do the attitudes of the woman, the hotel owner, and the servant differ with respect to the theft? *(Possible response: The woman feels sorry for the young man and considers the amount of money meaningless enough to warrant ignoring the crime; the hotel owner has no pity and wants to see the young man punished; the servant feels that it is his responsibility to bury his child, and so he is willing to bear the responsibility for his crime.)* **Analyzing**

dered up and down the dirty, littered streets. The only merchant who seemed to be doing a profitable business was the man who sold coffins. Mainly they were small coffins, rude little pine boxes with the nails I still visible and the edges rough and splintery. Men and women stood haggling with the merchant. In the woman's *reboza*[7] the current baby slept or cried, and the voices were muted. No one wept. The sound of the buses going to the villages filled the square with noise, and the blue smoke from their exhausts blocked out the snow-topped mountains.

We walked home without talking. There seemed nothing to say.

We divided the pineapple and crackers into lunch half and dinner half; we ate the lunch half at a table in the patio, where the sun coming through the green plastic made it seem like an aquarium. At dinnertime we opted for staying in our room, where we sat on the coppercolored bedspreads and extravagantly spread the last of our grainy Colombian peanut butter and drank our J carefully husbanded instant coffee. When the rain started, our ill-lit room seemed a SR-2▶ haven.

Next morning Julie counted our remain- K ing cash. "We've got enough for bus fare for two people—and 11 sucres left over. Dad and I will go to the bank, and you wait here until we get back, Mom."

"Why can't I go and you wait here?"

"You know my Spanish is better, and we'll have the usual hassle with the bank manager." I nodded; so did Cliff, and they left.

The owner knocked on the door and entered smiling. "How do you like it here, Señora?"

"We like the room, but we'll be leaving today."

"But why?"

"We've had some things stolen from us, so it seems better to leave."

"Stolen! Here? In my hotel? Impossible, Señora!"

"Unfortunately, it is not impossible. My husband and daughter have gone to the bank to get more money, and as soon as they return, we'll pay our bill and find another hotel."

"No! In my hotel guests are safe. They do not get stolen from. What was taken, if I may ask, Señora?"

"About 700 sucres and a few packs of cigarettes. It could not have been an accident, Señor, and we did not lose the money or make a mistake about where we put it. We've already considered these things." I was surprised at how good my Spanish was when it needed to be. The words came with no searching.

"Then, Señora, we will find the thief and return your possessions. Until we do, there will be no charge for your room." The aristocratic pride of his Spanish ancestry was suddenly present, and his faded maroon sweater could have been a doublet[8] of fine velvet. "We will talk further when the Señor returns." He turned and left the room. I wouldn't have been surprised if he had bowed from the waist. My smile was half amused, half admiring. L

The señora's shrill voice was the one I could hear most clearly. Her shrieking soprano seemed to clang against the stone walls. Most of the words were lost in the

7. ***reboza*** (rā bō′ sä): a wrap or shawl that can be used for carrying a baby.

8. **doublet** (dub′ lit): a man's closefitting jacket.

Words to Know and Use

haven (hā′ vən) *n.* a place of shelter or safety
soprano (sə pran′ ō) *n.* the highest singing voice

I. Reading Skill: INFERRING Ask students what the selling of so many small coffins indicates. *(Possible responses: Health conditions for babies and young children are poor. There is a high rate of infant mortality among the Indians of Ecuador.)*

J. LEP: Vocabulary Students may be able to use the context of the sentence to help them understand the word *husbanded.* If students have difficulty explaining its meaning, tell them that *husbanded* means "sparingly used" or "carefully measured out and conserved."

K. Reading Skill: CLARIFYING Ask students to explain the time frame of the story. First, have them identify when the tourists arrived at the hotel. *(on a Saturday)* Next, ask them to determine when the robbery occurred. *(probably on Saturday night when the family was out to dinner)* Finally, have them tell what day it is now. *(Monday morning)*

L. Literary Element: CHARACTERIZATION Point out that the hotel owner's words and manner, as well as the narrator's comments, reveal some things about his character. Have students explain what they have discovered about him. *(Possible response: He is of Spanish upper-class ancestry, and, although he may not be wealthy, he maintains a sense of personal dignity and of pride in his heritage.)*

Art Note

Diego Rivera (1886–1957) was a world-renowned Mexican artist and a champion of the laboring classes. He received many commissions to paint murals for public spaces in the United States. He delighted in any work that enabled him to bring meaningful art to all the people. *What qualities of character do you find in the face and attitude of this peasant holding his hat?*

M. Reading Skill: INFERRING Ask students who is accused of being the thief. *(the young Indian servant)* Have students explain whether the hotel owner seems more upset about the crime or the fact that he feels he personally has been disgraced. *(Possible responses: The hotel owner is most upset about what he perceives as his personal disgrace; the hotel owner is outraged that a thief is in his employ.)*

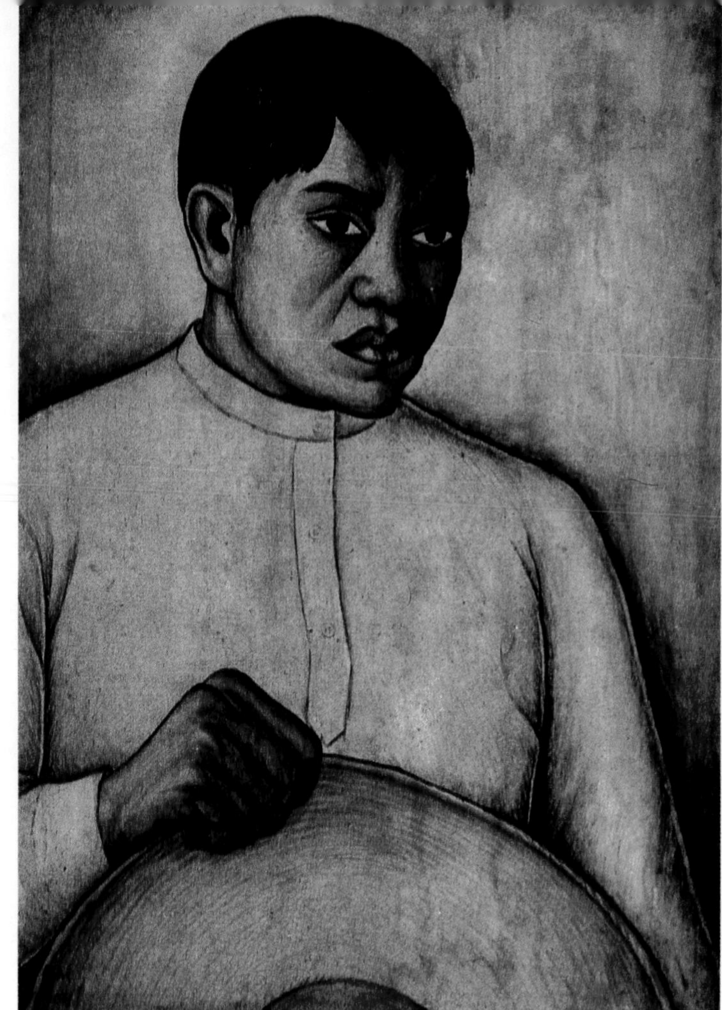

CAMPESINO CON SOMBRERO 1926
Diego Rivera Courtesy of Galería Arvil, Mexico City.

shrill echo, but the term "*ladrón*"[9] was unmistakable. It reminded me of the chipmunk records, and I wondered how anyone could take it seriously. I could not hear the voice of the young man with the clean white shirt. The owner spoke clearly, and his words came distinct across the empty patio. "*The man is a thief.* I want him arrested and I want the money returned. I have been disgraced in my own home, and justice must be done."

M

The policeman's voice sounded bored, and I could not hear his words from the kitchen. As he crossed the patio, he said, "I will be back this afternoon to arrest him if the sergeant says this complaint has been properly filled in. There are so many papers." The owner turned and strode to the kitchen off the patio.

The sound of a blow is like no other real

9. ***ladrón*** (lä drōn′): a thief.

REAL LIFE CONNECTIONS

Help students understand the tremendous power the European class had over the Indian class by pointing out the beating that the hotel owner gave to the Indian, who had no benefit of protection from the law. Discuss what students know about social inequities and civil and human rights violations in the world today.

sound. I had never heard anyone being beaten before. I wanted to turn off the sound, turn the channel, turn to a different station, close my ears. I ran the water in the little curtained-off bathroom and told myself it was not my fault. Most likely the kid did steal the money. What did I think would happen when I told the owner? How much
SR-3 ▶ in U.S. money was 700 sucres anyway?

When the noise stopped, I looked again out the shuttered window. The boy was walking slowly across the stone floor. The shirt was spattered with dirt and his face looked proud beneath the blood smears. I puzzled over the dignity he seemed to project. His bare feet made no sound, and he did not turn in the direction of our window.
N The owner's words came clear and carefully spaced. "I shall return from the police station with the order for your arrest, and you will go to prison. Go now to tell your wife."

The boy made a gesture which could have been a nod, or merely clearing his eyes of sweat and blood. He went silently out the door, and I noted idly that this was the first time I had ever seen an Indian servant using the front door. Shortly afterward I watched the owner stride out, wearing a tweed jacket over his maroon sweater and a brown felt hat.

Suddenly the room was unbearable. In
O impotent, irate rage I snatched up my coat, grabbed the key and marched out the door. The sun was intoxicating. I realized with a sense of delicious alarm that I had not one cent of money. There was a freedom in not having to worry about protecting my purse or feeling guilty when the beggars approached. I stalked up the steep incline, arms swinging and breathing deeply like a gym teacher showing off. When I got tired and out of breath, I slowed down and stopped to look where I was. I had left the European section of the city and was now in the Indian portion of the town. My blond *gringo*[10] head, reflected in the shop windows, was startling.

I turned the corner at the crest of the hill and discovered that I had walked to the site
P of the *feria*. It was quiet there now. Most of the vendors were back in their villages, building the chairs and tending the gardens for next Sunday's marketing. A few of the permanent shops were open, the owners standing, casually chatting and enjoying the sun, while the wives and assistants scurried about cleaning up the residue left from Sunday's market day. Mounds of <u>debris</u> were stacked in the street, and the small <u>urchins</u> pawed through in search of some discarded treasure. The blue buses were parked at the curb, and the loudspeaker announcing their destinations could be heard today when there was no crowd.

The coffin vendor's stall was open for business. Only one couple stood there. She was tall for an Ecuadorian. Her *reboza* was wrapped tightly around her shoulders despite the warm sun. I could not hear her voice over the din of the buses. He stood on the other side of the vendor. When the blue
Q bus was gone and the stillness returned, her voice was startlingly clear. "But the price of a baby's coffin has always been 650 sucres. Everyone in the village knows that. Now you want 750. We have only 700 sucres. That is all we have." She spoke Spanish with the careful <u>enunciation</u> of one who does not

10. ***gringo*** (griŋ′ gō): a Latin-American term for an American.

Words to Know and Use	**debris** (də brē′) *n.* trash, litter, or bits of rubbish **urchin** (ur′ chin) *n.* a small child **enunciation** (ē nun′ sē ā′ shən) *n.* the pronouncing of words distinctly

N. Critical Thinking: ANALYZING Point out that although the servant has just been beaten and the hotel owner has threatened his impending arrest, he is free to go to tell his wife about his circumstances. Ask students what this situation might reveal about the structure of the society. *(Possible response: There seem to be some societal rules of behavior that ensure the servant will not run away but rather will put his affairs in order and then be ready to accept his punishment. There also may not be any way to escape.)*

O. Literary Element: CHARACTERIZATION Ask students what the narrator's feelings reveal about her attitudes. *(Possible responses: She is upset about the beating but has limited sympathy for the Indian's situation; she is trying to cover up the guilt that she feels for the boy's being beaten after she reported the theft.)*

P. LEP: Setting Encourage students from foreign and urban cultures to share their knowledge of street markets. Ask volunteers to describe the scene here in their own words. *(Possible response: Sellers who set up temporary stalls on Sundays were home getting their wares ready. People were cleaning up from the last big market day, while children looked in the trash for things they could use.)*

Q. Reading Skill: PREDICTING Ask students what might be significant about this conversation. *(Possible response: The amount of money, 700 sucres, is the same amount that was stolen from the American tourists.)*

R. Critical Thinking: ANALYZING Ask students what the narrator's thoughts reveal about how her attitude has changed. *(Possible response: She seems finally to look at the servant as a human being and now feels sorry for him; her thoughts about the exchange value of 700 sucres suggests she is becoming aware of her former insensitivity and arrogance.)*

Art Note
Morris Rippel is a licensed architect as well as an artist and an amateur astronomer. His accurate pencil drawings of the surface of the moon once drew the attention of NASA, which offered him a position. He has lived all his life in New Mexico, where he finds all the inspiration for his work in tempera and watercolor. *What time of the day and what part of the world are evoked in this scene?*

use the language daily. Her voice was calm. She did not shout nor plead. She stated a logical fact without any emotion.

I don't know if I would have looked again if that number had not echoed so clearly. I really knew what I'd see even before I looked. His face was clean now, and the bruises were that much clearer. The shirt was still dirty. The somber dignity was still
SR-4 ▶ there.

Frantically, I hunted for a cab to take me back to the hotel. There was none. Then I realized I had no money for a cab if I did find one. I retraced my steps down the hills, reminding myself to watch carefully and not get lost this time. My alienness seemed more pronounced, and I noted in my haste that the sidewalks were broken and dangerous. As I strode, I rehearsed what I would say to the owner and the young man in the white shirt. What were the Spanish words for what I wanted? What were the local rules? What can the outsider offer to do without creating resentment? Would we have to appear at the police station to get charges dropped? How much exactly was 700 sucres in U.S. money? R

I reached the hotel and saw gratefully that the patio and hall were empty. Almost stealthily I climbed the stairs, opened our

SIDE STREET, SAN MIGUEL 1979 Morris Rippel Private collection.

Words to Know and Use	**stealthily** (stelth' ə lē) *adv.* in a secretive manner

door, entered and grabbed the Spanish-English dictionary. While I sat at the window watching the front door and patio, I checked to be sure I had the right words. I watched my hand tremble while I lit a cigarette and smiled aloofly as though it belonged to some other body. It was very quiet. I realized I was hungry and wished that Cliff and Julie would come home with money for lunch.

Finally the owner came in. He carried a brown over-sized envelope in one hand and his hat in the other. Beside him the policeman looked clumsy and miserable. Behind them walked the young man in his white shirt. His cheeks had the same pinkness I had noted yesterday, and they seemed incongruous blended with the discolored bruises. All three were silent.

Clutching the dictionary, I marched myself down the stairs and crossed the patio to where all three stood. I addressed the owner first. "Please, I didn't want to get him in trouble. Let's forget the 700 sucres. My husband has gone to the bank for more money, and we won't move at all. Just drop the charges against the young man." Even in my own ears I sounded prattling and foolish and I wished I could stop myself from chattering on so long. S

The owner looked at me. "You were lying then, Señora, when you told me this morning that you had been robbed in my hotel?"

"No. I didn't lie. The money was taken but it is not worth prison."

"Then there is no question. In my hotel the guests are not robbed. Forgive me, Señora, but this is not your concern." I envied the arrogance and dignity with which he crossed the patio and went into the kitchen. T

I turned next to the policeman. "Can I pay the young man's fine or give him money to return and thus erase the crime?" My American accent coupled with strange words puzzled him, and he asked me twice to repeat myself. I felt foolish saying the same thing over. When he understood, he said, "I don't know. I'll have to ask the sergeant." He turned to go out.

At that point the young man spoke. I was surprised at the timbre of his voice. I had expected it to be the near whisper which I had come to associate with Indian voices. He had a strong baritone and spoke in Spanish with an accent different from mine, but pronounced. "I do not need the American señora to bury my child. I am his father. I will bury him. If I pay for his funeral by spending six months in prison, that is my choice. I am the father. If the señora cannot understand this, it is not my concern. I am the father—I pay for my son's burial in my own way." U SR-5

He did deign to look at me, then turned and stalked to the door, and the policeman followed. They closed the door firmly. The rain began falling, making a gentle, mournful sound on the plastic roof. When Julie and Cliff came back, we took a cab out to the American sector of the city, where we had lunch at the Inter-American Hilton Hotel. Lunch cost 800 sucres. ❧ V W

Words to Know and Use

incongruous (in käŋ′ grōō əs) *adj.* not fitting; unsuitable

101

Data Bank

Ecuador has a long history of Spanish rule and divided classes. In 1534 the Spanish conquered the Inca Indians and set up large haciendas, or farming estates. The Spanish forced the Indians to work for them on these estates doing labor in the fields as well as other tasks of servitude. Although over the generations there were some intermarriages between Indians and Europeans, the haughty attitudes of the Spaniards toward the Indian classes never really changed. These attitudes were passed down through the generations and, as is shown in this story, are still apparent today.

Text Annotations

S. LEP: Language Encourage Spanish-speaking students to translate this dialogue into Spanish for the class.

T. Literary Element: CHARACTERIZATION Ask students to explain the hotel owner's attitude and what this reveals about him. *(Possible response: He has no sympathy for the Indian and sees no room for forgiveness. This indicates his harsh pride, his rigidity of character, and his contempt for the Indian.)*

U. Literary Element: CHARACTERIZATION Ask students what the Indian's attitude reveals about him. *(Possible response: He will not accept sympathy and does not want to have his actions excused; he wants to assume responsibility for his behavior. This indicates that he is a proud man with a strong sense of family duty and personal honor.)*

V. LEP: Support Encourage students who come from other countries to share what they know about attitudes of personal pride and honor. Ask them to give examples.

W. Literary Element: IRONY Ask students why they think the narrator chose to mention the price of the Americans' lunch at the Hilton. *(Possible response: to make a point about the differences in the meaning of money to different classes of people: 800 sucres is merely the cost of a pleasant lunch for Americans, while a lesser amount (750 sucres) is the price of a child's coffin for an Ecuadorean parent.)*

Check Test

1. What do the American tourists discover is missing from their hotel room? *(700 sucres and cigarettes)*

2. Who is the thief? *(a young Indian servant)*

3. Why does the thief steal the money? *(He needs to buy a coffin for his child.)*

4. What does the hotel owner do to the thief? *(He beats him and has him arrested.)*

5. What costs more—the coffin or the Americans' lunch at the Hilton Hotel? *(the lunch)*

Encouraging Independent Reading

"The Shoes," a short story by Grazia Deledda

"Thank You, M'am," a short story by Langston Hughes

"The Glass of Milk," a short story by Manuel Rojas

Student Responses

Responding to Reading

These questions are open-ended with no "right" or "wrong" answers. However, responses must be supported with information from the selection. Possible responses follow:

1. The choice of any character as most sympathetic should be considered valid.

2. Students may see the tourist's main problem as having the money stolen or having to grapple with whether the amount of money is worth sending a man to prison; the hotel owner's main problem as having to find the thief and make sure that he is punished or having to maintain his pride, dignity, and reputation; the young servant's main problem as needing money to bury his child or having to face prison for stealing the money he needs.

3. Students may say that the tourist's problem seems to indicate she is from a privileged background and has no knowledge of what it is like to be poor and needy. The hotel owner's problem reflects the pride and dignity of his upper-class Spanish ancestry and his contempt for the lower-class Indian. The servant's problem reflects the status of the Indian in the society, that of poverty, resignation, and servitude.

4. Some students may describe the young man as a good worker who takes pride in his appearance, his job, and his role as a parent; they may believe that even though he is driven to commit a crime in order to bury his child, he shows that he is an honorable man by his willingness to accept the consequences of his actions. Others may agree that the young man has a strong sense of honor, but may feel that he is weak and unresourceful since the only way he tries to get money is to steal it.

5. Some students may say that the hotel owner had to uphold the pride and dignity of his upper-class Spanish heritage and the reputation of his hotel. Others may feel that the owner had nothing but contempt for the Indian class and felt entitled to take advantage of an opportunity to punish one of them.

6. Some students may say that the young servant acted honorably by accepting responsibility for his crime and

Continued on page 103

e x p l a i n

Responding to Reading

First Impressions

1. With which character did you most sympathize? Why?

Second Thoughts

2. Look back at the chart you made showing the different problems of the American tourist, the hotel owner, and the young servant. What is each person's primary, or main, problem?

3. How does each main character's primary problem reflect his or her cultural background?

4. Describe the character of the young man.

   Think about
   - his actions and appearance before the robbery
   - why he stole and what he stole
   - his actions and response after he was caught

5. Why does the hotel owner insist that the young Indian be punished?

   Think about
   - the hotel owner's ancestry
   - how he makes his living
   - his feelings about the Indian

6. Think back to your earlier discussion about what an honorable act is. Which characters in this story act honorably?

7. The Americans do not seem to understand very much about the people of Ecuador at the beginning of the story. What do you think the Americans have learned about these people and about themselves?

Broader Connections

8. There are many situations in life when the line between honor and dishonor is unclear. What are some other instances in today's world when the line between honor and dishonor blurs?

Literary Concept: Irony

Irony occurs when a character or reader expects one thing to happen but something entirely different occurs. For example, in "The Fan Club," it is ironic that Laura gives a speech on discrimination and then turns around and joins the attack on Rachel. Why does the cost of lunch at the Hilton seem ironic to the Americans in "Honor"?

Literary Concept—Irony

The price of lunch at the Hilton was 800 sucres, while the price of a child's coffin was 750 sucres. The Americans would not expect their lunch to cost more than a child's coffin or expect that, for almost the same amount of money, they can enjoy lunch while another person faces a prison term.

Writing Options

1. The young man says to the narrator, "I am the father. If the señora cannot understand this, it is not my concern. I am the father—I pay for my son's burial in my own way." Write an explanation of what he suspects the "señora" cannot understand.

2. A police officer must write up a summary of a crime in a matter-of-fact style. Imagine an outcome for this case. Then write a crime report. Explain why the young man is a suspect, report the actions of the American lady and the hotel manager, and state how the case closed.

3. What if the narrator had not seen the young couple buying the coffin? Describe in a paragraph how she might have reacted when the police came to arrest the young man.

4. If you had been the young man, would you have risked going to jail in order to buy a coffin? Explain your answer in a short paragraph.

5. Think about the narrator, the hotel owner, and the young man. With which person would you choose to spend an evening? Explain your answer in writing.

Vocabulary Practice

Exercise Read the sentences below. On a separate sheet of paper, write the vocabulary word that best completes each sentence.

1. The rain flowed in little streams in the folds of the ____ roof.
2. The hotel was a(n) ____ building without an elevator.
3. The tourists had a small ____ of money safely hidden in a book.
4. The bruises on the young man's face seemed ____ with his pink cheeks.
5. The señora screamed in her high-pitched ____ voice.
6. The American spoke with careful ____ so that her Spanish would be understood.
7. Down a street in the Indian section ran a(n) ____, laughing and yelling.
8. She crept ____ back into her hotel room, hoping no one would see her.
9. The streets were littered with garbage and ____ after the Sunday market.
10. After the noise of the market, their room was a quiet ____.

Words to Know and Use

antiquated
cache
corrugated
debris
enunciation
haven
incongruous
soprano
stealthily
urchin

Continued from page 103

choosing to go to prison. Others may feel that the narrator acted honorably by offering to dismiss the crime after she found out the reason for it. Still others may feel that the hotel owner acted honorably by keeping his promise to find the thief and see that he is punished.

7. Some students may say that the Americans have learned how important pride and dignity are to the people of Ecuador, no matter what their economic status or cultural heritage. Others may feel that the Americans have realized how much they take money and their comfortable lifestyle for granted.

8. Possible situations that students may mention: Telling on someone who is taking drugs may be honorable in terms of trying to get help for the person but dishonorable in terms of not keeping the person's secret. Going to war can be honorable if it means defending one's country but dishonorable if it means aggression against another country.

Writing Options

The Writing Options are designed to meet varied student interests and abilities. Have each student choose one writing activity to complete. You may wish to guide some students to an option that requires less writing.

Journal Update Have students review their journal entries for "Honor." What new understandings of honor and of cultural differences can they add to their earlier writing?

Vocabulary Practice

1. corrugated
2. antiquated
3. cache
4. incongruous
5. soprano
6. enunciation
7. urchin
8. stealthily
9. debris
10. haven

Options for Learning

These activities suit a variety of learning styles and modes of expression. Allow students to review the options and then choose the one they wish to do. Many are excellent collaborative learning projects.

1. Be an Economist It might help to show students an example of a bar graph before they begin drawing theirs.

2. Artisan Display Suggest that students obtain brochures and posters from a local travel agency. Perhaps students of Latin American backgrounds could bring in some crafts for display.

3. Rediscover the Incas Students might refer to an atlas and a gazeteer to create a large illustrated map of Ecuador that could be incorporated into a presentation of their findings. Students may also want to create an illustrated time line of Incan history.

4. Sounds of the Andes Suggest to students that they might also refer to magazines and travel brochures to collect pictures of the instruments to show as they play their tapes.

Fact Finder

Ecuador is the Spanish word for *equator.* The equator crosses through the country and thus is the source of its name. Students can find this information in an atlas, an encyclopedia, or a book about Ecuador.

Additional Information About the Author

Betty Dahlin Betty Dahlin is a retired English teacher who now works as a part-time columnist and consultant. She lives in Seal Beach, California.

Closure

In "Honor," a young man commits a crime out of love and desperate need and *chooses* to pay the price to retain his honor.

Point out that students came to understand the characters in "Honor" by realizing how their cultural backgrounds influenced their behavior. Suggest that students consider how cultural background can influence the actions and choices of people they meet in their real lives.

e x t e n d

Options for Learning

1 • Be an Economist The standard of living in South America is much lower than in the United States. In an encyclopedia, atlas, or almanac, find out the average yearly income for an individual in the following countries: Ecuador, Peru, Colombia, Bolivia, Argentina, Venezuela, Brazil, and the United States. Then make a bar graph that illustrates these differences.

2 • Artisan Display Ecuador and other Latin American countries are famous for their native crafts, such as weaving, embroidery, pottery, and carving. Ask friends, teachers, or neighbors whether they have examples that you could display. Add travel posters and pictures from magazines to heighten your display's Latin American flavor. Be sure to label each item.

3 • Rediscover the Incas Most of the Indians in Ecuador live in the Andes Mountains. These people are descended from the ancient Inca Indians, who once controlled a vast empire in South America. Research the Indians of Ecuador to find out how, over the centuries, they fell from the Incas' position of immense wealth and power.

4 • Sounds of the Andes The folk music of the people of Ecuador and other South American countries is quite different from American music. Ecuadorean musicians often play various types of guitars and flutes. At a library or record store, find some examples of South American folk music. If possible, make a sample tape for the class to hear.

FACT FINDER

From what does Ecuador get its name?

Betty Dahlin

1925–

About writing, Betty Dahlin says, "I dream up the plot and characters, but I put them in real places." Many of those real places she knows from experience. For example, her book *Listen to the Roses* is set in Minnesota, where she grew up. After traveling in South America, Dahlin set her book *Lesson in Love* in Colombia. Her book *Roman Butterfly* reflects an extended vacation in Italy. Dahlin may love travel, but she hates airports. She once flew to Hawaii instead of New York City because she did not want to spend six hours waiting in Los Angeles for the weather to clear up on the East Coast. Dahlin has also worked as a teacher, waitress, model, secretary, and editor. She has three children and ten grandchildren.

Cross-Curricular Options

Students might work individually or in teams to complete any of the following activities.

Geography: Research the land of Ecuador and create a relief map to show the topographical variations.

Math: Find out more about the changing value of the sucre as compared to the American dollar over a period of time. Show the fluctuations on a comparison chart or track them on a double line graph.

English/Art: Create a word-and-image collage to show thoughts and feelings about the meaning of *honor.* Words, phrases, and images might be cut out from old magazines or handwritten or drawn in different-colored pens.

Health: Find out about the health-care situation of the Ecuadorean Indians. What are the problems? What is being done to improve conditions?

e x p l o r e

Autobiography

My Shirt Is for Church

DANIEL K. INOUYE (ĭn ō' ā)
with LAWRENCE ELLIOTT

Examine What You Know (Prior Knowledge)

Have you ever made a snap judgment of someone based on the clothes he or she was wearing? Discuss the following questions with your classmates.

1. How important is it to have and wear nice clothes?
2. What can clothes tell you about a person?
3. Is it fair to judge someone by his or her clothes?
4. How accurate are first impressions based on appearances?

Expand Your Knowledge (Building Background)

In the true story you are about to read, the main character is a Japanese American living in Hawaii. The first 149 Japanese in Hawaii were recruited from the slums of Japan's big cities in 1865 to work on the sugar plantations. Because these first recruits were not considered good farm laborers, no more Japanese were brought to Hawaii until 1885. By 1890, however, 7,600 Japanese were working on the plantations, and by the early 1940's, 25 percent of Hawaii's population was of Japanese descent. As the number of Japanese increased, so did prejudice against them. This excerpt is an account of the experiences of one Japanese-American teenager just before the outbreak of World War II.

Enrich Your Reading (Reading Skill)

Understanding Key Words In the selection you are about to read, the author uses two words that are especially important to the meaning of the story. *Nisei* (nē' sā') is the Japanese word for second-generation Japanese immigrants. *Haole* (hä' ō lā') is a Hawaiian term that refers to non-Polynesian Hawaiians. Understanding these words is crucial to understanding the story. As you read, be aware of the ring of authenticity that they add to a story told by a Japanese American growing up in Hawaii.

■ *A biography of the author can be found on page 113.*

Objectives

- To understand and analyze a short work of autobiography
- To recognize first-person point of view as an element of autobiography
- To recognize the use of key words and to understand how they affect the meaning of a story
- To express understanding of the work through a choice of writing options including a yearbook quotation, summarizing statements, a newspaper editorial, and a paragraph of comparison

Examine What You Know

Discussion Prompts: What does it mean to make a "snap judgment"? What possible problems might arise from making a snap judgment? On what other personal qualities besides clothing do people sometimes base their judgments of others?

Expand Your Knowledge

Discussion Prompts: Why do you think prejudice against the Japanese increased as their numbers increased? How might the situation for the Japanese differ today in Hawaii and in the rest of the United States?

Enrich Your Reading

Tell students to look for words printed in a type style different from the rest of the text. Words that are set off in some way are usually important. Remind students to look for explanations of key words in context clues in the surrounding text.

Thematic Link—Paying the Price

In "My Shirt Is for Church," Daniel Inouye recounts the price he paid for his unwillingness to behave as though he were white rather than Japanese—and how that price later proved to be a benefit.

Journal Writing

Daniel Inouye recalls the influence certain adults had on his life. Suggest these journal topics to students:

- Who in your life has most helped to shape your thoughts and attitudes? Write about that person and tell how she or he has influenced you.
- What things do you value most in life? Consider your family, education, friends, interests, and so on.

For other journal opportunities, refer students to Examine What You Know (p. 105) and Cultural Connections (p. T–109)

Additional Resources

UNIT ONE RESOURCE BOOK
Reader's Guidesheet, p. 43
Vocabulary Worksheet, p. 44
Selection and Vocabulary Check Tests, p. 45
Selection Test, pp. 46–47

Collaborative Learning

Opportunities for collaborative learning appear throughout the lesson and include Annotation D, Options for Learning activities 1 and 3 (p. 113), and Cross-Curricular Options (p. T–113).

Teaching Strategies

Vocabulary Preview

These vocabulary words are defined at the bottom of the selection page on which they appear. You may wish to discuss them briefly before students begin reading.

affluent wealthy or rich
bigotry prejudice
distraught extremely upset
encumbrance a burden
fawning flattering
inexorable impossible to change
ingenious clever, inventive
invariable constant
orthopedics the branch of medicine dealing with bones
pretense a false show

Support for Students of Limited English Proficiency

- Use **Reader's Guidesheet**, p. 43
- This selection provides a springboard for discussion of prejudice within students' own ethnic or cultural groups. Students may also identify with the author's feelings of being a second-class citizen in his own land. Allow students to share their experiences.
- Annotations D, J, and O provide support for LEP students.

Text Annotations

A. Literary Element: AUTOBIOGRAPHY/POINT OF VIEW Have students tell who is narrating the story and how they know. Have them identify the narrator's point of view. *(Possible responses: Daniel Inouye is telling his own story. The author credit and the use of the pronouns* I *and* my *in the title and opening sentence suggest that Inouye is the narrator, using the first person point of view.)*

B. Literary Element: SETTING Have students identify ways in which Inouye conveys a sense of the time and place. *(Possible responses: He identifies the time—his sophomore year in Mt. McKinley High; he describes the makeup of the class; and he contrasts his attitudes and style with those of his classmates.)*

C. Reading Skill: CLARIFYING Have students explain why McKinley High School was referred to as "Tokyo High." *(because, as Inouye explains, "nearly all of us there were of Japanese ancestry, and from the least affluent* nisei *families at that." Tokyo is Japan's largest city.*

My Shirt Is for Church

DANIEL K. INOUYE *with* LAWRENCE ELLIOTT

A It was in my sophomore year in high school that I first came under the warm and rewarding spell of Mrs. Ruth King, a teacher whose influence in my young life ranked just behind that of my mother and father. She certainly didn't look inspiring, a short, plump lady in her middle forties, with graying hair and eyes that seemed to look vaguely out from behind a pair of rimless glasses and to see practically nothing. But the truth was that she saw practically everything; surely nothing of any real importance that happened in her classroom escaped her notice. SR-1 ▶

B Hers was the top tenth-grade class at McKinley High. I don't know how I got into it, and from the very first day, I wanted out. In place of all my old live-and-let-live buddies from Moiliili and McCully,[1] I found myself rubbing shoulders with a breed of kids who kept trying to pretend that their skin was white and their eyes were blue. And there in the midst of this pretense, surrounded by all those starched white shirts and shined shoes, was rough-and-tumble Dan Inouye, to whom a necktie was a garrote[2] on the spirit and shoes an encumbrance to be suffered through at funerals and in church. ◀ SR-2

C In those days, McKinley High School was jokingly referred to as Tokyo High. Thanks to an ingenious system of segregation, nearly all of us there were of Japanese ancestry, and from the least affluent *nisei*[3] families at that. It worked through a device known as the English Standard School and neatly sidestepped the law that, theoretically, opened all the public schools to everyone, regardless of race, color, or creed. To be admitted to an English Standard School—which by invariable coincidence had better facilities and better faculties—one had to pass an examination. The written part was fair enough, since everyone had an equal chance. But the oral test D served as an automatic weeding-out factor, for rare indeed was the student of Asian

1. **Moiliili and McCully:** *nisei* neighborhoods in Hawaii.
2. **garrote** (gə rōt′): a Spanish instrument for strangling, often used for capital punishment.
3. ***nisei*** (nē′ sā′): North American–born children of Japanese-born families (literally "second generation").

Words to Know and Use

pretense (prē tens′) *n.* a false claim or show
encumbrance (en kum′ brəns) *n.* a burden or hindrance
ingenious (in jēn′ yəs) *adj.* clever or inventive
affluent (af′ lo͞o ənt) *adj.* wealthy or rich
invariable (in ver′ ē ə bəl) *adj.* constant or unchanging

106

Structured Reading for Less Proficient Students

These questions can help to guide students through the reading. Ask each question at the point of the selection where the SR number appears in the margin.

SR–1. Who is the subject of the autobiography? *(Daniel K. Inouye)* What time in his life is the author discussing? *(his sophomore year in high school)* **Literal recall**

SR–2. Contrast Inouye with his classmates. *(His classmates, trying to pretend they are white, wear starched white shirts and shined shoes, while Dan dresses casually and wears no shoes.)* **Comparing and contrasting**

Continued on page 108

parentage who could properly pronounce the *th* sound, the *r*, and the *l*. The obvious result was that the English Standard Schools became almost the exclusive province of Caucasian youngsters, and that handful of Japanese and Chinese whose parents could afford to give them private tutoring. Not until 1955 was the last of this subtle segregation eliminated from Hawaii's public school system.

I was too young and unknowing then to be troubled by the concept of "Tokyo High." Only my stiff-necked classmates bothered me, and sometimes it seemed that the only person who ever talked to me in that grade was Mrs. King. "Your grammar leaves something to be desired, Dan," she would say to me privately. "Why don't you stay after school today and we'll work on it?" And I would, happily, because to be in her presence was suddenly to glimpse something beyond the narrow horizons of the life I'd known, to sense that being a clerk, or even a beach boy, was not the ultimate and only hope for a kid like me. She took me seriously, which is something that no one, not even I myself, had ever done.

All at once, literature was exciting and history was real. Washington and Jefferson and Lincoln suddenly stepped out of some mythical haze and became men of flesh and blood, men with great problems and the great courage to face them. I felt the bitter cold and despair of that winter at Valley Forge.[4] I felt a sharp sense of personal loss at the death of Lincoln, the lost opportunity to bind up the nation's wounds. Whereas Japanese history had always sounded like some great, impersonal pageant, the story of America had the ring of an adventure in human progress, troubles, and setbacks and the inexorable march down to the present.

But most important of all, I came to believe that the giants who made American history were *my* forefathers. Always before, I had been a little embarrassed singing about the "land where my fathers died," and I always spoke of *the* fathers of *the* country. It was Mrs. King who, in some wonderfully subtle way, convinced me of the essential relationship between America's founding fathers and all of America's people.

In midyear, Mrs. King recommended me for membership in McKinley's two junior honor societies, the Torch Society and the McKinley Citizenship Club. My mother and father glowed with pride, and although I tried to pretend that it didn't matter to me one way or the other, the truth is that I was really excited by the prospect. On the appointed afternoon, beaming with good fellowship, I strode up before the Student Council for my interview. They sat behind a long table, four seniors trying to look as stern as bankers. They didn't ask me to sit down.

"Why do you think you belong in an honor society?" one of them asked.

I shrugged. "It was Mrs. King's idea. I . . ."

"Why don't you wear shoes?" another suddenly shot at me, a Japanese kid I'd known for at least five years.

"Because I only have one pair," I said to

4. **Valley Forge:** an area near Philadelphia where George Washington and his Revolutionary army spent the winter of 1777–1778.

Words to Know and Use

inexorable (in eks′ ə rə bəl) *adj.* impossible to influence, change, or persuade

107

D. LEP: Language Have students explain the system in Hawaii's schools that discriminated against Asians. *(Possible response: To get into the better schools, students had to pass an oral test, which Asians were unable to do because of differences in pronunciation between English and Asian languages.)* You may want to have students who are learning a second language discuss particular sounds they find difficult to pronounce.

E. Reading Skill: RECOGNIZING RELEVANT DETAILS Ask students to identify details that explain Inouye's strong feelings of warmth and respect for his teacher, Mrs. Ruth King. *(Possible responses: She gave him hope; took him seriously; made literature exciting and history come alive; and made him feel he was an American.)*

F. Literary Element: FIGURATIVE LANGUAGE/SIMILE Have students describe in their own words the picture formed in their minds by the simile *as stern as bankers*. *(Possible response: Council members sitting up straight, looking serious, showing no emotion, hands folded in front of them.)* Ask volunteers to pantomime their descriptions.

G. Reading Skill: INFERRING Ask students what it appears the Student Council is really concerned about, as indicated by their asking this type of question. *(Possible response: They are concerned about Inouye's appearance and about his lack of interest in trying to look white, as they do.)*

DATA BANK

Hawaii became a U.S. territory in 1900, and all foreign-born people there became American citizens. However, these people had no voting rights or political power. (Hawaii was ruled by a white governor appointed by the President of the United States.) Inouye was a high-school student in the late 1930's, a time when many Japanese continued to live in poverty. They had little say in running their lives, but they still wanted to feel and appear "American."

H. Literary Element: DIALOGUE Ask students why they think Inouye added dialogue to tell about this experience. *(Possible responses: to make the situation come alive; to help readers have a clearer picture of what he faced; to make his story more dramatic)*

I. Literary Element: THEME Ask students to explain in their own words what Inouye values. *(Possible responses: scholarship; honor; his friends; internal values rather than external appearances.)*

J. LEP Support: VOCABULARY Students may not be familiar with *lame* used in this context. Explain that it means "useless and ineffective." Have a volunteer give an example of a *lame explanation.*

K. Literary Element: IRONY Have students explain the ironic twist that results from Inouye's humiliation. *(Possible response: An unexpected result of Inouye's rejection by the four snobbish seniors is that it challenges him to prove himself and succeed.)*

him. "They have to last." It was a silly question; he knew I only had one pair. He probably even knew that they'd been bought two years ago, and bought two sizes too large so I wouldn't grow out of them, and that until only recently I'd had to stuff the toes with paper to keep the darned things on.

But the silly questions were only beginning. "Why don't you wear a white shirt?" they asked. "Why don't you wear a tie?"

I didn't know what to say. I looked from one to the other, a gathering fear inside me, like dirty fingers squeezing my stomach. What was this all about? I thought they were going to interview me about my interests and ideas, about my schoolwork maybe. Why did they care what I wore?

"Are you going to answer the question?"

"I don't know," I said. "My shirt is for church . . ."

"Don't you care how you look in school?"

Not wanting to, I looked down at my sports shirt and my denim pants and bare feet. "My clothes are clean," I mumbled. "I don't know what's wrong."

"What about your friends?" one of them barked, and rattled off a list of kids from my neighborhood. "Are *they* your friends?"

"Yes," I said, and all at once I knew that they were going to turn me down. "What's the matter with them?"

"Delinquents!"

"Because they don't wear shoes?" I said, and it was not a question. "Because they're poor? They're no more delinquents than I am. Or you are." All the disappointment, all the fear had suddenly boiled up in anger, and when they tried to interrupt me, I shouted them down: "Hey, listen, I thought this was an honor society—honor, scholarship. But if all you're looking for is guys who wear white shirts and shoes, you don't want me and I for sure don't want you. I wouldn't trade one of my friends for . . . for both your honor societies and all four of you, so just forget the whole thing!"

For a long, long time afterward, I would stiffen with an inner fury every time I remembered those moments of humiliation, and I remembered them often. Nor was that the end of it. Somehow I had to explain to my parents that I had not been accepted into the honor societies without telling them the real reasons, for they would then have blamed themselves. So I stammered and stuttered through some lame explanation that fooled them not a bit, and their eyes grew sad and there was no more for any of us to say. As for Mrs. King, who seemed to know everything there was to know about my unhappy encounter with the Council without my saying a word, she was so deeply hurt by their behavior that not once in my next year at McKinley High did she recommend another candidate for the Torch Society or the McKinley Citizenship Club.

But the most important effect of the entire episode was to convince me of the essential truth of that old saw[5] about its being an ill wind that blows no good. It left me enraged and a little confused, but most of all it left me with a fiery resolve to "show those guys!" Never before had I felt so challenged, nor so determined to make something of myself. As a matter of fact, I don't think it's unfair to say that those four snobbish seniors are at least partly responsible for whatever successes I subsequently enjoyed. Their faces stuck in my mind, and do to this day, and for years afterward, I charged at every obstacle in my path as though those four had personally put it there and it was absolutely essential for me

5. **saw:** an old saying.

Structured Reading for Less Proficient Students

Continued from page 106

SR–3. Why was Inouye rejected from membership in the honor society? *(The Student Council didn't like his refusal to dress and behave as though he were white.)* How did this affect Inouye? *(He was angry at the humiliation he suffered, but it left him with a determination to make something of himself.)* **Literal recall**

SR–4. Who else besides Inouye's parents and teacher had a positive influence on Inouye, and how? *(Possible responses: Dr. Sato and Dr. Craig, both of whom showed so much strength, comfort, and generosity that they inspired Inouye's desire to become a doctor.)* **Cause and effect**

L. Reading Skill: SUMMARIZING Ask students to summarize Inouye's rejection in their own words. *(Possible response: The students of the honor societies have rejected him for his blatant refusal to try to act white.)*

to overcome it to prove that shoes and neck-
SR-3 ▶ ties were no measure of a man.

I should explain that there was no racial prejudice connected with my rejection, unless it was a kind of reverse bigotry. It was not my Japanese ancestry that the panel attacked, but my refusal to make any attempt to hide it in slavish imitation of *haole*[6] dress and manner. And in this regard the Japanese members were my severest critics.
L They were very much in tune with a sizable segment of the Japanese community in Hawaii, which in their fawning anxiety to please their white neighbors, behaved as though they were white, too. They bought automobiles beyond their means, were sensitive to any change in *haole* fashions and mimicked them, and bitterly resented those of us who refused to conform to their twisted notions of what made an American. We were letting down all Japanese Americans, they cried, and never missed an opportunity to crack down on us, more severely than our *haole* neighbors ever did.

Daniel Inouye (2nd row, right) and family members. Daniel's high school ID card. Courtesy of Daniel Inouye, Hawaii.

My newfound ambition was soon channeled in a single direction, and a most unlikely one at that for the son of a poor *nisei* family: I had decided to become a doctor! I suppose the seeds of that dream had been sown years before when my grandmother was stricken with cancer. I remember the sad reliance of all the family on good Dr. Sato, not to save Grandmother's life, for we were all too painfully aware that the dread disease would take its inexorable course, but to ease her suffering and help her over that incredibly hard journey to final release. He came nearly every day over those long weeks and always found time for a word of comfort to the rest of us after he had seen to Grandmother's needs.

What nobler goal could a young man aspire to, I day-dreamed, than to minister to the sick and to provide strength when people most desperately needed it? Soon I was haunting the Library of Hawaii, reading everything about medicine and the men who practiced it that I could find. Without getting their hopes up, my parents encouraged me—to have a doctor in the family was the absolute peak of achievement to which a Japanese household could aspire—and my single Christmas gift for each of the next two years was a chemistry set.

My ambition was reinforced by a personal

6. ***haole*** (hä′ ō lā′): a non-Polynesian Hawaiian, usually a white person.

Words to Know and Use

bigotry (big′ ə trē) *n.* narrow-minded behavior or opinions; prejudice
fawning (fôn′ iŋ) *adj.* affectionate; flattering

CULTURAL CONNECTION

Students who have come to the United States from other countries may have experienced some conflicts in adapting to American ways of life. Since this may be a sensitive issue, you might focus a discussion on positive elements of students' assimilation into American culture, that is, success stories of students learning to adapt to the American way of life.

M. Critical Thinking: ANALYZING Have students discuss what Inouye means by an "odd sense of family shame." *(Possible responses: His parents have a strong code of family pride and feel their son's handicap is a physical deformity that reflects on them; his parents feel that others will blame them for not properly taking care of the arm when the accident first occurred.)*

N. Historical Sidelight The repair of Inouye's left arm is even more critical in light of his later years. In World War II, he joined the U.S. Army and fought with the famous 442nd combat team (an all-*nisei* unit). He lost his right arm during battle.

O. LEP: Cultural Differences Discuss the high costs of health care in our society today. Then point out that in the continental United States—in the days of pioneers and the settlement of the West—professional people, such as doctors and teachers, were often paid through a bartering system, an exchange of goods and services. Ask students who have newly arrived in the United States if such forms of payment were used in the places from which they came. Allow them an opportunity to describe health-care experiences in their former homes.

Check Test

1. Whose personal story is being told? *(Daniel K. Inouye's)*

2. Where did the narrator live and go to school? *(in Hawaii; McKinley High School)*

3. Why was the narrator rejected by the school honor society? *(He refused to behave as though he were white.)*

4. Who were great influences on Inouye's life? *(his parents; his teacher, Mrs. Ruth King; Dr. Sato; Dr. Craig)*

Encouraging Independent Reading

Yokahama, California, short stories by Toshio Mori

A Special Kind of Courage, nonfiction by Geraldo Rivera

"Of Dry Goods and Black Bow Ties," an autobiographical essay by Yoshiko Uchida

disaster. Some years before, playfully wrestling with my good friend Shigeto Kanemoto, I fell hard on my left arm and suffered a compound fracture. Mother rushed me to the only doctor she could think of, a fine eye, ear, nose, and throat man then treating my brother for an ear infection. He set the arm as best he could, but unhappily he had had little practice in orthopedics and his best was not good enough. The break was a tricky one, and when it finally mended, my arm hung limp and crooked, and I could barely move it.

M My mother and father were distraught. Of course they were not unmindful of my personal loss—bad enough—but there was also an odd sense of family shame involved: how would it look to the world for the Inouye's eldest son to turn out to be a cripple! It was too bitter a prospect to even contemplate, and they were absolutely determined that if there was any single thing on God's earth that they could do to prevent that happening, they would do it.

So began a bleak two-year period during which my mother took me from one doctor to another, seeking to have my misset fracture properly mended. Everywhere she asked who was the best orthopedic surgeon in Hawaii, and everywhere they told her someone different. Finally, one sunny morning Mother ordered me into my shoes and sole white shirt and took me to the Children's Hospital and asked for a doctor named Craig. He took only one look at my arm and said I would need an operation if I was to have any chance at all to regain its full use. Mother asked no questions, not how much the operation would cost, nor whether it was dangerous. She spoke only one sentence: "When can you do it?"

I remember little about my hospital stay or the actual surgery. Only Dr. Craig sticks in my mind, a white-headed, seamy-faced, ever-smiling man who always had a small joke for me—"You a baseball player? You better start learning to throw lefty, because when we get finished, your left arm will be stronger than your right." And it almost was. Soon after the operation I could bend it, and not long after that it was as tough as it had ever been. N

When I went back for my final checkup, Dr. Craig had still not said a word about his fee, but Mother was now ready to get down to cases. "We will not be able to pay you at once," she said, "but we will bring you a small amount each month until the whole amount is paid. I hope you will allow this and not worry, for we are grateful to you, and even if it takes a lifetime . . ."

"You owe me nothing," Dr. Craig said.

"Nothing?" Mother whispered.

"You will have to pay the hospital's costs—I believe that comes to $30—but the operation is my gift to Dan." He grinned at me. "You going to be a left-handed pitcher?"

"No," I said, unsmiling and never more serious in my life. "I'm going to be a doctor—like you." ◀SR-4

For a long time afterward, I made regular trips to his office, carrying produce from our little garden, eggs, now and then a freshly killed chicken, and not wanting to bother him, just left my basket in his waiting room. And often I saw on his table little baskets just like mine, and soon I understood that the Inouyes were not the only recipients of Dr. Craig's generosity. O

Words to Know and Use

orthopedics (ôr′ thō pē′ diks) *n.* the branch of medicine dealing with the bones and joints

distraught (di strôt′) *adj.* extremely upset or driven mad

DATA BANK

The English Standard Test played a large part in keeping Asians poor and powerless in Hawaii. Despite the segregation in schools and the prejudice that existed toward Asians in general, many Japanese still longed to feel and look "American." The bombing of Pearl Harbor created even more ill feelings. Ironically, even when the immigrants of Japan living in the continental United States (known as *issei*) and their *nisei* children were placed in relocation centers, the Japanese-Americans living in Hawaii remained at liberty.

e x p l a i n

Responding to Reading

First Impressions

1. What did you think when you realized the Student Council panel was judging Inouye by his appearance?

Second Thoughts

2. How did Inouye's teacher, Mrs. King, influence Inouye's life?

   Think about
   - his feelings about himself as a student
   - his feelings about being an American
   - her reaction to Inouye's interview with the Student Council

3. Compare and contrast Inouye's values with those of the Student Council members who interviewed him.

   Think about
   - what clothes represented to the Student Council members
   - how Inouye and how the members felt about their Japanese ancestry
   - Inouye's interests and achievements
   - Inouye's statement "My shirt is for church"

4. Inouye says, "I don't think it's unfair to say that those four snobbish seniors are at least partly responsible for whatever successes I subsequently enjoyed." Why does he say this?

5. How are Dr. Sato and Dr. Craig alike, and how are they different? Why did each have such a big influence on Inouye?

6. Consider the influence of Inouye's parents and decide which was more important in forming Inouye's character—his experiences with people outside his family or the values he received from his parents. Explain.

Broader Connections

7. Think about the important positions to which students are elected in your school, such as student body president or Student Council officers. How vital is appearance in attaining these positions?

Literary Concept: Autobiography

An **autobiography,** the account of a person's life written by that person, is usually narrated from the first-person point of view. The author must decide which facts and events are important enough to include. Why did Daniel Inouye group the particular episodes in the selection as part of a chapter in his life?

Literary Concept—Autobiography

Possible responses: Students may say that Inouye chose these particular episodes to show influences that were especially important in shaping his career choices and his success in life. Inouye grouped these episodes because they showed the people who were most influential in his life—his parents; his teacher, Mrs. Ruth King; the four seniors who rejected him; and the two doctors, Sato and Craig.

Student Response

Responding to Reading

These questions are open-ended with no "right" or "wrong" answers. However, students should support their responses with information from the selection. Possible answers follow:

1. All responses supported by the selection should be considered valid.

2. Possible responses: She helped him believe in himself by working with him on his English and other studies. She helped him feel that he was an American by making the history of America come alive. She showed that she respected his values by not nominating anyone else to the honor society after he was rejected.

3. Some students may note that the Student Council panel members felt the only way to be an American was to dress and behave as though they were white. To them, image was all-important. Other students may say that, in contrast, Inouye placed value on the internal qualities of a person, on the importance of friendship, honor, and pride in his ancestry.

4. Students may say that the seniors' attitudes so enraged Inouye that he became determined to be successful and show them how wrong they were; that the seniors' rejection of their ancestry only prompted Inouye to value his ancestry.

5. Possible responses: Both Dr. Sato and Dr. Craig are sources of strength and comfort to their patients and the families. Both doctors are also attentive and generous with their time. Their help in healing and easing suffering serve as inspiration to Inouye. In contrast, Dr. Craig is a specialist while Dr. Sato appears to be a family doctor.

6. Some students may feel that Inouye's parents were more influential because they raised him and gave him the basic strength and courage to cope with life. Other students may feel that the people outside Inouye's family were more important because those experiences gave him a broader understanding of the world.

7. Some students may believe that those who are sharp dressers and have a self-confident image are most likely to be elected class leaders. Other students may believe that qualities of character, personality, and leadership outweigh appearance.

Writing Options

The Writing Options are designed to meet varied student interests and abilities. Have each student choose one writing activity to complete. You may wish to guide some students to an option that requires less writing.

Journal Update Encourage students to review their journal entries for "My Shirt Is for Church." What new understandings do they have about their values and their judgments of others, or about important people in their lives? Ask students to add new insights to their earlier writing.

Vocabulary Practice

1. a	**5.** d	**8.** d
2. d	**6.** c	**9.** c
3. c	**7.** c	**10.** d
4. d		

Writing Options

1. Yearbooks often have memorable quotes under seniors' pictures. Using what you know about Inouye, write a suitable yearbook quotation for him. What would someone from the Student Council panel have written?

2. State three decisions that Inouye makes on the basis of the lessons he learns. These decisions may involve a new way of seeing himself, a new way of seeing others, or a new direction or purpose for his life.

3. Pretend that you are an angry Daniel Inouye and that you have just been turned down for membership in the honor society. Write an editorial for the school newspaper expressing your views.

4. How do the two doctors in this selection compare with doctors you have encountered? Jot down the character traits of Dr. Sato and Dr. Craig and then write a paragraph comparing these doctors with doctors you have known.

Vocabulary Practice

Exercise Read each set of words below. On a separate sheet of paper, write the letter of the word that is not related in meaning to the other words in the set.

1. (a) molecule (b) deformity (c) surgery (d) orthopedics
2. (a) unmoving (b) inexorable (c) unchanging (d) untried
3. (a) upset (b) confused (c) amused (d) distraught
4. (a) ingenious (b) original (c) clever (d) rare
5. (a) hoax (b) pretense (c) fraud (d) translation
6. (a) intolerance (b) prejudice (c) denial (d) bigotry
7. (a) constant (b) changeless (c) fluid (d) invariable
8. (a) rich (b) affluent (c) prosperous (d) virtuous
9. (a) fawning (b) flattering (c) forthright (d) pleasing
10. (a) burden (b) obstruction (c) encumbrance (d) confrontation

Words to Know and Use

affluent
bigotry
distraught
encumbrance
fawning
inexorable
ingenious
invariable
orthopedics
pretense

e x t e n d

Options for Learning

1 • Honor Society Interview In small groups, role-play Daniel Inouye's interview with the members of the Student Council. Create additional dialogue that you think might have occurred among these people. Look back at the selection for ideas of what each character might say. Also think about your earlier discussion about the importance of appearance. Ad-lib Inouye's interview in front of the class.

2 • Hawaii's History Hawaii was the fiftieth and last state admitted to the United States of America. Use a reference book or encyclopedia to discover why each of the following dates is important in Hawaiian history: 1778, 1795, 1835, 1898, 1941, 1959, 1982. Make a time line and add a sentence next to each date explaining why it is important.

3 • Careers in Medicine As a young man, Daniel Inouye dreamed of becoming a doctor. Make a chart listing at least six other types of jobs in health care. For each job, list the prerequisites for study, the number of years of training required, and the starting salary. Share your chart with your classmates.

FACT FINDER

Of how many islands does the state of Hawaii consist?

Daniel K. Inouye

1924–

If the Student Council members at McKinley High School could have gazed into the future, they might have changed their minds about admitting Daniel Inouye to membership in the honor society. After Inouye graduated from McKinley, he enrolled in a premedical program at the University of Hawaii but later dropped out to fight in World War II. His combat team, made up of Japanese Americans, was the most decorated unit in United States history. Though severely wounded in an attack against a German stronghold, Inouye kept firing hand grenades into the German machine gun nests and saved his unit. As a result of his injuries, Inouye's right arm had to be amputated. For his heroism and valor, Inouye earned the Distinguished Service Cross, the Bronze Star, and the Purple Heart.

Inouye returned to the University of Hawaii to study government and politics. "I had originally intended to study medicine, but the loss of my right arm caused me to go into the field of law; I had always been interested in politics." When Hawaii became a state in 1959, he was elected to the House of Representatives. He has been a United States Senator from Hawaii since 1962. Undaunted by the absence of a right arm, Inouye plays pool and the piano.

Options for Learning

These activities suit a variety of learning styles and modes of expressions. Allow students to review the options and then choose the one each wishes to do. Many are excellent collaborative learning projects.

1. Honor Society Interview Suggest that students tape record the interviews so they can evaluate their own effectiveness.

2. Hawaii's History Answers: 1778: discovered by British explorer James Cook; 1795: proclaimed a kingdom by Chief Kamehameha; 1835: established first sugar plantation; 1898: annexed by United States; 1941: Pearl Harbor attacked; 1959: became 50th U.S. state.

3. Careers in Medicine The school's career guidance counselor or health and hygiene teachers may have useful information on jobs in the health-care fields. Students might also contact a local community or technical college for information.

Fact Finder

Hawaii consists of 132 islands that are divided into three groups. One of the groups consists of eight main islands, and people live on seven of them. This information can be found in an encyclopedia, an almanac, or a book about Hawaii.

Additional Information About the Author

Inouye became well known to the American public during the Watergate hearings in the early 1970's. As a member of the investigating committee, Senator Inouye was seen daily on television, and his calm, dignified, yet unrelenting manner was appreciated by the public.

Closure

Like the young servant in "Honor," Inouye chooses to pay a price to retain a sense of self-respect and pride. Because of his refusal to pretend to be white Inouye is not accepted by other *nisei*. He pays the price of humiliation at the hands of the Student Council; however, the price ultimately benefits him because it makes him determined to be a success. Encourage students to consider and discuss how important it is to them to be accepted by others.

Cross-Curricular Options

Students might work individually or in teams to complete any of the following activities.

Social Studies: Research and report on Inouye's record as a senator. Look for information about committees that he has worked on and his voting record in the Senate. Also research the Watergate hearings to learn about the role he played in those proceedings.

Economics: Research and report on the economic situation of the Japanese living in Hawaii today.

Geography: Create an illustrated map of the Hawaiian Islands. Show locations of volcanoes and other various topographical features. Use picture symbols to represent those features.

Publishing: Compile the contributions of all teams. Display or make copies to distribute.

Writer's Workshop

Objectives

- To use a personal or literary experience as a springboard for writing a reflective essay
- To use small groups as a prewriting activity to share and evaluate important experiences
- To identify generalizations that can be drawn from specific experiences
- To map reflections about an experience
- To draft, revise, edit, and share a reflective essay
- To reflect on the writing process

Integrating . . .

Literature and Writing Point out that each of the main characters in this subunit experienced an important event—a turning point—for which he or she had to "pay the price." Yet each event taught the character a lesson about life. Ask students about personal experiences for which they have had to "pay a price." Discuss how people decide the meaning of and learn from an experience. Suggest that among other ways, they decide by reflecting on their experiences. Tell them that this Writer's Workshop will help them reflect on and draw conclusions about their own experiences or those of a literary character.

Writing and Language The Language Workshop in this subunit focuses on audience and purpose in writing. Explain the importance of making writing appropriate for a specific audience, and urge students to define their purpose before they begin writing. If students have difficulty shaping their writing to fit purpose and audience during the drafting stage, you may want to conduct a mini-lesson or review the material in the Language Workshop.

Writing and Study Skills This unit's Study Skills Workshop is a Vocabulary Workshop dealing with levels of language. Emphasize that both formal and informal English are acceptable as long as they suit the audience and purpose.

FIRST-PERSON NARRATIVE

After he was refused admission to the honor society because he wasn't properly dressed, Daniel Inouye was determined to "prove that shoes and neckties were no measure of a man." If we take the time to reflect on our own or other people's experiences, we often find in them an essential truth, or a meaning that extends beyond a particular experience.

For this assignment you will write a **reflective essay.** The primary aim of reflective writing is to connect a particular experience with an essential truth, or generalization, about life. Most reflective essays are written from the writer's viewpoint, that is, as first-person narratives. Reflective essays may also examine the personal experiences of others. In either case, a reflective essay uses an experience as a springboard to a more general statement about human experience.

GUIDED ASSIGNMENT: REFLECTIVE ESSAY

The main characters in the preceding selections come to a greater understanding about their lives because of their personal experiences. Choose one of these experiences and write a reflective essay that connects the experience with a truth about life. If you prefer, you may select an experience of your own and reflect on its meaning.

Here is your PASSkey to this assignment.

PURPOSE: To reflect on an essential truth
AUDIENCE: Yourself and your classmates
SUBJECT: An important incident
STRUCTURE: First-person essay

Prewriting

STEP 1 **Examine experiences** In small groups, discuss the main characters in the preceding selections. Choose the most important incident in each character's experience. Then share with your classmates an incident in your life that you feel had a great impact on your beliefs and behavior.

Additional Resources

UNIT ONE RESOURCE BOOK
Writer's Workshop Copy Master, p. 48
Peer and Self-Evaluation Guidelines, p. 49
Writing Assessment Guidelines, p. 50

ENRICHMENT MATERIALS
Thinking Skills Transparency and Worksheet
Fine Art Transparency and Writing Prompts
Revision, Proofreading, and Elaboration Worksheet
Writing Prompts for Assessment

One group of students came up with the following incident from "Marigolds." The second example is an experience chosen by a student that had a big effect on his life.

◀ STUDENT MODEL

Specific Incidents

—In "Marigolds," Lizabeth's attack on Lottie's marigolds is the most important incident.

—I bought a girl I liked lots of gifts so that she would like me.

STEP 2 Identify generalizations Ask what broad messages about life you learned from your own and each character's experiences. Write down each message as a generalization—a statement drawn from specific details that applies to a larger group.

◀ STUDENT MODEL

Specific Incident	Generalizations
-Lizabeth's attack on Lottie's marigolds	-Poverty breeds frustration and anger. -Young people have no respect for the old.
-Student buys gifts for a girl	-People will do anything for love. -You can't buy someone's affections.

STEP 3 Choose one generalization Decide which generalization you would like to explore in your essay. A good reflective essay focuses on one idea. If you have trouble selecting which generalization to write about, you might consider these questions:

- Which generalization best fits the incident?
- Which one do you understand the best?
- Which one sparks your interest?

STEP 4 Map your reflections Once you narrow your focus to one generalization, construct a rough map of your reflections. Add other incidents—drawn from literature or from your own life—that reflect this generalization. On the following page is a map of one student's thoughts on "You can't buy someone's affections."

Teaching Strategies

Introduction Have students turn to the Writer's Workshop for this subunit on page 114. Discuss with them how a reflective essay makes a generalization from a specific experience or experiences. Stress that this generalization must apply to a large number of people and must grow logically out of the experience.

Call students' attention to the Guided Assignment box on page 114, and explain that they will write a first-person essay about an experience. Make sure they understand that the essay must reflect on the general meaning of the experience. Point out that their audience will be themselves and their classmates.

Teaching Tip

Give students some practice in making generalizations about experience by asking them to recount short experiences that have happened to them, to someone they know, or to a fictional character. Ask the class to reflect on the experience, and then write their reflections on the board. Ask students to draw a broad lesson or idea from each reflection to generalize about the experience. Have LEP students work in a group, relating an experience and making a group map of their reflections. Then help them use the map to form a generalization about the experience.

Prewriting Help students focus on the general form for a reflective essay: recounting an experience, reflecting on it, and then forming a generalization about it.

Computer Tip

Suggest that students map their reflections on the computer. The ease of adding, deleting, and moving items around will encourage students to experiment until they find solid connections between their reflections and their generalization.

Drafting Remind students to use the map of their reflections when drafting their reflective essays. Stress that the drafting stage has three steps: relating a story, adding supporting information and reflections, and stating the generalization suggested by the experience.

Encourage students to add dialogue as they write, in much the same way as Daniel Inouye does in "My Shirt Is for Church." If they find this difficult, suggest that they reread the passage in which Inouye is interviewed for the honor society and use it as a model.

Teaching Tip
Have students number the paragraphs of the student model essay and compare them to steps 1, 2, and 3 in the drafting section of this Writer's Workshop. For LEP students, prepare a chart listing the steps of a reflective essay: *Tell the Story, Reflect on Its Meaning, Make a Generalization.* Have students draft the paragraphs of their essay directly on the chart, following the steps you have outlined.

Revising and Editing Help students find partners with whom to use the *Revision Checklist* on page 117. Tell students that this checklist will focus on the logic and clarity of their essays. You may want to have teacher conferences with some students if using the *Revision Checklist* reveals serious problems in their drafts. Focus on helping students improve the logic and clarity of their essays.

Teaching Tip
You may wish to have students number the paragraphs of their essays and then match them to the steps developed in the drafting section of this Writer's Workshop. Using this method, students can revise their essays to conform more closely to these steps, thus improving the clarity and logic of their work.

STUDENT MODEL ▶

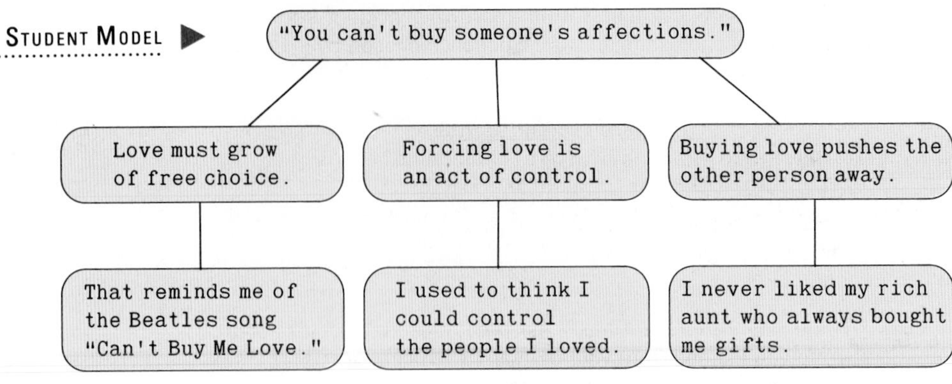

STEP 5 Check with a classsmate Ask a classmate to check your thinking so far by looking at your map. The connections between your reflections and the generalization should make sense to him or her.

Drafting

STEP 1 Tell the story Begin by describing the specific experience from your life or from the character's life. Zero in on the important details and omit any information that doesn't relate to the generalization suggested by the experience.

STUDENT MODEL ▶

Sheila sat in front of me in English class. Each day we talked before class began about the things we loved and hated. It wasn't long before I began to really care about her, but she seemed interested in other things and other people. How could I get her attention?

One day I noticed that she often talked about things she wanted—earrings, perfume, and stuff like that. I realized that this was a way to show my love. Each day I placed a little gift on her desk before she arrived. She was a bit embarrassed, but I thought that was natural. Then our conversations became strained. One week later she asked the teacher to change her seat.

STEP 2 Add supporting information Add to your draft any reflections from your prewriting map that support your generalization. Be sure to link incidents together through effective transition statements such as the first sentence on the next page.

ADDITIONAL WRITING AND RESEARCH TOPICS

The following provide added writing practice based on the selections in this subunit:

Reflective Essay

- Have you ever "paid a price" for something you did or said (or something you did not do or say)? In a brief narrative, tell what happened and what consequences followed. Reflect on the meaning of the experience and its outcome.
- "Marigolds" is told from Lizabeth's point of view. Rewrite the account of the flower-smashing incident from Miss Lottie's point of view. Try to infer Miss Lottie's feelings and thoughts as she reflects on her experience.

Other Topics

Opinion: Do you think the young man in "Honor" who stole the 700 sucres should serve a six-month prison sentence? Put yourself in the role of the judge who is trying his case, and write an opinion paper.

After Sheila moved, I was hurt. Then one day my rich aunt came to visit. I had never liked her; she was too eager to please people. Each day when I got home from school, she would have left some gift at my place at the table. I always thanked her, but I found myself avoiding her more and more.

◀ STUDENT MODEL

STEP 3 State your generalization To complete your essay, state the generalization about life suggested by your experience. Note how this student linked particular incidents to his generalization about life.

Then one day it hit me. My aunt was treating me just the way I had treated Sheila. Now I understood. You can't buy someone's love. It only pushes them away.

◀ STUDENT MODEL

Revising and Editing

Ask a classmate to respond to your draft. He or she may want to use the following checklist.

Revision Checklist

1. What is the generalization the writer has identified?
2. Is this generalization linked to a specific incident?
3. Does the writer explain ideas clearly and in depth?

Editing When you are satisfied with the content of your essay, work on refining your sentence structure, grammar, and spelling.

Publishing

As a class, put together a collection of generalizations about life.

Reflecting on Your Writing

Answer the following questions. Turn in your answers with your paper or place them in your writing portfolio.

1. What was the most difficult part of this assignment for you? Why?
2. What part of your paper got the most positive reaction from a classmate? Why do you think he or she liked this part best?

Presenting As an alternative to the *Presenting* suggestion in the pupil's edition, you might consider these ideas:

1. Have students prepare their reflective essays so that they can present them in the style of a traditional, oral storyteller. Remind students to include their experience, their reflections, and their generalization in their presentations.

2. Have students prepare their essays in the form of a picture book for young children, presenting their experience, their reflections on it, and their generalization in an entertaining way that is appropriate for young children.

Reflecting on Your Writing When you review students' portfolios, remember to respond to their answers to the reflecting questions.

Students should use these questions to evaluate their experience in writing a reflective essay and to evaluate the writing itself. Additional help may be appropriate if a majority of the class has a similar response to Question 1.

Closure

Before beginning the next subunit, be sure that students have internalized these concepts:

- A reflective essay examines personal experience in order to reflect on it and form some generalization about human experience
- The generalization in a reflective essay must be linked to the specific experience recounted

Language Workshop

Objectives

- To recognize the four main purposes of writing: expression, information, entertainment, and persuasion
- To identify the audience before beginning to write
- To determine the purpose for writing
- To use language appropriate to the purpose

Integrating . . .

Writing and Language Remind students that in the Writer's Workshop they wrote a reflective essay. Ask students what the purpose of the essay was. Lead them to conclude that they wanted to inform the reader about an essential truth. Explain that the purpose in writing generally dictates the kind of language to be used. Write the following topics on the board.

1. How to Make a Million Dollars
2. Hayley's Accidental Haircut
3. Our Children Need Clean Air!

Have volunteers read each topic and describe the kind of writing that would be generated by each. Discuss with students that 1 would tell how to do something, 2 would likely be humorous, and 3 would make a case against air pollution. Point out that by examining the topic, they can determine the kind of writing that will follow. Explain to students that this Language Workshop focuses on four main purposes of writing and the language used in each.

Teaching Strategies

Have students read the first three paragraphs on page 118 and the questions that follow. Remind students that knowing their audience makes it easier to choose appropriate language. Be sure to discuss the sidenote to the right of this section.

Teaching Tip

To help students become proficient at determining the audience and writing purpose, have them jot down a PASSkey for every story they read in the next several days and discuss them in class.

LANGUAGE WORKSHOP

AUDIENCE AND PURPOSE

After you have decided on a writing topic, but before you begin drafting, consider the following factors: Who is your intended **audience?** That is, who will read your writing? What is your **purpose** in writing? In other words, what do you want your audience to know, feel, or do?

Depending on who your audience is, the information you provide and the way you present it will vary. Before you can write about how to prepare a traditional Thanksgiving meal, for example, you need to determine whether your audience consists of experienced or beginning cooks.

Sometimes your audience is chosen for you. If you are running for student council president, your audience is the students in your school. At other times you may need to choose your audience yourself. If you were concerned about a pollution problem in your town, you might write a letter to the president of a local company that is polluting your town water, or you might write a letter to the editor of your home newspaper in hopes of reaching the general public. Once you determine who your readers will be, ask yourself questions like the following:

Choose a Tone ▶

For an audience you know well, choose an informal tone that is friendly and relaxed. For an audience who is less familiar to you, a formal tone is more appropriate.

1. What do my readers know about this subject? What further information do they need?
2. Which aspect of my subject will my readers find most interesting?
3. What style and tone would be most appropriate and effective?

Four Main Writing Purposes

There are four main purposes for writing: to express yourself, to inform, to entertain, and to persuade. Sometimes writing has only one of these purposes. For instance, the primary purpose of *Dandelion Wine* by Ray Bradbury is to entertain. Often a piece of writing has more than one purpose. Daniel Inouye's autobiography, "My Shirt Is for Church," is entertaining, but it is also informative and persuasive.

To determine your purpose for writing, ask yourself these questions:

Pronoun Choice ▶

Often the pronouns you choose reflect your purpose. Use the first-person pronoun *I* if you want a personal tone. Use *you* if you want to move your audience to action. The third person is most often used in formal writing. (For more about pronouns, see the Language Handbook.)

1. What do I want to accomplish in this piece of writing?
2. What effect do I want my writing to have on my audience?
3. How can I accomplish this?

The Writer's Workshops include a PASSkey feature, in which *P* and *A* stand for *purpose* and *audience*. The feature is intended to help you focus on these and other key elements in every writing assignment.

Additional Resources

UNIT ONE RESOURCE BOOK

Language Workshop Copy Master, p. 51

ENRICHMENT MATERIALS

Grammar and Usage Copy Masters

Exercise 1 Suppose the topic you are assigned to write about is "Why America Is Still the Land of Opportunity." For each purpose and audience given below, write two or three sentences that you might include in a paragraph written for that group.

1. To persuade adults to make a certain decision
2. To inform immigrants from Central America
3. To state an opinion to a government official
4. To entertain your friends

Exercise 2 The following list contains three subjects, and two possible audiences for each subject. Create a one-sentence purpose for each audience. For example, if your subject were the history of your hometown and your audience were local grade school children, your purpose might be to inform them and instill in them a sense of pride in their past. If your audience were potential visitors, your purpose might be to persuade them to visit.

1. Subject : a historic theater in poor condition
   Audience A: the preservation society
   Audience B: a developer of high-rise apartment buildings
2. Subject: the Amazon rain forest
   Audience A: a biology teacher
   Audience B: an environmental group
3. Subject: a famous movie star
   Audience A: newspaper readers
   Audience B: your best friend

Exercise 3 Style Review the literature in the first subunit of this book. Write down the title of each selection. Next to each title write what you think the author's purpose and intended audience were.

Exercise 4 Analyzing and Revising Your Writing

1. Take a piece of writing from your portfolio.
2. On a separate piece of paper, write what your purpose and intended audience were for the paper you chose.
3. Now reread your paper with your audience and purpose in mind.
4. In writing, explain how your paper does or does not match its audience and purpose, and how it could be improved.

Closure

Before beginning the next subunit, be sure students have internalized these concepts:

- The four main purposes of writing are to express, inform, entertain, and persuade.
- The audience and the purpose for writing determines content and style.
- The purpose in writing also determines the degree of formality and type of language used.

Additional Practice

This item provides practice in understanding audience and purpose. Write this paragraph. Then write the author's purpose and possible audience.

Writing a check is a simple process. On the first line, fill in the date. On the next line, write out the name of the person who will receive the money. In the box next to the dollar sign, write in numerals for the amount of money that the check is worth. Below that, write out the amount in words. check is worth. The final step is to write your signature at the bottom of the check.

Purpose: *(to inform about a process)*

Possible audience: *(a younger student)*

Now have students continue reading, stopping before Exercise 1. Ask a volunteer to read the sidenote and challenge students to find examples of first- and third-person pronouns in this subunit's selections about pronouns.

Teaching Tip

Check to see that Spanish-speaking students do not use a pronoun after a proper noun when they speak or write, as in the sentence "Mary, she went home late."

Assign Exercises 1 and 2 on page 119 for students to complete individually. Review the answers orally before proceeding. Then assign Exercises 3 and 4.

Exercise 1

Answers will vary. Sample answers include:
1. Enroll in post-graduate courses and take advantage of unlimited job opportunities.
2. Once you have registered you are eligible for the following services: . . .
3. Our city can be revitalized with your affirmative vote for the new budget.
4. Though I have had eleven different summer jobs, I welcome the challenge of finding new and exciting employment in the future.

Exercise 2

1A. To persuade them to put funds into rebuilding.
1B. To express an opinion about a developer's decision to tear down the theater.
2A. To inform the teacher about the vegetation.
2B. To express an opinion about the environmental importance of the rain forest.
3A. To entertain them with personal anecdotes.
3B. To inform the friend about the star's next appearance.

Exercise 3

1. "The Open Window": to entertain; readers
2. "The Fan Club": to entertain, express opinion; young readers
3. "Like Mexicans": to inform; non-Mexican readers
4. "A Kind of Murder": to entertain; young readers
5. "The Road Not Taken": to inform; poetry readers
6. "Choices": to express opinion; poetry readers

Exercise 4

Answers will vary.

Vocabulary Workshop

Objectives

- To understand the differences between formal and informal language
- To understand the appropriate uses of formal and informal language
- To choose appropriately between the use of formal and informal English
- To identify and use appropriate vocabulary, mechanics, and organization for both types of speech

Integrating . . .

Literature and Vocabulary Share with students that this workshop will help them use formal and informal language appropriately.

Teaching Strategies

Read through the material with students. Assign the exercise on page 120. Hold conferences with students to discuss their responses.

Closure

Before beginning the next subunit, be sure students have internalized these concepts:

- By considering audience and purpose, one can decide whether formal English or informal English is needed.
- After the level of language is chosen, one uses the appropriate vocabulary, mechanics, and organization.

Teaching Tip: LEP

LEP students may have difficulty understanding the difference in tone between formal and informal English. If possible, have students find examples from their native language in which essentially the same thought is expressed but the way it is said differs.

Exercise

(A possible response is given.)
I would like to be considered for your student exchange program with Ecuador. I am interested in learning about other countries and cultures. I believe that exchange programs build friendships between people and between countries. My two years of Spanish would allow me to adjust easily. I look forward to hearing from you.

LEVELS OF LANGUAGE

Standard English, which follows accepted rules of grammar, usage, and mechanics, can be grouped into two, somewhat overlapping categories: formal and informal. **Formal English** is used primarily in writing but is appropriate in any situation that is serious, dignified, or ceremonial. **Informal English,** also known as conversational or colloquial English, is appropriate in everyday situations. It is used in magazines, newspapers, casual letters, and conversation.

	Formal	Informal
Tone	• Serious, academic	• Personal, friendly
Vocabulary	• May use complicated words • Avoids contractions	• Uses simpler words • Often uses contractions; may use slang
Mechanics	• Uses correct grammar	• Uses correct grammar
Organization	• Longer, more carefully constructed sentences	• Similar to conversational English

Exercise Rewrite the following informal letter in formal English. You may invent further details about the applicant, if necessary.

Hi Folks,
My name is Alexandra Paganni, and I've always thought that living somewhere away from home would be cool. I guess Ecuador is a good place to try living without my folks and my obnoxious brother. I think the experience would be awesome because I could practice my Spanish. I think a foreign exchange program is a super way for countries to become pals with each other. Do you think I have a chance to get picked to go? I know I'd be a great rep for this school.

Additional Resources

UNIT ONE RESOURCE BOOK
Related Skills Copy Master, p. 52

ADDITIONAL PRACTICE

Rewrite the following informal sentences in formal English.

1. This dude Carlos had an awesome time down under last year. *(My friend Carlos had a wonderful time in Australia last year.)*
2. They had to push him into the plane to come home. *(He was reluctant to return.)*
3. He can't wait to hop a steamer heading back. *(He cannot wait for an opportunity to return.)*

A Matter of Life and Death

Most decisions you make revolve around simple day-to-day experiences. What will you wear to school? What courses will you take next year? There may come a time, however, when you face a decision that means life or death. Perhaps you are driving a car when an accident suddenly occurs in front of you, or maybe you are with a group of friends who decide to do something extremely dangerous. How do you think you might respond at such stressful moments?

The characters in the selections you are about to read are all faced with life-and-death decisions. When you read these selections, consider what other options the characters have. Ask yourself what decisions you might make in such matters of life and death.

Subunit Preview

Have students read the introduction to subunit 3, **A Matter of Life and Death.** Ask them to think how the stress of facing a life-or-death decision relates to the unit theme, **Decisions: Action or Apathy.** What might prompt someone to "tempt fate"? What might someone value more than life? What might be harder to face than death? Invite students to scan the subunit Table of Contents and ask them which selection that they think will be most interesting.

For Additional Challenge

The following selections offer extra challenge in the exploration of the subunit theme:

"They Called Her Moses," a biography by Robert De Cormier

"To Build a Fire," a short story by Jack London

Additional Resources

Subunit Test, pp. 75–76

Observation Assessment

Observing how students respond to the text, to the classroom instruction, and to peers is an important part of an assessment program. The following suggestions and the form in each Unit Resource Book can be used to implement observation assessment.

- As students work through the subunit, assess their use of reading strategies as they read. Do they use illustrations for help when they run into difficulty? Do they observe differences between their mental images of characters and setting and the illustrations?
- As they progress through the subunit, do they show growth in using strategies during reading?
- To evaluate students' ability to recognize a story's emotional tone, have them identify words and phrases that create mood.

Objectives

- To understand and analyze a modern short story
- To understand the use of internal dialogue
- To make and check predictions
- To express understanding of the work through a choice of writing forms, including explanation, letters, and narration
- To identify synonyms and antonyms

Prereading/Motivation

Examine What You Know

Discussion Prompts: What were your feelings about each choice? What were your feelings about the consequences of each? What factors helped you to find a solution?

Expand Your Knowledge

Discussion Prompts: What kinds of events may occur during a revolution? How might civilians help one side or the other during a revolution? What might a government do to end a revolutionary uprising?

Enrich Your Reading

Possible answers are:

Prediction 1 The barber will (not) take revenge.

Prediction 2 He will (not) betray his principles.

Prediction 3 He will (not) slit the captain's throat.

Thematic Link—A Matter of Life and Death
In this story, the main character must choose between taking or sparing the life of his enemy.

explore

Fiction

Lather and Nothing Else

HERNANDO TÉLLEZ (her nan′ dō tā′ lyās)

Examine What You Know (Prior Knowledge)

Like the main character in this story, we sometimes find ourselves in a dilemma. A dilemma is a choice between two unpleasant alternatives. For example, having to choose between going to a dance with someone you don't like or staying home alone is a dilemma. Recall a time you felt you were in a dilemma. In a chart like the one below, describe your two choices, their consequences, and your solution.

Choice A	Choice B
______	______
Consequences of A	Consequences of B
______	______

Your Solution

______

Expand Your Knowledge (Building Background)

"Lather and Nothing Else" takes place in a country undergoing a revolution. Though this story is set in South America, such conflicts have occurred all over the world. During a revolution it is often difficult to tell who is the enemy. Many fighters are civilians without uniforms. Consequently, the government under attack usually resorts to very harsh measures to keep the general population under control.

Enrich Your Reading (Reading Skill)

Predicting One way a writer creates suspense is by encouraging the reader to predict or guess what will happen next. In the story you are about to read, look for the questions in the text that ask you to make predictions. Each time you come to one of these boxes, predict how the barber will solve his dilemma. You may find that you change your mind as the story progresses.

■ *A biography of the author can be found on page 129.*

Journal Writing

The main character of this story faces conflicting choices. Suggest these journal topics to students:

- Discuss a time when you made a difficult choice.
- How do conflicts help you learn about yourself?
- Lather is "foam formed by soap and water." It also means "an agitated state," as in the phrase "in a lather." Knowing this, predict what the story "Lather and Nothing Else" might be about.
- For other journal opportunities, refer students to question #6 (p. 127).

Additional Resources

UNIT ONE RESOURCE BOOK
Reader's Guidesheet, p. 55
Vocabulary Worksheet, p. 56
Selection and Vocabulary Check Tests, p. 57
Selection Test, pp. 58–59

Collaborative Learning

Opportunities for collaborative learning appear throughout the lesson and include Options for Learning activities 1 and 4 and Cross-Curricular Options (p. T–129).

Lather and Nothing Else

HERNANDO TÉLLEZ

He came in without a word. I was stropping[1] my best razor. And when I recognized him, I started to shake. But he did not notice. To cover my nervousness, I went on honing the razor. I tried the edge with the tip of my thumb and took another look at it against the light.

A Meanwhile he was taking off his cartridge-studded belt with the pistol holster suspended from it. He put it on a hook in the wardrobe and hung his cap above it. Then he turned full around toward me and, loosening his tie, remarked, "It's hot as the devil. I want a shave." With that he
SR-1 ▶ took his seat.

I estimated he had a four-days' growth of
B beard, the four days he had been gone on the last foray after our men. His face looked
SR-2 ▶ burnt, tanned by the sun.

I started to work carefully on the shaving soap. I scraped some slices from the cake, dropped them into the mug, then added a
C little lukewarm water, and stirred with the brush. The lather soon began to rise.

"The fellows in the troop must have just about as much beard as I." I went on stirring up lather. "But we did very well, you know. We caught the leaders. Some of them we brought back dead; others are still alive. But they'll all be dead soon."

"How many did you take?" I asked.

"Fourteen. We had to go pretty far in to find them. But now they're paying for it. And not one will escape; not a single one."

He leaned back in the chair when he saw the brush in my hand, full of lather. I had not yet put the sheet on him. I was certainly flustered. Taking a sheet from the drawer, I tied it around my customer's neck.

He went on talking. He evidently took it for granted that I was on the side of the
existing regime. ◀ SR-3

"The people must have gotten a scare with what happened the other day," he said.

"Yes," I replied, as I finished tying the knot against his nape, which smelt of sweat.

"Good show, wasn't it?"

"Very good," I answered, turning my attention now to the brush. The man closed his eyes wearily and awaited the cool caress of the lather.

I had never had him so close before. The day he ordered the people to file through

1. **stropping:** using a thick leather band, called a strop, to sharpen.

Words to Know and Use	
	hone (hōn) *v.* to sharpen on a strop or whetstone
	foray (fôr′ ā) *n.* a raid or hunt
	regime (rə zhēm′) *n.* a political or ruling system
	nape (nāp) *n.* the back of the neck
	caress (kə res′) *n.* a gentle or affectionate touch

123

Teaching Strategies

Vocabulary Preview

These vocabulary words are defined at the bottom of the selection page on which they appear. You may wish to discuss them briefly before students begin reading.

caress a gentle touch
conscientious having a sense of what is right
emit to give forth
foray a raid or hunt
hone to sharpen
nape the back of the neck
regime a ruling system
rejuvenate to make young again
tranquil calm
whorl a spiral

Support for Students of Limited English Proficiency

- Use **Reader's Guidesheet**, p. 55.
- Explain that much of the story is a description of the thoughts and images that pass through a barber's mind as he faces a dilemma. Encourage students to visualize the setting as they read.
- Annotations **E** and **L** focus on troublesome terms.

Text Annotations

A. Literary Element: MOOD Ask students to identify the mood, or atmosphere, in the barbershop. *(The mood is ominous; there is much tension and fear.)* Elicit the details that create this mood. *(The barber is shaking with nervousness; the customer wears a pistol and cartridge belt.)*

B. Literary Element: POINT OF VIEW Elicit that the narrator, a village barber, tells the story from the first-person point of view. Point out that this lets the readers know his true feelings about the regime and the political struggle.

C. Literary Sidelight: SYMBOL Review the meaning of "to work oneself into a lather." (to become agitated or excited) Point out that the stirring up of lather in the cup symbolizes the barber's stirred-up emotions.

Structured Reading for Less Proficient Students

These questions can help to guide students through the reading. Ask each question at the point of the selection where the SR number appears in the margin.

SR–1. Why does the customer come into the narrator's shop? *(He wants a shave.)* **Literal recall**

SR–2. Where has the customer been for the last four days? *(He had been out on a foray to capture the leaders of the revolution.)* **Literal recall**

SR–3. Why is the narrator so nervous? *(He is a secret revolutionary and the enemy of the customer.)* **Literal recall**

SR–4. How do you think the narrator feels toward his customer? Explain why you think as you do. *(The narrator probably hates or is repulsed by the customer, because he has ordered the killing and mutilation of the narrator's comrades.)* **Making inferences**

SR–5. Why is the narrator giving Captain Torres such a good shave? *(The narrator is a conscientious barber and proud of his work.)* **Literal recall**

Continued on page 124

D. Reading Skill: PREDICTING *(Possible answers: The barber will slit the man's throat; will threaten to kill him to gain an advantage; will try to gain secret information from the man; will draw blood as he shaves the man; will simply shave him.)*

E. LEP: Vocabulary Discuss the meaning of *firing party. (a squad of soldiers detailed to shoot someone sentenced to die)* Ask volunteers to explain what the captain expects to happen in the evening. *(A few rebel leaders will be killed slowly, perhaps tortured.)*

F. Literary Element: INTERNAL DIALOGUE Point out that throughout the story the narrator shares the thoughts running through his head. Explain that the conversation the barber has with himself helps the readers to get to know him.

G. Reading Skill: PREDICTING *(Possible answers: The barber will be true to his principles and give the captain an excellent shave; he will follow his revolutionary instincts and take revenge on the captain.)*

H. Literary Element: CHARACTER Have students tell what this dialogue reveals about the kind of person Captain Torres is. *(Possible response: He is cruel and sadistic; he takes pleasure in the pain of his victims.)*

the schoolyard to look upon the four rebels hanging there, my path had crossed his briefly. But the sight of those mutilated bodies kept me from paying attention to the face of the man who had been directing it all and whom I now had in my hands. SR-4

D

predict What will the barber do?

It was not a disagreeable face, certainly. And the beard, which aged him a bit, was not unbecoming. His name was Torres. Captain Torres.

I started to lay on the first coat of lather. He kept his eyes closed.

"I would love to catch a nap," he said, "but there's a lot to be done this evening."

E

I lifted the brush and asked, with pretended indifference: "A firing party?"

"Something of the sort," he replied, "but slower."

"All of them?"

"No, just a few."

I went on lathering his face. My hands began to tremble again. The man could not be aware of this, which was lucky for me. But I wished he had not come in. Probably many of our men had seen him enter the shop. And with the enemy in my house I felt a certain responsibility.

F

I would have to shave his beard just like any other, carefully, neatly, just as though he were a good customer, taking heed that not a single pore should emit a drop of blood. Seeing to it that the blade did not slip in the small whorls. Taking care that the skin was left clean, soft, shining, so that when I passed the back of my hand over it not a single hair should be felt. Yes. I was secretly a revolutionary, but at the same time I was a conscientious barber, proud of the way I did my job. And that four-day beard presented a challenge.

G

What will the barber do? **predict**

I took up the razor, opened the handle wide, releasing the blade, and started to work, downward from one sideburn. The blade responded to perfection. The hair was tough and hard; not very long, but thick. Little by little the skin began to show through. The razor gave its usual sound as it gathered up layers of soap mixed with bits of hair. I paused to wipe it clean, and taking up the strop once more went about improving its edge, for I am a painstaking barber. SR-5

The man, who had kept his eyes closed, now opened them, put a hand out from under the sheet, felt of the part of his face that was emerging from the lather, and said to me, "Come at six o'clock this evening to the school."

H

"Will it be like the other day?" I asked, stiff with horror.

"It may be even better," he replied.

"What are you planning to do?"

"I'm not sure yet. But we'll have a good time."

Once more he leaned back and shut his eyes. I came closer, the razor on high.

"Are you going to punish all of them?" I timidly ventured.

"Yes, all of them."

The lather was drying on his face. I must hurry. Through the mirror, I took a look at the street. It appeared about as usual; there was the grocery shop with two or three customers. Then I glanced at the clock, two-thirty.

Words to Know and Use	**emit** (ē mit′) *v.* to give forth or send out **whorl** (hwôrl) *n.* anything that appears to whirl in circles, such as tufts of hair, or fingerprints; a spiral **conscientious** (kän′ shē en′ shəs) *adj.* having a sense of what is right

124

STRUCTURED READING FOR LESS PROFICIENT STUDENTS

Continued from page 123

SR–6. What difficult decision must the narrator make? *(He must decide whether or not to kill the captain with his razor.)* **Making inferences**

SR–7. What does the narrator decide to do? *(He decides not to kill him.)* What are the narrator's reasons for this decision? *(He knows it would lead to more bloodshed and his own death; killing the captain would violate the pride he takes in his work.)* **Summarizing**

SELF-PORTRAIT WITH A BARBER
1914–23 Nicolai Pavlovich Ulianov
The State Trerayakov Gallery, Moscow.

The razor kept descending. Now from the other sideburn downward. It was a blue beard, a thick one. He should let it grow like some poets, or some priests. It would suit him well. Many people would not recognize him. And that would be a good thing for him, I thought, as I went gently over all the throat line. At this point you really had to handle your blade skillfully, because the hair, while scantier, tended to fall into small whorls. It was a curly beard. The pores might open, minutely, in this area and let out a tiny drop of blood. A good barber like myself stakes his reputation on not permitting that to happen to any of his customers.

And this was indeed a special customer. How many of ours had he sent to their death? How many had he mutilated? It was best not to think about it. Torres did not know I was his enemy. Neither he nor the others knew it. It was a secret shared by very few, just because that made it possible for me to inform the revolutionaries about Torres's activities in the town and what he planned to do every time he went on one of his raids to hunt down rebels. So it was going to be very difficult to explain how it was that I had him in my hands and then let him go in peace, alive, clean-shaven.

His beard had now almost entirely disappeared. He looked younger, several years younger than when he had come in. I suppose that always happens to men who enter and leave barbershops. Under the strokes of my razor Torres was rejuvenated; yes, because I am a good barber, the best in this town, and I say this in all modesty.

A little more lather here under the chin, on the Adam's apple, right near the great vein. How hot it is! Torres must be sweating just as I am. But he is not afraid. He is a tranquil man, who is not even giving thought to what he will do to his prisoners this evening. I, on the other hand, polishing his skin with this razor but avoiding the drawing of blood, careful with every

Words to Know and Use

rejuvenate (ri jo͞o′ və nāt′) *v.* to bring back to youth or strength
tranquil (tran′ kwil) *adj.* calm, not agitated

125

Art Note

Russian artist Nikolai Pavlovich Ulianov (1875–1949) was interested for a time in the multiple images produced by mirrors on opposite walls. This painting seems to illustrate the thoughts of Captain Torres in *Lather and Nothing Else* as he contemplates several mirrored reflections of himself in a situation that may be fatal. *What might the artist intend by portraying the barber as a larger figure than his client?*

I. Reading Skills: INFERRING Have students tell why it would be a good thing for the captain to grow a beard and be less recognizable. *(If the captain was hard to recognize, his enemies among the rebels would be less likely to single him out for revenge.)*

J. Literary Element: THEME Ask students how the captain's actions and the narrator's thoughts illustrate the theme "A Matter of Life and Death." *(The captain has killed many rebels and will kill more. The barber is perhaps contemplating whether to kill the captain or let him live.)*

K. Literary Element: SUSPENSE Point out that the suspense is mounting because the barber is just about done shaving the captain and so must make a decision.

L. LEP: Vocabulary Explain that the cartilage of the larynx in the throat is called the Adam's apple. Have students feel their Adam's apples and tell them that the vein beneath it returns blood from the head to the heart.

Historical Sidelight At one time, barbers were also surgeons. The familiar red-and-white striped barber pole represents a red pole that a patient squeezed during bloodletting (believed to relieve fevers and headaches) to make the process go more smoothly. The white stripes represent the bandages used to wrap the patients' wounds.

REAL LIFE CONNECTIONS

In "Lather and Nothing Else," the narrator must decide whether or not to take the life of his enemy, a fateful decision on which his own life may also depend. Encourage students to name actual events from history in which military or political leaders were assassinated.

M. Literary Element: INTERNAL DIALOGUE Ask students to summarize the barber's thoughts here. *(Possible response: Killing the captain will do no good since it will just result in more and more killing. Even so, it would be easy to do it.)*

N. Reading Skill: PREDICTING *(Possible answers: The last few paragraphs suggest that the barber will kill the captain; the barber's earlier thoughts suggest he sees little point in killing the captain.)*

O. Literary Element: IRONY Point out that Torres has known all along about the barber's rebel sympathies. Explain that this ironic twist catches the barber and the reader unaware. Ask students how the ending changes their attitude toward Torres. *(Torres gains a measure of respect for facing death in such a cool, macho fashion).*

Check Test

1. What is the occupation of the narrator of the story? *(barber)*

2. Why is the narrator upset about shaving the captain? *(The narrator is a revolutionary; the captain is his enemy.)*

3. What does the narrator consider doing as he shaves the captain? *(He considers killing the captain.)*

4. In the end, what does the narrator do to the captain? *(He gives him a good shave and lets him live.)*

Encouraging Independent Reading

"A Horseman in the Sky," a short story by Ambrose Bierce
"The Guest," a short story by Albert Camus
"The Inspiration of Mr. Budd," a short story by Dorothy Sayers

stroke—I cannot keep my thoughts in order.

Confound the hour he entered my shop! I am a revolutionary but not a murderer. And it would be so easy to kill him. He deserves it. Or does he? No! No one deserves the sacrifice others make in becoming assassins. What is to be gained by it? Nothing. Others and still others keep coming, and the first kill the second, and then these kill the next, and so on until everything becomes a sea of blood. I could cut his throat, so, swish, swish! He would not even have time to moan, and with his eyes shut he would not even see the shine of the razor or the gleam in my eye. M

But I'm shaking like a regular murderer. From his throat a stream of blood would flow on the sheet, over the chair, down on my hands, onto the floor. I would have to close the door. But the blood would go flowing along the floor, warm, indelible, not to be staunched, until it reached the street like a small scarlet river.

I'm sure that with a good strong blow, a deep cut, he would feel no pain. He would not suffer at all. And what would I do then with the body? Where would I hide it? I would have to flee, leave all this behind, take shelter far away, very far away. But they would follow until they caught up with me. "The murderer of Captain Torres. He slit his throat while he was shaving him. What a cowardly thing to do!"

And others would say, "The avenger of our people. A name to remember"—my name here. "He was the town barber. No one knew he was fighting for our cause." N

And so, which will it be? Murderer or hero? My fate hangs on the edge of this razor blade.

What will the barber do? 

I can turn my wrist slightly, put a bit more pressure on the blade, let it sink in. The skin will yield like silk, like rubber, like the strop. There is nothing more tender than a man's skin, and the blood is always there, ready to burst forth. A razor like this cannot fail. It is the best one I have.

But I don't want to be a murderer. No, sir. You came in to be shaved. And I do my work honorably. I don't want to stain my hands with blood. Just with lather, and nothing else. You are an executioner; I am only a barber. Each one to his job. That's it. Each one to his job. ◀ SR-7

The chin was now clean, polished, soft. The man got up and looked at himself in the glass. He ran his hand over the skin and felt its freshness, its newness.

"Thanks," he said. He walked to the wardrobe for his belt, his pistol, and his cap. I must have been very pale, and I felt my shirt soaked with sweat. Torres finished adjusting his belt buckle, straightened his gun in its holster, and smoothing his hair mechanically, put on his cap. From his trousers pocket he took some coins to pay for the shave. And he started toward the door. On the threshold he stopped for a moment, and turning toward me, he said,

"They told me you would kill me. I came to find out if it was true. But it's not easy to kill. I know what I'm talking about." O

Professional Notebook

One of the most flattering things that ever happened to me as a teacher occurred when I received a postcard from a very good student on his first visit to Italy, who wrote, "You are not a professor of political philosophy but a travel agent." Nothing could have better expressed my intention as an educator. He thought I had prepared him to see. Then he could begin thinking for himself with something to think about. . . . Education in our times must try to find whatever there is in students that might yearn for completion, and to reconstruct the learning that would enable them autonomously to seek that completion.

Allan Bloom, *The Closing of the American Mind*

Responding to Reading

First Impressions

1. When you reflect on this story, what image first comes to mind? Why do you think this image occurred to you?

Second Thoughts

2. What is the barber's dilemma?
3. Why doesn't the barber kill Captain Torres?

   Think about
   - the barber's beliefs about his profession
   - the barber's role in the revolution
   - the barber's beliefs about killing
   - the predictions you made as you read the story
4. Even though the barber is holding a weapon and Captain Torres is defenseless, it is the barber who is nervous. Why is the barber nervous and Captain Torres calm?
5. Captain Torres risks his life for a shave. Is he totally at the mercy of the barber, or does he have some control over the situation?

   Think about
   - what Torres knows about killing and what he talks about
   - how the barber behaves during the shave
6. The barber solves his dilemma by choosing not to kill Captain Torres. Did he make the right decision? Explain.

Broader Connections

7. History is full of difficult decisions. For example, should the United States have dropped the atomic bomb on Japan? In a daily newspaper, find an article that discusses some hard choices being made about an issue. Share the article with your classmates.

Literary Concept: Internal Dialogue

Much of this story is told through characters speaking directly to each other in dialogue. However, we also hear the barber's thoughts, or **internal dialogue,** as he considers his dilemma. For example, the barber thinks, "But I don't want to be a murderer. No, sir. You came in to be shaved." Look back at the chart you made about a dilemma you have had. Write out the ideas as if they were an internal dialogue.

Literary Concept—Internal Dialogue

Answers will vary.

Student Response

Responding to Reading

These questions are open-ended with no "right" or "wrong" answers. However, responses must be supported with information from the selection. Possible answers follow:

1. Any image from the story is valid.

2. The barber's dilemma is deciding whether or not to kill the captain.

3. The barber doesn't kill the captain for several reasons. Students may say that he takes great pride in his work; killing a customer goes against his professionalism. They may also say that he is an undercover informer for the rebels and killing the captain would expose his rebel leanings. Or, the barber is a thoughtful and compassionate man; therefore, he knows that killing Torres would result in more bloodshed.

4. Some may say that the barber is nervous because he faces a difficult dilemma. He is also very afraid of the cruel captain. Students may say that Captain Torres seems calm because he does not believe the barber is capable of murder.

5. Some might suggest that Torres is at the mercy of the barber, since he has no way of knowing what decision the barber will make. Others might say that Torres senses that the barber is too nervous to kill him. Another opinion is that Torres knows the barber will not want to reveal his rebel sympathies by killing him.

6. Some might say that the barber makes the right decision in that he is free to carry on his undercover work. Others might say that the barber chooses wrongly, missing a chance to strike a mortal blow against the enemy.

7. Regarding the decision to drop the atomic bomb, some students will say this was the wrong decision in that thousands of innocent people were maimed and killed and a precedent for using nuclear weapons was set. Others will say it was the right decision in that it brought a quick end to the war, ultimately saving many lives.

For the newspaper articles, ask students to describe the hard choices that must be made and list the pros and cons of each choice.

Writing Options

The Writing Options are designed to meet varied student interests and abilities. Have each student choose one writing activity to complete. You may wish to guide some students to an option that requires less writing.

Journal Update Have students review their journal entries for "Lather and Nothing Else." What can they add to their ideas about the meaning of this story title? Have they any additional reflections on making difficult choices?

Vocabulary Practice

1. Synonyms
2. Antonyms
3. Antonyms
4. Synonyms
5. Synonyms
6. Antonyms
7. Synonyms
8. Synonyms
9. Synonyms
10. Synonyms

Writing Options

1. Recall these words of Captain Torres: "They told me you would kill me. I came to find out if it was true. But it's not easy to kill. I know what I'm talking about." Do you believe that Captain Torres really finds it difficult to kill? Explain your opinion in a brief paragraph.

2. The barber solves his dilemma by deciding to let Captain Torres live. Now he must explain his decision to the other revolutionaries who have likely lost family and friends because of the captain's past actions. Write a letter from the barber to his friends explaining why he did not kill Torres.

3. What do you think would have happened if the barber had killed Captain Torres? What would the barber have done next? Rewrite the ending of the story to include this new twist.

4. Consider the personal dilemma that you described earlier. How do you feel now about the choice you made? Think about the long-range effects of your decision. Is there any advice you might give the barber about making hard choices? Based on your experiences, write a short letter of advice to the barber about the best way to deal with any dilemma.

Vocabulary Practice

Exercise Decide whether the following pairs of words are synonyms or antonyms. On your paper, identify each pair as *Synonyms* or *Antonyms.* Remember that synonyms are words with nearly the same meaning. Antonyms have opposite meanings. Do not confuse words that describe different parts of something as antonyms. For example, the word *nape,* which describes the back of the neck, is not an antonym for the word *throat.*

1. tranquil—calm
2. caress—hit
3. conscientious—irresponsible
4. regime—government
5. foray—raid
6. tranquil—stormy
7. rejuvenate—revive
8. hone—sharpen
9. emit—discharge
10. whorl—spiral

Words to Know and Use

caress
conscientious
emit
foray
hone
nape
regime
rejuvenate
tranquil
whorl

Options for Learning

1 • Final Confessions Choose a partner with whom to act out the final scene of this story. Think about what the barber might say in response to Captain Torres's remark "They told me you would kill me." For his part, how far might Captain Torres push the barber into a confession that he is a revolutionary?

2 • Build a Barbershop Imagine you have been asked to design the set for a filming of this short story. Look back carefully at the story for clues as to how the set should look. Study pictures of old barbershops. Then draw or construct a model of the barbershop as you think it should appear on film.

3 • Business First Design a business card and stationery for either the barber or Captain Torres. Include a slogan that captures the man's beliefs about his occupation. Also include some type of small logo or graphic symbol that stands for his work.

4 • Leader of the People Imagine that you are the barber and have decided to speak out against Captain Torres in the town square. Make a list of the Captain's crimes against the people. Be sure to note that he represents a cruel regime, and include some of the wrongdoings of this government. Your speech should incite the townspeople to revolt, so when you rehearse, add emotion and enthusiasm. Then present a fiery speech to your classmates.

FACT FINDER

What is the name of the great vein right near the Adam's apple in your throat?

Hernando Téllez

1908–1966

"Lather and Nothing Else" incorporates two great interests of Hernando Téllez—writing and politics. Born in Bogotá, Colombia, Téllez entered politics as a career. He served in the Colombian Parliament and later as Colombia's ambassador to the United Nations Educational, Scientific, and Cultural Organization (UNESCO) in Paris. Téllez has written much about politics for newspapers and magazines, but he is also known as an accomplished short story writer. "Lather and Nothing Else" is from his book of short stories entitled *Cenizas para el Viento y Otras Historias (Ashes for the Wind and Other Stories).*

Options for Learning

These activities suit a variety of learning styles and modes of expression. Allow students to review the options and then choose the one they wish to do. Many are excellent collaborative learning projects.

1. Final Confessions Have students write out a draft of their script before acting it out.

2. Build a Barbershop Students might research by interviewing senior citizens in the community about their memories of old-fashioned barbershops.

3. Business First Suggest that students first collect business cards and stationery to guide them.

4. Leader of the People To support their views, students might create slogans ("Down with Tyranny," "Fight for Human Rights") and posters.

Fact Finder

Students may consult a physician, medical text, or an encyclopedia to find that this vein is called the jugular vein.

Additional Information About the Author

Hernando Telléz Hernando Telléz was in the forefront of a 1950s movement to convey a strong awareness of political and social problems. In 1950, when "Lather and Nothing Else" was published, Telléz's native Columbia was wracked by civil war. Unable to find a political solution to the internal strife, Telléz saw his writings as a call for reason and understanding in a desperate situation.

Closure

Suggest that at some point during the day students tune into their inner voices and write a paragraph of their thoughts as internal dialogue.

Cross-Curricular Options

Students should use the suggestions below to create a folder of "Background Notes" that includes ideas and information that provide context for the story.

Geography: Create a map of South America. Label countries, capitals, and other major cities. Provide a key explaining each map symbol.

Math: Find the per capita income of each South American country. Arrange the data on a chart in order from highest to lowest.

Social Studies: Locate facts about the government of each South American country. Write the name of the leader, his or her term of office, and the kind of government he or she heads.

Foreign Language: Identify and list the language spoken in each South American country. Use a Spanish-English dictionary to find the Spanish words for *barber, captain, revolutionary,* and other significant words from the story.

Publishing: Compile the contributions. Display or make copies to distribute.

Objectives

- To understand a true story from American history
- To recognize external and internal conflict
- To understand the use of contrast
- To express understanding of the work through a choice of writing options, including headlines, speeches, and paragraphs of comparison and contrast.

Prereading/Motivation

Examine What You Know

Discussion Prompts: What *beliefs* do people in your community hold? How do people show respect for the things and beliefs they value?

Expand Your Knowledge

Discussion Prompts: Why might white settlers have wanted the Indians' land? How did the settlers gain access to the land? How would you have settled the conflict between Cherokees and white settlers?

Enrich Your Reading

Have students copy the chart on page 130 and fill it in as they read. Possible answers: Cherokees: Treaty—The Cherokees could not believe that their chiefs had signed the treaty and did not support its terms. Gold—The Cherokees did not care about gold or the wealth it brought. Land—The Cherokees were deeply attached to their land and could not imagine leaving it. White Settlers: Treaty—The settlers supported the treaty because it opened the Cherokee land to them. Gold—The settlers were wildly excited at the thought of finding gold and getting rich. Land—The settlers were anxious to take the Cherokee land.

Thematic Link—A Matter of Life and Death
Tsali and his family must decide between giving up their ancestral lands or their lives.

e x p l o r e

Oral History

Tsali of the Cherokees

NORAH ROPER *as told to* ALICE MARRIOTT

Examine What You Know (Prior Knowledge)

In the story you are about to read, you will discover what two different groups of people value. In your journal or on a piece of paper, list the five things you value most. Then think of two people who are quite different from you but whom you know well, such as a brother and sister, an aunt and uncle, or two friends. How and why would their lists differ from yours?

Expand Your Knowledge (Building Background)

The Cherokees are an Indian tribe whose original home was the southeastern United States. In the early 1800's, the Cherokees were farmers and hunters who had established small manufacturing plants and schools and who even published a newspaper in their own language. White settlers, however, wanted the Indian land, and during the winter of 1838–1839, the Georgia militia forced approximately fifteen thousand Cherokees to leave their homes in the Great Smoky Mountains. So many Indians died on this forced march to Oklahoma that the route has become known as the Trail of Tears.

Enrich Your Reading (Reading Skill)

Contrast When you **contrast** characters, you look for differences. In this selection, the writer describes sharp differences between the white settlers and a group of Cherokees. As you read, use a chart like the one below to note these differences by indicating each group's attitude toward the subjects listed along the top.

	Treaty	Gold	Land
Cherokees			
White Settlers			

■ *A biography of the author can be found on page 141.*

Journal Writing

The Cherokee attitude toward the land and wealth was very different from that of white settlers. The clash of these two cultures became a matter of life and death. Suggest these journal topics:

- Discuss what makes a person rich in our culture.
- Discuss other forms of wealth.
- For other journal opportunities, refer students to Examine What You Know (p. 130) annotations C (p. T–131) and L (p. T–133) and Broader Connections (p. 139).

Additional Resources

UNIT ONE RESOURCE BOOK
Reader's Guidesheet, p. 60
Vocabulary Worksheet, p. 61
Selection and Vocabulary Check Tests, p. 62
Selection Tests, pp. 63–64

Collaborative Learning

Opportunities for collaborative learning appear throughout the lesson and include Real Life Connection (p. T–135) and Options for Learning and Cross-Curricular Options (p. T–141)

Tsali of the Cherokees

NORAH ROPER *as told to* ALICE MARRIOTT

In the time when their troubles began, the ordinary Cherokees did not at first understand that anything was really wrong. They knew that their tribal chiefs traveled back and forth to the white man's place called Washington more often than they used to do. They knew that when the chiefs came back from that place there were quarrels in the tribal council.

Up in the hills and the back country, where the *Ani Keetoowah*—the true Cherokees—lived, word of the changes came more slowly than the changes themselves came to the valley Cherokees. Many of the hill people never left their farm lands, and those who did went only to the nearest trading post and back. Few travelers ever came into the uplands, where the mists of the Smokies[1] shut out the encroaching world.

So, when the news came that some of the chiefs of the Cherokees had touched the pen, and put their names or their marks on a paper, and agreed by doing so that this was no longer Cherokee country, the *Ani Keetoowah* could not believe what they heard. Surely, they said to each other, this
B news must be false. No Cherokee—not even a mixed-blood—would sign away his own and his people's lands. But that was what the chiefs had done.

Then the word came that the chiefs were even more divided among themselves, and that not all of them had touched the pen. Some were not willing to move away to the new lands across the Mississippi and settle in the hills around Fort Gibson, Oklahoma.

"Perhaps we should hang on," the *Ani Keetoowah* said to one another. "Perhaps we will not have to go away after all." They waited and hoped, although they knew in their hearts that hope is the cruelest curse on mankind. C

One of the leaders of the *Ani Keetoowah* was Tsali. The white men had trouble pronouncing his name, so they called him "Charley" or "Dutch." Tsali was a full-blood, and so were his wife and their family. They were of the oldest *Keetoowah* Cherokee blood and would never have let themselves be shamed by having half-breed relatives.

Tsali and his four sons worked two hillsides and the valley between them, in the

1. **Smokies:** the Great Smoky Mountains (part of the Appalachian mountain system), in North Carolina and Tennessee.

Words to Know and Use	**encroaching** (en krōch′ iŋ) *adj.* advancing **encroach** *v.*

Teaching Strategies

Vocabulary Preview

These vocabulary words are defined at the bottom of the selection page on which they appear. You may wish to discuss them briefly before students begin reading.

askew to one side
encroaching advancing
loom a weaving machine
plunder to take by force
rheumatism illness that causes stiffness
smolder to burn without flame
sulkily resentfully
wrench to twist violently

Support for Students of Limited English Proficiency

- Use Reader's Guidesheet p. 60.
- The setting of "Tsali of the Cherokees," the Appalachian Mountains in the late 1830s, will present some difficulties to LEP students. In addition, the story is told from a Native-American perspective. Use encyclopedias, history texts, and other sources to build background for this setting and point of view.
- Annotations A, B, D, F, O, and R focus on troublesome vocabulary and details.

Text Annotations

A. LEP: Pronunciation The initial *ts* sound in *Tsali* may be unfamiliar to some. You might suggest that students can pronounce the name like "Zolly."

B. LEP: Vocabulary Elicit that a "mixed-blood" was a person with both Cherokee and white ancestors. Point out that the speaker, who prides herself on being a "true Cherokee," has little use for the mixed-bloods.

C. Critical Thinking: ANALYZING Ask students to explain how hope might be "a cruel curse." *(Possible response: Hope prevents people from making realistic adjustments to life's difficulties.)* Have them tell what this attitude toward hope reveals about the Cherokee culture. *(Possible response: The Cherokees were realists; they were very much rooted in the present.)*

Structured Reading for Less Proficient Students

These questions can help to guide students through the reading. Ask each question at the point of the selection where the SR number appears in the margin.

SR–1. How do Tsali and his family support themselves? *(They are farmers; they grow or make almost everything they need.)* **Summarizing**

SR–2. Why do the white settlers especially want Tsali's hillside land? *(Gold has been found there.)* **Literal recall**

SR–3. Why do soldiers come to Tsali's home? *(The soldiers come to remove Tsali's family and open the land to white settlers.)* **Summarizing**

SR–4. What do Tsali and his family do when the soldiers come to their farm? *(They escape into the woods.)* **Literal recall**

SR–5. What do the soldiers intend to do to Tsali and his family when they refuse to leave their land? *(They intend to shoot and kill them.)* **Literal recall**

D. LEP: Vocabulary The definition of *hollow*, a "low place between hills," may be unfamiliar.

E. Reading Skill: CONTRASTING Ask students to explain the term *worldly rich.* *(having money and many possessions)* Have them contrast Tsali's wealth with worldly wealth. (*Possible response: Tsali's wealth lay in his extended family, his farmland, his self-sufficient lifestyle, and his Cherokee traditions.*)

F. LEP: Comprehension Discuss the meaning of "the eternal fire that was the life of all Cherokees." Help students see that the fire symbolized the life of the tribe in the Cherokee religion.

G. Historical Sidelight Missionaries to the Cherokees were funded in part by the federal government. They taught farming, cooking, and the three R's. Few adult Cherokees gave up their native religion for Christianity. Cherokee children were often sent to distant mission schools.

H. Reading Skill: CONTRASTING Have students contrast the white man's attitude toward gold with Tsali's. *(Possible response: The missionary is "gold crazy"; he will do anything for gold. Tsali places no special value on gold, although he uses it to trade sometimes.)*

southern part of the hill country. Tsali and his wife and their youngest son lived in a log house at the head of the hollow. The others had their own homes, spread out along the hillsides. They grew corn and beans, a few English peas, squashes and pumpkins, tobacco and cotton, and even a little sugar cane and indigo.[2] Tsali's wife kept chickens in a fenced run[3] away from the house.

The women gathered wild hemp[4] and spun it; they spun the cotton, and the wool from their sheep. Then they wove the thread into cloth, and sometimes in winter when their few cattle and the sheep had been cared for and the chickens fed and there was not much else to do, the men helped at the looms which they had built themselves. The women did all the cutting and the making of garments for the whole family.

Tsali and his family were not worldly rich, in the way that the chiefs and some of the Cherokees of the valley towns were rich. They had hardly seen white man's metal money in their lives. But Tsali's people never lacked for food, or good clothing, or safe shelter.

The missionaries seldom came into the uplands then. Tsali took his sons and their wives, and his own wife, to the great dance ground where the seven *Keetoowah* villages gathered each month at the time of the full moon. There they danced their prayers in time to the beating of the women's terrapin-shell[5] leg rattles, around and around the mound of packed white ashes on top of which bloomed the eternal fire that was the life of all the Cherokees.

The occasional missionaries fussed over the children. They gave them white men's names, so by Tsali's time everyone had an Indian name and an English one. The Cherokees listened to the missionaries politely, for the missionaries were great gossips, and the Cherokees heard their news and ignored the rest of their words.

"You will have to go soon," said one white preacher to Tsali, "There's no hope this time. The lands have all been sold, and the Georgia troopers are moving in. You'll have to go west."

"We'll never leave," Tsali answered. "This is our land and we belong to it. Who could take it from us—who would want it? It's hard even for us to farm here, and we're used to hill farming. The white men wouldn't want to come here—they'll want the rich lands in the valleys, if the lowland people will give them up."

"They want these hills more than any other land," the missionary said. He sounded almost threatening. "Don't you see, you poor ignorant Indian? They are finding gold—gold, man, gold—downstream in the lower *Keetoowah* country. That means that the source of the gold is in the headwaters of the rivers that flow from here down into the valleys. I've seen gold dust in those streams myself."

"Gold?" asked Tsali. "You mean this yellow stuff?" And he took a buckskin pouch out of the pouch that hung from his sash, and opened it. At the sight of the yellow dust the pouch contained, the missionary seemed to go a little crazy.

2. **indigo:** a plant used to make blue dye.
3. **run:** an enclosed area for domestic animals.
4. **hemp:** a plant used to make rope.
5. **terrapin-shell:** turtle-shell.

Words to Know and Use

loom (lo͞om) *n.* a machine for weaving thread into cloth

Data Bank

Early treaties between the United States and the Cherokees punished the tribe for having sided with the British in the American Revolution. In the late 1700s, some Cherokees who opposed peaceful relations with whites moved west to Arkansas and Texas on their own accord. Unfair treaties forced other Cherokees to cede land and emigrate west in 1810 and again in 1817.

The traditionalist Cherokees who remained in the East resented white efforts to "civilize" them, efforts sometimes supported by mission-educated chiefs. The traditionalists viewed their homeland as the center of the world and a holy place. The West was the outer edge of the "island" where the spirits of the dead lived.

President Andrew Jackson pledged to "remove" remaining Cherokees and other tribes in the Southeast. The Treaty of New Echota, signed in 1835 by an unauthorized minority of Cherokee chiefs and protested by the entire Cherokee nation, gave the government authority to begin the removal now known as the Trail of Tears.

"That's it!" he cried. "Where did you get it? How did you find it? You'll be rich if you can get more."

"We find it in the rivers, as you said," Tsali replied. "We gather what we need to take to the trader. I have this now because I am going down to the valley in a few days, to get my wife some ribbons to trim her new dress."

I "Show me where you got it," the missionary begged. "We can all be rich. I'll protect you from the other white men, if you make me your partner."

"No, I think I'd better not," said Tsali thoughtfully. "My sons are my partners, as I was my father's. We do not need another partner, and, as long as we have our old squirrel guns, we do not need to be protected. Thank you, but you can go on. We are better off as we are." J

The missionary coaxed and threatened, but Tsali stood firm. In the end, the white man went away, without any gold except a pinch that Tsali gave him, because the missionary seemed to value the yellow dust even more than the trader did.

Then it was time to go to the trading post. K When Tsali came in the store, the trader said to him, "Well, Chief, glad to see you. I hear you're a rich man these days."

"I have always been a rich man," Tsali answered. "I have my family and we all have our good health. We have land to farm, houses to live in, food on our tables, and enough clothes. Most of all, we have the love in our hearts for each other and our friends. Indeed, you are right. We are very rich."

"That's one way of looking at it," said the trader, "but it isn't what I was thinking about. From what I hear, there's gold on your land. You've got a gold mine."

"A gold man?" repeated Tsali. "I never heard of a gold man."

"No!" shouted the trader. "A gold *mine,* I said. A place where you can go and pick up gold."

"Oh, that!" Tsali exclaimed. "Yes, we have some places like that on our land. Here's some of the yellow dust we find there."

And he opened the pouch to show the trader. The trader had seen pinches of Tsali's gold dust before, and taken it in trade, without saying much about it. Now he went as crazy as the missionary. "Don't tell anybody else about this, Charley," he whispered, leaning over the counter. "We'll just keep it to ourselves. I'll help you work it out, and I'll keep the other white men away. We'll all be rich." ◀SR-2

"Thank you," said Tsali, "but I don't believe I want to be rich that way. I just want enough of this stuff to trade you for ribbons and sugar."

"Oh, all right," answered the trader sulkily, "have it your own way. But don't blame me if you're sorry afterwards." L

"I won't blame anybody," said Tsali, and bought his ribbon.

A month later, when the Georgia militia[6] came riding up the valley to Tsali's house, the missionary and the trader were with them. The men all stopped in front of the house, and Tsali's wife came out into the dogtrot, the open-ended passage that divided the two halves of the house and made

6. **militia:** an army made up of ordinary citizens instead of professional soldiers.

Words to Know and Use

sulkily (sul' kə lē) *adv.* in a resentful or glum manner

I. Literary Element: IRONY Ask students why the missionary's behavior is unexpected. *(Possible response: We expect missionaries to be interested in spiritual and religious matters, not get-rich-quick schemes.)*

J. Historical Sidelight Cherokees disapproved of anyone who tried to produce more than was needed to survive. They killed game only when necessary. At the Green Corn Ceremony, held each year when the corn was first edible, they destroyed surplus food and goods in a gesture of renewal.

K. Reading Skill: PREDICTING Have students tell what they think will happen now that white people know there is gold on Tsali's land. *(Possible response: The whites will make an effort to remove him quickly and gain the land for themselves.)*

L. Critical Thinking: EVALUATING Have students discuss Tsali's attitudes toward wealth. Have them decide whether his ignoring the white men's interest in his gold is wise or foolish.

M. Reading Skill: CONTRASTING Ask students to contrast the way Amanda talks to the soldiers with the way they talk to her. *(Amanda is friendly and polite; the soldiers are condescending and rude.)*

Historical Sidelight According to other accounts of this incident, Tsali and his sons killed two soldiers involved in the Cherokee round-up. To punish them, General Winfield Scott enlisted the aid of a group of Cherokees called the Oconaluftee. In return for finding and executing Tsali, these Indians were allowed to remain in North Carolina. After Tsali's death, General Scott removed the soldiers from the area, and hundreds of other fugitive Cherokees came out of hiding. Their descendants are known as the Eastern Band of Cherokees.

N. Reading Skill: INFERRING Ask students what Amanda might have had in mind by giving her son Tsali's gun. *(Possible response: She wanted him to be armed in case he decided to resist the soldiers.)*

A Cherokee cabin
Smithsonian Institution, Washington, D.C.

a cool breezeway where the family sat in warm weather. She spoke to the men.

"Won't you come in and sit down?"

"Where's the old man?" the militia captain asked.

M "Why, he's working out in the fields," said Amanda. "Sit down and have a cool drink of water while I send the boy for him."

"Send the boy quickly," the captain ordered. "We'll wait in our saddles and not trouble to get down."

"All right, if you'd rather not," Amanda said. "Do you mind telling me why you're here?"

"We're here to put you off this place," said the captain. "Haven't you heard? This isn't Cherokee land any more; the chiefs signed it over to the government, and now it's open for settlement. One or the other of these two gentlemen will probably claim it."

SR-3 ▶ "They can't do that!" Amanda protested. "It's our land—nobody else's. The chiefs had no right to sign it away. My husband's father worked this place, and his father before him. This is our home. This is where we belong."

"No more," said the captain. "You belong in the removal camps down by the river, with the rest of the Indians. They're going to start shipping the Cherokees west tomorrow morning."

Amanda sat down on the bench in the dogtrot, with her legs trembling under her. "All of us?" she asked.

"Every one of you."

"Let me call my son and send him for his daddy," Amanda said.

"Hurry up!"

Amanda went into the house, calling to the boy, who was just fourteen and had been standing, listening, behind the door. She gave him his father's old squirrel gun, N and he sneaked his own blowgun and darts and slid out the back of the house. Amanda went back to the dogtrot and sat and waited. She sat there and waited, while the missionary, the trader, and the captain quarreled about which of their wives should cook in her kitchen. She let them quarrel and hoped her men were all right.

Tsali and his older sons were working the
O overhill corn field, when the boy came panting up, and told them what had happened.

"Is your mother all right?" Tsali asked.

"She was when I left," the boy answered.

"We'll hide in the woods till they're gone," Tsali told his older sons. "If they find us, they'll have to kill us to put us off this land."

"What about the women?" the oldest son asked.

"They'll be all right," Tsali answered. "Your mother's a quick-thinking woman; she'll take care of them. If we can hide in the caves by the river till dark, we'll go back then and get them."

They slipped away into the woods, downhill to the river, taking the boy with them, although he offered to go back and tell the white men he couldn't find his father.

All afternoon Amanda waited. Her daughters-in-law saw the strange men and horses in front of the big house and came to join her. At dusk, the captain gave up and ordered his men to make camp in the front yard. "We'll wait here until the men come back," he said.

With the white men camped all around the house, the women went into the kitchen and barred all the doors. It was a long time before the campfires made from the fence pickets ceased to blaze and began to smolder. It was a longer time until the women heard it—a scratch on the back door, so soft and so light that it would have embarrassed a mouse. Amanda slid back the bar, and Tsali and his sons slipped into the darkened room. There was just enough moonlight for them to make out each other's shapes.

"We came to get you," Tsali said. "Come quickly. Leave everything except your knives. Don't wait a minute."

Amanda and her daughters-in-law always wore their knives at their belts, so they were ready. One at a time, Tsali last, the whole family crept out of their home and escaped into the woods. ◀SR-4

In the morning, when the white men stretched and scratched and woke, the *Ani Keetoowah* were gone. P

It was spring, and the weather was warm, but the rain fell and soaked the Cherokees. They had brought no food, and they dared not fire a gun. One of the daughters-in-law was pregnant, and her time was close. Amanda was stiff and crippled with rheumatism. They gathered wild greens, for it was too early for berries or plums, and the men and boy trapped small animals and birds in string snares the women made by pulling out their hair and twisting it. Q

Day by day, for four weeks, the starving family listened to white men beating through the woods. The Cherokees were tired and cold and hungry, but they were silent. They even began to hope that in time the white men would go away and the Indians would be safe.

It was not to be. One trooper brought his dog, and the dog caught the human scent. So the dog, with his man behind him, came sniffing into the cave, and Tsali and his family were caught before the men could pick up their loaded guns.

The militiaman shouted, and other white

Words to Know and Use

smolder (smōl′ dər) *v.* to burn and smoke without flame
rheumatism (ro͞o′ mə tiz əm) *n.* an inflammation and stiffness of the joints and muscles

135

O. LEP: Vocabulary Call attention to the phrase *came panting up.* Ask students how people breathe after running a long way. Then have them define *panting.*

P. Critical Thinking: ANALYZING Have students discuss what the author implies about Tsali's family with the term *Ani Keetoowah,* or "true Cherokee." *(Possible response: Tsali's family is true to its heritage and traditions by refusing to cooperate with the removal plan.)*

Q. Literary Element: SETTING Have students tell how the weather and season worsen the family's plight. *(Wet weather soaks the Cherokees; in the early spring season, there is little wild food to gather.)*

REAL LIFE CONNECTIONS

Point out that Tsali and his family were willing to resist the militia, preferring death to the loss of their land. Ask students to think of other real-life examples in which people have courageously resisted a military force or a law that they considered unjust. *(Possible examples include abolitionists who helped runaway slaves, conscientious objectors who went to jail in wartime, and resistance fighters who fought against Nazi occupation.)* Have them discuss what leads some individuals to take such decisive action. Ask them whether they can imagine any situations in which they would risk jail, injury, or death for a belief or cause.

R. LEP: Comprehension Have students reread Tsali's words. Ask them to explain why they are written separated by dashes. *(Possible response: The separation of the words emphasizes Tsali's quiet determination.)*

men came thudding through the woods. They tied the Cherokee men's hands behind them and bound them all together along a rope. The militiamen pushed Tsali and his sons through the woods. The women followed, weeping.

At last, they were back at their own house, but they would not have recognized it. The troopers had plundered the garden, and trampled the plants they didn't eat. The door from the kitchen into the dogtrot hung askew, and the door to the main room had been wrenched off its hinges. Clothes and bedding lay in filthy piles around the yard. What the militiamen could not use, they ruined.

"Oh, my garden!" cried Amanda, and, when she saw the scattered feathers, "Oh, my little hens!"

"What are you going to do with us?" Tsali demanded.

"Take you down to the river. The last boat is loading today. There's still time to get you on it and out of here."

"I—will—not—go," Tsali said quietly. "You—nor you—nor you—nobody can make me go." R

"Our orders are to take all the Cherokees. If any resist, shoot them." ◀SR-6

"Shoot me, then!" cried Tsali. The captain raised his rifle.

"Stop!" Amanda screamed. She stepped over beside her husband. "If you shoot, shoot us both," she ordered. "Our lives have

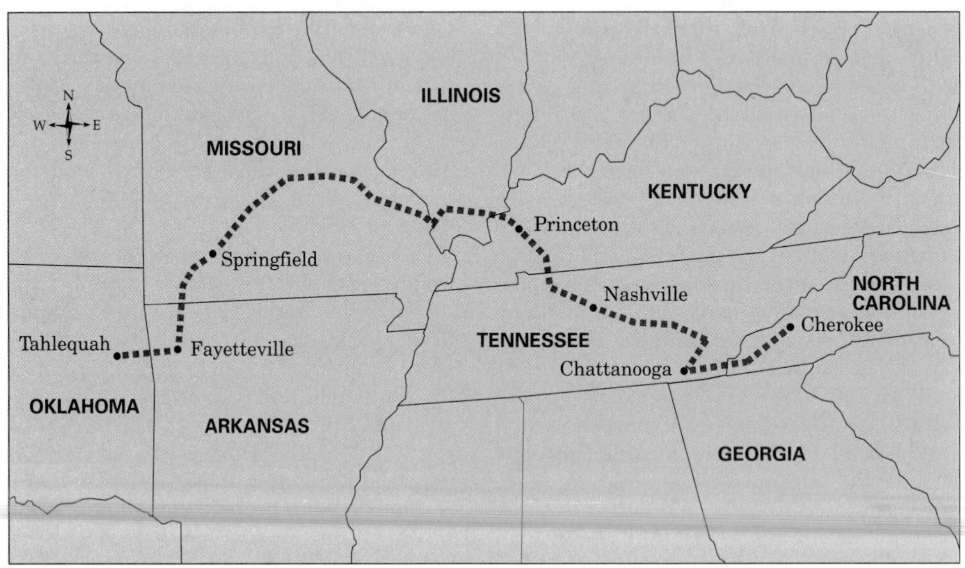

Dotted line indicates route of Trail of Tears from North Carolina to Oklahoma.

Words to Know and Use

plunder (plun′ dər) *v.* to take property by force for one's own purposes
askew (ə skyōō′) *adv.* to one side
wrench (rench *v.* to twist or pull violently

136

PROFESSIONAL NOTEBOOK

The more I teach, the more convinced I am that one of the essential roles of the teacher is to make it possible for even the most difficult and unhappy individuals to feel supported and welcome within a group of their peers. It frees them to learn and to share what they know in return for the welcome they receive. The difficult ones, once integrated into a group, provide the strength and spirit to the whole that for me as a teacher results in a challenging and yet congenial class.

Herbert Kohl, *Growing Minds: On Becoming a Teacher*

been one life since we were no older than our boy here. I don't want to go on living without my husband. And I cannot leave our home any more than he can. Shoot us both."

The four sons stepped forward. "We will die with our parents," the oldest one said. S "Take our wives to the boat, if that is the only place where they can be safe, but we stay here." He turned to his wife and the other young women.

"That is my order as your husband," Tsali's son said. "You must go away to the west and make new lives for yourselves while you are still young enough to do so." The wives sobbed and held out their arms, but the husbands turned their backs on the women. "We will stay with our parents," all the young men said.

The young boy, too, stood with his brothers, beside his father. "Let this boy go," Tsali said to the white men. "He is so young. A man grows, and plants his seed, and his seed goes on. This is my seed. I planted it. My older sons and I have had our chances. They will leave children, and their names will never be forgotten. But this boy is too young. His seed has not ripened for planting yet. Let him go to care for his sisters on the way to the west." T

"Very well," said the captain. "He can't do much harm if he does live." He turned to two militiamen. "Take the boy and the young women away," he ordered. "Keep them going till they come to the boats, and load them on board."

The young women and the boy, stunned and silenced, were driven down the road before they could say goodbye, nor would the troopers let them look back. Behind them, as they started on the long main road, they heard the sound of the shots. ❧

S. Historical Sidelight Boats carried some Cherokees down the Tennessee River to an assembly point for the long Trail of Tears. The Indians made the actual journey across Tennessee, Kentucky, Missouri, Arkansas, and Oklahoma in horsedrawn wagons or on foot.

T. Reading Skill: CLARIFYING Have students explain why Tsali sends his youngest son away. *(Possible response: Tsali wants his son to live long enough to have children, who will then carry on the family name.)*

Literary Sidelight Point out the byline of the story. Explain that Norah Roper, the granddaughter of the main character Tsali, was told this story by members of her family. Have students speculate on why she told it to the author, Alice Marriott. *(Possible response: She wanted it preserved in written form so it could reach a wider audience.)*

Check Test

1. What does Tsali have that the white men want? *(land and gold)*

2. Where do Tsali and his family hide from the militia? *(in a cave near the river)*

3. What do the militia plan to do with Tsali's family? *(They plan to send the family to the West.)*

4. What do Tsali, his wife, and sons choose to do? *(They choose to die rather than yield.)*

Encouraging Independent Reading

The Delight Makers, a novel by Adolph Bandelier
Bury My Heart at Wounded Knee, nonfiction by Dee Brown
The Trail of Tears: The Rise and Fall of the Cherokee Nation, nonfiction by John Ehle
The Way to Rainy Mountain, nonfiction by N. Scott Momaday

Art Note

Jerry Ingram (1941–) is a Choctaw Indian whose sculptures, designs and paintings are widely exhibited. Since his school days in Oklahoma, Ingram has been interested in the cultures and rituals of other tribes as well as those of the Choctaw. This watercolor depicts a Plains warrior who has fasted and prayed for spiritual power as represented by the eagle. *Why is the eagle an appropriate symbol?*

INSIGHT

Red Eagle

JANET CAMPBELL

Red eagle.
Cold, dead, noble, Red Eagle.
Tomorrow they will bury you in Black
  Hill.
They think you have left me forever.
When I grow lonely for you I will walk
  into the night and listen to your
  brother, the wind.
He will tell me if you want me.
I will follow the path through the forest
  upon which your moccasins have
  trod so many times.
I will hear the night sounds you have
  told me about.
I will walk into the valley of Minnelosa
  the sweet grass.
In the white moonlight I will pray.
I will pray to the spirits and they will
  speak to me as they have spoken
  to you before.
Then I will touch your tree and you
  will softly whisper to me.
From the wind, from the night, from
  the trees, from the sweet grass,
You will whisper to me, Red Eagle,
  Red Eagle,
  Upon the mountain.

WHEN THE EAGLE SPOKE TO ME 1979 Jerry Ingram
By permission of the artist.

Insight

This piece reflects on the ideas in the main selection and is suggested for students' independent reading. Optional discussion questions follow.

1. What event seems to have prompted the poet to write this poem? *(the death of Red Eagle)*

2. Why is the speaker convinced that Red Eagle hasn't left her forever? *(The speaker believes that through nature she can communicate with Red Eagle's spirit.)*

3. The poem suggests that nature is an important part of Native American religion. Explain. *(Possible response: The spirits of the dead seem to inhabit features of the landscape, such as trees and the mountain.)*

4. Recall that the story of Tsali was told by his granddaughter, Norah Roper. How do you think her feelings for Tsali are similar to the speaker's feelings for Red Eagle? *(Possible response: Both selections show love and respect for the dead; both speakers look to the dead for inspiration.)*

e x p l a i n

Responding to Reading

First Impressions

1. How do you feel about Tsali's fatal decision?

Second Thoughts

2. Why do Tsali and other Cherokees ignore the warnings about the need to leave their land?

   Think about
   - the disagreement among Cherokee chiefs
   - Tsali's attitude about the value of gold
   - Amanda's protest to the militia men who claim her home

3. What do Tsali and his family value?

4. How are the values of the white settlers different from those of the Indians?

5. Do Tsali, his wife, and their four sons make the right decision? Explain.

   Think about
   - the treaty the Cherokee chiefs had signed
   - Tsali's family's feelings about the land
   - the surviving son
   - what, if anything, was gained by their deaths

6. The writer says that "hope is the cruelest curse on mankind." How does the story support this view?

Broader Connections

7. People throughout history have been displaced from their homes when their land suddenly became valuable or needed for a specific purpose. Perhaps someone you know has been displaced in order to build a new state highway or sports stadium, for example. For what other purposes have people been displaced? Is such displacement ever justifiable? Why or why not?

Literary Concept: Conflict

The struggle between opposing forces in a story is called **conflict.** A struggle between characters or between a character and an outside force is an **external conflict. Internal conflict** is a mental struggle within a character. What is the main conflict in "Tsali of the Cherokees"? How is this conflict resolved or ended?

Literary Concept—Conflict
Some students may say that the main conflict is between Tsali and his family and the white soldiers. Others may say that the main conflict is between Tsali and the missionary and trader. Still others may say that the main conflict is between the Cherokees and the white settlers. In any case, students should say that this is an example of external conflict that is resolved with Tsali's death.

Student Response

Responding to Reading
These questions are open-ended with no "right" or "wrong" answers. However, responses must be supported with information from the selection. Possible answers follow:

1. Any response supported by the story is valid.

2. Some students may say that as a farmer in a remote area, Tsali was not really aware of the plan to remove the Indians. He did not realize the lengths to which white men would go for gold. Others may add that Tsali did not think the chiefs would serve their people so badly, nor could he imagine living elsewhere.

3. Tsali and his family value their love for each other, their home and land, and their traditional way of life.

4. While the Cherokees love their land for what it is, the whites value land for the gold or other wealth it can bring. The Cherokees see wealth as living simply in the traditional ways. The whites see wealth as having surplus money to buy things.

5. Some students might say that Tsali and his family did the right thing, standing up for their principles and traditions. Others might suggest that Tsali, Amanda, and their sons should not have given up their lives just because they had lost their land.

6. Students may say that Tsali hoped that the rumors about removal were wrong; he hoped that he could trust his white neighbors; later he hoped he could hide out until the soldiers went away. In all these hopes, he was cruelly disappointed.

7. Students' answers will vary concerning the purposes people have been displaced. Some students may say that displacement is justifiable if it is done within the legal system for the good of the community and if people are paid for the losses they suffer. Others may feel that people should not be displaced from their homes simply so that someone else can benefit financially. People faced with this situation should organize to block unwanted or unnecessary displacement.

Writing Options

The Writing Options are designed to meet varied student interests and abilities. Have each student choose one writing activity to complete. You may wish to guide some students to an option that requires less writing.

Journal Update Have students review their journal entries for the story. Ask them to add to their writings any reflections they may now have about the meaning of wealth.

Vocabulary Practice

1. Correct

2. Incorrect
Encroaching means "advancing"; a house cannot advance.

3. Incorrect
Wrench means "pull violently"; Tsali could not do this to his farm.

4. Incorrect
Smolder means "to burn"; rain would put out the smoldering fire.

5. Correct

6. Incorrect
Sulkily means "in a resentful manner," and the trader is speaking of happiness and excitement.

7. Correct

8. Correct

9. Correct

10. Incorrect
A *loom* is used for making cloth, not bread.

Writing Options

1. Like the white settlers of those times, the Cherokee people published their own newspaper in their own language. Imagine that both the Cherokee and the white newspapers have run a story on Tsali's death. For each story, write a headline that captures that paper's viewpoint.

2. Tsali gives his definition of a rich man in this story. Make two columns on a piece of paper. In one column list Tsali's ideas of what a rich man is. In the second column list your own ideas of what rich means. Then in a paragraph tell how the two lists are alike and different.

3. Imagine that the captain of the militia hires a public relations firm to help him convince the Cherokees to leave their land and go to Oklahoma. Write the speech that the public relations firm might prepare for the captain.

4. Tsali must make a life-and-death decision in this story. Compare Tsali's decision to the decision of the main character in "Lather and Nothing Else." Before you write your paragraph, think about these questions:
   - What forced each person into his choice?
   - What were the consequences?
   - How were others affected?

Vocabulary Practice

Exercise Read each sentence below. If the boldfaced word is used correctly, write *Correct*. If it is used incorrectly, write *Incorrect*. If a word is incorrect, explain why.

1. The door hung **askew** after the soldiers forced it open.
2. The Indians' house was left **encroaching** once the soldiers departed.
3. Tsali had to **wrench** his farm in the mountains.
4. The crops began to **smolder** after the spring rains.
5. Amanda was stiff from her **rheumatism.**
6. "I'd be excited and happy to have some of your gold," answered the trader **sulkily.**
7. When the Cherokees left their farm, they did not know that the soldiers would ruin and **plunder** everything.
8. Without any more wood, the fire was beginning to **smolder.**
9. In order to scare the Indians away, the soldiers would **wrench** the doors of the houses off their hinges.
10. The children worked hard at the **loom** making fresh bread for the family.

Words to Know and Use

askew
encroaching
loom
plunder
rheumatism
smolder
sulkily
wrench

e x t e n d

Options for Learning

1 • Stories Without Words Imagine that you are Tsali's surviving son. Draw the series of pictures that he might draw to tell the story of his family's tragedy.

2 • Stories with Words Like "Tsali of the Cherokees," Native American history is an oral history. In other words, facts about events have been passed down among family members and tribes through word of mouth rather than in written form. Retell this story using important details and some of the dialogue from the selection. If possible, tape-record your version of the story and share it with younger students.

3 • Native American Beliefs Early Native Americans had different feelings about the land than did European settlers. In your library, research the beliefs of the Cherokees or another Native American tribe about the land and nature. Write a short report telling how their beliefs and actions differed from the beliefs and actions of the European settlers.

4 • Round-Table Talk With five of your classmates, role-play a discussion among the following characters from the story: the captain of the militia, a Cherokee chief who signed the government treaty, Tsali's youngest son, a Cherokee woman who survived the Trail of Tears, the missionary, and the trader. Have each character express his or her opinion about the following statement: Tsali and his people should have obeyed the militia's orders.

FACT FINDER

How many Cherokees escaped the forced march to Oklahoma and remained in the Great Smoky Mountains of western North Carolina?

Alice Marriott

1905–

At the age of five, while visiting a grandfather who was the curator of Egyptology at Chicago's Field Museum, Alice Marriott wandered off by herself. To her delight, she discovered the museum's Indian totem poles. This early interest in ancient cultures blossomed at the University of Oklahoma, where she became the first woman to receive a degree in anthropology. From Oklahoma she traveled to Oregon to study American Indians. "We lived in tents, interviewed elderly Modoc Indians, and I fell completely and permanently in love with the desert country in general and Oregon in particular." Marriott later returned to Oklahoma and became "one of the lucky few who worked with Plains Indians while the last of the buffalo hunters were still around." She has written many books and articles on Native Americans including "Tsali of the Cherokees," which was told to her by Norah Roper, Tsali's granddaughter. Marriott now lives in Oklahoma City.

Options for Learning

These activities suit a variety of learning styles and modes of expression. Allow students to review the options and then choose the one they wish to do. Many are excellent collaborative learning projects.

1. Stories Without Words Suggest that students first look at examples of Indian history paintings.

2. Stories With Words Students should practice inflection and gestures that express feeling.

3. Native American Beliefs Suggest that students make an outline before they begin their first drafts. Students may also want to make a chart of their findings.

4. Round-Table Talk Students may want to prepare written opening statements for their characters.

Fact Finder

Approximately 1,000 Cherokees escaped the forced march by hiding in the remote mountains of western North Carolina, much as Tsali tried to do. These people came to be known as the Eastern Band of Cherokees. Students can find out about these people by looking up Eastern Band of Cherokees in an encyclopedia or reference book.

Additional Information About the Author

Alice Marriott Alice Marriott lived and worked for ten years with various Oklahoma Indian tribes, including the Kiowas and Cherokees. An adopted member of three Indian families, Ms. Marriott has become a skilled teller of Indian stories. Among her many books are *Indians on Horseback, The Ten Grandmothers,* and *Maria: The Potter of San Ildefonso.*

Closure

This selection focuses on a matter of life and death in that Tsali and his family choose death over giving up their land and way of life. Ask students to name other instances in American history when individuals have braved death in order to hold on to what is theirs.

Cross-Curricular Options

Students could work in groups to create an "Indian Facts Almanac," using details from the selection when possible. Suggestions include:

Geography: Create a map of the United States showing where selected Indian tribes lived. Indicate the route of the Trail of Tears.

Language Arts: Locate a copy of the Cherokee alphabet, or syllabary, created by Sequoyah. Practice writing a few words in Cherokee.

Social Studies: Collect samples of letters, diaries, and other primary sources that provide insight into traditional Indian life.

Foreign Languages: Make a list of place names that come from Indian languages. Include translations of the words, if possible.

Art History: Locate early paintings and photographs of traditional Indian life. Write captions for these pictures.

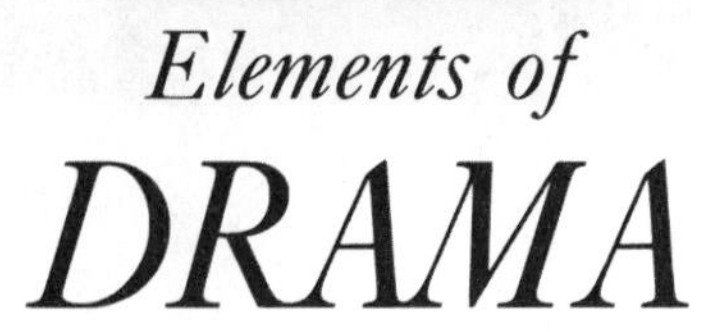

Elements of Drama

This feature gives students a common vocabulary with which to express their reactions to drama. The terms on these pages are covered in depth in the selections that follow.

Objectives

- To understand and appreciate drama
- To become familiar with the elements of drama
- To understand strategies for reading drama
- To explore the link between form and content in drama

Motivation

Allow students a few minutes to brainstorm a list of terms that they associate with drama, such as *actor* and *actress*. Then have volunteers come to the chalkboard to list a few of the words that they generated. Your list may look like this:

script	curtains
scenery	props
characters	dialogue

Complete the motivation by asking students the following questions: Which of these terms do you consider the most important? Why? Why do you think dramas are so popular with so many different people? Which dramas have you seen performed on TV, in movies, in videos, and on stage that you especially enjoyed?

Elements of *DRAMA*

When you hear the word *drama,* you probably think first of a play performed on stage before a live audience. Drama, however, takes many forms. Television programs, radio plays, and movies are also forms of drama. Drama, in fact, is any form of literature that is meant to be performed before an audience. All forms of drama, no matter where each is performed, share certain elements.

Understanding Drama

Script Drama begins with a **script**—the written form of the play. The playwright, or author of the play, creates the script from his or her imagination. However, the events may be based on real life. Like any story, a script has settings, characters, a plot, and one or more themes.

Cast of Characters The script usually begins with a list of the **cast**—the characters that will appear in the play. Often, a short description appears by each character's name. To help the audience recognize each character, the cast is listed in order of appearance rather than in order of each character's importance to the story.

Dialogue Most of the story of a play is told through the words, or **dialogue,** of the characters. The actors and actresses recite the dialogue written by the playwright. These conversations move the plot forward and show what the characters are like. As in the example below, from *The Monkey's Paw* (page 144), the words are written in lines next to the name of the character who will speak them.

Mrs. White. What's it for?

Sergeant. You wouldn't believe me, if I was to tell you.

Herbert. *I* will, every word.

Stage Directions Within the script, playwrights include a set of instructions, or **stage directions,** to help the actors, actresses, and audience comprehend the action. Stage directions normally appear in a different kind of type, such as italics, and are separated from the rest of the script by parentheses or brackets. These directions serve a number of functions. They may describe the **scenery,** or the decorations on stage that help show the setting of the play. They may describe **props**—the objects that the actors need—or they may describe lighting, costumes, music, or sound effects. Stage directions are most often used to explain how the characters should move and speak.

Look at the following stage directions taken from *The Monkey's Paw.* Notice that the directions explain how to read the dialogue and that they are set off from the rest of the text.

Sergeant *(impressively)***.** That there paw has had a spell put upon it!

Mr. White. No? *(In great alarm, he thrusts the paw back into Morris's hand.)*

Scene and Act The plot of a drama is divided into scenes. Each **scene** establishes a different setting, either in time or place. Long plays are divided into acts. Each **act** is a group of smaller scenes. *The Monkey's Paw* is a one-act play with three scenes.

Strategies for Reading Drama

1. **Preview the play.** Before you begin to read a play, preview, or look ahead at, the title, cast of characters, number of scenes and acts, any illustrations, and any opening stage directions. These details will help you mentally set the stage for the drama you are about to read.

2. **First read the play silently.** Plays are intended to be read aloud. However, silently reading the play before you read it aloud helps you to understand the plot and characters. Read to understand why the characters behave the way they do and what conflicts they are trying to resolve. Once you understand the plot line, you can concentrate on following stage directions when you read the play aloud.

3. **Take note of the stage directions.** The stage directions set the scene and describe how the characters look, move, and speak. When you first read a play, use the stage directions to help you visualize how the stage looks with its scenery and props. Imagine what the characters look like. Carefully read any directions following a character's name to see what emotions or movements the playwright wants used with the dialogue. Paying careful attention to the stage directions will help you picture the changing scenes of the play and the actions the playwright expects from the actors and actresses.

4. **Summarize and predict.** When you come to the end of a scene or an act, take a few moments to summarize, or restate, the major events of the section you have just read. Note what effect the conflict is having on each of the characters. Ask yourself if any of the characters seem to be changing as a result of their interactions with each other. If a character's words or actions are confusing, reread the section that is unclear. Then try to predict what you think will happen in the next scene. How will the main characters resolve their conflicts? How might the characters change in the process?

5. **Read the play aloud.** When you read the play aloud, remember to read only the dialogue and not the stage directions. Look ahead for your part, if you have been assigned one, so that you are ready to read when it is your turn. Take note of the stage directions, especially those that pertain to your tone of voice and actions. Think about how your character really feels about the events in the play, and let your facial expressions and body movements reflect your character's emotions.

Teaching Strategies

1. To introduce students to the elements of drama, read the first paragraph on page 142 aloud while students follow along silently. Then have students explain in their own words what you read.

Discussion Prompts: Why do you think so many people associate the word *drama* with plays performed on stage before a live audience? Do you prefer seeing dramas live, on TV, or in the movies? Or do you prefer listening to them over the radio? What do you find most enjoyable about any type of drama?

2. Next talk about the terms under the heading *Understanding Drama*. Highlight each of the examples. For reinforcement, have students find examples of each term from the other dramas in their text.

3. Discuss the reading strategies on page 143.

Closure

Have students briefly describe in their journals a drama that they have enjoyed. Urge students to use some of the terms that they just learned.

Objectives

- To understand a classic story retold in drama form
- To recognize and understand foreshadowing
- To recognize and understand the use of dialect
- To express understanding of the work through a choice of writing options, including morals and descriptions

Prereading/Motivation

Examine What You Know

Discussion Prompts: What needs and/or wants in your life could be fulfilled if you had three wishes? How would each wish improve your life? If your wishes were granted exactly as written, what unpleasant surprises might you face?

Expand Your Knowledge

Discussion Prompts: Name some fairy tales or other stories in which magic charms or the number three are important. What are the outcomes of any wishes made in these stories? Why do some people believe in magic charms while others do not?

Enrich Your Reading

Discuss the pronunciations and spelling patterns of the words on the list. Then have students take turns pronouncing them. Ask students to discuss any examples of regional dialects that they know.

Thematic Link—A Matter of Life and Death

This drama focuses on "a matter of life and death" as the characters use a magic charm with deadly results.

explore

Drama

The Monkey's Paw

W. W. JACOBS dramatized by LOUIS N. PARKER

Examine What You Know (Prior Knowledge)

A main character in this play is given three wishes. In a chart like the one below, list three wishes you would make if you knew they would come true. Then tell why you made each wish.

First Wish	Reason
Second Wish	Reason
Third Wish	Reason

Expand Your Knowledge (Building Background)

The play you are about to read contains a number of elements that are common in folklore. One is the use of a magic charm, in this case a monkey's paw. In India, monkeys are sacred animals that are highly honored and sometimes believed to have magical powers. Another magical element that occurs in this play is the number three, which many people and cultures believe has magic or supernatural qualities. The old saying that bad luck travels in threes reflects the latter belief.

Enrich Your Reading (Reading Skill)

Dialect The variety of language spoken in one place by a group of people is called a **dialect.** The dialect in "The Monkey's Paw" is that of working-class people on the outskirts of London. The writer spells words as they would be spoken. Before you begin reading the play, review the examples of dialect and their meanings below.

Lor, no!—Lord, no!	to've—to have	s'pose—suppose
d'you or d'ye—do you	'ooked—hooked	ha'—have
marm—ma'am *or* madam	'ee—ye *or* you	ay—yes
'ardship—hardship	'un—one	o'—of

■ *A biography of the author can be found on page 163.*

Journal Writing

A magic charm and how its owners use it is the focus of this drama based on a classic short story. Suggest these journal topics:

- Discuss any "lucky" or "magic" items that you or someone you know or have read about has used.
- Imagine that the monkey's paw in the title is a magic charm. Explain how the magic might work.

For other journal opportunities, refer students to annotation FF (p. T–159) and Broader Connections (p. 161).

Additional Resources

UNIT ONE RESOURCE BOOK

Reader's Guidesheet, p. 65
Vocabulary Worksheet, p. 66
Selection and Vocabulary Check Tests, p. 67
Selection Test, pp. 68–69.

Collaborative Learning

Opportunities for collaborative learning appear throughout the lesson and include Teaching Tip (p. T–150), Options for Learning (p. 163) and Cross-Curricular Options (p. T–163).

The Monkey's Paw

W. W. JACOBS *dramatized by* LOUIS N. PARKER

CHARACTERS

Mr. White

Mrs. White

Herbert

Sergeant-Major Morris

Mr. Sampson

Scene: *The living room of an old-fashioned cottage on the outskirts of Fulham. Set cornerwise in the left angle at the back a deep window; farther front, three or four steps lead up to a door. Farther forward a dresser, with plates, glasses, etc. At back an* alcove *with the street door fully visible. On the inside of the street door, a wire letter box. On the right a cupboard, then a fireplace. In the center a round table. Against the wall, an old-fashioned piano. A comfortable armchair each side of the fireplace. Other chairs. On the mantelpiece a clock, old china figures, etc. An air of comfort* pervades *the room.*

Scene 1

A *At the rise of the curtain,* Mrs. White, *a pleasant-looking old woman, is seated in the armchair below the fire, attending to a kettle which is steaming on the fire, and keeping a laughing eye on* Mr. White *and* Herbert. *These two are seated at the right angle of the table nearest the fire with a chessboard between them.* Mr. White *is evidently losing. His hair is ruffled; his spectacles are high up on his forehead.* Herbert, *a fine young fellow, is looking with satisfaction at the move he has just made.* Mr. White *makes several attempts to move but thinks better of them. There is a shaded lamp on the table. The door is tightly shut. The curtains of the window are drawn; but every now and then the wind is heard whistling outside.*

Mr. White *(moving at last, and triumphant).* There, Herbert, my boy! Got you, I think.

Herbert. Oh, you're a deep 'un, Dad, aren't you?

Mrs. White. Mean to say he's beaten you at last?

Herbert. Lor, no! Why, he's overlooked—

Mr. White *(very excited).* I see it! Lemme have that back!

Herbert. Not much. Rules of the game!

Mr. White *(disgusted).* I don't hold with them scientific rules. You turn what ought to be an innocent relaxation—

Mrs. White. Don't talk so much, Father. You put him off—[1]

Herbert *(laughing).* Not he!

1. **you put him off:** you upset him.

Words to Know and Use	**alcove** (al′ kōv′) *n.* a section of a room that is recessed and set apart **pervade** (pər vād′) *v.* to spread throughout

145

Teaching Strategies

Vocabulary Preview

These vocabulary words are defined at the bottom of the selection page on which they appear. You may wish to discuss them briefly before students begin reading.

addle to confuse
alcove a recessed area
bog a swamp
compensation a making up for
disclaim to refuse to claim
fret to worry
infernal fiendish
involuntary unintentional
pensively thoughtfully
pervade to spread throughout
reproachfully accusingly
rubbish trash
tempestuous violent; stormy
trifle a small amount
yarn an exaggerated story

Support for Students of Limited English Proficiency

- Use Reader's Guidesheet p. 65.
- *The Monkey's Paw* contains dialect and vocabulary that may prove troublesome to LEP students. Reading aloud dialectal terms and discussing unfamiliar words will be helpful.
- Annotations F, I, M, O, X, and DD focus on troublesome vocabulary and details.

Text Annotations

A. Literary Element: DRAMA Explain that *The Monkey's Paw* is a one-act play divided into three scenes. Have students tell the purpose of scenes. *(Scenes mark changes in the time or place of the setting.)*

Structured Reading for Less Proficient Students

These questions can help to guide students through the reading. Ask each question at the point of the selection where the SR number appears in the margin.

SR–1. Who are the members of the family and what are they doing in this scene? *(The family consists of Mr. and Mrs. White and son Herbert. Father and son are playing chess, while all await the arrival of a friend.* **Summarizing**

SR–2. How has Sergeant-Major Morris come to know some interesting yarns? *(He heard them while serving in the British military in India.* **Clarifying**

SR–3. How did the monkey's paw get its magic? *(A holy man in India placed a spell on it to show that fate ruled people.)* **Literal recall**

SR–4. How does Mr. White get the monkey's paw? *(When Morris throws the paw into the fire, Mr. White retrieves it.)* **Literal recall**

SR–5. What is Mr. White's first wish? What happens as he makes this wish? *(Mr. White first wishes for two hundred pounds to pay off the debt on his house. As he makes the wish, the paw moves.)* **Literal recall**

Continued on page T–146

B. Literary Sidelight The Whites live in a lonely, dreary location that will be revealed to be near a cemetery. This is an appropriate setting for a gothic tale, a style of writing that often emphasizes supernatural and/or grotesque events.

C. Reading Skill: DRAWING CONCLUSIONS Explain that dynamos are machines that generate electricity. Ask students what kind of job Herbert has. *(Possible response: He works at a power plant.)*

Mr. White *(trying to distract his attention)*. Hark[2] at the wind.

Herbert *(dryly)*. Ah! I'm listening. Check.[3]

Mr. White *(still trying to distract him)*. I should hardly think Sergeant-Major Morris'd come tonight.

Herbert. Mate.[4] *(rises)*

Mr. White *(with an outbreak of disgust and sweeping the chessmen off the board)*. That's the worst of living so far out. Your friends can't come for a quiet chat, and you addle your brains over a confounded—

SR-1 ▶ **Herbert.** Now, Father! Morris'll turn up all right.

B **Mr. White** *(still in a temper)*. Lover's Lane, Fulham! Ho! Of all the beastly, slushy, out-o'-the-way places to live in—! Pathway's a bog, and the road's a torrent. *(to* Mrs. White, *who has risen and is at his side)* What's the County Council[5] thinking of, that's what I want to know. Because this is the only house in the road, it doesn't matter if nobody can get near it, I s'pose.

Mrs. White. Never mind, dear. Perhaps you'll win tomorrow. *(She moves to back of table.)*

Mr. White. Perhaps I'll—perhaps I'll—! What d'you mean? *(bursts out laughing)* There! You always know what's going on inside o' me, don't you, Mother?

Mrs. White. Ought to, after thirty years, John. *(She goes to dresser and busies herself wiping tumblers on tray there. He rises, goes to fireplace, and lights pipe.)*

Herbert. And it's not such a bad place, Dad, after all. One of the few old-fashioned houses left near London. None o' your stucco villas.[6] Home-like, I call it. And so do you, or you wouldn't ha' bought it. *(rolls a cigarette)*

Mr. White *(growling)*. Nice job I made o' that, too! With two hundred pounds[7] owin' on it.

Herbert *(on back of chair)*. Why, I shall work that off in no time, Dad. Matter o' three years, with the raise promised me.

Mr. White. If you don't get married.

Herbert. Not me. Not that sort.

Mrs. White. I wish you would, Herbert. A good, steady, lad—*(She brings the tray with a bottle of whisky, glasses, a lemon, spoons, buns, and a knife to the table.)*

Herbert. Lots o' time, Mother. Sufficient for the day—as the sayin' goes. Just now my dynamos don't leave me any time for lovemaking. Jealous they are, I tell you!

Mr. White *(chuckling)*. I lay awake o' night often, and think: If Herbert took a nap, and let his what-d'you-call-ums—dynamos, run down, all Fulham would be in darkness. Lord! what a joke! C

Herbert. Joke! And me with the sack![8] Pretty idea of a joke you've got, I don't think.

(knock at outer door)

Mrs. White. Hark!

(knock repeated, louder)

2. **hark:** listen!
3. **check:** in chess, a move that places the opponent in danger.
4. **mate:** checkmate; in chess, the move that wins the game by capturing the opponent's king.
5. **County Council:** the local government.
6. **stucco villas:** small houses whose surface is cement or plaster.
7. **pounds:** the basic units of money in Great Britain.
8. **with the sack:** fired from a job.

Words to Know and Use

addle (ad''l) *v.* to confuse
bog (bäg) *n.* soggy ground; a swamp

STRUCTURED READING FOR LESS PROFICIENT STUDENTS

Continued from page T–145

SR–6. In Scene 2, what news does Mr. Sampson bring to the Whites? *(Herbert has been killed in an accident at the power plant.)* **Literal recall**

SR–7. How is Mr. White's first wish fulfilled? *(As compensation for Herbert's death, the Whites receive two hundred pounds.)* **Clarifying**

SR–8. In Scene 3, what wish does Mrs. White want to make with the paw? *(She wants to wish Herbert alive again.)* **Literal recall**

SR–9. Why doesn't Mr. White want his wife to open the door? *(He is afraid of what he and his wife will see there; he is afraid of what Herbert will look like after the accident and ten days in the grave.)* **Clarifying**

SR–10. What third and final wish does Mr. White make with the monkey's paw? *(He wishes for Herbert to be dead and at peace.)* **Literal recall**

THE EVENING MEAL © 1900 Henry Spernon Tozer From *Paradise Lost: Paintings of English Country Life and Landscape* by Christopher Wood.

Mr. White *(going toward door)*. That's him. That's the Sergeant-Major. *(He unlocks door, back.)*

Herbert *(removes chessboard)*. Wonder what yarn he's got for us tonight. *(places chessboard on piano)*

Mrs. White *(goes up right, busies herself putting the other armchair nearer fire, etc.)*. Don't let the door slam, John!

D (Mr. White *opens the door a little, struggling with it. Wind.* Sergeant-Major Morris, *a veteran with a distinct military appearance—left arm gone—dressed as a commissionaire, is seen to enter.* Mr. White *helps him off with his coat, which he hangs up in the outer hall.)*

Mr. White *(at the door)*. Slip in quick! It's as much as I can do to hold it against the wind.

Sergeant. Awful! Awful! *(busy taking off his cloak, etc.)* And a mile up the road—by the cemetery—it's worse. Enough to blow the hair off your head.

Mr. White. Give me your stick.

Sergeant. If 'twasn't I knew what a welcome I'd get—

Mr. White *(preceding him into the room)*. Sergeant-Major Morris!

Mrs. White. Tut! tut! So cold you must be! Come to the fire; do'ee, now.

Sergeant. How are you, marm? *(to* Herbert*)*

Words to Know and Use

yarn (yärn) *n.* an exaggerated story

D. Historical Sidelight A sergeant-major is the highest rank that a soldier who is not an officer can attain. This rank suggests that Morris was a career soldier of working-class background.

Art Note

Like other artists of his time, Henry Spernon Tozer (1850–1914) followed Victorian tastes in depicting pleasant cottage interiors. In *The Evening Meal* there can be seen a number of articles related to the lives of the inhabitants. Yet, the expressions of the elderly pair suggest that the clutter may not signify contentment. *What do you think their lives were really like?*

E. Literary Element: CHARACTERIZATION Point out that the sergeant is bragging about the hardships of military life. Ask students what this tells the reader about him. *(The sergeant takes pride in his military career, even its sacrifices, and looks down a little on the easy life of civilians.)*

F. LEP: Vocabulary Explain that a flywheel is a moving wheel on a steam generator. Discuss what the expression *gobble me up* means here. *(The machine might pull him in and crush him.)*

G. Reading Skill: SUMMARIZING Have students summarize the disagreement between Herbert and Morris. *(Possible response: Herbert says magic is fake; the sergeant-major says he has seen it work and believes it is real.)*

How's yourself, laddie? Not on duty yet, eh? Day-week, eh?

Herbert. No sir. Night week. But there's half an hour yet.

Sergeant *(sitting in the armchair above the fire, toward which* Mrs. White *is motioning him.* Mr. White *mixes grog*[9] *for* Morris*).* Thank'ee kindly, marm. That's good—hah! That's a sight better than the trenches at Chitral.[10] That's better than settin' in a puddle with the rain pourin' down in buckets and the natives takin' pot-shots at you.

Mrs. White. Didn't you have no umbrellas? *(Corner below fire, kneels before it, stirs it, etc.)*

Sergeant. Umbrell—? Ho! ho! That's good! Eh, White? That's good. Did ye hear what she said? Umbrellas!— *And* goloshes! *And* hot-water bottles!—Ho, yes! No offense, marm, but it's easy to see you was never a soldier.

E

Herbert *(rather hurt).* Mother spoke out o' kindness, sir.

Sergeant. And well I know it; and no offense intended. No, marm, 'ardship, 'ardship is the soldier's lot. Starvation, fever, and get yourself shot. That's a bit o' my own.

Mrs. White. You don't look to've taken much harm—except—*(Indicates his empty sleeve. She takes kettle to table, then returns to fire.)*

Sergeant *(showing a medal hidden under his coat).* And that I got this for. No, marm. Tough. Thomas Morris is tough. *(*Mr. White *is holding a glass of grog under the* Sergeant's *nose.)* And sober. What's this now?

Mr. White. Put your nose in it; you'll see.

Sergeant. Whisky? And hot? And sugar? And a slice o' lemon? No. I said I'd never—but seein' the sort o' night. Well! *(waving the glass at them)* Here's another thousand a year!

Mr. White *(also with a glass).* Same to you, and many of 'em.

Sergeant *(to* Herbert, *who has no glass).* What? Not you?

Herbert *(laughing and sitting across chair).* Oh! 'tisn't for want of being sociable. But my work don't go with it. Not if 'twas ever so little. I've got to keep a cool head, a steady eye, and a still hand. The flywheel might gobble me up. F

Mrs. White. Don't, Herbert. *(sits in armchair below fire)*

Herbert *(laughing).* No fear, Mother.

Sergeant. Ah! You electricians!—Sort o' magicians, you are. Light! says you—and light it is. And, power! says you—and the trams[11] go whizzin'. And, knowledge! says you—and words go 'ummin' to the ends o' the world. It fair beats me—and I've seen a bit in my time, too.

Herbert *(nudges his father).* Your Indian magic? All a fake, Governor. The fakir's[12] fake. G

Sergeant. Fake, you call it? I tell you, I've *seen* it.

Herbert *(nudging his father with his foot).* Oh, come, now! Such as what? Come, now!

Sergeant. I've seen a cove[13] with no more clothes on than a baby, *(to* Mrs. White*)* if you know what I mean—take an empty basket—empty, mind!—as empty as—as this here glass—

Mr. White. Hand it over, Morris. *(hands it to* Herbert, *who goes quickly behind table and fills it)*

9. **grog:** a warm rum drink.
10. **Chitral** (chi träl′): a city in what is now Pakistan.
11. **trams:** streetcars.
12. **fakir** (fə kir′): one who performs magic.
13. **cove:** British slang for boy or man.

CRITIC'S CORNER

Every one of Mr. [W. W.] Jacobs' stories is an amplified anecdote; that is to say, it is a thing with a complication and a climax, a climax which must be at once expected and unexpected. In this matter Mr. Jacobs is entirely in line with the oldest mirth of mankind. The great classic conception of a good story is that it should have a point, and that the principal character should sit down on it.

G. K. Chesterton, essay excerpted in *Twentieth-Century Literary Criticism*, edited by Dennis Poupard

Sergeant. Which was not my intentions, but used for illustration.

Herbert *(while mixing)*. Oh, *I've* seen the basket trick; and I've read how it was done. Why, I could do it myself, with a bit o' practice. Ladle out something stronger. *(*Herbert *brings him the glass.)*

H **Sergeant.** Stronger?—What do you say to an old fakir chuckin' a rope up in the air—in the *air,* mind you!—and swarming up it, same as if it was 'ooked on—and vanishing clean out o' sight?—I've seen *that. (*Herbert *goes to table, plunges a knife into a bun and offers it to the* Sergeant *with exaggerated politeness.)*

Sergeant *(eyeing it with disgust)*. Bun—? What for?

Herbert. That yarn takes it.[14] *(*Mr. *and* Mrs. White *delighted)*

Sergeant. Mean to say you doubt my word?

I **Mrs. White.** No, no! He's only taking you off.—You shouldn't, Herbert.

Mr. White. Herbert always was one for a bit o' fun!

*(*Herbert *puts bun back on table, comes round in front, and moving the chair out of the way, sits crosslegged on the floor at his father's side.)*

Sergeant. But it's true. Why, if I chose, I could tell you things—But there! You
SR-2► don't get no more yarns out o' *me.*

Mr. White. Nonsense, old friend. *(puts down his glass)* You're not going to get shirty about a bit o' fun. *(moves his chair nearer* Morris's*)* What was that you started telling me the other day about a monkey's paw or something? *(nudges* Herbert, *and winks at* Mrs. White*)*.

Sergeant *(gravely)*. Nothing. Leastways, nothing worth hearing.

Mrs. White *(with astonished curiosity)*. Monkey's *paw*—?

Mr. White. Ah—you was tellin' me—

Sergeant. Nothing. Don't go on about it. *(puts his empty glass to his lips—then stares at it) What?* Empty again? There! When I begin thinkin' o' the paw, it makes me that absent-minded—

Mr. White *(rises and fills glass)*. You said you always carried it on you.

Sergeant. So I do, for fear o' what might happen. *(sunk in thought)* Ay!—ay!

Mr. White *(handing him his glass refilled)*. There. *(sits again in same chair)*

Mrs. White. What's it for?

Sergeant. You wouldn't believe me if I was to tell you.

Herbert. *I* will, every word.

Sergeant. Magic, then! Don't you laugh!

Herbert. I'm not. Got it on you now?

Sergeant. Of course.

Herbert. Let's see it.

(Seeing the Sergeant *embarrassed with his glass,* Mrs. White *rises, takes it from him, places it on mantelpiece, and remains standing.)*

Sergeant. Oh, it's nothing to look at. *(hunting in his pocket)* Just an ordinary—little paw—dried to a mummy. *(produces it and holds it toward* Mrs. White*)* Here.

Mrs. White *(who has leant forward eagerly to see it, starts back with a little cry of disgust)*. Oh!

Herbert. Give us a look. *(*Morris *passes the paw* to Mr. White, *from whom* Herbert *takes it)* Why, it's all dried up!

Sergeant. I said so.

(wind)

Mrs. White *(with a slight shudder)*. Hark at the wind! *(sits again in her old place)*

Mr. White *(taking the paw from* Herbert*)*. And what might there be special about it?

14. **takes it:** takes the cake; beats everything.

H. Historical Sidelight At the time of the play, Britain ruled a large empire of which India was the leading colony. India was a land of both fabulous wealth and crushing poverty. Some Indians earned a living demonstrating tricks or feats of skill on public streets. These people charmed snakes in baskets, climbed ropes and vanished, lay on beds of nails, or stood on one leg for long periods of time. The British of that era saw India as a mysterious and romantic place.

I. LEP: Idiom Explain that the phrase *taking you off* is equivalent to "putting you on" or "teasing you."

DATA BANK

During the period of the British Empire (roughly 1600–1950), English writers often enriched their works with exotic elements from India and other British colonies. Sir Arthur Conan Doyle, for example, the creator of the Sherlock Holmes mysteries, included Asian elements in a number of stories, most notably "The Adventures of the Speckled Band." H. H. Munro, whose pen name was Saki, relied on Asian magic and mystery in such well-known tales as "The Lumber Room" and "Sredni Vashtar." The British author most closely associated with imperial India is, of course, Rudyard Kipling, whose Anglo-Indian childhood provided the inspiration for such works as *Kim* and *The Jungle Book.*

J. Reading Skill: CLARIFYING Have students restate the fakir's belief about fate. *(Possible response: People cannot change their fates, and if they try to do so, they might suffer some serious or tragic consequences.)*

Teaching Tip

If students are having difficulty with the British dialect of the play consider having them work in pairs or small groups to rewrite troublesome passages in their own words.

K. Reading Skill: INFERRING Ask students to suggest why the paw's previous owner wished for death on his third wish. *(Possible response: The unexpected results of his first two wishes were so horrible that he wanted to die.)*

Sergeant *(impressively)*. That there paw has had a spell put upon it!

Mr. White. No? *(In great alarm he thrusts the paw back into* Morris's *hand.)*

Sergeant *(pensively, holding the paw in the palm of his hand)*. Ah! By an old fakir. He was a very holy man. He'd sat all doubled up in one spot, goin' on for fifteen year; thinkin' o' things. And he wanted to show that fate ruled people. That everything was cut and dried from the beginning, as you might say. That there warn't no gettin' away from it. And that, if you tried to, you caught it hot. *(pauses solemnly)* So he put a spell on this bit of a paw. It might ha' been anything else, but he took the first thing that came handy. Ah! He put a spell on it, and made it so that three people *(looking at them and with deep meaning)* could each have three wishes. J SR-3 ▶

(All but Mrs. White *laugh rather nervously.)*

Mrs. White. Ssh! Don't!

Sergeant *(more gravely)*. But—! But, mark you, though the wishes was granted, those three people would have cause to wish they *hadn't* been.

Mr. White. But how *could* the wishes be granted?

Sergeant. He didn't say. It would all happen so natural, you might think it a coincidence if so disposed.

Herbert. Why haven't you tried it, sir?

Sergeant *(gravely, after a pause)*. I have.

Herbert *(eagerly)*. You've had your three wishes?

Sergeant *(gravely)*. Yes.

Mrs. White. Were they granted?

Sergeant *(staring at the fire)*. They were.

(a pause)

Mr. White. Has anybody else wished?

Sergeant. Yes. The first owner had his three wish—*(lost in recollection)* Yes, oh, yes, he had his three wishes all right. I don't know what his first two were, *(very impressively)* but the third was for death. *(All shudder.)* That's how I got the paw. K

(a pause)

Herbert *(cheerfully)*. Well! Seems to me you've only got to wish for things that *can't* have any bad luck about 'em—*(rises)*

Sergeant *(shaking his head)*. Ah!

Mr. White *(tentatively)*. Morris—if you've had your three wishes—it's no good to you, now—what do you keep it for?

Sergeant *(still holding the paw; looking at it)*. Fancy, I s'pose. I did have some idea of selling it, but I don't think I will. It's done mischief enough already. Besides, people won't buy. Some of 'em think it's a fairy tale. And some want to try it first and pay after.

(nervous laugh from the others)

Mrs. White. If you could have another three wishes, would you?

Sergeant *(slowly—weighing the paw in his hand and looking at it)*. I don't know—I don't know—*(suddenly, with violence, flinging it in the fire)* No! I'm damned if I would!

(movement from all)

Mr. White *(rises and quickly snatches it out of the fire)*. What are you doing? *(White goes to the fireplace.)*

Sergeant *(rising and following him and trying to prevent him)*. Let it burn! Let the infernal thing burn!

Words to Know and Use

pensively (pen′ siv lē) *adv.* in a thoughtful manner
infernal (in fur′ nəl) *adj.* hellish; fiendish

150

DATA BANK

Although the mummified monkey's paw seems to be W. W. Jacobs' own creation, this talisman draws upon a number of magical and supernatural beliefs. In India, the place of the paw's origin, the monkey is a sacred animal, and the monkey chieftain Hanuman plays a major role in the epic *Ramayana*. In another former British colony, Nigeria, dried monkey heads were thought to possess mysterious healing powers and were regularly offered for sale in the marketplaces. The monkey's paw is also reminiscent of the so-called hand of glory, the dried and pickled hand of a man who has been hanged. Throughout Europe, but especially in medieval England, these ghastly objects were valuable charms and used by witches for secret purposes. Supposedly the hands had the power to prevent people from waking up, and so were in much demand by house burglars.

Mrs. White *(rises)*. Let it burn, Father!

Mr. White *(wiping it on his coat sleeve)*. No. If you don't want it, give it to me.

SR-4 ▶

L

Sergeant *(violently)*. I won't! I won't! My hands are clear of it. I threw it on the fire. If you keep it, don't blame me, whatever happens. Here! Pitch it back again.

Mr. White *(stubbornly)*. I'm going to keep it. What do you say, Herbert?

Herbert *(laughing)*. I say, keep it if you want to. Stuff and nonsense, anyhow.

Mr. White *(looking at the paw thoughtfully)*. Stuff and nonsense. Yes. I wonder—*(casually)* I wish— *(He was going to say some ordinary thing, like "I wish I were certain.")*

Sergeant *(misunderstanding him; violently)*. Stop! Mind what you're doing. That's not the way.

Mr. White. What *is* the way?

Mrs. White *(moving away to back of table, and beginning to put the tumblers straight and the chairs in their places)*. Oh, don't have anything to do with it, John. *(takes glasses on tray to dresser, busies herself there, rinsing them in a bowl of water on the dresser, and wiping them with a cloth)*

Sergeant. That's what I say, marm. But if I warn't to tell him, he might go wishing something he didn't mean to. You hold it in your right hand, and wish aloud. But I warn you! I warn you!

Mrs. White. Sounds like the Arabian Nights.[15] Don't you think you might wish me four pair o' hands?

Mr. White *(laughing)*. Right you are, Mother!—I wish—

Sergeant *(pulling his arm down)*. Stop it! If you must wish, wish for something sensible. Look here! I can't stand this. Gets on my nerves. Where's my coat? *(goes into alcove)*

*(*Mr. White *crosses to fireplace and carefully puts the paw on mantelpiece. He is absorbed in it to the end of the tableau.)*

M

Herbert. I'm coming your way, to the works, in a minute. Won't you wait? *(helps* Morris *with his coat)*

Sergeant *(putting on his coat)*. No. I'm all shook up. I want fresh air. I don't want to be here when you wish. And wish you will as soon's my back's turned. I know. I know. But I've warned you, mind.

N

Mr. White *(helping him into his coat)*. All right, Morris. Don't you fret about us. *(gives him money)* Here.

Sergeant *(refusing it)*. No, I won't—

Mr. White *(forcing it into his hand)*. Yes, you will. *(opens door)*

Sergeant *(turning to the room)*. Well, good night all. *(to* White*)* Put it in the fire.

All. Good night.

(Exit Sergeant. Mr. White *closes door, comes toward fireplace, absorbed in the paw.)*

Herbert. If there's no more in this than there is in his other stories, we shan't make much out of it.

Mrs. White *(to* White*)*. Did you give him anything for it, Father?

Mr. White. A trifle. He didn't want it, but I made him take it.

Mrs. White. There, now! You shouldn't. Throwing your money about.

Mr. White *(looking at the paw which he has picked up again)*. I wonder—

15. **Arabian Nights:** a reference to *The Thousand and One Nights*, a famous work of literature containing, among others, the stories of Ali Baba and Sinbad.

Words to Know and Use

fret (fret) *v.* to worry
trifle (trī′ fəl) *n.* a small amount

L. Literary Element: FORESHADOWING
Ask the students what the sergeant-major's violent reaction suggests will happen if Mr. White uses the paw. *(Possible response: Morris seems convinced that some horrible tragedy will befall the Whites if they use the paw.)*

M. LEP: Vocabulary Explain that *tableau* is another word for scene. Ask students to suggest how Mr. White's staring at the paw for the rest of the scene might affect an audience at the play. *(Possible response: The audience will focus on the paw too, heightening tension and interest.)*

N. Literary Element: FORESHADOWING
Ask students what the sergeant-major's words suggest is to come. *(The Whites will use the paw right away, and it will not be a pleasant experience.)*

Professional Notebook

My experience as a reader and writer influences my beliefs about reading. I carry books with me everywhere in case a delay allows time for reading. I also carry a notebook in which I jot down quotes, observations, and ideas for writing. In the past few years, I have created a file of personal writing, vignettes, poems. Some I have shared with others. I immerse myself in a literate environment because print, the texts of others as well as my own, meets real needs in my life. I believe this is true for students as well.

Sandra Norris, *The Teaching of Reading, a Personal Statement*

O. LEP: Vocabulary Tell students that *henpecked* describes a husband ruled over by his wife. Explain that Herbert is teasing his mother for being bossy and that she is chasing him playfully.

P. Critical Thinking: ANALYZING Have students speculate on why Mr. White, who seems to have all he wants, decides to use the paw despite Morris's warnings. *(Possible responses: White is curious about the supernatural; he is bored and wants excitement.)*

Q. Reading Skill: CONTRASTING Have students contrast Herbert's attitude toward the paw with Mr. White's attitude. *(Herbert still treats the paw as a joke; Mr. White has sensed the paw's power and is badly shaken and afraid.)*

Herbert. What?

Mr. White. I wonder, whether we hadn't better chuck it on the fire?

Herbert *(laughing)*. Likely! Why we're all going to be rich and famous, and happy.

Mrs. White. Throw it on the fire, indeed, when you've given money for it! So like you, Father.

O **Herbert.** Wish to be an emperor, Father, to begin with. Then you can't be henpecked!

Mrs. White *(going for him front of table with a duster)*. You young—! *(follows him to back of table)*

Herbert *(running away from her, hiding behind table)*. Steady with that duster, Mother!

P **Mr. White.** Be quiet, there! *(Herbert catches Mrs. White in his arms and kisses her.)* I wonder—*(He has the paw in his hand.)* I don't know what to wish for, and that's a fact. *(He looks about him with a happy smile.)* I seem to've got all I want.

Herbert *(with his hands on the old man's shoulders)*. Old Dad! If you'd only cleared the debt on the house, you'd be quite happy, wouldn't you? *(laughing)* Well—go ahead!—wish for the two hundred pounds: that'll just do it.

Mr. White *(half laughing)*. Shall I?

Herbert. Go on! Here!—I'll play slow music. *(goes to piano)*

Mrs. White. Don't 'ee, John. Don't have nothing to do with it!

Herbert. Now, Dad! *(plays)*

Mr. White. I will! *(holds up the paw, as if half ashamed)* I wish for two hundred pounds. *(Crash on the piano. At the same instant Mr. White utters a cry and lets the paw drop.)*

Mrs. White *and* Herbert. What's the matter?

Mr. White *(gazing with horror at the paw)*. It moved! As I wished, it twisted in my hand like a snake. ◀SR-5

Herbert *(goes down and picks the paw up)*. Nonsense, Dad. Why, it's as stiff as a bone. *(lays it on the mantelpiece)*

Mrs. White. Must have been your fancy, Father.

Herbert *(laughing)*. Well—? *(looking round the room)* I don't see the money; and I bet I never shall.

Mr. White *(relieved)*. Thank God, there's no harm done! But it gave me a shock.

Herbert. Half past eleven. I must get along. I'm on at midnight. *(fetches his coat, etc.)* We've had quite a merry evening.

Mrs. White. I'm off to bed. Don't be late for breakfast, Herbert.

Herbert. I shall walk home as usual. Does me good. I shall be with you about nine. Don't wait, though.

Mrs. White. You know your father never waits.

Herbert. Good night, Mother. *(Kisses her. She lights candle on dresser, goes up stairs and exit.)*

Herbert *(coming to his father, who is sunk in thought)*. Good night, Dad. You'll find the cash tied up in the middle of the bed.

Mr. White *(staring, seizes Herbert's hand)*. It moved, Herbert. Q

Herbert. Ah! And a monkey hanging by his tail from the bedpost, watching you count the golden sovereigns.[16]

Mr. White *(accompanying him to the door)*. I wish you wouldn't joke, my boy.

Herbert. All right, Dad. *(opens door)* Lord! What weather! Good night. *(exit)*

(The old man shakes his head, closes the door, locks it, puts the chain up, slips the lower bolt, has some difficulty with the upper bolt.)

16. **sovereigns:** British gold coins.

Real Life Connections

Remind students that, in spite of the sergeant-major's repeated warnings, the Whites used the monkey's paw anyway. Ask them to discuss why some people ignore the advice of those who are better informed or more experienced. Students may want to recount incidents from their own experience in which they regretted ignoring good advice. Or, they may make the point that it is sometimes necessary to ignore advice, no matter how well intended it may be.

Mr. White. This bolt's stiff again! I must get Herbert to look to it in the morning. *(Comes into the room, puts out the lamp, crosses toward steps; but is irresistibly attracted toward the fireplace. Sits down and stares into the fire. His expression changes: he sees something horrible.)*

Mr. White *(with an* involuntary *cry)*. Mother! Mother!

Mrs. White *(appearing at the door at the top of the steps with candle)*. What's the matter?

Mr. White *(Mastering himself. Rises.)*. Nothing—I—haha!—I saw faces in the fire.

Mrs. White. Come along. *(She takes his arm and draws him toward the steps. He looks back frightened toward the fireplace as they reach the first step.)*

Tableau Curtain

Scene 2

R

Bright sunshine. The table, which has been moved nearer the window, is laid for breakfast. Mrs. White *is busy about the table.* Mr. White *is standing in the window looking off. The inner door is open, showing the outer door.*

Mr. White. What a morning Herbert's got for walking home!

Mrs. White. What's o'clock? *(looks at clock*

NIGHT LAMP 1950 Andrew Wyeth Private collection.

Words to Know and Use

involuntary (in väl′ ən ter′ ē) *adj.* unintentional; accidental

153

R. Reading Skill: PREDICTING As students begin to read Scene 2, ask them to predict whether the wish for two hundred pounds will come true, and if so, how. *(Answers will vary. Have students cite details from the play to support their responses.)*

Art Note

Andrew Wyeth (1917–), a consummate master in the portrayal of mysteriously lighted scenes, here shows us the actual source, a kerosene lamp. Yet, because we view it from the outside in the dark, the effect is that of a moment suspended in time, just before someting happens—a moment of absolute silence. *How does this painting illustrate certain passages in* The Monkey's Paw?

S. Literary Element: FORESHADOWING/IRONY When students have completed the play, you may want to discuss the irony of this clue. *(Herbert is indeed "just by" the cemetery, although not in the way Mr. White envisions.)*

T. Literary Element: SETTING/CHARACTER Ask students how the end of the storm and the dawning of a sunny morning mirror a change in Mr. and Mrs. White. *(Possible response: They seem to have forgotten the fear and horror caused by the paw the previous evening; they appear cheerful and rational.)*

on mantelpiece) Quarter to nine, I declare. He's off at eight. *(crosses to fire)*

S **Mr. White.** Takes him half an hour to change and wash. He's just by the cemetery now.

Mrs. White. He'll be here in ten minutes.

Mr. White *(coming to the table)*. What's for breakfast?

Mrs. White. Sausages. *(at the mantelpiece)* Why, if here isn't that dirty monkey's paw! *(Picks it up, looks at it with disgust, puts it back. Takes sausages in dish from before fire and places them on table.)* Silly thing! The idea of us listening to such nonsense!

T **Mr. White** *(goes up to window again)*. Ay—the Sergeant-Major and his yarns! I suppose all old soldiers are alike—

Mrs. White. Come on, Father. Herbert hates us to wait. *(They both sit and begin breakfast.)*

Mrs. White. How could wishes be granted, nowadays?

Mr. White. Ah! Been thinking about it all night, have you?

Mrs. White. You kept me awake, with your tossing and tumbling—

Mr. White. Ay, I had a bad night.

Mrs. White. It was the storm, I expect. How it blew!

Mr. White. I didn't hear it. I was asleep and not asleep, if you know what I mean.

Mrs. White. And all that rubbish about its making you unhappy if your wish *was* granted! How could two hundred pounds hurt you, eh, Father?

Mr. White. Might drop on my head in a lump. Don't see any other way. And I'd try to bear that. Though, mind you, Morris said it would all happen so naturally that you might take it for a coincidence, if so disposed.

Mrs. White. Well—it hasn't happened. That's all I know. And it isn't going to. *(A letter is seen to drop in the letter box.)* And how you can sit there and talk about it—*(Sharp postman's knock. She jumps to her feet.)* What's that?

Mr. White. Postman, o' course.

Mrs. White *(seeing the letter from a distance; in an awed whisper)*. He's brought a letter, John!

Mr. White *(laughing)*. What did you think he'd bring? Ton o' coals?

Mrs. White. John—! John—! Suppose—?

Mr. White. Suppose what?

Mrs. White. Suppose it was two hundred pounds!

Mr. White *(suppressing his excitement)*. Eh!—Here! Don't talk nonsense. Why don't you fetch it?

Mrs. White *(crosses and takes letter out of the box)*. It's thick, John—*(feels it)*—and—and it's got something crisp inside it. *(takes letter to* White*)*

Mr. White. Who—who's it for?

Mrs. White. You.

Mr. White. Hand it over, then. *(feeling and examining it with ill-concealed excitement)* The idea! What a superstitious old woman you are! Where are my specs?[17]

Mrs. White. Let me open it.

Mr. White. Don't you touch it. Where are my specs?

Mrs. White. Don't let sudden wealth sour your temper, John.

17. **specs:** eyeglasses.

Words to Know and Use

rubbish (rub′ ish) *n.* worthless material; trash

PROFESSIONAL NOTEBOOK

The typical curriculum of American schools was not designed to address differences in the learning styles of the various personality types. Educators today have inherited a mind set of what schooling is and should be, and that mind set favors some types and handicaps others. . . . Schools expect students to work quietly, sitting quietly in their own seats most of the time. School learning is regarded essentially as a private, interior mental effort. That expectation fits introverted types well, but neglects the extroverts who learn best when they can test ideas in talk and action. . . . That bias might be tolerable if extroverts were a small minority of the population: however, research reported in the Myers–Briggs Manual clearly shows that the typical school has 70 to 75 percent extroverts.

GORDON LAWRENCE *Personality Structure and Learning Style: Uses of the Myers–Briggs Type Indicator and Brain Behavior*, NATIONAL ASSOCIATION OF SECONDARY SCHOOL PRINCIPALS, 1982).

Mr. White. *Will* you find my specs?

Mrs. White *(taking them off mantelpiece).* Here, John, here. *(as he opens the letter)* Take care! Don't tear it!

Mr. White. Tear what?

Mrs. White. If it was banknotes, John!

Mr. White *(taking a thick, formal document out of the envelope and a crisp-looking slip).* You've gone dotty.[18]—You've made me nervous. *(reads)* "Sir,—Enclosed please find receipt for interest on the mortgage of £200 on your house, duly received." *(They look at each other.* Mr. White *sits down to finish his breakfast silently.* Mrs. White *goes to the window.)*

U

Mrs. White. That comes of listening to tipsy old soldiers.

Mr. White *(pettish).* What does?

Mrs. White. You thought there was banknotes in it.

Mr. White *(injured).* I didn't! I said all along—

Mrs. White. How Herbert will laugh, when I tell him!

Mr. White *(with gruff good humor).* You're not going to tell him. You're going to keep your mouth shut. That's what you're going to do. Why, I should never hear the last of it.

Mrs. White. Serve you right. I shall tell him. You know you like his fun. See how he joked you last night when you said the paw moved. *(She is looking through the window.)*

Mr. White. So it did. It did move. That I'll swear to.

Mrs. White *(Abstractedly; she is watching something outside.).* You thought it did.

Mr. White. I say it did. There was no thinking about it. You saw how it upset me, didn't you? *(She doesn't answer.) Didn't* you?—Why don't you listen? *(turns round)* What is it?

Mrs. White. Nothing.

Mr. White *(turns back to his breakfast).* Do you see Herbert coming?

Mrs. White. No.

Mr. White. He's about due. What *is* it?

Mrs. White. Nothing. Only a man. Looks like a gentleman. Leastways, he's in black, and he's got a top-hat on.

Mr. White. What about him? *(He is not interested; goes on eating.)*

Mrs. White. He stood at the garden gate as if he wanted to come in. But he couldn't seem to make up his mind.

Mr. White. Oh, go on! You're full o' fancies.

Mrs. White. He's going—no; he's coming back.

Mr. White. Don't let him see you peeping.

Mrs. White *(with increasing excitement).* He's looking at the house. He's got his hand on the latch. No. He turns away again. *(eagerly)* John! He looks like a sort of a lawyer.

Mr. White. What of it?

Mrs. White. Oh, you'll only laugh again. But suppose—suppose he's coming about the two hundred—

Mr. White. You're not to mention it again! You're a foolish old woman. Come and eat your breakfast. *(eagerly)* Where is he now?

Mrs. White. Gone down the road. He has turned back. He seems to've made up his mind. Here he comes! Oh, John, and me all untidy! *(Crosses to fire. There is a knock.)*

V

Mr. White *(to* Mrs. White, *who is hastily smoothing her hair).* What's it matter? He's made a mistake. Come to the wrong house. *(Goes to fireplace.* Mrs. White *opens the door.* Mr. Sampson, *dressed from head*

18. **dotty:** crazy.

U. Reading Skill: CLARIFYING Have a volunteer explain the contents of the letter. *(The letter is not the hoped-for money. Rather, it is a routine receipt for interest Mr. White paid on his two hundred pound mortgage loan.)*

V. Critical Thinking: SYNTHESIZING Point out that the man's uncertainty over whether to come or go builds suspense and parallels the Whites' own uncertainty about whether their wish will come true. Have students speculate on why the man hesitates, keeping in mind that the Whites' house is the only one in the area. *(Possible responses: He's not sure he has the right house; he needs time to prepare himself to see the Whites because the purpose for his visit is not a pleasant one.)*

W. Literary Element: SUSPENSE Point out that dramatic tension is heightened as the true reason for Sampson's visit is slowly revealed.

X. LEP: Vocabulary Some students may not be familiar with the word *instinctively.* Tell them that to move "instinctively" is to move without thinking about moving.

Y. Reading Skill: INFERRING Have students tell what Mrs. White realizes Mr. Sampson means. *(She realizes that Herbert is not in pain because he is dead.)*

Z. Literary Skill: FORESHADOWING Have students turn back to page 148, column 2, and find the clue in Herbert's lines that hint at his horrible death. *("I've got to keep a cool head. . . . The flywheel might gobble me up.")*

to foot in solemn black, with a top hat, stands in the doorway.)

Sampson *(outside)***.** Is this Mr. White's?

Mrs. White. Come in, sir. Please step in. *(She shows him into the room. He is awkward and nervous.)* You must overlook our being so untidy; and the room all anyhow; and John in his garden coat. *(to* Mr. White, *reproachfully)* Oh, John.

Sampson *(to* Mr. White*)***.** Morning. My name is Sampson.

Mrs. White *(offering a chair)* Won't you please be seated? *(*Sampson *stands quite still.)*

Sampson. Ah—thank you—no, I think not—I think not. *(pause)*

Mr. White *(awkwardly, trying to help him)***.** Fine weather for the time o' year.

Sampson. Ah—yes—yes—*(Pause; he makes a renewed effort.)* My name is Sampson—I've come—

Mrs. White. Perhaps you was wishful to see Herbert; he'll be home in a minute. *(pointing)* Here's his breakfast waiting—

Sampson *(interrupting her hastily)***.** No, no! *(pause)* I've come from the electrical works—

Mrs. White. Why, you might have come *with* him.

*(*Mr. White *sees something is wrong, tenderly puts his hand on her arm.)*

Sampson. No—no—I've come—*alone.*

Mrs. White *(with a little anxiety)***.** Is anything the matter?

W **Sampson.** I was asked to call—

Mrs. White *(abruptly)***.** Herbert! Has anything happened? Is he hurt? Is he hurt?

Mr. White *(soothing her)***.** There, there, Mother. Don't you jump to conclusions. Let the gentleman speak. You've not brought bad news, I'm sure, sir.

Sampson. I'm—sorry—

Mrs. White. Is he hurt? *(*Sampson *bows.)* Badly?

Sampson. Very badly. *(turns away)*

Mrs. White *(with a cry)***.** John—! *(She instinctively moves toward* White.*)* X

Mr. White. Is he in pain?

Sampson. He is not in pain.

Mrs. White. Oh, thank God! Thank God for that! Thank—*(She looks in a startled fashion at* Mr. White*—realizes what* Sampson *means, catches his arm and tries to turn him toward her.)* Do you mean—? Y

*(*Sampson *avoids her look; she gropes for her husband: he takes her two hands in his, and gently lets her sink into the armchair above the fireplace, then he stands on her right, between her and* Sampson.*)*

Mr. White *(hoarsely)***.** Go on, sir.

Sampson. He was telling his mates a story. Something that had happened here last night. He was laughing, and wasn't noticing and—and—*(hushed)* the machinery caught him— Z

(A little cry from Mrs. White; *her face shows her horror and agony.)*

Mr. White *(vague, holding* Mrs. White's *hand)***.** The machinery caught him—yes—and him the only child—it's hard, sir—very hard—

Sampson *(subdued)***.** The Company wished me to convey their sincere sympathy with you in your great loss— ◀SR-6

Mr. White *(staring blankly)***.** Our—great—loss—!

Words to Know and Use	**reproachfully** (ri prōch′ fə lē) *adv.* accusingly

Sampson. I was to say further—*(as if apologizing)* I am only their servant—I am only obeying orders—

Mr. White. Our—great—loss—

Sampson *(laying an envelope on the table and edging toward the door).* I was to say, the Company disclaims all responsibility, but in consideration of your son's services, they wish to present you with a certain sum as compensation. *(gets to door)*

Mr. White. Our—great—loss—*(suddenly, with horror)* How—how much?

AA **Sampson** *(in the doorway).* Two hundred pounds. *(exit)*

*(*Mrs. White *gives a cry. The old man takes no heed of her, smiles faintly, puts out his hands like a sightless man, and drops, a senseless heap, to the floor.* Mrs. White *stares at him blankly, and her hands go out helplessly toward him.)*

SR-7 ▶ *Tableau Curtain*

Scene 3

BB *Night. On the table a candle is flickering at its last gasp. The room looks neglected.* Mr. White *is dozing fitfully in the armchair.* Mrs. White *is in the window peering through the blind.* Mr. White *starts, wakes, looks around him.*

Mr. White *(fretfully).* Jenny—Jenny.

Mrs. White *(in the window).* Yes.

Mr. White. Where are you?

Mrs. White. At the window.

Mr. White. What are you doing?

Mrs. White. Looking up the road.

Mr. White *(falling back).* What's the use, Jenny? What's the use?

Mrs. White. That's where the cemetery is; that's where we've laid him.

Mr. White. Ay—ay—a week today—what o'clock is it?

Mrs. White. I don't know.

Mr. White. We don't take much account of time now, Jenny, do we? CC

Mrs. White. Why should we? He don't come home. He'll never come home again. There's nothing to think about—

Mr. White. Or to talk about. *(pause)* Come away from the window; you'll get cold.

Mrs. White. It's colder where *he* is.

Mr. White. Ay—gone for ever—

Mrs. White. And taken all our hopes with him—

Mr. White. And all our *wishes*—

Mrs. White. Ay, and all our—*(with a sudden cry)* John! *(She comes quickly to him; he rises.)*

Mr. White. Jenny! For God's sake! What's the matter?

Mrs. White *(with dreadful eagerness).* The *paw!* The monkey's paw!

Mr. White *(bewildered).* Where? Where is it? What's wrong with it?

Mrs. White. I want it! You haven't done away with it?

Mr. White. I haven't seen it—since—why?

Mrs. White. I want it! Find it! Find it!

Mr. White *(groping on the mantelpiece).* Here! Here it is! What do you want of it? *(He leaves it there.)*

Mrs. White. Why didn't I think of it? Why didn't *you* think of it?

Mr. White. Think of what?

Mrs. White. The *other two* wishes!

Mr. White *(with horror).* What?

Words to Know and Use

disclaim (dis klām′) *v.* to refuse to acknowledge or claim
compensation (käm′ pən sā′ shən) *n.* anything given to make up for something else

AA. Literary Skill: IRONY Have students explain the irony of the situation. *(If the Whites expected to get the money at all, they didn't expect to do so at the expense of their son's life.)*

BB. Reading Skill: PREDICTING Ask students to predict what might happen in the third scene. Have them tell whether they think Mr. White will wish again with the paw, and, if so, for what. *(Answers will vary. Students should support their answers with information from the story.)*

CC. Critical Thinking: ANALYZING Have the students tell why Mr. White now calls his wife Jenny. *(Possible response: Now that their only child is dead, it is too painful for them to call each other Mother and Father.)*

Art Note
Charles Edward Perugini sidestepped the preferred Victorian custom of portraying widows as appealingly young and pretty. Instead, he chose to show an old woman mourning, her lined face exhibiting a sorrow tempered with hard-learned patience. *Could this be a portrait of Mrs. White in* The Monkey's Paw*? If so, what might she be doing?*

DD. LEP: Vocabulary Tell students *paroxysm* means "a sudden outburst of emotion."

FAITHFUL Charles Edward Perugini National Museums and Galleries on Merseyside, Walker Art Gallery, Liverpool.

Mrs. White. We've only had one.

Mr. White *(tragically).* Wasn't that enough?

Mrs. White. No! We'll have one more. *(*White *crosses.* Mrs. White *takes the paw and follows him.)* Take it. Take it quickly. And wish—

Mr. White *(avoiding the paw).* Wish what?

Mrs. White. Oh, John! John! Wish our boy
SR-8 ▶ alive again!

Mr. White. Good God! Are you mad?

Mrs. White. Take it. Take it and wish. *(with a paroxysm of grief)* Oh, my boy! My boy! DD

Mr. White. Get to bed. Get to sleep. You don't know what you're saying.

Mrs. White. We had the first wish granted—why not the second?

Mr. White *(hushed).* He's been dead ten days, and—Jenny! Jenny! I only knew

EE him by his clothing—if you wasn't allowed to see him then—how could you bear to see him *now*?

Mrs. White. I don't care. Bring him back.

Mr. White *(shrinking from the paw)*. I daren't touch it!

Mrs. White *(thrusting it in his hand)*. Here! Here! Wish!

Mr. White *(trembling)*. Jenny!

Mrs. White *(fiercely)*. Wish. *(She goes on frantically whispering "Wish.")*

Mr. White *(shuddering, but overcome by her insistence)*. I—I—wish—my—son—alive again. *(He drops it with a cry. The candle goes out. Utter darkness. He sinks into a chair.* Mrs. White *hurries to the window and draws the blind back. She stands in the moonlight. Pause.)*

Mrs. White *(drearily)*. Nothing.

Mr. White. Thank God! Thank God!

FF **Mrs. White.** Nothing at all. Along the whole length of the road not a living thing. *(closes blind)* And nothing, nothing, nothing left in our lives, John.

Mr. White. Except each other, Jenny—and memories.

Mrs. White *(coming back slowly to the fireplace)*. We're too old. We were only alive in him. We can't begin again. We can't feel anything now, John, but emptiness and darkness. *(She sinks into armchair.)*

Mr. White. 'Tisn't for long, Jenny. There's that to look forward to.

Mrs. White. Every minute's long, now.

Mr. White *(rising)*. I can't bear the darkness!

Mrs. White. It's dreary—dreary.

Mr. White *(goes to dresser)*. Where's the candle? *(finds it and brings it to table)* And the matches? Where are the matches? We mustn't sit in the dark. 'Tisn't wholesome. *(Lights match; the other candlestick is close to him.)* There. *(turning with the lighted match toward* Mrs. White, *who is rocking and moaning)* Don't take on so, Mother.

Mrs. White. I'm a mother no longer.

Mr. White *(lights candle)*. There now; there now. Go on up to bed. Go on, now—I'm a-coming.

Mrs. White. Whether I'm here or in bed, or wherever I am, I'm with my boy, I'm with—

(a low single knock at the street door)

Mrs. White *(starting)*. What's that!

Mr. White *(mastering his horror)*. A rat. The house is full of 'em. *(A louder single knock; she starts up. He catches her by the arm.)* Stop! What are you going to do?

Mrs. White *(wildly)*. It's my boy! It's Herbert! I forgot it was a mile away! What are you holding me for? I must open the door!

(The knocking continues in single knocks at irregular intervals, constantly growing louder and more insistent.)

Mr. White *(still holding her)*. For God's sake!

Mrs. White *(struggling)*. Let me go!

Mr. White. Don't open the door! *(He drags her away.)*

Mrs. White. Let me go!

Mr. White. Think what you might see!

Mrs. White *(struggling fiercely)*. Do you think I fear the child I bore! Let me go! *(She wrenches herself loose and rushes to the door, which she tears open.)* I'm coming, Herbert! I'm coming!

Mr. White *(cowering in the extreme corner, left front)*. Don't 'ee do it! Don't 'ee do it! ◀SR-9

*(*Mrs. White *is at work on the outer door, where the knocking still continues. She slips the chain, slips the lower bolt, unlocks the door.)*

EE. Reading Skill: DRAWING CONCLUSIONS Ask students to conclude why the Whites weren't allowed to see their son after he died. *(Possible response: It would have been too upsetting to see Herbert's body, which had been mangled beyond recognition.)*

FF. Critical Thinking: EVALUATING Ask students whether they think Mr. and Mrs. White lived too much for their son and not enough for each other. Have them explain their answers. *(Possible responses: They did live too much for Herbert, and now they have nothing to live for. They did not live too much for Herbert; it is normal to feel such crushing grief at the loss of a beloved child.)*

CRITIC'S CORNER

. . . there are two or three [of Jacobs' short stories], notably "The Monkey's Paw" and "The Brown Man's Servant," which show him as a master of eerie mystery and horror, who challenges comparison with Poe; the effect of "The Brown Man's Servant" is heightened by a wry humour which Poe had not, and the uncanny grimness of "The Monkey's Paw" by a pathos that is wrought to a pitch of almost painful intensity when the knock comes on the door at night and the heart-broken mother, after struggling desperately with the bolts, flings the door open and there is nothing there. This, like "Beauty and the Barge" and other of his stories, has been as successful on the stage as in Jacobs' books. . . .

A. St. John Adcock, essay excerpted in Twentieth-Century Literary Criticism, edited by Dennis Poupard

GG. Literary Element: SUSPENSE Ask students how the playwright builds suspense at this point in the play. *(The constant knocking at the door and Mrs. White's inability to open the door create suspense.)*

HH. Literary Element: THEME Have students summarize how each wish on the monkey's paw became a matter of life and death. *(The first wish caused Herbert's death; the second wish resurrected him from death; the third wish returned him to a peaceful grave and possibly saved Mr. and Mrs. White's lives.)*

Check Test

1. From whom did the Whites get the paw? *(Sergeant-Major Morris)*

2. What is unusual about the monkey's paw? *(It has the magic power to grant three wishes.)*

3. What wish does Mr. White make first? *(He wishes for two hundred pounds.)*

4. What happens to make this first wish come true? *(The Whites' son is killed on the job and they receive two hundred pounds in compensation.)*

5. What is Mr. White's last wish? *(He wishes his son dead again and at peace.)*

Encouraging Independent Reading

"Miriam," a short story by Truman Capote

"The Last Seance," a short story by Agatha Christie

"Midas," a Greek myth retold by Bernard Evslin

"Autumn Heat," a short story by W. F. Harvey

"The Last Leaf," a short story by O. Henry

Mr. White *(suddenly)*. The paw! Where's the monkey's paw? *(He gets on his knees and feels along the floor for it.)*

Mrs. White *(tugging at the top bolt)*. John! The top bolt's stuck. I can't move it. Come and help. Quick!

Mr. White *(wildly groping)*. The paw! There's a wish left.

(The knocking is now loud, and in groups of increasing length between the speeches.)

GG **Mrs. White.** D'ye hear him? John! Your child's knocking!

Mr. White. Where is it? Where did it fall?

Mrs. White *(tugging desperately at the bolt)*. Help! Help! Will you keep your child from his home?

Mr. White. Where did it fall? I can't find it—I can't find—

(The knocking is now tempestuous, and there are blows upon the door as of a body beating against it.) GG

Mrs. White. Herbert! Herbert! My boy! Wait! Your mother's opening to you! Ah! It's moving! It's moving!

Mr. White. God forbid! *(finds the paw)* Ah!

Mrs. White *(slipping the bolt)*. Herbert!

Mr. White *(Has raised himself to his knees; he holds the paw high)*. I wish him dead. *(The knocking stops abruptly.)* I wish him dead and at peace! ◀ SR-1

Mrs. White *(flinging the door open simultaneously)*. Herb—

(A flood of moonlight. Emptiness. The old man sways in prayer on his knees. The old woman lies half swooning, wailing against the door-post.) HH

Curtain

Words to Know and Use

tempestuous (tem pes' cho͞o əs) *adj.* violent or stormy

Responding to Reading

First Impressions

1. What part of the play made the strongest impression on you?

Second Thoughts

2. How would you describe Mr. and Mrs. White and their son, Herbert, in the opening scene?

   Think about
   - what they say about their lives
   - how they treat each other
   - how they react to the sergeant-major's tales

3. Mr. White says, "I seem to've got all I want." Does he really feel this way?

   Think about
   - what Mr. White has
   - his interest in the monkey's paw
   - why Mr. White makes his first wish

4. Why does Mr. White hesitate to make his second wish?

5. Do the characters in this play act as you would expect real people to act? Find several examples to support your answer.

6. The fakir who put a spell on the monkey's paw did so to prove that people have no control over their lives. Based on the Whites' experiences, do you think the fakir proved his point? Explain.

Broader Connections

7. The sergeant-major says that the fakir wanted to prove "that fate ruled people." How much are people ruled by fate (however you may choose to define the term), and how much do they control their own destinies through conscious decisions and actions? Explain your answer.

Literary Concept: Foreshadowing

A writer's use of hints or clues to indicate events that will happen is called **foreshadowing.** In "The Monkey's Paw," the sergeant-major states that the first owner of the monkey's paw wished for death as his third wish. How does this comment foreshadow the Whites' tragedy? Find and explain one other example of foreshadowing in the play.

Student Response

Responding to Reading

The questions are open-ended with no "right" or "wrong" answers. However, responses must be supported with information from the selection. Possible answers follow:

1. Have students describe the part that made the sharpest impression on them.

2. The Whites are simple people who love each other and Herbert. Their lives are a bit routine, which may be why they are fascinated by the sergeant-major's tales.

3. Some students may say that Mr. White must feel a lack or else he would not be so interested in the power of the monkey's paw. Others may say that he really does believe he has all he wants and uses the paw simply to satisfy his curiosity.

4. Some students may say that he is frightened of the paw's power or that he is terrified of what Herbert will look like. Others may suggest that raising someone from the dead seems likes an evil or sacrilegious deed to him.

5. Some students may say yes and cite examples such as the Whites' doing something they were warned not to do or feeling deep grief over the loss of their son. Others may say no and cite examples such as the Whites' simplicity and gullibility.

6. Some students may say the fakir did prove his point because the Whites could not control their curiosity, used the paw in spite of warnings, and brought great tragedy upon themselves. Others may say he did not prove his point, since, in the end, Mr. White did control the outcome of events.

7. Possible response: No one can totally control the forces and circumstances of life that we call fate. However, people can control their own destinies to a great extent if they consciously set realistic goals and then work toward them consistently.

Literary Concept—Foreshadowing

Mr. White will also make his last wish for death, that of his son's. Some examples of foreshadowing that students may cite: Herbert's mentioning his need to keep "a cool head, a steady eye, and a still hand" at work foreshadows his death at the plant; Morris's urging Mr. White to throw the monkey's paw on the fire foreshadows the misery the Whites experience from wishing on the paw; Herbert's saying he never expects to see the money his father has wished for foreshadows Herbert's death; Mr. White's saying Herbert is "just by the cemetery" foreshadows the Whites' knowledge of Herbert's being dead.

Writing Options

The Writing Options are designed to meet varied student interests and abilities. Have each student choose one writing activity to complete. You may wish to guide some students to an option that requires less writing.

Journal Update Have students review their journal entries for *The Monkey's Paw.* Ask what they have learned about people's attitudes toward the role of luck in their lives. Have them write some ideas on their own beliefs about luck, fate, and the unforeseen consequences of wishes.

Vocabulary Practice

1. yarn
2. alcove
3. pervade
4. addle
5. rubbish
6. tempestuous
7. pensively
8. disclaim
9. involuntary
10. reproachfully
11. compensation
12. fret
13. trifle
14. infernal
15. bog

Writing Options

1. A moral is a lesson taught by a story. The lesson is usually stated in one sentence as a guideline for living. Examples are "Honesty is the best policy" and "Look before you leap." Think about the lesson that is taught by "The Monkey's Paw." Write a moral for this play.
2. The sergeant-major tells the Whites the history of the monkey's paw. Describe what you think the sergeant-major's three wishes might have been and the consequences of each wish. (Remember that he lost an arm as one consequence.)

Vocabulary Practice

Exercise On your paper, write the word that best completes each sentence below.

1. The sergeant captivated his audience with a clever ____.
2. Mrs. White stood in the ____ by the door, looking for her son.
3. A feeling of terror will ____ the room when the knocking begins.
4. The sergeant-major's strange tales began to ____ Mr. White's senses.
5. Mrs. White believed it was a lot of ____ that a wish on the monkey's paw would somehow make one unhappy.
6. The knocking increased until it sounded like a(n) ____ storm.
7. The sergeant-major stared into the fire, ____ mumbling his thoughts about the monkey's paw.
8. Mr. Sampson said that the company would ____ all responsibility for Herbert's accident.
9. Unable to stop himself, Mr. White gave a(n) ____ cry when he saw the faces in the fire.
10. Mrs. White looked ____ at her husband when he refused to make a second wish.
11. The power company gave the Whites two hundred pounds as ____ for their son's death.
12. When her son didn't return, Mrs. White began to ____ about his whereabouts.
13. The sergeant-major would take only a small amount, a(n) ____, for the monkey's paw.
14. Mr. White threw the evil and ____ paw into the fire.
15. The constant rain had turned the pathway into a(n) ____.

Words to Know and Use

addle
alcove
bog
compensation
disclaim
fret
infernal
involuntary
pensively
pervade
reproachfully
rubbish
tempestuous
trifle
yarn

Options for Learning

1 • Selling the Paw Imagine that you have been asked to create and present a radio advertisement for a company that is selling monkey paws. Assume that your audience consists of people who are trying to find quick ways to improve their lives. Play up the paws' positive aspects, but be sure to mention in the fine print that use of the paws might cause some problems. Create a catchy slogan such as "Need a little hand to get things done?" Read your advertisement to the class.

2 • Playing Ma and Pa The last scene of "The Monkey's Paw" contains the most exciting moment, or climax, of the play. With two partners, ad-lib the final scene, with this twist: change the ending by having Mrs. White open the door before Mr. White can make the last wish. Have the third person ad-lib the part of whoever or whatever is behind the door.

3 • Draw the Paw The monkey's paw disgusts Mrs. White when she first sees it. What do you think this small, mummified hand looks like? Draw your conception of the monkey's paw.

4 • Make a Wish Throughout time people have told stories about creatures and objects with magical powers that make dreams come true. Literature is full of characters, such as genies and fairies, that grant wishes. Research some of these mythological characters to answer the following questions:

- Who believed in them?
- What did they look like?
- What kinds of wishes did they grant?
- To whom did they grant these wishes?
- What price was exacted for the granting of a wish?

FACT FINDER

How much is two hundred English pounds in American currency?

W. W. Jacobs
1863–1943

William Wymark Jacobs spent much of his boyhood poking around the London docks where his father was a manager. Growing up around the wharves and ships greatly influenced his later writing career. At first, Jacobs was unable to make a living as a writer. To make ends meet, he took the civil service exam and acquired a job with the savings bank department of the General Post Office, but his heart wasn't in it. His first and deepest love was always writing. In 1896, Jacobs published his first book of sea stories, *Many Cargoes.* It was a tremendous success. One critic called Jacobs "one of the most permanently delightful short story writers who ever lived." Jacobs wrote nineteen more books including *Light Freights, Ship's Company,* and *Salthaven.*

Cross-Curricular Options

Students may create a "Background Notes" display for the play, using details from the selection where suitable.

Geography: Create a map of the British Isles. Locate London and Fulham. Label the bodies of water that surround the islands.

Social Studies: Prepare a profile of Great Britain in 1900. Include information on occupations, government, homes, cities, transportation, and culture.

Language: Create a Dictionary of Dialect. Include examples from the play as well as other British words not commonly used in the United States. Include respellings and definitions.

Art History: Locate turn-of-the-century photographs, paintings, and drawings of daily life in Britain. Write a caption for each.

Publishing: Compile all contributions and prepare a display.

Options for Learning

These activities suit a variety of learning styles and modes of expression. Allow students to review the options and then choose the one they wish to do. Many are excellent collaborative learning projects.

1. Selling the Paw Remind students that a radio advertisement is totally dependent on sounds to capture audience attention and sell a product. Suggest that students consider using sound effects and music in their advertisments and that they tape-record them.

2. Playing Ma and Pa Encourage students to use costumes and props to make their presentations more realistic.

3. Draw the Paw Students may use biology texts or encyclopedia pictures for reference.

4. Make a Wish Suggest that students research encyclopedia entries on folklore and mythology, as well as collections of fairy tales for children.

Fact Finder

Students can find the current value of major currencies in the financial section of the newspaper or at a bank. In a recent month, the British pound was worth $1.87; therefore, two hundred pounds would be worth about $374 dollars today. In 1900, the setting of the play, the pound was worth about $5. So the Whites received about $1000, about the annual salary of a working man at the turn of the century.

Additional Information About the Author

W. W. Jacobs W. W. Jacobs was primarily a humorist. It is a bit ironic, therefore, that Jacobs is most remembered, in the United States at least, as the author of a grim tale of gothic horror, "The Monkey's Paw."

Closure

The Monkey's Paw explores the theme "A Matter of Life and Death" in that after inadvertently contributing to his son's death, Mr. White literally wishes his son first to live again and then to die. Ask students to name other stories or films in which the characters' wishes have led to tragic consequences.

Writer's Workshop

Writer's Workshop

Objectives

- To write a descriptive essay about a literary character
- To use prewriting skills to choose a character, gather impressions, and diagram information about the character
- To choose a strategy for organizing diagrammed information
- To draft, revise, edit, and share a descriptive essay
- To publish a descriptive essay and reflect on the writing process

Integrating . . .

Literature and Writing Discuss with students how observing people making life-and-death decisions can reveal character. Ask why they think this is so. *(Possible response: because when confronted with such important decisions, people have no time to consider their petty everyday concerns, and onlookers can see the real person behind the veneer)* Have students describe people they have seen on TV news or in person who were making, or had just made, a life-and-death decision. What did they say and do, and what did this portray about their personality?

Literature and Writing The Language Workshop in this subunit is on using vivid modifiers. Stress that vivid modifiers give writing color and that they are particularly important in descriptive writing. Encourage students to use precise modifiers in their writing for this workshop.

Literature and Study Skills The Study Skills Workshop in this subunit involves different kinds of reading for accomplishing different goals. Suggest that after carefully reading each literature selection, students scan and skim the selection, in the *Prewriting* stage of their descriptive essays. They may want to skim—quickly read only the high points—to choose a character for their essay. They may want to scan—sweep their eyes across each page until they find what they're looking for—to check their first impressions about their character.

DESCRIPTION

If a friend wanted to arrange a blind date for you, you would probably insist that your friend describe the person. Naturally, you would want to know what the person looked like, but unless you simply planned to stare at your date all evening, you would need some other information as well. You might, for example, want to know about the person's interests, behavior, background, and values.

Whether writers describe real characters or fictional characters, they usually try to present an accurate, detailed picture of the person. A **description** paints a still-life picture of the character—a picture expressed through words.

Here is your PASSkey to this assignment.

GUIDED ASSIGNMENT: CHARACTER PORTRAIT

Choose one of the main characters in this subunit. Describe this character in detail, painting a portrait with your words.

PURPOSE: To describe a character
AUDIENCE: Your teacher and classmates
SUBJECT: A character from this subunit
STRUCTURE: A descriptive essay

Prewriting

STEP 1 Choose your character Select a character you're interested in describing. Perhaps one character intrigues you, or you identify with him or her in some way. Jot down your impressions of this character, noting both external and internal traits—that is, how the character appears and what he or she feels or believes. Here are some traits one student thought of as she recalled a character named Maggie:

STUDENT MODEL ▶

`trapped, isolated, artistic, no makeup, dissatisfied, wrinkled housecoat, vibrant, middle-aged, housewife`

STEP 2 Understand your character Review the list of traits and try to decide how they fit together to describe the person. Why does this person dress or behave the way he or she does? The student mentioned in Step 1 came up with this theory about Maggie:

Additional Resources

UNIT ONE RESOURCE BOOK
Writer's Workshop Copy Master, p. 70
Peer and Self-Evaluation Guidelines, p. 71
Writing Assessment Guidelines, p. 72

ENRICHMENT MATERIALS
Thinking Skills Transparency and Worksheet
Fine Art Transparency and Writing Prompts
Revision, Proofreading, and Elaboration Worksheet
Writing Prompts for Assessment

She's a vibrant, middle-aged woman with an artistic bent who feels trapped in her isolated role as housewife.

◀ STUDENT MODEL

STEP 3 Check your first impressions Review the story in which the character is featured, this time with the purpose of testing the truth of your first impression. As you look over the story, gather more information. You might want to create a diagram similar to the following one in which you can show how you elaborate on your original idea.

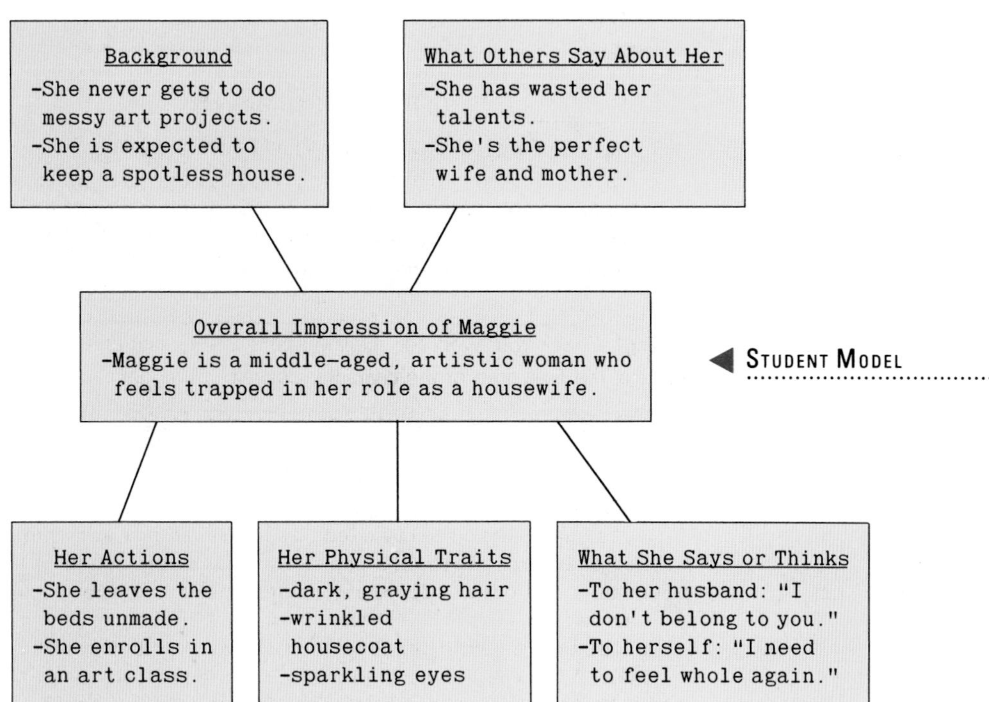

◀ STUDENT MODEL

STEP 4 Organize your information Character descriptions can be organized in one of two ways. You can begin with the person's physical features and then build up to his or her personal qualities, or you can begin with your overall impression and then fill in the details that created that impression. Whichever plan you choose, be sure to group related details together.

Prewriting Stress the importance of checking their first impressions by reviewing the story in which the character they have chosen to describe appears. Make sure they understand that this step can eliminate false impressions and generate useful ideas to use in their writing. Point out that the importance of elaborating their first impressions with additional information is to give them a full, rich group of ideas and details from which to choose. To accomplish this, they should try using a diagram like the one in the text.

Teaching Tip
Remind students that there are many other prewriting strategies (such as outlining, clustering, freewriting, and charting) that they can choose from to elaborate their ideas. Explain that they need not diagram, but may choose whichever prewriting strategy seems to best suit them and their topic. Emphasize that students have a choice about how to organize their information for the descriptive essay, but that whatever choice they make, they must group related details together.

Computer Tip
Students using a computer may want to try both organizational strategies and evaluate which works best for their essay. The capability of moving paragraphs and sentences will make trying different organizational strategies relatively easy.

Teaching Tip
Warn students not to go overboard by using too many modifiers. Urge them instead to use fresh, descriptive words.

Teaching Strategies

Introduction Have students turn to the Writer's Workshop for this subunit on page 164. Discuss with them the concept of descriptive writing as painting pictures with words.

Call students' attention to the Guided Assignment box on page 164. Be sure they understand that they will write a descriptive essay on a character from one of the literary selections in the subunit and that their audience will be their teacher and classmates. Emphasize that the assignment asks for a detailed description.

Drafting Suggest that students use whatever prewriting material they possess when drafting their descriptive essays. Remind them that the assignment calls for a detailed description and that referring to their diagram or other prewriting aids will help them create a full, detailed essay.

Revising and Editing Suggest that when students revise, they pay particular attention to choosing vivid modifiers and to making sure the details of their descriptive essays are arranged in related groups.

If students have difficulty using vivid modifiers in the revising stage of their descriptive essays, conduct a mini-lesson or review the material in the Language Workshop.

Drafting

Using the information you've gathered about the character and following the organizational plan you've chosen, draft your descriptive essay. Try to show the character's qualities through precise, concrete descriptions.

Revising and Editing

Share your draft with a classmate. Working as a pair, use the following checklist to evaluate and revise your draft.

Revision Checklist

1. Have you described both external and internal qualities?
2. Have you taken into account what the character says and does, what others say about him or her, and any background information?
3. Are the details organized in a meaningful order?
4. Have you described this character's qualities in precise language?

Editing Check your work for spelling errors, clarity, and punctuation.

This is the final draft of the character portrait of Maggie.

STUDENT MODEL ▶

Maggie is a passionate artist struggling to break free from the chains binding her to her home and family. Her creative instinct, buried long ago when her parents scolded her for messing up their house with her art projects, had never really died. It surfaced now and then in her colorful clothes, with their bright splashes of orange and purple flowers, in her sparkling eyes, and in her dark, slightly graying, luxuriant hair, which ran wildly down her shoulders when it wasn't tied up. But her husband liked her hair tied back; he expected the house to be in tiptop shape each day. She and the house were his possessions, like the new car he bought each year and locked in the garage. She had been the perfect wife and mother. But Maggie, now middle-aged, couldn't be locked in her home anymore. "I don't belong to you," she told her husband. The daily routines of ironing, cooking, and running errands for her family had left her with nothing more than a bare outline of herself. "You've wasted your talents," her friend Sari had told her, and Maggie knew

ADDITIONAL WRITING AND RESEARCH TOPICS

The following items provide additional writing practice based on the selections in this subunit:

Descriptive Essay

- Write a self-portrait—a description of yourself—from the third-person point of view. Describe both your external physical features and your internal qualities, using vivid, concrete language.
- Find a photograph or painted portrait of a person in a book or art gallery. Translate this visual picture into a "word picture" by describing the character in the picture.

Another Topic

Narration The barber in "Lather and Nothing Else" holds back his impulse to harm his enemy. Think of a time in your life when you were tempted to hurt someone but held back. In a first-person narrative, recount that experience.

this. She had given 99 percent of herself to her family and now felt incomplete. "I need to feel whole again," she said to herself. And so she woke up one morning, refused to make the beds, and went downtown to enroll in an art class. For a year she poured her soul into her paintings, waving her paintbrush like a bird flapping its wings for the first time. The fire within her burned on the canvas in passionate colors, erasing her years of bondage.

Publishing

Put together a literary "yearbook" featuring all of the character portraits written by your class.

Reflecting on Your Writing

Answer the following questions. Turn in your answers with your paper or place them in your writing portfolio.

1. Did you find support for your first impressions of your character or did you have to rethink your ideas?
2. Why did you organize your paper in the way you did?
3. What part was the most difficult to write? Why?

Publishing As an alternative to the *Publishing* suggestion in the pupil's edition, you might consider these ideas:

- Have students arrange a portrait gallery in the classroom or library. Suggest that each mount his or her descriptive essay on a poster, along with a drawing or magazine picture that portrays the character.
- Have students make an oral presentation of their descriptive essays and dress to resemble their characters.

Reflecting on Your Writing When you review students' portfolios, remember to respond to their answers for the *Reflecting* questions.

Students' answers to these questions should attempt to evaluate specific parts of the writing process used in writing their descriptive essays. If many students report the same difficulty in their answers to Question 3, you may wish to reteach some skills.

Closure

Before beginning the next subunit, be sure that students have internalized these concepts:

- A descriptive essay paints a picture with words.
- When writing about literature, check first impressions by reviewing the story.
- Descriptive essays can be organized from abstract to concrete qualities, or from concrete to abstract qualities.
- Details within a descriptive essay should be ordered in related groups.

Professional Notebook

The first writing skill that novices need to learn is reader awareness—that the reader is another person who cannot possibly share the writer's feelings, ideas, or memories unless the writer gives the reader enough information. This is a skill that precedes learning to write in sentences. The novice needs to understand what it means to develop an idea for the reader. It is never enough to write "More details" or "Lack of development." Novices think they have written enough and do not know what details the reader still needs. By asking genuine questions about the text, the teacher helps writers clarify meanings not only for readers but also for themselves. Students most often do not realize the possibilities of their subjects without a teacher's help. The act of writing is an act of discovering something.

Sydell Rabin, *"Reading Papers: A Teaching Response," English Journal*

Language Workshop

Objectives

- To understand that modifiers are words that limit the meanings of other words
- To identify adjectives modifying nouns or pronouns
- To identify adverbs modifying verbs, adjectives, or other adverbs
- To use modifiers correctly in writing
- To replace vague modifiers with more specific, vivid modifiers in writing

Integrating . . .

Writing and Grammar Remind students that in a character portrait such as the one they wrote in the Writer's Workshop, specific kinds of words can help to vividly describe the character. Then write the following phrases on the board:

1. a bad storm
   a tempestuous storm
2. an agonizing injury
   a bad injury
3. he drove skillfully
   he drove well

Have students read each pair of phrases and identify which paints a more vivid picture. Point out that vivid language creates interest while adding information.

Teaching Strategies

Have a volunteer read the focus statement in the box at the top of page 168. Point out that modifiers can enhance as well as limit the meanings of other words. Then have students continue reading up to "Using Adjectives." Discuss the two paragraphs about the diver, reminding students to read the *Punctuation Rule* to the right of the revised paragraph. Then orally demonstrate this rule by inserting *and* between two adjectives in the paragraph (cold and cruel ocean).

Teaching Tip

You may wish to distribute thesauruses to students and have them find vivid modifiers for vague words you name, such as *good, nice, hot, fun,* and *big.* Students may keep running lists in their journals of exceptional modifiers they discover.

LANGUAGE WORKSHOP

USING VIVID MODIFIERS

Words that limit the meanings of other words are called **modifiers.** An **adjective** is a word that modifies a noun or a pronoun. An **adverb** is a word that modifies a verb, an adjective, or another adverb.

A landscape painter usually begins a painting by laying down large areas of background color—blue for the sky and for water, gray for mountains, green for grass and for trees. Then the painter fills in the details. Of course, these details give the painting its interest and beauty. After all, anyone can paint the top half of a canvas blue, but it takes real talent to paint a realistic cloud or tree.

Among the details that authors add to make their writing vivid and concrete are modifiers—adjectives and adverbs. Compare the following paragraphs. Notice how much more vivid the second paragraph is because of the adjectives and adverbs that have been added.

Unrevised

Out of air, the diver surfaced and blew up his buoyancy vest so that he could float. He removed his face mask and looked around at the ocean stretching as far as his eyes could see. There was no boat there to meet him, only the waves! He felt as he had never felt before.

PUNCTUATION RULE

When one adjective follows another, a comma may be needed to separate them. If an *and* placed between the adjectives sounds natural, and if you can switch the order of the adjectives without changing the meaning of the sentence, then use a comma.

Revised

Out of air, the *weary* diver surfaced and *hurriedly* blew up his buoyancy vest so that he could float. He removed his face mask and looked around at the *cold, cruel* ocean stretching as far as his *strained, stinging, irritated* eyes could see. There was no *friendly* boat there to meet him, only the *relentlessly rocking* waves! He felt *more alone* than he had ever felt before.

Using Adjectives

An adjective tells *which one, what kind, how much,* or *how many* about a noun or a pronoun.

that razor   *lukewarm* water   *more* lather   *four* rebels

Additional Resources

UNIT ONE RESOURCE BOOK

Language Workshop Copy Master, p. 73

ENRICHMENT MATERIALS

Grammar and Usage Copy Masters

When choosing adjectives, look for ones that are original, fresh, and precise. Avoid adjectives that are vague or overused.

Vague The food was *bad.*
Precise The food *reeked.*

Overused A *gentle* breeze was blowing.
Fresh A *delicate* breeze was blowing.

Using Adverbs

An adverb tells *how, when, where,* or *to what extent* about a verb, an adjective, or another adverb.

The barber shaved *carefully.* (adverb modifying a verb)
He was an *extremely* flustered man. (adverb modifying an adjective)
I did *very* well on the test. (adverb modifying an adverb)

Reminder
Many adverbs are formed by adding *-ly* to adjectives:

Adj.	Adv.
slow	slowly
quick	quickly
hopeful	hopefully

One quality that makes for successful writing is the ability to communicate with just the right word. In most instances, avoid vague adverbs such as *really, very, well,* and *often.* Specific adverbs like *precisely, dramatically,* and *briefly* will add variety and vigor to your writing.

Exercise 1 Write down all the modifiers used in the revised paragraph about the diver on the preceding page. Tell whether each modifier is an *Adjective* or an *Adverb.* Then explain how the modifiers contribute to creating the mood of the piece.

Exercise 2 Rewrite each of the following sentences, adding the modifiers indicated in parentheses. Make sure that the modifiers you add are fresh, vivid, and precise.

1. The ____ (adjective) barber ____ (adverb) shaved the general with the ____ (adjective) blade.
2. The ____ (adjective) general spoke ____ (adverb) as he was being shaved.
3. The barber spoke ____ (adverb) to the ____ (adjective) customer.
4. Accustomed to brutality, General Torres talked of murder in a(n) ____ (adjective) way.
5. The government ____ (adverb) spied on the revolutionaries' ____ (adjective) activities.
6. He had a(n) ____ (adjective) face and a(n) ____ (adjective) manner of speaking.

Now have students read up to Exercise 1 and brainstorm other adjectives and adverbs to replace those given in the examples. Be sure students read the Reminder. Point out that the *-ly* ending does not always signal an adverb—for example, a *lively* dance, a *weekly* program, the *nightly* news, a *likely* story. Also point out that some words have the same form whether used as an adjective or an adverb, such as *a short skirt, cut short; a first date, arrived first.* Lead students to conclude that the way a word is used in a sentence determines its part of speech.

Teaching Tip

If students have difficulty in identifying a modifier as an adjective or adverb, suggest that they ask themselves what word is being modified. If a noun or pronoun is being modified, the word is an adjective. If a verb, adjective, or adverb is being modified, the word is an adverb.

Assign Exercises 1 and 2 on page 169 and review the answers with students. Then have them form small groups to complete Exercise 3. Offer help as needed during their group discussions. Assign Exercise 4, appointing one student in each group to record the modifiers. Finally, assign Exercise 5 to students, suggesting that they keep both the original piece and the revision in their portfolios to review later as a reference for improving their writing.

Answer Key
Exercise 1

1. weary—adjective
2. hurriedly—adverb
3. cold, cruel—adjectives
4. strained, stinging, irritated—adjectives
5. friendly—adjective
6. relentlessly rocking—adverb and adjective
7. more alone—adverb and adjective

Answers explaining modifiers' contribution to mood will vary but should indicate the gravity of the situation.

Exercise 2

(Answers will vary but may include the following:)

1. nervous, carefully, sharpened
2. opinionated, confidently
3. hesitantly, impatient
4. offhand
5. secretly, subversive
6. impressive, understated

Closure

Before beginning the next subunit, be sure students have internalized these concepts:

- Modifiers are words that limit and enhance the meanings of other words.
- Adjectives modify nouns or pronouns, and adverbs modify verbs, adjectives, or other adverbs.
- Vague modifiers can be replaced with more specific, interesting words that convey additional information.

Exercise 3

Answers will vary. Encourage students to think of modifiers to replace those in the paragraphs.

Exercise 4

(Answers will vary but may include the following:)

1. overtly
2. numerous
3. remarkably
4. close
5. ordinary
6. extraordinary
7. gravely urgent
8. raging, blazing
9. swollen, rushing

Exercise 5

Answers will vary, but students should replace vague adjectives and adverbs with vivid modifiers.

Exercise 3 Style Choose two paragraphs from "Lather and Nothing Else" or "Tsali of the Cherokees" that are particularly descriptive. Write down the modifiers used in each paragraph and label them *Adjective* or *Adverb.* Then, with other students in a small group, discuss the paragraphs you chose. Talk about what information is added by the modifiers, how they affect the mood, and whether they could be replaced with modifiers that are more original or more effective.

Exercise 4 Work in a small group to complete the following passage. As a group, brainstorm a list of vivid, precise modifiers to fill in the blanks. Try to avoid the most obvious choices (such as "*very* dangerous"). You may use a thesaurus if you wish. Compare your work with that of other groups in your class to see the variety of modifiers that writers have at their disposal.

> No one knows how he or she will act in a(n) ____ dangerous situation. There are ____ examples of people who reacted ____ when their ____ friends or children were in danger. Sometimes ____ people have shown ____ strength or courage in a ____ ____ situation. "Everyday heroes" have endured ____ , ____ fires and ____ , ____ rivers to rescue strangers.

Exercise 5 Analyzing and Revising Your Writing

1. Take a piece of writing from your portfolio.
2. Reread the piece, looking for vague, uninteresting adjectives and adverbs.
3. Choose two paragraphs and rewrite them with new modifiers.
4. Compare your revision with the original piece of writing. Which one do you prefer? Why?

LANGUAGE HANDBOOK

For review and practice, see Section 4, **Using Modifiers.**

ADDITIONAL PRACTICE

The following items provide additional practice on using vivid modifiers.

Write these sentences, replacing each underlined modifier with a fresher, more vigorous, or more precise one. Possible answers are given.

1. The <u>red</u> clay was piled on the <u>wooden</u> table. *brick-red; knotty pine*

2. A <u>few</u> people reported the <u>odd</u> noises to the police. *Three; weird*

Write this paragraph, adding vivid adjectives and adverbs to replace the blanks. Possible answers are given.

I've never seen such a group of *miserable* people as on the *unhappy* night that we lost the state championship. Our team had looked *so promising* just hours earlier. In fact, we sped to a(n) *significant* lead during the first period.

READING FOR DIFFERENT PURPOSES

To find a specific fact or definition, you can quickly **scan** a reading selection, sweeping your eye across each page until you spot what you're looking for.

To find the main idea in a piece of reading, or to get an overview of its content, you can **skim** fairly quickly, reading only the title, headlines, highlighted words or phrases, and topic sentences. If there's a summary section, slow down and read it more carefully.

Finally, to read for **in-depth learning,** read more slowly. Skim the entire piece first, noting the main ideas. Then, read carefully, making sure you understand the key words and concepts. Take notes as you read.

How to Scan

To train yourself to scan, try this method: (1) Choose a familiar textbook. (2) Place a folded paper or a three- by five-inch card over the first line of a page and move the paper quickly down the page. (3) Look for key words or phrases that indicate you are near the information you need. (4) When you locate such a clue, stop scanning and begin to read slowly.

Exercise Follow these directions step by step.

Step 1 Scan the following article to identify the Native American tribe that is mentioned. Write your answer.

Step 2 Skim the article, noting the topic sentence and the boldfaced words. Write one sentence summarizing the main idea of the passage.

Step 3 Read the article in depth. Write at least three facts or reasons that support the main idea of the article.

> The only person in modern history to invent an alphabet was **Sequoyah,** a member of the Cherokee tribe. Sequoyah was born in Tennessee sometime in the 1760's and as a child, received no education. As a young man, he decided that the way white people communicated by writing and reading would be useful to the members of his tribe. He decided to make up a system of letters that would enable the Cherokee people to communicate on paper. He referred to writing on paper as "talking leaves."
>
> It took Sequoyah twelve years to invent the **eighty-six-letter alphabet** that represented the sounds of Cherokee speech. A council of chiefs approved Sequoyah's work, and he began to teach the alphabet to his tribe. The alphabet was so **simple and logical** that a Cherokee speaker could learn it in a few days. Within a few months, thousands of illiterate Cherokees had become **literate in their own language.** Sequoyah traveled to Arkansas and to Oklahoma, where the Cherokees had been forced to relocate. Wherever he found his people, he taught them to read and write.

Study Skills Workshop

Objectives

- To use scanning to locate specific details quickly
- To use skimming to get a general idea of a passage
- To read in depth to understand detailed information

Integrating . . .

Reading, Writing, and Study Skills Share with students that this workshop discusses three kinds of reading, all of which are helpful for different purposes.

Teaching Strategies

Ask students to describe the type of reading they do when they preview a new chapter in a textbook. *(Possible response: quickly look at titles, subtitles, photos, and graphic aids)* Explain that this kind of reading is called skimming.

Then ask them to describe how they would read a magazine article to find the date a particular event happened. *(Possible response: look quickly over the pages searching for numbers)* Explain that this process is called scanning. Point out that there is a third type of reading in which every word is read so that the reader can grasp relationships and details.

Read through the material with students. Discuss and practice the scanning method described in the margin.

Assign the exercise on page 171. Have students read their answers.

Closure

Be sure students have internalized these concepts:

- Skimming allows a reader to note main points about a passage.
- Scanning is used to locate particular pieces of information.
- In-depth reading is used for a careful reading of a passage.

Exercise

1. Sequoyah invented a simple, eighty-six-letter alphabet that helped thousands of Cherokees become literate in their own language. **2.** Sequoyah saw that reading and writing helped people communicate. **3.** He developed a simple and logical eighty-six-letter alphabet and used it to teach the Cherokee people to read.

Additional Resources

UNIT ONE RESOURCE BOOK
Related Skills Copy Master, p. 74

ENRICHMENT MATERIALS
Standardized Test Practice Copy Masters

Additional Practice

1. Skim the workshop on page 120. Write one sentence that summarizes the main idea. *(The appropriate level of language should be used for each different communication need.)*

2. Scan the workshop to find four types of communication in which it is appropriate to use informal language. *(magazines, newspapers, casual letters, conversations)*

3. Reread the workshop in depth. Find three important supporting details.

Unit Two *Escapes: Triumphs and Retreats*

Objectives

Students will develop skills in the following areas. An asterisk (*) indicates a workshop topic.

Reading and Thinking

understanding italics	*p. 175*
observing form of a poem	*p. 183*
understanding dialect	*p. 188*
understanding dialogue	*p. 201*
understanding Briticisms	*p. 216*
clarifying	*pp. 243, 245, 247, 248, 253, 254*
making a timeline	*p. 268*
summarizing	*pp. 270, 272, 273, 274*
noting stage directions	*p. 290*

Vocabulary and Related Skills

analogies	*p. 182*
*dialect	*p. 214*
synonyms	*pp. 231, 257*
antonyms	*pp. 231, 257*
using words in context	*pp. 242, 276*
*context clues	*p. 266*

Literary Appreciation

jargon	*p. 181*
free verse	*p. 186*
rhyme scheme	*p. 186*
plot	*p. 198*
point of view	*pp. 198, 206*
symbolism	*p. 206*
plot	*p. 230*
subplot	*p. 230*
metaphor	*p. 230*
sensory details	*p. 241*
mood	*p. 242*
theme	*p. 256*
flashback	*p. 257*
biography	*p. 275*
conflict	*p. 275*
antagonist	*p. 288*
suspense	*p. 289*
minor characters	*p. 313*
setting	*p. 314*

Writing

newspaper article	*pp. 182, 289, 314*
conversation	*pp. 182, 199, 231, 242, 257*
postcard	*p. 186*
slogan	*p. 199*
monologue	*p. 207*
dialogue	*p. 207*
*persuasion on: letter of recommendation	*pp. 208–11*
letter	*pp. 231, 276, 314*
song lyrics	*p. 242*
report	*p. 257*
*creative expression: radio drama	*pp. 259–62*
similes	*p. 289*
editorial	*p. 289*
epilogue	*p. 314*
diary entry	*p. 314*
*exposition: biographical	*pp. 316–19*
*paraphrasing	*p. 323*

Language, Grammar, Usage, Mechanics

*double negatives	*pp. 212–13*
*using indefinite pronouns	*pp. 263–65*
*sentence combining	*pp. 320–22*

Planning the Unit

You may find the following information and lists of resources helpful in preparing for the unit.

Difficulty Level of Selections

In determining the accessibility of the selections in this unit, many factors, including reading level and comprehension difficulty, have been taken into account. The ranking can be used as a general guide in determining how much preparation and assistance students will require in order to master the selection. No selection should be included or eliminated from the course based merely on difficulty level. Basic students will derive a great deal of confidence and self-esteem by working through a *challenge* selection; conversely, advanced students may find pleasure, relevance, and important themes in a selection that is rated *easy*.

Selection	Level
Stowaway! *p. 175*	**average**
Song of the Open Road *p. 183*	**average**
Travel *p. 185*	**average**
Antaeus *p. 188*	**average**
Gaston *p. 201*	**average**
The Third-Floor Flat *p. 216*	**average**
The Treasure of Lemon Brown *p. 232*	**easy**
The Euphio Question *p. 243*	**challenge**
The Survival in the Forty-Ninth *p. 268*	**average**
The Death Trap *p. 278*	**average**
A Young Lady of Property *p. 290*	**average**

Classroom Resources

Videocassettes, Films, and Filmstrips

■ ***Kurt Vonnegut, Jr.: "Deadeye Dick,"*** 16mm film, video, Wombat Productions, 1984, (60 minutes). This biographical production eyes Vonnegut's life and samples his works.

■ ***Millay at Steepletop***, film, video, BFA, 1984, (25 minutes). A documentary which captures the spirit of Edna St. Vincent Millay and of the place that was special to her.

■ ***Murder on the Orient Express***, 16mm film, video, Paramount, 1974, (128 minutes). The Academy Award-winning film of Agatha Christie's classic with an all-star cast.

■ ***Walt Whitman—Endlessly Rocking***, 16mm film, video, Barr Films, 1986, (21 minutes). A unique film where Whitman "appears" to a classroom of students and reads his poetry to the best of contemporary music.

Audiocassettes, Tapes, and Records

Edna St. Vincent Millay, audiocassette, Wilcom, Inc. A dramatization of the life of the poet.

The Snow Goose, audiocassette, Listen for Pleasure, (120 minutes). From the book by Paul Gallico read by Sir John Mills.

Three Blind Mice, 2 audiocassettes, Listen for Pleasure, 1985, (150 minutes). A reading of the book by Agatha Christie.

William Saroyan, audiocassette, Pacifica Tape Library, (55 minutes). This offers Saroyan's comments on the experiences which make up the education of an individual.

Community Resources

Involving the resources of your community in lesson preparation can add insight and relevance to the text. Consider the following possibilities as you plan.

■ For "Stowaway," contact an airline for educational materials on safety features, equipment, training, and procedures.

■ For "Song of the Open Road" and "Travel," contact travel agencies for information on uncommon and adventurous travel opportunities.

■ For "Antaeus," invite a city spokesperson to discuss land use and preservation of open space.

■ For "Gaston," invite someone from the French Consulate to describe daily life in Paris.

■ For "The Third-Floor Flat," have a detective discuss procedures for solving real-life whodunits.

■ For "The Treasure of Lemon Brown," invite parents to join students in an open forum on preparing young people for success.

■ For "Survival in the Forty-Ninth," invite a forest ranger to discuss wilderness survival.

■ For "The Death Trap," invite a magician to perform and explain his or her craft to the class.

■ For "A Young Lady of Property," have an actor, actress, or director talk about careers in theater and film.

Unit Preview

Winning is rarely as clear-cut as it seems, and neither is losing. In Unit 2, **Escapes: Triumphs and Retreats**, students will meet a number of characters who experience both victory and surprise. The unit contains three subunits:

- Subunit 1: Seizing the Moment
- Subunit 2: The Best-Laid Plans
- Subunit 3: Beating the Odds

Art Note

In *A World Within #44* artist Humberto Calzada (1944–) has created an imaginary scene with structures within structures. Born in Cuba, Calzada likes to paint architecture similar to that seen in the Caribbean. This scene is reminiscent of surrealist art. *In what way does this work apply to the theme of Escape?*

About the Author

Tom Stoppard is among the best-known and most celebrated modern dramatists, winner of the Tony Award in 1968, 1976, and 1984. He was born in Czechoslovakia in 1937 and raised in England. To support himself while trying to sell his plays, Stoppard worked as a critic and journalist. He garnered both popular and critical success in 1966 with the production of his first major play, *Rosencrantz and Guildenstern Are Dead,* which was acclaimed by critic Harold Hobson as "the most important event in British professional theatre of the last nine years." The play introduced Stoppard's main theme, the absurdity of life, as well as his use of puns, paradox, and word play. In his later plays, including *Travesties* (1974), *Every Good Boy Deserves Favor* (1977), and *The Real Thing* (1982), Stoppard has increasingly voiced his commitment to personal and artistic freedom.

Unit Two

Escapes: Triumphs and Retreats

"Every exit is an entrance somewhere else."

Tom Stoppard

A WORLD WITHIN # 44
(detail) 1988 Humberto Calzada

Discussion Questions

To help students probe connections among the fine art, quotation, and unit theme, have them consider the following questions:

1. What do you think Tom Stoppard means here? How would you explain his quotation in your own words? *(Possible response: "Every ending is a beginning." Students might suggest that Stoppard means that life is a series of new beginnings, so there is little reason to be sad when something ends. Students might also say Stoppard means that endings are really new starts.)*

2. What "exits" in your life have led to new beginnings? *(Possible response: Students might say that leaving one class or school at the end of the year has signaled a new beginning in another class or school. They might also apply the quotation to relationships, jobs, or family moves.)*

3. Do you agree with the quotation? Discuss your reasons. *(Possible responses: Students who cite positive experiences with endings leading to new beginnings may agree that exits are really entrances. Others, for whom endings may not have resulted in fresh starts, might argue that many exits lead nowhere.)*

4. What relationship do you see among the quotation, the artwork, and unit title? *(Possible response: The picture could represent both an exit and an entrance, as described in the quotation. The picture seems to offer possibility for both triumph and retreat, as described in the unit title.)*

5. Based on the artwork, quotation, and unit title, what do you predict the selections in this unit will concern? *(Possible responses: Students might say that the selections will show characters who experience opportunity and defeat. They may also suggest that the unit will concern risktakers.)*

Subunit Preview

Have students read the introduction to subunit 1, **Seizing the Moment.** Ask them to consider how recognizing opportunities pertains to the broader unit theme, **Escapes: Triumphs And Retreats.** How does losing out on a rare opportunity feel? Can a person prepare for an unexpected opportunity? How? How might someone create opportunity? Ask students to look over the subunit Table of Contents and point out the selection that they expect to be the most interesting.

For Additional Challenge

The following selections offer extra challenge in the exploration of the subunit theme:

"After Twenty Years," a short story by O. Henry

"Shaving," a short story by Leslie Norris

Additional Resources

Subunit Test, pp. 26–27

SEIZING THE MOMENT

Can you control your own fate? Some people think not; they wait passively, letting life take its course. Yet others, in the same surroundings, know how to take advantage of every opportunity, even to create their own possibilities. "The moment" might be a job opening, an opportunity to make a new friend, a chance to travel, or a way to resolve a bad situation.

In this subunit, you will meet a number of characters who try to "seize the moment." As you read each selection, decide what opportunity presents itself and how the character tries to take advantage of that chance to influence his or her fate.

OBSERVATION ASSESSMENT

Observing how students respond to the text, to the classroom instruction, and to peers is an important part of an assessment program. The following suggestions and the form in each Unit Resource Book can be used to implement observation assessment.

- As students work through the subunit, assess how they respond to literature. Do they enjoy sharing interesting facts and details with others? Can they put factual material in a context that relates to them?
- As they work through the subunit, can you see increasing enjoyment of reading?
- To evaluate their response to the selections, observe their reactions as they read. Do they respond with comments, questions, facial expressions, or laughter? Do they express interest to know more at the end of a story?

e x p l o r e

Magazine Article

Stowaway!

ARMANDO SOCARRAS RAMÍREZ
(är män′ dō sō kär′ äs rä mē′ räz)

as told to D. FODOR *and* J. REDDY

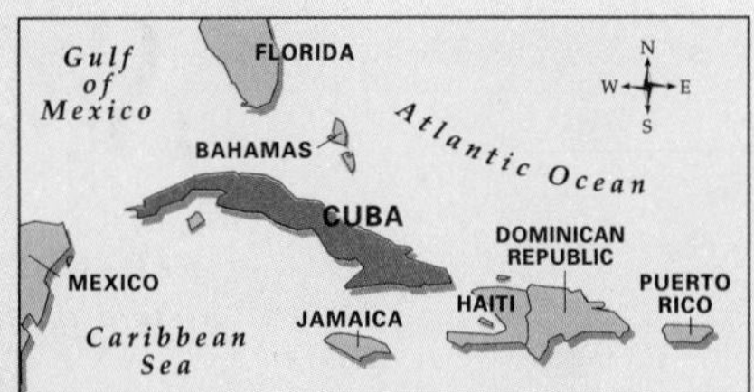

Examine What You Know (Prior Knowledge)

The personal narrative you are about to read is told by someone who was a stowaway. What do you know about stowaways? For what reasons might a person become a stowaway? Draw a word web on your paper as shown below. On the spokes around the word, write your associations with the word *stowaway*. Then, as you read, compare what you wrote with what you learn in the story.

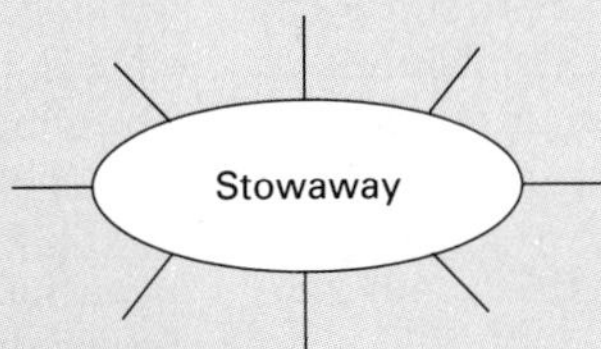

Expand Your Knowledge (Building Background)

The true story you are about to read begins in Cuba, an island about ninety miles south of Florida. Between 1957 and 1959, Cuba's government was overthrown in a violent revolution led by Fidel Castro. Since the beginning of Castro's communist regime, hundreds of thousands of people dissatisfied with the conditions in Cuba have left. An especially large emigration of refugees took place between April and September of 1980, when about 125,000 Cubans fled to the United States. Some refugees have been allowed to leave peacefully, but as you will see in this story, others have resorted to rather ingenious means to escape Castro's dictatorship.

Enrich Your Reading (Reading Skill)

Understanding Italics When you read this selection, you will notice that two large sections of the text are printed in a different style of type. This kind of type is called **italics.** Writers often use italics to emphasize a word or point. In this account, the writer uses italics to alert the reader that a different narrator is now telling the story.

Objectives

- To understand and analyze a magazine article
- To recognize the use of jargon
- To understand external and internal conflict
- To understand the use of italics to signal changes in the narrator
- To determine word meanings through the use of analogies
- To express understanding of the work through a choice of writing forms, including a letter, a list, a news report, and a dialogue

Prereading/Motivation

Examine What You Know

Discussion Prompts: What small words can you find within the word *stowaway*? What might prompt *you* to become a stowaway? If you were going to become a stowaway, where would you hide?

Expand Your Knowledge

Discussion Prompts: Why might people be dissatisfied living under a communist regime? What do you think refugees from Cuba might be seeking? What might they be escaping from? Why might some refugees be allowed to leave while others are detained?

Additional Background: In response to Castro's seizure of $1 billion in U.S.-owned properties, the United States imposed a trade embargo against Cuba in 1960. A complete break in diplomatic relations came in 1961. Relations were further strained that spring, when U.S.-supported anti-Castro exiles invaded the Bay of Pigs in southern Cuba, and then that fall, when the United States found Soviet-supplied missile sites in Cuba.

Enrich Your Reading

Before students start reading, mention that the title *Stowaway!* above is printed in italics. Then point out the italicized passages so that students are familiar with the appearance of those passages.

Thematic Link—Seizing the Moment

As recounted in this magazine article, Armando Ramírez seizes the moment to escape from Cuba by stowing away on a jet airplane bound for Spain.

Journal Writing

Suggest these journal topics to students:

- What dangers might exist for a stowaway?
- If you had to be a stowaway, would you rather be alone or with a friend? Explain your answer.
- Tell about a time when you had to choose between taking a risk or playing it safe.

For other journal opportunities, refer students to Examine What You Know (p. 175), Real-Life Connections (p. T–178), and Broader Connections (p. 181).

Additional Resources

UNIT TWO RESOURCE BOOK
Reader's Guidesheet, p. 1
Vocabulary Worksheet, p. 2
Selection and Vocabulary Check Tests, p. 3
Selection Test, pp. 4–5

Collaborative Learning

Opportunities for collaborative learning appear throughout the lesson and include Broader Connections (p. 181) and Writing Options 2 and 4 (p. 182).

Teaching Strategies

Vocabulary Preview

These vocabulary words are defined at the bottom of the selection page on which they appear. You may wish to discuss them briefly before students begin reading.

abyss depth beyond measurement
conduit pipe that holds wires
crescendo increase in loudness
disillusion disappoint
fuselage the body of an airplane
futile useless, hopeless
malfunction failure to operate
ration distribute in fixed amounts
retracting drawing in from an extended position
stationary not moving; still

Support for Students of Limited English Proficiency

■ Use Reader's Guidesheet, p. 1.

■ If possible, have students who are refugees from other countries share their experiences of how they escaped the countries they lived in formerly. Alert students to the fact that "Stowaway!" contains vocabulary, especially jargon related to airplanes and flying, that may be unfamiliar to them. Encourage them to review the footnotes and the definitions at the bottom of the pages. You may wish either to draw an airplane on the chalkboard or to use a picture of one to point out specific parts mentioned in the story. Students may want to share their native language terms for these words with the class.

■ Annotations E and L focus on unfamiliar vocabulary.

Text Annotations

A. Critical Thinking: ANALYZING Have students analyze why the writer begins at this moment in the story. *(Possible response: to build excitement and capture reader interest)*

B. Literary Element: IMAGERY Ask students to cite specific descriptive details and phrases that help create excitement in this scene. *(Possible response: dramatic sensory details such as "sweating with fear," "massive craft," "jet blast flattening the grass," and "shriek of the four jet engines.")*

C. Reading Skill: PREDICTING Have students predict what will happen to Armando. *(Possible responses: He will be badly crushed but survive; he will miraculously fit in the cramped space.)*

Stowaway!

ARMANDO SOCARRAS RAMÍREZ
as told to D. FODOR *and* J. REDDY

A

The jet engines of the Iberia Airlines DC-8 thundered in earsplitting crescendo as the big plane taxied toward where we huddled in the tall grass just off the end of the runway at Havana's[1] José Martí Airport. For months my friend Jorge Pérez Blanco[2] and I had been planning to stow away in a wheel well[3] on this flight, No. 904—Iberia's once-weekly, nonstop run from Havana to Madrid.[4] Now, in the late afternoon of last June 3 [1970], our mo-
SR-1 ▶ ment had come.

We realized that we were pretty young to be taking such a big gamble; I was seventeen, Jorge sixteen. But we were both determined to escape from Cuba, and our plans had been carefully made. We knew that departing airliners taxied to the end of the 11,500-foot runway, stopped momentarily after turning around, then roared at full throttle down the runway to take off. We wore rubbersoled shoes to aid us in crawling up the wheels and carried ropes to secure ourselves inside the wheel well. We had also stuffed cotton in our ears as protection against the shriek of the four jet B engines. Now we lay sweating with fear as the massive craft swung into its about face, the jet blast flattening the grass all around us. "Let's run!" I shouted to Jorge.

We dashed onto the runway and sprinted toward the left-hand wheels of the momentarily stationary plane. As Jorge began to scramble up the forty-two-inch-high tires, I saw there was not room for us both in the single well. "I'll try the other side!" I shouted. Quickly I climbed onto the right wheels, grabbed a strut[5] and, twisting and wriggling, pulled myself into the semidark well. The plane began rolling immediately, and I grabbed some machinery to keep from falling out. The roar of the engines nearly deafened me.

As we became airborne, the huge double wheels, scorching hot from takeoff, began folding into the compartment. I tried to flatten myself against the overhead as they C came closer and closer; then, in desperation, I pushed at them with my feet. But they pressed powerfully upward, squeezing me, terrifyingly against the roof of the well. Just when I felt that I would be crushed, the wheels locked in place and the bay doors beneath them closed, plunging me into

1. **Havana** (hə van′ ə): the capital of Cuba.
2. **Jorge Pérez Blanco** (hôr′ hā pē res bläŋ′ kô).
3. **wheel well:** the compartment into which an airplane wheel retracts.
4. **Madrid** (mä drid′): the capital of Spain.
5. **strut:** a brace.

Words to Know and Use	**crescendo** (kri shen′ dō′) *n.* a gradual increase in loudness **stationary** (stā′shə ner′ ē) *adj.* not moving; still

176

Structured Reading for Less Proficient Students

These questions can help to guide students through the reading. Ask each question at the point of the selection where the SR number appears in the margin.

SR–1. What do the narrator and Jorge plan to do? *(stow away in the wheel well of a DC-8 leaving Cuba for Madrid)* **Literal recall**

SR–2. What risks does Armando now realize that he faces in the wheel well? *(being crushed to death, falling from the aircraft, being spotted)* **Summarizing**

SR–3. Why doesn't Armando leave Cuba legally? *(The wait is very long, and attempting to leave legally will make his life even less bearable.)* **Clarifying**

SR–4. What risks does Armando face because the craft is miles above sea level? *(freezing to death and not getting enough oxygen to survive)* **Clarifying**

SR–5. How do the doctors explain Armando's survival? *(He went into a "deep-freeze" condition. His survival was a medical miracle.)* **Literal recall**

ASTROJET 1967 Richard Estes
Des Moines Art Center Purchased with funds from the Coffin Fine Arts Trust, Nathan Emory Coffin Collection of the Des Moines Art Center.

darkness. So there I was, my five-foot-four-inch, 140-pound frame literally wedged in amid a spaghetti-like maze of conduits and machinery. I could not move enough to tie myself to anything, so I stuck my rope behind a pipe.

Then, before I had time to catch my breath, the bay doors suddenly dropped open again and the wheels stretched out into their landing position. I held on for dear life, swinging over the abyss, wondering if I had been spotted, if even now the plane was turning back to hand me over to Castro's police. D ◀ SR-2

By the time the wheels began retracting again, I had seen a bit of extra space among all the machinery where I could safely squeeze. Now I knew there *was* room for me, even though I could scarcely breathe. After a few minutes, I touched one of the tires and found that it had cooled off. I swallowed some aspirin tablets against the

Words to Know and Use

conduit (kän′ do͞o it) *n.* a pipe that holds fluids or electric wires
abyss (ə bis′) *n.* a depth that seems beyond measurement
retracting (ri trakt′ iŋ) *n.* the act of drawing in from an extended position
retract *v.*

177

Art Note

Contemporary artist Richard Estes is one of the original Photorealists. Art critics in the early 1960's rejected the precise detail in the works of such painters. However, the movement has since gained adherents and admirers, and Estes is acknowledged as its preeminent practitioner. *Looking at this picture, what feelings do you think Armando had as he watched the jet taxi on the runway?*

D. Critical Thinking: EVALUATING Ask students to decide which aspect of Armando's escape as described thus far they find the most harrowing. *(Possible response: Some students may cite the physical dangers Armando faces; others may mention his chance of capture and punishment in Cuba.)*

Data Bank

The DC-8 was developed in the late 1950's for use in commercial long-distance runs. A narrow-bodied jet with four wing-mounted engines, it cruises at about 550 miles per hour and carries slightly over 100 passengers. It is similar in design to the 707. Today the DC-8 is rarely used in flights originating in the United States, although many other countries maintain these planes in their fleets.

E. LEP: Vocabulary Tell students that *fatigues* are the clothing worn by people in the armed forces when they are engaged in non-military duties. Explain that since fatigues are made of thin cotton cloth suitable for tropical Cuba, they would offer Armando little protection against the fierce cold he faces in the wheel well.

F. Reading Skill: ITALICS Ask volunteers to explain whose point of view is presented in the italicized passage. *(The italicized passages show the pilot's point of view from inside the airplane.)*

G. Critical Thinking: ANALYZING Ask students to analyze what the red light blinking out means. *(Possible responses: The red light blinks out because the right wheel has now closed correctly. Students should realize that this section presents the pilot's view of the same situation Armando has just described.)*

H. Teaching Tip

Explore with students why the authors provide the background into Armando's life at this point rather than presenting the story in strict chronological order. Guide them to see how the authors open with an exciting part of the narrative to capture their reader's attention and then present exposition in flashback to fill in space until the climax, when the plane lands and we learn whether Armando will survive his daring escape.

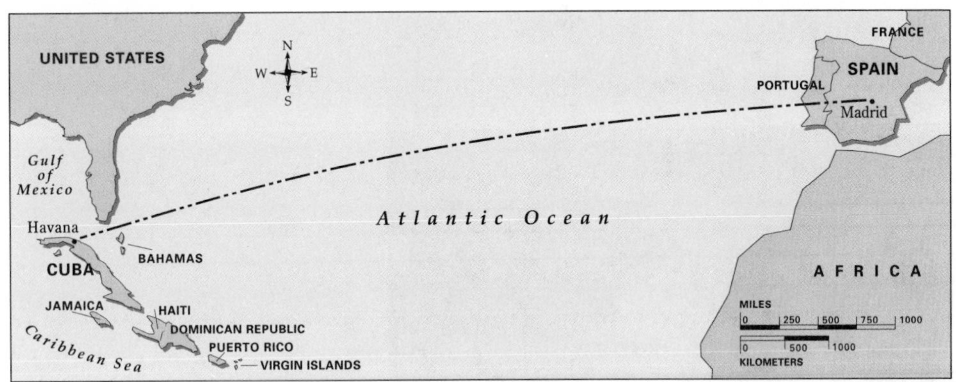

E head-splitting noise and began to wish that I had worn something warmer than my light sport shirt and green fatigues.

F *Up in the cockpit of Flight 904, Captain Valentín Vara del Rey, forty-four, had settled into the routine of the overnight flight, which would last eight hours and twenty minutes. Takeoff had been normal, with the aircraft and its 147 passengers, plus a crew of ten, lifting off at 170 mph. But, right after liftoff, something unusual had happened. One of three red lights on the instrument panel had remained lighted, indicating improper retraction of the landing gear.*

"Are you having difficulty?" the control tower asked.

"Yes," replied Vara del Rey. "There is an indication that the right wheel hasn't closed properly. I'll repeat the procedure."

G *The captain relowered the landing gear, then raised it again. This time the red light blinked out.*

Dismissing the incident as a minor malfunction, the captain turned his attention to climbing to assigned cruising altitude. On leveling out, he observed that the temperature outside was −41 degrees Fahrenheit. Inside, the pretty stewardesses began serving dinner to the passengers.

Shivering uncontrollably from the bitter cold, I wondered if Jorge had made it into the other wheel well and began thinking about what had brought me to this desperate situation. I thought about my parents H and my girl, María Esther, and wondered what they would think when they learned what I had done.

My father is a plumber, and I have four brothers and a sister. We are poor, like most Cubans. Our house in Havana has just one large room; eleven people live in it—or did. Food was scarce and strictly rationed. About the only fun I had was playing baseball and walking with María Esther along the seawall. When I turned sixteen, the government shipped me off to vocational school in Betancourt, a sugar-cane village in Matanzas Province.[6] There I was supposed to learn welding, but classes were often interrupted to send us off to plant cane.

Young as I was, I was tired of living in a I state that controlled *everyone's* life. I dreamed of freedom. I wanted to become

6. **Matanzas** (mä tän′ säs) **Province:** region on the northwest coast of Cuba.

Words to Know and Use	**malfunction** (mal fuŋk′ shən) *n.* a failure to operate properly **ration** (rash′ ən) *v.* to distribute in fixed amounts

Real Life Connections

To help students recognize similarities between Armando's conflicts and their own, explore with them what restrictions they feel society and government place on their lives. Which restrictions do they think are necessary for their safety and welfare? Which restrictions do they view as unnecessary or petty?

an artist and live in the United States, where I had an uncle. I knew that thousands of Cubans had gotten to America and done well there. As the time approached when I would be drafted, I thought more and more of trying to get away. But how? I knew that two planeloads of people are allowed to leave Havana for Miami each day, but there is a waiting list of 800,000 for these flights. Also, if you sign up to leave, the government looks on you as a *gusano*[7]—a worm—and life becomes even less bearable.

My hopes seemed futile. Then I met Jorge at a Havana baseball game. After the game we got to talking. I found out that Jorge, like me, was disillusioned with Cuba. "The system takes away your freedom—forever," he complained.

Jorge told me about the weekly flight to Madrid. Twice we went to the airport to reconnoiter.[8] Once a DC-8 took off and flew directly over us; the wheels were still down, and we could see into the well compartments. "There's enough room in there for me," I remember saying.

These were my thoughts as I lay in the freezing darkness more than five miles above the Atlantic Ocean. By now we had been in the air about an hour, and I was getting lightheaded from the lack of oxygen. Was it really only a few hours earlier that I had bicycled through the rain with Jorge and hidden in the grass? Was Jorge safe? My parents? María Esther? I drifted into unconsciousness.

The sun rose over the Atlantic like a great golden globe, its rays glinting off the silver-and-red fuselage of Iberia's DC-8 as it crossed the European coast high over Portugal. With the end of the 4,636-mile flight in sight, Captain Vara del Rey began his descent toward Madrid's Barajas Airport. Arrival would be at 8 A.M. local time, the captain told his passengers over the intercom, and the weather in Madrid was sunny and pleasant.

Shortly after passing over Toledo,[9] Vara del Rey let down his landing gear. As always, the maneuver was accompanied by a buffeting as the wheels hit the slipstream and a 200-mph turbulence swirled through the wheel wells. Now the plane went into its final approach; now a spurt of flame and smoke from the tires as the DC-8 touched down at about 140 mph.

It was a perfect landing—no bumps. After a brief postflight check, Vara del Rey walked down the ramp steps and stood by the nose of the plane waiting for a car to pick him up, along with his crew.

Nearby, there was a sudden, soft plop as the frozen body of Armando Socarras fell to the concrete apron beneath the plane. José Rocha Lorenzana, a security guard, was the first to reach the crumpled figure. "When I touched his clothes, they were frozen as stiff as wood," Rocha said. "All he did was make a strange sound, a kind of moan."

"I couldn't believe it at first," Vara del Rey said when told of Armando. "But then I went over to see him. He had ice over his nose and mouth. And his color . . ." *As he watched the unconscious boy being bundled into a truck, the captain kept exclaiming to himself, "Impossible! Impossible!"*

The first thing I remember after losing consciousness was hitting the ground at the

7. ***gusano*** (go͞o sän′ ō) *Spanish:* a worm.
8. **reconnoiter** (rek′ ə noit′ ər): to gather information by surveying or examining
9. **Toledo** (tō lā′ dō): a city in central Spain.

Words to Know and Use	**futile** (fyo͞ot′ ′l) *adj.* useless; hopeless **disillusion** (dis′ i lo͞o′ zhən) *v.* to make disappointed and, therefore, no longer interested or involved **fuselage** (fyo͞o′ sə lij′) *n.* the body of an airplane

179

I. Reading Skill: CLARIFYING Ask students to explain what factors motivated Armando finally to undertake his desperate plan. *(Possible responses: His desire for freedom, his desire to be an artist and to live in America, and the impending draft pushed him to undertake his escape.)*

J. Literary Element: CHARACTERIZATION Have students analyze Armando's character based on his planning and decision. Encourage them to cite specific details to support their responses. *(Possible responses: Based on the boys' two visits to the airport, some students may see Armando as a careful planner. Others, in contrast, may use this same evidence as proof of his reckless nature.)*

K. Literary Element: JARGON Have students search through these paragraphs for terms related particularly to aircraft and flying. *(fuselage, Iberia's DC-8, descent, Barajas Airport, arrival, intercom, landing gear, slipstream, turbulence, wheel wells, final approach, touched down)* Ask what would be missing from the story if such terms were not used. *(Possible response: a sense of realism)*

Professional Notebook

We too often get overly concerned in letting the students decide their 'own pace' when we, rightfully, try to teach diversity. The kids are not the experts; the adults are, or should be. It is patronizing to let a kid continue to learn at a painfully slow pace just because she has come to see herself as a 'slow' learner. Remember, the ultimate in tracking is individualized instruction. Kids need frequently to work with the group for many reasons: social, intellectual, academic. These kids are real people who can do real school work when their learning strengths are engaged.

Jerry Conrath, *Our Other Youth*

L. LEP: Language Ask Spanish-speaking volunteers to pronounce the name of the hospital for the class and to share any knowledge they may have of Madrid.

M. Critical Thinking: ANALYZING Ask students to analyze why so many people felt moved to write to Armando. *(Possible response: People felt profoundly moved by his willingness to risk his life for freedom.)*

N. Reading Skill: PREDICTING Have students, based on what they know of Armando from his account, predict his success in achieving his goals. *(Possible response: Armando's determination, bravery, and luck suggest that he will be able to achieve whatever he aspires to.)*

O. Critical Thinking: EVALUATING Have students debate whether they agree with Armando that the risk he took was worth it. *(Possible response: Some students may argue that freedom is worth any risk, even a mortal one. Others may say that Armando's attempt was foolhardy.)*

Check Test

1. Why did Armando stow away in the DC-8? *(He stowed away to escape to freedom from Cuba.)*

2. What could happen to Armando in the well when the wheels retract? *(He could be crushed to death.)*

3. What does Armando want to be and where does he want to live? *(He wants to be an artist in the United States.)*

4. How is Armando finally discovered? *(He falls out of the wheel well after the plane lands.)*

5. With whom does Armando live in America? *(He lives with his uncle.)*

Encouraging Independent Reading

The Great Excape, nonfiction by Paul Brickhill

The Long Walk: A Gamble for Life, nonfiction by Slavomir Rawicz

Kidnapped, a novel by Robert Louis Stevenson

The Trapp Family Singers, an autobiography by Maria von Trapp

L Madrid airport. Then I blacked out again and woke up later at the Gran Hospital de la Beneficencia in downtown Madrid, more dead than alive. When they took my temperature, it was so low that it did not even register on the thermometer. "Am I in Spain?" was my first question. And then, "Where's Jorge?" (Jorge is believed to have been knocked down by the jet blast while trying to climb into the other wheel well and to be in prison in Cuba.)

Doctors said later that my condition was comparable to that of a patient undergoing "deep-freeze" surgery—a delicate process performed only under carefully controlled conditions. Dr. José María Pajares, who cared for me, called my survival a "medical miracle," and, in truth, I feel lucky to be
SR-5 ▶ alive.

M A few days after my escape, I was up and around the hospital, playing cards with my police guard and reading stacks of letters from all over the world. I especially liked one from a girl in California. "You are a hero," she wrote, "but not very wise." My uncle, Elo Fernández, who lives in New Jersey, telephoned and invited me to come to the United States to live with him. The International Rescue Committee arranged my passage and has continued to help me.

N I am fine now. I live with my uncle and go to school to learn English. I still hope to study to be an artist. I want to be a good citizen and contribute something to this country, for I love it here. You can smell freedom in the air.

O I often think of my friend Jorge. We both knew the risk we were taking and that we might be killed in our attempt to escape Cuba. But it seemed worth the chance. Even knowing the risks, I would try to escape again if I had to. ❧

INSIGHT

Chance in a Million

Charles Glasgow, a vice-president of the Douglas Aircraft Company, which makes the DC-8, says there is "one chance in a million" that a man would not be crushed when the plane's huge double wheel retracts. "There is space for a man in there," he says, "but he would have to be a contortionist to fit himself in among the wheels, hydraulic pipes and other apparatus."

Armando should also have died from both the lack of oxygen and extreme cold. At the altitude of Flight 904 (29,000 feet), the oxygen content of the air was about half that at sea level, and the temperature was 41 degrees below zero. An expert at Brooks Air Force Base School of Aerospace Medicine in San Antonio, Texas, says that at that altitude, in an unpressurized, unwarmed compartment, a man would normally retain consciousness for only two or three minutes and live only a short while longer.

Perhaps a Spanish doctor summed up Armando Socarras's experience most effectively: "He survived with luck, luck, luck—many tons of luck."

Insight

This piece reflects on the ideas in the main selection and is suggested for students' independent reading. Optional discussion questions follow.

1. Why might Charles Glasgow from Douglas Aircraft be eager to cite the danger a stowaway would face in the wheel well of a DC-8? *(Glasgow would wish to discourage others from stowing away, because such a practice could lead to damage of the aircraft or to crashes that would give the DC-8 a bad reputation.)*

2. How would you explain Armando's survival? *(Students may attribute his survival to luck, to his will to survive, or to his youth and health.)*

3. Do you think that it would have made any difference to Armando even if he had been aware of all the dangers outlined in this article? Why or why not? *(Some students may think that Armando would have taken the risk regardless of the dangers because he longed for freedom. Other students may think that no sane person would take a million-to-one chance on his life knowingly.)*

Responding to Reading

First Impressions

1. Jot down your initial reaction to this true story of escape.

Second Thoughts

2. How do Armando's background and goals influence his wish to escape?
   Think about
   - what he says about his country
   - what he says about wanting to become an artist
3. Why do you think Armando did not tell his family and his girlfriend that he planned to escape?
4. Look back at the italicized sections of this selection. What effect do these sections have on the telling of the story?
5. "You are a hero," a girl writes to Armando, "but not very wise." Is she right? Explain your answer.
   Think about
   - the planning he and his friend had done
   - what they did not know about the airplane and the trip

Broader Connections

6. Many people in the world besides Cubans are attempting to leave their homelands because of harsh economic or political conditions. Look in newspapers and weekly news magazines to find out what other people are trying to escape bad conditions where they live.

Literary Concept: Jargon

Jargon is the specialized vocabulary used in a particular profession. "Stowaway!" contains much jargon related to airplanes and flying, such as *fuselage* and *turbulence*. Such terms add a feeling of authenticity to the story. Look back at "Stowaway!" and find other examples of jargon related to airplanes and flying.

Concept Review: Conflict External conflict is a struggle between characters or between a character and an outside force. A mental struggle within a character is called internal conflict. What types of conflicts occur in "Stowaway!"? Explain.

Student Response

Responding to Reading

These questions are open-ended with no "right" or "wrong" answers. However, responses must be supported with information from the selection. Possible answers follow:

1. Almost any initial reaction to the narrative, either negative or positive, is valid.

2. Some students may say that Armando's desire to become an artist was the main reason he decided to escape from Cuba. Others may cite his desire for freedom and unwillingness to serve in Cuba's military.

3. Some students may feel that Armando kept his plans secret to spare his family pain or to spare himself prosecution from Cuban authorities; others may argue that he feared his family might try to persuade him to stay in Cuba.

4. Some students may say that the italicized portions of the story helped them better understand what was happening by showing the viewpoints of both Armando and the pilot. Others may say that these portions helped reinforce the danger and terror of Armando's escape.

5. Some students may feel that the girl is right because Armando and Jorge did not plan thoroughly enough to understand the danger they faced. Others may argue that the girl was wrong because Armando and his friend did visit the airport twice to watch the plane take off and land.

6. Some students might mention the Vietnamese or Cambodian refugees who are coming to America to escape harsh political conditions in their home countries. Others might mention the Russians emigrating to America or Israel in search of freedom.

Literary Concept: Jargon

Other examples of jargon related to airplanes and flying included in this narrative are as follows: DC-8, taxied, wheel well, full throttle, runway, jet engines, jet blast, strut, takeoff, bay doors, landing position, cockpit, liftoff, landing gear, control tower, cruising altitude, leveling out, slipstream, and final approach. Also refer to annotation K.

Concept Review: Conflict External conflicts include Armando's struggles against the repressive communist system from which he wishes to escape; and his struggle to overcome the physical dangers of possibly being crushed to death or dying from lack of oxygen or extreme cold during his experience as a stowaway. The internal conflict occurs when Armando thinks of his desire to be with his family and his girlfriend, who are in Cuba, and his desire to live in freedom in the United States.

Writing Options

The Writing Options are designed to meet varied student interests and abilities. Have each student choose one writing activity to complete. You may wish to guide some students to an option that requires less writing.

Journal Update Have students review their journal entries for "Stowaway!" What have they learned about the reasons that people become stowaways? What new reflections can they add to their writing?

Vocabulary Practice

1. crescendo
2. retracting
3. conduit
4. abyss
5. fuselage
6. futile
7. disillusion
8. stationary
9. malfunction
10. ration

Writing Options

1. Take the part of Armando and create a letter to leave behind for your family or girlfriend. Explain why you left, what you hope to find in the United States, and why you kept your departure a secret.
2. Create a list of questions you would like to ask Armando about his experience. Think about the trip itself, the conditions in Cuba when he lived there, and his new life outside of Cuba.
3. Write a news report of the event. Be sure to include a lead paragraph that answers these questions: Who, What, When, Where, Why. Use quotes from the story.
4. Re-create the conversation between Jorge and Armando at the ballpark. Before writing the dialogue, set the scene by describing the park as you imagine it. Try to capture the sense of danger and excitement that this moment must have held for the two young Cubans.

Vocabulary Practice

Exercise For each set of words below, determine what the relationship is between the words in the first pair. Then decide which of the vocabulary words is needed to express a similar relationship in the second pair. The following is an example of a typical analogy question.

Example COLT : HORSE : : *fawn* : deer (A *colt* is a young *horse*; a *fawn* is a young *deer*.)

1. ACCELERATION : SPEED : : ____ : sound
2. EXTENDING : OUT : : ____ : in
3. PIPELINE : WATER : : ____ : wires
4. MOUNTAIN : HIGHLAND : : ____ : chasm
5. HULL : BOAT : : ____ : airplane
6. SAFE : DANGEROUS : : ____ : effective
7. DELIGHT : PLEASE : : ____ : disenchant
8. SELFISH : GENEROUS : : ____ : moving
9. LEAK : PLUMBER : : ____ : mechanic
10. SAVE : PENNIES : : ____ : water

Words to Know and Use

abyss
conduit
crescendo
disillusion
fuselage
futile
malfunction
ration
retracting
stationary

Closure

In *"Stowaway!"* a young man acts swiftly and decisively to seize his opportunity to find a better life. Ask students to consider what opportunities they have seized that have had an important impact on their lives.

e x p l o r e

Poetry

Song of the Open Road
WALT WHITMAN

Travel
EDNA ST. VINCENT MILLAY

Examine What You Know (Prior Knowledge)

Many people have dreams of going to far-off and exotic places. Think of the places you would like to visit if you could. In your journal or on a piece of paper, make a list of these places. Then explain your reasons for wanting to go to each place. Also note your reasons for wanting to leave your present life behind. As you read, compare your reasons for wanting to travel with those of the speakers in the next two poems.

Expand Your Knowledge (Building Background)

Americans' desire for travel and for "seizing the moment" are themes that occur again and again in American literature. Numerous literary classics such as Mark Twain's *The Adventures of Huckleberry Finn*, John Steinbeck's *Travels with Charlie*, or Jack London's *The Call of the Wild* recount the tales of those who have left their familiar surroundings to learn more about themselves and their world. The two poems you are about to read present two perspectives on the lure of travel and the adventure it offers.

Enrich Your Reading (Reading Skill)

Observing Form The distinctive look of a poem comes from its **form** and includes how the poem is arranged on the page; the lengths of the lines; the breaks between words, lines, and stanzas; and the grouping of ideas into visible units. A poet can create a poem with an orderly, regular arrangement of lines and verses or one that is free-form. A poet can also choose a particular rhyme scheme or compose a poem with no set rhyme pattern. The two poems you are about to read are a study in contrast. As you read, think about why each poet might have chosen the form that he or she did.

■ *Biographies of the authors can be found on page 187.*

Objectives

- To understand and analyze two classic poems
- To identify and contrast poetic forms
- To explore free verse
- To review rhyme scheme in poetry
- To express understanding of the work through a choice of writing forms, including an explanation and a postcard

Prereading/Motivation

Examine What You Know

Discussion Prompts: Would you prefer to visit distant, foreign places or undiscovered regions in your own area? How did you first learn of the places that you would like to visit: from friends? reading? television? movies? What do you find alluring about the places you are listing?

Expand Your Knowledge

Discussion Prompts: What in America's history might explain why we are drawn to travel? Why do people like books about other people who have "seized the moment"? What stories about travel have you read that were meaningful to you? Can you explain why?

Additional Background: "Seize the day" is a translation of the Latin phrase *carpe diem* by Horace. A famous version of this phrase is in Robert Herrick's poem "To the Virgins, to Make Much of Time," which begins: "Gather ye rosebuds while ye may,/ Old Time is still a-flying:/ And this same flower that smiles today,/ Tomorrow will be dying."

Enrich Your Reading

Explain to students that some poets prefer an orderly, regular arrangement of lines, while others express their ideas in poems with no set rhyme pattern. Remind students that neither form is "better"; in fact, some poets have written poems with a regular form and other poems in free-form verse, depending on their purpose.

Thematic Link—Seizing the Moment

In these two poems, the speakers seize the moment through travel.

Journal Writing

These two poems address travel-related themes. Suggest these journal topics to students:

- If you were to write a "Song of the Open Road," what things might you want to "sing" about?
- What do you find especially exciting about travel?

For other journal opportunities, refer students to Examine What You Know (p. 183), Responding to Reading question 1 (p. 184), and question 7 (p. 186).

Additional Resources

UNIT TWO RESOURCE BOOK
Reader's Guidesheet, p. 6
Vocabulary Worksheet, p. 7
Selection and Vocabulary Check Tests, p. 8
Selection Text, pp. 9–10

Collaborative Learning

Opportunities for collaborative learning appear throughout the lesson and include Cross-Curricular Options (p. T–187).

Teaching Strategies

Support for Students of Limited English Proficiency

- Use **Reader's Guidesheet**, p. 6.
- These poems contain settings and words that may be unfamiliar to some students. Remind them that the United States is a very large country, stretching from one ocean to another. Explain that in the days before widespread air and automobile travel, people frequently traveled on foot or by train or horse and buggy. Have students read the poems several times over silently, then ask for volunteers to read each poem aloud.
- **Annotation B** focuses on unfamiliar vocabulary.

Text Annotations

A. Literary Element: FREE VERSE Ask students to explain why this is considered a poem. *(Possible response: The words are arranged and chosen to create a certain effect—here, the excitement of travel.)*

B. LEP: Vocabulary Point out to students that *querulous* means "irritable" or "whining." Ask them to contrast the phrase *querulous criticisms* with the feeling expressed in the last line of the poem. *(Possible response: The feelings are opposites: One has a feeling of being irritable and closed in, the other of joy and expansiveness.)*

Song of the Open Road

WALT WHITMAN

Afoot and light-hearted I take to the open road,
A Healthy, free, the world before me,
The long brown path before me leading wherever I
 choose.

Henceforth I ask not good fortune, I myself am good
 fortune,
Henceforth I whimper no more, postpone no more,
 need nothing,
B Done with indoor complaints, libraries, querulous
 criticisms,
Strong and content I travel the open road.

5 ***Henceforth:*** from now on.

9 ***querulous:*** whining.

RISE OF FALL 1985 Chuck Forsman Tibor De Nagy Gallery, New York.

Student Response

Responding to Reading

These questions are open-ended with no "right" or "wrong" answers. However, responses must be supported with information from the selection. Possible answers follow:

1. Almost any picture that the student imagines, either negative or positive, is valid.

2. Some may say that the speaker wishes to travel for excitement and self-expression; others might feel that he just wants to escape his problems.

3. Some may say that the speaker now sees he can make his own luck through self-expression; others may say that he wants to rely on himself.

4. Some may say that the speaker wants to escape people who criticize him or gripe about life in general; others may say that he is fed up with his life.

Responding to Reading

First Impressions of "Song of the Open Road"

1. What pictures does this poem bring to mind? Draw one of these images.

Second Thoughts on "Song of the Open Road"

2. Why do you think the speaker wants to travel?

   Think about
   - the kind of person the speaker seems to be
   - what the speaker is leaving behind
   - the reasons you listed for wanting to travel

3. Think about the meaning of "good fortune." Then explain what the speaker means by saying "Henceforth I ask not good fortune, I myself am good fortune."

4. Why does the speaker wish to flee "indoor complaints"?

Travel

EDNA ST. VINCENT MILLAY

The railroad track is miles away,
  And the day is loud with voices speaking,
A Yet there isn't a train goes by all day
  But I hear its whistle shrieking.

All night there isn't a train goes by,
  Though the night is still for sleep and dreaming,
B But I see its cinders red on the sky,
  And hear its engine steaming.

My heart is warm with the friends I make,
  And better friends I'll not be knowing;
C Yet there isn't a train I wouldn't take,
  No matter where it's going.

Text Annotations

A. Critical Thinking ANALYZING Ask students to analyze what the railroad track and train might represent to the speaker. *(Possible responses: excitement, adventure, pleasure in the lure of going somewhere.)*

B. Literary Element: IMAGERY Have students identify the images in this passage and explain to what senses they appeal. *("Cinders red on the sky" appeals to the sense of sight; "engine steaming" appeals to hearing, sight, and perhaps smell.)*

C. Literary Element: RHYME SCHEME Have students describe the effect of the regular rhythm and rhyme scheme in this poem. *(Possible response: The regular rhyme suggests the flow of the train chugging down the track.)*

Check Test

1. By what means does the speaker in "Song of the Open Road" travel? *(on foot)*

2. What three things does he reject when he sets off on his travel? *(indoor complaints, libraries, querulous criticisms)*

3. How far is the track from the speaker in "Travel"? *(miles away)*

4. At the end of the poem "Travel," what train does the speaker say she would be willing to take? *(any one)*

Encouraging Independent Reading

Platero and I, prose poems by Juan Ramón Jiménez
On the Road, nonfiction by Jack Kerouac
Travels with Charley in Search of America, nonfiction by John Steinbeck
"Facing West from California's Shores," "I Hear America Singing," "Pioneers! O Pioneers!" "Song for All Seas, All Ships," and "There Was a Child Went Forth," poems by Walt Whitman

Art Note

Chuck Forsman (1944–) draws inspiration for his landscape paintings from scenes of the American West. In *Rise of Fall,* the Colorado hills are crossed by many lines—some natural, others imposed by people. *Explain whether you think this is a real or an imaginary landscape.*

PROFESSIONAL NOTEBOOK

One of the most difficult questions students ask is, "Why is poetry so important?" You might want to share Laurence Perrine's explanation with your students: "Poetry is as universal as language and almost as ancient. The most primitive people have used it, and the most civilized have cultivated it. In all ages, and in all countries, poetry has been written—and eagerly read or listened to—by all kinds and conditions of people. . . . Why? First, because it has given pleasure. . . . But this is not the whole answer. Poetry in all ages has been regarded as important, not simply as one of several alternative forms of amusement. . . . Rather, it has been regarded as something central to each man's existence, something having unique value to the fully realized life, something that he is better off for having and spiritually impoverished without."
LAURENCE PERRINE, *SOUND AND SENSE*

e x p l a i n

Responding to Reading

First Impressions of "Travel"

1. Without using the title, think of one word that describes what this poem is about. Compare your choice with the choices your classmates have made.

Second Thoughts on "Travel"

2. What do you think the speaker's life is like?

   Think about
   - how the speaker describes his or her day
   - the speaker's attitude toward his or her friends

3. What do you think is more important to the speaker, traveling or simply riding on a train? Why?

4. If the speaker has good friends at home, why does he or she want to leave?

Comparing the Poems

5. How are these two speakers alike or different in their reasons for longing to travel? Which speaker seems more apt to travel?

6. What purpose did each poet have in using a particular form? What kind of message was each trying to convey?

7. Which speaker would you rather meet? Why?

Literary Concept: Free Verse

Poetry that does not have regular rhyme, rhythm, or line length is called **free verse**. Walt Whitman's poetry was considered shocking in his time because it did not have regular rhyme, rhythm, or line length. Why does the poem still fit the definition of poetry?

Concept Review: Rhyme Scheme Which lines rhyme in Edna St. Vincent Millay's poem "Travel"?

Writing Options

1. Which do you look forward to more, traveling to a destination or arriving at and enjoying a new place? Explain.

2. Imagine you are the speaker in each poem. Write a postcard telling where you ended up and why you went there.

Student Response

Responding to Reading

1. Almost any word that students use to describe the poem is valid.

2. Some may say that the speaker has a happy life, as shown by her full days and close friends; others may say that her desire to travel shows that her life is not really that satisfying to her.

3. Those who see the train representing travel in the speaker's thoughts may say travel is more important to her or him. Those noting that the speaker thinks of taking any train might say that he or she sees riding on a train as more important.

4. Some may say that the speaker finds travel more important than her or his friends; others may feel that her or his life is not happy, despite her or his friends; still others may say that she or he would like some time to be alone.

5. The speaker in "Song of the Open Road" seems to long for adventure and the outdoors, while the speaker in "Travel" is tempted by "romantic" ideas of a train. Students citing the joy that the speaker in Whitman's poem finds at leaving "complaints" behind may say he or she is more willing to travel. Those noting that the speaker in Millay's poem is willing to leave friends may say he or she is more apt to travel.

6. Some may say that Whitman's free verse suggests the freedom of travel; others may say that the regular form of "Travel" suggests both the rhythm of a moving train and the constraints of the speaker's life.

7. Some might prefer Whitman's speaker, because he or she is taking action, doing what he or she wants to do; others might prefer Millay's speaker, because they know that she or he has warm friends.

Writing Options

The Writing Options are designed to meet varied student interests and abilities. Have each student choose one writing activity to complete. You may wish to guide some students to an option that requires less writing.

Journal Update Have students turn one of their journal entries about travel into a poem.

Literary Concept—Free Verse

Whitman's free verse still fits the description of poetry because the words are chosen and arranged to create certain effects—here, the excitement of travel, the freedom to seize the day. Refer to annotation A.

Concept Review: Rhyme Scheme In "Travel," the following lines rhyme: 1 and 3, 2 and 4, 5 and 7, 6 and 8, 9 and 11, and 10 and 12.

e x t e n d

Walt Whitman
1819–1892

Like many writers, Walt Whitman learned his craft while working as a journalist. After leaving school at the age of thirteen, he worked at a series of jobs, including office boy, typesetter, country schoolteacher, and printer's apprentice. By 1841, Whitman had decided to pursue a career in journalism. For the next twenty years he held various newspaper jobs in New York and Brooklyn. Whitman's main interest was writing poetry, however. His most famous body of poetry is called *Leaves of Grass*, a collection of twelve poems first published in 1855 that he continued to revise throughout his lifetime. During the Civil War, Whitman served as a volunteer nurse in military hospitals around Washington, D.C. In 1873 Whitman suffered a paralytic stroke and moved to Camden, New Jersey, where, despite his disability, the literary greats of England and America visited him throughout the last years of his life.

Edna St. Vincent Millay
1892–1950

Edna St. Vincent Millay began writing poetry while just a child. By the age of nineteen she had published her first poem, entitled "Renascence." Upon graduation from Vassar College in 1917, she moved to New York City's Greenwich Village. She lived there among many artists who were, as she said, "very, very poor and very, very merry." Millay did some of her best work when she was young, writing about themes of love and death and the rebelliousness of youth. Although many of her poems shocked older generations, her contemporaries enjoyed the simple meter and straightforward, down-to-earth language of her poetry. In 1923 she won a Pulitzer Prize for three works, including the collection of poems entitled *The Harp Weaver and Other Poems.* Millay also wrote several plays and the libretto for an opera. Some of her later poems dealt with the atrocities of World War II. Millay published more than twenty volumes of poetry before her death in 1950.

Additional Information About the Author

Walt Whitman Although today we recognize *Leaves of Grass* as a masterpiece, as with so many classics, its initial publication did little to improve its author's life. When weeks went by and the book continued to be ignored, Whitman resorted to writing his own favorable reviews—under assumed names, of course! To spark interest, he sent copies of the book to famous literary figures, such as Emerson and Longfellow. Ironically, attention in the United States came to the poet only after his genius was recognized in England by Alfred, Lord Tennyson, the poet laureate.

Edna St. Vincent Millay Despite her devotion to her writing—often at the expense of her health—Millay found the time and energy to support numerous social causes. In 1927, for example, she was a leading figure in protesting the trial and execution of Sacco and Vanzetti; in the late 1930's she was deeply concerned with the rise of totalitarianism in Europe. She spent much of her time writing propaganda for the democratic cause. Soon after, she suffered a nervous collapse from which she never fully recovered.

Closure

"Song of the Open Road" and "Travel" explore the importance of seizing the moment through travel. Have students explain how they like to "seize the moment."

Cross-Curricular Options

Students could create "The Ideal Travel Plan," incorporating the speakers' love of travel in these two poems. The following are suggestions:

Geography: Working on a large world map, trace the route to be taken, including a brief explanation of each stop.

Sociology: Assign students to investigate the culture of each major stop on the route. Include such topics as music, foods, art, and customs.

Literature: Have students locate other travel poems or write their own.

Math: Have students visit a travel agent to calculate the total cost of the trip, including food, lodging, bus fare, sightseeing, souvenirs.

Foreign Language: Have students list foreign-language phrases essential for travelers in each geographic area.

Publishing: Compile all contributions. Display or make copies to share.

Objectives

- To read and analyze a short story
- To trace the story's plot
- To review point of view
- To understand the use of dialect
- To express understanding of the work through a choice of writing forms, including a report card, a slogan, dialogue, and comparing and contrasting

Prereading/Motivation

Examine What You Know

Discussion Prompts: Do you think people are born with leadership abilities or do they learn these qualities? Explain your answer. Which leadership qualities do you think are the most important? Why? Have you ever been a leader among your friends? Describe your experiences.

Expand Your Knowledge

Discussion Prompts: In what ways might other people also derive strength from the land? What other stories do you know about Hercules?

Additional Background According to Greek mythology, Antaeus was the son of the goddess of Earth, Ge, and the god of the Sea, Poseidon. Antaeus was able to renew his strength as long as he was in contact with the earth, his mother.

Enrich Your Reading

Before students start reading, have them brainstorm examples of dialect they know. Then discuss the examples in the text so that students are familiar with their pronunciation and meaning.

Thematic Link—Seizing the Moment

In this short story, T. J. seizes the moment by leading a group of boys into creating an oasis in an urban environment—a roof garden in a slum.

e x p l o r e

Fiction *Antaeus*

BORDEN DEAL

Examine What You Know (Prior Knowledge)

Have you ever met someone who became a leader among your group of friends almost the first day he or she arrived? What qualities of leadership did this person possess? List a half dozen or more qualities that a person needs to become a leader in your school or among your circle of friends. As you read this story, compare the traits you have noted with the main character in "Antaeus."

Expand Your Knowledge (Building Background)

The title of this story comes from the Greek myth of Antaeus, a powerful giant who challenged all visitors to his kingdom to a wrestling match. If the visitors won, they could keep on living, but if they lost, Antaeus would kill them. Hercules, one of the most powerful of the Greek heroes, learned that Antaeus gained his strength from contact with the earth. By holding Antaeus off the ground, Hercules was able to weaken Antaeus and then strangle him to death. As you read, look for the lines that explain why Deal named his story "Antaeus."

Enrich Your Reading (Reading Skill)

Dialect In this story the main character speaks a dialect that is common in some parts of the rural South. His speech contains such ungrammatical phrases as "You mean you ain't got no fields to raise nothing in?" and nonstandard English such as "It'll be ourn [ours]." Don't be confused by dialect. In most cases it is easily understandable, especially if you read it aloud. In many cases, the character simply adds an unusual ending to a word (*ours* becomes *ourn*) or creates a new word from other words (*off of* becomes *offen*).

■ *A biography of the author can be found on page 200.*

Journal Writing

Suggest these journal topics to students:

- Imagine that you and your friends have "a secret place" where nobody else can go without permission. Write about such a place.
- Why is it important to some people to have their own land that nobody else can touch?

For other journal opportunities, refer students to Examine What You Know (p. 188), Annotation S, and question 7 (p. 198).

Additional Resources

UNIT TWO RESOURCE BOOK

Reader's Guidesheet, p. 11
Vocabulary Worksheet, p. 12
Selection and Vocabulary Check Tests, p. 13
Selection Test, pp. 14–15

Collaborative Learning

Opportunities for collaborative learning appear throughout the lesson and include annotation S, Real Life Connections (p. T-191), Cultural Connections (p. T-192), Options for Learning Activities 2 and 3 (p. 200), and Cross-Curricular Options (p. T–200).

Antaeus

BORDEN DEAL

A This was during the wartime, when lots of people were coming North for jobs in factories and war industries, when people moved around a lot more than they do now and sometimes kids were thrown into new groups and new lives that were completely different from anything they had ever known before. I remember this one kid; T. J. his name was, from somewhere down South, whose family moved into our building during that time. They'd come North with everything they owned piled into the back seat of an old-model

B sedan that you wouldn't expect could make the trip, with T. J. and his three younger

SR-1 ▶ sisters riding shakily atop the load of junk.

It was a secret place for us, where nobody else could go without our permission.

Our building was just like all the others there, with families crowded into a few rooms, and I guess there were twenty-five or thirty kids about my age in that one building. Of course, there were a few of us who formed a gang and ran together all the time after school, and I was the one who brought T. J. in and started the whole thing.

The building right next door to us was a factory where they made walking dolls. It was a low building with a flat, tarred roof that had a parapet[1] all around it about head high, and we'd found out a long time before that no one, not even the watchman, paid any attention to the roof because it was higher than any of the other buildings around. So my gang used the roof as a headquarters. We could get up there by crossing over to the fire escape from our own roof on a plank and then going on up. It was a secret place for us, where nobody else could go without our permission. ◀ SR-2

I remember the day I first took T. J. up there to meet the gang. He was a stocky, robust kid with a shock of white hair, nothing sissy about him except his voice—he talked different from any of us, and you noticed it right away. But I liked him anyway, so I told him to come on up.

We climbed up over the parapet and dropped down on the roof. The rest of the gang were already there.

"Hi," I said. I jerked my thumb at T. J.

1. **parapet** (par′ ə pet): a low wall along the edge of a fortress or balcony.

Words to Know and Use	**robust** (rō bust′) *adj.* strong, healthy

Structured Reading for Less Proficient Students

These questions can help to guide students through the reading. Ask each question at the point of the selection where the SR number appears in the margin.

SR–1. Where has T. J.'s family moved from and why have they come North? *(They have come from "somewhere down South," probably to obtain jobs in "factories and war industries.")* **Inferring**

SR–2. How do the members of the gang know each other? Where is their headquarters? *(All the boys live in the same building. Their headquarters is the roof of a next-door building.)* **Literal recall**

SR–3. What does T. J. suggest that he and the gang do on the roof? *(plant a garden)* **Literal recall**

SR–4. Why do the boys like T. J.'s idea? *(It makes them feel rich.)* **Clarifying**

SR–5. Who motivates the gang to keep the idea of a garden alive during the winter? *(T. J.)* **Literal recall**

Continued on page 190

Teaching Strategies

Vocabulary Preview

These vocabulary words are defined at the bottom of the selection page on which they appear. You may wish to discuss them briefly before students begin reading.

anonymous lacking unique features
cascade fall like a waterfall
contemplate think about
desecrated treated disrespectfully
dilating expanding
distracted having attention drawn away
domain area under one person's rule
enterprise undertaking or project
esoteric beyond the knowledge of most
inert inactive; motionless
laborious requiring much work
resolute determined; steady
robust strong, healthy
shrewd cunning; clever
stolid firm or unemotional

Support for Students of Limited English Proficiency

- Use **Reader's Guidesheet**, p. 11.
- The dialogue in "Antaeus" may be difficult for students. Encourage them to read troublesome passages aloud. Point out that writers use dialect to add a touch of realism to their stories, because dialect reflects the speech of people of a particular place and time. You may wish to write unusual examples of dialect on the chalkboard with a standard English translation beside them.
- **Annotations E** and **N** focus on dialect.
- **Annotations D, M, T, Y,** and **Z** focus on vocabulary, phrases, and aspects of culture that may be confusing.

Text Annotations

A. Literary Elements: SETTING Ask students if they can guess the time and place of the story from the information provided. *(It is early in the mid-1940s, during World War II, in the northern part of the United States.*

B. Reading Skill: RECOGNIZING RELEVANT DETAILS Have students describe T. J.'s economic status, citing details to support their conclusion. *(Possible response: Since their car is described as "an old model sedan" and their possessions are a "load of junk" piled in the car, the family is plainly poor.)*

C. Teaching Tip

To help students understand T. J.'s situation, have them role-play how they would approach a group of unfamiliar people their own age if they had just moved into a new neighborhood. Encourage students first to share their feelings about being in such a situation, especially their fear of rejection.

D. LEP: Vocabulary Explain to students that a *sissy* is someone who is timid or cowardly. The term was very popular in the 1940s and 1950s, but it is rarely used today.

E. Reading Skill: UNDERSTANDING DIALECT To help students understand T. J.'s Southern dialect, ask a volunteer to read this passage aloud. Then have students point out the specific words *(yonder, you-all)* and usage *(no woods)* that create the dialect.

F. Critical Thinking: ANALYZING Have students explain why people *would* want to grow things when everything that they need is available in stores. *(Possible response: Many people derive great pleasure from being able to make things grow. Some like to produce their own fruits and vegetables, while others enjoy creating beauty through trees, shrubs, and flowers.)*

G. Literary Element: POINT OF VIEW Ask students to explore the advantages of having the narrator tell the story many years after he was a participant. *(Possible response: As a participant, the narrator experienced the action firsthand. By telling the story many years later, he is able to analyze the events through the benefit of maturity and hindsight. This enables him to add richness and depth to his narration.)*

"He just moved into the building yesterday."

C He just stood there, not scared or anything, just looking, like the first time you see somebody you're not sure you're going to like.

"Hi," Blackie said. "Where you from?"

"Marion County," T. J. said.

We laughed. "Marion County?" I said. "Where's that?"

He looked at me like I was a stranger, too. "It's in Alabama," he said, like I ought to know where it was.

"What's your name?" Charley said.

"T. J.," he said, looking back at him. He had pale blue eyes that looked washed out, but he looked directly at Charley, waiting for his reaction. D He'll be all right, I thought. No sissy in him . . . except that voice. Who ever talked like that?

"T. J.," Blackie said. "That's just initials. What's your real name? Nobody in the world has just initials."

"I do," he said, "and they're T. J. That's all the name I got."

His voice was resolute with the knowledge of his rightness, and for a moment no one had anything to say. T. J. looked around at the rooftop and down at the black tar under his feet. E "Down yonder where I come from," he said, "we played out in the woods. Don't you-all have no woods around here?"

"Naw," Blackie said. "There's the park a few blocks over, but it's full of kids and cops and old women. You can't do a thing."

T. J. kept looking at the tar under his feet. "You mean you ain't got no fields to raise nothing in? No watermelons or nothing?"

F "Naw," I said scornfully. "What do you want to grow something for? The folks can buy everything they need at the store."

He looked at me again with that strange, unknowing look. "In Marion County," he said, "I had my own acre of cotton and my own acre of corn. It was mine to plant ever' year."

He sounded like it was something to be proud of, and in some obscure way it made the rest of us angry. "Heck!" Blackie said. "Who'd want to have their own acre of cotton and corn? That's just work. What can you do with an acre of cotton and corn?"

T. J. looked at him. "Well, you get part of the bale[2] offen[3] your acre," he said seriously. "And I fed my acre of corn to my calf."

G We didn't really know what he was talking about, so we were more puzzled than angry; otherwise, I guess, we'd have chased him off the roof and wouldn't let him be part of our gang. But he was strange and different, and we were all attracted by his stolid sense of rightness and belonging, maybe by the strange softness of his voice contrasting our own tones of speech into harshness.

He moved his foot against the black tar. "We could make our own field right here," he said softly, thoughtfully. "Come spring we could raise us what we want to . . . watermelons and garden truck and no telling what all."

"You'd have to be a good farmer to make these tar roofs grow any watermelons," I said. We all laughed.

But T. J. looked serious. "We could haul

2. **bale:** a large, bound bundle.
3. **offen:** *dialect,* off of.

Words to Know and Use

resolute (rez′ ə lo͞ot′) *adj.* determined; steady
stolid (stäl′ id) *adj.* firm or unemotional

190

STRUCTURED READING FOR LESS PROFICIENT STUDENTS

Continued from page 189

SR–6. On what key point concerning crops does T. J. give in? *(plant grass instead of a garden.)* **Literal recall**

SR–7. Describe the gang's attitude toward the grass. *(Possible response: respectful)* **Clarifying**

SR–8. What will the adult tell the gang? *(Possible responses: He will make them leave; he will praise their garden.)* **Predicting**

SR–9. Who is the man who gives orders? What does he order to be done with the garden, and why? *(He is the building owner. He orders that the garden be shoveled off the roof because he believes that the roof will sag under the weight of the dirt.)* **Summarizing**

SR–10. What does T. J. decide to do? *(destroy the garden)* **Literal recall**

SR–11. Where does T. J. go? *(He heads south for his old home.)* **Clarifying**

us some dirt up here," he said. "And spread it out even and water it and before you know it we'd have us a crop in here." He looked at us intently. "Wouldn't that be
SR-3 ▶ fun?"

"They wouldn't let us," Blackie said quickly.

"I thought you said this was you-all's roof," T. J. said to me. "That you-all could do anything you wanted up here."

"They've never bothered us," I said. I felt the idea beginning to catch fire in me. It was a big idea and it took a while for it to sink in, but the more I thought about it the better I liked it. "Say," I said to the gang, "he might have something there. Just make us a regular roof garden, with flowers and grass and trees and everything. And all ours, too," I said. "We wouldn't let anybody up here except the ones we wanted to."

H

"It'd take a while to grow trees," T. J. said quickly, but we weren't paying any attention to him. They were all talking about it suddenly, all excited with the idea after I'd put it in a way they could catch hold of it. Only rich people had roof gardens, we knew, and the idea of our own private domain excited
SR-4 ▶ them.

"We could bring it up in sacks and boxes," Blackie said. "We'd have to do it while the folks weren't paying any attention to us. We'd have to come up to the roof of our building and then cross over with it."

"Where could we get the dirt?" somebody said worriedly.

"Out of those vacant lots over close to school," Blackie said. "Nobody'd notice if we scraped it up."

I slapped T. J. on the shoulder. "Man, you had a wonderful idea," I said, and everybody grinned at him, remembering he had started it. "Our own private roof garden."

I

He grinned back. "It'll be ourn,"[4] he said. "All ourn." Then he looked thoughtful again. "Maybe I can lay my hands on some cotton seed, too. You think we could raise us some cotton?"

J

We'd started big projects before at one time or another, like any gang of kids, but they'd always petered out for lack of organization and direction. But this one didn't . . . somehow or other T. J. kept it going all through the winter months. He kept talking about the watermelons and the cotton we'd raise, come spring, and when even that wouldn't work he'd switch around to my idea of flowers and grass and trees, though he was always honest enough to add that it'd take a while to get any trees started. He always had it on his mind and he'd mention it in school, getting them lined up to carry dirt that afternoon, saying, in a casual way, that he reckoned a few more weeks ought to see the job through. ◀ SR-5

Our little area of private earth grew slowly. T. J. was smart enough to start in one corner of the building, heaping up the carried earth two or three feet thick, so that we had an immediate result to look at, to contemplate with awe. Some of the evenings T. J. alone was carrying earth up to the building, the rest of the gang distracted by other enterprises or interests, but T. J. kept plugging along on his own, and eventually we'd all

4. **ourn:** *dialect,* ours.

Words to Know and Use	**domain** (dō mān') *n.* an area under one person's rule or one group's control **contemplate** (kän' təm plāt') *v.* to look at closely; to think about **distracted** (di strakt' id) *adj.* having one's attention drawn away from **distract** *v.* **enterprise** (ent' ər prīz') *n.* an undertaking or project

H. Reading Skill: PREDICTING Have students predict whether the gang will adopt T. J.'s idea, citing specific details to support their position. *(Possible response: Those who think the gang will adopt T. J.'s idea might cite the narrator's enthusiasm as an indication that the others will follow; those who disagree might argue that T. J., as a newcomer, carries little weight within the gang.)*

I. Literary Sidelight Dialect is an especially effective way to portray and differentiate character. One of the most famous examples of this technique is in *The Adventures of Huckleberry Finn,* where Mark Twain uses a number of different dialects to delineate his characters. In the opening Explanatory, Twain carefully notes that the "shadings have not been done in a haphazard fashion, or by guesswork, but painstakingly." The same is true here, because T. J.'s dialect sets him off from the others and the narrator's elevated diction sets him off from his youth.

J. Critical Thinking: ANALYZING Ask students why the idea of the garden is so important to T. J. and how it might relate to his feelings about moving. *(Possible response: Although T. J. seems to accept the move to an urban environment with maturity and grace, he misses his rural home very deeply. The garden represents for him a little piece of his past.)*

Real Life Connections

To help students recognize similarities between T. J.'s situation and their own lives, have them share their experiences of moving to a new location or meeting a newcomer who has settled in their town. Ask students to discuss what they found especially difficult about moving: leaving relatives and friends behind? entering a new school? leaving their home and environment? getting used to a completely new place? Discuss what students found especially challenging about meeting a newcomer: finding out if the person would fit with the gang? helping the newcomer adjust to their friends? Finally, have students explain ways that they might be able to ease the problems associated with moving.

K. Teaching Tip
To help students, especially those from urban environments, understand T. J.'s expertise with soil, have volunteers explain how they demonstrate any expertise they have in a particular area. Students might explain how to judge the quality of a used car or how to apply acrylic nails, for example. Encourage students to draw parallels between their interests and T. J.'s.

L. Literary Element: FORESHADOWING Discuss with students whether the grown-ups might care about the gang's projects. Then ask students how this passage might foreshadow the story's climax. *(Possible response: Although some adults might praise the gang's effort to bring nature to the city, others might disapprove, thinking that the boys were creating a mess, that the gang might start trouble, that they were creating unsafe conditions for themselves or others, that they were damaging the building.)*

M. LEP: Paraphrasing Have students paraphrase this passage to help them better understand the meaning of the phrase *vision bright within us. (Possible response: T. J. helped us imagine how great the completed garden would look by giving us words of encouragement.)*

N. Reading Skill: DIALECT Ask a volunteer to read this passage aloud and then have students isolate the words that help create the dialect. *("mighty late"; "just about"; "wasn't never gonna")*

O. Reading Skill: COMPARING Ask students to compare T. J. to Antaeus and then explain what these parallels suggest about his fate. *(Possible response: Both T. J. and Antaeus gain their strength from contact with the earth; the title of the story suggests that T. J., like Antaeus, will be crushed by "the most powerful" which here would be the grown-ups.)*

come back to him again, and then our own little acre would grow more rapidly.

K He was careful about the kind of dirt he'd let us carry up there and more than once he dumped a sandy load over the parapet into the areaway below because it wasn't good enough. He found out the kinds of earth in all the vacant lots for blocks around. He'd pick it up and feel it and smell it, frozen though it was sometimes, and then he'd say it was good growing soil or it wasn't worth anything, and we'd have to go on somewhere else.

L Thinking about it now, I don't see how he kept us at it. It was hard work, lugging paper sacks and boxes of dirt all the way up the stairs of our own building, keeping out of the way of the grown-ups so they wouldn't catch on to what we were doing. They probably wouldn't have cared, for they didn't pay much attention to us, but we wanted to keep it secret anyway. Then we had to go through the trapdoor to our roof, teeter over a plank to the fire escape, then climb two or three stories to the parapet and drop down onto the roof. All that for a small pile of earth that sometimes didn't seem worth the effort. M But T. J. kept the vision bright within us, his words shrewd and calculated toward the fulfillment of his dream; and he worked harder than any of us. He seemed driven toward a goal that we couldn't see, a particular point in time that would be definitely marked by signs and wonders that only he could see.

The laborious earth just lay there during the cold months, inert and lifeless, the clods lumpy and cold under our feet when we walked over it. But one day it rained, and afterward there was a softness in the air, and the earth was alive and giving again with moisture and warmth. That evening T. J. smelled the air, his nostrils dilating with the odor of the earth under his feet.

"It's spring," he said, and there was a gladness rising in his voice that filled us all with the same feeling. "It's mighty late for it, but it's spring. I'd just about decided it wasn't never gonna get here at all." N

He was a new Antaeus, preparing his own bed of strength.

We were all sniffing at the air, too, trying to smell it the way that T. J. did, and I can still remember the sweet odor of the earth under our feet. It was the first time in my life that spring and spring earth had meant anything to me. I looked at T. J. then, knowing in a faint way the hunger within him through the toilsome[5] winter months, knowing the dream that lay behind his plan. He was a new Antaeus, preparing his own bed of strength. O

"Planting time," he said. "We'll have to find us some seed."

"What do we do?" Blackie said. "How do we do it?"

"First we'll have to break up the clods," T. J. said. "That won't be hard to do. Then we plant the seed, and after a while they come up. Then you got you a crop." He

5. **toilsome:** difficult.

Words to Know and Use

shrewd (shrōōd) *adj.* cunning; clever
laborious (lə bôr′ ē əs) *adj.* requiring much work; difficult
inert (in ʉrt′) *adj.* inactive; motionless
dilating (dī′ lāt′ iŋ) *adj.* expanding **dilate** *v.*

192

CULTURAL CONNECTION

In T. J.'s culture in the rural South during and before World War II, people valued knowledge of agriculture and farm management. Have students discuss whether these skills are valued within their culture as well. If so, ask them to cite specific details to support their responses. They might discuss the recognition that skilled farmers receive in county fairs or from agricultural associations. Encourage students to appreciate subtle applications of these skills, as in the cultivation of indoor plants and pets.

ILLINOIS LANDSCAPE SERIES II, #41 1982 Harold Gregor Collection of Glen Janss, Sun Valley, Idaho.

frowned. "But you ain't got it raised yet. You got to tend it and hoe it and take care of it and all the time it's growing and growing while you're awake and while you're asleep. Then you lay it by when it's growed and let it ripen, and then you got you a crop."

"There's those wholesale seed houses over on Sixth," I said. "We could probably swipe some grass seed over there."

P T. J. looked at the earth. "You-all seem mighty set on raising some grass," he said. "I ain't never put no effort into that. I spent all my life trying not to raise grass."

"But it's pretty," Blackie said. "We could play on it and take sunbaths on it. Like having our own lawn. Lots of people got lawns."

"Well," T. J. said. He looked at the rest of us, hesitant for the first time. He kept on looking at us for a moment. "I did have it in mind to raise some corn and vegetables. But we'll plant grass."

He was smart. He knew where to give in. And I don't suppose it made any difference to him, really. He just wanted to grow something, even if it was grass. Q ◀ SR-6

"Of course," he said, "I do think we ought to plant a row of watermelons. They'd be mighty nice to eat while we was a-laying on that grass."

We all laughed. "All right," I said. "We'll plant us a row of watermelons."

Things went very quickly then. Perhaps half the roof was covered with the earth, the half that wasn't broken by ventilators,[6] and we swiped pocketfuls of grass seed from the open bins in the wholesale seed house, mingling among the buyers on Saturdays and

6. **ventilators:** devices for removing foul air from a building.

Art Note
Harold Gregor (1929–) was born in Detroit and holds degrees from two Michigan universities and a Ph.D. from Ohio State. He has taught at San Diego State University and at Purdue. Since 1970 he has lived in rural Illinois. *In what ways, if any, do you think the artist and T. J. in "Antaeus" might have the same, or different, feelings about the farmlands of the Midwest?*

P. Historical Sidelight Historically, farmers have fought strenuously to reclaim the land from the encroachment of grasslands. The prairie grasses of the Midwest, for example, proved especially difficult for the homesteaders to tame in the mid- to late 1800s. Ironically, farmers have become so successful at cultivating these grasslands that prairies are now being saved as endangered lands. As a farmer, T. J. would be very familiar with the problems associated with making land workable for crops.

Q. Literary Element: CHARACTERIZATION Ask students what T. J.'s decision about the grass reveals about his character. *(Possible response: Some students might say that his concession about the crop reveals he is a natural leader, because he knows when to concede as well as press his point. Others might say that it shows he is intelligent and perceptive.)*

R. Critical Thinking: ANALYZING Ask students to analyze what the grass represents to the gang. *(Possible responses: beauty, hope, accomplishment, wealth, self-esteem, or self-respect)*

Professional Notebook

We should be sure our students know how to read carefully. A surprising number of students consider themselves to have prepared a text carefully if they have read it just once. . . . They don't know about rereading to identify key terms, search for transitions, or distinguish between major and minor points; they don't think to question the premises, assess the evidence, or explore an analysis—they don't . . . carry on a dialogue with the text.
KATHERINE K. GOTTSCHALK, *Teaching Prose* (1984)

S. Teaching Tip

To help students understand the reverence with which the gang holds the grass, ask volunteers to discuss a possession that they especially treasure. Why might some people feel more strongly about things that they have created themselves? Explore with students the special pride that comes with creating something of beauty, especially something natural or very difficult to create.

T. LEP: Culture Explain to students that each plant has many different varieties, each bred to achieve specific traits. For example, some varieties of watermelon are bred for size, others for hardiness, and still others for sweetness. Each different variety has a name, which usually indicates the qualities of that particular hybrid. Ask students what the name "Kleckley Sweets" suggests about that variety of watermelon. *(The name suggests that it was bred for sweetness.)*

U. Reading Skill: PREDICTING Ask students to predict who the men may be. *(Possible response: They may be inspectors looking for possible violations of the city's code for dwellings, or they may be the owners of the factory on whose roof the gang has planted their garden.)*

V. Literary Element: CONFLICT Have students explain the conflict that creates the rising action in this passage. *(The conflict is between the factory owner, who does not want the grass on the roof of his building, and T. J., who is shocked that anyone would object to the beauty he and the others have created.)*

during the school lunch hour. T. J. showed us how to prepare the earth, breaking up the clods and smoothing it and sowing the grass seed. It looked rich and black now with moisture, receiving of the seed, and it seemed that the grass sprang up overnight, pale green in the early spring.

We couldn't keep from looking at it, unable to believe that we had created this delicate growth. We looked at T. J. with understanding now, knowing the fulfillment of the plan he had carried alone within his mind. We had worked without full understanding of the task, but he had known all the time.

R

We found that we couldn't walk or play on the delicate blades, as we had expected to, but we didn't mind. It was enough just to look at it, to realize that it was the work of our own hands, and each evening the whole gang was there, trying to measure the growth that had been achieved that day.

SR-7

S

One time a foot was placed on the plot of ground . . . one time only, Blackie stepping onto it with sudden bravado. Then he looked at the crushed blades and there was shame in his face. He did not do it again. This was his grass, too, and not to be desecrated. No one said anything, for it was not necessary.

T. J. had reserved a small section for watermelons and he was still trying to find some seed for it. The wholesale house didn't have any watermelon seeds, and we didn't know where we could lay our hands on them. T. J. shaped the earth into mounds, ready to receive them, three mounds lying in a straight line along the edge of the grass plot.

We had just about decided that we'd have to buy the seeds if we were to get them. It was a violation of our principles, but we were anxious to get the watermelons started. Somewhere or other, T. J. got his hands on a seed catalog and brought it one evening to our roof garden.

"We can order them now," he said, showing us the catalog. "Look!"

We all crowded around, looking at the fat, green watermelons pictured in full color on the pages. Some of them were split open, showing the red, tempting meat, making our mouths water.

T

"Now we got to scrape up some seed money." T. J. said, looking at us. "I got a quarter. How much you-all got?"

We made up a couple of dollars between us and T. J. nodded his head. "That'll be more than enough. Now we got to decide what kind to get. I think them Kleckley Sweets. What do you-all think?"

He was going into esoteric matters, beyond our reach. We hadn't even known there were different kinds of melons. So we just nodded our heads and agreed that yes, we thought the Kleckley Sweets, too.

"I'll order them tonight," T. J. said. "We ought to have them in a few days."

SR-8

Then an adult voice said behind us: "What are you boys doing up here?"

U

It startled us, for no one had ever come up here before, in all the time we had been using the roof of the factory. We jerked around and saw three men standing near the trapdoor at the other end of the roof. They weren't policemen, or night watchmen, but three men in plump business suits, looking at us. They walked toward us.

"What are you boys doing up here?" the one in the middle said again.

Words to Know and Use

desecrated (des′ i krāt′ id) *adj.* treated disrespectfully **desecrate** *v.*
esoteric (es′ ə ter′ ik) *adj.* beyond the understanding or knowledge of most people

194

We stood still, guilt heavy among us, levied by the tone of voice, and looked at the three strangers.

The men stared at the grass flourishing behind us. "What's this?" the man said. "How did this get up here?"

"Sure is growing good, ain't it?" T. J. said conversationally. "We planted it."

The men kept looking at the grass as if they didn't believe it. It was a thick carpet over the earth now, a patch of deep greenness startling in the sterile industrial surroundings.

"Yes, sir," T. J. said proudly. "We toted that earth up here and planted that grass." He fluttered the seed catalog. "And we're just fixing to plant us some watermelon."

The man looked at him then, his eyes strange and faraway. "What do you mean, putting this on the roof of my building?" he V
said. "Do you want to go to jail?"

T. J. looked shaken. The rest of us were silent, frightened by the authority of his voice. We had grown up aware of adult authority, of policemen and night watchmen and teachers, and this man sounded

CHALK VINES 1988 Robert Vickrey Kennedy Galleries, New York.

Art Note

The remarkable glow of color in *Chalk Vines* is characteristic of the paintings of Robert Vickrey (1926–), who is considered "the world's most proficient craftsman in egg tempera painting." The subjects that he most likes to paint are nuns, bicycles, his wife, and his daughters and sons. *By considering the characters in "Antaeus," decide who the dreamer might be if this picture resembles a dream.*

W. Teaching Tip

To help students explore both sides of the conflict, divide students into three equal groups. Assign one group to represent the gang, another to represent the factory owner, and the third to represent a jury. Have the two sides (gang and factory owner) present their positions to the jury. After each side has argued its case, have the jury vote on which side is justified. Also have jury members decide if either side should have to make compensation to the other.

X. Literary Element: THEME Ask students to explain the story's theme, based on T. J.'s fierce assertion here. *(Possible responses: People draw their energy from the land, and to deny people contact with the land is to deny them their strength and selfhood. Everyone needs to feel that they can accomplish something in order to have a purpose in life.)*

Y. LEP: Paraphrasing To make sure that students understand what the land means to T. J., ask them to paraphrase the narrator's comments in this passage. *(Possible response: Thanks to T. J., we will remember the importance of the land forever.)*

Z. LEP: Vocabulary Point out to students how the adjective *dusky* comes from the noun *dusk*. Then ask students to describe what *dusky* means. Have them brainstorm a list of some other adjectives that were formed from nouns. *(Possible responses: reddish, red; bluish, blue)*

AA. Literary Element: PLOT Ask students to describe how the author builds suspense in this passage in preparation for the story's climax. *(T. J.'s decision that no one is "gonna lay a hand" on the land builds tension by implying that he is going to take some action to prevent the adults from despoiling the gang's creation.)*

BB. Literary Element: CLIMAX Have students explain why this is the story's climax. *(It is the turning point of the story, the point at which the conflict is resolved. In this instance, the climax has occurred because T. J. has decided that he would sooner destroy his creation than have the adults touch it.)*

like all the others. But it was a new thing to T. J.

"Well, you wan't[7] using the roof," T. J. said. He paused a moment and added shrewdly, "So we just thought to pretty it up a little bit."

"And sag it so I'd have to rebuild it," the man said sharply. He turned away, saying to a man beside him. "See that all that junk

SR-9 ▶ is shoveled off by tomorrow."

"Yes, sir," the man said.

T. J. started forward. "You can't do that," he said. "We toted it up here and it's our earth. We planted it and raised it and toted it up here."

The man stared at him coldly. "But it's my building," he said. "It's to be shoveled off tomorrow."

W "It's our earth," T. J. said desperately. "You ain't got no right!"

The men walked on without listening and descended clumsily through the trapdoor. T. J. stood looking after them, his body tense with anger, until they had disappeared. They wouldn't even argue with him, wouldn't let him defend his earth-rights.

He turned to us. "We won't let 'em do it," he said fiercely. "We'll stay up here all day tomorrow and the day after that and we won't let 'em do it."

> ***"It's our earth. It's our land. Can't nobody touch a man's own land."***

We just looked at him. We knew that there was no stopping it. He saw it in our faces and his face wavered for a moment before he gripped it into determination.

"They ain't got no right," he said. "It's our earth. It's our land. Can't nobody touch a man's own land." X

We kept on looking at him, listening to the words but knowing that it was no use. The adult world had descended on us even in our richest dream, and we knew there was no calculating the adult world, no fighting it, no winning against it.

We started moving slowly toward the parapet and the fire escape, avoiding a last look at the green beauty of the earth that T. J. had planted for us . . . had planted deeply in our minds as well as in our experience. Y We filed slowly over the edge and down the steps to the plank, T. J. coming last, and all of us could feel the weight of his grief behind us.

"Wait a minute," he said suddenly, his voice harsh with the effort of calling. We stopped and turned, held by the tone of his voice, and looked up at him standing above us on the fire escape.

"We can't stop them?" he said, looking down at us, his face strange in the dusky Z light. "There ain't no way to stop 'em?"

"No," Blackie said with finality. "They own the building."

We stood still for a moment, looking up at T. J., caught into inaction by the decision working in his face. He stared back at us and his face was pale and mean in the poor light, with a bald nakedness in his skin like cripples have sometimes.

"They ain't gonna touch my earth," he said fiercely. "They ain't gonna lay a hand AA on it! Come on."

He turned around and started up the fire escape again, almost running against the effort of climbing. We followed more slowly, not knowing what he intended. By the time we reached him, he had seized a

7. **wan't:** *dialect,* were not.

CRITIC'S CORNER

Bordon Deal . . . explores the tangled themes of race and politics in all his fourteen published novels. Deal's most significant contribution is his trilogy on Southern politics: *The Loser* (1964), *The Advocate* (1968), and *The Winner* (1973).

The protagonist of all three novels is John Bookman, a small town lawyer who combines politics with a legal career. Deal has an understanding of the politics he portrays, and his characters are well drawn. For most of his productive life Deal's vision has been shaped by his study of a belief in Jungian philosophy. This philosophy is the basis of the Bookman trilogy, in which Deal delineates and details the creation of a mythic hero out of an ordinary, fallible human being. *The Loser* is the first phase; *The Advocate* is the withdrawal of the hero and his denial of destiny; *The Winner* is the hero's acceptance of death and destiny.

O. B. Emerson, "Some Contemporary Literary Views of the Newest South," in *The Rising South*, p. 119.

board and thrust it into the soil, scooping it up and flinging it over the parapet into the areaway below. He straightened and looked us squarely in the face.

"They can't touch it," he said. "I won't let

SR-10 ► 'em lay a dirty hand on it!"

We saw it then. He stooped to his labor again and we followed it, the gusts of his anger moving in frenzied labor among us as we scattered along the edge of earth, scooping it and throwing it over the parapet, destroying with anger the growth we had nurtured with such tender care. The soil carried so laboriously upward to the light and the sun cascaded swiftly into the dark areaway, the green blades of grass crumpled and twisted in the falling.

BB

It took less time than you would think . . . the task of destruction is infinitely easier than that of creation. We stopped at the end, leaving only a scattering of loose soil, and when it was finally over, a stillness stood among the group and over the factory building. We looked down at the bare sterility of black tar, felt the harsh texture of it under the soles of our shoes, and the anger had gone out of us, leaving only a sore aching in our minds like overstretched muscles.

CC

T. J. stooped for a moment, his breathing slowing from anger and effort, caught into the same contemplation of destruction as all of us. He stooped slowly, finally, and picked up a lonely blade of grass left trampled under our feet, and put it between his teeth, tasting it, sucking the greenness out of it into his mouth. Then he started walking toward the fire escape, moving before any of us were ready to move, and disappeared over the edge while we stared after him.

We followed him, but he was already halfway down to the ground, going on past the board where we crossed over, climbing down into the areaway. We saw the last section swing down with his weight, and then he stood on the concrete below us, looking at the small pile of anonymous earth scattered by our throwing. Then he walked across the place where we could see him and disappeared toward the street without glancing back, without looking up to see us watching him.

They did not find him for two weeks. Then the Nashville police caught him just outside the Nashville freight yards. He was walking along the railroad track, still heading south, still heading home. ◄ SR-11

As for us, who had no remembered home to call us . . . none of us ever again climbed the escapeway to the roof. ❧

DD

Words to Know and Use	
	cascade (kas kād′) *v.* to fall like a waterfall
	anonymous (ə nän′ ə məs) *adj.* lacking unique features

CC. Literary Element: PLOT Ask students to explain the effects of the climax—T. J.'s decision to destroy the land rather than have the adults touch it. *(Possible response: The members of the gang feel empty of anger, left only with a "sore aching" in their minds.)*

DD. Reading Skill: INFERRING Ask students to infer why they think none of the gang members ever returns to the roof again. *(Possible response: Some students may feel that no gang members return to the roof because they too feel the emptiness caused by the loss of their earth; others may argue that the roof reminds them of T. J. and the good times they had together, and so the gang feels too lonely to return.)*

Check Test

1. How does the narrator get to know T. J.? *(T. J. and his family have moved north from Alabama, into the building in which the narrator lives.)*

2. What does T. J. propose that the gang do on the roof of the factory? *(He proposes that they plant a garden.)*

3. How does the gang get soil on to the roof? *(They dig it up from vacant lots and carry it in bags and boxes to the roof.)*

4. What crop does the gang actually grow? *(They grow grass.)*

5. Why must the garden be destroyed? Who destroys it? *(The owner of the building insists it be destroyed; T. J. and the gang destroy it.)*

6. Where does T. J. go at the end of the story? *(south to Nashville)*

Encouraging Independent Reading

The Dollmaker, a novel by Harriet Arnow
"The War of the Wall," a short story by Toni Cade Bambara
"Sweet Potato Pie," a short story by Eugenia Collier
Heidi, a novel by Johanna Spyri

Student Response

Responding to Reading

These questions are open-ended with no "right" or "wrong" answers. However, responses must be supported with information from the selection. Possible answers follow:

1. Any reaction is valid.

2. Some students may say that T. J. wants to create the roof garden because it reminds him of his rural home in the South, which he misses very much. Others may say that the garden gives him an escape from the city environment.

3. Some may feel that the gang members are different from T. J. because they are from the city, while he is from the country; T. J. understands how to grow things from the soil, while they do not. Other students may point out that, unlike T. J., the gang members are willing to let the factory owner remove the garden; T. J. is more independent and self-directed than the other boys are.

4. Some students may say that T. J. is a leader because he has a goal; he has the ability to persuade and inspire others with his enthusiasm; he has qualities of determination and persistence; he is not afraid of authority figures.

5. Some students may feel that to the gang, the roof garden represents a place to escape from life's pressures, while others may see it as a sign of their abilities and their worth.

6. Some students might say that T. J. runs away because he is hurt or angry, while others might suggest that he realizes he can never be happy if he is out of touch with the earth.

7. Some students may feel that the author choose the name "Antaeus" for the story because T. J., like the giant, had to be in contact with the earth or he lost his strength. Others may say that T. J. was a giant because he had leadership abilities that set him apart from others.

Responding to Reading

First Impressions

1. What part of the story affected you the most? Explain.

Second Thoughts

2. Why does T.J. want to create the roof garden?

Think about
- T.J.'s background
- how the city is different from his Southern home
- the importance of "escapes" in everyone's life

3. How are the gang members different from T.J.?

Think about
- their initial reaction to T.J. and his description of farming
- what the gang members want to grow
- how the gang members react to the order to remove the garden

4. What leadership qualities does T.J. possess?

Think about
- why he wants to create the roof garden
- how he presents his idea to the gang
- how he keeps the project going
- the notes you made in your journal on leadership "qualities"

5. What does the roof garden represent to the gang?

6. Why do you think T.J. runs away after destroying the roof garden?

7. Think about the Greek myth of Antaeus that you read about on page 188. Why did the author choose this name for the title of his story?

Literary Concept: Plot

The sequence of actions and events in a story is called the **plot.** One event logically follows the next until the turning point, or climax, of the story is reached. The events that build toward the climax of the story are called the rising action, and the events that follow the action are called the falling action. Using the plot diagram on page 18, tell what events in "Antaeus" make up the rising action, climax, and falling action.

Concept Review: Point of View Point of view refers to the person who is telling the story. A story may be written from the first-person or the third-person point of view. Who is telling the story in "Antaeus"?

Literary Concept—Plot

The rising action begins when the conflict develops between the factory owner and T. J. The rising action continues with T. J.'s decision that no one besides the boys is going to touch the garden. The climax occurs with T. J.'s decision that he would sooner destroy his creation than have the adults touch it. The falling action describes the aftermath of the destruction of the roof garden and tells what happens to the roof garden, T. J., and the gang.

Concept Review—Point of View: The story is told by one of the gang members who befriends T. J. It is told from the first-person point of view.

Writing Options

1. Design a report card for T.J. Begin by thinking back to your earlier discussion of leadership and your list of leadership qualities. Use these qualities as categories on the report card. Then grade T.J. on his performance in each category. Include comments that give your reasons for each grade.

2. Think of a slogan that would be appropriate for a sweatshirt designed for T.J.'s gang.

3. Write the conversation between T.J. and the police in Nashville who catch him walking along the railroad track. What will the men say when they find him? How will T.J. respond?

4. If you have read "Stowaway!," contrast Armando Ramírez with T.J. in this story. Which one is more realistic or practical in solving his problems? Explain.

Vocabulary Practice

Exercise Some words are frequently used in discussing certain subjects. For instance, *orbit* is a word you would expect to find in a book about space. Match each book title in the left-hand column with the word in the right-hand column that you would expect to find in that book. Write the matching word on another sheet of paper.

1. *How to Be Naturally Healthy*
2. *The Smart Shopper*
3. *Digging Rocks*
4. *The Secret Life of the Japanese Beetle*
5. *Waterfalls of Yosemite*
6. *Leaders Who Did Not Falter*
7. *Planning Successful Business Projects*
8. *Unsigned Poems*
9. *Flag Burners in History*
10. *The Boy Who Never Cried*
11. *The Ever-Expanding Eye*
12. *Deep in Thought*
13. *My Kingdom*
14. *Still Life*
15. *Ten Easy Ways to Keep Your Mind on Track*

Words to Know and Use

anonymous
cascade
contemplate
desecrated
dilating
distracted
domain
enterprise
esoteric
inert
laborious
resolute
robust
shrewd
stolid

Writing Options

The Writing Options are designed to meet varied student interests and abilities. Have each student choose one writing activity to complete. You may wish to guide some students to an option that requires less writing.

Journal Update Have students review their journal entries for "Antaeus." What have they learned about the effect of the land on people? What new reflections can they add to their writing?

Vocabulary Practice

1. robust
2. shrewd
3. laborious
4. esoteric
5. cascade
6. resolute
7. enterprise
8. anonymous
9. desecrated
10. stolid
11. dilating
12. contemplate
13. domain
14. inert
15. distracted

Options for Learning

These activities suit a variety of learning styles and modes of expression. Allow students to review the options and then choose the one they wish to do. Many are excellent collaborative learning projects.

1. Grow Your Own Suggest that students use graph paper to chart the growth of their plants.

2. Pro and Con Students might watch a brief television editorial for suggestions on format and tone.

3. T. J. Phone Home Students may role-play their conversations.

Fact Finder

The dirt would weigh 12,500 pounds, 250 multiplied by 50. Whether the building's owner had a right to be concerned depends on the roof's size and construction and how the soil is arranged. The roof of an average home most likely could not withstand that amount of weight, but a factory roof probably could. Students could determine this by contacting a building contractor.

Additional Information About the Author

The author was born in Mississippi and christened Loyse Youth Deal. Borden's family, along with many other cotton farmers, lost their land during the Depression, when the author was a boy. Through government aid, they bought two mules and joined a nearby commune. While still a student at the University of Alabama, Deal published his first story, "Exodus," later reprinted in *Best Short Stories of 1949.* He began writing full time in 1954, and by 1957 he had received national recognition, including a Guggenheim Fellowship.

Closure

"Antaeus" explores seizing the moment. Have students relate T. J.'s love of the earth to ways they find to spend time in nature, such as gardening, camping, and hiking.

e x t e n d

Options for Learning

1 • Grow Your Own Like T.J., many people in cities and towns grow their own fruits and vegetables. If you could grow one food crop, what would you plant? From books in the library, brochures, the backs of seed packets, or from someone you know who is a good gardener, find out how you would grow this crop. Determine what soils, lighting, and watering techniques are needed. How much produce will one plant yield? Draw a diagram to illustrate the stages of the plant's growth. Then share your findings with the class.

2 • Pro and Con Suppose a sympathetic TV reporter heard the story of the confrontation between the boys who created the roof garden and the men who ordered it destroyed. Think of the points he or she might want to include in a one-minute editorial applauding the boys' efforts and attacking the owner of the building as insensitive and lacking in imagination. Present your editorial to the class. Another classmate may want to present a one-minute rebuttal from the owner's viewpoint.

3 • T.J. Phone Home Imagine that the gang members find out a way to contact T.J. by telephone in the South. Think of reasons why the gang members want T.J. to return. Come up with other reasons why T.J. wants to stay down South. Then re-create a brief phone conversation between T.J. and the narrator of the story in which the narrator tries to convince T.J. to come back North.

FACT FINDER

Suppose that an average bushel of dirt weighs fifty pounds and that T.J.'s gang carted up 250 bushels of dirt onto the roof. How much would this amount weigh? Did the building's owner have a right to be concerned?

Borden Deal
1922–1985

Like T.J., many of Borden Deal's characters live in or come from the South. Deal once explained that his characters "live and work in real time in real places: raising horses, building highways and TVA (Tennessee Valley Authority) dams, running for public office, farming the southern earth." Deal's own life sounds like that of several of his characters. During the Great Depression he worked on his father's cotton farm. Later, as a young man, he traveled the country looking for any work he could find. His employers during this time included the U.S. Department of Labor, the telephone company, a film company, and the U.S. Navy. Deal was fascinated by ancient myths and believed that these stories "recur over and over again throughout the history of mankind." In all, Deal wrote more than one hundred stories, poems, and reviews. "Antaeus" was included in the *Best American Stories of the Year* of 1962.

Cross-Curricular Options

Georgraphy: Have students use a map to locate T. J.'s former home in Marion County, Alabama, and Nashville, Tennessee, where he is found at the end of the story.

Math: Suggest that students calculate what it would cost today to prepare a small home vegetable garden, including fertilizer and seeds.

History: Students might like to research the migration of Southerners to the North during World War II. Include a discussion of why these people came north, how they fared, and how many returned.

Art: Have students prepare a three-dimensional display of the factory and the gang's roof garden.

Publishing: Compile the contributions of all students. Display or make copies to distribute.

e x p l o r e

Fiction

Gaston

WILLIAM SAROYAN

Examine What You Know (Prior Knowledge)

Almost everyone has experienced being caught in the middle between the desires of two people. Think about a time this has happened to you. Then copy and fill out the diagram below. As you read the selection, think about how the girl in the story might fill out this chart.

Person Number 1 ________ Person Number 2 ________

Your Name ________

Wanted me to . . . ________ Wanted me to . . . ________

I finally decided to . . . ________

Expand Your Knowledge (Building Background)

One of the characters in this selection has chosen to leave the United States and live in Paris. People from one country who live in another are called *expatriates*. Some expatriates live abroad for business or political reasons, while others are simply lured by the romance and excitement of life in a foreign land. During the 1920's and 1930's many American artists and writers became expatriates living in Paris. These members of the "Lost Generation," as they were called, included such famous writers as Ernest Hemingway, Gertrude Stein, and Richard Wright.

Enrich Your Reading (Reading Skill)

Understanding Dialogue Much of this story is told through the dialogue between a father and his daughter. The writer, however, has often left out such tag lines as "he said" and "she said" to indicate who is speaking. To keep track of a two-character dialogue, remember these two guidelines. The two characters alternate speaking. A switch in speakers is indicated by a new paragraph.

■ *A biography of the author can be found in the Reader's Handbook.*

Objectives

- To explore and appreciate a short story
- To recognize symbolism
- To understand dialogue
- To review point of view
- To express understanding of the work through a choice of writing forms, including description, monologue, dialogue, and comparison

Prereading/Motivation

Examine What You Know

Discussions Prompts: Why were you caught in the middle of the situation? How do you feel about your decision? How do you suggest others resolve such conflicts?

Expand Your Knowledge

Discussion Prompts: Why might people choose to live in another country? What aspects of Paris are especially romantic or exciting? If you were to become an expatriate, where would you live and why?

Additional Background: There were many reasons Americans chose to settle abroad. Some expatriates relocated simply because it was cheaper to live in Europe. Others, such as the poet Archibald MacLeish, planned brief stays to sharpen their American identity and sift through traditions in an attempt to define their art. Still others, such as the poet Ezra Pound, gained importance abroad and at home partly through expatriation.

Enrich Your Reading

Before students start reading, isolate and discuss a portion of the dialogue so that they are familiar with its appearance.

Thematic Link—Seizing the Moment

In this short story, the father tries to seize the moment by making his time with his daughter special.

Journal Writing

This story explores a parent-child relationship. Suggest these journal topics to students:

- Write about an enjoyable time you spent with your parent or guardian when you were a young child.
- Invent a character named Gaston, telling the character's age, appearance, personality, and important relationships with others.

For other journal opportunities, refer students to Examine What You Know (p. 201), First Impressions and Broader Connections (p. 206), and Real Life Connections (p. T–205).

Additional Resources

UNIT TWO RESOURCE BOOK
Reader's Guidesheet, p. 16
Vocabulary Worksheet, p. 17
Selection Check Tests, p. 18
Selection Test, pp. 19–20

Collaborative Learning

Opportunities for collaborative learning appear throughout the lesson and include Writing Options 1 and 3 (p. 207).

Teaching Strategies

Support for Students of Limited English Proficiency

- Use Reader's Guidesheet, p. 16.
- This story is short and contains a great deal of dialogue, as well as fairly simple vocabulary and sentence structure. On a literal level, it is not difficult to understand, but its symbolism and deeper level of meaning may be difficult for students of limited English proficiency to comprehend. Suggest that these students read the story through twice, the second time looking for answers to question 3 on page 206: "How are the father and Gaston similar?"
- For help in understanding and pronouncing French words, encourage students to review the footnotes.
- Annotation I focuses on difficult vocabulary.

Text Annotations

A. Literary Element: POINT OF VIEW Have students identify the point of view. *(It is the third-person point of view because the story is told by someone outside the action.)*

B. Critical Thinking: ANALYZING Have students analyze the father's character, based on his appearance. *(Possible response: His unconventional appearance—huge mustache, striped pullover, and bare feet—suggests that he too is unconventional, a free spirit not interested in conforming.)*

C. Reading Skill: INFERRING Ask students what they can infer, up to this point in the story, about the father-daughter relationship. *(Possible response: Father and daughter have seen little of each other; they do not live together; she has a nicer home than he does.)*

D. Reading Skill: INFERRING Have students infer the father's feelings about his daughter from his choice of peaches. *(Possible response: Giving his daughter "the biggest and best looking peach" and then taking the flawed one for himself suggests that he loves her and wants her to have the best.)*

Gaston

WILLIAM SAROYAN

A They were to eat peaches, as planned, after her nap, and now she sat across from the man who would have been a total stranger except that he was in fact her father. They had been together again (although she couldn't quite remember when they had been together before) for almost a hundred years now, or was it only since day before yesterday? Anyhow, they were together again, and he was kind of funny. First, he had the biggest mustache she had ever seen on anybody, although to her it was not a mustache at all; it was a lot of red and brown hair under his nose and around the ends of his mouth. B Second, he wore a blue-and-white striped jersey, instead of a shirt and tie, and no coat. His arms were covered with the same hair, only it was a little lighter and thinner. He wore blue slacks, but no shoes and socks. He was barefoot, and so was she, of course.

He was at home. She was with him in his home in Paris,[1] if you could call it a home. He was very old, especially for a young man—thirty-six, he had told her; and she was six, just up from sleep on a very hot afternoon in August. SR-1 ▶

C That morning, on a little walk in the neighborhood, she had seen peaches in a box outside a small store and she had stopped to look at them, so he had bought a kilo.[2]

Now, the peaches were on a large plate on the card table at which they sat.

There were seven of them, but one of them was flawed. It *looked* as good as the others, almost the size of a tennis ball, nice red fading to light green, but where the stem had been there was now a break that went straight down into the heart of the seed.

D He placed the biggest and best-looking peach on the small plate in front of the girl, and then took the flawed peach and began to remove the skin. When he had half the skin off the peach he ate that side, neither of them talking, both of them just being there, and not being excited or anything—no plans, that is.

The man held the half-eaten peach in his fingers and looked down into the cavity, into the open seed. The girl looked, too.

While they were looking, two feelers poked out from the cavity. They were attached to a kind of brown knob-head, which followed the feelers, and then two large legs took a strong grip on the edge of the cavity and hoisted some of the rest of whatever it was out of seed, and stopped there a moment, as if to look around. ◀ SR-2

The man studied the seed dweller, and so, of course, did the girl.

The creature paused only a fraction of a second and then continued to come out of the seed to walk down the eaten side of the peach to wherever it was going.

1. **Paris:** the capital of France.
2. **kilo** (kē′ lō): one kilogram, or about two pounds.

STRUCTURED READING FOR LESS PROFICIENT STUDENTS

These questions can help to guide students through the readings. Ask each question at the point of the selection where the SR number appears in the margin.

SR–1. Where is the girl in this story and whom is she with? *(She is in her father's home in Paris.)* **Summarizing**

SR–2. What emerges from the man's peach? *(an insect)* **Clarifying**

SR–3. Why do you think the father tells his daughter that the insect is Gaston, the grand boulevardier? *(Possible response: so she won't be frightened, so she can appreciate nature's wonders)* **Inferring**

SR–4. What does the father leave to buy for his daughter? *(a bad peach)* **Clarifying**

Continued on page 203

The girl had never seen anything like it—a whole big thing made out of brown color, a knob-head, feelers, and a great many legs. It was very active, too. Almost businesslike, you might say. The man placed the peach back on the plate. The creature moved off the peach onto the surface of the white plate. There it came to a thoughtful stop.

"Who is it?" the girl said.

"Gaston."

"Where does he live?"

"Well, he *used* to live in this peach seed, but now that the peach has been harvested and sold, and I have eaten half of it, it looks as if he's out of house and home."

E "Aren't you going to squash him?"

"No, of course not, why should I?"

"He's a bug. He's *ugh*."

"Not at all. He's Gaston the grand boulevardier."[3]

"Everybody hollers when a bug comes out of an apple, but you don't holler or

SR-3 ▶ *anything*."

"Of course not. How would *we* like it if somebody hollered every time we came out of our house?"

"Why *would* they?"

"Precisely. So why should we holler at Gaston?"

"He's not the same as us."

F "Well, not exactly, but he's the same as a lot of other occupants of peach seeds. Now, the poor fellow hasn't got a home, and there he is with all that pure design and handsome form, and nowhere to go."

"Handsome?"

"Gaston is just about the handsomest of his kind I've ever seen."

"What's he saying?"

"Well, he's a little confused. Now, inside that house of his he had everything in order. Bed here, porch there, and so forth."

"Show me."

GIRL AT TABLE Xavier Valls.

The man picked up the peach, leaving Gaston entirely alone on the white plate. He removed the peeling and ate the rest of the peach.

"Nobody else I know would do that," the girl said. "They'd throw it away."

"I can't imagine why. It's a perfectly good peach."

He opened the seed and placed the two sides not far from Gaston. The girl studied the open halves.

"Is *that* where he lives?"

3. **boulevardier** (bo͞ol vär dyā′): someone who makes an effort to be seen; a "man about town."

E. Literary Element: CHARACTERIZATION
Ask students to explain what the father's explanation of "Gaston" reveals about the father's character. *(Possible response: He is creative, imaginative, playful, and adept at defusing a potentially frightening situation.)*

F. Teaching Tip

The father's explanation of why he doesn't "holler" at Gaston presents a natural way to discuss different sorts of prejudice with students. Make sure that students understand the little girl is talking about people hollering at the insect because of its appearance, not because it could do harm. Have volunteers share their experiences of misjudging something or someone at first glance. You might remind students of "The Fan Club" in Unit 1 if they have read that selection.

Art Note

In this painting, characteristic of the work of contemporary artist Xavier Valls, the composition seems formal, the scene almost solemn. Every object is clearly delineated. Yet there is a mood as of something veiled—perhaps in the attitude of the girl. *How might "Gaston" fit this picture?*

Structured Reading for Less Proficient Students

Continued from page 202

SR–5. What does the girl's mother tell her when she calls? *(She is sending the chauffeur to pick her up for a birthday party and that tomorrow they are returning to New York.)* **Literal recall**

SR–6. What does the girl do to Gaston after she speaks with her mother? *(squashes him)* **Clarifying**

SR–7. How does the father feel after his daughter leaves? *(sad and vulnerable; "like Gaston on the white plate")* **Inferring**

G. Literary Element: SYMBOLISM Ask students how Gaston's peach pit might symbolize the father's former home. *(Possible response: Neither can return home again, for their homes have been destroyed—Gaston's by the man eating the peach, the man's through divorce or separation.)*

H. Critical Thinking: ANALYZING Ask students why they think the father leaves instructions for his daughter to tell her mother that he has gone to buy a bad peach. *(Possible response: Some students may say that he cannot be serious, even when dealing with a serious matter. Others might see his remark as a subtle jab at his wife, who may consider him a "bad peach" or "bad apple" and regret that she ever married him.)*

I. LEP: Vocabulary Pronounce the word *chauffeur* for students and explain that it refers to a person employed to drive another person's automobile. Explain to students that the word comes from French. Then ask students what having a chauffeur suggests about the mother's lifestyle. *(that she has a wealthly, luxurious lifestyle)*

J. Reading Skill: CONTRASTING Have students contrast the girl's mother and father and explain how they are different. Encourage students to cite specific details to back up their points. *(Possible response: The father and mother are very different: The father's appearance and behavior suggest that he is a nonconformist who is creative and playful; the mother's conversation here suggests that she is realistic and controlled.)*

"It's where he used to live. Gaston is out in the world and on his own now. You can see for yourself how comfortable he was in there. He had everything."

"Now what has he got?"

"Not very much, I'm afraid."

"What's he going to do?"

"What are *we* going to do?"

"Well, we're not going to squash him, that's one thing we're *not* going to do," the girl said.

G "What *are* we going to do, then?"

"Put him back?"

"Oh, *that* house is finished."

"Well, he can't live in our house, can he?"

"Not happily."

"Can he live in our house *at all*?"

"Well, he could *try*, I suppose. Don't you want to eat a peach?"

"Only if it's a peach with somebody in the seed."

"Well, see if you can find a peach that has an opening at the top, because if you can, that'll be a peach in which you're likeliest to find somebody."

The girl examined each of the peaches on the big plate.

"They're all shut," she said.

"Well, eat one, then."

"No. I want the same kind that you ate, with somebody in the seed."

"Well, to tell you the truth, the peach I ate would be considered a bad peach, so of course stores don't like to sell them. I was sold that one by mistake, most likely. And so now Gaston is without a home, and we've got six perfect peaches to eat."

"I don't want a perfect peach. I want a peach with people."

"Well, I'll go out and see if I can find one."

"Where will I go?"

"You'll go with me, unless you'd rather stay. I'll only be five minutes."

"If the phone rings, what shall I say?"

"I don't think it'll ring, but if it does, say hello and see who it is."

"If it's my mother, what shall I say?"

"Tell her I've gone to get you a bad peach, and anything else you want to tell her." H

"If she wants me to go back, what shall I say?"

"Say yes if you want to go back."

"Do you want me to?"

"Of course not, but the important thing is what you want, not what I want."

"Why is *that* the important thing?"

"Because I want you to be where you want to be."

"I want to be here."

"I'll be right back."

He put on socks and shoes, and a jacket, and went out. She watched Gaston trying to find out what to do next. Gaston wandered around the plate, but everything seemed wrong, and he didn't know what to do or where to go. ◀SR-4

The telephone rang, and her mother said she was sending the chauffeur to pick her up because there was a little party for somebody's daughter who was also six, and then tomorrow they would fly back to New York. I ◀SR-5

"Let me speak to your father," she said.

"He's gone to get a peach."

"*One* peach?"

"One with people."

"You haven't been with your father two days and already you *sound* like him."

"There *are* peaches with people in them. I know. I saw one of them come out."

"A *bug*?" J

"Not a bug. Gaston."

"*Who?*"

"Gaston the grand something."

"Somebody else gets a peach with a bug in

PROFESSIONAL NOTEBOOK

Providing students time to process, clarify, and question about concepts presented during class is critical for learning. The traditional model of teaching and testing often ignores students' need to reflect on the information. If teachers offer 3–5 minutes during class for structured thinking about the topic, students learn and retain better. Indeed, research indicates that deeper understanding and greater retention occur when concepts and information are reviewed, summarized, discussed, and communicated to others.

***Journal of Reading*, VOL. 33, NO. 7 (APRIL 1990, P. 551)**

J it and throws it away, but not him. He makes up a lot of foolishness about it."

"It's not foolishness."

"All right, all right, don't get angry at me about a horrible peach bug of some kind."

"Gaston is right here, just outside his broken house, and I'm not angry at you."

"You'll have a lot of fun at the party."

"OK."

"We'll have fun flying back to New York, too."

"OK."

"Are you glad you saw your father?"

"Of course I am."

"Is he funny?"

"Yes."

"Is he crazy?"

K "Yes. I mean, no. He just doesn't holler when he sees a bug crawling out of a peach seed or anything. He just looks at it carefully. But it *is* just a bug, isn't it, *really*?"

"That's all it is."

"And we'll *have* to squash it?"

"That's right. I can't wait to see you, darling. These two days have been like two years to me. Goodbye."

The girl watched Gaston on the plate, and she actually didn't like him. He was all *ugh*, as he had been in the first place. He didn't have a home anymore, and he was wandering around on the white plate, and he was silly and wrong and ridiculous and useless and all sorts of other things. She cried a

L little, but only inside, because long ago she had decided she didn't like crying, because if you ever started to cry it seemed as if there was so much to cry about you almost couldn't stop, and she didn't like that at all. The open halves of the peach seed were wrong, too. They were ugly or something. They weren't clean.

The man bought a kilo of peaches but found no flawed peaches among them, so he bought another kilo at another store, and this time his luck was better, and there were *two* that were flawed. He hurried back to his flat and let himself in.

His daughter was in her room, in her best dress.

"My mother phoned," she said, "and she's sending the chauffeur for me because there's another birthday party."

"Another?"

"I mean, there's *always* a lot of them in New York."

"Will the chauffeur bring you back?"

"No. We're flying back to New York tomorrow."

"Oh."

"I liked being in your house."

"I liked having you here."

"Why do you live here?"

"This is my home."

"It's nice, but it's a lot different from our home."

"Yes, I suppose it is."

"It's kind of like Gaston's house."

"Where *is* Gaston?"

"I squashed him."

"Really? Why?"

"Everybody squashes bugs and worms."

"Oh. Well. I found you a peach."

"I don't want a peach anymore."

"OK." ◀SR-6

He got her dressed, and he was packing her stuff when the chauffeur arrived. He went down the three flights of stairs with his daughter and the chauffeur, and in the street he was about to hug the girl when he decided he had better not. They shook hands instead, as if they were strangers. M

He watched the huge car drive off, and then he went around the corner where he took his coffee every morning, feeling a little, he thought, like Gaston on the white plate. ❧ ◀SR-7

K. Critical Thinking: EVALUATING Ask students if they think the girl's father is crazy. Have them explain their answers. *(Possible response: He is not crazy; rather, he looks at things in a way that differs from the mother's.)*

L. Reading Skill: DRAWING CONCLUSIONS Have students conclude, based on the details in this passage, whether the daughter sides with her father or her mother. *(At this point she sides with her mother, as shown by her different attitude toward Gaston. Before, she was entranced by him; now she finds him disgusting.)*

M. Critical Thinking: ANALYZING Ask students to analyze why the father does not hug his daughter. *(Possible response: He realizes that the bond between them that he had established during their brief visit has now been broken.)*

Check Test

1. Who are the two main characters in the story? *(a six-year-old girl and her father)*

2. Who is Gaston? Where was his home? *(Gaston is an insect; his home was inside a peach.)*

3. Where and with whom does the daughter live? What is their lifestyle? *(She lives in New York with her mother; they are wealthy)*

4. What happens to Gaston? *(The daughter squashes him.)*

Encouraging Independent Reading

E = MC² Mon Amour, a novel by Patrick Calvin

"The Hiltons' Holiday," a short story by Sarah Orne Jewett

"A Fairy Tale," a poem by Leory V. Quintana

"Should Wizard Hit Mommy?" a short story by John Updike

Real Life Connections

Help students to recognize similarities between the little girl's situation and their own lives. Point out that children of even happily married parents sometimes become caught in minor disagreements between their parents. Then ask students how they react if caught in a minor or humorous conflict between their parents or guardians. What advice might students offer to the girl in dealing with her situation?

e x p l a i n

Responding to Reading

First Impressions

1. Write down your thoughts about the little girl's situation.

Second Thoughts

2. How would you describe the father?

   Think about
   - his living situation
   - his appearance
   - how he treats and reacts to his daughter

3. How are the father and Gaston similar?

   Think about
   - where they both used to live
   - where they live now
   - what happens to both at the end of the story

4. How does the daughter reflect the personalities of both parents?

   Think about
   - her response to her father's description of Gaston
   - her response to her mother's description of her father
   - her decision about what to do with Gaston

5. What is so special about the time that the father and daughter share together? In what sense do they seize the moment?

6. Do you think the man is a good father?

Broader Connections

7. The girl in the story is caught between two parents who each want her affection and loyalty but who have very different values and lifestyles. At what age should a child of divorced or separated parents be able to choose how long and how often to visit the parent with whom he or she is not living? Explain your reasoning.

Literary Concept: Symbolism

A **symbol** is a person, place, or object that stands for something beyond itself. In this story, Gaston can be seen as a symbol. Think about the similarities that exist between Gaston and the father. In what ways is the insect's life a mirror of the father's existence?

Student Response

Responding to Reading

These questions are open-ended with no "right" or "wrong" answers. However, responses must be supported with information from the selection. Possible answers follow:

1. Almost any thoughts about the little gir's situation, whether negative or positive, are valid.

2. Some students may describe the father as creative and loving, while others may see him as irresponsible and immature. Refer to Annotation B. Students should note that the father is living alone and does not seem to be as wealthy as the mother who lives in New York. His appearance seems that of a casual, free spirit.

3. Some students may say that Gaston and the father are similar because they both once had comfortable homes that they lost and now they are both out in the world on their own. Others may also note that both Gaston and the father are harshly judged by others. Some may also say that they are similar because they are both squashed in the end by the daughter, who kills the bug and rejects her father.

4. Some students may say that the daughter has her father's playful imagination but her mother's need for conformity and control.

5. Some students may feel that their time together is special because they share a moment of almost magical imagination. Students may note that because they live apart, they seize what could be a very routine moment and make it special by looking at life a little differently.

6. Some students might feel that the man is a good father because he loves his daughter and tries to make her happy, as shown by his attempt to buy more bad peaches. Others may feel that he is not a good father because he lives very far away from his daughter, does not seem to be in touch with her that often, and does not put up a fight to have her stay with him.

7. Some students might feel that an impartial outside party should judge when a child is mature and responsible enough to make such a decision; others may argue that even very young children have a right to make such decisions for themselves. Be sure students explain their feelings.

Literary Concept—Symbolism

The insect's life is a mirror of the father's life in that both have been displaced from their homes—the father by divorce, the insect by the father. In addition, both are "killed" at the daughter's hands—Gaston literally, the father symbolically as he loses the closeness they shared during her visit.

Concept Review: Point of View When the story is told by a major or minor character in the story, the story is told from the first-person point of view. When the story is told by someone outside the action, the story is told from the third-person point of view. Look back at "Gaston." From which point of view is this story told? Explain your answer.

Writing Options

1. Based on the phone conversation between the mother and the daughter, write a description of the mother. What do you think she looks like? What kind of clothes does she wear, how does she spend her time, and what does she value in other people?

2. How do you think Gaston views the scene with the father and daughter? Assume that you are Gaston and write a first-person monologue describing the events in the story.

3. Compose a dialogue between the father and the mother that takes place after the story ends. Make sure that they talk about the father's apartment, Gaston, their daughter, and the mother's lifestyle in New York.

4. Pretend you are the daughter in this story. Write a one-sentence description of your father at these moments in the story:
   - at the beginning
   - after opening up the peach
   - after telling him you are leaving
   - after you leave

5. Look back at the poem "Song of the Open Road" on page 184. In what ways might the father and the narrator of "Song of the Open Road" be similar?

6. Think back to your chart about being caught in the middle. Briefly describe how it felt to be in such a situation and how you feel about the decision you eventually made.

The story is told in the third-person point of view, by someone outside the action. Third-person pronouns and the fact that the thoughts of two different characters are given are among the clues to the point of view from which the story is told. Refer to **Annotation A.**

Writing Options
The Writing Options are designed to meet varied student interests and abilities. Have each student choose one writing activity to complete. You may wish to guide some students to an option that requires less writing.

Journal Update Have students review their journal entries for "Gaston." What new reflections about parents or about a character named Gaston can they add to their writing?

Closure

In this story the father seizes a special moment with his daughter. He turns what could have been a frightening or depressing experience into a "fun" time. Have students think of times in their lives when a frightening or difficult experience was turned into a pleasant or memorable occasion.

Writer's Workshop

Objectives

- To understand the goals of persuasive writing
- To familiarize students with different types of persuasion
- To formulate concrete examples of persuasive writing
- To locate evidence in drafting a letter of recommendation
- To draft, revise, edit, and share a persuasive letter of recommendation
- To reflect on the writing process

Integrating . . .

Literature and Writing Point out to students that a letter of recommendation from an influential person can be the difference between success and failure in obtaining employment. Ask them if they have ever needed to get a letter of recommendation for a job they sought. Ask them if they think it would be more difficult to write a letter of recommendation for Walt Whitman than one for T.J. in *Antaeus*.

Writing and Language The Language Workshop in this subunit focuses on avoiding double negatives. Point out to students that one of the essentials of a persuasive letter is good grammar. Explain that persuasive writing is almost totally undermined by poor use of language. Ask them what problems T.J. might have in drafting an effective letter of recommendation that others might not have.

Literature and Life Skills Have students clip actual want ads from the newspaper. Then ask how these ads differ from the ads in the Writer's Workshop. (Many want ads contain abbreviations.) Show students that most want ads identify the qualities that a suitable job candidate would possess. Ask them to circle the primary qualities mentioned in a want ad (e.g., "nonsmoker") and draw a square around the secondary ones (e.g., "driver's license a plus").

PERSUASION

It's difficult to get through a day without someone trying to persuade us to do something or to believe something. Television commercials and print ads try to persuade us to buy products. Various organizations fill our mailboxes with letters urging us to send donations. Before any political election, we are bombarded with ads and letters that aim to convince us to vote for a certain candidate. Although persuasive writing takes many complex forms, its purpose is simple: to convince an audience to agree with the writer's opinion.

While some persuasive writing, such as that used in advertising, may rely on emotional appeals or half-truths, the most effective persuasion is based on sound reasoning and solid evidence. If you hope to convince someone that your opinion is right, simply stating your opinion isn't enough. You have to justify it. The more reasons and factual evidence you can find to support your opinion, the more likely you will persuade others to accept it.

For this assignment you will write a persuasive letter. Once you have determined the subject of your letter, you will gather evidence that will convince your audience to agree with your opinion. The more reasons and factual evidence you find to support your opinion, the more likely you are to persuade others to accept it.

GUIDED ASSIGNMENT: LETTER OF RECOMMENDATION

The Help-Wanted ads that follow appeared in a local newspaper. Choose a character from one of the reading selections in this subunit who would qualify for one of the jobs described. Then write a letter of recommendation for this character.

Here is your PASSkey to this assignment.

PURPOSE: To persuade another person

AUDIENCE: An employer

SUBJECT: A character from your reading

STRUCTURE: A business letter

Help Wanted: Day-care center is now hiring responsible adults to supervise the 6-to-8-year-old group of after-school children. Applicants should be positive role models for children and have an understanding of kids' needs and interests. Minimum of 5 years experience caring for youngsters. Contact Mr. Nolan at the ABC Day-Care Center.

Additional Resources

UNIT TWO RESOURCE BOOK

Writer's Workshop Copy Master, p. 21
Peer and Self-Evaluation Guidelines, p. 22
Writing Assessment Guidelines, p. 23

ENRICHMENT MATERIALS

Thinking Skills Transparency and Worksheet
Fine Art Transparency and Writing Prompts
Revision, Proofreading, and Elaboration Worksheet
Writing Prompts for Assessment

Wanted: Goal-oriented young man or woman for management position in rising company. Good planning and organizational skills are essential. Must be able to work well with others, delegate responsibility, and oversee long-range projects. Contact: Mrs. Powers, WCO Corporation.

Help Wanted: Interested in travel opportunities? Then this position might be what you're looking for. Openings are now available in our international sales dept. The person should be a self-starter who loves adventure and is willing to spend time away from home. Must be adaptable to change. Send resume and letter to Mr. Tinker.

Prewriting

STEP 1 Choose a character Examine each of the ads carefully, noting the primary qualifications needed for each job. Now think about the characters in the reading selections, jotting down on a separate sheet of paper those characters you think might qualify for each job. Decide which character best meets the qualifications for one of the advertised positions.

STEP 2 Gather evidence Review the reading selection to gather evidence that will support the character's qualifications for the job. List this evidence on a separate sheet of paper.

STEP 3 Organize your evidence Organize your persuasive evidence, matching information about the character with each of the job qualifications given in the ad. You might want to organize your information in a chart similar to the following one. Here, a student has given details about Captain Torres from "Lather and Nothing Else" to match qualifications listed in the ad for the management position.

Organizational Skills	Delegates Responsibility	Oversees Long-Range Projects
-moves large numbers of men great distances -keeps his troops fed	-as Captain, continually dictates orders to his troops	-maintains control of the rebels for extended periods

◀ STUDENT MODEL

STEP 4 Organize your letter The sections of your letter should correspond to each of the job qualifications listed in the ad. Once you have outlined the sections, decide on the order in which you

Teaching Strategies

Introduction Ask students to turn to the Writer's Workshop for this subunit on page 208. Discuss with them the role of judgment and evaluation in persuasion. Be sure they understand the three elements of persuasive writing: a statement of the writer's judgment, strong supporting reasons for the judgment, and a statement convincing the reader that the judgment is sound.

Call students' attention to the Guided Assignment box on page 208, and be sure they understand that they will write a letter of recommendation for one of the characters in the subunit. Point out the PASSkey graphic, and read with them the purpose, audience, subject, and structure of the assignment. Emphasize the fact that their purpose is to persuade and that their audience is the prospective employer.

Prewriting Discuss with students why the effectiveness of their letters will depend on the qualities they choose to include in the text of their letters. Remind them that a good letter should not have sweeping generalizations. In order to be persuasive, a letter should rely on specifics.

Teaching Tip

As the class begins *Prewriting*, give them some practice in devising qualities. Follow these steps:

1. Read with the class Step 1 under *Prewriting* on page 209. Have students volunteer qualities that are generally required for any job (e.g. a sense of responsibility).

2. Ask students to explain why Walt Whitman and Edna St. Vincent Millay would be ideally suited for the international sales job. Elicit from students that both of them indicate a strong love of travel in their writing.

3. Review with students the qualities that make the fictional T.J. and the real Armando Soccarras Ramírez brothers under the skin.

Drafting Suggest that students make a simple outline before they begin drafting. An outline that discusses three outstanding qualifications for a job candidate would be appropriate for a business letter.

Computer Tip

Those who decide to make an outline might consider using a computer, which will make it easy to move the parts around as they work.

Have students number each outline idea that will become a separate paragraph. Here is an example for a three-paragraph letter:

1. Paragraph one, which introduces the writer and the job candidate.

2. Paragraph two, which gives at least two of the candidate's outstanding qualifications.

3. Paragraph 3, which sums up why the candidate is well-qualified for the particular job.

Remind students that the outline is simply a guide to keep them organized as they write. They should understand that if their method of writing makes an outline unnecessary, they certainly may omit it.

Be sure students keep in mind that a letter of recommendation must deal with specifics. Remind them that the strongest persuasive writing always avoids the use of sweeping generalizations. In order to convince an employer of a prospective employee's qualifications for a particular job, the writer must state exactly what makes the candidate an eminent prospect. Exaggeration and generalization weaken any persuasive message.

will arrange them. Some writers begin with the weakest evidence and progress to the strongest. In this case, however, you may want to begin with the strongest evidence in order to gain the prospective employer's attention and respect. The student whose chart is shown in Step 3 began with organizational skills because her evidence was the strongest for that qualification.

Drafting

STEP 1 Write an introductory paragraph Begin your letter with a standard salutation: Dear ______ (the name of the contact person in the ad). Then write your introduction—a brief paragraph expressing your opinion about the applicant's qualifications for the job. Here is one student's introduction. (For more information on correct business letter form, see the **Writer's Handbook.**)

STUDENT MODEL ▶

Dear Mr. Fritz:

According to your recent ad, your company is seeking a person who has good organizational skills, can delegate responsibility, and can oversee long-range projects. One man who fits this description and who would be an asset to your company is Captain Torres.

STEP 2 Write the body of your letter Following the order you chose, present one qualification at a time and support it with the evidence you gathered from the text. Even though you're writing about a literary character, you should treat the subject as if he or she were a real person. Remember, too, that this is a business letter, so your tone and style should be formal.

Special Tip

When you're trying to persuade someone, it's easy to get carried away and make sweeping generalizations such as "She's the most talented person in the world." Avoid exaggerating the truth.

STEP 3 Create a strong ending Conclude your letter on a strong, positive note and sign your name. Without repeating what you've already said, reaffirm the applicant's ability to do the job.

Revising and Editing

Share your draft with a classmate. Have him or her read it without looking at the ad to which you've responded. See if your classmate can figure out for which job you're recommending the character. If he or she can't figure it out, use the following checklist to guide your revision.

Revision Checklist

1. Is your purpose expressed clearly in the opening paragraph?
2. Have you provided persuasive evidence of the character's qualifications?
3. Are your points organized logically and effectively?
4. Do the tone and style of the letter sound professional?

Editing After you've revised your draft, edit it for grammar, spelling, and style. Make sure you have used correct business letter form.

Presenting

From among your classmates, select an employee review board to read all the letters of recommendation for each job. Based on the strength of the recommendations, decide which character will be hired for each job.

Reflecting on Your Writing

Answer the following questions. Turn in your answers with your paper.

1. Did Step 1 of the prewriting activity help you choose a character? Explain.
2. Why did you organize your letter the way you did?
3. How do you feel about your letter of recommendation? Why?

ADDITIONAL WRITING AND RESEARCH TOPICS

The following items provide additional writing practice based on the selections in this subunit.

Persuasion

- If your school could invite a famous musical group or singer to perform at a school dance, who should it be? Write your recommendation to the school activities committee.
- Write a letter of recommendation for Walt Whitman to be the graduation speaker at your school's commencement.

Other Topics

Narration: Write a chapter from your travel diary that details the sights and sounds of one of your favorite destinations.

Social Studies Research: "Stowaway" recounts one teenager's dramatic and dangerous flight from Cuba. Research the reasons that someone would be afraid to leave Cuba and, conversely, why they might be willing to stay.

Revising and Editing Suggest that as students revise their letters, they consider changing the order of the paragraphs. Research has shown that audiences best remember the last idea presented. Therefore, urge students to state their least persuasive point in their first paragraph and make their strongest, most persuasive point in the final paragraph.

Presenting As an alternative to the *Presenting* suggestion in the pupil's edition, you might consider this idea:

1. Allow small groups of students to select the letter that they find the most persuasive, and have the authors read these letters to the class. One student may role-play the person who decides which recommendation to choose.

Reflecting on Your Writing When you review students' writing portfolios, remember to respond to their answers for the *Reflecting* questions. Additional help may be appropriate if a majority of the class have similar responses for Question 1.

Teaching Tip: LEP

Have LEP students discuss which words in their own language they would use to express qualifications in a letter of recommendation. They will find that the qualities for a good candidate will be the same, or quite similar, in English. Remind them that a strong letter of recommendation will be based on their own proficiency in English, and that bilingual candidates for a particular job are often in strong demand by employers.

Closure

Before beginning the next subunit, be sure students have internalized these concepts:

- Persuasive writing involves evaluation.
- To evaluate something, the writer must select certain qualities that are appealing.
- After making an evaluation, the writer forms an opinion about the subject.
- The writer supports the opinion with specific examples.

Language Workshop

Objectives

- To identify double negatives in writing
- To avoid using double negatives in speech and writing
- To correctly express negative meanings

Integrating . . .

Grammar and Writing Review with students the importance of using correct grammar when they speak and write especially in formal situations.

Tell students that in this Language Workshop they will learn how to avoid a common grammatical error in their speech and writing: double negatives. Then write the following sentences on the board:

1. He has never given me a ride home.

2. I haven't any new clothes.

3. Why isn't she ever ready on time?

4. She didn't tell anyone.

Ask volunteers to read each sentence and tell which have negative meanings. (*all*) Then ask students to identify the negative word in each. (*never, haven't, isn't, didn't*) Point out that each sentence is correct as worded above. Then rewrite the sentences as follows:

1. He hasn't never given me a ride home.

2. I haven't no new clothes.

3. Why isn't she never ready on time?

4. She didn't tell no one.

Now ask students to read each sentence and determine if it is still correctly worded, and if not, to discuss the error. Lead students to identify the double negative in each sentence.

Teaching Strategies

Ask a volunteer to read the focus statement in the box at the top of page 212. Explain that not only are double negatives incorrect, they also obscure meaning. For example, have students discuss the meaning of the following sentence: I won't never quit my job.

DOUBLE NEGATIVES

Negatives are words such as *no, not, never, nothing,* and *none.* A **double negative** occurs when two negative words are used where only one is necessary. Avoid using double negatives in your speech and writing.

HINT

If you aren't sure whether you have used a double negative, say the sentence aloud and listen closely for two negative words. Turn any contraction into the two words from which the contraction was made (for example: *aren't = are not*).

When you are strongly opposed to something, you want the world to know. For example, you might say, "I will *never* quit school!" However, using two negatives does not add emphasis to your statement: "I will *not never* quit school!" Besides being incorrect, double negatives may actually mean the opposite of what you intend.

Always avoid using a negative word with a contraction, which contains a shortened form of the negative word *not.* Use words such as *any, anything,* or *ever* after negative contractions rather than words such as *none, nothing,* or *never.*

Incorrect We haven't met *no* people in our new neighborhood.

Correct We haven't met *any* people in our new neighborhood.

Three other negative words are *barely, scarcely,* and *hardly.* Do not use them with another negative word.

Incorrect I hardly *never* see girls my age in the neighborhood.

Correct I hardly *ever* see girls my age in the neighborhood.

Exercise 1 In the story "Antaeus," the new boy, T. J., uses a number of double negatives. The author chose to use these double negatives to make the dialogue sound realistic. Rewrite each of the following quotations from the story, correcting the double negatives and any other errors in the use of standard English.

NOTE

The word *ain't* is nonstandard English and should not be used in speech or writing. When it appears in dialogue or dialect, it is a contraction for *am not* or *have not.*

1. "Don't you have no woods around here?"
2. "No watermelons or nothing?"
3. "You mean you ain't got no fields to raise nothing in?"
4. "I ain't never put no effort into that."
5. "Can't nobody touch a man's own land."
6. "I'd just about decided it wasn't never gonna get here at all."

Now have students continue reading as you work through the lesson. Be sure to call attention to the *Hint* box to the right of this section before assigning Exercise 1.

Assign the exercises on pages 212–213 to students. In Exercise 3, have students form small groups, appointing one student to record the final corrections.

Additional Resources

UNIT TWO RESOURCE BOOK

Language Workshop Copy Master, p. 24

ENRICHMENT MATERIALS

Grammar and Usage Copy Masters

Exercise 2 Some of these sentences contain double negatives. Rewrite the sentences correctly. If a sentence contains no error, write *Correct.*

1. Do not never try to stow away in the wheel well of an airplane.
2. You couldn't barely expect to stay alive during takeoff.
3. How could you not be crushed as the wheel retracted?
4. If you survived takeoff, there wouldn't be hardly any air for you to breathe at twenty-nine thousand feet.
5. The temperature wouldn't never be above forty-one degrees below zero.
6. You would lose consciousness before the plane hadn't scarcely reached cruising altitude.
7. Armando Socarras is the one man to attempt this impossible feat.
8. Hardly nobody can understand how he survived the flight.
9. In his desire to leave Cuba and escape to Spain, he didn't never think he might be crushed just as the plane became airborne.
10. Nobody should never think they would survive a similar experience; there couldn't never be someone else as lucky as Socarras.

Exercise 3 Work in a group to proofread the following passage. Look carefully at the negatives in each sentence. As a group, correct any errors you find. Write the corrected sentences on a sheet of paper.

Walt Whitman is one of America's most widely read poets. You couldn't hardly find any collections of American poetry without his work. However, Whitman didn't never finish elementary school. He worked as a carpenter, printer, and teacher. His job as a newspaper editor hadn't scarcely begun when he was fired for criticizing the expansion of slavery into the newest American territories. Whitman couldn't find nothing right in this policy. In 1885 Whitman published a book of his poetry called *Leaves of Grass.* Whitman wrote in free verse; he didn't use no regular pattern of rhythm or rhyme. No one never had written such poems about American men and women before. There has hardly never been a poet as beloved as Walt Whitman.

Exercise 4 Analyzing and Revising Your Writing

1. Take a paper from your writing portfolio.
2. Reread the paper, looking for errors in the use of negatives.
3. Revise any errors you find.
4. Remember to check for double negatives in your future writing.

LANGUAGE HANDBOOK

For review and practice, see Section 4, Using Modifiers.

Teaching Tip: LEP

Because Spanish-speaking students often use double negatives in their speech, you may wish to tape sentences containing double negatives. Have LEP students listen to the tape as you assist them in identifying the errors.

Answer Key
Exercise 1

1. "Don't you have any woods around here?"
2. "No watermelons or anything?"
3. "You mean you don't have any fields to raise anything in?"
4. "I have never put any effort into that."
5. "Nobody can touch a man's own land."
6. "I'd just about decided it wasn't ever going to get here at all."

Exercise 2

(Some answers may vary.)

1. Do not ever try to stow away in the wheel well of an airplane.
2. You could barely expect to stay alive during takeoff.
3. Correct
4. If you survived takeoff, there would hardly be any air for you to breathe at twenty-nine thousand feet.
5. The temperature would never be above forty-one degrees below zero.
6. You would lose consciousness before the plane had scarcely reached cruising altitude.
7. Correct
8. Hardly anybody can understand how he survived the flight.
9. In his desire to leave Cuba and escape to Spain, he didn't ever think he might be crushed just as the plane became airborne.
10. Nobody should ever think they would survive a similar experience; there couldn't ever be someone else as lucky as Socarras.

Exercise 3

(Some answers may vary.)

Walt Whitman is one of America's most widely read poets. You could hardly find any collections of American poetry without his work. However, Whitman never finished elementary school. He worked as a carpenter, printer, and teacher. His job as a newspaper editor had scarcely begun when he was fired for criticizing the expansion of slavery into the newest American territories. Whitman couldn't find anything right in this policy. In 1885 Whitman published a book of his poetry called *Leaves of Grass.* Whitman wrote in free verse; he didn't use any regular pattern of rhythm or rhyme. No one had ever written such poems about American men and women before. There has hardly ever been a poet as beloved as Walt Whitman.

Exercise 4

Answers will vary, but no double negatives should appear.

Closure

Before beginning the next subunit, be sure students have internalized these concepts:

- Negatives are words such as *no, not, never, nothing,* and *none.*
- A double negative, or the use of two negative words, is incorrect in both speaking and writing.
- The words *barely, scarcely,* and *hardly* should not be used with another negative word in a sentence.

Additional Practice

The following items provide additional practice on avoiding double negatives.

Write these sentences using the correct form of the word in parentheses. Correct answers are underlined.

1. I (wasn't, <u>was</u>) scarcely able to see the dot.
2. Karen hardly (<u>ever</u>, never) says hello.
3. My mother (wouldn't, <u>would</u>) never miss a game.
4. Pat didn't bake (<u>anything</u>, nothing) for the sale.
5. Tina didn't speak to (nobody, <u>anybody</u>) in the room.

Vocabulary Workshop

Objective

- To understand that dialect is the distinct form of language spoken by a group of people

Integrating . . .

Literature, Grammar, and Vocabulary Share with students that this workshop will help them understand dialects.

Teaching Strategies

Have students discuss stories, books, movies, and television shows in which characters speak in dialect. Be sure that "Antaeus" is discussed. Ask why these writers chose to depart from standard English. *(Possible responses: to add realism; to help readers relate to characters)*

Read through the material with students, stopping to discuss and give examples of the different dialects represented in your classroom. Ask students for whom English is a second language to describe the dialects of their native languages.

Assign the exercise on page 214. Have students read aloud and discuss their responses.

Closure

Before beginning the next subunit, be sure students have internalized these concepts:

- Dialect is the form of language spoken by a particular group of people.
- Dialect may not be appropriate in formal settings.

Teaching Tip: LEP

Exposure to the meaning of various expressions in dialect will be helpful for LEP students. Be certain, however, that LEP students understand the difference between dialect and standard English. Pair LEP students with English-speaking students to complete the exercise.

Exercise

(Some students may substitute words or phrases from their own dialect. You can use this as an opportunity to reinforce the idea that dialect is not the same as standard English.)

Vocabulary Workshop

DIALECT

Hello! Hallo! Hullo! Hi, y'all! Depending on where you come from, one of these greetings might be your usual way of saying "hello." Most people who live in a certain geographic area—such as the South or Midwest—speak in ways that sound somewhat alike. These recognizable speech patterns are a part of what is known as dialect. A **dialect** is the distinct form of a language spoken in a particular region or by a certain social or ethnic group.

DIALECT DIFFERENCES

Are any of these words from your dialect?

Food eaten between meals: *bite, lunch, piece meal, snack*

Amusement park ride: *coaster, roller coaster, rolly-coaster*

Vehicle for small baby: *baby buggy, baby cab, baby carriage, baby coach*

Differences in pronunciation from one dialect region to another can vary greatly. *Pie* is pronounced like *pa* in much of the South, and *oil* is pronounced like *earl* in certain parts of New York. Another element of dialect is the use of different words for the same item. *Pop, tonic, soda,* and *soft drink* are all regional variations for the same drink.

There is no right or wrong in regional speech, but dialect often varies from standard English. In many informal situations, you can use the dialect you are most comfortable with. In more formal settings, however, be sure to use language your audience will understand and accept.

Exercise The following passages of dialogue are from the story "Antaeus," in which the main character, T.J., speaks in a rural Southern dialect. Read each of T.J.'s statements and then rewrite the sentences in standard English.

1. "Down yonder where I come from we played out in the woods."
2. "I had my own acre of cotton and my own acre of corn. It was mine to plant ever' year."
3. "Well, you get part of the bale offen your acre."
4. "Come spring we could raise us what we want to . . . watermelons and garden truck and no telling what all."
5. "Before you know it we'd have us a crop in here."
6. "I thought you said this was you-all's roof."
7. "It'll be ourn. All ourn."
8. "You-all seem mighty set on raising some grass."
9. "They'd be mighty nice to eat while we was a-laying on that grass."
10. "We toted that earth up here and planted that grass. And we're just fixing to plant us some watermelon."

Additional Resources

UNIT TWO RESOURCE BOOK

Related Skills Coppy Master, p. 25

ADDITIONAL PRACTICE

Find five more examples of dialect from "Antaeus." Rewrite each sentence in standard English. *(Responses will vary. Check that students have correctly identified examples of dialect. Check also that they rewrote the dialect correctly in standard English.)*

The Best-Laid Plans

Everyone makes plans—from what to do on an evening out to planning a life's career. Sometimes the planning is for positive goals; at other times the planning involves deception or manipulation. However, no matter how carefully people plan, things change, unexpected events occur, and only rarely does a plan work out perfectly.

This next subunit includes selections in which characters' "best-laid plans" take unexpected twists. As you read, notice how these characters react to new developments or revelations in their lives. Why did their best-laid plans fail?

Subunit Preview

Have students read the introduction to subunit 2, **The Best-Laid Plans.** Ask them to consider how encounters with the unexpected might relate to the larger theme, **Escapes: Triumphs And Retreats.** Can life be "planned"? Explain your answer. Would you enjoy a life that had no surprises? Why not? How might an obstacle be better than your plan? Ask students to read the subunit Table of Contents and predict which selection that they think will be the most interesting.

For Additional Challenge

The following selections offer further challenge in exploring the subunit theme:

"To a Mouse," a poem by Robert Burns

"The Interlopers," a short story by Saki

Additional Resources

Subunit Test, pp. 48–49

Observation Assessment

Observing how students respond to the text, to the classroom instruction, and to peers is an important part of an assessment program. The following suggestions and the form in each Unit Resource Book can be used to implement observation assessment.

- As students work through the subunit, assess their ability to interpret mood. Do they get a "general feeling" about the mood as they read a story or poem? Do they anticipate mood for various genres, such as mystery, realistic fiction, or fantasy?
- As they progress through the subunit, can you see increased facility in approaching the various genres?
- To check for appropriate response, have students verbally describe mood and identify details that create atmosphere.

Objectives

- To understand and analyze a mystery
- To identify and understand plot and subplots
- To identify and understand Briticisms and their contribution to meaning
- To identify metaphor
- To express understanding of the work through a choice of writing options, including a letter, evaluation, and dialogue

Prereading/Motivation

Examine What You Know

Discussion Prompts: What mysteries have you read or seen? What kinds of crimes were involved? What kinds of characters solved the crimes? Where and when did the action take place? What kinds of false leads or twists and turns kept you guessing "whodunit"?

Expand Your Knowledge

Discussion Prompts: What qualities do you think a person needs to be a good detective? What do you think makes a fictional detective memorable and popular? Why would millions of people want to read a series of mysteries featuring the same detective?

Enrich Your Reading

Review the terms with students. You may wish to ask them if they have heard of Agatha Christie and if they know why she included the Briticisms. Discuss the fact that the author was English and that the story is set in England.

Thematic Link—The Best-Laid Plans

In "The Third-Floor Flat," the meticulous and observant detective Hercule Poirot solves what was intended to be a well-planned and foolproof crime of murder.

e x p l o r e

Fiction

The Third-Floor Flat

AGATHA CHRISTIE

Examine What You Know (Prior Knowledge)

The selection you are about to read is a mystery—a whodunit. Think about mysteries you have read or seen and try to determine the qualities of a good mystery. Is the setting important? What are the characters like? How does the action unfold? Describe in your journal the ideal setting, characters, and plot of a good mystery. Then compare your ideas with the same elements in this story.

Expand Your Knowledge (Building Background)

A good mystery requires a good detective. Perhaps the world's most famous fictional sleuth is the Englishman Sherlock Holmes, who first appeared in a series of books by Sir Arthur Conan Doyle in the late 1800's. American detectives of renown include C. Auguste Dupin, created by Edgar Allan Poe in the early 1800's, and the cartoon character Dick Tracy, created by Chester Gould in 1931. In the following selection you will meet another famous detective—Hercule Poirot (er kül' pwä rō'). Poirot, a Belgian private detective, first appeared in 1920 in a novel called *The Mysterious Affair at Styles.* The book began the career of one of the most famous mystery writers ever, Dame Agatha Christie.

Enrich Your Reading (Reading Skill)

Briticisms A word or phrase that is peculiar to British English is called a **Briticism**. In the mystery you are about to read, you will come across a number of Briticisms. Don't be confused by these words and phrases. Before you begin reading, preview the following list of Briticisms taken from the story and their American equivalents.

sitting room—living room
to rootle—to dig around
solicitors—lawyers
perambulators—baby carriages
dustbin—a container for ashes or trash
flat—apartment
lift—elevator
torch—flashlight
wonky—crazy

■ *A biography of the author can be found in the Reader's Handbook.*

Journal Writing

Hercule Poirot uses his powers of observation and reasoning to solve a crime. Suggest these journal topics to students:

- Describe how you solved a tough problem.
- Invent a situation that could explain this sentence: "Two young men were looking at each other in silent horror."

For other journal opportunities, refer students to Examine What You Know (p. 216) and Broader Connections (p. 230).

Additional Resources

UNIT TWO RESOURCE BOOK
Reader's Guidesheet, p. 28
Vocabulary Worksheet, p. 29
Selection and Vocabulary Check Tests, p. 30
Selection Test, pp. 31–32

Collaborative Learning

Opportunities for collaborative learning appear throughout the lesson and include First Impressions (p. 230) and Cultural Connections (p. T–224).

The Third-Floor Flat

AGATHA CHRISTIE

A "Bother!" said Pat.

With a deepening frown she rummaged wildly in the silken trifle she called an evening bag. Two young men and another girl watched her anxiously. They were all standing outside the closed door of Patricia Garnett's flat.

"It's no good," said Pat. "It's not there. And now what shall we do?"

"What is life without a latchkey?" murmured Jimmy Faulkener.

He was a short, broad-shouldered young man, with good-tempered blue eyes.

Pat turned on him angrily. "Don't make jokes, Jimmy. This is serious."

"Look again, Pat," said Donovan Bailey. "It must be there somewhere."

He had a lazy, pleasant voice that matched his lean, dark figure.

"If you ever brought it out," said the other girl, Mildred Hope.

"Of course I brought it out," said Pat. "I believe I gave it to one of you two." She turned on the man accusingly. "I told Donovan to take it for me."

B But she was not to find a scapegoat so easily. Donovan put in a firm disclaimer, and Jimmy backed him up.

"I saw you put it in your bag, myself," said Jimmy.

"Well, then, one of you dropped it out when you picked up my bag. I've dropped it once or twice."

"Once or twice!" said Donovan. "You've dropped it a dozen times at least, besides leaving it behind on every possible occasion."

"I can't see why everything on earth doesn't drop out of it the whole time," said Jimmy.

"The point is—how are we going to get in?" said Mildred.

She was a sensible girl, who kept to the point, but she was not nearly so attractive as the impulsive and troublesome Pat.

All four of them regarded the closed door blankly.

"Couldn't the porter help?" suggested Jimmy. "Hasn't he got a master key or something of that kind?"

Pat shook her head. There were only two keys. One was inside the flat hung up in the kitchen and other was—or should be—in the maligned bag.

"If only the flat were on the ground floor," wailed Pat. "We could have broken open a window or something. Donovan, you wouldn't like to be a cat burglar, would you?"

Donovan declined firmly but politely to be a cat burglar. ◄SR-1

"A flat on the fourth floor is a bit of an undertaking," said Jimmy. C

Words to Know and Use	**disclaimer** (dis klām′ ər) *n.* a refusal to accept responsibility

217

Structured Reading for Less Proficient Students

These questions can help to guide students through the reading. Ask each question at the point of the selection where the SR number appears in the margin.

SR–1. What problem do Pat and her friends face? *(Pat has lost her key and cannot get into her flat with her friends.)* **Literal recall**

SR–2. How do Jimmy and Donovan decide to get into Pat's flat? *(by using the coal lift)* **Literal recall**

SR–3. What do the men discover when they turn on the light? *(They are in the wrong flat.)* **Literal recall**

SR–4. Once he is in Pat's flat, what strange discovery does Donovan make? *(Although he has not cut himself, his hand is covered with blood.)* **Summarizing**

SR–5. Why do the men return to the third-floor flat? What do they find there? *(They return to find the source of the blood. They find a dead woman.)* **Literal recall**

SR–6. Who lives in the same building as Pat? *(the famous detective Hercule Poirot)* **Literal recall**

Continued on page 219.

Teaching Strategies

Vocabulary Preview

These vocabulary words are defined at the bottom of the selection page on which they appear. You may wish to discuss them briefly before students begin reading.

admonition a mild warning
compromising risky
disclaimer a refusal to accept responsibility
discreet careful
fervent strongly felt
incriminate to make appear guilty
invalidate to remove the legal value
placidly peacefully
ruefully regretfully
ruse a trick

Support for Students of Limited English Proficiency

- Use Reader's Guidesheet, p. 28.
- In addition to the Briticisms explained in Enrich Your Reading, "The Third-Floor Flat" features the detective Hercule Poirot, who lapses into his native French from time to time. Explain that these French terms are italicized and footnoted. Also point out that Poirot's stilted and somewhat humorous-sounding dialogue is meant to suggest how a French-speaking man speaks English.
- Annotations D, J, W, DD, II, PP, and UU focus on language and ideas that need attention.

Text Annotations

A. Literary Element: PLOT Explain that the plot of an Agatha Christie mystery is like a difficult puzzle. Point out that at first the various plot events and clues seem not to fit the puzzle. In the end, however, the author presents an ingenious, surprising solution.

B. Literary Element: PLOT Point out that almost every incident in a short mystery story will have an important bearing on the plot. Suggest that Pat's missing key, for example, could be a key to understanding subsequent events.

C. Reading Skills: INFERRING Ask students whose apartment Jimmy is referring to. *(Pat's)* Then ask them why the story title refers to a different flat. *(Possible response: Something important happens in the apartment below Pat's.)*

Art Note

Pas de deux refers to a dance for two or to the interactions of two beings. In this very contemporary painting, the various expressions range from devoted attention to indifference. In elegant, nearly narrative style, Alex Katz presents his vision and leaves interpretation to the viewer. *Which of the characters in "The Third-Floor Flat" seem to fit those pictured in "Pas de Deux"? Explain.*

D. LEP: Clarifying Point out that the coal lift would be called a dumbwaiter in the United States. Elicit that the coal lift is a small platform operated by ropes and pulleys inside a shaft in the wall and used to raise coal to the apartments and lower garbage and ashes.

Teaching Tip

To help students follow the actions of the characters, suggest that they reread small portions and try to visualize what happens in the scene.

PAS DE DEUX (panels 2 and 3) 1983 Alex Katz Collection of Paul J. Schupf Courtesy of Marlborough Gallery, New York.

"How about a fire escape?" suggested Donovan.

"There isn't one."

"There should be," said Jimmy. "A building five stories high ought to have a fire escape."

"I daresay," said Pat. "But what should be doesn't help us. How am I ever to get into my flat?"

"Isn't there a sort of thingummybob?" said Donovan. "A thing the tradesmen send up chops and Brussels sprouts in?"

"The service lift,"[1] said Pat. "Oh, yes, but it's only a sort of wire-basket thing. Oh! wait—I know. What about the coal lift?" D

"Now that," said Donovan, "is an idea."

Mildred made a discouraging suggestion. "It'll be bolted," she said. "In Pat's kitchen, I mean, on the inside."

But the idea was instantly negatived.

"Don't you believe it," said Donovan.

"Not in *Pat's* kitchen," said Jimmy. "Pat never locks and bolts things."

1. **lift:** a British term for elevator.

REAL LIFE CONNECTIONS

Most students are familiar with elevators in apartment buildings. To help students understand the coal lift, ask them to picture a small elevator car with only the floor and a frame—no walls and no ceiling—and some ropes attached. Explain that the lift is not run by electricity, but rather by a system of ropes and pulleys. If possible, have volunteers share any knowledge they have about this kind of hauling system. Perhaps they have seen this in a commercial building, such as a restaurant or factory.

At one time or another, students may have misplaced or lost a key and been locked out of a house or apartment. Invite volunteers to share experiences of this nature and explain how they solved their problems.

"I don't think it's bolted," said Pat. "I took the dustbin[2] off this morning, and I'm sure I never bolted it afterward, and I don't think I've been near it since."

"Well," said Donovan, "that fact's going to be very useful to us tonight, but, all the same, young Pat, let me point out to you that these slack habits are leaving you at the mercy of burglars—non-feline—every night."

Pat disregarded these admonitions.

"Come on," she cried, and began racing down the four flights of stairs. The others followed her. Pat led them through a dark recess, apparently full to overflowing of perambulators,[3] and through another door into the well of the flats, and guided them to the right lift. There was, at the moment, a dustbin on it. Donovan lifted it off and stepped gingerly onto the platform in its place. He wrinkled up his nose.

"A little noisome,"[4] he remarked. "But what of that? Do I go alone on this venture or is anyone coming with me?"

"I'll come, too," said Jimmy.

He stepped on by Donovan's side.

"I suppose the lift will bear me," he added doubtfully.

E "You can't weigh much more than a ton of coal," said Pat, who had never been particularly strong on her weights-and-measures table.

"And, anyway, we shall soon find out," said Donovan cheerfully, as he hauled on the rope.

With a grinding noise they disappeared from sight.

"This thing makes an awful noise," remarked Jimmy, as they passed up through blackness. "What will the people in the other flats think?"

"Ghosts or burglars, I expect," said Donovan. "Hauling this rope is quite heavy work. The porter of Friars Mansions does more work than I ever suspected. I say, Jimmy, old son, are you counting the floors?" F

"Oh, Lord! No. I forgot about it."

"Well, I have, which is just as well. That's the third we're passing now. The next is ours."

"And now, I suppose," grumbled Jimmy, "we shall find that Pat did bolt the door after all."

But these fears were unfounded. The wooden door swung back at a touch, and Donovan and Jimmy stepped out into the inky blackness of Pat's kitchen. ◀SR-2

"We ought to have a torch[5] for this wild night work," explained Donovan. "If I know Pat, everything's on the floor, and we shall smash endless crockery before I can get to the light switch. Don't move about, Jimmy, till I get the light on."

He felt his way cautiously over the floor, uttering one fervent "Damn!" as a corner of the kitchen table took him unawares in the ribs. He reached the switch, and in another moment another "Damn!" floated out of the darkness.

"What's the matter?" asked Jimmy.

"Light won't come on. Dud bulb, I suppose. Wait a minute. I'll turn the sitting-room light on." G

The sitting room was the door immediately across the passage. Jimmy heard Donovan go out of the door, and presently fresh

2. **dustbin:** a British term for a container for ashes or trash.

3. **perambulators** (pər am′ byo͞o lāt′ ərz): a British term for baby carriages.

4. **noisome** (noi′ səm): smelly.

5. **torch:** a British term for flashlight.

Words to Know and Use

admonition (ad′ mə nish′ ən) *n.* a mild warning
fervent (fur′ vənt) *adj.* strongly felt and expressed

E. Literary Element: CHARACTERIZATION Elicit that the author characterizes Pat as a comic, hare-brained figure who is not sensible enough to realize that the men together do not weigh a ton, or 2,000 pounds.

F. Reading Skills: CLARIFYING Ask students what Donovan is accomplishing by hauling the rope. *(He is raising the lift.)*

G. Literary Element: PLOT Explain that Agatha Christie was a master of tricks and deceptions. As a result, readers of her mysteries learn to be on the lookout for even the simplest incidents that might prove to be significant clues later on. Suggest that this "dud" bulb might be a good example of such a clue.

STRUCTURED READING FOR LESS PROFICIENT STUDENTS

Continued from page 217

SR–7. Why is it curious that the light works for Poirot? *(Minutes earlier, Donovan said the light didn't work.)* **Recognizing relevant details**

SR–8. How was Mrs. Grant killed? *(She was shot with a pistol while at the table.)* **Literal recall**

SR–9. Why do the police think John Fraser killed Mrs. Grant? *(They found a note from him, and they found his handkerchief in the flat.)* **Literal recall**

SR–10. Why doesn't Poirot believe that Fraser killed Mrs. Grant? *(Poirot thinks that the real killer made up the clues about Fraser to divert attention.)* **Literal recall**

SR–11. Why did Donovan steal Pat's key? *(to have an excuse to use the coal lift to get into Mrs. Grant's apartment)* **Inferring**

SR–12. Why did Donovan kill Mrs. Grant? *(She was Donovan's wife. He killed her so that she would not tell Pat about their marriage.)* **Clarifying**

H. Reading Skill: PREDICTING Explain that a sentence from a story is sometimes featured to build suspense about what is going to happen. Have students speculate on why the men will soon look at each other in silent horror.

I. Literary Element: PLOT Point out that from the story title we can assume that the men's landing in the third-floor flat is significant. Have students speculate on how this incident might be important later.

J. LEP: Figurative Language Elicit that the author uses the phrase *another inky void* as a figurative expression emphasizing that the men are in total darkness as they climb off the lift into the apartment.

K. Reading Skill: CLARIFYING Explain that *malefactors* means "evildoers." Ask a volunteer to explain why Donovan says they could have been hauled off to a police station. *(Possible response: If Mrs. Grant had seen the men, she might have assumed they were burglars and called the police.)*

L. Literary Sidelight This short story exemplifies Agatha Christie's talent as a storyteller and her down-to-earth writing style. As in all her works, the descriptions are easy to follow, and her dialogue is ordinary and comfortable.

muffled curses reached him. He himself edged his way cautiously across the kitchen.

"What's the matter?"

H ***In another minute two young men were looking at each other in silent horror.***

"I don't know. Rooms get bewitched at night, I believe. Everything seems to be in a different place. Chairs and tables where you least expected them. Oh, hell! Here's another!"

But at this moment Jimmy fortunately connected with the electric-light switch and pressed it down. In another minute two young men were looking at each other in silent horror.

This room was not Pat's sitting room. SR-3 ▶ They were in the wrong flat.

To begin with, the room was about ten times more crowded than Pat's, which explained Donovan's pathetic bewilderment at repeatedly cannoning into chairs and tables. There was a large, round table in the center of the room covered with a baize cloth, and there was an aspidistra[6] in the window. It was, in fact, the kind of room whose owner, the young men felt sure, would be difficult to explain to. With silent horror they gazed down at the table, on which lay a little pile of letters.

"Mrs. Ernestine Grant," breathed Donovan, picking them up and reading the name. "Oh, help! Do you think she's heard us?"

"It's a miracle she hasn't heard you," said Jimmy. "What with your language and the way you've been crashing into the furniture. Come on, for the Lord's sake, let's get out of here quickly."

They hastily switched off the light and retraced their steps on tiptoe to the lift. Jimmy breathed a sigh of relief as they regained the fastness of its depths without further incident.

"I do like a woman to be a good, sound sleeper," he said approvingly. "Mrs. Ernestine Grant has her points."

"I see it now," said Donovan; "why we made the mistake in the floor, I mean. Out in that well we started up from the basement." He heaved on the rope, and the lift shot up. "We're right this time." I

"I devoutly trust we are," said Jimmy as he stepped out into another inky void. "My nerves won't stand many more shocks of this kind." J

But no further nerve strain was imposed. The first click of the light showed them Pat's kitchen, and in another minute they were opening the front door and admitting the two girls who were waiting outside.

"You have been a long time," grumbled Pat. "Mildred and I have been waiting here ages."

"We've had an adventure," said Donovan. "We might have been hauled off to the police station as dangerous malefactors."[7] K

Pat had passed on into the sitting room, where she switched on the light and dropped her wrap on the sofa. She listened with lively interest to Donovan's account of his adventures.

"I'm glad she didn't catch you," she commented. "I'm sure she's an old curmudgeon.[8] I got a note from her this morning—wanted to see me sometime—something she had to complain about—my piano, I suppose. People who don't like L

6. **aspidistra** (as′ pi dis′ trə): a houseplant with dark flowers and stiff, shiny leaves.

7. **malefactors** (mal′ ə fak′ tərz): criminals.

8. **curmudgeon** (kər muj′ ən): a rude, ill-tempered person.

PROFESSIONAL NOTEBOOK

The point, counterpoint response strategy . . . was developed as a way of helping students to build a repertoire of interpretive strategies that can be enlisted when dealing with complex short stories.

The key to this strategy is that students begin with their personal responses and move toward more public and generalized interpretations. Interpretive authority is shared among the teacher, the students, and the professional critics, but the final interpretations rest with individual students. Elements of the story are discussed in the context of the students' responses . . .

Stage One *Students read and respond to the story. They make notes pertaining to any questions, reactions, confusions, predictions, associations, or anything they feel is significant as they read. Then they write a preliminary response essay that includes these responses and possible themes they have constructed.*

Continued on page T–221

pianos over their heads shouldn't come and live in flats. I say, Donovan, you've hurt your hand. It's all over blood. Go and wash it under the tap."

M Donovan looked down at his hand in surprise. He went out of the room obediently and presently his voice called to Jimmy.

"Hullo," said the other, "what's up? You haven't hurt yourself badly, have you?"

"I haven't hurt myself at all."

There was something so queer in Donovan's voice that Jimmy stared at him in surprise. Donovan held out his washed hand and Jimmy saw that there was no mark or cut of any kind on it.

N "That's odd," he said, frowning. "There was quite a lot of blood. Where did it come from?" And then suddenly he realized what his quicker-witted friend had already seen. "By Jove," he said. "It must have come from that flat." He stopped, thinking over the possibilities his words implied. "You're sure it was—er—blood?" he said. "Not paint?"

Donovan shook his head. "It was blood, SR-4 ▶ all right," he said, and shivered.

They looked at each other. The same thought was clearly in each of their minds. It was Jimmy who voiced it first.

O "I say," he said awkwardly. "Do you think we ought to—well—go down again—and have—a—a look around? See it's all right, you know?"

"What about the girls?"

"We won't say anything to them. Pat's going to put on an apron and make us an omelet. We'll be back by the time they wonder where we are."

"Oh, well, come on," said Donovan. "I suppose we've got to go through with it. I daresay there isn't anything really wrong."

But his tone lacked conviction. They got into the lift and descended to the floor below. They found their way across the kitchen without much difficulty and once more switched on the sitting-room light.

"It must have been in here," said Donovan, "that—that I got the stuff on me. I never touched anything in the kitchen."

He looked round him. Jimmy did the same, and they both frowned. Everything looked neat and commonplace and miles removed from any suggestion of violence or gore.

Suddenly Jimmy started violently and caught his companion's arm.

"Look!"

Donovan followed the pointing finger, and in his turn uttered an exclamation. From beneath the heavy rep curtains there protruded a foot—a woman's foot in a gaping patent-leather shoe.

Jimmy went to the curtains and drew them sharply apart. In the recess of the window a woman's huddled body lay on the floor, a sticky dark pool beside it. She was dead, there was no doubt of that. Jimmy was attempting to raise her up when Donovan stopped him. P ◀ SR-5

"You'd better not do that. She oughtn't to be touched till the police come."

"The police. Oh! Of course. I say, Donovan, what a ghastly business. Who do you think she is? Mrs. Ernestine Grant?"

"Looks like it. At any rate, if there's anyone else in the flat they're keeping jolly quiet." Q

"What do we do next?" asked Jimmy. "Run out and get a policeman or ring up from Pat's flat?"

"I should think ringing up would be best. Come on, we might as well go out the front door. We can't spend the whole night going up and down in that evil-smelling lift."

Jimmy agreed. Just as they were passing through the door he hesitated. "Look here; do you think one of us ought to stay—just

M. Literary Element: PLOT Ask students if they are familiar with the phrase *the plot thickens.* Point out that it refers to the way in which a mystery author, like a cook, slowly adds the right ingredients to give a story its shape. Elicit that Mrs. Grant's desire for a meeting with Pat and the blood on Donovan's hand are clues that help shape the plot.

N. Reading Skills: PREDICTING Have students predict where the blood on Donovan's hand might have come from. *(Possible response: He touched something bloody in the flat below.)*

O. Reading Skill: BRITICISMS Point out the expression *I say* and elicit that it is often used by Britons to express surprise or other strong emotion. Have students suggest an American equivalent. *(Possible response: Oh, my; Dear me; Oh, boy.)* Point out that the British character says "have a look around," while an American would simply say "look around."

P. Literary Element: PLOT Point out that we are more than one-third through the mystery before the crime—a murder—is revealed. Also point out that although there is no obvious suspect or motive so far, the author is bound to provide a solution to the puzzle by story's end. Have students speculate on possible suspects or motives.

Q. Reading Skill: BRITICISMS Note the use of the expression *jolly quiet.* Ask students what the slang word *jolly* means. *(very)*

PROFESSIONAL NOTEBOOK

Continued from page T–220

Stage Two *In preparation for a class discussion based on the students' written responses, the teacher skims the response essays and categorizes them according to themes. . . . The teacher asks students to elaborate on the various themes and explain how they constructed them. The teacher may point out the various strategies used to develop themes (drawing on personal responses to characters, . . . the title, imagery, narrative conflict, etc.). The teacher may also want to bring in professional critical pieces to further illustrate the range of interpretive strategies used. . . .*

Stage Three *The students construct interpretive essays based on their preliminary response essays and on the responses and themes that were discussed. . . .*

THERESA ROGERS, "A POINT COUNTERPOINT RESPONSE STRATEGY FOR COMPLEX SHORT STORIES," *Journal of Reading,* DECEMBER/JANUARY 1990/1991; PP. 278–279.

R. Literary Element: SUBPLOT Point out that the main plot of the story deals with the murder of Mrs. Grant in the third-floor flat. Suggest that the rivalry between Donovan and Jimmy for Pat's affections, described here, forms a sort of subplot that reveals something about the main characters and their relationships.

S. Literary Sidelight The sudden appearance of the "little man with a very fierce mustache and an egg-shaped head" is repeated in many of Agatha Christie's stories. For Christie fans, nothing else is needed to identify her famous detective, Hercule Poirot.

T. Literary Element: GENRE Point out that the limited length of the short-story form leads the author to rely on a coincidence—having the famed detective Hercule Poirot live in the same building in which the murder has occurred. Elicit that this allows the plot to proceed without interruption.

U. Literary Element: CHARACTERIZATION Point out that Agatha Christie conveys much about her characters through their words and actions. Ask students what they can tell about Poirot so far. *(Possible responses: He is very courteous; he is smart; he dresses well; he seems foreign from his speech; he seems very gentle.)*

V. Literary Element: PLOT Have students speculate on why the light works now but not when Donovan tried it earlier. Have them share any suspicions they might have.

Historical Sidelight Hercule Poirot appears in more than sixty of Agatha Christie's stories, including her very first book, *The Mysterious Affair at Styles.* Christie informed readers that Poirot's knowledge of crime came from his experience as an inspector with the Belgian police force. The author thought it amusing that the physically small Poirot should be named for Hercules, the hero of Greek myths. Also tell students that *poirot* is a French word meaning "buffoon."

to keep an eye on things—till the police come?"

"Yes, I think you're right. If you'll stay I'll run up and telephone."

He ran quickly up the stairs and rang the bell of the flat above. Pat came to open it, a very pretty Pat with a flushed face and a cooking apron on. Her eyes widened in surprise.

"You? But how—Donovan, what is it? Is anything the matter?"

He took both her hands in his. "It's all right, Pat—only we've made a rather unpleasant discovery in the flat below. A woman—dead."

"Oh!" She gave a little gasp. "How horrible. Has she had a fit or something?"

"No. It looks—well—it looks rather as though she has been murdered."

"Oh, Donovan!"

"I know. It's pretty beastly."

Her hands were still in his. She had left them there—was even clinging to him. Darling Pat—how he loved her. Did she care at all for him? Sometimes he thought she did. Sometimes he was afraid that Jimmy Faulkener—remembrances of Jimmy waiting patiently below made him start guiltily.

"Pat, dear, we must telephone to the police."

"Monsieur is right," said a voice behind him. "And in the meantime, while we are waiting their arrival, perhaps I can be of some slight assistance."

They had been standing in the doorway of the flat, and now they peered out onto the landing. A figure was standing on the stairs a little way above them. It moved down and into their range of vision.

They stood staring at a little man with a very fierce mustache and an egg-shaped head. He wore a resplendent dressing gown and embroidered slippers. He bowed gallantly to Patricia.

"Mademoiselle!" he said. "I am, as perhaps you know, the tenant of the flat above. I like to be up high—the air—the view over London. I take the flat in the name of Mr. O'Connor. But I am not an Irishman. I have another name. That is why I venture to put myself at your service. Permit me." With a flourish he pulled out a card and handed it to Pat. She read it.

"M. Hercule Poirot.[9] Oh!" She caught her breath. "*The* M. Poirot? The great detective? And you will really help?"

"That is my intention, mademoiselle. I nearly offered my help earlier in the evening."

Pat looked puzzled.

"I heard you discussing how to gain admission to your flat. Me, I am very clever at picking locks. I could, without doubt, have opened your door for you, but I hesitated to suggest it. You would have had the grave suspicions of me."

Pat laughed.

"Now, monsieur," said Poirot to Donovan. "Go in, I pray of you, and telephone to the police. I will descend to the flat below."

Pat came down the stairs with him. They found Jimmy on guard, and Pat explained Poirot's presence. Jimmy, in his turn, explained to Poirot his and Donovan's adventures. The detective listened attentively.

"The lift door was unbolted, you say? You emerged into the kitchen, but the light it would not turn on."

He directed his footsteps to the kitchen as he spoke. His fingers pressed the switch.

"*Tiens! Voilá ce qui est curieux!*"[10] he said as the light flashed on. "It functions perfectly now. I wonder—"

He held up a finger to insure silence and

9. **M. Hercule Poirot** (mə syö′ er kül′ pwȧ *r*ō′).

10. ***Tiens! Voilà ce qui est curieux!*** (tya*n* vwȧ lȧ′ skē e kü *r*yö′) *French:* Hold on! That's curious!

REAL LIFE CONNECTIONS

Poirot's awareness that if he had picked the lock on Pat's door, she and her friends might have been suspicious of him is a point well taken about human behavior. Ask students how they might respond to a stranger who offered to help them do something similar. Have them explain what their suspicions would be and why.

Broaden the discussion to include students' own real experiences of hearing about or observing behavior that seemed out of the ordinary. Perhaps students have observed someone trying to break into a locked car. Did they assume that the person was a thief trying to break in or the owner who had been locked out?

listened. A faint sound broke the stillness—the sound of an unmistakable snore.

"Ah!" said Poirot. "*La chambre de domestique.*"[11]

He tiptoed across the kitchen into a little pantry, out of which led a door. He opened the door and switched on the light. The room was the kind of dog kennel designed by the builders of flats to accommodate a human being. The floor space was almost entirely occupied by the bed. In the bed was a rosy-cheeked girl lying on her back with her mouth wide open, snoring placidly.

Poirot switched off the light and beat a retreat.

"She will not wake," he said. "We will let her sleep till the police come."

He went back to the sitting room. Donovan had joined them.

"The police will be here almost immediately, they say," he said breathlessly. "We are to touch nothing."

Poirot nodded. "We will not touch," he said. "We will look, that is all."

> ***"I never went near the window—how did the blood come on my hand?"***

He moved into the room. Mildred had come down with Donovan, and all four young people stood in the doorway and watched him with breathless interest.

"What I can't understand, sir, is this," said Donovan. "I never went near the window—how did the blood come on my hand?"

"My young friend, the answer to that stares you in the face. Of what color is the tablecloth? Red is it not? And doubtless you did put your hand on the table."

"Yes, I did. Is that—" He stopped.

Poirot nodded. He was bending over the table. He indicated with his hand a dark patch on the red.

"It was here that the crime was committed," he said solemnly. "The body was moved afterward."

Then he stood upright and looked slowly round the room. He did not move, he handled nothing, but nevertheless the four watching felt as though every object in that rather frowsty place gave up its secret to his observant eye.

Hercule Poirot nodded his head as though satisfied. A little sigh escaped him. "I see," he said.

"You see what?" asked Donovan curiously.

"I see," said Poirot, "what you doubtless felt—that the room is overfull of furniture."

Donovan smiled ruefully. "I did go barging about a bit," he confessed. "Of course, everything was in a different place to Pat's room, and I couldn't make it out."

"Not everything," said Poirot.

Donovan looked at him inquiringly.

"I mean," said Poirot apologetically, "that certain things are always fixed. In a block of flats the door, the window, the fireplace—they are in the same place in the rooms which are below each other."

"Isn't that rather splitting hairs?" asked Mildred. She was looking at Poirot with faint disapproval.

"One should always speak with absolute

11. ***la chambre de domestique*** (lȧ shäm' br' də dô mes tēk') *French:* the maid's room.

Words to Know and Use

placidly (plas' id lē) *adv.* peacefully
ruefully (ro͞o' fəl lē) *adv.* in a way that shows regret over some previous comment or action

223

W. LEP: Cultural Discussion Explain that although Poirot speaks English most of the time, he sometimes lapses into French. Elicit that this reveals that French, not English, is his native language. Point out that the French phrases and Poirot's somewhat stilted English add color and humor to the dialogue at times. Ask any student of French in your class to pronounce the phrase.

X. Literary Element: METAPHOR Elicit that Agatha Christie is using a metaphor, a comparison that says one thing is actually another. On page 230 under Concept Review, students will be asked to locate this metaphor. Have students suggest what the comparison of the room to a dog kennel is meant to suggest about the room. *(Possible response: The room is small, boxlike, and claustrophobic; the room lacks grace and comfort.)*

Y. Literary Element: CHARACTERIZATION Have students tell what more they have learned about Poirot from his words and his investigation. *(Possible response: He is observant, thoughtful, and thorough.)*

Z. Reading Skills: CLARIFYING Have students paraphrase what Poirot means here. *(Possible response: Apartments that are directly above or below one another usually have physical structures that are symmetrical.)* Be sure students understand that Poirot's comments indicate he is not completely satisfied with Donovan's explanation.

Professional Notebook

Don't use a chainsaw to do the job intended for dental floss. Don't over-react to the discouraged learner. We, too often, focus on ''appropriate'' or inappropriate behavior in moralistic tones, not in a framework of learning. Building (or rebuilding) self-esteem, confidence, and internal responsibility is our primary objective; then skills, everything else, with discouraged learners at least, comes a distant third.

Use a chainsaw to do the job intended for a chainsaw. Be tough, determined, clear in your priorities, and keep in mind with everything you do that the most important work in the world is going on: learning, gaining self-reliance, participating in the culture.
Jerry Conrath, *Our Other Youth*

AA. Literary Element: CHARACTERIZATION Elicit the meaning of *reverential* and what this type of greeting indicates about the police's attitude toward Poirot. *(Possible response: He is such a famous detective that the police are in awe of him, viewing him in an almost superhuman light.)*

BB. Reading Skill: BRITICISMS Point out that Britons use the adverb *frightfully* to mean "very."

CC. Literary Element: PLOT Explain that the plot of a mystery often presents a superficial explanation of events that the police are apt to accept. Suggest that in order to discover the real solution, the careful reader, like Poirot, must look beneath the surface.

DD. LEP: Cultural Discussion Ask students what they know about how the news media in their native countries treat the reporting of crimes. You may wish to tie this in with the suggestions for discussion mentioned in Cultural Connections below.

accuracy. That is a little—how do you say?—fad of mine."

There was the noise of footsteps on the stairs, and three men came in. They were a police inspector, a constable, and the divisional surgeon. The inspector recognized Poirot and greeted him in an almost reverential manner. Then he turned to the others. AA

"I shall want statements from everyone," he began, "but in the first place—"

Poirot interrupted. "A little suggestion. We will go back to the flat upstairs and mademoiselle here shall do what she was planning to do—make us an omelet. Me, I have a passion for the omelets. Then, *M. l'Inspecteur,*[12] when you have finished here, you will mount to us and ask questions at your leisure."

It was arranged accordingly, and Poirot went up with them.

"M. Poirot," said Pat, "I think you're a perfect dear. And you shall have a lovely omelet. I really make omelets frightfully well." BB

"That is good. Once, mademoiselle, I loved a beautiful young English girl, who resembled you greatly—but alas!—she could not cook. So perhaps everything was for the best."

There was a faint sadness in his voice, and Jimmy Faulkener looked at him curiously.

Once in the flat, however, he exerted himself to please and amuse. The grim tragedy below was almost forgotten.

The omelet had been consumed and duly praised by the time that Inspector Rice's footsteps were heard. He came in accompanied by the doctor, having left the constable below.

"Well, Monsieur Poirot," he said. "It all seems clear and aboveboard—not much in your line, though we may find it hard to catch the man. I'd just like to hear how the discovery came to be made." CC

Donovan and Jimmy between them recounted the happenings of the evening. The inspector turned reproachfully to Pat.

"You shouldn't leave your lift door unbolted, miss. You really shouldn't."

"I shan't again," said Pat, with a shiver. "Somebody might come in and murder me like that poor woman below."

"Ah! but they didn't come in that way, though," said the inspector.

"You will recount to us what you have discovered, yes?" said Poirot.

"I don't know as I ought to—but seeing it's you, M. Poirot—"

"Précisément,"[13] said Poirot. "And these young people—they will be discreet."

"The newspapers will get hold of it, anyway, soon enough," said the inspector. "There's no real secret about the matter. DD Well, the dead woman's Mrs. Grant, all right. I had the porter up to identify her. Woman of about thirty-five. She was sitting at the table, and she was shot with an automatic pistol of small caliber, probably by someone sitting opposite her at table. She fell forward, and that's how the bloodstain came on the table." ◀SR-8

"But wouldn't someone have heard the shot?" asked Mildred.

"The pistol was fitted with a silencer. No, you wouldn't hear anything. By the way, did you hear the screech the maid let out when we told her her mistress was dead?

12. ***M. l'Inspecteur*** (lan spek tör′) *French:* Mister Inspector.

13. **précisément** (pre sēz e män′) *French:* precisely.

Words to Know and Use	**discreet** (di skrēt′) *adj.* careful about what one says or does

CULTURAL CONNECTION

Mention to students that some British newspapers have been thought to be overzealous on occasion in their attempts to get stories. Point out that some American newspapers and media also at times appear to be unconcerned with people's privacy. If the situations raised are not too sensitive, encourage volunteers to share any experiences or observations concerning this issue. Also encourage students to share their views on the rights of the press and of free speech versus the right to privacy.

RED COAT 1982 Alex Katz Private collection Courtesy of Marlborough Gallery, New York.

No. Well, that just shows how unlikely it was that anyone would hear the other."

"Has the maid no story to tell?" asked Poirot.

"It was her evening out. She's got her own key. She came in about ten o'clock. Everything was quiet. She thought her mistress had gone to bed."

"She did not look in the sitting room, then?"

"Yes, she took the letters in there which had come by the evening post,[14] but she saw nothing unusual—any more than Mr. Faulkener and Mr. Bailey did. You see, the murderer had concealed the body rather neatly behind the curtains."

"But it was a curious thing to do, don't you think?"

Poirot's voice was very gentle, yet it held something that made the inspector look up quickly. **EE**

"Didn't want the crime discovered till he'd had time to make his getaway."

"Perhaps—perhaps—but continue with what you were saying."

"The maid went out at five o'clock. The doctor here puts the time of death as—roughly—about four to five hours ago. That's right, isn't it?"

The doctor, who was a man of few words, contented himself with jerking his head affirmatively.

"It's a quarter to twelve now. The actual time can, I think, be narrowed down to a fairly definite hour." **FF**

He took out a crumpled sheet of paper.

"We found this in the pocket of the dead woman's dress. You needn't be afraid of handling it. There are no fingerprints on it."

Poirot smoothed out the sheet. Across it some words were printed in small, prim capitals.

I WILL COME TO SEE YOU THIS EVENING AT HALF PAST SEVEN.—J. F. **GG**

"A compromising document to leave behind," commented Poirot, as he handed it back.

"Well, he didn't know she'd got it in her

14. **evening post:** the evening mail.

Words to Know and Use

compromising (käm′ prə mīz′ iŋ) *adj.* causing suspicion; risky **compromise** *v.*

Art Note

Alex Katz makes large-scale paintings that, like motion-picture closeups, capture our attention. His "grand impersonal style" reflects the appearances of modern life. Just as Manet painted the world he saw, Katz responds to the life and art he sees. He believes that his "art . . . can mean different things to different people." *Can you guess the thoughts of the woman in the red coat?*

EE. Reading Skill: INFERRING Ask students what they think this dialogue seems to suggest. Ask if they think Poirot might know who the murderer is. *(Possible response: He seems to have a good idea since he asks such pointed questions in a tone of voice that catches the inspector's attention. Poirot also seems to stop himself from saying something that might give away his thinking.)*

FF. Reading Skill: CLARIFYING Ask students to use the doctor's information to decide when the murder was committed. *(somewhere between a quarter to seven and a quarter to eight)*

GG. Critical Thinking: ANALYZING Ask students to whom the initials J. F. seem to point. *(Jimmy Faulkener)* Ask whether they think the note is a true clue or a false clue introduced by the criminal to divert attention from himself or herself. *(Possible response: It seems like a false clue, since the solution to a mystery story is not likely to be so easy.)*

DATA BANK

Much has been written about Agatha Christie and the incredible number of novels, short stories, plays, and poems she created during her lifetime. However, one of the most unusual and baffling Christie-related stories was a real-life incident that occurred in early December 1926. On the evening of December 3, Agatha Christie drove off in her car, supposedly to go to Yorkshire. She had left letters for her husband and secretary and had sent a letter to the police constable saying that she feared for her life. The next day her car was found with her suitcase and her expired driver's license.

The newspapers covered the story, police were brought in from several countries, and a major search for Agatha Christie was launched. She was eventually found two weeks later in a hotel under another name. Doctors issued a statement that she had suffered amnesia. Others claimed that she had planned her disappearance because of marital problems. She never fully explained her disappearance.

HH. Literary Element: PLOT Ask students to suggest how Poirot would reconstruct the criminal's actions during and after the murder. *(Possible response: After shooting Mrs. Grant, the murderer removed his or her own fingerprints from the gun and then deliberately placed on the body the note from J. F. and dropped the handkerchief with John Fraser's name to divert attention from himself or herself.)*

II. LEP: Vocabulary Elicit that the word *flurried* means "nervous and confused." Explain that it is a synonym for *flustered.*

JJ. Literary Element: PLOT Point out that the timing, or chronology, of events is often significant in the plot of a mystery. Have students recall when the murder occurred. *(between 6:45 and 7:45)* Point out that since Donovan, Jimmy, Pat, and Mildred did not leave until seven, their night out does not really provide them with an air-tight alibi.

KK. Literary Element: MOTIVE Point out that motive, the reason(s) why a character acts the way he or she does, is especially important in a mystery. Suggest that one reason this mystery is so puzzling is that there is no hint so far of any character having a motive for killing Mrs. Grant.

LL. Literary Element: CHARACTERIZATION Have students tell what personality traits Poirot shows here. *(Possible responses: politeness; consideration; charm; sentimentality)*

pocket," said the inspector. "He probably thought she'd destroyed it. We've evidence that he was a careful man, though. The pistol she was shot with we found under the body—and there again no fingerprints. They'd been wiped off very carefully with a silk handkerchief."

"How do you know," said Poirot, "that it was a silk handkerchief?"

"Because we found it," said the inspector triumphantly. "At the last, as he was drawing the curtains, he must have let it fall unnoticed."

He handed across a big white silk handkerchief—a good-quality handkerchief. It did not need the inspector's finger to draw Poirot's attention to the mark on it in the center. It was neatly marked and quite legible. Poirot read the name out.

"John Fraser."

"That's it," said inspector. "John Fraser—J. F. in the note. We know the name of the man we have to look for, and I daresay when we find out a little about the dead SR-9 ▶ woman, and her relations come forward, we shall soon get a line on him."

"I wonder," said Poirot. "No, *mon cher,*[15] somehow I do not think he will be easy to find, your John Fraser. He is a strange HH man—careful, since he marks his handkerchiefs and wipes the pistol with which he has committed the crime—yet careless since he loses his handkerchief and does not search for a letter that might incriminate II him."

"Flurried, that's what he was," said the inspector.

"It is possible," said Poirot. "Yes, it is possible. And he was not seen entering the building?"

"There are all sorts of people going in and out at that time. These are big blocks. I suppose none of you"—he addressed the four collectively— "saw anyone coming out of the flat?" JJ

Pat shook her head. "We went out earlier—about seven o'clock."

"I see." The inspector rose. Poirot accompanied him to the door.

"As a little favor, may I examine the flat below?"

"Why, certainly, M. Poirot. I know what they think of you at headquarters. I'll leave you a key. I've got two. It will be empty. The maid cleared out to some relatives, too scared to stay there alone."

"I thank you," said M. Poirot. He went back into the flat, thoughtful.

"You're not satisfied, M. Poirot?" said KK Jimmy.

"No," said Poirot. "I am not satisfied."

Donovan looked at him curiously. "What is it that—well, worries you?"

Poirot did not answer. He remained silent for a minute or two, frowning, as though in thought, then he made a sudden impatient movement of shoulders.

"I will say good night to you, mademoiselle. You must be tired. You have had much cooking to do—eh?"

Pat laughed. "Only the omelet. I didn't do dinner. Donovan and Jimmy came and called for us, and we went out to a little LL place in Soho."

"And then without doubt, you went to a theater?"

"Yes. 'The Brown Eyes of Caroline.'"

"Ah!" said Poirot. "It should have been blue eyes—the blue eyes of mademoiselle."

He made a sentimental gesture, and then

15. ***mon cher*** (mōn sher) *French:* my dear.

Words to Know and Use	**incriminate** (in krim′ i nāt′) *v.* to make appear guilty of a crime or fault

226

PROFESSIONAL NOTEBOOK

Success in school is strongly related to students' knowledge of words. Because instruction is composed of descriptions, explanations, demonstrations, and definitions that assume an increasingly sophisticated receptive vocabulary, learners with relatively limited vocabularies find themselves at a considerable disadvantage. With each year of schooling, texts take on a larger role in instruction, and factors that may inhibit comprehension of these texts, such as a lack of vocabulary knowledge, can be expected to have increasingly detrimental effects on achievement.

"TWO APPROACHES TO VOCABULARY INSTRUCTION . . ." *Reading Research Quarterly*, 1989, VOLUME XXIV, NUMBER 2.

once more wished Pat good night, also Mildred, who was staying the night by special request, as Pat admitted frankly that she would get the horrors if left alone on this particular night.

The two young men accompanied Poirot. When the door was shut and they were preparing to say goodbye to him on the landing, Poirot forestalled them.

"My young friends, you heard me say that I was not satisfied? *Eh bien,*[16] it is true—I am not. I go now to make some little investigations of my own. You would like to accompany me—yes?"

MM An eager assent greeted this proposal. Poirot led the way to the flat below and inserted the key the inspector had given him in the lock. On entering, he did not, as the others had expected, enter the sitting room. Instead he went straight to the kitchen. In a little recess,[17] which served as a scullery,[18] a big iron bin was standing. Poirot uncovered this and, doubling himself up, began to rootle in it with the energy of a ferocious terrier. NN

Both Jimmy and Donovan stared at him in amazement.

Suddenly with a cry of triumph he emerged. In his hand he held aloft a small stoppered bottle.

"*Violà!*"[19] he said. "I find what I seek." He sniffed at it delicately. "Alas! I am *enrhumé*[20]—I have the cold in the head."

Donovan took the bottle from him and sniffed in his turn, but could smell nothing. He took out the stopper and held the bottle to his nose before Poirot's warning cry could stop him.

OO Immediately he fell like a log. Poirot, by springing forward, partly broke his fall.

"Imbecile!" he cried. "The idea. To remove the stopper in that foolhardy manner! Did he not observe how delicately I handled it? Monsieur—Faulkener—is it not? Will you be so good as to get me a little brandy? I observed a decanter in the sitting room." OO

Jimmy hurried off, but by the time he returned, Donovan was sitting up and declaring himself quite all right again. He had to listen to a short lecture from Poirot on the necessity of caution in sniffing at possibly poisonous substances.

"I think I'll be off home," said Donovan, rising shakily to his feet. "That is, if I can't be any more use here. I feel a bit wonky still." PP

"Assuredly," said Poirot. "That is the best thing you can do. M. Faulkener, attend me here a little minute. I will return on the instant."

He accompanied Donovan to the door and beyond. They remained outside on the landing talking for some minutes. When Poirot at last re-entered the flat he found Jimmy standing in the sitting-room gazing round him with puzzled eyes.

"Well, M. Poirot," he said, "what next?"

"There is nothing next. The case is finished." QQ

"What?"

"I know everything—now."

Jimmy stared at him. "That little bottle you found?"

"Exactly. That little bottle."

Jimmy shook his head. "I can't make head or tail of it. For some reason or other I can see you are dissatisfied with the evidence against this John Frazer, whoever he may be."

16. ***eh bien*** (e byàn') *French:* oh well.
17. **recess:** a nook or alcove.
18. **scullery** (skul' ər ē): a small room off a kitchen where pots and pans are stored.
19. ***Voilà!*** (vwä lä') *French:* There it is!
20. ***enrhumé*** (än rü mā') *French:* sick with a cold.

MM. Literary Skill: PLOT Point out that the story is more than two-thirds over and rapidly approaching its climax, or high point. Explain that, as is often the case in mysteries, the climax comes when the detective reveals the solution. Point out that the revelation is usually surprising to readers who are struggling to make sense of clues in the plot.

NN. Reading Skill: BRITICISMS If students have difficulty with *rootle,* ask them for the context clues that suggest it means "to dig around." *(Poirot is doubled over a sort of kitchen garbage bin; his actions are like a terrier, a dog that likes to dig.)*

OO. Reading Skill: INFERRING Ask students if they can guess what is going on here. Ask if they think Poirot has really found an important clue or is playing a trick. *(Answers may vary.)*

PP. LEP: Vocabulary Have students explain why Donovan feels *wonky* or crazy. *(Possible response: He has just been knocked unconscious by sniffing some powerful, and perhaps poisonous, substance.)*

QQ. Reading Skill: PREDICTING Ask students to predict what Poirot now knows and whom he will accuse of murdering Mrs. Grant.

DATA BANK

Agatha Christie (1890–1976) was raised in a middle-class Victorian family. She was educated at home by her mother. Later she was sent to classes for art, singing, cooking, piano lessons, Swedish exercises, and so on.

The Victorian world of England inspired Agatha's romantic imagination but also created in her a high regard for British law. Yet her feelings did not prevent her in her writings from making police officers or judges murderers if it suited her purposes.

RR. Literary Element: THEME Have students recall the subunit theme "The Best-Laid Plans." Point out that Poirot has seen through the murderer's plan to create a fictional suspect named John Fraser. Suggest that as this plan unravels, we naturally look for suspects closer to home.

SS. Literary Element: PLOT Point out that Poirot now begins to reconstruct the crime for Jimmy and the equally baffled readers. Explain that this section of the plot, in which the solution to the mystery is made clear, is called the *denouement* (dā' nōō män'), a French word that means "untying."

TT. Literary Element: PLOT Remind students that on the first page of the story Pat accused Donovan of taking her key. Point out that this seemingly inconsequential detail was actually an important clue.

UU. LEP: Clarifying Ask a volunteer to clarify why Donovan took Pat's key. *(For some reason, he wanted to get into Mrs. Grant's apartment in an unsuspicious manner; he took the key knowing that he could then suggest using the lift; on the way up, he deliberately got off in Mrs. Grant's flat.)*

VV. Literary Element: CHARACTERIZATION Ask students what Poirot's ruse suggests about him. *(Possible responses: He is a clever judge of people and knows how to manipulate people; he is willing to take unusual and irregular steps to get necessary evidence and information.)*

"Whoever he may be," repeated Poirot softly. "If he is anyone at all—well, I shall be surprised."

"I don't understand."

"He is a name—that is all—a name carefully marked on a handkerchief!"

"And the letter?"

RR "Did you notice that it was printed? Now, why? I will tell you. Handwriting might be recognized, and a typewritten letter is more easily traced than you would imagine—but if a real John Fraser wrote that letter those two points would not have appealed to him! No, it was written on purpose, and put in the dead woman's pocket for us to find. SR-10 ▶ There is no such person as John Fraser."

Jimmy looked at him inquiringly.

"And so," went on Poirot, "I went back to the point that first struck me. You heard me say that certain things in the room were always in the same place under given circumstances. I gave three instances. I might have mentioned a fourth—the electric-light switch, my friend."

Jimmy still stared uncomprehendingly. Poirot went on.

SS "Your friend Donovan did not go near the window—it was by resting his hand on this table that he got it covered in blood! But I asked myself at once—why did he rest it there? What was he doing groping about this room in darkness? For remember, my friend, the electric-light switch is always in the same place—by the door. Why, when he came to this room, did he not at once feel for the light and turn it on? That was the natural, the normal thing to do. According to him, he tried to turn on the light in the kitchen, but failed. Yet when I tried the switch it was in perfect working order. Did he, then, not wish the light to go on just then? If it had gone on, you would both have seen at once that you were in the wrong flat. There would have been no reason to come into this room."

"What are you driving at, M. Poirot? I don't understand. What do you mean?"

"I mean—this."

Poirot held up a Yale door key.

"The key of this flat?"

"No, *mon ami,*[21] the key of the flat above. Mademoiselle Patricia's key, which M. Donovan Bailey abstracted from her bag sometime during the evening." TT

"But why—why?"

"*Parbleu!*[22] so that he could do what he wanted to do—gain admission to this flat in a perfectly unsuspicious manner. He made sure that the lift door was unbolted earlier in the evening." UU ◀ SR-11

"Where did you get the key?"

Poirot's smile broadened. "I found it just now—where I looked for it—in M. Donovan's pocket. See you, that little bottle I pretended to find was a ruse. M. Donovan is taken in. He does what I knew he would do—unstoppers it and sniffs. And in that little bottle is ethyl chloride, a very powerful instant anesthetic. It gives me just the moment or two of unconsiousness I need. I take from his pocket the two things that I knew would be there. This key was one of them—the other—" VV

He stopped and then went on.

"I questioned at the time the reason the inspector gave for the body being concealed

21. ***mon ami*** (mōn à mē') *French:* my friend.
22. ***Parbleu!*** (pár blö') *French:* You bet!

Words to Know and Use	**ruse** (rōōz) *n.* a trick

CRITIC'S CORNER

Agatha Christie "was essentially, and aimed to be, a popular writer, a good teller of tales. . . . Our main requirement is that the author gets on with the story and doesn't allow anything to interfere with the narrative flow, and this she invariably does. Similarly with characterization and setting . . .: in the tale they must be subordinate to the incidents; they must support them but not obtrude themselves into too independent an existence. . . . she places the interest fair and square where in popular literature it belongs—in the narration of events.

. . . And the beauty of that narrative . . . is that, like a bud opening into flower, we have a sense of initial mystery and concealment which gradually unfolds to reveal a design of patterned intricacy and beauty. . . . Her books are the literary equivalent of that most universal human curiosity, the desire to penetrate the secrets of our fellow humans' lives."

ROBERT BARNARD, *A Talent to Deceive, an Appreciation of Agatha Christie,* P. 124.

behind the curtain. To gain time? No, there was more than that. And so I thought of just one thing—the post, my friend. The evening post that comes at half past nine or thereabouts. Say the murderer does not find something he expects to find, but that something may be delivered by post later. Clearly, then, he must come back. But the crime must not be discovered by the maid when she comes in, or the police would take possession of the flat, so he hides the body behind the curtain. And the maid suspects nothing and lays the letters on the table as usual."

"The letters?"

"Yes, the letters." Poirot drew something from his pocket. "This is the second article I took from M. Donovan when he was unconscious." He showed the superscription—a typewritten envelope addressed to Mrs. Ernestine Grant. "But I will ask you one thing first, M. Faulkener, before we look at the contents of this letter. Are you or are you not in love with Mademoiselle Patricia?" WW

"I care for Pat damnably—but I've never thought I had a chance."

"You thought that she cared for M. Donovan? It may be that she had begun to care for him—but it was only a beginning, my friend. It is for you to make her forget—to stand by her in her trouble."

"Trouble?" said Jimmy sharply.

"Yes, trouble. We will do all we can to keep her name out of it, but it will be impossible to do so entirely. She was, you see, the motive."

He ripped open the envelope that he held. An enclosure fell out. The covering letter was brief and was from a firm of solicitors.[23]

Dear Madam,

The document you enclose is quite in order, and the fact of the marriage having taken place in a foreign country does not invalidate it in any way.

Yours truly, etc.

Poirot spread out the enclosure. It was a certificate of marriage between Donovan Bailey and Ernestine Grant, dated eight years ago.

"Oh, my God!" said Jimmy. "Pat said she'd had a letter from the woman asking to see her, but she never dreamed it was anything important." XX

Poirot nodded. "M. Donovan knew—he went to see his wife this evening before going to the flat above—a strange irony, by the way, that led the unfortunate woman to come to this building where her rival lived—he murdered her in cold blood—and then went on to his evening's amusement. His wife must have told him that she had sent the marriage certificate to her solicitors and was expecting to hear from them. Doubtless he himself had tried to make her believe that there was a flaw in the marriage." YY ◀SR-12

"He seemed in quite good spirits, too, all the evening. M. Poirot, you haven't let him escape?" Jimmy shuddered.

"There is no escape for him," said Poirot gravely. "You need not fear."

"It's Pat I'm thinking about mostly," said Jimmy. "You don't think—she really cared."

"*Mon ami,* that is your part," said Poirot gently. "To make her turn to you and forget. I do not think you will find it very difficult!" ❧ ZZ

23. **solicitors:** in England, members of the legal profession who may not plead cases in the superior courts.

Words to Know and Use

invalidate (in val′ ə dāt′) *v.* to take away the legal value of something

Historical Sidelight Explain that during much of this century, Londoners enjoyed three mail deliveries daily—morning, afternoon, and evening. Within the city, letters would usually be delivered the same day they were mailed.

WW. Literary Element: SUBPLOT Have students recall that the story's subplot concerned Donovan's and Jimmy's romantic interests in Pat. Point out that this subplot had seemed separate from the main plot of Mrs. Grant's murder. Elicit that Poirot is now showing how details of the subplot reveal the killer's motive in the main plot.

XX. Reading Skill: INFERRING Ask students to infer why Mrs. Grant wanted to see Pat. *(Possible response: Mrs. Grant probably wanted to tell Pat that she was married to Donovan Bailey, in an effort to break off her husband's growing relationship with Pat.)*

YY. Literary Element: CONFLICT Ask students to name the main source of conflict in the story. *(Possible response: Donovan was unable to dissolve his marriage to Mrs. Grant in order to marry Pat.)* Point out that this conflict, although it is not revealed until the very end, has caused most of the events of the plot.

Check Test

1. Who are the main characters in the story? *(Pat, Donovan, Jimmy, Poirot)*

2. What was the first problem in the story? *(Pat was locked out of her apartment.)*

3. Whose apartment is the "Third-Floor Flat"? What happened in it? *(Mrs. Grant's apartment; she was murdered in it.)*

4. Who solved the crime? *(Poirot)*

5. Who was the murderer? *(Donovan)*

6. What was the murderer's motive? *(He was in love with Pat and wanted to be free of Mrs. Grant, who was really his wife.)*

Real Life Connections

Students may have heard of or read about a similar kind of crime, one often referred to as "a crime of passion." Encourage volunteers to share knowledge about such crimes.

You may also wish to invite students' reactions to Poirot's comments to Jimmy about making Pat turn to him and helping her to forget. Ask students if they feel that this is realistic. Have them tell what they know about human nature that makes them feel as they do.

Encouraging Independent Reading

Cards on the Table, The Murder of Roger Ackroyd, Murder on the Orient Express, and *Peril at End House,* novels by Agatha Christie

The Labors of Hercules and *Poirot Investigates,* short stories by Agatha Christie

The Adventures of Sherlock Holmes, short stories by Arthur Conan Doyle

Ten Great Mysteries by Edgar Allan Poe, short stories by Edgar Allan Poe edited by Groff Conklin

Student Response

Responding to Reading

These questions are open-ended with no "right" or "wrong" answers. However, responses must be supported with information from the selection. Possible answers follow:

1. Any response is valid.

2. Students may say that on Donovan's return to the scene of the crime, he does and says things that cause him to be a suspect rather than make him appear innocent; that the way he handles the electric light switches makes him suspect. Alert students may point out, however, that had Donovan not returned, the letter from the solicitors would have made him suspect.

3. Students may say that he is a pleasant and courteous man who is meticulous in his method of observation and demanding in his thoroughness and accuracy.

4. Some students may say that at that time Poirot still does not know the motive for the killing, nor does he have any solid evidence, and that he needs to keep Donovan unaware in order to trick him and find the evidence. Other students may say that Jimmy would have been taken by complete surprise had Poirot accused Donovan in Grant's kitchen and that this could have provided an opportunity for Donovan to escape or to murder again.

5. Students' answers will vary, depending on what they wrote earlier.

6. Students' opinions will vary. Some students may feel that we live in a violent society, so it is only natural that the arts reflect that violence. Others may believe that showing violence on screen in graphic detail or describing in books and magazines some of the more extreme and sickening cases of violence can spark violence in people who are already out of tune with society.

Responding to Reading

First Impressions

1. What was your reaction when you found out that Donovan had committed the murder? Check with your classmates to see how many predicted the outcome correctly.

Second Thoughts

2. According to an old saying, the criminal always returns to the scene of the crime. How does Donovan's return explain his downfall?

3. What kind of man is Poirot?

Think about
- how he treats others
- what he observes and what he questions that others do not

4. Why doesn't Poirot accuse Donovan in Grant's kitchen?

Think about
- how this decision would have affected the story
- the danger he would be creating for himself and Jimmy

5. Think again about the elements of a good mystery that you described earlier. Explain the differences and similarities between your ideas and the setting, characters, and plot of this story.

Broader Connections

6. This story is about a murder. Acts of violence are the subjects of many books, movies, and TV shows. Some people say that such works are entertainment and simply reflect what is happening in society. Others insist that the violence in books, TV, and films actually encourages more violent acts. What is your opinion on this issue?

Literary Concept: Plots and Subplots

Mysteries normally have complex plots. Often there is a smaller story, or subplot, within the main story. The subplot may reveal how characters have been involved with each other prior to the beginning of the main plot. The main plot of this mystery involves finding out who killed Mrs. Grant. Briefly summarize the subplot.

Concept Review: Metaphor A **metaphor** is a comparison between two unlike things that have something in common. Agatha Christie uses a metaphor to describe the maid's room in Mrs. Grant's apartment. Look back at the story and find this metaphor.

Literary Concept—Plots and Subplots

Possible response: The subplot of the story concerns the love triangle between Pat, Jimmy, and Donovan. Details reveal that both Jimmy and Donovan are attracted to Pat and that Pat seems to prefer Donovan. The importance of this subplot becomes clear only at the end of the story, when we learn that Donovan was married to Ernestine Grant and that he indeed killed her in order to prevent her from telling Pat about his marriage.

Refer to annotations R and WW.

Concept Review: Metaphor Agatha Christie compares the maid's room to a dog kennel in order to convey its small size, boxy shape, and general lack of comfort. The metaphor can be found in paragraph 2 on page 223.

Refer to annotation X.

Writing Options

1. Imagine that you are Poirot and you are writing a letter to a friend describing the third-floor flat. In your letter, list all the clues that you used to solve the crime.

2. In this story Donovan's "best laid plans" are foiled. Knowing what you now do about the characters, how could he have prevented anyone from solving the crime?

3. Write Mrs. Grant's and Donovan's conversation leading up to the murder. Use what you have learned from Poirot to create what you think they might have said to each other. Remember that after the conversation, Donovan decides he has no choice but to murder her.

Vocabulary Practice

Exercise Read the pairs of words below. On your paper, write *Synonyms* if the pair are synonyms. Write *Antonyms* if they are antonyms. Remember that synonyms are words with almost the same meaning. Antonyms have opposite meanings.

1. disclaimer—denial
2. admonition—warning
3. fervent—unemotional
4. placidly—peacefully
5. ruefully—regretfully
6. discreet—careless
7. compromising—risky
8. incriminate—blame
9. ruse—trick
10. invalidate—legalize

Words to Know and Use

admonition
compromising
disclaimer
discreet
fervent
incriminate
invalidate
placidly
ruefully
ruse

Writing Options

The Writing Options are designed to meet varied student interests and abilities. Have each student choose one writing activity to complete. You may wish to guide some students to an option that requires less writing.

Journal Update Have students review their journal entries for "The Third-Floor Flat." What qualities in this story do students feel make it a good mystery? What skills and abilities have students discovered are most helpful to the detective in this story? What new reflections can students add to their earlier writing?

Vocabulary Practice

1. Synonyms
2. Synonyms
3. Antonyms
4. Synonyms
5. Synonyms
6. Antonyms
7. Synonyms
8. Synonyms
9. Synonyms
10. Antonyms

Closure

Explain that many people voraciously read mystery novels as a favorite pastime and escape. Ask students whether this small taste of mystery could turn them into mystery-novel fans. Have them explain their responses.

Objectives

- To understand and analyze a short work of fiction
- To understand and review the use of sensory details
- To recognize how a writer creates mood
- To express understanding of the work through a choice of writing options, including dialogue, an analysis, song lyrics, and a character sketch

Prereading/Motivation

Examine What You Know

Discussion Prompts: What factors would make you consider an item valuable? Would you ever consider parting with something you regarded as a treasure, or would you want to keep it through the years? Why?

Expand Your Knowledge

Discussion Prompts: For what reasons do people become homeless? Why do some people choose to remain homeless on the street rather than accept the services of shelters? How do you feel about the issue of homelessness?

Thematic Link—The Best-Laid Plans

In "The Treasure of Lemon Brown," a character finds that his plans for life do not work out as he had hoped, and his treasure is a reminder of the people and things he loved and lived for.

Art Note

A museum book on the work of Philip Reisman is aptly subtitled *People Are His Passion.* Reisman's art portrays the experiences of working people—and of others whose lives are degraded by squalor and deprivation. "84 Madison II" is a view of a tenement building and some of its inhabitants. *How do you visualize the interior of this old but essentially strong and beautiful structure?*

e x p l o r e

Fiction

The Treasure of Lemon Brown

WALTER DEAN MYERS

Examine What You Know (Prior Knowledge)

One of the characters in the story you are about to read says that "Every man got a treasure." Treasures tell a lot about what someone values in life. Make a list of six items that are of great value to you. Are your treasures valuable in terms of money or because of the sentiment you attach to them? Explain the significance of each item, and then read to find out what Lemon Brown's treasure is and why it is important.

Expand Your Knowledge (Building Background)

One of the main characters in this story is a homeless person. Homelessness is a growing worldwide problem. The United Nations reports that there are 100 million homeless people in the world. In the United States, estimates of the number of homeless people range from 250,000 to 3 million. Some of these people may be homeless temporarily, but others live permanently on the streets, under bridges, in subways, in cheap hotels, in church shelters, or wherever else they can find a place to survive. What do you know about homelessness? What have you observed in your community?

Write Before You Read (Journal Writing)

The words and phrases listed below convey images, feelings, or sounds found in the story you are about to read. These details, called story impressions, are listed in the order that they appear in the story. Use these words in the order given to predict the plot of "The Treasure of Lemon Brown." Then read to see how closely your ideas resemble the writer's.

unhappy boy—angry father—rainy evening—
old tenement house—homeless person—blues singer—
neighborhood thugs—howling—personal treasure—home

■ *A biography of the author can be found in the Reader's Handbook.*

Additional Journal Writing

In "The Treasure of Lemon Brown," a man protects personal possessions that are important to him. Suggest these journal topics to students:

- For what reason might a person be willing to fight to protect personal treasures or mementos?
- What important memory has an older person shared with you? Tell about it.

For other journal opportunities, refer students to Examine What You Know (p. 232) and First Impressions and Broader Connections (p. 241).

Additional Resources

UNIT TWO RESOURCE BOOK

Reader's Guidesheet, p. 33
Vocabulary Worksheet, p. 34
Selection and Vocabulary Check Tests, p. 35
Selection Test, pp. 36–37

Collaborative Learning

Opportunities for collaborative learning appear throughout the lesson and include Broader Connections (p. 241) and Cultural Connections (p. T-239).

The Treasure of Lemon Brown

WALTER DEAN MYERS

A The dark sky, filled with angry, swirling clouds, reflected Greg Ridley's mood as he sat on the stoop of his building. His father's voice came to him again, first reading the letter the principal had sent to the house, then lecturing endlessly about his poor efforts in math.

"I had to leave school when I was thirteen," his father had said. "That's a year younger than you are now. If I'd had half the chances that you have, I'd . . ."

Greg had sat in the small, pale-green kitchen listening, knowing the lecture would end with his father saying he couldn't play ball with the Scorpions. He had asked his father the week before, and his father had said it depended on his next report card. It wasn't often the Scorpions took on new players, especially fourteen-year-olds, and this was a chance of a lifetime for Greg. He hadn't been allowed to play high-school ball, which he had really wanted to do, but playing for the Community Center team was the next best thing. Report cards were due in a week, and Greg had been hoping for the best. But the principal had ended the suspense early when she sent that letter saying Greg would probably fail math if he didn't spend more time studying.

"And you want to play *basketball?*" His father's brows knitted over deep brown eyes. "That must be some kind of a joke. Now you just get into your room and hit those books." B

That had been two nights before. His father's words, like the distant thunder that now echoed through the streets of Harlem,[1] still rumbled softly in his ears. ◀SR-1

It was beginning to cool. Gusts of wind made bits of paper dance between the parked cars. There was a flash of nearby lightning, and soon large drops of rain splashed onto his jeans. C He stood to go upstairs, thought of the lecture that probably awaited him if he did anything except shut himself in his room with his math book, and started walking down the street instead. Down the block there was an old tenement that had been abandoned for some months. Some of the guys had held an impromptu checker tournament there the week before, and Greg had noticed that the door, once boarded over, had been slightly ajar.

Pulling his collar up as high as he could,

1. **Harlem:** a neighborhood in New York City.

Words to Know and Use

impromptu (im prämp' to͞o') *adj.* without preparation or forethought

233

Teaching Strategies

Vocabulary Preview

These vocabulary words are defined at the bottom of the selection page on which they appear. You may wish to discuss them briefly before students begin reading.

commence begin
impromptu without preparation
ominous threatening
tentatively with hesitation
vault leap over

Support for Students of Limited English Proficiency

- Use Reader's Guidesheet, p. 33.
- "The Treasure of Lemon Brown" contains some vocabulary that may interfere with students' understanding of the sensory descriptions. Help students use context clues where possible and define terms when necessary. Have students restate ideas in their own words.
- Annotations B, D, I, L, and T focus on terms and ideas that may need attention.

Text Annotations

A. Literary Element: MOOD Note that the author uses a description of the sky to convey the boy's mood and give the reader a feeling about the story. Have students identify the feeling. *(Possible response: angry, depressed, restless)*

B. LEP: Vocabulary Students may not be familiar with the way *knitted* is used here. Explain that here it means "came together into wrinkles." Point out that knitted brows indicate someone has a serious concern or is worried. Ask a volunteer to demonstrate the facial expression.

C. Literary Concept: SENSORY DETAILS Explain that a writer can choose words that help readers use one or more of their senses to picture what is being described. Ask students what words help them see, hear, and feel the weather. *("Gusts of wind made bits of paper dance"; "a flash of nearby lightning"; "large drops of rain splashed onto his jeans")*

STRUCTURED READING FOR LESS PROFICIENT STUDENTS

These questions can help to guide students through the reading. Ask each question at the point of the selection where the SR number appears in the margin.

SR–1. What is the problem between Greg and his father? *(Greg has a chance to play on a basketball team, but his father won't let him because Greg is failing math and his father wants him to study.)* **Summarizing**

SR–2. What does Greg do instead of studying? *(He walks down the block to an abandoned old tenement.)* **Literal recall**

SR–3. Whom does Greg meet and what does the person look like? *(Greg meets Lemon Brown, an old black man with a wrinkled face and white hair and whiskers, who is wearing layers of dirty coats and rags.)* **Literal recall**

SR–4. What does Lemon Brown tell about his past and present? *(Brown had been a traveling musician who played the blues. He fell on hard times. He is staying in the abandoned tenement, and he has a treasure.)* **Summarizing**

Continued on page 234

D. LEP: Vocabulary Students may have seen graffiti on buildings, walls, and so on, but may not be familiar with the term *graffiti.* You may want to ask volunteers to define the term. If necessary, explain that *graffiti* consists of names, messages, and drawings that have usually been spray-painted on some public surface. You may wish to discuss the reasons why people write graffiti, its effects, and other ways to obtain recognition.

E. Literary Element: SENSORY DETAILS Have students identify the details that help them understand the room and its contents and name the senses to which these details appeal. *(Possible responses: sense of sight: "squarish patch of light on the floor," "old table on its side," "pile of rags or a torn mattress in the corner," "couch, with one side broken," "blinking neon sign"; sense of smell: "musty smell"; sense of hearing: "creaky" couch)*

F. Literary Element: SENSORY DETAILS From these details have students describe in a phrase the kind of night it is. *(Possible response: a dark, stormy, windy night)*

G. Literary Element: FIGURATIVE LANGUAGE Ask students what the author conveys about the man's voice by comparing it to "dry twigs being broken." *(Possible response: The voice is dry, scratchy, old, worn, and perhaps weak.)*

he checked for traffic and made a dash across the street. He reached the house just as another flash of lightning changed the D night to day for an instant, then returned the graffiti-scarred building to the grim shadows. He vaulted over the outer stairs SR-2 ▶ and pushed tentatively on the door. It was open, and he let himself in.

The inside of the building was dark except for the dim light that filtered through the dirty windows from the streetlamps. There was a room a few feet from the door, and from where he stood at the entrance, Greg could see a squarish patch of light on the floor. He entered the room, frowning at the musty smell. It was a large room that might have been someone's parlor at one time. Squinting, Greg could see an old table on its E side against one wall, what looked like a pile of rags or a torn mattress in the corner, and a couch, with one side broken, in front of the window.

He went to the couch. The side that wasn't broken was comfortable enough, though a little creaky. From this spot he could see the blinking neon sign over the bodega[2] on the corner. He sat a while, watching the sign blink first green, then red, allowing his mind to drift to the Scorpions, then to his father. His father had been a postal worker for all Greg's life and was proud of it, often telling Greg how hard he had worked to pass the test. Greg had heard the story too many times to be interested now.

For a moment Greg thought he heard something that sounded like a scraping against the wall. He listened carefully, but it was gone.

Outside the wind had picked up, sending the rain against the window with a force F that shook the glass in its frame. A car passed, its tires hissing over the wet street and its red tail lights glowing in the darkness.

Greg thought he heard the noise again. His stomach tightened as he held himself still and listened intently. There weren't any more scraping noises, but he was sure he had heard something in the darkness—something breathing!

He tried to figure out just where the breathing was coming from; he knew it was in the room with him. Slowly he stood, tensing. As he turned, a flash of lightning lit up the room, frightening him with its sudden brilliance. He saw nothing, just the overturned table, the pile of rags, and an old newspaper on the floor. Could he have been imagining the sounds? He continued listening, but heard nothing and thought that it might have just been rats. Still, he thought, as soon as the rain let up he would leave. He went to the window and was about to look out when he heard a voice behind him.

"Don't try nothin' 'cause I got a razor here sharp enough to cut a week into nine days!"

Greg, except for an involuntary tremor in his knees, stood stock still. The voice was G high and brittle, like dry twigs being broken, surely not one he had ever heard before. There was a shuffling sound as the person who had been speaking moved a step closer. Greg turned, holding his breath, his eyes straining to see in the dark room.

The upper part of the figure before him

2. **bodega** (bō dā′ gə): a small grocery store.

Words to Know and Use	
	vault (vôlt) *v.* to leap over
	tentatively (ten′ tə tiv lē) *adv.* with hesitation or uncertainty

Structured Reading for Less Proficient Students

Continued from page 233

SR–5. Who comes into the tenement? What do they want? *(three neighborhood thugs who are after Lemon Brown's treasure)* **Literal recall**

SR–6. How do Greg and Lemon Brown fight the thugs? *(They hide upstairs; then Greg howls at the thugs and Brown hurls himself down the stairs at the men, who are scared off.)* **Literal recall**

SR–7. What is Lemon Brown's treasure and what does it represent to him? *(old clippings about his being a blues singer and harmonica player and an old harmonica; his treasure represents who he was and what he had accomplished in life)* **Clarifying**

SR–8. What does Lemon Brown teach Greg about parent-child relationships? *(that knowing what a parent accomplished can help a child achieve in life; that the most important thing a parent has is what he can pass on to his children)* **Clarifying**

OVER THERE 1988
Doug Safranek Courtesy of Schmidt Bingham Gallery, New York.

was still in darkness. The lower half was in the dim rectangle of light that fell unevenly from the window. There were two feet, in cracked, dirty shoes from which rose legs that were wrapped in rags.

"Who are you?" Greg hardly recognized his own voice.

"I'm Lemon Brown," came the answer. "Who're you?"

"Greg Ridley."

"What you doing here?" The figure shuffled forward again, and Greg took a small step backward.

"It's raining," Greg said.

"I can see that," the figure said.

The person who called himself Lemon Brown peered forward, and Greg could see him clearly. He was an old man. His black, heavily wrinkled face was surrounded by a halo of crinkly white hair and whiskers that seemed to separate his head from the layers of dirty coats piled on his smallish frame. His pants were bagged to the knee, where they were met with rags that went down to the old shoes. The rags were held on with strings, and there was a rope around his middle. Greg relaxed. He had seen the man before, picking through the trash on the corner and pulling clothes out of a Salvation Army box. There was no sign of the razor that could "cut a week into nine days." ◄ SR-3

"What are you doing here?" Greg asked.

"This is where I'm staying," Lemon Brown said. "What you here for?"

"Told you it was raining out," Greg said, leaning against the back of the couch until he felt it give slightly.

"Ain't you got no home?"

"I got a home," Greg answered.

"You ain't one of them bad boys looking for my treasure, is you?" Lemon Brown cocked his head to one side and squinted one eye. "Because I told you I got me a razor."

Art Note
Contemporary artist Douglas Safranek studied at Boston College and the University of Wisconsin. He paints with tempera, a difficult medium, for which he carefully mixes dry color pigments with egg yolk; he applies the mixture to a smooth panel. The figures in his New York cityscapes add definition to the buildings and the littered streets. *Where might you find Lemon Brown in this scene?*

H. Literary Element: SENSORY DETAILS Point out that the author uses many details to help readers "see" Lemon Brown. Have students identify the details here. *(Possible responses: "black, heavily wrinkled face," "halo of crinkly white hair and whiskers," "layers of dirty coats," "smallish frame," "pants . . . bagged to the knee," "rags that went down to old shoes," "rope around his middle.")*

I. LEP: Cultural Discussion Explain that the Salvation Army is an organization that helps the poor and the homeless by providing food and clothing. Have students discuss organizations that help the poor and homeless in their community. Extend the discussion to include mention of organizations that help the poor and homeless in other countries.

J. Reading Skill: CLARIFYING Note the use of nonstandard English in the dialogue. Discuss the standard English equivalents for the following: "What you here for?" *("Why are you here?")*; "Ain't you got no home?" *("Don't you have a home?")*; "I got a home." *("I have a home.")*; "You ain't one of them bad boys . . .?" *("You aren't one of those bad boys . . .?)*

REAL LIFE CONNECTIONS

Students who live in cities or large towns may be familiar with the situation of the boy, Greg Ridley, and the story setting—city streets, tenements, abandoned buildings, and homeless people around. You may wish to have them compare their neighborhood or community to the one in the story. If students know of or have heard about people living in abandoned buildings, they might share this knowledge.

Students may identify with Greg's feelings of restlessness and wanting to get out of their home when they feel frustrated or upset. Have students discuss what they do or where they go when they are overcome by frustration and anger.

K. Historical Sidelight The blues is a form of musical expression about the misery, sorrow, and hardships of life, usually sung by an individual and presenting his or her personal problems. The blues developed in America from a mixture of many sources: remnants of African music passed down from the slaves brought to the New World in the 1600's, work songs of generations of African-American slaves, the "hard-luck tales" and "love themes" of freed African-American field laborers, the mournful songs of wanderers, and the sorrowful songs of the spirituals.

L. LEP: Vocabulary Point out to students that a *knot* can mean a problem or a tangle in hair. Ask what meanings "knotty-headed" may have here. *(Possible responses: It may mean "difficult to understand,"* or *"too complicated to figure out" or it may refer to the boy's appearance.)*

M. Reading Skill: INFERRING Ask students what they think Lemon Brown means about Greg having moon eyes. *(Possible response: You can see different things when you look at the moon, but you can never be sure that you are right, just as when you look at Greg's eyes you can't figure out for sure what he is thinking or feeling.)*

N. Reading Skill: CLARIFYING Have students explain what Lemon means in light of the information on the blues presented in Annotation K, the Historical Sidelight. *(Possible response: Blues songs are about hardships and misery, but Lemon Brown was successful, so there was no reason for him to continue to sing the blues.)*

"I'm not looking for your treasure," Greg answered, smiling. "*If* you have one."

"What you mean, *if* I have one," Lemon Brown said. "Every man got a treasure. You don't know that, you must be a fool!"

"Sure," Greg said as he sat on the sofa and put one leg over the back. "What do you have, gold coins?"

"Don't worry none about what I got," Lemon Brown said. "You know who I am?"

"You told me your name was orange or lemon or something like that."

"Lemon Brown," the old man said, pulling back his shoulders as he did so, "they used to call me Sweet Lemon Brown."

"Sweet Lemon?" Greg asked.

K "Yessir. Sweet Lemon Brown. They used to say I sung the blues so sweet that if I sang at a funeral, the dead would commence to rocking with the beat. Used to travel all over Mississippi and as far as Monroe, Louisiana, and east on over to Macon, Georgia. You mean you ain't never heard of Sweet Lemon Brown?"

"Afraid not," Greg said. "What . . . what happened to you?"

"Hard times, boy. Hard times always after a poor man. One day I got tired, sat down to rest a spell, and felt a tap on my shoulder. Hard times caught up with me."

"Sorry about that."

"What you doing here? How come you didn't go on home when the rain come. Rain don't bother you young folks none."

L "Just didn't," Greg looked away.

"I used to have a knotty-headed boy just like you." Lemon Brown had half walked, half shuffled back to the corner and sat down against the wall. "Had them big eyes like you got. I used to call them moon eyes.

M Look into them moon eyes and see anything you want."

"How come you gave up singing the blues?" Greg asked.

"Didn't give it up," Lemon Brown said. "You don't give up the blues; they give you up. After a while you do good for yourself, and it ain't nothing but foolishness singing about how hard you got it. Ain't that right?" N

"I guess so." ◀ SR-4

"What's that noise?" Lemon Brown asked, suddenly sitting upright.

Greg listened, and he heard a noise outside. He looked at Lemon Brown and saw the old man was pointing toward the window.

Greg went to the window and saw three men, neighborhood thugs, on the stoop. One was carrying a length of pipe. Greg looked back toward Lemon Brown, who moved quietly across the room to the window. The old man looked out, then beckoned frantically for Greg to follow him. For a moment Greg couldn't move. Then he found himself following Lemon Brown into the hallway and up darkened stairs. Greg followed as closely as he could. They reached the top of the stairs, and Greg felt Lemon Brown's hand first lying on his shoulder, then probing down his arm until he finally took Greg's hand into his own as they crouched in the darkness.

"They's bad men," Lemon Brown whispered. His breath was warm against Greg's skin.

"Hey! Rag man!" A voice called. "We know you in here. What you got up under them rags? You got any money?"

Silence.

"We don't want to have to come in and hurt you, old man, but we don't mind if we have to."

Words to Know and Use

commence (kə mens') *v.* to begin

DATA BANK

During the 1950's, homelessness in America was usually associated with run-down sections of cities known as *skid rows*. The people in such areas were often elderly, poor white men. Many were alcoholics. Since the 1970's, however, the homeless population has been growing, changing, and expanding to all sections of cities.

Today the homeless population includes large numbers of young men and women (and their children) who are without jobs and sometimes skills and are unable to afford housing. Also in the homeless population are former psychiatric patients who have been released into the general community without adequate support.

Lemon Brown squeezed Greg's hand in his own hard, gnarled fist.

There was a banging downstairs and a light as the men entered. They banged around noisily, calling for the rag man.

"We heard you talking about your treasure," the voice was slurred. "We just want to see it, that's all."

"You sure he's here?" One voice seemed to come from the room with the sofa.

"Yeah, he stays here every night."

"There's another room over there; I'm going to take a look. You got that flashlight?"

"Yeah, here, take the pipe too."

Greg opened his mouth to quiet the sound of his breath as he sucked it in uneasily. A beam of light hit the wall a few feet opposite him, then went out.

"Ain't nobody in that room," a voice said. "You think he gone or something?"

"I don't know," came the answer. "All I know is that I heard him talking about some kind of treasure. You know they found that shopping bag lady with that money in her bags."

"Yeah. You think he's upstairs?"

O "HEY, OLD MAN, ARE YOU UP THERE?"

Silence.

SR-5 ▶ "Watch my back, I'm going up."

P There was a footstep on the stairs, and the beam from the flashlight danced crazily along the peeling wallpaper. Greg held his breath. There was another step and a loud crashing noise as the man banged the pipe against the wooden banister. Greg could feel his temples throb as the man slowly neared them. Greg thought about the pipe, wondering what he would do when the man reached them—what he *could* do.

Then Lemon Brown released his hand and moved toward the top of the stairs. Greg looked around and saw stairs going up to the next floor. He tried waving to Lemon Brown, hoping the old man would see him in the dim light and follow him to the next floor. Maybe, Greg thought, the man wouldn't follow them up there. Suddenly, though, Lemon Brown stood at the top of the stairs, both arms raised high above his head.

"There he is!" A voice cried from below.

"Throw down your money, old man, so I won't have to bash your head in!"

Lemon Brown didn't move. Greg felt himself near panic. The steps came closer, and still Lemon Brown didn't move. He was an eerie sight, a bundle of rags standing at the top of the stairs, his shadow on the wall looming over him. Maybe, the thought came to Greg, the scene could be even eerier.

Greg wet his lips, put his hands to his mouth and tried to make a sound. Nothing came out. He swallowed hard, wet his lips once more and howled as evenly as he could.

"*What's that?*"

As Greg howled, the light moved away from Lemon Brown, but not before Greg saw him hurl his body down the stairs at the men who had come to take his treasure. There was a crashing noise, and then footsteps. A rush of warm air came in as the downstairs door opened, then there was only an ominous silence. Q R ◀ SR-6

Greg stood on the landing. He listened, and after a while there was another sound on the staircase.

Words to Know and Use	**ominous** (äm′ ə nəs) *adj.* threatening

O. Reading Skill: INFERRING Ask students why these words are in capital letters. *(Possible response: to convey that the man is shouting)*

P. Literary Element: SENSORY DETAILS Have students identify the details that help them step into the world being described and to name the senses they use in understanding the scene. *(Possible responses: sight—"beam from the flashlight danced crazily," "peeling wallpaper," "wooden banister"; sound—"footstep on the stairs," "loud crashing noise," "man banged the pipe"; touch—"temples throb.")*

Q. Critical Thinking: ANALYZING Ask students what they think Lemon Brown is trying to accomplish by hurling himself at the intruders. *(Possible response: He is trying to use his body as a weapon, hoping the force of his movement will knock them over and scare them into leaving.)*

R. Reading Skill: INFERRING Ask students what they think has happened. *(Possible responses: Lemon scared the intruders off; Lemon has been hurt.)*

Professional Notebook

In the protected environment of the classroom, we can take risks in teaching that allow our students the latitude to take risks in thinking. When we share our own reasons and reservations, we allow our students to see that the solutions to problems are always tentative and that we must work cooperatively to succeed. . . . Power is having the strength and ability to design questions from conventional givens and the courage to let the answers change over time.

Only educators who have power can give power. Those who are able to take risks and to challenge the obvious must define and redefine this line between caregiver and liberator. For those who are up to it, for those who discover how to give power away, there is a limitless supply. There is enough power for every student every day.

La Vergne Rosow, "Consumer Advocacy, Empowerment, and Adult Literacy," *Journal of Reading*, December/January 1990/1991.

Art Note
James Reed, a contemporary African-American realist painter, is noted for his compelling portraits in which the subjects seem to tell us about their lives. As in *"Depressed,"* each image conveys its personal message of human experience and a commentary on society as a whole. *If this were a picture of Lemon Brown, what do you suppose he would say to us?*

S. Reading Skill: PREDICTING Ask students what they think Lemon Brown's treasure might be. *(Answers will vary but might include an album of some kind, since students know that he had been a successful blues singer.)*

T. LEP: Phrasing Point out the example of nonstandard English in the phrase ". . . see what them scoundrels be doing." Encourage students to restate the phrase in standard English. *(". . . see what those scoundrels are doing.")*

Teaching Tip
Students might enjoy drawing their own pictures of Lemon Brown or illustrating scenes from the story.

DEPRESSED 1950 James Reed Courtesy of Atlanta University Art Exhibition, Georgia.

"Mr. Brown?" he called.

"Yeah, it's me," came the answer. "I got their flashlight."

Greg exhaled in relief as Lemon Brown made his way slowly back up the stairs.

"You O.K.?"

"Few bumps and bruises," Lemon Brown said.

"I think I'd better be going," Greg said, his breath returning to normal. "You'd better leave, too, before they come back."

"They may hang around outside for a while," Lemon Brown said, "but they ain't getting their nerve up to come in here again. Not with crazy old rag men and howling spooks. Best you stay awhile till the coast is clear. I'm heading out West tomorrow, out to East St. Louis."[3]

"They were talking about treasures," Greg said. "You *really* have a treasure?"

"What I tell you? Didn't I tell you every man got a treasure?" Lemon Brown said. "You want to see mine?" S

"If you want to show it to me," Greg shrugged.

"Let's look out the window first, see what them scoundrels be doing," Lemon Brown said. T

3. **East St. Louis:** Illinois city located across the Mississippi River from St. Louis, Missouri.

REAL LIFE CONNECTIONS

Students may have been victims of assaults or may have seen others attacked. If the situations are not too sensitive, have volunteers share experiences. Lead students in a discussion of what they know about reasons for attacks and what can be done to prevent them.

They followed the oval beam of the flashlight into one of the rooms and looked out the window. They saw the men who had tried to take the treasure sitting on the curb near the corner. One of them had his pants leg up, looking at his knee.

"You sure you're not hurt?" Greg asked Lemon Brown.

U "Nothing that ain't been hurt before," Lemon Brown said, "When you get as old as me, all you say when something hurts is, 'Howdy, Mr. Pain, sees you back again.' Then when Mr. Pain see he can't worry you none, he go on mess with somebody else."

Greg smiled.

"Here, you hold this." Lemon Brown gave Greg the flashlight.

He sat on the floor near Greg and carefully untied the strings that held the rags on his right leg. When he took the rags away, Greg saw a piece of plastic. The old man carefully took off the plastic and unfolded it. He revealed some yellowed newspaper clippings and a battered harmonica.

"There it be," he said, nodding his head. "There it be."

Greg looked at the old man, saw the distant look in his eye, then turned to the clippings. They told of Sweet Lemon Brown, a blues singer and harmonica player who was appearing at different theaters in the South. One of the clippings said he had been the hit of the show, although not the headliner. All of the clippings were reviews of shows Lemon Brown had been in more than fifty years ago. Greg looked at the harmonica. It was dented badly on one side, with the reed holes on one end nearly closed. V

"I used to travel around and make money for to feed my wife and Jesse—that's my boy's name. Used to feed them good, too. Then his mama died, and he stayed with his mama's sister. He growed up to be a man, and when the war come he saw fit to go off and fight in it. I didn't have nothing to give him except these things that told him who I was and what he come from. If you know your pappy did something, you know you can do something too. W

"Anyway, he went off to war, and I went off still playing and singing. 'Course by then I wasn't as much as I used to be, not without somebody to make it worth the while. You know what I mean?"

"Yeah," Greg nodded, not quite really knowing.

"I traveled around, and one time I come home, and there was this letter saying Jesse got killed in the war. Broke my heart, it truly did.

"They sent back what he had with him over there, and what it was is this old mouth fiddle and these clippings. Him carrying it around with him like that told me it meant something to him. That was my treasure, and when I give it to him he treated it just like that, a treasure. Ain't that something?" X ◀SR-7

"Yeah, I guess so," Greg said.

"You *guess* so?" Lemon Brown's voice rose an octave as he started to put his treasure back into the plastic. "Well, you got to guess 'cause you sure don't know nothing. Don't know enough to get home when it's raining."

"I guess . . . I mean, you're right."

"You O.K. for a youngster," the old man said as he tied the strings around his leg, "better than those scalawags what come here looking for my treasure. That's for sure."

"You really think that treasure of yours was worth fighting for?" Greg asked. "Against a pipe?"

"What else a man got 'cepting what he can pass on to his son, or his daughter, if she be

U. Reading Skill: PARAPHRASING Ask students to restate in their own words what Lemon Brown says about pain. *(Possible response: If you don't let pain bother you, it will pass.)* Ask if they agree with this attitude. *(Possible responses: Yes, if you ignore pain it will go away; no, some pain may be too great to ignore.)*

V. Historical Sidelight The blues gained popularity in the early 1900's when a band leader by the name of W. C. Handy began adapting the sad songs of traditional African-American music into his own new compositions. Among the most well known blues singers were Bessie Smith, Gertrude "Ma" Rainey, Blind Lemon Jefferson, and Robert Johnson.

W. Critical Thinking: ANALYZING Point out that just a short while before, Greg and Lemon Brown were strangers, yet now Lemon is sharing some very personal information with Greg. Ask students why they think Lemon is sharing all of this with Greg. *(Possible responses: They have gone through a scary situation together, and this has made them feel close; Lemon has no one left to share anything with and he is lonely for company; earlier, Lemon asked Greg why he didn't go home—perhaps he senses Greg has family problems and he hopes to give Greg a better understanding of the importance of family ties.)*

X. Reading Skill: INFERRING Have students explain what Lemon's son, Jesse, conveyed to his father by treating the mementos as treasures, too. *(Possible response: Jesse conveyed that he loved his father and was proud of him.)*

CULTURAL CONNECTION

The blues are very much part of African-American history and experience in the United States. Ask students of various ethnic backgrounds and cultures to think about their cultures and how those cultures are expressed in music or art or drama. Encourage students to explore what the arts reflect about their culture. Perhaps some students have family mementos that reveal something of their cultural heritages. If possible, have students bring in the mementos and share the history of them with the class.

Y. Critical Thinking: ANALYZING Ask students what Greg's words reveal about his feelings for Lemon Brown. *(Possible response: that he likes him and cares about him)*

Z. Literary Element: MOOD Have students explain what the details at the beginning of this paragraph suggest about whether Lemon Brown and Greg will be O.K. *(Possible response: The night becoming warmer and the rain ending suggest a mood that is lighter and more hopeful than the dark, stormy mood at the beginning of the story.)*

Check Test

1. Why is Greg angry at the beginning of the story? *(He isn't allowed to play on a basketball team because he is flunking math.)*

2. What does he do instead of studying? *(goes out)*

3. Whom does Greg meet? *(Lemon Brown, a former blues singer who is now a homeless person living in an abandoned building)*

4. Who comes after them in the abandoned building? *(neighborhood thugs who want Lemon Brown's treasure)*

5. How do Greg and his new acquaintance stop the intruders? *(Lemon Brown hurls himself at the thugs, and Greg howls.)*

6. What is Lemon Brown's treasure? *(newspaper clippings and an old, dented harmonica)*

his oldest?" Lemon Brown said. "For a bigheaded boy you sure do ask the SR-8 ▶ foolishest questions."

Lemon Brown got up after patting his rags in place and looked out the window again.

"Looks like they're gone. You get on out of here and get yourself home. I'll be watching from the window so you'll be all right."

Lemon Brown went down the stairs behind Greg. When they reached the front door, the old man looked out first, saw the street was clear, and told Greg to scoot on home.

Y "You sure you'll be O.K.?" Greg asked.

"Now didn't I tell you I was going to East St. Louis in the morning?" Lemon Brown asked. "Don't that sound O.K. to you?"

"Sure it does," Greg said. "Sure it does. And you take care of that treasure of yours."

"That I'll do," Lemon said, the wrinkles about his eyes suggesting a smile. "That I'll do."

Z The night had warmed and the rain had stopped, leaving puddles at the curbs. Greg didn't even want to think how late it was. He thought ahead of what his father would say and wondered if he should tell him about Lemon Brown. He thought about it until he reached his stoop and decided against it. Lemon Brown would be O.K., Greg thought, with his memories and his treasure.

Greg pushed the button over the bell marked Ridley, thought of the lecture he knew his father would give him, and smiled. ❧

INSIGHT

Miss Rosie

LUCILLE CLIFTON

When I watch you
wrapped up like garbage
sitting, surrounded by the smell
of too old potato peels
or
when I watch you
in your old man's shoes
with the little toe cut out
sitting, waiting for your mind
like next week's grocery
I say
when I watch you
you wet brown bag of a woman
who used to be the best looking gal in
  Georgia
used to be called the Georgia Rose
I stand up
through your destruction
I stand up

Encouraging Independent Reading

"Lucas and Jake," a short story by Paul Darcy Boles
Great Expectations, a novel by Charles Dickens
"To Dah-dum, in Memoriam," a short story by Paule Marshall
Fallen Angels, a novel by Walter Dean Myers
My Sweet Charlie, a novel by David Westheimer

Insight

This piece reflects on the ideas in the main selection and is suggested for students' independent reading. Optional discussion questions follow.

1. What is Miss Rosie's situation? *(Possible response: She is a homeless person)*

2. Do you think the speaker admires or despises Miss Rosie? Why? *(Possible response: She seems to admire Rosie because she remembers what Rosie used to be. The speaker says she stands up, implying that seeing Rosie's destruction makes the speaker feel respectful and also want to achieve more.)*

3. In what ways are Rosie and Lemon Brown similar? *(Possible response: They were both once successful, popular people who lost their way and became homeless.)*

e x p l a i n

Responding to Reading

First Impressions

1. Jot down your thoughts about Lemon Brown in your journal. Be prepared to discuss your impressions with your classmates.

Second Thoughts

2. Why does Lemon Brown consider his mementos a treasure?

   Think about
   - how Lemon Brown once made a living
   - what happened to Lemon Brown's son
   - the treasures you listed before you read the story

3. Lemon Brown says: "If you know your pappy did something, you know you can do something too." How does this statement make Greg feel?

   Think about
   - Lemon Brown's relationship with his son
   - Greg's relationship with his father
   - what Greg knows about his dad's work

4. What has Greg learned by the end of the story that causes him to smile?

5. Read the poem "Miss Rosie" on page 240. Compare this poem to "The Treasure of Lemon Brown."

6. As the number of homeless people in the world continues to increase, governments, church and community service groups, and compassionate individuals are attempting to help bring about an end to this problem. Think back to what you have learned about the homeless. Whose responsibility is it to help them?

Literary Concept: Sensory Details

To create images and feelings in their readers, writers use words that appeal to the senses, or **sensory details.** These words help the reader see, hear, taste, smell, and feel the world the writer is describing. Walter Dean Myers uses many sensory details in this short story. For example, when Greg walks into the abandoned building, he sees a "squarish patch of light on the floor" and frowns "at the musty smell." Make a chart with a heading for each of the senses, and then list the examples of sensory details that you find in this story.

Student Response

Responding to Reading

These questions are open-ended with no "right" or "wrong" answers. However, responses must be supported with information from the selection. Possible answers follow:

1. All responses are valid.

2. Some may say that they remind him of a happier, successful time in his life. Others may say that they were given with love and a feeling of pride to his son, who treated them in the same way, which let Lemon know that his son loved him in return and was proud of him.

3. Most students will recognize that it makes Greg feel good because he understands that his father has worked hard and has accomplished a lot with little help from anyone. He begins to understand that if his father succeeded, so can he.

4. Some may say that Greg has learned that his father loves him and wants him to succeed. Others may say that Greg realizes that his father is not going to change, so it is up to him to change.

5. Possible response: Both selections are about homeless people who once were part of life in a more mainstream society.

6. Answers will vary. Some students may feel that it is a shared responsibility between city, state, and federal governments. Others may feel that individuals in a community and charities should try to help the homeless.

Literary Concept—Sensory Details

There are numerous sensory details. Some possible examples include these:

Sight dark sky filled with angry, swirling clouds; pale green kitchen; squarish patch of light on the floor; blinking neon sign; pile of rags and newspapers on the floor; black, heavily wrinkled face; halo of crinkly white hair and whiskers; peeling wallpaper; yellowed newspaper clippings; battered harmonica.

Sound creaky couch; scraping against the wall; car tires hissing; breathing, shuffling; high, brittle voice, like dry twigs being broken; Greg howled; crashing noise, footsteps.

Smell musty smell.

Touch wooden banister; throbbing temples.

Refer to annotations C, E, F, H, and P.

Writing Options

The Writing Options are designed to meet varied student interests and abilities. Have each student choose one writing activity to complete. You may wish to guide some students to an option that requires less writing.

Journal Update Have students review their journal entries for "The Treasure of Lemon Brown." How did the events of the story compare with their predictions? What new reflections can they add to their writing?

Vocabulary Practice

1. ominous
2. impromptu
3. commence
4. tentatively
5. vault

Closure

Have students look back at the list of treasures they created. Ask them if, in light of the story, there are any items that they would add to or subtract from their lists.

Concept Review: Mood The feeling or attitude that the writer creates in the reader is called **mood**. A writer uses descriptive and sensory details to create a mood. Look back at the beginning of this selection. What mood is created for the reader? What details help create this mood?

Writing Options

1. What do you think happens when Greg goes back home? Write the conversation Greg has with his father when he returns. Remember what concerns the father has about his son. Also, consider what Greg has learned about fathers and sons from Lemon Brown.
2. The teenage character in this selection learns an important lesson from an older person. Write about something important that you have learned from someone much older than yourself. What effect has this information had on your actions?
3. The blues is a kind of music with slow jazz rhythms and melancholy words. Blues singers often sing about broken hearts, family problems, or just hard times. Try your hand at writing the blues. Write song lyrics that express what either Greg or Lemon might be feeling after their encounter.
4. Create a list of ten adjectives that describe Lemon Brown. Then, based on this list, write a brief character sketch of him.

Vocabulary Practice

Exercise On your paper, write the word from the list that best completes each sentence below.

1. The quiet in the abandoned building was ____ and frightening.
2. Greg's dad made a long and ____ speech about math homework.
3. When Lemon Brown would ____ to play and sing, a hush would fall on the room.
4. Greg spoke ____ into the darkness, "Who's there?"
5. He hoped he could ____ over the railing if he needed to get away.

Words to Know and Use

commence
impromptu
ominous
tentatively
vault

Concept Review—Mood *Possible response: The mood is depressed and angry. These are details that create the mood: dark sky, angry, swirling clouds; father lecturing, letter saying Greg would probably flunk math*

Refer to Annotation A.

e x p l o r e

Fiction

The Euphio Question

KURT VONNEGUT, JR. (vän' ə gut)

Examine What You Know (Prior Knowledge)

"The Euphio Question" tells of an amazing machine that helps people forget all their troubles. The machine thus creates an escape from reality. In real life, people find many kinds of safe escapes, such as movies and sports, but they also find escapes that are dangerous. Make a list of ways, both safe and dangerous, that people use to escape the stresses of their world. Then, as you read, compare these escapes to the one in the story.

Expand Your Knowledge (Building Background)

The story you are about to read is science fiction, yet it is based on some of the actual space exploration research done in the 1950's. Since interplanetary space travel and satellites were then still in the future, scientists had to view the planets and stars through giant telescopes in observatories on earth. One valuable tool they used was the radio telescope, an instrument that picks up impulses called radio waves from objects in space that ordinary telescopes cannot see. The picture on this page shows a modern-day radio telescope. Notice how the scientist in "The Euphio Question" uses his radio telescope.

Enrich Your Reading (Reading Skill)

Clarify While reading a challenging selection like "The Euphio Question," you may want to stop occasionally to clarify, or make clear, important developments in the plot. Notice the questions labeled *clarify* throughout this story. When you come to these questions, think about what you have just read. If you are unable to answer the question, reread that part of the story to make sure you understand what has taken place.

■ *A biography of the author can be found on page 258.*

Objectives

- To understand and analyze a short work of fiction
- To identify and understand theme
- To recognize the use of flashback
- To use clarifying as a strategy for understanding story plot.
- To express understanding of the work through a choice of writing options, including dialogue, a report, explanation, and song titles

Prereading/Motivation

Examine What You Know

Discussion Prompts: What have you done to relieve the pressure or stress created by a problem? What have you observed or learned about other people's ways of escaping stress? How do you determine whether an escape is healthy or possibly harmful or dangerous?

Expand Your Knowledge

Discussion Prompts: What kinds of information do you think radio waves can give about objects in space? Why is it important to our world to focus on space exploration?

Enrich Your Reading

Questions are posed at various points of the selection. Have students stop and answer them. Allow students to reread parts of the story if necessary.

Thematic Link—The Best-Laid Plans

In "The Euphio Question," a man plans to market a machine that produces instant happiness but that leads to disastrous results for individuals and society.

Journal Writing

In "The Euphio Question," a machine offers an escape from reality by providing "instant happiness." Suggest these journal topics to students:

- What activities and experiences make you happy?
- In what ways do machines increase or decrease your happiness and well-being?

For other journal opportunities, refer students to Examine What You Know (p. 243), First Impressions and Broader Connections (p. 256), and Real Life Connections (p. T-255).

Additional Resources

UNIT TWO RESOURCE BOOK

Reader's Guidesheet, p. 38
Vocabulary Worksheet, p. 39
Selection and Vocabulary Check Tests, p. 40
Selection Test, pp. 41–42

Collaborative Learning

Opportunities for collaborative learning appear throughout the lesson and include Options for Learning activities 2 and 4 (p. 258) and Cross-Curricular Options (p. T-258).

Teaching Strategies

Vocabulary Preview

These vocabulary words are defined at the bottom of the selection page on which they appear. You may wish to discuss them briefly before students begin reading.

adversity hardship
anarchist one who challenges rules
apathetically without enthusiasm
appalled shocked
exploitation the taking advantage of
forte something one does well
haranguing scolding
invincible unbeatable
maudlin foolishly sentimental
monopoly complete control
monotonous lacking variety
oblivion nothingness
stamina ability to do a great deal
synthetic artificial
unscrupulous not concerned with right

Support for Students of Limited English Proficiency

- Use Reader's Guidesheet, p. 38.
- "The Euphio Question" contains some difficult terminology and concepts. Encourage peer support for answering the clarifying questions inserted in the text. You may also find it helpful to refer to the Structured Reading questions.
- Annotations E, G, H, N, S, V, DD, EE, and KK focus on troublesome terms and concepts.

Text Annotations

A. Literary Element: SETTING Ask students if the story is set in the past, present, or future, and how they can tell. *(Possible response: the world of the future, because a machine that provides tranquility does not exist in today's world).*

B. Literary Element: FLASHBACK Note that the narrator switches from talking about the present to talking about something that happened a while before to create a kind of story within a story. Have students identify the time referred to. *(six months before)*

The Euphio Question

KURT VONNEGUT, JR.

Ladies and gentlemen of the Federal Communications Commission,[1] I appreciate this opportunity to testify on the subject before you.

I'm sorry—or maybe *heartsick* is the word—that news has leaked out about it. But now that word is getting around and coming to your official notice, I might as well tell the story straight and pray to God that I can convince you that America doesn't want what we discovered.

I won't deny that all three of us—Lew Harrison, the radio announcer, Dr. Fred Bockman, the physicist, and myself, a sociology professor—found peace of mind. We did. And I won't say it's wrong for people to seek peace of mind. But if somebody thinks he wants peace of mind the way we found it, he'd be well advised to seek coronary thrombosis[2] instead. SR-1

A Lew, Fred, and I found peace of mind by sitting in easy chairs and turning on a gadget the size of a table-model television set. No herbs, no golden rule, no muscle control, no sticking our noses in other people's troubles to forget our own; no hobbies, Taoism,[3] push-ups or contemplation of a lotus.[4] The gadget is, I think, what a lot of people vaguely foresaw as the crowning achievement of civilization: an electronic something-or-other, cheap, easily mass produced, that can, at the flick of a switch, provide tranquillity. I see you have one here. SR-2

B My first brush with synthetic peace of mind was six months ago. It was also then that I got to know Lew Harrison, I'm sorry to say. Lew is chief announcer of our town's only radio station. He makes his living with his loud mouth, and I'd be surprised if it were anyone but he who brought this matter to your attention.

Lew has, along with about thirty other shows, a weekly science program. Every week he gets some professor from Wyandotte College and interviews him about his particular field. Well, six months ago Lew worked up a program around a young

1. **Federal Communications Commission:** the government body that regulates and licenses all radio and television operations.
2. **coronary thrombosis** (kôr′ ə ner′ ē thräm bō′ sis): a blood clot in the heart.
3. **Taoism** (dou′ iz′ əm): Chinese philosophy and religion that stresses simplicity, patience, and harmony.
4. **contemplation of a lotus:** a reference to the Hindu religious practice of meditation.

Words to Know and Use	**synthetic** (sin thet′ ik) *adj.* not natural; artificial

244

STRUCTURED READING FOR LESS PROFICIENT STUDENTS

These questions can help to guide students through the reading. Ask each question at the point of the selection where the SR number appears in the margin.

SR–1 Who is the narrator of the story? Where is he? *(a sociology professor; at a Federal Communications Commission meeting)* **Literal recall**

SR–2 Who are Lew Harrison and Dr. Fred Bockman? How did they and the narrator attain tranquility? *(a radio announcer and a physicist; sitting in easy chairs and turning on a gadget)* **Literal recall**

SR–3 What is Lew interviewing Fred about? *(signals from outer space picked up by Fred's radio telescope)* **Recognizing relevant details**

SR–4 Why do the signals affect even those who have not listened to the broadcast? *(Amplified by the broadcast, the signals are so powerful that nobody within range can escape them.)* **Cause and effect**

Continued on page 245

dreamer and faculty friend of mine, Dr. Fred Bockman. I gave Fred a lift to the radio station, and he invited me to come on in and watch. For the heck of it, I did.

Fred Bockman is thirty and looks eighteen. Life has left no marks on him because he hasn't paid much attention to it. What he pays most of his attention to, and what Lew Harrison wanted to interview him about, is this eight-ton umbrella of his that he listens to the stars with. It's a big radio antenna rigged up on a telescope mount. The way I understand it, instead of looking at the stars through a telescope, he aims this thing out in space and picks up radio signals coming from different heavenly bodies.

Of course, there aren't people running radio stations out there. It's just that many of the heavenly bodies pour out a lot of
C energy and some of it can be picked up in the radio-frequency band. One good thing Fred's rig does is to spot stars hidden from telescopes by big clouds of cosmic dust. Radio signals from them get through the
SR-3 ▶ clouds to Fred's antenna.

That isn't all the outfit can do, and, in his interview with Fred, Lew Harrison saved the most exciting part until the end of the
D program. "That's very interesting, Dr. Bockman," Lew said. "Tell me, has your radio telescope turned up anything else about the universe that hasn't been revealed by ordinary light telescopes?"

This was the snapper. "Yes, it has," Fred said. "We've found about fifty spots in space, *not hidden by cosmic dust,* that give off powerful radio signals. Yet no heavenly
E bodies at all seem to be there."

"Well!" Lew said in mock surprise. "I should say that *is* something! Ladies and gentlemen, for the first time in radio history, we bring you the noise from Dr. Bockman's mysterious voids." They had strung a line out to Fred's antenna on the campus. Lew waved to the engineer to switch in the signals coming from it. "Ladies and gentlemen, the voice of nothingness!" E

What unusual signals has Fred Bockman discovered with his radio telescope?

F

The noise wasn't much to hear—a wavering hiss, more like a leaking tire than anything else. It was supposed to be on the air for five seconds. When the engineer switched it off, Fred and I were inexplicably grinning like idiots. I felt relaxed and tingling. Lew Harrison looked as though he'd stumbled into the dressing room at the Copacabana.[5] He glanced at the studio clock, appalled. The monotonous hiss had been on the air for five minutes! If the engineer's cuff hadn't accidentally caught on the switch, it might be on yet. G

Fred laughed nervously, and Lew hunted for his place in the script. "The hiss from nowhere," Lew said. "Dr. Bockman, has anyone proposed a name for these interesting voids?"

"No," Fred said. "At the present time they have neither a name nor an explanation."

The voids the hiss came from have still to be explained, but I've suggested a name for them that shows signs of sticking: "Bockman's Euphoria." We may not know what the spots are, but we know what they do, so the name's a good one. Euphoria, since it means a sense of buoyancy and well-being, is really the only word that will do. H

5. **Copacabana** (kō′ pə kə ban′ ə): a famous nightclub.

Words to Know and Use

appalled (ə pôld′) *adj.* shocked **appall** *v.*
monotonous (mə nät′ ′n əs) *adj.* lacking variety; tiresome

245

C. Historical Sidelight An American engineer, Karl G. Jansky, discovered radio waves (a type of electromagnetic wave) from space in 1931. The first radio telescope was built in the late 1930's by an American amateur radio operator. However, a British astronomer, Sir Bernard Lovell, built the first giant radio telescope in 1957 in Manchester, England.

D. Literary Element: DIALOGUE Have students tell how the narrative changes at this point. *(Possible response: The narrative jumps from the narrator's observations to the actual radio show interview about Fred's radio telescope.)*

E. LEP Support: Vocabulary The concept of *voids* may be confusing to students. Explain that a *void* is an "empty area in space where there are no stars or other heavenly bodies."

F. Clarifying Answer: *(radio waves)*

G. LEP Support: Subtle Humor To help students understand Lew's facial expression, explain that women performed in shows at the Copacabana nightclub in very flimsy costumes. The women obviously wouldn't be wearing very much in their dressing rooms.

H. LEP Support: Vocabulary The meaning of *buoyancy* may not be clear to students. Explain that, as used here, it means "vivacity" or "tendency to float." Students may wish to describe the feeling of euphoria and tell of times they have experienced this "natural high."

Structured Reading for Less Proficient Students

Continued from page 244

SR–5 What does the prospect of marketing the euphio machine reveal about the values and personalities of Fred and Lew? *(Fred is cautious and doesn't feel right about marketing the machine; Lew is a conniver who cares only about money.)* **Inferring**

SR–6 What conclusions can you draw so far about how the machine affects people? *(The machine removes people's motivation to act and turns sensible people into giggling idiots.)* **Drawing conclusions**

SR–7 Summarize some of the effects the machine has on people. *(It takes away awareness of danger; people's ability to protect themselves; their awareness of time and ability to care for their needs.)* **Summarizing**

SR–8 What happens to the euphio machine? *(Fred and the narrator smash it.)* **Literal recall**

SR–9 How do you know that the world has not seen the last of the euphio machine? *(During the narrator's plea to ban euphio, another euphio machine is turned on, and the narrator loses touch with reality.)* **Drawing conclusions**

I. Reading Skill: INFERRING Ask students why they think Fred, Lew, and the narrator are embarrassed by the emotion they feel. *(Possible responses: They are not used to feeling so happy and carefree; they do not understand why they feel so good and are confused.)*

J. Reading Skill: PREDICTING Ask students to speculate on what the narrator's hunch may be. *(Possible response: that his family has also been subjected to the radio signals; that the radio signals somehow caused happy, carefree feelings and unusual behavior)*

K. Reading Skill: INFERRING Ask students if they believe Marion really lied. Have them explain their answers. *(Possible response: Marion probably did not lie, since the radio waves seem to have caused a lot of unusual behavior.)*

After the broadcast, Fred, Lew, and I were cordial to one another to the point of being maudlin.

"I can't remember when a broadcast has been such a pleasure," Lew said. Sincerity is not his forte, yet he meant it.

"It's been one of the most memorable experiences of my life," Fred said, looking puzzled. "Extraordinarily pleasant."

I We were all embarrassed by the emotion we felt and parted company in bafflement and haste. I hurried home for a drink, only to walk into the middle of another unsettling experience.

The house was quiet, and I made two trips through it before discovering that I was not alone. My wife, Susan, a good and lovable woman who prides herself on feeding her family well and on time, was lying on the couch, staring dreamily at the ceiling. "Honey," I said tentatively, "I'm home. It's suppertime."

"Fred Bockman was on the radio today," she said in a faraway voice.

"I know. I was with him in the studio."

"He was out of this world," she sighed. "Simply out of this world. That noise from space—when he turned that on, everything just seemed to drop away from me. I've been lying here, just trying to get over it."

"Uh-huh," I said, biting my lip. "Well, guess I'd better round up Eddie." Eddie is my ten-year-old son and captain of an apparently invincible neighborhood baseball team.

"Save your strength, Pop," said a small voice from the shadows.

"You home? What's the matter? Game called off on account of atomic attack?"

"Nope. We finished eight innings."

"Beating 'em so bad they didn't want to go on, eh?"

"Oh, they were doing pretty good. Score was tied, and they had two men on and two outs." He talked as though he were recounting a dream. "And then," he said, his eyes widening, "everybody kind of lost interest, just wandered off. I came home and found the old lady curled up here, so I lay down on the floor."

"Why?" I asked incredulously.

"Pop," Eddie said thoughtfully, "I'm damned if I know."

"Eddie!" his mother said.

"Mom," Eddie said, "I'm damned if *you* know either."

I was damned if anybody could explain it, but I had a nagging hunch. I dialed Fred Bockman's number. "Fred, am I getting you up from dinner?" J

"I wish you were," Fred said. "Not a scrap to eat in the house, and I let Marion have the car today so she could do the marketing. Now she's trying to find a grocery open."

"Couldn't get the car started, eh?"

"Sure she got the car started," said Fred. "She even got to the market. Then she felt so good she walked right out of the place again." Fred sounded depressed. "I guess it's a woman's privilege to change her mind, but it's the lying that hurts."

"Marion lied? I don't believe it." K

"She tried to tell me everybody wandered out of the market with her—clerks and all."

"Fred," I said, "I've got news for you. Can I drive out right after supper?" ◀ SR-4

When I arrived at Fred Bockman's farm, he was staring, dumbfounded, at the evening paper.

"The whole town went nuts!" Fred said. "For no reason at all, all the cars pulled up

Words to Know and Use	
	maudlin (môd′ lin) *adj.* foolishly sentimental; corny
	forte (fôrt) *n.* something a person does especially well
	invincible (in vin′ sə bəl) *adj.* unbeatable

REAL LIFE CONNECTIONS

To help students understand the idea of the effect of a signal being sent through a radio, ask them if they have ever heard a radio station doing a test by broadcasting one tone for about a minute. If so, ask students how they reacted to it. Perhaps some may have felt that the sound put them into a kind of trance.

Talk about listening to other continuous sounds and the effects they have on the mind. Some students may use a specific sound to help them meditate. Invite those students to explain what happens to them during this exercise. Invite discussion about why the mind relaxes as a result. Suggest that a possible explanation may be that the tone obliterates all other stimuli, thus causing the brain to relax or focus.

to the curb like there was a hook and ladder going by. Says here people shut up in the middle of sentences and stayed that way for five minutes. Hundreds wandered around in the cold in their shirt sleeves, grinning like toothpaste ads." He rattled the paper. "This *is* what you wanted to talk to me about?"

I nodded. "It all happened when that noise was being broadcast, and I thought maybe—"

"The odds are about one in a million that there's any maybe about it," said Fred. "The time checks to the second."

"But most people weren't listening to the program."

L "They didn't have to listen, if my theory's right. We took those faint signals from space, amplified them about a thousand times, and rebroadcast them. Anybody within reach of the transmitter would get a good dose of the stepped-up radiations, whether he wanted to or not." He shrugged. "Apparently that's like walking past a

SR-5 ▶ field of burning marijuana."

M **clarify** What effects have these strange radio signals had on people?

"How come you never felt the effect at work?"

"Because I never amplified and rebroadcast the signals. The radio station's transmitter is what really put the sock into them."

"So what're you going to do next?"

Fred looked surprised. "Do? What is there to do but report it in some suitable journal?"

Without a preliminary knock, the front door burst open, and Lew Harrison, florid and panting, swept into the room and removed his great polo coat with a bullfighterlike flourish. "You're cutting him in on it, too?" he demanded, pointing at me. N

Fred blinked at him. "In on what?"

"The millions," Lew said. "The billions."

"Wonderful," Fred said. "What are you talking about?"

"The noise from the stars!" Lew said. "They love it. It drives 'em nuts. Didja see the papers?" He sobered for an instant. "It *was* the noise that did it, wasn't it, Doc?"

"We think so," Fred said. He looked worried. "How, exactly, do you propose we get our hands on these millions or billions?"

"Real estate!" Lew said raptly. " 'Lew,' I said to myself, 'Lew, how can you cash in on this gimmick if you can't get a monopoly on the universe? And, Lew,' I asked myself, 'how can you sell the stuff when anybody can get it free while you're broadcasting it?' " O

"Maybe it's the kind of thing that shouldn't be cashed in on," I suggested. "I mean, we don't know a great deal about—"

"Is happiness bad?" Lew interrupted.

"No," I admitted.

"Okay, and what we'd do with this stuff from the stars is make people happy. Now I suppose you're going to tell me that's bad?"

"People ought to be happy," Fred said.

"Okay, okay," Lew said loftily. "That's what we're going to do for the people. And the way the people can show their gratitude is in real estate." He looked out the window. "Good—a barn. We can start right there. We set up a transmitter in the barn, run a line out to your antenna, Doc, and we've got a real-estate development."

"Sorry," Fred said. "I don't follow you.

Words to Know and Use

monopoly (mə näp′ ə lē) *n.* complete control of the sale of a product or service

247

L. Reading Skill: CONTEXT CLUES Have students use clues in the paragraph to explain the meaning of *amplified*. *(Possible responses: The meaning is "made louder and stronger"; context clues: "faint signals," "thousand times," "stepped-up," "good dose")*

M. Clarifying Answer: *The strange radio signals put people in a dreamlike state; made them stop what they were doing; and put them out of touch with reality.*

N. LEP Support: Vocabulary The word *florid* may be troublesome for students. Explain that it means "reddish or rosy in color." Note that it refers to Lew's face looking flushed from excitement. Ask students what words they have in their native languages that have a similar meaning.

O. Literary Element: CHARACTER Have students describe the kind of man Lew appears to be, based on his pitch to Fred and the narrator. *(Possible responses: a selfish man who sees only the money side of the discovery; a manipulator)*

Literary Sidelight According to author Dr. Stanley Shatt, "Vonnegut's scientists frequently discover that they have unwittingly opened a modern version of Pandora's box, and the question becomes whether or not mankind has the emotional, spiritual, and moral strength to match its technological progress." After students finish reading, talk about how this statement applies to this story.

P. Literary Element: SATIRE Ask students if they feel the narrator is being serious when he comes up with the name "Euphoria Heights" or is ridiculing Lew's sales pitch. *(Possible response: Students may feel that the narrator is being sarcastic.)*

Q. Reading Skill: INFERRING Ask students what Fred is implying about Lew's suggestion by his comment to Lew. *(Possible response: He feels that it is not morally right to do what Lew is suggesting.)*

R. Clarifying Answer: *His plans are to use the transmitter sets to send the signals into people's homes. Lew wants to handle the "business end," and is intent on making a lot of money from the venture.*

This place wouldn't do for a development. The roads are poor, no bus service or shopping center, the view is lousy, and the ground is full of rocks."

Lew nudged Fred several times with his elbow. "Doc, Doc, Doc—sure it's got drawbacks, but with that transmitter in the barn, you can give them the most precious thing in all creation—happiness." P

"Euphoria Heights," I said.

"That's great!" said Lew. "I'd get the prospects, Doc, and you'd sit up there in the barn with your hand on the switch. Once a prospect set foot on Euphoria Heights, and you shot the happiness to him, there's nothing he wouldn't pay for a lot."

"Every house a home, as long as the power doesn't fail," I said.

"Then," Lew said, his eyes shining, "when we sell all the lots here, we move the transmitter and start another development. Maybe we'd get a fleet of transmitters going." He snapped his fingers. "Sure! Mount 'em on wheels."

"I somehow don't think the police would think highly of us," Fred said.

"Okay, so when they come to investigate, you throw the old switch and give *them* a jolt of happiness." He shrugged. "Hell, I might even get bighearted and let them have a corner lot."

Q "No," Fred said quietly. "If I ever joined a church, I couldn't face the minister."

"So we give *him* a jolt," Lew said brightly.

"No," Fred said. "Sorry."

"Okay," Lew said, rising and pacing the floor. "I was prepared for that. I've got an alternative, and this one's strictly legitimate. We'll make a little amplifier with a transmitter and an aerial on it. Shouldn't cost over fifty bucks to make, so we'd price it in the range of the common man—five hundred bucks, say. We make arrangements with the phone company to pipe signals from your antenna right into the homes of people with these sets. The sets take the signal from the phone line, amplify it, and broadcast it through the houses to make everybody in them happy. See? Instead of turning on the radio or television, everybody's going to want to turn on the happiness. No casts, no stage sets, no expensive cameras—no nothing but that hiss."

"We could call it the euphoriaphone," I suggested, "or 'euphio' for short."

"That's great, that's great!" Lew said. "What do you say, Doc?"

"I don't know." Fred looked worried. "This sort of thing is out of my line." ◀SR-6

"We all have to recognize our limitations, Doc," Lew said expansively. "I'll handle the business end, and you handle the technical end." He made a motion as though to put on his coat. "Or maybe you don't want to be a millionaire?"

"Oh, yes, yes indeed I do," Fred said quickly. "Yes indeed."

"All righty," Lew said, dusting his palms, "the first thing we've gotta do is build one of the sets and test her."

What are Lew Harrison's plans for this new discovery?

R

This part of it *was* down Fred's alley, and I could see the problem interested him. "It's really a pretty simple gadget," he said. "I suppose we could throw one together and run a test out here next week."

The first test of the euphoriaphone, or euphio, took place in Fred Bockman's living room on a Saturday afternoon, five days after Fred's and Lew's sensational radio broadcast.

There were six guinea pigs—Lew, Fred and his wife Marion, myself, my wife Susan,

DATA BANK

Most radio telescopes are described as having a parabolic bowl-shaped reflector to collect the radio waves from space. The reflectors are constructed with wires or metal sheets and are turned by motors toward different areas of the sky. The reflector of the telescope focuses the radio waves on a small radio antenna that changes them into an electric signal.

At that point, an astronomer uses a radio receiver to receive the electric signals and tune in only the ones that he or she wants to study. The receiver amplifies the signals so that they can be recorded—either as wavy lines on paper or as data on a tape. The data on tape can be analyzed by a computer.

and my son Eddie. The Bockmans had arranged chairs in a circle around a card table, on which rested a gray steel box.

Protruding from the box was a long buggy-whip aerial that scraped the ceiling. While Fred fussed with the box, the rest of us made nervous small talk over sandwiches and beer. Eddie, of course, wasn't drinking beer, though he was badly in need of a sedative. He was annoyed at having been brought out to the farm instead of to a ball game and was threatening to take it out on the Bockmans' Early American furnishings. He was playing a spirited game of flies and S grounders with himself near the French doors, using a dead tennis ball and a poker.

"Eddie," Susan said for the tenth time, "please stop."

"It's under control, under control," Eddie said disdainfully, playing the ball off four walls and catching it with one hand.

Marion, who vents her maternal instincts on her immaculate furnishings, couldn't hide her distress at Eddie's turning the place into a gymnasium. Lew, in his way, was trying to calm her. "Let him wreck the dump," Lew said. "You'll be moving into a palace one of these days."

"It's ready," Fred said softly.

T We looked at him with queasy bravery. Fred plugged two jacks from the phone line into the gray box. This was the direct line to his antenna on the campus, and clockwork would keep the antenna fixed on one of the mysterious voids in the sky—the most potent of Bockman's Euphoria. He plugged a cord from the box into an electrical outlet in the baseboard, and rested his hand on a switch. "Ready?"

"Don't, Fred!" I said. I was scared stiff.

"Turn it on, turn it on," Lew said. "We U wouldn't have the telephone today if Bell hadn't had the guts to call somebody up."

"I'll stand right here by the switch, ready to flick her off if something goes sour," Fred said reassuringly. There was a click, a hum, and the euphio was on.

A deep, unanimous sigh filled the room. The poker slipped from Eddie's hands. He moved across the room in a stately sort of waltz, knelt by his mother, and laid his head in her lap. Fred drifted away from his post, humming, his eyes half closed.

Lew Harrison was the first to speak, continuing his conversation with Marion. "But who cares for material wealth?" he asked earnestly. He turned to Susan for confirmation.

"Uh-uh," said Susan, shaking her head dreamily. She put her arms around Lew, and kissed him for about five minutes.

"Say," I said, patting Susan on the back,

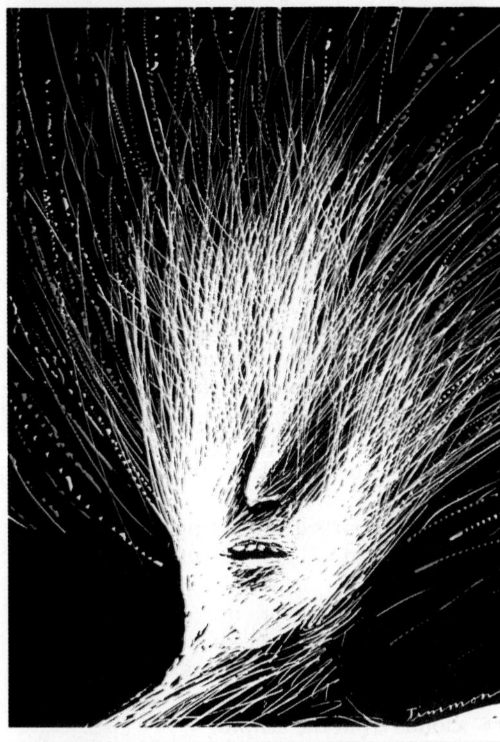

© 1987 Bonnie Timmons/Image Bank, Chicago.

Art Note
Bonnie Timmons is an award-winning contemporary illustrator and a writer. Her book *Orville's Outing* was published in 1983. For several years, she worked as a medical illustrator with the Peace Corps in Nairobi, Kenya. In this apparently electrified head, the artist portrays a devastating effect like that of a powerful drug. *How is this painting similar to what happens to Bockman and the others in "The Euphio Question"?*

S. LEP Support: Language Students may not understand the references to *flies and grounders* and to *French doors.* Give students the opportunity to explain what they think Eddie is doing. If necessary, explain that he is hitting balls in the air and on the ground. Also explain that the doors are double doors that open from the center and are made mostly of glass.

T. Reading Skill: INFERRING
Have students tell what the narrator conveys about the feelings of most of the group, Lew excepted. *(Possible response: that they are feeling a little shaky and uncertain, although they are trying to be brave)*

U. Historical Sidelight Some students may not understand the reference to Bell. If necessary, explain that Lew is referring to Alexander Graham Bell, who invented the telephone.

V. LEP Support: Language It may not be clear to students that Lew has fallen on the stone hearth and hit his head on a metal log support. Discuss the seriousness of what has happened to him and compare this to his reaction.

W. Literary Element: IMAGERY Point out the narrator's words, "warm fog of silence." Ask students what they imagine from this description. *(Possible response: being in a fog so thick that you can't see or hear anything and feeling warm and cozy)*

X. Literary Sidelight Note the state trooper's reference to his gun being "just like Hoppy's." He is referring to Hopalong Cassidy, a TV cowboy who rode a white horse and was very popular during the 1950's.

"you kids get along swell, don't you? Isn't that nice, Fred?"

"Eddie," Marion said solicitously, "I think there's a real baseball in the hall closet. A *hard* ball. Wouldn't that be more fun than that old tennis ball?" Eddie didn't stir.

Fred was still prowling around the room, smiling, his eyes now closed all the way. His heel caught in a lamp cord, and he went sprawling on the hearth, his head in the ashes. "Hi-ho, everybody," he said, his eyes still closed. "Bunged my head on an andiron."[6] He stayed there, giggling occasionally. V

"The doorbell's been ringing for a while," Susan said. "I don't suppose it means anything."

"Come in, come in," I shouted. This somehow struck everyone as terribly funny. We all laughed uproariously, including Fred, whose guffaws blew up little gray clouds from the ashpit. SR-7▶

A small, very serious old man in white had let himself in, and was now standing in the vestibule, looking at us with alarm. "Milkman," he said uncertainly. He held out a slip of paper to Marion. "I can't read the last line in your note," he said. "What's that say about cottage cheese, cheese, cheese, cheese, cheese . . ." His voice trailed off as he settled, tailor-fashion, to the floor beside Marion. After he'd been silent for perhaps three quarters of an hour, a look of concern crossed his face. "Well," he said apathetically, "I can only stay for a minute. My truck's parked out on the shoulder, kind of blocking things." He started to stand. Lew gave the volume knob on the euphio a twist. The milkman wilted to the floor.

"Aaaaaaaaaaah," said everbody.

"Good day to be indoors," the milkman said. "Radio says we'll catch the tail end of the Atlantic hurricane."

"Let 'er come," I said. "I've got my car parked under a big, dead tree." It seemed to make sense. Nobody took exception to it. I lapsed back into a warm fog of silence and thought of nothing whatsoever. These lapses seemed to last for a matter of seconds before they were interrupted by conversation of newcomers. Looking back, I see now that the lapses were rarely less than six hours. W

I was snapped out of one, I recall, by a repetition of the doorbell's ringing. "I said come in," I mumbled.

"And I did," the milkman mumbled.

The door swung open, and a state trooper glared in at us. "Who the hell's got his milk truck out there blocking the road?" he demanded. He spotted the milkman. "Aha! Don't you know somebody could get killed, coming around a blind curve into that thing?" He yawned, and his ferocious expression gave way to an affectionate smile. "It's so damn' unlikely," he said, "I don't know why I ever brought it up." He sat down by Eddie. "Hey, kid—like guns?" He took his revolver from its holster. "Look—just like Hoppy's." X

Eddie took the gun, aimed it at Marion's bottle collection and fired. A large blue bottle popped to dust and the window behind the collection splintered. Cold air roared in through the opening.

"He'll make a cop yet," Marion chortled.

6. **andiron** (and′ ī′ ərn): one of the two metal supports for logs in a fireplace.

Words to Know and Use

apathetically (ap′ ə thet′ ik lē) *adv.* without enthusiasm

250

Professional Notebook

In a set of recent studies . . . I focused on the meaning-making process itself—examining how students think when they read for literary purposes (in response to short stories and poems). My work indicates that there is a series of changing relations that the reader adopts toward a text, with each aspect of the reader/text relationship adding a somewhat different dimension to the reader's understanding of the entire piece. These stances are not linear, have the potential to recur at any point in the reading, and are a function of varying interactions between the reader and the text. . . . The four major stances in the process of interpretation are:

Being Out and Stepping In *In this stance readers make initial contacts with the genre, content, structure, and language of the text by using prior knowledge and surface features to get sufficient information to begin to build an envisionment. . . .*

Continued on page 251

"God, I'm happy," I said, feeling a little like crying. "I got the swellest little kid and the swellest bunch of friends and the swellest old wife in the world." I heard the gun go off twice more, and then dropped
Y into heavenly oblivion.

Again the doorbell roused me. "How many times do I have to tell you—for Heaven's sake, come in," I said, without opening my eyes.

"I *did*," the milkman said.

I heard the tramping of many feet, but had no curiosity about them. A little later, I noticed that I was having difficulty breathing. Investigation revealed that I had slipped to the floor, and that several Boy Scouts had bivouacked[7] on my chest and abdomen.

"You want something?" I asked the tenderfoot whose hot, measured breathing was in my face.

"Beaver Patrol wanted old newspapers, but forget it," he said. "We'd just have to carry 'em somewhere."

"And do your parents know where you are?"

"Oh, sure. They got worried and came after us." He jerked his thumb at several couples lined up against the baseboard, smiling into the teeth of the wind and rain lashing in at them through the broken window.

"Mom, I'm kinda hungry," Eddie said.

"Oh, Eddie—you're not going to make your mother cook just when we're having
Z such a wonderful time," Susan said.

Lew Harrison gave the euphio's volume knob another twist. "There, kid, how's that?"

"Aaaaaaaaaaah," said everybody.

When awareness intruded on oblivion again, I felt around for the Beaver Patrol and found them missing. I opened my eyes to see that they and Eddie and the milkman and Lew and the trooper were standing by a picture window, cheering. The wind outside was roaring and slashing savagely and driving raindrops through the broken window as though they'd been fired from air rifles. I shook Susan gently, and together we went to the window to see what might be so entertaining.

"She's going, she's going, she's going," the milkman cried ecstatically.

Susan and I arrived just in time to join in the cheering as a big elm crashed down on our sedan.

"Kee-*runch*!" said Susan, and I laughed until my stomach hurt.

"Get Fred," Lew said urgently. "He's gonna miss seeing the barn go!"

"H'mm?" Fred said from the fireplace.

"Aw, Fred, you missed it," Marion said.

"Now we're really gonna see something," Eddie yelled. "The power line's going to get it this time. Look at that poplar lean!"

The poplar leaned closer, closer, closer to the power line; and then a gust brought it down in a hail of sparks and a tangle of wires. The lights in the house went off.

Now there was only the sound of the wind. "How come nobody cheered?" Lew said faintly. "The euphio—it's off!"

A horrible groan came from the fireplace. "God, I think I've got a concussion."

Marion knelt by her husband and wailed. "Darling, my poor darling—what happened to you?"

7. **bivouacked** (biv′ wakt′): camped out.

Words to Know and Use

oblivion (ə bliv′ ē ən) *n.* nothingness

251

Y. Literary Sidelight Vonnegut is known for his use of humor to convey a very pessimistic view of life. On the surface, the situations created by the effects of the euphio machine are quite laughable. However, what Vonnegut is showing is his view of society "willing itself to its own inevitable destruction, or man as a hapless pawn in an arbitrary and incomprehensible world," as critic Peter J. Reed has said. You may wish to share this information with students now as it relates to the events of the story and to Lew's behavior (see annotation Z), or you may include it later in a discussion about the story's theme.

Z. Reading Skill: INFERRING Point out how Lew raises the euphio volume in response to human need and ask students what the author may be saying about the human situation. *(Possible responses: that people cannot always be trusted to do the right thing; that a machine can be dangerous in the hands of the wrong person)*

PROFESSIONAL NOTEBOOK

Continued from page 250

Being In and Moving Through *In this stance readers are immersed in the text world . . . They take new information and immediately use it to go beyond what they already understand—asking questions about motivation, causality, and implications.*

Being In and Stepping Out *In this stance readers use their text knowledge to reflect on personal knowledge. They use what they read . . . to reflect on their own lives, on the lives of others, or on the human condition.*

Stepping Out and Objectifying the Experience *In this stance readers distance themselves from the text world, reflecting on and reacting to both the content and the experience. They objectify the text, judge it, and relate it to other texts or experiences. . . .*

JUDITH A. LANGER, "UNDERSTANDING LITERATURE," *Language Arts*, DECEMBER 1990.

Art Note

Screenprinting, the method used by contemporary artist Linda Smith for *At Home,* may produce as many as 200 prints of one picture. Using a stenciled screen on which areas not to be printed are blocked with a resistant substance, the printmaker forces pigment through the mesh onto the paper placed under it. For more than one color, additional screens are used. *How many objects can you identify in this picture?*

AA. Reading Skill: CONTEXT CLUES Have students identify the clues that explain what a *hag* is. *(Possible responses: "dreadful, dirty old"; "red eyes sunk deep in her head"; "hair like Medusa's"; "witch")*

BB. Reading Skill: INFERRING Ask students what seems to happen to people's senses when they are under the influence of the euphio machine. *(Possible responses: Their sensory impressions become scrambled or reversed and are misinterpreted by the brain.)*

AT HOME 1988 Linda Smith Screenprint Courtesy of Schwartz Cierlak Gallery, Santa Monica, California.

I looked at the woman I had my arms around—a dreadful, dirty old hag, with red
AA eyes sunk deep in her head and hair like Medusa's.[8] "Ugh," I said, and turned away in disgust.

"Honey," wept the witch, "it's me—Susan."

Moans filled the air, and pitiful cries for food and water. Suddenly the room had become terribly cold. Only a moment before I had imagined I was in the tropics. BB

"Who's got my damn' pistol?" the trooper said bleakly.

8. **hair like Medusa's:** In Greek mythology, Medusa's hair was a tangle of snakes.

REAL LIFE CONNECTIONS

Students may realize that the actions of the people under the effect of the euphio machine are in some ways similar to those of a mentally disturbed person or to those of a person heavily influenced by alcohol or drugs. Talk with students about stories they have read or films they have seen where people behave in a similar manner.

A Western Union boy I hadn't noticed before was sitting in a corner, miserably leafing through a pile of telegrams and making clucking noises.

I shuddered. "I'll bet it's Sunday morning," I said. "We've been here twelve hours!" It was Monday morning.

The Western Union boy was thunderstruck. "Sunday morning? I walked in here on a Sunday night." He stared around the room. "Looks like them newsreels of SR-8 ▶ Buchenwald,[9] don't it?"

The chief of the Beaver Patrol, with the incredible stamina of the young, was the hero of the day. He fell in his men in two ranks, haranguing them like an old Army top-kick. While the rest of us lay draped around the room, whimpering about hunger, cold, and thirst, the patrol started the furnace again, brought blankets, applied compresses to Fred's head and countless barked shins, blocked off the broken window, and made buckets of cocoa and coffee.

CC **clarify** What happens during the test of the machine at Fred's house?

Within two hours of the time that the power and the euphio went off, the house was warm and we had eaten. The serious respiratory cases—the parents who had sat near the broken window for twenty-four hours—had been pumped full of penicillin and hauled off to the hospital. The milkman, the Western Union boy, and the trooper had refused treatment and gone home. The Beaver Patrol had saluted smartly and left. Outside, repairmen were working on the power line. Only the original group remained—Lew, Fred and Marion, Susan and myself, and Eddie. Fred, it turned out, had some pretty important-looking contusions and abrasions,[10] but no concussion.

Susan had fallen asleep right after eating. Now she stirred. "What happened?"

"Happiness," I told her. "Incomparable, continuous happiness—happiness by the kilowatt."

Lew Harrison, who looked like an anarchist with his red eyes and fierce black beard, had been writing furiously in one corner of the room. "That's good—happiness by the kilowatt," he said. "Buy your happiness the way you buy light."

"Contract happiness the way you contract influenza," Fred said. He sneezed. DD

Lew ignored him. "It's a campaign, see? The first ad is for the long-hairs: 'The price of one book, which may be a disappointment, will buy you sixty hours of euphio. Euphio never disappoints.' Then we'd hit the middle class with the next one—" EE

"In the groin?" Fred said.

"What's the matter with you people?" Lew said. "You act as though the experiment had failed."

"Pneumonia and malnutrition are what we'd *hoped* for?" Marion said.

"We had a cross-section of America in this room, and we made every last person happy," Lew said, "not for just an hour, not

9. **Buchenwald** (bo͞o′ k'n wôld'): site of a Nazi concentration camp in Germany near Weimar.

10. **contusions** (kən ty͞o͞o′zhənz) **and abrasions** (ə brā′zhənz): bruises and scrapes.

Words to Know and Use

stamina (stam′ ə nə) *n.* the ability to do a great deal without getting tired
haranguing (hə raŋ′ iŋ) *adj.* delivering a lengthy, noisy, or scolding speech **harangue** *v.*
anarchist (an′ ər kist′) *n.* someone who challenges society's rules or accepted standards of behavior

CC. Clarifying Answer: *People lose control of their minds, become destructive, lose all initiative, and are not able to react except to laugh or to stare as though in a fog.*

DD. LEP Support: Language Students may not understand the sarcasm in Fred's comment. Have a volunteer speak Fred's words, using the tone of voice that Fred might use, to help students determine whether Fred is being serious or is ridiculing Lew.

EE. LEP Support: Subtle Humor Explain that the *long-hairs* Lew refers to are the intellectuals of society.

DATA BANK

Radio telescopes not only can receive signals but also can send powerful radio waves to the moon and the planets. The radio telescope then picks up the radio echoes coming back from the moon or planet. This technique is called *radar astronomy* because it operates on the same principle as radar. The technique is useful to astronomers, who can use the echoes to make a map of the moon or planet that shows very minute details.

FF. Literary Element: IRONY Remind students that writers can use irony to convey an attitude or belief that is opposite in meaning to that which is stated. Ask students what the irony is in Lew's comments about the euphio machine bringing families together and saving the American home. *(Possible response: The euphio machine cannot bring families together because it dehumanizes people and leaves them unable to think and communicate in the real world.)*

GG. Literary Concept: THEME Have students explain the author's message. *(Possible response: He is warning about the dangers of turning to machines in search of profit, comfort, or freedom from cares. They might seem wonderful but could prove to be deadly to humanity.)*

HH. Reading Skill: INFERRING Ask students what Marion realizes at this point. *(The return of electricity would mean that the euphio machine would be on again.)*

II. Clarifying Answer: Fred and the narrator realize how dangerous the machine is, and they don't feel that the public should be exposed to it.

for just a day, but for two days without a break." He arose reverently from his chair. "So what we do to keep it from killing the euphio fans is to have the thing turned on and off with clockwork, see? The owner sets it so it'll go on just as he comes home from work; then it'll go off again while he eats supper; then it goes on after supper, off again when it's bedtime; on again after breakfast, off when it's time to go to work, then on again for the wife and kids."

He ran his hands through his hair and rolled his eyes. "And the selling points—my God, the selling points! No expensive toys for the kids. For the price of a trip to the movies, people can buy thirty hours of euphio. For the price of a fifth of whisky, they can buy sixty hours of euphio!"

"Or a big family bottle of potassium cyanide,"[11] Fred said.

FF "Don't you see it?" Lew said incredulously. "It'll bring families together again, save the American home. No more fights over what TV or radio program to listen to. Euphio pleases one and all—we proved that. And there is no such thing as a dull euphio program."

A knock on the door interrupted him. A repairman stuck his head in to announce that the power would be on again in about two minutes.

GG "Look, Lew," Fred said, "this little monster could kill civilization in less time than it took to burn down Rome.[12] We're not going into the mind-numbing business, and that's that."

"You're kidding!" Lew said, aghast. He turned to Marion. "Don't you want your husband to make a million?"

"Not by operating an electronic opium den," Marion said coldly.

Lew slapped his forehead. "It's what the public wants. This is like Louis Pasteur[13] refusing to pasteurize milk."

HH "It'll be good to have the electricity again," Marion said, changing the subject. "Lights, hot-water heater, the pump, the—oh, Lord!"

The lights came on the instant she said it, but Fred and I were already in mid-air, descending on the gray box. We crashed down on it together. The card table buckled, and the plug was jerked from the wall socket. The euphio's tubes glowed red for a moment, then died.

Expressionlessly, Fred took a screwdriver from his pocket and removed the top of the box.

"Would you enjoy doing battle with progress?" he said, offering me the poker Eddie had dropped.

In a frenzy, I stabbed and smashed at the euphio's glass and wire vitals. With my left hand, and with Fred's help, I kept Lew from throwing himself between the poker and the works. ◀ SR-9

How do Fred and the narrator feel about the euphio machine now?

II

"I thought you were on my side," Lew said.

---

11. **potassium cyanide** (pō tas′ ē əm sī′ ə nīd): a deadly poison.

12. **burn down Rome:** According to legend, while Rome was burning in A.D. 60, the cruel, self-obsessed emperor, Nero, fiddled.

13. **Louis Pasteur** (lo͞o′ ē pas tur′): French chemist who discovered that harmful microorganisms in food could be killed with heat.

PROFESSIONAL NOTEBOOK

In American reading instruction, the onus for success or failure has often been placed on books. The assumption that materials teach children is, of course, fallacious. However, it is also clear that some materials are better than others in fostering lifelong literacy. As educators have realized in the past and are learning again, students require numerous experiences with literature to become readers and writers. . . . Through literary connections, a fundamental goal of schooling is reached as students think and reflect.

LINDA S. LEVSTIK, "RESEARCH DIRECTIONS: MEDIATING CONTENT THROUGH LITERARY TEXTS," *Language Arts*, DECEMBER 1990.

"If you breathe one word about euphio to anyone," I said, "what I just did to euphio I will gladly do to you."

JJ And there, ladies and gentlemen of the Federal Communications Commission, I thought the matter had ended. It deserved to end there. Now, through the medium of Lew Harrison's big mouth, word has leaked out. KK He has petitioned you for permission to start commercial exploitation of euphio. He and his backers have built a radio telescope of their own.

Let me say again that all of Lew's claims are true. Euphio will do everything he says it will. The happiness it gives is perfect and unflagging in the face of incredible adversity. Near tragedies, such as the first experiment, can no doubt be avoided with clockwork to turn the sets on and off. I see that this set on the table before you is, in fact, equipped with clockwork.

LL The question is not whether euphio works. It does. The question is, rather, whether or not America is to enter a new and distressing phase of history where men no longer pursue happiness but buy it. This is no time for oblivion to become a national craze. The only benefit we could get from euphio would be if we could somehow lay down a peace-of-mind barrage on our enemies while protecting our own people from it.

In closing, I'd like to point out that Lew Harrison, the would-be czar of euphio, is an unscrupulous person, unworthy of public trust. It wouldn't surprise me, for instance, if he had set the clockwork on this sample euphio set so that its radiations would addle your judgments when you are trying to make a decision.

MM In fact, it seems to be whirring suspiciously at this very moment, and I'm so happy I could cry. I've got the swellest little kid and the swellest bunch of friends and the swellest old wife in the world. And good old Lew Harrison is the salt of the earth, believe me. I sure wish him a lot of good luck with his new enterprise. ❧ ◂SR-10

Words to Know and Use	
	exploitation (eks' ploi tā' shən) *n.* the taking advantage of something for one's own advantage or profit
	adversity (ad vʉr'sə tē) *n.* hardship
	unscrupulous (un skrōō' pyə ləs) *adj.* not concerned with what is right

255

Real Life Connections

Although initially hailed as wonderful examples of technological progress, video games also have been criticized for their ''mindnumbing'' qualities—especially if a person spends hours and hours at the screen. Invite students to discuss the positive and negative effects of this invention or others with regard to the individual, the family, and society.

JJ. Literary Element: FLASHBACK Have students tell how the story changes at this point. *(Possible response: It returns to the present time when the narrator is at the FCC meeting.)*

KK. LEP Support: Cultural Discussion Talk with students about the idea of commercial exploitation. Ask if they think it is present in all cultures or is most evident in consumer societies like that of the United States.

LL. Literary Concept: THEME Ask students to put into their own words what warning the author is making here. *(Possible response: Trying to buy happiness and to escape from reality through the new technology will destroy our country.)*

MM. Literary Sidelight Vonnegut's pessimistic view of self-destructive humanity is once again reflected in the story's ending.

Check Test

1. Who are the main characters in this story? *(Lew, Fred, and the narrator)*

2. What is the euphio machine and what are its effects? *(a machine that transmits radio signals from space that numb people's minds and make them feel a "happy" oblivion)*

3. Where does the narrator tell the story? *(at an FCC meeting)*

4. What is the euphio question? *(whether America is to enter a phase of history in which people no longer pursue happiness but buy it and, in the process, expose themselves to a machine that could destroy humanity)*

Encouraging Independent Reading

The Body Snatchers, a novel by Jack Finney
"Life-Line," a short story by Robert Heinlein
"The Little Black Bug," a short story by Cyril Kornbluth
Cat's Cradle, a novel by Kurt Vonnegut, Jr.
"Harrison Bergeron," a short story by Kurt Vonnegut Jr.

Student Response

Responding to Reading

These questions are open-ended with no "right" or "wrong" answers. However, responses must be supported with information from the selection. Possible answers follow:

1. Any response is valid.

2. Some students may say that Fred Bockman is a quiet, soft-spoken scientist and dreamer. Lew Harrison is a loud-mouthed radio announcer and host who, although intelligent, is more concerned with himself and with making money than anything else. Some students may say that Fred and Lew are alike in that both are interested in science and would like to be millionaires, but they differ in that Fred would not consider making money at the expense of other people's lives, welfare, or safety.

3. Students may say that the narrator knows the effect of the machine—it numbs people's minds and prevents them from dealing with reality; that he believes the machine could destroy civilization.

4. Some students may be in favor of its use because it could stop wars and suffering. Others may be opposed because selfish people might use it to control society.

5. Many students may say that Lew's plan cannot be successful because people would not want to give up all the other things they enjoy in life and because of the danger in something going wrong with the clockwork.

6. Some students may say that Daniel Inouye would be among the least likely to use the machine. Perhaps Lavinia in *Dandelion Wine* would be likely to use the euphio machine because she is not satisfied with her life and takes chances to change it.

7. Discussion Prompt Ask for examples of how facing up to a problem makes one a stronger person in the long run.

e x p l a i n

Responding to Reading

First Impressions

1. In your journal or on a piece of paper, jot down your reaction to the euphio machine.

Second Thoughts

2. Describe the characters of Fred Bockman and Lew Harrison. What, if anything, do they have in common? How do they differ?

   Think about
   - their professions
   - the things they say and what they really mean
   - their ideas and plans for the machine

3. Why do you think the narrator wants the euphio machine banned?

4. If the euphio machine really existed, would you be in favor of its use? Explain.

   Think about
   - situations where the machine could serve a useful purpose
   - the dangers involved with its use

5. Our "best laid plans" do not always succeed. Evaluate Lew's plan for the euphio machine and the chances for the plan's success.

6. Think of all the characters you have read about so far in this book. Which one would be most likely to use the euphio machine? Who would be least likely? Explain your answers.

Broader Connections

7. With a euphio machine, people no longer have to face real life or real problems. Instead, they have—at least temporarily—a safe and comfortable escape. Yet, often, the best lessons and the best experiences come from facing up to life and its obstacles. Recount an incident in which you faced up to a serious problem or obstacle. What was the outcome and what did you learn?

Literary Concepts: Theme and Flashback

The **theme** is the message a story carries. A writer rarely states the theme directly. Instead, the reader must infer the theme after carefully reading the selection. State the theme of "The Euphio Machine" in one or two sentences. Then, list three events or statements from the story that support your idea of the theme.

Literary Concepts—Theme and Flashback

The overall *theme* of "The Euphio Question" concerns the dangerous consequences of turning to machines instead of relying on our own minds to help us cope with life and its obstacles. This message is reinforced in the following ways:

1. The chaos and injury that occur as a result of the test of the euphio machine at Fred's house.

2. Fred's likening the buying of euphio hours to buying a big bottle of potassium cyanide and telling Lew that "this little monster could kill civilization in less time than it took to burn down Rome."

3. The narrator's plea to the Federal Communications Commission for the euphio machine to be banned.

A **flashback** is the point in a story where the action moves from one time period backward into another. The main action of this story takes place at a meeting of the Federal Communications Commission. At this meeting, the speaker tells of an event that happened in the past. "My first brush with synthetic peace of mind was six months ago," he says as the flashback begins. Try to identify the point in this story where the flashback ends.

Writing Options

1. Write a conversation among some of the story's minor characters about their euphio machine experiences. Try to describe a variety of possible attitudes, feelings, and experiences.
2. What would happen if the euphio machine was turned on during the FCC meeting? Write the committee report that might result. Think about the tone this report might have.
3. Fred exclaims that "this little monster could kill civilization." Tell what you think Fred means. Explain the effect the euphio machine could have on businesses, families, and schools, for example.
4. Write a list of titles for possible songs that could express this story's theme.

Vocabulary Practice

Exercise Decide if the following pairs of words or phrases are synonyms or antonyms. On a separate sheet of paper, identify each pair as *Synonyms* or *Antonyms*.

1. natural—synthetic
2. shocked—appalled
3. monotonous—varying
4. forte—weakness
5. monopoly—control
6. stamina—endurance
7. anarchist—rebel
8. adversity—hardship
9. maudlin—overly sentimental
10. powerless—invincible
11. apathetically—enthusiastically
12. oblivion—nothingness
13. haranguing—praising
14. exploitation—taking advantage
15. unscrupulous—honest

Words to Know and Use

adversity
anarchist
apathetically
appalled
exploitation
forte
haranguing
invincible
maudlin
monopoly
monotonous
oblivion
stamina
synthetic
unscrupulous

The point in the story where the *flashback* ends is paragraph 1 on page 255, with the narrator warning Lew not to breathe a word about the euphio machine. The narrator then addresses the "ladies and gentlemen of the Federal Communications Commission."

Writing Options

The Writing Options are designed to meet varied student interests and abilities. Have each student choose one writing activity to complete. You may wish to guide some students to an option that requires less writing.

Journal Update Have students review their journal entries for "The Euphio Question." What have they learned about happiness? What new reflections can they add to their writing?

Vocabulary Practice

1. Antonyms
2. Synonyms
3. Antonyms
4. Antonyms
5. Synonyms
6. Synonyms
7. Synonyms
8. Synonyms
9. Synonyms
10. Antonyms
11. Antonyms
12. Synonyms
13. Antonyms
14. Synonyms
15. Antonyms

e x t e n d

Options for Learning

These activities suit a variety of learning styles and modes of expression. Allow students to review the options and then choose the one they wish to do. Many are excellent collaborative learning projects.

1. Draw a Euphio Machine
Have students reread the description of the euphio machine hookup on page 249 to refresh their memories.

2. From Serious to Euphoric
Students should first brainstorm and list the kinds of people they want to portray, along with several appropriate behavior characteristics. Remind students that since they cannot use words in a pantomime, their actions will have to be exaggerated to convey the intended meaning.

3. Selling the Machine
Suggest that students review Lew's comments on pages 253 and 254 to remind them of his ideas for a campaign.

4. Euphio or Not?
Students should choose a point of view and then separate into teams to prepare their arguments and possible responses.

Fact Finder

The name of one of the large radio telescopes in the United States is the Very Large Array (VLA) telescope, located near Socorro, New Mexico. This information can be found in an encyclopedia.

Additional Information About the Author

Kurt Vonnegut, Jr. Vonnegut's midwestern background, his parents, and his experiences writing for his high-school newspaper were strong influences in his life. The high-school paper was published daily, so he had constant feedback on his writing. "It just turned out," he said, "that I could write better than a lot of other people."

Closure

Discuss with students what this story conveys about intentions and plans formed in the name of progress. Invite students to share their feelings about the possible benefits and dangers of technological progress.

Options for Learning

1 • Draw a Euphio Machine Draw a set of plans based on your impression of the euphio machine. Create front and back views, and a close-up.

2 • From Serious to Euphoric Perform a small-group pantomime about serious people experiencing the euphio machine.

3 • Selling the Machine Write and present a radio commercial that Lew Harrison might give for the euphio machine if the FCC accepts it.

4 • Euphio or Not? Stage a debate among the FCC members about whether or not to approve the euphio machine. Along with people expressing the views of Lew, Fred, and the narrator, include new points of view that you think should be represented.

FACT FINDER

Find out the name and location of one of the large radio telescopes in the United States.

Kurt Vonnegut, Jr.

1922–

Welcome to the Monkey House, Slapstick, Breakfast of Champions—these are some of the unusual works by Kurt Vonnegut that numerous readers have enjoyed. Yet Vonnegut did not always plan to be a writer. In fact, his education trained him to be a scientist and an anthropologist.

Vonnegut served in the army during World War II. He was taken prisoner by the Germans and forced to work in a slaughterhouse (a place where animals are butchered) in Dresden, Germany. Vonnegut was in Dresden as American and British planes bombed and destroyed the city, killing 135,000. Later, Vonnegut wrote a novel called *Slaughterhouse Five* about this harrowing experience.

Vonnegut first became widely read in 1963, when he published his comic novel *Cat's Cradle.* Science-fiction fans enjoy Vonnegut's futuristic subjects like the euphio machine and time travel. A wider audience also reads Vonnegut's work, fascinated by his stories that depict real-life issues such as greed and love and are often told in a humorous and satirical vein.

Of all his fans, though, Vonnegut feels a special closeness with high school readers. "High school," he says, "is closer to the core of the American experience than anything else I can think of."

Cross-Curricular Options

Students might work individually or on teams to complete any of the following optional activities.

Science: Research a recent technological development and prepare a report on it. Consider the positive side as well as the negative side.

Social Studies: Focus on a problem in society and invent a machine that might "cure" that problem. Prepare a presentation that includes drawings and/or diagrams to support the explanation.

Economics Research the process of marketing a new product (costs to a company, percentage of markup, and so forth) and prepare a presentation explaining your findings.

English: Research information about Kurt Vonnegut, Jr.'s life and works. Prepare an interview that he might give and present it in TV or radio program format.

CREATIVE EXPRESSION

Although all writing involves creativity on some level, the term "creative expression," or "creative writing," usually means producing an original short story, novel, poem, or play. One type of play is a radio drama. In the days before television, families often gathered around the radio to listen to these plays. Since they were designed for radio, the productions were different from plays performed in theaters. Sound was everything. Radio studios contained elaborate sound rooms where all sorts of special effects could be produced to make the experience as realistic as possible for the audience.

Naturally, any physical movements by the actors were lost on a radio audience. Consequently, script writers had to make sure the dialogue itself told listeners whatever they needed to know. Playwrights frequently included instructions to the actors telling them how a particular line should be delivered. To help the audience imagine the setting, playwrights sometimes opened a play with a narrator describing the scene before the actors took over. Many of the old-time radio plays were adapted from short stories with exciting plots that would interest audiences. The selections in this subunit all have plots suitable for rewriting as strong radio drama.

Here is your PASSkey to this assignment.

GUIDED ASSIGNMENT: OLD-TIME RADIO DRAMA

Turn one of the stories from "The Best-Laid Plans" into a radio drama.

PURPOSE: To write expressively
AUDIENCE: People who enjoy exciting drama
SUBJECT: A short story from this subunit
STRUCTURE: A radio drama

Prewriting

STEP 1 **Select a story to adapt** In small groups, discuss what qualities a story should have to make it a good radio drama. Then review the stories in this subunit. Select the one you think would make the best radio play.

Writer's Workshop

Objectives

- To understand the goals of writing drama
- To determine how to write dialogue
- To determine the importance of sound effects
- To draft, revise, edit, and present a radio drama

Integrating . . .

Literature and Writing Ask students what the selections in the subunit have in common. Elicit from them that all the selections have exciting plots. Discuss radio plays, explaining that before television was invented, people listened to the radio for entertainment. Since the action of a radio play could not be seen, the words had to convey the meaning. Explain that old-time radio plays had to have exciting plots to keep listeners interested.

Tell students that in this subunit they will adapt a selection as a radio play. Have students begin by visualizing the stories, imagining them as drama that will only be heard.

Writing and Grammar The Language Workshop in this subunit focuses on using indefinite pronouns. Mastering indefinite pronouns is important, since the suspense in a radio play often hinges on the unknown. If students incorporate indefinite pronouns into their plays, they will be able to build suspense and increase the dramatic effect. Explain that students will lose points with an audience if the pronouns are not used correctly.

Writing and Vocabulary The Vocabulary Workshop in this subunit relates to context clues. Tell students that familiarity with context clues will help make their radio plays more interesting. As students revise their work, have them pay attention to the context clues to determine if they are clear and make sense.

Explain to LEP students that their languages also depend on context clues to convey meaning. Have LEP students supply examples of this.

Additional Resources

UNIT TWO RESOURCE BOOK
Writer's Workshop Copy Master, p. 43
Peer and Self-Evaluation Guidelines, p. 44
Writing Assessment Guidelines, p. 45

ENRICHMENT MATERIALS
Thinking Skills Transparency and Worksheet
Fine Art Transparency and Writing Prompts
Revision, Proofreading, and Elaboration Worksheet
Writing Prompts for Assessment

Teaching Strategies

Introduction Have students turn to the Guided Assignment box on page 259. Point out the PASSkey graphic. Discuss how vital it is that the written word convey all meaning. Explain that their radio play will be read to an audience that will be unable to see the action. Emphasize that their written words must be strong enough to convey plot as well as action.

Tell students that in this assignment they will become familiar with writing dialogue. Remind them that they are already familiar with dialogue because of their ability to speak. Explain that dialogue is just written speech.

Prewriting Review each of the prewriting steps with the students. Discuss scenes in the selections that do not need to be included. Explain that every scene is not necessary and does not further the plot. As students write dialogue, encourage them to infer what they think the characters might have said. Allow students the creative freedom to adapt the stories loosely, and include scenes that do not exist in the stories. Stress, however, that the final result is important. Students should create a radio script that an audience can listen to and understand.

Computer Tip
Encourage students to outline their scenes and plan their dialogue on a computer. Explain that a computer will allow them to move their ideas and notes around. Remind them that they will also be able to store this material and refer to it later. Allow students to decide whether they are more comfortable working on a computer or with pencil and paper.

STEP 2 Outline the scenes Begin your adaptation by deciding which of the story's scenes are essential and which are not. Essential scenes will be those that introduce characters and show their development, contain important plot details, develop the conflict, and present the story's resolution. Long passages of description can be left out unless they are crucial to the story's plot or meaning. On a separate piece of paper, briefly summarize each scene you will use and give it a number. Include in your summary any required sound effects. Decide whether or not you should have a narrator. Note on your list when the narrator should speak, and summarize what he should say. Here is the first part of an outline one student wrote for "Stowaway!"—a selection from a previous subunit.

STUDENT MODEL ▶

Scene 1: Sound effects of jet engines. The narrator tells the audience that the setting is the airport at Havana. He also introduces Jorge and Armando.
Scene 2: Jorge and Armando climb inside the wheel well of the jet.
Scene 3: Flashback—Jorge and Armando talk over plans for stowing away.
Scene 4: The cockpit crew discusses the difficulties they're having in getting the landing gear closed properly.

STEP 3 Plan the play's dialogue In the short story you chose, important conversations may have been summarized by the author, as was the case for Scene 3 of the student model in Step 2. Review the scenes you've decided to include. Place a star by those for which you will need to write dialogue during the drafting phase. For most of the scenes on your list, you will be able to use dialogue from the original story. Look over those scenes in the story and decide which lines are crucial and which might be eliminated.

Drafting

Using your list of required scenes and other notes, write a rough draft of your radio play.

STEP 1 Use the proper format for writing drama Looking over the plays in this book will give you good ideas about how to write drama. For example, include instructions, or stage directions, in parentheses, as in the following model:

JORGE (shouting above the roar of the engines). Let's run!

◀ STUDENT MODEL

STEP 2 **Decide if you need a narrator** A narrator can describe different characters, settings, or scene changes. Details and sentences from the original story will supply some dialogue for a narrator. Feel free to add other information that will clarify the situation and the setting for your audience. Here is the introduction a student wrote for "Stowaway!"

NARRATOR. It is late in the afternoon on June 3, 1970. Iberia Airlines' once-weekly nonstop Flight 904 bound for Madrid is about to take off from Havana's José Martí Airport. Though the pilot and his crew don't know it, they have two extra passengers—stowaways. Jorge and Armando, two Cuban teenagers, are determined to begin new lives of freedom.

◀ STUDENT MODEL

STEP 3 **Create needed dialogue** Invent dialogue for your play using information from the original story. One student used the following paragraph from the story "Stowaway!" as the basis for a scene in a radio play.

> Then I met Jorge at a Havana baseball game. After the game we got to talking. I found out that Jorge, like myself, was disillusioned with Cuba. "The system takes away your freedom—forever," he complained.

Here is a portion of the student's version of the scene as adapted for the play.

ARMANDO (tiredly). I wish they wouldn't interrupt my classes to send me off to plant sugar cane.
JORGE. I know what you mean. It isn't fair. Nothing is.
ARMANDO. All I want to do is become an artist.
JORGE (dejectedly). Well, forget it. You know there's no chance. You have to do what they tell you to do. (with bitterness in his voice) The system takes away your freedom—forever.

◀ STUDENT MODEL

Revising and Editing

Once you have completed the rough draft of your radio play, ask a classmate to review your work according to the following checklist.

Drafting Instruct students to work closely with their prewriting outlines as they begin to write. Tell them to change their outlines as they see fit. Explain that often writers get a clearer idea of what they want to say as they write. Assure them that the outline is not etched in stone but should serve merely as a helpful organizational guide. Remind students to include adequate stage directions, narration, and sound effects, in their plays. Refer those students who are having trouble to other plays in this book.

Revising and Editing If students revise their radio plays with a partner, you might suggest that one student read the radio play to the other. In this way, the student can determine if the true goals of a radio play have been achieved. Tell students to judge the radio plays according to the questions in the *Revision Checklist.*

Have students edit their plays for grammar, mechanics, usage, and spelling.

Presenting As an alternative to the *Presenting* suggestion in the pupil's edition, you might consider these ideas:

- Select three or four radio plays and present them in the school auditorium to other classes. Each student in the class should get a part. Put one student in charge of sound effects and another in charge of lighting. You might consider inviting family members to watch the plays.
- Invite members of a local theater group to watch the class plays. If possible, invite someone who is familiar with radio. Have these people give tips on acting and describe the difficulties they encounter as they work with plays.

Reflecting on Your Writing You may wish to discuss the answers to *Reflecting on Your Writing* with the entire class. It helps students to discover that others have encountered the same problems as they did. As students answer Question 3, determine if they would benefit from reworking their plays or certain parts of them. Some students may wish to continue working on this project for extra credit.

Closure

Before beginning the next subunit, be sure students have internalized these concepts:

- Stories with exciting plots can be adapted into radio plays.
- Writing that is to be heard differs from writing that is to be read.
- Sound effects are used to provide clarity and to further the plot.
- Context clues clarify confusing words or ideas.
- Indefinite pronouns can be used to create suspense.

Revision Checklist

1. Does the radio play include the essential scenes from the short story?
2. If necessary, has dialogue been written to replace the original author's summaries? Does the dialogue match the personality of the character?
3. If a narrator is used, is the narration clear and true to the original story?
4. Is the play organized in a sensible manner? Do the scenes flow together well?
5. Does the play include instructions for delivering lines?
6. Is the play written in a proper format?

Editing When you have finished revising your play, proofread for spelling, clarity, and mechanics.

Presenting

Ask some classmates to join you in performing your play. If possible, select appropriate music and tape-record your performance, to play back later for the rest of the class. You may want to set up a tape center in the library so that other students can enjoy your work.

Reflecting on Your Writing

Answer the following questions. Turn in your answers with your paper or place them in your writing portfolio.

1. How did you decide which scenes from the original story to include and which to omit?
2. Was drama harder or easier for you to write than other types of writing?
3. If you had more time to work on your play, what aspects of it would you improve? Why?

Additional Writing and Research Topics

The following items provide additional writing practice based on the selections in this subunit:

Creative Expression

- Choose one of the selections in the subunit that you did not use to write your radio play. Select a scene from this selection and write a list of sound effects for it. Be sure that the sound effects either further the plot or create a mood.
- Write one page of dialogue in which Jimmy explains the truth to Pat.

Other Topics

Personal Narrative: In "The Third-Floor Flat," Pat is about to find out something about Donovan that she did not previously know. Write about a time when you found out something about someone close to you. This could be something happy and exciting.

Persuasion: Convince a friend or family member that you should be the first one on your block to buy Kurt Vonnegut's "Euphio."

USING INDEFINITE PRONOUNS

Indefinite pronouns do not refer to a specific person or thing. Some are singular, some are plural, and some can be either.

The chart below lists indefinite pronouns. Notice that many of the singular indefinite pronouns end with *-body* or *-one.* Also notice that some indefinite pronouns are singular, some are plural, and some can be either.

Indefinite Pronouns	
Singular ▶	another anybody anyone anything each either everybody everyone everything neither nobody no one one somebody someone something
Plural ▶	both few many several
Singular or Plural ▶	all any most none some

Indefinite Pronouns as Subjects

Like a noun or a personal pronoun, an indefinite pronoun can be the subject of a sentence. When an indefinite pronoun acts as a subject, it must agree with the verb.

No one is happy all the time. (The singular pronoun *no one* is the subject of the singular verb *is.*)

Few are unhappy all the time. (The plural pronoun *few* is the subject of the plural verb *are.*)

Occasionally, people commit an error in agreement with an indefinite pronoun because they are confused by words that appear between the pronoun and the verb. Consider this example:

Incorrect *Each* of the science fiction writers *tell* about the future.

Correct *Each* of the science fiction writers *tells* about the future.

Additional Resources

UNIT TWO RESOURCE BOOK

Language Workshop Copy Master, p. 46

ENRICHMENT MATERIALS

Grammar and Usage Copy Masters

Language Workshop

Objectives

- To understand that indefinite pronouns do not refer to a specific person or thing
- To identify indefinite pronouns as singular or plural or both
- To use correct indefinite pronoun agreement when the pronoun is a subject or an antecedent

Integrating . . .

Writing and Grammar Remind students that when they proofread their radio dramas from the preceding Writer's Workshop, they might find errors in subject/verb agreement. Explain that when the subject is singular, the verb form must also be singular. Write the following sentences on the board:

1. Michael follow Ed to the mall.

2. Tanya and Mikki sings loudly in the choir.

Ask students to read each sentence, tell why the subject and verb do not agree, and make the necessary corrections. *(follows, sing)* Then write the following sentences on the board:

3. Everybody loves to hear Jennifer giggle.

4. Neither character in the story was very strong-willed.

Have volunteers identify the subject of each sentence, helping them to see that although the subjects are not nouns, each must still agree with the verb.

Teaching Strategies

Ask a volunteer to read the focus statement in the box at the top of page 263. Then have the next paragraph read aloud and call students' attention to the list of indefinite pronouns. Be sure that students realize that some indefinite pronouns may be either singular or plural. Have students give an example of the same pronoun being used as singular and then as plural. For example: "*All* of my homework is complete" (singular); "*All* of the students are tired" (plural).

Continue having students read, working through the section on indefinite pronouns as subjects.

Teaching Tip: LEP

To assist LEP students who might have difficulty with indefinite pronouns, point out that most indefinite pronouns express the idea of quantity, such as *few, all, most, none, some, several.* Then have students decide "how many" the indefinite pronoun refers to in order to make it agree with the verb.

Before assigning Exercise 1, have students form three groups. Assign each group one of these titles: *Singular, Plural,* and *Singular or Plural.* Have the students in each group select four pronouns from the list on page 263 and write it as a subject in a sentence using correct verb agreement. Have each group appoint someone to record their responses, and then share them with the class.

Now assign Exercise 1 to students. Have volunteers read aloud their responses. Encourage discussion and clarification as needed. Be sure students can explain why sentence 9 is correct, identifying *all* as the indefinite pronoun that agrees with *lead.*

Continue working through the lesson, having students read and discuss the section on indefinite pronouns as antecedents, stopping before Exercise 2. Call students' attention to the sidenote on the use of *his* or *her.* Point out that some writers use *his* as a generic term, meaning *his or her.*

Exercise 1

1. Everyone discusses favorite stories in our English class.
2. Most of the students enjoy mystery stories.
3. One of my favorite mystery writers is Agatha Christie.
4. Everybody agrees that Hercule Poirot is a great detective.
5. Several of my classmates like Miss Marple better than Monsieur Poirot.
6. No one in class disagrees with the notion that a great mystery is difficult to write.
7. Each of the characters has to have a reason for the actions they take.
8. Few predict the end of a good mystery novel.
9. Correct.
10. Some of the world's famous detectives use intuition as well as logic to solve mysteries.

To check agreement with an indefinite pronoun, remove the phrase that comes between it and the subject: *Each . . . tells. Each* is singular. Therefore, you need a singular verb.

Exercise 1 Some of these sentences contain errors in indefinite pronoun-verb agreement. On your paper rewrite the sentences correctly. If a sentence contains no error, write *Correct.*

1. Everyone discuss favorite stories in our English class.
2. Most of the students enjoys mystery stories.
3. One of my favorite mystery writers are Agatha Christie.
4. Everybody agree that Hercule Poirot is a great detective.
5. Several of my classmates likes Miss Marple better than Monsieur Poirot.
6. No one in class disagree with the notion that a great mystery is difficult to write.
7. Each of the characters have to have a reason for the actions he or she takes.
8. Few predicts the end of a good mystery novel.
9. However, all of the events in a well-written mystery lead logically to the conclusion.
10. Some of the world's famous detectives uses intuition as well as logic to solve mysteries.

Indefinite Pronouns as Antecedents

The noun or pronoun that a pronoun stands for is called its **antecedent.** Consider the following example:

Sweet Lemon Brown was playing *his* harmonica.

The pronoun *his* stands for *Sweet Lemon Brown.* Therefore, *Sweet Lemon Brown* is the antecedent of *his.* Now consider this example:

Someone was playing *his* harmonica.

In this case the indefinite pronoun *someone* is the antecedent of *his.*

Always make sure that any pronoun that refers back to an indefinite pronoun agrees in number with that indefinite pronoun. If the indefinite pronoun is singular, then the pronoun that refers to it must also be singular.

His or Her?

Notice that the phrase *his or her* may be used when the person referred to could be either male or female.

Incorrect *Everyone* on the team cast *their* vote.

Correct *Everyone* on the team cast *his or her* vote.

If the indefinite pronoun is plural, then the pronoun that refers to it must also be plural.

Incorrect *Both* had *his* opinions about whether Greg should play.

Correct *Both* had *their* opinions about whether Greg should play.

The pronouns *all, any, some, most,* and *none* may be either singular or plural, depending on their meaning in the sentence. Remember: To tell whether one of these pronouns is singular or plural, find the word to which the pronoun refers. Consider these examples:

None of the *players* were in trouble with *their* teachers. (The word *none* refers to the plural word *players,* so use the plural pronoun *their.*)

None of his *work* has ever been shown on the air, but *it* may be, one of these days. (The word *none* refers to the singular word *work,* so use the singular pronoun *it.*)

Exercise 2 Write the indefinite pronoun in each sentence. Then write the correct pronoun from the choices in parentheses.

1. Few of the early blues musicians earned (their, his or her) living easily.
2. Many of these people spent (their, his or her) lives on the road.
3. Few of those artists kept (their, his or her) health during the long trips.
4. Some of the musicians ended (their, her) careers as Sweet Lemon Brown did.
5. Everyone in a jazz band wants (his or her, their) own "sound."
6. All of these musicians build (his or her, their) music on the blues.
7. No one sang (his or her, their) personal brand of the blues better than Bessie Smith.
8. None of her music has lost (their, its) impact.
9. Even on a scratchy old record, each of her notes burns (their, its) haunting message into your soul.
10. Everyone remembers (their, his or her) introduction to this unforgettable musical artist.

Exercise 3 Analyzing and Revising Your Writing
Reread a piece of writing from your portfolio. Check for indefinite pronoun agreement and correct any errors that you find.

LANGUAGE HANDBOOK

For review and practice, see Section 3, Using Pronouns.

Have students form three small groups. Make sure that LEP students are evenly distributed. Assign one of the following titles to each group: *Singular, Plural, Singular or Plural.* Direct students to look through the selections in this subunit to find five examples of the type of indefinite pronoun indicated by their group's title. Have a group member record the sentences. Allow groups to discuss how the pronouns are used (as a subject or antecedent). Finally, have students identify the word(s) with which the pronoun agree(s). Have groups then share their sentences.

Now assign Exercise 2 to students. Have volunteers share their answers. Finally, assign Exercise 3, making sure that students' work reflects correct indefinite pronoun agreement.

Closure

Before beginning the next subunit, be sure students have internalized these concepts:

- Indefinite pronouns do not refer to a specific person or thing.
- Some indefinite pronouns are singular; some are plural; and some, such as *all, any, most, none,* and *some,* may be either.
- When indefinite pronouns act as subjects, they must agree with the verbs. When a pronoun refers back to an indefinite pronoun, it must agree in number with that indefinite pronoun.

Exercise 2

1. Few; their
2. Many; their
3. Few; their
4. Some; their
5. Everyone; his or her
6. All; their
7. No one; his or her
8. None; its
9. Each; its
10. Everyone; his or her

Exercise 3

Answers will vary, but the entire piece should contain indefinite pronoun agreement.

ADDITIONAL PRACTICE

The following items provide additional practice in the use of indefinite pronouns.

Write these sentences using the correct word.

1. Some of the stores (is, <u>are</u>) open at night.
2. Both of the cars (<u>need</u>, needs) new mufflers.
3. Everybody tried (<u>his or her</u>, their) best.
4. Each of the women wore (<u>her</u>, their) tag.
5. None of the commercials (is, <u>are</u>) very clever.
6. Some of the fruit (taste, <u>tastes</u>) sour.

Write these sentences correctly. Underline the antecedent of each indefinite pronoun.

7. <u>All</u> of the students waits patiently. *wait*
8. <u>Everyone</u> wore their uniform for the big game. *his or her*
9. <u>Few</u> of my friends have made his or her vacation plans. *their*
10. <u>Nobody</u> remembered what their assignment was. *his or her*

Vocabulary Workshop

Objectives

- To understand that the meaning of an unfamiliar word can be derived from words and sentences near it
- To identify and use context clues such as restatement examples, and inference to determine the meaning of an unfamiliar word

Integrating . . .

Literature and Vocabulary Share with students that this workshop will help them use three types of context clues to figure out the meanings of unfamiliar words.

Teaching Strategies

Ask students to identify strategies they use to figure out unfamiliar words in their reading. *(Possible responses: skip over them, look for clues, use the glossary, ask someone)*

Read through the material with students. Assign the exercise on page 266. Call on students to read definitions, and have volunteers point out the context clues.

Closure

Before beginning the next subunit, be sure students have internalized these concepts:

- Using context clues helps a reader to determine the word's meaning.
- In restatement clues, a definition is directly stated.
- Example and inference clues require readers to use related information.

Teaching Tip: LEP

Words with multiple meanings are especially difficult for LEP students. These students will benefit from the application of context clues strategies to figure out the intended uses of words with multiple meanings. Point out that each time they encounter multiple-meaning words, they should re-examine the context to be certain of which use is intended.

Exercise

(Possible answers are given.)
1. dreamer. **2.** odd. **3.** without explanation. **4.** curious. **5.** unbeatable.

Vocabulary Workshop

CONTEXT CLUES

Often you can figure out an unfamiliar word by studying the **context clues**—the words and sentences around a word. When a writer follows a word with another way of stating the same idea, this context clue is called a **restatement** clue. Restatement clues are often signaled by *or, that is,* and *in other words,* and by commas and dashes.

The euphio box offered *synthetic,* or man-made, tranquility.

The word *synthetic* is followed by a word that restates it.

Example clues that help explain a word are often signaled by *such as, for example,* and *for instance.*

The happiness created by this machine worked even in the face of incredible *adversity,* such as sickness or poverty.

Although *adversity* is not directly restated, the two examples suggest that adversity is a state of trouble.

Sometimes you will need to piece together several **inference clues,** or hints throughout the larger context, that help you figure out what the word means.

People were *mesmerized* by the effects of the machine. People felt calmed, carefree—as if they were under a magician's spell.

The sentence that follows *mesmerized* helps the reader to infer that being mesmerized is like being hypnotized.

Exercise Write your definition of each underlined word.

1. Fred Bockman was the visionary, or starry-eyed dreamer, who invented the euphio machine.
2. This bizarre, or odd, machine picked up radio signals from different heavenly bodies.
3. The hiss from the machine inexplicably made people feel happy and peaceful; that is, no one could explain why they felt so tranquil.
4. The narrator's wife was very inquisitive; she kept asking questions to try to understand how the machine worked.
5. Eddie, the narrator's ten-year-old son, was the captain of an invincible baseball team; no other team had ever beaten Eddie's powerful team.

Additional Resources
UNIT TWO RESOURCE BOOK
Related Skills Copy Master, p. 47

ADDITIONAL PRACTICE

Use context clues to define each underlined word.

1. The enticement, or attraction, of making money has prompted many new products. *(attraction)*

2. Of course, some unscrupulous inventors have taken others' ideas, ran misleading advertisements, or misused investors' money. *(dishonest)*

3. Although infringement on copyrights and patents is illegal, some inventors regularly steal other inventors' ideas. *(violation)*

Beating the Odds

Everyone loves to hear of people who beat the odds—who succeed when their chances seem hopeless, or who manage to escape from intolerable situations. Such tales can be inspirational reminders of what people can do or of how circumstances can change. In some cases you may even identify with the main character's struggle.

This group of selections tells of people who seemed to accomplish the impossible. As you read, think about the qualities that help each character succeed.

Subunit Preview

Have students read the introduction to subunit 3, **Beating the Odds.** Ask them to reflect on how challenging the "impossible" relates to the unit theme, **Escapes: Triumphs and Retreats.** Why would someone attempt the impossible? What is to be gained from knowing someone else's achievements? Which is usually the larger part of success—determination or luck? Explain your answer. Have students scan the subunit Table of Contents and ask them which selection that they think will be most interesting.

For Additional Challenge

The following selections offer further challenge in exploring the subunit theme:

Annapurna, a nonfiction adventure by Maurice Herzog

"The Quiet Man," a short story by Maurice Walsh

Additional Resources

Subunit Test, pp. 70–71

Observation Assessment

Observing how students respond to the text, to the classroom instruction, and to peers is an important part of an assessment program. The following suggestions and the form in each Unit Resource Book can be used to implement observation assessment.

- As students work through the subunit, assess how they use prereading strategies. Do they draw on prior experience to predict probable story lines and outcomes? Do prereading strategies seem to motivate and encourage them? Do they see prereading strategies as an important part of reading?
- Can you see growing ease with using prereading strategies as students work through the subunit?
- To evaluate students' sense of genre and story, observe how they use various cues to distinguish between nonfiction and fiction. Do they use their "story" sense based on their knowledge of genre to make predictions?

Objectives

- To understand and analyze a biographical magazine article
- To use a time line to sequence events
- To summarize important events in a biographical work
- To identify the conflict
- To express understanding of the work through a choice of writing options, including survival tips, a thank-you letter, a paragraph of opinion, and dialogue

Prereading/Motivation

Examine What You Know

Discussion Prompts: What immediate needs do people face when they are lost in the wilderness? What one item would you want to be sure to have with you in the wilderness?

Expand Your Knowledge

Discussion Prompts: What other facts do you know about the Alaskan wilderness? Do you think it would be possible to develop this wilderness with roads and other facilities? What would the benefits of development be? What would be the drawbacks?

Additional Background Prior to 1867, the Alaskan wilderness was owned by czarist Russia. On May 30 of that year, Alaskan natives learned that their land had been sold to the United States for $7.2 million. This amounted to about two cents per acre of land.

Enrich Your Reading

Students should include the following events: 1) Crane bails out; 2) He camps on the river waiting to be rescued; 3) He finds Berail's cabin, leaves after one day; 4) He almost dies in search of civilization and returns to cabin; 5) He gathers strength in cabin, leaves as food runs out; 6) He finds another abandoned, stocked cabin and then the cabin of his rescuers.

Thematic Link—Beating the Odds

In this biographical article, a soldier lost in the Alaskan wilderness beats the odds by managing to survive the cold and other hardships.

explore

Magazine Article

Survival in the Forty-Ninth

JOHN McPHEE

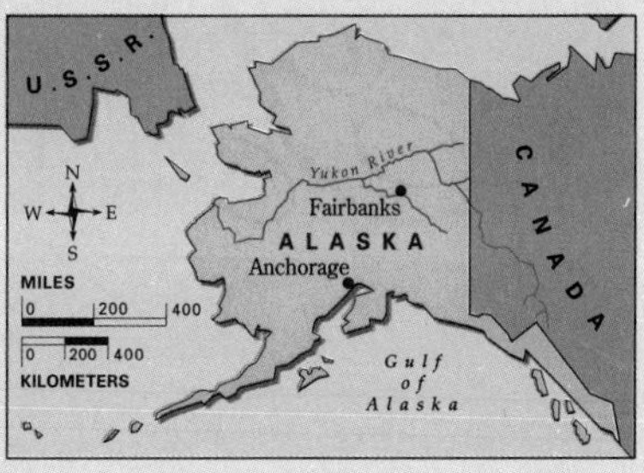

Examine What You Know (Prior Knowledge)

What images do you associate with the idea of wilderness survival? Perhaps you picture someone alone and terrified in the jungle or crawling across the scorching desert. In your journal or on a piece of paper, describe the images that the words *wilderness* and *survival* create for you. Then see if this story gives you any new images.

Expand Your Knowledge (Building Background)

Although Alaska became the forty-ninth state in 1959, it is still a wild and sparsely populated piece of America. In fact, many people still consider this beautiful state the last wilderness in the United States. Near the Arctic Circle, where this story takes place, Alaska's mountainous landscape is especially forbidding. Temperatures can drop to a dangerous fifty degrees below zero, the snow can be waist deep, and the gusting wind can easily knock a person over. Once the wind stops blowing, you can hear the threatening howl of wolves. Alaska is the least populated state in the nation; yet in area, it is by far the largest state.

Enrich Your Reading (Reading Skill)

Making a Time Line The author of the following selection switches back and forth between the survival story of Leon Crane and a conversation that Crane and the author are having. Use a time line like the one below to record the important events in Crane's story. The questions that interrupt the text will also help you keep track of and summarize the important events.

Crane survives crash of the airplane. — Crane makes his way to river to await rescue. — • — •

■ *A biography of the author can be found on page 277.*

Journal Writing

Suggest these journal topics to students:

- Describe a situation in which you needed survival skills.
- Some people choose vacations in which they must find their way out of a wilderness area. Would you choose such a vacation? Why or why not?

For other journal opportunities, refer students to Examine What You Know (above), Annotations H and X, and Broader Connections (p. 275).

Additional Resources

UNIT TWO RESOURCE BOOK

Reader's Guidesheet, p. 50
Vocabulary Worksheet, p. 51
Selection and Vocabulary Check Tests, p. 52
Selection Test, pp. 53–54

Collaborative Learning

Opportunities for collaborative learning appear throughout the lesson and include Options for Learning activities (p. 277) as well as creating a wilderness survival kit in Cross-Curricular Options (p. T–277).

Survival in the Forty-Ninth

JOHN McPHEE

While flying in a helicopter over Alaska, John McPhee spotted the wreckage of an old World War II bomber. Curious about whether there had been any survivors, McPhee began an investigation into the incident. After some clever detective work, he located the sole survivor and interviewed him. The following account relates this survivor's adventure.

The *Liberator,* making cold-weather propeller tests above twenty thousand feet, went into a spin, dived toward the earth, and, pulling out, snapped its elevator controls.[1] It then went into another spin, and the pilot gave the order to abandon ship. There were five aboard. Leon Crane was the copilot. He was twenty-four, and he had been in Alaska less than two months. Since the plane was falling like a swirling leaf, he had to drag himself against
A heavy centrifugal force toward the open bomb bay. He had never used a parachute. The outside air temperature was at least thirty degrees below zero. When he jumped, he forgot his mittens. The day was December 21.

The plane fiercely burned, not far away from where he landed, and he stood watching it, up to his thighs in snow. He was wearing a hooded down jacket, a sweater, winter underwear, two pairs of trousers, two pairs of socks, and felt-lined military mukluks.[2] He scanned the mountainsides but could see nothing of the others. He thought he had been the second one to go out of the plane, and as he fell he thought he saw a parachute open in the air above him. He shouted into the winter silence. Silence answered. Months later, he would learn that there had been two corpses in the aircraft. Of the two other fliers no track or trace was ever found. "Sergeant Pompeo, B
the crew chief, had a hell of a thick set of glasses. He must have lost them as soon as

1. **elevator controls:** cockpit controls that raise or lower flaps located on the horizontal part of the tail of a plane, allowing a pilot to make the plane go up or down.

2. **mukluks** (muk′ luks′): high moccasin boots resembling those worn by Eskimos.

Words to Know and Use

centrifugal (sen trif′ yo͞o gəl) *adj.* displaying a tendency to move away from the center

269

Teaching Strategies

Vocabulary Preview

These vocabulary words are defined at the bottom of the selection page on which they appear. You may wish to discuss them briefly before students begin reading.

aeronautical having to do with airplanes
centrifugal showing tendency to move away from center
meandering following a winding path
refurbishment renovation
vigilance watchfulness

Support for Students of Limited English Proficiency

- Use Reader's Guidesheet, p. 50
- "Survival in the Forty-Ninth" contains references to arctic life, the military, and aeronautics that may be obscure to some students. You may want to create graphic organizers on the board for each topic and add terms to the proper categories as students read.
- Annotations B, E, K, and O focus on troublesome terms and concepts.

Text Annotations

A. Literary Element: BIOGRAPHY Ask students why the facts the author gives about Crane are important. *(Possible response: They show he was relatively unprepared for survival in Alaska.)*

B. LEP: Vocabulary Students of limited English proficiency may not recognize the meanings of *track* and *trace* in this context. Explain that both mean a trail or sign of someone's passage. Also help them pronounce the word *Sergeant* and explain that it is a military rank.

Structured Reading for Less Proficient Students

These questions can help to guide students through the reading. Ask each question at the point of the selection where the SR number appears in the margin.

SR–1. How many people survived the crash? *(just one, Leon Crane)* **Literal recall**

SR–2. What dangerous weather condition threatens Crane's survival? *(temperatures thirty to fifty degrees below zero)* What does Crane do to stay warm? *(He lights a fire and lies wrapped up in his parachute.)* **Literal recall**

SR–3. What does Crane do to try to obtain food? Is he successful? *(He makes a spear, a bow and arrow, and a slingshot out of his parachute and tries to hunt; he is not successful. He chews moss but swallows little of it.)* **Summarizing**

SR–4. What does Crane conclude when he finds a stocked cabin? *(that civilization is just around the corner)* What mistake does this conclusion lead him to make? *(He leaves the cabin after only one day and almost dies.)* **Clarifying**

Continued on page 270

C. Critical Thinking: EVALUATION Have students evaluate Crane's chances of survival, given his supplies and amount of experience in Alaska. *(Possible responses: His chances are not very good, because he's only been in Alaska two months, and he has no food, no easy means of obtaining food, no sleeping bag, no mittens, and little knowledge of where he is.)*

D. Literary Sidelight Point out the irony and symbolism in Crane's burning his father's letter. The letter might be seen as a symbol of Crane's last tie to civilization. Burning it further intensifies his sense of isolation.

E. LEP: Experiential Background Students from some climates might not appreciate how cold the temperatures mentioned here are. On the board, draw a thermometer scale that goes from 100° F to −50° F. Point out that water freezes at 32° F and that spending extended time outside in temperatures below 0° F can be life-threatening.

F. Reading Skill: SUMMARIZING *(Crane's dilemma: He is lost in the frozen wilderness without food or shelter. He got into the dilemma as a result of surviving an airplane crash.)*

G. Literary Element: BIOGRAPHY Ask students how long after the true-life adventure the author interviewed Crane. *(much later; Crane was only twenty-four when the event happened; his hair was graying when McPhee interviewed him.)*

H. Discussion Have students discuss their own possible reactions to being in the predicament Crane was in. Ask if they think they would have been able to control their fear.

I. Critical Thinking: EVALUATING Have students evaluate Crane's ingenuity and his skills as an outdoorsman. *(Possible response: He showed some ingenuity in thinking of ways to hunt food, but little skill in applying them.)*

he hit the airstream. Without them, he really couldn't see. What was he going to do when he got down there?"

C For that matter, what was Crane going to do? He had no food, no gun, no sleeping bag, no mittens. The plane had been meandering in search of suitable skies for the tests. Within two or three hundred miles, he had no idea where he was. SR-1

Two thousand feet below him, and a couple of miles east, was a river. He made his way down to it. Waiting for rescue, he stayed beside it. He had two books of matches, a Boy Scout knife. D He started a fire with a letter from his father and for the first eight days he did not sleep more than two hours at a time in his vigilance to keep the fire burning. The cold awakened him anyway. Water fountained from a gap in the river ice, and that is what he lived on. His hands, which he to some extent protected with parachute cloth or in the pockets of his jacket, became cut and abraded from tearing at spruce boughs. When he spread his fingers, the skin between them would split. E Temperatures were probably ranging between a high of thirty below zero and a low around fifty. The parachute, as much as anything, kept him alive. It was twenty-eight feet in diameter, and he wound it around him so that he was at the center of a great cocoon. Still, he said, his back would grow cold while his face roasted, and sparks kept igniting the chute. SR-2

G He was telling me some of this on a sidewalk in Philadelphia when I asked him how he had dealt with fear.

He stopped in surprise and looked contemplatively up the street toward Independence Hall,[3] his graying hair wisping out to the sides. He wore a business suit and a topcoat, and he had bright, penetrating eyes. He leaned forward when he walked. H "Fear," he repeated. "I wouldn't have used that word. Think about it: there was not a hell of a lot I could do if I were to panic. Besides, I was sure that someone was going to come and get me."

All that the search-and-rescue missions had to go on was that the *Liberator* had last been heard from above Big Delta, so the search area could not be reduced much below forty thousand square miles. Needless to say, they would not come near finding him. He thought once that he heard the sound of an airplane, but eventually he realized that it was a chorus of wolves. I In his hunger, he tried to kill squirrels. He made a spear and threw it awkwardly as they jumped and chattered in the spruce boughs. He made a bow and arrow, using a shroud line[4] from his parachute, but when he released the arrow, it shot off at angles ridiculously oblique to the screeching, maddening squirrels. There was some rubber involved in the parachute assembly, and he used that to make a slingshot, which was worse than the bow and arrow. When he fell asleep by the fire, he dreamed of milkshakes, dripping beefsteaks, mashed po-

summarize

F What is Leon Crane's dilemma and how has he gotten into it?

3. **Independence Hall:** a landmark building in Philadelphia where the Declaration of Independence and the U.S. Constitution were adopted.
4. **shroud** (shroud) **line:** one of the lines that connect a parachute and its harness.

Words to Know and Use

meandering (mē an′dər iŋ) *adj.* following a random, winding path
vigilance (vij′ ə ləns) *n.* watchfulness

270

STRUCTURED READING FOR LESS PROFICIENT STUDENTS

Continued from page 269

SR–5. Why does Crane leave the cabin the second time? *(His food is running out.)* **Literal recall**

SR–6. What does Crane follow in his quest to find civilization? *(the Charley River)* **Literal recall**

SR–7. To what two Alaskans does Crane owe his life? *(Al Ames, at whose occupied cabin he ended up, and Phil Berail, whose abandoned, but stocked cabin kept Crane alive for weeks)* **Literal recall**

tatoes, and lamb chops, with lamb fat running down his hands. Awake, he kicked aside the snow and found green moss. He put it in his mouth and chewed, and chewed some more, but scarcely swallowed any. Incidentally, he was camped almost exactly where, some twenty-five years later, Ed and Virginia Gelvin would build a cabin from
SR-3 ▶ which to trap and hunt.

J Crane is a thoroughly urban man. He grew up in the neighborhood of Independence Hall, where he lives now, with an unlisted number. That part of the city has undergone extensive refurbishment in recent years, and Crane's sons, who are residential builders and construction engineers, have had a part in the process. Crane, more or less retired, works for them, and when I visited him, I followed him from building to building as he checked on the needs and efforts of carpenters, bricklayers, plumbers. He professed to have no appetite for wild country, least of all for the expanses of the north. As a boy, he had joined a city Scout troop and had become a First Class Scout, but that was not to suggest a particular knowledge of wilderness. When he flew out of Fairbanks that morning in 1943, his lifetime camping experience consisted of one night on the ground—with his troop, in Valley Forge. K

THE TRAPPER 1921 Rockwell Kent Oil on canvas 34″ × 44″ Collection of Whitney Museum of American Art, New York Purchase 31,258.

He decided on the ninth day that no help was coming. Gathering up his parachute, he began to slog his way downriver, in snow sometimes up to his waist. It crossed his mind that the situation might be hopeless, but he put down the thought, as he moved from bend to bend, by telling himself to keep going because "right around that curve is what you're looking for." In fact, he was about sixty miles from the nearest human being, almost a hundred from the nearest group of buildings large enough to be called a settlement. Around the next bend, he saw more mountains, more bare, jagged rock, more snow-covered sweeps of alpine tundra,[5] contoured toward another L

5. **alpine tundra:** a large, fairly flat, treeless area located at a very high elevation.

Words to Know and Use

refurbishment (ri fur′ bish mənt) *n.* a polishing up; renovation

Art Note

Rockwell Kent (1882–1971) was an American painter, graphic artist, and illustrator. In *The Trapper,* he limited his palette to the cold blues and whites of distant mountains and sky and the shadows nearby. This technique intensifies the sense of isolation of the man and his dog in the barren landscape. *How does this scene relate to Leon Crane's experience?*

J. Reading Skill: INFERRING Ask students how well they think Crane's upbringing in Philadelphia prepared him for his ordeal in Alaska. *(Possible response: Being a "thoroughly urban" man, he may not have had an opportunity to learn any wilderness skills.)*

K. LEP: Cultural References Immigrants from some cultures may not be familiar with the Boy Scouts of America. Have students familiar with scouting explain the organization's goals, what a troop is, and what a First Class Scout might be.

L. Literary Element: CONFLICT Have students explain what external and internal conflicts Crane faces. *(His external conflict is staying alive in a cold, rugged country in which food is hard to come by; his internal conflict is fighting his own sense of hopelessness and motivating himself to keep going, even though the odds are against him.)*

Teaching Tip

To help students with the time lines assigned in Enrich Your Reading, suggest they draw small illustrations to accompany key events, for example, a parachute to show Crane's bailout, a trail through snow to suggest his search for shelter, and so on.

PROFESSIONAL NOTEBOOK

In her eighteen years as a teacher in a one-room schoolhouse, Sybil Marshall was able to witness the educational growth of her students from a fairly unique perspective. She writes of her experience as follows in An Experiment in Education:

I had learned to respect the intelligence, integrity, creativity and capacity for deep thought and hard work latent somewhere in every child; they had learned that I differed from them only in years and experience, and that as I, an ordinary human being, loved and respected them. . . . I expected payment in kind.

M. Reading Skill: CLARIFYING Ask students why the cabin "was like the lamb chops" to Crane. *(It seemed too good to be true, so he thought it might be just a vivid dream, like the one he had had about lamb chops.)*

N. Critical Thinking: DRAWING CONCLUSIONS Ask students why Alaskans have such a custom. *(They live in a dangerous wilderness where houses are far apart and people get stranded.)* Ask what the "prepared shavings" were for. *(wood shavings for starting a fire)* Finally, ask students how long they would stay in the cabin if they were in Crane's predicament. *(Answers will vary, depending on students' conclusions about the best survival strategy.)*

O. LEP: Idioms Help students of limited English proficiency interpret the idioms *right around the corner* ("very near, though not yet in sight") and *home free* ("sure of success").

P. Reading Skill: SUMMARIZING *(During the ninth day, Crane decides that no one is coming for him, so he sets off in search of food and shelter. The cabin he finds indicates to him that he is near civilization.)*

Q. Literary Element: AUTHOR'S PURPOSE Ask students how they can tell that the author means to entertain readers as well as to inform them about one man's survival. *(He tells this true story very suspensefully; he portrays Crane as an interesting "character," with both flaws and strengths.)*

R. Reading Skill: PREDICTING Ask students if they think Crane will venture out into the wilderness again or wait in the cabin for someone to find him. *(Possible response: When his food runs out, he will need to go out unless he develops a way to find new food.)*

S. Literary Element: TONE Ask what tone students would use to read this section aloud. *(Possible responses: joyful, relieved, hopeful)*

river bend. "Right around that curve is what you're looking for," he told himself again. Suddenly, something was there. First, he saw a cache, high on legs in the air, and then a small cabin, with a door only three feet high. It was like the lamb chops, with the grease on his fingers, but when he pushed at the door, it was wood and real. The room inside was nine by ten: earth floor, low ceiling, a bunk made of spruce. It was Alaskan custom always to leave a cabin open and stocked for anyone in need. Split firewood was there, and matches, and a pile of prepared shavings. On a table were sacks of dried raisins, sugar, cocoa, and powdered milk. There was a barrel stove, frying pans on the wall. He made some cocoa and, after so long a time without food, seemed full after a couple of sips. Then he climbed a ladder and looked in the cache, lifting a tarp to discover hammers, saws, picks, drills, coiled rope, and two tents. No one, he reasoned, would leave such equipment far off in the wilderness. "I figured civilization was right around the corner. I was home free."

summarize

How does Crane's plan of action change after the ninth day? What happens to encourage him?

So he stayed just a night and went on down the river, anxious to get back to Ladd Field. The moon came up after the brief light of day, and he kept going. He grew weak in the deep cold of the night, and when the moon went below the mountains, he began to wander off the stream course, hitting boulders. He had been around many corners, but no civilization was there. Now he was sinking into a dream-hazy sleepwalking numbed-out oblivion; but fear, fortunately, struck through and turned him, upriver. He had not retraced his way very far when he stopped and tried to build a fire. He scraped together some twigs, but his cut and bare hands were shaking so—at roughly fifty below zero—that he failed repeatedly to ignite a match. He abandoned the effort and moved on through the snow. He kept hitting boulders. He had difficulty following his own tracks. He knew now that he would die if he did not get back to the cabin, and the detached observer within him decided he was finished. Left foot, right foot—there was no point in quitting, even so. About noon, he reached the cabin. With his entire body shaking, he worked at a fire until he had one going. Then he rolled up in his parachute and slept almost continuously for three full days. ◀ SR-4

In his excitement at being "right around the corner from civilization," he had scarcely looked in the cache, and now he found rice, flour, beans, powdered eggs, dried vegetables, and beef—enough for many weeks, possibly months. He found mittens. He found snowshoes. He found long johns, socks, mukluks. He found candles, tea, tobacco, and a corncob pipe. He found ammunition, a .22. In the cabin, he mixed flour, peas, beans, sugar, and snow, and set it on the stove. That would be his basic gruel—and he became enduringly fond of it. Sometimes he threw in eggs and vegetables. He covered his hands with melted candle wax, and the bandage was amazingly effective. He developed a routine, with meals twice a day, a time for hunting, a fresh well chopped daily through the four-foot river ice. He slept eighteen hours a day, like a wintering bear—not truly hibernating, just lying there in his den. He felt a need to hear a voice, so he talked to himself. The day's high moment was a pipeful of tobacco puffed while he looked

DATA BANK

Hikers in the wilderness can take advantage of methods used by Native Americans to ascertain direction even when the sun and stars are not visible. To use this method, three or four trees must be available in an open region.

1. Examine tree foliage. In the northern hemisphere the south side of each tree—where sunlight is more constant—should appear to have distinctly more foliage.

2. Examine the tree tops. They almost always lean toward sunlight, in a south or southeast direction.

3. Examine the tree bark. The north side—away from the sun—should appear duller and darker.

4. Examine a tree stump. Rings will be thicker on the north and thinner on the south side.

5. Moss or lichen will almost always appear on the north side of a tree.

through ten-year-old copies of *The Saturday Evening Post.* He ransacked the magazines for insights into the woods lore he did not know. He learned a thing or two. In a wind, it said somewhere in the *Post,* build your fire in a hole. He shot and ate a ptarmigan[6] and had the presence of mind to look in its stomach. He found some overwintering berries there, went to the sort of bushes they had come from, and shot more ptarmigan. Cardboard boxes, the magazines, and other items in the cabin were addressed to "Phil Berail, Woodchopper, Alaska." Contemplating these labels, Crane decided that Alaska was a fantastic place—where someone's name and occupation were a sufficient address. One day, an old calendar fell off the wall and flipped over on its way to the floor. On the back was a map of Alaska. He stared at it all day. He found Woodchopper, on the Yukon, and smiled at his foolishness. From the terrain around (T) him, the northward flow of the stream, the relative positions of Fairbanks and Big Delta, he decided—just right—that he was far up the Charley River. The smile went back where it came from.

summarize

(U) **How does Crane manage to survive in the cabin?**

(V) He decided to wait for breakup, build a raft, and in late May float on down to the Yukon. After five or six weeks, though, he realized that his food was going to give out in March. There was little ammunition with which to get meat, and he had no confidence anyway in his chances with the rifle. SR-5 ▶ If he stayed, he would starve. He felt panic now, but not enough to spill the care with which he was making his plans. He had set off willy-nilly once before and did not want to repeat the mistake. He patched his clothes with parachute cloth, sewing them with shroud lines. He made a sled from some boards and a galvanized tub. He figured closely what the maximum might be that he could drag and carry. On February 12 he left. The sled would scarcely budge at first, and snow bunched up before it. Wearing a harness he had made, he dragged the sled slowly downriver. Berail's snowshoes had Indian ties. Try as he would, he could not understand how to secure them to his feet. The snowshoes were useless. Up to his knees, and sometimes to his hips, he (W)

Leon Crane

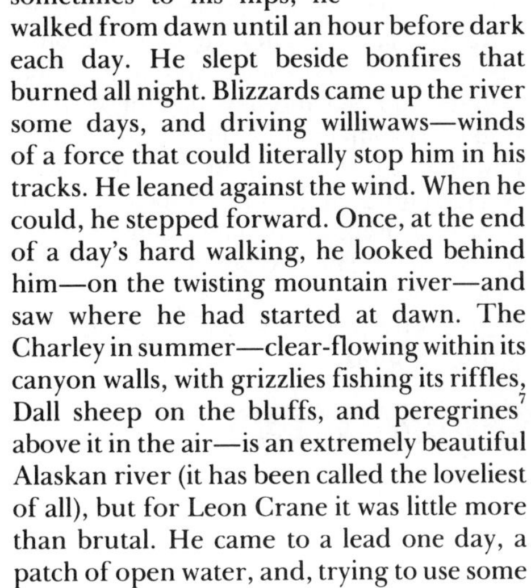

walked from dawn until an hour before dark each day. He slept beside bonfires that burned all night. Blizzards came up the river some days, and driving williwaws—winds of a force that could literally stop him in his tracks. He leaned against the wind. When he could, he stepped forward. Once, at the end of a day's hard walking, he looked behind him—on the twisting mountain river—and saw where he had started at dawn. The Charley in summer—clear-flowing within its canyon walls, with grizzlies fishing its riffles, Dall sheep on the bluffs, and peregrines[7] above it in the air—is an extremely beautiful Alaskan river (it has been called the loveliest of all), but for Leon Crane it was little more than brutal. He came to a lead one day, a patch of open water, and, trying to use some (X)

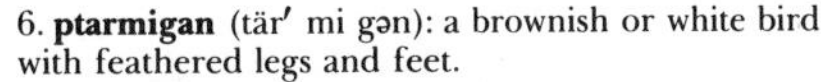

6. **ptarmigan** (tär′ mi gən): a brownish or white bird with feathered legs and feet.

7. **peregrines** (per′ ə grinz): falcons.

T. Critical Thinking: DRAWING CONCLUSIONS Ask students to explain why reading the map causes Crane's spirits to drop. *(At first he thinks "Woodchopper" is the cabin owner's occupation. From the map he realizes that it is a town located in the middle of nowhere.)*

U. Reading Skill: SUMMARIZING *(He rations his supplies, hunts, heals his hands with wax, and burns wood for warmth.)*

V. Reading Skill: USING CONTEXT CLUES Have students figure out the meaning of *breakup* from the context of the sentence. *(early spring, when the ice on the river begins breaking up and melting)*

W. Critical Thinking: ANALYZING Ask students if Crane shows an ability to learn from his mistakes. *(Yes, the first time he set off from the cabin, he did so without a plan and without adequate supplies, and he almost died. This time he prepares and thinks through the strategy for his trip carefully.)*

X. Discussion Ask students to comment on the contrast between the general perception of the Charley River as beautiful and Crane's idea of it as "brutal." Ask for other examples of widely varying points of view on a place, and have students explain why two views can vary so greatly.

Y. Literary Element: AUTHOR'S PURPOSE Ask students why they think the author decided to include this direct quotation from Crane. Ask what it shows about Crane. *(Possible response: It breaks the tension because it is a humorous understatement of what Crane has been through; it shows that he has considerable grace under pressure.)*

Z. Reading Skill: SUMMARIZING *(He makes a sled from his parachute, then goes downriver. Then he finds a cabin, stays a few days, and finally makes his way to the Ames's cabin.)*

AA. Literary Element: THEME Crane knows that he has survived against overwhelming odds. Have students discuss factors that were in his favor and factors that were against him. *(Possible response: In his favor: he had warm clothes and a parachute, he was resourceful, was not injured, didn't panic. Against him: life-threatening weather, he had no idea of his location, no food, shelter, or clear path of action, no wilderness experience)*

Check Test

1. Where was Crane stranded and why? *(in the wilderness of Alaska; his plane crashed)*

2. Where did he camp for the first nine days? *(beside a river)*

3. What shelter did he find when he set off down the river? *(a fully stocked cabin)* How long did he stay there the first time? *(just one day)*

4. Why did Crane retrace his steps back to the shelter? *(He knew he would die if he didn't.)*

5. Who were the first people Crane saw as he drew near civilization? *(Al Ames, a trapper, and his wife and children)*

Encouraging Independent Reading

The Incredible Journey, a novel by Sheila Burnford
Kon-Tiki, nonfiction by Thor Heyerdahl
"Love of Life" and "To Build a Fire," short stories by Jack London
Coming into the Country, and *The Survival of the Bark Canoe,* nonfiction by John McPhee
The Swiss Family Robinson, a novel by Johann Wyss

boulders as stepping stones, he fell in up to his armpits. Coming out, barging through snowdrifts, he was the center of a fast-forming block of ice. His matches were dry. Shaking as before, he managed this time to build a fire. All day, he sat steaming beside it, removing this or that item of clothing, drying it a piece at a time. SR-6 ▸

After a couple of weeks on the river, he found another cabin, with a modest but welcome food cache—cornmeal, canned vegetables, Vienna sausage. He sewed himself a backpack and abandoned his cumbersome sled. Some seven or eight days on down the river, he came around a bend at dusk and found cut spruce tops in parallel rows stuck in the river snow. His aloneness, he sensed, was all but over. It was the second week of March, and he was eighty days out of the sky. The arrangement of treetops, obviously, marked a place where a plane on skis might land supplies. He looked around in near darkness and found a toboggan trail. He camped and next day followed the trail to a cabin—under smoke. He shouted toward it. Al Ames, a trapper, and his wife, Neena, and their children appeared in the doorway. "I am Lieutenant Leon Crane, of the United States Army Air Forces," he called out. "I've been in a little trouble." Ames took a picture, which hangs on a wall in Philadelphia. Y

summarize

Z How does Crane make his way from Berail's cabin to civilization?

Crane remembers thinking, Somebody must be saving me for something, but I don't know what it is. His six children, who owe themselves to that trip and to Phil Berail's fully stocked Charley River cabin, are—in addition to his three sons in the construction business—Mimi, who is studying engineering at Barnard; Rebecca, who is in the master's program in architecture at Columbia; and Ruth, a recent graduate of the Harvard Medical School. Crane himself went on to earn an advanced degree in aeronautical engineering at the Massachusetts Institute of Technology and spent his career developing helicopters for Boeing Vertol. AA

"It's a little surprising to me that people exist who are interested in living on that ground up there," he told me. "Why would anyone want to take someone who wanted to *be* there and throw them out? Who the hell could *care*?"

Al Ames, who had built his cabin only two years before, harnessed his dogs and mushed Crane down the Yukon to Woodchopper, where a plane soon came along and flew him out.

Crane met Phil Berail at Woodchopper and struggled shyly to express to him his inexpressible gratitude. Berail, sixty-five, was a temporary postmaster and worked for the gold miners there. He had trapped from his Charley River cabin. He was pleased that it had been useful, he said. For his part, he had no intention of ever going there again. He had abandoned the cabin four years before. ◂ SR-7

Words to Know and Use	**aeronautical** (er' ō nôt' i kəl) *adj.* having to do with airplanes

Responding to Reading

First Impressions

1. What visual image of Crane's efforts to survive do you recall most strongly? Why?

Second Thoughts

2. What do you think is the most crucial decision Leon Crane makes when he first faces the wilderness alone? Explain.

   Think about
   - where he decides to walk
   - how he builds a fire
   - how he handles his emotions
   - how he uses the parachute
   - how and where he finds food

3. Is Crane unusually lucky, or does he make his own luck to survive? Review the events on your time line for help.

   Think about
   - what he happens to have with him when he parachutes
   - how he finds the cabin
   - what he finds in the cabin
   - the qualities that help Crane beat the odds and survive

4. What other character whom you have read about in this book might have survived in Crane's situation? Explain.

Broader Connections

5. Faced with Alaska's frigid wilderness, Leon Crane found that he had the qualities needed for survival in that particular setting. What are the most important survival qualities in your world? Explain.

Literary Concept: Biography

A **biography** is a true story about a person's life written by another person, the biographer. The biographer's job is to learn about real events. Think about the biographical research that John McPhee did to write this account. What are three specific details that helped this story seem real?

Concept Review: Conflict At the beginning of a typical story, an author usually sets up the conflict, or struggle, a character faces. What was the conflict in this selection?

Student Resonse

Responding to Reading

These questions are open-ended with no "right" or "wrong" answers. However, responses must be supported with information from the selection. Possible answers follow:

1. Any reasonable response based on the article is acceptable.

2. Some students may say his most crucial decision is not to panic and to assume he can survive. Others may say it is to make his way down to the river, where he has access to drinking water. Still others may say it is his decision to keep his parachute and use it for warmth, or his decision to keep a fire going.

3. Some students may say he is lucky because he isn't injured in the crash, he has matches, and he finds the cabin just before he is beginning to starve. Others may say he makes his own luck by using the parachute for warmth, following the river to the cabin, and not panicking.

4. Some students may say the Great Armando would have survived in Crane's situation because he is strong, clever, and resourceful. Others might name the stowaway in "The Stowaway" as a good survivor. Still others may name yet another character. Be sure students support their responses.

5. Some students may feel that in today's world, education is the most important survival skill. With it, you can get a job that pays enough to provide food and shelter. Without it, you lack the skills necessary to function in today's job market. Others may say the ability to adapt to change is the most important skill to acquire in this fast-paced world. Students may supply other answers.

Literary Concept—Biography

Possible response: The fact that the author tracked down Leon Crane, the subject of the biography, made this story seem real. Crane's thoughts about fear could only have come from a man who had been lost in the wilderness. Similarly, his use of the parachute as a sleeping bag, a sled, a slingshot, and a bow and arrow (using parts from the parachute) lent the story an air of authenticity.

Concept Review: Conflict *Possible response:* Crane must struggle to survive in the wilderness. His internal conflicts involve whether to stay put or move on, how to find food, and how to prevent despair, fear, and boredom from overcoming him.

Writing Options

The Writing Options are designed to meet varied student interests and abilities. Have each student choose one writing activity to complete. You may wish to guide some students to an option that requires less writing.

Journal Update Have students review their journal entries. Ask them to write about what they have learned about survival from reading "Survival in the Forty-Ninth." Suggest they take stock of their own survival skills. How would they fare in a situation like the one experienced by Leon Crane?

Vocabulary Practice

1. c **2.** b **3.** d **4.** b **5.** a

Writing Options

1. Use the information you have learned from reading this story to write a tip-sheet of five to ten items on "How to Survive in the Wilderness." Assume that your audience is made up of people who are about to travel to the Arctic Circle. Use Crane's experiences as a guide but feel free to use your own ideas as well.
2. Imagine that you are Crane. Write a letter to Phil Berail expressing your thanks for the fully stocked cabin.
3. Crane keeps telling himself that help is "right around that curve." Do you think such a belief is helpful or a problem in a difficult situation? Explain.
4. When Crane reaches the cabin after weeks in the wilderness, he says to Ames, "I've been in a little trouble." Describe what *you* would have said if you had been Crane.

Vocabulary Practice

Exercise Use your understanding of the boldfaced word to complete each of the following sentences. Write the letter of the correct answer on your paper.

1. Crane's **aeronautical** engineering degree led to a career in developing (a) automobiles (b) boats (c) helicopters (d) skyscrapers.
2. **Centrifugal** force kept Crane from (a) eating (b) moving quickly (c) talking (d) sleeping.
3. A **meandering** trail follows a path that is (a) shortest (b) direct (c) straight (d) winding.
4. An important part of a cabin's **refurbishment** would be (a) tearing it down (b) fixing its plumbing (c) learning its history (d) finding new tenants.
5. Crane needed to maintain constant **vigilance** to (a) keep his fire from going out (b) fall asleep (c) relax (d) amuse himself.

Words to Know and Use

aeronautical
centrifugal
meandering
refurbishment
vigilance

Options for Learning

1 • Design a Wilderness Book Recreate Crane's wilderness experience as a picture book for youngsters. Relate the entire story, using only simple sentences to tell the tale. If possible, read your book to a class of elementary school students.

2 • Trace Crane's Adventure Study the map of Alaska on page 268 and other maps of Alaska if necessary. Find exactly where Crane traveled. Draw a simplified map on which you can show your classmates the crash location, the cabins, the river, and other places vital to Crane's story. Calculate how many miles he trekked.

3 • Survival Gear Visit a sporting goods store to find out about the contributions of modern technology to cold-weather gear. How do people keep warm today in the world's most frigid climates? Present your findings in an oral report to the class.

FACT FINDER

On average, what is the coldest place in the United States?

John McPhee
1931–

NYT Pictures

"I'm a working journalist," John McPhee once told an interviewer, "and I've got to go out and work." No truer statement about John McPhee can be found, for he is one of the most productive of all American writers. Ever since 1965, when he published his first book (a study of basketball player Bill Bradley), he has published something practically every year.

McPhee's books cover a remarkable range of subjects. "John McPheeland," noted one critic, "is a small nation populated almost entirely by canoe makers, basketball players, inspired tinkerers, back yard inventors, restaurant owners, vegetable growers, and geologists."

While this seems like an incredible range of writing, McPhee has a simple explanation: "Just about everything I've written touches on subjects that interested me as a kid."

McPhee spent his years as a kid in Princeton, New Jersey, where his father served as doctor for the Princeton University athletic teams. As a boy, McPhee enjoyed basketball, canoeing, and many other sports. He did well in school, especially in an English class that required him to write three compositions each week. He later attended Princeton University, lived in England, and worked in New York City. McPhee now lives in his hometown of Princeton, but he travels widely to research his many writing projects. To write *Coming into the Country* (of which "Survival in the Forty-Ninth" is a part), McPhee spent many months living in Alaska.

Options for Learning
These activities suit a variety of learning styles and modes of expression. Allow students to review the options and then choose the one they wish to do. Many are excellent collaborative learning projects.

1. Design a Wilderness Book Students may obtain a book about Alaska to help visualize the landscape in which Leon Crane was lost. Encourge students to use other nonfiction picture books as models.

2. Trace Crane's Adventure Show students how to use the map scale on the maps they study to calculate distances. Then have them decide on a scale for their own maps and compute how far apart they should show various places.

3. Survival Gear Students may obtain a catalog from a well-known outdoors store such as L. L. Bean or Eddie Bauer. Catalogs often explain the function and theory behind the latest outdoor equipment.

Fact Finder
Barrow, Alaska, has the lowest mean temperature in the United States. In January the average temperature is −15 degrees Fahrenheit. A good source for temperature data is a world almanac.

Additional Information About the Author
John McPhee John McPhee notes that the ideas for most of his books "originate when they strike an echo from my earlier experience." McPhee's motto is "You hope that some subject will interest you and then you will have to deal with it on its own terms."

Closure
"Survival in the Forty-Ninth" presents a character who must "beat the odds" to survive. Leon Crane's predicament is not one of his own making. To prevail, he must use every bit of his intelligence and resourcefulness. Have students think about the qualities of character that are important to survival in a life-or-death situation and whether it is possible to cultivate these qualities in oneself.

Cross-Curricular Options

Students could create a survival kit for the Alaskan wilderness, working individually, in pairs, or in teams.

Biology/Math: Study the nutritional needs of a normal person in a high-stress environment. Calculate how many calories are needed and what is the most efficient way to allocate them.

Writing: Read resource books on survival skills. Write a pamphlet summarizing the strategies that work best in the arctic.

Geography: Construct a map of the region that is waterproof and easy to read.

Economics: Price equipment at various outdoor outlets. Students might compete to see who can obtain a specified list of survival goods at the lowest prices.

Objectives

- To understand and analyze a short story
- To identify the antagonist in a story and analyze his traits
- To analyze techniques used to create suspense
- To express understanding of the work through a choice of writing options, including a description, similes, a news story, and an editorial

Prereading/Motivation

Examine What You Know

Discussion Prompts: How does understanding how a trap works help a person escape from the trap? Are there some traps that are impossible to escape from?

Expand Your Knowledge

Discussion Prompts: Do you believe these escapes are real, or are they fixed in some way? Why are people interested in watching performers such as Houdini risk their lives?

Additional Background Harry Houdini prided himself on being able to withstand a punch from anyone. This proved to be his undoing, when, in 1926, a man recognized Houdini offstage and punched him in the chest without warning. Without being able to prepare himself for the blow, Houdini was injured gravely and died shortly thereafter.

Thematic Link—Beating the Odds

In this story, love enables a character to beat the odds and escape a death trap.

Fiction

The Death Trap

PAUL GALLICO

Examine What You Know (Prior Knowledge)

The title of the next selection is "The Death Trap." What do you think of when you hear the word *trap*? Name as many kinds of traps as you can think of. Discuss any experiences you may have had with traps, including any experiences you may have had with being trapped yourself. Compare your experiences with those of the characters in the next story.

Expand Your Knowledge (Building Background)

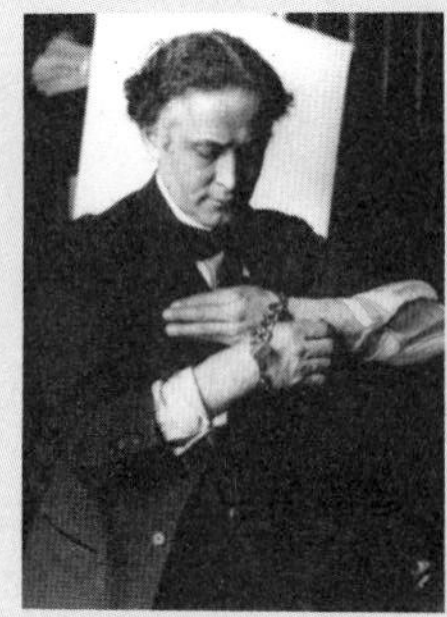

Harry Houdini

In the story you are about to read, the main character earns his living as an escape artist, a person who executes amazing escapes from supposedly escape-proof devices. While the hero of this story is a fictional character, he may have been modeled after the most famous escape artist of all—Harry Houdini (1874-1926). The son of a Hungarian rabbi, Houdini performed incredible feats, freeing himself in seconds from such devices as leg irons, jail cells, sealed boxes, and even ten pairs of handcuffs. His most famous trick involved escaping from an airtight tank filled with water. In another trick he would have himself handcuffed, tied up with a rope, and stuffed into a box. The box would then be padlocked and dropped into water. Moments later Houdini would emerge.

Write Before You Read (Journal Writing)

Two of the characters in the next selection believe in love at first sight. What do you think of this idea? Is love at first sight a myth or the way love often happens? Write your opinion.

■ *A biography of the author can be found in the Reader's Handbook.*

Additional Journal Writing

- Suggest these additional Journal topics to students. "The first time I get a real bad scare, I'll quit . . ." says one character in the story. When does it make sense to let a "scare" make you quit? When does it make sense to stick out a bad situation?
- Can a psychological trap be as deadly as a physical one? Explain.

For other journal opportunities, refer students to Examine What You Know (above), Real Life Connections (page T–286), and First Impressions and Broader Connections (page 288).

Additional Resources

UNIT TWO RESOURCE BOOK
Reader's Guidesheet, p. 55
Vocabulary Worksheet, p. 56
Selection and Vocabulary Check Tests, p. 57
Selection Test, pp. 58–59

Collaborative Learning

Opportunities for collaborative learning appear throughout the lesson and include the Examine What You Know activity (above) and Cross-Curricular Options (page T–289).

The Death Trap

PAUL GALLICO

There's no such thing as magic. You know that. You've seen a lot of magic shows from out front where the magician performs the apparently impossible. Well, it not only seems impossible; it is. There's a gaff to everything.

Gaff is the carnival word for the gimmick, the trick, the concealed device, the common-sense explanation of how it is done. And usually the gaff is something so simple you don't want to believe it. You'd see the Great Armando buried handcuffed in a stone sarcophagus,[1] and three minutes later he'd be out of it, taking his bow. Common sense would tell you he couldn't do it unless he had super-human powers or assistance. But the kind of showmanship he'd give you would make you want to believe in the superhuman powers. That's what you paid SR-1 ▶ your money for.

A Yet in nine cases out of ten, he had assistance. I provided it. With my help he escaped from a sealed subway caisson,[2] a time vault in the subtreasury, a four-thousand-year-old Greek stone coffin, the punishment cell at Alcatraz,[3] and countless types of manacles and restraining jackets.

But don't forget, he had moxie[4] along with it. Even if you know the gimmicks, it B takes guts to let them lace you into a straitjacket, stuff you into a government mailbag, padlock it, nail you into a packing case bound with rope, and drop you into an icy river in mid-winter.

The only one to come near the Great Armando was Houdini, and everything Houdini did, Armando did better. Houdini did the river-escape trick, only he used handcuffs that he could get out of in ten seconds. Nobody but Armando dared to do it with the straitjacket and letting an expert truss[5] him up.

C Yet, as I wrote in my diary, the straitjacket finished him—leastways, the gimmick in it. And a woman put it there. The only woman he ever loved.

He was a queer duck, was Joe Ferris. Nobody ever knew him or got close to him, not even me, and I was his trusted partner. I suppose that was the Polish in him. Often he was moody and suspicious. He kept his money stashed away in cash in safe-deposit boxes under different names that I never D even knew. He thought only of his reputation and the myth of the Great Armando. He said to me, "Remember this. Whatever happens, the Great Armando never fails."

Yet he was no fool, either, and knew the

1. **sarcophagus** (sär käf′ ə gəs): a coffin or tomb.
2. **caisson** (kā′ sən): a watertight enclosure used for doing construction work under water.
3. **Alcatraz** (al′ kə traz′): an island prison in San Francisco Bay.
4. **moxie** (mäks′ ē): slang for courage.
5. **truss:** to tie.

Teaching Strategies

Vocabulary Preview

These vocabulary words are defined at the bottom of the selection page on which they appear. You may wish to discuss them briefly before students begin reading.

cowed timid; frightened
delirium mental confusion
devoid completely without
drudge one who does difficult, thankless work
imperceptibly without being noticed
insoluble unsolvable
interstices cracks; crevices
plaited braided or woven
submissive showing no resistance
vindictive revengeful

Support for Students of Limited English Proficiency

- Use Reader's Guidesheet, p. 55.
- "The Death Trap" has slang and carnival terms that students of limited English proficiency may find hard to understand. Have them list confusing terms as they read and then share their lists in a class discussion.
- Annotations B, E, G, P, X, and II focus on troublesome terms.

Text Annotations

A. Literary Element: POINT OF VIEW Ask whether the story is told from first- or third-person point of view *(first).*

B. LEP: Vocabulary Students of limited English proficiency may not know what a straitjacket is. Have volunteers describe the device and tell what it is used for. *(an outer garment that binds the body; used to restrain a violent prisoner or patient)*

C. Literary Element: FORESHADOWING Ask what hints this gives about the plot and what questions it raises. *(It hints that Armando may get trapped in a straitjacket; it raises the question of why the one he loved would sabotage him.)*

D. Reading Skill: PREDICTING Ask what Armando might do if he had to choose between risking his life and his reputation. *(Possible response: He would risk his life.)*

Structured Reading for Less Proficient Students

These questions can help to guide students through the reading. Ask each question at the point of the selection where the SR number appears in the margin.

SR–1. What is a gaff? *(The common-sense explanation for a trick)* Why is the gaff important to Armando? What kind of act does he have? *(He is an escape artist. The gaff is the trick that makes him seem to have superhuman powers.)* **Clarifying**

SR–2. According to Armando, when will he quit his act? *(the first time he gets a real scare)* **Literal recall**

SR–3. Why do Armando and the narrator always investigate the restraining devices in advance? *(to figure out how to open them)* **Clarifying**

SR–4. With whom does Armando fall in love? *(with Tina, the sheriff's wife)* **Literal recall**

SR–5. Why does the sheriff have a grudge against Armando? *(The sheriff had tried to extort money from a carnival Armando once traveled in, and Armando had helped beat him up.)* **Literal recall**

Continued on page T–280

E. LEP: Idioms/Slang Show how students can infer that *gander* means "look" from the context of the preceding sentence. Then point out how the noun *gaff* from the previous page has been changed into *gaffed,* a verb. Discuss the colloquial use of nouns as verbs, and give examples such as *to video, to muscle, to okay.*

F. Critical Thinking: ANALYZING Ask students in what sense the sheriff's wife might be in a trap. *(She might be trapped in a brutal marriage and afraid to leave.)*

G. LEP: Slang Ask students to guess the meaning of the expression "to make a monkey out of," based on what they know about the behavior of monkeys. *(to make a fool of)* Then ask if there are any expressions in their native languages that compare human behavior to animal behavior.

H. Reading Skill: CLARIFYING Make sure students understand what signing a release implies and in what sense Armando's "murder" could be "for free." *(Before doing his stunts, Armando signs a paper relieving the authorities of any responsibility for what happens to him; therefore, the sheriff could ensure Armando's death without fear of punishment.)*

I. Literary Element: ANTAGONIST Ask students who Armando's antagonist is *(the sheriff)* and to speculate on what type of antagonist he will be. *(Possible response: a dangerous, clever one, who will fight to the death with no scruples)*

risks he was running. He once told me, "The first time I get a real bad scare, I'll quit and nobody'll ever hear of the Great Armando again. But up to now I haven't seen anything we can't beat." **SR-2**

But that was before we met up with Sheriff Jules Massin of Ossowo County in the tough River Rouge section of Detroit, where we were doing the water escape as preliminary publicity to Armando's being booked into the Michigan Palace Theater in Detroit. The sheriff had taken up our challenge to lace Armando into a straitjacket from which he could not escape.

"The first time I get a real bad scare, I'll quit and nobody'll ever hear of the Great Armando again."

On the face of it, it was routine. There was no straitjacket made that Armando couldn't get out of in less than a minute. But we never took chances. It was a condition that Armando guaranteed to get out of any restraining device provided he could inspect it first. The padlock on the mail sack had to be closed and opened in our presence. This gave me the necessary gander at the key. And the packing case had to go on exhibition in the lobby of the theater before and after the stunt. That's when we gaffed it. **E** **SR-3**

We thought we had every angle covered. Only we never figured to come up against a man with murder in his heart.

There was a crowd in the sheriff's office the day we went there to inspect the restraints and set up the stunt: deputies, detectives, police, reporters, and photographers. The sheriff's wife was there, too. His office was on the ground floor of his home. At first I didn't notice her. She had a scarf bound around her head, European style. She had pale cheeks and prominent gray-green eyes that seemed absolutely devoid of expression. They did not even flicker when the sheriff, noticing her in the forefront of those crowding around his desk, snarled, "What the hell you doin' here, Tina? Can't you see I'm busy?"

She was submissive to his abuse; every line of her body proclaimed her to be cowed and hopeless. Yet she did not go, and soon other matters claimed the sheriff's attention. **F**

The sheriff was a mean man. Mean, dirty, and dangerous. He wasn't a copper for nothing. He liked it. We meet all kinds in our racket, from plain smart alecks who think it is fun to make a monkey out of a performer to cops and jailers who don't like to see you make a monkey out of them. But we'd never run up against a guy nursing murder in his heart because it was for free. Armando always signed a release. **G** **H**

That was the sheriff. I knew him for a killer, a killer inside the law from the moment I walked into his office. He was over six feet tall, fat, burly, and dirty. His clothes were dirty, as were his skin, his fingernails, and his teeth. His breath was bad. He wore a fancy gun in a belt holster, silver- and ivory-handled. You could see he loved the power it gave him. **I**

Massin threw a straitjacket onto his desk and sneered, "Anything wrong with that?"

Words to Know and Use

devoid (di void') *adj.* completely without
submissive (sub mis' iv) *adj.* displaying no resistance
cowed (koud) *adj.* timid; frightened **cow** *v.*

STRUCTURED READING FOR LESS PROFICIENT STUDENTS

Continued from page T-279

SR-6. How does the sheriff trick Armando? *(He has plaited straw finger grips sewn into the straitjacket after Armando has inspected it.)* **Literal recall**

SR-7. What dilemma does Armando face? *(If he goes ahead with the stunt, he will probably die; if he doesn't, he might as well be dead, because he'll lose his reputation.)* **Clarifying**

SR-8. Why does the narrator say that Armando's greatest trick was also his last? *(Because when the packing case is brought up, it is clear that Armando has escaped, but no trace of him can be found, so it is assumed that he died trying to come up out of the water.)* **Summarizing**

SR-9. Who does the narrator think he sees thirty years later? *(Armando and Tina)* What do they say to him? *(that they are Mr. and Mrs. Vernon Howard)* **Literal recall**

SR-10. How had Armando managed to escape the finger grips? *(Tina had cut them slightly so that they were easy to get out of.)* **Literal recall**

J It was an ordinary violence-restraint jacket with straps and buckles, the easiest type for Armando, for the canvas was not unusually thick. No matter how strong the manipulator, Armando, by swelling his muscles, could always reserve enough slack to get his arms over his head. Then he opened the buckles *through* the canvas. I told you he had the most powerful fingers in the world. In that department he was superhuman. That's why he was called great.

I picked up the jacket to show Armando. But he wasn't looking. Something strange had happened. He was staring instead at Tina Massin, and on his face was an expression such as I had never seen there before.

I had to catch my breath. Her head cloth had fallen back upon her neck, revealing hair so ash blond it was almost white and the perfect oval of her face. She looked like the pale, imprisoned princess in the book of Grimm's fairy tales[6] I had when I was a kid. The impression she made upon me at that moment was one I would never forget.

K Have you ever known it to happen that you see someone for the first time and in that moment you know his life story almost as though you had read it in a book? She was of foreign extraction, maybe Polish or Finnish. I guessed she had been taken from an institution or orphanage into the sheriff's establishment, as household drudge. She had no doubt first been abused and later married, because it was more convenient to own a wife than a servant. There are some women who become the hopeless, submissive captives to the most appalling men. Such a one was Tina Massin.

They were caught up in one another's eyes, these two utterly different and contrasting strangers, the showman with the long black hair and piercing glance, the pale girl with the silken-thick hair and eyes that were for the first time alive and filled with a kind of pleading. Any moment it would become obvious that two people had found one another, had fallen in love, and were attempting to communicate. L

I created a diversion by tossing the jacket back onto the desk. "That's okay," I said.

The sheriff sniggered unpleasantly. "It's the way I strap 'em into it," he said. I was satisfied to let Armando deal with that. The post-office inspector produced the mailbag. I bent over to examine the thickness, fittings, and padlock. I had a dozen keys that would open it. Armando would have two of them concealed on his person attached to a fine wire. Once out of the straitjacket, a matter of sixty seconds, he would push out the key and manipulate it, again through the material of the sack. M

It was okay. Nevertheless, I made them open and shut the lock several times to make sure it hadn't been gaffed with shot or sand. Mrs. Massin dropped her handkerchief. Armando stooped to pick it up as did she. Their fingers touched for an instant. I was still bent over, examining the mailbag. I heard her whisper to him, "For God's sake, don't do it. . . ."

The time set was ten the next morning at the Western and Lakes railroad pier, where there was a big traveling crane. The document releasing the sheriff's office and Detroit police from all responsibility was

6. **Grimm's fairy tales:** well-known collections of stories for children—including "Snow White" and "Hansel and Gretel"—published by two German brothers, Jakob and Wilhelm Grimm.

Words to Know and Use	**drudge** (druj) *n.* someone who performs difficult, thankless work

J. Reading Skill: SUMMARIZING Ask students to summarize how Armando escapes from a straitjacket. Have a volunteer use pantomime to demonstrate his escape method. *(Possible response: He flexes his chest and arm muscles, creating slack (a loose space); pulls his arms up, then opens the buckles through the jacket material.)*

K. Critical Thinking: INFERRING/EVALUATING Ask students how they think Carl is able to figure out so much about Tina Massin just by looking at her. Ask if they think such first impressions are usually accurate. *(Possible response: He has known people who resemble her in the past; he can't imagine someone as wholesome as she is voluntarily associating with Massin. Answers about the accuracy of such assessments will vary. Have students give examples from their own experience.)*

L. Literary Element: ANTAGONIST Ask students how Armando's encounter with Tina might make the sheriff a more dangerous antagonist. *(Possible response: If the sheriff suspects their love, he will be even more determined to kill Armando; Armando's love may make him reckless, careless, or susceptible to being tricked by the sheriff through Tina.)*

M. Reading Skill: DRAWING CONCLUSIONS Ask students what kind of job they think Carl the narrator might have had before he became Armando's partner. *(Possible response: locksmith)*

Professional Notebook

Don't use a chainsaw to do the job intended for dental floss. Don't over-react to the discouraged learner. We, too often, focus on ''appropriate'' behavior in moralistic tones, not in a framework of learning. Building (or re-building) self-esteem, confidence, and internal responsibility is our primary objective; then skills; everything else, with discouraged learners at least, comes a distant third.

JERRY CONRATH, ***Our Other Youth***

Art Note
Richard Lindner (1901–   ) was born in Hamburg and studied art in Nuremberg and Munich. In 1933 he left Germany for Paris, and, in 1941, came to the United States, where he worked for a time as a highly paid illustrator and an instructor. In *The Visitor,* the stylized figures and bright colors suggest magic—or fate—in an atmosphere of carnival. *Describe how the painting illustrates The Death Trap.*

N. Critical Thinking: INFERRING Ask students why they think Tina is so despairing. *(Possible response: She fears that Armando, the man she loves, will die; she knows that her husband, the sheriff, is going to trick Armando.)*

O. Literary Element: SATIRE Ask students how Carl satirizes the sheriff. (He uses the word *fragrant* when he really means foul.)

P. LEP: Slang The terms *shakedown, shelled out,* and *hand-out* may be puzzling to some students. Tell students the terms are related. Have students infer the meanings of *shelled out* (paid) and *hand-out* (bribe or payoff) from the context. Then have them use these meanings to conclude what a *shakedown* is. (forced payment; extortion) Say that *grift* refers to dishonest gambling.

Q. Historical Sidelight Traveling carnival shows were a major form of entertainment in the United States of the 1920s, before movies became the dominant pastime. Some shows were known for bordering on the illegal, featuring gambling and fraud.

produced, and the photographers jostled for position. Somebody handed Armando a pen. Mrs. Massin made a slight gesture with her hand. Their eyes met once more. She licked dry lips and, almost imperceptibly, shook her head. The sheriff missed the byplay, but sniggered again. "Going to welsh?"[7] he asked and then, addressing everyone in general, said, "I say all greasers are yellow."

Joe Ferris flourished the pen dramatically. "Armando he nevaire[8] welsh," he said and signed. The light in Tina Massin's eyes was extinguished. All the life went from her. She was hopeless, despairing, submissive. She turned and went out of the room.

N

SR-4

I went to see Harry Hopp, an old-time reporter friend on the *Free Press.* I told you we never left anything to chance. I didn't like the setup for two cents. I asked, "What's the background on your fragrant sheriff of Ossowo County?"

O

Hopp said, "Can't tell you anything good about him. And as long as you're asking, he hates carnivals and the carny crowd. They can't get the time of day in his county. You better watch out for that baby."

"Yeah," I said, "I got that. But why?"

"Shakedown," he replied. "There was a carnival through here five or six years ago really loaded with grift.[9] They shelled out plenty to the sheriff to operate, but when he came back again for a second hand-out, they beat him up and threw him out. Maybe your boyfriend even was with the carny and saw it happen. He's death on anything connected with traveling shows or midways."

P

That night I said to Armando, "Lissen,

THE VISITOR 1953 Richard Lindner © 1990 ARS, New York/ADAGP.

Joe. Were you ever with a grift show that beat up a sheriff around here before you started in with me?"

He reflected and then said slowly, "So that's where I know him from. When he tried to shake me down, I poked him, and that started it."

Q

7. **welsh:** slang for evade, break a promise.
8. **nevaire:** *dialect,* never.
9. **grift:** unfair or rigged games of chance.

Words to Know and Use

imperceptibly (im' pər sep' tə blē) *adv.* without being noticed

282

R I said, "I don't like it. He's got it in for you. Let's call it off. We can do it in Cleveland next week."

He looked at me as if I were out of my mind and asked, "Have we got all the angles covered?"

I went back over things in my mind. There was nothing that could happen that we hadn't thought of. "Yes," I said.

"Okay," he said, "we go. We can't afford
SR-5 ▶ to back out."

S But I was wrong. There was something I hadn't thought of, something so simple and elementary as a means of destroying Armando that it never dawned on me until it was too late.

The day of the test was damp, cold, and sunless. There were chunks of ice floating in the river. In spite of the raw, blustery weather, the pier and several adjoining docks were black with people. We'd had a big press in advance of the attempt. . . .

The stunt was routine, and we'd done it a dozen times before. The gaff was this: as soon as they started to nail the cover onto the box, Armando would start working his way out of the straitjacket and the mailbag, while I'd stall, suggesting putting in more nails or tying the rope tighter until I got a signal from Armando that he was out of the restraints. The crate had been gimmicked by us the night before with a concealed sliding panel in one side. Fifteen seconds after the box disappeared beneath the surface, he'd be out of it.

T It was that simple—like all stage or escape illusions, except it was the way Armando did it that made it look so good. It is a part of the showmanship in that kind of an act that when you really think a guy is in danger, he's as safe as he'd be at home in bed. The real deadly stuff doesn't show. Like staying under holding your breath for more than three minutes in freezing water and then coming up amidst ice floes or risking being carried away under the ice by the current. He had a right to call himself the Great Armando and to be proud of his rep.[10] T

She wasn't pretty anymore. Her face was tear stained and filled with fear.

U When Armando and I arrived, there was a big bunch of reporters including Harry Hopp, several sob sisters, a horde of photographers, and newsreel movie men. Captain Harry Stevens of the river police was giving directions to a police launch that was to pick Armando up if and when he appeared. He was not too pleased at being used for a publicity stunt and greeted us sourly. He said, "Okay, okay, let's get going and get out of here. You fellows signed a release, didn't you?"

Sheriff Massin, wearing a big sheepskin-lined coat, said, "Yup. Got it right here."

Armando slipped out of his cloak. Underneath he was wearing trousers and a sweatshirt of light, warm wool, and sneakers. The sheriff stepped over with the straitjacket, a nasty, self-satisfied smile on his face. Tina Massin was there in the front row. She wasn't pretty anymore. Her face was tear stained and filled with fear. Her eyes were fixed upon the jacket.

I spotted something about the sleeves that had not been there the day before. My stomach started to sink. I said, "Here, wait a minute. Let me see that jacket. It's been gimmicked."

10. **rep:** short for *reputation.*

R. Critical Thinking: EVALUATING Ask students to evaluate the morality of the sheriff's attitude toward Armando. Ask if he has a right to "have it in for" Armando. Have them support their opinions with arguments. *(Possible responses: The carnival deserved harsh treatment because it was dishonest; the sheriff was equally dishonest by trying to profit from a shakedown and deserved the treatment he got for his blackmail attempt.)*

S. Literary Element: SUSPENSE Ask how the author builds suspense in this part of the story. *(by dropping hints that keep us guessing about what exactly will be the means of destroying Armando)*

T. Literary Element: THEME Ask students to explain how the odds the public thinks Armando usually beats are not the true odds stacked against him. *(Possible response: The true odds Armando usually faces are not in escaping from the trap but in risking the icy water and in making the scene seem dangerous and entertaining.)*

U. Historical Sidelight Remind students that before the days of daily television news, people relied on newspapers and newsreels (short films about news events, which were shown in movie theaters before the main feature) for information about current events. "Sob sisters" were reporters who specialized in emotional human-interest stories.

DATA BANK

Like the Great Armando, the escape artist Harry Houdini made a thorough study of locks, studying drawings of their mechanisms, which he obtained from locksmiths. One of Houdini's favorite ways of getting publicity was to challenge local police departments to find a jail or handcuff that he could not escape from. Police departments would be embarrassed and angry when Houdini escaped from their jails, seeming to make a mockery of their security systems. Sir Arthur Conan Doyle, the author of the Sherlock Holmes stories, was convinced that Houdini used some kind of supernatural powers in his escapes, but Houdini insisted that all his escapes were based on easily explainable techniques. In the 1920s Houdini exposed the ''gaffs'' used by many so-called spiritualists and mediums who claimed to contact the dead.

V. Literary Element: IRONY Ask why the means of Armando's destruction is surprising and ironic. *(No one would expect a great escape artist to be defeated by an innocent child's toy.)*

W. Reading Skill: CLARIFYING Ask if this information clarifies any of Tina's earlier behavior. *(Possible responses: She tried to warn Armando about the trick because she knew about the finger traps; she knew her husband had a trick planned, though she may not have known what it was.)*

X. LEP: Language Point out that the phonetic spellings *feller (fellow)* and *hadda (had to)* allow the reader to "hear" how the sheriff speaks and help characterize him. Explain that the word *loony* is a disrespectful term for an insane person and that *greaseball* is a derogatory ethnic slur. Ask how Massin's use of these words also helps characterize him. *(They reinforce our image of him as a foul, despicable person with no concern for others' feelings.)*

Y. Discussion Have students discuss the pros and cons of Armando's backing down at this point. Then ask how Hopp's offer affects the conflict. *(Possible response: Hopp seems to offer a way out, but the sheriff's insistence on the word* welsh *[to cheat by refusing to pay off a bet] makes it clear that there is no way for Armando to resolve the conflict without costing either his life or his reputation.)*

Z. Literary Element: SUSPENSE Have students point out how the author creates suspense in this passage. *(Possible response: He keeps the reader waiting to find out whether Armando will accept the challenge.)*

The sheriff said, "They're stalling," but handed it over.

I turned out the sleeves. Inside, ten finger grips of plaited strips of colored straw had been sewn to the canvas lining. You've seen them in any magic or trick store, or child's magic set. Once they are slipped over a finger, the harder you pull, the more tightly they grip. A device also used commercially for hoisting, there is no possible way of tearing loose from it. The secret of escape is to push against the grips. The plaits then contract and enlarge so that the finger can be removed. But fastened inside the long, narrow sleeve of the jacket, there was no leverage to push. And deprived of the use of his fingers, the Great Armando was as good as dead. SR-6 ▶

I saw Armando's eyes narrow when he saw the deadly trap and the sweat bands form on his upper lip and under his eyes. It was the first time I ever saw Joe Ferris afraid. I said, "What the hell is this? Those things weren't in there yesterday when we inspected the jacket."

Massin sniggered. "Well, they're in there now." Tina Massin seemed about to faint. I had a picture of her sitting up all night with the sheriff standing over her, sewing in those terrible devices designed to kill a man for free.

Captain Stevens came over, took the str¬itjacket and looked at it and the innocent-looking toy finger grips plaited in reds, yellows, greens, and purples. "What's the idea, Sheriff?" he asked.

Massin bustled truculently and replied loudly so that all the press could hear. "This feller says he can get out of anything, don't he? I had a man once I hadda take to the loony house. Killed three guys. He got out of the jacket. He had hands like a gorilla. I fixed him up like this. He didn't get out. Okay, so let this greaseball put up or shut up. They seen them kinds of grips a dozen times before in their racket."

Captain Stevens looked doubtful, but I could sense that he was secretly pleased, in a way, that a performer who had put them to a lot of needless trouble was going to be shown up. He said to us, "What about it, boys? You don't have to go through with it if you don't want to, but make up your minds and let's get out of here."

Harry Hopp, the *Free Press* reporter, said, "Don't let him do it, Carl. It's sheer murder. I'll see that he doesn't get the worst of it in the papers."

Massin laughed his loud, dirty laugh. "I knew the four-flusher would welsh."

"Welsh nothing!" I shouted. "Our contract clearly stated—"

"Quiet, everyone!" It was Armando. And even in that crisis, he didn't forget the phony Mexican accent. "Shut up, Carl." But he wasn't looking at me. He was looking straight at Tina Massin and she at him. There was no mistake. They were in love, all right. They had found and lost each other in the same moment. They were saying goodbye, for there was no hope for them. She was the wife of a brute who would never let her go. And he was faced with an insoluble dilemma. Because if he went through with the stunt, he was a dead man, and if he backed out, he might as well be dead because he would never again be the Great Armando. ◀ SR-7

He said, "All right, Sheriff, I am ready."

The sheriff stepped forward, laughing.

Words to Know and Use

plaited (plāt′ id) *adj.* braided or interwoven **plait** *v.*
insoluble (in säl′ yo͞o bəl) *adj.* unsolvable

284

Critic's Corner

A critic once described Paul Gallico as "a teller of tales, a dreamer of dreams, a romantic." Ask students if this assessment seems to apply in the story they are reading. You might ask them twice, once in the middle of the story and then again after they finish it.

"So long, sucker. You asked for it." Things moved fast then as he went about his for-free murder, forcing each finger of Armando's hands deep into the plaits of the straw finger grips, then pushing his knee into Armando's back in order to haul the straps tighter.

And all the time Joe Ferris continued to look only on the white face of this girl he had come to love in such a strange manner and who had been forced to become his executioner. Her eyes were lost in his. Her lips moved, though no sound came, but I would have sworn they were communicating for the last time.

When four men lifted the mailbag with Armando inside it into the packing case and the electric crane traveled over and lowered the lid into the top, Tina Massin gave a soft cry and crumpled to the pier in a dead faint. The sheriff laughed, saying, "Now, what the hell's the matter with her?" A newsreel cameraman shouted, "Hey, Sheriff, willya look out! You're in the way of the shot." I felt like it was me who was going to die.

I jumped up onto the box to stall as long as I could and give him a chance even though I knew it was hopeless. There was no signal from him as usual to let me know he was out of the jacket and sack waiting for the plunge with his finger on the gaffed panel that would slide open and free him as soon as he sank beneath the surface.

Then he hadn't got out. The child's toy had defeated him. The legend of the Great Armando was a thing of the past. But I was determined to save the life of Joe Ferris.

The sheriff cried "Lower away!" and there was a cheer from the crowd as the steel cable paid out. The weighted crate went in with a splash and began to settle as the water poured in through the <u>interstices</u>.

I had a sickening vision of Armando trussed up like a mummy in the horrid canvas jacket, his fingers helplessly trapped in the straw grips, the icy water pouring into the case, the mail sack filling up, his last gasp for oxygen, then the hopeless, last-minute struggle, tugging against the inexorable grips, and the final bubble bursting from the tortured lungs. And after that silence.

Air was rushing up in a dirty surface swirl as the case sank with its burden. When my stopwatch showed two minutes and there was no sign of an arm or dark head breaking the gray river surface, I bawled in panic, "Haul away! Get him up out of there. Something's gone wrong! Get him up, do you hear!"

There was some confused shouting, and I could see the police captain shouting futilely at the man in the hanging operator's booth of the crane. But there was no rattle of machinery or running of steel cable over the wheel. Something had happened to the crane or the power, for I could see the operator wrestling with his levers.

I went over the side of the pier into the water. Men and women were screaming. I had a crazy idea I could swim down, work the panel, and get him out of there, sack and all, and up to the surface. I fought the cable and my bursting lungs. Then the police launch came and fished me out. After ten minutes the power came on again and the crate was raised. But there was not a chance in the world that the Great Armando was still alive. The sheriff had won.

Workmen attacked the case with axes and

Words to Know and Use

interstices (in tur′ stə siz′) *n.* cracks; crevices

AA. Critical Thinking: ANALYZING Have students compare and contrast the reactions of various members of the crowd to the grim event. *(Only Carl and Tina seem upset; the sheriff is in high spirits, and the reporters seem concerned only about getting a good story.)*

BB. Reading Skill: USING CONTEXT CLUES Ask students what *paid* means in this context. Have them explain what clues they used to figure out its meaning. *(It means "slowly unwound and lowered." Clues include the words "Lower away!" and the description of the electric crane in the next column.)*

CC. Literary Element: STYLE Ask students why the author has the narrator describe Armando's possible fate in such detail. *(Possible responses: to show how closely Carl identified with Armando; to help readers imagine the horror of what Armando is experiencing)*

DD. Reading Skill: PREDICTING Ask students if they think Carl is right and that Armando will be found dead in the crate. *(Answers will vary. Have students give reasons for their opinions.)*

EE. Literary Element: CLIMAX Have students explain why this is the turning point of the story. *(Until now, we have been suspensefully waiting to see how the conflict between Armando and his antagonist would turn out. Now we know that Armando has escaped the trap but has probably died anyway. It seems that both men have won and both have lost.)*

FF. Critical Thinking: DRAWING CONCLUSIONS Ask students if they can figure out how Armando escaped from the finger grips. *(Some students will say he found a way to push against them; others may suspect he had help of some kind or that the grips were not as foolproof as they appeared to be.)*

GG. Reading Skill: UNDERSTANDING CAUSE AND EFFECT Ask students to infer why Carl ends up in the hospital in a state of delirium. *(From diving into the freezing water, he developed pneumonia.)*

crowbars. Interns from an ambulance, their white trousers showing beneath their dark overcoats, stood by with a pulmotor. With a splintering and wrenching the side of the case broke away, revealing the locked mail sack.

And I was the first one to see that it wasn't full enough!

With a yell I broke away from Harry Hopp, seized the key from the postal inspector, and opened the padlock.

EE It was empty! No, not quite empty. Inside, buckled as though it had never been unfastened, the terrible finger grips still in place, was the straitjacket neatly folded. But of the Great Armando there was no sign. He had accomplished his greatest escape!

It was his last, too, for he was never seen again. The police dredged, grappled, and dived for three days, but his body was never recovered. He had defeated the vicious finger grips, the jacket, the mail sack, and the case and got out, and then perhaps at the last moment, exhausted from the struggle, his strength exhausted, he had drowned and been swept down river or under a pier. FF ◀ SR-8

I went to a hospital myself with pneumonia. They said I swore in my delirium I'd kill Sheriff Massin for murdering my friend and partner. It turned out it wasn't necessary. Six months after the disappearance of the Great Armando, I read in a newspaper that Jules Massin was shot to death in a saloon by the saloonkeeper he had attempted to shake down. I never heard what became of Mrs. Massin after that. GG

A couple of months after I got out of the hospital, Captain Stevens of the river police sent me the straitjacket complete with the sheriff's deadly gaff as a souvenir. I

Words to Know and Use

delirium (di lir' ē əm) *n.* a state of mental confusion

286

REAL LIFE CONNECTIONS

To help students understand the Great Armando's behavior, discuss the idea of "quitting while you're ahead." Ask a volunteer to explain the idea. Then have students bring up incidents from their own lives where they had the opportunity to quit while they were ahead. Ask them how they came to this decision, whether they were tempted to keep going, and whether they now regret having come to the decision.

couldn't bear to look at it and put it away with my diary of how it all happened, in the bottom of my trunk. Then I went back into the locksmith business.

HH All that was thirty years ago. Now I am holding the jacket in my fingers again, for two days ago I saw Joe Ferris, the Great Armando! And with him was Tina Massin! I'll swear it! I couldn't have been mistaken, even though his hair was white and his features changed. She looked almost the same, except happy. It was coming out of a movie house in Athens, Georgia.

I said, "Joe! Joe Ferris! And Tina Massin!"

They denied it. They stopped politely, but their expressions remained blank. The man said, "You must be mistaking us for someone else. My name is Vernon Howard, and this is Mrs. Howard here. I'm in the grain and feed business. Anyone in Athens knows me. And now if you'll excuse Mrs. Howard and myself . . ."

Vernon Howard's Grain and Feed Store was at the corner of Boulevard and Pecan streets. When I instituted inquiries as to II how long it had been there, the invariable answer was, "Oh, 'bout as long as I kin remember. . . ." But when I got down to cases, no one seemed to remember them back for SR-9 ▶ *thirty years, or longer.*

When I returned to New York, I dug out the straitjacket of Sheriff Massin. I hadn't touched it since the day I thought it had killed the Great Armando. The color on the finger grips of plaited straw had run, but otherwise they were exactly as they had been on that fatal day. I examined them. Then I took a magnifying glass. I tried them out by putting my fingers in and yanking. They pulled loose. And after that I knew the secret of how the Great Armando had escaped from the inescapable trap laid for him by vindictive Sheriff Massin. The finger stalls had been subtly and efficiently gaffed, by his wife.

The straw plaits had been cut with scissors in such a way as to defy casual inspection, but in every case destroying the tension of the plaits so that they no longer pulled against one another. ◀ SR-10

I remembered the look between them, the money he had stashed away in safe-deposit boxes, and his remark: "If I ever get a real scare, I'll quit and nobody'll ever hear of the Great Armando again." And how JJ easily he could have swam ashore under cover of the panic and excitement, and vanished, to return when he read that Sheriff Massin was dead.

Yeah, we'd thought of everything, except one thing. And in the end it was Joe Ferris, the Great Armando, who had the guts to put his faith in love as a gimmick. ❧

INSIGHT

Love Is Not Concerned

ALICE WALKER

love is not concerned
with whom you pray
or where you slept
the night you ran away
from home
love is concerned
that the beating of your heart
should kill no one.

Words to Know and Use

vindictive (vin dik' tiv) *adj.* revengeful

HH. Discussion Have students discuss whether they were surprised to find out that Armando was still alive and was with Tina.

II. LEP: Dialect Have a volunteer read the quotation from the feed store owner in a Southern accent so that students for whom English is a second language can understand that *'bout* is dialect for *about* and *kin* is dialect for *can.*

JJ. Critical Thinking: ANALYZING Ask students if they think Armando and Tina planned his escape together or whether Armando was surprised to find the finger grips cut. *(Answers will vary. Have students search the story for clues that suggest Armando knew or did not know he was in no real danger.)*

Check Test

1. What is the narrator's job? *(assistant to the Great Armando)*

2. What kinds of things is Armando supposed to escape from in Detroit? *(a straitjacket, a mail sack, and a packing case)*

3. Who warns Armando not to try the stunt? *(the sheriff's wife)*

4. What does the sheriff add to the straitjacket? *(plaited strips of straw, or finger grips)*

5. What was found in the packing case when it was brought up? *(only the straitjacket)*

Encouraging Independent Reading

The Magic Makers, nonfiction by I. G. Edmonds
The Great Houdini, a biography by Beryl Williams and Samuel Epstein
The Hand of Mary Constable and *The Poseidon Adventure,* novels by Paul Gallico
"The Wit of Porportuk," a short story by Jack London
"The Lady, or the Tiger?" a short story by Frank R. Stockton

Insight

This feature reflects on the ideas in the main selection and is suggested for students' independent reading. Optional discussion questions follow.

1. What does the poem mean when it says love is not concerned with whom you pray or where you slept? *(Possible response: Love does not care about who you are, or what you do; race, religion, and financial status do not matter.)*

2. According to the poem, with what is love concerned? *(Possible response: Love is concerned that your actions should not hurt anyone else.)*

3. How does this poem represent the attitudes of the Great Armando and Tina? *(Possible response: Armando doesn't care that Tina is unavailable or that she lives with a monster. Their plan to run away together is based on their love for each other, not on vengeance against the sheriff. They also run away to be together.)*

e x p l a i n

Responding to Reading

First Impressions

1. What were your first thoughts after the story ended? Record your impressions in your journal or on a piece of paper.

Second Thoughts

2. Why is "The Death Trap" an appropriate title for this story?

   Think about
   - how the sheriff rigs the straitjacket
   - what kind of a life Tina has with the sheriff
   - how Tina and Armando get "caught up in one another's eyes"
   - your knowledge and experiences of traps

3. Why do you think Armando continues with the stunt even though he knows the straitjacket is rigged?

4. It is probably Tina and Armando whom the narrator sees years later in Georgia. What reasons might they have for hiding their identities?

5. The narrator says, "There's no such thing as magic." Does his story prove his point? Explain.

   Think about
   - the narrator's explanation of "magic" and gimmicks
   - Tina and Armando's first meeting
   - Armando's "faith in love as a gimmick"
   - what you wrote earlier about love at first sight

6. Think again about the different traps in which one can be caught. In your opinion, which character was in the worst trap? Explain.

Broader Connections

7. Tina is typical of the kind of women who become "the hopeless, submissive captives to the most appalling men." What escapes do women in such relationships have today that didn't exist in the 1920's when this story takes place?

Literary Concept: Antagonist

The **antagonist** of a story is the character or force working against the main character. Who is the antagonist in "The Death Trap"? What evil characteristics does the writer give this character?

Student Response

Responding to Reading

These questions are open-ended with no "right" or "wrong" answers. However, responses must be supported with information from the selection. Possible answers follow:

1. Accept any reasonable response.

2. Some students may say that the title is appropriate because the sheriff rigs the straitjacket so that Armando will not be able to get out of it and will die trapped underwater. Others may say that both Armando and Tina are trapped in lives they do not want to lead. To escape, both must risk death—Tina from her murderous husband and Armando from his stunt.

3. Some students may say Armando's pride prevents him from backing down from a challenge. Others may say Armando knows that Tina has rigged the plaits and that he is in no real danger.

4. Some students may say the couple fears that the sheriff's family will track them down and accuse them of being responsible for the sheriff's death. Others may say that Armando doesn't want his standing in the community threatened by his questionable past or pressure to perform again.

5. Some students may say that the explanations Carl gives for Armando's stunts prove that magic does not exist. Others may say that the power of love contradicts the narrator's assertion: The real magic of love overcomes the sheriff when the fake magic of Armando could not.

6. Some students may say Armando is caught in the worst trap. He is a victim of his own pride, which causes him to seek new challenges and take ever greater risks. Sooner or later, he will slip up and be caught in a trap he can't escape from. Others may say Tina is caught in a worse trap—being married to an abusive man.

7. Some students may note that women can be more independent in today's world. They are able to get an education and hold a job of their own. Others may note that today courts, churches and social service agencies are more aware of the problems women face in abusive relationships and can offer shelter and counseling. Other students may feel that women really have not made that many advances in the historically male-dominated cultures of the world.

Literary Concept—Antagonist

Possible response: Sheriff Massin, the antagonist in the story, is made out to be dishonest (he shakes down the carnival twice); cruel and abusive (he yells at his wife, pushes people around, uses abusive language); murderous and a cheater (not only does he try to kill the Great Armando, he does it in an unfair way); foul and dirty; calious to suffering (that of his wife or of Armando trapped in the box); vindictive (he waits years to get back at Armando); and weak (Armando beat him up easily years earlier). Refer to annotations I and L.

Concept Review: Suspense In "The Death Trap," the author creates suspense as much by what he leaves out as by what he tells. Give some examples of important omissions that add suspense.

Writing Options

1. Imagine what it must have been like to be Armando when he was underwater, struggling with the straitjacket. Describe what you see, feel, think, and do.
2. When the narrator says that Tina was like a princess, he is using a simile. By making this comparison, the writer encourages you to think about Tina in a certain way. Create your own similes for describing Armando's hands, the sheriff, the straitjacket, and the feelings between Tina and Armando.
3. Pretend that you are the reporter, Harry Hopp. Write a news story about "The End of the Great Armando." Make sure to begin with a lead paragraph that answers *who, what, when, where,* and *why.*
4. Using details from Armando's apparent death, write an editorial expressing your opinion about whether there should be laws forbidding payment of money to or publicity for people who perform life-threatening stunts.

Vocabulary Practice

Exercise On your paper, write the letter of the unrelated word in each group below.

1. (a) cowed (b) timid (c) unbothered (d) frightened
2. (a) sanity (b) delirium (c) lunacy (d) madness
3. (a) full (b) populated (c) devoid (d) crowded
4. (a) drudge (b) slave (c) servant (d) hero
5. (a) imperceptibly (b) obviously (c) invisibly (d) subtly
6. (a) solvable (b) explainable (c) decipherable (d) insoluble
7. (a) interstices (b) openings (c) cracks (d) peaks
8. (a) braided (b) singular (c) plaited (d) woven
9. (a) yielding (b) submissive (c) resistant (d) obedient
10. (a) vindictive (b) forgiving (c) vengeful (d) avenging

Words to Know and Use

cowed
delirium
devoid
drudge
imperceptibly
insoluble
interstices
plaited
submissive
vindictive

Cross-Curricular Options

History: In newspapers and newsreels of the 1920s, research stories of Houdini and other magicians to see how these entertainers were covered.

Science/Technology: Find out how long people can stay alive underwater. Study diagrams of locks to discover how they work.

Art: If there are any budding magicians in class, produce a magic show.

History/Art/Music: Students can recreate the 1920s traveling carnival in class. Suggestions: research and report on the traveling shows; display photographs of carnivals past and present; draw, paint, or sculpt carnival performers and scenes; find and play appropriate carnival music.

Concept Review: Suspense Possible response: Early in the story (p. 280) the narrator lets on that the Great Armando was unbeatable until he met up with Jules Massin. The reader immediately wants to know what Massin did. A little later, he gives more information (p. 283) by saying Massin was able to destroy the Great Armando. But the reader does not find out what destroys him for some time. Later, the reader is kept in suspense about whether or not Armando will accept the challenge; what happens to him inside the box; and finally—what ultimately becomes of him. Refer to annotations S and Z.

Writing Options

The Writing Options are designed to meet varied student interests and abilities. Have each student choose one writing activity to complete. You may wish to guide some students to an option that requires less writing.

Journal Update Have students review their journal entries. Suggest that they write about how their attitudes toward traps have changed as a result of reading the story. What new aspects of traps or escapes from traps are they now aware of?

Vocabulary Practice

1. c
2. a
3. c
4. d
5. b
6. d
7. d
8. b
9. c
10. b

Closure

Armando and Tina's love overcomes great odds. Have students summarize some of the dangers and obstacles they overcame. *(Possible responses: Tina overcame her fear of her husband and "fixed" the finger grips; Armando overcame the death trap; the obstacle of the sheriff was removed when he died; they managed to find each other; they managed to disappear and conceal their identities.)*

Objectives

- To understand and analyze a play
- To follow stage directions
- To understand how minor characters influence the action in a play
- To show understanding of the work through a choice of writing forms, including an article, an epilogue, a diary entry, a thank-you note, an explanation, and a description

Prereading Motivation

Examine What You Know

Discussion Prompts: What features does this place have that are unique? What has happened there that was important to you? What is your favorite part of the place? How would you feel if this place were somehow destroyed or changed in some fundamental way?

Expand Your Knowledge

Discussion Prompts: How would you prepare for taking a screen test? What do you suppose directors and producers look for in screen tests? How likely is it that someone taking a screen test would get hired or become a star?

Additional Background: The movies were a relatively new phenomenon in 1925, when *A Young Lady of Property* takes place. The glamour of the Hollywood studios was renowned throughout America, and the myth of the young unknown catapulted to stardom through a successful screen test had a grip on the American imagination. As in the play, many unscrupulous enterprepreneurs capitalized on these dreams with phony screen tests.

Enrich Your Reading

Encourage students, as they read, to visualize the set and the appearances and movements of the actors on the stage. Some students may wish to sketch the set and the action to help them follow the play.

Thematic Link—Beating the Odds

In this story, a character beats the odds by finding happiness in a situation that she had thought was hopeless.

e x p l o r e

Drama

A Young Lady of Property

HORTON FOOTE

Examine What You Know (Prior Knowledge)

A young girl in this play has a special feeling about a house she lived in when she was little. On paper, describe a home or some other place that has a special meaning for you. Then, as you read, compare your reasons with the main character's.

Expand Your Knowledge (Building Background)

The main character in this play dreams about escaping her small-town existence for Hollywood and stardom. Taking a screen test is one of the steps associated with breaking into the movie world. During a screen test, an actor or actress performs a short scene while being filmed. The director then reviews the film to see whether the person is suited for a movie role.

Enrich Your Reading (Reading Skill)

Stage Directions Stage directions describe how to set the stage and where the actors are to move throughout the play. Study the diagram below and refer to it as you read the play.

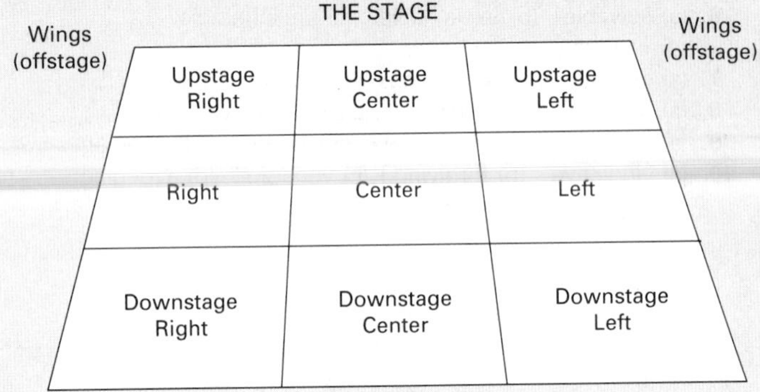

■ *A biography of the author can be found on page 315.*

Journal Writing

Suggest these journal topics to students:

- How do you picture a "young lady of property"? How does property elevate a person's social status, power, or self-image?
- Can anyone own property? What does owning property have to do with a person being free or independent?

For other journal opportunities, refer students to Examine What You know (above), Real Life Connections (p. T–293), and Broader Connections (p. 313).

Additional Resources

UNIT TWO RESOURCE BOOK

Reader's Guidesheet, p. 60
Vocabulary Worksheet, p. 61
Selection and Vocabulary Check Tests, p. 62
Selection Test, pp. 63–64

Collaborative Learning

Opportunities for collaborative learning appear throughout the lesson and include Options for Learning activities 2 and 4 (page 315) and Cross-Curricular Options (page T–315).

A Young Lady of Property

HORTON FOOTE

CHARACTERS

A

Miss Martha Davenport	**Lester Thompson**
Mr. Russell Walter Graham	**Mrs. Leighton**
Wilma Thompson	**Minna Boyd**
Arabella Cookenboo	**Miss Gert**

Man

Place: Harrison, Texas

Time: Late spring, 1925

B *The stage is divided into four areas. Area one, directly across the front of the stage, is a sidewalk. Area two, just above the sidewalk left of center, is part of a kitchen. A table, with a portable phonograph on it, and four chairs are placed here. Area three is above the sidewalk right of center. It has a yard swing in it. Area four is directly upstage center. In it is a post office window.*

The lights are brought up on the post office window. It is attended by two people, Miss Martha Davenport, *who is inside the window, and* Mr. Russell Walter Graham, *who is leaning on the outside ledge of the window. It is about three-thirty of a late spring day.* Miss Martha *and* Mr. Russell Walter *look very sleepy. Two girls around fifteen come in with schoolbooks in their arms. They are* Wilma Thompson *and* Arabella Cookenboo. *Wilma is a handsome girl with style and spirit about her.* Arabella *is gentle looking, so shy about growing into womanhood that one can't really tell yet what she is to look like or become. She is Wilma's shadow and obviously her adoring slave. They go up to the window.* Mr. Russell Walter *sees them and punches* Miss Martha. B

Russell. Look who's here, Miss Martha. The Bobbsey twins.

*(*Miss Martha *gives a peal of laughter that sounds as if she thinks* Mr. Russell Walter *the funniest man in five counties.)*

Teaching Strategies

Support for Students of Limited English Proficiency

- Use **Reader's Guidesheet** p. 60
- *A Young Lady of Property* is set in the rural South of the 1920's, a time and place of old-fashioned values and a culture remote from the lives of many of today's students. The play contains many Southern colloquialisms and idioms that may be unfamiliar to students with limited English proficiency, such as *ma'm, hogtied, Oh, my cow,* and *I do declare.* To infer the meaning of these terms, encourage students to study the surrounding text and try to find the connection between the image created by each word or phrase and the context of the play.
- **Annotations C, K, T, AA, EE, NN, SS, WW, DDD,** and **III** focus on troublesome terms and syntax.

Text Annotations

A. Literary Element: CAST OF CHARACTERS Have students write the cast of characters on a separate sheet. As they read, you may wish to have them write next to each name a brief description of the character as he or she appears in the play. As the play progresses, students can amend their entries to reflect new traits revealed by characters. *(Sample response: Arabella Cookenboo: A shy fifteen-year-old girl, devoted friend of Wilma; does not want to become a movie star)*

B. Literary Element: STAGE DIRECTIONS Have students summarize the information in the stage directions. Have them indicate the location of each character in the diagram on the facing page. *(Possible response: The stage has four regions—a sidewalk, a kitchen, a yard, and a post office. Martha and Russell are inside the post office window. Wilma and Arabella are outside the window.)*

STRUCTURED READING FOR LESS PROFICIENT STUDENTS

These questions can help to guide students through the reading. Ask each question at the point of the selection where the SR number appears in the margin.

SR–1. With whom does Wilma live and why might this be? *(her Aunt Gertrude; because her mother is dead)* **Clarifying**

SR–2. What is the property that Wilma owns? *(the house she lived in when she was younger)* How did Wilma come to own it? *(When her mother was dying, she bequeathed the house to Wilma.)* **Literal recall**

SR–3. Describe the change in Wilma's feelings about her father. *(Wilma had hated her father because his gambling upset her mother, but now she loves him and wants to live with him.)* **Summarizing**

SR–4. What has Wilma's father neglected to tell her? *(that he is marrying Mrs. Leighton, selling the house, and quitting his job)* **Literal recall**

SR–5. What is Wilma waiting for? *(a letter from Mr. Delafonte)* **Literal recall**

Continued on page T–292

C. LEP: Humor Students might be puzzled by Russell's attempt at humor here, making plays with the words *special deliveries, ones,* and *twos.* Remind them that this is a post office where jargon specific to the job would be common. Show how the addition of the word *stamp* (and *cent*) to each term makes the meaning more clear. Tell students that one- and two-cent stamps were more common in 1925. For example: special delivery stamps. Point out that Martha's use of the word *tease* makes a noun out of verb.

D. Reading Skill: CLARIFYING Ask students to explain what Wilma is trying to persuade Russell Walter to do. Ask why he is reluctant to submit to her wishes. *(Possible response: She is trying to persuade him to look through the pile of General Delivery mail for her letter. He doesn't want to do it because the chances it will be there are exceedingly slim.)*

E. Reading Skill: DRAWING CONCLUSIONS Ask students what conclusion they draw from Martha's statement and Wilma's reaction to her statement. *(Possible response: Wilma's father is not married, but is romantically involved with Mrs. Leighton. Wilma is not pleased about their relationship.)*

Miss Martha *(again giggling).* Now, Mr. Russell Walter, don't start teasing the young ladies. How are you, girls?

Wilma ***and*** **Arabella.** Fine.

C

Russell. Can I sell you any stamps? We have some lovely special deliveries today. Our ones and twos are very nice too.

Martha *(giggling).* Isn't he a tease, girls?

Wilma. Mr. Russell Walter, when's the next train in from Houston?

Russell. Why? Going on a trip?

Martha *(rolling at his wit).* Now, Mr. Russell Walter, stop teasing the young ladies. The next mail doesn't come in on the train, dear ones; it comes in on the bus. And that will be at six. Although the Houston mail is usually very light at that time, there are a few special deliveries. Do you think your letter might come by special delivery, Wilma?

Wilma. No ma'am. Regular.

Martha. Oh. Well, in that case I don't hold out much hope for it on that delivery. It's usually mostly second-class mail. You know, seed catalogs and such. The next Houston mail heavy with first-class is delivered at five tomorrow morning.

Russell. Which she knows better than you.

Martha *(giggling).* Now, Mr. Russell Walter, stop teasing the young ladies.

Wilma. Arabella and I were discussing coming here from school, Mr. Russell Walter, that the mail sometimes gets in the wrong box.

Russell. Rarely, Miss Wilma. Rarely.

Wilma. Arabella says that once a Christmas card meant for her got put by mistake in Box 270, instead of her box, which is 370, and she didn't get it back until the third of January.

Russell. Well, if that happens, nothing we can do about it until the person whose box it got into by mistake returns it.

Wilma. Yes sir. *(a pause)* I don't suppose any mail has been put in my box since my Aunt Gert was here last.

Russell. Well, seeing as she was here just a half hour ago, I don't think so.

Martha. Who are you expecting a letter from, young lady?

Wilma. Somebody very important. Come on, Arabella. *(They start out. They pause. She goes back to the window.)* Mr. Russell Walter, once I had a movie star picture, Ben Lyons I think, that was addressed to Wilma Thomas instead of Thompson, and if you remember, Mr. Peter was new at the time and put it into General Delivery, and it wasn't until two weeks later that you discovered it there and figured it belonged to me.

D

Russell. Well, Mr. Peter isn't new here now.

Wilma. But I thought maybe accidentally someone put my letter in General Delivery.

Russell. Nope.

Martha. Oh, Mr. Walter. Go ahead and look. It won't hurt you.

Russell. Now, Miss Martha . . .

Martha. Now just go ahead . . . *(She hands him a stack of letters.)*

Russell. All right. . . . Anything to please the ladies. *(He goes over to the letters and starts looking into them.)*

E

Martha. Wilma, I saw your daddy and Mrs. Leighton at the picture show together again last night. Maybe you'll be having a new mother soon.

Wilma. Well, I wouldn't hold my breath waiting if I were you.

Martha. I was saying to Mr. Russell Walter, I see the tenants have left the Thompson house. Maybe they were asked to leave so

STRUCTURED READING FOR LESS PROFICIENT STUDENTS

Continued from page T-291

SR–6. Why is Wilma feeling scared and where does she want to go when she feels scared? *(She is scared that her father will marry Mrs. Leighton; she wants to go to her house.)* **Clarifying**

SR–7. Why does Wilma change her mind about going to Hollywood and what does she decide she'd rather do? *(She realizes she wanted to be a movie star out of loneliness rather than genuine desire and she'd rather marry and live in her house.)* **Literal recall**

SR–8. What does Wilma think of when she goes to her house that make it so important to her? *(She remembers times there with her mother)* **Clarifying**

SR–9. Why can Mr. Lester sell Wilma's house? *(Nothing in writing legally makes it her house.)* **Clarifying**

SR–10. How is the sale of the house stopped? *(Wilma tells Mrs. Leighton how much the house means to her and Mrs. Leighton persuades her father not to sell it.)* **Summarizing**

Mr. Thompson might move in with a bride.

Wilma. They were asked to leave because they were tearing it to pieces. They had weeds growing in the yard and had torn off wallpaper. My Aunt Gert asked them to leave. . . .

Martha. Oh, of course. They didn't take any pride in it at all. Not like when your mother was living. Why, I remember your mother always had the yard filled with flowers, and . . . *(The phone rings.)* Excuse me. *(Miss Martha answers it.)* Post office. Yes. Yes. She's here. Yes, I will. *(She puts the phone down.)* That was your Aunt Gertrude, Wilma. She said you were to come right home.

Wilma. All right.

F **Martha.** Found any mail for Wilma, Mr. Russell Walter?

Russell. Nope, Miss Wilma. No mail and no female either.

Martha *(giggling)*. Isn't he a sight? You come back at six, Wilma. Maybe we'll have something then.

SR-1 ▶ **Wilma.** Yes ma'm. Come on, Arabella.

(They go outside the area and walk directly down the center of the stage and pause at the apron, looking up and down. They are now on the sidewalk area.)

G **Wilma.** I'd like to scratch that old cat's eyes out. The idea of her saying old lady Leighton is going to be my mother. She's so nosy. I wonder how she'd like it if I asked her if Mr. Russell Walter was going to ask her to marry him after she's been chasing him for fifteen years.

Arabella. Well, just ignore her.

Wilma. I intend to.

Arabella. What are you going to do now, Wilma?

Wilma. Fool around until the six o'clock mail.

Arabella. Don't you think you ought to go home like your aunt said?

Wilma. No.

Arabella. Have you told your Aunt Gert about the letter you're expecting yet?

Wilma. No.

Arabella. When are you going to tell her?

Wilma. Not until it comes. I think I'll go over and see my house. Look at how those tenants left it. I may have to sell it yet to get me to Hollywood. . . . H

Arabella. Wilma, is that house really yours?

Wilma. Sure it's mine. My mother left it to me.

Arabella. Well, do you get the rent for it and tell them who to rent to like Papa does his rent houses?

Wilma. No. But it's understood it's mine. My mother told Aunt Gert it was mine just before she died. Daddy had put it in her name because he was gambling terrible then, and Aunt Gert says Mama was afraid they'd lose it. I let Daddy rent it and keep the money now. Aunt Gert says I should, as he is having a very hard time. His job at the cotton gin[1] doesn't pay hardly anything. Of course, I feel very lucky having my own house. I ◀ SR-2

Arabella. Well, I have a house.

Wilma. Do you own it yourself?

Arabella. No. But I live in it.

Wilma. Well, that's hardly the same thing. I own a house, which is very unusual, Aunt Gert says, for a girl of fifteen. I'm a young lady of property, Aunt Gert says. Many's the time I thought I'll just go and

1. **cotton gin:** a machine used to separate cotton fiber from the seeds.

F. Literary Element: HUMOR Ask students to explain what is humorous about Russell's remark. Have them tell the type of humor it is and whether they think it is funny. *(Possible response: The remark is a play on the homonym of* mail *which is spelled* male. *Student opinions of the joke will vary.)*

G. Critical Thinking: ANALYZING Have students discuss the real cause of Wilma's anger toward Martha. Also have them reveal a possible motive that Martha would have for being so indiscreet. *(Possible response: Wilma is probably more angry with her father than with Martha. Martha may have brought up the topic of marriage more for Russell's ears than Wilma's.)*

H. Literary Element: MINOR CHARACTERS Ask students how Arabella's questions add to the play. *(Possible responses: She gives Wilma a chance to supply information to the audience with her responses; she helps Wilma reveal her own personality by contrast.)*

I. Teaching Tip

Have students keep track of clues to the personalities of different characters as they are revealed in the dialogue of the play. For example, here Lester's weakness for gambling and lack of worldly success are alluded to. Point out that in a play characters are defined either by their own words and actions, or by the words of some other character.

REAL LIFE CONNECTIONS

To help students understand Wilma's attitude toward Mrs. Leighton, have volunteers talk about attitudes toward parents who remarry. Ask them to think of reasons it is common for children initially to resent stepparents. Ask whether it is natural for stepparent/stepchild relationships to be troubled at first. Then have students think about how they would feel if they were the stepparent or the remarrying natural parent. Have them compose a speech they would make to the children to explain the new arrangement and reassure them that things were going to be okay.

J. Literary Element: CHARACTER Ask students to sketch the character of Wilma's mother from what they know about her so far. Then ask them how accurate they think their portrayal is. *(Possible response: She was kind, gentle, sweet, and saintly. The description is probably not entirely accurate due to the tendency of people to remember lost loved ones in an extremely positive light.)*

K. LEP: Idioms Ask students to explain the meaning of the term *hogtied* and the phrase *isn't good enough to shine my mother's shoes.* Point out the rural roots in *hogtied*, which literally means "tied up like a hog prepared for slaughter," and indicate that speakers from the "old" South, which was a rural culture, are more likely to use terms like this. Call attention to the attitude revealed in the phrase *isn't good enough to shine my mother's shoes,* implying that some people are better than others.

L. Literary Element: DRAMA Ask students to indicate what Wilma's turning away from her father and Mrs. Leighton might express. *(Possible response: She turns away from them in person in the same way she rejects the idea of their marriage.)*

live in it all by myself. Wouldn't Harrison sit up and take notice then? Once when I was thirteen and I was very fond of my Cousin Neeley I thought I'd offer it to him to get through law school. But I'm glad I didn't, since he turned out so hateful. *(a pause)* Do you remember when I used to live in my house?

Arabella. No.

Wilma. Well, it's a long time ago now, but I still remember it. My mama and I used to play croquet[2] in the yard under the pecan trees. We'd play croquet every afternoon just before sundown, and every once in a while she'd stop the game and ask me to run to the corner without letting the neighbors know what I was doing, to see if my father was coming home. She always worried about his getting home by six, because if he wasn't there by then she knew it meant trouble. My mother always kept me in white starched dresses. Do you remember my mother?

Arabella. No. But my mother does. She says she was beautiful, with the disposition of a saint.

J **Wilma.** I know. Her name was Alice. Isn't that a pretty name?

Arabella. Yes. It is.

Wilma. There's a song named "Sweet Alice Ben Bolt." Aunt Gert used to sing it all the time. When Mama died, she stopped. My mama died of a broken heart.

Arabella. She did?

Wilma. Oh, yes. Even Aunt Gert admits that. Daddy's gambling broke her heart. Oh, well. What are you gonna do about it? Boy, I used to hate my daddy. I used to dream about what I'd do to him when I grew up. But he's sorry now and reformed, so I've forgiven him.

Arabella. Oh, sure. You shouldn't hate your father.

Wilma. Well, I don't know. Do you know something I've never told another living soul?

Arabella. What?

Wilma. Swear you won't tell?

Arabella. I swear.

Wilma. I love him now. Sometimes I think I'd give up this whole movie-star business if I could go back to our house and live with Daddy and keep house for him. But Aunt Gert says under the circumstances that's not practical. I guess you and everybody else know what the circumstances are. Mrs. Leighton. She's got my daddy hogtied. Aunt Gert says she isn't good enough to shine my mother's shoes, and I think she's right. K ◀SR-3

(Miss Martha *comes out of the post office area upstage center. She walks halfway down the center of the stage.)*

Martha. Are you girls still here?

Wilma. Yes ma'am.

Martha. Minna called this time, Wilma. She said you were to come home immediately. *(*Miss Martha *goes back inside the post office area and into her window upstage center.)*

Arabella. Now come on, Wilma. You'll just get in trouble.

Wilma. All right. *(They start off right.* Wilma *stops. She looks panicky.)* Wait a minute, Arabella. Yonder comes my daddy walking with that fool Mrs. Leighton. I'd just as soon I didn't have to see them. Let's go the other way. *(They turn around and start left. A man's voice calls in the distance:* "Wilma, Wilma." Wilma *and* Arabella *stop.* Wilma *whispers:)* That's the kind of L

2. **croquet** (krō kā′): an outdoor game in which wooden balls are driven through a series of small arches by players with mallets.

PROFESSIONAL NOTEBOOK

Students are often concerned with how "real" a work of literature is—whether the author mentions the right songs, hairstyles, fashions, and the like. In *The Educated Imagination*, Northrup Frye addresses this issue:

*There are trick-pictures—*trompe l' oeil, *the French call them, where the resemblance to life is very strong. A painter of this school [once painted one of his wife's] best napkins so expertly that she grabbed at the canvas trying to* pull it off. But a painting as realistic as that isn't a reality but an illusion: it has the glittering unnatural clarity of a hallucination. The real realities, so to speak, are things that don't remind us directly of our own experience, but are such things as the wrath of Achilles or the jealousy of Othello, which are bigger and more intense experiences than anything we can reach—except in our imagination . . .

NORTHRUP FRYE, *The Educated Imagination*

THE ARTIST IN HER ROOM IN PARIS 1907–09
Gwen John private collection.

luck I have. He saw me. Now I'll have to speak to old lady Leighton.

Arabella. Don't you like her?

Wilma. Do you like snakes?

Arabella. No.

Wilma. Well, neither do I like Mrs. Leighton and for the same reason.

M (Lester Thompson *and* Mrs. Leighton *enter from downstage right.* Lester *is a handsome, weak man in his forties.* Mrs. Leighton *is thirty-five or so, blond, pretty, and completely unlike Wilma's description. There is a warmth about her that we should wish that Wilma might notice.* Lester *goes over to* Wilma.)

Lester *(as he leaves* Mrs. Leighton*).* Excuse me, Sibyl. Wilma . . .

Wilma. Yes sir.

Lester. Say hello to Mrs. Leighton.

Wilma *(most ungraciously).* Hello, Mrs. Leighton.

Mrs. Leighton *(most graciously).* Hello, Wilma.

Lester. What are you doing hanging around the streets, Wilma?

Wilma. Waiting to see if I have a letter.

Lester. What kind of letter, Wilma?

Wilma. About getting into the movies. Arabella and I saw an ad in the *Houston Chronicle* about a Mr. Delafonte who is a famous Hollywood director. N

Lester. Who is Mr. Delafonte?

Wilma. The Hollywood director I'm trying to tell you about. He's giving screen tests in Houston to people of beauty and talent, and if they pass they'll go to Hollywood and be in the picture shows. O

Art Note

Gwen John (1876–1939) was born in Wales and attended the Slade School of Fine Art in London. At the age of twenty-seven, she went to France where she spent the rest of her life, forming close friendships with other prominent artists, particularly with the sculptor Auguste Rodin, whom she loved. *Taking this picture as an illustration of* A Young Lade of Property, *what do you suppose the young woman is thinking?*

M. Literary Element: STAGE DIRECTIONS Have students refer back to the information about stage directions on page 290. Point out that it is unusual for a stage direction to describe characters as this one does. Discuss how such things as "warmth" or "weakness" are conveyed to an audience. *(Possible response: Most stage directions do not voice opinions, or speak directly to the reader, as this one does. The audience is typically made aware of characters' "warmth" or "weakness" through the actions, body language, and words of the actors.)*

N. Literary Element: SUSPENSE Ask students to describe how the issue of the letter creates suspense in the reader's mind. *(Possible response: The reader learns early in the play that the letter is important to Wilma, but does not find out what it is about until now.)*

O. Literary Element: THEME Ask students to indicate what kind of odds Wilma and Arabella must beat to become movie stars. *(Possible response: At fifteen, untrained as actresses, and knowing no one in show business, they must beat odds that seem very great.)*

P. Literary Element: DIALOGUE Have students describe how the relationship between Wilma and her father is revealed through dialogue. *(Possible response: Here we learn that Lester is very protective of Wilma, but also that he doesn't know her very well and does not have much sympathy for her hopes and dreams.)*

Q. Literary Element: MINOR CHARACTERS Ask students what Mrs. Leighton is adding to the play. *(Possible responses: Her questions allow Lester to share some "private" information; her connection to Lester suggests she may play a role in the decision about whether to sell the house.)*

R. Reading Skill: INFERRING Ask students to describe Minna's relationship to Wilma's family. Have them indicate what clues they used to make this inference. *(Possible response: Minna feels like part of the family. Clues—She takes personal interest in Wilma's behavior.)*

S. Literary Sidelight The glitter of Hollywood stands in opposition to Wilma's dreams of a warm home life in the play. To Wilma, Hollywood represents the "outer" world, which is flashy and alluring but ultimately empty. Conversely, her house, which is solid and plain, represents the "inner" world of family and stability that Wilma eventually chooses. As the play progresses, the reader begins to see that even at fifteen, Wilma is aware that behind Hollywood's superficial shine there is little substance.

Lester. Well, that's all a lot of foolishness, Wilma. You're not going to Houston to take anything.

Wilma. But, Daddy . . . I . . .

Lester. You're fifteen years old and you're gonna stay home like a fifteen-year-old girl should. There'll be plenty of time to go to Houston.

Wilma. But, Daddy, Mr. Delafonte won't be there forever.

Lester. Go on home, Wilma.

Wilma. But, Daddy . . .

P

Lester. Don't argue with me. I want you to march home just as quick as you can, young lady. I'm going to stand right here until you turn that corner, and if I ever catch you hanging around the streets again, it will be between you and me.

Wilma. Yes sir. Come on, Arabella.

(She and Arabella *walk out left.* Lester *stands watching.* Sibyl Leighton *comes up to him.)*

Mrs. Leighton. Have you told her we're getting married, Lester?

Lester. No, I'm telling Gert tonight.

Mrs. Leighton. Aren't you going to tell Wilma?

Lester. No. Gert's the one to tell her. Wilma and I have very little to say to each other. Gert has her won over completely.

Q

Mrs. Leighton. They must be expecting it. Why would they think you're selling your house and quitting your job?

Lester. I don't think they know that either. I'll explain the whole thing to Gert tonight. Come on. She's turned the corner. I think she'll go on home now.

SR-4 ▶

(They walk on and off. The lights are brought up downstage left in area 2. It is part of the kitchen in Gertrude Miller's house. Minna Boyd, *a thin, strong Negro woman in her middle forties, is seated at the table. She has a portable, hand-winding Victrola*[3] *on the table. She is listening to a jazz recording.* Wilma *and* Arabella *come in upstage center of the kitchen area.)*

Minna. Well, here's the duchess. Arrived at last. Where have you been, Wilma? What on earth do you mean aggravating us this way? Your Aunt Gert was almost late for her card party worrying over you.

Wilma. You knew where I was. You called often enough. I was at the post office waiting for the mail.

R

Minna. How many times has Miss Gert told you not to hang around there? Where's your pride? You know Mr. Russell Walter called and told her you were about to drive them crazy down at the post office. He said when you get your letter, he's gonna be so relieved he'll deliver it in person. Your aunt says you're to get right to your room and study.

Wilma. We're just going. Come on, Arabella.

S

Minna. And without Arabella. I know how much studying you and Arabella will do. You'll spend your whole time talking about Hollywood and picture shows. Clara Bow this and Alice White[4] that. You go in there and learn something. The principal called your auntie this morning and told her you were failing in your typing and shorthand.

Wilma *(very bored)*. Well, I don't care. I hate them. I never wanted to take them anyway.

Minna. Never mind about that. You just get in there and get to it. *(Wilma pays no attention. She goes deliberately and sits in a chair, scowling.)* Wilma . . .

3. **Victrola:** an early record player.

4. **Clara Bow . . . and Alice White:** two stars of silent films.

Wilma. What?

T **Minna.** Now why do you want to act like this?

Wilma. Like what?

Minna. So ugly. Your face is gonna freeze like that one day and then you're gonna be in a nice how-do-you-do.

Arabella. I'd better go, Wilma.

Wilma. All right, Arabella. Someday soon I'll be established in my own house, and then you won't be treated so rudely.

Minna. You come back some other time.

Arabella. Thank you, I will.

Wilma. I'll never get out of the house again today, Arabella, so will you check on the six o'clock mail?

Arabella. All right.

Wilma. Come right over if I have a letter.

Arabella. All right. Goodbye.

U *(*Arabella *goes out upstage center of the kitchen area and goes offstage.* Wilma *plucks an imaginary guitar and sings, in an exaggerated hillbilly style,* "Write me a letter. Send it by mail. Send it in care of Birmingham jail."*)*

Minna. Wilma, what is that letter about you're expectin'? Have you got a beau[5] for yourself?

Wilma. Don't be crazy.

Minna. Look at me.

Wilma. I said no, and stop acting crazy. I'm expecting a letter from Mr. Delafonte.

Minna. Mr. who?

Wilma. Mr. Delafonte, the famous movie director.

Minna. Never heard of him.

V **Wilma.** Well, I wouldn't let anyone know if I was that ignorant. The whole world has heard of Mr. Delafonte. He has only directed Pola Negri and Betty Compson and Lila Lee[6] and I don't know who all.

Minna. What are you hearing from Mr. Delafonte about?

Wilma. A Hollywood career.

Minna. What are you going to do with a Hollywood career?

Wilma. Be a movie star, you goose. First he's going to screen-test me, and then I'll go to Hollywood and be a Wampus baby star.

Minna. A what?

Wilma. A Wampus baby star. You know. That's what you are before you are a movie star. You get chosen to be a Wampus baby star and parade around in a bathing suit and get all your pictures in the papers and the movie magazines.

Minna. I want to see Miss Gert's face when you start parading around in a bathing suit for magazines. And what's all this got to do with a letter?

Wilma. Well, I read in a Houston paper where Mr. Delafonte was in Houston interviewing people at his studio for Hollywood screen tests. So Arabella and I wrote him for an appointment.

Minna. And that's what your letter is all about? No gold mine. No oil well. Just Mr. Delafonte and a movie test.

Wilma. Yes. And if you be nice to me, after I win the screen test and sell my house I might take you out with me. ◄SR-5

Minna. Sell your what?

Wilma. My house.

W **Minna.** Wilma . . . why don't you stop talking like that? . . .

Wilma. Well, it's my house. I can sell it if I want to.

Minna. You can't.

5. **beau** (bō): a boyfriend.

6. **Pola Negri and Betty Compson and Lila Lee:** early movie actresses.

T. LEP: Language Have students explain what is implied by Minna saying . . . *why do you want to act like this?* instead of "Why are you acting like this?" *(It implies Wilma is deliberately trying to upset everyone.)* Then go on to define *gonna ("going to")* and a *nice how-do-you-do ("a difficult situation")*

U. Literary Element: STAGE DIRECTIONS You may wish to have a volunteer read the stage directions and role-play Wilma singing and strumming an imaginary guitar. Ask what Wilma is "saying" with this song. *(She is expecting a letter. She is letting Minna know she resents being told what to do.)*

V. Literary Element: IRONY Ask students what is ironic about Wilma telling Minna she is ignorant. *(Possible response: Wilma is the one who is ignorant here, as common sense would indicate that she has little chance, at fifteen, through the mail, of becoming a movie star.)*

W. Literary Element: CONFLICT Point out to students that a focal point of the conflict in this play will be the house, or "property."

X. Reading Skill: PREDICTING Have students predict what may be the real cause of Gert's headache. Have them support their predictions with evidence from the text. *(Possible response: Gert may be upset because she has learned that Lester plans to marry Mrs. Leighton. Evidence: We have heard Lester say he plans to tell Gert. Gert bursts out crying after she comes in, indicating that her pain is not solely physical.)*

Y. Literary Element: SYMBOLISM Ask students to explain what the house might represent to Wilma in this passage. *(Possible response: The house may represent independence and a refuge from reality for Wilma. She thinks she can stay in it like the lady of mystery and avoid the problems of real life.)*

Z. Reading Skill: UNDERSTANDING CAUSE AND EFFECT Ask students to explain what they think causes Wilma to be afraid. *(Possible responses: She may fear the change that will come with her father's marriage to Mrs. Leighton; she may fear that when her father remarries he will completely forget her mother. She wants to return to the house where she lived with her parents.)*

Wilma. I can.

Minna. That house wasn't give to you to sell. A fifteen-year-old child. Who do you think is gonna let you sell it?

Wilma. Haven't you told me the house was mine? Hasn't Aunt Gert?

Minna. Yes, but not to sell and throw the money away. And besides, it looks like to me the house is gonna be having permanent visitors soon.

Wilma. Who?

Minna. What you don't know won't hurt you.

Wilma. If you mean my daddy and old lady Leighton, I'd burn it down first.

Minna. Wilma.

Wilma. I will, I'll burn it down right to the ground.

*(*Miss Gert *comes in downstage left of the kitchen area. She is in her forties, handsome and tall.)*

Minna. Hello, Miss Gert. . . .

Gert. Hello, Minna. Hello, Wilma.

Minna. How was the party?

X **Gert.** All right. Minna, Neeley is going to be away tonight, so don't fix any supper for him, and we had refreshments at the party, so I'm not hungry. *(She suddenly bursts out crying and has to leave the room. She goes running out downstage left of the kitchen area.)*

Wilma. Now what's the matter with her?

Minna. Sick headache likely. You stay here, I'll go see.

Wilma. All right. If she wants any ice, I'll crack it.

*(*Minna *goes out downstage left of the kitchen area.* Wilma *turns on the phonograph and plays a popular song of the 1920's.)*

Minna *(comes back in)*. We better turn that off. She's got a bad one. First sick headache she's had in three years. I remember the last one.

Wilma. Does she want any cracked ice? . . .

Minna. No.

Wilma. Did she hear any bad news?

Minna. I don't know.

Wilma. Can I go in to see her?

Minna. Nope. You can please her, though, by getting into your studying.

Wilma. If you won't let me sell my house and go to Hollywood, I'll just quit school and move over there and rent out rooms. Support myself that way.

Minna. You won't do nothin' of the kind. You go in there now and study.

Wilma. Why do I have to study? I have a house . . . and . . .

Minna. Wilma, will you stop talking crazy?

Wilma. I'm not talking crazy. I could think of worse things to do. I'll rent out rooms and sit on the front porch and rock and be a lady of mystery, like a lady I read about once that locked herself in her house. Let the vines grow all around. Higher and higher until all light was shut out. She was eighteen when the vines started growing, and when she died and they cut the vines down and found her she was seventy-three, and in all that time she had never put her foot outside once. All her family and friends were dead. . . . Y

Minna. I know you're crazy now.

Wilma. Minna . . . Minna . . . *(She runs to her.)* I'm scared. I'm scared.

Minna. What in the name of goodness are you scared of?

Wilma. I'm scared my daddy is going to marry Mrs. Leighton. Z

Minna. Now . . . now . . . *(holds her)*

Wilma. Minna, let me run over to my house for just a little bit. I can't ever go over there when there's tenants living in it. I feel the need of seeing it. I'll come right back.

Minna. Will you promise me to come right back?

Wilma. I will.

Minna. And you'll get right to your studying and no more arguments?

Wilma. No more.

Minna. All right, then run on.

AA **Wilma.** Oh, Minna. I love you. And you know what I'm going to do? I'm going to be a great movie star and send my chauffeur and my limousine to Harrison and put you in it and drive you all the way to Hollywood.

Minna. Thank you.

Wilma. H.O.B.

Minna. H.O.B.? What's H.O.B.?

Wilma. Hollywood or bust! . . . *(She goes running out upstage center of the kitchen area.* Minna *calls after her:)*

SR-6 ▶ **Minna.** Don't forget to get right back.

BB *(We hear* Wilma's *voice answering in the distance:* "All right." *The lights are brought down. The lights are brought immediately up in the kitchen, a half-hour later.* Aunt Gert *comes in downstage left of the area. She has on a dressing gown. Twilight is beginning. She switches on a light. She looks around the room. She calls:)*

Gert. Minna, Minna. *(A pause. She calls again:)* Minna. Minna.

(In comes Arabella *upstage center of the area. She is carrying two letters.)*

Arabella. Hello, Miss Gertrude.

Gert. Hello, Arabella.

Arabella. Where's Wilma?

Gert. I don't know. The door to her room was closed when I went by. I guess she's in there studying.

Arabella. Yes'm. *(She starts out of the room downstage left of the area.)*

Gert. Arabella.

*(*Arabella *pauses.)*

Arabella. Yes'm.

Gert. Wilma's gotten behind in her schoolwork, so please don't ask her to go out anyplace tonight, because I'll have to say no, and . . .

Arabella. Oh, no ma'am. I just brought her letter over to her. She asked me to get it if it came in on the six o'clock mail, and it did.

Gert. Is that the letter she's been driving us all crazy about?

Arabella. Yes ma'am, I got one too. *(She holds two letters up. Puts one on the table.)*

Gert. Oh. Well . . . *(*Arabella *starts out again downstage left of the area.)* Arabella, what is in that letter?

Arabella. Hasn't Wilma told you yet?

Gert. No.

Arabella. Then you'd better find out from her. She might be mad if I told you.

Gert. All right. *(*Arabella *starts out of the room.)* You didn't see Minna out in the backyard as you were coming in, did you?

Arabella. No.

Gert. I wonder where she can be. It's six-fifteen and she hasn't started a thing for supper yet.

*(*Arabella *goes out downstage left of the area and looks out an imaginary window right center. She comes back in the room.)* CC

Arabella. Wilma isn't in the bedroom.

Gert. She isn't?

Arabella. No ma'am. Not in the front room either. I went in there. DD

Gert. That's strange. Isn't that strange? *(*Minna *comes in upstage center of the area. She has a package in her hand.)* Oh, there you are, Minna.

AA. LEP: Language Have volunteers describe how a *chauffeur* and *limousine* fit into the typical movie-star stereotype. Point out that to most Americans, French words connote the impression of being "high-class." Ask students how serious Wilma's boast of driving all the way to Hollywood is.

BB. Literary Element: STAGE DIRECTIONS Ask students what important information the stage directions are conveying here. *(the passage of a half-hour, expressed through the lights going down and coming up)*

CC. Literary Sidelight Discuss "real time" versus the actual time it takes to act out a scene in a play. Point out that this interlude acts as an "accordion" scene with respect to time: if the play is running short, Arabella's search for Wilma may be extended in real time. On the other hand, the scene could be played out in only a few seconds if the director feels it is necessary.

DD. Literary Element: SUSPENSE Have students explain how the playwright creates suspense in this scene. *(Possible response: Wilma is supposed to be in her room but she isn't. The reader is curious to find out where she went.)*

Art Note

Paintings of the Connecticut countryside by Peter Poskas present a possible world of peace and tranquillity. In this scene, the sunlight on the trees and the details of the farmhouse are so true and natural that we can almost feel the wooden porch floor beneath our feet and smell the earth and the spring air. *In what ways might this be a picture of the Thompson house in* A Young Lady of Property?

EE. LEP: Idioms Have students explain what the expression *Give her an inch and she'll take a mile* means. *("Give her a little leeway and she'll take advantage of it.")* Ask if students think this is a fair characterization of Wilma. *(Many will say yes, based on her behavior in the post office and her determination to go after what she wants.)*

FF. Literary Concept: MINOR CHARACTERS Ask students what role Martha seems to have in the play. *(Possible response: Martha is a minor character. She serves as an example of the typical Harrison townsperson—warm, informal, folksy, and somewhat overly concerned with other people's business. Her role is to provide information.)*

Minna. I had to run to the store for some baking soda. How do you feel? *(Minna puts the package on the table.)*

Gert. Better. Where's Wilma?

Minna. You don't mean she's not back yet?

Gert. Back? Where did she go?

Minna. She swore to me if I let her go over to her house for a few minutes she'd be back here and study with no arguments.

Gert. Well, she's not here.

EE **Minna.** That's the trouble with her. Give her an inch and she'll take a mile.

Gert. Arabella, would you run over to Wilma's house and tell her to get right home?

Arabella. Yes ma'am.

(She picks the letter up off the table and takes it with her as she goes out downstage left of the area. A knock is heard offstage.)

Gert. *(calling)*. Come in. *(Miss Martha comes in upstage center of the area.)* Oh, hello, Miss Martha.

Martha. Hello, Gert. Hello, Minna.

Minna. Hello, Miss Martha. . . .

Martha. I thought you'd be back here. I knocked and knocked at your front door, and no one answered, but I knew somebody must be here this time of day, so I just decided to come on back. FF

Gert. I'm glad you did. We can't hear a knock at the front door back here. Sit down, won't you?

Martha. I can't stay a second. I just wanted to tell Wilma that her letter arrived on the six o'clock bus.

Gert. She knows, thank you, Miss Martha. Arabella brought it over to her.

Martha. Oh, the address on the back said

SPRING PLOWING, JOHNSON FARM 1987 Peter Poskas Courtesy of Schmidt-Bingham Gallery, New York.

the Delafonte Studio. I wonder what that could be?

Gert. I don't know.

GG

Minna. I knows. It's the moving pictures. She wrote about getting into them.

Gert. I do declare. She's always up to something.

Martha. Well, I never heard of moving pictures in Houston. I just heard the news about Lester. Was I surprised! Were you?

Gert. Yes, I was.

Martha. When's the wedding taking place?

Gert. I don't know.

Martha. Oh, I see. Well, I have to run on now.

Gert. All right, thank you, Miss Martha, for coming by. I know Wilma will appreciate it.

Martha. I'll just go out the back way if you don't mind. It'll save me a few steps.

Gert. Of course not.

Martha. Good night.

Gert. Good night, Miss Martha. *(She goes out upstage center of the area.)*

Minna. What news is this?

HH

Gert. Oh, you must know, Minna. Lester and Mrs. Leighton are getting married at last. That's why I came home from the party all upset. I had to hear about my own brother's marriage at a bridge party. And I know it's true. It came straight from the county clerk's office. They got their license this morning.

Minna. Well, poor Wilma. She'll take this hard.

Gert. She's going to take it very hard. But what can you do? What can you do?

(They both sit dejectedly at the table. The lights fade in the area downstage left as they come up on the area downstage right. Wilma *comes in from upstage center of the downstage right area. It is the yard of her house. She sits in the swing rocking back and forth, singing "Birmingham Jail" in her hillbilly style.* Arabella *comes running in right center of the yard area.)*

Wilma. Heh, Arabella. Come sit and swing.

Arabella. All right. Your letter came.

Wilma. Whoopee. Where is it?

Arabella. Here. *(She gives it to her.* Wilma *tears it open. She reads:)*

Wilma. "Dear Miss Thompson: Mr. Delafonte will be glad to see you anytime next week about your contemplated screen test. We suggest you call the office when you arrive in the city, and we will set an exact time. Yours truly, Adele Murray." Well . . . Did you get yours?

Arabella. Yes.

Wilma. What did it say?

Arabella. The same.

Wilma. Exactly the same? II

Arabella. Yes.

Wilma. Well, let's pack our bags. Hollywood, here we come.

Arabella. Wilma . . .

Wilma. Yes?

Arabella. I have to tell you something . . . Well . . . I . . .

Wilma. What is it?

Arabella. Well . . . promise me you won't hate me, or stop being my friend. I never had a friend, Wilma, until you began being nice to me, and I couldn't stand it if you weren't my friend any longer. . . .

Wilma. Oh, my cow. Stop talking like that. I'll never stop being your friend. What do you want to tell me?

Arabella. Well . . . I don't want to go to see Mr. Delafonte, Wilma. . . .

Wilma. You don't?

Arabella. No. I don't want to be a movie star. I don't want to leave Harrison or my

GG. Cultural Sidelight Point out that Minna's use of *I knows* and Gert's use of *I do declare* are examples of Southern dialect. Emphasize that pronunciation and usage are slightly different in a dialect. Point out that linguistic experts now generally agree that there is no "right" or "wrong" in language. Any phrase is technically "correct" if it is actually used by native speakers. Emphasize, however, that the mainstream culture expects educated individuals to conform to standard English. Have students discuss how value judgments are made about a person based on his or her mastery of standard English.

HH. Reading Skill: UNDERSTANDING CAUSE AND EFFECT Ask students to explain the cause of Gert's headache when she came home from her bridge party earlier and to notice if their predictions were correct. *(Possible response: She was upset about the news that Lester and Mrs. Leighton are getting married.)*

II. Reading Skill: PREDICTING Ask students to predict what kind of director Mr. Delafonte will turn out to be. *(Possible responses: He may turn out to be some kind of swindler, or he may be a very warm and caring person.)*

JJ. Reading Skill: COMPARE AND CONTRAST Have students think of words to compare and contrast Wilma's and Arabella's personalities. *(Possible response: Wilma—confident, outgoing, emotional, fiery; Arabella—insecure, withdrawn, shy, timid).*

KK. Literary Element: THEME Ask students to explain how fig trees seem to beat the odds. Have them point out the connection between the trees and Wilma's view of her own predicament. *(Possible response: Fig trees rise from a tangle of weeds, a seemingly difficult, if not impossible, feat; Wilma sees her plight as a similar one—she is a victim of difficult circumstances, which have stacked the odds against her, but like the fig tree nevertheless struggles to overcome these unfavorable odds.)*

LL. Critical Thinking: ANALYZING Ask students to explain the real reason why Wilma's house looks lonesome, and why she thinks living there will help matters. *(Possible response: It is lonesome because she is lonesome. She longs for a connection to her mother and the way things used to be, and thinks living in the house, the location of all her fond memories, will restore some of the feelings of togetherness she used to have.)*

MM. Discussion Have students discuss their own views of Arabella's mother's opinion. Ask if they think there is such a thing as a "normal life" and whether all women find marriage and children fulfilling. Discuss how this statement reflects feelings of 1925, and how people's ideas have changed since then.

mother or father. . . . I just want to stay here the rest of my life and get married and settle down and have children.

Wilma. Arabella . . .

Arabella. I just pretended like I wanted to go to Hollywood because I knew you wanted me to, and I wanted you to like me. . . .

Wilma. Oh, Arabella . . .

JJ

Arabella. Don't hate me, Wilma. You see, I'd be afraid . . . I'd die if I had to go to see Mr. Delafonte. Why, I even get faint when I have to recite before the class. I'm not like you. You're not scared of anything.

Wilma. Why do you say that?

Arabella. Because you're not. I know.

Wilma. Oh, yes, I am. I'm scared of lots of things.

Arabella. What?

Wilma. Getting lost in a city. Being bitten by dogs. Old lady Leighton taking my daddy away. . . . *(a pause)*

Arabella. Will you still be my friend?

Wilma. Sure. I'll always be your friend.

Arabella. I'm glad. Oh, I almost forgot. Your Aunt Gert said for you to come on home.

Wilma. I'll go in a little. I love to swing in my front yard. Aunt Gert has a swing in her front yard, but it's not the same. Mama and I used to come out here and swing together. Some nights when Daddy was out all night gambling, I used to wake up and hear her out here swinging away. Sometimes she'd let me come and sit beside her. We'd swing until three or four in the morning. *(A pause. She looks out into the yard.)* The pear tree looks sickly, doesn't it? The fig trees are doing nicely though. I was out in back and the weeds are near knee high, but fig trees just seem to thrive in the weeds. The freeze must have killed off the banana trees. . . . *(A pause.* Wilma *stops swinging—she walks around the yard.)* Maybe I won't leave either. Maybe I won't go to Hollywood after all.

KK

Arabella. You won't?

Wilma. No. Maybe I shouldn't. That just comes to me now. You know sometimes my old house looks so lonesome it tears at my heart. I used to think it looked lonesome just whenever it had no tenants, but now it comes to me it has looked lonesome ever since Mama died and we moved away, and it will look lonesome until some of us move back here. Of course, Mama can't, and Daddy won't. So it's up to me.

LL

Arabella. Are you gonna live here all by yourself?

Wilma. No. I talk big about living here by myself, but I'm too much of a coward to do that. But maybe I'll finish school and live with Aunt Gert and keep on renting the house until I meet some nice boy with good habits and steady ways, and marry him. Then we'll move here and have children, and I bet this old house won't be lonely anymore. I'll get Mama's old croquet set and put it out under the pecan trees and play croquet with my children, or sit in this yard and swing and wave to people as they pass by.

MM

Arabella. Oh, I wish you would. Mama says that's a normal life for a girl, marrying and having children. She says being an actress is all right, but the other's better.

Wilma. Maybe I've come to agree with your mama. Maybe I was going to Hollywood out of pure lonesomeness. I felt so alone with Mrs. Leighton getting my daddy and my mama having left the world. Daddy could have taken away my lonesomeness, but he didn't want to or couldn't. Aunt Gert says nobody is lonesome with a house full of children, so maybe that's what I just ought to stay here and have. . . .

Arabella. Have you decided on a husband yet?

Wilma. No.

Arabella. Mama says that's the bad feature of being a girl; you have to wait for the boy to ask you and just pray that the one you want wants you. Tommy Murray is nice, isn't he?

Wilma. I think so.

Arabella. Jay Godfrey told me once he wanted to ask you for a date, but he didn't dare because he was afraid you'd turn him down.

Wilma. Why did he think that?

Arabella. He said the way you talked he didn't think you would go out with anything less than a movie star.

Wilma. Maybe you'd tell him different. . . .

Arabella. All right. I think Jay Godfrey is very nice. Don't you?

Wilma. Yes, I think he's very nice and Tommy is nice. . . .

Arabella. Maybe we could double-date sometimes.

Wilma. That might be fun.

Arabella. Oh, Wilma. Don't go to Hollywood. Stay here in Harrison and let's be friends forever. . . .

Wilma. All right. I will.

Arabella. You will?

Wilma. Sure, why not? I'll stay here. I'll stay and marry and live in my house.

Arabella. Oh, Wilma. I'm so glad. I'm so very glad. SR-7 ▶

(Wilma *gets back in the swing. They swing vigorously back and forth. . . . A man comes in right center of the yard area.)*

Man. I beg your pardon. Is this the Thompson house?

(They stop swinging.)

Wilma. Yes sir.

Man. I understand it's for sale. I'd like to look around.

Wilma. No sir. It's not for sale. It's for rent. I'm Wilma Thompson. I own the house. My daddy rents it for me. . . .

Man. Oh, well, we were told by Mr. Mavis . . .

Wilma. I'm sure. Mr. Mavis tries to sell everything around here. He's pulled that once before about our house, but this house is not for sale. It's for rent. NN

Man. You're sure?

Wilma. I'm positive. We rent it for twenty-seven fifty a month. You pay lights, water, and keep the yard clean. We are very particular over how the yard is kept. I'd be glad to show it to you. . . .

Man. I'm sorry. I was interested in buying. There must have been a mistake.

Wilma. There must have been.

Man. Where could I find your father, young lady?

Wilma. Why do you want to see him?

Man. Well, I'd just like to get this straight. I understood from Mr. Mavis . . .

Wilma. Mr. Mavis has nothing to do with my house. My house is for rent, not for sale.

Man. All right. *(The* Man *leaves. He goes out right center of the yard area.)* OO

Wilma. The nerve of old man Mavis putting out around town that my house is for sale. Isn't that nervy, Arabella?

(Arabella *gets out of the swing.)*

NN. LEP: Idiom Students with limited English proficiency might not understand the phrase *he pulled that once before.* Have a volunteer explain what *pulling* refers to in this context *("playing a trick").*

OO. Literary Element: MINOR CHARACTERS Have students explain the function of the man in the play. *(Possible response: His function is to signal that the house is for sale.)*

PP. Reading Skill: COMPARE AND CONTRAST Ask students to compare and contrast Wilma's reaction to the news that her father is getting married and the news that the house is for sale. Suggest reasons her reactions are different. *(Possible response: She is unexcited about the marriage, but extremely upset about the house being sold, perhaps because she has conceded that her father's actions are out of her control, but has all along assumed that the house is something that no one could meddle with without her approval.)*

QQ. Literary Element: CHARACTER Ask students to indicate how Lester's failure to tell Wilma about the marriage fits in with what we know of his character. *(Possible response: He is selfish, shortsighted, and does not live up to his responsibilities; since telling Wilma about the marriage is one of his responsibilities, his failure to do so is consistent with his character.)*

Arabella. We'd better go. It'll be dark soon. The tree frogs are starting.

Wilma. It just makes me furious. Wouldn't it make you furious?

Arabella. Come on. Let's go.

Wilma. Wouldn't it make you furious?

Arabella. Yes.

Wilma. You don't sound like you mean it.

Arabella. Well . . .

Wilma. Well . . . what? . . .

Arabella. Nothing. . . . Let's go.

Wilma. Arabella, you know something you're not telling me.

Arabella. No, I don't. Honest, Wilma . . .

Wilma. You do. Look at me, Arabella . . .

Arabella. I don't know anything. I swear . . .

Wilma. You do. I thought you were my friend.

Arabella. I am. I am.

Wilma. Well, then why don't you tell me?

Arabella. Because I promised not to.

Wilma. Why?

Arabella. Well . . . I . . .

Wilma. What is it? Arabella, please tell me.

Arabella. Well . . . Will you never say I told you?

Wilma. I swear.

Arabella. Well, I didn't tell you before because in all the excitement in telling you I wasn't going to Hollywood and your saying you weren't going, I forgot about it . . . until that man came . . .

Wilma. What is it, Arabella? What is it?

Arabella. Well, I heard my daddy tell my mother that Mr. Lester had taken out a license to marry Mrs. Leighton.

Wilma. Oh, well. That doesn't surprise me too much. I've been looking for that to happen.

Arabella. But that isn't all, Wilma. . . .

Wilma. What else?

Arabella. Well . . .

Wilma. What else?

Arabella. Well . . .

Wilma. What else, Arabella? What else? . . .

Arabella. Well . . . My daddy heard that your daddy had put this house up for sale. . . .

Wilma. I don't believe you. . . .

Arabella. That's what he said, Wilma. . . . I . . . He said Mr. Lester came to him and wanted to know if he wanted to buy it. . . .

Wilma. Well. He won't do it. Not my house. He won't do it! *(*Wilma *has jumped out of the swing and runs out of the yard upstage center.)* PP

Arabella. Wilma . . . Wilma . . . Please . . . don't say I said it. . . . Wilma . . .

(She is standing alone and frightened as the lights fade. The lights are brought up in the area left of center. Minna *is mixing some dough on the table.* Miss Gert *comes in.)*

Gert. She's not back yet?

Minna. No. I knew when Arabella took that letter over there she wouldn't be here until good dark.

Gert. I just put in a call for Lester. . . . He is going to have to tell her about the marriage. It's his place. Don't you think so? QQ

Minna. I certainly do. I most certainly do.

*(*Wilma *comes running in upstage center of the kitchen area.)*

Wilma. Aunt Gert, do you know where I can find my daddy?

Gert. No, Wilma . . . I . . .

Wilma. Well, I've got to find him. I went over to the cotton gin, but he'd left. I called out to his boardinghouse and he wasn't there. . . .

Gert. Well, I don't know, Wilma. . . .

Wilma. Is he gonna sell my house?

Gert. Wilma . . .

Wilma. Is he or isn't he?

Gert. I don't know anything about it. . . .

Wilma. Well, something's going on. Let me tell you that. I was sitting in the swing with Arabella when a man came up and said he wanted to buy it, and I said to rent, and he said to buy, that Mr. Mavis had sent him over, and I told him he was mistaken, and he left. Well, I was plenty mad at Mr. Mavis and told Arabella so, but she looked funny, and I got suspicious, and I finally got it out of her that Daddy was going to marry old lady Leighton and was putting my house up for sale. . . . *(*Gert *is crying.)* Aunt Gert. Isn't that my house?

Gert. Yes. I'd always thought so. . . .

RR

Wilma. Then he can't do it. Don't let him do it. It's my house. It's all in this world that belongs to me. Let Mrs. Leighton take him if she wants to but not my house. Please, please, please. *(She is crying.* Minna *goes to her.)*

Minna. Now, come on, honey. Come on, baby. . . .

SS

SR-8 ▶

Wilma. I wouldn't sell it, not even to get me to Hollywood. I thought this afternoon, before the letter from Mr. Delafonte came, I'd ask Aunt Gert to let me sell it, and go on off, but when I went over there and sat in my yard and rocked in my swing and thought of my mama and how lonesome the house looked since we moved away . . . I knew I couldn't . . . I knew I never would. . . . I'd never go to Hollywood before I'd sell that house, and he can't. . . . I won't let him. I won't let him.

PORTRAIT OF JOSEPH CRAWHALL 1884 E.A. Walton
Scottish National Portrait Gallery, Edinburgh.

Art Note

Edward A. Walton (1860–1922) was associated with the Glasgow (Scotland) school of painters. Primarily a landscape artist, he also excelled at portraiture, particularly of children. In this painting of a friendly rival, he spelled out their differences in the upper right portion of the picture. *What, if anything, about this portrait reminds you of Lester Thompson in* A Young Lady of Property?

RR. Critical Thinking: SYNTHESIZING Ask students to look back at Gert's actions and statements. Ask whether Gert agrees with Wilma that the house shouldn't be sold without Wilma's approval. If so, ask students to speculate about why she doesn't tell Wilma she will help her do something about the situation. *(Possible response: Gert is on Wilma's side. She may feel it is not her place to interfere in a father–daughter relationship; she may feel there is nothing she can do; she may want to maintain a good relationship with her brother.)*

SS. LEP: Syntax Help students understand that the ellipses represent sentences that Wilma is failing to complete and that she allows to trail off. If possible, have a student do a dramatic reading of this passage, pausing as though overcome with emotion when he or she reaches the ellipses. Encourage students to imagine the missing words that Wilma fails to say, and to speculate about why she does not say them.

TT. Reading Skill: CLARIFYING Ask students to clarify what Gert is saying here. Have them explain how her words are critically important to Wilma. *(Possible response: Wilma's mother made an oral request that the house be left to Wilma, but nothing to that effect was actually written in her will. Thus Wilma may be morally but not legally entitled to the house.)*

UU. Critical Thinking: EVALUATING Ask students to judge whether Minna is correct in saying that Wilma is being stolen from. *(Possible responses: Yes, she is being stolen from. Legally, the house has not been established as hers, but morally there is no question that Wilma has a right to it. Others may uphold the legal rights of ownership.)*

VV. Literary Element: MINOR CHARACTERS Ask students how Lester's character affects the plot of the play. *(Possible response: His cowardly avoidance of responsibility means that the other characters are moved to action; a more dominant or responsible character might take decisive action to move the plot in another direction or to prevent action from the other characters.)*

Minna. Now, honey . . . honey . . . Miss Gert, do you know anything about this?

Gert *(wiping her eyes).* Minna, I don't. I heard at the card party that he was marrying Mrs. Leighton . . . but I heard nothing about Lester's selling the house. . . .

Minna. Well, can he? . . .

Gert. I don't know. I just never thought my brother, my own brother . . . Oh, I just can't stand things like this. You see, it's all so mixed up. I don't think there was anything said in writing about Wilma's having the house, but it was clearly Alice's intention. She called me in the room before Lester and made him promise just before she died that he would always have the house for Wilma. . . . TT

Minna. Well, why don't we find out? . . .

Gert. Well . . . I don't know how. . . . I left a message for Lester. I can't reach him.

Minna. I'd call Mr. Bill if I were you. He's a lawyer.

Gert. But, Minna, my brother.

Minna. I'd call me a lawyer, brother or no brother. If you don't, I will. I'm not gonna have what belongs to this child stolen from her by Mr. Lester or anybody else. . . . UU

Gert. All right. I will. I'll go talk to Bill. I'll

SR-9 ▶ find out what we can do legally.

(She starts out downstage left of the area. Lester *comes in upstage center of the area.* Minna *sees him coming.)*

Minna. Miss Gert.

*(*Gert *turns and sees him just as he gets inside the area.)*

Lester. Hello, Gert.

Gert. Hello, Lester.

Lester. Hello, Wilma.

Wilma. Hello . . .

Gert. Wilma, I think you'd better leave. . . .

Wilma. Yes'm. . . . *(She starts out.)*

Lester. Wait a minute, Gert. I've something to tell you all. I want Wilma to hear. . . .

Gert. I think we know already. Go on, Wilma.

Wilma. Yes'm.

*(*Wilma *leaves downstage left of the area.* Minna *follows after her. A pause.)*

Gert. We've heard about the marriage, Lester.

Lester. Oh, well. I'm sorry I couldn't be the one to tell you. We only decided this morning. There was a lot to do, a license and some business to attend to. I haven't told anyone. I don't know how the news got out. VV

Gert. You didn't really expect them to keep quiet about it at the courthouse?

Lester. Oh. Well, of course I didn't think about that. *(a pause)* Well, the other thing is . . . You see . . . I've decided to sell the house.

Gert. I know. Wilma just found out about that, too.

Lester. Oh. Well, I'll explain the whole thing to you. You see, I felt . . . *(*Gert *starts to cry.)* Now what's the matter with you, Gert?

Gert. To think that my brother, my own brother, would do something like this.

Lester. Like what? After all it's my house, Gert.

Gert. There's some dispute about that. The least I think you could have done, the very least, was come to tell your own child.

Lester. Well, I'm here now to do that. I only put it up for sale at noon today. I've nothing to hide or be ashamed of. The house

PROFESSIONAL NOTEBOOK

A young girl spends an hour with an examiner. She is asked a number of questions that probe her store of information (Who discovered America? What does belfry *mean?). Some time afterward, the examiner scores her responses and comes up with a single number. . . . This number is likely to exert appreciable effect upon her future, influencing the way in which her teachers think of her and determining her eligibility for certain privileges. Many observers are not happy with this state of affairs.*

There must be more to intelligence than short answers to short questions. . . . [But] only if we expand and reformulate our view of what counts as human intellect will we be able to devise more appropriate ways of assessing [human intelligence] and more effective ways of educating it.

Howard Gardner, *Frames of Mind, The Theory of Multiple Intelligences*

is in my name. Sibyl, Mrs. Leighton, doesn't like Harrison. You can't blame her. People have been rotten to her. We're moving to Houston. I'm selling this house to pay down on one in Houston. That'll belong to Wilma just the same, someday. Sibyl's agreed to that, and Wilma will really get a better house in time. And we always want her to feel like it's her home, come and visit us summers . . . and like I say when something happens to me or Sibyl, the house will be hers. . . .

Gert. That's not the point, Lester. . . .

Lester. What do you mean?

Gert. You know very well.

Lester. I can't make a home for her over there, can I? She'll be grown soon and marrying and having her own house. I held on to this place as long as I could. . . . Well, I'm not going to feel guilty about it. . . .

Gert. I'm going to try to stop you, Lester. . . .

Lester. Now look, Gert. For once try and be sensible. . . .

Gert. Legally I'm going to try and stop you. I'm going . . .

Lester. Please, Gert . . .

WW **Gert.** . . . to call Bill and tell him the whole situation and see what we can do. If we have any rights I'll take it to every court I can. Brother or no brother. . . .

Lester. Now look, don't carry on like this. Maybe I've handled it clumsily, and if I have I'm sorry. I just didn't think. . . . I should have, I know . . . but I . . .

Gert. That's right. You didn't think. You never do. Well, this time you're going to have to. . . .

XX **Lester.** Can't you look at it this way? Wilma is getting a better house and . . .

Gert. Maybe she doesn't want a better house. Maybe she just wants this one. But that isn't the point either. The sickening part is that you really didn't care what Wilma thought or even stopped for a moment to consider if she had a thought. You've never cared about anyone or anything but yourself. Well, this time I won't let you without a fight. I'm going to a lawyer.

Lester. Gert . . .

Gert. Now get out of my house. Because brother or no, I'm through with you. YY

Lester. All right. If you feel that way.

(He leaves upstage center of the area. Gert *stands for a moment, thinking what to do next.* Minna *comes in downstage left of the area.)*

Minna. I was behind the door and I heard the whole thing.

Gert. Did Wilma hear?

Minna. No, I sent her back to her room. Now you get right to a lawyer.

Gert. I intend to. He's gotten me mad now. I won't let him get by with it if I can help it. I think I'll walk over to Bill's. I don't like to talk about it over the telephone. ZZ

Minna. Yes'm.

Gert. You tell Wilma to wait here for me.

Minna. Yes'm. Want me to tell her where you've gone?

Gert. I don't see why not. I'll be back as soon as I finish.

Minna. Yes'm. *(*Gert *leaves upstage center of the area.* Minna *goes to the door and calls:)* Wilma. Wilma. You can come here now. *(She fills a plate with food and puts it on the table.* Wilma *comes in downstage left of the area.)* You better sit down and try to eat something.

Wilma. I can't eat a thing.

Minna. Well, you can try.

WW. LEP: Syntax Once again, the characters are speaking in broken sentences, as represented by ellipses. Help students to see that Gert's dialogue continues across Lester's interruption. Have students read the dialogue aloud and speculate on the missing words.

XX. Reading Skill: PREDICTING Ask students to predict whether Lester will make good on his promise to get a better house for Wilma. Have them support their predictions with evidence from the text. *(Possible response: No, he will not get her a better house. In the past, he's run out of money and ended up taking advantage of people, and it is likely he would do this again in the future.)*

YY. Reading Skill: INFERRING Ask students to explain why Gert is not willing to see Lester's side of the issue and whether she is being unfair to him. *(Possible response: Gert is reacting to Lester's past history of squandering money and manipulating people. She is being as fair as she can, but she has seen Wilma hurt too much in the past, and doesn't want to see it happen again.)*

ZZ. Teaching Tip

Have students draw a vertical line down the center of a piece of paper. On one side, list arguments in favor of Lester being able to sell the house. On the other side, list arguments against. Take a poll to see whether the class thinks Lester has a right to sell the house.

AAA. Literary Element: ANTAGONIST Ask students which character in the play serves as the antagonist. Ask what problem this character causes for Wilma. *(Possible response: Lester is the antagonist. By putting up the house for sale he causes Wilma great anguish and indecision about her future.)*

BBB. Literary Element: CONFLICT Ask students what conflict Wilma is trying to resolve here. *(Possible response: Her conflict concerns her future. She can't decide whether she should stay home with things she is familiar with, or strike out into the unknown world.)*

CCC. Reading Skill: PREDICTING Ask the class what kind of person they think Mrs. Leighton will turn out to be. Have them explain their opinions. *(Possible responses: Some may remember the extremely positive stage direction and think favorably of her. Others may go along with Gert, Minna, and Wilma's negative feelings about her.)*

DDD. LEP: Vocabulary Some students may have trouble with the word *bluff.* To aid them, have volunteers give examples of how a bluff can be used as a tactic in games and sports. For example, in baseball, a catcher might bluff a throw to one base, only to throw to another base to catch a runner off-guard. Have them show how a legal bluff is used in a similar way.

Wilma. No. It would choke me. What happened?

Minna. Your aunt told him not to sell the house, and he said he would, and so she's gone to see a lawyer.

Wilma. Does she think she can stop him?

Minna. She's gonna try. I know she's got him scared. . . .

AAA

Wilma. But it's my house. You know that. He knows that. . . . Didn't she tell him?

Minna. Sure she told him. But you know your daddy. Telling won't do any good; we have to prove it.

Wilma. What proof have we got?

Minna. Miss Gert's word. I hope that's enough. . . .

Wilma. And if it isn't?

Minna. Then you'll lose it. That's all. You'll lose it.

Wilma. I bet I lose it. I've got no luck.

Minna. Why do you say that?

Wilma. What kind of luck is it takes your mama away, and then your daddy, and then tries to take your house? Sitting in that yard swinging I was the happiest girl in the world this afternoon. I'd decided not to go in the movies and to stay in Harrison and get married and have children and live in my house. . . .

Minna. Well, losing a house won't stop you from staying in Harrison and getting married. . . .

BBB

Wilma. Oh, yes. I wouldn't trust it with my luck. With my kind of luck I wouldn't even get me a husband. . . . I'd wind up like Miss Martha working at the post office chasing Mr. Russell Walter until the end of time. No mother and no father and no house and no husband and no children. No, thank you. I'm just tired of worrying over the whole thing. I'll just go on into Houston and see Mr. Delafonte and get on out to Hollywood and make money and get rich and famous. *(She begins to cry.)*

Minna. Now, honey. Honey . . .

Wilma. Minna, I don't want to be rich and famous. . . . I want to stay here. I want to stay in Harrison. . . .

Minna. Now, honey. Try to be brave.

Wilma. I know what I'm gonna do. *(She jumps up.)* I'm going to see old lady Leighton. She's the one that can stop this. . . .

CCC

Minna. Now, Wilma. You know your aunt don't want you around that woman.

Wilma. I can't help it. I'm going. . . .

Minna. Wilma . . . you listen to me . . . *(*Wilma *runs out upstage center of the area.)* Wilma . . . Wilma . . . you come back here. . . .

(But Wilma *has gone.* Minna *shakes her head in desperation. The lights fade. When the lights are brought up, it is two hours later.* Minna *is at the kitchen table reading the paper.* Gert *comes in upstage center of the area.)*

Gert. Well, we've won.

Minna. What do you mean?

Gert. I mean just what I say. Lester is not going to sell the house.

Minna. What happened?

DDD

Gert. I don't know what happened. I went over to see Bill and we talked it all through, and he said legally we really had no chance, but he'd call up Lester and try to at least bluff him into thinking we had. And when he called Lester, he said Lester wasn't home, and so I suggested his calling you know where.

Minna. No. Where?

Gert. Mrs. Leighton's. And sure enough he was there, and then Bill told him why he was calling, and Lester said, well, it didn't matter as he'd decided not to sell the house after all.

Minna. You don't mean it?

Gert. Oh, yes, I do. Where's Wilma?

Minna. She's over there with them.

Gert. Over where with them?

Minna. At Mrs. Leighton's.

Gert. Why, Minna . . .

Minna. Now don't holler at me. I told her not to go, but she said she was going, and then she ran out that door so fast I couldn't stop her.

(Wilma *comes running in upstage center of the area.)*

Wilma. Heard the news? House is mine again.

Minna. Do you know what happened?

Wilma. Sure. Mrs. Leighton isn't so bad. Boy, I went running over there expecting the worst . . .

EEE **Gert.** Wilma, what do you mean going to that woman's house? Wilma, I declare . . .

Wilma. Oh, she's not so bad. Anyway we've got her to thank for it.

Minna. Well, what happened? Will somebody please tell me what happened?

Wilma. Well, you know I was sitting here and it came to me. It came to me just like that. See Mrs. Leighton. She's the one to stop it and it's got to be stopped. Well, I was so scared my knees were trembling the whole time going over there, but I made myself do it, walked in on her, and she looked more nervous than I did.

Gert. Was your father there?

FFF **Wilma.** No ma'am. He came later. Wasn't anybody there but me and Mrs. Leighton. I'm calling her Sibyl now. She asked me to. Did Arabella come yet?

Minna. Arabella?

Wilma. I called and asked her to come and celebrate. I'm so excited. I just had to have company tonight. I know I won't be able to sleep anyway. I hope you don't mind, Aunt Gert. . . .

Minna. If you don't tell me what happened . . .

Wilma. Well . . . Mrs. Leighton . . . I mean Sibyl . . . *(*Arabella *comes in upstage center of the area.* Wilma *sees her.)* Oh, come on in, Arabella.

Arabella. Hi. I almost didn't get to come. I told my mama it was life or death, and so she gave in. But she made me swear we'd be in bed by ten. Did you hear about Mr. Delafonte?

Wilma. No? What?

Arabella. He's a crook. It was in the Houston papers tonight. He was operating a business under false pretenses. He had been charging twenty-five dollars for those screen tests and using a camera with no film in it. GGG

Wilma. My goodness.

Arabella. It was in all the papers. On the second page. My father said he mustn't have been very much not to even get on the front page. He wasn't a Hollywood director at all. He didn't even know Lila Lee or Betty Compson.

Wilma. He didn't?

Arabella. No.

Minna. Wilma, will you get back to your story before I lose my mind?

Wilma. Oh. Yes . . . I got my house back, Arabella.

Arabella. You did?

Wilma. Sure. That's why I called you over to spend the night. A kind of celebration.

Arabella. Well, that's wonderful.

Minna. Wilma . . .

Wilma. All right. Where was I?

EEE. Cultural Sidelight Point out that in the etiquette in this part of the country in the 1920's, spontaneous visits to the residence of a gentleman or lady were frowned upon. People were not supposed to call without an invitation or prior notice. This could be one reason why Gert is upset with Wilma here.

FFF. Literary Element: SYMBOLISM Discuss with students the meaning of Wilma's now calling Mrs. Leighton "Sybil". *(Possible response: She and Mrs. Leighton are now friends.)*

GGG. Reading Skill: USING CONTEXT CLUES Have students define the term *false pretenses* using clues from the context of the play. If they need a clue, ask them to think of a verb that is similar to the word *pretense. (pretend)* Point out that *pretense* and this word have a common root. *(Possible response: "false pretenses" are acts of pretending.)*

Art Note

British painter and stage designer Duncan Grant (1886–1978) who was born in Scotland, became known during his lifetime as the outstanding artist of the Bloomsbury Group, a circle of authors and artists living in London. In this painting, Grant evokes the pleasant atmosphere of the room by a softly lighted focus on a well-used, comfortably cushioned armchair. *Name other articles shown that emphasize contentment and ease.*

HHH. Literary Element: SYMBOLISM Ask students to explain how this dialogue sums up what the house represents for Wilma. *(Possible responses: The house represents a connection with her mother and with a happy family life; the house represents security and love.)*

III. LEP: Language Some students may have trouble deciphering Wilma's long run-on sentences. Have a volunteer break up her statement here and in her earlier dialogue into separate sentences, adding missing or implied information into the text as needed. Point out that breeches of standard sentence structure are acceptable here because they are part of dialogue.

JJJ. Reading Skill: DRAWING CONCLUSIONS Ask students whether Wilma had made a mistake in her initial judgment of Mrs. Leighton. Have them support their conclusions with evidence from the text. *(Possible response: Yes, Wilma severely misjudged Mrs. Leighton. She thought Mrs. Leighton was a crass enemy when actually she is a sympathetic friend, as evidenced by her threat to stop the marriage if Lester doesn't take the house off the market.)*

ARTIST'S STUDY AT CHARLESTON 1967 Duncan Grant
The Metropolitan Museum of Art Gift of Arthur W. Cohen, 1985.

Gert. You were at Mrs. Leighton's.

Wilma. Oh, yes. Sibyl's. I'm calling her Sibyl now, Arabella. She asked me to.

Minna. Well . . . what happened? Wilma, if you don't tell me . . .

Wilma. Well, I just told her the whole thing.

Minna. What whole thing?

HHH **Wilma.** Well, I told her about my mother meaning for the house to always be mine, and how I loved the house, and how I was lonely and the house was lonely, and that I had hoped my daddy and I could go there and live someday but knew now we couldn't, and that I had planned to go to Hollywood and be a movie star but that this afternoon my friend Arabella and I decided we didn't really want to do that, and that I knew then that what I wanted to do really was to live in Harrison and get married and live in my house and have children so that I wouldn't be lonely anymore and the house wouldn't. And then she started crying. HHH

Gert. You don't mean it.

Wilma. Yes ma'am. And I felt real sorry for her, and I said I didn't hold anything against her, and then Daddy came in, and she said why didn't he tell her that was my house, and he said because it wasn't. And then she asked him about what Mother told you, and he said that was true but now I was going to have a better house, and she said I didn't want to have a better house, but my own house, and that she wouldn't marry him if he sold this house, and she said they both had jobs in Houston and would manage somehow, but I had nothing, so then he said all right. III

Gert. Well. Good for her.

Minna. Sure enough, good for her.

Wilma. And then Mr. Bill called and Daddy told him the house was mine again, and then she cried again and hugged me and asked me to kiss her and I did, and then Daddy cried and I kissed him, and then I cried. And they asked me to the wedding and I said I'd go and that I'd come visit them this summer in Houston. And then I came home. JJJ

Minna. Well. Well, indeed.

KKK

Gert. My goodness. So that's how it happened. And you say Mrs. Leighton cried?

Wilma. Twice. We all did. Daddy and Mrs. Leighton and me. . . .

Gert. Well, I'm glad, Wilma, it's all worked out.

Wilma. And can I go visit them this summer in Houston?

Gert. If you like.

Wilma. And can I go to the wedding?

Gert. Yes, if you want to.

Wilma. I want to.

Minna. Now you better have some supper.

Wilma. No. I couldn't eat, I'm still too excited.

Minna. Miss Gert, she hasn't had a bite on her stomach.

Gert. Well, it won't kill her this one time, Minna.

Wilma. Aunt Gert, can Arabella and I go over to my yard for just a few minutes and swing? We'll be home by ten. . . .

Gert. No, Wilma, it's late.

Wilma. Please. Just to celebrate. I have it coming to me. We'll just stay for a few minutes.

Gert. Well . . .

Wilma. Please . . .

Gert. Will you be back here by ten, and not make me have to send Minna over there?

Wilma. Yes ma'am.

Gert. All right.

Wilma. Oh, thank you. *(She goes to her aunt and kisses her.)* You're the best aunt in the whole world. Come on, Arabella.

Arabella. All right. *(They start upstage center of the area.* Gert *calls after them:)*

Gert. Now remember. Back by ten. Arabella has promised her mother. And you've promised me.

Wilma *(calling in distance)***.** Yes ma'am.

*(*Gert *comes back into the room.)*

Gert. Well, I'm glad it's ending this way.

Minna. Yes ma'am.

Gert. I never thought it would. Well, I said hard things to Lester. I'm sorry I had to, but I felt I had to.

Minna. Of course you did.

Gert. Well, I'll go to my room. You go on when you're ready.

Minna. All right. I'm ready now. The excitement has wore me out.

Gert. Me too. Leave the light on for the children. I'll keep awake until they come in.

Minna. Yes'm.

Gert. Good night. ◀SR-10

Minna. Good night.

*(*Gert *goes out downstage left of the area.* Minna *goes to get her hat. The lights fade. The lights are brought up in the downstage right area.* Wilma *and* Arabella *come in upstage center of the area and get in the swing.)*

LLL

Wilma. Don't you just love to swing?

Arabella. Uh huh.

Wilma. It's a lovely night, isn't it? Listen to that mockingbird. The crazy thing must think it's daytime.

Arabella. It's light enough to be day.

Wilma. It certainly is.

MMM

Arabella. Well, it was lucky we decided to give up Hollywood with Mr. Delafonte turning out to be a crook and all.

Wilma. Wasn't it lucky?

Arabella. Do you feel lonely now?

NNN

Wilma. No, I don't feel nearly so lonely. Now I've got my house and plan to get married. And my daddy and I are going to see each other, and I think Mrs. Leighton is going to make a nice friend. She's crazy about moving pictures.

KKK. Critical Thinking: EVALUATING Ask students what Gert's reaction to this news is and have them explain how an actress would convey this on stage. *(Possible responses: surprise, disbelief, genuine pleasure, confusion; reactions would be shown through body language and tone of voice.)*

LLL. Literary Element: SYMBOLISM Ask students to describe Wilma's mood. *(happy, carefree)* Then ask what swinging may symbolize for Wilma. *(Possible response: Swinging symbolizes that she is free to be a kid again and does not have to worry about grown-up problems.)*

MMM. Literary Element: HUMOR Ask students to explain what is humorous about Arabella and Wilma giving up on Hollywood. *(Possible response: It is almost certain that neither of them had any chance of becoming movie stars, anyway, even if Mr. Delafonte hadn't turned out to be a crook.)*

NNN. Literary Element: RESOLUTION Ask students to summarize how Wilma's conflict is resolved. *(Possible response: She has decided she will not leave Harrison. She will accept her father's marriage and accept Mrs. Leighton as a stepmother.)*

OOO. Critical Thinking: ANALYZING
Ask students to explain the significance of the cloud passing over the moon and why it scares Wilma. *(Possible response: The cloud is a reminder of how quickly a person's life can change, from happiness to tragedy.)*

PPP. Reading Skill: DRAWING CONCLUSIONS Ask students to explain the significance of Wilma no longer being able to visualize her mother's face. *(Possible response: It shows that she is beginning to accept that her mother is gone and that she must get on with her life.)*

QQQ. Critical Thinking: EVALUATING
Ask students whether Lester's putting up the house for sale was ultimately a good or a bad thing. *(Possible response: It was a good thing, for two reasons: it inadvertently caused Wilma to seek help from her new stepmother and in the process find out that they could be friends; and it helped force Wilma to realize the kind of future she really wanted for herself.)*

Check Test

1. What letter is Wilma waiting for and why is it important to her? *(It is a letter from Mr. Delafonte telling her about having a screen test so she can go to Hollywood and be in movies.)*

2. Who gave Wilma the right to her house? *(her mother)*

3. Why does Wilma's father want to sell the house? *(He is planning to marry Mrs. Leighton and move to Houston. He needs the money to buy a house in Houston.)*

4. Who persuades Lester to keep the house? *(Mrs. Leighton)*

5. What are Wilma's plans for her future at the end of the play? *(to get married and have a family and live in her house)*

Encouraging Independent Reading

"Home," a short story by Gwendolyn Brooks
The Trip to Bountiful, a play by Horton Foote
A Raisin in the Sun, a play by Lorraine Hansberry
"Oxenhope," a short story by Sylvia Townsend Warner
Our Town, a play by Thornton Wilder

Arabella. Funny how things work out.

Wilma. Very funny.

Arabella. Guess who called me on the telephone.

Wilma. Who?

Arabella. Tommy . . . Murray.

Wilma. You don't say.

Arabella. He asked me for a date next week. Picture show. He said Jay was going to call you.

Wilma. Did he?

Arabella. I asked him to tell Jay that you weren't only interested in going out with movie actors.

Wilma. What did he say?

Arabella. He said he thought Jay knew that. *(A pause.* Wilma *jumps out of the swing.)* Wilma. What's the matter with you? Wilma . . . *(She runs to her.)*

OOO **Wilma.** I don't know. I felt funny there for a minute. A cloud passed over the moon and I felt lonely . . . and funny . . . and scared. . . .

Arabella. But you have your house now.

Wilma. I know . . . I . . . *(A pause. She points offstage right.)* I used to sleep in there. I had a white iron bed. I remember one night Aunt Gert woke me up. It was just turning light out, and she was crying. "I'm taking you home to live with me," she said. "Why?" I said. "Because your mama's gone to heaven," she said. *(a pause)* I can't remember my mama's face anymore. I can hear her voice sometimes calling me far off: "Wilma, Wilma, come home." Far off. But I can't remember her face. I try and I try, but finally I have to go to my bureau drawer and take out her picture and look to remember. . . . Oh, Arabella. It isn't only the house I wanted. It's the life in the house. My mama and me and even my daddy coming in at four in the morning. . . . PPP

Arabella. But there'll be life again in this house.

Wilma. How?

Arabella. You're gonna fill it with life again, Wilma. Like you said this afternoon.

Wilma. But I get afraid.

Arabella. Don't be. You will, I know you will.

Wilma. You think I can do anything. Be a movie star. . . . Go to Hollywood. *(a pause)* The moon's from behind the cloud. *(A pause. In the distance we can hear the courthouse clock strike ten.)* Don't tell me it's ten o'clock already. I'll fill this house with life again. I'll meet a young man with steady ways and nice habits. . . . *(Far off* Aunt Gert *calls:* "Wilma. Wilma." Wilma *calls back:)* We're coming. You see that pecan tree out there? QQQ

Arabella. Uh huh.

Wilma. It was planted the year my mother was born. It's so big now I can hardly reach around it. *(Aunt Gert calls again:* "Wilma. Wilma." Wilma *calls back:)* We're coming.

(She and Arabella *sit swinging.* Wilma *looks happy and is happy as the lights fade.)*

REAL LIFE CONNECTIONS

In the play, Wilma decides that she will stay in Harrison and get married. Ask the students if they think a person of fifteen in real life should be making decisions like this. Should Wilma be held to her decision?

In general, does a person need to make up his or her mind about the future by the age of fifteen? If not fifteen, then when? How can making up one's mind about the future at an early age help with decisions like whether or not to go to college? How can an unwise decision hurt a person's later life?

Have students discuss their own plans for the future.

Responding to Reading

First Impressions

1. What was your reaction to the way the play turned out? Explain.

Second Thoughts

2. What do you learn about Wilma early in the play?

   Think about
   - how she is compared with Arabella in the stage directions
   - how she interacts with Martha and Russell at the post office
   - what makes her angry

3. Describe Wilma's feelings about Mrs. Leighton for most of the play. Is Wilma being fair?

   Think about
   - what happened to Wilma's own mother
   - what Wilma thinks of her father
   - why she might fear Mrs. Leighton

4. Why is being "a young lady of property" so important to Wilma?

5. Why does Wilma give up her dream of becoming a star? Does she make the right decision?

6. Has Wilma changed by the end of the play? Explain your answer.

   Think about
   - how she feels about Mrs. Leighton and her father
   - why she doesn't want to go to Hollywood
   - what she plans to do with the house

Broader Connections

7. Owning a home is a goal for many Americans. Think about the reasons you gave earlier for your attachment to a particular home or place. Did your special feeling for this place have anything to do with owning it? Why is owning property—particularly a home—important to many people?

Literary Concept: Minor Characters

Minor characters play a secondary role in a story or play. Though they are rarely at the center of the action, they may have an important influence on a character who is, or deliver crucial information to move the plot forward. In your notebook, explain how Minna influences both the characters and the action of this play.

Student Response

Responding to Reading

The following questions are open-ended with no "right" or "wrong" answers. However, responses must be supported with information from the selection. Possible answers follow:

1. Any sincere response is valid.

2. Some students may say that she is aggressive and emotional. Others may say she is a confident person with strong opinions who knows what she wants and is determined to do her best to obtain it.

3. Students may say that for most of the play Wilma calls Mrs. Leighton "old lady," despises her, and refuses to accept Mrs. Leighton's relationship to her father. They may say Wilma is being fair because her father is unreliable and irresponsible and may be making a bad choice and because she does not want him to try to replace her mother. Others may say she is unfair because she should be able to pick up on what the stage directions indicate about Mrs. Leighton: that she is "warm" and "gracious."

4. Some students may say the property is like an insurance policy for Wilma's future, as well as part of her identity. Others may say it is important because she remembers how happy she was in the house when her mother was alive.

5. Some students may say the only reason Wilma dreamed of being a star was because she was lonely. Others may say her dream is a symbol of her independence. Many students may think that a future in Harrison sounds dull, and Wilma is hasty in giving up her dream. Others may say that her chances of becoming a star were miniscule, and she was right to give up her dream.

6. Some students may say that Wilma is the same feisty individual at the end of the play that she was at the beginning. Others may say she has learned that she needs people more than she thought; she has become more realistic.

7. Possible response: Owning property is a form of security to people. When they own something they know no one can take it away from them. Owning property also makes people feel like members of an upper social class, as a person with property is important and respected by the community.

Literary Concept—Minor Characters

Possible response: Minna influences the characters and action of the play in several ways. She is instrumental in reminding Wilma that she must act like a lady and remember her pride. Her questions about Mr. Delafonte cause Wilma to reassess her ideas about becoming a movie star. She comforts Gert when she feels bad, and helps Gert sort out her thoughts about Wilma, her brother, and the house. Perhaps the most important way in which she affects the play's action is to insist that Gert call the lawyer. She is the only one with the courage to admit what Lester is doing—stealing his daughter's house. Refer to annotations M and HHH.

Concept Review—Setting Possible response: If the play were set in a large city in the present day, some changes might include: more sophisticated characters; Wilma waiting for a phone call or a fax message from a TV casting agent or a video or music producer rather than for a letter; dialogue that included current slang, rather than rural expressions; Wilma's property being a townhouse or a condominium.

Writing Options

The Writing Options are designed to meet varied student interests and abilities. Have each student choose one writing activity to complete. You may wish to guide some students to an easier option that requires less writing.

Journal Update Have students review their journal entries. Ask them what emotions the play made them feel. Now that they have read the play, does the title seem to suit it? Have them explain why or why not.

Concept Review: Setting The setting for this play is a small town in Texas in 1925. How might this play be different if the setting were a large urban city in the present day?

1. Write the article that appears in the paper on the day after Mr. Delafonte's arrest. In it, link him to several other crimes that you imagine he could have committed. Include some facts about Mr. Delafonte's life that he might have told a reporter to make himself look good. Finally, be sure to include some quotes from Mr. Delafonte declaring his innocence.

2. Write a brief epilogue, or closing section, explaining what you think happens to Wilma after the play ends. Describe her new relationship with her stepmother and her father. Tell whether or not she settles down, whether she plans any other escapes from small-town life, and what she does with the rest of her life.

3. At the beginning of the play Wilma longs to escape Harrison, Texas. Create a diary entry in which she explains what she wants to leave, why she wants to leave it, and what she is looking for.

4. Imagine that you are Wilma. Write a note to Mrs. Leighton thanking her for understanding your situation and persuading your father not to sell the house. Apologize for your earlier rudeness toward her and express your interest in getting to know her better. Include a reference to your mother that clearly indicates that you are looking for a friend, not another mother.

5. Look back at what you wrote for Examine What You Know and then think about Wilma's feelings about the home of her childhood. In a paragraph, explain what the house symbolizes for Wilma.

6. The theme of this unit is "Escapes: Triumphs and Retreats." Write about a dream of escape of yours—a situation you would like to leave behind and a dream that you would like to pursue. Include one step that you could take right now toward making your dream a reality.

e x t e n d

Options for Learning

1 • Future Aspirations Conduct a survey of the girls at your school to find out their life goals. Include questions like these:

- What professional and personal goals do you have?
- How do you hope to attain these goals?
- Do you have an alternative plan?

Present your findings to the class.

2 • Dialogue What if Lester had sold the house? With several classmates, ad-lib a dialogue involving Wilma, Arabella, Minna, and Aunt Gert. Have each explain her reaction to Lester's action.

3 • Design Your Dream House If you could design the perfect home for you, what would it be like? Describe your dream house. Then draw a detailed picture of your house to share with the class.

4 • Be a Star Organize a role-playing activity that demonstrates a screen test. The participants should include the director, the director's assistant, and several young actors hoping to be discovered. Each actor will need a short script to audition. If possible, videotape the audition to play back for the class.

FACT FINDER

What famous actress was discovered at age 15 in a drug store across from her high school?

Horton Foote
1916–

Horton Foote did not wait for a screen test. At the age of sixteen he left his home in Wharton, Texas, to study acting in Pasadena, California. From there he went to New York City to continue acting and to begin writing. Since then he has written plays for radio, TV, film, and stage. As a screen writer he won Oscars for the screenplays of *To Kill a Mockingbird* and *Tender Mercies*.

About writing, Foote says: "I believe deeply in the human spirit, and I have an awe about it because I don't know how people carry on." He started to learn about struggling people as a boy growing up in Texas. While the other boys played ball, young Foote stayed inside listening to the stories of the old-timers. "One thing I was given in life," he says, "is a deep desire to listen. I've spent my life listening. When we were children, my brother—who preferred baseball—asked me why I fooled around with all those things. I said I didn't know, but I was just fascinated." Not surprisingly, many of Foote's plays take place in the small fictional town of Harrison, Texas. "I did not choose this task, this place, or these people to write about so much as they chose me, and I try to write about them with honesty," he says.

Options for Learning

These activities suit a variety of learning styles and modes of expression. Allow students to review the options and then choose the one they wish to do. Many are excellent collaborative learning projects.

1. Future Aspirations Suggest that students conduct the survey so respondents can rate how much they agree or disagree with a statement. For example, students might ask: "Is making a lot of money important to you?" A response of "5" might mean "strongly agree," while a response of "1" might mean "strongly disagree."

2. Dialogue A tape recorder or video camera can help students edit their dialogues and improve them.

3. Design Your Dream House Home improvement or architecture magazines, such as *Architecture Today, House Beautiful,* or *House and Garden,* might contain helpful suggestions.

4. Be a Star Students may use a scene from the play for the screen test. Consult the school drama teacher for pointers.

Fact Finder

Lana Turner was discovered at a soda fountain in Schwab's drug store by a Hollywood reporter. Students can find this fact in a book about the history of Hollywood.

Additional Information About the Author

Horton Foote "From the beginning," Foote writes, "most of my plays have taken place in the imaginary town of Harrison, Texas, and it seems to me a more unlikely subject could not be found in these days of Broadway and world theatre, than this attempt of mine to recreate a small Southern town and its people."

Closure

A Young Lady of Property is about growing up. Wilma Thompson feels that nothing is stable in her life except her house. When that is threatened, Wilma needs to decide who she is and who she wants to be. First she chooses independence so that no one can hurt her. Then she learns that being grown up requires taking the risk of reaching out and depending on others. Have students discuss what growing up means to them.

Cross-Curricular Options

Have students plan a renovation and addition for an old house similar to the one owned by Wilma Thompson.

Art: Make either drawings or plans for how the house looks now and how it will look after the renovation.

Math: Figure out a budget for the entire job. Then look into how much materials and labor will cost for the house. Consult local hardware, lumber, and building supply stores, as well as contractors.

Social Studies: Look into the legal aspect of improving a house. Call a lawyer, if you have access to one. Call City Hall and find out what permits and legal documents will be needed.

Literature: A house is more than just a place to live. Read about how houses are built and what they mean to the people who own them. An excellent source is *House* by Tracy Kidder. Then prepare a class report on "What Houses Mean to Us."

Science: Investigate the most efficient ways to heat, cool, and insulate the house.

Writer's Workshop

Objectives

- To select an interesting subject for biographical exposition
- To research a biographical topic using facilities in the library
- To organize biographical notes
- To use sentence combining and paraphrasing
- To draft, revise, edit, and share a biographical exposition
- To reflect on the writing process

Integrating . . .

Literature and Writing Share with students that each of the protagonists in the reading selections would make an interesting topic for a biography. Leon Crane, The Great Armando, and Wilma all are strong characters who overcome different sets of obstacles, different kinds of odds.

Writing and Language The Language Workshop in this subunit focuses on sentence combining. Point out to students that one of the pitfalls in nonfiction writing is using sentences that are too clipped or too flat. One of the qualities of good writing, such as John McPhee's, is the use of sentences that express a series of thoughts or images.

Discuss with LEP students the problems of writing in a new language, especially using simple words or sentences. Ask them to write down in their own language a simple and a complex word that have similar meanings. Then ask them to translate the words they have chosen into English. Then guide them in a more challenging exercise with sentences: have them write down a simple sentence and a complex sentence in their own language and then translate both into English: They will see that English is not so different in sentence structure from their native language.

Writing and Life Skills The Study Skills Workshop in this subunit deals with paraphrasing. Point out to students the importance of paraphrasing when taking notes for biographical writing.

WRITER'S WORKSHOP

EXPOSITION

When you're interested in a particular sports figure, movie celebrity, or musical performer, you probably enjoy reading about that person's life. After all, the more we know about people, the better we understand them. A book or article written about an individual's life is called a **biography** (the prefix *bio-* means "life," and the suffix *-graphy* means "written"). Sometimes biographies are written by a friend or relative who personally knows the subject. More often, biographies are written by authors who learn about the subject's life through research. For example, "Tsali of the Cherokees" was written by Alice Marriott from her interviews with Norah Roper. In either case, the biographer's purpose is to present an informative account of the person's life, highlighting that person's special qualities and accomplishments.

For this assignment you will write a brief biography of a famous person. Because it would be impossible to cover your subject's entire life, be selective in deciding what information to include.

GUIDED ASSIGNMENT: "WHO'S WHO FOR TEENS"

Select a famous person who interests you and who you think would interest your classmates. Collect data about this person and write a brief biography.

Here is your PASSkey to this assignment.

PURPOSE: To inform
AUDIENCE: Other teenagers
SUBJECT: A famous person
STRUCTURE: Biographical article

Prewriting

STEP 1 Select a subject Select a person whom you would like to learn more about and whom other teenagers might find interesting. You might consider a performer, an athlete, someone in an unusual career, or someone with a special talent.

STEP 2 What do you want to know? Before you begin your research, take a few minutes to note, first, what you already know about the person (or think you know) and, second, what you would

Additional Resources

UNIT TWO RESOURCE BOOK

Writer's Workshop Copy Master, p. 61
Peer and Self-Evaluation Guidelines, p. 62
Writing Assessment Guidelines, p. 63

ENRICHMENT MATERIALS

Thinking Skills Transparency and Worksheet
Fine Art Transparency and Writing Prompts
Revision, Proofreading, and Elaboration Worksheet
Writing Prompts for Assessment

like to find out about him or her. From these notes, make a list of the general categories that you will research. You can add to this list or modify it later. One student who chose to write a biography of the athlete Ben Johnson came up with these categories:

◀ STUDENT MODEL

```
a. Olympic competition        e. keys to his success
b. drug use                   f. income
c. his future as a runner     g. what he does now
d. early training             h. family influence
```

STEP 3 Begin your research In the library, identify possible sources of information about your subject. A good place to start is the *Biography Index,* which lists magazine articles and books containing biographical information about the people indexed. You might also check the *Readers' Guide to Periodical Literature.*

STEP 4 Gather information from your sources Refer to the "Guide for Research and Report Writing" in the **Writer's Handbook** for specific information about doing research. In general, be selective in taking notes. Use your notes from Step 2 and your list of categories as a guide to research. On the top of an index card, write the author and title of the source from which you're taking notes. Remember that writers must give credit to sources they "borrow" information from. Don't take someone else's ideas and pass them off as your own or you will be guilty of *plagiarism,* the theft of words or ideas.

Although it may be tempting to simply copy the information directly from the source onto your notecards, it is better to paraphrase or summarize the information, restating it in your own words. To give a particular point emphasis, you may want to copy the information word-for-word. To safeguard against plagiarism, be sure to copy this quote exactly and to enclose it in quotation marks. Note how the student writing about Ben Johnson paraphrased a sentence.

◀ STUDENT MODEL

Original Text	Student's Notecard
"Another key to Johnson's success was Francis's unorthodox coaching methods."	Current Biography Yearbook, 1988 Ben's success was partly due to his coach's unusual training techniques.

STEP 5 Categorize your information Write the category on the back of each card after you've written your note on the front. Feel free to add to or modify your categories. Use at least two different sources for each category to be as objective as possible.

Teaching Strategies

Introduction Have students turn to the **Writer's Workshop** on page 316. Point out that they may already be familiar with some forms of written biography if they read "celebrity" magazines or tabloid newspapers. Have students share with the class the strong and weak points of this kind of biographical writing. For example, the topics may be interesting but the facts are often distorted or exaggerated.

Direct students to the **Guided Assignment** box on page 316. Explain that they may choose a famous person from any field (sports, movies, music, politics, etc.) as the subject of their biography. Point out the PASSkey graphic and stress that the audience for the biography is other teenagers.

Prewriting Discuss with students why it is important to select a biographical subject that is interesting not just to them but to the whole class.

Teaching Tip
Have students brainstorm possible subjects for their biographies. Write the most frequently mentioned figures on the board, along with the qualities that make them most interesting to students: celebrity, notoriety, accomplishment, etc.

Share with students the importance of research in writing an interesting biography. Explain that richness of detail enhances the quality of biographical writing and engages the reader in the subject's story. Point out that other sources for biographical research besides the ones given in the *Prewriting* section can be found in the *Subject Guide* volumes of *Books in Print.* Many biographies written especially for young adults are listed in these directories.

Computer Tip

Those students who have access to a computer might consider numbering their subtopics. With this technique they will be able to focus on the relevant points of their subject's life by moving the various paragraphs around.
For example, someone's birthplace might be of paramount importance in determining the most interesting aspects of his or her life. This could be subtopic number 1. The parentage of a famous or accomplished person might be a governing factor in his or her life. This might be subtopic number 2.

Drafting Point out to students that a good biography follows the rules of journalism: it incorporates who, what, when, where, and why. It is especially important to include as many of these topics as possible in the introduction, covering what the person is noted for. For example, Leon Crane is most famous for having survived for 80 days in the frozen Alaskan wilderness. Point out to the class that it is almost mandatory for them to include the "why" in their introduction because it incorporates the focal point of the subject's life.

Stress the importance of objectivity in expressing the person's significance. A good biography does not rest on feelings and opinions; it is grounded in fact and substance. For example, someone who is writing a biography of the magician Houdini (the inspiration for the character of "The Great Armando" in *The Death Trap*) need only cite the daring feats he achieved in order to write a strong introduction to his life.

Point out to students that drafting a solid introduction makes biography writing proceed more smoothly. Often, a writer must simply amplify the facts given in the first part of the biography.

STEP 6 Organize your notes When your notes are completed, sort the cards into piles according to the category you've written on the back. The categories will be the subtopics of your paper. Then arrange the piles in the order in which you will present the information in your biography. The simplest way to organize a biography is chronologically, moving from the past to the present. Another option is to organize the data into two sections—the personal life and the professional career of the subject.

STEP 7 Establish a theme Identify a dominant theme or quality of your subject's life. For example, the student researching Ben Johnson felt that his story was one of a brilliant rise to fame and a sudden fall because of drugs.

STEP 8 Create a topic outline Using the order in which you arranged your notecards, make a brief topic outline. Each subtopic or category of information should be listed. Here is the student's outline for the biography of Ben Johnson.

STUDENT MODEL ▶

I. Introduction: Johnson's rise and fall
II. His upbringing
III. His early training
IV. Keys to his success
V. Olympic competition
VI. His future plans

Drafting

STEP 1 Write a strong introduction To capture your audience's attention, come up with an exciting opening. You may want to highlight the dominant theme or quality of your subject in your introduction. Note how this student introduced her biography by summarizing her theme—the rise and fall of Ben Johnson.

STUDENT MODEL ▶

When he broke the world record for the 100-meter dash in the 1987 Olympics, Canada's Ben Johnson had finally fulfilled his lifelong dream. But his dream turned into a nightmare when it was discovered that he used steroids. Within a week, Johnson lost his gold medal and everything he had worked for since he started running.

STEP 2 Write your draft With your focus in mind, draft your biography, using your notecards and your outline. Since your purpose is informative, write in the third person and avoid expressing your feelings or opinions. For each new subtopic, begin a new paragraph.

STEP 3 **Write your bibliography** List the sources you used in preparing your article. Include the author's name (if given), the title, the publisher and place of publication, and the copyright date.

Revising and Editing

Read over your draft as if you were reading it for the first time. Use the following checklist to guide your revision.

Revision Checklist

1. Will my introduction catch the audience's attention?
2. Did I focus on a dominant theme or special quality of my subject's life?
3. Have I included enough specific information to inform my readers? If not, what information should I add?
4. Have I included any irrelevant information?
5. Is my biography logically developed and easy to follow?
6. Will my biography appeal to other teens?

Editing After revising the content and form, proofread your composition for clarity, spelling, sentence structure, and punctuation.

Publishing

Put together a book titled "Who's Who for Teens" featuring all of the biographical articles written by your class. Elect a team of editors to organize the book (alphabetically or by subject matter), and perhaps enlist the aid of art students to draw illustrations (or find photos to go with each biography).

Reflecting on Your Writing

1. What did you learn about your writing while working on this assignment?
2. What part of your paper contains your best writing? Why?
3. What part of this assignment was the most difficult for you to carry out? Why?

Teaching Tip

Review the *Revision Checklist* with students.

1. Did they include at least two of the journalistic "w's" in their introductions?

2. Did they elaborate the reasons for the importance of their biographical subject?

3. Were they specific about their subject's life—his or her sports triumphs, medical invention, or political power? Are more facts needed?

4. Are extraneous details being substituted for necessary facts in the students' writing?

5. Does the biography follow a chronological or thematic order?

6. Is the subject one that is accessible to most teenagers?

Revising and Editing

Publishing Ask students to put together a list of the class's biographies arranged by subject (sports figures, rock stars, movie stars, political figures, etc.), as in the *Subject Guide to Books in Print*. Divide the class into groups according to the subjects of their biographies. Have each group choose the best biography from their group to present to the class. Then have the class select the most interesting, best-written, or most revealing biography.

Reflecting on Your Writing When you review students' writing samples, remember to respond to their answers to the *Reflecting* questions. Additional help may be appropriate if a majority of the class have similar responses for Question 3.

Closure

Before beginning the next subunit, be sure students understand and internalize these concepts:

- An interesting biography is well researched.
- A well-written biography uses complex sentences, not simple declarative statements, to relate a person's life.
- A theme and a topic outline facilitate the writing of a biography.
- A complete bibliography is essential to a biography.

Additional Writing and Research Topics

The following topics provide additional writing practice based on the selections in the subunit:

- Write a biography of one of Wilma's children. Do you think they would value their house as much as Wilma did? Give some reasons in your biography why they would or would not.
- Write a biography of Armando and Tina's children. Do you think they would lead an exciting or a quiet life?

Other Topics

Narration: Write a chapter for your diary that relates one of the bravest or most exciting moments in your life.

Social Studies Research: "A Young Lady of Property" takes place in a small town that is similar to the town in "The Death Trap." Ask students to compare and contrast the two towns in terms of the types of people who live there.

Language Workshop

Objectives

- To use coordinating conjunctions to combine sentence parts
- To vary sentence length in written work

Integrating . . .

Writing and Language Remind students that in the Writer's Workshop part of the revision and editing process includes checking that the biography is easy to follow, appealing, and contains proper sentence structure. Read the following sentences to students: *The long trip was boring. It was uneventful.* Point out that the short, choppy sentences can be made more appealing by combining them into a longer sentence: *The long trip was boring and uneventful.* Then write the following on the board:

1. There was no trace of the airplane. There were no survivors.

2. Mounds of snow littered the parking lot. The snow was dirty.

Ask volunteers to read the sentences aloud and explain how they could be revised by combining. Point out that sentences that are too long should also be revised. Write the following on the board and have a volunteer read it:

Brad looked up. His eyes widened in surprise. His mouth fell open. He swallowed a gasp. On the cafeteria steps was the tallest girl Brad had ever seen wearing the brightest purple lizard-skin cowboy boots topped by a leather suit and a toothy grin that stretched for miles.

Ask volunteers to give their opinions about the kinds of sentences this writer used. Then ask students to revise the sentences to make the paragraph more interesting. Finally, tell students that this Language Workshop focuses on sentence combining.

LANGUAGE WORKSHOP

SENTENCE COMBINING I

Crane opened the door. He stepped inside. He closed the door behind him. He walked to the window. He looked around at the stocked cabin. He was relieved.

As you can see, a series of short sentences one after the other can become irritating. When you write, try to vary your sentence length by combining short, related sentences to make longer sentences.

Joining Sentence Parts

REMINDER

In writing, not all sentences should be joined. Your goal should be a variety of sentence lengths.

Sometimes the ideas in two sentences are so closely related that the sentences use some of the same words or ideas. You can combine sentences like these by eliminating repeated words or ideas and joining the remaining sentence parts. To join sentence parts, use a coordinating conjunction such as *and, but,* or *or.*

To join similar sentence parts, use *and.* (Notice that the italicized words are eliminated in the combined sentence.)

The lone survivor had no food. *He also had* no sleeping bag.
The lone survivor had no food **and** no sleeping bag.

To join contrasting sentence parts, use *but.*

He scanned the mountainside. *He* saw no other signs of life.
He scanned the mountainside **but** saw no other signs of life.

When the sentence parts present a choice, use *or.*

Leon Crane could sleep. *He* could keep his fire going.
Leon Crane could sleep **or** keep his fire going.

Exercise 1 Combine each pair of sentences. Use the words given in parentheses and eliminate the italicized words.

1. Leon Crane jumped from the diving plane. *He* landed in the Alaskan wilderness. (and)
2. The lone survivor hiked down to a river. *He* built a fire. (and)
3. He made a spear. *He* couldn't catch any squirrels. (but)
4. Would Crane survive? *Would he* succumb to nature? (or)
5. He found a stocked cabin. *He* only stayed there one night. (but)

Additional Resources

UNIT TWO RESOURCE BOOK
Language Workshop Copy Master, p. 68

ENRICHMENT MATERIALS
Grammar and Usage Copy Master

6. Crane left the cabin. *He* later decided to retrace his steps. (but)
7. He stayed at that cabin. *He* waited for spring to arrive. (and)
8. Crane could stay and hunt. *He could* leave to find help. (or)
9. Crane followed a toboggan trail. *He* found a cabin owned by a trapper and his family. (and)
10. The trapper harnessed his dogs. *He* took Crane to the town. (and)

Adding Words to Sentences

Sometimes you can compare two related sentences and find that much of the second sentence merely repeats the first sentence. Often, only one word from the second sentence is essential. In such cases you can transfer that one word to the first sentence and then delete the second sentence altogether. When you transfer a word, make sure to place it close to the person, thing, or action it describes in the new sentence.

Leon Crane found a cabin. *It was a* small *cabin.*

Leon Crane found a **small** cabin.

Sometimes you can combine more than two sentences in this way.

The survivor lived in the cabin. *The survivor was* lonely. *His cabin was* tiny.

The **lonely** survivor lived in the **tiny** cabin.

Sometimes when adding a word you will have to use a comma.

It was a dark night. *It was a* cold *night.*

It was a **cold,** dark night.

When you combine sentences by adding a word, you sometimes need to change the form of the added word. Usually this means adding an ending such as *-y, -ed, -ing, -ly, -able,* or *-ably.*

Crane lived in the cabin for six weeks. *He lived in* comfort.

Crane lived **comfortably** in the cabin for six weeks.

Exercise 2 Combine each pair of sentences by eliminating the italicized words. Sometimes you will need to change the form of a word. Use commas when necessary.

1. The Yukon River is the most important river in Alaska. *It is the* longest.
2. The Yukon cuts across Alaska from east to west. *The Yukon is* treacherous. *Alaska is* frigid.

Teaching Strategies

Ask a volunteer to read the first section of the lesson, stopping before Exercise 1. Call students' attention to the *Reminder.*

Ask students if they can think of other connecting words. Students may mention other coordinating conjunctions such as *nor, for, yet, so*; correlative conjunctions such as *both . . . and, either . . . or, not only . . . but also*; subordinating conjunctions such as *after, before, although, if, because, since, while, that*; or conjunctive adverbs such as *however, nevertheless, therefore, consequently.*

Assign Exercise 1 to students, reminding them to delete unnecessary punctuation and capital letters. Have students share their responses. Then continue working through the lesson.

Before assigning Exercise 2, form four groups and assign one selection from this subunit to each group. Challenge students to find three different examples of short sentences that could be combined and then share their findings and combinations with the class. Remind students that their primary goal is to create smooth, well-written sentences.

Teaching Tip

Point out that when combining short, choppy sentences, it is often necessary to change the word order. Assure students that this is permissible, but remind them to be sure they do not alter the original meaning.

Next assign Exercise 2. Encourage the use of dictionaries to check the spelling of any word whose form changes. Review the exercise, and then form small groups to complete Exercise 3. Ask one student in each group to rewrite and read the final paragraph. Then assign Exercise 4.

Closure

Before beginning the next subunit, be sure students have internalized these concepts:

- Two short, related sentences can often be combined, but the original meaning must be retained.
- When joining sentence parts, be sure to use the correct coordinating conjunction, such as *and*, *but*, and *or*.
- Varying sentence length when writing helps to create interest.

Answer Key
Exercise 1

1. Leon Crane jumped from the diving plane and landed in the Alaskan wilderness.
2. The lone survivor hiked down to a river and built a fire.
3. He made a spear but couldn't catch any squirrels.
4. Would Crane survive or succumb to nature?
5. He found a stocked cabin but only stayed there one night.
6. Crane left the cabin but later decided to retrace his steps.
7. He stayed at that cabin and waited for spring to arrive.
8. Crane could stay and hunt or could leave to find help.
9. Crane followed a toboggan trail and found a cabin owned by a trapper and his family.
10. The trapper harnessed his dogs and took Crane to the town.

Exercise 2

1. The Yukon River is the longest, most important river in Alaska.
2. The treacherous Yukon cuts across frigid Alaska from east to west.
3. Yukon river steamers journey slowly across Alaska to the Bering Sea.
4. This mighty river is icebound much of the year.
5. Alaskans predict when the solid ice will break up and flow rapidly out to sea.

Exercise 3

My great-aunt Lily tells wonderful stories and makes beautiful paintings. She once traveled up into Alaska on a slow steamer from Oregon. Her father bought land near Ketchikan and built a log cabin for his family. He fished and logged. Lily loved her simple, happy life. Her father raised huskies and sold them at trading posts. Aunt Lily remembers the smallest details about each of their dogs. She painted a detailed picture of her favorite husky sitting next to their cabin. Her flawless memory and extraordinary talent allowed Aunt Lily to recreate that scene.

Exercise 4

Answers will vary, but students' work should reflect the sentence-combining techniques of this workshop.

3. Yukon river steamers journey across Alaska to the Bering Sea. *The steamers' journey is* slow.
4. This river is icebound much of the year. *The river is* mighty.
5. Alaskans predict when the ice will break up and flow out to sea. *The ice is* solid. *The ice flow will be* rapid.

Exercise 3 Work in a small group to rewrite the following passage, using the combining techniques in this workshop. Eliminate the words in italics and combine the sentences in parentheses.

> (My great-aunt Lily tells wonderful stories. *She also* makes beautiful paintings.) (She once traveled up into Alaska on a steamer from Oregon. *The steamer was* slow.) (Her father bought land near Ketchikan. *Her father also* built a log cabin for his family.) (He fished. *He also* logged.) (Lily loved her life. *Her life was* simple. *Her life was* happy.) (Her father raised huskies. *He* sold them at trading posts.) (Aunt Lily remembers each of their dogs. *She remembers* the smallest details about *them.)* (She painted a picture of her favorite husky sitting next to their cabin. *The picture had* detail.) (Her memory and her talent allowed Aunt Lily to recreate that scene. *Her memory was* flawless. *Her talent was* extraordinary.)

Exercise 4 Analyzing and Revising Your Writing

1. Take a paper from your writing portfolio.
2. Rewrite one or two paragraphs, using the sentence-combining skills you have learned.
3. Check to see that you have punctuated correctly.
4. Remember to check for related sentences that might be combined the next time you are revising your work.

LANGUAGE HANDBOOK

For review and practice, see Section 7, **Sentence Structure.**

ADDITIONAL PRACTICE

The following items provide additional practice in combining sentences.

Combine each pair of sentences using *,and* or *,but* or *,or.*

1. Joe took the escalator. Vi took the elevator. *, and*
2. Will you drive to the football game? Is your car still in the shop? *, or*
3. Bill likes anchovy pizza. No one else does. *, but*
4. Cassie wants to go to the rehearsal. She has an appointment at the orthodontist. *, but*

Combine these sentences, using the correct punctuation and changing word forms whenever necessary.

5. The koala bear sat in the tree. It was a eucalyptus tree. *. . . in the eucalyptus tree.*
6. Peacocks strutted around the garden. They were graceful. *Graceful peacocks . . .*
7. The sound of the cannon woke the soldiers. The cannon boomed. *The sound of the booming cannon . . .*
8. Molly put the cheese on the pizza. The cheese was grated. *. . . the grated cheese . . .*

PARAPHRASING

Every report you write will include information taken from other sources, usually written. One of the best ways to present this material is to use a **paraphrase.**

When you write a paraphrase, you put someone else's ideas into your own words. A paraphrase usually simplifies a selection; generally, although not always, it also shortens it.

Like notes that you take, a paraphrase records the essential information in a selection. Unlike notes, a paraphrase is organized in sentences and paragraphs. Here's how it's done.

Step 1 Locate the main idea Read the selection carefully and think about what it means. Find the sentence that states the main idea and put that idea into your own words.

Step 2 List supporting details In your own words, list all the details, points, and arguments that support the main idea. List these items in the same order in which they appear in the original.

Step 3 Simplify the vocabulary Remember that in a paraphrase you must use your own words to express and simplify the ideas from the selection. One way to do this is to replace difficult words in the original selection with more familiar synonyms.

Step 4 Revise the paraphrase Once you have written a draft of your paraphrase, reread it and make revisions. Make sure you have put the material into your own words. Check to see that you have shortened long sentences and simplified the vocabulary. Read the paraphrase one last time to be sure that it expresses the idea of the original selection. Proofread your paraphrase to eliminate any errors in grammar and punctuation. Finally, be sure to identify your source.

Exercise Write a paraphrase of the workshop on dialect on page 214 of this book. Follow the steps discussed above. Be sure to proofread your finished paraphrase.

Study Skills Workshop

Objective

- To understand what a paraphrase is and how it is written

Integrating . . .

Literature and Study Skills Share with students that this workshop will show them a useful method of including information from other sources when they write reports.

Teaching Strategies

Ask a volunteer to summarize "Survival in the Forty-Ninth." Ask students to explain the process the volunteer used to shorten the piece. Explain that this process is very similar to paraphrasing.

Read through the material with students. As you discuss Step 4, point out that it may be helpful to use the tips from the **Language Workshop** when combining sentences. Stress that students must credit their sources.

Assign the exercise on page 323. Hold conferences with individual students to review their paraphrases.

Closure

Before beginning the next subunit, be sure students have internalized these concepts:

- A paraphrase is an individual's version of information from another source.
- A paraphrase consists of the main idea of the selection and supporting details.
- The vocabulary in a paraphrase is usually simpler than that of the original.

Teaching Tip: LEP

Whenever possible, provide LEP students with materials that may be highlighted or written on. By highlighting key material, students receive visual clues about the structure of the text.

Exercise

(A possible answer is given.)
Dialect is the distinct form of language spoken by a particular group of people. The pronunciations of words and the names for items may vary in different dialects. While dialect may be appropriate in informal situations, standard English should be used in formal settings.

Additional Resources

UNIT TWO RESOURCE BOOK
Related Skills Copy, p. 69

ENRICHMENT MATERIALS
Standardized Test Practice Copy Masters

ADDITIONAL PRACTICE

Write a paraphrase of this workshop following the guidelines.
(A possible response is given.)

A paraphrase is an individual's version of information from another source. A paraphrase begins with the main idea of the original source and then gives supporting details. A paraphrase is usually shorter and simpler than the original.

Unit Three *Challenges: Winners and Losers*

Objectives

Students will develop skills in the following areas. An asterisk (*) indicates a workshop topic.

Reading and Thinking

drawing conclusions *pp. 327, 328, 329, 330, 332, 334*
noting literal and figurative language *p. 351*
understanding dialect *p. 366*
noting punctuation in poetry *p. 380*
predicting *p. 392*
inferring *pp. 410, 423, 427, 428*
identifying problem and solution *p. 436*

Vocabulary and Related Skills

using words in context *pp. 344, 400, 442*
*using a thesaurus *p. 365*
*critical listening *p. 408*
synonyms *p. 430*
antonyms *p. 430*
*public speaking *p. 451*

Literary Appreciation

figurative language *p. 335*
conflict *p. 335*
descriptive details *p. 343*
autobiography *p. 343*
personification *pp. 356, 384, 441*
character motivation *p. 377*
sensory details *p. 377*
word choice *p. 384*
author's purpose *p. 391*
falling action *p. 399*
resolution *p. 399*
suspense *p. 399*
setting *p. 429*
foreshadowing *p. 429*
climax *p. 441*

Writing

speech *pp. 336, 344*
conversation *pp. 336, 442*
letter *pp. 344, 350, 400*
poem *pp. 344, 356, 384*
metaphors *p. 344*
personal narrative *p. 350*
*creative expression: poem *pp. 358–61*
summary *p. 378*
report *p. 391*
diary entry *p. 391*
*literary analysis: analyzing theme *pp. 401–403*
obituary *p. 430*
credo *p. 435*
personification *p. 442*
*persuasion: statement to a jury *pp. 444–47*

Language, Grammar, Usage, Mechanics

*using specific nouns and verbs *pp. 362–64*
*making subjects and verbs agree *pp. 405–407*
*using pronouns correctly *pp. 448–50*

Planning the Unit

You may find the following information and lists of resources helpful in preparing for the unit.

Difficulty Level of Selections

In determining the accessibility of the selections in this unit, many factors, including reading level and comprehension difficulty, have been taken into account. The ranking can be used as a general guide in determining how much preparation and assistance students will require in order to master the selection. No selection should be included or eliminated from the course based merely on difficulty level. Basic students will derive a great deal of confidence and self-esteem by working through a *challenge* selection; conversely, advanced students may find pleasure, relevance, and important themes in a selection that is rated *easy*.

Classroom Resources

Videocassettes, Films, and Filmstrips

■ ***Anne Sexton***, 16mm film, Indiana University Audio-Visual Center, 1966, (30 minutes). An introduction to Anne Sexton and a view of her poetry.

■ ***My Left Foot***, 16mm film, video, Miramax Films/HBO Home Video, 1989, (103 minutes). An Academy Award-winning adaptation of Christy Brown's book.

■ ***A Native Son***, video, Mississippi Center for Educational TV, 1975, (30 minutes). Mississippi authors discuss the life and works of Richard Wright.

■ ***Rudyard Kipling—The Road from Mandalay***, 16mm film, video, Centron Educational Films, 1978, (30 minutes). This film re-creates through flashbacks one day in the life of Rudyard Kipling.

Audiocassettes, Tapes, and Records

Amy Tan Reads the Joy Luck Club, 2 audiocassettes, Japanese American Curriculum Project, (156 minutes). The author's reading of her award-winning first publication.

Anne Sexton Reads her Poetry, audiocassette, Caedmon. Features the poet reading from her work.

John Updike—Poetry and Prose, audiocassette, Jeffrey Norton Publishers, (47 minutes). The writer reads from and comments on his work.

Native Son, audiocassette, Caedmon. Condensation of Richard Wright's novel, read by James Earl Jones.

Community Resources

Involving the resources of your community in lesson preparation can add insight and relevance to the text. Consider the following possibilities as you plan.

■ For "My Left Foot," invite an activist for the rights of handicapped people to discuss recent advances and plans for the future.

■ For "Test," plan an informational field trip to the Department of Motor Vehicles.

■ For "If" and "Courage," invite a poet to talk about writing and having poetry published.

■ For "Rules of the Game," contact a community organization that sponsors chess tournaments for a schedule of classes and matches.

■ For "Fast Break" and "Ex-Basketball Player," invite former basketball stars from your school to discuss their favorite memories.

■ For "Wilma," plan a field trip to a public library to use periodical literature to research women gold medalists in the Olympics.

■ For "The Most Dangerous Game," invite a hunter and an animal rights activist to debate hunting.

■ For "All I Really Need to Know I Learned in Kindergarten," plan a field trip to a kindergarten to observe children's skills and tactics of "survival."

■ For "The Rights to the Streets of Memphis," invite a law enforcement officer from the juvenile division to talk about "street smarts" and juvenile crime.

Unit Preview

How can we tell the winners from the losers? Can you win and lose at the same time? In Unit 3, **Challengers: Winners and Losers,** students will explore the questions of winning and losing. The unit contains three subunits:

- Subunit 1: Tests of Courage
- Subunit 2: Who Wins?
- Subunit 3: Strategies for Survival

Art Note

Theophilus Brown (1919–) studied at Yale, with Amédée Ozenfant in New York, with Fernand Léger in Paris, and at the University of California, Berkeley. He later taught at Berkeley, at the California School of Fine Arts, and at the University of California at Davis. His approach is neither abstract nor fully representational—surrealistic, yet immediate. *Why are the blurred, off-register colors so effective in Football Painting #2?*

About the Author

Short-story writer and poet Sandra Cisneros is in the forefront of contemporary Chicano literature. As the recipient of the first major publishing contract ever awarded to a work of fiction by and about Chicanos, Cisneros has opened the door for other Chicano writers. "I'm excited about the whole generation of Chicana writers," she remarked in a recent magazine interview. Cisneros won the Before Columbus American Book Award for her collection *The House on Mango Street.* From her home in San Antonio, Texas, Cisneros continues to write, publish, and help others understand and appreciate Chicano literature.

Unit Three

CHALLENGES: WINNERS AND LOSERS

"I've managed to do a lot of things in my life I didn't think I was capable of."

Sandra Cisneros

FOOTBALL PAINTING #2 (detail) 1956 William Theophilus Brown Collection of the Santa Barbara Museum of Art Gift of Paul Wonner.

325

Discussion Questions

To help students probe connections among the fine art, quotation, and unit theme, have them consider the following questions:

1. What do you think Sandra Cisneros means by her statement? What things might she have accomplished that she didn't think she could do? *(Possible response: Students may suggest that Cisneros felt she could not succeed in some areas because she or others doubted her ability.)*

2. What challenges have you met that have made you a winner? *(Possible response: Students may suggest that they succeeded in a course they initially thought was too difficult, mastered a sports skill or craft, or worked to overcome a disability.)*

3. How might the quotation and unit title be linked? *(Possible response: Students may suggest that winners accomplish things they did not think they could do; losers do not challenge themselves. Students might further suggest that you cannot be a loser if you try, even if you do not succeed.)*

4. What relationship do you see among the artwork, quotation, and unit title? *(Possible responses: Students might suggest that the figures in the picture are struggling against challenges. They are trying to accomplish great things in an effort to become winners.)*

5. What do you think the selections in this unit will be about, based on the artwork, quotation, and unit title? *(Possible responses: Students may suggest the selections will challenge them to decide for themselves how to define winning and losing.)*

Subunit Preview

Have students read the introduction to subunit 1, **Tests of Courage.** Ask them to explore how one's attitude toward facing a challenge is relevant to the unit theme, **Challenges: Winners and Losers.** Why do some people accept challenges so creatively or courageously? What positive aspects of a person's character does a challenge bring out? Invite students to read the subunit Table of Contents and predict which selection will be the most interesting.

For Additional Challenge

The following selections offer extra challenge in the exploration of the subunit theme:

"Through the Tunnel," a short story by Doris Lessing

"With All Flags Flying," a short story by Anne Tyler

Additional Resources

Subunit Test, pp. 26–27

TESTS OF COURAGE

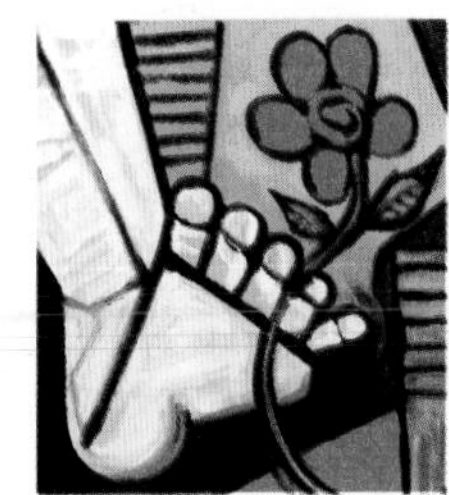

How do you deal with an unexpected challenge—a difficulty you hadn't counted on? Some people panic, then slowly adjust to the new trial. Others move ahead boldly, ready to handle whatever comes their way. Challenge often brings out the best in people by forcing them to think creatively and to develop resources they did not even know they had. In this way, challenges help an individual to grow.

This subunit tells of people who experience challenges that test their courage. As you read each selection, decide what unknown challenge each main character faces and how he or she handles it.

OBSERVATION ASSESSMENT

Observing how students respond to the text, to the classroom instruction, and to peers is an important part of an assessment program. The following suggestions and the form in each Unit Resource Book can be used to implement observation assessment.

- As students work through the subunit, assess their use of postreading strategies. Can they identify the key events? Can they explain characters' motivations? Can they verbalize what the story means to them?
- As students work through the subunit, can you see gains in the use of postreading strategies?
- To evaluate students' ability to see relationships between a story and prior experience, ask them what places, people, and events occur to them as they read. Ask them to explain the connection. Can they relate a selection to another story, a poem, a film, or a TV show?

e x p l o r e

Fiction

The Street of the Cañon

JOSEPHINA NIGGLI (nig′ lē)

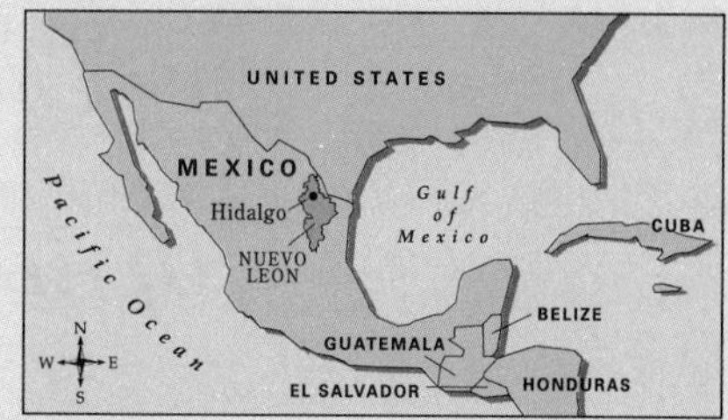

Examine What You Know (Prior Knowledge)

In the story you are about to read, a young man risks bodily harm for a young woman he wants to meet. Can you imagine something similar happening in real life, or does this occur only in books and movies? Share your opinion with your classmates. Then read to see whether the young man's behavior is heroic or foolish.

Expand Your Knowledge (Building Background)

"The Street of the Cañon" takes place in the valley of the Sabinas River in the Mexican state of Nuevo León (nwe′ vô le ôn′), the author's birthplace. Although Niggli spent most of her life in the United States, she returned to the Sabinas Valley from time to time to collect stories and impressions. These ideas grew into her book *Mexican Village*, of which "The Street of the Cañon" is a part. Although the story might be fictional, the places, situations, and values held by the characters are real. The town of Hidalgo, for example, is a real village, named after Miguel Hidalgo y Costilla (mē gel′ ē däl′ gô ē kôs tē′ yä), a priest who in 1810 led an uprising that triggered Mexico's War of Independence with Spain.

Enrich Your Reading (Reading Skill)

Drawing Conclusions To **draw conclusions,** you must combine inferences with facts from the story and your own experiences and insights. Use the questions that appear throughout the story you are about to read to help you draw conclusions about its characters and events.

■ *A biography of the author can be found in the Reader's Handbook.*

Objectives

- To read and analyze a short story
- To draw conclusions about the meaning of a story
- To identify and understand figurative language
- To recognize conflict in a story
- To show understanding of the work through a choice of writing options, including a story episode, a speech, dialogue, a compromise, and an analysis

Prereading/Motivation

Examine What You Know

Discussion Prompts: Have you ever tried to attract someone's attention by showing off? Did you risk making a fool of yourself or worse? Are characters and events more dramatic in stories than in real life? If so, why? In what ways are heroes and fools sometimes alike?

Expand Your Knowledge

Discussion Prompts: How might living in a small village where everyone knows one another limit a person's opportunities? How might it increase opportunities? Are the basic concerns of people who live in small villages different from those of city dwellers? Explain.

Enrich Your Reading

As students read "The Street of the Cañon," ask them to draw conclusions about these topics: the identity of the stranger, the contents of the stranger's package, what the stranger did in the past, the stranger's motives for meeting Sarita, the real owner of the bones of Don Rómolo. Explain that students may have to change their conclusions as the story progresses and more facts and details are revealed.

Thematic Link—Tests of Courage

In this story, a young man puts himself through a great and unusual test of courage.

Journal Writing

The distrust that can exist between neighboring communities is central to "The Street of the Cañon." Suggest these journal topics to students:

- Have you ever disliked or distrusted someone because of where he or she lived? Tell about it.
- Have you ever gone out of your way to meet someone from another community? Tell what happened.

For other journal opportunities, refer students to Examine What You Know (p. 327) and Real Life Connections (p. T–331).

Additional Resources

UNIT THREE RESOURCE BOOK
Reader's Guidesheet, p. 1
Vocabulary Worksheet, p. 2
Selection and Vocabulary Check Tests, p. 3
Selection Test, pp. 4–5

Collaborative Learning

Opportunities for collaborative learning appear throughout the lesson and include Examine What You Know (p. 327).

Teaching Strategies

Vocabulary Preview

These vocabulary words are defined at the bottom of the selection page on which they appear. You may wish to discuss them briefly before students begin reading.

apprehension an uneasy feeling
audaciously boldly
disdain contempt
intricate full of complexity
nonchalantly casually
plausibility believability
prominent noticeable
propriety being proper
pungent having a strong smell
virtuous righteous

Support for Students of Limited English Proficiency

- Use Reader's Guidesheet, p. 1.
- "The Street of the Cañon" is set in Mexico and contains a number of Spanish terms. Ask Spanish-speaking volunteers to help with the pronunciation of these terms.
- Annotations A, N, O, and X focus on troublesome terms and concepts.

Text Annotations

A. LEP: Vocabulary Have a volunteer pronounce the terms *San Juan Iglesias, Don Roméo Calderón,* and *Cañon.* Point out the meaning of *cañon* (canyon) and *iglesias* (churches). Explain that *Don* is a title meaning "Sir."

B. Literary Element: MOOD Point out that the author creates a mood of mystery by having the unnamed man slip from shadow to shadow, clutching an unspecified package and hiding from the barking dog.

C. Reading Skill: DRAWING CONCLUSIONS *The people of San Juan Iglesias hate the people of Hidalgo; they are bitter enemies.*

The Street of the Cañon

JOSEPHINA NIGGLI

It was May, the flowering thorn was sweet in the air, and the village of San Juan Iglesias[1] in the Valley of the Three Marys was celebrating. The long, dark streets were empty because all of the people, from the lowest-paid cowboy to the mayor, were helping Don Roméo Calderón[2] celebrate his daughter's eighteenth birthday. A

On the other side of the town, where the Cañon Road led across the mountains to the Sabinas Valley, a tall, slender man, a package clutched tightly against his side, slipped from shadow to shadow. Once a dog barked, and the man's black suit merged into the blackness of a wall. But no voice called out, and after a moment he slid into the narrow, dirt-packed street again. B

The moonlight touched his shoulder and spilled across his narrow hips. He was young, no more than twenty-five, and his black curly head was bare. He walked swiftly along, heading always for the distant sound of guitar and flute. If he met anyone now, who could say from which direction he had come? He might be a trader from Monterrey or a buyer of cow's milk from farther north in the Valley of the Three Marys. Who would guess that an Hidalgo[3] man dared to walk alone in the moonlit streets of San Juan Iglesias? ◀SR-1

drawing conclusions

How do the people of San Juan Iglesias feel about the people of Hidalgo? C

Carefully adjusting his flat package so that it was not too prominent, he squared his shoulders and walked jauntily across the street to the laughter-filled house. Little boys packed in the doorway made way for him, smiling and nodding to him. The long, narrow room with the orchestra at one end was filled with whirling dancers. Rigid-backed chaperones were gossiping together, seated in their straight chairs against the plaster walls. Over the scene was the yellow glow of kerosene lanterns, and the air was hot with the too-sweet perfume of gardenias, tuberoses, and the pungent scent of close-packed humanity.

1. **San Juan Iglesias** (sän hwän ē gle′ sē äs).
2. **Don Roméo Calderón** (dôn rō me′ ô käl de rôn′).
3. **Hidalgo** (ē däl′ gô).

Words to Know and Use	**prominent** (präm′ ə nənt) *adj.* noticeable **pungent** (pun′ jənt) *adj.* having a strong smell

328

Structured Reading for Less Proficient Students

These questions can help to guide students through the reading. Ask each question at the point of the selection where the SR number appears in the margin.

SR–1. Where does the tall, slender man come from? *(Hidalgo)* Where is he now? *(in San Juan Iglesias)* **Literal recall**

SR–2. Does anyone at the party recognize the man? How do you know? *(No; if they recognized him, they would turn on him like snarling cats.)* **Inferring**

SR–3. Why doesn't Don Roméo's daughter recognize the stranger? *(She was very angry and upset when she saw him last and also could not see his face clearly in the moonlight.)* **Clarifying**

SR–4. Why do the villagers think the people of Hidalgo are wicked? *(People from Hidalgo tried to steal the bones of Don Rómolo Balderas.)* **Literal recall**

Continued on page 329

The man in the doorway, while trying to appear at ease, was carefully examining every smiling face. If just one person recognized him, the room would turn on him like a den of snarling mountain cats, but so far all the laughter-dancing eyes were friendly.

Suddenly a plump, officious little man, his round cheeks glistening with perspiration, pushed his way through the crowd. His voice, many times too large for his small body, boomed at the man in the doorway, "Welcome, stranger, welcome to our house." Thrusting his arm through the stranger's, and almost dislodging the package, he started to lead the way through the maze of dancers. "Come and drink a toast to my daughter—to my beautiful Sarita.[4] She is eighteen this night."

In the square patio the gentle breeze ruffled the pink and white oleander bushes. A long table set up on sawhorses[5] held loaves of flaky-crusted French bread, stacks of thin, delicate *tortillas,*[6] plates of barbecued beef, and long red rolls of spicy sausages. But most of all there were cheeses, for the Three Marys was a cheese-eating valley. There were yellow cheese and white cheese and curded cheese from cow's milk. There was even a flat white cake of goat cheese from distant Linares,[7] a delicacy too expensive for any but feast days.

To set off this feast were bottles of beer floating in ice-filled tin tubs, and another table was covered with bottles of mescal, of tequila, of maguey wine.

Don Roméo Calderón thrust a glass of tequila into the stranger's hand. "Drink, friend, to the prettiest girl in San Juan. As pretty as my fine fighting cocks, she is. On her wedding day she takes to her man, and by the Blessed Ribs may she find him soon, the best fighter in my flock. Drink deep, friend. Even the rivers flow with wine."

drawing conclusions

How does the father feel about his daughter?

The Hidalgo man laughed and raised his glass high. "May the earth be always fertile beneath her feet."

Someone called to Don Roméo that more guests were arriving, and with a final delighted pat on the stranger's shoulder, the little man scurried away. As the young fellow smiled after his retreating host, his eyes caught and held another pair of eyes—laughing black eyes set in a young girl's face. The last time he had seen that face it had been white and tense with rage, and the lips clenched tight to prevent an outgushing stream of angry words. That had been in February, and she had worn a white lace shawl over her hair. Now it was May, and a gardenia was a splash of white in the glossy, dark braids. The moonlight had mottled his face that February night, and he knew that she did not recognize him. He grinned impudently back at her, and her eyes widened, then slid sideways to one of the chaperones. The fan in her small hand snapped shut. She tapped its parchment tip against her mouth and slipped away to join the dancing couples in the front room. The gestures of a fan translate into a coded language on the frontier. The stranger raised one eyebrow as he interpreted the signal.

4. **Sarita** (sä rē′ tä).
5. **sawhorses:** racks used to support wood while it is being sawed.
6. ***tortillas:*** flat, round cornmeal or flour cakes.
7. **Linares** (lē nä′ res).

D. Literary Element: FIGURATIVE LANGUAGE Review that the word *like* indicates the author is using a simile to compare the guests to a den of mountain cats.

E. Reading Skill: PREDICTING Ask students to predict why the stranger from Hidalgo has come to Sarita's birthday party. Ask what students think he plans to do.

Cultural Sidelight Point out the details describing the food and drink at the party. Explain that the author, Josefina Niggli, used traditional Mexican customs and folklore in her stories to breathe life into characters and events.

F. Reading Skill: DRAWING CONCLUSIONS *He adores his daughter and feels she is beautiful and deserves the best; he is anxious that she marry well.*

G. Literary Element: PLOT Have students summarize the information about the past and present that the stranger's memory provides here. *(The stranger and the young woman have seen each other before, in February, when the stranger did something that enraged the woman. Although he remembers her, she does not recognize him.)*

STRUCTURED READING FOR LESS PROFICIENT STUDENTS

Continued from page 328

SR–5. Who was Don Rómolo Balderas? *(the greatest historian in Mexico)* **Literal recall**

SR–6. Who was the leader of the three men who opened Don Rómolo's grave? *(Pepe Gonzalez)* **Literal recall**

SR–7. What does the stranger ask Sarita to do with him? What does this suggest? *(He asks her to walk around the plaza with him on Sunday; this suggests he wants to marry her.)* **Literal recall**

SR–8. According to Tío Daniel, who made the delicious cheese that mysteriously appeared at the party? *(Timotéo Gonzalez of Hidalgo, the father of Pepe Gonzalez)* **Literal recall**

SR–9. Who does Sarita suspect is the stranger with whom she danced? *(Pepe Gonzalez)* **Literal recall**

H. Literary Element: FIGURATIVE LANGUAGE Point out that the stranger does not actually kiss the woman's hands and feet. Elicit the meaning of his figurative expression. *(Possible response: "I show you the highest regard and respect, Senora.")*

I. Literary Element: CHARACTERIZATION Ask the students for words that describe the stranger based on his interaction with the old chaperone. *(Possible responses: bold, playful, disrespectful, charming, dashing)*

J. Reading Skill: DRAWING CONCLUSIONS *The young man is talking with the older chaperone so that she will allow him to speak and dance with her charge, young Sarita.*

K. Literary Element: FIGURATIVE LANGUAGE Elicit that the chaperone is using metaphors, saying she is a sheep and Sarita a lamb. Point out that Sarita later uses the metaphor of a dragon to describe the older woman.

L. Critical Thinking: ANALYZING Ask students to explain why the song has two different names and why the stranger requests that it be played. *(Possible response: Hidalgo people like the song and so give it a "nice" name; the villagers of San Juan Iglesias give the song an unflattering name to express contempt for Hidalgans. The stranger requests the song as a crowning touch to his own boldness.)*

But he did not move toward her at once. Instead, he inched slowly back against the table. No one was behind him, and his hands quickly unfastened the package he had been guarding so long. Then he nonchalantly walked into the front room.

The girl was sitting close to a chaperon. As he came up to her, he swerved slightly toward the bushy-browed old lady.

H "Your servant, señora. I kiss your hands and feet."

The chaperon stared at him in astonishment. Such fine manners were not common to the town of San Juan Iglesias.

"Eh, you're a stranger," she said. "I thought so."

I "But a stranger no longer, señora, now that I have met you." He bent over her, so close she could smell the faint fragrance of talcum on his freshly shaven cheek. "Will you dance the *parada* with me?"

This request startled her eyes into popping open beneath the heavy brows. "So, my young rooster, would you flirt with me, and I old enough to be your grandmother?"

"Can you show me a prettier woman to flirt with in the Valley of the Three Marys?" he asked audaciously.

drawing conclusions

J **Why is the young man talking with the older chaperone?**

She grinned at him and turned toward the girl at her side. "This young fool wants to meet you, my child."

The girl blushed to the roots of her hair and shyly lowered her white lids. The old woman laughed aloud.

"Go out and dance, the two of you. A man clever enough to pat the sheep has a right to play with the lamb."

The next moment they had joined the circle of dancers, and Sarita was trying to control her laughter. K

"She is the worst dragon in San Juan. And how easily you won her!"

"What is a dragon," he asked imperiously, "when I longed to dance with you?"

"Ay," she retorted, "you have a quick tongue. I think you are a dangerous man."

In answer he drew her closer to him and turned her toward the orchestra. As he reached the chief violinist, he called out, "Play 'The *Virgencita*,'[8] 'The Shy Young Maiden.'"

The violinist's mouth opened in soundless surprise. The girl in his arms said sharply, "You heard him, 'The *Borachita*,'[9] 'The Little Drunken Girl.'"

With a relieved grin the violinist tapped his music stand with his bow, and the music swung into the sad farewell of a man to his sweetheart: L

Farewell, my little drunken one,
I must go to the capital
To serve the master
Who makes me weep for my return.

The stranger frowned down at her. "Is this a joke, señorita?" he asked coldly.

"No," she whispered, looking about her quickly to see if the incident had been observed. "But 'The *Virgencita*' is the favorite song of Hidalgo, a village on the other side of the mountains in the next valley. The

8. ***virgencita*** (vēr hen sē′ tä).
9. ***borachita*** (bô rä chē′ tä).

Words to Know and Use

nonchalantly (nän′ shə länt′ lē) *adv.* casually; unemotionally
audaciously (ô dā′ shəs lē) *adv.* boldly

330

Critic's Corner

The reason for *Mexican Village*'s success is undoubtedly Niggli's ability to tell a good story well. But the life she infused into the book because of her understanding of the people, their customs, personalities, dress, and language, make it a book to learn from as well as enjoy. One reviewer called *Mexican Village* a remarkable achievement because one could understand so much about Mexico from a single book. The same could still be said today. While reviewers in 1945 remarked that the book seemed a bit idyllic and romanticized, all agreed that Niggli's skillful storytelling makes the characters and settings seem alive. Mildred Adams of *The New York Times* pointed out a noteworthy aspect of Niggli's work: Many things make this volume memorable in the modern spate of tales about Mexico. Not the least is the fact that it has no axe to grind, it demands no ideological bias on the part of the reader.

Paula Shirley, *Dictionary of Literary Biography*

people of Hidalgo and San Juan Iglesias do not speak."

"That is a stupid thing," said the man from Hidalgo as he swung her around in a large turn. "Is not music free as air? Why should one town own the rights to a song?"

The girl shuddered slightly. "Those people from Hidalgo—they are wicked monsters. Can you guess what they did not six months since?"

The man started to point out that the space of time from February to May was three months, but he thought it better not to appear too wise. "Did these Hidalgo monsters frighten you, señorita? If they did, I personally will kill them all."

She moved closer against him and tilted her face until her mouth was close to his ear. "They attempted to steal the bones of Don Rómolo Balderas."[10]

"Is it possible?" He made his eyes grow round and his lips purse up in disdain. "Surely not that! Why, all the world knows that Don Rómolo Balderas was the greatest historian in the entire republic.[11] Every school child reads his books. Wise men from Quintana Roo to the Rio Bravo[12] bow their heads in admiration to his name. What a wicked thing to do!" He hoped his virtuous tone was not too virtuous for plausibility, but she did not seem to notice.

"It is true! In the night they came. Three devils!"

10. **Don Rómolo Balderas** (dôn rô′ mô lô bäl de′ räs).

11. **the entire republic:** Mexico.

12. **from Quintana Roo to the Rio Bravo:** from the territory on the east Yucatán Peninsula of southeast Mexico to the Rio Grande, the river running along the Texas-Mexico boundary into the Gulf of Mexico.

TEHUANTEPEC DANCE 1935
Diego Rivera Los Angeles County Museum of Art Gift of Mr. and Mrs. Milton W. Lipper from the Milton W. Lipper Estate.

Words to Know and Use

disdain (dis dān′) *n.* contempt
virtuous (vʉr′ choo̅ əs) *adj.* righteous
plausibility (plô′ zə bil′ ə tē) *n.* believability

331

M. Literary Element: CONFLICT Point out that the main conflict, or struggle, in the story results from the way in which the historic animosity between the two villages affects the relationship between the stranger and Sarita. Point out the irony of Sarita's dancing cheek to cheek with someone whom she has just called a monster.

N. LEP: Comprehension Elicit that to "steal the bones" means to dig up a grave and take the remains of a body.

O. LEP: Vocabulary Have a Spanish-speaking volunteer pronounce the names *Don Rómolo Balderas, Quintana Roo,* and *Río Bravo.* Have them translate *Río Bravo (Brave River).* Discuss how the accent mark in *Rómolo* affects the pronunciation.

Art Note

Diego Rivera (1886–1957) was one of Mexico's most famous artists. As a youth, he worked and studied in Paris, where he experimented with simplified forms. In this painting, however, the figures are precisely drawn: the onlookers and the dancers in the background as well as the pair in the foreground. *How do the images of the two main dancers illustrate the characters in "The Street of the Cañon"?*

REAL LIFE CONNECTIONS

Point out that Latin American villages have a much less fragmented lifestyle than do most American communities. Explain that villages in which the same families have lived for generations develop great stability and a strong sense of shared traditions and culture. Develop a discussion of the possible advantages of living a "village" lifestyle. *(Possible benefits include the emotional comfort of belonging to a large group in which one has "roots"; the convenience of having relatives and neighbors to share burdens and responsibilities; freedom from alienation and isolation.)* Also discuss some disadvantages of the "village" lifestyle. *(Possible drawbacks include lack of privacy, limited economic and social mobility, and the necessity of conforming with prevailing provincial attitudes.)*

P. Reading Skill: SUMMARIZING Have students summarize the events that caused such an uproar in the village the previous May. *(Three men from Hidalgo came to the graveyard in San Juan to dig up Don Rómolo's bones. The blacksmith spotted them, called for help, and a fight broke out. The three men escaped, one with a broken arm. Their leader was named Pepe Gonzalez.)*

Q. Reading Skill: DRAWING CONCLUSIONS *The stranger is one of the three men, probably the leader, Pepe Gonzalez.*

R. Critical Thinking: EVALUATING Ask students to determine which village has the better claim to Don Rómolo's bones. *(Possible response: Since Don Rómolo was born in Hidalgo and died in San Juan Iglesias, both villages seem to have an equal claim. Students might suggest that since Don Rómolo moved from Hidalgo to San Juan, he might have preferred to be buried there too.)*

S. Literary Element: THEME Point out that Pepe Gonzalez seems to enjoy setting tests of courage for himself. Elicit how his present escapade, attending Sarita's party, is a test of courage. *(Possible response: If he is recognized, he could be jailed, beaten, or killed.)* Have students suggest why he has set this test of courage for himself. *(Possible response: He seems to have fallen in love with Sarita at first sight and wanted to see her again.)*

"Young devils, I hope."

"Young or old, who cares? They were devils. The blacksmith surprised them even as they were opening the grave. He raised such a shout that all of San Juan rushed to his aid, for they were fighting, I can tell
P you. Especially one of them—their leader."

"And who was he?"

"You have heard of him doubtless. A proper wild one named Pepe Gonzalez."[13]

"And what happened to them?"

"They had horses and got away, but one,
SR-6 ▶ I think, was hurt."

The Hidalgo man twisted his mouth, remembering how Rubén the candymaker had ridden across the whitewashed line high on the cañon trail that marked the division between the Three Marys and the Sabinas sides of the mountains and then had fallen in a faint from his saddle because his left arm was broken. There was no candy in Hidalgo for six weeks, and the entire Sabinas Valley resented that broken arm as fiercely as did Rubén.

drawing conclusions

Q **How does the young man know about the incident Sarita is describing?**

The stranger tightened his arm in reflexed anger about Sarita's waist as she said, "All the world knows that the men of Hidalgo are sons of the mountain witches."

"But even devils are shy of disturbing the honored dead," he said gravely.

R "'Don Rómolo was born in our village,' Hidalgo says. 'His bones belong to us.' Well, anyone in the valley can tell you he died in San Juan Iglesias, and here his bones will stay! Is that not proper? Is that not right?" R

To keep from answering, he guided her through an intricate dance pattern that led them past the patio door. Over her head he could see two men and a woman staring with amazement at the open package on the table.

His eyes on the patio, he asked blandly, "You say the leader was one Pepe Gonzalez? The name seems to have a familiar sound."

"But naturally. He has a talent." She tossed her head and stepped away from him as the music stopped. It was a dance of two *paradas.* He slipped his hand through her arm and guided her into place in the large oval of parading couples. Twice around the room and the orchestra would play again.

"A talent?" he prompted.

"For doing the impossible. When all the world says a thing cannot be done, he does it to prove the world wrong. Why, he climbed to the top of the Prow, and not even the long-vanished Joaquín Castillo had ever climbed that mountain before. And this same Pepe caught a mountain lion with nothing to aid him but a rope and his two bare hands." S

"He doesn't sound such a bad friend," protested the stranger, slipping his arm around her waist as the music began to play the merry song of the soap bubbles:

Pretty bubbles of a thousand colors
That ride on the wind
And break as swiftly
As a lover's heart.

13. **Pepe Gonzalez** (pe′ pä gôn sä′ les).

Words to Know and Use

intricate (in′ tri kit) *adj.* full of complex detail

The events in the patio were claiming his attention. Little by little he edged her closer to the door. The group at the table had considerably enlarged. There was a low murmur of excitement from the crowd.

"What has happened?" asked Sarita, attracted by the noise.

"There seems to be something wrong at the table," he answered, while trying to peer over the heads of the people in front of him. Realizing that this might be the last moment of peace he would have that evening, he bent toward her.

"If I come back on Sunday, will you walk around the plaza with me?"

She was startled into exclaiming, "Ay, no!"

"Please. Just once around."

T "And you think I'd walk more than once with you, señor, even if you were no stranger? In San Juan Iglesias, to walk around the plaza with a girl means a

SR-7 ▶ wedding."

"Ha, and you think that is common to San Juan alone? Even the devils of Hidalgo respect that law." He added hastily at her puzzled upward glance. "And so they do in all the villages." To cover his lapse he said softly, "I don't even know your name."

A mischievous grin crinkled the corners of her eyes. "Nor do I know yours, señor. Strangers do not often walk the streets of San Juan."

Before he could answer, the chattering in the patio swelled to louder proportions. Don Roméo's voice lay on top, like thick cream on milk. "I tell you it is a jewel of a cheese. Such flavor, such texture, such whiteness. It is a jewel of a cheese."

"What has happened?" Sarita asked of a woman at her elbow.

U "A fine goat's cheese appeared as if by magic on the table. No one knows where it came from."

"Probably an extra one from Linares," snorted a fat, bald man on the right.

"Linares never made such a cheese as this," said the woman decisively.

"Silence!" roared Don Roméo. "Old Tío[14] Daniel would speak a word to us."

A great hand of silence closed down over the mouths of the people. The girl was standing on tiptoe trying vainly to see what was happening. She was hardly aware of the stranger's whispering voice, although she remembered the words that he said. "Sunday night—once around the plaza." V

She did not realize that he had moved away, leaving a gap that was quickly filled by the blacksmith.

Old Tío Daniel's voice was a shrill squeak, and his thin, stringy neck jutted forth from his body like a turtle's from its shell. "This is no cheese from Linares," he said with authority, his mouth sucking in over his toothless gums between his sentences. "Years ago, when the great Don Rómolo Balderas was still alive, we had such cheese as this—ay, in those days we had it. But after he died and was buried in our own sainted ground, as was right and proper. . . ."

"Yes, yes," murmured voices in the crowd. He glared at the interruption. As soon as there was silence again, he continued:

"After he died, we had it no more. Shall I tell you why?"

"Tell us, Tío Daniel," said the voices humbly.

"Because it is made in Hidalgo!"

The sound of a waterfall, the sound of a wind in a narrow cañon, and the sound of an angry crowd are much the same. There

14. **tío** (tē′ ō): uncle.

Teaching Tip

After the students finish reading, have them go back and find clues to the stranger's intentions. For example, in the first paragraph on page 333 the stranger edges closer to the door because he realizes he must soon make a quick getaway.

T. Reading Skill: CLARIFYING Ask a student to explain what, in effect, the stranger is asking Sarita. *(He is asking her to become engaged to marry him.)* Point out that the author has foreshadowed this possibility on page 329 when Sarita's father tells the stranger that he hopes his daughter finds a husband soon.

U. Reading Skill: INFERRING Have students infer how the fine cheese got there. *(It was the package that the stranger placed there.)*

V. Reading Skill: PREDICTING Ask students to predict whether Sarita will go once around the plaza with the stranger on the following Sunday. *(Possible responses: No, once the villagers recognize him, they will not allow him to return; no, Sarita may not be willing to become engaged to someone from Hidalgo; yes, Sarita has fallen in love with his charm.)*

Critic's Corner

Mexican Village has been called both a novel and a collection of tales. Although the stories follow separate plot lines, the same characters appear throughout the work, making it seem that the protagonist is actually the whole village, an idea which is also suggested by the title. . . . Each story bears as title a street or section of the town.

The individual tales have warmth, charm, irony, laughter, and sometimes tragedy. The element of trickery . . . is frequently present and surprises abound. In depicting the human comedy of life in the Sabinas Valley . . . the action concerns itself with courtship, marriage, death, family relations, and local entertainment such as cockfighting. Niggli employs Mexican folklore in *Mexican Village* as a means of bringing the people to life. The book is filled with legends, traditions, superstitions, and proverbs of the folk it describes.

Paula Shirley, *Dictionary of Literary Biography*

W. Reading Skill: DRAWING CONCLUSIONS *The young man is none other than wild Pepe Gonzalez.*

X. LEP: Vocabulary Ask a volunteer to pronounce these Spanish names. Students might also locate the Mexican cities on a map.

Y. Reading Skill: INFERRING Ask the students why Sarita would be expected to feel anger. *(Possible response: The stranger Pepe Gonzalez tricked her; he has made her look foolish.)* Have them suggest why she feels apprehensive. *(Possible response: She realizes she cares about Pepe and is concerned for his safety. She worries about what the villagers might do if they catch Pepe.)*

Check Test

1. Where is everyone when the stranger arrives? *(at Sarita's birthday party)*

2. Whom does the stranger come to see? *(Sarita)*

3. What gift does the stranger bring with him? *(the finest goat cheese)*

4. Where do the villagers finally suspect the stranger is from? *(from the village of Hidalgo)*

5. What does the stranger do just before the villagers realize where he is from? *(He disappears.)*

Encouraging Independent Reading

Tevye's Daughters, interconnected short stories by Sholom Aleichem
Kalasanda, interconnected short stories by Barbara Kimenye
Mexican Village, a novel by Josephina Niggli
"Long Walk to Forever," a short story by Kurt Vonnegut, Jr.

were no distinct words, but the sound was enough.

"Are you certain, Tío?" boomed Don Roméo.

"As certain as I am that a donkey has long ears. The people of Hidalgo have been famous for generations for making cheese like this—especially that wicked one, that owner of a cheese factory, Timotéo Gonzalez, father to Pepe, the wild one, whom we have good cause to remember." SR-8 ▶

drawing conclusions

W | Who is the young man?

"We do, we do," came the sigh of assurance.

"But on the whole northern frontier there are no vats like his to produce so fine a product. Ask the people of Chihuahua, of Sonora. Ask the man on the bridge at Laredo, or the man in his boat at Tampico, '*Hola,*[15] friend, who makes the finest goat cheese?' X

"And the answer will always be the same, 'Don Timotéo of Hidalgo.'"

It was the blacksmith who asked the great question. "Then where did that cheese come from, and we haters of Hidalgo these ten long years?"

No voice said, "The stranger," but with one fluid movement every head in the patio turned toward the girl in the doorway. She also turned, her eyes wide with something that she realized to her own amazement was more apprehension than anger. Y

But the stranger was not in the room. When the angry, muttering men pushed through to the street, the stranger was not on the plaza. He was not anywhere in sight. A few of the more religious crossed themselves for fear that the Devil had walked in their midst. "Who was he?" one voice asked another. But Sarita, who was meekly listening to a lecture from Don Roméo on the propriety of dancing with strangers, did not have to ask. She had a strong suspicion that she had danced that night within the circling arm of Pepe Gonzalez. ❧ ◀ SR-9

15. ***hola*** (ō' lä): hello.

INSIGHT

She Loved Him All Her Life

LYNNE ALVAREZ

She loved him all her life
and when she thought he might die
she tied her wrist to his at night
so that his pulse would not flutter
away from her suddenly
and leave her stranded

Words to Know and Use

apprehension (ap' rē hen' shən) *n.* an uneasy feeling; anxiety
propriety (prō prī' ə tē) *n.* the quality of being proper according to accepted standards

334

Insight

This piece reflects on the ideas in the main selection and is suggested for students' independent reading. Optional discussion questions follow.

1. What is the woman in the poem most afraid of? *(She fears being left alone when her husband dies.)*

2. How does the love described in the poem contrast with the love that is suggested in "The Street of the Cañon"? *(The love in the poem is the mature love of a married couple, a love that has lasted a lifetime and is about to be interrupted by death. In the story, the love between Sarita and Pepe Gonzalez, if it is indeed love, is just beginning; it has not yet had a chance to grow.)*

3. Can you imagine Sarita reciting such a poem some day for Pepe? *(Answers will vary. Some students may say that it is likely that Sarita will defy her village, marry Pepe, and live with him until they are old.)*

Responding to Reading

First Impressions

1. What one word captures the personality of Pepe Gonzalez? Explain briefly why you chose this word.

Second Thoughts

2. What is important to the people of San Juan Iglesias?

   Think about
   - how they celebrate special birthdays
   - what the bones of Don Rómolo Balderas mean to them
   - how they view the citizens of Hidalgo
   - how they treat strangers

3. What kind of man does Pepe Gonzalez seem to be?

4. Why do you think Pepe brings the fine goat's cheese to the birthday party?

5. Sarita calls the people from Hidalgo "wicked monsters." Do you think she changes her opinion by the end of the evening? Explain.

6. If you have read "The Death Trap," compare the Great Armando with Pepe Gonzalez.

   Think about
   - how they have built their reputations
   - the reasons they both risk their lives

Literary Concept: Figurative Language

Language that communicates ideas beyond the ordinary meanings of words is called **figurative language.** The words in a figurative expression are not literally true, but rather paint vivid pictures and ideas in the mind of the reader. The most common types of figurative expressions are simile, metaphor, and personification. When Sarita's chaperon allows Sarita to dance with Pepe, the chaperon says, "A man clever enough to pat the sheep has a right to play with the lamb." What does this mean?

Concept Review: Conflict In stories, conflict can exist within a character, between characters, or between a character and an outside force such as nature. What are the conflicts in "The Street of the Canōn"?

Student Response

Responding to Reading

These questions are open-ended with no "right" or "wrong" answers. However, responses must be supported with information from the selection. Possible answers follow:

1. Any thoughtful response is acceptable.

2. Some students may say that a sense of community with shared values and traditions is most important to the people of San Juan Iglesias. Others may suggest that pride in themselves and their village is most important.

3. Some students may say Pepe is a bold hero who values love and honor above the petty squabbles of the villagers. Others may say that Pepe is a fool who takes needless risks. Some may suggest he is a peacemaker, hoping to build bridges between the two villages. Others may say he is a misfit, unable to abide by the customs and traditions of his village.

4. Some may say he brings the cheese as an offering from the people of Hidalgo to show they are not all bad. Others may suggest he brings it to honor the occasion of Sarita's birthday. Some might say he simply wanted to annoy the people of San Juan, to let them know an enemy from Hidalgo slipped into their party undetected.

5. Some students may say that Sarita has changed her opinion about the people of Hidalgo since she has obviously found the stranger from Hidalgo to be very attractive. Other students might say that Pepe's secretive and somewhat disrespectful behavior will corroborate Sarita's opinion that the people of Hidalgo are wicked monsters.

6. Some students may say that both Pepe Gonzalez and the Great Armando feel truly alive only when they are taking a risk. Others may focus on how impetuous Pepe is in comparison with the Great Armando's calculating way of approaching risk: Pepe just came to San Juan Iglesias without knowing what would happen, while the Great Armando never took a risk without knowing exactly what he was getting himself into.

Literary Concept—Figurative Language

Possible response: *The chaperone is using metaphors, comparing herself to a sheep and young Sarita to a lamb. One might pat a sheep in order to gain its confidence and so be able to play with its lamb. Pepe has just been complimenting the chaperone, asking her to dance and telling her she is the prettiest woman in the valley, in order to make her like him and so feel comfortable about his dancing with Sarita.* Refer to annotations D, H, and K.

Concept Review: Conflict Possible response: The main conflict is the animosity between the villagers of Hidalgo and those of San Juan Iglesias and their argument over the bones of Don Rómolo. As a result of this struggle, Pepe feels internal struggle as he wonders whether to carry out his plan to see Sarita. Similarly, Sarita will feel internal conflict over whether to meet Pepe again.

Writing Options

The Writing Options are designed to meet varied student interests and abilities. Have each student choose one writing activity to complete. You may wish to guide some students to an option that requires less writing.

Journal Update Have students review their journal entries for this selection. Ask them what insights they have gained from this story—for example, from the hatred between the two towns and from Pepe's bold behavior.

Vocabulary Practice

1. audaciously
2. pungent
3. virtuous
4. disdain
5. plausibility
6. intricate
7. prominent
8. nonchalantly
9. propriety
10. apprehension

Closure

Pepe Gonzalez, the main character of "The Street of the Cañon," puts his courage to the test by secretly venturing into a village that is hostile to him in order to see the beautiful Sarita once again. In the end, Sarita also faces a test of courage as she must decide whether to see Pepe again against the wishes of her village. Ask students if they have ever tested their own courage in a similar fashion, by taking an action that opposed popular or majority opinion.

Writing Options

1. What do you think will happen next to the two lovers? Write the next episode.
2. What if the people at the party had discovered Pepe's true identity, and Sarita's chaperon had stood up for him? Write her short speech in defense of Pepe.
3. If you could eavesdrop on the conversation between Sarita and Don Roméo at the end of the story, what would you hear? Write their conversation.
4. Imagine that you are an outside arbitrator brought in to settle the "Bone Dispute" between Hidalgo and San Juan Iglesias. You have listened to both sides and developed a compromise for the two towns. Write the compromise solution that you will deliver to both town councils.
5. Look at the *Insight* poem "She Loved Him All Her Life." What image or emotion does the word *stranded* bring to mind? Could this word describe what Pepe might do to Sarita? Why or why not?

Vocabulary Practice

Exercise On your paper, write the vocabulary word that is opposite in meaning to each word in the list below.

1. timidly: ____
2. bland: ____
3. sinful: ____
4. respect: ____
5. improbability: ____
6. simple: ____
7. inconspicuous: ____
8. anxiously: ____
9. misbehavior: ____
10. unconcern: ____

Words to Know and Use

apprehension
audaciously
disdain
intricate
nonchalantly
plausibility
prominent
propriety
pungent
virtuous

e x p l o r e

Autobiography

from My Left Foot

CHRISTY BROWN

Examine What You Know (Prior Knowledge)

One of the characters in the story you are about to read demonstrates an incredible faith, despite all evidence to the contrary. What does it mean to have faith and how would you define it? Discuss this subject with your classmates and come up with three or four brief definitions of the word *faith.* As you read the selection, see if any of your definitions come close to describing the kind of faith portrayed.

Expand Your Knowledge (Building Background)

Christy Brown, the author of the selection you are about to read, suffered from cerebral palsy, a medical condition caused by disease or injury to a baby's brain before or during birth or in early infancy. Cerebral palsy's major symptom is a lack of muscle control. In some cases the condition is mild and barely noticeable, but in others there may be constant jerking motions, an inability to walk or use the hands and arms, and great difficulty in speaking. Cerebral palsy may also damage sight, hearing, and intelligence, though many people with the condition have average or above-average intelligence. No cure exists for cerebral palsy, but physical therapists can teach patients to move with greater ease.

Christy Brown

Write Before You Read (Journal Writing)

In your journal, describe one or more actual examples of someone overcoming a handicap to accomplish something seemingly impossible. These could be experiences you have witnessed firsthand or experiences you have heard or read about. Study what you have written down and then make a list of the qualities it takes to overcome a handicap.

■ *A biography of the author can be found in the Reader's Handbook.*

Objectives

- To read and analyze an excerpt from an autobiography
- To recognize how descriptive details help a reader form vivid pictures of a scene
- To express understanding of the work through a choice of writing options, including a speech, an explanation, a poem, and a metaphor

Prereading/Motivation

Examine What You Know

Discussion Prompts: Is faith always, sometimes, or never opposed to common sense? Why do people need faith? Why don't they just believe in what they can see, know, and prove with logic?

Expand Your Knowledge

Discussion Prompts: Have you ever known anyone with cerebral palsy? How might the hopes and dreams of a person with cerebral palsy be different from those of a normal person? How might they be the same? What emotional hardships might people with cerebral palsy suffer? How can those hardships be softened or avoided?

Additional Background Cerebral palsy names a group of disorders caused by damage to motor areas of the brain during birth or early life. If the German measles infection is contracted by a mother during pregnancy, it can cause damage to the brain of the fetus that results in cerebral palsy.

Thematic Link—Tests of Courage
In this excerpt, a mother and son test their courage as they learn to cope with the boy's debilitating handicap.

Additional Journal Writing

With faith and courage, the main characters of *My Left Foot* work to overcome a handicap. Suggest this additional journal topic for students:

- Imagine that you are unable to walk, speak, or use your hands. Explain the system you might devise to communicate with others.

For other journal opportunities, refer students to Examine What You Know (p. 337), Broader Connections (p. 343), and Real Life Connections (p. T–341).

Additional Resources

UNIT THREE RESOURCE BOOK
Reader's Guidesheet, p. 6
Vocabulary Worksheet, p. 7
Selection and Vocabulary Check Tests, p. 8
Selection Test, pp. 9–10

Collaborative Learning

Opportunities for collaborative learning appear throughout the lesson and include Examine What You Know (p. 337).

Teaching Strategies

Vocabulary Preview

These vocabulary words are defined at the bottom of the selection page on which they appear. You may wish to discuss them briefly before students begin reading.

bondage a limiting of movement
conviction a strong belief
impertinence a lack of respect
momentous very important
volition will or choice

Support for Students of Limited English Proficiency

- Use Reader's Guidesheet, p. 6.
- *My Left Foot* contains some figurative language and Irish terms and idioms that may be difficult for students with limited English ability. Encourage students to use context clues to determine the meaning of unfamiliar terms.
- Annotations A, E, I, and R focus on troublesome terms and concepts.

Text Annotations

A. LEP: Vocabulary Ask students to infer the meaning of "a whole army of relations queued up" from the story's context. Bring out that Brown is using the word *army* metaphorically to mean "a great many."

B. Literary Element: AUTOBIOGRAPHY Have students list clues that identify the selection as autobiography. *(Possible responses: The author writes from the first-person point of view in a factual tone, organizes the account chronologically from birth, and mentions family members.)*

from My Left Foot

CHRISTY BROWN

I was born in the Rotunda Hospital on June 5th, 1932. There were nine children before me and twelve after me, so I myself belong to the middle group. Out of this total of twenty-two, seventeen lived, but four died in infancy, leaving thirteen still to hold the family fort.

Mine was a difficult birth, I am told. Both
A mother and son almost died. A whole army of relations queued up outside the hospital until the small hours of the morning, waiting for news and praying furiously that it would be good.

After my birth, Mother was sent to recuperate for some weeks, and I was kept in the hospital while she was away. I remained there for some time, without name, for I wasn't baptized until my mother was well enough to bring me to church.

B It was Mother who first saw that there was something wrong with me. I was about four months old at the time. She noticed that my head had a habit of falling backward whenever she tried to feed me. She attempted to correct this by placing her hand on the back of my neck to keep it steady. But when she took it away, back it would drop again. That was the first warning sign. Then she became aware of other defects as I got older. She saw that my hands were clenched nearly all of the time and were inclined to twine behind my back, my mouth couldn't grasp the teat of the bottle because even at that early age my jaws would either lock together tightly, so that it was impossible for her to open them, or they would suddenly become limp and fall loose, dragging my whole mouth to one side. At six months I could not sit up without having a mountain of pillows around me. At twelve months it was the same. SR-1

Very worried by this, Mother told my father her fears, and they decided to seek medical advice without any further delay. I was a little over a year old when they began to take me to hospitals and clinics, convinced that there was something definitely wrong with me, something which they could not understand or name, but which was very real and disturbing.

Almost every doctor who saw and examined me labeled me a very interesting but also a hopeless case. Many told Mother very gently that I was mentally defective and would remain so. That was a hard blow to a young mother who had already reared five healthy children. The doctors were so very sure of themselves that Mother's faith in me seemed almost an impertinence. They assured her that nothing could be done for me. SR-2

Words to Know and Use	**impertinence** (im purt' 'n əns) *n.* the quality of not showing proper respect

338

Structured Reading for Less Proficient Students

These questions can help to guide students through the reading. Ask each question at the point of the selection where the SR number appears in the margin.

SR–1. What were the first warning signs that young Christy was not normal? *(His head kept dropping; his hands were clenched much of the time; his jaws would lock; he could not sit up at six months)* **Literal recall**

SR–2. What did the doctors say about Christy's condition? *(They said he was a hopeless case and mentally defective; they said nothing could be done for Christy.)* **Summarizing**

SR–3. What evidence did Mrs. Brown have for believing her son's mind was not impaired by his handicap? *(She had no evidence; she simply knew.)* **Clarifying**

SR–4. Why did Christy's mother decide to treat him like her other children? *(She believed that would be best for Christy's development.)* **Clarifying**

Continued on page 339

She refused to accept this truth, the inevitable truth—as it then seemed—that I was beyond cure, beyond saving, even beyond hope. She could not and would not believe that I was an imbecile, as the doctors told her. She had nothing in the world to go by, not a scrap of evidence to support her conviction that, though my body was crippled, my mind was not. In spite of all the doctors and specialists told her, she would not C agree. I don't believe she knew why—she just knew, without feeling the smallest SR-3 ▶ shade of doubt.

Finding that the doctors could not help in any way beyond telling her not to place her trust in me, or, in other words, to forget I was a human creature, rather to regard me as just something to be fed and washed and then put away again, Mother decided there and then to take matters into her own hands. I was *her* child, and therefore part of the family. No matter how dull and incapable I might grow up to be, she was determined to treat me on the same plane as the others, and not as the "queer one" in the back room who was never spoken of when SR-4 ▶ there were visitors present.

That was a momentous decision as far as my future life was concerned. It meant that I would always have my mother on my side to help me fight all the battles that were to come, and to inspire me with new strength when I was almost beaten. But it wasn't easy for her because now the relatives and friends had decided otherwise. They contended that I should be taken kindly, sympathetically, but not seriously. That would be a mistake. "For your own sake," they told her, "don't look to this boy as you would to the others; it would only break your heart in the end." Luckily for me, Mother and Father held out against the lot of them. But Mother wasn't content just to say that I was not an idiot: she set out to prove it, not because of any rigid sense of duty, but out of love. That is why she was so successful. D

At this time she had the five other children to look after besides the "difficult one," though as yet it was not by any means a full house. They were my brothers, Jim, Tony, and Paddy, and my two sisters, Lily and Mona, all of them very young, just a year or so between each of them, so that they were almost exactly like steps of stairs.

Four years rolled by, and I was now five, and still as helpless as a newly born baby. While my father was out at bricklaying, earning our bread and butter for us, Mother was slowly, patiently pulling down the wall, brick by brick, that seemed to thrust itself between me and the other children, slowly, patiently penetrating beyond the thick curtain that hung over my mind, separating it from theirs. It was hard, heart-breaking work, for often all she got from me in return was a vague smile and perhaps a faint gurgle. I could not speak or even mumble, nor could I sit up without support on my own, let alone take steps. But I wasn't inert or motionless. I seemed, indeed, to be convulsed with movement, wild, stiff, snakelike movement that never left me, except in sleep. My fingers twisted and twitched continually, my arms twined backwards and would often shoot out suddenly this way and that, and my head lolled and sagged sideways. I was a queer, crooked little fellow. ◀ SR-5

Mother tells me how one day she had been sitting with me for hours in an upstairs room, showing me pictures out of a great

Words to Know and Use

conviction (kən vik′ shən) *n.* strong belief or opinion
momentous (mō men′ təs) *adj.* very important

C. Literary Element: THEME Ask students to discuss how Christy's mother's decision would be a test of her courage. *(Possible response: It took great courage for Mrs. Brown to maintain her convictions about Christy's mind against the advice of the doctors.)*

D. Literary Element: CHARACTERIZATION Have students list character traits of Christy's mother. *(Possible responses: loving, faithful, patient, determined, persevering, hard-working, long-suffering)*

E. LEP: Figurative Learning Elicit that *earning our bread and butter* is an idiom meaning "earning money to meet our basic needs." Point out that Brown uses the images of a brick wall and a curtain as metaphors to describe the way in which his disability has cut him off from his family and normal life.

F. Literary Element: DESCRIPTIVE DETAILS Have students list the details in this passage that help them picture Christy. *(Possible responses: wild, stiff, snakelike movements; twisted fingers; arms shooting out or twined backward; head that lolled and sagged sideways)*

Structured Reading for Less Proficient Students

Continued from page 338

SR–5. How did Christy change over his first five years? *(He changed very little; at age five, he was still as helpless as a baby; he could not speak, walk, or even sit up.)* **Literal recall**

SR–6. Why did Christy's mother leave the room crying after reading to him? *(She was discouraged that he could make no sign to her that he understood her; perhaps she was beginning to doubt that he was intelligent.)* **Clarifying**

SR–7. Why did the family seem so tense once Christy took the chalk in his foot? *(The family wanted to believe that Christy was attempting to communicate but feared he may not have been.)* **Clarifying**

SR–8. Why was Christy's writing the letter *A* important to his family? *(It proved that he was intelligent and able to communicate; it justified their faith in him.)* **Clarifying**

SR–9. Why was writing the *A* important to Christy? *(He finally could express himself.)* **Literal recall**

G. Reading Skills: CLARIFYING Have a volunteer explain why Mrs. Brown is so eager for Chris to give her a sign that he liked the book. *(Possible response: She desparately needed reassurance that his mind was normal and that he could think and feel normally.)*

H. Critical Thinking: ANALYZING Ask students why they think Brown's relatives want young Christy to be put into an institution. *(Possible response: They thought Christy was putting too great a strain on Mrs. Brown and the other family members.)*

I. LEP: Euphemism Explain that *natural habits* is a euphemism, a mild expression used in place of one that is considered too direct. Point out that Brown is telling us that he had control over his bladder and bowels but needed his father's help to use the toilet.

Literary Sidelight Christy Brown's autobiographical *My Left Foot* made quite a splash when it was first published in 1954. The author typed the entire manuscript with his toes, a unique accomplishment. More important, Brown's mordant style, deft sense of humor, and amazing perspective on worldly matters were hailed as revolutionary. The book inspired many other handicapped individuals to express themselves more fully and demand equal opportunities.

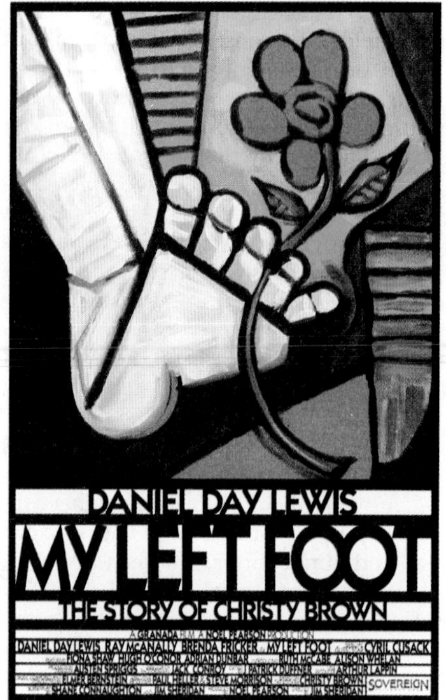

Movie poster for *My Left Foot* Everett Collection, Miramax, New York.

big storybook that I had got from Santa Claus last Christmas and telling me the names of different animals and flowers that were in them, trying without success to get me to repeat them. This had gone on for hours while she talked and laughed with me. Then at the end of it she leaned over me and said gently into my ear:

G "Did you like it, Chris? Did you like the bears and the monkeys and all the lovely flowers? Nod your head for yes, like a good boy."

But I could make no sign that I had understood her. Her face was bent over mine hopefully. Suddenly, involuntarily, my queer hand reached up and grasped one of the dark curls that fell in a thick cluster about her neck. Gently she loosened the clenched fingers, though some dark strands were still clutched between them.

Then she turned away from my curious stare and left the room, crying. The door closed behind her. It all seemed hopeless. It looked as though there was some justification for my relatives' contention that I was an idiot and beyond help. ◀SR-6

They now spoke of an institution. H

"Never!" said my mother almost fiercely, when this was suggested to her. "I know my boy is not an idiot. It is his body that is shattered, not his mind. I'm sure of that."

Sure? Yet inwardly, she prayed God would give her some proof of her faith. She knew it was one thing to believe but quite another thing to prove.

I was now five, and still I showed no real sign of intelligence. I showed no apparent interest in things except with my toes—more especially those of my left foot. Although my natural habits were clean, I could not aid myself, but in this respect my father took care of me. I used to lie on my back all the time in the kitchen or, on bright warm days, out in the garden, a little bundle of crooked muscles and twisted nerves, surrounded by a family that loved me and hoped for me and that made me part of their own warmth and humanity. I was lonely, imprisoned in a world of my own, unable to communicate with others, cut off, separated from them as though a glass wall stood between my existence and theirs, thrusting me beyond the sphere of their lives and activities. I longed to run about and play with the rest, but I was unable to break loose from my bondage. I

Words to Know and Use

bondage (bän′ dij) *n.* a way of limiting one's freedom to move around

CRITIC'S CORNER

After completing *My Left Foot* [in 1954], Brown did not have anything published until 1970, when *Down All the Days* appeared. The work, which was published in fifteen countries, received wide critical attention, much of it favorable. . . .

An impressionistic work, *Down All the Days* is essentially plotless, though many of the events are clearly recreations of the anecdotes included in *My Left Foot.* Brown later dismissed the early work as "the kind of book they expected a cripple to write—too sentimental and corny." The narrator of *My Left Foot* is essentially an adolescent—all hope and naiveté, still somewhat astounded by the relative success of his painful struggle. In *Down All the Days,* an older, somewhat embittered Brown seems intent on exploring the pain involved in that struggle and in the more general struggle of lower-class Dublin life.

CATHLEEN DONNELLY, UNIVERSITY OF DELAWARE

K Then, suddenly, it happened! In a moment everything was changed, my future life molded into a definite shape, my mother's faith in me rewarded and her secret fear changed into open triumph.

It happened so quickly, so simply after all the years of waiting and uncertainty, that I can see and feel the whole scene as if it had happened last week. It was the afternoon of a cold, gray December day. The streets outside glistened with snow, the white sparkling flakes stuck and melted on the windowpanes and hung on the boughs of the trees like molten silver. The wind howled dismally, whipping up little whirling columns of snow that rose and fell at every fresh gust. And over all, the dull, murky sky stretched like a dark canopy, a vast infinity of grayness. L

Inside, all the family were gathered round the big kitchen fire that lit up the little room with a warm glow and made giant shadows dance on the walls and ceiling.

In a corner Mona and Paddy were sitting, huddled together, a few torn school primers[1] before them. They were writing down little sums onto an old chipped slate, using a bright piece of yellow chalk. I was close to them, propped up by a few pillows against the wall, watching.

M It was the chalk that attracted me so much. It was a long, slender stick of vivid yellow. I had never seen anything like it before, and it showed up so well against the black surface of the slate that I was fascinated by it as much as if it had been a stick of gold.

N Suddenly, I wanted desperately to do what my sister was doing. Then—without thinking or knowing exactly what I was doing, I reached out and took the stick of chalk out of my sister's hand—with my left foot.

I do not know why I used my left foot to do this. It is a puzzle to many people as well as to myself, for, although I had displayed a curious interest in my toes at an early age, I had never attempted before this to use either of my feet in any way. They could have been as useless to me as were my hands. That day, however, my left foot, apparently by its own volition, reached out and very impolitely took the chalk out of my sister's hand. N

I held it tightly between my toes, and, acting on an impulse, made a wild sort of scribble with it on the slate. Next moment I stopped, a bit dazed, surprised, looking down at the stick of yellow chalk stuck between my toes, not knowing what to do with it next, hardly knowing how it got there. Then I looked up and became aware that everyone had stopped talking and was staring at me silently. Nobody stirred. O Mona, her black curls framing her chubby little face, stared at me with great big eyes and open mouth. Across the open hearth, his face lit by flames, sat my father, leaning forward, hands outspread on his knees, his shoulders tense. I felt the sweat break out on my forehead.

My mother came in from the pantry with a steaming pot in her hand. She stopped midway between the table and the fire, feeling the tension flowing through the room. P She followed their stare and saw me in the corner. Her eyes looked from my face down

1. **primers** (prim′ ərz): simple books for teaching reading to those who are just beginning to learn to read.

Words to Know and Use

volition (vō lish′ ən) *n.* will or choice

341

J. Literary Element: FIGURATIVE LANGUAGE Point out that Brown earlier used the images of a brick wall and a thick curtain to describe how his handicap cut him off from others. Now he describes it as a glass wall. Suggest that the barrier between Christy and the others is becoming less impregnable.

K. Reading Skill: PREDICTING Ask students to predict what will happen. Ask how they think Christy's life will be changed and his mother's faith rewarded.

L. Literary Element: SETTING Point out that descriptive details of the setting outside—the wind howling dismally, the whirling snow, the dull, dark canopy of sky—evoke Christy's state of mind as he is cut off from his family behind a glass wall. Suggest that the details of the inside setting—the family gathered round the warm glow of the fire—evoke the contentment he would feel if he could break through the wall.

M. Literary Element: DESCRIPTIVE DETAILS Point out that sensory details, such as the vivid yellow color of the chalk and the chipped black surface of the slate, help us to envision this all-important scene.

N. Discussion Ask students to suggest some reasons why Christy is probably better off at home than in an institution.

O. Reading Skill: CAUSE AND EFFECT Ask students to explain why everyone stops talking to stare at Christy. *(Possible responses: Christy has never attempted to write or communicate before; everyone is surprised and anxious to see what he will do.)*

REAL LIFE CONNECTIONS

Explain that during the first half of this century large families were more common than they are today. Point out that Christy Brown was one of thirteen surviving children. If any students in the class come from large families, have them describe their experiences. Then have students contrast large families with small families, listing the benefits and drawbacks of each. Ask students to list reasons that explain why fewer couples have chosen to raise large families in recent years.

Point out that Christy Brown persevered in his desire to write. Typing entirely with his left foot, he wrote books that became world famous.

Ask students how important they think perseverance, or staying power, is to success in the world. For example, do they think talent or perseverance is more important?

Urge students to recall instances in which they persevered, overcoming obstacles and discouragement, to reach a desired goal.

P. Literary Element: SUSPENSE Point out that the suspense mounts as we, like Mrs. Brown and her family, become caught in the tension of the moment and wonder what Christy is about to do.

Q. Literary Element: THEME Ask volunteers to suggest how Christy is now facing a test of courage. *(Possible response: He must be brave enough to try something new and difficult at the risk of disappointing himself and his family.)*

R. LEP: Figurative Language Have volunteers paraphrase these colorful phrases into everyday language: "the room was full of flame and shadow"; "lulled my taut nerves into a sort of waking sleep"; "the hiss and crackle of the logs on the open hearth."

S. Critical Thinking: ANALYZING Ask students to compare Christy's feelings at this moment with his mother's feelings. *(Possible response: Christy feels a sense of accomplishment and exhilaration; his mother feels as if her faith has been rewarded; she feels relief and gratitude.)*

T. Literary Element: SYMBOL Elicit that the letter *A*, the beginning of the alphabet, symbolizes a new beginning for Christy's life.

Check Test

1. Who almost died when Christy was born? *(mother and son)*

2. What did the doctors say about Christy's mind? *(They said he was mentally defective.)*

3. Who never doubted that Christy had a good mind? *(his mother)*

4. What was the first thing Christy ever wrote and how did he write it? *(Holding a piece of chalk in his left foot, he wrote the letter A.)*

Encouraging Independent Reading

Of Snails and Skylarks, poetry by Christy Brown
I Never Promised You a Rose Garden, a novel by Hannah Green
Little, Little, a novel by M. E. Kerr
Karen, a biography by Marie Killelea
Under the Eyes of the Clock, an autobiography by Christopher Nolan

to my foot, with the chalk gripped between
SR-7 ▶ my toes. She put down the pot.

Then she crossed over to me and knelt down beside me, as she had done so many times before.

"I'll show you what to do with it, Chris," she said, very slowly and in a queer, choked way, her face flushed as if with some inner excitement.

Taking another piece of chalk from Mona, she hesitated, then very deliberately drew, on the floor in front of me, *the single letter "A."*

"Copy that," she said, looking steadily at me. "Copy it, Christy."

I couldn't.

Q I looked about me, looked around at the faces that were turned toward me, tense, excited faces that were at that moment frozen, immobile, eager, waiting for a miracle in their midst.

R The stillness was profound. The room was full of flame and shadow that danced before my eyes and lulled my taut[2] nerves into a sort of waking sleep. I could hear the sound of the water tap dripping in the pantry, the loud ticking of the clock on the mantelshelf, and the soft hiss and crackle of the logs on the open hearth.

I tried again. I put out my foot and made a wild jerking stab with the chalk which produced a very crooked line and nothing more. Mother held the slate steady for me.

"Try again, Chris," she whispered in my ear. "Again."

I did. I stiffened my body and put my left foot out again, for the third time. I drew one side of the letter. I drew half the other side. Then the stick of chalk broke and I was left with a stump. I wanted to fling it away and give up. Then I felt my mother's hand on my shoulder. I tried once more. Out went my foot. I shook, I sweated and strained every muscle. My hands were so tightly clenched that my fingernails bit into the flesh. I set my teeth so hard that I nearly pierced my lower lip. Everything in the room swam till the faces around me were mere patches of white. But—I drew it—*the letter "A."* There it was on the floor before me. Shaky, with awkward, wobbly sides and a very uneven center line. But it *was* the letter "A." I looked up. I saw my mother's S face for a moment, tears on her cheeks. Then my father stooped and hoisted me on to his shoulder. ◀ SR-8

I had done it! It had started—the thing that was to give my mind its chance of expressing itself. True, I couldn't speak with my lips. But now I would speak through something more lasting than spoken words —written words.

That one letter, scrawled on the floor with a broken bit of yellow chalk gripped between my toes, was my road to a new world, my key to mental freedom. It was to T provide a source of relaxation to the tense, taut thing that was I, which panted for expression behind a twisted mouth. ❧ ◀ SR-9

2. **taut:** tense.

Responding to Reading

First Impressions

1. Jot down several words that express your feelings as Christy slowly draws the letter "A."

Second Thoughts

2. What do you think of Christy Brown's mother? Support your opinions with facts from the story.

   Think about
   - her faith in the soundness of her son's mind
   - things she does for him
   - her frustrations and successes

3. Why is writing the letter "A" such a momentous event in Christy Brown's life?

4. What do you think Christy Brown's purpose was in writing this account of his life?

Broader Connections

5. In recent years the U.S. government has enacted legislation to expand the physical world of the physically handicapped. This legislation mandates braille pads on elevators and access to restrooms for wheelchair-bound, among other requirements. How do you feel about legislation that forces businesses and other institutions to make physical accommodations for the handicapped despite the high cost this involves?

Literary Concept: Descriptive Details

Descriptive details help readers picture important scenes. To highlight the scene in which he draws the letter "A," Brown uses a great many descriptive details, such as "My hands were so tightly clenched that my fingernails bit into the flesh. I set my teeth so hard I nearly pierced my lower lip." What other descriptive details help make this central moment stand out?

Concept Review: Autobiography How might this story be different if it were a biography written by an objective observer instead of an autobiography? Explain.

Student Response

Responding to Reading

These questions are open-ended with no "right" or "wrong" answers. However, responses must be supported with information from the selection. Possible answers follow:

1. Any sincere reflection on the story is acceptable.

2. Some students may say that Mrs. Brown was a model of courage, faith, and patience. Some may suggest that she was an ideal mother, doing her utmost for her child. Others may say that she was especially intuitive and insightful to see the intelligence in Christy's eyes that no one else perceived.

3. Some students may point out that Christy's writing *A* establishes that Christy was intelligent and not an "idiot." Others may point out that the *A* was his first communication with the outside world. Some may suggest it was the symbolic beginning of Christy's development as a writer.

4. Some students may say that Christy Brown wanted to share his interesting experiences with others. Some may suggest he hopes to encourage others similarly to overcome their handicaps.

5. Many students will say that the special legislation is necessary if handicapped people are to have the same access to opportunities as nonhandicapped. Some students may point out that although such items as ramps and elevators are expensive, they allow the handicapped to work and become more productive citizens in general.

Literary Concept—Descriptive Details

Possible responses: *Brown uses details to establish the setting—a windy, wintry day outside, a "warm glow" from the kitchen fire inside. Details such as the torn primers, the chipped slate, and the bright yellow chalk help readers envision the children doing their homework. By comparing the chalk to a stick of gold, Brown helps us feel the great attraction he had for it. Later, Brown uses details to accentuate the tension of the moment—his mother's wide-open eyes, his father leaning forward with tense shoulders, the sweat breaking out on his own forehead. Sound details, such as the tick of the clock and the dripping water tap, suggest the eerie stillness that has descended on the family during this great event.* Refer to annotations F, L, and M.

Concept Review: Autobiography Were the excerpt a biography, it would probably be written from the third-person point of view. A biography would not include as many of Christy Brown's feelings and sense impressions.

Writing Options

The Writing Options are designed to meet varied student interests and abilities. Have each student choose one writing activity to complete. You may wish to guide some students to an option that requires less writing.

Journal Update Have students review their journal entries for this selection. Ask them about the insights they gained from the ending of *My Left Foot*. For example, they might discuss whether a person's "outside" is always a good indicator of what is going on "inside."

Vocabulary Practice

1. c
2. b
3. a
4. a
5. a

Closure

Both main characters in this selection face tests of courage. Mrs. Brown courageously stands by her conviction that her son's mind is normal, despite the contrary opinions of doctors and relatives. At the end of the excerpt, Christy bravely tests his own ability to communicate, breaking through the wall that has isolated him for so long. Ask students to name people in the news who have recently undergone tests of courage.

Writing Options

1. Write a speech to nominate Christy's mother for "Mother of the Year."
2. You know the first letter Christy wrote. If you were Christy, what would your first sentence be? Write the sentence; then explain why this would be your first message.
3. Write a poem about Christy Brown to illustrate the personal qualities that helped him overcome his handicap.
4. Christy uses many metaphors and other figures of speech to describe his feelings of loneliness and isolation. For example, he sees his mother as "pulling down the wall, brick by brick, that seemed to thrust itself between me and the other children." Create your own metaphor to describe another feeling Christy Brown has in this selection.

Vocabulary Practice

Exercise On your paper, write the letter of the word or phrase that best completes the sentence.

1. The student's **impertinence** made the teacher feel (a) proud (b) calm (c) angry (d) honored.
2. A **momentous** event in your life is one you are likely to (a) forget (b) remember (c) ignore (d) miss.
3. A person with strong **convictions** about a topic is likely to be (a) opinionated (b) undecided (c) uninterested (d) hesitant.
4. When Christy Brown describes his illness as a form of **bondage,** he means that the illness limits his (a) freedom (b) size (c) intelligence (d) beliefs.
5. When you do something under your own **volition,** you do it because you (a) want to (b) have to (c) are forced to (d) should have done it earlier.

Words to Know and Use

bondage
conviction
impertinence
momentous
volition

e x p l o r e

Fiction

Test

THEODORE L. THOMAS

Examine What You Know (Prior Knowledge)

What words and phrases do you associate with the word *test*, which is also the title of this selection? Complete a word web similar to the one below. Include your feelings, as well as facts, about tests. Then, as you read the selection, think about why the author chose this title.

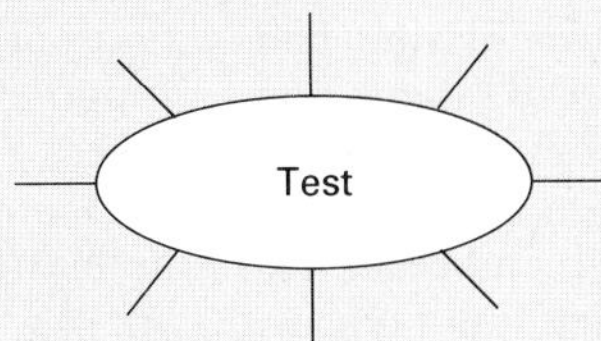

Expand Your Knowledge (Building Background)

How good a driver do you think you are or will be? The selection you are about to read raises the issue of teenage driving safety. On average, there are about 19 million motor vehicle accidents in the United States each year. About 50,000 Americans are killed in these accidents. The highest percentage of those killed are young people between the ages of fourteen and twenty-four. For example, in 1988, 14,800 people in this age group died on U.S. roads.

Write Before You Read (Journal Writing)

Describe the most important test you have ever taken. Perhaps it was a test in school or at a place of employment. Maybe it was a tryout for an athletic team or a school play. Explain how you prepared for the test and what your feelings were before, during, and after the experience? What was the outcome and how has it influenced your life?

■ *A biography of the author can be found in the Reader's Handbook.*

Objectives

- To read and understand a short story
- To express understanding of the work through a choice of writing options, including a business letter and a personal narrative

Prereading/Motivation

Examine What You Know

Discussion Prompts: What images first came to mind when you saw the word *test?* Looking at your word web, how would you summarize your feelings about the word *test?* By using only your word web, how would you define the word *test?*

Expand Your Knowledge

Discussion Prompts: Why do you think such a high number of young people are killed on our highways? What do you think are some major causes of motor vehicle accidents? Would making it harder for young people to get a driver's license be an effective means of making roads safer? Why or why not?

Thematic Link—Tests of Courage

In "Test," the main character faces an ordeal that tests his skill, character, and courage.

Additional Journal Writing

The main character must pass a test that requires no study or skill, but may predict his chances for survival. Use these ideas for journal writing:

- Does getting high scores on written tests assure you of success in life? Why or why not?
- Some say life is a test. How might that be so?

For other journal opportunities, refer students to Examine What You Know (above), Broader Connections (page 350) and Real Life Connections (page T–348).

Additional Resources

UNIT THREE RESOURCE BOOK

Reader's Guidesheet, p. 11
Vocabulary Worksheet, p. 12
Selection Check Tests, p. 13
Selection Test, pp. 14–15

Collaborative Learning

Opportunities for collaborative learning appear throughout the lesson and include Annotation C, Teaching Tip (page T–347), and Real Life Connections (page T–348).

Teaching Strategies

Support for Students of Limited English Proficiency

- Use **Reader's Guidesheet,** p. 11.
- "Test" contains several vivid "picture" verbs, such as *slewed, careen,* and *loomed,* which may be unfamiliar to students. Have students use context clues and recall their own experience as drivers or passengers to understand these words.
- Use **Annotations C, D,** and **E** to help students with language.

Text Annotations

A. Literary Element: EXPOSITION Have students find details that develop the idea that "it was a good day for driving." *(Details include: It is a lightly traveled road; Robert is relaxed and not tired; the sun is bright but not glaring; the air is fresh and clean.)*

B. Literary Element: CHARACTER Ask students why they might feel at ease in a car with Robert driving. *(Possible reasons: he feels relaxed and confident, pays attention to other vehicles, knows and takes pride in his own car, and isn't in a hurry.)*

C. Reading Skill: VISUALIZING Explain that the meaning of *slewed* is *turned and skidded.* Have volunteers at the chalkboard draw a quick diagram, showing an aerial view of the road and indicating the placement and movement of each vehicle as Robert tries to pass.

Test

THEODORE L. THOMAS

A Robert Proctor was a good driver for so young a man. The turnpike curved gently ahead of him, lightly traveled on this cool morning in May. He felt relaxed and alert. Two hours of driving had not yet produced the twinges of fatigue that appeared first in the muscles in the base of the neck. The sun was bright but not glaring, and the air smelled fresh and clean. He breathed it in deeply and blew it out noisily. It was a good day for driving.

He glanced quickly at the slim, gray-haired woman sitting in the front seat with him. Her mouth was curved in a quiet smile. She watched the trees and the fields slip by on her side of the pike. Robert Proctor immediately looked back at the road. He said, "Enjoying it, Mom?"

"Yes, Robert." Her voice was as cool as the morning. "It is very pleasant to sit here. I was thinking of the driving I did for you when you were little. I wonder if you enjoyed it as much as I enjoy this."

He smiled, embarrassed. "Sure I did."

She reached over, patted him on the arm, and then turned back to the scenery.

B He listened to the smooth purr of the engine. Up ahead he saw a great truck, spouting a geyser of smoke as it sped along the turnpike. Behind it, not passing it, was a long blue convertible, content to drive in the wake of the truck. Robert Proctor noted the arrangement and filed it in the back of his mind. He was slowly overtaking them, but he would not reach them for another minute or two.

He listened to the purr of the engine, and he was pleased with the sound. He had tuned that engine himself over the objections of the mechanic. The engine idled rough now, but it ran smoothly at high speed. You needed a special feel to do good work on engines, and Robert Proctor knew he had it. No one in the world had a feel like his for the tune of an engine. B SR-1

It was a good morning for driving, and his mind was filled with good thoughts. He pulled nearly abreast of the blue convertible and began to pass it. His speed was a few miles per hour above the turnpike limit, but his car was under perfect control. The blue convertible suddenly swung out from behind the truck. It swung out, without warning and struck his car near the right front fender, knocking his car to the shoulder on the left side of the turnpike lane.

Robert Proctor was a good driver, too wise to slam on the brakes. He fought the steering wheel to hold the car on a straight path. The left wheels sank into the soft left shoulder, and the car tugged to pull to the left and cross the island and enter the lanes carrying the cars heading in the opposite direction. He held it, then the wheel struck a rock buried in the soft dirt, and the left front tire blew out. The car slewed, and it was then that his mother began to scream. C

The car turned sideways and skidded part of the way out into the other lanes.

STRUCTURED READING FOR LESS PROFICIENT STUDENTS

These questions can help to guide students through the reading. Ask each question at the point of the selection where the SR number appears in the margin.

How does Robert feel about his ability as a motorist? *(Possible response: confident, proud, skillful)* **Drawing conclusions**

What problems arise that Robert can't control? *(The convertible swings out and hits him; his left wheels sink in the dirt and tug him to the left; a blowout causes his car to skid.)* **Summarizing**

Where is Robert's car, and what is the immediate danger? *(in the left lane for oncoming traffic; a car is bearing down on him)* **Clarifying**

What disturbs Robert most about the imagined accident? *(the death of the trusting and helpless sleeping girl)* **Inferring**

What do the two grooves worn into the floor indicate? *(Many people fail the test and are dragged away.)* **Drawing conclusions**

Robert Proctor fought against the steering wheel to straighten out the car, but the drag of the blown tire was too much. The scream rang steadily in his ears, and even as he strained at the wheel one part of his mind wondered cooly how a scream could so long be sustained without a breath. An oncoming car struck his radiator from the side and spun him viciously, full into the left-hand SR-2 ▶ lanes.

He was flung into his mother's lap, and she was thrown against the right door. It held. With his left hand he reached for the steering wheel and pulled himself erect against the force of the spin. He turned the wheel to the left and tried to stop the spin and careen out of the lanes of oncoming traffic. His mother was unable to right herself. She lay against the door, her cry rising and falling with the spin of the car.

The car lost some of its momentum. During one of the spins he twisted the wheel straight, and the car wobblingly stopped spinning and headed down the lane. Before Robert Proctor could turn it off the pike to safety a car loomed ahead of him, bearing down on him. There was a man at the wheel of that other car, sitting rigid, unable to move, eyes wide and staring and filled with fright. Alongside the man was a girl, her

DEMOLISHED VEHICLE 1970 John Salt Housatonic Museum of Art, Bridgeport, Connecticut.

Teaching Tip

Have students find passages that describe Robert struggling to control his car. Ask for volunteers to act out his actions as another student reads those passages aloud.

D. Reading Skill: UNDERSTANDING WORD CHOICE Explain that *to careen* means *to lean.* Have students identify other action words that tell Robert's movements as he tries to regain control. *(Words include* reached, pulled, turned, tried to stop*)*

E. LEP: Vocabulary Explain that the word *loomed* means *appeared as large and distorted.* It also implies that something is about to happen. Ask students to suggest the feelings that the word *loomed* connotes. *(possible response: terror, dread, foreboding, horror)*

Art Note

English artist John Salt (1937–) studied at the Slade School of Fine Arts, London, and the Maryland Institute College of Art, Baltimore. His work is widely exhibited in the United States and abroad. This photo-realist painting brings the viewer almost inside the car, with just enough distance to fully perceive the wreckage. *How are you affected by details of the painting, such as the steering wheel and the newspaper?*

F. LEP: Comprehension Ask students what words might describe Robert's feelings at the instant before the unavoidable collision. *(Possible words: helpless, sorry)* Have them point out specific information in the story that supports their answer. *(Only the trusting helplessness of the sleeping girl reaches his mind.)*

G. Critical Thinking: ANALYZING Ask students if they are surprised by the outcome of Robert's "accident." If not, ask why. *(Possible clues: He heard no crash, survived a head-on collision, and felt a painless wrench. The prolonged scream and Robert's ability to see clearly the people in the oncoming car speeding toward him create an unreal, nightmarish quality.)*

H. Literary Element: CHARACTER Ask students what the lingering image of the sleeping girl may suggest about Robert's character. *(Possible response: He is very disturbed at the idea of causing someone's death even though it happened only in his imagination; he cares about other people.)*

Art Note

George Clair Tooker, Jr. (1920–) grew up in rural surroundings on Long Island, New York. He majored in English literature at Harvard and, after serving briefly with the Marines, studied at the Art Students League in New York. *Farewell* was inspired by Tooker's recollection of a corridor in the hospital where his mother died. *Why do you suppose the artist placed the woman at a distance and made her form vague?*

head against the back of the seat, soft curls framing a lovely face, her eyes closed in easy sleep. It was not the fear in the man that reached into Robert Proctor. It was the trusting helplessness in the face of the sleeping girl. The two cars sped closer to each other, and Robert Proctor could not change the direction of his car. The driver of the other car remained frozen at the wheel. At the last moment Robert Proctor sat motionless staring into the face of the onrushing, sleeping girl, his mother's cry still sounding in his ears. He heard no crash when the two cars collided head-on at a high rate of speed. He felt something push into his stomach, and the world began to go gray. Just before he lost consciousness he heard the scream stop, and he knew then that he had been hearing a single, short-lived scream that had only seemed to drag on and on. There came a painless wrench, and then darkness. SR-3 ▶

Robert Proctor seemed to be at the bottom of a deep black well. There was a spot of faint light in the far distance, and he could hear the rumble of a distant voice. He tried to pull himself toward the light and the sound, but the effort was too great. He lay still and gathered himself and tried again. The light grew brighter and the voice louder. He tried harder, again, and he drew closer. Then he opened his eyes full and looked at the man sitting in front of him.

"You all right, son?" asked the man. He wore a blue uniform, and his round, beefy face was familiar.

Robert Proctor tentatively moved his head and discovered he was sitting in a reclining chair, unharmed and able to move his arms and legs with no trouble. He looked around the room, and he remembered.

The man in the uniform saw the growing intelligence in his eyes, and he said, "No harm done, son. You just took the last part of your driver's test."

Robert Proctor focused his eyes on the man. Though he saw the man clearly, he seemed to see the faint face of the sleeping girl in front of him.

The uniformed man continued to speak. "We put you through an accident under hypnosis—do it to everybody these days before they can get their driver's licenses. Makes better drivers of them, more careful drivers the rest of their lives. Remember it now? Coming in here and all?"

Robert Proctor nodded, thinking of the sleeping girl. She never would have awakened. She would have passed right from a sweet, temporary sleep into the dark, heavy sleep of death, nothing in between. His mother would have been bad enough; after all, she was pretty old. The sleeping girl was downright waste. ◀ SR-4

FAREWELL 1966 George Tooker Hood Museum of Art, Dartmouth College, Hanover, New Hampshire

Real Life Connections

Despite his "fatal accident," Robert's reactions to the emergency show some important attributes of good drivers, such as fast reflexes and the ability to think under pressure. Have the class brainstorm other important qualities of good drivers that may not show up on a driving test but could mean the difference between life and death. Have students form small groups to choose one or two traits they consider essential to safe driving and discuss ways to determine if a person is qualified to drive.

The uniformed man was still speaking. "So you're all set now. You pay me the ten-dollar fee and sign this application, and we'll have your license in the mail in a day or two." He did not look up.

Robert Proctor placed a ten-dollar bill on the table in front of him, glanced over the application, and signed it. He looked up to find two white-uniformed men, standing one on each side of him, and he frowned. He started to speak, but the uniformed man spoke first. "Sorry, son. You failed. You're sick. You need treatment."

The two men lifted Robert Proctor to his feet, and he said, "Take your hands off me. What is this?"

I The uniformed man said, "Nobody should want to drive a car after going through what you just went through. It should take months before you can even think of driving again, but you're ready right now. Killing people doesn't bother you. We don't let your kind run around loose in society any more. But don't you worry now, son. They'll take good care of you, and they'll fix you up." He nodded to the two men, and they began to march Robert Proctor out.

At the door he spoke, and his voice was so urgent the two men paused. Robert Proctor said, "You can't really mean this. I'm still dreaming, aren't I? This is still part of the test, isn't it?"

The uniformed man said, "How do any of us know?" And they dragged Robert Proctor out the door, knees stiff, feet dragging, his rubber heels sliding along the two grooves worn into the floor. ❧ J

◀ SR-5

INSIGHT

Love Poem

JOYCE CAROL OATES

Taking the curve of the road too fast
the car swerves, tires hit gravel,
fence posts never seen before lurch
crazily
then are righted again.
A miracle.
Our pulses now race in a single spasm:
other curves lie ahead.
If we die today we die together.

I. Critical Thinking: EVALUATING Ask students why they think Robert is or is not being misjudged. *(Any opinion that is supported by examples from the story is valid.)*

J. Literary Element: THEME Ask students what comment this story makes about "tests of courage." *(Possible response: Even on an ordinary day, when everything seems familiar and under control, we may face a test of courage.)*

Check Test

1. What kind of test was Robert taking? *(a driving test)*

2. How did Robert escape death in the head-on collision? *(He was hypnotized; it never happened.)*

3. What did Robert expect to get for paying a ten-dollar fee? *(a driver's license)*

Encouraging Independent Reading

"Along the Scenic Route," a short story by Harlan Ellison
"The Signature," a short story by Elizabeth Enright
Street Rod, a novel by Henry Gregor Felson
"Blue Eyes Far Away," a short story by MacKinlay Kantor
1984, a novel by George Orwell

Insight

This piece reflects on the ideas in the main selection and is suggested for students' independent reading. Optional discussion questions follow.

1. How are the experiences of Robert and the speaker in the poem similar? *(Similarities include going too fast, losing control, taking others with them, being ready to continue.)*

2. Why might this poem be titled "Love Poem"? *(Possible response: The car speeding out of control, miraculously escaping ruin, and continuing, despite hazards ahead, describes a love relationship—it is a metaphor.)*

Student Response

Responding to Reading

These questions are open-ended with no "right" or "wrong" answers. However, responses must be supported with information from the selection. Possible answers follow:

1. Any reaction is valid.

2. Students may say that Robert is confused, because he tried to do the right thing but failed anyway; that he feels he's been tricked and he's angry.

3. Some may say Robert could not have passed his driving test because it was set up to test character, not skills. Others may say that had Robert revealed his horror after the test he might have passed.

4. Students may say that it is fair, as Robert cared more about the fun than the responsibility of driving; that it is unfair, as the accident was imagined and Robert felt worse about the people involved than about being in trouble.

5. Some may say that Robert will get therapy until he responds to death as expected. Others may say that his "treatment" will be continuing nightmares of the horror he experienced.

6. Students may speculate that the remark indicates everyone in the story is being tested or that the whole story is a hypnotic dream.

7. Some possible steps: Student drivers should be shown at-the-scene videos of fatal highway accidents; driving instructors should bring in survivors and relatives of victims of fatal automobile accidents to meet student drivers.

Writing Options

The Writing Options are designed to meet varied student interests and abilities. Have each student choose one writing activity to complete. You may wish to guide some students to an option that requires less writing.

Journal Update Ask students to look over their earlier journal entries for "Test." What insights have they gained about tests that they can add to their writing?

Closure

In this story, the main character fails a test because he doesn't quite understand the rules. Ask students if they have ever been confused by the rules of any test—whether in school or not—and whether they were able to pass the test anyway.

Responding to Reading

First Impressions

1. How did you react to Robert's test? Explain your answer.

Second Thoughts

2. What feelings do you think Robert has about his test?

   Think about
   - his driving skills
   - the manner in which the test is conducted
   - his reactions to failing the test
   - the word web on tests that you filled out earlier

3. Is there any way that Robert could have passed his driving test?

4. Is the decision to take Robert away for treatment fair? Explain.

   Think about
   - the teenage accident statistics you read about earlier
   - how Robert performs during the crisis
   - his feelings about the young girl in the oncoming car
   - why he failed the test

5. What kind of treatment do you think is in store for Robert?

6. "How do any of us know?" replies the uniformed man when Robert asks if being taken away is part of the test. What might the man mean by this?

Broader Connections

7. Local, state, and federal agencies have developed many ways to impress driving safety on young drivers. If you were named traffic commissioner of your state, what steps would you take to make teenagers safer drivers?

Writing Options

1. Imagine that Robert is released from custody and is upset about the test he was given. Assume his point of view and write an angry letter of complaint to the director of driver's licensing for your state. Explain why the test is unfair and why Robert deserves his license.

2. If you have completed your driver's license exam, describe your experience. Begin by listing all that you recall about the setting, the examiner, and your feelings and experiences during the test. Develop these notes into a short personal narrative.

e x p l o r e

Poetry

If
RUDYARD KIPLING

Courage
ANNE SEXTON

Examine What You Know (Prior Knowledge)

What does *courage* mean to you ? Is it standing up for what you believe in, risking your life to save someone else's, or simply keeping your spirits up in whatever circumstances you find yourself? In your journal or on a piece of paper, create a definition of courage based on your own experiences and observations. Keep your definition in mind as you read these two poems.

Expand Your Knowledge (Building Background)

While both of these poems portray courage, they have many differences, arising perhaps from the contrasting personalities of the poets and from the times in which they lived. Rudyard Kipling (1865-1936) grew up in an era when Britain's military might helped it colonize lands across the globe. Kipling staunchly defended Britain's empire, and his writing glorified the spread of British power. On a personal level, Kipling praised qualities such as hard work and loyalty and believed in the duty of humans to be strong and self-reliant. Unlike Kipling, American poet Anne Sexton (1928–1974) was an introspective person who questioned authority on all levels. Looking deep inside herself for answers to life's perplexities, she found only more questions. All of this she turned into poetry filled with distinctly personal images and symbols.

Enrich Your Reading (Reading Skill)

Literal and Figurative Language Words can have a literal meaning, a figurative meaning, or both, depending on the author's purpose. **Literal** means that the words mean what they ordinarily mean. A house is a house, and a walk to town is exactly that. **Figurative** means that the words are *not* used in their ordinary sense, but in some new, creative, symbolic, or thought-provoking way. Sexton, for example, describes a child's first step as being "as awesome as an earthquake." Notice the combination of literal and figurative language in these poems.

■ *Biographies of the authors can be found on page 357.*

Objectives

- To recognize the common theme in different poems
- To identify personification
- To distinguish between literal and figurative language
- To express understanding of the poems through a choice of writing options, including a definition and a poem

Prereading/Motivation

Examine What You Know

Discussion Prompts: What are the risks of standing up for what you believe in? Does risking your life to help someone else require the same kind of courage as standing up for your beliefs? Why or why not? How is keeping up your spirits despite circumstances an act of courage? What definition of courage would apply to all these situations?

Expand Your Knowledge

Discussion Prompts: What different kinds of courage are there? How do you determine whether or not an action or a decision is an act of courage?

Enrich Your Reading

Point out some of the figurative language in each poem. For example, Kipling refers to "Triumph and Disaster" as "two imposters," and Sexton speaks of "wringing out" despair "like a sock." Encourage students to make up figurative language of their own. They might begin by simply describing something as "awesome as a. . . ."

Thematic Link—Tests of Courage

In these poems, courage is tested in the everyday lives of ordinary people.

Journal Writing

These poems tell about the courage it takes to live an ordinary life and achieve maturity. Some journal topics follow:

- Explain which you think is a better description of courage—*proceeding with* or *without fear.*
- Is courage part of your everyday life? How so?
- Why is it important to have courage?

For other journal opportunities, refer students to Examine What You Know (above), annotation E for "Courage," and Real Life Connections (page T–354).

Additional Resources

UNIT THREE RESOURCE BOOK

Reader's Guidesheet, p. 16
Vocabulary Worksheet, p. 17
Selection Check Tests, p. 18
Selection Test, pp. 19–20

Collaborative Learning

Opportunities for collaborative learning appear throughout the lesson and include Support for Students of Limited English Proficiency (page T–352), Cultural Connections (page T–352), and Real Life Connections (page T–354).

Teaching Strategies

Support for Students of Limited English Proficiency

- Use Reader's Guidesheet, p. 16.
- "If" and "Courage" contain figurative language and expressions from other times and cultures that may confuse some students. Have students make a simple classroom glossary for troublesome words and phrases. Encourage them to use context clues, dictionaries, and discussion to determine meanings. Here is a sample glossary:

A Poet's Way	Our Way
keep your head	stay calm
deal in lies	be a liar
with a banner	with pride
wallowing up	taking delight in

- Annotations A and D for "If" and B, I, and F for "Courage" focus on figurative language and unusual usage.

Text Annotations

A. LEP: Paraphrasing Ask students to suggest a phrase that explains what the poet means by the word *it. (Possibilities include* the trouble *or* the problem.) Have them restate the first two lines of "If" in their own words. *(One possibility: If you stay cool when everyone else freaks and blames everything on you.)*

B. Literary Element: THEME Ask students how the idea of rebuilding after a loss or disappointment requires courage. *(Possible response: You rebuild on faith, with no guarantee that your efforts will turn out as planned.)*

C. Literary Element: PERSONIFICATION Ask students to identify the word that suggests that "Will" has the human ability to act. *(says)* Ask students in what way will, or determination, is like a person. *(Possible response: The will to succeed, or carry on, can seem to take over on its own when other motivations are crushed.)*

D. Literary Element: FIGURATIVE LANGUAGE Ask students what it means to "walk with Kings." *(Possible responses: achieve great success, attain fame, hobnob with high society)*

E. Reading Skill: UNDERSTANDING WORD CHOICE Have students suggest words to replace *man and son* in the last line that would apply to women too and not change the meaning of the poem. *(adult, child)*

If

RUDYARD KIPLING

A If you can keep your head when all about you
Are losing theirs and blaming it on you;
If you can trust yourself when all men doubt you,
But make allowance for their doubting too:
If you can wait and not be tired by waiting,
Or, being lied about, don't deal in lies,
Or being hated don't give way to hating,
And yet don't look too good, nor talk too wise;

If you can dream—and not make dreams your master;
If you can think—and not make thoughts your aim,
If you can meet with Triumph and Disaster
And treat those two impostors just the same:
If you can bear to hear the truth you've spoken
Twisted by knaves to make a trap for fools,
Or watch the things you gave your life to, broken,
B And stoop and build 'em up with worn-out tools;

If you can make one heap of all your winnings
And risk it on one turn of pitch-and-toss,
And lose, and start again at your beginnings,
And never breathe a word about your loss:
If you can force your heart and nerve and sinew
C To serve your turn long after they are gone,
And so hold on when there is nothing in you
Except the Will which says to them: "Hold on!"

If you can talk with crowds and keep your virtue,
D Or walk with Kings—nor lose the common touch,
If neither foes nor loving friends can hurt you,
If all men count with you, but none too much:
If you can fill the unforgiving minute
With sixty seconds' worth of distance run,
Yours is the Earth and everything that's in it,
E And—which is more—you'll be a Man, my son!

14 ***knaves*** (nāvz)*:* dishonest or tricky persons.

Cultural Connection

Point out that the tradition of giving advice to the young is universal.

- Ask students which piece of advice in "If" sounds the most familiar to them. Have students restate Kipling's advice in the same words such advice has been given to them.
- Have students make up one or more mottos appropriate for their generation, using Kipling's idea and their own language.

PORTRAIT OF HERBERT JACOBY 1905 Mary Cassatt Collection of Mr. and Mrs. Everett Reese, Ohio.

Responding to Reading

First Impressions of "If"

1. Which lines in this poem do you find memorable? Explain.

Second Thoughts on "If"

2. Is the advice in this poem relevant to a modern audience? Why or why not?
3. Why does Kipling say that triumph and disaster are "imposters" who should be treated "just the same"?
4. What is the most important quality a young man needs, according to Kipling? Could this apply equally well to a young woman?

Art Note

Mary Cassatt (1845–1926) was well known for her representations of children. This portrait is in pencil on rice paper, the background enhanced very lightly with blue water color. Although the damask-upholstered chair and the boy's clothing provide some information about him, they are lightly sketched in comparison with the definite drawing of his face. *Can you explain why?*

Student Response

Responding to Reading

These questions are open-ended with no "right" or "wrong" answers. However, responses must be supported with information from the selection. Possible answers follow:

1. Any response is valid. Invite students to share their reasons.

2. Some students may say that the advice in "If" is too old to be useful; that at least half the people in the world are not men; that anyone who followed the advice would be phony or would collapse. Other students may say that the advice is mostly good, for both women and men; that the poem mainly says to take charge of your life, be cool, and grow up—good advice any time.

3. Students may say that triumph and disaster are deceivers who can fool you into thinking you are better or worse than you really are; that triumph and disaster don't last very long and can be different from or even the opposite of what they seem.

4. Some may say that Kipling implies that the most important quality a young man can have is the courage to stand on his own and not be controlled by others' opinions and actions or by the ups and downs in life. Others may say that Kipling mainly says a young man should be responsible for his own life and believe in himself. All of his advice applies to women as well as men.

Text Annotations

A. Literary Element: SIMILE Ask what the simile "as awesome as an earthquake" suggests about a child's first step. *(Possible response: It is an enormous, life-changing event.)* Ask how it expresses courage. *(Possible response: A first step is a bold and daring step that fear could keep one from taking.)*

B. LEP: Comprehension Ask students what feeling(s) the poet describes with the words "your heart went on a journey all alone." *(Possible responses: loneliness, separation, rejection)* Ask how getting a first spanking calls for courage. *(Possible responses: You have to endure the disapproval of someone whose love and approval you need.)*

C. Reading Skill: INFERRING Ask students to identify the words in the first stanza that could feel like acid and to explain why. *(crybaby, poor, fatty, crazy; they are put-downs.)*

D. Reading Skill: UNDERSTANDING WORD CHOICE Point out that *fondle* means *to handle with tender care.* Ask what the poet is saying about the person who doesn't fondle his weakness. *(Possible response: He doesn't give into it or make special allowances for himself.)*

E. Discussion Ask students if they think love and courage are related and to explain how they are alike or different. Have them relate their opinions to the poem and to life.

Courage

ANNE SEXTON

It is in the small things we see it.
F The child's first step,
as awesome as an earthquake.
The first time you rode a bike,
wallowing up the sidewalk.
G The first spanking when your heart
went on a journey all alone.
When they called you crybaby
or poor or fatty or crazy
and made you into an alien,
H you drank their acid
and concealed it.

Later,
if you faced the death of bombs and bullets
you did not do it with a banner,
you did it with only a hat to
cover your heart.
I you did not fondle the weakness inside you
though it was there.
Your courage was a small coal
that you kept swallowing.
J If your buddy saved you,
and died himself in so doing,
then his courage was not courage,
it was love; love as simple as shaving soap.

REAL LIFE CONNECTIONS

Point out that "Courage" divides life into four stages. The first stanza focuses on childhood, when courage occurs spontaneously and may not be recognized as courage by the child. Discuss with students how each experience depicted in the first stanza is an example of courage. Have them categorize those four experiences under labels such as "Pleasure" and "Pain." Then have students form small groups to discuss other childhood firsts and add them to each category. Each addition must meet these criteria:

A. The experience required courage.
B. Everyone in the group can relate some aspect of the experience to his or her childhood.

Later,
if you have endured a great despair,
then you did it alone,
getting a transfusion from the fire,
picking the scabs off your heart,
then wringing it out like a sock.
Next, my kinsman, you powdered your sorrow,
you gave it a back rub
K and then you covered it with a blanket
and after it had slept a while
it woke to the wings of the roses
and was transformed.

Later,
when you face old age and its natural conclusion
your courage will still be shown in the little ways,
each spring will be a sword you'll sharpen,
those you love will live in a fever of love,
and you'll bargain with the calendar
and at the last moment
L when death opens the back door
you'll put on your carpet slippers
and stride out.

SUSAN COMFORTING THE BABY 1881 Mary Cassatt Columbus Museum of Art, Ohio Bequest of Frederick W. Schumacher, 1957.

F. Literary Element: PERSONIFICATION Ask students what image comes to mind as they read the passage describing the care given to sorrow. *(Possible responses: a baby, young child, someone in need of loving attention)*

G. Literary Element: THEME Have students compose a statement that uses the word *courage* and relates to the poet's image of dying. *(One possible response: Death is certain and as common as going out the back door, but facing it takes courage.)*

Check Test

1. What does Kipling say you must do when everyone doubts you? *(trust yourself)*

2. What are the rewards of behaving as Kipling advises? *(the Earth: being a Man)*

3. What does Sexton say is as "awesome as an earthquake" for a child? *(a child's first step)*

4. What makes courage become love? *(dying in order to save another)*

5. What does striding out the back door symbolize? *(death)*

Encouraging Independent Reading

"No coward soul is mine," a poem by Emily Brontë
"Say not, the struggle naught availeth," a poem by Arthur Hugh Clough
"Invictus," a poem by William Ernest Henley
Inclusive Verse, poetry by Rudyard Kipling
All My Pretty Ones, poetry by Anne Sexton

Art Note

American artist Mary Cassatt (1845–1926) began her art education in Philadelphia but soon went to live in Paris, where she became a member of the group of French painters called Impressionists. Her portraits of motherhood are as lovely and as beloved as some of the famous madonnas of an earlier period. *What are some of the remarkably realistic features in* Susan Comforting the Baby?

e x p l a i n

Responding to Reading

First Impressions of "Courage"

1. What mood or feeling did this poem evoke in you? Compare your answer with those of your classmates.

Second Thoughts on "Courage"

2. Why do you think Anne Sexton calls her poem "Courage"?
   Think about
   - what you have already written about courage
   - the examples of courage that she cites

3. What does this poem teach about dealing with despair and sorrow? Explain.

4. Sexton uses figurative language to talk about death. What images does her description of death bring to your mind? How do these images add to your appreciation of the poem?

Comparing the Poems

5. Compare the tone, or attitude, of these two poets toward the subject of courage.

6. Compare the forms of these two poems. Describe how form helps convey each poem's message and each poet's purpose.
   Think about
   - what each poem looks like on the page
   - what makes up a stanza in each poem

7. Which poem gives the best advice for "facing the unknown"?

Literary Concept: Personification

Personification is a figure of speech in which human qualities are given to animals, objects, ideas, or feelings. What examples of personification can you find in these two poems?

Writing Options

1. Write a definition of *courage* as each poet might express it.
2. Write your own poem about courage.

Student Response

Responding to Reading

These questions are open-ended with no "right" or "wrong" answers. However, responses must be supported with information from the selection. Possible answers follow:

1. Any response is valid.

2. Students may say that ordinary things in life—such as taking a first step, loving, overcoming defeat, and accepting death—takes courage; that the poem is about the courage it takes to do the things we are expected to do.

3. Some may say that despair and sorrow should be allowed time to run their course. Others may say that we should experience sorrow as part of life—neither deny it nor refuse to let it go.

4. Some students may say that Sexton's description shows dying as an ordinary event that calls for courage like learning to walk. Others may say that even though death is natural, it's "awesome as an earthquake" for each person and therefore requires courage.

5. Students may say that "If" is bold and direct, while "Courage" is subtle and introspective; or that "If" instructs and challenges like a pep talk, while "Courage" describes and reflects on life just as it's lived.

6. Possible response: "If" looks like brave soldiers standing at attention with its stanzas of uniform length formed by alternating long and short lines. "Courage" appears to flow as thoughts do with its stanzas and lines of varying lengths.

7. Any answer is valid that relates the poem to real life.

Writing Options

The Writing Options are designed to meet varied student interests and abilities. Have each student choose one writing activity to complete. You may wish to guide some students to an option that requires less writing.

Journal Update Have students to review journal entries for "If" and "Courage." What other thoughts about courage can they add to their earlier comments?

Literary Concept—Personification

Possible responses: Examples of personification in "If" include: dreams as a master; Triumph and Disaster depicted as impostors; Will that says "Hold on!" and "the unforgiving minute." Examples of personification in "Courage" include: a heart going on a journey; weakness that may be fondled; a heart with scabs; sorrow that is powdered, rubbed, and covered and that sleeps and wakes; a calendar that bargains; and death that opens the back door.

Refer to annotations C for "If" and G for "Courage."

extend

Rudyard Kipling
1865–1936

Rudyard Kipling was born to a British family in Bombay, India, in the days when Britain controlled India and many other lands around the world. When he was six, Kipling's parents sent him to live in England with a foster family that treated him cruelly. At twelve, Kipling entered a boarding school, where he faced beatings and teasing from school bullies and where school rules were harsh. After graduation, at seventeen, he returned to India to work as a newspaper reporter and to write poems and short stories. By twenty-four, Kipling had returned to England, already a well-known writer. Throughout his career, Kipling was known for his tales of India, his children's stories, and his glorification of the British Empire. His works include *The Jungle Books, Captains Courageous,* and the *Just So Stories.* Later, Kipling lost popularity, as fewer people agreed with his belief in Britain's right to colonize the world.

Anne Sexton
1928–1974

"My themes," said Anne Sexton, "are life, death, insanity, daughterhood, motherhood, and love." Sexton's poems relate these intimate topics in a very personal way, revealing experiences from her own troubled life.

Born in Newton, Massachusetts, Sexton began writing poems in high school. She doubted her ability, though, and soon stopped writing. Not until the age of twenty-eight, in 1957, did she find the courage to write once again. By 1960 she had published a collection of poems, *To Bedlam and Part Way Back,* telling of her struggle with mental illness. Her 1966 volume, *Live or Die,* which explores the feeling of love, won a Pulitzer Prize. In addition to being a writer, Sexton also worked as a fashion model, a high school teacher, and a university professor.

Cross-Curricular Options

Art: Create a collage on the theme of courage, incorporating images and ideas from "If" and "Courage."

History: Research and report on social or political trends in the United States during Anne Sexton's lifetime, 1928–1974, that may have influenced her attitudes, just as British military strength and colonialism affected Kipling's views.

Home Arts: Research and report on current theories of how to raise children to become confident and self-reliant, or courageous, in life.

Social Studies: Create a bulletin-board display showing how various cultures have encouraged, shown, or rewarded courage throughout the history of humankind.

Additional Information about the Authors

Rudyard Kipling At age sixteen Rudyard Kipling produced his first book of verse, "School Boy Lyrics," a privately distributed collection of satire and humor. His writing career began in earnest at seventeen in the hubbub of a newspaper office where his father's influence gained him employment. There, he seized the scraps of time between his duties of sorting telegrams and writing editorials to sketch out his own stories. Learning to write under pressure, he became a master "phrase-maker." One critic has commented, "No other storyteller was ever able to put so much as Kipling into so little space." In 1907, Kipling received the Nobel prize for literature.

Anne Sexton Anne Sexton grew up in wealth with every advantage except the feeling of being wanted. In grade school, where she distinguished herself as the "class rogue"—flamboyant, rebellious, popular, but trying—her teachers recognized her as brilliant but disturbed. As a young wife and mother, she began a lifelong battle against depression. Her poetry grew out of her therapy as she began writing her thoughts, feelings, and dreams. Critics called her poetry "confessional," a label Sexton long resented and finally accepted, sayng that she may be the only confessional poet. Her life, marked by professional success but personal torment and tragedy, ended in suicide.

Closure

"If" offers advice for the human condition, while "Courage" describes it. Both poems, however, explore and celebrate the courage people show in facing everyday life. Have the class make a list of ordinary situations at school that require and test their courage. Ask them to explain how these poems relate to those familiar situations.

Writer's Workshop

Objectives

- To establish the goals of expressive writing
- To generate concrete words that evoke vivid images
- To determine how poems are used as a vehicle for expression
- To draft, revise, edit, present, and publish a poem that expresses intense feelings
- To reflect on the writing process

Integrating . . .

Literature and Writing Discuss with students the recurring themes in the Subunit 1 literature. Elicit from them that each theme deals with strong emotion. Explain that the literary selections in the pupil edition illustrate one way of expressing strong emotion and that poetry is another form of expression.

Writing and Language The Language Workshop in this subunit deals with the use of specific nouns and verbs. Discuss the use of nouns and verbs to paint pictures with words, explaining that the more exact the noun or verb used, the clearer the picture will be. Point out that this is true for prose writing assignments as well as the poetry assignment for this Writer's Workshop. To emphasize this point, have one student create a sentence consisting of a vague noun and verb, and ask another student what pictures these words paint. Then have the first student replace the noun and verb with more vivid words, and allow the second student to explain what pictures these words evoke. Have students continue this exercise until they understand that vivid and exact words make writing come alive.

Writing and Vocabulary The Vocabulary Workshop in this subunit deals with using a thesaurus. Have students practice using the thesaurus, explaining that this book will be helpful when they look for vivid words for their poems.

WRITER'S WORKSHOP

CREATIVE EXPRESSION

Personal, expressive writing allows you to reach deep into your experiences, emotions, and thoughts. In the process, you may discover new ways of looking at old ideas and experiences, or you may learn something new about yourself.

In addition to diaries, journals, and personal essays, poetry is a common form of expressive writing. Although some poets write to entertain or persuade others, most poems are primarily expressions of the poet's feelings and thoughts. Instead of stating their feelings directly, however, as the writer of a diary might do, poets use their imagination to express emotions and ideas in a variety of original ways, using sounds, images, rhythms, and unusual combinations of words.

For this assignment you will write an original poem, expressing your feelings, thoughts, or experiences in imaginative ways.

GUIDED ASSIGNMENT: POET'S CORNER

The two *Insight* poems in this subunit express the intense feelings two poets have about the people they love. Compose a poem about any idea, feeling, or experience that is meaningful to you.

Here is your PASSkey to this assignment.

PURPOSE: To express your feelings
AUDIENCE: Yourself
SUBJECT: An emotion or experience
STRUCTURE: A poem

Prewriting

STEP 1 Brainstorm possible topics Jot down all topics that come to mind. You might want to write about one of the ideas suggested by this subunit's reading selections: love, fear, courage, hidden dangers, or perseverance. If these ideas don't excite you, skim the Table of Contents or look through a newspaper or magazine for an idea that is familiar to you and interests you. From your list, select the topic that intrigues you the most.

STEP 2 Map your ideas Write your topic in the middle of a piece of paper. Then write down everything that this topic makes

Additional Resources

UNIT THREE RESOURCE BOOK
Writer's Workshop Copy Master, p. 21
Peer and Self-Evaluation Guidelines, p. 22
Writing Assessment Guidelines, p. 23

ENRICHMENT MATERIALS
Thinking Skills Transparency and Worksheet
Fine Art Transparency and Writing Prompts
Revision, Proofreading, and Elaboration Worksheet
Writing Prompts for Assessment

you think of. Cluster these ideas around your central topic, and connect related ideas by joining them with a line. Here is the cluster map or word web one student created when she brainstormed her topic: rejection.

STUDENT MODEL

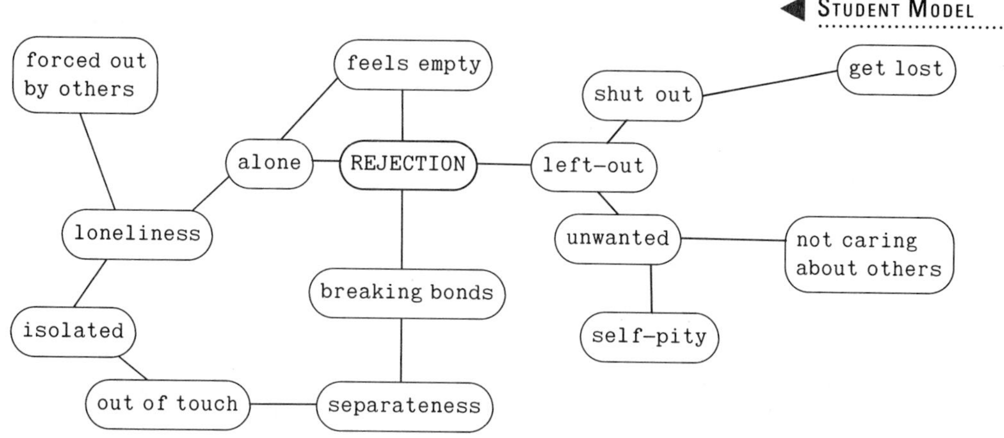

STEP 3 Examine your map Sometimes writers discover an offshoot of their original idea that provides better subject matter for a poem. Decide if your original idea is still your favorite. For example, the student who chose "rejection" decided to focus on "loneliness" instead.

STEP 4 Organize your ideas When you have chosen the topic for your poem, create a new map with your ideas organized around the five senses. Ask yourself, What does ______ (your topic) look, sound, feel, smell, and taste like? Don't worry if you can't think of images for all five senses. Note how this student has organized her ideas.

STUDENT MODEL

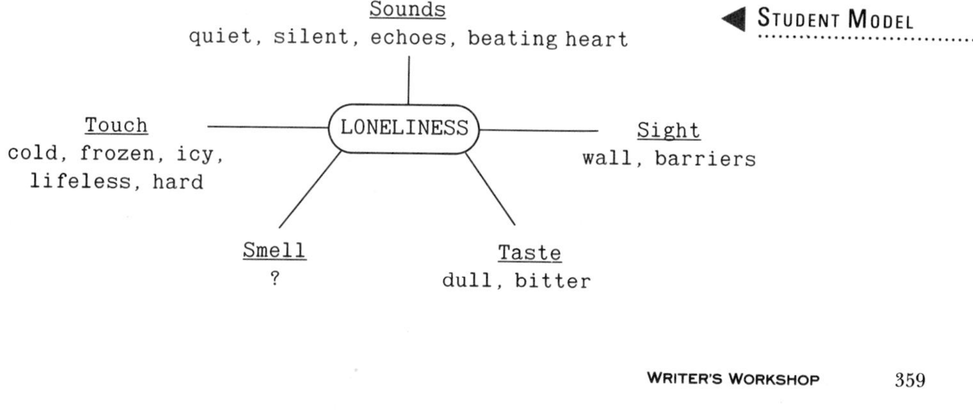

Prewriting Refer students to the list of recurring themes that they created in *Integrating Literature and Writing.* Encourage students to use this list as a springboard for formulating writing ideas, and have them brainstorm other topics to add to the list. Suggest that students explore an emotion that is now of great interest to them. Explain to students that poetry is not as structured as other writing modes, and that they should have fun and be creative with the assignment. In fact, stress that they should not view this exercise as an assignment, but as a creative way of sharing their emotions.

Computer Tip

For those students who have access to a computer, suggest organizing their lists on the computer. Point out that using a computer might also be a good way to create their prewriting clusters. Explain that computers allow writers to edit and move around the different components of their map easily. Have students determine whether they would be more comfortable using a computer or writing out the clusters by hand. Discuss the benefits and drawbacks of each method.

Teaching Tip

Students may need extra help in mapping their ideas. If necessary, review the use of clusters, or maps, with the class. You may wish to provide samples on the board for students to refer to as they write. Have the students themselves provide the ideas for these clusters. If necessary, detail the prewriting steps for each cluster. This will serve as additional brainstorming for the students.

As students fine-tune each cluster, cross out rather than erase any changes. This allows students to see the process clearly as they attempt to create their own clusters. Encourage students either to use or to slightly change the topics on the board if they get stuck when thinking of their own topics.

Teaching Strategies

Introduction Direct students to page 358. Discuss the meaning of the words "creative expression." Have students brainstorm creative and vivid words that capture a variety of emotions. Write these words on the board so that students can refer to them as they write their poems. Outline the different kinds of poems, explaining to students that poetry can take many forms and that most poems do not rhyme. You might want to provide examples of various forms of poetry, including haiku and concrete poems. Explain that a concrete poem is a good example of a literary work that paints both a verbal and a visual picture.

Remind students that a song also is a type of poem, and that they have already memorized dozens of these. Encourage students to list some of the songs that they have committed to memory.

Direct students to the Guided Assignment box on page 358. Explain that this assignment allows them to write any type of poem they wish, as long as it expresses intense feelings or emotion. Point out the PASSkey graphic, and stress that students are writing their poems for themselves. Assure students that there are no "right" or "wrong" poems.

Drafting Discuss with students that the precise use of language is the most important thing to remember as they get ready to write their poems. Remind them that if they carefully choose each word in their poem, the poem will more accurately convey the emotion and message they intend to express. Tell students to keep in mind that each word used in a poem evokes a specific image and that vivid words provide the exact image needed to bring a poem to life. Encourage them to again visualize each noun and verb they select, to make sure their words reflect specific emotions.

Teaching Tip

Tell students not to revise and or edit their poems as soon as they finish writing them. Explain that it might be a good idea to take a short break in order to distance themselves from their poems. Assure them that when they return to their poems, they can revise and edit them with a fresh eye. Tell students that a short break could be as little as a day, or as long as they feel is necessary.

Revising and Editing Suggest that students revise their work with the help of a partner. Have each student allow a partner to read his or her poem. After the partner finishes the poem, encourage the partner to explain it to the student who wrote it. This will ensure that the partner understood all of the similes and metaphors. Since the poem should have a beginning, middle, and an end, the partner may wish to explain the poem in the form of a story. Allow the poet to acknowledge whether the partner has perceived the poem accurately.

After the student revises the poem for clarity of words and ideas, he or she can edit the poem for spelling and mechanics. Explain that while a poem allows for a freer creative process than a story or report, the writer still must follow spelling and punctuation rules. As the students revise, direct them to the *Revision Checklist* on page 361.

STEP 5 **Create similes and metaphors** Similes and metaphors are the unusual comparisons that make poetry interesting to read. Begin by asking yourself, What objects or experiences does ______ (your topic) remind me of? and, What are the similarities in each comparison? Consider these comparisons to loneliness.

STUDENT MODEL ▶

Loneliness is like . . .	Loneliness is . . .
-an island cut off from the world	-a cold, empty hallway
-a statue that can't speak	-a cold, frozen lake in winter

Drafting

STEP 1 **Experiment with your ideas** You probably now have enough material for a good poem. Begin drafting by experimenting with different arrangements of words and phrases. You don't have to use every sensory image, simile, and metaphor you've created. Also, don't worry about making your poem rhyme or have a regular rhythm unless you want it to. Blend related ideas together. If necessary, add new phrases that complete a thought or feeling you're trying to express.

STEP 2 **Arrange your ideas** Reread what you have written thus far and decide if a different arrangement of ideas is needed. Your poem need not tell a story, but like any composition, it should have a beginning, a middle, and an end. Look at other poems in the book for ideas about arranging and structuring your poem.

Special Tip

If you have trouble concluding your poem, try returning to the idea or image with which you began.

Revising and Editing

Like other kinds of writing, poems require revision. You might begin by sharing your poem with a classmate. Ask your reader what he or she likes best and least about your poem and what effect the poem has on him or her. Use your reader's reactions as a guide to your revision. Also use the following checklist.

Revision Checklist

1. Does the poem express the feelings you intended it to?
2. Are the parts arranged in the best order? Is there a beginning, a middle, and an end?
3. Are there images that appeal to the senses?
4. Will the reader understand the similes and metaphors in the poem?

Editing Proofread for spelling, clarity, and mechanics.

Presenting and Publishing

You may wish to read your poem to the class. If not, your class might put together a booklet of poems with illustrations. If your school has a magazine, consider submitting your poem for publication. Here is the final version of the student's poem on loneliness.

STUDENT MODEL

Loneliness

A new student in a new school,
I'm like a statue in a cold museum.
Visitors stroll by with sidelong glances.
They look at me, but don't see me.
I reach for them, but they fear my touch may
be hard and icy.
I call to them, but they hear only the voices
of those they know,
And my voice echoes against their walls.
My loneliness becomes heavy, silent,
Like the statue after dark.

Reflecting on Your Writing

1. Which image or comparison in your poem do you like best? Why?
2. Do you feel your poem captures the ideas you intended to express? Why or why not?
3. Do you find poetry writing harder or easier than other kinds of writing? Explain.

Presenting Students may wish to illustrate their poems. Suggest that students share their poems with an audience for whom the poem was not intended (for example, with a friend not in the student's class). Students may even wish to share their poems with their families.

Reflecting on Your Writing Direct students to the Reflecting questions. Discuss these with each student to elicit further thoughts about his or her poem.

Closure

As students finish this subunit, it is important that they fully understand the following concepts:

- Poetry is an excellent vehicle for expression.
- Vivid and exact words are needed in order to allow a poem to paint a picture with words.
- Revision gives students the opportunity to make sure each word and idea in the poem functions as it should.
- Allowing others to interpret the poem helps the poet to recognize vague or misleading words or phrases.

ADDITIONAL WRITING AND RESEARCH TOPICS

The following items provide additional writing practice based on the selections in this subunit.

Creative Expression

- Imagine you are Christy Brown, the author of *My Left Foot.* Write a poem expressing how you felt when you succeeded in writing your first letter.
- Choose one of your favorite songs and write additional stanzas for it.

Other Topics

Narrative: Write a poem completing the story "The Street of the Cañon." Include the outcome of a Sunday meeting between Sarita and the Hidalgo man. Be sure to include Sarita's feelings about the events as well as about the man.

Memoir: Write a poem about an event from your past that required perseverance. Be sure the poem chronicles the event as it occurred.

Language Workshop

Objectives

- To use precise nouns and verbs in speaking and writing
- To replace general nouns and verbs in writing to create interest and make writing clearer

Integrating . . .

Writing and Language Remind students that one purpose in writing is to express a feeling, as in the previous Writer's Workshop. Ask students to discuss any word changes they made during the revision process. Have volunteers explain their reasons for changing specific words in their own poems. Explain that part of the challenge of writing is to find the right word to convey a specific feeling. Write the following sentences from "The Street of the Cañon" on the board.

1. The long, narrow room with the orchestra at one end was filled with whirling dancers.

2. Suddenly a plump, officious little man, his round cheeks glistening with perspiration, pushed his way through the crowd.

3. In the square patio the gentle breeze ruffled the pink and white oleander bushes.

Call students' attention to the phrase "whirling dancers" in sentence 1 and model your thoughts aloud: "Since the story is set in Mexico, the phrase 'whirling dancers' makes me think of lively music and dancing, like the flamenco dancers I've seen in the movies." Discuss the other sentences, encouraging students to identify the words that create vivid images and to describe the images created. Point out that this Language Workshop focuses on using specific nouns and verbs.

Answer Key
Exercise 1

Answers will vary, but students should identify six precise nouns used in the sentences they choose.

LANGUAGE WORKSHOP

USING SPECIFIC NOUNS AND VERBS

If you stop to think about it, almost all writing and speech is about things or about actions. To speak and write about things, such as people or objects, we use **nouns.** To speak and write about actions, we use **verbs.** One way to improve your communication is to be careful about what nouns and verbs you use.

Using Specific Nouns

One of the choices that you have as a writer is between general nouns and specific ones. Consider the following examples:

General Noun	Specific Nouns
athlete	swimmer, linebacker, pole-vaulter
vehicle	tractor, flying saucer, submarine
food	hamburger, tofu, carrot

General nouns don't provide much information. Notice how replacing a general noun with a specific noun improves the following sentence:

General Noun The *plant* was sweet in the air.
Specific Noun The *honeysuckle* was sweet in the air.

HINT

One place to look if you can't think of any precise or strong replacements for nouns and verbs is a thesaurus. See the vocabulary workshop **Using a Thesaurus.**

Exercise 1 Style In a group skim the selections in this unit, looking for precise nouns. Choose six sentences and discuss how the writers used precise nouns to convey their ideas clearly. Ask one group member to take notes.

Using Specific Verbs

Just as you can often choose between a general noun and a specific one, you can also choose between a general verb and a specific verb. Strong, vivid verbs help to grab your reader's interest by creating strong images in his or her mind.

General Verbs Robert was *moved* into his mother's lap, and she was *sent* against the door.
Specific Verbs Robert was *flung* into his mother's lap, and she was *thrown* against the door.

Additional Resources
UNIT THREE RESOURCE BOOK
Language Workshop Copy Master, p. 24
ENRICHMENT MATERIALS
Grammar and Usage Copy Masters

Try to visualize the action in the first sentence. Why is the image clearer and more powerful in the second sentence?

Writers use specific verbs to convey their ideas as clearly as possible. Consider the following alternatives to the verb *said.*

shouted	pleaded	muttered	whined	snapped
promised	replied	cackled	mumbled	whispered
whimpered	stammered	explained	ordered	called

Exercise 2 Replace each of the italicized verbs with a stronger, more precise one. Choose verbs that help to create vivid images.

1. I was covered in sweat when I *walked* into the examination room to take my driver's test.
2. Later in the parking lot, the officer *looked* at my mother's purple and silver 1942 Packard.
3. I put the car in neutral on a hill, and we *went* halfway down the street before I shifted to drive.
4. My last assignment was to *go* on the highway for five miles. However, it was raining and I never turned on the wipers.
5. When the officer told me I had passed, I *said,* "It can't be true!"

Exercise 3 Work in groups to rewrite the following passage. For each italicized verb, brainstorm a list of precise, powerful verbs to replace it. Use a thesaurus to strengthen your lists. Then choose the verb from each list that expresses the strongest image in that position. Compare your work with that of the other groups in your class to see the wealth of possible verbs.

> Christy Brown's mother *thought* about a way to help him communicate. Her relatives *said* she would never succeed. Christy *tried* to answer his mother's questions, but he could neither speak nor control his limbs. Then he *saw* his left foot and began to move it. One day he *took* his sister's chalk with his left foot and began to *mark* her chalkboard.

Exercise 4 Analyzing and Revising Your Writing

1. Take a piece of writing from your portfolio.
2. Replace the weak words with strong, precise nouns and verbs that will create powerful images in your reader's mind.
3. Check for vivid and precise nouns and verbs in your future writing.

LANGUAGE HANDBOOK

For review and practice, see Section 2, **Using Nouns,** and Section 5, **Using Verbs.**

Teaching Strategies

Ask a volunteer to read the introductory paragraph on page 362. Point out that nouns and verbs are the building blocks of our language and that all sentences are built upon them.

Teaching Tip

To reinforce this concept, try having students orally communicate an idea without using nouns or verbs. For example, challenge students to explain what they will do after school today or how to make a pizza.

Next read and discuss the section on specific nouns. Have students form small groups to complete Exercise 1, reminding them to read the Hint box first. You may assign a specific selection to each group or allow them to use any they wish. Have groups share their responses.

Now read and discuss the remainder of the lesson and assign Exercise 2. Have students form small groups to complete Exercise 3. Then ask them to share their lists with the class. Finally, assign Exercise 4.

Closure

Before beginning the next subunit, be sure students have internalized this concept:

- Precise nouns and verbs not only enhance speaking and writing but also help make images clearer for the listener and reader.

Exercise 2

Answers will vary but might include:
1. inched **2.** glared **3.** coasted **4.** drive **5.** stammered

Exercise 3

Answers will vary but might include the following:
thought—deliberated
said—vowed
tried—struggled
saw—discovered
took—gripped
mark—scrawl on

Exercise 4

Answers will vary, but students' work should reflect strong, precise nouns and verbs.

ADDITIONAL PRACTICE

The following items provide additional practice in using specific nouns and verbs.

Have students rewrite the sentences, replacing the italicized word with a more vivid word. Possible answers are given.

1. The brakes *sounded* when the car came to a halt.
2. Amy winced at the *scent* of the rotten meat.
3. Did you hear the *noise* when the big mirror fell?
4. A calling hawk *flew* into view.
5. The blue parrot *spoke* all night long.
6. The large snake *went* under the porch.

Vocabulary Workshop

Objective

- To use a thesaurus to find vivid and precise replacements for words

Integrating . . .

Writing, Language, and Vocabulary Share with students that this workshop will introduce them to the thesaurus. The thesaurus is a reference tool that can be used for the Writer's Workshop poetry assignment, the Language Workshop on nouns and verbs, as well as all other types of writing.

Teaching Strategies

Write the words *said* and *nice* on the chalkboard. Explain that these are two examples of words that are overused in writing. Have students suggest other words that might replace them.

Read through the material with students, noting the example shown on the page. Model use of the index. Then have students work in groups to use a thesaurus to find additional synonyms for *said* and *nice*.

Assign the exercise on page 364.

Closure

Before beginning the next subunit, be sure students have internalized this concept:

- A thesaurus is a reference source in which vivid and precise replacements for words can be found.

Teaching Tip

Point out that some words create feelings in addition to their meanings. Tell them that these feelings are called a word's *connotation*. As an example, ask whether students would rather know someone who is *clever* or someone who is *sly*.

Exercise

(An example is given.)
Line of poetry: The *smell moves* down from the flower. *Smell:* fragrance, odor, scent, perfume, aroma, essence; *moves:* drifts, rides, floats, wanders. Revised line: The *fragrance drifts* down from the flower.

VOCABULARY WORKSHOP

USING A THESAURUS

REMINDER

The thesaurus lists antonyms as well as synonyms and related words. An **antonym** is a word that is opposite in meaning. For example, *cold* is an antonym for *hot*.

If you can't think of a word that's like what you want to say, perhaps you can think of one that is opposite. If you can, then you can look that word up to find antonyms that suit your purpose.

When you need to replace a word with one that is more vivid or precise, look up the word in a **thesaurus**—a reference work that lists words related in meaning. Suppose, for example, that you have written the following sentence:

> The man in the doorway, while trying to appear at ease, was carefully *looking at* every smiling face.

What you really want to convey about the man's looking is that it is very intense. To find a word to convey this meaning, you can turn to a thesaurus to find synonyms for the word *look.* **Synonyms** are words that are similar in meaning. Remember that when you use a thesaurus, you usually need to look up the **base word**—the basic part of the word, without any added prefixes or suffixes. For example, you would look up the base word *look* rather than the word *looking*.

There are two kinds of thesaurus. In a **traditional thesaurus** you look up your base word in the index at the back of the book. The index will refer you to a numbered entry in the main part of the book. In a **dictionary thesaurus,** which is easier to use, you simply look up the base word in alphabetical order, as you would do in a dictionary. In this second type of thesaurus, you would find an entry like the following:

> **look,** *v.* & *n.*—*v.* behold; perceive, discern; examine, inspect, scan; stare; seem, appear. See VISION, APPEARANCE, ATTENTION.
> —*n.* glance, view; APPEARANCE, aspect. See VISION.

Since *examine* conveys your meaning better than does *look,* you try it in the sentence:

> The man in the doorway, while trying to appear at ease, was carefully *examining* every smiling face.

If you had not found a suitable word by looking at the first part of the entry, you could have looked up other words that you found in the entry (*appearance* or *vision,* for example).

LANGUAGE HANDBOOK

For review and practice, see Section 2, **Using Nouns,** Section 4, **Using Modifiers,** and Section 5, **Using Verbs.**

Exercise Look at the poetry you wrote for the Writer's Workshop on the preceding pages. Find two or three words that you would like to change. Look up these words in a dictionary thesaurus. Write down all the possible replacements and choose the most precise and vivid words to revise your poetry.

Additional Resources

UNIT THREE RESOURCE BOOK
Related Skills Copy, p. 25

ADDITIONAL PRACTICE

Use a thesaurus to replace each of the underlined words with a more precise synonym.

The Hawks beat the Chiefs in yesterday's game at Municipal Field. A spectator said "That was the most interesting game I've ever seen!" While Hawks fans were happy after the game, Chiefs fans seemed sad. *(Possible responses are given.)*

1. *demolished*
2. *exclaimed*
3. *amazing*
4. *elated*
5. *despondent*

Who Wins?

Winning and losing may seem as different as black and white, but sometimes the distinctions are not so clear. You may lose a game or fail at some task or relationship but learn a lesson that makes you a winner later on. On the other hand, you might dwell so much on past victories that you soon lose your "winning edge." In the long run, some winners are losers, and some losers are winners.

As you read each selection, think of what defines a winner and who the winners and losers are. What qualities are most necessary in a winner's character?

Subunit Preview

Have students read the introduction to subunit 2, **Who Wins?** Ask them to consider how reactions to wins and losses may relate to the unit theme, **Challenges: Winners and Losers.** How might a defeat be used to an advantage? How might an easy victory become an obstacle? To what extent does *how* you win or lose matter? Encourage students to read the subunit Table of Contents and predict which selection will interest them most.

For Additional Challenge

The following selections offer extra challenge in the exploration of the subunit theme:

"nobody loses all the time," a poem, by E. E. Cummings

"The Lottery," a short story by Shirley Jackson

Additional Resources

Subunit Test, pp. 53–54

Observation Assessment

Observing how students respond to the text, to the classroom instruction, and to peers is an important part of an assessment program. The following suggestions and the form in each Unit Resource Book can be used to implement observation assessment.

- As students work through this subunit, assess their general attitude toward reading. When presented with a new story, do they show interest? flip through it? look at the illustrations? begin reading parts that catch their eye? want to share their reactions?
- As students work through the subunit, can you see increased interest—rereading favorite parts on their own or initiating further reading on a subject?
- To evaluate their use of postreading strategies, have students verbalize their personal response to the story and support their views with specific examples.

Objectives

- To analyze a contemporary short story
- To understand character motivation
- To understand the use of dialect in a short story
- To identify sensory details
- To express understanding of the work through a choice of writing forms, including narration, a summary, a definition, and description

Prereading/Motivation

Examine What You Know

Discussion Prompts: What life principle did you follow in this instance? Why did this principle help you to play well? In what ways did you plan ahead or help your team?

Expand Your Knowledge

Discussion Prompts: Why do you think that many Chinese—and other immigrants—settle together? Why might Chinatown be an especially popular tourist attraction? What special pressures might exist for the sons and daughters of Chinese immigrants?

Additional Background: Today, San Francisco's Chinatown covers 24 blocks and contains 35,000 of the city's 60,000 Chinese residents.

Enrich Your Reading

Discuss with students other dialects they may have encountered. You might want them to list words from each dialect to define and discuss.

Thematic Link—Who Wins?

In this story, the narrator wonders who wins when she experiences conflicts with her mother and conflicting feelings about excelling at chess.

Fiction

Rules of the Game

AMY TAN

Examine What You Know (Prior Knowledge)

Think about a time when you played well in a game because you followed some important life principle. Maybe you won a Scrabble game because you took the time to plan ahead or helped your basketball team win because you placed the good of the team over your own desires. Summarize this event in your journal or on a piece of paper, and keep it in mind while you read this story.

Expand Your Knowledge (Building Background)

"Rules of the Game" takes place in San Francisco's Chinatown, the largest Chinese settlement outside Asia and one of San Francisco's main tourist attractions. California's first Chinese settlers arrived in 1848 during the gold rush era. During the next ten years, twenty-five thousand more Chinese came to California hoping for sudden wealth in the gold mines. Many did go to the mines, but the majority eventually settled in San Francisco, where they sold items imported from China, peddled vegetables, fished, or worked as servants. By 1885, Chinatown, or "Little China," covered ten blocks. The Chinatown of today, where this story takes place, was rebuilt after the earthquake of 1906. Most of San Francisco's Chinese live there.

Enrich Your Reading (Reading Skill)

Dialect refers to the speech patterns of specific groups or regions. In "Rules of the Game," the mother speaks English in the dialect of a recent Chinese immigrant. Notice the mother's dialect as she speaks to her daughter and as she offers wise, old Chinese sayings. Think about how the author's use of dialect helps bring the mother's character to life.

■ *A biography of the author can be found on page 379.*

Journal Writing

Suggest these journal topics to students:

- What are your family's "rules of the game"? How are they different from the "rules" elsewhere?
- The narrator says, "A light wind began blowing past my ears. It whispered secrets only I could hear." What secrets might the wind whisper?
- For other journal opportunities, refer students to Examine What You Know (p. 366) and Real-Life Connections (p. T–371).

Additional Resources

UNIT THREE RESOURCE BOOK

Reader's Guidesheet, p. 28
Vocabulary Worksheet, p. 29
Selection and Vocabulary Check Tests, p. 30
Selection Test, pp. 31–32

Collaborative Learning

Opportunities for collaborative learning appear throughout the lesson and include Cultural Connection (p. T–375), Options for Learning (p. 379) and Cross-Curricular Options (p. T–379).

Rules of the Game

AMY TAN

I was six when my mother taught me the art of invisible strength. It was a strategy for winning arguments, respect from others, and eventually, though neither of us knew it at the time, chess games.

"Bite back your tongue," scolded my mother, when I cried loudly, yanking her hand toward the store that sold bags of salted plums. At home she said, "Wise guy, he not go against wind. In Chinese we say, Come from South, blow with wind—poom!—North will follow. Strongest wind
SR-1 ▶ cannot be seen."

The next week I bit back my tongue as we entered the store with the forbidden candies. When my mother finished her shopping, she quietly plucked a small bag of plums from the rack and put in on the counter with the rest of the items.

My mother imparted her daily truths so she could help my older brothers and me rise above our circumstances. We lived in San Francisco's Chinatown.[1] Like most of the other Chinese children who played in the back alleys of restaurants and curio[2] shops, I didn't think we were poor. My bowl was always full, three five-course meals every day, beginning with a soup full of mysterious things I didn't want to know the names of.

We lived on Waverly Place, in a warm, clean, two-bedroom flat that sat above a small Chinese bakery specializing in steamed pastries and dim sum.[3] In the early morning, when the alley was still quiet, I could smell fragrant red beans as they were cooked down to a pasty sweetness. By daybreak our flat was heavy with the odor of fried sesame balls and sweet curried-chicken crescents. From my bed I would listen as my father got ready for work, then locked the door behind him, one-two-three clicks. A ◀ SR-2

At the end of our two-block alley was a small, sandlot playground with swings and slides well-shined down the middle with use. The play area was bordered by wood-slat benches, where old-country[4] people sat cracking roasted watermelon seeds with their golden teeth and scattering the husks to an impatient gathering of gurgling pigeons. The best playground, however, was the dark alley itself. It was crammed with daily mysteries and adventures. My

1. **Chinatown:** the Chinese section of any city outside China.

2. **curio** (kyoor′ ē ō′): any unusual item.

3. **dim sum** (dim′ tsoom′): a small dumpling filled with vegetables or meats and cooked by steaming.

4. **old-country:** of or from the country of an immigrant's origin (in this case, China).

Teaching Strategies

Vocabulary Preview

These vocabulary words are defined at the bottom of the selection page on which they appear. You may wish to discuss them briefly before students begin reading.

adversary opponent
benevolently kindly
concession a privilege
deftly skillfully
etiquette accepted behavior
humility absence of vanity
obscure to conceal from view
prodigy a child with awe-inspiring talent
replica reproduction
successive one after another

Support for Students of Limited English Proficiency

- Use **Readers' Guidesheet**, p. 28.
- "Rules of the Game" contains examples of Chinese-American dialect, such as Mrs. Jong's comments and the cries of the butchers, that students may find difficult to understand upon first reading. Direct them to paraphrase such dialogue into standard spoken English to help them better grasp its meaning.
- Annotations C, H, K, N, Q, V, and X focus on dialect and specialized vocabulary.

Text Annotations

A. Literary Element: SENSORY DETAILS
Ask students to isolate details that appeal to specific senses in this passage. *("fragrant red beans"—smell; "pasty sweetness"—taste; "odor of fried sesame balls and sweet curried-chicken crescents"—smell/taste; "one-two-three clicks"—sound)*

Structured Reading for Less Proficient Students

These questions can help to guide students through the reading. Ask each question at the point of the selection where the SR number appears in the margin.

SR–1. What does the narrator learn from her mother? *(the "art of invisible strength")* How can she use this knowledge? *(to win arguments, respect, and chess games)* **Literal recall**

SR–2. Where does the family live? *(in San Francisco's Chinatown)* Who is in the family? *(the narrator, her mother, father, older brothers)* **Clarifying**

SR–3. How did Waverly's family receive the chess set? *(It was given to them by the missionary ladies at Christmas.)* **Literal recall**

SR–4. What problem has Mrs. Jong had with "rules"? *(Possible responses: Mrs. Jong finds the "rules" or laws and customs of a foreign country strange and unclear, if not unfair.)* **Clarifying**

SR–5. How does Waverly become better at chess? *(An elderly Chinese man teaches her.)* **Literal recall**

Continued on page 368

B. Cultural Sidelight As opposed to Western medicine, which views disease as caused by bacteria or viruses—invading organisms that come from outside the body—Chinese medicine is based on a theory of balance of elements within the body. Medicinal herbs are supposed to help correct the imbalance of elements—such as wind, wood, metal, water—that is responsible for the dis-ease.

C. LEP: Dialect Since students might mistake "pet" for a verb rather than a noun, have them paraphrase this dialect. *(Possible response: "The fish in this store are to be eaten as food, not to be bought as pets.")*

D. Literary Element: CHARACTER MOTIVATION Ask what Mrs. Jong's story reveals about her character. *(Possible responses: She is caring and concerned about her children in the face of the realisitc dangers of urban life; she is overly protective and negative.)*

Market in Chinatown, San Francisco © F. Grehan/Photo Researchers, New York.

brothers and I would peer into the medicinal herb[5] shop, watching Old Li dole out onto a stiff sheet of white paper the right amount of insect shells, saffron-colored[6] seeds, and pungent leaves for his ailing customers. It was said that he once cured a woman dying of an ancestral curse that had eluded the best of American doctors. Next to the pharmacy was a printer who specialized in gold-embossed wedding invitations and festive red banners.

Farther down the street was Ping Yuen Fish Market. The front window displayed a tank crowded with doomed fish and turtles struggling to gain footing on the slimy, green-tiled sides. A handwritten sign informed tourists, "Within this store, is all for food, not for pet." Inside, the butchers with their bloodstained white smocks deftly gutted the fish while customers cried out their orders and shouted, "Give me your freshest," to which the butchers always protested, "All are freshest." On less-crowded market days we would inspect the crates of live frogs and crabs, which we were warned not to poke, boxes of dried cuttlefish, and row upon row of iced prawns,[7] squid, and slippery fish. The sand dabs[8] made me shiver each time; their eyes lay on one flattened side and reminded me of my mother's story of a careless girl who ran into a crowded

5. **medicinal herb:** any plant used for its healing properties.
6. **saffron-colored:** orangey yellow in color.
7. **prawns** (prôns): large shrimps.
8. **sand dabs:** various small, edible flatfish.

Words to Know and Use	**deftly** (deft′ lē) *adv.* skillfully

STRUCTURED READING FOR LESS PROFICIENT STUDENTS

Continued from page 367

SR–6. What strategy does Waverly use to get her mother's permission to play in tournaments? *(She pretends she does not want to play.)* **Inferring**

SR–7. Why does Mrs. Jong give Waverly special privileges? *(Mrs. Jong is proud of Waverly and wants her to be a champion.)* **Inferring**

SR–8. Why does Waverly ask her mother to stop bragging? *(Possible response: She is angry at being displayed like an object.)* **Drawing conclusions**

SR–9. Predict what will happen to Waverly. *(Possible responses: her mother will punish her severely for her behavior; she and her mother will have a heart-to-heart talk.)* **Predicting**

SR–10. What does Waverly imagine? *(She imagines that her mother's black chessmen are marching across the plain, sending her white pieces scurrying. As her mother's pieces move closer to the edge, Waverly escapes by growing lighter.)* **Analyzing**

D street and was crushed by a cab. "Was smash flat," reported my mother.

At the corner of the alley was Hong Sing's, a four-table café with a recessed stairwell in front that led to a door marked Tradesmen. My brothers and I believed the bad people emerged from this door at night. Tourists never went to Hong Sing's, since the menu was printed only in Chinese. A Caucasian[9] man with a big camera once posed me and my playmates in front of the restaurant. He had us move to the side of the picture window so the photo would capture the roasted duck with its head dangling from a juice-covered rope. After he took the picture, I told him he should go into Hong Sing's and eat dinner. When he smiled and asked me what they served, I shouted, "Guts and duck's feet and octopus gizzards!" Then I ran off with my friends, shrieking with laughter as we scampered across the alley and hid in the entryway grotto of the China Gem Company, my heart pounding with hope that he would chase us.

E My mother named me after the street that we lived on: Waverly Place Jong, my official name for important American documents. But my family called me Meimei,[10] "Little Sister." I was the youngest, the only daughter. Each morning before school, my mother would twist and yank on my thick black hair until she had formed two tightly wound pigtails. One day, as she struggled to weave a hard-toothed comb through my disobedient hair, I had a sly thought.

I asked her, "Ma, what is Chinese torture?" My mother shook her head. A bobby pin was wedged between her lips. She wetted her palm and smoothed the hair above my ear, then pushed the pin in so that it nicked sharply against my scalp.

"Who say this word?" she asked without a trace of knowing how wicked I was being. I shrugged my shoulders and said, "Some boy in my class said Chinese people do Chinese torture."

"Chinese people do many things," she said simply. "Chinese people do business, do medicine, do painting. Not lazy like American people. We do torture. Best torture." F

My older brother Vincent was the one who actually got the chess set. We had gone to the annual Christmas party held at the First Chinese Baptist Church at the end of the alley. The missionary ladies had put together a Santa bag of gifts donated by members of another church. None of the gifts had names on them. There were separate sacks for boys and girls of different ages.

One of the Chinese parishioners had donated a Santa Claus costume and a stiff, paper beard with cotton balls glued to it. I think the only children who thought he was the real thing were too young to know that Santa Claus was not Chinese. When my turn came up, the Santa man asked me how old I was. I thought it was a trick question; I was seven according to the American formula and eight by the Chinese calendar. I said I was born on March 17, 1951. That seemed to satisfy him. He then solemnly asked if I had been a very, very good girl this year and did I believe in Jesus Christ and obey my parents. I knew the only answer to that. I nodded back with equal solemnity. G

Having watched the other children opening their gifts, I already knew that the big gifts were not necessarily the nicest ones. One girl my age got a large coloring book of

9. **Caucasian** (kô kā′ zhən): referring to a member of what is loosely called the white race.

10. **Meimei** (mā′ mā).

E. Reading Skill: INFERRING Ask students what they can infer from the fact that the Jongs named their daughter after their street rather than giving her a Chinese name. *(Possible response: They thought such an "official" name might help Waverly succeed in America and rise above her circumstances.)*

F. Literary Element: CHARACTER MOTIVATION Ask what motivates Mrs. Jong's comments about the Chinese. *(Possible responses: She is motivated by ethnic pride and a desire to spark that pride in her daughter. Or, she has a sense of humor and is joking with her daughter.)*

G. Cultural Sidelight By the "Chinese calendar," Waverly is referring to the fact that Chinese give the age of "one" to newborns, whereas Americans start counting age at "zero."

H. LEP: Dialect Ask students to clarify Mrs. Jong's dialect: "Too good. Cost too much." *(This present is too good because it costs too much.)* Then ask what effect the use of dialect has here. *(Possible responses: It reminds us that Mrs. Jong is not on home ground; it emphasizes the difference in status between her and the missionaries.)*

I. Historical Sidelight Chess originated in India in the 6th century A.D. First known as *Chaturanga*("army game"), it spread rapidly along the routes of commerce and conquest, reaching Europe between 700 and 900 A.D. Until the 18th and 19th centuries, chess was mainly the game of royalty. Then it moved into the coffeehouses and universities.

biblical characters, while a less greedy girl who selected a smaller box received a glass vial of lavender toilet water. The sound of the box was also important. A ten-year-old boy had chosen a box that jangled when he shook it. It was a tin globe of the world with a slit for inserting money. He must have thought it was full of dimes and nickels, because when he saw that it had just ten pennies, his face fell with such undisguised disappointment that his mother slapped the side of his head and led him out of the church hall, apologizing to the crowd for her son who had such bad manners he couldn't appreciate such a fine gift.

The chess board seemed to hold elaborate secrets waiting to be untangled.

As I peered into the sack, I quickly fingered the remaining presents, testing their weight, imagining what they contained. I chose a heavy, compact one that was wrapped in shiny silver foil and a red satin ribbon. It was a twelve-pack of Life Savers, and I spent the rest of the party arranging and rearranging the candy tubes in the order of my favorites. My brother Winston chose wisely as well. His present turned out to be a box of intricate plastic parts; the instructions on the box proclaimed that when they were properly assembled he would have an authentic miniature replica of a World War II submarine.

Vincent got the chess set, which would have been a very decent present to get at a church Christmas party except it was obviously used, and, as we discovered later, it was missing a black pawn and a white knight. My mother graciously thanked the unknown benefactor, saying, "Too good. Cost too much." At which point an old lady with fine, white, wispy hair nodded toward our family and said with a whistling whisper, "Merry, merry Christmas." H

When we got home, my mother told Vincent to throw the chess set away. "She not want it. We not want it," she said, tossing her head stiffly to the side with a tight, proud smile. My brothers had deaf ears. They were already lining up the chess pieces and reading from the dog-eared instruction book.

I watched Vincent and Winston play during Christmas week. The chess board seemed to hold elaborate secrets waiting to be untangled. The chessmen were more powerful than Old Li's magic herbs that cured ancestral curses. And my brothers wore such serious faces that I was sure something was at stake that was greater than avoiding the tradesmen's door to Hong Sing's. I

"Let me! Let me!" I begged between games when one brother or the other would sit back with a deep sigh of relief and victory, the other annoyed, unable to let go of the outcome. Vincent at first refused to let me play, but when I offered my Life Savers as replacements for the buttons that filled in for the missing pieces, he relented. He chose the flavors: wild cherry for the black pawn and peppermint for the white knight. Winner could eat both.

As our mother sprinkled flour and rolled out small, doughy circles for the steamed dumplings that would be our dinner that night, Vincent explained the rules, pointing

◀SR-3

Words to Know and Use

replica (rep′ li kə) *n.* reproduction

to each piece. "You have sixteen pieces and so do I. One king and queen, two bishops, two knights, two castles, and eight pawns. The pawns can only move forward one step, except on the first move. Then they can move two. But they only take men by moving crossways like this, except in the beginning, when you can move ahead and take another pawn."

"Why?" I asked as I moved my pawn. "Why can't they move more steps?"

J "Because they're pawns," he said.

"But why do they go crossways to take other men? Why aren't there any women and children?"

"Why is the sky blue? Why must you always ask stupid questions?" asked Vincent. "This is a game. These are the rules. I didn't make them up. See. Here. In the book." He jabbed a page with a pawn in his

K hand. "Pawn. P-A-W-N. Pawn. Read it yourself."

My mother patted the flour off her hands. "Let me see book," she said quietly. She scanned the pages quickly, not reading the foreign English symbols, seeming to search deliberately for nothing in particular.

"This American rules," she concluded at last. "Every time people come out from foreign country, must know rules. You not know, judge say, Too bad, go back. They not telling you why so you can use their way go forward. They say, Don't know why, you find out yourself. But they knowing all the time. Better you take it, find out why yourself." She tossed her head back with a satis-

SR-4 ▶ fied smile.

I found out about all the whys later. I read the rules and looked up all the big words in a dictionary. I borrowed books from the Chinatown library. I studied each chess piece, trying to absorb the power each contained.

I learned about opening moves and why it's important to control the center early on: the shortest distance between two points is straight down the middle. I learned about the middle game and why tactics between two adversaries are like clashing ideas; the one who plays better has the clearest plans for both attacking and getting out of traps. I learned why it is essential in the endgame to have foresight, a mathematical understanding of all possible moves, and patience; all weaknesses and advantages become evident to a strong adversary and are obscured to a tiring opponent. I discovered that for the whole game one must L gather invisible strengths and see the endgame before the game begins.

I also found out why I should never reveal "why" to others. A little knowledge withheld is a great advantage one should store for future use. That is the power of chess. It is a game of secrets in which one must show and never tell.

I loved the secrets I found within the sixty-four black and white squares. I carefully drew a handmade chessboard and pinned it to the wall next to my bed, where at night I would stare for hours at imaginary battles. Soon I no longer lost any games or Life Savers, but I lost my adversaries. Winston and Vincent decided they were more interested in roaming the streets after school in their Hopalong Cassidy[11] cowboy hats.

On a cold spring afternoon, while walking

11. **Hopalong Cassidy:** a fictional Western hero created in 1910 by novelist Clarence Mulford.

Words to Know and Use

adversary (ad′ vər ser′ ē) *n.* an opponent
obscure (əb skyoor′) *v.* to conceal from view

371

J. Literary Element: CHARACTER MOTIVATION Ask students what motivates Waverly to ask these questions. *(Possible response: curiosity, a lively intelligence; she wants recognition from her brothers; she wants "women and children" to be equal to "men"; she is rebellious and cannot accept rules.)*

K. LEP: Vocabulary Explain that a *pawn* is one of eight chess pieces of the same color and with the lowest value. The term is also used to refer to a person who is manipulated to further another's purpose. Ask students to discuss examples of people they know or have heard about who have become "pawns." *(Possible responses: Friends tricked into passing notes or helping someone evade punishment or responsibility.)*

L. Critical Thinking: ANALYZING Ask students what Waverly means by "invisible strengths" and how she learned the technique. *(Possible response: "Invisible strengths" suggests self-control, intelligence, and cunning, which she learned from her mother, as explained in the first paragraph of the story.)*

Real Life Connections

To help students understand Mrs. Jong's efforts to help her daughter rise above her circumstances, explore with students the aspirations their parents, grandparents, elder siblings, and other relatives might have for them. Include in the discussion such goals as education, status, economic security, respect, job satisfaction, and marriage and children. Ask students to explain the specific ways their relatives have helped them to achieve these goals. Relate this information to the life the Jongs have created for their children by dint of their hard work and vigilance. Then ask students what some of the costs of these efforts might be—to their relatives, their families, and themselves.

M. Reading Skill: PREDICTING Ask students to predict why Waverly runs home and grabs the chess set and Life Savers. *(Possible responses: She wants to bribe the men to play with her; she wants to show off her possessions.)*

N. LEP: Vocabulary Make sure students understand that each of these phrases is the name of a chess strategy. Then ask volunteers to explain what the name of each strategy suggests about it. *(Possible responses: "The Double Attack"—attacking from two sides; "Throwing Stones"—finishing off an opponent or sending decoys to sides of board; "The Sudden Meeting"—pieces massed together; "The Surprise"—a surprise move; "The Humble Servant"—a pawn eliminating the king; "Sand in the Eyes"—diversionary tactics; "A Double Killing"—insuring the elimination of two pieces with one move.)*

home from school, I detoured through the playground at the end of our alley. I saw a group of old men, two seated across a folding table playing a game of chess, others smoking pipes, eating peanuts, and watching. I ran home and grabbed Vincent's chess set, which was bound in a cardboard box with rubber bands. I also carefully selected two prized rolls of Life Savers. I came back to the park and approached a man who was observing the game. M

"Want to play?" I asked him. His face widened with surprise, and he grinned as he looked at the box under my arm.

"Little sister, been a long time since I play with dolls," he said, smiling benevolently. I quickly put the box down next to him on the bench and displayed my retort.

Lau Po, as he allowed me to call him, turned out to be a much better player than my brothers. I lost many games and many Life Savers. But over the weeks, with each diminishing roll of candies, I added new secrets. Lau Po gave me the names. The Double Attack from the East and West Shores. Throwing Stones on the Drowning Man. The Sudden Meeting of the Clan. The Surprise from the Sleeping Guard. The Humble Servant Who Kills the King. Sand in the Eyes of Advancing Forces. A Double Killing Without Blood. N

There were also the fine points of chess etiquette. Keep captured men in neat rows, as well-tended prisoners. Never announce "Check" with vanity, lest someone with an unseen sword slit your throat. Never hurl pieces into the sandbox after you have lost a game, because then you must find them again, by yourself, after apologizing to all around you. By the end of the summer, Lau Po had taught me all he knew, and I had become a better chess player. ◀SI

Jeff Reed//The Stock Shop, New York.

Words to Know and Use	**benevolently** (bə nev′ ə lənt lē) *adv.* kindly **etiquette** (et′ i kit) *n.* accepted behavior

A small weekend crowd of Chinese people and tourists would gather as I played and defeated my opponents one by one. My mother would join the crowds during these O outdoor exhibition games. She sat proudly on the bench, telling my admirers with proper Chinese humility, "Is luck."

A light wind began blowing past my ears. It whispered secrets only I could hear.

A man who watched me play in the park suggested that my mother allow me to play in local chess tournaments. My mother smiled graciously, an answer that meant nothing. I desperately wanted to go, but I bit back my tongue. I knew she would not let me play among strangers. So as we P walked home I said in a small voice that I didn't want to play in the local tournament. They would have American rules. If I lost, I would bring shame on my family.

Q "Is shame you fall down nobody push SR-6 ▶ you," said my mother.

During my first tournament my mother sat with me in the front row as I waited for my turn. I frequently bounced my legs to unstick them from the cold metal seat of the folding chair. When my name was called, I leapt up. My mother unwrapped something in her lap. It was her *chang*,[12] a small tablet of red jade which held the sun's fire. "Is luck," she whispered, and tucked it into my dress pocket. I turned to my opponent, a fifteen-year-old boy from Oakland. He looked at me, wrinkling his nose.

As I began to play, the boy disappeared, the color ran out of the room, and I saw only my white pieces and his black ones waiting on the other side. A light wind began blowing past my ears. It whispered secrets only I could hear.

"Blow from the South," it murmured. "The wind leaves no trail." I saw a clear path, the traps to avoid. The crowd rustled. "Shhh! Shhh!" said the corners of the room. The wind blew stronger. "Throw sand from the East to distract him." The knight came forward ready for the sacrifice. The wind hissed, louder and louder. "Blow, blow, blow. He cannot see. He is blind now. Make him lean away from the wind so he is easier to knock down."

"Check," I said, as the wind roared with laughter. The wind died down to little puffs, my own breath.

My mother placed my first trophy next to a new plastic chess set that the neighborhood Tao society[13] had given to me. As she wiped each piece with a soft cloth, she said, "Next time win more, lose less."

"Ma, it's not how many pieces you lose," I said. "Sometimes you need to lose pieces to get ahead."

"Better to lose less, see if you really need."

At the next tournament, I won again, but it was my mother who wore the triumphant grin. R

"Lost eight pieces this time. Last time was eleven. What I tell you? Better off lose less!" I was annoyed, but I couldn't say anything.

12. ***chang*** *Chinese:* an object thought to bring good luck to its holder.

13. ***Tao Society:*** a society based on religious beliefs that advocate simplicity and selflessness.

Words to Know and Use

humility (hyo͞o mil' ə tē) *n.* the absence of vanity

373

O. Literary Element: **CHARACTER MOTIVATION** Ask students what motivates Mrs. Jong's comment. *(Possible responses: proper Chinese humility; false humility that is really pride)*

P. Historical Sidelight The first chess tournaments were held in the 18th and 19th centuries, as prominent players developed schools and followers. The first international chess tournament, held in London in 1851, was won by a German. Six years later, the first American chess genius, Paul Morphy, proceeded to defeat most of Europe's major players. Recent world tournament winners include Russian Boris Spassky (1969–72), American Bobby Fischer (1972–75), and Russian Anatoli Karpov.

Q. LEP: Dialect Ask students to clarify Mrs. Jong's response by restating it in their own words. *(It's a shame to lose only if you haven't tried.)*

R. Literary Element: **IRONY** Have students explain the irony in Mrs. Jong's comments. *(Possible response: She does not understand that the number of pieces a player loses is no indication of the success of the game; this parallels the irony of her trying to teach Waverly to be successful in America while still playing by Chinese "rules" of obedience and family pride.)*

Professional Notebook

There is one other kind of borrowing, beyond genre, topic, and technique, that I haven't touched on. . . . It is the way literature permeates the lives of kids who write and read. They borrow from their reading not just for their writing; the ways they walk, talk, and look at the world are subtly altered. Literature seeps into their waking hours—and their sleeping hours, too. I laughed when I read Jane's latest letter to me:

". . . I looked up and saw my friend Hillary Smith. She was a ghost. I was really scared now. So I ran into a room that had candles all around it. . . . Over in the corner was a rocking chair. The chair was the very one Mrs. Tomgallon's ancestor died in. It started to give me the creeps because I was going to have to sleep in that room. . . . As I blew the candles out, the windows were rattling, the bed was shaking, and . . .

'Jane! Get up! Time to go to school!' It was my mother. Ms. Atwell, I walked into my book.

In the Middle **BY NANCIE ATWELL**

Art Note
From Metamorphosis III exemplifies the graphic sleight-of-hand for which M.C. Escher (1898–1972) is so well known. *Metamorphose* means "to become transformed." Viewed from right to left, the words become a grid, which turns into a chessboard—and the pieces suggest a castle, which then devolves into geometric shapes and, finally, into organic ones. *Describe the difference when the print is viewed from left to right.*

S. Historical Sidelight In 1914 a major tournament was held in St. Petersburg (now called Leningrad), Russia. At the end of the tournament, Czar Nicholas II created the title of "grand master of chess" and awarded it to the five finalists. Today, many serious chess players gather points toward grand master status by competing in local, regional, and national chess tournaments.

T. Literary Element: SENSORY DETAILS
Ask students to isolate details from this passage that appeal to the senses of sound, sight, and smell. *(Sound—"echoed with phlegmy coughs," "squeaky rubber knobs . . . sliding across freshly waxed wooden floors"; Sight—"freshly waxed wooden floors," "sweaty brow"; Smell—"malodorous suit")*

METAMORPHOSIS (detail) 1967–68 M. C. Escher © 1990 M. C. Escher heirs/Cordon Art, Baarn, Holland.

I attended more tournaments, each one farther away from home. I won all games, in all divisions. The Chinese bakery downstairs from our flat displayed my growing collection of trophies in its window, amidst the dust-covered cakes that were never picked up. The day after I won an important regional tournament, the window encased a fresh sheet cake with whipped-cream frosting and red script saying, "Congratulations, Waverly Jong, Chinatown Chess Champion." Soon after that, a flower shop, headstone engraver, and funeral parlor offered to sponsor me in national tournaments. That's when my mother decided I no longer had to do the dishes. Winston and Vincent had to do my chores.

"Why does she get to play and we do all the work?" complained Vincent.

"Is new American rules," said my mother. "Meimei play, squeeze all her brains out for win chess. You play, worth squeeze towel."

S By my ninth birthday, I was a national chess champion. I was still some 429 points away from grandmaster status, but I was touted as the Great American Hope, a child prodigy and a girl to boot. They ran a photo of me in *Life* magazine next to a quote in which Bobby Fischer[14] said, "There will never be a woman grandmaster." "Your move, Bobby," said the caption.

The day they took the magazine picture I wore neatly plaited braids clipped with plastic barrettes trimmed with rhinestones. I was playing in a large high school auditorium that echoed with phlegmy[15] coughs and the squeaky rubber knobs of chair legs sliding across freshly waxed wooden floors. Seated across from me was an American man, about the same age as Lau Po, maybe fifty. I remember that his sweaty brow seemed to weep at my every move. He wore a dark, malodorous[16] suit. One of his pockets was stuffed with a great white kerchief on which he wiped his palm before sweeping his hand over the chosen chess piece with a great flourish. T

In my crisp pink-and-white dress with scratchy lace at the neck, one of two my mother had sewn for these special occasions, I would clasp my hands under my chin, the delicate points of my elbows poised lightly on the table in the manner my mother had shown me for posing for the press. I would swing my patent leather shoes back and forth like an impatient child riding on a school bus. Then I would pause,

14. **Bobby Fischer:** World Chess Champion from 1972 to 1975.
15. **phlegmy** (flem′ ē): characterized by a mucous discharge from the throat, as during a cold.
16. **malodorous:** having a bad smell.

Words to Know and Use
prodigy (präd′ ə jē) *n.* a person, particularly a child, with awe-inspiring talent

DATA BANK

Recalling Mrs. Jong's pride in her Chinese ancestry, students might be interested in knowing that Europeans take credit for an invention first discovered by the Chinese. In Europe, the major breakthrough in the history of printing was Johann Guttenberg's invention of movable type, the creation of a stamp for each letter so the letters could be assembled to print a page. Guttenberg, who lived from circa 1400 to 1468, is best known for his most famous printed book, the so-called Guttenberg Bible.

Although Guttenberg is given the credit for inventing movable type and thus making books commonly available, the process was already known in China. However, it was seldom used there because of the large number of Chinese characters and the lack of a suitable ink.

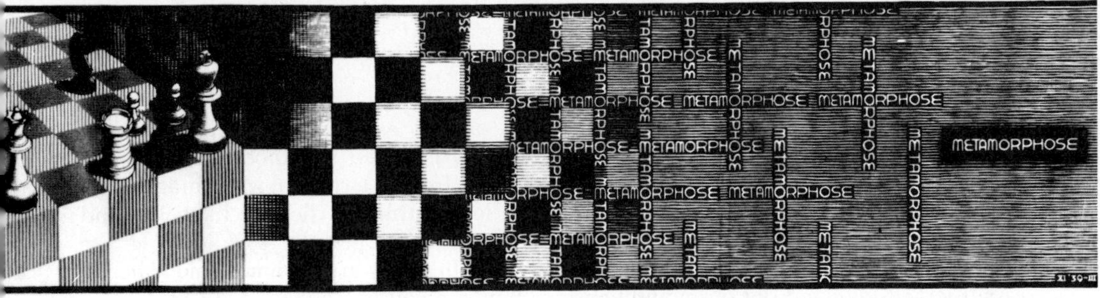

suck in my lips, twirl my chosen piece in midair as if undecided, and then firmly plant it in its new, threatening place, with a triumphant smile thrown back at my opponent for good measure.

I no longer played in the alley of Waverly Place. I never visited the playground where the pigeons and old men gathered. I went to school, then directly home to learn new chess secrets, cleverly concealed advantages, more escape routes.

But I found it difficult to concentrate at home. My mother had a habit of standing over me while I plotted out my games. I think she thought of herself as my protective ally. Her lips would be sealed tight, and after each move I made, a soft "Hmmm-mph" would escape from her nose.

U "Ma, I can't practice when you stand there like that," I said one day. She retreated to the kitchen and made loud noises with the pots and pans. When the crashing stopped, I could see out of the corner of my eye that she was standing in the doorway. "Hmmmph!" Only this one came out of her tight throat.

My parents made many concessions to allow me to practice. One time I complained that the bedroom I shared was so noisy that I couldn't think. Thereafter, my brothers slept in a bed in the living room facing the street. I said I couldn't finish my rice; my head didn't work right when my stomach was too full. I left the table with half-finished bowls and nobody complained. But there was one duty I couldn't avoid. I had to accompany my mother on Saturday market days when I had no tournament to play. My mother would proudly walk with me, visiting many shops, buying very little. "This my daughter Wave-ly Jong," she said to whoever looked her way. ◀SR-7

One day after we left a shop, I said under my breath, "I wish you wouldn't do that, telling everybody I'm your daughter." My mother stopped walking. Crowds of people with heavy bags pushed past us on the sidewalk, bumping into first one shoulder, then another.

"Aiii-ya. So shame be with mother?" She grasped my hand even tighter as she glared at me. V

I looked down. "It's not that, it's just so obvious. It's just so embarrassing."

"Embarrass you be my daughter?" Her voice was cracking with anger.

"That's not what I meant. That's not what I said."

"What you say?"

I knew it was a mistake to say anything more, but I heard my voice speaking. "Why do you have to use me to show off? If you

Words to Know and Use

concession (kən sesh′ən) *n.* a privilege granted

U. Literary Element: CHARACTER MOTIVATION Ask students to explain what motivates Mrs. Jong to make such a racket in the kitchen. *(Possible response: Angry and frustrated that Waverly has rejected her "help," she seeks to vent her feelings and perhaps attract some sympathy from her daughter.)*

V. LEP: Dialect Ask students to paraphrase Mrs. Jong's comment in their own words. *(Possible response: Oh, my. Are you so ashamed to be seen with your mother?)*

CULTURAL CONNECTION

The narrator stresses the extent to which her family requires certain responsibilities of her. Until she became a famous chess player, she had chores at home, and was obligated to eat all of her food. Before and after her fame, she is expected to keep from shaming her family (as shown in the incident of the boy whose mother punished him at the Christmas party) and in fact, to bring glory upon it (as shown in her parents' reactions to her fame). Ask students what they think of these family "rules," and have them compare and contrast the Jongs' expectations with those of families in their own cultures. Students of Chinese heritage might contribute their perspectives on how accurately Waverly's experience reflects their own sense of their culture.

W. Discussion Ask students how they think Waverly should have handled her feelings. *(Possible response: Some will support Waverly's rebellion; others might say that Waverly should have spoken to her mother privately about her feelings; others, that she should have swallowed her anger and allowed her mother her moment of reflected glory, considering Mrs. Jong's sacrifices.)*

X. LEP: Dialect Have students paraphrase these comments. *(Possible response: "We are not concerned with this girl. This girl has no importance for us.")*

Y. Literary Element: THEME Ask students why Waverly sees her mother as her opponent. *(Possible response: Waverly is fighting against her mother for independence. She sees her as an invincible adversary.)*

Check Test

1. Where does Waverly live? *(in San Francisco's Chinatown)*
2. Who receives the chess set as a Christmas gift? *(Waverly's brother)*
3. Who is Lau Po? *(He is an elderly man who teaches Waverly chess strategies.)*
4. Why does Waverly hate to go shopping on Saturdays with her mother? *(because Mrs. Jong introduces her to everyone)*
5. What is Waverly doing at the end of the story? *(planning what she will do next or pondering her next move)*

Encouraging Independent Reading

"The Good Deed," a short story by Pearl S. Buck
"Spelling Bee," a short story by Laurene Chambers Chinn
The Woman Warrior, an autobiography by Maxine Hong Kingston
The Joy Luck Club, a novel by Amy Tan

W SR-8 ▶ want to show off, then why don't you learn to play chess."

My mother's eyes turned into dangerous black slits. She had no words for me, just sharp silence.

I felt the wind rushing around my hot ears. I jerked my hand out of my mother's tight grasp and spun around, knocking into an old woman. Her bag of groceries spilled to the ground.

"Aii-ya! Stupid girl!" my mother and the woman cried. Oranges and tin cans careened down the sidewalk. As my mother stooped to help the old woman pick up the escaping food, I took off.

I raced down the street, dashing between people, not looking back as my mother screamed shrilly, "Meimei! Meimei!" I fled down an alley, past dark, curtained shops and merchants washing the grime off their windows. I sped into the sunlight, into a large street crowded with tourists examining trinkets and souvenirs. I ducked into another dark alley, down another street, up another alley. I ran until it hurt and I realized I had nowhere to go, that I was not running from anything. The alleys contained no escape routes.

My breath came out like angry smoke. It was cold. I sat down on an upturned plastic pail next to a stack of empty boxes, cupping my chin with my hands, thinking hard. I imagined my mother, first walking briskly down one street or another looking for me, then giving up and returning home to await my arrival. After two hours, I stood up on
SR-9 ▶ creaking legs and slowly walked home.

The alley was quiet, and I could see the yellow lights shining from our flat like two tiger's eyes in the night. I climbed the sixteen steps to the door, advancing quietly up each so as not to make any warning sounds. I turned the knob; the door was locked. I heard a chair moving, quick steps, the locks turning—click! click! click!—and then the door opened.

"About time you got home," said Vincent. "Boy, are you in trouble."

He slid back to the dinner table. On a platter were the remains of a large fish, its fleshy head still connected to bones swimming upstream in vain escape. Standing there waiting for my punishment, I heard my mother speak in a dry voice.

"We not concerning this girl. This girl not have concerning for us." X

Nobody looked at me. Bone chopsticks clinked against the insides of bowls being emptied into hungry mouths.

I walked into my room, closed the door, and lay down on my bed. The room was dark, the ceiling filled with shadows from the dinnertime lights of neighboring flats.

In my head I saw a chessboard with sixty-four black and white squares. Opposite me was my opponent, two angry black slits. She wore a triumphant smile. "Strongest wind cannot be seen," she said. Y

Her black men advanced across the plane, slowly marching to each successive level as a single unit. My white pieces screamed as they scurried and fell off the board one by one. As her men drew closer to my edge, I felt myself growing light. I rose up into the air and flew out the window. Higher and higher, above the alley, over the tops of tiled roofs, where I was gathered up by the wind and pushed up toward the night sky until everything below me disappeared and
I was alone. ◀ SR-10

I closed my eyes and pondered my next move. ❧

Words to Know and Use	**successive** (sək ses' iv) *adj.* following one after another

376

REAL LIFE CONNECTIONS

Point out to students that Waverly gives up a great many things to excel at chess—leisure time, friendships, family interaction, for example. Do they think her sacrifices were worth it? In real life, do they think it is worth giving up the usual pleasure of childhood for the sake of excelling in something such as music or athletics? Why or why not?

Responding to Reading

First Impressions

1. What do you think Waverly's next move will be? Why? Write your prediction in your journal or on a piece of paper.

Second Thoughts

2. Why is Waverly able to become such an accomplished chess player?

   Think about
   - what she was like before learning chess
   - what special skills chess requires
   - the help and support she receives from her mother and others
   - how she reacts to challenges

3. What kind of person is Waverly's mother?

   Think about
   - what rules and lessons she teaches her children
   - her reaction to the used chess set
   - her relationship with Waverly

4. Why does Waverly get angry with her mother and run off?

5. Explain why, in the last paragraphs of the story, Waverly describes her relationship with her mother as a chess game.

6. Do you think Waverly is successful in proving herself? Explain.

Broader Connections

7. People who move to a new country may find themselves caught between two sets of rules—their own and those of their adopted country. Waverly's mother tells her daughter to follow the American rules. What do you think she means by this and why might immigrants find these rules difficult to follow?

Literary Concept: Character Motivation

Character motivation refers to the reasons for the behavior of people in a story. Readers are not likely to find a story believable if they cannot see the motivation behind the characters' actions. Review this story and give some reasons to explain the behavior of Waverly and her mother.

Concept Review: Sensory Details Throughout the early parts of this story, Amy Tan brings alive the market and the alley with sensory details. Write down what stands out most vividly in these early scenes.

Student Response

Responding to Reading

These questions are open-ended with no "right" or "wrong" answers. However, responses must be supported with information from the selection. Possible answers follow:

1. Any response based on the story is valid.

2. Possible answers: Waverly's curiosity and intelligence; her love of strategy, sharpened by her dealings with her mother; the support of her mother, family, and community; her rebellious desire to succeed at any challenge.

3. Some students may say that Waverly's mother is caring and loving, trying to teach her children how to succeed in a hostile environment. Others may say she is ruthless and ambitious, demanding that Waverly succeed to bring her glory. Other students may note that she is proud, refusing to accept charity but also refusing to behave badly in public.

4. Some students may say Waverly runs off because she feels like an object whom her mother possesses and resents sharing her triumph with her mother. Others may say she is embarrassed at her outburst.

5. Some students may say she sees every relationship as a combat. Others may note that she sees that both activities require strategy, winning, and losing or that she feels outclassed by a master strategist, her mother.

6. Possible responses: Yes—she has succeeded at chess. No—she gives up something she loves and is good at to spite her mother, from whom she is not yet independent.

7. Some students may say she means that Waverly should succeed at activities that Americans value and understand what Americans require so that they can't claim she is falling short. Such rules may be difficult because they conflict with an immigrant's own culture, impulses, and support systems; "winning" at these rules may feel like "losing" oneself or one's culture.

Literary Concept—Character Motivation
Possible motivations: Waverly—rebelliousness, need for independence and own identity, wish to work out an American identity as opposed to her family's Chinese ways, desire for fame; Mother—protectiveness, fear of the new country, desire to preserve Chinese heritage, pride, placing high value on community respect, wish to succeed in the new country, wish to seek glory through children, wish to help children do better than she has done. Refer to annotation D, F, J, O, and U.

Concept Review—Sensory Details *Responses will vary; possible details—soup full of mysterious things; smells of red beans, sesame balls, and chicken crescents; people cracking watermelon seeds and scattering the husks; dark, mysterious alley; images of herbs in Old Li's shop; gold invitations and red banners; fish and turtles crammed in slimy green tank; bloody white smocks; crates and boxes of dead and live seafood. Refer to annotations A and T.*

Writing Options

The Writing Options are designed to meet varied student interests and abilities. Have each student choose one writing activity to complete. You may wish to guide some students to an option that requires less writing.

Journal Update Have students review their journal entries and add more details in light of their experience of reading the story. Ask them in particular to focus on the idea of "rules of the game," and new thoughts they have on this idea after reading the selection.

Vocabulary Practice

1. replica
2. deftly
3. prodigy
4. etiquette
5. obscure
6. humility
7. benevolently
8. adversary
9. concession
10. successive

Writing Options

1. "Wise guy, he not go against wind," Waverly's mother says. In a sentence or two, summarize what you think she means by this saying. Then write a true or made-up story that proves this statement either true or false.
2. Think back to your answer for First Impressions, and write a brief summary of the next chapter of Waverly's life.
3. Write a definition of the word *winner* based on Waverly's story.
4. Recall what you wrote in Examine What You Know and explain what playing chess teaches Waverly about life. To do this, describe another occupation in which she might be successful using the skills she gains in this story.

Vocabulary Practice

Exercise Write the word from the list that is most clearly related to the situation conveyed in the sentence.

1. Winston's present was a copy of a World War II submarine.
2. The Chinese butcher skillfully gutted the fish.
3. Everyone was amazed that a young girl could demonstrate such brilliance at chess.
4. Waverly learned that throwing chess pieces was bad manners.
5. The weaknesses of a move were no longer hidden to Waverly's observant eye.
6. Modestly, Waverly told others that she won because of luck.
7. The old man smiled kindly as he helped her learn the game.
8. Waverly faced a challenging opponent in each tournament.
9. Mrs. Jong granted Waverly many favors so that she had time to practice her game.
10. Each match became more difficult than the previous one.

Words to Know and Use

adversary
benevolently
concession
deftly
etiquette
humility
obscure
prodigy
replica
successive

Options for Learning

1 • A Chinatown Scene Using the author's vivid details for inspiration, and any art books you may find depicting San Francisco's Chinatown, draw one of the street scenes from the story. Begin by using the sensory imagery that Amy Tan uses to describe the scenes, but add some of your own details.

2 • Interview the Champion Role-play a press conference held for Waverly after she wins the Junior World Chess Championship. Along with Waverly herself, you should have several reporters and Bobby Fischer or some other chess champion on hand. Make sure her mother is in the audience in case Waverly needs help.

3 • "How to . . ." Write a how-to paper on chess or some other game that you know. Briefly describe the rules for playing the game. Explain *your* rules and strategies for winning.

4 • For Mrs. Jong Design a Mother's Day card that Waverly might send her mother. This card should show Waverly's appreciation for her mother's support and reveal a little of Waverly's unique personality.

FACT FINDER

How many people of Chinese origin live in the United States?

Amy Tan
1952–

While this story is not autobiographical, it does reflect parts of Amy Tan's own life. She was born in Oakland, California, two and a half years after her parents moved from China. Like Waverly in "Rules of the Game," Tan grew up much more attuned to American ways than her parents were. "When I was growing up, I blamed everything on the fact that my mother was Chinese while I thought of myself as totally American," says Tan. Although she did not become the neurosurgeon or concert pianist her parents had hoped for, Tan has become a successful author. Her novel *The Joy Luck Club,* of which "Rules of the Game" is a chapter, was on the bestseller list for many months. Tan has also returned to China to meet her many relatives there and to gather ideas for more stories. Her husband is an Italian American. "We have a lot of humorous arguments about whether ravioli is a version of the Chinese dumpling or the reverse," Tan quips.

Cross-Curricular Options

Students may supplement their reading of the selection with the following research projects, which may be done individually, in pairs, or in groups.

History: Research the history of Chinese immigration to America, beginning with the exodus of Chinese to America in 1848. Consider such factors as why the Chinese came to America, where they settled, and how they enriched American culture.

Social Studies: Report on the status of the most recent Chinese immigrants to America. Consider for example job opportunities, pay rates, language problems, and Chinese self-help organizations.

Art: Find pictures or actual samples of different chess sets, including those made by master artisans in such materials as wood, ivory, precious metals, crystal, and china, as well as wooden, plastic, and electronic sets.

Home Economics: Prepare elements of a Chinese meal. Provide recipes as well as food to share with classmates.

Options for Learning

These activities suit a variety of learning styles and modes of expression. Allow students to review the options and then choose the one they wish to do. Many are excellent collaborative learning projects.

1. A Chinatown Scene Students may want to obtain brochures on Chinatown in New York or San Francisco from a local travel agency.

2. Interview the Champion To obtain ideas, have students watch a press conference on television.

3. "How To . . ." Have students first list the steps in their process analysis.

4. For Mrs. Jong Students might look at cards in a local drugstore or card shop to get ideas.

Fact Finder

Currently, the Chinese constitute one percent of the nation's foreign-stock population, with an estimated 500,000 Chinese Americans in America (third generation and beyond). Students can find this information in an almanac.

Additional Information About the Author

Amy Tan was born in Oakland, two years after her parents emigrated from China to the United States. Her parent's ambition for Tan was that she would be a neurosurgeon and concert pianist on the side. Instead, she became a consultant to programs for disabled children. She did not become a professional writer until later. She made her first visit to China in 1987. Describing her feelings, Tan has said: "As soon as my feet touched China, I became Chinese."

Closure

As with other stories in this subunit, "Rules of the Game" urges students to examine who wins in a conflict. In this story, Waverly Jong must decide who wins when she gives up something she loves to spite her mother. Suggest that students review her motivation, then go on to examine the motivations of characters who behave similarly in other literary works, movies, and television shows.

Objectives

- To understand and analyze two contemporary poems
- To recognize the importance of word choice in poetry
- To apply the rules of punctuation to poetry
- To review personification
- To express understanding of the works through a choice of writing forms, including a poem and a radio broadcast

Prereading/Motivation

Examine What You Know

Discussion Prompts: Do you know about basketball from playing the game, seeing it live or on TV, or hearing it broadcast on the radio? What words first come to mind when you think of basketball? What aspects of basketball might explain its popularity?

Expand Your Knowledge

Discussion Prompts: Which of these terms are commonly used in daily life? Are their usual meanings and their meanings in basketball the same or different? Explain your answer.

Additional Background: Basketball was invented in 1891 by Canadian James Naismith, then a teacher, who was seeking a vigorous game suitable for playing indoors during the winter. The first teams had nine players, and the goals were wooden peach baskets nailed to the walls. The game spread rapidly throughout Canada and America. During World War I, servicemen popularized the sport in many other countries.

Enrich Your Reading

You may wish to have partners read the poems aloud to each other, carefully following the punctuation as they read.

Thematic Link—Who Wins?
These poems explore the nature of winning and its potential legacy.

e x p l o r e

Poetry

Fast Break

In Memory of Dennis Turner, 1946–1984

EDWARD HIRSCH

Ex-Basketball Player

JOHN UPDIKE

Examine What You Know (Prior Knowledge)

You are about to read two poems about basketball. One captures an exciting moment in a game; the other describes a former star. Before you read these poems, list ten things about the game of basketball. Think about rules, players, equipment, and styles of play, as well as emotions and other associations you have to the game.

Expand Your Knowledge (Building Background)

Like most sports, basketball has its own specialized vocabulary, or jargon. To better understand these two poems, review the definitions of the basketball terms below.

fast break—a play in which one team rushes down the court before the other team has assembled its defenders
hook shot—a one-handed shot in which a player brings the ball over the head, tossing the ball toward the basket
rim—the metal hoop that holds the net
center—the player, often the tallest on a team, who generally stays in the middle at each end of the court
boxes out—blocks out
outlet—a player who runs down the court ahead of the other players to set up a play
guard—the player who normally brings the ball down the court
dribble—to bounce the ball on the court
forward—a player who usually takes a front position on the court
bucketed—scored

Enrich Your Reading (Reading Skill)

Punctuation To understand a poem, follow the same rules of punctuation that you would follow when reading prose. Add short pauses for commas and longer pauses for semicolons and periods. Notice the different effects that punctuation—or the lack of it—produces in these two poems.

■ *Biographies of the authors can be found on page 385.*

Journal Writing

Suggest these journal topics to students:

- Describe a typical basketball player. Include psychological as well as physical characteristics.
- How would you explain the appeal of basketball to those who do not follow the game?
- How is basketball similar to and different from other sports?

For other journal opportunities, refer students to Examine What You Know (above).

Additional Resources

UNIT THREE RESOURCE BOOK
Reader's Guidesheet, p. 33
Vocabulary Worksheet, p. 34
Selection in Check Test, p. 35
Selection Test, pp. 36–37

Collaborative Learning

Opportunities for collaborative learning appear throughout the lesson and include the teaching suggestions for Enrich Your Reading (at left, above).

Fast Break

In Memory of Dennis Turner, 1946–1984

EDWARD HIRSCH

A
B
C
D

A hook shot kisses the rim and
hangs there, helplessly, but doesn't drop,

and for once our gangly starting center
boxes out his man and times his jump

perfectly, gathering the orange leather
from the air like a cherished possession

and spinning around to throw a strike
to the outlet who is already shovelling

an underhand pass toward the other guard
scissoring past a flat-footed defender

who looks stunned and nailed to the floor
in the wrong direction, trying to catch sight

of a high, gliding dribble and a man
letting the play develop in front of him

in slow-motion, almost exactly
like a coach's drawing on the blackboard,

both forwards racing down the court
the way that forwards should, fanning out

and filling the lanes in tandem, moving
together as brothers passing the ball

Teaching Strategies

Support for Students of Limited English Proficiency

■ Use Reader's Guidesheet, p. 33.
Both poems contain examples of the specialized vocabulary inherent in the sport of basketball. You may wish to show a part of a videotape of a basketball game to supply a visual image of these terms.

Text Annotations

A. Reading Skill: ANALYZING Ask a volunteer to explain what happens in lines 1–6. *(The center—the tall middle player—blocks his opponent, executes a perfectly timed jump and catches the ball.)*

B. Literary Element: WORD CHOICE Ask students to describe their reaction to the word "scissoring." *(Possible responses: It sounds like the player is moving in a fast, zigzagging, or dangerous way.)*

C. LEP: Vocabulary Explain that coaches frequently draw pictures of the plays on the blackboard to help players understand their moves. Discuss the advantages of this method of learning and ask volunteers to explain how the word *slow-motion* relates to the play as well as the drawing. *(The play, like the drawing, unfolds slowly.)*

D. Literary Element: PUNCTUATION Ask a volunteer to read lines 19–22, pausing where appropriate. Ask why there isn't any punctuation between "them" and "without". *(Possible response: to mimic the fluidity of the pass and capture its rhythm.)*

E. Literary Element: THEME Ask students which player wins in this poem. *(Possible responses: the "power-forward" because he shoots for a basket; the two forwards because they pass the ball perfectly, the center because he boxed out his man, or the entire offensive team.)*

Responding to Reading

These questions are open-ended with no "right" or "wrong" answers. However, responses must be supported with information from the selection. Possible answers follow:

1. Almost any response related to the poem or basketball is valid.

2. Some students may say that a fast break involves speed and excitement for one team and confusion and a sense of slow motion or stop action for the other. Other students may say that a fast break involves five men working in unison, jumping, blocking, catching, dribbling, passing, and shooting with great skill and speed. Others may say a fast break involves elements of surprise, speed, and hours of practice.

3. Some students may say that the speaker expresses feelings of pleasure, excitement, and tension. Others may say that the speaker expresses feelings of anticipation.

Art Note

To illustrate the excitement and energy of basketball, artist LeRoy Neiman (1927–) has chosen to portray a leaping trio of players at a basket. Neiman has placed them in an almost balletic pose that shows both grace and power. In this serigraph, or silkscreen, the figures seem sketched, or hastily worked on the spot. *What features has Neiman exaggerated to indicate energy?*

D between them without a dribble, without
a single bounce hitting the hardwood

until the guard finally lunges out
and commits to the wrong man

E while the power-forward explodes past them
in a fury, taking the ball into the air

BASKETBALL 1972 LeRoy Neiman By permission of the artist.

Responding to Reading

First Impressions of "Fast Break"

1. What sensation did you get when you read this poem? Discuss your reaction with your classmates.

Second Thoughts on "Fast Break"

2. What are the elements of a fast break?

3. What feelings does the speaker express in this poem?

   Think about
   - the moment being described
   - the speaker's feelings about the team
   - the speaker's feelings about basketball in general

CRITIC'S CORNER

Punctuation: what is it, after all, but another way of cutting up time, creating or negating relationships, telling words when to take a rest, when to get on with their relentless stories, when to catch their breath?
KAREN ELIZABETH GORDON, *The Well-Tempered Sentence*

Ex-Basketball Player

JOHN UPDIKE

Pearl Avenue runs past the high-school lot,
Bends with the trolley tracks, and stops, cut off
Before it has a chance to go two blocks,
At Colonel McComsky Plaza. Berth's Garage
Is on the corner facing west, and there,
Most days, you'll find Flick Webb, who helps Berth out.

Flick stands tall among the idiot pumps—
Five on a side, the old bubble-head style,
Their rubber elbows hanging loose and low.
One's nostrils are two S's, and his eyes
An E and O. And one is squat, without
A head at all—more of a football type.

Once Flick played for the high-school team, the Wizards.
He was good: in fact, the best. In '46
He bucketed three hundred ninety points,
A county record still. The ball loved Flick.
I saw him rack up thirty-eight or forty
In one home game. His hands were like wild birds.

He never learned a trade, he just sells gas,
Checks oil, and changes flats. Once in a while,
As a gag, he dribbles an inner tube,
But most of us remember anyway.
His hands are fine and nervous on the lug wrench.
It makes no difference to the lug wrench, though.

Off work, he hangs around Mae's Luncheonette,
Grease-gray and kind of coiled, he plays pinball,
Sips lemon cokes, and smokes those thin cigars;
Flick seldom speaks to Mae, just sits and nods
Beyond her face toward bright applauding tiers
Of Necco Wafers, Nibs, and Juju Beads.

DATA BANK

The placement of a comma once saved a man's life. Czar Alexander III had signed a death warrant reading: "Pardon impossible, to be sent to Siberia." Being sent to Siberia was inevitably a death sentence. In this instance, however, Czarina Maria Fyodorovna saved the man by altering the message to read: "Pardon, impossible to be sent to Siberia."

Text Annotations

A. Literary Element: WORD CHOICE Ask students how the description of the cut-off road might relate to the title "Ex-Basketball Player." *(Possible response: The poem is about an "ex-player," so the cut-off road may relate to a cut-off playing career.)*

B. Literary Element: PERSONIFICATION Ask students to explain the comparison. *(Possible response: The gasoline pumps are being compared to people who are bubble-headed idiots, the pumps' rubber hoses are compared to "elbows hanging loose.")*

C. Reading Skill: CLARIFYING Ask students to evaluate Flick's performance in high school basketball. *(He was the best player ever; his 1946 record still stands.)*

D. Literary Element: THEME Ask students if they think Flick had choices to be a winner in life. *(Possible response: Some who see Flick as "bubble-headed" like the pumps will say he had no real choices; others may think he wasted his talents and opportunities.)*

E. LEP: Vocabulary Point out that Necco Wafers, Nibs, and Juju Beads are brands of candies. Flick's only audience now are the mute rows ("tiers") of candies. Ask students what feeling this imagery conveys. *(Possible responses: sad, lonely, heartbreaking)*

Check Test

1. What do the two forwards in "Fast Break" do with the ball? *(pass it back and forth between them)*

2. What does Flick Webb do for a living? *(sells gas, checks oil, changes flats)*

Encouraging Independent Reading

Basketball's Magnificent Bird: The Larry Bird Story, a biography by Frederick L. Corn
Lou Gehrig: Pride of the Yankees, a biography by Paul Gallico
"Foul Shot," a poem by Edwin A. Hoey
Basketball My Way, nonfiction by Nancy Lieberman and Harvey Frommer
"Casey at the Bat," a poem by Ernest Lawrence Thayer

Student Response

Responding to Reading

These questions are open-ended with no "right" or "wrong" answers. However, responses must be supported with information from the selection. Possible answers follow:

1. Almost any response based on the poem is valid.

2. Some students, citing Flick's county record, may say that he is a loser because he had the natural ability to go on to a career in semi-pro or pro ball and did not. Others may argue that Flick is a winner because he was a great high school star.

3. Possible responses: A basketball player's hands are like wild birds because they are strong, agile, quick, and often in motion; because the hands dribbling the ball move like the wings of a bird; because the hands, like wild birds, cannot be tamed.

4. Some students may say that the last two lines are ironic because Flick has gone from an audience of cheering people to one of mute candies; others, that the word "applauding" conveys irony.

5. Some may say that Hirsch rarely uses punctuation at the end of the lines in "Fast Break" to convey the flow and excitement of the game; others, that Updike uses frequent commas and periods at the end of lines to mirror the cutting off of Flick's success.

6. Some may see a hopeful message in "Fast Break"; others may see "Ex-Basketball Player" as despairing.

Writing Options

The Writing Options are designed to meet varied student interests and abilities. Have each student choose one writing activity to complete. You may wish to guide some students to an option that requires less writing.

Journal Update Suggest that students review their journal entries and add any new insights they have about basketball from the reading of the poems.

e x p l a i n

Responding to Reading

First Impressions of "Ex-Basketball Player"

1. What primary image do you receive from this poem?

Second Thoughts on "Ex-Basketball Player"

2. Is Flick Webb a winner or a loser? Explain.

   Think about
   - Flick's natural talents
   - what choices Flick might have made after high school

3. Why would a basketball player's hands be compared to wild birds (line 18)?
4. What is ironic about the last two lines of the poem?

Comparing the Poems

5. Look again at the punctuation of these two poems. How do the different uses of punctuation affect the sound and meaning of each poem?
6. How do the themes or messages of these two poems differ?

Literary Concept: Word Choice

A poet chooses words very carefully. For example, in "Fast Break" the poet chooses to describe the center as "gangly." In the second poem, the poet describes Flick as "grease-gray and kind of coiled." What reactions do you have to these particular word choices? What other interesting word choices stand out for you?

Concept Review: Personification These two poems contain figures of speech that give objects human qualities. For example, each gas pump in "Ex-Basketball Player" is described as having a "bubble-head" with "rubber elbows hanging loose and low." What other examples of personification can you find in the poems?

Writing Options

1. Write a poem about a sports activity. Select a familiar image or scene and describe it from a player's point of view.
2. Rewrite the events in "Fast Break" as if a radio announcer were describing them live. Give names to the players and set the game in a real place.

Literary Concept—Word Choice

Possible responses: Students may think "gangly" appropriate for describing a center because a center must be tall to jump high enough to tap the ball. They may suggest that "grease-gray" is a good description for a broken man who pumps gas; that "coiled" may suggest he is hunched up and turned inward or angry and ready to spring or hunched over in the way some tall people are. Have students explain other interesting word choices.

Concept Review: Personification *Examples include: "Fast Break": "A hook shot kisses the rim and hangs there, helplessly". "Ex-Basketball Player": "Pearl Avenue runs . . . Bends . . . cut off/Before it has a chance to go two blocks,"; "the idiot pumps" described throughout the second stanza; the lug wrench; the "bright, applauding tiers" of candies.*

Edward Hirsch
1950–

Edward Hirsch's writing reflects two important influences in his life—his time spent in urban settings, principally Chicago and Detroit, and his inability to sleep. Hirsch's poetry often reflects urban environments, and he has found "that late at night is not only a good time for writing and thinking but also for setting poems." Such late-night work has brought him numerous awards for poetry. Hirsch has this to say about his writing, Hirsch says, "I want to write poems that are imaginative, astonishing, playful, mysterious, and extreme."

John Updike
1932–

John Updike is one of America's most prolific and highly regarded writers. After an unsuccessful attempt at a career in art and a brief but highly successful career as a staff writer for *The New Yorker* magazine, Updike moved to a small Massachusetts town. Since 1958 he has produced twenty-five volumes of fiction, poetry, and criticism. Many of his characters are like Flick Webb—ordinary people doing ordinary things. As Updike states, "The idea of a hero is aristocratic. Now either nobody is a hero or everyone is. I vote for everyone."

Additional Information About the Authors

Edward Hirsch Hirsch was born in Chicago, Illinois, and educated at Grinnell College and the University of Pennsylvania. In addition to writing, he has enjoyed a long career as a teacher, most recently as an associate professor of English at the University of Houston in Texas. Critic Carolyn Kizer praised Hirsch's poetry in a review in the *Washington Post Book World*, claiming that his "great strength lies in his descriptive powers." Writing in *Poetry* magazine, Peter Stitt claimed that as Hirsch "learns to administer with lighter touch his considerable linguistic fertility, he will surely grow into one of the important writers of our age."

John Updike Updike was born in Reading, Pennsylvania, an only child. After graduating with honors from Harvard University, he studied art in England for a year. Eventually he settled in Massachusetts to devote himself full time to writing. He has been called the most significant creator of "middleness" in American writing since William Dean Howells, devoting himself to describing people like Flick Webb.

Closure

Suggest that students form their own ideas about the importance of winning and losing in sports. Ask them to think about whether it is the playing of the game or winning it that matters most to them as players or as spectators.

Objectives

- To understand and analyze autobiographical writing
- To explore the author's purpose
- To express understanding of the work through a choice of writing forms, including a scouting report and diary entries

Prereading/Motivation

Examine What You Know

Discussion Prompts: What psychological traits might Olympic champions need to succeed? What do you consider the most important quality or skill that Olympic athletes share? What distinguishes champions from those who almost win?

Expand Your Knowledge

Why do you think Wilma Rudolph decided to become a runner? In what ways might her family have helped her to succeed? Do you think she faced any special pressures as a woman athlete? Explain your answer.

Additional Background: Wilma Rudolph's triumph was the first time in the history of the Olympic Games that an American woman won three gold medals in running. When she returned home, Americans went wild over their newest heroine, rewarding her with banquets, awards, and adoration. Europeans as well praised her accomplishments, and throngs of admirers jostled just to catch a glimpse of her. More than any other athlete, Rudolph is credited with attracting women to competitive track. Noted one contemporary, "Wilma's accomplishments opened up the real door for women in track because of her grace and beauty. People saw her as beauty in motion."

Thematic Link—Who Wins?

In this story, Wilma Rudolph learns that the secret of winning is learning from your losses.

explore

Autobiography

Wilma

WILMA RUDOLPH

Examine What You Know (Prior Knowledge)

What personal qualities and skills do you think it takes to become an Olympic athlete? Consider running, swimming, skiing, boxing, gymnastics, and other sports included in the Olympics. Discuss with your classmates the qualities and abilities that champions in these sports share. Then compare your ideas with what you learn about Wilma Rudolph.

Expand Your Knowledge (Building Background)

This selection is taken from the autobiography of Wilma Rudolph, one of America's great track champions. In 1956, at age sixteen, Rudolph won a bronze medal at the Olympics. Four years later, she won three gold medals. In 1961 she held the world records in the one-hundred-meter and two-hundred-meter races.

These are remarkable achievements for a girl who could not walk until she was eight years old and who required a special shoe until she was eleven. Yet because of her inner drive, her natural talents, and her devoted family, "Skeeter" Rudolph overcame her handicap to become one of America's greatest runners.

Write Before You Read (Journal Writing)

Think about something you have—either a possession or a talent—that you have worked very hard to acquire or develop. Briefly explain why you wanted this possession or skill and what kept you from giving up in your pursuit of it. How did you feel once you had achieved your goal?

A biography of the author can be found in the Reader's Handbook.

Additional Journal Writing

In this excerpt from her autobiography, Wilma Rudolph explains an important lesson she learned that taught her how to be a winner. Suggest these additional journal topics to students:

- What lesson have you learned that you would like to teach to someone else?
- What athletic aspirations have you ever had? Why?

For other journal opportunities, refer students to Real Life Connections (p. T–389).

Additional Resources

UNIT THREE RESOURCE BOOK

Reader's Guidesheet, p. 38
Vocabulary Worksheet, p. 39
Selection Check Tests, p. 40
Selection Test, pp. 41–42

Collaborative Learning

Opportunities for collaborative learning appear throughout the lesson and include Real Life Connections on page T–389.

Wilma

WILMA RUDOLPH

A So, it's 1956, and I'm a fifteen-year-old high school sophomore, and my life has never been better. I couldn't remember being happier. School was fun then. I remember the television show *American Bandstand* was very big with the kids, and once a week somebody would come into the school with a bunch of records and we'd have our own *American Bandstand* show after school. They would B give out records to kids who won dance contests doing the latest dances, and I even won a couple myself. All the girls were wearing long, tight skirts, the ones that ended just below the knees, and bobby socks and padded bras. They wore chains around their necks with their boyfriends' rings on them, and if you were going steady with an athlete, the girl wore the guy's letter sweaters or their team jackets. Little Richard[1] was big, and Chuck Berry[2] was big, but truthfully, Elvis Presley had no effect whatsoever. Burt High School was all black, and we just didn't have any kids in the school C who identified with Elvis Presley. The black kids sort of knew that he was just a white guy singing black music, but no black kids had motorcycles or leather jackets, probably because they didn't have the money to buy them.

We had all sorts of little special groups in the school but none that could be described D as being like white greasers. One group was the dressers, the kids who came from fairly affluent homes and who showed it off by wearing the best clothes all the time, even to the point where some of the guys in this group came to school wearing suits and ties. The next group was the regulars, the kids who were looked upon as being regular kids, nothing special, just everyday happy kids. Athletes were another group, and they usually stuck with other athletes. The funniest group was the "process" guys. They would go to barber shops and get their hair straightened, and everybody would talk about how the barbers used lye[3] to straighten out their hair. Then they would slick back the straightened hair, and this slick look became known as the process look. The guys thought it gave them a worldly image, the image of being real slick dudes who hung around in nightclubs and traveled with the fastest company. E But most of them did just the opposite; they traveled with other process guys only. ◄ SR-1

My whole life at the time revolved around basketball and my family. Robert was my boyfriend; we went out on dates, and when there was nothing else to do, we'd all go

1. **Little Richard:** Richard Penniman, who figured prominently in the development, during the 1950's, of rock and roll as the dominant form of American popular music.

2. **Chuck Berry:** a key figure in the development of rock music during the 1950's and the originator of the rock guitar style popularized by such groups as the Beatles and the Rolling Stones.

3. **lye:** a strong, alkaline solution.

Teaching Strategies

Support for Students of Limited English Proficiency

- Use Reader's Guidesheet, p. 38.
- "Wilma" contains vocabulary and slang phrases from the South such as "I paid them no mind" that may be far removed from the experiences of many urban students. Encourage them to figure out the meaning of unfamiliar words and phrases through context clues.
- Annotations D and G focus on unfamiliar vocabulary.

Text Annotations

A. Literary Element: POINT OF VIEW Explain that Wilma Rudolph is telling this story through her own eyes. Ask students to explore some of the advantages of the first-person point of view. *(Possible responses: a sense of immediacy and intimacy; a feeling of identification since there is no intervening narrator)*

B. Critical Thinking: ANALYZING Ask students to analyze what qualities would make Wilma a good dancer. *(Possible responses: grace, suppleness, athletic ability, keen sense of beat and music)*

C. Literary Element: SETTING Based on details provided here, have students describe the setting. *(mid-fifties, an all-black school in the deep South)*

D. LEP: Vocabulary Explain that *greasers* were so named because they slicked back their hair with greasy pomades. In emulation of such figures as Elvis Presley and actor James Dean, they wore black leather motorcycle jackets, white t-shirts, and blue jeans.

E. Critical Thinking: EVALUATING Have students explain Wilma's attitude toward the "process" guys. *(Possible response: She regards them with amusement and gentle contempt.)*

Structured Reading for Less Proficient Students

These questions can help to guide students through the reading. Ask each question at the point of the selection where the SR number appears in the margin.

SR–1. Identify the social groups in Wilma's school. *("dressers," affluent students who dress well; "regulars," happy kids; athletes; "process" guys, boys who have straightened hair)* **Literal recall**

SR–2. Summarize the reasons for Wilma's happiness. *(She is involved in activities she enjoys; she has a loving family, friends and a boyfriend.* **Summarizing**

SR–3. What details suggest Wilma's love of running? *(She considers a future in track; she cuts classes to run, risking her father's wrath; she is the first out and last in at practice.)* **Literal recall**

SR–4. What did Wilma realize after losing? *(that she could not win on natural ability alone; that she was being tested as a person)* **Literal recall**

SR–5. What did Wilma learn about losing? *(If you can pick yourself up after defeat, you are going to be a champion.)* **Literal recall**

F. Literary Sidelight The coach from Austin Peay College was not the only one who saw Wilma's talent early on and encouraged her. At the Penn Relays one year, Jackie Robinson, the athlete who had broken the color barrier in baseball in 1947, told the then unknown young runner: ". . . don't let anything, or anybody, keep you from running. Keep running."

G. LEP: Vocabulary Explain that "cutting classes" means being absent from class without an excuse.

H. Reading Skill: INFERRING Ask students why Wilma might have thought that she would not get caught. *(Possible responses: Perhaps she honestly thought that her absence would go unnoticed. More likely, she believed that her teachers and principal would ignore her absences to allow her to run.)*

I. Critical Thinking: ANALYZING Ask students to analyze Wilma's feelings about the upcoming meet. *(Possible response: While she is very excited, she does not seem nervous at all.)*

J. Literary Sidelight Tuskegee Institute, in Alabama, is among America's most renowned professional and technical universities. Founded for black students in 1881, Tuskegee was headed by the famed black educator Booker T. Washington until his death in 1915. Tuskegee is also noted for its extensive archives devoted to black history; the George Washington Carver Museum; and an experimental natural sciences research center.

hang out at the local teenage club. Life SR-2 ▶ seemed so uncomplicated, and happy, then.

As soon as the basketball season ended, I had my track stuff on, and I was running. There was a kid in school everybody called Sundown; the reason he was called that was because he was so black. His real name was Edward. Anyway, he and I used to skip out of classes almost every day, and we'd sneak off across the street to the municipal stadium, and we'd throw our books over the big wall that surrounded the stadium. Then we'd climb the fence and run over to the track and do some running. If we heard any strange sounds, like somebody was coming, we'd run underneath the stands and hide.

Sometimes, when the college track team from Austin Peay College was using the stadium, the place would be filled with these white guys practicing. Sundown and I would show up out of the clear blue sky, and they would look and sort of blink and then go back about their business. The coach of the college team, this white guy, sort of knew that I was skipping out of classes to practice running; he would give me this little wink, like he knew what was F going on but like he also had a little bit of admiration for me because I was so in love with running. Whenever he talked to his team, I would sort of hang around on the fringes and listen, hoping to pick up a pointer or two for free. I think he noticed that, too, and when he saw me sort of hanging around, it always seemed he would start talking a little louder than before.

That taste of winning I had gotten the year before never left me. I was more serious about track now, thinking deep down inside that maybe I had a future in the sport G if I tried hard enough. So I thought nothing of cutting classes and going out to run. But one day I got a call to report to the principal's office. I went in, and he said, "Wilma, all of us here know just how important running track is to you. We all know it, and we are all hoping that you become a big success at it. But you can't keep cutting H classes and going out to run." I was, well, mortified;[4] the principal had found me out. He finally said that if I continued cutting classes, he would have to tell my father, and I knew what that meant. So I stopped. Even so, I was the first girl out there at practice and the last one to leave, I loved it so. We had some more of those playday-type meets early that season, and I kept on winning all the races I was in. I felt unbeatable. ◀ SR-3

Then came the big meet at Tuskegee, Alabama. It was the big meet of the year. Girls from all over the South were invited down there to run, and the competition was the best for high school kids. It was a whole weekend type of thing, and they had dances and other things planned for the kids when they weren't out running. Coach Gray was going to drive us all down there to I Tuskegee Institute, where the meet was held, and I remember we brought our very best dresses. We all piled into his car until there wasn't an inch of empty space in that car. Mrs. Allison, my old teacher, came with us; she was going to chaperon us at the big dance after the meet.

All the way down to Alabama, we talked and laughed and had a good time, and Coach Gray would tell us how tough the competition was going to be, especially the girls from Atlanta, Georgia, because they had a lot of black schools down there, and they had these track programs that ran the whole year because of the warm weather. When we got there, all of us were over- J whelmed, because that was the first college

4. **mortified:** humiliated.

Professional Notebook

Writing in Our Other Youth, *author Jerry Conrath provides suggestions for reaching discouraged learners: "Behavior that distracts is unacceptable. We preach about 'inappropriate' behavior in moralistic terms; we need to be more clear on what behavior is acceptable and helpful to learning, and what rules must be made to facilitate learning. Because we adults often are not clear on the purpose of school and reasons for rules and expectations, we often communicate to kids a very fuzzy sense of why things must be done. Why do we have school? To teach our kids to be participants, and not simply spectators, of their culture. Even discouraged kids know when they are with an adult who has thought that through. Then when they ask, 'Why do we have to do this?' they receive a rational answer. That shocks them, but they know they are in a serious, not frivolous, classroom."*

Rudolph sets a world record at the 1960 Olympic Games in Rome AP/Wide World Photos, Inc., New York.

campus any of us ever saw. We stayed in this big dorm, and I remember just before the first competition, I started getting this nervous feeling that would stay with me for the rest of my running career. Every time K before a race, I would get it, this horrible feeling in the pit of my stomach, a combination of nerves and not eating.

When we got to the track, these girls from Georgia really looked like runners, but I paid them no mind because, well, I was a L little cocky. I did think I could wipe them out because, after all, I had won every single race I had ever been in up to that point. So what happens? I got wiped out. It was the absolute worst experience of my life. I did not win a single race I ran in, nor did I qualify for anything. I was totally crushed. The girls from Georgia won everything. It was the first time I had ever tasted defeat in track, and it left me a total wreck. I was so despondent[5] that I refused to go to any of M the activities that were planned, including the big dance. I can't remember ever being so totally crushed by anything.

On the ride back, I sat in the car and didn't say a word to anybody, I just thought to myself about how much work was ahead of me and how I would like nothing better

5. **despondent:** hopeless.

Teaching Tip
To help students understand Wilma's horrible nervous feeling before the race, ask them to generate a list of adjectives that describe their feelings before an especially nerve-wracking event such as a competition, performance, major exam, or driving test. Compare their descriptions to Wilma's in this passage.

L. Reading Skill: PREDICTING Ask students to predict how Wilma will do in the meet and support their predictions with specific reasons from the essay. *(Possible responses: Some students might predict that Wilma will lose because she is nervous and cocky; others, that she will win because she has practiced constantly, is naturally talented, and has great desire and motivation to win.*

M. Critical Thinking: EVALUATING Discuss in what ways this crushing defeat might turn out to be an advantage for Wilma and in what ways it might be a disadvantage. *(Possible response: It might be an advantage because it would caution her against future overconfidence; it might be a disadvantage because it could crush her spirit and turn her away from track.)*

Real Life Connections

Point out to students how crushed Wilma Rudolph was by her unexpected defeat, yet she was able to turn her loss into something positive. Ask students what lessons they think could be learned from a personal defeat. In what ways might a defeat be even more valuable than a victory?

N. Reading Skill: UNDERSTANDING MAIN IDEA Ask what Wilma means when she says that "there was more to track than just running fast". *(Possible response: She means that track calls for training and such qualities as discipline, courage, determination, and maturity.)*

O. Critical Thinking: EVALUATING Ask students if they agree with the teachers' actions. *(Possible responses: Yes, because Wilma was so obviously talented and motivated that she should be given her chance to succeed; no, because her education should come before anything else.)*

P. Literary Element: AUTHOR'S PURPOSE Ask students what "tremendous effect" Wilma Rudolph might want this essay to have on her audience. *(Possible responses: to persuade her readers to learn from their mistakes; to express her opinions about a turning point in her life and career.)*

Q. Literary Element: THEME Ask students if they consider Wilma a winner or a loser. *(Most will agree that she is a winner because she did not let losing defeat her. Instead, she turned defeat into victory by overcoming her disappointment.)*

Check Test

1. What sport beside track does Wilma enjoy? *(basketball)*

2. How does Wilma find extra time to run? *(She skips classes)*

3. How many races does Wilma win at Tuskegee? *(none)*

4. What does Wilma learn from defeat? *(to try again)*

Encouraging Independent Reading

"Raymond's Run," a short story by Toni Cade Bambara

I Always Wanted to Be Somebody, an autobiography by Althea Gibson

Jesse: The Man Who Outran Hitler, an autobiography by Jesse Owens with Paul Niemark

"The Perfect Game," a short story by Sergio Ramírez

"April Showers," a short story by Edith Wharton

in the whole world than to come back to Tuskegee the next year and win everything. When I got home, my father knew immediately what had happened, and he didn't say anything. Every time I used to come home after a meet, I would rush into the house all excited and bubble over with, "I won . . . I won." This time I didn't say a word. I just walked in quietly, nodded to my father, who was sitting there, and went into my room and unpacked.

After so many easy victories, using natural ability alone, I got a false sense of being unbeatable. But losing to those girls from Georgia, who knew every trick in the book, that was sobering. It brought me back down to earth, and it made me realize that I couldn't do it on natural ability alone, that N there was more to track than just running fast. I also realized it was going to test me as a person—could I come back and win again SR-5 after being so totally crushed by a defeat?

When I went back to school, I knew I couldn't continue to cut classes to practice or else I'd be in big trouble. So I would fake sickness, tell the teacher that I didn't feel well and could I please go home? They would let me go, and then I would go over to the track and run. When that stopped working, when they realized that I looked pretty good for being sick all the time, I simply asked them point-blank, "Look, O could I cut this class today and go out and run?" Believe it or not, a lot of teachers said, "Okay, Wilma, go, but don't tell anybody."

I ran and ran and ran every day, and I acquired this sense of determination, this sense of spirit that I would never, never give up, no matter what else happened. P That day at Tuskegee had a tremendous effect on me inside. That's all I ever thought about. Some days I just wanted to go out and die. I just moped around and felt sorry for myself. Other days I'd go out to the track with fire in my eyes and imagine myself back at Tuskegee, beating them all. Losing as badly as I did had an impact on my personality. Winning all the time in track had given me confidence; I felt like a winner. But I didn't feel like a winner any more after Tuskegee. My confidence was shattered, and I was thinking the only way I could put it all together was to get back the next year and wipe them all out.

But looking back on it all, I realized somewhere along the line that to think that way wasn't necessarily right, that it was kind of extreme. I learned a very big lesson for the rest of my life as well. The lesson was, winning is great, sure, but if you are really going to do something in life, the secret is learning how to lose. Nobody goes undefeated all the time. Q If you can pick up after a crushing defeat and go on to win again, you are going to be a champion someday. But if losing destroys you, it's all over. You'll never be able to put it all back together again. SR-5

I did, almost right away. There were more playdays scheduled, and I won all the rest of the races I was in the rest of that season. But I never forgot Tuskegee. In fact, I was thinking that anybody who saw me lose so badly at the meet would write me off immediately. I was wrong. One day, right after the track season ended that year, Coach Gray came over to me and he said, "Wilma, Ed Temple, the referee who is the women's track coach at Tennessee State, is going to be coming down to Clarksville to talk with your mother and father."

"What about?" I asked.

"Wilma," he said, "I think he wants you to spend the summer with him at the college, learning the techniques of running." ❧

DATA BANK

Not long after the events described, Wilma Rudolph went on to achieve a stunning victory in the 1960 Olympics and inspire a generation of athletes.

The Olympics are an international athletic competition held every four years at a different location. Restricted to amateurs, the Olympics were begun in 1896 by French sportsman Baron Pierre de Coubertin, who had worked for years gathering the aid of various individuals and organizations to hold a competition for athletes of all nations. Athletes from thirteen nations attended the first Olympics, held at Athens, and competed in forty-two events.

Since then, there have been a number of important developments. One major change has been the notable increase of Olympic competition among women, no doubt due to athletes like Wilma Rudolph. In addition, the number of events open to competition has increased steadily, today including such sports as fencing, team handball, judo, and volleyball.

Responding to Reading

First Impressions

1. Would you want Wilma as a friend? Why or why not?

Second Thoughts

2. How does Wilma change by the end of the selection?

   Think about
   - how Wilma feels about her running before she races at Tuskegee
   - what happens at Tuskegee
   - what she learns from losing
   - what you know about her later career

3. Wilma says that "the secret is learning how to lose." What do you think she means?

4. Think back to the personal qualities and abilities of an Olympic athlete as you described them earlier. Compare and contrast your list and the qualities and abilities that Wilma possesses.

5. How is Wilma like or different from Waverly in the story "Rules of the Game"?

   Think about
   - what goals each person has
   - how each works to achieve her goals
   - what each learns from her achievements

Literary Concept: Author's Purpose

Authors write for four main purposes: to entertain, to inform, to express opinions, and to persuade. They may combine two or three purposes in one piece, but one purpose is usually the most important. For what purposes do you think Wilma Rudolph wrote this? Which of these purposes do you think was most important to her and why?

Writing Options

1. Imagine that you are a scout from Tennessee State. Write a scouting report about Wilma Rudolph. Assess her strengths and weaknesses and give your opinion of her potential.

2. Write three entries from Wilma's diary. First imagine it is a few days before the meet at Tuskegee and describe your feelings. Then describe the actual event and how you felt a few days afterwards.

Literary Concept—Author's Purpose

Possible responses: Students may say that Wilma Rudolph wrote this autobiographical excerpt to inform readers of her life and career, to express herself and her views about running and about life, to persuade people not to give up, but to pick themselves up and try again after a defeat. Some students may think that her most important purpose was to share the lesson she learned about losing and thus to inspire and persuade others to be winners in life.

Student Response

Responding to Reading

These questions are open-ended with no "right" or "wrong" answers. However, responses must be supported with information from the selection. Possible answers follow:

1. Almost any response is valid. Have students explain why they feel as they do.

2. Some students may say that Wilma changes when she comes to realize after her defeat at Tuskegee that the secret of winning is learning how to lose. Others might claim that Wilma learns, based on her feelings before and after Tuskegee, that she cannot be cocky. Based on what they learn about her career, still others may argue that Wilma sees she is exceptionally talented.

3. Possible responses: Wilma means that only by coping with defeat can people learn the psychological skills they need to win; that losing teaches people where they went wrong and how to do better the next time.

4. Some students may include such qualities as natural talent, determination, or stubbornness on their lists. Others may cite such qualities and abilities as a sense of humor or a cheerful, balanced temperament.

5. Some students may say that both characters are determined to win, hard-working and focused, and flexible enough to learn from their errors. Others might argue that while Wilma learns from her defeat, Waverly does not show any change in attitude toward her mother.

Writing Options

The Writing Options are designed to meet varied students interests and abilities. Have each student choose one writing activity to complete. You may wish to guide some students to an option that requires less writing.

Journal Update Have students review their journal entries for "Wilma." What similarities and differences do they see between their pursuit of goals and Wilma's?

Objectives

- To understand and analyze a contemporary short story
- To recognize the resolution of a short story
- To predict what will happen in a short story
- To review the building of suspense
- To express understanding of the work through a choice of writing forms, including narration, exposition, a moral and notes
- To recognize synonyms and antonyms

Prereading/Motivation

Examine What You Know

Discussion Prompts: What was peculiar about the behavior you are describing? How long did the peculiar behavior last? What ended the crush?

Expand Your Knowledge

Discussion Prompts: How might summer tourists be different from year-round residents? Why might some people adore fishing and others detest it? What kind of relationships could exist between tourists and year-round residents?

Additional Background: Tourism is second only to manufacturing in its importance to New Hampshire's economy. The state's lakes, mountains, and fine climate have made it a major tourist attraction since the early 19th century. Lake Winnipesaukee is among the leading tourist areas, and numerous other lakes and the Connecticut River valley also attract many visitors.

Enrich Your Reading

There are a number of places where students might make predictions. These include when the narrator invites Sheila out, when he notices his fishing equipment, and when he must decide to reel in the fish or cut his line.

> **Thematic Link—Who Wins?**
> In this story, the narrator wonders who wins when he chooses between conflicting feelings.

explore

Fiction

The Bass, the River, and Sheila Mant

W. D. WETHERELL

Examine What You Know (Prior Knowledge)

The narrator of "The Bass, the River, and Sheila Mant" tells of a time when he became infatuated with an older girl. Infatuation is a strong, sudden feeling of affection for someone else—a crush, in other words. People with crushes often behave in strange ways. In your journal, drawing on your own experiences or your observations, describe an example of peculiar behavior brought on by a crush. Then think about what you have written as you read the upcoming story.

Expand Your Knowledge (Building Background)

The story you are about to read takes place in the lake country of New Hampshire. The characters are modeled after tourists who travel there every summer from Boston, New York, and other urban areas to sail, relax, and enjoy nature. Many of the tourists fish, not just for bass, as the boy in the story does, but also for trout, salmon, pickerel, perch, whitefish, and bullheads. The popularity of fishing helps make tourism one of New Hampshire's largest industries.

Enrich Your Reading (Reading Skill)

Predicting The boy in the story you are about to read faces a difficult choice. In fact, much of this story focuses directly on his decision. As you read, you will find yourself asking, "What's he going to do now?" At the places in the story where you wonder this, make predictions about what will happen.

■ *A biography of the author can be found in the Reader's Handbook.*

Journal Writing

Suggest these journal topics to students:

- Describe an infatuation in your own words?
- Do you think that age makes a difference, or are people of any age equally likely to become infatuated?
- Describe a time when an infatuation caused you or a friend to act in a certain way.

For other journal opportunities, refer students to Examine What You Know (p. 392), Real-Life Connections (p. T–398), and Broader Connections (p. 399).

Additional Resources

UNIT THREE RESOURCE BOOK
Reader's Guidesheet, p. 43
Vocabulary Worksheet, p. 44
Selection and Vocabulary Check Tests, p. 45
Selection Test, pp. 46–47

Collaborative Learning

Opportunities for collaborative learning appear throughout the lesson.

The Bass, the River, and Sheila Mant

W. D. WETHERELL

A There was a summer in my life when the only creature that seemed lovelier to me than a largemouth bass was Sheila Mant. I was fourteen. The Mants had rented the cottage next to ours on the river; with their parties, their frantic games of softball, their constant comings and goings, they appeared to me denizens[1] of a brilliant existence. "Too noisy by half," my mother quickly decided, but I would have given anything to be invited to one of their parties, and when my parents went to bed I would sneak through the woods to their hedge and stare enchanted at the candlelit swirl of white dresses and bright, paisley skirts.

Sheila was the middle daughter—at seventeen, all but out of reach. She would spend her days sunbathing on a float my Uncle Sierbert had moored in their cove, and before July was over I had learned all her moods. If she lay flat on the diving board with her hand trailing idly in the water, she was pensive, not to be disturbed. On her side, her head propped up by her arm, she was observant, considering those around her with a look that seemed queenly and severe. Sitting up, arms tucked around her long, suntanned legs, she was approachable, but barely, and it was only in those glorious moments when she stretched herself prior to entering the water that her various suitors found the courage to come near. ◀SR-1

These were many. The Dartmouth heavyweight crew would scull[2] by her house on their way upriver, and I think all eight of them must have been in love with her at various times during the summer; the coxswain[3] would curse at them through his megaphone, but without effect—there was always a pause in their pace when they passed Sheila's float. I suppose to these jaded twenty-year-olds she seemed the incarnation of innocence and youth, while to me she appeared unutterably suave, the epitome of sophistication. I was on the swim team at school and to win her attention would do endless laps between my house and the Vermont shore, hoping she would notice the beauty of my flutter kick, the B

1. **denizens:** inhabitants.

2. **scull:** to move a boat by means of light oars mounted on each side of the craft. In this reference, the crew propels a light and narrow racing boat, each member rowing with a single oar.

3. **coxswain** (käk'sən): the person who calls out the rowing rhythm for a crew.

Words to Know and Use

incarnation (in' kär nā' shən) *n.* a person representing a particular concept
suave (swäv) *adj.* having a smooth manner
epitome (ē pit' ə mē') *n.* the ideal or essence of a particular quality

Teaching Strategies

Vocabulary Preview

These vocabulary words are defined at the bottom of the selection page on which they appear. You may wish to discuss them briefly before students begin reading.

aura a quality that surrounds a person
conspicuous easy to see
dubious hesitating
epitome the ideal
incarnation a person who represents a particular concept
overcompensate to make more than the necessary adjustment
suave having a smooth manner

Support for Students of Limited English Proficiency

- Use Readers' Guidesheet, p. 43
- "The Bass, the River, and Sheila Mant" contains examples of elevated diction, such as "jaded" and "unutterably," that students may find difficult to understand upon first reading. Encourage them to use context clues to help grasp the meaning of such unfamiliar words.
- Annotations B, H, and M focus on troublesome vocabulary.

Text Annotations

A. Literary Element: THEME Ask students to describe how the narrator feels about Sheila and what detail(s) led to their conclusion. *(Possible response: He is infatuated with her, as shown by the descriptions "lovelier to me" and "brilliant existence.")*

B. LEP: Vocabulary The words "jaded" and "unutterably" may be troublesome. Discuss them and have volunteers paraphrase the passage. *(Possible response: To these bored young men of twenty, she seemed to represent innocence and youth, while to me she seemed very smooth, the ideal of sophistication.)*

Structured Reading for Less Proficient Students

These questions can help to guide students through the reading. Ask each question at the point of the selection where the SR number appears in the margin.

SR–1. Why is the narrator so aware of Sheila's moods? *(Possible response: He considers her the loveliest creature alive; he watches her and wants to be near her.)* **Clarifying**

SR–2. Contrast the narrator's feelings with Sheila's feelings. *(The narrator is bashful and frightened; Sheila is unaware of him.)* **Compare and contrast**

SR–3. How does the narrator prepare for his date with Sheila? *(cleans and polishes his canoe)* **Literal recall**

SR–4. Why does the narrator want to be rid of his fishing equipment? *(because Sheila thinks fish are "boring" and "dumb" and more than anything else he wants to please her)* **Literal recall**

Continued on page 395

C. Reading Skill: INFERRING Ask students what they can infer from the fact that the narrator asks Sheila out in late August. *(Possible responses: It took him all summer to get up his nerve; it is his last chance.)*

D. Discussion Since Sheila's behavior indicates that she is not interested in the narrator, ask students why she might agree to go on a date with him. *(Possible responses: She is bored. She is using him to get to the dance.)*

Historical Sidelight People have fished since the Stone Age, using bones as hooks and vines as lines. Sportfishing began in the late 15th century when the prioress of an abbey published a book explaining how to make hooks, rods, and artificial lures. In 1653, Izaak Walton helped fishing become an art as well as a science in his book, *The Compleat Angler.* Sport fishing continues to enjoy great popularity today. Bass are among the most popular game fish because of their abundance and fighting ability.

E. Reading Skill: PREDICTING Ask students to predict what may happen with the rod and fishing line. *(Possible responses: The narrator may catch a fish or snag something else; the line may break; someone may be injured.)*

power of my crawl. Finishing, I would boost myself up onto our dock and glance casually over toward her, but she was never watching, and the miraculous day she was, I immediately climbed the diving board and did my best tuck and a half for her and continued diving until she had left and the sun went down and my longing was like a madness and I couldn't stop.

C It was late August by the time I got up the nerve to ask her out. The tortured will-I's, won't-I's, the agonized indecision over what to say, the false starts toward her house and embarrassed retreats—the details of these have been seared from my memory, and the only part I remember clearly is emerging from the woods toward dusk while they were playing softball on their lawn, as bashful and frightened as a unicorn.

Sheila was stationed halfway between first and second, well outside the infield. She didn't seem surprised to see me—as a matter of fact, she didn't seem to see me at all. SR-2

"If you're playing second base, you should move closer," I said.

She turned—I took the full brunt of her long red hair and well-spaced freckles.

"I'm playing outfield," she said, "I don't like the responsibility of having a base."

"Yeah, I can understand that," I said, though I couldn't. "There's a band in Dixford tomorrow night at nine. Want to go?"

One of her brothers sent the ball sailing over the left fielder's head; she stood and watched it disappear toward the river.

D "You have a car?" she said, without looking up.

I played my master stroke. "We'll go by canoe."

I spent all of the following day polishing it. I turned it upside down on our lawn and rubbed every inch with Brillo, hosing off the dirt, wiping it with chamois[4] until it gleamed as bright as aluminum ever gleamed. About five, I slid it into the water, arranging cushions near the bow so Sheila could lean on them if she was in one of her pensive moods, propping up my father's transistor radio by the middle thwart so we could have music when we came back. Automatically, without thinking about it, I mounted my Mitchell reel on my Pfleuger spinning rod and stuck it in the stern. SR-3

I say automatically, because I never went anywhere that summer without a fishing rod. When I wasn't swimming laps to impress Sheila, I was back in our driveway practicing casts, and when I wasn't practicing casts, I was tying the line to Tosca, our springer spaniel, to test the reel's drag, and when I wasn't doing any of those things, I was fishing the river for bass.

E Too nervous to sit at home, I got in the canoe early and started paddling in a huge circle that would get me to Sheila's dock around eight. As automatically as I brought along my rod, I tied on a big Rapala plug, let it down into the water, let out some line, and immediately forgot all about it.

It was already dark by the time I glided up to the Mants' dock. Even by day the river was quiet, most of the summer people preferring Sunapee or one of the other nearby lakes, and at night it was a solitude difficult to believe, a corridor of hidden life that ran between banks like a tunnel. Even the stars were part of it. They weren't as sharp anywhere else; they seemed to have chosen the river as a guide on their slow wheel toward morning, and in the course of the summer's fishing, I had learned all their names.

4. **chamois** (sham′ ē): soft leather used as a polishing cloth.

CULTURAL CONNECTION

To help students understand the gulf between summer tourists and year-round residents in a resort town, explore with them the differences between the two groups. You might want to begin by pointing out that people able to afford a summer at a lake resort town would be well off, underscoring your point with the narrator's perception of the Mants' "brilliant existence" described in the first paragraph of the story. The year-round residents, in contrast, would provide the essential services for the tourists and so might often be in a subordinate position. Relate this information to the comment the narrator's mother makes about the Mants' parties.

I was there ten minutes before Sheila appeared. I heard the slam of their screen door first, then saw her in the spotlight as she came slowly down the path. As beautiful as she was on the float, she was even lovelier now—her white dress went perfectly with her hair and complimented her figure even more than her swimsuit.

It was her face that bothered me. It had on its delightful fullness a very dubious expression.

"Look," she said. "I can get Dad's car."

"It's faster this way," I lied. "Parking's tense up there. Hey, it's safe. I won't tip it or anything."

F She let herself down reluctantly into the bow. I was glad she wasn't facing me. When her eyes were on me, I felt like diving in the river again from agony and joy.

I pried the canoe away from the dock and started paddling upstream. There was an extra paddle in the bow, but Sheila made no move to pick it up. She took her shoes off, and dangled her feet over the side.

Ten minutes went by.

G "What kind of band?" she said.

"It's sort of like folk music. You'll like it."

"Eric Caswell's going to be there. He strokes number four."[5]

"No kidding?" I said. I had no idea whom she meant.

"What's that sound?" she said, pointing toward shore.

"Bass. That splashing sound?"

"Over there."

"Yeah, bass. They come into the shallows at night to chase frogs and moths and things. Big largemouths. *Micropetrus salmonides*,"[6] I added, showing off.

"I think fishing's dumb," she said, making a face. "I mean, it's boring and all. Definitely dumb."

H Now I have spent a great deal of time in the years since wondering why Sheila Mant should come down so hard on fishing. Was her father a fisherman? Her antipathy[7] toward fishing nothing more than normal filial[8] rebellion? Had she tried it once? A messy encounter with worms? It doesn't matter. What does is that at that fragile moment in time I would have given anything not to appear dumb in Sheila's severe and unforgiving eyes.

I She hadn't seen my equipment yet. What I *should* have done, of course, was push the canoe in closer to shore and carefully slide the rod into some branches where I could pick it up again in the morning. Failing that, I could have surreptitiously[9] dumped the whole outfit overboard, written off the forty or so dollars as love's tribute. What I actually *did* do was gently lean forward, and slowly, ever so slowly, push the rod back through my legs toward the stern where it would be less conspicuous. ◀SR-4

It must have been just exactly what the bass was waiting for. Fish will trail a lure sometimes, trying to make up their mind whether or not to attack, and the slight pause in the plug's speed by my adjustment was tantalizing enough to overcome the bass's inhibitions. My rod, safely out of sight at last, bent double. The line, tightly coiled,

5. **strokes number four:** rows in the fourth position on a sculling crew.

6. ***Micropetrus salmonides:*** actually *Micropterus salmoides,* the Latin name for the largemouth bass.

7. **antipathy** (an tip′ ə thē): strong dislike.

8. **filial:** of or due from a son or daughter.

9. **surreptitiously:** secretly.

Words to Know and Use

dubious (do͞o′ bē əs) *adj.* hesitating; doubtful
conspicuous (kən spik′ yo͞o əs) *adj.* easy to see; obvious

395

F. Reading Skill: INFERRING Ask students to explain why the narrator feels like diving into the river when Sheila looks at him. *(He is so infatuated with her that he can barely stand her glance.)*

G. Reading Skill: DRAWING CONCLUSIONS Ask students why they think Sheila mentions Eric Caswell. *(Possible response: Sheila has a crush on Eric. It is the same situation as the narrator faces: being in love with someone a few years older and seemingly more experienced.)*

H. LEP: Vocabulary Students may find the phrase "fragile moment in time" difficult to understand. Discuss how the boy's infatuation leaves him open to pain and humiliation. Then explain that the moment is fragile because Sheila has the ability to destroy the boy with her "severe and unforgiving eyes."

I. Reading Skill: PREDICTING Have students predict what the boy will do. *(Possible responses: He may throw the rod into the water; confess his interest in fishing to Sheila; do nothing and hope for the best.)*

STRUCTURED READING FOR LESS PROFICIENT STUDENTS

Continued from page 393

SR–5. What is Sheila mainly interested in? *(Possible response: herself, her future, her appearance)* **Clarifying**

SR–6. What two things is the narrator torn between and which does he choose? *He is torn between Sheila and the bass he has caught; he lets the bass go.)* **Literal recall**

SR–7. What happens to Sheila? *She leaves the narrator and goes home in a Corvette with Eric Caswell.)* **Literal recall**

Art Note
Contemporary artist Louise Cherwak says, "I believe it is important to protect our wilderness areas so that not only we but also future generations can enjoy them, as my son Chris—the boy in the canoe—did in the Ocala National Forest in Florida." Graphite, or pencil, drawings often communicate more form and substance than oil paintings or watercolors. *Can you explain why?*

J. Literary Element: CONFLICT Ask students to explain why the narrator faces a difficult choice. *(Possible response: He loves fishing and has just hooked his biggest bass. However, he knows Sheila detests fishing and he wants her good opinion above all else.)*

K. Critical Thinking: ANALYZING Ask the class to analyze the connection between the fish on the rod and the relationship between Sheila and the narrator. *(Possible responses: Some students might say that Sheila is the "fish" that the narrator has hooked on the rod; others, that the narrator is hooked on Sheila's line.)*

THE BOY IN A CANOE 1987 Louise Cherwak Collection of the artist.

peeled off the spool with the shrill, tearing zip of a high-speed drill.

J Four things occurred to me at once. One, that it was a bass. Two, that it was a big bass. Three, that it was the biggest bass I had ever hooked. Four, that Sheila Mant must not know.

"What was that?" she said, turning half around.

"Uh, what was what?"

"That buzzing noise."

"Bats."

K She shuddered, quickly drew her feet back into the canoe. Every instinct I had told me to pick up the rod and strike back at the bass, but there was no need to—it was already solidly hooked. Downstream, an awesome distance downstream, it jumped clear of the water, landing with a concussion heavy enough to ripple the entire river. For a moment, I thought it was gone, but then the rod was bending again, the tip dancing into the water. Slowly, not making any motion that might alert Sheila, I reached down to tighten the drag.[10]

10. **tighten the drag:** increase the tension of the fishing line to make it more difficult for the fish to swim away with the bait.

DATA BANK

Among the favored fishing tactics are bait fishing, spin fishing, fly-fishing, and trolling. In trolling, the method the narrator uses here, anglers drag a baited hook or lure about thirty yards or more behind the stern. Once a fish hits a lure and becomes hooked, the boat is stopped and the fish is reeled in. The angler then lands it with a net or gaff (a sharp, hooklike instrument).

While all this was going on, Sheila had begun talking, and it was a few minutes before I was able to catch up with her train of thought.

"I went to a party there. These fraternity men. Katherine says I could get in there if I wanted. I'm thinking more of UVM or Bennington.[11] Somewhere I can ski."

The bass was slanting toward the rocks on the New Hampshire side by the ruins of Donaldson's boathouse. It had to be an old bass—a young one probably wouldn't have known the rocks were there. I brought the canoe back out into the middle of the river, hoping to head it off.

"That's neat," I mumbled. "Skiing. Yeah, I can see that."

"Eric said I have the figure to model, but I thought I should get an education first. I mean, it might be a while before I get started and all. I was thinking of getting my hair styled, more swept back? I mean, Ann-Margret?[12] Like hers, only shorter."

L She hesitated. "Are we going backwards?"

We were. I had managed to keep the bass in the middle of the river away from the rocks, but it had plenty of room there, and for the first time a chance to exert its full strength. I quickly computed the weight necessary to draw a fully loaded canoe backwards—the thought of it made me feel faint.

"It's just the current," I said hoarsely. "No sweat or anything."

I dug in deeper with my paddle. Reassured, Sheila began talking about something else, but all my attention was taken up now with the fish. I could feel its desperation as the water grew shallower. I could see the extra strain on the line, the frantic way it cut back and forth in the water. I could visualize what it looked like—the gape of its mouth, the flared gills and thick, vertical tail. The bass couldn't have encountered many forces in its long life that it wasn't capable of handling, and the unrelenting tug at its mouth must have been a source of great puzzlement and mounting panic.

M Me, I had problems of my own. To get to Dixford, I had to paddle up a sluggish stream that came into the river beneath a covered bridge. There was a shallow sandbar at the mouth of this stream—weeds on one side, rocks on the other. Without doubt, this is where I would lose the fish.

"I have to be careful with my complexion. I tan, but in segments. I can't figure out if it's even worth it. I wouldn't even do it, probably. I saw Jackie Kennedy[13] in Boston, and she wasn't tan at all." ◀SR-5

Taking a deep breath, I paddled as hard as I could for the middle, deepest part of the bar. I could have threaded the eye of a needle with the canoe, but the pull on the stern threw me off and I overcompensated—the canoe veered left and scraped bottom. I pushed the paddle down and shoved. A moment of hesitation . . . a moment more. . . . The canoe shot clear into the deeper water of the stream. I immediately looked down at the rod. It was bent in the same tight arc—miraculously, the bass was still on.

11. **UVM or Bennington:** the University of Vermont or Bennington College in Bennington, Vermont.

12. **Ann-Margret:** 1941– ; a movie star, singer, and dancer famous at the time of this story.

13. **Jackie Kennedy:** 1929– ; the wife of President John F. Kennedy. The public admired Jackie Kennedy's sense of style.

Words to Know and Use

overcompensate (ō′ vər käm′ pən sāt′) *v.* to make more than the necessary adjustment or action

L. Literary Element: SUSPENSE Ask students to explain how the writer creates suspense in this passage. *(Possible responses: The writer creates suspense by causing the reader to wonder if the canoe will capsize or if Sheila will learn of the fish; the narrator's own tension—"the thought of it made me feel faint"—also helps create suspense.)*

M. LEP: Vocabulary Have a volunteer define *sandbar (a compound word that describes a strip of sand formed in a river or sea by the action of the currents or tides).* Ask students why sandbars would be dangerous to sailors. *(because they snag the bottom of boats and cause them to tip or run aground.)*

N. Literary Element: CONFLICT Ask students to describe what the narrator is feeling in this passage. *(Possible responses: He is torn between his longing for Sheila and his love for fishing and nature.)*

O. Literary Element: CLIMAX Ask students to explain how the narrator's action represents a turning point. *(The narrator's conflict over having to choose between Sheila and the fish is decided when he chooses Sheila and cuts the fish loose.)*

P. Discussion Ask students what mistake they think the narrator made. *(Possible responses: Sacrificing himself for another; not following his innermost desires.)*

Check Test

1. What are the ages of the narrator and Sheila? *(He is fourteen, and she is seventeen.)*

2. What are the narrator's major summer activities? *(fishing and watching Sheila Mant)*

3. What is Sheila's attitude toward fishing? *(She thinks it is "boring" and "dumb.")*

4. What does the narrator catch on the canoe trip? *(a large bass)*

5. What does Sheila do at the end? *(She leaves with another boy.)*

Encouraging Independent Reading

"He Thinks He's Wonderful," a short story by F. Scott Fitzgerald
"A White Heron," a short story by Sarah Orne Jewett
"Homage for Isaac Babel," a short story by Doris Lessing
"The Trout," a short story by Sean O'Faolain
"Thirteen," a short story by Jessamyn West

The moon was out now. It was low and full enough that its beam shone directly on Sheila there ahead of me in the canoe, washing her in a creamy, luminous glow. I could see the lithe,[14] easy shape of her figure. I could see the way her hair curled down off her shoulders, the proud, alert tilt of her head, and all these things were as a tug on my heart. Not just Sheila, but the aura she carried about her of parties and casual touchings and grace. Behind me, I

N could feel the strain of the bass, steadier now, growing weaker, and this was another tug on my heart, not just the bass but the beat of the river and the slant of the stars and the smell of the night, until finally it seemed I would be torn apart between longings, split in half. Twenty yards ahead of us was the road, and once I pulled the canoe up on shore, the bass would be gone, irretrievably gone. If instead I stood up, grabbed the rod and started pumping, I would have it—as tired as the bass was, there was no chance it could get away. I reached down for the rod, hesitated, looked up to where Sheila was stretching herself lazily toward the sky, her small breasts rising beneath the soft fabric of her dress, and

O the tug was too much for me, and quicker than it takes to write down, I pulled a penknife from my pocket and cut the line in

SR-6 ▶ half.

With a sick, nauseous feeling in my stomach, I saw the rod unbend.

"My legs are sore," Sheila whined. "Are we there yet?"

Through a superhuman effort of self-control, I was able to beach the canoe and help Sheila off. The rest of the night is much foggier. We walked to the fair—there was the smell of popcorn, the sound of guitars. I may have danced once or twice with her, but all I really remember is her coming over to me once the music was done to explain that she would be going home in Eric Caswell's Corvette.

"OK," I mumbled.

For the first time that night she looked at me, really looked at me.

"You're a funny kid, you know that?" ◀ SR-7

Funny. Different. Dreamy. Odd. How many times was I to hear that in the years to come, all spoken with the same quizzical, half-accusatory tone Sheila used then. Poor Sheila! Before the month was over, the spell she cast over me was gone, but the memory of that lost bass haunted me all summer and P haunts me still. There would be other Sheila Mants in my life, other fish, and though I came close once or twice, it was these secret, hidden tuggings in the night that claimed me, and I never made the same mistake again. ❧

14. **lithe** (līth): limber; flexible.

Words to Know and Use

aura (ô′ rə) *n.* a quality that seems to surround a person

Real Life Connections

Point out to students that Sheila describes the narrator as a "funny kid." He then remarks that in the years to come, many people will use the same "quizzical, half accusatory" tone to describe him as funny, different, or dreamy. In real life, why might people use these terms and tone to describe people? Do students think these are positive or negative terms? Do these terms describe positive or negative character traits? Have students explain their answers.

e x p l a i n

Responding to Reading

First Impressions

1. What single word describes your feelings when the boy cuts the line? Explain.

Second Thoughts

2. Would the boy and Sheila have made a good match?

   Think about
   - their interests
   - their similarities and differences
   - how they get along with each other

3. Other than cutting the line, what could the boy have done? What did you predict he would do?

4. Why do you think Sheila calls the boy a "funny kid"?

5. Do you consider the boy in this story a winner, a loser, or something in between? Explain.

   Think about
   - his obsession with Sheila
   - his age at the time of the story
   - his skills
   - his reflections at the end of the story

Broader Connections

6. To make himself acceptable to Sheila, the boy conceals an important interest that he has. When, if ever, do you think it is right to put aside part of your own personality—such as your interests—for the sake of a relationship? Give examples to support your view.

Literary Concepts: Falling Action and Resolution

Falling action is that part of the plot following the climax in which the story draws to a conclusion. For example, in this story the climax occurs when the boy cuts the line. What is the falling action?

The **resolution** is the last part of the plot. The loose ends of the story are tied up in the resolution. Any remaining questions that the reader might have are answered. What is the resolution in this story?

Concept Review: Suspense The author creates a growing sense of excitement or suspense as the story unfolds. How does he accomplish this?

Student Response

Responding to Reading

These questions are open-ended with no "right" or "wrong" answers. However, responses must be supported with information from the selection. Possible answers follow:

1. Almost any response that is based on the story is valid.

2. Some students may say that the boy and Sheila would have made a good match because opposites attract, while others will feel that the two would have been a very poor match because they share no common interests and don't get along especially well.

3. Possible responses: the boy could have dumped his line overboard; he could have reeled in the fish.

4. Some may say that Sheila feels that he is "funny" because he seemed preoccupied and worried; others may say that she is surprised and taken aback because he did not seem to care that she was going home with another boy.

5. Some may believe that he is a loser because he seems to regret his actions in the end. Others may see him as a winner because he learned from his experiences. Still others may think that he both wins and loses because he learned about himself but lost Sheila.

6. Some students may say it is *never* right to sacrifice part of your personality for the sake of a relationship because you will come to regret it; you will blame and resent the other person for causing you to give up a part of yourself. Other students may say that to make a relationship work each person must at times put aside some of his or her interests for the other.

Literary Concept—Falling Action and Resolution

The falling action in this story is the description of the boy's beaching the canoe and the events of the fair, which include Sheila's calling the boy a "funny kid" and her leaving with Eric Caswell.

The resolution of the story is in the last paragraph of the story, in which the narrator describes his getting over Sheila, but not the loss of the bass, and tells how the experience has affected his life.

Concept Review—Suspense

The writer builds suspense by having the narrator choose between the two things that at that time matter most to him in his life—Sheila Mant and the biggest bass he has ever hooked. Suspense is increased by the boy's trying to hide the fish from Sheila as the reader wonders if she will see it. Suspense is also created through the dragging out of the boy's decision, and the descriptions of his infatuation with Sheila and his love for nature and the bass.

Writing Options

The Writing Options are designed to meet varied student interests and abilities. Have each student select one writing activity to complete. You may wish to guide some students to an option that requires less writing.

Journal Update Have students review and revise their journal entries for "The Bass, The River, and Sheila Mant." What have they learned about the way infatuated people behave?

Vocabulary Practice

Exercise A

1. (b)
2. (c)
3. (a)
4. (a)
5. (a)

Exercise B

1. Antonyms
2. Synonyms
3. Synonyms
4. Synonyms
5. Antonyms

Writing Options

1. Write your version of what might have happened if the boy had reeled in the bass. Would Sheila have been impressed or disgusted? Would the story have ended differently?
2. Tell how the following fishing terms and expressions might apply to the characters in the story: *bait; hooked; lure; hook, line, and sinker; the one that got away.*
3. Write a brief moral for this story.
4. Write two notes that the boy might have written to Sheila but never delivered. The first note should be written before the canoe incident. In this note, he should tell her how he feels about her. In the second note, written after the dance, he should express his feelings about the evening they spent together.

Vocabulary Practice

Words to Know and Use

aura
conspicuous
dubious
epitome
incarnation
overcompensate
suave

Exercise A On your paper, write the letter of the word or phrase that best completes each sentence.

1. To say Sheila has an **aura** of beauty means that she has (a) a plan to become beautiful (b) the qualities that seem to surround a beautiful person (c) no chance of being beautiful.
2. If the boy was **dubious** about asking out Sheila Mant, then (a) he was confident (b) he was curious (c) he was doubtful.
3. To avoid being **conspicious,** the boy (a) hid his fishing rod (b) laughed out loud (c) wore bright clothing.
4. If Sheila is the **incarnation** of innocence, she is (a) very innocent (b) the opposite of innocent (c) slightly innocent.
5. When the bass pulled the canoe to one side, the narrator did not intend to **overcompensate** by turning his canoe (a) too much (b) too quickly (c) completely over.

Exercise B Decide whether the following pairs of words are synonyms or antonyms. On your paper, identify each pair as *Synonyms* or *Antonyms.*

1. dubious—trusting
2. suave—smooth
3. epitome—essence
4. dubious—doubtful
5. conspicuous—hidden

LITERARY ANALYSIS

When scientists observe an unfamiliar occurrence, they develop a **hypothesis,** or theory, to explain it and then test their hypothesis through further observation and research. They analyze the occurrence by breaking it down into smaller components and figuring out how the parts relate to each other.

When you're writing about ideas in literature, you operate much like a scientist. While you're reading, or after you've finished, you form a hypothesis, or possible idea, about the meaning of the work. Sometimes the meaning, or **theme,** is clearly stated. More often, you must analyze clues provided in the text to identify the theme.

For this assignment you will write a literary analysis of a theme from your reading. Since most works of literature suggest more than one theme, don't worry about getting a "right answer." If the clues in the text support your idea, then you'll know you're on the right track.

GUIDED ASSIGNMENT: ANALYZING THEME

Write a multi-paragraph essay analyzing a major theme of one of the reading selections in this subunit. Support your interpretation with evidence from the text.

Here is your PASSkey to this assignment.

PURPOSE: To analyze a literary theme
AUDIENCE: Your classmates
SUBJECT: A literary selection
STRUCTURE: A multi-paragraph essay

Prewriting

STEP 1 Choose a selection Decide which of the following literary selections you would like to analyze: (1) "The Bass, the River, and Sheila Mant"; (2) "Rules of the Game"; (3) "Ex-Basketball Player." Make sure that you choose a selection that interests you and that you understand well.

STEP 2 Summarize the text Begin by writing a simple summary of the text, which may provide clues to a theme. You may need to reread the story or poem with the purpose of identifying a major

Writer's Workshop

Objectives

- To understand the goals of literary analysis
- To determine the theme or themes of a literary work
- To determine and analyze the clues that support a theme
- To understand thesis statements and topic sentences
- To draft, revise, edit, and present an essay that analyzes a literary theme
- To reflect on the writing process

Integrating . . .

Literature and Writing Ask students to provide a definition of the word *theme.* Have students generate a list of themes prevalent in literature. (These might include loyalty, perseverance, courage, and unrequited love.) Point out that many themes found in literature are recurring. Discuss the idea that only a few themes appear repeatedly in stories throughout history. Explain that in this subunit students will analyze literary themes using the literature in the subunit.

Writing and Grammar The Language Workshop in this subunit is on subject-verb agreement. Explain that in order for the meaning of a sentence to be clear, the subject and verb must agree. Have students provide examples in which the subject and verb do not agree, and discuss why this could lead a reader to misread or misunderstand a sentence or a selection.

Writing and Speaking and Listening The Speaking and Listening Workshop addresses critical listening. Point out that the development of good listening skills is important to effective group and partner work such as that required in the Writer's Workshops and other activities. Note also that critical listening will be essential during the presentation of speeches in the next Writer's Workshop, which begins on page 444.

Additional Resources

UNIT THREE RESOURCE BOOK

Writer's Workshop Copy Master, p. 48
Peer and Self-Evaluation Guidelines, p. 49
Writing Assessment Guidelines, p. 50

ENRICHMENT MATERIALS

Thinking Skills Transparency and Worksheet
Fine Art Transparency and Writing Prompts
Revision, Proofreading, and Elaboration Worksheet
Writing Prompts for Assessment

Teaching Strategies

Introduction Share with students that a piece of literature can have more than one theme. You might wish to illustrate this by providing an example of a piece of literature with which the students are familiar. A good example might be "The Bass, The River, and Sheila Mant." Elicit from students the story's underlying themes of first love, confusion, and the fight with the bass, and write these on the board for future reference. You may want students to think of other works with multiple themes as well, until they are confident in determining a selection's theme.

Explain that in this workshop students will analyze a piece of literature from the unit and focus on only one theme.

Direct students to the Writer's Workshop on page 401. Read aloud the guided assignment and the PASSkey graphic. Be sure that students understand that they should carefully choose a literary theme, making certain that there is sufficient evidence in the selection to back up their choice.

> **Teaching Tip**
> Write the titles of two or three selections from previous subunits in separate columns on the chalkboard. Have the class brainstorm a number of themes for each selection, and write them in the correct column. This will reinforce that most selections have more than one theme and that students will not be wrong to focus on any single theme as the subject of their essay. Be sure to examine clues that are not initially clear. Show students how to analyze a piece of literature to uncover its underlying theme.
>
> Point out to LEP students that these themes are universal and are most likely found in literature in their own language. Provide LEP students with the opportunity to share with the class prevalent themes from their literature. This may help students to find themes in their literature that they otherwise might have missed.

theme running through the whole work. For example, a student summarized the text of the poem "Courage" as follows:

STUDENT MODEL ▶

```
The poem is about a man's courage: how he showed it as a
child, as a young soldier, and finally as an old man about
to die.
```

STEP 3 Identify the topic of the work What central idea or subject is the work about? In the Sexton poem, for example, the topic is clearly stated in the title "Courage." In other works, you may have to infer the topic.

STEP 4 Review the text Identify important messages and events that relate to the central topic. To evaluate the importance of a specific part of the text, ask yourself, Does this matter to the text as a whole? and, If so, why or how? You may want to organize your ideas into a chart similar to the one this student began:

STUDENT MODEL ▶

Courage

Important Passages/Events	Why/How They're Important
"It's in the small things we see it."	It's the first line; "small" is emphasized.
"child's first step . . . awesome as an earthquake."	Small things, like first steps, seem big.
"Your courage was a small coal . . ."	Image emphasizes the smallness of courage.
Poem begins with child and ends with an old man.	Span of time suggests that courage comes in all stages of life.

STEP 5 Look for patterns or themes Examine your list of important passages and events and the reasons you think they're important. With these ideas in mind, ask yourself this question: What does this story or poem say about the topic? Jot down several possible statements of theme in response to the question. The student writing about "Courage" came up with these.

STUDENT MODEL ▶

```
(a) Courage is found in the little steps one takes
    throughout life.
(b) Courage is facing life's hardships alone.
(c) A child is just as courageous as an adult.
```

STEP 6 Write a thesis statement From your list of possible themes, select the one that you think best fits the details of the story or poem. Or, combine several of your original statements into a

Prewriting Emphasize the importance of choosing a piece of literature with which students are comfortable. Explain that if a literary theme does not come to light initially, it might become clear if they write the summary of the piece. Also explain that, in some cases, readers may have to infer the theme. Discuss the notion of inference until students are comfortable using this skill.

Tell the students that charting is a simple prewriting strategy that helps them organize their thoughts and keep them handy as they write.

new one. Then write a clear and precise statement of the text's theme that can serve as the focus of your essay. Your thesis statement should not summarize the text. Instead, it should express the conclusion you've reached about the text's theme, or meaning. Here is the thesis statement for the literary analysis of "Courage."

> Thesis: Ann Sexton's poem "Courage" suggests that courage isn't found in big, adventurous leaps, but in the little struggles one encounters throughout life.

◀ STUDENT MODEL

STEP 7 **Organize your evidence** Categorize the important passages and events you listed in STEP 4 by grouping together related information. Then write a general statement that summarizes the information in each group. These general statements will serve as **topic sentences** in your essay. Note how this student grouped one set of key details from "Courage" and wrote a topic sentence that links these details to the thesis:

> Topic Sentence: Courage is found in the little struggles all children go through as they grow up.
>
> -Taking first step -Getting spanked
> -Learning to ride a bike -Being teased by kids

◀ STUDENT MODEL

Then arrange your topic sentences in a logical order. This grouping will serve as a rough outline for your essay.

Drafting

STEP 1 **Write your introduction** In your first paragraph, introduce the work you have chosen to analyze. Then state the thesis you have formed about the work's theme.

STEP 2 **Draft the body of your essay** Use the topic sentences you constructed to guide your organization, beginning a new paragraph with each topic sentence. Develop each paragraph in as much detail as possible, using all the important evidence from the text that supports the topic sentence. Keep in mind that a good expository essay has a beginning, a middle, and an end. Finally, write a conclusion that summarizes your key points.

Revising and Editing

Trade papers with a classmate and have him or her respond to your composition, using the following questions as a guide.

Computer Tip
Students with access to a computer may wish to create their prewriting chart on the computer.

As you work through the prewriting steps with the students, take time during step 6 to discuss thesis statements thoroughly. Have students create thesis statements for familiar stories. Quickly review topic sentences and outline their relationship to thesis statements. Explain and discuss the different types of order. For example, you might talk about sequential and spatial order.

Drafting Encourage students to keep their prewriting charts by their sides as they begin drafting. They may even wish to circle those items that they definitely want to include, to make sure that they do not forget them. This will encourage students to think further about which details to include and how to pare the list.

Run through the drafting steps with the students. Encourage students to read each completed paragraph carefully and ask themselves if each sentence relates strongly to the topic sentence. Have them delete any sentences with weak ties to the topic sentence.

Revising and Editing Suggest that each student revise his or her essay with a partner. Have the partner read the essay, keeping the *Revision Checklist* in mind. Encourage the partner to provide a written response to the checklist and to explain why he or she responded in such a way. Encourage students to put their essays aside for a time before revising them so that they can correct their papers with a fresh eye. Have students edit their own papers for structure, spelling, and mechanics. Tell students to review the Language Workshop if they have trouble with subject-verb agreement.

Presenting After students have formed three groups and analyzed their essays, each group might read highlights of their essays to the class. This will demonstrate that each selection has many themes and that each student interpreted the selection in a slightly different way.

To provide the class with more insight into the literature, students may wish to share their essays with another class that has read the same literature.

Since the students' essays may have focused on different themes for each selection, you might instruct students to create a theme chart. This could consist of the selections, the themes found in each selection, and even each thesis statement. Have volunteers create the chart, allowing them to be as creative as they wish. The chart could be hung in the classroom and incorporated into a future lesson.

Reflecting on Your Writing If several students answer the *Reflecting* questions in a similar way, you may wish to review these questions. Discussing them as a group may provide students with more insight into the assignment.

Closure

As this subunit draws to a close, determine that students have grasped the following concepts:

- Literary works can contain more than one theme
- Themes often need to be inferred
- Thesis statements must be supported with evidence from the text

Revision Checklist

1. Is the thesis a clear statement of theme?
2. Is the thesis supported with sufficient evidence?
3. Does each topic sentence directly support the thesis?
4. Does each paragraph address a different aspect of the thesis?
5. Are the paragraphs arranged in a logical order?

Editing Edit for sentence structure, spelling, and mechanics.

Presenting

Form three groups, based on which reading selection each class member analyzed. In each group, participants should discuss their analysis of the work's theme. It will be interesting to see the similarities and differences reached in conclusions about the work.

Reflecting on Your Writing

After your group discussion, answer the following questions. Place your answers with a copy of your final draft in your writing portfolio.

1. How difficult was it for you to discover the theme of this work?
2. How did your thesis statement compare with those of your classmates?
3. Which part of this assignment do you feel you did very well? Why?
4. Which part of this assignment gave you the most trouble? Why?

Additional Writing and Research Topics

The following items provide additional writing practice based on the selections in this subunit.

Analysis of Theme

- Think of three songs whose themes are similar to those found in the literature in this unit. Write an essay analyzing one song's theme. Be sure to write a thesis statement and list supporting details.
- Write a narrative that changes the ending of "The Bass, The River, and Sheila Mant." Come up with a new theme based on your ending.

Other Topics

Social Studies Research: Research two great runners who have won medals in the Olympics. Write a report about one of these great runners. Draw parallels beween this runner's life and that of Wilma Rudolph.

First Person Narrative: Step into the story "The Rules of the Game." Help Waverly work out her problems with her mother. Write down the things you would tell Waverly to help her solve her problems.

MAKING SUBJECTS AND VERBS AGREE

A verb must agree with its subject in number.

Have you ever tried to paddle a canoe with a friend? If the two of you don't work together to find the right rhythm, the canoe will go in circles. In the same way, the subject and verb in a sentence need to work together.

If the subject of a sentence is singular, its verb must also be singular. If a subject is plural, its verb must also be plural. This correspondence of subject and verb is called **subject-verb agreement.**

The *runner* (singular) **paces** (singular) before each race.

The *runners* (plural) **pace** (plural) before each race.

The *s* at the end of a verb, as in *paces, leaps,* or *answers,* shows that the verb is singular. To form the plural, most verbs drop the *s.*

You will usually be able to hear when the subject and verb of a sentence are in agreement. For example, "The runner pace before each race" probably sounds incorrect to you, and it is. Sometimes, though, you may not be able to hear whether the singular or the plural verb is correct.

REMINDERS

1. The pronoun *you* can be singular or plural, but it always takes a plural verb.
2. Except in *I am* and *I was,* the pronoun *I* always takes a plural verb.

Dealing with Phrases

A prepositional phrase between the subject and verb can make it difficult to tell whether a singular or plural verb is required. Remember that you will only find the subject *outside* the prepositional phrase.

The subject of the verb is never found in a prepositional phrase.

The *runner* with the braids *practices* for hours. (*Runner,* not *braids,* is the subject.)

The *timers* at the race *are* in their positions. (*Timers,* not *race,* is the subject.)

Language Workshop

Objectives

- To use correct subject-verb agreement in writing
- To understand that the subject of a verb is not found in phrases
- To identify compound subjects and use correct verb agreement with them

Integrating . . .

Writing, Listening, and Grammar Review with students the importance of using correct grammar when they speak and write, especially in formal situations such as the literary analysis they wrote for the preceding Writer's Workshop. Also mention that being able to hear an error in speech is evidence that they have internalized grammatical concepts. Read the following sentences to students, asking them to listen for errors.

1. Stars gives off their own light.

2. Some stars shines more brightly than others.

3. Several of my friends likes to look for constellations like the Big Dipper and Orion.

Have volunteers make corrections in each sentence; reread them if necessary. Call attention to the types of errors students found, pointing out that this Language Workshop focuses on making subjects and verbs agree.

Teaching Strategies

Ask a volunteer to read the focus statement at the top of page 405. Point out that the sentences about the stars were incorrect because the subjects and verbs did not agree.

Have students read up to the section called *Dealing with Phrases.* Call their attention to the *Reminder box* on page 405, and ask volunteers for examples of each.

Additional Resources

UNIT THREE RESOURCE BOOK
Language Workshop Copy Master, p. 51

ENRICHMENT MATERIALS
Grammar and Usage Copy Masters

Teaching Tip
Tell students that an -s ending often signals a plural noun, as in *shoes, cabbages,* and *basketballs.* However, some nouns, such as *economics* and *mathematics,* though ending in an s, must be used with a singular verb. Have students try to think of additional singular nouns that end in s. (*Checkers, chess*) Point out that these must be used with singular verbs.

Now have students read the section *Dealing with Phrases,* making sure they discuss the *Hint* box. Point out that the number of the subject will not be changed by a phrase that follows it.

Teaching Tip: LEP
Have LEP students read aloud the sample sentences in this section, leaving out the phrases between the subject and the verb. (*The runner practices for hours. The timers are in their positions. Wilma Rudolph travels by bus. Her class-mates have come to watch.*)

Assign Exercise 1 to students. When all are finished, review the correct responses.

Answer Key
Exercise 1

1. am
2. are
3. wish
4. watch
5. is
6. hurl
7. weighs
8. tosses
9. runs
10. participate

Ask a volunteer to read the first focus statement on compound subjects, and discuss the example. Then have another volunteer read the next focus statement and the examples below it. For students who are having difficulty understanding this concept, have volunteers make up additional examples of sentences with compound subjects using *and, or,* and *nor.* Then have students work individually to complete Exercise 2, reviewing their responses when they are finished.

HINT

To help decide which word is the subject, say the sentence without the phrase. If you have chosen the correct word as the subject, the sentence will make sense without the phrase.

Phrases that begin with the words *with, together with, including, as well as,* or *in addition to* are not part of the subject.

Wilma Rudolph, together with her teammates, *travels* by bus.

Her *classmates,* in addition to her teacher, *have come* to watch.

Exercise 1 Choose the verb that agrees with the subject.

1. I (am, is) a fan of track and field events.
2. Events held on an outdoor track (is, are) exciting.
3. I (wish, wishes) I could have seen some of the great runners like Wilma Rudolph.
4. My friends (watch, watches) the New York Marathon every year.
5. Another event that (is, are) interesting is the javelin throw.
6. The athletes at a meet (hurl, hurls) the light spears as far as they can.
7. The discus (weigh, weighs) almost four and one-half pounds.
8. Each contestant (toss, tosses) the discus in a body-whirling release.
9. My father, in addition to my uncles, (run, runs) in masters' events for older athletes.
10. You can (participate, participates) in track and field as long as you stay fit.

Dealing with Compound Subjects

A **compound subject** is two or more subjects used with the same verb. Compound subjects that contain the word *and* are plural and take a plural verb.

Exploring and chess are Waverly Jong's favorite activities.

When the parts of a compound subject are connected by the conjunction *or* or *nor,* the verb agrees with the subject nearer the verb.

Neither Waverly nor her *brothers know* how to play chess.

Either her brothers or her *mother does* the chores.

Exercise 2 Some of the following sentences contain errors in subject-verb agreement. Rewrite these sentences correctly. If a sentence has no error, write *Correct.*

1. Waverly Jong and her parents lives in San Francisco.
2. Their apartment above a Chinese bakery is warm and clean.
3. Waverly and her brothers plays in the back alleys.
4. The back alleys are full of mysteries and adventure.
5. Life Savers and a chess set is the best Christmas presents.
6. Either Waverly or her brothers reads the chess rule book.
7. Chinese neighbors and tourists gathers to watch Waverly play chess.
8. Neither Waverly nor the other players realizes how talented she is.
9. Sometimes Waverly and her mother argues about life in America.
10. In Waverly's mind the chess pieces represents her and her mother.

Exercise 3 Read the following passage. Look at the subject-verb agreement in each sentence and correct any errors. Write the corrected sentences on your paper.

Many cities and towns has a section called Chinatown. The cities with the largest Chinatowns are New York, San Francisco, and Los Angeles. The architecture in these neighborhoods are inspired by the buildings in the cities and villages of China. The roofs, as well as an occasional storefront, is made of tiles. Even the telephone booths looks unique. Neither local people nor tourists can stops from examining the vast array of food displayed outside. Many of the fruits and vegetables is unfamiliar to non-Chinese. The delicious smell from restaurants tempt all who pass by. Chinese food, as well as Southeast Asian cuisines, is offered in many restaurants.

Exercise 4 Analyzing and Revising Your Writing

1. Take a paper from your writing portfolio. Choose a passage to analyze.
2. Reread the passage, looking for errors in subject-verb agreement. Look carefully wherever you have used a prepositional phrase or a compound subject.
3. Revise any errors in subject-verb agreement.
4. Compare your revision to the original. Note how the corrected sentences sound better.
5. Remember to check for errors in subject-verb agreement the next time you proofread your work.

LANGUAGE HANDBOOK

For review and practice, see Section 6, Subject-Verb Agreement.

ADDITIONAL PRACTICE

The following items provide additional practice in subject-verb agreement.

Write these sentences, choosing the correct word from each pair in parentheses. Underline each subject twice.

1. Flares from the sun (affects, affect) the earth's weather.

2. The water in the tanks (was, were) changed yesterday.

3. The seats in the minibus (is, are) comfortable.

4. Jane, with her sisters, (goes, go) to Curie High.

Write these sentences, choosing a word from the pair in parentheses to agree with the compound subject. Draw two lines under each part of the compound subject.

5. A newspaper and a magazine (was, were) stuffed into the mailbox.

6. Your calendar and your map (is, are) out of date.

7. The books and this album (belongs, belong) to Ruthie.

8. Either the speakers or the microphone (wasn't, weren't) working.

For additional practice have students form small groups. Ask each group to choose one selection from this subunit and find three interesting sentences, rewriting them with incorrect subject-verb agreement. When each group has their examples, have them take turns writing them on the board for the class to discuss and correct. Then assign Exercises 3 and 4.

Closure

Before beginning the next subunit, be sure students have internalized these concepts:

- A verb must agree with its subject in number.
- The subject of a sentence is never found in a prepositional phrase.
- Compound subjects joined with *and* take plural verbs.
- When compound subjects are formed with *or* or *nor*, the verb agrees with the subject nearer the verb.

Exercise 2

1. Waverly Jong and her parents live in San Francisco.
2. correct
3. Waverly and her brothers play in the back alleys.
4. correct
5. Life Savers and a chess set are the best Christmas presents.
6. Either Waverly or her brothers read the chess rule book.
7. Chinese neighbors and tourists gather to watch Waverly play chess.
8. Neither Waverly nor the other players realize how talented she is.
9. Sometimes Waverly and her mother argue about life in America.
10. In Waverly's mind the chess pieces represent her and her mother.

Exercise 3

Many cities and towns have a section called Chinatown. The cities with the largest Chinatowns are New York, San Francisco, and Los Angeles. The architecture in these neighborhoods is inspired by the buildings in the cities and villages of China. The roofs, as well as an occasional storefront, are made of tiles. Even the telephone booths look unique. Neither local people nor tourists can stop from examining the vast array of food displayed outside. Many of the fruits and vegetables are unfamiliar to non-Chinese. The delicious smell from restaurants tempts all who pass by. Chinese food, as well as Southeast Asian cuisines, is offered in many restaurants.

Exercise 4

Answers will vary, but students' work should reflect correct subject-verb agreement.

Speaking and Listening Workshop

Objectives

- To understand the difference between one-way and two-way listening
- To learn guidelines for becoming an attentive and critical listener

Integrating . . .

Literature and Speaking and Listening Explain that critical listening is an important lifelong skill.

Teaching Strategies

Have students work in pairs. Ask one person to describe in two minutes his or her ideal vacation. Then ask the partner to retell as much as he or she can remember. Have students switch roles and repeat the exercise. Ask students to discuss their observations.

Read through the material with students. Assign the exercise on page 408.

Closure

Before beginning the next subunit, be sure students have internalized these concepts:

- A critical listener keeps an open mind and stays focused on the speaker.
- A critical listener identifies the speaker's purpose and main idea and tries to predict what will be said next.
- A critical listener summarizes the speaker's main ideas.

Teaching Tip

Videotape segments from television news shows. Have students practice the guidelines with the tapes.

Exercise

(An abridged set of guidelines is given.)

1. Keep an open mind about the speaker and the topic.
2. Stay focused on the speaker.
3. Identify the purpose and main ideas.
4. Listen and watch for special elements.
5. Anticipate what comes next.
6. Summarize the speaker's main points.

SPEAKING AND LISTENING WORKSHOP

CRITICAL LISTENING

There are two kinds of listening: In **two-way listening** the listener can stop the speaker to ask questions. You participate in this kind of listening in conversations or in classroom discussions. In **one-way listening** the listener cannot respond to the speaker. Think about the way you listen to the news on television or to a political speech. In these one-way listening situations you only have one chance to receive the information. To listen well, follow these guidelines:

1. **Keep an open mind** Don't decide beforehand what you are going to like or dislike about the topic or the speaker.
2. **Stay focused** Your mind can listen four times faster than anyone can speak. Don't spend the resulting free time daydreaming. Instead, spend it thinking about what the speaker is saying. Hold a dialogue with yourself about the speaker's statements. Pose questions to yourself about the topic.
3. **Identify the speaker's purpose and main ideas** Pay attention to the introduction and conclusion of any presentation. These are places where the speaker's purpose is often stated. Ask yourself whether the speaker is trying to motivate, to inform, or to fulfill some other purpose. You will often be able to identify the speaker's main ideas by paying attention to signals such as intonation, gestures, and facial expressions.
4. **Listen and watch** Another reason to watch carefully for gestures and expressions is so that you will not miss any humor or irony in the presentation. People communicate with gestures as well as with words. Pay special attention also to any visual aids.
5. **Anticipate and predict** Carry on an imaginary conversation with the speaker. Write down any questions that come to mind. Predict what the speaker will say next or what the conclusion will be.
6. **Summarize** Keep track of the speaker's main ideas as you listen. Note these if possible, but don't get bogged down in details. Instead, summarize the speaker's statements.

HINT

Listen for words such as *next, as a result, second,* and *in conclusion.* These are signal words that help you follow the speaker's main points.

ASK QUESTIONS

If possible, ask the questions you have written in your notes. If the situation is one in which questions are not appropriate, perhaps you can approach the speaker with your questions later.

Exercise Plan to use these listening strategies the next time you listen to a lecture in class. Keep an abridged copy of these guidelines with you and consciously follow them as you listen. See whether you can infer the speaker's purpose and predict the main points as you listen.

Additional Resources

UNIT THREE RESOURCE BOOK

Related Skills Copy Master, p. 52

ENRICHMENT MATERIALS

Oral Communications Booklet

ADDITIONAL PRACTICE

Use the critical listening guidelines to listen to a television documentary. Rate yourself.

	good	fair	poor
1. I kept an open mind.			
2. I remained focused.			
3. I identified the purpose and main idea.			
4. I looked for special elements.			
5. I made predictions.			
6. I summarized main points.			

STRATEGIES FOR SURVIVAL

One of life's greatest challenges is simply to survive—from moment to moment, day to day, year to year. One person may survive the danger of war or the sadness of a miserable childhood. In some instances, survival seems to be more a matter of luck than of anything else. But in other circumstances, the person's survival is directly related to some strategy that he or she devises. Others fight to survive hunger, poverty, tyranny, prejudice, or injustice.

In this subunit, you will meet people who develop their own strategies for survival. Read each selection to discover the strategy that each main character uses to survive.

Subunit Preview

Have students read the introduction to subunit 3, **Strategies for Survival.** Ask them to consider how responses to threatening situations relate to the unit theme, **Challenges: Winners and Losers.** Ask students to list these "weapons" in the order of most to least effective in a fight for survival: *physical strength, ability to think, size, courage, foresight,* and *speed.* Have them explain their reasoning. Suggest that students read the subunit Table of Contents and indicate which selection that they expect to be the most interesting.

For Additional Challenge

The following selections offer extra challenge in the exploration of the subunit theme:

"The Dinner Party," a short story by Mona Gardner

"You Need to Go Upstairs," a short story by Rumer Godden

Additional Resources

Subunit Test, pp. 75–76

OBSERVATION ASSESSMENT

Observing how students respond to the text, to the classroom instruction, and to peers is an important part of an assessment program. The following suggestions and the form in each Unit Resource Book can be used to implement observation assessment.

- As students work through this subunit, assess how they keep on track as they read. Do they stop occasionally to make sure that they understand what is happening? Do they go back and reread to figure out *why* something is happening?
- As they progress through this subunit, can you see growth in their ability to make new predictions when their initial ones aren't working out?
- To evaluate how well students understand visual cues, see if they refer to captions, heads, titles, illustrations, callouts, and editorial notes.

Objectives

- To understand and analyze a classic short story
- To recognize the importance of setting in a story
- To understand how an author uses inferences
- To understand an author's use of foreshadowing
- To express understanding of the work through a choice of writing forms, including an account, questions, description, and an obituary.

Prereading/Motivation

Examine What You Know

Discussion Prompts: What is your definition of the word *game*? How might others' definitions differ? At what point does a game stop being fun? What might make a game dangerous?

Expand Your Knowledge

Discussion Prompts: Do you think most hunters share certain character traits? Explain. Why do you think big-game hunting was a sport of the wealthy? What animals might have been especially prized catches and why? Do you think attitudes about big-game hunting might be changing today? Explain.

Enrich Your Reading

Students answers may include:

Inference: Zaroff hunts humans. **Clues:** Zaroff insists that hunting begins to bore him, that the animals no longer present a challenge; now he hunts the only animal that can reason.

Inference: Ivan was killed in the trap. **Clues:** When he heard the dogs stop barking, Rainsford knew that his knife-trap had worked. He saw far away that Zaroff was on his feet, but Ivan was not. **Inference:** Rainsford killed Zaroff and threw him to the dogs.

Clues: Zaroff says one of them will be fed to the dogs. Rainsford is alive at the end.

> **Thematic Link—Strategies for Survival**
>
> In this story of a life-and-death struggle, an individual uses all of his wit and skill as strategies to survive.

e x p l o r e

Short Story

The Most Dangerous Game

RICHARD CONNELL

Examine What You Know (Prior Knowledge)

Start a word web with the word *game* in the center. Then consider the title of the story you are about to read. Does the title suggest additional ideas for the word web? Predict the kind of game that this story will be about.

Expand Your Knowledge (Building Background)

Before many species became endangered, big-game hunting had been a popular sport among certain wealthy people. In fact, during the nineteenth and early twentieth centuries, some individuals devoted almost all of their time to tracking down rare and dangerous animals. Successful hunters brought back trophies, the stuffed heads or the horns of the animals they had killed. These were displayed with great pride.

Enrich Your Reading (Reading Skill)

Inference At times in this story the author hints at something that happens but does not directly tell about the event. To get the most out of the story, you must examine the evidence the author provides and make a logical guess, or an **inference,** about what happened. For example, in the story the main character is on a ship when he grabs for his falling pipe, loses his balance, and then feels the warm water close over his head. You can infer that he has fallen overboard. At certain points in the story, you will be asked to make other inferences. Write your responses in your journal or on a piece of paper, using a chart like the one below.

Inference Clues	Inference
grabs for pipe; loses balance; water closes over him	Rainsford fell overboard

■ *A biography of the author can be found on page 431.*

Journal Writing

Suggest these journal topics to students:

- What are your opinions about hunting as a sport? Explain your feelings.
- What is "the most dangerous game" you can imagine?
- Explain whether you agree or disagree with this statement: "The world is made up of two classes—the hunters and the huntees."

For other journal opportunities, refer students to Enrich Your Reading (p. 410), First Impressions and Broader Connections (p. 429).

Additional Resources

UNIT THREE RESOURCE BOOK

Reader's Guidesheet, p. 55
Vocabulary Worksheet, p. 56
Selection and Vocabulary Check Tests, p. 57
Selection Test, pp. 58–59

Collaborative Learning

Opportunities for collaborative learning appear throughout the lesson and include annotation ss, Real-Life Connections (p. T–413), and Options for Learning (p. 431), and Cross-Curricular Options (p. T–431).

The Most Dangerous Game

RICHARD CONNELL

A "Off there to the right—somewhere—is a large island," said Whitney. "It's rather a mystery—"

"What island is it?" Rainsford asked.

"The old charts call it 'Ship-Trap Island,'" Whitney replied. "A suggestive name, isn't it? Sailors have a curious dread of the place. I didn't know why. Some superstition—"

"Can't see it," remarked Rainsford, trying to peer through the dank tropical night that was palpable as it pressed its thick, warm blackness in upon the yacht.

"You've good eyes," said Whitney, with a laugh, "and I've seen you pick off a moose moving in the brown fall bush at four hundred yards; but even you can't see four
B miles or so through a moonless Caribbean night."

"Nor four yards," admitted Rainsford. "Ugh! It's like moist black velvet."

"It will be light in Rio," promised Whitney. "We should make it in a few days. I hope the jaguar guns have come from Purdey's. We should have some good hunt-
SR-1 ▶ ing up the Amazon. Great sport, hunting."

"The best sport in the world," agreed Rainsford.

"For the hunter," amended Whitney. "Not for the jaguar."

"Don't talk rot, Whitney," said Rainsford. "You're a big-game hunter, not a philosopher. Who cares how a jaguar feels?"

"Perhaps the jaguar does," observed Whitney.

"Bah! They've no understanding."

> **"The world is made up of two classes—the hunters and the huntees."**

"Even so, I rather think they understand one thing—fear. The fear of pain and the fear of death."

"Nonsense," laughed Rainsford. "This hot weather is making you soft, Whitney. C
Be a realist. The world is made up of two classes—the hunters and the huntees. Luckily, you and I are hunters. Do you think we've passed that island yet?"

"I can't tell in the dark. I hope so."

"Why?" asked Rainsford.

"The place has a reputation—a bad one."

"Cannibals?" suggested Rainsford.

"Hardly. Even cannibals wouldn't live in such a Godforsaken place. But it's gotten into sailor lore, somehow. Didn't you notice

Structured Reading for Less Proficient Students

These questions can help to guide students through the reading. Ask each question at the point of the selection where the SR number appears in the margin.

SR–1. Where are Whitney and Rainsford going? *(hunting up the Amazon)* **Clarifying**

SR–2. What reaction does everyone but Rainsford have to "Ship-Trap Island"? *(They consider it evil; it frightens them.)* **Summarizing**

SR–3. How does Rainsford fall overboard? *(When he leaps to the railing to track the gunshot, his pipe gets knocked out of his mouth and he falls overboard lunging for it.)* **Drawing conclusions**

SR–4. How does Rainsford manage to find land after falling from the boat? *(He swims in the direction from which he earlier heard shots.)* **Literal recall**

SR–5. What details suggest General Zaroff's wealthy lifestyle? *(His home, servant, clothing, table setting, food, reading, collection of game animal heads.)* **Recognizing relevant details**

Continued on page 412

Teaching Strategies

Vocabulary Preview

These vocabulary words are defined at the bottom of the selection page on which they appear. You may wish to discuss them briefly before students begin reading.

amenity comfort, convenience
condone to overlook, forgive
cultivated refined
deplorable regrettable
disarm to remove suspicions
grotesque distorted; strange
imprudent showing poor judgment
indolently lazily
naive unsophisticated
opaqueness quality of not letting light through
protruding sticking out
quarry animal being hunted
specimen a sample or example
tangible able to be felt by touch
zealous enthusiastic

Support for Students of Limited English Proficiency

- Use Reader's Guidesheet, p. 55
- "The Most Dangerous Game" contains vocabulary that may be troublesome for some students. Annotations E, F, J, N, P, S, Y, NN, and PP focus on unfamiliar vocabulary.

Text Annotations

A. Critical Thinking: ANALYZING Have students analyze why Connell begins the story with Whitney's remarks. *(to build suspense and establish a tense, mysterious atmomsphere)*

B. Teaching Tip

Ask volunteers to point out the Caribbean Sea on the map. Indicate what its boundaries are—from the western tip of Cuba twelve hundred miles east to the Virgin Islands, south five hundred miles to South America and west five hundred miles along the coast of Venezuela. Navigation is open and clear, making the Caribbean a major trade route to Latin American countries. The Caribbean is a popular vacation spot because of its warm waters and mild tropical climate.

C. Literary Element: CHARACTER Have students describe Rainsford's character. *(Possible responses: tough, realistic, unsentimental, hard.)*

D. Literary Element: FORESHADOWING Ask students what Whitney's feelings in this passage might foreshadow. *(Possible response: His feelings might foreshadow evil, frightening, and dreadful things to come.)*

E. LEP: Vocabulary Pronounce *yacht* aloud for students. Suggest that they look up the pronunciation of other unfamiliar words they encounter in the text. Also discuss the word *yacht* and what it connotes about Rainsford's socioeconomic status.

F. LEP: Vocabulary Ask students what *doggedly* means and how they can figure this out from the context. (Doggedly *means "persistently, stubbornly." The clue to meaning is "slow, deliberate strokes . . . seemingly endless time he fought the sea," which conveys his persistent effort.)*

that the crew's nerves seemed a bit jumpy today?"

"They were a bit strange, now you mention it. Even Captain Nielsen—"

"Yes, even that tough-minded old Swede, who'd go up to the devil himself and ask him for a light. Those fishy blue eyes held a look I never saw there before. All I could get out of him was: 'This place has an evil name among seafaring men, sir.' Then he said to me, very gravely, 'Don't you feel anything?'—as if the air about us was actually poisonous. Now, you mustn't laugh when I tell you this—I did feel something like a sudden chill.

D "There was no breeze. The sea was as flat as a plate-glass window. We were drawing near the island then. What I felt was a—a mental chill; a sort of sudden dread."

"Pure imagination," said Rainsford. "One superstitious sailor can taint the whole ship's company with his fear."

"Maybe. But sometimes I think sailors have an extra sense that tells them when they are in danger. Sometimes I think evil is a tangible thing—with wavelengths, just as sound and light have. An evil place can, so to speak, broadcast vibrations of evil. Anyhow, I'm glad we're getting out of this zone.
SR-2 ▶ Well, I think I'll turn in now, Rainsford."

"I'm not sleepy," said Rainsford. "I'm going to smoke another pipe up on the afterdeck."

"Good night, then, Rainsford. See you at breakfast."

"Right. Good night, Whitney."

E There was no sound in the night as Rainsford sat there but the muffled throb of the engine that drove the yacht swiftly through the darkness, and the swish and ripple of the wash of the propeller.

Rainsford, reclining in a steamer chair, indolently puffed on his favorite briar. The sensuous drowsiness of the night was on him. "It's so dark," he thought, "that I could sleep without closing my eyes; the night would be my eyelids—"

An abrupt sound startled him. Off to the right he heard it, and his ears, expert in such matters, could not be mistaken. Again he heard the sound, and again. Somewhere, off in the blackness, someone had fired a gun three times.

Rainsford sprang up and moved quickly to the rail, mystified. He strained his eyes in the direction from which the reports had come, but it was like trying to see through a blanket. He leaped upon the rail and balanced himself there, to get greater elevation; his pipe, striking a rope, was knocked from his mouth. He lunged for it; a short, hoarse cry came from his lips as he realized he had reached too far and had lost his balance. The cry was pinched off short as the blood-warm waters of the Caribbean Sea closed over his head. F ◀ SR-3

He struggled up to the surface and tried to cry out, but the wash from the speeding yacht slapped him in the face, and the salt water in his open mouth made him gag and strangle. Desperately he struck out with strong strokes after the receding lights of the yacht, but he stopped before he had swum fifty feet. A certain coolheadedness had come to him; it was not the first time he had been in a tight place. There was a chance that his cries could be heard by someone aboard the yacht, but that chance was slender and grew more slender as the yacht raced on. He wrestled himself out of his clothes and shouted with all his power.

Words to Know and Use	**tangible** (tan′ jə bəl) *adj.* that can be felt by touch; having actual form **indolently** (in′ də lənt lē) *adv.* lazily

412

STRUCTURED READING FOR LESS PROFICIENT STUDENTS

Continued from page 411

SR–6. Why has General Zaroff become bored with hunting animals? *(The animals are not cunning enough, so he always gets his quarry.)* **Clarifying**

SR–7. What new animal does General Zaroff now hunt? *(men)* **Clarifying**

SR–8. What trick does Rainsford try first and what is its outcome? *(He weaves an intricate trail; Zaroff finds him but saves him for another day's sport.)* **Clarifying**

SR–9. What does Rainsford try next and what happens? *(He sets a Malay man-catcher which slightly wounds Zaroff's shoulder.)* **Clarifying**

SR–10. What is Rainsford's third plan and how does it work? *(He builds a Burmese tiger pit, which claims one of Zaroff's best dogs.)* **Clarifying**

SR–11. What do you think will happen to Rainsford? *(He will either drown, be picked up by a passing ship, or somehow return to kill Zaroff.)* **Predicting**

The lights of the yacht became faint and ever-vanishing fireflies; then they were blotted out entirely by the night.

G Rainsford remembered the shots. They had come from the right, and doggedly he swam in that direction, swimming with slow, deliberate strokes, conserving his strength. For a seemingly endless time he fought the sea. He began to count his strokes; he could do possibly a hundred more and then—

H Rainsford heard a sound. It came out of the darknesss, a high screaming sound, the sound of an animal in an extremity of anguish and terror.

He did not recognize the animal that made the sound. He did not try to. With fresh vitality, he swam toward the sound. He heard it again; then it was cut short by another noise, crisp, staccato.

"Pistol shot," muttered Rainsford, swimming on.

I SR-4 ▶ Ten minutes of determined effort brought another sound to his ears—the most welcome he had ever heard—the muttering and growling of the sea breaking on a rocky shore. He was almost on the rocks before he saw them; on a night less calm he would have been shattered against them. With his remaining strength he dragged himself from the swirling waters. Jagged crags appeared to jut up into the opaqueness; he forced himself upward, hand over hand. Gasping, his hands raw, he reached a flat place at the top. Dense jungle came down to the very edge of the cliffs. What perils that tangle of trees and underbrush might hold for him did not concern Rainsford just then. All he knew was that he was safe from his enemy, the sea, and that utter weariness was on him. He flung himself down at the jungle edge and tumbled headlong into the deepest sleep of his life.

When he opened his eyes, he knew from the position of the sun that it was late in the afternoon. Sleep had given him new vigor; a sharp hunger was picking at him. He looked about him almost cheerfully.

"Where there are pistol shots, there are men. Where there are men, there is food," he thought. But what kind of men, he wondered, in so forbidding a place? An unbroken front of snarled and ragged jungle fringed the shore.

He saw no sign of a trail through the closely knit web of weeds and trees; it was easier to go along the shore, and Rainsford floundered along by the water. Not far from where he had landed, he stopped.

Some wounded thing, by the evidence a large animal, had thrashed about in the underbrush. The jungle weeds were crushed down, and the moss was lacerated; J one patch of weeds was stained crimson. A small, glittering object not far away caught Rainsford's eye, and he picked it up. It was an empty cartridge.

"A twenty-two," he remarked. "That's odd. It must have been a fairly large animal, too. The hunter had his nerve to tackle it with a light gun. It's clear that the brute put up a fight. I suppose the first three shots I heard were when the hunter flushed[1] his quarry and wounded it. The last shot was when he trailed it here and finished it."

He examined the ground closely and found what he had hoped to find—the print of hunting boots. They pointed along the cliff in the direction he had been going. Eagerly he hurried along, now slipping on a rotten log or a loose stone, but making

1. **flushed:** raised from hiding.

Words to Know and Use

opaqueness (ō pāk′ nəs) *n.* the quality of not letting light pass through
quarry (kwôr′ ē) *n.* prey; an animal being hunted, often with the help of dogs or hawks

413

G. Critical Thinking: ANALYZING Have students analyze how the details in this passage build suspense. *(Possible responses: The anguished, terrified scream adds to the tense mood. In addition, the inability of Rainsford, an expert hunter, to recognize the anguished animal adds to the suspense by hinting that some unfamiliar, unusual creature is being hunted.)*

H. Literary Element: SETTING Ask students to explain how this particular setting is essential to the story. *(Possible response: The setting is essential because the story has to take place in a dangerous environment to convey its suspense, drama, and tension. The setting makes Rainsford's near-death much more plausible.)*

I. Reading Skill: DRAWING CONCLUSIONS Ask students to summarize what Rainsford concludes has happened, and list his evidence for drawing this conclusion. *(A hunter shot three times to wound his prey. It struggled before the hunter finally killed it with a fourth shot. The prey was large and the hunter bold. Evidence: jungle weeds "crushed," moss "lacerated," indicating a struggle; weeds stained indicates a wound; cartridge indicates the fourth shot; small caliber indicates a bold hunter, large area disturbed indicates a large prey).*

Real Life Connections

To help students recognize similarities between Rainsford's reactions and their own, first point out to students how Rainsford retains his composure however difficult his situation may be. Then ask students about instances when they have, or have not, kept their composure under pressure. Ask volunteers to share their situations and reactions. For example, students may wish to discuss a time when they took an important test, faced a driving emergency, or had a medical emergency.

J. LEP: Vocabulary Ask volunteers to look up and read to the class the definitions of *mirage* and *gargoyle.* For the latter, mention that a gargoyle can be a decoration. Sometimes a gargoyle functions as a gutter, the rain water flowing from the figure's mouth. To help students remember the word, you might want to add that *gargoyle* comes from an Old French word meaning "throat," and point out the link to our word *gargle.*

headway; night was beginning to settle down on the island.

Bleak darkness was blacking out the sea and jungle when Rainsford sighted the lights. He came upon them as he turned a crook in the coastline, and his first thought was that he had come upon a village, for there were many lights. But as he forged along, he saw to his great astonishment that all the lights were in one enormous building—a lofty structure with pointed towers plunging upward into the gloom. His eyes made out the shadowy outlines of a palatial château;[2] it was set on a high bluff, and on three sides of it, cliffs dived down to where the sea licked greedy lips in the shadows.

"Mirage," thought Rainsford. But it was no mirage he found when he opened the tall, spiked iron gate. The stone steps were real enough; the massive door with a leering gargoyle for a knocker was real enough; yet about it all hung an air of unreality. K

2. **château:** a castle or large country house.

DATA BANK

Tracking is one of the oldest and most difficult hunting skills. To illustrate how clever trackers like Zaroff or Rainsford operate in the wild, consider this situation. Footprints from individuals A and B are left in the dirt, side by side. How can you tell if A and B walked (a.) together or (b.) by themselves at different times? And, if they walked alone, who came first?

The experienced tracker looks for instances where footprints are stamped over one another. Does A's footprint exclusively appear on top of B's? This means B came first and A followed.

Similarly, if B's prints always appear on top, then A came first and B followed.

Finally, if A's prints are sometimes on top, and B's are on top at other times, then A and B must have walked together.

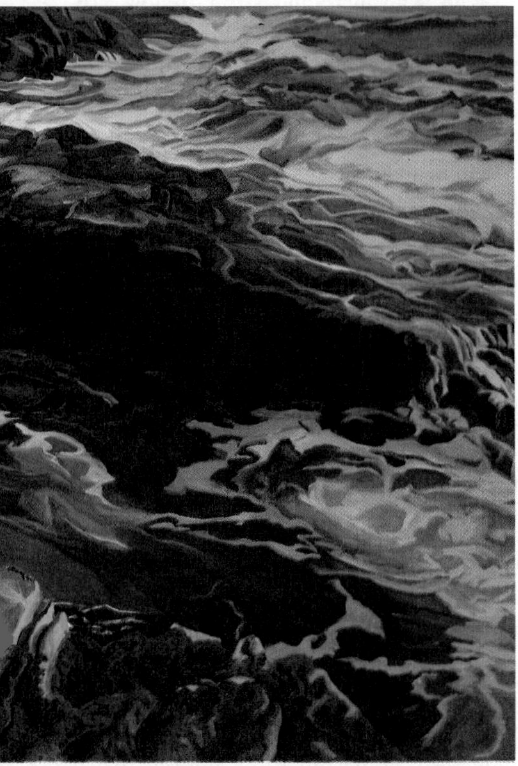

ICE BLUE 1981 Susan Shatter Fischbach Gallery, New York.

He lifted the knocker, and it creaked up stiffly, as if it had never before been used. He let it fall, and it startled him with its booming loudness. He thought he heard steps within; the door remained closed. Again Rainsford lifted the heavy knocker and let it fall. The door opened then, opened as suddenly as if it were on a spring, and Rainsford stood blinking in the river of glaring gold light that poured out. The first thing Rainsford's eyes discerned was the largest man Rainsford had ever seen—a gigantic creature, solidly made and black-bearded to the waist. In his hand the man held a long-barreled revolver, and he was pointing it straight at Rainsford's heart. L

Out of the snarl of beard, two small eyes regarded Rainsford.

"Don't be alarmed," said Rainsford, with a smile which he hoped was disarming. "I'm no robber. I fell off a yacht. My name is Sanger Rainsford of New York City."

The menacing look in his eyes did not change. The revolver pointed as rigidly as if the giant were a statue. He gave no sign that he understood Rainsford's words or that he M

Words to Know and Use	**disarm** (dis ärm′) *v.* to remove suspicions

Art Note

This oil painting of the sea rushing toward a rocky shore reveals the inhospitable nature of the land as well as the ocean. Contemporary artist Susan Shatter realizes every aspect of the water's waves, swirls and rebounds. She emphasizes its power by contrast with the placid tidal pool it has left in the upper left corner of the scene. *How does the title* Ice Blue *suggest the ocean's hazards?*

K. Teaching Tip

To help students visualize this dramatic scene, have them discuss movies or television shows with similar figures and settings. Spy movies, thrillers, and adventures often feature such scenes.

L. Reading Skill: QUESTIONING Point out the servant's odd behavior and ask students why he might be acting in this manner. *(Possible responses: he might be extremely well trained to resist all distractions; he might be unable to hear or speak.)*

M. Literary Element: CHARACTER Ask students to characterize General Zaroff. *(Possible responses: Although "singularly handsome," his appearance is nonetheless "bizarre." The contrast between his "vivid white" hair and "black as the night" eyes, eyebrows, and mustache suggests conflicting elements in his character.)*

N. LEP: Vocabulary Point out that *dumb* means "unable to speak," not "witless."

O. Literary Sidelight "Duke" is the highest heredity title outside the royal family, ranking immediately below a prince. Thus Zaroff's tailor serves only royalty and the nobility just below royalty.

P. LEP: Vocabulary Point out that a refectory table is a long narrow table with two trestle supports at the ends. A score is twenty, so twoscore would be forty, suggesting the huge length of the table and room. Discuss how these words add to the impact of the setting.

Q. Reading Skills: PREDICTING Ask students to predict why the general might be appraising Rainsford. *(Possible responses: The general might want to see if Rainsford would be a suitable hunting partner, business partner, or long-term guest. The general might also have something less savory in mind for Rainsford.)*

M had even heard them. He was dressed in uniform, a black uniform trimmed with gray astrakhan.[3]

"I'm Sanger Rainsford of New York," Rainsford began again. "I fell off a yacht. I am hungry."

The man's only answer was to raise with his thumb the hammer of his revolver. Then Rainsford saw the man's free hand go to his forehead in a military salute, and he saw him click his heels together and stand at attention. Another man was coming down the broad, marble steps, an erect, slender man in evening clothes. He advanced to Rainsford and held out his hand.

In a cultivated voice marked by a slight accent that gave it added precision and deliberateness, he said: "It is a very great pleasure and honor to welcome Mr. Sanger Rainsford, the celebrated hunter, to my home."

Automatically Rainsford shook the man's hand.

"I've read your book about hunting snow leopards in Tibet, you see," explained the man. "I am General Zaroff."

Rainsford's first impression was that the man was singularly handsome; his second was that there was an original, almost bizarre quality about the general's face. He was a tall man past middle age, for his hair was a vivid white; but his thick eyebrows N and pointed military mustache were as black as the night from which Rainsford had come. His eyes, too, were black and very bright. He had high cheek bones, a sharp-cut nose, a spare, dark face, the face of a man used to giving orders, the face of an aristocrat. Turning to the giant in uniform, the general made a sign. The giant put away his pistol, saluted, withdrew.

"Ivan is an incredibly strong fellow," remarked the general, "but he has the misfortune to be deaf and dumb. A simple fellow O but, I'm afraid, like all his race, a bit of a savage."

"Is he Russian?"

"He is a Cossack,"[4] said the general, and his smile showed red lips and pointed teeth. "So am I."

"Come," he said, "we shouldn't be chatting here. We can talk later. Now you want clothes, food, rest. You shall have them. This is a most restful spot."

Ivan had reappeared, and the general spoke to him with lips that moved but gave forth no sound.

"Follow Ivan, if you please, Mr. Rainsford," said the general. "I was about to have my dinner when you came. I'll wait for you. You'll find that my clothes will fit you, I think."

It was to a huge, beam-ceilinged bedroom with a canopied bed big enough for six men that Rainsford followed the silent giant. Ivan laid out an evening suit, and Rainsford, as he put it on, noticed that it came from a London tailor who ordinarily cut and sewed for none below the rank of P duke.

The dining room to which Ivan conducted him was in many ways remarkable. There was a medieval magnificence about it. It suggested a baronial hall of feudal times with its oaken panels, its high ceiling, its vast refectory table where twoscore men Q could sit down to eat. About the hall were

3. **astrakhan:** fur from young lambs.

4. **Cossack:** a member of the people of southern Russia, famous as horsemen.

Words to Know and Use

cultivated (kul' tə vāt' id) *adj.* refined and cultured

Professional Notebook

Many kind, loving adults overdose on "warm fuzzies" in place of serious work. Gooey experiences to help youngsters feel good about themselves are inadequate. Warmth is fine. But students, even discouraged ones, come to feel good about themselves through demonstrable achievement, even if small. Some of our most acclaimed alternative schools patronize students by putting patty-cake work/play sheets in front of teenagers and gush over how wonderfully the work is done. Work that isn't worth doing—from which no real learning takes place—is not worth doing well. Sloppy expectations invite sloppy performance.

Jerry Conrath, "Our Other Youth"

the mounted heads of many animals—lions, tigers, elephants, moose, bears; larger or more perfect specimens Rainsford had never seen. At the great table the general was sitting, alone.

"You'll have a cocktail, Mr. Rainsford," he suggested. The cocktail was surpassingly good; and, Rainsford noted, the table appointments were of the finest—the linen, the crystal, the silver, the china.

They were eating borscht, the rich red soup with sour cream so dear to Russian palates. Half apologetically General Zaroff said, "We do our best to preserve the amenities of civilization here. Please forgive any lapses. We are well off the beaten track, you know. Do you think the champagne has
SR-5 ▶ suffered from its long ocean trip?"

"Not in the least," declared Rainsford. He was finding the general a most thoughtful and affable host, a true cosmopolite.[5]
R But there was one small trait of the general's that made Rainsford uncomfortable. Whenever he looked up from his plate he found the general studying him, appraising him narrowly.

"Perhaps," said General Zaroff, "you were surprised that I recognized your name. You see, I read all books on hunting published in English, French, and Russian. I have but one passion in my life, Mr. Rainsford, and it is the hunt."

"You have some wonderful heads here," said Rainsford as he ate a particularly well cooked filet mignon. "That Cape buffalo is the largest I ever saw."

"Oh, that fellow. Yes, he was a monster."

"Did he charge you?"

"Hurled me against a tree," said the general. "Fractured my skull. But I got the brute."

"I've always thought," said Rainsford, "that the Cape buffalo is the most dangerous of all big game."

For a moment the general did not reply; he was smiling his curious, red-lipped smile. Then he said slowly, "No. You are wrong, sir. The Cape buffalo is not the most dangerous big game." He sipped his wine. "Here in my preserve on this island," he said in the same slow tone, "I hunt more dangerous game." S

Rainsford expressed his surprise. "Is there big game on this island?"

The general nodded. "The biggest."

"Really?"

"Oh, it isn't here naturally, of course. I have to stock the island." T

"What have you imported, general?" Rainsford asked. "Tigers?"

The general smiled. "No," he said. "Hunting tigers ceased to interest me some years ago. I exhausted their possibilities, you see. No thrill left in tigers, no real danger. I live for danger, Mr. Rainsford."

The general took from his pocket a gold cigarette case and offered his guest a long black cigarette with a silver tip; it was perfumed and gave off a smell like incense.

"We will have some capital hunting, you and I," said the general. "I shall be most glad to have your society." U

"But what game—" began Rainsford.

"I'll tell you," said the general. "You will be amused, I know. I think I may say, in all modesty, that I have done a rare thing. I have invented a new sensation. May I pour you another glass of port, Mr. Rainsford?"

"Thank you, general."

The general filled both glasses and said,

5. **cosmopolite:** a person who is comfortable anywhere in the world.

Words to Know and Use

specimen (spes′ ə mən) *n.* a sample or example of a whole group
amenity (ə men′ ə tē) *n.* anything that adds to one's comfort or convenience

417

R. Critical Thinking: EVALUATING Ask students to consider what animal might be more dangerous than the Cape buffalo. List their suggestions on the board. *(Possible responses: tigers, bears, wolves, lions)*

S. LEP: Vocabulary Explain to students that by "stocking the island" the general means that he imports specimens to hunt and places them in strategic places in the jungle. To help students better understand the term, use it in other contexts as well, as in "to stock the shelves with food."

T. Literary Element: FORESHADOWING Ask students to consider in what sense the general's remark might be an indication of things to come. *(Possible response: It seems that the general has made up his mind that Rainsford will participate in his hunting plans. There is a sense of danger awaiting Rainsford.)*

Teaching Tip

Acronyms and other mnemonic devices are an especially useful and fun way to help students remember important information. The acronym DIME, for example, can help students remember four important reading skills:

D Learn *D*etails
I Make *I*nferences and Draw Conclusions
M Get the *M*ain Idea
E Make an *E*valuation or Judgment

Write the acronym and explanation on the board and discuss it with students. Then have them apply this information to their reading of "The Most Dangerous Game" and other assignments they may have. You may also wish to isolate specific passages from the story as illustrations of each letter.

U. Historical Sidelight Explain that Zaroff is alluding to the fate of some Russian emigrés, forced by their changing fortunes to adopt menial jobs. Many such emigres relocated to Monte Carlo or Paris.

V. Reading Skill: SUMMARIZING Have students summarize what Zaroff tells of his life. *(Trained from childhood to hunt, Zaroff entered the Czar's cavalry as expected. After the Russian Revolution, he returned to hunting. However, hunting now bores him because he always outwits his prey.)*

W. Critical Thinking: EVALUATING Ask students if they agree with Zaroff's conclusion about the boredom of perfection. *(Possible responses: Perfection is boring because it removes all challenge; perfection is desirable for its sense of achievement and completion.)*

"God makes some men poets. Some He makes kings, some beggars. Me He made a hunter. My hand was made for the trigger, my father said. He was a very rich man with a quarter of a million acres in the Crimea, and he was an ardent sportsman. When I was only five years old, he gave me a little gun, specially made in Moscow for me, to shoot sparrows with. When I shot some of his prize turkeys with it, he did not punish me; he complimented me on my marksmanship. I killed my first bear in the Caucasus[6] when I was ten. My whole life has been one prolonged hunt. I went into the army—it was expected of noblemen's sons—and for a time commanded a division of Cossack cavalry, but my real interest was always the hunt. I have hunted every kind of game in every land. It would be impossible for me to tell you how many animals I have killed."

The general puffed at his cigarette.

"After the debacle[7] in Russia, I left the country, for it was imprudent for an officer of the Czar to stay there. Many noble Russians lost everything. I, luckily, had invested heavily in American securities, so I shall never have to open a tearoom in Monte Carlo or drive a taxi in Paris. Naturally, I continued to hunt —grizzlies in your Rockies, crocodiles in the Ganges,[8] rhinoceroses in East Africa. It was in Africa that the Cape buffalo hit me and laid me up for six months. As soon as I recovered, I started for the Amazon to hunt jaguars, for I had heard they were unusually cunning. They weren't." The Cossack sighed. "They were no match at all for a hunter with his wits about him, and a high-powered rifle. I was bitterly disappointed. I was lying in my tent with a splitting headache one night when a terrible thought pushed its way into my mind. Hunting was beginning to bore me! And hunting, remember, had been my life. I have heard that in America, businessmen often go to pieces when they give up the business that has been their life." W SR-6

"Yes, that's so," said Rainsford.

The general smiled. "I had no wish to go to pieces," he said. "I must do something. Now, mine is an analytical mind, Mr. Rainsford. Doubtless that is why I enjoy the problems of the chase."

"No doubt, General Zaroff."

"So," continued the general, "I asked myself why the hunt no longer fascinated me. You are much younger than I am, Mr. Rainsford, and have not hunted as much, but you perhaps can guess the answer."

"What was it?"

"Simply this: hunting had ceased to be what you call 'a sporting proposition.' It had become too easy. I always got my quarry. Always. There is no greater bore than perfection." X

The general lit a fresh cigarette.

"No animal had a chance with me any more. That is no boast; it is a mathematical certainty. The animal had nothing but his legs and his instinct. Instinct is no match for reason. When I thought of this, it was a tragic moment for me, I can tell you."

Rainsford leaned across the table, absorbed in what his host was saying.

"It came to me as an inspiration what I must do," the general went on.

6. **Crimea . . . Caucasus:** regions in the southern U.S.S.R.

7. **debacle:** a bad defeat (a reference to the Russian Revolution).

8. **Ganges:** a river in northern India.

Words to Know and Use

imprudent (im pro͞od′ 'nt) *adj.* showing poor judgment

DATA BANK

Buffalo is the everyday name for wild or domesticated oxen. Like cattle, buffalo have cloven hooves and chew their cud, but buffalo are far more powerful than cattle. American buffalo are more correctly called *bison.*

The Cape buffalo, which Rainsford and General Zaroff discuss, is indeed a fierce fighting opponent. It inhabits southern and central Africa and is very large, measuring to almost six feet as the shoulder. It is noted for horns that are massive at the base, forming a helmet over the forehead and reaching a length of about three feet.

Cape buffalo fell victim to disease early in the twentieth century. Almost the entire population was wiped out. The survivors, according to hunting old-timers, do not possess the same fierce fighting ability that their ancestors had in the 1890s.

"And that was?"

The general smiled the quiet smile of one who has faced an obstacle and surmounted it with success. "I had to invent a new animal to hunt," he said.

"A new animal? You're joking."

"Not at all," said the general. "I never joke about hunting. I needed a new animal. I found one. So I bought this island, built this house, and here I do my hunting. The island is perfect for my purposes—there are jungles with a maze of trails in them, hills, swamps—"

"But the animal, General Zaroff?"

"Oh," said the general, "it supplies me with the most exciting hunting in the world. No other hunting compares with it for an instant. Every day I hunt, and I never grow bored now, for I have a quarry with which I can match my wits."

Rainsford's bewilderment showed in his face.

"I wanted the ideal animal to hunt," explained the general. "So, I said: 'What are the attributes of an ideal quarry?' And the answer was, of course: 'It must have courage, cunning, and, above all, it must be able to reason.'"

Y "But no animal can reason," objected Rainsford.

"My dear fellow," said the general, "there is one that can."

"But you can't mean—" gasped Rainsford.

"And why not?"

"I can't believe you are serious, General Zaroff. This is a grisly joke."

"Why should I not be serious? I am speaking of hunting."

"Hunting? General Zaroff, what you speak of is murder." ◄ SR-7

The general laughed with entire good nature. He regarded Rainsford quizzically. "I refuse to believe that so modern and civilized a young man as you seem to be harboring romantic ideas about the value of human life. Surely your experiences in the war—"

"Did not make me condone cold-blooded murder," finished Rainsford stiffly.

Laughter shook the general. "How extraordinarily droll you are!" he said. "One does not expect nowadays to find a young man of the educated class, even in America, with such a naive, and, if I may say so, mid-Victorian point of view. It's like finding a snuffbox in a limousine. Ah, well, doubtless you had Puritan ancestors. So many Americans appear to have had. I'll wager you'll forget your notions when you go hunting with me. You've a genuine new thrill in store for you, Mr. Rainsford."

"The weak of the world were put here to give the strong pleasure."

"Thank you. I'm a hunter, not a murderer."

"Dear me," said the general, quite unruffled. "Again that unpleasant word. But I think I can show you that your scruples are quite ill-founded." Z

"Yes?"

"Life is for the strong, to be lived by the strong and, if need be, taken by the strong. The weak of the world were put here to give the strong pleasure. I am strong. Why AA

Words to Know and Use

condone (kən dōn′) *v.* to overlook an offense; forgive
naive (nä ēv′) *adj.* unsophisticated

419

X. Critical Thinking: INFERRING Ask students to infer from the interchange between the two what Zaroff actually hunts. Then ask them how this relates to the double meaning in the story's title. *(Possible response: He hunts humans; a game is both sport and prey. The most dangerous "game" (quarry) is a human, and the most dangerous "game" as a sport is the hunting of humans.)*

Y. LEP: Vocabulary Explain that *scruples* are moral considerations and that Rainsford is objecting to the General's plan to hunt human beings.

Z. Critical Thinking: EVALUATING Have students evaluate the validity of Zaroff's beliefs. *(Possible response: The general is mistaken: the strong were put on the earth to help the weak, not harm them.)*

DATA BANK

The Russian revolution of 1917 was capped off when Lenin's Bolsheviks seized power and declared a dictatorship of the proletariat. Opposing the new regime were liberals, bourgeois, Constitutional Democrats, rival socialist parties, and tsarist reactionaries like Zaroff. Because they had been in power so long, the tsarist aristocrats were deeply resented by most of the other anti-Bolshevik groups. This was one of the main reasons the anti-Bolsheviks never united and were never a serious threat to Lenin.

In 1920 civil war broke out in the Soviet Union, followed by the ''Red Terror'' in which citizens were rounded up and killed (or imprisoned) if they were suspected of being against the regime. Tsarists like Zaroff scattered to all corners of the globe, taking what they could of their wealth, never to see their native country again.

Art Note

Casanova is a generic term of contempt for a man whose behavior toward women is unscrupulous. Such a person is considered to be without a moral sense, and therefore dangerous. In this oil painting, Cuban American artist Julio Larraz depicts such a man in sinister light and in a setting rife with the remains of creatures he has caught and killed. *Can you imagine the thoughts of the seated man?*

CASANOVA 1987 Julio Larraz Private collection Courtesy of Nohra Haime Gallery, New York.

should I not use my gift? If I wish to hunt, why should I not? I hunt the scum of the earth—sailors from tramp ships—lascars, blacks, Chinese, whites, mongrels—a thoroughbred horse or hound is worth more than a score of them."

"But they are men," said Rainsford hotly.

"Precisely," said the general. "That is why I use them. It gives me pleasure. They can reason, after a fashion. So they are dangerous."

"But where do you get them?"

The general's left eyelid fluttered down in a wink. "This island is called Ship-Trap," he answered. "Sometimes an angry god of the high seas sends them to me. Sometimes, when Providence is not so kind, I help Providence a bit. Come to the window with me."

Rainsford went to the window and looked out toward the sea.

"Watch! Out there!" exclaimed the general, pointing into the night. Rainsford's eyes saw only blackness, and then, as the general pressed a button, far out to sea Rainsford saw the flash of lights.

The general chuckled. "They indicate a channel," he said, "where there's none; giant rocks with razor edges crouch like a sea monster with wide-open jaws. They can crush a ship as easily as I crush this nut." He

CULTURAL CONNECTION

Zaroff's philosophy that "life is for the strong" has most likely been influenced by the social Darwinists, who thrived in the late nineteenth and early twentieth centuries and was promoted in the United States by William Graham Sumner. Social Darwinists shaped Darwin's evolutionary theory to explain social behavior.

The core of their beliefs held that society should not be protected from competition, or "natural selection." People should compete with one another for resources, weeding out the strong from the weak. Those who couldn't compete successfully would die out, leaving the human race more "fit."

These distortions of Darwin's original ideas were used to justify a variety of barbarous acts including the war crimes committed by Nazi Germany in the 1930s and 40s.

dropped a walnut on the hardwood floor and brought his heel grinding down on it. "Oh, yes," he said, casually, as if in answer to a question, "I have electricity. We try to be civilized here."

"Civilized? And you shoot down men?"

A trace of anger was in the general's black eyes, but it was there for but a second, and he said, in his most pleasant manner, "Dear me, what a righteous young man you are! I assure you I do not do the thing you suggest. That would be barbarous. I treat these visitors with every consideration. They get plenty of good food and exercise. They get into splendid physical condition. You shall see for yourself tomorrow."

"What do you mean?"

BB "We'll visit my training school," smiled the general. "It's in the cellar. I have about a dozen pupils down there now. They're from the Spanish bark *San Lucar*, which had the bad luck to go on the rocks out there. A very inferior lot, I regret to say. Poor specimens and more accustomed to the deck than to the jungle."

He raised his hand, and Ivan, who served as waiter, brought thick Turkish coffee. Rainsford, with an effort, held his tongue in check.

CC "It's a game, you see," pursued the general blandly. "I suggest to one of them that we go hunting. I give him a supply of food and an excellent hunting knife. I give him three hours' start. I am to follow, armed only with a pistol of the smallest caliber and range. If my quarry eludes me for three whole days, he wins the game. If I find him"—the general smiled—"he loses."

"Suppose he refuses to be hunted?"

"Oh," said the general, "I give him his option, of course. He need not play that game if he doesn't wish to. If he does not wish to hunt, I turn him over to Ivan. Ivan once had the honor of serving as official knouter[9] to the Great White Czar, and he has his own ideas of sport. Invariably, Mr. Rainsford, invariably they choose the hunt." DD

"And if they win?"

The smile on the general's face widened. "To date I have not lost," he said.

Then he added, hastily: "I don't wish you to think me a braggart, Mr. Rainsford. Many of them afford only the most elementary sort of problem. Occasionally I strike a tartar. One almost did win. I eventually had to use the dogs." EE

"The dogs?"

"This way, please. I'll show you."

The general steered Rainsford to a window. The lights from the windows sent a flickering illumination that made grotesque patterns on the courtyard below, and Rainsford could see moving about there a dozen or so huge black shapes. As they turned toward him, their eyes glittered greenly.

"A rather good lot, I think," observed the general. "They are let out at seven every night. If anyone should try to get into my house—or out of it—something extremely regrettable would occur to him." He hummed a snatch of song from the Folies Bergère.[10]

"And now," said the general, "I want to show you my new collection of heads. Will you come with me to the library?"

9. **knouter** (nout′ ər): a person who whipped criminals in Russia.

10. **Folies Bergère** (fô lē ber zher′) *French:* an elaborately costumed French theatrical revue consisting of musical skits and dancing.

Words to Know and Use | **grotesque** (grō tesk′) *adj.* characterized by distorted shapes; twisted, strange

421

AA. Reading Skill: INFERRING Ask students to infer the general's meaning in this passage. *(He means that sometimes travelers suitable for use as hunting prey do crash on the shores of his island. At other times, however, when his "stock" runs low, he creates artificial traps to lure his victims.)*

Teaching Tip

Point out to students the words and phrases Zaroff uses to dehumanize his victims: "very inferior lot" and "poor specimens." You might want to explain how other tyrants have stripped people of their humanity to justify their victimization. Examples: Slave-traders referred to Africans as "animals"; Nazis referred to Jews and gypsies as "racially inferior"; whites referred to Native Americans as "savages."

BB. Critical Thinking: EVALUATING Ask students if they think the General's "game" is fair. Have them explain their decisions. *(Possible response: The game is not fair because the General is armed with a pistol; his quarry, with a knife. Further, the General knows the topography, while his quarry has only been on the island once, when he was captured.)*

CC. Reading Skill: INFERRING Have students infer from this passage what Ivan considers "sport." *(Possible responses: He enjoys torturing his victims before he kills them.)*

DD. Literary Sidelight Explain to students that a Tartar is a member of any of the various tribes, chiefly Mongolian or Turkish, that overran Asia and much of Eastern Europe in the Middle Ages. The word *tartar* has thus been used to mean "a savage and intractable fighter."

Data Bank

The extinction of animals such as the dodo bird led to the passing of laws in several countries protecting certain animals. Wildlife conservationists categorize threatened species in the following manner.

Endangered Species are the most severely threatened by extinction; their members are so few that they can be counted individually. Due to the destruction of habitat and the vagaries of breeding, these species require human intervention in order to be maintained. The California condor is an example.

Threatened species face dangers from the environment and human interference, but still breed successfully and are abundant in some areas. Examples include the gray wolf, which is plentiful in some places, but whose numbers are diminishing yearly.

Rare species have diminished populations but their numbers are constant or increasing. They live in protected environments. Examples include the American bison.

EE. Literary Element: SETTING Ask students how the setting reinforces Rainsford's feelings. *(Possible response: The "dark and silent" night illuminated only by the "fragment of sallow moon" casting a "wan light" reinforces his isolation and desperation.)*

FF. Literary Sidelight Pronounce *ennui* (än wē') for students and explain its French origin and its meaning ("boredom"). Also explain that *crêpes suzette* is a thin dessert pancake. Point out that familiarity with French is often regarded as a sign of a civilized person.

GG. Literary Element: FORESHADOWING Have students trace the hints planted throughout the story that made this outcome inevitable. *(Possible responses: Both Whitney and Zaroff noted Rainsford's fame as a big-game hunter, making him a worthy adversary; Zaroff repeatedly expressed boredom with his usual prey and his need for a suitable quarry.)*

"I hope," said Rainsford, "that you will excuse me tonight, General Zaroff. I'm really not feeling at all well."

"Ah, indeed?" the general inquired solicitously. "Well, I suppose that's only natural, after your long swim. You need a good, restful night's sleep. Tomorrow you'll feel like a new man, I'll wager. Then we'll hunt, eh? I've one rather promising prospect—"

Rainsford was hurrying from the room.

"Sorry you can't go with me tonight," called the general. "I expect rather fair sport—a big, strong fellow. He looks resourceful—Well, good night, Mr. Rainsford; I hope you have a good night's rest."

The bed was good, and the pajamas of the softest silk, and he was tired in every fiber of his being, but nevertheless Rainsford could not quiet his brain with the opiate of sleep. He lay, eyes wide open. Once he thought he heard stealthy steps in the corridor outside his room. He sought to throw open the door; it would not open. He went to the window and looked out. His room was high up in one of the towers. The lights of the château were out now, and it was dark and silent; but there was a fragment of sallow moon, and by its wan light he could see, dimly, the courtyard. There, weaving in and out in the pattern of shadow, were black, noiseless forms. The hounds heard him at the window and looked up, expectantly, with their green eyes. Rainsford went back to the bed and lay down. By many methods he tried to put himself to sleep. He had achieved a doze when, just as morning began to come, he heard, far off in the jungle, the faint report of a pistol.

General Zaroff did not appear until luncheon. He was dressed faultlessly in the tweeds of a country squire. He was solicitous[11] about the state of Rainsford's health.

"As for me," sighed the general, "I do not feel so well. I am worried, Mr. Rainsford. Last night I detected traces of my old complaint."

To Rainsford's questioning glance the general said: "Ennui. Boredom."

Then, taking a second helping of crêpes suzette, the general explained: "The hunting was not good last night. The fellow lost his head. He made a straight trail that offered no problems at all. That's the trouble with these sailors; they have dull brains to begin with, and they do not know how to get about in the woods. They do excessively stupid and obvious things. It's most annoying. Will you have another glass of Chablis, Mr. Rainsford?"

"General," said Rainsford firmly, "I wish to leave this island at once."

The general raised his thickets of eyebrows; he seemed hurt. "But, my dear fellow," the general protested, "you've only just come. You've had no hunting—"

"I wish to go today," said Rainsford. He saw the dead black eyes of the general on him, studying him. General Zaroff's face suddenly brightened.

He filled Rainsford's glass with venerable Chablis from a dusty bottle.

"Tonight," said the general, "we will hunt—you and I."

Rainsford shook his head. "No, general," he said. "I will not hunt."

The general shrugged his shoulders and delicately ate a hothouse grape. "As you wish, my friend," he said. "The choice rests entirely with you. But may I not venture to suggest that you will find my idea of sport more diverting than Ivan's?"

He nodded toward the corner to where the giant stood, scowling, his thick arms crossed on his hogshead of chest.

11. **solicitous:** showing concern.

II **infer** What choice does Zaroff offer Rainsford?

"You don't mean—" cried Rainsford.

"My dear fellow," said the general, "have I not told you I always mean what I say about hunting? This is really an inspiration. I drink to a foeman worthy of my steel—at last."

The general raised his glass, but Rainsford sat staring at him.

"You'll find this game worth playing," the general said enthusiastically. "Your brain against mine. Your woodcraft against mine. Your strength and stamina against mine. Outdoor chess! And the stake is not without value, eh?"

"And if I win—" began Rainsford huskily.

"I'll cheerfully acknowledge myself defeated if I do not find you by midnight of the third day," said General Zaroff. "My sloop will place you on the mainland near a town."

The general read what Rainsford was thinking.

JJ "Oh, you can trust me," said the Cossack. "I will give you my word as a gentleman and a sportsman. Of course you, in turn, must agree to say nothing of your visit here."

"I'll agree to nothing of the kind," said Rainsford.

"Oh," said the general, "in that case—but why discuss that now? Three days hence we can discuss it over a bottle of Veuve Cliquot, unless—"

The general sipped his wine.

Then a businesslike air animated him. "Ivan," he said to Rainsford, "will supply you with hunting clothes, food, a knife. I suggest you wear moccasins; they leave a poorer trail. I suggest, too, that you avoid a big swamp in the southeast corner of the island. We call it Death Swamp. There's quicksand there. One foolish fellow tried it. The deplorable part of it was that Lazarus followed him. You can imagine my feelings, Mr. Rainsford. I loved Lazarus; he was the finest hound in my pack. Well, I must beg you to excuse me now, I always take a siesta after lunch. You'll hardly have time for a nap, I fear. You'll want to start, no doubt. I shall not follow till dusk. Hunting at night is so much more exciting than by day, don't you think? Au revoir, Mr. Rainsford, au revoir."[12] KK

General Zaroff, with a deep, courtly bow, strolled from the room.

From another door came Ivan. Under one arm he carried khaki hunting clothes, a haversack of food, a leather sheath containing a long-bladed hunting knife; his right hand rested on a cocked revolver thrust in the crimson sash about his waist. . . .

Rainsford had fought his way through the bush for two hours. "I must keep my nerve. I must keep my nerve," he said through tight teeth.

He had not been entirely clearheaded when the château gates snapped shut behind him. His whole idea at first was to put distance between himself and General Zaroff, and, to this end, he had plunged along, spurred on by the sharp rowels of something very like panic. Now he had got a grip on himself, and stopped, and was taking stock of himself and the situation.

12. **au revoir** (ō' rə vwär') *French:* until we meet again; goodbye.

Words to Know and Use **deplorable** (dē plôr' ə bəl) *adj.* extremely regrettable

HH. Reading Skill: INFERRING *(Zaroff offers the choice of being hunted by him or tortured by Ivan.)*

II. Literary Element: IRONY Ask students to explain the irony in the general's comment. *(The general is neither a gentleman nor a sportsman. Killing fellow humans is against everything that a "gentleman" believes. In the same way, Zaroff cannot be a sportsman; he does not give his victims an even chance.)*

JJ. Literary Element: CHARACTER Ask students to explain what Zaroff's reactions in this passage reveal about his character. *(Possible response: The contrast between his disregard for the "foolish fellow" and his concern for his hunting dog reveals that he places little value on human life but deeply values his animals.)*

KK. Teaching Tip

Connell omits the details of Rainsford's preparation, cutting instead directly to the hunt. This serves to increase suspense by plunging the reader right into a more dramatic part of the story. Explain how by doing this Connell shows the action rather than telling about it, one of the hallmarks of effective writing.

LL. Literary Element: SETTING Ask students if they think the events could have taken place in another setting. *(Possible response: Since Rainsford's options would be different if he was not on a small, isolated, and densely foliaged island, the setting is integral to the story.)*

MM. Reading Skill: INFERRING Based on what students know of Zaroff's character, have them infer why Zaroff turns away. *(Possible response: He wants to prolong the hunt.)*

NN. LEP: Vocabulary Explain to students that *uncanny* means "beyond the ordinary or normal," and implies a mysterious, supernatural power.

LL He saw that straight flight was futile; inevitably it would bring him face to face with the sea. He was in a picture with a frame of water, and his operations, clearly, must take place within that frame.

"I'll give him a trail to follow," muttered Rainsford, and he struck off from the rude paths he had been following into the trackless wilderness. He executed a series of intricate loops; he doubled on his trail again and again, recalling all the lore of the fox hunt and all the dodges of the fox. Night found him leg-weary, with hands and face lashed by the branches, on a thickly wooded ridge. He knew it would be insane to blunder on through the dark, even if he had the strength. His need for rest was imperative, and he thought, "I have played the fox, now I must play the cat of the fable." A big tree with a thick trunk and outspread branches was nearby, and taking care to leave not the slightest mark, he climbed up into the crotch and, stretching out on one of the broad limbs, after a fashion, rested. Rest brought him new confidence and almost a feeling of security. Even so zealous a hunter as General Zaroff could not trace him there, he told himself; only the devil himself could follow that complicated trail through the jungle after dark. But, perhaps, the general was a devil—

An apprehensive night crawled slowly by like a wounded snake, and sleep did not visit Rainsford, although the silence of a dead world was on the jungle. Toward morning, when a dingy gray was varnishing the sky, the cry of some startled bird focused Rainsford's attention in that direction. Something was coming through the bush, coming slowly, carefully, coming by the same winding way Rainsford had come. He flattened himself down on the limb, and through a screen of leaves almost as thick as tapestry, he watched. The thing that was approaching was a man.

It was General Zaroff. He made his way along with his eyes fixed in utmost concentration on the ground before him. He paused, almost beneath the tree, dropped to his knees, and studied the ground. Rainsford's impulse was to hurl himself down like a panther, but he saw that the general's right hand held something metallic—a small automatic pistol.

The hunter shook his head several times, as if he were puzzled. Then he straightened up and took from his case one of his black cigarettes; its pungent, incenselike smoke floated up to Rainsford's nostrils.

Rainsford held his breath. The general's eyes had left the ground and were traveling inch by inch up the tree. Rainsford froze there, every muscle tensed for a spring. But the sharp eyes of the hunter stopped before they reached the limb where Rainsford lay; a smile spread over his brown face. Very deliberately he blew a smoke ring into the air; then he turned his back on the tree and walked carelessly away, back along the trail he had come. The swish of the underbrush against his hunting boots grew fainter and fainter. MM

The pent-up air burst hotly from Rainsford's lungs. His first thought made him feel sick and numb. The general could follow a trail through the woods at night; he could follow an extremely difficult trail. He must have uncanny powers. Only by the merest chance had the Cossack failed to see his quarry. NN

Words to Know and Use	**zealous** (zel′ əs) *adj.* intensely devoted and enthusiastic

Real Life Connections

To help students understand Rainsford's desperation, have them recast his predicament into situations they have encountered that inspired a similar terror and fear. For example, being unable to escape might translate into the feeling students have when they sit down to a surprise test or quiz for which they are completely unprepared.

Rainsford's second thought was even more terrible. It sent a shudder of cold horror through his whole being. Why had the general smiled? Why had he turned back?

Rainsford did not want to believe what his reason told him was true, but the truth was as evident as the sun that had by now pushed through the morning mists. The general was playing with him! The general was saving him for another day's sport! The Cossack was the cat; he was the mouse. OO SR-8 ▶ Then it was that Rainsford knew the full meaning of terror.

"I will not lose my nerve. I will not."

He slid down from the tree and struck off again into the woods. His face was set, and he forced the machinery of his mind to function. Three hundred yards from his hiding place he stopped where a huge, dead tree leaned precariously on a smaller, living one. Throwing off his sack of food, Rainsford took his knife from its sheath and began to work with all his energy.

The job was finished at last, and he threw himself down behind a fallen log a hundred feet away. He did not have to wait long. The cat was coming again to play with the mouse.

Following the trail with the sureness of a bloodhound came General Zaroff. Nothing escaped those searching black eyes, no crushed blade of grass, no bent twig, no mark, no matter how faint, in the moss. So intent was the Cossack on his stalking that he was upon the thing Rainsford had made before he saw it. His foot touched the protruding bough that was the trigger. Even as he touched it, the general sensed his danger and leaped back with the agility of an ape. But he was not quite quick enough; the dead tree, delicately adjusted to rest on the cut living one, crashed down and struck the general a glancing blow on the shoulder as it fell; but for his alertness, he must have been smashed beneath it. He staggered, but he did not fall; nor did he drop his revolver. He stood there, rubbing his injured shoulder, and Rainsford, with fear again gripping his heart, heard the general's mocking laugh ring through the jungle. ◀ SR-9

"Rainsford," called the general, "if you are within sound of my voice, as I suppose you are, let me congratulate you. Not many men know how to make a Malay mancatcher. Luckily for me, I too have hunted in Malacca. You are proving interesting, Mr. Rainsford. I am going now to have my wound dressed; it's only a slight one. But I shall be back. I shall be back."

When the general, nursing his bruised shoulder, had gone, Rainsford took up his flight again. It was flight now, a desperate, hopeless flight, that carried him on for some hours. Dusk came, then darkness, and still he pressed on. The ground grew softer under his moccasins; the vegetation grew ranker, denser; insects bit him savagely. PP Then, as he stepped forward, his foot sank into the ooze. He tried to wrench it back, but the muck sucked viciously at his foot as if it were a giant leech. With a violent effort, he tore his foot loose. He knew where he was now. Death Swamp and its quicksand. QQ

His hands were tight closed as if his nerve were something tangible that someone in the darkness was trying to tear from his grip. The softness of the earth had given him an idea. He stepped back from the quicksand a dozen feet or so and, like some huge prehistoric beaver, he began to dig.

Words to Know and Use | **protruding** (prō tro͞od′ iŋ) *adj.* sticking or jutting out **protrude** *v.*

425

OO. Critical Thinking: ANALYZING Ask students to analyze why Rainsford now feels "the full meaning of terror." *(He now realizes that Zaroff has the upper hand and that he has only a slim chance of succeeding against him.)*

PP. LEP: Vocabulary Tell students that *ranker* means *"more excessive or lush."* The word also implies an offensively strong smell. Have students explain why the word is especially effective in this description. *(Possible response: It implies a moral as well as physical revulsion.)*

QQ. Literary Element: SETTING Have students explore how this particular setting builds suspense. *(Possible responses: The very name "Death Swamp" foreshadows doom; also, Zaroff's warning of the Swamp's dangers leads one to anticipate a brutal battle for survival.)*

Real Life Connections

To help students sort out their feelings about hunting, have them discuss this quote. Does Ms. Markham's assertion have validity? Ask students to support their positions with logical arguments.

"As to the brutality of elephant-hunting, I cannot see that it is any more brutal than ninety per cent of all human activities. I suppose there is nothing more tragic about the death of an elephant than there is about the death of a Hereford steer—certainly not in the eyes of the steer. The only difference is that the steer has neither the ability nor the chance to outwit the gentleman who wields the slaughter-house snickersnee, while the elephant has both of these to put against the hunter."

Beryl Markham, *West with the Night*

RR. Reading Skill: PREDICTING Have students predict who has been captured in the trap. *(Possible responses: General Zaroff, Ivan, one of the fierce hunting dogs.)*

SS. Teaching Tip

To help students visualize the intensity of these scenes with their stark shadings of light and dark, dramatic voice-overs, and tense action, have volunteers role-play a portion. Consider using appropriate background music and props such as flashlights to enhance the suspense.

Art Note

Frederic Edwin Church (1826–1900) was born in Hartford, Connecticut. He traveled widely in wilderness areas. His scientific accuracy and devotion to nature gave life and meaning to his landscape paintings. This scene of a Jamaican rain forest typifies his splendid treatments of the atmosphere of the tropics. *How does this island jungle compare with that in "The Most Dangerous Game"?*

Rainsford had dug himself in in France when a second's delay meant death. That had been a placid pastime compared to his digging now. The pit grew deeper; when it was above his shoulders, he climbed out, and from some hard saplings cut stakes and sharpened them to a fine point. These stakes he planted in the bottom of the pit with the points sticking up. With flying fingers he wove a rough carpet of weeds and branches, and with it he covered the mouth of the pit. Then, wet with sweat and aching with tiredness, he crouched behind the stump of a lightning-charred tree.

He knew his pursuer was coming; he heard the padding sound of feet on the soft earth, and the night breeze brought him the perfume of the general's cigarette. It seemed to Rainsford that the general was coming with unusual swiftness; he was not feeling his way along, foot by foot. Rainsford, crouching there, could not see the general, nor could he see the pit. He lived a year in a minute. Then he felt an impulse to cry aloud with joy, for he heard the sharp crackle of the breaking branches as the cover of the pit gave way; he heard the sharp scream of pain as the pointed stakes found their mark. He leaped up from his place of concealment. Then he cowered back. Three feet from the pit a man was standing, with an electric torch in his hand. RR

"You've done well, Rainsford," the voice of the general called. "Your Burmese tiger pit has claimed one of my best dogs. Again you score. I think, Mr. Rainsford, I'll see

RAIN FOREST, JAMAICA, WEST INDIES 1865 Frederic E. Church Cooper-Hewitt Museum, Smithsonian Institution/Art Resource, New York.

DATA BANK

Both Rainsford and Zaroff adopt classic hunting techniques to foil their adversary. Zaroff employs methods called "still-hunting" and "driving" that game hunters use for large prey such as deer. Still-hunting involves tracking the prey until it is cornered. Zaroff employs this method as he follows Rainsford through the jungle. Toward the end of the story, Zaroff uses driving when he has his dogs flush Rainsford out of the jungle so he can try to shoot him.

When Rainsford plays the role of the hunter he sticks primarily to typical duck-hunting methods. Duck hunters use waterfowl calls and wooden ducks to attract their prey into a trap or duck "blind" from which they shoot. Rainsford modifies this basic plan by using his own trail to lure Zaroff into his Malay man-catcher, his Burmese tiger pit, and his springing sapling trap.

what you can do against my whole pack. I'm going home for a rest now. Thank you for a
SR-10 ▶ most amusing evening."

At daybreak, Rainsford, lying near the swamp, was awakened by a sound that made him know that he had new things to learn about fear. It was a distant sound, faint and wavering, but he knew it. It was the baying of a pack of hounds.

SS Rainsford knew he could do one of two things. He could stay where he was and wait. That was suicide. He could flee. That was postponing the inevitable. For a moment he stood there, thinking. An idea that held a wild chance came to him, and tightening his belt, he headed away from the swamp.

The baying of the hounds grew nearer, then still nearer, nearer, ever nearer. On a ridge Rainsford climbed a tree. Down a watercourse, not a quarter of a mile away, he could see the bush moving. Straining his eyes, he saw the lean figure of General Zaroff. Just ahead of him Rainsford made out another figure, whose wide shoulders surged through the tall jungle weeds. It was the giant Ivan, and he seemed pulled forward by some unseen force. Rainsford knew that Ivan must be holding the pack in leash.

They would be on him any minute now.
TT His mind worked frantically. He thought of a native trick he had learned in Uganda. He slid down the tree. He caught hold of a springy young sapling, and to it he fastened his hunting knife, with the blade pointing down the trail. With a bit of wild grapevine he tied back the sapling. Then he ran for his life. The hounds raised their voices as
UU they hit the fresh scent. Rainsford knew now how an animal at bay feels.

He had to stop to get his breath. The baying of the hounds stopped abruptly, and Rainsford's heart stopped too. They must have reached the knife.

He shinnied excitedly up a tree and looked back. His pursuers had stopped. But the hope that was in Rainsford's brain when he climbed died, for he saw in the shallow valley that General Zaroff was still on his feet. But Ivan was not. The knife, driven by the recoil of the springing tree, had not wholly failed.

What happened to Ivan? **infer** VV

Rainsford had hardly tumbled to the ground when the pack took up the cry again.

"Nerve, nerve, nerve!" he panted, as he dashed along. A blue gap showed between the trees dead ahead. Ever nearer drew the hounds. Rainsford forced himself on toward that gap. He reached it. It was the shore of the sea. Across the cove he could see the gloomy gray stone of the château. Twenty feet below him the sea rumbled and hissed. Rainsford hesitated. He heard the hounds. Then he leaped far out into the ◀ SR-11
sea. . . .

When the general and his pack reached the place by the sea, the Cossack stopped. For some minutes he stood regarding the blue-green expanse of water. He shrugged his shoulders. Then he sat down, took a drink of brandy from a silver flask, lit a perfumed cigarette, and hummed a bit from *Madame Butterfly*.[13]

General Zaroff had an exceedingly good dinner in his great paneled dining hall that evening. With it he had a bottle of Pol Roger and half a bottle of Chambertin. Two slight annoyances kept him from perfect

13. ***Madame Butterfly:*** an opera composed by Giacomo Puccini.

TT. Critical Thinking: ANALYZING Ask students to analyze this passage and explain why humans are "the most dangerous game." *(because they can reason and think)*

UU. Literary Sidelight Explain that Uganda has large game, including elephant, lion, rhinoceros, and leopard. Have a volunteer locate this country of East Africa on a map.

VV. Literary Element: THEME Ask students to explain how Rainsford's feelings about hunted animals may have changed. *(Possible response: In the beginning of the story, Rainsford had no sympathy for his prey, even denying they felt "the fear of pain and the fear of death." Now, he understands how the quarry feels.)*

WW. Reading Skill: *(He was killed in the trap.)*

XX. Literary Element: IRONY Ask students to explain what is unexpected about Zaroff's thoughts. *(Possible response: He salves his ego by thinking that Rainsford has not played fairly when it is really he—armed with guns, dogs, Ivan, and rest—who has cheated.)*

YY. Reading Skill: RECOGNIZING RELEVANT DETAILS Have students locate the details that indicate Rainsford would be capable of this feat. *(Possible response: His strength as a swimmer was shown after he fell overboard; his cunning was shown in each instance he built a trap.)*

ZZ. Reading Skill INFERRING *(Rainsford killed him and threw him to the dogs.)*

Check Test

1. How does Rainsford fall overboard? *(Lunging for his pipe, he loses his balance and falls overboard.)*

2. How do the sailors feel about Ship-Trap Island? *(They dread it.)*

3. Who is Ivan? *(Zaroff's servant)*

4. Where does General Zaroff get the humans he hunts? *(He uses shipwrecked sailors.)*

5. Who becomes Zaroff's quarry when he refuses to participate in Zaroff's hunt? *(Rainsford)*

6. What happens to Zaroff? *(Rainsford kills him.)*

Encouraging Independent Reading

"Lucero," a short story by Oscar Castro Z.
"Rikki-tikki-tavi," a short story by Rudyard Kipling
The Call of the Wild, and "Lost Face," fiction by Jack London.
"The Pit and the Pendulum" a short story by Edgar Allan Poe
"Leiningen versus the Ants," a short story by Carl Stephenson

enjoyment. One was the thought that it would be difficult to replace Ivan; the other was that his quarry had escaped him. Of course, the American hadn't played the game—so thought the general as he tasted his after-dinner liqueur. In his library he read, to soothe himself, from the works of Marcus Aurelius.[14] At ten he went up to his bedroom. He was deliciously tired, he said to himself as he locked himself in. There was a little moonlight, so, before turning on his light, he went to the window and looked down at the courtyard. He could see the great hounds, and he called: "Better luck next time" to them. Then he switched on the light.

WW

A man, who had been hiding in the curtain of the bed, was standing there.

"Rainsford!" screamed the general. "How did you get here?"

XX

"Swam," said Rainsford. "I found it quicker than walking through the jungle."

The general sucked in his breath and smiled. "I congratulate you," he said. "You have won the game."

Rainsford did not smile. "I am still a beast at bay," he said, in a low, hoarse voice. "Get ready, General Zaroff."

The general made one of his deepest bows. "I see," he said. "Splendid! One of us is to furnish a repast[15] for the hounds. The other will sleep in this very excellent bed. On guard, Rainsford. . . ."

He had never slept in a better bed, Rainsford decided. ❧

What happened to Zaroff? 

YY

14. **Marcus Aurelius:** a Roman emperor and philosopher.
15. **repast:** meal.

PROFESSIONAL NOTEBOOK

Dag Hammarskjöld, Swedish statesman and Secretary General of the United Nations from 1953 to 1961, believed that education is intended to develop truer, simpler, quieter, firmer, and, therefore, wiser and stronger young.

Responding to Reading

First Impressions

1. In your journal or on a piece of paper, jot down words and phrases that describe your feelings about the end of this story.

Second Thoughts

2. Zaroff claims to be a civilized person. Do you agree or disagree?

   Think about
   - descriptions of Zaroff's lifestyle and background
   - Zaroff's attitude toward life

3. After Rainsford has jumped into the sea, Zaroff concludes that Rainsford "hadn't played the game." Do you agree? Explain.

4. Instead of ambushing Zaroff or trying to capture him, Rainsford insists on a fight to the death. Why, do you think, does he do this?

5. At one point Rainsford says hunting is "the best sport in the world." How do you think he feels about hunting at the end of the story?

   Think about
   - Rainsford's comments about hunting at the beginning of the story
   - his experiences as the hunted instead of the hunter
   - his treatment of Zaroff at the end of the story

6. Does Rainsford have the right to kill Zaroff? Before deciding, consider what rules Rainsford should follow: Zaroff's rules? the laws of civilized society? the rules of warfare? religious guidelines?

Broader Connections

7. Zaroff's dangerous game was played between two men on a small island. What dangerous games are played on a national or an international scale?

Literary Concept: Setting

Some stories work well in any setting. Other stories, such as works of historical fiction, are tied to a specific time and place. In such cases, the setting is said to be essential or integral to the story. How integral is the setting in "The Most Dangerous Game"? Explain your answer.

Concept Review: Foreshadowing Whitney's discussion of how sailors fear Ship-Trap Island is an example of foreshadowing. Find at least three other examples of foreshadowing on pages 412–413 of the story.

Student Response

Responding to Reading

These questions are open-ended with no "right" or "wrong" answers. However, responses must be supported with information from the selection. Possible answers follow:

1. Almost any response is valid.

2. Some students may say that in manner, dress, education, and social habits, Zaroff appears highly civilized. Others may say that while Zaroff initially treats Rainsford with great kindness, he soon reveals that he values humans only as objects of prey. Zaroff's sophisticated appearance masks his savage, coldblooded interior.

3. Some students may say that Rainsford broke the rules because he jumped into the sea and thus left the island. Others may point out that the "game" is defined by Zaroff's rules, which are hardly fair.

4. Some students may say that Rainsford may want to fight to the death to see the look of surprise on Zaroff's face; to maintain his sense of fair play; or to finish the game fairly. Some students may argue that perhaps Rainsford is not that much more civilized than Zaroff.

5. Some students may say that Rainsford's fondness for hunting may have faded, now that he understands it from the point of view of the hunted. In the beginning of the story he claims that the quarry has no feelings. Since he experienced intense feelings as a quarry, he may think twice the next time he hunts. Others may say that Rainsford's enjoyment of Zaroff's bed indicates that Rainsford has "replaced" Zaroff as the new hunter on the island. Zaroff has lost the game but won Rainsford over to the sport of hunting humans.

6. Some students may say that since Zaroff hunted Rainsford, the latter had the right to kill Zaroff. Others may argue that despite Zaroff's behavior, Rainsford had no right to kill the general but should have brought him to justice.

7. Students may mention the political games that countries play with each other regarding nuclear power and other issues or the power games that politicians, heads of state, and special interest groups play to further their own interests.

Literary Concept—Setting

Possible response: Setting is an integral part of "The Most Dangerous Game": if Rainsford were not trapped on an isolated island, he would not be prey to Zaroff. Further, the island's rocky shore makes shipwrecks likely, which enables Zaroff to find fresh victims; the island's thick foliage makes flight and the illusion of a hunt possible.

Concept Review—Foreshadowing: Examples of foreshadowing on pages 412–413 include Rainsford's hearing while on the yacht the startling sound of gunshots; the description of the Caribbean Sea as "blood-warm waters" that close over Rainsford's head; the high screaming sound of an anguished animal and the pistol shot that Rainsford hears while swimming; the mention of "perils" that might be in store for him; Rainsford's wondering what kind of men inhabit such a forbidding place.

Writing Options

The Writing Options are designed to meet varied student interests and abilities. Have each student choose one writing activity to complete. You may wish to guide some students to an option that requires less writing.

Journal Update Have students review their journal entries for "The Most Dangerous Game." What new reflections can be added to their earlier writing?

Vocabulary Practice

1. Synonyms
2. Antonyms
3. Synonyms
4. Antonyms
5. Synonyms
6. Synonyms
7. Antonyms
8. Synonyms
9. Antonyms
10. Antonyms
11. Synonyms
12. Antonyms
13. Synonyms
14. Synonyms
15. Antonyms

Writing Options

1. Write a brief account of what you think Rainsford might do after the story ends. Think about where he will live, what he will do with Zaroff's possessions, and how he will earn a living.
2. Suppose you had the opportunity to spend an evening with Rainsford or Zaroff. Which person would you choose? Write at least five questions that you might ask.
3. General Zaroff says, "The weak of the world were put here to give the strong pleasure." Describe someone from the news or history who uses or did use others.
4. Using facts from the story plus your imagination, write an obituary for General Zaroff. Try to imitate the structure and style of the obituary column of your local paper.

Vocabulary Practice

Exercise Read the pairs of words below. On your paper, write *Synonyms* if the pair are synonyms. Write *Antonyms* if they are antonyms.

1. imprudent—unwise
2. grotesque—beautiful
3. naive—childlike
4. quarry—hunter
5. condone—forgive
6. cultivated—trained
7. deplorable—acceptable
8. amenity—convenience
9. zealous—calm
10. disarming—annoying
11. protruding—bulging
12. tangible—untouchable
13. indolently—lazily
14. specimen—sample
15. opaqueness—transparency

Words to Know and Use

amenity
condone
cultivated
deplorable
disarming
grotesque
imprudent
indolently
naive
opaqueness
protruding
quarry
specimen
tangible
zealous

extend

Options for Learning

1 • Become a Cartographer A cartographer is someone who creates maps. Draw a map of Zaroff's island. Label the locations listed below. Where possible, use descriptions from the story for help in determining locations.

- the rocky coast where Rainsford was washed ashore
- Zaroff's castle
- the tree where Rainsford spent the first night of the hunt
- Death Swamp
- the Malay man-catcher
- the Burmese tiger pit
- the springing tree trap
- the cliff off which Rainsford jumped at the end

2 • The People's Court Imagine that Zaroff survives and is charged with the attempted murder of Sanger Rainsford. Hold the trial in your classroom. Class members should play the parts of judge, jury, defending and prosecuting attorneys, Zaroff, Rainsford, and any witnesses the lawyers need. The jury should decide Zaroff's fate.

3 • Technical Drawing Do detailed drawings of the three traps Rainsford makes during the hunt. Label all the parts and write a brief explanation of how each trap works.

4 • Gamesmanship Invent a board game based on "The Most Dangerous Game." Use incidents from the story and make up additional ones. Make or gather any equipment needed to play. Write clear instructions and invite class members to play the completed game.

FACT FINDER

If Rainsford can kill a moose from four hundred yards away, is he a good shot? Measure from the door of your school.

Richard Connell

1893–1949

You might almost say that Richard Connell was born with an editing pen in his hand. At age ten he was covering baseball and basketball games for the newspaper his father edited. At sixteen, he was an editor himself, working on a local newspaper. During college at Harvard, he edited both the college newspaper and *Lampoon*, Harvard's wild and wacky humor magazine. Connell served in World War I, and the brutal reality of battle influenced his later writing. After the war Connell settled in California, where he wrote more than one hundred short stories, in addition to film scripts and novels. "The Most Dangerous Game" is his most famous work.

Options for Learning

These activities suit a variety of learning styles and modes of expression. Allow students to review the options and then choose the one they wish to do. Many are excellent collaborative learning projects.

1. Become a Cartographer Suggest that students use graph paper and a ruler to accurately establish distances. Suggest also that students use an encyclopedia to learn what cartographers do and the different types of maps they create. This may give students novel ideas for their maps of Zaroff's island.

2. The People's Court Students might find it helpful to watch a courtroom drama or speak with someone who has served on a jury.

3. Technical Drawing Students might first consult a book on mechanical drawing for suggestions.

4. Gamesmanship Students could begin by reviewing the rules and layout of standard board games.

Fact Finder

Have students measure four hundred yards on a school playing field or nearby park to get a feel for the distance. They can decide whether they think Rainsford is a good shot.

Closure

"The Most Dangerous Game" explores strategies for survival. Ask students to compare Rainsford's survival techniques in this story to the way Richard Wright survived in "The Rights to the Streets of Memphis."

Cross-Curricular Options

Geography: Rainsford and Zaroff have traveled the world in search of game. List each of the places mentioned in the story and tell whether each is a city, country, state, or topographical feature such as a river or mountain range. Locate these places on a map. Display your findings for the class.

Science: Rainsford gets caught in the quicksand that "sucked viciously at his foot as if it were a giant leech." Compose a "Fact and Fiction" chart that answers the following questions: What is quicksand? What causes it? What are the myths associated with it? How can quicksand be identified? What is the best way to escape from it?

Ecology: Make a comparison of four or more endangered species, listing each species' habitat, numbers, and the reasons it is endangered.

Objectives

- To understand and analyze an essay
- To express understanding of the work through a choice of writing forms, including a credo, description, and exposition

Prereading/Motivation

Examine What You Know

Discussion Prompts: What kindergarten activities did you especially enjoy? Which activities taught you how to get along better with your peers? How did kindergarten help prepare you for taking care of yourself?

Expand Your Knowledge

Discussion Prompts: Why might people be actively looking for personal advice today? Which topics might people most want advice about? What advice have you found useful enough to pass on to others?

Additional Background: Fulghum's *All I Really Need to Know I Learned in Kindergarten* has sold more than 900,000 hardcover copies and has had 13 foreign-language editions. Fulghum received a record-breaking $2.1 million advance for paperback rights. The essays that make up this runaway bestseller originally were biweekly columns that Fulghum wrote between 1960 and 1984 for a small Unitarian church newsletter. Church members sent his mimeographed musings around the world before the essays were formally published. Rabbi Harold S. Kushner explains Fulghum's popularity this way: "In a world of complex ethical decisions, he cuts through the details and says, 'at the heart are a very few simple rules. You *can* be a moral person; it's not as complicated as it seems.'"

Thematic Link—Strategies for Survival

In this essay, Robert Fulghum offers uncomplicated strategies for surviving in the complex modern world.

e x p l o r e

Essay

from All I Really Need to Know I Learned in Kindergarten

ROBERT FULGHUM (fu̇l′ gum)

Examine What You Know (Prior Knowledge)

Close your eyes and take a memory trip back to your kindergarten days. Can you recall the sights, sounds, and smells of your classroom? What did you actually do during class? In small groups discuss some of your kindergarten activities. What do you think you learned from these experiences? Use a chart like the one below to record your ideas.

Activity	What I Learned

Expand Your Knowledge (Building Background)

The essay you are about to read was published in 1986. It is a short, apparently simple piece, yet it has become amazingly popular. People of all ages and from all walks of life have read and appreciated it. It has been quoted, copied, hung on bulletin boards, and sent to family and friends. As you read, try to determine why so many people have enjoyed this selection and have wanted to share it with others.

Write Before You Read (Journal Writing)

The world is full of advice givers. Parents, friends, teachers, ministers, newspaper and magazine columnists, and even the author of this selection have suggestions about what you should do and how you should act. Think about the advice you have received over the years. In your journal or on a piece of paper, briefly describe the best or worst advice you ever got. Explain what the advice was, who gave it to you, and why you did or did not benefit from it.

■ *A biography of the author can be found in the Reader's Handbook.*

Journal Writing

- Suggest these additional journal topics to students:
- If someone asked you to write a list of advice called "All I Really Need to Know I Learned in Kindergarten," what strategies would you include?
- Discuss a strategy for survival that you learned in kindergarten and have used often since.
- Why might kindergarten be an especially memorable time in a child's life?

For other journal opportunities, refer students to Broader Connections (p. 435).

Additional Resources

UNIT THREE RESOURCE BOOK

Reader's Guidesheet, p. 60
Vocabulary Worksheet, p. 61
Selection Check Tests, p. 62
Selection Test, pp. 63–64

Collaborative Learning

Opportunities for collaborative learning appear throughout the lesson and include Examine What You Know (p. 432).

from All I Really Need to Know I Learned in Kindergarten

ROBERT FULGHUM

All I really need to know about how to live and what to do and how to be I learned in kindergarten. Wisdom was not at the top of the graduate-school mountain but there in the sandpile at Sunday SR-1 ▶ School. These are the things I learned:

Share everything.
Play fair.
Don't hit people.
Put things back where you found them.
Clean up your own mess.
Don't take things that aren't yours.
Say you're sorry when you hurt somebody.
Wash your hands before you eat.
Flush.
Warm cookies and cold milk are good for you.
Live a balanced life—learn some and think some and draw and paint and sing and dance and play and work every day some.
Take a nap every afternoon.

When you go out into the world, watch out for traffic, hold hands, and stick together.

Be aware of wonder. Remember the little seed in the Styrofoam cup: The roots go down and the plant goes up and nobody really knows how or why, but we are all like that.

Goldfish and hamsters and white mice and even the little seed in the Styrofoam cup—they all die. So do we.

And then remember the Dick-and-Jane[1] books and the first word you learned—the biggest word of all—LOOK. ◀ SR-2

Everything you need to know is in there somewhere. The Golden Rule[2] and love and basic sanitation. Ecology and politics and equality and sane living.

1. **Dick-and-Jane books:** elementary reading books widely used in the 1950's and 1960's.
2. **Golden Rule:** "Do unto others as you would have them do unto you" (from the Bible).

STRUCTURED READING FOR LESS PROFICIENT STUDENTS

These questions can help to guide students through the reading. Ask each question at the point of the selection where the SR number appears in the margin.

SR–1. According to Fulghum, where did he learn the rules of ethical behavior? *(in kindergarten, in the sandpile, at Sunday School)* **Literal recall**

SR–2. Summarize Fulghum's advice. *(Play fairly with people; strive for balance; take care of yourself and others; appreciate life and its mysteries.)* **Summarizing**

SR–3. How does Fulghum want his audience to use his advice? *(He wants people to apply it to their own lives.)* **Analyzing**

Teaching Strategies

Support for Students of Limited English Proficiency

- Use **Reader's Guidesheet**, p. 60.
- Although Fulghum's advice is easy to read, students may find it hard to understand. To facilitate their comprehension, have them paraphrase Fulghum's aphorisms. Urge them to support their paraphrases with examples from their lives.
- **Annotation C** focuses on humor.

Text Annotations

A. Critical Thinking: ANALYZING Ask students to analyze how Fulghum's advice might apply to the adult world. *(People might learn to respect the environment; you might try to leave the world a better place than you found it; nations might learn to cooperate and get along with each other.)*

B. Literary Sidelight Robert Fulghum advises his readers to rearrange their lives to achieve self-fulfillment. Fulghum's life shows evidence that he takes his own advice seriously. Fulghum changed careers many times seeking self-fulfillment. First he was an IBM executive, then he was a Unitarian minister, then he studied at a Zen Buddhist monastery in Japan, and finally he worked as an art teacher. He tried, he has said, "to do the things I really care about."

C. LEP: Humor Students with limited English proficiency who have not attended kindergarten might not appreciate the warm humor in Fulghum's tone. Here he compares human growth to the growth of a seed in a Styrofoam cup—something that most kindergarteners study as an "experiment." Point out the sense of wonder that Fulghum is trying to rekindle in his readers' minds. Ask former kindergarteners to relate how they felt when their seeds grew into real plants. Point out how the silliness in Fulghum's message helps drive home the point that life really isn't all that complicated.

D. Literary Element: Mood Ask students how they would describe the mood of this passage. *(Possible responses: hopeful, upbeat, positive)*

E. Literary Element: THEME Ask students what strategy for a good life Fulghum suggests here. *(Use his guidelines, rephrased in complex terms, to deal with all your problems.)*

F. Critical Thinking: Evaluating Ask students to summarize and evaluate Fulghum's advice. *(He advises using decency, kindness, consideration, and common sense when dealing with others and yourself. Some students may find his advice logical and long overdue, while others may see it as simplistic and overly optimistic.)*

Check Test

1. What does Fulghum mean by "a balanced life"? *(a life with variety and creativity in which you learn and think, draw and paint, sing and dance, work and play)*
2. What example does Fulghum use when he advises us to "be aware of wonder"? *(the little seed in the Styrofoam cup)*
3. What "biggest word of all" can people learn from the Dick-and-Jane books? *(LOOK)*
4. What does Fulghum advise people to do, no matter how old they are, when they go out in the world? *(hold hands and stick together)*

Encouraging Independent Reading

Jonathan Livingston Seagull, a novel by Richard S. Bach

All I Really Need to Know I Learned in Kindergarten and *It Was on Fire When I Lay Down On It,* nonfiction by Robert Fulghum

The Prophet, poetry by Kahlil Gibran

E Take any one of those items and extrapolate[3] it into sophisticated adult terms and apply it to your family life or your work or your government or your world, and it holds true and clear and firm. Think what a better world it would be if we all—the whole world—had cookies and milk about three o'clock every afternoon and then lay down with our blankies for a nap. Or if all governments had as a basic policy to always put things back where they found them and to clean up their own mess. ◀ SR-3

F And it is still true, no matter how old you are—when you go out into the world, it is best to hold hands and stick together. ❧

3. **extrapolate** (ek strap′ ə lāt′): to make conclusions based on inferences from known facts or observations.

© 1990 Jeffrey Myers/FPG International, New York.

Critic's Corner

Robert Fulghum is one of his own best critics. An article in the *New York Times* magazine sums up the thoughts of Fulghum and others:

"Fulghum, a voracious reader, is the first to admit that 'Kindergarten' is not great literature. Some of it, he freely admits, is the 'worst kind of heart-rending daddy drivel imaginable,' the literary equivalent of happy-face buttons . . .

"Rabbi Harold S. Kushner . . . believes that Fulghum's popularity can be explained thus: 'In a world of complex ethical decisions, [he] cuts through the details and says 'at the heart are a few simple rules. You *can* be a moral person; it's not as complicated as it seems' . . .'

"[Fulghum] has thought quite a bit about 'the fame thing.' He regards it as an episodic incident, like a play, and he will know when it is over. 'And I will take a bow and say, 'Thank you very much',' he said. 'Episode closed. I have other lives to live.' "

Responding to Reading

First Impressions

1. What is your reaction to the advice in the essay? Compare your impressions with those of your classmates.

Second Thoughts

2. The author of "All I Really Need to Know . . ." lists sixteen strategies for dealing with life. Could these strategies be of use to you?

   Think about
   - which ideas seem practical and sensible
   - which ideas would not work in your life
   - which ideas you disagree with

3. In the essay, simple ideas are used as substitutes for complex issues. What might some of these simple concepts stand for?

   Think about
   - cookies and milk
   - traffic
   - holding hands
   - "blankies"

Broader Connections

4. Envision a world where all people live by Fulghum's **credo,** or code for living. How would nations have to have changed in order to live by this code?

Writing Options

1. Write your own credo. Try using Robert Fulghum's essay as a model. Use simple words and sentences to state your ideas.
2. Think again about your memories of kindergarten. Describe a particular incident in which you learned something important. Be sure to describe how you felt then and why you think you still remember this event.
3. Take one of the ideas in Fulghum's credo and extrapolate it into both family life and government policy. (When you extrapolate you apply known facts or observations to a new situation in order to clarify or explain it.) First state the idea that you have chosen to extrapolate. Explain how applying this idea could make your family life better. Finally, explain how the idea could improve an existing policy of your local or national government.

Student Response

Responding to Reading

These questions are open-ended with no "right" or "wrong" responses. However, responses must be supported with information from the selection. Possible answers follow:

1. Any reasonable reaction to Fulghum's advice is valid. Encourage students to provide specific reasons to back up their reactions.

2. Some students may say that a number of Fulghum's strategies would indeed be useful to them, while others may see no relevance in his advice. Those who support Fulghum's credo may cite his suggestions about sharing, playing fair, and cleaning up as especially useful. Those who do not like his advice might say that napping is impractical or living a balanced life is impossible.

3. Some students may say that "cookies and milk" represent special treats; others may see them as necessary comforts. For some, "traffic" could represent life's dangers; for others it could mean inconvenience. "Holding hands" might show love for some people but might indicate caring and friendship for others. Finally, some students may see "blankies" as symbols of comfort while others may see them as representing aid and assistance.

4. Possible suggestions for world change might include better distribution of wealth, peace for all nations, and respect for the environment.

Closure

Ask students to consider (1) whether there is one piece of advice that they could take from Fulghum's essay and apply to their own lives or (2) what they have learned as sophomores that they could use to help them succeed in life.

Writing Options

The Writing Options are designed to meet varied student interests and abilities. Have each student choose one writing activity to complete. You may wish to guide some students to an option that requires less writing.

Journal Update Have students review their journal entries for "All I Really Need to Know I Learned in Kindergarten." How does Fulghum's advice compare to the advice that they describe in their journals?

explore

Objectives

- To understand and analyze an autobiographical selection
- To identify a story's climax
- To complete a problem/solution outline
- To identify personification
- To express understanding of the work through a choice of writing forms, including dialogue, narration, autobiography, and personification.

Prereading/Motivation

Examine What You Know

Discussion Prompts: When does a group of people become a "gang"? Why do you think people act like bullies? Is it better to face down a gang or a bully yourself, to seek help, or to do nothing?

Expand Your Knowledge

Discussion Prompts: How do childhood experiences affect someone's later life? Discuss some of the problems Wright might have faced growing up in a single-parent household.

Additional Background: As a child, the only thing that gave Wright hope was his reading, but Memphis libraries refused to issue library cards to blacks. Wright got around this by having a white friend check out books for him. He later said, "It had been only through books—at best, no more than vicarious cultural transfusions—that I had managed to keep myself alive."

Enrich Your Reading

Possible answers are: **Who:** Richard Wright; **What:** going grocery shopping for his family; **Why:** the gang of neighborhood bullies beat him and steal the grocery money; **Attempted Solutions:** 1. trying to shop a second time; 2. beating the bullies with a stick; **Results:** 1. his money is stolen again; 2. he wins; **End Result:** He learns how to survive on the streets.

> **Thematic Link—Strategies for Survival**
> In this story, Wright learns a brutal strategy for survival in the ghetto.

Autobiography

The Rights to the Streets of Memphis

RICHARD WRIGHT

Examine What You Know (Prior Knowledge)

What comes to mind when you think of the words *gang* and *bully*? In small groups discuss ways of dealing with people who threaten you.

Expand Your Knowledge (Building Background)

The following selection is from an autobiography called *Black Boy*, which tells about the difficulties of author Richard Wright's early years. Wright's father left home when the boy was five, and although Wright's mother worked hard to support the family, she was periodically forced to put her son in an orphanage.

Enrich Your Reading (Reading Skill)

Problem/Solution The main character in this selection attempts a number of solutions to solve a problem. The chart below can be used to represent the events in this real-life account. Familiarize yourself with the chart before reading the selection. Then as you read think about the following questions: Who has the problem and what is it? Why is it a problem? What attempts are made to solve the problem?

Problem	Who ______	
	Why ______	
	What ______	
Solution	Attempted Solutions	Results
	1. ______	1. ______
	2. ______	2. ______
	End Result ______	

■ *A biography of the author can be found on page 443.*

Journal Writing

Suggest these journal topics to students:

- Which people have "the rights to the streets" in your neighborhood? Explain your answer.
- What are some positive as well as negative ways people go about earning the rights to the streets?
- What methods for getting along in your community have you learned?

For other journal opportunities, refer students to Real-Life Connections (p. T–442).

Additional Resources

UNIT THREE RESOURCE BOOK

Reader's Guidesheet, p. 65
Vocabulary Worksheet, p. 66
Selection and Vocabulary Check Tests, p. 67
Selection Test, pp. 68–69

Collaborative Learning

Opportunities for collaborative learning appear throughout the lesson and include Examine What You Know (p. 436), Options for Learning (p. 443), and Cross-Curricular Options (p. T–443).

The Rights to the Streets of Memphis

RICHARD WRIGHT

Hunger stole upon me so slowly that at first I was not aware of what hunger really meant. Hunger had always been more or less at my elbow when I played, but now I began to wake up at night to find hunger standing at my bedside, staring at me gauntly. The hunger I had known before this had been no grim, hostile stranger; it had been a normal hunger that had made me beg constantly for bread, and when I ate a crust or two I was satisfied. But this new hunger baffled me, scared me, made me angry and insistent. Whenever I begged for food now, my mother would pour me a cup of tea which would still the clamor in my stomach for a moment or two; but a little later I would feel hunger nudging my ribs, twisting my empty guts until they ached. I would grow dizzy and my vision would dim. I became less active in my play, and for the first time in my life, I had to pause and think of what was happening
SR-1 ▶ to me.

"Mama, I'm hungry," I complained one afternoon.

A "Jump up and catch a kungry," she said, trying to make me laugh and forget.

"What's a "*kungry?*"

"It's what little boys eat when they get hungry," she said. A

"What does it taste like?"

"I don't know."

"Then why do you tell me to catch one?"

"Because you said that you were hungry," she said, smiling.

I sensed that she was teasing me, and it made me angry. B

"But I'm hungry. I want to eat."

"You'll have to wait."

"But I want to eat now."

"But there's nothing to eat," she told me.

"Why?"

"Just because there's none," she explained. C

"But I want to eat," I said, beginning to cry.

"You'll just have to wait," she said again.

"But why?"

"For God to send some food."

"When is He going to send it?"

"I don't know."

"But I'm hungry!"

She was ironing, and she paused and looked at me with tears in her eyes.

"Where's your father?" she asked me.

I stared in bewilderment. Yes, it was true that my father had not come home to sleep

Words to Know and Use

baffle (baf′ əl) *v.* to confuse
clamor (klam′ ər) *n.* a loud complaint
bewilderment (bē wil′ dər mənt) *n.* confusion

437

Teaching Strategies

Vocabulary Preview

These vocabulary words are defined at the bottom of the selection page on which they appear. You may wish to discuss them briefly before students begin reading.

abreast alongside
baffle to confuse
bewilderment confusion
clamor loud complaint
dispirit to discourage
flay to whip
hostile unfriendly; warlike
retaliate to strike back at
stark sheer and utter
taunt to provoke

Support for Students of Limited English Proficiency

- Use Readers' Guidesheet p. 65.
- Encourage students to try to figure out unknown words through context clues.
- Annotations A, E, H; and M focus on challenging vocabulary.

A. LEP: Vocabulary Explore why Mrs. Wright picked the word "kungry." *(She made up a silly-sounding rhyme for hungry to distract Richard from his hunger, which she cannot satisfy.)*

B. Reading Skill: INFERRING Have students infer what Mrs. Wright is like from her behavior here. *(Possible responses: patient, loving, kind.)*

C. Historical Sidelight In 1914, there were few social programs. Aid to dependent children, part of Social Security, was created in 1935 as part of Roosevelt's Second New Deal.

STRUCTURED READING FOR LESS PROFICIENT STUDENTS

These questions can help to guide students through the reading. Ask each question at the point of the selection where the SR number appears in the margin.

SR–1. Explain how Richard's hunger has changed. *(Before, he experienced normal childhood hunger; now, he is starving.)* **Clarifying**

SR–2. Why isn't there any food in the Wright household? *(Mr. Wright has left the family and Mrs. Wright has not yet found a job.)* **Literal recall**

SR–3. How does Mrs. Wright's attitude toward her situation change? *(She loses her good humor, becoming tired and despairing.)* **Analyzing**

SR–4. What does the gang do to Richard? *(Twice they grab him, knock him down, and steal his grocery money.)* **Literal recall**

SR–5. Why does Mrs. Wright send Richard out to fight? *(Stated: She wants him to learn to stand up for himself. Unstated: She is desperate.)* **Analyzing**

SR–6. What does Richard do to the gang? *(In a frenzy, he beats them with his stick.)* **Literal recall**

Art Note
This Romare Bearden (1914–1988) collage of photographs and paint is an eclectic sampling of life in Harlem in the 1920's. It combines familiar urban images, such as laundry hung out to dry on tenement fire escapes, with African masks that evoke the heritage of many Harlem residents. *What feeling about city life does this painting give you?*

D. Reading Skill: PROBLEM/SOLUTION Explore with students the depth of Mrs. Wright's problems and the various solutions open to her. *(Possible responses: Her problems include finding a job that pays enough to support her family, locating suitable child care, and dealing with her own and her children's grief at being abandoned; solutions might include moving in with family or friends or giving her children over to the care of others.)*

E. LEP: Vocabulary Explain to students that *flat* is the British word for apartment. It is also used by some Americans. The term refers to the fact that most apartments are on a single floor; they are "flat."

F. Reading Skill: PREDICTING Ask students to predict how Richard's life will change without his father present. *(Possible responses: He will have to assume greater responsibilities around the house; he will no longer have any time to play; he will suffer economic hardships.)*

BLACK MANHATTAN 1969
Romare Bearden Schomburg Center for Research in Black Culture, Art and Artifacts Division, The New York Public Library Photograph by Dawoub Bey.

D for many days now, and I could make as much noise as I wanted. Though I had not known why he was absent, I had been glad that he was not there to shout his restrictions at me. But it had never occurred to me that his absence would mean that there would be no food.

"I don't know," I said.

"Who brings food into the house?" my mother asked me.

"Papa," I said. "He always brought food."

"Well, your father isn't here now," she said.

"Where is he?"

"I don't know," she said.

"But I'm hungry," I whimpered, stomping my feet.

"You'll have to wait until I get a job and buy food," she said. ◀SR-2

As the days slid past, the image of my father became associated with my pangs of hunger, and whenever I felt hunger, I thought of him with a deep, biological bitterness.

My mother finally went to work as a cook and left me and my brother alone in the flat each day with a loaf of bread and a pot of tea. When she returned at evening, she would be tired and dispirited and would cry a lot. Sometimes, when she was in despair, she would call us to her and talk to us for hours, telling us that we now had no father, that our lives would be different from those of other children, that we must learn as E F

Words to Know and Use

dispirit (di spir′ it) *v.* to discourage

soon as possible to take care of ourselves, to dress ourselves, to prepare our own food; that we must take upon ourselves the responsibility of the flat while she worked. Half-frightened, we would promise solemnly. We did not understand what had happened between our father and our mother, and the most that these long talks did to us was to make us feel a vague dread. Whenever we asked why father had left, she would tell us that we were too young to
SR-3 ▶ know.

One evening my mother told me that thereafter I would have to do the shopping for food. She took me to the corner store to show me the way. I was proud; I felt like a grown-up. The next afternoon I looped the basket over my arm and went down the pavement toward the store. When I reached the corner, a gang of boys grabbed me, knocked me down, snatched the basket, took the money, and sent me running home in panic. That evening I told my mother what had happened, but she made no comment; she sat down at once, wrote another note, gave me more money, and sent me out to the grocery again. I crept down the steps and saw the same gang of boys playing down the street. I ran back into the house. G

"What's the matter?" my mother asked.

"It's those same boys," I said. "They'll beat me."

"You've got to get over that," she said. "Now, go on."

"I'm scared," I said.

"Go on and don't pay any attention to them," she said.

I went out of the door and walked briskly down the sidewalk, praying that the gang would not molest me. But when I came abreast of them, someone shouted. H

"There he is!"

They came toward me and I broke into a wild run toward home. They overtook me and flung me to the pavement. I yelled, pleaded, kicked, but they wrenched the money out of my hand. They yanked me to my feet, gave me a few slaps, and sent me home sobbing. My mother met me at the door. I

"They b-beat m-me," I gasped. "They t-t-took the m-money." ◀ SR-4

I started up the steps, seeking the shelter of the house.

"Don't you come in here," my mother warned me.

I froze in my tracks and stared at her.

"But they're coming after me," I said.

"You just stay right where you are," she said in a deadly tone. "I'm going to teach you this night to stand up and fight for yourself." J

She went into the house, and I waited, terrified, wondering what she was about. Presently she returned with more money and another note; she also had a long, heavy stick.

"Take this money, this note, and this stick," she said. "Go to the store and buy those groceries. If those boys bother you, then fight."

I was baffled. My mother was telling me to fight, a thing that she had never done before. K

"But I'm scared," I said.

"Don't you come into this house until you've gotten those groceries," she said.

"They'll beat me; they'll beat me," I said.

"Then stay in the streets; don't come back here!" ◀ SR-5

I ran up the steps and tried to force my way past her into the house. A stinging slap came on my jaw. I stood on the sidewalk, crying.

Words to Know and Use	**abreast** (ə brest′) *adv.* alongside

G. Critical Thinking: EVALUATING Ask students to evaluate Mrs. Wright's success in handling the situation. *(Possible responses: Citing the "vague dread" her words inspire in her children, some students may argue that Mrs. Wright handled the situation poorly. Others may agree with her methods, believing that five-year-old Richard was indeed too young to understand the truth.)*

H. LEP: Vocabulary Tell students that *molest* is a verb primarily used to mean "to bother or annoy" and that the word is not used here in a sexual sense.

I. Reading Skill: PREDICTING Ask students to predict what Richard's mother will do, given her earlier behavior, Richard's age, and her changed circumstances. *(Possible responses: Her initial kindness toward Richard suggests that she would comfort him, but the brutal circumstances argue for her teaching him to defend himself.)*

J. Literary Element: THEME Ask students what strategy for survival Mrs. Wright is teaching her son. *(She is teaching him to use physical force to defend himself.)*

K. Critical Thinking: SYNTHESIZING Ask students why Mrs. Wright is now advocating physical violence, which she had never before endorsed. *(Possible responses: She may now realize that the fatherless boy must know how to defend himself against bullies; she has become desperate.)*

Professional Notebook

To know how to suggest is the great art of teaching. To attain it we must be able to guess what will interest; we must learn to read the childish soul as we might a piece of music.
H. F. Amiel, Journal, 1864

The secret of teaching is to appear to have known all your life what you learned this afternoon.
Author unidentified, quoted by H. L. Mencken

Teaching of others teacheth the teacher.
Thomas Fuller, Gnomologia, 1732

L. Literary Element: CLIMAX Have students explain how this scene prepares for the story's climax. *(It builds suspense by leading to the moment of greatest intensity and interest, as readers wonder first what choice Richard will make, and second, what will happen when he once again confronts the mob.)*

M. Reading Skill: VOCABULARY Explain that the word *lam* is slang. Here, Wright is using the verb form, which means "to beat or thrash." The term *on the lam,* however, means "fleeing or making a getaway, as from the police."

N. Literary Element: CLIMAX Ask students to explain why this is the turning point of the story. *(The story builds to its point of greatest interest and intensity as we see Wright's response to his conflict.)*

O. Literary Element: THEME Ask students what strategies for survival Wright has learned. *(Possible responses: He must fight for what he wants; life is full of brutal choices.)*

Check Test

1. Why does Richard's mother have no food for him? *(His father has left and she has not yet found a job.)*

2. What chore does Mrs. Wright assign to Richard? *(shopping for food)*

3. What does the gang steal from Richard? *(the food money)*

4. How does Richard finally succeed in shopping for groceries? *(He beats the bullies with a stick.)*

Encouraging Independent Reading

"Tenement Room: Chicago," a poem by Frank Marshall Davis
The Dream Keeper, poetry by Langston Hughes
Song of Solomon, a novel by Toni Morrison
Stories from El Barrio, short stories by Piri Thomas
"The Man Who Lived Underground," a short story by Richard Wright

"Please, let me wait until tomorrow," I begged.

"No," she said. "Go now! If you come back into this house without those groceries, I'll whip you!"

L She slammed the door and I heard the key turn in the lock. I shook with fright. I was alone upon the dark, hostile streets, and gangs were after me. I had the choice of being beaten at home or away from home. I clutched the stick, crying, trying to reason. If I were beaten at home, there was absolutely nothing that I could do about it; but if I were beaten in the streets, I had a chance to fight and defend myself. I walked slowly down the sidewalk, coming closer to the gang of boys, holding the stick tightly. I was so full of fear that I could scarcely breathe. I was almost upon them now.

"There he is again!" the cry went up.

They surrounded me quickly and began to grab for my hand.

"I'll kill you!" I threatened.

M They closed in. In blind fear I let the stick fly, feeling it crack against a boy's skull. I swung again, lamming another skull, then another. Realizing that they would retaliate if I let up for but a second, I fought to lay them low, to knock them cold, to kill them so that they could not strike back at me. I flayed with tears in my eyes, teeth clenched, stark fear making me throw every ounce of my strength behind each blow. N I hit again and again, dropping the money and the grocery list. The boys scattered, yelling, nursing their heads, staring at me in utter disbelief. They had never seen such frenzy. I stood panting, egging them on, taunting them to come on and fight. When they refused, I ran after them and they tore out for their homes, screaming. The parents of the boys rushed into the streets and threatened me, and for the first time in my life I shouted at grown-ups, telling them that I would give them the same if they bothered me. I finally found my grocery list and the money and went to the store. On my way back I kept my stick poised for instant use, but there was not a single boy in sight. That night I won the right to the streets of Memphis. O ❧

◀SR-6

INSIGHT

Mother to Son

LANGSTON HUGHES

Well, son, I'll tell you:
Life for me ain't been no crystal stair.
It's had tacks in it,
And splinters,
And boards torn up,
And places with no carpet on the floor—
Bare.
But all the time
I'se been a-climbin' on,
And reachin' landin's,
And turnin' corners,
And sometimes goin' in the dark
Where there ain't been no light.
So boy, don't you turn back.
Don't you set down on the steps
'Cause you finds it's kinder hard.
Don't you fall now—
For I'se still goin', honey,
I'se still climbin',
And life for me ain't been no crystal stair.

Words to Know and Use

hostile (häs′ təl) *adj.* unfriendly and warlike
retaliate (ri tal′ ē āt′) *v.* to strike back in return for an injury
flay (flā) *v.* to whip
stark (stärk) *adj.* sheer and utter
taunt (tônt) *v.* to provoke or mock

440

Insight

This piece reflects on the ideas in the main selection and is suggested for students' independent reading. Optional discussion questions follow.

1. What might the tacks, splinters, and bare spots on the staircase represent? *(difficulties, unmet needs)*

2. What do you think the speaker means when she advises her son not to turn back? *(She is urging him to keep trying despite problems and setbacks.)*

3. What similarities and differences do you see between the speaker in this poem and Mrs. Wright in "The Rights to Streets of Memphis"? *(Both are poor women, trying to teach their sons how to live and survive. Mrs. Wright may be tougher than the mother in the poem.)*

e x p l a i n

Responding to Reading

First Impressions

1. What part of the selection made the deepest impression on you? Jot down how you felt at that point.

Second Thoughts

2. Describe the character of Richard's mother. Does she change?

   Think about
   - Mrs. Wright's response when Richard says that he is hungry
   - her evening talks with the boys after returning from work
   - her response to Richard after he is robbed the first time
   - her response the second time he is robbed

3. Do you approve of Mrs. Wright's forcing Richard out to face the gang with a stick? Why or why not?

4. What do you think of Richard's behavior during the fight scene? Does he do more than is called for or just enough to ensure his present and future safety? Read the scene again before you answer.

5. Do you think Richard's life will be different after he wins the fight?

   Think about
   - possible changes in his relationships with his mother and brother
   - possible changes in his relationships with neighbors and with other neighborhood children
   - possible changes in his feelings about himself

Broader Connections

6. The event in this selection occurred around 1913. Could the same thing happen today? If it did, what would be the same and what would be different?

Literary Concept: Climax

The **climax,** or turning point, is the moment in a work of dramatic or narrative literature when interest and intensity peak. For example, in "The Bass, the River, and Sheila Mant," the climax occurs when the young boy must decide whether to reel in the fish or cut it loose. What is the climax of Richard Wright's real-life experience on the street?

Concept Review: Personification What is personified in the first paragraph of this selection? What words and phrases does the author use to make this thing seem human? What effect does this have on the story?

Literary Concept—Climax
The climax of this story comes when Richard beats the bullies with a stick, scattering them so he can go grocery shopping.

Concept Review: Personification
Wright personifies his hunger in the first paragraph. It had "been at my elbow," "stalking at my bedside, staring at me gauntly." It was a "grim, hostile stranger." Students may say that this personification of hunger increases the drama of the story as it clearly depicts the young boy's terror.

Student Response

Responding to Reading
These questions are open-ended with no "right" or "wrong" answers. However, responses must be supported with information from the selection. Possible answers follow:

1. Almost any part of the selection is a valid choice. Encourage students to be specific about the impressions and feelings that specific part brought out.

2. Comparing her initial playful teasing to her final determination that Richard defend himself, some students may claim that Mrs. Wright changes from a patient, loving, good-humored, and kind woman in the beginning of the story to a dispirited, hardened, and cruel person at the end. Others, in contrast, might argue that she remains the same throughout.

3. Some students may agree with Mrs. Wright's tactics, claiming that she was right because Richard did indeed learn to defend himself. Others might strongly object to her actions because she risked her son's life.

4. Some students may say that Richard fought harder than he had to, citing such phrases as "utter disbelief" and "frenzy." Others, in contrast, might argue that he fought just enough to make sure that he was never bothered by the gang again.

5. Those who say that Richard's life will be different after the fight might say that he has earned the respect of his mother, brother, neighbors, and himself. Others might argue that his life will indeed be different, but not better, for now everyone is afraid of him and he is no longer the same kind of person he was before the fight.

6. Some students may say that people may experience similar problems today. Others may point out a variety of available social services that can provide help for the poor and hungry. Some students may mention factors that would complicate the problem further such as drugs or AIDS.

Writing Options

The Writing Options are designed to meet varied student interests and abilities. Have each student select one writing activity to complete. You may wish to guide some students to an option that requires less writing.

Journal Update Have students review their journal entries for "The Rights to the Streets of Memphis." After reading the selection, how might they revise their writing?

Vocabulary Practice

1. dispirited
2. clamor
3. baffle
4. bewilderment
5. hostile
6. abreast
7. taunt
8. stark
9. retaliate
10. flay

Writing Options

1. Look again at the personification the author uses in the opening paragraph. Then make up your own personification to describe fear.
2. If you have not already done so, read the poem "Mother to Son" on page 440. Now imagine a conversation between the mother in the poem and Richard Wright's mother in which they discuss their ideas on raising children. Write this conversation in dialogue form. Use the Richard Wright selection as a model of correct punctuation and paragraphing.
3. How might things have changed if Richard had not been victorious? Imagining that Richard lost the fight and the grocery money, write a conclusion describing the consequences.
4. When Richard went out to face the neighborhood gang, he was so frightened that he could hardly breathe. Describe a time when you were frightened. Explain why you were afraid, how you felt, and what you did.

Vocabulary Practice

Exercise On your paper write the vocabulary word that best completes each sentence.

1. Ready to give up, Richard's mother came home tired and ____ from work each day.
2. The ____ in Richard's stomach was a constant reminder to him of his hunger.
3. The confusing and conflicting demands of Richard's mother would ____ him.
4. Richard stared in ____ upon hearing his mother's order.
5. It was obvious from their sneers and cries that the gang of boys had ____ intentions.
6. The gang members walked two ____ down the sidewalk, forcing everyone else to go around them.
7. The gang began to ____ Richard with insults as he drew near.
8. You could see the ____ terror in his eyes as he neared the gang.
9. After having been attacked once, Richard grew angry and decided to ____.
10. He began to ____ at the boys with the stick, cracking one of them on the head.

Words to Know and Use

abreast
baffle
bewilderment
clamor
dispirited
flay
hostile
retaliate
stark
taunt

Real Life Connections

To help students understand the love Mrs. Wright has for her son, point out how she tries to distract Richard from his hunger pangs by joking with him. Ask students to discuss ways their parents have tried to ease their pain. Which methods did they find most successful? Ask why the effort might be as important as the outcome.

Point out to students that Richard was in a very difficult situation. Do they think he made the right choice in deciding to face down the gang rather than enduring his mother's punishment? In real life, have students ever faced a dilemma as difficult as Richard's?

Options for Learning

1 • At Your Service In this selection Mrs. Wright is forced to leave her young children at home alone. Today, working parents still face many problems regarding child care. Research day-care facilities in your community and report your findings in an oral presentation. Use charts, diagrams, and other graphic aids to make your information clear. Here are some questions to consider.

- How many families in your community need or use day-care facilities?
- What day-care facilities are available in your community?
- What do these services cost?
- Is there a shortage of day-care facilities?
- What problems do working parents have with day care? Interview some parents if possible.
- What improvements could be made in your community to help working parents with young children?

2 • Capture a Kungry Mrs. Wright often told her children to catch a kungry to eat. Create a folk tale, song, or rap about the kungry and perform your creation for your class.

3 • Try a Triptych A triptych (trip′ tik) is a work of art with three hinged panels, each panel showing a different scene. Create a triptych that shows Richard before, during, and after his battle with the neighborhood bullies.

FACT FINDER

Where is Memphis? Find it on a map.

Richard Wright
1908–1960

No one who knew Richard Wright during his early years could have predicted that he would become a world-famous author. Wright, the grandson of slaves, was born into poverty in rural Mississippi. When he was five, his father left home. When he was ten, his mother became paralyzed, and Richard was sent to live with one poor relative after another. None of them could discipline the brilliant but troubled young man.

At fifteen Wright struck out across the country supporting himself with odd jobs until the Great Depression forced him onto the welfare rolls. Ironically, it was the depression that led to Wright's first chance to write professionally. Through the Federal Writers' Project, Wright and other unemployed writers were engaged to produce books that would give the country "a detailed portrait of itself." Wright's stories about racial prejudice soon won him respect and awards. After World War II, Wright moved to Paris, where he continued to write until his death. His most famous works include *Native Son* and another autobiography, *American Hunger*.

Options for Learning

These activities suit a variety of learning styles and modes of expression. Allow students to review the options and then choose the one they wish to do. Many are excellent collaborative learning projects.

1. At Your Service Suggest that students list the resources available to them. These might include looking up recent newspaper and magazine articles, calling local childcare agencies and workers, and interviewing parents.

2. Capture a Kungry First telling their story aloud might help students capture the flavor of their folktale, song, or rap.

3. Try a Triptych Students might find it helpful to review the story first, arranging details about Richard in three columns labeled *before, during,* and *after.*

Fact Finder

Students can find the location of Memphis by checking an atlas. Memphis is located in the extreme southwest corner of Tennessee.

Additional Information About the Author

Richard Wright Richard Wright won the Springarn Award of the National Association for the Advancement of Colored People in 1940 for *Native Son,* his first novel. Five years later, the publication of his autobiographical *Black Boy* brought him financial security and international fame.

Closure

Suggest that students compare and contrast the strategies for survival outlined by the selections in this subunit. Have them evaluate which strategies seem to them most realistic for their world today.

Cross-Curricular Options

History: Research the history of the Social Security Administration, focusing on the development of programs that help families and children. Explain what assistance was available when the program was begun in 1935, how the aid has changed, and what is currently offered to people in need.

Social Studies: Report on the migration of blacks to the North in the early part of the twentieth century. Explain who traveled north and their reasons for relocating. Consider as well job opportunities, pay rates, and cultural differences.

Psychology: Research the psychology of gangs and relate your findings to the behavior in this story.

Art: Find pictures or photographs of participants in the Harlem Renaissance that took place in New York City in the 1920's. Use the pictures to get a sense of how people looked in black communities before 1935, and the pride they had in their community. Consider, for example, Langston Hughes and Countee Cullen.

Math: Research how much money a family of four would have needed to survive in a big city at the turn of the century.

Writer's Workshop

Objectives

- To understand the goals of persuasive writing
- To determine how writing differs when it is to be read orally
- To uncover evidence to support arguments
- To understand the concept of inference
- To draft, revise, edit, and present a persuasive speech
- To reflect on the writing process

Integrating . . .

Literature and Writing Explain to students that in literature, things are not always as they appear. Motives, actions, and results are often ambiguous, and the reader must interpret and infer.

Explain that inferences are educated guesses based on facts. Tell students that in this subunit they will write a persuasive speech about one of the selections based on inference.

Writing and Grammar The Language Workshop in this subunit focuses on using pronouns correctly. Explain the importance of pronouns as a means of varying language, especially when speaking rather than writing. As an example, have students create and read aloud a paragaph without any pronouns. Then ask them to determine where monotonous repetition occurs.

LEP students may need special help with pronouns. For example, they may have problems with the correct usage of *I* and *me*.

Writing and Speaking and Listening The Speaking and Listening Workshop focuses on public speaking. You might wish to review the guidelines first so that students can internalize them before writing their speeches. Write the guidelines on the board so that students can study them to help dispel their fears about public speaking.

WRITER'S WORKSHOP

PERSUASION

Think about the last time you had a long talk with someone. How much of that conversation involved one or both of you attempting to persuade the other to do something? The purpose of speaking and writing is often to persuade.

The writing you will do next is a persuasive speech. You will write the opening statement to a jury, in which you will give a summary of your case. Your goal will be to persuade the jury of a defendant's guilt or innocence. The speech will explain why you think the defendant is guilty or innocent and how you will prove it.

This writing will differ from other kinds you have done because it will be written to be presented orally. When you write, you must think about how your words will sound to your audience. Since your purpose is to persuade, you will need to use strong arguments to convince the jury. To be effective, these statements must be supported by evidence.

GUIDED ASSIGNMENT: OPENING STATEMENT TO A JURY

Certain characters in the preceding selections could be tried for possible crimes. Write a persuasive speech to convince a jury of the guilt or innocence of one of these characters.

Here is your PASSkey to this assignment.

- **P**URPOSE: To persuade
- **A**UDIENCE: The jury
- **S**UBJECT: The fate of the defendant
- **S**TRUCTURE: A written speech

Prewriting

STEP 1 **Choose a defendant** You are a criminal lawyer. Your job is to defend or prosecute one of the following characters. Select the character for whom you feel you can build the best case based on what you learned in the selection.

- Sanger Rainsford: accused of the murder of General Zaroff
- General Zaroff: accused of the attempted murder of Sanger Rainsford
- Richard Wright: accused of assault and battery on a group of youths

Additional Resources

UNIT THREE RESOURCE BOOK

Writer's Workshop Copy Master, p. 70
Peer and Self-Evaluation Guidelines, p. 71
Writing Assessment Guidelines, p. 72

ENRICHMENT MATERIALS

Thinking Skills Transparency and Worksheet
Fine Art Transparency and Writing Prompts
Revision, Proofreading, and Elaboration Worksheet
Writing Prompts for Assessment

Teaching Strategies

Introduction Ask students to turn to the Writer's Workshop on page 444. Read the guided assignment to students and explain the PASSkey graphic. Discuss how writing a speech differs from writing prose that will not be read aloud. If possible, provide examples of both types of writing.

Emphasize that speeches must capture and sustain the attention of the audience. At this time, you may wish to brainstorm some persuasive words that students can use in their speeches. These words can be written on the board for future use.

STEP 2 **State your purpose** To make sure you are clear about the reason for writing, draft a statement of purpose. This will keep your work focused. Here is the statement of a student who wrote about a character different from those listed above.

◀ STUDENT MODEL

```
I will defend Richard Wright's mother. She is accused of
encouraging her son to commit a violent act. I will
persuade the jury that she is innocent.
```

STEP 3 **Identify your arguments** Reread the selection to find possible arguments you can use in your case. Then brainstorm your ideas with a classmate to create a list of your strongest arguments.

STEP 4 **Support your arguments** When your purpose is to persuade, your arguments must be backed by evidence. Evidence can include facts, statistics, observations, and expert opinions. Find evidence for each of your arguments. To help keep this information organized, use a chart like the one this student writer made.

◀ STUDENT MODEL

Argument	Evidence
She is not a violent person.	Use sons and neighbors as witnesses.
She could not afford to have the money stolen.	Sons could tell how little their dad left them with.
She could not do the shopping herself.	Her employer could tell what hours she worked.
Her son could get badly hurt if he didn't fight back.	Son could tell about beatings from gang.
She encouraged self-defense, not violence.	Self-defense is not a crime.

Drafting

STEP 1 **Organize your ideas** Arguments in the body of a persuasive piece of writing are usually organized in order of importance. For greatest effect, begin with your least important argument and save your strongest argument for last.

STEP 2 **Write a draft of your speech** Begin your draft with an introduction that states your purpose. Your introduction should greet the jury, telling them who you are and whom you are prosecuting or defending. Then draft the body of your speech, using the information from your chart as a guide. Start a new paragraph for each argument.

Teaching Tip
If students have trouble uncovering evidence, you may wish to make this exercise a cooperative activity. Divide the class into four groups. Assign one story to the first two groups and the other story to the remaining group. Have two students in each group take notes: one student can write down the arguments while the other documents the evidence. Encourage students to raise all points and not to discard any ideas as too trivial. Explain that through brainstorming, evidence might be uncovered that would otherwise have remained buried.

Computer Tip
Students with access to computers may wish to write their drafts on a computer. This assignment requires students to order their arguments in order of importance, and working on a computer will facilitate the organizational process. As students draft their speeches, they may decide to change the order of their arguments. Allow students to decide whether they will write longhand, on a typewriter, or on a computer.

Prewriting Discuss each prewriting step. Emphasize the importance of choosing a selection that students enjoy. Stress that once students write their prewriting statements, these statements should be available at all times. Encourage students to gather information for evidence from outside sources. Be sure to stress that students document information and cite its source.

Drafting Have students rework their argument list to place the items in order of importance. Encourage students to discuss with a partner which points are the most important.

Briefly explain the difference between fact and opinion and elicit examples from students. Explain that the distinction is important because some evidence may be based on the opinions of a witness, and witnesses often incorporate opinions into their description of events. Tell students that opinions carry a lot of weight when character witnesses give their testimony. Students may wish to have character witnesses contribute to their evidence.

Revising and Editing Have students revise their speeches with a partner. Ask each student to read his or her speech aloud to a partner, who will serve as a juror. Have the juror create a chart from the Revision Checklist and fill it out as he or she listens to the speech. Encourage both students to look for opportunities in which changing a word or two will provide a stronger case and influence the jury. Explain the importance of loaded language in this instance. (Refer students to the Thinking Skills Workshop on page 547.) Then have the jurors provide their verdicts.

Ask students to edit their speeches for spelling and mechanics.

Presenting Emphasize that it is essential for students to rehearse sufficiently before presenting their speeches. Remind them that while what they have written is extremely important, their delivery is also important—half of the job is acting. Have students practice at home with family members and with friends before they attempt their speeches in front of the class. You might have each student practice with an additional partner first. Some other presenting ideas include the following:

- Arrange a "court" day for other tenth graders who have read the literature. Have these students serve as jurors as your students perform their speeches.
- Videotape each student as he or she gives the speech. This helps the student see for herself or himself how well the speech was delivered.
- Recreate a courtroom and videotape the entire proceedings. Have the class serve as the jury for each student.

STEP 3 **Draft a conclusion** End your written speech with a brief conclusion that summarizes the main points of your argument in a final paragraph.

Revising and Editing

Remember that you are writing a speech. Your words should sound smooth and natural when spoken. Read your speech aloud to test it. Also note that it is fair to appeal to the jury's emotions as well as to their intelligence (see Loaded Language in the Thinking Skills Workshop on page 547). Look over your draft carefully. Use the following checklist to help you refine your work.

Revision Checklist

1. Is your purpose stated clearly in the introduction?
2. Are your facts accurate?
3. Do your arguments make sense?
4. Do you have enough strong, clear evidence to persuade a jury?

Editing When you have finished your revision, check for spelling and mechanical errors. Here is the final version of one student's speech.

STUDENT MODEL ▶

Ladies and Gentlemen of the Jury:

My name is Alicia Alvarez, and I am here today to defend Mrs. Wright against the ridiculous charge of encouraging her son Richard to commit a violent act.

I will prove to you that Mrs. Wright is not a violent person or a bad parent. In fact, just the opposite is true. Witnesses will tell you that she has always been a gentle, caring, hard-working person. They will describe how she was abandoned by her husband and how she has wept many tears of sadness and desperation wondering how she could feed her hungry young sons.

But, ladies and gentlemen, Mrs. Wright did not stay home and cry or beg for help. You will hear of the long hours she worked. You will hear of Mrs. Wright's fear when her son Richard was attacked and robbed by a group of violent young thugs who had been terrorizing the neighborhood. Richard himself will describe the beatings and show you the bruises that still remain.

Ladies and gentlemen, Mrs. Wright feared for her son's safety, and in her desperation, she did what any parent would do. She refused to let her son be hurt again, and she gave him the means to defend himself. Ladies and gentlemen, we all have the right to defend ourselves against violence!

In summary, I repeat again that Mrs. Wright is a gentle, hard-working mother forced into difficult situations. She encouraged self-defense, and, ladies and gentlemen of the jury, self-defense is not a crime!

Presenting

Practice reading the final copy of your speech several times. If possible, tape-record your speech or rehearse it with a friend and ask for feedback. Then present your speech to the class.

Reflecting on Your Writing

Answer the following questions. Then attach your answers to your final draft to be placed in your writing portfolio.

1. How was speech writing different from other types of writing you have done?
2. What is the strongest part of your speech? Why?
3. Do you feel your speech is convincing? Why or why not?

Reflecting on Your Writing Assess students' written responses to the *Reflecting* questions. Determine whether students have adequately mastered the objectives of the subunit. Compare responses to determine if students are experiencing similar feelings.

Teaching Tip

You may wish to have students discuss in class their answers to the *Reflecting* questions. This might work best if conducted informally. Have students arrange their chairs in a semicircle. Encourage one student to begin discussing reactions to the writing assignment. Then ask students to take turns voicing opinions. Designate one student as the notetaker. Have students read parts of their speeches as they answer Questions 2 and 3.

Closure

As you complete this subunit, make sure students fully understand these concepts:

- Writing that will be read aloud requires different criteria from other forms of writing.
- Speakers must provide sufficient evidence to support arguments.
- Inferential skills are essential when analyzing literature.
- In a persuasive piece of writing, arguments are ordered according to importance.
- Familiarity with "loaded" language is helpful when writing a persuasive essay.

Additional Writing and Research Topics

The following items provide additional writing practice.

Persuasion

- Convince a group of friends which movie they should see this weekend. Since everyone will have a different opinion, it is up to you to persuade the entire group. Write a persuasive note to the group.
- Write a letter persuading a shop owner in your neighborhood to give you a part-time job. Convince this person that you are responsible, qualified, and eager to work. Be sure to include facts to back up your arguments.

Other Topics

Social Studies Research: Research a famous court case that occurred during the 1960's. Decide which side you agree with and write a persuasive essay to the jury, detailing your arguments.

Narration: Choose a "hot" issue and write a letter to the editor of your local newspaper defending your opinions on the topic.

Language Workshop

Objectives

- To identify a pronoun as a word that replaces a noun or another pronoun
- To understand the nominative, objective, and possessive forms of pronouns
- To use pronouns correctly in writing

Integrating . . .

Writing and Grammar Remind students that in the preceding Writer's Workshop they wrote a statement to persuade a jury about the guilt or innocence of a character in one of the subunit selections. Point out how monotonous the statement would become if students did not use pronouns. To illustrate this point, write the following paragraph on the chalkboard:

> General Zaroff hunted animals, but General Zaroff soon became bored. "The Most Dangerous Game" is a story that describes General Zaroff and General Zaroff's reasons for no longer hunting animals. In this story the reader learns that General Zaroff now hunts humans. Is General Zaroff guilty of murder, or is General Zaroff simply engaging in a legal sport?

Ask volunteers to replace General Zaroff's name with appropriate pronouns, discussing each substitution. Explain that this Language Workshop focuses on using pronouns correctly and effectively.

LANGUAGE WORKSHOP

USING PRONOUNS CORRECTLY

A **pronoun** is a word that replaces a noun or another pronoun. When choosing pronouns, consider your point of view and whether the pronoun is the subject or object of the sentence.

Have you ever been on the second string of an athletic team? If you have, you can understand what a pronoun does. A pronoun stands in for a noun the way a second stringer stands in for a first stringer on a team. Since you don't want to have to repeat the noun, you can use a pronoun, such as *I* or *she,* instead. Following is a list of personal pronouns.

	Nominative	Objective	Possessive
First Person	I, we	me, us	my, mine, our, ours
Second Person	you	you	your, yours
Third Person	he, she, it, they	him, her, it, them	his, her, hers, its, their, theirs

Using the Nominative Form of Pronouns

As you can see from the chart, all the first- and third-person pronouns can be used in any of three forms: nominative, objective, or possessive.

Nominative pronouns are used as subjects of verbs.

> *I* started up the steps, seeking the shelter of the house. (The subject of the verb *started* is the pronoun *I.*)
>
> *He* examined the ground closely. (The subject of the verb *examined* is the pronoun *he.*)

Use the nominative form of a pronoun even if two or more pronouns or a noun and a pronoun are used as a compound subject.

> *He* and *I* were left alone in the flat each day.
>
> *General Zaroff* and *he* ate dinner at the great table.

Additional Resources

UNIT THREE RESOURCE BOOK

Language Workshop Copy Master, p. 73

ENRICHMENT MATERIALS

Grammar and Usage Copy Masters

Use the nominative form of a pronoun when the pronoun is used together with a noun as the subject of a sentence.

We brothers learned to take care of ourselves.

Using the Objective Form of Pronouns

Objective pronouns are used as direct objects, indirect objects, and objects of prepositions. The **direct object** is the person or thing that receives the action of the verb. The **indirect object** tells to whom or for whom the action of the verb is done; it always comes before the direct object in a sentence. An **object of a preposition** comes after a preposition, such as *at, to, from, under,* or *around.*

LANGUAGE HANDBOOK

For review of these sentence parts, see Section 7, **Sentence Structure.**

My mother asked *me* to do the food shopping. (*Me* is the direct object of the verb *asked.*)

Ivan supplied *him* with hunting clothes, food, and a knife. (*Him* is the indirect object of the verb *supplied.*)

Could General Zaroff follow the complicated trail to *him?* (*Him* is the object of the preposition *to.*)

Use the objective form of a pronoun even if two or more pronouns or a noun and a pronoun are used as a compound object in a sentence.

My mother did not have any food for my brother and *me.* (*Me* is an object of the preposition *for.*)

Exercise 1 Write the correct pronoun from those given in parentheses.

1. (We, Us) brothers hadn't had enough food for days.
2. My brother and (I, me) didn't understand that our father had left for good.
3. Soon my mother left (him, he) and (I, me) alone together every day.
4. She went to work as a cook, and the responsibility of the apartment was left to (I, me).
5. While (she, her) was working, my brother and (I, me) would eat bread and tea.
6. One day my mother said she had something important to tell (I, me).
7. (She, Her) had decided that (she, her) didn't have enough time for food shopping.
8. She took (I, me) to the corner to show (I, me) the way.
9. The next day (I, me) went to the store with money and a basket.

Read the following phrases to students, asking them to tell if the pronoun is correct.

1. I helped he
2. Brett and him went
3. Alex and me drove
4. Us girls giggled

Have students correct the pronouns and discuss reasons for each correction. Then continue working through the lesson, stopping before you assign Exercise 1. Write the following sentences on the chalkboard:

1. She and I ate lunch at a new restaurant.
2. The cashier gave too much change back to her and me.

Have students identify the pronouns used in each sentence and discuss how the pronouns changed their forms. Point out that in the first sentence, the pronouns are the subjects. In the second sentence, the pronouns follow the preposition *to.* Explain that looking at the position of the pronoun as well as the way it is used can help students know which form to use.

Now have students form small groups. Assign each group one of the following titles: *Nominative Pronouns, Objective Pronouns,* and *Possessive Pronouns.* Challenge students to pick a selection from this subunit and find and copy five sentences with their particular form of pronoun. Remind students to jot down the page number on which they find each example. When all groups have found their examples, invite them to take turns coming to the chalkboard and writing a sentence, omitting the pronoun. Then have volunteers supply an appropriate pronoun that satisfies the correct form and sentence content. When students have had sufficient practice, assign Exercise 1 and review their responses.

Teaching Strategies

Ask a volunteer to read the focus statement at the top of page 448. Point out that the point of view determines the kind of pronoun to be used. Have students read the next paragraph and study the chart that follows. Discuss with students the kinds of pronouns that would be used with each of the following: biography, autobiography, journal, business letter, nonfiction article, and persuasive speech. Then have students work through the section on nominative forms of pronouns. Point out that if students are having difficulty determining which pronoun to use in a compound subject, they might try each subject separately with the verb. Explain that often they will hear which form is correct.

Now assign Exercise 2. Explain to students that they should be aware of the point of view they use when they write to determine the form of pronouns to be used. Remind students that much of what they write every day is informal.

Teaching Tip

Point out to students that they may encounter the pronoun *whom* in their reading. Explain that *whom* is a more formal word choice, and not usually used in informal language. However, you may wish to display on the chalkboard several examples of its correct use in sentences or find illustrative passages from selections in this text. Point out that *whom* is the objective form of *who*.

Closure

Before beginning the next subunit, be sure that students have internalized these concepts:

- Pronouns are words that replace nouns or other pronouns.
- There are three forms of pronouns: nominative, objective, and possessive. Nominative pronouns are used as the subjects of verbs, as in *I flew.* Objective pronouns are used as direct or indirect objects and objects of prepositions. Possessive pronouns show ownership.

Answer Key
Exercise 1

1. We	**11.** her
2. I	**12.** them
3. him, me	**13.** her
4. me	**14.** I
5. she, I	**15.** me
6. me	**16.** them, they
7. She, she	**17.** I
8. me, me	**18.** me
9. I	**19.** We
10. they	**20.** her

You may wish to have students share their reasons for each choice.

Exercise 2

Answers will vary, but students' work should reflect correct use of pronouns.

10. A gang of boys grabbed me and snatched the basket, and then (they, them) took all the money.

11. When my mother came home I told (she, her) and my brother what had happened.

12. "If I go outside, I'll see (they, them) again!" I said.

13. She sent me out again; nothing I said made (she, her) change her mind.

14. The gang and (I, me) faced each other again; I ran home.

15. That's when my mother told (I, me) to stand up and fight.

16. She gave me a stick to hit (they, them) with when (they, them) grabbed me.

17. I was not to return until (I, me) had bought the groceries.

18. My mother had never told my brother and (I, me) to fight before.

19. (We, Us) brothers needed to be stronger with our father gone.

20. That night I won the right to the streets of Memphis, thanks to (she, her).

LANGUAGE HANDBOOK

For review and practice, see Section 3, **Using Pronouns.**

Exercise 2 Analyzing and Revising Your Writing Find a piece of first-person writing in your portfolio. Rewrite one passage from this piece of writing using the third person. Which do you prefer, the first-person version or the third-person version? Remember that you will usually have a choice between writing in the first person or writing in the third person. The first person is often used for informal writing, while the third person is often used for formal writing.

ADDITIONAL PRACTICE

The following items are additional exercises to help students with using pronouns correctly.

Write these sentences, choosing the correct pronoun from each pair in parentheses.

1. The nurse asked (they, them) to speak more quietly.

2. Our new class president is (she, her).

3. (Us, We) were startled by the siren.

4. Please give this message to (he, him).

5. (They, Them) hiked to the top of the hill for a picnic.

6. I don't think that was (he, him).

7. Lynn helped Scott and (I, me)

SPEAKING AND LISTENING
WORKSHOP

PUBLIC SPEAKING

Do you have nightmares the night before you are scheduled to present an oral report at school? If so, you are not alone: public speaking is high on most people's list of fears. However, thorough preparation can lessen your anxiety. These tips will help you to pull off a speech like a pro.

1. **Prepare carefully.**
   - **Choose a topic that interests you.** It's hard to capture an audience's attention with a topic that you find boring.
   - **Collect more information than you will need.** You'll feel more comfortable if you are well versed in your topic.
   - **Organize your speech so that it is clear and easy to follow.** One good way to do this is to write your major points and supporting examples on sturdy index cards.
2. **Rehearse thoroughly.**
   - **Practice makes perfect.** Give your speech over and over. Once you have the speech almost memorized, work a little bit on the tone so that you can sound natural.
   - **Get a practice audience.** Get someone you trust to listen to your speech.
3. **Deliver with vigor.**
   - **Begin with energy.** Take a deep breath, smile, and look into the faces of your audience. Then simply begin your speech, delivering it with energy and enthusiasm.
   - **Speak directly to your audience.** Look into the eyes of at least a few people in your audience. This will accomplish two things: (1) it will make you feel more comfortable, as though you were having a one-on-one conversation, and (2) it will keep you in touch with your audience. If people seem distracted, try to capture their attention again. Change your voice or, if appropriate, skip to your next point.
   - **End with power.** Summarize your main ideas. Then close with a statement that your audience will remember, such as a joke, an anecdote, or a quotation.

LIMIT YOUR TOPIC

Make sure that you choose a topic that you can cover adequately in the time allowed for your speech.

HINT

Prepare a few interesting charts or other visual aids. They'll give your audience something to look at in addition to you!

TIP

If possible, tape-record your speech. Even if your voice sounds tinny on tape, using a tape recorder will help you get rid of all those *um's* and *ah's*, and it will tell you where to slow down and where to use more emphasis.

Exercise Choose a very specific topic. Prepare, rehearse, and deliver a two-minute speech on that topic. Follow the suggestions above, and you will be able to sleep well the night before your speech.

Speaking and Listening Workshop

Objectives

- To prepare for speaking by choosing an interesting topic, collecting information, organizing the speech, and choosing visual aids
- To rehearse a speech by practicing and giving it first to a friendly audience

Integrating . . .

Writing and Speaking Tell students that almost every speaker faces fear and nervousness at one time or another. Share with students that this workshop will improve their public speaking skills and help to ease their nervousness.

Teaching Strategies

Have students brainstorm characteristics of the speakers they most enjoy listening to. *(Possible responses: funny, interesting, makes eye contact, enthusiastic)* Then ask them to analyze how a speaker becomes accomplished in each of these traits.

Read through the material with students. Assign the exercise on page 451.

Closure

Before beginning the next subunit, be sure students have internalized this concept:

- Preparing carefully, rehearsing, and maintaining enthusiasm are key ingredients for a successful speech.

Teaching Tip: LEP

LEP students may be more fearful about speaking to groups. Once they have drafted their notes, have them work with English-speaking partners to organize and rehearse their speeches.

Exercise

(A checklist of behaviors to observe is given.)
1. The topic was appropriate.
2. Information was complete and well organized.
3. The speech showed evidence of practice.
4. The speaker had a strong start and finish.
5. The speaker maintained eye contact and delivered the speech with vigor.

Additional Resources

UNIT THREE RESOURCE BOOK
Related Skills Copy, p. 74

ENRICHMENT MATERIALS
Oral Communications Booklet

ADDITIONAL PRACTICE

Prepare and give a short speech titled "How You Can Overcome Your Fear of Public Speaking." *(Responses will vary. Be sure that speeches are well organized and show evidence of practice and that speakers maintain eye contact and enthusiasm.)*

Unit Four *Human Rights: Pain and Pride*

Objectives

Students will develop skills in the following areas. An asterisk (*) indicates a workshop topic.

Reading and Thinking

identifying assumptions	*p. 455*
understanding nonstandard English	*p. 460*
reading poetry orally	*p. 476*
identifying main idea	*p. 481*
identifying the topic sentence	*p. 481*
*separating fact from opinion	*p. 493*
appreciating descriptive details	*p. 495*
recognizing cause and effect	*p. 508*
comparing and contrasting	*p. 526*
*recognizing propaganda techniques	*p. 547*
*notetaking	*p. 549*

Vocabulary and Related Skills

synonyms	*pp. 474, 485*
using words in context	*p. 518*
*evaluating and making judgments	*p. 599*

Literary Appreciation

tone	*p. 473*
details	*p. 474*
imagery	*p. 480*
personification	*p. 480*
persuasive essay	*p. 484*
mood	*p. 505*
irony	*p. 505*
primary source	*p. 517*
secondary source	*p. 517*
internal conflict	*p. 517*
external conflict	*p. 517*
oral history	*p. 526*
denotation	*p. 539*
connotation	*p. 539*
protagonist	*p. 575*
antagonist	*p. 575*
stereotype	*p. 589*
climax	*p. 589*

Writing

letter	*pp. 459, 506, 526*
dialogue	*p. 474*
speech	*p. 485*
summary	*pp. 485, 575*
persuasive essay	*p. 485*
*exposition: supporting an opinion	*pp. 486–89*
poem	*pp. 506, 518*
newspaper article	*pp. 518, 590*
proverb	*p. 540*
Venn diagram	*p. 540*
*argumentation: point-counterpoint essay	*pp. 541–44*
*exposition: comparison/contrast essay	*pp. 592–95*

Language, Grammar, Usage, Mechanics

*avoiding fragments and run-ons	*pp. 490–92*
*using effective transitions	*pp. 545–46*
*making correct comparisons	*pp. 596–98*

Planning the Unit

You may find the following information and lists of resources helpful in preparing for the unit.

Difficulty Level of Selections

In determining the accessibility of the selections in this unit, many factors, including reading level and comprehension difficulty, have been taken into account. The ranking can be used as a general guide in determining how much preparation and assistance students will require in order to master the selection. No selection should be included or eliminated from the course based merely on difficulty level. Basic students will derive a great deal of confidence and self-esteem by working through a *challenge* selection; conversely, advanced students may find pleasure, relevance, and important themes in a selection that is rated *easy*.

Selection	Level
After You, My Dear Alphone p. 455	**easy**
A Start in Life p. 460	**average**
Not Knowing, in Aztlan p. 476	**average**
Indian Children Speak p. 478	**average**
Darkness at Noon p. 481	**average**
Tanforan: A Horse Stall for Four p. 495	**challenge**
Montgomery Boycott p. 508	**average**
Day Work p. 520	**average**
Chee's Daughter p. 527	**average**
Twelve Angry Men p. 549	**average**

Classroom Resources

Videocassettes, Films, and Filmstrips

■ ***Come Along with Me***, video, Coronet/MTI, 1986. A television adaptation from an unfinished novel by Shirley Jackson.

■ ***The Lottery***, 16mm film, video, Britannica, 1969, (18 minutes). A dramatization of Shirley Jackson's short story.

■ ***Martin Luther King, Jr. (Second Edition)***, 16mm film, video, Britannica, 1982, (24 minutes). Using documentary footage, the film examines King's career and beliefs.

■ ***Twelve Angry Men***, 16mm film, video, Key Video, 1957, (95 minutes). Based on the classic drama, starring Henry Fonda, E. G. Marshall, Jack Klugman, and Jack Warden.

■ ***Twelve Angry Men***, 16mm film, CRM Films, 1957, (25 minutes). Features an excerpt from the film and emphasizes writing techniques.

Audiocassettes, Tapes, and Records

The Lottery and Other Stories, record, audiocassette, Caedmon. Maureen Stapleton reads four of Shirley Jackson's stories.

My Life with Martin Luther King, audiocassette, Caedmon. Features Coretta Scott King reading from her account of her life with her husband.

Martin Luther King Jr.—The Prolonged Dream, audiocassette, National Public Radio, 1984, (30 minutes). A tribute to the civil rights leader.

Community Resources

Involving the resources of your community in lesson preparation can add insight and relevance to the text. Consider the following possibilities as you plan.

■ For "After You, My Dear Alphonse," invite a spokesperson for the NAACP to discuss racism.

■ For "A Start in Life," invite job or school counselors to discuss job stereotypes.

■ For "Not Knowing, In Aztlan" and "Indian Children Speak," invite a Native American to discuss what it is like being a Native American in the United States.

■ For "Darkness at Noon," have a blind person discuss ways to interact with the blind.

■ For "Tanforan," invite a Japanese American who experienced relocation to speak to the class.

■ For "Montgomery Boycott," have an older black person share memories of the civil rights movement in the 1960's.

■ For "Chee's Daughter," plan a field trip to Native American reservation or cultural center.

■ For *Twelve Angry Men,* invite a trial lawyer to discuss jury selection strategy; have former jury members share their experiences; or take a field trip to a courthouse to see a trial in progress.

Unit Preview

Why can't people see beyond the surface and know us for what we really are? Unit 4, **Human Rights: Pain and Pride,** explores the pain and pride of being human. The unit contains three subunits:

- Subunit 1: How Others See Me
- Subunit 2: Grace Under Pressure
- Subunit 3: Passing Judgments

Art Note

Ruben De Anda is a San Diego artist whose watercolor collage portrays the people and events involved in the human rights struggle. De Anda combines images of the American past with two of the most powerful symbols of freedom in this country: the Statue of Liberty and the American flag. *Which images relate to the pain and pride of the human rights struggle?*

About the Author

Martin Luther King, Jr., experienced injustice firsthand. The famous civil rights leader was born in Atlanta, Georgia, in 1929, the first son of a Baptist minister. Ordained a Baptist minister, King completed additional study before becoming a pastor in a Montgomery, Alabama, church in 1954. That same year, the Supreme Court outlawed all segregated public education. King organized a bus boycott to protest enforced racial segregation on public transportation. During the nearly 400-day protest, King was jailed and his home was bombed. The boycott ended when the Supreme Court outlawed segregated public transportation. King emerged from this victory a highly respected leader. He adapted Gandhi's principles of nonviolent protest to organize other successful civil rights campaigns and was awarded the Nobel Peace Prize in 1964. On April 4, 1968, he was assassinated in Memphis, Tennessee.

HUMAN RIGHTS: PAIN AND PRIDE

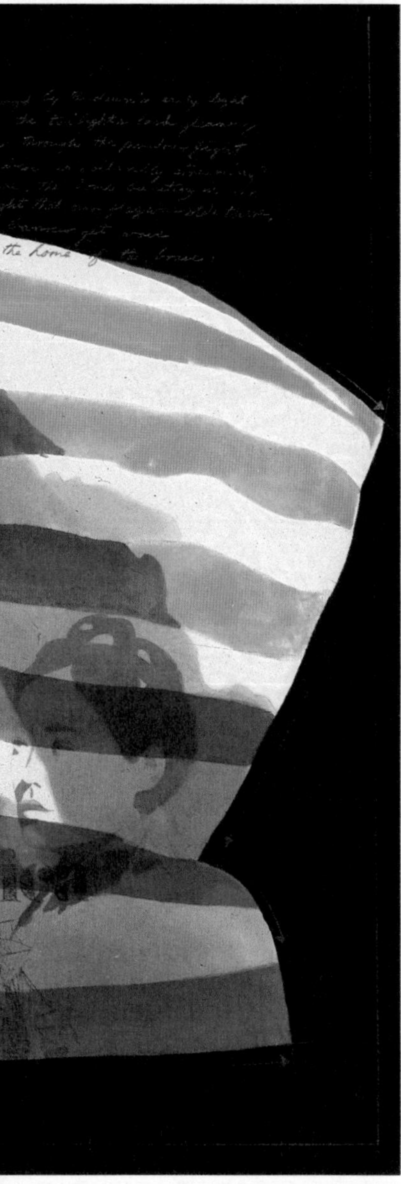

"Injustice anywhere is a threat to justice everywhere."

Martin Luther King, Jr.

U.S. FLAG COLLAGE (detail) 1986 Ruben De Anda © Ruben De Anda, San Diego, California.

Discussion Questions

To help students probe connections among the fine art, quotation, and unit theme, have them consider the following questions:

1. Do you agree with the quotation? Support your response with examples from your reading or experiences. *(Possible response: Students may agree with King that justice cannot truly exist as long as there is injustice in the world. Others may argue that the existence of injustice does not necessarily threaten justice. Encourage students to use specific examples to make their points.)*

2. How would you define *justice* and *injustice*? How might your definition compare to King's definition? *(Possible response: Students may define* injustice *as unfairness, prejudice, or bias. They may say that* justice *is fairness, equal rights, or decency. Some students may say that King is referring to prejudice.)*

3. What connections can you draw between the quotation and the title of this unit? *(Possible responses: Students may suggest that injustice results when human rights are violated and feel that such violations can threaten justice anywhere in the world.)*

4. Discuss how this picture reinforces the quotation and unit title. *(Possible responses: Students might suggest that an American flag superimposed by representative multicultural images implies that America is a land where justice and human rights are valued and fought for.*

5. Based on the artwork, quotation, and unit title, what do you predict the selections in this unit will be about? *(Possible responses: Students may suggest the selections will explore true and fictional examples of human rights.)*

Subunit Preview

Have students read the introduction to subunit 1, **How Others See Me.** Ask them to reflect on how the experience of being stereotyped is related to the unit theme, **Human Rights: Pain and Pride.** How do you expect someone who is prejudged to feel? What aspect(s) of being prejudged would bother you the most? Whom do you learn most about from prejudice—*the one who prejudges* or *the one who is prejudged*? How so? Invite students to read the subunit Table of Contents and predict which selection will be the most interesting.

For Additional Challenge

The following selections offer further challenge in exploring the subunit theme:

The Snow Goose, a novella by Paul Gallico

"The Hen and the Oriole," a poem by Don Marquis

Additional Resources

Subunit Test, pp. 26–27

How Others See Me

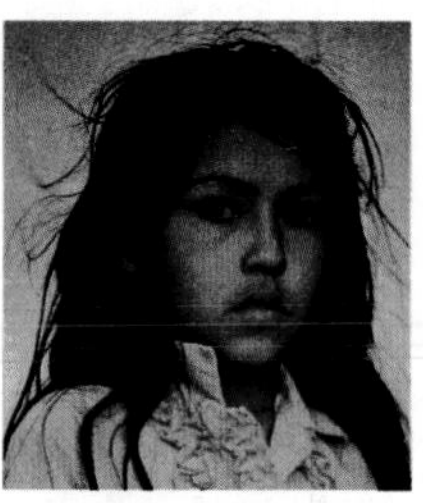

How many times a day do you hear a critical remark about someone based on his or her appearance? People often judge one another by appearances. Though most would agree that such superficial judgments are unfair or inaccurate, it's still easy to make assumptions about people's values, beliefs, and worth because of the color of their skin or the clothes they wear. Perhaps one of the most basic human rights should be the right to be judged not by our appearance but by our words and actions.

The main characters in this subunit are judged by their appearances. As you read the selections, decide why these judgments are unfair.

Observation Assessment

Observing how students respond to the text, to the classroom instruction, and to peers is an important part of an assessment program. The following suggestions and the form in each Unit Resource Book can be used to implement observation assessment.

- As students work through this subunit, assess their reaction when presented with a longer selection. Do they give up? start but quickly lose track? read the entire piece and recall nothing? Or do they identify with characters and situations? make comments to themselves or others while reading? go back and reread immediately when they lose track?

- To evaluate how well students connect with a selection, have them draw an analogy between the character's situation an a situation from life. Have them explain why a character's feelings are or are not believable.

e x p l o r e

Fiction

After You, My Dear Alphonse

SHIRLEY JACKSON

Examine What You Know (Prior Knowledge)

As you will see in this selection, prejudice is not always an open act of discrimination. Falsely assuming something about someone can be a subtle form of prejudice. Make up an example that illustrates an instance in which someone makes false judgments about another person. Share your example with your classmates.

Expand Your Knowledge (Building Background)

The title of this selection, "After You, My Dear Alphonse," is an expression that comes from *Alphonse and Gaston,* an American comic strip that first appeared in 1905. The words describe a situation in which two people, out of respect for each other, both suggest that the other go first. Often the expression is used to describe a comic situation, such as two baseball players letting a pop fly fall between them.

Enrich Your Reading (Reading Skill)

Identifying Assumptions When you make an assumption, you are supposing that something is a fact with little or no evidence to back up your belief. One of the characters in the story you are about to read makes many false assumptions concerning black people. Identify these assumptions as you read Shirley Jackson's short story.

■ *A biography of the author can be found in the Reader's Handbook.*

Objectives

- To read and understand a short story
- To identify assumptions
- To express understanding of the work through a choice of writing options, including a letter, a description, and a title

Prereading/Motivation

Examine What You Know

Discussion Prompts: What kinds of information do people use to make assumptions about other people? Why do people feel the need to make assumptions about other people?

Expand Your Knowledge

Discussion Prompts: What expressions from popular entertainment, such as TV, movies, and comics, do you use? Describe the situations in which you use these expressions.

Enrich Your Reading

Have students create charts in which they record the facts about Boyd and his family and the corresponding false assumptions that Mrs. Wilson makes. Possible answers include these:
Information: Boyd is carrying all the wood. *Assumptions:* Johnny made him do all the work; Johnny is making Boyd do all the work because Boyd is black.
Information: Boyd's father works in a factory. *Assumption:* Boyd's father is a laborer.
Information: Boyd is black. *Assumptions:* Boyd's family is large and poor; Boyd's mother works; Boyd doesn't get enough to eat; Boyd's family needs charity.

Thematic Link—How Others See Me
In this story, one character's false assumptions prevent her from seeing another individual as he really is.

Journal Writing

Communication plays an important role in "After You, My Dear Alphonse." Suggest these journal topics to students:

- Give examples of special phrases or "in-jokes" you use when talking with your friends.
- Give examples of times you have made false assumptions about others and tell how your assumptions were corrected.

For other journal opportunities, refer students to Broader Connections (p. 459).

Addditional Resources

UNIT FOUR RESOURCE BOOK
Reader's Guidesheet, p. 1
Vocabulary Worksheet, p. 2
Selection Check Tests, p. 3
Selection Test, pp. 4–5

Collaborative Learning

Opportunities for collaborative learning appear throughout the lesson and include Cultural Connections (p. T–457).

Teaching Strategies

Support for Students of Limited English Proficiency

- Use **Reader's Guidesheet,** p. 1.
- "After You, My Dear Alphonse" contains numerous references to traditional stereotypes about blacks. Read aloud the first three columns of the story and encourage students to take a critical look at the ideas underlying Mrs. Wilson's false assumptions. Have students evaluate Mrs. Wilson's behavior by deciding whether she is reacting on the basis of reality or stereotype. Be sure students understand that Mrs. Wilson's behavior is changed when she sees that Boyd is a "Negro."
- **Annotation H** focuses on an aspect of culture.

Text Annotations

A. Literary Element: CHARACTER Ask students what they can infer about Mrs. Wilson based on her dialogue here and earlier and what details support their conclusions. *(Possible responses: She is strict, since she scolds her son for being late and for not being polite; she values proper manners, since she insists on politeness; she is formal, since she speaks in complete sentences and has lunch at a set time.)*

B. Literary Element: SETTING Ask students what details indicate the time during which the story takes place. *("He was a Negro boy" suggests a time before the 1960's: "Dead Japanese" suggests World War II and the 1940's.)*

C. Reading Skill: IDENTIFYING ASSUMPTIONS Have students identify the assumption(s) Mrs. Boyd has made. *(She has assumed that Johnny made Boyd carry the wood; perhaps she has assumed that Johnny orders Boyd because Boyd is black.)*

D. Reading Skill: INFERRING Ask students how they would describe the relationship between the two boys. *(Possible response: The boys seem to be good friends, with a relationship built on feelings of equality and respect.)*

After You, My Dear Alphonse

SHIRLEY JACKSON

Mrs. Wilson was just taking the gingerbread out of the oven when she heard Johnny outside talking to someone.

"Johnny," she called, "you're late. Come in and get your lunch."

"Just a minute, Mother," Johnny said. "After you, my dear Alphonse."

"After *you,* my dear Alphonse," another voice said.

"No, after *you,* my dear Alphonse," Johnny said.

Mrs. Wilson opened the door. "Johnny," she said, "you come in this minute and get your lunch. You can play after you've eaten."

Johnny came in after her, slowly. "Mother," he said, "I brought Boyd home for lunch with me."

"Boyd?" Mrs. Wilson thought for a moment. "I don't believe I've met Boyd. Bring him in, dear, since you've invited him. Lunch is ready."

"Boyd!" Johnny yelled. "Hey, Boyd, come on in!"

"I'm coming. Just got to unload this
SR-1 ▶ stuff."

"Well, hurry, or my mother'll be sore."

A "Johnny, that's not very polite to either your friend or your mother," Mrs. Wilson said. "Come sit down, Boyd."

As she turned to show Boyd where to sit, she saw he was a Negro boy, smaller than Johnny but about the same age. His arms were loaded with split kindling wood. "Where'll I put this stuff, Johnny?" he asked.

Mrs. Wilson turned to Johnny. "Johnny," B
she said, "what did you make Boyd do? What is that wood?"

"Dead Japanese," Johnny said mildly. "We stand them in the ground and run over
them with tanks." ◀ SR-2

"How do you do, Mrs. Wilson?" Boyd said.

"How do you do, Boyd? You shouldn't let Johnny make you carry all that wood. Sit
down now and eat lunch, both of you." C

"Why shouldn't he carry the wood, Mother? It's his wood. We got it at his place."

"Johnny," Mrs. Wilson said, "go on and eat your lunch."

"Sure," Johnny said. He held out the dish of scrambled eggs to Boyd. "After you, my dear Alphonse."

"After *you,* my dear Alphonse," Boyd D
said.

"After *you,* my dear Alphonse," Johnny said. They began to giggle.

"Are you hungry, Boyd?" Mrs. Wilson asked.

"Yes, Mrs. Wilson."

STRUCTURED READING FOR LESS PROFICIENT STUDENTS

These questions can help to guide students through the reading. Ask each question at the point of the selection where the SR number appears in the margin.

SR–1 Who are the characters in the story? What are their relationships? *(Mrs Wilson, Johnny, Boyd; Mrs. Wilson is Johnny's mother, Boyd is Johnny's friend)* **Literal recall**

SR–2 How do the boys intend to use the wood that Boyd is carrying? *(to play war; the logs represent "dead Japanese")* **Clarifying**

SR–3 What kind of work does Mrs. Wilson think Boyd's father does? *(factory labor)* What is the father's actual position? *(factory foreman)* **Literal recall**

SR–4 What does Mrs. Wilson want to give Boyd for himself and his family? *(used clothing)* Why does Boyd refuse to take it? *(He has plenty of clothes; his family buys what they want.)* **Literal recall**

SR–5 What does Mrs. Wilson do that shows she is angry with Boyd? *(removes the gingerbread as he is about to take a piece)* **Inferring**

"Well, don't you let Johnny stop you. He always fusses about eating, so you just see that you get a good lunch. There's plenty of food here for you to have all you want."

"Thank you, Mrs. Wilson."

"Come on, Alphonse," Johnny said. He pushed half the scrambled eggs onto Boyd's plate. Boyd watched while Mrs. Wilson put a dish of stewed tomatoes beside his plate.

"Boyd don't eat tomatoes, do you, Boyd?" Johnny said.

"*Doesn't* eat tomatoes, Johnny. And just because you don't like them, don't say that about Boyd. Boyd will eat *anything*."

"Bet he won't," Johnny said, attacking his scrambled eggs.

"Boyd wants to grow up and be a big, strong man so he can work hard," Mrs. Wilson said. "I'll bet Boyd's father eats stewed tomatoes."

"My father eats anything he wants to," Boyd said.

"So does mine," Johnny said. "Sometimes he doesn't eat hardly anything. He's a little guy, though. Wouldn't hurt a flea."

"Mine's a little guy, too," Boyd said.

"I'll bet he's strong, though," Mrs. Wilson said. She hesitated. "Does he . . . work?"

"Sure," Johnny said. "Boyd's father works in a factory."

"There, you see?" Mrs. Wilson said. "And he certainly has to be strong to do that—all that lifting and carrying at a factory."

"Boyd's father doesn't have to," Johnny said. "He's a foreman."

Mrs. Wilson felt defeated. "What does your mother do, Boyd?"

"My mother?" Boyd was surprised. "She takes care of us kids."

"Oh. She doesn't work, then?"

"Why should she?" Johnny said through a mouthful of eggs. "You don't work."

"You really don't want any stewed tomatoes, Boyd?"

"No, thank you, Mrs. Wilson," Boyd said.

"No, thank you, Mrs. Wilson, no, thank you, Mrs. Wilson, no, thank you, Mrs. Wilson," Johnny said. "Boyd's sister's going to work, though. She's going to be a teacher."

"That's a very fine attitude for her to have, Boyd." Mrs. Wilson restrained an impulse to pat Boyd on the head. "I imagine you're all very proud of her?"

"I guess so," Boyd said.

"What about all your other brothers and sisters? I guess all of you want to make just as much of yourselves as you can."

"There's only me and Jean," Boyd said. "I don't know yet what I want to be when I grow up."

"We're going to be tank drivers, Boyd and me," Johnny said. "Zoom." Mrs. Wilson caught Boyd's glass of milk as Johnny's napkin ring, suddenly transformed into a tank, plowed heavily across the table.

"Look, Johnny," Boyd said. "Here's a foxhole. I'm shooting at you."

Mrs. Wilson, with the speed born of long experience, took the gingerbread off the shelf and placed it carefully between the tank and the foxhole.

"Now eat as much as you want to, Boyd," she said. "I want to see you get filled up."

ON THE RED TABLE 1 1983
Daniel Quintero Private collection Courtesy of Marlborough Gallery, New York.

Art Note

Spanish artist Daniel Quintero (1949–), who worked for a time in England and Ireland, now lives in Spain. In this portrait, the pensive boy seems unaware of another young person close by. His face is dramatized by the framing effect of the supporting pole, and the power of his mood is heightened by the deep primary colors used. *Might this be a picture of Boyd in "After You, My Dear Alphonse"? Why or why not?*

E. Reading Skill: COMPARING Elicit from students similarities that they notice between Boyd and Johnny. *(Neither boy likes stewed tomatoes; both see their fathers as eating anything they wish and as being little.)*

F. Reading Skill: IDENTIFYING ASSUMPTIONS Ask students what assumption Mrs. Wilson has made here. *(that Boyd's father is a laborer because he works in a factory and is black)* Ask why she may be feeling defeated. *(because her stereotyped ideas about Boyd are proving to be untrue)*

G. Reading Skill: INFERRING Ask students what Mrs. Wilson's attitude toward Boyd and his family is. *(She feels she is superior to them; her attitude is condescending.)*

H. LEP: Culture Explain that the boys are playing war, imitating the soldiers of World War II. Have a volunteer describe a foxhole. *(a shallow pit hastily dug by soldiers for refuge during enemy fire)* You may wish to have students from various cultures tell about other games children play based on activities that they see in adult life.

Cultural Connection

To help students understand the causes of some of Mrs. Wilson's false assumptions, have them identify the classic stereotypes the writer is exploring in this selection. Some such stereotypes are that blacks are generally servants, laborers, poor and hungry, and have large uneducated families. Discuss with students the possible roots of these stereotypes and how our cultural system tends to sustain them.

I. Reading Skill: IDENTIFYING ASSUMPTIONS Have students identify the assumptions Mrs. Wilson has made here about Boyd's family. *(Possible responses: She has assumed that they are poor, do not have enough clothing, need charity, and will accept hand-me-downs, and that the mother can sew.)*

J. Reading Skill: INFERRING Ask students why they think Mrs. Wilson removes the plate of gingerbread. *(Possible response: She is angry at Boyd because he has not lived up to her assumptions; he has defeated all her fixed thinking about what a black boy should be like.)* Ask students what they can infer about Mrs. Wilson from her reaction. *(Possible response: She is rigid, narrow-minded, bigoted, and unable to change; she is unable to see Boyd as the individual he is.)*

K. Reading Skill: INFERRING Have students tell what they can infer about Boyd's experience with prejudice. *(Possible response: Boyd has apparently experienced little prejudice; he seems puzzled by Mrs. Wilson's behavior.)* Ask how students can tell that Boyd is not prejudiced. *(Possible response: He treats Mrs. Wilson and Johnny as individuals; he regards Johnny as a friend and equal.)*

Check Test

1. Whom does Johnny bring home for lunch? *(a black friend named Boyd)*
2. What is Boyd's father's job? *(factory foreman)*
3. How many children are in Boyd's family? *(two; he and his sister, Jean)*
4. Why does Mrs. Wilson say she is disappointed in Boyd? *(because he does not want the clothes Mrs. Wilson offers)*

Encouraging Independent Reading

"Any Human to Another," a poem by Countee Cullen
"Mother Dear and Daddy," a short story by Junius Edwards
"The Test," a short story by Angelica Gibbs
"The Bones of Lovella Brown," a short story by Ann Petry
Bless the Beasts and Children, a novel by Glendon F. Swarthout

"Boyd eats a lot, but not as much as I do," Johnny said. "I'm bigger than he is."

"You're not much bigger," Boyd said. "I can beat you running."

Mrs. Wilson took a deep breath. "Boyd," she said. Both boys turned to her. "Boyd, Johnny has some suits that are a little too small for him, and a winter coat. It's not new, of course, but there's lots of wear in it still. And I have a few dresses that your mother or sister could probably use. Your mother can make them over into lots of things for all of you, and I'd be very happy to give them to you. Suppose before you leave I make up a big bundle and then you and Johnny can take it over to your mother right away . . ." Her voice trailed off as she saw Boyd's puzzled expression. I

"But I have plenty of clothes, thank you," he said. "And I don't think my mother knows how to sew very well, and anyway I guess we buy about everything we need.
SR-4 ▶ Thank you very much, though."

"We don't have time to carry that old stuff around, Mother," Johnny said. "We got to play tanks with the kids today."

Mrs. Wilson lifted the plate of gingerbread off the table as Boyd was about to take another piece. "There are many little boys like you, Boyd, who would be very grateful for the clothes someone was kind
SR-5 ▶ enough to give them." J

"Boyd will take them if you want him to, Mother," Johnny said.

"I didn't mean to make you mad, Mrs. Wilson," Boyd said.

"Don't think I'm angry, Boyd. I'm just disappointed in you, that's all. Now let's not say anything more about it."

She began clearing the plates off the table, and Johnny took Boyd's hand and pulled him to the door. "'Bye, Mother," Johnny said. Boyd stood for a minute, staring at Mrs. Wilson's back.

"After you, my dear Alphonse," Johnny said, holding the door open.

"Is your mother still mad?" Mrs. Wilson heard Boyd ask in a low voice. K

"I don't know," Johnny said. "She's screwy sometimes."

"So's mine," Boyd said. He hesitated. "After *you*, my dear Alphonse." ❧

INSIGHT

Incident

COUNTEE CULLEN

Once riding in old Baltimore,
  Heart-filled, head-filled with glee,
I saw a Baltimorean
  Keep looking straight at me.

Now I was eight and very small,
  And he was no whit bigger,
And so I smiled, but he poked out
  His tongue and called me, "Nigger."

I saw the whole of Baltimore
  From May until December:
Of all the things that happened there
  That's all that I remember.

Insight

This piece reflects on the ideas in the main selection and is suggested for students' independent reading. Optional discussion questions follow.

1. Have students tell what the speaker of the poem and Boyd from the short story have in common. *(They are both young, small and black and suffer the prejudice of others.)*

2. Have students tell why the incident described is "all" that the speaker remembers. *(Possible response: Incidents that are so insulting to a person are painful, and painful experiences are often the ones that stand out most in a person's mind.)*

3. Ask students which is more harmful—the outright expression of prejudice in "Incident" or Mrs. Wilson's phony politeness and friendliness. *(Possible responses: Outright expressions are more harmful because they are so blatant and purposely hurtful. Mrs. Wilson's type of prejudice is just as bad because it is based on phoniness and it perpetuates stereotypes.)*

Responding to Reading

First Impressions

1. How do you respond to the character of Mrs. Wilson? Explain your answer.

Second Thoughts

2. What does Mrs. Wilson believe is true about all black people? Look back at the assumptions you identified as you were reading.

3. How would you describe the friendship between Johnny and Boyd?

   Think about
   - what the title suggests
   - how they play together
   - how they react to Mrs. Wilson

4. Why doesn't Boyd get angry at Mrs. Wilson?

   Think about
   - Boyd and Johnny's friendship
   - what Boyd does and doesn't understand about Mrs. Wilson
   - what we know about Boyd's family

5. Why do you think that Mrs. Wilson becomes angry and disappointed with Boyd?

Broader Connections

6. What are some subtle forms of prejudice that you have seen or experienced?

Writing Options

1. Imagine that after Boyd gets home he tells his mother about the offer of clothes and about other happenings at the Wilsons. Compose a letter that Boyd's mother mails to Mrs. Wilson.

2. Through Boyd's answers to Mrs. Wilson, you learn a number of facts about his family. Expanding on these details, describe Boyd's family and home.

3. What would have happened had Mrs. Wilson convinced Boyd to take home the clothes? Describe the thoughts that run through his mind as he walks home carrying these handouts.

4. Write a new title for this story. Explain why your title helps a reader understand and appreciate the story.

Student Response

Responding to Reading

These questions are open-ended with no "right" or "wrong" answers. However, responses must be supported with information from the story. Possible answers follow:

1. Almost any response is acceptable.

2. Students may say that Mrs. Wilson believes black people are poor, uneducated, and servile; that they have large families and are in need of food and clothing; that they accept charity; that they are all alike. Students may also suggest that Mrs. Wilson feels obligated to act a certain way toward black people because of the assumptions she has made.

3. Students may say that the friendship between Johnny and Boyd is based on the real knowledge each boy has of the other; that their friendship is based on shared interests rather than on formal obligations; that they genuinely like and respect each other.

4. Some students may say that Boyd's manners and respect for elders prevent him from reacting angrily to Mrs. Wilson. Others may suggest that Boyd realizes that Mrs. Wilson is a well-meaning but ignorant woman. Others may say that Boyd doesn't want to lose Johnny as a friend and therefore is polite to his mother. Still others may point out that Boyd is puzzled by Mrs. Wilson's behavior and, since he himself is not prejudiced, he does not recognize that she is prejudiced towards him.

5. Some students may say that Mrs. Wilson becomes angry with Boyd because he fails to act in accordance with her stereotypical notions. Others may say that she is angry because Boyd does not respond to her offers of generosity.

Closure

Ask students what this story has taught them about false assumptions and ways of seeing and understanding other people.

Writing Options

The Writing Options are designed to meet varied student interests and abilities. Have each student choose one writing activity to complete. You may wish to guide some students to an option that requires less writing.

Journal Update Have students review their journal entries for "After You, My Dear Alphonse." What have they learned about communication and prejudice? What new reflections can they add to their earlier writing?

Objectives

- To read and understand a short story
- To recognize nonstandard English
- To recognize the use of tone
- To understand the importance of details
- To express understanding of the work through a choice of writing options, including words of advice, dialogue, predictions, lists, and comparison

Prereading/Motivation

Examine What You Know

Discussion Prompts: What goals led you to look for work? How did your work experience change the way you thought about yourself?

Expand Your Knowledge

Discussion Prompts: How do you think life in rural Iowa in the 1920s differed from your life today? What types of work opportunities most likely were available to young people in the 1920s?

Enrich Your Reading

You may wish to have students rewrite each phrase in standard English. Possible examples are these: "Oh, ain't it somewheres around?" *("Oh, isn't it somewhere?")* "They ain't all dirty, are they?" *("They aren't all dirty, are they?")* "We ain't got any suitcase." *("We don't have a suitcase.")*

Thematic Link—How Others See Me

In this story, the main character's new start in life leads her to understand that others see her in a way that is very different from the way she has viewed herself.

explore

Fiction

A Start in Life

RUTH SUCKOW (so͞o' kou)

Examine What You Know (Prior Knowledge)

Try to remember the first time you worked for someone else. Maybe you delivered newspapers or groceries. Perhaps you washed dishes or windows or hauled packages or golf bags. Can you recall how you felt as you performed this first job and how you felt about your employer? Jot down what went through your mind. Compare your feelings to those of the girl in the story as she begins her first job.

Expand Your Knowledge (Building Background)

"A Start in Life" takes place in Iowa in the 1920's. These were good times for business, and many Iowans enjoyed the national boom. The state built many new roads, bridges, railroads, and dams to help the economy grow. However, such giant steps forward did not help everyone. The Switzer family in the story is typical of Iowans who struggled to survive in the 1920's.

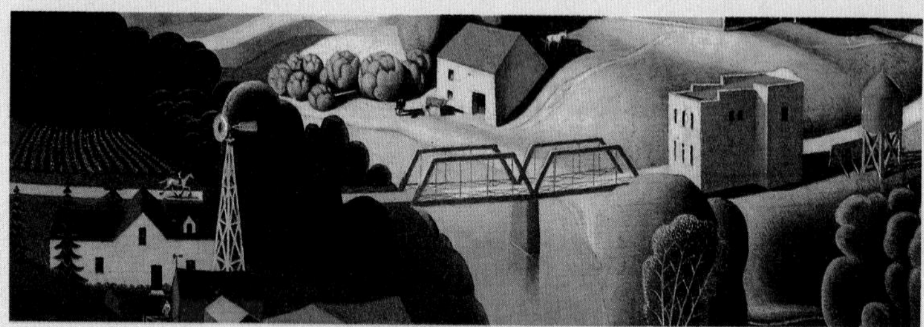

Enrich Your Reading (Reading Skill)

Nonstandard English is English that does not conform to accepted standards of grammar, usage, and mechanics. Expressions like *he don't* and words like *ain't* are nonstandard. Nonstandard English is a spoken form of English and usually appears in literature as dialogue. Notice that some of the characters in "A Start in Life" use nonstandard English frequently. For example, the mother asks about a missing belt: "Ain't it somewheres around?" As you read, note other instances of nonstandard English.

■ *A biography of the author can be found on page 475.*

Journal Writing

The notion of change is central to the story. Suggest these journal topics to students:

- Identify a time when you or your family made a new "start in life." Tell about some things that changed and others that remained the same.
- Think about several objectives that you are eager to accomplish in your life. Explain how each "new start" will mean the end of something else.

For other journal opportunities, refer students to Examine What You Know (p. 460) and Real Life Connections (p. T-469).

Additional Resources

UNIT FOUR RESOURCE BOOK

Reader's Guidesheet, p. 6
Vocabulary Worksheet, p. 7
Selection and Vocabulary Check Tests, p. 8
Selection Test, pp. 9–10

Collaborative Learning

Opportunities for collaborative learning appear throughout the lesson and include Options for Learning activity 4 (p. 475), annotations N and X, Teaching Tip (p. T-466) and Cross-Curricular Options (p. T-475).

A Start in Life

RUTH SUCKOW

The Switzers were scurrying around to get Daisy ready by the time that Elmer Kruse should get through in town. They had known all week that Elmer might be in for her any day. But they hadn't done a thing until he appeared. "Oh, it was so rainy today, the roads were so muddy, they hadn't thought he'd get in until maybe next week." It would have been the same any other day.

Mrs. Switzer was trying now at the last moment to get all of Daisy's things into the battered telescope[1] that lay on the bed. The bed had not "gotten made"; and just as soon as Daisy was gone, Mrs. Switzer would have to hurry off to the Woodworths', where she was to wash today. Daisy's things were scattered over the dark brown quilt and the rumpled sheet, which were dingy and clammy in this damp weather. So was the whole bedroom with its sloping ceiling and old-fashioned square-paned windows, the commode[2] that they used for a dresser littered with pin tray, curlers, broken comb, ribbons, smoky lamp, all mixed up together; the door of the closet open, showing the confusion of clothes and shabby shoes. . . . They all slept in this room—Mrs. Switzer and Dwight in the bed, the two girls in the cot against the wall.

A

B

"Mama, I can't find the belt to that plaid dress."

"Oh, ain't it somewheres around? Well, I guess you'll have to let it go. If I come across it, I can send it out to you. Someone'll be going past there."

She had meant to get Daisy all mended and "fixed up" before she went out to the country. But somehow . . . oh, there was always so much to see to when she came home. Gone all day, washing and cleaning for other people; it didn't leave her much time for her own home.

C

She was late now. The Woodworths liked to have her get the washing out early so that she could do some cleaning too before she left. But she couldn't help it. She would have to get Daisy off first. She had already had on her wraps ready to go, when Elmer came—her cleaning cap, of a blue faded almost into gray, and the ancient black coat with gathered sleeves that she wore over her work dress when she went out to wash.

"What's become of all your underclothes? They ain't all dirty, are they?"

"They are, too. You didn't wash for us last week, Mama."

"Well, you'll have to take along what you've got. Maybe there'll be some way of getting the rest to you."

"Kruses come in every week, don't they?" Daisy demanded.

"Yes, but maybe they won't always be bringing you in."

1. **telescope:** an adjustable traveling bag consisting of two cases, the larger over the smaller.

2. **commode:** a small, low table that has drawers or cabinet space, usually used as a washstand.

Teaching Strategies

Vocabulary Review

These vocabulary words are defined at the bottom of the selection page on which they appear. You may wish to discuss them briefly before students begin reading.

condolence a showing of sympathy
curt brief
desolate lonely and sad
ecstatic joyful
forlornness hopelessness
genially in a friendly way
imposing impressive
piteously arousing pity
preening primping
subdued holding back feelings

Support for Students of Limited English Proficiency

- Use **Reader's Guidesheet**, p. 6.
- "A Start in Life" contains terms, expressions, and nonstandard dialect that may pose difficulties for some students. Reading aloud to them some examples of dialogue with nonstandard English will help students to "hear" the characters as they read on their own.
- **Annotations C, G, L, R, BB,** and **KK** focus on troublesome language.

Text Annotations

A. Literary Element: MOOD Have students tell the mood described by this passage. Ask them to give details to support their ideas. *(Possible responses: gloomy, depressing, disorganized. Details: clothes scattered over dingy, clammy dark brown quilt and rumpled sheet)*

B. Reading Skill: INFERRING Ask students what they can infer about the Switzers based on this description. *(Possible responses: They are poor; their lives are rushed and disorganized; Mrs. Switzer is an overworked single parent.)*

C. LEP: Language The meaning of the phrase "get Daisy all mended and 'fixed up'" may be unclear to some students. Discuss it and have volunteers paraphrase the passage. *(Possible response: to mend Daisy's clothes and make sure she has everything she needs)*

Structured Reading for Less Proficient Students

These questions can help to guide students through the reading. Ask each question at the point of the selection where the SR number appears in the margin.

SR–1. Why is Mrs. Switzer getting Daisy's things together? *(Daisy is going away with Elmer Kruse.)* **Clarifying**

SR–2. In what ways is Daisy "important in her small world"? *(She is the oldest child, she gets her choice of hand-me-down clothes, her sister and brother envy her.)* **Literal recall**

SR–3. What does Mrs. Switzer know that makes her worried about Daisy? *(Daisy is going off to work for other people for the first time and doesn't know what to expect.)* **Clarifying**

SR–4. What does Daisy see as she leaves in the car with Elmer? *(the small house that is her home, the yard, her brother and sister, her mother, her playthings)* **Literal recall**

SR–5. What mixed feelings does Daisy have on the car ride? *(She feels proud and forlorn.)* **Literal recall**

Continued on page 462

D. Reading Skill: NOTING DETAILS Have students identify details that describe Daisy. *("skinny," "pale, sharp eyes set close together," and "thin, stringy reddish hair")*

E. Critical Thinking: SYNTHESIZING Have students give opinions about things Daisy "ought to be told." *(Possible response: Going to work for someone and visiting are not the same. People will expect different behavior. She will live by different rules.)*

F. Literary Element: CHARACTERIZATION Have students describe how Daisy sees herself. *(Possible responses: She is proud of herself and feels important and confident.)*

G. LEP: Language Have students discuss what the writer means when she says Mrs. Switzer's face "was working." *(Possible response: She was trying to keep from crying, trying not to show how sad she felt about Daisy's leaving.)* Have students discuss what Mrs. Switzer knows that Daisy does not. *(what it is like to work for someone else)*

She jammed what she could into the telescope, thinking with her helpless, anxious fatalism[3] that it would have to do somehow.

"Daisy, you get yourself ready now."

"I am ready, Mama; I want to put on my other ribbon."

"Oh, that's 'way down in the telescope somewhere. You needn't be so anxious to fix yourself up. This ain't like going SR-1 ▶ visiting."

D Daisy stood at the little mirror preening herself—such a homely child, "all Switzer," skinny, with pale, sharp eyes set close together and thin, stringy, reddish hair. But she had never really learned yet how homely she was. She was the oldest, and she got the pick of what clothes were given to the Switzers. Goldie and Dwight envied her. She was important in her small world. She was proud of her blue coat that had belonged to Alice Brooker, the town lawyer's daughter. It hung unevenly about her bony little knees, and the buttons came down too far. Her SR-2 ▶ mother had tried to make it over for her.

E Mrs. Switzer looked at her, troubled, but not knowing how she could tell her all the things she ought to be told. Daisy had never been away before except to go to her Uncle Fred's at Lehigh. She seemed to think that this would be the same. She had so many things to learn. Well, she would find them out soon enough—only too soon. Working for other people—she would learn what that meant. Elmer and Edna Kruse were nice young people. They would mean well enough by Daisy. It was a good chance for her to start in. But it wasn't the same.

F Daisy was so proud. She thought it was quite a thing to be "starting in to earn." She thought she could buy herself so much with that dollar and a half a week.[4] The other children stood back watching her, round-eyed and impressed. They wished that they were going away, like Daisy.

They heard a car come splashing through the mud on low. "There he is back! Have you got your things on? Goldie—go out and tell him she's coming."

"No, me tell him, me!" Dwight shouted jealously.

"Well—both of you tell him. Land! . . ."

She tried hastily to put on the cover of the bulging telescope and to fasten the straps. One of them broke.

"Well, you'll have to take it the way it is."

It was an old thing, hadn't been used since her husband, Mert, had "left off canvassing"[5] before he died. And he had worn it all to pieces.

G "Well, I guess you'll have to go now. He won't want to wait. I'll try and send you out what you ain't got with you." She turned to Daisy. Her face was working. There was nothing else to do, as everyone said. Daisy would have to help, and she might as well learn it now. Only, she hated to see Daisy go off, to have her starting in. She knew what it meant. "Well—you try and work good this summer, so they'll want you to stay. I hope they'll bring you in sometimes." ◀ SR-3

Daisy's homely little face grew pale with awe, suddenly, at the sight of her mother

3. **fatalism:** the acceptance that events are beyond human control.

4. **dollar and a half a week:** in the 1920's, when the events of this story take place, this amount could buy more than the same amount today, but it was still a low wage.

5. **canvassing:** working as a traveling salesman.

Words to Know and Use	**preening** (prēn′ iŋ) *adj.* primping; grooming and dressing oneself in a fussy way **preen** *v.*

STRUCTURED READING FOR LESS PROFICIENT STUDENTS

Continued from page 461

SR–6. Describe the members of the Kruse family and tell what the parents do for a living. *(Edna and Elmer Kruse are a young couple who farm; they have two babies, both boys.)* **Summarizing**

SR–7. How does Edna show that she is not pleased with Daisy's performance? *(makes a face, tells Daisy she must help and must watch, whispers to Elmer, becomes impatient, has a tightly closed mouth, is cool to Daisy)* **Literal recall**

SR–8. What has happened to cause Edna to scold Daisy? *(Daisy has put Billy into a corner of the room, far away from the blocks, because he knocked down the building she made; Billy then cried.)* **Summarizing**

SR–9. What does Daisy realize about why she has been left alone? *(The Kruses did not want to take her in the car. In the Kruse family, she is an outsider.)* **Clarifying**

THE FARMER'S DAUGHTER 1943 Thomas Hart Benton Collection of Mr. and Mrs. Stuart Slavin, Ladue, Missouri.

crying, at something that she dimly sensed in the pressure of her mother's thin, strong arms. Her vanity in her new importance was somehow shamed and dampened.

Elmer's big, new Buick, mud-splashed but imposing, stood tilted on the uneven road. H Mud was thick on the wheels. It was a bad day for driving, with the roads a yellow mass, water lying in all the wheel ruts. This little road that led past these few houses on the outskirts of town and up over the hill had a cold, rainy loneliness. Elmer sat in the I front seat of the Buick, and in the back was a big box of groceries.

"Got any room to sit in there?" he asked genially. "I didn't get out, it's so muddy here."

"No, don't get out," Mrs. Switzer said hastily. "She can put this right on the floor there in the back." She added, with a timid

Words to Know and Use

imposing (im pō′ ziŋ) *adj.* impressive
genially (jēn′ yəl lē) *adv.* in a friendly way

Art Note
Thomas Hart Benton (1889–1975) began a chronicle of rural America in the 1920's. His paintings frequently called attention to the hardships of daily life, as in *The Farmer's Daughter:* the sagging house shored up with logs; the outdoor root cellar that suggests the family's winter diet; the lean and wiry dog; and the thinly clad girl who pumps water. *How might this picture describe Daisy Switzer's feelings?*

H. Reading Skill: COMPARING AND CONTRASTING Ask students to note the comparison between the car and its surroundings. *(The Buick is big, new, and imposing, while the surroundings are muddy, shabby, and bleak.)*

I. Reading Skill: PREDICTING Ask students to note the mood at the beginning of Daisy's new life. *("cold, rainy loneliness")* Have students predict how her new life will be. *(Possible responses: Her life will improve; the Kruses' new Buick indicates that she will be in more affluent surroundings. Her life will be lonely and sad; she is leaving her family.)*

J. Literary Sidelight The author writes that Mrs. Switzer "hinted" about Elmer's bringing Daisy whenever he comes to the Switzers. Later, Suckow writes that Daisy intends to "hint" to her new employers about things she wants, such as the pineapple and the movies. This lack of assertiveness may be due in part to the way in which these two characters see themselves in relation to the Kruses, that is, inferior and subservient.

K. Reading Skill: NOTING DETAILS Have students identify details the author uses to describe Daisy's home. *(Details include "weathered," "dim color," "gnawed look," "littered," "shaggy, long grass")*

L. Literary Element: TONE Discuss with students the feelings they have from this passage about Daisy's leaving home. *(Possible responses: sadness, depression)* Ask students what they think the author's attitude is toward the Switzer family. *(Possible responses: caring, understanding)*

M. LEP: Vocabulary Students who are from warm, dry climates may not be familiar with the word *chains* in connection with automotive vehicles. Explain that chains are sometimes used on the tires of vehicles that must operate in severe conditions, such as mud, snow, and ice, to prevent skidding.

N. Reading Skill: VISUALIZING Have collaborative groups use the details the writer gives to construct maps showing the location of Daisy's house, the town, the Dunkels' house, the pasture, and the main road.

attempt at courtesy, "Ain't the roads pretty bad out that way?"

"Yes, but farmers get so they don't think so much about the roads."

"I s'pose that's so."

He saw the signs of tears on Mrs. Switzer's face, and they made him anxious to get away. She embraced Daisy hastily again. Daisy climbed over the grocery box and scrunched herself into the seat.

J "I guess you'll bring her in with you sometime when you're coming," Mrs. Switzer hinted.

"Sure. We'll bring her."

He started the engine. It roared, half died down as the wheels of the car spun in the thick, wet mud.

K In that moment, Daisy had a startled view of home—the small house standing on a rough rise of land, weathered to a dim color that showed dark streaks from the rain; the narrow, sloping front porch whose edge had a soaked, gnawed look; the chickens, grayish-black, pecking at the wet ground; their playthings, stones, a wagon, some old pail covers littered about; a soaked, discolored piece of underwear hanging on the line in the back yard. The yard was tussocky[6] and overhung the road with shaggy, long grass where the yellow bank was caved in under it. Goldie and Dwight were gazing at her solemnly. She saw her mother's face—a thin, weak, loving face, drawn with neglected weeping, with its reddened eyes and poor teeth . . . in the old coat and heavy shoes and cleaning cap, her work-worn hand with its big knuckles clutching at her coat. She saw the playthings they had used yesterday, and the old swing that hung from one of the trees, the ropes sodden, the seat in crooked. . . .

L The car went off, slipping on the wet clay. She waved frantically, suddenly understanding that she was leaving them. They waved at her.

Mrs. Switzer stood there a little while. Then came the harsh rasp of the old black iron pump that stood out under the box elder tree. She was pumping water to leave for the children before she went off to work.

◀ SR-4

Daisy held on as the car skidded going down the short clay hill. Elmer didn't bother with chains. He was too used to the roads. But her eyes brightened with scared excitement. M When they were down and Elmer slowed up going along the tracks in the deep, wet grass that led to the main road, she looked back, holding on her hat with her small, scrawny hand.

Just down this little hill—and home was gone. The big car, the feel of her telescope under her feet, the fact that she was going out to the country changed the looks of everything. She saw it all now.

Dunkels' house stood on one side of the road. A closed-up white house. The windows stared blank and cold between the old shutters. There was a chair with a broken straw seat under the fruit trees. The Dunkels were old Catholic people who seldom went anywhere. In the front yard was a clump of tall pines, the rough brown trunks wet, the green branches, dark and shining, heavy with rain, the ground underneath mournfully sodden and black.

The pasture on the other side. The green grass, lush, wet and cold, and the outcroppings of limestone that held little pools of rainwater in all the tiny holes. Beyond, the low hills gloomy with timber against the lowering sky. N

They slid out onto the main road. They bumped over the small wooden bridge above the swollen creek that came from the

6. **tussocky:** full of clumps of grass or twigs.

Cultural Connection

In the Switzer household, Daisy enjoys a great deal of prestige and responsibility as the oldest *child*. In other cultures, the oldest *son* might enjoy this privileged status. Have students discuss ways in which sex and birth order affect family roles in their cultures.

pasture. Daisy looked down. She saw the little swirls of foam, the long grass that swished with the water, the old rusted tin cans lodged between the rocks.

O She sat up straight and important, her thin, homely little face strained with excitement, her sharp eyes taking in everything. The watery mud holes in the road, the little thickets of plum trees, low and wet, in dark interlacings. She held on fiercely but made no sound when the car skidded.

P She felt the grandeur of having a ride. One wet Sunday, Mr. Brooker had driven them all home from church, she and Goldie and Dwight packed tightly into the back seat of the car, shut in by the side curtains, against which the rain lashed, catching the muddy scent of the roads. Sometimes they could plan to go to town just when Mr. Pattey was going to work in his Ford. Then they would run out and shout eagerly, "Mr. Pattey! Are you going through town?" Sometimes he didn't hear them. Sometimes he said, with curt good nature, "Well, pile in"; and they all hopped into the truck back. "He says we can go along with him."

She looked at the black, wet fields through which little leaves of bright green corn grew in rows, at showery bushes of sumac along the roadside. A gasoline engine pumping water made a loud, desolate sound. There were somber-looking cattle in the wet grass, and lonely, thick-foliaged trees growing here and there in the pastures. She felt her telescope on the floor of the car, the box of groceries beside her. She eyed these with a sharp curiosity. There was a fresh pineapple—something the Switzers didn't often get at home. She wondered if Edna would have it for dinner. Maybe she could hint a little to Edna.

She was out in the country. She could no longer see her house even if she wanted to—standing dingy, streaked with rain, in its rough grass on the little hill. A lump came into her throat. She had looked forward to playing with Edna's children. But Goldie and Dwight would play all morning without her. She was still proud of being the oldest, of going out with Elmer and Edna; but now there was a forlornness in the pride. ◄SR-5

Q She wished she were in the front seat with Elmer. She didn't see why he hadn't put her there. She would have liked to know who all the people were who lived on these farms, how old Elmer's babies were, and if he and Edna always went to the movies when they went into town on Saturday nights. Elmer must have lots of money to buy a car like this. He had a new house on his farm, too, and Mrs. Metzinger had said that it had plumbing. Maybe they would take her to the movies, too. She might hint about that.

When she had gone to visit Uncle Fred, she had had to go on the train. She liked this better. She hoped they had a long way to go. She called out to Elmer:

"Say, how much farther is your place?"

"What's that?" He turned around. "Oh, just down the road a ways. Scared to drive in the mud?"

"No, I ain't scared. I like to drive most any way."

She looked at Elmer's back, the old felt hat crammed down carelessly on his head, the back of his neck with the golden hair on the sunburned skin above the blue of his shirt collar. Strong and easy and slouched

Words to Know and Use

curt (kurt) *adj.* brief; in a manner of being to the point
desolate (des′ ə lit) *adj.* lonely and sad
forlornness (fôr lôrn′ nes) *n.* hopelessness; sadness; feelings of abandonment **forlorn** *adj.*

O. Literary Sidelight The image of riding in an automobile has powerful significance in this story. Daisy associates the automobile with grandeur as it whisks her away to a new start. The automobile trip foreshadows the notion that she is on a one-way ride, leaving her family—as the conclusion of the story confirms.

P. Literary Element: CHARACTER The author describes the Switzers' strategy for getting rides from Mr. Pattey. Ask students to give their opinion of what this strategy suggests about the Switzers. *(Possible response: The Switzers are poor but clever; the Switzers are manipulative people and freeloaders.)*

Q. Reading Skill: INFERRING Have students explain the significance of the fact that Daisy is sitting in the back seat of Elmer's car. *(Possible response: Hers is a formal arrangement; if she were family, or even a friend, she'd probably sit with Elmer; Daisy is as important as the groceries, which are also in the back seat.)*

R. LEP: Rhetorical Questions Some students may be puzzled by Edna Kruse's way of greeting Daisy. Make it clear to students that Edna is expecting Daisy and that her question is appropriate, even though she already knows the answer.

S. Literary Element: MOOD Have students identify the feelings they associate with the Kruses' house. Ask them to give details that support their ideas. *(Possible responses: kind, fond, happy, playful. Details: the exchanges between Elmer and Edna and between Elmer and his children.)*

Teaching Tip

Students may enjoy working in small groups to rewrite in dramatic form the portion of the story beginning with Edna's greeting to Daisy on Daisy's arrival at the Kruses' house to the portion ending with Edna's remainder to Daisy that Daisy has to help her. Remind students to include stage directions. Allow groups who wish to do so to present their scenes to the class.

a little over the steering wheel that he handled so masterly. Elmer and Edna were just young folks; but Mrs. Metzinger said that they had more to start with than most young farmers did and that they were hustlers. Daisy felt that the pride of this belonged to her too, now.

"Here we are!"

"Oh, is this where you folks live?" Daisy cried eagerly.

The house stood back from the road, beyond a space of bare yard with a little scattering of grass just starting—small, modern, painted a bright new white and yellow. The barn was new, too, a big, splendid barn of frescoed brick, with a silo of the same. There were no trees. A raw, desolate wind blew across the back yard as they drove up beside the back door.

Edna had come out on the step. Elmer grinned at her as he took out the box of groceries, and she slightly raised her eyebrows. She said kindly enough:

R "Well, you brought Daisy. Hello, Daisy, are you going to stay with us this summer?"

"I guess so," Daisy said importantly. But she suddenly felt a little shy and forlorn as she got out of the car and stood on the bare ground in the chilly wind.

"Yes, I brought her along," Elmer said.

"Are the roads very bad?"

"Kind of bad. Why?"

"Well, I'd like to get over to Mama's sometime today."

"Oh, I guess they aren't too bad for that."

Daisy pricked up her sharp little ears. Another ride. That cheered her.

"Look in the door," Edna said in a low, fond voice, motioning with her head.

S Two little round, blond heads were pressed tightly against the screen door. There was a clamor of "Daddy, Daddy!" Elmer grinned with a half-bashful pride as he stood with the box of groceries, raising his eyebrows with mock surprise and demanding: "Who's this? What you shoutin' 'Daddy' for? You don't think Daddy's got anything for you, do you?" He and Edna were going into the kitchen together, until Edna remembered and called back hastily: S

"Oh, come in, Daisy!"

Daisy stood, a little left out and solitary, there in the kitchen, as Billy, the older of the babies, climbed frantically over Elmer, demanding candy, and the little one toddled smilingly about. Her eyes took in all of it. She was impressed by the shining blue-and-white linoleum, the range with its nickel and enamel, the bright new woodwork. Edna was laughing and scolding at Elmer and the baby. Billy had made his father produce the candy. Daisy's sharp little eyes looked hungrily at the lemon drops until Edna remembered her.

"Give Daisy a piece of your candy," she said. T

He would not go up to Daisy. She had to come forward and take one of the lemon drops herself. She saw where Edna put the sack, in a dish high in the cupboard. She hoped they would get some more before long.

"My telescope's out there in the car," she reminded them.

"Oh, Elmer, you go and get it and take it up for her," Edna said.

"What?"

"Her valise—or whatever it is—out in the car."

"Oh, sure," Elmer said with a cheerful grin.

"It's kind of an old telescope," Daisy said conversationally. "I guess it's been used a lot. My papa used to have it. The strap broke when Mama was fastening it this morning. We ain't got any suitcase. I had to

PROFESSIONAL NOTEBOOK

How can high levels of literacy be accomplished in a short period of time? As an important beginning step, we need to learn about each student's reading style and about how style affects the way the child processes and retains information. Both the quickest and most honorable path toward creating a literate society is to make learning to read what it should be: natural, easy, and enjoyable. Only then will our students choose to devote substantial time and effort to reading—and only then are they likely to become truly literate.

MARIE CARBO, "IGNITING THE LITERACY REVOLUTION THROUGH READING STYLES," *Educational Leadership*, OCTOBER 1990.

take this because it was all there was in the house, and Mama didn't want to get me a new one."

T Edna raised her eyebrows politely. She leaned over and pretended to spat the baby as he came toddling up to her, then rubbed her cheek against his round head with its funny fuzz of hair.

Daisy watched solemnly. "I didn't know both of your children was boys. I thought one of 'em was a girl. That's what there is at home now—one boy and one girl."

"Um-hm," Edna replied absently. "You can go up with Elmer and take off your things, Daisy," she said. "You can stop and unpack your valise now, I guess, if you'd like to. Then you can come down and help me in the kitchen. You know we got you to help me," she reminded.

Daisy, subdued, followed Elmer up the bright new stairs. In the upper hall, two strips of very clean rag rug were laid over the shining yellow of the floor. Elmer had put her telescope in one of the bedrooms.

"There you are!"

She heard him go clattering down the stairs, and then a kind of murmuring and laughing in the kitchen. The back door slammed. She hurried to the window in time to see Elmer go striding toward the

SR-6 ▶ barn.

She looked about her room with an intense curiosity. It, too, had a bright varnished floor. She had a bed all her own—a small, old-

U fashioned bed, left from some old furnishings, that had been put in this room that had the pipes and the hot water tank. She had to see everything, but she had a stealthy look as she tiptoed about, started to open the drawers of the dresser, looked out of her window. She put her coat and hat on the bed. She would rather be down in the kitchen with Edna then unpack her telescope now.

She guessed she would go down where the rest of them were.

Elmer came into the house for dinner. He brought in a cold, muddy, outdoor breath with him. The range was going, but the bright little kitchen seemed chilly, with the white oil cloth on the table, the baby's varnished high chair and his little fat, mottled[7] hands.

Edna made a significant little face at Elmer. Daisy did not see. She was standing back from the stove, where Edna was at work, looking at the baby. V

"He can talk pretty good, can't he? Dwight couldn't say anything but 'Mama' when he was that little."

Edna's back was turned. She said meaningly:

"Now, Elmer's come in for dinner, Daisy; we'll have to hurry. You must help me get on the dinner. You can cut bread and get things on the table. You must help, you know. That's what you are supposed to do." W

Daisy looked startled, a little scared and resentful. "Well, I don't know where you keep your bread."

"Don't you remember where I told you to put it this morning? Right over in the cabinet, in that big box. You must watch, Daisy, and learn where things are."

Elmer, a little embarrassed at the look that Edna gave him, whistled as he began to wash his hands at the sink. X

7. **mottled:** having an appearance that is blotchy or spotted with different colors or shades.

Words to Know and Use

subdued (sub do͞od′) *adj.* hiding or holding back feelings **subdue** *v.*

T. Critical Thinking: ANALYZING After Daisy explains about her broken suitcase, Edna "raised her eyes politely." Have students tell what Edna's response might mean. *(Possible response: Daisy might have been a bit too familiar with Edna, who was still a stranger and her employer.)*

U. Literary Element: CHARACTER Have students find details that describe how Daisy behaved as she explored her new room. Ask their opinions about what the writer might mean to suggest about Daisy. *(Possible response: She looks with "intense curiosity," "a stealthy look," she "tiptoed about." Daisy may feel she doesn't belong there.)*

V. Reading Skill: CLARIFYING Have students explain what Edna's "significant little face" is meant to convey to Elmer. *(Possible response: It is meant to convey disapproval of Daisy without wishing to hurt her feelings.)*

W. Literary Element: THEME Have students tell the type of relationship Edna is trying to establish with Daisy. *(an employee-employer relationship, not a family relationship)* Have students identify the words the author uses to summarize how Edna sees Daisy. *("You must help, you know. That's what you are supposed to do.")*

X. Discussion Have students discuss the dialogue the author might have written if she had wanted Elmer and Edna to have a conversation instead of just a silent exchange. Students may wish to compose such a dialogue and share it with the rest of the class.

Art Note

Grant Wood (1892–1942) was born in Iowa, and many of his portraits drawn from midwestern American life are chillingly plain and severe. With *Stone City,* however, he realized his talent for stylization. He imposed on the little village, the site of an abandoned stone quarry, an unrealistic orderliness, making of the scene a sort of fantasy. *Which features of the landscape did the artist change?*

Y. Reading Skill: CLARIFYING Have students explain what Daisy's "queer ache" might be. *(Possible response: Daisy might be feeling anxious, alone, nervous, or frightened as she begins to realize the "difference between the position of herself and of the two babies.")*

Z. Critical Reading: EVALUATING Ask students to tell whether they think it is fair of Edna to be impatient with Daisy. Have them explain their answers. *(Students who think Edna is being fair may say that since Daisy knew that she was coming to the Kruses' to work, she should do so without being told. Students who think Edna is being unfair may say that it is unreasonable of her to expect Daisy to pitch right in when the girl is so new to and unfamiliar with the Kruses and their household.)*

STONE CITY, IOWA 1930 Grant Wood Joslyn Art Museum, Omaha, Nebraska.

"How's Daddy's old boy?" he said loudly, giving a poke at the baby's chin.

As Edna passed him, she shook her head and her lips just formed, "Been like that all morning!"

He grinned comprehendingly. Then both their faces became expressionless.

Y Daisy had not exactly heard, but she looked from one to the other, silent and dimly wondering. The queer ache that had kept starting all through the morning, under her interest in Edna's things and doings, came over her again. She sensed something different in the atmosphere than she had ever known before—some queer difference between the position of herself and of the two babies, a faint notion of what Mama had meant when she had said that this would not be visiting. Y

"I guess I'm going to have the toothache again," she said faintly.

No one seemed to hear her.

Edna whisked off the potatoes, drained the water. . . ."You might bring me a dish, Daisy." Daisy searched a long time while Edna turned impatiently and pointed. Edna Z put the rest of the things on the table herself. Her young, fresh, capable mouth was tightly closed, and she was making certain resolutions.

Daisy stood hesitating in the middle of the room, a scrawny, unappealing little figure. Billy—fat, blond, in funny, dark blue union-alls[8]—was trotting busily about the kitchen. Daisy swooped down upon him and tried to bring him to the table. He set up a howl. Edna turned, looked astonished, severe.

"I was trying to make him come to the table," Daisy explained weakly.

"You scared him. He isn't used to you. He doesn't like it. Don't cry, Billy. The girl didn't mean anything."

"Here, Daddy'll put him in his place," Elmer said hastily.

AA Billy looked over his father's shoulder at Daisy with suffused, resentful blue eyes. She did not understand it and felt strangely at a loss. She had been left with Goldie and Dwight so often. She had always made Dwight go to the table. She had been the boss.

Edna said in a cool, held-in voice, "Put these things on the table, Daisy."

They sat down. Daisy and the other children had always felt it a great treat to eat away from home instead of at their own scanty, hastily set table. They had hung around Mrs. Metzinger's house at noon, hoping to be asked to stay, not offended when told that "it was time for them to run off now." Her pinched little face had a hungry look as she stared at the potatoes and fried ham and pie. But they did not watch and urge her to have more, as Mrs. Metzinger did, and Mrs. Brooker when she took pity on the Switzers and had them there. Daisy wanted more pie. But none of them seemed to be taking more, and so she said nothing. She remembered what her mother had said, with now a faint comprehension. "You must remember you're out working for other folks, and it won't be like it is at home."

After dinner Edna said, "Now you can wash the dishes, Daisy." ◀SR-7

She went into the next room with the children. Daisy, as she went hesitatingly about the kitchen alone, could hear Edna's low contented humming as she sat in there rocking the baby in her lap. The bright kitchen was empty and lonely now. Through the window, Daisy could see the great barn looming up against the rainy sky. She hoped that they would drive to Edna's mother's soon.

She finished as soon as she could and went into the dining room where Edna was sewing on the baby's rompers. Edna went on sewing. Daisy sat down disconsolately. That queer, low ache went all through her. She said in a small, dismal voice: BB

"I guess I got the toothache again."

Edna bit off a thread.

"I had it awful hard awhile ago. Mama come pretty near taking me to the dentist."

"That's too bad," Edna murmured politely. But she offered no other condolence. She gave a little secret smile at the baby asleep on a blanket and a pillow in one corner of the shiny leather davenport.[9] CC

"Is Elmer going to drive into town tomorrow?"

8. **union-alls:** one-piece underwear.
9. **davenport:** a large sofa.

Words to Know and Use

condolence (kən dō′ ləns) *n.* something said or otherwise communicated to show sympathy and understanding to another who is suffering

AA. Reading Skill: CONTRASTING Have students explain the difference between Daisy's role at home and her role at the Kruses'. *(At home, Daisy "had been the boss"; this is not the case at the Kruses'.)*

BB. LEP: Vocabulary Some students may find the term *rompers* unfamiliar. Explain that *rompers* are one-piece baby outfits.

CC. Critical Thinking: ANALYZING Have students compare Edna's reaction to Daisy's complaint with her reaction to her baby. *(Possible responses: Edna shows more concern for her sleeping baby than she does for Daisy. Her maternal feelings are focused on her own child.)*

Real Life Connections

The writer gives several examples that indicate the difference in status that exists between the Switzers and the Kruses. Some of these examples might be labeled "material"; others may be categorized as "outlook." Students might be interested in identifying them and discussing whether these examples (cars, plumbing, living space, food, privacy, intact families, working mothers, and so on) carry the same status values today. Students might suggest items and attitudes that confer or deny status today.

DD. Literary Element: TONE Have students name the "strange lonesome ache" that Daisy is experiencing. *(homesickness, heartache)* Then ask them to name an adjective to describe the author's attitude toward Daisy here. *(sympathetic)*

EE. Literary Element: THEME Edna reminds Daisy that she is to help her with the children. Ask students to consider how this role fits with the way Daisy sees herself. *(Possible response: As the oldest child, Daisy is used to looking after the younger children. This role is in keeping with the way she sees herself.)*

FF. Reading Skill: NONSTANDARD ENGLISH Ask students to tell other ways to express the same question in standard English. *(Possible responses: "Shall we play blocks, Billy?"; "Do you want to play blocks, Billy?")*

GG. Critical Thinking: EVALUATING Have students evaluate Daisy's behavior as a baby sitter. *(Some students may think that Daisy is a good baby sitter; she wants to "make something really wonderful with these blocks," presumably to entertain Billy. Other students may think that Daisy is not a good baby sitter; she does not allow Billy to participate in the activity.)*

"Tomorrow? I don't suppose so."

"Mama couldn't find the belt of my plaid dress, and I thought if he was, maybe I could go along and get it. I'd like to have it."

DD Daisy's homely mouth drooped at the corners. Her toothache did not seem to matter to anyone. Edna did not seem to want to see that anything was wrong with her. She had expected Edna to be concerned, to mention remedies. But it wasn't toothache, that strange lonesome ache all over her. Maybe she was going to be terribly sick. Mama wouldn't come home for supper to be told about it.

She saw Mama's face as in that last glimpse of it—drawn with crying, and yet trying to hold a smile, under the old cleaning cap, her hand holding her coat together. . . .

Edna glanced quickly at her. The child was so mortally unattractive, unappealing even in her forlornness. Edna frowned a little but said kindly:

"Now you might take Billy into the kitchen out of my way, Daisy, and amuse him."

"Well, he cries when I pick him up," Daisy said faintly.

EE "He won't cry this time. Take him out and help him play with his blocks. You must help me with the children, you know."

"Well, if he'll go with me."

"He'll go with you, won't he, Billy boy? Won't you go with Daisy, sweetheart?"

Billy stared and then nodded. Daisy felt a thrill of comfort as Billy put his little fat hand in hers and trotted into the kitchen beside her. He had the fattest hands, she thought. Edna brought the blocks and put the box down on the floor beside Daisy.

"Now, see if you can amuse him so that I can get my sewing done."

"Shall you and me play blocks, Billy?" Daisy murmured. FF

He nodded. Then he got hold of the box with one hand, tipped out all the blocks on the floor with a bang and a rattle, and looked at her with a pleased, proud smile.

"Oh no, Billy. You musn't spill out the blocks. Look, you're too little to play with them. No, now—now wait! Let Daisy show you. Daisy'll build you something real nice—shall she?"

He gave a solemn nod of consent.

Daisy set out the blocks on the bright linoleum. She had never had such blocks as these to handle before. Dwight's were only a few old, unmatched, broken ones. Her spirit of leadership came back, and she firmly put away that fat hand of Billy's whenever he meddled with her building. GG She could make something really wonderful with these blocks.

"No, Billy, you musn't. See, when Daisy's got it all done, then you can see what the lovely building is."

She put the blocks together with great interest. She knew what she was going to make—it was going to be a new house; no, a new church. Just as she got the walls up, in came that little hand again, and then with a delighted grunt Billy swept the blocks pell-mell[10] about the floor. At the clatter, he sat back, pursing his mouth to give an ecstatic "Ooh!"

"Oh, Billy—you mustn't, the building

10. **pell-mell:** in a disorderly way.

Words to Know and Use	**ecstatic** (ek stat′ ik) *adj.* joyful

470

wasn't done! Look, you've spoiled it. Now, you've got to sit 'way off here while I try to build it over again."

Billy's look of triumph turned to surprise and then to vociferous protest as Daisy picked him up and firmly transplanted him to another corner of the room. He set up a tremendous howl. He had never been set aside like that before. Edna came hurrying out. Daisy look at Edna for justification, but instinctively on the defensive.

"Billy knocked over the blocks. He spoiled the building."

"Wah! Wah!" Billy gave loud heartbroken sobs. The tears ran down his fat cheeks, and he held out his arms piteously toward his mother.

HH "I didn't hurt him," Daisy said, scared.

"Never mind, lover," Edna was crooning. "Of course he can play with his blocks. They're Billy's blocks, Daisy," she said. "He doesn't like to sit and see you put up buildings. He wants to play, too. See, you've made him cry now."

"Do' wanna stay here," Billy wailed.

"Well, come in with Mother then." She picked him up, wiping his tears.

"I didn't hurt him," Daisy protested.

II "Well, never mind now. You can pick up the blocks and then sweep up the floor, Daisy. You didn't do that when you finished the dishes. Never mind," she was saying to Billy. "Pretty soon Daddy'll come in and we'll have a nice ride."

Daisy soberly picked up the blocks and got the broom. What had she done to Billy? He had tried to spoil her building. She had always made Dwight keep back until she had finished. Of course it was Daisy, the oldest, who should lead and manage. There had been no one to hear her side. Everything was different. She winked back tears as she swept, poorly and carelessly. ◀ SR-8

Then she brightened up as Elmer came tramping up on the back porch and then through the kitchen.

"Edna!"

"She's in there," Daisy offered.

"Want to go now? What? Is the baby asleep?" he said blankly.

Edna gave him a warning look and the door was closed.

JJ Daisy listened hard. She swept very softly. She could catch only a little of what they said—"Kind of hate to go off . . . I know, but if we once start . . . not a thing all day . . . what we got her for. . . ." She had no real comprehension of it. She hurried and put away the broom. She wanted to be sure and be ready to go.

Elmer tramped out, straight past her. She saw from the window that he was backing the car out from the shed. She could hear Edna and Billy upstairs, could hear the baby cry a little as he was wakened. Maybe she ought to go out and get her wraps, too.

Elmer honked the horn. A moment later Edna came hurrying downstairs, in her hat and coat, and Billy in a knitted cap and a red sweater crammed over his union-alls, so that he looked like a little brownie. The baby had his little coat, too.

KK Edna called out, "Come in and get this boy, Daddy." She did not look at Daisy but said hurriedly, "We're going for a little ride, Daisy. Have you finished the sweeping? Well, then, you can pick up those pieces in the dining room. We won't be gone so very long. When it's a quarter past five, you start the fire, like I showed you this noon, and

Words to Know and Use

piteously (pit′ ē əs lē) *adv.* in a way to arouse pity and understanding

471

HH. Critical Thinking: ANALYZING Have students tell what Daisy might be afraid of. *(Possible responses: She might be afraid of being sent back home as a failure; she might be afraid of being punished physically or by deprivation.)*

II. Critical Thinking: ANALYZING Have students explain what Edna's telling Daisy to sweep the floor suggests about the different expectations held by Daisy and Edna about Daisy's responsibilities. *(Possible response: Edna has expectations that she has not made clear to Daisy. Daisy still does not seem to realize fully her responsibility in the Kruses' home.)*

JJ. Reading Skill: DRAWING CONCLUSIONS Have students tell what Elmer and Edna are arguing about and what position each is taking. *(Possible response: As the family is getting ready to go for a ride, Elmer is reluctant to leave Daisy behind on her first day. Edna seems to be reminding him that Daisy is not part of the family and that she hasn't acted like a house worker all day.)*

KK. LEP: Language Explain to students that in some families, husbands and wives refer to each other as "Mommy" and "Daddy" instead of by their first names.

PROFESSIONAL NOTEBOOK

Cultural codes refer to the type of information that allows readers to construct a fictional world, to orient themselves in it, and to understand the characters and their actions. The more culturally at home in a text students become, the less dependent they will be on guidance from teachers, suggesting that reading teachers need to examine literature from more than a linguistic perspective. In other words, the author's philosophy or perspective guides the conscious selection of characters, setting, plot, and theme. An important part of literary interpretation is understanding how cultural codes influence the underlying meaning of a selection.

CHARLES W. PETERS AND MARILYN CARLSEN, *Children's Comprehension of Text*

LL. Literary Element: THEME Ask students to explain what Daisy has realized about her status in the family and about how family members see her. *(She does not belong with them. They see her as an outsider.)* Ask what clues led Daisy to this conclusion. *(She was not invited on the ride, although "there was room" and "there wasn't anything, really, to be done at home.")*

MM. Literary Element: TONE Have students describe the feelings they have at the end of the story. *(Possible responses: sadness, helplessness, bitterness)* Then ask how they think the author viewed the character of Daisy. *(Possible responses: with concern, sympathy, compassion)*

Check Test

1. How is Daisy going to spend the summer? *(working in the Kruses' house)*

2. Who does Daisy leave at home? *(her mother, sister, and brother)*

3. What things about the Kruses impress Daisy? *(their car, their home, their food)*

4. What chores does Edna expect Daisy to do? *(help get meals, set the table, wash dishes, baby sit, sweep, clean up)*

5. How and why does Daisy make Billy cry over the incident with the blocks? *(After he knocks the blocks over, she sets him down in a corner.)*

6. in the end, how do the Kruses show Daisy that she is not part of their family? *(They drive off without her.)*

Encouraging Independent Reading

Jane Eyre, a novel by Charlotte Brönte
"A Goatherd at Lunch," a short story by Italo Calvino
"The Doll's House," a short story by Katherine Mansfield
"The Magistrate's Daughter," a short story by Alan Paton
"The Osage Orange Tree," a short story by William Stafford

slice the potatoes that were left, and the meat. And set the table."

The horn honked again.

"Yes! Well, we'll be back, Daisy. Come, lover, Daddy's in a hurry."

Daisy stood looking after them. Billy clamored to sit beside his daddy. Edna took the baby from Elmer and put him beside her on the back seat. There was room—half of the big back seat. There wasn't anything, really, to be done at home. That was the worst of it. They just didn't want to take her. They all belonged together. They didn't want to take anyone else along. She was an outsider. They all—even the baby—had a freshened look of expectancy. LL SR-9

The engine roared—they had started; slipping on the mud of the drive, then forging straight ahead, around the turn, out of sight.

She went forlornly into the dining room. The light from the windows was dim now in the rainy, late afternoon. The pink pieces from the baby's rompers were scattered over the gay rug. She got down on her hands and knees, slowly picking them up, sniffing a little. She heard the Big Ben clock in the kitchen ticking loudly.

That dreadful ache submerged her. No one would ask about it, no one would try to comfort her. Before, there had always been Mama coming home, anxious, scolding sometimes, but worried over them if they didn't feel right, caring about them. Mama and Goldie and Dwight cared about her—but she was away out in the country, and they were at home. She didn't want to stay here, where she didn't belong. But Mama had told her that she must begin helping this summer.

Her ugly little mouth contorted into a grimace of weeping. But silent weeping, without any tears; because she already had the cold knowledge that no one would notice or comfort it. ❧ MM

REAL LIFE CONNECTIONS

Have students discuss their first work experiences and point out resemblances they can see between themselves and Daisy in relation to work.

Discussion prompts: Were students well-prepared for their first work experiences or taken by surprise? What kinds of jobs did they do? Did they notice any differences between their employers' expectations and their own expectations of what the job entailed? Were they ever scolded for doing the wrong thing or for not doing enough? Based on what they have learned through experience, how would they advise a young person who is just getting started in the working world?

Responding to Reading

First Impressions

1. Which moment in the story affected you the most? Why? Compare your answer with those of your classmates.

Second Thoughts

2. Why is Daisy so proud and excited about leaving for the Kruses'?
   Think about
   - what she thinks she is leaving behind
   - what she imagines about the Kruses
   - how leaving influences her status in her family
3. Why do you think Daisy's work at the Kruses does not go well?
   Think about
   - the experiences and expectations Daisy brings to the job
   - how Edna treats her
4. Has Daisy changed by the end of the story? Explain.
5. How do different people in the story see Daisy?
   Think about
   - how her brother and sister look up to her
   - how her mother feels about her leaving
   - how the Kruses act toward her
6. The word *start* can mean beginning, but it can also mean surprise. Which meaning or meanings fit the story? Explain.

Broader Connections

7. In the 1920's, household workers like Daisy were generally at the mercy of their employers. In modern times, even though domestic workers are not unionized, they are probably more aware of their rights. What are the rights of domestic workers and what laws, if any, should be passed to further protect these workers?

Literary Concept: Tone

Tone is the writer's attitude toward the subject. For example, a writer's tone could be amused, ironic, serious, sarcastic, or sympathetic. How would you describe the writer's tone toward Daisy and her family? How would you characterize the overall tone of "A Start in Life"?

Literary Concept—Tone
Possible response: The writer's tone toward Daisy and her family is sympathetic and serious. The overall tone is understanding and compassionate.

Student Response

Responding to Reading
These questions are open-ended with no "right" or "wrong" answers. However, responses must be supported with information from the selection. Possible answers follow:

1. Almost any response is valid.

2. Some students may say that Daisy is eager to leave the impoverished environment of her home and become part of this relatively affluent and capable family. Others may say that going away to work and earn money makes Daisy feel important and adult.

3. Students may suggest that Daisy lacks the world experience and work experience to do well; that she expects to be part of the family; that she is probably too young to be working; that Edna is also unprepared to handle Daisy; and that Edna's expectations do not match Daisy's abilities.

4. Students who say that Daisy has changed may support their opinion by citing her realization that working in another home is different from visiting that home and her recognition that she is an outsider in the Kruse family. They may also suggest that Daisy now has a greater appreciation for her own family. Students who think that Daisy has not changed may support their opinion by saying that, just as she enjoyed a position of prestige in her own home, Daisy wants to have a similar position in the Kruses' home; and that, although Daisy now realizes her status, she has not grown in her ability to handle her new position in life.

5. Students may say that her brother and sister see Daisy as mature and capable, that her mother loves her but considers her ill-prepared for work, and that the Kruses view her as a nearly hopeless employee.

6. Students may say that both meanings can apply to the events in this story; that Daisy made a new beginning by leaving home to go to work for the Kruses; and that Daisy experienced several surprise "starts," as she learned about her new role.

7. Students may suggest that modern domestic workers should expect reasonable working conditions, including a fair number of hours, a reasonable set of responsibilities, and, if they live in their employers' homes, decent food and shelter. Have students explain their opinions regarding the need for laws.

Concept Review: Details The author describes the Switzers' bedroom with these details: The bed is not made and has Daisy's things "scattered over the dark brown quilt and the rumpled sheet," and the quilt, sheet, and "whole bedroom" are "dingy and clammy"; the bedroom has a "sloping ceiling and square-paned windows"; a small table serves as a dresser and it is "littered with pin tray, curlers, broken comb, ribbons, smoky lamp"; the closet door is open, revealing "the confusion of clothes and shabby shoes." The description indicates that the family is poor and disorganized.

Writing Options

The Writing Options are designed to meet varied student interests and abilities. Have each student choose one writing activity to complete. You may wish to guide some students to an option that requires less writing.

Journal Update Have students review their journal entries for "A Start in Life." What have they learned about change and new beginnings? What new reflections can they add to their earlier writings?

Vocabulary Practice

Exercise A

1. c
2. a
3. d
4. e
5. b

Exercise B

1. d
2. c
3. b
4. d
5. b

Concept Review: Details What details does the author use to describe the bedroom at the Switzers'? What information does the description give you about the family?

Writing Options

1. Daisy's mother had no time to give Daisy advice before she left for the Kruses'. What advice should Daisy's mother have given? Write this advice in the mother's own words.
2. Review the talk between Edna and Elmer on page 471. Then, use your imagination to fill in the dialogue from the fragments that Suckow gives us.
3. Predict what the end of summer will bring for Daisy. What will she have learned? How will she have changed?
4. List important details about the two houses—the Switzers' and the Kruses'. Include descriptions of each place as well as descriptions of the people who live there, the way they relate to each other, and their daily routines. Then use the lists to compare and contrast life at the two households.

Vocabulary Practice

Words to Know and Use

condolence
curt
desolate
ecstatic
forlornness
genially
imposing
piteously
preening
subdued

Exercise A On your paper, write the letter of the situation that best matches the boldfaced word on the left.

1. **desolate**
2. **condolence**
3. **curt**
4. **imposing**
5. **ecstatic**

a. sending a sympathy card when someone dies
b. shouting with joy
c. seeing a bleak expanse of desert
d. hearing a brief news report
e. seeing a seven-foot-tall basketball player

Exercise B On your paper, write the letter of the word that is not related in meaning to the other words.

1. (a) preening (b) primping (c) grooming (d) ruining
2. (a) neighborly (b) genially (c) cautiously (d) kindly
3. (a) hopelessness (b) hopefulness (c) sadness (d) forlornness
4. (a) subdued (b) quiet (c) unemotional (d) angry
5. (a) sadly (b) admirably (c) piteously (d) regretfully

Options for Learning

1 • Drawing Miss Daisy Imagine that you are Daisy. Make pencil sketches of your bedroom at home, the Kruses' car, your new bedroom, Edna's kitchen, and Billy with his blocks. Use many of the details from the story but add some of your own. Under each sketch, write a short caption.

2 • Help Wanted If you perform a service for someone, you are said to be in the service industry. Study the want ads in your local newspaper to discover how many service jobs are available. What are they called? What are the duties? What is the pay? What education is necessary? Report back to the class.

3 • Auto Research Write a brief report about automobiles of the 1920's. Include pictures in your report. If possible draw lines labeling the cars' important features.

4 • Phone Tap Imagine that both the Kruses and Switzers have telephones. Role-play the phone conversation Daisy and her mother might have had once the Kruses left the house on that first day.

FACT FINDER

Find out how much a Model T Ford cost in 1925.

Ruth Suckow
1892–1960

Known as a local-color author, Ruth Suckow wrote stories and novels about German-American families living in Iowa early in the century. Like the story you have just finished, her works tend to be highly realistic, often with a sad tone. Some Iowans even criticized her for making life in the state look so depressing.

Yet other people praised Suckow's writing. H. L. Mencken, an important critic of the time, liked her realistic characters, settings, and stories. More recently, Suckow has been applauded for accurately showing the difficult lives of women in rural America.

Suckow was the daughter of an Iowa minister. In 1929, she married Ferner Nuhn, another Iowa writer. In addition to writing stories and novels, Suckow worked as a beekeeper.

Options for Learning

These activities suit a variety of learning styles and modes of expression. Allow students to review the options and then choose the one they wish to do. Many are excellent collaborative learning projects.

1. Drawing Miss Daisy Students may refer to pictures in old magazines or in reference works that depict home decorations and furnishings of the 1920s.

2. Help Wanted Students may find it helpful to organize the information they find into a chart that compares and contrasts different types of service occupations.

3. Auto Research Students may have access to model-car kits that detail features of these automobiles.

4. Phone Tap Some students may wish to listen to recordings of rural speech made during this period in an effort to reproduce some of the realistic, nonstandard dialects.

Fact Finder

According to the 1989 edition of the *World Book Encyclopedia,* when the Model T was introduced in 1908 it sold for $850. However, because Ford was able to improve productivity through the use of assembly-line techniques, the price dropped to $260 in 1925.

Additional Information About the Author

Between 1924 and 1952, Suckow published seven novels and several collections that include stories and memoirs. In her somewhat autobiographical works, she realistically depicts the experiences of German immigrant families in small-town Iowa as they become Americanized.

Closure

In some ways, Daisy's transition from home to work mirrors her transition from childhood to young adulthood. During this period of change, her perceptions of herself and of her world undergo transformation. Have students tell how starting a new chapter of one's life can alter one's self-image.

Cross-Curricular Options

Geography Create a relief map that shows the geographical features that make Iowa so well suited to agriculture.

Math Devise a 1920s budget for spending a regular weekly income of $1.50. Then create a 1990s budget to show differences in costs and types of expenses.

Music/Dance Research and collect popular songs from the 1920s and demonstrate various dances of the period.

Art Set up a gallery of reprints of famous paintings (such as Grant Wood's *American Gothic*) depicting life in rural America and provide relevant background information for the class.

Objectives

- To understand poetry
- To identify imagery in poetry
- To recognize personification
- To experience poetry through oral reading
- To express understanding of the works through a choice of writing options, including a poem and dialogue

Prereading/Motivation

Examine What You Know

Discussion Prompts: What words would you use to identify your feelings about the experience? How might it have affected your behavior?

Expand Your Knowledge

Discussion Prompts: In what way might it be said that the Spanish soldiers never really destroyed the Mexican culture? How might the Pima feel today about people outside their culture?

Enrich Your Reading

Demonstrate how oral reading affects the meaning of a poem by reading aloud the first fifteen lines of "Indian Children Speak." Have students explain how the expression with which you read the lines makes them feel.

Thematic Link—How Others See Me

Each poem expresses the idea that people from different cultures have perceptions and prejudices that affect the way they see each other and the way others see them.

e x p l o r e

Poetry

Not Knowing, in Aztlán

TINO VILLANUEVA
(vēl yän wä' vä)

Indian Children Speak

JUANITA BELL

Examine What You Know (Prior Knowledge)

Describe to your classmates a time when you were misunderstood by an authority figure such as a parent, teacher, coach, or boss. Explain your true intentions and how your actions were wrongly perceived. Then read to see how the speakers of these two poems are misunderstood.

Expand Your Knowledge (Building Background)

The term *Aztlán,* from the title in the first poem, refers to the mythological home of the Aztec Indians. In the fifteenth and sixteenth centuries, the Aztecs of central Mexico had a highly advanced civilization with cities as large as any in Europe. In 1521, however, their society was conquered and finally destroyed by Spanish explorers. Nevertheless, Aztlán has remained a unifying idea for many people of Mexican and Indian heritage.

The author of the second poem, Juanita Bell, is a Pima Indian. Known as "River People," the Pima Indians farmed in southern Arizona using long irrigation canals to raise wheat and other crops. The Pima civilization collapsed when settlers began to deplete the rivers on which Pima life depended. Today, about ten thousand Pimas live on reservations near Phoenix, Arizona.

Enrich Your Reading (Reading Skill)

Oral Reading Poetry is meant to be read aloud. Poets choose words for their sounds as well as for their meaning. A poet often arranges words so that their sounds form a pattern or rhythm that is pleasing, startling, or interesting in some way. The way a reader speaks the lines affects the poem's meaning. After you have read each of the following poems once to yourself, read them aloud. Repeat the poems slowly several times as you experiment with the expression you put into your reading. Notice how changes in your tone of voice affect the meaning of the poem.

■ *A biography of Villanueva can be found in the Reader's Handbook.*

Journal Writing

These poems concern other people's perceptions of the speakers or subjects. Suggest these journal topics:

- What could a stranger tell about you from your outward appearance? What important things about you could the stranger not detect?
- When Indian children speak, what do you imagine they might say?

For other journal opportunities, refer students to Examine What You Know (p. 476), First Impressions (p. 477), and Real Life Connections (p. T–478)

Additional Resources

UNIT FOUR RESOURCE BOOK

Reader's Guidesheet, p. 11
Vocabulary Worksheet, p. 12
Selection and Vocabulary Check Tests, p. 13
Selection Test, pp. 14–15

Collaborative Learning

Opportunities for collaborative learning appear throughout the lesson and include Cultural Connections (p. T–479).

Not Knowing, in Aztlán

TINO VILLANUEVA

the way they look at you
                the schoolteachers
the way they look at you
                the City Hall clerks
the way they look at you   A
                the cops
                the airport marshals
the way they look at you   B

                you don't know if it's something you did   C

                                        or something you are

Responding to Reading

First Impressions of "Not Knowing, in Aztlán"

1. Can you identify with the "you" of this poem? What situations make you feel looked at in the same way?

Second Thoughts on "Not Knowing, in Aztlán"

2. What, according to the poem, is the "way" that certain authority figures look at the speaker?

Think about

- who the speaker is
- who the observers are
- how else people can look at each other

3. What is your interpretation of the last two lines?

4. With what tone of voice did you read this poem aloud? Why did you choose this tone of voice?

Teaching Strategies

Support for Students of Limited English Proficiency

- Use **Reader's Guidesheet**, p.11.
- Students may be unfamiliar with the reverence for nature that is characteristic of Native American peoples. Discuss this aspect of Native American culture with them, or, if possible, ask a student of Native American ancestry or another Native American to do so. The importance of nature to Native American peoples is especially prominent in "Indian Children Speak." Note the references to the moon, the sunset, the wild animal, and others.

Text Annotations

A. Reading Skill: ORAL READING Ask students which word in this repeated line they would emphasize in reading the poem aloud. *(Answer may vary. The words* way, they, look, *and* you *are possibilities. Students may suggest changing the emphasis when the line is repeated.)*

B. Reading Skill: DRAWING CONCLUSIONS Ask students who "they" in the poem are and what these people generally represent. *("They" are schoolteachers, clerks, cops, marshals; they represent authority.)*

C. Critical Thinking: ANALYZING Ask students to tell which they think is worse—to be scorned because of "something you did" or because of "something you are." Have them explain their answers. *(Most students will think it is worse to be scorned because of "something you are," saying that you cannot change what you are, but you can change what you do.)*

Student Response

Responding to Reading

These questions are open-ended with no "right" or "wrong" answers. However, responses must be supported with information from the selection. Possible answers follow:

1. Any response is valid.

2. Students may say that the speaker is a young person or student, or a stranger in the society, or someone who looks "different" from most others; that the figures seem unfriendly, suspicious, or resentful; the figures that might have offered sympathetic looks or looks of wanting to help.

3. Students may offer interpretations such as these: You wonder if authority figures are criticizing your behavior or your existence; the way certain people look at you or treat you makes you doubt yourself.

4. Some students may say they used a bewildered tone of voice because they are confused about the basis on which they are being judged. Other students may say they used a tone of resentment because they have had similar experiences.

Text Annotations

A. LEP: Using Context Clues Some students may not understand *ragged* and *confided.* Ask them to try to find context clues to figure out the meanings. *(for* ragged, *"My dress is old"; for* confided, *the word* softly *and Pansy's dialogue)* Then discuss how Pansy's beautiful words contradict what people say about Indian children.

B. Literary Element: IMAGERY Point out how powerfully this imagery expresses feelings and ask volunteers to explain what Ramon means. *(Possible response: Since my mother died, I feel overcome by wild, uncontrollable feelings.)* Then discuss how Ramon contradicts the idea that Indian children are not affectionate. *(He takes the speaker's hand; he expresses love for his mother.)*

C. Literary Element: IMAGERY Have students tell what the tree hanging down reminds them of. *(Possible response: a person who is ashamed or who does not want to be noticed)*

Indian Children Speak

JUANITA BELL

People said, "Indian children are hard to teach.
Don't expect them to talk."
One day stubby little Boy said,
"Last night the moon went all the way with me,
When I went out to walk."
People said, "Indian children are very silent.
Their only words are no and yes."
A But, ragged Pansy confided softly,
"My dress is old, but at night the moon is kind;
Then I wear a beautiful moon-colored dress."
People said, "Indian children are dumb.
They seldom make a reply."
Clearly I hear Delores answer,
"Yes, the sunset is so good, I think God is throwing
A bright shawl around the shoulders of the sky."
People said, "Indian children have no affection.
They just don't care for anyone."
B Then I feel Ramon's hand and hear him whisper,
"A wild animal races in me since my mother sleeps
under the ground. Will it always run and run?"
People said, "Indian children are rude.
They don't seem very bright."
Then I remember Joe Henry's remark,
"The tree is hanging down her head because the sun
C is staring at her. White people always stare.
They do not know it is not polite."

REAL LIFE CONNECTIONS

Most students will be able to connect their own experiences with the experiences of the young people in the two poems. Have them discuss or write in their journals about how people have sometimes judged them solely on the basis of what they looked like or how they behaved. Ask them to express how they have felt when someone saw them only as people belonging to a particular group, rather than as individuals. Ask students if they have ever judged other people in this prejudiced way. Discuss the stereotyped ideas people may hold about others based on age, race, sex, size, or other qualities.

People said, "Indian children never take you in,
Outside their thoughts you'll always stand."
I have forgotten the idle words that People said,
But treasure the day when iron doors swung wide,
And I slipped into the heart of Indian Land.

D

Suzanne Anderson Page From *Song of the Earth Spirit* by Suzanne Anderson Page, McGraw-Hill Publishing Company.

D. Literary Element: THEME Ask students to summarize the ways in which white people see Indian children. *(unintelligent, silent, unaffectionate, rude, distant)*

Historical Sidelight The Aztec King Montezuma II believed in the legend of Quetzalcoatl, a white-feathered serpent "god." According to the legend, Quetzalcoatl would return someday to the land of the Aztecs. When the Spanish explorer Cortez arrived on the western coast of Mexico, his white-sailed ships seemed to fly on the water, and Montezuma believed that the god had returned to rule. He welcomed Cortez into the capital city of Tenochtitlán (now Mexico City), where Cortez took him prisoner and quickly conquered the Aztecs.

Check Test

1. Name the four kinds of people the speaker of the first poem says are looking at him. *(schoolteachers, City Hall clerks, cops, airport marshals)*

2. Who went walking with little Boy? *(the moon)*

3. What does the speaker of the second poem say guards the heart of Indian Land? *(iron doors)*

Encouraging Independent Reading

Hispanics in the United States: An Anthology of Creative Literature, poetry and prose edited by Gary D. Keller and Francisco Jiménez

Carriers of the Dream Wheel: Contemporary Native American Poetry, edited by Duane Niatum

Voices of the Rainbow: Contemporary Poetry by American Indians, edited by Kenneth Rosen

CULTURAL CONNECTION

Confronting prejudice often results in strengthening the bonds among people of the same culture. These people may form cultural-pride organizations to counteract prejudice, to raise their self-esteem, and to promote their cultural interests. Critics frequently say that such organizations only result in reinforcing differences among people. Have students give their views regarding the role of cultural pride in a multicultural American society.

Student Responses

Responding to Reading

These questions are open-ended with no "right" or "wrong" answers. However, responses must be supported with information from the selection. Possible answers follow:

1. Any response is valid.

2. Students may say that all these remarks present a negative view of Indian children based on prejudiced ideas.

3. Students may say that these examples provide stronger images and drive home their points better than intellectual argument would; that the examples reach the reader's emotions, not just the intellect.

4. Possible responses: Ramon's mother has died. In contrast to the stereotype offered, his mother's death has caused Ramon to have wild feelings of grief, sadness, and rage. He feels lost without her and wonders if he'll ever feel safe again.

5. Students may say that these remarks reveal that Native American children have strong feelings and reflect on what they see; that they are sensitive, perceptive, intelligent, and articulate; that they relate many ideas to nature.

6. Students may say that both poets wanted to refute stereotyped ideas about young Native American people.

7. Students may say that the speaker of the second poem, unlike the first speaker, knows that the Indian children are being judged on the basis of their race and identity; that the second speaker knows the value of his or her Native American identity.

Writing Options

The Writing Options are designed to meet varied student interests and abilities. Have each student choose one writing activity to complete. You may wish to guide some students to an option that requires less writing.

Journal Update Have students review their journal entries and add new reflections about the way others see us.

e x p l a i n

Responding to Reading

First Impressions of "Indian Children Speak"

1. What image stands out as you think back over this poem?

Second Thoughts on "Indian Children Speak"

2. What do all the things that people say about Indian children have in common?
3. Why does the speaker use examples instead of intellectual arguments?
4. What has happened to Ramon's mother? What does Ramon's statement and question say about his relationship with her?
5. What do Ramon and the other children's remarks reveal about them?
   Think about
   - what they talk about
   - how they use language

Comparing the Poems

6. Compare the poets' purposes for writing these two poems.
7. Compare the endings of both poems. What does the speaker of the second poem know that the first speaker does not?

Literary Concept: Imagery

Description that makes an object or experience so real that a reader can easily imagine it is called **imagery.** What details create vivid imagery in "Indian Children Speak"?

Concept Review: Personification What examples of personification can you find in the poem "Indian Children Speak?"

Writing Options

1. Make a list of the inaccurate things that people say about you. Use these quotes in a poem entitled "It Isn't So."
2. Expand "Not Knowing, in Aztlán" by adding thoughts and/or words for the schoolteacher, clerk, cop, and airport marshal.

Literary Concept—Imagery

Possible responses: "stubby little Boy," "a beautiful moon-colored dress,"; " 'God is throwing/A bright shawl around the shoulders of the sky,' "; " 'A wild animal races in me since my mother sleeps/under the ground./Will it always run and run?' "; " 'The tree is hanging down her head because the sun is staring at her.' "; "iron doors swung wide,/And I slipped into the heart of Indian Land."

Concept Review: Personification Examples: " 'the moon went all the way with me,' " "the moon is kind"; "the sunset is so good"; " 'The tree is hanging down her head because the sun is staring at her.' "

e x p l o r e

Persuasive Essay

Darkness at Noon

HAROLD KRENTS

Examine What You Know (Prior Knowledge)

What would it be like to be blind? Do you think that the way people act toward you would change if you were blind? In your journal or on a piece of paper, jot down the answers to these two questions. Then compare your responses to the experiences of those described in the next selection.

Expand Your Knowledge (Building Background)

Harold Krents accomplished much in a short lifetime—especially considering that he was one of the approximately 500,000 people in the United States who are classified as legally blind. People are considered legally blind when they can only see, with glasses or contact lenses, at twenty feet what someone else can see at two hundred feet. Until the middle of the twentieth century, most blind persons were educated in special schools. Today more than 60 percent of the blind go to regular schools and many go on to college. Krents himself graduated with honors from Harvard University. He was so adept at functioning with his blindness that he was classified as 1-A (fit for duty) by the draft board, who doubted that he was really blind.

Enrich Your Reading (Reading Skill)

Main Idea The **main idea** is the one idea to which the sentences in a paragraph relate. When the main idea is stated directly, it is often found as the first sentence of a paragraph. The sentence containing the main idea is called the **topic sentence.** Main ideas do not occur in every paragraph, and when they do, they are not always directly stated. They may be implied, and the reader will have to infer the main ideas from the information provided. As you read the following essay, look for the main ideas the author presents about blindness.

■ *A biography of the author can be found in the Reader's Handbook.*

Objectives

■ To understand the structure and purpose of a persuasive essay

■ To identify main ideas

■ To express understanding of the work through a choice of writing options, including a speech, a summary, an anecdote, and a persuasive essay

Prereading/Motivation

Examine What You Know

Discussion Prompts: How would being blind change the way you did your favorite activities? How might being blind change the way you felt about yourself?

Expand Your Knowledge

Discussion Prompts: What are some ways that our society responds to the needs of blind people? Why might blind people be better able to find productive opportunities today than at any time in the past?

Additional Background: The Rehabilitation Act of 1973 requires federally funded businesses to hire qualified handicapped people and prohibits their unfair treatment in government-run programs. The Education for All Handicapped Children Act of 1975 requires states to provide free education for all school-aged handicapped children.

Enrich Your Reading

Model the use of a graphic organizer on which students can record main ideas and details as they read. Possibilities include the following: **1.** Things the writer says about sighted people's reactions to blind people. **2.** Ways that being blind made it difficult for this writer to achieve some goals.

Thematic Link—How Others See Me
This essay presents a blind writer's reaction to how other people see him.

Journal Writing

This essay presents a personal point of view regarding the effects of a physical disability. Suggest these journal topics to students:

■ In what way is the title of the selection contradictory? What might you expect to read about in an essay with this title?

■ Recall any experiences you have had with disabled people. What were your thoughts and feelings?

For other journal opportunities, refer students to Examine What You Know (p. 481).

Additional Resources

UNIT FOUR RESOURCE BOOK
Reader's Guidesheet, p. 16
Vocabulary Worksheet, p. 17
Selection and Vocabulary Check Tests, p. 18
Selection Test, pp. 19–20

Collaborative Learning

Opportunities for collaborative learning appear throughout the lesson and include Closure (p. T–485).

Teaching Strategies

Vocabulary Review

These vocabulary words are defined at the bottom of the selection page on which they appear. You may wish to discuss them briefly before students begin reading.

conversely in the opposite way
disposition mood
graphically realistically
mandate require
misconception a mistaken idea

Support for Students of Limited English Proficiency

- Use **Reader's Guidesheet**, p. 16.
- "Darkness at Noon" contains descriptions of behavior at several settings—the airport, the restaurant, and a hospital. Have students verbalize ways patrons of these places are generally treated. Help them compare this with the way the writer is treated. Then, to help students understand how some people behave toward the writer, acting as though he is unable to hear and speak, review first-, second-, and third-person pronouns.
- **Annotation B** focuses on language.

Text Annotations

A. Literary Element: THEME Ask students to read the opening paragraph and rephrase the writer's statement about the importance of how others see him. *(Possible response: To know what he looks like, the writer must depend on others' views. He can tell by the way other people treat him that they don't think positively about him.)*

B. LEP: Language Students who are not proficient in English terms may find this sentence difficult to understand. Explain that *Kit* is the writer's wife and that the waiter is asking her what the writer wants, rather than addressing the writer directly. Explain that the writer is speaking sarcastically to the waiter when he says that "indeed *he* would."

Darkness at Noon

HAROLD KRENTS

A

Blind from birth, I have never had the opportunity to see myself and have been completely dependent on the image I create in the eye of the observer. To date it has not been narcissistic.[1]

SR-1 ▶ There are those who assume that since I can't see, I obviously also cannot hear. Very often people will converse with me at the top of their lungs, enunciating each word very carefully. Conversely, people will often whisper, assuming that since my eyes don't work, my ears don't either.

For example, when I go to the airport and ask the ticket agent for assistance to the plane, he or she will invariably pick up the phone, call a ground hostess and whisper: "Hi, Jane, we've got a 76 here." I have concluded that the word *blind* is not used for one of two reasons: Either they fear that if the dread word is spoken, the ticket agent's retina will immediately detach,[2] or they are reluctant to inform me of my condition, of which I may not have been previously aware.

B

On the other hand, others know that of course I can hear, but believe that I can't talk. Often, therefore, when my wife and I go out to dinner, a waiter or waitress will ask Kit if "*he* would like a drink" to which I

SR-2 ▶ respond that "indeed *he* would."

This point was graphically driven home to me while we were in England. I had been given a year's leave of absence from my Washington law firm to study for a diploma in law degree at Oxford University. During the year I became ill and was hospitalized. Immediately after admission, I was wheeled down to the X-ray room. Just at the door sat an elderly woman—elderly I would judge from the sound of her voice. "What is his name?" the woman asked the orderly who had been wheeling me.

"What's your name?" the orderly repeated to me.

"Harold Krents," I replied.

"Harold Krents," he repeated.

"When was he born?"

"When were you born?"

"November 5, 1944," I responded.

"November 5, 1944," the orderly intoned.

C

This procedure continued for approximately five minutes, at which point even my saint-like disposition deserted me. "Look," I finally blurted out, "this is absolutely ridiculous. Okay, granted I can't see,

1. **narcissistic:** in a way that shows complete interest only in one's self.

2. **retina will immediately detach:** refers to a medical condition that results in blurred vision because of a separation of the layers of the innermost part of the eye, the retina.

Words to Know and Use

conversely (kän vurs' lē) *adv.* in the opposite way; vice versa
graphically (graf' ik lē) *adv.* vividly, realistically
disposition (dis' pə zish' ən) *n.* frame of mind; mood

482

Structured Reading for Less Proficient Students

These questions can help to guide students through the reading. Ask each question at the point of the selection where the SR number appears in the margin.

SR–1. How has the writer's image of himself been formed? *(by the ways others see him)* **Clarifying**

SR–2. What are two assumptions sighted people often make about blind people? *(People who can't see probably can't speak or hear.)* **Literal recall**

SR–3. What is one of the most disillusioning experiences in the writer's life? *(his difficulty in getting a job, not because of his ability but because of his disability)* **Summarizing**

SR–4. What event changed the way employers began to view disabled people? *(In 1976 the Department of Labor mandated equal opportunities for the handicapped.)* **Literal recall**

SR–5. How does the writer feel about future employment opportunities for disabled people? *(He's optimistic; he hopes that disabled workers will be viewed the same as others.)* **Inferring**

CONSCIOUSNESS 1980 Winifred Nicholson © Estate of Winifred Nicholson.

but it's got to have become pretty clear to both of you that I don't need an interpreter." C

"He says he doesn't need an interpreter," the orderly reported to the woman.

The toughest misconception of all is the view that because I can't see, I can't work. I was turned down by over forty law firms because of my blindness, even though my qualifications included a cum laude degree[3] from Harvard College and a good ranking in my Harvard Law School class. D

The attempt to find employment, the continuous frustration of being told that it was impossible for a blind person to practice law, the rejection letters, not based on my lack of ability but rather on my disability, will always remain one of the most
SR-3 ▶ disillusioning experiences in my life.

Fortunately, this view of limitation and exclusion is beginning to change. On April 16, [1976,] the Department of Labor issued regulations that mandate equal-employment opportunities for the handicapped. By and large, the business community's response to offering employment to the disabled has been enthusiastic. ◀ SR-4

I therefore look forward to the day, with the expectation that it is certain to come, when employers will view their handicapped workers as a little child did me years ago when my family still lived in Scarsdale.

I was playing basketball with my father in our back yard according to procedures we had developed. My father would stand beneath the hoop, shout, and I would shoot over his head at the basket attached to our garage. Our next-door neighbor, aged five, wandered over into our yard with a playmate. "He's blind," our neighbor whispered to her friend in a voice that could be heard distinctly by Dad and me. Dad shot and missed; I did the same. Dad hit the rim; I missed entirely. Dad shot and missed the garage entirely. "Which one is blind?" whispered back the little friend. E

I would hope that in the near future when a plant manager is touring the factory with the foreman and comes upon a handicapped and nonhandicapped person working together, his comment after watching them work will be, "Which one is disabled?" ❧ ◀ SR-5

3. **cum laude** (ko͞om lou′dä): a Latin phrase signifying above-average academic ranking at the time of graduation from a college or university.

Words to Know and Use

misconception (mis′ kən sep′ shən) *n.* a mistaken idea or belief
mandate (man′ dāt′) *v.* to order with authority; to require

483

Data Bank

Technology has provided blind people with several important devices. Most library collections contain such items as braille editions and talking books or tape-recorded readings. Such devices as the opticon and the optical scanner also enable blind people to read printed matter. An opticon creates an enlarged image of each letter, and the blind person reads by feeling the image. An optical scanner, a computer equipped with a voice synthesizer, reads printed forms out loud. One recently developed device was derived from nature. Following the example of a skill perfected by the bat, inventors have created a sonar-equipped device that is worn by the blind person. The device emits radio waves that then echo off any objects in the person's path.

Art Note

English painter and writer Winifred Nicholson (1893–1981) devoted her life to exploring colors. For example, she observed that "when . . . the red car I drive comes into the electric [light of the town] my car becomes neutral dun. . . . " In *Consciousness,* on a background of black she has given all the colors of the rainbow to an invisible essence. *Why might this painting reflect the theme of "Darkness at Noon?"*

C. Literary Element: PERSUASIVE ESSAY Have students tell the writer's purpose for including this hospital experience. *(Possible response: He hopes this anectdote will help readers to see vividly the ridiculous way in which a handicapped person is sometimes treated and will win readers over to his viewpoint.)*

D. Reading Skill: RECOGNIZING RELEVANT DETAILS Ask students to explain how these details support the main idea of the paragraph. *(Possible response: The writer's background is so excellent that readers can see he is well-qualified to work. The fact that he was turned down by 40 firms supports how hard it is to change people's misconceptions.)*

E. Reading Skill: MAIN IDEA Have students state the main idea of this paragraph. *(Possible response: Disabled people are as capable as able-bodied ones.)*

Check Test

1. When was Harold Krents blinded? *(He was born blind.)*

2. Name three common misconceptions about blind people. *(They can't hear, speak, or work.)*

3. Where did Krents attend law school? *(Harvard)*

4. What kind of regulations did the Department of Labor issue in 1976? *(equal opportunity employment)*

Encouraging Independent Reading

Butterflies Are Free, a play by Leonard Gershe

"You Need to Go Upstairs," a short story by Rumer Godden

Of Such Small Differences, a novel by Joanne Greenberg

The Story of My Life, an autobiography by Hellen Keller

e x p l a i n

Responding to Reading

First Impressions

1. What single word or phrase would you use to describe Harold Krents?

Second Thoughts

2. Why do people treat Krents the way that they do?

   Think about
   - the assumptions they make
   - your observations and experiences with or around blind persons

3. What is Krents's attitude toward his blindness?

   Think about
   - how he is treated by others
   - how even ordinary tasks become complicated
   - how he responds to the way he is treated

4. Krents achieved a great deal before his death at 42. What do you think was responsible for his success?

5. If you have read "After You, My Dear Alphonse," compare the kinds of assumptions Mrs. Wilson makes to the assumptions that Krents cites in his essay.

6. Krents hopes that people will someday focus on handicapped people's abilities rather than on their disabilities. Is this a realistic hope? Why or why not?

Broader Connections

7. Think about your initial responses to what it might be like to be blind and how others might treat you. Does this essay change your attitude toward blind or disabled people or affect how you might respond to them in the future? Explain.

Literary Concept: Persuasive Essay

In a **persuasive essay,** a writer presents facts and opinions that support a particular point of view. The goal of the writer of persuasion is to win the reader over to his or her viewpoint. How does Krents bring his viewpoints to life?

Student Response

Responding to Reading

These questions are open-ended with no "right" or "wrong" answers. However, responses must be supported with information from the selection. Possible answers follow:

1. Almost any response is valid.

2. Some students may say that people treat Krents as they do out of fear; or because they lack experience with blind people; or because they assume that blind people cannot hear or speak or are less intelligent than most people.

3. Some students may say that Krents has accepted his blindness; although he is annoyed by people's reactions to him, he has learned to be patient. Other students may say that Krents does not view himself as handicapped by blindness and does not allow his blindness to prevent him from any achievement.

4. Students may say that his intelligence, sense of humor, and determination were responsible for his success.

5. Students may say that in both cases the assumptions made are based on stereotypes and lack of personal experience; that both Mrs. Wilson and the people cited by Krents were making assumptions about a person based on their misconceptions and prejudiced ideas, rather than on knowledge of the individual.

6. Students may say that, based on recent labor laws, this is a realistic hope; they may cite personal observations of the way our society has already changed its treatment of blind people to support their opinions. Other students may believe that because handicaps make individuals seem "different," many people will continue to focus primarily on these disabilities.

7. Students who respond that the essay changed their attitudes may say that the writer's use of realistic examples gave them new insights into what it might be like to be blind. Other students may say they already share Krents's point of view and the essay only confirmed their opinions regarding blind people.

Literary Concept—Persuasive Essay

Possible response: Krents brings his viewpoint to life through factual evidence: humorous anecdotes about the way he has been treated by people who behave as though he cannot hear, speak, reason, or work simply because he is unable to see; facts about his own abilities and qualifications for work; and facts about government regulations regarding employment opportunities for the handicapped. Krents also offers his opinions, citing the frustrations and disillusionments that he has endured and offering his hope that future employers will not distinguish between handicapped and nonhandicapped employees.

Writing Options

1. Imagine that you have been asked to write a speech introducing Harold Krents at a benefit devoted to raising money for handicapped children. In your speech, summarize Krents's contributions to his profession and to society as a whole. Refer to the biography in the Reader's Handbook.

2. Krents tells three personal anecdotes to make his points about the treatment of blind persons. Briefly summarize these three short accounts.

3. Describe a misconception that you have held about someone else. Explain why you held this belief in the first place. Relate what happened to change your mind.

4. Imagine someone who says of teenagers: "They're all alike—whiners. They don't know how good they have it. Theirs is the easiest life of any group in society." Write a short persuasive essay using personal experiences to show that this person is wrong.

Vocabulary Practice

Exercise Read the pairs of words below. On your paper, write *Synonyms* if the pair are synonyms. Write *Antonyms* if they are antonyms.

1. conversely—similarly
2. disposition—mood
3. graphically—vividly
4. mandate—require
5. misconception—understanding

Words to Know and Use

conversely
disposition
graphically
mandate
misconception

Writing Options

The Writing Options are designed to meet varied student interests and abilities. Have each student choose one writing activity to complete. You may wish to guide some students to an option that requires less writing.

Journal Update Have students review their journal entries for "Darkness at Noon." What have they learned about disabilities? What new reflections can they add to their earlier writing?

Vocabulary Practice

1. antonyms
2. synonyms
3. synonyms
4. synonyms
5. antonyms

Closure

In this selection, the writer describes the stereotyped ways in which other people see him. Suggest that each student decide on one visible thing to change about himself or herself—the color of hair or eyes, the need for glasses, the use of a crutch, hearing ability, and so on. Then have students form small groups to discuss how each might be seen differently with this one change.

Writer's Workshop

Objectives

- To understand the goals of supporting an opinion
- To establish criteria
- To use criteria as a basis for comparison
- To develop supporting evidence for criteria
- To draft, revise, edit, and present an expository essay
- To reflect on the writing process

Integrating . . .

Literature and Writing Discuss with students the idea of preconceived notions and of forming opinions without facts to back them up. For example, in "After You, My Dear Alphonse," the mother has a misconception about Boyd and his background. Have students relate the concept of preconceived notions to their own world and to other literature. Stress the importance of keeping an open mind for both readers and writers.

Tell students that in this subunit they will write an essay that uses supporting details to back up an opinion.

Students may wish to continue the discussion of unsupported opinions. Have students form groups and discuss instances where they have jumped to the wrong conclusions because of a lack of concrete facts. Have the groups share their findings with the class.

Writing and Language Direct students to the Language Workshop on page 490. Explain to students that it is important to avoid fragments and run-on sentences when they write. Remind them that their audience will judge not only what they say but how they say it.

Writing and Thinking The Thinking Skills workshop deals with fact and opinion. Explain the differences between the two. Have the students come up with their own examples of each. Explain that they will use facts to support their opinions when they write their essays.

EXPOSITION: SUPPORTING AN OPINION

Everybody has an opinion about something. Whether it's about the food in the cafeteria, the latest fashions, the role of U.S. armed forces abroad, or just the weather, everyone has a belief or feeling that he or she wants to discuss with others. Our opinions, however, are not necessarily held by those we share them with. To convince someone else of your opinions, you often need to back up your beliefs with supporting evidence. Supporting evidence usually comes from people's ideas and experiences. For example, your opinion that high-top tennis shoes are more stylish than low-top sneakers might be based on what you've seen in the latest catalogs and in television ads, what your friends say, or what the "coolest" people in school are wearing.

For this assignment you will be asked to decide who should receive a scholarship award donated by a local millionaire and then to support your opinion. The nominees are characters from some of the stories in this subunit.

GUIDED ASSIGNMENT: SCHOLARSHIP AWARD

Use what you have learned about certain characters in this subunit to form and support an opinion about which character should receive a scholarship grant. Then write an essay defending your choice.

Here is your PASSkey to this assignment.

PURPOSE: To support your opinion
AUDIENCE: The scholarship committee
SUBJECT: A character in need of financial aid
STRUCTURE: An expository essay

Prewriting

STEP 1 Review the candidates The following characters have been chosen as candidates to receive a thirty-thousand-dollar scholarship to a school of their choice: Boyd from "After You, My Dear Alphonse," Daisy from "A Start in Life," and Harold from "Darkness at Noon." Write some brief notes about each character. You might consider answering the following questions.

Additional Resources

UNIT FOUR RESOURCE BOOK

Writer's Workshop Copy Master, p. 21
Peer and Self-Evaluation Guidelines, p. 22
Writing Assessment Guidelines, p. 23

ENRICHMENT MATERIALS

Thinking Skills Transparency and Worksheet
Fine Art Transparency and Writing Prompts
Revision, Proofreading, and Elaboration Worksheet
Writing Prompts for Assessment

- What kind of person do you think the character is?
- What hardships or problems has each character faced?
- How has the character handled these difficulties?
- What chance for success would the character have if he or she did not receive the scholarship?

STEP 2 Develop criteria To judge these three characters fairly, you will need to establish some uniform criteria to use as a basis of comparison. For example, you might consider the two most important qualifications to be that the person needs financial aid and that he or she will use the award wisely. Ask yourself what other criteria are important and write them down. Then identify actions and attitudes that fit these criteria. Note how one student developed two criteria for a "Best Teacher" award and then listed qualifications for meeting each criterion.

STUDENT MODEL

The "Best Teacher" must . . .

Be sensitive to student needs	Know how to teach
1. Understand students' weaknesses 2. Listen to students' ideas 3. Help students achieve their potential	1. Make learning interesting 2. Be excited about his or her subject 3. Know his or her subject well

STEP 3 Select your nominee Now apply your criteria to each of the three candidates. First review your notes on each character. Then write each character's name or initials next to those criteria he or she fulfills. If you happen to think of other criteria during this process, add them to your list. The character who meets most of your criteria will be your nominee for the scholarship.

STEP 4 Add supporting details Since you may have to defend your choice, you'll need supporting evidence. Review your notes about your nominee and reread the story in which he or she appears, if necessary. List specific details that show how the person you selected meets your criteria. The student defending her choice of best teacher, for example, came up with the following evidence in support of her two criteria.

Teaching Strategies

Introduction Direct students to the Writer's Workshop on page 486. Explain that they will write an expository essay that gives an opinion and provides supporting evidence. Remind students that facts provide the best supporting evidence. Advise students to reread the literature in order to get a clearer picture of each character. As they read, instruct them to jot down the details about each character that might sway the scholarship-award vote in his or her favor.

Direct students to the Guided Assignment box and the PASSkey graphic. Stress the importance of keeping the purpose and audience in mind throughout the writing process.

Prewriting Before students begin, you may wish to read all of the prewriting steps aloud. Tell students that it is essential for them to choose both a story and character that they like and are familiar with. You may want to help students by brainstorming some character traits and writing them on the chalkboard. Discuss the four questions from Step 1 orally with the students.

Before students attempt Step 2, discuss how to develop criteria. You may wish to choose as an example a character from another literature selection with which they are familiar. At this time, you can distribute the worksheet "Generating Criteria." They can complete this worksheet individually, or you can work through it with them.

Step 2 lends itself well to a cooperative activity. Have students work in pairs or small groups of three or four. Have groups develop the criteria and list the qualifications as shown.

Explain that the more carefully they choose criteria, the easier it will be to write their essays. Advise students not to rush through this step.

Computer Tip
Students might want to organize their criteria and qualifications on a computer. This would make it easier for the groups to brainstorm and revise their work. Students can then store this material and update it throughout the writing process. Students should be encouraged to become comfortable with the computer and use it to enhance their creativity.

Encourage students to complete all of the stages of the writing process on the computer. Be sure that they save each stage so that they have an accurate record.

Drafting Encourage students to choose an organizational device before they begin to draft their essays. You might want to go over a few with the class. Outlines work for defining criteria and qualifications. A list or word web are other organizational devices that might be helpful. Allow students to choose the device with which they are most comfortable.

Revising and Editing Encourage students to consider revising the order of the paragraphs in their essays when they begin to revise the actual wording. Students who have organized their essays with a criterion beginning each paragraph may want to rethink the order. Stress that the order of paragraphs should make sense, whether the strongest criterion comes first or last.

Finally, have students edit their papers for spelling, grammar, and mechanics. Stress once more the importance of avoiding run-ons and fragments.

STUDENT MODEL ▶

Mr. Thomas is sensitive to students' needs.	Mr. Thomas knows how to teach.
a. He asks whether the homework is too demanding. b. He meets with students outside of class to discuss their problems. c. He's aware of individual differences.	a. He uses lots of resources to expand each lesson. b. He knows the answers to most students' questions. c. He connects his lessons to real-life experiences.

Drafting

STEP 1 Organize your evidence Decide how you want to present your supporting evidence. You may want to begin by listing all the criteria for receiving a scholarship and then stating how your candidate meets these criteria. On the other hand, you might discuss each criterion and its supporting evidence separately.

STEP 2 Write an introduction Begin by explaining the purpose of the scholarship. Then summarize the process you went through to select a nominee. Finally, note who the candidates are, and introduce your nominee.

STEP 3 Draft the body and conclusion In the body of the essay, support your opinion by describing how your nominee meets all or most of the criteria you have established. Begin a new paragraph when discussing either a new criterion or new evidence, depending on your method of organization. Conclude your essay with a brief summary of your evidence. Here is the first paragraph from the body of the student's essay on the "Best Teacher" award.

STUDENT MODEL ▶

A good teacher must be sensitive to students' needs. Mr. Thomas excels in this respect. Every week or so he checks with us to make sure we're not overburdened with homework. If we tell him the homework is too demanding, he tries to find out why and then gives us time to catch up. Mr. Thomas also takes time to talk to us outside of class, especially when we have problems. For example, when I told him I had trouble taking notes in class, he let me move my desk closer to the blackboard and showed me how to follow an outline.

Revising and Editing

Reread your paper with the following questions in mind. Then revise your essay accordingly.

Revision Checklist

1. Does the introduction clearly state the purpose of my essay?
2. Have I established appropriate criteria on which to base my opinion?
3. Have I presented sufficient evidence to support my opinion?
4. Is the essay organized logically?
5. Does my conclusion summarize my evidence?

Editing Edit your paper for spelling, grammar, and mechanics.

Presenting

Have a panel of students play the role of the scholarship committee. Read your essay aloud to the panel. Once the panel has heard arguments for all three characters, they will vote to award the grant.

Reflecting on Your Writing

Answer the following questions. Place the answers, along with a copy of your essay, in your writing portfolio.

1. What was the most difficult part of this assignment for you? Why?
2. How did you feel about opinions that differed from yours concerning who should receive the grant?
3. What is the strongest part of your essay?

Presenting Encourage students to practice reading their essays before they read them to the "scholarship committee." Explain the importance of reading the essay in a natural and comfortable way. Stress that their goal is to put the committee at ease and convince them who should receive the scholarship. Have students turn to the guidelines to review an oral report that they followed in an earlier subunit. Encourage them to take this opportunity to do a little acting.

As an alternative, have students form groups based on which character they chose. Read the essays to the groups and have the group members act as the committee.

Reflecting on Your Writing As you review students' writing portfolios, you may wish to compare the answers to the *Reflecting* questions. If they are similar, it might be a good idea to discuss them in class. At this time, students may wish to read parts of their essays in answer to Question 3.

Closure

Before beginning the next subunit, be sure students have internalized these concepts:

- Criteria must be chosen before evaluation can occur.
- Comparison is an important part of the evaluation process.
- Opinions should be supported with examples.
- The strength of a presentation can convince someone of an argument.

Additional Writing and Research Topics

The following items provide additional writing practice based on the selections in this subunit:

Persuasion

- If you could persuade the mayor of your city to allocate funds to a specific city agency, which agency would you choose? Write your recommendations to the mayor.
- Write a note to a relative explaining why you should be allowed to get a pet.

Other Topics

Narration: Write a group of letters supporting your position about what you want to do this summer. Be as creative as you wish. You should, however, make sure that your supporting arguments are strong. For instance, you may wish to begin a dog-grooming company. Convince someone why you could make a success of this.

AVOIDING FRAGMENTS AND RUN-ONS

A group of words that is only part of a sentence is a **sentence fragment.** Two or more sentences written incorrectly as one are a **run-on sentence.**

Sentence Fragments

What would be the first question you would ask if somebody told you that a murder had been committed in your neighborhood last night? You would probably ask who was murdered. Then you might ask who did the murder. The reason you would ask those questions is that you can't understand an event without knowing something about both the **act** itself and the **people** involved. If the act interests you, you want to know who did it, that is, who the murderer was. On the other hand, if you know that somebody did something special, you want to know what he or she did.

Language is organized to answer both questions about a reported event—Who did it? and What happened? Every complete sentence has an actor and an action. The actor is the **subject;** the action is the **verb.** When either the subject or the verb is missing from a sentence, the result is a sentence fragment. To correct a sentence fragment, you must add the missing information.

Fragment Was blind from birth. (In this case the subject is missing, and the reader is left wondering, *Who was blind from birth?*)

Sentence Harold Krents was blind from birth.

Fragment Harold Krents, in spite of lifelong blindness. (Now the reader is left confused because the verb is missing. He or she is left wondering, *What did Harold Krents do in spite of his blindness?*)

Sentence Harold Krents, in spite of lifelong blindness, received law degrees from Harvard Law School and Oxford University.

There are a few cases in which a group of words has a subject and a verb and yet still is not a sentence. Consider the following example.

Language Workshop

Objectives

- To understand that a sentence has a subject and a verb and expresses a complete thought
- To recognize sentence fragments and correct them by supplying missing information
- To recognize run-on sentences and revise them by separating them or by connecting them correctly

Integrating . . .

Grammar and Writing Remind students that in the Writer's Workshop they were asked to write an essay defending their choice of the character they believed most deserved a scholarship to attend college. Explain that in order to present convincing arguments, they must be able to express themselves in complete thoughts. Otherwise, the most important part of their arguments could be lost. Write the following on the board:

1. Responsibility for younger brother and sister.

2. Daisy is intelligent and eager.

Ask students to identify the group of words that expresses a complete thought about Daisy's character. Point out that in order to convince others of our opinions, we must be able to convey clear messages through written and spoken language. This Language Workshop focuses on the importance of avoiding fragments and run-on sentences.

Teaching Strategies

Ask a volunteer to restate the definition of a sentence. Have students identify the subjects and verbs in the example sentences.

Teaching Tip

Some students may incorrectly identify imperative sentences as sentence fragments. Give an example of an imperative sentence and help students distinguish between an understood subject and a missing subject.

Additional Resources

UNIT FOUR RESOURCE BOOK

Language Workshop Copy Master, p. 24

ENRICHMENT MATERIALS

Grammar and Usage Copy Masters

Fragment Although he was blind. (The group of words has a subject, *he,* and a verb, *was,* but it does not express a complete thought. *Although he was blind, what?*)

Sentence Although he was blind, Harold was very successful.

> A **sentence** has a subject and a verb and expresses a complete idea or thought.

Exercise 1 Write *S* for each group of words that is a sentence and *F* for each fragment. Then add words to make each fragment a sentence.

1. Although most museums now have wheelchair ramps.
2. Wide elevators, with room for a wheelchair and an attendant.
3. Printed in Braille next to the paintings and other works of art.
4. Many museums offer audio tours for blind or hearing-impaired people.
5. Especially enjoy hands-on sculpture exhibitions.

Note

Fragments are acceptable for some types of personal writing, such as note taking or recording journal entries. Professional writers also use fragments, on occasion, when writing dialogue. Fragments make dialogue sound more realistic, because people often use fragments in conversation. In most writing, however, complete sentences should be used.

Run-on Sentences

A run-on sentence is the opposite of a sentence fragment. Instead of having too little information, a run-on has too much. A run-on occurs when two or more sentences are written incorrectly as one.

Do you know people who talk so fast they hardly stop to take a breath? A run-on sentence that goes on and on without a punctuation break can create the same effect. Eventually, the listener or reader becomes confused because the connections between ideas—between subjects, verbs, and objects—are unclear.

You may encounter two kinds of run-ons. In the first kind two or more sentences are strung together without any punctuation marks to separate them. In the second kind the writer uses a comma instead of a period or a semicolon to separate two complete ideas. A run-on caused by a comma used in place of a period is called a **comma splice.**

Comma Splice Daisy was given a lot of responsibility and respect within her family, she expected the same from the Kruce family.

Sentence Daisy was given a lot of responsibility and respect within her family; she expected the same from the Kruce family.

Say It Aloud

Sometimes you can spot run-on sentences by reading your writing aloud. Notice where you pause naturally at the end of a complete thought. Be sure you have used the correct punctuation at that point.

Work through the lesson, but stop before students reach Exercise 1. Divide the class into three groups, *Subjects, Verbs,* and *Sentences.* A person from the first group suggests a subject; a person from the second group suggests a verb that fits the subject; a person from the third group uses the subject and verb in a sentence, a fragment, or a run-on sentence.

Call on other students to identify the third group of words as a sentence fragment, a run-on sentence, or a sentence. Then have students suggest corrections if necessary.

Answer Key
Exercise 1

All of the groups of words are fragments, except item 4.

Discuss the use of fragments in professional writing, especially in dialogue. Provide examples from the stories students have read. For example, "After you, my dear Alphonse," is a phrase used throughout Shirley Jackson's story. Although the phrase conveys meaning, it is a sentence fragment. Ask students to suggest occasions when the use of sentence fragments is acceptable.

Teaching Tip

Students may have difficulty identifying run-on sentences because in their minds they may "fill in" the missing punctuation or connecting words. Overdramatize the reading of run-on sentences to help students notice the lack of pauses or breaks.

Teaching Tip: LEP

Provide a sentence in English and ask Spanish-speaking students to say the same sentence in Spanish. Point out to students that in Spanish, the verb precedes the subject but that in English, more often, the subject precedes the verb. Provide several examples so that all students can see how the sentence structures differ.

Discuss the two kinds of run-on sentences and the various ways of correcting them. Write these sentences on the board.

Mrs. Wilson became angry, Boyd rejected her offer of old clothes.

First revision: Mrs. Wilson became angry because Boyd rejected her offer of old clothes.

Second revision: Mrs. Wilson became angry. Boyd rejected her offer of old clothes.

Point out that the first revision of the run-on sentence is preferable to the second, since it makes clear the relationship between the two ideas. Have students discuss when it might be preferable to split a run-on sentence into two separate sentences.

Assign exercises 2 and 3.

Teaching Tip

Point out that some conjunctions, such as *and* and *therefore,* show a cause-and-effect or sequential relationship between ideas. Other conjunctions, such as *however,* show contrast. Emphasize the importance of understanding the relationship between the parts of a run-on sentence before deciding how to connect them.

Closure

Before beginning the next subunit, be sure students have internalized these concepts:

- A sentence fragment is a group of words that does not express a complete idea.
- Two or more sentences written incorrectly as one are a run-on sentence.
- A sentence fragment can be corrected by adding information to form a complete thought.
- Run-on sentences can be corrected in a variety of ways. Separate sentences can be created, or correct punctuation and appropriate conjunctions can be used to link complete thoughts.

Exercise 2

Answers will vary. Make sure students' answers are correctly punctuated. Make sure coordinating and subordinating conjunctions are used appropriately.

Exercise 3

Answers will vary.

There are several ways to correct run-on sentences. You can end the first complete thought with a period, a question mark, or an exclamation mark and then start the next word with a capital letter. You can connect the two sentences with a semicolon. You can connect them with a comma and a coordinating conjunction, such as *and, or, nor, for, but, so,* or *yet.* Or you can connect them with a semicolon and a subordinating conjunction, such as *however* or *therefore,* followed by a comma.

Run-on	Some people have help getting a good start in life Daisy Switzer was not one of those people.
Sentence	Some people have help getting a good start in life; Daisy Switzer was not one of those people.
Sentence	Some people have help getting a good start in life, but Daisy Switzer was not one of those people.
Sentence	Some people have help getting a good start in life; however, Daisy Switzer was not one of those people.

Exercise 2 Correct the following run-on sentences. Be sure you punctuate the revised sentences correctly. Experiment with various ways of correcting run-ons. Compare your corrections to those done by other students to see some of the ways in which run-ons can be fixed.

1. Taking a job can often be a difficult adjustment, having a boss is not easy.
2. It is exciting to get the first paycheck it often seems smaller than you expected.
3. A new job means new responsibilities, it means a new set of friends, too.
4. Many teenagers are working after school and on weekends parents worry that they don't have enough time to have fun.
5. Work experience is important, however, one shouldn't let a part-time job get in the way of one's studies.

Exercise 3 Analyzing and Revising Your Writing

1. Take a paper from your writing portfolio.
2. Skim your work, looking for sentence fragments and run-on sentences.
3. Rewrite any fragments or run-ons that you find, using correct punctuation.
4. Remember to check for fragments and run-ons the next time you proofread your work.

LANGUAGE HANDBOOK

For review and practice, see Section 1, Writing Complete Sentences.

ADDITIONAL PRACTICE

The following items provide additional practice in avoiding sentence fragments and run-ons.

Write these fragments and run-on sentences correctly. Possible answers are given.

1. Even Donna in her lovely silk dress *looked drab next to Dorothy.*

2. Sam and Ramon, the tallest boys in the class , *don't like to play basketball.*

3. Ate almost all of the spaghetti in the bowl *Ryan ate . . . bowl.*

Write these word groups. Identify each as a sentence fragment or a run-on sentence.

4. After all the joys and sorrows *(sentence fragment)*

5. No one, not even the loyal, hardworking, and optimistic coach *(sentence fragment)*

6. Please help with these books they're heavy *(run-on sentence)*

7. Never saw that one heading for me *(sentence fragment)*

THINKING SKILLS WORKSHOP

FACT AND OPINION

A **fact** is a statement that can be proved. An **opinion** is a statement that cannot be proved; often, an opinion expresses a person's viewpoint or judgment.

HINT

Words such as *all, none, best,* and *worst* often signal opinions rather than facts.

When you read or listen to persuasive arguments or when you use them yourself, you must be able to separate facts from opinions.

Fact Countee Cullen was born in 1903.
Opinion Countee Cullen was the best poet of the Harlem Renaissance.

To tell whether a statement is a fact, ask yourself whether it can be proved. If it can be proved, it is a fact. If not, it is an opinion. How can a statement be proved? Facts can be proved in one or more of the following ways: (1) by personal observation, (2) by asking an expert, or (3) by checking an up-to-date and reliable reference work such as an encyclopedia. You can sometimes recognize opinions because they contain **judgment words**—words that express personal feelings.

JUDGMENT WORDS

awful	magnificent
bad	terrible
beautiful	terrific
excellent	valuable
fine	clever
good	intelligent
interesting	wonderful
likable	brilliant

Remember, though, that opinions don't always contain judgment words. Sometimes an opinion is expressed as though it were a fact, and you can only recognize that it is not a fact by questioning it. Ask yourself, Can this statement be proved? If so, it is a fact. If not, it is an opinion.

Exercise Identify the following statements as *Fact* or *Opinion*. If the statement is a fact, write how you could prove it. If it is an opinion, identify any judgment words it contains.

1. Baltimore is the friendliest city in America.
2. Most Native Americans live on tribal reservations.
3. Louis Braille was himself blind.
4. Men and women in wheelchairs have participated in marathon races.
5. A woman would make a better United States President than a man.

Thinking Skills Workshop

Objectives

- To understand the distinction between facts and opinions
- To understand how facts can be proved
- To identify opinions by recognizing judgment words

Integrating . . .

Literature and Thinking Skills
Share with students that this workshop will help them distinguish fact from opinion.

Teaching Strategies

Ask students to identify where they are most likely to encounter opinions. *(Possible responses: in newspaper editorials and letters, political speeches, advertisements)* Then have them discuss why people need to distinguish between facts and opinions. *(Possible response: to make informed decisions)*

Read through the material with students. Then read and discuss the Judgment Words and the signal words in the Hint box.

Assign the exercise on page 493. Have students share their answers and discuss the reasoning they used.

Closure

Before beginning the next subunit, be sure students have internalized these concepts:

- Facts can be proved by observation, verification by an expert, or reference materials.
- Readers can evaluate opinions by deciding whether or not they are supported by facts.

Teaching Tip

Choose a certain period of time during which students may discuss a topic but may not include any opinions. After the discussion, have students think about why the activity was difficult.

Exercise

(Possible responses are given.)
1. opinion; *friendliest.* **2.** fact; verify in the 1990 census. **3.** fact; check a biographical source. **4.** fact; check newspaper files. **5.** opinion; *better.*

Additional Resources

UNIT FOUR RESOURCE BOOK
Related Skills Copy, p. 25

ADDITIONAL PRACTICE

Write *fact* or *opinion* after each statement. If it is a fact, write how it could be proved.

1. Washington, DC is the most interesting capital city in the world. *(opinion)*

2. The National Zoological Park covers almost 200 acres. *(fact; You could measure it or check an almanac.)*

3. Pandas sit upright with their hind legs stretched out when they eat. *(fact; You could check by observation.)*

Subunit Preview

Have students read the introduction to subunit 2, **Grace Under Pressure.** Ask them to consider how countering an insult with dignity relates to the broader unit theme, **Human Rights: Pain and Pride.** How can you tell if compliance with injustice shows strength or weakness? Can patience with injustice be an effective strategy? How so? Can retaliation win respect? Why or why not? Ask students to look over the subunit Table of Contents and point out the selection that they think will be the most interesting.

For Additional Challenge

The following selections offer further challenge in exploring the subunit theme:

"The Base Stealer," a poem by Robert Francis

"I Will Fight No More Forever," a speech by Chief Joseph

Additional Resources

Subunit Test, pp. 53–54

Grace Under Pressure

Imagine you've just been told that you cannot drive until you are twenty-one years old. Naturally you feel your rights have been denied. What do you do? Do you strike out in anger? Do you refuse to comply and drive anyway hoping the authorities won't catch you? Or do you bite your tongue, bide your time, and perhaps begin looking for ways to regain the right denied? Chances are your reaction will influence the outcome.

In the following selections you will meet characters who attempt to react with patience and grace when their human rights are denied. As you read, ask yourself whether you would react in the same manner.

Observation Assessment

Observing how students respond to the text, to the classroom instruction, and to peers is an important part of an assessment program. The following suggestions and the form in each Unit Resource Book can be used to implement observation assessment.

- As students work through this subunit, observe how they approach a nonfiction piece. Do they set a purpose before a reading? Can they relate their reading to themselves and to their purpose? Do they share their reactions to interesting or surprising information?
- As they work through the subunit, can you see growth in the ability to draw analogies between a story and personal experience?
- To evaluate how well students use postreading strategies, see if they can explain what they have learned from a story. Can they summarize key events and ideas? Can they explain what the story means to them?

explore

Autobiography

Tanforan: A Horse Stall for Four

YOSHIKO UCHIDA
(yō' shē ko͞o chē' də)

Examine What You Know (Prior Knowledge)

In the true account you are about to read, a family of American citizens is labeled a security risk by the federal government and ordered to gather a few possessions in preparation for removal to a detention camp. If you were suddenly pulled from your home, what possessions would you want to take? On a sheet of paper, list which ten items you would choose. As you read this story, note how these items compare with the items most missed or treasured by the author's family.

Expand Your Knowledge (Building Background)

During World War II, President Franklin D. Roosevelt issued an executive order that imprisoned Japanese Americans in relocation camps. The government decided that Japanese-American citizens were a threat to national security, despite the fact that twenty thousand Japanese Americans were fighting for the United States in the war. Although the Allies fought against Germany and Italy as well as against Japan, German and Italian Americans were not detained.

Relocation camps for Japanese Americans were usually in out-of-the-way places and generally consisted of little more than hastily constructed barracks allowing little privacy. Although the U.S. Supreme Court upheld the government's decision in 1944, the nation acknowledged in 1988 that it had acted illegally. The government made apologies and agreed to pay damages to the Japanese Americans it had imprisoned.

Enrich Your Reading (Reading Skill)

Appreciating Descriptive Details Writers include precise **details** that describe sights, sounds, smells, tastes, and touch in order to help readers visualize a particular scene, event, or character. In the upcoming selection, the writer provides many details to illustrate the dreariness of the detention camp. An example is "dust, dirt, and wood shavings covered the linoleum that had been laid over manure-covered boards." As you read, look for details that make the camp seem real.

■ *A biography of the author can be found on page 507.*

Objectives

- To understand an autobiographical excerpt
- To identify the mood of a selection
- To recognize irony
- To appreciate descriptive details
- To express understanding of the work through a choice of writing options, including letters, a list, and a poem

Prereading/Motivation

Examine What You Know

Discussion Prompts: What criteria did you use to choose each item on your list? What might your emotional state be under these extraordinary circumstances? Would this affect your choices?

Expand Your Knowledge

Discussion Prompts: What kinds of hardships do you think relocation caused the Japanese Americans? Why do you think German and Italian Americans were not interned during the war?

Additional Background: In March of 1942, the United States began to notify Japanese Americans that they would have to leave their homes. At that time there were about 125,000 Japanese Americans living along the Pacific Coast, of whom seven out of ten were Nisei, or second generation American born Japanese. Many detainees were given only a few days to sell their possessions and report for a trip to an unknown destination. The majority of these Japanese Americans were farmers who were forced to abandon their crops and thus incurred tremendous losses. By August of that year, 110,000 Japanese Americans were removed from the west coast to ten inland camps.

Enrich Your Reading

Suggest that students create a sensory details chart with five columns headed sight, sound, smell, taste, and touch. Have students note sensory details from the selection that appeal to the senses in the appropriate columns.

Thematic Link—Grace Under Pressure

In this selection, the main characters adjust gracefully to the pressures of living in a relocation camp.

Journal Writing

- How might a person who is "overwhelmed with a longing for home" feel?
- "It was everyone for himself or herself." Describe a personal experience which shows this behavior.

For other journal opportunities, refer students to Examine What You Know (above), Broader Connections (page 505), and Teaching Tip (p. T–500).

Additional Resources

UNIT FOUR RESOURCE BOOK
Reader's Guidesheet, p. 28
Vocabulary Worksheet, p. 29
Selection and Vocabulary Check Tests, p. 30
Selection Test, pp. 31–32

Collaborative Learning

Opportunities for collaborative learning appear throughout the lesson and include Options for Learning activities 2 and 3 (page 507), Real-Life Connections (p. T–500), and Cross-Curricular Options (page T–507).

Teaching Strategies

Vocabulary Preview

These vocabulary words are defined at the bottom of the selection page on which they appear. You may wish to discuss them briefly before students begin reading.

adept skilled; expert
communal of or in a group of people
destitute those without food, clothing, and shelter
erratic uncertain; irregular
inevitable unavoidable
ludicrous ridiculous
obsessive very preoccupied
ravenously hungrily; greedily
sporadically now and then

Support for Students of Limited English Proficiency

- Use Reader's Guidesheet, p. 28.
- Yoshiko Uchida, the author of "Tanforan: A Horse Stall for Four," does not openly or loudly state her feelings about the ordeal she was forced to endure. Rather, she uses descriptive details to let us see the contrast between circumstances in the camp and what she was accustomed to at home. Encourage LEP students to share their feelings about the contrast between their homelands and the United States. Use annotations C, E, J, K, U and W. Annotations D, F, M, R, T, and W focus on terms and concepts.

Text Annotations

A. Literary Element: POINT OF VIEW Ask students to identify the point of view from which the story is told and to explain how they know. *(first person point of view; pronouns* I, we, our, *and* us*)*

B. Literary Element: CHARACTERIZATION Ask students what they can tell about Ms. Uchida from the fact that she always dresses in her best to venture outside. *(Possible responses: She is formal and proper; she takes great pride in herself.)*

Tanforan: A Horse Stall for Four

YOSHIKO UCHIDA

SR-1 ▶ *The following excerpt is from a memoir by Yoshiko Uchida called* Desert Exile: The Uprooting of a Japanese American Family. *During World War II, the author, then a senior in college, and her family were suddenly uprooted and sent to a detention camp because of their Japanese heritage. Yoshiko's father had been sent to a prisoner-of-war camp in Missoula, Montana. In this excerpt Yoshiko describes how the rest of the family endures their first days in a camp located at the Tanforan racetrack in California.*

As the bus pulled up to the grandstand, I could see hundreds of Japanese Americans jammed along the fence that lined the track. These people had arrived a few days earlier and were now watching for the arrival of friends or had come to while away the empty hours that had suddenly been thrust upon them.

A As soon as we got off the bus, we were directed to an area beneath the grandstand where we registered and filled out a series of forms. Our baggage was inspected for contraband,[1] a cursory[2] medical check made, and our living quarters assigned. We were to be housed in Barrack 16, Apartment 40. Fortunately, some friends who had arrived earlier found us and offered to help us locate our quarters.

It had rained the day before, and the hundreds of people who had trampled on the track had turned it into a miserable mass of slippery mud. We made our way on it carefully, helping my mother, who was dressed just as she would have been to go to church. She wore a hat, gloves, her good coat, and her Sunday shoes, because she would not have thought of venturing outside our house dressed in any other way. B

Everywhere there were black tar-papered barracks that had been hastily erected to house the eight thousand Japanese Americans of the area who had been uprooted from their homes. Barrack 16, however, was not among them, and we couldn't find it until we had traveled half the length of

1. **contraband:** goods brought in illegally.
2. **cursory:** hasty.

STRUCTURED READING FOR LESS PROFICIENT STUDENTS

These questions can help to guide students through the reading. Ask each question at the point of the selection where the SR number appears in the margin.

SR–1. Why have the Uchidas been uprooted from their home? *(They are Japanese Americans and considered a threat during World War II.)* **Clarifying**

SR–2. What type of housing were the Uchidas given at Tanforan Racetrack? *(They were housed in a ten-foot by twenty-foot horse stall.)* **Literal recall**

SR–3. How did the Uchidas feel about living at Tanforan? *(Yoshiko felt degraded, humiliated, and homesick; her mother was unutterably sad.)* **Literal recall**

SR–4. In what ways were the conditions at Tanforan depressing? *(Possible responses: People had little recreation; there were lines for meals, washing clothes, bathing; the food was bad; the stall was poorly lit and drafty; there was little privacy; conditions were unsanitary.* **Summarizing**

SR–5. What good news comes to the Uchidas at the end of the selection? *(Their father will join them.)* **Literal recall**

Boarding the bus for Tanforan National Archives, Washington, D.C.

the track and gone beyond it to the northern rim of the racetrack compound.

Finally one of our friends called out, "There it is, beyond that row of eucalyptus trees." Barrack 16 was not a barrack at all, but a long stable raised a few feet off the
C ground with a broad ramp the horses had used to reach their stalls. Each stall was now numbered, and ours was number 40. That the stalls should have been called "apartments" was a euphemism[3] so ludicrous it was comical. D

When we reached stall number 40, we

3. **euphemism** (yo͞o′ fə miz′ əm): a mild expression used instead of one that is unpleasantly direct.

Words to Know and Use	**ludicrous** (lo͞o′ di krəs) *adj.* ridiculous

C. Reading Skill: VISUALIZING Encourage students to visualize the well-groomed, well-dressed Mrs. Uchida in contrast to the stable. Have them consider how they would feel in her place. *(Possible responses: angry, horrified, insulted, worried)*

D. LEP: Euphemisms Develop the concept of euphemisms by asking students to name some common euphemisms. *(Possible responses: "powder room" or "lavatory" for bathroom; "passed away" for died; "preowned" for used)*

DATA BANK

That your own country would put you behind barbed wire without any trial, simply because of race, is a real tragedy. I know many young Japanese-Americans today blame us for having acquiesced, as they see it. But the world was a different place. Our thought was to show that we were loyal Americans. We believed we could prove this by doing what the government asked.

Most Japanese responded with a great deal of dignity. Yes, we were angry, but I think we should distinguish between anger and bitterness. I always feel that when you're bitter, you're only destroying yourself. This is something I hope to convey in my writing.

YOSHIKO UCHIDA

E. Literary Element: MOOD Ask students to tell the feeling that the descriptive details in this passage create. *(Possible responses: disgust, sadness)*

F. Cultural Sidelight A Dutch door is one that has separate upper and lower halves that can be opened independently of each other.

G. Literary Element: IRONY Ask students if the Uchidas really seem like a threat to the nation's security. Elicit that the author is masking her anger over the accommodations with irony.

H. Literary Element: AUTHOR'S PURPOSE Ask students what the author's main purpose might have been for writing this selection, based on what they have read so far. *(Possible response: She wants to inform her audience about conditions in the camps.)*

I. Literary Element: TONE Point out that the author compares the inevitability of long lines at Tanforan to the inevitability of the north wind. Ask students what this comparison reveals about the author's attitude toward her detention. *(She feels that it is beyond her control, just as the wind is.)*

pushed open the narrow door and looked uneasily into the vacant darkness. The stall was about ten by twenty feet and empty except for three folded army cots lying on the floor. Dust, dirt, and wood shavings covered the linoleum that had been laid over manure-covered boards, the smell of horses hung in the air, and the whitened corpses of many insects still clung to the hastily whitewashed walls.

High on either side of the entrance were two small windows, which were our only source of daylight. The stall was divided into two sections by Dutch doors worn down by teeth marks, and each stall in the stable was separated from the adjoining one only by rough partitions that stopped a foot short of the sloping roof. The space, while perhaps a good source of ventilation for the horses, deprived us all of but visual privacy, and we couldn't even be sure of that because of the crevices and knotholes in the dividing walls.

Because our friends had already spent a day as residents of Tanforan, they had become adept at scrounging for necessities. One found a broom and swept the floor for us. Two of the boys went to the barracks where mattresses were being issued, stuffed the ticking with straw themselves, and came back with three for our cots.

Nothing in the camp was ready. Everything was only half-finished. I wondered how much the nation's security would have been threatened had the army permitted us to remain in our homes a few more days until the camps were adequately prepared for occupancy by families.

By the time we had cleaned out the stall and set up the cots, it was time for supper. Somehow, in all the confusion, we had not had lunch, so I was eager to get to the main mess hall,[4] which was located beneath the grandstand.

I felt degraded, humiliated, and overwhelmed with a longing for home.

The sun was going down as we started along the muddy track, and a cold, piercing wind swept in from the bay. When we arrived, there were six long, weaving lines of people waiting to get into the mess hall. We took our place at the end of one of them, each of us clutching a plate and silverware borrowed from friends who had already received their baggage.

Shivering in the cold, we pressed close together trying to shield Mama from the wind. As we stood in what seemed a bread line for the destitute, I felt degraded, humiliated, and overwhelmed with a longing for home. And I saw the unutterable sadness on my mother's face.

This was only the first of many lines we were to endure, and we soon discovered that waiting in line was as inevitable a part of Tanforan as the north wind that swept in from the bay, stirring up all the dust and litter of the camp.

Once we got inside the gloomy, cavernous mess hall, I saw hundreds of people eating at wooden picnic tables, while those who had already eaten were shuffling aimlessly over the wet cement floor. When I reached

4. **mess hall:** an area used for the serving and eating of meals.

Words to Know and Use

adept (ə dept') *adj.* skilled; expert
destitute (des' tə to͞ot') *n.* those without food, clothing, and shelter
inevitable (in ev' i tə bəl) *adj.* unavoidable

the serving table and held out my plate, a cook reached into a dishpan full of canned sausages and dropped two onto my plate with his fingers. Another man gave me a boiled potato and a piece of butterless bread.

J With five thousand people to be fed, there were few unoccupied tables, so we separated from our friends and shared a table with an elderly man and a young family with two crying babies. No one at the table spoke to us, and even Mama could seem to find no friendly word to offer as she normally would have done. We tried to eat, but the food wouldn't go down.

"Let's get out of here," my sister suggested.

We decided it would be better to go back to our barrack than to linger in the depressing confusion of the mess hall. It had grown dark by now, and since Tanforan had no lights for nighttime occupancy, we had to pick our way carefully down the slippery track.

My sister and I worried about Mama, for she wasn't strong . . .

K Once back in our stall, we found it no less depressing, for there was only a single electric light bulb dangling from the ceiling, and a one-inch crevice at the top of the north wall admitted a steady draft of the cold night air. We sat huddled on our cots, bundled in our coats, too cold and miserable even to talk. My sister and I worried about Mama, for she wasn't strong and had recently been troubled with neuralgia,[5] which could easily be aggravated by the cold. She in turn was worrying about us, and of course we all worried and wondered about Papa.

Suddenly we heard the sound of a truck stopping outside.

"Hey, Uchida! Apartment 40!" a boy shouted.

I rushed to the door and found the baggage boys trying to heave our enormous "camp bundle" over the railing that fronted our stall.

L "What ya got in here anyway?" they shouted good-naturedly as they struggled with the unwieldy bundle. "It's the biggest thing we got on our truck!"

I grinned, embarrassed, but I could hardly wait to get out our belongings. My sister and I fumbled to undo all the knots we had tied into the rope around our bundle that morning and eagerly pulled out the familiar objects from home.

M We unpacked our blankets, pillows, sheets, tea kettle, and, most welcome of all, our electric hot plate. I ran to the nearest washroom to fill the kettle with water, while Mama and Kay made up the army cots with our bedding. Once we hooked up the hot plate and put the kettle on to boil, we felt better. We sat close to its warmth, holding our hands toward it as though it were our fireplace at home.

Before long some friends came by to see us, bringing with them the only gift they had—a box of dried prunes. Even the day before, we wouldn't have given the prunes a second glance, but now they were as welcome as the boxes of Maskey's chocolates my father used to bring home from San Francisco.

Mama managed to make some tea for our friends, and we sat around our steaming kettle, munching gratefully on our prunes. We spent most of the evening talking about

5. **neuralgia** (no͞o ral′ jə): a pain along a nerve path.

J. Reading Skill: UNDERSTANDING MAIN IDEA The main idea of this paragraph and the preceding one is implied, not stated. Have students give a sentence that directly states the main idea the author wants to convey about the first meal at the camp. *(Possible response: Bad food, unpleasant surroundings, and unhappy people made eating impossible.)*

K. Literary Element: MOOD Point out that the author uses the word *depressing* to describe the atmosphere of the stall. Have students identify the details that convey this atmosphere. *(Details: "single electric light bulb dangling," "steady draft of the cold night air," "huddled . . . bundled, too cold and miserable even to talk")*

L. Literary Element: DIALOGUE Point out that this is one of the few examples of dialogue in the selection. Ask why the author includes so little dialogue. *(Possible responses: She is concerned mainly with describing her own memories and feelings. Lack of dialogue intensifies the mood. Details of conversation are unimportant to her.)*

M. LEP: Vocabulary Some students may not know what an electric hot plate is. Explain that it is a portable device that people use to boil water or prepare simple meals. Ask students why the electric hot plate is the "most welcome of all" the author's familiar objects from home. *(Possible responses: It offers the Uchida family a little warmth and hot water; it is a luxury they have control over in the camp.)*

PROFESSIONAL NOTEBOOK

This teaching of youth is always exciting, . . . Often they ask us questions that we think are a little crazy: sometimes we laugh at them! And in some instances we have given our questioners silly answers. And a few of us have been stupid enough to tell students they cannot succeed in this or that. This is dangerous. After many years of teaching and associating with young people, I have learned to respect the ideas of my students, particularly the ideas I didn't understand. And I have learned never to tell a student he cannot succeed in this or that.
JESSE STUART, *To Teach, To Love*

Teaching Tip

You might ask students to recall times when they were homesick. Have them describe their feelings when they received letters or packages from home.

N. Reading Skill: INFERRING Have students tell why they think signs of strain began to appear in family life at the camp. *(Possible responses: Family members were deprived of jobs, homes, and friends; normal roles and relationships were disrupted; families no longer got support from community organizations—churches, clubs, and schools.)*

O. Reading Skill: UNDERSTANDING ORGANIZATION Ask students how Uchida uses "space order" to organize her writing. *(She describes one area of the camp at a time; first the stall, then the mess hall, next the stables, and now the washrooms.)*

P. Literary Element: THEME Point out that the woman who improvises and shares a bathtub is one example of how internees show "grace under pressure." Ask students to name another example. *(Possible response: The friends who swept the floor for the Uchidas and brought them mattresses before the family arrived.)*

food and the lack of it, a concern that grew obsessive over the next few weeks, when we were constantly hungry.

Our stable consisted of twenty-five stalls facing north, which were back to back with an equal number facing south, so we were surrounded on three sides. Living in our stable were an assortment of people—mostly small family units—that included an artist, my father's barber and his wife, a dentist and his wife, an elderly retired couple, a group of Kibei bachelors (Japanese born in the United States but educated in Japan), an insurance salesman and his wife, and a widow with two daughters. To say that we all became intimately acquainted would be an understatement. It was, in fact, communal living, with semiprivate cubicles provided only for sleeping.

Our neighbors on one side spent much of their time playing cards, and at all hours of the day we could hear the sound of cards being shuffled and money changing hands. Our other neighbors had a teenage son who spent most of the day with his friends, coming home to his stall at night only after his parents were asleep. Family life began to show signs of strain almost immediately, not only in the next stall but throughout the entire camp. N

One Sunday our neighbor's son fell asleep in the rear of his stall with the door bolted from inside. When his parents came home from church, no amount of shouting or banging on the door could awaken the boy.

"Our stupid son has locked us out," they explained, coming to us for help.

I climbed up on my cot and considered pouring water on him over the partition, for I knew he slept just on the other side of it. Instead I dangled a broom over the partition and poked and prodded with it, shouting, "Wake up! Wake up!" until the boy finally bestirred himself and let his parents in. We became good friends with our neighbors after that.

About one hundred feet from our stable were two latrines[6] and two washrooms for our section of camp, one each for men and women. The latrines were crude wooden structures containing eight toilets, separated by partitions but having no doors. The washrooms were divided into two sections. In the front section was a long tin trough spaced with spigots of hot and cold water, where we washed our faces and brushed our teeth. To the rear were eight showers, also separated by partitions but lacking doors or curtains. The showers were difficult to adjust, and we either got scalded by torrents of hot water or shocked by an icy blast of cold. Most of the Issei[7] were unaccustomed to showers, having known the luxury of soaking in deep, pine-scented tubs during their years in Japan, and found the showers virtually impossible to use. O

Our card-playing neighbor scoured the camp for a container that might serve as a tub and eventually found a large wooden barrel. She rolled it to the showers, filled it with warm water, and then climbed in for a pleasant and leisurely soak. The greatest compliment she could offer anyone was the use of her private tub. P

6. **latrines** (lə trēnz′): toilets for the use of a large number of people, as in an army camp.

7. **Issei** (ē′ sā): Japanese who came to the United States after the Oriental exclusion act of 1907 and were thus not granted citizenship until 1952.

Words to Know and Use	**obsessive** (əb ses′ iv) *adj.* having the nature of an abnormal preoccupation with some feeling or idea **communal** (käm′ yo͞o nəl) *adj.* of or in a group of people living together

REAL LIFE CONNECTIONS

Ask students to suggest current situations in which people's rights seem to be violated by their governments. Do they think government should have the power to overrule or violate certain rights? Ask them to present possible scenarios in which such action might be permissible. Also have them discuss ways in which people can protect their rights against government violations. Encourage students to bring in newspaper and magazine clippings that explore these issues.

Q. Reading Skill: UNDERSTANDING MAIN IDEA Explain that the author directly states a main idea of the selection. Have students suggest details that support this main idea. *(Any details of the dismal conditions presented in the selection will suffice.)*

R. LEP: Vocabulary Some students may have trouble with the word *morale.* Explain that one's morale is his or her mental ability to withstand hardship, in this case the hardship of the camp. Have students give examples from contemporary life in which it might be important to have a good morale. *(Possible responses: when one has a lasting illness; when one has been unemployed for a long time)*

The lack of privacy in the latrines and showers was an embarrassing hardship especially for the older women, and many would take newspapers to hold over their faces or squares of cloth to tack up for their own private curtain. The army, obviously ill-equipped to build living quarters for women and children, had made no attempt to introduce even the most common of life's civilities into these camps for us. Q

During the first few weeks of camp life, everything was erratic and in short supply. Hot water appeared only sporadically, and the minute it was available, everyone ran for the showers or the laundry. We had to be clever and quick just to keep clean, and my sister and I often walked a mile to the other end of the camp, where hot water was in better supply, in order to boost our morale with a hot shower. R

In the early days, at least, it was everyone for himself or herself.

Even toilet paper was at a premium, for new rolls would disappear as soon as they were placed in the latrines. The shock of the evacuation compounded by the short supply of every necessity brought out the baser[8] instincts of the internees,[9] and there was little inclination for anyone to feel responsible for anyone else. In the early days, at least, it was everyone for himself or herself.

One morning I saw some women emptying bed pans into the troughs where we washed our faces. The sight was enough to turn my stomach, and my mother quickly made several large signs in Japanese cautioning people against such unsanitary practices. We posted them in conspicuous spots in the washroom and hoped for the best.

Across from the latrines was a double barrack, one containing laundry tubs and the other equipped with clotheslines and ironing boards. Because there were so many families with young children, the laundry tubs were in constant use. The hot water was often gone by 9:00 A.M., and many women got up at 3:00 and 4:00 in the morning to do their wash, all of which, including sheets, had to be done entirely by hand.

We found it difficult to get to the laundry before 9:00 A.M., and by then every tub was taken and there were long lines of people with bags of dirty laundry waiting behind each one. When we finally got to a tub, there was no more hot water. Then we would leave my mother to hold the tub while my sister and I rushed to the washroom, where there was a better supply, and carried back bucketfuls of hot water, as everyone else learned to do. By the time we had finally hung our laundry on lines outside our stall, we were too exhausted to do much else for the rest of the day. ◀SR-4

For four days after our arrival, we continued to go to the main mess hall for all our meals. My sister and I usually missed breakfast because we were assigned to the early shift, and we simply couldn't get there by 7:00 A.M. Dinner was at 4:45 P.M., which

8. **baser:** less honorable.

9. **internees:** those forced to remain in a certain place, especially during wartime.

Words to Know and Use

erratic (er rat' ik) *adj.* uncertain; irregular
sporadically (spə rad' ik lē) *adv.* now and then; not in a regular, dependable way

DATA BANK

Over 110,000 Japanese Americans were interned in ten different camps in California, Arizona, Idaho, Utah, Colorado, and Arkansas. The western camps were in desolate, windswept locations; the Arkansas camps were in swampy lowlands.

The camps resembled towns; each had its own schools, churches, and newspapers. Private business was barred, but cooperative stores and service shops were set up. Internees grew their food on camp farms. War materials were manufactured in some camps.

Camps were governed by elected councils. Only Nisei could run for office. This caused bitterness among the Issei, who were the older, first generation, and used to governing their communities.

S. Historical Sidelight Meat, butter, and other foodstuffs were in short supply during World War II. Families were issued ration tickets that allowed them to buy limited amounts of food and other goods. Explain that this may have been one reason for the starchy diet at the camp.

T. LEP: Chronological Order Point out that the author jumps around in time in order to describe how conditions in camp life improved.

One of these horse stalls at Tanforan racetrack housed the Uchida family. National Archives, Washington, D.C.

was a terrible hour, but not a major problem, as we were always hungry. Meals were uniformly bad and skimpy, with an abundance of starches such as beans and bread. I wrote to my non-Japanese friends in Berkeley shamelessly asking them to send us food, and they obliged with large cartons of cookies, nuts, dried fruit, and jams. S

We looked forward with much anticipation to the opening of a half dozen smaller mess halls located throughout the camp. But when ours finally opened, we discovered that the preparation of smaller quantities had absolutely no effect on the quality of the food. We went eagerly to our new mess hall only to be confronted at our first meal with chili con carne, corn, and butterless bread. To assuage[10] our disappointment, a friend and I went to the main mess hall, which was still in operation, to see if it had anything better. Much to our amazement and delight, we found small lettuce salads, the first fresh vegetables we had seen in many days. We ate ravenously and exercised enormous self-control not to go back for second and third helpings.

The food improved gradually, and by the time we left Tanforan five months later, we T

10. **assuage** (ə swāj′): to ease; calm.

Words to Know and Use — **ravenously** (rav′ ə nəs lē) *adv.* hungrily; greedily

502

PROFESSIONAL NOTEBOOK

Decisions. In addition to everything else, a good discussion involves a lot of fast decisions by the person who leads it. In fact, a good discussion calls for more decisions than I could count. I know because I tried counting them once. Actually I decided I would try to chronicle all the decisions I made in the course of a half-period discussion. I soon found that even that modest goal was too ambitious. I got as far as a half minute. I counted twelve decisions in all. If this is a typical half minute, then, figuring that I spend six hours with students in a day, that's 8,640 decisions per day.

JAMES NEHRING, *Why Do We Gotta Do This Stuff, Mr. Nehring?*

T had fried chicken and ice cream for Sunday dinner. By July tubs of soapy water were installed at the mess hall exits so we could wash our plates and utensils on the way out. Being slow eaters, however, we usually found the dishwater tepid and dirty by the time we reached the tubs, and we often rewashed our dishes in the washroom.

U Most internees got into the habit of rushing for everything. They ran to the mess halls to be first in line; they dashed inside for the best tables and then rushed through their meals to get to the washtubs before the suds ran out. The three of us, however, seemed to be at the end of every line that formed and somehow never managed to be first for anything.

V One of the first things we all did at Tanforan was to make our living quarters as comfortable as possible. A pile of scrap lumber in one corner of camp melted away like snow on a hot day as residents salvaged whatever they could to make shelves and crude pieces of furniture to supplement the army cots. They also made ingenious containers for carrying their dishes to the mess halls, with handles and lids that grew more and more elaborate in a sort of unspoken competition. V

W Because of my father's absence, our friends helped us in camp, just as they had in Berkeley, and we relied on them to put up shelves and build a crude table and two benches for us. We put our new camp furniture in the front half of our stall, which was our "living room," and put our three cots in the dark, windowless rear section, which we promptly dubbed "the dungeon." We ordered some print fabric by mail and sewed curtains by hand to hang at our windows and to cover our shelves. Each new addition to our stall made it seem a little more like home.

X One afternoon about a week after we had arrived at Tanforan, a messenger from the administration building appeared with a telegram for us. It was from my father, telling us he had been released on parole from Montana and would be able to join us soon in camp. Papa was coming home. The wonderful news had come like an unexpected gift, but even as we hugged each other in joy, we didn't quite dare believe it until we actually saw him. ❧ ◄ SR-5

After five months at Tanforan, the Uchidas were transferred to a guarded camp in the Utah desert. Yoshiko taught school at the camp until 1943, when she was released to accept a fellowship for graduate study at Smith College. Her parents were released later that year.

U. Critical Thinking: EVALUATING Ask students whether they think the government meant to punish the Japanese by providing poor conditions or whether they think the government simply did not have time to create a more comfortable camp. *(Possible response: That the food gradually improved suggests that the government did not mean to punish the internees.)*

V. Literary Element: THEME Ask students how the homemade furniture and containers illustrate the idea of "grace under pressure." *(Possible response: The internees did whatever they could to improve their surroundings and make themselves comfortable instead of complaining about their dismal living conditions.)*

W. LEP: Vocabulary Review the meaning of *dungeon.* Ask students to suggest what the rear section of the stall had in common with a dungeon. *(Both lack light and fresh air.)*

X. Literary Element: IRONY Have students explain the irony in the statement "Papa was coming home." *(Possible response: The place where he is going, Tanforan, is nothing like home.)* Ask them to tell in what way Tanforan is Papa's home. *(Possible response: It is where his family is.)*

Check Test

1. Why are the Japanese-Americans relocated at Tanforan Racetrack? *(They are considered a threat to national security.)*

2. Where is the Uchida family forced to live? *(in a former horse stall)*

3. Why are the washroom facilities at the camp inadequate? *(There is no privacy; there is a shortage of hot water and soap; there are no tubs.)*

4. What happens to the Uchida family after their stay at Tanforan? *(They are moved to a permanent detention center.)*

DATA BANK

In April 1988 the United States Congress passed a restitution act to provide $20,000 compensation to each Japanese American internee. The act was also an official apology and provided pardons for individuals who had been convicted of not cooperating with the various evacuation orders. Unfortunately, half of the internees, nearly 60,000 people, had already died by the time this act was passed.

Encouraging Independent Reading

Concentration Camps, U.S.A.: Japanese Americans and World War II, nonfiction by Roger Daniels.
Diary of a Young Girl, a diary by Anne Frank
Desert Exile: The Uprooting of a Japanese American Family, nonfiction by Yoshiko Uchida

INSIGHT

In Response to Executive Order 9066: All Americans of Japanese Descent Must Report to Relocation Centers

DWIGHT OKITA (ō kē′ tə)

Dear Sirs:
Of course I'll come. I've packed my galoshes
and three packets of tomato seeds. Janet calls them
"love apples." My father says where we're going
they won't grow.

I am a fourteen-year-old girl with bad spelling
and a messy room. If it helps any, I will tell you
I have always felt funny using chopsticks
and my favorite food is hot dogs.
My best friend is a white girl named Denise—
we look at boys together. She sat in front of me
all through grade school because of our names:
O'Connor, Ozawa. I know the back of Denise's head very well.
I tell her she's going bald. She tells me I copy on tests.
We're best friends.

I saw Denise today in Geography class.
She was sitting on the other side of the room.
"You're trying to start a war," she said, "giving secrets away
to the Enemy, Why can't you keep your big mouth shut?"
I didn't know what to say.
I gave her a packet of tomato seeds
and asked her to plant them for me, told her
when the first tomato ripens
to miss me.

Insight

This piece reflects on the ideas in the main selection and is suggested for students' independent reading. Optional discussion questions follow.

1. What does the fourteen-year-old girl who is the speaker in the poem have in common with Yoshiko Uchida, the author of "Tanforan"? *(Both are female Japanese Americans who are forced to leave their homes and enter relocation centers during World War II.)*

2. What do you think the girl's father means when he says the love apples won't grow where they're going? *(They will probably be relocated to some dry desert region; there is also the symbolic notion that love will not blossom under the circumstances.)*

3. Why do you think the poet portrays the girl as a typical American teenager? *(to point out the absurdity of relocating her; to show that despite her ancestry she is an American)*

4. The speaker says Denise O'Connor is her best friend. Is Denise a good friend? Explain. *(No; Denise betrays their friendship, making outrageous accusations based on wartime propaganda.)*

Responding to Reading

First Impressions

1. What do you think of the Uchida family? Jot down a few sentences.

Second Thoughts

2. Did the Uchidas show grace under pressure? Explain.

   Think about
   - the different pressures they felt
   - how they responded to these pressures
   - how other internees responded

3. Think again about the descriptive details the author uses in this selection. What would be the most grueling aspect of the camp for you? Why?

4. Look again at the list you made of possessions you would take to a detention camp. Why are these possessions so important in such a place? Having read this selection, how would you change your list?

5. How might Yoshiko Uchida and the speaker in the *Insight* poem at the end of this selection be similar?

   Think about
   - what details emphasize their Japanese heritage
   - what details make them seem typically American
   - what both are accused of
   - how much each understands the situation

Broader Connections

6. Give other examples of people who have endured detention without having done wrong. How should these people be compensated for their loss of freedom and property?

Literary Concept: Mood

Mood is the feeling that the writer creates for the reader. Writers use descriptive details to create mood. What mood does this selection create in you? What details help to convey this feeling?

Concept Review: Irony What is ironic about the detention of both the Uchida family and the speaker of the *Insight* poem?

Student Response

Responding to Reading

These questions are open-ended with no "right" or "wrong" answers. However, responses must be supported with information from the selection. Possible answers follow:

1. Almost any response is valid.

2. The Uchidas were under a great deal of pressure. They were separated from father and husband; they had lost their home and their possessions; they were in an unpleasant environment. Some students may say they bravely endured these pressures by keeping a sense of humor and taking small pleasures where they could. Others may say they were too passive, giving in when they should have rebelled. Students may point out that the other internees responded in much the same way.

3. Some may suggest that the dark, drafty, and smelly stall-housing would be most grueling, since so much time was spent there. Other students may feel the inadequate food or the washing facilities would be more of a problem, since they were potential health hazards.

4. Some items on the list may be important because they are unavailable at the camp; others because they allow the owners to continue certain interests, jobs, or hobbies or to create a feeling of home.

5. Like Yoshiko Uchida, the speaker in the poem is a female Japanese American who must leave her home for a relocation camp. Both accept the situation in a somewhat passive and uncomplaining way. Both have non-Japanese friends and typical American tastes and interests. Both are accused of being security risks.

6. Examples include: Jews in concentration camps during World War II; the hostages held in the Middle East, most notably in Iran, Lebanon, and Iraq; travelers held hostage by terrorist groups. Compensation might include: money, land, other types of property.

Literary Concept—Mood
The author creates a depressing, hopeless mood. Details include: the description of the horse stall that is small and drafty, smells like horses, is poorly lit, and has bugs whitewashed to the walls; the description of the mess hall with its wet floor, diners waiting in long lines, starchy and unappetizing food; the description of the washrooms and latrines in which there is no privacy and little hot water. Refer to annotations **E** and **K**.

Concept Review: Irony *Both the Uchida family and the speaker of the Insight poem were detained in relocation camps because as Japanese Americans they were considered to be security risks. This is ironic because both the young girl in the poem and the Uchidas were loyal American citizens.*

Writing Options

The Writing Options are designed to meet varied student interests and abilities. Have each student choose one writing activity to complete. You may wish to guide some students to an option that requires less writing.

Journal Update Have students revise their journal entries for "Tanforan: Horse Stall for Four." What have they learned about adjusting to difficult circumstances? What new reflections about grace under pressure can be added to their earlier writings?

Vocabulary Practice

1. ravenously
2. sporadically
3. communal
4. destitute
5. adept
6. inevitable
7. ludicrous
8. obsessive
9. erratic
10. communal

Writing Options

1. As Yoshiko, write a letter to a friend back in Berkeley. Explain how you feel about being imprisoned. Also report the latest news around camp.
2. As an internee at a relocation camp, write a letter to your representatives in Congress explaining why you feel you should be set free. You may want to refer to the Bill of Rights as part of your defense.
3. Using information from the selection, make up a list of rules that the residents might have had for themselves in order to survive their ordeal.
4. Pretend that you are Yoshiko's mother. Write a short poem that expresses the "unutterable sadness" that Yoshiko sees on your face. Use the *Insight* poem as a model.

Vocabulary Practice

Exercise On your paper, write the word from the list that best completes each sentence. One word is used twice.

1. Hungry for fresh vegetables, the Uchida family ate the salads ____.
2. Fresh vegetables and salads were served only ____ at the camp.
3. Hundreds of people ate together in ____ mess halls.
4. Since they had few belongings, everyone felt poor, like the ____.
5. Prisoners at Tanforan became ____ at making the stalls more homelike.
6. The search for hot water was an ____ part of camp life.
7. Today it seems ____ that American citizens were imprisoned because their ancestors were Japanese.
8. There was an ____ interest in food at the camps because it was always in short supply.
9. At first the flow of goods to the camp was ____; no one knew when or whether supplies might arrive.
10. The ____ latrines and showers caused embarrassment for many of the women prisoners.

Words to Know and Use

adept
communal
destitute
erratic
inevitable
ludicrous
obsessive
ravenously
sporadically

e x t e n d

Options for Learning

1 • I Was There Interview either a Japanese American who was interned in a relocation camp or another American citizen, such as a farmer or housewife, who remained in this country during World War II. Ask your subject about his or her memories of life in the States during wartime. Tape-record or videotape your interview for the class.

2 • Payment Due Research the history of the American government's official view of Japanese-American internees. In 1976, for example, President Ford said, "Not only was the evacuation wrong, but Japanese Americans were and are loyal Americans." Learn more about this speech and also about the 1983 Commission of Wartime Relocation. Share your findings with your classmates.

3 • Campsites Draw a blueprint of the camp. Include the stalls, the mess hall, and other structures mentioned in the selection.

4 • Talk It Out Read other chapters of *Desert Exile* to get a more complete picture of life in the relocation camps.

FACT FINDER

How many Japanese Americans were interned in relocation camps?

Yoshiko Uchida
1921–

Although she is now a productive and successful writer, Yoshiko Uchida had a hard time getting started after completing her graduate work at Smith College. She mailed dozens of short stories to well-known magazines but received only printed rejection slips. Finally, an editor at *The New Yorker* magazine suggested that she write about her detention camp experiences. Uchida followed this advice. She also began to explore her other experiences as an American-born daughter of Japanese parents. In 1952 she visited Japan, where she gained a new respect and admiration for her family's heritage.

When Uchida isn't relating her own experiences in books like *Desert Exile,* she is writing about other Japanese topics—often in children's books, such as *Takao and Grandfather's Sword, Rokubei and the Thousand Rice Bowls,* and *Sumi's Prize.* Uchida says, "Through my books I hope to give young Asian Americans a sense of their past and to reinforce their self-esteem and self-knowledge."

Options for Learning

These activities suit a variety of learning styles and modes of expression. Allow students to review the options and then choose the one they wish to do. Many are excellent collaborative learning projects.

1. I Was There Remind students to prepare their interview questions in advance.

2. Payment Due *Manzanara* by John Armor and Peter Wright, with photographs by Ansel Adams and commentary by John Hersey, will be helpful to students.

3. Campsites Students may want to consult the photographs found in **Desert Exile** in order to complete their drawings.

4. Talk It Out Suggest that volunteers read to the class excerpts from Ms. Uchida's memoir.

Fact Finder

By August of 1942 approximately 110,000 Japanese American civilians had been sent to relocation camps.

Additional Information About the Author

Yoshiko Uchida The author was a senior at the University of California, Berkeley, when her family was interned in 1942. Although she earned a master's degree in education, she taught only briefly, finding that the occupation severely limited her time for writing.

Uchida is the author of more than twenty books on Japanese culture. Best known perhaps are her award-winning retellings of Japanese folktales for students in the middle grades.

Closure

Like other selections in this subunit, "Taforan: Horse Stall for Four" explores how people react with "grace under pressure." The Uchidas gracefully accept conditions at the camp and try to make the best of a very bad situation. Have students give examples of behavior that would not have exemplified grace under pressure on the part of the Uchidas.

Cross-Curricular Options

Social Studies: Students might research historical immigration laws and policies, such as the Gentleman's Agreement of 1907, the Asian Barred Zone of 1917, the Exclusion Act of 1923, and the national origins systems, which deliberately restricted immigration from Japan to the United States during this century.

Math: Ask students to research the number of Japanese immigrants living in California between 1870 and 1940 and plot a graph showing their findings.

Art: Ask volunteers to design a poster that might have been used during World War II to protest the internment of Japanese Americans. Other students could create a poster that protests a current issue.

Language: Students might present an oral reading, dramatization, or dance based on a Japanese folktale found in one of Ms. Uchida's collections, such as the *Dancing Kettle and Other Japanese Folk Tales* or *The Magic Listening Cap—More Folk Tales from Japan.*

e x p l o r e

Autobiography

Montgomery Boycott

CORETTA SCOTT KING

Examine What You Know (Prior Knowledge)

You certainly recognize the words *civil rights,* but how much do you know about the subject? Either individually or as a class use a chart like the one below to summarize what you know about civil rights. In the middle column, list the questions that you would like answered about this topic. In the last space, fill in any new knowledge you gain as you read Coretta Scott King's account of the Montgomery boycott of 1955.

What I (We) Know	What I (We) Want to Learn	What I (We) Learned

Expand Your Knowledge (Building Background)

Although slavery ended with Abraham Lincoln's Emancipation Proclamation of 1863, discrimination and segregation did not cease. Former slaves remained at the bottom of the economic and social ladders. In the 1890's, with the rise of a new generation of African Americans who had never been slaves, laws were passed in certain states to ensure the separation of races in public places. These were called Jim Crow laws—named after a black character in an old song. Jim Crow laws remained in existence until they were challenged by African Americans in courts of law. The Supreme Court decisions of the 1950's and 1960's and the Civil Rights Act of 1964 struck down most of these laws.

Enrich Your Reading (Reading Skill)

Cause and Effect One event can bring about, or cause, multiple effects. In the following selection, a woman refuses to give up her seat on a bus. Read to see what multiple effects this decision has on the residents of Montgomery, Alabama, and on the course of the civil rights movement.

■ *A biography of the author can be found on page 519.*

Objectives

- To understand and analyze an excerpt from an autobiography
- To distinguish primary sources from secondary sources
- To identify cause-and-effect relationships
- To review internal and external conflict
- To express understanding of the work through a choice of writing forms, including newspaper reports, a character analysis, protest signs, and a poem

Prereading/Motivation

Examine What You Know

Discussion Prompts: What civil rights leaders and events have you read or heard about? What civil rights issues are you curious about? What opinions and attitudes do you have about the civil rights movement?

Expand Your Knowledge

Discussion Prompts: Does a person have the right to disobey an unfair law? How might the injustices of the past affect people's attitudes about race and equality today? How might the experiences of African Americans in the civil rights movement help other groups today?

Additional Background: *Segregation* refers to the separation of the races in housing, schools, and public facilities, either by law or because of social pressure. *Discrimination* is the denial of basic rights and opportunities to a person because of his or her race, creed, color, or other social characteristics.

Enrich Your Reading

The chain of cause and effect that resulted from one woman's refusing to give up her seat on a bus led to the boycott of the bus company and the launching of the civil rights movement with Martin Luther King, Jr. as its leader.

Thematic Link—Human Rights: Grace Under Pressure

In this selection, the civil rights leaders and other African Americans of Montgomery show admirable grace under pressure as they proudly fight for their human rights.

Journal Writing

Suggest these journal topics to students:

- In this selection, a leader says, "This is no time to talk, it is a time to act." What kinds of situations demand action rather than just words?
- Tell about a time when you behaved in a fearless manner even though you were scared.

For other journal opportunities, refer students to Cultural Connection (page T–512), Real-Life Connections (page T–513), annotations D, H, and P, and Broader Connections (page 517).

Additional Resources

UNIT FOUR RESOURCE BOOK

Reader's Guidesheet, p. 33
Vocabulary Worksheet, p. 34
Selection and Vocabulary Check Tests, p. 35
Selection Test, pp. 36–37

Collaborative Learning

Opportunities for collaborative learning appear throughout the lesson and include Options for Learning activities 1 and 3 (p. 519), as well as Cross-Curricular Options (page T–519).

Montgomery Boycott

CORETTA SCOTT KING

Of all the facets of segregation in Montgomery, the most degrading were the rules of the Montgomery City Bus Lines. This Northern-owned corporation outdid the South itself. Although seventy percent of its passengers were black, it treated them like cattle—worse than that, for nobody insults a cow. The first seats on all buses were reserved for whites. Even if they were unoccupied and the rear seats crowded, Negroes would have to stand at
A the back in case some whites might get aboard; and if the front seats happened to be occupied and more white people boarded the bus, black people seated in the rear were forced to get up and give them their seats. Furthermore—and I don't think Northerners ever realized this—Negroes had to pay their fares at the front of the bus, get off, and walk to the rear door to board again. Sometimes the bus would drive off without them after they had paid
B their fare. This would happen to elderly people or pregnant women, in bad weather or good, and was considered a great joke by the drivers. Frequently the white bus drivers abused their passengers, called them niggers, black cows, or black apes. Imagine what it was like, for example, for a black man to get on a bus with his son and be subjected to such treatment. ◀SR-1

There had been one incident in March 1955 when fifteen-year-old Claudette Colvin refused to give up her seat to a white passenger. The high school girl was handcuffed and carted off to the police station. At that time Martin served on a committee to protest to the city and bus-company officials. The committee was received politely—and nothing was done. ◀SR-2

The fuel that finally made that slow-burning fire blaze up was an almost routine incident. C On December 1, 1955, Mrs. Rosa Parks, a forty-two-year-old seamstress whom my husband aptly described as "a charming person with a radiant personality," boarded a bus to go home after a long day working and shopping. The bus was crowded, and Mrs. Parks found a seat at the beginning of the Negro section. At the next stop more whites got on. The driver ordered Mrs. Parks to give her seat to a white man who boarded; this meant that she would have to stand all the way home. Rosa Parks was not in a revolution- D ary frame of mind. She had not planned to do what she did. Her cup had run over. As she said later, "I was just plain tired, and my feet hurt." So she sat there, refusing to get

Words to Know and Use

degrading (dē grād' iŋ) *adj.* that which lowers dignity **degrade** *v.*

509

Structured Reading for Less Proficient Students

These questions can help to guide students through the reading. Ask each question at the point of the selection where the SR number appears in the margin.

SR–1. Which aspect of segregation in Montgomery does King call "the most degrading"? *(the rules of the Montgomery City Bus Lines)* **Literal recall**

SR–2. According to King, what was the general feeling of city and bus company officials about injustices on the bus lines? *(polite indifference)* **Inferring**

SR–3. Why did the Montgomery bus boycott receive such rapid support from the town's black citizens? *(People's frustrations with segregation had been building up for a long time, and they pounced on the chance to finally take action.)* **Clarifying**

SR–4. How did people in Montgomery find out about the coming boycott? *(The white press published angry articles about it, and black ministers preached about it.)* **Summarizing**

Continued on page 510

Teaching Strategies

Vocabulary Review

These vocabulary words are defined at the bottom of the selection page on which they appear. You may wish to discuss them briefly before students begin reading.

coercion act of forcing someone to do something
coherently showing clear thinking
degrading lowering dignity
irate very angry
serene calm

Support for Students of Limited English Proficiency

- Use **Reader's Guidesheet**, p. 33.
- "Montgomery Boycott" contains references to leaders and organizations in the civil rights movement. African American students may be more familiar with these terms than other students are. Encourage students with this knowledge to share it.
- Annotations A, E, and Q focus on troublesome terms.

Text Annotations

A. LEP: Cultural Terms Students from some cultures may not know the significance of racial terms in the selection. In the 1950's *Negroes* was the socially accepted term for *African Americans,* which is the preferred term today. *Blacks* and *black people* are also accepted terms. *Niggers* was then—and is now—an insulting racial slur.

B. Reading Skill: SUMMARIZING Have students summarize how African Americans were treated on the city bus lines. *(They had to pay in the front, then get off the bus and enter the rear. They could sit only in the rear. They had to give up their seats to whites when asked. They were insulted.)*

C. Literary Element: FIGURATIVE LANGUAGE Ask students to explain the comparison being made here. *(The anger of African Americans at their unjust treatment is compared to a fire that intensifies as a result of what happened to Parks.)*

D. Discussion Have students discuss whether they would have had the courage to do as Parks did.

Historical Sidelight The Brotherhood of Sleeping Car Porters is a union of railroad porters that was founded in 1925. It was one of the first unions to organize African American workers.

E. LEP: Idiom/Figurative Language Explain that the idiom "had had enough" means "could not tolerate any more abuse." Have students compare the metaphor "It was spontaneous combustion" to the figurative language noted in Annotation C on page 509.

F. Literary Element: PRIMARY AND SECONDARY SOURCES Have students determine from this passage whether the historical account they are reading is a primary or secondary source. Have them give evidence for their conclusion. *(It is a primary source. Possible evidence: The use of the words* we *and* my husband *indicate that the writer was a participant in the events she describes.)*

G. Reading Skill: UNDERSTANDING CAUSE AND EFFECT Ask students what caused Mr. Nixon to start talking about a bus boycott. *(in general, a history of unfair treatment of blacks on the buses; in particular, the arrest of Rosa Parks for refusing to give up her seat to a white man)*

H. Critical Thinking: EVALUATING In their journals, have students evaluate Dr. King's views on religion

up. The driver called a policeman, who arrested her and took her to the courthouse. From there Mrs. Parks called E. D. Nixon, who came down and signed a bail bond for her.

Mr. Nixon was a fiery Alabamian. He was a Pullman porter[1] who had been active in A. Philip Randolph's Brotherhood of Sleeping Car Porters and in civil-rights activities. Suddenly he also had had enough; suddenly, it seemed, almost every Negro in Montgomery had had enough. It was spontaneous combustion. Phones began ringing all over the Negro section of the city. The Women's Political Council suggested a one-day boycott of the buses as a protest. E. D. Nixon courageously agreed to organize it.

The first we knew about it was when Mr. Nixon called my husband early in the morning of Friday, December 2. He had already talked to Ralph Abernathy. After describing the incident, Mr. Nixon said, "We have taken this type of thing too long. I feel the time has come to boycott the buses. It's the only way to make the white folks see that we will not take this sort of thing any longer."

Martin agreed with him and offered the Dexter Avenue Church as a meeting place. After much telephoning, a meeting of black ministers and civic leaders was arranged for that evening. Martin said later that as he approached his church Friday evening, he was nervously wondering how many leaders would really turn up. To his delight, Martin found over forty people, representing every segment of Negro life, crowded into the large meeting room at Dexter. There were doctors, lawyers, businessmen, federal-government employees, union leaders, and a great many ministers. The latter were particularly welcome, not only because of their influence, but because it meant that they were beginning to accept Martin's view that "Religion deals with both heaven and earth. . . . Any religion that professes to be concerned with the souls of men and is not concerned with the slums that doom them, the economic conditions that strangle them, and the social conditions that cripple them, is a dry-as-dust religion." From that very first step, the Christian ministry provided the leadership of our struggle, as Christian ideals were its source.

> **"*This is no time to talk; it is time to act.*"**

The meeting opened with brief devotions. Then, because E. D. Nixon was away at work, the Reverend L. Roy Bennett, president of the Interdenominational Ministerial Alliance, was made chairman. After describing what had happened to Mrs. Parks, Reverend Bennett said, "Now is the time to move. This is no time to talk; it is time to act."

Martin told me after he got home that the meeting was almost wrecked because questions or suggestions from the floor were cut off. However, after a stormy session, one thing was clear: however much they differed on details, everyone was unanimously for a boycott. It was set for Monday, December 5. Committees were organized; all the ministers present promised to urge their congregations to take part. Several thousand leaflets were printed on the church mimeograph machine[2] describing the reasons for the boycott and urging all

1. **Pullman porter:** a railroad employee who waits on people in a passenger car with seats that can be converted into beds.

2. **mimeograph machine:** a machine for making copies of written, drawn, or typewritten material.

STRUCTURED READING FOR LESS PROFICIENT STUDENTS

Continued from page 509

SR–5. What conflict did Martin Luther King feel about the planned boycott and why? *(He wondered if it was unchristian because it involved threatening the bus company with bankruptcy, which he saw as a kind of force; Dr. King was opposed to any use of force.)* **Analyzing**

SR–6. Why were the Kings so excited the first morning of the boycott? *(They saw empty buses pass their house, and knew the boycott was working.)* **Clarifying**

SR–7. What do you think the MIA will decide about whether or not to be a secret society, and why? *(Possible responses: Open, because that is in keeping with the spirit of protest; secret, because conditions are dangerous.)* **Predicting**

SR–8. How would you summarize the main principles Dr. King expressed in his speech? *(Possible response: Fight for justice, do no evil to your enemies, act with dignity and love.)* **Summarizing**

Martin Luther King, Jr., in Montgomery, 1956 Dan Weiner Courtesy of Sandra Weiner.

Negroes not to ride buses "to work, to town, to school, or anyplace on Monday, December 5." Everyone was asked to come to a mass meeting at the Holt Street Baptist Church on Monday evening for further instructions. The Reverend A. W. Wilson had offered his church because it was larger than Dexter and more convenient, being in the center of the Negro district.

Saturday was a busy day for Martin and the other members of the commitee. They hustled around town talking with other leaders, arranging with the Negro-owned taxi companies for special bulk fares and with the owners of private automobiles to get the people to and from work. I could do little to help because Yoki was only two weeks old, and my physician, Dr. W. D. Pettus, who was very careful, advised me to stay in for a month. However, I was kept busy answering the telephone, which rang continuously, and coordinating from that central point the many messages and arrangements.

Our greatest concern was how we were going to reach the fifty thousand black people of Montgomery, no matter how hard we worked. The white press, in an outraged exposé,[3] spread the word for us in a way that would have been impossible with only our resources.

As it happened, a white woman found one of our leaflets, which her Negro maid

3. **exposé** (eks′ pō zā′): an account of a wrongdoing that is made known to the public.

I. Reading Skill: INFERRING Ask students how they can tell that housing in Montgomery was segregated. *(The author refers to the "Negro district" of town.)*

J. Critical Thinking: EVALUATING Ask students whether the author played an important part in the boycott. *(Possible responses: Yes, she helped coordinate messages and arrangements from home; or no, her role was limited because she had to stay home with her baby.)*

K. Reading Skill: UNDERSTANDING CAUSE AND EFFECT Ask students to identify the effects of a maid's leaving a leaflet in her employer's kitchen. *(The employer got angry; she phoned the white press; the press spread the word of the protestors' plans; many more protestors joined the boycott after reading about it in the white press.)*

L. Historical Sidelight The NAACP (National Association for the Advancement of Colored People) is an interracial civil rights organization that was founded in 1909, when concerned blacks and whites united in common cause to fight discrimination and segregation.

M. Literary Sidelight Henry David Thoreau (1817–1862) wrote an essay called *Civil Disobedience,* in which he claimed that people were not obligated to obey unjust laws. His ideas inspired the Indian leader Mohandas Gandhi, who in turn inspired King to promote nonviolent resistance (civil disobedience) to fight unjust laws.

N. Reading Skill: CLARIFYING Ask students why it was important to Dr. King to think of his movement as noncooperation, rather than as a boycott. *(He wanted to emphasize that his goal was not to destroy the bus company [as the word boycott might suggest] but to win freedom for his people through nonviolent action [as the word noncooperation might suggest].)*

O. Critical Thinking: ANALYZING Ask students to identify the connection between the empty bus and the boycotters' dreams of winning their rights. *(The empty bus showed that the boycott could be a success, that people were willing to use nonviolent collective action to win their rights.)*

had left in the kitchen. The irate woman immediately telephoned the newspapers to let the white community know what the blacks were up to. We laughed a lot about this, and Martin later said that we owed them a great debt.

On Sunday morning, from their pulpits, almost every Negro minister in town urged people to honor the boycott.

Martin came home late Sunday night and began to read the morning paper. The long articles about the proposed boycott accused the NAACP of planting Mrs. Parks on the bus—she had been a volunteer secretary for the Montgomery chapter—and likened the boycott to the tactics of the White Citizens' Councils.[4] This upset Martin. That awesome conscience of his began to gnaw at him, and he wondered if he were doing the right thing. Alone in his study, he struggled with the question of whether the boycott method was basically unchristian. Certainly it could be used for unethical ends. But, as he said, "We are using it to give birth to freedom . . . and to urge men to comply with the law of the land. Our concern was not to put the bus company out of business, but to put justice in business." He recalled Thoreau's words, "We can no longer lend our cooperation to an evil system," and he thought, "He who accepts evil without protesting against it is really cooperating with it." Later Martin wrote, "From this moment on I conceived of our movement as an act of massive noncooperation. From then on I rarely used the word *boycott.*

Serene after his inner struggle, Martin joined me in our sitting room. We wanted to get to bed early, but Yoki began crying and the telephone kept ringing. Between interruptions we sat together talking about the prospects for the success of the protest. We were both filled with doubt. Attempted boycotts had failed in Montgomery and other cities. Because of changing times and tempers, this one seemed to have a better chance, but it was still a slender hope. We finally decided that if the boycott was 60 percent effective we would be doing all right, and we would be satisfied to have made a good start.

A little after midnight we finally went to bed, but at five-thirty the next morning we were up and dressed again. The first bus was due at 6 o'clock at the bus stop just outside our house. We had coffee and toast in the kitchen; then I went into the living room to watch. Right on time, the bus came, headlights blazing through the December darkness, all lit up inside. I shouted, "Martin! Martin, come quickly!" He ran in and stood beside me, his face lit with excitement. There was not one person on that usually crowded bus!

We stood together waiting for the next bus. It was empty too, and this was the most heavily traveled line in the whole city. Bus after empty bus paused at the stop and moved on. We were so excited we could hardly speak coherently. Finally Martin said, "I'm going to take the car and see what's happening in other places in the city."

He picked up Ralph Abernathy, and they cruised together around the city. Martin

4. **White Citizens' Councils:** groups that originated in Mississippi in 1954 and spread throughout much of the South trying to discourage the supporters of desegregation.

Words to Know and Use	**irate** (ī rāt′) *adj.* very angry; incensed **serene** (sə rēn′) *n.* peaceful; calm **coherently** (kō hir′ ənt lē) *adv.* in a manner showing clear thinking and understandable speech

512

CULTURAL CONNECTION

The selection contains references to several different names for African Americans, some of which are or were considered terms of respect and one of which is considered an insult. Have students write in their journals about the power of names to confer respect or give insult to social groups. What name do they prefer for their own ethnic group? Have they ever been hurt by an ethnic slur used against them? Why do people use such slurs?

told me about it when he got home. Everywhere it was the same. A few white people and maybe one or two blacks in otherwise empty buses. Martin and Ralph saw extraordinary sights—the sidewalks crowded with men and women trudging to work; the students of Alabama State College walking or thumbing rides; taxi cabs with people clustered in them. Some of our people rode mules; others went in horse-drawn buggies. But most of them were walking, some making a round trip of as much as twelve miles. Martin later wrote, "As I watched them I knew that there is nothing more majestic than the determined courage of individuals willing to suffer and sacrifice for their freedom and dignity." P

Martin rushed off again at nine o'clock that morning to attend the trial of Mrs. Parks. She was convicted of disobeying the city's segregation ordinance and fined ten dollars and costs. Her young attorney, Fred D. Gray, filed an appeal. It was one of the first clearcut cases of a Negro being convicted of disobeying the segregation laws—usually the charge was disorderly conduct or some such thing. Q

The leaders of the movement called a meeting for three o'clock in the afternoon to organize the mass meeting to be held that night. Martin was a bit late, and as he entered the hall, people said to him, "Martin, we have elected you to be our president. Will you accept?" R

It seemed that Rufus A. Lewis, a Montgomery businessman, had proposed Martin, and he had been unanimously elected. The people knew, and Martin knew, that the post was dangerous, for it meant being singled out to become the target of the white people's anger and vengeance. Martin said, "I don't mind. Somebody has to do it, and if you think I can, I will serve." S

Then other officers were elected. Rev. L. Roy Bennett became vice-president; Rev. E. N. French, corresponding secretary; Mrs. Erna A. Dungee, financial secretary; and E. D. Nixon, treasurer. After that they discussed what to call the organization. Someone suggested the Negro Citizens' Committee. Martin did not approve, because that sounded like an organization of the same spirit as the White Citizens' Council. Finally, Ralph Abernathy proposed calling the organization the Montgomery Improvement Association, the MIA, and this name was unanimously approved. T

"We'd better decide now if we are going to be fearless men or scared little boys."

Fear was an invisible presence at the meeting, along with courage and hope. Proposals were voiced to make the MIA a sort of secret society, because if no names were mentioned it would be safer for the leaders. E. D. Nixon opposed that idea. "We're acting like little boys," he said. "Somebody's name will be known, and if we're afraid, we might just as well fold up right now. The white folks are eventually going to find out anyway. We'd better decide now if we are going to be fearless men or scared little boys." U ◀SR-7

That settled that question. It was also decided that the protest would continue until certain demands were met. Ralph Abernathy was made chairman of the committee to draw up the demands.

Martin came home at six o'clock. He said

P. Discussion Point out to students that Martin Luther King is famous for his eloquent speeches and writings on the subject of freedom. Have students discuss or write in their journals about why this gift probably helped him become a leader.

Q. LEP: Cultural References Students new to the United States may not be familiar with its court system. Ask volunteers to explain the significance of filing an appeal. *(A convicted person often has the right to have his or her case heard again in a new trial, with the possibility of having the conviction overturned.)*

R. Literary Element: PRIMARY SOURCES Because Mrs. King was a participant in the boycott and married to its leader, she can give us behind-the-scenes details about an important moment in American history, as Dr. King assumes his first position of leadership in the civil rights movement.

S. Critical Thinking: EVALUATING Have students evaluate Dr. King's character, based on his words and actions here. *(Possible response: He was brave, determined, humble.)*

T. Reading Skill: CLARIFYING Ask students why Dr. King did not want the group to have a name similar to the White Citizens' Council *(because that group has a reputation for unfair tactics, and he didn't want people to think his own organization used similar tactics to win civil rights)*

U. Historical Sidelight Students may not realize how much the protestors had to be afraid of. Civil rights demonstrators in the South often faced police brutality. Their churches and homes were bombed, and some organizers were even murdered by angry whites.

REAL LIFE CONNECTIONS

The selection describes the excitement of people working together for a common cause they believed in. Have students share any experiences they have had in working together with other people for a cause.

V. Reading Skill: INFERRING Ask students why Dr. King might be nervous about telling his wife about his new position. *(Possible response: He knew she would be worried about him and feared she might ask him not to take the position because his family needed him.)*

W. Literary Element: INTERNAL CONFLICT Ask students if they think all great leaders have moments of panic and doubt. *(Answers will vary.)*

Rosa Parks on the bus
UPI/Bettmann Newsphotos, New York.

V later that he was nervous about telling me he had accepted the presidency of the protest movement, but he need not have worried, because I sincerely meant what I said when I told him that night, "You know that whatever you do, you have my backing."

Reassured, Martin went to his study. He was to make the main speech at the mass meeting that night. It was now six-thirty, and—this was the way it was usually to be—he had only twenty minutes to prepare what he thought might be the most decisive speech of his life. He said afterward that thinking about the responsibility and the reporters and television cameras, he almost panicked. Five minutes wasted and only fifteen minutes left. At that moment he turned to prayer. He asked God "to restore my balance and be with me in a time when I need Your guidance more than ever." W

PROFESSIONAL NOTEBOOK

. . . the techniques of cooperative learning cannot be mastered by reading about them. They have to be tried, tested, and modified. . . . Both teachers and students may need time to get used to somewhat higher levels of noise in the classroom, to increased student movement, to greater student autonomy, and to less reliance on the teacher as an authority figure and a font of knowledge. Both teachers and students will have to learn to feel at ease with new patterns . . .

The potential benefits of cooperative learning for Native American students are clear. Cooperative learning appears to improve student achievement and it also matches such traditional Indian values and behaviors as respect for the individual, development of an internal locus of control, cooperation, sharing, and harmony.

LEE LITTLE SOLDIER, "COOPERATIVE LEARNING AND THE NATIVE AMERICAN STUDENT," *Phi Delta Kappan*, OCTOBER, 1989

How could he make his speech both militant enough to rouse people to action and yet devoid of hate and resentment? He was determined to do both.

Martin and Ralph went together to the meeting. When they got within four blocks of the Holt Street Baptist Church, there was an enormous traffic jam. Five thousand people stood outside the church listening to loudspeakers and singing hymns. Inside it was so crowded, Martin told me, the people had to lift Ralph and him above the crowd and pass them from hand to hand over their heads to the platform. The crowd and the singing inspired Martin, and God answered his prayer. Later Martin said, "That night I understood what the older preachers meant when they said, 'Open your mouth and God will speak for you.'"

First the people sang "Onward, Christian Soldiers" in a tremendous wave of five thousand voices. This was followed by a prayer and a reading of the Scriptures. Martin was introduced. People applauded; television lights beat upon him. Without any notes at all he began to speak. Once again he told the story of Mrs. Parks, and rehearsed some of the wrongs black people were suffering. Then he said, "But there comes a time when people get tired. We are here this evening to say to those who have mistreated us so long that we are tired, tired of being segregated and humiliated, tired of being kicked about by the brutal feet of oppression."

The audience cheered wildly, and Martin said, "We have no alternative but to protest. We have been amazingly patient . . . but we come here tonight to be saved from the patience that makes us patient with anything less than freedom and justice."

Taking up the challenging newspaper comparison with the White Citizens' Council and the Klan,[5] Martin said, "They are protesting for the perpetuation of injustice in the community; we're protesting for the birth of justice . . . their methods lead to violence and lawlessness. But in our protest there will be no cross burnings; no white person will be taken from his home by a hooded Negro mob and brutally murdered . . . we will be guided by the highest principles of law and order."

Having roused the audience for militant action, Martin now set limits upon it. His study of nonviolence and his love of Christ informed his words. He said, "No one must be intimidated to keep them from riding the buses. Our method must be persuasion, not coercion. We will only say to the people, 'Let your conscience be your guide.' . . . Our actions must be guided by the deepest principles of the Christian faith. . . . Once again we must hear the words of Jesus, 'Love your enemies. Bless them that curse you. Pray for them that despitefully use you.' If we fail to do this, our protest will end up as a meaningless drama on the stage of history, and its memory will be shrouded in the ugly garments of shame. . . . We must not become bitter and end up by hating our white brothers. As Booker T. Washington[6] said, 'Let no man

5. **Klan:** refers to the group patterned after the Ku Klux Klan, founded in Tennessee in 1866, which tries to establish white power and authority by unlawful and violent methods directed against minority groups.

6. **Booker T. Washington:** 1856–1915; the organizer and head of the black normal school that later became Tuskegee Institute. Washington himself was the son of a black slave and a white father.

Words to Know and Use

coercion (kō ʉr′ shən) *n.* the act of forcing someone to do something through the use of power or threats

X. Literary Element: STYLE Ask what details Mrs. King uses to help readers imagine the excitement of the meeting. *(the traffic jam, the five thousand singing people, the fact that her husband had to be lifted over the crowd)*

Y. Critical Thinking: ANALYSIS Have students analyze the pattern of comparison and contrast Dr. King uses in his speech. *(He contrasts point by point the goals and tactics of the White Citizens' Council with the goals and tactics of his own movement.)*

Z. Critical Thinking: EVALUATING Have students evaluate Dr. King's speech to see if it achieved his goal of being "militant enough to rouse people to action and yet devoid of hate." *(Possible responses: Yes, he says he is tired of being kicked, but he also asks his followers to "love their enemies"; no, it was too passive; no, it was too angry.)*

AA. Literary Element: FIGURATIVE LANGUAGE Ask volunteers to explain the musical terms *keynote* and *tempo* and tell how the terms could apply to a speech and a social movement. *(The keynote, the first note of a scale, determines all the other notes; it also describes the guiding principle of a speech or policy. Tempo refers to the speed and rhythm of music; the term could apply to Dr. King's rhythmic speaking style, as well as to the feverish rhythm of change that the boycott started in civil rights.)*

Check Test

1. Why was Rosa Parks arrested on the bus? *(She refused to give up her seat to a white man.)*

2. What did the leaders organize in order to protest the incident with Mrs. Parks? *(a bus boycott)*

3. Who became the leader of the protestors? *(Dr. Martin Luther King, Jr.)*

4. What relationship did the author of the selection have to the protest leader? *(She was his wife.)*

5. How did the first bus the Kings saw on the first day of the protest indicate the success of the boycott? *(No one was on the bus.)*

6. What methods of protest did Dr. King favor over violence and bloodshed? *(persuasion; nonviolence)*

Encouraging Independent Reading

Parting the Waters: America in the King Years, nonfiction by Taylor Branch
Martin Luther King, a biography by Robert E. Jakoubek
"I Have a Dream," a speech by Martin Luther King Jr.
Eyes on the Prize, an oral history by Juan Williams

pull you so low as to make you hate him.'"

Z Finally, Martin said, "If you will protest courageously, and yet with dignity and Christian love, future historians will say, 'There lived a great people—a black people—who injected new meaning and dignity into the veins of civilization.' This is our challenge and our overwhelming responsibility." Z ◀ SR-8

AA As Martin finished speaking, the audience rose cheering in exaltation. And in that speech my husband set the keynote and the tempo of the movement he was to lead from Montgomery onward. ❧

INSIGHT

It Happened in Montgomery

PHIL W. PETRIE

For Rosa Parks

BUS 1941 Jacob Lawrence Terry Dintenfass Gallery, New York.

Then he slammed on the brakes—
Turned around and grumbled.

But she was tired that day.
Weariness was in her bones.
And so the thing she's done yesterday,
And yesteryear,
On her workdays,
Churchdays,
Nothing-to-do-guess-I'll-go-and-visit
  Sister Annie Days—

She felt she'd never do again.

And he growled once more.
So she said:
No sir . . . I'm stayin' right here.

And he gruffly grabbed her,
Pulled and pushed her—
Then sharply shoved her through the
  doors.

The news slushed through the littered
  streets—
Slipped into the crowded churches,
Slimmered onto the unmagnolied side
  of town
While the men talked and talked and
  talked.

She—
Who was tired that day,
Cried and sobbed that she was glad
  she'd done it,
That her soul was satisfied.

That Lord knows,
A little walkin' never hurt anybody;

That in one of those unplanned,
  unexpected,
Unadorned moments—
A weary woman turned the page of
  History.

Insight

This piece reflects on the ideas in the main selection and is suggested for students' independent reading. Optional discussion questions follow.

1. What thing has Rosa Parks been doing all her life, but will never do again? *(gotten up from her seat on the bus to give it to a white person)*

2. What reason does the poem give for Parks's action? *(weariness)*

3. How does the characterization of Parks in the poem compare with the portrayal of her in "Montgomery Boycott"? *(The portraits are similar, describing her as weary, brave, and determined.)*

e x p l a i n

Responding to Reading

First Impressions

1. What were your thoughts as you finished "Montgomery Boycott"?

Second Thoughts

2. How would you describe Martin Luther King, Jr.?

   Think about
   - what you knew already about him
   - his dreams of freedom for African Americans
   - his doubts about himself and his actions
   - how the boycott changes his life

3. How do the words *spontaneous combustion* describe the events leading up to the boycott?

   Think about
   - what the words *spontaneous combustion* mean
   - how Mr. E. D. Nixon and others respond to Rosa Parks's arrest

4. What do you think of Rosa Parks and her accomplishments?

   Think about
   - what kind of person she is
   - what she does on the bus and why
   - whether she really "turned the page of history" as Petrie's poem says

Broader Connections

5. A boycott is one tactic that a group or individual can use to apply economic pressure in order to change a law, a policy, a way of producing goods, or a way of doing business. Can you think of any boycotts that are occurring today? What is their purpose and how effective do you think they are?

Literary Concept: Primary and Secondary Sources

When an account of an event is written by someone who experienced the event firsthand, that account is said to be a **primary source.** In contrast, when an account is written by someone who did not experience the event firsthand but learned about it through conversation or some form of research, that account is said to be a **secondary source.** Is "Montgomery Boycott" a primary or a secondary source of information? Explain.

Concept Review: Internal and External Conflict What internal and external conflicts does Martin Luther King, Jr., experience during the Montgomery boycott?

Literary Concept—Primary and Secondary Sources

"Montgomery Boycott" is a primary source; it is written by someone who experienced the boycott firsthand. Parts of the selection however were from secondary sources as evidenced by Mrs. King's statements, "Martin told me . . . ."

Concept Review: Internal and External Conflict Martin Luther King, Jr. experiences external conflict with the discriminatory attitudes and threats of white society; he experiences internal conflict as he struggles to accept a boycott as a form of nonviolent noncooperation and as he struggles to write a speech that will inspire people to nonviolent action.

Student Response

Responding to Reading

These questions are open-ended with no "right" or "wrong" answers. However, responses must be supported with information from the selection. Possible answers follow:

1. Accept any answer. All first impressions are valid.

2. Students' previous knowledge of Dr. King may have been minimal, but encourage knowledgeable students to share their information. Students may say that King was courageous, religious, and compassionate. Some students may mention that he was also a man of great integrity, conviction, and vision, a good organizer, a great speech-maker, a natural leader, and a peacemaker.

3. Make sure students understand that *spontaneous combustion* refers to a fire that suddenly ignites without anyone lighting it, as a result of the accumulation of combustible materials in a certain environment. The events in the selection were like spontaneous combustion because the African Americans of Montgomery, who had suffered years of abuse and discrimination, suddenly "ignited" into a fire of angry resistance without needing anyone to "fire them up."

4. Students may say that Rosa Parks was not a revolutionary leader who acted to defend a principle; she was an ordinary working person who was tired of being abused. Others may say that she was also a person of great courage, who was willing to take an action that involved great personal risk and hardship. She "turned the page of history" because her action set in motion a chain of events that got the civil rights movement going and launched the careers of two of its greatest leaders, Martin Luther King, Jr., and Ralph Abernathy.

5. Encourage students to read newspapers and news magazines, to watch television newscasts, and to talk to family members to find information about current boycotts. Promote a discussion of the issues involved in each boycott.

Writing Options

The Writing Options are designed to meet varied student interests and abilities. Have each student choose one writing activity to complete. You may wish to guide some students to an option that requires less writing.

Journal Update Have students review their journal entries of "Montgomery Boycott." Have them consider whether their views of civil disobedience have changed as a result of reading the selection. Would they be willing to take actions as bold as those of Rosa Parks and Martin Luther King, Jr. to stand up for something they believe in?

Vocabulary Practice

1. coercion
2. irate
3. coherently
4. serene
5. degrading

Writing Options

1. Write two newspaper reports of the Montgomery boycott that might have appeared the day after its occurrence. Write one from the perspective of a black-owned newspaper and the second from the perspective of a white-owned paper. Keep a professional tone in each report.

2. Through her courage, Rosa Parks helps make her "dreams of freedom" a reality. What other character have you read about in this book who has the courage of Rosa Parks? Explain why you think this character is similar.

3. Create several protest signs for demonstrators to carry on the day of the boycott. Some of these should be written for those blacks who need to know what the boycott is all about. Other signs should be designed to educate whites. Use catchy phrases to carry your message.

4. Look again at Phil Petrie's poem about Rosa Parks. Using a similar style, create your own poem about Martin Luther King, Jr.

Vocabulary Practice

Exercise Write the word from the list that best completes the meaning of the sentence.

1. For years those in power used ____ to keep blacks afraid and to deprive them of political power.
2. Some blacks were ____ after Rosa Parks's arrest and wanted to react violently.
3. Martin Luther King, Jr., explained his boycott plan so ____ that few people had doubts about what he planned to accomplish.
4. The peaceful and ____ lives of many townspeople were disrupted by the furor over Rosa Parks's arrest.
5. The humiliating and ____ rules of the Montgomery City Bus Lines were, in fact, instituted by a Northern-owned corporation.

Words to Know and Use

coercion
coherently
degrading
irate
serene

e x t e n d

Options for Learning

1 • Moments in History Research news stories and magazine articles that reported the Montgomery boycott. Make photocopies of the headlines, stories, and pictures that depict this important moment in civil rights history. Then design a "Moment in History" display or bulletin board that captures the facts and the emotional impact of this event.

2 • "I Have a Dream" At your school or local library, find and listen to recordings of several speeches by Martin Luther King, Jr. Play your favorite for the class. Explain when and where he made the speech and why this speech is significant to you.

3 • It's About Time Draw a time line of the civil rights movement beginning with the Montgomery boycott. Along the base of your time line, briefly describe the important events and the people that made them happen.

FACT FINDER

What is the origin of the word boycott*?*

Coretta Scott King

1927–

As a child in Heiberger, Alabama, Coretta Scott had to walk five miles a day to a one-room schoolhouse while white children rode past her on a school bus. Such experiences made Coretta Scott determined to make something of herself and be treated as an equal in society. A good student, she followed in her sister's footsteps by attending Antioch College in Ohio. After graduating from Antioch, she moved to Boston to study music and eventually met Martin Luther King, Jr. They were married in 1953, two years before the Montgomery boycott.

King has shown great determination and courage in her fight for civil rights. In 1956 her home was bombed, and in 1968 her husband was assassinated in Memphis, Tennessee. The day before his funeral, she led a march of striking Memphis garbage workers. The next year she began to write *My Life with Martin Luther King, Jr.*, the book from which "Montgomery Boycott" is taken. Currently, she is the president and chief executive officer of the Martin Luther King, Jr., Center for Nonviolent Social Change. Coretta Scott King was once quoted as saying, "It's interesting how a movement is somehow triggered at a certain moment in history." Perhaps she was thinking of Rosa Parks and Montgomery, Alabama.

Options for Learning

These activities suit a variety of learning styles and modes of expression. Allow students to review the options and then choose the one they wish to do. Many are excellent collaborative learning projects.

1. Moments in History Back issues of *Ebony, Time, Newsweek, Life,* and *Look* magazines from the 1950's and 1960's, as well as Time-Life photo books on the period, may be good sources of photos and articles on the civil rights movement.

2. "I Have a Dream" Students may find excerpts from key King speeches in films or videotapes on the civil rights movement, including the PBS series *Eyes on the Prize,* which chronicles the movement.

3. It's About Time Students may use the *Eyes on the Prize* series, the book based on it, other library books, or encyclopedia articles as sources of important events and dates in the civil rights movement.

Fact Finder

The word *boycott* comes from Charles C. Boycott, a rent collector in Ireland in the 1880's. When rents in his area became too high, tenants ostracized Boycott, refusing to talk to him or sell him goods. Students may find this information in a dictonary, an encyclopedia, or a book on word origins.

Additional Information About the Author

Coretta Scott King Coretta Scott King is an optimistic person known for her great composure in times of crisis. "It seems that when there's a crisis, I call upon all my energy, my resources," she once remarked. "There is no problem that we can't solve if we can corral our resources." Ask students if they share King's sense of optimism and determination.

Closure

In "Montgomery Boycott," African Americans of Montgomery, Alabama, face the pain of segregation with proud demands for their human rights. Ask students which person in the excerpt they admire most, and why.

Cross-Curricular Options

History: Have students research other nonviolent techniques used by Dr. King and his followers in the civil rights movement. Have them debate the effectiveness of such techhniques in bringing about social change.

Social Studies: Have students research the Civil Rights Acts of the 1960's and find out how they are enforced. Have them role-play the opposing lawyers in an actual civil rights case.

Math: Have students prepare graphs showing the increase in registered African American voters in the North and in the South from 1950 to the present.

Music: Have students set the Insight poem "It Happened in Montgomery" to music and perform it in a school assembly.

Objectives

- To understand a work of nonfiction
- To recognize an oral history
- To express understanding of the work through a choice of writing options, including a comparison and a letter

Prereading/Motivation

Examine What You Know

Discussion Prompts: How did you feel when you were falsely accused? Were you able to communicate these feelings to your accuser? Why do you think that you were falsely accused? How do you feel about the outcome now?

Expand Your Knowledge

Discussion Prompts: What does the phrase *the American dream* mean to you? How might you make this dream come true? A difficult childhood causes some people to strive hard for success in later life. Other people seem unable to overcome their early unhappiness. Why do you think this might be true?

Additional Background. Remind students that few job opportunities were open to African-Americans for much of this century. Laws in the South and local traditions and prejudices in the North closed entry-level jobs to blacks in both private industry and government. To survive, African-Americans were often forced to take low-paying jobs, such as laborers or domestic workers. Black women often had no choice but to work for white families as maids, cooks, housecleaners, or babysitters.

Thematic Link—Grace Under Pressure
In this selection, the main character gracefully maintains her dignity under the pressure of being falsely accused of stealing.

e x p l o r e

Oral History *Day Work*

JAMES P. COMER

Examine What You Know (Prior Knowledge)

In the next selection the author's mother tells about a time when she was falsely accused. Can you recall such a time in your own life? On a chart like the one below, jot down a few notes about this memory. Compare your experience to the experience of the author's mother.

The Accusation	My Accuser	My Reaction	The Outcome

Expand Your Knowledge (Building Background)

This selection is taken from the book *Maggie's American Dream: The Life and Times of a Black Family*. In the book the author, James Comer, tells about the hard work and perseverance demonstrated by members of his family, especially his mother, Maggie Comer, who grew up in the rural South. Her father died when she was young, and her mother remarried and moved the family to Memphis to live with their new stepfather. Maggie's stepfather turned out to be a cruel man who beat both his wife and children. Maggie's older brothers left home at sixteen—the age at which they could legally leave. When Maggie turned sixteen, she too left home. She headed north for Chicago, where she met Hugh Comer—"as near perfect a man as there can be." Maggie later married Hugh, and they devoted their lives to raising and educating five children, who eventually earned a total of thirteen university degrees.

Write Before You Read (Journal Writing)

Think about someone in your life of whom you feel proud. It might be a parent, grandparent, sibling, or friend. In your journal or on a piece of paper, describe a moment or an incident in which you felt especially proud of this person.

■ *A biography of the author can be found in the Reader's Handbook.*

Additional Journal Writing

Suggest these additional journal topics to students:

- Predict what "day work" might be. What might such work reveal about a character?
- Discuss an incident in which you felt that you were being treated unfairly by an employer.
- Describe your reaction to a situation in which you faced discrimination. How would you react now?

For other journal opportunities, refer students to Examine What You Know (p. 520), Broader Connections (p. 526), and Cultural Connection (p. T–524).

Additional Resources

UNIT FOUR RESOURCE BOOK
Reader's Guidesheet, p. 38
Vocabulary Worksheet, p. 39
Selection Check Test, p. 40
Selection Test, pp. 41–42

Collaborative Learning

Opportunities for collaborative learning appear throughout the lesson and include Cultural Connection (p. T–524).

Day Work

JAMES P. COMER

A In those days they called it "day work." You work maybe today or two days, sometimes three for one person. At one time I was working for three to four persons a week. That was cleaning their whole house. I worked for Dr. and Mrs. McDonald maybe on a Monday. Maybe on Tuesdays I would go to Dr. Matthews's. I would go to the Van Horns' and do a day's work. The Van Horns' was a house with
SR-1 ▶ three lawyers.

B I patterned my life after things that I learned. So many people would just work and pay no attention to what's going on. I didn't just cook and clean. I worked with my eyes and ears open. I watched and listened to them and the way they lived. For me it was like going to school. I have no complaint about most because they were very beautiful people, willing to help and teach you along. I would ask them about this thing or that thing I would see them do.

C Little helpful hints they had, they would pass it on to me. As they shopped they would say, "Maggie, do you ever do this or that? We do it this way." Those women would also tell you how to know that you were getting a good deal and what sort of stores to go to. At the lawyers' house they would discuss the business right over the breakfast table. That's where they did the most talk together. After they would leave—she was a beautiful woman too—she would sit down and have coffee with me and talk. "Well, Maggie if you ever get into a lawsuit or problem of any kind, handle it this way." Their main thing was you should never try to handle a case by yourself. Always see a lawyer.

I learned the cuts of meat at the Brisseys' house. I worked for her when I was seventeen years old. She had this cookbook, which I had never see before. It showed the pictures of the different cuts of meat—rump roast center cut and chops and calf's liver and so on. So when I was shopping for myself, I would go to the store and ask for that cut of meat. They were always surprised because, as a rule, our people would go in and say, I want a dollar's worth of pork chops, or a dollar's worth of this or that. They could get the best cut for the same money, but they didn't know any better.

I learned the advantage of buying good clothing. You might pay a few cents more, but it paid off in the end because it lasted and always looked good. I noticed people that bought from the cheaper stores, and my children's clothes outwore them two to one. I remember the shoes that I bought for my children. My children's feet never looked bad. I wanted that because I knew what happened to mine as a child, and I didn't want it to happen to my children. You only needed one pair a season. I know some of my neighbors would buy shoes two or three to every one pair my children had, and their feet never looked as good. ◀ SR-2

Teaching Strategies

Support for Students of Limited English Proficiency

- Use **Reader's Guidesheet** p. 38
- As oral history, "Day Work" is written in an informal, conversational style. To help LEP students appreciate the tone, ask volunteers to read the story aloud, pretending to be Maggie Comer relating her experiences to her son.
- A number of expressions used in the selection may be unfamiliar to LEP students. Review the expressions below and their meanings:

1. My children's clothes outwore theirs two to one. (twice as long) (p. 521)

2. She spelled down those nineteen whites. (outspelled) (p. 522)

3. I don't eat after other people (eat from other people's plates) (p. 523)

4. Maggie wouldn't have anything you have in this house. (want) (p. 523)

- For additional LEP support, refer to **Annotations K** and **N.**

Text Annotations

A. Literary Element: AUTHOR'S PURPOSE Point out that the author is telling his mother's story using the mother's own words. Ask students to suggest the author's purpose. *(Possible response: to inform readers of what life was like for his mother and other African-American women early in this century)*

B. Reading Skill: INFERRING Ask students to supply adjectives that describe Dr. Comer's mother. *(Possible response: She is intelligent, alert, and eager to learn.)*

C. Literary Element: ORAL HISTORY Point out that the selection has a conversational tone. Ask students to point out examples of informal phrases and sentence structures. Suggest that the author may have tape-recorded his mother's reminiscenses.

Structured Reading for Less Proficient Students

These questions can help to guide students through the reading. Ask each question at the point of the selection where the SR number appears in the margin.

SR–1. What is day work? *(Day work was a term for part-time paid housework. Day workers worked for an employer by the day, not full time.)* **Literal recall**

SR–2. Why was day work like "going to school" for Maggie Comer? *(She learned a great deal about how to shop and manage a household wisely.)* **Clarifying**

SR–3. What was the real reason for Mrs. Tucker accusing Maggie of stealing coffee? *(Mrs. Tucker was so surprised to learn that Maggie owned property that she assumed Maggie must have stolen things in order to afford it.)* **Clarifying**

SR–4. Why did Maggie leave her job at the Tuckers'? *(She didn't want to work for someone who didn't trust her.)* **Clarifying**

D. Reading Skill: UNDERSTANDING ORGANIZATION Point out that this brief paragraph represents a transition in the selection. Explain that up to the point Comer has listed positive aspects of her day work. Ask students what they can expect in the upcoming paragraphs. *(Possible response: She will tell about problems she encountered and negative aspects of the work.)*

E. Reading Strategies: DRAWING CONCLUSIONS Ask students who they think Louise is. *(She is probably Maggie's daughter and the author's sister.)* Also ask them what they think a "posture contest" might be. *(It might have been a little like a beauty contest in which contestants were judged on posture and overall grace of movement.)*

F. Critical Thinking: ANALYZING Ask students why this information about the spelling contest is set off in parentheses. *(Possible response: Maggie Comer has gone off on a tangent here. The author wants us to know that this information doesn't help develop the main idea of the passage. It is only related in that it tells about another contest Louise won; it could be left out without changing the meaning.)*

(left) Maggie and her husband (below) The author's birthplace Penguin, U.S.A.

D I learned a great deal from some of the people I worked for. But—well, there were problems.

In the tenth grade Louise won the posture contest of about one hundred girls. She was the only one black. They had all white judges. They didn't use any blacks because there wasn't any blacks in the school system at the time. I told you how E tiny and cute she was. She wore cuban-heel shoes, and I dressed her up for the part.

(Louise got another award like that way back when she was a little girl—in a spelling contest like the one they have today over the country. They spelled down to twenty F girls in the finals. She was the only black, nineteen whites. She spelled those nineteen whites down and won.)

That night after the posture contest, I was catering[1] a party for this lady. It had been in

1. **catering:** providing food, supplies, and service for.

PROFESSIONAL NOTEBOOK

American education is structured to serve children who have had the average family experience or better. Teachers are not trained to work with children who have not had such an experience. . . . As a result, when children present themselves to the school with behavior that is useful to them on the playground or in a housing project but gets them in trouble in school, they are often viewed as bad rather than underdeveloped. . . . Without training, the [teacher's] response is to punish the bad behavior rather than close the developmental gap.

JAMES P. COMER, *Maggie's American Dream*

the paper who won the contest, and some of her guests had seen it. I went in to take something to the table, and one of the G guests said to this other woman, "Did you see a little nigger girl won the posture contest?" Those women turned all colors. I heard the woman I was working for whispering, "Shh, that's her mother; that was Maggie's daughter."

H I didn't say anything. I just acted like I didn't hear. But when I went back to the table everybody was quiet. They were looking at me. It really put a damper on[2] the party. And I was sorry for that because this lady I was working for, Mrs. Forsberg, and I called ourselves very good friends. Before that incident it was, "Maggie, bring this or that." After that she didn't have me come in to the table much more.

I I worked for another family, the Friedmans. They were very nice, but they worked you awfully hard. I would eat at noon like for ten minutes.

One day I was working, and I happened to see her getting my lunch ready after her son had had his. He left part of his soup, and she poured some more soup in there and called me in to lunch. I didn't eat the soup. Her daughter came in—she worked at the store, and they took different lunch periods. She saw I didn't eat the soup, and she wanted to know why. I told her that her mother just poured in some of Myron's soup and I don't eat after other people. Of course, that upset the whole family. They were very angry with their mother. Many, many years after that they were still trying to apologize to me.

One time my husband's two sisters and mother came to visit us, and I wanted to take off for the couple of weeks they were going to be visiting. So I sent a friend of mine to work in my place.

This lady I worked for said to this friend,

Maggie's passport photo, 1970 Penguin, U.S.A.

"I hope you're going to be like Maggie. She doesn't take anything. She doesn't take my sheets and doesn't take this."

J This friend, knowing what I had, said, "Maggie wouldn't have anything you have in this house. She has a new piano, and she just furnished a house with new furniture."

When I went back, this woman was spouting tears. She said, "I think I insulted your friend."

I asked her how.

"I told her that you didn't take anything, and she said you wouldn't have anything that I have here."

"I wouldn't. I'm sorry that you thought that of her."

"You got a piano?"

"Yes."

K She went on, you have this, you have that? After that she got so tight I quit working for her.

The same kind of thing happened when I

2. **put a damper on:** ruined the mood of.

G. Critical Thinking: EVALUATING Ask students what the guest's use of the phrase *nigger girl* suggests about her. *(She was prejudiced and insensitive; she was annoyed that an African-American had won the contest.)* Have students explain how they know that the guests knew they should not use this term. *(They all appeared embarrassed when Maggie overheard.)*

H. Literary Element: THEME Maggie pretends not to hear the offensive remark about her daughter. Ask students how this demonstrates "grace under pressure." *(Possible response: Maggie endures gracefully the pressure of hearing her child referred to as "a little nigger girl" by refraining from speaking up so as not to make a scene that would embarrass her employer.)*

I. Literary Sidelight The structure of this selection is anecdotal. That is, Maggie recalls one colorful true story after another about her experiences as a day worker.

J. Literary Element: IRONY Ask a volunteer to explain the irony of this situation. *(Possible response: One would expect a housecleaner or maid to be financially less well off than his or her employer. Yet, in reality, the hardworking Maggie is better off than her employer and owns newer and finer possessions.)*

K. LEP: Vocabulary Discuss the meaning of the phrase *she got so tight. (She became much more careful about spending money.)* Ask students why the employer suddenly got so tight. *(She was jealous that Maggie was better off than she; she decided that she had been paying Maggie too much.)*

DATA BANK

As a child, Maggie rarely went to school. At age sixteen, in Chicago, she was placed in a class of eight-year-olds so that she could learn to read and write.

Dr. James P. Comer, Maggie's son, graduated from Howard University and Indiana University Medical School. Today he is a child psychiatrist and dean at the Yale School of Medicine. He has written a number of books, including *Beyond Black and White* and *School Power*. He is a leading proponent of parent involvement in schools and writes a regular column in *Parents* magazine.

L. Literary Sidelight Maggie's employers have a stereotyped view of their black dayworkers. They assume, for example, that dayworkers will not own their own homes or have nice furniture. Point out that Maggie feels she must play along with the stereotype to some extent. She knows that running counter to the social norms might jeopardize her job.

M. Literary Element: THEME Ask students to discuss how Maggie acts with grace under pressure here. *(Possible responses: She isn't flustered by her employer's accusations; her resignation and the way she offers to pay for any missing items is a graceful way to show how offended she is by the accusation.)*

N. LEP: Language Read the sentence "She really got on Mrs. Tucker" and elicit that *got on* is slang for "criticize." Ask students to suggest any other slang expressions with which they are familiar.

worked for another woman, Mrs. Tucker, the beautician. Her husband had to be in a wheelchair all the time. He would be taken every morning to his shoe store, and she would do hair. She and I just got along beautiful. We'd have coffee every morning, and then I'd do up the house. She'd send me to the bank to take her evening's money and never missed a penny. Finally the banker's wife, someone I had worked for, came to get her hair done.

L I was there cleaning and she said, just making conversation, "Oh Maggie, did you get your taxes paid? My husband told me you were in the bank the other day."

I said, "Yes," kind of quiet. Because working like that I wasn't expected to own property.

The next morning I went and Mrs. Tucker was all sullen. Finally she said, "Maggie, this coffee can is very low. I thought you just opened it yesterday."

"I did."

"It looks like maybe a half cup of coffee was taken out of the can."

"The can comes like that when it sits on the shelf so long and has been handled about. They're not full. The weight is there but the can is not full."

She knew that. But this was because she was wondering how I could afford property. She seemed to think that I had taken coffee. I had to tell her that we didn't drink coffee at home—my husband never drinks coffee, and I only drink it when I am out with someone else. ◀ SR-

The next payday I told her, "Mrs. Tucker, I won't be back."

She got awfully nervous then. "What's wrong?"

"It seems that you're accusing me of taking coffee. The fact that you would think that I would take coffee, you might think that I would take something else. So you look good to see if you miss anything before I go. If you do, I want to pay you for it." M ◀ SR-

By this time I really didn't need to work. We had saved money from the beginning of our marriage, built two homes, and had this little store. And your dad worked throughout the depression, and I had worked right along from right after Louise came.

She said, "Oh no, nothing like that!"

She tried to talk me into staying but she couldn't. When I left, she said, "Don't tell Mrs. Jackson, or any of those people that I know, what I said about the coffee."

"Oh yes, I'll tell them. Mrs. Jackson got me to work for you."

Mrs. Jackson felt so bad when I told her. She really got on Mrs. Tucker, "Maggie works for us, takes care of our silver, takes care of the dishes, never breaks dishes . . . !" Oh, they felt terrible. I never met Mrs. Tucker again, but I understand that she felt awfully bad about it. N

CULTURAL CONNECTION

Discuss the following observation by Maggie Comer:

"Even as a little barefoot girl in the country, I had this dream. I had this gift from inside to want something. I thought to myself that if this one could do it and that one could do it, I could do it. And when I couldn't go on, I said my children would do it. People would say black folks can't do this and can't do that—I wouldn't have any of it. . . . I just wanted a chance. . . ."

INSIGHT

1910

PAT MORA

In Mexico they bowed
their heads when she passed.
Timid villagers stepped aside
for the Judge's mother, Doña Luz,

who wore her black shawl, black
gloves whenever she left her home—
at the church, the *mercado,* and the *plaza*
in the cool evenings when she strolled
barely touching her son's wrist
with her fingertips.

who wore her black shawl, black
gloves in the carriage that took her
and her family to Juarez, border town, away
from Villa laughing at their terror when
he rode through the village shouting,
spitting dust.

who wore her black shawl, black
gloves when she crossed the Rio Grande to
El Paso, her back straight, chin high,
never watching her feet,

who wore her black shawl, black
gloves into Upton's Five-and-Dime,

who walked out, back straight, lips quivering,
and slowly removed her shawl and gloves,
placed them on the sidewalk with the other
shawls and shopping bags
"You Mexicans can't hide
things from me," Upton would say.
"Thieves. All thieves.
Let me see those hands."

who wore her black shawl, black
gloves the day she walked, chin high,
never watching her feet, on the black

beams and boards, still smoking,
that had been Upton's Five-and-Dime.

Check Test

1. What was day work? *(working as a cook or housecleaner by the day, not full time)*

2. What sorts of things did Maggie enjoy learning as a dayworker? *(She liked to learn helpful hints about running a household and shopping wisely.)*

3. How does Maggie react when she hears her daughter called a "nigger girl" by a guest of her employer? *(She pretends not to have heard it; she ignores it.)*

4. What did Mrs. Tucker accuse Maggie of doing? *(She accused her of stealing coffee.)*

Encouraging Independent Reading

"Oh, Madam . . . ," a short story by Elizabeth Bowen

"The Pocketbook Game," a short story by Alice Childress

Working: People Talk About What They Do All Day and How They Feel About What They Do, nonfiction by Studs Terkel

American Mosaic: An Oral History of Immigration, nonfiction by Joan Morrison and Charlotte Fox Zabusky

Insight

This piece reflects on the ideas in the main selection and is suggested for students' independent reading. Optional discussion questions follow.

1. Have students tell how they know that Doña Luz is highly respected in her Mexican village. *(People bow and step aside when she passes. She is the mother of a judge.)*

2. Ask students to identify the unfair experiences that both Doña Luz and Maggie Comer experience. *(Like Maggie Comer, Doña Luz is unfairly accused of theft. In both cases, the accusation was prompted by racial prejudice.)*

3. Have students discuss the ending of the poem and tell why they think Upton's store burned down. *(Possible response: Perhaps people were so angry that Upton had called Doña Luz a thief that they burned down his store.)*

Student Response

Responding to Reading

These questions are open-ended with no "right" or "wrong" answers. However, responses must be supported with information from the selection. Possible answers follow:

1. Any response is valid. Various words, including *determined, self-confident,* and *success-oriented,* may describe Maggie Comer.

2. Students may say that Maggie views life as an ongoing learning experience; that her philosophy emphasizes self-advancement and providing opportunities for her children; that getting along well with others is part of life.

3. Students should point to various day-work situations in which Maggie responds to insults. Some students might refer to the way Maggie pretends not to have heard a racial slur about her daughter, gracefully defusing a tense situation. Others will point to how she resigns her job at the Tuckers' after being unfairly accused of theft.

4. Some students may suggest that Maggie acted more gracefully than they did, in that she refused to engage in arguments, name-calling, or recriminations. Others might say that they stood up for themselves more forcefully than Maggie did.

5. Some students might suggest that in "After You, My Dear Alphonse" the woman made incorrect assumptions about a black family having few possessions and being poor and needy, just as Mrs. Tucker assumed Maggie would not be a home owner. Students may notice that, in both works, prejudiced people show their inability to accept black people as their equals. In "After You, My Dear Alphonse," however, unlike in "Day Work," a white boy and a black boy show their blindness to prejudice. Other students may point out that in "Montgomery Boycott," as in "Day Work," black people are treated as inferior. However, "Day Work" deals with prejudiced employers, while "Montgomery Boycott" deals with prejudiced laws which treated black people who stood up for their rights as criminals. In both works, black people acted against prejudice with grace and skill.

6. Although the qualities mentioned as being shared will vary, they should all be of a positive nature, worthy of evoking a feeling of pride.

Responding to Reading

First Impressions

1. What single word would you use to describe Maggie? Before you answer, think about her actions and what she values.

Second Thoughts

2. How would you describe Maggie's philosophy of life?

   Think about
   - what she says about learning
   - her attitudes about work and her employers
   - how she responds to problems

3. How does Maggie demonstrate grace under pressure?

4. Think again about how you reacted when you were falsely accused. How would you compare your reaction to Maggie's?

5. If you have read either "After You, My Dear Alphonse" or "Montgomery Boycott," compare and contrast the prejudice portrayed in either of these stories with the prejudice presented in "Day Work."

Broader Connections

6. Think again about the person you named as someone of whom you are proud. What qualities do this person and Maggie Comer share?

Literary Concept: Oral History

Oral history is stories about real events passed by word of mouth from one generation to the next. In this part of his book, James Comer uses the words of his mother to tell her story. What questions do you think he asked his mother that prompted her to tell about the events in "Day Work"? What other questions would you like to ask Maggie Comer?

Writing Options

1. Compare Maggie with Doña Luz in the poem "1910," on page 525. How have they both been misjudged? For what reason have they been misjudged? How has each reacted?

2. Imagine that you are Mrs. Tucker. After rethinking your actions, you write Maggie a letter of apology. In it explain why you misjudged her.

Literary Concept—Oral History

Students may suggest that Comer asked his mother questions such as these: What did you like about day work? Did you learn any valuable lessons doing day work? Did you have problems with your employees? Did you experience racial discrimination? Questions that students would like to ask will vary.

Writing Options

The Writing Options are designed to meet varied student interests and abilities. Have each student choose one writing activity to complete. You may wish to guide some students to an option that requires less writing.

Journal Update Have students revise their journal entries. What new things can they add about grace and prejudice?

Closure

In this selection, Maggie Comer shows grace in the face of prejudice, racial slurs, and a false accusation of theft. Ask students if grace is the best weapon against such obstacles or what alternative responses they might suggest.

e x p l o r e

Short Story

Chee's Daughter

JUANITA PLATERO and SIYOWIN MILLER

Examine What You Know (Prior Knowledge)

In this selection two families want custody of the same child. Child custody cases are often settled when one parent or family is judged a better care provider than another. What personal qualities do you think are most needed to raise a healthy child? List them. Then compare your list to the qualities of the two families in this story.

Expand Your Knowledge (Building Background)

Chee, the main character in this story, is a member of the Navaho Indian tribe, the largest Indian tribe in the United States. The Navaho settled in the southwestern part of the United States around 1000 A.D. Like many Native Americans, they saw the land as a source of both physical and spiritual support. In the 1800's, the Navaho fought to keep their lands from white settlers. The U.S. Army, however, destroyed the Navaho farms and marched 8,000 Navaho three hundred miles to a government camp. More than 2,000 Navaho died on the march, which has been called the Long Walk. Today about 95,000 Navaho live on a reservation that covers sixteen million acres in Arizona, New Mexico, and Utah.

Enrich Your Reading (Reading Skill)

Compare/Contrast The type of diagram below, called a Venn diagram, was developed to show likenesses and differences between two subjects. Copy the diagram on your paper. Then, as you read this selection, note on the diagram the similarities and differences between Chee and Old Man Fat.

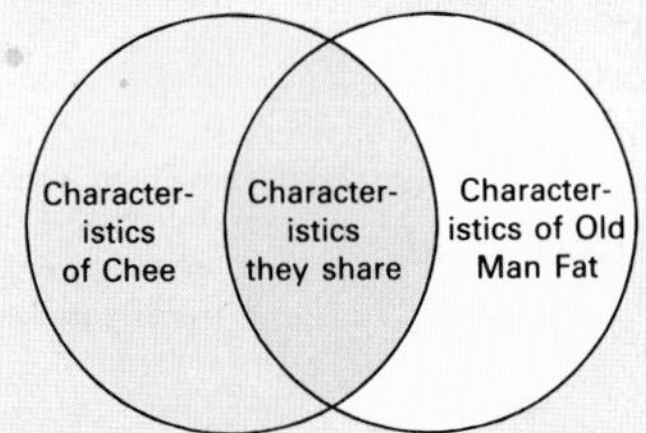

■ *Biographies of the authors can be found in the Reader's Handbook.*

Objectives

- To understand a short story
- To understand denotations and connotations
- To compare and contrast
- To express understanding of the work through a choice of writing options, including a lullaby, a proverb, a plan of action, and a Venn diagram.

Prereading/Motivation

Examine What You Know

Discussion Prompts: If you were a judge, on what basis would you decide a question of child custody? What issues were involved in child custody cases you know about?

Expand Your Knowledge

Discussion Prompts: What do you know about the land and climate of the southwestern United States? How might this region have affected Navaho life? Describe what you think life is like on a reservation.

Additional Background: About 1,000 years ago, the Navaho people migrated to the Southwest from what is now Alaska and Canada. Their Pueblo neighbors taught them to farm. In the 1600's, the Navaho began to raise sheep. Today the mining of vast coal deposits on the Navaho reservation is the tribe's major source of income.

Enrich Your Reading

Possible answers are these:

Chee:

- respects Navaho customs
- farmer
- hardworking and successful
- loves Little One

Old Man Fat:

- prefers white men's customs
- trader and entrepreneur
- lazy
- loves Little One

Characteristics they share:

- both love Little One

Thematic Link—Grace Under Pressure

The main character shows grace as he grieves for his wife and copes with the pressure of being separated from his daughter.

Journal Writing

- Freewrite about all the things that you associate with being someone's daughter or someone's son.
- Describe a situation in which you returned home to find a family member weeping. How did you feel?

For other journal opportunities, refer students to Examine What You Know (p. 527), Broader Connections (p. 539), and Real-Life Connections (pp. T-532 and T-537).

Additional Resources

UNIT FOUR RESOURCE BOOK

Reader's Guidesheet, p. 43
Vocabulary Worksheet, p. 44
Selection and Vocabulary Check Tests, p. 45
Selection Test, pp. 46–47

Collaborative Learning

Opportunities for collaborative learning appear throughout the lesson and include First Impressions (p. 539).

Teaching Strategies

Vocabulary Preview

These vocabulary words are defined at the bottom of the selection page on which they appear. You may wish to discuss them briefly before students begin reading.

belligerently in a quarrelsome way
deference respect for another
furrow groove cut by a plow
gaudy cheap and showy
surmise guess; conclude

Support for Students of Limited English Proficiency

- Use Reader's Guidesheet, p. 43
- At several points in "Chee's Daughter," the text includes quotations from a Navaho chant traditionally sung at corn-planting time. For example, "In the middle of the wide field . . . Yellow Corn Boy. . . . He has started both ways." Explain that Yellow Corn Boy is the corn itself. Point out that the quotes indicate that the land and agriculture had great religious significance in the Navaho world.
- Annotations C, L, P, X, BB, JJ and NN provide support on culture and vocabulary.

Text Annotations

A. Literary Element: SENSORY DETAILS Point out that the author uses imagery, language that appeals to our senses. Ask students to tell how the sensory details help them experience the story. *(Possible response: The reader can almost feel the touch of the sun, hear the "he he he heya" of the song, see the snow on distant mountains.)*

B. Literary Element: SETTING Have students identify how the author describes Chee's home. *("this wide place in the canyon—levels of jagged rock and levels of rich red earth")* Elicit that the details about the earth, the trees, and so on are important because they establish Chee's close connection to the land.

C. LEP: Culture Explain to students that, as a staple of the Navaho diet, corn is all-important. Therefore, as they plant, Navaho farmers sing songs and offer prayers to the gods to guarantee a good harvest.

Chee's Daughter

JUANITA PLATERO *and* SIYOWIN MILLER

The hat told the story, the big black drooping Stetson.[1] It was not at the proper angle, the proper rakish angle for so young a Navaho. There was no song, and that was not in keeping either. There should have been at least a humming, a faint, all-to-himself "he he he heya," for it was a good horse he was riding, a slender-legged, high-stepping buckskin
A that would race the wind with light knee urging. This was a day for singing, a warm winter day, when the touch of the sun upon the back belied[2] the snow high on distant mountains.

Wind warmed by the sun touched his high-boned cheeks like flicker feathers, and still he rode on silently, deeper into Little Canyon, until the red rock walls rose straight upward from the stream bed and only a narrow piece of blue sky hung above. Abruptly the sky widened where the canyon walls were pushed back to make a wide place, as though in ancient times an angry stream had tried to go all ways at once.

This was home—this wide place in the canyon—levels of jagged rock and levels of
B rich red earth. This was home to Chee, the rider of the buckskin, as it had been to many generations before him.

He stopped his horse at the stream and sat looking across the narrow ribbon of water to the bare-branched peach trees. He was seeing them each springtime with their age-gnarled limbs transfigured[3] beneath veils of blossom pink; he was seeing them in autumn laden with their yellow fruit, small and sweet. Then his eyes searched out the indistinct furrows of the fields beside the stream, where each year the corn and beans and squash drank thirstily of the overflow from summer rains. Chee was trying to outweigh today's bitter betrayal of hope by gathering to himself these reminders of the integrity of the land. Land did not cheat! His mind lingered deliberately on all the days spent here in the sun caring for the young plants, his songs to the earth and to the life springing from it—"In the middle of the wide field . . . Yellow Corn Boy . . .
He has started both ways . . ."—then the harvest and repayment in full measure. C
Here was the old feeling of wholeness and of oneness with the sun and earth and growing things.

Chee urged the buckskin toward the family compound where, secure in a recess of overhanging rock, was his mother's dome-

1. **Stetson:** a hat, usually of felt, having a broad brim and a high, soft crown and most often worn by Westerners.
2. **belied:** gave the wrong idea or impression of.
3. **transfigured:** changed in appearance.

Words to Know and Use	**furrow** (fur' ō) *n.* a long, narrow groove cut in the earth by a plow

528

Structured Reading for Less Proficient Students

These questions can help to guide students through the reading. Ask each question at the point of the selection where the SR number appears in the margin.

SR–1. What has happened to Chee's wife? *(She died of the coughing illness.)* **Inferring**

SR–2. Why do Chee's in-laws come after his daughter? *(It is Navaho custom for girl children to belong to their mother's people.)* **Literal recall**

SR–3. Summarize the basic difference between Chee and his father-in-law. *(Chee reveres Navaho traditions and the land. Old Man Fat has little respect for tradition, despises agriculture, and tries to exploit tourists.)* **Summarizing**

SR–4. Why does Chee go to his in-laws' after his wife's death? Does he accomplish his goal? *(He wants to get his daughter back; he is not successful.)*

SR–5. Why does Chee consider leaving his home at Little Canyon? *(He is so upset about the loss of his daughter that he begins to lose his faith in traditional ways and the land.)* **Clarifying**

Continued on page 530

shaped hogan,[4] red rock and red adobe[5] like the ground on which it nestled. Not far from the hogan was the half circle of brush like a dark shadow against the canyon wall—corral for sheep and goats. Farther from the hogan, in full circle, stood the horse corral made of heavy cedar branches sternly interlocked. Chee's long, thin lips curved into a smile as he passed his daughter's tiny hogan squatted like a round Pueblo[6] oven beside the corral. He remembered the summer day when together they sat back on their heels and plastered wet adobe all about the circling wall of rock and the woven dome of pinyon[7] twigs. How his family laughed when the Little One herded the bewildered chickens into her tiny hogan as the first snow fell.

> ***"Someone has told them," he thought, "and they are inside weeping."***

Then the smile faded from Chee's lips, and his eyes darkened as he tied his horse to the corral post and turned to the strangely empty compound. "Someone has told them," he thought, "and they are inside weeping." He passed his mother's deserted loom on the south side of the hogan and pulled the rude wooden door toward him, bowing his head, hunching his shoulders to get inside.

His mother sat sideways by the center fire, her feet drawn up under her full skirts. Her hands were busy kneading dough in the chipped white basin. With her head down, her voice was muffled when she said, "The meal will soon be ready, son."

Chee passed his father sitting against the wall, hat over his eyes as though asleep. He passed his older sister, who sat turning mutton[8] ribs on a crude wire grill over the coals, noticed tears dropping on her hands. "She cared more for my wife than I realized," he thought.

Then, because something must be said sometime, he tossed the black Stetson upon a bulging sack of wool and said, "You have heard, then." He could not shut from his mind how confidently he had set the handsome new hat on his head that very morning, slanting the wide brim over one eye: he was going to see his wife and today he would ask the doctors about bringing her home; last week she had looked so much better.

His sister nodded but did not speak. His mother sniffled and passed her velveteen sleeve beneath her nose. Chee sat down, leaning against the wall. "I suppose I was a fool for hoping all the time. I should have expected this. Few of our people get well from the coughing sickness.[9] But *she* seemed to be getting better."

His mother was crying aloud now and blowing her nose noisily on her skirt. His father sat up, speaking gently to her.

Chee shifted his position and started a cigarette. His mind turned back to the Little One. At least she was too small to understand what had happened, the Little One who had been born three years before in the sanitarium where his wife was being treated for the coughing sickness, the Little

4. **hogan** (hō′ gôn′): a typical Navaho shelter, built with logs and covered with earth.

5. **adobe** (ə dō′ bē): sun-baked clay bricks.

6. **Pueblo** (pweb′ lō): in the style common to certain Native American villages in the southwestern United States.

7. **pinyon** (pin′ yən): pine.

8. **mutton:** meat from a sheep.

9. **the coughing sickness:** tuberculosis, a disease that affects the lungs and is characterized by persistent coughing.

D. Literary Element: DENOTATION AND CONNOTATION Have students look up the meaning of *nestled* as it pertains to this passage. *(Possible response: settled)* Then ask them to tell how the word *nestled* makes them feel. *(Possible responses: warm, safe, comfortable)*

E. Reading Skill: INFERRING Ask students what this passage reveals about the family's feelings toward Little One. Have them cite the details on which they based their answers. *(Possible responses: They love her very much; she is a source of joy to them. Details: Chee smiles as he passes Little One's hogan and thinks about a particular day they spent together; "his family laughed when the Little One herded . . . ")*

F. Reading Skill: PREDICTING Ask students to predict what the family has been told to cause them to weep. *(Possible response: Someone they love is sick or hurt or dead.)*

G. Literary Element: MOOD Ask students to imagine a movie version of "Chee's Daughter." Have them describe background music that would convey the appropriate mood for this scene.

H. Historical Sidelight Once ranked among the world's worst killers, tuberculosis, referred to here as "the coughing sickness," is now treated successfully with modern drugs. However, during the late 1800's and first half of the 1900's, TB patients were often isolated in health resorts called sanitariums. With bed rest, fresh air, and a healthy diet, many patients overcame the disease. Because of this information we can assume the story is set no later than the 1940's.

DATA BANK

A hogan has a circular shape to symbolize the sun. Its door traditionally faces east to greet the rising Father Sun, one of the main Navaho gods. Inside, the south side of the hogan belongs to the women and the north side to the men. If someone dies in a hogan, it is abandoned.

Traditional Navaho family life is matriarchal, or mother-based. The Navaho woman owns the hogan, the land, the children, and the livestock. Her husband owns only what he has inherited or purchased with outside earnings. Under this system, if a mother should die, her children usually go to their maternal grandmother if she is still alive.

I. Reading Skill: **COMPARING AND CONTRASTING** Have students compare and contrast Chee's and his sister's reactions. *(Possible response: Although both Chee and his sister are very upset, they express their feelings differently. Chee denies that things are as bad as they are and momentarily can make no sound. His sister sobs, openly acknowledging how bad things are.)*

J. Reading Skills: **INFERRING** Review that the hogan traditionally faces east to greet the sun, a much-revered god among the Navaho. Ask students what not observing this custom might suggest about Chee's in-laws. *(They do not observe the old customs; perhaps they want to be like modern white Americans.)*

K. Literary Element: **CONFLICT** Ask students what the central conflict, or struggle, of the plot will be. *(The central conflict will be between Chee and his in-laws over the custody of the Little One.)*

L. LEP: Culture/Setting In the Navaho culture, earth and its various land forms are closely connected to people's lives. If possible, show students pictures of the canyons, buttes, and mesas of America's Southwest, which may not be familiar to immigrants or to students from other areas of the United States.

M. Literary Element: **DENOTATION AND CONNOTATION** Point out that the authors describe the trading post as "sprawled in mushroom growth." Ask students what emotional response this phrase evokes in them. *(The word* sprawling *suggests overly large and perhaps sloppy; the word* mushroom *suggests the growth is rapid but perhaps unhealthy or short-lived.)*

One he had brought home to his mother's hogan to be nursed by his sister whose baby was a few months older. As she grew fat cheeked and sturdy legged, she followed him about like a shadow; somehow her baby mind had grasped that of all those at the hogan who cared for her and played with her, he—Chee—belonged most to her. She sat cross-legged at his elbow when he worked silver at the forge; she rode before him in the saddle when he drove the horses to water; often she lay wakeful on her sheep pelts until he stretched out for the night in the darkened hogan and she could snuggle warm against him.

Chee blew smoke slowly, and some of the sadness left his dark eyes as he said, "It is not as bad as it might be. It is not as though we are left with nothing."

I Chee's sister arose, sobs catching in her throat, and rushed past him out the doorway. Chee sat upright, a terrible fear possessing him. For a moment his mouth could make no sound. Then: "The Little One! Mother, where is she?"

His mother turned her stricken face to him. "Your wife's people came after her this morning. They heard yesterday of their daughter's death through the trader at Red Sands."

Chee started to protest, but his mother shook her head slowly. "I didn't expect they would want the Little One either. But there is nothing you can do. She is a girl child and be-
SR-2 ▶ longs to her mother's people; it is custom."

J Frowning, Chee got to his feet, grinding his cigarette into the dirt floor. "Custom! When did my wife's parents begin thinking about custom? Why, the hogan where they live doesn't even face the East!" He started toward the door. "Perhaps I can overtake them. Perhaps they don't realize how much we want her here with us. I'll ask them to give my daughter back to me. Surely, they won't refuse."

K His mother stopped him gently with her outstretched hand. "You couldn't overtake them now. They were in the trader's car. Eat and rest, and think more about this."

"Have you forgotten how things have always been between you and your wife's people?" his father said.

That night, Chee's thoughts were troubled—half-forgotten incidents became disturbingly vivid—but early the next morning he saddled the buckskin and set out for the settlement of Red Sands. Even though his father-in-law, Old Man Fat, might laugh, Chee knew that he must talk to him. There were some things to which Old Man Fat might listen.

L Chee rode the first part of the fifteen miles to Red Sands expectantly. The sight of sandstone buttes[10] near Cottonwood Spring reddening in the morning sun brought a song almost to his lips. He twirled his reins in salute to the small boy herding sheep toward many-colored Butterfly Mountain, watched with pleasure the feathers of smoke rising against tree-darkened western mesas from the hogans sheltered there. M But as he approached the familiar settlement sprawled in mushroom growth along the highway, he began to feel as though a scene from a bad dream was becoming real.

Several cars were parked around the trading store, which was built like two log hogans side by side, with red gas pumps in front and a sign across the tarpaper roofs: *Red Sands Trading Post—Groceries Gasoline Cold Drinks Sandwiches Indian Curios.* Back of the trading post an unpainted frame house

10. **buttes** (byōōts): steep hills in the western United States, having flat tops and standing alone.

STRUCTURED READING FOR LESS PROFICIENT STUDENTS

Continued from page 528

SR–6. What new undertaking does Chee begin in spring? *(He plants a large new field.)* **Literal recall**

SR–7. At the end of summer, when Chee visits Old Man Fat, why has the trading post closed? *(Due to the new cut-off, cars no longer pass the post.)* **Literal recall**

SR–8. What changes does Chee see in Old Man Fat and his lifestyle? *(Old Man Fat seems friendlier and sadder; he has little money.)* **Literal recall**

SR–9. What has Chee brought to Old Man Fat and his wife? *(Chee has brought a winter's supply of corn, meat, and other food items.)* **Literal recall**

SR–10. What does Chee hope to achieve by bringing these things to Old Man Fat? *(He hopes his in-laws will let him have his daughter.)* **Clarifying**

SR–11. Does Chee achieve his goal in the end? *(Yes, Old Man Fat gives Little One to Chee)* **Literal recall**

and outbuildings squatted on the drab, treeless land. Chee and the Little One's mother had lived there when they stayed with his wife's people. That was according to custom—living with one's wife's people—but Chee had never been convinced that it was custom alone which prompted Old Man Fat and his wife to insist that their daughter bring her husband to live at the trading post.

Beside the Post was a large hogan of logs, with brightly painted pseudo-Navaho[11] designs on the roof—a hogan with smoke-smudged windows and a garish blue door, which faced north to the highway. Old Man Fat had offered Chee a hogan like this one. The trader would build it if he and his wife would live there and Chee would work at his forge making silver jewelry where tourists could watch him. But Chee had asked instead for a piece of land for a cornfield and help in building a hogan far back from the highway and a corral for the sheep he had brought to this marriage.

A cold wind blowing down from the mountains began to whistle about Chee's ears. It flapped the gaudy Navaho rugs which were hung in one long, bright line to attract tourists. It swayed the sign *Navaho Weaver at Work* beside the loom where Old Man Fat's Wife sat hunched in her striped blanket, patting the colored thread of a design into place with a wooden comb. Tourists stood watching the weaver. More tourists stood in a knot before the hogan where the sign said: *See Inside a Real Navaho Home 25¢.*

Then the knot seemed to unravel as a few people returned to their cars; some had cameras; and there against the blue door Chee saw the Little One standing uncertainly. The wind was plucking at her new purple blouse and wide green skirt; it freed truant strands of soft, dark hair from the meager queue[12] into which it had been tied with white yarn.

A PRIVATE PERFORMANCE Lois Johnson
From *Contemporary Western Artists* by Peggy and Harold Samuels.

11. **pseudo-Navaho** (so͞o′ dō nav′ ə hō): imitation Navaho.

Words to Know and Use

gaudy (gôd′ ē) *adj.* cheap and showy; in poor taste

Art Note

Lois Johnson (1942–) has lived in Flagstaff, Arizona, since 1965. Of her portraits of Navaho and Hopi Indians, she says, "I attempt to recreate on canvas their humor and their dignity," and, of the children who are most often her subjects, "I respond to their innocence." The little girl in this picture seems delighted to be dancing. *What connection can you make between this painting and "Chee's Daughter"?*

N. Reading Skill: INFERRING Ask students what, in addition to custom, might prompt Old Man Fat to insist that Chee live at the trading post. *(Possible response: He probably wanted Chee to work in some money-making scheme of his.)*

O. Literary Element: CONNOTATION AND DENOTATION Ask students what the word *pseudo-Navaho* suggests about Old Man Fat. *(*Pseudo-Navaho *suggests Old Man Fat is not true to his culture and upbringing.* Pseudo-Navaho *carries the connotation of something fake and phony.)*

PROFESSIONAL NOTEBOOK

Gardening helps remind me how growing happens. Your job as a gardener or as an educator is to know that the potential is there and that it will unfold. Your job is to plant good seeds and nurture them until they get big enough to grow up, and not to smother them while they are growing. You shouldn't overwater them, overfertilize them or overwork them. And when bugs get on the plants, you've got to get rid of them so the plants can continue to grow.
MYLES HORTON, THE LONG HAUL

P. LEP: Vocabulary Some students will be familiar with the word *truant* meaning "a student who stays away from school." Explain that here the word means "straying." Ask students how the two meanings are related. *(A student who stays away from school has strayed from where he or she should be.)*

Q. Literary Element: CHARACTER Ask students what the tightening of Chee's lips suggests about how he feels. Have them tell why he feels this way. *(Possible response: He is upset because he sees that the Navaho traditions and customs are being cheapened by Old Man Fat for his own profit, and he doesn't want Little One to be corrupted by the old man's greed.)*

R. Literary Element: CONFLICT Elicit that the conflict between Chee and Old Man Fat exemplifies the conflict between the traditional and the modern. Ask students for words that describe Old Man Fat's behavior in this argument. *(Possible responses: mean, belligerent, aggressive, offensive)* Ask for words that describe Chee's behavior. *(Possible responses: gentle, steady, moderate, reasonable)*

S. Critical Thinking: ANALYZING Ask students to suggest reasons why Old Man Fat seems so angry about Chee's traditional Navaho lifestyle. *(Possible responses: He is uncomfortable with his own heritage; he wants the Navaho to imitate white people.)*

"Isn't she cunning!" one of the women tourists was saying as she turned away.

Chee's lips tightened as he began to look around for Old Man Fat. Finally he saw him passing among the tourists, collecting coins.

Then the Little One saw Chee. The uncertainty left her face, and she darted through the crowd as her father swung down from his horse. Chee lifted her in his arms, hugging her tight. While he listened to her breathless chatter, he watched Old Man Fat bearing down on them, scowling.

As his father-in-law walked heavily across the graveled lot, Chee was reminded of a statement his mother sometimes made: "When you see a fat Navaho, you see one who hasn't worked for what he has."

Old Man Fat was fattest in the middle. There was indolence in his walk even though he seemed to hurry, indolence in his cheeks so plump they made his eyes squint, eyes now smoldering with anger.

Some of the tourists were getting into their cars and driving away. The old man said belligerently to Chee, "Why do you come here? To spoil our business? To drive people away?"

"I came to talk with you," Chee answered, trying to keep his voice steady as he faced the old man.

"We have nothing to talk about," Old Man Fat blustered and did not offer to touch Chee's extended hand.

"It's about the Little One." Chee settled his daughter more comfortably against his hip as he weighed carefully all the words he had planned to say. "We are going to miss her very much. It wouldn't be so bad if we knew that *part* of each year she could be with us. That might help you too. You and your wife are no longer young people, and you have no young ones here to depend upon." Chee chose his next words remembering the thriftlessness of his wife's parents, and their greed. "Perhaps we could share the care of this little one. Things are good with us. So much snow this year will make lots of grass for the sheep. We have good land for corn and melons."

Chee's words did not have the expected effect. Old Man Fat was enraged. "Farmers, all of you! Long-haired farmers! Do you think everyone must bend his back over the short-handled hoe in order to have food to eat?" His tone changed as he began to brag a little. "We not only have all the things from cans at the trader's, but when the Pueblos come past here on their way to town we buy their salty jerked mutton, young corn for roasting, dried sweet peaches."

Chee's dark eyes surveyed the land along the highway as the old man continued to brag about being "progressive." *He* no longer was tied to the land. He and his wife made money easily and could *buy* all the things they wanted. Chee realized too late that he had stumbled into the old argument between himself and his wife's parents. They had never understood his feeling about the land—that a man took care of his land and it in turn took care of him. Old Man Fat and his wife scoffed at him, called him a Pueblo farmer, all during that summer when he planted and weeded and har-

12. **queue** (kyo͞o): a braid of hair worn hanging from the back of the head.

Words to Know and Use	**belligerently** (bə lij′ ər ənt lē) *adv.* in a quarrelsome way

532

REAL LIFE CONNECTIONS

Use these prompts to discuss the role of traditions in students' lives.

- In what ways do traditions make our lives better, easier, or more fulfilling?
- Do traditions ever stand in the way of progress? Give some examples.
- When is it all right to break traditions? For example, is Chee justified in trying to break the tradition of having Little One go to her mother's people?

vested. Yet they ate the green corn in their mutton stews, and the chili paste from the fresh ripe chilies, and the tortillas from the cornmeal his wife ground. None of this working and sweating in the sun for Old Man Fat, who talked proudly of his easy way of living—collecting money from the trader who rented his strip of land beside the highway, collecting money from the
SR-3 ▶ tourists.

Yet Chee had once won that argument. His wife had shared his belief in the integrity of the earth, that jobs and people might fail one but the earth never would. After that first year she had turned from her own people and gone with Chee to Little Canyon.

Old Man Fat was reaching for the Little One. "Don't be coming here with plans for
U my daughter's daughter," he warned. "If you try to make trouble, I'll take the case to the government man in town."

The impulse was strong in Chee to turn and ride off while he still had the Little One in his arms. But he knew his time of victory would be short. His own family would uphold the old custom of children, especially girl children, belonging to the mother's people. He would have to give his daughter
V up if the case were brought before the Headman of Little Canyon, and certainly he would have no better chance before a strange white man in town.

He handed the bewildered Little One to her grandfather, who stood watching every movement suspiciously. Chee asked, "If I brought you a few things for the Little One, would that be making trouble? Some velvet for a blouse, or some of the jerky she likes so well . . . this summer's melon?"

Old Man Fat backed away from him. "Well," he hesitated, as some of the anger disappeared from his face and beads of greed shone in his eyes. "Well," he repeated. Then as the Little One began to squirm in his arms and cry, he said. "No! No! Stay away from here, you and all your family." ◀ SR-4

The sense of his failure deepened as Chee rode back to Little Canyon. But it was not until he sat with his family that evening in the hogan, while the familiar bustle of meal preparing went on about him, that he began to doubt the wisdom of the things he'd always believed. He smelled the coffee boiling and the oily fragrance of chili powder dusted into the bubbling pot of stew; he watched his mother turning round, crusty fried bread in the small black skillet. All around him was plenty—a half of mutton hanging near the door, bright strings of chili drying, corn hanging by the braided husks, cloth bags of dried peaches. Yet in his heart was nothing.

He heard the familiar sounds of the sheep outside the hogan, the splash of water as his father filled the long drinking trough from the water barrel. When his father came in, Chee could not bring himself to tell a second time of the day's happenings. He watched his wiry, soft-spoken father while his mother told the story, saw his father's queue of graying hair quiver as he nodded his head with sympathetic exclamations.

Chee's doubting, acrid[13] thoughts kept forming: Was it wisdom his father had passed on to him, or was his inheritance only the stubbornness of a long-haired Navaho resisting change? Take care of the land and it will take care of you. True, the land had always given him food, but now W
food was not enough. Perhaps if he had

13. **acrid:** irritating; upsetting.

T. Critical Thinking: SYNTHESIZING Ask students if they think that the reverse of this statement is true; that is, if you don't take care of your land, your land won't take care of you. Ask for examples drawn from people's concern for the environment.

U. Reading Skill: PREDICTING Have students predict what Chee might do next. *(Possible responses: He might take his daughter in spite of custom; he might ride away quietly; he might ride away but threaten old Man Fat.)*

V. Historical Sidelight Historically, the Bureau of Indian Affairs, an agency of the U.S. Department of the Interior, has enforced the law, provided welfare services, and run the schools on Native American reservations. Today, many tribes are taking over some or all of these responsibilities themselves. At the time of this story, however, white employees of the Bureau had a great deal of control over the Indians.

PROFESSIONAL NOTEBOOK

[Teachers] have begun to acknowledge more fully the importance of having students read literature that enhances self-image, that develops a sense of pride in the cultural heritage, and that demonstrates clearly the contribution of a group to American culture. But we have not gone far enough. Minority literature is too often peripheral, an extra, an option to what some see as the real or mainstream literature; it is separate but not equal. Ethnic literature should not exist just as an extra for those who are interested in it or who ''need'' it. We think the literature of different cultural groups in this country has the potential for enriching the curriculum immeasurably. . . .

STEPHEN N. JUDY and SUSAN J. JUDY,
THE ENGLISH TEACHER'S HANDBOOK

W. Literary Element: **INTERNAL CONFLICT** Have students explain the conflict in Chee's mind. *(Chee struggles to decide whether his traditional ways are indeed better than the modern ways and education of white people.)*

X. LEP: Vocabulary Review the meaning of the term *forage* as it is used here. *(edible wild plants for livestock)* Have students paraphrase the sentence.

Y. Critical Thinking: **SYNTHESIZING** Ask students what the authors mean when they say Chee "had forsaken his brotherhood with earth and sun and growing things." *(Answers should reflect the idea that Chee is losing faith in his traditional Navaho beliefs; he is beginning to doubt that the earth will take care of him if he takes care of it.)*

Z. Reading Skill: **PREDICTING** Ask students if they think Chee will leave Little Canyon and to explain their answers. *(Possible responses: He will leave, because he sees that his traditional ways in Little Canyon have cost him his daughter. He will not leave, because he cannot bring himself to abandon his cultural heritage—even for his daughter.)*

AA. Literary Element: **MOOD** Point out that the story setting has changed from a dreary winter to a lovely spring. Have students suggest how the mood of the story will change. *(Possible response: It will become brighter and more positive.)*

W gone to school he would have learned a different kind of wisdom, something to help him now. A schoolboy might even be able to speak convincingly to this government man whom Old Man Fat threatened to call, instead of sitting here like a clod of earth itself—Pueblo farmer indeed. What had the land to give that would restore his daughter?

Take care of the land and it will take care of you.

X In the days that followed, Chee herded sheep. He got up in the half light, drank the hot coffee his mother had ready, then started the flock moving. It was necessary to drive the sheep a long way from the hogan to find good winter forage. Sometimes Chee met friends or relatives who were on their way to town or to the road camp where they hoped to get work; then there was friendly banter and an exchange of news. But most of the days seemed endless; he could not walk far enough or fast enough from his memories of the Little One or from his bitter thoughts. Sometimes it seemed his daughter trudged beside him, so real he could almost hear her footsteps—the muffled pad-pad of little feet clad in deer hide. In the glare of a snow bank he would see her vivid face, brown eyes sparkling. Mingling with the tinkle of sheep bells he heard her laughter.

Y When, weary of following the small, sharp hoof marks that crossed and recrossed in the snow, he sat down in the shelter of a rock, it was only to be reminded that in his thoughts he had forsaken his brotherhood with the earth and sun and growing things. If he remembered times when he had flung himself against the earth to rest, to lie there in the sun until he could no longer feel where he left off and the earth began, it was to remember also that now he sat like an alien against the same earth; the belonging together was gone. The earth was one thing and he was another.

Z It was during the days when he herded sheep that Chee decided he must leave Little Canyon. Perhaps he would take a job silversmithing for one of the traders in town. Perhaps even though he spoke little English, he could get a job at the road camp with his cousins; he would ask them about it. SR-5

AA Springtime transformed the mesas.[14] The peach trees in the canyon were shedding fragrance and pink blossoms on the gentled wind. The sheep no longer foraged for the yellow seeds of chamiso but ranged near the hogan with the long-legged new lambs, eating tender young grass.

Chee was near the hogan on the day his cousins rode up with the message for which he waited. He had been watching with mixed emotions while his father and his sister's husband cleared the fields beside the stream.

"The boss at the camp says he needs an extra hand, but he wants to know if you'll be willing to go with the camp when they move it to the other side of the town?" The tall cousin shifted his weight in the saddle.

BB The other cousin took up the explanation. "The work near here will last only until the new cut-off beyond Red Sands is finished. After that, the work will be too far away for you to get back here often."

14. **mesas** (mā′ səz): small, high plateaus with flat tops and steep sides.

DATA BANK

Juanita Platero and Siyowin Miller, the authors of the selection, were well acquainted with the Navaho way of life. Platero herself was a Navaho who lived with her husband on the reservation. Miller was not a Native American, but she had a life-long interest in Native American affairs. In fact, her adopted name *Siyowin* means "Prairie Chicken Woman" in Lakota.

In 1929 Miller and Platero were introduced to each other by Standing Bear, a Lakota chief and a writer. In 1940 the team worked to produce a novel, *The Winds Erase Your Footsteps.* Later, they wrote a number of short stories, including "Chee's Daughter."

That was what Chee had wanted—to get away from Little Canyon—yet he found himself not so interested in the job beyond town as in this new cut-off which was almost finished. He pulled a blade of grass, split it thoughtfully down the center as he asked questions of his cousins. Finally he said: "I need to think more about this. If I decide on this job, I'll ride over."

Before his cousins were out of sight down the canyon, Chee was walking toward the fields, a bold plan shaping in his mind. As the plan began to flourish, wild and hardy as young tumbleweed, Chee added his own voice softly to the song his father was singing: ". . . In the middle of the wide field . . . Yellow Corn Boy . . . I wish to put in."

Chee walked slowly around the field, the rich red earth yielding to his footsteps. His plan depended upon this land and upon the things he remembered most about his wife's people.

CC Through planting time Chee worked zealously and tirelessly. He spoke little of the large, new field he was planting because he felt so strongly that just now this was something between himself and the land. The first days he was ever stooping, piercing the ground with the pointed stick, placing the corn kernels there, walking around the field and through it singing, ". . . His track leads into the ground . . . Yellow Corn Boy . . . his track leads into the ground." After that, each day Chee walked through his field watching for the tips of green to break through; first a few spikes in the center and then more and more until the corn in all parts of the field was above ground. Surely, Chee thought, if he sang the proper songs, if he cared for this land faithfully, it would not forsake him now, even though through the lonely days of winter he had betrayed the goodness of the earth in his thoughts. ◀SR-6

Through the summer Chee worked long days, the sun hot upon his back, pulling weeds from around young corn plants; he planted squash and pumpkin; he terraced a small piece of land near his mother's hogan and planted carrots and onions and the moisture-loving chili. He was increasingly restless. Finally he told his family what he hoped the harvest from this land would bring him. Then the whole family waited with him, watching the corn: the slender, graceful plants that waved green arms and bent to embrace each other as young winds wandered through the field, the maturing plants flaunting their pollen-laden tassels in the sun, the tall and sturdy parent corn with new-formed ears and a froth of purple, red and yellow corn beards against the dusty emerald of broad leaves. DD

Summer was almost over when Chee slung the bulging packs across two pack ponies. His mother helped him tie the heavy rolled pack behind the saddle of the buckskin. Chee knotted the new yellow kerchief about his neck a little tighter, gave the broad black hat brim an extra tug, but these were only gestures of assurance and he knew it. The land had not failed him. That part was done. But this he was riding into? Who could tell?

When Chee arrived at Red Sands, it was as he had expected to find it—no cars on the highway. His cousins had told him that even the Pueblo farmers were using the new cut-off to town. The barren gravel around the Red Sands Trading Post was deserted. A sign banged against the dismantled gas pumps, *Closed Until Further Notice.* EE FF ◀SR-7

Old Man Fat came from the crude summer shelter built beside the log hogan from a few branches of scrub cedar and the sides

BB. LEP: Vocabulary Explain that a *cut-off* is a new road, a shortcut, that connects two existing roads.

CC. Literary Element: PLOT Point out that the pace of the action is beginning to quicken. Remind students that the events of the plot will rise to a high point, or climax. Ask students to suggest what it might be. *(Answers will probably reflect the notion that Chee will again confront his in-laws about regaining custody of his daughter.)*

DD. Literary Element: PERSONIFICATION Have students identify examples of personification. *(The corn plants "waved green arms," "bent to embrace each other," and "flaunted" their tassels as the winds "wandered through the field.")*

EE. Literary Element: SUSPENSE Ask students why the authors have not told us exactly what Chee is up to. (Possible response: *They want to keep the reader guessing, to maintain the reader's interest.)*

Professional Notebook

The question that the teacher must always be ready to address is this: How do I use this student's response to teach him how to read, and thus learn from, texts? How do I use this student's response to push him into deeper and more critical engagement with the claims of the author and with his own reaction to those claims? We ask this question because of our initial assumption that the great works constituting our literary heritage contain more wisdom than most of us can generate on our own. The point is to teach the student how to extract some of that wisdom so that he can put it to use in his own thinking.

ROBERT T. FANCHER, "ENGLISH TEACHING AND HUMANE CULTURE"

FF. Reading Skill: CLARIFYING Ask students to explain why the once-busy trading post is now deserted. *(The new cut-off has changed the traffic flow; most cars no longer pass the trading post on the way to town.)*

GG. Reading Skill: CONTRASTING Have students contrast how Old Man Fat acts and appears now with how he acted and appeared the previous fall. *(He seems friendlier; his voice is gentler and less threatening; hard times have left him thinner.)*

Art Note

Walter Ufer (1876–1936), painter of the American West and the Indians of New Mexico, was born in Louisville, Kentucky. As a boy he worked at menial jobs and despaired of ever being able to afford an education in art. However, an employer and a Chicago mayor helped and encouraged him. Ufer saw the Native Americans as sadly deprived of their culture. *How is this painting different from other portraits of Native Americans?*

THE CORN PICKER
Walter Ufer Eiteljorg Museum of American Indian and Western Art, Indianapolis, Indiana.

of wooden crates. He seemed almost friendly when he saw Chee.

GG "Get down, my son," he said, eyeing the bulging packs. There was no bluster in his voice today and his face sagged, looking somewhat saddened; perhaps because his cheeks were no longer quite full enough to push his eyes upward at the corners. "You are going on a journey?"

Chee shook his head. "Our fields gave us so much this year, I thought to sell or trade this to the trader. I didn't know he was no longer here."

Old Man Fat sighed, his voice dropping to an injured tone. "He says he and his wife are going to rest this winter; then after that he'll build a place up on the new highway."

Chee moved as though to be traveling on, then jerked his head toward the pack ponies. "Anything you need?"

"I'll ask my wife," Old Man Fat said as he led the way to the shelter. "Maybe she has a little money. Things have not been too good with us since the trader closed. Only a few tourists come this way." He shrugged his shoulders. "And with the trader gone—no credit." ◀SR-8

Chee was not deceived by his father-in- HH

law's unexpected confidences. He recognized them as a hopeful bid for sympathy and, if possible, something for nothing. Chee made no answer. He was thinking that so far he had been right about his wife's parents: their thriftlessness had left them with no resources to last until Old Man Fat found another easy way of making a living.

HH

Old Man Fat's Wife was in the shelter working at her loom. She turned rather wearily when her husband asked with noticeable deference if she would give him money to buy supplies. Chee surmised that the only income here was from his mother-in-law's weaving.

She peered around the corner of the shelter at the laden ponies, and then she looked at Chee. "What do you have there, my son?"

Chee smiled to himself as he turned to pull the pack from one of the ponies, dragged it to the shelter where he untied the ropes. Pumpkins and hard-shelled squash tumbled out, and the ears of corn—pale yellow husks fitting firmly over plump, ripe kernels, blue corn, red corn, yellow corn, many-colored corn, ears and ears of it—tumbled into every corner of the shelter. ◀SR-9

"Yoooooh," Old Man Fat's Wife exclaimed as she took some of the ears in her hands. Then she glanced up at her son-in-law. "But we have no money for all this. We have sold almost everything we own—even the brass bed that stood in the hogan."

II

Old Man Fat's brass bed. Chee concealed his amusement as he started back for another pack. That must have been a hard parting. Then he stopped, for coming from the cool darkness of the hogan was the Little One, rubbing her eyes as though she had been asleep. She stood for a moment in the doorway, and Chee saw that she was dirty, barefoot, her hair uncombed, her little blouse shorn of all its silver buttons. Then she ran toward Chee, her arms outstretched. Heedless of Old Man Fat and his wife, her father caught her in his arms, her hair falling in a dark cloud across his face, the sweetness of her laughter warm against his shoulder.

JJ

It was the haste within him to get this slow waiting game played through to the finish that made Chee speak unwisely. It was the desire to swing her before him in the saddle and ride fast to Little Canyon that prompted his words. "The money doesn't matter. You still have something. . . ."

KK

Chee knew immediately that he had overspoken. The old woman looked from him to the corn spread before her. Unfriendliness began to harden in his father-in-law's face. All the old arguments between himself and his wife's people came pushing and crowding in between them now. ◀SR-10

Old Man Fat began kicking the ears of corn back onto the canvas as he eyed Chee angrily. "And you rode all the way over here thinking that for a little food we would give up our daughter's daughter?"

Chee did not wait for the old man to reach for the Little One. He walked dazedly to the shelter, rubbing his cheek against her soft dark hair and put her gently into her grandmother's lap. Then he turned back to the horses. He had failed. By his own haste he had failed. He swung into the saddle, his hand touching the roll behind it. Should he ride on into town?

LL

Then he dismounted, scarcely glancing at

Words to Know and Use	**deference** (def′ ər əns) *n.* respect for the wishes or opinion of another **surmise** (sər mīz′) *v.* to guess or conclude

537

HH. Literary Element: CHARACTER Ask students what Chee's scheme reveals about him. *(Possible responses: he is bright and clever; he is a problem solver; he is willing to work hard to fulfill his goals.)*

II. Literary Element: THEME Ask students how this scene illustrates this idea: Take care of the land and the land will take care of you. *(Old Man Fat and his wife, who abandoned their land for the tourist trade, are left with nothing. Chee, who farmed all summer, is now being "taken care of" by the land.)*

JJ. LEP: Vocabulary Tell students that *heedless* means "without paying attention to" or "unmindful of."

KK. Reading Skill: INFERRING Ask students what the something is that Chee refers to. *(The something is his daughter.)* Have students suggest why Chee believes he has "overspoken." *(He has "tipped his hand"; he has let his in-laws know that he has really come to bargain for his daughter.)*

LL. Literary Element: CLIMAX Point out that the story is rapidly reaching its high point, or climax. Explain that the author continues to build suspense by making it appear that Chee's efforts are in vain.

Real Life Connections

Ask students to compare Chee's strong desire to support and raise his child with the attitudes and practices of real-life fathers they know. Possible discussion prompts include these:

- What are a father's responsibilities to his children?
- Why do some fathers in our culture who live apart from their children fail to provide the necessary support for their children?
- How would you describe the ideal father?

MM. Reading Skills: PREDICTING Have students tell why they think Chee brings the rest of the food into the hogan when his in-laws have already refused to give him Little One. Have students predict how the story will end. *(Possible responses: He feels sympathy for them; he still hopes to change their minds. Possible predictions: They will be moved by Chee's generosity to share The Little One or to give her up.)*

NN. LEP: Vocabulary Explain that meat is jerked, or preserved, by cutting it into strips and drying it in the sun. Students might be interested to know that the word *jerky* comes from a Spanish word *charqui,* which, in turn, was borrowed from a southwestern Native American language.

OO. Literary Element: CLIMAX AND RESOLUTION Ask students if the ending of the story is in keeping with Old Man Fat's character. Have them explain their answers. *(Yes, his greed is greater than his love for his granddaughter or his concern for tradition. He gives up his granddaughter.)*

Check Test

1. What happens to Chee's wife? *(She dies of tuberculosis in a sanitarium.)*

2. With whom does Chee's daughter go to live? *(with her mother's parents)*

3. Why doesn't Chee respect his father-in-law? *(His father-in-law does not uphold traditional Navaho values.)*

4. Why does Old Man Fat's tourist business suddenly end? *(After a new road is built, tourists no longer pass the trading post.)*

5. Why does Chee grow extra food during the summer? *(to give as a gift to his in-laws to persuade them to let him see or have his daughter)*

Encouraging Independent Reading

"Wild Bird," a short story by Florence Parry Heide

Kramer vs. Kramer, a novel by Avery Korman

The Milagro Beanfield War, a novel by John Treadwell Nichols

The Winds Erase Your Footprints, a novel by Juanita Platero and Siyowin Miller

The Light in the Forest, a novel by Conrad Richter

Old Man Fat, who stood uncertainly at the corner of the shelter, listening to his wife. MM "Give me a hand with this other pack of corn, Grandfather," Chee said, carefully keeping the small bit of hope from his voice.

Puzzled but willing, Old Man Fat helped carry the other pack to the shelter, opening it to find more corn as well as carrots and round pale yellow onions. Chee went back for the roll behind the buckskin's saddle and carried it to the entrance of the shelter, where he cut the ropes and gave the canvas a nudge with his toe. Tins of coffee rolled out, small, plump cloth bags; jerked meat NN from several butcherings spilled from a flour sack, and bright red chilies splashed like flames against the dust.

"I will leave all this anyhow," Chee told them. "I would not want my daughter nor even you old people to go hungry."

Old Man Fat picked up a shiny tin of coffee, then put it down. With trembling hands he began to untie one of the cloth bags—dried sweet peaches.

The Little One had wriggled from her grandmother's lap and was on her knees, digging her hands into the jerked meat.

"There is almost enough food here to last all winter." Old Man Fat's Wife sought the eyes of her husband.

Chee said, "I meant it to be enough. But that was when I thought you might send the Little One back with me." He looked down at his daughter noisily sucking jerky. Her mouth, both fists were full of it. "I am sorry that you feel you cannot bear to part with her."

Old Man Fat's Wife brushed a straggly wisp of gray hair from her forehead as she turned to look at the Little One. Old Man Fat was looking too. And it was not a thing to see. For in that moment the Little One OO ceased to be their daughter's daughter and became just another mouth to feed.

"And why not?" the old woman asked wearily.

Chee was settled in the saddle, the barefooted Little One before him. He urged the buckskin faster, and his daughter clutched his shirt-front. The purpling mesas flung back the echo: ". . . My corn embrace each other. On the middle of the wide field . . . Yellow Corn Boy, embrace each other." ❧ ◄SR-

Responding to Reading

First Impressions

1. Think about the characters you encountered in this story. Discuss with your classmates some of the impressions you now have about the Navaho.

Second Thoughts

2. Think back to the qualities you listed as important for raising a child. Which character, Chee or Old Man Fat, has more of these qualities? Explain.
3. Why is the land so special to Chee?

   Think about
   - how he describes the land
   - what his father taught him about the land
   - what the land gives him
4. Look again at the notes you wrote in the Venn diagram comparing Chee and Old Man Fat. In what ways are these two Navaho different?
5. What reasons might Old Man Fat and his wife have for keeping the Little One?
6. How might you explain the change in Old Man Fat's and his wife's attitudes about keeping the Little One?

   Think about
   - what has happened to the trading post
   - what Chee offers them
   - what fears they may have of the future

Broader Connections

7. Chee has been taught, "Take care of the land and it will take care of you." What values have you been taught about taking care of the land? How do your beliefs affect your actions?

Literary Concept: Denotation and Connotation

The dictionary definition of a word is its **denotation.** The emotional response that a word evokes is its **connotation.** Old Man Fat is described as coming out of "the crude summer shelter." In this context the word *crude* means "unfinished or rough," but it also evokes the idea of something that is tasteless and sloppy. Find other examples of such carefully chosen words to describe Old Man Fat and his surroundings.

Student Response

Responding to Reading

These questions are open-ended with no "right" or "wrong" answers. However, responses must be supported with information from the selection. Possible answers follow:

1. Any responses are valid.

2. Chee, because he shows the ability to work hard, love, plan ahead, and maintain his relationships with his community and traditions.

3. Some students might point out that Chee often sees himself as part of the land. He knows the land well and loves it. Furthermore, it is Chee's care of the land that brings him what he wants most—his daughter.

4. Students may suggest that Old Man Fat despises Navaho traditions, while Chee respects them; that Old Man Fat is basically lazy and opportunistic, while Chee is hard-working and generous.

5. Possible reasons: Old Man Fat and his wife actually love the girl; they want her to hurt Chee or to remove her from what they consider a backward environment; they want the girl because she might attract tourists to their roadside attractions.

6. The drastic decline in business at the trading post makes it difficult for Old Man Fat to support the child, so Chee's disguised offer of food for the girl is hard to resist. Old Man Fat probably wants to be on good terms with Chee in case he has to call on him for more help later.

7. Possible response: It is important to take care of the land because it is a limited resource on which not only humans but also all other life on earth depend. Actions might include recycling trash, planting trees, and participating in other environmental causes.

Literary Concept—Denotation and Connotation

Old Man Fat's hogan is described as painted with "pseudo-Navaho designs." The connotation is that Old Man Fat, like the designs on his hogan, is "imitation" Navaho. The description of its "garnish blue door" indicates that it is out of place on the "drab treeless land."

Writing Options

The Writing Options are designed to meet varied student interests and abilities. Have each student choose one writing activity to complete. You may wish to guide some students to an option that requires less writing.

Journal Update Have students revise their journal entries for "Chee's Daughter." What new reflections can they add to their earlier writings about family or people's responsibilities to the land?

Vocabulary Practice

1. a
2. c
3. c
4. d
5. c

Closure

In this story, a young Navaho father exhibits patience, restraint, an understanding of people, and grace as he works to regain custody of his daughter. Suggest that students be alert to child-custody cases reported in the media and to contrast the way the people involved handled the problem with Chee's handling of the problem.

Writing Options

1. Imagine that you are Chee and are about to leave your daughter behind with Old Man Fat. Compose a lullaby for her filled with soothing images of the land. Choose words that will help calm the child through both their meaning and their sound.

2. A proverb is a short, wise saying, such as "Haste makes waste." Write a proverb to explain why Chee was able to regain his daughter.

3. What if the trading post had not moved? How would Chee have managed to get his daughter back? Think of Chee's options and then devise a strategy that he might consider. Make sure that these plans are consistent with his character.

4. Draw and fill in a Venn diagram (see page 527) that compares and contrasts Chee and Christy Brown's mother in the excerpt from *My Left Foot* on page 337.

Vocabulary Practice

Exercise Write the letter of the word that is not related in meaning to the other words in each set.

1. (a) belligerently (b) peacefully (c) serenely (d) calmly
2. (a) deference (b) respect (c) hostility (d) reverence
3. (a) furrow (b) groove (c) mound (d) rut
4. (a) gaudy (b) tacky (c) tasteless (d) conservative
5. (a) surmise (b) guess (c) forget (d) infer

Words to Know and Use

belligerently
deference
furrow
gaudy
surmise

ARGUMENTATION

To present their opinions on controversial issues, writers often compose argumentative essays. For example, a newspaper editorial promotes a particular writer's views on an issue in order to persuade readers to adopt the same viewpoint. Editorials, however, can present only one side of an issue. The strongest arguments are those that examine fairly both sides of a controversy and then reach a conclusion as to the best position to support.

Each of the selections in this subunit presents conflicting views on a human rights issue. In this writing assignment, you will have the opportunity to present both sides of an issue in a "Point-Counterpoint" essay and to state which side of the issue you support.

GUIDED ASSIGNMENT: POINT-COUNTERPOINT ESSAY

In a point-counterpoint essay, present both sides of a controversial issue that interests you. Then argue to persuade your readers to support the side you favor.

Here is your PASSkey to this assignment.

PURPOSE: To persuade

AUDIENCE: People who are interested in your topic

SUBJECT: A controversial issue

STRUCTURE: An argumentative essay

Prewriting

STEP 1 Select a controversial issue To find ideas for your essay, scan newspapers and magazines, and watch national and local news reports. In choosing a controversial issue to debate, it is important to avoid topics that are purely matters of personal taste or that are too broad to cover in a brief essay. In a small group, brainstorm a list of controversial topics. You may find it useful to frame your issues as "should" questions and to categorize them under several headings. Here is part of the list one group made.

◀ STUDENT MODEL

```
Global: Should the United States give the Soviet Union
        money to help it improve its economy?
National: Should the federal government allow logging in
          national forests?
```


Writer's Workshop

Objectives

- To understand the goals of argumentation
- To determine the difference between "pro" and "con" arguments
- To take a side on a controversial issue
- To provide sufficient evidence to back up an opinion
- To draft, revise, edit, and present an argumentative essay
- To reflect on the writing process

Integrating . . .

Literature and Writing Share with students that the selections in this subunit deal with controversial issues. Conflicting views are presented, and the reader must determine how he or she feels about each issue.

Tell students that in this subunit they will write a point-counterpoint essay in which they present both sides of a controversial issue, take a stand, and try to convince the reader to agree with their opinion.

Writing and Language The Language Workshop in this subunit deals with using effective transitions. Students should understand the importance of smooth transitions. Explain that if writers use transitional words or phrases carefully, readers will interpret their writing correctly. Direct students to the list of transitional words in the Language Workshop. Suggest that students keep this list handy as they write their essays.

Discuss transitional words with LEP students, and determine if these words exist in their languages. This will probably be the case.

Writing and Thinking The Thinking Skills Workshop deals with propaganda techniques. Define propaganda for the students. Explain that propaganda techniques are faulty arguments, and that they have no place in their essays.

Additional Resources

UNIT FOUR RESOURCE BOOK

Writer's Workshop Copy Master, p. 48
Peer and Self-Evaluation Guidelines, p. 49
Writing Assessment Guidelines, p. 50

ENRICHMENT MATERIALS

Thinking Skills Transparency and Worksheet
Fine Art Transparency and Writing Prompts
Revision, Proofreading, and Elaboration Worksheet
Writing Prompts for Assessment

Teaching Strategies

Introduction Direct students to the Writer's Workshop on page 541. Point out the PASSkey graphic. Tell students that they are about to become embroiled in a controversial issue. Explain that they will scrutinize both sides of an issue and try to refrain from making judgments until they have sufficient evidence. Then, they will take a stand and try to convince others to agree with them. Explain that when controversial issues are brought into the light, they often lead to heated discussion. Assure students that the next few days will not be dull. Encourage them to keep an open mind as they enter the world of controversy.

Teaching Tip
You may want to provide some guidelines as students search for their controversial issues. If you wish to help students in their choice of topics, bring in newspapers, magazines, and journals. Explain to students that they need not focus on a current issue. They can write their essays about issues that occurred at any time throughout history. The steps and procedures are the same regardless of the era of the issue. Share the following instructions with the students:

1. Research a number of topics before choosing one.
2. Keep an open mind as you decide on a topic.
3. Pick a topic that interests you.
4. Pick a topic that you know little about.
5. Pick a topic that you do not yet have an opinion about.
6. Keep an open mind as you research your topic.
7. Don't begin writing or even forming a firm opinion until you have sufficient research to back up your opinion.

Prewriting Before students begin, review the prewriting steps with them. Emphasize the importance of choosing a topic carefully. Have students brainstorm topics. Encourage them to find unique topics, so that presenting them will be more interesting to the class. Stress that this is an opportunity to learn about a number of new subjects.

Local: Should the city council raise taxes to pay for improving the park system?
School: Should upperclassmen be excused from study hall?

STEP 2 Find support for both sides Good arguments use specific evidence in the form of facts, examples, and expert opinions. Depending on your topic, you may need to do some research in order to become informed about the complexities of your topic. If the issue you've selected is from the "Local" or "School" division of your brainstorming list, consider conducting interviews with individuals who are especially knowledgeable in that area. Complete a "Pro and Con" chart to keep track of the opposing sides of the issue. *Pro* means "in favor of," and *con* means "opposed to." Here is part of the chart one student made on the topic "Should upperclassmen be excused from study hall?"

STUDENT MODEL ▶

Pro	Con
1. They are mature enough to use their free time responsibly. 2. They deserve special privileges.	1. Such a policy would be unfair to other students. 2. The schoolwork of some upperclassmen would suffer.

STEP 3 Collect evidence Copy the data from your pro and con chart on a separate piece of paper. Beneath each statement, list facts, details, and explanations that support your reasoning. Below is some of the evidence one student collected.

STUDENT MODEL ▶

Con #2—The schoolwork of some upperclassmen would suffer.
—Many students say that they get most of their homework done in study hall.
—If upperclassmen did not have to go to study hall, some of them would not complete their homework, and their grades would suffer.
—Mr. James, a math teacher, says: "This school tried a 'no study hall' policy ten years ago, and parents complained."

STEP 4 Decide which position you will support Review all of the reasons and evidence you've collected. Weigh the merits of each reason that's listed on your pro and con chart. Then decide which side of the issue you want to support.

Drafting

STEP 1 **Introduce your topic** Explain why the issue you've selected is important to both you and your readers. Then, as in the model below, briefly describe the two opposing viewpoints and state which side you support.

STUDENT MODEL

Students at our high school are concerned about the issue of excusing upperclassmen from study hall. Many juniors and seniors believe that they have earned this privilege. Other students and faculty members believe that the loss of study hall will create both academic and administrative problems. This essay will explore both sides of this controversial issue and show that, indeed, excusing upperclassmen from study hall presents problematic rather than positive consequences.

STEP 2 **Write a draft of your argument** Using your chart and notes, write the body of your essay, dividing it between pro and con sections. Start with whichever position you plan to argue *against*. State each argument and the evidence you have found to support it. Present both sides of the issue fairly and completely.

STEP 3 **Conclude with your position** The final paragraph of your paper should persuade readers to accept the position you favor. Refer to specific evidence and reasons presented in the earlier sections of your essay. Focus on describing the weaknesses of the opposing view and on highlighting the strengths of your position.

Revising and Editing

Once you have completed the rough draft of your essay, ask a classmate to review your work according to the following checklist.

Revision Checklist

1. Does the introduction clearly describe the issue and its two sides?
2. Does the body of the essay contain both pro and con sections? Does each section include specific reasons and evidence in support of that side?
3. Does the last paragraph successfully persuade readers to favor the side of the issue that the writer supports?

Explain to students that after they choose their topics, they should carefully choose specific evidence. Tell students that specific evidence does not include opinions. Facts are needed to form an airtight argument. Make sure students are familiar with the idea of pro and con arguments.

Computer Tip

Encourage students to use a computer if they have access to one. A computer is a good tool to help organize their lists of controversial issues. It will also be useful as they begin to assemble their arguments. Students using computers will have the ability to expand ideas and topics as they work.

Drafting Before students begin to write, be sure that they have taken a stand on their topic. Encourage them to think the matter through carefully and be completely sure which side they are on. Read each drafting step aloud before the students begin to write, and clear up any confusion about how to organize their arguments. Tell students to stop writing periodically to make sure they are presenting both sides fairly. Encourage students to include as much information as is necessary to win their argument, and assure them that there are no length restrictions.

Revising and Editing Suggest that students pair up to revise their essays. Encourage them to choose partners who know little about their topic and nothing about their opinion. In this way, students will read each other's work completely objectively. Have the students look closely at the **Revision Checklist** as they read the essays. Have each student admit whether or not he or she was persuaded by the essay.

Have the students edit their essays for spelling, grammar, and mechanics.

Presenting Try the following presenting ideas with the class:

- Set up a point-counterpoint debate in the classroom. Have each student choose a position from one of the essays in class. If this becomes too one-sided, write each position on a slip of paper and have students pick the position they will debate. Explain to students that debaters need not always agree with the side they are taking. If the arguments in the essays are strong enough, it should be easy for students to do well.

- Have students organize a "debate day" for other classes. After the essays are presented, students from the other classes may wish to respond. Run through some of the guidelines for these students. If the other classes wish, they may research the topics and provide their responses at a later date.

Reflecting on Your Writing If many students want to make their essays more persuasive, consider setting aside time for this process. Ask students if they are still 100-percent certain about the position they have taken. Allow students to revise their essays according to their new positions. Remind them that they will have to rewrite the summary paragraphs.

Closure

Before beginning the next subunit, make sure students understand the following:

- An argumentation essay includes facts to back up opinions.
- Sufficient evidence is needed to back up an opinion.
- It is important to provide both sides of an argument in order for a fair choice to be made.
- Propaganda techniques are faulty arguments.

Editing When you have finished revising your essay, proofread it for spelling, clarity, and mechanics.

Presenting

Share your paper with two classmates. Ask them to act out your essay in a point-counterpoint debate in front of the class. Then have the rest of the class vote to see which side of the issue they support. Have students describe how the debate affected their opinions on the issue you explored.

Reflecting on Your Writing

Answer the following questions about this assignment. Place the answers and your paper in your writing portfolio.

1. Did you have a hard time deciding which position to take? Why or why not? Did you change your mind as you explored your issue?
2. What was the most difficult part of writing this essay? Why?
3. How persuasive do you think your essay is? How would you make it more persuasive?

Additional Writing and Research Topics

The following items provide additional writing practice based on the selections in this subunit:

Argumentation
Write an argument convincing the president of the United States that war is not good for anyone. Be sure to back up this opinion with concrete facts. You may wish to go to the library to get statistics that corroborate this belief.

Other Topics
Historical Research: Research a historical conflict. (It does not have to involve the United States.) Explore the feelings that both sides had about the issue. For example, you might want to explore the events that led up to the Revolutionary War. Include as many facts as you can. At the bottom of your essay, write a sentence or two explaining what position you would have taken had you been involved in the conflict.

USING EFFECTIVE TRANSITIONS

A **transition** is a word or phrase that shows how ideas are related or connected.

Transitions make writing clearer by showing the relationships that exist between ideas. Consider the following sentences.

Chee's lips tightened as he began to look around for Old Man Fat. *Finally* he saw him passing among the tourists, collecting coins.

The word *finally* tells you how the events in the two sentences are related in time. A transition at the beginning of a sentence can relate that sentence to the preceding one. A transition within a sentence can relate the parts of the sentence to one another.

Often she lay wakeful on her sheep pelts *until* he stretched out for the night.

The transition *until* tells you that the event described in the first half of the sentence stops when the event described in the second half begins.

Transitions can be used for many different purposes. Here are some common transitions and the purposes for which they are used.

To Show Time	after, before, during, finally, first, meanwhile, sometimes, when, whenever, immediately
To Show Place	above, around, beneath, down, here, there
To Show Order of Importance	first, second, mainly, most important
To Show Cause and Effect	as a result, because, therefore, so, for that reason, consequently, since, although
To Show Contrast	on the other hand, yet, but, however, by contrast
To Show Comparison	as, than, in the same way, similarly, likewise

Language Workshop

Objectives

- To understand that transition words and phrases help make writing clearer
- To understand that transition words help show relationships between ideas
- To use transition words in writing

Integrating . . .

Writing and Language Remind students that in the **Writer's Workshop** they wrote argumentative essays. Explain that when they write such essays, it is important to present their ideas in a clear and logical manner. Tell students that using effective transition words and phrases can help them do that. Read the following excerpt from "Montgomery Boycott":
Attempted boycotts had failed in Montgomery and other cities. Because of changing times and tempers, this one seemed to have a better chance, but it was still a slender hope. We finally decided that if the boycott was 60 percent effective we would be doing all right, and we would be satisfied to have made a good start.

Point out to students that the use of the word *because* signals a cause and effect relationship, and that the word *finally* suggests that the decision was made after a considerable length of time. Encourage students to give other examples of relationships between ideas. This **Language Workshop** focuses on effective use of transition words to make the relationship between ideas clear.

Teaching Strategies

Ask a volunteer to read the focus statement in the box on page 545. Work through the lesson, making sure that students understand how transition words are used in writing. You might like to refer to the selection "Montgomery Boycott" to demonstrate transitions related to time.

Additional Resources

UNIT FOUR RESOURCE BOOK
Writer's Workshop Copy Master, p. 51

ENRICHMENT MATERIALS
Grammar and Usage Copy Masters

Point out that sometimes the kinds of transition words and phrases one uses depend upon the nature of the topic. For example, if students write an essay presenting arguments against a local tax increase, they might use transition words that show order of importance. If they write about why the United States should or should not increase spending on education, they might use transition words and phrases that show cause and effect.

Teaching Tip: LEP

Check to see that LEP students understand the meaning of sentences that contain the word *before* or *after* in transitional phrases. For example, in the sentence *Before Julie left for school, she wrote her sister a note,* make sure students understand that Julie wrote the note before leaving for school, even though leaving for school is mentioned first.

Closure

Before beginning the next subunit, be sure students have internalized these concepts:

- Transitions are words or phrases that show how ideas are related. Some examples of transition words are *finally, because, but, although,* and *while.*
- Transitions help readers follow the presentation of events or ideas in a written work.
- Transitions can be used for many purposes. Relationships that show time, place, order of importance, cause and effect, contrast, and comparison can all be clarified with transition words and expressions.

Answer Key
Exercise 1

1. After
2. For that reason
3. Because
4. However

Exercise 2

Answers will vary. Look for transitions showing time in the first paragraph. Transitions showing cause and effect would clarify relationships among ideas in the second and third paragraphs.

Exercise 3

Answers will vary.

Exercise 1 Read the following passage. Write the correct transition from the two in parentheses.

Chee and his family were deeply saddened by Chee's wife's death. 1. (*After* or *During*) Chee's wife died, Chee's mother- and father-in-law took Chee's daughter to live with them. 2. (*For that reason,* or *Most important,*) Chee and his family were saddened even more than they had been already. 3. (*Because* or *As a result,*) Chee knew that his daughter would be raised at a trading post instead of on the land, he wanted to get her back. 4. (*However,* or *Sometimes*) Chee's in-laws wanted to keep the little girl because they thought she would attract customers to their shop.

Peer Review

It's sometimes a good idea to have someone you trust read your writing to check for transitions. You may know what you want to say so well that you can't see the need for connections between your ideas.

Exercise 2 Read the following paragraphs. Working in a small group, add transitions. Try to make stronger links between the ideas within the paragraphs and between the paragraphs. Compare your work with that done by other groups to see the diversity of transitions used in good writing.

Ancestors of the Navaho lived in northwestern Canada and Alaska. One thousand years ago they began migrating south. They reached the area that is part of the southwestern United States. The people living in the area were the Pueblo Indians. The Pueblo Indians were farmers. The Navaho learned how to plant fruits and vegetables from them.

In the 1600's the Spanish settled in the Southwest. The Navaho joined the Pueblo and Apache peoples in their struggle against the Spanish. The tribes did not want to become servants or prisoners of the Spanish people.

In the 1800's Navaho fought to keep their land from Americans looking for silver and gold. Narvona, an important leader, was killed by United States soldiers. The tribe attacked Fort Defiance in Arizona. The government decided to take action. More than eight thousand Navaho were forced to leave their land and walk three hundred miles across New Mexico. This deadly march has been called the Long Walk by the Navaho people and others.

Language Handbook

For review and practice, see Section 7, **Sentence Structure.**

Exercise 3 Style With others in a small group, skim one of the stories you have read in this unit, looking for transitional words or phrases. When you find a transition, discuss why the writer might have chosen to use a transition at that point and tell what purpose the transition serves.

Additional Practice

The following items are additional exercises to help students use transitions in their writing.

Write these sentences, replacing each blank with an appropriate transition. Possible answers.

1. Lancelot glanced out the tiny tower window. Below lay the gardens of the duke.
2. A moving shadow caught his eye. Was that Anne, the duchess, there by the wall?
3. Then the shadow vanished. Consequently, Lancelot began to think he had imagined it.

Write this description. Insert transitions wherever they would be appropriate. Note that the paragraph moves from nearby to far away. Check placement and accuracy of students' transitions.

The snow stopped falling. The sun rose. A squirrel scampered about, looking for food. Two sparrows found the bird feeder and began to eat hungrily. The horses whinnyed softly in their stalls, waiting to be fed. The branches of the apple trees swayed under their burden of snow. A lone pickup truck struggled to make its way through the pale drifts. The hills looked sleek and elegant, their fir trees outlined sharply.

PROPAGANDA TECHNIQUES

Sometimes persuasive writers and speakers present reasonable arguments. At other times they use faulty arguments such as the following **propaganda techniques.**

Loaded Language Loaded language is words and phrases chosen specifically to appeal to the emotions. Loaded language is often based on the connotations of words. The **connotation** of a word is an emotional meaning associated with it in addition to its dictionary definition, or **denotation.** The connotation of a word may be positive or negative. For example, you might feel differently about a gang of *kids,* than you would about a gang of *thugs. Thugs* is an example of negative loaded language.

Circular Reasoning Normally, a person presenting an argument backs it up with supporting evidence, as in, "You should learn how to interview because you will need this skill to get a job." Sometimes, however, instead of offering evidence, people simply restate their initial statement in different words, as in, "You should learn how to interview because learning to interview is something young people should do." This statement is circular; it adds no new supporting ideas.

Either/Or Fallacy An argument that presents only two of many alternatives is making use of the either/or fallacy. The statement "Either you support your President or you don't" is an example. It ignores a third alternative: that you support some of the President's policies but not all.

Overgeneralization Generalizations are statements that apply to a number of persons, places, or things. If a statement is too broad to be proved, it is called an overgeneralization. The statement "Today's students know nothing about World War II" is an overgeneralization because many students do, in fact, know something about the war.

Bandwagon/Snob Appeal Statements like "Every fashionable senior this year is wearing a piece of Navaho jewelry" urge you to step in line with the crowd. Snob appeal is a form of bandwagon appeal. The statement "Only a chosen few will be admitted to the Navaho Club" is an example of snob appeal.

Exercise Work with other students to find examples of each kind of propaganda technique in advertisements from magazines and newspapers. Make a bulletin board or collage of these for the class.

Thinking Skills Workshop

Objective

- To identify and read beyond propaganda techniques such as loaded language, circular reasoning, the either/or fallacy, overgeneralizations, the bandwagon approach, and snob appeal

Integrating . . .

Literature and Thinking Skills
Share with students that unlike persuasive arguments, propaganda may ask the reader to ignore logic and react emotionally.

Teaching Strategies

Ask students to discuss the negative effects that propaganda can have. *(Possible responses: can mislead people; can cause people to make unwise decisions)*

Read through the material with students. Assign the exercise on page 547 as homework.

Closure

Before beginning the next subunit, be sure students have internalized this concept:

- Propaganda techniques encourage people to react emotionally instead of logically.

Teaching Tip: LEP
Ask LEP students to tell about advertising in their native cultures. Compare how various cultures use and react to propaganda techniques. Ask them to share their opinions about the effectiveness of propaganda techniques in American advertising on people whose primary language is not English.

Exercise

(Responses will vary. Be sure that groups can name the technique used in each of the advertisements they included in their collages.)

Additional Resources

UNIT FOUR RESOURCE BOOK
Related Skills Copy, p. 52

ADDITIONAL PRACTICE

Work in a group to create a product and an advertisement for the product. In your advertisement, use at least one of the techniques discussed in the workshop. *(Responses will vary. Be sure that groups can name the technique used in their advertisements.)*

Subunit Preview

Have students read the introduction to subunit 3, **Passing Judgments.** Ask how having the obligation to judge another relates to the broader unit theme, **Human Rights: Pain and Pride.** Is is possible for a human being to be objective? Why or why not? Do feelings and opinions make a just decision possible? If factual data could be sorted and analyzed by a computer, would the verdict be more or less fair than the verdict reached after a trial by jury? Explain your answer. Ask students to read the subunit introduction and predict which aspect of the play will be most interesting.

For Additional Challenge

The following selections offer extra challenge in the exploration of the subunit theme:

"The Devil and Daniel Webster," a short story by Stephen Vincent Benét

"The Masque of the Red Death," a short story by Edgar Allan Poe

PASSING JUDGMENTS

Who has the right to judge you? You may feel that no one does, but if someone accuses you of committing a crime, our society reserves the right to judge you in court. America's legal system is designed to protect the rights of the accused. In our court system, you are presumed innocent until proven guilty. To ensure that your trial is fair and objective, you are judged by a jury of your peers. But does this system of justice always produce a fair outcome? Who are these peers who will judge you, and how sure can you be of their motives for judging you?

In the next subunit, you will meet twelve men who must pass judgment on a young man. As you read, judge for yourself how secure our human rights seem to be under America's legal system.

OBSERVATION ASSESSMENT

Observing how students respond to the text, to the classroom instruction, and to peers is an important part of an assessment program. The following suggestions and the form in each Unit Resource Book can be used to implement observation assessment.

- As students read the play, note which strategies they use during reading. Do they use illustrations to identify the characters? Do they use stage directions to visualize movement? Do they use their own experience to make inferences about what the characters might feel and do?

e x p l o r e

Drama

Twelve Angry Men

REGINALD ROSE

Examine What You Know (Prior Knowledge)

As the members of the jury in a murder trial, the twelve characters in this selection must decide on a man's guilt or innocence. Jot down on paper five things you know about our nation's jury system. Then compare your notes with what you learn in reading *Twelve Angry Men.*

Expand Your Knowledge (Building Background)

Our system of trial by jury was first brought to this country by English colonists. A system of trial by jury similar to the English system was written into our Constitution. The Fifth Amendment guarantees due process—that each trial will follow the law. The Sixth Amendment guarantees "a speedy and public trial." Jurors must be undecided as to the defendant's guilt or innocence before the trial begins and must be chosen from the community where the crime occurred. An accused person may choose to be tried by a judge rather than a jury. Whether judge or jury is chosen, the law states that in a criminal trial, a person is presumed innocent until proven guilty "beyond a reasonable doubt." Without sufficient proof, the judge or jury must acquit, or find not guilty, the person who is accused.

Enrich Your Reading (Reading Skill)

Notetaking Use a chart like the one below to note the major events in this courtroom drama. As you read the play, identify the three pieces of evidence that are brought into question. For each piece of evidence, identify the act in which it is introduced, the act in which it is questioned and by whom, and any weaknesses found in it by the jurors.

Evidence	When Introduced	When Questioned	Questioning Juror(s)	Weakness(es)

Objectives

- To read and understand a three-act play
- To recognize the uses of stage directions in a play
- To apply notetaking skills to the reading of a play
- To identify the protagonist and antagonist in a play
- To recognize sterotypes
- To identify the climax of a play
- To review suspense
- To express understanding of the work through a choice writing options, including lists, summaries, charts, a news article and paragraphs of opinion and explanation

Prereading/Motivation

Examine What You Know

Discussion Prompts: Have you ever heard an adult discuss jury duty? What did he or she say? How do the courts select people to serve on juries? Why might the members of a jury disagree on a case?

Expand Your Knowledge

Discussion Prompts: How can the courts make sure that potential jurors are open-minded and undecided about a case? How would you explain the phrase *beyond a reasonable doubt?*

Enrich Your Reading

Have students copy the chart and fill it in as they read. Teaching Tips throughout the play will alert you to points where new evidence is discussed and brought into question.

Thematic Link—Passing Judgment

In this play, the twelve characters are the members of a jury who must judge whether a young man is guilty of murder "beyond a reasonable doubt."

Journal Writing

The characters of *Twelve Angry Men* serve as a judge. Suggest these journal topics to the students:

- Why is serving on a jury a serious responsibility?
- Why might the twelve members of a jury be described as "angry men"?
- What feelings would you have if you were called to serve on a jury for a murder trial?

For other journal opportunities, refer students to Real Life Connections (pp. T–555) and Broader Connections (p. 589).

Additional Resources

UNIT FOUR RESOURCE BOOK

Reader's Guidesheets, pp. 56, 59, and 62
Vocabulary Worksheets, pp. 57, 60, and 63
Selection and Vocabulary Check Tests, pp. 58, 61, and 69
Selection Test, pp. 70–73

Collaborative Learning

Opportunities for collaborative learning appear throughout the lesson and include Options for Learning activities 2 and 3 (p. 591) and Cross-Curricular Options (p. T–591).

Teaching Strategies

Vocabulary Preview

These vocabulary words are defined at the bottom of the selection page on which they appear. You may wish to discuss them briefly before students begin reading.

alibi excuse
abstain withhold one's vote
conceivable believable
defendant person accused in court
discrepancy lack of agreement
intimidate make afraid
motive reason for doing
prosecution side that brings the case against a person accused of a crime
tenement old apartment building
writhing twisting

Support for Students of Limited English Proficiency

- Use **Reader's Guidesheets**, pp. 56, 59, and 62
- *Twelve Angry Men* is set in a courthouse jury room in a large American city during a recent decade. Students may be unfamiliar with many of the specialized judicial terms used in the play or with America's trial-by-jury system in general. Have students from other countries share descriptions of their systems of justice first. You may then want to show a short educational film on our court system if one is available from your local library or school media services. It may also prove beneficial to show parts of the 1957 version of *Twelve Angry Men* as students finish reading aloud each act.
- **Annotations C, D, L, P, U, Y, CC, II, JJ** in **Act One, annotations C, G, I, N, U, V, X, CC, and EE** in Act Two, and annotations **B, F, G, L, O, Q, Y, BB, II, and LL** in Act Three focus on terms and phrases that may trouble LEP students.

Text Annotations

A. Literary Element: AUTHOR'S PURPOSE Point out that the characters, who are jurors, have no names, only numbers. Explain that this anonymity helps the audience or readers focus on the issues the jurors must decide.

B. Literary Element: CHARACTERIZATION Explain that these characterizations, or descriptions of each juror, are intended to help the actors interpret the roles.

C. LEP: Vocabulary Explain to students that *sadism* is a desire to hurt others. Ask students what type of behavior they might expect from Juror Three. *(Possible response: He will be a source of conflict.)*

Twelve Angry Men

REGINALD ROSE

CHARACTERS

A

Foreman of the Jury	**Juror No. Seven**
Juror No. Two	**Juror No. Eight**
Juror No. Three	**Juror No. Nine**
Juror No. Four	**Juror No. Ten**
Juror No. Five	**Juror No. Eleven**
Juror No. Six	**Juror No. Twelve**

Guard (bit part)
Judge (bit part) } offstage voices
Clerk (bit part) }

B

NOTES ON CHARACTERS AND COSTUMES

Foreman: He is a small, petty man who is impressed with the authority he has and handles himself quite formally. He is not overly bright, but dogged.

Juror No. Two: He is a meek, hesitant man who finds it difficult to maintain any opinions of his own. He is easily swayed and usually adopts the opinion of the last person to whom he has spoken.

C **Juror No. Three:** He is a very strong, very forceful, extremely opinionated man within whom can be detected a streak of sadism. Also, he is a humorless man who is intolerant of opinions other than his own and accustomed to forcing his wishes and views upon others. C

Juror No. Four: He seems to be a man of wealth and position and a practiced speaker who presents himself well at all times. He seems to feel a little bit above the rest of the jurors. His only concern is with the facts in this case, and he is appalled with the behavior of the others.

Juror No. Five: He is a naive, very frightened young man who takes his obligations in this case very seriously but who

STRUCTURED READING FOR LESS PROFICIENT STUDENTS

These questions can help to guide students through the reading. Ask each question at the point of the selection where the SR number appears in the margin.

SR–1. Who is the defendant in the trial? What is the crime? *(The defendant is a "kid"; the crime is murder in the first degree, for the defendant is accused of stabbing his father to death.)* **Literal recall**

SR–2. In the first vote taken among themselves, how do the twelve jurors vote? *(Eleven jurors vote "guilty"; one votes "not guilty.")* **Literal recall**

SR–3. Describe the defendant. *(He is nineteen; he comes from a slum; his mother is dead; he is tough and angry.)* **Literal recall/summarizing**

SR–4. What does Juror Twelve see as the purpose of the jury members who voted "guilty"? *(They must convince Juror Eight to change his vote to "not guilty.")* **Literal recall**

Continued on page 551

finds it difficult to speak up when his elders have the floor.

Juror No. Six: He is an honest but dull-witted man who comes upon his decisions slowly and carefully. He is a man who finds it difficult to create positive opinions but who must listen to and digest and accept those opinions offered by others which appeal to him most.

Juror No. Seven: He is a loud, flashy, glad-handed salesman type who has more important things to do than to sit on a jury. He is quick to show temper and equally quick to form opinions on things about which he knows nothing. He is a bully and, of course, a coward.

Juror No. Eight: He is a quiet, thoughtful, gentle man—a man who sees all sides of every question and constantly seeks the truth. He is a man of strength tempered with compassion. Above all, he is a man who wants justice to be done and will fight to see that it is.

Juror No. Nine: He is a mild, gentle old man, long since defeated by life, and now merely waiting to die. He recognizes himself for what he is and mourns the days when it would have been possible to be courageous without shielding himself behind his many years.

Juror No. Ten: He is an angry, bitter man—a man who antagonizes almost at sight. He is also a bigot who places no values on any human life save his own. Here is a man who has been nowhere and is going nowhere and knows it deep within him. D

Juror No. Eleven: He is a refugee from Europe. He speaks with an accent and is ashamed, humble, almost subservient to the people around him. He will honestly seek justice because he has suffered through so much injustice.

Juror No. Twelve: He is a slick, bright advertising man who thinks of human beings in terms of percentages, graphs, and polls, and has no real understanding of people. He is a superficial snob, but trying to be a good fellow.

Guard: This is a bit part. He can be any age and wears a uniform.

Costumes: The jurors wear everyday business clothes suitable for summer. Juror No. Five wears an expensively tailored suit. Juror No. Seven's clothes are flashy. Juror No. Twelve dresses smartly but in good taste.

Place: *A jury room.* E

Time: *The present. Summer.*

Synopsis

Act One: Late afternoon.

Act Two: A second or two later.

Act Three: Immediately following Act Two.

ACT ONE

At Rise of Curtain: *The curtain comes up on a dark stage; then, as the lights start to come up on the scene, we hear the voice of the Judge, offstage.*

Judge *(offstage)*. Murder in the first degree . . . premeditated homicide[1] . . . is the most serious charge tried in our criminal courts. You have heard a long and complex case, gentlemen, and it is now your duty to sit down to try and separate F

1. **premeditated homicide:** first degree murder; a planned, purposeful murder.

D. LEP: Vocabulary Students may be unfamiliar with the word *bigot.* Explain that a bigot is a person who is intolerant of people who hold opinions that differ from his or her own. A bigot, then, is a person who harbors prejudices toward other people.

Historical Sidelight Students may be interested to learn that there are theories about the origins of drama. One theory suggests that drama grew out of a natural love of storytelling and the reenactment of victorious hunts or battles. According to a second theory, drama arose out of the hymns of praise sung at the tombs of dead heroes. Others believe that drama originated with ancient religious ceremonies performed to win favor from the gods.

E. Literary Element: SETTING Have students note details that identify the setting. *(jury room; present time; summer)*

F. Literary Element: PLOT Explain that at the end of a trial, the judge instructs the jury as to the exact nature of its responsibility. This is called "the charge to the jury." Point out that the playwright uses this charge to set forth the basic dramatic situation of the play.

Structured Reading for Less Proficient Students

Continued from page 550

SR–5. Who are the two witnesses to the murder? What did they see and hear? *(The man downstairs heard the boy say that he was going to kill his father; he also heard the body fall and saw the boy run away. The woman across the street watched the murder through the windows of a passing el train.)* **Literal recall/summarizing**

SR–6. Describe Juror Eight's "peculiar feeling" about the trial. *(He feels that the defense counsel did not cross-examine properly, and, as a result, many questions were left unasked.)* **Literal recall**

SR–7. What point does Juror Eight make by bringing his own switchblade knife to the jury room? *(He shows that such knives are readily available in the boy's community and that merely because the boy has such a knife does not prove his guilt.)* **Clarifying**

SR–8. What happens in the vote at the end of Act One? *(One of the jurors who originally voted "guilty" changes his vote to "not guilty.")* **Literal recall**

G. Literary Element: STAGE DIRECTIONS Remind students that these stage directions are given from the actors' point of view. For example, the door is on the actors' left as they face the audience. To the audience, the door would appear on the right side of the set.

H. Reading Skill: CLARIFYING Ask students to explain the guard's comment. *(Possible response: The case against the accused murderer is so strong that he is sure to be found guilty.)*

Teaching Tip

From time to time, refer students back to the notes on pages 550–551 to refresh their memories about each of these characters.

I. Literary Element: MOOD Ask students how the talk of heat and sweating symbolizes the mood in the jury room. *(Possible response: The jurors are in a "hot spot" because they must decide whether a man is to live or die. Having to make this difficult decision would make anyone "sweat.")*

F the facts from the fancy. One man is dead. The life of another is at stake. If there is a reasonable doubt in your minds as to the guilt of the accused—then you must declare him not guilty. If—however—there is no reasonable doubt, then he must be found guilty. Whichever way you decide, the verdict must be unanimous. I urge you to deliberate honestly and thoughtfully. You are faced with a grave responsibility. Thank you, gentlemen.

G *(There is a long pause. The lights are now up full in the jury room. There is a door left and a window in the right wall of the room. Over the door left is an electric clock. A water cooler is downstage right, with a wastebasket beside it. A container with paper cups is attached to the wall nearby. A long conference table is slightly upstage of center stage. About it are twelve uncomfortable-looking straight chairs. There is a chair at either end of the table, seven at the upstage side and three at the downstage side of the table. [*Note: *This arrangement of the chairs about the table will enable most of the action to be directed toward the audience, with a minority of the characters placed with their backs toward the audience.] There are two more straight chairs against the wall downstage left and one in the upstage right corner of the room. It is a bare, unpleasant room. After the pause, the door left opens and the* Guard *walks in. As he opens the door the lettering "Jury Room" can be seen on the outside of the door. The* Guard *walks across the room and opens the window right as a clerk drones out, offstage left.)*

Clerk *(offstage left)*. The jury will retire.[2]

H **Guard** *(surveying room, shaking his head)*. He doesn't stand a chance. *(moves left again)*

(The Jurors *file in left. The* Guard *stands upstage of the door and counts them. Four or five of the jurors light cigarettes as they enter the room.* Juror Five *lights a pipe, which he smokes constantly.* Jurors Two, Nine, *and* Twelve *go to the water cooler for a drink.* Juror Seven *goes to the window and opens it wider. The rest of the* Jurors *begin to take seats around the table, though some of them stand and lean forward, with both hands on the back of the chair.* Juror Seven *produces a pack of gum and offers a piece to the men by the water cooler.)*

Seven. Chewing gum? Gum? Gum?

Nine. Thank you, but no. *(*Jurors Two *and* Twelve *shake their heads.)*

Seven. Y'know something?

Twelve. I know lots of things. I'm in advertising.

Seven *(tugging at collar)*. Y'know, it's hot.

Twelve *(to* Two, *mildly sarcastic)*. I never would have known that if he hadn't told me. Would you?

Two *(missing sarcasm)*. I suppose not. I'd kind of forgotten.

Twelve. All I've done all day is sweat.

Three *(calling out)*. I bet you aren't sweating like that kid who was tried.

Seven. You'd think they'd at least air-condition the place. I almost dropped dead in court. I

Twelve. My taxes are high enough.

Seven. This should go fast, anyway. *(moves to table, as* Eight *goes to window)*

Nine *(nodding to himself, then, as he throws his paper water cup into the wastebasket)*. Yes, it's hot.

2. **retire:** to withdraw to a private place; here, the term refers to the jury's leaving the courtroom to decide on a verdict in the jury room.

J **Three.** Did he lock that door?

Guard. Okay, gentlemen. Everybody's here. If there's anything you want, I'm right outside. Just knock. *(Goes out left, closing door. They all look at door, silently. The lock is turned.)*

Four. Yes, he did.

Three. What do they think we are, crooks?

Foreman *(seated at left end of table).* They lock us up for a little while. . . .

Three *(breaking in).* And then they lock that kid up forever and that's okay by me.

Five *(motioning toward door).* I never knew they did that.

Ten *(blowing his nose).* Sure, they lock the door. What did you think?

Five *(a bit irritated).* I just didn't know. It never occurred to me.

Four. Shall we all admit right now that it is hot and humid and our tempers are short?

K **Eight** *(turning from window).* It's been a pretty hard week. *(turns back and continues looking out)*

Three. I feel just fine.

Twelve. I wonder what's been going on down at the office. You know how it is in advertising. In six days my job could be gone, and the whole company, too. They aren't going to like this. (Jurors *start to take off their suit coats and hang them over backs of chairs.)*

Foreman. Well, figure this is our duty.

Twelve. I didn't object to doing my duty. I just mentioned that I might not have a job by the time I get back. *(He and* Nine *move to table and take their places.* Nine *sits near right end of table.)*

Three *(motioning to* Four*).* Ask him to hire you. He's rich. Look at the suit!

Foreman *(to* Four, *as he tears off slips of paper for a ballot).* Is it custom-tailored?

Four. Yes, it is.

Foreman. I have an uncle who's a tailor. *(*Four *takes his jacket off, places it carefully over back of chair and sits.)*

Four. How does he do?

Foreman *(shaking his head).* Not too well. Y'know, a friend of his, that's a friend of my uncle, the tailor—well—this friend wanted to be on this jury in my place.

Seven. Why didn't you let him? I would have done anything to miss this.

Foreman. And get caught, or something? Y'know what kind of a fine you could pay for anything like that? Anyway, this friend of my uncle's was on a jury once, about ten years ago—a case just about like this one.

Twelve. So what happened?

Foreman. They let him off. Reasonable doubt. And do y'know, about eight years later they found out that he'd actually done it, anyway. A guilty man—a murderer—was turned loose in the streets.

Three. Did they get him?

Four. They couldn't.

Three. Why not?

Four. A man can't be held in double jeopardy. Unless it's a hung jury, they can't try a man twice for the same crime. L

Seven. That isn't going to happen here.

Three. Six days. They should have finished it in two. *(slapping back of one hand into palm of other)* Talk! Talk! Talk! *(gets up and starts for water cooler)* Did you ever hear so much talk about nothing?

Two *(laughing nervously).* Well—I guess—they're entitled. . . .

Three. Everybody gets a fair trial. . . . *(shakes his head)* That's the system. *(downs his drink)* Well, I suppose you can't say anything against it. *(Tosses his water cup toward wastebasket and misses.* Two

J. Literary Element: MOOD Ask students how the locking of the jury room's door affects the atmosphere in the room. *(Possible response: It adds to the intensity and seriousness of the situation. With the heat, the room now resembles a pressure cooker.)*

K. Reading Skill: CONTRASTING Have students contrast the reactions of Jurors Three and Eight to the week-long trial. What do their reactions suggest about them? *(Possible response: It has been a hard week for Eight, but Three feels "just fine." This suggests that Eight is taking the case more seriously.)*

L. LEP: Vocabulary Explain that in legal terms, *jeopardy* is the danger of being convicted and punished when tried for a crime. Our legal system precludes double jeopardy—being tried for the same crime twice.

Literary Sidelight Point out how the playwright uses the discussion of a previous case to introduce naturally concepts such as reasonable doubt and double jeopardy. The audience needs to know about these concepts in order to understand the play better.

Critic's Corner

Rose's early years as a television writer shaped and colored his entire career. During his emergence in the 1950s, a golden age for original television drama . . . Rose tailored his craft to the particular strengths of the medium. His scripts were topical and controversial; he used narrow, often indoor settings, and he centered conflicts on small but crucial individual moral choices. As a writer of motion pictures, Rose has continued to produce the kind of social, timely, personal dramas he created for television. Rose's main subjects are crime; juvenile delinquency; the problems of children and adolescents; and contemporary social issues, including bigotry, poverty, and urban blight. . . . at its best Rose's work is powerful, committed, intense.

Carola Kaplan, ***Dictionary of Literary Biography***

M. Literary Element: CHARACTER Have a student tell how Juror Seven's speech here is in keeping with his description on page 550. *(Possible response: His plans to go to a play are more important than his duty to dispense justice; he considers the proceedings a "show.")*

N. Reading Skill: CLARIFYING Have a student restate Juror Four's comment in order to make its meaning clearer. *(Possible response: We must decide the case on the facts and not be swayed by prejudices.)*

O. Critical Thinking: ANALYZING Ask students to suggest how Juror Eight feels being the only one to vote "not guilty." *(Possible responses: isolated, unpopular, uncertain)*

picks cup up and puts it in wastebasket as Three *returns to his seat.)*

Seven *(to* Ten*)***.** How did you like that business about the knife? Did you ever hear a phonier story?

Ten *(wisely)***.** Well, look, you've gotta expect that. You know what you're dealing with. . . .

Seven. He bought a switch knife[3] that night. . . .

Ten *(with a sneer)***.** And then he lost it.

Seven. A hole in his pocket.

Ten. A hole in his father.

Two. An awful way to kill your father—a knife in his chest. *(crosses to table)*

Ten. Look at the kind of people they are—you know them. *(gets handkerchief out again)*

Seven. What's the matter? You got a cold?

Ten *(blowing)***.** A lulu! These hot weather colds can kill you.

Seven. I had one last year, while I was on vacation, too.

Foreman *(briskly)***.** All right, gentlemen. Let's take seats.

Seven. Right. This better be fast. I've got tickets to—*(Insert name of any current Broadway hit.)*—for tonight. I must be the only guy in the world who hasn't seen it yet. *(laughs and sits down, as do others still not seated)* Okay, your honor, start the show.

Foreman *(to* Eight *who is still looking out window)***.** How about sitting down? *(*Eight *doesn't hear him.)* The gentleman at the window. *(*Eight *turns, startled.)* How about sitting down?

Eight. Oh, I'm sorry. *(sits at right end of table, opposite* Foreman*)*

Ten. It's tough to figure, isn't it? A kid kills his father. Bing! Just like that. Well, it's the element. They let the kids run wild. Maybe it serves 'em right.

Four. There are better proofs than some emotion you may have—perhaps a dislike for some group.

Seven. We all agreed that it was hot.

Nine. And that our tempers will get short.

Three. That's if we disagree—but this is open and shut. Let's get it done.

Foreman. All right. Now—you gentlemen can handle this any way you want to. I mean, I'm not going to make any rules. If we want to discuss it first and then vote, that's one way. Or we can vote right now and see how we stand.

Seven. Let's vote now. Who knows, maybe we can all go home.

Ten. Yeah. Let's see who's where.

Three. Right. Let's vote now.

Eight. All right. Let us vote.

Foreman. Anybody doesn't want to vote? *(Looks around table. There is a pause as all look at each other.)*

Seven. That was easy.

Foreman. Okay. All those voting guilty raise your hands. *(Jurors* Three, Seven, Ten *and* Twelve *put their hands up instantly. The* Foreman *and* Two, Four, Five *and* Six *follow a second later. Then* Eleven *raises his hand and a moment later* Nine *puts his hand up.)* Eight—nine—ten—eleven—that's eleven for guilty. Okay. Not guilty? *(*Eight's *hand goes up. All turn to look at him.)*

Three. Hey, you're in left field![4]

Foreman. Okay. Eleven to one. Eleven guilty, one not guilty. Now we know where we stand.

---

3. **switch knife:** a switchblade; a knife whose blade is hidden in the handle and springs out at the push of a button.

DATA BANK

A critically successful film version of *Twelve Angry Men* appeared in 1957. The film's screenplay, an Academy Award nominee, was adapted by Reginald Rose from his earlier teleplay. Directed by Sidney Lumet, the movie's star-studded cast included Henry Fonda, Lee J. Cobb, E. G. Marshall, Jack Warden, Ed Begley, Jack Klugman, and Martin Balsam.

P. LEP: Vocabulary Explain that calculus is a form of math usually taught in college. Elicit that Juror Twelve is being sarcastic, poking fun at what he perceives to be Juror Eight's lack of intelligence.

Q. Literary Element: THEME Ask students to tell on what basis Juror Three and Juror Ten seem to judge the defendant. *(Possible response: They judge him based on his appearance.)*

Film stills from the 1957 United Artists movie, *Twelve Angry Men,* with Henry Fonda, Lee J. Cobb, and Martin Balsam.

Three *(rising, to* Eight*)***.** Do you really believe he's not guilty?

Eight *(quietly)***.** I don't know.

Seven *(to* Foreman*)***.** After six days, he doesn't know.

P **Twelve.** In six days I could learn calculus. This is A, B, C.

Eight. I don't believe that it is as simple as A, B, C.

Three. I never saw a guiltier man in my life. *(sits again)*

Eight. What does a guilty man look like? He is not guilty until we say he is guilty. Are we to vote on his face?

Three. You sat right in court and heard the same things I did. The man's a dangerous killer. You could see it. Q

Eight. Where do you look to see if a man is a killer?

4. **in left field:** an expression meaning way off, or far from the truth or the accepted belief.

Real Life Connections

Point out that it is a basic rule of group behavior for people to want to identify with and be part of the majority. Ask students if they agree that it takes great personal courage and uncommonly strong conviction to hold to an unpopular view, as Juror Eight does in the play. Ask students to discuss real-life incidents in which they have held opinions opposed by the majority. Have them describe the pressure that they felt from the group. Ask students if they made any efforts to persuade others to adopt their points of view and whether these efforts met with success.

R. Literary Element: CONFLICT Point out that the central conflict in the play is the question of if there is reasonable doubt about whether the defendant murdered his father. Ask students how this question has caused for Juror Eight an internal conflict that puts him in external conflict with the rest of the jury. *(Juror Eight is unsure in his own mind about the defendant's guilt, whereas the other jurors are sure the defendant is guilty.)*

S. Critical Thinking: SYNTHESIZING Ask students to tell how the passage relates to the title of the play. *(Possible response: As the jurors describe the hardships they experience, some of which don't really seem so hard, they reveal themselves to be angry men indeed.)*

T. Reading Skill: INFERRING Ask students who Juror Ten is referring to when he talks about " 'em," the people he has lived among all his life. *(Possible response: slum kids who are probably members of some ethnic minority)* Ask students what conclusions they can draw about Juror Ten. *(Possible response: He is prejudiced and engages in stereotyping.)*

U. LEP: Vocabulary Some students may be unfamiliar with the meaning of the word *monopoly.* Explain that a monopoly is the exclusive control or possession of something—in this case, the truth. Have students paraphrase the sentence. *(Possible response: You're not the only one who knows what truth is.)*

Three *(irritated by him)***.** Oh, well! . . .

Eight *(with quiet insistence)***.** I would like to know. Tell me what the facial characteristics of a killer are. Maybe you know something I don't know.

Four. Look! What is there about the case that makes you think the boy is innocent? R

Eight. He's nineteen years old.

Three. That's old enough. He knifed his own father. Four inches into the chest. An innocent little nineteen-year-old kid.

Four *(to* Three*)***.** I agree with you that the boy is guilty, but I think we should try to avoid emotionally colored arguments.

Three. All right. They proved it a dozen different ways. Do you want me to list them?

Eight. No.

Ten *(rising, putting his feet on seat of chair and sitting on back of it, then, to* Eight*)***.** Well, do you believe that stupid story he told?

Four *(to* Ten*)***.** Now, now.

Ten. Do you believe the kid's story?

Eight. I don't know whether I believe it or not. Maybe I don't.

Seven. So what'd you vote not guilty for?

Eight. There were eleven votes for guilty—it's not so easy for me to raise my hand and send a boy off to die without talking about it first.

Seven. Who says it's easy for me?

Four. Or me?

Eight. No one.

Foreman. He's still just as guilty, whether it's an easy vote or a hard vote.

Seven *(belligerently)***.** Is there something wrong because I voted fast?

Eight. Not necessarily.

Seven. I think the guy's guilty. You couldn't change my mind if you talked for a hundred years.

Eight. I don't want to change your mind.

Three. Just what are you thinking of?

Eight. I want to talk for a while. Look—this boy's been kicked around all his life. You know—living in a slum—his mother dead since he was nine. That's not a very good head start. He's a tough, angry kid. You know why slum kids get that way? Because we knock 'em over the head once a day, every day. I think maybe we owe him a few words. That's all. *(Looks around table. He is met by cold looks.* Nine *nods slowly while* Four *begins to comb his hair.)*

Four. All right, it's hard, sure—it was hard for me. Everything I've got I fought for. I worked my way through college. That was a long time ago, and perhaps you do forget. I fought, yes, but I never killed.

Three. I know what it's like. I never killed nobody. S

Twelve. I've been kicked around, too. Wait until you've worked in an ad agency and the big boy that buys the advertising walks in. We all know.

Eleven *(who speaks with an accent)***.** In my country, in Europe, kicking was a science, but let's try to find something better than that.

Ten *(to* Eight*)***.** I don't mind telling you this, mister. We don't owe the kid a thing. He got a fair trial, didn't he? You know what that trial cost? He's lucky he got it. Look, we're all grown-ups here. You're not going to tell us that we're supposed to believe him, knowing what he is. I've lived among 'em all my life. You can't believe a word they say. You know that. T

Nine *(to* Ten, *very slowly)***.** I don't know that. What a terrible thing for a man to believe! Since when is dishonesty a group characteristic? You have no monopoly on the truth! U

DATA BANK

If the jurors in a case cannot reach a unanimous decision among themselves, they are said to be a "hung jury." In this event, the judge declares a mistrial, and an entirely new trial must be scheduled. Since trials are time-consuming and expensive, it is in everyone's interest, if at all possible, for jurors to reach unanimity.

Three *(interrupting)*. All right. It's not Sunday. We don't need a sermon.

V **Nine** *(not heeding)*. What this man says is very dangerous. *(*Eight *puts his hand on* Nine's *arm and stops him.* Nine *draws a deep breath and relaxes.)*

Four. I don't see any need for arguing like this. I think we ought to be able to behave like gentlemen.

Seven. Right!

Twelve *(smiling up at* Four*)*. Oh, all right, if you insist.

Four *(to* Twelve*)*. Thank you.

Twelve. Sure.

Four. If we're going to discuss this case, why, let's discuss the facts.

Foreman. I think that's a good point. We have a job to do. Let's do it.

Eleven. If you gentlemen don't mind, I'm going to close the window. *(gets up and does so; then, apologetically as he moves back to table)* It was blowing on my neck. *(*Ten *blows his nose fiercely as he gets down from back of chair and sits again.)*

Seven. If you don't mind, I'd like to have the window open.

Eleven. But it was blowing on me.

Seven. Don't you want a little air? It's summer—it's hot.

Eleven. I was very uncomfortable.

Seven. There are twelve of us in this room; it's the only window. If you don't mind!

Eleven. I have some rights, too.

Seven. So do the rest of us.

Four *(to* Eleven*)*. Couldn't you trade chairs with someone at the other end of the table?

Eleven. All right, I will open the window, if someone would trade. *(Goes to window and opens it.* Two *gets up and goes to* Eleven's *chair, near right end of table.)*

Two *(motioning)*. Take my chair.

Eleven. Thank you. *(goes to* Two's *chair, near left end of table)*

Foreman. Shall we get back to the case?

Three. Yeah, let's.

Twelve. I may have an idea here. I'm just thinking out loud now, but it seems to me that it's up to us to convince this gentleman—*(motioning toward* Eight*)*—that we're right and he's wrong. Maybe if we each talk for a minute or two. You know—try it on for size. W

Foreman. That sounds fair enough.

Four. Very fair.

Foreman. Supposing we go once around the table.

Seven. Okay—let's start it off.

Foreman. Right. *(to* Two*)* We'll start with you.

Two *(timidly)*. Oh. Well . . . *(There is a long pause.)* I just think he's guilty. I thought it was obvious.

Eight. In what way was it obvious?

Two. I mean that nobody proved otherwise.

Eight *(quietly)*. Nobody has to prove otherwise; innocent until proven guilty. The burden of proof is on the prosecution. The defendant doesn't have to open his mouth. That's in the Constitution. The Fifth Amendment.[5] You've heard of it.

Four. Everyone has.

---

5. **Fifth Amendment:** one of the provisions of the Fifth Amendment to the Constitution is that a defendant is not required to testify against himself or herself.

Words to Know and Use

prosecution (präs' i kyo͞o' shən) *n.* in a criminal case, the side that brings the case against a person accused of committing a crime

defendant (dē fen' dənt) *n.* in a court case, the person accused of a crime

V. Literary Element: CHARACTERIZATION Point out that each character reveals his personality traits through his own words: Juror Three's comment about sermons shows his cynicism; Juror Four again insists on decorum; and so on.

W. Critical Thinking: EVALUATING Ask students whether they think that Juror Twelve's suggestion is a good one. That is, should the jurors begin by trying to convince Juror Eight that he is wrong? *(Possible response: The jurors might do better by simply discussing the facts of the case.)*

X. Critical Thinking: EVALUATING Ask students how the jurors are doing so far in their effort to convince Juror Eight that he is wrong. *(Most students will say that the jurors are not doing well and may cite Juror Eight's observation that, so far, they have presented him "No reasons—just guilty.")*

Y. LEP: Vocabulary Explain that *flimsy* means "weak" or "lacking seriousness or sense."

Z. Literary Sidelight: CLARIFYING Point out that Juror Ten is hardly paying Juror Eight a compliment when he says that he is a "pretty smart fellow." Rather, it is more of a veiled threat. Juror Ten is furious that Eight has made him look foolish by pointing out the inconsistency of his bigotry.

X

Two *(flustered)*. Well, sure—I've heard of it. I know what it is . . . I . . . what I meant . . . well, anyway . . . I think he's guilty!

Eight *(looking at* Two, *shaking his head slowly)*. No reasons—just guilty. There is a life at stake here.

Three. Okay, let's get to the facts. Number one: let's take the old man who lived on the second floor right underneath the room where the murder took place. At ten minutes after twelve on the night of the killing, he heard loud noises in the upstairs apartment. He said it sounded like a fight. Then he heard the kid say to his father, "I'm gonna kill you." A second later he heard a body falling, and he ran to the door of his apartment, looked out and saw the kid running downstairs and out of the house. Then he called the police. They found the father with a knife in his chest.

Foreman. And the coroner[6] fixed the time of death at around midnight.

Three. Right. Now what else do you want?

Eight. It doesn't seem to fit.

Y

Four. The boy's entire story is flimsy. He claimed he was at the movies. That's a little ridiculous, isn't it? He couldn't even remember what picture he saw.

Three. That's right. Did you hear that? *(to* Four*)* You're absolutely right.

Five. He didn't have any ticket stub.

Eight. Who keeps a ticket stub at the movies?

Four *(to* Five*)*. That's true enough.

Five. I suppose, but the cashier didn't remember him.

Three. And the ticket taker didn't, either.

Ten. Look—what about the woman across the street? If her testimony don't prove it, then nothing does.

Twelve. That's right. She saw the killing, didn't she?

Foreman *(rapping on table)*. Let's go in order.

Ten *(loudly)*. Just a minute. Here's a woman who's lying in bed and can't sleep. It's hot, you know. *(gets up and begins to walk around at left stage, blowing his nose and talking)* Anyway, she wakes up and she looks out the window, and right across the street she sees the kid stick the knife into his father.

Eight. How can she really be sure it was the kid when she saw it through the windows of a passing elevated train? ◀SR-

Ten *(pausing downstage left)*. She's known the kid all his life. His window is right opposite hers—across the el[7] tracks—and she swore she saw him do it.

Eight. I heard her swear to it.

Ten. Okay. And they proved in court that you can look through the windows of a passing el train at night and see what's happening on the other side. They proved it.

Eight. Weren't you telling us just a minute or two ago that you can't trust *them?* That you can't believe *them.*

Ten *(coldly)*. So?

Eight. Then I'd like to ask you something. How come you believed her? She's one of *them,* too, isn't she? *(*Ten *crosses up to* Eight.*)*

Ten. You're a pretty smart fellow, aren't you? Z

6. **coroner:** a public official who runs an investigation to determine causes of deaths seemingly not due to natural causes.

7. **el:** elevated train, that is, a train with tracks that are above the ground so that cars and people can travel underneath them.

Foreman *(rising)*. Now take it easy. *(Three gets up and goes to* Ten.*)*

Three. Come on. Sit down. *(leads* Ten *back to his seat)* What're you letting him get you all upset for? Relax. *(*Ten *and* Three *sit down.)*

Four. Gentlemen, they did take us out to the woman's room and we looked through the windows of a passing el train—*(to* Eight*)*—didn't we?

Eight. Yes. *(nods)* We did.

Four. And weren't you able to see what happened on the other side?

Eight. I didn't see as well as they told me I would see, but I did see what happened on the other side.

Ten *(snapping at* Eight*)*. You see—do you see?

Foreman *(sitting again)*. Let's calm down now. *(to* Five*)* It's your turn.

Five. I'll pass it.

Foreman. That's your privilege. *(to* Six*)* How about you?

Six *(slowly)*. I don't know. I started to be convinced, you know, with the testimony from those people across the hall. Didn't they say something about an argument between the father and the boy around seven o'clock that night? I mean, I can be wrong.

Eleven. I think it was eight o'clock. Not seven.

Eight. That's right. Eight o'clock.

AA

Four. They heard the father hit the boy twice and then saw the boy walk angrily out of the house.

Six. Right.

Eight. What does that prove?

Six. Well, it doesn't exactly prove anything. It's just part of the picture. I didn't say it proved anything.

Foreman. Anything else?

Six. No. *(rises, goes to water cooler for a drink and then sits again)*

BB

Seven. I don't know—most of it's been said already. We can talk all day about this thing, but I think we're wasting our time.

Eight. I don't.

Four. Neither do I. Go on.

Seven. Look at the kid's record. He stole a car. He's been arrested for mugging. I think they said he stabbed somebody in the arm.

Four. They did.

Seven. He was picked up for knife fighting. At fifteen he was in reform school.

Three. And they sent him to reform school for stabbing someone!

Seven *(with sarcasm)*. This is a very fine boy. CC

Eight. Ever since he was five years old his father beat him up regularly. He used his fists.

Seven. So would I! On a kid like that.

DD

Three. You're right. It's the kids. The way they are—you know? They don't listen. *(bitterly)* I've got a kid. When he was eight years old, he ran away from a fight. I saw him. I was *so* ashamed. I told him right out, "I'm gonna make a man out of you or I'm gonna bust you up into little pieces trying." When he was fifteen, he hit me in the face. He's big, you know? I haven't seen him in three years. Rotten kid! I hate tough kids! You work your heart out. . . . *(pauses)* All right. Let's get on with it. . . . *(gets up and goes to window, very embarrassed)*

Four. We're missing the point here. This boy—let's say he's a product of a filthy neighborhood and a broken home. We can't help that. We're not here to go into the reasons why slums are breeding

AA. Critical Thinking: SYNTHESIZING Ask students why the prosecutor of the case might have introduced the neighbors' testimony about the father hitting the son. *(Possible response: The boy's desire for revenge on his father for the beating might be seen as a motive for the murder.)*

BB. Literary Element: CHARACTER MOTIVATION Remind students that Juror Seven wants a quick verdict so that he can use his theater tickets that night.

CC. LEP: Sarcasm Review that sarcasm is the use of language to ridicule or hurt someone. Explain that when Juror Seven says "This is a very fine boy" he means the exact opposite.

DD. Literary Element: IRONY Have students explain the irony of Juror Three's statement. *(He claims to hate "tough kids," yet he threatened to beat up his own son for trying to avoid a fight. Eventually his son hit him.)* Have students suggest how Juror Three's anger may influence his decision in the case. *(Possible response: He may take out his anger toward his son on the defendant.)*

EE. Literary Element: CHARACTER Point out that Juror Ten misses no opportunity to vent his bigotry.

FF. Literary Element: MOOD Suggest that the locked jury room is becoming more and more like a pressure cooker. As the pressure to reach a verdict rises, tension mounts, and we see angry emotional outbursts by various jurors. Elicit that this helps to clarify the title, *Twelve Angry Men.*

GG. Literary Element: CHARACTER Point out that Juror Eight continues to seek the truth, even though it means he must ask unpleasant questions that challenge the prejudices of the other jurors.

grounds for criminals; they are. I know it. So do you. The children who come out of slum backgrounds are potential menaces to society.

EE **Ten.** You said it there. I don't want any part of them, believe me. *(There is a dead silence for a moment, and then* Five *speaks haltingly.)*

Five. I've lived in a slum all my life. . . .

Ten. Now wait a second!

Five. I used to play in a back yard that was filled with garbage. Maybe it still smells on me.

Foreman. Now, let's be reasonable. There's nothing personal—

FF **Five** *(rising, slamming his hand down on table)***.** There is something personal! *(Then he catches himself, and, seeing everyone looking at him, sits down, fists clenched.)*

Three *(turning from window)***.** Come on, now. He didn't mean you, feller. Let's not be so sensitive. *(There is a long pause.)*

GG **Eight** *(breaking silence)***.** Who did he mean?

Eleven. I can understand this sensitivity.

Foreman. Now let's stop the bickering.

Twelve. We're wasting time.

Foreman *(to* Eight*)***.** It's your turn.

Eight. All right. I had a peculiar feeling about this trial. Somehow I felt that the defense counsel never really conducted a thorough cross-examination.[8] Too many questions were left unasked. SR-6 ▶

Four. While it doesn't change my opinion about the guilt of the kid, still, I agree with you that the defense counsel was bad.

Three. So-o-o-o? *(crosses back to table and sits)*

Eight. This is a point.

Three. What about facts?

Eight. So many questions were never answered.

Three *(annoyed)***.** What about the questions that were answered? For instance, let's talk about that cute little switch knife. You know, the one that fine upright kid admitted buying.

Eight. All right, let's talk about it. Let's get it in here and look at it. I'd like to see it again, Mr. Foreman. *(*Foreman *looks at him questioningly and then gets up and goes to door left.)*

(During the following dialogue, the Foreman *knocks. The* Guard *unlocks the door and comes in left and the* Foreman *whispers to him. The* Guard *nods and leaves, locking the door. The* Foreman *returns to his seat.)*

Three. We all know what it looks like. I don't see why we have to look at it again. *(to* Four*)* What do you think?

Four. The gentleman has a right to see exhibits in evidence.

Three *(shrugging)***.** Okay with me.

Four *(to* Eight*)***.** This knife is a pretty strong piece of evidence, don't you agree?

Eight. I do.

Four. Now let's get the sequence of events right as they relate to the switch knife.

Twelve. The boy admits going out of his house at eight o'clock, after being slapped by his father.

Eight. Or punched.

Four. Or punched. *(gets up and begins to pace at right stage, moving downstage right to upstage right and back again)* He went to a neighborhood store and bought a switch

8. **cross-examination:** the questioning of a witness in court.

HH knife. The storekeeper was arrested the following day when he admitted selling it to the boy.

Three. I think everyone agrees that it's an unusual knife. Pretty hard to forget something like that.

II **Four.** The storekeeper identified the knife and said it was the only one of its kind he had in stock. Why did the boy get it?

Seven *(sarcastically)*. As a present for a friend of his, he says.

Four *(pausing in his pacing)*. Am I right so far?

Eight. Right.

Three. You bet he's right. *(to all)* Now listen to this man. He knows what he's talking about.

Four *(standing at right stage)*. Next, the boy claims that on the way home the knife must have fallen through a hole in his coat pocket, that he never saw it again. Now there's a story, gentlemen. You know what actually happened. The boy took the knife home, and a few hours later stabbed his father with it and even remembered to wipe off the fingerprints.

(The door left opens and the Guard *walks in with an oddly designed knife with a tag on it.*

HH. Reading Skill: INFERRING Ask students why the storekeeper might have been arrested for selling the knife to the boy. *(Possible response: It is illegal to sell switchblade knives; it is illegal to sell them to minors under twenty-one years old.)*

II. LEP: Vocabulary Explain that to have something *in stock* is to have it on hand so that a customer can buy it.

JJ. LEP: Vocabulary Explain that *ad lib* means "made up on the spot." The actors here are supposed to make up appropriate comments to reflect their surprise and excitement.

KK. Literary Element: CONFLICT Point out that Jurors Eight and Three have come to represent the opposite sides of the conflict over the boy's guilt. Have students characterize the positions of these men. *(Juror Three is convinced of the boy's guilt, no matter what. Juror Eight is determined at all costs to present the possibility of the boy's innocence.)*

Four *crosses left and takes the knife from him. The* Guard *goes out left, closing and locking the door.)*

Four *(at left center, holding up knife)*. Everyone connected with the case identified this knife. Now are you trying to tell me that someone picked it up off the street and went up to the boy's house and stabbed his father with it just to be amusing?

Eight. No. I'm saying that it's possible that the boy lost the knife and that someone else stabbed his father with a similar knife. It's possible. *(Four flips knife open and jams it into wall just downstage of door left.)*

Four *(standing back to allow others to see)*. Take a look at that knife. It's a very strange knife. I've never seen one like it before in my life. Neither had the storekeeper who sold it to him. *(Eight reaches casually into his pocket and withdraws an object. No one notices him. He stands up.)* Aren't you trying to make us accept a pretty incredible coincidence?

Eight *(moving toward* Four*)*. I'm not trying to make anyone accept it. I'm just saying it's possible.

Three *(rising, shouting)*. And I'm saying it's not possible! *(Eight swiftly flicks open blade of a switch knife, jams it into wall next to first knife and steps back. They are exactly alike. There are several gasps, and everyone stares at knife. There is a long silence.* Three *continues, slowly, amazed.)* What are you trying to do?

JJ **Ten** *(loudly)*. Yeah, what is this? Who do you think you are? *(A flow of ad lib conversation bursts forth.)*

Five. Look at it! It's the same knife!

Foreman. Quiet! Let's be quiet. *(Jurors quiet down.* Three *sits again.)*

Four. Where did you get it?

Eight. I got it in a little junk shop around the corner from the boy's house. It cost two dollars.

Three. Now listen to me!

Eight *(turning to him)*. I'm listening.

Three. You pulled a real smart trick here, but you proved absolutely zero. Maybe there are ten knives like that, so what?

Eight. Maybe there are. KK

Three. The boy lied and you know it.

Eight *(crossing back to his seat, sitting)*. And maybe he didn't lie. Maybe he did lose the knife and maybe he did go to the movies. Maybe the reason the cashier didn't see him was because he sneaked into the movies, and maybe he was ashamed to say so. *(looks around)* Is there anybody here who didn't sneak into the movies once or twice when they were young? *(There is a long silence.)* ◄SR-7

Eleven. I didn't.

Four. Really, not even once?

Eleven. We didn't have movies.

Four. Oh. *(crosses back to his place and sits)*

Eight. Maybe he did go to the movies—maybe he didn't. And—he may have lied. *(to* Ten*)* Do you think he lied?

Ten *(violently)*. Now that's a stupid question. Sure, he lied!

Eight *(to* Four*)*. Do you?

Four. You don't have to ask me that. You know my answer. He lied.

Eight *(to* Five*)*. Do you think he lied? *(Five can't answer immediately. He looks around nervously.)*

Five. I—I don't know.

Seven. Now wait a second. What are you—the guy's lawyer? Listen—there are still eleven of us who think he's guilty. You're alone. What do you think you're going to accomplish? If you want to be stubborn and hang this jury[9] he'll be tried again, and found guilty sure as he's born.

Eight. You're probably right.

Seven. So what are you going to do about it? We can be here all night.

LL **Nine.** It's only one night. A man may die.

Seven. Oh, now. Come on.

Eight *(to* Nine*)*. Well, yes, that's true.

Foreman. I think we ought to get on with it now.

Three. Right. Let's get going here.

Ten *(to* Three*)*. How do you like this guy? *(*Three *shrugs and turns to* Eight.*)*

Three. Well, what do you say? You're the one holding up the show.

Four *(to* Eight*)*. Obviously you don't think the boy is guilty.

Eight. I have a doubt in my mind.

Four. But you haven't really presented anything to us that makes it possible for us to understand your doubt. There's the old man downstairs. He heard it. He heard the kid shriek it out. . . .

Three. The woman across the el tracks—she saw it!

MM **Seven.** We know he bought a switch knife that night and we don't know where he really was. At the movies?

Foreman. Earlier that night the kid and his father did have a fight.

Four. He's been a violent kid all the way, and while that doesn't prove anything. . . .

Ten. Still, you know. . . .

Eight *(standing)*. I've got a proposition to make. *(*Five *stands and puts his hands on back of his chair. Several jurors glare at him. He sinks his head down a bit, then sits down.)* I want to call for a vote. I want you eleven men to vote by secret ballot. I'll abstain. If there are still eleven votes for guilty, I won't stand alone. We'll take in a guilty verdict right now.

Seven. Okay. Let's do it.

Foreman. That sounds fair. Is everyone agreed?

Four. I certainly am.

Twelve. Let's roll it.

Eleven *(slowly)*. Perhaps this is best. *(*Eight *walks over to window and stands there for a moment looking out, then turns as* Foreman *passes ballot slips down table to all of them.* Eight *tenses as* Jurors *begin to write. Then folded ballots are passed back to* Foreman. *He flips through folded ballots, counts them to be sure he has eleven and then he begins to open them, reading verdict each time.)*

Foreman. Guilty. Guilty. Guilty. Guilty. Guilty. Guilty.

Three. That's six.

Foreman. Please. *(fumbles with one ballot)* Six guilty. Guilty. Guilty. Guilty. *(pauses for a moment at tenth ballot and then reads)* Not guilty. *(*Three *slams his hand down hard on table.* Eight *starts for table, as* Foreman *reads final ballot.)* Guilty. ◀SR-8

Ten *(angrily)*. How do you like that!

Seven *(standing, snarling)*. Who was it? I think we have a right to know. *(Looks about. No one moves.)* NN

Curtain

9. **hang this jury:** to deadlock the jury by one's vote. When a jury cannot reach a unaminous opinion or clear majority on a case, it is called a hung jury, which results in the case having to be tried again, with a new jury.

Words to Know and Use

abstain (ab stān′) *n.* to withhold one's vote in an election or a group decision

563

LL. Literary Element: PLOT Point out that Juror Five's earlier comment about not knowing if the boy lied and Juror Nine's statement here that "A man may die" suggest that Juror Eight is persuading his co-jurors to open their minds a bit.

MM. Literary Element: DIALOGUE Have students tell the purpose of this dialogue. *(It sums up the case presented thus far against the boy)*

NN. Literary Element: DRAMA Point out that the playwright builds up tension in the final moments and brings down the curtain just as the outcome of the vote is revealed. Explain that during the intermission, as the playgoers wait for the second act to begin, they will also be trying to figure out "Who was it?"

Check Test

1. What crime is the defendant, the teen-aged boy, accused of? *(the first-degree murder of his father)*

2. At first, how many of the twelve jurors think the defendant is guilty? *(eleven)*

3. Which juror thinks there is a reasonable doubt about the boy's guilt in the murder? *(Juror Eight)*

4. How many jurors change their minds about the boy's guilt during Act One? *(one juror)*

PROFESSIONAL NOTEBOOK

Teachers who want their students to grow need to accept their students' tastes. Often it seems to teachers that what students appreciate is stereotypic and even simplistic. It's important to recognize, however, that students in secondary school are in a stage of development in which they are establishing their identity, breaking away from authoritarian ties, and trying to develop their relationships with the world out there. They are looking for answers. They are using literature for their own ends, and to undercut that is to underrate the importance of literature as experience.

Stephen N. and Susan J. Judy, ***The English Teacher's Handbook***

Student Response

Responding to Reading

These questions are open-ended with no "right" or "wrong" answers. However, responses must be supported with information from the selection. Possible answers follow:

1. Any response based on the play is valid.

2. Some students may say that the weight of evidence and eyewitness testimony strongly suggest that the boy is guilty. Others may suggest that a strong element of prejudice is influencing the jurors.

3. Some students may say that Juror Eight has a great desire to see justice; others may point out that he realizes the boy is not getting a fair deal and so stands up to the majority to force them to examine their opinions more closely; others may say that he has some other special information or idea, such as he had with the knife, that will help show reasonable doubt.

4. Some students may suggest that Juror Ten is acting unfairly, since he is so prejudiced against the boy. Others may say that Juror Three is unfair, that his bad relationship with his own son is coloring his opinion. Others may point out that Jurors Seven and Twelve are unfair in their eagerness to end deliberations quickly with a "guilty" vote so they can return to their families and jobs.

5. Some might suggest that it indicates he suspects one of the other jurors has changed his mind; or perhaps he simply is gambling that someone else will come to his aid to prolong the discussion. Some students might suggest that his decision shows he is not trying to obstruct the others if they honestly believe in the boy's guilt.

Responding to Reading

First Impressions

1. Which juror makes the strongest impression on you? Compare your reactions with those of your classmates.

Second Thoughts

2. Why do you think all the jurors but one immediately agree on a guilty verdict?

3. Why does Juror Eight stand up against the majority?

4. Which jurors seem to be acting unfairly?

Think about
- what you know about trial by jury
- why some jurors dislike the boy
- why some jurors want a quick decision

5. What do you think of Juror Eight's decision to abstain from voting at the end of Act One?

Literary Concept: Stage Directions

Stage directions are notes included in the scripts of plays to guide actors and to help readers picture the action and the setting. At the beginning of this play, on pages 550 and 551, descriptions of the characters are provided. How do these "Notes on Characters and Costumes" help you better understand the play?

Writing Options

1. Make a list of the legal terms and concepts referred to in Act One.

2. Imagine that you are Juror Thirteen. Explain where you stand concerning the boy's guilt or innocence.

3. What is the difference between proving that someone is guilty or proving that someone is innocent? Why do you think this distinction is such an important concept in our legal system?

Reading On

Based on what you have learned about the jurors, who do you think changed his vote to "not guilty"?

Literary Concept—Stage Directions

Possible response: Twelve characters are a lot to keep track of and the notes serve as a quick and useful reference for better understanding the characters. Since the characters do not have names, supplying background descriptions help the audience associate who is who with so many viewpoints presented.

Writing Options

The Writing Options are designed to meet varied student interests and abilities. Have each student choose one writing activity to complete. You may wish to guide some students to an option that requires less writing.

Reading On

Some students may say that Juror Two has changed his opinion, since he is so easily swayed. Others may say that it is Juror Four, since he seems so displeased with most of the other jurors. Students may also point to Juror Nine, suggesting that he is making a last-gasp effort to be courageous.

ACT TWO

A At Rise of Curtain: *It is only a second or two later. The* Jurors *are in the same positions as they were at the end of Act One.*

Three *(after a brief pause)*. All right! Who did it? What idiot changed his vote?

Eight. Is that the way to talk about a man's life? *(sits at his place again)*

Three. Whose life are you talking about? The life of the dead man or the life of a murderer?

Seven. I want to know. Who?

Three. So do I.

Eleven. Excuse me. This was a secret ballot.

B **Three.** No one looked while we did it, but now I want to know.

Eleven. A secret ballot; we agreed on that point, no? If the gentleman wants it to remain a secret—

Three *(standing up angrily)*. What do you mean? There are no secrets in here! I know who it was. *(turns to* Five*)* What's the matter with you? You come in here and you vote guilty and then this—*(nods toward* Eight*)*—slick preacher starts to C tear your heart out with stories about a poor little kid who just couldn't help becoming a murderer. So you change your vote. If that isn't the most sickening— *(*Five *edges away in his chair.)*

Foreman. Now hold it. *(*Seven *sits again slowly.)*

Four *(to* Three*)*. I agree with you that the man is guilty, but let's be fair.

Three. Hold it? Be fair? That's just what I'm saying. We're trying to put a guilty man into the chair where he belongs—and all of a sudden we're paying attention to fairy tales.

Five. Now, just a minute—

Three *(bending toward* Five*, wagging finger at him)*. Now, you listen to me—

Foreman *(rapping on table)*. Let's try to keep this organized, gentlemen.

Four. It isn't organized, but let's try to be civilized.

Eleven. Please. I would like to say something here. I have always thought that a man was entitled to have unpopular opinions in this country. This is the reason I came here. I wanted to have the right to disagree.

Three. Do you disagree with us?

Eleven. Usually, I would. In this one case I agree with you, but the point I wish to make is that in my own country, I am ashamed to say—

Ten. Oh, now-w-w, what do we have to listen to—the whole history of your country? *(*Three *sits again in disgust.)*

Four. It's always wise to bear in mind what has happened in other countries, when people aren't allowed to disagree; but we are, so let's stick to the subject. D

Seven. Yeah, let's stick to the subject. *(to* Five*)* I want to ask you, what made you change your vote?

Three. I want to know, too. You haven't told us yet.

Five. Why do you think I did change my vote?

Seven. Because I do. Now get on with it.

Nine *(quietly)*. There's nothing for him to tell you. He didn't change his vote. I did. *(all look at* Nine.*)*

Five *(to* Three*)*. I was going to tell you, but you were so sure of yourself.

Three. Sorry. *(to* Nine*)* Okay now. . . .

Nine. Maybe you'd like to know why.

Three *(not giving him a chance)*. Let me tell you why that kid's a—

Foreman. The man wants to talk. *(*Three *subsides.)*

Text Annotations

A. Literary Element: SETTING/ACT Point out that a new act usually marks a change in the time or place of the setting. In this play, however, there are no time lapses between the acts, and all the action is set in the same jury room.

B. Critical Thinking: ANALYZING Have students discuss why Juror Three is so anxious to learn which of the other jurors has changed his vote. *(Possible response: He wants to criticize and perhaps even threaten this juror.)*

C. LEP: Sarcasm Point out that Juror Three uses the word *preacher* sarcastically in order to ridicule Juror Eight's sympathy for the defendant's poverty.

D. Literary Element: IRONY Point out how ironic it is that Jurors Three, Four, and Ten—although automatically asserting that people in this country have the right to disagree—are doing all they can to stifle and intimidate the other jurors who disagree with them.

STRUCTURED READING FOR LESS PROFICIENT STUDENTS

These questions can help to guide students through the reading. Ask each question at the point of the selection where the SR number appears in the margin.

SR–1. What reason for changing his vote does Juror Nine give at the opening of Act Two? *(Nine admires Eight's courage and wants to support him; he wants to hear more discussion about the case.)* **Literal recall**

SR–2. Why does an el train's passing by the apartment make the old man's testimony doubtful? *(Since the el train makes such a roaring sound, it's doubtful the old man could have heard the boy say "I'm going to kill you.")* **Summarizing**

SR–3. What reason does Juror Nine give for why the old man might have lied in his testimony? *(Juror Nine suspects that the old man had a need to be listened to and quoted at least once in his uneventful life; the old man was willing to lie to get some attention.)* **Clarifying**

Continued on page 566

E. Critical Thinking: ANALYZING Have the students reread the description of Juror Nine on page 551. Ask them to suggest why a "mild old man" who is "defeated by life" is now courageous enough to stand up and disagree with ten of the jurors. *(Possible response: He sses this as one last chance to make a difference.)*

F. Literary Element: STAGE DIRECTIONS Explain that actors talk "in pantomime" by gesturing and only pretending to speak. This leads the audience to focus on the dialogue between Jurors Two and Four, who are standing upstage by the water cooler.

G. LEP: Idiom If necessary, review the meaning of *clutching at straws* as "trying anything in desperation."

H. Reading Skill: CLARIFYING Have students tell what Juror Three is referring to here. *(He is referring to the comments he made earlier about slums, which offended Juror Five.)*

Nine *(to* Foreman*).* Thank you. *(points at* Eight*)* This gentleman chose not to stand alone against us. That's his right. It takes a great deal of courage to stand alone, even if you believe in something very strongly. He left the verdict up to us. He gambled for support and I gave it to him. I want to hear more. The vote is ten to two. *(*Jurors Two *and* Four *get up at about the same instant and walk to water cooler as* Ten *speaks.)*

Ten. That's fine. If the speech is over, let's go on. *(*Foreman *gets up, goes to door left, pulls tagged knife from wall and then knocks on door.)*

(The door is opened by the Guard*. The* Foreman *hands the* Guard *the tagged switch knife. The* Guard *goes out and the* Foreman *takes the other switch knife, closes it and puts it in the middle of the table. He sits again. The other* Jurors *talk on, in pantomime, as* Two *and* Four *stand by the water cooler.)*

Four *(filling cup).* If there was anything in the kid's favor, I'd vote not guilty.

Two. I don't see what it is.

Four *(handing cup to* Two*, then drawing drink for himself).* Neither do I. They're clutching at straws.

Two. As guilty as they get—that's the kid, I suppose.

Four. It's that one juror that's holding out, but he'll come around. He's got to, and, fundamentally, he's a very reasonable man.

Two. I guess so.

Four. They haven't come up with one real fact yet to back up a not guilty verdict.

Two. It's hard, you know.

Four. Yes, it is. And what does "guilty beyond a reasonable doubt" really mean?

Two. What's a reasonable doubt?

Four. Exactly. When a life is at stake, what is a reasonable doubt? You've got to have law and order; you've got to draw the line somewhere; if you don't, everyone would start knifing people.

Two. Not much doubt here.

Four. Two men think so. I wonder why. I really wonder why.

Two. You do hear stories about innocent men who have gone to jail—or death, sometimes—then years later things turn up.

Four. And then on the other hand some killers get turned loose and they go and do it again. They squeeze out on some technicality[10] and kill again. *(Throws his cup into wastebasket, walks back and sits. We then hear* Three *say to* Five*.)*

Three. Look buddy, now that we've kind of cooled off, why—ah—I was a little excited a minute ago. Well, you know how it is—I didn't mean to get nasty. Nothing personal. *(*Two *trails back to his place and sits again.)*

Five *(after staring at* Three *for a moment).* Okay.

Seven *(to* Eight*).* Look. Supposing you answer me this. If the kid didn't kill him, who did?

Eight. As far as I know, we're supposed to decide whether or not the boy on trial is guilty. We're not concerned with anyone else's motives here.

Seven. I suppose, but who else had a motive?

10. **technicality:** in a court case, a small loophole in the legal system (e.g., evidence obtained without a search warrant) that causes the trial to be stopped and the defendant to be set free.

Words to Know and Use	**motive** (mōt′ iv) *n.* reason for doing something

566

STRUCTURED READING FOR LESS PROFICIENT STUDENTS

Continued from page 565

SR–4. According to Juror Eight, why does saying "I'm going to kill you" not necessarily connect the boy to the murder? *(People often use this phrase to express anger; if the boy was really going to murder his father, he would not scream out his intention to do so.)* **Literal recall**

SR–5. Why does Juror Eight suspect the old man's statement that he went to the door in fifteen seconds? *(The old man is crippled and needs two canes to walk; he was in bed, down the hall from the door when he heard the murder.)* **Summarizing**

SR–6. How does Juror Eight try to disprove the old man's statement about how long it took him to reach the door? *(He measures the distances the man walked and then times the trip to the door.)* **Summarizing**

SR–7. Why does Juror Eight say that Juror Three disgusts him? *(Juror Eight is furious that Juror Three refuses to look at any of the facts, because he is so anxious for the boy to be executed.)* **Literal recall**

I **Eight.** The kid's father was along in years; maybe an old grudge.

Nine. Remember, it is "guilty beyond a reasonable doubt." This is an important thing to remember.

J **Three** *(to* Ten*).* Everyone's a lawyer. *(to* Nine*)* Supposing you explain to us what your reasonable doubts are.

Nine. This is not easy. So far, it's only a feeling I have. A feeling. Perhaps you don't understand.

Three *(abruptly).* No. I don't.

Ten. A feeling! What are we gonna do, spend the night talking about your feelings? What about the facts?

Three. You said a mouthful. *(to* Nine*)* Look, the old man heard the kid yell, "I'm gonna kill you." A second later he heard the father's body falling, and he saw the boy running out of the house fifteen seconds after that.

Seven. Where's the reasonable doubt in that?

Twelve. That's right. And let's not forget the woman across the street. She looked into the open window and saw the boy stab his father. She saw it!

Three. Now, if that's not enough for you—

Eight *(quietly firm).* It's not enough for me. K

Four. What is enough for you? I'd like to know.

Seven. How do you like him? It's like talking into a dead phone.

Four. The woman saw the killing through the windows of a moving elevated train. The train had five cars, and she saw it through the windows of the last two cars. She remembers the most insignificant details.

Three. Well, what have you got to say about that?

I. LEP: Vocabulary Review the meaning of *grudge* as "ill will" or "a feeling of anger."

J. Critical Thinking: SYNTHESIZING Ask students what Juror Three means by his comment "Everyone's a lawyer". *(He is being sarcastic; he is putting down Juror Nine's efforts to understand the legal aspects of the jury's task.)*

K. Critical Thinking: EVALUATING Ask students whether Jurors Eight and Nine have adequately explained their "not guilty" votes. Ask whether the frustration that Jurors Three, Seven, and Twelve feel is justified at this point. *(Students should be encouraged to give cogent reasons in support of their ideas.)*

CULTURAL CONNECTION

Read the following excerpt aloud and ask students to discuss whether its insights seem to apply to the characters in *Twelve Angry Men.*

Thus, it is the "ordinariness" of the jury that finally emerges as its unique strength. What sets the jury system apart from all the other methods of determining guilt or innocence is that ideally it alone allows a person to be judged by others just like him—people who come from the same community and share its values, people who have had similar experiences, people who have been tempted and have not always resisted, people who feel remorse for what they have done and perhaps regret for what they have not done, people who know how thin the line between guilt and innocence sometimes is.

MELVYN BERNARD ZERMAN, *Beyond a Reasonable Doubt*

L. Literary Elements: CHARACTER Ask students what Juror Eight's gesture here—grabbing Juror Three's tic-tac-toe paper—reveals about him. *(Possible response: He is very serious and decisive; he will not stand for Juror Three's efforts to ridicule the jury's duty.)*

M. Literary Element: PROTAGONIST AND ANTAGONIST Have students tell to whom Juror Three is referring with the word *him. (Juror Eight)* Tell students to look for further heated exchanges between Jurors Three and Eight that suggest they are the principal characters in conflict.

Teaching Tip
Suggest that students use their copies of the chart given on page 550 to take notes on this new el train evidence that Juror Eight is introducing.

N. LEP: Vocabulary Elicit a definition of *testimony* as it is used here. *(statement given in a court and used for evidence or proof)*

Eight. I don't know. It doesn't sound right to me.

Three. Well, supposing you think about it. *(to* Twelve*)* Lend me your pencil. *(*Twelve *hands him a pencil.)* Let's play some tic-tac-toe. *(draws an X on a piece of paper, then hands pencil and paper to* Twelve*)* We might as well pass the time.

L **Eight.** This isn't a game. *(Rises and snatches paper away.* Three *jumps up.)*

Three. Now, wait a minute!

Eight. This is a man's life.

Three *(angrily)*. Who do you think you are?

Seven *(rising)*. All right, let's take it easy. *(*Eight *sits again.)*

M **Three.** I've got a good mind to walk around this table and belt him one!

Foreman. Now, please. I don't want any fights in here.

Three. Did you see him? The nerve! The absolute nerve!

Ten. All right. Forget it. It don't mean anything.

Six. How about sitting down?

Three. "This isn't a game." Who does he think he is? *(*Six *and* Ten *urge* Three *back into his seat.* Seven *sits again, and all are seated once more.)*

Four *(when quiet is restored)*. Weren't we talking about elevated trains?

Eight. Yes, we were.

Four. So?

Eight. All right. How long does it take an elevated train going at top speed to pass a given point?

Four. What has that got to do with anything?

Eight. How long would it take? Guess.

Four. I wouldn't have the slightest idea.

Seven. Neither would I.

Nine. I don't think they mentioned it.

Eight *(to* Five*)*. What do you think?

Five. About ten or twelve seconds—maybe.

Eight. I'd say that was a fair guess. *(looks about)* Anyone else?

Eleven. I would think about ten seconds, perhaps. . . .

Two *(reflectively)*. About ten seconds, yes.

Four. All right, we're agreed. Ten seconds. *(to* Eight*)* What are you getting at?

Eight. This. An el train passes a given point in ten seconds. That given point is the window of the room in which the killing took place. You can almost reach out of the window of that room and touch the el. Right?

Foreman. That's right. I tried it.

Four. So?

Eight. All right. Now let me ask you this. Did anyone here ever live right next to the el tracks?

Five. I've lived close to them.

Eight. They make a lot of noise, don't they? *(*Five *nods.)* I've lived right by the el tracks. When your window is open, and the train goes by, the noise is almost unbearable. You can't hear yourself think.

Ten *(impatiently)*. Okay. You can't hear yourself think. Get to the point.

Eight. The old man who lived downstairs heard the boy say—

Three *(interrupting)*. He didn't *say it,* he screamed it.

Eight. The old man heard the boy scream, "I'm going to kill you," and one second later he heard a body fall. *(slight pause)* One second. That's the testimony. Right? N

Two. Right.

Eight. The woman across the street looked through the windows of the last two cars of the el and saw the body fall. Right?

Four. Right.

Twelve. So?

REAL LIFE CONNECTIONS

Point out that the seriousness of the jury's task is greatly heightened by the fact that a man's life is at stake; that is, if the jury finds the defendant guilty, the young man may be executed. Use the following prompts to lead a class discussion on the subject of capital punishment.

- Do you believe that the fear of capital punishment might prevent criminals from committing certain crimes? Why or why not?
- Do you think the imposition of the death sentence violates the Eighth Amendment to the Constitution, which forbids cruel and unusual punishment?

Interested students might do library research in preparation for a debate on the issue.

Eight *(slowly)*. The last two cars. *(slight pause, then repeats)* The last two cars.

Ten. What are you giving us here?

Eight. An el train takes ten seconds to pass a given point, or two seconds per car. That el had been going by the old man's window for at least six seconds and maybe O more *before the body fell,* according to the woman. The old man would have had to hear the boy say "I'm going to kill you" while the front of the el was roaring past his nose. It's not possible that he could SR-2 ▶ have heard it.

Three. What do you mean! Sure, he could have heard it.

Eight. With an el train going by?

Three. He said the boy yelled it out.

Eight. An el train makes a lot of noise.

Three. It's enough for me.

Four. It's enough for me, too.

Nine. I don't think he could have heard it.

P **Two.** Maybe the old man didn't hear it. I mean with the el noise. . . .

Three. What are you people talking about? Are you calling the old man a liar?

Eight *(shaking his head)*. Something doesn't fit.

Five. Well, it stands to reason—

Three. You're crazy! Why would he lie? What's he got to gain?

Nine. Attention . . . maybe.

Three. You keep coming up with these bright sayings. Why don't you send one in to a newspaper? They pay two dollars.

Eight *(hard, to* Three*)*. What does that have to do with a man's life? *(then, to* Nine*)* Why might the old man have lied? You have a right to be heard.

Nine *(after moment's hesitation)*. It's just that I looked at him for a very long time. The seam of his jacket was split under his arm. Did you notice that? He was a very old man with a torn jacket, and he carried two canes. *(gets up, moves right and leans against wall)* I think I know him better than anyone here. This is a quiet, frightened, insignificant man who has been nothing all his life—who has never had recognition—his name in the newspapers. Nobody knows him after seventy-five years. This is a very sad thing. A man like this needs to be recognized—to be questioned, and listened to, and quoted just once. This is very important. . . . Q ◀ SR-3

Twelve. And you're trying to tell us he lied about a thing like this just so he could be important?

Nine. No, he wouldn't really lie. But perhaps he'd make himself believe that he heard those words and recognized the boy's face.

Three. Well—*(loud and brassy)*—that's the most fantastic story I've ever heard. How can you make up a thing like that?

Nine *(doggedly)*. I'm not making it up.

Three. You must be making it up. People don't lie about things like that.

Nine. He made himself believe he told the truth.

Three. What do you know about it?

Nine *(low but firm)*. I speak from experience.

Seven. What!

Nine. I am the same man. R

Four. I think we all understand now. Thank you. *(*Nine *moves slowly back to table and sits.)*

Three *(as* Nine *sits)*. If you want to admit you're a liar, it's all right by me.

Eight. Now, that is too much!

Three. He's a liar. He just told us so.

Eight. He did not say he was a liar; he was explaining.

O. Literary Element: DIALOGUE Ask the students why these words are in italic type. Ask how an actor might say these words in a performance. *(Possible response: The words are in italic type to emphasize that the noise was occurring before and during the murder. An actor would stress the words by saying them slowly or loudly.)*

P. Literary Element: CHARACTER Ask students why Juror Two might be expected to agree with Jurors Eight and Nine. If necessary, refer them to the notes on page 551. *(Possible response: Juror Two is meek and easily swayed; he usually adopts the opinion of the last person he has spoken to.)*

Q. Reading Skill: INFERRING Ask students to suggest how Juror Nine seems to know so much about the motive for the old man's testimony. *(Possible response: Juror Nine identifies with the old man; Nine, too, wants a moment of glory before he dies, and he suspects the same of the old man.)*

R. Discussion Have students discuss Juror Nine's admission that "I am the same man." Ask them whether admitting that was a courageous thing for Juror Nine to do. *(Possible response: Students may say that admitting any vulnerability in such a hostile atmosphere takes courage.)*

S. Critical Thinking: SYNTHESIZING Ask students to speculate on why the playwright included this incident, in which Juror Two offers cough drops to the others. *(Possible response: All the jurors except Eight ignore or brush aside Two's offer, making Two look a bit ridiculous; Eight shows compassion for Two by accepting his well-intended, if perhaps inappropriate, offer.)*

T. Literary Element: IRONY Have students explain the irony in this situation. *(Juror Ten uses ungrammatical English to complain about the defendant's bad English.)*

U. LEP: Vocabulary Elicit that *glower* means to "stare angrily" or "scowl." Have students explain why Juror Ten is so angry at Juror Eleven. *(He doesn't like having his grammar corrected.)*

Three *(to* Nine*)*. Didn't you admit that you're a liar?

Eight *(to* Three*)*. Please—he was explaining the circumstances so that we could understand why the old man might have lied. There is a difference.

Three. A liar is a liar, that's all there is to it.

Eight. Please—have some compassion.

Foreman. Gentlemen, please, we have our job and our duty here.

Four. I think they've covered it.

Eight. I hope we have.

Foreman *(to* Eight*)*. All right. Is there anything else? *(*Two *holds up a box of cough drops and speaks to* Foreman.*)*

Two. Cough drop?

Foreman *(waving it aside)*. No, thank you.

S

Two *(hesitantly)*. Anybody—want a cough—drop? *(offers box around)*

Foreman *(sharply)*. Come on. Let's get on with it.

Eight. I'll take one. *(*Two *hands him box.)* Thank you. *(takes one and returns box)* Now—there's something else I'd like to point out here. I think we proved that the old man couldn't have heard the boy say "I'm going to kill you."

Three. Well, I disagree.

Four *(to* Three*)*. Let's hear him through, anyway.

Eight. But supposing the old man really did hear the boy say "I'm going to kill you." This phrase—how many times has each of you used it? Probably hundreds. "If you do that once more, Junior, I'm going to murder you." "Come on, Rocky, kill him!" We say it every day. This doesn't mean that we're really going to kill someone.

SR-4 ▶

Four. Don't the circumstances alter that somewhat?

Twelve. The old man was murdered.

Three. One thing more. The phrase was "I'm going to kill you." And the kid screamed it out at the top of his lungs.

Four. That's the way I understand it.

Three. Now don't try and tell me he didn't mean it. Anybody says a thing like that the way he said it—they mean it.

Ten. And how they mean it!

Eight. Well, let me ask you this. Do you really think the boy would shout out a thing like that so the whole neighborhood would hear it? I don't think so. He's much too bright for that.

Ten *(exploding)*. Bright! He's a common ignorant slob. He don't even speak good English! T

Eleven *(slowly)*. He *doesn't* even speak good English.

Four. The boy is clever enough. *(*Four's *line is spoken as* Ten *rises and glowers at* Eleven. *There is a momentary pause.* Ten *sits again as* Five *gets up and looks around. He is nervous.)* U

Five. I'd like to change my vote to not guilty. *(*Three *slams his fist into his hand, then walks to window and does it again.)*

Foreman. Are you sure?

Five. Yes. I'm sure.

Foreman. The vote is nine to three in favor of guilty.

Four *(to* Five*)*. I'd like to know why you've changed your vote.

Five. I think there's a doubt.

Three *(turning abruptly from window, snarling)*. Where? What is the doubt?

Five. There's the knife. . . .

Seven *(slamming his hand down on the table)*. Oh, fine!

Ten. He—*(motioning at* Eight*)*—he talked you into believing a fairy tale.

REAL LIFE CONNECTIONS

Point out that on page 570, Juror Ten claims that the defendant is "a common ordinary slob" and supports this statement with the comment, "He *don't* even speak good English." Lead a discussion about the advantages of speaking gramatically and the disadvantages of speaking ungrammatically. Ask students to describe incidents in which they have drawn conclusions about people based on their use of language. Have students discuss whether it is useful or misleading to make decisions about a person's character based on his or her command of English.

Four *(to* Five*).* Go on. Give us the reasons.

Five. The old man, too. Maybe he didn't lie, but then just *maybe* he did. Maybe the old man doesn't like the kid.

V **Seven.** Well, if that isn't the end.

Five. I believe that there is reasonable doubt. *(sits again)*

Seven. What are you basing it on? Stories that this guy—*(indicates* Eight*)*—made up! He ought to write for Amazing Detective Monthly. He'd make a fortune. Listen, the kid had a lawyer, didn't he? Why didn't his lawyer bring up all these points? W

Five. Lawyers can't think of everything.

Seven. Oh brother! *(to* Eight*)* You sit in here and pull stories out of thin air. Now we're supposed to believe that the old man didn't get out of bed, run to the door and see the kid beat it downstairs fifteen seconds after the killing.

Four. That's the testimony, I believe.

Seven. And the old man swore to this—yes—he swore to this only so he could be important. *(looks over at* Nine*)*

Five. Did the old man say he *ran* to the door?

Seven. Ran. Walked. What's the difference? He got there.

Five. I don't remember what he said. But I don't see how he could run.

Four. He said he *went.* I remember it now. He *went* from his bedroom to the front door. That's enough, isn't it?

Eight. Where was his bedroom, again?

Ten *(disinterested)*. Down the hall somewhere.

Eight *(mad)*. Down the hall! Are we to send a man off to die because it's down the hall *somewhere?*

Ten. I thought you remembered everything. Don't you remember that?

Eight. No, I don't.

Nine. I don't remember, either.

Eight. Mr. Foreman, I'd like to take a look at the diagram of the apartment.

Seven. Why don't we have them run the trial over just so you can get everything straight?

Eight. The bedroom is down the hall somewhere. Do you *know*—do you know exactly where it is? Please. A man's life is at stake. Do you *know?*

Seven. Well, ah . . .

Eight. Mr. Foreman.

Foreman *(rising)*. I heard you. *(goes to door left and knocks on door)*

(During the ensuing dialogue, the Guard *opens the door left. The* Foreman *whispers to him. The* Guard *nods and then closes the door.)*

Three *(stepping away from window, moving a few steps toward* Eight*)*. All right. What's this one for? How come you're the only one in the room who wants to see exhibits all the time? X

Five. I want to see this one, too.

Nine. So do I.

Three. And I want to stop wasting time.

Four. Are we going to start wading through all that nonsense about where the body was found?

Eight. We're not. We're going to find out how a man who's had two strokes in the past three years and who walks with a pair of canes could get to his front door in fifteen seconds. ◀SR-5

Three. He said twenty seconds.

Two. He said fifteen.

Three. How does he know how long fifteen seconds is? You can't judge that kind of thing.

Nine. He said fifteen. He was very positive about it.

V. LEP: Idiom Elicit the meaning of the line, "Well, if that isn't the end." *(Possible response: That is beyond belief; that is too much to take.)*

W. Reading Skill: CLARIFYING Ask a volunteer to clarify what Juror Seven means when he says that Juror Eight "ought to write for Amazing Detective Monthly." *(Possible response: He suggests that Juror Eight has an overactive imagination or that his ideas are too fantastic for real life.)*

Teaching Tip

Direct students to use their charts to list details about this new piece of evidence the jury has unearthed—whether or not the old man could have reached the door in time to see the boy.

X. LEP: Vocabulary Explain that an *exhibit* is an item of evidence that has been tagged and shown, or exhibited, to a jury during a trial.

PROFESSIONAL NOTEBOOK

We all know what happens when parts are assigned and deadpan Jane runs monotone through every passage, despite preparation. We also know how tedious it is to hear a scene that students have carefully read first on their own massacred by poor classroom readers, then played on record, and finally dissected endlessly in class until it has lost all appeal. Here again a compromise must be made so that students have opportunities to cultivate skills in oral reading without killing all pleasure for the others in the class. The best solution is to make specific assignments in oral reading: students could be asked to select and read key scenes, passages revealing character, or moments of climax—all of which require careful selection, yet which are brief enough to retain classroom interest.

DWIGHT BURTON, ***Literature Study in the High Schools***

Y. Reading Skill: CLARIFYING Have students explain what Juror Three's "blunder" is. *(Possible response: By saying the old man is confused and perhaps not positive about anything, Juror Three casts all the man's testimony about the murder into doubt, thereby strengthening Juror Eight's argument that there may be reasonable doubt.)*

Z. Literary Element: STAGE DIRECTIONS Note that the stage directions call for all the jurors, except Three, Seven, and Ten, to show some interest in the floorplan. Ask students what the playwright intends to suggest with these directions. *(Possible response: Three, Seven, and Ten seem to have closed minds on the case; nothing will sway them from their belief in the boy's guilt.)*

AA. Critical Thinking: EVALUATING Have students voice their opinions on whether this would have been possible.

Three *(angrily)*. He's an old man. You saw that. Half the time he was confused. How could he be positive about—anything? *(looks around sheepishly, unable to cover his blunder)* Well, ah—you know. Y

Eight. No, I don't know. Maybe you know.

(The door left opens and the Guard *walks in carrying a large pen-and-ink diagram of the apartment done on heavy drawing board stock. It is a railroad flat.*[11] *A bedroom faces the el tracks. Behind it is a series of rooms off a long hall. In the front bedroom there is a mark where the body was found. At the back of the apartment, we see the entrance into the apartment hall from the building hall. We see a flight of stairs in the building hall. The diagram is clearly labeled, and included in the information on it are the various dimensions of the various rooms. The* Guard *gives the diagram to the* Foreman, *who has remained by the door left.)*

Guard. Is this what you wanted?

Foreman. That's right. Thank you.

Guard. Sure, that's my job. *(Nods and goes out left, closing and locking door as he goes.* Eight *rises and starts toward* Foreman.*)*

Foreman. You want this?

Eight. Yes, please. *(*Foreman *nods.* Eight *takes diagram and crosses upstage right. He takes chair from upstage right corner and brings it right center, half facing table. He sets diagram up on chair so that all can see it.* Eight *looks it over. Several* Jurors *get up to see it better.* Foreman *comes over to look.* Three, Ten *and* Seven, *however, barely bother to look at it.* Three *sits abruptly again at table.)* Z

Seven *(to* Ten*)*. Do me a favor. *(slumps in chair)* Wake me up when this is over.

Ten. I looked at that diagram for two hours; enough is enough.

Four. Some of us are interested. Go ahead.

Eight. All right. This is the apartment in which the killing took place. The old man's apartment is directly beneath it, and exactly the same. *(pointing)* Here are the el tracks. The bedroom. Another bedroom. Living room. Bathroom. Kitchen. And this is the hall. Here's the front door to the apartment, and here are the steps. *(points to front bedroom and then to front door)* Now, the old man was in bed in this room. He says he got up, went out into the hall, down the hall to the front door and opened it and looked out just in time to see the boy racing down the stairs. Am I right?

Four. That's the story.

Seven. That's what happened!

Eight. Fifteen seconds after he heard the body fall.

Eleven. Correct. *(*Foreman *and other* Jurors *who have come over to look at diagram now drift back to table and sit again.)*

Eight *(still by diagram at right center)*. His bed was at the window. *(looking closer)* It's twelve feet from his bed to the bedroom door. The length of the hall is forty-three feet six inches. He had to get up out of bed, get his canes, walk twelve feet, open the bedroom door, walk forty-three feet and open the front door—all in fifteen seconds. Do you think this is possible? AA

Ten. You know it's possible.

Four. I don't see why not.

Three. He would have been in a hurry. He did hear the scream.

Eleven. He can only walk very slowly. They had to help him into the witness chair.

Three. You make it sound like a long walk.

11. **railroad flat:** an apartment with a series of narrow rooms arranged in a line.

Critic's Corner

Rose's work is noteworthy for his willingness to take on difficult social issues and to deal with the darker aspects of human psychology, for his deep commitment to social justice, for his in-depth characterizations and sharp, compact scenes. Yet his writing shows an unwillingness to probe beyond a certain point: his desire to see justice done sometimes creates happy endings that are unconvincing, and his general optimism seems unjustified. In an overall view of Rose's screenplays, one must ask whether he tries to appease his audience in limiting the complexity of the issues he asks them to consider. As Rose himself describes it, "In all my work, . . . my main purpose has always been to protect my own view of good and evil—and this is the essence of controversy."
CAROLA KAPLAN, *Dictionary of Literary Biography*

It's not. *(*Eight *goes downstage left and takes two chairs. He crosses downstage right, near water cooler, and puts them together to indicate a bed.)*

Nine. For an old man who uses canes it's a long walk.

Three *(to* Eight*)*. What are you doing?

Eight. I want to try this thing. Let's see how long it took him. I'm going to pace off twelve feet—the length of the bedroom. *(begins to do so, pacing from downstage right, across stage, toward downstage center)*

Three. You're crazy! You can't re-create a thing like that.

Eleven. Perhaps if we could see it—this is an important point.

Three *(angrily)*. It's a ridiculous waste of time!

Six. Let him do it.

Four. I can't see any harm in it. Foolish, but go ahead.

Eight. Hand me a chair, please. *(*Nine *pushes chair from right end of table to* Eight *and then sits again.)* All right. *(places chair at point he has paced off)* This is the bedroom door. How far would you say it is from here to the door of this room?

Six *(as all look)*. I'd say it was twenty feet. *(Several* Jurors, *excluding* Three, Seven *and* Ten, *rise and stand near their places, watching.)*

Two. Just about.

Eight. Twenty feet is close enough. All right, from here to the door and back is about forty feet. It's shorter than the length of the hall the old man had to move through. Wouldn't you say that?

Nine. A few feet, maybe.

Ten. Look, this is absolutely insane. What makes you think you can do this?

Foreman. We can't stop him.

Eight. Do you mind if I try it? According to you, it'll only take fifteen seconds. We can spare that. *(walks over to two chairs and lies down on them)* Who's got a watch with a second hand?

Two. I have. *(indicates wristwatch)*

Eight. When you want me to start, stamp your foot. That'll be the body falling.

Two. We'll time you from there.

Eight *(lying down on two chairs)*. Let's say he keeps his canes right at his bedside. Right?

Four. Right!

Eight. Okay. I'm ready.

Two *(explaining)*. I'm waiting for the hand to get to sixty. *(All watch carefully; then* Two *stamps his foot, loudly.* Eight *begins to get up. Slowly, he swings his legs over edges of chairs, reaches for imaginary canes and struggles to his feet.* Two *stares at his watch.* Eight *walks as a crippled old man would walk now. He goes toward chair which is serving as bedroom door. He gets to it and pretends to open it.)* BB

Ten *(shouting)*. Speed it up. He walked twice as fast as that. *(*Eight, *not having stopped for this outburst, begins to walk simulated forty-foot hallway, to door left and back to chair.)*

Eleven. This is, I think, even more quickly than the old man walked in the courtroom.

Three. No, it isn't.

Eight. If you think I should go faster, I will.

Four. Speed it up a little. *(*Eight *speeds up his pace slightly. He reaches door left and turns now, heading back, hobbling as an old man would hobble, bent over his imaginary canes. All watch him tensely. He hobbles back to chair, which also serves as front door. He stops there and pretends to unlock door. Then he pretends to push it open.)* CC ◀SR-6

Eight *(loudly)*. Stop.

BB. Critical Thinking: EVALUATING You might want to suggest that the students reenact the exact details of this scene for themselves and determine how long they think it would have taken the old man to walk this distance.

CC. LEP: Vocabulary If necessary, have a volunteer demonstrate how one hobbles.

DD. Literary Element: DIALOGUE Have students discuss what Juror Seven might be expected to say here. Have them suggest why the playwright has Juror Seven's comment trail off. *(Possible response: Seven wants a quick guilty vote, so he'd like to say something to discount Eight's experiment. By having Seven try but fail to say anything meaningful, the playwright suggests that Eight's findings cannot be contradicted.)*

EE. LEP: Idiom and Slang Point out that *bleeding heart* and *heart bleeding all over the floor* are informal expressions that suggest someone is overly or insincerely sympathetic. Explain that *burn* is a slang expression for "be executed in an electric chair."

FF. Literary Element: IRONY Point out that Juror Three stated earlier that if someone said, "I'm going to kill you," then he or she meant it. Ask students if they think Juror Three really would kill Juror Eight. *(Responses will vary.)* Then ask students if they think Juror Eight set him up to lose his temper. *(Students might see this is one way Juror Eight can get Juror Three to discredit himself.)*

Check Test

1. Why do some of the jurors suspect that the old man could not have heard the murder? *(A loud el train was passing the apartment at the time of the murder.)*

2. Why does one juror suspect the old man lied on the witness stand? *(He thinks the old man lied in order to get attention.)*

3. How does Juror Eight use the floor plan of the old man's apartment? *(to reenact the man's testimony and to determine whether the old man could have seen the defendant fifteen seconds after the murder)*

4. How does Juror Three threaten Juror Eight at the end of the act? *(He threatens to kill him.)*

Two *(his eyes glued to watch).* Right.

Eight. What's the time?

Two. Fifteen—twenty—thirty—thirty-five—thirty-nine seconds, exactly. *(Moves toward* Eight. *Other* Jurors *now move in toward* Eight, *also.)*

Three. That can't be!

Eleven. Thirty-nine seconds!

Four. Now, that's interesting.

DD **Seven** *(looking at* Jurors*).* Hey, now—you know. . . .

Nine. What do you think of that!

Eleven *(nodding).* Thirty-nine seconds. Thirty-nine.

Four. And the old cripple swore, on his oath, that it was fifteen.

Eleven *(pointing to* Eight*).* He may have been a little bit off on the speed that the old cripple moved at—but twenty-four seconds off . . . well, now you know. . .

Foreman. Far be it from me to call anyone a liar, and even allowing for quite a difference in speed between the old man and you . . . *(motions at* Eight*)* Why, still, there's quite a—

Four. Quite a discrepancy.

Eight. It's my guess that the old man was trying to get to the door, heard someone racing down the stairs and *assumed* that it was the boy.

Six. I think that's possible.

Three *(infuriated).* Assumed? Now, listen to me, you people. I've seen all kinds of dishonesty in my day—but this little display takes the cake.

Eight. What dishonesty?

Three *(to* Four*).* Tell him! *(*Four *turns away downstage right and sits silently in one of the two chairs there.* Three *looks at him and then he strides to* Eight.*)* You come in here with your heart bleeding all over the floor about slum kids and injustice and you make up these wild stories, and you've got some soft-hearted old ladies listening to you. Well, I'm not. I'm getting real sick of you. *(to all)* What's the matter with you people? This kid is guilty! He's got to burn! We're letting him slip through our fingers. EE

Eight *(calmly).* Our fingers. Are you his executioner?

Three *(raging).* I'm one of 'em!

Eight. Perhaps you'd like to pull the switch.

Three *(shouting).* For this kid? You bet I'd like to pull the switch!

Eight *(shaking his head sadly).* I'm sorry for you.

Three *(shouting).* Don't start with me!

Eight. What it must feel like to want to pull the switch!

Three. Shut up!

Eight. You're a sadist. . . .

Three *(louder).* Shut up!

Eight *(his voice strong).* You want to see this boy die because you personally want it—not because of the facts. *(spits out words)* You are a beast. You disgust me. ◀ SR-7

Three *(shouting).* Shut up! *(Lunges at* Eight, *but is caught by two of the* Jurors *and is held. He struggles as* Eight *watches calmly. Then he screams.)* Let me go! I'll kill him! I'll kill him! FF

Eight *(softly).* You don't really mean you'll kill me, do you? *(*Three *stops struggling now and stares at* Eight, *and all the* Jurors *watch in silence, as:)*

Curtain

Words to Know and Use	**discrepancy** (di skrep′ ən sē) *n.* lack of agreement

e x p l a i n

Responding to Reading

First Impressions

1. What words express how the debate among the jurors is making you feel? Share your feelings with your classmates.

Second Thoughts

2. Is your opinion of the young man's guilt or innocence changing? Explain.
3. What unique perspectives do you see in Jurors Nine, Ten, and Eleven?
4. What kind of a man is Juror Three?

   Think about
   - what you learn in the opening notes
   - the incident he relates about his son
   - how he reacts to other jurors

5. How does Juror Eight try to influence the opinions of others?

Literary Concepts: Protagonist and Antagonist

The **protagonist** is the main character in a work of fiction around whom the action centers. The **antagonist** is the character who opposes or competes with the protagonist. Who do you think are the protagonist and the antagonist in this play? Why?

Writing Options

1. Look back at your chart to examine the evidence presented thus far. Summarize any new evidence given in Act Two.
2. Might the inclusion of women on the jury have made a difference in this play? Explain.
3. Make two lists of jurors. On one list, write the numbers of the jurors you think bow to peer pressure. On the other list, write the numbers of those who are independent thinkers.

Reading On

How do you think Juror Three's outburst will affect the other jurors?

Student Response

Responding to Reading

These questions are open-ended with no "right" or "wrong" answers. However, responses must be supported with information from the selection. Possible answers follow:

1. Any response based on the play is valid.

2. Some students may say that the young man's guilt seems less obvious now that the old man's testimony has been questioned. Some may say that there is definitely a reasonable doubt about the defendant's guilt. Others may maintain that the bulk of the evidence still points to the defendant's guilt.

3. Some students will suggest that Juror Nine, who considers himself a frightened failure of a man, is using the case to prove himself courageous. Students should point out that Ten is a bigot whose prejudices prevent him from examining or thinking about the facts of the case. Students might indicate that Eleven, a recent refugee, has the perspective of someone who is anxious to see if his adopted country's legal ideals are effective when put to the test in an actual trial.

4. Students should point out that Juror Three is a forceful, opinionated, intolerant man. Some might say that the incident with his son shows his violent nature and lack of compassion and feeling. Students might suggest that his cynical and sarcastic remarks to jurors who disagree with him show him to be very bitter. His overwhelming desire that the defendant "burn" and his thwarted attack on Eight also show his violence.

5. Students should point out that Juror Eight tries to influence the opinions of the other jurors with his open-minded interpretation of the evidence. Others might point to the interesting and intelligent arguments about inconsistencies in the testimony. Students might note that he treats his co-jurors in a kind and fair-minded way. Others might note that he presses the most narrow-minded jurors into stating their opinions so that in this way they discredit themselves.

Literary Concept—Protagonist and Antagonist

Juror Eight is the protagonist. He initiates the major incidents in the plot, with the result that the action tends to center around him.

Juror Three is the antagonist in the play. His personality is the opposite of Juror Eight's. Also, Juror Three constantly argues with or ridicules each point that Eight makes.

Writing Options

The Writing Options are designed to meet varied student interests and abilities. Have each student choose one writing activity to complete. You may wish to guide some students to an option that requires less writing.

Reading On

Possible answer: Three's outburst may lead some jurors to vote "not guilty" since it puts Three, the leading proponent of a "guilty" vote, in a negative light.

Text Annotations

A. Reading Skill: SUMMARIZING Have students summarize the events that led up to this confrontation between Jurors Three and Eight. *(Juror Eight expresses his belief that Juror Three wants to see the defendant die because of personal reasons and not because of the facts. Juror Three, angry at this remark, threatens to kill Juror Eight and attempts to strike him.)*

B. LEP: Dialogue Point out that the playwright has Juror Eleven, a recent immigrant from Europe, speak in a somewhat formal and stilted manner. Explain that this emphasizes the irony: It requires a newcomer to remind the native-born Americans of the strengths of their democratic system.

C. Reading Skill: PREDICTING Have students recall that in the last vote, nine jurors voted "guilty" and three voted "not guilty." Ask them to predict the outcome of this next vote and explain their reasons. *(Most students will predict that this time there will be more "not guilty" votes. Their reasons may include the convincing argument Juror Eight has put forth and any dialogue by Jurors Two, Six, and Eleven indicating that they are changing their minds.)*

ACT THREE

A At Rise of Curtain: *We see the same scene as at the end of Act Two. There has been no time lapse.* Three *glares angrily at* Eight. *He is still held by two* Jurors. *After a long pause,* Three *shakes himself loose and turns away. He walks to the window. The other* Jurors *move away and stand around the room now; they are shocked by this display of anger. There is silence. Then the door left opens and the* Guard *enters. He looks around the room.*

Guard. Is there anything wrong, gentlemen? I heard some noise.

Foreman. No. There's nothing wrong. *(points to large diagram of apartment)* You can take that back. We're finished with it. *(*Guard *nods and takes diagram. He looks curiously at some of* Jurors *and then goes out.* Jurors *still are silent; some of them begin to sit down slowly at table.* Four *is still seated downstage right.* Three *still stands at window. He turns around now.* Jurors *look at him.)*

Three *(loudly)*. Well, what are you looking at? *(They turn away. He goes back to his seat now.* Eight *puts his chair back at right end of table. Silently, rest of* Jurors, *including* Four *but excluding* Eleven, *take their seats.* Twelve *begins to doodle on a piece of paper.* Eleven *moves downstage left and leans reflectively against wall.* Ten *blows his nose but no one speaks. Then, finally.)*

Four. I don't see why we have to behave like children here.

B **Eleven.** Nor do I. We have a responsibility. This is a remarkable thing about democracy. That we are—what is the word? . . . ah, notified! That we are notified by mail to come down to this place—and decide on the guilt or innocence of a man; of a man we have not known before. We have nothing to gain or lose by our verdict. This is one of the reasons why we are strong. We should not make it a personal thing. . . . B

Nine *(slowly)*. Thank you, very much.

Eleven *(slight surprise)*. Why do you thank me?

Nine. We forget. It's good to be reminded. *(*Eleven *nods and leans against wall again.)*

Four. I'm glad that we're going to be civilized about this.

Twelve. Well, we're still nowhere.

Eight. No, we're somewhere, or getting there—maybe.

Four. Maybe.

Twelve. Who's got an idea?

Six. I think maybe we should try another vote. *(turns to* Foreman*)* Mr. Foreman?

Foreman. It's all right with me. Anybody doesn't want to vote? *(Looks around table. Most of them shake their heads.* Eleven *has moved to table and takes his seat.)*

Four. Let's vote.

Twelve. Yes, vote.

Seven. So all right, let's do it.

Three. I want an open ballot. Let's call out our votes. I want to know who stands where. C

Foreman. That sounds fair. Anyone object? *(Looks around. There is a general shaking of heads.)* All right. I'll call off your jury numbers. *(takes a pencil and paper and makes marks in one of two columns after each vote)* I vote guilty. Number two?

Two. Not guilty.

Foreman. Three?

Three. Guilty.

Foreman. Four?

Four. Guilty.

Foreman. Five?

Five. Not guilty.

Foreman. Six?

STRUCTURED READING FOR LESS PROFICIENT STUDENTS

These questions can help to guide students through the reading. Ask each question at the point of the selection where the SR number appears in the margin.

SR–1. How many jurors vote "not guilty" at the opening of Act Three? *(six jurors)* **Literal recall**

SR–2. Why do the jurors reconstruct the actual murder? *(They want to see if it could have taken thirty to forty seconds; if it did, the old man's testimony would be more believable.)* **Summarizing**

SR–3. What point does Juror Eight make about the lighting in the old man's tenement that casts further doubt on his testimony? *(Since there is so little light in the tenement halls, the old man would have had difficulty identifying the defendant.)* **Literal recall**

SR–4. What is it about the knife wound that leads some jurors to think the defendant may not have been the murderer? *(The man was killed with a downward stab of the knife, which was held overhand; like other knife fighters, the boy would have slashed underhand and upward.* **Clarifying**

Continued on page 577.

Six. Not guilty.

Foreman. Seven?

Seven. Guilty.

Foreman. Eight?

Eight. Not guilty.

Foreman. Nine?

Nine. Not guilty.

Foreman. Ten?

Ten. Guilty.

Foreman. Eleven?

Eleven. Not guilty.

Foreman. Twelve?

Twelve. Guilty.

Four. That's six to six.

D **Ten** *(mad)*. I'll tell you something. The crime is being committed right in this room.

SR-1 ▶ **Foreman.** The vote is six to six.

Three. I'm ready to walk into court right now and declare a hung jury. There's no point in this going on any more.

Four *(to* Eleven*)*. I'd like to know why you changed your mind. *(to* Two*)* And why you changed your mind. *(to* Six*)* And why you did. There are six men here who think that we may be turning a murderer loose in the streets. Emotion won't do. Why? *(*Two, Eleven *and* Six *look at each other.)* E

Six. It would seem that the old man did not see the boy run downstairs. I do not think it likely that the old man heard someone scream "I'm going to kill you." Old men dream. And if the boy did scream that he was going to kill, then we have the authority of this man—*(motions at* Three*)*—to prove that it might not really mean he's going to kill.

Seven. Why don't we take it in to the judge and let the kid take his chances with twelve other guys? F

Foreman. Six to six. I don't think we'll ever agree—on anything.

D. Reading Skill: CLARIFYING Ask a volunteer to explain what Juror Ten means when he says that a "crime" is being committed in the jury room. *(Possible response: It seems criminal to Juror Ten that five jurors no longer believe the boy is guilty. He thinks that it will be a crime if the boy is not found guilty and punished.)*

E. Critical Thinking: EVALUATING Ask students to tell how they would vote if they were members of this jury. Have them give reasons for their votes.

F. LEP: Comprehension Explain that Juror Seven is suggesting that they declare themselves a hung jury. Review that when a jury cannot reach a unanimous decision, the judge might declare a mistrial. In that event, the case would have to be retried before a new jury.

Structured Reading for Less Proficient Students

Continued from page 576

SR–5. How does Juror Ten explain why he believes the boy is guilty? *(Juror Ten stereotypes all the people in the boy's ethnic group as violent liars and murderers.)* **Clarifying**

SR–6. What does Juror Eight point out about the eyewitness across the street that casts her testimony into doubt? *(He points out that the woman across the street in all likelihood was not wearing her glasses when she witnessed the murder and so could not be sure of what she saw.)* **Literal recall**

SR–7. What decision do the twelve jurors make at the end of the play? *(At the end of the play, the twelve jurors vote "not guilty.")* **Literal recall**

G. LEP: Grammar Point out that Juror Three uses a double negative—"there *isn't no* doubt." Explain that people sometimes use double negatives to emphasize a point, even though this usage is incorrect.

H. Literary Element: FORESHADOWING Point out the simple confidence with which Juror Eight makes this remark. Have students discuss what outcome this might suggest for the play. *(It suggests that the entire jury will reach a unanimous verdict.)*

I. Critical Thinking: ANALYZING Point out that the jurors who voted "guilty" think the jury is hung, while those who voted "not guilty" think it is not hung. Ask students if this vote suggests that one side is more convinced of the strength of their position than the other side is. *(Possible response: By saying the jury is not hung, the jurors who voted "not guilty" seem to imply that they can convince the others that there is indeed a shadow of a doubt.)*

J. Literary Element: CHARACTER Point out that Juror Four's vote change is consistent with his honest interest in uncovering the facts in the case. Elicit that in this he is unlike the other jurors, who seem less interested in the facts than in a "guilty" verdict.

Three. It's got to be unanimous—*(motioning at* Eight*)*—and we're never going to convince him.

Eight. At first I was alone. Now five others agree; there is a doubt.

G **Three.** You can't ever convince me that there's a doubt, because I know there isn't no doubt.

Twelve. I tell you what, maybe we are a hung jury. It happens sometimes.

H **Eight.** We are not going to be a hung jury.

Seven. But we are, right now, a perfect balance. Let's take it in to the judge.

Four *(to* Eight*).* If there is a reasonable doubt, I don't see it.

Nine. The doubt is there, in my mind.

Foreman. Maybe we should vote.

Twelve. What do you mean—vote?

Three. Not again!

Ten. I still want to know. Vote on what?

Foreman. Are we or aren't we a hung jury?

Eight. You mean that we vote yes, we are a hung jury, or no, we are not a hung jury?

Foreman. That's just what I was thinking of.

Eleven *(bitterly).* We can't even agree about whether or not the window should be open.

Foreman. Let's make it a majority vote. The majority wins.

Four. If seven or more of us vote yes, that we are a hung jury, then we take it in to the judge and tell him that we are a hung jury.

Foreman. Right. And if seven or more vote no, that means that we aren't a hung jury, and we go on discussing it.

Four. It doesn't seem quite right to me.

Three. It's the only solution.

Seven. I agree, it's the only way.

Twelve. Anything to end this.

Foreman *(looking around table).* Are we agreed then? Seven or more vote yes and we take it in to the judge. *(all nod)*

Three. Let's call our votes out.

Foreman. I vote yes, we're a hung jury. *(makes a mark on a sheet of paper)* Two?

Two. No.

Foreman. Three?

Three. Yes.

Foreman. Four?

Four. Yes.

Foreman. Five?

Five. No.

Foreman. Six?

Six. No.

Foreman. Seven?

Seven. Yes.

Foreman. Eight?

Eight. No.

Foreman. Nine?

Nine. No.

Foreman. Ten?

Ten. Yes.

Foreman. Eleven?

Eleven. No.

Foreman. Twelve?

Twelve. Yes.

Three *(with a groan).* Oh, no! I

Foreman. It's six to six.

Nine. We can't even get a majority to decide whether or not we're a hung jury.

Four *(rising).* I went along with the majority vote on this question. And I didn't agree with voting that way, not really, and I still don't. So I'm changing my vote. I say no, we are not a hung jury. I believe that the boy is guilty beyond a reasonable doubt. There are some things I want to find out from those gentlemen that changed their minds. *(sits again)* J

Foreman. Then we aren't a hung jury—so we go on.

Eight. Good! We go on.

Four *(to* Two*)*. Why did you change your mind?

Two *(hesitating a moment)*. He—*(points to* Eight*)*—he seems so sure. And he has made a number of good points. While he—*(points to* Three*)*—only gets mad and insults everybody.

K

Four. Does the anger and the insult change the guilt of the boy? He did do it. Are you going to turn a murderer loose because one of the jurors gets angry when he thinks a murderer is being turned loose?

Two. That's true.

Five. There is a doubt.

Four. I don't think so. The track is straight in front of the window. Let's take that point. So the el train would have made a low rumbling noise. El trains screech when they go around curves. So the old man could have heard a scream, which is high-pitched. And it is a tenement and they have thin walls.

Three. Good. Good. That's it. That's it.

Four. And what if the old man was wrong about the time it took him to get to the door but right about whom he saw? Please remember that there weren't any fingerprints on the knife, and it is summer, so gloves seem unlikely.

L

Three *(to* Eight*)*. Now I want you to listen to this man. *(motions at* Four*)* He's got the goods.

Four. And it might have taken a few seconds to get a handkerchief out and wipe the fingerprints away.

Eight. This is a point.

Three. Why don't we just time this one, to see?

Five. Just what are we timing?

Eight. Yes, let's be exact, please.

M

Four. I am saying that the old man downstairs might have been wrong about how long it took him to get to the door but that he was right about whom he saw running down the stairs. Now it may have taken the murderer about thirty-nine seconds to wipe away all the fingerprints and get down the stairs to the place where the old man saw him—the boy, that is.

Three. This is right.

Foreman. We reconstructed the old man getting out of bed and going to the door, and we timed that; now let's reconstruct the actual crime.

Nine. As well as we can reconstruct it.

Seven. I think a murderer could use up thirty or forty seconds pretty easily at that point.

Four. Let's reconstruct the killing.

Seven. Yes, let's.

Three *(taking knife from table, giving it to* Eight*)*. Here, you do the stabbing.

Four *(taking knife)*. No, I'll do it.

Three *(to* Seven*)*. Why don't you be the one that gets stabbed? You're younger than I am. And don't forget, you take one second to fall.

Four *(rising, moving toward right, turning)*. And he was found on his side—his right side—so fall and roll onto your right side. *(to* Eight*)* If someone hates another person enough to kill them, don't you think that it's reasonable to suppose that the murderer would look at his victim for a second or two?

Twelve *(to* Eight*)*. Divorce yourself from this particular case—just human nature.

Words to Know and Use

tenement (ten′ ə mənt) *n.* an apartment building; often a very old and run-down building

K. Critical Thinking: EVALUATING Ask students whether they agree that Juror Two has changed his mind on the vote for the wrong reasons. *(Possible response: Yes, Juror Two should base his vote on the facts of the case and not on the personalities of the jurors.)*

L. LEP: Slang Explain that here the slang phrase *He's got the goods* means "He's reached the right conclusions."

M. Literary Element: PLOT Point out that, so far, the momentum of events has moved the jurors steadily away from a "guilty" to a "not guilty" verdict. Explain that the playwright now varies the pacing of the plot by having Juror Four offer some excellent arguments in favor of a "guilty" verdict.

PROFESSIONAL NOTEBOOK

Great teachers have left no record of their pedagogical accomplishments. The effect of their work has been rather like that of opera singers before the advent of recordings; there was, that is to say, no trace of their work beyond the circle of their auditors. It does not do to overemphasize the comparison, but there is a sense in which teaching, like opera, is a performing art. Not only must the teacher get up his subject, but he must get it across. There is many a tried, but no true, method for doing this. . . . What all the great teachers appear to have in common is love of their subject, an obvious satisfaction in arousing this love in their students, and an ability to convince them that what they are being taught is deadly serious.

JOSEPH EPSTEIN, *Masters: Postcards of Great Teachers*

N. Literary Element: PROTAGONIST Ask students to note that Juror Eight is open-minded and polite to Juror Three, even though the latter is trying to discount Eight's argument.

O. LEP: Comprehension Ask a volunteer to clarify this exchange between Jurors Three and Four. *(Possible response: Juror Four reminds Three that they are not simply creating a story that sounds better; rather, they are honestly trying to determine the facts of the case.)*

P. Reading Skill: SUMMARIZING Have a volunteer summarize the importance of what Juror Four has just demonstrated. *(Possible response: He has demonstrated that it took thirty to forty seconds to commit the murder. This is the same amount of time that it would have taken the old man to reach his door. So although the old man was wrong about the time, his testimony about seeing the boy could well be true.)*

Eight. Yes, it seems reasonable.

Three. Hey, wait a minute! *(all look at* Three*)* He falls and he ends up on his right side, the father did, but stabbing someone isn't like shooting them, even when it's right in the heart. The father would have worked around for a few seconds—lying there on the floor—writhing, maybe.

Four. That's quite possible. There would have been enough oxygen in his system to carry him for two or three seconds, I should think.

Eleven. Wouldn't the father have cried out?

Three. Maybe the kid held his mouth.

N **Eight.** That also seems possible.

Four. Also, there's another point we might bring out. Anyone who is clear enough mentally to wipe the fingerprints away after murdering someone, well, that person is also clear enough mentally to look around the apartment, or the room in this case, to see if there are any other clues. It would be just for a second or two, I should think, but still he would look around.

Three. This gets better and better.

O **Four.** We're trying to make it clear. One doesn't talk about quality when murder is involved. Well, let's do it.

Foreman. About this on the fingerprints—the kid wiped the fingerprints off the knife. Well, what about the doorknob? If I saw a man coming into my home, a man that hated me, and he was wiping the doorknob with a handkerchief as he came in, it would give me an uneasy feeling. *(all smile)* So the doorknobs must have been wiped after the killing, and this, too, would take some time.

Four *(to* Two*)***.** You timed the last one. Why don't you time this one, too?

Two. All right.

Four *(as* Seven *takes his position in front of* Four *at right stage;* Four *has knife in his hand)***.** Stamp your foot when you want me to start.

Two *(waiting a few seconds)***.** I want the hand to be at sixty. *(waits another second, then stamps foot)*

Four *(not screaming, but still loud)***.** I'm going to kill you. *(Brings knife down, overhand. Blade is collapsed.* Seven *catches knife in his hands and falls to floor a second after shout. He writhes a bit, then rolls onto his right side.* Four *stares at him for a few moments, then digs into his pocket and produces a handkerchief. It takes him a moment or two to unfold handerchief; then he bends down and wipes handle of knife. He looks about, as though checking to be sure that he has done everything. Then he rushes to door left that leads out of jury room and wipes doorknob. Then he turns around a full circle and wipes knob again.)* He would have wiped both knobs. *(Then he rushes right and goes back to door of jury room and repeats double process on doorknob. Then he stamps his foot and cries out.)* Stop!

Two *(checking watch)***.** Twenty—yeah, twenty, twenty-five—twenty-nine—about twenty-nine and a half seconds, I'd say.

Four *(moving to behind* Foreman's *chair at left end of table)***.** And whoever did murder the old man, and I think it was the kid, he still had to run down the hall and down the stairs—at least one flight of stairs. P

Three. You see! You see! *(*Seven *rises from floor and dusts himself off.)*

Four. The old man downstairs may have

Words to Know and Use

writhing (rīth′ iŋ) *adj.* twisting one's body around, usually in severe pain
writhe *v.*

been wrong on the time, but in view of this I think it's quite reasonable to assume that he did see the kid run downstairs. SR-2 ▶

Q

Twelve *(to* Eight*)***.** So now both time sequences check—the one you did and the one we did; what with running downstairs and everything, it does pretty much check out on times.

Seven. Sure—he's an old man who wants attention. . . . *(motions at* Nine*)* He's probably right, but the old man feels the way everyone does—a life is at stake. *(sits again at table, placing knife back on table)*

Four. So the story of the old man may well be true.

Eight. Except for the fact that he absolutely swore, under oath, that it was only fifteen seconds.

Nine. We seem to all agree that it was twenty-five to forty seconds later.

Eight. You are now admitting that the old man lied in one case and told the truth in the other. I admit that this does tend to confirm the story of the old man, but in part he is now a proven liar—and this is by your own admission.

Two *(to* Eight*)***.** That may be true, the old man lies in part, but I think it will change my vote once more. *(to* Foreman*)* Guilty.

Three *(to* Six*)***.** What about you? What do you think now?

R

Six *(getting up, crossing to water cooler)***.** I'm not just sure what I think. I want to talk some more. At first I thought guilty, then I changed. Now—I'm sort of swinging back to guilty. *(takes a drink)*

Three *(to* Eleven*)***.** And what about you?

Eleven. No. *(shakes his head)* I am now in real doubt—real doubt. . . .

Five. I say guilty. I was right the first time.

Three. Now we're beginning to make sense in here.

Foreman. It seems to be about nine guilty to three not guilty. *(Four sits again.)*

Eight. One more question about the old man downstairs. How many of you live in apartment buildings? *(Eight hands go up, including his own.)*

Eleven *(to* Eight*)***.** I don't know what you're thinking, but I know what I'm thinking.

Four *(to* Eleven*)***.** What's that?

Eleven. I do not live in a tenement, but it is close and there is just enough light in the hall so you can see the steps, no more—the light bulbs are so small—and this murder took place in a tenement. Remember how we stumbled on the steps?

Eight. The police officers were using big bulbs and one even had a flashlight. Remember? ◀ SR-3

Eleven. An old man who misjudged the time by twenty seconds, on this we all agree, this old man looked down the dark hallway of a tenement and recognized a running figure?

Eight. He was one hundred percent wrong about the time; it took twice as long as he thought.

Eleven. Then could not the old man be one hundred percent wrong about who he saw? S

Three. That's the most idiotic thing I've ever heard of. You're making that up out of thin air.

Twelve. We're a hung jury. Let's be honest about it.

Eleven *(to* Seven*)***.** Do you truly feel that there is no room for reasonable doubt?

Seven. Yes, I do.

Eleven. I beg your pardon, but maybe you don't understand the term "reasonable doubt."

Seven *(angrily)***.** What do you mean, I don't understand it? Who do you think you are

Q. LEP: Vocabulary Review the meaning of *sequence* as "a series of connected events."

R. Literary Element: SUSPENSE Point out that Juror Two has changed his vote from "not guilty" to "guilty" and that Juror Six may be about to do the same. Ask students how this creates suspense. *(Possible response: For a while, it seemed as if Juror Eight would persuade all the others to vote "not guilty." This new development makes the outcome uncertain and creates more interest about the boy's fate.)*

S. Critical Thinking: EVALUATING Ask students to decide whether in the end they would consider the old man's testimony valid or not. *(Students should support their ideas with sound reasons.)*

REAL LIFE CONNECTIONS

The search for justice and the struggle against injustice should be a real part of everyday life. Use the following quotations to develop a discussion on justice.

No man suffers injustice without learning, vaguely but surely, what justice is.
ISAAC ROSENFIELD

People who live in a narrow circle are kind, perhaps, but rarely just. Only an open and varied life educates us to share many points of view, and so to become capable of justice.
CHARLES HORTON COOLEY

Justice is what we get when the decision is in our favor.
JOHN W. RAPER

Men are always invoking justice; and it is justice which should make them tremble.
MADAME SWETCHINE

T. Literary Sidelight With the line "He comes over here running for his life," the playwright alludes to the flight of the Jews and other persecuted minorities from Europe to escape Nazi extermination.

U. Reading Skill: CLARIFYING Ask a volunteer to explain why Juror Eight wants Juror Seven to apologize to Juror Eleven. *(Possible response: Juror Seven seems to suggest that since Eleven was born in Europe, he is somehow less American or has less right to express his opinions; such opinions are repulsive to Juror Eight's belief in justice and fairness.)*

Teaching Tip

Alert students that the knife wound will be an important piece of evidence. Ask them to take notes that they can include on their evidence chart.

V. Literary Element: CONFLICT Point out that this scene dramatizes the conflict between Jurors Eight and Three, the protagonist and antagonist, respectively. Three, who in a fit of anger claimed that he would like to kill Eight, now has the chance to do so.

T to talk to me like that? *(to all)* How do you like this guy? He comes over here running for his life, and before he can even take a big breath, he's telling us how to run the show. The arrogance of him!

Four. No one here is asking where anyone came from.

Seven. I was born right here.

Four. Or where your father came from. *(looks at* Seven, *who looks away)*

Eight. Maybe it wouldn't hurt us to take a few tips from people who came running here! Maybe they learned something we don't know. We're not so perfect.

Eleven. Please. . . . I am used to this. . . . It's all right. Thank you.

U **Eight.** It's not all right.

Seven. Okay—okay—I apologize. Is that what you want?

Eight *(grimly)***.** That's what I want.

Foreman. All right. Let's stop the arguing. Who's got something constructive to say?

Two *(hesitantly)***.** Well, something's been bothering me a little. This whole business about the stab wound, and how it was made—the downward angle of it, you know?

Three. Don't tell me we're going to start that. They went over it and over it in court.

Two. I know they did—but I don't go along with it. The boy is five feet eight inches tall. His father was six feet two inches tall. That's a difference of six inches. It's a very awkward thing to stab *down* into the chest of someone who's half a foot taller than you are. *(*Three *grabs knife from the table and jumps up)*

Three *(moving left center)***.** Look, you're not going to be satisfied till you see it again. I'm going to give you a demonstration. Somebody get up. *(Looks toward table.* Eight *stands up and walks toward him.* Three *closes knife and puts it in his pocket. They stand face to face and look at each other for a moment.)* Okay. *(to* Two*)* Now watch this. I don't want to have to do it again. *(crouches down until he is quite a bit shorter than* Eight*)* Is that six inches?

Twelve. That's more than six inches.

Three. Okay, let it be more. *(Reaches into his pocket and takes out knife. He flicks it open, changes its position in his hand and holds knife aloft, ready to stab. He and* Eight *look steadily into each other's eyes. Then he stabs downward, hard.)* V

Two *(shouting)***.** Look out! *(Reaches short just as blade reaches* Eight's *chest.* Three *laughs.)*

Six. That's not funny. *(crosses back to table and sits)*

Five. What's the matter with you?

Three. Now just calm down. Nobody's hurt, are they?

Eight *(low)***.** No. Nobody's hurt. *(turns, crosses back to his place but does not sit)*

Three. All right. There's your angle. Take a look at it. *(illustrates)* Down and in. That's how I'd stab a taller man in the chest, and that's how it was done. *(crosses back to his place at table)* Take a look at it, and tell me I'm wrong. *(*Two *doesn't answer.* Three *looks at him for a moment, then jams knife into table and sits down. All look at knife.)*

Six. Down and in. I guess there's no argument. *(*Eight *picks knife out of table and closes it. He flicks it open and, changing its position in his hand, stabs downward with it.)*

Eight *(to* Six*)***.** Did you ever stab a man?

Six. Of course not.

Eight *(to* Three*)***.** Did you?

Three. All right, let's not be silly.

CRITIC'S CORNER

The theater [has] a very basic advantage: the directness of contact between actor and public. The laughter of the public cannot reach the film comedian. The television star can never perceive the tears of his audience. We hear voices from the radio, but they are without echo and without modulation. The decisive moment for a work of art is the moment of contact—of contact with those for whom it was created. . . . Nothing speaks more for the immortality of the theater than this characteristic—this present moment which is more than any actuality.

SIEGFRIED MELCHINGER, *The Concise Encyclopedia of Modern Drama*

Eight *(insistently)***.** Did you?

Three *(loudly)***.** No. I didn't!

Eight. Where do you get all your information about how it's done?

Three. What do you mean? It's just common sense.

Eight. Have you ever seen a man stabbed?

W **Three** *(pausing, looking around rather nervously, finally)***.** No.

Eight. All right. I want to ask you something. The boy was an experienced knife-fighter. He was even sent to reform school for knifing someone. Isn't that so?

Twelve. That's right.

Eight. Look at this. *(closes knife, flicks it open and changes position of knife so that he can stab overhand)* Doesn't it seem like an awkward way to handle a knife?

Three. What are you asking me for? *(Eight closes blade and flicks it open, holding knife ready to slash underhanded.)* X

Five. Wait a minute! What's the matter with me? Give me that knife. *(reaches out for knife)*

Eight. Have you ever seen a knife fight?

Five. Yes, I have.

Eight. In the movies? *(passes knife to* Five*)*

Five. In my backyard. On my stoop. In the vacant lot across the street. Too many of them. Switch knives came with the neighborhood where I lived. Funny that I didn't think of it before. I guess you try to forget those things. *(flicks knife open)* Anyone who's ever used a switch knife would never have stabbed downward. You don't handle a switch knife that way. You use it underhanded. *(illustrates)*

W. Literary Element: STAGE DIRECTIONS Have students discuss what the playwright might have intended with these stage directions. *(Possible response: Juror Three's nervousness suggests that he is lying; the stage directions suggest that he has stabbed someone or at least witnessed a stabbing.)*

X. Reading Skill: CLARIFYING Ask a student to use a pen or other knife-shaped object to reenact Juror Eight's demonstration.

Y. LEP: Vocabulary Elicit that *mumbo jumbo* means "foolish or meaningless talk."

Z. Literary Element: CHARACTER MOTIVATION Remind students that Juror Seven is very eager to be sure he gets to use his theater tickets.

AA. Literary Element: FIGURATIVE LANGUAGE Point out that a chip shot is a short golf stroke used to get on the green, which is the location of the hole—the golfer's final destination. Elicit that Juror Twelve is making this comparison to describe the process by which Juror Eight suggests ideas that will lead the jury closer to its final decision.

Eight. Then he couldn't have made the kind of wound that killed his father.

Five. I suppose it's conceivable that he could have made the wound, but it's not likely, not if he'd ever had any experience with switch knives, and we know that the kid had a lot of experience with switch knives.

Three. I don't believe it.

Y **Ten.** Neither do I. You're giving us a lot of mumbo jumbo.

Eight *(to* Twelve). What do you think?

Twelve *(hesitantly)*. Well—I don't know.

Eight *(to* Seven*)*. What about you?

Z **Seven.** Listen, I'll tell you all something. I'm a little sick of this whole thing already. We're getting nowhere fast. Let's break it up and go home.

Eight. Before we decide anything more, I would like to try to pull this together.

Three. This should be good.

Four. He has a right. Let him go ahead.

Two. Do you want me to time this, too? *(*Eight *looks at* Two.*)*

Foreman. Let's hear him.

AA **Twelve** *(getting comfortable)*. I'm in advertising. I'm used to the big shots pulling things together. Let's chip up a few shots to see if any of them land on the green.

Eight. I want you all to look at this logically and consistently.

Three. We have. Guilty.

Eight. I want to know—is the kid smart or is the kid dumb?

Four. What do you mean?

Eight *(moving upstage center, so that he is standing back of men at upstage side of table)*. This is a kid who has gone to the reform school for knife fighting. The night of the murder he bought a knife, a switch knife. It would then take a very stupid kid to go and murder a man, his father, with an instrument that everyone would associate with the kid.

Three. I quite agree, he's dumb.

Eight. However, if he were dumb, then why did he make the kind of wound that an inexperienced man would make with a knife?

Foreman. I'm not sure I understand.

Eight. To murder someone must take a great emotion, great hatred. *(moves over to left of* Foreman*)* And at that moment he would handle the knife as best he could, and a trained knife-fighter would handle it as he had been trained, underhand. . . . *(makes underhanded motion)* A man who had not been trained would go overhand. . . . *(makes overhanded motion)* But the kid is being very smart. Everyone knows that he is an experienced knife-fighter—so he is smart enough at that moment to make the wound that an amateur would make. That man is a smart man. Smart enough to wipe the fingerprints away, perhaps even smart enough to wait until an el train was going by in order to cover the noise. Now, is the kid smart, or is he dumb? *(looks around)* ◀ SR-4

Three. Hey, now, wait a minute!

Nine. Well, the woman across the el tracks saw the murder through the el train, so someone in that el train could have seen the murder, too.

Eight. A possibility, but no one did that we know of.

Nine. It would take an awfully dumb man to take that chance, doing the murder as the train went by.

Words to Know and Use	**conceivable** (kən sēv′ ə bəl) *adj.* believable; able to be imagined or accepted

DATA BANK

In the 1950's many television series, such as *Studio One, The U.S. Steel Hour, Kraft Television Theater,* and *Pulitzer Prize Playhouse,* showcased the talents of young actors and directors in a live dramatic format. An extraordinary group of screenwriters, including Reginald Rose, Paddy Chayefsky, Rod Serling, and Gore Vidal, also emerged during this period. Rose's 1954 play *Twelve Angry Men* was produced live for *Studio One* in an actual jury room. Like other *Studio One* productions, it emphasized bold camera techniques and dramatic innovation.

Television's move from New York to Hollywood spelled the end of live television drama. But as creator of *The Defenders* series, which ran from 1961 to 1965, Reginald Rose provided a haven for many actors, directors, and producers from the 1950's. *The Defenders* sought to enlighten viewers about the law and dealt with difficult issues, such as capital punishment, mercy killing, and criminal insanity.

Eight. Exactly. A dumb man, a very stupid man, a man swept by emotion. Probably he heard nothing; he probably didn't even hear the train coming. And whoever did murder the father did it as well as he could.

Four. So?

Eight *(moving back to his place, at right end of table, not sitting)*. The kid is dumb enough to do everything to associate himself with the switch knife—a switch knife murder—and then a moment after the murder he becomes smart. The kid is smart enough to make a kind of wound that would lead us to suspect someone else, and yet at the same instant he is dumb enough to do the killing as an el train is going by, and then a moment later he is smart enough to wipe fingerprints away. To make this boy guilty you have to say he is dumb from eight o'clock until about midnight, and then about midnight he is smart one second, then dumb for a few seconds and then smart again and then once again he becomes stupid, so stupid that he does not think of a good alibi. Now is this kid smart or is he dumb? To say that he is
BB guilty you have to toss his intelligence like a pancake. There is doubt, doubt, doubt. *(beats table with fist as he emphasizes the word* doubt*)*

Four. I hadn't thought of that.

Eight. And the old man downstairs. On the stand he swore that it was fifteen seconds; he insisted on fifteen seconds, but we all agree that it must have been almost forty seconds.

Nine. Does the old man lie half the time and then does he tell the truth the other half of the time?

Eight. For the kid to be guilty he must be stupid, then smart, then stupid and then smart and so on, and, also, for the kid to be guilty the old man downstairs must be a liar half of the time and the other half of the time he must tell the truth. You can reasonably doubt. *(Sits again. There is a moment of silence.)*

Seven *(breaking silence)*. I'm sold on "reasonable doubt." CC

Two. I think I am, too.

Six. I wanted more talk, and now I've had it.

Eight *(fast)*. I want another vote.

Foreman. Okay, there's another vote called for. I guess the quickest way is a show of hands. Anybody object? *(No one does.)* All right. All those voting not guilty raise your hands. *(Jurors* Two, Five, Six, Seven, Eight, Nine, Eleven *and* Twelve *raise their hands immediately.* Foreman *looks around table carefully and then he, too, raises his hand. He looks around table, counting silently.)* Nine. *(hands go down)* All those voting guilty. *(Jurors* Three, Four *and* Ten *raise their hands.)* Three. *(They lower their hands.)* The vote is nine to three in favor of acquittal.[12]

Ten. I don't understand you people. How can you believe this kid is innocent? Look, you know how those people lie. I don't have to tell you. They don't know what the truth is. And let me tell you, they—*(*Five *gets up from table, turns his back to it and goes to window.)*—don't need any real big reason to kill someone, either. You know, they get drunk, and bang, someone's lying in the gutter. Nobody's blaming them. That's how they DD

12. **acquittal:** a verdict of not guilty.

Words to Know and Use

alibi (al' ə bī') *n.* a story told by an accused criminal that supposedly proves he or she was somewhere else at the time of the crime

585

Teaching Tip
Ask a volunteer to read aloud Juror Eight's long speech on page 585. Ask students to comment on the speaker's expression and gestures.

BB. LEP: Figurative Language Point out that Juror Eight uses a vivid simile—". . . you have to toss his intelligence like a pancake"—in order to emphasize the inconsistencies in the testimony.

CC. Literary Element: PLOT Point out that Juror Eight's speech marks the turning point in the plot. As a result of his argument here, a decisive change takes place in the minds of six jurors and events can now move forward.

DD. Literary Element: STEREOTYPE Point out that Juror Ten, who is described as a bigot in the notes on page 550, is making a generalization about the ethnic group to which the defendant belongs.

EE. Literary Element: STAGE DIRECTIONS Ask students to speculate on why the playwright has various jurors go to the window as Juror Ten continues his speech. *(Possible response: The jurors who get up show that they disagree with Juror Ten and don't want to hear his bigoted comments.)*

FF. Literary Element: STEREOTYPE Point out that the playwright does not have Juror Ten name the specific group to which he is ascribing general tendencies. Have students tell what point Rose may be trying to make. *(Possible response: He may be suggesting that any group can have generalizations made about it and that such generalizations are always unfair.)*

GG. Literary Element: CHARACTER Ask students why Juror Four's comment about splitting Ten's skull is shocking. *(Prior to now, Juror Four has always been formal, cool-tempered, and rational.)*

Teaching Tip

Ask students to take notes on the jurors' discussion of the eyewitness's testimony. Have them include these details on their chart.

HH. Literary Element: STAGE DIRECTIONS Point out how the playwright uses stage directions here and below to bring up the subject of eyeglasses and vision. Explain that these details lead naturally to a discussion of the witness's eyesight.

are. You know what I mean? Violent! *(*Nine *gets up and goes to window and looks out. He is followed by* Eleven.*)* Human life don't mean as much to them as it does to us. Hey, where are you all going? Look, these people're drinking and fighting all the time, and if somebody gets killed, so somebody gets killed. They don't care. Oh, sure, there are some good things about them, too. Look, I'm the first to say that. *(*Eight *gets up and then* Two *and* Six *follow him to window.)* I've known a few who were pretty decent, but that's the exception. Most of them, it's like they have no feelings. They can do anything. What's going on here? *(*Foreman *gets up and goes to window, followed by* Seven *and* Twelve.*)* I'm speaking my piece, and you—listen to me! They're no good. There's not a one of 'em who's any good. We better watch out. Take it from me. This kid on trial . . . *(*Three *sits at table toying with knife as* Four *gets up and starts toward* Ten. *All the other* Jurors *have their backs turned on* Ten.*)* Well, don't you know about them? Listen to me! What are you doing? I'm trying to tell you something. . . . *(*Four *stands over him as he trails off. There is a dead silence. Then* Four *speaks softly.)*

SR-5

Four. I've had enough. If you open your mouth again, I'm going to split your skull. *(Stands there and looks at him. No one moves or speaks.* Ten *looks at* Four *and then looks down at table.)*

Ten *(softly)***.** I'm only trying to tell you. . . . *(There is a long pause as* Four *stares down at* Ten.*)*

Four *(to* Jurors *at window)***.** All right. Sit down, everybody. *(All move back to their seats. When they are all seated,* Four *takes a stand behind men on upstage side of table. He speaks quietly.)* I still believe the boy is guilty of murder. I'll tell you why. To me, the most damning evidence was given by the woman across the street who claimed she actually saw the murder committed.

Three. That's right. As far as I'm concerned, that's the most important testimony.

Eight. All right. Let's go over her testimony. What exactly did she say?

Four *(moving toward window)***.** I believe I can recount it accurately. She said that she went to bed at about eleven o'clock that night. Her bed was next to the open window, and she could look out of the window while lying down and see directly into the window across the street. She tossed and turned for over an hour, unable to fall asleep. Finally she turned toward the window at about twelve-ten, and, as she looked out, she saw the boy stab his father. As far as I can see, this is unshakable testimony.

Three. That's what I mean. That's the whole case. *(*Four *takes off his eyeglasses and begins to polish them as they all sit silently watching him.)*

Four *(to all of them)***.** Frankly, in view of this, I don't see how you can vote for acquittal. *(to* Twelve *as he sits again)* What do you think about it?

Twelve. Well—maybe. . . . There's so much evidence to sift. . . .

Three. What do you mean, maybe? He's absolutely right. You can throw out all the other evidence.

Four. That was my feeling. I don't deny the validity of the points that he has made. *(motions at* Eight*)* Shall we say that on one side of the tracks there is doubt? But what can you say about the story of the woman? She saw it. *(*Two, *while he is polishing his glasses, too, squints at clock.)*

Two. What time is it?

Eleven. Ten minutes of six.

Six. You don't suppose they'd let us go home and finish it in the morning. I've got a kid with mumps. . . .

Five. Not a chance.

Eight *(to* Two*).* Can't you see the clock without your glasses?

Two. Not clearly.

Eight. Oh.

Four. Glasses are a nuisance, aren't they?

Eight *(an edge of excitement in his tone).* Well, what do you all do when you wake up at night and want to know what time it is?

Two. I put my glasses on and look at the clock.

Four. I just lie in bed and wait for the clock to chime. My father gave it to me when we married, my wife and I. It was ten years before we had a place to put it.

Eight *(to* Two*).* Do you wear your glasses to bed?

Two. Of course not. No one wears eyeglasses to bed.

Eight. The woman who testified that she saw the killing wears glasses. What about her?

Four. Did she wear glasses?

II **Eleven** *(excitedly).* Of course! The woman wore bifocals. I remember this very clearly. They looked quite strong.

Nine. That's right. Bifocals. She never took them off.

Four. Funny. I never thought of that.

Eight. I think it's logical to say that she was not wearing her glasses in bed, and I don't think she'd put them on to glance casually out the window. . . . She testified that the murder took place the instant she looked out and that the lights went out a split second later. She couldn't have had time to put on her glasses then. Now perhaps this woman honestly thought she saw the boy kill his father. *(rises)* I say that she only saw a blur. ◀ SR-6

Three. How do you know what she saw? Maybe she's farsighted.[13] . . . *(Looks around. No one answers. Loudly.)* How does he know all these things? *(There is silence.)*

Eight. Does anyone think there still is not a reasonable doubt? *(Looks around room, then squarely at* Ten. Ten *looks down at table for a moment; then he looks up at* Eight.*)*

Ten. I will always wonder. But there is a reasonable doubt.

Three *(loudly).* I think he's guilty!

Eight *(calmly).* Does anyone else?

Four *(quietly).* No. I'm convinced now. There is a reasonable doubt.

Eight *(to* Three*).* You're alone. JJ

Foreman. Eleven votes, not guilty; one, guilty.

Three. I don't care whether I'm alone or not! I have a right. . . .

Eight. Yes, you have a right. *(All stare at* Three.*)*

Three. Well, I told you. I think the kid's guilty. What else do you want? KK

Eight. Your arguments. *(All look at* Three *after glancing at* Eight.*)*

Three. I gave you my arguments.

Eight. We're not convinced. We're waiting to hear them again. We have time. *(Sits down again.* Three *runs to* Four *and grabs his arm.)*

Three *(pleading).* Listen. What's the matter with you? You're the guy. You made all the arguments. You can't turn now. A guilty man's going to be walking the

13. **farsighted:** able to see faraway objects more clearly than objects close at hand.

II. LEP: Vocabulary Explain that bifocals are eyeglasses with two lenses for each eye. The upper lens is for distant vision; the lower lens is for near vision.

JJ. Literary Element: IRONY Point out the irony of situation: The vote at the end of the play is the exact opposite of what it was at the beginning.

KK. Literary Element: CLIMAX Explain that the play has now reached its point of highest interest. Have a volunteer state the question whose solution will determine the outcome. *(Will Juror Three vote "not guilty" or will he hold to his "guilty" vote and hang the jury?)*

Real Life Connections

Have students discuss any benefits or drawbacks of the following recent innovations in the jury system around the country.

- As a result of a 1970 Supreme Court ruling, more than two-thirds of the states now permit six-member juries in many cases.
- Some states no longer require juries to reach unanimous decisions. In Oregon, ten out of twelve is sometimes enough for a verdict, while nine out of twelve is sufficient in Louisiana.
- In some courts, juries do not attend the trial. Instead the judge provides a videotape of the trial. (Material that jurors should disregard is deleted.) Juries view the tape and then proceed with their deliberations.

LL. LEP: Comprehension Ask a volunteer to clarify what Juror Eight means by this remark. *(Possible response: Eight suggests that Three will be unable to sleep due to a guilty conscience if he hangs the jury.)*

MM. Literary Element: THEME Point out that at long last the jury has passed judgment on the defendant with a unanimous verdict of "not guilty."

Check Test

1. Why do some of the jurors reenact the murder? *(They want to make the old man's testimony more believable by proving the murder took thirty to forty seconds—the amount of time it took the old man to reach the door and see the defendant.)*

2. Why does Juror Eight think that the boy did not inflict the knife wound? *(The murderer held the knife overhanded and slashed downward; the boy, an experienced knife fighter, would have held the switchblade underhanded and stabbed upward.)*

3. Why do most of the jurors suspect the woman across the street could not be sure she saw the defendant kill his father? *(The woman was in bed and not wearing her glasses, so she could not have seen anything but a blur.)*

4. How does the jury vote in the end? *(the jury reaches a unanimous vote of "not guilty.")*

Encouraging Independent Reading

Fair Trial: Fourteen Who Stood Accused from Anne Hutchinson to Alger Hiss, nonfiction by Richard Morris

"The Lady, or the Tiger?" a short story by Frank R. Stockton

QB-VII, a novel by Leon Uris

The Caine Mutiny Court-Martial, a play by Herman Wouk

Beyond a Reasonable Doubt: Inside the American Jury System, nonfiction by Melvyn Bernard Zerman

streets. A murderer! He's got to die! Stay with me! . . .

Four *(rising)*. I'm sorry. I'm convinced. I don't think I'm wrong often, but I guess I was this once. *(crosses right)* There is a reasonable doubt in my mind.

Eight. We're waiting. . . . *(*Three *turns violently on him.)*

Three *(shouting)*. You're not going to intimidate me! *(They are all staring at* Three.*)* I'm entitled to my opinion! *(No one answers him.)* It's gonna be a hung jury! *(turns abruptly and sits in his chair again)* That's it!

LL **Eight.** There's nothing we can do about that except hope that some night, maybe in a few months, why, you might get some sleep.

Five. You're all alone.

Nine. It takes a great deal of courage to stand alone.

Four *(moving back to table, sitting)*. If it is a hung jury, there will be another trial and some of us will point these things out to the various lawyers. *(*Three *looks around table at all of them. As* Three's *glance goes from juror to juror, each one of them shakes his head in his direction. Then, suddenly,* Three's *face contorts and he begins to pound on table with his fist. He seems about to cry.)*

Three *(thundering)*. All right! *(Jumps up quickly and moves downstage right, his back to all of them as* Foreman *goes to door left and knocks. The other* Jurors *now rise.)* MM

(The Guard *opens the door left and looks in and sees them all standing. The* Guard *holds the door open for them as they all file past and out left; that is, all except* Three *and* Eight. *The* Guard *waits for them.* Eight *moves toward the door left, pausing at left center.)*

Eight *(to* Three*)*. They're waiting. *(*Three *sees that he is alone. He moves to table and pulls switch knife out of table and walks over to* Eight *with it.* Three *is holding knife in approved knife-fighter fashion.* Three *looks long and hard at juror* Eight *and weaves a bit from side to side as he holds knife with point of it in direction of* Eight's *belly.* Eight *speaks quietly, firmly.)* Not guilty. *(*Three *turns knife around and* Eight *takes it by handle.* Eight *closes knife and puts it away.)*

Three. Not guilty! *(*Three *walks out of room.* Eight *glances around quickly, sighs, then turns and moves out through door.* Guard *goes out, closing door.)* ◀ SR-7

Curtain

Words to Know and Use

intimidate (in tim′ ə dāt′) *v.* to make afraid; overpower

e x p l a i n

Responding to Reading

First Impressions

1. How do you feel about the outcome of the play?

Second Thoughts

2. Why is Juror Eight so determined not to have a hung jury, in which case the young man would have to be retried?

   Think about
   - the evidence you have recorded on your chart
   - what Juror Eight means by "reasonable doubt"
   - his comments about poverty, prejudice, and society

3. Which of the jurors is the most objective? Give examples of that juror's comments and actions that demonstrate objectivity.

4. Near the end of the act, jurors Three, Four, and Ten are the only jurors voting guilty. Compare and contrast their personalities and motives.

5. In your opinion, why does Juror Three finally change his verdict?

Broader Connections

6. Based on this play and on any experiences you may have had with the legal system, do you think the trial-by-jury system guarantees a fair trial? Why or why not?

Literary Concepts: Stereotype and Climax

A **stereotype** is a broad and unfair generalization about a particular ethnic, racial, political, social, or religious group. In the play, Juror Ten engages in stereotyping when he says, "Look, these people're drinking and fighting all the time, and if somebody gets killed, so somebody gets killed. They don't care." Look back at the playwright's descriptions of the jurors on pages 550 and 551. Which of these descriptions might be considered stereotypes? Why?

The **climax** is the turning point or high point of interest in a story or drama, the moment of greatest emotional intensity. Soon after the climax occurs, the outcome of the story becomes clear. What is the climax in *Twelve Angry Men?*

Concept Review: Suspense In *Twelve Angry Men,* the feeling of tension, or suspense, begins when Juror Eight does not go along with the majority vote to find the accused guilty. What keeps the suspense growing throughout this play?

Student Response

Responding to Reading

These questions are open-ended with no "right" or "wrong" answers. However, responses must be supported with information from the selection. Possible answers follow:

1. Any response based on the play is valid. Ask students to point to specific elements of the play that have affected them.

2. Some students may say that Juror Eight feels it is quite obvious from the evidence that reasonable doubt exists and that it would be a waste of time and money to hold a second trial. Some students might suggest that Eight is afraid that another jury, without someone to champion the cause of a poor kid from the slums, might not give the boy as fair a hearing as the present one.

3. Many students will say that Juror Eight is the most objective because he considers all the facts carefully, brings up interesting points, and is open-minded to the arguments of his opponents. Other students might suggest that Juror Four is the most objective because he approaches the task analytically and refuses to let passions and personal feelings enter into the deliberations. He also changes his mind when the facts warrant it.

4. Students should point out that Juror Ten is a bigot who bases his guilty vote on stereotyped views of the defendant's ethnic group. Juror Four is calm and objective; his motive is to see justice done, and he honestly believes that the boy is guilty for most of the deliberations. Some students may say that Juror Three is hardest to understand. He is highly opinionated, violent, and sadistic. Students might suggest that his terrible relationship with his own son is a motive for his determination to find the boy guilty; that is, perhaps he wishes somehow to punish his son by convicting the defendant.

Possible answers continued on page T–590.

Literary Concepts—Stereotypes and Climax

Possible responses: The playwright uses Juror Seven to stereotype salesmen as being loud, flashy, and opinionated. Juror Four is a stereotype of wealthy people feeling "above the rest" of the people. Juror Twelve—slick, snobbish, and superficial—is a stereotype of the advertising man.

The climax of the play comes on page 587, when all the jurors except Juror Three have voted "not guilty," and it is unclear whether Three will change his vote.

Concept Review: Suspense

Possible response: The subsequent votes in which jurors change their minds is one major source of suspense in the play. The ultimate question—whether the boy will be found guilty or not guilty, or whether the jury will be hung—also provides suspense.

5. Students might suggest that Juror Three does not have the courage or strength of character to stand alone and maintain the boy's guilt. Others may say that the weight of evidence may have finally convinced Juror Three that there is reasonable about the boy's role in the murder.

6. Since the defendant came so close to being judged guilty when there was clearly a reasonable doubt, students might suggest that the jury system does not guarantee a fair trial. Other students might point out that by providing jurors who share common experiences and values with the defendant, the system builds in a certain amount of fairness. Students might also point out that in pretrial screening, lawyers try to eliminate jurors who might be prejudiced or hostile to a defendant.

Writing Options

The Writing Options are designed to meet varied student interests and abilities. Have each student choose one writing activity to complete. You may wish to guide some students to an option that requires less writing.

Journal Update Have students review their journal entries for *Twelve Angry Men.* Ask them to add any new reflections on our jury system to their writing.

Vocabulary Practice

1. c
2. b
3. c
4. c
5. c
6. b
7. b
8. c
9. c
10. b

Writing Options

1. Imagine a press conference with several of the jurors, including Juror Three. Each explains his not guilty decision in a brief comment. Write a news article for the local paper that summarizes these jurors' opinions. Be sure to identify the jurors you choose.

2. Make a list of questions that a defense attorney might have asked prospective jurors in order to identify and excuse the jurors least likely to be fair.

3. You are told that Juror Twelve is an advertising man. What might be the professions of the other jurors? Make a list.

4. Think back to some of the characters in earlier selections in this book who have made an impression on you. Which characters would have sided with Juror Three and which would have sided with Juror Eight?

5. At the beginning of Act Three, Juror Eleven says, "We have nothing to gain or lose by our verdict. This is one of the reasons we are strong." Explain what you think he means and whether or not you agree.

6. Why is this play called *Twelve Angry Men?* Why did the playwright use the word *angry?*

Vocabulary Practice

Exercise Write the letter of the unrelated word in each group below.

1. (a) defendant (b) accused (c) inspector
2. (a) motive (b) question (c) reason
3. (a) tenement (b) apartment (c) trial
4. (a) conceivable (b) believable (c) reliable
5. (a) intimidate (b) frighten (c) inspire
6. (a) writhing (b) talking (c) twisting
7. (a) prosecution (b) client (c) defense
8. (a) discrepancy (b) difference (c) likeness
9. (a) abstain (b) decline (c) indulge
10. (a) alibi (b) farewell (c) excuse

Words to Know and Use

abstain
alibi
conceivable
defendant
discrepancy
intimidate
motive
prosecution
tenement
writhing

Options for Learning

1 • Draw Twelve Draw caricatures of the twelve jurors using the medium of your choice. Review the descriptions of the characters on pages 550 and 551 and skim through the play to find mannerisms and other hints that will help you visualize each character.

2 • Tried in Class In groups of thirteen, plan and rehearse an act from *Twelve Angry Men.* Note any stage directions that describe the set and the characters' movements and voice inflections. Then stage your production for your classmates.

3 • Cast the Show Which present-day actors would you cast for the parts in *Twelve Angry Men?* In small groups, decide who will play which parts. Use the descriptions of the characters on pages 550 and 551 to help you make your choices.

4 • Map the Scene Draw or construct a 3-D model of the murder scene. Include the tenements on both sides of the el tracks, as well as a detailed drawing or construction of the room where the murder took place.

5 • Go a Courtin' Visit a nearby courtroom to observe a trial in progress. Before you go, make a list of things you expect to see. During your visit, take notes on the proceedings. Share your observations with your classmates.

FACT FINDER

What is double indemnity?

Reginald Rose
1920–

Reginald Rose's early careers included clerk, publicity writer, and advertising copywriter. In the 1950's, however, he began writing in a format that eventually won him fame. Rose began writing plays for stage and screen. His first big hit, in 1954, was *Twelve Angry Men,* for which he won a television Emmy award. In 1962 and 1963, Rose won Emmy awards for a courtroom drama series he created called *The Defenders.* While working on *The Defenders* series, he read hundreds of scripts by unknown writers. Rose tried to give these writers a break in a field in which it is difficult to make a living. He found, however, that television offered few opportunities for young writers. "There's just too much at stake for a network or sponsor to take a chance on an unknown."

Rose continues to write with great regularity. He often writes six days a week, producing four or five pages a day. Some of his more recent film scripts include *The Sea Wolves, Whose Life Is It Anyway?* and *Escape from Sobibor,* a play about concentration camps that appeared on network television in 1987.

Options for Learning

These activities suit a variety of learning styles and modes of expression. Allow students to review the options and then choose the one they wish to do. Many are excellent collaborative learning projects.

1. Draw Twelve Show examples of caricatures in cartoons. Remind students that they will want to exaggerate particular qualities of each juror.

2. Tried in Class Suggest that students make a list of props that they will require for each act. Instruct them to follow stage directions closely while rehearsing.

3. Cast the Show You may want to show portions of the movie version of the play so that students can see how actors of the 1950's interpreted their roles.

4. Map the Scene Refer students to that part of Act Two in which the dimensions and layout of the murdered man's apartment are given.

5. Go a Courtin' Arrange a field trip for interested students. Have them report on their experiences. If this is not possible, arrange for a judge or trial lawyer to speak to the class about our trial-by-jury system.

Fact Finder

A dictionary will reveal that double indemnity is a clause in an insurance policy stating that the beneficiary of the policy will be paid twice the normal amount in the event of certain specified losses.

Additional Information About the Author

Reginald Rose Reginald Rose grew up the son of a lawyer, so it isn't surprising that much of his early work had urban and legal themes. In recent years, Rose has scripted many films. The father of six sons, Rose lives in London, England.

Closure

Twelve Angry Men explores the process by which a jury of ordinary men passes judgment on a young defendant accused of murder. Ask students to discuss situations in which they have "passed judgment" too hastily on a person or situation.

Cross-Curricular Options

Suggest that interested students complete the following activities:

Social Studies: Compile a list of the five most widely publicized trials in your community or region over the last decade. Find out which evidence or testimony was most influential in convicting or freeing the defendant(s).

Language: Compile a list of legal terms that are frequently used in courtrooms. Devote one section of the list to words borrowed directly from Latin.

Language Arts: Interview someone who has served on a jury that tried a serious crime. Ask questions about the deliberation process and tape-record the person's recollections.

Mathematics: Locate and present statistics that indicate the costs of administering justice in the community and state.

Dramatics: Organize a production of *Twelve Angry Men* for the school or community. Design and build an appropriate set.

Writer's Workshop

Objectives

- To understand the goals of expository writing
- To evaluate literary characters
- To use comparison and contrast in presenting characters
- To draft, revise, edit, and share an expository essay
- To reflect on the writing process

Integrating . . .

Literature and Writing Tell students that characters from varied backgrounds can share the same beliefs. Stress that, conversely, characters from the same background also can violently oppose one another. For example, in *Twelve Angry Men,* jurors number four and eight seem to be similar kinds of men, but they hold totally different opinions until the play's final scene.

Writing and Grammar The Language Workshop in this subunit focuses on making correct comparisons with adjectives and adverbs. Point out to students that strong expository writing makes judicious use of positive, comparative, and superlative adjectives and adverbs. Writing that relies solely on one degree to convey meaning is not effective.

Discuss with LEP students the ways they form comparisons in their own language. Ask them to write down positive, comparative, and superlative forms of an adjective or adverb in their own language. Then ask them to translate these into English. They will see that, with some exceptions, the formations are similar in English.

Literature and Life Skills The Thinking Skills workshop in this subunit deals with evaluating and making judgments. Point out to students the importance of establishing criteria for evaluating and measuring the item they are judging. Stress the need for relevance in formulating objective criteria. For example, *Twelve Angry Men* is solely concerned with establishing objective criteria for a young man's guilt or innocence.

EXPOSITION: COMPARING AND CONTRASTING

As you can see from the play *Twelve Angry Men,* people can hold very different opinions about the same subject. You experience this same phenomenon on a daily basis. Your opinions differ from those of your friends about all sorts of things, such as the difficulty of a math test or a referee's call in a basketball game. Yet, at the same time, one of the reasons you are probably friends is that you also hold similar beliefs about a number of other subjects.

Your opinions are largely based on your previous experiences and on what other people have told you. Reginald Rose included in his play characters with varied backgrounds who hold both similar and different beliefs about justice and human rights. Such characters provide ample material for dramatic conflict.

For this next writing assignment, you will have the opportunity to compare and contrast the backgrounds of two characters from *Twelve Angry Men.* Examining these characters will help you better understand how their backgrounds influence their beliefs.

GUIDED ASSIGNMENT: JUDGING THE JURY

The jurors in the play *Twelve Angry Men* have many similarities and differences. Write a comparison/contrast essay that explains how the backgrounds of two of the characters influence their beliefs.

Here is your PASSkey to this assignment.

PURPOSE: To explain
AUDIENCE: Other readers of *Twelve Angry Men*
SUBJECT: Two characters from the play
STRUCTURE: A comparison/contrast essay

Prewriting

STEP 1 **Examine the jurors** Remember that your purpose in this essay is to show how the backgrounds of two different jurors influence their beliefs. Look back at the characters in *Twelve Angry Men* to see what information the playwright gives you about each juror. Make a chart like the one below to keep track of information about each character.

Additional Resources

UNIT FOUR RESOURCE BOOK

Writer's Workshop Copy Master, p. 66
Peer and Self-Evaluation Guidelines, p. 67
Writing Assessment Guidelines, p. 68

ENRICHMENT MATERIALS

Thinking Skills Transparency and Worksheet
Fine Art Transparency and Writing Prompts
Revision, Proofreading, and Elaboration Worksheet
Writing Prompts for Assessment

Juror	Background	Attitudes/Actions
One		
Two		

◀ STUDENT MODEL

STEP 2 Select two jurors When you compare two things, you note likenesses. When you contrast two things, you identify differences. Review your chart and decide which two jurors will best suit a comparison/contrast essay.

STEP 3 Gather information Review the play again and list specific actions and dialogue that illustrate the backgrounds and attitudes of the two jurors you have chosen. Circle any traits that the characters share. These details will be compared in your essay. Put stars next to the qualities that they do not share. These will be contrasted.

STEP 4 Organize your evidence There are two ways to organize a comparison/contrast essay. One way, called a block pattern, is to describe one of the subjects in the first part of the essay. The second part of the essay discusses the second subject and points out similarities and differences between that subject and the first. A second method, known as an alternating pattern, describes the similarities and differences between the two subjects point by point. The writer groups differences and similarities under general areas, and alternates his or her discussion of the subjects according to each point. One student diagrammed his options for organization as follows.

Block Pattern	Alternating Pattern
-Description of the background, actions, and attitudes of Juror A -Description of the background, actions, and attitudes of Juror B as compared and contrasted with those of Juror A	-Description of the background of Juror A as compared and contrasted with the background of Juror B. -Description of the actions of Juror A as compared and contrasted with the actions of Juror B.

◀ STUDENT MODEL

Teaching Strategies

Introduction Have students turn to the Writer's Workshop on page 592. Ask students to share contrasting and comparative opinions on topics of relevance to the play (for example, popular TV shows that have strongly opposed protagonists and antagonists). Some students may admire a villain for a self-imposed code of honor; others may despise a law-enforcement official for the corruption that governs his or her life.

Direct students to the Guided Assignment box on page 592. Explain that they will have to make close, individual evaluations of several jurors in order to write a successful comparison/contrast essay about two of them. Point out that students will have to concentrate on the jurors' backgrounds in order to complete the assignment.

Prewriting Explain the importance of establishing criteria for evaluating characters' backgrounds when preparing student essays. Point out the PASSkey graphic, and note again that the subject of the essay will be two characters from the play.

Teaching Tip

Write the words *criterion* and *criteria* on the board. Point out that the first is the singular form and the second, is the plural. Tell students that both come from a Greek word meaning *to judge* or *to decide*.

Point out that it is important for students to take notes about the jurors as they read the play. Some jurors (for example, numbers four and eight) may seem quite similar but may actually take two different sides of the case. Jurors number four and eight would be interesting contrasts for the essay, as would jurors number three and eight, who are very different character types. Although their parts are smaller, jurors number seven and twelve lend themselves well to comparison essays because of their similar backgrounds and outlooks on life and their roles in the legal system.

Drafting Remind students that when creating the introduction for their essay, they should be as specific as possible about the similarities or differences between the two jurors they have chosen. Suggest that they cite at least one quality that unites or separates the two men.

Computer Tip
Students who have access to a computer might benefit from trying the following during their drafting process:

1. Code the notes you have taken on each juror.
2. Code the qualities you have listed for the two jurors you are comparing or contrasting.
3. Using only the computer codes, not the juror numbers, see if you have developed sufficient contrasting or comparative qualities to create a substantive essay.

Stress with students the importance of writing strong topic sentences for their essays. You may want to review the function of a topic sentence. Explain why a topic sentence is of particular importance when drafting a convincing essay that is thematically tied to comparison/contrast. Students may find it helpful to use actual speeches from the play to underline their concluding points about the two jurors they have chosen. The use of actual text helps clarify the importance of specificity in good writing, especially in exposition. Students should remember that their comparisons/contrasts rely on details derived from the play itself. Point out that they must be as patient and tenacious in sifting through characters' qualities as juror number eight is in sifting through evidence in the murder trial.

Revising and Editing Once students have completed the rough drafts of their essays, divide them into groups of two in order to review one another's work. Stress the importance of the *Revision Checklist* in this step of the writing process. Encourage students to consider the following:

1. Is the introduction specific and clear? Does it include a strong topic sentence?

Drafting

STEP 1 **Write an introduction** Begin with a statement that describes the purpose of your essay, that is, why you are comparing and contrasting the two jurors. One student wrote the following introduction.

STUDENT MODEL ▶

Of the twelve jurors in the play *Twelve Angry Men*, Jurors Seven and Eleven appear at first to hold similar viewpoints. As the play unfolds, however, it is evident that these two men are very distinct individuals. An examination of the similarities and differences in the backgrounds of these two characters shows why these two jurors hold the opinions that they do.

STEP 2 **Write the body and conclusion** Use the organizational plan you have chosen to write the body of your essay. Be sure to include a topic sentence in each paragraph to let your readers know which character trait you are discussing. Use the notes you took on each juror to show how the likenesses and differences in the characters' backgrounds influence their beliefs. You may want to include actual speeches made by these jurors to support your findings. Conclude your paper with a brief summary of your findings.

Revising and Editing

Once you have completed the rough draft of your essay, ask a classmate to review your work according to the following checklist. Then revise your paper based on his or her comments.

Revision Checklist

1. Does the introduction establish the purpose of the paper and state which characters are being compared and contrasted?
2. Is the organizational plan of the paper clear?
3. Does the writer include appropriate information from the play to support the comparisons and contrasts being made?
4. Has the writer left out any important areas of comparison and contrast that should be included?
5. Does the writer conclude with a brief summary of the main points of the essay?

2. Have students followed the Block Pattern or Alternating Pattern consistently? Or have they mixed up the two techniques in writing their essays?
3. Details such as clothes and speaking style are often as telling as actual dialogue in rendering characters in dramatic writing.
4. Have students referred to their original notes when writing their essays? Checking initial notes is a way of making certain that all relevant points of comparison and contrast have been covered.
5. When reviewing one another's essay summaries, students should keep in mind the image of a lawyer summing up his case for the jury. The summary is the final opportunity to present one's "case" to the reader/listener.

Remind students who have access to computers that the spell-check capability is a valuable tool for proofreading.

Editing When you have finished your revision, proofread your essay for spelling, grammar, and mechanics.

Presenting

In small groups, read your essays aloud. Note the major similarities and differences mentioned about the pairs of characters. Also note the method of organization each writer chose. Decide as a group which pair of characters makes the most interesting comparison/contrast essay and why.

Reflecting on Your Writing

Answer the following questions about this assignment. Place the answers and a copy of your essay in your writing portfolio.

1. Of those essays you heard in your group, which did you like the best? How does that essay differ from yours?
2. Why did you choose the method of organization that you did? Would a different organizational plan have improved or weakened your paper?
3. Compare the difficulty of writing this essay with writing the other writer's workshops you have completed. Explain the differences.

Presenting Ask a "jury" of students chosen from small groups to read aloud the essay from their group that best accomplishes the comparison/contrast essay.

Reflecting When reviewing students' writing portfolios, remember to respond to their answers for the *Reflecting* questions. The class may need additional help at this stage if a majority of students found difficulty in answering Question 2.

Closure

Before beginning the next subunit, be sure students have internalized the following concepts:

- Comparing and contrasting involves evaluation.
- To evaluate something, the writer must select criteria upon which to base the evaluation.
- After making an evaluation, the writer forms an opinion about the subject.
- The writer supports the opinion with specific examples from the text.

Additional Writing and Research Topics

The following items provide additional writing practice based on the literary selection and techniques presented in this subunit.

Exposition: Comparing and Contrasting

- Write an expository essay comparing and contrasting two characters from your favorite TV show. Remember to support your opinions with specific qualities evident in each character's speech, clothing, and manner.

Other Topics

Narration: Write a chapter for your own book entitled *Who I Am*. Using either the Alternating Pattern or Block Pattern, write down the qualities about yourself that would fall into similar categories (e.g., funny/outgoing or shy/quiet) as opposed to contrasting qualities (e.g., smart but I sometimes make mistakes).

Social Studies Research: *Twelve Angry Men* presents characters from various sociological backgrounds. Write a sociological portrait (family background, education, financial status, religious beliefs, etc.) of one of the characters.

Language Workshop

Objectives

- To understand the use of the three degrees of adjectives and adverbs
- To form the degrees of adjectives and adverbs correctly
- To use modifiers correctly in writing

Integrating . . .

Writing and Grammar Remind students that in the Writer's Workshop they wrote an essay comparing and contrasting the backgrounds of two of the characters in *Twelve Angry Men.* Explain that part of their success in writing comparison/contrast essays depends on their use of comparative adjectives and adverbs. Write these sentences on the chalkboard:

1. Juror Three is more opinionated than Juror Two.

2. Juror Eight is quieter than Juror Seven.

Point out that the words *more opinionated* and *quieter* are forms of the adjectives *opinionated* and *quiet* used to compare the two individuals in each sentence. Ask students to review the descriptions of the characters at the beginning of the play and to think of sentences comparing one of the jurors to the juror described in each of the following sentences:

1. Juror Five takes his responsibilities seriously.

2. Juror Eleven is polite.

Explain that this Language Workshop focuses on the forms of adjectives and adverbs that are used to make comparisons.

Teaching Tip

Point out to students that sometimes spelling changes must be made in adding *-er* or *-est* to an adjective or adverb. Have them look at the following examples: hot, hotter, hottest, lively, livelier, liveliest.

Review the list of irregular modifiers in the box on page 597. Call on volunteers to use some of these modifiers in sets of sentences that illustrate positive, comparative, and superlative degrees.

MAKING CORRECT COMPARISONS

> Adjectives and adverbs have three forms, or degrees: **positive, comparative,** and **superlative.** These forms allow us to make precise, accurate comparisons.

I like dramas *better* than musicals.

Today's rehearsal was the *shortest* of the week.

You use adjectives and adverbs to make comparisons every day. You say things like "This pillow is softer," or "That cheese is sharper." Most of the time when you make these comparisons, you choose the correct form of the modifier. Occasionally, however, you may run into difficulty.

There are three degrees of comparison. In the **positive degree,** an adjective or adverb describes people, places, things, ideas, or actions but does not make a comparison. In the **comparative degree,** an adjective or adverb compares two of anything. In the **superlative degree,** an adjective or adverb compares three or more of anything.

Positive This murder trial is *long.*

Comparative This murder trial is *longer* than the murder trial last week.

Superlative This murder trial is the *longest* one I've ever attended.

A phrase like "all other" or "any other" makes the noun that it refers to one unit or one group. Use the comparative form rather than the superlative form to compare this group to something else:

Incorrect This juror is *angriest* than any of the others.

Correct This juror is *angrier* than any of the others.

Most modifiers form their comparative and superlative degrees in regular ways.

1. A one-syllable modifier forms the comparative and superlative by adding *-er* and *-est.*

Positive	Comparative	Superlative
big	bigger	biggest
old	older	oldest

Additional Resources

UNIT FOUR RESOURCE BOOK

Language Workshop Copy Master, p. 69

ENRICHMENT MATERIALS

Grammar and Usage Copy Masters

2. Most two-syllable modifiers form the comparative and superlative by adding *-er* and *-est.* Sometimes a two-syllable modifier sounds awkward when *-er* or *-est* is added. In such cases use *more* or *most* to form the comparative or superlative. Two-syllable adverbs that end in *-ly* form comparisons by using *more* and *most.*

Positive	Comparative	Superlative
strong	stronger	strongest
clumsy	clumsier	clumsiest
helpful	more helpful	most helpful
boldly	more boldly	most boldly

3. Modifiers of three or more syllables use *more* or *most* to form the comparative and superlative.

Positive	Comparative	Superlative
dangerous	more dangerous	most dangerous
important	more important	most important
colorful	more colorful	most colorful
carefully	more carefully	most carefully

Some modifiers use completely different words for their comparative and superlative forms. Study the chart on the side of the page to learn about these irregular modifiers.

REMINDER

To make a negative comparison, use *less* and *least* before the positive form of the modifier: *hopeful, less hopeful, least hopeful; funny, less funny, least funny.*

IRREGULAR COMPARISONS

Pos.	Comp.	Super.
good	better	best
well	better	best
bad	worse	worst
much	more	most
many	more	most
little	less *or* lesser	least

Exercise 1 Find the errors in comparison in the following sentences and write each sentence correctly. If a sentence has no errors, write *Correct.*

1. The play *Twelve Angry Men* is the grippingest drama I have ever seen.
2. I saw it performed by the most talented amateur actors you could imagine.
3. The costumes were realisticer than the set, though.
4. The set was the most bleakest room to watch for two hours.
5. The most hard part of watching was waiting to see what the verdict would be.
6. Of all the characters, Juror Number Three was the less appealing.
7. He was by far the most loud and most angriest.
8. The actor who played Juror Number Eleven had the most convincing accent.
9. I think I held my breath through most of the more tenser confrontations.
10. Despite the tension, *Twelve Angry Men* is the hopefullest play I've seen in years.

Teaching Strategies

Ask a volunteer to read the focus statement in the box at the top of page 596. Remind students that adjectives describe nouns and pronouns and that adverbs describe verbs, adjectives, and other adverbs. Work through the lesson, asking students to provide other examples of adjectives and adverbs, especially words that students have encountered in their reading of *Twelve Angry Men.* As students suggest words and their comparative and superlative forms, record them on a chart similar to the one below.

Positive	Comparative	Superlative
loud	louder	loudest
strong	stronger	strongest

Teaching Tip: LEP

Spanish forms of comparison are different from English forms. For example, *more cold* is correct in Spanish. Check to see that Spanish-speaking students and other ESL students understand how comparisons are formed in English.

Teaching Tip

Explain to students that it is necessary to use *other* or *else* when comparing one thing (or person) within a group of which it is a part. Show them the following examples:

Correct: The Nile River is longer than any other river in the world.

Correct: The pitcher performed better than anyone else on the team.

Assign the exercises beginning on page 597. Divide the class into groups before having students begin Exercise 3.

Answer Key for Exercise 1

1. most gripping
2. Correct
3. more realistic
4. bleakest
5. hardest
6. least appealing
7. loudest and angriest
8. Correct
9. tenser
10. most hopeful

ADDITIONAL PRACTICE

The following items are additional exercises to help students with comparative and superlative forms of adjectives and adverbs.

Write these sentences, choosing the correct modifier from each pair in parentheses.

1. Please talk (more quiet, more quietly).
2. The rumbling sound arose (suddenly, more suddenly) from beneath the car.
3. The pineapple cake is (less sweet, least sweet) of all.

Rewrite these sentences, correcting the errors in degrees of comparison.

4. Of the two cities, New York is farthest from here. *(farther)*
5. Baseball goes more slowly than almost any sport. *(any other)*
6. This mask looks worst than yours. *(worse)*
7. Much least sugar would be better for you. *(Much less)*

Exercise 2

1. most difficult
2. smallest
3. more
4. hardest
5. more closely
6. less
7. more difficult
8. deepest
9. most interesting and most educational
10. fairest

Exercise 3

My experiences in the world of the theater are more diverse than you might imagine. I began acting in student dramas when I was less shy than I am now. As an elementary student I sang and danced better than any of the other "butterflies" and "snowflakes." In eighth grade I became more interested in writing plays. The drama class put on their most exciting production using my play, *First Date*. I found that I was happier than I had ever been hearing my own words from the actors' lips.

Closure

Before completing this final subunit in Unit 4, be sure that students understand the following concepts:

▪ Adjectives and adverbs have three degrees of comparison: positive, comparative, and superlative. The positive degree is used to describe without making a comparison. The comparative degree is used when comparing two things. The superlative degree is used when comparing three or more things.

▪ In a regular comparison, *-er* is added to a one-syllable modifier and to most two-syllable modifiers to form the comparative degree. The superlative degree is formed by adding *-est*. Some two-syllable modifiers, modifiers of three or more syllables, and two-syllable adverbs ending in *-ly* use *more* and *most* to form the comparative and superlative degrees.

▪ For some irregular modifiers, such as *good, bad,* and *many*, the word itself changes to form the comparative and superlative degrees.

Exercise 2 On your paper, write the form of the modifier given in parentheses.

1. A jury in a murder trial has the (difficult—superlative) job you can imagine.
2. They must be sure without even the (small—superlative) doubt that the defendant is guilty.
3. It often takes (many—comparative) days than one to come to a decision.
4. The members of the jury have to make one of the (hard—superlative) decisions of their lives.
5. The jurors have to listen to the evidence (closely—comparative) than they have ever listened to anything.
6. Twelve people who know one another (little—comparative) than they know their local mail carriers must agree on a verdict.
7. When the case occurs in a state that allows capital punishment, jurors have a (difficult—comparative) decision than they might otherwise have.
8. Someone who is a member of such a jury may feel some of the (deep—superlative) emotions he or she has ever felt.
9. Most jurors who have decided a murder case feel it was the (interesting—superlative) and (educational—superlative) experience of their lives.
10. That may be why many experts believe that the American justice system is one of the (fair—superlative) in the world.

Collaborative Learning

This exercise may be done in groups. One person should record the revised sentences. ▶

Exercise 3 The following paragraph contains errors in the use of comparisons. Work with other students to rewrite the paragraph, correcting all errors.

My experiences in the world of the theater are diverser than you might imagine. I began acting in student dramas when I was less shyer than I am now. As an elementary student I sang and danced more well than any of the other "butterflies" and "snowflakes." In eighth grade I became interesteder in writing plays. The drama class put on their excitingest production using my play, *First Date*. I found that I was most happiest listening to my own words than listening to the words that another playwright had produced.

Language Handbook

For review and practice, see Section 4, Using Modifiers.

EVALUATING AND MAKING JUDGMENTS

Whenever you see a performance like a play, a movie, or a concert, you can evaluate it and make a judgment about its quality. When you judge anything—a piece of writing, an idea, or a candidate for office—you are expressing the reasons why you like it or dislike it.

Use the following steps when you make an evaluation.

1. Establish standards, or **criteria,** for measuring the thing that you are evaluating. For example, criteria for judging a story might be the following: Are the characters believable? Is the plot intriguing?
2. Gather data to see whether the subject meets your criteria.
3. Organize the evidence you've gathered.
4. Draw a conclusion about the subject based on your evaluation.

The most important step in any evaluation is establishing logical criteria. No matter how carefully you have gathered your evidence, if you use the wrong criteria, your judgment may not be reasonable. If you judge a restaurant by the size of the parking lot, an actor by how many times he has married, or a book by the picture on its cover, your judgment will be of little value. Make sure the criteria you choose are relevant to the subject.

Here are examples of conclusions you might reach if you use relevant criteria to judge political candidates, a play, and a restaurant.

1. Yes, I will vote for her, because she has a record of acting to improve environmental legislation in Congress.
2. No, I don't recommend that play, because the actors were not able to portray their characters believably.
3. No, I don't recommend that restaurant, because it is overpriced in comparison to others with the same caliber of service and food.

Exercise Write criteria for evaluating, and then make a judgment about (1) the food and atmosphere in the high school cafeteria, (2) the foreign language program in your school, (3) the last concert you attended, and (4) the last story that you read.

Thinking Skills Workshop

Objectives

- To understand that judgments are expressions of the reasons for liking or not liking something
- To establish appropriate criteria in order to make judgments

Integrating . . .

Literature and Thinking Skills
Share with students that this workshop will help them learn how to make well-informed judgments about what they read.

Teaching Strategies

Ask students to identify the types of things in their lives they make judgments about. *(Possible responses: food, books, movies, music, other people)*

Read through the material with students. Discuss how criteria are developed and how criteria vary from person to person.

Assign the exercise on page 599. Have students share their answers with their classmates and discuss how different criteria lead to different judgments.

Closure

Before beginning the next subunit, be sure students have internalized these concepts:

- Judgments are expressions of the reasons for liking or not liking something.
- Establishing good criteria is essential for making reasonable judgments.
- Comparing evidence about the subject to the criteria allows an evaluator to draw conclusions.

Teaching Tip
You may wish to examine students' lists of criteria before they complete the exercise. Have students expand or revise their lists if necessary.

Exercise
(Possible criteria are given. Students' judgments will vary.)
1. fresh, healthful, tasty, comfortable **2.** good instruction, enough textbooks, interesting use of A-V materials **3.** loud, involves audience, energetic **4.** suspenseful, realistic, moving

Additional Resources
UNIT FOUR RESOURCE BOOK
Related Skills Copy, p. 70

ADDITIONAL PRACTICE

Write criteria for evaluating, and then make a judgment about each of the following. Give data related to the criteria.

1. a movie you saw recently
2. the President's last televised speech
3. a recent sporting event

(Responses will vary. Check that students established reasonable criteria.)

Unit Five *The Future: Hopes and Fears*

Objectives

Students will develop skills in the following areas. An asterisk (*) indicates a workshop topic.

Reading and Thinking

evaluating a character	*p. 603*
examining titles	*p. 614*
outlining	*p. 622*
authors' purpose	*p. 639*
clarifying	*pp. 644, 648, 649, 652, 653*
visualizing	*p. 661*
understanding cause and effect	*p. 679*
noting stereotypes	*p. 684*
predicting	*p. 690*

Vocabulary and Related Skills

using words in context	*p. 612*
*filling out applications	*p. 637*
*telephone techniques	*p. 672*
synonyms	*p. 716*
antonyms	*p. 716*
*analogies	*p. 725*

Literary Appreciation

science fiction	*p. 611*
characterization	*p. 611*
rhetorical question	*p. 618*
allusion	*p. 628*
letter	*pp. 643, 683*
satire	*p. 654*
exaggeration	*p. 654*
dramatic irony	*p. 654*
repetition	*p. 664*
suspense	*p. 678*
simile	*p. 683*
metaphor	*p. 683*
humorous essay	*p. 688*
writer's purpose	*p. 715*
characterization	*p. 715*

Writing

summary	*pp. 612, 643, 655, 716*
weather report	*p. 612*
slogan	*p. 618*
poem	*pp. 618, 664*
newspaper article	*p. 622*
fantasy story	*p. 622*
essay	*p. 622*
conversation	*p. 628*
*exposition: letter with proposed solution	*pp. 631–33*
letter	*pp. 643, 660, 683*
advertisement	*p. 655*
postcard	*p. 664*
description	*p. 664*
*exposition magazine article	*pp. 666–69*
editorial	*p. 688*
moral	*pp. 678, 683*
travel article	*p. 716*
*exposition: prediction essay	*pp. 718–21*

Language, Grammar, Usage, Mechanics

*problems with modifiers	*pp. 634–36*
*vary sentence beginnings	*pp. 670–71*
*using verb tenses correctly	*pp. 722–24*

Planning the Unit

You may find the following information and lists of resources helpful in preparing for the unit.

Difficulty Level of Selections

In determining the accessibility of the selections in this unit, many factors, including reading level and comprehension difficulty, have been taken into account. The ranking can be used as a general guide in determining how much preparation and assistance students will require in order to master the selection. No selection should be included or eliminated from the course based merely on difficulty level. Basic students will derive a great deal of confidence and self-esteem by working through a *challenge* selection; conversely, advanced students may find pleasure, relevance, and important themes in a selection that is rated *easy*.

Selection	Level
Searching for Summer *p. 603*	**average**
Improved Farm Land *p. 614*	**average**
Hard Questions *p. 617*	**average**
A Couple of Really Neat Guys *p. 619*	**average**
David Meets Goliath at City Hall *p. 623*	**average**
The Weapon *p. 639*	**average**
The Feeling of Power *p. 644*	**challenge**
The Suspected Shopper *p. 657*	**average**
Building Boom *p. 661*	**average**
All Watched Over by Machines of Loving Grace *p. 663*	**challenge**
Four O'Clock *p. 674*	**easy**
A Letter to God *p. 679*	**average**
Diablo Country *p. 684*	**average**
Visit to a Small Planet *p. 690*	**average**

Classroom Resources

Videocassettes, Films, and Filmstrips

- ***Isaac Asimov***, video, PBS, 1988, (60 minutes). Bill Moyers interviews this prolific and important author.
- ***Atomic Artist***, 16mm film, video, Icarus, 1983, (29 minutes). Portrait of Tony Price, painter and sculptor who has been turning nuclear scraps into works of art.
- ***Carl Sandburg: Poet of the People***, 16mm film, video, Aims, 1983, (23 minutes). With Hugh Downs viewers relive the life of this earthy poet.

Audiocassettes, Tapes, and Records

Buchwald Stops Here, 7 audiocassettes, Audio Book Company. Presents the American humorist and satirist, Art Buchwald.

Carl Sandburg Reading Cool Tombs and Other Poems, audiocassette, Caedmon. The poet reading from his works, including "The Windy City" and "Prairie Waters by Night."

The Feeling of Power, audiocassette, Audio Book Company. A reading of Isaac Asimov's work of the same title.

A Necklace of Raindrops and Other Stories, record, audiocassette, Caedmon. Joan Aiken reads six of her stories.

Visits to a Small Planet, Where the Artist is the Enemy, 3¾ IPS 1 Track audiotape, National Center for Audio Tapes, 1961, (30 minutes). Gore Vidal's drama, from the series, Ideas and the Theater.

Community Resources

Involving the resources of your community in lesson preparation can add insight and relevance to the text. Consider the following possibilities as you plan.

- For "Improved Farm Land" and "Hard Questions," invite a real estate developer and an environmentalist to debate suburban growth.
- For "A Couple of Really Neat Guys," have students tour their city to score its "environmental IQ."
- For "David Meets Goliath at City Hall," have an environmental activist talk about activism.
- For "The Weapon," invite an environmental engineer to discuss the dilemma of nuclear waste.
- For "The Feeling of Power," have a computer expert discuss whether human beings control computers or vise versa.
- For "The Suspected Shopper," invite a shopping mall manager to discuss store security systems.
- For "Building Boom" and "All Watched Over by Machines of Loving Grace," contact a historical society for "Then and Now" photographs of your town or city.
- For "A Letter to God," invite a religious leader to discuss the different kinds of faith people exhibit.
- For "Diablo Country," invite a spokesperson from an environmental advocacy organization to discuss grass-roots activism.
- For "Visit to a Small Planet," organize a panel of persons who claim to have seen UFOs to share their experiences and speculations.

Unit Preview

What kind of world are we leaving to future generations? The selections in Unit 5, **The Future: Hopes and Fears** focus attention on our dreams and concerns for the future. The unit contains three subunits:

- Subunit 1: Saving the Environment
- Subunit 2: The Price of Technology
- Subunit 3: In Whose Hands?

Art Note

American artist and environmentalist Wyland lives on the Hawaiian island of Oahu and, in winter, dives with the whales off Maui. His underwater research is reflected in his paintings. He has made life-size whale paintings for walls in the United States, Canada, Europe, and Japan, and plans 100 murals as part of his project, *The Art of Saving Whales. How many forms of life do you find in this underwater scene?*

Unit Five

THE FUTURE: HOPES AND FEARS

"You can't take sides when you know the earth is round."

Patricia Sun

DOLPHIN PARADISE (detail)
Wyland Wyland Galleries,
Oahu, Hawaii.

601

Discussion Questions

To help students probe connections among the fine art, quotation, and unit theme, have them consider the following questions:

1. Rephrase the quotation in your own words and explain what it means. *(Possible response: "It's impossible to be on one side or the other regarding helping the environment because we are all sharing the same planet.")*

2. What are some of your hopes and fears for the future? *(Possible response: Students may hope for such things as personal achievement, greater understanding between people, and the eradication of disease. They may fear such things as personal failure, the breakdown of relationships, widespread destruction of the environment and war.)*

3. Describe what you see in the picture. What part of it do you find especially effective and why? *(Possible response: Students may describe how the sky, land, and sea blend into one another. They may find the picture of marine life particularly effective. Encourage them to support their choice with specific reasons.)*

4. What relationship do you see among the quotation, the unit title, and the artwork? *(Possible response: Students may suggest that all three concern some aspect of saving the environment. The quotation probes taking sides about such issues; the unit title concerns our hopes and fears for the future; and the picture illustrates one aspect of the environment that is both beautiful and endangered. Students may also note that the picture is round and the quotation discusses the earth's roundness.)*

Subunit Preview

Have students read the introduction to subunit 1, **Saving the Environment.** Ask them to consider how protests against the destruction of nature relate to the unit theme, **The Future: Hopes and Fears.** Can one person affect the quality of the earth's environment? How so? Who is responsible for protecting nature? What do people living now owe to future generations? Have students scan the subunit Table of Contents and predict which selection will be the most interesting.

For Additional Challenge

The following selections offer extra challenge in the exploration of the subunit theme:

The Green Lifestyle Handbook: 1001 Ways You Can Save the Earth, nonfiction by Jeremy Rifkin

"Ninety-sixth Psalm"

Additional Resources

Subunit Test, pp. 26–27

SAVING THE ENVIRONMENT

Throughout most of history, people have considered the world a place of unlimited abundance. How could we ever run out of land when there is so much of it? How could we ever pollute the air when the earth's atmosphere stretches miles above the globe? Water covers three-fourths of the earth's surface. How could we ever contaminate such vast quantities?

As you will see in the following selections, the hopes and fears for the future depend on our ability to avoid destroying the earth through nuclear war, uncontrolled development, or pollution. As you read these selections, discover what the writers are trying to say about saving our environment.

OBSERVATION ASSESSMENT

Observing how students respond to the text, to the classroom instruction, and to peers is an important part of an assessment program. The following suggestions and the form in each Unit Resource Book can be used to implement observation assessment.

- As students work through this subunit, observe how they use postreading strategies. Do they make attempts to summarize the most important ideas of a selection? Do they make judgments about the selection and know how to support their opinions? Do they relate the selection to their own experience?
- As students work through this subunit, can you see growth in their evaluating of information?
- To evaluate how well they activate prior knowledge, ask what connections they can draw between a selection and what they have learned from newspapers, magazines, TV, or other classes.

explore

Fiction

Searching for Summer

JOAN AIKEN (ā′ kin)

Examine What You Know (Prior Knowledge)

This selection is a work of science fiction. What do the words *science fiction* mean to you? In your journal or on a piece of paper, write what you know about science fiction by describing the setting, characters, and plot of a science fiction story.

Expand Your Knowledge (Building Background)

The story you are about to read takes place after a war sometime in the future. In many ways the physical features of the setting described resemble the features of what some scientists call a nuclear winter. The theory behind nuclear winter is that the firestorms unleashed by a nuclear war would fill the skies with clouds of waste and smoke for an extended period of time. Scientists estimate that the decrease in sunlight caused by such clouds might lower the average global temperature at least ten degrees. Such a temperature change, along with reduced sunlight, would have profound effects on all plant and animal life on earth.

Enrich Your Reading (Reading Skill)

Evaluating a Character One way to evaluate a character in a story is to judge his or her personality in terms of good and bad qualities. As you read "Searching for Summer," use a chart like the one below to note both stated and inferred facts about Mr. Noakes, a minor, but important, character in the story. Then write a brief evaluation of this character.

Character	Stated Facts	Inferred Facts
Mr. Noakes		
Evaluation: ______		

■ *A biography of the author can be found on page 613.*

Objectives

- To explore a short story
- To appreciate a work of science fiction
- To review characterization
- To evaluate a character
- To express understanding of the work through a choice of writing forms, including summary, description, reporting, and opinion

Prereading/Motivation

Examine What You Know

Discussion Prompts: What science-fiction movies have you seen? Which of these have been adapted from short stories or novels? Why do you think many people enjoy science fiction so much?

Expand Your Knowledge

Discussion Prompts: How would the plants and animals on earth be affected by a nuclear winter? What do you think would be the most severe effect? Are people justified to fear the stockpiling of nuclear weapons?

Additional Background: The first atomic bomb was tested on July 16, 1945, at Alamogordo, New Mexico. A baseball-sized bomb produced an explosion equal to that caused by 20,000 tons of TNT. Subsequent bombs range in power from a fraction of a kiloton (1000 tons of TNT) to many megatons (1 million tons of TNT).

Enrich Your Reading

Have students copy the chart and fill it in as they read. These are possible answers:

Stated Facts: Mr. Noakes is a repulsive-looking pub owner who would exploit any sunny land; **Inferred Facts:** He is a cruel, vicious man. **Evaluation:** Mr. Noakes is a repulsive-looking pub owner who would do anything to further his own fortunes.

Thematic Link—Saving the Environment

In this science-fiction story, Tom and Lily save a small piece of the environment by not telling others about the beauty they've found.

Journal Writing

"Searching for Summer" describes some of the changes that might occur after vast nuclear explosions. Suggest these journal topics to students:

- With what moods do you associate sunshine?
- How do you imagine you would feel if you could never see the sun or experience summer again?

For other journal opportunities, refer students to Examine What You Know (p. 603), First Impressions (p. 611), Broader Connections (p. 611), Real-Life Connections (p. T–608), and Closure (p. T–613).

Additional Resources

UNIT FIVE RESOURCE BOOK

Reader's Guidesheet, p. 1
Vocabulary Worksheet, p. 2
Selection and Vocabulary Check Tests, p. 3
Selection Test, pp. 4–5

Collaborative Learning

Opportunities for collaborative learning appear throughout the lesson and include Options for Learning activities 1 and 3 (p. 613) and Cross-Curricular Options and Closure (p. T–613).

Teaching Strategies

Vocabulary Preview

These vocabulary words are defined at the bottom of the selection page on which they appear. You may wish to discuss them briefly before students begin reading.

commiserate express pity
dour gloomy; forbidding
grimacing distorting one's face in pain, disgust, or anger
indomitable strong; undefeatable
omen a thing or event that foretells the future
proprietor owner of a business
rudimentary underdeveloped
scoundrel a mean or wicked person
tawny tan-colored
wizened shriveled; dried up

Support for Students of Limited English Proficiency

- Use Reader's Guidesheet, p. 1.
- "Searching for Summer" contains British terms and dialect that may be difficult for students.
- You may wish to read sections of dialogue written in dialect aloud to your students to aid their comprehension of the material. Annotations B, H, J, R, W, and X focus on and explain specific words and phrases written in dialect.

Text Annotations

A. Literary Element: SCIENCE FICTION Ask students to explain the real or imagined scientific developments that form the basis of the setting. *(The imagined development is that nuclear bombs were exploded in the past, leaving the sky gray and overcast. The scientific theory that a "nuclear winter" would result from the explosion of nuclear weapons forms the basis of the setting.)*

B. LEP: Dialect Explain to students that the characters in this story are British, thus they speak with British accents. The author has re-created the sound of their speech through dialect, spelling the words as they sound. Have students pronounce *liddle 'un* and explain it. *("little one," a child)*

C. Critical Thinking: ANALYZING Ask students to analyze what they can tell about the environment from the scene at the grave. *(Possible response: Even in August it is cold, the grass is still withered, and the leaves have not yet blossomed on the trees.)*

Searching for Summer

JOAN AIKEN

SR-1 ▶ Lily wore yellow on her wedding day. In the 'eighties people put a lot of faith in omens and believed that if a bride's dress was yellow, her married life would be blessed with a bit of sunshine.

A It was years since the bombs had been banned, but still the cloud never lifted. Whitish gray, day after day, sometimes darkening to a weeping slate-color, or, at the end of an evening, turning to smoky copper, the sky endlessly, secretively brooded.

How could the sky ever have been blue?

B Old people began their stories with the classic, fairy-tale opening: "Long, long ago, when I was a liddle 'un, in the days when the sky was blue . . ." and children, listening, chuckled among themselves at the absurd thought, because, *blue,* imagine it! How could the sky ever have been *blue*? You might as well say, "In the days when the grass was pink."

Stars, rainbows, and all other such heavenly sideshows had been permanently withdrawn, and if the radio announced that there was a blink of sunshine in such and such a place, where the cloud belt had thinned for half an hour, cars and buses would pour in that direction for days in an unavailing search for warmth and light.

After the wedding, when all the relations were standing on the church porch, with Lily shivering prettily in her buttercup nylon, her father prodded the dour and withered grass on a grave—although it was August, the leaves were hardly out yet—and said, "Well, Tom, what are you aiming to do now, eh?" C

"Going to find a bit of sun and have our honeymoon in it," said Tom. There was a general laugh from the wedding party. ◀ SR-2

"Don't get sunburned," shrilled Aunt Nancy.

"Better start off Bournemouth[1] way. Paper said they had a half hour of sun last Wednesday week," Uncle Arthur weighed in heavily.

1. **Bournemouth** (bôrn′ məth): a seaside resort in south-central England.

Words to Know and Use	**omen** (ō′ mən) *n.* a thing or event which foretells the future **dour** (door) *adj.* gloomy; forbidding

Structured Reading for Less Proficient Students

These questions can help to guide students through the reading. Ask each question at the point of the selection where the SR number appears in the margin.

SR–1. Why does Lily wear yellow for her wedding? *(People think it is lucky and will bless the couple's life with a bit of sunshine.)* **Literal recall**

SR–2. What are Tom and Lily going to do on their honeymoon? *(try to find sun)* **Clarifying**

SR–3. Who is Mr. Noakes? *(He is the owner of the Rising Sun pub.)* **Literal recall**

SR–4. What would Mr. Noakes do if he could find a sunny place? *(buy the land and erect a trailer camp, country club, and resort)* **Clarifying**

SR–5. Why does Lily want to visit Mrs. Hatchings? *(to return her purse)* **Literal recall**

Continued on page 605

"We'll come back brown as—as this grass," said Tom, and ignoring the good-natured teasing from their respective families, the two young people mounted on their scooter, which stood ready at the churchyard wall, and chugged away in a shower of golden confetti. When they were out of sight, and the yellow paper had subsided on the gray and gritty road, the Whitemores and Hoskinses strolled off, sighing, to eat wedding cake and drink currant[2] wine; and old Mrs. Hoskins spoiled everyone's pleasure by bursting into tears as she thought of her own wedding day when everything was so different.

D

Meanwhile Tom and Lily buzzed on hopefully across the gray countryside, with Lily's veil like a gilt banner floating behind. It was chilly going for her in her wedding things, but the sight of a bride was supposed to bring good luck, and so she stuck it out, although her fingers were blue to the knuckles. Every now and then they switched on their portable radio and listened to the forecast. Inverness had seen the sun for ten minutes yesterday, and Southend[3] for five minutes this morning, but that was all.

E

"Both those places are a long way from here," said Tom cheerfully. "All the more reason we'd find a nice bit of sunshine in these parts somewhere. We'll keep on going south. Keep your eyes peeled, Lil, and tell me if you see a blink of sun on those hills ahead."

But they came to the hills and passed them, and a new range shouldered up ahead and then slid away behind, and still there was no flicker or patch of sunshine to be seen anywhere in the gray, winter-ridden landscape. Lily began to get discouraged, so they stopped for a cup of tea at a drive-in.

"See the sun lately, mate?" Tom asked the proprietor.

He laughed shortly. "Notice any buses or trucks around here? Last time I saw the sun was two years ago September; came out just in time for the wife's birthday."

F

"It's stars I'd like to see," Lily said, looking wistfully at her dust-colored tea. "Ever so pretty they must be."

"Well, better be getting on, I suppose," said Tom, but he had lost some of his bounce and confidence. Every place they passed through looked nastier than the last, partly on account of the dismal light, partly because people had given up bothering to take pride in their boroughs.[4] And then, just as they were entering a village called Molesworth, the dimmest, drabbest, most insignificant huddle of houses they had come to yet, the engine coughed and died on them.

G

"Can't see what's wrong," said Tom, after a prolonged and gloomy survey.

"Oh, Tom!" Lily was almost crying. "What'll we do?"

"Have to stop here for the night, s'pose." Tom was short-tempered with frustration. "Look, there's a garage just up the road. We can push the bike there, and they'll tell us if there's a pub where we can stay. It's nearly six anyway."

H

They had taken the bike to the garage, and the man there was just telling them that

2. **currant:** small, sour, seedless berry that grows on shrubs and is used to make jams, jellies, and wine.

3. **Inverness** (in′ vər nes′) . . . **Southend:** two resort cities in the British Isles.

4. **boroughs:** small, self-governing towns in England that send representatives to Parliament.

Words to Know and Use

proprietor (prō prī′ ə tər) *n.* a person who owns and manages a business

605

D. Reading Skill: CLARIFYING Ask students to explain why Mrs. Hoskins cries. *(She is sad at the thought of how the world has changed for the worse; she was married before the bombs exploded and the sky clouded over.)*

E. Teaching Tip

To help familiarize students with the places mentioned in the story, post a large map of Great Britain on the bulletin board and have students locate Inverness and Southend.

F. Reading Skill: PREDICTING Ask students to predict, based on the reactions Tom and Lily get to their queries, whether Tom and Lily will see the sun. *(Possible response: Some may say the couple stands little chance of seeing the sun because it so rarely appears; others may feel that because they are newlyweds they might have some luck.)*

G. Literary Sidelight Notice how the story follows the traditional organization of a fairy tale: A pair of innocents embark on a hopeful voyage into the world; on their way, they encounter progressively meaner and more dangerous places until they arrive at the most miserable place of all, usually by accident. Often, the most dangerous place is the forest. Aiken puts an interesting twist to the genre by making the woods the site of great goodness rather than evil.

H. LEP: Dialect Explain to students that *pub* is an expression commonly used in England; *pub* is short for a *public house,* a tavern.

STRUCTURED READING FOR LESS PROFICIENT STUDENTS

Continued from page 604

SR–6. What astonishing thing do Tom and Lily find at the Hatchings? *(the sun)* **Clarifying**

SR–7. How do the Hatchings treat the newlyweds? *(with warmth and kindness)* **Inferring**

SR–8. Where does Tom tell Mr. Noakes he and Lily have been? *(miles away, beyond Brinsley)* **Literal recall**

I. Literary Element: IRONY Ask students to explain how the pub's name might be ironic. *(Possible response: The sun never rises over the pub.)*

J. LEP: Dialect Have students recast Mrs. Hatching's dialogue into standard written English. *(Possible response: "George, be careful with my son, William.")*

K. Literary Element: CHARACTERIZATION Ask students to explain what Mr. Noakes's comments about the Hatchings reveal about his character. *(Possible response: His lack of patience and understanding reveal him to be selfish and narrow-minded; his comment that they ought to be killed reveals him as cruelly vicious as well.)*

L. Reading Skill: INFERRING Ask students what they can infer about Mr. Noakes's character from his appearance. Have them cite specific details to back up their inferences. *(Possible response: His red face suggests that he is often angry; his wet, full lips suggest that he is lascivious; his bulging eyes suggest that he is greedy.)*

M. Literary Sidelight Another well-known science-fiction story that uses the symbol of the sun to suggest hope and possibility is Ray Bradbury's "All Summer in a Day." In this story, the sun appears on schedule once a year, but cruel and thoughtless school children deny one of their own the chance to see it.

N. Historical Sidelight For many people who lived through World War II, margarine is a symbol of the deprivation that they endured on the home front through food rationing and shortages. Students may not know that at that time margarine was considered a poor substitute for butter. It came in white slabs, and people could add yellow food coloring if they desired.

I the only pub in the village was the Rising Sun, where Mr. Noakes might be able to give them a bed, when a bus pulled up in SR-13 ▶ front of the petrol[5] pumps.

"Look," the garage owner said, "there's Mr. Noakes just getting out of the bus now. Sid!" he called.

But Mr. Noakes was not able to come to them at once. Two old people were climbing slowly out of the bus ahead of him: a blind man with a white stick, and a withered, frail old lady in a black satin dress and hat. J "Careful now, George," she was saying, "mind ee be careful with my son, William."

"I'm being careful, Mrs. Hatching," the conductor said patiently, as he almost lifted the unsteady old pair off the bus platform. The driver had stopped his engine, and everyone on the bus was taking a mild and sympathetic interest, except for Mr. Noakes just behind, who was cursing irritably at the delay. When the two old people were on the narrow pavement, the conductor saw that they were going to have trouble with a bicycle that was propped against the curb just ahead of them; he picked it up and stood holding it until they had passed the line of petrol pumps and were going slowly off along a path across the fields. Then, grinning, he put it back, jumped hurriedly into the bus, and rang his bell.

K "Old nuisances," Mr. Noakes said furiously. "Wasting public time. Every week that palaver[6] goes on, taking the old man to Midwick Hospital Out Patients and back again. I know what *I'd* do with 'em. Put to sleep, that sort ought to be."

Mr. Noakes was a repulsive-looking individual, but when he heard that Tom and Lily wanted a room for the night, he changed completely and gave them a leer that was full of false goodwill. He was a big, red-faced man with wet, full lips, bulging pale gray bloodshot eyes, and a crop of stiff, greasy black hair. He wore tennis shoes. L "Honeymooners, eh?" he said, looking sentimentally at Lily's pale prettiness. They followed Mr. Noakes glumly up the street to the Rising Sun.

While they were eating their baked beans, Mr. Noakes stood over their table grimacing at them. Lily unwisely confided to him that they were looking for a bit of sunshine. Mr. M Noakes's laughter nearly shook down the ramshackle building.

"Sunshine! That's a good 'un! Hear that, Mother?" he bawled to his wife. "They're looking for a bit of sunshine. Heh-heh-heh-heh-heh-heh! Why," he said, banging on the table till the baked beans leaped about, "if I could find a bit of sunshine near here, permanent bit that is, dja know what I'd do?"

The young people looked at him inquiringly across the bread and margarine. N

"Lido,[7] trailersite, country club, holiday camp—you wouldn't know the place. Land around here is dirt cheap; I'd buy up the lot. Nothing but woods. I'd advertise—I'd have people flocking to this little dump from all over the country. But what a hope, what a hope, eh? Well, feeling better? Enjoyed your tea? Ready for bed?" ◀ SR-4

Avoiding one another's eyes, Tom and Lily stood up.

5. **petrol:** a British term for gasoline.
6. **palaver** (pe lav′ ər): useless and idle talk.
7. **lido** (lē′ dō): a British term for a public outdoor swimming pool.

Words to Know and Use	**grimacing** (gri′ mās iŋ) *adj.* distorting one's face because of pain, disgust, or anger **grimace** *v.*

606

Professional Notebook

The high-tech information age is shaping and changing our lives like few other milestones in human history. What are we doing about the impact of this new era in the field of education? Are we preparing students to live and work in a high-tech information society? Specific skills and knowledge areas must be developed, added, or emphasized in our school curriculum in order to prepare our students to perform adequately in the high-technology information age. With a focus on developing skills for lifelong learning, information-processing skills and proficiency with computers must be become 'new basics.'

Gail A. Caissey, "Skills for the Information Age" (*The Education Digest*, February 1990)

O. Critical Thinking: ANALYZING Ask students to analyze why Lily wants to go for a walk. *(Possible reasons: She detests Mr. Noakes, and his lewd insinuations make her extremely uncomfortable.)*

O "I—I'd like to go for a bit of a walk first, Tom," Lily said in a small voice. "Look, I picked up that old lady's bag on the pavement. I didn't notice it till we'd done talking to Mr. Noakes, and by then she was out of sight. Should we take it back to her?"

"Good idea," said Tom, pouncing on the suggestion with relief. "Do you know where she lives, Mr. Noakes?"

"Who, old Ma Hatching? Sure I know. She lives in the wood. But you don't want to go taking her bag back, not this time o' the evening you don't. Let her worry. She'll come asking for it in the morning."

"She walked so slowly," said Lily, holding the bag gently in her hands. It was very old, made of black velvet on two ring-handles, and embroidered with beaded roses. "I think we ought to take it to her, don't you, Tom?"

◀SR-5

"Oh, very well, very well, have it your own way," Mr. Noakes said, winking at Tom. "Take that path by the garage. You can't go wrong. I've never been there meself, but

SUNBURST Gordon Parks
By permission of the photographer.

DATA BANK

The concerns of science fiction have been found even in ancient literature. For example, the Greek myth of Daedalus deals with flying, and Lucian of Samosata's *True History* (c. A.D. 160) deals with a trip to the moon. Trips to the moon reappear later, in the seventeenth century, in works by figures as different as the French writer Cyrano de Bergerac and the German astronomer Johannes Kepler. Another frequent subject of science fiction, the creation of better worlds, goes back at least to the fourth century B.C. with Plato's *Republic*. The theme reappeared in 1516 with Sir Thomas More's *Utopia*. Perhaps the finest story of an imaginary voyage is Swift's *Gulliver's Travels* (1726). The first great science-fiction writer, however, is generally accepted to be Jules Verne. His *Journey to the Center of the Earth* (1864), *A Trip to the Moon* (1865), and *20,000 Leagues Under the Sea* (1870) have retained their appeal to this day.

P. Reading Skill: CLARIFYING Have students explain what type of vacation Tom had planned for his honeymoon. *(He planned that they would find a bit of sun to enjoy, not trek through a dismal forest after their motor scooter broke down in a miserable, ill-kept town.)*

Q. Reading Skill: INFERRING Have students infer what the runner beans and overgrown vines on the porch suggest. *(There must be a great deal of sun to support beans and flowers, both hot-weather crops that thrive best in full sun.)*

R. LEP: Dialect Ask a volunteer to paraphrase Mrs. Hatching's words in standard English. *(Possible response: "It's the pretty bride. I saw you this afternoon when we were coming home from the hospital.")*

S. Reading Skill: UNDERSTANDING WORD CHOICE Have students explain the significance of Tom's phrase "My wife's hurt her foot—" *(Possible response: Neither Tom nor Lily is used to being married. Hearing the phrase "my wife" reminds them and the readers that the couple is newly married and thus inexperienced with living as a couple.)*

T. Teaching Tip

Explain to students that today nylon is an inexpensive fabric, rarely used in this country for fine wedding dresses. Often well-off brides select richer fabrics, such as silk, satin, or taffeta. That Lily's nylon dress should excite such comment suggests again the deprivation experienced by those in the story after the devastation.

they live somewhere in that wood back o' the village. You'll find it soon enough."

They found the path soon enough, but not the cottage. Under the lowering sky they walked forward endlessly among trees that carried only tiny and rudimentary leaves, wizened and poverty-stricken. Lily was still wearing her wedding sandals, which had begun to blister her. She held onto Tom's arm, biting her lip with the pain, and he looked down miserably at her bent brown head; everything had turned out so differently from what he had planned. P

By the time they reached the cottage, Lily could hardly bear to put her left foot to the ground, and Tom was gentling her along. "It can't be much farther now, and they'll be sure to have a bandage. I'll tie it up, and you can have a sit-down. Maybe they'll give us a cup of tea. We could borrow an old pair of socks or something. . . ." Hardly noticing the cottage garden, beyond a vague impression of rows of runner beans, they made for the clematis-grown[8] porch and knocked. There was a brass lion's head on the door, carefully polished. Q

"Eh, me dear!" It was the old lady, old Mrs. Hatching, who opened the door, and her exclamation was a long-drawn gasp of pleasure and astonishment. "Eh, me dear! 'Tis the pretty bride. See'd ye s'arternoon when we was coming home from hospital." R

"Who be?" shouted a voice from inside.

"Come in, come in, me dears. My son William'll be glad to hear company; he can't see, poor soul, nor has this thirty year, ah, and a pretty sight he's losing this minute—"

"We brought back your bag," Tom said, putting it in her hands, "and we wondered if you'd have a bit of plaster[9] you could kindly let us have. My wife's hurt her foot—"

My wife. Even in the midst of Mrs. Hatching's voluble welcome, the strangeness of these words struck the two young people, and they fell quiet, each of them, pondering, while Mrs. Hatching thanked and commiserated, all in a breath, and asked them to take a seat on the sofa and fetched a basin of water from the scullery;[10] and William from his seat in the chimney corner demanded to know what it was all about. S

> ***"The sun? Is it really the sun?"***

"Wot be doing? Wot be doing, Mother?"

"'Tis a bride, all in's finery," she shrilled back at him, "an's blistered her foot, poor heart." Keeping up a running commentary for William's benefit, she bound up the foot, every now and then exclaiming to herself in wonder over the fineness of Lily's wedding dress, which lay in yellow nylon swathes around the chair. "There, me dear. Now us'll have a cup of tea, eh? Proper thirsty you'm fare to be, walking all the way to here this hot day." T

Hot day? Tom and Lily stared at each other and then around the room. Then it was true, it was not their imagination, that a great, dusty golden square of sunshine lay

8. **clematis** (klem′ ə tis) **grown:** covered with vines of the buttercup family that bear brightly colored flowers.

9. **plaster:** a British term for adhesive tape or bandage.

10. **scullery:** a British term for a room where pans are kept and dirty kitchen work is done.

Words to Know and Use

rudimentary (ro͞o′ də men′ tər ē) *adj.* underdeveloped; of the most simple kind
wizened (wiz′ ənd) *adj.* shriveled, dried up
commiserate (kə miz′ ər āt′) *v.* to express pity; sympathize

REAL LIFE CONNECTIONS

To help students recognize parallels between Tom's feelings and their own experiences, ask them how they felt when they planned a special treat for someone they care for—a relative or a friend, perhaps—and their plans went awry. For example, they might have tried to take to the beach a relative who lives inland and it rained for a whole week, or they might have prepared a special dinner and the meal became burnt. Ask volunteers to write about their experiences or share them with the class.

on the fireplace wall, where the brass pendulum of the clock at every swing blinked into sudden brilliance? That the blazing geraniums on the windowsill housed a drove of murmuring bees? That through the window the gleam of linen hung in the sun to whiten suddenly dazzled their eyes?

"The sun? Is it really the sun?" Tom said,
SR-6 ▶ almost doubtfully.

U "And why not?" Mrs. Hatching demanded. "How else'll beans set, tell me that? Fine thing if sun were to stop shining." Chuckling to herself she set out a Crown Derby[11] tea set, gorgeously colored in red and gold, and a baking of saffron[12] buns. Then she sat down and, drinking her own tea, began to question the two of them about where they had come from, where they were going.

V The tea was tawny and hot and sweet; the clock's tick was like a bird chirping; every now and then a log settled in the grate. Lily looked sleepily around the little room, so rich and peaceful, and thought, I wish we were staying here. I wish we needn't go back to that horrible pub. . . . She leaned against Tom's comforting arm.

"Look at the sky," she whispered to him. "Out there between the geraniums. Blue!"

"And ee'll come up and see my spare bedroom, won't ee now?" Mrs. Hatching said, breaking off the thread of her questions—which indeed was not a thread, but merely a savoring of her pleasure and astonishment

W at this unlooked-for visit—"Bide here, why don't ee? Mid as well. The lil un's fair wore out. Us'll do for ee better'n rangy old Noakes, proper old scoundrel 'e be. Won't us, William?"

"Ah," William said appreciatively, "I'll sing ee some o' my songs."

A sight of the spare room settled any doubts. The great white bed, huge as a prairie, built up with layer upon solid layer of mattress, blanket, and quilt, almost filled the little shadowy room in which it stood. Brass rails shone in the green dimness. "Isn't it quiet," Lily whispered. Mrs. Hatching, silent for the moment, stood looking at them proudly, her bright eyes slowly moving from face to face. Once her hand fondled, as if it might have been a baby's downy head, the yellow brass knob.

And so, almost without any words, the matter was decided.

Three days later they remembered that they must go to the village and collect the scooter, which must, surely, be mended by now.

They had been helping old William pick a basketful of beans. Tom had taken his shirt off, and the sun gleamed on his brown back; Lily was wearing an old cotton print, which Mrs. Hatching, with much chuckling, had shortened to fit her. ◀ SR-7

It was amazing how deftly, in spite of his blindness, William moved among the beans, feeling through the rough, rustling leaves for the stiffness of concealed pods. He found twice as many as Tom and Lily, but then they, even on the third day, were still stopping every other minute to exclaim over the blueness of the sky. At night they sat on the back doorstep while Mrs. Hatching clucked inside as she dished the supper,

11. **Crown Derby:** a fine porcelain made during the 1800's, imprinted with a crown.

12. **saffron:** exquisite, orange-colored herb often used in baked goods and rice.

Words to Know and Use

tawny (tô′ nē) *adj.* tan-colored
scoundrel (skoun′ drəl) *n.* a mean or wicked person

U. Reading Skill: INFERRING Have students infer from Mrs. Hatching's comments how often the sun shines and with what strength. *(It shines strongly all the time.)*

V. Reading Skill: CONTRAST Ask students to contrast the Hatchings' home to the pub, paying special attention to the mood of each. *(Possible response: The Hatchings' home is comfortable and welcoming, with a warm, homey mood. The pub is depressing and grim, with a strained, awkward mood.)*

W. LEP: Dialect Ask a volunteer to paraphrase Mrs. Hatching's words in standard English. *(Possible response: "Stay here, why don't you? Might as well. The little one is wore out. Our hospitality will be better than mean old Mr. Noakes, the scoundrel he is. Won't we, William?")*

X. LEP: Dialect Have a volunteer paraphrase Mrs. Hatching's comments. *(Possible response: "You'll be star-struck! Come inside before the soup is cold. The stars have never vanished.")*

Y. Literary Element: CHARACTERIZATION Have students discuss what aspects of Mr. Noakes's character they find most repulsive. *(Possible responses: his false heartiness, shown by his greeting; his bad taste, shown by his tasteless joke about their possible death; or his lewdness, shown toward Lily)*

Z. Critical Thinking: SYNTHESIZING To help students synthesize science fiction, characterization, and symbolism, ask volunteers to explain if they think the sun shines only on the Hatchings, and if so, why. If not, have them explain where else it might shine and why. *(Possible responses: It might shine only on those who are good, on little pockets of people scattered throughout the world. It might shine only on the Hatchings because of some atmospheric fluke. Some may even suggest that the Hatching's are a dream of Tom and Lily's imaginations.)*

AA. Critical Thinking: EVALUATING Ask students if they agree with Tom's decision to lie to Mr. Noakes, and why. *(Possible responses: Tom did the right thing to preserve the Hatchings' idyllic life; Tom did the wrong thing because he should have given Mr. Noakes a chance to prosper.)*

Check Test

1. Why is the sky no longer blue? *(Since nuclear war, clouds have covered the sun, leaving the sky gray or copper.)*
2. Where are Lily and Tom going? *(on their honeymoon, to look for the sun)*
3. Who is Mr. Noakes? *(the owner of the village pub; a nasty person)*
4. Where do Lily and Tom discover the sun? *(at the Hatchings')*
5. Why does Tom lie to Mr. Noakes? *(Tom does not want him to learn that the sun shines at the Hastings'.)*

Encouraging Independent Reading

The Martian Chronicles, interrelated short stories by Ray Bradbury
"A Boy and His Dog," a short story by Harlan Ellison
A Canticle for Liebowitz, a novel by Walter M. Miller
On the Beach, a novel by Nevil Shute

X "Star-struck ee'll be! Come along in, do-ee, before soup's cold. Stars niver run away yet as I do know."

"Can we get anything for you in the village?" Lily asked, but Mrs. Hatching shook her head.

"Baker's bread and suchlike's no use but to cripple thee's innardses wi' colic.[13] I been living here these eighty years wi' out troubling doctors, and I'm not faring to begin now." She waved to them and stood watching as they walked into the wood, thin and frail beyond belief, but wiry, <u>indomitable</u>, her black eyes full of zest. Then she turned to scream menacingly at a couple of pullets[14] who had strayed and were scratching among the potatoes.

Almost at once they noticed, as they followed the path, that the sky was clouded over.

"It *is* only there on that one spot," Lily said in wonder. "All the time. And they've never even noticed that the sun doesn't shine in other places."

"That's how it must have been all over the world, once," Tom said.

At the garage they found their scooter ready and waiting. They were about to start back when they ran into Mr. Noakes.

Y "Well, well, well, well, *well!*" he shouted, glaring at them with ferocious good humor. "How many wells make a river, eh? And where did you slip off to? Here's me and the missus was just going to tell the police to have the rivers dragged. But hullo, hullo, what's this? Brown, eh? Suntan? Scrumptious," he said, looking meltingly at Lily and giving her another tremendous pinch. "Where'd you get it, eh? That wasn't all got in half an hour, *I* know. Come on, this means money to you and me, tell us the big secret. Remember what I said; land around these parts is dirt cheap."

Tom and Lily looked at each other in horror. They thought of the cottage, the bees humming among the runner beans, the sunlight glinting in the red-and-gold teacups. At night, when they had lain in the huge, sagging bed, stars had shone through the window, and the whole wood was as quiet as the inside of a shell. Z

"Oh, we've been miles from here," Tom lied hurriedly. "We ran into a friend, and he took us right away beyond Brinsley." AA And as Mr. Noakes still looked suspicious and unsatisfied, he did the only thing possible. "We're going back there now," he said; "the sunbathing's grand." And opening the throttle he let the scooter go. They waved at Mr. Noakes and chugged off toward the gray hills that lay to the north. ◀SR-8

"My wedding dress," Lily said sadly. "It's on our bed."

They wondered how long Mrs. Hatching would keep tea hot for them, who would eat all the pastries.

"Never mind, you won't need it again," Tom comforted her.

At least, he thought, they had left the golden place undisturbed. Mr. Noakes never went into the wood. And they had done what they intended; they had found the sun. Now they, too, would be able to tell their grandchildren, when beginning a story, "Long, long ago, when we were young, in the days when the sky was blue. . . ." ❧

13. **colic:** sharp abdominal pain caused by disturbances in the digestive system.
14. **pullets:** young hens.

Words to Know and Use	**indomitable** (in däm′ i tə bəl) *adj.* strong; undefeatable

Responding to Reading

First Impressions

1. What are your feelings about Tom and Lily? Jot down your impressions.

Second Thoughts

2. What effects has the war had upon the environment of the story and upon people's personalities and actions?
3. Why do you think the old people's memories about sunshine are so important?
4. What do Tom and Lily learn from the Hatchings?

   Think about
   - what Tom and Lily believe before meeting them
   - how the Hatchings differ from people like Mr. Noakes
   - how the Hatchings have adapted to the world
5. Why don't Tom and Lily return to the Hatchings' cottage?
6. What do you think was the author's purpose in writing "Searching for Summer"?

Broader Connections

7. Recently we have witnessed many events that seem to have eased the threat of nuclear war. The Berlin Wall has come down, and governments in Eastern Europe and the Soviet Union have been changing rapidly. At the same time, however, new tensions have arisen, and more and more countries have access to nuclear weapons. What thoughts do you have in these changing times about the possibility of nuclear war?

Literary Concept: Science Fiction

Fiction that is based on real or imagined scientific developments is called **science fiction.** Science fiction is normally set in the future. Look back at your own description of the setting, characters, and plot of a typical science fiction story. How does "Searching for Summer" compare with your ideas and with the definition above?

Concept Review: Characterization Look back at your notes on Mr. Noakes. What actions, thoughts, and words portray this character's personality?

Student Response

Responding to Reading

These questions are open-ended, with no "right" or "wrong" answers. However, responses must be supported with information from the selection. Possible answers follow:

1. Almost any feelings about Tom and Lily, whether negative or positive, are valid.

2. Possible response: Nuclear explosions have caused clouds to form, which cover the sun. As a result, the sky is always various shades of gray or copper, the grass is brown and withered, and the landscape is gray. Some students may say that the effects of the war have made people worship the sun. Others may say that the effects of the war have made people sad, angry, or bitter. When the sun does appear briefly in a particular spot, people throng there to see it.

3. Some students may say that the old people's memories about the sun are so important because they help keep alive the hope of the sun returning; others may feel that the memories are a warning about the dangers of nuclear war.

4. Before Tom and Lily meet the Hatchings, they are gradually becoming sad and gloomy over their future. Some may say that the Hatchings teach Tom and Lily that there are kind people left in the world and that not everyone is greedy like Mr. Noakes. Others may say that the Hatchings teach the couple to adjust better to their life and that the Hatchings represent that bit of sunshine one can find by not losing faith and looking for it.

5. Some students may point out that Tom and Lily are afraid Mr. Noakes will follow them to the cottage, exploit the sun's appearance, and ruin the Hatchings' lives. Other students may feel that Tom and Lily realize that they have to be part of the world; others may say that they want their time in the sun to be special by being brief.

6. Some might feel that the author wanted to warn people about the dangers of nuclear war; others might say that she was writing to entertain.

7. Some students might feel that with the breakdown of communism, nuclear war is much less likely; others might say that growing tensions in the Mideast increase the possibility of a nuclear confrontation.

Literary Concept—Science Fiction

Possible response: Answers will vary depending on students' description of a typical science-fiction plot. Some may note that the story is set in the future, typical of science fiction. Others may say that it deals with a blend of scientific fact and fiction, in that nuclear bombs are real and that scientists theorize the prospect of a nuclear winter. Refer to Annotations A and Z.

Concept Review—Characterization *Possible response: His determination to exploit any sunlight for personal profit and his nasty remarks about the Hatchings reveals his greedy and vicious character.* Refer to Annotations K and Z.

Writing Options

The Writing Options are designed to meet varied student interests and abilities. Have each student choose one writing activity to complete. You may wish to guide some students to an option that requires less writing.

Journal Update Have students review their journal entries for "Searching for Summer." What new reflections about the sun can be added to their writing?

Vocabulary Practice

1. commiserate
2. proprietor
3. dour
4. indomitable
5. omen
6. scoundrel
7. rudimentary
8. grimacing
9. tawny
10. wizened

Writing Options

1. Write a summary of what might have happened before this story begins. How might the war have started? Who was involved? What weapons were used, and how did the war finally end? Is this a nuclear winter that is described, or is it something else?
2. Write about Tom and Lily's next few months. Describe how their experiences with the Hatchings affect their lives.
3. Create a typical weather report for Molesworth, England, during the time of this story. Since the weather there is almost always the same, come up with some entertaining angle that will make your report more interesting than another forecaster's.
4. How would you feel if you lived in a world like Tom and Lily's? Describe how you think such conditions would affect you.

Vocabulary Practice

Exercise On your paper, write the word from the list that best completes each sentence.

1. Mrs. Hatching is someone who likes to ____ over another person's problems.
2. The ____ of the hotel is willing to give Tom and Lily a room for the night.
3. Mr. Noakes is always in a gloomy, ____ mood.
4. Mrs. Hatching is known for her courage and ____ spirit.
5. People think it is a good ____ for a bride to wear a yellow dress on her wedding day.
6. By explaining his scheme to get rich, Mr. Noakes shows what a(n) ____ he is.
7. Ever since the war, even the most simple and ____ crops have been hard to grow.
8. Angry and impatient at having to wait, Mr. Noakes could be seen ____ at the old couple as he got off the bus.
9. When milk is added to tea, the hot liquid takes on a(n) ____ color.
10. The lack of sunlight caused the fruit to become dry and ____.

Words to Know and Use

commiserate
dour
grimacing
indomitable
omen
proprietor
rudimentary
scoundrel
tawny
wizened

Options for Learning

1 • Story Time Rewrite this story as a children's book. Begin by making a brief outline of the plot. Expand this outline into complete sentences. Include vivid images so that your audience can picture the setting. Be sure to show through words or actions the personalities of the important characters. If possible, illustrate your book; then read it to a group of young children.

2 • Noakes's Sunny Nook Imagine that Mr. Noakes finds out about the Hatchings' place in the sun. Design the billboard he might create to advertise the area to the public. Include his ideas for a swimming pool, trailer site, country club, and holiday camp. Remember that Mr. Noakes's primary concern is money. Use images and words that reflect his values and personality.

3 • Blue Skies How many songs can you think of that mention the sun, blue skies, or stars? Play or sing a medley of these songs for the class.

4 • Cloudy Canvas Draw or paint a landscape of the countryside around Molesworth, including the Hatchings' spot in the sun.

FACT FINDER

What is the average amount of rainfall for your state each year?

Joan Aiken
1924–

Like the young couple in this story, Joan Aiken faced a crisis early in her life. At the age of twenty, she became a widow with two children. Her husband had left her with many debts. "So I worked like a beaver selling stories." As the daughter of a famous poet, Conrad Aiken, she had been encouraged to write, but now she needed to write in order to survive.

Aiken eventually became a successful author of books for both adults and children. Looking back at her work, she noted: "With over sixty books listed on the British Public Lending Register I feel I have achieved my ambition to be a professional writer." As a writer of children's books, she invented "unhistorical romances," which combine fairy tale and myth set during the reign of an imaginary king, James the Third. Aiken is also known for mysteries and thrillers written for readers of all ages. As one critic remarked, "A thriller by Joan Aiken is like an ice-cream cone. Both must be consumed at a single sitting and both leave a cold but pleasurable feeling in the pit of the stomach."

Options for Learning

These activities suit a variety of learning styles and modes of expression. Allow students to review the options and then choose the one they wish to do. Many are excellent collaborative learning projects.

1. Story Time Suggest that students review some children's books for guidelines as to length, vocabulary, and number of illustrations.

2. Noakes's Sunny Nook Students might first brainstorm a list of words that reflect Mr. Noakes's concerns and personality.

3. Blue Skies Many libraries have record, videotape, and cassette tape collections that students can access.

4. Cloudy Canvas Have students first reread the description of the town and the Hatching's cottage.

Fact Finder

The answer will vary depending on the state in which students live. Almanacs list average rainfall by state.

Additional Information About the Author

Joan Aiken Joan Aiken recalls that she wrote her first stories and poems when she was five years old and promptly decided that writing was the career for her. She published her first poems while still in school. After her husband's death she published many stories, but soon she came to feel that she wanted to write longer works that would earn her more money. With that goal in mind, she revised the manuscript of a novel that she had written at seventeen. It became her first published novel, *The Kingdom and the Cave*. Her first big success came soon after with *The Wolves of Willoughby Chase*. Marketed as a children's book, it was hailed by adults as well.

Cross-Curricular Options

Science: Have students compare the average number of sunny days in a major British city to the average number of sunny days in a large city in their state.

Social Science: Suggest that students report on modern wedding superstitions, like Lily's yellow dress in the story.

History: Students might like to research the growth of nuclear capabilities among countries of the world from 1945 to the present.

Geography: Have students map out a week-long honeymoon trip to any place in the United States that includes a great deal of sun and can be reached comfortably on a motor scooter.

Publishing: Compile the contributions of all students. Display or make copies to distribute.

Closure

"Searching for Summer" can be read as a plea to save the environment. Ask students to list ways they think science and technology can help preserve their environment rather than destroy it. *(Students might mention such developments as solar energy, recycling, and methods to clear the earth's air and water.)*

Objectives

- To explore and appreciate two poems
- To identify rhetorical questions
- To examine titles
- To express understanding of the work through a choice of writing forms, including slogans, poetry, and letters

Prereading/Motivation

Examine What You Know

Discussion Prompts: What products made from trees can you find in your home and school? Which of these products do you think make life easier? What trees do you feel are especially beautiful? How do trees make you feel?

Expand Your Knowledge

Discussion Prompts: Should we extend existing conservation laws? Why or why not? Do you think we should harvest more or less timber from our forests than we do now? Explain your answer. How can individuals conserve the national forests on a daily basis?

Additional Background: Among the first significant steps in conservation history was the development of the national park system in 1872, starting with the creation of Yellowstone National Park. Next was the establishment of the federal forest reserves, later called the national forests, in 1891 and the founding of the U.S. Soil Survey in 1899. Much significant legislation has been enacted since that time. The establishment of the Environmental Protection Agency in 1970 is considered especially important.

Enrich Your Reading

Have students discuss their predictions of the poems' content.

Thematic Link—Saving the Environment
In these two poems, the poets question humanity's effect on the environment.

e x p l o r e

Poetry

Improved Farm Land

CARL SANDBURG

Hard Questions

MARGARET TSUDA (so͞o' də)

Examine What You Know (Prior Knowledge)

The two poems you are about to read express two poets' feelings about trees and other aspects of nature. Jot down some thoughts you have about the value of trees on a chart like the one below. Consider what products we get from trees (practical value) as well as how trees affect our senses and emotions (aesthetic value).

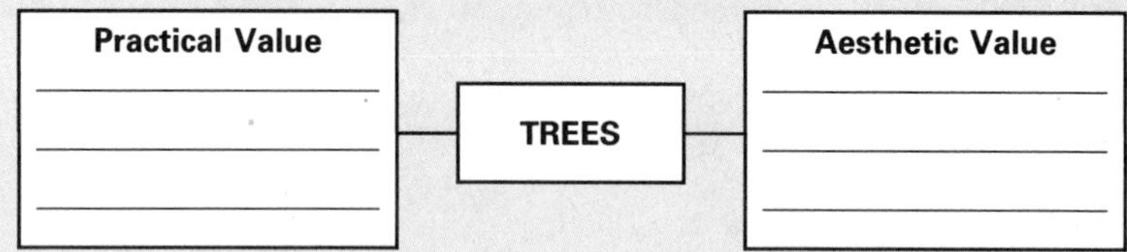

Expand Your Knowledge (Building Background)

At one time in this country, huge forests were consumed or cleared with little or no concern for the future. With the establishment of the U.S. Forest Service in 1905, however, the federal government began to set aside areas called forest reserves to preserve American forests. Throughout this century, Congress has continued to pass laws that provide increased protection of our forests. The Wilderness Act of 1964, for example, establishes Wilderness Areas where roads, buildings, and timber harvesting are prohibited. Even so, about half the national forest acreage is labeled "commercial forestland," which allows private companies to harvest timber. By 1971, 40 percent of the timber cut in America came from our national forests.

Enrich Your Reading (Reading Skill)

Examining Titles Titles help a reader predict what a particular work is about. Based on the titles of the next two poems and the information presented above, jot down a brief prediction of what you think each of these poems will be about.

■ *Biographies of the authors can be found in the Reader's Handbook.*

Journal Writing

Both "Improved Farm Land" and "Hard Questions" express how the poets feel about the land. Suggest these journal topics to students:

- What might the term *improved farm land* mean?
- What "hard questions" about the environment are especially important to you?

For other journal opportunities, refer students to Examine What You Know (p. 614), First Impressions (p. 616), and Real-Life Connections (p. T–616).

Additional Resources

UNIT FIVE RESOURCE BOOK
Reader's Guidesheet, p. 6
Vocabulary Worksheet, p. 7
Selection Check Test, p. 8
Selection Test, pp. 9–10

Collaborative Learning

Opportunities for collaborative learning appear throughout the lesson and include Real-Life Connections (p. T–616).

Improved Farm Land

CARL SANDBURG

SEEDTIME AND HARVEST 1937 Grant Wood Collection of Hirschl & Adler Galleries, Inc., New York.

A Tall timber stood here once
here on a corn belt farm along the Monon.
Here the roots of a half mile of trees
B dug their runners deep in the loam
for a grip and a hold against windstorms.
Then the axmen came and the chips flew
C to the zing of steel and handle—
the lank railsplitters cut the big ones first,
the beeches and the oaks, then the brush.

2 ***Monon:*** railroad line in Indiana.

4 ***loam:*** rich, dark soil.

Teaching Strategies

Support for Students of Limited English Proficiency

- Use **Reader's Guidesheet**, p. 6
- Point out to students that both of these poems are written in free verse; consequently, neither has rhyme nor rhythm. Read the poems aloud to the students after they have read them silently to themselves. Ask them to visualize images from the poems as you read. "Improved Farm Land" and "Hard Questions" contain some vocabulary terms, especially farming terms and the names of wild animals, that may be unfamiliar to students.
- **Annotations B** and **E** in "Improved Farm Land" and **C** in "Hard Questions" focus on difficult vocabulary.

Art Note

Writing about American artist Grant Wood (1891–1942), critic Larry Woiwode tells that after two summers in France, Wood said he "realized that all the really good ideas I'd ever had came to me while I was milking a cow. So I went back to Iowa." In *Seed Time and Harvest,* Wood eliminated details in order to stress the beauty of forms in the landscape. *What do you think is this farmer's chief crop?*

Text Annotations

A. Literary Element: ALLITERATION Have students define the term *alliteration* and identify the example of it in this passage. *(Alliteration is the repetition of a consonant sound at the beginning of words. "Tall timber" is alliterative.)* Then ask them to describe the word picture created for them by the alliteration. *(Some students might say that the alliteration creates a feeling of majesty or splendor; others may feel an impression of a canopy of trees.)*

B. LEP: Vocabulary Point out to students the definition of *loam* and tell them it is very good for growing many crops.

C. Literary Element: ONOMATOPOEIA Ask students to define *onomatopoeia* and find the example of it in this passage. *(Onomatopoeia is the use of words that imitate sounds. "Zing" is the example of onomatopoeia here.)*

D. Reading Skill: SUMMARIZING Have students summarize this passage. *(Cleared of its timber, the soil is now fine farm land.)*

E. LEP: Vocabulary Explain to students that *fodder* is animal food; here, it means crops grown especially to feed the animals.

F. Literary Element: PERSONIFICATION Have students identify the personification in this passage and explain how it contributes to the poem's theme. *(Possible response: Personifying trees as a "great singing family" conveys their humanity and grandeur, reinforcing the theme that progress is a double-edged sword.)*

Check Test

1. Who cut down the trees first? *(the "axmen" and "lank railsplitters")*

2. How was the land cleared? *(with dynamite, wagons, and horses)*

3. What would be hard for the improved farm land to remember? *(that it once had been covered in trees)*

Student Response

Responding to Reading

These questions are open-ended, with no "right" or "wrong" answers. However, responses must be supported with information from the selection. Possible answers follow:

1. Almost any image from the poem, whether negative or positive, is valid.

2. Some students may feel that the speaker supports improved farm land because now farmers can raise crops; others may feel that the speaker is against improving the land because doing so destroyed the majestic "tall timber."

3. Some students may say that the phrase means the trees were like a family of people; others may say that the trees seemed to sing as they swayed in the prairie wind. Others may say that unlike humans, the trees lived harmoniously as a part of nature.

4. Some students may say that the title is ironic because the speaker believes the land has not been improved by the destruction of its trees.

Dynamite, wagons and horses took the stumps—
D the plows sunk their teeth in—
now it is first-class corn land—improved
property—
E and the hogs grunt over the fodder crops.
It would come hard now for this half mile of
improved farm land
along the Monon corn belt,
on a piece of Grand Prairie,
to remember once it had a great singing family of
F trees.

Responding to Reading

First Impressions of "Improved Farm Land"

1. With what image does "Improved Farm Land" leave you? Describe this image in your journal or on notebook paper.

Second Thoughts on "Improved Farm Land"

2. How do you think the speaker feels about improved farm land? Why?

3. What does the speaker mean by a "great singing family of trees"?

Think about
- where this phrase appears in the poem
- what qualities trees and families share
- what images "singing" suggests

4. What is ironic about the title of this poem?

REAL LIFE CONNECTIONS

To help students draw connections between their own lives and the speaker's feelings about changes in the land, ask students how they feel when they see a part of nature such as a big tree or open field removed to make way for something else. Ask students if they would feel the same way even if the replacement would serve their needs better. Compare and contrast the feelings of students from urban, suburban, and rural areas.

Hard Questions

MARGARET TSUDA

A Why not mark out the land
into neat rectangles
squares and clover leafs?

Put on them cubes of
varying sizes
according to use—
dwellings
    singles/multiples
complexes
    commercial/industrial.

Bale them together with
bands of roads.

What if a child shall cry
B "I have never known spring!
I have never seen autumn!"

What if a man shall say
"I have never heard
silence fraught with living as
in swamp or forest!"
What if the eye shall never see
C marsh bird and muskrats?

Does not the heart need
wildness?
Does not the thought need
something
to rest upon
not self-made by man,
a bosom
not his own?

Comstock, New York.

18 ***fraught:*** filled or charged.

Text Annotations

A. Literary Element: RHETORICAL QUESTION Have students explain what point the poet wishes to emphasize through this rhetorical question. *(Possible response: that the land has been overdivided into geometric shapes)*

B. Critical Thinking: ANALYZING Have students analyze how it might be possible for a child never to know spring or autumn. *(Possible response: because all the trees, which show the change of seasons, have been lost to homes and commercial buildings)*

C. LEP: Vocabulary Explain that a muskrat is a foot-long rodent with a thick light-brown fur. Muskrats live in burrows or piles of vegetation in freshwater or saltwater.

Check Test

1. How are the cubes of land connected? *(with bands of roads)*

2. What does the speaker worry that the child will not know? *(the seasons)*

3. What does the speaker feel that the heart needs? *(wildness)*

4. What does the speaker feel that the thought needs? *(something not self-made by man)*

Encouraging Independent Reading

Watership Down, a novel by Richard Adams
"I am the Land. I Wait," a poem by Marina de Bellagente
"Flower-Fed Buffaloes," "Factory Windows Are Always Broken," and "The Ghost of the Buffaloes," poems by Vachel Lindsay
"Buffalo Dusk," "Illinois Farmer," and "Plowboy," poems by Carl Sandburg
"Dandelions," a poem by Will Stanton

PROFESSIONAL NOTEBOOK

Reading aloud to students introduces them to good literature, encourages language development, and demonstrates that wonderful experiences can come from books. . . . Reading aloud is not just for younger children. Middle schoolers, high schoolers, and even college students love to hear good literature. Teacher educators read to their students both to model effective reading and to reinforce how beneficial and enjoyable reading aloud can be. . . . Reading aloud should be considered an important part of the language arts program. It is the third leg on the reading program tripod of direct instruction, sustained silent reading or book contact, and reading aloud.

EDWARD J. DWYER AND REBECCA ISBELL, "READING ALOUD TO STUDENTS," *The Education Digest,* SEPT. 1990, P. 70.

Student Response

Responding to Reading

1. Any question is valid.

2. Some students may feel that the speaker is describing the transformation of fields into commercial and residential property; others might see the creation of farms and highways from wilderness.

3. The speaker's tone changes in the fourth stanza. Some students may say that the speaker's matter-of-fact tone changes to an outcry, an exclamation. Other students may say that a second speaker is introduced in the fourth stanza.

4. Some may say the questions are hard because they have no easy answers, while others may argue that the answers exist but are very complex. Still other students may point out that the questions are hard because human beings need farm land, homes, and commercial properties as well as wilderness. Still others may say that there is a need to take a hard look now before the wilderness and many species of life on earth disappear.

5. Some students may say the line means that people need undeveloped land in which to wander; others may feel that people need freedom and an untouched natural setting to be happy.

6. Some students may say that both poems discuss the advantages and disadvantages of developing wilderness land; others may feel that both poets are in favor of leaving some portion of the land undeveloped.

Writing Options

The Writing Options are designed to meet varied student interests and abilities. Have each student choose one writing activity to complete. You may wish to guide some students to an option that requires less writing.

Journal Update Have students review their journal entries for these two poems. What new reflections about the environment can be added to their writing?

Responding to Reading

First Impressions of "Hard Questions"

1. Which of the questions in this poem do you find most thought-provoking? Why?

Second Thoughts on "Hard Questions"

2. What kind of development might the speaker be describing in the beginning of the poem?
3. Where and how does the speaker's tone change in this poem?
4. Why are the questions in the poem hard questions?
5. The poem asks, "Does not the heart need wildness?" What does this mean and how would you respond to the question? Explain.

Comparing the Poems

6. How similar are the themes of these poems?

   Think about
   - what subjects the poems deal with
   - what the speakers have said about these subjects

Literary Concept: Rhetorical Question

A **rhetorical question** is a question asked only for effect, often to emphasize a point. An answer is usually not expected. Which questions in Margaret Tsuda's poem seem to be rhetorical questions?

Writing Options

1. Review your comparison of the poems' themes. Create three or four environmental slogans that the speakers of both poems might support.
2. Think again about the practical and aesthetic values of trees. Based on these ideas, create a short poem about trees.
3. Assume you are a land developer or lumberjack. Write a letter to the speaker of "Hard Questions." Explain why it is necessary to cut down some forests.

Literary Concept—Rhetorical Question

These questions in Margaret Tsuda's poem seem to be rhetorical questions: *"Why not mark out the land/into neat rectangles/squares and clover leafs?" "What if a child shall cry/'I have never known spring! I have never seen autumn!'" "What if a man shall say/'I have never heard/silence fraught with living as/in swamp or forest!'" "What if the eye shall never see/marsh birds and muskrats?" "Does not the heart need/wildness?/" "Does not the thought need/something/to rest upon/not self-made by man,/a bosom/not his own?"*

Humorous Essay

A Couple of Really Neat Guys

DAVE BARRY

Examine What You Know (Prior Knowledge)

You are about to read a humorous newspaper article about the serious problem of littering. In small groups, discuss the questions below.

- What words do you associate with littering?
- Is littering wrong? Why or why not?
- When, if ever, do you litter?
- What should be done to solve the litter problem?

Expand Your Knowledge (Building Background)

Littering is a worldwide problem, the size and seriousness of which is not adequately conveyed by the term *litterbug.* Along the highways and roadsides in America, 20 million cubic yards of litter is collected each year. In the cities of many countries, the problem may be even worse. A government commission in London, England, for example, called that city "dirty, degrading and depressing." The commission went on to suggest 120 ways to clean up London, including bigger litter bins and special garbage crews. Litter, and the pollution it brings, has also become a major problem in the world's oceans. Environmentalists estimate that one pound of litter per person is dumped overboard on a typical boating day trip. In 1988, a two-month cleanup along America's ocean beaches gathered up 904 tons of litter. This included plastics, glass, bottles, styrofoam, metals, paper, wood, and clothing. Spread out ankle high, this would cover ninety city blocks. Piled up, it would fill 9½ average-size houses.

Write Before You Read (Journal Writing)

Think about the worst litterer you have ever encountered. In your journal compose a letter you might write to this litterbug.

■ *A biography of the author can be found in the Reader's Handbook.*

Objectives

- To understand and appreciate a humorous newspaper article
- To express understanding of the work through a choice of writing forms, including a news account, a fantasy, and a serious essay

Prereading/Motivation

Examine What You Know

Discussion Prompts: What types of litter are found most frequently in your neighborhood? What places do you think are most seriously affected by litter? Explain your answer. What steps do you think people like yourself can take to combat littering?

Expand Your Knowledge

Discussion Prompts: Why might the problem of littering be worse in cities than in rural areas? Do you think the suggestions of the London commission would make a significant improvement in the litter problem? Why or why not? Do you think that littering has become a more serious problem in recent years? Explain your answer.

Thematic Link—Saving the Environment
In this essay, columnist Dave Barry uses humor to explain how he has tried to save the environment.

Additional Journal Writing

In "A Couple of Really Neat Guys," Dave Barry humorously discusses the problem of littering. Suggest these journal topics to students:

- How do you think "A Couple of Really Neat Guys" would act? How would they look?
- How can the title "A Couple of Really Neat Guys" have two different meanings?

For other journal opportunities, refer students to Examine What You Know (p. 619) and annotation G.

Additional Resources

UNIT FIVE RESOURCE BOOK
Reader's Guidesheet, p. 11
Vocabulary Worksheet, p. 12
Selection and Vocabulary Check Test, p. 13
Selection Test, pp. 14–15

Collaborative Learning

Opportunities for collaborative learning appear throughout the lesson and include Examine What You Know (p. 619) and Closure.

Teaching Strategies

Support for Students of Limited English Proficiency

- Use **Reader's Guidesheet** p. 11.
- Students may not understand the term *litter.* Explain this term and then have students share the word in their native language that means the same.
- "A Couple of Really Neat Guys" also contains some vocabulary words that students may not have encountered previously. Encourage students to use context clues to figure out their meanings.
- Annotations D and H focus on difficult vocabulary.

Text Annotations

A. Literary Element: Essay Ask students to decide, based on the opening, whether this is a formal or informal essay. *(It is an informal essay because it is personal and light-hearted in tone.)*

B. Critical Thinking: Analyzing Have students analyze how Barry creates humor in this passage. *(Possible response: He creates humor through exaggeration, as in "nuclear-powered radio and enough food to supply several Canadian provinces." He also juxtaposes unlikely images, as when he joins "Picnic" to "People from Hell."*

C. Teaching Tip In this essay, Barry uses many techniques that we tell our students to avoid: misused capitals, slang, and exaggeration. Trace with students examples of these techniques and then explain how Barry uses them with great skill to create specific stylistic effects. Explain that in less skilled hands, Barry's techniques might be ineffective.

D. LEP: Vocabulary Guide students to figure out the meaning of *avenger* from its context in the sentence. See also if they can think of other words that sound the same, such as *vengeance.*

A Couple of Really Neat Guys

DAVE BARRY

A If you were to ask me how I came to be running after litterbugs in downtown Miami while wearing bright-red women's tights, I would have to say that the turning point was a visit to my optometrist.[1]

My optometrist is named Dr. Jeffrey Jeruss, and although he looks like a normal human being, only slightly larger, it turns out that when it comes to littering he is—and I mean this as a compliment—insane. So am I. I HATE littering. I hate it when you go to a park or the beach and the day is suddenly destroyed by the arrival of: The Picnic People from Hell. You know these people. B They have a large nuclear-powered radio and enough food to supply several Canadian provinces, and they immediately transform themselves into a high-output litter machine, cranking out potato-chip bags and beer cans and sandwich wrappers and chicken bones and dirty diapers weighing more than the infant that generated them. SR-1 ▶

And when it's time to leave, these people simply . . . leave. They pick nothing up. They just WALK AWAY from what looks like the scene of a tragic dumpster[2] explosion. And on the way home they flick their cigarette butts out of the car window. Of course! You wouldn't want to mess up a sharp-looking ashtray interior, not when the entire planet is available! Ha ha! Good thinking, you SLIME-EXCRETING MORONS. WHY DON'T YOU TAKE YOUR CIGARETTE BUTTS AND— C

Forgive me. I get carried away. But I never did anything about it except mutter and seethe[3] until my fateful visit to Dr. Jeruss for an eye exam. He was shining his little light into my eyeballs and making that "hmmmmm" noise that doctors are trained to make, when I happened to mention littering. Suddenly Jeffrey started stomping around the examination room, neck muscles bulging, denouncing the beer-can tossers of the world and waving his eyeball light around like the Hammer of Thor.[4] Watching him, I realized I had finally found the perfect sidekick for: Captain Tidy. ◀SR-2

Captain Tidy is a concept I have fantasized about for many years. He is a masked avenger for the forces of neatness. D When a person litters, Captain Tidy comes

1. **optometrist:** a specialist who examines eyes and prescribes glasses or contact lenses but who cannot prescribe drugs or perform surgery.

2. **dumpster:** a large, metal garbage container which is transferred by truck to a garbage dump.

3. **seethe** (sēth): to be on the verge of an angry outburst.

4. **Hammer of Thor:** weapon used by the Norse god of thunder.

Structured Reading for Less Proficient Students

These questions can help to guide students through the reading. Ask each question at the point of the selection where the SR number appears in the margin.

SR–1. Describe the speaker's attitude toward litter. *(He hates it.)* **Literal recall**

SR–2. What is Dr. Jeffrey Jeruss's feelings about litter? *(He also hates it.)* **Clarifying**

SR–3. What do the speaker and Dr. Jeruss do in an attempt to combat litter? *(They dress up as superheroes, rent a car, and drive around Miami trying to convince people not to litter.)* **Summarizing**

SR–4. What effect do their actions have? *(Their actions have little effect on the litter bugs, but Jeff Jeruss and Dave Barry feel better.)* **Clarifying**

swooping out of nowhere and explains to the litterer, in polite terms, that he or she is being a jerk. What kept me from acting out this fantasy was the fear of being embarrassed, by which I mean having my nose punched into my brain. But I knew that if Captain Tidy had a SIDEKICK, a LARGE sidekick, a large TRAINED OPTOMETRIST sidekick, that would be a whole different story.

And thus Jeff and I became: Captain Tidy and Neatness Man. We assembled costumes consisting of the aforementioned red tights (size triple-extra large), plus red Superman-style boots, plus blue shorts and shirts with our superhero names professionally lettered on them, plus white gloves, plus capes made from garbage bags, plus utility belts from which were suspended feather dusters, dustpans and rubber gloves.

Also, of course, we wore hoods and masks to preserve our Secret Identities. If you had seen us wearing our outfits and standing in our official superhero stance—hands on hips, chests thrust out, garbage bags blowing out dramatically behind—your only possible reaction would have been to say, with genuine emotion in your voice, "What a pair of dorks."

But we didn't care. We were on a mission. We rented a black Tidymobile with very dark windows, and we spent a day cruising the streets. When we saw people litter, we'd leap out, rush up to the perpetrators,[5] pick up their litter, hand it back to them and say, with deep but polite superhero voices, "Sir, you don't want to litter, DO YOU?" Inevitably, they'd look ashamed, take their litter back and dispose of it properly. One possible explanation for this, of course, is that they thought we were dangerous escaped perverted tights-wearing lunatics. But I like to think that they were genuinely impressed

Reprinted by permission, Tribune Media Services, Orlando, Florida.

with our message. At one point, a tough-looking street crowd actually APPLAUDED us for making a man pick up his cigarette butt. And remember, this was in MIAMI, a city where armed robbery is only a misdemeanor.

By the end of the day, thanks to our efforts, Miami had been transformed from a city with crud all over the streets into a city with crud all over the streets. But at least SOME litterers had been chastised,[6] and Jeff and I felt a LOT better. I strongly recommend that you consider becoming a litter avenger in your particular city or town or random suburban area. What's the worst that could happen to you? OK, death. But probably you'd do fine. Just remember to be polite. "Speak softly and carry a large sidekick"—that's Rule Two of the Captain Tidy Code. Rule One, of course, is: "Always visit the bathroom BEFORE you put on your tights." ❧

5. **perpetrators:** people committing offensive acts.
6. **chastised:** condemned sharply.

Text Annotations

E. Reading Skill: PREDICTING Ask students whether they think that Captain Tidy and his sidekick will be effective in combatting litter. *(Possible responses: Students who see Barry as simply trying to bring attention to the problem of littering might argue that he cannot help but be successful. Those who take Barry literally might argue that he and his sidekick will fail, for few people find middle-aged men in superhero costumes threatening.)*

F. Reading Skill: VISUALIZING Ask students to isolate the details that help them visualize Captain Tidy and Neatness Man. *(Possible responses: "red Superman-style boots," "blue shorts and shirts," "capes made from garbage bags")*

G. Literary Element: AUTHOR'S PURPOSE Have students explain, based on the actions of Captain Tidy and Neatness Man in this passage, what the author's purpose is. *(His main purpose is to persuade people to stop littering, but he is also interested in entertaining us.)*

H. LEP: Vocabulary Explain to students that a *misdemeanor* is a relatively minor criminal offense.

I. Literary Element: AUTHOR'S PURPOSE Ask students to isolate the line where Barry directly states his purpose. *("I strongly recommend that you consider becoming a litter avenger in your particular city or town or random suburban area.")*

Check Test

1. Who is Dr. Jeffrey Jeruss? *(Dave Barry's optometrist)*
2. Who are Captain Tidy and Neatness Man? *(Jeff and Dave)*
3. What are Captain Tidy's and Neatness Man's functions? *(to stop people from littering)*
4. What does Barry ask his readers to become? *(litter avengers)*

Encouraging Independent Reading

Slumgullion Stew: An Edward Abbey Reader, nonfiction by Edward Abbey
Dave Barry's Greatest Hits, humorous essays by Dave Barry
"Fresh Air Will Kill You" in *Have I Ever Lied to You?,* humorous essays by Art Buchwald

PROFESSIONAL NOTEBOOK

There is a tension between academic achievement and social acceptance that educators must take seriously. For teenagers, the high school is not simply a place where they learn but a place where they live. *As educators, we can no longer afford to argue that our responsibilities begin and end with classroom instruction. We also need to help high school students structure a social system in which "living" and learning are compatible activities, one in which excelling academically does not mark a student for social isolation.*

B. Bradford Brown and Laurence Steinberg, from *National Center on Effective Secondary Schools Newsletter* (reprinted in *The Education Digest,* March 1990)

Student Response

Responding to Reading

These questions are open-ended with no "right" or "wrong" answers. However, responses must be supported with information from the selection. Possible answers follow:

1. Almost any reaction to Captain Tidy and Neatness Man, whether negative or positive, is valid.

2. Some students may say that Barry did convince them; others may say that reading the essay did not change their opinions on littering.

3. Students might note that the very idea of two grown men dressing up and chasing litterbugs is humorous. Some students may also cite his use of exaggeration, as in the picnic scene. Others may explain how he uses capital letters and slang to create humor, as in "MORONIC SLIME-EXCRETING PUKE-HEADS."

4. Students who feel humor can change people's opinions might argue that the essay would be very effective; others, citing social indifference, might claim that the essay would have little effect.

5. Some students may feel that the concept is wild and would have little effect; others might argue that it could be an effective public relations idea.

6. Some students might suggest the names of those who clean up litter be printed in the newspaper or that litter bugs be made to spend many hours cleaning up litter in parks and along streams and highways.

Writing Options

The Writing Options are designed to meet varied student interests and abilities. Have each student choose one writing activity to complete. You may wish to guide some students to an option that requires less writing.

Journal Update Have students review their journal entries for "A Couple of Really Neat Guys." Can they add some new thoughts to their letters or descriptions?

Closure

Students might wish to form litter avenger teams. First, have them brainstorm effective ideas for discouraging littering and for cleaning up litter. Some may wish to campaign against littering.

Responding to Reading

First Impressions

1. What do you think of Captain Tidy and Neatness Man? Explain.

Second Thoughts

2. Take a look at what you wrote earlier about littering. Compare your ideas with Dave Barry's. Has he changed your mind at all? Explain.
3. How does Barry use humor to make his points? Give examples.
4. Could this article change people's minds about littering?

   Think about
   - whether or not humor is effective in changing attitudes
   - how people you know might be affected
5. What if Captain Tidy and Neatness Man were real people instead of Barry's fantasy? Could such a team have a positive impact on the littering problem, or is this concept strictly a wild idea?

Broader Connections

6. Give some original suggestions on how to enforce existing laws against littering. Can you, for example, think of either incentives to make people *want* to clean up or some punishments that "fit the crime" of littering?

Writing Options

1. Write a straightforward news account of a confrontation that might occur between the Neat Guys and "The Picnic People from Hell," whose litter "looks like the scene of a tragic dumpster explosion."
2. Write an original fantasy about how to get people to stop littering. Make yourself the hero. Give yourself any powers necessary to solve the problem. Perhaps, like Barry, you will want to model yourself around an existing superhero.
3. Write a serious essay about the problem of littering. In the first paragraph, describe a variety of littering that is particularly offensive to you and give your reasons for writing about it. In the paragraphs that follow, explain more fully why this problem is serious and how it might be solved.

e x p l o r e

Article

David Meets Goliath at City Hall

ANDREW HOLLEMAN

Examine What You Know (Prior Knowledge)

The high school student who wrote the following magazine article tells about a cause he defended. What is something that you believe in strongly enough to defend? What would have to happen before you took a stand? What action would you take? Share your ideas with your classmates in a brief discussion.

Expand Your Knowledge (Building Background)

The subject of the following article is an endangered wetland. As the name suggests, wetlands—also called swamps or marshes—are areas of land where the water level is near or above the land surface. Some of the best known wetlands are the Florida Everglades, the Okefenokee Swamp, and the Louisiana bayous. For a long time people treated wetlands as needless nuisances and drained them to make room for farmland, highways, and urban development. As a consequence, 35 percent of the wetlands in this country had been destroyed by the 1970's. Wetlands, however, perform invaluable functions as wildlife preserves and water purification systems. Marshes and swamps filter water that drains off farmland. This process removes excess fertilizers and pesticides before these chemicals reach reservoirs. Because wetlands store water and only gradually release it, they also reduce flooding in the areas in which they are located. Realizing the environmental importance of wetlands, the federal government has begun to pass laws to protect these areas.

Enrich Your Reading (Reading Skill)

Outlining Outlining can be a useful tool for reading and understanding nonfiction. When you make such an outline, look for topic sentences that state the writer's main ideas. Following the topic sentences should be supporting details. As you read this essay, make an outline of the writer's main ideas and supporting details.

■ *A biography of the author can be found on page 629.*

Objectives

- To understand a magazine article
- To identify an allusion
- To practice outlining
- To express understanding of the work through a choice of writing options, including a prophecy and dialogue

Prereading/Motivation

Examine What You Know

Discussion Prompts: Why is this cause especially important to you? Which of your actions do you think would be most effective, and why?

Expand Your Knowledge

Discussion Prompts: Do you think people who exploit the wetlands are fully aware of the area's importance?

Additional Background: The Everglades cover a total area of 2,746 square miles in southern Florida. The Okefenokee Swamp is small in comparison, covering 631 square miles mainly in southeastern Georgia, with a slight overlap into Florida. The swamp drains mostly to the southwest into the Gulf of Mexico.

Enrich Your Reading

You may wish to point out the following main ideas and having students find the supporting details.

- Holleman receives a registered letter concerning the development of a wetland area near his home and expresses his anger over this.
- Holleman initiates a campaign to save the wetland area.
- Holleman presents his views at a public meeting.
- Holleman steps up his fight by broadening his campaign.
- Through a state test, the land is declared unsuitable for building.
- Holleman asks for citizen involvement in saving the environment.

Thematic Link—Saving the Environment

In this article, Andrew Holleman describes how he saved an endangered natural area from development.

Journal Writing

In "David Meets Goliath at City Hall," Andrew Holleman describes how he saved an area of wetlands from commercial development. Suggest these journal topics to students:

- What does the title "David Meets Goliath at City Hall" make you think about?
- Describe a time when the "little guy," or underdog, defeated someone more powerful.

For other journal opportunities, refer students to Examine What You Know (p. 623) and Broader Connections (p. 628).

Additional Resources

UNIT FIVE RESOURCE BOOK

Reader's Guidesheet, p. 16
Vocabulary Worksheet, p. 17
Selection Check Test, p. 18
Selection Test, pp. 19–20

Collaborative Learning

Opportunities for collaborative learning appear throughout the lesson and include Options for Learning activities, and 2 (p. 629), Cross-Curricular Options (p. T–629), and annotation D.

Teaching Strategies

Support for Students of Limited English Proficiency

- Use Reader's Guidesheet, p. 16.
- Students from other countries may want to share environmental concerns that exist in their former homelands. Provide them with opportunities to share this information with the class. You might also bring in pictures of the Everglades, Louisiana bayous, Okefenokee Swamp, or other wetlands for students to study.
- "David Meets Goliath at City Hall" contains humor and references to commerce and government that may be unfamiliar to students.
- Annotations C, E, G, I, and K focus on unfamiliar references.

Text Annotations

A. Literary Element: ALLUSION Ask students to explain a possible meaning of the title. *(Possible response: An underdog, like David, overcomes someone more powerful, like the Philistine giant Goliath, through local politics.)*

B. Literary Element: DIALOGUE Ask students to provide some reasons why Holleman begins his essay with dialogue. *(Possible responses: It captures the reader's interest; it helps plunge the reader into the narrative.)*

C. LEP: Reference Explain to students that a *condominium* is an apartment house in which each apartment is individually owned. In most cases, owners can sell or rent their apartments without the approval of the other owners.

D. Teaching Tip

Have teams of students research each of the species mentioned in this passage and share their findings with the class in an oral report. Students may want to illustrate their reports with pictures, slides, or posters.

E. LEP: Humor Ask volunteers to define a *fish story*. *(A fish story is a tall tale, an exaggeration.)*

A

David Meets Goliath at City Hall

ANDREW HOLLEMAN

B

"Mom, I've got to go to the library. Can you drive me?" That was the first thing I said after I read a registered letter that my parents got. It concerned the development of land near my home and stated that a meeting about it would be held at the town hall.

It made me mad. "How could this be happening?" I asked myself. I knew these woods—I had loved, studied, explored them; I practically grew up there. Now an $11 million, 180-unit condominium complex was going to be built on one privately owned parcel (sandwiched between two pieces of preserved conservation land). That parcel was almost half wetlands. It contained wood turtles, blue-spotted salamanders (both declining species rated "of special concern" by wildlife authorities), great blue herons, various hawks, lady's-slippers, and mountain laurel.

C

D

I was angry because this beautiful piece of land and wildlife habitat was about to be destroyed. Weren't people aware of their environment after being informed every day from so many sources that our world is at stake?

I also had so many memories based in that area. When I was very young, I took nature walks there with my family and even remember having a winter picnic in the snow by a stream with them. Later, when I was older, I went there with my friend on our own nature walks or to go ice-skating on a pond in the woods.

Now I go there to sit and think for hours on end. There are times I just sit and watch the deer, fox, and other animals. I go fishing sometimes in the ice-skating pond and have caught a twelve-inch bass (this is not a fish story). E

I guess I was just plain angry that "my land" was going to be destroyed and that it was one more insult to the environment. I had to do something. ◀SR-1

At the library, I looked up the Hatch Act, the Massachusetts law that protects wetlands. I also read the town Master Plan. It listed the acreage of the site and noted which parts were wetland, poor soil, or developable. There I found the ammunition I needed: Only 2.2 acres of the 16.3-acre site were considered sound enough to be developed.

After leaving the library, I wrote a petition and took it to neighbors to get signatures from registered voters and to tell people about the developer's meeting and the harm that this complex could do to our woods. ◀SR-2

Much to my surprise, most people

Structured Reading for Less Proficient Students

These questions can help to guide students through the reading. Ask each question at the point of the selection where the SR number appears in the margin.

SR–1. Why is Holleman angry about the planned condominium? *(Beautiful land and a wildlife habitat will be destroyed; he enjoys the land personally.)* **Summarizing**

SR–2. How does Holleman begin his campaign to save the wetland? *(He researches the law and writes and circulates a petition.)* **Clarifying**

SR–3. What kind of support does Holleman get at the town meeting? *(more than 250 attend)* **Literal recall**

SR–4. What does Holleman tell the town meeting audience in his speech? *(that this development would destroy the animals and plants; that the stream would become polluted and taint town wells; that another suitable site is available)* **Summarizing**

SR–5. What was the deep-hole test and what were its results? *(The test determines whether land will drain suitably for building. The land was found unsuitable.)* **Clarifying**

showed a lot of interest and were happy to sign. I collected about 150 signatures (only two adults said no) and also started a petition for students to sign.

It wasn't always easy going from door to door. One day, while crossing my beloved wetlands to reach another part of the neighborhood, I slipped on a rotted log and sent myself and the petition flying into a small, muddy stream. It took a while for the petition to dry and for my mother to iron out the papers. That was the last time I went through the swamp with anything important that wasn't waterproofed.

When the night came for the meeting, my parents and I were directed to a room that could hold about 50 people (the developer had sent his original notification to the 50 F families whose homes abutted the property). Within twenty minutes we were moved to a larger room in the town hall because it was obvious that many more people would show up. Finally, it became apparent that we needed a larger room still.

A half hour later, more than 250 people had gathered in the hall's basement gymnasium, ready to hear about the proposed project and its impact on our community. A number of times during the meeting, the developer took credit for inviting the people there to hear about his proposal. The crowd, just as often, reminded him that I was the one who had actually invited most
SR-3 ▶ of them.

After the developer discussed his project plans, I made my speech. You can't have stage fright at a moment like this—you have to just get up and tell your side of the story. Holding the shell of a wood turtle I'd found in the woods, I spoke about how this development would destroy the animal and plant life. I told how the stream on the land would eventually become polluted and carry its pollution into nearby town wells. I also suggested another site the developer might use, one that would better withstand the environmental impact. (Interestingly enough, the developer has already started constructing a condominium on the alternative site that I had originally suggested. It was the old drive-in movie lot here in town.) ◀ SR-4

After that night, I wrote letters to many state representatives and senators and also to a local TV anchorwoman, hoping to gain more support. I included my petition in the letters. I then telephoned the Massachusetts Audubon Society "Helpline" and spoke with Dr. Dorothy Arvidson, a biologist and now a good friend. G

She told me to keep my fight local, that I should approach the town representatives because national and state organizations wouldn't be much help. She was telling me other things to do when I interrupted to say I was only twelve years old. "Well, that's no excuse," she said, and went on giving me information. H

From that point on, meetings were held every week for seven months so the developer could present his proposal to conservation commissions, appeal boards, and selectmen—just to name a few. These meetings often took place on school nights and sometimes lasted up to three and a half hours. Somehow I managed to attend every one and still get good grades. I

Later we formed a neighborhood association to keep people up-to-date and to raise money for a lawyer and an environmental scientist. My dad and I became members of the Concord Road Neighborhood Association. The public supported us, donating nearly $16,000 to stop the condominium project.

I was told that "you can't fight city hall" and that the developer was a "townie" who

F. Reading Skill: INFERRING Have students infer why so many people turned out for the community meeting. *(Possible response: The overwhelming turnout suggests that people feel strongly about one side or the other of the debate, that people are curious about the controversy, and that Holleman was successful in raising support for his side.)*

G. LEP: Reference Explain to students that the Audubon Society is a national conservation organization devoted to "promoting the conservation of wildlife and the natural environment and educating man regarding his relationship with, and his place within, the natural environment as an ecological system." For further information, see the Data Bank feature on the bottom of p. T-626.

H. Critical Thinking: ANALYZING Have students analyze Holleman's character in light of this new information about his age. *(Possible response: On learning that Holleman is only twelve, some students may say that he is even more mature, knowledgeable, and responsible than they thought before. Others may cite his intelligence and determination.)*

I. LEP: Reference Explain to students that selectmen are members of a board of town officials chosen to manage certain public affairs.

Art Note

Carl Schwartz (1935–   ), educated at the School of the Art Institute, Chicago, is inspired by the patterns of light found among plants and in water. This painting of a wilderness area beautifully demonstrates the effect of sunlight on the tangled tree trunks and low-lying plants, and its absence in the deep darkness of the foreground. *What reasons would you give for preserving wetlands like this from development?*

J. Reading Skill: UNDERSTANDING MAIN IDEA Ask students to use Holleman's comments in this passage to state the main idea of the article. *(Possible response: Stand up for your beliefs, because even if you don't win, you will know that you have tried.)*

WET WOODLAND (detail) Carl Schwartz By permission of the artist.

always got his way. But my feeling is you shouldn't get discouraged if you hear statements like that. If you believe in something, you have to stand up for it. Don't ever give J up the fight against a poorly sited development, pollution, or anything environmentally dangerous. If you do, you are giving up on the world. Even if you don't win, at least you will have tried.

After nine months and much hard work, the developer, the neighborhood association, the state Department of Environmental Quality Engineering, and others showed up to give the site a deep-hole test to find out if it was suitable for building. The test checks the soil's drainage by seeing if a deeply dug hole will fill with water. I was fairly confident that the site would fail, be-

Data Bank

Named for the American naturalist John James Audubon, the first Audubon Society was founded in 1886. Audubon societies were soon formed in many areas of the country, and in 1905 they were consolidated into a national organization headquartered in New York City. The Society has many functions. Among the most well known is a sanctuary program that provides protection for fifty different areas of land and water. It also offers nature centers, summer workshops, and educational publications. Publications include *Audubon* magazine, which deals with conservation and wildlife; *American Birds,* a journal about North American birds; and a newsletter on conservation legislation and related matters. The society also underwrites field research and provides expert advice and testimony on behalf of conservation legislation.

cause I had known that land a long time. But I can tell you that when the test confirmed my beliefs, I was excited and relieved. (Even if the site had passed the test, I

SR-5 ▶ would have kept fighting anyway.)

The town of Chelmsford then officially "denied comprehensive permit," a legal step that ensured the development would not be built and that nothing of the same magnitude could ever be constructed there. So the land is safe—for the time being. I'm

K now trying to get funding from the state to buy the site outright to protect it.

To all of the people who read this article, I challenge you to come to the defense of the environment. It is not just the destruction of the rain forests, the acid rain,[1] and the ozone layer[2] that should concern us, but also our own communities. We can work to stop building developments that are hazardous to life and land. We can recycle plastics, glass, and paper. We can save water and use far less energy than we do.

It is not all that hard to help in the fight to save our planet, Earth. If we are all a little more caring and careful, we will be much closer to saving our environment for ourselves and for future generations. ❧

1. **acid rain:** rain that has a high concentration of acids as a result of the burning of fuels such as gasoline and oil. Acid rain has a destructive effect on plant and animal life and even on buildings.

2. **ozone layer:** a layer of the atmosphere in which there is a concentration of ozone, which absorbs much ultraviolet radiation and prevents some heat loss from the earth.

I N S I G H T

Birdfoot's Grampa

JOSEPH BRUCHAC

The old man
must have stopped our car
two dozen times to climb out
and gather into his hands
the small toads blinded
by our lights and leaping,
live drops of rain.

The rain was falling,
a mist about his white hair
and I kept saying
you can't save them all,
accept it, get back in
we've got places to go.

But, leathery hands full
of wet brown life,
knee deep in the summer
roadside grass,
he just smiled and said
they have places to go to
too.

K. LEP: Reference Make sure that students understand that by buying the site "outright" Holleman means that he is trying to purchase the land so that he can preserve it.

Check Test

1. What does the builder want to put on the wetland? *(a condominium)*

2. Give two reasons why Holleman is upset about the proposed destruction of the wetland. *(because the wildlife habitat will be destroyed; because of his personal enjoyment of the area)*

3. How does Holleman get other people involved in fighting plans for the development? *(by going door to door to inform them of the problem and of the meeting and to get signatures on a petition)*

4. What test did the development site fail to pass? *(the deep-hole test)*

Encouraging Independent Reading

Silent Spring, nonfiction by Rachel Carson
A Bill of Rights for Future Generations, nonfiction by Jacques-Yves Cousteau
Fifty Simple Things You Can Do To Save the Earth, nonfiction by the Earth Works Group
Gorillas in the Mist, nonfiction by Dian Fossey
Save the Earth! nonfiction by Betty Miles
Never Cry Wolf, nonfiction by Farley Mowat

Insight

This piece reflects on the ideas in the main selection and is suggested for students' independent reading. Optional discussion questions follow.

1. Why does the old man get out of the car to gather the toads? *(Possible responses: so they don't run over them with the car; because he values all living things)*

2. How do you feel about the old man's efforts to gather the toads? *(Possible responses: Some students may support his efforts as humane, while others might reject them as futile.)*

3. What parallels can you draw between Andrew Holleman and the old man in "Birdfoot's Grampa"? *(Possible responses: They both respect the environment and the life it supports and want to protect it; neither gives up because someone else says the effort is useless.)*

Student Response

Responding to Reading

These questions are open-ended with no "right" or "wrong" answers. However, responses must be supported with information from the selection. Possible answers follow:

1. Any impression based on the selection is valid.

2. Some may think that Andrew is successful because he is determined and because he cares so much; others may see his success as a result of his effectiveness as a speaker or the support of adults.

3. Some may say that Andrew shows how the water would become polluted; others may feel that he proves that the animals and plants found in the wetlands would be destroyed. Others may note that Andrew's feelings are personal and subjective and that others may not agree.

4. Some may say Andrew would succeed because their communities face similar problems and because he is so committed and determined and articulate; others may say that he would not succeed because their community leaders would not be receptive to a young person's suggestions.

5. Students may feel that Grampa would support Andrew's efforts, as they are similar to his own; others might feel that Grampa would not be interested in battling authority as Andrew does. Students may say that the poem's speaker does not have Grampa's patience or determination; is concerned about his or her own goals, rather than sharing Grampa's concern about the toads; and may not share Grampa's belief in the worthwhileness of one individual's efforts.

6. Students might say that they can help save endangered birds or trees or help protect lakes or streams from pollution. They may suggest taking actions similar to Andrew's.

Writing Options

The Writing Options are designed to meet varied student interests and abilities. Have each student choose one writing activity to complete. You may wish to guide some students to an option that requires less writing.

Journal Update Have students review their journal entries. What new reflections can they add to their writing?

Responding to Reading

First Impressions

1. What is your impression of Andrew?

Second Thoughts

2. Why is it possible for Andrew to be successful in preserving the wetland area near his home?

   Think about
   - what Andrew values
   - what special skills he possesses
   - who supports him in his fight

3. What actual evidence does Andrew provide that the building of the condominium would be an "insult to the environment"?

4. How successful might Andrew be solving a similar problem in your town?

   Think about
   - what problems he might face in your community
   - how your community leaders would react to a young person's suggestions

5. If you have not already done so, read the *Insight* poem entitled "Birdfoot's Grampa." How do you think Grampa would view Andrew's efforts? How does the poem's speaker differ from Grampa?

Broader Connections

6. As you look around your community, what animal, plant, or natural resource needs protection or cleanup? What actions might you take?

Literary Concept: Allusion

An **allusion** is a reference to a person, place, or event with which the reader is expected to be familiar. The title "Antaeus" is an allusion to a mythological character. To whom does the title of this selection allude?

Writing Options

1. What do you think Andrew Holleman will do as an adult? Write a prophecy describing what the writer will become when he is older.

2. Imagine that Andrew meets Neatness Man from "A Couple of Really Neat Guys" in the previous selection. Write the conversation the two might have on the question of saving the environment.

Literary Concept—Allusion

The title alludes to the biblical story of David defeating the giant Goliath. "David" refers to Andrew Holleman, the underdog who triumphs at the end. "Goliath" refers to the developer, the one who seemingly has the upper hand but is defeated at the end.

e x t e n d

Options for Learning

1 • Land Debate Stage a debate among classmates in the roles of Andrew and several other people, all of whom have definite views on the preservation of wetlands. Include people such as the condominium developer, a contractor who builds hospitals, a highway engineer, and a state park ranger.

2 • Save the Earth Select an environmental concern about which you know relatively little, such as acid rain, the destruction of the rain forests or ozone layer, or overpopulation. Make a list of questions that you would like to have answered. Then research your topic and build a display that informs the public about this issue.

3 • Speak Up Write the speech Andrew might have made at the town meeting. Look back at the article to see what points he covered. Then deliver your speech to your classmates.

4 • Film Outline A storyboard is a series of sketches that show the major scenes of a television show or movie. Using the main points from the outline you made of this article, draw a storyboard to illustrate Andrew's successful battle.

FACT FINDER

How many square feet are in an acre? How does an acre compare to a football field?

Andrew Holleman

1974–

Andrew Holleman developed his love of nature from his parents and from his reading. At twelve years old he first began his crusade to save the wooded wetland near his home in Chelmsford, Massachusetts. Though the land is presently safe from development, Holleman is still struggling to find the money with which to buy it. Pleas to state agencies and officials have been unsuccessful due to budget restraints.

Holleman has continued his environmental work by speaking to groups of school children and concerned citizens. He has also addressed the board members of the Peabody Museum in Salem, Massachusetts, regarding a tract of land they were attempting to save from development. After high school Holleman is considering a career in environmental law. He has learned that one person can make a difference, that "we may not be able to single-handedly save the rain forests or find the solution to the acid rain problem, but we can contribute to the protection of our world by recycling, conserving energy, and helping others become aware of the need to protect our heritage."

Options for Learning

These activities suit a variety of learning styles and modes of expression. Allow students to review the options and then choose the one they wish to do. Many are excellent collaborative learning projects.

1. Land Debate Suggest that students role-play their positions before they begin the actual debate.

2. Save the Earth Students might create a cluster diagram or word web to generate questions.

3. Speak Up Before they write, have students refer back to the selection and their outline for ideas.

4. Film Plan Have students draw their sketches in pencil so that they can adjust for space.

Fact Finder

An acre contains 43,560 square feet. A football field measures 160 feet by 360 feet (including the end zone), for a total of 57,600 square feet. The size of an acre and football field can be found in most reliable dictionaries.

Additional Information About the Author

Andrew Holleman Andrew Holleman later won an Environmental Protection Agency Regional Merit Award for his work in saving the wetland area. He is the youngest person ever to receive this award.

Closure

"David Meets Goliath at City Hall" explores saving the environment. Have students isolate headlines from daily newspapers that illustrate efforts similar to Holleman's in their communities.

Cross-Curricular Options

History: Students might like to research the history of the conservation movement in the United States. Have them include a discussion of important organizations, legislation, and leaders.

Math: Have students research the cost of the average condominium in their area. Then tell them to calculate, using the 16.3 acres available, how many units the builder could produce and what he would charge for each.

Geography: Suggest that students research the Florida Everglades, the Okefenokee Swamp, or the Louisiana bayous. Have them locate each area on a map, discuss its topography and important geographic features, and highlight relevant conservation measures.

Science: Have students select any one endangered species and prepare an oral report on it.

Publishing: Compile the contributions of all students. Display or make copies to distribute.

Writer's Workshop

Objectives

- To understand the goals of writing a proposal letter
- To analyze problems and discover solutions
- To draft, revise, edit, and publish a formal letter

Integrating . . .

Literature and Writing Tell students that the literature in this subunit deals with the environment. Have students relate events in the literature to their own lives. For example, in "Searching for Summer," the characters search for a glimmer of sunshine. Ask students how they would feel if the sun disappeared today. Ask if there are things in nature that they have heard of or read about that they will never be able to see. Discuss whether students have ever thought about taking an active role in cleaning up the environment.

Tell students that in this subunit, they will take an active stand. They will uncover a problem in their community and write a letter to the town council offering a solution.

Writing and Grammar Direct students to the Language Workshop on problems with modifiers. Explain the importance of mastering confusing modifiers. Stress that the town council will judge what they say as well as how they say it. Explain that writing their letters correctly will give them an edge. LEP students should pay special attention to these modifiers, because they will not have had contact with them in their languages.

Writing and Life Skills The Life Skills Workshop in this unit focuses on filling out applications. Explain that we are confronted with applications every day, and mastering them now will make life easier. Tell students that they may have to fill out applications or similar forms when they elicit information for their letters.

EXPOSITION: PROBLEM—SOLUTION

In conference rooms around the world, men and women huddle around tables trying to solve the world's troubles. Poverty, disease, war, crime, oppression, and pollution are just a few of the many critical issues tackled by these expert problem solvers. With the world's greatest minds at work, you would think someone, somewhere, would have discovered solutions by now. Unfortunately, there are no quick fixes to the world's crises. Solutions often call for money and resources that are not available, and some solutions create more problems than they solve.

Despite the difficulty and uncertainty of problem solving, human progress depends on it. Where would we be today if scientists hadn't found the cure for many diseases, or if machinery hadn't been invented to make our lives more safe, productive, and comfortable? Even people who aren't experts—for example, Dave Barry and Andrew Holleman in the preceding reading selections—have come up with ways to deal with some of the problems facing our society. For this assignment you, too, will have the opportunity to propose a solution to a real-life problem.

GUIDED ASSIGNMENT:
PROPOSAL TO TOWN COUNCIL

Choose a problem that exists in your community. Write a letter to your town council explaining how you think this problem can be solved.

Here is your PASSkey to this assignment.

PURPOSE: To propose a solution to a problem
AUDIENCE: Your town council
SUBJECT: A problem in your community
STRUCTURE: A formal letter

Prewriting

STEP 1 Choose a problem Think about the problems you've noticed in your community. If you are stuck for ideas, look through a local newspaper, ask parents or relatives for suggestions, or talk to local government officials or teachers. Review your ideas and choose a problem for which you feel you may have some solutions.

Additional Resources

UNIT FIVE RESOURCE BOOK
Writer's Workshop Copy Master, p. 21
Peer and Self-Evaluation Guidelines, p. 22
Writing Assessment Guidelines, p. 23

ENRICHMENT MATERIALS
Thinking Skills Transparency and Worksheet
Fine Art Transparency and Writing Prompts
Revision, Proofreading, and Elaboration
Writing Prompts for Assessment

STEP 2 Define the problem clearly To give boundaries to the problem you've chosen, state why it is a problem and who is affected by it. For example, a statement such as "Real estate development is a problem" isn't as useful as "New real estate developments are forcing many poor people out of their homes."

STEP 3 Discover the cause Before you can solve your problem, you need to know what caused it. If the cause isn't obvious, you'll need to do some research. Think about the people involved whom you might interview. Are there any local agencies affected that could provide information? Has anything already been written about this problem in a local paper or magazine that you could read? The student concerned about real estate development found these probable causes.

◀ STUDENT MODEL

- Real estate developers want to build new houses to make more money.
- People whose houses are being torn down have lived in them most of their lives and don't want to move.
- These same people have a very limited income and probably can't afford to move.
- The city officials say they feel sorry for these residents, but they need the tax money the new development will bring.
- The people who move into this new development will be resented.

After you have listed possible causes, weed out any items that don't account for how the problem came about. In the above example, the student eliminated the last statement because it shows an effect of the problem instead of a cause.

STEP 4 Brainstorm for solutions List as many solutions as you can. Solutions can often be found by eliminating one or more of the causes, by creating a compromise between two opposing forces, or by reducing the extent of the problem's effects. Don't criticize or eliminate any solution at this point.

STEP 5 Examine your solutions To decide on the best solution to your problem, predict the effects each solution might have. Then determine whether these effects are positive or negative. The solution with the least harmful effects is probably the best to propose. On the next page are some possible solutions to the real estate problem and their potential effects. The student marked each positive effect with a (+) and each negative effect with a (−).

Teaching Strategies

Introduction Have students turn to the **Writer's Workshop** for this subunit. Explain that for this exercise they should focus on a problem that affects a large number of people. (Noisy neighbors bothering one family would not be a good example.) Emphasize that even though many of today's problems affect the environment, students are not limited to this area in their writing. Encourage them to choose issues about which they feel strongly.

Call students' attention to the **Guided Assignment** box on page 630. Remind students that they will have to research and determine solutions to their problems. Point out the PASSkey graphic and stress the importance of keeping their audience in mind.

Prewriting Read each of the *Prewriting* steps with the students. Encourage them to choose their problems carefully. Have students begin by making a list of issues about which they feel strongly.

Remind students that finding the cause of their problem might not be easy. Encourage them to be patient and to take logical steps to uncover the information. You may need to help students plan their investigation and draw their conclusions.

Explain to students that the stronger their arguments, the more impact their letters will have. Have students brainstorm solutions with other students. Tell them to be as creative as they wish with their solutions. Remind them, however, that since these are real problems, they should attempt to find logical solutions. Encourage students to be objective as they examine each potential solution. Tell them to be realistic in their choices if they want the city council to take their letters seriously.

Computer Tip

Encourage students with access to a computer to use it during the *Prewriting* stage. Suggest they use the computer to organize their research, make lists, store information they collect, highlight solutions, and finally rework their lists of ideas. Stress that it is important to be comfortable as they work. For some students, using a computer will be ideal. For others, it will be easier to write out their ideas by hand.

Teaching Tip

Before students draft their letters, you may wish to discuss formal letter writing. Tell students that this process differs from writing friendly letters. Provide students with an example of a proper business letter.

Explain that a formal business letter has a different format and a different tone. To familiarize students with the concept of tone, you may wish to brainstorm and write on the board words that convey authority and seriousness. Explain that writers must always use correct English, never slang words that are unbusinesslike. Explain that if they wish to be taken seriously, they need to sound serious.

Drafting Some students may wish to organize their ideas in outline form before they begin to write. Tell students that this can be a good organizational device and may remind them to include all their important points in a sensible order. Some students may wish to begin with their strongest points. Others may feel that ending with their strongest points would provide more impact. Let students decide what works best for them. Remind students to pay close attention to language as they write. Stress accuracy and tone.

Revising and Editing Students may wish to revise their letters with a partner. Direct students to keep the *Revision Checklist* close at hand as they read the letters. Students may wish to write out the answers to the checklist. Tell students not to write "yes" or "no" answers, but to explain why they feel that their letters meet the criteria. These written responses will become a valuable tool as the students revise their letters.

Have students decide if the order of their paragraphs makes sense. Ask those students who put the strongest points last if the letter builds in intensity. Have them determine if it has a strong impact.

Have students edit their letters for spelling, grammar, and mechanics. Check that the correct business form was used. Have them check if they used confusing modifiers correctly.

STUDENT MODEL ▶

Possible Solutions	Potential Effects
1. Find other ways for the city to make money so it wouldn't need taxes from real estate developments. (eliminating a cause)	1. Developers would lose money (−); residents might have to pay higher taxes (−); residents wouldn't have to move (+).
2. Real estate developers could use vacant land in these neighborhoods to build on. (compromise)	2. Residents wouldn't have to move (+); developers would still make money (+); land used for parks or playgrounds would be taken (−).
3. The real estate company could pay residents more for their property. (reducing effects)	3. Residents could afford to move to nicer homes (+); they still would be forced out (−); cost to developers would be higher (−).

STEP 6 Choose the best solution Decide on the best solution and then plan how it should be carried out. Think about what must be done for the solution to work. In the real estate case, the student decided that solution 2 was the best because it had the least harmful effects to both parties.

Drafting

Using the information you've gathered, write a draft of your proposal letter. Start with the salutation "Dear Ladies and Gentlemen of the ______ Council." Define the problem as you did earlier. Then discuss the causes of the problem and propose your solution. Be sure to explain how you plan to make your solution work. Remember to begin a new paragraph for each new topic and use a formal tone, since this is a business letter.

Revising and Editing

Read your letter to a group of classmates who are posing as the town council. Ask them to evaluate your letter based on the following criteria. Use their comments to guide your revision.

Revision Checklist

1. Is the problem clearly defined?
2. Have all probable causes of the problem been identified?
3. Does the proposed solution make sense?
4. Has the plan for carrying out the solution been clearly explained?
5. Is the tone appropriate for a business letter?

Editing After you have listened to the comments of your classmates and made revisions, edit your letter for spelling, grammar, and mechanics. Be sure to use correct business letter form (see the **Writer's Handbook.**)

Publishing

Send your letter to your town council. You may also want to send a copy to the editor of your local newspaper.

Reflecting on Your Writing

Answer the following questions. Attach your answers to a copy of your letter to be placed in your writing portfolio.

1. What weaknesses in your solution were pointed out by your classmates? How did you respond?
2. What was the most difficult part of this assignment for you? Why?
3. What response do you expect from your letter? Why?

Publishing As an alternative to the publishing suggestion in the pupil's edition, you may want to suggest these ideas:

- Send a copy of the letters to the school newspaper.
- Organize a "problem solving campaign" in your school.
- Send letters to parents and neighbors in the community.
- Videotape students reading their letters, and send the tape and the letters to the town or city council.
- Organize a "problem-solving day" in your school. Have interested citizens attend a reading of the letters.
- Have students choose one letter and send signed petitions supporting it to the town council.

Reflecting on Your Writing You may wish to have students discuss their feelings about *Reflecting,* Question 3. Explain that the town council is very busy, and a response is not mandatory. Suggest that they follow up the letters with a note or even a phone call. Determine whether or not the students desire to continue with the assignment.

Closure

Before beginning the next subunit, be sure students have internalized these concepts:

- Close analysis of problems may uncover realistic solutions.
- Facts are needed to add weight to allegations.
- Problem solvers should concentrate on finding the most sensible solution to their problem.
- A business letter has a different structure and tone than a friendly letter.

Additional Writing and Research Topics

These items provide writing practice based on the selections in this subunit:

Problem–Solution

- The characters in "A Couple of Really Neat Guys" have a problem dealing with litter. Write a letter to these characters offering them a solution to their problem.
- In "Searching for Summer," the newlyweds leave in order to preserve the peace of the spot. How could they have allowed others to share in its beauty without commercializing it? Write a letter to the couple with your suggestions.

Other Topics

Social Studies Research: "David Meets Goliath at City Hall" deals with one young man's fight against the system. Research other cases where one person has taken a stand and made a difference. Write your findings in a brief report.

Character Portrait: The selections in this subunit provide many exciting and interesting characters. Select one character and write a profile of his or her life. If the character is real, you can research the facts you don't have. If the character is fictional, make up the missing facts.

Language Workshop

Objectives

- To understand that certain modifiers are often used incorrectly by speakers and writers
- To identify errors in the use of modifiers
- To use modifiers—*good* and *well, bad* and *badly, this* and *that, them* and *those,* and *here* and *there*—correctly in writing

Integrating . . .

Writing and Grammar Remind students that in the Writer's Workshop they wrote a letter to their town council stating a problem that exists in their community. Remind them that in writing such a letter, it is important for them to define the problem clearly, be aware of the cause, and offer possible solutions. Explain that the success they will have in getting results from such a letter depends partly on using correct grammar. Write these sentences on the board.

1. The proposal for the school funding budget was not planned good.

2. Town council felt badly about this here accusation.

Invite students to change the modifiers *good* (to *well*), *badly* (to *bad*) and to delete the word *here*. Help students see that using incorrect modifiers can create a poor impression and get unwanted results. This Language Workshop focuses on correct use of modifiers.

LANGUAGE WORKSHOP

PROBLEMS WITH MODIFIERS

Certain modifiers are often used incorrectly by speakers and writers. The following guidelines will help you remember the correct way to use the confusing modifiers *good* and *well, bad* and *badly, this* and *that, them* and *those,* and *here* and *there.*

Good and *Well*

LINKING VERBS

Linking verbs include *be, sound, taste, appear, feel, look, smell, become, remain, seem, stay* and *grow.*

Good is always an adjective. It is used to modify nouns and pronouns, and it often appears after linking verbs.

That band sounded really good. (The adjective *good* modifies the noun *band.*)

Well can be an adjective meaning "in good health" or an adverb meaning "expertly" or "properly." When used as an adjective, it modifies a noun or a pronoun. When used as an adverb, it modifies a verb, an adjective, or another adverb.

The patient looks well today. (Here *well* is an adjective meaning "in good health"; it modifies the noun *patient.*)

You sing very well. (Here *well* is an adverb meaning "expertly"; it modifies the verb *sing.*)

Good is never an adverb; it should never be used to modify a verb, an adjective, or another adverb.

Incorrect Tom and Lily had not planned their honeymoon *good.* (Here *good* is being used incorrectly as an adverb to modify the verb *planned.*)

Correct Tom and Lily had not planned their honeymoon *well.* (Here *well* is used correctly as an adverb.)

Bad and *Badly*

Bad is an adjective; it modifies a noun or a pronoun. *Badly* is an adverb; it modifies a verb, an adjective, or another adverb.

Never use *badly* after a linking verb such as *is, was, seemed,* or *felt.* Instead, use the adjective *bad.*

Additional Resources

UNIT FIVE RESOURCE BOOK

Language Workshop Copy Master, p. 24

ENRICHMENT MATERIALS

Grammar and Usage Copy Masters

Incorrect The couple felt *badly* about leaving the wedding dress behind. (Here the adverb *badly* incorrectly follows a linking verb.)

Correct The couple felt *bad* about leaving the wedding dress behind. (Here the adjective *bad* is correctly used, after the linking verb *felt,* to modify the noun *couple.*)

This and *That; These* and *Those*

This and *that* are adjectives that modify singular nouns. *These* and *those* modify plural nouns. Be especially careful when these modifiers are used with words such as *kind, sort,* and *type.*

Incorrect *Those* kind of honeymoons are more romantic. (*Kind* is singular, so it should be modified by either of the singular adjectives *this* or *that.*)

Correct *That* kind of honeymoon is more romantic. (Here, *that* correctly modifies the singular noun *kind.* Notice that the noun *honeymoon* and the verb *is* have also been made singular.)

Incorrect *These* sort of sunny days are rare.

Correct *This* sort of sunny day is rare.

The decision between *this* or *that* is also sometimes a difficult one. Remember that if you're talking about something that is close to you in time or space, you use *this.* If you're talking about something that is distant in time or space, you use *that.*

Them and *Those*

Those can be either a pronoun or an adjective. *Them* is always a pronoun and should never be used as an adjective.

Incorrect Where did you put *them* pastries?

Correct Where did you put *those* pastries? (adjective)

Correct Where did you put *them?* (pronoun)

Correct *Those* are my pastries. (pronoun)

Here and *There*

Avoid using "this here and "that there." The words *this* and *that* include the ideas of *here* and *there.* So, using these words together is repetitious.

Teaching Strategies

Work through the lesson with students, but stop before students reach the exercises. Ask them to provide sentences with each of the modifiers as you proceed through the lesson. Encourage students to demonstrate their understanding by using modifiers in personal opinion sentences about the selections they have read. For example, students might say, *It is good that forest reserves were established to preserve American forests.*

Teaching Tip

If students have difficulty distinguishing between adjectives and adverbs, have them use the following chart:

An Adverb Answers	An Adjective Answers
How?	What kind?
When?	Which one?
Where?	Whose?
To what extent?	How many?
About a Verb, Adjective or Another Adverb	About a Noun or Pronoun

Assign the exercises on p. 636 and suggest that students look back at the lesson if they are uncertain about the use of modifiers as they proceed through the exercises.

Teaching Tip: LEP

You may wish to assign a "reference person" to each LEP student. Explain that the "reference person" (who is one of your more capable students) should be available to help out with any difficult sections of the exercises.

Closure

Before beginning the next subunit, be sure students have internalized these concepts:

- There are some modifiers that are often used incorrectly by speakers and writers.
- *Good* is always used as an adjective; *well* can be used as an adverb to mean "expertly" or "properly" and as an adjective to mean "in good health."
- *Bad* is an adjective and modifies a noun or a pronoun. *Badly* is an adverb and modifies a verb, adjective, or another adverb.
- *This* and *that* are adjectives that modify singular nouns; *these* and *those* modify plural nouns.
- *Those* can be either a pronoun or adjective; *them* is always a pronoun.
- *This* and *here* should never be used together.

Answer Key
Exercise 1

1. delete "here"
2. *those* sunny days
3. correct
4. look *well*
5. feel *good*
6. correct
7. planned *badly*
8. feel *bad*
9. Those
10. correct
11. *that* type of *place*
12. fit her foot *well*
13. so *bad*
14. feel *good*
15. delete "there"
16. *those* gray clouds
17. felt so *well*
18. sleep *well*
19. seemed *good*
20. *This* kind of science fiction story

Exercise 2

Encourage students to share how they have used what they have learned about modifiers to improve their own writing.

Incorrect *This here* garden is beautiful.
Correct *This* garden is beautiful.

Exercise 1 Correct the errors in the use of modifiers in these sentences. If a sentence is correct, write *Correct.*

1. In "Searching for Summer," by Joan Aiken, this here planet has become a gray, dreary place.
2. The people in the story wish them sunny days would return.
3. They realize that the grayness was caused by the bombs, but they would like to make that kind of weather disappear.
4. Because there hasn't been any sunshine for years, people don't look good.
5. Tom and Lily feel well about their wedding and honeymoon.
6. They think that they have a good chance of finding some sunshine somewhere.
7. It turns out that their journey was planned bad.
8. They feel badly when the only place to stay is a dreary pub.
9. Them places are not meant for young people.
10. Tom thinks that Lily's idea to take a walk is a good suggestion.
11. The path leads them to those type of places they had dreamed about.
12. Lily's sandal does not fit her foot good.
13. By the time they find the cottage, her foot feels so badly she needs to sit down.
14. Mrs. Hatching makes them feel well about being her guests.
15. The couple wonders where the Hatchings got those there tans.
16. Tom and Lily soon forget about them gray clouds.
17. The warm sun feels well on their faces.
18. They eat and sleep good at Mrs. Hatching's cottage.
19. When the sun was out, life seemed well.
20. These kind of science fiction stories can entertain and warn readers.

Exercise 2 Analyzing and Revising Your Writing

1. Take a piece of writing from your portfolio.
2. Reread one or two paragraphs, looking for incorrectly used modifiers.
3. Correct any modifier errors that you find.
4. Remember to check for incorrectly used modifiers the next time you proofread your writing.

LANGUAGE HANDBOOK

For review and practice, see Section 4, **Using Modifiers.**

Additional Practice

The following items are additional exercises to help students with correct use of problem modifiers.

Rewrite these sentences using *good, well, bad,* and *badly* correctly.

1. The banana bread tasted (good, well).
2. At least Al can bat (good, well).
3. Ms. Sims hasn't looked (good, well) since she had the flu.
4. The milkshakes here are usually (good, well).

Rewrite these sentences using *this, that, these, those, here,* and *there* correctly.

5. The disc jockey plays (them, those) old songs often.
6. Somebody from the last class left (this, this here) book.
7. Jo listened to (that, those) advice.
8. I have met (them, those) twins before.
9. (This, This here) fog is really a low cloud.

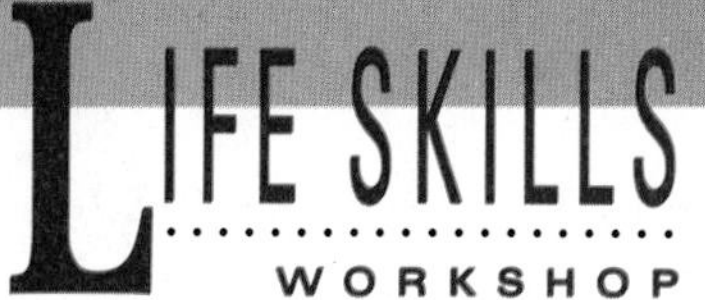

FILLING OUT APPLICATIONS

Whether you're applying for a job or filing a petition, you will need to fill out an application form. Keep these guidelines in mind.

1. Read all the directions carefully *before* you write anything down. Pull together the information you don't know by heart, such as your references, social security number, your mother's maiden name, or dates of previous employment or classes.
2. Fill out the application line by line. Before filling in a line, read the directions for that line again. Plan ahead to make sure your writing will fit on the line. If you make a mistake, you can either start again or carefully draw a single neat line through the error and write the correct information above the line.
3. If at all possible, complete every line. You can write "Does not apply" if an item does not apply to you. You can also use the abbreviation "NA" (for "not applicable"). Check the application for accuracy, spelling, and completeness when you have finished.

JOB APPLICATIONS

On job applications, you will often be asked to list previous employers and to provide references. References are people who know you well and who will be willing to discuss your abilities. Ask permission in advance from people whom you want to use as references. Make sure that they are prepared to say good things about you. Also ask for their daytime telephone numbers and complete addresses, including ZIP Codes.

Exercise Imagine that you are asked to complete an application form, part of which appears below. Copy this form onto a sheet of paper and fill it out.

REMINDER

Use a good pen or a typewriter, and be neat. Never use a pencil unless you are told to do so.

GYM-BO'S HEALTH CLUB, APPLICATION FORM

Personal Information

Name________________________
last first middle

Social Security Number____________ Date______

Address________________________
street city state/ZIP

Telephone__________ Date of Birth____/____/____

Emergency Contact____________ ____________
name telephone

What Class Do You Wish to Take?

Class____________ Level____________

Life Skills Workshop

Objectives

- To understand how to fill out an application

Integrating . . .

Writing and Life Skills Share with students that this workshop will help them fill out applications more easily.

Teaching Strategies

Ask students to identify times when people must fill out application forms. *(Possible responses: when applying for jobs or to schools; when filing petitions with the government)*

Read through the material with students. Emphasize that they should read over a completed application to check for accuracy, spelling, and completeness. Read the note at the side of the page about references, stressing that one should always ask permission before using a person as a reference.

Assign the exercise on page 637.

Closure

Before beginning the next subunit, be sure students have internalized these concepts:

- Filling out applications is an important part of everyday life.
- It is helpful to read all directions before starting, to write neatly, to fill out each line completely, and to be prepared for standard questions.

Teaching Tip

Discuss with students that it is worth their time to prepare a sheet with the basic information they will need for filling out applications.

Additional Resources

UNIT FIVE RESOURCE BOOK
Related Skills Copy, p. 25

ADDITIONAL PRACTICE

Fill out this form to apply for the Frequent Flosser Club. *(Possible responses are given)*

Name (last, first) Rosado, Melanie
Street Address 1818 Oak Avenue
City, State ZIP Plainview, NY 11803
Number of Flossings Per Week 14
Number of Dental Clinic Visits Last Year 2

Answer Key for Exercise

(An example of a completed form is given.)
Name Fuentes, Robert Mark
SSN 012-34-5678 Date May 1, 1992
Address 42 Spruce St., Smithtown, NY 11787
Telephone (518) 555-2185
Date of Birth 9/8/76
Emergency Contact Ruth Fuentes (518) 555-3753
Class first aid Level beginning

Subunit Preview

Have students read the introduction to subunit 2, **The Price of Technology.** Ask them to explore how feelings of loss in the course of progress are related to the unit theme, **The Future: Hopes and Fears.** Does modern technology mostly *serve* or *rule* people? How so? Has the computer made the brain obsolete? Why or why not? Some say that wisdom has not kept pace with technology. What does that mean? Why is it a problem? Invite students to look over the subunit Table of Contents and point out the selection that they expect to be the most interesting.

For Additional Challenge

The following selections offer further challenge in exploring the subunit theme:

"By the Waters of Babylon," a short story by Stephen Vincent Benét

Frankenstein, a novel by Mary Wollstonecraft Shelley

Additional Resources

Subunit Test, pp. 53–54

THE PRICE OF TECHNOLOGY

Advances in science and technology have helped make possible a standard of living that would have been unimaginable to our ancestors. These advances, however, have brought their own set of problems. Nuclear power, for instance, holds the promise of supplying a large part of the world's energy needs while nuclear waste and nuclear war threaten the world's future.

The following selections explore this dual nature of technology—the good and the bad consequences of progress. As you read these selections, examine your own views about the price of technology.

OBSERVATION ASSESSMENT

Observing how students respond to the text, to the classroom instruction, and to peers is an important part of an assessment program. The following suggestions and the form in each Unit Resource Book can be used to implement observation assessment.

- As students work through the subunit, observe their attitudes when approaching a selection. Do they first distinguish whether it is nonfiction or fiction? Does glancing at the format of a selection give them an idea about what they are going to read?
- As they work through this subunit, can you see growth in their ability to use visual cues?
- To evaluate how well students makes inferences, have them state the purpose of a selection. Can they recognize humor or irony as a means to convey a serious message?

e x p l o r e

Fiction

The Weapon

FREDRIC BROWN

Examine What You Know (Prior Knowledge)

What does the word "weapon" mean to you? Does a single image appear in your mind, or do you see several images all at once? Copy and complete the diagram below. Then compare your ideas with both your classmates and with the weapons described in this story.

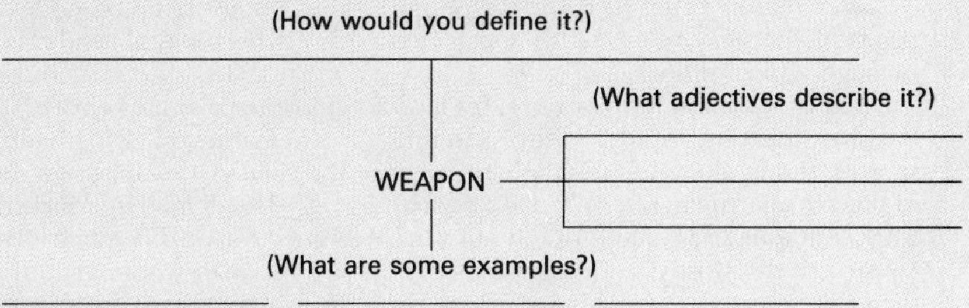

Expand Your Knowledge (Building Background)

What is the best way to ensure world peace? On one side are people whose beliefs are characterized in the slogan "peace through strength." "Hawks," as they are sometimes called, support new weapons research and the maintenance of a large military force, even in times of peace. They believe that other countries are unlikely to attack a country or its allies if that country's defenses are strong and if an overwhelming counterattack is likely. On the other side are the "doves," who believe that huge military build-ups always lead to war. These people argue that huge defense spending is both immoral and a poor use of money that could be used for important social programs.

Enrich Your Reading (Reading Skill)

■ *A biography of the author can be found in the Reader's Handbook.*

Author's Purpose Authors write for one or more of four main purposes: to entertain, to inform, to express opinions, and to persuade. As you read, think about what purposes the author might have had for writing "The Weapon."

Objectives

- To understand and explore a short story
- To analyze author's purpose
- To examine the significance of the title of a selection
- To express understanding of the work through a choice of writing options, including a letter, a summary, and a diagram

Prereading/Motivation

Examine What You Know

Discussion Prompts: What weapons might not be physical? In what instances might nonphysical weapons be more harmful than physical ones? What do you consider the most dangerous weapon? Why?

Possible definition: something to fight with; **descriptive adjectives:** dangerous, harmful, lethal; **examples:** a gun, a knife, scathing words

Expand Your Knowledge

Discussion Prompts: What images does the word *hawks* convey? What do you think of when you hear the word *doves?* Would you describe yourself as a *hawk* or a *dove?* Explain your answer.

Enrich Your Reading

Before students begin to read, review the four main purposes for writing. Ask them to give examples of writing for each purpose from a newspaper. *(Possible responses: to entertain—comics, a humorous column; to inform—news articles; to express opinions—editorials, book and movie reviews; to persuade—advertisements, editorials column)*

Thematic Link—The Price of Technology

In this short story, Frederic Brown explores the potentially disastrous price of weapons technology.

Journal Writing

In "The Weapon," Frederic Brown explores the implications of the "ultimate weapon." Suggest these journal topics to students:

- What do you imagine is "the weapon"?
- How might "the weapon" affect the world?
- Who do you think does more for world peace, hawks or doves? Why?

For other journal opportunities, refer sutdents to Examine What You Know and Expand Your Knowledge (p. 639), and to Broader Connections (p. 643).

Additional Resources

UNIT FIVE RESOURCE BOOK

Reader's Guidesheet, p. 28
Vocabulary Worksheet, p. 29
Selection and Vocabulary Check Tests, p. 30
Selection Test, pp. 31–32

Collaborative Learning

Opportunities for collaborative learning appear throughout the lesson and include First Impressions (p. 643).

Teaching Strategies

Support for Students of Limited English Proficiency

■ Use Reader's Guidesheet, p. 28

■ The message in this story about the danger of nuclear weapons concerns young people of all cultures; many feel strongly about it. Suggest that students set as their purpose for reading the discovery of the author's message. Also obtain a library copy of the children's story "Chicken Little" and read it aloud; ask students if there are similar stories in their native cultures. Have them read to discover the role "Chicken Little" plays in the selection.

■ Annotations C and I offer specific help for LEP students.

Text Annotations

A. Critical Thinking: ANALYZING Ask students to locate clues suggesting that Dr. Graham's work will be important in the story. *(the mention of his being a "key" scientist on a "very important" project; the fact that although he is at home, he is at work.)*

Teaching Tip

Explain that mental retardation is characterized by an inability to learn normally. People having an IQ of less than 70 (100 being the norm) are considered retarded to some degree. Although early intervention can help individuals to reach their potential, many are unable to live independently.

B. Reading Skill: PREDICTING Inform students that the word *niemand* means "nobody" in German. Ask students to predict, based on this and on what Graham thinks of the man, whether they think the stranger will prove to be harmless or perhaps the opposite. You may wish to remind students that Odysseus, in the classic Greek story, called himself "nobody" to trick his opponent.

C. LEP: Language Ask students why a person might be called a "crackpot." *(Possible response: A person might be thought of as a "cracked pot" if his brain seemed slightly fractured.)* Ask a volunteer to define the word. *(a lunatic, an eccentric person)*

The Weapon

FREDRIC BROWN

A The room was quiet in the dimness of early evening. Dr. James Graham, key scientist of a very important project, sat in his favorite chair, thinking. It was so still that he could hear the turning of pages in the next room as his son leafed

SR-1 ▶ through a picture book.

Often Graham did his best work, his most creative thinking, under these circumstances, sitting alone in an unlighted room in his own apartment after the day's regular work. But tonight his mind would not work constructively. Mostly he thought about his mentally arrested[1] son—his only son—in the next room. The thoughts were loving thoughts, not the bitter anguish he had felt years ago when he had first learned of the boy's condition. The boy was happy; wasn't that the main thing? And to how many men is given a child who will always be a child, who will not grow up and leave him? Certainly that was rationalization,[2] but what is wrong with rationalization when—the

SR-2 ▶ doorbell rang.

Graham rose and turned on lights in the almost-dark room before he went through the hallway to the door. He was not annoyed; tonight, at this moment, almost any interruption to his thoughts was welcome.

He opened the door. A stranger stood there. He said, "Dr. Graham? My name is Niemand. I'd like to talk to you. May I come in a moment?"

Graham looked at him. He was a small man, nondescript,[3] obviously harmless—possibly a reporter or an insurance agent.

But it didn't matter what he was. Graham found himself saying, "Of course. Come in, Mr. Niemand." A few minutes of conversation, he justified himself by thinking, might divert his thoughts and clear his mind. B

"Sit down," he said, in the living room. "Care for a cup of coffee?"

Niemand said, "No, thank you." He sat in the chair; Graham sat on the sofa.

The small man interlocked his fingers; he leaned forward. He said, "Dr. Graham, you are the man whose scientific work is more likely than that of any other man to end the human race's chance for survival."

> ***"But, Dr. Graham, is humanity ready for an ultimate weapon?"***

A crackpot, Graham thought. Too late now he realized that he should have asked the man's business before admitting him. It would be an embarrassing interview—he C

1. **mentally arrested:** halted in intellectual development.
2. **rationalization:** a superficially reasonable excuse for a thing or event that covers up a more accurate but less appealing explanation.
3. **nondescript:** plain; uninteresting.

Structured Reading for Less Proficient Students

These questions can help to guide students through the reading. Ask each question at the point of the selection where the SR number appears in the margin.

SR–1. Who is Dr. Graham? *(He is the key scientist of a very important project.)* **Literal recall**

SR–2. What is wrong with Dr. Graham's son? *(He is mentally retarded.)* **Clarifying**

SR–3. What does Niemand want to talk to Dr. Graham about? *(the weapon Dr. Graham is working on)* **Literal recall**

SR–4. How does Harry respond to Mr. Niemand? *(Harry likes Niemand; he takes the man's hand.)* **Literal recall**

SR–5. What is Dr. Graham's position about the weapon? *(He is unconcerned about its results; he sees it as a byproduct of the advancement of science.)* **Clarifying**

SR–6. What "gift" does Niemand give Harry? *(a loaded revolver)* **Literal recall/Clarifying**

disliked being rude, yet only rudeness was effective.

"Dr. Graham, the weapon on which you
SR-3 ▶ are working—"

The visitor stopped and turned his head as the door that led to a bedroom opened and a boy of fifteen came in. The boy didn't notice Niemand; he ran to Graham.

"Daddy, will you read to me now?" The boy of fifteen laughed the sweet laughter of a child of four.

Graham put an arm around the boy. He looked at his visitor, wondering whether he
D had known about the boy. From the lack of surprise on Niemand's face, Graham felt sure he had known.

"Harry"—Graham's voice was warm with affection—"Daddy's busy. Just for a little while. Go back to your room; I'll come and read to you soon."

"'Chicken Little'?[4] You'll read me 'Chicken Little'?"

"If you wish. Now run along. Wait, Harry, this is Mr. Niemand."

The boy smiled bashfully at the visitor. Niemand said, "Hi, Harry," and smiled back at him, holding out his hand. Graham, watching,
E was sure now that Niemand had known: the smile and the gesture were for the boy's mental age, not his physical one.

The boy took Niemand's hand. For a moment it seemed that he was going to climb into Niemand's lap, and Graham pulled him back gently. He said, "Go to your room now, Harry."

The boy skipped back to his bedroom, not
SR-4 ▶ closing the door.

Niemand's eyes met Graham's and he said, "I like him," with obvious sincerity. He
F added, "I hope that what you're going to read to him will always be true."

Graham didn't understand. Niemand said, "'Chicken Little,' I mean. It's a fine
G story—but may 'Chicken Little' always be wrong about the sky falling down."

Graham suddenly had liked Niemand when Niemand had shown liking for the boy. Now he remembered that he must close the interview quickly. He rose in dismissal.

He said, "I fear you're wasting your time and mine, Mr. Niemand. I know all the arguments; everything you can say I've heard a thousand times. Possibly there is truth in what you believe, but it does not concern me. I'm a scientist, and only a scientist. Yes, it is public knowledge that I am

SELF-PORTRAIT 1981 James Valerio Collection of Joseph D. and Janet M. Shein, Philadelphia.

4. **Chicken Little:** a children's story in which Chicken Little is hit on the head by an acorn and falsely concludes that the sky is falling. Her cries of alarm throw her whole village into chaos.

D. Literary Element: FORESHADOWING Have students predict how Niemand might use his knowledge of Dr. Graham's son to convince Dr. Graham that the weapon is dangerous. *(Possible response: He might kidnap the child; he might speak with the child to help him sway his father.)*

E. Reading Skill: INFERRING Ask students why they think the author keeps stressing Niemand's awareness of Harry's condition. *(Possible responses: It may be crucial to the development of the plot. The author wants to show that Niemand is a gentle person.)*

F. Reading Skill: CLARIFYING Ask students to explain Niemand's remark that he hopes what Dr. Graham tells his son "will always be true." *(Possible response: Niemand hopes that the total destruction of the ultimate weapon will always be a false alarm, like Chicken Little's.)*

G. Critical Thinking: EVALUATING Ask students to evaluate whether Niemand is a rational man justified in his fears or a "crackpot" alarmist. *(Possible response: Some students may feel that the threat of world destruction is very real, and so Niemand is justified. Others might argue that the world is in very little danger of being destroyed, and so Niemand is a "crackpot.")*

Teaching Tip

Have students present arguments that they think might persuade Dr. Graham that he is wrong to develop his weapon. Consider organizing a class debate so that students can more fully explore their positions and articulate their points.

Art Note

James Valerio (1938–) was born in Chicago and attended the School of the Art Institute, where he received many honors for his work. His paintings are realistic and detailed: the folds and drape of clothing, the reflections of light on metal and glass surfaces, and the character lines in a face all are meticulously rendered. *Which details in this picture refer to the work of the scientist in The Weapon?*

PROFESSIONAL NOTEBOOK

If at-risk students are to become successful in the classroom, teachers need to help them learn the secrets of how to become good readers. Good readers become good learners. The teacher's major role is to teach in such a way that students accept the challenge of learning. Patiently explain, give examples, explain again. Provide support and encouragement. Teach students through your words and actions during practice. Their eventual success will teach them that effort pays off. Give students meaningful and challenging but attainable assignments, then demonstrate effective ways to accomplish these. Model, demonstrate, talk through, and clearly explain every step required. . . . The more classroom tasks are related to the interests and background of the student, the more motivated students are to work.

***The Journal of Reading*, VOL. 33, NO. 7 (APRIL 1990), P. 550**

H. Reading Skill: AUTHOR'S PURPOSE Have students define the author's purpose based on this passage. *(Possible response: Students might argue that this passage shows the author is concerned with persuading his audience rather than expressing his opinion.)*

I. LEP: Cultural Reference Explain to students that even though Niemand is a virtual stranger, Dr. Graham readily offers him a cup of coffee, as such hospitality is part of his cultural tradition. Ask students whether they would offer such hospitality to a stranger, especially to one with whom they disagreed on an important matter.

J. Reading Skill: PREDICTING Ask students to predict the gift Niemand left for Harry. *(Possible response: He could have left something good, such as a book or a toy, or something bad, such as poison or some sort of weapon.)*

K. Critical Thinking: ANALYZING Have students analyze why Niemand gave the loaded gun to Harry. *(Possible response: Niemand is warning Dr. Graham that giving the weapon to humanity is like giving a loaded gun to a retarded child.)*

Check Test

1. What is Dr. Graham's job? *(He is a scientist.)*
2. Who is Harry and what is his handicap? *(Graham's son; he is mentally retarded.)*
3. What project is Dr. Graham working on? *(developing the ultimate weapon)*
4. What does Niemand want Dr. Graham to do? *(stop developing the weapon)*
5. What does Niemand give to Harry? *(a loaded revolver)*

Encouraging Independent Reading

Fail Safe, a novel by Eugene Burdick and Harvey Wheeler
"The Portable Phonograph," a short story by Walter Van Tilburg Clark
"Prometheus, the Fire Bringer," a Greek myth retold by Jeremy Ingalls
Cat's Cradle, a novel by Kurt Vonnegut Jr.

working on a weapon, a rather ultimate one. But, for me personally, that is only a byproduct of the fact that I am advancing science. I have thought it through, and I have found that that is my only concern." SR-5 ▶

H "But, Dr. Graham, is humanity ready for an ultimate weapon?"

Graham frowned. "I have told you my point of view, Mr. Niemand."

Niemand rose slowly from the chair. He said, "Very well, if you do not choose to discuss it, I'll say no more." He passed a hand across his forehead. "I'll leave, Dr. Graham. I wonder, though . . . may I change my mind about the coffee you offered me?" I

Graham's irritation faded. He said, "Certainly. Cream and sugar?"

"Please."

Graham went into the kitchen. He got the coffee, cream, and sugar.

When he returned to the living room, Niemand was just leaving the boy's bedroom. He heard Niemand's, "Good night, Harry," and Harry's happy, "Night, Mr. Niemand."

Graham poured the coffee. Later, Niemand declined a second cup and started to leave.

J Niemand said, "I took the liberty of bringing a small gift to your son, Doctor. I gave it to him while you were getting the coffee for us. I hope you'll forgive me."

"Of course. Thank you. Good night."

Graham closed the door; he walked through the living room into Harry's room. He said, "All right, Harry. Now I'll read to—"

There was sudden sweat on his forehead, but he forced his face and his voice to be calm as he stepped to the side of the bed. "May I see that, Harry?" When he had it safely, his hands shook as he examined it.

He thought, *only a madman would give a loaded revolver to a retarded child.* ❧ K ◀ SR-6

INSIGHT

A Poison Tree

WILLIAM BLAKE

I was angry with my friend:
I told my wrath, my wrath did end.
I was angry with my foe:
I told it not, my wrath did grow.

And I watered it in fears,
Night and morning with my tears;
And I sunnèd it with smiles,
And with soft deceitful wiles.

And it grew both day and night,
Till it bore an apple bright;
And my foe beheld it shine,
And he knew that it was mine,

And into my garden stole
When the night had veiled the pole:
In the morning glad I see
My foe outstretched beneath the tree.

Insight

This piece reflects on the ideas in the main selection and is suggested for students' independent reading. Optional discussion questions follow.

1. What happens when the speaker tells his friend that he is angry? What happens when he does not express his feelings? *(When he tells his friend how he feels his anger ends; when he withholds his feelings his anger grows.)*
2. Why did his foe die? *(He ate the poisoned apple, the fruit of his friend's wrath.)*
3. Do you think that the speaker in "A Poison Tree" would agree with Niemand's actions? *(Possible responses: Yes, because both opposed their foes, had strong feelings, and were willing to harm others and to act deceitfully to make their point; no, because the speaker in the poem would not tell his enemy directly what was on his mind.)*

e x p l a i n

Responding to Reading

First Impressions

1. How did this story affect you? Share with your classmates your feelings about the people and the events in this story.

Second Thoughts

2. What kind of man is Dr. James Graham?

   Think about
   - what he has accomplished
   - how he defends his work as a nuclear scientist
   - how he treats and responds to his son

3. Is Niemand a madman?

   Think about
   - your own idea of what a madman is
   - why Dr. Graham calls Niemand a madman
   - what motivates Niemand's actions throughout the story

4. Think again about the author's purposes for writing. How does the last line of the story explain the author's purpose?

5. Why is "The Weapon" an appropriate title? What other titles can you think of for this story?

Broader Connections

6. Think about the issues raised in Expand Your Knowledge and this story. With whom would you be more likely to agree, Dr. Graham or Niemand?

Writing Options

1. Do you think this incident will change Dr. Graham? Write a letter from him to Niemand one year later.

2. Summarize the "Chicken Little" story. Then explain why the author might have chosen to include a reference to this children's nursery tale.

3. Dr. Graham is working on the ultimate weapon. Look again at the diagram you made in which you defined the word *weapon*. Then make a new diagram that defines Dr. Grahams "ultimate weapon."

Student Response

Responding to Reading

These questions are open-ended, with no "right" or "wrong" answers. However, responses must be supported with information from the selection. Possible answers follow:

1. Any reaction to the story, whether negative or positive, is valid.

2. Students may see Dr. Graham as a successful scientist and loving father or as an intellectual who is out of touch with the reality and consequences of his work.

3. Some students may say Niemand is a madman because he gives the loaded revolver to a retarded boy; others may see him as sane because he is acting in a cause that could save humanity and because he has a rational plan for making his point.

4. Students may say the author's purpose is to convince his readers to oppose weapons development or to express his opinion that such weapons research is wrong. In the last line, the author conveys the idea that scientists are insane to place the ultimate weapon they have developed into the hands of people who are not mature or responsible enough to handle it wisely.

5. Students may feel the title is appropriate either because the story concerns the "ultimate weapon" or because of Niemand's gift to Harry. Almost any title students suggest may be suitable, such as "A Child's Toy," which could refer to Dr. Graham, to Niemand, or to Harry.

6. Students may agree with Niemand that weapons research can only harm people, or they may say that any and all scientific research has value.

Writing Options

The Writing Options are designed to meet varied student interests and abilities. Have each student choose one writing activity to complete. You may wish to guide some students to an option that requires less writing.

Journal Update Have students review their journal entries for "The Weapon." What new reflections can they add about their feelings on weapons development?

Objectives

- To understand a short story
- To explore satire
- To review dramatic irony
- To practice clarifying meaning
- To express understanding of the work through a choice of writing options, including a summary, a "how-to" paper, an ad, and a story

Prereading/Motivation

Examine What You Know

(*Answers to problems:* Multiplication problem answer is 321,372; division problem answer is 2.97)

Discussion Prompts: What might people in the future puzzle over simple mathematical problems? What may have convinced people that they needed computers to do even simple math? Did you find these two problems easy or hard?

Expand Your Knowledge

Discussion Prompts: What are some of the advantages of computers? What are some of their disadvantages? What firsthand experience have you had with computers?

Additional Background: Computers are defined as electronic, mechanical, or electromechanical devices that can automatically perform at high-speed a sequence of logical, arithmetic, or textual operations. Calculators can also perform high-speed instructions, but computers are able to vary the sequence of such instructions by themselves based on decisions the machines make as a result of incoming data.

Enrich Your Reading

Discussion Prompts: Why might clarifying questions help you to follow the plot? Might clarifying questions be compared to a road map that will help you from taking a "wrong turn"? Do you think clarifying questions are useful in a technological selection?

Thematic Link—The Price of Technology

In this short story, Asimov describes the potential effects of technology on people's ability to reason mathematically.

e x p l o r e

Fiction

The Feeling of Power

ISAAC ASIMOV

Examine What You Know (Prior Knowledge)

Throughout the next story, various members of a future society puzzle over simple mathematical problems. In fact, you will meet adults who cannot perform the simplest mathematical calculation and who think multiplication is something only calculators and computers can do. On a piece of paper, complete the following math problems. Do not use a calculator. After you have finished, write a short explanation of what you did to get the right answer for each.

$$\begin{array}{r} 474 \\ \times\ \underline{678} \end{array} \qquad 93\overline{)276}$$

Expand Your Knowledge (Building Background)

In "The Feeling of Power," Isaac Asimov invents a "self-directing war computer." Such an invention seems within the realm of possibility, considering the amazing progress in computer technology over the past forty years. The first computer, built in 1944, occupied an entire building at Harvard University, and even computers of the 1950's took up entire rooms. These massive machines had slow response times and small memories by today's standards and were so expensive that only large corporations and governments could afford them. In the 1960's, computers became smaller, faster, and less expensive due to the development of a new miniature power source called the *transistor.* In the mid-1980's, a microscopic device called the *chip* further revolutionized the computer industry. Speed and memory were increased and cost was reduced to a point where millions of Americans could afford to buy their own.

Enrich Your Reading (Reading Skill)

Clarifying As you read "The Feeling of Power," you may need to stop from time to time to clarify what you are reading. The *clarify* questions that appear with this story will help you keep up with the plot, follow the motives of the characters, and understand the theme.

■ *A biography of the author can be found on page 656.*

Journal Writing

In "The Feeling of Power," Asimov satirically explores the effect of computers on society. Suggest these journal topics to students:

- In what ways do computers give people power?
- What gives you a "feeling of power"?

For other journal opportunities, refer students to First Impressions and Broader Connections (p. 654), Real Life Connections (p. T-648), and annotation S.

Additional Resources

UNIT FIVE RESOURCE BOOK

Reader's Guidesheet, p. 33
Vocabulary Worksheet, p. 34
Selection and Vocabulary Check Test, p. 35
Selection Test, pp. 36–37

Collaborative Learning

Opportunities for collaborative learning appear throughout the lesson and include Cross-Curricular Options (p. T-656), as well as Teaching Tips on pp. T-647, T-648, T-651, and T-653.

The Feeling of Power

ISAAC ASIMOV

A Jehan Shuman was used to dealing with the men in authority on long-embattled Earth. He was only a civilian, but he originated programming patterns that resulted in self-directing war computers of the highest sort. Generals consequently listened to him. Heads of congressional committees, too.

B There was one of each in the special lounge of New Pentagon. General Weider was space-burnt and had a small mouth puckered almost into a cipher.[1] Congressman Brant was smooth cheeked and clear eyed. He smoked Denebian tobacco with the air of one whose patriotism was so notorious, he could be allowed such liberties.

Shuman, tall, distinguished, and Programmer-first-class,
SR-1 ▶ faced them fearlessly.

He said, "This, gentlemen, is Myron Aub."

C "The one with the unusual gift that you discovered quite by accident," said Congressman Brant placidly. "Ah." He inspected the little man with the egg-bald head with amiable curiosity.

The little man, in return, twisted the fingers of his hands anxiously. He had never been near such great men before. He was only an aging, low-grade Technician who had long ago failed all tests designed to smoke out the gifted ones among mankind and had settled into the rut of unskilled labor. There was just this hobby of his that the great Programmer had found out about and was now making such a frightening fuss over.

General Weider said, "I find this atmosphere of mystery childish."

"You won't in a moment," said Shuman. "This is not something we can leak to the first comer. —Aub!" There was something imperative about his manner of biting off that one-syllable name, but then he was a great Programmer speaking to a mere Technician. "Aub! How much is nine times seven?" D

Aub hesitated a moment. His pale eyes glimmered with a feeble anxiety. "Sixty-three," he said.

Congressman Brant lifted his eyebrows. "Is that right?"

"Check it for yourself, Congressman."

The congressman took out his pocket

1. **cipher** (sī′ fər): something that is shaped like an *O*.

Words to Know and Use	**notorious** (nō tôr′ ē əs) *adj.* well-known, but in an unfavorable way; infamous **imperative** (im per′ ə tiv) *adj.* commanding; having a forceful nature

Structured Reading for Less Proficient Students

These questions can help to guide students through the reading. Ask each question at the point of the selection where the SR number appears in the margin.

SR–1. Why is Jehan Shuman important? *(He created programs for the most advanced self-directing war computers.)* **Clarifying**

SR–2. What is Aub able to do? *(Multiply 17 and 23 mentally without using a computer.)* **Literal recall**

SR–3. To what use does Congressman Brant want to put Aub's skills? *(to winning the war)* **Inferring**

SR–4. Who is Loesser? *(He is the man in control of the West European computer combine.)* **Literal recall**

SR–5. What arguments does Shuman use to persuade Loesser to join Project Number? *(He argues that the human mind must have computed before the invention of computers, that doing away with computers will prove efficient, that the project is patriotic, and that it will be an intellectual adventure.)* **Summarizing**

Continued on page 646

Teaching Strategies

Vocabulary Preview

These vocabulary words are defined at the bottom of the selection page on which they appear. You may wish to discuss them briefly before students begin reading.

capricious unpredictable; erratic
catastrophic disastrous
finite having a beginning and end
haggard disheveled in appearance
imperative commanding
melancholy gloom; depression
notorious well known; infamous
recalcitrant unruly; defiant
sordid miserable; depressing
subside pull back, quiet down

Support for Students of Limited English Proficiency

- Use Reader's Guidesheet, p. 33.
- Students may not understand at first that this science-fiction selection takes place in the future. Refer to annotation B, which asks students to note the elements of science fiction that are evident.
- "The Feeling of Power" also contains satirical humor that may be hard for students to understand.
- Annotations A, F, N, T, and Y focus on satirical humor.

Text Annotations

A. LEP: Satirical Humor Point out to students the satirical humor and mocking irony in the phrase *only a civilian,* which implies that people in the military look down on those not in the service.

B. Literary Element: SCIENCE FICTION Ask students to explain the real or imagined scientific developments that form the basis of the setting. *(Possible responses: The story is set in the fictional "New Pentagon," implying that it is the future; Asimov has invented new words to describe new phenomena, such as* space-burnt *and* Denebian *tobacco.)*

C. Reading Skill: PREDICTING Ask students to predict what Myron Aub's "unusual gift" might be. *(Possible responses: flying, telepathy, a new weapon)*

D. Reading Skill: CLARIFYING Have students explain what Aub can do that the others apparently cannot. *(solve simple multiplication problems in his head)*

Art Note

Born in Augusta, Georgia, Jasper Johns (1930–) studied at the University of South Carolina. Considered one of the original Pop artists, he paints and sculpts well-known objects of everyday life. In this painting he combined newspaper and encaustic, a substance made by mixing paint with hot wax. The paste-like paint forms an interesting surface texture. *What important reality does this picture portray?*

E. Literary Element: SATIRE Have students explain how Asimov uses exaggeration to teach a lesson or improve society. *(Possible response: By exaggerating the General's astonishment with Aub's ability to perform elementary mathematical calculations, Asimov might be suggesting that we rely too much on machines, especially pocket calculators and computers, and that our society would be better if we made more use of our mental abilities.)*

F. LEP: Satirical Humor Point out to students how Asimov satirically underscores the effort Aub must expend to perform a simple multiplication problem by describing his forehead as "corrugated" and his marks as "painstaking." Make sure that students understand the satirical humor of an entire society able to construct sophisticated computers yet unable to do elementary math.

NUMBERS IN COLOR (detail) 1958–59 Jasper Johns Albright-Knox Art Gallery, Buffalo, New York.

computer, nudged the milled edges twice, looked at its face as it lay there in the palm of his hand, and put it back. He said, "Is this the gift you brought us here to demonstrate. An illusionist[2]?"

"More than that, sir. Aub has memorized a few operations and with them he computes on paper."

"A paper computer?" said the general. He looked pained.

"No, sir," said Shuman patiently. "Not a paper computer. Simply a sheet of paper. General, would you be so kind as to suggest a number?"

"Seventeen," said the general.

"And you, Congressman?"

"Twenty-three."

"Good! Aub, multiply those numbers and please show the gentlemen your manner of doing it."

"Yes, Programmer," said Aub, ducking his head. He fished a small pad out of one shirt pocket and an artist's hairline stylus out of the other. His forehead corrugated as he made painstaking marks on the paper.

General Weider interrupted him sharply. "Let's see that."

Aub passed him the paper, and Weider said, "Well, it looks like the figure seventeen."

Congressman Brant nodded and said, "So it does, but I suppose anyone can copy fig-

2. **illusionist:** a performer who tricks observers into believing in magical or false images and objects.

STRUCTURED READING FOR LESS PROFICIENT STUDENTS

Continued from page 645

SR–6. What is the goal of the Project Number? *(to eliminate the computer and thus defeat the Denebians)* **Clarifying**

SR–7. What was the result of Aub's killing himself? *(Tribute was paid to him for his discovery, but the project went on without him.)* **Literal recall**

SR–8. How does Shuman feel after he solves a multiplication problem in his head? *(He feels amazingly powerful.)* **Literal recall**

ures off a computer. I think I could make a passable seventeen myself, even without practice."

"If you will let Aub continue, gentlemen," said Shuman without heat.

Aub continued, his hand trembling a little. Finally he said in a low voice, "The answer is three hundred and ninety-one."

Congressman Brant took out his computer a second time and flicked it, "By Godfrey, so it is. How did he guess?"

"No guess, Congressman," said Shuman. "He computed that result. He did it on this sheet of paper."

"Humbug," said the general impatiently. "A computer is one thing and marks on paper are another."

"Explain, Aub," said Shuman.

"Yes, Programmer. —Well, gentlemen, I write down seventeen and just underneath it, I write twenty-three. Next, I say to myself: seven times three—"

The congressman interrupted smoothly, "Now, Aub, the problem is seventeen times twenty-three."

"Yes, I know," said the little Technician earnestly, "but I *start* by saying seven times three because that's the way it works. Now seven times three is twenty-one."

"And how do you know that?" asked the congressman.

"I just remember it. It's always twenty-one on the computer. I've checked it any number of times."

"That doesn't mean it always will be, though, does it?" said the congressman.

"Maybe not," stammered Aub. "I'm not a mathematician. But I always get the right answers, you see."

"Go on."

"Seven times three is twenty-one, so I write down twenty-one. Then one times three is three, so I write down a three under the two of twenty-one."

"Why under the two?" asked Congressman Brant at once.

"Because—" Aub looked helplessly at his superior for support. "It's difficult to explain."

Shuman said, "If you will accept his work for the moment, we can leave the details for the mathematicians."

Brant subsided.

Aub said, "Three plus two makes five, you see, so the twenty-one becomes a fifty-one. Now you let that go for a while and start fresh. You multiply seven and two, that's fourteen, and one and two, that's two. Put them down like this and it adds up to thirty-four. Now if you put the thirty-four under the fifty-one this way and add them, you get three hundred and ninety-one and that's the answer." ◄SR-2

There was an instant's silence and then General Weider said, "I don't believe it. He goes through this rigmarole[3] and makes up numbers and multiplies and adds them this way and that, but I don't believe it. It's too complicated to be anything but hornswoggling."[4]

"Oh no, sir," said Aub in a sweat. "It only *seems* complicated because you're not used to it. Actually, the rules are quite simple and will work for any numbers."

"Any numbers, eh?" said the general. "Come then." He took out his own computer (a severely styled GI model) and

3. **rigmarole** (rig′ ə mə rōl′): complicated, time-wasting series of steps in a procedure.

4. **hornswoggling:** trickery.

Words to Know and Use

subside (səb sīd′) *v.* to pull back, quiet down

647

G. Reading Skill: CLARIFYING Ask students what the Congressman's comment reveals about his ability to write numbers. *(He cannot write numbers.)*

Teaching Tip

To underscore Asimov's satire, have small groups of students go to the chalkboard and explain to the rest of the class how to perform the four basic arithmetic functions: addition, subtraction, multiplication, and division.

H. Historical Sidelight Students might be interested in knowing that the Congressman's question was answered by the ancient Greeks, the first people to appreciate the importance of proving the validity of mathematical results. In the sixth century, B.C. the philosopher Thales devised mathematical proofs. The most famous of the early Greek mathematicians, however, is Euclid, a fourth-century B.C. philosopher whose *Elements* established standards for mathematicians thereafter.

I. Literary Element: SATIRE Ask students to explain the satire in Shuman's comment. *(The mathematicians in this future society do not know how to do basic arithmetic.)*

J. Critical Thinking: ANALYZING Have students analyze the society in which this story takes place, based on General Weider's comments. *(Possible response: They are narrow-minded and resistant to new ideas, even when such ideas are clearly explained.)*

DATA BANK

The physical equipment that makes up a computer is called hardware; the programs that run the hardware are called software. Such programs can involve several million instructions and often cost more than the computer itself. Below is part of a simple program to add a series of numbers. It is written in BASIC, a common computer language, and tells the computer to add series of values (V) into the sum (S) and print the sum when the value of 0 is typed in.

```
10      REM ZERO THE S.
15 LET S = Ø
20      REM READ A VALUE INTO V
25 INPUT V
30      REM INCLUDE V INTO THE S
40 LET S = S + V
50      REM RETURN IF NEEDED
60 IF V <> Ø, GO TO 25
```

K. Literary Element: IRONY Ask students to explain how the ability to do arithmetic might indeed be "magic." *(Possible response: It gives people a feeling of power as well as actual power, because an understanding of math allows them to manipulate their world through numbers.)*

L. Reading Skill: CLARIFYING *He can compute numbers without using a computer; the others are amazed because none of them can do basic arithmetic without a computer.*

M. Critical Thinking: EVALUATING Ask students to evaluate the Congressman's remarks. *(Possible response: Some might agree that computers are only tools for manipulating information and that people can handle data in the same way. Some might argue that computers are superior because they can work more quickly, while others might claim that the brain is superior because it can reason.)*

N. LEP: Satirical Humor Explain to students that the Congressman's remark is satirically humorous on two levels. First, Asimov exaggerates the amount of time it took the Congressman to learn basic arithmetic to satirize the sorry condition of the future society. Second, the Congressman's remark is humorous because it is such blatant flattery.

Teaching Tip

Form student teams to debate the superiority of the computer over pen-and-paper calculations. See if students can agree on which method is the most useful: If they could only select one, which would it be and why? Encourage them to use specific examples in their arguments.

struck it at random. "Make a five seven three eight on the paper. That's five thousand seven hundred and thirty-eight."

"Yes, sir," said Aub, taking a new sheet of paper.

"Now," (more punching of his computer), "seven two three nine. Seven thousand two hundred and thirty-nine."

"Yes, sir."

"And now multiply those two."

"It will take some time," quavered Aub.

"Take the time," said the general.

"Go ahead, Aub," said Shuman crisply.

K Aub set to work, bending low. He took another sheet of paper and another. The general took out his watch finally and stared at it. "Are you through with your magic-making, Technician?"

"I'm almost done, sir. —Here it is, sir. Forty-one million, five hundred and thirty-seven thousand, three hundred and eighty-two." He showed the scrawled figures of the result.

General Weider smiled bitterly. He pushed the multiplication contact on his computer and let the numbers whirl to a halt. And then he stared and said in a surprised squeak, "Great Galaxy, the fella's right."

L 

What is Aub's gift and why are the others so amazed by it?

The President of the Terrestrial Federation had grown haggard in office, and, in private, he allowed a look of settled melancholy to appear on his sensitive features. The Denebian war, after its early start of vast movement and great popularity, had trickled down into a sordid matter of maneuver and countermaneuver, with discontent rising steadily on Earth. Possibly, it was rising on Deneb, too.

And now Congressman Brant, head of the important Committee on Military Appropriations, was cheerfully and smoothly spending his half-hour appointment spouting nonsense.

"Computing without a computer," said the president impatiently, "is a contradiction in terms."

"Computing," said the congressman, "is only a system for handling data. A machine might do it, or the human brain might. Let me give you an example." And, using the new skills he had learned, he worked out sums and products until the president, despite himself, grew interested. M

"Does this always work?"

"Every time, Mr. President. It is foolproof."

"Is it hard to learn?"

"It took me a week to get the real hang of it. I think you would do better." N

"Well," said the president, considering, "it's an interesting parlor game, but what is the use of it?"

"What is the use of a newborn baby, Mr. President? At the moment there is no use, but don't you see that this points the way toward liberation from the machine? Consider, Mr. President"—the congressman rose and his deep voice automatically took on some of the cadences[5] he used in public debate— "that the Denebian war is a war of computer against computer. Their computers forge an impenetrable shield of countermissiles against our missiles, and ours

5. **cadences** (kād′ 'ns iz): the risings and fallings in voice tone during speaking.

Words to Know and Use	**haggard** (hag′ ərd) *adj.* disheveled and worn in appearance **melancholy** (mel′ ən käl′ ē) *n.* gloom; depression **sordid** (sôr′ did) *adj.* despicable; grasping

REAL LIFE CONNECTIONS

To help students recognize similarities between the president's situation and their own, have them describe a time when they realized that something they were learning in school could be of great use to them in their lives. Have volunteers name the subject they were learning and why they felt it was important. For example, students might suggest that learning to read maps in social studies was important because they knew they would one day like to travel. List the subjects and the reasons on the chalkboard for all to share.

forge one against theirs. If we advance the efficiency of our computers, so do they theirs, and for five years a precarious and profitless balance has existed.

"Now we have in our hands a method for going beyond the computer, leapfrogging it, passing through it. We will combine the mechanics of computation with human thought; we will have the equivalent of intelligent computers; billions of them. I can't predict what the consequences will be in detail, but they will be incalculable. And if Deneb beats us to the punch, they may be unimaginably catastrophic."

The president said, troubled, "What would you have me do?"

"Put the power of the administration behind the establishment of a secret project on human computation. Call it Project Number, if you like. I can vouch for my committee, but I will need the administration behind me."

"But how far can human computation go?"

"There is no limit. According to Programmer Shuman, who first introduced me to this discovery—"

"I've heard of Shuman, of course."

"Yes. Well, Dr. Shuman tells me that in theory there is nothing the computer can do that the human mind cannot do. The computer merely takes a finite amount of data and performs a finite number of operations upon them. The human mind can duplicate the process."

The president considered that. He said, "If Shuman says this, I am inclined to believe him—in theory. But, in practice, how can anyone know how a computer works?"

Brant laughed genially. "Well, Mr. President, I asked the same question. It seems that at one time computers were designed directly by human beings. Those were simple computers, of course, this being before the time of the rational use of computers to design more advanced computers."

"Yes, yes. Go on."

"Technician Aub apparently had, as his hobby, the reconstruction of some of these ancient devices, and in so doing he studied the details of their workings and found he could imitate them. The multiplication I just performed for you is an imitation of the workings of a computer."

"Amazing!"

The congressman coughed gently. "If I may make another point, Mr. President—the further we can develop this thing, the more we can divert our Federal effort from computer production and computer maintenance. As the human brain takes over, more of our energy can be directed into peacetime pursuits, and the impingement[6] of war on the ordinary man will be less. This will be most advantageous for the party in power, of course."

What advantage do these men see to human computation?

"Ah," said the president, "I see your point. Well, sit down, Congressman, sit down. I want some time to think about this. —But meanwhile, show me that multiplication trick again. Let's see if I can't catch the point of it."

6. **impingement** (im pinj′ mənt): effect.

Words to Know and Use

catastrophic (kat′ ə sträf′ ik) *adj.* disastrous on a huge scale
finite (fī′ nīt′) *adj.* having a beginning and an ending

649

O. Literary Element: SATIRE Ask students how Asimov is making fun of the society that he has created—and ours—in this passage. Ask what lesson he might be teaching. *(Possible response: Both societies intended the computer to go beyond pen-and-paper calculations; the people in the story now realize that in some ways human thought is far superior to machine calculations. Asimov is satirizing our reliance on machines and our distrust of human thought and might be suggesting that we "return to basics" and rely on our own abilities.)*

P. Reading Skill: PREDICTING Have students predict the purpose of "Project Number." *(Possible response: to teach everyone in the society to calculate by hand; to use the power of hand calculations to defeat the Denebians.)*

Q. Literary Element: DRAMATIC IRONY Ask students what they know about the computers that the characters in the story do not. *(Students know that humans invented the computers. This makes the passage highly ironic.)*

Teaching Tip

Suggest that students give speeches explaining how various common mechanical devices work. They might want to demonstrate a clock or motor, for example. If possible, have them use the device in their speech.

R. Reading Skill: CLARIFYING *They will be able to out-think the Denebians and defeat them in war. They can then direct more of their energy to peacetime pursuits.*

PROFESSIONAL NOTEBOOK

Recent research has also transformed our understanding of how literacy is acquired. . . . The picture of literacy development that emerges from these studies is that children learn most effectively through participation in meaningful joint activities in which their performance is assisted and guided by a more competent member of the culture. Simply telling students to read more critically or make their point more effectively in writing will be of no help unless they have developed an understanding of the mental activities involved. For this to happen, they need to participate jointly in reading and writing events with their teacher or more competent peers, in which these internal activities are externalized—and thus made available for appropriation—in talk about the text.

GORDON WELLS, "THE CONDITIONS THAT ENCOURAGE LITERATE THINKING," *The Education Digest*, VOL. LV, NO. 9 (MAY 1990, P. 25)

S. Critical Thinking: ANALYZING Have students analyze some of the advantages of the human mind *not* giving the same answer every time. *(Possible response: The ability to look at a problem and come up with different responses is invaluable in problem solving. Many important discoveries have been made by people able answer a common problem in an uncommon way.)*

T. LEP: Satirical Humor Point out to students the satiric humor here: The mind can duplicate the computer because the mind *created* the computer.

U. Historical Sidelight The earliest known written mathematics dates from about 2000 B.C. and is preserved on papyrus scrolls from Egypt and on clay tablets from Mesopotamia. Some scrolls contain rudimentary formulas for computing areas or volumes and for solving such arithmetic problems as the division of wages among workers. The Nile's annual flooding required accurate surveying, which the Egyptians perfected through geometric techniques.

V. Literary Element: DRAMATIC IRONY Ask students to explain the dramatic irony in Shuman's remarks. *(The reader knows that people did indeed invent computers, using their knowledge of computation. Just because the word Shuman coined to descibe arithmetic—*graphitics*—derives from a European word does not mean that his reasoning is correct.)*

W. Reading Skill: INFERRING Have students describe life in the future, according to this story. *(Possible responses: Mass-transference has replaced conventional transportation, communication is faster and more efficient, people rely on machines.)*

Programmer Shuman did not try to hurry matters. Loesser was conservative, very conservative, and liked to deal with computers as his father and grandfather had. Still, he controlled the West European computer combine, and if he could be persuaded to join Project Number in full enthusiasm, a great deal would be accomplished.

But Loesser was holding back. He said, "I'm not sure I like the idea of relaxing our hold on computers. The human mind is a capricious thing. The computer will give the same answer to the same problem each time. What guarantee have we that the human mind will do the same?"

"The human mind, Computer Loesser, only manipulates facts. It doesn't matter whether the human mind or a machine does it. They are just tools."

"Yes, yes. I've gone over your ingenious demonstration that the mind can duplicate the computer, but it seems to me a little in the air. I'll grant the theory, but what reason have we for thinking that theory can be converted to practice?"

"I think we have reason, sir. After all, computers have not always existed. The cave men with their triremes,[7] stone axes, and railroads had no computers."

"And possibly they did not compute."

"You know better than that. Even the building of a railroad or a ziggurat[8] called for some computing, and that must have been without computers as we know them."

"Do you suggest they computed in the fashion you demonstrate?"

"Probably not. After all, this method—we call it 'graphitics,' by the way, from the old European word *grapho,* meaning 'to write'—is developed from the computers themselves, so it cannot have antedated[9] them. Still, the cave men must have had *some* method, eh?"

"Lost arts! If you're going to talk about lost arts—"

"No, no. I'm not a lost art enthusiast, though I don't say there may not be some. After all, man was eating grain before hydroponics,[10] and if the primitives ate grain, they must have grown it in soil. What else could they have done?"

"I don't know, but I'll believe in soil-growing when I see someone grow grain in soil. And I'll believe in making fire by rubbing two pieces of flint together when I see that, too."

Shuman grew placative.[11] "Well, let's stick to graphitics. It's just part of the process of etherealization.[12] Transportation by means of bulky contrivances is giving way to direct mass-transference. Communications devices become less massive and more efficient constantly. For that matter, compare your pocket computer with the massive jobs of a thousand years ago. Why not, then, the last step of doing away with computers altogether? Come, sir, Project Number is a going concern; progress is already headlong. But we want your help. If patriotism doesn't move you, consider the intellectual adventure involved."

7. **triremes** (trī′ rēmz′): ancient warships, with three sets of oars on each side.

8. **ziggurat** (zig′ oo rat′): pyramid-shaped structure (of ancient Assyrians and Babylonians).

9. **antedated** (an′ ti dāt′ id): occurred earlier than.

10. **hydroponics:** the science of growing plants in nutrient-fortified solutions or inert material instead of in soil.

11. **placative:** appeased, calm; not angry.

12. **etherealization** (ē thir′ ē əl i zā′ shən): process of making something unearthly; treating something new and unknown as unearthly.

Words to Know and Use | **capricious** (kə prish′ əs) *adj.* unpredictable; erratic

650

DATA BANK

The storage area in modern computers is called a RAM, for random access memory. The amount of memory a computer can store is measured in "bytes," each of which usually contains eight bits of information. RAM ranges in size from a few hundred bytes in the smallest microprocessors to several million bytes in the large "mainframe" computers. Most computers have a memory section called ROM (read only memory), reserved for storing permanent programs or information.

MANDRIX 1977
Ed Paschke Phyllis Kind Gallery, Chicago.

Loesser said skeptically, "What progress? What can you do beyond multiplication? Can you integrate a transcendental function?"

"In time, sir. In time. In the last month I have learned to handle division. I can determine, and correctly, integral quotients and decimal quotients."

"Decimal quotients? To how many places?"

Programmer Shuman tried to keep his tone casual. "Any number!"

Loesser's lower jaw dropped. "Without a computer?" X

"Set me a problem."

"Divide twenty-seven by thirteen. Take it to six places."

Five minutes later, Shuman said, "Two point oh seven six nine two three."

Loesser checked it. "Well, now, that's

Art Note
Chicago painter Ed Paschke expresses his view of modern humanity by altering forms and endowing them with glowing electronic colors. In *Mandrix,* the man appears masked, his head elongated, his nose defined by a triangle, black eyesockets circled as if with tiny lights. Yet his cry of anguish or anger is painfully real. *If the subject is counting with his fingers, which character in The Feeling of Power might he represent?*

Teaching Tip
Have small groups of students define and demonstrate integral quotients and decimal quotients by going to the chalkboard and solving brief problems. Then ask them to give examples of when such information would be of use in their daily lives.

X. Literary Element: SATIRE Have students explain how Asimov uses exaggeration in this passage to satirize the society that he describes. *(Possible response: Loesser's exaggerated response to Shuman's knowledge of division pokes fun at a society that can build war computers but not handle basic arithmetic.)*

Y. LEP: Satirical Humor Point out to students the satirical humor in using business jargon such as *tricky points* and *licked the bugs* to describe manipulating square roots. Have students suggest other terms that would create the same effect, such as *ironed out the kinks.*

Z. Reading Skill: CLARIFYING *Shuman demonstrates his ability to use decimals in division and tells Loesser that Aub has almost figured out how to determine square and cube roots.*

AA. Reading Skill: INFERRING Ask students what the General means by *fundamentals. (He means a basic knowledge of arithmetic.)*

BB. Critical Thinking: EVALUATING Have students evaluate General Weider's plans for "Project Number." *(Possible responses: Some students may agree with the General that a speedy end to the war might be the best for all involved, while others may argue that he and the others who back him are perverting this new knowledge to evil ends.)*

CC. Historical Sidelight Before World War II, guided missiles were limited to experimental, pilotless aircraft controlled by radio. Today guided missiles are grouped into four launch-to-target categories: surface-to-surface, surface-to-air, air-to-surface, and air-to-air—"surface" in each case signifying on as well as below the surface of the land or sea. Missiles can also be grouped by the area of operation or flight characteristics. There are no manned missiles.

amazing. Multiplication didn't impress me too much because it involved integers[13] after all, and I thought trick manipulation might do it. But decimals—"

"And that is not all. There is a new development that is, so far, top secret and that, strictly speaking, I ought not to mention. Still—we may have made a breakthrough on the square root front."

"Square roots?"

Y "It involves some tricky points and we haven't licked the bugs yet, but Technician Aub, the man who invented the science and who has an amazing intuition in connection with it, maintains he has the problem almost solved. And he is only a Technician. A man like yourself, a trained and talented mathematician, ought to have no difficulty."

"Square roots," muttered Loesser, attracted.

"Cube roots, too. Are you with us?"

Loesser's hand thrust out suddenly,

SR-5 ▶ "Count me in."

Z **clarify** How does Shuman overcome Loesser's doubts about graphitics?

General Weider stumped his way back and forth at the head of the room and addressed his listeners after the fashion of a savage teacher facing a group of recalcitrant students. It made no difference to the general that they were the civilian scientists heading Project Number. The general was the overall head, and he so considered himself at every waking moment.

He said, "Now square roots are all fine. I can't do them myself and I don't understand the methods, but they're fine. Still, the Project will not be sidetracked into what some of you call the fundamentals. You can play with graphitics any way you want to after the war is over, but right now we have specific and very practical problems to solve." AA

In a far corner, Technician Aub listened with painful attention. He was no longer a Technician, of course, having been relieved of his duties and assigned to the Project, with a fine-sounding title and good pay. But, of course, the social distinction remained and the highly placed scientific leaders could never bring themselves to admit him to their ranks on a footing of equality. Nor, to do Aub justice, did he, himself, wish it. He was as uncomfortable with them as they with him.

The general was saying, "Our goal is a simple one, gentlemen; the replacement of the computer. A ship that can navigate space without a computer on board can be constructed in one-fifth the time and at one-tenth the expense of a computer-laden ship. We could build fleets five times, ten times as great as Deneb could if we could but eliminate the computer. BB ◀ SR-6

"And I see something even beyond this. It may be fantastic now, a mere dream, but in the future I see the manned missile!" CC

There was an instant murmur from the audience.

The general drove on. "At the present time, our chief bottleneck is the fact that missiles are limited in intelligence. The computer controlling them can only be so large, and for that reason they can meet the

13. **integers:** the set of positive and negative whole numbers, including 0, such as 2 or –5.

Words to Know and Use

recalcitrant (ri kal′ si trənt) *adj.* unruly and stubbornly defiant of authority

CULTURAL CONNECTION

Ask students from other cultures as well as those who are native born to explain whether people in their culture value knowledge mainly for its own sake or primarily because it has some practical application. For example, do people in their culture more highly respect those who study fields such as philosophy and ancient languages for the pleasure it gives them or those who are able to use that knowledge to achieve something concrete? Ask volunteers to share specific examples. You might then want to ask students to agree or disagree with the way "graphitics" is used in "Project Number."

changing nature of anti-missile defenses in an unsatisfactory way. Few missiles, if any, accomplish their goal, and missile warfare is coming to a dead end—for the enemy, fortunately, as well as for ourselves.

"On the other hand, a missile with a man or two within, controlling flight by graphitics, would be lighter, more mobile, more intelligent. It would give us a lead that might well mean the margin of victory. Besides which, gentlemen, the exigencies[14] of war compel us to remember one thing. A man is much more dispensable than a computer. Manned missiles could be launched in numbers and under circumstances that no good general would care to undertake as far as computer-directed missiles are concerned—" DD

EE 

What is General Weider's plan for graphitics?

He said much more, but Technician Aub did not wait.

Technician Aub, in the privacy of his quarters, labored long over the note he was leaving behind. It read finally as follows:

"When I began the study of what is now called graphitics, it was no more than a hobby. I saw no more in it than an interesting amusement, an exercise of mind.

"When Project Number began, I thought that others were wiser than I; that graphitics might be put to practical use as a benefit to mankind, to aid in the production of really practical mass-transference devices perhaps. But now I see it is to be used only for death and destruction.

"I cannot face the responsibility involved in having invented graphitics."

He then deliberately turned the focus of a protein-depolarizer on himself and fell instantly and painlessly dead.

What is Aub saying in his note?

 FF

They stood over the grave of the little Technician while tribute was paid to the greatness of his discovery.

Programmer Shuman bowed his head along with the rest of them but remained unmoved. The Technician had done his share and was no longer needed, after all. He might have started graphitics, but now that it had started, it would carry on by itself overwhelmingly, triumphantly, until manned missiles were possible with who knew what else. ◀SR-7

Nine times seven, thought Shuman with deep satisfaction, is sixty-three, and I don't need a computer to tell me so. The computer is in my own head. GG

And it was amazing the feeling of power that gave him. ❧ ◀SR-8

14. **exigencies** (eks′ ə jen sēz): immediate demands.

DD. Literary Element: SATIRE Have students discuss how this passage is satirical. *(Possible response: Asimov is satirizing a society that would decide a machine is more important than a person.)*

EE. Reading Skill: CLARIFYING *He wants to use it to design manned missiles to defeat the Denebians.*

Teaching Tip

Have students role-play a confrontation between Aub and world leaders in which he tries to convince them that "graphitics" has more valuable uses than warfare. First, have students brainstorm how this society might use such an invention.

FF. Reading Skill: CLARIFYING *He is saying that he cannot face the horrifying use to which graphitics is being put and his responsibility for the death and destruction that will result.*

GG. Critical Thinking: EVALUATING Ask students if they agree with Shuman's feelings. *(Possible responses: Yes, because knowledge is power; no, because knowledge should be useful to be worthwhile.)*

Check Test

1. What does Aub discover? *(how to do arithmetic without a computer)*

2. Why is everyone so amazed by Aub's discovery? *(No one else can do it.)*

3. What is Project Number? *(a secret project designed to use Aub's discovery for war)*

4. What happens to Aub at the end of the story? *(He kills himself.)*

Encouraging Independent Reading

"The Fun They Had," a short story by Isaac Asimov
I, Robot, interrelated short stories by Isaac Asimov
2001: A Space Odyssey, a novel by Arthur C. Clarke
"The Virtuoso," a short story by Herbert Goldstone

Student Response

Responding to Reading

These questions are open-ended, with no "right" or "wrong" answers. However, responses must be supported with information from the selection. Possible answers follow:

1. Any impression of the society, negative or positive, is valid.

2. Students may think that people have become dependent on computers because they are lazy or because so much time has passed since their invention that people have forgotten there was ever another way.

3. Students may say that Aub's gift is valuable because of the pleasure derived from being able to reason; because it allows people to be independent of machines; or because it can be used to wage war. In any case, the value of Aub's gift is an increased feeling of power.

4. Students may say that the story makes fun of how the military can use the new gift only to make war or that it mocks the pointlessness of the war between Earth and Deneb.

5. Some students may say that Aub, unlike Graham, is horrified by the destruction his invention will cause if it's misused; others may note that both men create new inventions with the potential to cause vast destruction.

6. Students might say that learning how to drive a car or learning to speak a foreign language has given them a feeling of power.

Responding to Reading

First Impressions

1. What do you think of the society in which this story takes place?

Second Thoughts

2. Why do you think the people in this story have become so dependent on computers?
3. What is the value of Aub's gift?

   Think about
   - its value to Aub
   - its value to Shuman
   - its value to others like Brant, the President, Loesser, and General Weider
4. What general failings of the human race are pointed out and made fun of in this story?

   Think about
   - the military's vision for how to use this new gift
   - the situation on the Earth and the planet Deneb
5. Compare and contrast the situations and reactions of Aub in this story and Dr. Graham in "The Weapon."

Broader Connections

6. At the end of the story, Shuman experiences a "feeling of power" because he has gained control over something that at one time seemed to master him. Make a list of ways that something you have learned might give you "a feeling of power."

Literary Concept: Satire

"A Feeling of Power" is a **satire,** a kind of writing that pokes fun at its subject in order to teach a lesson or improve society. **Exaggeration** is one of the satirist's main tools. The adult characters in this story cannot solve a third-grade problem. Find other exaggerations in the story. How do these contribute to the satire?

Concept Review: Dramatic Irony A reader of a story may learn information that certain characters do not know. Such an instance is called **dramatic irony.** Describe an instance of dramatic irony in this story.

Literery Concept—Satire

Possible responses: General Weider's astonishment at Aub's abilities, Loesser's humorous response to the idea of growing food in soil, and his amazement that Shuman can use decimals in division are also examples of exaggeration used to make a point or teach a lesson. Refer to annotations **E, I, O, X,** and **DD.**

Concept Review: Dramatic Irony *Possible response: Readers learn before Aub does the uses to which his invention will be put.* Refer to annotations **Q** and **V.**

Writing Options

1. "The Feeling of Power" deals with a computer's ability to calculate. What if the story concentrated instead on a computer's ability to store information? In this version, humans would have weak memories because of computer-dependence. Write a summary of the story with this new plot.

2. Select a problem in mathematics. Write a "how to" paper explaining to a young audience the steps in solving a problem. Make sure to use the second-person "you" voice. Point out tricky places in the process.

3. Pretend that you have been hired to write ads for graphitics. Make a list of the selling points such as "ease" and "self-fulfillment." Build your ads around these selling points. Remember that you will be directing ads at people who cannot perform any mathematical operations on their own.

4. What if Aub had given his secret to the Denebians? Rewrite the story with this change.

Vocabulary Practice

Exercise Read each phrase below and write the word from the list suggested by the phrase.

1. a villain who is infamous
2. appearing old and worn
3. a hurricane of monstrous size
4. in a demanding and commanding way
5. a rebellious student who refuses to obey authority
6. someone who is unpredictable
7. in a limited way
8. a dirty affair
9. in a gloomy mood
10. quiet down

Words to Know and Use

capricious
catastrophic
finite
haggard
imperative
melancholy
notorious
recalcitrant
sordid
subside

Writing Options

The Writing Options are designed to meet varied student interests and abilities. Have each student choose one writing activity to complete. You may wish to guide some students to an option that requires less writing.

Journal Update Have students review their journal entries for "The Feeling of Power." What new reflections can they add to their concepts of power?

Vocabulary Practice

1. notorious
2. haggard
3. catastrophic
4. imperative
5. recalcitrant
6. capricious
7. finite
8. sordid
9. melancholy
10. subside

e x t e n d

Options for Learning

These activities suit a variety of learning styles and modes of expression. Allow students to review the options and then choose the one they wish to do. Many are excellent collaborative learning projects.

1. Technical Crossword Suggest that students list terms from the story and then plot their crosswords on graph paper.

2. Math Whiz Students might create a chart to illustrate their findings.

3. Computer Job Search Interviews can be conducted with a tape recorder. Students may want to chart their findings.

4. Take a Hike Students can create a cluster diagram to generate ideas.

Fact Finder

The first true computer, a mechanical adding machine, was invented by French philosopher Blaise Pascal in 1642. Students can find this information in an encyclopedia.

Additional Information About the Author

Isaac Asimov Asimov decided to pursue the dual careers of science and writing when at age fifteen he entered Columbia University. At eighteen he sold his first story, "Marooned off Vesta," to *Amazing Stories.* After serving in World War II, he earned a Ph.D. from Columbia in 1948. He then joined the faculty of Boston University School of Medicine, rising to professor of biochemistry. Ten years later he turned to writing full-time, and by 1980 he had published 225 books for both young and adult readers.

Closure

"The Feeling of Power" explores the negative price of technology. Have students find instances from daily life where technology has provided great benefits to people.

Options for Learning

1 • Technical Crossword Design a crossword puzzle using mathematical and other technical terms from "The Feeling of Power." Use additional terms as needed.

2 • Math Whiz Check each math problem in the story to be sure the answer is correct. Do each on paper and by calculator. Time each process and compare its speed. If you know of any shortcuts for figuring calculations, share them with the class.

3 • Computer Job Search Research some of the most recent developments in computer technology. If possible, interview someone from this field regarding future job potential within the industry. Report your findings to the class.

4 • Take a Hike People in our society have become automobile-dependent just as people in the story are computer-dependent. Write an essay describing the many ways life would change if people drove cars only in emergencies.

FACT FINDER

Who invented the first computer?

Isaac Asimov

1920–

"It seems fair to say," notes Isaac Asimov, "that no one has written more books on more subjects than I." Who could argue with someone who has published more than 400 books on dozens and dozens of subjects?

Asimov was born in Russia, but his parents soon moved to Brooklyn, New York. There, his interest in writing began as he read science-fiction magazines that his parents sold at their candy store. He studied science in school, but developed many other interests, and now writes about a wide range of subjects.

Asimov is best known as a science-fiction writer for works such as *Pebble in the Sky* and the *Foundation* trilogy. In his science-fiction, he has often predicted future realities such as the computer revolution. He has also written on numerous other subjects. His history books include *The Roman Empire* and *The Golden Door: The United States From 1865 to 1917.* His other books range from *Asimov's Guide to the Bible* and *Asimov's Guide to Shakespeare* to his *Treasury of Humor,* and countless students refer to his *Encyclopedia of Science* and other factual science books. Of his astounding output of writing, Asimov says simply, "It's not my fault. I like to write and people seem willing to let me."

Cross-Curricular Options

Math: Have students write a basic computer program and demonstrate it for the class.

History: Students might like to research the history of computers, detailing the specific milestones in the development of key machines.

Science: Have students select an aspect of the space program and prepare an oral report on it.

English: Suggest that students read another science-fiction story, or a book or article by Asimov, and compare it to "The Feeling of Power." Have them explain how the two works are similar and different.

Publishing: Compile the contributions of all students. Display or make copies to distribute.

e x p l o r e

Essay

The Suspected Shopper

ELLEN GOODMAN

Examine What You Know (Prior Knowledge)

Imagine that you have been made manager of a medium-sized variety store in your community. The store is popular, and sales are excellent, but in recent times the store has experienced a dramatic increase in loss of profits through shoplifting. The problem, in fact, is so serious that you have been told that you must either drastically reduce shoplifting or raise prices in order to stay in business. Make a list of the ways that you plan to reduce shoplifting. Remember, however, that your goal is to lower the chances of shoplifting without reducing the number of shoppers.

Expand Your Knowledge (Building Background)

Store owners today have good reason to be concerned about shoplifting. About 2 million Americans are charged annually for this crime. For every arrest, however, police estimate that thirty-five shoplifters are never caught. Of those caught, 75 percent are from middle or higher-economic brackets, and 80 percent have the cash or credit cards in their pockets to pay for their stolen goods. Each year the value of these stolen items comes to approximately 35 billion dollars. Retailers have no choice but to pass this loss on to the consumers. For example, a family of four spends about three hundred dollars more than it should each year to cover the cost of merchandise that has "walked" out of stores.

Write Before You Read (Journal Writing)

Imagine that you are an experienced store detective. What signs do you look for to spot shoplifters? Do shoplifters wear certain clothes? Do they have a certain body language that gives them away? Briefly describe the cues you use to identify suspicious behavior.

■ *A biography of the author can be found in the Reader's Handbook.*

Objectives

- To understand a persuasive essay
- To express understanding of the work through a choice of writing options, including a letter, an essay, and a list of creative ideas

Prereading/Motivation

Examine What You Know

Discussion Prompts: What are some methods to stop shoplifting that you've seen used in other stores? Which of the ways on your list do you think will be the most effective? Why? Which method do you think will do the least to discourage shoppers? Explain your answer.

Expand Your Knowledge

Discussion Prompts: Why do you think such a high percentage of shoplifters come from the middle- or high-economic brackets? How would you explain the fact that most people arrested have the money with them to pay for their goods? In light of this information, decide why you think people shoplift.

Thematic Link—The Price of Technology

In this article, Ellen Goodman describes how technology affects the price and experience of shopping.

Additional Journal Writing

Suggest these additional journal topics to students:

- What does the title "The Suspected Shopper" make you think the essay will be about?
- What do you think the "suspected shopper" might be suspected of doing?
- What is it like to be wrongly suspected of doing something against the rules?

For other journal opportunities, refer students to Examine What You Know (p. 657) and Broader Connections (p. 660).

Additional Resources

UNIT FIVE RESOURCE BOOK

Reader's Guidesheet, p. 38
Vocabulary Worksheet, p. 39
Selection and Vocabulary Check Tests, p. 40
Selection Test, pp. 41–42

Collaborative Learning

Opportunities for collaborative learning appear throughout the lesson and include Examine What You Know and Write Before You Read (p. 657).

Support for Students of Limited English Proficiency

- Use **Reader's Guidesheet,** p. 38
- "The Suspected Shopper" contains allusions to warfare that may be unfamiliar to students.
- **Annotations B and C** focus on unfamiliar allusions to warfare.
- In addition, some students may be unfamiliar with the anti-theft devices described in the essay. Encourage such students to work with partners who can explain these shopping experiences. Urge students from other cultures to tell the class of other methods of shopping besides stores and malls.

Text Annotations

A. Literary Element: SIMILE Have students isolate the simile in this passage and analyze its effect. *(The simile "spread their wares like plush welcome mats across the pages of my newspaper" suggests that the stores are warm and inviting places, contrasting with the "warnings and wariness" that the author finds when she shops.)*

Teaching Tip

Trace with students Goodman's catalog technique as she lists the security devices that she encounters while shopping. Have students analyze how such a list of examples is especially convincing and explain that they can use the same technique in their own writing. If time permits, have them add to Goodman's list by brainstorming more examples.

B. LEP: Allusions Ask students why Goodman would use an allusion to warfare when writing about shopping. *(Possible response: to indicate that shopping has become like a war, with the consumer pitted against the merchant and everyone suffering as a result.)*

C. LEP: Allusions Explain to students that Goodman is here alluding to instances during war when innocent bystanders are mistakenly shot by their own side. Tell students about a prize-winning book on the subject, *Friendly Fire* by Frances Fitzgerald.

The Suspected Shopper

ELLEN GOODMAN

A It is Saturday, Shopping Saturday, as it's called by the merchants who spread their wares like plush welcome mats across the pages of my newspaper.

But the real market I discover is a different, less eager place than the one I read about. On this Shopping Saturday I don't find welcomes, I find warnings and wariness.

At the first store, a bold sign of the times confronts me: SHOPLIFTERS WILL BE PROSECUTED TO THE FULL EXTENT OF THE LAW.

At the second store, instead of a greeter, I find a doorkeeper. It is his job, his duty, to bar my entrance. To pass, I must give up the shopping bag on my arm. I check it in and check it out.

At the third store, I venture as far as the dressing room. Here I meet another worker paid to protect the merchandise rather than to sell it. The guard of this dressing room counts the number of items I carry in and will count the number of items I carry out.

In the mirror, a long, white, plastic security tag juts out from the blouse tucked into the skirt. I try futilely to pat it down along my left hip, try futilely to zip the skirt. SR-1

Finally, during these strange gyrations,[1] a thought seeps through years of dulled consciousness, layers of denial. Something has happened to the relationship between shops and shoppers. I no longer feel like a woman in search of a shirt. I feel like an enemy at Checkpoint Charlie.[2] B

I finally, belatedly, realize that I am treated less like a customer these days and more like a criminal. And I hate it. This change happened gradually, and understandably. Security rose in tandem[3] with theft. The defenses of the shopkeepers went up, step by step, with the offenses of the thieves.

But now as the weapons escalate, it's the average consumer, the innocent bystander, who is hit by friendly fire. C SR-2

I don't remember the first time an errant[4] security tag buzzed at the doorway, the first time I saw a camera eye in a dress department. I accepted it as part of the price of living in a tight honesty market.

In the supermarket, they began to insist on a mug shot before they would cash my check. I tried not to take it personally. At the drugstore, the cashier began to staple my bags closed. And I tried not to take it personally. SR-3

1. **gyrations:** twisting motions.
2. **Checkpoint Charlie:** a guarded point along the Berlin Wall, which used to separate East and West Berlin. Travelers had to obtain permission from both East German and American border authorities at this point to pass from one side of the city to the other.
3. **in tandem:** together; as a pair.
4. **errant:** wandering or traveling from the correct path.

STRUCTURED READING FOR LESS PROFICIENT STUDENTS

These questions can help to guide students through the reading. Ask each question at the point of the selection where the SR number appears in the margin.

SR–1. Summarize Goodman's experiences shopping. *(She sees a sign warning that shoplifters will be prosecuted, she must relinquish her packages before entering a store, a checker counts the items she wishes to try on, and she cannot judge how a skirt fits because of the security tag.)* **Summarizing**

SR–2. What does she hate about shopping? *(She hates being treated as a criminal rather than a customer.)* **Literal recall**

SR–3. What happens in the supermarket? *(They insist on taking her picture before they will cash her check.)* **Literal recall**

SR–4. What effect does Goodman say thievery has had on shopping? *(Merchant distrust has infected everyone; no one trusts anyone else.)* **Clarifying**

SR–5. How does Goodman feel when she finishes shopping? *(resentful)* **Literal recall**

D Now, these experiences have accumulated until I feel routinely treated like a suspect. At the jewelry store, the door is unlocked only for those who pass judgment. In the junior department, the suede pants are permanently attached to the hangers. In the gift shop, the cases are only opened with a key.

I am not surprised anymore, but I am finally aware of just how unpleasant it is to be dealt with as guilty until we prove our innocence. Anyplace we are not known, we are not trusted. The old slogan, "Let the Consumer Beware," has been replaced with a new slogan: "Beware of the Consumer."

It is no fun to be Belgium[5] in the war between sales and security. Thievery has changed the atmosphere of the marketplace. Merchant distrust has spread
E through the ventilation system of a whole
SR-4 business, a whole city, and it infects all of us.

At the cashier counter today, with my shirt in hand, I the Accused stand quietly while the saleswoman takes my credit card. I watch her round up the usual suspicions. In front of my face, without a hint of embarrassment, she checks my charge number against the list of stolen credit vehicles. F While I stand there, she calls the clearinghouse of bad debtors.

Having passed both tests, I am instructed to add my name, address, serial number to the bottom of the charge. She checks one signature against another, the picture against the person. Only then does she release the shirt into my custody.

And so this Shopping Saturday I take home six ounces of silk and a load of resentment. ❧ G SR-5

5. **It . . . Belgium:** the country of Belgium incorporates an area fiercely fought over during both World War I and World War II.

PROFESSIONAL NOTEBOOK

How to create classroom communities of literate thinkers is the challenge that faces us. . . . the solution rests with the encouragement of teachers to act as literate thinkers themselves: using the evidence from observations in their own classrooms as texts to empower their own planned curriculum change and development.

GORDON WELLS, "THE CONDITIONS THAT ENCOURAGE LITERATE THINKING," *Educational Leadership* Reprinted in *The Education Digest* (MAY 1990, P. 26)

D. Literary Element: ESSAY Ask students to explain whether this is a formal or informal essay and explain their conclusion. *(It is an informal essay because it is not rigidly organized and it includes personal accounts, such as the two examples here.)*

E. Historical Sidelight Goodman's metaphor is an allusion to Legionnaires' Disease, a severe form of pneumonia. The name comes from an outbreak of the disease at an American Legion convention at a Philadelphia hotel in 1976. Other outbreaks were later traced to the same cause: bacteria transmitted through ventilation systems.

F. Critical Thinking: ANALYZING Review different methods of arranging details, such as order of importance and chronological order, and analyze Goodman's method of arranging her details here. *(She uses chronological order, from the beginning of the shopping trip to the end.)*

G. Literary Element: AUTHOR'S PURPOSE Have students analyze Goodman's purpose in this essay. Remind them that authors may have more than one purpose. *(Possible responses: She is expressing her opinion on the change in merchants' outlook and resulting consumer discontent; she is trying to persuade the reader to help stop shoplifting. She wants to entertain the reader with her informal, humorous writing style.)*

Check Test

1. What is attached to the skirt Goodman tries on? *(a security tag)*

2. What is the writer upset about? *(the way she is treated as a criminal instead of welcomed as a consumer)*

3. What does she buy? *(a shirt)*

4. What does she feel after she finishes shopping? *(resentment)*

Encouraging Independent Reading

"The Unknown Citizen," a poem by W. H. Auden

Aunt Erma's Cope Book, humorous essays by Erma Bombeck

"The Signature," a short story by Elizabeth Enright

"My Life with R. H. Macy," a short story by Shirley Jackson

Student Response

Responding to Reading

These questions are open-ended with no "right" or "wrong" answers. However, responses must be supported with information from the selection. Possible answers follow:

1. Students may or may not identify with any part of the essay.

2. Students may think that Goodman represents the view of the honest shopper resentful of the security changes brought about by shoplifters or the view of shoppers in a hurry annoyed by the added inconvenience of anti-theft devices.

3. Students may say that the writer is resentful because store owners have assumed that, as a consumer, she is likely to be a thief or because she no longer enjoys shopping because of increased security.

4. Some students may say that the writer's feelings of resentment are justified because she seems to be honest. Others may argue that her feelings are not justified because of the enormous costs of shoplifting to both storeowners and consumers.

5. Some students may feel that teenagers have been unfairly accused, while others may see the charges as justified.

Writing Options

The Writing Options are designed to meet varied student interests and abilities. Have each student choose one writing activity to complete. You may wish to guide some students to an option that requires less writing.

Journal Update Have students review their journal entries for the selection. What new reflections can they add to their writing about "The Suspected Shopper"?

Responding to Reading

First Impressions

1. Did you identify with any part of this essay? Why?

Second Thoughts

2. What view of the average shopper does the writer present? Do you agree with this view?

3. Why does the writer carry home a "load of resentment" after shopping?

Think about
- what store owners and employees have assumed about her
- how increased security has changed shopping

4. Do you think the writer's feelings of resentment are justified? Why or why not?

Think about
- what kind of person the writer seems to be
- what you know about the costs of shoplifting to storeowners and consumers

Broader Connections

5. Teenagers are often suspected of many kinds of wrongdoing, including shoplifting. Is this suspicion justified?

Writing Options

1. Write a letter from a storeowner to Ellen Goodman. Explain why you have decided to add modern security devices to combat shoplifting and employee theft. Look back at the list of security measures you developed in Examine What You Know. Express your sensitivity to her feelings but help her see your viewpoint.

2. Why do you think there is so much shoplifting, especially if most shoplifters can pay for what they steal? Write what you think the shoplifting epidemic says about today's society.

3. How might someone like Dave Barry, the author of "A Couple of Really Neat Guys" on pages 620–621, deal with shoplifters? Come up with five creative ways he or someone else might stop shoplifting.

e x p l o r e

Poetry

Building Boom

CHARLES REZNIKOFF

All Watched Over by Machines of Loving Grace

RICHARD BRAUTIGAN

Examine What You Know (Prior Knowledge)

The next two poems contrast scenes of natural beauty with modern technology. Have you ever come across a power line in a quiet forest or a bulldozer on a deserted beach? In your journal, describe such a scene or one that you can imagine. Then compare your thoughts with those of your classmates and the two poems that follow.

Expand Your Knowledge (Building Background)

The word *cybernetic* appears in one of the poems you are about to read. Cybernetic is the adjective form of the word *cybernetics,* the science that studies and compares the body's control centers—the brain and nervous system—with complex electronic control systems. Cybernetics was first introduced by one of the most well-known mathematicians of the 20th century, Norbert Wiener, who noted that both people and machines can use feedback to monitor their progress and adjust their behavior. Knowledge of cybernetics has helped scientists develop computers for machines such as robots that can analyze data and make decisions.

Enrich Your Reading (Reading Skill)

Visualizing When you **visualize** as you read, you create mental pictures of what the writer describes. Taking the time to imagine what a person, event, or scene looks like makes reading more enjoyable. As you read the next two poems, visualize the scenes that the poets describe. If possible, sketch one or two of these scenes.

■ *Biographies of the authors can be found on page 665.*

Objectives

- To understand and analyze two contemporary poems
- To explore the use of repetition in poetry
- To practice visualizing
- To express understanding of the work through a choice of writing options, including a postcard, a poem, and a descriptive paragraph

Prereading/Motivation

Examine What You Know

Discussion Prompts: What aspects of such scenes impressed you the most? Have you seen many such scenes? a few? none at all? How was your journal entry similar to and different from your classmates' entries?

Expand Your Knowledge

Discussion Prompts: Give some examples of when you used feedback to monitor your progress. How might you use feedback to adjust your behavior? What movies or TV shows can you think of that had robots analyzing data and making decisions?

Additional Background: Cybernetics grew out of the problems scientists encountered during World War II while developing electronic brains and automatic-control mechanisms for devices such as bombsights. Cybernetics has also been applied to the study of psychology, economics, systems engineering, and various social systems.

Enrich Your Reading

Encourage students to describe what they have visualized and to share any sketches that they may make.

Thematic Link—The Price of Technology

In these poems, the price of technology is the destruction of the natural environment.

Journal Writing

These two poems contrast scenes of natural beauty with modern technology. Suggest these journal topics:

- What is a "building boom"?
- What do you think happens to nature during a "building boom"?
- How could people be "all watched over by machines of loving grace"?

For other journal opportunities, refer students to Examine What You Know (p. 661) and Real-Life Connections (p. T–663).

Additional Resources

UNIT FIVE RESOURCE BOOK

Reader's Guidesheet, p. 43
Vocabulary Worksheet, p. 44
Selection Check Test, p. 45
Selection Test, pp. 46–47

Collaborative Learning

Opportunities for collaborative learning appear throughout the lesson and include Real Life Connections (p. T–663) and Cross-Curricular Options (p. T–665).

Teaching Strategies

Support for Students of Limited English Proficiency

- Use **Reader's Guidesheet**, p. 43.
- Students may find the titles confusing and the poetry hard to follow. Ask students to explain what they think each title means. Then encourage them to paraphrase difficult passages in the poems.
- **Annotation B** from "Building Boom" and **annotation A** from "All Watched Over By Machines of Loving Grace" focus on paraphrasing.

Text Annotations

A. Reading Skill: VISUALIZING Ask students to visualize the scene the poet describes here and then share their mental pictures by describing them. *(Possible response: The willows form a tall, straight row, like a fence, but they look out of place sitting amid new apartment houses.)*

B. LEP: Paraphrasing Ask students to paraphrase these two lines. *(Possible response: Even though the trees are not spoiled by the litter all around them, the apartments somehow reduce their size, making them seem small and perhaps insignificant.)*

C. Critical Thinking: EVALUATING Ask students if they feel that beauty is a sufficient reason for existence. *(Possible responses: Some might argue that things such as trees need only be beautiful; others might say that even trees should serve a purpose, such as providing shade or giving fruit.)*

Student Response

Responding to Reading

These questions are open-ended with no "right" or "wrong" answers. However, responses must be supported with information from the selection. Possible answers follow:

1. Any image from the poem is valid.

2. Some students may say that the poem is about the destruction of a row of willow trees to provide room for an apartment house. Other students may say that the poem is about how human carelessness and negligence destroys the natural environment.

3. Some students may say that the speaker feels sad or resigned. Others may say that the speaker feels disgusted with people who pollute and destroy nature.

4. Students may say that beautiful things should be saved when they give pleasure or have great value. They may mention such things as jewelry, paintings, and antiques; the state and national forests; landmark buildings; and photographs and films that capture and preserve the beauty of the natural world.

Building Boom

CHARLES REZNIKOFF

The avenue of willows leads nowhere:
A it begins at the blank wall of a new apartment house
and ends in the middle of a lot for sale.
Papers and cans are thrown about the trees.
B The disorder does not touch the flowing branches;
but the trees have become small among the new houses,
and will be cut down—
C their beauty cannot save them.

Responding to Reading

First Impressions of "Building Boom"

1. What single image does this poem leave in your mind? Why do you suppose this image, and not another one, is what you recall?

Second Thoughts on "Building Boom"

2. In a sentence or two, summarize what this poem is about.

3. How does the speaker feel about the scene that he or she describes?

4. The speaker notes that the beauty of the willow trees "cannot save them." When is beauty a reason for saving anything?

All Watched Over by Machines of Loving Grace

RICHARD BRAUTIGAN

I like to think (and
the sooner the better!)
A of a cybernetic meadow
where mammals and computers
live together in mutually
programming harmony
like pure water
touching clear sky.

B I like to think
  (right now, please!)
of a cybernetic forest
filled with pines and electronics
where deer stroll peacefully
past computers
as if they were flowers
with spinning blossoms.

I like to think
  (it has to be!)
of a cybernetic ecology
where we are free of our labors
and joined back to nature,
C returned to our mammal
brothers and sisters,
and all watched over
by machines of loving grace.

THE ANGEL OF THE MOUNTAIN 1977 Ladislav Novak
Watercolor on paper, 13¾" × 9¾" Courtesy of Stuart Levy Gallery, New York.

REAL LIFE CONNECTIONS

In many communities and neighborhoods, housing and commercial developments have caused the destruction of the natural environment and of animal habitats. The machinery of technology has encroached on the lives of people, to the degree that many people interact more with machines—such as TVs, VCRs, radios, telephones, and computers—than they do with other people. Have students consider, discuss, and write in their journals about the impact of development and electronics on their community and on their personal lives. Have them consider how their lives would be changed if every machine they now use were suddenly to disappear.

Text Annotations

A. LEP: Paraphrasing Have students paraphrase this passage to capture its meaning and tone. *(Possible response: I can imagine a field of machines and people getting along together.)*

B. Literary Element: REPETITION Ask students to locate the other places where this phrase appears and discuss its effect. *(Possible responses: The repetition appears in the first line of each stanza. It creates rhythm; emphasizes the ironic tone; and underscores the poem's theme—the dangers of technology.)*

Art Note

Czech artist Ladislav Novák (1925–) makes his magical pictures by froissage: He crumples paper, rubs it with diluted inks, then spreads it flat to find the lines formed by the ink. In these markings he sees shapes which he then reinforces with colors and a title. My main concern is . . . transforming . . . the commonplace into something extraordinary," he explains. *How does this picture express the idea of the poem?*

C. Reading Skill: VISUALIZING Ask students how they visualize the world described in this stanza. *(Possible response: brightly colored, artificial, frightening)*

Check Test

1. Where does the avenue of willows lead in "Building Boom"? *(nowhere)*

2. What is going to happen to the willows? *(They will be cut down.)*

3. In the second poem, what do the deer stroll past in the cybernetic forest? *(computers)*

4. Who or what watches over the cybernetic ecology? *(machines of loving grace)*

Encouraging Independent Reading

"Cargoes," a poem by John Masefield
"Song of the Open Road," a poem by Ogden Nash
"Apartment House," a poem by Gerald Raftery
"Southbound on the Freeway," a poem by May Swenson
"Telephone Poles," a poem by John Updike

Student Response

Responding to Reading

1. Any impression based on the poem is valid.

2. Students may say that the speaker thinks technology has already taken control over nature or that it very shortly will; that the speaker fears technology will destroy nature and people's relationship with nature; and that the speaker would like to turn back "progress."

3. Some students may say that the speaker is sarcastic, as shown by the words in parentheses. Others may see him as serious, as shown by his description of the machines.

4. Students may say the contrasting images create the poem's sarcastic tone or ironic overtones; that the idea of "Machines of Loving Grace" is a contradiction that jolts the reader into awareness; and that the contrast between electronics and mammals makes the reader aware of the high price paid for technology.

5. Students may say that both poets respect nature and are sorry for its destruction. Some may feel that Reznikoff feels more deeply for nature than Brautigan does because of the sarcastic tone of Brautigan's poem.

6. Some students may say that the first poem has a serious tone, while the second is ironic or sarcastic. Others may see the first poem as having a sad tone, the second as being happy or wistful.

7. Students may argue that both poems say humans pay a very high price for technology. Others may say that the second poem sees the technological control greater and more frightening than the first.

Writing Options

The Writing Options are designed to meet varied student interests and abilities. Have each student choose one writing activity to complete. You may wish to guide some students to an option that requires less writing.

Journal Update Have students review their journal entries for these two poems. What new reflections about nature and technology can they add to their writing?

Responding to Reading

First Impressions of "All Watched Over . . ."

1. What do you think of the creatures in Richard Brautigan's forest?

Second Thoughts on "All Watched Over . . ."

2. What does the speaker seem to think of nature, technology, and progress?

   Think about
   - whether nature or technology seems to be in control
   - the feeling provided by the words written in parentheses

3. Do you think the speaker is serious or sarcastic? Explain.

4. What effect does contrast have on this poem?

   Think about
   - the title
   - contrasting images throughout the poem

Comparing the Poems

5. How similar are the poets' views of nature?

6. How would you contrast the tones of the two poems?

7. What does each of these poems have to say about the price humans pay for technological progress?

Literary Concept: Repetition

Repetition is the method of using a sound, word, phrase, or line two or more times. Poets might use repetition to emphasize ideas or to create rhythm in a poem. What is repeated in Richard Brautigan's poem? Why do you think the poet created this repetition?

Writing Options

1. Pretend that you are camped out in a cybernetic forest. Write a postcard describing the sites and how you feel about them.

2. Think again about contrasts you have seen between nature and technology. Use these ideas as a basis for your own poem.

3. Write a short descriptive paragraph that tells what might have once stood by the "avenue of willows" mentioned in "Building Boom."

Literary Concept—Repetition

Possible Response: The phrase *I like to think* is repeated. The poet uses repetition to create rhythm; emphasize the sarcastic or ironic tone; and emphasize the poem's theme—the dangers posed by technology.

© Layle Silbert

Charles Reznikoff
1894–1976

Charles Reznikoff's career was much longer and steadier than Richard Brautigan's—but not nearly as sensational. Reznikoff's poetry first appeared after World War I. Highly respected by his fellow poets, he is perhaps best known for his clear and simple imagery. As is evident in "Building Boom," Reznikoff often provides a distinct picture in his poetry. Labeled "the dean of Jewish-American poets," Reznikoff used his cultural heritage as the basis of many of his poems. In a collection published in 1929, *By the Waters of Manhattan,* the poet based his poems on the Old Testament. In these poems Reznikoff wrote in the first-person voices of such biblical subjects as "Israel" and "King David." In these and other poems written between 1918 and 1936, Reznikoff departed from the single image poem choosing instead to work with a loose story line or series of character sketches. Reznikoff continued to write poetry until his death at the age of eighty-one.

Richard Brautigan
1935–1984

Richard Brautigan is often thought of as a hero of the hippie generation of the 1960's. During this decade he reached the peak of his popularity with the publication of his novel, *Trout Fishing in America,* which sold more than two million copies. In this novel Brautigan captured the disillusionment felt by many young people when he described how the great American outdoors was being turned into a junkyard.

Brautigan was quite familiar with the outdoor life, having grown up fishing and hunting in the Pacific Northwest. He came from a poor family and began writing poetry as a teenager. He once said about his early writing, "I wrote poetry for seven years to learn how to write a sentence because I really wanted to write a sentence because I really wanted to write novels and I figured that I couldn't write a novel until I could write a sentence." One of his first books, called *Please Plant This Book,* was made up of eight seed packets with a poem printed on each.

At the age of twenty he moved to San Francisco where he enjoyed much success as a writer. In the 1970's, however, interest in Brautigan's work declined and the author became increasingly depressed, committing suicide in September of 1984.

Additional Information About the Author

Charles Reznikoff Reznikoff began writing poetry when he was thirteen. A brilliant student, he graduated from high school when he was fifteen. A year later, in 1910, he enrolled in the School of Journalism at the University of Missouri but left soon after when he discovered that he was interested in writing, not in news. After a stint in his parents' hat company, he entered New York University's Law School. In 1915 he received his degree and was second in his class. He practiced law only briefly, quickly turning to writing poetry. In 1918 he printed his first book himself on a press in his parents' basement.

Richard Brautigan Brautigan did not freely disclose information about himself. He described his father as a "common laborer," his mother as a housewife. He married in 1957, divorced in 1970: The union produced a daughter, Ianthe, in 1960. In 1967 he was poet-in-residence at the California Institute of Technology, although he had never gone to college himself. His writing first attracted attention in California in the 1960's on the heels of a popular movement often referred to as "The Greening of America." Initially such books as *Trout Fishing in America, In Watermelon Sugar,* and *The Pill Versus the Springhill Mine Disaster* sold astonishingly well. Perhaps their appeal at that time came from Brautigan's belief in the power of the imagination to transform reality.

Closure

Each of these poems expresses its author's concerns over the impact of technology on the environment. Have students share with the class one of their concerns with respect to the effect of technological progress on nature.

Cross-Curricular Options

Science: Suggest that students research cybernetics and prepare brief oral reports for the class. Some students might want to include a discussion of robotics in their reports.

History: Have students look into the building booms of the late 1940s and early 1950s. Ask them to include a discussion of the effects of the mass building on the ecology.

Math: Suggest that students research the cost of the average home computer and detail its specific capabilities.

Publishing: Compile the contributions of all students. Display or make copies to distribute.

Writer's Workshop

Objectives

- To understand the goals of expository writing
- To select specifics in supporting a generalization
- To use varied sentence beginnings in expository writing
- To draft, revise, edit, and share a magazine article
- To reflect on the writing process

Integrating . . .

Literature and Writing Tell students that the literature in this subunit deals with the achievements and frustrations of modern technology. In "The Suspected Shopper," Ellen Goodman tells about the nuisance of coping with products of new technology that make her feel like a criminal. Ask students to write down instances when they have been frustrated or thwarted by electronic or automatic devices. This will help them focus their ideas for the Guided Assignment.

Writing and Language Direct students to the Language Workshop on varying sentence beginnings. Point out to them that a successful magazine article needs to capture and hold the reader's attention through rhythmic writing. Stress that the popular magazines they read are often fairly well written. Ask them to bring to class one of their favorite magazines, and then have them indicate how often they can locate varying types of sentence beginnings in the magazine's articles. (Check off with a pen or pencil each sentence that begins in a different style than the previous one.)

Literature and Life Skills The variable workshop in this subunit deals with *Speaking and Listening* in general, and *Telephone Techniques* in particular. Explain to students that their success in the professional world will depend to a great extent on how well they can use the telephone. Stress that a professional and courteous manner, speaking clearly and correctly, and accurately taking notes can save time and get positive results in phone relationships.

EXPOSITION: SUPPORTING A GENERALIZATION

Technology has brought great improvements to our way of life. Today, for example, you can fly in a supersonic jet from New York to London in less than four hours. Along the way you can listen to digitally recorded music over stereo headphones or watch a feature movie while eating a meal heated in a microwave oven. If you're really ambitious, you can type on your laptop personal computer and make phone calls from the plane thirty thousand feet up. In the air or on the ground, every day you use products designed to make your life more efficient and more enjoyable. Isn't progress sweet—or is it?

If you live in a city, or anyplace where cars are parked overnight, you probably have lain awake fuming while a car alarm ripped through the night air. Or perhaps you recently purchased something that has been "shrink-wrapped" and consequently lost time, not to mention two fingernails, trying to free your purchase from its mummy-like plastic wrapping. One could certainly generalize that many new "helpful" products also bring new headaches with them.

Selections like Ellen Goodman's piece on shoplifting show how technological advances can become technological annoyances. In the next writing assignment, you can express your own frustration with progress.

GUIDED ASSIGNMENT: TAKING ON HIGH TECH

What price have you had to pay for technology? Write an article for *Technological Annoyances* magazine expressing your frustration at some new consumer product or procedure.

Here is your PASSkey to this assignment.

PURPOSE: To support a generalization
AUDIENCE: Readers of a magazine
SUBJECT: The annoyances of technology
STRUCTURE: A magazine article

Prewriting

STEP 1 **Brainstorm modern annoyances** In a small group, brainstorm a list of modern technological advances that cause

Additional Resources

UNIT FIVE RESOURCE BOOK
Writer's Workshop Copy Master, p. 48
Peer and Self-Evaluation Guidelines, p. 49
Writing Assessment Guidelines, p. 50

ENRICHMENT MATERIALS
Thinking Skills Transparency and Worksheet
Fine Art Transparency and Writing Prompts
Revision, Proofreading, and Elaboration Worksheet
Writing Prompts for Assessment

you frustration. Note the intended good effects of each product or procedure and also how each causes you problems.

STEP 2 Narrow your focus Choose one product or procedure that you would like to focus on. Remember that Ellen Goodman's article did not discuss all of technology but rather its impact on one area of everyday life—her shopping.

STEP 3 Make a generalization Formulate a general statement about the impact of this product or technological advance on your life. This will be your thesis statement. Here is the thesis statement formulated by one student.

STUDENT MODEL

> Car phones enable business people to be productive while driving in their automobiles, but at the same time this communication marvel makes driving unsafe.

STEP 4 Collect evidence You now need evidence to support your generalization. There are many ways to collect evidence. Like Ellen Goodman, you might make specific observations. You might also interview others with experiences similar to yours or find actual research that supports your thesis statement. For example, the student who chose to write on cellular phones decided it was important to find out how many of these devices had been installed in cars during the past year. The *Readers' Guide to Periodical Literature* lists recent magazine articles on such topics. The student also decided to contact the state police to see if any statistics had been kept on accidents resulting from people using phones while driving.

Drafting

STEP 1 Organize your evidence Review the facts and opinions you've collected that support your thesis statement. Decide the order in which you'd like to present this information. For example, you may want to start with a personal anecdote told to you by someone you interviewed and then progress to some hard facts found in your research.

STEP 2 Write your introduction A magazine article needs an exciting introduction to catch the reader's interest. Like the student writer of the model on the following page, you might want to begin with a personal story that leads into your thesis statement.

Teaching Strategies

Introduction Have students turn to the Writer's Workshop for this subunit on page 666. Explain that they will be writing about a generalization dealing with technology. Be sure that they understand that they will need to cite specifics in order to write a convincing and interesting article, and that they cannot rely on generalizations to support a generalization.

Have students look at the Guided Assignment box on page 666. Be sure that they note the PASSkey graphic, indicating that they will write a magazine article supporting a generalization on the annoyances of technology.

Prewriting Read each step of the *Prewriting* process with the class. While they are brainstorming, you might point out how many areas of their lives are affected by modern technology. They use technology for communication (telephones), information retrieval (computers), entertainment (movies, TVs, VCRs, CDs), and even for simple math computations (calculators). Like the mammals and computers that Richard Brautigan imagines, today's students are not too far removed from a world in which they are "All Watched Over by Machines of Loving Grace."

Be sure that students understand the importance of forming a thesis statement about the everyday annoyances that result from the interaction between humans and machines. Discuss with them the particular chemistry that exists between people and technologies. People expect machines to be foolproof and ever accommodating, and become incredibly frustrated when machines exhibit any glitch.

Computer Tip
Students with access to a computer might use it to brainstorm ideas for different types of technological devices they come into contact with. Such students may want to organize categories by frequency of use, complexity of the device, uses of the device (e.g., a computer can perform many more activities than a microwave oven), and levels of expectations for each item of technology.

Using this method, students should find it easier to organize their evidence for a thesis statement.

Drafting Direct LEP students to write a description of some of their country's most and least reliable technological devices. Ask them to give the names in their own language of devices such as television, video recorder, cassette tape and deck, compact disc, or radio. Very often, the English word is quite similar to the foreign-language word. It will be culturally reassuring to LEP students to see that technological devices (and their annoyances) exist in other countries too. Discuss the fact that technological names often know no nationality, and technological devices have their own language.

Drafting Point out to students the importance of writing a strong opening paragraph for their magazine article. Suggest that they begin with a startling statistic, such as the failure rate of some kinds of technology (e.g., how many times a day computers are "down" in businesses throughout the United States) or some personal anecdote, such as what feelings or calamitous result occurred because of a technological failure that happened to them. For example, did they leave an important message on a friend or employer's answering machine that was "eaten up and swallowed" with disastrous results for all parties?

Revising and Editing Point out to students that it might be helpful for them to ask a partner to review their article. Remind students to refer to the *Revision Checklist* as they review one another's work. Students may find it helpful to respond to each of the checklist questions with a specific answer. By analyzing *why* an introduction is strong (because it is startling, shocking, or ironic, etc.) students will see that a specific detail has gone into creating an eye-opening beginning statement.

Discuss how the strength of Ellen Goodman's article comes not only from its overall message, but from its intriguing opening. Instead of encountering friendly merchants on "Shopping Saturday," she finds "warnings and wariness." These words beckon readers to continue.

Remind students that they must give specific examples to support their generalization. Advise them to present these details—whether they are feelings, incidents, or accidents—in a logical order. It is important during the revising and editing process to remember that the article should employ varying sentence beginnings.

Stress with students the importance of proofreading their work for spelling, clarity, and mechanics.

STUDENT MODEL ▶

I never liked walking to school, especially now that I'm old enough to drive. But lately it's not only a drag, it's downright dangerous.

Two days ago I stood patiently waiting for the WALK signal at the stoplight. After it changed, I stepped off the curb into the street. A screeching noise behind me caused me to glance over my right shoulder. In the corner of my eye I saw a red blur heading my way fast. I leaped back at the last second as a Porsche with a businessman behind the wheel flashed past. Through the car window I could see him shouting angrily. Was he yelling at me? The nerve of him—and I waited for the light!

Then I replayed the scene in my mind, and this time I realized why he never saw me. Mr. Big Businessman was too occupied with his cellular phone to watch for an ordinary person trying to cross the street. Car phones may enable business people to be productive while driving in their automobiles, but these conveniences also create a new driving hazard.

STEP 3 **Write the body of your draft** Write the rest of your draft using the information you gathered. Follow the order you established earlier for presenting your evidence. To connect your evidence with your thesis statement, incorporate comments that explain how your observations, interviews, and research illustrate your generalization. Conclude with a summarizing statement that restates your thesis.

Revising and Editing

Ask a classmate to review your work according to the following checklist. Use his or her comments as a guide to your revision.

Revision Checklist

1. Does the introduction catch the reader's interest?
2. Is the generalization about technology clearly stated in a thesis statement?
3. Does the order in which the evidence is presented seem logical?
4. Is there enough evidence to adequately support the generalization?
5. Is the writer's viewpoint convincing? Why or why not?

ADDITIONAL WRITING AND RESEARCH TOPICS

The following topics provide additional writing practice based on the selections in the subunit:

- Write a short play or scene that focuses on two characters: Ellen Goodman and the manager of security in one of the stores she patronizes.
- Dr. James Graham is scheduled to appear on your TV show. Write a series of questions for him to answer on the topic of nuclear armament.

Additional Topics

Creative Writing Write a short magazine article on the topic "Generalizations Are Always Insupportable."

Biographical Research Write a biographical essay on Isaac Asimov, supporting his belief that there is no alternative life form to ours in outer space. Use *The Reader's Guide to Periodical Literature* or *Contemporary Authors* for your research.

Editing After you have revised your article, proofread your work for spelling, clarity, and mechanics.

Publishing

Produce a magazine called *Technological Annoyances* that consists of articles collected from your classmates. Form an editorial board to organize the articles into a logical sequence. If possible, have student artists illustrate your magazine and place a copy in the library for other students to review.

Reflecting on Your Writing

Place the answers to the following questions in your writing portfolio.

1. Were you satisfied with your introduction? Why or why not?
2. If you had more time, how might you make the support for your generalization stronger?
3. What has working on this article taught you about your writing?

Publishing In addition to placing a copy of the magazine *Technological Annoyances* in the school library, students may want to submit their best articles to the school newspaper. (They might also consider inaugurating an ongoing column on the subject in the school newspaper.)

Have the class select its best article and then submit it to a national technology magazine.

Reflecting on Your Writing Students may wish to discuss Question 3 because it explores the clarity and certainty with which they have accomplished their assignment.

Closure

Before beginning the next subunit, be sure students understand and internalize these concepts:

- A magazine article must have a strong beginning.
- Good writing includes the use of varying sentence beginnings.
- In an interesting magazine article, a generalization must be supported by specifics.
- Good nonfiction writing must include thorough research.

Language Workshop

Objectives

- To understand that varying sentence beginnings can add interest to writing
- To develop and use strategies for varying sentence beginnings
- To identify sentences to be revised by varying their beginnings

Integrating . . .

Writing and Language Remind students that in the Writer's Workshop they wrote a magazine article expressing their frustration at some technological annoyance. Explain that in order to capture an audience and maintain their interest, it is helpful to vary the sentence beginnings. Choose a sentence from a selection and ask students to suggest ways its beginning could be changed. For example, you might choose the sentence *The boy smiled bashfully at the visitor,* and students might suggest the variation *Bashfully, the boy smiled at the visitor.*

Teaching Strategies

Point out to students that a writer's style can often influence our interest in reading his or her work. Work through the lesson, but stop before students reach the exercises. As students proceed through the strategies, ask them to find examples of each strategy in the selections they have read. If students are unable to find good examples, have them choose sentences in the selections and suggest ways that the beginnings might be varied.

Teaching Tip

Point out to students that although they have learned how to write grammatically correct sentences, repeating technically correct, simple sentences can be monotonous and uninteresting to a reader. You might want to suggest using adjectives as a strategy for varying sentence beginnings—for example: *Exhausted and weary, the friends completed their ambitious climb.* Invite students to describe events from the past few days using sentences with adjective beginnings.

LANGUAGE WORKSHOP

VARYING SENTENCE BEGINNINGS

HINT

Try reading your own writing aloud, and listen for a variety of sentence rhythms and styles.

Some writers use one sentence structure throughout a piece of writing. This kind of writing is tedious to read. For example, a writer may always begin a sentence with the subject. Consider the following:

> I was in a hurry as I left the department store. I had bought a pair of gold earrings to wear to a dance. I told the clerk I didn't need a bag and put the earrings into my purse. I knew that I would put them on as soon as I left the store. I tried to rush through the exit. A security guard blocked my way. He said, "You're under arrest for shoplifting."

Every sentence begins with the subject (usually *I*), followed by the verb. If you change the sentence beginnings, you can enliven the paragraph.

> *Hurriedly,* I left the department store. I had bought a pair of gold earrings to wear to a dance. *Telling the clerk I didn't need a bag,* I put the earrings into my purse. *As soon as I left the store,* I planned to put them on. *A woman in a hurry,* I tried to rush through the exit. A security guard blocked my way. *"You're under arrest for shoplifting,"* he said.

Of course, you don't have to change every sentence. You just need to introduce some variety. Try some of the following suggestions for using sentence structures other than subject-verb.

Strategies for Varying Sentence Beginnings

1. Begin with a **quote.**

   "I read every night to my son," Dr. Graham told the visitor.

2. Begin with an **appositive,** a phrase that identifies or describes the subject.

   A dedicated father, Dr. Graham read diligently to his son every evening.

3. Begin with an infinitive phrase. An **infinitive** is a verb form that begins with the word *to.*

   To entertain his son, Dr. Graham read diligently to him every evening.

Additional Resources

UNIT FIVE RESOURCE BOOK

Language Workshop Copy Master, p. 51

ENRICHMENT MATERIALS

Grammar and Usage Copy Masters

4. Begin with a single adverb modifier. An **adverb** modifies a verb and usually ends in *-ly.*

   Diligently, Dr. Graham read to his son every evening.

5. Begin with a **subordinate clause,** a clause that starts with a subordinating conjunction such as *since, because,* or *although.*

   Since Dr. Graham wanted to entertain his child, he read diligently to him every evening.

6. Begin with one or more prepositional phrases. A **prepositional phrase** begins with a preposition, such as *with, on, at,* or *in.*

   At the end of the day, Dr. Graham always read to his son.

7. Begin with a participial phrase. A **participle** is an adjective formed by adding *-ing* to a verb.

   Reading diligently, Dr. Graham entertained his son every evening.

Exercise 1 Rewrite the following sentences, beginning each with the form suggested in parentheses.

1. "The Feeling of Power" is a story about the future, that shows us a future society dominated by computers. (appositive that describes "The Feeling of Power")
2. Myron Aub was a technician with a low rating on intelligence tests. (prepositional phrase)
3. He could multiply any number if he had time. (subordinate clause beginning with *if*)
4. The government, consequently, was interested in him. (adverb)
5. Shuman used Aub to prove that anyone could learn multiplication and division. (infinitive)
6. Shuman enticed the government officials with the idea of manned missiles and finally convinced them. (participial phrase beginning with *Enticing*)

Exercise 2 Analyzing and Revising Your Writing
Take a piece of writing from your portfolio and revise it to increase the variety of sentence beginnings.

LANGUAGE HANDBOOK

For review and practice, see Section 1, **Writing Complete Sentences,** and Section 4, **Using Modifiers.**

Teaching Tip: LEP
While working through Strategies for Varying Sentence Beginnings, with LEP students, provide an example of each sentence with a varied beginning and without. For example, point out that the sentence *Dr. Graham told the visitor that she reads every night to her son* does not have a varied beginning. Then show students how the sentence can be changed, using the example on the pupil page. Continue in this way to complete the instruction on strategies.

Teaching Tip
Point out that too many varied sentence beginnings could make a piece of writing more difficult to read. The sentence structure would not follow the pattern we are most accustomed to reading, and the rhythm would continually be interrupted by brief pauses. Explain to students that they need only use a few varied sentence beginnings to introduce some variety in their writing.

Closure

Before beginning the next subunit, be sure students have internalized these concepts:

- Varying sentence beginnings can add interest to a piece of writing.
- Strategies for varying sentence beginnings include beginning with a quote, an appositive, an infinitive phrase, a single adverb modifier, a subordinate clause, a prepositional phrase, and a participle.

Answer Key
Exercise 1

Answers will vary. Allow students to refer back to the strategies if they wish. Ask students to share their responses with classmates. Point out variations in the way students changed sentence beginnings.

Exercise 2

Answers will vary. Encourage students to share their responses with classmates, noting the variety of strategies students found.

ADDITIONAL PRACTICE

The following items are additional exercises to help students vary their sentence beginnings.

Vary the beginnings of these sentences by using quotes, appositives, or infinitives. *Possible answers are given.*

1. John grumbled. *"I'll beat Rosie at cards next time,"* . . .

2. Avery used his binoculars. *To see the players up close,* . . .

3. Dorothy beat her opponent easily. *A whiz at chess,* . . .

Vary the beginnings of these sentences by using an adverb modifier, a subordinate clause, a prepositional phrase, or a participial phrase.

4. Tomas eventually became a wealthy man. *Although he was a poor Haitian immigrant,* . . .

5. I found the largest pine cones I've ever seen. *Under this Florida fir* . . .

6. Frances completed the puzzle in only an hour. *Working diligently,* . . .

Speaking and Listening Workshop

Objectives

- To utilize effective telephone techniques for making business calls
- To research the names or titles of people before calling
- To explain the purpose of the call and be prepared with relevant information
- To monitor tone of voice
- To make follow-up calls

Integrating . . .

Writing and Speaking and Listening Share with students that this workshop will help them make effective business calls.

Teaching Strategies

Have students name qualities of people with whom they like to speak on the telephone. *(Possible responses: courteous, easy to understand, helpful)*

Read through the material with students. Assign the exercise on page 672. Check students' written notes to be sure they have recorded pertinent information.

Closure

Before beginning the next subunit, be sure students have internalized these concepts:

- Effective telephone techniques make it easier to gain information from a telephone call.
- Being prepared and using a pleasant tone of voice help a caller achieve the purpose of the call.
- Taking notes during a call is essential, especially when using the telephone for a job search.

Exercise

(A sample response is given.)
Smith's Nursery, 225 Turner Rd.; owned by Charles Smith; 10 full-time employees plus 5 for seasonal business; employees care for plants, arrange baskets and dish gardens, make deliveries to florists. My qualifications: horticulture course, member of 4-H Club, placed 2nd in flower arranging at county fair.

SPEAKING AND LISTENING WORKSHOP

TELEPHONE TECHNIQUES

COURTESY FIRST!

Whatever happens while you are on the telephone, remain courteous. Do so even if you are placed on hold for a long time or transferred from person to person. Maintaining a courteous tone will go a long way toward winning the support and confidence of the people to whom you are speaking.

You already know how to use the telephone for social purposes. You probably know some basic courtesy guidelines, such as identifying yourself if you are the caller. When you use the telephone to do business, there are a few other points you need to keep in mind.

General Guidelines for Using the Telephone

1. **Research your call** Try to find out, before you call, the name or title of the person to whom you need to speak. This will help you avoid spending hours on hold as you are transferred from department to department. Remember, it's often useful to get the names of people who give you important information. That way, you can refer to them later.
2. **Explain your purpose** Many people make a few notes before they make any business call. If you do this, it will help you organize your thoughts so that you can quickly explain what you want. Make sure that you have all the relevant material or information in front of you. For example, if you're calling about a delayed order of merchandise, have model numbers, receipts or invoices, and previous correspondence in front of you.
3. **Be aware of your tone** Speak clearly, slowly, and as pleasantly as possible. Remember that you are being judged solely on your words and how you communicate through them. Even if you are calling to register a complaint, keep your tone of voice reasonable.
4. **Make follow-up calls** Many business people keep a log of their telephone conversations. Then, when and if they have to make follow-up calls, they have all the information from past communications at hand.

LEAVE A PAPER TRAIL

Ideas can be miscommunicated on the telephone, and people sometimes forget what they said. Therefore, when you discuss important matters on the telephone, it's often a good idea to follow up your conversation with a letter confirming the details discussed and agreed to. At the very least, you should take notes during the call and keep these notes for later reference.

Exercise Choose a local business where you might be interested in working. Do research to find out whom to call. Write down all the appropriate information about the company and your interests and qualifications as if you were actually intending to call for job information.

Additional Resources

UNIT FIVE RESOURCE BOOK
Related Skills Copy, p. 52

ENRICHMENT MATERIALS
Oral Communications Booklet

ADDITIONAL PRACTICE

Use the guidelines to make an actual call to find out some information. Rate your telephone skills using this checklist.

	good	fair	poor
1. I researched the call.			
2. I explained the purpose.			
3. My tone of voice was ____.			
4. I made follow-up calls.			

IN WHOSE HANDS?

Who controls your future? In most daily activities, you have a fair amount of control over your life. There are, however, greater powers that can dictate your future. Often people you know, such as parents or teachers, make decisions for you. On a grander scale, politicians, or even nature, can change your plans for the future.

In the following selections, people's hopes and fears for the future are at times controlled by themselves and at other times taken over by greater forces. As you read, observe both how the people in these selections exercise control over their own lives, and how they respond when that control falls into someone else's hands.

Subunit Preview

Have students read the introduction to subunit 3, **In Whose Hands?** Invite them to explore how questions about whom to trust relate to the broader unit theme, **The Future: Hopes and Fears.** Why might people let others think for them? Should ordinary people question authority? Why or why not? Who controls the future of the world? Are you comfortable with your answer? Why or why not? Ask students to review the subunit Table of Contents and predict which selection will be the most interesting.

For Additional Challenge

The following selections offer extra challenge in the exploration of the subunit theme:

"Maud Martha Spares the Mouse," a short story by Gwendolyn Brooks

"The Twenty-third Psalm"

Additional Resources

Subunit Test, pp. 80–81

OBSERVATION ASSESSMENT

Observing how students respond to the text, to the classroom instruction, and to peers is an important part of an assessment program. The following suggestions and the form in each Unit Resource Book can be used to implement observation assessment.

- As students work through the subunit, observe their use of reading strategies to stay on track. Do they discuss things that are unclear? Do they check the meanings of unfamiliar words? Do they subvocalize or read aloud difficult parts of a selection?
- As they work through this subunit, can you see growth in students' self-monitoring for comprehension?
- To determine how well students evaluate information, see if they can distinguish between details that add color or interest and details that are essential to understanding the main idea. Can they state the theme of a selection in words of their own?

Objectives

- To read and understand a short story
- To recognize the use of suspense
- To express understanding of the work through a variety of writing options, including morals and descriptive scenes

Prereading/Motivation

Examine What You Know

Discussion Prompts: How would you define the term *evil?* Are evil people completely evil, or are they partly good? What causes people to be evil? Why do evil people sometimes change their ways for the better?

Expand Your Knowledge

Discussion Prompts: What is twilight? When does it occur? What are your associations with this time of day? Have you ever seen any rebroadcasts of original *Twilight Zone* episodes? Can you recall a specific plot?

Additional Information: Before creating *The Twilight Zone,* playwright Rod Serling was a prolific contributor of fine dramas for live TV productions. His most famous play is *Requiem for a Heavyweight.* In addition to hosting *The Twilight Zone,* Serling wrote many of the scripts for the show. The show specialized in unusual and offbeat stories that often ended with ironic twists.

Thematic Link—In Whose Hands?

In this story, the fates of countless people rest in the hands of a man with unusual powers.

Fiction

Four O'Clock

PRICE DAY

Examine What You Know (Prior Knowledge)

What kind of a person would you categorize as evil? Think of villains in movies you have seen, corrupt and vicious people you have read about in books and newspapers, or even people you have known. With a small group of your classmates, develop a list of qualities that might describe an evil person. Keep these qualities in mind as you read this story.

Expand Your Knowledge (Building Background)

This selection is a teleplay from one of the most popular series in the history of television, *The Twilight Zone.* Created by Rod Serling, this series began on CBS in 1959 and ran for five seasons. On the average, 18 million viewers watched this program each week—a program that one critic called a "flower blossoming in a television desert." Unlike earlier television shows that re-created real-life drama and situation comedy, *The Twilight Zone* created nightmarish worlds of fantasy and science fiction. The characters, however, were ordinary people very much like the viewers themselves. As you begin to read this story, you might take heed of Rod Serling's famous warning: "You're traveling through another dimension, a dimension not only of sight and sound, but of mind; a journey into a wondrous land whose boundaries are that of imagination—Next stop, *The Twilight Zone!*"

Write Before You Read (Journal Writing)

If you had a special power to do one thing for humanity, what would you do? Before answering, consider what aspect of human life or of the human personality you think most needs help or changing. In a paragraph, describe what you would do and what would be the far-reaching effects of your good work.

■ *A biography of the author can be found in the Reader's Handbook.*

Additional Journal Writing

Suggest these additional journal topics to students:

- Based on the title, what do you think this story is about?
- Write a brief plot outline for a story with the title "Four O'Clock."
- What eerie things do you imagine at twilight? Describe a few.

For other journal opportunities, refer students to First Impressions (p. 678).

Additional Resources

UNIT FIVE RESOURCE BOOK

Reader's Guidesheet, p. 55
Vocabulary Worksheet, p. 56
Selection Check Test, p. 57
Selection Test, pp. 58–59

Collaborative Learning

Opportunities for collaborative learning appear throughout the lesson and include Examine What You Know (p. 674), annotation J, and Writing Options (p. 678).

Four O'Clock

PRICE DAY

A

B The hands of the alarm clock on the table in front of Mr. Crangle stood at 3:47, on a summer afternoon.

"You're wrong about that, you know," he said, not taking his eyes from the face of the clock. "You're quite wrong, Pet, as I have explained to you often enough before. The moral angle presents no difficulties at all." C

The parrot, in the cage hanging above him, cocked her head and looked down with a hard, cold, reptilian eye, an ancient eye, an eye older by age upon age than the human race.

D She said, "Nut."

Mr. Crangle, his eye still on the clock, took a peanut from a cracker bowl at his elbow and held it above his head, to the bars of the cage. Pet clutched it in a leathery claw. The spring-steel muscles opened the horny beak. She clinched the peanut and crushed it, the sound mingling in the furnished room with the big-city sounds coming through the open window—cars honking, feet on the sidewalk, children calling to each other, a plane overhead like a contented, industrious bee.

"It is quite true," Mr. Crangle said at 3:49, "that only someone above all personal emotions, only someone who can look at the whole thing as if from the outside, can be trusted morally to make such a decision." As the big hand reached 3:50, he felt a sense of power surge deeply through him. E "Think, Pet. In ten minutes. In ten little minutes, when I say the word, all the evil people all over the world will become half their present size, so they can be known. All the uncaught murderers and the tyrants and the proud and sinful, all the bullies and the wrongdoers and the blackmailers and nicotine fiends and transgressors." His eyes blazed with omnipotence. "All of them, every one." F SR-1

Pet said, "Nut."

Mr. Crangle gave her one.

"I know you don't agree fully with the half-size solution," he said, "but I do believe it to be the best one, all things considered." G

He had studied over the alternatives day and night since that morning three weeks ago when, as he sat on a bench in the park, looking at the pictures in the clouds across the lake, it came to him that he had the power to do this thing, that upon him at that moment had been bestowed the gift of putting a mark on all the bad people on earth, so that they should be known. SR-2

The realization surprised him not at all. Once before, such a thing had happened. He had once held the power to stop wars. That was when the radio was telling about the big air raids on the cities. In that case

Structured Reading for Less Proficient Students

These questions can help to guide students through the reading. Ask each question at the point of the selection where the SR number appears in the margin.

SR–1. What does Mr. Crangle plan to do at four o'clock? *(He plans to make all the evil people in the world half their present size.)* **Literal recall**

SR–2. How did Mr. Crangle get his power? *(It simply came to him.)* Why does he want to use the power? *(He wants the evil people to be known.)* **Literal recall**

SR–3. In the past, what two powers did Mr. Crangle have but not use? *(power to stop wars by making airplane propellers limp; power to stop traffic accidents by making wheels square)* **Literal recall**

SR–4. What special traits does Mr. Crangle think he has *(He believes he has knowledge of good and evil and is all-knowing.)* **Literal recall**

SR–5. What happens to Mr. Crangle when he finally uses his power? How do you know this? *(After feeling a great shock, he is suddenly half his size. He can no longer reach the bird cage.)* **Literal recall and Inference**

Teaching Strategies

Support for Students of Limited English Proficiency

- Use **Reader's Guidesheet**, p. 55.
- Tell students that "Four O'Clock" is a work of science fiction with a fantastic premise. If possible, show students a segment of *The Twilight Zone* movie or one of the older black-and-white episodes made for television. This will help students from other cultures understand the nature of the program and the background material presented.
- **Annotations F and I** focus on troublesome terms and concepts.

Text Annotations

A. Literary Element: TITLE Elicit that the title "Four O'Clock" focuses our attention on a specific time of day and causes us to wonder about its significance.

B. Literary Element: SETTING Note the exact time given in the opening paragraph: 3:47. Point out that the changing time of the setting is all-important in the story.

C. Literary Element: FORESHADOWING Elicit that Mr. Crangle is talking to his pet parrot. Point out that the mention of a disagreement over a "moral angle" suggests that Crangle is up to something that may be objectionable or unethical.

D. Literary Element: CHARACTERIZATION Explain that although Pet is asking for a nut to eat, there is also a suggestion that she is calling Crangle a nut. Elicit that the author uses the play on words to suggest that Crangle is not sane.

E. Literary Element: SUSPENSE Point out that references to time—first 3:47, then 3:50—as well as the inference that a big decision is about to be made heighten interest in the story.

F. LEP: Summarizing Elicit that *nicotine fiends* are heavy smokers and *transgressors* are people who break laws or rules. Have students sum up what Mr. Crangle plans to do to the people he names. *(He plans to reveal them.)*

G. Critical Thinking: EVALUATING Have students evaluate Mr. Crangle's plan of action and name some possible objections.

H. Literary Element: FIGURATIVE LANGUAGE Point out the similes in the paragraph—"crews bundled like children against cold" and "props hanging limp, like empty banana skins." Elicit that these similes add color and humor to the description.

I. LEP: Comprehension Elicit that a jet airplane has no prop, or propeller; rather, it gets its forward thrust from the powerful jet of burning gas that passes out through the rear of the engine.

J. Critical Thinking: EVALUATING Ask students to pretend for a moment that they are psychologists or psychiatrists. Ask what evaluation they might make of Mr. Crangle's mental and emotional state.

K. Literary Element: CHARACTERIZATION Point out that authors sometimes use a character's name to give us some hints about his or her personality. Point out that Crangle sounds a little like *crank* meaning an "ill-tempered person with strange ideas."

L. Literary Element: IRONY Ask students to point out the irony of Mr. Crangle's professed hatred of violence. *(Possible response: Crangle's plan will cause violent changes in the bodies and lives of countless people.)*

the particular thing he could do was to take the stiffness out of airplane propellers, so that some morning when the crews, bundled like children against cold, went out to get in their planes, they would find the props hanging limp, like empty banana skins. H

That time, he had delayed too long, waiting for just the right time and just the right plan, and they had outwitted him, unfairly. They had invented the jet, to which his power did not apply. I

Then, too, there had been the thing about wheels. The thing about wheels came to him in a coffee place as he was looking at a newspaper photograph of a bad traffic accident, three killed. The power, that was, to change all the wheels in the world from round to square, or even to triangular if he wished, so they would stub in the asphalt and stop. But he wasn't allowed to keep that power. Before he could work out a plan and
SR-3 ▶ a time, he had felt it taken from him.

The power over bad people had stayed. It had even grown stronger, if power like that could grow stronger. And this time he had hurried, though of course there were certain problems to be thought through. J

First, who was to decide what people were evil? That wasn't too hard, really, in spite of Pet's doubts. An evil person was a person who would seem evil to a man who held within himself the knowledge of good and evil, if that man could know all the person's innermost secrets. An evil person was a person who would seem evil to an all-knowing K
SR-4 ▶ Mr. Crangle.

Then, how to do it, the method? Mark them on the forehead, or turn them all one color, say purple? But then they would simply be able to recognize each other the more readily, and to band together in their wickedness.

When at last he hit upon the idea of a

Yellow-fronted Amazon parrot Photograph by Horst Mueller.

change in size, what came to him first was the thought of doubling the height and bulk of all the bad people. That would make them inefficient. They couldn't handle delicate scientific instruments or typewriters or adding machines or telephone dials. In time they would expire from bigness, like the dinosaurs in the article in the Sunday paper. But they might first run wild, with their great weight and strength, and hurt other people. Mr. Crangle wouldn't have liked that. He hated violence. L

Half-size people, it was true, might be able to manipulate some of the machines. They could also be dangerous. But it would take them a long time to develop tools and weapons to their scale, and think how ridiculous they would be, meanwhile, with their clothes twice too big and their hats falling down over their ears.

At 3:54, Mr. Crangle smiled at the thought of how ridiculous they would be.

"Nut," Pet said.

He reached up and gave her one, his eyes still on the clock.

"I think," he said, "that the most interesting place to be would be at a murder trial where nobody knew whether the accused was guilty or not. And then at four o'clock, if he was guilty—"

Mr. Crangle's breath was coming faster. The clock hands stood at 3:56.

M "Or watching the drunkards in a saloon," he said.

"Nut," Pet said, and he gave her one.

"Oh," he said, "there are so many places, so many places to be. But I'd rather be with you when it happens, Pet. Right here alone with you."

He sat tense in his chair. He could actually see the big hand of the clock move, in the tiniest little jerkings, leaving a hairline of white between itself and the black 3:57 dot, and moving to the 3:58 dot, narrowing the space, until it touched that dot, and then stood directly on it, and then moved past toward the 3:59 dot.

"At first," Mr. Crangle said, "the newspapers won't believe it. Even though some of it will happen right in the newspaper offices, they won't believe it. At first they won't. And then when they begin to understand that it has happened to a lot of people everybody knows are evil, then they'll see the design."

The clock said 3:59.

"A great story," Mr. Crangle said. "A great newspaper story. And nobody will know who did it, Pet, nobody but you and me." N

The point of the big hand crept halfway past the 3:59 dot. Mr. Crangle's heart beat hard. His eyes were wide, his lips parted. He whispered, "Nobody will know." O

The tip of the big hand touched the dot at the top of the clock face. The alarm went off. Mr. Crangle felt a great surge of strength, like water bursting a dam, and a great shock, as of a bolt of lightning. He closed his eyes.

"Now!" he said softly, and slumped exhausted.

By going to the window and looking down at the crowd in the street, he could have seen whether it had worked or not. He did not go to the window. He did not need to. He knew.

The alarm bell ran down.

Pet cocked her head and looked at him with an eye like polished stone.

"Nut," she said.

His hand, as he stretched it up, failed by a full foot and a half to reach the cage. ❧ ◀SR-5

M. Literary Element: DIALOGUE Elicit that Pet is the only other character in the story, and her dialogue consists of only one word. Point out that this refrain, "Nut," serves as a humorous counterpoint to Crangle's feverish imaginings.

N. Literary Element: THEME Point out that the theme of the subunit is "In Whose Hands?" Ask students how "Four O'Clock" develops this theme. *(Possible response: The story presents a situation in which countless people are unknowingly in the hands of an anonymous madman who plans to use his incredible power to mete out a drastic punishment.)*

O. Literary Element: CLIMAX Point out that the author uses a break in the text to indicate that the climax, the four o'clock deadline, has come. The tension reaches its peak as we are about to learn the final outcome.

Check Test

1. What does Mr. Crangle plan to do at four o'clock? *(He plans to make all the evil people in the world one-half their original size.)*

2. How did Mr. Crangle get his unusual power? *(It just came to him; he suddenly realized he had the power, and it had even grown stronger over time.)*

3. What happens to Mr. Crangle at the end of the story? What does this suggest about his plan? *(At the end, Mr. Crangle is suddenly half his former size; this suggests that he is evil.)*

Encouraging Independent Reading

"The Chaser," a short story by John Collier
"Dr. Heidegger's Experiment," a short story by Nathaniel Hawthorne
"A Canary's Ideas," a short story by Joaquim Maria Machado de Assis
"The Eclipse," a short story by Augusto Monterroso

Student Response

Responding to Reading

These questions are open-ended with no "right" or "wrong" answers. However, responses must be supported with information from the selection. Possible answers follow:

1. Any response based on the story is valid.

2. Some students might suggest that he is cranky and strange. Others might say that he is lonely. Students should also suggest that he is one-sided, arrogant, judgmental, and self-righteous.

3. Many students will suggest that Crangle's decision is insane. Some may point out that he is taking the law into his own hands rather than letting society punish evil-doers. Others may suggest that his plan to punish all in the same way shows a complete disregard for justice.

4. Some students might suggest that he might have eliminated the bombing raids and traffic accidents that bothered him so much. Others might suggest that the sudden loss of airplanes and cars would have disrupted the modern world, possibly creating violent reactions among people.

5. Students might say that the author has included the parrot as a foil to highlight the distinctive characteristics of Mr. Crangle. Other students might say that the parrot's one word—Nut—seems to be as much a comment on Mr. Crangle's mental state as a request for food.

6. Students might point out that Mr. Crangle is among those who are shrunk because, due to his lack of compassion and by virtue of his tyrannical use of power, he is evil.

e x p l a i n

Responding to Reading

First Impressions

1. How did you react to the ending? Compare your reaction with the reactions of your classmates.

Second Thoughts

2. What kind of person is Mr. Crangle?
3. What do you think of Mr. Crangle's decision to shrink the evil people in the world?

   Think about
   - why he feels it is necessary to do this
   - what kind of people he labels as evil
   - your own criteria for deciding who is evil
4. What if Crangle's plans to take the stiffness out of airplane propellers or to change the shape of all the wheels in the world had succeeded? What might have been the consequences?
5. Why do you think the writer put the parrot into the play?

   Think about
   - the physical qualities of the parrot that the writer emphasizes
   - how the parrot and Mr. Crangle interact
   - the ending of the story
6. Why is Mr. Crangle among those who are shrunk?

Literary Concept: Suspense

Suspense is the excitement or tension that readers feel as they become involved in a story and are eager to know the outcome of a conflict. In this story, the writer builds suspense by continually reminding you that something will happen soon. What detail does the writer add to create this suspense?

Writing Options

1. A moral states a lesson about life. Write a moral for this story.
2. What do you think might happen next in this story? Write the next scene. Be sure to include Mr. Crangle's explanation of what has happened to him and what he does about it.

Literary Concept—Suspense

Possible response: Details having to do with time heighten the suspense in the story. The author informs us early on that the extraordinary event is to occur at four o'clock. As we watch the minutes tick by, our interest in the final outcome heightens. The climax adds to the suspense by not stating directly what happens at four o'clock.

Writing Options

The Writing Options are designed to meet varied student interests and abilities. Have each student choose one writing activity to complete. You may wish to guide some students to an option that requires less writing.

Journal Update Have students review their journal entries for "Four O'Clock." Ask them to add to their writing any new reflections that have been prompted by the end of the story.

explore

Fiction

A Letter to God

GREGORIO LÓPEZ Y FUENTES
(grā gō' rē ō lō' pez ē fwen'tes)

Examine What You Know (Prior Knowledge)

Imagine for a moment that your home has been hit by a natural disaster such as a fire, a tornado, or an earthquake. Whom might you and your family turn to for help? Compare your list with your classmates' and keep these possible sources of help in mind as you read the story.

Expand Your Knowledge (Building Background)

Among the many types of disasters that can befall the farmer, none is more dreaded than a sudden hailstorm. In a quarter of an hour, a whole crop and an entire year's livelihood can be destroyed. Although most hailstones are smaller than an inch in diameter, some have been found to be the size of baseballs or larger. Hail can severely damage buildings, dent cars and airplanes, and in severe situations, injure or kill both people and animals.

Enrich Your Reading (Reading Skill)

Understanding Cause and Effect When you look back over a story, you should be able to see how each event has been caused by an earlier one and how it, in turn, causes something else to happen. As you read "A Letter to God," fill in a cause and effect chart like the one below. The first sequence has been filled in for you.

Cause and Effect Chart

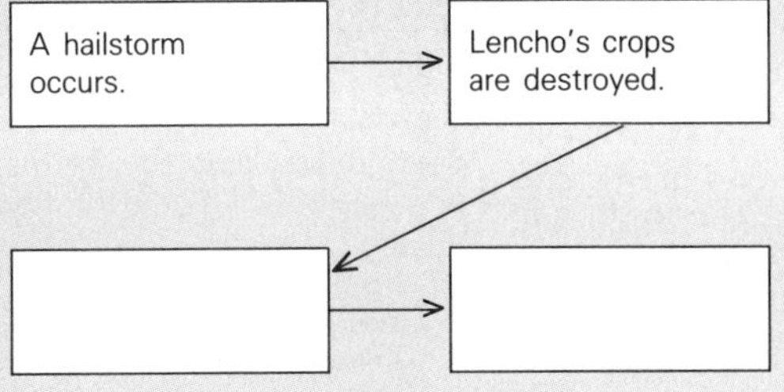

■ *A biography of the author can be found in the Reader's Handbook.*

Objectives

- To read and understand a short story
- To recognize similes and metaphors
- To understand cause and effect
- To express understanding of the work through a variety of writing options, including morals and letters

Prereading/Motivation

Examine What You Know

Discussion Prompts: Do you know of anyone who lost a home to fire or flood? What institutions and agencies provide help to people during such emergencies? What sorts of emotional problems might result when a family loses its home or its livelihood?

Expand Your Knowledge

Discussion Prompts: Do you know how hail is formed? Have you ever been caught in a hailstorm? Why might hailstorms, which normally occur in spring, be especially dangerous to crops?

Enrich Your Reading

Have students copy the chart and fill it in as they read. Direct them to add additional boxes as necessary. Possible answers: A hailstorm occurs—Lencho's crops are destroyed; Lencho writes a letter to God asking for 100 pesos—the postmaster is moved by Lencho's faith; the postmaster, pretending to be God, sends 60 pesos to Lencho—Lencho becomes angry that there are only 60 pesos and not 100; he writes back to God asking for the rest, warning God not to use the post office, since the employees stole some of the money.

Thematic Link—In Whose Hands?

In this story, the main character affirms that he is in the hands of God.

Journal Writing

Faith and respect for faith motivate the main characters in "A Letter to God." Suggest these journal topics to students:

- What circumstances might prompt an individual to write a letter to God?
- What does the phrase *the help of God* mean to you? What forms might such help take?

For other journal opportunities, refer students to annotation **D** and Broader Connections (p. 683).

Additional Resources

UNIT FIVE RESOURCE BOOK
Reader's Guidesheet, p. 60
Vocabulary Worksheet, p. 61
Selection Check Test, p. 62
Selection Test, pp. 63–64

Collaborative Learning

Opportunities for collaborative learning appear throughout the lesson and include Examine What You Know (p. 679) and Writing Options (p. 683).

Teaching Strategies

Support for Students of Limited English Proficiency

- Use **Reader's Guidesheet**, p. 60.
- Tell students that "A Letter to God" is set in rural Mexico some decades ago. Point out that the main characters are simple peasants who have no contact with the outside world. Students who have come from or know about rural areas of Mexico may want to describe the people and places there to the rest of the class. Allow them opportunities to share prior experiences with other students.
- **Annotations G and K** focus on troublesome terms.

Text Annotations

A. Literary Element: SIMILE Point out that the author compares the hill to a truncated pyramid.

B. Literary Element: MOOD Elicit that this description of the beautiful and productive landscape creates a mood of well-being and harmony with nature.

C. Literary Element: DIALOGUE Point out that the dialogue of Lencho and his family is comprised of simple words and short sentences, what one might expect of a peasant family who has little contact with the outside world. The wife's comment shows her basic piety.

D. Discussion Ask students if they ever enjoy just standing in the rain. Ask what feelings being rained on evokes?

E. Literary Element: METAPHOR Ask students in what ways the rain drops are like coins. *(Possible responses: They are round and glisten like new coins; they are as valuable as money because they make the crops grow and give Lencho his livelihood.)*

F. Literary Element: CONFLICT Review that conflict can occur between man and man or between man and nature, as in this case with the hailstorm.

A Letter to God

GREGORIO LÓPEZ Y FUENTES

A The house—the only one in the whole valley—stood at the top of a low hill that looked like one of those primitive, truncated[1] pyramids some wandering tribes abandoned when they moved on. From there you could see the meadows, the river, the stubble pasture, and next to the corral the field of ripe corn with beans blossoming purple among the stalks—the unmistakable sign of a good crop. B The only thing the earth needed was a good rain, or at least one of those heavy showers that form puddles between the rows. To doubt that it would rain would have been the same as mistrusting the experience of veteran farmers who believed in planting on a certain day of the year.

Lencho, who knew the country well, had spent the morning scanning the sky to the northeast.

C "Now at last the rain is really coming, old girl."

And his wife, who was cooking dinner, replied: "May God grant it."

The older children worked in the field while the younger ones played near the house until their mother called to them all: "Come for dinner . . . !"

It was during the meal that great drops of rain began to fall, as Lencho had predicted. Mountainous masses of clouds could be seen coming from the northeast, and the air was fresh and cool. The man went out to fetch some implements that had been left on a stone fence, just to feel the pleasurable sensation of the rain on his body. When he came in he exclaimed: D

"These are not drops of water falling from the sky, they are bright coins: the big drops are ten-centavo[2] coins, and the little drops are the fives. . . ." E

And he gazed with contented eyes at the field of ripe corn and beans in blossom, all veiled in the filmy curtain of rain. But suddenly a strong wind began to blow, and hailstones as big as acorns started to come down with the raindrops. These indeed looked like new silver coins. The children dashed out into the rain to pick up the largest of the icy pearls.

"This is really very bad," the man exclaimed with chagrin.[3] "Let's hope it stops soon."

. . . there was one hope—the help of God.

But it did not stop soon. For an hour the hail came down upon the house, the garden, the mountain, the corn, and the whole valley. The field was white, as if covered with salt; the trees were left leafless, the corn destroyed, the beans left without a F

1. **truncated:** cut off at the top.
2. **ten-centavo** *Spanish:* one-tenth of a peso.
3. **chagrin:** annoyance.

STRUCTURED READING FOR LESS PROFICIENT STUDENTS

These questions can help to guide students through the reading. Ask each question at the point of the selection where the SR number appears in the margin.

SR–1. What destroys Lencho's corn and other crops? *(a heavy hailstorm)* **Literal recall**

SR–2. What does Lencho ask for in his letter to God? *(He asks for 100 pesos to sow a new crop and live on.)* **Literal recall**

SR–3. Why does the postmaster decide to answer Lencho's letter to God? *(He doesn't want Lencho to lose his faith, to become disillusioned.)* **Literal recall**

SR–4. Why does the postmaster send about half the money Lencho requested? *(It was impossible to accumulate the full amount.)* **Literal recall**

SR–5. Why does Lencho write a second letter to God? *(Lencho is angry that he didn't get the full 100 pesos. He writes for the rest, warning God not to use the post office, since the employees are dishonest.)* **Literal recall**

blossom. And Lencho's heart was filled with grief.

After the storm had passed, Lencho told his children as he stood in the middle of the field: "A cloud of locusts would have left more than this; the hailstorm left nothing. This year we'll have no corn or beans. . . ."

The night was one of weeping.

"All our work for nothing!"

"And no one to help us!"

"This year we shall be hungry!"

But in the hearts of all who lived in that solitary house in the middle of the valley there was one hope—the help of God.

"Don't be so upset, even though it's a hard blow. Remember that being hungry never kills anybody!"

"That's what they say—being hungry never kills anybody."

And during the night Lencho thought a great deal about what he had seen in the village church on Sundays: a triangle, and inside the triangle an eye. An eye that seemed very big, an eye—as they had explained it to him—which sees everything, even what is in the depths of one's conscience.

Lencho was an uncouth[4] peasant who worked hard in the fields, but he knew how to write. At daybreak the following Sunday, having strengthened himself in the conviction that there is Someone who watches over us, he began to write a letter that he would carry personally into town and drop in the mail. It was nothing less than a letter to God!

"Dear God," he wrote, "if You do not help me, I and my whole family will be hungry

4. **uncouth** (un ko͞oth′): not cultured.

SAN YSIDRO 1986 Félix A. López By permission of the artist.

G. LEP: Vocabulary Tell students that locusts are large, grasshopperlike insects that fly in great swarms, or clouds. Explain that locusts often devour entire crops along their migration routes.

H. Reading Skill: DRAWING CONCLUSIONS Ask students what conclusions they can draw about Lencho and his family from the information in these paragraphs. *(Possible responses: They have a strong religious faith; they are optimistic; they minimize their difficulties.)*

I. Literary Element: THEME Review that the theme of the subunit is "In Whose Hands?" Point out that Lencho, in his time of need, strengthens his conviction that he is in the hands of God, that "Someone who watches over us."

Art Note

Felix A. Lopez (1942–) is a native of the Santa Fe region of New Mexico. Drawing his inspiration from the very old Hispanic-American religious culture, he taught himself the art of woodworking. He makes his beautiful color pigments from such natural substances as soot, crushed rocks, clay, and plants; the wood, he gathers in nearby forests. *How is the figure of San Ysidro like the letter writer in the story?*

J. Reading Skill: UNDERSTANDING CAUSE AND EFFECT Ask students what causes the post office employee to laugh. *(He gets a letter addressed to God.)*

K. LEP: Vocabulary Explain to students that *not to disillusion that abundant faith* means "not to weaken Lencho's strong faith" or "not to cause Lencho to begin to doubt God."

L. Critical Thinking: EVALUATING Ask students to decide whether the postmaster was wise to answer the letter. Ask what they can say about the postmaster's decision and what objections they have.

Check Test

1. Why did Lencho ask God for 100 pesos? *(His crops had been destroyed by hail, and he needed the money to live on and to plant again.)*

2. Why did the postmaster answer Lencho's letter? *(He admired Lencho's faith and didn't want Lencho to become disillusioned.)*

3. How much money did the postmaster send? *(about 60 pesos)*

4. Why was Lencho angry when he got the letter from "God"? *(Lencho was angry that there were only 60 pesos; since he knew God would not make a mistake, he concluded that the post office employees had stolen the rest of his money.)*

Encouraging Independent Reading

"The Shoes," a short story by Grazia Deledda

"Borrowing Fire," a short story by Ingeborg Refling Hagen

"The Cop and the Anthem" and "A Lickpenny Lover," short stories by O. Henry

"Ann and the Cow," a short story by Johannes V. Jensen

"The (*or* A) Piece of String," a short story by Guy de Maupassant

this year. I need a hundred pesos to sow again and to live on while the new crop is growing, because the hailstorm . . ."

He wrote "To God" on the envelope, put the letter inside, and went into town, still worried. At the post office he put a stamp on the letter and dropped it into the mailbox.

An employee who was a mailman and also an assistant at the post office came over to his boss and, laughing heartily, showed him the letter addressed to God. Never in all his days as a mailman had he come upon that house. The postmaster, fat and jolly, began to laugh, too, but suddenly became serious; and as he tapped the table with the letter he observed, "What faith! Oh, that I had the faith of the man who wrote this letter! To believe as he believes; to wait with the confidence he feels as he waits; to start corresponding with God!"

And in order not to disillusion that abundant faith, revealed by a letter that could not be delivered, the postmaster had an idea: to answer the letter. But when he opened it, he found that in order to do so, something more would be needed than goodwill, paper, and ink. He kept on with his plan, however. He asked his helper for some money, he himself gave part of his salary, and several friends of his were induced to give something "for a charitable cause."

It was impossible for him to accumulate the hundred pesos requested by Lencho, and he could send the peasant only a little over half. He put the bills into an envelope addressed to Lencho, and with them a letter that had only one word, as a signature: God.

The following Sunday Lencho came in, a little earlier than usual, to ask if there was a letter for him. It was the mailman himself who handed him the letter while the postmaster, with the happy glow of a man who has done a good deed, watched through the door from his office. Lencho showed not the slightest surprise when he saw the bills—so very sure was he—but became angry when he counted the money. God could not have made a mistake or have denied what Lencho had requested!

He went at once to the window and asked for paper and ink. At the public desk he began to write, wrinkling his brow because of the effort it cost him to express his thoughts. When he had finished, he went up and bought a stamp, licked it with his tongue, and then stuck it on with a bang of his fist.

As soon as the letter fell into the drop, the postmaster got it and opened it up. It said:

"Dear God: You know that money I asked you for? Only sixty pesos reached me. Please send me the rest; I need it badly. But don't send it through the post office, because the employees are very dishonest. Lencho." ❧

Responding to Reading

First Impressions

1. What was your reaction to the story's ending? Compare your reaction with your classmates'.

Second Thoughts

2. What is your opinion of the postmaster's actions?
   Think about
   - how he reacts to the letter
   - what his other choices might be
   - how his actions affect Lencho
3. Look back at the cause and effect chart you created for this story. What choices does Lencho have, and what do the choices he makes reveal about him?
4. How might Lencho respond if he discovers the real source of the money?
5. Why is the ending of this story ironic?

Broader Connections

6. In the United States, people who lose property through natural disasters such as tornadoes, hurricanes, and earthquakes are often viewed as more deserving of help than families who are plagued by grinding poverty or other difficult circumstances. Why do you think this might be so? Is this attitude fair?

Literary Concept: Simile and Metaphor

Fuentes's description of the opening scene contains both similes and metaphors. In the first sentence of the story, Fuentes uses a **simile,** a comparison using the word *like* or *as,* to describe the hill. Later in the story, Lencho uses a **metaphor,** a comparison that does not use the word *like* or *as,* when he says to his children that the raindrops "are bright coins." Find one other simile from the first half of the story.

Writing Options

1. Write a moral for this story.
2. Write the postmaster's next letter. If you feel his attitude may have changed, be sure to show this change in your letter.

Student Response

Responding to Reading

These questions are open-ended with no "right" or "wrong" answers. However, responses must be supported with information from the selection. Possible answers follow:

1. Any response based on the story is valid.

2. Some students might suggest that the postmaster's action was well-intentioned and generous. Others might suggest that his actions were ill-advised since he was deceiving Lencho and in a sense playing with Lencho's faith. Some might point out that he was dishonest, as Lencho warned.

3. Some students might point out that once his crop is destroyed, Lencho chooses to call on God for help, revealing his faith in Him. Being poor, Lencho had few other alternatives. When Lencho receives less money than he asks for, he writes back to God, again revealing his faith. Some students might note that his comments about the postal workers reveal he is suspicious of his fellow man.

4. Some students might say that Lencho would be angry if he learned the postmaster had opened his letter and then played the role of God. Others might conclude that Lencho would be grateful to the postmaster.

5. Some students might point out that the ending is ironic because the postal workers who have contributed money to Lencho are accused by him of being dishonest.

6. Some students might point out that the poor are said to be responsible for their low economic status due to their lack of ambition or some moral failing. As a result, there is often little sympathy for people in poverty. On the other hand, people who are made poor by an act of God are viewed as deserving victims of forces that they couldn't control. Students might suggest that this divided attitude is not fair; a truly compassionate society would work to eliminate poverty regardless of its causes.

Literary Concept—Simile and Metaphor

Possible response: Fuentes uses the simile *hailstones as big as acorns.* In the same paragraph he says "These indeed looked like new silver coins." Also see annotation A.

Writing Options

The Writing Options are designed to meet varied student interests and abilities. Have each student choose one writing activity to complete. You may wish to guide some students to an option that requires less writing.

Journal Update Have students review their journal entries for "A Letter to God." Ask them to add to their writing any new reflections that have been prompted by the ending of the story.

e x p l o r e

Humorous Essay

Diablo Country

ART BUCHWALD

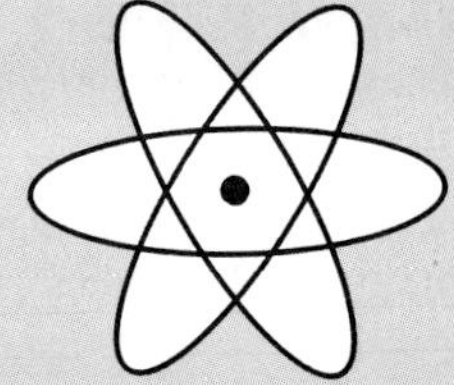

Examine What You Know (Prior Knowledge)

The author of this selection examines his feelings about the safety and necessity of nuclear power. Set up graphs like the ones below and circle the numbers that indicate how safe and how necessary you think nuclear energy is. Then explain your choices to your classmates.

Nuclear Energy

1	2	3	4	5	6	7	8	9	10
Safe				Not Sure					Hazardous

1	2	3	4	5	6	7	8	9	10
Necessary				Not Sure					Unnecessary

Expand Your Knowledge (Building Background)

Nuclear energy is created when atoms of uranium are split in a process called fission. The splitting of these atoms releases a tremendous amount of heat, which is used to produce steam. The steam then drives a turbine, which creates electricity. About 15 percent of the electricity used in the United States is produced this way.

Much less fuel is required to produce nuclear energy than to produce energy by the burning of fossil fuels. Also, nuclear energy production does not release solid pollutants into the atmosphere. On the other hand, nuclear power plants are very expensive to build, and they produce radioactive wastes that remain toxic for thousands of years. Because of these problems, the federal government established the Nuclear Regulatory Commission (NRC) in 1974 to oversee the nuclear power industry.

Enrich Your Reading (Reading Skill)

Stereotypes A **stereotype** is a fixed notion about someone or something that does not allow for any individual differences. As you read "Diablo Country," look to see which groups of people the writer describes in terms of stereotypes.

■ *A biography of the author can be found on page 689.*

Objectives

- To read and understand a humorous essay
- To recognize an author's use of stereotypes
- To express understanding of the work through a variety of writing options, including editorials and signs

Prereading/Motivation

Examine What You Know

Discussion Prompts: Are there any nuclear-power plants in your region? If so, do people voice any objections to them? What are the advantages and disadvantages of nuclear-power plants?

Expand Your Knowledge

Discussion Prompts: Why have many utility companies cancelled plans to build new nuclear-power plants? What associations do you have with the names Chernobyl and Three Mile Island? Why is it so difficult to find suitable storage sites for radioactive waste?

Enrich Your Reading

Have students form two columns: one headed *Stereotype 1: Nuclear Power Protestors* and one with the heading *Stereotype 2: Nuclear Advocates.* Ask students to note details and generalizations about each group that the author provides to establish each stereotype.

Thematic Link—In Whose Hands?

In this essay, the author casts doubt on the hands that control the nuclear industry.

Journal Writing

The selection describes the author's reactions to opponents and supporters of a nuclear power plant being built at Diablo Canyon in California. Suggest these journal topics to students:

- The word *diablo* means "devil." What problems have bedeviled the nuclear-power industry?
- Discuss a time when having a stereotyped opinion of someone led you to make a wrong conclusion.

For other journal opportunities, refer students to First Impressions and Broader Connections (p. 688).

Additional Resources

UNIT FIVE RESOURCE BOOK

Reader's Guidesheet, p. 65
Vocabulary Worksheet, p. 66
Selection Check Tests, p. 67
Selection Test, pp. 68–69

Collaborative Learning

Opportunities for collaborative learning appear throughout the lesson and include annotation G, Options for Learning (p. 689), and Cross-Curricular Options (p. T–689).

A

Diablo Country

ART BUCHWALD

B I pride myself on having a very open mind on things such as nuclear energy as long as they don't build a plant near my home.

So when I saw the Diablo Canyon demonstration in California a while ago, I watched it with the calm impartiality which I reserve for all things that
SR-1 ▶ don't affect me personally.

C On one side were scruffy, unshaven, unshod protestors. On the other were well-dressed state troopers and clean, good-looking spokesmen for the power company. The dispute, as I understand it, was the scruffy unbathed people claimed that the people in the white hats didn't know what they were doing. They had built a billion-dollar nuclear plant near the San Andreas fault,[1] which everyone says is going to cause
SR-2 ▶ an earthquake in California sooner or later.

My wife, who doesn't know the first thing about nuclear energy, asked me one evening as we watched the scruffies being hauled off in sheriffs' vans, "Why would they build a nuclear plant next to an earthquake center?"

"Because it obviously makes sense. The people who construct those plants know what they're doing. If you had been listening to the nice, clean-cut men in white shirts, ties, and dark suits, you would know that the power company has done exhaustive tests, and the nuclear plant can withstand any earthquake shock known to man. Besides, we have a Nuclear Regulatory Commission that has the last word on whether a plant is safe or not. They would never have given their OK to open one if there was the slightest question that building a nuke plant next to an earthquake fault could hurt the environment." D

"Then why are the people in the scruffy clothes willing to be arrested for trying to close down the plant?" she asked.

"Because they have an unrealistic fear of nuclear power. They don't understand it, and therefore they're against it. Many of them are students who enjoy getting involved in civil disobedience. But they're willing to go to jail for their beliefs."

"Whose side are you on?"

"I'm afraid I have to be on the side of those wearing the ties and coats. After all, they've been dealing with nuclear power all their lives and they should know if it's safe or not." E ◀ SR-3

"A few years ago, you would have been on the side of the unwashed."

"I guess age does that to you. At some point in time you have to say that just because a person needs a shave doesn't make

1. **San Andreas fault:** active rift in the Earth's crust extending approximately 600 miles (966 km) from Southern California to the northwest American coast.

Teaching Strategies

Support for Students of Limited English Proficiency

- Use **Reader's Guidesheet**, p. 65.
- Tell students that "Diablo Country" is a humorous column based on real incidents in California. Ask students from other countries to share their feelings or knowledge about nuclear-energy production in their native lands.
- **Annotations A, F,** and **H** focus on troublesome terms and concepts.

Text Annotations

A. LEP: Title After students have read the column, you might point out that the word *diablo* is Spanish for "devil."

B. Literary Element: GENRE Explain that tone is the attitude an author takes toward his or her subject matter. Point out that the tone of Buchwald's essay is humorous. Here, for example, he pokes fun at himself for being open-minded and impartial on issues that don't affect him personally.

C. Literary Element: STEREOTYPE Point out that Buchwald stereotypes the opponents of nuclear power as being *scruffy, unshaven,* and *unshod.*Students may need to know that *unshod* means "without shoes." He stereotypes supporters of the power plant as *well-dressed, clean,* and *good-looking.*

D. Reading Skills: INFERRING Point out the stereotypes of clean-cut men in suits and ties. Ask students what assumptions Buchwald, and many others, make about such people. *(Possible response: We assume that conservatively dressed, clean-cut people have good information and make wise decisions.)*

E. Literary Element: DIALOGUE Point out that Buchwald uses the form of a dialogue with his wife to present his ideas in a natural and fun-to-read form.

STRUCTURED READING FOR LESS PROFICIENT STUDENTS

These questions can help to guide students through the reading. Ask each question at the point of the selection where the SR number appears in the margin.

SR–1. Who is the narrator in the essay? *(the author, Art Buchwald)* **Inferring**

SR–2. Who are the groups of people on the two different sides of the Diablo Country nuclear plant issue? *(scruffy, unshaven, unshod protestors; state troopers and clean, good-looking spokesmen for the power company)* **Literal recall**

SR–3. At first, on whose side is the author? *(on the side of those wearing the ties and coats)* **Literal recall**

SR–4. How does the author's attitude change? *(He now thinks that the scruffy people may have been right.)* **Inferring**

F. LEP: Clarifying Explain that during the 1960's in the United States a counterculture developed whose members wore long hair and colorful casual clothes, proposed radical economic and social changes, and often opposed the spokespeople of big business and government. Art Buchwald suggests that he and his wife once sympathized with the ideals of this counterculture, but, with the passage of time, have adopted more traditional and conservative views.

G. Discussion Have students discuss their attitudes toward science and technology. Do they think people tend to place too much faith in the powers of scientists and technicians? Can they cite reasons that might lead one to lack faith in some aspect of the scientific establishment?

H. LEP: Idiom Review that the idiom *making a mountain out of a molehill* means "making a big fuss over something unimportant."

I. Literary Element: IRONY Have students explain why this outcome is ironic. *(Possible response: As Buchwald says, we would expect the engineers who build nuclear-power plants to be very careful. It is most unexpected, almost inconceivable, that they would get their drawings mixed up and install the wrong pipes throughout the plant.)*

J. Literary Element: THEME Ask students how the selection develops the theme "In Whose Hands?" *(Buchwald is no longer so confident of the hands that control the nuclear industry; he seems to have less confidence in the clean-cut advocates of nuclear power and is willing to give more credit to the scruffy protestors.)*

(right) Inside a nuclear reactor © Arthus-Bertrand/Peter Arnold, Inc., New York (inset) The Diablo Canyon Nuclear power plant AP/Wide World Photos, Inc., New York.

F him right—and just because a person has short hair and dresses properly doesn't make him wrong."

"That's a stupid reason for taking one side over the other."

"There's more to it than that. The people who build nuclear plants are scientists, trained in our finest technical institutions. They work with computers and consult with famous experts who have an answer for G every problem. The engineers and designers take extraordinary steps to see that not one bolt is put in wrongly. If they say a nuclear plant can survive an earthquake, I have to accept their word for it.

"This is not to say I am unsympathetic with the poor souls who are willing to go to jail because they lack faith in our great scientific establishment. But in this case, I believe they're making a mountain out of a H molehill. I would bet my All Savers Bank Account that they are wrong."

Well, you can imagine my surprise when a week later the evening news announced that the Diablo Canyon nuclear reactor could not go into service because someone had gotten the drawings all mixed up, and the wrong pipes had been installed in the wrong sections of the plant. I It meant that every pipe had to be personally inspected and replaced if it was discovered that it didn't belong there.

A man from the power company in a nice white shirt, tie, and blue suit explained it wasn't a very serious mistake and could have happened to anybody.

Another well-dressed man from the Nuclear Regulatory Commission said he was appalled at the sloppy engineering and was J ordering an immediate investigation.

They didn't put on any scruffy people for comment. I wish they had, because I wanted to find out where to send them my All Savers Bank Account. ❧ ◀ SR-4

CRITIC'S CORNER

Aside from being entertaining, a collection of Buchwald's columns forms a unique social history, conveying the essence and spirit of our times more accurately than any dry analysis of current events. Buchwald hears with perfect pitch the babble of cockamamie politicians and bureaucrats, the twaddle of assorted "newsmakers," and the cacophony of our latest fads, trends, and media hype. . . . [He] manages with startling consistency to turn this dross of news into satiric gold. Virtuoso that he is, he makes the devilish job of writing humor look easy.

VIC SUSSMAN, FROM *Contemporary Authors*, NEW REVISION SERIES, VOL. 21

INSIGHT

Don't Can Your Aluminum

THE EARTH WORKS GROUP

BACKGROUND

Aluminum is the most abundant metal on earth, but it was only discovered in the 1820's. At that time it was worth $1,200 a kilogram, more than gold. According to Worldwatch Institute, "Since its first use as a toy rattle for Napoleon's son, aluminum's use has escalated. The first all-aluminum beverage can appeared in 1963 and today accounts for the largest single use of aluminum. . . . In 1985 more than 70 billion beverage cans were used, of which almost 66 billion—or 94%—were aluminum."

YES YOU CAN-CAN

- If you throw an aluminum can out of your car window, it will still litter the Earth up to 500 years later.
- If you throw away 2 aluminum cans, you waste more energy than is used daily by each of a billion human beings in poorer lands.
- According to the Aluminum Association, Americans recycled 42.5 billion aluminum cans in 1988.
- In 1988 alone, aluminum can recycling saved more than 11 billion kilowatt hours of electricity, enough to supply the residential electric needs of New York City for six months.
- The energy saved from one recycled aluminum can will operate a television set for three hours.
- Recycling aluminum cuts related air pollution by 95%.
- Making aluminum from recycled aluminum uses 90% less energy than making aluminum from scratch.

SIMPLE THINGS TO DO

Because recycling aluminum is so profitable for manufacturing companies (they make $2 million *every day* from recycling), there probably are more different ways to recycle aluminum than any other material. Check to see which programs exist in your area.

RESULTS

- According to Recycle America's statistics, if only 250 people (including you, of course) each recycled one can a day, we would save the energy equivalent of 1,750–3,500 gallons of gasoline every year. Now try that calculation with 250,000 people; just one can a day could save the energy equivalent of between 1.75 and 3.5 million gallons of gas. And *that's* only .1% of the U.S. population, with a single can apiece.
- If we recycle, we mine fewer raw materials. To produce one ton of aluminum from raw materials, it takes a phenomenal 8,760 pounds of bauxite and 1,020 pounds of petroleum coke. But according to Aluminum Association estimates, this figure is cut down by 95% when recycled aluminum is used.

—from *50 Simple Things You Can Do to Save the Earth*

Check Test

1. Why were the scruffy people protesting the Diablo Canyon Nuclear Plant? *(They said that the people building it didn't know what they were doing; they said that an earthquake could destroy the plant.)*

2. Why does Art Buchwald at first think the protestors are wrong? *(He has faith in the nuclear industry and the NRC; he believes that the scientists and engineers would never build an unsafe plant.)*

3. What happens at the plant to make Buchwald question his earlier beliefs? *(Due to a mix-up, the wrong pipes are installed throughout the plant; the NRC describes the plant's engineering as sloppy.)*

Encouraging Independent Reading

You Can Fool All of the People All of the Time, a collection of humor by Art Buchwald

Recycling, nonfiction by James and Lynn Hahn

Nuclear Energy at the Crossroads, nonfiction by Irene Kiefer

Save the Earth! nonfiction by Betty Miles

Insight

This piece reflects on the ideas in the main selection and is suggested for students' independent reading. Optional discussion questions follow.

1. Describe how the Earth Works Group's approach to the nation's need for energy differs from that of the clean-cut men described in "Diablo Country." *(The Earth Works Group advocates recycling as a major way to save energy; the clean-cut men of "Diablo Country" advocate building nuclear-power plants to generate more electricity to meet the nation's energy needs.)*

2. What is the largest single use of aluminum today? *(beverage cans)*

3. Which of the facts in the article do you find most startling? Why? *(Accept all reasonable responses.)*

Student Response

Responding to Reading

These questions are open-ended with no "right" or "wrong" answers. However, responses must be supported with information from the selection. Possible answers follow:

1. Any response is valid.

2. Most students will point out that the speaker is not really open-minded, since he would object to a plant near his home. Other students might say that the speaker's description of himself as open-minded is intended as tongue-in-cheek humor: he is more open-minded than we first believe.

3. He believes their comments are based on the latest, most accurate scientific information. Students may also point out that many people associate a suit and tie with success, authority, or knowledge.

4. Buchwald agrees with the NRC regulator who viewed the mistake as appalling. Some students might say that even if the pipe incident was not a serious error, any mistake at a nuclear-power plant greatly undermines public confidence.

5. Some students will say that the article suggests that we have placed nuclear power in the hands of people who are overconfident and perhaps unreliable. Others might suggest that the piece says we must take a more hands-on approach to the issues of science and technology that affect our lives.

6. Some students might say the author wanted to entertain us with a humorous account of how stereotypes tend to mask the truth. Other students may suggest that Buchwald means to persuade us that the nuclear power industry faces serious credibility problems.

7. Accept any response. Some students might point out that a cheap new fuel would raise living standards dramatically by decreasing the amount we spend on fuels. Others might point to the economic dislocation that would occur among workers and communities who derive their incomes from industries based on other fuels, such as oil.

e x p l a i n

Responding to Reading

First Impressions

1. As you read this essay, with which side did you find yourself agreeing? Why?

Second Thoughts

2. The speaker announces in the first sentence that he has "a very open mind on things." Does he?

Think about
- what it means to be open-minded
- what stereotypes he makes

3. Why does the writer place his trust in the "nice, clean-cut men in white shirts, ties, and dark suits"?

4. A spokesman for the power company explains that installing the wrong pipes was not a very serious mistake. What does Buchwald think, and with which man do you agree? Explain.

5. How does this story relate to the subunit title "In Whose Hands?"

Think about
- who makes this country's decisions about nuclear energy
- how much influence the average citizen has over these decisions

6. What purposes might the writer have had for writing this piece?

Broader Connections

7. What if something very ordinary, like water, became a fuel? What effects would this have on your life and on the nation's economy?

Literary Concept: Humorous Essay

An essay is a brief nonfiction work that deals with a single subject, often in a personal way. Sometimes, as in "Diablo Country," a writer adds humor to make his ideas and opinions more entertaining. How do the stereotypes in this essay add to the humor of the piece?

Writing Options

1. Read the *Insight* on page 687. Using the information from this page, write a one-minute editorial urging people to recycle aluminum.

2. Make up signs for the Diablo Canyon protestors to carry.

Literary Concept—Humorous Essay

Possible response: Colorful adjectives such as *scruffy, unwashed,* and *unshod* help create a humorous image of the stereotypical nuclear protester. The sharp and doubtlessly exaggerated contrast between these protesters and the "nice, clean-cut men in white shirts"; adds humor, too. Most of the humor results from the ironic turnaround in the author's estimation of these two groups. That is, news of the company's mix-up suddenly makes the scruffy unwashed seem quite knowledgeable, while the clean-cut spokesmen appear incompetent and less than honest.

Writing Options

The Writing Options are designed to meet varied student interests and abilities. Have each student choose one writing activity to complete. You may wish to guide some students to an option that requires less writing.

Journal Update Have students review their journal entries. Ask them to note whether the events Buchwald describes affect their opinions of nuclear power.

e x t e n d

Options for Learning

1 • Nuclear Debate With several of your classmates, research and present a debate on the pluses and minuses of nuclear energy. Try to include one or two visual aids, such as charts, maps, or graphs, in your presentation. Ask the class to vote on which side presents the most logical and effective argument.

2 • The Way It Works Check an encyclopedia or a science book or talk to a science teacher or some other authority to find out how nuclear energy is created. Draw a diagram or prepare a model that demonstrates the process and share your results with the class.

3 • Nuclear Time Line Set up a time line that shows important dates in the development of nuclear energy and the scientists who contributed to that development. Begin your time line with the discovery of natural radioactivity in 1896.

4 • Major Meltdowns Create a display of photocopied newspaper and magazine articles that explain what happened at the nuclear plant breakdown at Three Mile Island in 1979 or at Chernobyl in 1986. Begin by checking for relevant articles for those years in the *Readers' Guide to Periodical Literature.*

FACT FINDER

When and where was atomic fission first successfully demonstrated?

Art Buchwald
1925–

Although he is now considered one of America's funniest writers, Art Buchwald had a childhood that was anything but fun. His mother died when Buchwald was very young, and his father, unable to support the family, was forced to place his young son in several foster homes in New York City. Buchwald also stayed at the Hebrew Orphan Asylum for a time. After dropping out of high school at seventeen, Buchwald joined the Marine Corps. "I felt that the Marines were the only ones I had ever cared about or who had cared about me." As a Marine, he fought in the Pacific during World War II.

After the war, Buchwald moved to Europe and began writing a column about Paris life. The column was so popular that it eventually appeared in eighty-five newspapers in the United States. Despite his success in Europe, Buchwald returned to the States in 1961 in order to write political humor. Since then, he has won praise for his wit, his writing, and his concern about serious problems. One critic notes that Buchwald is "at his best when he is morally outraged at some new hypocrisy or cruelty." In 1982 he won a Pulitzer Prize.

CROSS-CURRICULAR OPTIONS

Social Studies: Find Art Buchwald columns in newspapers or in his published collections. Choose one column to read aloud to the class. Provide background information, if necessary.

Geography: Prepare a map of the United States showing the location of nuclear-power plants. On a political map of the world, show the countries most dependent on nuclear energy.

Science: Investigate a source of energy—solar power, wind power, or geothermal energy—that is proposed as an environmentally sound alternative to nuclear power.

Language: Collect oral histories in which people share their feelings about nuclear power.

Math: Contrast the costs of nuclear-generated electricity with power produced by coal- and oil-burning plants or hydroelectric plants.

Options for Learning

These activities address a variety of learning styles and modes of expression. Allow students to review the options and then choose the one they wish to do. Many are excellent collaborative learning projects.

1. Nuclear Debate Establish the debate format, including the number of constructive and rebuttal speeches, and the time allocated for each.

2. The Way It Works Students might speak with the utility officials in the area to find out about nearby nuclear reactors.

3. Nuclear Time Line Refer students to the encyclopedia for important dates.

4. Major Meltdowns Students might also investigate minor accidents at other nuclear facilities.

Fact Finder

Most encyclopedia articles on nuclear energy will reveal that in 1942 scientists at the University of Chicago were the first to demonstrate atomic fission.

Additional Information About the Author

Art Buchwald Art Buchwald is among the most widely read political humorists in the country. He is often called a modern-day court jester, someone who can extract humor from even the most humdrum news story or lighten the frustration caused by the most intractable issues of the day.

Closure

In whose hands should we place responsibility for important issues, such as nuclear power, that affect our lives and environment? Without attempting to answer that question directly, "Diablo Country" warns us against stereotypical thinking. Specifically, we see that clean-cut, engineering types may make serious mistakes, while scruffy, protesting types may have valuable insights. Ask students to name other highly charged issues in society today and suggest ways in which stereotypes can cloud the thinking on these issues.

Objectives

- To read and understand a three-act play
- To identify the author's purposes for writing a play
- To review characterization in a play
- To make predictions
- To express understanding of the work through a choice of writing options, including travel articles, bumper stickers, stage directions, summaries, and paragraphs of opinion

Prereading/Motivation

Examine What You Know

Discussion Prompts: What would seem odd or unusual to an alien observing each of these facets of life on earth? How do anthropologists and other social scientists study primitive societies here on earth? What serious problems now facing earth might a more advanced culture be able to solve?

Expand Your Knowledge

Discussion Prompts: Why do you think the members of a community are sometimes frightened by the arrival of outsiders or strangers? What movies or books about alien invaders have you seen or read recently? For what purpose did the aliens come? How were they received?

Enrich Your Reading

Have students copy the questions on page 690. Then, after they have answered the questions, have them share their responses.

Thematic Link—In Whose Hands?

In this play, an alien from another dimension comes to the United States. As a few human beings begin to experience his extraordinary superhuman powers, they begin to wonder in whose hands their fate now rests.

Drama

Visit to a Small Planet

GORE VIDAL

Examine What You Know (Prior Knowledge)

The characters in the following play learn what an alien from an advanced world in outer space thinks of Earth. Imagine that you are a visitor from an advanced world. In your "Space Journal," comment on the following facets of life on earth. Then compare your views with those of your classmates and the alien in the play.

- Technological achievements
- Eating and drinking habits
- Transportation and entertainment
- International relations

Expand Your Knowledge (Building Background)

Alien visits are a favorite topic for science fiction writers. One of the most famous of these stories is *War of the Worlds* by H. G. Wells. Written in 1898, the story describes an alien invasion from Mars. Forty years later, an actor named Orson Welles produced a radio version of this book that was so convincing thousands of listeners believed Martians had actually landed. In panic, citizens fled from their homes, believing they were in mortal danger. More recently, films such as Steven Spielberg's *E.T.* and *Close Encounters of the Third Kind* have provided less horrifying versions of alien visitors.

Enrich Your Reading (Reading Skill)

Predicting Good readers make predictions about characters and plot before and during their reading. Use the following questions to make your own predictions about the alien in this play.

1. Why has the alien come?
2. Who will the alien want to talk to?
3. How will people react to his visit?
4. What will happen as a result of the alien's visit?

■ *A biography of the author can be found on page 717.*

Journal Writing

The characters of *Visit to a Small Planet* find themselves in the hands of an all-powerful alien. Suggest these journal topics to students:

- Why might an alien from another solar system consider earth to be a small planet?
- Describe how you think you'd react if a flying saucer landed in your front yard.

For other journal opportunities, refer Students to Examine What You Know (p. 690), Broaden Connections (p. 715), and **Annotation HH.**

Additional Resources

UNIT FIVE RESOURCE BOOK

Reader's Guidesheet, p. 70
Vocabulary Worksheet, p. 71
Selection and Vocabulary Check Tests, p. 72
Selection Test, pp. 73–74

Collaborative Learning

Opportunities for collaborative learning appear throughout the lesson and include Options for Learning, (p. 717) and Cross-Curricular Options (p. T–717).

A

Visit to a Small Planet

GORE VIDAL

CHARACTERS

Kreton	**John Randolph**
Roger Spelding	**General Powers**
Ellen Spelding	**Aide**
Mrs. Spelding	**Paul Laurent**
Two Technicians	**Second Visitor**

President of Paraguay

ACT ONE

(Stock shot: The night sky, stars. Then slowly a luminous object arcs into view. As it is almost upon us, dissolve to the living room of the Spelding house in Maryland.

Superimpose card: "The Time: The Day After Tomorrow."

B *The room is comfortably balanced between the expensively decorated and the homely.* Roger Spelding *is concluding his TV broadcast. He is middle-aged, unctuous,*[1] *resonant. His wife, bored and vague, knits passively while he talks at his desk. Two technicians are on hand, operating the equipment. His daughter,* Ellen, *a lively girl of twenty, fidgets as she listens.)*

C **Spelding** *(into microphone)*. . . . and so, according to General Powers . . . who should know if anyone does . . . the flying object which has given rise to so much irresponsible conjecture is nothing more than a meteor passing through the earth's orbit. It is not, as many believe, a secret weapon of this country. Nor is it a spaceship, as certain lunatic elements have suggested. General Powers has assured me that it is highly doubtful there

1. **unctuous** (uŋk' cho͞o əs): in a smug or dishonest manner, as in someone pretending to be earnest when trying to persuade another.

Words to Know and Use | **conjecture** (kən jek' chər) *n.* speculation; guess

Teaching Strategies

Vocabulary Preview

These vocabulary words are defined at the bottom of the selection page on which they appear. You may wish to discuss them briefly before students begin reading:

conjecture speculation; guess
lurid violently passionate
malevolence feeling of ill will or hatred toward others
patronizing in a superior manner
philanthropist a person who gives to charities
predatory characterized by robbing others

Support for Students of Limited English Proficiency

- Use **Reader's Guidesheet**, p. 70.
- The setting of *Visit to a Small Planet,* a suburban Maryland home in the mid-1950's, should present few difficulties to LEP students. Allow students to read the play silently first before the class reads it aloud. You may wish to have a drama or advanced English class record the play so that LEP students can listen to the script individually while following along with the text.
- **Annotations D, K, Q, U, V, W, DD, GG, KK, and NN** in Act One; **annotations B, E, I, O, S, and X** in Act Two; and **annotations A, J, and L** in Act Three focus on items that may prove troublesome.

Text Annotations

A. Literary Element: TITLE Point out that Earth, along with Mars, Venus, and Mercury, are the four small terrestrial planets. Explain that the so-called major planets, Jupiter, Saturn, Uranus, and Neptune, are much larger. Ask students to suggest some connotations of *small* that have to do with qualities other than size. *(unimportant; lacking quality or development; petty)*

B. Literary Element: CHARACTERIZATION Point out the adjectives used to characterize the members of the Spelding family—*unctuous, bored, vague,* and *lively.* Have students use these descriptions to speculate on what they might expect of each character.

C. Reading Skills: INFERRING Ask students to infer what Roger Spelding does for a living. *(He is a TV announcer; he is a news commentator.)*

Structured Reading for Less Proficient Students

These questions can help to guide students through the reading. Ask each question at the point of the selection where the SR number appears in the margin.

SR–1. As Act 1 opens, what does Roger Spelding assure his TV audience? *(He assures them that the object in the sky is a meteor, not a spaceship.)* **Literal recall**

SR–2. What actually lands in the garden in back of the Speldings' house? *(A mysterious spacecraft lands in the garden; inside is a being from another galaxy.)* **Summarizing**

SR–3. What reason does Kreton give at first for coming to earth? *(He claims that he has been studying it and wanted to make a visit.)* **Literal recall**

SR–4. What does the fact that there is no instrument board in Kreton's spaceship suggest? *(He comes from a planet that is so advanced that it no longer needs technology.)* **Inferring**

Continued on page 692

Historical Sidelight A sudden flap of UFO sightings in the late 1940's and early 1950's led the U.S. Air Force to investigate. Using code names, such as Project Blue Book, the Air Force continued the investigation for twenty years without significant findings. Critics maintain that the Air Force was engaged in a public-relations efforts designed to debunk the UFO phenonmena as groundless.

D. LEP: Metaphor Elicit that Spelding is referring to Washington, D.C. as "the warm pulsebeat of the nation." Explain that he is likening the capital of the country to the human heart.

E. Literary Element: STAGE DIRECTIONS Ask students what the stage directions reveal about Spelding's character. *(Possible response: He is a bit of a phony; he isn't as happy and hearty as he pretends on TV.)*

F. Literary Sidelight The correct quotation from Shakespeare's *King Lear* is this: "How sharper than a serpent's tooth it is/To have a thankless child." Point out that the sentiment isn't really appropriate, since Ellen isn't ungrateful; she is merely in love with someone who holds values different from her father's.

G. Literary Element: CONFLICT Point out that the conflict over Ellen fiancé's supposed lack of "get-up-and-go" suggests that the hard-driving, ambitious Mr. Spelding values worldly success over personal happiness.

H. Literary Element: DIALOGUE Elicit that this comment characterizes Mr. Spelding as close-minded and self-important. He does not want to be corrected, even in small factual matters.

is any form of life on other planets capable of building a spaceship. "If any traveling is to be done in space, we will do it first." And those are his exact words. . . . Which winds up another week of news. *(crosses to pose with wife and daughter)* This is Roger Spelding, saying good night to Mother and Father America from my old homestead in Silver Glen, Maryland, close to the warm pulsebeat of the nation. D SR-1

Technician. Good show tonight, Mr. Spelding.

Spelding. Thank you.

Technician. Yes sir, you were right on time.

*(*Spelding *nods wearily, his mechanical smile and heartiness suddenly gone.)* E

Mrs. Spelding. Very nice, dear. Very nice.

Technician. See you next week, Mr. Spelding.

Spelding. Thank you, boys.

*(*Technicians *go.)*

Spelding. Did you like the broadcast, Ellen?

Ellen. Of course I did, Daddy.

Spelding. Then what did I say?

Ellen. Oh, that's not fair.

Spelding. It's not very flattering when one's own daughter won't listen to what one says while millions of people . . .

Ellen. I always listen, Daddy, you know that.

Mrs. Spelding. We love your broadcasts, dear. I don't know what we'd do without them.

Spelding. Starve.

Ellen. I wonder what's keeping John?

Spelding. Certainly not work.

Ellen. Oh, Daddy, stop it! John works very hard and you know it.

Mrs. Spelding. Yes, he's a perfectly nice boy, Roger. I like him.

Spelding. I know. I know: he has every virtue except the most important one: he has no get-up-and-go.

Ellen *(precisely)*. He doesn't want to get up and he doesn't want to go because he's already where he wants to be on his own farm, which is exactly where *I'm* going to be when we're married.

Spelding. More thankless than a serpent's tooth is an ungrateful child. F

Ellen. I don't think that's right. Isn't it "more deadly . . ."

Spelding. Whatever the exact quotation is, I stand by the sentiment.

Mrs. Spelding. Please don't quarrel. It always gives me a headache.

Spelding. I never quarrel. I merely reason, in my simple way, with Miss Know-it-all here.

Ellen. Oh, Daddy! Next you'll tell me I should marry for money.

Spelding. There is nothing wrong with marrying a wealthy man. The horror of it has always eluded me. However, my only wish is that you marry someone hardworking, ambitious, a man who'll make his mark in the world. Not a boy who plans to sit on a farm all his life, growing peanuts . . . G

Ellen. English walnuts.

Spelding. Will you stop correcting me? H

Ellen. But, Daddy, John grows walnuts . . .

*(*John *enters breathlessly.)*

John. Come out! Quickly. It's coming this way. It's going to land right here!

Spelding. *What's* going to land?

John. The spaceship. Look!

Spelding. Apparently you didn't hear my broadcast. The flying object in question is a meteor, not a spaceship.

*(*John *has gone out with* Ellen, Spelding *and* Mrs. Spelding *follow.)*

Structured Reading for Less Proficient Students

Continued from page 691

SR–5. Why does General Powers declare martial law and complete censorship? *(Powers wants to keep the event secret until he decides or is told what to do.)* **Clarifying**

SR–6. Why is it hard for the characters to keep secrets from Kreton? *(He is a mindreader; he hears their thoughts.)* **Literal recall**

SR–7. What happens when General Powers orders his men to take apart Kreton's spaceship? *(He erects an invisible wall around it.)* **Literal recall**

SR–8. What does Kreton seem to like most about the people on earth? *(He likes their primitiveness; he enjoys sensing their raw and interesting emotions.)* **Literal recall**

SR–9. What goal does Kreton announce at the end of the act? *(He announces that he plans to take over the entire world.)* **Literal recall**

Mrs. Spelding. Oh, my! Look! Something *is* falling! Roger, you don't think it's going to hit the house, do you?

Spelding. The odds against being hit by a falling object that size are, I should say, roughly, ten million to one.

John. Ten million to one or not, it's going to land right here and it's *not* falling.

Spelding. I'm sure it's a meteor.

I **Mrs. Spelding.** Shouldn't we go down to the cellar?

Spelding. If it's not a meteor, it's an optical illusion . . . mass hysteria.

Ellen. Daddy, it's a real spaceship. I'm sure it is.

Spelding. Or maybe a weather balloon. Yes, that's what it is. General Powers said only yesterday . . .

John. It's landing!

Spelding. I'm going to call the police . . . the army!

(bolts inside)

Ellen. Oh, look how it shines!

John. Here it comes!

Mrs. Spelding. Right in my rose garden!

Ellen. Maybe it's a balloon.

J **John.** No, its a spaceship and right in your own back yard.

Ellen. What makes it shine so?

John. I don't know, but I'm going to find out.

(runs off toward the light)

Ellen. Oh, darling, don't! John, please! John, John, come back!

(Spelding, *wide-eyed, returns.)*

Mrs. Spelding. Roger, it's landed right in my rose garden.

K **Spelding.** I got General Powers. He's coming over. He said they've been watching this thing. They . . . they don't know what it is.

Ellen. You mean it's nothing of ours?

Spelding. They believe it . . . *(swallows hard)* . . . it's from outer space. L

Ellen. And John's down there! Daddy, get a gun or something.

Spelding. Perhaps we'd better leave the house until the army gets here.

Ellen. We can't leave John.

Spelding. I can. *(peers nearsightedly)* Why, it's not much larger than a car. I'm sure it's some kind of meteor.

Ellen. Meteors are blazing hot.

Spelding. This is a cold one . . .

Ellen. It's opening . . . the whole side's opening! *(Shouts)* John! Come back! Quick. . . .

Mrs. Spelding. Why, there's a man getting out if it! *(sighs)* I feel much better already. I'm sure if we ask him, he'll move that thing for us. Roger, you ask him.

Spelding *(ominously)*. If it's really a man?

Ellen. John's shaking hands with him. *(calls)* John darling, come on up here . . .

Mrs. Spelding. And bring your friend . . .

Spelding. There's something wrong with the way that creature looks . . . if it is a man and not a . . . not a monster. M

Mrs. Spelding. He looks perfectly nice to me.

(John *and the* Visitor *appear. The* Visitor *is in his forties, a mild, pleasant-looking man with side-whiskers and dressed in the fashion of 1860. He pauses when he sees the three people, in silence for a moment. They stare back at him, equally interested.)* ◀SR-2

Visitor. I seem to've made a mistake. I *am* sorry. I'd better go back and start over again.

I. Literary Element: WRITER'S PURPOSE Elicit that Spelding, unwilling to accept the obvious, is mouthing the various official explanations that are given when people claim to see UFO's. Explain that Gore Vidal's purpose is to poke fun at officialdom's close-mindedness.

J. Literary Element: DRAMA Ask students to suggest some visual effects and sound effects that they might use offstage to simulate the rocket landing.

K. LEP: Word Play Point out the wordplay in the name General Powers. A general is the most powerful rank in the army and has wide-ranging, or general, powers.

L. Literary Element: DIALOGUE Have a volunteer read Spelding's lines. Point out that the ellipsis points and the stage directions are meant to convey that Spelding is so shocked by developments that he can hardly speak.

M. Literary Element: THEME Point out that the Speldings' disagreement over whether the visitor is "perfectly nice" or "a monster" suggests the theme "In Whose Hands?" That is, no one can be sure who the visitor is or what his purpose might be.

Critic's Corner

The 1957 stage version of *Visit to a Small Planet* had a Broadway run of 338 performances and an extended national tour. These comments are from the reviews of leading critics:

" . . . in both the writing and the playing, 'Visit to a Small Planet' is a topsy-turvy lark that has a lot of humorous vitality. The tone is low; the entertainment is highly enjoyable."
Brooks Atkinson, *The New York Times*

" . . . Within its limitations, [Vidal's] play is a remarkably lively and agreeable piece of work."
Wolcott Gibbs, *The New Yorker*

Art Note

Will Barnet (1911–) is a master of the art of abstraction. His images are clear and uncluttered. They describe a scene, a person, or an object in colors or with symbols that suggest an idea. This striking painting may call to mind the machinery of a piston engine or any mechanism that sends and receives impulses, incuding the human system. *Why is it an apt illustration for A Visit to a Small Planet?*

N. Literary Element: FORESHADOWING Ask students if they have any associations with the name Kreton. Elicit that it sounds like *cretin,* a term for someone suffering from a certain type of mental retardation. Suggest that this name might be a clue to things to come.

O. Literary Sidelight Point out that a rose garden might symbolize a perfect place, one without any problems. Explain that by having the ship land in the center of the rose garden, the author signals that the Speldings' comfortable little world is in for a drastic change.

P. Reading Skill: INFERRING Ask students to make some inferences about Kreton and his culture, based on the details presented so far. Have them suggest why he is evasive when asked about his home. *(Possible response: Kreton is from a highly intelligent and advanced culture. His evasiveness may be due to his belief that the Speldings won't understand his explanation.)*

KIESLER AND WIFE 1963–65 Will Barnet The Metropolitan Museum of Art, New York Purchase, Roy R. and Marie S. Neuberger Foundation, Inc. Gift and George A. Hearn Fund, 1966.

Spelding. My dear sir, you've only just arrived. Come in, come in. I don't need to tell you what a pleasure this is . . . Mister . . . Mister . . .

N **Visitor.** Kreton . . . This *is* the wrong costume, isn't it?

Spelding. Wrong for what?

Kreton. For the country, and the time.

Spelding. Well, it's a trifle old-fashioned.

Mrs. Spelding. But really awfully handsome.

Kreton. Thank you.

O **Mrs. Spelding** *(to husband)*. Ask him about moving that thing off my rose bed.

(Spelding *leads them all into living room.)*

Spelding. Come on in and sit down. You must be tired after your trip.

Kreton. Yes, I am a little. *(looks around delightedly)* Oh, it's better than I'd hoped!

Spelding. Better? What's better?

Kreton. The house . . . that's what you call it? Or is this an apartment?

Spelding. This is a house in the State of Maryland, U.S.A.

Kreton. In the late twentieth century! To think this is really the twentieth century. I must sit down a moment and collect myself. The *real* thing! *(He sits down.)*

Ellen. You . . . you're not an American, are you?

Kreton. What a nice thought! No, I'm not.

John. You sound more English.

Kreton. Do I? Is my accent very bad?

John. No, it's quite good.

Spelding. Where *are* you from, Mr. Kreton? P

Kreton *(evasively)*. Another place.

Spelding. On this earth of course.

Kreton. No, not on this planet.

DATA BANK

The number of science-fiction movies produced in the United States mushroomed during the 1950's, and a large number of these films developed the theme of alien invasion. A filmography of the period includes such titles as *It Came from Outer Space* and *Invasion of the Body Snatchers*.

Many of these films follow a predictable pattern. The protagonist, often a scientist, spots the invaders but cannot persuade anyone else of their presence. When strange events and crime occur, society fruitlessly searches for a logical explanation. Meanwhile, the scientist begins a lonely battle against the invader. Eventually, the invader makes its presence known, usually by some horrible destruction. The once-skeptical society then turns to the scientist, who presents a plan of action. A struggle then occurs in which the invader is destroyed or at least repelled.

Ellen. Are you from Mars?

Kreton. Oh dear no, not Mars. There's nobody on Mars . . . at least no one I know.

Q **Ellen.** I'm sure you're testing us, and this is all some kind of publicity stunt.

Kreton. No, I really am from another place.

Spelding. I don't suppose you'd consent to my interviewing you on television?

Kreton. I don't think your authorities will like that. They are terribly upset as it is.

Spelding. How do you know?

R **Kreton.** Well, I . . . pick up things. For instance, I know that in a few minutes a number of people from your army will be here to question me and they . . . like you . . . are torn by doubt.

Spelding. How extraordinary!

Ellen. Why did you come here?

Kreton. Simply a visit to your small planet. I've been studying it for years. In fact, one might say, you people are my hobby. Especially this period of your development. R-3 ▶

John. Are you the first person from your . . . your planet to travel in space like this?

S **Kreton.** Oh my no! Everyone travels who wants to. It's just that no one wants to visit you. I can't think why. *I* always have. You'd be surprised what a thorough study I've made. *(recites)* The planet, Earth, is divided into five continents with a number of large islands. It is mostly water. There is one moon. Civilization is only just beginning. . . .

Spelding. Just beginning! My dear sir, we have had. . . .

Kreton *(blandly)*. You are only in the initial stages, the most fascinating stage as far as I'm concerned . . . I do hope I don't sound patronizing.

Ellen. Well, we are very proud.

Kreton. I know, and that's one of your most endearing, primitive traits. Oh, I can't believe I'm here at last!

(General Powers, *a vigorous product of the National Guard, and his* Aide *enter.)*

T **Powers.** All right, folks. This place is surrounded by troops. Where is the monster?

Kreton. I, my dear General, am the monster.

Powers. What are you dressed up for, a fancy-dress party?

Kreton. I'd hoped to be in the costume of the period. As you see, I am about a hundred years too late.

Powers. Roger, who is this joker?

Spelding. This is Mr. Kreton . . . General Powers. Mr. Kreton arrived in that thing outside. He is from another planet.

Powers. I don't believe it.

Ellen. It's true. We saw him get out of the flying saucer.

Powers *(to* Aide). Captain, go down and look at that ship. But be careful. Don't touch anything. And don't let anybody else near it. *(*Aide *goes.)* So you're from another planet.

U **Kreton.** Yes. My, that's a very smart uniform, but I prefer the ones made of metal, the ones you used to wear, you know: with the feathers on top.

Powers. That was five hundred years ago. . . . Are you *sure* you're not from the Earth?

Kreton. Yes.

Words to Know and Use	**patronizing** (pā′ trən īz′ iŋ) *adj.* in a haughty, snobbish, or superior manner **patronize** *v.*

Q. LEP: Vocabulary Elicit that a publicity stunt is a scheme or trick designed to get media attention, or publicity. Such stunts are used to promote various products, services, and celebrities. Ask students for examples.

R. Critical Thinking: SYNTHESIZING Ask students how Kreton might "pick up" things. Ask how he knows people from the army are coming to question him. *(Possible response: He can read people's minds telepathically; he has ESP.)*

S. Critical Thinking: ANALYZING Ask students why no other members of Kreton's culture have chosen to visit earth. Have them suggest what this might tell us about Kreton. *(Possible response: The people in Kreton's world think earth an undesirable place to visit for some reason; Kreton is different from the others in his society—more curious and adventuresome perhaps.)*

T. Literary Element: WRITER'S PURPOSE Suggest that the author uses the character of General Powers to satirize a tendency among military men to jump to conclusions and use undue force prematurely.

U. LEP: Clarifying Ask students what Kreton means by metal uniforms with feathers on top. *(suits of armor with plumes on the helmets)*

V. LEP: Vocabulary Point out that *tall* in Western dialects can be used to mean "serious" or "difficult."

W. LEP: Vocabulary Point out that the Chief of Staff is the senior officer of the Army or Air Force of the United States.

X. Reading Skill: CLARIFYING Have students explain why Roger Spelding wants the story first. *(He wants a scoop for his TV broadcast.)* Have students explain what Powers means when he says "Complete censorship" and "martial law." *(Possible response: The military has decided to keep Kreton's arrival a secret, or classified; under martial law, the military suspends people's ordinary rights and privileges in order to deal with an emergency situation.)*

V **Powers.** Well, I'm not. You've got some pretty tall explaining to do.

Kreton. Anything to oblige.

Powers. All right, which planet?

Kreton. None that you have ever heard of.

Powers. Where is it?

Kreton. You wouldn't know.

Powers. This solar system?

Kreton. No.

Powers. Another system?

Kreton. Yes.

Powers. Look, Buster, I don't want to play games: I just want to know where you're from. The law requires it.

Kreton. It's possible that I could explain it to a mathematician, but I'm afraid I couldn't explain it to you, not for another five hundred years, and by then of course *you'd* be dead, because you people do die, don't you?

Powers. What?

Kreton. Poor fragile butterflies, such brief little moments in the sun. . . . You see *we* don't die.

Powers. You'll die all right if it turns out you're a spy or a hostile alien.

Kreton. I'm sure you wouldn't be so cruel.

*(*Aide *returns; he looks disturbed.)*

Powers. What did you find?

Aide. I'm not sure, General.

Powers *(heavily)***.** Then do your best to describe what the object is like.

Aide. Well, it's elliptical,[2] with a fourteen-foot diameter. And it's made of an unknown metal which shines, and inside there isn't anything.

Powers. Isn't anything?

Aide. There's nothing inside the ship: No instruments, no food, nothing.

Powers *(to* Kreton*)***.** What did you do with your instrument board?

Kreton. With my what? Oh, I don't have one. ◀SR-4

Powers. How does the thing travel?

Kreton. I don't know.

Powers. You don't know. Now look, Mister, you're in pretty serious trouble. I suggest you do a bit of cooperating. You claim you traveled here from outer space in a machine with no instruments . . .

Kreton. Well, these cars are rather common in my world, and I suppose, once upon a time, I must've known the theory on which they operate, but I've long since forgotten. After all, General, we're not mechanics, you and I.

Powers. Roger, do you mind if we use your study?

Spelding. Not at all. Not at all, General.

Powers. Mr. Kreton and I are going to have a chat. *(to* Aide *)* Put in a call to the Chief of Staff. W

Aide. Yes, General.

*(*Spelding *rises, leads* Kreton *and* Powers *into next room, a handsomely furnished study, many books, and a globe of the world.)*

Spelding. This way, gentlemen.

*(*Kreton *sits down comfortably beside the globe, which he twirls thoughtfully. At the door,* Spelding *speaks in a low voice to* Powers.*)*

I hope I'll be the one to get the story first, Tom.

Powers. There isn't any story. Complete censorship. I'm sorry, but this house is under martial law. I've a hunch we're in trouble. X

(He shuts the door. Spelding *turns and rejoins his family.)* ◀SR-5

Ellen. I think he's wonderful, whoever he is.

---

2. **elliptical:** oval.

Mrs. Spelding. I wonder how much damage he did to my rose garden . . .

John. It's sure hard to believe he's really from outer space. No instruments, no nothing . . . boy, they must be advanced scientifically.

Mrs. Spelding. Is he spending the night, dear?

Spelding. What?

Mrs. Spelding. Is he spending the night?

Spelding. Oh yes, yes, I suppose he will be.

Y **Mrs. Spelding.** Then I'd better go make up the bedroom. He seems perfectly nice to me. I like his whiskers. They're so very . . . comforting. Like Grandfather Spelding's.

(She goes.)

Spelding *(bitterly)*. I *know* this story will leak out before I can interview him. I just know it.

Ellen. What does it mean, we're under martial law?

Spelding. It means we have to do what General Powers tells us to do. *(He goes to the window as a soldier passes by.)* See?

John. I wish I'd taken a closer look at that ship when I had the chance.

Ellen. Perhaps he'll give us a ride in it.

John. Traveling in space! Just like those stories. You know: intergalactic drive stuff.

Spelding. *If* he's not an impostor.

Ellen. I have a feeling he isn't.

John. Well, I better call the family and tell them I'm all right.

(He crosses to telephone by the door which leads into hall.)

Z **Aide.** I'm sorry, sir, but you can't use the phone.

Spelding. He certainly can. This is my house . . .

Aide *(mechanically)*. This house is a military reservation until the crisis is over: Order of General Powers. I'm sorry.

John. How am I to call home to say where I am?

Aide. Only General Powers can help you. You're also forbidden to leave this house without permission.

Spelding. You can't do this!

Aide. I'm afraid, sir, we've done it.

Ellen. Isn't it exciting!

(cut to study) AA

Powers. Are you deliberately trying to confuse me?

Kreton. Not deliberately, no.

Powers. We have gone over and over this for two hours now, and all that you've told me is that you're from another planet in another solar system . . .

Kreton. In another dimension. I think that's the word you use.

Powers. In another dimension and you have come here as a tourist.

Kreton. Up to a point, yes. What did you expect?

Powers. It is my job to guard the security of this country.

Kreton. I'm sure that must be very interesting work.

BB **Powers.** For all I know, you are a spy, sent here by an alien race to study us, preparatory to invasion.

Kreton. Oh, none of my people would *dream* of invading you.

Powers. How do I know that's true?

Kreton. You don't, so I suggest you believe me. I should also warn you: I can tell what's inside.

Powers. What's inside?

Kreton. What's inside your mind.

Y. Literary Element: CHARACTER Ask students to describe the character of Mrs. Spelding in a few words. *(Possible responses: superficial, simple, accepting, hospitable)*

Z. Literary Element: CONFLICT Point out that Kreton's arrival has begun to interrupt the Speldings' lives. Have students speculate on how this might lead to conflict. *(Possible response: It could lead to conflict between Mr. Spelding and General Powers.)*

AA. Literary Element: SETTING Explain that this drama was originally written as a TV play not a stage play. Point out that the phrase *cut to study* alerts the director and camera operator that the setting now changes from the living room to the study. Also note that the time of the setting has changed: It is now two hours later.

BB. Critical Thinking: EVALUATING Ask students to discuss Kreton's motives. Ask if they believe he has come simply as a tourist or are they, like General Powers, suspicious of his intentions.

CC. Literary Element: THEME Point out that Vidal's attitude toward his characters is cynical and satirical. For example, in the middle of this momentous event, Powers is concerned mainly with getting a promotion; similarly, Spelding cares only about the glory that will come from breaking the story to his TV audience. Explain that Vidal has said that his plays describe a society that "bores and appalls" him.

DD. LEP: Vocabulary Explain that *gad about* means "to travel around in a carefree or purposeless way."

EE. Literary Element: CHARACTER Point out that although we know nothing about Kreton's people, these remarks establish that he is unlike them. He is less formal and more impulsive. Elicit that *impromptu* means "something done without thought or preparation."

FF. Literary Element: CONFLICT Point out that as the act progresses, Kreton reveals more and more of his incredible powers. This places him in increasing conflict with Powers and the military, who are used to having all power.

Powers. You're a mind reader?

Kreton. I don't really read it. I hear it.

Powers. What am I thinking?

Kreton. That I am either a lunatic from the Earth or a spy from another world. SR-6 ▶

Powers. Correct. But then you could've guessed that. *(frowns)* What am I thinking now?

CC **Kreton.** You're making a picture. Three silver stars. You're pinning them on your shoulder, instead of the two stars you now wear.

Powers *(startled)*. That's right. I was thinking of my promotion.

Kreton. If there's anything I can do to hurry it along, just let me know.

Powers. You can. Tell me why you're here.

Kreton. Well, we don't travel much, my people. We used to, but since we see everything through special monitors and recreators, there is no particular need to travel. However, *I* am a hobbiest. I love to gad about. DD

Powers *(taking notes)*. Are you the first to visit us?

Kreton. Oh, no! We started visiting you long before there were people on the planet. However, we are seldom noticed on our trips. I'm sorry to say I slipped up, coming in the way I did . . . but then this visit was all rather impromptu. *(laughs)* I am a creature of impulse, I fear. EE

*(*Aide *looks in.)*

Aide. Chief of Staff on the telephone, General.

Powers. *(Picks up phone)*. Hello, yes, sir. Powers speaking. I'm talking to him now. No, sir. No, sir. No, we can't determine what method of power was used. He won't talk. Yes, sir. I'll hold him there. I've put the house under martial law . . . belongs to a friend of mine, Roger Spelding, the TV commentator. Roger Spelding, the TV . . . What? Oh, no; I'm sure he won't say anything. Who . . . oh, yes, sir. Yes, I realize the importance of it. Yes, I will. Goodbye. *(hangs up)* The President of the United States wants to know all about you.

Kreton. How nice of him! And I want to know all about him. But I do wish you'd let me rest a bit first. Your language is still not familiar to me. I had to learn them all, quite exhausting.

Powers. You speak *all* our languages?

Kreton. Yes, all of them. But then it's easier than you might think, since I can see what's inside.

Powers. Speaking of what's inside, we're going to take your ship apart.

Kreton. Oh, I wish you wouldn't.

Powers. Security demands it.

Kreton. In that case *my* security demands you leave it alone. FF

Powers. You plan to stop us?

Kreton. I already have . . . Listen.

(Far-off shouting. Aide *rushes into the study.)*

Aide. Something's happened to the ship, General. The door's shut and there's some kind of wall around it, an invisible wall. We can't get near it.

Kreton *(to camera)*. I hope there was no one inside.

Powers *(to* Kreton*)*. How did you do that?

Kreton. I couldn't begin to explain. Now if you don't mind, I think we should go in and see our hosts. ◀ SR-7

(He rises, goes into living room. Powers *and* Aide *look at each other.)*

Powers. Don't let him out of your sight.

(Cut to living room as Powers *picks up phone.* Kreton *is with* John *and* Ellen.*)*

Kreton. I don't mind curiosity, but I really can't permit them to wreck my poor ship.

Ellen. What do you plan to do, now you're here?

Kreton. Oh, keep busy. I have a project or two . . . *(sighs)* I can't believe you're real!

John. Then we're all in the same boat.

Kreton. Boat? Oh, yes! Well, I should have come ages ago but I . . . I couldn't get away until yesterday.

John. Yesterday? It took you a *day* to get here?

Kreton. One of *my* days, not yours. But then you don't know about time yet.

John. Oh, you mean relativity.[3]

Kreton. No, it's much more involved that that. You won't know about time until . . . now let me see if I remember . . . no, I don't, but it's about two thousand years.

John. What do we do between now and then?

Kreton. You simply go on the way you are, living your exciting primitive lives . . . you have no idea how much fun you're having now.

Ellen. I hope you'll stay with us while you're here.

Kreton. That's very nice of you. Perhaps I will. Though I'm sure you'll get tired of having a visitor underfoot all the time.

Ellen. Certainly not. And Daddy will be deliriously happy. He can interview you by the hour.

John. What's it like in outer space?

Kreton. Dull.

Ellen. I should think it would be divine!

(Powers *enters.)*

Kreton. No, General, it won't work.

Powers. What won't work?

Kreton. Trying to blow up my little force field. You'll just plough up Mrs. Spelding's garden. II

(Powers *snarls and goes into study.)*

Ellen. Can you tell me what we're *all* thinking?

Kreton. Yes. As a matter of fact, it makes me a bit giddy. Your minds are not at all like ours. You see, we control our thoughts while you . . . well, its extraordinary the things you think about!

Ellen. Oh, how awful! You can tell *everything* we think?

Kreton. Everything! It's one of the reasons I'm here, to intoxicate myself with your primitive minds . . .with the wonderful rawness of your emotions! You have no idea how it excites me! You simply seethe with unlikely emotions. JJ

Ellen. I've never felt so sordid. ◀SR-8

John. From now on I'm going to think about agriculture.

Spelding *(entering)*. You would.

Ellen. Daddy!

Kreton. No, no. You must go right on thinking about Ellen. Such wonderfully *purple* thoughts! KK

Spelding. Now see here, Powers, you're carrying this martial law thing too far . . .

Powers. Unfortunately, until I have received word from Washington as to the final disposition of this problem, you must obey my orders: no telephone calls, no communication with the outside.

Spelding. This is unsupportable.

Kreton. Poor Mr. Spelding! If you like, I

3. **relativity:** part of the theory of Albert Einstein and H. A. Lorenz that states that time and space are not absolute; different individuals at separate vantage points may experience and measure time and space in different ways.

GG. LEP: Idiom Elicit that although Kreton has taught himself all earth's languages, he is unfamiliar with the idiom *We're all in the same boat,* meaning "in the same position or condition."

HH. Discussion Ask students what Kreton might mean when he says people on earth won't know about time for many years. Have volunteers offer some suggestions about what there might be to know about time.

II. Literary Element: HUMOR Elicit that Kreton has read General Powers' mind. Point out that the author uses Kreton's telepathy as a ready source of humor throughout the play.

JJ. Literary Element: THEME Explain that in addition to being a science-fiction fantasy, the play has the moral element of a fable. Elicit that through Kreton the playwright seeks to remind us that our lives are fun and exciting and filled with wonderful raw emotions. The playwright also suggests that these qualities, often taken for granted, can be lost over time.

KK. LEP: Vocabulary Have students list their associations with the word *purple.* Explain that the word can mean "ornate and elaborate."

DATA BANK

People have witnessed bizarre objects in the sky throughout history and in all countries. However the number of reported UFO sightings increased dramatically during and after World War II.

The Air Force investigated more than 12,000 UFO reports that occurred from 1947 to 1969 under the code names Project Sign, Project Grudge, and Project Blue Book. Fully 95 percent of the sightings were explained in terms of identifiable phenomena. For example, aircraft, rockets, weather balloons, cloud formations, lightning, birds, and even swarming insects have been reported as UFO's. Optical illusions, caused by special atmospheric conditions, and airplane exhaust trails, seen under unusual lighting conditions, explained other sightings. Government investigators also suggested that sightings resulted from psychological delusions, mass hysteria, and deliberate hoaxes.

LL. Literary Element: CHARACTER Elicit that the false face Spelding puts on to woo his TV public cannot fool Kreton. The playwright uses Kreton's telepathy to unmask Spelding's hypocrisy.

MM. Literary Element: IRONY Explain that both Powers and Spelding are deeply suspicious and afraid of the people they believe have sent Kreton to spy on earth. Elicit that it is therefore ironic when Kreton assures the men that earth is far too primitive to interest any extraterrestrials other than himself.

NN. LEP: Idiom Point out that *to go native* is "to adopt the customs and attitudes of those who live in a place to which one has moved." Ask students to discuss whether Kreton will actually "go native."

OO. Reading Skill: PREDICTING Stress that the playwright has ended Act 1 with a startling plot development: Kreton plans to take over the entire world! Have students predict whether or not he will achieve this goal.

shall go. That would solve everything, wouldn't it?

Powers. You're not going anywhere, Mr. Kreton, until I've had my instructions.

Kreton. I sincerely doubt if you could stop me. However, I put it up to Mr. Spelding. Shall I go?

LL

Spelding. Yes! *(*Powers *gestures a warning.)* Do stay, I mean, we want you to get a good impression of us . . .

Kreton. And of course you still want to be the first journalist to interview me. Fair enough. All right, I'll stay on for a while.

Powers. Thank you.

Kreton. Don't mention it.

Spelding. General, may I ask our guest a few questions?

Powers. Go right ahead, Roger. I hope you'll do better than I did.

Spelding. Since you read our minds, you probably already know what our fears are.

Kreton. I do, yes.

Spelding. We are afraid that you represent a hostile race.

Kreton. And I have assured General Powers that my people are not remotely hostile. Except for me, no one is interested in this planet's present stage.

Spelding. Does this mean you might be interested in a *later* stage?

MM

Kreton. I'm not permitted to discuss your future. Of course, my friends think me perverse to be interested in a primitive society, but there's no accounting for tastes, is there? You are my hobby. I love you. And that's all there is to it.

Powers. So you're just here to look around . . . sort of going native.

NN

Kreton. What a nice expression! That's it exactly. I am going native.

Powers *(grimly)*. Well it is my view that you have been sent here by another civilization for the express purpose of reconnoitering prior to invasion.

Kreton. That *would* be your view! The wonderfully primitive assumption that all strangers are hostile. You're almost too good to be true, General.

Powers. You deny your people intend to make trouble for us?

Kreton. I deny it.

Powers. Then are they interested in establishing communication with us? Trade? That kind of thing?

Kreton. We have always had communication with you. As for trade, well, we do not trade . . . that is something peculiar only to your social level. *(quickly)* Which I'm not criticizing! As you know, I approve of everything you do.

Powers. I give up.

Spelding. You have no interest then in . . . well, trying to dominate the Earth.

Kreton. Oh, yes!

Powers. I thought you just said your people weren't interested in us.

Kreton. *They're* not, but *I* am.

Powers. You!

Kreton. Me . . . I mean I. You see I've come here to take charge.

Powers. Of the United States?

OO

Kreton. No, of the whole world. I'm sure you'll be much happier, and it will be great fun for me. You'll get used to it in no time.

Powers. This is ridiculous. How can one man take over the world?

Kreton. Wait and see!

Powers *(to* Aide*)*. Grab him!

*(*Powers *and* Aide *rush* Kreton *but within a foot of him they stop, stunned.)*

Kreton. You can't touch me. That's part of the game. *(He yawns.)* Now, if you don't mind, I shall go up to my room for a little lie-down.

Spelding. I'll show you the way.

Kreton. That's all right, I know the way. *(touches his brow)* Such savage thoughts! My head is vibrating like a drum. I feel quite giddy, all of you thinking away. *(He starts to the door; he pauses beside* Mrs. Spelding.*)* No, it's not a dream, dear lady. I shall be here in the morning when you wake up. And now, good night, dear, wicked children. . . . ◀ SR-9

(He goes as we fade out.)

Responding to Reading

First Impressions

1. What do you think of Kreton? Share your reactions with your classmates.

Second Thoughts

2. What kind of person is Roger Spelding?

   Think about
   - what he does for a living
   - how he gets along with his family
   - what he considers to be the most important virtue

3. What impression does Kreton have of earth?

   Think about
   - his view of the stage of development of life on earth
   - his thoughts about and attitudes toward human beings

4. Which character's reaction to Kreton do you find the most interesting? Why?

5. Think back to the predictions you made earlier about an alien visiting Earth. How do these predictions compare with what you have read thus far?

Student Response

Responding to Reading

These questions are open-ended with no "right" or "wrong" answers. However, responses must be supported with information from the selection. Possible answers follow:

1. Any response based on the play is valid.

2. Some students may say that Roger Spelding is an ambitious and successful man. As a TV commentator, he is very concerned with outward appearances, hiding his negative feelings beneath a facade of engaging warmth and wisdom. Others may note that his relationships with his wife and daughter seem not very warm or loving, perhaps because he places such high importance on a successful career.

3. Some students may note that, in general, earth impresses Kreton as a very exciting place where people live highly emotional and fun-filled lives. Kreton attributes this to the primitive level of human development. Others may note that although Kreton is friendly enough in his dealings with people, he does take a somewhat condescending attitude toward them.

4. Any response is valid. Students might say that Ellen and John have the most interesting reactions to Kreton, accepting the alien for what he is and trying to learn all they can from him. Others will be interested in General Powers' reactions, as his various efforts to destroy or control Kreton are thwarted. Students might be amused at Roger Spelding, who views the alien as a sure boost to his career. Mrs. Spelding's vague reaction, treating Kreton like an unexpected but welcome visiting in-law, is also interesting.

5. Have students compare the events of Act 1 with the predictions they made for Enrich Your Reading.

Text Annotations

A. Literary Element: PLOT Point out that the three acts of a drama usually divide the plot into beginning, middle, and end. Act 1 introduces the characters and sets up the story. Act 2 presents obstacles and confrontations that develop the conflict. In Act 3, the conflict is finally resolved. Ask students to look for the sources of conflict in Act 2.

B. LEP: Clarifying Ask a volunteer to clarify what is happening in this opening scene. *(Possible response: Kreton is able to read the cat's thoughts and so carries on a conversation with it.)*

C. Literary Element: DIALOGUE Elicit that the ellipsis points indicate the time during which Kreton reads the cat's thoughts. Ask students to supply examples of what the cat might be "saying."

D. Reading Skills: PREDICTING Ask students to predict Kreton's secret. Ask what they think he plans to do when and if he takes over the world. *(Accept any reasonable responses.)*

ACT TWO

A *(Fade in on* Kreton's *bedroom next morning. He lies fully clothed on bed with cat on his lap.)*

Kreton. Poor cat! Of course I sympathize with you. Dogs *are* distasteful. What? Oh, I can well believe they do: yes, yes, how disgusting. They don't ever groom their fur! But you do *constantly,* such a fine coat. No, no, I'm not just saying that. I really mean it: exquisite texture. Of course, I wouldn't say it was *nicer* than skin but even so. . . . What? Oh, no! They *chase* you! Dogs chase you for no reason at all except pure malice? You poor creature. Ah, but you *do* fight back! That's right! Give it to them: slash, bite, scratch! Don't let them get away with a trick. . . . No! Do dogs really do that? Well, I'm sure *you* don't. What . . . oh, well, yes I completely agree about mice. They *are* delicious! (Ugh!) Pounce, snap and there is a heavenly dinner. No, I don't know any mice yet . . . they're not very amusing? But after all, think how you must terrify them because you are so bold, so cunning, so beautifully predatory!

B

C

(knock at door)

Come in.

Ellen *(enters).* Good morning. I brought you your breakfast.

Kreton. How thoughtful! *(examines bacon)* Delicious, but I'm afraid my stomach is not like yours, if you'll pardon me. I don't eat. *(removes pill from his pocket and swallows it)* This is all I need for the day. *(indicates cat)* Unlike this creature, who would eat her own weight every hour, given a chance.

Ellen. How do you know?

Kreton. We've had a talk.

Ellen. You can *speak* to the cat?

Kreton. Not speak exactly, but we communicate. I look inside, and the cat cooperates. Bright red thoughts, very exciting, though rather on one level.

Ellen. Does kitty like us?

Kreton. No, I wouldn't say she did. But then she has very few thoughts not connected with food. Have you, my quadruped[4] criminal? *(He strokes the cat, which jumps to the floor.)*

Ellen. You know you've really upset everyone.

Kreton. I supposed that I would.

Ellen. Can you really take over the world, just like that?

Kreton. Oh, yes.

Ellen. What do you plan to do when you *have* taken over?

Kreton. Ah, that is my secret. D

Ellen. Well, I think you'll be a very nice President, *if* they let you, of course.

Kreton. What a sweet girl you are! Marry him right away.

Ellen. Marry John?

Kreton. Yes, I see it in your head *and* in his. He wants you very much.

Ellen. Well, we plan to get married this summer, if Father doesn't fuss too much.

Kreton. Do it before then. I shall arrange it all if you like.

Ellen. How?

Kreton. I can convince your father.

Ellen. That sounds awfully ominous. I

4. **quadruped:** a four-footed creature.

Words to Know and Use	**predatory** (pred′ ə tôr′ ē) *adj.* characterized by robbing, exploiting, or killing others

702

STRUCTURED READING FOR LESS PROFICIENT STUDENTS

These questions can help to guide students through the reading. Ask each question at the point of the selection where the SR number appears in the margin.

SR–1. Why does Kreton send for the president? *(He wants to discuss the process by which he will take over the world.)* **Clarifying**

SR–2. What mistake does Kreton make when he sends for the president? *(By mistake, he sends for the President of Paraguay, not the President of the United States.)* **Literal recall**

SR–3. Who is Paul Laurent? Why does the government of the United States turn the problem of Kreton over to Laurent? *(Paul Laurent is the Secretary General of the World Council. The U.S. government feels that the Kreton problem is too big for one country to handle.)* **Literal recall**

Continued on page 703

FRIEDA'S DREAM Monte Dolack Courtesy of the artist.

think you'd better leave poor Daddy alone.

Kreton. Whatever you say. *(sighs)* Oh, I love it so! When I woke up this morning, I had to pinch myself to prove I was really here.

E

Ellen. We were all doing a bit of pinching too. Ever since dawn we've had nothing but visitors and phone calls and troops outside in the garden. No one has the faintest idea what to do about you.

Kreton. Well, I don't think they'll be confused much longer.

Ellen. How do you plan to conquer the world?

Kreton. I confess I'm not sure. I suppose I must make some demonstration of strength, some colorful trick that will

F

E. LEP: Vocabulary Point out that "pinching yourself" is supposedly a way to make sure you are not dreaming. Kreton says that he had to pinch himself in order to let Ellen know how wonderful he finds life on earth to be. Ellen is "doing a bit of pinching" because Kreton's arrival and the ensuing events seem so fantastic.

F. Literary Element: CHARACTERIZATION Point out that Kreton's remarks reveal him to be whimsical and a bit irrational. His momentous decision to take over the earth seems like a frivolous afterthought.

Art Note

Contemporary artist Monte Dolack creates posters for various uses, including films and museums as well as environmental groups. Of particular interest are his humorous pictures of animals intruding on the lives of humans. In this poster, Frieda the cat is apparently very much a part of a household. She gazes from her comfortable indoor perch out at the sky. *What do you think Frieda sees in the clouds?*

STRUCTURED READING FOR LESS PROFICIENT STUDENTS

Continued from page 702

SR–4. In his conversation with Laurent, how does Kreton say he plans to take over the world? What example of this does he provide for Laurent? *(Kreton says he will use a number of demonstrations and tricks to persuade people. He demonstrates by having all the guns of all the world's soldiers suddenly fly through the air.)* **Literal recall**

SR–5. Why does Paul Laurent think at first that Kreton's plan to take over the world might be wonderful? *(He imagines that Kreton will unify the world and help people overcome problems with his superior knowledge.)* **Summarizing**

SR–6. What project does Kreton plan to begin first once he becomes world leader? *(He plans to start a "splendid war.")* **Literal recall**

SR–7. According to Kreton, how do most humans actually feel about war? *(Kreton thinks that most people truly find war pleasurable; he thinks it is the one thing people do well.)* **Summarizing**

G. Literary Element: CHARACTERIZATION Point out that the playwright is making a comparison between Kreton and the cat. Elicit that just as a cat catches and plays with mice, so Kreton feels free to catch and play with people, whether they are presidents or ordinary people like Ellen and her father.

H. Literary Element: WRITER'S PURPOSE Review that Gore Vidal used this play to address certain political issues of the day. Have students speculate on the point Vidal makes by having General Powers read *The Atom and You,* while contemplating using a fission bomb. *(Possible response: Vidal suggests that the military is apt to use weapons whose destructive powers they do not fully understand.)*

I. LEP: Camera Directions Explain that to "dissolve" is to shift scenes by having one scene fade out while the next appears behind it and grows clearer as the first dims.

J. Literary Element: CHARACTERIZATION Point out that despite the momentous events occurring all around her, Mrs. Spelding seems concerned only about the spaceship's effect on her garden. Ask students what this suggests about her. *(Possible response: She is out of touch with the real world and the larger issues affecting her.)*

K. Reading Skills: CLARIFYING Have students clarify what Mr. Spelding means by saying, "The rest of our lives, if something isn't done." Ask if he expects the crisis to go on indefinitely, or expects their lives to end soon, or is he referring to John's unwelcome status as his future son-in-law. *(Accept reasonable answers that are supported by the play.)*

frighten everyone . . . though I much prefer taking charge quietly. That's why I've sent for the President.

Ellen. The President? *Our* President?

Kreton. Yes, he'll be along any minute now.

Ellen. But the President just doesn't go around visiting people.

G **Kreton.** He'll visit me. *(chuckles)* It may come as a surprise to him, but he'll be in this house in a very few minutes. I think we'd better go downstairs now. *(to cat)* No, I will not give you a mouse. You must get your own. Be self-reliant. Beast! SR-1

(Dissolve to the study. Powers *is reading book entitled* The Atom and You. *Muffled explosions off stage.)*

H **Aide** *(entering)***.** Sir, nothing seems to be working. Do we have the General's permission to try a fission bomb on the force field?

Powers. No . . . no. We'd better give it up.

Aide. The men are beginning to talk.

Powers *(thundering)***.** Well, keep them quiet! *(contritely)* I'm sorry, Captain. I'm on edge. Fortunately, the whole business will soon be in the hands of the World Council.

Aide. What will the World Council do?

Powers. It will be interesting to observe them.

Aide. You don't think this Kreton can really take over the world, do you?

Powers. Of course not. Nobody can.

I *(Dissolve to living room.* Mrs. Spelding *and* Spelding *are alone.)*

Mrs. Spelding. You still haven't asked Mr. Kreton about moving that thing, have you?

Spelding. There are too many important things to ask him.

J **Mrs. Spelding.** I hate to be a nag, but you know the trouble I have had getting anything to grow in that part of the garden . . .

John *(enters)***.** Good morning.

Mrs. Spelding. Good morning, John.

John. Any sign of your guest?

Mrs. Spelding. Ellen took his breakfast up to him a few minutes ago.

John. They don't seem to be having much luck, do they? *(to* Spelding*)* I sure hope you don't mind my staying here like this.

*(*Spelding *glowers.)*

Mrs. Spelding. Why, we love having you! I just hope your family aren't too anxious.

John. One of the G.I.'s finally called them, said I was staying here for the week end.

K **Spelding.** The rest of our lives, if something isn't done soon.

John. Just how long do you think that'll be, Dad?

Spelding. Who knows?

*(*Kreton *and* Ellen *enter.)*

Kreton. Ah, how wonderful to see you again! Let me catch my breath. . . . Oh, your minds! It's not easy for me, you know: so many crude thoughts blazing away! Yes, Mrs. Spelding, I will move the ship off your roses.

Mrs. Spelding. That's awfully sweet of you.

Kreton. Mr. Spelding, if any interviews are to be granted, you will be the first, I promise you.

Spelding. That's very considerate, I'm sure.

Kreton. So you can stop thinking *those* particular thoughts. And now where is the President?

Spelding. The President?

Kreton. Yes, I sent for him. He should be here. *(goes to terrace window)* Ah, that must be he.

Critic's Corner

Vidal's versatility extends beyond the world of the novel, as he has also achieved fame as playwright, critic, essayist, mystery writer, screenwriter, and almost, politician. Despite his many abilities Vidal may be best known as a successful, flamboyant, and eccentric talk-show guest who exhibits an irrepressible urge to debate. Vidal *has* managed to endure, both as "public figures" and "artist"; an examination of his life and works will indicate that his artistic achievements and commercial successes are compatible, for he has shown from the beginning of his career an insight into contemporary themes and an ability to construct novels in effective ways.

Robert Graalman, *Dictionary of Literary Biography*

(A swarthy man in uniform with a sash across his chest is standing, bewildered, on the terrace. Kreton *opens the glass doors.)*

Kreton. Come in, sir! Come in, Your Excellency. Good of you to come on such short notice.

(Man *enters.)*

Man *(in Spanish accent)***.** Where am I?

Kreton. You *are* the President, aren't you?

Man. Of course I am the President. What am I doing here? I was dedicating a bridge and I find myself . . .

L **Kreton** *(aware of his mistake)***.** Oh, dear! Where was the bridge?

Man. Where do you think, you idiot, in Paraguay!

Kreton *(to others)***.** I seem to've made a mistake. Wrong President. *(gestures and the* man *disappears)* Seemed rather upset, didn't he?

John. You can make people come and go just like that?

SR-2 ▶ **Kreton.** Just like that.

(Powers *looks into the room from the study.)*

Powers. Good morning, Mr. Kreton. Could I see you for a moment?

Kreton. By all means.

(He crosses to the study.)

M **Spelding.** I believe I am going mad.

(Cut to study. The Aide *stands at attention while* Powers *addresses* Kreton.*)*

Powers. . . . and so we feel, the government of the United States feels, that this problem is too big for any one country. Therefore, we have turned the whole affair over to Paul Laurent, the Secretary-General of the World Council.

SR-3 ▶ **Kreton.** Very sensible. I should've thought of that myself.

Powers. Mr. Laurent is on his way here now. And may I add, Mr. Kreton, you've made me look singularly ridiculous.

Kreton. I'm awfully sorry. *(pause)* No, you can't kill me.

Powers. You were reading my mind again.

Kreton. I can't really help it, you know. And such *black* thoughts today, but intense, very intense. N

Powers. I regard you as a menace.

Kreton. I know you do, and I think it's awfully unkind. I do mean well.

Powers. Then go back where you came from and leave us alone.

Kreton. No, I'm afraid I can't do that just yet . . .

(Telephone rings; Aide *answers it.)*

Aide. He's outside? Sure, let him through. *(to* Powers*)* The Secretary-General of the World Council is here, sir.

Powers *(to* Kreton*)***.** I hope you'll listen to *him.* O

Kreton. Oh, I shall, of course. I love listening.

(The door opens and Paul Laurent, *middle-aged and serene, enters.* Powers *and his* Aide *stand to attention.* Kreton *goes forward to shake hands.)*

Laurent. Mr. Kreton?

Kreton. At your service, Mr. Laurent.

Laurent. I welcome you to this planet in the name of the World Council.

Kreton. Thank you, sir, thank you.

Laurent. Could you leave us alone for a moment, General?

Powers. Yes, sir.

(Powers *and* Aide *go.* Laurent *smiles at* Kreton.*)*

Laurent. Shall we sit down?

Kreton. Yes, yes I love sitting down. I'm

L. Literary Element: DRAMA Explain that a *farce* is a dramatic composition that uses highly improbable plot events or characters for humorous effect. Point out that incidents such as this, in which Kreton mistakenly summons the President of Paraguay instead of the President of the United States, are farcical.

M. Critical Thinking: ANALYZING Have students suggest what it is about Kreton's arrival and the subsequent events that lead Spelding to believe he is going mad. *(Possible response: Kreton's arrival and subsequent events seem impossible. They are fantastic and defy logic.)*

N. Critical Thinking: SYNTHESIZING Point out that Kreton earlier described the cat's thoughts as "red." Now he says the general's thoughts are "black." Ask students to tell what Kreton means by these colors. Ask them to suggest some examples of red thoughts and black thoughts.

O. LEP: Denotation and Connotation Point out that although Kreton knows the denotations, or literal meanings, of words, he is not familiar with their connotations, or the emotional values the words convey. For example, Powers uses *listen* here to connote that Kreton should pay close attention to Laurent and follow his advice. This is lost on Kreton, who loves to listen to people because it is a new experience for him.

PROFESSIONAL NOTEBOOK

. . . dramatics recommends itself to the attention of adults who want to help young people structure their inner experience. From their earliest years, young people should have extensive opportunity to participate in a process which over many centuries has provided for mankind some of the deepest symbols of his condition and of his relationship to the universal. . . . creative dramatics provides much of what was provided, in primitive societies, by the rites of passage at puberty. It provides the opportunity for the youngster to move toward the new thing, at a time when, for a complex of reasons, he cannot or dare not actually become the new thing. . . .

Richard Crosscup, *Children and Dramatics*

Art Note
Will Barnet (1911–), writing in 1966 about his work, said, "a portrait, becomes . . . the *idea* of a person." Barnet is concerned with color and the relationships of forms, but also with meaning. Because he eliminates detail, his work is called abstract. However, it vividly portrays states of mind and emotions. *In this portrait, what do you see that suggests the personality of Mrs. Spelding or of her husband?*

P. Literary Element: TONE Elicit that this comment by Laurent is in keeping with the playwright's satirical and somewhat sarcastic tone. Vidal is making fun of diplomats, suggesting that they normally talk at great length without getting to the point.

Q. Reading Skill: CLARIFYING Ask students to clarify Laurent's comment about attending many conferences. *(Possible response: As a diplomat who takes part in many negotiations, Laurent has probably trained himself not to reveal his inner feelings, since that might weaken his bargaining position.)*

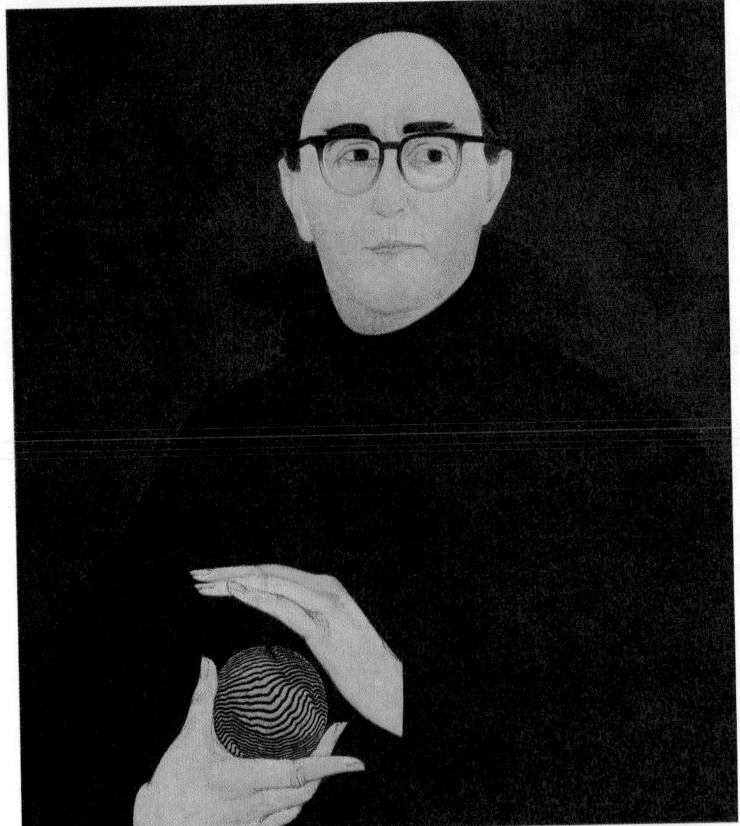

PORTRAIT OF HENRY PEARSON 1967 Will Barnet The Metropolitan Museum of Art, New York Gift of Mrs. Will Barnet, 1981.

afraid my manners are not quite suitable, yet.

(They sit down.)

P **Laurent.** Now, Mr. Kreton, in violation of all the rules of diplomacy, may I come to the point?

Kreton. You may.

Laurent. Why are you here?

Kreton. Curiosity. Pleasure.

Laurent. You are a tourist then in this time and place?

Kreton *(nods)*. Yes. Very well put.

Laurent. We have been informed that you have extraordinary powers.

Kreton. By your standards, yes, they must seem extraordinary.

Laurent. We have also been informed that it is your intention to . . . to take charge of this world.

Kreton. That is correct. . . . What a remarkable mind you have! I have difficulty looking inside it.

Laurent *(laughs)*. Practice. I've attended so many conferences. . . . May I say that your conquest of our world puts your status of tourist in a rather curious light? Q

REAL LIFE CONNECTIONS

Elicit that Gore Vidal means to suggest the United Nations when he describes the World Council of which Paul Laurent is Secretary General. Ask students to share their knowledge and opinions about the United Nations. Students might, for example, read current events articles having to do with U.N.-sponsored efforts around the world. Or, arrange a discussion of how having a world forum is important to address problems and relieve tensions. Ask students to cite instances in which the U.N. has effectively dealt with crises. Have them discuss whether disarmament could be carried out effectively under U.N. auspices. Students might also speculate on what a unified world under U.N. leadership would be like.

Kreton. Oh, I said nothing about *conquest.*

Laurent. Then how else do you intend to govern? The people won't allow you to direct their lives without a struggle.

Kreton. But I'm sure they will if I ask them to.

Laurent. You believe you can do all this without, well, without violence?

Kreton. Of course I can. One or two demonstrations and I'm sure they'll do as I ask. *(smiles)* Watch this.

(Pause. Then shouting. Powers *bursts into room.)*

Powers. Now what've you done?

Kreton. Look out the window, Your Excellency.

R *(*Laurent *goes to window. A rifle floats by, followed by an alarmed soldier.)*

Nice, isn't it? I confess I worked out a number of rather melodramatic tricks last night. Incidentally, all the rifles of all the soldiers in all the world are now floating in the air. *(gestures)* Now they have R-4 ▶ them back.

Powers *(to* Laurent*).* You see, sir, I didn't exaggerate in my report.

Laurent *(awed).* No, no, you certainly didn't.

S **Kreton.** You were skeptical, weren't you?

Laurent. Naturally. But now I . . . now I think it's possible.

Powers. That this . . . this gentleman is going to run everything?

T **Laurent.** Yes, yes I do. And it might be wonderful.

Kreton. You *are* more clever that the others. You begin to see that I mean only good.

Laurent. Yes, only good. General, do you realize what this means? We can have one government. . . .

Kreton. With innumerable bureaus, and intrigue. . . . U

Laurent *(excited).* And the world could be incredibly prosperous, especially if he'd help us with his superior knowledge. ◀ SR-5

Kreton *(delighted).* I will, I will. I'll teach you to look into one another's minds. You'll find it devastating but enlightening: all that self-interest, those lurid emotions. . . .

Laurent. No more countries. No more wars. . . .

Kreton *(startled).* What? Oh, but I like a lot of countries. Besides, at this stage of your development you're supposed to have lots of countries and lots of wars . . . innumerable wars . . . V

Laurent. But you can help us change all that.

Kreton. *Change* all that! My dear sir, I am your friend.

Laurent. What do you mean?

Kreton. Why, your deepest pleasure is violence. How can you deny that? It is the whole point to you, the whole point to my hobby . . . and you are my hobby, all mine. W

Laurent. But our lives are devoted to *controlling* violence, and not creating it.

Kreton. Now, don't take me for an utter fool. After all, I can see into your minds. My dear fellow, don't you *know* what you are?

Laurent. What are we?

Kreton. You are savages. I have returned to the dark ages of an insignificant planet simply because I want the glorious excitement of being among you and reveling in

Words to Know and Use	**lurid** (lo͝or′ id) *adj.* violently passionate; shocking

707

R. Literary Element: WRITER'S PURPOSE Point out that one purpose of every drama is to entertain. Point out that farcical events, such as the floating gun, draw big laughs from audiences while stressing Kreton's incredible powers.

S. LEP: Vocabulary Explain to students that *skeptical* means "doubtful."

T. Literary Element: PLOT Explain that the playwright changes the pacing and direction of events here by having the influential Laurent suggest that a world ruled by Kreton could be wonderful. Point out that before this point everyone had been looking for ways to stop or control Kreton.

U. Critical Thinking: ANALYZING Ask students why Kreton looks forward to a government with "innumerable bureaus, and intrigue". *(Possible response: Such a situation will produce endless confusion, anger, and other strong emotions that Kreton finds so thrilling.)*

V. Literary Element: THEME Point out that Laurent at first imagines that he is placing the world's future in the hands of someone who shares his own idealistic values. Have students suggest how Kreton would actually manipulate events once he had the world in his hands. *(Answers will vary but should be consistent with Kreton's character as it has been revealed thus far.)*

W. Critical Thinking: EVALUATING Ask students to evaluate Kreton's assertion that violence is humankind's deepest pleasure. Ask for historical evidence that supports or counters this view.

Critic's Corner

The play [*Visit to a Small Planet*] is pervaded by such good humor and speeded by such inventive stage business that a number of genuine satirical pricks are gone almost before they draw blood. Almost. For although Mr. Vidal has gone nowhere near as far with his initial idea as a real social critic could, he has managed to kid, if not the pants, then the socks off a number of previous American concepts. . . .
Marya Mannes, "Satire Comes to Broadway," ***Reporter XVI*** **(March 7, 1957)**

X. **LEP: Vocabulary** Explain that the word *intoxicates*, meaning "makes drunk," suits Kreton's mood well as the act progresses. Point out that the more negative emotions Kreton absorbs, the more he seems to want, causing him to become increasingly out of control.

Y. **Literary Element: THEME** Suggest that Kreton envisions a world in which he, like a master puppeteer, will pull the strings, while ordinary people will have no idea whose hands control their destinies.

Historical Sidelight This teleplay was written and produced when fear of nuclear war was the overriding concern of most Americans. The first hydrogen bomb was detonated by the United States in 1952. Vastly more powerful than the fission bombs dropped on Japan during World War II, the new fusion weapon was widely rumored to be a doomsday machine that could set off a chain reaction that would consume the earth. These apocalyptic fears were heightened the following year when the Soviet Union developed a hydrogen bomb.

Z. **Literary Element: TITLE** Point out the reference to humans as a "little race." Remind students of the word *small* in the play's title. Ask students what the author, through Kreton, is criticizing here. *(the level of humankind's emotional and intellectual development)*

AA. **Literary Element: CONFLICT** Point out that Act 2 ends on an exciting note by revealing the full nature of the conflict between Kreton and the other characters. Ask students to speculate on how this conflict might be resolved in the third and final act.

X your savagery! There is murder in all your hearts and I love it! It intoxicates me!

Laurent *(slowly)***.** You hardly flatter us.

Kreton. I didn't mean to be rude, but you did ask me why I am here, and I've told you.

Laurent. You have no wish then to . . . to help us poor savages.

Kreton. I couldn't even if I wanted to. You won't be civilized for at least two thousand years, and you won't reach the level of my people for about a million years.

Laurent *(sadly)***.** Then you have come here only to . . . to observe?

Y **Kreton.** No, more than that. I mean to regulate your pastimes. But don't worry: I won't upset things too much. I've decided I don't want to be known to the people. You will go right on with your countries, your squabbles, the way you always have, while I will *secretly* regulate things through you.

Laurent. The World Council does not govern. We only advise.

Kreton. Well, I shall advise you, and you will advise the governments, and we shall have a lovely time.

Laurent. I don't know what to say. You obviously have the power to do as you please.

Kreton. I'm glad you realize that. Poor General Powers is now wondering if a hydrogen bomb might destroy me. It won't, General.

Powers. Too bad.

Kreton. Now, Your Excellency, I shall stay in this house until you have laid the groundwork for my first project.

Laurent. And what is that to be?

Kreton. A war! I want one of your really splendid wars, with all the trimmings, all the noise and the fire . . . ◀SR-

Laurent. A war! You're joking. Why at this moment we are working as hard as we know how *not* to have a war.

Kreton. But secretly you want one. After all, it's the one thing your little race does well. You'd hardly want me to deprive you of your simple pleasures, now would you? Z ◀SR-

Laurent. I think you must be mad.

Kreton. Not mad, simply a philanthropist. Of course I myself shall get a great deal of pleasure out of a war (the vibrations must be incredible!), but I'm doing it mostly for you. So, if you don't mind, I want you to arrange a few incidents, so we can get one started spontaneously.

Laurent. I refuse.

Kreton. In that event, I shall select someone else to head the World Council. Someone who *will* start a war. I suppose there exist a few people here who might like the idea. AA

Laurent. How can you do such a horrible thing to us? Can't you see that we don't want to be savages?

Kreton. But you have no choice. Anyway, you're just pulling my leg! I'm sure you want a war as much as the rest of them do, and that's what you're going to get: the biggest war you've ever had!

Laurent *(stunned)***.** Heaven help us!

Kreton *(exuberant)***.** Heaven won't! Oh, what fun it will be! I can hardly wait! *(He strikes the globe of the world a happy blow as we fade out.)*

Words to Know and Use

philanthropist (fə lan′ thrə pist) *n.* a person of goodwill, often wealthy, who donates gifts to charities and humanitarian institutions

Responding to Reading

First Impressions

1. Has your impression of Kreton changed? If so, how?

Second Thoughts

2. Look back at Kreton's conversation with the cat. Why do you think the playwright opens Act Two this way?

3. What kind of man is Laurent?

Think about

- how he reacts to Kreton at first
- what Laurent says about humanity
- how Laurent reacts to Kreton at the end of Act Two

4. Which character seems the most humorous to you? Why?

ACT THREE

(Fade in on the study, two weeks later. Kreton *is sitting at desk on which a map is spread out. He has a pair of dividers, some models of jet aircraft. Occasionally he pretends to dive-bomb, imitating the sound of a bomb going off.* Powers *enters.)*

Powers. You wanted me, sir?

A **Kreton.** Yes, I wanted those figures on radioactive fallout.

Powers. They're being made up now, sir. Anything else?

Kreton. Oh, my dear fellow, why do you dislike me so?

Powers. I am your military aide, sir: I don't have to answer that question. It is outside the sphere of my duties.

Kreton. Aren't you at least happy about your promotion?

Powers. Under the circumstances, no, sir.

Kreton. I find your attitude baffling.

Powers. Is that all, sir?

Kreton. You have never once said what you thought of my war plans. Not once have I got a single word of encouragement from you, a single compliment . . . only black thoughts.

Powers. Since you read my mind, sir, you know what I think.

Kreton. True, but I can't help but feel that deep down inside of you there is just a twinge of professional jealousy. You don't like the idea of an outsider playing your game better than you do. Now confess!

Powers. I am acting as your aide only under duress.[5]

Kreton *(sadly)***.** Bitter, bitter . . . and to think I chose you especially as my aide. Think of all the other generals who would give anything to have your job.

Powers. Fortunately, they know nothing about my job.

Kreton. Yes, I do think it wise not to advertise my presence, don't you? B

5. **duress:** compulsion; pressure.

Student Response

Responding to Reading

These questions are open-ended with no "right" or "wrong" answers. However, responses must be supported with information from the selection. Possible answers follow:

1. Any response based on the play is valid.

2. Some students might point out that this is a humorous conversation that emphasize Kreton's incredible telepathy. Others will suggest that Vidal wants to stress certain aspects that Kreton has in common with the cat, such as boldness and cunning.

3. Students might suggest that Paul Laurent is a noble and idealistic man. He is fair and openminded in the way he welcomes Kreton to earth. Others may note that his utter horror at Kreton's plan to start a war shows him to be humane and compassionate.

4. Many students will suggest that Kreton is most humorous due to his offbeat and cynical view of humankind, his incredible telepathic powers, and his startling and often silly comments and reactions. Others might suggest that General Powers is most humorous, due to the inappropriate and ineffective methods by which he tries to control Kreton. Accept any response that students support.

Text Annotations

A. LEP: Vocabulary Explain that radioactive fallout is the slow descent of radioactive particles after the explosion of a nuclear weapon in the atmosphere. Elicit that from Kreton's request, we can infer that he is planning to use nuclear weapons in his war.

Structured Reading for Less Proficient Students

These questions can help to guide students through the reading. Ask each question at the point of the selection where the SR number appears in the margin.

SR–1. What size war is Kreton planning to wage? *(He is planning to wage a war that will destroy a few dozen cities and kill quite a few million people.)* **Literal recall**

SR–2. How is Mr. Spelding helping to fulfill Kreton's plans? *(Spelding is handling Kreton's public relations.)* **Literal recall**

SR–3. According to Ellen, how is Kreton like a vampire? *(Ellen says that he sacrifices people in order to drink in, or experience, their emotional vibrations.)* **Clarifying**

SR–4. When does Kreton plan to begin the war? *(the night in which the act takes place)* **Literal recall**

SR–5. What unexpected event interrupts Kreton's plans to begin the war? *(a visitor from Kreton's planet arrives at the Speldings.)* **Clarifying**

Continued on page 710

B. Literary Element: THEME Suggest that the theme "In Whose Hands?" takes on a conspiratorial dimension here. That is, only a few people know that the entire world has been taken over by an alien from another dimension.

C. Critical Thinking: ANALYZING Ask students to compare and contrast the emotions of love and hate. Challenge them to suggest reasons for why Kreton might not be able to distinguish between the vibrations of these two strong emotions.

D. Literary Element: CHARACTERIZATION Ask students why they shouldn't be surprised to hear that Spelding has decided to handle Kreton's public relations. *(Possible response: Spelding's career and his need for power always take precedence over his family and other people; he is superficial and doesn't hesitate to manipulate the truth.)*

E. Literary Element: FORESHADOWING Remind students that Ellen's realization here and indeed Kreton's behavior were foreshadowed by the alien's conversation with the cat at the opening of Act 2.

Powers. I can't see that it makes much difference, since you seem bent on destroying our world.

Kreton. I'm not going to destroy it. A few dozen cities, that's all, and not very nice cities, either. Think of the fun you'll have building new ones when it's over.

Powers. How many millions of people do you plan to kill?

Kreton. Well, quite a few, but they love this sort of thing. You can't convince me they don't. Oh, I know what Laurent says. But he's a misfit, out of step with this time. Fortunately, my new World Council is SR-1 ▶ more reasonable.

Powers. Paralyzed is the word, sir.

Kreton. You don't think they like me either?

Powers. You *know* they hate you, sir.

C **Kreton.** But love and hate are so confused in your savage minds and the vibrations of the one are so very like those of the other that I can't always distinguish. You see, we neither love nor hate in my world. We simply have hobbies. *(He strokes the globe of the world tenderly.)* But now to work. Tonight's the big night: first, the sneak attack, then: boom! *(He claps his hands gleefully.)*

(Dissolve to the living room, to John *and* Ellen.)

Ellen. I've never felt so helpless in my life.

John. Here we all stand around doing nothing while he plans to blow up the world.

Ellen. Suppose we went to the newspapers.

John. He controls the press. When Laurent resigned, they didn't even print his speech.

(a gloomy pause)

Ellen. What are you thinking about, John?

John. Walnuts.

(They embrace.)

Ellen. Can't we do anything?

John. No, I guess there's nothing.

Ellen *(vehemently)***.** Oh! I could kill him!

*(*Kreton *and* Powers *enter.)*

Kreton. Very good, Ellen, *very* good! I've never felt you so violent.

Ellen. You heard what I said to John?

Kreton. Not in words, but you were absolutely bathed in malevolence.

Powers. I'll get the papers you wanted, sir.

*(*Powers *exits.)*

Kreton. I don't think he likes me very much, but your father does. Only this morning he offered to handle my public relations, and I said I'd let him. Wasn't that nice of him? D

John. I think I'll go get some fresh air. ◀ SR-2

(He goes out through the terrace door.)

Kreton. Oh, dear! *(sighs)* Only your father is really entering the spirit of the game. He's a much better sport than you, my dear.

Ellen *(exploding)***.** Sport! That's it! You think we're sport. You think we're animals to be played with: well, we're not. We're people, and we don't want to be destroyed. E

Kreton *(patiently)***.** But *I* am not destroying you. You will be destroying one another of your own free will, as you have always done. I am simply a . . . a kibitzer.[6]

6. **kibitzer** (kib′ its ər): a person who meddles in another's affairs or gives unwanted advice.

Words to Know and Use	**malevolence** (mə lev′ ə ləns) *n.* a feeling of ill will or hatred toward others

710

STRUCTURED READING FOR LESS PROFICIENT STUDENTS

Continued from page 709

SR–6. According to the Visitor, where is Kreton from and what rule has he broken? *(The visitor and Kreton are from the distant future; Kreton has broken the rule of never interfering with the past.)* **Summarizing**

SR–7. What does the Visitor tell the humans about Kreton that explains the alien's actions? *(Kreton is mentally and morally retarded.)* **Literal recall**

SR–8. Why is it that the Speldings in the end have no recollection of Kreton's visit? *(The Visitor turns back time to the moment before Kreton arrived.)* **Clarifying**

F

Ellen. No, you are a vampire!

Kreton. A vampire? You mean I drink blood? Ugh!

Ellen. No, you drink emotions, our emotions. You'll sacrifice us all for the sake of your . . . your vibrations!

SR-3 ▶

Kreton. Touché.[7] Yet what harm am I really doing? It's true I'll enjoy the war more than anybody; but it will be *your* destructiveness after all, not mine.

Ellen. You could stop it.

Kreton. So could you.

Ellen. I?

Kreton. Your race. They could stop altogether, but they won't. And I can hardly intervene in their natural development. The most I can do is help out in small, practical ways.

Ellen. We are not what you think. We're not so . . . so primitive.

G

Kreton. My dear girl, just take this one household: your mother dislikes your father, but she is too tired to do anything about it, so she knits and she gardens and she tries not to think about him. Your father, on the other hand, is bored with all of you. Don't look shocked: he doesn't like you any more than you like him. . . .

Ellen. Don't say that!

Kreton. I am only telling you the truth. Your father wants you to marry someone important; therefore he objects to John while you, my girl . . .

Ellen *(with a fierce cry, grabs vase to throw).* You devil! *(Vase breaks in her hand.)*

Kreton. You see? That proves my point perfectly. *(gently)* Poor savage, I cannot help what you are. *(briskly)* Anyway, you will soon be distracted from your personal problems. Tonight is the night. If you're a good girl, I'll let you watch the bombing.

SR-4 ▶

H

(Dissolve to study: Eleven forty-five. Powers *and the* Aide *gloomily await the war.)*

Aide. General, isn't there anything we can do?

Powers. It's out of our hands.

I

*(*Kreton, *dressed as a Hussar with shako,*[8] *enters.)*

Kreton. Everything on schedule?

Powers. Yes, sir. Planes left for their targets at twenty-two hundred.

Kreton. Good . . . good. I myself shall take off shortly after midnight to observe the attack firsthand.

Powers. Yes, sir.

*(*Kreton *goes into the living room, where the family is gloomily assembled.)*

Kreton *(enters from study).* And now the magic hour approaches! I hope you're all as thrilled as I am.

Spelding. You still won't tell us who's attacking whom?

Kreton. You'll know in exactly . . . fourteen minutes.

Ellen *(bitterly).* Are we going to be killed too?

Kreton. Certainly not! You're quite safe, at least in the early stages of the war.

Ellen. Thank you.

J

Mrs. Spelding. I suppose this will mean rationing again.

Spelding. Will . . . will we see anything from here?

Kreton. No, but there should be a good picture on the monitor in the study. Powers is tuning in right now.

---

7. **touché** (to͞o shā′) an interjection acknowledging a witty or insightful remark or insult.

8. **shako** (shăk′ ō): a stiff, flat-topped military hat, often adorned with a plume.

F. Literary Element: CHARACTERIZATION Ask students what Ellen's description of Kreton as an emotion-vampire reveals about her character. *(Possible response: It shows her to be insightful and imaginative.)*

G. Critical Thinking: EVALUATING Ask students whether they think Kreton's description of the Spelding family is accurate. Have them suggest what comment the playwright seems to be making about typical American family life. *(Accept all reasonable answers, which should be supported by details from the play.)*

H. Literary Element: DRAMA Point out that the playwright shifts the scenes regularly to provide variety and to move the plot. For example, first there is a scene between Kreton and Powers, then we see John and Ellen alone, next Kreton talks with Ellen, then it is back to Kreton and Powers, and so on.

I. Reading Skill: UNDERSTANDING VOCABULARY Explain that a *hussar* was a European cavalry officer.

J. LEP: Vocabulary Review that *rationing* is the process by which governments limit the amounts of scarce goods that citizens can have during wartime.

REAL LIFE CONNECTIONS

In the play, Gore Vidal touches on the question of marriage. As Kreton observes, Mrs. Spelding dislikes her husband, but is too tired to do anything about it. Mr. Spelding thinks that a person should marry for wealth and position and so objects to Ellen's engagement to a farmer, John Randolph.

Encourage students to discuss their concerns about marriage. For what reasons should people marry? Why is the divorce rate so high? What aspects of marriage, if any, should be reexamined?

K. Reading Skills: PREDICTING Ask students to predict why another spacecraft might be coming to the Speldings. *(Possible responses: to help Kreton with his plan; to stop Kreton from carrying out his plan)*

L. LEP: Vocabulary Tell students that *inadvertently* means "without meaning to" or "unintentionally."

M. Literary Element: STAGE DIRECTIONS Ask students what they can infer about Kreton's feelings toward the newcomer by the details in these stage directions. *(Possible responses: Kreton is afraid of the newcomer; the newcomer has authority over Kreton.)*

N. Literary Element: PLOT Introduce the term *deus ex machina*, explaining that its literal meaning is "god from a machine" and pointing out that it describes a person or event that comes just in time to solve a difficulty in a story. Elicit that only such a Visitor would have the power to counter Kreton and so bring about the resolution of the central conflict.

O. Literary Element: WRITER'S PURPOSE Point out that the author gets in a final dig at the intelligence level of humans by letting us know that the seemingly all-powerful Kreton is, on his own planet, morally and mentally retarded.

K **John** *(at window)*. Hey look, up there! Coming this way!

*(*Ellen *joins him.)*

Ellen. What is it?

John. Why . . . it's *another* one! And it's going to land.

Kreton *(surprised)*. I'm sure you're mistaken. No one would dream of coming here.

(He has gone to the window, too.)

Ellen. It's landing!

Spelding. Is it a friend of yours, Mr. Kreton?

Kreton *(slowly)*. No, no, not a friend . . .

L *(*Kreton *retreats to the study; he inadvertently drops a lace handkerchief beside the sofa.)*

John. Here he comes.

Ellen *(suddenly bitter)*. Now we have two of them.

SR-5 ▶ **Mrs. Spelding.** My poor roses.

M *(The new* Visitor *enters in a gleam of light from his ship. He is wearing a most futuristic costume. Without a word, he walks past the awed family into the study.* Kreton *is cowering behind the globe.* Powers *and the* Aide *stare, bewildered, as the* Visitor *gestures sternly and* Kreton *reluctantly removes shako and sword. They communicate by odd sounds.)*

Visitor *(to* Powers*)*. Please leave us alone.

(Cut to living room as Powers *and the* Aide *enter from the study.)*

Powers *(to* Ellen*)*. Who on earth was that?

Ellen. It's another one, another visitor.

Powers. Now we're done for.

Ellen. I'm going in there.

Mrs. Spelding. Ellen, don't you dare!

Ellen. I'm going to talk to them.

(starts to door)

John. I'm coming, too.

Ellen *(grimly)*. No, alone. I know what I want to say.

(Cut to interior of the study, to Kreton *and the other* Visitor *as* Ellen *enters.)*

Ellen. I want you both to listen to me . . .

Visitor. You don't need to speak. I know what you will say.

Ellen. That you have no right here? That you mustn't . . .

Visitor. I agree. Kreton has no right here. He is well aware that it is forbidden to interfere with the past. N

Ellen. The past?

Visitor *(nods)*. You are the past, the dark ages: we are from the future. In fact, we are *your* descendants on another planet. We visit you from time to time, but we never interfere, because it would change *us* if we did. Fortunately, I have arrived in time. ◀ SR-6

Ellen. There won't be a war?

Visitor. There will be no war. And there will be no memory of any of this. When we leave here, you will forget Kreton and me. Time will turn back to the moment before his arrival.

Ellen. Why did you want to hurt us?

Kreton *(heartbroken)*. Oh, but I didn't! I only wanted to have . . . Well, to have a little fun, to indulge my hobby . . . against the rules of course.

Visitor *(to* Ellen*)*. Kreton is a rarity among us. Mentally and morally he is retarded. He is a child, and he regards your period as his toy. O ◀ SR-7

Kreton. A child, now really!

Visitor. He escaped from his nursery and came back in time to you. . . .

Kreton. And *every*thing went wrong, everything! I wanted to visit 1860 . . . that's my

P *real* period, but then something happened to the car and I ended up here, not that I don't find you nearly as interesting but . . .

Visitor. We must go, Kreton.

Kreton *(to* Ellen*)***.** You did like me just a bit, didn't you?

Ellen. Yes, yes I did, until you let you hobby get out of hand. *(to* Visitor*)* What is the future like?

Visitor. Very serene, very different . . .

Kreton. Don't believe him: it is dull, dull, dull beyond belief! One simply floats through eternity: no wars, no excitement . . .

Visitor. It is forbidden to discuss these matters.

Kreton. I can't see what difference it makes, since she's going to forget all about us anyway.

Ellen. Oh, how I'd love to see the future . . .

Visitor. It is against . . .

Kreton. Against the rules: how tiresome you are. *(to* Ellen*)* But, alas, you can never pay us a call because you aren't born yet! I mean where we are, you are not. Oh, Ellen, dear, think kindly of me, until you forget.

Ellen. I will.

Q **Visitor.** Come. Time has begun to turn back. Time is bending.

(He starts to door. Kreton *turns conspiratorially to* Ellen.*)*

Kreton. Don't be sad, my girl. I shall be back one bright day, but a bright day in 1860. I dote on the Civil War, so exciting . . .

Visitor. Kreton!

Kreton. Only next time I think it'll be more fun if the *South* wins! *(He hurries after the* Visitor.*)*

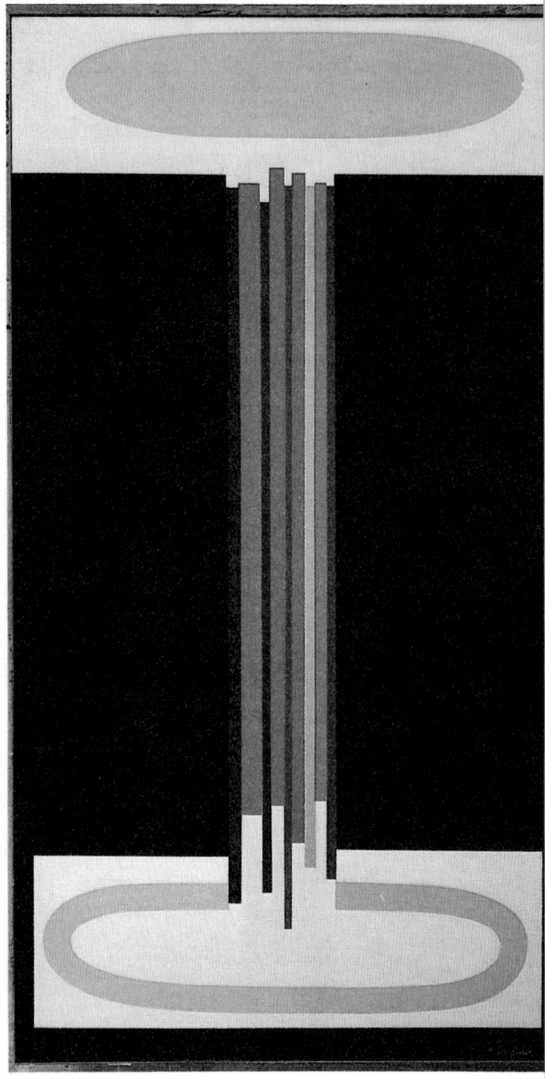

IMPULSE 1964 Will Barnet By permission of the artist.

Art Note

In his portraits, Will Barnet (1911–) clearly denotes the features of his subjects, but, in addition, he may include some references to their occupations. For example, in this painting of the artist Henry Pearson, Barnet carefully delineates the sensitive hands that hold the globe-shaped object in the foreground. *Which character in A Visit to a Small Planet might this figure represent, and why?*

P. Literary Element: FORESHADOWING Ask students if they can think of any hints in the play that foreshadowed the fact that Kreton might be retarded. *(Possible responses: His name sounds like cretin; no one else on his planet would even dream of visiting earth; he couldn't explain the advanced technology of his car or use it correctly to land in 1860.)*

Q. Discussion Students might want to discuss this outcome with other stories involving time travel. Have them prepare a list of common themes.

(*Cut to clock as the hands spin backwards. Dissolve to the living room, exactly the same as the* SR-8 ▶ *first scene:* Spelding, Mrs. Spelding, Ellen.*)*

Spelding. There is nothing wrong with marrying a wealthy man. The horror of it has always eluded me. However, my only wish is that you marry someone hard-working, ambitious, a man who'll make his mark in the world. Not a boy who plans to sit on a farm all his life, growing peanuts . . .

Ellen. English walnuts! And he won't just sit there.

Spelding. Will you stop contradicting me?

Ellen. But, Daddy, John grows walnuts . . .

(John *enters.)*

John. Hello, everybody.

Mrs. Spelding. Good evening, John.

Ellen. What kept you, darling? You missed Daddy's broadcast.

John. I saw it before I left home. Wonderful broadcast, sir.

Spelding. Thank you, John.

(John *crosses to window.)*

John. That meteor you were talking about, well, for a while it looked almost like a spaceship or something. You can just barely see it now.

(Ellen *joins him at window. They watch, arms about one another.)*

Spelding. Spaceship! Nonsense! Remarkable what some people will believe, *want* to believe. Besides, as I said in the broadcast: if there's any traveling to be done in space, we'll do it first.

(He notices Kreton's *handkerchief on sofa and picks it up. They all look at it, puzzled, as we cut to stock shot of the starry night, against which two spaceships vanish in the distance, one serene in its course, the other erratic, as we fade out.)* R

R. Literary Element: STAGE DIRECTIONS Elicit that the erratic spaceship is of course Kreton. Point out that tiny details like this add to the entertainment value of the play.

Check Test

1. Who lands in the Speldings' rose garden? *(Kreton, an alien from another dimension)*

2. What does Kreton plan to do? *(He plans to take over the entire world.)*

3. What does Kreton decide will be his first project as world ruler? *(He will bring about a war.)*

4. According to the second Visitor, what is wrong with Kreton? *(He is mentally and morally retarded.)*

5. At the end of the play, why can't the Speldings remember Kreton's visit? *(The Visitor turns back time to the moment before Kreton's arrival.)*

Encouraging Independent Reading

Childhood's End, a novel by Arthur C. Clarke
Stranger in a Strange Land, a novel by Robert A. Heinlein
Brave New World, a novel by Aldous Huxley
E.T.: The Extraterrestrial, a novel by William Kotzwinkle
The Best Man, a play by Gore Vidal

Literary Concept—Writer's Purpose

Possible response: The playwright uses the play to criticize a number of aspects of American life in the 1950's. The play criticizes the military, in the person of General Powers, for being heavy-handed, prone to using censorship and martial law, and apt to use nuclear weapons. With Roger Spelding, Gore Vidal criticizes TV news and newscasters. Spelding is more concerned with his career than he is in broadcasting the truth. Through the positive character of Paul Laurent, Vidal tries to persuade us that world government is a possible solution to war.

Concept Review: Characterization *Possible response:* The playwright's description of Mrs. Spelding as "vague" and "bored" is borne out by her seeming obliviousness to the world-shaking events occurring in her home. Her constant concern for her roses shows that she is childlike, living in her own little world, with little or no meaningful dialogue with her husband or daughter.

Responding to Reading

First Impressions

1. What is your impression of Kreton now?

Second Thoughts

2. Kreton said in Act One that Earth's "civilization is only just beginning." Do you agree?

   Think about
   - what he considers undeveloped about life on Earth
   - what qualities you think a highly civilized society has
   - how civilized you think Kreton is

3. Compare and contrast the way Ellen and her father respond to Kreton. What do their responses reveal about their personalities and their values?

4. What hopes and fears about the future does this play address?

5. Suppose you could travel to Kreton's world. What would you find most and least appealing?

Broader Connections

6. For Kreton, "savage" is the best word to describe the people that live on Earth because their "deepest pleasure is violence." Do you agree with Kreton's remarks? Explain your answer using examples from history and your experience.

7. Kreton's world is peaceful, in part because people "neither love nor hate." They "simply have hobbies." Are emotions the root of humanity's problems, and would eliminating emotions improve the ability of humans to live together peaceably? Explain.

Literary Concept: Writer's Purpose

Writer's have many purposes: for example, to inform, to entertain, to persuade, and to express themselves. Besides entertaining his audiences with *Visit to a Small Planet*, what other purposes might the playwright have had for writing this play?

Concept Review: Characterization How would you describe Mrs. Spelding? What techniques of characterization does the playwright use to depict her?

Student Response

Responding to Reading

These questions are open-ended with no "right" or "wrong" answers. However, responses must be supported with information from the selection. Possible answers follow:

1. Any response based on the play is valid.

2. Many students will disagree, pointing out that civilization has been steadily developing for thousands of years and technological development has been especially rapid in the last century. Students might agree that certain features one would expect to find in a highly civilized society are absent from our own; as examples, students might point out a lack of harmony with the environment, unhealthy lifestyles, and lack of concern for the plight of fellow humans. Other students may point out that Kreton is not a proper judge of what is civilized.

3. Students might point out that Ellen initially thinks Kreton is wonderful and admires his special powers; later, when Kreton reveals his war plans, Ellen is deeply angered and offended. These reactions show her to be open-minded, fair, compassionate, and peace-loving. Students should point out that Mr. Spelding, by contrast, although repelled by Kreton, uses the alien to advance his own career. This shows Spelding to be cynical and selfish.

4. Some students will point out that the play addresses the fear of war, especially nuclear war, and man's general inhumanity to man. There is also a fear of powerful leaders who act secretly or without the support of the people. Students may point out that the play addresses the hope that people can unite to stop wars, through organizations such as the United Nations. The play also implies that people might someday develop to a point at which they will not deliberately hurt each other.

Continued on page 716

Continued from page 715

5. Some students might say that they would like the peace and serenity of Kreton's world, a place where there would be no physical struggle for existence and no emotional or psychic pain. Other students might agree with Kreton that a planet where people show few intense emotions would be highly unsatisfying. Students might also suggest that the number of rules in force in Kreton's world suggests a place that would be uncomfortably rigid.

6. Accept all reasonable responses. Many students will disagree with Kreton's remark, pointing out that the majority of people are not violent. Some might suggest that people choose violence as a last resort. Students may point to other aspects of life, such as love, friendship, entertainment, good food, and so on that seem to provide far more pleasure than violence. Others might point out that constant warfare on our globe as well as growing crime rates does suggest human beings are "savage."

7. Accept all reasonable responses. Some students might say that negative emotions—such as anger, hatred, and jealousy—are indeed the causes of many problems—such as war, bigotry, abuse, and addiction. Students might also point out, however, that positive emotions, such as love and compassion, bring out many good things on earth and indeed help to solve many problems. Students might point out that being in touch with our emotions is a meaningful and rewarding part of being human; therefore, eliminating emotions, if it were possible, might create a monotonous and unfeeling race of people who were dangerourly one-sided.

Writing Options

1. In one sentence, sum up Kreton's feelings about Earth. Then rephrase this sentence as a bumper sticker for his spaceship.
2. Write a travel article for a visitor who might want to venture to Kreton's land. Remember what he says about ambition, pride, eating, and emotions.
3. Gore Vidal includes useful stage directions throughout most of the play. Find five to ten lines of the play for which very few stage directions are given. Add directions that state how you think the actors should play their parts.
4. Imagine that this play is going to be shown on television. Write a brief summary for *TV Guide*.
5. Explain how you feel about science fiction. Use elements of this play and of any other science fiction stories you have read in this book to support your opinions.
6. What might Kreton think about other characters from this unit? Write his feelings about either Birdfoot's Grampa, Dr. Graham from "The Weapon," Programmer Shuman from "The Feeling of Power," Mr. Crangle from "Four O'Clock," or Lencho from "A Letter to God."

Vocabulary Practice

Exercise Read the pairs of words below. On your paper, write *Synonym* if the pair are synonyms. Write *Antonym* if they are antonyms. Some words will appear more than once.

1. malevolence—friendliness
2. predatory—thievish
3. conjecture—guess
4. lurid—shocking
5. philanthropist—miser
6. patronizing—snobbish
7. conjecture—certainty
8. malevolence—malice
9. philanthropist—contributor
10. lurid—appalling

Words to Know and Use

conjecture
lurid
malevolence
patronizing
philanthropist
predatory

Writing Options

The Writing Options are designed to meet varied student interests and abilities. Have each student choose one writing activity to complete. You may wish to guide some students to an option that requires less writing.

Journal Update Have students review and update their journal entries for *Visit to a Small Planet.*

Vocabulary Practice

1. Antonym
2. Synonym
3. Synonym
4. Synonym
5. Antonym
6. Synonym
7. Antonym
8. Synonym
9. Synonym
10. Synonym

Options for Learning

1 • Cast the Show Find pictures in newspapers and magazines of people that look like the characters in this play as you picture them. Then create a poster that advertises a local production of the show, using your photos to publicize the members of the cast.

2 • Alien Encounters Watch a video of another science fiction story about aliens who visit Earth, such as *War of the Worlds, The Day the Earth Stood Still, Invaders from Mars, E.T.,* or *Close Encounters of the Third Kind.* Afterwards, write a movie review that compares the film with Vidal's play.

3 • Comic Characters Re-create a small episode from this play in comic strip form. Select a short dialogue involving at least three characters. Then draw comic strip boxes that picture this scene.

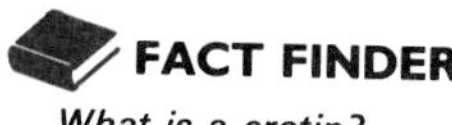

FACT FINDER

What is a cretin?

Gore Vidal

1925–

"We all have a story, and mine is blindness," says Gore Vidal. "I was brought up in the house of a blind man." The man was his grandfather, Senator Thomas Gore of Oklahoma. "I was taught to read early so that I could read to him, and I read him the newspapers, the Congressional Record, history." Years later Vidal would change his name from Eugene to Gore in honor of this man.

Vidal wrote his first novel at the age of nineteen. In the 1950's, he began writing television and film plays, among them *Visit to a Small Planet.* During his three decades of writing, Vidal has also earned a reputation as a controversial personality. He has run for several political offices in the United States. A frequent guest on talk shows, he seems to take pleasure in angering his audience and alienating other guests. He once said of himself, "I'm exactly as I appear. There is no warm lovable person inside. Beneath my cold exterior, once you break the ice, you find cold water."

Though Vidal may profess a lack of warmth, he is also capable of acts of great charity. From his estate in the mountains south of Naples, Italy, he arranged for a blind girl from a nearby Italian town to have an eye operation in Boston. Despite a life that has taken him far from Oklahoma, his early experiences with his grandfather have had a lasting effect on Vidal's life.

Cross-Curricular Options

Students might enjoy forming groups of alien spies on a reconnoitering mission from space to earth. Their mission is to locate important information preparatory to a large-scale alien invasion. Some suggestions for the groups include these:

Geography Group Decide which of earth's countries would be the best place to land initially and to launch a drive for world domination. Support your decision with maps and charts.

Math Group Investigate the number and power of nuclear and tactical weapons held by earth's major nations. Show this information in graph form.

Language Group Write official memos explaining the objectives of the alien invasion and the best methods for meeting these objectives.

Art Group Prepare propaganda posters to persuade earth's people that it is in their best interests to cooperate with the alien invaders.

Options for Learning

These activities suit a variety of learning styles and modes of expression. Allow students to review the options and then choose the one they wish to do. Many are excellent collaborative learning projects.

1. Cast the Show Suggest that students compile a list of adjectives that describe each character. Then have them name actors who often portray these traits.

2. Alien Encounters Suggest that students first list the points about the movie and play that they will compare in their reviews. Possible points include type of alien, reason for visiting Earth, and responses of earthlings.

3. Comic Characters Point out that the stage directions or camera instructions often mark the beginnings and endings of scenes in the play.

Fact Finder

Any dictionary or encyclopedia will enable students to discover that a *cretin* is "someone who suffers from cretinism, a congenital deficiency in the thyroid gland causing severe mental and physical retardation."

Additional Information About the Author

Gore Vidal was born and raised at West Point, and is the son of a military academy instructor. In the early 1950's, in need of income, Vidal began to write movie scripts and teleplays, and in five years he reached his goal of becoming independently wealthy.

Closure

In whose hands does the fate of the human race rest? That is one important theme that *Visit to a Small Planet* explores. The play asserts that in an age of nuclear weapons and pushbutton wars, we cannot risk being manipulated by foolish or power-hungry leaders. Ask students to name current events that have led them to believe that the human race is or is not "in good hands."

Writer's Workshop

Objectives

- To understand the goals of expository writing
- To research a topic for an expository essay
- To write about a single theme using verb tenses correctly
- To incorporate analogies into writing
- To draft, revise, edit, and share an expository essay
- To reflect on the writing process

Integrating . . .

Literature and Writing Share with students that the literature in this subunit deals directly or indirectly with power over one's fate. For example, Art Buchwald and The Earth Works Group imply that awareness of one's relationship with the environment can positively affect the planet's ecology. In contrast, Fuentes' and Vidal's works deal with powers that are beyond humanity's control. Ask students how much control they think they will have over their lives in the future. Tell them that in the next writing assignment they will get to make predictions about the future.

Writing and Language Direct students to the Language Workshop on using verb tenses correctly. Point out to them that the mastery of good writing involves knowing how and when to shift tenses within an essay or story. Ask students to circle the past-tense verbs in "Diablo Country" and to draw a square around those in the present tense. They will see that accomplished writers, such as Buchwald, shift tenses to achieve effect in their writing.

Writing and Vocabulary Point out to students that the Vocabulary Workshop in this subunit deals with analogies: pairs of words that are related to one another. Stress that practice with analogies is essential in understanding concept relationships that they might use in their writing.

EXPOSITION

Human beings have always been curious about what the future will bring. Writers of science fiction have responded to this curiosity by providing us with their visions of future worlds. Sometimes these imaginative glimpses of tomorrow are optimistic portraits of a world in which many of today's problems have been solved. Hunger and poverty have been eliminated, and the nations of the earth live in perfect harmony, aided by miraculous advances in technology. Space travel may have opened up new and exciting frontiers, with humans establishing colonies on the planets of distant stars.

Other science fiction writers, however, conceive of a future that is not nearly so pleasant. They see, for example, a devastated planet earth, crippled by pollution or nuclear war, in which technological skill has not been matched by moral wisdom. Regardless of whether they see the future in a positive or negative light, science fiction writers usually begin by asking themselves, What if . . . ? They look at aspects of the world today and use their imaginations to sketch pictures of the world tomorrow. Their answers to the What if? question form the predictions on which their stories are based.

Here is your PASSkey to this assignment.

GUIDED ASSIGNMENT: PREDICTIONS FOR 2050

Write an essay in which you predict what you think life will be like in the year 2050.

PURPOSE: To make predictions
AUDIENCE: Your classmates
SUBJECT: Life in the year 2050
STRUCTURE: An expository essay

Prewriting

STEP 1 Choose your topic In a small group, brainstorm areas of human experience as possible topics for your essay. Consider such areas as the environment, technology, fashion, entertainment, government, sports, and education. Then identify the one you find most interesting.

Additional Resources

UNIT FIVE RESOURCE BOOK

Writer's Workshop Copy Master, p. 81
Peer and Self-Evaluation Guidelines, p. 82
Writing Assessment Guidelines, p. 83

ENRICHMENT MATERIALS

Thinking Skills Transparency and Worksheet
Fine Art Transparency and Writing Prompts
Revision, Proofreading, and Elaboration Worksheet
Writing Prompts for Assessment

STEP 2 **Identify subtopics** Break down your chosen topic into any subtopics that come to mind. Here are the divisions made by one student who picked transportation as her topic.

◀ STUDENT MODEL

—Personal transportation: bikes, motorcycles, cars, trucks
—Air and sea travel: airplanes, ocean liners, hydrofoils
—Mass transit: buses, subways, and trains
—New developments: space shuttle, high-speed trains, supersonic airliners

STEP 3 **Make predictions about each subtopic** Use your imagination to predict how each of your subtopics might change in the future. You might want to make a chart like the one below. In the "Now" column, describe or summarize briefly how things are today. In the "Year 2050" column, predict how things might change. You may need to consult reference materials, especially current magazines, that deal specifically with scientific and technological advances. Make reasonable predictions by keeping in mind that you are being asked to look only as far as the year 2050. For instance, predicting that people will travel by a molecular transporter device might be reasonable for the year 2400, but it is unlikely, given the present state of technology, that we will have advanced that far by 2050.

PERSONAL TRANSPORTATION

Now	Year 2050
Cars require gasoline. Most families have one car, but some have two or more. People often drive by themselves. Motorcycles and bikes are used mainly for recreation.	Because of pollution, riding alone in a gasoline-powered car is illegal. Solar and electric cars are available but expensive. Bicycle routes have been established within all cities and suburbs.

Drafting

STEP 1 **Introduce your topic** Tell the reader what you will be making predictions about, including the main topic and the various subtopics you selected. Also explain what current problems and

Prewriting Read each step of the prewriting process with the class. Remind students that a predictive essay logically flows from the known to the theoretical.

Stress with students the necessity of identifying and choosing a subtopic for their predictive essay. Remind them that they will write best if they choose a topic (and subtopic) that has some personal relevance. Computer experts might be drawn to the capabilities of that technology (for example, the advances in virtual reality), while biology students might be more interested in the advances in and future implications of genetic engineering.

Computer Tip

Students with access to a computer might want to transfer their notes onto their computer. This will allow them to more easily access research details on their subtopics. It will also give them the opportunity to cross-reference parallel advances in related fields. For example, if they have chosen transportation as a topic and cars, motorcycles, and bikes as subtopics, they will discover in their research that solar power might be widespread enough in the year 2050 to have an impact on *all* forms of transportation—on air, sea, and land.

LEP students may want to approach their essay from the point of view of their native culture. Some of them may come from countries where they have "seen the future"—that is, places where environmental problems have forced the people or government to confront challenges that other countries might not face for years. LEP students might want to predict life in the year 2050 based on the particular problems and solutions of their native experience.

Teaching Strategies

Introduction Have students turn to the Writer's Workshop for this subunit on page 718. Explain to them that they will be writing an essay dealing with the future. Emphasize that they must conduct careful research into the background of their topic in order to extrapolate theories for their essays. Call students' attention to the Guided Assignment box on page 718. Be sure to note the PASSkey graphic indicating that they will be writing an expository essay for their classmates about life in the year 2050.

Drafting During the drafting process, remind students that they will be using techniques of comparison/contrast that they studied in earlier units. Each area being discussed will probably begin with a statement about an aspect of modern life that will then be compared and contrasted with the same aspect in the year 2050.

Stress with students that when they write their conclusions, it is important for them to be specific in their statements about life in the year 2050. Expository writing relies on background research that sets forth facts in detail. Explain that while their essays are predictive and theoretical, they nevertheless must flow from detailed answers to the questions listed in Step 3.

Revising and Editing Students may find it helpful to have a classmate review their essays. Before following the revision checklist, students might want to keep in mind that good predictive writing flows from the familiar.

Remind students that following the *Revision Checklist* will help them analyze the strengths and weaknesses of one another's writing. Stress that a good introduction should contain a clear statement about the essay's topic. Make sure students understand that the introductory paragraph should also contain an intriguing fact or prediction.

Be sure that students devote at least one paragraph to each area discussed and stress that the essay should include a summary of the effects of the predicted changes on people's lives. Conclusions should be specific, based on the earlier research from the *Prewriting* stage.

Remind students to check one another's work for spelling, clarity, and mechanics.

new developments lead you to your predictions. Here is the introduction composed by the student writing about transportation.

STUDENT MODEL ▶

By the year 2050, the way people get around will be very different. All forms of transportation, from personal vehicles to mass transportation systems, will have undergone major changes as a result of the problems and developing technologies of the late twentieth century. Concerns about safety, pollution, and dwindling fuel supplies will make us change the way we travel. New technologies will create new forms of transportation that will alter the speed and safety with which we travel and the distances we are able to cover.

STEP 2 **Write your draft** Using your chart and notes from any research you did, draft the rest of your paper. Create a separate paragraph for each subtopic. Begin each paragraph by briefly describing how things are today. Then describe how you think things will change, citing any research that supports your prediction.

STEP 3 **Write a conclusion** Conclude your essay by summarizing the effects that your predicted changes will have on people's lives. Answer such questions as the following: Will the world be a safer place? Will the environment be cleaner? Will these changes create more problems than they solve? Can people afford to pay for them? Would money be better spent in other areas of development?

Revising and Editing

Once you have completed the rough draft of your essay, ask a classmate to review your work according to the following checklist. Revise your work based on the classmate's answers to these questions.

Revision Checklist

1. Does the introduction explain the general area about which predictions will be made?
2. Do the subtopics discussed in the paper cover all aspects of the general topic?
3. Is each subtopic adequately covered, in at least one paragraph?
4. Does the essay conclude with a summary of the effects of the predicted changes on people's lives in the year 2050?

Editing When you have finished revising your essay, proofread for spelling, clarity, and mechanics.

Presenting

Read your essay to the class but omit the final paragraph. Lead a discussion in which your classmates debate (1) whether your predictions are likely to come true and (2) whether your predictions will make the world a better place. Then read your final paragraph aloud.

Reflecting on Your Writing

Answer the following questions about this assignment. Place the answers and your paper in your writing portfolio.

1. What was the best feedback you received from the classmate who read your paper?
2. Which aspect of writing this essay did you find most difficult? Why?
3. If you had more time for revision, what parts of your essay would you change? Why?

Presenting/Publishing Students may want to collect the most interesting, essays into a magazine called *Future-watch,* which they may donate to the school library.

Reflecting on Your Writing When reviewing student's writing portfolios, you may wish to promote further discussion if many students had similar answers to Question 2 (the difficulty of writing the essay).

Closure

Before beginning the next subunit, be sure that students understand and internalize those concepts:

- An expository essay explains one's opinions about something.
- A predictive essay should flow logically from present events or a present context.
- Using verb tenses correctly is essential to good writing.
- The proper use of analogies can enrich the writing process.

Additional Writing and Research Topics

The following items provide additional writing practice based on the selections in this subunit:

Creative Writing/Exposition

- What current invention would you like to see improved in the year 2050? What capabilities would it have that it does not now?
- Based on your own predictive essay, write about an invention that you think will be indispensable in the year 2050.

Language Workshop

Objectives

- To understand that there are different forms, or tenses, of verbs
- To understand that every verb has two tenses for each of three categories—past, present, and future
- To use verb tenses correctly to show when events take place at a single time and when events take place at different times

Integrating . . .

Writing and Grammar In the Writing Workshop students wrote an essay in which they predicted what life might be like in the year 2050. Explain that using the correct verb tenses to show past, present, and future can help when they write such an essay. Write these sentences on the board.

1. Life in 2050 will bring solar-powered cars and supersonic airliners.
2. The year 2050 brings with it solar-powered cars and supersonic airliners.
3. The year 2050 brought solar-powered cars and supersonic airliners.

Point out that although all of the sentences above refer to the year 2050, a different time period is suggested in each. Ask students to identify the time period in each sentence. Point out that in writing and speaking, the tense of a verb communicates the time of an action, condition, or event. This Language Workshop focuses on using verb tenses correctly.

Answer Key
Exercise 1

1. had watched
2. wrote
3. have (has) submitted
4. will have squawked
5. will pray

Sentences will vary. Check also for subject-verb agreement.

LANGUAGE WORKSHOP

USING VERB TENSES CORRECTLY

Infants live only in the present. The adult view of time, however, has three basic divisions—the past, the present, and the future. When you refer to these different times in your speaking or writing, you use different forms, or **tenses,** of verbs.

Every verb has two tenses for each of these three categories of time—two for the past, two for the present, and two for the future.

PROGRESSIVE FORMS

Each of the verb tenses also has a progressive form used to describe ongoing action.
Past progressive: They *were wishing.*
Past perfect progressive: They *had been wishing.*
Present progressive: They *are wishing.*
Present perfect progressive: They *have been wishing.*
Future progressive: They *will be wishing.*
Future perfect progressive: They *will have been wishing.*

Tenses of the Verb *Recycle*

Past Tenses		
Simple Past	They *recycle.*	Used for past action
Past Perfect	They *had recycled.*	Used for action completed before some other action in the past
Present Tenses		
Simple Present	They *recycle.*	Used for a present or habitual action
Present Perfect	They *have recycled.*	Used for an action completed in the past or an action that started in the past and continues in the present
Future Tenses		
Simple Future	They *will recycle.*	Used for a future action
Future Perfect	They *will have recycled.*	Used for action completed before some other action in the future

Exercise 1 Rewrite the following verbs in the form indicated in parentheses. Then write a complete sentence using the verb in that tense.

1. watch (past perfect)
2. write (simple past)
3. submit (present perfect)
4. squawk (future perfect)
5. pray (simple future)

Additional Resources

UNIT FIVE RESOURCE BOOK
Language Workshop Copy Master, p. 84

ENRICHMENT MATERIALS
Grammar and Usage Copy Masters

Writing About a Single Time

When the events you are writing about all take place in one time, make sure that your verbs all refer to that time.

Sometimes when you tell a story, you are talking about things that all happened in the past. On the other hand, when you write an essay, you may be writing about things that are all going on in the present. A political campaign speech might be all about things that the candidate plans for the future. Make sure that you do not shift from one tense to another when writing about a single time.

Incorrect Jonah *piles* the papers and *stuffed* them in bags. (The tense shifts from the present, *piles,* to the past, *stuffed.*)

Correct Jonah *piled* the papers and *stuffed* them in bags. (Both verbs are in the past tense.)

SPECIAL NOTE

You may notice when you read a review of a book or movie that the writer always uses the present tense in referring to the events in the story. This is a **convention,** or customary practice. Reviewers use it partly to avoid confusion when relating fictional events.

Writing About a Sequence of Events

When the events you are writing about take place at different times, use verbs that show the sequence of these events.

When you are writing or speaking about a sequence of events, you will *need* to shift your verb tense. For example, the sentence below describes a sequence of two events: (1) Jonah finishes the recycling, and (2) the center closes. Notice how the verb tense changes to show this sequence.

Jonah *will have finished* (future perfect) the recycling by the time the center *closes* (present).

You need to be especially careful when you're shifting tenses. Make sure that the sequence makes sense.

Incorrect By the time the clock *reaches* four o'clock, Mr. Crangle's wish *had come* true.

Correct By the time the clock *reaches* four o'clock, Mr. Crangle's wish *will have come* true.

As you proofread, check to make sure that you have used verb tenses correctly. Use a single tense for events that all occur at a single time. Shift tenses to describe events that occur in sequence.

Teaching Strategies

As you proceed through the lesson, ask volunteers to read the focus statements in the boxes. Remind students that by using the correct form of a verb, one can communicate whether something is happening now, has happened in the past, or is expected to happen in the future. Work through the lesson, giving special emphasis to the Tenses of the Verb *Recycle* chart on page 722. Explain to students that the chart is a listing of all the forms for the six tenses of the verb *recycle*. Have students conjugate the verb *recycle* for the six tenses of a verb. (*I recycled; you recycled; he, she, it recycled; etc.*)

Teaching Tip

Some students might have difficulty remembering the six verb tenses. Once students have read the Tenses of the Verb *Recycle* chart on page 722, have them use the chart as a guide to review the forms of other verbs. For example, students might complete the chart using such verbs as *talk, work, learn*.

Teaching Tip: LEP

Discuss with LEP students how other languages indicate verb tenses. For example, in Spanish a change in tense is indicated by changing the ending of the verb. The first person singular of *speak,* for example, would be *hablo* in the present, *hablé* in the past, and *hablaré* in the future tense. Check to see that students are not confused by the differences in verb tense formation between their native language and English.

Teaching Tip

Work with students to conjugate the verb *wish* in its progressive forms. Use the side note next to the chart as a reference. Students' conjugations should look like the following:

Past Progressive

Singular	*Plural*
I was wishing	We were wishing
You were wishing	You were wishing
He/she/it was wishing	They were wishing

Closure

Before completing the final subunit in Unit 5, be sure students have internalized these concepts:

- There are six different forms, or tenses, of verbs: the simple past and past perfect, the simple present and present perfect, and the simple future and future perfect.
- When writing about events that all take place in one time, verbs should all refer to that time.
- When writing about events that take place at different times, verbs should show the sequence of these events.

Exercise 2

Check student responses. Check variations among student responses when a shift in tense was required. Items 2, 7, and 10 are correct.

Exercise 3

Answers will vary. Ask volunteers to read the passage they chose, pointing out the tense of the verbs in the passage. Invite all students to offer possible reasons for the change in verb tense.

Exercise 4

Encourage students to share how they have used what they have learned about verb tenses and the shifting of verb tenses to improve their writing.

Exercise 2 Rewrite each sentence to correct any error in verb tense. If a sentence needs no correction, write *Correct.*

1. Everyone recycles aluminum cans, so there was less litter.
2. Wash out all the cans and save aluminum foil and frozen-food trays.
3. They had picked up cans along the road and have kept the environment cleaner.
4. You can recycle glass because you found a glass-recycling center.
5. The energy we will save from recycling one glass bottle will have lit a 100-watt light bulb for four hours.
6. I had kept two boxes for green and clear glass, but I had forgotten about brown glass.
7. I have voted in every town election to begin curbside recycling.
8. Americans will use 2.5 million plastic bottles every hour, and most of those they will have thrown away rather than recycle.
9. You can line up all the Styrofoam cups made in one day, and they will have reached around the planet.
10. Try to reuse or recycle something every day because every positive action helps.

Exercise 3 Style Choose a passage from one of the pieces you have read in this subunit. The passage should be two or three paragraphs long. List each verb in the passage and write its tense. If a shift in tense occurs, give a reason the writer might have had for choosing a different tense at that point.

LANGUAGE HANDBOOK

For review and practice, see Section 5, **Using Verbs.**

Exercise 4 Analyzing and Revising Your Writing Review a piece of your own writing, looking for improper shifts in verb tense. Correct any errors that you find.

ADDITIONAL PRACTICE

The following items are additional exercises to help students use verb tenses correctly.

Write these sentences correctly.

1. Bob Fosse produces and directed this movie. *(produced)*

2. The candidate researches and wrote his own speeches. *(researched)*

3. This plan landed and refuels in Los Angeles. *(lands)*

Write these sentences about a sequence of events correctly by changing the second verb.

4. By the time Marge returns, I finish my lunch. *(will have finished)*

5. Sam will have closed the shop by the time Tina will return. *(returns)*

6. Before Dad comes home we finished the dishes. *(will finish)*

7. Saul will cut the grass as soon as Ken will have eaten breakfast. *(has eaten)*

ANALOGIES

Choose the lettered pair of words that best expresses a relationship similar to that of the original words.

____ RIVER : WATER :: (a) parrot : bird (b) dress : fabric (c) animal : vegetarian (d) horse : mane

Questions like this one often appear on standardized tests. This is an **analogy** question. You are given two words that are related in some way. To solve the analogy, you need to figure out how they are related. Then you can find the two other words that have the same relationship. Use the following strategy to answer analogy questions:

1. Think of a sentence that tells the relationship between the first pair of words: "A river is made of water."
2. Take the first word pair out of the sentence: "A ____ is made of ____."
3. Try out the possible answers in the blanks until you find one that makes sense. The word pair that makes the most sense in the sentence is the answer.

   "A horse is made of mane." (This doesn't make sense; therefore, it isn't the correct answer.)

   "A dress is made of fabric." (This makes sense; *b* is the answer.)

Exercise Answer the following analogy questions using the method described above. Look up any words you don't know in a dictionary.

1. ____ RABBIT : BURROW :: (a) cottage : dwelling (b) human : house (c) filly : mare (d) trumpet : musician
2. ____ OVERWORK : STRESS :: (a) relaxation : anxiety (b) advertising : sales (c) play : work (d) dreaming : sleep
3. ____ NURTURE : CHILD :: (a) feed : pet (b) misbehave : punishment (c) befriend : enemy (d) teach : school
4. ____ NAVIGATE : BOAT :: (a) travel : train (b) paint : brush (c) steer : car (d) eat : kitchen
5. ____ ARTIST : STUDIO :: (a) teacher : children (b) actor : theater (c) spoon : scoop (d) starch : bread

KINDS OF ANALOGIES

Type	Example
cause to effect	rain : wetness
part to whole	lettuce : salad
object to purpose	stove : cook
action to object	shovel : snow
object to environment	baby : crib
object to characteristic	silk : smooth
word to synonym	anger : fury
word to antonym	sweet : sour
object to material	cheese : milk
worker to product	writer : book
worker to tool	sculptor : clay
time sequence	morning : afternoon
spatial order	front : back

Vocabulary Workshop

Objective

- To understand that an analogy question involves understanding the relationship between a pair of words and choosing another pair with the same relationship

Integrating . . .

Literature and Vocabulary Share with students that this workshop will help them answer the analogy questions that appear on standardized tests such as the PSAT and the SAT I.

Teaching Strategies

Ask students to look at the analogy question at the top of the page. Read through the material with students. Assign the exercise on page 725.

Closure

Before beginning the next subunit, be sure students have internalized these concepts:

- An analogy is two pairs of words with the same relationship.
- There are many different kinds of analogies.
- In order to answer an analogy question, one must determine the relationship of the first two words and choose another pair with the same relationship.

Teaching Tip: LEP

Explain that the format of an analogy question may vary. For example, sometimes a complete analogy is given, with one of the four words left out. Creating sentences using analogy words makes the analogy relationships more visible.

Additional Resources

UNIT FIVE RESOURCE BOOK

Related Skills Copy, p. 85

ADDITIONAL PRACTICE

Write one analogy for each of the following.

1. cause to effect
2. part to whole
3. word to synonym
4. word to antonym
5. object to characteristic
6. time sequence
7. spatial order

Exercise

1. b
2. b
3. a
4. c
5. b

Unit Six *The Classic Tradition*

Objectives

Students will develop skills in the following areas. An asterisk (*) indicates a workshop topic.

Reading and Thinking

recognizing blank verse	*p. 730*
noting iambic pentameter	*p. 730*
understanding figures of speech	*p. 731*
recognizing allusions	*p. 731*
understanding word play	*p. 731*

Vocabulary and Related Skills

*critical viewing	*p. 845*

Literary Appreciation

characterization	*pp. 752, 816*
soliloquy	*p. 752*
suspense	*p. 772*
foreshadowing	*p. 772*
plot	*p. 772*
exposition	*p. 772*
rising action	*p. 772*
climax	*pp. 772, 797*
falling action	*pp. 772, 816*
resolution	*p. 772*
rhetorical question	*p. 797*
conflict	*p. 816*
tragedy	*p. 834*
theme	*p. 834*

Writing

list	*p. 753*
diary entry	*p. 773*
newspaper article	*p. 798*
letter	*p. 817*
interview	*p. 817*
story	*p. 835*
speech	*p. 835*
*exposition: newspaper article examining cause and effect	*pp. 837–40*
*self-assessment	*p. 840*

Language, Grammar, Usage, Mechanics

*sentence combining: inserting word groups	*pp. 842–44*

Planning the Unit

You may find the following information and lists of resources helpful in preparing for the unit.

Presenting *Julius Caesar*

The language and poetic form of *Julius Caesar* may be especially challenging for some students. Assure them that as they read, Shakespeare's language will become more familiar and less difficult. Also point out that this text offers these features to help them understand the play.

1. A **synopsis** of every scene that previews the plot developments.
2. Extensive **side notes** that explain difficult words, passages, puns or jokes, allusions or references, and sometimes staging.
3. Occasional **side note questions** in blue type to help direct students' thinking.
4. A short set of **Responding to Reading** questions at the end of each scene or pair of scenes that allow students to reflect on plot developments before continuing.
5. A full set of **Explain** questions and activities at the end of each act.
6. A wide variety of **Options for Learning** activities at the end of each act which allow students other modes of response to the literature.

Encourage students to read each synopsis before beginning the scene. Then have them read the scene, using the side notes as needed. Stress that simply reading the side notes will not give them the story. The sides notes are not a translation of the whole play but rather an aid to understanding certain difficult words and passages. As often as possible, have students read aloud.

Classroom Resources

Videocassettes, Films, and Filmstrips

■ ***Julius Caesar***, 16mm film, video, Republic Pictures, 1970, (116 minutes). An adaptation of Shakespeare's play starring Charlton Heston, John Gielgud, and others.

■ ***Julius Caesar: An Introduction***, 16 mm film, video, Phoenix/BFa, 1969, (28 minutes). Brief narrative bridges connect the performances of key scenes.

■ ***Rappin' with the Bard***, video, Beacon, 1988, (43 minutes). Familiar images are used to introduce Shakespearen language and stories.

■ ***Shakespeare: The Man and His Times***, video with teacher's guide, Educational Audio Visual, 1989, (38 minutes). Period paintings, prints, and woodcuts show major events of Shakespeare's life.

Audiocassettes, Tapes, and Records

Julius Caesar, audiocassette, Spoken Arts. The Dublin Gate Theatre performs, with Hilton Edwards and Michael MacLiammoir.

Julius Caesar—A Series, 3 audiocassettes, Listening Library. The Shakespeare Recording Society presents this version, with Anthony Quayle, John Mills, and Ralph Richardson.

William Shakespeare—A Portrait in Sound, audiocassette, National Public Radio, 1979, (116 minutes). Recreates the environment of sixteenth century England and depicts Shakespeare at the peak of his dramatic power.

Community Resources

Involving the resources of your community in lesson preparation can add insight and relevance to the text. Consider the following possibilities as you plan.

■ For *Julius Caesar,* invite members of a theater company to discuss various aspects of a stage production, such as acting, directing, sets, scenery, lighting, costumes, scripts; take a backstage tour of a local theater; or visit a museum that exhibits art of ancient Rome or of the European Renaissance.

Unit Preview

How does a hunger for power affect a leader and those around him? Shakespeare's *Julius Caesar,* the selection in Unit 6, **The Classic Tradition**, explores that very question.

Art Note

Andrea Mantegna (1431–1506) was a distinguished northern Italian artist famous for his religious and historical paintings. *The Triumph of Caesar* is a series of nine paintings on canvas-backed paper. In this final painting of the series, Caesar is a monumental figure, seated on a pedestal and holding the scepter of authority. Yet, Mantegna has given him an almost sorrowful expression of contemplation.

About the Author

For more information on William Shakespeare, see pupil's edition page 836.

Additional Resources

UNIT SIX RESOURCE BOOK

Selection Test, pp. 21–24

THE CLASSIC TRADITION

"*I do fear the people choose Caesar for their king.*"

William Shakespeare

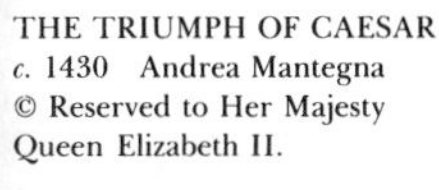

THE TRIUMPH OF CAESAR
c. 1430 Andrea Mantegna

Discussion Questions

To help students probe connections among the fine art, quotation, and unit theme, have them consider the following questions:

1. Why do you think the speaker is afraid that the people will choose Caesar for their king? *(Possible response: students might suggest that the speaker believes or is certain that Caesar is unfit to govern. They may also suggest that the speaker has had a falling out with Caesar that might bring him some personal danger.)*

2. What mood or atmosphere does this quotation suggest? Explain your response. *(Possible response: Citing the word fear, students may suggest that the quotation sets a tense or fearful mood.)*

3. Based on this quotation, what do you think this play might be about? *(Possible response: Students might predict that the play concerns lust for power, abuse of power, or the problems of poor government.)*

4. What elements of the picture reinforce the mood of the quotation? *(Possible response: Students may suggest that the figures' somber expressions echo the quotation's fearful mood. They may say that the figures are wearing clothing and jewelry and carrying items that suggest their royal positions.)*

5. What does the quotation suggest may be some reasons why Shakespeare is considered a "classic" writer, as the unit title suggests? *(Possible response: Students may suggest that Shakespeare is considered classic because his themes, such as greed, power, and passion, have remained constant throughout the ages.)*

OBSERVATION ASSESSMENT

Observing how students respond to the text, to the classroom instruction, and to peers is an important part of an assessment program. The following suggestions and the form in each Unit Resource Book can be used to implement observation assessment.

- As students progress through the play, assess their use of prereading strategies. Can they identify characters and events depicted in the illustrations? Can they recognize events described in the scene summaries as they unfold in the play?
- As they work through this unit, do they use their prior knowledge to draw conclusions about what the characters might feel and do?
- As they work through this unit, can you see growth in their use of prereading strategies?
- To evaluate how well students understand the Guide for Reading annotations, see if they refer to them when they encounter difficulty with the text. Can they paraphrase a passage by using the annotations for help with unfamiliar words and wording? Do the annotations help them read aloud with appropriate expression?

Objectives

- To understand a play
- To understand blank verse
- To understand Shakespeare's language
- To understand Shakespeare's style, including figures of speech, allusions, and word play
- To understand characterization
- To understand suspense and foreshadowing
- To understand climax
- To understand conflict
- To understand tragedy
- To understand theme
- To express understanding of the work through a choice of writing options, including speeches, wanted posters, newspaper stories, letters, and dialogue

Prereading/Motivation

Examine What You Know

Discussion Prompts: Encourage students to discuss other figures from history who were famous for their hunger for power: for example, Genghis Khan or Adolf Hitler. Students can also discuss power-hungry characters from popular fiction, films, and television.

In the discussion of friendship, encourage students to identify situations in which friendship might be severely tested, or in which loyalty to friends might conflict with other, more important values. Ask students to think of times when friends can get each other into trouble or convince each other to do something dangerous. Ask whether it can ever be a good thing for a friend to encourage another friend to join in a cause that might be dangerous or unpopular.

e x p l o r e

Drama *Julius Caesar*

WILLIAM SHAKESPEARE

Examine What You Know (Prior Knowledge)

In *Julius Caesar,* William Shakespeare (1564-1616) tells a story about the hunger for power—a story based on real people and events from the days when Rome ruled much of the world. Think of stories—fictional or true—you've read or seen about people who hunger for power. Tell of two or three such stories. Where were they set? Who were the power-hungry individuals? What happened to them? If you're familiar with such stories, you know something about the main theme of *Julius Caesar.*

Like all of Shakespeare's plays, however, *Julius Caesar* deals with many other themes. One of these is friendship. You'll find some interesting views on friendship in the play you're about to read. For example, is it right to persuade a close friend to do something dangerous? This drama also deals with such universal themes as ambition, vanity, envy, and revenge.

In fact, you might find it helpful to forget, for the time being, how long ago Shakespeare lived. You will be surprised to learn how modern many of his situations, characters, and themes are.

Expand Your Knowledge (Building Background)

Julius Caesar Julius Caesar was a Roman general and politician who lived from about 100 to 44 B.C. One of the greatest military leaders in Roman history, Caesar conquered most of Gaul, a land that covered the areas now known as France and Belgium. He also brought Roman civilization into Britain and later led his army in a takeover of Egypt.

Caesar gained so much military power that the Roman Senate feared he would try to control the government. To keep that from happening, the Senate ordered him to disband his army around 50 B.C. Caesar refused and led his army into Italy, the peninsula where Rome lay. There he fought a civil war against the armies of his former friend and ally, Pompey. The battles spread as far as Spain and Egypt, ending with Caesar's victory in 45 B.C.

Caesar's military successes made him popular among the citizens of Rome. They showed their respect by granting him a title no one had ever held before in Rome—dictator for life. Some Roman leaders saw this as the possible end of the Roman republic. They began to think of ways to stop Caesar.

Journal Writing

Among the chief motivations for the characters in *Julius Caesar* are honor, ambition, and pride. Suggest these journal topics to students:

- Discuss a time when someone urged you to do something but you refused because you thought such an action would conflict with your code of "honor." What does being "honorable" mean, in your opinion?
- What are some of the ways that ambition can be a good motivating force in people? What are some of the ways it can be a bad motivation? Discuss a situation from your experience in which you became sharply aware of the difference between "good" and "bad" ambition.
- Pride is sometimes called an especially dangerous vice because it may blind people to reality and prevent them from correcting their errors or mistakes. Do you agree? Why or why not? For other journal opportunities, refer students to the Writing Options for Act II (page 772) and to Journal Update (page 835).

This is the point at which *Julius Caesar* begins. The year is 44 B.C., and Caesar stands at the height of his powers. The mighty ruler sees himself almost as a god. He does not know that several men around him are plotting to end his rule—and his life.

Shakespeare's Society William Shakespeare lived in England during a time when artists of all types were held in high esteem. Elizabeth I was the Queen of England, and the period of her reign, from 1558 to 1603, has become known as the Elizabethan Age. Elizabeth supported all the arts—literature, painting, sculpture, music, and theater. Her support led to the creation of some of the greatest works England has ever produced.

Several outstanding dramatists appeared during the Elizabethan Age, but no other as notable as Shakespeare. His works offered something for everyone; rich and poor, educated and uneducated, all attended and enjoyed Shakespeare plays. His works range from broad humor to pathetic tragedy (sometimes within the same play). A Shakespearean play is quite likely to include comic characters, bloody fights, and interesting observations about human nature.

Such a mixture was important to Shakespeare. As a serious playwright, he wanted to explore human behavior, to understand how different people deal with life's universal problems. Yet he also wrote for an audience that wanted to see action. So he worked hard to keep his plays from being a collection of long speeches. He made sure that the plays included enough noise, movement, and violence to keep anyone interested.

Shakespeare's Theater Besides being a writer, Shakespeare was also part owner of the Globe Theatre, where most of his plays were first performed. The Globe was a typical Elizabethan theater, built for outdoor performances. The theater had no roof, but an overhang partially protected some of its seats from wind and rain. A few people could afford to pay for these seats, but most of the audience stood in the open area, or *pit,* near the stage.

(left) Wenceslaus Hollar's 1647 view of London shows the Globe Theatre and a "bear-baiting" arena. However, Hollar has mistakenly reversed the labels of the theater (right) and the arena.

Expand Your Knowledge

Discussion Prompts on Julius Caesar: Ask students how military success and political popularity are related. Encourage students to discuss the effect that a tremendously popular military leader might have in American today. Ask what circumstances might make such a leader become so popular that he or she would be made a dictator. Ask how such a ruler might come to feel about himself or herself. Then encourage students to imagine how others might fear such a ruler and ask what actions they might turn to.

Discussion Prompts on Shakespeare's Society: Ask students what popular forms of entertainment today offer "something for everyone; rich and poor, educated and uneducated." Ask how a play can be both serious and entertaining at the same time, and encourage students to give examples of plays, films, or television shows that are so. Remind students of the elements Shakespeare introduces—"comic characters, bloody fights, and interesting observations about human nature"—and ask what forms today include these elements. Then ask students how different people might enjoy the same entertainment in different ways and for different reasons. Encourage them to give specific examples from plays, films, and television shows with which they are familiar (for example, a serious action film or political thriller in which some people mainly enjoy the fight scenes while others are interested in the underlying message). Ask students how they themselves respond to works that have both a "serious message" and a lot of action or comedy.

Discussion Prompts on Shakespeare's Theater: Ask students to share their own experiences with theater. Ask how it differed from film or television, focusing especially on the need for imagination.

Additional Resources

UNIT SIX RESOURCE BOOK

Reader's Guidesheet, pp. 1, 4, 7, 10, and 13
Vocabulary Worksheet, pp. 2, 5, 8, 11, and 14
Selection and Vocabulary Check Tests, pp. 3, 6, 9, 12, and 15
Selection Test, pp. 21–24

Collaborative Learning

Opportunities for collaborative learning appear throughout the lesson and include many of the Extend activities (pp. 753, 773, 797, 817, 835).

Enrich Your Reading

Blank Verse Encourage students to read a passage of blank verse aloud. First, make sure students understand the content of what they are reading. Explain all unfamiliar words and make sure that any figurative language is clear to students. Encourage students to paraphrase the passage in their own words, so that they feel comfortable with its sense.

Then encourage various students to read the passage aloud. After they have done so, and have become comfortable with this practice, model for them a reading that exaggerates the stressed syllables. Encourage students to read the passage in this exaggerated way, and to have fun with the exaggeration and distortion. Ask students which words "leap out" at them when the passage is exaggerated in this way. Encourage them to discuss whether these are particularly important words or ideas.

Then have students go back to reading the passage aloud in a normal way. Ask if they can now hear the more subtle rhythms. Point out that while much of iambic pentameter falls into a regular, repetitive rhythm (da-DUM, da-DUM, da-DUM, etc.), sometimes Shakespeare will vary the rhythm, such as by starting a line with a stress (as in "FRIENDS, RO-mans, COUN-try-men) or by putting two strong stresses or two unstressed syllables next to each other (as in the same example). Encourage them to see that these variations imitate "ordinary conversation" while helping Shakespeare to bring out important words, shift the mood, or suggest character. Ask, for example, what audiences might think about a character who uses many strong, abrupt stresses, as opposed to a character whose speech is more rhythmic and flowing.

The people in the pit were the ones likely to be looking for action and broad humor in a play. They would cheer when the hero won a swordfight, yell insults at the villain, and laugh loudly at the jokes.

The performances these audiences saw were somewhat different from plays of today. For example, women never appeared in plays. Instead, teenage boys played all the female parts. In addition, the stage had no scenery. Sometimes a sign on a wall told the audience where the scene was taking place; often the playwright would include lines of dialogue to identify the setting. With no scenery, the Elizabethan audience needed a vivid imagination to picture bloody battlefields, galloping horses, splendid palaces, and the like.

Enrich Your Reading (Reading Skill)

Blank Verse Elizabethan playwrights wrote dialogue in the form of poetry. Shakespeare used a type of poetry that was popular among English writers—**blank verse,** or poetry with lines that do not rhyme.

Blank verse has lines written in a pattern called **iambic pentameter.** An *iamb* is a pair of syllables in which the second syllable is stressed more than the first one. *Pentameter* comes from two Greek words that mean "five measures." Thus, a line written in iambic pentameter has five pairs of syllables (ten syllables in all). Each pair follows the pattern unstressed/stressed.

Read the following iambic pentameter line from *Julius Caesar.* The mark (˘) indicates an unstressed syllable, and (ʹ) indicates a stressed syllable.

Thĕ ángry̆ spót dŏth glów ŏn Cáesăr's brów

Many people consider iambic pentameter the most natural poetic pattern for English, a language that is based on stressed and unstressed syllables. Decide for yourself by reading some of Shakespeare's lines aloud. Be sure not to put *too much* emphasis on the accented syllables. Then decide if the lines sound like ordinary conversation.

Shakespeare's Language As you read *Julius Caesar,* keep two things in mind about Shakespeare's language. First, since his dialogue is written as blank verse, he sometimes changed the order of words to fit the pattern of syllables. As a result, some lines require a reader to slow down and think about exactly what the character means.

Keep in mind also that Shakespeare's language belongs to the Elizabethan Age. Four hundred years ago, English was different from what it is today. A play by Shakespeare will thus include words that are no longer used in English; it will also include words whose meanings have changed since Shakespeare's day.

Shakespeare's Language Remind students that the marginal notes are there to help with difficulties in Shakespeare's language. You might model the use of these notes for students, as well as modeling the use of context clues and other clues to the meaning of a word. For example, you might read through a passage, encourage students to guess at its meaning, have them identify which words they do not understand, have them identify context or other clues to help them determine meaning, and then have them check the marginal notes. Finally, you might have students reread the passage with their new knowledge, paraphrasing it if necessary. You might also suggest that in some cases, students might find it easiest to read straight through, checking the marginal notes only when they hit a roadblock.

As you read, refer to the notes in the margins of the pages. These will help you understand many words and passages in the play. More important, the notes will gradually help you get used to Shakespeare's language and thus make the reading easier and easier.

Shakespeare's Style Shakespeare's audience expected a playwright to use certain literary techniques. As you read *Julius Caesar,* look for examples of each of the following features of Shakespeare's style.

1. **Figures of Speech** A figure of speech is an expression that is not meant to be taken word for word. It usually involves a comparison between two things that are not really alike. The purpose of a figure of speech is to bring an image to the reader's or listener's mind in order to describe something in a more vivid, memorable way. Similes and metaphors, for example, are figures of speech. Read the following example from *Julius Caesar.* Notice the comparison Marc Antony uses below when he describes the wounds in Caesar's body. What two things does he compare?

   Over thy wounds now do I prophesy
   (Which, like dumb mouths, do ope their ruby lips
   To beg the voice and utterance of my tongue),
   A curse shall light upon the limbs of men.

2. **Allusions** An allusion is a reference to a well-known person, place, thing, or event. Many people in Shakespeare's audience were familiar with the cultures of ancient Greece and Rome. As a result, Shakespeare often made allusions to those ancient cultures. For example, in Act One, Scene 2, Cassius compares himself to Aeneas (ē nē′ əs), a character from Roman mythology. You will find explanations of Shakespeare's allusions in the marginal notes.

3. **Word Play** Shakespeare liked to please his audience by using one of their favorite types of jokes—the **pun.** A pun is a joke that makes use of two different meanings of a word, or of two words that sound alike. The opening scene of *Julius Caesar* includes several puns on words having to do with shoes. A shoemaker, for example, calls himself "a mender of bad soles," meaning it to sound like "a mender of bad souls."

As you read *Julius Caesar,* remember these comments about Shakespeare's language and style. Use the notes in the margins as an aid in understanding the dialogue. Before long, the play will become easier to follow, and you will find yourself getting more from your reading.

■ *A biography of the author can be found on page 836.*

2. Allusions
Remind students that the allusions in Shakespeare's plays would have been familiar to his audience although they are strange to us. Encourage students to think of allusions that they might make that would be unfamiliar to audiences of a hundred years or four hundred years from now (possible examples: "He thinks he's as great as Superman," "She's as cool as Madonna.")

3. Word Play
Remind students that puns are often difficult for those who are not native speakers. Encourage LEP students to share puns from their native language and to attempt to "translate" or explain these puns. This experience might help all students feel more comfortable with their own difficulties with Shakespeare's puns, which are in fact written in "another language" from the English we speak today.

Thematic Link

Julius Caesar, a drama in the classic tradition, contains a number of classic themes interwoven throughout the play. Among these themes are friendship, revenge, authority, ambition, the uses and misuses of persuasion, and the tragic dilemma of those with good intentions who deceive themselves into believing that noble ideals justify any means, no matter how violent.

Shakespeare's Style

1. Figures of Speech
Remind students about the different types of figures of speech. Use the passage cited on this page to review simile and metaphor, pointing out the simile of "like dumb mouths" and the metaphor of "do ope their ruby lips." Ask students to think of similes and metaphors that they use in their daily lives, to remind them that these are figures that we all use instinctively, all the time. You might wish to discuss with students the "pros" and "cons" of a playwright using these figures (pro—makes the language richer, more interesting, more vivid; con—harder to understand, less like "real life").

Cast of Characters Some students may have difficulties with the large numbers of characters, particularly since characters have Latin names that may be unfamiliar to most students. The following suggestions may be helpful:

First, read through the various names with students. Make sure they are comfortable pronouncing the Latin names. See the pronunciation key below and on page 733 for all the names. It may be helpful to point out some of the common Latin endings: *ius, us, a,* and *o.* It may also be helpful to point out that these are all *masculine* endings; that is, they denote men. Encourage students to notice that the two female characters' names both end in *ia.*

Next, students may appreciate knowing that charaters are grouped in various categories. Encourage them to make a cluster chart with the figure of Julius Caesar at the center, to help them visualize the different relationships. They might make this chart ahead of time, based on the information on this page, or you may prefer to have them make the chart as they read.

In either case, you may want to make sure that students understand what each category means, as in the following list:

Triumvirs: rulers who share power as a threesome

Senators: members of the Roman Senate, a ruling body that had some power but would have been subordinate to Caesar as dictator

Conspirators: people who join together in a *conspiracy,* or secret plot

Tribunes of the people: Whereas the Senate represented nobility and landowners, tribunes represented the common people; however, their power was limited.

Julius Caesar

WILLIAM SHAKESPEARE

CHARACTERS

Julius Caesar

Octavius Caesar, **Marcus Antonius**, **M. Aemilius Lepidus** — Triumvirs after the death of Julius Caesar

Cicero, **Publius**, **Popilius Lena** — Senators

Marcus Brutus, **Cassius**, **Casca**, **Trebonius**, **Ligarius**, **Decius Brutus**, **Metellus Cimber**, **Cinna** — Conspirators against Julius Caesar

Flavius and Marullus, Tribunes of the people

Artemidorus of Cnidos, a teacher of Rhetoric

A Soothsayer

Cinna, a poet

Another Poet

Lucilius, **Titinius**, **Messala**, **Young Cato**, **Volumnius** — Friends to Brutus and Cassius

Varro, **Clitus**, **Claudius**, **Strato**, **Lucius**, **Dardanius** — Servants to Brutus

Pindarus, servant to Cassius

Calpurnia, wife to Caesar

Portia, wife to Brutus

The Ghost of Caesar

Senators, Citizens, Guards, Attendants, Servants, etc.

Time: 44 B.C.

Place: Rome; the camp near Sardis; the plains of Philippi

Pronunciations of Characters' Names

Julius Caesar (jool′ yəs sē zər)
Octavius Caesar (äk tā′ vē əs sē′ zər)
Marcus Antonius (mär′ kəs an tō′ nē əs)
M. Aemilius Lepidus (ə mēl′ yəs lep′ i dəs)
Cicero (sis′ə rō)
Publius (po͞o′ blē əs)
Popilius Lena (pō pil′ ē əs lē′ nə)
Marcus Brutus (mär′ kəs bro͞o′ təs)
Cassius (kash′ əs)
Casca (kas′ kə)
Trebonius (trə bō′ nē əs)
Ligarius (li gar′ ē əs)
Decius Brutus (dē′ shəs bro͞o′ təs)
Metellus Cimber (mə tel′ əs cim′ bər)
Cinna (sin′ ə)
Flavius (flā′ vē əs)
Marullus (mə ro͞ol′ əs)
Artemidorus (är′ tə mə dôr′ əs)
Lucilius (lo͞o si′ lē əs)
Titinius (tī tin′ ē əs)
Messala (məs a′ lə)
Cato (kā′ tō)
Volumnius (və lo͞om′ nē əs)

ACT ONE

Scene 1 *A street in Rome.*

The play begins on February 15, the religious feast of Lupercal. Today the people have a particular reason for celebrating. Julius Caesar has just returned to Rome after a long civil war in which he defeated the forces of Pompey, his rival for power. Caesar now has the opportunity to take full control of Rome.

In this opening scene, a group of workmen, in their best clothes, celebrate in the streets. They are joyful over Caesar's victory. The workers meet Flavius and Marullus, two tribunes—government officials—who supported Pompey. The tribunes express their anger at the celebration, and one worker responds with puns. Finally, the two tribunes scatter the crowd.

Flavius. Hence! home, you idle creatures, get you home!
B Is this a holiday? What, know you not,
Being mechanical, you ought not walk
Upon a laboring day without the sign
Of your profession? Speak, what trade art thou?

First Commoner. Why, sir, a carpenter.

Marullus. Where is thy leather apron and thy rule?
What dost thou with thy best apparel on? You, sir, what trade are you?

C **Second Commoner.** Truly sir, in respect of a fine workman I am but, as you would say, a cobbler.

Marullus. But what trade art thou? Answer me directly.

Second Commoner. A trade, sir, that I hope I may use with a safe conscience, which is indeed, sir, a mender of bad soles.

Marullus. What trade, thou knave? Thou naughty knave, what trade?

Second Commoner. Nay, I beseech you, sir, be not out with me. Yet if you be out, sir, I can mend you.

D **Marullus.** What mean'st thou by that? Mend me, thou saucy fellow?

Second Commoner. Why, sir, cobble you.

Flavius. Thou art a cobbler, art thou?

Second Commoner. Truly, sir, all that I live by is with

GUIDE FOR READING

A **3–6 *What, know . . . profession:*** Since you are workers ***(mechanical)***, you should be carrying the tools of your trade ***(sign / Of your profession)***. *What is Flavius' attitude toward these workers?*

11–31 In this conversation, the ***cobbler*** (shoemaker) makes several puns, which all go over the head of Marullus. Imagine the workmen laughing, as Marullus gets angrier and angrier, wondering what's so funny.

18–19 Marullus accuses the commoner of being a wicked, sly person ***(naughty knave)***, but the commoner begs arullus not to be angry with him ***(be not out with me)***.

22–23 Marullus thinks the cobbler means "I can mend your behavior." He accuses the cobbler of being disrespectful ***(saucy)***.

26 The cobbler jokes about the

Varro (var′ ō)
Clitus (clī′ təs)
Claudius (claw′ dē əs)
Strato (strä′ tō)
Lucius (lo͞o′ shəs)
Dardanius (där dā′ nē əs)
Pindarus (pin dar′ əs)
Calpurnia (kal pur′ nē ə)
Portia (por′ shə)

Teaching Strategies

Support for Students of Limited English Proficiency

- Use **Reader's Guidesheet**, p. 1.

- *Julius Caesar* Act I contains vocabulary items that may be difficult or challenging for some students. For example, some words are archaic. In addition, a proper appreciation of the playwright's use of puns depends on recognizing two possible meanings for a single word—one or both of which may not be in current usage. Help LEP students over the rough spots by using the annotations.

- **Annotations C** and **I** (Scene 1); **E, N, P, AA,** and **II** (Scene 2); **B, J,** and **R** (Scene 3) focus on vocabulary, allusion, word play, and irony.

Text Annotations

A. Answer: *Flavius' attitude toward the workers seems proud and contemptuous.*

B. Reading Skill: VISUALIZING Have students use clues in the dialogue to visualize this scene. Ask students to describe the crowd and Flavius' movements, gestures, and tone of voice. *(Possible response: The workers are happily milling about; Flavius sounds angry, possibly poking or shoving crowd members.)*

C. LEP: Pun Tell students that, just as many words in modern English have multiple meanings, the word "cobbler" in Shakespeare's time had a specific meaning (a person who repaired shoes) and a more general meaning (any clumsy worker). Marullus, thinking of the second meaning, asks the shoemaker again about his trade.

D. Literary Element: TONE Ask students what adjective they would choose to describe the commoner's tone toward the tribune in this passage. *(Possible responses: humorous, sly, insolent, sarcastic)*

E. Historical Sidelight Shakespeare's audiences apparently took a great delight in puns. Several other Shakespearean plays, including *Romeo and Juliet,* open with scenes that include many plays on words. Possibly the playwright used this technique to "warm up" his audience at the beginning of a performance.

F. Literary Element: DIALOGUE Ask students to comment on the form of the characters' dialogue here. What distinction can they draw between the commoner's speech and Marullus' speech? *(Possible response: The commoner speaks in prose, while Marullus speaks in verse.)* Which form of speech do they believe is used for more lofty, dignified content? *(verse)*

G. Literary Element: THEME Ask students what Marullus implies about the mob here. *(Possible response: that they are fickle, cruel, and ungrateful)*

H. Literary Element: PERSONIFICATION Ask students to explain the use of personification in these lines. *(Possible response: The river is personified as a woman who can "hear" sounds and who "trembles.")*

the awl. I meddle with no tradesman's matters nor women's matters, but with all. I am indeed, sir, a surgeon to old shoes. When they are in great E danger, I recover them. As proper men as ever trod upon neat's leather have gone upon my handiwork.

Flavius. But wherefore art not in thy shop today?
Why dost thou lead these men about the streets?

Second Commoner. Truly, sir, to wear out their shoes, to get myself into more work. But indeed, sir, we make holiday to see Caesar and to rejoice in his F triumph.

Marullus. Wherefore rejoice? What conquest brings he home?
What tributaries follow him to Rome
To grace in captive bonds his chariot wheels?
You blocks, you stones, you worse than senseless things!
O you hard hearts, you cruel men of Rome!
Knew you not Pompey? Many a time and oft
Have you climbed up to walls and battlements,
G To tow'rs and windows, yea, to chimney tops,
Your infants in your arms, and there have sat
The livelong day, with patient expectation,
To see great Pompey pass the streets of Rome.
And when you saw his chariot but appear,
Have you not made an universal shout,
That Tiber trembled underneath her banks
H To hear the replication of your sounds
Made in her concave shores?
And do you now put on your best attire?
And do you now cull out a holiday?
And do you now strew flowers in his way
That comes in triumph over Pompey's blood?
Be gone!
Run to your houses, fall upon your knees,
Pray to the gods to intermit the plague
That needs must light on this ingratitude.

Flavius. Go, go, good countrymen, and for this fault
Assemble all the poor men of your sort;
Draw them to Tiber banks, and weep your tears
Into the channel, till the lowest stream
Do kiss the most exalted shores of all.

similarity of ***awl*** (a shoemaker's tool) to the word *all. Do you or any of your friends ever make up puns?*

31 *neat's leather:* calfskin, used to make expensive shoes. The cobbler means that even rich people come to him for shoes.

32 *wherefore:* why.

40–41 *What . . . wheels:* What captured prisoners march chained to the wheels of his chariot?

45 *Pompey:* a former Roman ruler defeated by Caesar in 48 B.C. Pompey was murdered a year after his defeat.

53 *Tiber:* a river that runs through Rome.

54 *replication:* echo.

57 *cull out:* select.

59 *Pompey's blood:* Caesar is returning to Rome in triumph after defeating Pompey's sons in Spain.

62–63 *intermit . . . ingratitude:* hold back the deadly illness that might be just punishment for your behavior.

66–68 *weep . . . of all:* Weep into the Tiber River until it overflows.

734 UNIT SIX THE CLASSIC TRADITION

CULTURAL CONNECTION

In Julius Caesar's time, not all Romans believed literally in the existence of the pagan gods. The traditional religion, however, was supported by the state, and the various gods were worshiped regularly at temples throughout the city. Ask students to compare this attitude toward religion to our attitude today, in the United States. Ask whether we have an official religion, and whether we freely accept a rejection of religion in our political leaders. Encourage students from other countries to share their experiences with official religions and the connections between religion and politics.

[Exeunt all the Commoners.*]*

I See, whe'r their basest metal be not moved.
They vanish tongue-tied in their guiltiness.
Go you down that way towards the Capitol;
The way will I. Disrobe the images
If you do find them decked with ceremonies.

Marullus. May we do so?
You know it is the feast of Lupercal.

Flavius. It is no matter. Let no images
Be hung with Caesar's trophies. I'll about
And drive away the vulgar from the streets
So do you too, where you perceive them thick.
These growing feathers plucked from Caesar's wing
Will make him fly an ordinary pitch,
Who else would soar above the view of men
And keep us all in servile fearfulness.

[Exeunt.]

Exeunt *(Latin):* They leave.

69 Flavius and Marullus are now alone, having shamed the workers into leaving the street. Flavius says that they will now see if they have touched ***(moved)*** the workers' poor characters ***(basest metal).***

72–73 *Disrobe . . . ceremonies:* Strip the statues of any decorations you find on them.

77–79 *I'll about . . . thick:* I'll go around and scatter the rest of the commoners. Do the same yourself wherever they are forming a crowd.

80–83 *These . . . fearfulness:* Flavius compares Caesar to a bird. He hopes that turning away some of Caesar's supporters ***(growing feathers)*** will prevent him from becoming too powerful.

Responding to Reading

1. Do you sympathize with Flavius and Marullus or with the commoners who are celebrating Caesar's victory? Explain.

2. What attitudes do the two tribunes and the commoners seem to have toward each other? Support your opinion with evidence.

3. Do you think this scene is as funny today as it might have been in Shakespeare's time? Explain.

4. Do you think it might be dangerous for Flavius and Marullus to take the decorations from the statues? Why or why not?

I. LEP: Vocabulary Help students with this line by explaining that "metal" in Shakespeare's time could refer, in a metaphorical sense, to a person's character. Even today, we may use the related word "mettle" in the same fashion.

J. Reading Skill: CLARIFYING What do Flavius and Marullus think of Caesar? *(Possible response: Flavius and Marullus think that Caesar does not deserve the support of the people, since he has not done nearly as much for the good of Rome as Pompey. They suspect that Caesar plans to rule as a dictator.)*

K. Literary Element: CONFLICT Have students sum up the external conflicts that are revealed in this first scene. *(Possible response: Caesar is in conflict with some of the city tribunes, who favor Pompey; these tribunes, in turn, are in conflict with the people, who favor Caesar.)*

Student Response

Responding to Reading

These questions are open-ended with no "right" or "wrong" answers. However, responses must be supported with information from the selection. Possible answers follow:

1. Answers will vary. Some students might sympathize with Flavius and Marullus, but many will probably sympathize with the commoners, who are intelligent and witty.

2. Possible response: It will be dangerous for the tribunes to remove the decorations because the commoners, who are out in the streets for a festival, may become violent in their support of Caesar. In addition, Caesar's forces may arrest the tribunes for such actions.

3. Students may say that the tribunes appear arrogant and scornful toward the commoners, while the commoners respond by being flippant, willy, and irreverant.

4. Answers will vary but students may point to puns such as the word "cobbler" which are no longer funny today without explanation.

Text Annotations

A. Historical Sidelight Julius Caesar had a daughter named Julia by a previous marriage; Julia had, in fact, been married to Pompey when he and Caesar were allies. But Caesar had failed to produce a son and male heir, which was important for every prominent Roman. For this reason, he had taken the precaution of adopting Octavius, his great-nephew, as his son and heir. This explains his concern that Calpurnia "shake off" her "sterile curse" and produce an heir.

B. Answer: *Antony is ready to obey all of Caesar's commands immediately. He seems to regard Caesar as a great leader, worthy of respect and total obedience.*

C. Literary Element: FORESHADOWING Ask students how the members of Shakespeare's audience might have reacted to these lines. *(Possible response: The audience might have recognized these lines as a foreshadowing of his murder.)*

Scene 2 *A public place in Rome.*

As Caesar attends the traditional race at the festival of Lupercal, a soothsayer warns him to beware of the ides of March, or March 15. (The middle day of each month was called the ides.) When Caesar leaves, Cassius and Brutus speak. Cassius tries to turn Brutus against Caesar by using flattery, examples of Caesar's weaknesses, and sarcasm about Caesar's power. Caesar passes by again, expressing his distrust of Cassius. Cassius and Brutus learn of Caesar's rejection of a crown the people of Rome have offered him. They agree to meet again to discuss what must be done about Caesar.

[A flourish of trumpets announces the approach of Caesar. *A large crowd of* Commoners *has assembled; a* Soothsayer *is among them. Enter* Caesar, *his wife,* Calpurnia, Portia, Decius, Cicero, Brutus, Cassius, Casca, *and* Antony, *who is stripped for running in the games.]*

Caesar. Calpurnia.

Casca. Peace, ho! Caesar speaks.

Caesar. Calpurnia.

Calpurnia. Here, my lord.

Caesar. Stand you directly in Antonius' way
When he doth run his course. Antonius.

Antonius. Caesar, my lord?

A **Caesar.** Forget not in your speed, Antonius,
To touch Calpurnia; for our elders say
The barren, touched in this holy chase,
Shake off their sterile curse.

Antonius. I shall remember.
When Caesar says "Do this," it is performed.

Caesar. Set on, and leave no ceremony out.

[Flourish of trumpets. Caesar *starts to leave.]*

Soothsayer. Caesar!

Caesar. Ha! Who calls?

Casca. Bid every noise be still. Peace yet again!

Caesar. Who is it in the press that calls on me?
I hear a tongue shriller than all the music
Cry "Caesar!" Speak. Caesar is turned to hear.

C **Soothsayer.** Beware the ides of March.

5–11 ***Stand . . . curse:*** Antony ***(Antonius)*** is about to run in a race that is part of the Lupercal celebration. Caesar refers to the superstition that a ***sterile*** woman (one unable to bear children) can become fertile if touched by one of the racers.

12–13 ***I shall . . . performed:*** *What do these lines tell you about Antony's attitude toward Caesar?* B

15–17 Remember that the crowd is cheering constantly. The ***soothsayer*** (fortuneteller), who calls out Caesar's name can hardly be heard. Casca tells the crowd to quiet down.

18 ***press:*** crowd.

21 ***ides:*** the middle day of the month.

Professional Notebook

Students tend to read for plot. If they do not find it easily, they lose interest. I find it helpful to have them read the first two pages silently in class and then to ask some questions. The author may give a clue to character in italics. More can be learned by what the characters say about other characters soon to appear. The essence: can we guess what is to come from careful reading of these two pages? A one-page writing assignment is appropriate: "From the first twenty-five lines of dialogue, what can you surmise about one of the characters? What do you based your judgment on?"

John Sweet, *Notes on the Teaching of Drama*

Caesar. What man is that?

Brutus. A soothsayer bids you beware the ides of March.

Caesar. Set him before me; let me see his face.

Cassius. Fellow, come from the throng; look upon Caesar.

Caesar. What say'st thou to me now? Speak once again.

Soothsayer. Beware the ides of March.

Caesar. He is a dreamer; let us leave him. Pass.

[Trumpets sound. Exeunt all but Brutus *and* Cassius.*]*

Cassius. Will you go see the order of the course?

30–33 Cassius asks if Brutus is going to watch the race ***(the order of the course),*** but Brutus says he is not fond of sports ***(gamesome).***

"Beware the ides of March."

Photographs from the 1953 Metro Goldwyn-Mayer film version of *Julius Caesar*, starring Louis Calhern, Marlon Brando, and Deborah Kerr.

D. Literary Element: CHARACTERIZATION Have students explain what contrast Brutus draws between his own personality and that of Antony in these lines. *(Possible response: Brutus admits that he is not lively and fond of sports, like Antony.)*

E. LEP: Vocabulary Explain to students that this passage contains several familiar words that were used in Shakespeare's time with different meanings. For example, "passions" simply means "emotions"; "difference" here means "conflict"; "conceptions" means "ideas." The word "soil" implies a planting metaphor; the idea is that Brutus' melancholy behavior "takes root" from the conflicting emotions that are troubling him.

F. Literary Element: CONFLICT To what kind of conflict does Brutus explicitly refer in these lines? *(Possible response: He says he is suffering from internal conflict, "with himself at war.")*

G. Answer: *Cassius is trying to tell Brutus that Brutus himself should be the leader of Rome, rather than Caesar.*

H. Critical Thinking: ANALYZING Have students explain whether they think Cassius is flattering Brutus here in order to win him over to the opposition against Caesar. *(Possible response: Cassius may be flattering Brutus, whom he calls "noble.")*

Brutus. Not I.

Cassius. I pray you do.

D **Brutus.** I am not gamesome. I do lack some part
Of that quick spirit that is in Antony.
Let me not hinder, Cassius, your desires.
I'll leave you.

Cassius. Brutus, I do observe you now of late;
I have not from your eyes that gentleness
And show of love as I was wont to have.
You bear too stubborn and too strange a hand
Over your friend that loves you.

Brutus. Cassius,
Be not deceived. If I have veiled my look,
I turn the trouble of my countenance
Merely upon myself. Vexed I am
E Of late with passions of some difference,
Conceptions only proper to myself,
Which give some soil, perhaps, to my behaviors;
But let not therefore my good friends be grieved
(Among which number, Cassius, be you one)
Nor construe any further my neglect
F Than that poor Brutus, with himself at war,
Forgets the shows of love to other men.

Cassius. Then, Brutus, I have much mistook your passion,
By means whereof this breast of mine hath buried
Thoughts of great value, worthy cogitations.
Tell me, good Brutus, can you see your face?

Brutus. No, Cassius, for the eye sees not itself
But by reflection, by some other things.

Cassius. 'Tis just.
And it is very much lamented, Brutus,
That you have no such mirrors as will turn
Your hidden worthiness into your eye,
That you might see your shadow. I have heard
H Where many of the best respect in Rome
(Except immortal Caesar), speaking of Brutus
And groaning underneath this age's yoke,
Have wished that noble Brutus had his eyes.

Brutus. Into what dangers would you lead me, Cassius,
That you would have me seek into myself
For that which is not in me?

37–39 *I do observe . . . to have:* Lately I haven't seen the friendliness in your face that I used to see ***(was wont to have).*** *Can you sometimes look into a friend's eyes and tell how he or she is feeling?*

44–53 *I turn . . . other men:* I have been frowning at myself, not at you. I have been troubled ***(Vexed)*** lately by mixed emotions ***(passions of some difference).*** They are personal matters that are, perhaps, marring my good manners. I hope my friends won't interpret ***(construe)*** my actions as anything more than my own private concerns. *Do you ever avoid your friends when you have a lot on your mind?*

54–57 *I have . . . cogitations:* I have misunderstood your feelings. As a result, I have kept certain thoughts to myself.

62–69 *it is . . . eyes:* It is too bad you don't have a mirror that would show you your inner qualities ***(hidden worthiness).*** In fact, many respected citizens suffering under Caesar's rule ***(this age's yoke)*** have wished that Brutus could see how much better he is than Caesar. *What is Cassius trying to tell Brutus?* G

Cassius. Therefore, good Brutus, be prepared to hear;
And since you know you cannot see yourself
I So well as by reflection, I, your glass,
Will modestly discover to yourself
That of yourself which you yet know not of.
And be not jealous on me, gentle Brutus.
Were I a common laugher, or did use
To stale with ordinary oaths my love
To every new protester; if you know
That I do fawn on men and hug them hard,
J And after scandal them; or if you know
That I profess myself in banqueting
To all the rout, then hold me dangerous.

[Flourish and shout.]

Brutus. What means this shouting? I do fear the people
Choose Caesar for their king.

K **Cassius.** Ay, do you fear it?
Then must I think you would not have it so.

Brutus. I would not, Cassius, yet I love him well.
But wherefore do you hold me here so long?
What is it that you would impart to me?
If it be aught toward the general good,
Set honor in one eye and death i' the other,
L And I will look on both indifferently;
For let the gods so speed me as I love
The name of honor more than I fear death.

Cassius. I know that virtue to be in you, Brutus,
As well as I do know your outward favor.
Well, honor is the subject of my story.
I cannot tell what you and other men
Think of this life, but for my single self,
I had as lief not be as live to be
In awe of such a thing as I myself.
I was born free as Caesar, so were you;
We both have fed as well, and we can both
Endure the winter's cold as well as he.
For once, upon a raw and gusty day,
The troubled Tiber chafing with her shores,
Caesar said to me, "Dar'st thou, Cassius, now
Leap in with me into this angry flood
And swim to yonder point?" Upon the word,
Accoutered as I was, I plunged in
And bade him follow. So indeed he did.

73–77 *Therefore . . . not of:* Listen, Brutus, since you cannot see yourself, I will be your mirror ***(glass)*** and show you what you truly are.

78 *jealous on me:* suspicious of me.

79–85 *Were I . . . dangerous:* If you think I am a fool ***(common laugher)*** or someone who pretends to be the friend of everyone I meet; or if you believe that I show friendship and then talk evil about my friends ***(scandal them)*** behind their backs, or that I try to win the affections of the common people ***(all the rout),*** then consider me dangerous and don't trust me.

88–89 *do you . . . it so:* Imagine Cassius blurting out this line, maybe a little more eagerly than he had intended. He is trying to find a meaning in Brutus' words that may or may not be there.

93–95 *If it . . . indifferently:* If what you have in mind concerns the good of Rome ***(the general good),*** I would face either honor or death to do what must be done.

99 *outward favor:* physical appearance.

103–104 *I had . . . I myself:* I would rather not live, than to live in awe of someone no better than I am.

109 *troubled . . . shores:* The Tiber River was rising in the middle of a storm.

113 *Accoutered:* dressed.

I. Literary Element: FIGURATIVE LANGUAGE Have students explain what is being compared in Cassius' metaphor. *(Possible response: Cassius compares himself to a mirror that will reveal Brutus' true self.)*

J. Literary Element: THEME Ask students how Cassius attempts to prove in this passage that he is a true friend. *(Possible response: He says that he must be a true friend, since he does not fawn on people and then slander them behind their backs, nor does he curry favor with the mob.)* Do students think that these arguments really "prove" that Cassius is a true friend? *(Possible response: The proofs may not be sufficient, since there are many other ways that friendship could be false.)*

K. Cultural Sidelight The seventh and last Roman king, Tarquin the Proud, was driven out of the city in 509 B.C. and a republic was established. During the nearly five centuries of the republic, down to the time of Julius Caesar, the Romans had a deep-seated horror of kingship as an institution. They equated the word "king" with the idea of tyranny.

L. Literary Element: CHARACTERIZATION Ask students to explain what this passage implies about Brutus' most important value in life. *(Possible response: His most important value is "honor.")*

M. Literary Element: ALLUSION Make sure students can follow this allusion to the story of Aeneas carrying his aged father Anchises out of the burning city of Troy after the Greeks had conquered it. Then ask students what point Cassius is making with this comparison. *(Possible response: He is painting Caesar as old and sick, while he himself is young and heroic.)*

N. LEP: Irony Have students identify Cassius' intention in referring to Caesar as a god here. Point out the contrast between the image of a powerful god and that of a weak man who "did shake" from fever.

"I do fear the people choose Caesar for their king."

The torrent roared, and we did buffet it
With lusty sinews, throwing it aside
And stemming it with hearts of controversy.
But ere we could arrive the point proposed,
Caesar cried, "Help me, Cassius, or I sink!"
I, as Aeneas, our great ancestor,
M Did from the flames of Troy upon his shoulder
The old Anchises bear, so from the waves of Tiber
Did I the tired Caesar. And this man
Is now become a god, and Cassius is
A wretched creature and must bend his body
If Caesar carelessly but nod on him.
He had a fever when he was in Spain,
And when the fit was on him, I did mark
N How he did shake. 'Tis true, this god did shake.
His coward lips did from their color fly,
And that same eye whose bend doth awe the world
Did lose his luster. I did hear him groan.
Ay, and that tongue of his that bade the Romans
Mark him and write his speeches in their books,

115–117 *we did . . . controversy:* We fought the tide with strong muscles ***(lusty sinews),*** conquering it with our spirit of competition ***(hearts of controversy).***

118 *ere:* before.

120–123 *I, as Aeneas . . . Caesar:* Aeneas (in nē′ əs), the mythological founder of Rome, carried his father, Anchises (an kī′ sēz), out of the burning city of Troy. Cassius says he did the same for Caesar when Caesar could no longer swim in the raging river.

125 *bend his body:* bow.

130 *His coward . . . fly:* His lips turned pale.

131 *bend:* glance.

Alas, it cried, "Give me some drink, Titinius,"
As a sick girl! Ye gods! it doth amaze me
A man of such a feeble temper should
So get the start of the majestic world
And bear the palm alone.

[Shout. Flourish.]

Brutus. Another general shout?
I do believe that these applauses are
For some new honors that are heaped on Caesar.

Cassius. Why, man, he doth bestride the narrow world
Like a Colossus, and we petty men
Walk under his huge legs and peep about
To find ourselves dishonorable graves.
Men at some time are masters of their fates.
The fault, dear Brutus, is not in our stars,
But in ourselves, that we are underlings.
"Brutus," and "Caesar." What should be in that "Caesar?"
Why should that name be sounded more than yours?
Write them together: yours is as fair a name.
Sound them, it doth become the mouth as well.
Weigh them, it is as heavy. Conjure with 'em:
"Brutus" will start a spirit as soon as "Caesar."
Now in the names of all the gods at once,
Upon what meat doth this our Caesar feed
That he is grown so great? Age, thou are shamed!
Rome, thou hast lost the breed of noble bloods!
When went there by an age since the great Flood
But it was famed with more than with one man?
When could they say (till now) that talked of Rome
That her wide walls encompassed but one man?
Now is it Rome indeed, and room enough,
When there is in it but one only man!
O, you and I have heard our fathers say
There was a Brutus once that would have brooked
The eternal devil to keep his state in Rome
As easily as a king.

Brutus. That you do love me I am nothing jealous.
What you would work me to, I have some aim.
How I have thought of this, and of these times,
I shall recount hereafter. For this present,

133–139 *that tongue . . . alone:* The same tongue that has led Romans to memorize his speeches cried out in the tone of a sick girl. I'm amazed that such a weak man should get ahead of the rest of the world and appear as the victor ***(bear the palm)*** all by himself. (A palm leaf was a symbol of victory in war.)

140–142 *Another . . . on Caesar:* The shouts of the crowd are coming from offstage. Brutus is troubled by this cheering for Caesar, worried about where it might lead.

143–145 *he doth . . . Colossus:* Cassius compares Caesar to Colossus, the huge statue of the Greek god Apollo at Rhodes. The statue supposedly spanned the entrance to the harbor and was so high that ships could sail through the space between its legs. *What is Cassius' tone in these lines?*

149–150 *The fault . . . underlings:* It is not the stars that have determined our fate; we are inferiors through our own fault.

156 *Conjure:* call up spirits.

160 *Age . . . shamed:* It is a shameful time ***(Age)*** in which to be living.

169–171 *There was . . . a king:* Cassius is referring to an ancestor of Brutus who drove invading kings from Rome.

172 *am nothing jealous:* am sure.

173 *have some aim:* can guess.

174–177 *How I have . . . moved:* I will tell you later ***(recount hereafter)***

O. Answer: *Cassius' tone is bitter and envious.*

P. LEP: Vocabulary Have students use context clues in this passage to determine the meaning of "sound" ("pronounce") and "doth become" ("is fitting for") in this line.

Q. Historical Sidelight In Shakespear's time, the word "room" was pronounced the same way as the word "Rome." However, the vowel sound in both was pronounced more like the vowel sound in *thought* and not the long *o* sound we use today for *Rome.* Cassius is playing on the sound of the words to make a sarcastic pun.

R. Reading Skill: INFERRING Ask students to explain what inferences might be drawn about Brutus' character from this passage. *(Possible response: Brutus' swift acceptance of Cassius' profession of friendship may indicate that he is naive. His apparently nervous refusal to discuss the matter further now may indicate that he is cautious or indecisive.)*

S. Answer: *Brutus hints that he basically agrees with Cassius' description of the "hard conditions" in Rome. By saying that he would "rather be a villager" than live in Rome, he hints that he might be prepared to take action against Caesar.*

T. Literary Element: IRONY Have students explain why Cassius' words here might be intended as ironic. *(Possible responses: He describes his previous words as "weak," whereas in fact he has passionately argued his case. He refers to Brutus' reactions as "but thus much show of fire," that is, he acts as though Brutus' response has been passionate, whereas in fact Brutus has put him off by saying he will not fully discuss the subject until later.)*

U. Literary Element: SOUND EFFECTS Have students identify the use of alliteration and consonance in this passage. *(Possible response: alliteration and consonance are evident in the repeated hard "c" sound of "Calpurnia's cheek," the repeated soft "c" and "s" sounds in "Cicero looks with such . . . and such," the repeated "f" sounds in "ferret and . . . fiery," and the repeated hard "c" sounds in "Capitol . . . crossed in conference.")*

V. Literary Element: CHARACTERIZATION Have students explain how this passage characterizes Caesar, Antony, and Cassius at the same time. *(Possible response: Caesar's words show that he is a shrewd judge of character, while Antony's judgment shows that he is not very perceptive. Cassius is characterized by Caesar as "hungry" and "dangerous." Caesar's second speech also reveals that he is extremely self-confident, perhaps even boastful.)*

W. Answer: *He boasts that he is not afraid.*

I would not (so with love I might entreat you)
Be any further moved. What you have said
I will consider; what you have to say
I will with patience hear, and find a time
Both meet to hear and answer such high things.
Till then, my noble friend, chew upon this:
Brutus had rather be a villager
Than to repute himself a son of Rome
Under these hard conditions as this time
Is like to lay upon us.

Cassius. I am glad
That my weak words have struck but thus much show
Of fire from Brutus.

[Voices and Music are heard approaching.]

Brutus. The games are done, and Caesar is returning.

Cassius. As they pass by, pluck Casca by the sleeve,
And he will (after his sour fashion) tell you
What hath proceeded worthy note today.

[Reenter Caesar *and his train of followers.]*

Brutus. I will do so. But look you, Cassius!
The angry spot doth glow on Caesar's brow,
And all the rest look like a chidden train.
Calpurnia's cheek is pale, and Cicero
Looks with such ferret and such fiery eyes
As we have seen him in the Capitol,
Being crossed in conference by some senators.

Cassius. Casca will tell us what the matter is.

*[*Caesar *looks at* Cassius *and turns to* Antony.*]*

Caesar. Antonius.

Antonius. Caesar?

Caesar. Let me have men about me that are fat,
Sleek-headed men, and such as sleep o' nights.
Yond Cassius has a lean and hungry look;
He thinks too much, such men are dangerous.

Antonius. Fear him not, Caesar, he's not dangerous.
He is a noble Roman, and well given.

Caesar. Would he were fatter! But I fear him not.
Yet if my name were liable to fear,

my thoughts about this topic. For now, I ask you as a friend not to try to convince me further.

180 ***meet:*** appropriate.

183 ***repute himself:*** present himself as.

185 *What do you think Brutus might be prepared to do?*

190 The private conversation is now over. Caesar and his admirers return, with the crowd following close behind.

193 ***worthy note:*** worth remembering.

196 ***chidden train:*** a group of followers who have been scolded.

197–200 ***Cicero . . . senators:*** Cicero was a highly respected senator. Brutus says he has the angry look of a ***ferret*** (a fierce little animal), the look he gets when other senators disagree with him at the Capitol.

202–226 Brutus and Cassius take Casca aside. The conversation Caesar has with Antony is not heard by any of the other characters around them.

209 ***well given:*** Antony says that Cassius, despite his appearance, is a supporter of Caesar.

PROFESSIONAL NOTEBOOK

One of the persistent problems in teaching Shakespeare in high school is that students too frequently perceive this subject as being "high-brow" or "intellectual". . . .

This rather forbidding image of Shakespeare may be at least partly the result of high school teachers having typically taught this subject from the point of view of the gentlemen's boxes, *as if the Elizabethan theater had been patronized entirely by intellectual, literary, and* suppressed *audiences.*

Yet there is little doubt that both the writing and the presenting of the plays were very much affected by those ever-present habitués of the theater—the groundlings. Noisy, garrulous, unkempt, chewing on bits of food, rolling dice—the groundlings were far different from the polite, restrained, seated audiences of today's theater. . . .

. . . I decided to try giving students the opportunity to interact *with the play and the*

Continued on page 743

I do not know the man I should avoid
So soon as that spare Cassius. He reads much,
He is a great observer, and he looks
Quite through the deeds of men. He loves no plays
As thou dost, Antony; he hears no music.
Seldom he smiles, and smiles in such a sort
As if he mocked himself and scorned his spirit
That could be moved to smile at anything.
Y Such men as he be never at heart's ease
Whiles they behold a greater than themselves,
And therefore are they very dangerous.
I rather tell thee what is to be feared
Than what I fear, for always I am Caesar.
Come on my right hand, for this ear is deaf,
And tell me truly what thou think'st of him.

[Trumpets sound. Exeunt Caesar *and all his train except* Casca, *who stays behind.]*

Casca. You pulled me by the cloak. Would you speak with me?

Brutus. Ay, Casca. Tell us what hath chanced today
That Caesar looks so sad.

Casca. Why, you were with him, were you not?

Brutus. I should not then ask Casca what had chanced.

AA **Casca.** Why, there was a crown offered him; and being offered him, he put it by with the back of his hand, thus. And then the people fell a-shouting.

Brutus. What was the second noise for?

Casca. Why, for that too.

Cassius. They shouted thrice. What was the last cry for?

Casca. Why, for that too.

Brutus. Was the crown offered him thrice?

BB **Casca.** Ay, marry, was't! and he put it by thrice, every time gentler than other; and at every putting-by mine honest neighbors shouted.

Cassius. Who offered him the crown?

Casca. Why, Antony.

212–215 ***I do not . . . of men:*** Caesar labels Cassius dangerous and, at the same time, one who can see through people and understand their secrets. Caesar makes a boast about himself. *What does he boast of?*

222 *What is Caesar's opinion of Cassius? Why does he feel this way?* X

225 *What does Caesar reveal about himself in this line?* Z

227 Now only Brutus, Cassius, and Casca remain on stage.

229 ***hath chanced:*** has happened.

235 ***put it by:*** pushed it aside.

243 ***Ay, marry, was't:*** Yes, indeed, it was. *Marry* was a mild oath used in Shakespeare's time (but not in ancient Rome). The word means "by the Virgin Mary."

X. Answer: Caesar believes that Cassius is a bitter, mocking person with no ability to enjoy life. *Caesar thinks Cassius is dangerous because Cassius will never be content as long as he beholds a greater man than himself.*

Y. Literary Element: THEME According to Caesar here, what vice tends to corrupt friendship and social stability? *(Possible response: envy of other people's superior talents or abilities)*

Z. Answer: *Caesar reveals that he is deaf in one ear.*

AA. LEP: Vocabulary Ask students to pantomime the events described here, showing that they understand the meaning of "put it by" ("waved it away") and "fell a-shouting" ("began to shout").

BB. Reading Skill: INFERRING Ask students what inference they can draw from the fact that it was Antony who offered Caesar the crown. *(Possible response: Antony is loyal to Caesar, perhaps to the extent of idolizing him.)* Then ask what Brutus' request for information implies about his reactions. *(Possible response: He is greatly disturbed.)*

PROFESSIONAL NOTEBOOK

Continued from page 743

players, much as the groundlings did in the Globe Theater of the 1600's. This was accomplished by having them play the role of the groundlings during the introductory phase of the unit. I focused this opening on the spectacle and antics of the groundlings, rather than on the play itself. By this means, I hoped to get students to begin perceiving Shakespeare differently.

. . . I tried to describe the scene by appealing to the senses of smell, taste, sound, and sight. The purpose of this earthy approach was to develop an attitude toward Shakespeare that would motivate students to identify with the groundlings and thus become emotionally involved in the subject.

RICHARD J. MUELLER, *A Groundling's Approach to Shakespeare*

CC. Critical Thinking: SEPARATING FACT AND OPINION Have students explain how Casca combines objective facts with his own opinions in this passage. *(Possible response: Casca describes objectively how Antony repeatedly offered a coronet to Caesar and how Caesar rejected it. Casca also adds his own opinion that Caesar really wanted to accept the coronet.)*

DD. Literary Element: DIALOGUE Have students note that Casca's speeches in this scene are in prose, whereas Cassius and Brutus speak in verse. Why might Shakespeare have organized the dialogue this way? *(Possible response: Prose in Shakespeare's drama was used primarily for humorous or satirical scenes involving "low" characters; verse was used for loftier characters and themes. Prose is thus appropriate for Casca's mocking description of the mob, and for Casca's down-to-earth character.)*

EE. Reading Skill: COMPARE AND CONTRAST Have students comment on the similarities they note between Casca and Cassius. *(Possible response: Both characters are opposed to Caesar; they both hold low opinions of the Roman mob; they are both skilled in ironic, mocking speech.)*

FF. Critical Thinking: ANALYZING Ask why students think Caesar offered to commit suicide to the crowd. *(Possible response: to curry favor with the mob, to dramatize his devotion to the common people)* Ask students what they believe was the cause for Caesar's epileptic incident. *(Possible response: The cause may have been Caesar's disappointment or anguish that the crowd became joyful when he rejected the coronet.)*

Brutus. Tell us the manner of it, gentle Casca.

Casca. I can as well be hanged as tell the manner of it. It was mere foolery; I did not mark it. I saw Mark Antony offer him a crown—yet 'twas not a crown neither, 'twas one of these coronets—and, as I told you, he put it by once. But for all that, to my thinking, he would fain have had it. Then he offered it to him again; then he put it by again; but to my thinking, he was very loath to lay his fingers off it. And then he offered it the third time. He put it the third time by; and still as he refused it, the rabblement hooted, and clapped their chapped hands, and threw up their sweaty nightcaps, and uttered such a deal of stinking breath because Caesar refused the crown that it had, almost, choked Caesar; for he swounded and fell down at it. And for mine own part, I durst not laugh, for fear of opening my lips and receiving the bad air.

Cassius. But soft, I pray you. What, did Caesar swound?

Casca. He fell down in the market place and foamed at mouth and was speechless.

Brutus. 'Tis very like. He hath the falling sickness.

Cassius. No, Caesar hath not it; but you, and I, and honest Casca, we have the falling sickness.

Casca. I know not what you mean by that, but I am sure Caesar fell down. If the tag-rag people did not clap him and hiss him, according as he pleased and displeased them, as they use to do the players in the theater, I am no true man.

Brutus. What said he when he came unto himself?

Casca. Marry, before he fell down, when he perceived the common herd was glad he refused the crown, he plucked me ope his doublet and offered them his throat to cut. An I had been a man of any occupation, if I would not have taken him at a word I would I might go to hell among the rogues. And so he fell. When he came to himself again, he said, if he had done or said anything amiss, he desired their worships to think it was his infirmity. Three or four wenches where I stood cried, "Alas, good soul!" and

252 ***coronets:*** small crowns made out of laurel branches twisted together. A coronet was less of an honor than the kind of crown a king would wear.

254 ***fain:*** gladly.

256 ***loath:*** reluctant.

258–259 ***rabblement:*** unruly crowd.

263 ***swounded:*** fainted.

266 ***soft:*** Wait a moment.

268–270 There is some historical evidence that Caesar had epilepsy. In Shakespeare's time, this illness was known as the falling sickness (because someone having an epileptic seizure is likely to fall to the floor).

272 Cassius sarcastically uses the phrase ***falling sickness*** to refer to the tendency to bow down before Caesar.

281 ***ope his doublet:*** open his jacket.

282–284 ***An . . . rogues:*** If ***(An)*** I had been a worker with a proper tool, may I go to hell with the sinners ***(rogues)*** if I would not have done as he asked ***(taken him at a word).***

286 ***amiss:*** wrong.

287 ***infirmity:*** sickness.

288 ***wenches:*** common women.

DATA BANK

Shakespeare's principal source for *Julius Caesar* was the *Lives of the Noble Greeks and Romans* by the ancient historian Plutarch. Plutarch wrote in Greek, however, and Shakespeare probably read his *Life of Caesar, Life of Brutus,* and *Life of Antonius* in a translation into Elizabethan English by Sir Thomas North, published in 1579. Here is Plutarch's account of Caesar's distrust of lean men:

"Caesar also had Cassius in great jealousy, and suspected him much: whereupon he said on a time to his friends, 'what will Cassius do, think ye? I like not his pale looks.' Another time when Caesar's friends complained . . . he answered them again, 'As for those fat men and smooth-combed heads . . . I never reckon of them; but these pale-visaged and carrion-lean people, I fear them most,' meaning Brutus and Cassius." *(Life of Caesar)*

GG forgave him with all their hearts. But there's no heed to be taken of them. If Caesar had stabbed their mothers, they would have done no less.

Brutus. And after that, he came thus sad away?

Casca. Ay.

Cassius. Did Cicero say anything?

HH **Casca.** Ay, he spoke Greek.

Cassius. To what effect?

Casca. Nay, an I tell you that, I'll ne'er look you i' the face again. But those that understood him smiled at one another and shook their heads; but for mine own part, it was Greek to me. I could tell you more news, too. Marullus and Flavius, for pulling scarfs off Caesar's images, are put to silence. Fare you well. There was more foolery yet, if I could remember it.

Cassius. Will you sup with me tonight, Casca?

Casca. No, I am promised forth.

Cassius. Will you dine with me tomorrow?

II **Casca.** Ay, if I be alive, and your mind hold, and your dinner worth eating.

Cassius. Good. I will expect you.

Casca. Do so. Farewell both.

[Exit.]

Brutus. What a blunt fellow is this grown to be!
He was quick mettle when he went to school.

Cassius. So is he now in execution
Of any bold or noble enterprise,
However he puts on this tardy form.
This rudeness is a sauce to his good wit,
Which gives men stomach to digest his words
With better appetite.

Brutus. And so it is. For this time I will leave you.
Tomorrow, if you please to speak with me,
I will come home to you; or if you will,
Come home to me, and I will wait for you.

Cassius. I will do so. Till then, think of the world.

[Exit Brutus.*]*

302 *put to silence:* This may mean that the two tribunes have been put to death or that they have been barred from public life.

305 *I am promised forth:* I have another appointment.

312 *quick mettle:* clever, intelligent.

313–318 *So is . . . appetite:* Cassius says that Casca can still be intelligent in carrying out an important project. He only pretends to be slow ***(tardy).*** His rude manner makes people more willing to accept ***(disgest)*** the things he says.

GG. Literary Element: THEME Have students discuss what this passage implies about the Roman people's political judgment. *(Possible response: The people are blind and irrational: Caesar is now so popular with them that he could stab their mothers and they would still hail him as a hero.)*

HH. Cultural Sidelight Many upper-class, educated Romans in Caesar's time spoke Greek as fluently as Latin. Greek was considered the international language of elite "culture," much as French was regarded in the nineteenth and early twentieth century. Here it is possible that Cicero spoke Greek so that the common people nearby would not understand him.

II. LEP: Irony Explain to students that by the phrase "if your mind hold" Casca does not mean that Cassius may shortly go insane; he means, rather, "if your intention is still the same"—namely, if the invitation is still good. Help students see the cynical, ironic way in which Casca replies; refusing to commit himself to a definite *yes,* he must point out possible failings in Cassius' hospitality.

Real Life Connections

In recalling for Brutus and Cassius the scene in the marketplace, Casca emphasizes the absolute devotion the commoners hold for Caesar by saying that they would have forgiven him even if he had stabbed their mothers. Have students compare situations in modern times in which leaders have gained such power over people that, no matter what the circumstance, the devotion is complete. Encourage students to explore topics such as:

- What makes people become so devoted that they suspend their judgment and sense of reason?
- Have the rewards of such devotion usually been positive or negative for the leader? For the people? In what ways?
- In the future, will there be other leaders who are able to gain such power and devotion? Why or why not?

JJ. Literary Element: THEME Ask students what Cassius' cynical words imply about the ways that even "noble" people can make errors in judgment. *(Possible response: Cassius reflects that, with sufficient persuasion, even good and noble men can be "wrought" or fashioned to steer another course.)*

KK. Literary Element: THEME Ask students to explain whether these words show that Cassius is conscious of being a false friend to Brutus. *(Possible response: By envisioning a reversal of roles, Cassius seems to show that he knows how he has tricked Brutus; Cassius may believe that tricking Brutus is being his true friend, since he believes in the conspiracy.)*

LL. Literary Sidelight This short speech of Cassius on stage alone is an example of a Shakespearean *soliloquy* (see page 752), in which a character reviews his or her private thoughts or feelings. Other soliloquies in *Julius Caesar* occur at the beginning of Act II (Brutus) and toward the end of Act III, Scene 1 (Antony). The rhyming *couplet* (two lines) at the end of Cassius' speech was a device Shakespeare often used to signal the end of a scene.

Student Response

Responding to Reading

These questions are open-ended with no "right" or "wrong" answers. However, responses must be supported with information from the selection. Possible answers follow:

1. Cassius' purpose is to persuade Brutus that Caesar has grown too powerful and has become a dictator who should be deposed. To convince Brutus that Caesar is a mere mortal, Cassius tells him the stories about Caesar almost drowning in the Tiber and almost dying from a fever in Spain. Cassius also implies that Brutus himself would be a respected leader.

JJ Well, Brutus, thou art noble; yet I see
Thy honorable mettle may be wrought
From that it is disposed. Therefore it is meet
That noble minds keep ever with their likes;
For who so firm that cannot be seduced?
KK Caesar doth bear me hard, but he loves Brutus.
If I were Brutus now and he were Cassius,
He should not humor me. I will this night,
In several hands, in at his windows throw,
As if they came from several citizens,
Writing, all tending to the great opinion
That Rome holds of his name; wherein obscurely
Caesar's ambition shall be glanced at.
LL And after this let Caesar seat him sure,
For we will shake him, or worse days endure.
[Exit.]

324–338 Now Cassius is alone on stage. The thoughts he expresses in this speech are thoughts he would not want Brutus to know about.

325–326 *Thy . . . disposed:* Your honorable nature can be manipulated ***(wrought)*** into something not quite so honorable.

329 *bear me hard:* hold a grudge against me.

331 *He should . . . me:* I wouldn't let him get away with fooling me.

331–335 *I will . . . his name:* Cassius plans to leave messages at Brutus' home that appear to be from several people.

338 *we will . . . endure:* We will remove Caesar from his high position or suffer the consequences.

Responding to Reading

1. What is Cassius' purpose in talking to Brutus about Caesar? Give examples to support your opinion.

2. Briefly describe the personalities of Brutus and Cassius. Find lines in the scene to support each of your descriptions.

3. What is your impression of Caesar? Explain.

Think about

- his actions and what he says about himself and others
- what others say about him

4. On the Explore pages, you thought about stories you knew that dealt with the hunger for power. So far in this play, which character seems the most hungry for power? Explain and give examples.

Scene 3 *A street in Rome.*

It is the night of March 14. Amid violent thunder and lightning, a terrified Casca fears that the storm and other omens predict terrible events to come. Cassius interprets the storm as a sign that Caesar must be overthrown. Cassius and Casca agree that Caesar's rise to power must be stopped by any means. Cinna, another plotter, enters, and they discuss how to persuade Brutus to follow their plan.

2. Possible response: Brutus is meditative (lines 42–48), devoted to honor (lines 94–97), and patriotic (lines 181–185). Cassius is proud (lines 101–104), envious (lines 133–139), sarcastic (lines 271–272), and manipulative (lines 324–338).

3. Possible response: Caesar is proud and confident, perhaps even imperious. He says he fears no one. From Casca's account of Caesar's actions, Caesar seems to curry the people's favor. Although the people treat him as a hero, Caesar has a number of physical infirmities, including deafness and epilepsy. Caesar is the kind of leader who inspires strong reactions of love and hate. Men like Antony are devoted to him; others, such as Casca and Cassius, hold him in contempt. Caesar shows that he is very intelligent when he sums up Cassius' personality traits.

4. Possible responses: Cassius seems the most hungry for power, as illustrated by his numerous sarcastic references to Caesar's unworthiness to lead Rome; Caesar seems the most hungry for power, as illustrated by his possible desire to accept the coronet and his fear of Cassius' threat to his power.

[Thunder and lightning. Enter, from opposite sides, Casca, *with his sword drawn, and* Cicero.*]*

Cicero. Good even, Casca. Brought you Caesar home?
Why are you breathless? and why stare you so?

Casca. Are not you moved when all the sway of earth
Shakes like a thing unfirm? O Cicero,
I have seen tempests when the scolding winds
Have rived the knotty oaks, and I have seen
The ambitious ocean swell and rage and foam
To be exalted with the threat'ning clouds;
But never till tonight, never till now,
Did I go through a tempest dropping fire.
A Either there is a civil strife in heaven,
Or else the world, too saucy with the gods,
Incenses them to send destruction.

Cicero. Why, saw you anything more wonderful?

Casca. A common slave—you know him well by sight—
Held up his left hand, which did flame and burn
Like twenty torches joined; and yet his hand,
Not sensible of fire, remained unscorched.
Besides—I ha' not since put up my sword—
Against the Capitol I met a lion,
B Who glared upon me, and went surly by
Without annoying me. And there were drawn
Upon a heap a hundred ghastly women,
Transformed with their fear, who swore they saw
Men, all in fire, walk up and down the streets.
And yesterday the bird of night did sit
Even at noonday upon the market place,
Hooting and shrieking. When these prodigies
Do so conjointly meet, let not men say,
"These are their reasons, they are natural,"
C For I believe they are portentous things
Unto the climate that they point upon.

Cicero. Indeed it is a strange-disposed time.
But men may construe things after their fashion,
Clean from the purpose of the things themselves.
Comes Caesar to the Capitol tomorrow?

Casca. He doth, for he did bid Antonius
Send word to you he would be there tomorrow.

3 *sway of earth:* the natural order of things.

5 *tempests:* storms.

6 *rived:* torn.

8 *To be exalted with:* to raise themselves to the level of.

11–13 *Either . . . destruction:* Such a terrible storm could be caused by only two things—a civil war ***(strife)*** in heaven or angry gods destroying the world.

14 *saw . . . wonderful:* Did you see anything else that was strange?

19 *Not sensible of fire:* not feeling the fire.

20–21 *I ha' not . . . lion:* I haven't put my sword back into its scabbard since I saw a lion at the Capitol building.

23 *drawn / Upon:* huddled together.

27 *bird of night:* the owl, usually seen only at night.

29–33 *When these . . . upon:* When strange events ***(prodigies)*** like these happen at the same time ***(conjointly meet),*** no one should say there are natural explanations for them. I believe they are bad omens ***(portentous things)*** for the place where they happen.

34–36 *Indeed . . . themselves:* Cicero does not accept Casca's superstitious explanation of events. He agrees that the times are strange. But he says people can interpret events the way they want to, no matter what actually causes the events.

Text Annotations

A. Literary Element: SETTING Ask students to explain how the setting of this scene is appropriate to the atmosphere, or mood, of the play at this point. *(Possible response: The violence of the storm corresponds with the potentially violent conflicts in the Roman state, as first the tribunes and then Cassius try to stir up opposition to Caesar.)*

B. LEP: Mood Remind students who are challenged by the word "surly" ("ill-tempered") that they can use the context clue provided by "glared" in the same line to guess at the meaning. In Elizabethan times, the word "annoying" had a stronger meaning than it does now; in this context, it means "physically harming." Encourage students to see how these strong words create a mood of foreboding and danger.

C. Cultural Sidelight In both ancient Rome and Elizabethan England, portents, omens and "prodigies" were taken seriously by many people as signs of future events.

D. Answer: *Cassius might do this to show that he does not fear any danger.*

E. Literary Element: CHARACTERIZATION Ask students what Cassius' words and behavior in this passage reveal about his personality. *(Possible response: Cassius is ready to take dangerous risk; his evidently exaggerated pleasure in the storm also hints that he has a flare for the melodramatic.)*

F. Critical Thinking: ANALYZING Have students compare these lines with Cassius' assessment of Casca's character to Brutus in Act I, Scene 2, lines 313–318. Ask whether these passages are consistent. *(Possible response: The passages are inconsistent, since Cassius had earlier praised Casca as ready to undertake any "bold" and noble" enterprise; now he reproaches Casca for "dullness.")* Ask students what might be the explanation for any inconsistency. *(Possible response: Cassius was earlier trying to hint to Brutus that Casca would join the opposition to Caesar; now, however, he is trying to persuade Casca to do so.)*

G. Critical Thinking: EVALUATING Ask how skillful Cassius is in his persuasion of Casca here. Have students evaluate Cassius' argument. *(Possible response: Cassius is quite skillful, since he plays on Casca's superstitious nature by seeming to agree that the portents are significant; he tries to persuade him, however, that the omens really mean that Caesar must be overthrown.)*

Cicero. Good night then, Casca. This disturbed sky
Is not to walk in.

Casca. Farewell, Cicero.

[Exit Cicero.*]*

[Enter Cassius.*]*

Cassius. Who's there?

Casca. A Roman.

Cassius. Casca, by your voice.

Casca. Your ear is good. Cassius, what night is this!

Cassius. A very pleasing night to honest men.

Casca. Who ever knew the heavens menace so?

Cassius. Those that have known the earth so full of faults.
For my part, I have walked about the streets,
Submitting me unto the perilous night,
And, thus unbraced, Casca, as you see,
Have bared my bosom to the thunder-stone;
And when the cross blue lightning seemed to open
The breast of heaven, I did present myself
Even in the aim and very flash of it.

Casca. But wherefore did you so much tempt the heavens?
It is the part of men to fear and tremble
When the most mighty gods by tokens send
Such dreadful heralds to astonish us.

Cassius. You are dull, Casca, and those sparks of life
That should be in a Roman you do want,
Or else you use not. You look pale, and gaze,
And put on fear, and cast yourself in wonder,
To see the strange impatience of the heavens.
But if you would consider the true cause
Why all these fires, who all these gliding ghosts,
Why birds and beasts, from quality and kind;
Why old men fool and children calculate;
Why all these things change from their ordinance,
Their natures, and preformed faculties,
To monstrous quality, why, you shall find
That heaven hath infused them with these spirits
To make them instruments of fear and warning
Unto some monstrous state.

43 *Who's there:* Cassius probably has his sword out. Remember, with no light other than moonlight, it could be dangerous to come upon a stranger in the street.

51–57 *For my . . . flash of it:* Cassius brags that he offered himself to the dangerous night, with his coat open ***(unbraced),*** exposing his chest to the thunder and lightning. *Why might he do this?*

60–62 *It is . . . astonish us:* Men are supposed to tremble when the gods use signs ***(tokens)*** to send frightening messengers ***(heralds)*** to scare us.

64 *want:* lack.

68–77 Cassius insists that heaven has brought about such things as birds and animals that change their natures ***(from quality and kind),*** children who predict the future ***(calculate);*** all these beings that act unnaturally ***(change from their ordinance / Their natures, and preformed faculties).*** Heaven has done all this, he says, to warn the Romans of an evil condition that they should correct.

PROFESSIONAL NOTEBOOK

Students should surely be given opportunity to read passages aloud and perform sections, but not to the endless boredom of other class members or to the desecration of the given text. Perhaps too much classroom time is presently given over to indiscriminate or unprepared student readings. Students might be better assigned to prepare "key scenes" from contemporary plays and work up gradually to the Shakespearean scenes, which can be best illuminated at first by professional actors on record or film or by the teacher. . . .

GLADYS VEIDEMANIS, *Shakespeare in the High School Classroom*

Now could I, Casca, name to thee a man
Most like this dreadful night
That thunders, lightens, opens graves, and roars
As doth the lion in the Capitol;
A man no mightier than thyself or me
In personal action, yet prodigious grown
And fearful, as these strange eruptions are.

Casca. 'Tis Caesar that you mean. Is it not, Cassius?

Cassius. Let it be who it is. For Romans now
Have thews and limbs like to their ancestors.
But woe the while! our fathers' minds are dead,
And we are governed with our mothers' spirits,
Our yoke and sufferance show us womanish.

Casca. Indeed, they say the senators tomorrow
Mean to establish Caesar as king,
And he shall wear his crown by sea and land
In every place save here in Italy.

Cassius. I know where I will wear this dagger then;
Cassius from bondage will deliver Cassius.
Therein, ye gods, you make the weak most strong;
Therein, ye gods, you tyrants do defeat.
Nor stony tower, nor walls of beaten brass,
Nor airless dungeon, nor strong links of iron,
J Can be retentive to the strength of spirit;
But life, being weary of these worldly bars,
Never lacks power to dismiss itself.
If I know this, know all the world besides,
That part of tyranny that I do bear
I can shake off at pleasure.

[Thunder still.]

Casca. So can I.
So every bondman in his own hand bears
The power to cancel his captivity.

Cassius. And why should Caesar be a tyrant then?
Poor man! I know he would not be a wolf
K But that he sees the Romans are but sheep;
He were no lion, were not Romans hinds.
Those that with haste will make a mighty fire
Begin it with weak straws. What trash is Rome,
What rubbish and what offal, when it serves
For the base matter to illuminate

83 prodigious grown: become enormous and threatening. *To whom does Cassius refer in lines 76–82?* H

86–90 *Romans . . . womanish:* Modern Romans have muscles ***(thews)*** and limbs like our ancestors, but we have the minds of our mothers, not our fathers. Our acceptance of a dictator ***(yoke and sufferance)*** shows us to be like women, not like men. (In Shakespeare's time—and in ancient Rome—women were considered weak creatures.)
93–94 *he shall . . . Italy:* The senators will make Caesar the king of all Roman territories except ***(save)*** Rome itself ***(Italy),*** since Romans would never let their own land be ruled by a king.
95–96 *I know . . . deliver Cassius:* I will free myself from slavery ***(bondage)*** by killing myself ***(wear this dagger).***
97–103 Cassius shouts these lines toward the sky, trying to be heard over the thunder. Only through suicide, he says angrily, do the gods make the weak strong and able to defeat tyrants. The strong spirit cannot be imprisoned by tower, metal walls, dungeons, or iron chains. The reason is that one can always commit suicide ***(life . . . Never lacks power to dismiss itself).*** *Do you think Cassius would really kill himself?* I

110–118 *And why . . . as Caesar:* Cassius goes into a tirade about Caesar, saying things for which he could be put to death. He says the only reason for Caesar's strength is the weakness of the Romans. They are ***hinds*** (female deer) and trash ***(offal)*** for allowing such a person as Caesar to come to power.

H. Answer: *Cassius refers to Caesar.*

I. Answer: *Answers will vary. Most students will say that Cassius seems too hungry for power at this point to commit suicide before Caesar is deposed.*

J. LEP: Vocabulary Remind students that in modern English, the first "nor" in this series would be "neither." The phrase "retentive to" may cause students difficulty; here it means "able to imprison."

K. Literary Element: FIGURATIVE LANGUAGE Have students explain the two metaphors in this passage and to tell who is compared to what. *(Possible response: Caesar is compared to a wolf and the common Romans to sheep in the first metaphor; in the second Caesar is compared to a lion and the Romans are compared to hinds, or cowering female deer.)*

L. Critical Thinking: EVALUATING Ask students how sincere Cassius is in this speech and what his motivation might be. *(Possible response: Cassius is feigning fear of Casca's loyalty in order to get Casca to insist upon his own loyalty to Cassius and the anti-Caesar cause.)*

M. Literary Sidelight Shakespeare often uses storms in his plays to suggest a connection between upheavals in nature and highly emotional conflicts between characters or within a single character. Some famous examples include the storm on the heath at the opening of *Macbeth* and the storm in *King Lear*. Literary critics have given the name "pathetic fallacy" to this technique of emphasizing human emotions and actions through natural occurrences.

N. Reading Skill: INFERRING Ask why "old Brutus' statue" would be an appropriate location for one of the letters. *(Possible response: It would remind Brutus of his heroic ancestor, who drove a tyrannical king out of Rome.)*

So vile a thing as Caesar! But, O grief,
Where hast thou led me? I, perhaps, speak this
Before a willing bondman. Then I know
L
My answer must be made. But I am armed,
And dangers are to me indifferent.

Casca. You speak to Casca, and to such a man
That is no fleering telltale. Hold, my hand.
Be factious for redress of all these griefs,
And I will set this foot of mine as far
As who goes farthest.

Cassius. There's a bargain made.
Now know you, Casca, I have moved already
Some certain of the noblest-minded Romans
To undergo with me an enterprise
Of honorable-dangerous consequence;
And I do know, by this they stay for me
In Pompey's Porch; for now, this fearful night,
There is no stir or walking in the streets,
And the complexion of the element
M
In favor's like the work we have in hand,
Most bloody, fiery, and most terrible.

[Enter Cinna.*]*

Casca. Stand close awhile, for here come one in haste.

Cassius. 'Tis Cinna. I do know him by his gait.
He is a friend. Cinna, where haste you so?

Cinna. To find out you. Who's that? Metellus Cimber?

Cassius. No, it is Casca, one incorporate
To our attempts. Am I not stayed for, Cinna?

Cinna. I am glad on't. What a fearful night is this!
There's two or three of us have seen strange sights.

Cassius. Am I not stayed for? Tell me.

Cinna. Yes, you are.
O Cassius, if you could
But win the noble Brutus to our party—

Cassius. Be you content. Good Cinna, take this paper
And look you lay it in the praetor's chair,
Where Brutus may but find it, and throw this
N
In at his window. Set this up with wax
Upon old Brutus' statue. All this done,

118–120 ***But, O . . . bondman:*** Cassius pretends that he did not mean to speak so freely. Maybe, he says, he has been speaking to a happy slave ***(willing bondman)*** of Caesar.

124 ***fleering telltale:*** sneering tattletale.

125–127 ***Be factious . . . farthest:*** Form a group, or faction, to correct ***(redress)*** these wrongs, and I will go as far as any other man.

133–134 ***by this . . . Porch:*** Right now, they wait ***(stay)*** for me at the entrance to the theater Pompey built.

136–138 ***the complexion . . . terrible:*** The sky ***(element)*** looks like the work we have ahead of us—bloody, full of fire, and terrible.

140 ***gait:*** manner of walking.

143–144 ***it is . . . stayed for:*** This is Casca, who is now part of our plan ***(incorporate / To our attempts)***. Are they waiting for me?

151–155 Cassius gives Cinna several notes addressed to Brutus, along with instructions about where each note should be placed.

152 ***lay it . . . chair:*** Place this paper in the judge's ***(praetor's)*** seat.

Repair to Pompey's Porch, where you shall find us.
Is Decius Brutus and Trebonius there?

Cinna. All but Metellus Cimber, and he's gone
To seek you at your house. Well, I will hie
And so bestow these papers as you bade me.

Cassius. That done, repair to Pompey's Theater.

[Exit Cinna.*]*

Come, Casca, you and I will yet ere day
See Brutus at his house. Three parts of him
Is ours already, and the man entire
Upon the next encounter yields him ours.

Q **Casca.** O, he sits high in all the people's hearts,
And that which would appear offense in us,
His countenance, like richest alchemy,
Will change to virtue and to worthiness.

Cassius. Him and his worth and our great need of him
You have right well conceited. Let us go,
R For it is after midnight, and ere day
We will awake him and be sure of him.

[Exeunt.]

159–160 ***I will . . . bade me:*** I'll hurry ***(hie)*** to place ***(bestow)*** these papers as you instructed me.

163–165 ***Three parts . . . yields him ours:*** We've already won over three parts of Brutus. The next time we meet him, he will be ours completely. *Do you think Brutus will fall for this trick?* O

166–169 ***he sits . . . worthiness:*** The people love Brutus. What would seem offensive if we did it will, like magic ***(alchemy),*** become good and worthy because of his involvement. *Do you agree with Casca?* P

172 ***conceited:*** judged.

Responding to Reading

1. What meaning does Casca give to the thunder and lightning? What does this tell you about him?
2. How does Cassius interpret the meaning of the violent storm and the other unusual events? Do you think Cassius believes what he says? Explain.
3. What more can you infer about Cassius' opinion of Caesar and about what Cassius plans to do?
4. Can Cassius' plans be successful without Brutus? Why or why not?

O. Answer: *Predictions will vary. Many students will say that Brutus will join the conspiracy in the end, since he has already indicated in the previous scene that he basically agrees with Cassius. Brutus has also said that he fears that Caesar will be crowned king. Others may believe Brutus loves Caesar too much, or is too fearful.*

P. Answer: *Students may point out that murder is still murder, whatever the reputation of the person who commits the crime. Others may believe some murder is politically justified.*

Q. Literary Element: THEME Ask students how this passage relates to the themes of ambition for power and the manipulation of the people in the play. *(Possible response: Casca cynically suggests that Brutus' reputation for honor can give the conspirators' action a good public "image.")*

R. LEP: Vocabulary Urge students to use the context clue provided by "after midnight" to guess that "ere" in Shakespeare's time meant "before."

Check Test

1. Why do the tribunes scold the common people in Scene 1? *(because the crowd is rejoicing in Caesar's triumph and the tribunes support Pompey)*

2. What does the soothsayer tell Caesar in Scene 2? *(to beware the ides of March)*

3. According to Casca, how did Caesar react when Mark Antony offered him a crown? *(He rejected it.)*

4. What trick does Cassius plan in order to convince Brutus to join him against Caesar? *(Cassius will plant several anonymous letters so that Brutus will find them.)*

5. In Scene 3, whom does Cassius recruit to join the conspirators? *(Casca)*

Student Response

Responding to Reading

These questions are open-ended with no "right" or "wrong" answers. However, responses must be supported with information from the selection. Possible answers follow:

1. Casca interprets the storm as a sign of the gods' anger at Rome—possibly an indication that Casca is superstitious or feeling guilty.

2. Cassius interprets the storm as a warning to the Romans that they should rid themselves of Caesar's dictatorship. He may believe this literally, or he may be simply trying to play on Casca's superstitious nature in order to recruit him to the conspiracy.

3. Cassius does not just envy Caesar; he also despises him as a dictator. He plans to go to any length—including murder or suicide—to throw off Caesar's yoke.

4. Cassius' plans will benefit immensely from Brutus' support, since Brutus' reputation for honor might make the conspiracy more acceptable to the common people.

Student Response

Responding to Reading

These questions are open-ended with no "right" or "wrong" answers. However, responses must be supported with information from the selection. Possible answers follow:

1. Possible responses: Cassius—sarcastic, envious, devious; Brutus—noble, naive, patriotic, indecisive; Casca—ironic, superstitious; Antony—loyal, fun-loving; Caesar—proud, arrogant, confident, perceptive.

2. Possible response: Caesar inspires strong loves and hates among the common people and the nobility of Rome; he is self-confident, egotistical, and perceptive; he rules like a dictator, but he is shrewd enough not to seem to be ambitious.

3. Possible responses: No—Brutus is basically loyal to Caesar and loves him; Yes—the persuasive Cassius has planted serious doubts in Brutus' mind about Caesar's intentions to seize power.

4. Possible responses: Cassius—he has the largest number of lines in Act I and is the driving force behind the conspiracy against Caesar; Brutus—his support of the conspirators will be critical; Caesar—he is the focus of the action.

5. Answers will vary. Encourage students to support their answers with reasons and examples.

Writing Options

The Writing Options are designed to meet varied student interests and abilities. Have each student choose one writing activity to complete. You may wish to guide some students to an option that requires less writing.

Responding to Reading

First Impressions

1. Write one or two adjectives that describe each of these men: Cassius, Brutus, Casca, Antony, and Caesar. Compare your descriptions with those of your classmates.

Second Thoughts

2. What is your opinion of Julius Caesar in this act?

   Think about
   - the exchange between the tribunes and the commoners
   - Caesar's appearances and what he says
   - what others say about him

3. Do you think Cassius will be successful in winning over Brutus to his secret plan? Explain.

4. Who do you think is the most important character in this play up to now? Explain your answer.

5. Does any character in Act One remind you of any other character in this book? Explain and give examples.

Literary Concepts: Characterization and Soliloquy

Characterization refers to the techniques a writer uses to create and develop characters. In drama, important characterization techniques include the following:

- showing a character's actions
- revealing dialogue spoken by the character
- showing reactions of other characters

Choose one important character from Act One. List what you learn about the character from his or her actions and dialogue and from the reactions of others.

A **soliloquy** is a speech given by a character who is alone on the stage or among other characters who are ignored temporarily. The character giving the soliloquy may speak to himself or herself or address the audience directly. The soliloquy reveals thoughts and intentions of the character that cannot be shared with other characters at that point. Which character gives a soliloquy at the end of Scene 2? What does the soliloquy reveal? What events and actions might this soliloquy lead you to expect later in the play?

Characterization

Possible responses: Caesar—actions include refusing the crown; dialogue includes worry about Cassius and insistence on his own courage; other characters' reactions includes Casca's cynicism about Caesar's motives in refusing the crown and Cassius' story about Caesar's weakness; we learn that Caesar is not universally loved, that he is vain and loves dramatic gestures, and that he may or may not be brave, depending on whose account we believe. Brutus—actions include refusing to listen to Cassius' plans; dialogue includes expressions of concern about Caesar and Cassius' observations; other characters' reactions include Cassius asserting that Brutus is highly respected and Cassius' soliloquy that Brutus is easily manipulated; we learn that Brutus cares about honor, Rome, and Caesar and that he is probably easily manipulated, even though highly respected.

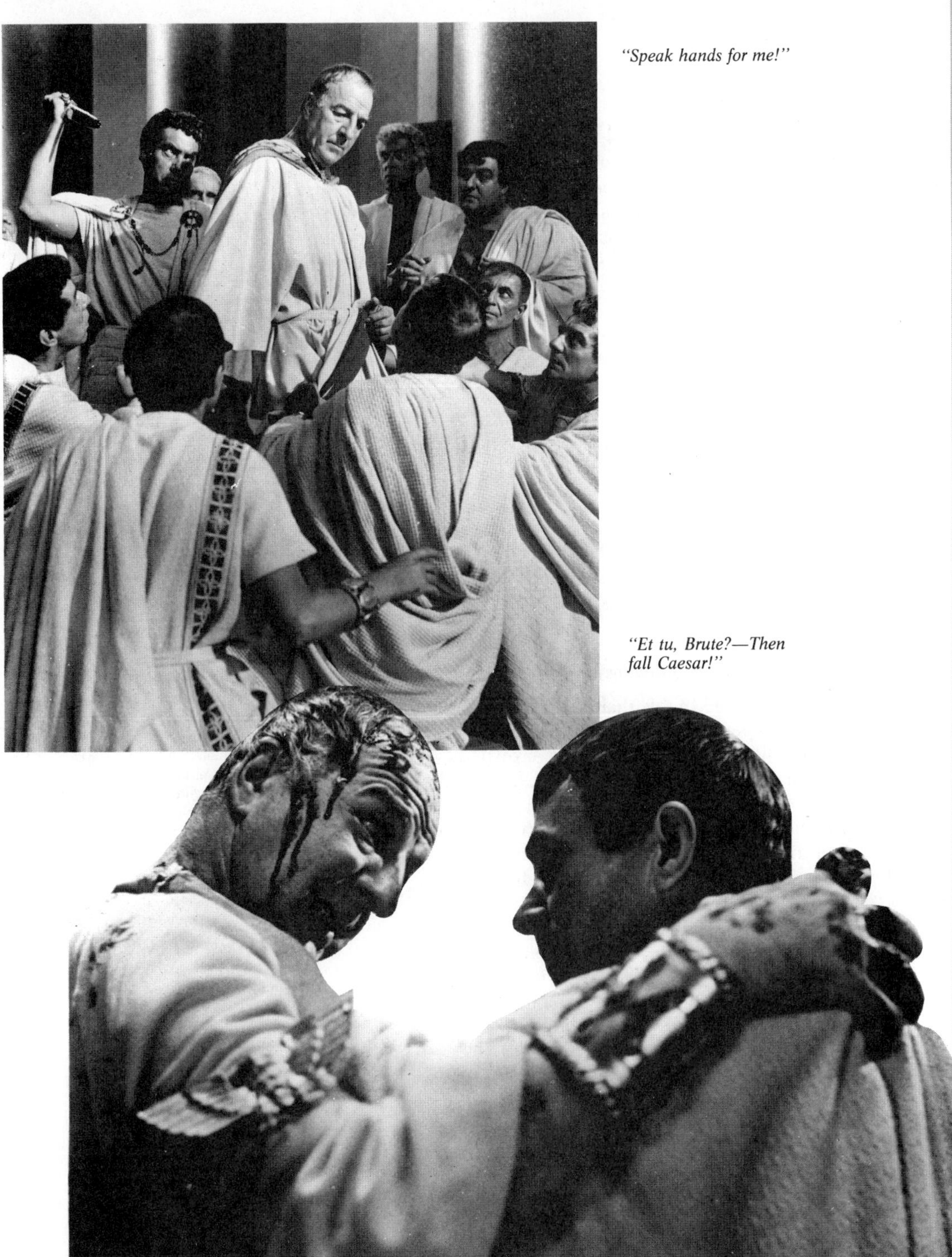

"Speak hands for me!"

"Et tu, Brute?—Then fall Caesar!"

Options for Learning

These activities suit a variety of learning styles and modes of expression. Allow students to review the options and then choose the one they wish to do. Many are excellent collaborative learning projects.

1. Research Caesar Advise students to consult a detailed but not overly specialized encyclopedia article, such as the entry in *World Book.*

2. Bring a Scene to Life Advise students to make a chart of stage directions for the scene they choose. Students should note sound effects (for example, off-stage shouts or the noise of a storm) on their charts.

3. Roman Life Students may consult books such as J. Carcopino, *Daily Life in Ancient Rome* or the *Oxford History of the Classical World.*

4. A Shakespearean Summary Advise students to start this assignment by writing a brief summary in prose. Then remind them to reread the discussions in the Explore pages of blank verse and iambic pentameter. Encourage students by reminding them that this meter is very close to the natural rhythms of ordinary English speech.

Literary Concepts—Soliloquy

Cassius gives a soliloquy at the end of Scene 2. It reveals his plan to win Brutus over to his side in the plot against Caesar. Students may say that this will lead to an overthrow of Caesar or perhaps a conflict between Cassius and Brutus.

Teaching Strategies

Support for Students of Limited English Proficiency

- Use **Reader's Guidesheet**, p. 4.
- *Julius Caesar* Act II contains some figurative language that may be challenging to students who are not used to Shakespeare's elaborate similes and metaphors. Use the annotations to help students to clarify the meaning of these passages.
- **Annotations B, E, I, T, AA, GG,** and **MM** (Scene 1); **G** and **O** (Scene 2); and **B** (Scene 3) focus on figurative language and irony.

Text Annotations

A. Reading Skill: INTERPRETIVE ORAL READING Have students read Brutus' opening lines in Act II aloud, observing the punctuation and varying their tone and volume to indicate the places where Brutus calls to his servant and where he speaks to himself.

B. LEP: Figurative Language Help students to understand that Brutus is comparing Caesar to an adder, a kind of poisonous snake. Adders were popularly believed to come out of their holes on "bright" sunny days; in this extended metaphor, Brutus compares such a day to the act of crowning Caesar. The crown itself then becomes the adder's "sting"—a powerful weapon that Caesar may abuse.

C. Answer: *Brutus thinks that Caesar may forget lowly people and abuse his power. He may scorn the "base degrees" once he is made a king.*

ACT TWO

Scene 1 *Brutus's orchard in Rome.*

It is a few hours before dawn on March 15—the ides of March. Brutus, unable to sleep, walks in his garden. He faces a crucial decision: either to continue living under the tyranny of Caesar or to kill Caesar and thus end his rule. While considering the problem, Brutus receives an anonymous letter (from Cassius) suggesting that Brutus take action against Caesar. Shortly after, Cassius and the conspirators visit Brutus, and they all agree to assassinate Caesar that day.

Brutus. What, Lucius, ho!
I cannot by the progress of the stars
A Give guess how near to day. Lucius, I say!
I would it were my fault to sleep so soundly.
When, Lucius, when? Awake, I say! What, Lucius!

[Enter Lucius *from the house.]*

Lucius. Called you, my lord?

Brutus. Get me a taper in my study, Lucius.
When it is lighted, come and call me here.

Lucius. I will, my lord.

[Exit.]

[Brutus *returns to his brooding.]*

Brutus. It must be by his death; and for my part,
I know no personal cause to spurn at him,
But for the general. He would be crowned.
How that might change his nature, there's the question.
It is the bright day that brings forth the adder,
And that craves wary walking. Crown him that,
B And then I grant we put a sting in him
That at his will he may do danger with.
The abuse of greatness is when it disjoins
Remorse from power. And to speak truth of Caesar,
I have not known when his affections swayed
More than his reason. But 'tis a common proof
That lowliness is young ambition's ladder,
Whereto the climber-upward turns his face;
But when he once attains the upmost round,
He then unto the ladder turns his back,
Looks in the clouds, scorning the base degrees
By which he did ascend. So Caesar may.

GUIDE FOR READING

2–3 *I cannot . . . day:* There are no stars in the sky to tell me how near it is to morning.

4 *I would . . . soundly:* I wish I could sleep so soundly.

7 *taper:* candle.

10–35 Brutus, alone again, thinks out loud about the problem of Caesar. In general, Brutus fears that Caesar will become too powerful.

10–12 *It must . . . general:* It can only be solved by Caesar's death. I have no personal grudge against him; I'm thinking only of the general welfare.

15–16 *It is . . . walking:* Sunshine brings out the poisonous snake ***(adder)***, so walk carefully.

19–28 *The abuse . . . may:* Greatness is misused when it separates pity ***(disjoins / Remorse)*** from power. I have never known Caesar to be ruled by his heart rather than his head. *What does Brutus think Caesar will do if he gets to the top of **ambition's ladder?** What will Caesar's attitude be toward those at the ladder's lower rungs **(base degrees)?*** C

Critic's Corner

"The soliloquy in which Brutus finally arrives at his decision and thereby makes the murder of Caesar possible, is so riddled with implicit contradictions that some students of the play have judged it incomprehensible. It is, however, thoroughly in character. Brutus, not himself an evil man, is about to perform an act which will release evil impulses whose true nature he persistently fails to grasp. . . . 'I know no personal cause to spurn at him': the admission is, for a man who sincerely values friendship, personal relationships, serious enough; but since another side of Brutus's nature craves abstract consistency, the wedding of high principle to effective action, he turns this recognition into an argument for clearing himself of dubious personal motives and seeks to place the burden of justification squarely upon an appeal to the 'general' good."

DEREK TRAVERSI, *Julius Caesar: The Roman Tragedy*

D Then lest he may, prevent. And since the quarrel
Will bear no color for the thing he is,
Fashion it thus: that what he is, augmented,
Would run to these and these extremities;
And therefore think him as a serpent's egg,
E Which, hatched, would as his kind grow mischievous,
And kill him in the shell.

[Reenter Lucius *with a letter.]*

Lucius. The taper burneth in your closet, sir.
Searching the window for a flint, I found
This paper, thus sealed up, and I am sure
It did not lie there when I went to bed.

[Gives him the letter.]

Brutus. Get you to bed again; it is not day.
Is not tomorrow, boy, the ides of March?

F **Lucius.** I know not, sir.

Brutus. Look in the calendar and bring me word.

Lucius. I will, sir.

[Exit.]

Brutus. The exhalations, whizzing in the air,
Give so much light that I may read by them.

[Opens the letter and reads.]

"Brutus, thou sleep'st. Awake, and see thyself!
Shall Rome, etc. Speak, strike, redress!"
"Brutus, thou sleep'st. Awake!"
Such instigations have been often dropped
Where I have took them up.
"Shall Rome, etc." Thus must I piece it out:
Shall Rome stand under one man's awe? What, Rome?
My ancestors did from the streets of Rome
G The Tarquin drive when he was called a king.
"Speak, strike, redress!" Am I entreated
To speak and strike? O Rome, I make thee promise,
If the redress will follow, thou receivest
Thy full petition at the hand of Brutus!

[Reenter Lucius.*]*

Lucius. Sir, March is wasted fifteen days.

29 *lest . . . shell:* Rather than let Caesar do that, I should take steps to prevent it. Since our case against Caesar is weak ***(Will bear no color)*** at present, we must shape ***(Fashion)*** our argument against him in the following way: We know what kind of person Caesar is now. If his true nature were allowed to develop ***(augmented),*** it would reach terrible extremes. So we must treat him as a serpent's egg and kill him before he hatches.

36 *closet:* private room.

45 *exhalations:* meteors.

47–48 *etc.:* and so forth; ***redress:*** right a wrong. The letter is meant to suggest certain things to Brutus, without actually spelling them out.
50 *instigations:* suggestions.

52 *Thus . . . out:* I must guess the rest of the sentence.

53 *Shall . . . awe:* Should Rome have such fear and respect for just one man?

55–56 *My ancestors . . . king:* Brutus refers to his ancestor who drove out Rome's last king. After that, rule by the Senate was established.

58–60 *I make . . . Brutus:* I promise you, Rome, if a remedy for our troubles can follow from my action, you will get what you need from Brutus.

D. Critical Thinking: EVALUATING Ask students whether Brutus is morally justified in taking action now to "prevent" tyranny in the future. Encourage them to decide whether he has good reason to fear that Caesar will be a tyrant. *(Possible responses: Brutus is motivated more by his opinion than by facts and is not justified in planning a murder that may cause civil chaos; Brutus has good reason to fear tyranny and to wonder how to prevent it.)*

E. LEP: Figurative Language Be sure students understand Caesar is being compared to the "egg" of a poisonous serpent, which must be killed before it hatches. Remind students that this figure of speech extends Brutus' earlier metaphor of Caesar as a poisonous adder.

F. Literary Element: FORESHADOWING Ask students to explain why Brutus' question about the calendar is an example of foreshadowing, in light of the mention of the "ides of March" in Act I. *(Possible response: In Act I the soothsayer warned Caesar to beware the ides of March. The audience will thus already know that something terrible may happen on this day.)*

G. Historical Sidelight King Tarquin, called "the Proud" because of his lawlessness and arrogance, murdered his father-in-law in the sixth century B.C. to gain the throne. Eventually, the Romans, led by Brutus' ancestor Lucius Junius Brutus, rebelled against Tarquin and drove him out. Lucius Brutus was thus popularly held to be the founder of the Roman Republic, and he was revered for his unflinching devotion to the republic. When his own sons plotted to restore the monarchy, Lucius Brutus had them executed.

H. Answer: *Brutus is divided between his personal love and loyalty to Caesar and his fear that Caesar may become tyrannical and destroy the state.*

I. LEP: Figurative Language Help students to chart the terms of this comparison on the chalkboard or on a piece of paper as follows: the interval between conceiving an idea and carrying it out = hideous dream; a person's inner frame of mind = a little kingdom being torn apart by revolt or civil war.

J. Literary Element: TONE Ask students to explain Brutus' tone as he reflects on the nature of conspiracy. If students were speaking these lines, what tone would they use? Regretful? Ironic? Melancholy? Triumphant? *(Possible response: The tone would probably combine irony and regret, given Brutus' character.)*

[Knocking within.]

Brutus. 'Tis good. Go to the gate, somebody knocks.

[Exit Lucius.*]*

Since Cassius first did whet me against Caesar,
I have not slept.
Between the acting of a dreadful thing
And the first motion, all the interim is
Like a phantasma or a hideous dream.
I The genius and the mortal instruments
Are then in council, and the state of man,
Like to a little kingdom, suffers then
The nature of an insurrection.

63 ***whet me:*** sharpen my appetite.

65–71 ***Between . . . insurrection:*** The time between the earliest thought of a terrible act and the actual performance of it is a nightmare. The soul ***(genius)*** and body ***(mortal instruments)*** debate the subject, while the man himself feels like a kingdom undergoing a civil war. *What is Brutus' internal conflict?* H

[Reenter Lucius.*]*

Lucius. Sir, 'tis your brother Cassius at the door,
Who doth desire to see you.

72 ***brother:*** Cassius, the husband of Brutus' sister, is his brother-in-law.

Brutus. Is he alone?

Lucius. No, sir, there are more with him.

Brutus. Do you know them?

Lucius. No, sir. Their hats are plucked about their ears
And half their faces buried in their cloaks,
That by no means I may discover them
By any mark of favor.

79–80 ***by no . . . favor:*** There is no way I can tell who they are.

Brutus. Let 'em enter.

[Exit Lucius.*]*

They are the faction. O conspiracy,
Sham'st thou to show thy dang'rous brow by night,
When evils are most free? O, then by day
Where wilt thou find a cavern dark enough
J To mask thy monstrous visage? Seek none, conspiracy,
Hide it in smiles and affability!
For if thou path, thy native semblance on,
No Erebus itself were dim enough
To hide thee from prevention.

82–91 ***O conspiracy . . . prevention:*** If these plotters are afraid to be seen at night, how will they keep these terrible plans from showing on their faces during the day? They must smile and show friendliness ***(affability).*** If they go out showing their true natures ***(native semblance),*** even the dark gateway to hell ***(Erebus*** erʹ ə bəs***)*** couldn't hide them.

[Enter the conspirators, Cassius, Casca, Decius, Cinna, Metellus Cimber, *and* Trebonius.*]*

Cassius. I think we are too bold upon your rest.
Good morrow, Brutus. Do we trouble you?

92 ***I think . . . rest:*** I think we may have come too early.

CRITIC'S CORNER

" . . . if ever Shakespeare left anything beyond doubt it is that this particular man Brutus should never have had anything to do with this particular deed. Practically every scene of the play contributes something toward this conclusion. So true is it indeed that Julius Caesar, *if you care to take it so, becomes a sort of manual on the art of knowing what your soul is telling you to do, or not to do, of finding out what you think in contrast with what you think you think.*

Brutus is an exceptional man. Yet Brutus is Everyman in the sense that every man is Brutus at some hour of his life. Whoever is aware of the disparity between what he would be and what the world seems bent on making him is a Brutus in a general sense. More specifically, Brutus is the man of sensitive nature who, outraged by the cruelty and tyranny around him, sadly and reluctantly concludes that there is no way to oppose the world but with the world's

Continued on page 757

Brutus. I have been up this hour, awake all night.
Know I these men that come along with you?

Cassius. Yes, every man of them; and no man here
But honors you; and every one doth wish
You had but that opinion of yourself
Which every noble Roman bears of you.
This is Trebonius.

Brutus. He is welcome hither.

Cassius. This, Decius Brutus.

Brutus. He is welcome too.

Cassius. This, Casca; this, Cinna; and this, Metellus
Cimber.

Brutus. They are all welcome.
What watchful cares do interpose themselves
Betwixt your eyes and night?

Cassius. Shall I entreat a word?

[They whisper.]

Decius. Here lies the east. Doth not the day break
here?

Casca. No.

Cinna. O, pardon, sir, it doth; and yon grey lines
That fret the clouds are messengers of day.

Casca. You shall confess that you are both deceived.
Here, as I point my sword, the sun arises,
Which is a great way growing on the south,
Weighing the youthful season of the year.
Some two months hence, up higher toward the north
He first presents his fire; and the high east
Stands as the Capitol, directly here.

*[*Brutus *and* Cassius *rejoin the others.]*

Brutus. Give me your hands all over, one by one.

Cassius. And let us swear our resolution.

Brutus. No, not on oath. If not the face of men,
The sufferance of our souls, the time's abuse—
If these be motives weak, break off betimes,
And every man hence to his idle bed.
So let high-sighted tyranny range on

107–108 *What watchful . . . night:* What troubles keep you awake at night?

109 *Shall I entreat a word:* Cassius asks Brutus to step aside and talk privately with him. While they talk, the others chatter about the sky (lines 108–118), pretending to be not at all interested in what Cassius and Brutus are discussing.

114 *fret:* stripe.

117–118 *Which is . . . year:* from a southerly direction, since it is still early in the year.

124–129 *If not . . . lottery:* We do not need to swear our loyalty to one another. The sadness of people's faces, our own suffering, and the awful time we live in—if these aren't strong enough to hold us together, then let us all go back to bed. In that case, let tyranny live, while we die off, one at a time, by chance ***(by lottery)***.

K. Literary Element: CHARACTERIZATION Ask which character traits Cassius might be appealing to when he uses the words "honor" and "noble." *(Possible response: to Brutus' love of honor and sense of his own noble ancestry.)* Then ask what the use of these words shows about Cassius. *(Possible response: that he is perceptive and manipulative, especially with Brutus)* Finally, ask whether Brutus is really above flattery. *(Possible response: Brutus probably thinks he is, but Cassius' manipulation of him shows otherwise.)*

L. Literary Element: STAGE DIRECTIONS Ask students why they think Cassius draws Brutus aside for a private conversation here. *(Possible responses: He wants to know Brutus' final decision; he wants Brutus to feel close to him.)*

M. Literary Element: SUSPENSE Ask students how this apparently trivial conversation serves to heighten the suspense at this point in the play. *(Possible response: As the conspirators argue about a relatively minor matter, the tension in the audience mounts over whether Brutus will decide to join the plot.)*

N. Reading Skill: INFERRING Ask students to contrast Brutus' attitude toward the oath with that of Cassius. What can students infer from this contrast about the character of each man? *(Possible responses: Cassius is distrustful of others, while Brutus is trusting, perhaps even naive; he not only trusts, but has an overwhelming need to attribute only the best motives to his "partners in crime," perhaps to rationalize his own action and motives.)*

CRITIC'S CORNER

Continued from 756

weapons, that fire must drive out fire and force force.

The lofty character of the end intended, the preservation of the liberties of Rome, blinds Brutus to the low character of the means proposed. He represses, but he cannot eradicate, that abhorrence of force which, by definition, must be inherent in every lover of liberty. The result is war in that psychological realm where all war begins."

HAROLD GODDARD, *The Meaning of Shakespeare*

O. Answer: *Brutus believes that the honesty of the conspirators' cause—ridding Rome of a potential tyrant—is stronger than any oath. Students' opinions will vary. Many students will point out that the conspirators' cause will involve assassination, so it can hardly be called "honest." Others will agree that the plot is so risky that oaths will hardly make it any safer.*

P. Answer: *Students may observe that Brutus' high-minded attitude toward the conspiracy and his sense of honor in not breaking a promise may not be shared by Cassius and the others. Cassius, in particular, has shown himself to be envious, bitter, and manipulative. Some students may point out that Brutus seems to need to believe that the conspirators are better than they are, to be willing to go along with them.*

Q. Literary Element: THEME Ask students to explain how these lines shed light on Brutus' concept of friendship. *(Possible response: Brutus believes that every Roman must be trusted as sincere when he gives his promise or his word. He believes that friendship depends on believing that his friends are motivated by as strong a sense of honor as he is.)*

R. Literary Element: THEME Ask students how this passage relates to the themes of ambition and manipulation of the mob in the play. *(Possible response: Metellus cynically proposes that Cicero be invited to join the conspirators so that his age and reputation for dignity and respect will sway the mob into believing that the cause of the plotters is just.)*

Till each man drop by lottery. But if these
(As I am sure they do) bear fire enough
To kindle cowards and to steel with valor
The melting spirits of women, then, countrymen,
What need we any spur but our own cause
To prick us to redress? what other bond
Than secret Romans that have spoke the word
And will not palter? and what other oath
Than honesty to honesty engaged
That this shall be, or we will fall for it?
Swear priests and cowards and men cautelous,
Old feeble carrions and such suffering souls
That welcome wrongs; unto bad causes swear
Such creatures as men doubt; but do not stain
The even virtue of our enterprise,
Nor the insuppressive mettle of our spirits,
To think that or our cause or our performance
Did need an oath when every drop of blood
Q That every Roman bears, and noble bears,
Is guilty of a several bastardy
If he do break the smallest particle
Of any promise that hath passed from him.

Cassius. But what of Cicero? Shall we sound him?
I think he will stand very strong with us.

Casca. Let us not leave him out.

Cinna. No, by no means.

Metellus. O, let us have him! for his silver hairs
Will purchase us a good opinion
And buy men's voices to commend our deeds.
R It shall be said his judgment ruled our hands;
Our youths and wildness shall no whit appear,
But all be buried in his gravity.

Brutus. O, name him not! Let us not break with him,
For he will never follow anything
That other men begin.

Cassius. Then leave him out.

Casca. Indeed he is not fit.

Decius. Shall no man else be touched but only Caesar?

Cassius. Decius, well urged. I think it is not meet
Mark Antony, so well beloved of Caesar,
Should outlive Caesar. We shall find of him

133–138 *What does Brutus believe is even stronger than any oath the men could take together? Do you agree?* O

136 *palter:* go back on our word.

139–150 *Swear . . . from him:* Swearing oaths is for priests, cowards, crafty ***(cautelous)*** men, old dying men ***(feeble carrions),*** and unhappy people who enjoy lying. Such people do not have our unfailing courage ***(insuppressive mettle).*** What we believe or what we are about to do ***(or our cause or our performance)*** does not need oaths, since our blood would not be truly Roman (would be ***guilty of a several bastardy***) if any of us were to break his word. Brutus seems to believe that the other conspirators are as honorable as he is. *Do you agree with him?* P

151 *sound him:* see what he thinks of the matter.

155–160 *let us . . . gravity:* Let us get Cicero to join us. His age ***(silver hairs)*** will win us popular support. People will say our youth and wildness were ruled by his sound judgment. So let us tell him of our plan.

167–173 *I think . . . together:* Shall we also kill Mark Antony, Caesar's good friend? He is a clever plotter

DATA BANK

In the *Life of Brutus*, Plutarch writes as follows about the exclusion of Cicero from the conspiracy:

"After that time they began to feel all their acquaintance whom they trusted, and laid their heads together . . . and did not only pick out their friends, but all those also whom they thought stout enought to attempt any desperate matter, and that were not afraid to lose their lives. For this cause they durst not acquaint Cicero with their conspiracy . . . for they were afraid that he being a coward by nature, and age also having increased his fear, he would quite turn and alter all their purpose, and quench the heat of their enterprise . . ."

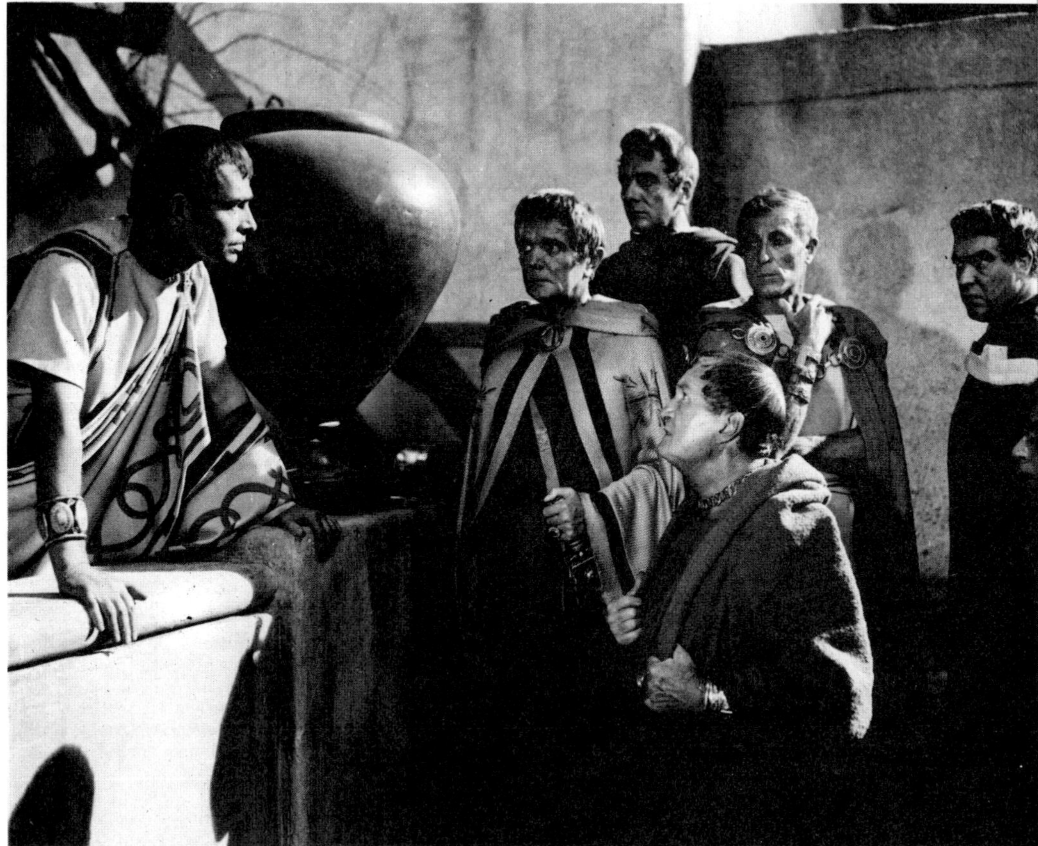

"Let us be sacrificers, but not butchers, Caius."

A shrewd contriver; and you know, his means,
If he improve them, may well stretch so far
As to annoy us all; which to prevent,
Let Antony and Caesar fall together.

Brutus. Our course will seem too bloody, Caius
Cassius,
To cut the head off and then hack the limbs,
Like wrath in death and envy afterwards;
T For Antony is but a limb of Caesar.
Let us be sacrificers, but not butchers, Caius.
We all stand up against the spirit of Caesar,
And in the spirit of men there is no blood.

(shrewd contriver), and if we had more power ***(his means / If he improve them),*** he could be trouble for us.

179 *How does this line reveal a contrast between Brutus' and Cassius' attitudes toward the plot?* S

S. Answer: *Brutus' line implies that he thinks of the conspiracy as a sacred task that is approved by the gods, as opposed to Cassius' more practical—and bloody—approach.*

T. LEP: Figurative Language Tell students that the figurative language in this speech involves another extended metaphor. Anthony is like one "limb" of Caesar's body, says Brutus; that is, Anthony is as dependent on Caesar as an arm or a leg is dependent on a body. Ask students to note how this metaphor of Caesar's "body" is continued and varied in the speech.

U. Literary Element: IRONY Remind students of Casca's comment just before the end of Act I that the addition of Brutus to the conspiracy would help to win over the crowd. Then ask what is ironic about Brutus' words here. *(Possible response: Brutus now voices similar sentiments as he emphasizes his concern with the "image" the conspiracy will have with the crowd.)*

V. Answer: *Some students will agree, citing Brutus' remarks about Antony's irresponsibility and general dependence on Caesar. Other students may disagree, citing Cassius' suspicions about Antony's shrewdness and his "ingrafted love" of Caesar, which may prompt him to become an avenger of his leader's death.*

W. Literary Element: STAGE DIRECTIONS In light of the fact that the ancient Romans had no striking clocks, why do students think that Shakespeare included this obvious anachronism in the stage directions here? *(Possible response: The striking of a clock dramatically underlines that time is growing short. The stage direction increases the suspense.)*

X. Reading Skill: CLARIFYING Ask students to review Cassius' speech and then to explain what two reasons Cassius offers for Caesar's possible failure to appear at the Capitol. *(Possible response: He says that Caesar has grown superstitious and may be frightened by the unusual omens of that night, and he adds that Caesar's augurers may persuade him to stay home.)*

O that we then could come by Caesar's spirit
And not dismember Caesar! But, alas,
Caesar must bleed for it! And, gentle friends,
Let's kill him boldly, but not wrathfully;
Let's carve him as a dish fit for the gods,
Not hew him as a carcass fit for hounds.
And let our hearts, as subtle masters do,
Stir up their servants to an act of rage
And after seem to chide 'em. This shall make
Our purpose necessary, and not envious;
U Which so appearing to the common eyes,
We shall be called purgers, not murderers.
And for Mark Antony, think not of him;
For he can do no more than Caesar's arm
When Caesar's head is off.

Cassius. Yet I fear him,
For in the ingrafted love he bears to Caesar—

Brutus. Alas, good Cassius, do not think of him!
If he love Caesar, all that he can do
Is to himself—take thought, and die for Caesar.
And that were much he should; for he is given
To sports, to wildness, and much company.

Trebonius. There is no fear in him. Let him not die,
For he will live and laugh at this hereafter.

[Clock strikes.]

Brutus. Peace! Count the clock.

W **Cassius.** The clock hath stricken three.

Trebonius. 'Tis time to part.

Cassius. But it is doubtful yet
Whether Caesar will come forth today or no;
For he is superstitious grown of late,
Quite from the main opinion he held once
Of fantasy, of dreams, and ceremonies.
It may be these apparent prodigies,
The unaccustomed terror of this night,
X And the persuasion of his augurers
May hold him from the Capitol today.

Decius. Never fear that. If he be so resolved,
I can o'ersway him; for he loves to hear
That unicorns may be betrayed with trees
And bears with glasses, elephants with holes,

182–183 ***O that . . . Caesar:*** Brutus wishes they could remove Caesar's soul without having to destroy his body.

187 ***Not . . . hounds:*** Let's not chop him up like the body of an animal to be fed to dogs.

188–193 ***let our hearts . . . murderers:*** Let our hearts treat our hands ***(servants)*** the way sly masters do; we will let our hands do our dirty work, then later scold ***(chide)*** them for what they have done. This attitude will make us seem to the public ***(common eyes)*** to be healers ***(purgers)*** instead of murderers.

198 ***ingrafted:*** deep-rooted.

202–203 ***And that . . . company:*** Mark Antony isn't likely to kill himself; he loves sports, wildness, and socializing too much to do such a thing. V

204 ***There is no fear in him:*** We have nothing to fear from Antony. *Do you agree?*

209–217 ***But it is . . . Capitol today:*** We don't know if Caesar will leave his house ***(come forth)*** today. Lately he has become superstitious, in contrast to the strong views ***(main opinion)*** he once had of such beliefs. The cause may be these strange events and the arguments of his fortunetellers ***(augurers).*** These things may keep him from coming to the Capitol today.

219 ***o'ersway him:*** change his mind.

220–224 ***That unicorns . . . flattered:*** Decimus tells of ways to trap shrewd

PROFESSIONAL NOTEBOOK

While Shakespeare fills his plays with considerable attractions for the "groundlings"—murders, quarrels, suicides, duels, insanity, slapstick comedy, patriotic fervor, and spectacle—his essential appeal is to the ear, to the mind, to refined perception. . . . To begin with, students must learn that a play can be enjoyable even when the plot is known in advance. Like the more sophisticated members of the Greek or Elizabethan audience, they must learn to anticipate and enjoy the unique treatment of a previously worked subject and to let language more than spectacle and action work upon their imagination and emotions.
GLADYS VEIDEMANIS, *Shakespeare in the High School Classroom*

Lions with toils, and men with flatterers;
But when I tell him he hates flatterers,
Y He says he does, being then most flattered.
Let me work,
For I can give his humor the true bent,
And I will bring him to the Capitol.

Cassius. Nay, we will all of us be there to fetch him.

Brutus. By the eighth hour. Is that the uttermost?

Cinna. Be that the uttermost, and fail not then.

Metellus. Caius Ligarius doth bear Caesar hard,
Who rated him for speaking well of Pompey.
I wonder none of you have thought of him.

Z **Brutus.** Now, good Metellus, go along by him.
He loves me well, and I have given him reasons.
Send him but hither, and I'll fashion him.

Cassius. The morning comes upon's. We'll leave you, Brutus.
And, friends, disperse yourselves; but all remember
What you have said and show yourselves true Romans.

Brutus. Good gentlemen, look fresh and merrily.
Let not our looks put on our purposes,
AA But bear it as our Roman actors do,
With untired spirits and formal constancy.
And so good morrow to you every one.

[Exeunt all but Brutus.*]*

Boy! Lucius! Fast asleep? It is no matter.
Enjoy the honey-heavy dew of slumber.
Thou hast no figures nor no fantasies
Which busy care draws in the brains of men;
Therefore thou sleep'st so sound.

[Enter Portia, Brutus' *wife.]*

Portia. Brutus, my lord!

Brutus. Portia! What mean you? Wherefore rise you now?
BB It is not for your health thus to commit
Your weak condition to the raw cold morning.

Portia. Nor for yours neither. Y' have ungently, Brutus,
Stole from my bed. And yesternight at supper

animals. He says that Caesar, who loves to hear such stories, can also be trapped—by flattery.

226 ***I can give . . . true bent:*** I can get him into the right mood.

229 ***By the . . . uttermost:*** By eight o'clock. Do we all agree that eight is the latest we will be there?

231–233 ***Caius . . . of him:*** Caius Ligarius has a grudge against Caesar, who criticized him for supporting Pompey. I don't know why you haven't asked him to join our plot.

236 ***fashion:*** persuade.

243 ***Let not . . . purposes:*** Let's not let our appearances give away ***(put on)*** what we are planning to do.

246 All the other conspirators leave, and Brutus is once again alone in his garden.

252 As you read the conversation between Brutus and his wife, think about the kind of relationship they have.

Y. Literary Element: CHARACTERIZATION Ask what this passage suggests about Caesar's personality, and about the personality of Decius. *(Possible response: Caesar may be boastful and lacking in self-knowledge. Decius is very perceptive and quick to take advantage of the character flaws of others.)*

Z. Literary Element: THEME Ask students to explain how this passage adds a new perspective on Brutus' concept of friendship. *(Possible response: Brutus had spoken earlier of friendship in terms of sacred trust and honor; now, however, he seems confident that he can persuade Ligarius simply because Ligarius dislikes Caesar and because Ligarius owes Brutus favors. Brutus implies that he will manipulate Ligarius, and manipulation of a friend is a new dimension of Brutus' ideas of friendship.)*

AA. LEP: Figurative Language Be sure that students understand Brutus' comparison: the conspirators should be like actors on the ancient Roman stage, who mask their true feelings as they play their assigned parts.

BB. Critical Thinking: ANALYZING Do students think that Brutus is sincerely concerned about Portia's health in this passage, or is he apprehensive that Portia may have overheard some of the details of the conspiracy? *(Possible response: Brutus may have both motives for his reaction here.)*

CC. Cultural Sidelight In both ancient Rome and Elizabethan England, the idea of "humors" was an important concept in medicine. This theory held that the balance of various fluids in the body—blood, phlegm, black bile, and yellow bile—had an important influence on people's health and emotions.

DD. Answer: *Brutus probably lies because he fears that Portia may convince him to change his mind or may worry about his involvement in the conspiracy.*

EE. Literary Element: CHARACTERIZATION Ask what this passage implies about Portia's personality. *(Possible response: She is observant and intelligent, since she shrewdly guesses that Brutus suffers from mental or psychological, rather than physical, distress.)*

FF. Reading Skill: ANALYZING Ask students what this interchange reveals about Portia's and Brutus' relationship. *(Possible response: The two must have a fairly egalitarian relationship, since Portia insists that Brutus share his secrets with her.)*

You suddenly arose and walked about,
Musing and sighing with your arms across;
And when I asked you what the matter was,
You stared upon me with ungentle looks.
I urged you further, then you scratched your head
And too impatiently stamped with your foot.
Yet I insisted, yet you answered not,
But with an angry wafture of your hand
Gave sign for me to leave you. So I did,
Fearing to strengthen that impatience
Which seemed too much enkindled, and withal
CC Hoping it was but an effect of humor,
Which sometime hath his hour with every man.
It will not let you eat nor talk nor sleep,
And could it work so much upon your shape
As it hath much prevailed on your condition,
I should not know you Brutus. Dear my lord,
Make me acquainted with your cause of grief.

Brutus. I am not well in health, and that is all.

Portia. Brutus is wise and, were he not in health,
He would embrace the means to come by it.

Brutus. Why, so I do. Good Portia, go to bed.

Portia. Is Brutus sick, and is it physical
To walk unbraced and suck up the humors
Of the dank morning? What, is Brutus sick,
And will he steal out of his wholesome bed
To dare the vile contagion of the night,
EE And tempt the rheumy and unpurgéd air,
To add unto his sickness? No, my Brutus.
You have some sick offense within your mind,
Which by the right and virtue of my place
I ought to know of; and upon my knees
I charm you, by my once commended beauty,
By all your vows of love, and that great vow
Which did incorporate and make us one,
That you unfold to me, yourself, your half,
Why you are heavy, and what men tonight
Have had resort to you; for here have been
Some six or seven, who did hide their faces
Even from darkness.

FF **Brutus.** Kneel not, gentle Portia.

Portia. I should not need if you were gentle Brutus.

265 ***Yet:*** still.

266 ***wafture:*** gesture.

269 ***withal:*** also.

270 ***humor:*** mood.

273–275 ***And could . . . you Brutus:*** If a mood like that could change your appearance ***(shape)*** the way it changes your personality ***(condition),*** I would not recognize you.

277 *Why do you think Brutus lies to Portia?* DD

281–287 ***Is Brutus . . . sickness:*** Do you expect me to believe that you're sick? Is it healthy to walk without a coat ***(unbraced)*** and breathe the air of a damp morning or the unhealthy night air that is not yet cleansed ***(unpurged)*** by the sun?

288–290 ***You have . . . know of:*** You have a sickness of the mind; as your wife, I have a right to know what it is.

295 ***heavy:*** sad.

Within the bond of marriage, tell me, Brutus,
Is it excepted I should know no secrets
That appertain to you? Am I yourself
But, as it were, in sort or limitation?
To keep with you at meals, comfort your bed,
And talk to you sometimes? Dwell I but in the
GG suburbs
Of your good pleasure? If it be no more,
Portia is Brutus' harlot, not his wife.

Brutus. You are my true and honorable wife,
As dear to me as are the ruddy drops
That visit my sad heart.

Portia. If this were true, then should I know this
secret.
I grant I am a woman, but withal
A woman that Lord Brutus took to wife.
HH I grant that I am a woman, but withal
A woman well reputed, Cato's daughter.
Think you I am no stronger than my sex,
Being so fathered and so husbanded?
Tell me your counsels; I will not disclose 'em.
I have made strong proof of my constancy,
Giving myself a voluntary wound
Here, in the thigh. Can I bear that with patience,
And not my husband's secrets?

Brutus. O ye gods,
Render me worthy of this noble wife!

[Knocking within.]

Hark, hark! one knocks. Portia, go in awhile,
JJ And by-and-by thy bosom shall partake
The secrets of my heart.
All my engagements I will construe to thee,
All the charactery of my sad brows.
Leave me with haste.

[Exit Portia.*]*

Lucius, who's that knocks?

[Reenter Lucius *with* Caius-Ligarius.*]*

Lucius. Here is a sick man that would speak with you.

Brutus. Caius Ligarius, that Metellus spake of.
Boy, stand aside. Caius Ligarius, how?

303 *appertain:* relate.

304 *in sort or limitation:* only in part.

311–312 *the ruddy . . . heart:* my blood.

319–325 *Think you . . . secrets:* How can you consider me merely a typical woman, when I am the daughter of Cato (a highly respected Roman) and the wife of Brutus? So tell me your secret. I have proven my strength by wounding myself here in the thigh. If I can put up with that pain, I can certainly deal with my husband's secrets. *Should Brutus tell Portia his secret?* II

331–332 *All my . . . brows:* I will explain all my dealings and the reason for my sad looks.

GG. LEP: Figurative Language Point out to students that this figure of speech involves a strikingly modern word, "suburbs." Clarify Portia's meaning: that, as Brutus' wife, she should not be banished to his outer circle.

HH. Cultural Sidelight Although the ancient Roman legal system gave very few rights to women (at least in the Republican period), the honor and respect accorded to a Roman *matrona* (married mother of children) were considerable. A woman's lineage was also considered very important; Portia reminds Brutus that she is the daughter of Cato, an incorruptible and widely admired Roman leader who had committed suicide in 46 B.C. rather than surrender to Caesar in the war with Pompey.

II. Answer: *Some students may argue that Brutus should take Portia into his confidence, treating her as an equal. Other students may argue that no purpose would be served by telling the secret; in fact, if the plot should fail, Portia's prior knowledge of it might endanger her safety. Still others may point out that Portia would probably talk Brutus out of participating, or at least play on his guilt to make participation more difficult.*

JJ. Literary Element: SUSPENSE Ask students to explain how Shakespeare increases the suspense here. *(Possible response: Brutus hurriedly interrupts the conversation with Portia when he hears knocking at the door. The audience wonders who the visitor is, and also whether or not Brutus will keep his promise to share his secret with his wife.)*

Cultural Connection

Ask students to identify the type of relationship that Portia seems to expect with Brutus. Note especially her insistence that if Brutus does not deal respectfully with her, she is "Brutus' harlot, not his wife." Note also Portia's admission that she is "but a woman"—that is, less worthy of respect than a man (according to Roman ways).

Then ask students to compare this image of marriage with their own ideas about male-female relations. Ask them what they think husbands and wives or boyfriends and girlfriends should expect of each other. Ask, also, whether they think that ideas about the status of women, or about male-female relations, have changed since Shakespeare's time. You might point out that in Shakespeare's time, relationships of equality were very rare among any two people; instead, hierarchy (lord and servant, master and apprentice, king and nobles) was more the order of the day. How do students believe these attitudes might have affected attitudes towards marriage?

KK. Irony Share with students that the figurative language in this passage also involves irony. Caius Ligarius is not literally "sick"; he is wearing a "kerchief" around his head to disguise himself.

LL. Answer: *Caius means that there are some men (especially Caesar) who must die ("be made sick").*

MM. LEP: Irony Point out to students that Ligarius and Brutus are using a kind of ironic "code" in these lines, playing on the notions of sickness and "wholeness," or health. Ask students to explain what they really mean. *(Possible response: Brutus means that their plan will heal the suffering state; Caius answers that the plan will also involve making some "whole men"—namely Caesar—"sick".)*

NN. Critical Thinking: EVALUATING Ask students to evaluate Caius Ligarius' words here. Is he acting rationally? *(Possible response: No, since he blindly follows Brutus, with no specific idea about what the plan involves or what its consequences may be)*

Student Response

Response to Reading

These questions are open-ended with no "right" or "wrong" answers. However, responses must be supported with information from the selection. Possible answers follow:

1. Some students may say that Brutus' argument is convincing, since he knows Caesar's personality and temperament; others may feel that Brutus' argument is not persuasive, because he tries to rationalize an assassination based on what he thinks Caesar may potentially do in the future and currently has no proof that Caesar will actually become a tyrant.

2. Some students may believe that Brutus' reaction shows that he is extremely patriotic and highly conscious of the role his ancestors played in freeing the city from the tryannical king Tarquin. Others may just see him as naive and gullible.

Caius. Vouchsafe good morrow from a feeble tongue.

Brutus. O, what a time have you chose out, brave Caius,
To wear a kerchief! Would you were not sick!

KK **Caius.** I am not sick if Brutus have in hand
Any exploit worthy the name of honor.

Brutus. Such an exploit have I in hand, Ligarius,
Had you a healthful ear to hear of it.

Caius. By all the gods that Romans bow before,
I here discard my sickness! Soul of Rome!
Brave son, derived from honorable loins!
Thou like an exorcist has conjured up
My mortified spirit. Now bid me run,
And I will strive with things impossible;
Yea, get the better of them. What's to do?

Brutus. A piece of work that will make sick men whole.

MM **Caius.** But are not some whole that we must make sick? LL

Brutus. That must we also. What it is, my Caius,
I shall unfold to thee as we are going
To whom it must be done.

Caius. Set on your foot,
NN And with a heart new-fired I follow you,
To do I know not what; but it sufficeth
That Brutus leads me on.

[Thunder.]

Brutus. Follow me then.

[Exeunt.]

338 *Vouchsafe . . . tongue:* Accept a good morning from a sick man.

341 *kerchief:* a covering to protect the head during sickness.

343 *exploit:* deed.

347 *I here discard my sickness:* I declare myself cured.
348 *derived . . . loins:* descended from noble Romans.
349 *exorcist:* someone who can call up spirits.

355 *What does Caius mean?*

360 *Set on your foot:* Lead the way.

362 *it sufficeth:* It is enough.

Responding to Reading

1. At the beginning of this scene, Brutus sorts out his ideas about why Caesar must die. Does he make a convincing argument? Explain.
2. Think of the letter Brutus receives and the effect it has on him. What does this tell you about Brutus?
3. On the Explore pages, you learned that friendship is an important theme in this play. Do you think Brutus and Cassius are truly friends? Explain.

3. Some students may say that Cassius and Brutus are not friends because they have such different conceptions of what friendship means: Brutus is idealistic and honest, whereas Cassius is practical and manipulative. Others may say that Cassius and Brutus are friends: they trust and rely on one another.

Scene 2 *Caesar's house in Rome.*

It is now past dawn on March 15. Like everyone else in Rome, Caesar and his wife have slept badly because of the storm. There is still some lightning and thunder. Caesar prepares to go to the Capitol, but because of the many threatening omens, his wife Calpurnia insists that he stay home. Caesar agrees, for Calpurnia's sake. He changes his mind when Decius, one of the conspirators, persuades him that he must not seem swayed by his wife's superstitions. Although Caesar doesn't know it, the other conspirators are on their way to his house to make sure he does not decide to stay at home.

[Enter Caesar *in his nightgown.]*

Caesar. Nor heaven nor earth have been at peace tonight.
Thrice hath Calpurnia in her sleep cried out
"Help, ho! They murder Caesar!" Who's within?

[Enter a Servant.*]*

Servant. My lord?

Caesar. Go bid the priests do present sacrifice,
And bring me their opinions of success.

Servant. I will, my lord.

[Exit.]

[Enter Caesar's *wife* Calpurnia, *alarmed.]*

Calpurnia. What mean you, Caesar? Think you to walk forth?
You shall not stir out of your house today.

Caesar. Caesar shall forth. The things that threatened me
Ne'er looked but on my back. When they shall see
The face of Caesar, they are vanished.

Calpurnia. Caesar, I never stood on ceremonies,
Yet now they fright me. There is one within,
Besides the things that we have heard and seen,
Recounts most horrid sights seen by the watch.
A lioness hath whelped in the streets,
And graves have yawned and yielded up their dead.
Fierce fiery warriors fought upon the clouds
In ranks and squadrons and right form of war,
Which drizzled blood upon the Capitol.
The noise of battle hurtled in the air,
Horses did neigh, and dying men did groan,

6–7 *Go bid . . . success:* Roman priests would kill an animal as a sacrifice to the gods. Then they would cut the animal open and examine its internal organs for signs of future events.

12–62 As you read this conversation, think about Caesar's view of himself. Remember the way he talked of himself to Antony in Act One. Look for new evidence of Caesar's view of his own importance and his power.

12–14 *The things . . . vanished:* When I turn to face the things that threaten me, they disappear.

15–28 *Caesar, I never . . . fear them:* Calpurnia tells Caesar that she has never before believed in omens ***(stood on ceremonies)***, but now she is frightened. She describes the terrible things she has heard of from the men who were on guard during the night.

Text Annotations

A. Literary Element: Irony Ask what is unintentionally ironic about Caesar's words in light of the action of the preceding scene. *(Possible response: His words are truer than he knows, since the conspirators have just finished plotting his assassination)*

B. Literary Element: CHARACTERIZATION Ask what these words imply about Caesar's character. *(Possible response: Caesar is courageous, boastful, and over-confident; also he has the grandiose habit of referring to himself in the third person.)*

C. Reading Skill: VISUALIZING Ask students to describe these images in their own words, or possibly to draw them or represent them artistically in some other way. Musical students may find or compose music to convey the mood evoked by these images. Then have students discuss why Shakespeare has Calpurnia recount these stories, encouraging them to grasp the mood of supernatural horror created here.

D. Historical Sidelight The ancient historian Plutarch, whose *Lives of the Noble Greeks and Romans* served as one of Shakespeare's sources, reports numerous omens on the evening before Caesar's assassination. Many cultures have clung to the belief that unusual events, especially comets, are supernatural signs of bad fortune for rulers or leaders.

E. Literary Element: CHARACTERIZATION Ask how this speech adds a new perspective to Caesar's characterization. *(Possible response: Caesar seems sensible and philosophical in this passage, rather than boastful or over-confident as he has seemed before.)*

F. Cultural Sidelight The Roman profession of augury was widely respected and exceedingly complex. Basically, it involved foretelling the future by two methods: observation of the flights of birds and (as here) a kind of "autopsy" performed on the remains of sacrificed animals. A beast without a heart would be considered a major omen of bad fortune.

G. LEP: Figurative Language Be sure students understand that these lines include two separate figures of speech. In the first, "danger" is personified as an inferior enemy of Caesar. In the second, Caesar uses a metaphor to compare danger and himself to two lions from the same litter, with danger again the weaker and Caesar the "elder and more terrible."

And ghosts did shriek and squeal about the streets.
O Caesar, these things are beyond all use,
And I do fear them!

Caesar. What can be avoided
Whose end is purposed by the mighty gods?
Yet Caesar shall go forth, for these predictions
Are to the world in general as to Caesar.

Calpurnia. When beggars die there are no comets seen;
D The heavens themselves blaze forth the death of
princes.

Caesar. Cowards die many times before their deaths;
The valiant never taste of death but once.
Of all the wonders that I yet have heard,
It seems to me most strange that men should fear,
E Seeing that death, a necessary end,
Will come when it will come.

[Reenter Servant.*]*

What say the augurers?

Servant. They would not have you to stir forth today.
F Plucking the entrails of an offering forth,
They could not find a heart within the beast.

Caesar. The gods do this in shame of cowardice.
Caesar should be a beast without a heart
If he should stay at home today for fear.
No, Caesar shall not. Danger knows full well
That Caesar is more dangerous than he.
G We are two lions littered in one day,
And I the elder and more terrible,
And Caesar shall go forth.

Calpurnia. Alas, my lord!
Your wisdom is consumed in confidence.
Do not go forth today. Call it my fear
That keeps you in the house and not your own.
We'll send Mark Antony to the Senate House,
And he shall say you are not well today.
Let me upon my knee prevail in this.

Caesar. Mark Antony shall say I am not well,
And for thy humor I will stay at home.

[Enter Decius.*]*

Here's Decius Brutus, he shall tell them so.

27 *beyond all use:* unlike anything we are accustomed to.

29–32 Caesar insists that, if these are omens and if the gods have destined that certain things will happen, no one can avoid them. He will go out, since the predictions, he believes, apply to the whole world, not only to Caesar.

51 *littered in one day:* born at the same time.

CRITIC'S CORNER

"Calpurnia's dream is one of the play's cruxes. By this time in the course of the drama an internal convention has been established regarding dreams and omens: whatever their source, they are true, and it is dangerous to disregard them. Shakespeare's audience would certainly have been familiar with the story of Julius Caesar, and such a collection of portents and premonitions would have seemed to them, as it does to us, to be infallibly leading to the moment of murder. . . . Unlike the events narrated by Casca, those reported by Calpurnia are not specified in Plutarch; it is noteworthy how much more *Shakespearean* they are, and how economically chosen to foreshadow, metaphorically, the later events of the play."
MARJORIE B. GARBER, "Dream and Interpretation: *Julius Caesar*"

Decius. Caesar, all hail! Good morrow, worthy Caesar!
I come to fetch you to the Senate House.

Caesar. And you are come in very happy time
To bear my greetings to the senators
And tell them that I will not come today.
Cannot, is false; and that I dare not, falser.
I will not come today. Tell them so, Decius.

Calpurnia. Say he is sick.

Caesar. Shall Caesar send a lie?
Have I in conquest stretched mine arm so far
To be afeard to tell greybeards the truth?
Decius, go tell them Caesar will not come.

Decius. Most mighty Caesar, let me know some cause,
Lest I be laughed at when I tell them so.

Caesar. The cause is in my will: I will not come.
That is enough to satisfy the Senate;
But for your private satisfaction,
Because I love you, I will let you know.
Calpurnia here, my wife, stays me at home.
She dreamt tonight she saw my statue,
Which, like a fountain with an hundred spouts,
Did run pure blood, and many lusty Romans
Came smiling and did bathe their hands in it.
And these does she apply for warnings and portents
And evils imminent, and on her knee
Hath begged that I will stay at home today.

Decius. This dream is all amiss interpreted;
It was a vision fair and fortunate.
Your statue spouting blood in many pipes,
In which so many smiling Romans bathed,
Signifies that from you great Rome shall suck
Reviving blood, and that great men shall press
For tinctures, stains, relics, and cognizance.
This by Calpurnia's dream is signified.

Caesar. And this way have you well expounded it.

Decius. I have, when you have heard what I can say:
And know it now, the Senate have concluded
To give this day a crown to mighty Caesar.
If you shall send them word you will not come,
Their minds may change. Besides, it were a mock
Apt to be rendered, for some one to say

72–75 *Shall . . . not come:* Caesar is appalled by his wife's suggestion that he lie to a bunch of old men ***(greybeards)*** about his reason for not going to the Senate. *How might an actor say these lines?*

87 *portents:* signs of evil to come.

90–97 Decius has to think fast. He promised the others that he could flatter Caesar into believing anything. Now he must give Caesar a new interpretation of Calpurnia's dream, one that will get him out of the house.
90 *amiss:* wrongly.
95–96 *great men . . . cognizance:* Great men will come to you for honors and souvenirs to remember you by.

103–104 *it were . . . rendered:* It's likely that someone will make a sarcastic comment.

H. Answer: *An actor might use a proud and slightly contemptious tone for these lines.*

I. Literary Sidelight Point out to students that Caesar refers to himself both in the first and in the third person here. In his *Commentaries,* the history Caesar wrote of his own military campaigns, he regularly used the third person to refer to himself. In Shakespeare's time, royalty might also use the third person.

J. Literary Element: CHARACTERIZATION Have students comment on what these lines reveal about Caesar's personality. *(Possible response: These lines imply that Caesar is arrogant and holds the Senate in contempt.)*

K. Critical Thinking: EVALUATING Invite students to evaluate Decius' skill and ingenuity in his interpretation of the dream. *(Possible response: Decius is ingenious, since he interprets the dream in a way that is likely to appeal to Caesar's conception of himself as the fearless head of state.)*

L. Reading Skill: INTERPRETIVE ORAL READING Encourage students to read this passage aloud. Students should practice altering their tone, rate, volume, and pitch as they render Decius' "quotations" of what various senators might say.

M. Answer: *Decius argues that the Senate may change its mind about crowning Caesar; he says that some senators may mock Caesar for being overly influenced by a superstitious wife; and he even adds that some people may accuse Caesar of being cowardly.*

N. Critical Thinking: ANALYZING Ask students to explain which of Decius' arguments they think is most important in changing Caesar's mind. *(Possible response: Probably Decius' final argument—implying that Caesar might be called a coward—has been the most decisive, since Caesar now refers to Calpurnia's "fears" as "foolish" and says that he is "ashamed" to have yielded to her.)*

O. LEP: Irony Make sure students see the irony in Caesar's wishing to "remember" a man who intends to murder him, in Trebonius' joke about standing near, and in Caesar's trusting reference to "friends."

"Break up the Senate till another time,
When Caesar's wife shall meet with better dreams."
If Caesar hide himself, shall they not whisper
"Lo, Caesar is afraid"?
Pardon me, Caesar, for my dear dear love
To your proceeding bids me tell you this,
And reason to my love is liable.

Caesar. How foolish do your fears seem now,
Calpurnia!
I am ashamed I did yield to them.
Give me my robe, for I will go.

[Enter Brutus, Ligarius, Metellus, Casca, Trebonius, Cinna, *and* Publius.*]*

And look where Publius is come to fetch me.

Publius. Good morrow, Caesar.

Caesar. Welcome Publius.
What Brutus, are you stirred so early too?
Good morrow, Casca. Caius Ligarius,
Caesar was ne'er so much your enemy
As that same ague which hath made you lean.
What is't o'clock?

Brutus. Caesar, 'tis strucken eight.

Caesar. I thank you for your pains and courtesy.

[Enter Antony.*]*

See! Antony, that revels long o'nights,
Is notwithstanding up. Good morrow, Antony.

Antony. So to most noble Caesar.

Caesar. Bid them prepare within.
I am to blame to be thus waited for.
Now, Cinna, now, Metellus. What, Trebonius!
I have an hour's talk in store for you;
Remember that you call on me today;
Be near me, that I may remember you.

Trebonius. Caesar, I will. *[Aside]* And so near will I be
That your best friends shall wish I had been further.

Caesar. Good friends, go in and taste some wine with
me,
And we (like friends) will straightway go together.

109–111 ***my dear . . . liable:*** My sincere interest in your career ***(proceeding)*** makes me tell you this. My feeling for you overtakes my intelligence ***(reason).*** *What argument does Decimus use to change Caesar's mind?*

122 ***ague:*** sickness.

126–127 ***Antony . . . up:*** Even Antony, who parties ***(revels)*** late into the night, is up early today.

135 ***Aside:*** privately, in a way that keeps the other characters from hearing what is said. Think of it as a whisper that the audience happens to overhear.

PROFESSIONAL NOTEBOOK

Will [students] be able to make sense of the archaic vocabulary, the blank verse, the puns, the classical and anachronistic allusions, the confusion of names, the distortions of history? Given the meaningful possibilities of this play, each teacher must decide whether or not his class is able to break through the difficulties to effect some communication with the play. That judgment, I think, must be based not on reading rate or vocabulary count or spelling ability, but on a subjective estimate of the imaginative courage of the class. Class and teacher must be willing to take a risk, to go beyond the printed words not minding if they stumble over the first "Hence!"

EDWARD RYERSON, "*Julius Caesar* Once Again"

Brutus. *[Aside]* That every like is not the same, O Caesar,
The heart of Brutus yearns to think upon.

[Exeunt.]

140–142 ***That every . . . upon:*** The fact that we behave like friends doesn't mean we are friends. My heart grieves ***(earns)*** to think of it. *What is Brutus saying about his friendship with Caesar?*

Responding to Reading

1. Do Caesar's words and actions in this scene cause you to change the opinion you have of him? Why or why not?

   Think about
   - his response to the predictions of evil
   - his conversation with Calpurnia
   - the fact that he is persuaded to go to the Capitol
   - his conversation with the conspirators at the end of this scene

2. Contrast the relationship between Caesar and Calpurnia with the relationship between Brutus and Portia.

Scene 3 *A street in Rome near the Capitol.*

In this brief scene, Caesar has still another chance to avoid the path that leads to his death. Artemidorus, a supporter of Caesar, has learned about the plot. He reads a letter he has written to warn Caesar. Then he waits in the street for Caesar to pass by on his way to the Capitol.

[Enter Artemidorus, *reading a paper.]*

Artemidorus. "Caesar, beware of Brutus; take heed of Cassius; come not near Casca; have an eye to Cinna; trust not Trebonius; mark well Metellus Cimber; Decius Brutus loves thee not; thou hast wronged Caius Ligarius. There is but one mind in all these men, and it is bent against Caesar. If thou beest not immortal, look about you. Security gives way to conspiracy. The mighty gods defend thee!
"Thy Lover,
"ARTEMIDORUS."
Here will I stand till Caesar pass along
And as a suitor will I give him this.
My heart laments that virtue cannot live
Out of the teeth of emulation.

9 ***lover:*** devoted friend.

13–14 ***My heart . . . emulation:*** My heart is sad that Caesar's greatness cannot escape jealousy ***(the teeth of emulation).***

P. Literary Element: THEME Ask students what outlook Trebonius and Brutus now express on friendship. *(Possible response: They both openly acknowledge that friendship may be false.)* Ask whether both Trebonius and Brutus seem to have the same inner emotions when they express this outlook. *(Possible response: No, since Trebonius seems hard and scornful, while Brutus seems regretful)*

Q. Answer: *Brutus is saying that his friendship with Caesar has grown to be hypocritical, since despite appearances he has joined the conspiracy.*

Text Annotations

A. Literary Element: SUSPENSE Ask students how Shakespeare's presentation of Artemidorus reading his "petition" serves to increase the suspense. *(Possible response: The audience is now aware that news of the plot has leaked, so there is a possibility that Caesar may be warned about it in time. On the other hand, the audience wonders whether Artemidorus will succeed in presenting his petition to Caesar.)*

B. LEP: Figurative Language Be sure that students understand that "emulation" (which means "envy" here) is envisioned in Artemidorus' metaphor to be like a person or beast with sharp, vicious "teeth." Artemidorus is sad because virtue in some people is always vulnerable to the "bite" of envy in others.

Student Response

Responding to Reading

These questions are open-ended with no "right" or "wrong" answers. However, responses must be supported with information from the selection. Possible answers follow:

1. Possible response: Caesar is more fully characterized in this scene. His responses to the predictions of evil show that he is rational and courageous, but he also seems overly confident and egotistical when he speaks of himself in the third person. Decius' success in persuading him to go to the Capitol shows that Caesar may be afraid of being called cowardly or subservient to his wife. His conversation with the conspirators shows that he suspects nothing.

2. Whereas Brutus is evasive and (at first) lies to Portia, Caesar is more open with his wife. Although both men are persuaded by their wives, Caesar later changes his mind.

Text Annotations

A. Literary Element: DIALOGUE Have students note how choppy the dialogue is here, as Portia first addresses Lucius, then calls on "constancy" as she talks to herself, and finally calls again to the servant. The abrupt changes in the dialogue effectively convey Portia's acutely nervous state.

B. Answer: *Many students will disagree with the statement, or at least with the implication that it is easier for men than women to keep a secret. Ask students to explain their reasons.*

C. Literary Element: FORESHADOWING Ask students what this reference to "suitors" pressing on Caesar foreshadows about the assassins' plans, in light of the fact that Portia apparently knows of the conspiracy. *(Possible response: They will probably try to crowd around Caesar under the pretext of presenting "suits," or petitions.)*

If thou read this, O Caesar, thou mayst live;
If not, the Fates with traitors do contrive.

[Exit.]

16 *contrive:* plot.

Scene 4 *In front of Brutus's house.*

Shakespeare continues to build suspense with another short scene. This one involves Brutus' wife, Portia, who feels anxious about the conspiracy. Portia nervously orders the servant Lucius to go and see what is happening at the Capitol. She next meets the soothsayer, who makes her even more anxious as he continues to predict danger for Caesar.

[Enter Portia *and* Lucius.*]*

Portia. I prithee, boy, run to the Senate House.
Stay not to answer me, but get thee gone!
Why dost thou stay?

Lucius. To know my errand, madam.

Portia. I would have had thee there and here again
Ere I can tell thee what thou shouldst do there.
O constancy, be strong upon my side,
A Set a huge mountain 'tween my heart and tongue!
I have a man's mind, but a woman's might.
How hard it is for women to keep counsel!
Art thou here yet?

5–6 *I would have . . . do there:* I would have had you travel there and back without telling you what I wanted you to do. (Portia is upset with herself for acting foolishly.)

10 *keep counsel:* keep a secret. *What do you think of Portia's (or Shakespeare's) statement that it is hard for a woman to keep a secret?* B

Lucius. Madam, what should I do?
Run to the Capitol and nothing else?
And so return to you and nothing else?

Portia. Yes, bring me word, boy, if thy lord look well,
C For he went sickly forth; and take good note
What Caesar doth, what suitors press to him.
Hark, boy! What noise is that?

17 *what suitors press to him:* what people stand near him.

Lucius. I hear none, madam.

Portia. Prithee, listen well.
I heard a bustling rumor like a fray,
And the wind brings it from the Capitol.

Lucius. Sooth, madam, I hear nothing.

21 *I heard . . . fray:* Portia imagines that she has heard a noise like a battle ***(fray)***.

23 *Sooth:* truthfully.

[Enter the Soothsayer.*]*

Portia. Come hither, fellow. Which way hast thou
been?

24 The soothsayer is the same fortuneteller who warned Caesar to

CRITIC'S CORNER

"Portia is one of the first of a number of Shakespearean heroines who have brief roles of supreme importance. Speaking to Brutus, she refers to herself as 'your self, your half.' [See her speech on page 762, line 294.] The phrase 'better half' as applied to a wife has been so prostituted to jocosity that it is scarcely possible to use it seriously. Yet it describes precisely Portia's relation to Brutus. The point is underlined by the fact that Calpurnia bears somewhat the same relation to Caesar. These women through their dreams and intuitions draw from deeper springs of wisdom than any to which their husbands have access. And Caesar because of his vanity and his nature, Brutus because of a strain of cold rationalism that runs through his nature, are in peculiar need of the insight of their wives."

HAROLD GODDARD, *The Meaning of Shakespeare*

Soothsayer. At mine own house, good lady.

Portia. What is't o'clock?

Soothsayer. About the ninth hour, lady.

Portia. Is Caesar yet gone to the Capitol?

Soothsayer. Madam, not yet. I go to take my stand,
To see him pass on to the Capitol.

Portia. Thou hast some suit to Caesar, hast thou not?

Soothsayer. That I have, lady. If it will please Caesar
D To be so good to Caesar as to hear me,
I shall beseech him to befriend himself.

Portia. Why, know'st thou any harm's intended
towards him?

Soothsayer. None that I know will be, much that I
fear may chance.
Good morrow to you. Here the street is narrow.
The throng that follows Caesar at the heels,
Of senators, of praetors, common suitors,
E Will crowd a feeble man almost to death.
I'll get me to a place more void and there
Speak to great Caesar as he comes along.

[Exit.]

Portia. I must go in. Ay me, how weak a thing
The heart of woman is! O Brutus,
The heavens speed thee in thine enterprise—
Sure the boy heard me.—Brutus hath a suit
That Caesar will not grant.—O, I grow faint.—
F Run, Lucius, and commend me to my Lord;
Say I am merry. Come to me again
And bring me word what he doth say to thee.

[Exeunt severally.]

beware the ides of March. He is now on his way to the street near the Capitol building where he usually sits.

32 *Thou hast . . . Caesar:* Have you some favor to ask of Caesar?

38–39 *None . . . chance:* I'm not sure of any danger, but I fear that some may chance to happen.

49–50 *Brutus hath . . . not grant:* Brutus has a favor to ask that Caesar will not give him.
51 *commend . . . lord:* Give my husband my good wishes.
severally: in different directions.

Responding to Reading

1. Imagine you are watching a performance of this play. What might be the effect on the audience of two such brief scenes?
2. Considering what you already know about Caesar, how might he react to Artemidorus' letter? Support your view with examples from the play.
3. From her words and behavior, what emotions do you think Portia is feeling in Scene 4?

D. Literary Element: SUSPENSE How does Shakespeare combine suspense on the part of the audience with suspense on the part of Portia here? *(Possible response: The audience's tension increases when the soothsayer seems to imply that he knows of some harm that may come to Caesar. At the same time, Portia nervously infers from the soothsayer's words that he may know the specific details of the plot, thus putting Brutus in danger.)*

E. Reading Skill: VISUALIZING Urge students to try to visualize the soothsayer's description of the crowded street along which Caesar will pass. Ask what event might furnish a modern parallel to this scene. *(Possible responses: a presidential motorcade or a parade for a championship sports team)*

F. Reading Skill: INTERPRETIVE ORAL READING Encourage students to read this passage aloud. Students should alter their pitch, rate, and volume in order to convey Portia's distracted agitation.

Check Test

1. What major decision do the conspirators take concerning Caesar in Scene 1? *(to murder him)*

2. How does Portia succeed in persuading Brutus to confide his plans to her? *(She reminds him that she has given herself a wound in the thigh to prove her courage and constancy.)*

3. In Scene 2, who tries to persuade Caesar not to go to the Capitol and whose arguments change Caesar's mind? *(Calpurnia, Decius)*

4. In Scene 3, how does Artemidorus plan to warn Caesar of the plot? *(by giving Caesar a letter as he passes on the street)*

5. In Scene 4, what does Portia order Lucius to do? *(to run to the Capitol and to bring her news of Brutus)*

Student Response

Responding to Reading

These questions are open-ended with no "right" or "wrong" answers. However, responses must be supported with information from the selection. Possible answers follow:

1. Students may say that the two short scenes would help quicken the pace of the action and build suspense.

2. Students may say that Caesar might ignore the warnings of Artemidorus, either because he is overconfident about his own power and prestige (compare his emphasis on his own "will" in Scene 2) or because he cannot bring himself to believe that his trusted friends would betray him (compare his friendly conversation with the conspirators at the end of Scene 2).

3. Students may say that Portia's confused words and flustered behavior suggest that she is extremely apprehensive about the plot.

e x p l a i n

Responding to Reading

First Impressions

1. Whom do you side with at this point, Caesar or the conspirators? Why?

Second Thoughts

2. How would you describe the relationship between Brutus and Portia?
3. Do Brutus and Cassius have different motives for wanting to kill Caesar? Explain.
4. What is your opinion of the plot against Caesar? Do the plotters have enough evidence to back up their claims? Do their plans seem justified? Explain.
5. Who is the true leader of the conspirators? Support your opinion with facts from the play.
6. Who do you think would make a better replacement for Caesar as a leader of Rome—Brutus or Cassius? Explain.
7. Do you think Caesar has any suspicion that there is a plot to kill him? Explain your answer and what it says about Caesar as a ruler.

Literary Concepts: Suspense and Plot

Suspense is the tension or excitement readers (or audiences) feel as they become drawn into the story and eager to learn the outcome. One method Shakespeare uses to create suspense is **foreshadowing.** As you read Scene 2, how did you respond to Calpurnia's dream of Caesar's murder? How did Caesar's response make you feel? What other ways does Shakespeare build suspense in Act Two?

The **plot** is the sequence of actions in a literary work. Most plots center on a conflict or problem the characters struggle to resolve. A plot in a classical piece of literature usually follows a specific pattern consisting of five stages: **exposition, rising action, climax, falling action,** and **resolution.** In a five-act play, the first act usually presents the exposition—the background information—and introduces the characters, the setting, and the conflict. The second act then presents the rising action—the part of the story where the conflict becomes obvious, suspense builds, and characters struggle to resolve their problems. Do Acts One and Two of *Julius Caesar* conform to this pattern? Explain and give examples.

Student Response

Responding to Reading

These questions are open-ended with no "right" or "wrong" answers. However, responses must be supported with information from the selection. Possible answers follow:

1. Any reasonable answer is valid. Some students will side with Caesar, arguing that there is very little evidence to prove Caesar is a tyrant. Others may side with the conspirators, citing Caesar's arrogance and egotism.

2. Some students may say that the relationship is one-sided, since Brutus does not at first trust Portia enough to be honest with her about the conspiracy; others may say the relationship is somewhat egalitarian, since Portia feels free to make demands on Brutus and to reproach him.

3. Students may feel that Brutus acts out of high-minded patriotism and for what he conceives to be the general good. On the other hand, although Cassius often refers to the bondage of the Roman people, his motives also seem to include personal envy, bitterness, and revenge.

4. Some students may say that the plotters have evidence that Caesar will not be crowned in the Senate on the ides of March, but they do not have convincing evidence that Caesar will become more tyrannical; hence their plans for Caesar's assassination do not seem justified. Others may say the plotters have good reason to fear Caesar's egotism, ambition, and popularity with the volatile rabble, so their plans are justified.

5. Possible response: Although some students may say that Cassius was the driving force in Act I, others may insist that Brutus emerges as the true leader, since his reputation for honor is critical to the plotters' success. The conspirators are also swayed by his arguments to exclude Cicero and to spare Antony.

6. Some students may say that Brutus would make a better replacement, since he is motivated by the general good; others may choose Cassius, since he appears to be more practical and clever.

7. Most students will argue that Caesar has no suspicion, since he treats the conspirators in a friendly way at the end of scene 2 and ignores Calpurnia's warnings. Although Caesar has identified Cassius as "dangerous" in Act I, his lack of suspicions now may suggest that he is an egotistical, overconfident leader.

Writing Options

The Writing Options are designed to meet varied student interests and abilities. Have each student choose one writing activity to complete. You may wish to guide some students to an option that requires less writing.

Writing Options

1. Imagine that you are a prominent citizen of Rome and Cassius asks you to join the conspiracy to kill Caesar. Write a response with an explanation of your decision.
2. Pretend you are Cassius. Write an entry in your journal describing your feelings about the plan to kill Caesar.
3. When the plotters approach Caesar to kill him, they expect Mark Antony to be at his side. What do you predict Antony will do? Explain.
4. What if Caesar had not gone to the Senate that day? What would the plotters have done? Would they have killed him at home, put off the plot, lost their nerve? Write an explanation of your opinion.
5. Caesar says, "Cowards die many times before their deaths / The valiant never taste of death but once." What does this quote mean to you? Do you agree with it? Explain.

e x t e n d

Options for Learning

1 • Rome's Government Use the library to find out about the government of Rome at the time of Caesar's death. Report to the class on the role the Senate played, the powers Caesar had, and the voice the people of Rome had in selecting members of their government. Explain how the government structure affects developments in this play.

2 • Music for a Tragedy Suppose you were selecting music for a movie or television production of *The Tragedy of Julius Caesar*. Find one piece of music for each of the following scenes:

- Brutus examines the reasons why Caesar has to die, Act Two, Scene 1.
- Brutus speaks with Portia, Act Two, Scene 1.
- Portia speaks to Lucius and the soothsayer, Act Two, Scene 4.

Play each selection for the class, and explain why you think it is appropriate for the scene it accompanies.

3 • Brutus' Use the library to find out what the home and orchard of a man like Brutus might have looked like. Then draw a picture or build a model of the scene in which Brutus and the other conspirators discuss the details of their plan.

4 • Interpret a Character With a group of students, perform part of Act Two for the class. Remember to recite your lines as blank verse. Try to interpret your character's personality, motives, and feelings. After the performance, ask for a critique from the class.

Options for Learning

These activities suit a variety of learning styles and modes of expression. Allow students to review the options and then choose the one they wish to do. Many are excellent collaborative learning projects.

1. Rome's Government Suggest that students consult encyclopedia articles under the heading "Roman Republic" or "Ancient Rome: Republican Period" for this assignment.

2. Music for a Tragedy Suggest that students reread each scene and then write one adjective that best describes each scene's overall mood, or atmosphere. Then students can choose musical selections that convey this mood.

3. Brutus' House Advise students to consult illustrations of the ancient Roman houses excavated at Pompeii or Herculaneum.

4. Interpret a Character Remind students that their recitations of blank verse should follow the punctuation of the lines.

Literary Concepts—Foreshadowing and Suspense

Students should point out devices such as the soothsayer's references to the ides of March, the storm and strange omens, Calpurnia's dream, the role of Artemidorus, and Portia's agitation as the act concludes.

Literary Concept: Plot

Students will probably say that Acts One and Two do conform to the pattern. They may point out that Act One does in fact introduce the characters, setting, and the basic conflict—whether Romans should put up with the growing power of Caesar. They may next point out that, in Act Two, the conspirators' words and actions make the conflict obvious, omens and other foreshadowing build suspense, and Brutus struggles to resolve his inner conflict.

Teaching Strategies

Support for LEP Students of Limited English Proficiency

- Use **Reader's Guidesheet**, p. 7.
- *Julius Caesar* Act Three contains some archaic words and words with archaic meanings that may be challenging for some students. Help students to identify and understand these archaisms by using the relevant annotations below.
- **Annotations E, F, N, T, BB, CC, JJ,** and **KK** (Scene 1), and **E, AA,** and **HH** (Scene 2), focus on archaic words and meanings.

Text Annotations

Scene 1

A. Literary Element: FORESHADOWING Ask students how the soothsayer manages to foreshadow a disaster. *(Possible response: The soothsayer answers that the ides of March "are not gone," meaning that there is still time for some catastrophe to happen.)*

B. Literary Element: SUSPENSE Ask students how Shakespeare creates and maintains suspense in this brief exchange. *(Possible answer: When Artemidorus steps forward, the audience will inevitably feel the suspense, since they know Artemidorus is familiar with the details of the conspiracy. Decius deftly interposes with another "suit," however. The conspirators are safe from discovery, at least for the moment.)*

C. Reading Skill: VISUALIZING You might wish to stage this part of the action in class, so that students can experience for themselves the effect of seeing the man who could have saved Caesar forced out of his reach. In any case, encourage students to visualize the impact of the action as indicated by the stage directions.

ACT THREE

Scene 1 *The Capitol in Rome.*

Outside the Capitol, Caesar refuses to look at Artemidorus' letter of warning. Caesar next moves into the Capitol. There, the conspirators surround him, pretending to plead a case. Suddenly, they stab him to death. Mark Antony flees, but Brutus persuades the conspirators to let him live. Brutus himself promises to explain the killing and its reasons to the Roman people. Antony returns and pretends to be an ally of the conspirators. Secretly, however, he plans to strike back with help from Octavius Caesar, who is now on his way to Rome.

[The Senate sits on a higher level, waiting for Caesar *to appear.* Artemidorus *and the* Soothsayer *are among the crowd. A flourish of trumpets. Enter* Caesar, Brutus, Cassius, Casca, Decius, Metellus, Trebonius, Cinna, Antony, Lepidus, Popilius, *and others.* Caesar *stops in front of the* Soothsayer.*]*

A **Caesar.** The ides of March are come.

Soothsayer. Ay, Caesar, but not gone.

*[*Artemidorus *steps up to* Caesar *with his warning.]*

Artemidorus. Hail, Caesar! Read this schedule.

*[*Decius *steps up quickly with another paper.]*

Decius. Trebonius doth desire you to o'erread
(At your best leisure) this his humble suit.

Artemidorus. O Caesar, read mine first, for mine's a suit
B That touches Caesar nearer. Read it, great Caesar!

Caesar. What touches us ourself shall be last served.

*[*Caesar *pushes the paper aside and turns away.]*

Artemidorus. Delay not, Caesar! Read it instantly!

Caesar. What, is the fellow mad?

Publius. Sirrah, give place.

*[*Publius *and other conspirators force* Artemidorus *away from* Caesar.*]*

C **Cassius.** What, urge you your petitions in the street?
Come to the Capitol.

*[*Caesar *goes into the Senate House, the rest following.* Popilius *speaks to* Cassius *in a low voice.]*

GUIDE FOR READING

3 *schedule:* document.

4–13 Artemidorus is the man who has prepared a written warning for Caesar to read ***(o'erread)*** about the men plotting against him. The conspirators suspect this and do not want him to get to Caesar. Decius steps in front of Artemidorus and offers a written request from someone else. Then Publius (who is not a conspirator) and Cassius push Artemidorus aside.

11 *Sirrah:* a form of address used toward a servant or inferior, often to express anger or disrespect; ***give place:*** get out of the way.

D **Popilius.** I wish your enterprise today may thrive.
Cassius. What enterprise, Popilius?
Popilius. Fare you well.

[Advances to Caesar.*]*

Brutus. What said Popilius Lena?

Cassius. He wished today our enterprise might thrive.
I fear our purpose is discovered.

Brutus. Look how he makes to Caesar. Mark him.

E **Cassius.** Casca, be sudden, for we fear prevention.
Brutus, what shall be done? If this be known,
Cassius or Caesar never shall turn back,
For I will slay myself.

Brutus. Cassius, be constant.
Popilius Lena speaks not of our purposes,
For look, he smiles, and Caesar doth not change.

Cassius. Trebonius knows his time, for look you, Brutus,
He draws Mark Antony out of the way.

[Exeunt Antony *and* Trebonius.*]*

Decius. Where is Metellus Cimber? Let him go
And presently prefer his suit to Caesar.

F **Brutus.** He is addressed. Press near and second him.

Cinna. Casca, you are the first that rears your hand.

*[*Caesar *seats himself in his high Senate chair.]*

Caesar. Are we all ready? What is now amiss
That Caesar and his Senate must redress?

Metellus. Most high, most mighty, and most puissant Caesar,
Metellus Cimber throws before thy seat
An humble heart.

[Kneeling.]

Caesar. I must prevent thee, Cimber.
These couchings and these lowly courtesies
Might fire the blood of ordinary men
And turn preordinance and first decree
Into the law of children. Be not fond
To think that Caesar bears such rebel blood
That will be thawed from the true quality
With that which melteth fools—I mean, sweet words,

14 *I wish . . . thrive:* I hope your venture is successful.

20–27 *Look how . . . change:* Brutus and Cassius watch Popilius Lena talk privately with Caesar. They fear he is telling Caesar of their plot. Then, seeing Popilius Lena smile, they know they were mistaken.

31 *prefer . . . Caesar:* ask his favor of Caesar.
32 *Press . . . him:* Get near him (Metullus Cimber) and back up his request.

36 *puissant:* powerful.

40–53 *I must prevent . . . satisfied:* Caesar claims that, unlike ordinary men, he cannot be moved by bowing and scraping. He will not let such things change the laws of the country ***(preordinance and first decree).*** His heart cannot be melted by sweet words, bowing ***(curtsies),*** and behavior fit for a dog ***(base spaniel fawning).***

D. Literary Element: **SUSPENSE** Ask students how Popilius Lena's words help build suspense. *(Possible response: Popilius Lena's vague phrase, "your enterprise," could refer to the conspiracy; or it might be an innocuous reference to some other project. Cassius is set on edge by Lena's words, thinking that he may have discovered the plot and that he may warn Caesar.)*

E. LEP: Archaic Words and Meanings The word *prevention* here is used in a slightly different meaning from its familiar modern denotation. Here it means "discovery."

F. LEP: Archaic Words and Meanings Be sure students realize that the word *addressed* means "ready." In the same line, *second* as a verb means "to support." You might remind students of the phrase, "I second the motion."

G. Literary Element: FIGURATIVE LANGUAGE Ask students what comparison is being made here. *(Petitioners are compared to fawning dogs.)* Then help students identify the two words in this passage that furnish the key to the metaphor. *("spaniel" and "cur")*

H. Answer: *Many students will point out that Caesar's evaluation of his own personality conflicts with the fact that he was swayed by Decius Brutus' arguments and flattery in Act Two, Scene 2.*

I. Literary Element: IRONY Ask students to explain what is ironic about Brutus' speech to Caesar in this context. *(Possible response: Brutus is hardly sincere when he says that he does not flatter Caesar when he kisses his hand. In fact, he is playing his role in the conspirators' plan to crowd around Caesar under the pretext of begging him to grant a petition, so that they can assassinate him with their daggers.)*

J. Literary Element: FIGURATIVE LANGUAGE Ask students what Caesar compares himself to in this simile. *(to the constant Northern Star)* Then have them identify the quality in himself he wants to emphasize by this comparison. *(Possible response: his firmness and determination)*

K. Answer: By emphasizing his own firmness and constancy, Caesar certainly seems to be bragging.

L. Literary Element: THEME Ask students how Caesar's last words relate to the theme of friendship in the play and what this line reveals about Caesar's feelings as he dies. *(Possible response: Caesar's last words imply that Brutus' betrayal of his friendship is the real blow that makes Caesar surrender his life.)*

Low-crookèd curtsies, and base spaniel fawning.
Thy brother by decree is banished.
H If thou dost bend and pray and fawn for him,
I spurn thee like a cur out of my way.
Know, Caesar doth not wrong, nor without cause
Will he be satisfied.

Metellus. Is there no voice more worthy than my own,
To sound more sweetly in great Caesar's ear
For the repealing of my banished brother?

Brutus. I kiss thy hand, but not in flattery, Caesar,
I Desiring thee that Publius Cimber may
Have an immediate freedom of repeal.

Caesar. What, Brutus?

Cassius. Pardon, Caesar! Caesar, pardon!
As low as to thy foot doth Cassius fall
To beg enfranchisement for Publius Cimber.

Caesar. I could be well moved, if I were as you;
If I could pray to move, prayers would move me;
But I am constant as the Northern Star,
J Of whose truth-fixed and resting quality
There is no fellow in the firmament.
The skies are painted with unnumbered sparks,
They are all fire, and every one doth shine;
But there's but one in all doth hold his place.
So in the world: 'tis furnished well with men.
And men are flesh and blood, and apprehensive,
Yet in the number I do not know but one
That unassailable holds on his rank,
Unshaked of motion; and that I am he,
Let me a little show it, even in this,
That I was constant Cimber should be banished
And constant do remain to keep him so.

Cinna. O Caesar!

Caesar. Hence! Wilt thou lift up Olympus?

Decius. Great Caesar!

Caesar. Doth not Brutus bootless kneel?

Casca. Speak hands for me!

[They stab Caesar. Casca, *the others in turn, then* Brutus.*]*

L **Caesar.** *Et tu, Brute?*—Then fall Caesar!

M *[Dies.]*

Metellus Cimber's brother, Caesar says, has been banished by law. Begging won't change that. G

59 *freedom of repeal:* the right to return to Rome from exile.

60–63 Caesar is surprised that Brutus, would beg for freedom ***(enfranchisement)*** for Publius Cimber. Actually, Brutus, like the rest of the conspirators, is only looking for an excuse to carry out their plan.

64–81 *I could be . . . Olympus:* Caesar says he is too strong to be moved by begging, even when it comes from these respected men. He compares himself to the North Star, which sailors use for direction because it always appears at the same place in the sky. Like that star, Caesar says, which has no equal in the sky ***(fellow in the firmament),*** he cannot be moved. They might as well try to lift Mount Olympus (the mountain where the Greek gods were believed to live). K

83 *Doth not . . . kneel:* Can't you see that even Brutus' kneeling doesn't sway me? ***Bootless*** means "without any effect," like a kick from a foot that has no boot.

85 *Et tu, Brute?:* Even you, Brutus?

CRITIC'S CORNER

"In the seventy lines or so that remain before the assassination, Shakespeare deliberately alienates some of the sympathy and admiration that his Caesar has awakened in us. This is essential if we are not to feel that the stabbing is mere senseless butchery. It is that, of course, as we are very soon to realize, but for the moment we must not be allowed to feel so, or we shall lose the sense of dramatic conflict. Some balance of sympathy must be maintained, as it has hitherto been maintained by the shifting emphasis laid upon the faults and virtues both of the conspirators and of Caesar. The envy and fanaticism of Cassius have been set off by the honest if misguided motives of Brutus, the arrogance of Caesar by his nobility.

Now the arrogance takes the upper hand. For a few minutes we forget our admiration, as we are intended to do, and it is only the agony of his last cry . . . that reawakens our sympathy."

T.S. DORSCH, *The Arden Shakespeare/Julius Caesar*

"Speak hands for me!"

"Et tu, Brute?—Then fall Caesar!"

M. Teaching Tip

You might encourage students to make a list of the betrayals of friendship that take place in this play. So far, such a list might include Cassius' betrayal of Brutus through manipulation, and Brutus' betrayal of Caesar by assassination. Future betrayals among the conspirators and triumvirs will add to the list. When the whole play has been read, you might have students write about or discuss how each betrayal leads to the next, or rate the betrayals and explain why some are more serious than others.

Real Life Connections

The question of political assassination is key in *Julius Caesar*. The conspirators justify their deed by claiming that Caesar is such a potentially dangerous—and popular—tyrant that assassination is the only way to prevent dictatorship. Ask students what they think of these arguments as they apply to situations in the modern world. Do students believe that assassination is ever justified? Do they believe that sometimes it may be the only way, or do they think that there are always better alternatives? Encourage students both to speculate about hypothetical situations and to give actual examples from history or contemporary politics. Also encourage students to speculate about the aftermath of political assassinations. Ask what type of reaction such an action is likely to provoke. Ask if students believe that conspirators or assassins can organize to prevent negative reactions or to affect in any way the outcome of their acts.

N. Reading Skill: VISUALIZING Encourage students to give a visual description of the action in the senate house, as it is described in these lines. *(Possible response: Brutus shouts to the fleeing senators to calm themselves; two of the conspirators swiftly urge Brutus and Cassius to go outside to the "pulpit," or public speaking rostrum; Brutus tries to find out where Publius is in the confusion.)*

O. LEP: Archaic Words and Meanings Students may be puzzled by Brutus' exhortation to "talk not of standing." The word "stand" here connotes "standing fast," as in Metellus' speech in the previous line. Some of the conspirators fear that they may have to defend themselves against friends of Caesar, and Brutus is trying to reassure them that they will not have to stand fast, as there is no danger.

P. Critical Thinking: EVALUATING Ask students how they evaluate Brutus' comment here about having released Caesar from the fear of death. You might ask whether Brutus is sincere. *(Possible answer: The comment seems to be a rationalization to excuse the murder, especially since Caesar said specifically in Act Two that he did not fear death.)* Then ask students what their evaluations reveal about Brutus' character. *(Possible response: He has a desperate need to believe that he is right and that he is not harming anyone, even a man he has killed.)*

Cinna. Liberty! Freedom! Tyranny is dead!
Run hence, proclaim, cry it about the streets!

Cassius. Some to the common pulpits and cry out
"Liberty, freedom, and enfranchisement!"

Brutus. People and Senators, be not affrighted.
Fly not; stand still. Ambition's debt is paid.

N **Casca.** Go to the pulpit, Brutus.

Decius. And Cassius, too.

Brutus. Where's Publius?

Cinna. Here, quite confounded with this mutiny.

Metellus. Stand fast together, lest some friend of Caesar's
Should chance—

O **Brutus.** Talk not of standing! Publius, good cheer.
There is no harm intended to your person
Nor to no Roman else. So tell them, Publius.

Cassius. And leave us, Publius, lest that the people,
Rushing on us, should do your age some mischief.

Brutus. Do so, and let no man abide this deed
But we the doers.

[Reenter Trebonius.*]*

Cassius. Where is Antony?

Trebonius. Fled to his house amazed.
Men, wives, and children stare, cry out, and run,
As it were doomsday.

Brutus. Fates, we will know your pleasures.
That we shall die, we know; 'tis but the time,
And drawing days out, that men stand upon.

Cassius. Why, he that cuts off twenty years of life
Cuts off so many years of fearing death.

Brutus. Grant that, and then is death a benefit.
So are we Caesar's friends, that have abridged
P His time of fearing death. Stoop, Romans, stoop,
And let us bathe our hands in Caesar's blood
Up to the elbows and besmear our swords.
Then walk we forth, even to the market place,
And waving our red weapons o'er our heads,
Let's all cry, "Peace, freedom, and liberty!"

88 *Some . . . pulpits:* Some of you go to the speakers' platforms. The scene is now chaos—people yelling, screaming, and running in fear. Cassius and Brutus are trying to avoid a riot.

101–102 *leave . . . mischief:* Cassius wants Publius, an old man, to leave before he gets hurt by the crowd.
103 *abide:* suffer for.

116–121 Brutus leads the others in covering themselves with Caesar's blood. He wants the Romans to think of their act as a public one, an act they are not trying to hide.

Cassius. Stoop then and wash. How many ages hence
Shall this our lofty scene be acted over
In states unborn and accents yet unknown!

Q

Brutus. How many times shall Caesar bleed in sport,
That now on Pompey's basis lies along
No worthier than the dust!

Cassius. So oft as that shall be.
So often shall the knot of us be called
The men that gave their country liberty.

Decius. What, shall we forth?

Cassius. Ay, every man away.
Brutus shall lead, and we will grace his heels
With the most boldest and best hearts of Rome.

[Enter a Servant.*]*

Brutus. Soft! who comes here? A friend of Antony's.

Servant. Thus, Brutus, did my master bid me kneel;
Thus did Mark Antony bid me fall down;
And being prostrate, thus he bade me say:
Brutus is noble, wise, valiant, and honest;
Caesar was mighty, bold, royal, and loving.
S
Say I love Brutus and I honor him;
Say I feared Caesar, honored him, and loved him.
If Brutus will vouchsafe that Antony
May safely come to him and be resolved
How Caesar hath deserved to lie in death,
Mark Antony shall not love Caesar dead
So well as Brutus living, but will follow
The fortunes and affairs of noble Brutus
Thorough the hazards of this untrod state
With all true faith. So says my master Antony.

Brutus. Thy master is a wise and valiant Roman.
I never thought him worse.
Tell him, so please him come unto this place,
He shall be satisfied and, by my honor,
Depart untouched.

Servant. I'll fetch him presently.

[Exit]

Brutus. I know that we shall have him well to friend.

V **Cassius.** I wish we may. But yet have I a mind

125 *How many . . . sport:* This scene will often be performed as a play in the future in countries and languages that don't even exist now. *Why do you think Shakespeare added this line?* R

126 *Pompey's basis:* the foot of Pompey's statue.

136-149 Fearful for his own life, Antony sends a message with his servant. Lying face down on the floor ***(being prostrate),*** the servant begs for assurance that Brutus will promise ***(vouchsafe)*** Antony's safety so that he may come and be given an explanation ***(be resolved)*** for Caesar's murder. Then Antony will agree to follow Brutus through the dangers of this new, untried government ***(the hazards of this untrod state).***

153-155 *What promise does Brutus tell the servant to relay to Antony?* T

156 *presently:* immediately.

158-160 *But yet . . . purpose:* Unlike Brutus, Cassius doesn't trust Antony. He adds that his doubts ***(misgiving)*** in

Q. Literary Element: SCENERY Ask students why the reference to the base of Pompey's statue here is especially effective in visual terms. *(Possible response: Pompey was Caesar's greatest enemy; ironically, Caesar's blood now stains the base of Pompey's statue.)*

R. Answer: *Shakespeare may have added this line to underline for the Elizabethan audience the dramatic, historic importance of the events they were seeing portrayed in the play; or simply as an ironic reference to the fact that this is, in truth, a play.*

S. Literary Element: DIALOGUE Ask students to comment on their impression of Antony's intentions as they read the flowery, rhetorical dialogue in this passage. *(Possible response: Antony's intentions are hard to gauge, since he seems to accord the same respect to Brutus and to Caesar. Perhaps Antony is deliberately ambiguous, until he learns more about his status with the conspirators. Students may note that Antony has no way of knowing that the conspirators have decided to spare his life.)*

T. Answer: *Brutus promises that Antony will not be harmed and that the conspirators will provide him with satisfactory justification for their murder of Caesar.*

U. Answer: *Since this is the second time that Cassius has expressed misgivings about Antony, Shakespeare may be hinting that Cassius is correct to distrust him.*

V. LEP: Archaic Words and Meanings Students may be challenged by Cassius' use of the phrase, "my misgiving falls shrewdly to the purpose." In this passage, *misgiving* means "suspicion"; *falls shrewdly to the purpose* means "sees the matter correctly."

W. Answer: *Antony may be honest to the degree that he is so loyal to Caesar that he would consider death by the same hands as an honor. On the other hand, students may find his words difficult to believe and they may wonder whether his true intention is to avenge Caesar's assassination.*

X. Reading Skills: VISUALIZING Ask students to visualize Antony's entrance as they read this passage. Encourage them to imagine what gestures Antony might make during the first lines of his speech. *(Possible response: As he enters, Antony might glimpse the body of Caesar and then bend down over it as he addresses his fallen leader in the first three lines. In the next two lines, he might rise and address the conspirators directly.)*

Y. Reading Skill: IDENTIFYING SIGNIFICANT DETAILS After students have read Antony's offer to die, ask them if they remember which other characters in the play so far have made similar offers. *(Possible responses: Casca reported in Act One that Caesar offered his life to the crowd; Cassius said he was ready to commit suicide in Act One.)* Ask students what effect these offers to die have. *(Possible responses: They make it clear that the stakes are very high; they show that suicide and honor are closely related in this play.)*

V
That fears him much; and my misgiving still
Falls shrewdly to the purpose.

[Reenter Antony.*]*

Brutus. But here comes Antony. Welcome, Mark Antony.

Antony. O mighty Caesar! Dost thou lie so low?
Are all thy conquests, glories, triumphs, spoils,
X
Shrunk to this little measure? Fare thee well.
I know not, gentlemen, what you intend,
Who else must be let blood, who else is rank.
If I myself, there is not hour so fit
As Caesar's death's hour; nor no instrument
Of half that worth as those your swords, made rich
With the most noble blood of all this world.
I do beseech ye, if you bear me hard,
Now, whilst your purpled hands do reek and smoke,
Fulfill your pleasure. Live a thousand years,
I shall not find myself so apt to die;
Y
No place will please me so, no mean of death,
As here by Caesar, and by you cut off,
The choice and master spirits of this age.

Brutus. O Antony, beg not your death of us!
Though now we must appear bloody and cruel,
As by our hands and this our present act
You see we do, yet see you but our hands
And this the bleeding business they have done.
Our hearts you see not. They are pitiful;
And pity to the general wrong of Rome
(As fire drives out fire, so pity pity)
Hath done this deed on Caesar. For your part,
To you our swords have leaden points, Mark Antony.
Our arms in strength of malice, and our hearts
Of brothers' temper, do receive you in
With all kind of love, good thoughts, and reverence.

Cassius. Your voice shall be as strong as any man's
In the disposing of new dignities.

Brutus. Only be patient till we have appeased
The multitude, beside themselves with fear,
And then we will deliver you the cause
Why I, that did love Caesar when I struck him,
Have thus proceeded.

matters like this are usually accurate. Who do you think is right, Cassius or Brutus? U

163-178 The sight of Caesar's body causes Antony to break down. Keep in mind that he truly loved Caesar, almost as a son loves his father.

167–178 *Who else . . . this age:* Who else is so diseased ***(rank)*** that he must be "cured" by the knives of the men who just killed Caesar? Antony says he would be honored to be killed at the same time, with the same weapons, and by the same blood-stained ***(purpled)*** hands that killed Caesar. He adds that the honor would come partly from being killed by such great men ***(the choice and master spirits of this age).*** Do you believe that Antony is being honest here? W

186 *As fire . . . pity:* As one fire consumes another, our sorrow for Rome became greater than our sorrow for Caesar.

188–193 *To you . . . dignities:* As far as you're concerned, Antony, our swords are harmless ***(have leaden points).*** Our arms, even though they seem cruel ***(in strength of malice),*** and our hearts, full of brotherly feeling, welcome you. You will have as much to say as anyone in handing out honors from the new government.

DATA BANK

"We must not forget how widespread was the longing for unshakable rule and how overwhelming was the dread of civil war at the time *Julius Caesar* was first performed. Elizabeth I had come to the throne in 1558 when the country was in such a state of rebellion and confusion that it seemed likely to slip back into the horrors of the War of the Roses. Elizabeth had given her subjects peace, and the nation had prospered; for many years she had been a strong ruler, despite the repeated Catholic claims that she was illegitimate and therefore not a true successor. Attempts at assassination had been made by many. By 1599 she was old and visibly failing. She had no direct heir; there was no one whose claim to the throne after her was beyond dispute. Childless like Caesar, she could pass on the office only by naming an heir, and this she refused to do, perhaps in order to prevent the growth of factions.

WILLIAM AND BARBARA ROSEN, ***The Tragedy of Julius Caesar***

Antony. I doubt not of your wisdom.
Let each man render me his bloody hand.
First, Marcus Brutus, will I shake with you;
Z Next, Caius Cassius, do I take your hand;
Now, Decius Brutus, yours; now yours, Metellus;
Yours, Cinna; and, my valiant Casca, yours.
Though last, not least in love, yours, good
Trebonius.
Gentlemen all—Alas, what shall I say?
My credit now stands on such slippery ground
That one of two bad ways you must conceit me,
Either a coward or a flatter.
That I did love thee, Caesar, O, 'tis true!
If then thy spirit look upon us now,
Shall it not grieve thee dearer than thy death
To see thy Antony making his peace,
Shaking the bloody fingers of thy foes,
Most noble! in the presence of thy corse?
Had I as many eyes as thou hast wounds,
Weeping as fast as they stream forth thy blood,
It would become me better than to close
In terms of friendship with thine enemies.
Pardon me, Julius! Here wast thou bayed, brave hart;
Here didst thou fall; and here thy hunters stand,
Signed in thy spoil, and crimsoned in thy lethe.
AA O world, thou wast the forest to his hart;
And this indeed, O world, the heart of thee!
How like a deer, strucken by many princes,
Dost thou here lie!

Cassius. Mark Antony—

Antony. Pardon me, Caius Cassius.
The enemies of Caesar shall say this;
Then, in a friend, it is cold modesty.

Cassius. I blame you not for praising Caesar so;
But what compact mean you have with us?
Will you be pricked in number of our friends,
Or shall we on, and not depend on you?

Antony. Therefore I took your hands; but was indeed
BB Swayed from the point by looking down on Caesar.
Friends am I with you all, and love you all,
Upon this hope, that you shall give me reasons
Why and wherein Caesar was dangerous.

208 *credit:* reputation.

209 *conceit:* think of.

212–227 These lines are addressed to the corpse ***(corse)*** of Caesar. Antony is so upset that he temporarily forgets who is with him.

221 *Here . . . hart:* This is the place where you were trapped ***(bayed)*** like a hunted deer ***(hart).***

223 *Signed . . . lethe:* Marked with your blood ***(spoil)*** and red in your death. At this point, Antony is probably having difficulty speaking through his tears.

229–231 With these lines, Antony regains control of himself. He points out that even Caesar's enemies will say such things as he has just said.

233 *compact:* agreement.

234 *pricked:* listed; marked by punching a hole in a wax tablet.

236 *Therefore . . . hands:* That is why I shook hands with all of you (because I intend to be counted as an ally of yours).

Z. Reading Skill: PREDICTING Remind students that in Act Two, Scene I, Brutus sealed his membership in the conspiracy by taking each member by the hand. Then ask students to predict what Antony's shaking hands signifies here. *(Possible response: Antony draws attention to the fact that each hand is "bloody"—with the blood of his friend Caesar. He may be contemplating revenge under the guise of friendship.)*

AA. Literary Element: FIGURATIVE LANGUAGE Ask students who is being compared to what in this speech. *(Caesar is being compared to a deer that was slain by hunters.)* Draw students' attention to the pun Antony makes in lines 224–225, as he plays on "hart"—a deer—and "heart."

BB. Literary Element: THEME Ask students what they think of Antony's mention of "friendship." *(Possible response: Seen against Antony's repeated outbursts of grief for Caesar, his mention of friendship with the conspirators may suggest he is being hypocritical or that he is torn with indecision.)* Ask why students think that the conspirators continue to trust Antony. *(Possible response: The conspirators may be hoping that they can win Antony over which would be useful to their cause.)*

CC. LEP: Archaic Words and Meanings
Explain that *suitor* here means "petitioner" or "pleader,"—one who asks permission. *Produce his body to the market place* means "bring his body into the public square."

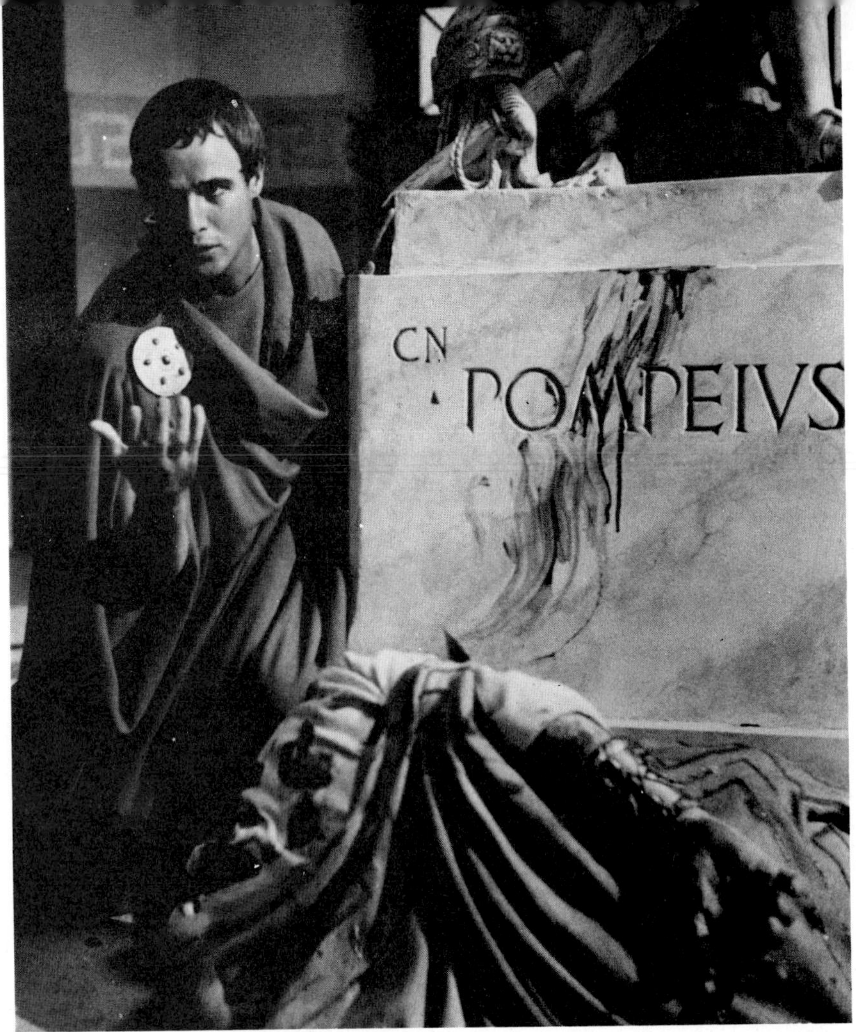

"Woe to the hand that shed this costly blood!"

Brutus. Or else were this a savage spectacle.
Our reasons are so full of good regard
That were you, Antony, the son of Caesar,
You should be satisfied.
Antony. That's all I seek;
CC And am moreover suitor that I may
DD Produce his body to the market place

241 ***Or else . . . spectacle:*** If we could not give you reasons for what we have done, it would be nothing but an uncivilized show.

246–255 ***That's all . . . utter:*** Antony asks permission to carry Caesar's body

DD And in the pulpit, as becomes a friend,
Speak in the order of his funeral.

Brutus. You shall, Mark Antony.

Cassius. Brutus, a word with you.

[Aside to Brutus.*]*

You know not what you do. Do not consent.
That Antony speak in his funeral.
Know you how much the people may be moved
By that which he will utter?

Brutus. By your pardon,

[Aside to Cassius.*]*

I will myself into the pulpit first
And show the reason of our Caesar's death.
What Antony shall speak, I will protest
He speaks by leave and by permission,
And that we are contented Caesar shall
Have all true rites and lawful ceremonies.
It shall advantage more than do us wrong.

Cassius.

[Aside to Brutus.*]*

EE I know not what may fall. I like it not.

Brutus. Mark Antony, here, take you Caesar's body.
You shall not in your funeral speech blame us,
But speak all good you can devise of Caesar,
And say you do't by our permission.
Else shall you not have any hand at all
About his funeral. And you shall speak
FF In the same pulpit whereto I am going,
After my speech is ended.

Antony. Be it so.
I do desire no more.

Brutus. Prepare the body then, and follow us.

[Exeunt all but Antony, *who looks down at* Caesar's *body.]*

GG **Antony.** O, pardon me, thou bleeding piece of earth,
That I am meek and gentle with these butchers!
Thou art the ruins of the noblest man
That ever lived in the tide of times.
Woe to the hand that shed this costly blood!
Over thy wounds now do I prophesy

outside and make a funeral speech in his honor. Brutus agrees, but Cassius fears that Antony's words might incite the people in Caesar's favor.

259 *protest:* explain.

263 *It shall . . . wrong:* His speech will do us more good ***(advantage more)*** than harm.

277–298 Now that Antony is alone with Caesar's corpse, he speaks truthfully. His speech shows what he really thinks of the men who have just left and what he intends to do about the murder.
280 *in the tide of times:* in all of history.

DD. LEP: Archaic Words and Meanings *Pulpit* refers to the rostrum or lectern from which public officials addressed the Romans. *As becomes a friend* means "as is fitting for a friend."

EE. Literary element: CLIMAX Suggest to students that Cassius' line "I know not what may fall" serves as a clue for identifying what may be the true climax of Shakespeare's play: Antony's speech. Ask them to note whether the events of the play's falling action seem to stem from the assassination or from Antony's speech. Mention the importance and the risk in Brutus' decision to let Antony speak at Caesar's funeral.

FF. Critical Thinking: ANALYZING Ask students if they think Brutus is wise to allow Antony to speak second, rather than first. Remind them that in public debates, last place in the order of speakers is generally considered to be the most advantageous. Encourage students to speculate about why Brutus makes the choice he does. *(Possible responses: he is overconfident; he is naive; he feels guilty; his need to trust Antony and the rabble overwhelms his judgment; his need to believe that everyone thinks he is honorable overwhelms his judgment.)*

GG. Literary Element: CHARACTERIZATION Ask students how Antony's personality and tone abruptly change at the beginning of this soliloquy. *(Possible response: Antony suddenly reveals his true opinion of the conspirators; he calls them "butchers." He is no longer meek and submissive; he seems almost savagely vengeful.)*

HH. Literary Element: FIGURATIVE LANGUAGE Ask what is being compared to what in this simile. *(Caesar's wounds are compared to "mouths" that are unable to speak that beg Antony to speak for them.)*

II. Literary Element: THEME Ask students to explain how this passage relates to the theme of the consequences of civil violence. *(Possible response: Antony predicts that Caesar's assassination will lead inevitably to social chaos and to the horrors of civil war; in fact, Antony himself will help this to happen.)*

JJ. Historical Sidelight At the time of Julius Caesar's assassination, Octavius, Caesar's grandnephew and chosen heir, was a youth of nineteen.

KK. LEP: ARCHAIC WORDS AND MEANINGS In these lines, the verb *try* means "to test"; the noun *issue* refers to the conspirators' bloody deed or its outcome.

LL. Answer: Predictions may vary, but students should be able to predict that Antony's speech will be eloquent, based on his words so far in this scene. They may also predict that Antony will skillfully play on the crowd's emotions, now that he has tricked the conspirators.

HH (Which, like dumb mouths, do ope their ruby lips
To beg the voice and utterance of my tongue),
A curse shall light upon the limbs of men;
Domestic fury and fierce civil strife
Shall cumber all the parts of Italy;
Blood and destruction shall be so in use
And dreadful objects so familiar
That mothers shall but smile when they behold
Their infants quartered with the hands of war,
All pity choked with custom of fell deeds;
II And Caesar's spirit, ranging for revenge,
With Até by his side come hot from hell,
Shall in these confines with a monarch's voice
Cry "Havoc!" and let slip the dogs of war,
That this foul deed shall smell above the earth
With carrion men, groaning for burial.

[Enter Octavius' Servant.*]*

You serve Octavius Caesar, do you not?

Servant. I do, Mark Antony.

Antony. Caesar did write for him to come to Rome.

Servant. He did receive his letters and is coming,
And bid me say to you by word of mouth—
O Caesar!

Antony. Thy heart is big. Get thee apart and weep.
Passion, I see, is catching, for mine eyes,
Seeing those beads of sorrow stand in thine,
Began to water. Is thy master coming?

Servant. He lies tonight within seven leagues of Rome.

JJ **Antony.** Post back with speed and tell him what hath chanced.
Here is a mourning Rome, a dangerous Rome,
No Rome of safety for Octavius yet.
Hie hence and tell him so. Yet stay awhile.
Thou shalt not back till I have borne this corse
KK Into the market place. There shall I try
In my oration how the people take
The cruel issue of these bloody men,
According to the which thou shall discourse
To young Octavius of the state of things.
Lend me your hand.

[Exeunt with Caesar's *body.]*

286–292 *Domestic fury . . . deeds:* Rome ***(Italy)*** will be torn by civil war. People will become so accustomed to horrible sights that mothers will simply smile when they see their children cut into pieces ***(quartered).*** Pity will disappear among so much cruelty.

294 *Até* (ā' tē): the Greek goddess of revenge.

296 *"Havoc!":* a battle cry signaling mass killings.

298 *With carrion . . . burial:* like rotting corpses begging to be buried.

299 Antony is interrupted by a servant of Octavius, an ally of Caesar. The servant begins to relay a message, then sees the bleeding corpse on the floor.

309 *He lies . . . Rome:* Octavius will set up camp tonight about twenty-one miles ***(seven leagues)*** outside Rome.

310–321 *Post back . . . your hand:* Antony tells the servant to hurry back and tell Octavius what has happened. Then he tells the servant to wait. He wants the servant to listen to his funeral speech and report to Octavius how the crowd responds to it. LL

Critic's Corner

"Left alone with his thoughts, [Antony's] last speech in this scene is a further revelation of character. Couched in the facile rhetoric which comes so readily to him, it apostrophizes the dead Caesar as 'thou bleeding piece of earth' and goes on to speak of 'costly blood' and to characterize his wounds as 'dumb mouths' and 'ruby lips.' In a world so fluent in feeling, where emotion swells in accordance with the forms of rhetoric, intensely rather than deeply, like the blood which issues from the wounds it contemplates, Antony's oratory is perfectly at home. It issues, however, in a vision of chaos."

Derek Traversi, *"Julius Caesar: The Roman Tragedy"*

Responding to Reading

1. What effects, if any, do the appearances of Artemidorus, and Popilius Lena have as this scene opens? Explain.
2. Do you get any new impressions of Caesar's personality from his words before the assassination attempt? Explain and give examples.
3. As he is being killed, Caesar says, "Et tu, Brute?—Then fall Caesar!" What do you think is going through his mind as he says these words? What might be going through Brutus' mind at the same time? Explain.
4. Evaluate Antony's methods for striking back at the assassins. What does his strategy tell you about him? Support your view with examples from the play.
5. What do you think Shakespeare might be trying to tell us about the theme of friendship in this scene?

   Think about
   - the friendship of Brutus and Caesar
   - the friendship of Antony and Caesar

Scene 2 *The Forum in Rome.*

Brutus speaks before a group of "citizens," or common people of Rome. He explains why Caesar had to be slain for the good of Rome. Then, Brutus leaves and Antony speaks to the citizens. A far better judge of human nature than Brutus, Antony cleverly manages to turn the crowd against the conspirators by telling them of Caesar's good works and his concern for the people, as proven by the slain ruler's will. He has left all his wealth to the people. As Antony stirs the citizens to pursue the assassins and kill them, he learns that Octavius has arrived in Rome and that Brutus and Cassius have fled.

A *[Enter* Brutus *and* Cassius *and a throng of* Citizens, *disturbed by the death of* Caesar.*]*

Citizens. We will be satisfied! Let us be satisfied!

Brutus. Then follow me and give me audience, friends.
B Cassius, go you into the other street
And part the numbers.
Those that will hear me speak, let 'em stay here;
Those that will follow Cassius, go with him;

2–8 ***give me audience:*** Listen to me. Brutus is shouting, trying to get the crowd to quiet down so he can speak. He asks Cassius to divide the crowd ***(part the numbers)*** and speak to another group. We will tell the people

Student Response

Responding to Reading

These questions are open-ended with no "right" or "wrong" answers. However, responses must be supported with information from the selection. Possible answers follow:

1. The appearances increase suspense as audience and conspirators wonder whether Caesar will discover the plot.

2. Caesar appears determined and perhaps boastful as he abruptly rejects the proposal of a reprieve for Publius Cimber and then compares himself to the northern star.

3. Possibly Caesar surrenders to shock and despair when he sees that one of his closest friends has joined the conspiracy. Brutus may be experiencing anguish because his love of country has caused him to betray Caesar.

4. Antony counts on his eloquence with the mob and on joining forces with Octavius, revealing that he is quick-witted, manipulative, and loyal to Caesar.

5. Shakespeare may be suggesting that friendship is subject to many conflicting pressures. Brutus and Cassius, for example, start to argue almost immediately after the assassination; Antony must pretend that he is ready to join the conspirators, apparently betraying his friendship with Caesar.

Text Annotations

Scene 2

A. Teaching Tip
It may be useful to chart with students the changing mood of the crowd throughout the scene. It may also be helpful to encourage students to think of contemporary parallels of crowds' moods changing, at such events as boxing matches and other sports spectacles as well as in political contexts. Students might enjoy improvising a contemporary version of a fickle crowd whose mood is changed first by one speaker or performer, then by another.

B. Literary Element: MOOD Ask students what the exclamations of the citizens and orders of Brutus imply about the mood of the people as this scene opens. *(Possible response: The people are angry and threatening.)*

C. Answer: *In the first part of his speech, Brutus tries to appeal to the reason of his audience, rather than to their emotions. In the second part, however, when he feels that the crowd is with him, he emotionally offers his own life to the people when the good of Rome will require it. From Brutus' words, it is reasonable to infer that he really believes that the killing was justified.*

D. Critical Thinking: **DISTINGUISHING: FACT AND OPINION** Ask students to distinguish between fact and opinion in this portion of Brutus' speech. *(Possible response: Brutus is relying almost entirely on opinion in his appeal to the people. There is no evidence that Caesar would have made the people slaves. Even the judgment of Caesar as "ambitious" relies more on opinion than on fact.)*

E. LEP: Archaic Words and Meanings A number of words in this passage may be challenging for some students. Have them review the marginal note for the passage in order to understand the difficult words. Then ask them to paraphrase the passage in their own words.

And public reasons shall be rendered
Of Caesar's death.

First Citizen. I will hear Brutus speak.

Second Citizen. I will hear Cassius, and compare their reasons when severally we hear them rendered.

[Exit Cassius, *with some of the* Citizens. Brutus *goes into the pulpit.]*

Third Citizen. The noble Brutus is ascended. Silence!

Brutus. Be patient till the last. Romans, countrymen, and lovers, hear me for my cause, and be silent, that you may hear. Believe me for mine honor, and have respect to mine honor, that you may believe. Censure me in your wisdom, and awake your senses, that you may the better judge. If there be any in this assembly, any dear friend of Caesar's, to him I say that Brutus' love to Caesar was no less than his. If then that friend demand why Brutus rose against Caesar, this is my answer: Not that I loved Caesar less, but that I loved Rome more. Had you rather Caesar were living, and die all slaves, than that Caesar were dead, to live all freemen? As Caesar loved me, I weep for him; as he was fortunate, I rejoice at it; as he was valiant, I honor him; but—as he was ambitious, I slew him. There is tears for his love; joy for his fortune; honor for his valor; and death for his ambition. Who is here so base that would be a bondman? If any, speak, for him have I offended. Who is here so rude that would not be a Roman? If any, speak, for him have I offended. I pause for a reply.

All. None, Brutus, none!

Brutus. Then none have I offended. I have done no more to Caesar than you shall do to Brutus. The question of his death is enrolled in the Capitol; his glory not extenuated, wherein he was worthy, nor his offenses enforced, for which he suffered death.

[Enter Antony *and others, with* Caesar's *body.]*

Here come his body, mourned by Mark Antony, who though he had no hand in his death, shall receive the benefit of his dying, a place in the commonwealth, as which of you shall not? With this I depart,

our reasons ***(public reasons shall be rendered)*** for killing Caesar, he says.

14–40 As you read Brutus' speech, think about the kinds of arguments he uses to persuade the crowd. *Does he try to appeal to their emotions? Do you think he truly believes that the killing was justified?* C

14 ***lovers:*** friends.

17 ***Censure me:*** Judge me.

30–31 ***Who is . . . bondman:*** Which of you is so low that you would prefer to be a slave?

32 ***rude:*** uncivilized.

37–40 ***The question . . . death:*** The reasons for his death are on record in the Capitol. We have not belittled ***(extenuated)*** his accomplishments or overemphasized ***(enforced)*** the failings for which he was killed.

DATA BANK

As has been pointed out in annotation D, there is no evidence that Caesar would have made the people slaves. And, in fact, Caesar had actually accomplished some good for the people—including protecting poor tenants in Rome from gouging landlords, establishing full citizenship as a reward for military service, limiting the provincial governors' terms of office to one or two years in order to protect the provincials from exploitation. However, Caesar also was known for his fierce and often rash behavior in his military leadership as well as his political rule of Rome.

Possibly the greatest fear of Caesar came from his actions of placing his statue with the statues of the gods at the public games with the inscription "to the unconquerable god," giving his friends, many of whom were not even Romans, new posts in the Senate and forbidding people from spending too much money on luxuries while he himself wore purple garments and sat on a gold throne in the Senate House.

that, as I slew my best lover for the good of Rome, I have the same dagger for myself when it shall please my country to need my death.

All. Live, Brutus! live, live!

First Citizen. Bring him with triumph home unto his house.

Second Citizen. Give him a statue with his ancestors.

G **Third Citizen.** Let him be Caesar.

Fourth Citizen. Caesar's better parts
Shall be crowned in Brutus.

First Citizen. We'll bring him to his house with shouts and clamors.

Brutus. My countrymen—

Second Citizen. Peace! silence! Brutus speaks.

First Citizen. Peace ho!

Brutus. Good countrymen, let me depart alone,
And, for my sake, stay here with Antony.
Do grace to Caesar's corpse, and grace his speech
H Tending to Caesar's glories which Mark Antony,
By our permission, is allowed to make.
I do entreat you, not a man depart,
Save I alone, till Antony have spoke.

[Exit]

First Citizen. Stay, ho! and let us hear Mark Antony.

Third Citizen. Let him go up into the public chair.
We'll hear him. Noble Antony, go up.

Antony. For Brutus' sake I am beholding to you.

[Goes into the pulpit.]

Fourth Citizen. What does he say of Brutus?

Third Citizen. He says for Brutus' sake
He finds himself beholding to us all.

Fourth Citizen. 'Twere best he speak no harm of Brutus here!

First Citizen. This Caesar was a tyrant.

Third Citizen. Nay, that's certain.
We are blest that Rome is rid of him.

48–58 *What is the mood of the crowd as Brutus finishes his speech?* F

62 *grace his speech:* Listen to him respectfully.

66 *Save:* except.

67 *Is Brutus wise to depart before Antony makes his speech?* I

68 *public chair:* speaker's platform.

70 *beholding:* indebted.

71–78 Notice what the people are now saying about Caesar, only minutes after they were crying for him. Antony hears all this. *How do you think he will respond?* J

F. Answer: *As Brutus finished his speech, the people solidly support him, shouting that they will honor him like Caesar.*

G. Literary Element: THEME Ask students what the reaction of the crowd to Brutus' speech suggests about the ability of the people in a crowd to analyze and think logically. *(Suggested response: The crowd's frenzied approval, provoked almost entirely by Brutus' appeals to emotions, suggests that the crowd of people is fickle and stupid.)*

H. Literary Element: VERSE Point out to students that Brutus' speech to the crowd has been in prose, but his response to their approval is in poetry. Encourage them to speculate about the reasons for this shift. *(Possible response: Brutus' appeal was dull, plodding, and reasonable, but his relief at the crowd's approval sends him into poetry—his emotions are more sincere at this point than when he was struggling to rationalize his actions and persuade the crowd.)*

I. Answer: *Given the warnings of Cassius, Brutus may not be wise to depart so soon.*

J. Answer: *Students may point out that Antony will have to persuade the people cleverly that Caesar was not, in fact, a tyrant, but rather a just, heroic, and generous ruler.*

K. Literary Element: DIALOGUE Ask students to identify the contrast in form between Antony's oration and that of Brutus. The first two lines of Brutus' speech furnish the necessary clue. *(Possible response: Brutus' speech was in prose, whereas Antony's speech is in verse.)* Have students speculate about what this contrast suggests about the effects of each speech on the crowd. *(Possible response: Since Shakespeare generally uses verse for lofty, solemn themes, Antony's speech may have the more powerful effect on the crowd.)*

L. Literary Element: IRONY Ask what use of repetition underlines Antony's use of irony in these lines. *(Possible responses: "ambition" and "ambitious"; "Brutus is an honorable man.")*

M. Answer: Antony may want to gauge the crowd's reaction, to collect his thoughts, or to frame a strategy for the second part of his speech. Meanwhile, the dramatic gesture of bending over Caesar's body serves as a bit of visual "body language" to play on the sympathies of the crowd.

N. Critical Thinking: EVALUATING Encourage students to evaluate the crowd's reactions to Antony. Ask whether, although the people are fickle, there is some truth in their observations. Help students to sort out various evaluations of the crowd.

Second Citizen. Peace! Let us hear what Antony can say.

Antony. You gentle Romans—

All. Peace, ho! Let us hear him.

Antony. Friends, Romans, countrymen, lend me your ears;
I come to bury Caesar, not to praise him.
The evil that men do lives after them;
The good is oft interred with their bones.
So let it be with Caesar. The noble Brutus
Hath told you Caesar was ambitious.
If it were so, it was a grievous fault,
And grievously hath Caesar answered it.
Here, under leave of Brutus and the rest
(For Brutus is an honorable man;
So are they all, all honorable men),
Come I to speak in Caesar's funeral.
He hath brought many captives home to Rome,
Whose ransoms did the general coffers fill.
Did this in Caesar seem ambitious?
When that the poor have cried, Caesar hath wept;
Ambition should be made of sterner stuff.
Yet Brutus says he was ambitious;
And Brutus is an honorable man.
You all did see that on the Lupercal
I thrice presented him a kingly crown,
Which he did thrice refuse. Was this ambition?
Yet Brutus says he was ambitious;
And sure he is an honorable man.
I speak not to disprove what Brutus spoke,
But here I am to speak what I do know.
You all did love him once, not without cause.
What cause withholds you then to mourn for him?
O judgment, thou art fled to brutish beasts,
And men have lost their reason! Bear with me,
My heart is in the coffin there with Caesar,
And I must pause till it come back to me.

First Citizen. Methinks there is much reason in his sayings.

Second Citizen. If thou consider rightly of the matter,
Caesar has had great wrong.

Third Citizen. Has he, masters?
I fear there will a worse come in his place.

82–149 Antony's words at Caesar's funeral make up one of the most famous speeches in all of Shakespeare's plays. Remember that Antony wants to stir the people into a civil war. He must work on them gradually, since they are now supporters of Brutus. One gradual change is in his use of the word *honorable.* As the speech goes on, the word becomes more and more sarcastic.

85 *interred:* buried.

84–86 *The evil . . . Caesar:* Let Caesar's good deeds die with him; let him be remembered by his faults.

88 *grievous:* serious.

90 *under leave of:* with the permission of.

95 *general coffers:* the Roman government's treasury.

102 *thrice:* three times.

111–113 *Bear with . . . to me:* Antony stops speaking and turns to the corpse. He says he is overcome with grief ***(My heart is in the coffin)*** and needs to pause for a while. *What other reasons might Antony have for pausing at this point in his speech?*

Fourth Citizen. Marked ye his words? He would not take the crown;
Therefore 'tis certain he was not ambitious.

O

First Citizen. If it be found so, some will dear abide it.

Second Citizen. Poor soul! his eyes are red as fire with weeping.

123 *some will dear abide it:* Some will pay dearly for it.

O. Literary Element: CLIMAX Ask students how they know the play is approaching a climax here. *(Possible response: This passage shows the first, highly significant shift of sympathy by the crowd. Their growing fury against the conspirators and sympathy for Caesar will prove decisive if these emotions continue.)*

"My heart is in the coffin there with Caesar."

P. Literary Sidelight Antony's use of the word *masters* here is archaic: in Shakespeare's time, the word was applied to working-class people.

Q. Literary Element: PROPS Aside from the conspirators' weapons, Caesar's will is possibly the most important prop in the play. Encourage students to visualize how Antony uses this prop in the course of the rest of his speech.

R. Literary Sidelight Antony here avails himself of a rhetorical device made famous by the Roman orator Cicero. The Latin technical term for this devise is *praeteritio,* (prē′ tə rish′ ē ō) in which a speaker claims that he will not discuss a subject but then actually says a good deal about it in an indirect fashion. Encourage students to identify the irony in that device.

S. Literary Element: IRONY Ask students to explain Antony's use of irony here. *(Possible response: He means the opposite of what he says, since he has shown already that he hardly considers the conspirators "honorable." His graphic reminder of the daggers that "stabbed Caesar" is further irony in relation to the "honorable men.")*

Third Citizen. There's not a nobler man in Rome than Antony.

Fourth Citizen. Now mark him. He begins again to speak.

Antony. But yesterday the word of Caesar might
Have stood against the world. Now lies he there,
And none so poor to do him reverence.
P O masters! If I were disposed to stir
Your hearts and minds to mutiny and rage,
I should do Brutus wrong, and Cassius wrong,
Who, you all know, are honorable men.
I will not do them wrong. I rather choose
To wrong the dead, to wrong myself and you,
Than I will wrong such honorable men.
But here's a parchment with the seal of Caesar.
Q I found it in his closet; 'tis his will.
Let but the commons hear this testament,
Which (pardon me) I do not mean to read,
And they would go and kiss dead Caesar's wounds
And dip their napkins in his sacred blood;
Yea, beg a hair of him for memory,
And dying, mention it within their wills,
Bequeathing it as a rich legacy
Unto their issue.

Fourth Citizen. We'll hear the will! Read it, Mark Antony.

All. The will, the will! We will hear Caesar's will!

Antony. Have patience, gentle friends, I must not read it.
It is not meet you know how Caesar loved you.
You are not wood, you are not stones, but men;
R And being men, hearing the will of Caesar,
It will inflame you, it will make you mad.
'Tis good you know not that you are his heirs,
For if you should, O, what would come of it?

Fourth Citizen. Read the will! We'll hear it, Antony! You shall read us the will, Caesar's will!

Antony. Will you be patient? Will you stay awhile?
I have o'ershot myself to tell you of it.
S I fear I wrong the honorable men
Whose daggers have stabbed Caesar; I do fear it.

130 ***But:*** only.

136 ***honorable men:*** By this point, Antony is using the term more as an insult than a compliment. He spits it out angrily, wanting the crowd to know that he doesn't believe for a second that it describes the assassins.

140 ***parchment:*** document.

143 ***Which . . . read:*** Mark Antony is manipulating the crowd here. He has every intention of reading the will, but wants the crowd to force him to do so.

145 ***napkins:*** handkerchiefs.

148–149 ***Bequeathing . . . issue:*** People would leave it (a hair from Caesar's head) in their wills for their children ***(issue)***.

154 ***meet:*** proper.

163 ***I have . . . of it:*** I have gone too far in even mentioning it to you.

CULTURAL CONNECTION

Shakespeare's portrayal of the crowd in *Julius Caesar* is quite negative. Encourage students to see Shakespeare's view as one person's opinion, which came out of a particular loyalty that Shakespeare himself felt to the ruling monarch and political system of England, and a particular idea of "commoners" as uneducated and unreliable. Encourage students to see that the idea of every citizen deserving a voice in government was totally unknown in Shakespeare's time.

To get at the concept of how opinions might influence a writer, ask students to think of examples of times that crowds have been negatively portrayed by some and positively portrayed by others. Students might consider some of the following examples: a crowd of teenagers on Saturday night; a protest march for a political cause; the "home team" supporters at a sporting event. Encourage students to imagine how different observers with different points of view might portray these situations.

Fourth Citizen. They were traitors. Honorable men!

All. The will! the testament!

Second Citizen. They were villains, murderers! The will! Read the will!

Antony. You will compel me then to read the will?
Then make a ring about the corpse of Caesar
And let me show you him that made the will.
Shall I descend? and will you give me leave?

All. Come down.

Second Citizen. Descend.

Third Citizen. You shall have leave.

*[*Antony *comes down.]*

Fourth Citizen. A ring! Stand round.

First Citizen. Stand from the hearse! Stand from the body!

Second Citizen. Room for Antony, most noble Antony!

Antony. Nay, press not so upon me. Stand far off.

All. Stand back! Room! Bear back!

Antony. If you have tears, prepare to shed them now.
You all do know this mantle. I remember
The first time ever Caesar put it on.
'Twas on a summer's evening in his tent,
That day he overcame the Nervii.
Look, in this place ran Cassius' dagger through.
See what a rent the envious Casca made.
Through this the well-beloved Brutus stabbed;
And as he plucked his cursed steel away,
Mark how the blood of Caesar followed it,
As rushing out of doors to be resolved
If Brutus so unkindly knocked or no;
For Brutus, as you know, was Caesar's angel.
Judge, O you gods, how dearly Caesar loved him!
This was the most unkindest cut of all;
For when the noble Caesar saw him stab,
Ingratitude, more strong than traitors' arms,
Quite vanquished him. Then burst his mighty heart;
And in his mantle muffling up his face,
Even at the base of Pompey's statue
(Which all the while ran blood) great Caesar fell.

173 *Shall I . . . leave:* Will you give me permission to come down? Antony pretends to be at the mercy of the crowd. *Why do you think he does this?* T

184 *mantle:* Caesar's toga.

187 *the Nervii:* a Belgian tribe that Caesar defeated thirteen years earlier.

189 *rent:* tear, hole.

192 *Mark:* notice.

193–194 *As rushing . . . or no:* Antony says Caesar's blood rushed out of that opening to find out if it really was Brutus who had made the wound.

200 *vanquished:* defeated.

T. Answer: Antony pretends to be at the mercy of the crowd in order to imply that he is their servant—rather than a spokesperson for the cause of a dictatorial ruler. Antony wants his image—and that of Caesar—to appear democratic.

U. Literary Element: STAGE DIRECTIONS Ask students what Antony's purpose might be in "descending" from the pulpit and in urging the people to make a ring around the corpse. *(Possible response: Antony may want to establish more intimate contact with the people. At the same time, he may be counting on the people to be shocked when they see Caesar's body at close range.)*

V. Critical Thinking: ANALYZING Ask students how they would analyze Antony's purpose in these remarks about Caesar's mantle. *(Possible response: Antony is once again appealing to the crowd's emotions. His remarks help to draw a highly effective contrast between Caesar's former military glory and the pathetic gashes in his mantle.)*

W. Literary Element: CLIMAX Ask students how this passage represents another step closer to the play's climax. *(Possible response: First, Antony has won the crowd to a new sympathy with Caesar. Now he has taken them to a new level—hatred of the man who has betrayed Caesar—Brutus, the conspirator whom they had most respected. If the crowd continues to despise Brutus, the conspirators will have no support.)*

X. Literary Element: CLIMAX Although Antony's dramatic removal of the cloak might seem to coincide with the climax of his speech, he still has another card to play. Have students predict what this may be. *(Possible response: reading Caesar's will)*

Y. Critical Thinking: EVALUATING Once again, have students evaluate the reactions of the crowd. Ask to what extent they find these reactions reasonable, and to what extent they seem fickle, irrational reactions.

O, what a fall was there, my countrymen!
Then I, and you, and all of us fell down,
Whilst bloody treason flourished over us.
O, now you weep, and I perceive you feel
The dint of pity. These are gracious drops.
Kind souls, what, weep you when you but behold
Our Caesar's vesture wounded? Look you here!
X Here is himself, marred, as you see, with traitors.

[Pulls the cloak off Caesar's *body.]*

First Citizen. O piteous spectacle!

Second Citizen. O noble Caesar!

Third Citizen. O woeful day!

Y **Fourth Citizen.** O traitors, villains!

208 dint: force.

209-211 *weep you . . . traitors:* Do you cry when you look only at his wounded clothing ***(vesture)?*** Here, look at his body! (Antony pulls Caesar's toga aside and reveals the knife wounds.) The people find the sight repulsive, and it makes them angry.

"If you have tears, prepare to shed them now."

DATA BANK

"But when they opened Caesar's testament, and found a liberal legacy of money bequeathed unto every citizen of Rome, and that they saw his body (which was brought into the market-place) all bemangled with gashes of swords, then there was no order to keep the multitude and common people quiet, but they plucked up forms, tables, and stools, and laid them all about the body; and setting them afire, burnt the corse. Then when the fire was well kindled, they took the fire-brands, and went unto their houses that had slain Caesar, to set them afire. Others also ran up and down the city to see if they could meet with any of them, to cut them in pieces: howbeit they could meet with never a man of them, because they had locked themselves up safely in their houses."
PLUTARCH, *Life of Caesar*

First Citizen. O most bloody sight!

Second Citizen. We will be revenged.

All. Revenge! About! Seek! Burn! Fire! Kill! Slay!
Let not a traitor live!

Antony. Stay, countrymen.

First Citizen. Peace there! Hear the noble Antony.

Second Citizen. We'll hear him, we'll follow him, we'll die
with him!

Antony. Good friends, sweet friends, let me not stir you up
To such a sudden flood of mutiny.
They that have done this deed are honorable.
What private griefs they have, alas, I know not,
That made them do it. They are wise and honorable,
And will no doubt with reasons answer you.
I come not, friends, to steal away your hearts.
I am no orator, as Brutus is,
But (as you know me all) a plain blunt man
That love my friend; and that they know full well
That gave me public leave to speak of him.
For I have neither wit, nor words, nor worth,
Action, nor utterance, nor the power of speech
To stir men's blood. I only speak right on.
I tell you that which you yourselves do know,
Show you sweet Caesar's wounds, poor poor dumb mouths,
And bid them speak for me. But were I Brutus,
And Brutus Antony, there were an Antony
Would ruffle up your spirits, and put a tongue
In every wound of Caesar that should move
The stones of Rome to rise and mutiny.

All. We'll mutiny.

First Citizen. We'll burn the house of Brutus.

Third Citizen. Away then! Come, seek the conspirators.

Antony. Yet hear me, countrymen. Yet hear me speak.

All. Peace, ho! Hear Antony, most noble Antony!

Antony. Why, friends, you go to do you know not what.
Wherein hath Caesar thus deserved your loves?
Alas, you know not! I must tell you then.
You have forgot the will I told you of.

All. Most true! The will! Let's stay and hear the will.

231–233 ***I am no . . . friend:*** This is another speaker's trick. Antony has just shown himself to be a much better speaker ***(orator)*** than Brutus. *Why, then, does he say he is "no orator"?*

235 ***wit:*** intelligence.

Z. Reading Skill: INFERRING Ask students what this statement implies about the consequences of Caesar's murder for the Roman people. *(Possible response: A civil war between the conspirators and their supporters and Antony and his followers may be imminent, if these citizens are ready to "die with" Antony.)*

AA. LEP: Archaic Words and Meanings The word *griefs* here means "grievances" or "causes for complaint."

BB. Answer: *Antony probably says this to make the crowd believe that he is a straightforward, honest man like any of them. He wants to avoid seeming "political," particularly now, when he is at his most "political" and manipulative.*

CC. Literary Element: IRONY Ask students to explain the irony in Antony's words here. *(Possible response: He pretends not to be a practiced orator, like Brutus in spite of the skillful and persuasive speech he has given.)*

DD. Reading Skill: INTERPRETIVE ORAL READING Encourage students to read the conclusion of this speech aloud, observing the punctuation. Ask how students would alter their volume, rate, and pitch as they pronounce these lines. *(Possible response: Students might try to experiment with a gradual crescendo in volume and with slowing the rate down gradually in order to deliver the word "mutiny" with climactic force.)*

EE. Cultural Sidelight This bequest was probably equivalent to about a year's pay for an average working man.

FF. Literary Element: CLIMAX Have students identify why this is the climax of the play. *(Possible response: The crowd's mood has completely shifted. It is now allied with Antony and against the conspirators to the point of being ready for violence.)*

GG. Literary Element: CHARACTER Ask what seems to be Antony's attitude toward the critical change he has brought about in the crowd after Caesar's murder. *(Possible response: He seems smug and vengeful, prepared for whatever events may happen, no matter how catastrophic.) Ask if students think that Antony reveals any ambition for his own power at this point. (Possible response: He does not hint here that he is eager to seize control of Rome; on the other hand, he seems confident about his ability to sway the people.)*

HH. LEP: Archaic Words and Meanings In this passage, the adjective *merry* means "favorable," rather than "cheerful." *Notice of the people* refers to the conspirators' observations of the people's reactions.

Antony. Here is the will, under Caesar's seal.
EE To every Roman citizen he gives,
To every several man, seventy-five drachmas.

Second Citizen. Most noble Caesar! We'll revenge his
death!

Third Citizen. O royal Caesar!

Antony. Hear me with patience.

All. Peace, ho!

Antony. Moreover, he hath left you all his walks,
His private arbors, and new-planted orchards,
On this side Tiber; he hath left them you,
And to your heirs for ever—common pleasures,
To walk abroad and recreate yourselves.
Here was a Caesar! When comes such another?

First Citizen. Never, never! Come, away, away!
We'll burn his body in the holy place
And with the brands the traitors' houses.
Take up the body.

FF **Second Citizen.** Go fetch fire!

Third Citizen. Pluck down benches!

Fourth Citizen. Pluck down forms, windows, anything!

[Exeunt Citizens *with the body.]*

GG **Antony.** Now let it work. Mischief, thou art afoot,
Take thou what course thou wilt.

[Enter a Servant.*]*

How now, fellow?

Servant. Sir, Octavius is already come to Rome.

Antony. Where is he?

Servant. He and Lepidus are at Caesar's house.

Antony. And thither will I straight to visit him.
He comes upon a wish. Fortune is merry,
And in this mood will give us anything.

HH **Servant.** I heard him say Brutus and Cassius
Are rid like madmen through the gates of Rome.

Antony. Belike they had some notice of the people,
How I had moved them. Bring me to Octavius.
[Exeunt.]

258 *drachmas:* silver coins, worth quite a bit to poor people such as those in the crowd.

264–268 Reading from the will, Antony tells the crowd that Caesar has left all his private parks and gardens on this side of the Tiber River to be used by the public.

272 *brands:* pieces of burning wood.

277–278 *Now let . . . wilt:* Alone, Antony gloats over what he has just accomplished. Let things take their course, he says. Whatever happens, happens.

283 *thither . . . him:* I will go right there to see him.

284–285 *He comes . . . anything:* Octavius has arrived just as Antony hoped; Antony believes that Fortune, the goddess of fate, is on his side.

287 *Are rid:* have ridden.

288 *Belike:* probably.

*R*esponding to Reading

1. Contrast the speeches given by Brutus and Antony in this scene.

   Think about
   - the purpose of each speech
   - tone and methods (e.g., sarcasm)
   - effectiveness
   - what each speech shows about its speaker

2. A tragic hero is a basically good and noble central character who makes fatal errors in judgment that contribute to the hero's downfall. Who, if anyone, is the tragic hero of this story? Explain.

3. What image does Shakespeare present of the "citizens," or common people, of Rome in this scene? Explain and provide examples.

Scene 3 *A street in Rome.*

This scene involves a famous Roman poet named Cinna. (He is not the same Cinna who took part in the assassination.) The angry Roman mob comes upon the poet, believing he is Cinna the conspirator. Soon, they realize this is the wrong man, yet they are so enraged that they slay him anyway. Then, they rush through the city after the true killers of Caesar.

A *[Enter* Cinna, *the* poet, *and after him the* Citizens, *armed with sticks, spears, and swords.]*

Cinna. I dreamt tonight that I did feast with Caesar,
And things unluckily charge my fantasy.
I have no will to wander forth of doors,
Yet something leads me forth.

First Citizen. What is your name?

Second Citizen. Whither are you going?

Third Citizen. Where do you dwell?

B **Fourth Citizen.** Are you a married man or a bachelor?

Second Citizen. Answer every man directly.

First Citizen. Ay, and briefly.

Fourth Citizen. Ay, and wisely.

Third Citizen. Ay, and truly, you were best.

2 things . . . fantasy: Recent events have caused me to imagine awful things.

6 Whither: where.

CRITIC'S CORNER

"The scene of Cinna the poet is in many ways the most symbolically instructive of the whole play. . . . The taking of the name for the man—a thematically important element throughout this play, where Caesar is at once a private man and a public title—is symbolic of the overt confusion manifest in much of the action. Cinna's dream is a legitimate cause for anxiety, which he chose to ignore at peril to himself. Plutarch supplied him with a practical motive: 'When he heard that they carried Caesar's body to burial, being ashamed not to accompany his funerals, he went out of his house'; in Shakespeare's version the cause is deliberately less exact, more psychological than circumstantial. The warning is given and ignored; the plebians do not care that they attack the wrong man. In one short scene of less than forty lines the whole myth of the play is concisely expressed."

MARJORIE B. GARBER, ***Dream and Interpretation: Julius Caesar***

Student Response

Responding to Reading

These questions are open-ended with no "right" or "wrong" answers. However, responses, must be supported with information from the selection. Possible answers follow:

1. Brutus wants to justify the conspirators' actions and calm the crowd, while Antony wants to incite the people to mutiny; Brutus speaks straightforwardly, while Antony pretends to speak frankly but includes many sarcastic references to the conspirators; Antony's speech, coming second, is more effective; Antony speaks in eloquent verse, while Brutus speaks in pedestrian prose; Brutus' speech is idealistic, while Antony's is that of a master manipulator.

2. Students may say that Brutus is a tragic hero. Brutus is a basically good and noble character who has made several disastrous errors in judgement, that force him to flee from Rome and lead to his downfall.

3. Shakespeare's crowd is easily persuaded and violently emotional; they are fickle, and easily roused to anger, as may be seen by their reactions to Brutus' and Antony's speeches.

Text Annotations

Scene 3

A. Teaching Tip

You may feel it is useful to have the class pause here and predict the types of actions the angry and unruly crowd might take. You may also want to continue your earlier discussion of Shakespeare's negative portrayal of the crowd. Ask if students agree with his portrait, or have other opinions of crowds.

B. Reading Skill: **INTERPRETIVE ORAL READING** Students may enjoy reading the passage aloud and conveying the almost comic extent of Cinna's harassment.

C. LEP: Irony Encourage students to see the irony of Cinna presenting this information, as though it could possibly be relevant or helpful. Ask students how people being interrogated in frightening circumstances might react.

D. Literary Element: THEME Ask students how this scene relates to the play's theme of the consequences of a breakdown in legitimate authority. *(Possible response: Within hours of Caesar's assassination, Rome has been plunged into social chaos, and the crowd irrationally tears apart an innocent man.)*

E. Answer: *Students might cite political protests or unruly sports events.*

Check Test

1. What is Caesar's reaction when Brutus stabs him? *(He cries, "Et tu Brute?" and then falls down dead.)*

2. Why does Cassius object to allowing Antony to speak at Caesar's funeral? *(He fears that Antony will move the people.)*

3. What charge does Brutus make against Caesar in his speech to the people? *(He says that Caesar was too ambitious.)*

4. What document plays a major role in Antony's speech to the people? *(Caesar's will)*

5. What action of the people in scene 3 shows that they are violently inflamed against the conspirators? *(They kill Cinna the poet because he has the same name as a conspirator.)*

Student Response

Responding to Reading

These questions are open-ended with no "right" or "wrong" answers. However, responses must be supported with information from the selection. Possible answers follow:

1. This scene shows that the citizens are angry and dangerous. The portrayal of the crowd in scene 2, which revealed the commoners as fickle and highly emotional, has to some extent prepared the audience for their violence in this scene.

2. Possible response: Rome needs stable, firm leadership that the people will acknowledge as a legitimate authority. It seems doubtful now that Rome will receive this leadership soon, since the conspirators are arrayed against Antony and Octavius in what is likely to develop into a civil war.

C **Cinna.** What is my name? Whither am I going? Where do I dwell? Am I a married man or a bachelor? Then, to answer every man directly and briefly, wisely and truly: wisely I say, I am a bachelor.

Second Citizen. That's as much to say they are fools that marry. You'll bear me a bang for that, I fear. Proceed—directly.

Cinna. Directly I am going to Caesar's funeral.

First Citizen. As a friend or an enemy?

Cinna. As a friend.

Second Citizen. That matter is answered directly.

Fourth Citizen. For your dwelling—briefly.

Cinna. Briefly, I dwell by the Capitol.

Third Citizen. Your name, sir, truly.

Cinna. Truly, my name is Cinna.

First Citizen. Tear him to pieces! He's a conspirator.

Cinna. I am Cinna the poet! I am Cinna the poet!

Fourth Citizen. Tear him for his bad verses! Tear him for his bad verses!

Cinna. I am not Cinna the conspirator.

Fourth Citizen. It is no matter; his name's Cinna! Pluck but his name out of his heart, and turn him going.

Third Citizen. Tear him, tear him!

D *[They attack* Cinna.*]*

Come, brands, ho! To Brutus', to Cassius'! Burn all! Some to Decius' house and some to Casca's; some to Ligarius'! Away, go!

[Exeunt all the citizens.]

17–18 *That's . . . fear:* This response shows that Cinna is in danger. The citizen threatens to beat him ***(You'll bear me a bang),*** even though Cinna's comment was not meant to be insulting.

34–35 *Pluck . . . going:* Let's just tear the name out of his heart and send him away.

36 The citizens murder Cinna the poet. *Can you think of other examples—from real life or literature—of crowds that have gotten out of control?* E

Responding to Reading

1. What does this scene show about the citizens of Rome? Did their actions in Scene 2 prepare you for such behavior? Explain.
2. What does the city of Rome need at this point? Do you think it will get what it needs? Why or why not?

Responding to Reading

First Impressions

1. Did you find this act exciting and suspenseful? Why or why not?

Second Thoughts

2. What do the conspirators believe they have accomplished by killing Caesar? Do you agree? Explain.
3. Why does Brutus trust Antony? What does his trust tell you about him?

   Think about
   - what Brutus expects of Antony
   - Antony's relationship with Caesar
   - clues that Brutus might not be seeing
4. Why do you think the citizens are so easily swayed from one side to the other?

   Think about
   - their response after the killing
   - their reaction to Brutus' speech
   - their reaction to Antony's speech
   - their killing of Cinna the poet

Literary Concepts: Climax and Rhetorical Question

In this play, as in most of Shakespeare's tragedies, the **climax,** or turning point, occurs in Act Three. The climax is the high point of interest or suspense. All the events before the climax make up the rising action, in which the central conflict is developed. The climax then marks the beginning of the falling action, or the events leading to the tragic ending for the protagonist. Which event in Act Three is the climax of this tragedy?

Notice that Marc Antony asks a number of questions in his speech at Caesar's funeral. For example:

> You all did see on the Lupercal
> I thrice did present him a kingly crown,
> Which he did thrice refuse. Was this ambition?

Such a question is a **rhetorical question,** one that does not call for an answer because the answer is obvious. A skilled speaker can use rhetorical questions to make a point or create an emotional effect. What do you think Antony hopes to accomplish with the above question? Find other rhetorical questions in Antony's funeral speech. Does he use these questions skillfully? Explain.

Student Response

Responding to Reading

These questions are open-ended with no "right" or "wrong" answers. However, responses must be supported with information from the selection. Possible answers follow:

1. Students may agree that the act is exciting and suspenseful, citing the murder of Caesar and all the suspense around it, the speeches of Brutus and Antony, and the volatile reactions of the crowd to these speeches.

2. The conspirators believe they have delivered Rome from bondage to a tyrant. Some students will agree with their action, citing Caesar's arrogance and ambition. Others will note that the conspirators' plot has plunged Rome into violence and civil war.

3. Brutus trusts Antony because he believes that Antony loves freedom and honor as much as he does, and perhaps because he needs to block out others' bad motives to rationalize his own guilt. He expects Antony to keep his promise but does not take into account Antony's deep love for Caesar. In addition, Brutus may not suspect that Antony is capable of playing on the crowd's emotions to advance his own ambitions for power. Students may say that this all shows Brutus to be naive and too focused on the idea of "honor".

4. The citizens are portrayed as easily persuaded by emotional arguments. Simplistic slogans like "freedom," "Caesar," "ambition," and "honor" are used by the speakers to manipulate the crowd. The people's reactions to Brutus' and Antony's speeches show that they will readily believe the last person they hear; Antony, therefore, has reaped a crucial advantage in speaking second, after Brutus. By the time the people encounter Cinna the poet, they are completely irrational in their rage and their thirst for revenge.

Literary Concept—Climax

Possible response: Antony's speech is the climax. To help students understand climax, remind the class that the climax of a play is the turning point, or pivot, around which the rising action and the falling action of the plot are placed. Suggest to students that Shakespeare underlines the climax of this play—Antony's successful incitement of the crowd to violence—by having the crowd move forward in a series of steps. First they return to their love for Caesar, then they begin to despise Brutus, then the reading of the will inflames them to all-out violence that will later lead to civil war.

Literary Concept—Rhetorical Question

With the above question he hopes to get the crowd to admit that Caesar was not ambitious, in spite of Brutus' claims. Other rhetorical questions are "Did this in Caesar seem ambitious?" (line 96) and "What cause withholds you then to mourn for him?" (line 109). Students may say that Antony uses these rhetorical questions skillfully, as he brings out the listeners' emotions and gets them to feel they are coming to these conclusions on their own.

Writing Options

The Writing Options are designed to meet varied student interests and abilities. Have each student choose one writing activity to complete. You may wish to guide some students to an option that requires less writing.

Options for Learning

These activities suit a variety of learning styles and modes of expression. Allow students to review the options and then choose the one they wish to do. Many are excellent collaborative learning projects.

1. Design the Sets Suggest that students look at illustrated reconstructions of the buildings in the ancient Roman Forum for this assignment. Students might use the following references: *Pictorial Dictionary of Ancient Rome* by Ernest Nash; *A History of Architecture* by Sir Bannister Fletcher.

2. Performing the Play Encourage students to pay special attention to blocking (the position and movements of each character on stage during a scene) and gestures as they play their performances.

3. A Skilled Speaker Remind students that Antony's speech is divided into four fairly lengthy parts, as well as a number of shorter exchanges with the citizens in the crowd. Urge students to plan how they will maintain a variety in pitch, volume, and tone during their renditions of Antony's speech.

4. Who was Octavious? Direct students to a good encyclopedia or to a reference volume such as the *Oxford Classical Dictionary* to research Octavius, who was Caesar's great-nephew and his adopted son—and was later to rule Rome as the Emperor Augustus (27 B.C.–A.D.14).

Writing Options

1. Is Brutus truly an "honorable man" or not? Write a brief explanation of your opinion.
2. Write a newspaper account of the killing of Caesar and the events that followed. Make up some eyewitness quotes. Give your article a headline with a total of thirty-two letters and spaces.
3. Most readers' image of Mark Antony changes a number of times during Act Three. List, in order, the changes in your own impression of Antony as you read the act. Explain whether any of the changes surprised you.
4. Create a "wanted poster" that Antony and Octavius might pass out to help find the fleeing conspirators. The poster should tell who is "wanted" and provide a brief description. It should also tell of their crimes and perhaps where they were last seen. In addition, you may want to offer a reward (in drachmas).

e x t e n d

Options for Learning

1 • Design the Sets Sketch possible sets for Act Three. Include sets for Scene 1 (the Capitol), Scene 2 (the Forum), and Scene 3 (a street in Rome). Remember that in Shakespeare's time sets were either bare or quite simple. Decide how detailed you want your sets to be. If necessary, do some research to learn what these Roman scenes really looked like.

2 • Performing the Play With a group of students, plan and perform one scene from Act Three for your classmates. After the performance, allow class members to offer and discuss critical suggestions about how the performance might be improved.

3 • A Skilled Speaker Read Antony's funeral speech to the class, stopping at points to comment on the speaker's purpose and methods of manipulating his audience.

4 • Who Was Octavius? Do some library research to find out who Octavius was and why he might have been so willing to help Antony. Report your findings to the class.

ACT FOUR

Scene 1 *At a table in Antony's house in Rome.*

Antony, Octavius, and Lepidus now rule Rome as a triumvirate—a committee of three. The scene opens on the triumvirate, meeting to draw up a list of their enemies who must be killed. They also discuss changing Caesar's will. As Lepidus goes to fetch the will, Antony expresses his low opinion of Lepidus as a leader. Then, Antony and Octavius begin to discuss how to defeat the armies of Brutus and Cassius.

Antony. These many, then, shall die; their names are
pricked.

A **Octavius.** Your brother too must die. Consent you,
Lepidus?

Lepidus. I do consent.

Octavius. Prick him down, Anthony.

Lepidus. Upon condition Publius shall not live,
Who is your sister's son, Mark Antony.

Antony. He shall not live. Look, with a spot I damn him.
But Lepidus, go you to Caesar's house.
Fetch the will hither, and we shall determine
How to cut off some charge in legacies.

Lepidus. What? shall I find you here?

Octavius. Or here or at the Capitol.

[Exit Lepidus.]

Antony. This is a slight unmeritable man,
C Meet to be sent on errands. Is it fit,
The threefold world divided, he should stand
One of the three to share it?

Octavius. So you thought him,
And took his voice who should be pricked to die
In our black sentence and proscription.

Antony. Octavius, I have seen more days than you;
And though we lay these honors on this man
To ease ourselves of divers sland'rous loads,
He shall but bear them as the ass bears gold,
D To groan and sweat under the business,
Either led or driven as we point the way;

GUIDE FOR READING

9 *with a spot . . . him:* I condemn him by marking him on this list.

11–12 *Fetch . . . legacies:* Bring Caesar's will here, so we can decide how to alter the amounts the people get. *Does this statement change your opinion of Antony? Explain.* B

15–31 *This is . . . commons:* Now that Antony and Octavius are alone, Antony says what he really thinks of Lepidus. He does not believe Lepidus is worthy of being one of three men in control of Rome's lands in Europe, Asia, and Africa ***(the threefold world).*** Lepidus, he says, is fit ***(Meet)*** for running errands. Antony admits that they have accepted Lepidus' opinion about who should be put on the list of those who will die ***(black sentence and proscription),*** but they have done that only so he will take the blame for the many unpopular things ***(divers sland'rous loads)*** they plan to do.

Teaching Strategies

Support for Students of Limited English Proficiency

- Use **Reader's Guidesheet**, p. 10.
- *Julius Caesar* Act Four contains some irregular syntax that may be difficult for some students. Help students who are puzzled by Shakespeare's occasional use of ellipses and inverted sentence structure by using the annotations as appropriate.
- **Annotations F** and **H** (Scene 1); **C** and **H** (Scene 2); **J, M, T, CC, HH,** and **MM** (Scene 3) focus on syntax, context, and irony.

Text Annotations

Scene 1

A. Literary Element: CONFLICT Ask students to describe how the conflict has widened in Rome at the beginning of this act. *(Possible response: In Act Three the conflict was between the conspirators and Caesar and his supporters. Now the conflict has widened to become full-scale civil war, which even divides the families of the triumvirs.)*

B. Answer: *Most students will agree that a new, cynical side of Antony's character is revealed here. Antony used Caesar's will to get the crowd on his side in Act Three; now he is trying to cheat the people by changing the terms of the will.*

C. Literary Element: THEME Ask students to explain how this speech relates to the themes of friendship and ambition in the play. *(Possible response: Antony reveals that he is hypocritical in his alliance with Lepidus. He also implies that he is reluctant to share any more power than necessary, especially with an "unworthy" partner like Lepidus. The speech hints that Antony may have been corrupted by ambition.)*

D. Literary Element: **FIGURATIVE LANGUAGE** Ask students what Antony contemptuously compares Lepidus to in this simile. *(Possible response: to an ass)* Then ask how Antony expands the simile. *(Possible response: He describes the beast groaning and sweating as it bears its owners' treasure; he then envisions the ass being turned out to graze, once it has finished its work.)* Finally, ask students what this comparison implies. *(Possible response: Antony is scornful of Lepidus and, having made use of him, does not want to share power with him.)*

E. Teaching Tip

It might help students to make a chart of who is in power and who is in conflict with whom in each act, such as the following:

	IN POWER	IN CONFLICT
Act One	Caesar	Caesar vs. conspirators Brutus vs. Cassius
Act Two	same	same
Act Three	Brutus and Cassius	Antony vs. Conspirators
Act Four	Antony, Octavius, and Lepidus	Antony and Octavius vs. Lepidus Triumvirs vs. conspirators

"Therefore let our alliance be combined . . ."

And having brought our treasure where we will,
Then take we down his load, and turn him off
D (Like to the empty ass) to shake his ears
And graze in commons.

Octavius. You may do your will;
E But he's a tried and valiant soldier.

Antony. So is my horse, Octavius, and for that
I do appoint him store of provender.
It is a creature that I teach to fight,
To wind, to stop, to run directly on,
His corporal motion governed by my spirit.
And, in some taste is Lepidus but so.
He must be taught, and trained, and bid go forth:
A barren-spirited fellow; one that feeds
On objects, arts and imitations
Which, out of use and staled by other men,
Begin his fashion. Do not talk of him,
But as a property. And now, Octavius,
Listen great things. Brutus and Cassius
Are levying powers. We must straight make head.
Therefore let our alliance be combined,
Our best friends made, and our best means stretched out;
And let us presently go sit in council
How covert matters may be best disclosed
And open perils surest answered.

Octavius. Let us do so; for we are at the stake
And bayed about with many enemies;
And some that smile have in their hearts, I fear,
Millions of mischiefs.

[Exeunt.]

34–35 ***So is my . . . property:*** Antony compares Lepidus to a horse who is given food ***(provender)*** and taught how to behave. Antony also says that Lepidus is interested in ***(feeds / On)*** unimportant things ***(objects, arts, and imitations)*** that he learns of from other people, and these things attract his attention ***(Begin his fashion)*** after others have lost interest in them.

46–47 ***Listen . . . head:*** Listen to important ***(great)*** matters. Brutus and Cassius are raising an army ***(levying powers).*** We must move fast ***(straight make head)*** to build up our own army.

51–53 ***let us . . . answered:*** Let us decide the best way to uncover hidden ***(covert)*** dangers and to deal with the threats we know about.

54–57 ***for we are . . . mischiefs:*** We are like a bear tied to a stake and taunted by barking dogs. Some of the people who smile at us may have evil intentions ***(mischiefs)*** in mind for us. *What do these lines tell you about Octavius' state of mind?*

Responding to Reading

1. Has this scene changed your opinion of Antony? Explain and give examples.
2. Octavius speaks only a few lines in this scene. What impression do you get of him from these lines?
3. You know little of Lepidus besides what Antony says. Do you think Lepidus might be as unworthy as Antony insists?

   Think about
   - how honest Antony is
   - Antony's purposes
   - Antony's persuasive abilities

F. LEP: Irony Make sure students realize that Antony's mention of his horse is an ironic insult to Lepidus, whose import Antony goes on to explain: like a horse, Lepidus may be brave enough to fight but he is hardly wise enough to rule.

G. Literary Element: CHARACTERIZATION Ask students to comment on what these lines he says about Lepidus may reveal about Antony's own character. *(Possible responses: Antony seems cold, imperious, and manipulative.)* Given Antony's own behavior immediately after Caesar's murder in Act III, ask what is ironic about his accusation that Lepidus follows the fashions of others. *(Possible response: Antony carefully hedged his bets with the conspirators, pretending at first to follow their lead.)*

H. LEP: Syntax Point out to students that in line 54 the word "be" has been omitted before "surest." When you have explained this ellipsis, ask students to notice that lines 53 and 54 exhibit parallel syntax. Ask students to paraphrase these lines in their own words. *(Possible response: "how we can uncover hidden dangers and deal with open threats in the best way.")*

I. Answer: *These lines suggest that Octavius is distrustful and apprehensive.*

Student Response

Responding to Reading

These questions are open-ended with no "right" or "wrong" answers. However, responses must be supported with information from the selection. Possible answers follow.

1. Most students will comment that Antony is shown in a bad light. He cynically prepares to cheat the people of their inheritance under Caesar's will, and he is scornful of Lepidus behind his back. Power seems to have corrupted Antony—or revealed his true nature.

2. Octavius seems straightforward and direct. He does not hesitate to disagree with Antony, reminding him that he had earlier approved of Lepidus' promotion to the triumvirate.

3. Given Antony's skill at persuasion, his dishonesty over the will, and his hunger for power, he is probably slandering Lepidus unfairly to avoid sharing any more power than necessary.

Text Annotations

Scene 2

A. Literary Element: SETTING Ask students how the setting for this scene presents a contrast with the setting for the first three acts of the play and for the first scene of Act Four. *(Possible response: The setting has shifted to a location far away from Rome and from the civic, public world. Now the play is set in the military world. The sound of drums and the brisk orders reinforce the setting of a military camp.)*

B. Answer: *Brutus probably thinks that his officer's report can furnish reliable clues about Cassius' true state of mind and intentions.*

C. LEP: Syntax Point out to students that this passage contains elliptical syntax. Students have to supply several words to make sense of Brutus' speech. Be sure that students can paraphrase the passage roughly as follows: "Lucilius, tell me how he greeted you. Let me be informed."

D. Literary Element: THEME Ask students to paraphrase Brutus' observation about friendship in these lines. *(Possible response: He says that friends who are growing apart, or "cooling," start to use a hypocritical, polite show of friendship, or "enforced ceremony," with each other.)* Ask if students think that Brutus' observation is sound. *(Possible response: Many students will agree that some people use ultra-politeness to mask feelings of disapproval or distaste.)*

Scene 2 *A military camp near Sardis. In front of Brutus' tent.*

Brutus seems displeased at the way events are developing, and he tells his servant about Cassius' new cold and distant attitude. Cassius arrives, and he and Brutus go into the tent to talk about their disagreements.

[Sound of drums. Enter Brutus, Lucilius, Lucius, *and* Soldiers. Titinius *and* Pindarus, *from* Cassius' *army, meet them.]*

Brutus. Stand ho!

Lucilius. Give the word, ho! and stand!

Brutus. What now, Lucilius? Is Cassius near?

Lucilius. He is at hand, and Pindarus is come
To do you salutation from his master.

Brutus. He greets me well. Your master, Pindarus,
In his own change, or by ill officers,
Hath given me some worthy cause to wish
Things done undone; but if he be at hand,
I shall be satisfied.

Pindarus. I do not doubt
But that my noble master will appear
Such as he is, full of regard and honor.

Brutus. He is not doubted. A word, Lucilius,
How he received you. Let me be resolved.

Lucilius. With courtesy and with respect enough,
But not with such familiar instances
Nor with such free and friendly conference
As he hath used of old.

Brutus. Thou has described
A hot friend cooling. Ever note, Lucilius,
When love begins to thicken and decay
It useth an enforced ceremony.
There are no tricks in plain and simple faith;
But hollow men, like horses hot at hand,
Make gallant show and promise of their mettle;

[Low march within.]

But when they should endure the bloody spur,
They fall their crests, and like deceitful jades
Sink in the trial. Comes his army on?

5 *do you salutation:* bring you greetings.

6–10 *He greets . . . satisfied:* Cassius sends a good man to greet me. Pindarus, your master has either had a change of heart or is surrounded by incompetent ***(ill)*** officers. Whatever the reason, he has made me wish that certain things had never happened ***(Things done undone).*** But if he is here ***(at hand),*** I will find out for myself ***(be satisfied).***

14–15 *A word . . . resolved:* Brutus takes his officer aside and asks him privately how he was treated when he met Cassius. *Why does Brutus want to know this?*

18 *conference:* conversation.

21–29 *Ever note . . . trial:* Brutus tells Lucilius never to forget ***(Ever note)*** that when affection begins to cool, it turns into awkward politeness ***(enforced ceremony).*** Honest relationships, he says, do not involve tricks. Insincere ***(hollow)*** men, like eager horses, make a great show of courage ***(mettle).*** But when they get the signal ***(spur)*** to fight, they drop their heads ***(fall their crests)*** and fail, like worn-out horses ***(jades).***

Lucilius. They mean this night in Sardis to be quartered.
The greater part, the horse in general,
Are come with Cassius.

Brutus. Hark! He is arrived.
March gently on to meet him.

E *[Enter* Cassius *and his army.]*

Cassius. Stand, ho!

Brutus. Stand, ho! Speak the word along.

First Soldier. Stand!

Second Soldier. Stand!

Third Soldier. Stand!

Cassius. Most noble brother, you have done me wrong.

F **Brutus.** Judge me, you gods! wrong I mine enemies?
And if not so, how should I wrong a brother?

Cassius. Brutus, this sober form of yours hides wrongs,
And when you do them—

Brutus. Cassius, be content.
Speak your griefs softly. I do know you well.
Before the eyes of both our armies here
(Which should perceive nothing but love from us)
Let us not wrangle. Bid them move away.
Then in my tent, Cassius, enlarge your griefs,
And I will give you audience.

H **Cassius.** Pindarus,
Bid our commanders lead their charges off
A little from this ground.

Brutus. Lucilius, do you the like, and let no man
Come to our tent till we have done our conference.
Let Lucius and Titinius guard our door.

[Exeunt.]

30 ***They . . . quartered:*** Cassius and his army intend to stay here (in Sardis) tonight.

31 ***horse in general:*** entire cavalry.

37–39 The soldiers are passing the order to stop marching ***(Stand)*** along the lengthy column that has followed Cassius into camp.

43 ***sober form:*** serious manner.

45–51 ***be content . . . audience:*** Brutus tells Cassius to stay calm and keep his voice down. He says they should not argue ***(wrangle)*** in front of their soldiers. Then he invites Cassius into his tent, where he will listen to him ***(give you audience).*** *Why does Brutus want to hide his and Cassius' disagreements from the soldiers?* G

Responding to Reading

1. Has the relationship between Brutus and Cassius changed since the murder of Caesar? Support your opinion with evidence from this scene.
2. Is there any evidence in this scene that Brutus himself has changed since the last time he appeared?

E. Literary Element: STAGE DIRECTIONS Encourage students to visualize the impact of an entire army coming onstage with Cassius. Help students see how much information a production might convey with this image. For example, Cassius' army might be larger or smaller than Brutus' telling us about the relative power of the two men; the army might be fierce and disciplined, tired and bedraggled, or sullen and desperate, in each case conveying a different image of Cassius' leadership and his fortunes.

F. Literary Element: CONFLICT Ask students whether they think that the audience has been prepared for the violent quarrel between Brutus and Cassius. *(Possible response: Most students will agree that the argument has been foreshadowed: Brutus and Cassius, for example, have had several disagreements about the conspirators' strategy, and Brutus has just finished voicing his suspicion that Cassius' friendship for him has cooled.)*

G. Answer: *Brutus probably feels that it would be undignified for the commanders to argue openly. Furthermore, such conflict might lessen the fighting morale of the troops.*

H. LEP: Syntax Be sure that students understand that Cassius is giving Pindarus an order to pass along to the commanders. They are to move their troops ("charges") away from Brutus' tent so that the generals will not be disturbed.

Student Response

Responding to Reading

These questions are open-ended with no "right" or "wrong" answers. However, responses must be supported with information from the selection. Possible answers follow:

1. The relationship has changed, because the stresses of exile, civil war, and possibly guilt have made Brutus and Cassius tense and distrustful with each other. Brutus suspects that Cassius friendship is cooling, and Cassius charges Brutus with wronging him.

2. Some evidence suggests that Brutus has changed. He now seems nervous, rather than calm and confident. His language comparing false friends to unreliable horses is particularly harsh—and it seems to echo Antony's harsh comparison of Lepidus to a horse in scene 1.

Text Annotations

Scene 3

A. Critical Thinking: EVALUATING Ask students to summarize and evaluate the two sides in this quarrel. Ask who the students think has more right on his side, Cassius or Brutus. *(Possible response: Cassius' position is that Brutus should not have punished Pella for taking bribes, since Cassius personally supported him and since the offense is trivial. Brutus' position is that both Pella and Cassius were guilty of injustice. Some students will support Brutus' idealism, while others may support Cassius' pragmatic attitude.)*

B. Reading Skill: INFERRING Ask students why they think Cassius allows Brutus to say such things about him. *(Possible response: Cassius probably allows Brutus to say such things because he has a deep need for Brutus' friendship. On a more practical level, he needs Brutus' support to do battle with the conspirators' enemies.)*

C. LEP: Syntax Be sure students understand that current standard word order and verb form here would be, "Or else, by the gods, this speech would be your last."

D. Literary Element: CHARACTERIZATION Ask how Brutus refers to Caesar in these lines. Then ask what this suggests about Brutus. *(Possible response: Brutus refers to Caesar as "the foremost man of all this world," bleeding for the cause of justice. These lines suggest that Brutus still holds Caesar in awe, but also that he still believes in the justice and honor of the conspirators' cause. He feels that the conspirators must live up to ideals of justice and nobility; otherwise, Caesar's murder will have been in vain.)*

E. Literary Element: DIALOGUE Point out to students that Brutus uses a series of rhetorical questions—questions to which the speaker really does not expect an answer. Have students note that each question in the series is longer than the preceding one and encourage them to see how this helps Brutus build intensity. Ask students whether they themselves ever use rhetorical questions when they speak forcefully or angrily, and ask for examples.

Scene 3 *Inside Brutus' tent at Sardis.*

Brutus and Cassius argue angrily, as Brutus accuses Cassius of corruption and greed. After a while, though, they calm down and become friendly once again. Brutus informs Cassius of Portia's death. Soon after, Massala enters. He tells of all the killings in Rome and of Antony and Octavius approaching with their armies. Brutus persuades Cassius that their forces must meet the enemy at Philippi in Greece. Later, as Brutus reads, the ghost of Caesar appears and promises to see Brutus at Philippi.

[*Enter* Brutus *and* Cassius.]

Cassius. That you have wronged me doth appear in this:
You have condemned and noted Lucius Pella
For taking bribes here of the Sardians;
Wherein my letters, praying on his side,
Because I knew the man, were slighted off.

A **Brutus.** You wronged yourself to write in such a case.

Cassius. In such a time as this it is not meet
That every nice offense should bear his comment.

Brutus. Let me tell you, Cassius, you yourself
Are much condemned to have an itching palm,
To sell and mart your offices for gold
To undeservers.

Cassius. I an itching palm?
B You know that you are Brutus that speaks this,
C Or, by the gods, this speech were else your last!

Brutus. The name of Cassius honors this corruption,
And chastisement doth therefore hide his head.

Cassius. Chastisement?

Brutus. Remember March; the ides of March remember.
Did not great Julius bleed for justice' sake?
D What villain touched his body that did stab
And not for justice? What, shall one of us,
That struck the foremost man of all this world
E But for supporting robbers—shall we now
Contaminate our fingers with base bribes,
And sell the mighty space of our large honors
For so much trash as may be grasped thus?
I had rather be a dog and bay the moon
Than such a Roman.

2 *noted:* publicly disgraced.

5 *slighted off:* ignored.

7–8 *it is not . . . comment:* It is not appropriate for every tiny ***(nice)*** offense to be criticized.

10 *to have an itching palm:* to be always looking for bribes.
11 *mart:* market.

13–15 *I an . . . last:* Cassius is almost speechless at the insult Brutus has just hurled at him. If anyone other than Brutus said such a thing to me, Cassius says, I would kill him on the spot.
16–17 *The name . . . head:* Because Cassius' name is linked to the bribery ***(corruption),*** no one dares talk about punishment ***(chastisement)*** for those who accept the bribes.

24 *But for supporting robbers:* because he (Caesar) protected robbers from punishment. This is not one of the charges the conspirators originally made against Caesar.
28 *bay:* howl at.

CRITIC'S CORNER

T. S. Dorsch has written the following about the portrayal of Brutus in the second half of the play:

"Caesar grows in stature as the play proceeds; Brutus deteriorates. In his quarrel with Cassius he is irritable, undignified, and unjust; he is more intolerant of the meddlesome poet than Cassius; and though he vehemently disputes Cassius' claim to be the abler soldier, his reasons for engaging the enemy at Philippi are less convincing than those of Cassius for deferring the battle. It is impossible to reconcile Shakespeare's presentation of Brutus with the common Renaissance view of him as the great liberator and patriot, the second of his name to free the Romans from the tyrant's yoke."

Cassius. Brutus, bait not me!
I'll not endure it. You forget yourself
To hedge me in. I am a soldier, I,
Older in practice, abler than yourself
To make conditions.

Brutus. Go to! You are not, Cassius.

Cassius. I am.

Brutus. I say you are not.

Cassius. Urge me no more! I shall forget myself.
Have mind upon your health, tempt me no farther.

Brutus. Away, slight man!

Cassius. Is't possible?

Brutus. Hear me, for I will speak.
Must I give way and room to your rash choler?
Shall I be frighted when a madman stares?

Cassius. O ye gods, ye gods! Must I endure all this?

Brutus. All this? Ay, more! Fret till your proud heart break.
Go show your slaves how choleric you are
And make your bondmen tremble. Must I budge?
Must I observe you? Must I stand and crouch
Under your testy humor? By the gods,
You shall digest the venom of your spleen,
Though it do split you; for from this day forth
I'll use you for my mirth, yea, for my laughter,
When you are waspish.

Cassius. Is it come to this?

Brutus. You say you are a better soldier;
Let it appear so. Make your vaunting true,
And it shall please me well. For mine own part,
I shall be glad to learn of noble men.

Cassius. You wrong me every way! You wrong me, Brutus!
I said an elder soldier, not a better.
Did I say "better"?

Brutus. If you did, I care not.

Cassius. When Caesar lived he durst not thus have moved me.

30–34 bait not me . . . conditions: Do not try to provoke ***(bait)*** me into fighting. I will not put up with ***(endure)*** it. Since I am the more experienced soldier, I should be the one to make decisions ***(conditions)***.

43–52 Must . . . spleen: Brutus refers to Cassius' quick temper ***(rash choler)***, to the fact that he is so angry ***(choleric)***, and to his irritable mood ***(testy humor)***. You can swallow the poison of your own anger ***(spleen)***, he says. (People once believed that the spleen, an organ near the stomach, was the source of certain emotions, such as anger and spite.)

55 waspish: ill tempered.

58 vaunting: bragging; *What challenge does Brutus make?*

61–63 You wrong . . . better: Cassius now controls his anger and tries to soften some of the things he said earlier. He will soon become angry again, though, since Brutus does not stop insulting him.

66–67 he durst . . . me: Even Caesar would not have dared to provoke me this way.

F. Reading Skill: INTERPRETIVE ORAL READING Encourage students to experiment with pace, pitch, and tone of voice when they read these lines aloud. Ask how Brutus' tone might change and why. *(Possible response: Brutus might say "Away, slight man!" in a calm voice, but he then might change to a more forceful tone with the line, "Hear me, for I will speak," as his anger builds.)* Ask how Cassius' tone might change. *(Possible response: Cassius might be extremely forceful in his first speech, beginning "Urge me no more!" He then might sound incredulous, perhaps using a near whisper, in the line "Is't possible?")*

G. Literary Element: FIGURATIVE LANGUAGE Ask students to explain Brutus' use of metaphor in this passage. *(Possible response: Brutus' metaphor compares Cassius' anger to a poisonous liquid, or "venom," that is producuced by the spleen and that Cassius will have to swallow, or "digest." Remind students that the Elizabethans believed that fluids, or humors, produced by various organs created temperaments and moods. Spleen was associated with bitterness and resentment.)*

H. Answer: *He challenges Cassius to prove his boast that he is the better soldier on the battlefield.*

I. Literary Element: IRONY Ask students to explain why Brutus might pronounce these lines in an ironic tone of voice. *(Possible response: Brutus probably does not believe that Cassius is a better soldier. Given his pride in his own dedication to nobility, he also probably uses the word "noble" in an ironic sense here.)*

J. Literary Element: DIALOGUE Ask students to identify features of the dialogue here that hint that the quarrel may be reaching a dangerous climax. *(Possible response: The choppy division of lines between speakers and the repetitions of the word "durst" (dare) hint that Brutus and Cassius are becoming highly agitated. "Durst" sounds like a "fighting word" in this passage.)*

K. Literary Element: FIGURATIVE LANGUAGE Ask students to identify the specific idea that is the basis for Brutus' metaphor here. *(The metaphor compares Brutus' heart to a mint; the drops of blood pumped through his heart are then compared to coins, or drachmas.)* Ask students how Brutus' use of this metaphor affects their impression of him. *(Possible response: Some students may admire Brutus' devotion to honesty and self-sacrifice; other students may comment that the metaphor makes Brutus seem somewhat self-righteous.)*

L. LEP: Syntax Be sure that students understand that *When* in this passage is used for "If" and that Brutus is speaking of himself rhetorically in the third person.

M. Literary Element: THEME Ask students to identify what is happening to Brutus' and Cassius' friendship at this point. *(Possible response: From manipulating Brutus, Cassius now seems to need his support; from leaning on Cassius, Brutus now seems to be scorning and criticizing him.)*

Brutus. Peace, peace! You durst not so have tempted
him.

J **Cassius.** I durst not?

Brutus. No.

Cassius. What, durst not tempt him?

Brutus. For your life you durst not.

Cassius. Do not presume too much upon my love.
I may do that I shall be sorry for.

Brutus. You have done that you should be sorry for.
There is no terror, Cassius, in your threats;
For I am armed so strong in honesty
That they pass by me as the idle wind,
Which I respect not. I did send to you
For certain sums of gold, which you denied me,
For I can raise no money by vile means—
K By heaven, I had rather coin my heart
And drop my blood for drachmas than to wring
From the hard hands of peasants their vile trash
By any indirection. I did send
To you for gold to pay my legions,
Which you denied me. Was that done like Cassius?
Should I have answered Caius Cassius so?
When Marcus Brutus grows so covetous
L To lock such rascal counters from his friends,
Be ready, gods, with all your thunderbolts,
Dash him to pieces!

Cassius. I denied you not.

Brutus. You did.

Cassius. I did not. He was but a fool that brought
M My answer back. Brutus hath rived my heart.
A friend should bear his friend's infirmities,
But Brutus makes mine greater than they are.

Brutus. I do not, till you practice them on me.

Cassius. You love me not.

Brutus. I do not like your faults.

Cassius. A friendly eye could never see such faults.

Brutus. A flatterer's would not, though they do appear
As huge as high Olympus.

82–86 *For I can . . . indirection:* I cannot raise money by dishonest ***(vile)*** methods. I would rather make coins out of my heart and blood than steal money from peasants by lying ***(indirection).***

87 *legions:* armies.

89–93 *Should . . . pieces:* Would I have answered a request from you in the same way? When I become such a miser ***(so covetous)*** as to deny cheap coins ***(rascal counters)*** to my friends, may the gods destroy me.

97 *rived:* torn apart.

98 *infirmities:* shortcomings.

Cassius. Come, Antony, and young Octavius, come!
Revenge yourselves alone on Cassius.
For Cassius is aweary of the world:
N Hated by one he loves; braved by his brother;
Checked like a bondman, all his faults observed,
O Set in a notebook, learned and conned by rote
To cast into my teeth. O, I could weep
My spirit from mine eyes! There is my dagger,
And here my naked breast; within, a heart
Dearer than Pluto's mine, richer than gold:
If that thou be'st a Roman, take it forth.
I, that denied thee gold, will give my heart.

106–121 *Come . . . lov'dst Cassius:* Cassius speaks these lines loudly, as though calling to Antony and Octavius, who are far away. He says they might as well kill him. He has been bullied ***(braved)*** by his true friend ***(brother)*** and scolded ***(Checked)*** like a slave; his faults have been written in a notebook and memorized ***(conned by rote)*** to be thrown into his face ***(cast into my teeth).*** Cassius then turns to Brutus and offers Cassius' knife to plunge into his own heart.

"There is no terror, Cassius, in your threats . . ."

N. Reading Skill: CLARIFYING Ask what is Cassius' purpose in this dramatic speech. *(Possible response: Cassius' purpose seems to be to inspire sympathy for himself. He offers to commit suicide, and he bitterly reproaches Brutus for loving Caesar more than he loves him.)*

O. Literary Element: CONFLICT Ask students to read this speech closely and then to describe some of the internal conflicts that it suggests in Cassius. *(Possible response: Cassius seems to want Brutus' friendship desperately, but he fears that Brutus despises him. His melodramatic offer to commit suicide probably springs from mixed emotions of shame, anger, and frustration. His yearning for friendship with Brutus seems also to be complicated by an envious suspicion that Brutus will never be as close a friend to him as Brutus was to Caesar.)*

P. LEP: Syntax Be sure that students can sort out the complicated syntax in these figures of speech. Brutus first compares himself to a lamb, meaning that he is a mild man. He then compares his own anger to flint that produces only brief sparks of fire.

Q. Literary Element: DIALOGUE Point out to students that the device of dividing one line of dialogue between speakers is often used by Shakespeare for moments of strong emotion. Then ask what stage in the argument the use of this device signals here. *(Possible response: It signals that the crisis is past and that the moment of reconciliation is at hand; the shared dialogue implies the closeness of shared thoughts.)*

R. Literary Element: HUMOR Ask students to explain the basis of Brutus' mild joke here. *(Possible response: He says that he will pretend that whenever Cassius grows angry it is really his ill-tempered mother who is speaking through him.)*

S. Answer: *Most students will agree that the argument and its ending are believable. The two friends are at first on edge, then flare up against each other. Cassius' pathetic plea for the restoration of their friendship touches Brutus, who then admits that he has been "ill-tempered," and the argument subsides, with Brutus making a light-hearted joke about Cassius' mother.*

Strike as thou didst at Caesar; for I know,
When thou didst hate him worst, thou lov'dst him
better
Than ever thou lov'dst Cassius.

Brutus. Sheathe your dagger.
Be angry when you will; it shall have scope.
Do what you will; dishonor shall be humor.
O Cassius, you are yoked with a lamb
That carries anger as the flint bears fire;
Who, much enforced, shows a hasty spark,
And straight is cold again.

Cassius. Hath Cassius lived
To be but mirth and laughter to his Brutus
When grief and blood ill-tempered vexeth him?

Brutus. When I spoke that, I was ill-tempered too.

Cassius. Do you confess so much? Give me your hand.

Brutus. And my heart too.

Cassius. O Brutus!

Brutus. What's the matter?

Cassius. Have you not love enough to bear with me
When that rash humor which my mother gave me
Makes me forgetful?

Brutus. Yes, Cassius, and from henceforth,
When you are over-earnest with your Brutus,
He'll think your mother chides, and leave you so.

[Enter a Poet *followed by* Lucilius, Titinius, *and* Lucius.*]*

Poet. Let me go in to see the generals!
There is some grudge between 'em. 'Tis not meet
They be alone.

Lucilius. You shall not come to them.

Poet. Nothing but death shall stay me.

Cassius. How now? What's the matter?

Poet. For shame, you generals! What do you mean?
Love and be friends, as two such men should be,
For I have seen more years, I'm sure, than ye.

Cassius. Ha, ha! How vilely doth this cynic rhyme!

Brutus. Get you hence, sirrah! Saucy fellow, hence!

122–128 ***Sheathe . . . cold again:*** Put away ***(Sheathe)*** your knife. Let your anger run free ***(have scope).*** Your insults ***(dishonor)*** will be taken as coming from a bad mood ***(humor).*** Cassius, you are tied to ***(yoked with)*** a mild man ***(lamb);*** anger to me is like the flint to fire. Strike it hard, and it will produce sparks; then it will cool immediately.

129–131 ***Hath Cassius . . . him:*** Have I lived so long only to become a joke to you when sadness and sickness trouble ***(vexeth)*** you?

134 The two men embrace in friendship, glad to be over their anger with each other.

137–139 ***Have you . . . forgetful:*** Don't you love me enough to put up with me when I lose control because of that bad temper I inherited from my mother?

142 ***He'll think . . . so:*** I will say it is your mother, not you, showing bad temper, and will forget about it. *Do you find Shakespeare's portrayal of this argument and its ending believable? Explain.*

143–158 The two men are briefly interrupted by a poet, who comes to persuade them to end their arguments and insists that nothing will stop ***(stay)*** him. These lines show that the tension between Brutus and Cassius is now completely gone. They joke about what a terrible poet this rude fellow ***(cynic)*** is and finally send him away. Once the silly poet is gone, Brutus and Cassius—friends once again—become serious.

CULTURAL CONNECTION

The concept of honor is an important one in *Julius Caesar.* Remind students that, although the play is set in ancient Rome, Shakespeare is writing about his own and his society's ideas. Encourage students to identify what honor seemed to mean in Shakespeare's time. *(Possible responses: never allowing an insult to pass; being willing to avenge one's honor with fighting unto death or with suicide; living up to certain standards of honesty and morality)* Then encourage students to discuss some of our own concepts of honor. You might particularly encourage students from other cultures to share with the class the concepts of honor in their societies, and to share whether they or their families' ideas have changed or been challenged by their experiences in the United States.

Cassius. Bear with him, Brutus. 'Tis his fashion.

Brutus. I'll know his humor when he knows his time.
T What should the wars do with these jigging fools?
Companion, hence!

Cassius. Away, away, be gone!

[Exit Poet.*]*

Brutus. Lucilius and Titinius, bid the commanders
Prepare to lodge their companies tonight.

Cassius. And come yourselves, and bring Messala with you
Immediately to us.

[Exeunt Lucilius *and* Titinius.*]*

Brutus. Lucius, a bowl of wine.

[Exit Lucius.*]*

Cassius. I did not think you could have been so angry.

Brutus. O Cassius, I am sick of many griefs.

U **Cassius.** Of your philosophy you make no use
If you give place to accidental evils.

Brutus. No man bears sorrow better. Portia is dead.

Cassius. Ha! Portia?

Brutus. She is dead.

Cassius. How scaped I killing when I crossed you so?
V O insupportable and touching loss!
Upon what sickness?

Brutus. Impatient of my absence,
And grief that young Octavius with Mark Antony
W Have made themselves so strong—for with her death
That tidings came—with this she fell distract,
And (her attendants absent) swallowed fire.

Cassius. And died so?

Brutus. Even so.

Cassius. O ye immortal gods!

[Reenter Lucius, *with wine and tapers.]*

Brutus. Speak no more of her. Give me a bowl of wine.
In this I bury all unkindness, Cassius.

[Drinks.]

167–168 Of your . . . evils: You aren't making use of your philosophy if you let chance happenings get you down. (Brutus was a Stoic, one who believed that pain and suffering should be endured calmly and that self-control was all-important.)

170 Ha: Cassius is not laughing but is so shocked by the news of Portia's death that he gasps.

172 How . . . so: How did I escape being killed when I angered you, with such a terrible thing on your mind?

175–179 Impatient . . . fire: She was worried about my absence and about the armies of Antony and Octavius. These things made her depressed ***(she fell distract).*** When her servants were not around, she swallowed a hot coal and choked.

T. Literary Element: Characterization Ask students to note the character changes that the two men seem to have undergone and to speculate on their origins. *(Possible response: Brutus has gone from thinking well of everyone, even his enemies, to spiteful impatience; Cassius has gone from scorning and despising everyone, even his friend Brutus, to making excuses for someone's behavior.)* Then ask students to explain Cassius' last few words. *(Possible response: To curry favor with Brutus, Cassius falls in with his mood.)*

U. Cultural Sidelight Many educated men of Julius Caesar's time were attracted by the Greek philosophical doctrine of stoicism, referred to in this passage. Stoicism was based on the concept of not allowing either the pleasures or the pains of this world to disturb a person's spiritual serenity.

V. Critical Thinking: EVALUATING Have students evaluate Cassius' response. Ask what it reveals about him. *(Possible response: an unexpected sensitivity and selflessness)* Ask students how, in light of this moment, they would now evaluate the men's friendship. *(Possible response: In light of the unusual strain on Brutus, perhaps this friendship is more solid than it earlier appeared.)*

W. LEP: Syntax Help students to sort out Brutus' meaning here by offering them a condensed paraphrase: "Impatience with my absence and anxiety about the strength of our enemies . . . made her insane, and . . . she committed suicide by swallowing a hot coal." Remind students that the contorted syntax of these lines may be due to Brutus' own grief and agitation.

X. Reading Skill: PREDICTING Ask what students believe will happen next in Brutus' and Cassius' friendship. *(Possible responses: The two men will go forth, united in their troubles; the next strain will lead to new cracks in the friendship.)*

Y. Reading Skill: INTERPRETIVE ORAL READING Encourage students to experiment with shifts of volume and tone as they read this passage aloud.

Z. Historical Sidelight After the formation of the triumvirate, Cicero had bitterly denounced Antony and argued for the preservation of the Republic. Antony took a savage revenge after Cicero's execution, ordering that the famous orator's head and hands be cut off and attached to the speaker's rostrum in Rome.

AA. Literary Sidelight This scene has puzzled critics and commentators, since it seems to imply that Brutus is only now learning of Portia's death. Some readers have argued that Brutus is deliberately shown to react to the tragic news in two contexts, first privately and sadly, and then publicly in a way that falsely shows him to handle it as a stoic.

Cassius. My heart is thirsty for that noble pledge.
X Fill, Lucius, till the wine o'erswell the cup.
I cannot drink too much of Brutus' love.

[Drinks. Exit Lucius.*]*

[Reenter Titinius, *with* Messala.]

Brutus. Come in, Titinius! Welcome, good Messala.
Now sit we close about this taper here
And call in question our necessities.

Cassius. Portia, art thou gone?

Y **Brutus.** No more, I pray you.
Messala, I have here received letters
That young Octavius and Mark Antony
Come down upon us with a mighty power,
Bending their expedition toward Philippi.

Messala. Myself have letters of the selfsame tenure.

Brutus. With what addition?

Messala. That by proscription and bills of outlawry
Octavius, Antony, and Lepidus
Have put to death an hundred senators.

Brutus. Therein our letters do not well agree.
Mine speak of seventy senators that died
By their proscriptions, Cicero being one.

Cassius. Cicero one?

Z **Messala.** Cicero is dead,
And by that order of proscription.
Had you your letters from your wife, my lord?

Brutus. No, Messala.

Messala. Nor nothing in your letters writ of her?

Brutus. Nothing, Messala.

Messala. That methinks is strange.

Brutus. Why ask you? Hear you aught of her in yours?

Messala. No, my lord.

Brutus. Now as you are a Roman, tell me true.

AA **Messala.** Then like a Roman bear the truth I tell,
For certain she is dead, and by strange manner.

186 ***o'erswell:*** overflow.

189–190 ***Now sit . . . necessities:*** Let's sit around this candle and talk about what we must do.

191–193 Cassius is distracted from the business that has to be discussed. He is having trouble believing that Portia is dead. Brutus asks him to stop talking about the painful topic.

196 ***Bending . . . Philippi:*** leading their armies to Philippi (a city in northern Greece).

197 ***Myself . . . tenure:*** I have received letters that say the same thing.

199 ***proscription . . . outlawry:*** official statements that declare certain acts to be criminal.

DATA BANK

Plutarch reported the death of Portia in his *Life of Brutus:*

"And for Porcia, Brutus' wife, Nicolaus the Philosopher and Valerius Maximus do write that she, determining to kill herself (her parents and friends carefully looking to her to keep her from it), took hot burning coals and cast them into her mouth, and kept her mouth so close that she choked herself. There was a letter of Brutus found written to his friends, complaining of their negligence, that his wife being sick, they would not help her, but suffered her to kill herself; choosing to die, rather than to languish in pain. Thus it appeareth that Nicolaus knew not well that time, sith the letter (at the least if it were Brutus' letter) doth plainly declare the disease and love of this lady, and also the manner of her death."

William and Barbara Rosen, ed. ***The Tragedy of Julius Caesar***

Brutus. Why, farewell, Portia. We must die, Messala.
With meditating that she must die once,
I have the patience to endure it now.

Messala. Even so great men great losses should endure.

BB **Cassius.** I have as much of this in art as you,
But yet my nature could not bear it so.

Brutus. Well, to our work alive. What do you think
Of marching to Philippi presently?

Cassius. I do not think it good.

Brutus. Your reason?

Cassius. This it is:
'Tis better that the enemy seek us.
So shall he waste his means, weary his soldiers,
Doing himself offense, whilst we, lying still,
Are full of rest, defense, and nimbleness.

Brutus. Good reasons must of force give place to better.
DD The people 'twixt Philippi and this ground
Do stand but in a forced affection,
For they have grudged us contribution.
The enemy, marching along by them,
By them shall make a fuller number up,
Come on refreshed, new-added, and encouraged;
From which advantage we cut him off
If at Philippi we do face him there,
These people at our back.

Cassius. Hear me, good brother.

Brutus. Under your pardon. You must note beside
That we have tried the utmost of our friends,
Our legions are brimful, our cause is ripe.
The enemy increaseth every day;
We, at the height, are ready to decline.
There is a tide in the affairs of men
Which, taken at the flood, leads on to fortune;
Omitted, all the voyage of their life
FF Is bound in shallows and in miseries.
On such a full sea are we now afloat,
And we must take the current when it serves
Or lose our ventures.

Cassius. Then, with your will, go on.
We'll along ourselves and meet them at Philippi.

222 ***in art:*** in theory, in my beliefs.

229–232 *How would you rephrase Cassius' reasons for not wanting to attack the armies of Antony and Octavius?* CC

233–242 ***Good . . . our back:*** Good reasons have to give way to better ones. The people between ***('twixt)*** here and Philippi are friendly only because they have to be ***(stand but in a forced affection).*** They have given us aid grudgingly. If the enemy marches through, they will find recruits. If we face them at Philippi, we'll eliminate this advantage and keep these unfriendly people behind us.

244–248 ***Under . . . decline:*** Brutus cuts Cassius off and insists on his own position. Their army, he says, is as good as it is ever going to get, while the enemy is getting stronger every day. *Do you agree with Brutus or Cassius? Why?* EE

245 ***tried the utmost:*** received all we can expect.

249–255 ***There is . . . ventures:*** Brutus compares life to a voyage on a ship. Following the high tide can lead to good fortune. Those who do not follow the tide might spend the rest of their lives in shallow water and misery. Our tide comes now, he insists, and we must act now.

BB. Critical Thinking: EVALUATING Have students give their impressions of Brutus' response to Portia's death here. *(Possible responses: He is too cold and detached, turning too quickly from his emotions to the business of war; he feels so deeply that he must cover his feelings by acting calm and changing the subject; he is overwhelmed by guilt; he is fulfilling his genuine military responsibilities.)*

CC. Answer: *If our enemies are forced to come to us, Cassius argues, they will suffer from lack of provisions and fatigue; we, on the other hand, will be rested and prepared for the battle.*

DD. Literary Element: CONFLICT Ask students how the element of conflict between Brutus and Cassius is reintroduced here. *(Possible response: Brutus' abrupt dismissal of Cassius' arguments hints that the earlier tension between them may be resurfacing.)*

EE. Possible Response: *If Brutus' facts are correct, he seems to have the stronger argument here.*

FF. LEP: Syntax Help students to understand the syntactic key to these famous lines: that Shakespeare uses the past participles *taken* and *omitted* in parallel structure. If necessary, offer students a paraphrase: "Men achieve success when they take advantage of a high tide in their affairs; if men omit or fail to take such an opportunity, they spend the rest of their lives in failure."

GG. Literary Element: SETTING Ask stuudents how the introduction of night into the setting affects the mood. *(Possible response: It introduces the ominous sense of endings, darkness, confusion, and exhaustion.)*

HH. Literary Element: CHARACTERIZATION Ask students to explain how these lines may shed light on Brutus' character. *(Possible response: Brutus is favorably characterized in these lines, since he is solicitous about Lucius and invites his military subordinates to share his tent.)*

GG **Brutus.** The deep of night is crept upon our talk
And nature must obey necessity,
Which we will niggard with a little rest.
There is no more to say?

Cassius. No more. Good night.
Early tomorrow will we rise and hence.

Brutus. Lucius!

[Reenter Lucius.*]*

My gown.

[Exit Lucius.*]*

Farewell, good Messala.
Good night, Titinius. Noble, noble Cassius,
Good night and good repose!

Cassius. O my dear brother,
This was an ill beginning of the night!
Never come such division 'tween our souls!
Let it not, Brutus.

[Reenter Lucius, *with the gown.]*

Brutus. Everything is well.

Cassius. Good night, my lord.

Brutus. Good night, good brother.

Titinius and Messala. Good night, Lord Brutus.

Brutus. Farewell every one.

[Exeunt all but Brutus *and* Lucius.]

Give me the gown. Where is thy instrument?

Lucius. Here in the tent.

Brutus. What, thou speak'st drowsily?
HH Poor knave, I blame thee not, thou art o'erwatched.
Call Claudius and some other of my men;
I'll have them sleep on cushions in my tent.

Lucius. Varro and Claudius!

[Enter Varro *and* Claudius.]

Varro. Calls my lord?

Brutus. I pray you, sirs, lie in my tent and sleep.

260 *Which . . . rest:* We will reluctantly satisfy ***(niggard)*** nature by getting a little bit of rest.

265 *gown:* nightgown.

278 *Where is thy instrument:* One of Lucius' duties as a personal servant is to play music that will help Brutus get to sleep.

280–281 *What . . . o'erwatched:* I see you're sleepy. It's no wonder, since you've been watching and waiting for so long.

Real Life Connections

The mood of this scene is low-key, with Brutus expressing his discouragement and despair after Cassius leaves. Ask students to identify times they or people they know have shared these feelings, particularly after the types of setbacks Brutus has experienced—lack of success in a major project (the war), death of a loved one (Portia), a quarrel and widening rift with a friend (Cassius). Students might evaluate how Brutus handles the situation, whether they agree that Shakespeare's portrayal is realistic, and whether they perceive other alternatives, either for Brutus or for people today.

It may be I shall raise you by-and-by
On business to my brother Cassius.

Varro. So please you, we will stand and watch your
pleasure.

Brutus. I will not have it so. Lie down, good sirs.
It may be I shall otherwise bethink me.

*[*Varro *and* Claudius *lie down.]*

Look, Lucius, here's the book I sought for so;
I put it in the pocket of my gown.

Lucius. I was sure your lordship did not give it me.

II **Brutus.** Bear with me, good boy, I am much forgetful.
Canst thou hold up by thy heavy eyes awhile,
And touch thy instrument a strain or two?

Lucius. Ay, my lord, an't please you.

Brutus. It does, my boy.
I trouble thee too much, but thou art willing.

Lucius. It is my duty, sir.

Brutus. I should not urge thy duty past thy might.
I know young bloods look for a time of rest.

Lucius. I have slept, my lord, already.

Brutus. It was well done; and thou shalt sleep again;
I will not hold thee long. If I do live,
I will be good to thee.

JJ *[Music, and a song.* Lucius *falls asleep as he sings.]*

This is a sleepy tune. O murd'rous slumber!
Layest thou thy leaden mace upon my boy,
That plays thee music? Gentle knave, good night.
I will not do thee so much wrong to wake thee.
If thou dost nod, thou break'st thy instrument;
I'll take it from thee; and, good boy, good night.
Let me see, let me see. Is not the leaf turned down
KK Where I left reading? Here it is, I think.

[Sits.]

[Enter the Ghost of Caesar.*]*

How ill this taper burns! Ha! Who comes here?
LL I think it is the weakness of mine eyes
That shapes this monstrous apparition.
It comes upon me. Art thou anything?

287–292 *It may . . . bethink me:* Brutus wants them to be handy in case he needs to send a message to Cassius. Varro offers to stand guard all night. Brutus insists the men sleep, not stand guard. He says he may change his mind ***(otherwise bethink me)*** about sending messages to Cassius.

310 *mace:* a rod used as a symbol of authority. Brutus is addressing slumber as though it were an officer of the law who has arrested Lucius.

317 *How . . . burns:* How poorly this candle burns. Everyone in the tent is asleep, except Brutus. At first he thinks the thing he sees is only the result of poor eyesight. Then he realizes that something is really there.

II. Literary Element: CHARACTERIZATION Ask students what this passage reveals about Brutus. *(Possible response: He is tired and almost pathetic in his need for reassurance; alone with a harmless underling, he can finally let his guard down.)*

JJ. Literary Element: MOOD Ask students to use one or two adjectives to describe the mood that the setting and dialogue create at this point in the scene. *(Possible answers: "weary," "sleepy," "foreboding.")*

KK. LEP: Syntax Be sure that students understand the ellipsis in the phrase *I left* (off) *reading;* i.e., "I stopped reading."

LL. Literary Element: STAGE DIRECTIONS Ask students whether they think an audience in the theater should actually see a ghostlike figure on stage here, or whether a director might prefer to have Brutus staring into empty air. *(Possible response: Some students may argue that Brutus' vivid dialogue should be allowed to "carry" the scene on its own; others that the actual ghost might make the scene more powerful.)*

MM. Literary Element: FORESHADOWING
Ask what students think the ghost may be implying about the imminent battle at Philippi in these lines. *(Possible response: The ghost may be foreshadowing Brutus' defeat and death.)*

> **NN. Teaching Tip**
> You may find it useful to have students act out this scene, focusing on the shifts in mood and tone: Brutus and Cassius' quarrel, their reconciliation, Brutus' reaction to Portia's death, Brutus' kindness to his servant, and finally, Brutus' reaction to Caesar's ghost.

OO. Answer: *Shakespeare may have added the ghost as a foreshadowing of doom, as a reminder of Brutus' feelings of guilt, or as a device to excite and interest his audience.*

Act Four, Scene 3 of *Julius Caesar* painted by R. Westall The Folger Shakespeare Library, Washington, D.C.

". . . thou shalt see me at Philippi."

Art thou some god, some angel, or some devil,
That mak'st my blood cold and my hair to stare?
Speak to me what thou art.

Ghost. Thy evil spirit, Brutus.

Brutus. Why com'st thou?

Ghost. To tell thee thou shalt see me at Philippi.

MM **Brutus.** Well; then I shall see thee again?

Ghost. Ay, at Philippi.

Brutus. Why, I will see thee at Philippi then.

[Exit Ghost.*]*

Now I have taken heart thou vanishest.
NN Ill spirit, I would hold more talk with thee.
Boy! Lucius! Varro! Claudius! Sirs! Awake!
Claudius!

330 *Now . . . vanishest:* Now that I have my courage back, you disappear. *What might have been Shakespeare's purpose in adding a ghost to this play?* OO

DATA BANK

"Brutus was a careful man, and slept very little, both for that his diet was moderate, as also because he was continually occupied. . . . But now whilst he was in war, and his head ever busily occupied to think of his affairs and what would happen, after he had slumbered a little after supper, he spent all the rest of the night in despatching of his weightiest causes; and after he had taken order for them, if he had any leisure left him, he would read some book . . . One night very late (when all the camp took quiet rest) as he was in his tent with a little light . . . he thought he heard one come into him, and, casting his eye toward the door of his tent, that he saw a wonderful strange and monstrous shape of a body coming towards him, and said never a word. So Brutus boldly asked what he was, a god or a man, and what cause brought him thither? The spirit answered him, 'I am thy evil spirit, Brutus: and thou shalt see me by the city of Philippes.''
PLUTARCH, *Life of Brutus*

Lucius. The strings, my lord, are false.

QQ **Brutus.** He thinks he still is at his instrument.
Lucius, awake!

Lucius. My lord?

Brutus. Didst thou dream, Lucius, that thou so criedst out?

Lucius. My lord, I do not know that I did cry.

Brutus. Yes, that thou didst. Didst thou see anything?

Lucius. Nothing, my lord.

Brutus. Sleep again, Lucius. Sirrah Claudius!
[To Varro*]*
Fellow thou, awake!

RR **Varro.** My lord?

Claudius. My lord?

Brutus. Why did you so cry out, sirs, in your sleep?

Both. Did we, my lord?

Brutus. Ay. Saw you anything?

Varro. No, my lord, I saw nothing.

Claudius. Nor I, my lord.

Brutus. Go and commend me to my brother Cassius.
Bid him set on his powers betimes before,
SS And we will follow.

Both. It shall be done, my lord.

[Exeunt.]

334 *false:* out of tune. Lucius, only half awake, thinks he is playing the instrument that Brutus took from him earlier. *Why does Brutus accuse Lucius, Claudius, and Varro of crying out in their sleep?* PP

352 *commend me:* give my respects to.

353 *Bid . . . before:* Tell him to get his army ***(pow'rs)*** moving early in the morning.

Responding to Reading

1. Describe the manner in which Brutus speaks to Cassius as they argue. Do you think Cassius deserves such treatment from Brutus? Why or why not?
2. In the disagreement about whether to attack the enemy army, Brutus gets his way. Does this show a change in his relationship with Cassius? Explain your answer.
3. Has Brutus really seen a ghost? How would you explain the incident?

PP. Answer *Brutus wants to know whether they have seen the ghost.*

QQ. LEP: Context Make sure LEP students understand that Lucius is talking in his sleep, dreaming that he is still playing the lute ("at his instrument") and that the strings are out of tune ("false").

RR. Critical Thinking: ANALYZING If Brutus' purpose has been to test the men to see if they too have seen a ghost, what effect do students think that the men's denial may have on Brutus? *(Possible response: He may doubt the existence of the ghost; on the other hand, he may draw the unnerving conclusion that the ghost's message was meant for him and no one else.)*

SS. Literary Element: SUSPENSE Ask students how these lines create suspense in the falling action of the play. *(Possible response: They create suspense by quickening the pace of the action. The battle between the enemy armies will probably take place sooner than expected.)*

Student Response

Responding to Reading

These questions are open-ended with no "right" or "wrong" answers. However, responses must be supported with information from the selection. Possible answers follow:

1. Some students may say that Brutus treats Cassius as if he were a disobedient inferior. Some may agree that he deserves this treatment for his corrupt behavior and melodramatic threats; others may feel that Brutus is condescending.

2. Yes—the two then reconcile as Cassius pacifies Brutus for the first time; no—Brutus' judgment has prevailed before: for example, in the exclusion of Cicero from the conspiracy and in the decisions to spare Mark Antony and to allow him to speak at Caesar's funeral.

3. Yes—many people in Shakespeare's time literally believed in ghosts; no—the ghost symbolizes Brutus' guilt for the assassination.

Check Test

1. What opinion does Antony hold of Lepidus in scene 1? *(that he is weak, foolish, unworthy to be a triumvir)*

2. In scene 2, what does Brutus suspect about Cassius? *(that his friendship is cooling)*

3. What accusations does Brutus make against Cassius during their quarrel in scene 3? *(that Cassius is corrupt and that he denied Brutus money for military pay)*

4. According to Brutus, how did Portia die? *(she committed suicide by swallowing fire)*

5. What does the Ghost of Caesar predict to Brutus? *(that he will see him at Philippi)*

Student Response

Responding to Reading

These questions are open-ended with no "right" or "wrong" answers. However, responses must be supported with information from the selection. Possible answers follow:

1. Students' opinions will vary. Some students may prefer the conspirators' side, because they oppose Antony's ruthlessness, and believe in the conspiracy's republican ideals. Others may see the triumvirs as representing the better chance of restoring order, since Octavius is Caesar's rightful successor as his closest male relative and since the conspirators seem weak and divided.

2. If Antony alters Caesar's will and continues in his arrogance and ambition, the Romans may be worse off.

3. Some students may say that Antony has changed: He is now portrayed as harsh, cynical, scornful, and ambitious for power. He criticizes Lepidus behind his back and tries to change Caesar's will to give the people less money. Others may say that Antony has not really changed, since his cynicism and ambition were shown in his manipulation of the crowd to create civil war.

4. Brutus, in his own mind at least, remains devoted to honor and justice. His treatment of Cassius, however, suggests that he has changed under the pressures of civil war, exile, and the suicide of Portia. He is harsher, more anxious, and more distrustful. He is also unnerved by the appearance of the ghost. Students' opinions of Brutus may vary.

5. Some students may agree that Cassius is more likeable—he is sincere and less priggish; others may think Brutus is more likeable—he is sadder, more mature, less melodramatic.

Writing Options

The Writing Options are designed to meet varied student interests and abilities. Have each student choose one writing activity to complete. You may wish to guide some students to an option that requires less writing.

Responding to Reading

First Impressions

1. Think about the two groups preparing for war. Which side would you rather be on? Write a sentence explaining your reasons.

Second Thoughts

2. Do the Romans seem better or worse off under the triumvirate than they were under Julius Caesar? Explain your answer.
3. Has Antony changed since Act Three? Explain and give examples.
4. Compare and contrast your opinion of Brutus in Act One with your view of him now. Has your opinion changed? Why or why not?
5. Many people think that Cassius becomes a more likable character than Brutus by Scene 3. Do you agree or disagree? Support your answer with facts from the scene.

Literary Concepts: Conflict and Falling Action

Conflict, or struggle between opposing forces, forms the basis of plot structure in literature. Think back, for example, to some conflicts in this play—the argument between the tribunes and the workers, Brutus' internal struggles, the central conflict between the conspirators and Caesar. Has the play prepared us for the conflicts that appear in Act Four? How do you think the various conflicts might be resolved?

The **falling action** in a work of fiction or drama reveals the effects of the climax. As the falling action begins, the suspense is over but the result of the decision that led to the climax are not yet fully worked out. The falling action usually occurs in Acts Four and Five.

In *Julius Caesar,* for example, Act Four opens by showing that Antony, Octavius, and Lepidus now rule Rome—a result of Caesar's assassination. What are some other important effects of the climax that are revealed in Act Four? What still needs to be worked out? Support your answers with evidence from the play.

Concept Review: Characterization Does Shakespeare show any new aspects to the character of either Brutus or Cassius in this act? Explain and give examples.

Literary Concept—Conflict

Most students will feel that the play has indeed prepared us for the intensity and bitterness of the conflicts in Act Four, citing, the growing seriousness of the previous conflicts: from the comic tribune-commoner conflict, to Brutus' inner conflict and the conspirators' conflict with Caesar, to the assassination, and toward eventual civil war. Such a progression would seem to prepare us for even more intense conflict—internal, within camps, and between enemy forces.

Literary Concept—Falling Action

Other important effects of the climax revealed in Act Four are the civil war, the conflicts between Cassius and Brutus, and the impending battle. The major issue that still must be worked out is who will ultimately rule Rome.

Concept Review: Characterization Students may point out Brutus' irritability he now shows toward Cassius and the poet. They may also mention the dishonesty displayed in comparing Brutus "public" and "private" responses to Portia's death. Students may now see Cassius as more human, since he is so hurt by Brutus' criticisms and seems to fear defeat and death in the battle.

Writing Options

1. Pretend you are Brutus' young servant, Lucius. Write a letter to your parents telling them of the events of Scenes 2 and 3 from your own (Lucius') point of view.
2. Figures of speech are important to Shakespeare's writing style. Choose three similes or metaphors in Act Four. Explain what each means and its relevance to developments in the play.
3. Imagine you are a journalist about to interview Antony or Octavius just before the battle against Brutus and Cassius. Write a list of questions you might ask.
4. In literature, a *symbol* is a person, place, or object that represents something else, often an idea. A warm, cozy house, for example, may symbolize security and family values. What does Caesar's ghost symbolize? Write an explanation of your opinion.

e x t e n d

Options for Learning

1 • What Really Happened? Do library research on the historical events upon which Shakespeare based Act Four. For example, how did the triumvirate gain power? How long after Caesar's death did this happen? One helpful book might be *Asimov's Guide to Shakespeare* by Isaac Asimov. Report on your findings.

2 • Lights, Camera Make a video of a small part (about forty or fifty lines) of Act Four. Choose actors and discuss with them the best way to present their lines. Create a simple set and draw storyboards, a series of sketches showing what your video will look like. Then make your video and show it to classmates for their comments.

3 • Brutus' Changes Imagine you are an actor portraying Brutus. Explain and demonstrate to the class how you would change your appearance from Act Three to Act Four. Keep in mind the differences in Brutus' situation and his personal grief.

4 • A Ghostly Mood Draw a picture of the moment Brutus sees the ghost of Caesar. Use the description from the play and your own imagination. In your drawing, try to create the mood of this dramatic meeting.

Options for Learning

These activities suit a variety of learning styles and modes of expression. Allow students to review the options and then choose the one they wish to do. Many are excellent collaborative learning projects.

1. What Really Happened? Suggest to students that they make a chronological chart listing the important events between 44 and 42 B.C. (the date of the battle of Philippi).

2. Lights, Camera, . . . Remind students that they can break the scene into smaller segments for shooting. Storyboards can be very simple sketches, as long as they make clear what the shot should look like and how much dialogue each shot should cover.

3. Brutus' Changes Suggest to students that they consult a drama teacher or coach familiar with costumes and makeup.

4. A Ghostly Mood Encourage students to think of the wide variety of visual elements that create mood: color, shape, design, light and shadow, subject matter.

Teaching Strategies

Support for Students with Limited English Proficiency

- Use Reader's Guidesheet, p. 13.
- *Julius Caesar* Act Five contains many plays on words and interesting uses of repetition that may be difficult for students of limited English proficiency to grasp. Encourage students to read these passages aloud and, for ESL students, to translate them into their own languages.
- Annotations F, I, and P (Scene 1), K and S (Scene 3), and H and N (Scene 5) focus on plays on words, repetition, and rhyme.

Text Annotations

A. Literary Element: Characterization Ask students to comment on Antony's speech here. Ask what personality traits he reveals in his answer to Octavius. *(Possible response: Antony evades Octavius' reproach, pretending that he has a superior insight into the enemy's motives. He seems tricky and egotistical.)*

B. Answer Octavius wins the argument.

C. Literary Element: Conflict Ask what this brief exchange suggests about the relationship of Antony and Octavius. *(Possible response: The dialogue here suggests that conflict between them lies just beneath the surface. Notice that Octavius, although he is young and untested, proves more than a match for Antony.)*

ACT FIVE

Scene 1 *The plains of Philippi in Greece.*

Antony and Octavius enter the battlefield with their army. Brutus and Cassius enter with their forces. The four leaders meet, but they only exchange insults and taunts. Antony and Octavius leave to prepare for battle. Cassius expresses his fears to Messala. Finally, Brutus and Cassius say their final farewells, in case they should die in battle.

[Enter Octavius, Antony, *and their Army.]*

Octavius. Now Antony, our hopes are answered.
You said the enemy would not come down
But keep the hills and upper regions.
It proves not so, their battles are at hand.
They mean to warn us at Philippi here,
Answering before we do demand of them.

Antony. Tut! I am in their bosoms and I know
Wherefore they do it. They could be content
To visit other places, and come down
A With fearful bravery, thinking by this face
To fasten in our thoughts that they have courage.
But 'tis not so.

[Enter a Messenger.*]*

Messenger. Prepare you, generals,
The enemy comes on in gallant show;
Their bloody sign of battle is hung out,
And something to be done immediately.

Antony. Octavius, lead your battle softly on
Upon the left hand of the even field.

Octavius. Upon the right hand I. Keep thou the left.

C **Antony.** Why do you cross me in this exigent?

Octavius. I do not cross you; but I will do so.

[March.]

[Drum. Enter Brutus, Cassius, *and their Army;* Lucilius, Titinius, Messala, *and others.]*

Brutus. They stand and would have parley.

Cassius. Stand fast, Titinius. We must out and talk.

Octavius. Mark Antony, shall we give sign of battle?

GUIDE FOR READING

3 ***keep . . . regions:*** stay in the higher areas (where they could defend themselves more easily).

5 ***warn:*** challenge.

7–11 ***I am . . . courage:*** I know their secrets ***(am in their bosoms)*** and why they have done this. They would rather be in other places, not here fighting us. They come down with a show of bravery, thinking they will convince us they have courage.

15 ***sign of battle:*** a red flag symbolizing readiness for battle.

17–21 Antony and Octavius have a small argument about whose soldiers will fight on each side of the field. *Who wins this argument?* B

20 ***exigent:*** moment of crisis.

22 ***They . . . parley:*** They are standing and waiting for a conference.

"The enemy comes on in gallant show; their bloody sign of battle is hung out."

D **Antony.** No, Caesar, we will answer on their charge.
Make forth. The generals would have some words.

Octavius. Stir not until the signal.

*[*Brutus, Cassius, Octavius, *and* Antony *meet in the center of the stage.]*

Brutus. Words before blows. Is it so, countrymen?

E **Octavius.** Not that we love words better, as you do.

Brutus. Good words are better than bad strokes, Octavius.

Antony. In your bad strokes, Brutus, you give good words;
Witness the hole you made in Caesar's heart,
Crying "Long live! Hail, Caesar!"

Cassius. Antony,
The posture of your blows are yet unknown;
But for your words, they rob the Hybla bees,
And leave them honeyless.

F **Antony.** Not stingless too.

Brutus. O yes, and soundless too!
For you have stol'n their buzzing, Antony,
And very wisely threat before you sting.

25 *answer on their charge:* respond to their attack.

37–39 *The posture . . . honeyless:* We don't know yet how effective you'll be as a soldier, but your words are sweeter than honey. (Hybla is a mountain in Sicily known for its sweet honey.)

D. Literary Element: ALLUSION Be sure that students understand the allusion in Antony's use of the term *Caesar.* Antony is referring now to Octavius as Julius Caesar's heir and giving his ally the title of *Caesar,* which means "ruler." You might explain that both the German *Kaiser* and the Russian *Tsar* come from this title.

E. Critical Thinking: ANALYZING Ask students to explain the situation here. *(Possible response: Brutus seems to want to negotiate, while Octavius seems scornful of "words" and prefers "blows.")* Then ask students to speculate on why each side has the views it does. *(Possible response: Perhaps Brutus is losing, and so wants to negotiate; perhaps, too, Brutus is genuinely devoted to peace and honor while Octavius wants only power.)*

F. LEP: Suffixes Point out the play between honey*less,* sting*less,* and sound*less.* Make sure students understand that this suffix means "without." You might have them think of other words with this suffix, or create new words with it. You might also ask ESL students for the equivalent suffix in their languages, and see if English-speaking students can identify the repeated sounds as they hear them in various foreign words.

G. Literary Element: FIGURATIVE LANGUAGE Ask students to identify the common element in three out of four of Antony's short similes here for the conspirators. *(Possible response: Except for the reference to "bondmen," all the comparisons refer to mimicking or fawning animals.)*

H. Literary Element: CHARACTERIZATION Ask what students conclude about Octavius' personality from these lines. *(Possible responses: He is bluntly direct and determined; he prefers action to words; he is arrogant.)*

I. LEP: Play on Words Make sure students follow Cassius' plays on Brutus' words. Brutus speaks of dying "honorable," whereas Cassius speaks of "honor"; Brutus calls Octavius "Young man," whereas Cassius calls him a "school boy." Encourage students to speculate on what this reveals about Cassius' and Brutus' relationship. *(Possible response: Cassius is subordinate to Brutus and taking his lead from him.)*

J. Answer: *The sarcastic, bitter insults between the leaders of the opposing sides may seem believable, but the meeting accomplishes nothing.*

Antony. Villains! you did not so when your vile daggers
Hacked one another in the sides of Caesar.
You showed your teeth like apes, and fawned like hounds,
G And bowed like bondmen, kissing Caesar's feet;
Whilst damned Casca, like a cur, behind
Struck Caesar on the neck. O you flatterers!

Cassius. Flatterers? Now, Brutus, thank yourself!
This tongue had not offended so today
If Cassius might have ruled.

Octavius. Come, come, the cause! If arguing make us sweat,
H The proof of it will turn to redder drops.
Look,
I draw a sword against conspirators.
When think you that the sword goes up again?
Never, till Caesar's three-and-thirty wounds
Be well avenged, or till another Caesar
Have added slaughter to the sword of traitors.

Brutus. Caesar, thou canst not die by traitors' hands
Unless thou bring'st them with thee.

Octavius. So I hope.
I was not born to die on Brutus' sword.

Brutus. Oh, if thou wert the noblest of thy strain,
Young man, thou couldst not die more honorable.

I **Cassius.** A peevish schoolboy, worthless of such honor,
Joined with a masker and a reveller!

Antony. Old Cassius still.

Octavius. Come, Antony. Away!
Defiance, traitor, hurl we in your teeth.
If you dare fight today, come to the field;
If not, when you have stomachs.

[Exeunt Octavius, Antony, *and their Army.]*

Cassius. Why, now blow wind, swell billow, and swim bark!
The storm is up, and all is on the hazard.

Brutus. Ho, Lucilius! Hark, a word with you.

*[*Lucilius *and* Messala *stand forth.]*

Lucilius. My lord?

*[*Brutus *and* Lucilius *converse apart.]*

44–50 *You did not so . . . neck:* You didn't give warning before you killed Caesar. Instead, you acted like loving pets and slaves while Casca, like a dog ***(cur),*** stabbed Caesar in the neck.

51–53 *Now . . . ruled:* Cassius angrily tells Brutus that they wouldn't be listening to these insults if he had had his way ***(Cassius might have ruled)*** when arguing that Antony should be killed.

54–56 *Come . . . drops:* Get to the point ***(cause).*** Arguing is tiresome. We will settle it by shedding blood.

61–62 *or till . . . traitors:* or until a second Caesar (that is, Octavius himself—Caesar's grandnephew and adopted son) has been killed by the traitors.

63–64 *Caesar . . . with thee:* Brutus here refers to Octavius, who took that name. The only way you'll die from a traitor's hands is if you kill yourself, Brutus insists.

70–71 *masker . . . still:* Cassius is insulting Antony by calling him a party-goer and a playboy. Same old Cassius ***(Old Cassius still),*** Antony replies.

75 *stomachs:* enough nerve.

Does the prebattle meeting seem believable? Has anything been accomplished? J

78 *all . . . hazard:* Everything is at stake.

Critic's Corner

There is no leading or floating image in the play; one feels it was not written under the particular stress of emotion or excitement which gives rise to a dominating image. There is, however, a certain persistence in the comparison of the characters to animals: Caesar is a wolf, a lion, a falcon, a serpent's egg, an adder, a stricken deer; the Romans are sheep and hinds and bees; the conspirators are apes and hounds; Brutus is a lamb; Lepidus is an ass, a horse; Metellus and Casca are curs; Cassius is a showy, mettlesome steed which fails at the moment of trial; and Octavius and Antony are bears tied to the stake.

Caroline Spurgeon, *Shakespeare's Imagery*

"Villians! you did not so when your vile daggers hacked one another in the sides of Caesar."

Critic's Corner

Highest among those who have exhibited human nature stands Shakespeare. His variety is like the variety of nature, endless diversity. . . . The characters of which he has given us an impression, as vivid as that which we receive from the characters of our own associates, are to be reckoned by scores. Yet in all those scores hardly one character is to be found which deviates widely from the common standard and which we should call very eccentric if we met it in real life. The silly notion that every man has one ruling passion, and that this clue once known unravels all the mysteries of his conduct, finds no countenance in the plays of Shakespeare. There man appears as he is, made up of a crowd of passions, which contend for the mastery over him and govern him in turn. **Thomas Babington Macaulay**

K. Answer: *Cassius means that the results of the battle will be critical for the cause of the conspirators.*

L. Literary Element: **FORESHADOWING** Ask what Cassius fears in this passage. *(Possible response: that the army will be defeated and slaughtered)* Then ask what the audience might think of as it hears the phrase "give up the ghost". *(Possible response: of the ominous appearance of Caesar's ghost in Act IV)*

M. Literary Element: **TRAGEDY** Have students explain how Cassius' outlook here hints at the tragedy to come. *(Possible response: Cassius realistically admits that the "affairs of men" are subject to uncertainty, and he envisions the worst that might happen.)*

N. Literary Element: **ALLUSION** Be sure that students understand that Brutus is referring to his own philosophical creed—stoicism—which is opposed to suicide. Remind students that the famous Roman Cato, who committed suicide because he was opposed to Caesar, was Portia's father and Brutus' father-in-law.

Cassius. Messala.

Messala. What says my general?

Cassius. Messala,
This is my birthday; as this very day
Was Cassius born. Give me thy hand, Messala.
Be thou my witness that against my will
(As Pompey was) am I compelled to set
Upon one battle all our liberties.
You know that I held Epicurus strong
And his opinion. Now I change my mind
And partly credit things that do presage.
Coming from Sardis, on our former ensign
Two mighty eagles fell, and there they perched,
Gorging and feeding from our soldiers' hands,
Who to Philippi here consorted us.
This morning are they fled away and gone,
And in their steads do ravens, crows, and kites
Fly o'er our heads and downward look on us
L As we were sickly prey. Their shadows seem
A canopy most fatal, under which
Our army lies, ready to give up the ghost.

Messala. Believe not so.

Cassius. I but believe it partly,
For I am fresh of spirit and resolved
To meet all perils very constantly.

Brutus. Even so, Lucilius.

Cassius. Now, most noble Brutus,
The gods today stand friendly, that we may,
Lovers in peace, lead on our days to age!
But since the affairs of men rest still incertain,
M Let's reason with the worst that may befall.
If we do lose this battle, then is this
The very last time we shall speak together.
What are you then determined to do?

Brutus. Even by the rule of that philosophy
N By which I did blame Cato for the death
Which he did give himself—I know not how,
But I do find it cowardly and vile,
For fear of what might fall, so to prevent
The time of life—arming myself with patience
To stay the providence of some high powers
That govern us below.

86–88 *against . . . liberties:* I am forced to gamble the freedom of Rome on one battle. *What does he mean?* K

89–101 *I held . . . give up the ghost:* Epicurus was a philosopher who did not believe omens. Cassius says that he once was a follower of this philosophy, but now he sometimes believes in things that predict the future ***(credit things that do presage).*** Cassius then tells Messala of two eagles that accompanied the army from Sardis to Philippi. The eagles have been replaced by ravens, crows, and hawks ***(kites)***—birds that symbolize death.

92 *former ensign:* the flag that was carried at the head of the army's march.

105 *constantly:* with determination.

111 *Let's . . . befall:* Let's think about the worst that might happen to us.

115–122 Even . . . govern us below: Brutus reminds Cassius that Brutus' philosophy (Stoicism) says people should endure their troubles. Therefore, Brutus should not believe in suicide. He mentions Cato, a famous Roman who killed himself after Pompey lost to Caesar.

Cassius. Then, if we lose this battle,
O You are contented to be led in triumph
Through the streets of Rome.

Brutus. No, Cassius, no. Think not, thou noble Roman,
That ever Brutus will go bound to Rome.
He bears too great a mind. But this same day
Must end that work the ides of March begun,
And whether we shall meet again I know not.
Therefore our everlasting farewell take.
For ever and for ever farewell, Cassius!
If we do meet again, why, we shall smile;
P If not, why then this parting was well made.

Cassius. For ever and for ever farewell, Brutus!
If we do meet again, we'll smile indeed;
If not, 'tis true this parting was well made.

Brutus. Why then, lead on. O that a man might know
The end of this day's business ere it come!
But it sufficeth that the day will end,
And then the end is known. Come, ho! Away!

[Exeunt]

131 *our . . . take:* Let's make a final farewell to each other.

Responding to Reading

1. Which side do you hope will win the upcoming battle? Why?
2. Which side seems more confident about winning the battle? Support your view with examples.
3. Who do you think wins the battle of insults before the real battle? Explain.

Scene 2 The battlefield.

Brutus sends Messala with orders for the forces across the field.

[Alarum. Enter Brutus *and* Messala.*]*

Brutus. Ride, ride, Messala, ride, and give these bills
Unto the legions on the other side.

1–2 *give . . . side:* Give these orders to our soldiers on that side of the field.

O. Historical Sidelight Cassius here alludes to the triumphal processions at Rome that were held in honor of victorious generals. On such occasions, the defeated enemy leaders who had been taken alive were paraded through the streets so that the crowds could jeer at them.

P. LEP: Repetition Help students to identify the repetition of such words as "ever," "farewell," "well," "for." Have them read the passage aloud, stressing the repeated words and syllables. Then have them speculate about the effect of such repetition. *(Possible response: It gives the scene a funereal, ritual quality; it stresses the idea of death and parting "forever" and "everlasting.")*

Student Response

Responding to Reading

These questions are open-ended with no "right" or "wrong" answers. However, responses must be supported with information from the selection. Possible answers follow:

1. Some students will side with Antony and Octavius, arguing that the conspirators have discredited themselves by resorting to violence in the assassination. Other students will side with Brutus and Cassius, arguing that Antony and Octavius are power-hungry and do not seem devoted to justice.

2. Antony and Octavius seem more confident. Cassius gloomily reports to Messala his anxiety stemming from evil omens that morning, and Brutus seems tired and discouraged.

3. Many students may observe that the battle of insults seems fairly even, with both sides scoring some points. Others may favor Brutus and Cassius, pointing out that they get in the last insult (lines 67–70); still others may point out that Octavius and Antony have the last word, even though a weak word.

Text Annotations

A. Answer Brutus, who has perceived some weakness among Octavius' troops, seems to feel confident at this point.

B. Reading Skill: VISUALIZING
Encourage studuents to visualize the sights and sounds on stage during this brief scene. *(Possible response: Students should mention the loud alarm, the swift entrance and exit of Brutus and Messala, and the horses.)*

C. Answer: *Cassius seems to feel angry and dismayed.*

D. Literary Element: CHARACTERIZATION
Ask what this incident reveals about Cassius. *(Possible response: He is desperate enough to have killed one of his own men who was fleeing from the battle.)*

[Loud alarum.]

B Let them set on at once; for I perceive
But cold demeanor in Octavius' wing,
And sudden push gives them the overthrow.
Ride, ride, Messala! Let them all come down.

[Exeunt.]

4 *cold demeanor:* lack of courage. *How does Brutus feel about the battle at this point?* A

Scene 3 *Another part of the battlefield.*

Cassius retreats, losing the battle to Antony's forces. He sends Titinius to see if nearby forces are friend or enemy. From a hill, Pindarus believes he sees Titinius killed. Completely discouraged, Cassius asks Pindarus to kill him. Titinius returns to find Cassius' body and kills himself. Brutus and others arrive, having defeated Octavius' army. Messala has brought them to see the body of Cassius. Now they see that Titinius is also dead. Brutus mourns the two, but also looks to a second battle with his enemies.

[Enter Cassius *and* Titinius.*]*

D **Cassius.** O, look, Titinius, look! The villains fly!
Myself have to mine own turned enemy.
This ensign here of mine was turning back;
I slew the coward and did take it from him.

Titinius. O Cassius, Brutus gave the word too early,
Who, having some advantage on Octavius,
Took it too eagerly. His soldiers fell to spoil,
Whilst we by Antony are all enclosed.

[Enter Pindarus.*]*

Pindarus. Fly further off, my lord! fly further off!
Mark Antony is in your tents, my lord.
Fly, therefore, noble Cassius, fly far off!

Cassius. This hill is far enough. Look, look, Titinius!
Are those my tents where I perceive the fire?

Titinius. They are, my lord.

Cassius. Titinius, if thou lovest me,
Mount thou my horse and hide thy spurs in him

1–4 *The villains . . . him:* Cassius is watching his men run away ***(fly)*** from the battle. He killed his own flag-bearer (the dead ***ensign*** lying on the ground near him) when he saw the man running away. *How does Cassius seem to feel about the battle?* C

7 *His . . . spoil:* Brutus' soldiers began looting (instead of fighting the enemy).

16–19 *Mount . . . enemy:* Ride my horse to those troops over there, and

DATA BANK

Of all the writers in the world, William Shakespeare has had the most universal recognition and acceptance, and today only the Bible is available in more languages than Shakespeare. In a report for the years 1958–60, the Memorial Library in Birmingham, England, which makes a specialty of preserving translations of Shakespeare, announced that it possessed versions in seventy-four languages, including Albanian, Armenian, Bengali, Chinese, Croatian, Japanese, Georgian, Marathi, Punjabi, Tatar, Turkish, Ukrainian, and Xhosa. This listing is hardly complete. The Folger Library [in Washington, D.C.] has received at least a fragment of Shakespeare in Pidgin English and has some other exotic versions not included in the foregoing list.

LOUIS B. WRIGHT, "SHAKESPEARE FOR EVERYMAN" IN *English Journal*, APRIL 1964

Till he have brought thee up to yonder troops
And here again, that I may rest assured
Whether yond troops are friend or enemy.

come back to tell me if they are friend or enemy.

Titinius. I will be here again even with a thought.

[Exit.]

20 even with a thought: as fast as you can think of it.

Cassius. Go, Pindarus, get higher on that hill.
My sight was ever thick. Regard Titinius,
And tell me what thou not'st about the field.

*[*Pindarus *ascends the hill.]*

F This day I breathed first. Time is come round,
And where I did begin, there shall I end.
My life is run his compass. Sirrah, what news?

26 is run his compass: has come full circle (that is, my life is complete). *What is Cassius planning to do?* E

Pindarus.

[Above.]

O my lord!

Cassius. What news?

Pindarus.

[Above.]

Titinius is enclosed round about
With horsemen that make to him on the spur.
Yet he spurs on. Now they are almost on him.
G Now, Titinius!
Now some light. O, he lights too! He's ta'en.

31–37 From a distance, Pindarus describes the capture of Titinius.

[Shout.]

And hark!
They shout for joy.

Cassius. Come down; behold no more.
O coward that I am to live so long
To see my best friend ta'en before my face!

40 ta'en: taken (captured).

[Enter Pindarus *from above.]*

Come hither, sirrah.
In Parthia did I take thee prisoner,
And then I swore thee, saving of thy life,
That whatsoever I did bid thee do,
Thou shouldst attempt it. Come now, keep thine oath.
Now be a freeman, and with this good sword,
That ran through Caesar's bowels, search this bosom.

42–50 In Parthia . . . the sword: When I saved your life in Parthia (an ancient Asian land), you swore to do whatever I asked. Now keep your oath and become a free man. I'll cover my face as you stab me ***(search this bosom)*** with the same knife that killed Caesar. Don't argue ***(Stand not to***

E. Answer: *Cassius hints that he is planning to kill himself.*

F. Reading Skill: CLARIFYING Be sure that students understand that Cassius is again referring to his birthday, which he mentioned to Messala at line 84 of Act V, Scene 1. Cassius hints that his life is like a circle; he was born and will die on the same day of the year.

G. Reading Skill: INTERPRETIVE ORAL READING Ask students to experiment with rate, pitch, volume, and pauses in dramatic oral readings of Pindarus' report. To further convey drama, have some students shout for joy as indicated.

H. Answer: *He decides to kill himself because he thinks that his best friend Titinius has been captured by the enemy.*

I. Literary Element: DIALOGUE Remind students that, although Caesar is killed at the halfway point of the play, his "presence" is so important in the second half that he might almost be considered a character. Ask how Cassius reinforces that presence here. *(Possible response: He addresses Caesar just as he kills himself, implying that Caesar has exacted vengeance for the assassination.)*

J. Literary Element: CONFLICT Ask students to explain what Shakespeare's purpose might be in making the conflict of the battle evenly balanced at this point. *(Possible response: The standoff helps to build suspense.)*

K. LEP: Play on Words Help students see the plays on words in this passage: the repetition of "lies" and the shifts between "is" and "was." You might encourage ESL students to translate these lines into their own languages to fully appreciate the effect of this type of wordplay.

L. Literary Element: FIGURATIVE LANGUAGE Ask students to explain the analogy drawn in this metaphor. *(Possible responses: Cassius, drenched in his own blood, is like the red setting "sun" of Rome. Now that Cassius is dead, the day of Roman glory is over, just as the red sun sets.)*

Stand not to answer. Here, take thou the hilts,
And when my face is covered, as 'tis now,
Guide thou the sword.

[Pindarus *stabs him.]*

I —Caesar, thou are revenged
Even with the sword that killed thee.

[Dies.]

Pindarus. So, I am free, yet would not so have been,
Durst I have done my will. O Cassius!
Far from this country Pindarus shall run,
Where never Roman shall take note of him.

[Exit.]

[Reenter Titinius *with* Messala.*]*

J **Messala.** It is but change, Titinius; for Octavius
Is overthrown by noble Brutus' power,
As Cassius' legions are by Antony.

Titinius. These tidings will well comfort Cassius.

Messala. Where did you leave him?

Titinius. All disconsolate,
With Pindarus his bondman, on this hill.

Messala. Is not that he that lies upon the ground?

Titinius. He lies not like the living. O my heart!

K **Messala.** Is not that he?

Titinius. No, this was he, Messala,
But Cassius is no more. O setting sun,
As in thy red rays thou dost sink to night,
So in his red blood Cassius' day is set!
L The sun of Rome is set. Our day is gone;
Clouds, dews, and dangers come; our deeds are done!
Mistrust of my success hath done this deed.

Messala. Mistrust of good success hath done this deed.
O hateful Error, Melancholy's child,
Why dost thou show to the apt thoughts of men
The things that are not? O Error, soon conceived,
Thou never com'st unto a happy birth,
But kill'st the mother that engend'red thee!

Titinius. What, Pindarus! Where art thou, Pindarus?

answer). *Why does Cassius finally decide to kill himself?* H

53–54 ***So . . . will:*** I am free; but I wouldn't have been if I had done what I wanted (that is, refused to kill Cassius).

57–59 ***It is . . . Antony:*** It's an even exchange. Just as Antony has defeated Cassius, Brutus has defeated Octavius.

62 ***disconsolate:*** extremely sad.

75–79 ***O hateful . . . thee:*** Why do mistaken beliefs, which come from sadness ***(Melancholy's child),*** always seem so true when they are false? A mistake is easily born but always kills its mother at birth.

CRITIC'S CORNER

From a slightly different perspective, the final scenes at Philippi might be a comedy of errors. Military bungles and mistaken identities follow quickly on each other's heels; the number of suicides, especially, seems excessive. Of the suicide of Titinius, a relatively minor character, Granville-Barker asks, 'why, with two suicides to provide for, Shakespeare burdened himself with this third?' The answer . . . must be found, I believe, in the context of false sacrifice throughout the play. Caesar's death was one such false sacrifice; Cinna the poet's a horrible mistake; the political murders by the triumvirate continued the chain; and now Cassius sacrifices himself on the basis of a mistake, while Titinius follows out of loyalty to the dead Cassius."

LAWRENCE N. DANSON, "RITUAL AND *JULIUS CAESAR*, PUBLISHED IN *William Shakespeare's Julius Caesar*, EDITED BY HAROLD BLOOM

Messala. Seek him, Titinius, whilst I go to meet
The noble Brutus, thrusting this report
Into his ears. I may say "thrusting" it;
M For piercing steel and darts envenomed
Shall be as welcome to the ears of Brutus
As tidings of this sight.

Titinius. Hie you, Messala,
And I will seek for Pindarus the while.

[Exit Messala.*]*

*[*Titinius *looks at* Cassius.*]*

Why didst thou send me forth, brave Cassius?
Did I not meet thy friends, and did not they
N Put on my brows this wreath of victory
And bid me give it thee? Didst thou not hear their shouts?
Alas, thou hast misconstrued everything!
But hold thee, take this garland on thy brow.
Thy Brutus bid me give it thee, and I
Will do his bidding. Brutus, come apace
And see how I regarded Caius Cassius.
By your leave, gods. This is a Roman's part.
Come, Cassius' sword, and find Titinius' heart.

[Dies.]

[Alarum. Enter Brutus, Messala, young Cato, Strato, Volumnius, *and* Lucilius.*]*

Brutus. Where, where, Messala, doth his body lie?

Messala. Lo, yonder, and Titinius mourning it.

Brutus. Titinius' face is upward.

Cato. He is slain.

Q **Brutus.** O Julius Caesar, thou art mighty yet!
Thy spirit walks abroad and turns our swords
In our own proper entrails.

[Low alarums.]

Cato. Brave Titinius!
Look whe'r he have not crowned dead Cassius.

Brutus. Are yet two Romans living such as these?
The last of all the Romans, fare thee well!
It is impossible that ever Rome
Should breed thy fellow. Friends, I owe more tears

84 *darts envenomed:* poisoned darts.

87 *Hie you:* Hurry.

94 *misconstrued:* misunderstood. *What was the mistake that led to Cassius' suicide?* O

95 Titinius removes the laurel wreath his friends put on his head to symbolize his victory. In his grief, he puts the wreath on Cassius' head.

97 *apace:* quickly.

99 *This . . . part:* This (killing myself) is the proper thing for a brave Roman to do. *Why does Titinius believe this is the right thing to do?* P

109 *whe'r:* whether.

110–113 *Are yet . . . fellow:* Are there two Romans still living who are as good as these two? I bid you both farewell. Rome will never see your equal ***(breed thy fellow).***

M. Reading Skill: PREDICTING Ask students how they think Brutus will react to the news of Cassius' suicide. *(Possible response: Given Brutus' character, he may be unnerved or depressed, but he will probably try to endure this misfortune stoically.)*

N. Literary Element: IRONY Ask whether, in addition to the ironic mistake Titinius describes here, there is also a broader, unintentional irony in his words, "Alas, thou hast misconstrued everything." *(Possible response: These words could possibly be applied to Cassius' motives and actions from the beginning of the conspiracy. His bitter envy of Caesar has resulted in chaos for the state and disaster for himself.)*

O. Answer: *The mistake was that Pindarus had misinterpreted the fate of Titinius. In the confusion of the battle, Pindarus mistakenly inferred that Titinius had been captured by enemy troops; in fact, Titinius had been joyfully welcomed by his own men.*

P. Answer: *Titinius may believe that this is the right thing to do because he thinks he has been indirectly responsible for Cassius' death.*

Q. Literary Element: TRAGEDY Ask students how this passage relates to the idea of tragedy. *(Possible response: Brutus seems belatedly to recognize that the assassination of Caesar has resulted in violence and chaos. All of Brutus' efforts to preserve Rome and his own honor have in fact led to trouble for Rome, the loss of honor, and his own destruuction: "our swords [turning]/In our own proper entrails.")*

R. Literary Element: CHARACTERIZATION Point out Brutus' quick shift from speaking to the dead Cassius to ordering his men on toward another battle. Ask students if this is generally consistent with Brutus' style, and why they feel this way. *(Possible response: Most students may feel that it is consistent because Brutus tends to keep his sadness and mourning private and behave in a way that will yield the most good for all.)*

S. LEP: Rhyme Have students read this final couplet aloud in order to hear the rhythm and rhyme. Help students to see that this sound effect creates a mood of determination and finality for the scene's end.

Student Response

Responding to Reading

These questions are open-ended with no "right" or "wrong" answers. However, responses must be supported with information from the selection. Possible answers follow:

1. Any honest impressions are valid. The scene's brevity may increase the audience's tension and excitement. The sound effects and sudden commands in the dialogue may also increase suspense and tension.

2. Some students may disagree with Cassius' behavior, arguing that he surrenders too easily to despair. One alternative he might have had was to verify the report of Titinius' death. Others may see his despair as justified by the larger picture of a losing battle.

3. Some students may agree with Brutus' evaluation, commenting that Cassius' advice to Brutus has been extremely valuable all along. Brutus now regrets that he has ignored that advice and realizes that he should weep for his friend. Other students may argue that Brutus is overly sentimental, given the fact that Cassius cynically manipulated him into joining the conspiracy in the first place.

4. Cassius' death must certainly be regarded as a serious blow. On the other hand, Brutus has been successful against Octavius' troops, so this may not be the end for the conspirators. Brutus himself looks forward to a second fight, and he is careful to protect the morale of his troops.

To this dead man than you shall see me pay.
I shall find time, Cassius; I shall find time.
Come therefore, and to Thasos send his body.
R His funerals shall not be in our camp,
Lest it discomfort us. Lucilius, come;
And come, young Cato. Let us to the field.
Labeo and Flavius set our battles on.
'Tis three o'clock; and, Romans, yet ere night
S We shall try fortune in a second fight.

[Exeunt.]

116 ***Thasos*** **(thā' säs'):** an island near Philippi.

122 ***We shall . . . fight:*** We'll try our luck in a second battle.

Responding to Reading

1. Scene 2 has only six lines of dialogue, all spoken by Brutus. How does this brief scene affect you? List your impressions.
2. Do you agree with Cassius' behavior in Scene 3, or should he have acted differently?

   Think about
   - how discouraged he becomes
   - his suicide
   - alternatives he might have
3. Brutus mourns the dead Cassius as a man to whom he owes more tears than he cay pay. Do you agree with Brutus' evaluation of Cassius? Why or why not?
4. Is Cassius' death the end for the conspirators?

   Think about
   - Brutus' reactions
   - your own predictions about the battle

Scene 4 *Another part of the field.*

During the battle, young Cato is killed and Lucilius taken prisoner. Brought to Antony, Lucilius insists that Brutus will never be taken alive.

[Another part of the field. Alarum. Enter Brutus, Messala, Young Cato, Lucilius, *and* Flavius.*]*

Brutus. Yet, countrymen, O, yet hold up your heads!

Cato. What fellow doth not? Who will go with me?
I will proclaim my name about the field.
I am the son of Marcus Cato, ho!
A foe to tyrants, and my country's friend.
I am the son of Marcus Cato, ho!

[Enter Soldiers *and fight.]*

Brutus. And I am Brutus, Marcus Brutus I!
Brutus, my country's friend! Know me for Brutus!

[Exit.]

*[*Young Cato *falls.]*

Lucilius. O young and noble Cato, art thou down?
Why, now thou diest as bravely as Titinius,
And mayst be honored, being Cato's son.

First Soldier. Yield, or thou diest.

Lucilius. Only I yield to die.

[Offering money.]

There is so much that thou wilt kill me straight.
Kill Brutus, and be honored in his death.

First Soldier. We must not. A noble prisoner!

[Enter Antony.*]*

Second Soldier. Room ho! Tell Antony Brutus is ta'en.

First Soldier. I'll tell the news. Here comes the general.
Brutus is ta'en! Brutus, is ta'en, my lord!

Antony. Where is he?

Lucilius. Safe, Antony; Brutus is safe enough.
I dare assure thee that no enemy
Shall ever take alive the noble Brutus.
B The gods defend him from so great a shame!
When you do find him, or alive or dead,
He will be found like Brutus, like himself.

Antony. This is not Brutus, friend; but, I assure you,
A prize no less in worth. Keep this man safe;
D Give him all kindness. I had rather have
Such men my friends than enemies. Go on,
And see whe'r Brutus be alive or dead;
And bring us word unto Octavius' tent
How everything is chanced.

[Exeunt.]

4 *Marcus Cato:* Portia's father, a greatly respected Roman.

12 *Yield:* surrender.

14–15 *There is . . . death:* This money is for you, if you will kill me immediately ***(straight).*** If you kill Brutus, you will win honor for it. Lucilius pretends to be Brutus and fools the soldier.

21–23 *Do you agree with Lucilius that Brutus will never be taken alive?* A

27–29 *Why do you think Antony is being so merciful to Lucilius?* C

Text Annotations

A. Answer: *Lucilius is probably correct; students should cite lines 126–128 of scene 1, where Brutus told Cassius that he would never "go bound to Rome."*

B. Reading Skill: INTERPRETIVE ORAL READING Have students experiment with various tones (for example, defiant or proud) as they read this speech aloud.

C. Answer Lucilius' bravery and intelligence would be valuable assets for Antony. Antony does not want such a man as his enemy.

D. Literary Element: THEME Ask what students believe this passage reveals about Antony's concept of friendship. *(Possible response: Antony's concept of friendship now seems to be purely political or strategic. If a person could be dangerous to Antony as an enemy, he would prefer to take him as a "friend.")*

E. Reading Skill: INFERRING Ask students what Brutus' line implies about his state of mind here. *(Possible response: Brutus is weary and pessimistic about the battle.)*

F. Literary Element: SUSPENSE Have students explain how Shakespeare organizes the dialogue here to build suspense. *(Possible response: The playwright builds suspense through the whispering, the gaps in conversation, and the indirect references to an unspecified, horrible "deed.")*

G. Literary Element: FIGURATIVE LANGUAGE Have students explain what liquid "runs over" from the "vessel" in this metaphor. *(Brutus' tears)*

H. LEP: Detail Be sure students grasp that Caesar's ghost has appeared to Brutus twice, even though he only appears once in the actual play. Have students imagine how Brutus feels about these apparitions. *(Possible responses: guilty, frightened, discouraged)*

Scene 5 Another part of the battlefield.

Facing defeat, Brutus' forces rest. Brutus feels that all is lost. He asks three men to kill him, but each refuses. Finally, Strato agrees to hold the sword as Brutus kills himself on it. Antony, Octavius, and others arrive. Antony mourns Brutus, calling him the "noblest Roman." Octavius promises him a noble funeral as the play ends.

[Enter Brutus, Dardanius, Clitus, Strato, *and* Volumnius.*]*

E **Brutus.** Come, poor remains of friends, rest on this rock.

Clitus. Statilius showed the torchlight but, my lord,
He came not back. He is or ta'en or slain.

Brutus. Sit thee down, Clitus. Slaying is the word.
It is a deed in fashion. Hark thee, Clitus.

[Whispers.]

Clitus. What, I, my lord? No, not for all the world!

F **Brutus.** Peace then. No words.

Clitus. I'll rather kill myself.

Brutus. Hark thee, Dardanius.

[Whispers.]

Dardanius. Shall I do such a deed?

Clitus. O Dardanius!

Dardanius. O Clitus!

Clitus. What ill request did Brutus make to thee?

Dardanius. To kill him, Clitus. Look he meditates.

Clitus. Now is that noble vessel full of grief,
G That it runs over even at his eyes.

Brutus. Come hither, good Volumnius. List a word.

Volumnius. What says my lord?

Brutus. Why this, Volumnius.
The ghost of Caesar hath appeared to me
H Two several times by night—at Sardis once,
And this last night here in Philippi fields.
I know my hour is come.

Volumnius. Not so, my lord.

Brutus. Nay, I am sure it is, Volumnius.

2–3 *Statilius . . . slain:* Statilius (our scout) signaled with his torch that all was well at our camp. But since he hasn't come back, he has been either captured or killed.

4–10 Brutus says that it has become fashionable to kill, not to capture. Then he whispers something to Clitus, who seems shocked by what Brutus has asked him to do. Brutus whispers the same request to Dardanius, who reacts the same way. After this, Brutus walks away from the two men.

17 *List:* listen to.

21 *Two several times:* twice.

J Thou seest the world, Volumnius, how it goes.
Our enemies have beat us to the pit.

[Low alarums.]

It is more worthy to leap in ourselves
Than tarry till they push us. Good Volumnius,
Thou know'st that we two went to school together.
Even for that our love of old, I prithee
K Hold thou my sword-hilts whilst I run on it.

Volumnius. That's not an office for a friend, my lord.

[Alarum still.]

Clitus. Fly, fly, my lord! There is no tarrying here.

Brutus. Farewell to you; and you; and you, Volumnius.
Strato, thou hast been all this while asleep.
Farewell to thee too, Strato. Countrymen,
My heart doth joy that yet in all my life
I found no man but he was true to me.
I shall have glory by this losing day
More than Octavius and Mark Antony
By this vile conquest shall attain unto.
So fare you well at once, for Brutus' tongue
Hath almost ended his life's history.
Night hangs upon mine eyes; my bones would rest,
That have but labored to attain this hour.

[Alarum. Cry within:]

Fly, fly, fly!

Clitus. Fly, my lord, fly!

Brutus. Hence! I will follow.

[Exeunt Clitus, Dardanius, *and* Volumnius.*]*

I prithee, Strato, stay thou by thy lord.
Thou art a fellow of a good respect;
Thy life hath had some smatch of honor in it.
Hold then my sword, and turn away thy face
While I do run upon it. Wilt thou, Strato?

Strato. Give me your hand first. Fare you well, my lord.

M **Brutus.** Farewell, good Strato. Caesar, now be still.
I killed not thee with half so good a will.

[Dies.]

27 *pit:* a hole into which hunted animals are forced. *How does Brutus seem to feel about the battle now?* I

29 *tarry:* wait.

31–32 *I prithee . . . on it:* I beg you to hold my sword (on the ground, with the blade pointing up) while I fall onto it.

33 *That's . . . friend:* That's no duty for a friend to perform.

38–39 Think about how Brutus sums up his life in these two lines. Then think about the way Cassius manipulated him in Act One, and the way Antony fooled him into letting Antony speak to the crowd. *What can you conclude about Brutus' understanding of people?* L

45–46 *my bones . . . hour:* My tired bones have worked to bring me to this final hour of rest.

52 *smatch:* little bit.

57 *I killed . . . will:* I didn't kill you (Caesar) half as willingly as I kill myself.

I. Answer: *Brutus feels that the battle is lost.*

J. Literary Element: FIGURATIVE LANGUAGE Be sure that students understand that the allusion here is to hunting. Brutus means that he and his soldiers have been trapped, like wild animals in a pit, by their enemies.

K. Literary Element: THEME Ask students how Volumnius' line might poignantly recall an earlier event in the play where the theme of friendship was also evoked. *(Possible response: This line might make the audience think of Caesar's dying words, "Et tu Brute?", when he was stabbed by a man he believed was his friend.)*

L. Answer: *One can conclude that Brutus is naive, since he believes that everyone else is as honorable and devoted to the general good as he is.*

M. Literary Element: TRAGEDY A tragic hero has been defined as a basically good or noble individual who makes a disastrous error in judgment that leads to catastrophe, usually the hero's own death. Ask if students think that Brutus qualifies as a tragic hero. *(Possible responses: Yes, since he is portrayed as basically good but disastrously mistaken in his decision to join the conspiracy; no, his mistakes reveal a trivial and naive nature, not a noble one.)*

N. LEP: Play on Words Help students see the ominous mood created by the repetition of *master* and *man,* and to grasp the irony of the words *free* and *bondage,* used to refer both to the bondage of servitude (a man must serve his master) and to the bondage of life itself, from which Brutus is now "free."

O. Teaching Tip

It may help students to make a chart of each death in *Julius Caesar,* including who performs each killing and why. For example:

Death	Perpetrator	Reason
Caesar	Conspirators	Fear of tyranny
Cinna	Mob	Hysteria
Portia	Portia	Fear and despair
. . .	. . .	. . .

Encouraging Independent Reading

A Man for All Seasons, a play by Robert Bolt
Shakespeare of London, a biography by Marchette Chute
"Caesar" in *Lives of the Noble Romans* (a volume of *Parallel Lives*), biographical essays by Plutarch
"Julius Caesar" in *The Twelve Caesars,* biographical essays by Suetonius
Macbeth, a play by William Shakespeare

[Alarum. Retreat. Enter Octavius, Antony, Messala, Lucilius, *and the Army.]*

Octavius. What man is that?

N **Messala.** My master's man. Strato, where is thy master?

Strato. Free from the bondage you are in, Messala.
The conquerors can but make a fire of him;
For Brutus only overcame himself,
O And no man else hath honor by his death.

59 ***man:*** servant.

"This was the noblest Roman of them all."

Lucilius. So Brutus should be found. I thank thee, Brutus,
That thou hast proved Lucilius' saying true.

Octavius. All that served Brutus, I will entertain them.
Fellow, wilt thou bestow thy time with me?

Strato. Ay, if Messala will prefer me to you.

Octavius. Do so, good Messala.

Messala. How died my master, Strato?

Strato. I held the sword, and he did run on it.

Messala. Octavius, then take him to follow thee,
That did the latest service to my master.

Antony. This was the noblest Roman of them all.
All the conspirators save only he
Did that they did in envy of great Caesar;
He, only in a general honest thought
And common good to all, made one of them.
His life was gentle, and the elements
So mixed in him that Nature might stand up
And say to all the world, "This was a man!"

Octavius. According to his virtue let us use him,
With all respect and rites of burial.
Within my tent his bones tonight shall lie,
Most like a soldier, ordered honorably.
So call the field to rest, and let's away
To part the glories of this happy day.

[Exeunt.]

64–66 *So Brutus . . . true:* That is just how Brutus should be found. Thank you, Brutus, for proving me correct (in saying you would never be taken alive).
67–68 *All . . . me:* All those who served Brutus will now be welcome in my army. Strato ***(Fellow),*** will you join me?

69 *prefer:* recommend.

73–74 *Octavius . . . master:* Octavius, I recommend him for your army; he performed the last favor for Brutus ***(my master).***
75–82 Now that the war is won, Antony pays a final tribute to Brutus. *What good qualities of Brutus does Antony mention in this tribute?*
76 *save:* except.

79 *made one of them:* joined the conspirators.

83 *According . . . him:* Let us treat him as he deserves.

88 *part:* divide up.

Responding to Reading

1. Describe your own image of the way this battle appears on the stage.
2. Why do you think Lucilius poses as Brutus when he is captured in Scene 4?
3. Does Brutus have any alternative besides killing himself? Explain.
4. Do you think Antony is sincere when he praises Brutus and calls him "the noblest Roman of them all"?

   Think about
   - what you know about Antony's personality
   - what Antony might hope to accomplish

P. Answer: *Antony says that Brutus was not motivated by envy, but rather by what he believed to be the general good. He was a gentle man who displayed all the balanced qualities that a true man should possess.*

Q. Literary Element: TRAGEDY Ask students to consider whether the real tragedy of the play is the death of Brutus, or whether Shakespeare might have intended another message in these lines. *(Possible response: The real tragedy may not be the death of Brutus, but rather the moral blindness and ambition of nearly all the characters, which led to suffering and chaos.)*

Student Response

Responding to Reading

These questions are open-ended with no "right" or "wrong" answers. However, responses must be supported with information from the selection. Possible answers follow:

1. The battle is a noisy, fast-paced, confusing event, with troops dashing to and fro across the stage.

2. Lucilius poses as Brutus to gain time for Brutus to assault or retreat.

3. Some students may suggest that Brutus could have retreated. Other students, however, may counter that this would not be compatible with Brutus' sense of honor, and that he would still have been risking capture.

4. Antony is sincere—now that Brutus is dead and the battle won, Antony can afford to be sincere in his praise; Antony is not sincere—once again, he is using his persuasive eloquence in the service of his own ambition, since he hopes by praising Brutus to convert the dead commander's troops to his cause.

Check Test

1. In Scene 1, why does Cassius feel apprehensive about the battle? *(He has seen bad omens.)*

2. In Scene 2, why does Brutus feel encouraged? *(He has spotted weakness among Octavius' troops.)*

3. What causes Cassius to despair and kill himself in Scene 3? *(the mistaken report of Titinius' capture)*

4. How does Lucilius trick the enemy soldiers when he is captured in Scene 4? *(He pretends to be Brutus.)*

5. Who wins the battle in Scene 5? *(Antony and Octavius)*

Student Response

Responding to Reading

These questions are open-ended with no "right" or "wrong" answers. However, responses must be supported with information from the selection. Possible answers follow:

1. Any reasonable answer is valid.

2. Students may say that Antony had hoped to unnerve Brutus by his insults in Scene 1, when he called him a "villain," "ape," "hound," and "cur"; by the time Brutus is dead, however, Antony can afford to pay his enemy a sincere tribute, calling him "the noblest Roman of them all." Other students may say that Antony only pretends to pay Brutus tribute in Scene 5 because he hopes to win over Brutus' remaining forces.

3. Many students will comment that the issue of Rome's freedom seems irrelevant to both sides. Antony and Octavius are interested in gaining power, while Cassius and Brutus are in a defensive position, fighting for survival.

4. Students should cite the description of a tragic hero as a basically good man who commits a fatal error in judgment that leads to his destruction. Many students will argue that Brutus fits this description, with his fatal error being the decision to join the conspiracy. Evidence from Act V that could be cited to support the view of Brutus as a tragic hero includes his military success, his "honorable" suicide, his acknowledgment that he regrets killing Caesar, and Antony's tribute. Other students, however, may object that Brutus' tactical errors and naiveté keep him from heroic status.

5. Caesar's assassination is the reason the armies fight. Antony recalls Caesar's murder in Scene 1; Octavius invokes his memory in the same scene; Brutus says in Scene 5 that the ghost has reappeared the previous evening; and both Cassius and Brutus call on Caesar at the moment of death.

6. Most students will comment that Brutus seems to be the most heroic character, but some may mention Caesar, Cassius, Antony, or Octavius.

7. Candidates for villain may include Cassius (for manipulating Brutus), Caesar (for his arrogance and egotism), and Antony (for his dishonesty and cynicism). Some students may point out that there are no clear heroes or villains.

Responding to Reading

First Impressions

1. Write a sentence describing how you feel about the way this play ends.

Second Thoughts

2. Contrast Antony's insults toward Brutus in Scene 1 to his praise for Brutus in Scene 5. How would you explain the change?
3. Are the leaders of the two armies concerned more for Rome's freedom or for their own power? Explain.
4. On page 795, you first thought about whether or not Brutus was the tragic hero of this story. How would you answer that question now? Support your view with evidence from Act Five.
5. Julius Caesar dies in Act Three but remains an important character in the play. How is he important to Act Five?

   Think about
   - why the armies fought
   - what Antony, Cassius, and Brutus say about him
   - the reappearance of his ghost
6. Who is the most heroic character in this play? Explain why and then compare that character to a hero from another story in this book.
7. Who, if anyone, is the villain of this play? Explain.

Literary Concept: Tragedy

The ancient Greek philosopher Aristotle identified the main characteristics of tragedy. He explained that **tragedy** is a series of actions that have disastrous consequences for the main character or characters; usually the actions are presented in poetic, dramatic form. All true tragedies arouse pity and fear in an audience: pity because the audience feels sorry for the tragic characters and hates to see them suffer; and fear because the viewers realize that, if circumstances were different, they too could be caught up in a web of tragic events. Do any scenes in *Julius Caesar* inspire pity and fear in you? Do you feel depressed because of the waste of human life, or perhaps relieved that the tension has ended and order has been restored?

Concept Review: Theme Power, greed, and ambition are some of the themes in *Julius Caesar.* Is the type of political leader who is the most successful also the most admirable? Explain. What might be Shakespeare's message about political control and responsibility?

Literary Concept: Tragedy

Possible response: the character of Brutus and his destruction inspired emotions of pity and fear.

Concept Review: Theme *Possible responses: Successful political leaders are not necessarily admirable. An example is Antony in the play, who is portrayed as a successful and persuasive manipulator. Shakespeare's message may be that those who possess political control must also display a corresponding sense of responsibility to be worthy of exercising power.*

Writing Options

1. What if Antony had been killed along with Julius Caesar, as Cassius wanted? Write an explanation of how this story might have been different.
2. Write some ideas for a modern-day story based on *Julius Caesar.*
3. Write a speech for Octavius to deliver at Brutus' funeral. Include criticism of Brutus' actions and praise for his good qualities.

e x t e n d

Options for Learning

1 • Improvise a Scene Select any one of the following situations from Act Five, and, with one or more classmates, improvise a scene for the class according to the instructions.

- Scene 1, after Antony and Octavius leave Brutus and Cassius. Improvise a conversation between Antony and Octavius about their enemies in the upcoming battle.
- Scene 3, after Titinius rides away from Cassius. Improvise the scene Titinius might actually have ridden into.
- Scene 5, after Antony and Octavius have praised the dead Brutus. Improvise a private conversation they might have had.

2 • Make a Video With a small group of your classmates, select one scene or part of a scene that you think could have a particularly dramatic impact on an audience. Discuss this scene with your classmates, and determine the mood and emphasis you want to achieve. Consider adding music and other sound effects. If possible, use a video camera and shoot the scene from several angles.

3 • Draw a Character Draw a character or a scene from *Julius Caesar.* Refer to the pictures throughout the play, or research other sources to find how people and the setting might have looked.

4 • The Next Chapter Use an encyclopedia and history books to find out what happened to Antony and Octavius after the deaths of Brutus and Cassius. Report to the class on your findings.

Writing Options

The Writing Options are designed to meet varied student interests and abilities. Have each student choose one writing activity to complete. You may wish to guide some students to an option that requires less writing.

Journal Update Have students review their journal entries for *Julius Caesar.* Ask what new insights the play has suggested about honor, ambition, and pride, and encourage students to record their new reflections in their journals.

Options for Learning

These activities suit a variety of learning styles and modes of expression. Allow students to review the options and then choose the one they wish to do. Many are excellent collaborative learning projects.

1. Improvise a Scene Remind students that they should examine the text of the play for clues about the relationships between the various characters.

2. Make a Video Suggest to students that they use a cassette tape recorder to record their music and sound effects. They can then dub the effects onto the edited videotape, or play the audio recorder while recording visually.

3. Draw a Character Advise students to consult the school or local library for photographs of famous productions of the play, such as those by the Royal Shakespeare Company at Stratford-on-Avon, England.

4. The Next Chapter Provide students with these two figures' dates as follows: Antony—82 B.C.–30 B.C. and Octavius—63 B.C.–14 A.D. Suggest that useful encyclopedia articles can be found under the headings "Actium" (Battle of), "Cleopatra," and "Augustus."

Cross-Curricular Options

Students might engage in a number of collaborative or independent projects relating to *Julius Caesar:*

History: Students might research the daily lives of the Romans under Caesar's rule, with particular attention to government, the role of women, and the era's military ideals. Students might enjoy reading Howard Fast's novel *Spartacus* for a literary way of researching history.

Geography: Have students prepare a map showing the extent of the Roman Empire during Caesar's time, superimposed over modern geographic boundaries. Students might enjoy making several maps, showing the rise and fall of the empire, perhaps also identifying various modern languages related to Latin.

Music: Students might find various themes for each act or each scene of *Julius Caesar,* conveying the mood shifts within the play.

Art: Some students may want to research both Roman dress and theatrical costumes in order to design their own costumes for various characters in the play.

Additional Information About the Author

Shakespeare wrote two other tragedies with ancient Roman settings: *Antony and Cleopatra* (1606) and *Coriolanus* (1608). *Antony and Cleopatra* may be of particular interest to students, since its plot dramatizes the famous love affair of Antony with Queen Cleopatra of Egypt and Antony's struggle with Octavius for supreme power. In fact, *Antony and Cleopatra* might even be seen as a sequel to *Julius Caesar.*

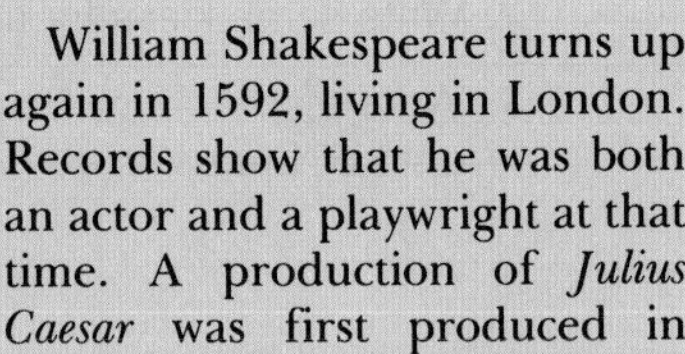

William Shakespeare

1564–1616

The works of William Shakespeare have probably been seen or read by more people worldwide than the works of any other writer. The man who wrote these works, however, is something of a mystery, even among scholars who have devoted much of their lives to studying his life and writing.

The mystery begins with Shakespeare's birth, since no record exists of the actual date. A baby named William Shakespeare was baptized in a church at Stratford-on-Avon on April 26, 1564. Babies at the time were baptized three days after birth, so scholars today believe that Shakespeare was born on April 23.

Although there are no records about his education, Shakespeare probably went to a local school in Stratford. Students in those days studied Latin and read the works of ancient Roman writers. Thus, by the time he was an adult, Shakespeare probably knew about the Roman culture of Julius Caesar's day.

A 1582 marriage record shows that Shakespeare married Anne Hathaway. Birth records indicate that Shakespeare and Hathaway had a daughter in 1583 and twins in 1585. Scholars can find no evidence of what Shakespeare did for the next seven years.

William Shakespeare turns up again in 1592, living in London. Records show that he was both an actor and a playwright at that time. A production of *Julius Caesar* was first produced in 1599, the eighteenth of Shakespeare's thirty-seven plays.

By the time *Julius Caesar* was first performed, Shakespeare was a rich man. He was part owner of the company of actors that produced his plays and of the Globe Theatre in which they performed. He also made money as a playwright, and he had published several books of poetry.

During these years, Shakespeare seems to have spent most of his time in London. There is some evidence, however, that he occasionally traveled to Stratford to be with his family. He continued living this way until 1613, when he completed his last play. After that, he probably moved back to live in Stratford permanently.

No one knows for sure just when, where, or how Shakespeare died. His grave at Holy Trinity Church in Stratford has a monument that gives the date of death as April 23, 1616. However, there are no records to prove that he actually died on that date.

Shakespeare had four grandchildren, but all died without having children of their own. As a result, his lineage ended when his last living grandchild died in 1670.

Closure

Mention that *Julius Caesar* is considered remarkable for many reasons and very much fits the unit theme "The Classic Tradition": its factual density—the richness of detailed action described and implied with great economy; its beauty of language—spare yet explicit, functional yet rich; its tribute to a man's noble intentions and the bequeathing of the "memory of an ideal." Encourage students to comment on these various aspects of *Julius Caesar* and offer their own personal feelings about it. Invite them to discuss how Shakespeare's themes are ever present in the world today.

EXPOSITION: CAUSE AND EFFECT

When we read newspaper reports of violent crimes or natural disasters, we're usually not satisfied with knowing just the details of how the crime was committed or how the disaster struck. Our need to make sense of incomprehensible events usually drives us to ask "Why did this happen?" or "What caused such a tragedy?" We also want to know the effects of the event on the victims, their families, and the environment.

Sometimes, however, causes and effects are not easily understood. Ask ten people what caused the Vietnam War, and you may get ten different answers. For such events it may be possible to infer only probable causes. Likewise, the effects of a cause may not be immediately apparent without investigation and may require making inferences.

For this assignment you will examine the causes and effects of an incident from Shakespeare's play *Julius Caesar*. Using the information you gather, you will then write a news story about the event.

Here is your PASSkey to this assignment.

GUIDED ASSIGNMENT: *ROMAN DAILY NEWS* ARTICLE

Numerous events in *Julius Caesar* are examples of cause-effect relationships. Write a news story based on one of these events.

PURPOSE: To inform
AUDIENCE: Roman citizens in Caesar's time
SUBJECT: A newsworthy event in the play
STRUCTURE: A news story

Prewriting

STEP 1 **Choose an event** Consider the events from *Julius Caesar* listed below as possible items for a news story. Remember that you will want to report the circumstances of the event and its probable causes and effects. Based on both your understanding of and interest in these events, choose one to report on.

- the violent storm in the first act
- Caesar's assassination
- the slaying of Cinna

Writer's Workshop

Objectives

- To understand the relationships between causes and effects
- To identify and gather facts for a news article
- To organize material for a news article from most to least important
- To draft, revise, edit, and share a news article
- To reflect on the writing process

Integrating . . .

Literature and Writing Have the class recall some of the most action-filled scenes of *Julius Caesar.* Then have them imagine that they are Roman citizens who were away when the events of the play occurred. Ask them what they would want to know about the incidents mentioned.

Tell students that in this workshop they will use their inference skills plus their knowledge of cause and effect to write about an event from the play.

Writing and Grammar Share with students that reporters not only write the facts of a story but also write complex, well-developed sentences that indicate relationships. For this reason, sentence-combining skills are essential to effective reporting. Tell students that the Language Workshop in this subunit will focus on sentence combining as an aid to news writing.

Literature and Thinking Skills Ask students what they think about in watching a play or movie. *(Possible responses: Is this a "good guy" or a "bad guy"? What will happen next?)* Point out that people usually enjoy a performance if they are active and critical viewers. Tell students that in the Thinking Skills Workshop in this subunit they will study some valuable hints for critical viewing.

Additional Resources

UNIT SIX RESOURCE BOOK
Writer's Workshop Copy Master, p. 16
Peer and Self-Evaluation Guidelines, p. 17
Writing Assessment Guidelines, p. 18

ENRICHMENT MATERIALS
Thinking Skills Transparency and Worksheet
Fine Art Transparency and Writing Prompts
Revision, Proofreading, and Elaboration Worksheet
Writing Prompts for Assessment

Teaching Strategies

Introduction Have students turn to the Writer's Workshop on page 837. Read with them the first three paragraphs and answer any questions on the use of inference to determine cause and effect.

Call attention to the Guided Assignment box on the same page and make sure that students understand they are to write a news article based on *Julius Caesar*. Point out the PASSkey graphic and read with students the purpose, audience, subject, and structure of the assignment. Emphasize the fact that they are to inform and their audience is to be the citizens of Rome in 44 B.C.

Prewriting To supplement the text on the subject of news gathering, you may want to use the following suggestion.

> **Teaching Tip**
>
> **1.** Have students role-play a newsworthy event, such as an accident or a robbery. Ask what questions they would ask the spokesperson about the event and write the questions on the chalkboard. Stop when you have listed a *what, where, when, who, why,* and *how* question. Point out that these are the basic news-gathering questions, often called "5 Ws and *H*.
>
> **2.** Distribute copies of news stories, such as brief crime reports, and have students read at least one of them to locate all five *Ws* and the *H*. Have students share their findings with the rest of the class.

Point out that the *why* question is not mentioned in the text, but that it is useful for determining a cause. Add that *what, who,* and *how* questions will help students state the effects of an event. Encourage the class to use both graphic organizers as they work through the *Prewriting* steps.

- the civil war between Antony's and Brutus' forces
- Portia's suicide
- Cassius' suicide

STEP 2 Identify the "hard facts" Reread the play to discover the actual facts surrounding the incident you've chosen. Find answers to the questions *who, what, when, where,* and *how*. Then construct a map similar to the student model below based on a murder in Shakespeare's *Macbeth*.

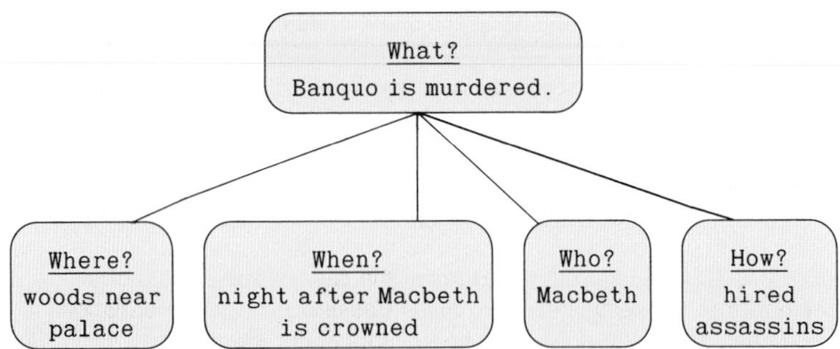

STEP 3 Consider the causes In some cases the causes of an event may be clearly stated. In other cases, you may have to infer the causes by piecing together what you know about the circumstances surrounding the event. Don't assume that if one event precedes another, the first event causes the second. The following checklist will help you make sure there is a logical connection between the causes you have identified and the event.

1. Are the causes stated in the text?
2. If not, what information do you have concerning characters and events surrounding the incident under investigation?
3. Do the causes explain *why* the event occurred?
4. Have you accounted for all possible causes?

STEP 4 Examine the effects Remember that one cause may have multiple effects. Some effects may be immediate and clearly stated. Other effects may occur later on and must be inferred. Again, don't assume that any event following an incident is an effect of that incident. You must be able to show how the incidents are linked through cause and effect. When you've identified the effects, add both the causes and effects to your map as this student did.

STUDENT MODEL

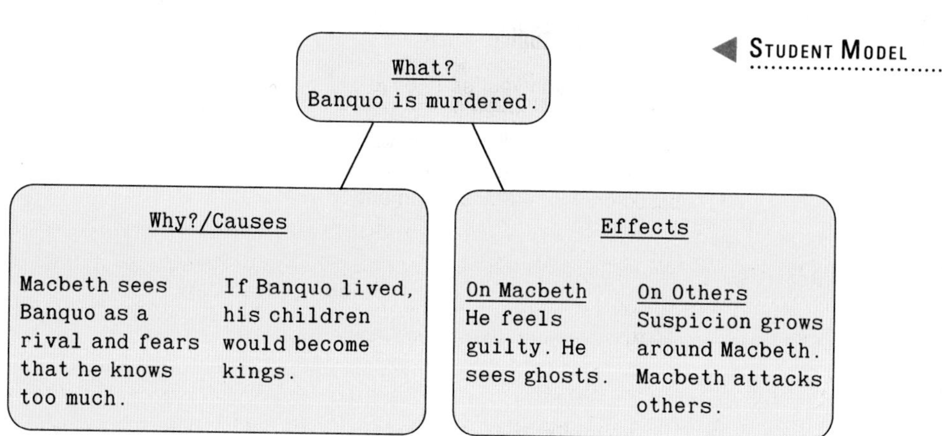

Drafting

STEP 1 Organize your information To determine what to say in your opening paragraph, number each feature in your map from most important to least important. For example, you might label "Why?" as 1 for most important and label "Who?" 2 for less important.

STEP 2 Write your lead The **lead** is the opening paragraph of your news story. It differs from typical introductions in that it briefly summarizes the most important features of the incident, usually answering most, but not all, of the questions you've set forth in your map. Following the order you've established, assemble the information into a lead, stating the most important information first. The lead is typically short, often less than forty words. The student writing about Macbeth decided to feature the *why, who, what,* and *how* information.

> Hoping to secure his reign as King of Scotland (why), Macbeth (who) had Banquo murdered (what) by hired assassins (how).

STEP 3 Draft the body Expand on the features you emphasized in your lead and account for all the information in your map. Pay particular attention to the causes and effects, showing their logical connections to the *what* of your story. Like the lead, the body should present information in the order of most to least important, not in time-order sequence. If, for example, the effects of the incident are more important than the causes, then present the effects first.

Drafting As students begin drafting their article, ask how the order of their middle paragraphs differs from that used in persuasive writing. *(Possible response: In news articles, the middle paragraphs are arranged from most to least important; in persuasive essays the opposite is often true.)* Ask students why they think this is the case. *(Possible response: because people read articles mainly for the most important information and sometimes don't get all the way to the end; however, people must read to the end of persuasive writing to reach the final argument)*

To give students help in drafting the lead of their article, refer them to the one-sentence model on page 839. Ask them why news writers don't just put all the information in their lead. *(Possible response: because there are often many important, although not essential, details that couldn't possibly fit in a lead)*

Remind students of the criteria for an effective lead: (1) it summarizes the most important features of the story (the 5 *Ws* and *H*); (2) it contains fewer than 40 words; and (3) it is usually one or two sentences long.

Revising and Editing As students check their causes and effects in the revising process, remind them to check for the answer to the *why* question, which does not appear in the checklist.

Computer Tip
Students who use a computer for revising will find it useful in changing sentence order as well as in combining sentences.

Encourage students to edit for correct punctuation in their combined sentences as well as in their article in general.

Publishing Instead of following the *Publishing* suggestion in the pupil's edition, you may want to consider this idea:

- Allow each student to publish a separate edition of *Rome Daily News*, using their article as the lead story. Have students write a few other short pieces giving related news and feature information, such as the time and place of Caesar's funeral, the people who will attend, and some of the stipulations of Caesar's will. Have students do their own layout and maybe even add a black-and-white drawing for effect.

Reflecting on Your Writing When you review students' writing portfolios, remember to respond to their answers for the *Reflecting* questions.

Closure

Be sure that students have internalized these concepts:

- Effects are events that happen; causes are whatever factors make the effects happen. An event that happens after another event is not necessarily caused by the first event.
- Causes may be inferred from effects.
- The facts for a news article should answer the questions *what, where, when, who, why,* and *how.*
- Facts in news articles proceed from the most important to the least important.

Revising and Editing

Read through your story once or twice to make sure that you haven't left out any important information and that you've organized the information logically. Then have a classmate act as an editor and read your news story, using the following checklist as a guide. Make revisions based on your editor's comments.

STUDENT MODEL ▶

Revision Checklist

1. Is the information accurate?
2. Does the lead emphasize the most newsworthy feature of the incident?
3. Are the *who, what, where, when,* and *how* features clearly presented?
4. Does the story develop those features in detail?
5. Does the story explain the causes and effects of the incident?
6. Is the information organized from most to least important?

Publishing

Select an editorial board who will evaluate all the news stories and select the best one covering each event. These can be published in your version of the *Roman Daily News* and placed in the library for review.

Reflecting on Your Writing

Answer the following questions. Place your answers with a copy of your paper in your writing portfolio.

1. What part of this assignment did you enjoy the most?
2. What is different about your news story in comparison with other stories written on the same incident? Which version do you like best?
3. How do you feel about journalistic writing in comparison with other types of writing that you have done in this book? Why?

ADDITIONAL WRITING AND RESEARCH TOPICS

The following items provide additional writing practice based on the selections in this subunit.

Cause and Effect: The United States has witnessed several assassinations in the last three decades. For example, John F. Kennedy, Martin Luther King, Jr., and John Lennon were victims of assassination. Research one of these assassinations, investigating both its causes and its effects, and write a report of your findings.

Another Topic

Reflective Essay: In trying to win Brutus to his side, Cassius tells him "The fault, dear Brutus, is not in our stars, But in ourselves . . . (I, ii). This often-quoted line from the play suggests a general truth about human nature. Reflect on this passage, exploring its meaning for you and for the human race. Think of examples from your own experiences and observations that illustrate this meaning. Write an essay developing your ideas.

SELF-ASSESSMENT
Year-End Portfolio Review

Most writers find it very helpful to review their work, even long after the last revision has been completed, because it gives them a chance to examine their progress and to set goals for future writing. The Writer's Workshops in this book all include a section called Reflecting on Your Writing at the end of the assignment. The questions in these sections have asked you to analyze and evaluate your work.

You will now use the answers to these questions to help you write a one-page essay reporting on your achievement this year as a writer and setting goals for the future.

Prewriting As you look through your responses in your Writing Portfolio, take notes. Look for weaknesses in your writing that you identified in the beginning of the year, strengths you've demonstrated, areas of improvement you or others have observed, and areas still needing improvement. You might want to make a chart like the one below.

Weaknesses	Strengths	Areas of Improvement	Areas Needing Improvement

Drafting Using your notes and chart, write a draft that describes your assessment of your best writing over the year. Include the following:

- an introduction that sets a purpose and is interesting to read
- topic sentences that present new ideas being discussed
- specific details (facts, observations, quotations, summaries) that support and illustrate each main point
- effective, logical organization

Conclude your essay with your goals for next year's writing.

Revising and Editing Design your own Revision Checklist for this assignment and use it to review your essay as honestly as you can. Write a final draft. Edit for spelling, clarity, and mechanics.

Writer's Workshop

Objectives

- To review the writing done during the past year
- To assess one's progress and set goals for future writing
- To analyze and evaluate one's writing, identifying weaknesses, strengths, and improvements
- To draft, revise, and edit an assessment of one's writing in the form of an expository composition

Teaching Strategies

Introduction Have students turn to the Writer's Workshop on page 841. Have them read through the first two paragraphs to get an idea of the content and format of their last assignment of the school year.

Prewriting Discuss with students that the focus of this assessment should not be on their accumulated grades but on their development as writers. To this end, encourage students to use the graphic organizer on page 841 as a place to begin.

Drafting Point out the four drafting reminders on page 842. Ask students what kind of composition these tips indicate. *(Possible response: an expository composition)*

Computer Tip
You might once again suggest drafting on a computer. Using a computer will enable students to rearrange their pieces of information into whichever paragraph each fits best.

Although you should not dictate to students the length of their assessment, you might want to suggest separate paragraphs for their weaknesses, strengths, and areas of improvement.

Revising and Editing As students revise, encourage them to be as honest as they can in writing their self-assessment, because otherwise, the only ones they delude will be themselves.

Have students edit carefully for correct punctuation in transitions and for accurate titles of selections and compositions.

Presenting Have students place their assessment at the front of their portfolio, followed by their year's worth of work in the order in which it was produced.

Assure the class that this portfolio, even with all its weaknesses, represents an immense undertaking and a great struggle to understand and improve. Point out that students should be happy with whatever they've learned and be confident that they will continue to improve in the coming year.

Closure

Be sure that students have internalized these concepts:

- This last composition is a review of the writing each student has done during the past year.
- The purpose of the last composition is for each student to examine his or her own progress and set goals for future writing.
- In the body of the composition each student analyzes and evaluates his or her writing, identifying weaknesses, strengths, and areas of improvement.

Language Workshop

Objectives

- To combine simple sentences to make writing smoother and less repetitive
- To combine sentences by inserting word groups preceded by *who, that,* or *which*
- To use punctuation correctly when adding word groups for sentence combining

Integrating . . .

Writing and Language Remind students that in the Writer's Workshop they wrote a news story based on cause and effect relationships. Explain that part of their success lies in writing sentences that show readers the events have a cause and effect relationship. Write these sentences on the chalkboard:

Rebecca did not finish reading the Shakespearean play.
She was not eligible for free tickets at Summer Theater.

Ask students how the above sentences could be combined to show a cause and effect relationship. Students might suggest the following:

Because Rebecca did not finish reading the Shakespearean play, she was not eligible for free tickets at Summer Theater.

Explain to students that the word *because* signals a cause and effect relationship. This Language Workshop focuses on combining sentences to show relationships among ideas.

LANGUAGE WORKSHOP

SENTENCE COMBINING II

You already know that combining sentences can make your writing smoother and less repetitive. You learned in an earlier workshop how to combine sentences in two ways: (1) by using the conjunctions *and, or,* and *but,* and (2) by inserting a key word or phrase from one sentence into another. Here are some other ways to combine sentences.

Inserting Word Groups

Use *who* to add information about a person or a group of persons. Use *that* or *which* to add information about a place, an idea, or a thing.

William Shakespeare was a British playwright. He wrote the play *Julius Caesar.*

William Shakespeare, who wrote the play *Julius Caesar,* was a British playwright.

You can see that there are commas around the *who* clause in the combined sentence. This is because the clause supplies additional information but is not absolutely necessary to explain who William Shakespeare was. A reader could read the sentence without the clause and not wonder whom the writer is talking about. Now look at another combined sentence.

John Doe was the British playwright. He wrote the play *Cheese Nose.*

John Doe was the British playwright *who* wrote the play *Cheese Nose.*

No commas are needed around the clause beginning with *who* in this combined sentence. The clause is essential to the meaning of the sentence because it helps identify John Doe. Without the clause, the reader might ask, "The British playwright who did what?"

One trick for remembering which kind of clause requires commas is to think about it this way: The commas form handles that the writer can use to pluck the clause out of the sentence. The writer can do this because the clause is not necessary.

Additional Resources

UNIT SIX RESOURCE BOOK

Language Workshop Copy Master, p. 22

ENRICHMENT MATERIALS

Grammar and Usage Copy Masters

Two other words that can be used to combine word groups are *that* and *which.* Use *which* in a clause that is not essential to the meaning of the sentence. Use *that* in a clause that is essential to the meaning of the sentence.

> Rome was a huge empire two thousand years ago. Caesar ruled the Roman Empire.
>
> Rome, *which* was a huge empire two thousand years ago, was ruled by Caesar.

Because the added information is not necessary to the sentence, the writer used *which* and set the clause off with commas. A clause beginning with *which* always requires a comma. A clause beginning with *that* never requires a comma.

> Calpurnia had a dream. The dream kept Caesar at home that morning.
>
> The dream *that* Calpurnia had kept Caesar at home that morning.

The added information in the combined sentence tells which dream kept Caesar at home, so the writer used *that.*

Exercise 1 Combine each pair of sentences by eliminating the word in italics. Remember to use correct punctuation.

1. Brutus plotted against Caesar. *Brutus* pretended to be Caesar's friend. (Use *who* and commas.)
2. Cassius joins with Brutus to plot Caesar's murder. *Cassius* has no sense of humor. (Use *who* and commas.)
3. The senator is Cicero. *Cicero* hears Casca's warnings on the stormy night. (Use *who* and no commas.)
4. The Globe Theatre was a typical Elizabethan theater. *The Globe Theatre* was built for outdoor performances. (Use *which* and commas.)
5. Friendship is one of the themes of this play. *Friendship* is sometimes false. (Use *that* and no commas.)

Showing Relationships

When two sentences contain related ideas, you can often combine them by using a combining word that shows *when, why,* and *under what conditions* something occurs.

Teaching Strategies

Ask a volunteer to read the material in the *Focus* box on page 842. Remind students that sentence combining can be used to make writing smoother and less repetitious and to show relationships among ideas.

Work through the lesson, but stop before students begin the exercises. Explain to students that writers vary sentence structure to add interest and coherence to their work and to help readers see relationships among ideas. You might want to compare a piece of writing to a piece of music. The same verbal rhythm or musical beat throughout would be dull and monotonous.

Have students, working in pairs, write sentences that use *who* to add information about a person or a group of persons and *that* or *which* to add information about a place, an idea, or a thing. One partner writes two simple sentences and the other combines them using, *who, which,* or *that.* Have partners then switch roles and repeat the activity. Tell them that the primary focus should be to show relationships between or among ideas. Ask partners to share their sentences and compare the many variations.

Assign the exercises. Have students refer to the instructional lesson on their pages as they proceed through the exercises. You may wish to teach a mini-lesson on pronouns if students have difficulty with this concept. Use Section 3 of the **Language Handbook** on page 899.

Teaching Tip: LEP

Encourage students to read the sentences in the exercises aloud to hear how the sentences sound together. After they combine the sentences, have them say the sentence out loud again, this time noting the changes that were made due to the combining. Distribute LEP students throughout the groups formed to complete Exercises 1–2. Allow students to help each other as they proceed through the exercises.

Closure

Before completing the Unit 6 subunit, be sure that students have internalized these concepts:

- Sentences can be combined to make one's writing smoother and less repetitive and to show relationships among ideas.
- Sentences can be combined by inserting word groups preceded by *who, that,* and *which.*
- Punctuation is sometimes needed when adding word groups for sentence combining.

Answer Key
Exercise 1

1. Brutus, who plotted against Caesar, pretended to be Caesar's friend.
2. Cassius, who has no sense of humor, joins with Brutus to plot Caesar's murder.
3. Cicero is the senator who hears Casca's warnings on the stormy night.
4. The Globe Theatre, which was a typical Elizabethan theatre, was built for outdoor performances.
5. Friendship that is sometimes false is one of the themes of this play.

Exercise 2

Compare group answers. Point out any variations in rewritten paragraphs.

Reminders

You can use words that show relationships—such as *when, after, because,* and *although*—to vary your sentence beginnings. See the workshop **Varying Sentence Beginnings** for more help.

Here are some words that can express relationships of *time, cause,* and *condition.*

Time	Cause	Condition
after	because	if
until	since	unless
while		whether

Words such as *when, after,* and *before* show when something happened. Words like *because* and *since* show why something happened. You can use words like *although* and *if* to explain under what conditions something occurred. Notice how the combining word shows the connection between two ideas in the following sentences:

Caesar was murdered. Caesar returned as a ghost.

After Caesar was murdered, he returned as a ghost.

Brutus pretended to be Caesar's friend. Brutus wanted to take Caesar by surprise.

Brutus pretended to be Caesar's friend *because* he wanted to take Caesar by surprise.

Notice that you can choose to reverse the order of the ideas when you use a word to combine them.

Brutus felt remorse as Caesar lay dying. Brutus planned Caesar's murder.

Although Brutus planned Caesar's murder, he felt remorse as Caesar lay dying.

Word groups that explain *when, why,* and *under what conditions* are called **subordinate clauses.** Sometimes the subordinate clause may be placed at the beginning of the sentence, followed by a comma.

Although he had control of the Roman Empire, Caesar could be betrayed by a single man.

Exercise 2 Work in a small group to combine each pair of sentences, using the word enclosed in parentheses. Eliminate the boldfaced words or replace them with pronouns.

1. Shakespeare was the greatest of all English playwrights. He grew up in a working-class family and had little schooling. (although) 2. Shakespeare wrote plays that have been performed around the world for five hundred years. **Shakespeare** was born and raised in a small town in England. (who) 3. His plays are about human emotions. **These emotions** are experienced by everyone. (that) 4. Shakespeare's plays were commercially successful in his day. **Shakespeare's plays** appealed to everyone. (which) 5. Some individuals believe that Shakespeare could not have written these plays. **Shakespeare** did not have much formal education. (because) 6. These individuals express this lack of faith in natural abilities. They are being close-minded. (when)

Language Handbook

For review and practice, see Section 1, **Writing Complete Sentences,** and Section 7, **Sentence Structure.**

Additional Practice

The following items are additional exercises to help students with inserting word groups to combine sentences and sentence parts.

Combine these sentence pairs with *who, that,* or *which.*

1. The Romans became great rulers. They learned from the Greeks. *(. . . Romans, who learned from the Greeks, became . . .)*

2. The ancient Romans built the Appian Way. It connected Rome to other cities in the empire. *(. . . Appian Way, which connected . . .)*

Combine these sentences to show the relationships between their parts.

3. The Battle of Philippi was fought. Antony became one of the rulers of Rome. *(After the Battle . . .)*

4. Caesar went to the capitol. Calpurnia had a bad dream. *(Before Caesar went . . .)*

5. Caesar had stayed home. The course of history might have been different. *(If Caesar . . . home, the course . . .)*

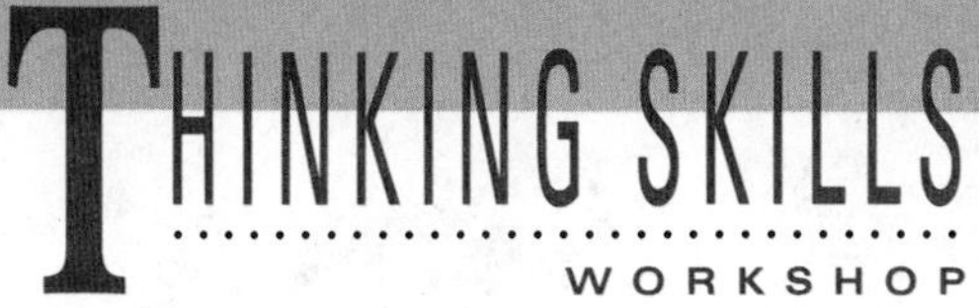

CRITICAL VIEWING

When you listen to the news on television, you are engaged in one-way listening. You only have one opportunity to grasp what is being said.

It is important to be aware of how television producers use special techniques to get more viewers to watch their news programs. As a part of the audience, you must learn to distinguish fact from opinion.

Since much of the information on current events comes through television newscasts, you need to be able to view and listen to the news accurately and critically. Keep the following points in mind:

1. **The whole story has not been told.** Because of time limitations, TV news shows present summaries and simplified versions of events. Make a habit of asking yourself what facts may have been omitted and what other information you need.
2. **Most issues and problems are not as simple as they appear.** TV reports frequently contrast two extreme views on an issue. However, there are more than two sides to most issues.
3. **Strong emotions and visual images can fool you.** News reports often focus, through both words and pictures, on people who are angry, hurt, or victimized. Realize that your feelings don't always help you to use sound judgment.
4. **News that seems too good (or bad) to be true must be questioned.** News reporters try to create a sense of excitement, but sometimes they stretch the truth in doing so.
5. **News reports may contain hidden editorializing.** "Hidden editorializing" means that opinion is represented as fact. Sometimes news stations present one-sided views of events unintentionally because they have time to present only a small part of a story.

Exercise Choose a current event that interests you. Prepare a list of questions you have about the situation. Then do a survey of how the event is being portrayed on television networks, in newspapers, and in radio news broadcasts. Watch three prime-time news shows, including one on public television. Write a short essay on whether it makes sense to depend exclusively on television as a news source. Try to conclude which medium answered your questions most thoroughly. In your essay, rate the various media and networks on how much they seem to present opinion as fact.

Thinking Skills Workshop

Objective

- To become aware of the way information is presented in television news reports

Integrating . . .

Literature and Thinking Skills
Share with students that following the guidelines will help them become critical viewers.

Teaching Strategies

Ask students what the purpose of television news should be. *(Possible response: Television news should give clear, concise, factual information about world events.)* Ask them to assess the importance of television news to viewers, and discuss the negative impact that subjective television reporting can have. *(Possible response: If people are misinformed, they may make poor decisions.)*

Read through the material with students. Assign the exercise on page 845.

Closure

Before beginning the next subunit, be sure students have internalized these concepts:

- Sometimes information is omitted from television news reports.
- Most issues are more complex than they seem on television.
- News reports may focus on the emotions in a situation rather than the facts.
- There may be hidden editorializing in a news report.

Teaching Tip
Students can use video recordings of themselves as "reporters" along with footage recorded from news programs to create an exposé of the television news industry.

Exercise
(Answers will vary. Check to see that students surveyed all three media.)

Additional Resources
UNIT SIX RESOURCE BOOK
Related Skills Copy, p. 20

ADDITIONAL PRACTICE

Choose another issue that interests you, and choose three different news magazines for your survey. Again, conclude which of the three treated the issue most completely. Write a short essay in which you generalize about the editorial philosophy of each magazine.

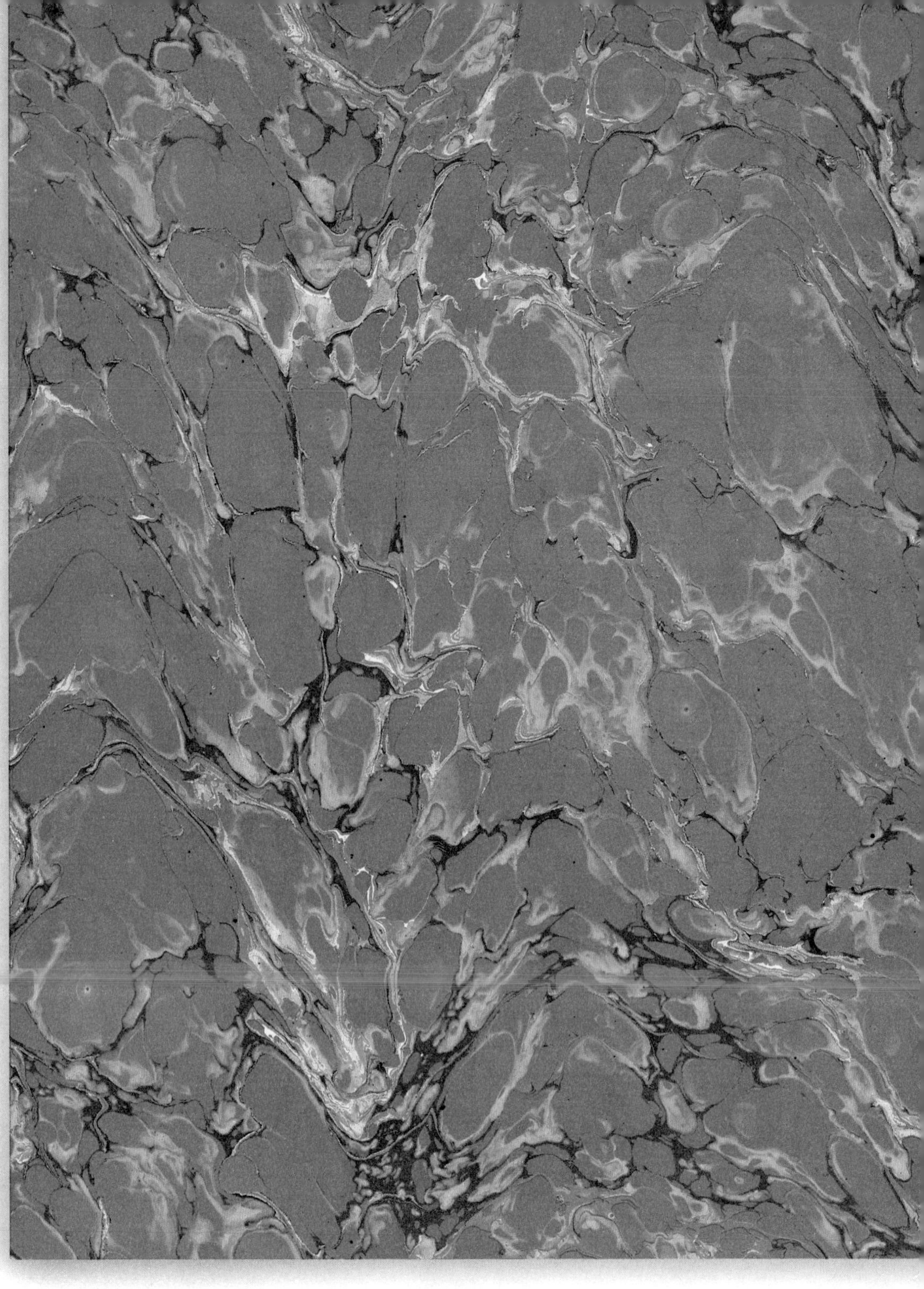

Handbook Contents

GLOSSARY

The **glossary** is an alphabetical listing of words from the selections, with meanings. The glossary gives the following information:

1. **The entry word broken into syllables.**
2. **The pronunciation of each word.** The **respelling** is shown in parentheses. The Pronunciation Key on the next page shows the symbols for the sounds of letters and key words that contain those sounds.

   A **primary accent** ′ is placed after the syllable that is stressed the most when the word is spoken. A **secondary accent** ′ is placed after a syllable that has a lighter stress.
3. **The part of speech of the word.** These abbreviations are used:

   n. noun *v.* verb *adj.* adjective *adv.* adverb
4. **The meaning of the word.** The definitions listed in the glossary apply to selected ways a word is used in these selections.
5. **Related forms.** Words with suffixes such as *-ing, -ed, -ness,* and *-ly* are often listed under the base word.

1. entry word **2. respelling**
3. part of speech **4. meaning**

def er en tial (def′ ər en′ shəl) *adj.* showing courteous regard or respect

Pronunciation Key

Symbol	Key Words	Symbol	Key Words	Symbol	Key Words	Symbol	Key Words
a	**a**t, g**a**s	**o͞o**	t**oo**l, cr**ew**		**a** in **a**go	**ch**	**ch**in
ā	**a**pe, d**ay**	**o͝o**	l**oo**k, p**u**ll		**e** in ag**e**nt	**sh**	**sh**e
ä	c**a**r, l**o**t	**yo͞o**	**u**se, c**u**te, f**ew**	**ə**	**i** in san**i**ty	**th**	**th**in
e	**e**lf, t**e**n	**yo͝o**	c**u**re		**o** in c**o**mply	***th***	**th**en
ē	**e**ven, m**e**	**oi**	**oi**l, c**oi**n		**u** in foc**u**s	**zh**	lei**s**ure
i	**i**s, h**i**t	**ou**	**ou**t, s**ou**r			**ŋ**	ri**ng**
ī	b**i**te, f**i**re	**u**	**u**p, c**u**t	**ər**	p**er**haps, murd**er**	**'**	**a**ble (ā'b'l)
ō	**o**wn, g**o**	**ur**	f**ur**, b**ir**d				
ô	l**aw**, h**o**rn						
			Foreign Symbols	**à**	s**a**lle	***n***	mo**n**
				ë	c**oeu**r	**ô̂**	abuel**o**s
				ö	f**eu**	***r***	grin**g**os
				ü	r**u**e		

A

a breast (ə brest') *adv.* alongside

ab stain (ab stān') *v.* to withhold one's vote in an election or a group decision

a byss (ə bis') *n.* a depth that seems beyond measurement

ad dle (ad' 'l) *v.* to confuse

a dept (ə dept') *adj.* skilled; expert

ad mo ni tion (ad' mə nish' ən) *n.* a mild warning

ad ver sar y (ad' vər ser'ē) *n.* an opponent

ad ver si ty (ad vur' sə tē) *n.* hardship

aer o nau ti cal (er' ō nôt' i kəl) *adj.* having to do with airplanes

af flu ent (af' lo͞o ənt) *adj.* wealthy or rich

al cove (al' kōv') *n.* a section of a room that is recessed and set apart

al i bi (al' ə bī') *n.* a story told by an accused criminal that supposedly proves he or she was somewhere else at the time of the crime

a men i ty (ə men' ə tē) *n.* anything that adds to one's comfort or convenience

a mi a ble (ā' mē ə bəl) *adj.* appearing friendly and pleasant

an ar chist (an' ər kist') *n.* someone who challenges society's rules or accepted standards of behavior

a non y mous (ə nän' ə məs) *adj.* lacking unique features

an ti quat ed (an' ti kwāt' id) *adj.* old or obsolete

ap a thet i cal ly (ap' ə thet' ik lē) *adv.* without enthusiasm

ap palled (ə pôld') *adj.* shocked **appall** *v.*

ap pre hen sion (ap' rē hen' shən) *n.* an uneasy feeling; anxiety

a skew (ə skyo͞o') *adv.* to one side

au da cious ly (ô dā' shəs lē) *adv.* boldly

au ra (ô' rə) *n.* a quality that seems to surround a person

B

baf fle (baf' əl) *v.* to confuse

bel lig er ent ly (bə lij' ər ənt lē) *adv.* in a quarrelsome way

ben e fac tor (ben' ə fak' tər) *n.* a person who gives help, especially financial aid

be nev o lent ly (bə nev' ə lənt lē) *adv.* kindly

be wil der ment (bē wil' dər mənt) *n.* confusion

big ot ry (big' ə trē) *n.* narrow-minded behavior or opinions; prejudice

bog (bäg) *n.* soggy ground; a swamp

bond age (bän' dij) *n.* a way of limiting one's freedom to move around

bra va do (brə vä′ dō) *n.* pretending to have courage when one really has little or none

C

cache (kash) *n.* a place where food or supplies are hidden

ca coph o ny (kə käf′ ə nē) *n.* loud, jarring sound

ca pri cious (kə prish′ əs) *adj.* unpredictable; erratic

ca ress (kə res′) *n.* a gentle or affectionate touch

car i ca ture (kar′ i kə chər) *n.* a picture that exaggerates certain characteristics

cas cade (kas kād′) *v.* to fall like a waterfall

cat a stroph ic (kat′ə sträf′ ik) *adj.* disastrous on a huge scale

cen trif u gal (sen trif′ yo͞o gəl) *adj.* displaying a tendency to move away from the center

clam or (klam′ ər) *n.* a loud complaint

co er cion (kō ʉr′ shən) *n.* the act of forcing someone to do something through the use of power

co her ent ly (kō hir′ ənt lē) *adv.* in a manner showing clear thinking and understandable speech

com mence (kə mens′) *v.* to begin

com mis er ate (kə miz′ ər āt′) *v.* to express pity; sympathize

com mu nal (käm′ yo͞o nəl) *adj.* of or in a group of people living together

com pact (käm′ pakt) *n.* treaty, agreement between two parties

com pen sa tion (käm′ pən sā′ shən) *n.* anything given to make up for something else

com pro mis ing (käm′ prə mīz′ iŋ) *adj.* causing suspicion; risky **compromise** *v.*

con ceiv a ble (kən sēv′ ə bəl) *adj.* believable; able to be imagined or accepted

con ces sion (kən sesh′ ən) *n.* a privilege granted

con do lence (kən dō′ ləns) *n.* something said or otherwise communicated to show sympathy and understanding to another who is suffering

con done (kən dōn′) *v.* to overlook an offense; forgive

con duit (kän′ do͞o it) *n.* a pipe that holds fluids or electric wires

con geal (kən jēl′) *v.* to thicken

con jec ture (kən jek′ chər) *n.* speculation; guess

con sci en tious (kän′ shē en′ shəs) *adj.* having a sense of what is right

con spic u ous (kən spik′ yo͞o əs) *adj.* easy to see; obvious

con tem plate (kän′ təm plāt′) *v.* to look at closely; to think about

con tempt (kən tempt′) *n.* a feeling of scorn toward someone or something

con tri tion (kən trish′ ən) *n.* a bad or guilty feeling from having done something wrong

con verse ly (kən vʉrs′ lē) *adv.* in the opposite way; vice versa

con vic tion (kən vik′ shən) *n.* strong belief or opinion

cor dial (kôr′ jəl) *adj.* warm, friendly

cor ru gat ed (kôr′ ə gāt′ id) *adj.* folded to form a wavy surface

cowed (koud) *adj.* timid; frightened **cow** *v.*

cre scen do (kri shen′ dō′) *n.* a gradual increase in loudness

cul ti vat ed (kul′ tə vāt′ id) *adj.* refined and cultured

curt (kʉrt) *adj.* brief; in a manner of being to the point

cyn i cal (sin′ i kəl) *adj.* possessing a negative attitude; sneering

D

de bris (də brē′) *n.* trash, litter, or bits of rubbish

de fend ant (dē fen′ dənt) *n.* in a court case, the person accused of a crime

def er ence (def′ ər əns) *n.* respect for the wishes or opinion of another

deft ly (deft′ lē) *adv.* skillfully

de grad ing (dē grād′ iŋ) *adj.* that which lowers dignity **degrade** *v.*

de lir i um (di lir′ ē əm) *n.* a state of mental confusion

de mise (dē mīz′) *n.* death

de plor a ble (dē plôr′ ə bəl) *adj.* extremely regrettable

des e crat ed (des′ i krāt′ id) *adj.* treated disrespectfully **desecrate** *v.*

des o late (des′ ə lit) *adj.* lonely and sad

des ti tute (des′ tə to͞ot′) *n.* those without food, clothing, and shelter

de void (di void′) *adj.* completely without

di lat ing (dī′ lāt′ iŋ) *adj.* expanding **dilate** *v.*

dis arm (dis ärm′) *v.* to remove suspicions

dis claim er (dis klām′ ər) *n.* a refusal to accept responsibility **disclaim** *v.*

dis creet (di skrēt′) *adj.* careful about what one says or does

dis crep an cy (di skrep′ ən sē) *n.* lack of agreement

dis crim i na tion (di skrim' i nā' shən) *n.* the act of showing favoritism or differential treatment; bias

dis dain (dis dān') *n.* contempt

dis il lu sion (dis' i lo͞o' zhən) *v.* to make disappointed and, therefore, no longer interested or involved

dis pir it (di spir' it) *v.* to discourage

dis po si tion (dis' pə zish' ən) *n.* frame of mind; mood

dis tract ed (di strakt' id) *adj.* having one's attention drawn away from **distract** *v.*

dis traught (di strôt') *adj.* extremely upset or driven mad

do main (dō mān') *n.* an area under one person's rule or one group's control

dour (do͝or) *adj.* gloomy; forbidding

drone (drōn) *v.* to talk in a monotonous, boring manner

drudge (druj) *n.* someone who performs difficult, thankless work

du bi ous (do͞o' bē əs) *adj.* hesitating; doubtful

dy na mo (dī' nə mō') *n.* a machine that generates electricity

E

ec stat ic (ek stat' ik) *adj.* joyful

ee rie (ir' ē) *adj.* weird, scary

e mit (ē mit') *v.* to give forth or send out

en croach ing (en krōch' iŋ) *adj.* advancing **encroach** *v.*

en cum brance (en kum' brəns) *n.* a burden or hindrance

en ter prise (ent' ər prīz') *n.* an undertaking or project

e nun ci a tion (ē nun' sē ā' shən) *n.* the pronouncing of words distinctly

e pit o me (ē pit' ə mē') *n.* the ideal or essence of a particular quality

er rat ic (er rat' ik) *adj.* uncertain, irregular

es o ter ic (es' ə ter' ik) *adj.* beyond the understanding or knowledge of most people

et i quette (et' i kit) *n.* accepted behavior

ex clu sive (eks klo͞o' siv) *adj.* private; not admitting others

ex ploi ta tion (eks' ploi tā' shən) *n.* the taking advantage of something for one's own advantage or profit

F

fal set to (fôl set' ō) *adj.* unusually high-pitched

fawn ing (fôn' iŋ) *adj.* affectionate; flattering

fer vent (fʉr' vənt) *adj.* strongly felt and expressed

fi nite (fī' nīt') *adj.* having a beginning and an ending

flay (flā) *v.* to whip

for ay (fôr' ā) *n.* a raid or hunt

for lorn ness (fôr lôrn' nes) *n.* hopelessness; sadness; feelings of abandonment **forlorn** *adj.*

forte (fôrt) *n.* something a person does especially well

fret (fret) *v.* to worry

fur row (fʉr' ō) *n.* a long, narrow groove cut in the earth by a plow

fu se lage (fyo͞o' sə lij') *n.* the body of an airplane

fu tile (fyo͞ot' 'l) *adj.* useless; hopeless

G

gaud y (gôd' ē) *adj.* cheap and showy; in poor taste

gen i al ly (jēn' yəl lē) *adv.* in a friendly way

graph i cal ly (graf' ik lē) *adv.* vividly, realistically

gri mac ing (gri' mis iŋ) *adj.* distorting one's face because of pain, disgust, or anger **grimace** *v.*

gro tesque (grō tesk') *adj.* characterized by distorted shapes; twisted, strange

H

hag gard (hag' ərd) *adj.* disheveled and worn in appearance

ha rangu ing (hə raŋ' iŋ) *adj.* delivering a lengthy, noisy, or scolding speech **harangue** *v.*

ha ven (hā' vən) *n.* a place of shelter or safety

hone (hōn) *v.* to sharpen on a strop or whetstone

hos tile (häs' təl) *adj.* unfriendly and warlike

hu mil i ty (hyo͞o mil' ə tē) *n.* the absence of vanity

I

im per a tive (im per' ə tiv) *adj.* commanding; having a forceful nature

im per cep ti bly (im' pər sep' tə blē) *adv.* without being noticed

im per ti nence (im pʉrt' 'n əns) *n.* the quality of not showing proper respect

im pos ing (im pō' ziŋ) *adj.* impressive

im po tent (im' pə tənt) *adj.* powerless or ineffective

im pov er ished (im päv' ər isht) *adj.* poor

im promp tu (im prämp′ to͞o′) *adj.* without preparation or forethought
im pru dent (im pro͞od′ ′nt) *adj.* showing poor judgment
in car na tion (in′ kär nā′ shən) *n.* a person or thing representing a particular concept
in con gru ous (in käŋ′ gro͞o əs) *adj.* not fitting; unsuitable
in crim i nate (in krim′ i nāt′) *v.* to make appear guilty of a crime or fault
in do lent ly (in′ də lənt lē) *adv.* lazily
in dom i ta ble (in däm′ i tə bəl) *adj.* strong; undefeatable
in ert (in ʉrt′) *adj.* inactive; motionless
in ev i ta ble (in ev′ i tə bəl) *adj.* unavoidable
in ex o ra ble (in eks′ ə rə bəl) *adj.* impossible to influence, change, or persuade
in fer nal (in fʉr′ nəl) *adj.* hellish; fiendish
in fir ma ry (in fʉr′ mə rē) *n.* a room or building where the sick or injured are cared for
in gen ious (in jēn′ yəs) *adj.* clever or inventive
in sol u ble (in säl′ yo͞o bəl) *adj.* unsolvable
in ter sti ces (in tʉr′ stə siz′) *n.* cracks; crevices
in tim i date (in tim′ ə dāt′) *v.* to make afraid; overpower
in tri cate (in′ tri kit) *adj.* full of complex detail
in val i date (in val′ ə dāt′) *v.* to take away the legal value of something
in var i a ble (in ver′ ē ə bəl) *adj.* constant or unchanging
in vin ci ble (in vin′ sə bəl) *adj.* unbeatable
in vol un tar y (in väl′ ən ter′ ē) *adj.* unintentional; accidental
i rate (ī rāt′) *adj.* very angry; incensed

L

la bo ri ous (lə bôr′ ē əs) *adj.* requiring much work; difficult
loom (lo͞om) *n.* a machine for weaving thread into cloth
lu di crous (lo͞o′ di krəs) *adj.* ridiculous
lu rid (lo͞or′ id) *adj.* violently passionate; shocking

M

ma lev o lence (mə lev′ ə ləns) *n.* a feeling of ill will or hatred toward others
mal func tion (mal fuŋk′ shən) *n.* a failure to operate properly
ma li cious (mə lish′ əs) *adj.* hateful; intended to do harm
man date (man′ dāt′) *v.* to order with authority; to require
maud lin (môd′ lin) *adj.* foolishly sentimental; corny
me an der ing (mē an′ dər i) *adj.* following a random, winding path
mel an chol y (mel′ ən käl′ ē) *n.* gloom; depression
men ace (men′ əs) *n.* threat
mis con cep tion (mis′ kən sep′ shən) *n.* a mistaken idea or belief
mock (mäk) *adj.* false; imitation
mo men tous (mō men′ təs) *adj.* very important
mo nop o ly (mə näp′ ə lē) *n.* complete control of the sale of a product or service
mo not o nous (mə nät′ ′n əs) *adj.* lacking variety; tiresome
mo tive (mōt′ iv) *n.* reason for doing something

N

na ive (nä ēv′) *adj.* unsophisticated
nape (nāp) *n.* the back of the neck
non cha lant ly (nän′ shə länt′ lē) *adv.* casually; unemotionally
no to ri ous (nō tôr′ ē əs) *adj.* well-known, but in an unfavorable way; infamous

O

ob liv i on (ə bliv′ ē ən) *n.* nothingness
ob scure (əb skyoor′) *v.* to conceal from view
ob ses sive (əb ses′ iv) *adj.* having the nature of an abnormal preoccupation with some feeling or idea
o men (ō′ mən) *n.* a thing or event which foretells the future
om i nous (äm′ ə nəs) *adj.* threatening
o paque ness (ō pāk′ nəs) *n.* the quality of not letting light pass through
or tho pe dics (ôr′ thō pē′ diks) *n.* the branch of medicine dealing with the bones and joints
o ver com pen sate (ō′ vər käm′ pən sāt′) *v.* to make more than the necessary adjustment or action
o ver wrought (ō′ vər rôt′) *adj.* overexcited; upset; hysterical

P

pa tron iz ing (pā′ trən īz′ i) *adj.* in a haughty, snobbish, or superior manner **patronize** *v.*
pen sive ly (pen′ siv lē) *adv.* in a thoughtful manner
per vade (pər vād′) *v.* to spread throughout
per verse (pər vʉrs′) *adj.* improper or wicked

phi lan thro pist (fə lan′ thrə pist) *n.* a person, often wealthy, who donates gifts to charities and humanitarian institutions
pit e ous ly (pit′ ē əs lē) *adv.* in a way to arouse pity and understanding
plac id ly (plas′ id lē) *adv.* peacefully
plait ed (plāt′ id) *adj.* braided or interwoven **plait** *v.*
plau si bil i ty (plô′ zə bil′ ə tē) *n.* believability
plum met ing (plum′ it i) *adj.* falling or dropping very quickly **plummet** *v.*
plun der (plun′ dər) *v.* to take property by force for one's own purposes
poign ant ly (poin′ yənt lē) *adv.* in a painful or sensitive manner
pre car i ous ly (prē ker′ ē əs lē) *adv.* in a risky or dangerous manner
pred a to ry (pred′ ə tôr′ ē) *adj.* robbing, exploiting, or killing others
preen ing (prēn′ i) *adj.* primping; grooming and dressing oneself in a fussy way **preen** *v.*
pre tense (prē tens′) *n.* a false claim or show
prod i gy (präd′ ə jē) *n.* a person, particularly a child, with awe-inspiring talent
prom i nent (präm′ ə nənt) *adj.* noticeable
pro pri e tor (prō prī′ ə tər) *n.* a person who owns and manages a business
pro pri e ty (prō prī′ ə tē) *n.* the quality of being proper according to accepted standards
pros e cu tion (präs′ i kyōō′ shən) *n.* in a criminal case, the side that brings the case against a person accused of committing a crime
pro trud ing (prō trōōd′ i) *adj.* sticking or jutting out **protrude** *v.*
pul ver ize (pul′ vər īz′) *v.* to crush or destroy
pun gent (pun′ jənt) *adj.* having a strong smell

Q

quad ran gle (kwä′ dra ′ gəl) *n.* an area, at a school or college, that is surrounded on four sides by buildings
quar ry (kwôr′ ē) *n.* prey; an animal being hunted, often with the help of dogs or hawks
quest (kwest) *n.* a search or hunt for something

R

ra tion (rash′ ən) *n.* to distribute in fixed amounts
rav en ous ly (rav′ ə nəs lē) *adv.* hungrily; greedily
ra vine (rə vēn′) *n.* a deep ditch worn in the earth's surface by a stream
re cal ci trant (ri kal′ si trənt) *adj.* unruly and stubbornly defiant of authority
re fur bish ment (ri fur′ bish mənt) *n.* a polishing up; renovation
re gime (rə zhēm′) *n.* a political or ruling system
re ju ve nate (ri jōō′ və nāt′) *v.* to bring back to youth or strength
rep li ca (rep′ li kə) *n.* a reproduction
re proach ful ly (ri prōch′ fə lē) *adv.* accusingly
res o lute (rez′ ə lōōt′) *adj.* determined; steady
re tal i ate (ri tal′ ē āt′) *v.* to strike back as return for an injury
re tract ing (ri trakt′ i) *n.* the act of drawing in from an extended position **retract** *v.*
ret ri bu tion (re′ trə byōō′ shən) *n.* punishment for a wrongdoing
rheu ma tism (rōō′ mə tiz′ əm) *n.* an inflammation and stiffness of the joints and muscles
ro bust (rō bust′) *adj.* strong, healthy
rub bish (rub′ ish) *n.* worthless material; trash
ru di men ta ry (rōō′ də men′ tər ē) *adj.* underdeveloped; of the most simple kind
rue ful ly (rōō′ fəl lē) *adv.* in a way that shows regret over some previous comment or action
ruse (rōōz) *n.* a trick

S

sad ist (sād′ ist) *n.* a person who gets pleasure from hurting others
scorched (skôrcht) *adj.* burned or parched by heat **scorch** *v.*
scoun drel (skoun′ drəl) *n.* a mean or wicked person
se rene (sə rēn′) *n.* peaceful; calm
shrewd (shrōōd) *adj.* cunning; clever
smol der (smōl′ dər) *v.* to burn and smoke without flame
so pra no (sə pran′ ō) *n.* the highest singing voice
sor did (sôr′ did) *adj.* despicable; grasping
spec i men (spes′ ə mən) *n.* a sample or example of a whole group
spo rad i cal ly (spə rad′ ik lē) *adv.* now and then; not in a regular, dependable way
squal or (skwäl′ ər) *n.* filth; dirtiness
squeam ish (skwēm′ ish) *adj.* easily nauseated
stam i na (stam′ ə nə) *n.* the ability to do a great deal without getting tired
stark (stärk) *adj.* sheer and utter
sta tion ar y (stā′ shə ner′ ē) *adj.* not moving; still

stealth i ly (stelth′ ə lē) *adv.* in a secretive manner
sto i cism (stō′ i siz′ əm) *n.* the act of not showing emotion
stol id (stäl′ id) *adj.* firm or unemotional
strick en (strik′ ən) *adj.* suffering from hurt or pain
stu por (sto͞o′ pər) *n.* a state in which one's mind is dulled or senseless
suave (swäv) *adj.* having a smooth manner
sub dued (sub do͞od′) *adj.* hiding or holding back one's feelings **subdue** *v.*
sub mis sive (sub mis′ iv) *adj.* displaying no resistance
sub side (səb sīd′) *v.* to pull back, quiet down
suc ces sive (sək ses′ iv) *adj.* following one after another
sulk i ly (sul′ kə lē) *adv.* in a resentful or glum manner
sur mise (sər mīz′) *v.* to guess or conclude
swath (swäth) *n.* a long strip of cloth
syn thet ic (sin thet′ ik) *adj.* not natural; artificial

T

tan gi ble (tan′ jə bəl) *adj.* that can be felt by touch; having actual form
taunt (tônt) *v.* to provoke or tease
taw ny (tô′ nē) *adj.* tan-colored
tem pes tu ous (tem pes′ cho͞o əs) *adj.* violent or stormy
ten e ment (ten′ ə mənt) *n.* an apartment building; often a very old and run-down building
ten ta tive ly (ten′ tə tiv lē) *adv.* with hesitation or uncertainty
tran quil (tran′ kwil) *adj.* calm, not agitated
trem or (trem′ ər) *n.* a shaking or trembling motion
tri fle (trī′ fəl) *n.* a small amount
tur bu lent (tur′ byo͞o lənt) *adj.* violently agitated; stormy
tyr an ny (tir′ ə nē) *n.* harshness; cruel or unjust use of power

U

un scru pu lous (un skro͞o′ pyə ləs) *adj.* not concerned with what is right
ur chin (ur′ chin) *n.* a small child

V

val or (val′ ər) *n.* bravery or courage
va por (vā′ pər) *n.* any visible moisture or gas, such as mist, fog, smoke, or steam
vault (vôlt) *v.* to leap over
veered (vird) *adj.* turned away **veer** *v.*
vig i lance (vij′ ə ləns) *n.* watchfulness
vin dic tive (vin dik′ tiv) *adj.* revengeful
vir tu ous (vur′ cho͞o əs) *adj.* righteous
vo li tion (vō lish′ ən) *n.* will or choice

W

whorl (hwôrl) *n.* anything that appears to whirl in circles, such as tufts of hair, or fingerprints; a spiral
wiz ened (wiz′ ənd) *adj.* shriveled; dried up
wrench (rench) *v.* to twist or pull violently
writh ing (rīth′ i) *adj.* twisting one's body around, usually in severe pain **writhe** *v.*

Y

yarn (yärn) *n.* an exaggerated story

Z

zeal ous (zel′ əs) *adj.* intensely devoted and enthusiastic

LITERARY TERMS

Act An act is a major unit of action in a play. Acts in a play are comparable to chapters in a book. Each act may contain several scenes. A one-act play usually has a small cast of characters. The plot centers on a single conflict that builds quickly to a climax. Louis Parker's *The Monkey's Paw* has only one act, while Shakespeare's *Julius Caesar* contains five acts.

Alliteration The repetition of consonant sounds at the beginning of two or more words is called alliteration. Poets use alliteration to emphasize words, to tie lines together, to reinforce tone and meaning, and to add sound effects. Note the alliteration of the *w* sound in Jenny Joseph's "Warning":

When I am an old woman I shall wear purple

Allusion An allusion is a reference to a well-known work of literature, person, place, thing, or event with which the reader is assumed to be familiar. In Act One, Scene 2, of *Julius Caesar,* Cassius makes an allusion to the Colossus, a statue of the Greek god Apollo.

Antagonist The antagonist of a short story, novel, drama, or narrative poem is the force working against the protagonist, or main character. The antagonist may be another character, society, nature, or an internal force within the protagonist.

See *Protagonist.*

Aside An aside is a remark spoken in an undertone by a character in a play. The remark is heard by the audience but not by the other characters on stage. Asides tell the audience what a character is thinking or feeling.

Assonance Assonance is the repetition of vowel sounds within two or more words. Notice the assonance of the long *o* sound in "Red Eagle" by Janet Campbell:

Red Eagle.
Cold, dead, noble Red Eagle,

Author's Purpose Authors write for any of four main purposes: to entertain, to inform, to express an opinion, or to persuade. An author may have several of these purposes for writing, but one is usually more important than the others.

Autobiographical Essay See *Autobiography.*

Autobiography An autobiography is a factual account of a person's life written by that person. It is usually written from the first-person point of view and is intended to give the reader insight into the person's character, feelings, and attitudes.

An autobiographical essay highlights certain events in the writer's life and reflects on how those events affected him or her. An example of an autobiographical essay is Daniel Inouye's "My Shirt Is for Church."

Biography A biography is a form of nonfiction in which a writer gives a factual account of someone else's life. A biography may tell about either a person's whole life or only a part of the person's life. It is written in the third person. "Survival in the Forty-Ninth" by John McPhee is a biographical piece.

Blank Verse Blank verse is unrhymed poetry with lines of ten syllables, five of which are accented. Each unaccented syllable, marked below with (˘), is followed by an accented one, marked below with (ʹ). Shakespeare's plays are written mainly in blank verse, as in this example from *Julius Caesar:* Act Two, Scene 1, lines 92-93.

I think we are too bold upon your rest.
Good morrow, Brutus. Do we trouble you?

See *Iambic Pentameter.*

Briticism A word or phrase that is peculiar to British English is called a Briticism. In the mystery "The Third Floor Flat" by Agatha Christie, the reader finds a number of Briticisms, such as *lift* fo elevator and *wonky* for crazy.

Cast of Characters In a play, the cast of characters is given at the beginning of the script, before the first act. It is a list of all the characters in the play, usually in order of appearance.

Catastrophe The resolution of the plot in a tragedy is called the catastrophe. It usually falls within the last act of a play and often involves the death of a hero, such as the suicide of Brutus in Act Five of *Julius Caesar.*

See *Tragedy.*

Character A character is a person or animal who takes part in the action of a work of literature. Generally, the plot of a story, novel, or play focuses on one or more main characters.

Main characters are those who are most important. The other characters are called **minor characters;** their most important role is to keep the plot moving along.

Characterization Characterization refers to the techniques a writer uses to create and develop a character. The reader learns about a character through the character's words, actions, and feelings; through descriptions of the character; and through what others in the work say about the character and how they react toward him or her.

Chronological Order The progression of events in the order in which they occur in time is called chronological order, or time order. Chronological order is a common way to organize the details in a piece of writing.

Climax The climax is the turning point in the plot of a literary work. It is at this peak of interest and intensity when the outcome of the conflict in the plot becomes clear. The climax usually results in a change in a character or a solution to a problem. The dramatic climax of *Julius Caesar,* for example, is the killing of Caesar.

See *Plot.*

Colloquialism Colloquialisms are informal words and phrases used in everyday conversation. An example is the word *litterbug* in Dave Barry's "A Couple of Really Neat Guys."

Comic Relief Comic relief is a humorous scene, incident, or speech that occurs in the course of a serious or tragic literary work. In drama, it is sometimes used to relieve the emotional intensity of a previous scene, as in Act Four, Scene 3, of *Julius Caesar* when a poet tries to break into the argument between Brutus and Cassius.

Conflict Conflict is the struggle between opposing forces that is the basis of the plot of a drama or work of fiction. **External conflict** occurs between a character and any force outside himself or herself, such as another character, society, or some force of nature. **Internal conflict** occurs when a character has an inner struggle within himself or herself, for example, when trying to make a decision. Some stories have multiple conflicts, or more than one conflict.

Connotation The emotional response that a word evokes is its connotation. This contrasts with its denotation, or simple dictionary definition. In "All Watched Over by Machines of Loving Grace," Richard Brautigan uses the word *cybernetic,* which means "comparing the brain to a computer." In addition to having this meaning, the word evokes the idea of something that is inhuman and sterile.

Consonance Consonance is the repetition of consonant sounds within and at the ends of words. The vowels that precede the like consonants differ, as in scream and lamb. An example of consonance is the *t* sound in "She Loved Him All Her Life" by Lynne Alvarez:

> She loved him all her life
> and when she thought he might die
> she tied her wrist to his at night
> so that his pulse would not flutter
> away from her suddenly
> and leave her stranded

Contrast Contrast is a stylistic technique in which one element is shown in opposition to another. These elements may be contrasting ideas or images, such as the two different views of Indian children in Juanita Bell's "Indian Children Speak."

Writers might use contrast to clarify ideas or to elicit an emotional response from the reader.

Denotation Denotation is the dictionary definition of a word.

See *Connotation.*

Description Description is writing that creates a picture of a scene, event, or character. To create description, writers often use sensory images—words and phrases that appeal to the reader's senses—and figurative language. Sometimes a description provides details about the actions or attitudes of a character. Notice the descriptive details in this passage from "Rules of the Game" by Amy Tan:

> At the end of our two-block alley was a small, sandlot playground with swings and slides well-shined down the middle with use. The play area was bordered by wood-slat benches, where old-country people sat cracking roasted watermelon seeds with their golden teeth and scattering the husks to an impatient gathering of gurgling pigeons.

See *Imagery* and *Figurative Language.*

Descriptive Details See *Description.*

Details See *Description* and *Sensory Details.*

Dialect Dialect is the particular variety of a language spoken in one geographical area by a certain group of people. Dialect includes the pronunciations, vocabulary, and grammatical constructions that are typical of a region. Notice the dialect in this example from Walter Dean Myer's "The Treasure of Lemon Brown":

> "What you doing here? How come you didn't go home when the rain come? Rain don't bother you young folks none."

Dialogue Dialogue is conversation between characters. It helps advance the plot and reveal the traits of the characters.

In drama the words each character says are written in lines next to the character's name, as in this excerpt from *Twelve Angry Men* by Reginald Rose. ("Four" refers to juror number four.)

> **Four.** If we're going to discuss this case, why, let's discuss the facts.
>
> **Foreman.** That's a good point. We have a job to do. Let's do it.

In other kinds of writing, the words each character speaks are commonly set off by quotation marks.

See *Internal Dialogue.*

Drama Drama is literature that is meant to be performed for an audience. In a drama, or play, actors play the roles of the characters, telling the story through words and actions. Like fiction, drama has four basic elements: character, setting, plot, and theme.

A drama is made up of one or more acts. Each act may contain several scenes. The script for a drama usually includes both a list of the characters and stage directions that tell the actors how to move or speak their lines. These directions also provide suggestions for special effects, music, lighting, and scenery.

See *Act, Cast of Characters, Dialogue, Scene,* and *Stage Directions.*

Essay An essay is a short nonfiction work that deals with one subject. In an essay the author might give an opinion, try to persuade, or simply narrate an interesting event. Harold Krents's "Darkness at Noon" is a persuasive essay.

Essays can also be formal or informal. Formal essays examine a topic in a thorough, serious, and highly organized manner. Informal essays are lighter in tone and reflect the writer's feelings and personality. An example of an informal essay is the excerpt from Robert Fulghum's *All I Really Need to Know I Learned in Kindergarten.* Some informal essays may also be humorous, such as Dave Barry's "A Couple of Really Neat Guys."

Exaggeration An exaggeration, or overstatement, is a statement in which a description of a person, event, or idea is magnified or overemphasized to an extreme degree. Writers often use exaggeration to emphasize a point. In Kurt Vonnegut's "The Euphio Question," the narrator momentarily sees his wife as "a dreadful, dirty old hag."

See *Hyperbole.*

Exposition The exposition in a drama or work of fiction is the part of the plot that provides background information and introduces the characters, setting, and conflict. The exposition usually occurs at the beginning of a literary work. The first four paragraphs of Joan Aiken's "Searching for Summer" introduce Lily, tell of the upcoming wedding, and introduce the main problem—a lack of sunshine and blue skies as a result of "the bombs."

See *Plot.*

External Conflict See *Conflict.*

Falling Action The falling action occurs after the climax in a work of fiction or drama and shows the effects of the climax, or turning point. As the falling action begins, the suspense is over but the results of the decision or action that caused the climax are not yet fully worked out.

See *Climax, Plot,* and *Resolution.*

Fiction Fiction refers to imaginative works of prose, including the novel and the short story. Even though fiction comes from the imagination of the writer, it may be based on actual events and real people. The main purpose of fiction is to entertain, but it often serves to instruct or enlighten.

See *Novel* and *Short Story.*

Figurative Language Language that conveys meaning beyond the literal meaning of the words is called figurative language. Figurative means that the words are used not in their ordinary sense but in some new symbolic or thought-provoking way. Writers use figurative language to create effects, to emphasize ideas, and to call upon emotions. Four special types of figurative language, called figures of speech, are the simile, the metaphor, hyperbole, and personification.

See *Hyperbole, Literal Language, Metaphor, Personification,* and *Simile.*

Figures of Speech See *Figurative Language.*

First-Person Point of View See *Point of View.*

Flashback A flashback is an interruption in the chronological order of events in a story in order to present a conversation or event that happened before the beginning of the story. This background information helps explain the present actions or attitude of a character. Much of Kurt Vonnegut's "The Euphio Machine" is told as a flashback.

Foreshadowing Foreshadowing is the technique of hinting about an event that will occur later in a story. For example, in *Julius Caesar* the soothsayer's warnings foreshadow the fate of Caesar. The use of foreshadowing creates suspense.

Form Form refers to the shape of a poem, that is, the way the words and lines are arranged. The lines may or may not be complete sentences. In many poems, lines are grouped into stanzas.

See *Stanza.*

Formal Essay See *Essay.*

Free Verse Free verse is poetry without regular patterns of rhythm, rhyme, or line length. It often sounds like everyday conversation when it is read aloud. Alice Walker's "Love Is Not Concerned" is a poem written in free verse.

See *Meter, Rhyme.*

Genre Genre refers to the distinct types or categories into which literary works are grouped. The four main literary genres are fiction, nonfiction, poetry, and drama.

Humor Humor in literature takes many forms. It might involve amusing description, exaggeration, or sarcasm. Humor is often created by the use of hyperbole or irony or through the writer's tone. "Diablo Country" by Art Buchwald is an example of a work that contains several forms of humor.

See *Hyperbole, Irony,* and *Tone.*

Humorous Essay See *Essay.*

Hyperbole Hyperbole is a figure of speech in which an exaggeration is made for emphasis or humorous effect. The title of Hugh Pentecost's "A Kind of Murder" is an example of hyperbole, since Silas Warren was not really murdered.

See *Figurative Language.*

Iamb See *Iambic Pentameter.*

Iambic Pentameter Iambic pentameter is the most common metrical, or rhythmic, pattern in English poetry. Each line has five iambs, or feet. Each iamb is a basic unit of rhythm consisting of an unstressed syllable (marked (˘) below) followed by a stressed syllable (marked (′) below) as shown in these lines from Shakespeare's *Julius Caesar,* spoken by Octavius in Act Five, Scene 1.

I draw a sword against conspirators.
When think you that the sword goes up again?

Idiom An idiom is a common phrase or expression that has a meaning different from the literal, or actual, meaning of its individual words. For example, "We're up against a brick wall" means "There's nothing more we can do."

Imagery Imagery refers to words and phrases that appeal to the reader's senses, often in a startling way. Most imagery appeals to the sense of sight, but imagery can appeal to other senses as well. These lines from Richard Connell's "The Most Dangerous Game" appeal to the senses of hearing and smell:

> . . . he heard the padding sound of feet on the soft earth, and the night breeze brought him the perfume of the General's cigarette.

Informal Essay See *Essay.*

Internal Conflict See *Conflict.*

Internal Dialogue Sometimes a character's thoughts are revealed through internal dialogue. For example, the barber in Hernando Téllez's "Lather and Nothing Else" thinks, "But I don't want to be a murderer. No, sir. You came in to be shaved."

See *Dialogue.*

Irony Irony is the contrast between what is expected and what really happens. Situational irony occurs when a reader or character expects one thing to happen, but something entirely different occurs. For example, the reader does not realize that Robert Proctor in Theodore Thomas's story "Test" is actually taking a strange driving exam under hypnosis.

Verbal irony occurs when a character or narrator says one thing but means another. In *Julius Caesar,* for example, Marc Antony uses verbal irony at Caesar's funeral when he calls Brutus an honorable man, yet means the opposite.

A third type of irony, dramatic irony, occurs when the reader or audience learns information that certain characters do not know.

Jargon The specialized vocabulary of a job or profession is called jargon. For example, *wheel well, strut,* and *fuselage* are aircraft jargon from Armando Ramírez's "Stowaway!"

Literal Language Words can have a literal meaning, a figurative meaning, or both, depending on the author's purpose. Literal denotes that the words mean what they ordinarily do; a dog is a dog, and a ride to the lake is exactly that.

See *Figurative Language.*

Main Character See *Character* and *Protagonist.*

Main Idea The main idea of a piece of writing is the central message it attempts to convey—the idea that controls or drives the entire work. For example, the main idea of Harold Krents's "Darkness at Noon" might be stated as "People with disabilities are much more able and talented than we realize."

Metaphor A metaphor is a figure of speech comparing two unlike things that have something in common. Unlike similes, metaphors do not use the word *like* or *as.* An example of a metaphor is "the ravine was a dynamo that never stopped running" from Ray Bradbury's *Dandelion Wine.*

See *Figurative Language.*

Meter Meter is the regular pattern of stressed and unstressed syllables in a line of poetry. The meter of a poem emphasizes the musical quality of the language. In addition, it may serve to call attention to particular words or ideas or to create a particular mood.

See *Blank Verse, Iambic Pentameter,* and *Rhythm.*

Minor Character See *Character.*

Mood Mood is the feeling—such as sadness or hope—that the writer evokes in the reader through carefully selected details and words. The use of connotation, dialogue, imagery, figurative language, foreshadowing, setting, and rhythm all help the writer create a mood. A writer often sets the mood in the opening paragraphs. For example, the beginning of Rona Maynard's "The Fan Club" introduces a mood of discomfort, self-consciousness, and dread.

Moral A moral is a lesson about human nature that a story teaches. For example, the moral of Fredric Brown's "The Weapon" is that humans are not able to control weapons that can potentially destroy the world.

Motivation The moving force behind a character's actions is referred to as the character's motivation. To understand a character's motivation, the reader can look at psychological and cultural factors as well as the circumstances surrounding the character. In Paul Gallico's "The Death Trap," for example, the Great Armando is motivated by his love for Tina Massin.

See *Character* and *Characterization.*

Murder Mystery Mysteries are stories with certain traditional ingredients: a murder victim, a murder scene, an investigator, suspects, and clues—any information that helps reconstruct the crime and reveal the killer. The detective—along with the reader—uses the clues to make inferences and draw conclusions about the identity of the murderer.

Myth A myth is a traditional story, usually about some superhuman being or unlikely event, that was once widely believed to be true. Many myths try to explain natural phenomena, such as the changing of the seasons. The title of the story "Antaeus" by Borden Deal comes from a Greek myth about a giant with that name.

Narrative A narrative is any writing that tells a story. A narrative tells a reader about something that happened by recounting a series of related events. The events of a narrative can be real or imaginary. Some common types of narrative are autobiographies, biographies, myths, narrative poems, novels, and short stories.

Narrator The narrator is the teller of a story. Sometimes the narrator is a character in the story. At other times, the narrator is an outside voice created by the writer.

See *Point of View.*

Nonfiction Nonfiction is prose writing about real people, places, things, events, and ideas. Biographies and autobiographies, histories, diaries, editorial articles, essays, journals, research reports, and news articles are all examples of nonfiction.

See *Autobiography, Biography,* and *Essay.*

Nonstandard English Nonstandard English does not conform to accepted standards of grammar, usage, or mechanics. For example, expressions such as "he don't" and "I ain't" are nonstandard. Nonstandard English is chiefly a form of spoken English; it is not used in writing except in passages of dialogue.

See *Standard English.*

Novel A novel is an extended work of fiction with a complex plot about the actions, feelings, and motivations of a group of characters. It is much longer and more complex than a short story.

Oral History Stories about real events passed by word of mouth from one generation to the next make up oral history. "Tsali of the Cherokees" is an example of oral history.

Personification Personification is a figure of speech in which human qualities are attributed to an object, animal, or idea. For example, Richard Wright personifies hunger in "The Rights to the Streets of Memphis": "I began to wake up at night to find hunger standing at my bedside, staring at me gauntly."

See *Figurative Language.*

Persuasive Essay See *Essay.*

Play See *Drama.*

Plot The sequence of actions and events in a drama or work of fiction is called the plot. Almost all plots center on at least one conflict or problem, which the characters struggle to resolve. Plots usually follow a specific pattern consisting of five stages: exposition, rising action, climax, falling action, and resolution.

Long literary works frequently have subplots as well as a main plot. In *Julius Caesar,* for example, the main plot focuses on Caesar's assassination and its results. A subplot involves the relationship between Brutus and Cassius.

See *Climax, Conflict, Exposition, Falling Action, Resolution,* and *Rising Action.*

Poetry Poetry is a special type of writing in which words are chosen and arranged to suggest meanings beyond the literal meanings of the words. Poets carefully select words for their sounds and meanings and combine them in different and unusual ways in order to communicate feelings, experiences, and different points of view. Poets use form, rhyme, rhythm, alliteration, assonance and consonance, imagery, figurative language, speaker, and theme—known collectively as the elements of poetry—to convey the sounds, emotions, pictures, and ideas they want to express. Poems can also tell stories. Some poems follow strict rules for form, rhythm, and rhyme, while those that follow no rules are said to be written in free verse.

Point of View Point of view is the perspective from which a story is told. The two basic points of view are first person and third person.

In first-person point of view, the narrator, usually a character in the story, recounts the story using the pronouns *I* and *me.* "Rules of the Game" by Amy Tan is told from the first-person point of view.

In a story told from a third-person point of view, the narrator is outside the story and uses the pronouns *he, she,* and *they.* "A Start in Life" by Ruth Suckow is an example of a story told from the third-person point of view.

Primary Source See *Sources.*

Propaganda Propaganda is biased, one-sided communication meant to influence the thoughts and actions of an audience. Methods used in propaganda are much stronger than those used in persuasion. A propagandist may conceal contradictory information and discourage debate. Propagandists may also lie, distort facts, and rely on very simple and repetitive messages. At the same time, the propagandist works to gain the audience's trust. Powerful symbols and loaded language, or the use of the connotative meanings of words to manipulate the audience, are tools of the propagandist. The speeches of Brutus and Marc Antony at Caesar's funeral in *Julius Caesar* are examples of propaganda.

See *Connotation.*

Prose Prose refers to all forms of written or spoken language that are logically organized and that lack the regular rhythmic patterns characteristic of poetry.

Protagonist The main character in a literary work is called the protagonist. The protagonist is always involved in the central conflict and often changes after the climax of the plot. Sometimes a work has more than one protagonist, as in Walter Myers's "The Treasure of Lemon Brown."

See *Antagonist.*

Pun A pun is a joke that makes use of two different meanings of a word or of two words that sound alike. Shakespeare liked to entertain his audience by using puns. The opening scene of *Julius Caesar* includes a number of puns on words having to do with shoes. A shoemaker, for example, calls himself "cobbler," which also meant in Shakespeare's time "someone who botches things up."

Realism See *Realistic Fiction.*

Realistic Fiction Realistic fiction is a type of fiction that imitates actual life. The characters act like real people and use ordinary human abilities to deal with problems typical of contemporary society.

Repetition The literary technique in which a word or group of words is repeated throughout a selection is called repetition. Writers often repeat a word or phrase to give special emphasis to a thought or action.

Resolution The final part of the plot of a drama or work of fiction is called the resolution. The resolution, which often blends with the falling action, explains how the conflict is resolved and may also answer the reader's remaining questions about the plot.

See *Falling Action* and *Plot.*

Rhetorical Question A rhetorical question does not call for an answer because the answer is obvious, as when Brutus asks the mourners at Julius Caesar's funeral, "Who is here so vile that will not love his country?" A speaker uses such questions to make a point or to create an emotional effect.

Rhyme Rhyme is the repetition of syllable sounds at the ends of words. When rhyme comes at the end of a line of poetry, it is called end rhyme, as in this example from "Incident" by Countee Cullen. Note the end rhyme in lines two and four.

I saw the whole of Baltimore
From May until December:
Of all the things that happened there,
That's all that I remember.

Rhyme Scheme Rhyme scheme is the pattern of end rhyme in a poem and can be charted by assigning a letter to each rhyming sound. The rhyme scheme for a stanza from Edna St. Vincent Millay's "Travel" is shown below.

My heart is warm with the friends I <u>make.</u> a
And better friends I'll not be <u>knowing;</u> b
Yet there isn't a train I wouldn't <u>take,</u> a
No matter where it's <u>going.</u> b

Rhythm The pattern of accented and unaccented syllables in poetry is called rhythm. Rhythm brings out the musical quality of language. It can also create mood and emphasize ideas. The accented, or stressed, syllables are marked with (ʹ), while the unaccented syllables are marked with (˘). The pattern these syllables make in a line of poetry can be divided into units. Each unit is called a foot.

See *Iambic Pentameter* and *Meter.*

Rising Action In fiction and drama, the rising action forms the second stage in the development of the plot. During the rising action, the conflict in a story becomes obvious. Complications arise and suspense begins to build as the main characters struggle to resolve their problem.

See *Plot.*

Satire Satire is a literary technique that combines a critical attitude with humor. Through the ridicule and mockery of satire, writers try to make their readers think about faults in society. Exaggeration is one of the satirist's main tools. *Visit to a Small Planet* by Gore Vidal uses satire.

Scene Scenes are the episodes into which the action of a play is divided. The setting of each scene differs in time, in place, or in both time and place. In long plays, scenes are grouped into acts. For example, while Louis Parker's play *The Monkey's Paw* has just one scene, Shakespeare's *Julius Caesar* has five scenes in the last act alone.

Science Fiction Science fiction is fiction based on real or possible scientific developments. It frequently presents both an imaginary view into the future and the writer's concerns about problems in today's society. Kurt Vonnegut's "The Euphio Machine" is an example of science fiction.

Secondary Source See *Sources.*

Sensory Details To evoke images and feelings in readers, writers use sensory details—words that appeal to the senses. These words help the reader see, hear, taste, smell, and feel the world the writer is describing. Josephina Niggli uses many sensory details in "The Street of the Cañon." For example, when the stranger entered the village, "the moonlight touched his shoulder" as he headed "for the distant sound of guitar and flute."
See *Imagery.*

Setting The setting of a drama or work of fiction is the time and place in which the action occurs. A work may be set in the past, the present, or the future; during the day or at night; during a particular time of year or in a certain historical period. The place may be real or imaginary. Sometimes the setting is clear and well-defined; at other times it is left to the reader's imagination.
Setting—along with plot, character, and theme—is one of the main elements of fiction.

Short Story A short story is a work of fiction that can be read in one sitting. It usually tells about one or two major characters and one major conflict. The four elements of a short story are character, plot, setting, and theme. An example of a short story is "Four O'Clock" by Price Day.
See *Fiction.*

Simile A simile is a comparison of two unlike things using the word *like* or *as.* In "Ex-Basketball Player" John Updike says of Flick Webb:

His hands were like wild birds.

Writers use similes to intensify emotional responses, to create vivid images, and to help the reader look at a familiar object in a new way.
See *Figurative Language.*

Slang Slang is very informal English that consists of colorful words and expressions, often created and used by a particular group. Slang terms can be new words or established words and phrases that have taken on new meanings. Slang terms usually go out of date quickly. An example of outdated slang is the expression "don't bug me."
See *Informal Language.*

Soliloquy A soliloquy is a speech made by a character in a play when he or she is alone on the stage or among other characters who are ignored temporarily. Its purpose is to let the audience know what the character is thinking. A soliloquy is given by Brutus in Act Two, Scene 1, of *Julius Caesar.*

Sound Devices See *Alliteration, Assonance, Consonance, Rhyme,* and *Rhythm.*

Sources When an account of an event is written by someone who experienced the event firsthand, that account is said to be a primary source. In contrast, when an account is written by someone who did not experience the event firsthand but learned about it through conversation or research, that account is a secondary source. "Tanforan" by Yoshiko Uchida is a primary source. John McPhee's "Survival in the Forty-Ninth" is a secondary source.

Speaker In poetry, the speaker is the voice that "talks" to the reader. The speaker of a poem might be compared to the narrator of a work of fiction. Although the speaker often expresses feelings that the poet wants to convey, the speaker may or may not be the voice of the poet.

Specialized Vocabulary See *Jargon.*

Stage Directions Stage directions are instructions included in the script of a play to the actors and director. They help the readers of the script to visualize the setting and imagine how the actors would move and speak. Stage directions also provide suggestions for props, lighting, music, and sound effects. They often appear in italics and are commonly set off from the dialogue by parentheses or brackets.

Standard English English is divided into two main levels: standard and nonstandard. Standard English is language that is acceptable at all

times and in all places. It conforms to accepted standards of grammar, usage, and mechanics.
See *Nonstandard English.*

Stanza A group of lines that forms a unit in a poem is called a stanza. A stanza is comparable to a paragraph in prose. The number of lines may vary or be uniform from stanza to stanza.

Stereotype A stereotype is an over-simplified idea of something or someone that allows for no individuality. Often a stereotype is a mental picture that members of a group believe typifies all members of some other group. In Shirley Jackson's "After You, My Dear Alphonse," Mrs. Wilson treats Boyd as a stereotype.

Style Style is the particular way in which a writer expresses his or her ideas. It refers not to what is said, but rather to how it is said. Every writer has a unique style. Elements that make up a writer's style are sentence length, use of descriptive language, tone, point of view, use of dialogue, use of irony, and methods of characterization.

Subplot See *Plot.*

Surprise Ending A surprise ending is an unexpected plot twist at the conclusion of a play or work of fiction. "The Third-Floor Flat" by Agatha Christie is a story with a surprise ending.

Suspense Suspense is the tension or excitement felt by the reader as he or she becomes involved in a drama or work of fiction and grows eager to know the outcome of the conflict. In "Lather and Nothing Else" by Hernando Téllez, for example, the reader wants to know whether the barber will kill the hated Captain Torres, whom he is shaving. The reader may even respond to the increasing suspense by reading faster and faster.

Symbolism A symbol is a person, place, or thing that represents something beyond itself. In literature, objects and images are often used to symbolize abstract ideas. For example, the house owned by Wilma in Horton Foote's *A Young Lady of Property* can symbolize both her freedom and memories of her mother.

Theme The theme of a literary work is the message or insight about life or human nature that the writer presents to the reader. Although some works are written purely for entertainment and do not have a clear-cut theme, in most serious works the writer has at least one theme.

Since the theme of a piece is not usually stated directly, the reader has to figure it out. One way to discover the theme is to consider what happens to the main character. The importance of that event, stated in general terms.

Third-Person Point of View See *Point of View.*

Time Order See *Chronological Order.*

Tone The tone of a work of literature is the writer's attitude toward his or her subject. It might be humorous, admiring, sad, angry, or bitter. The writer's word choice often indicates tone.

Tragedy A tragedy is a drama that begins peacefully and ends in violence, often with the death or ruin of one or more of the main characters. While fate is a major cause of the tragic ending, weaknesses or flaws within the characters also contribute significantly. The resolution of the plot is called the catastrophe. *Julius Caesar* is a tragedy.
See *Catastrophe* and *Resolution.*

Tragic Hero A tragic hero is the basically good and noble central character in a tragedy who makes fatal errors in judgment that contribute to his or her downfall.

Word Choice Word choice, or diction, involves a writer's selection of the proper language—words, phrases, figures of speech—to best express particular thoughts, feelings, and perceptions. Effective word choice helps a writer create characters and images that are clear and memorable.

Word Play See *Pun.*

BIOGRAPHIES OF AUTHORS

Dave Barry *(born 1947)* is an American humorist who lives in Coral Gables, Florida, and writes for the *Miami Herald.* His irreverent columns have become so popular that 150 other newspapers now run his commentaries about modern life in America. Barry has applied his comic wit to a variety of topics like "Scientific Stuff," "Household Perils," and "The Sporting Life." In 1988 he was awarded the Pulitzer Prize for commentary.

DAVE BARRY

Christy Brown *(1932–1981)* of Dublin, Ireland, was born with cerebral palsy. Raised in a slum as one of twenty-two children, Brown was unable to walk or talk and needed help to eat and drink. With the help of his family, he nevertheless learned to read and write. Using just his left little toe, he typed a novel over a period of fifteen years. Brown developed into a poet and artist as well as the author of seven published books. He has been ranked with the outstanding writers of his generation.

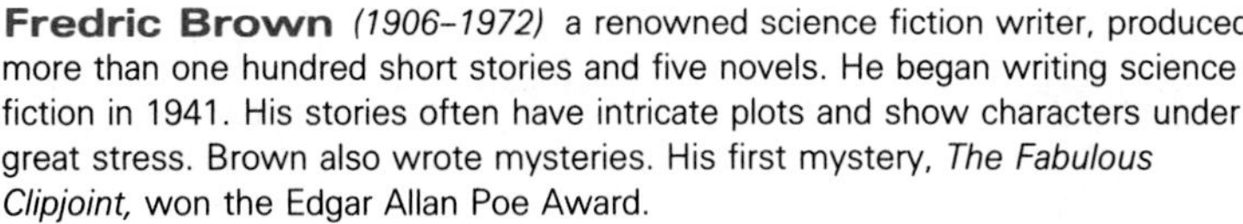

Fredric Brown *(1906–1972)* a renowned science fiction writer, produced more than one hundred short stories and five novels. He began writing science fiction in 1941. His stories often have intricate plots and show characters under great stress. Brown also wrote mysteries. His first mystery, *The Fabulous Clipjoint,* won the Edgar Allan Poe Award.

FREDRIC BROWN

Joseph Bruchac *(born 1942)* is a poet and storyteller of Abenaki ancestry. He has been a teacher at the State University of New York at Albany and writer-in-residence at Hamilton College of Columbia University. Bruchac appears at festivals throughout the country, combining music, poetry, and storytelling to relate ghost stories, tall tales, and Iroquois and Abenaki lore. He holds a black belt in the martial arts.

Janet Campbell *(born 1946)* was born in Riverside, California, but soon moved to the Coeur d'Alene Indian Reservation in northern Idaho, where she lived until she was ten years old. Later she lived with her family on the Colville and Yakima reservations. Though she dropped out of high school, Campbell won a scholarship to the novel-writing workshop at the University of California. She later attended City College in San Francisco.

AGATHA CHRISTIE

Agatha Christie *(1890–1976)* wrote sixty-seven novels, sixteen short story collections, and sixteen plays and was awarded such honors as that of Dame Commander in the Order of the British Empire and Grand Master of the Mystery Writers of America. Her most famous characters are Hercule Poirot, a Belgian detective who debuted in her first detective novel; and Miss Jane Marple, an elderly English gentlewoman who solved many of Christie's mysteries. Christie's play *The Mousetrap* is the longest-running drama in theater history.

JAMES P. COMER

Lucille Clifton *(born 1936)* writes with love, warmth, and humor about the vitality of African-American life. She grew up in DePew, New York, and attended Howard University and Fredonia State Teachers College. Her simple, straightforward poetry and prose have earned many awards and prizes, including a grant from the National Endowment for the Arts. Clifton also co-authored the Emmy Award-winning television program *Free to Be You and Me.*

James P. Comer *(born 1934)* is a professor of child psychiatry at Yale and founder of the Solomon Fuller Institute, a research center in Cambridge, Massachusetts. He has written many books dealing with problems that face children of ethnic minorities. His programs for teaching minority children are in use throughout the United States. His own story, *Maggie's American Dream,* emphasizes the importance of education as well as the roles of family, love, and community in changing the African-American experience.

ROBERT FULGHUM

Countee Cullen *(1903–1946)* grew up in Harlem. By high school he had already begun to accumulate literary honors and public prizes. Cullen continued to win writing honors at New York University, where he was elected to Phi Beta Kappa. In the 1920's he became a leader in the African-American arts movement known as the Harlem Renaissance. Cullen's writing expresses both the nobility of African culture and the author's hopes for the end of racism.

Price Day *(1907–1978)* began his career in journalism as a cartoonist and reporter. He earned his greatest fame as a foreign correspondent during and after World War II. Among his most notable assignments were covering the surrender of the German army in France and the independence of India. Day was the last interviewer of Mahatma Gandhi before Gandhi was assassinated. In 1949 Day won the Pulitzer Prize for international reporting.

PAUL GALLICO

Gregorio López y Fuentes *(1897–1966)* was a Mexican novelist, short story writer, poet, editor, and journalist who wrote mainly about the Mexican Revolution of 1910 and its effect on Indian traditions and rights. In his novel *Tierra,* he recounts the story of Zapata's ten-year struggle on behalf of Indian rights. In *El indio,* often considered Fuentes's masterpiece, he describes life in a remote Indian village after the revolution.

Robert Fulghum says he is still working on what he wants to be when he grows up. His humorous book *All I Really Need to Know I Learned in Kindergarten,* a bestseller in the United States, is scheduled for publication in nineteen more countries around the world. Fulghum has been an artist, folk singer, minister, salesman, and teacher, as well as a writer.

Paul Gallico *(1897–1976)* worked at a variety of writing jobs, including those of sports columnist, editor, and movie critic. He is best remembered, however, for his children's books, fables, ghost stories, and screenplays, particularly that for the movie *The Poseidon Adventure.* In the interest of authenticity, Gallico often read as many as thirty books on a subject before writing about it.

Ellen Goodman *(born 1941)* whose columns appear in more than 250 newspapers across the country, writes not about politics or government but about what she calls "life-and-death issues" such as parenting, the family, feminism, divorce, and alternative lifestyles. An honors graduate of Radcliffe College, Goodman has won a number of awards, including a Neiman Fellowship at Harvard University and the 1980 Pulitzer Prize for commentary.

LANGSTON HUGHES

Langston Hughes *(1903–1967)* was the first African American to earn his living solely from writing. Although he also wrote novels, short stories, plays, song lyrics, and radio scripts, Hughes is best known for his poetry. It uses strong blues rhythms and dialect to describe the people of Harlem. In his works Hughes expressed his views against racism and tried to encourage other African-American writers. His poetry has been translated into at least six languages, and some of his poems have been set to music.

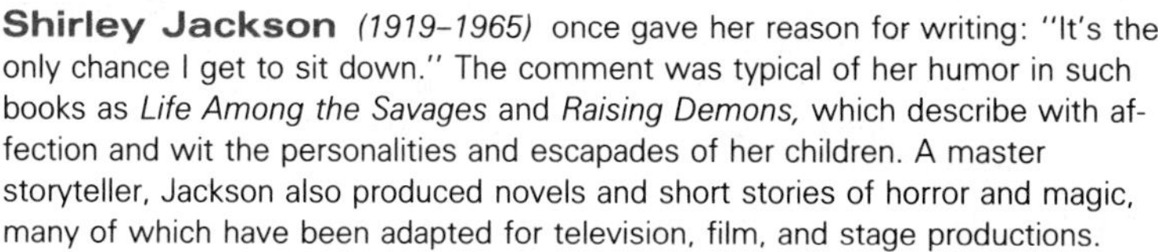

Shirley Jackson *(1919–1965)* once gave her reason for writing: "It's the only chance I get to sit down." The comment was typical of her humor in such books as *Life Among the Savages* and *Raising Demons,* which describe with affection and wit the personalities and escapades of her children. A master storyteller, Jackson also produced novels and short stories of horror and magic, many of which have been adapted for television, film, and stage productions.

PAT MORA

Jenny Joseph *(born 1932)* was born in Birmingham, England, and has written poetry since childhood. After graduating with honors from Oxford University, she worked as a newspaper journalist, traveled, and taught adult-education classes. Many of her poems have been read on the radio, and tapes and records have been made of her work. Joseph has also written six children's books.

Harold Krents *(1944–1987)* was blind from birth but nevertheless graduated with honors from Harvard University and went on to receive law degrees from Harvard and Oxford. His life inspired the hit Broadway play and film *Butterflies Are Free.* His autobiography, *To Race the Wind,* was adapted for television in 1972. Krents also served on the President's Committee on Employment of the Handicapped.

WALTER MYERS

Pat Mora *(born 1942)* was born and raised in El Paso, Texas, where she experienced a blending of Mexican and American cultures. She writes about the heritage of Mexican Americans because, she says, "I believe that Hispanics need to take their rightful place in American literature." Mora's poetry collections have received numerous awards, and in 1987 she received a national fellowship from the Kellogg Foundation.

Walter Dean Myers *(born 1937)* never expected to earn his living by writing. "Writing had no practical value for a black child," he recalls. Now that his twenty-five books have won wide popularity among young people, he says he needs to show African-American youngsters the possibilities that exist for them that did not exist for him. Myers believes that "there is always one more story to tell, one more person whose life needs to be held up to the sun."

WILMA RUDOLPH

Josephina Niggli *(born 1910)* is an award-winning playwright, poet, and prose writer who was born in Mexico and came to the United States with her parents in 1913. While still in her teens, Niggli began publishing short stories and poems. She later enrolled at the University of North Carolina to study play writing. Niggli's writing reflects her extensive knowledge of Mexican traditions and history.

Joyce Carol Oates *(born 1938)* wrote stories and put together two-hundred-page books in elementary school. At Syracuse University, from which she graduated with honors, she produced a novel per semester. The recipient of numerous awards for her work, Oates has said that she has an "ambition to get the whole world into a book." She serves on the faculty of Princeton University.

CARL SANDBURG

Dwight Okita *(born 1958)* is a Japanese-American poet turned playwright. His most recent plays are *The Rainy Season* and *In One Art and Out the Other.* This latter piece is part of a program called Poetry Under the Lights, in which musicians and poets describe their migration from one art form to another. Okita was educated at the University of Illinois at Chicago and writes a weekly theater column for the *Skyline,* a Chicago newspaper.

Phil Petrie *(born 1937)* was born in Clarksville, Tennessee, and educated at Tennessee State University in Nashville. Besides writing poetry and fiction, Petrie has edited a high school anthology of short stories drawn from African-American literature. He has also been the director of public affairs for Kings County Hospital in Brooklyn, New York.

WILLIAM SAROYAN

Juanita Platero, a Navaho Indian, lived with her husband on a reservation in New Mexico. Standing Bear, a Lakota chief, introduced Platero to **Siyowin Miller,** a writer with a strong interest in Native American culture. In 1940 the two women began collaborating, producing short stories as well as a novel, *The Winds Erase Your Footprints.*

Wilma Rudolph *(born 1940)* was nicknamed Skeeter by her high school coach because she was "always buzzing around." A superior athlete in high school, Rudolph scored 803 points in just twenty-five basketball games during her sophomore year. She went on to win three gold medals in track events at the 1960 Olympic games in Rome—a remarkable feat considering that an illness she contracted at age four had left her unable to walk without help until age eleven.

Carl Sandburg *(1878–1967)* born in Illinois to Swedish immigrant parents, was a poet, journalist, historian, author of children's books, and guitar-playing traveler who collected American folk songs. In his writing Sandburg paid homage to America and its common people. His *Chicago Poems* made him famous. Though critics praised his powerful free verse, they also criticized his use of slang and street language. Sandburg was awarded two Pulitzer Prizes—one for his poetry and one for his six-volume biography of Abraham Lincoln.

William Saroyan *(1908–1981)* the son of Armenian immigrants, wrote of the lives of working-class people. He left school after eighth grade to help support his family. Saroyan produced an incredibly large body of work, writing more than five hundred stories in one six-year period alone. His novel, *The Human Comedy,* was made into a movie, and his play *The Time of Your Life* won a Pulitzer Prize. Saroyan refused the prize, saying that art should be judged by the common people, not by representatives of wealth and big business.

THEODORE THOMAS

Gary Soto *(born 1952)* writes about the lives of Mexican Americans, about nature, and about personal dreams. A 1974 honors graduate of California State University, Soto continued his studies at the University of California, Irvine, while publishing his poems in magazines across the country. He has won many awards for his later works, including the 1976 United States Award of the International Poetry Forum for *The Elements of San Joaquin.*

Theodore Thomas *(born 1920)* is a graduate of the Massachusetts Institute of Technology and holds a degree in law from Georgetown University. With such diverse training, Thomas has held jobs as varied as those of chemical engineer and patent lawyer. Despite his work schedule, he produces a steady volume of writing. Thomas has contributed short stories to twenty anthologies and has contributed another seventy-five stories and articles to magazines.

TINO VILLANUEVA

Margaret Tsuda *(born 1921)* is a freelance writer and artist. She was educated at Hunter College in New York City. Her books *Cry Love Aloud* and *Urban River* are illustrated by the author using ink and a bamboo pen called a *taki.* Tsuda's poems have been translated into eight different languages, including Hindi. Her work has been published in the *Christian Science Monitor, Living Wilderness* magazine, the *Sentinel,* and *Bodhi* magazine.

Tino Villanueva *(born 1941)* in San Marcos, Texas, spent most of his early years moving around with his parents who were migrant farm workers. Villaneuva's love of sports persuaded him to stick with high school until he was drafted into the army. After finishing his military service, he enrolled at Southwest Texas State University and began to write poetry. Villaneuva uses his childhood experiences and rich Mexican-American heritage in his writing.

W. D. WETHERELL

Alice Walker *(born 1944)* is best known for her Pulitzer Prize-winning novel *The Color Purple,* which was published in 1982 and later made into a film. Walker was born in Eatonton, Georgia. Before becoming a successful writer, she registered voters in her home state, worked in a Head Start program in Missisippi, and for the New York City welfare department. Walker's novels, poems, stories, and essays are chiefly concerned with the role of African-American women.

W. D. Wetherell *(born 1948)* a novelist and short story writer, is a native of Long Island, New York. Wetherell won the Drue Heinze Literature Prize for his short story collection *The Man Who Loved Levittown.* He has also been awarded two fellowships by the National Endowment for the Arts, and his work has appeared in the *New York Times,* the *Atlantic,* and various literary magazines.

THE WRITING PROCESS

Everyone who reads and writes belongs to a special community, a community of readers and writers. You, too, are part of this community. When you read, you discover meaning that reflects who you are as well as what the writer is trying to communicate. When you write, you discover ideas about yourself, about the world, and about what you read.

On the following pages you will find practical information that you can apply in many different writing situations.

The Reader's Journal

Like all readers, you observe, question, predict, and make connections as you read. You experience feelings such as excitement and amusement. One place to record these responses to literature is in a Reader's Journal. Your journal then can provide you with a rich source of writing ideas. Your journal can also serve as the place to record notes as you prepare for a writing assignment.

Here are some tips for keeping a journal:

- Carry your journal with you or keep it in a convenient place.
- Date and label your journal entries.
- Record words, passages, and lines that trigger ideas, along with your response to these ideas.
- Set aside part of your journal for the journal writing that is suggested throughout this book.
- Set aside another part of your journal for observations, quotations, and imaginative writing that is not tied to a literary selection.

The Writing Process

Writing is a process unique to each writer and to each writing experience. However, the following activities need to take place during most writing experiences.

- **Exploring ideas** reflecting on what you know, what you need to know, and where you might find what you need
- **Gathering material** remembering, imagining, reading, observing, interviewing, discussing
- **Making connections** finding the way ideas fit together, letting new ideas surface, elaborating and pushing ideas to their limits
- **Clarifying communication** rethinking content, reorganizing structure, correcting mechanics and usage

In most books about writing, each of these activities is tied to a specific stage of the writing process. The traditional stages are listed below in the same order that they appear in the Writer's Workshops in this text. It is important to understand, however, that the stages are only guides. Any activity can take place at any point in the process. The more you write, the more you should develop your own personal process, moving in and out of the writing stages in the manner that works best for you.

Stage 1. Prewriting This is the planning stage where you think of ideas, do research, and organize your material.

Stage 2. Drafting When you draft, you begin to put your ideas on paper, following any notes, graphics, or outlines you have made. Drafting is a time to let ideas flow without concern for spelling and punctuation. These errors can be corrected later.

Stage 3. Revising and Editing When you revise, you refine your draft by improving word choice, and sentence structure, clarifying organization, eliminating unnecessary details, and adding new ideas when necessary. When you are satisfied with your revision, you edit, or proofread your work looking for errors in capitalization, punctuation, grammar, and spelling.

Stage 4. Publishing or Presenting This is the time to share your writing with others.

The Writer as Decision-Maker

During the writing process, writers make a series of decisions that give direction or redirection to their writing. These decisions concern the key issues of purpose, audience, subject, and structure. These elements are highlighted in the **PASSkey** to writing that accompanies each Writer's Workshop in this text. In order to keep your writing focused, you may find it helpful to create a **PASSkey** when you are writing for other classes, as well. Following is a list of questions to guide you in thinking about these issues as you write.

Purpose

Is a purpose stated in the assignment?
What do I really want to accomplish in this piece: to express ideas or feelings? to inform? to entertain? to analyze? to persuade?
How do I want my audience to respond?

Audience

Who will read my writing?
What do my readers know or need to know?
What might they find interesting?

Subject

What information must I pull together or research?
Will I need to fill in details from my imagination?
How detailed will I need to be for my audience?

Structure

Is a structure or form named in the assignment?
What is the most effective organization to accomplish my purpose?
What should the final product look like?

The Writer as Problem-Solver

Everyone's writing process is personal. Many writers, however, experience the same kinds of difficulties. The questions they ask tend to sound like these:

1. Where do I start? Where do I get ideas? What do I do with them?
2. Who can help me? When should I ask for help?
3. How do I know what's wrong with my writing? How do I fix it?

On the following pages are some strategies to help you deal with these common problems.

Strategies: Word Webs and Brainstorming The notes in your journal can be a good starting point for many writing assignments. When you need to explore ideas further, generate new ideas, or discover connections among ideas, you might want to try using a **word web.** A word web is a diagram showing a central idea and related ideas. Here is an example.

This word web shows the central idea "Laura" surrounded by words and phrases that describe her qualities. It would be useful for writing a character sketch on Laura.

To create a word web like the one above, write a central idea in the middle of a page and draw a circle around it. Outside the circle, write related ideas. Circle each one and draw a line connecting it to the central idea. Do the same for each related idea.

Brainstorming is similar to making a word web. In brainstorming, though, you write down every idea that comes to mind, whether it is related or not. Brainstorming can be done alone, but it is even more productive when done in a group.

Strategies: Charts and Diagrams Charts and diagrams can help you discover connections as well as pinpoint where you need to gather more material. You will discover a wide variety of useful charts and diagrams in this book—both on the Explore pages and with the Writer's Workshop assignments.

Strategies: Peers as Partners Because you are part of a community of readers and writers, you can work with a partner at any point in the writing process. You can co-develop a writing plan, bounce ideas off a friend, ask a classmate to read a rough draft or a cleaned-up copy, or in some cases team-write a piece. Involving peers in your problem-solving process can help you in exploring and clarifying ideas, in seeing a subject from a different point of view, and in identifying and eliminating problems in communication.

When you want some feedback on a piece of writing, you can read it aloud to a classmate and then ask that person two simple questions: What do you like? What don't you like?

A way to get more detailed feedback, especially for longer pieces, is to give a classmate the piece of writing along with the following questions. You can use the answers to these questions as a guide for talking about your writing with your partner.

- What did you like the best? the least?
- What message do you think I am trying to get across? Summarize it for me.
- What do you want to know more about? What parts went on too long?
- Did the beginning work for you? Did the ending?
- Did you have any trouble following my ideas?

Strategies: Self-Evaluation Sometimes a first draft of a piece of writing needs little revision. Other times you may have to write several drafts, perhaps going back to do more research or to rethink the ideas. When trying to figure out what's wrong with a piece of writing that just isn't working, you can start with a quick check like the following:

- The main point I am trying to make is ________.
- I want my reader to respond to my writing by thinking or feeling that ________.
- In looking back over the piece, I like ________.
- I don't like ________.

At this point you'll want to review the personal goals you set when identifying the purpose of your writing and to decide how close you've come to meeting your goals. One good evaluation strategy is to read your writing aloud. As you read, listen for the following problems:

- ideas that are unclear or unnecessary
- ideas that don't make logical connections
- abrupt transitions from one idea to the next
- a dull or choppy style
- words that don't sound quite right or aren't right for your audience

Strategies: The Final Edit It would be wonderful to know all the rules of grammar, spelling, capitalization, punctuation, and usage, all the synonyms for every word, all the meanings for every word you read or hear. The next best thing is to know where to get the information you need to refine your writing. Here are some ideas.

- **To check spelling** dictionary, spelling dictionary, computer spellchecker
- **To check punctuation, capitalization, grammar, and usage** the Language Handbook in this text
- **To check word meanings and synonyms** dictionary, thesaurus

One point to check carefully when writing about literature is the accuracy of your quotations and the correct spellings of any names and titles. The literature itself is your source for this information.

When you edit your writing or that of a peer partner, use the proofreading symbols shown on the next page.

Proofreading Symbols

Symbol	Meaning	Example
^	insert	le^son (s)
≡	capitalize	douglass
/	lower case	History
~	transpose	veiw
ℓ	take out	lots of
¶	paragraph	¶The
⊙	add a period	slavery⊙
^,	add a comma	Finally^,

The Writer as Learner

After you have completed a piece of writing, take time to think about your writing process. Questions like these can help you to focus on various aspects of the writing and learning experience:

- Am I pleased with my final product?
- Did I become involved in my topic?
- Did I learn something from writing about this topic?
- Which aspects of the writing were easiest for me? Which were the most difficult?
- What aspect of writing is becoming easier?
- What was the biggest problem I encountered? How did I solve the problem? How might I avoid the problem next time?
- When I compare this piece of writing with others in my working folder or portfolio, can I see changes in my writing style? in my writing skill?
- Have I seen anything in the writing done by my peers or by professional writers that I would like to try myself?

Another way to learn from a writing experience is through an objective evaluation of your final product. The evaluation may be conducted by a teacher or a peer reader. The goal is the same: to contribute to your growth as a writer and to heighten your sense of writing as communication.

Strategies: The Evaluation Task Each kind of writing has certain characteristics unique to that writing. An evaluator, however, can assess the strengths and weaknesses of most writing using general guidelines in three key areas:
(1) content
(2) form
(3) grammar, usage, and mechanics.

The following is a description of a well-developed piece of writing, which you might use when you are acting as a peer evaluator and when judging whether your own work is ready for a final evaluation or in need of further revision.

Content

The content of a well-developed piece of writing:

- Is clearly focused throughout the piece
- Keeps a consistent tone and point of view
- Uses precise verbs, nouns, and modifiers
- Elaborates on ideas with supporting details, examples, and summaries, as appropriate
- Demonstrates a clear sense of purpose
- Demonstrates a clear sense of audience through choice of language and details

Form

The form of a well-developed piece of writing:

- Shows clear relationships among ideas through effective transitions
- Includes sentences with a variety of structures

Grammar, Usage, and Mechanics

The final draft of a well-developed piece of writing:

- Contains few if any minor errors in grammar and usage
- Contains few if any minor errors in spelling, capitalization, and punctuation

The Writer as Communicator

When the time comes to share your writing, you have many choices. A few of these choices are listed below:

- Trade papers with the classmate who helped you refine your ideas.
- Trade papers with a classmate unfamiliar with your work.
- Read your writing aloud to a small group of classmates or to the class.
- Ask a classmate to read your writing aloud.
- Read your writing to younger children or to adults in your family or community.
- Discuss the ideas explored in your writing and the conclusions you arrived at.
- Choose appropriate ideas to share in a discussion and save others for future use.
- Present a dramatic reading with sound effects.
- Tape record a reading of the piece.
- Stage your work as simple Readers Theater or as a more elaborate performance.
- Publish a booklet of your own writing or of writing by many contributors.
- Display your writing in the class or school.
- Submit your writing to the school newspaper or literary magazine.
- Mail your writing to a magazine or newspaper with a wider circulation.
- Add your writing to your notebook or portfolio for later sharing

Whatever option you choose, share your work in the spirit of learning and growing in your role as communicator.

WRITING WITH COMPUTERS

In this age of "electronic miracles," we've become accustomed to having computers help us out. Computers can help us drive our automobiles and cook our food. Thanks to computer technology, we can phone a next-door neighbor or a friend on another continent. Now the same technology can make the task of writing easier, faster, and more effective.

What Is a Word Processor?

A computer becomes a word processor when a word-processing software program is loaded into it. Programs for word-processing are contained on a storage device, such as a floppy disk. The computer works in combination with a printer, which on command will print on paper any text that has been composed. Although computers vary and individual word-processing programs may differ in the features they offer, all word processing offers certain benefits to assist writers.

Type Without Knowing How

Perhaps the simplest and most elementary benefit of word processing is that it allows non-typers to produce printed words on a page. It's true that the computer's keyboard is like a typewriter and that to word process you must key in the words. However, because the word processor makes it so easy to correct errors and automatically takes care of many of the spacing and formatting decisions, it is not necessary to possess extensive typing skills.

Face the Blank Page Bravely

Even during the beginning stages of writing, when you're still thinking about a writing topic, word processing can help make your job easier. The screen light on many computers is adjustable and can be dimmed. Try free-writing with the screen dimmed, typing any ideas that come to mind. Not being able to see what you're typing frees you from concerns about form and correctness. It also keeps you from trying to re-write prematurely. After you've exhausted your supply of ideas, turn up the monitor screen and review what you've written. Then, you can tell the computer to store your ideas, print them out, or both.

Extend Your Memory

A computer can store, or "remember," a great deal of material. You can use this fact to your advantage both while you're organizing your ideas and while you're composing. In a computer, a body of information is called a file. Word processors store written material as files. For example, if you have a list of questions that helps you explore writing ideas, you can create a file to store it. If you'd like to keep an ongoing list of ideas, you can give it a file of its own, calling it up and adding to it as needed.

Some word processors let you work on more than one file at a time. This allows you to move back and forth between drafting and prewriting while the computer stores the other file for you. For example, suppose a great idea hits you during the drafting stage. Simply call up your idea file, store the inspiration, and return to your drafting. Later, you can refer to your idea file, pull out the idea, and insert it in the appropriate place in your text.

Handle Words with Confidence

Word processing simplifies adding or deleting material and moving words or passages around on the page. "Cut-and-paste" commands allow you to arrange and rearrange items in a writing plan or outline. You can also develop the points in your outline in order, or skip around as you fill in material. You can update and correct information quickly and without mess.

Throughout the planning and drafting stages, you have the option of working on-screen or making a paper copy (called a *hard copy*) of your text.

Find Your Own Drafting Style

The cut-and-paste feature is extremely useful

during the drafting stage as well because it allows the word processor to accommodate alternative writing styles.

If you work best by first organizing and then writing, you could review your idea file on-screen or print out your ideas on paper to form prewriting notes. Then, use the cut-and-paste command to form a plan. Finally, expand your plan into sentences.

An alternative drafting method is to write and organize as you go. Produce text quickly and experiment on the spot with several ways of expressing an idea, or with several plans for developing it. Later, you can delete unneeded text or reorganize your draft.

The word processor also gives you the flexibility to use different approaches in your writing. For example, you may want to follow the outline as you write, or you may want to write parts of the composition out of order—say, the conclusion first or the middle sections interspersed with the introduction and the conclusion.

Be Two People at Once

Competent writers are constantly aware of—and concerned with—the impact of their words on the reader. Word processing enables you to become author and audience at the same time. In fact, some word-processing programs have a "split-screen" feature that permits you to view onscreen more than one file at a time. The split screen is divided into separate sections called *windows,* and each window displays a portion of a file. You can move back and forth between windows and make changes, creating two versions of text simultaneously. You can experiment by moving words and even entire passages around. You can try a variety of locations for the same paragraph. The split screen allows you to test the merits of several versions and choose the one you consider to be the most effective.

Choose the Best Word

Word-processing programs have a "search and replace" function that indicates the number of times a given word is used in the text. If in revising your writing you suspect that you've overused a word, use this function to learn how many times it's mentioned in your text. (Some programs even display the location in the text of each occurrence.) Then, you can decide in each case whether to keep the word or to replace it with another.

Some word-processing programs have a built-in thesaurus to help you find a synonym. If yours does not, use your own thesaurus or a dictionary.

Produce a Perfect Paper

One of the best features of the word processor is its ability, at the stroke of a key, to produce a hard copy that is free of deletions, inserts, carets, smudges, and other marks. You can edit your writing onscreen or the "old-fashioned" way—with pencil on paper.

If you prefer, the word processor can print a copy with wide spacing and/or wide margins so that you can easily pencil in corrections. In this case, after careful proofreading you would add each of your corrections onto the screen and then print out a clean final version.

Spell Perfectly

Another feature of many processors, the *spelling checker,* automatically scans the text for misspelled or unfamiliar words. Spelling checkers call up each questionably spelled word so that you can check it against a built-in dictionary or one of your own.

Become a More Effective Writer

Without a doubt, word processors make composing and revising easier. They enable you to concentrate your efforts on the most important aspect of writing: saying what you have to say in the best possible way.

GUIDELINES FOR RESEARCH AND REPORT WRITING

A private eye summarizes an investigation. A sportswriter explains the academic probation of a star player. A student uses the library to write a term paper about the influence of Caribbean music on popular music in the United States. All these people have conducted research to find and evaluate information. Despite differences in style and purpose, each person has written a report or research paper that presents information to others.

The following section provides an overview of the steps needed to complete a formal research paper. Though the focus is on writing a paper for school, this process may be adapted to any kind of research task.

Discovering a Topic

Finding the right topic is crucial for success. Use the suggestions in The Writing Process, page 870 to explore possibilities.

Evaluating a Topic

Once you have possible topics, you need to eliminate the unsuitable ones, using questions such as the following to trim your list.

1. Do you really want to learn more about the topic you have chosen? Are you interested enough in the topic to spend a long time with it?
2. Is there enough information available on it? A subject that is too recent or too technical may not have enough materials.
3. Is the topic too simple? If you can learn everything you need to know in one article, the topic does not need research.
4. Is the topic too broad? Some topics, such as the Vietnam War, the rise and fall of the Roman Empire, or Native American life before Columbus, are just too big to handle in a short paper.

Limiting a Topic

Once you have chosen what you think is a good topic, you need to narrow its scope; otherwise, you'll be overwhelmed with information. You can begin by reading about your subject in an encyclopedia or other reference book, looking for ways to whittle down your topic. For example, you might begin by exploring the immigrant experience throughout U.S. history, then narrow your topic to the experiences of Chinese immigrants during the late 1800's.

As you limit your topic, try to focus on the purpose of your paper. If you were interested in personal computers, deciding whether to evaluate their latest advances or to report the history of their development would help focus your hunt for information.

Finding Sources

After narrowing your topic, you need to search for and collect information, using the tools listed below.

The Card Catalog The card catalog provides a guide to all material in the library, using three categories, **title cards, author cards,** and **subject cards.** Begin by looking up your subject, but don't give up if it doesn't seem to be there. You may have to look up a variety of headings before you strike gold.

Many public libraries offer a **computerized catalog system** that is more compact and often easier to use than the card catalog. If you know the author, title, or subject of a book, the computer will tell you if the library has that book. If you need a listing of the books the library has on a certain subject, type in the subject and the computer will list titles and call numbers of books available.

Readers' Guide to Periodical Literature This source will list current magazine articles on your subject.

Encyclopedias Generally, encyclopedias are a good starting point. They provide basic information and often suggest other books and articles. There are general encyclopedias as well as sets of special-purpose references that focus on one subject. Here is a partial listing.

- *The World Book Encyclopedia*
- *Encyclopaedia Britannica*
- *Collier's Encyclopedia*
- *The Baseball Encyclopedia*
- *Harper Encyclopedia of Science*

Specialized Reference Books The reference section of your library contains all kinds of books that may prove helpful. The librarian can point you in the right direction.

- **Almanacs and Yearbooks** provide up-to-date facts and statistics. The *Guinness Book of World Records* is an example.
- **Specialized Dictionaries** focus on a particular field of knowledge or part of the language. You can find dictionaries on such subjects as architecture, ballet, botany, biographies, slang, and many others.
- **Atlases** contain maps as well as other information on topics such as population, temperatures, weather, and so on.

People in the Know Interviews with people who are knowledgeable about your topic can add fresh insight. You'll be surprised at how cooperative such people can be if approached in the right way.

Evaluating Possible Sources

Researching a report can be time-consuming. To make the best use of your time, you should learn to quickly review the parts of a book to determine whether it will be a useful source of information.

Title Page This page gives the complete title of the book, the names of authors or editors, the name of the publisher, and the place of publication.

Copyright Page On this page you will find the date of publication. You can then decide if the material in the book is current enough for your purpose. For example, a 1965 copyright date on a book about nuclear energy would indicate that the information in that particular book is probably out of date.

Foreward, Preface, or Introduction These pages contain important background information, such as the author's purpose in writing the book or the method used in collecting the information.

Table of Contents This is a summary or outline of the contents of the book, arranged in order of appearance. These pages are especially important because they quickly tell you whether the book discusses your topic and whether the coverage is detailed enough for your purposes.

Text This is the body of the book. Look briefly at the text of any book you are interested in using. Can you understand the language and the level of discussion? Don't bother using a book that is too technical or too scholarly.

Appendices Some books may have appendices at the back which contain additional information such as maps, charts, tables, illustrations, or graphs.

Notes and Bibliography Here the author credits the sources used in the preparation of the book and lists other books that may be of interest to readers who need further information.

Glossary This is a dictionary at the back of the book that lists unusual or technical terms used in the text.

Index This is an alphabetical list of subjects covered in the book. Each entry is followed by page numbers that enable you to locate specific information. If your research subject is part of a chapter listed in the table of contents, a look at the index will tell you where it is located and how many pages are devoted to it.

Creating Bibliography Cards

Use bibliography cards to keep track of your sources. Once you have looked through an article or book and decided it may be useful, record essential information on a 3" × 5" index card, using a separate card for each source. You need to include the full title, complete names of authors, and complete publishing information. Carefully record your information in the exact format used in the bibliography, described on pages 882-883. If you get all the details in the right order now, you'll save time and effort later on.

Also list the library call number on each card; if you use more than one library, give the name as well. Finally, since your cards will also serve as a way of coding your notes, assign a number to each card and put it in the upper-right hand corner.

Sample Bibliography Card

McCunn, Ruthanne Lum. *An Illustrated History of the Chinese in America*. San Francisco: Design Enterprises of San Francisco, 1979.
973.951

Taking Notes

Format Most researcher write notes on 4" × 6" index cards to avoid confusing them with the smaller bibliography cards. The notes should be in the following format: 1) a heading, which gives the general idea, 2) the body of the note, 3) a page reference, and 4) a source number which matches the note card to the bibliography card. Use a separate card for each note.

Sample Note Card

Heading Note **Source Number**

Opportunities for the Chinese 4
Between 1860 and 1890, Chinese immigrants worked in all aspects of agriculture in California.
36

Page Reference

Knowing When Deciding when to take a note is difficult. The basic question you need to ask is: How important is this information for my topic? Here are some things to look for:

1. The main concepts of the topic
2. Results of research or studies
3. Important dates and facts
4. Key people involved
5. Interesting examples or stories
6. Contrasting opinions of experts
7. Special terms

Quoting or Summarizing Whenever possible, you should summarize the information you find in your own words. Keep your emphasis on what is important, being careful not to get bogged down in details. Also, label opinions; if you are reporting what Dr. Jones thinks, be sure to say so in your note.

Statements that are memorable, clever, famous, or written in an interesting way should be quoted directly. Copy them word for word and mark the beginning and end with quotation marks. If the quotation is too long to copy completely, you can combine summary with direct quotation.

Plagiarism The uncredited use of someone else's ideas or words is called plagiarism. This occurs when a direct quote is presented as if it were your own words or when someone's ideas are summarized without credit being given. Your teacher can further explain this important subject.

Organizing Your Material

State Your Controlling Purpose

Once you've assembled your information, you need a game plan for your paper. The first step is to state a controlling purpose, a sentence that sums up the aim of your paper. Your controlling purpose will help you move in the right direction as you organize and write your paper.

Examples

To describe the experiences of early Chinese immigrants in the United States.

To show how events like the Montgomery Boycott helped bring about a widespread and successful civil rights movement during the 1950's and 1960's.

To compare U.S. and Soviet accomplishments in space exploration.

Constructing an Outline Outlining can help you think through a paper before the writing starts. Though some writers work better without outlines, many find them necessary.

One way to begin an outline is to turn your controlling purpose into a question. This can help you break down your topic into its major parts, which then become the main headings of an outline.

Then review your notes again, paying special attention to the headings on the note cards. Group the notes into separate piles, putting similar ones together. Your groups can help you organize your outline into headings and subheadings.

Example

Chinese Immigrants to the United States: 1845-1900

I. In Search of Work
    A. Contract labor
    B. Conditions on ships
    C. Jobs
        1. Plantations
        2. Mines
II. New Opportunities
    A. The Gold Rush
        1. Work as Miners
        2. Services to Miners
    B. Railroad Building
        1. Transcontinental Railroads
        2. Accomplishments of Chinese Workers
    C. Agriculture
    D. Fishing and Shipping
    E. Industries in California
        1. Types
        2. Post-Civil War Economic Slump
III. Resistance to the Chinese
    A. Reasons
    B. Local anti-Chinese Laws
    C. Violence against the Chinese
    D. The Exclusion Laws

Writing from Your Outline Your main purpose now is to get your ideas down in writing. In the draft don't aim for perfect, error-free writing; simply get your ideas down in a form that you will be able to follow when it's time for revision.

Use your outline the way a contractor would use a blueprint. Build from it, but don't hesitate to make changes if something isn't working.

Incorporating Your Notes

You'll need to decide how best to present the information from your notes. Usually, you should use only key phrases, weaving them into your own sentences. Summarize as much as possible in your own words.

Sometimes you may wish to quote an entire passage. Longer quotations—those more than four typed lines—should be set off from the text. Indent the entire quote ten characters in from the left margin. Note that in this case no quotation marks are needed.

Phrases

Roosevelt spoke of "the need to find a program that uplifts rather than degrades."

Whole Sentences

The next step was to produce an airplane that could go faster than sound, but, according to Isaac Asimov, "There was talk of the *sound barrier* as though it were something physical that could not be approached without destruction."

Long Passages

In *Psychology: A Biographical Approach*, Malinda Jo Levin presents an interesting way of looking at dreams:

> Recently it has become popular to talk of dreams in relation to creativity. Elias Howe supposedly perfected the sewing machine while in a dream state, and Robert Louis Stevenson dreamed complete stories.

Be careful not to let quotations overrun your paper. You need to put the information together in a clear, easy-to-follow way.

Documenting Your Sources

Any information that you use from your sources must be documented, or credited to its original source. To accomplish this, you can use **parenthetical documentation.** In most cases, you will list only the author's last name and a page reference in parentheses after the paraphrased, summarized, or quoted material. Refer to the following example and guidelines.

Example

The Exclusion Law of 1882 severely restricted Chinese immigration to the United States. In 1881, more than 40,000 Chinese had come to the United States; in 1887, only ten Chinese immigrated here (McCunn 87).

Guidelines for Documentation

1. **Works by one author.** Give the author's last name in parentheses at the end of a sentence, followed by the page numbers (Jones 58).
2. **Work by more than one author.** List all the last names in parentheses, or give one last name followed by *et al.* (Smith, Jones, and Wilcox 87) or (Smith *et al.* 87).
3. **Works with no author listed.** When citing an article that does not identify the author, use the title of the work or a shortened version of it ("Cochise" 398).
4. **Two works by the same author.** If you use more than one work by the same author, give the title, or a shortened version, after the author's last name (Jones, *Indian Wars* 398).
5. **Two works cited at the same place.** If you use more than one source to support a point, use a semicolon to separate the entries (Jones 398; Smith 87).

Compiling the Bibliography

Once you have completed your draft, gather the bibliography cards for every source you have cited.

Use these cards to create your Bibliography or Works Cited, following the guidelines and sample entries below.

Guidelines for Final Bibliography

1. Arrange all bibliography entries by the last name of the author or editor.
2. If no author or editor is provided, alphabetize each entry by the first word of the title. If the first word is *A, An,* or *The,* begin with the second word of the title.
3. Begin the first line of each entry at the left margin. If the entry runs to a second or third line, indent those lines five spaces.
4. Single-space each bibliography entry, but double-space between entries.
6. Bibliography entries contain page numbers only when they refer to parts within whole works.

Sample Bibliography Entries

Whole Books

A. One author

Webster, Charles. *From Paracelsus to Newton: Magic and the Making of Modern Science.* Cambridge: Cambridge UP, 1983.

B. Two authors

Gilbert, Sandra M., and Susan Gubar. *The Madwoman in the Attic: The Woman Writer and the Nineteenth Century Literary Imagination.* New Haven: Yale UP, 1979.

C. Two or more authors

Gatto, Joseph, *et al. Exploring Visual Design.* 2nd ed. Worcester: Davis, 1987.

Use *et al.,* Latin for *and others,* instead of listing all authors.

D. No author given

Literary Market Place: The Directory of American Book Publishing. 1984 ed. New York: Bowker, 1984.

E. An editor, but no single author

Saddlemyer, Ann, ed. *Letters to Molly: John Millington Synge to Maire O'Neill.* Cambridge: Harvard UP, 1984.

When you have cited several works from a collection, you may write one entry for the entire collection or list each work separately.

F. Two or three editors

Emanuel, James A., and Theodore L. Gross, eds. *Dark Symphony: Negro Literature in America.* New York: Macmillan, 1968.

Parts Within Books

A. A poem, short story, essay, or chapter from a collection of works by one author

Angelou, Maya. "Remembering." *Poems.* New York: Bantam, 1986. 11.

B. A poem, short story, essay, or chapter from a collection of works by several authors

Welty, Eudora. "The Corner Store." *Prose Models.* Ed. Gerald Levin. New York: Harcourt, 1984. 20-22.

C. A novel or play from a collection under one cover

Serling, Rod. *Requiem for a Heavyweight. Twelve American Plays.* Ed. Richard Corbin and Miriam Balf. New York: Scribner's, 1973. 57-89.

The Red Pony. The Short Novels of John Steinbeck. New York: Viking, 1963. 355-649.

Magazines, Encyclopedias, Newspapers, Interviews

A. An article from a quarterly or monthly magazine

Batten, Mary. "Life Span." *Science Digest* Feb. 1984: 46-51.

B. An article from a weekly magazine

Powell, Bill. "Coping with the Markets." *Newsweek* 27 Apr. 1987: 54.

C. A magazine article with no author given

"How the New Tax Law Affects America." *Nation's Accountants* 24 Sept. 1986: 66-69.

D. An article from a daily newspaper

James, Noah. "The Comedian Everyone Loves to Hate." *New York Times* 22 Jan. 1984, sec. 2: 23.

E. An encyclopedia article
"Western Frontier Life." *World Book Encyclopedia.* 1991 ed.

F. A signed review
Ludlow, Arthur. "Glass Houses." Rev. of *Rolling Breaks and Other Movie Business,* by Aljean Harmetz. *Movies* Aug. 1983: 76.

G. An unsigned, untitled review
Rev. of *Harry and Son. American Film* Mar. 1984: 78.

H. An interview
Farquharson, Reginald W. Personal interview. 26 May 1988.

Revising

Research papers almost always need revising before they fully meet the needs of the writer and reader. To get ideas for revision, find someone to read your paper carefully, then the two of you can discuss the following questions as a guide.

1. Is the purpose for writing clear?
2. Are ideas presented clearly, one at a time?
3. Is more information needed anywhere?
4. Should some of the information be cut out?
5. Are there too many quotes or too few?

The Final Edit

After making all the necessary changes, read through the paper once more, correcting mistakes in usage, spelling, and mechanics. Be sure that you've used quotation marks correctly and that you've followed the right format for your documentation and bibliography.

Manuscript Form

Legibility If possible type or word process your papers. If you write by hand, use a pen with dark blue or black ink.

Corrections Insert missing words by writing them neatly above the line in which they should appear. Use a caret (‸) to indicate where they should be read in the text. You may make neat corrections by drawing a line through words and writing above them or by deleting a word or phrase with correction fluid and writing in the space. If there are several corrections on a page, recopy it.

Labeling Follow the instructions given by your teacher for identifying yourself as the author of the paper. Usually, you will be asked to put your name in the top right-hand corner of the first page. Below your name, you will place the name or number of the course. Below that, you will put the date.

Title The title of your paper should appear only once—on the first page. Center the title two lines below the last line of your heading. Leave two lines between the title and the first line of your first paragraph.

The first word of your title must be capitalized. Also capitalize any other important words in the title. Use initial capitals only. Do not capitalize every letter or underline your title. Use quotation marks in the title only if you are quoting some other source.

Teachers sometimes require a separate title page for long papers. A title page contains a heading in the upper right-hand corner and the title centered on the page.

CORRECT BUSINESS LETTER FORM

Business letters are written for a specific purpose, such as requesting information, ordering a product, or applying for a job. An effective letter is one that achieves its desired result. If you want your letter to get results, you should pay careful attention to its physical appearance and format. A neat, attractive letter will be easier to read. It will also create a favorable impression, and your reader will be more receptive to your message.

Use the following guidelines in writing business letters.

1. Use plain white paper, preferably 8½ by 11 inches.
2. Type your letter and envelope if possible. If you cannot type, write legibly in ink.
3. Frame your letter like a picture, allowing a margin at least 1¼ inches on all sides.
4. Be sure your letter is error free and clean.
5. Make a photocopy of your letter for your records.

The Parts of a Letter

Every business letter has six parts. These parts are used to present information in an organized and predictable way.

Heading The heading consists of three lines at the top of the page. The first line gives your street address (or your rural route or post office box number) and, if applicable, your apartment number. The second line lists your city, state, and ZIP code. The third line gives the date.

413 Acacia Avenue, 3A	P.O. Box 1782051
Palo Alto, California 94306	St. Louis, Missouri 63141
June 26, 19--	August 31, 19--

If you live in a small town that does not use street addresses or post office box numbers for mailing purposes, the name of your town should be placed on the first line and your state and ZIP code on the second line.

Inside Address The inside address follows the heading after a line of space. The name and title of the person to whom you are writing (or the name of the department if you do not know the person's name) go on the first line, the name of the company or organization goes on the second line, the street address or post office box number goes on the third line, and the city, state, and ZIP code go on the fourth line.

Ms. Sara Lemoine, Director
Youth Employment Agency
816 West Flournoy Avenue
Oak Park, Illinois 60304

Customer Service Department
SCM Office Suppliers
2409 West Second Street
Marion, Indiana 46952

If possible, you should direct your letter to a specific person, using his or her full name and correct title.

Salutation The salutation is placed beneath the inside address with a line of space between them. It begins with *Dear,* is followed by the name of the person to whom you are writing, and ends with a colon. If you do not know the person's name, address the department or position within the company or organization. The following forms are acceptable:

Dear Mr. Hammond:	Dear Sir or Madam:
Dear Representative:	Dear Editor:

Body The body, in which you convey your central message, begins beneath the salutation. Leave a line of space between them. Single-space between the lines in each paragraph and double-space between paragraphs. If your letter is very short, you may choose to double-space the entire body.

Closing The closing is placed two lines below the body. Only the first word is capitalized. The last word is followed by a comma.

Sincerely, Cordially,
Very truly yours, Respectfully yours,
Sincerely yours, Yours truly,

Signature The signature should be written in ink beneath the closing. If your letter is typed, you should also type your name below your signature, four spaces below the closing. Otherwise, print your name beneath the signature.

The business envelope is a standard nine by four inches. The address should be placed near the center of the envelope front. The return address is positioned in the upper left-hand corner.

Forms of Business Letters

The two most frequently used forms of business letters are full block and modified block. In full block form, all parts of the letter begin at the left margin. Paragraphs are not indented, but a line of space is left between them. An example of this form is given below.

Full Block Form

413 Acacia Avenue, 3A **Heading**
Palo Alto, California 94306
February 7, 19--

Service Representative **Inside Address**
Leisure Time Publishing Company
P.O. Box 87345
Walnut Creek, California 94597

Dear Service Representative: **Salutation**

I am writing to seek correction of a mistake that your company made. On January 15 I ordered the book *Great Moments in Rock and Roll* by Bill Fender from your company. I included a money order for $21.95. However, I have neither heard from your company nor received the book. **Body**

Please either send me the book or refund my money as soon as possible. I have enclosed a copy of my money order and a copy of my original order letter.

Yours truly, **Closing**

Rosa M. Ortega

Rosa M. Ortega **Signature**

Modified Block Form In modified block form, paragraphs are indented with a line of space left between them. As you can see in the example below, the heading, closing, and signature are aligned near the right margin.

718 Heffron Drive Winona, Minnesota 55987 March 29, 19——	**Heading**
Order Department Music Alive! P.O. Box 216735 Minneapolis, Minnesota 55428	**Inside Address**
Dear Order Department:	**Salutation**
I am interested in becoming a member of your Compact Disc Discount Club. Please send me an application form and a copy of your catalog.	**Body**
Sincerely,	**Closing**
Robert Costello Robert Costello	**Signature**

LANGUAGE HANDBOOK

USING THE LANGUAGE HANDBOOK

This language handbook outlines some of the common errors people make in both written and spoken English. The handbook does not focus on learning rules and terms. Its goal is to provide concentrated review and practice in the areas where usage problems often occur.

THE PARTS OF SPEECH

While terminology is not emphasized in this book, it is important to have a basic knowledge of the parts of speech so that you can communicate about language. Here is a quick review.

Noun. A noun is a word that names a person, place, thing, or idea.
athlete Los Angeles basketball faith

Pronoun. A pronoun is a word used in place of a noun or another pronoun.
we your itself someone who which

Verb. A verb is a word that tells about an action, or a state of being.
jump study felt is

Adjective. An adjective is a word that modifies a noun or a pronoun.
large orange terrific little

Adverb. An adverb is a word that modifies a verb, an adjective, or another adverb.
really completely early away actually

Preposition. A preposition is a word used with a noun or a pronoun to show how the noun or pronoun is related to some other word in the sentence.
up among before to near beside

Conjunction. A conjunction is a word that connects words or groups of words.
for but as indeed therefore

Interjection. An interjection is a word or group of words that shows feeling or emotion.
great oh hello ouch help

SECTION 1 WRITING COMPLETE SENTENCES

A *sentence* is a group of words that expresses a complete thought. Every sentence begins with a capital letter and ends with a period, a question mark, or an exclamation mark.

Sentence Parts

Every group of words that forms a sentence has a subject and a verb. A sentence may also have other elements, such as objects, that complete its meaning.

You probably already know the basic parts of a sentence. The following diagrams will help you review your knowledge of sentence parts.

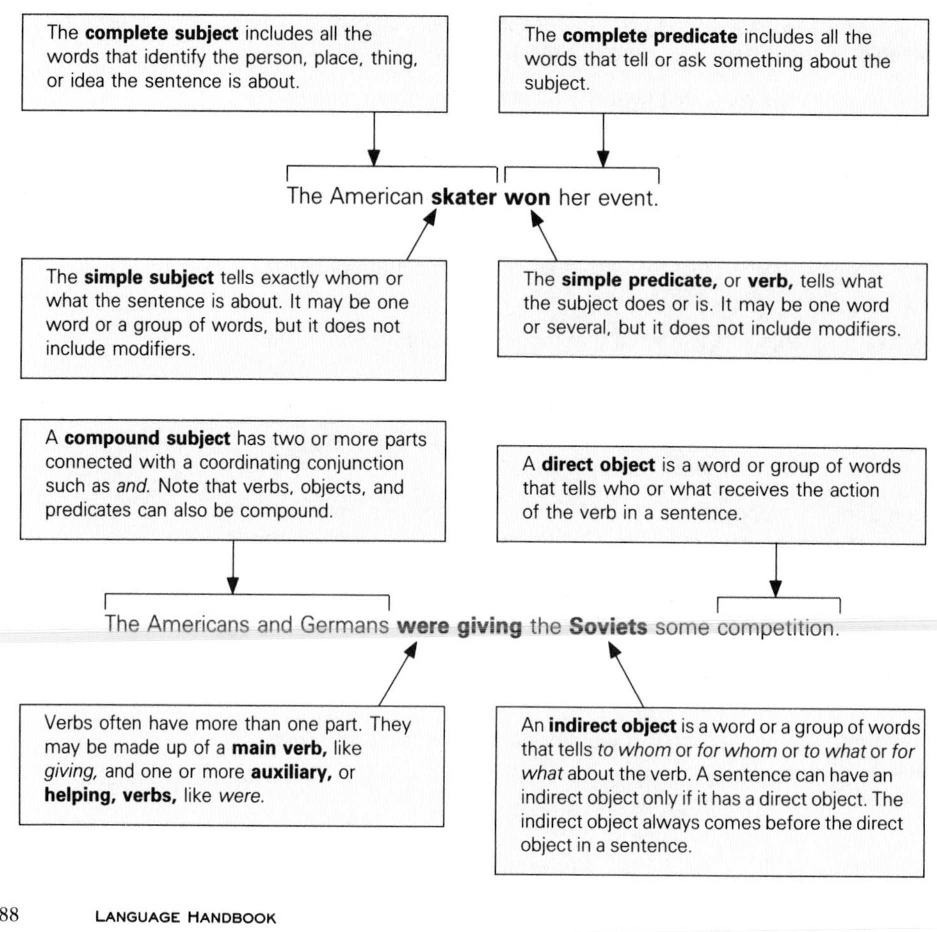

Additional Resources

GRAMMAR AND USAGE COPY MASTERS

- Exercises
- Tests

Sentence Fragments

A *sentence fragment* is a group of words that does not express a complete thought.

A group of words is a fragment if additional words are required in order to complete the idea. You can correct a sentence fragment by adding the missing words.

Fragment Spent twenty years in a South African jail. (Who or what spent twenty years in jail? The subject is missing.)
Sentence Nelson Mandela spent twenty years in a South African jail.

Fragment After the Reds won the series. (What happened after the Reds won the series? Additional words are needed to complete the idea.)
Sentence After the Reds won the series, the Cincinnati fans rejoiced.

Fragment The Komodo dragons on the Galápagos Islands. (What about the Komodo dragons? The verb is missing.)
Sentence The Komodo dragons on the Galápagos Islands like to bask in the sun all day.

QUICK TIP To check for sentence fragments in a composition, try reading the last sentence aloud, then the next to the last sentence, and so on. By reading the sentences in reverse order, you can concentrate on each by itself. When reading each sentence, ask yourself, does this group of words express a complete thought?

Exercise 1 Sentence Fragments On your paper, write each group of words. If the word group is a sentence, add the necessary capitalization and end punctuation. If the word group is a fragment, add whatever is necessary to make it a complete sentence.

Example a stand-up comedian
Answer A stand-up comedian has a difficult job.

1. make people laugh
2. come up with original gags and funny stories
3. Bob Goldthwaite, Louie Anderson, and Paula Poundstone
4. in comedy clubs around the country
5. after a comedian has appeared on *The Tonight Show* or a cable television special
6. attend acting schools or simply learn by watching other comedians

RULES ARE MADE TO BE BROKEN

In some situations the rule against using fragments can be broken. Fragments are acceptable in conversation and in written dialogue (which is, after all, an imitation of conversation). When taking notes, you should use fragments because you don't have time to write complete sentences.

Exercise 1

Answers will vary. Probable answers are provided.

1. Comedians love to make people laugh.
2. Comedians need to come up with original gags and funny stories.
3. Bob Goldthwaite, Louie Anderson, and Paula Poundstone are all stand-up comedians.
4. They appear in comedy clubs around the country.
5. After a comedian has appeared on *The Tonight Show* or a cable television special, he or she may become very popular.
6. Comedians attend acting schools or simply learn by watching other comedians.

7. They need to learn the tricks of the trade, such as raising one's voice at the end of a punch line.
8. Every comic must contend with hecklers.
9. Learn what to do and say when there are hecklers in the audience. (If students think this is a fragment, do a mini-review of imperative sentences.)
10. What is the best way to deal with a heckler?

Exercise 2

1. High in the Andes mountain range in Peru is the city of Cuzco. This was the ancient capital of the Inca empire.
2. The great period of the empire began when a neighboring tribe threatened to invade Inca land. The Incas met their neighbors on the battlefield and overpowered them.
3. When they conquered an area, the Incas enlisted its men into their army. Thus the Inca army grew to mighty proportions.

7. tricks of the trade, such as raising one's voice at the end of a punch line
8. every comic must contend with hecklers
9. learn what to do and say when there are hecklers in the audience
10. the best way to deal with a heckler

Run-on Sentences

A *run-on sentence* is two or more sentences written as one.

When ideas are run together, readers can become confused. You can avoid confusing run-on sentences by putting a period or other end mark at the end of each complete sentence. Of course, each sentence should begin with a capital letter.

Run-on The California sea otters were endangered now their numbers are increasing.
Correct The California sea otters were endangered. Now their numbers are increasing.

Run-ons also occur when writers use commas instead of periods to separate complete thoughts. When a writer uses a comma between two sentences, he or she commits the error known as a **comma splice** or **comma fault.** Correct a comma splice in the same way you would correct any other run-on.

Comma Splice A helicopter arrived, it rescued the flood victims.
Correct A helicopter arrived. It rescued the flood victims.

Exercise 2 Run-on Sentences Correct the following sentences that are run-ons by adding capitalization and punctuation to show where each complete thought begins and ends. If a sentence is not a run-on, write *Correct.*

Example Long ago in South America, the Incas ruled a vast empire, it stretched for most of the length of South America.
Answer Long ago in South America, the Incas ruled a vast empire. It stretched for most of the length of South America.

1. High in the Andes mountain range in Peru is the city of Cuzco, this was the ancient capital of the Inca empire.
2. The great period of the empire began when a neighboring tribe threatened to invade Inca land, the Incas met their neighbors on the battlefield and overpowered them.
3. When they conquered an area, the Incas enlisted its men into their army, thus the Inca army grew to mighty proportions.

4. The Incas built magnificent temples and palaces, they also built a system of roads throughout their empire.
5. By the late 1400's the empire was at its height its ruler was named Huayna Capac.
6. Huayna Capac had two sons, the older, Huáscar, was supposed to become ruler of the Incas after his father died.
7. Huayna Capac gave half the empire to Huáscar the other half he gave to his younger son, Atahualpa.
8. After Huayna Capac died, the two brothers declared war on each other each raised an enormous army.
9. The brothers' armies met at the Río Bamba their battle left thousands of warriors dead.
10. Then, a few years later, Atahualpa defeated Huáscar for good in an even greater battle.
11. Atahualpa then went to a resort area to relax and enjoy the hot baths.
12. While he was relaxing and enjoying himself, he heard a strange report, some old-looking bearded men had arrived.
13. The Incas had never seen Europeans before, they thought that Francisco Pizarro and his Spanish conquistadors must be gods.
14. Pizarro captured Atahualpa and held him for ransom, he promised to release the Inca king if his subjects would fill a ransom room with gold.
15. The Incas filled the room with gold, however, Pizarro simply took the gold and killed the Inca leader anyway.

Exercise 3 Complete Sentences Tell whether each group of words is a *Sentence, Fragment,* or *Run-on.* Then write each group of words. Add to the sentences any necessary punctuation. Correct the fragments by adding words to make complete sentences. Correct the run-ons, including comma splices, by adding capitalization and punctuation.

1. Langston Hughes, one of the leading writers of the Harlem Renaissance
2. Born in 1902 in Joplin, Missouri, at the beginning of a new century and of a new age in African-American culture
3. From an early age, he devoured the poetry of Carl Sandburg and Walt Whitman, he himself began publishing poetry at the age of nineteen
4. Hughes studied at Columbia University after one year he left school and became a sailor on a freighter
5. Hughes ended up in Paris there he listened to jazz in crowded nightclubs

4. The Incas built magnificent temples and palaces. They also built a system of roads throughout their empire.
5. By the late 1400s the empire was at its height. Its ruler was named Huayna Capac.
6. Huayna Capac had two sons. The oldest, Huascar, was supposed to become head of the Incas after his father died.
7. Huayna Capac gave half of the empire to Huascar. The other half he gave to his younger son, Atahualpa.
8. After Huayna Capac died, the two brothers declared war on each other. Each raised an enormous army.
9. The brothers' armies met at the Río Bamba. Their battle left thousands of warriors dead.
10. Correct
11. Correct
12. While he was relaxing and enjoying himself, he heard a strange report. Some old-looking bearded men had arrived.
13. The Incas had never seen Europeans before. They thought that Francisco Pizarro and his Spanish conquistadors must be gods.
14. Pizarro captured Atahualpa and held him for ransom. He promised to release the Inca king if his subjects would fill a ransom room with gold.
15. The Incas filled the room with gold. However, Pizarro simply took the gold and killed the Inca leader anyway.

Exercise 3

Answers will vary. Probable answers are provided.
1. Fragment–Langston Hughes, one of the leading writers of the Harlem Renaissance, lived a fascinating life.
2. Fragment–Born in 1902 in Joplin, Missouri, at the beginning of a new century and of a new age in African-American culture, Hughes began writing when he was quite young.
3. Run-on–From an early age, he devoured the poetry of Carl Sandburg and Walt Whitman. He himself began publishing poetry at the age of nineteen.
4. Run-on–Hughes studied at Columbia University. After one year he left school and became a sailor on a freighter.
5. Run-on–Hughes ended up in Paris. There he listened to jazz in crowded nightclubs.

6. Run-on–Hughes's first book of poetry was published in 1926. That same year Hughes enrolled at Lincoln University.
7. Run-on–Hughes's first novel, *Not Without Laughter,* portrayed everyday African-American life. It was a great success.
8. Fragment–in 1937, working as a reporter covering the Spanish Civil War, Hughes saw the reality of war for the first time.
9. Sentence–When he returned home, he founded the Harlem Suitcase Theater.
10. Fragment–His own one-act play, entitled *Don't You Want to Be Free?,* was performed there.
11. Fragment–Hughes continued writing superb poetry, much of it involving elements of the African-American tradition.
12. Fragment–Hughes wrote poetry containing short verses and repeated choruses like the old-fashioned spirituals and poetry containing the exciting rhythms of jazz music.
13. Run-on–In 1934 he worked as a columnist for a Chicago newspaper. His columns were later collected into five books.
14. Sentence–Hughes wrote in many different formats; he wrote poetry, plays, children's books, short stories, articles, biographies, movie scripts, and autobiographical material.
15. Fragment–Among his greatest works were the poems "A Negro Speaks of Rivers" and "Song of a Dark Girl."

PUNCTUATION

Material that appears in italics when printed in a book should be underlined when handwritten or typewritten, as follows:

Hughes's first novel, Not Without Laughter

6. Hughes's first book of poetry was published in 1926 that same year Hughes enrolled at Lincoln University
7. Hughes's first novel, *Not Without Laughter,* portrayed everyday African-American life it was a great success
8. In 1937, working as a reporter covering the Spanish Civil War
9. When he returned home, he founded the Harlem Suitcase Theater
10. His own one-act play, entitled *Don't You Want to Be Free?*
11. Continued writing superb poetry, much of it involving elements of the African-American tradition
12. Poetry containing short verses and repeated choruses like the old-fashioned spirituals and poetry containing the exciting rhythms of jazz music
13. In 1934 he worked as a columnist for a Chicago newspaper, his columns were later collected into five books
14. Hughes wrote in many different formats; he wrote poetry, plays, children's books, short stories, articles, biographies, movie scripts, and autobiographical material
15. Among his greatest works the poems "A Negro Speaks of Rivers" and "Song of a Dark Girl"

Sentence Combining

Whenever you revise your writing, you should check for sentence fragments and run-ons. You should also check to make sure that you do not have too many short, choppy sentences. In other words, you should vary both the lengths and the types of sentences you use. To come up with longer, varied sentences, you can combine by joining related sentences or by adding sentence parts.

When combining by joining related sentences, use a comma and a coordinating conjunction.

Separate Sentences	Rodney Fox is an expert on sharks. He is famous for his work with Dr. Eugenie Clark.
Combined Sentences	Rodney Fox is an expert on sharks**, and** he is famous for his work with Dr. Eugenie Clark.

COORDINATING CONJUNCTIONS

The coordinating conjunctions are *and, or, nor, for, but, so,* and *yet.*
An effective memorization tip is to think of them as the parts of a Russian-sounding name:

Andor Norfor Butsoyet

When combining by adding sentence parts, use a coordinating conjunction. Combined sentence parts are called **compound** parts. Here are a few of the different parts that can be combined. (Notice that the italicized words are deleted.)

Compound Subject	Whale sharks are large, deep-sea creatures. + Great whites *are large, deep-sea creatures.* = Whale sharks **and** great whites are large, deep-sea creatures.

Compound Verb	Rodney Fox was attacked by a great white shark. + *He was also* bitten *by the great white shark.* = Rodney Fox was attacked **and** bitten by a great white shark.
Compound Predicate	Fox struggled free. + *He* then swam back to his dive boat. = Fox struggled free **and** then swam back to his dive boat.
Compound Object	When Fox reached the boat, he had a crushed rib cage. + *He also had* a punctured lung. = When Fox reached the boat, he had a crushed rib cage **and** a punctured lung.

> **QUICK TIP** When you revise your writing, look for ways to combine some sentences to add variety in sentence type and length. Leave some sentences short for emphasis.

Exercise 4 Combining Sentences Combine sentences by following the directions in parentheses. Eliminate the italicized words.

1. Woolly mammoths lived over ten thousand years ago. *They* inhabited North America, Europe, and Asia. (Combine by adding the predicate from the second sentence.)
2. Long tusks were characteristic of the mammoths. Enormous size *was also characteristic of the mammoths.* (Add the subject from the second sentence.)
3. Modern elephants stand about ten feet high at the shoulder. Mammoths stood about thirteen feet high. (Combine by joining the sentences using a comma and the conjunction *but.*)
4. Years ago, scientists in Siberia discovered a peculiar mammoth. *They also* excavated *it.* (Combine by adding the verb from the second sentence.)
5. The mammoth was frozen. *It* had buttercups in its mouth. (Combine by adding the predicate from the second sentence.)
6. Thousands of years ago, something had frozen the mammoth. *This force had also frozen* the fresh green plants it was eating. (Combine by adding the object, *plants,* and its modifying words and phrases.)
7. The fresh green plants mean that the weather must have been warm. The freezing of the mammoth required a sudden, fierce cold. (Join the sentences using a comma and the conjunction *yet.*)
8. For years now, scientists have speculated about what might have caused the sudden deep freeze of the Siberian mammoth. Crackpots *have also speculated about what caused this deep freeze.* (Combine by adding the subject from the second sentence.)

Exercise 4

1. Woolly mammoths lived over ten thousand years ago and inhabited North America, Europe, and Asia.
2. Long tusks and enormous size were characteristics of the mammoths.
3. Modern elephants stand about ten feet high at the shoulder, but mammoths stood about thirteen feet high.
4. Years ago, scientists in Siberia discovered and excavated a peculiar mammoth.
5. The mammoth was frozen and had buttercups in its mouth.
6. Thousands of years ago, something had frozen the mammoth and the fresh, green plants it was eating.
7. The fresh, green plants mean that the weather must have been warm, yet the freezing of the mammoth required a sudden, fierce cold.
8. For years now, scientists and crackpots have speculated about what might have caused the sudden deep freeze of the Siberian mammoth.

9. To this day, no one has solved this mystery; furthermore, no one has a clue how to go about solving it.
10. Somehow that mammoth and those buttercups were warm one moment and frozen solid the next moment!

Exercise 5

Answers may vary. Probable answers are provided.
1. Fragment–American football, a game derived from the English games of rugby and soccer, has a fascinating history.
2. Run-on–The early games were violent. In one year–1905–there were eighteen deaths and 159 serious injuries.
3. Sentence–As a result, President Theodore Roosevelt threatened to ban the game.
4. Run-on–Representatives from various colleges met. They revised the rules.
5. Fragment–They made the game safer.
6. Sentence–For example, they required the use of linemen.
7. Run-on–This changed tackling considerably; tackles couldn't get a long running start.
8. Fragment–That modified game was still not like modern football.
9. Fragment–Passing, which was made a major part of the game by Notre Dame's Gus Dorais and Knute Rockne, was soon added.
10. Run-on–Passing increased spectator interest. Consequently, football is now one of the most popular of all sports.

Exercise 6

Answers may vary. Probable answers are provided.
American football, a game derived from the English games of rugby and soccer, has a fascinating history. The early games were violent. In one year–1905–there were eighteen deaths and 159 serious injuries. As a result, President Theodore Roosevelt threatened to ban the game. Representatives from various colleges met and revised the rules. They made the game safer; for example, they required the use of linemen. This changed tackling considerably; tackles couldn't get a long running start. That modified game was still not like modern football. Passing, which was made a major part of the game by Notre Dame's Gus Dorais and Knute Rockne, was soon added and it increased spectator interest. Consequently, football is now one of the most popular of all sports.

9. To this day, no one has solved this mystery. No one has a clue as to how to go about solving it. (Join the two sentences using a semicolon, the conjunctive adverb *furthermore,* and a comma.)
10. Somehow that mammoth was warm one moment and frozen solid the next moment! Those buttercups *were also warm one moment and frozen solid the next moment!* (Combine by adding the subject from the second sentence.)

Exercise 5 Sentence Review Tell whether each group of words is a *Sentence,* a *Fragment,* or a *Run-on.* Then write each group of words. Correct fragments by adding missing parts. Correct run-ons by making separate sentences or combining sentence parts. Add capitalization or punctuation as necessary.

1. American football, a game derived from the English games of rugby and soccer
2. The early games were violent, in one year—1905—there were eighteen deaths and 159 serious injuries
3. As a result, President Theodore Roosevelt threatened to ban the game
4. Representatives from various colleges met they revised the rules
5. Made the game safer
6. For example, they required the use of linemen
7. This changed tackling considerably tackles couldn't get a long running start
8. Still not like modern football
9. Passing, which was made a major part of the game by Notre Dame's Gus Dorais and Knute Rockne
10. Passing increased spectator interest consequently, football is now one of the most popular of all sports

Exercise 6 Combining Review Write the sentences of the preceding exercise as a paragraph. Combine two pairs of sentences in the paragraph to make longer sentences. Use the sentence-combining techniques that you have learned.

SECTION 2 USING NOUNS

A *noun* is a word that names a person, place, thing, or idea.

Persons William Shakespeare, aunt, teacher
Places San Antonio, river, museum, Mars
Things camera, coat, book, pencil
Ideas hope, democracy, happiness, prejudice

Noun Classes

Nouns can be classified into six groups, as shown in the following list.

Common Noun. A general name, such as *city, game, palace, lake, writer.*

Proper Noun. A specific name, such as *Rochester, Super Bowl, Buckingham Palace, Lake Michigan, E. B. White.* Note that proper nouns are always capitalized.

Concrete Noun. Anything that can be seen, heard, smelled, touched, or tasted, such as *cashew, pueblo, fern, cleat, bell.*

Abstract Noun. Something that cannot be directly seen, touched, tasted, or smelled, such as *goodness, defeat, peacefulness, duty.*

Compound Noun. A noun made of two or more words, such as *earthworm, great-uncle, ice hockey, Main Street.* Some compounds are written as one word, some as two words, and others with a hyphen.

Collective Noun. A noun that names a group of people or things, such as *Cherokee, committee, family, society, class, team.*

SPELLING

The spellings of proper nouns can be checked in reference works such as atlases, encyclopedias, and biographical dictionaries.

Compound nouns can be confusing. Some are spelled solid *(highland)*; some are spelled as two words *(high jump)*; and some are hyphenated *(high-rise)*. To find out how to spell a particular compound, check a dictionary.

Noun Usage

In most cases, the form of a noun changes to indicate that it is plural or possessive.

Plural Nouns

A noun is **singular** if it names one thing. It is **plural** if it names more than one thing. Follow these rules when forming the plurals of nouns:

1. Most nouns form the plural by simply adding *-s* to the singular.

jar	tulip	wave	satellite	file
jars	tulips	waves	satellites	files

REMINDER

Some nouns have no singular form. For example, one can't have a single *scissor.* One always uses the plural, *scissors.*

Additional Resources
GRAMMAR AND USAGE COPY MASTERS
- Exercises
- Tests

2. **Nouns that end in *-s, -sh, -ch, -x,* or *-z* form the plural by adding *-es.*** Even if you forget this exact rule, you can see from the following examples that adding *-es* to such words just looks and sounds right.

glass	dish	watch	ax	waltz
glasses	dishes	watches	axes	waltzes

3. **If a noun ends in *-o* preceded by a vowel, add *-s* to form the plural. Some nouns that end in *-o* preceded by a consonant form the plural with *-s.* Others form the plural with *-es.* Consult a dictionary to determine which are which.**

ratio	duo	silo	veto	hero
ratios	duos	silos	vetoes	heroes

4. **If a noun ends in *-y* preceded by a vowel, add *-s* to form the plural. If the *-y* follows a consonant, change the *-y* to *-i* and add *-es.***

pulley	attorney	envoy	duty	party
pulleys	attorneys	envoys	duties	parties

SPELLING

There is no general rule covering all nouns ending in *-f* or *-fe.* Some form the plural with *-s,* others by changing the *-f* to *-v* and adding *-s* or *-es.* Use a dictionary to check the plurals of words with these endings.

5. **For most nouns ending in *-f* or *-fe,* change the *-f* to *-v* and add *-es* or *-s.***

wharf	elf	life	loaf	sheaf
wharves	elves	lives	loaves	sheaves

For some nouns ending in *-f* or *-fe,* just add *-s* to make the plural.

reef	safe	giraffe	roof	carafe
reefs	safes	giraffes	roofs	carafes

6. **Some nouns have the same form for both singular and plural.**

trout	corps	moose	fish	tuna
trout	corps	moose	fish	tuna

7. **For some nouns the plural is formed in a unique way.**

medium	mouse	crisis	man	goose
media	mice	crises	men	geese

8. **If a compound noun is written as one word, form the plural by changing the last word in the compound to its plural form.**

rosebush	shovelful
rosebushes	shovelfuls

If the compound is written as separate words or is hyphenated, change the most important word to the plural form.

bill of sale	brother-in-law
bills of sale	brothers-in-law

Exercise 1 Plural Nouns Write the plural form of each noun. If you need help, check a dictionary.

1. shelf	**6.** chimney	**11.** swish	**16.** tomato
2. wife	**7.** treaty	**12.** jelly	**17.** piano
3. sheep	**8.** watch	**13.** county	**18.** photo
4. fox	**9.** brush	**14.** mouse	**19.** teaspoonful
5. child	**10.** orderly	**15.** witch	**20.** passer-by

Exercise 2 Plural Nouns Change the italicized singular nouns to their correct plural forms.

1. The *life* of artists can be difficult.
2. For many *man* and *woman* artistic talent can be a burden.
3. Many *society* do not encourage their artists.
4. In many *country* artistic dreams are considered *luxury*.
5. *Artist* are rarely called *hero*.
6. During the Renaissance, *belief* about artists changed.
7. *City* such as Florence, Italy, became filled with artists and writers.
8. People called patrons built vast *studio* in which *artist* could work.
9. *Sculptor* were paid to create *work* from marble or clay.
10. *Artist* won *prize* for painting vast public *mural*.

Possessive Nouns

A **possessive noun** is one that shows ownership or belonging. Follow these rules when forming the possessives of nouns:

1. **If a noun is singular, add an apostrophe and *-s* to form the possessive.**

Luisa	law	cobra	beret	Ms. Ruiz
Luisa's	law's	cobra's	beret's	Ms. Ruiz's

2. **If a noun is plural and ends in *-s*, add just the apostrophe.**

parents	players
parents' advice	players' coaches

THE CHOICE IS YOURS

Sometimes, instead of writing a possessive using an apostrophe, you may want to use a prepositional phrase. A prepositional phrase consists of a preposition, such as *at* or *of,* and an object.

For example, instead of writing *the airplane's propellers,* write *the propellers of the airplane.*

Exercise 1

1. shelves	**11.** swishes
2. wives	**12.** jellies
3. sheep	**13.** counties
4. foxes	**14.** mice
5. children	**15.** witches
6. chimneys	**16.** tomatoes
7. treaties	**17.** pianos
8. watches	**18.** photos
9. brushes	**19.** teaspoonfuls
10. orderlies	**20.** passers-by

Exercise 2

1. lives
2. men, women
3. societies
4. countries, luxuries
5. Artists, heroes
6. beliefs
7. Cities
8. studios, artists
9. Sculptors, works
10. Artists, prizes, murals

Exercise 3

1. students'
2. Shakespeare's
3. Lee's
4. class's
5. teenagers'
6. Teens'
7. Rome's
8. people's
9. families'
10. high school's

Exercise 4

Answers will vary. Probable answers are provided.

1. Roberta's cat–Roberta's cat is old.
2. the scientists' report–The scientists' reports were interesting.
3. the pitchers' styles–The pitchers' styles were quite different.
4. a captain's job–A captain's job is demanding.
5. Nicholas's answer–Nicholas's answer was correct.
6. some of the drivers' licenses–Some of the drivers' licenses were expired.
7. the radios' prices–The radios' prices had gone up.
8. an actress's career–An actress's career can be quite varied.
9. the fish's gills–The fish's gills are delicate.
10. two grandchildren's pictures–She hung her two grandchildren's pictures over the mantle.

REMINDER

Writers sometimes confuse the rules for singular nouns that end in *-s* and plural nouns that end in *-s.* Remember that singular nouns that end in *-s* form the possessive by adding an apostrophe and *-s.* Plural nouns that end in *-s* form the possessive by adding just an apostrophe.

3. If a noun is plural and does not end in *-s,* add an apostrophe and *-s.*

geese	women
geese's feathers	women's goals

Exercise 3 Possessive Nouns Change the italicized nouns to their correct possessive forms. (Leave the nouns singular or plural, as shown.)

1. The *students* interest in the city of Rome was formed by reading a Shakespearean play about the life of Julius Caesar.
2. *Shakespeare* tragedy deals with a conspiracy against Caesar.
3. *Lee* idea was fantastic! He wanted a class trip to Rome!
4. The *class* decision was unanimous in favor of the trip.
5. The idea was discussed with all the *teenagers* teachers and parents.
6. To raise money for the trip, the class created a company that they called Busy *Teens* Work Force, Inc.
7. *Rome* statues and fountains seemed far away to the hardworking students.
8. The young *people* fondest thoughts were on that special goal: Rome in July.
9. Their *families* good-byes were barely heard.
10. The *high school* busy sophomores were on their way to Rome!

Exercise 4 Noun Usage Review Write the possessive form of the italicized word in the singular or plural as indicated. Then write a sentence using the phrase.

Item the officer (singular) message
Answer the officer's message
The officer's message was, "Be brave!"

1. *Roberta* (singular) cat
2. the *scientist* (plural) reports
3. the *pitcher* (plural) styles
4. a *captain* (singular) job
5. *Nicholas* (singular) answer
6. some of the *driver* (plural) licenses
7. the *radio* (plural) prices
8. an *actress* (singular) career
9. the *fish* (plural) gills
10. two *grandchild* (plural) pictures

SECTION 3 USING PRONOUNS

A *pronoun* is a word that is used in place of a noun or another pronoun. The word to which a pronoun refers is its *antecedent*.

Deep in the woods, a dove was singing its sad song. (The pronoun *its* refers to the noun *dove*. *Dove* is the antecedent of *its*.)

Classes of Pronouns

A class is a group of similar things. Pronouns can be divided into a number of different classes, as shown in the following chart.

Classes of Pronouns
Personal
I, you, he, she, it, we, they, me, her, him, us, them, my, mine, your, yours, hers, his, its, our, ours, their, theirs
Reflexive and Intensive
myself, yourself, himself, herself, itself, ourselves, yourselves, themselves
Demonstrative
this, that, these, those
Interrogative
who, whose, whom, which, what
Relative
who, whose, whom, which, what, that
Indefinite
all, another, any, anybody, anyone, anything, both, each, either, everybody, everyone, everything, few, many, more, most, much, neither, nobody, none, no one, nothing, one, other, several, some, somebody, someone, something, such

Pronoun Usage

One of the reasons why it's important for you to learn how to use pronouns correctly is that they are used so often. For example, the preceding sentence itself contains four pronouns!

There are only a few situations in which pronouns are particularly confusing. By mastering these, you can avoid the problems that many people have in using pronouns.

Additional Resources

GRAMMAR AND USAGE COPY MASTERS

- Exercises
- Tests

Exercise 1

1. Their–Plural, Possessive
   them–Plural, Objective
2. I–Singular, Nominative
   my–Singular, Possessive
   me–Singular, Objective
   We–Plural, Nominative
   he–Singular, Nominative
   his–Singular, Possessive
   your–Singular, Possessive
   him–Singular, Objective

Personal Pronouns

Personal pronouns take their name from the fact that most of them are used to refer to persons. There are three different types, or **cases,** of personal pronouns. These are the **nominative case,** the **objective case,** and the **possessive case.**

SPEAKING PERSONALLY

Yet another way of classifying personal pronouns is by the person or persons to whom they refer.

First-person pronouns: *I, me, my, mine, we, us, our, ours*

Second-person pronouns: *you, your, yours*

Third-person pronouns: *he, she, it, him, her, his, hers, its, they, them, their, theirs*

Forms of Personal Pronouns

	Nominative	Objective	Possessive
Singular	I	me	my, mine
	you	you	your, yours
	she, he, it	her, him, it	her, hers, his, its
Plural	we	us	our, ours
	you	you	your, yours
	they	them	their, theirs

Exercise 1 Personal Pronouns Write the italicized pronouns from the following passages. For each pronoun, tell whether it is *Singular* or *Plural.* Then tell whether it is *Nominative, Objective,* or *Possessive.*

1. "The people of Pompeii knew that doom was at hand now. *Their* fears were doubled when an enormous rain of hot ashes began to fall on *them,* along with more lapilli."

   —"Pompeii," Robert Silverberg

2. "Within a few days *I* received a letter from *my* brother. This brother could not endure *me. We* had parted over a difference of opinion: he considered me a selfish parasite, incapable of self-sacrifice, and for this *he* despised me. In *his* letter he now wrote: 'Dear brother, I love you, and you cannot imagine what hellish torture our quarrel has caused me. Let us make it up. Let us each extend a hand to the other, and may peace triumph! I beg you! Awaiting *your* reply, I embrace you and remain your most loving and affectionate brother, Yevlampy.' Oh, my dear brother! I answered him saying that I embraced *him* and rejoiced."

   —"The Confession," Anton Chekhov

Uses of Personal Pronouns

Use *nominative pronouns* as subjects and as predicate pronouns.

You have seen that the nominative pronouns are *I, we, you, he, she, it,* and *they.* These pronouns are used as the subjects of sentences. The **subject** is what does the action of a sentence.

He swam the Channel. *They* filmed his crossing.

Nominative pronouns are also used as predicate pronouns. A **predicate pronoun** is one that comes after a linking verb and repeats or renames the subject.

It is *I.* The secretary of the drama club is *he.*

Use *objective pronouns* as direct objects, indirect objects, and objects of prepositions.

You have seen that the objective pronouns are *me, us, you, him, her, it,* and *them.* These pronouns are used as direct objects. A **direct object** is what receives the action of a verb.

Do you know *her?* Take *them* away.

Objective pronouns are also used as indirect objects. An **indirect object** tells *to whom* or *for whom* or *to what* or *for what* the action of the sentence is done.

The doctor gave *her* a checkup. That girl left *him* a note.

Objective pronouns are also used as objects of prepositions. The **object of a preposition** is a word that follows a preposition.

Powell is next in command under *him.*
The order came directly from *him* to *us.*

PREPOSITIONAL PHRASES

A prepositional phrase includes a preposition, its object, and any modifiers of the object:

to the ends of the earth
in the final analysis

Use *possessive pronouns* to show ownership or belonging.

Remember that the possessive pronouns are *my, mine, our, ours, your, yours, his, her, hers, its, their,* and *theirs.* Possessive pronouns can be used by themselves. They may also be used before nouns.

The strangest float in the parade is *theirs.*
Their float is in the shape of a giant lobster.

QUICK TIP How do you know whether to use a possessive, an objective, or a nominative pronoun? Just ask yourself, How will the pronoun be used? If it will be used to show ownership or belonging, a possessive pronoun is correct. If it will be used as an object, an objective pronoun is correct. If it will be used as a subject or predicate pronoun, a nominative pronoun is correct.

Exercise 2

1. Possessive
2. Nominative, Subject
3. Possessive
4. Nominative, Subject
5. Nominative, Predicate Pronoun
6. Possessive
7. Possessive
8. Objective
9. Nominative, Subject
10. Objective

Exercise 2 Uses of Personal Pronouns Tell whether each italicized pronoun is *Nominative, Objective,* or *Possessive.* Then, for each nominative pronoun, tell whether it is a *Subject* or a *Predicate Pronoun.*

1. *Our* country sent scientists to Lake Baykal in the Soviet Union.
2. *You* may know that Lake Baykal is the deepest lake in the world.
3. Kathleen Crane, the chief scientist, had *her* own reasons for exploring Lake Baykal.
4. *She* believed that the lake might contain a hot vent—a deep-water hot spring with unique life forms.
5. It was *she* who found the site of the hot vent.
6. *Her* efforts were supported by mapmaker Vladimir Golubev.
7. In *my* opinion, this was a unique and wonderful expedition.
8. Scientists had floating sleds that carried *them* along the lake walls.
9. *They* used a pressurized submersible to take them to the five-thousand-foot-deep hot vent.
10. Now we know that Baykal holds more than 2,600 forms of life, and half of *them* are found nowhere else on earth.

Common Problems with Personal Pronouns

You probably use personal pronouns correctly most of the time. However, there are a few situations in which personal pronouns can cause problems. These are described below.

Personal Pronouns as Predicate Pronouns. Never use objective pronouns as predicate pronouns. After a linking verb, such as *is* or *was,* always use a nominative pronoun.

Incorrect It was *them* who flew the first shuttle mission.
Correct It was *they* who flew the first shuttle mission.

Incorrect The student directors will be Mac and *her.*
Correct The student directors will be Mac and *she.*

Between Friends

In informal speech between friends, it's common for people to use objective pronouns as predicate pronouns, as in *I'm her* or *It is me.* However, in formal speech and writing, retain the proper nominative forms, as in *I'm she* or *It is I.*

QUICK TIP To tell which pronoun to use, try reversing the subject and the pronoun. The reversed sentence should still make sense.

Incorrect The first shuttle astronauts were *them.*
Them were the first shuttle astronauts.

Correct The first shuttle astronauts were *they.*
They were the first shuttle astronauts.

Personal Pronouns as Objects of Prepositions. Never use a nominative pronoun as the object of a preposition. A pronoun used as the object of a preposition should be in the objective case.

Incorrect Is this letter from you and *he?*

Correct Is this letter from you and *him?*

Personal Pronouns in Compounds. A pronoun can be joined with a noun or another pronoun to make a **compound.** Such compounds as the following occasionally confuse people.

Marita and she	Marita and her
I and they	me and them

Remember: the pronouns in a compound should be used like ordinary pronouns. That is, subjects and predicates should be in the nominative case. Objects should be in the objective case.

Incorrect Kim and *her* are going to be math tutors. (*Kim* and *her* are the subjects of the verb *are.* Therefore, the pronoun is incorrect.)

Correct Kim and *she* are going to be math tutors.

Incorrect The math teacher sent *she* and Kim a notice. (*She* and *Kim* are indirect objects of the verb *sent.* Therefore, the pronoun is incorrect.)

Correct The math teacher sent *her* and Kim a notice.

> **QUICK TIP** To tell which pronoun to use in a compound, try the pronoun by itself, without the other part of the compound. "The teacher sent *she* a notice" sounds odd and is incorrect.

***We* and *Us* Before Nouns.** Sometimes the pronouns *we* and *us* are used as modifiers before nouns. If the modified noun is a subject or predicate noun, use *we.* If the noun is an object, use *us.*

Incorrect *Us* windsurfers love the sun. (*Windsurfers* is the subject of the verb *love.* Therefore, you need to use *we.*)

Correct *We* windsurfers love the sun.

Incorrect However, the sun can give *we* windsurfers terrible burns. (*Windsurfers* is the object of the verb *give.* Therefore, you need to use *us.*)

Correct However, the sun can give *us* windsurfers terrible burns.

REMINDER

Remember that the nominative pronouns are *I, you, he, she, it, we,* and *they.* The objective pronouns are *me, you, him, her, it, us,* and *them.*

Exercise 3

1. We
2. me
3. he
4. he
5. them
6. them
7. they
8. he
9. us
10. he

QUICK TIP To determine which pronoun to use, try using the pronoun by itself. "The sun can give *we* terrible burns" sounds odd. "The sun can give *us* terrible burns" sounds right, and it is.

Exercise 3 Problem Personal Pronouns Choose the correct pronoun from those in parentheses.

1. (We, Us) hobbyists don't always gain national recognition.
2. Between you and (I, me), George E. Slye is an interesting retiree.
3. It is (he, him) who has more than one hundred miniature models of North American skyscrapers in his basement in New Hampshire.
4. His modelers and (he, him) work in balsa, basswood, and plastic, at a scale of one inch to two hundred feet.
5. He writes to owners of new skyscrapers, asking (they, them) and the architects for drawings.
6. The architects feel that Slye is honoring (they, them) and their drawings.
7. The owners and (they, them) gladly send Slye their plans.
8. His modelers and (he, him) sometimes finish a model before the actual building is complete.
9. Slye told (we, us) journalists that he didn't have any labor problems or government regulations to deal with.
10. Therefore, it is (he, him) alone who controls his production schedule!

USES OF *WHO* AND *WHOM*

Who and *whom* are sometimes used as **interrogative pronouns,** to ask questions.

Who was that?

Sometimes they are used to introduce subordinate clauses. A **subordinate clause** is a group of words with a subject and a verb that cannot stand on its own as a sentence.

He was the dictator *who* invaded Kuwait. (The subordinate clause is *who invaded Kuwait.*)

Using *Who* and *Whom*

Use *who* as the subject of a verb or as a predicate pronoun. Use *whom* as a direct object, an indirect object, or an object of a preposition.

Use *who* and *whom* exactly as you use personal pronouns. *Who* is a nominative pronoun. It is used as a subject or as a predicate pronoun. *Whom* is an objective pronoun. It is used as an object.

Subject	*Who* designed the first hot-air balloon?
Predicate Pronoun	The designers were *who?*
Direct Object	*Whom* did the first balloon carry?
Object of a Preposition	By *whom* was the first balloon flown?

Who and *whom* are often used in questions. They also appear as part of longer statements, like this one:

She is the architect (who, whom) designed the Vietnam Veterans Memorial.

To determine which pronoun to use, isolate the group of words to which the pronoun belongs:

(who, whom) designed the Vietnam Veterans Memorial.

Since the pronoun is being used as the subject of the verb *designed, who* is correct.

She is the architect *who* designed the Vietnam Veterans Memorial.

Exercise 4 ***Who* and *Whom*** Choose the correct pronoun from those given in parentheses.

1. (Who, Whom) has recently gone to Vietnam from the United States?
2. American scientists, (whom, who) Vietnamese researchers invited, have gone to Vietnam.
3. One of those who issued the invitation was a Vietnamese researcher to (who, whom) one flock of cranes owes a great deal.
4. The researcher was the one (who, whom) first found the flock feeding in an artificial pond.
5. The researcher was worried about the local farmers, to (who, whom) the cranes are not very important.
6. The farmers, (who, whom) were poor, had turned the cranes' usual water supply into rice paddies.
7. The American scientists (who, whom) are studying the flock want to protect the cranes' habitat.
8. There are several international wildlife benefactors from (who, whom) the scientists receive financial support.
9. The local authorities, (who, whom) have already set up a nature preserve, will receive a plan from the scientists.
10. The scientists hope that the people to (who, whom) they give the plan will help protect these rare and beautiful cranes.

Reflexive and Intensive Pronouns

Use reflexive and intensive pronouns only when they have an antecedent in the same sentence.

Reflexive and intensive pronouns are created by adding *-self* or *-selves* to certain personal pronouns.

Singular	myself	yourself	himself, herself, itself
Plural	ourselves	yourselves	themselves

Hisself and *theirselves* are not acceptable. They are nonstandard. The preceding are the only reflexive and intensive pronouns.

Exercise 4

1. Who
2. whom
3. whom
4. who
5. whom
6. who
7. who
8. whom
9. who
10. whom

Exercise 5

1. In the eleventh century, a Chinese astrologer named Yan Wei-Te prostrated himself before his emperor to share an amazing discovery.
2. The emperor and he marveled at his discovery, a new star in the heavens.
3. Tim and I learned that the new "star" was actually the supernova known as the Crab Nebula.
4. Correct
5. Some American Indians saw the supernova themselves at the same time that the Chinese did.
6. Recently, a professor and his student were themselves examining an ancient American Indian bowl.
7. They found that it contained a picture of a rabbit kicking a twenty-three-pointed star.
8. Correct
9. Correct
10. Correct

Incorrect Pedro knows *hisself* very well.

Correct Pedro knows *himself* very well.

When a reflexive or intensive pronoun appears in a sentence, the word that it refers to—its antecedent—must appear in the same sentence.

Correct *Sam* sent *himself* a love letter. (*Sam* is the antecedent of *himself.*)

Never use one of these pronouns without an antecedent.

Incorrect Susan and *myself* built the set. (*Myself* does not refer to another word in the sentence.)

Correct Susan and I built the set.

Exercise 5 Reflexive Pronouns Rewrite the following sentences, correcting any errors in the use of reflexive or intensive pronouns. If a sentence does not contain an error, write *Correct.*

1. In the eleventh century, a Chinese astrologer named Yan Wei-Te prostrated hisself before his emperor to share an amazing discovery.
2. The emperor and himself marveled at his discovery, a new star in the heavens.
3. Tim and myself learned that the new "star" was actually the supernova known as the Crab Nebula.
4. The nebula itself is sixty-five hundred light years from Earth, in the constellation Taurus.
5. Some American Indians saw the supernova theirselves at the same time that the Chinese did.
6. Recently, a professor and his student were theirselves examining an ancient American Indian bowl.
7. They found that itself contained a picture of a rabbit kicking a twenty-three-pointed star.
8. The number was itself significant because the Chinese had said that the Crab Nebula appeared for twenty-three days.
9. Archaeologists, who themselves study ancient societies, date the Indian bowl to the eleventh century.
10. Perhaps a thousand years ago, the Chinese astrologer himself had a fellow stargazer in the North American Southwest.

Indefinite Pronouns

If an indefinite pronoun is singular, its verb and any pronouns that refer to it must be singular. If an indefinite pronoun is plural, its verb and any pronouns that refer to it must be plural.

An **indefinite pronoun** is one that does not refer to a definite person or thing. Some indefinite pronouns are singular.

another	either	neither	other
anybody	everybody	nobody	somebody
anyone	everyone	no one	someone
anything	everything	nothing	something
each	much	one	

Some are plural:

both	few	many	several

Some can be either singular or plural, depending on their use.

all	enough	most	plenty
any	more	none	some

Singular *Most* of the lake was dried up. (*Most* refers to the singular word *lake.* Therefore, it is singular and takes a singular verb, *was.*)

Plural *Most* of the lakes in the area are low. (*Most* refers to the plural word *lakes.* Therefore, it is plural and takes a plural verb, *are.*)

When an indefinite pronoun is used as a subject, the verb must agree with the pronoun.

Incorrect *Neither* of the game shows *were* renewed this season. (*Neither* is the subject in this sentence. Since *neither* is singular, its verb should be singular. *Were* is plural.)

Correct *Neither* of the game shows *was* renewed this season.

QUICK TIP Don't be confused by a prepositional phrase between the subject and the verb. A verb never agrees with a word in a prepositional phrase.

Exercise 6

1. In the winter most of the humpback whales gather near Hawaii to bear their young.
2. When warmer months come, each of them travels several thousand miles in search of her feeding grounds.
3. Some of them travel to the California coast.
4. Others in the group choose to go north to Alaska's shores.
5. Each of the whales seems to return to the same feeding ground year after year.
6. Everyone in the scientific community has his or her own opinion about how whales choose a feeding ground.
7. Correct.
8. All of the specimens show that whales choose the same feeding grounds that their mothers choose.
9. Correct.
10. Perhaps many in the whale community have family ties as people do.

REMINDER

The gender of a pronoun can be male (*he*), female (*she*), or neuter (*it*). Note that some pronouns can refer to either males or females (*they, their, them*).

When a personal pronoun refers to an indefinite pronoun, the two pronouns must agree.

Incorrect Did *anyone* find *their* equipment yet?
(*Anyone* is singular, so the pronoun that refers to it should also be singular.)

Correct Did *anyone* find *his* equipment yet?
Did *anyone* find *her* equipment yet?
Did *anyone* find *his or her* equipment yet?

> **QUICK TIP** The phrase "his or her" is singular and can be used in place of *his* or *her* alone when the **gender,** or sex, of the person referred to is not known.

Exercise 6 Indefinite Pronouns Rewrite the following sentences, correcting any errors in the use of pronouns and in subject-verb agreement. If a sentence contains no errors, write *Correct.*

1. In the winter most of the humpback whales gather near Hawaii to bear her young.
2. When warmer months come, each of them travels several thousand miles in search of their feeding grounds.
3. Some of them travels to the California coast.
4. Others in the group chooses to go north to Alaska's shores.
5. Each of the whales seem to return to the same feeding ground year after year.
6. Everyone in the scientific community have their own opinion about how whales choose a feeding ground.
7. One of the scientists, C. Scott Baker, uses a dart to collect a substance called DNA from whales.
8. All of the specimens show that whales choose the same feeding grounds that his or her mothers choose.
9. None of the scientists point to scientific reasons for this.
10. Perhaps many in the whale community has family ties as people do.

Other Problems with Pronouns

Ambiguous Pronoun Reference. A word or a phrase is **ambiguous** if it could be taken more than one way. You should always be able to tell what word a pronoun refers to. If you can't—if the pronoun could refer as easily to one word as to another—then you need to rewrite the sentence to make it clear what the pronoun refers to.

Unclear The jeweler took the stone out of the setting and examined *it.* (Does the pronoun *it* refer to *setting* or to *stone?*)

Clear After removing the stone, the jeweler examined *its* setting.

Clear The jeweler removed the stone and examined *it.*

Indefinite Antecedent. As you know, the antecedent is the word to which a pronoun refers. A reader or listener should always be able to tell what the antecedent of a pronoun is.

Unclear The movie director wasn't happy, but he said *it* could be redone. (What was the director unhappy about? What does the pronoun *it* refer to? The antecedent is unclear.)

Clear The movie director wasn't happy with the shot, but he said *it* could be redone.

Pronouns and Contractions. A **contraction** is formed when two words are joined together in a special way. One or more of the letters in the second word are replaced by an apostrophe. These are some of the most common contractions:

it's = it + is	they're = they + are
you're = you + are	who's = who + is

Do not confuse these contractions with the possessive pronouns *its, their, your,* and *whose.*

Incorrect *Whose* going to show me how to operate this computer?

Correct *Who's* going to show me how to operate this computer?

LOOKING AT WORDS

They're, their, and *there* are **homonyms**—words that sound alike but mean different things.

> **QUICK TIP** To decide whether a contraction is correct in a sentence, substitute the words for which the contraction stands. In the example above, "Who is going to show me" sounds correct and is.

Them* and *Those. *Them* is a pronoun and is used only as an object. It is not used as a subject or to modify a noun.

Incorrect *Them* are my favorite movies. (*Them* is incorrectly used as the subject of the verb *are.*)

Correct *Those* are my favorite movies.

Incorrect Have you seen *them* movies? (*Them* is incorrectly used to modify *movies.*)

Correct Have you seen *those* movies?

Exercise 7

1. It's very hard to think about children being hungry.
2. Dick Gregory was one of those hungry children.
3. Correct
4. Who's going to find a better mother than Dick Gregory's Momma was?
5. But Dick never learned hate or shame at home; he learned those emotions at school.

Exercise 8

1. we	**9.** me
2. I	**10.** it's
3. me	**11.** I
4. he	**12.** Correct
5. Correct	**13.** Correct
6. Correct	**14.** whom
7. himself	**15.** their
8. whose	

1. We teenagers just love those creepy villains and monsters.
2. My sister and I have seen Boris Karloff as Frankenstein at least twenty times!
3. Will you come to the theater with Lindsay and me next time we go to see *Frankenstein?*
4. Boris Karloff played Frankenstein, and it was he who played the lead in the 1932 film called *The Mummy.*
5. Correct
6. Correct
7. Other actors have played Dracula, too, but for me, Bela Lugosi was Dracula himself.
8. Another actor whose voice was captivating was Vincent Price.
9. Who agrees with my sister and me that the cutest villain ever created was King Kong?
10. It's still a treat to see King Kong climb up the Empire State Building with Fay Raye in his hands.
11. My friends and I never believed that King Kong was really a mechanical model.
12. Jane and Tanika watched King Kong's giant mouth and jaws open and seem about to speak to them.
13. Correct
14. What whom do you think I'd like to cook up a batch of popcorn, turn down the lights, and be consumed by fright?
15. Some of our friends can join us and bring their favorite horror movies to play.

Exercise 7 Other Pronoun Problems Rewrite the following sentences, correcting all errors in pronoun usage. If a sentence has no errors, write *Correct.*

1. Its very hard to think about children being hungry.
2. Dick Gregory was one of them hungry children.
3. His mother worked as hard as she could, but her children suffered deeply.
4. Whose going to find a better mother than Dick Gregory's Momma was?
5. But Dick never learned hate or shame at home; he learned them emotions at school.

Exercise 8 Pronoun Usage Review Rewrite the following sentences, correcting any errors in the use of pronouns. If a sentence has no error, write *Correct.*

1. Us teenagers just love those creepy villains and monsters.
2. My sister and myself have seen Boris Karloff as Frankenstein at least twenty times!
3. Will you come to the theater with Lindsay and I next time we go to see *Frankenstein?*
4. Boris Karloff played Frankenstein, and it was him who played the lead in the 1932 film called *The Mummy.*
5. His voice itself could make me run out of the theater.
6. My brother loves vampire stories; it was he who said that Bela Lugosi played Dracula perfectly.
7. Other actors have played Dracula, too, but for me, Bela Lugosi was Dracula hisself.
8. Another actor who's voice was captivating was Vincent Price.
9. Who agrees with my sister and I that the cutest villain ever created was King Kong?
10. Its still a treat to see King Kong climb up the Empire State Building with Fay Raye in his hands.
11. My friends and myself never believed that King Kong was really a mechanical model.
12. Jane and Tanika watched his giant mouth and jaws open and seem about to speak to them.
13. Fay Raye was who? Was she the first actress to play King Kong's leading lady?
14. With who do you think I'd like to cook up a batch of popcorn, turn down the lights, and be consumed by fright?
15. Some of our friends can join us and bring his or her favorite horror movies to play.

SECTION 4 USING MODIFIERS

Modifiers are words that change or limit the meaning of other words. Two kinds of modifiers are adjectives and adverbs.

Adjectives

An *adjective* is a word that modifies a noun or a pronoun.

An adjective answers one of these questions: Which one? What kind? How many? How much?

this horn, *pine* tree, *several* days, *fewer* books

Classes of Adjectives

The following chart shows the various types of adjectives:

Articles *A, an,* and *the* are adjectives referred to as articles. The article *the* is the **definite article** because it points out a specific person, place, thing, or group.

A and *an* are **indefinite articles** because they do not refer to specific items. Use *an* before a vowel sound. Use *a* before a consonant sound. Remember, it is the sound, not the spelling, that determines the correct choice: *an* ear, *an* heir, *an* oboe, *a* house.

Proper Adjectives These adjectives are formed from proper nouns and are always capitalized: *Italian* ice, *Napoleonic* wars.

Predicate Adjectives These adjectives follow linking verbs and describe the subject of the sentence: Her feet are *cold.* The room looks *peaceful.*

Nouns as Adjectives Nouns become modifiers when they describe nouns: *blood* pressure, *rock* garden, *infant* seat.

Adverbs

An *adverb* modifies a verb, an adjective, or another adverb.

Adverbs tell *where, when, how,* or *to what extent.*

called *there* move *now* laughed *heartily*
very sadly *intensely* wild *nearly* awake *slightly* ill

SPELLING NOTE

Adverbs are often formed by adding *-ly* to an adjective. Notice that the addition of *-ly* may cause a change in spelling:

happy + -ly = happily

Additional Resources

GRAMMAR AND USAGE COPY MASTERS

- Exercises
- Tests

Many adverbs are formed by adding *-ly* to an adjective.

bright + *-ly* = brightly merry + *-ly* = merrily

Here is a list of commonly used adverbs that do not end in *-ly*.

Commonly Used Adverbs				
afterward	fast	low	often	there
almost	forth	more	seldom	today
already	hard	near	slow	tomorrow
also	here	never	soon	too
back	instead	next	still	well
even	late	not	straight	yesterday
far	long	now	then	yet

Modifier Usage

Adjectives and adverbs help you create strong, lively images. The following lessons will help you use them properly.

Adjective or Adverb?

If you can't decide whether to use an adjective or an adverb in a sentence, ask yourself the following questions:

1. Which word does the modifier describe? Use an adverb if the modified word is an action verb, adjective, or adverb. Use an adjective if the modified word is a noun or pronoun.
2. What does the modifier tell about the word it describes? Use an adverb if the modifier tells *how, when, where,* or *to what extent.* Use an adjective if the modifier tells *which one, what kind, how many,* or *how much.*

Which modifier correctly completes the following sentence—the adjective *real* or the adverb *really?*

She was ______________ upset about the change of plans.

The adverb *really* is the correct choice because the modifier describes the adjective *upset.*

Exercise 1 Adjective or Adverb? Choose the correct modifier from the two in parentheses. Then write the word or words it modifies and whether the modifier is an *Adjective* or an *Adverb.*

Example The train raced (quick, quickly) toward its destination.

Answer quickly raced Adverb

1. A city like Rome offers (extraordinary, extraordinarily) evidence of the talent and suffering of human beings.
2. The Caesars, who ruled Rome in its early days, worked (tireless, tirelessly) to create a vast empire.
3. During that time great artists designed the city's (fabulous, fabulously) temples, palaces, monuments, and fountains.
4. Most citizens lived in (miserable, miserably) conditions.
5. The rulers (cleverly, clever) provided free food and entertainment to Rome's residents, hoping that this "bread and circus" would calm the desperate citizens.
6. The wealth of this ancient city was built (large, largely) by human slavery and suffering.
7. Every third person in Caesar's Rome suffered (deep, deeply) as a slave.
8. In the summer of A.D. 64, a fire raged (uncontrollable, uncontrollably) throughout the city for ten days.
9. Rome was destroyed (frequent, frequently) by natural disasters including floods, earthquakes, and plagues.
10. Despite Rome's history of disasters and wars, it has survived (magnificently, magnificent) as one of the world's greatest cities.

Adverb or Predicate Adjective?

Use an adverb to modify an action verb. Use an adjective after a linking verb.

Most verbs are action verbs and so can be modified by adverbs. Linking verbs, such as *be* or *seem,* however, don't usually take modifiers. They are often followed by an adjective, which actually modifies the subject, not the verb. An adjective used in this way is called a **predicate adjective.**

The dress is *elegant.* (*Elegant* is a predicate adjective modifying *dress.*)

The men seemed *angry.* (*Angry* is a predicate adjective modifying *men.*)

Verbs like *appear, look, sound, feel, taste, grow,* and *smell* can be

Exercise 1

1. extraordinary; evidence; adjective
2. tirelessly; worked; adverb
3. fabulous; temples, palaces, monuments, and fountains; adjective
4. miserable; conditions; adjective
5. cleverly; provided; adverb
6. largely; built; adverb
7. deeply; suffered; adverb
8. uncontrollably; raged; adverb
9. frequently; destroyed; adverb
10. magnificently; survived; adverb

Exercise 2

1. quickly
2. careful
3. suddenly
4. magnificent
5. dramatically
6. quickly
7. weak
8. fearful
9. wonderfully
10. perfect

used either as action verbs or as linking verbs. An action verb is modified by an adverb. A linking verb connects a subject with an adjective that describes the subject. For help in deciding whether to use an adjective or an adverb, think about which word will be modified. Use an adjective to modify the subject. Use an adverb to modify the verb.

The horse looked *nervous* before the race. (The predicate adjective *nervous* modifies the subject, *horse,* not the linking verb *looked.*)

The horse looked *nervously* at the jockey. (Here the adverb *nervously* modifies the action verb *looked.*)

QUICK TIP If you are uncertain about whether to use an adverb or an adjective after a verb like *feel, sound, smell,* or *look,* ask yourself the following questions:

1. Can you substitute *is* or *was* for the verb? If you can, use an adjective.

   The coin *appeared* rare. The coin *is* rare.

2. Does the modifier tell *how, when, where,* or *to what extent* about an action verb? If it does, use an adverb.

Exercise 2 Adverb or Predicate Adjective? Choose the correct modifier for each of the following sentences.

1. Sarah looked (quick, quickly) around the museum.
2. She seemed (careful, carefully) about following the museum's map.
3. Sarah saw Matisse's cutouts (sudden, suddenly) as she entered the room.
4. The giant murals looked (magnificent, magnificently) on the museum walls.
5. The bright colors contrasted (dramatic, dramatically) with the white walls.
6. Sarah (quick, quickly) read the notes about Matisse's cutouts.
7. The French artist felt (weak, weakly) toward the end of his life.
8. He was (fearful, fearfully) about losing his ability to paint.
9. Matisse began to ''draw'' with scissors; his giant cutouts expressed his feelings (wonderful, wonderfully).
10. These spectacular cutouts suggest the (perfect, perfectly) combination of all five sensations—taste, smell, touch, sight, and sound.

Prepositional Phrases as Modifiers

You have already learned about single-word modifiers. Groups of words can also modify. Sometimes nouns and verbs are modified by groups of words that begin with prepositions.

Prepositions are words like *on* or *near* that help show how one word is related to another word. Prepositions often introduce groups of related words called **phrases.** Consider these sentences.

The pencil is *in the desk.*
The pencil is *on the desk.*
The pencil is *under the desk.*

Before lunch she worked.
During lunch she worked.
After lunch she worked.

Each sentence contains a **prepositional phrase,** shown in italics. The prepositional phrase consists of a preposition, its object, and any modifiers. In the first sentence, *in* is the preposition and *desk* is the object. In the first group of sentences, you can see that the words *in, on,* and *under* show the spatial relationship of the *desk* to the *pencil.* In the next group, *before, after,* and *during* show the time relationship between lunch time and the act of working.

Here is a list of words that are often used as prepositions. Most of these prepositions show relationships of place or time. Some show other relationships among people and things. Study the prepositions and notice the relationship that each shows.

Commonly Used Prepositions

about	at	down	near	to
above	before	during	of	toward
across	behind	except	off	under
after	below	for	on	underneath
against	beneath	from	onto	until
along	beside	in	out	up
among	between	inside	over	upon
around	but (except)	into	since	with
as	by	like	through	without

Exercise 3

Answers will vary. Possible prepositional phrases are provided.

1. What is the street after Elm Street?
2. Here is a list of chemicals the company dumped into the river.
3. I sat by the old oak along the road.
4. I wore my jacket with the fleece lining.
5. The irritating noise rang in her ears.
6. What will be the first prize claimed after the contest?
7. Please get the wrench from my toolbox.
8. The musicians played along the lakeshore.
9. He thought he left the notebook inside his briefcase.
10. They were the cheeriest patients on our floor.
11. Please don't remove the pillow from my bed.
12. That was the first mention of an exam she had heard during the class.
13. Slowly, the soldiers crept toward the monster.
14. You sound like a myna bird in a cage.
15. Donna was swimming near the cottage.

Prepositional phrases function either as adjectives or as adverbs in a sentence.

A prepositional phrase that modifies a noun or pronoun is called an *adjective phrase.*

The town *on the mountain* is Jaffrey.
She rode the horse *with the red saddle.*
The cave *under the gift shop* was astonishing.

Like adjectives, adjective phrases tell *which one, what kind, how many,* or *how much.*

A prepositional phrase that modifies a verb is called an *adverb phrase.*

They argued *until spring.*
They traveled *to Texas.*
The willow fell *into the river.*

Like adverbs, adverb phrases tell *how, when, where,* and *to what extent* about verbs.

Exercise 3 Prepositional Phrases Add prepositional phrases to the following nouns and verbs. Do not use the same preposition more than twice. Then use the noun or verb and your phrase in a sentence.

Example coins

Answer coins in the fountain
The couple threw coins in the fountain.

1. street	**6.** claimed	**11.** pillow
2. dumped	**7.** wrench	**12.** had heard
3. oak	**8.** played	**13.** crept
4. jacket	**9.** notebook	**14.** myna bird
5. rang	**10.** patients	**15.** was swimming

Modifiers in Comparisons

Comparing people, things, and actions is part of everyday life. You might say, for example, "The Bears are a *better* team than the Dolphins. Their defense is *better,* and they have *faster* runners." Or you might say, "The Dolphins run *quickly,* but the Bears run *more quickly.*"

In comparisons, modifiers have special forms or spellings.

The Comparative

When you compare one person, thing, or action with another, use the **comparative** form of the modifier.

China is *larger* than Japan.
Samantha runs *faster* than Bob.

The comparative form is generally made in two ways:

1. For short modifiers like *calm* and *soon,* add *-er.*

cold + -er = colder   thin + -er = thinner
juicy + -er = juicier   bold + -er = bolder

2. For longer modifiers like *interesting* and *beautiful,* use *more.*

more interesting   more beautiful

Most modifiers ending in *-ful* or *-ous* form the comparative with *more.*

more fearful   more bulbous   more soulfully

QUICK TIP Most two-syllable modifiers form the comparative with *-er.* However, a word like *softly* uses *more.* You can usually tell which form to use because the correct form will sound better. For example, you wouldn't say *softlier.*

REMINDER

Some modifiers cannot form comparisons. For example, something that is *unique* is one of a kind. It cannot be more or less unique than something else. Some other modifiers that cannot form comparisons are *equal, fatal, final,* and *absolute.*

The Superlative

Whenever you compare a person, thing, or action with more than one other person, thing, or action, use the **superlative** form of the modifier.

Karl is the *shyest* musician in the band.
Cathy runs most *energetically* in the morning.

The superlative form of modifiers is generally made by adding *-est* (for short modifiers) or by using *most* (for longer modifiers). For modifiers that take *-er* in the comparative, add *-est* for the superlative. Those that use *more* to form the comparative use *most* for the superlative.

Many people use the superlative incorrectly to compare two things. Consider the following examples:

Incorrect She's the *fastest* of the two swimmers.

Correct She's the *faster* of the two swimmers.

Exercise 4

1. Correct
2. Jessie likes Davy Crockett better than any other character in American folklore.

Modifier	Comparative	Superlative
smooth	smoother	smoothest
cute	cuter	cutest
loud	louder	loudest
intricate	more intricate	most intricate
sweetly	more sweetly	most sweetly

Irregular Comparisons

Some modifiers make their comparative and superlative forms by complete word changes.

Modifier	Comparative	Superlative
good	better	best
well	better	best
bad	worse	worst
little	less *or* lesser	least
much	more	most
many	more	most
far	farther	farthest

FEW AND LESS

Few (fewer, fewest) is used for things that can be counted: *I have a few books to finish reading. Less (lesser, least)* is used for things that cannot be counted: *There seems to be less smog this summer than there was last summer.*

To make a negative comparison, use *less* or *least* before the modifier: *careful, less careful, least careful.*

Exercise 4 Comparisons Find the errors in comparison in the following sentences and write the sentences correctly. If a sentence has no errors, write *Correct.*

Example Folklore is amusinger than any other form of literature.

Answer Folklore is more amusing than any other form of literature.

1. Often students enjoy reading folklore more than reading history.
2. Jessie likes Davy Crockett best than any other character in American folklore.

3. To Jessie, stories about Davy Crockett were the excitingest of all the tales.
4. Of all the tall tales that Lynn has read, she thinks that tales about Paul Bunyan are the worse.
5. Bunyan was more strong than any other lumberjack in America.
6. His blue ox, Babe, was the powerfulest ox in the entire world.
7. Paul Bunyan had a more large appetite than any other person alive.
8. His stove was the larger stove in the world—twenty-four feet long and five feet wide.
9. Of all the cowboys of the Southwest, Pecos Bill was the finer bronco rider.
10. Of all the entrants in the rodeo, Pecos Bill threw a rope the more accurately; legends say that he once roped a train!
11. Sam likes the character Sluefoot Sue more better than Pecos Bill.
12. Pecos Bill loved Sluefoot Sue the best of all the women in the Southwest.
13. Johnny Appleseed was a more friendlier character than Pecos Bill.
14. Johnny Appleseed was a real person, and he was strongest than any of the tales about him said he was.
15. The students in Jessie's class voted on their favoritest folk character: Babe, the blue ox, won unanimously!

Exercise 5 Review of Comparisons Choose the correct modifier from the two in parentheses.

1. Of all the different kinds of folklore, noodlehead stories are Ben's (most favorite, favoritest).
2. Ben spoke (more clearly, clearer) when he told the crazy stories than at other times.
3. Noodlehead stories are (sillier, more silly) than tall tales.
4. Noodleheads are people who act (more foolishly, foolishlier) than other people.
5. The (most funniest, funniest) things happen in noodlehead stories.
6. Some people laugh (loudest, louder) when they read noodlehead stories than when they read comic strips.
7. Because of the stories, Ben feels (weller, better) than he did yesterday.
8. Jenny, who is (quieter, more quieter) than Ben, said that she would love to hear an Indian noodlehead story.
9. Ben says that of all the countries in the world, India had the (earlier, earliest) noodlehead stories.
10. In a famous Indian story, a teacher spoke (most wisely, more wisely) than anyone had before to his silly pupils.

3. To Jessie stories about Davy Crockett were the most exciting of all the tales.
4. Of all the tall tales that Lynn has read, she thinks that tales about Paul Bunyan are the worst.
5. Bunyan was stronger than any other lumberjack in America.
6. His blue ox, Babe, was the most powerful ox in the entire world.
7. Paul Bunyan had a larger appetite than any other person alive.
8. His stove was the largest stove in the world—twenty-four feet long and five feet wide.
9. Of all the cowboys of the Southwest, Pecos Bill was the finest bronco rider.
10. Of all the entrants in the rodeo, Pecos Bill threw a rope the most accurately; legends say that he once roped a train!
11. Sam likes the character Sluefoot Sue better than Pecos Bill.
12. Correct
13. Johnny Appleseed was a friendlier character than Pecos Bill.
14. Johnny Appleseed was a real person, and he was stronger than any of the tales about him said he was.
15. The students in Jessie's class voted on their most favorite folk character: Babe, the blue ox, won unanimously!

Exercise 5

1. most favorite
2. more clearly
3. sillier
4. more foolishly
5. funniest
6. louder
7. better
8. quieter
9. earliest
10. more wisely

Exercise 6

1. Of all the different kinds of fiction, mysteries may be the easiest to read.
2. I can read mysteries faster than my older brother can.
3. Agatha Christie is the cleverest writer.
4. Correct
5. Christie created two memorable sleuths; I like Miss Jane Marple better than Hercule Poirot, the vain Belgian detective.
6. Poirot's career as an amateur sleuth is more important than his career on the Belgian police force was.
7. Miss Marple is the shrewdest senior citizen in the world.
8. Miss Marple's fascination with murders seems stranger than her fascination with the cozy English village of St. Mary Mead.
9. Miss Marple, by using the insights she gathered from observation of her fellow villagers, solved crimes more quickly than the local police force.
10. I think that *And Then There Were None* was the scariest book that Agatha Christie ever wrote.

Avoiding Double Comparisons

Do not use *-er* and *more* or *-est* and *most* at the same time.

Incorrect Wood is *more stronger* than plastic.

Correct Wood is *stronger* than plastic.

Incorrect The triathlon is the *most hardest* of all endurance events.

Correct The triathlon is the *hardest* of all endurance events.

Exercise 6 Double Comparisons Rewrite each incorrect sentence below, correcting the error in comparison. If a sentence is correct, write *Correct.*

1. Of all the different kinds of fiction, mysteries may be the most easiest to read.
2. I can read mysteries more faster than my older brother can.
3. Agatha Christie is the most cleverest writer.
4. This British detective story writer is one of the most popular authors in the English language.
5. Christie created two memorable sleuths; I like Miss Jane Marple more better than Hercule Poirot, the vain Belgian detective.
6. Poirot's career as an amateur sleuth is more importanter than his career on the Belgian police force was.
7. Miss Marple is the most shrewdest senior citizen in the world.
8. Miss Marple's fascination with murders seems more stranger than her fascination with the cozy English village of St. Mary Mead.
9. Miss Marple, by using the insights she gathered from observation of her fellow villagers, solved crimes more quicker than the local police force.
10. I think that *And Then There Were None* was the most scariest book that Agatha Christie ever wrote.

Avoiding Illogical Comparisons

Do not make illogical or confusing comparisons.

When you first read an illogical comparison, it may seem correct, but if you look or listen more closely, you may see that its meaning is not quite clear. One kind of illogical comparison occurs when a person, thing, or idea is compared to the group to which it belongs.

James Beard was a better chef than any in his kitchen.

Since James Beard was himself a chef in his kitchen, this sentence really means that he is better than himself! To avoid this kind of mistake, use the word *other* in such a comparison.

James Beard was a better chef than any other in his kitchen.

Sometimes an illogical comparison occurs because the correct comparison is not clearly stated. Even though it may seem correct at first, this kind of comparison can confuse a reader.

Confusing Sarah was more afraid of the roller coaster than Ann. (Did the roller coaster and Ann both frighten Sarah?)

Clear Sarah was more afraid of the roller coaster than Ann was.

Exercise 7 Illogical Comparisons Rewrite the following sentences, correcting the errors in comparison. If a sentence is already correct, write *Correct.*

1. Melissa likes plays better than Joey.
2. She thinks that live drama is better than any kind of performance.
3. Joey shares his ideas more forcefully than Melissa.
4. "I like folk music better than other music!" Joey shouts at Melissa.
5. "Folk music is a better expression of the common person's experience than other music," Joey says.
6. "Concerts demand more audience participation than any kind of performances," he says.
7. Melissa is a more careful listener than any student in her class.
8. Disagreeing with Joey, she says that good acting is harder than any kind of work.
9. "Have you ever been so engrossed in a play," Melissa asks, "that you liked the main character more than your date?"
10. "I'm sure you liked him better than I," Joey says. "You both should have gone to a concert instead!"

Special Problems with Modifiers

Some adjectives and adverbs can be especially confusing; in everyday speech you may hear these modifiers used incorrectly. In the following pages you will learn how to avoid some common mistakes.

Them and *Those*

***Them* is always a pronoun. It is never used as a modifier. *Those* is a pronoun when used alone; it is an adjective when followed by a noun.**

Exercise 7

1. Melissa likes plays better than Joey does.
2. She thinks that live drama is better than any other kind of performance.
3. Joey shares his ideas more forcefully than Melissa does.
4. Correct
5. "Folk music is a better expression of the common person's experience than other music is," Joey says.
6. "Concerts demand more audience participation than any other kind of performances," he says.
7. Melissa is a more careful listener than any other student in her class.
8. Disagreeing with Joey, she says that good acting is harder than any other kind of work.
9. "Have you ever been so engrossed in a play," Melissa asks, "that you liked the main character more than you liked your date?"
10. "I'm sure you liked him better than I did," Joey says. "You both should have gone to a concert instead!"

With *them* and *those,* the most common mistake is using *them* as an adjective. Remember that *them* is always a pronoun; use *those,* not *them,* as a modifier.

Incorrect What happened to all of *them* elephants?

Correct What happened to all of *those* elephants?

This and *That, These* and *Those*

Use *this* and *that* to modify singular nouns. Use *these* and *those* to modify plural nouns.

The adjectives *this* and *that* modify singular nouns. *These* and *those* modify plural nouns. When these modifiers are used with words such as *kind, sort,* and *type,* be especially careful to use them correctly.

Incorrect *Those* kind of apples are more delicious. (*Kind* is singular, so it should be modified by either *this* or *that.*)

Correct *That* kind of apple is more delicious. (Notice that the noun *apple* has become singular as well.)

Bad and *Badly*

Use *bad* as an adjective. Use *badly* as an adverb.

Bad is an adjective, so it should only be used to modify nouns and pronouns. Like other adjectives, *bad* sometimes follows a linking verb. *Badly* is always an adverb, so it should never be used with a linking verb.

Incorrect He feels *badly* about making us late.

Correct He feels *bad* about making us late.

Good and *Well*

***Good* is always an adjective. *Well* is usually an adverb.**

Many people believe that they can interchange the words *good* and *well.* The two words do have similar meanings, but *good* is always an adjective, modifying a noun or a pronoun. *Good* is never used to modify a verb.

Incorrect Amy painted the kitchen *good.*

Correct Amy painted the kitchen *well.*

Using *well* correctly can be more difficult than using *good* correctly.

Well usually functions as an adverb meaning "expertly" or "properly." But it may also mean "in good health"; when it does, it is an adjective, used after a linking verb.

After the fever passed, my brother seemed *well.* (adjective)
We cared for him *well* during his recovery. (adverb)

QUICK TIP Since *good* and *well* can both be adjectives, they can both be used as predicate adjectives after linking verbs. To decide which word to use in a sentence, remember that *well* refers to health, while *good* refers to happiness, comfort, or pleasure.
Marc stayed home from school because he didn't feel *well.*
Luisa felt *good* after she saved the rabbit's life.

Exercise 8 Problem Modifiers Choose the correct modifier from those in parentheses.

1. Gina's family took an auto trip to see the spectacular art of the Southwestern Indians; the family's ten-year-old jalopy ran (well, good) throughout the twelve-hundred-mile journey.
2. Gina's great-grandmother had been ill and was not (good, well) enough to join them on their trip.
3. Gina felt (bad, badly) about her great-grandmother's having to stay home.
4. After the long trip the family felt (good, well) about reaching their destination.
5. They went to see (them, those) rock pictures that are on the smooth surfaces of cliffs throughout the Southwest.
6. (This, These) kind of Indian art has been preserved in the dry Southwestern desert for thousands of years.
7. Gina loves (that, those) sort of woven blanket that is made by the Navajos.
8. Sometimes figures copied from (them, those) sand paintings are woven into the rugs.
9. Gina's sister preferred (those, that) kinds of woven baskets that are shaped like dolls.
10. (Them, Those) kachina masks and dolls were magnificent to see.
11. Pueblo artists do (good, well) at painting dramatic faces on their masks and dolls.
12. Gina's brother felt (bad, badly) about missing a kachina masked-dance ceremony.
13. Her parents loved (that, those) kinds of belts that are inlaid with turquoise and coral designs.

Exercise 8

1. well
2. well
3. bad
4. good
5. those
6. This
7. that
8. those
9. those
10. Those
11. well
12. bad
13. those

14. that
15. bad

Exercise 9

1. The Statue of Liberty has never disappointed her visitors.
2. She wasn't designed by an American, though.
3. The French architect, named Frédéric Bartholdí, could barely have built her without help. (*or* could not have)
4. His helper, Alexandre Gustave Eiffel, was no amateur; he designed the Eiffel Tower in Paris. (*or* was not an amateur)
5. The American government could scarcely refuse such a magnificent gift. (*or* could not refuse)
6. The gift was no ordinary gift. (*or* was not an ordinary)

14. It takes a master silversmith to create (that, those) kind of intricate silver work.
15. Gina and her family were overwhelmed by the richness and beauty of Indian art and culture; they all felt (bad, badly) about leaving the Southwest.

The Double Negative

Do not use two negatives together.

The most common negative words are *no, not, never, nothing,* and *none.* Sometimes you will hear people use two negative words together, especially with a contraction such as *didn't* or *couldn't.* This kind of error is called a **double negative.**

Incorrect The girl couldn't find no scissors in the closet.

Correct The girl couldn't find any scissors in the closet.

Correct The girl could find no scissors in the closet.

Remember that the *-n't* in a contraction means "not." If you pair a contraction containing *-n't* with another negative word, you end up with a double negative.

Hardly, barely, and *scarcely* are often used as negative words. Do not use them after contractions like *haven't* or *couldn't.*

Incorrect The children *couldn't barely* hear the music.

Correct The children *could barely* hear the music.

Exercise 9 Double Negatives Rewrite the sentences below, correcting the double negatives. If a sentence contains no double negatives, write *Correct.*

Example We couldn't hardly ask him to carry all the camping gear.

Answer We could hardly ask him to carry all the camping gear.

1. The Statue of Liberty has hardly never disappointed her visitors.
2. She wasn't designed by no American, though.
3. The French architect, named Frédéric Bartholdi, couldn't barely have built her without help.
4. His helper, Alexandre Gustave Eiffel, wasn't no amateur; he designed the Eiffel Tower in Paris.
5. The American government couldn't scarcely refuse such a magnificent gift.
6. The gift wasn't no ordinary gift.

7. The statue wasn't built by the rich for the rich neither.
8. Ordinary working people in France paid for it to be built, and ordinary working people in America paid for it to be erected in New York Harbor.
9. It wasn't no small feat collecting all the nickels and French francs necessary to complete the project.
10. Miss Liberty isn't hardly any lightweight.
11. She measures 151 feet to the top of her torch, and she's not made of no balsa wood but of granite and marble.
12. The Statue of Liberty bears a beautiful inscription on her base.
13. She doesn't hardly speak to Donald Trump when she says, "Give me your tired, your poor, / Your huddled masses yearning to breathe free."
14. She's not talking about no Wall Street moguls when she says, "Send these, the homeless, tempest-tost to me."
15. Remember when you visit her that she was built by the poor to welcome the working people of the world, and she's hardly speaking to no one else when she says, "I lift my lamp beside the golden door!"

Exercise 10 Modifier Usage Review Complete the following sentences with the correct word or words from those in parentheses.

1. Hardly (no, any) musical instrument is as well loved as the violin.
2. The violin sounds (beautiful, beautifully) with the piano.
3. The viola is slightly (larger, more large) than the violin.
4. Because the violin is smaller, it has a (higher, more high) pitch than the viola does.
5. Famous composers like Mozart have been (real, really) attracted by the high notes of the violin.
6. The double bass has the (deepest, most deeply) pitch of all the instruments in the string family.
7. The lute is the (ancientest, most ancient) ancestor of the guitar and the violin.
8. Many people in Shakespeare's time played the lute (good, well).
9. Some people think the piano is the (noblest, most noble) instrument ever invented.
10. Both the stringed instruments and the piano sound (magnificent, magnificently) in an orchestra.

7. The statue wasn't built by the rich for the rich either.
8. Correct
9. It was no small feat collecting all the nickels and French francs necessary to complete the project. (*or* wasn't a small feat)
10. Miss Liberty is hardly any lightweight. (*or* isn't any lightweight)
11. She measures 151 feet to the top of her torch, and she's not made of balsa wood but of granite and marble.
12. Correct
13. She doesn't speak to Donald Trump when she says, "Give me your tired, your poor, / Your huddled masses yearning to breathe free." (*or* hardly speaks)
14. She's not talking about Wall Street moguls when she says, "Send these, the homeless, tempest-tost to me."
15. Remember when you visit her that she was built by the poor to welcome the working people of the world, and she's speaking to no one else when she says, "I lift my lamp beside the golden door!" (*or* hardly speaking to anyone else)

Exercise 10

1. any
2. beautiful
3. larger
4. higher
5. really
6. deepest
7. most ancient
8. well
9. most noble
10. magnificent

SECTION 5 USING VERBS

A *verb* is a word that expresses an action or a state of being.

A robot *welded* the parts together.
Robots *are* perfect for dangerous jobs.

Classes of Verbs

These two sentence charts illustrate and define the different kinds of verbs.

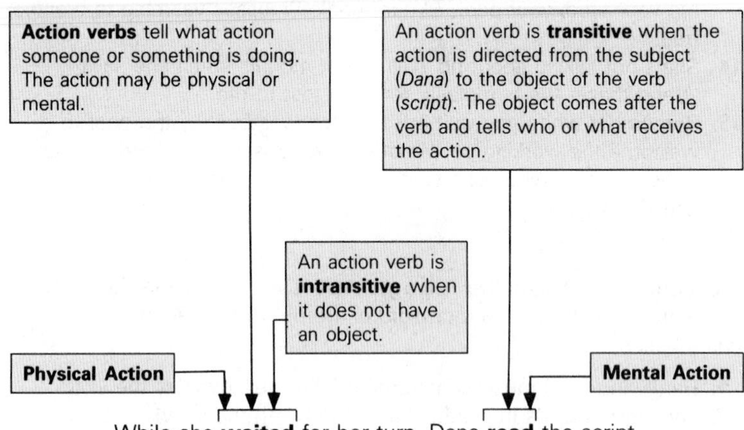

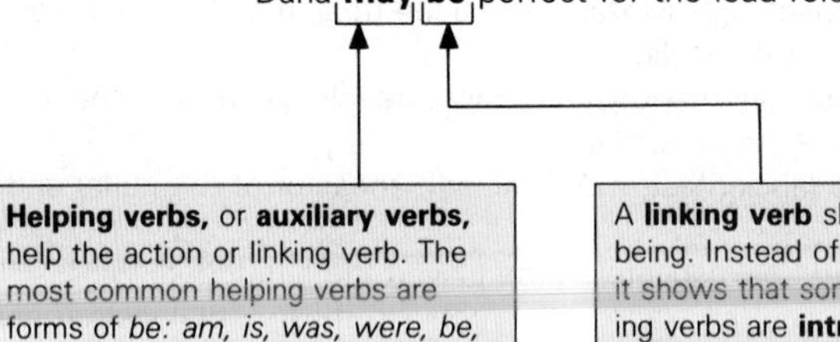

Helping verbs, or **auxiliary verbs,** help the action or linking verb. The most common helping verbs are forms of *be: am, is, was, were, be, been, being;* forms of *have: have, has, had;* forms of *do: do, does, did;* and *can, could, will, would, shall, should, may, might,* and *must.*

A **linking verb** shows a state of being. Instead of expressing action, it shows that something exists. Linking verbs are **intransitive** because they never take an object. A linking verb (*be*) links the subject (*Dana*) to a word in the predicate (*perfect*). In addition to the forms of *be,* the most common linking verbs are *look, smell, taste, feel, appear, sound, seem, become,* and *grow.*

Additional Resources

GRAMMAR AND USAGE COPY MASTERS
- Exercises
- Tests

Verb Usage

A sentence is not a sentence unless it has a verb. In fact, a verb is the only part of speech that can be a sentence on its own.

Stop! Look! Listen!

In most of your speaking and writing, you probably use verbs correctly without even thinking about it. In some cases, however, choosing the right verb might be confusing. This section will help you to avoid common errors in verb usage.

The Principal Parts of Verbs

Every verb has four basic forms. These are known as the principal parts of a verb. The following are the principal parts of the verb *knit.*

Present	Present Participle	Past	Past Participle
knit	(is) knitting	knitted	(have) knitted

Here are the principal parts of some other common verbs:

Present	Present Participle	Past	Past Participle
subtract	(is) subtracting	subtracted	(have) subtracted
drop	(is) dropping	dropped	(have) dropped
fry	(is) frying	fried	(have) fried
howl	(is) howling	howled	(have) howled

Exercise 1 Principal Parts Copy the following chart onto a piece of paper. Fill in the principal parts.

Present	Present Participle	Past	Past Participle
1. enjoy	______	______	______
2. work	______	______	______
3. fold	______	______	______
4. add	______	______	______
5. talk	______	______	______

Regular Verbs

If you study the verbs that you've seen so far in this section, you'll see that they form their principal parts in similar ways. To form the present participle, you add *-ing.* To form the past and past participles, you add

Exercise 1

1. (is) enjoying enjoyed (have) enjoyed
2. (is) working worked (have) worked
3. (is) folding folded (have) folded
4. (is) adding added (have) added
5. (is) talking talked (have) talked

-ed. Verbs that form their principal parts in these ways are called **regular verbs.** They are called regular because they are formed in the ordinary, or regular, way.

All regular verbs use the same form *(-ed)* for the past and past participle. The only difference is that the past participle is preceded by a helping verb (a form of *have* or *be).*

Principal Parts of Regular Verbs

Present	Present Participle	Past	Past Participle
rip	(is) ripping	ripped	(have) ripped
check	(is) checking	checked	(have) checked
bomb	(is) bombing	bombed	(have) bombed
dry	(is) drying	dried	(have) dried
move	(is) moving	moved	(have) moved

Quick Tip Note that a few regular verbs, such as *rip* and *dry,* change their spelling slightly when *-ing* or *-ed* is added.

IRREGULAR VERBS

An **irregular verb** is one that doesn't follow the usual pattern for verbs. Here are all of the present forms of one irregular verb, *be:*

I *am* we *are*
you *are* you *are*
he, she, it *is* they *are*

Irregular Verbs Verbs that do not add *-ed* or *-d* to the present to form the past and the past participle are **irregular verbs.**

Present	Present Participle	Past	Past Participle
put	(is) putting	put	(have) put
say	(is) saying	said	(have) said
tear	(is) tearing	tore	(have) torn
ring	(is) ringing	rang	(have) rung
throw	(is) throwing	threw	(have) thrown
go	(is) going	went	(have) gone
freeze	(is) freezing	froze	(have) frozen

Because the principal parts of irregular verbs are formed in a variety of ways, you must either memorize these parts or refer to a dictionary. Most dictionaries list the principal parts of irregular verbs.

Present Past Past Participle Present Participle

throw (thrō) ***vt.*** **threw, thrown, throw'ing** [ME *throwen,* to twist, wring, hurl ‹ OE *thrawan,* to throw, twist, akin to Ger *drehen,* to twist, turn ‹ IE base **ter-,* to rub, rub with turning motion, bore › THRASH, THREAD, Gr *teirein, terere,* to rub **1** to twist strands of (silk, etc.) into thread or yarn **2** to cause to fly through the air by releasing from the hand while the arm is in rapid motion; cast; hurl **3** to discharge through the air from a catapult, pump, gun, etc. **4** to hurl violently, as in anger, etc.; dash **5** to cause to fall; upset; overthrow; dislodge [*thrown* by a horse]

Exercise 2 Principal Parts in Dictionaries Make a chart with these headings: *Present, Present Participle, Past,* and *Past Participle.* List the principal parts from the following dictionary entries. Then, write a sentence using each principal part.

Example **throw** (thrō) *vt.* **threw, thrown, throw'ing** [ME *throwen,* to twist, wring, hurl ‹ OE *thrawan,* to throw, twist, akin to Ger *drehen,* to twist, turn ‹ IE base **ter-,* to rub, rub with turning motion, bore › THRASH, THREAD, Gr *teirein, terere,* to rub 1 to twist strands of (silk, etc.) into thread or yarn 2 to cause to fly through the air

Answer	Present	Present Participle	Past	Past Participle
	throw	(is) throwing	threw	(have) thrown

1. Please throw that switch.
2. Pico threw the ball to the shortstop.
3. The team had thrown the game.
4. The girls were throwing some practice pitches.

1. **freeze** (frēz) ***vi.*** **froze, fro'zen, freez'ing** [ME *fresen* ‹ OE *freosan,* akin to OHG *friosan* (Ger *frieren*) ‹ IE base **preus-,* to freeze, burn like cold › L *pruina,* hoarfrost, *pruna,* glowing coals] 1 to be formed into ice; be hardened or solidified by cold 2 to become clogged with ice 3 to be or become very cold
2. **tear** (ter) ***vt.*** **tore, torn, tear'ing** [ME *teren* ‹ OE *teran,* to rend, akin to Ger *zehren,* to destroy, consume ‹ IE base **der-,* to skin, split › DRAB, DERMA] 1 to pull apart or separate into pieces by force; rip or rend (cloth, paper, etc.) 2 to make or cause by tearing or puncturing [to *tear* a hole in a dress] 3 to wound by tearing; lacerate [skin *torn* and bruised]

Types of Irregular Verbs Irregular verbs fall into five groups.

Group 1 The easiest irregular verbs to remember are the ones that keep the same form for the present, past, and past participle forms.

Present	Present Participle	Past	Past Participle
burst	(is) bursting	burst	(have) burst
cost	(is) costing	cost	(have) cost
put	(is) putting	put	(have) put
set	(is) setting	set	(have) set

Here are some sentences using verbs from Group 1:

Please *put* ice in the lemonade.
The pipes *burst* in the cold.
I *have* already *set* the books on his desk.

Exercise 2

Possible sentences are provided.

freeze freezing froze have frozen

1. Don't freeze the milk.
2. I am freezing in this jacket.
3. The ground froze last night.
4. My shoes have frozen to the ground!

tear tearing tore have torn

1. Try not to tear the pages.
2. I am tearing this material.
3. Sue tore her dress.
4. The children have torn open their gifts.

Exercise 3

1. lost
2. put
3. sat
4. said
5. led
6. cost
7. caught
8. set
9. burst
10. brought

Group 2 These irregular verbs are fairly easy to remember. They have the same form for both the past and the past participle.

Present	Present Participle	Past	Past Participle
bring	(is) bringing	brought	(have) brought
catch	(is) catching	caught	(have) caught
lead	(is) leading	led	(have) led
lend	(is) lending	lent	(have) lent
lose	(is) losing	lost	(have) lost
say	(is) saying	said	(have) said
sit	(is) sitting	sat	(have) sat

These sentences use verbs from Group 2:

> I *say* exactly what I think.
> We *caught* the dripping water in a bucket.
> Some of us *have brought* friends along.

Exercise 3 Irregular Verbs Choose the correct past or past participle of each verb in parentheses.

1. The child had been (lose) for hours.
2. Our art supplies were (put) away.
3. We (sit) in the rumble seat of the Model T.
4. Have you (say) anything about your plans?
5. The group had (lead) off the set with a hit from the fifties.
6. That album (cost) less in the downtown store.
7. Wendy (catch) her addition error.
8. Kareem (set) his sculpture on its base.
9. A dam in the Southwest (burst).
10. The advertisement (bring) many customers.

Group 3 This group of irregular verbs makes the past participle by adding *-n* or *-en* to the past form.

Present	Present Participle	Past	Past Participle
break	(is) breaking	broke	(have) broken
choose	(is) choosing	chose	(have) chosen
freeze	(is) freezing	froze	(have) frozen
speak	(is) speaking	spoke	(have) spoken
steal	(is) stealing	stole	(have) stolen
tear	(is) tearing	tore	(have) torn
wear	(is) wearing	wore	(have) worn

These sentences use verbs from Group 3:

Mike *wears* a hat all the time.
The mayor *spoke* at the meeting.
The radio knob *has broken* off.

Exercise 4 Irregular Verbs Choose the correct form of the verb from the forms given.

1. Carlos has (broke, broken) his appointment with the dentist.
2. The cat usually (wore, worn) a flea collar.
3. Nick's little brother (stole, stolen) the show.
4. Monday was (chose, chosen) as the meeting date.
5. Nearly the entire lake has (froze, frozen).
6. A shredding machine (tore, torn) the paper to bits.
7. The President has (spoke, spoken) with his aides about the economy.
8. The knees of my jeans are (wore, worn) out.
9. All winter the ground was (froze, frozen) solid.
10. Britt (chose, chosen) a different math class.

Group 4 One group of irregular verbs changes only a vowel. The vowel is *i* in the present form, *a* in the past form, and *u* in the past participle form.

Present	Present Participle	Past	Past Participle
begin	(is) beginning	began	(have) begun
drink	(is) drinking	drank	(have) drunk
ring	(is) ringing	rang	(have) rung
sing	(is) singing	sang	(have) sung
swim	(is) swimming	swam	(have) swum

These sentences use verbs from Group 4:

I *swim* only the backstroke.
The concert *began* with a jazz number.
The lunch bell *has* already rung.

Exercise 5 Irregular Verbs Choose the correct past or past participle of each verb in parentheses.

1. The blood drive (begin) last Wednesday.
2. The boxer did not realize the bell had (ring).
3. The city has (begin) its summer festival.

Exercise 4

1. broken
2. wore
3. stole
4. chosen
5. frozen
6. tore
7. spoken
8. worn
9. frozen
10. chose

Exercise 5

1. began
2. rung
3. begun

4. rang
5. swam
6. drank
7. sung
8. swum
9. sang
10. drunk

Exercise 6

1. grown
2. written
3. done
4. threw
5. taken
6. saw
7. came

4. Bells (ring) in the new year.
5. Goldfish (swim) in the garden pool.
6. We (drink) homemade root beer.
7. Our choir has (sing) in three states.
8. Angela has (swim) in two relays.
9. Bill (sing) and played the drums.
10. Kit has never (drink) pineapple juice.

Group 5 Another group of irregular verbs forms the past participle from the present form rather than from the past form. The present and past participle are either the same or similar.

Present	Present Participle	Past	Past Participle
come	(is) coming	came	(have) come
do	(is) doing	did	(have) done
eat	(is) eating	ate	(have) eaten
fall	(is) falling	fell	(have) fallen
give	(is) giving	gave	(have) given
go	(is) going	went	(have) gone
grow	(is) growing	grew	(have) grown
know	(is) knowing	knew	(have) known
ride	(is) riding	rode	(have) ridden
run	(is) running	ran	(have) run
see	(is) seeing	saw	(have) seen
take	(is) taking	took	(have) taken
throw	(is) throwing	threw	(have) thrown
write	(is) writing	wrote	(have) written

Here are some sentences using verbs from Group 5:

Karen *rides* the subway to her job.
Monica *ran* the movie projector.
The Dolphins *have taken* second place in their division.

Exercise 6 Irregular Verbs Choose the correct past or past participle form of the verb from the forms given.

1. Potatoes are (grew, grown) in Idaho.
2. *Shane* was (wrote, written) by Jack Schaefer.
3. The gymnasts have (did, done) their routines dozens of times.
4. Gleason (threw, thrown) the ball to third base.
5. Organizing the meet has (took, taken) a long time.
6. From the airplane we (saw, seen) fireworks.
7. The fleeing prisoner (came, come) to a roadblock.

8. fell
9. gone
10. run
11. eaten
12. given
13. rode
14. known
15. did

8. Several of the most beautiful trees (fell, fallen) during the storm.
9. Vanessa had already (went, gone) to the library.
10. Many of them have (ran, run) in marathons.
11. Have you ever (ate, eaten) corn dogs?
12. The volunteers have (gave, given) away most of the food.
13. The cavalry (rode, ridden) across the wide plain.
14. Jerryl should have (knew, known) the facts.
15. Jill (did, done) a somersault in the water.

Verb Tenses

Verbs are time-telling words. They not only tell of an action or a state of being. They also tell *when* the action takes place. They tell whether the action or state of being is past, present, or future.

Verbs tell time in two ways:

1. changing their spelling
   walk → walked sleep → slept
2. using helping verbs
   will creep has crept had crept

Verbs express six different times. Each verb has a form to express each of these six different times. The forms of a verb used to indicate time are called the **tenses** of a verb.

The Tenses of Verbs

Tense	Form	Use
Present	Add *-s* or *-es* for third person singular.	To show an action that happens now: *Let's leave.* To tell about something that happens regularly: *The geyser erupts every ninety minutes.* To tell about constant action: *The earth revolves around the sun.*
Past	Add *-d* or *-ed* to the present. If the verb is irregular, use the past form.	To show an action that was completed in the past: *The Druids built Stonehenge.*
Future	Use *will* or *shall* with the present form.	To show an action that will occur in the future: *Computers will speak English some day.*

PROGRESSIVE FORMS

Every verb tense can be written in a **progressive** form to show continuous action. To form the progressive, you add a form of the verb *be* to the verb's present participle.

Normal Form
he *sang*
he *sings*
he *will sing*
he *had sung*
he *has sung*
he *will have sung*

Progressive Form
he *was singing*
he *is singing*
he *will be singing*
he *had been singing*
he *has been singing*
he *will have been singing*

Exercise 7

1. had hoped
2. was
3. is delaying
4. will . . . do
5. has done
6. will call
7. works
8. will have rewritten
9. has . . . completed
10. are

Present Perfect	Use *has* or *have* with the past participle.	To show an action that was completed at an indefinite time in the past or that began in the past and continues into the present: *The pyramids have stood for thousands of years.*
Past Perfect	Use *had* with the past participle.	To show an action in the past that came before another action in the past: *We had seen lightning shortly before the fire began.*
Future Perfect	Use *will have* or *shall have* with the past participle.	To show an action in the future that will happen before another future action or time: *Perhaps we shall have eradicated poverty by the year 2001.*

Exercise 7 Verb Tense Write each sentence, filling in the blank or blanks with the correct form of the verb described in parentheses.

Example Today's students of writing ______ tomorrow's movies and television programs. (future of *create*)

Answer Today's students of writing will create tomorrow's movies and television programs.

1. The director ______ to start shooting next week's episode yesterday. (past perfect of *hope*)
2. However, the script for the episode ______ terrible. (past of *be*)
3. This terrible script ______ filming and is costing a lot of money. (present perfect of *delay*)
4. What ______ the director ______? (future of *do*)
5. She will do what she ______ in the past. (present perfect of *do*)
6. She ______ in her story editors. (future of *call*)
7. A story editor is a professional screenplay editor who ______ on the staff of a television program. (present of *work*)
8. By the time the director is ready to start shooting the episode the following morning, the story editors ______ the screenplay several times. (future perfect of *rewrite*)
9. There is no professional story editor who ______ not ______ many such rushed revisions. (present perfect of *complete*)
10. Screenwriters and story editors ______ under a great deal of pressure because of the demands from producers, directors, actors, marketing people, network executives, and just about everyone else! (present of *be*)

Commonly Confused Verbs

Do not confuse *lie* and *lay*, *rise* and *raise*, or *sit* and *set*.

Some verbs are confusing because, while having different meanings, they are similar in form. Three of these confusing verb pairs are described in the following chart.

	Present	Present Participle	Past	Past Participle
Lie and *Lay*	lie	(is) lying	lay	(have) lain
	lay	(is) laying	laid	(have) laid
Rise and *Raise*	rise	(is) rising	rose	(have) risen
	raise	(is) raising	raised	(have) raised
Sit and *Set*	sit	(is) sitting	sat	(have) sat
	set	(is) setting	set	(have) set

Lie means "to rest in a flat position," "to be in a certain place," or "to exist." *Lie* never has a direct object.

The puppy *was lying* on the front lawn.

Lay means "to place." It almost always has a direct object.

The bathers *laid* their towels on the hot sand. (*Towels* is the direct object.)

Rise means "to go upward." *Rise* never has a direct object.

Oil dumped into water *rises* quickly to the surface.

Raise means "to lift" or "to make something go up." *Raise* almost always has a direct object.

The federal government *raised* taxes again. (*Taxes* is the direct object.)

Sit means "to occupy a seat." *Sit* never has a direct object.

The first violinist *sits* near the conductor.

Set means "to place." *Set* almost always has a direct object.

Please *set* those logs down by the fireplace. (*Logs* is the direct object.)

Other Confusing Verbs

Learn means "to gain knowledge or skill." *Teach* means "to help someone learn."

Did you *learn* to dive?
That diving school *teaches* beginners.

Let means "to allow or permit." *Leave* means "to place or deposit and cause to remain behind one."

Let the children stay.
Leave your cap and scarf at the front door.

May refers to permission or to something that is possible. *Can* refers to ability.

May we go outside?
Janet *can* play the flute.

Here are all the present forms of one regular verb, *sing:*

I sing we *sing*
You *sing* you (plural) *sing*
he, she, it *sings* they *sing*

Notice that the form with *he, she,* and *it* has an *-s* added to the end of it.

Exercise 8

1. sit
2. raise
3. lies
4. lay
5. sits
6. lays
7. risen
8. laid
9. risen
10. Set

Exercise 9

1. frozen
2. caught
3. worn
4. drank
5. run
6. said
7. came
8. lay
9. rising
10. sitting

Exercise 8 Confusing Verbs Write the correct verb form of the two given in parentheses.

1. If you (sit, set) next to me, we can share my poetry book.
2. Could you (raise, rise) the shade so we can see better?
3. My dog has a terrible new habit: he (lay, lies) right in front of the refrigerator!
4. Yesterday that sly old pooch (lay, laid) there almost all day!
5. Usually he (sits, sets) next to me on the porch early in the morning and we read poetry.
6. My brother (lays, lies) the chess pieces on the board each morning and waits for someone to challenge him to a game.
7. The sun has (raised, risen) already—it's going to be a hot day.
8. My father should have (laid, lain) my favorite book of poems on the table last night so I would be sure to find it.
9. If I can't find the book by noon, my anger will have (risen, raised) dramatically!
10. (Set, Sit) the iced tea on the table and let's pick out some poems to read.

Exercise 9 Verb Usage Review Choose the correct verb form from those given in parentheses.

1. We looked for the hole in the ice, but the pond had (froze, frozen) over.
2. After the runner had (catched, caught) her breath, she continued the race.
3. The guests have (wore, worn) out their welcome, and the holiday is only half over!
4. The astronauts (drank, drunk) from plastic bags and tubes.
5. How many times had William Jennings Bryan (ran, run) for President before the Scopes trial?
6. He just walked into the studio and (says, said), "Well, let's make an album."
7. After the hikers had explored the cave, they (come, came) back to tell us about the bats.
8. The mountain gorilla (lay, laid) down on his bed of leaves for a nap.
9. While the bread was (raising, rising), he put in a load of laundry.
10. The Old English epic poem *Beowulf* describes monsters (sitting, setting) around a table at a banquet.

SECTION 6 SUBJECT/VERB AGREEMENT

A verb must agree in number with its subject.

When the subject of a sentence is singular, its verb must also be singular. When the subject is plural, its verb must also be plural. This is called **subject-verb agreement.**

The hiker (singular) rests (singular) on a large rock near the trail.
The hikers (plural) rest (plural) on a large rock near the trail.

Most of the time, the singular and plural forms of verbs will not cause problems for you.

Verb Forms

	Singular		**Plural**	
First Person	I	work	we	work
Second Person	you	work	you	work
Third Person	he, she, it	works	they	work

However, the verb *be* does not follow the usual pattern. In the following chart, notice that *be* has special forms in both the present and the past tenses in all three persons.

Forms of *Be*

	Present Tense		**Past Tense**	
	Singular	**Plural**	**Singular**	**Plural**
First Person	I am	we are	I was	we were
Second Person	you are	you are	you were	you were
Third Person	he, she, it is	they are	he, she, it was	they were

QUICK TIP The most common errors involving forms of the verb *be* are using the words *you, we,* and *they* with the singular verb *was.* Remember to avoid saying or writing *you was, we was,* and *they was.*

Exercise 1 Agreement in Number Write the form of the verb that agrees in number with the subject of each of the following sentences. Then tell whether the verb form is singular or plural.

Example Museum lectures (are, is) often very interesting.

Answer are plural

REMINDER

When a word refers to one thing, it is **singular.** When it refers to more than one thing, it is **plural.** The **number** of a word refers to whether the word is singular or plural.

VERB FORMS

Except for the verb *be,* the only difference between singular and plural verbs is in the third-person present, which always ends in *-s.*

Additional Resources

GRAMMAR AND USAGE COPY MASTERS

- Exercises
- Tests

Exercise 1

1. were, plural
2. were, singular
3. were, plural
4. dates, singular
5. have, plural
6. reflects, singular
7. shows, singular
8. are, plural
9. depict, plural
10. portrays, singular
11. is, singular
12. were, plural
13. are, plural
14. is, singular
15. is, singular

1. We (were, was) fortunate to hear a Chinese art historian speak at the museum last night.
2. It's too bad that you (was, were) ill because you would have enjoyed this lecturer.
3. We (was, were) sorry when she ended her fascinating presentation about ancient China.
4. The Chinese civilization (date, dates) back more than four thousand years and is the oldest living civilization in the world.
5. The Chinese people (have, has) a deep respect for their ancestors.
6. Chinese art (reflects, reflect) this appreciation of history.
7. For example, modern-day pottery (show, shows) us what early Chinese villages looked like.
8. Chinese artists (is, are) very fond of landscapes.
9. Hanging scrolls (depicts, depict) scenes of nature, such as a mountain studded with pine trees overlooking a river.
10. A typical scroll, painted in watercolors, (portrays, portray) village life along a river.
11. Calligraphy (is, are) brush writing; it is another one of the many forms of Chinese art.
12. We (were, was) very interested in the lecturer's slides of Chinese porcelain, which was decorated with fierce, glaring dragons.
13. Beautifully embroidered silk robes (are, is) also examples of Chinese art.
14. Silk is valuable, but jade (is, are) the most precious of all Chinese materials.
15. Jade (is, are) too hard to be cut or carved; it must be shaped by slow grinding and rubbing.

Phrases Between a Subject and a Verb

Do not be fooled by other nouns in a sentence. Be sure that the verb agrees with its subject.

PREPOSITIONS

Commonly used prepositions include the following: *about, above, across, after, as, at, before, between, by, during, for, from, in, inside, into, like, near, of, off, on, over, since, through, to, until, up, upon, with, without.*

You are more likely to have a problem with subject-verb agreement if you cannot identify the subject in a sentence. To find the subject, first find the verb and then ask *who* or *what* before it.

The flower with bright red petals is a geranium. (Since *is* is the verb, ask, What is? *Flower,* not *petals,* is the subject.)

In the preceding sentence, "with bright red petals" is a **prepositional phrase.** Be especially careful when a prepositional phrase falls between the subject and the verb. Do not be fooled by the noun that appears in the phrase. Make the verb agree in number with the subject.

The books on the shelf are all mysteries. (*Books,* not *shelf,* is the subject.)

QUICK TIP To decide which word is the subject, say the sentence without the phrase. If you have chosen the correct word as the subject, the sentence will make sense without the phrase.

Exercise 2 Sentences with Phrases Choose the verb that agrees with the subject.

1. Tests of any kind (seem, seems) difficult to many people.
2. Students in high school (fear, fears) tests and exams more than they fear dental visits!
3. Anxiety about tests (is, are) distressing.
4. Characteristics of test anxiety (include, includes) headaches, sweaty palms, and feelings of panic.
5. Students with test anxiety (spend, spends) more time worrying than studying.
6. To relieve anxiety, students of all ages (need, needs) to learn to relax.
7. Relaxation classes after school (help, helps) students learn how to replace anxiety with calmness.
8. The teachers in this type of class (explain, explains) relaxation techniques.
9. A student with fears (try, tries) deep-breathing techniques.
10. Fearful students in this class (learn, learns) how to replace negative thoughts with positive ones.
11. Students with anxious behaviors (recognize, recognizes) the symptoms and learn to control them.
12. A class about study skills also (helps, help) reduce test anxiety.
13. Preparations for a test (is, are) very important; students learn to improve their study habits, so that they feel truly "ready" to be tested.
14. Students like Sean (feel, feels) secure when they have learned how to relax before a test.
15. Successful results on a test (is, are) sometimes the best way to relieve test anxiety!

Indefinite Pronouns as Subjects

Use a singular verb with a singular indefinite pronoun, and use a plural verb with a plural indefinite pronoun.

MEMORY TRICK

One way to remember which indefinite pronouns are singular is to look at the word endings that refer to one thing: *-other, -one, -body, -thing.* Also, many of the singular pronouns are compound—for example, *anything, someone;* none of the plural pronouns is compound.

Exercise 2

1. seem
2. fear
3. is
4. include
5. spend
6. need
7. help
8. explain
9. tries
10. learn
11. recognize
12. helps
13. are
14. feel
15. are

Indefinite pronouns do not refer to a definite person or thing. Some indefinite pronouns are singular, some are plural, and some can be either.

NEITHER/NOR

Remember that *nor* is almost always used with *neither.*

Incorrect The shoes nor the purse is my style.

Correct Neither the shoes nor the purse is my style.

	Indefinite Pronouns
Singular	another anybody anyone anything each either everybody everyone everything neither nobody no one one somebody someone something
Plural	both few many several
Singular or Plural	all any most none some

For the indefinite pronouns that are always singular or plural, the correct verb choice will often be the one that sounds right to you.

Incorrect Everyone have a project to complete.

Correct Everyone has a project to complete. (*Everyone* is singular; it takes a singular verb, *has.*)

Incorrect Both of the movies is in French.

Correct Both of the movies are in French. (*Both* is plural; it takes a plural verb, *are.*)

The indefinite pronouns that are either singular or plural cause the most difficulties in subject-verb agreement. If the pronoun refers to one thing, it is singular and requires a singular verb. If the pronoun refers to several things or to things that can be counted, it is plural and requires a plural verb.

Singular All of the food was eaten. (*All* refers to a single quantity of food, so it requires the singular verb *was.*)

Plural All of the dishes were washed. (*All* refers to several dishes, so it requires the plural verb *were.*)

QUICK TIP Remember that *none* can be plural. It is plural if it refers to more than one person, place, or thing. It is singular if it refers to only one person, place, or thing. For example, a quantity of sky is singular, but a quantity of clouds is plural.

Incorrect None of the clouds is visible from the city street.

Correct None of the clouds are visible from the city street.

Exercise 3 Indefinite Pronouns Rewrite the following sentences, correcting any errors in subject-verb agreement. If a sentence is correct, write *Correct.*

1. Everyone have a favorite classic of children's literature.
2. Both of my brothers loves *Treasure Island.*
3. Most of the characters in this adventure story was searching for buried treasure.
4. All of the treasure was found with the help of a marooned sailor named Ben Gunn.
5. One of my favorite classics are *The Wind in the Willows.*
6. None of the animals in this wonderful fantasy acts like animals—they all live like British country folks!
7. One of the animals drive a shiny red automobile.
8. Several of my cousins adores *The Wizard of Oz.*
9. Most of my younger relatives shrieks when I read the section about the wicked witch.
10. Everybody clap when Dorothy and Toto arrive back in Kansas.

Exercise 4 Review Write the subject of each of the following sentences. Then write the verb that agrees in number with the subject.

Example Many of the art forms (speaks, speak) to me.

Answer Many speak

1. Many great artists (was, were) living and working in Italy in the fifteenth century.
2. The paintings from this period in history (hang, hangs) on museum walls everywhere in the world.
3. Everyone in my art class (recognizes, recognize) the name of Leonardo da Vinci.
4. Most of da Vinci's artistic achievements (reflects, reflect) the brilliance of his curious mind.
5. Few of my classmates (know, knows) that da Vinci was the leading scientist of his age.
6. Several of my teachers (explain, explains) that da Vinci sought to understand the inner workings of everything he painted.
7. Because Leonardo da Vinci worked on so many kinds of projects simultaneously, many of his projects (were, was) never completed.
8. One of his artistic achievements (are, is) called *chiaroscuro,* meaning "clear-dark" in Italian.
9. This artistic technique, involving the use of light and background shadow, (makes, make) people seem realistic.
10. Everyone in the art world (understands, understand) the value of da Vinci's legacy.

Exercise 3

1. Everyone has a favorite classic of children's literature.
2. Both of my brothers love *Treasure Island.*
3. Most of the characters in this adventure story were searching for buried treasure.
4. Correct
5. One of my favorite classics is *The Wind in the Willows.*
6. None of the animals in this wonderful fantasy act like animals–they all live like British country folks!
7. One of the animals drives a shiny red automobile.
8. Several of my cousins adore *The Wizard of Oz.*
9. Most of my younger relatives shriek when I read the section about the wicked witch.
10. Everybody claps when Dorothy and Toto arrive back in Kansas.

Exercise 4

1. artists were
2. paintings hang
3. Everyone recognizes
4. Most reflect
5. Few know
6. Several explain
7. many were
8. One is
9. technique makes
10. Everyone understands

Exercise 5

1. love
2. understands
3. decide
4. is
5. is
6. develop
7. appear
8. seem
9. help
10. know

Compound Subjects

Use a plural verb with most compound subjects joined by *and*. Use a verb that agrees with the subject nearer the verb when the words in a compound subject are joined by *or* or *nor*.

REMINDER

If a compound subject is preceded by *each, every,* or *many a,* use a singular verb.

Each brother and sister receives a prize.

Many a cat and dog has found a new home.

A compound subject is two or more subjects used with the same verb. Most compound subjects that contain the word *and* are plural and take a plural verb.

Track and swimming are my favorite sports.
Speed and endurance help an athlete to excel.

REMINDER

Remember that nouns ending in *-s* are usually plural, whereas verbs ending in *-s* are usually singular.

When the parts of a compound subject are connected by the conjunction *or* or *nor,* you need to look at the subject that is closer to the verb to decide if the verb should be singular or plural.

Neither Lois nor her other friends work after school.
Either the gymnasts or the cyclist appear next.

Exercise 5 Compound Subjects Write the form of the verb that agrees with the subject.

1. Liz and her classmates (loves, love) to read mysteries.
2. Neither Liz nor her friend (understand, understands) the difficulties of writing a mystery novel.
3. Liz and Matt (decides, decide) to write a mystery.
4. Most people don't realize that neither the characters nor the plot (is, are) easily created.
5. Amateur sleuths or a private detective (is, are) essential in any good mystery.
6. Liz and Matt (develops, develop) a plot that revolves around a grizzly murder, of course!
7. A victim and many suspects (appears, appear) in different chapters of their story.
8. Both obvious clues and red herrings always (seems, seem) to lead the reader to a solution.
9. Strong dialogue and interesting plot developments (help, helps) to build suspense and keep the reader wondering what will happen next.
10. Neither the authors nor their classmates (know, knows) yet how the mystery will be solved!

Exercise 6

1. don't
2. don't
3. don't
4. don't
5. doesn't
6. doesn't
7. doesn't
8. don't
9. don't
10. don't

Agreement Problems with *Doesn't* and *Don't*

Use *doesn't* with singular subjects and with the personal pronouns *he, she,* and *it.* Use *don't* with plural subjects and with the personal pronouns *I, we, you,* and *they.*

For many writers, the words *doesn't* and *don't* create agreement problems. Keep in mind that these words are contractions for *does not* and *do not.*

Incorrect	*Doesn't* the stars seem brilliant tonight?
Correct	*Don't* the stars seem brilliant tonight?
Incorrect	*Don't* the moon seem eery tonight?
Correct	*Doesn't* the moon seem eery tonight?

> **QUICK TIP** If you remember that *does* is a singular verb and *do* is a plural verb, you will have fewer problems.

Exercise 6 *Doesn't* and *Don't* Choose the form of the verb that agrees in number with the subject.

1. Since the members of my family (doesn't, don't) agree about music, the room where we keep our CD player has become a battlefield.
2. Other people (doesn't, don't) understand the problem unless they live in this household for at least a week.
3. My grandparents (doesn't, don't) like loud music at all.
4. My mother and my older sister (doesn't, don't) like country music.
5. It (doesn't, don't) matter to me—I listen to country music whenever I'm in the mood.
6. My older brother (doesn't, don't) like classical music, but my younger sister turns up Beethoven full blast whenever she can.
7. My younger brother (doesn't, don't) listen to anything *I* say, but he has listened to the same sing-along-with-Mr.-Rogers tape at least one thousand times.
8. My brother and I (doesn't, don't) understand why anyone would like opera, but my father sings along with *Madame Butterfly.*
9. My family and I (doesn't, don't) agree about any music except elevator music: we all hate it!
10. Our neighbors (doesn't, don't) enjoy our varied musical tastes; they'd prefer the sound of silence instead.

SECTION 7 SENTENCE STRUCTURE

A *sentence* is a group of words that expresses a complete thought. A sentence may be *simple, compound,* or *complex.*

Simple Sentences

Throughout this book you have been studying sentences. You know that a sentence has two basic parts, the **subject** and the **predicate.**

Subject	Predicate
Officer	studied
The officer in the tent	studied the map of the area.

You also know that all the parts of a sentence may be **compound.** That is, they may have more than one part.

Compound Subject	The *teacher* and the *students* discussed the lesson.
Compound Verb	The dolphins *swam* and *jumped.*
Compound Object	The storm brought *ice* and *snow.*

You can see that each of these sentences expresses one main idea. These sentences are called **simple** sentences.

A simple sentence is a sentence that contains only one subject and one predicate. Remember, however, that the subject and predicate, or any part of the subject or predicate, may be compound.

Compound Sentences

Create a *compound sentence* by joining two or more simple sentences together.

When you join together two or more simple sentences, the result is a **compound sentence.**

Simple Sentences	The Shepherds adopted a little girl. They named her Molly.
Compound Sentence	The Shepherds adopted a little girl, and they named her Molly.

Simple sentences can be joined in one of three ways.

You can join simple sentences by using a comma and a coordinating conjunction.

Additional Resources

GRAMMAR AND USAGE COPY MASTERS

- Exercises
- Tests

Simple Sentences The car overheated. We made it to Lake Tahoe anyway.

Compound Sentence The car overheated**, but** we made it to Lake Tahoe anyway.

You can also join simple sentences by using a semicolon.

Compound Sentence The car overheated**;** we made it to Lake Tahoe anyway.

You can also join simple sentences by using a semicolon, a conjunctive adverb, such as *however* or *therefore,* and a comma.

Compound Sentence The car overheated**; however,** we made it to Lake Tahoe anyway.

QUICK TIP Two simple sentences should be joined together only if they are related in meaning. Do not join sentences that are unrelated.

Incorrect The Hubble Space Telescope is a sophisticated machine, and I have been studying sentence combining.

Exercise 1 Compound Sentences Combine each pair of simple sentences, following the directions given in parentheses.

Example The moon was full. It was hidden by clouds. (Combine with a comma and *but.*)

Answer The moon was full**, but** it was hidden by clouds.

1. In 1988, surgeons were very busy. They transplanted 9,123 kidneys and 1,647 hearts. (Combine with a semicolon.)
2. Every person has over nine thousand tastebuds. In adults, some of these do not work very well. (Combine with a comma and *but.*)
3. People actually have more than five senses. Most people do not make full use of any of their senses. (Combine with a semicolon, the conjunctive adverb *however,* and a comma.)
4. Human rabies is almost unheard of in the United States. In 1989 there was only one reported case. (Combine with a semicolon, the conjunctive adverb *indeed,* and a comma.)
5. Eating less fat can make you healthier. You will also lose weight. (Combine with a comma and *and.*)

Simple Sentence Review

To make a simple sentence, you can start with one of the simple sentence patterns. Then, you can do any of the following:

1. **Substitute pronouns for nouns.**
2. **Substitute infinitives for nouns.**
3. **Substitute *-ing* words for nouns.**
4. **Make nouns or verbs compound.**
5. **Add single-word modifiers, either adjectives or adverbs.**
6. **Add an infinitive phrase modifier.**
7. **Add an *-ing* phrase modifier.**

Exercise 1

1. In 1988, surgeons were very busy; they transplanted 9,123 kidneys and 1,647 hearts.
2. Every person has over nine thousand tastebuds, but in adults, some of these do not work very well.
3. People actually have more than five senses; however, most people do not make full use of any of their senses.
4. Human rabies is almost unheard of in the United States; indeed, in 1989 there was only one reported case.
5. Eating less fat can make you healthier, and you will also lose weight.

Clauses and Complex Sentences

A **clause** is a group of words that has a subject and a verb.

The boy (S) ran (V). who (S) called (V) here yesterday

after the rains (S) came (V) and they (S) lived (V) happily ever after

There are two kinds of clauses. **Independent clauses** are ones that can stand alone as sentences. All simple sentences are independent clauses.

The movie was wonderful. Matthew called.

Subordinate clauses are ones that cannot stand alone as sentences. Consider the following examples:

which is called El Niño in Spanish until the package is sent

Each has a subject and a verb, but more information is needed. Can you identify the subject and verb of each of the preceding clauses?

A clause may be introduced by a pronoun such as *who, whoever, whom, whomever, whose, what, whatever, that,* or *which.* It may also be introduced by one of the following subordinating conjunctions:

Subordinating Conjunctions	
Time	after, as, as long as, as soon as, before, since, until, when, whenever, while
Manner	as, as if
Place	where, wherever
Cause or Reason	because, since
Comparison	as, as much as, than
Condition	although, as long as, even if, even though, if, provided that, though, unless, while
Purpose	in order that, so that, that

To make a subordinate clause into a sentence, you have to add an independent clause (a sentence) to it. A sentence that is made up of one or more subordinate clauses and an independent clause is called a **complex sentence.**

We must wait (Independent Clause) +
until the package is sent (Subordinate Clause) =
We must wait until the package is sent. (Complex Sentence)

To summarize, a complex sentence is what you get when you add a clause to a simple sentence.

Exercise 2 Complex Sentences Copy the following complex sentences onto your paper. Underline each independent clause once and each subordinate clause twice.

Example This is the book that I told you about.

Answer This is the book that I told you about.

1. This is the place where the astronauts train.
2. Kate snapped a photo as we fell into the pool.
3. Dad insists that Teresa drives too fast.
4. Steve felt better after he had talked to his girlfriend.
5. The manager asked Donna if she would work on Tuesday.
6. Kevin sleeps during the day because he works at night.
7. When orders increase, the factory hires more workers.
8. We conserved water because a drought had reduced the supply.
9. Chicago is the place where deep-dish pizza was developed.
10. Adrienne admits that she is not a good loser.

Exercise 3 Sentence-Building Review Exercise Rewrite each of the following clauses, adding an independent clause. Then, underline each independent clause once and each subordinate clause twice. Tell whether the sentence that you created is a *Compound Sentence* (with two independent clauses) or a *Complex Sentence* (with one independent clause and one subordinate clause).

Example although no one was injured by the tremor

Answer Although no one was injured by the tremor many people were scared by it. (Complex Sentence)

Example you can go

Answer You can go, or you can stay here. (Compound Sentence)

1. when the lights went out
2. the party ended
3. it rained on Saturday
4. because there wasn't enough time
5. if that dog were properly trained
6. the fire was put out
7. who wrote that story
8. as long as you are satisfied
9. it was very foggy
10. since the twenty-first century is almost here

Exercise 2

1. This is the place where the astronauts train.
2. Kate snapped a photo as we fell into the pool.
3. Dad insists that Teresa drives too fast.
4. Steve felt better after he had talked to his girlfriend.
5. The manager asked Donna if she would work on Tuesday.
6. Kevin sleeps during the day because he works at night.
7. When orders increase, the factory hires more workers.
8. We conserved water because a drought had reduced the supply.
9. Chicago is the place where deep-dish pizza was developed.
10. Adrienne admits that she is not a good loser.

Exercise 3

Answers will vary. Probable answers are provided.

1. When the lights went out, the game ended abruptly. (complex)
2. The party ended after the music ended. (complex)
3. It rained on Saturday, and we stayed home. (compound)
4. We didn't finish the game because there wasn't enough time. (complex)
5. If that dog were properly trained, he would live indoors. (complex)
6. Once the firefighters arrived, the fire was put out. (complex)
7. I was the person who wrote that story. (complex)
8. As long as you are satisfied, let's finish the job. (complex)
9. It was very foggy, but the game was held nevertheless. (compound)
10. Since the twenty-first century is almost here, can we celebrate early? (complex)

SECTION 8 CAPITALIZATION

Rules of Capitalization

One of the purposes of capitalization is to call attention to particularly important words. Of course, you use capitalization at the beginning of sentences and for names. However, there are some other capitalization rules that writers need to know in order to distinguish certain words or groups of words. Most words that are capitalized fall into one of two broad categories: proper nouns and adjectives, and first words in groups of words. Listed below are some more-specific rules and examples of capitalization. You can use this section as a reference when you are in doubt about whether to capitalize a word.

Proper Nouns and Adjectives

Capitalize proper nouns and adjectives.

A **proper noun** is the name of a specific person, place, thing, or idea. Proper nouns are capitalized, and common nouns are not. A **proper adjective** is an adjective formed from a proper noun; it is also capitalized.

Common Noun	Proper Noun	Proper Adjective
mountains	**A**ndes	**A**ndean

Names and Titles of People

Capitalize people's names, and initials that stand for names.

C. Everett **K**oop   **C**lara **B**arton   **P**hil **D**onahue

Capitalize titles and abbreviations of titles when used before people's names or in direct address.

Professor **S**usan **H**ill   **M**s. **C**arla **S**mith   **D**r. **R. S**hepherd

Capitalize a title used without a person's name if it refers to a head of state or a person in another important position.

the **P**resident of the **U**nited **S**tates   the **P**ope
the **S**ecretary of **S**tate   the **Q**ueen of **E**ngland

Family Relationships

Capitalize words indicating family relationships when the words are used as names or parts of names.

Additional Resources

GRAMMAR AND USAGE COPY MASTERS

- Exercises
- Tests

Dad and Nana are looking forward to the arrival of **U**ncle **H**al.

If the word is preceded by an article or a possessive adjective, it is not capitalized.

My aunt gave me a big hug when I told her the news.
The brother of my friend has gone to Peru.

The Pronoun *I*

Always capitalize the pronoun *I*.

Joanne and **I** cooked the curried vegetables.

The Supreme Being and Sacred Writings

Capitalize all words referring to God and religious scriptures.

God	**B**uddha	the **B**ible
the **K**oran	**M**ohammed	the **T**orah

Exercise 1 Rewrite the following sentences, correcting any capitalization errors.

1. Would you tell mom i'll be a little late for dinner?
2. The first book of the bible is genesis.
3. The new teacher is from paris, france.
4. He is a parisian.
5. Our government is sometimes called a jeffersonian democracy.
6. She said, "Please ask dr. hernandez to call me."
7. My mother asked aunt rose if tad and maria could stay for lunch.
8. Please take this message to the principal, lynn.
9. It was captain sherman who gave sue and ted the booklets on bicycle safety.
10. Two names for god are jehovah and the almighty.

Geographical Names

In a geographical name, capitalize the first letter of each word except articles and prepositions.

Continents	**N**orth **A**merica	**E**urope	**A**frica
Bodies of Water	**N**orth **S**ea	**L**ake **E**rie	**P**acific **O**cean
Landforms	**U**ral **M**ountains	**D**eath **V**alley	**S**ahara **D**esert
World Regions	**C**entral **A**merica	the **Y**ukon	**M**iddle **E**ast

Exercise 1

1. Would you tell Mom I'll be a little late for dinner?
2. The first book of the Bible is Genesis.
3. The new teacher is from Paris, France.
4. He is a Parisian.
5. Our government is sometimes called a Jeffersonian democracy.
6. She said, "Please ask Dr. Hernandez to call me."
7. My mother asked Aunt Rose if Tad and Maria could stay for lunch.
8. Please take this message to the principal, Lynn.
9. It was Captain Sherman who gave Sue and Ted the booklets on bicycle safety.
10. Two names for God are Jehovah and The Almighty.

Exercise 2

1. Lake Bakal is the world's deepest freshwater lake.
2. The lake is in Siberia, in the Soviet Union.
3. Next week we elect the representative from the Eighth Congressional District.
4. The group of explorers left for the Galapagos Islands.
5. The island of Capri is in the Bay of Naples.
6. The Blue Grotto is a famous tourist attraction on Capri.
7. The Trans-Canada Highway crosses Western Canada.
8. Of the seven continents, Asia and Africa are the largest.
9. We had our family picnic at the Lincoln Park Zoo last week.
10. Last summer we drove along the Gulf of Mexico to New Orleans and then north to Memphis.

Public Areas	**O**ld **F**aithful	**R**ed **S**quare	**M**achu **P**icchu
Political Units	**F**rance	**N**ew **J**ersey	**Z**aire
Roads and Highways	**O**ak **S**treet	**H**ighway 1	**F**ifth **A**venue

Directions and Sections

Capitalize names of sections of the country or the world, and any adjectives that come from those names.

The **S**outh sustained heavy casualties during the Civil War.
The **M**idwestern town was devastated by a tornado.

Do not capitalize compass directions or adjectives that merely indicate direction or a general location.

The birds fly south in November.
The westward wind carried the little raft out to sea.

Exercise 2 Rewrite the following sentences, correcting any errors in capitalization.

1. Lake baykal is the world's deepest freshwater lake.
2. The lake is in siberia, in the soviet union.
3. Next week we elect the representative from the eighth congressional district.
4. The group of explorers left for the galapagos islands.
5. The island of capri is in the bay of naples.
6. The blue grotto is a famous tourist attraction on capri.
7. The trans-canada highway crosses western canada.
8. Of the seven continents, asia and africa are the largest.
9. We had our family picnic at the lincoln park zoo last week.
10. Last summer we drove along the gulf of mexico to new orleans and then north to memphis.

Organizations and Institutions

Capitalize the names of organizations and institutions and their abbreviations.

Democratic **N**ational **C**ommittee **J**efferson **H**igh **S**chool **U**.**N**.

Events, Documents, and Periods of Time

Capitalize the names of historical events, documents, and periods of time.

Korean **W**ar the **M**iddle **A**ges **D**eclaration of **I**ndependence

Months, Days, and Holidays

Capitalize the names of months, days, and holidays but not the names of seasons.

May **F**riday **T**hanksgiving **D**ay **s**pring

Races, Languages, Nationalities, and Religions

Capitalize the names of races, languages, nationalities, and religions and any adjectives formed from these names.

Cherokee	**F**rench	**C**atholicism	**H**ispanic
Hinduism	**P**eruvian	**O**riental	**A**merican

Exercise 3 Rewrite, correcting any errors in capitalization.

1. The fourth of july is an important date in american history.
2. The declaration of independence was adopted on july 4, 1776.
3. My sister is a student at pulaski high school.
4. In 1898 the treaty of paris ended the spanish-american war.
5. The first woman to fly solo across the atlantic ocean was amelia earhart.
6. The prophet mohammed founded the religion of islam.
7. Mohammed's followers are called moslems or muslims.
8. He has studied spanish, russian, french, and german.
9. I'm glad to see that a hispanic woman is running for mayor in our town.
10. Alice's sister was born at bloomington hospital.

School Subjects and Class Names

Do not capitalize the general names of school subjects unless they are names of languages. Do capitalize the titles of specific courses and of courses that are followed by a number. School subjects that are languages are always capitalized.

Russian **g**eometry **I**ntroduction to **S**ociology

Capitalize class names only when they refer to a specific group or event or when they are used in direct address.

The juniors are holding a carwash to make money for the **J**unior **P**rom.

Exercise 3

1. The Fourth of July is an important date in American history.
2. The Declaration of Independence was adopted on July 4, 1776.
3. My sister is a student at Pulaski High School.
4. In 1898 the Treaty of Paris ended the Spanish-American War.
5. The first woman to fly solo across the Atlantic Ocean was Amelia Earhart.
6. The prophet Mohammed founded the religion of Islam.
7. Mohammed's followers are called Moslems or Muslims.
8. He has studied Spanish, Russian, French, and German.
9. I'm glad to see that a Hispanic woman is running for mayor in our town.
10. Alice's sister was born at Bloomington hospital.

Exercise 4

1. I registered for Ancient History I, Business Math II, social studies, English, and music.
2. My favorite subjects, home economics and shop, are held at 2:00 P.M.
3. In 44 B.C. Julius Caesar was assassinated.
4. The Planet Mars was visible on the horizon in November.
5. The Hancock Building in Boston is next to Trinity Church.

Structures

Capitalize the names of specific monuments, bridges, and buildings.

the **E**iffel **T**ower the **T**appan **Z**ee **B**ridge
the **V**ietnam **V**eterans **M**emorial

Bodies of the Universe

Capitalize the names of the planets in the solar system and other objects in the universe, except words like *sun* and *moon*.

the eclipsed sun **J**upiter **O**rion

QUICK TIP Capitalize the word *earth* only when it is used in conjunction with the names of other planets. The word *earth* is not capitalized when the article *the* precedes it.

The earth is the third planet away from the sun in our solar system.

Time Abbreviations

Capitalize the abbreviations *B.C., A.D., A.M.,* and *P.M.*

Our school day ends at 3:10 **P.M.**

Exercise 4 Rewrite, correcting any errors in capitalization.

1. I registered for ancient history I, business math II, social studies, english, and music.
2. My favorite subjects, home economics and shop, are held at 2:00 p.m.
3. In 44 b.c. Julius Caesar was assassinated.
4. The Planet mars was visible on the horizon in November.
5. The hancock building in Boston is next to trinity church.

First Words

Capitalize the first word of every sentence.

After six silent years, the child spoke one word.

In general, capitalize the first word of every line of poetry. (In some modern poetry, lines do not begin with a capital letter.)

The cow is of the bovine ilk,
One end is moo, the other, milk.
"The Cow,"—Ogden Nash

Capitalize the first word of a direct quotation.

FDR said, "**W**e have nothing to fear but fear itself."

Capitalize the first word in the greeting of a letter. Also capitalize the title, the person's name, and words such as *Sir* and *Madam*.

Dear **S**ir or **M**adam: **D**ear **D**r. **T**emple:

Capitalize only the first word in the complimentary close.

Sincerely, **T**ruly yours,

Capitalize the first word of each item in an outline and letters that introduce major subsections.

I. **A**nimals
 A. **D**ogs
  1. **C**ollies
  2. **T**erriers

Capitalize the first word, the last word, and all other important words in titles. Do not capitalize conjunctions, articles, or prepositions with fewer than five letters.

Book Title	*Veracruz*	**Short Story**	"**T**o **B**uild a **F**ire"
Newspaper	*The* ***P****ost*	**Song**	"**D**ay by **D**ay"
Play	*Pygmalion*	**Work of Art**	the ***M****ona* ***L****isa*
Television Series	***C****heers*		

The word *the* at the beginning of a title and the word *magazine* are capitalized only when they are part of the formal name.

L*ife* magazine *The* ***W****all* ***S****treet* ***J****ournal* *Smithsonian* ***M****agazine*

Exercise 5 Rewrite, correcting any errors in capitalization.

1. Steve Martin hosted *saturday night live* last week on TV.
2. the famous humorist Will Rogers said, "all i know is what i read in the papers."
3. I. american history
   a. the war for independence
    1. battle of bunker hill
4. for my birthday I got a subscription to *seventeen.*
5. very sincerely yours,

Exercise 5

1. Steve Martin hosted *Saturday Night Live* last week on TV.
2. The famous humorist Will Rogers said, "all I know is what I read in the papers."
3. American history
 A. The War for Independence
  1. Battle of Bunker Hill
4. For my birthday I got a subscription to *Seventeen.*
5. Very sincerely yours,

SECTION 9 PUNCTUATION

When reading a selection in this book, you probably pay little attention to the punctuation used. If that punctuation were missing, however, reading would be a struggle. Consider this passage from Rona Maynard's "The Fan Club," without the original punctuation.

> Dianne Goddard was saying Itll be a riot I just cant wait to see her face when she finds out Laura flushed painfully Were they talking about her What a scream Cant wait to hear what she says Silently she hurried past and submerged herself in the stream of students heading for the lockers

As you can see, punctuation marks are essential. They are signals for a reader. They indicate pauses and show points of emphasis. They tell who is speaking and where ideas begin and end. If you want your readers to understand what you write, you need to use punctuation marks correctly.

Kinds of Punctuation Marks

In this section you will learn how to use the following kinds of punctuation marks:

1. End marks (.!?)
2. Commas (,)
3. Semicolons (;)
4. Colons (:)
5. Hyphens (-)
6. Apostrophes (')
7. Quotation marks ("")
8. Underlining (___)

End Marks

The punctuation marks that show where sentences end are called end marks. They are **periods, question marks,** and **exclamation points.** **Use a *period* at the end of a declarative sentence.**

A **declarative sentence** is a sentence that makes a statement. It is the most basic kind of sentence used for reporting information.

Palermo is in Sicily. My middle name is Pilar.

Use a period at the end of an imperative sentence.

An **imperative sentence** is one that requests or orders someone to do something.

Leave your shoes at the door. Help me with this.

Additional Resources

GRAMMAR AND USAGE COPY MASTERS

- Exercises
- Texts

Use a period at the end of an indirect question.

An **indirect question** tells what someone asked. However, it does not give the exact words of the person who asked the question.

The senator asked whether the country would give foreign aid.

Use a period after most abbreviations and initials.

An abbreviation is a shortened form of a word. An initial is a single letter that stands for a word or name.

Dr. Herbert A. Simon = Doctor Herbert Alexander Simon
Seattle, Wash., U.S.A. = Seattle, Washington, United States of America
123 E. Main St. = 123 East Main Street
Rev. Martin Luther King, Jr. = the Reverend Martin Luther King, Junior
1 gal., 6 oz. = one gallon, six ounces

Periods are omitted in some abbreviations. If you are not sure whether to use periods, look up the abbreviation in a dictionary.

FM (frequency modulation)	VT (Vermont)
UN (United Nations)	IN (Indiana)
FBI (Federal Bureau of Investigation)	TX (Texas)

Note that a period is not used after a standard, two-letter United States Post Office state abbreviation. (See list.) A period is used after an informal state abbreviation, such as Calif., for California, or Ill., for Illinois.

Use a period after each number or letter that shows a division of an outline or that precedes an item in a list.

List
1. Gather your information.
2. Take notes.
3. Make an outline.

Outline
I. Telescopes
A. Light telescopes
B. Radio telescopes

In numerals use a period between dollars and cents and before a decimal.

$18.98 2.853

Use a *question mark* at the end of an interrogative sentence.

An **interrogative sentence** is one that asks a question.

Does Saturn's moon Titan really have geysers on it?

State Abbreviations

Alabama	AL
Alaska	AK
Arizona	AZ
Arkansas	AR
California	CA
Colorado	CO
Connecticut	CT
Delaware	DE
District of Columbia	DC
Florida	FL
Georgia	GA
Hawaii	HI
Idaho	ID
Illinois	IL
Indiana	IN
Iowa	IA
Kansas	KS
Kentucky	KY
Louisiana	LA
Maine	ME
Maryland	MD
Massachusetts	MA
Michigan	MI
Minnesota	MN
Mississippi	MS
Missouri	MO
Montana	MT
Nebraska	NE
Nevada	NV
New Hampshire	NH
New Jersey	NJ
New Mexico	NM
New York	NY
North Carolina	NC
North Dakota	ND
Ohio	OH
Oklahoma	OK
Oregon	OR
Pennsylvania	PA
Rhode Island	RI
South Carolina	SC
South Dakota	SD
Tennessee	TN
Texas	TX
Utah	UT
Vermont	VT
Virginia	VA
Washington	WA
West Virginia	WV
Wisconsin	WI
Wyoming	WY

Exercise 1

1. I was supposed to meet Tom at 10:30 A.M.
2. Dr. James Coogan, Jr. is going to talk about lifesaving.
3. What is Dr. Harrigan's telephone number?
4. Where is Sgt. Leslie's office located?
5. Help! I can't get this door open.
6. I. Types of computer software
A. Word-processing software
B. Database software
C. Accounting and spreadsheet software
D. Games
7. Wow! That was quite a football game!
8. Mary, look out!
9. Our art supplies will cost less than ten dollars, but they'll be more than $825.
10. Please bring these items with you to the orienteering workshop:
1. a canteen
2. a compass
3. some nylon rope
11. UNICEF is the children's organization of the UN.
12. Please send your requests to Franklin's Inc., P.O. Box 552, New York, NY.

The above sentence gives the exact words of the person who asked the question. It is called a **direct question.** A question mark is used only with a direct question.

Do not use a question mark with an indirect question. Instead use a period.

Kelly asked whether Titan had geysers on it.

Use an exclamation point at the end of an exclamatory sentence.

How great that looks!

Use an exclamation point after an interjection or after any other exclamatory expression.

An **interjection** is a word or group of words used to express strong feeling. It may be a real word or simply a group of letters used to represent a sound. It is one of the eight parts of speech.

Wow! Hurrah! Ugh!

Exercise 1 End Marks Rewrite the following items, adding the necessary punctuation.

1. I was supposed to meet Tom at 10:30 AM
2. Dr James Coogan, Jr is going to talk about lifesaving
3. What is Dr Harrigan's telephone number
4. Where is Sgt Leslie's office located
5. Help I can't get this door open
6. **I** Types of computer software
A Word-processing software
B Database software
C Accounting and spreadsheet software
D Games
7. Wow That was quite a football game
8. Mary, look out
9. Our art supplies will cost less than ten dollars, but they'll be more than $825
10. Please bring these items with you to the orienteering workshop:
1 a canteen,
2 a compass, and
3 some nylon rope
11. UNICEF is the children's organization of the UN
12. Please send your requests to Franklin's, Inc, PO Box 552, New York, NY

13. Will you mail these coupons to the Clark Company, Ltd, 301 E Walton Place, Miami, Florida 33152
14. Sen Mark M Butler, Jr, will be the guest speaker
15. Mindy asked whether you were interested in going to the football game

The Comma

Use a comma after every item in a series except the last.

A series consists of three or more words, phrases, or clauses.

Words The flag is red, white, and blue.

Phrases The dog ran out the door, down the steps, and across the lawn.

Clauses How baboons forage for food, establish leadership, and find mates are all explained in this book.

Use commas after the adverbs *first, second, third,* and so on, when these adverbs introduce parallel items in a series.

There are three ways to get good grades: first, pay attention; second, take notes; and third, study.

Use commas between two or more adjectives of equal rank that modify the same noun.

They drove away in a bright, shiny, expensive car.

QUICK TIP To decide whether adjectives are of equal rank, try placing the word *and* between them. If the *and* sounds natural and if you can reverse the order of the adjectives without changing the meaning, then a comma is needed.

Use a comma to separate an introductory word, phrase, or clause from the rest of the sentence.

Yes, the ozone layer does protect us from the harmful ultraviolet rays of the sun.
However, the ozone layer does not block all the sun's ultraviolet rays.
On hot days during the summer, many people get sunburns.
When you go out into the sunshine, you may have to wear sunblock.

The comma may be left out if there would be little pause in speaking.

No Commas

Commas are not needed when all the items in a series are joined by *and, or,* or *nor.*

Rain nor sleet nor dark of night...

13. Will you mail these coupons to the Clark Company, Ltd., 301 E. Walton Place, Miami, Florida 33152?
14. Sen. Mark M. Butler, Jr. will be the guest speaker.
15. Mindy asked whether you were interested in going to the football game.

Exercise 2

1. Are the colors of the Italian flag red, white, and green?
2. A northerly wind swept the wet, thick snow against the front door.
3. The race car lost its right front tire, skidded a hundred feet, and did a complete turn.
4. To finish the stage set, do the following: first, put the risers in place; second, finish painting the backdrop; and third, move the flats onto the stage.
5. Was that a rabbit that scooted across our doorstep, through the evergreens, and under the back porch?
6. A long, sleek, black limousine pulled up in front of the bank.
7. Although the championship game had been postponed, we practiced every morning and evening.
8. The latest weather report, however, has predicted rain.
9. The official language of Saudi Arabia is, by the way, Arabic.
10. No, you cannot have someone else take the SAT for you.
11. Bowling, skating, and running are my favorite activities.
12. In the plaza in the front of the government building, a large, angry crowd gathered.
13. Yes, Margaret Thatcher was Prime Minister of Great Britain for eleven years.
14. After the smog became too oppressive, the city passed an ordinance requiring car pooling.
15. When you tune a guitar, follow these steps: first, sound the corresponding note on the pitch pipe; second, turn the tuning peg until the note of the string matches the note of the pipe; third, repeat this process with the remaining strings.

SENTENCE INTERRUPTERS

The following interrupters are quite common:
however
I suppose
I think
I believe
nevertheless
by the way
fortunately
on the one hand
in contrast

At first the sunshine simply feels good on the skin. Then the burns come.

Use commas to set off words or groups of words that interrupt the flow of thought in a sentence.

Grimm's Fairy Tales, to tell the truth, are too scary for young children. Some of these tales, moreover, contain stereotyping of men and women.

Exercise 2 Commas and End Marks Rewrite the following sentences, adding the necessary punctuation.

1. Are the colors of the Italian flag red white and green
2. A northerly wind swept the wet thick snow against the front door
3. The race car lost its right front tire skidded a hundred feet and did a complete turn
4. To finish the stage set, do the following: first put the risers in place; second finish painting the backdrop; and third move the flats onto the stage
5. Was that a rabbit that scooted across our doorstep through the evergreens and under the back porch
6. A long sleek black limousine pulled up in front of the bank
7. Although the championship game had been postponed we practiced every morning and evening
8. The latest weather report however has predicted rain
9. The official language of Saudi Arabia is by the way Arabic
10. No you cannot have someone else take the SAT for you
11. Bowling skating and running are my favorite activities
12. In the plaza in the front of the government building a large angry crowd gathered
13. Yes Margaret Thatcher was Prime Minister of Great Britain for eleven years
14. After the smog became too oppressive the city passed an ordinance requiring car pooling.
15. When you tune a guitar follow these steps: first sound the corresponding note on the pitch pipe; second, turn the tuning peg until the note of the string matches the note of the pipe; third repeat this process with the remaining strings.

Use commas to set off nouns of direct address.

The name of someone directly spoken to is a noun of **direct address.**

If you look through the microscope, Peggy, you'll see the round, green chloroplasts.
Sarah, you won the election!

Use commas to set off the speaker's tags used with direct quotations.

When you repeat someone's exact words, you make a **direct quotation.** A direct quotation is usually accompanied by explanatory words known as **speaker's tags.** Examples of speaker's tags include "Tina said," "Christie answered," and "Javier asked."

The pilot said, "We shall land in approximately twenty-three minutes."
"We shall land in approximately twenty-three minutes," the pilot said.
"We shall land," the pilot said, "in approximately twenty-three minutes."

Do not use commas with indirect quotations.

The pilot said that the plane would land in a few minutes.

Use a comma before the conjunction that joins the two main clauses in a compound sentence.

Kimberly seemed to agree, and no one else objected.

QUICK TIP Make sure that the two parts being joined are, indeed, complete clauses. A comma is not needed to separate compound predicates.

Compound Predicate	Sal turned on the radio and sat down to listen to it.
Compound Sentence	Sal turned on the radio, and then he sat down to listen to it.

Exercise 3 Commas Rewrite the following sentences, adding commas where needed. If no comma is needed, write *Correct.*

1. When you are finished Kurt will you help with this project?
2. "The music is not in some instrument but in you" wrote Stephanie Judy.
3. Lewis Carroll was a professional mathematician but he is best remembered for his children's books.
4. Kennedy said "Ask not what your country can do for you. Ask what you can do for your country."
5. "We have nothing to fear but fear itself" said Franklin D. Roosevelt.
6. Night fell over the lake and the loons began their crazy calling in the distance.
7. Tell me Marti about your journey.
8. The geologist predicted that an earthquake would occur in ten years.

SPEAKER'S TAGS

Common speaker's tags include the following:

she replied	she answered
she asked	she demanded
she warned	she questioned
she inquired	she wondered
she said	she explained

There are, of course, many others. Speaker's tags often reveal a great deal about the speaker's state of mind and tone of voice.

Exercise 3

1. When you are finished, Kurt, will you help with this project?
2. "The music is not in some instrument but in you," wrote Stephanie Judy.
3. Lewis Carroll was a professional mathematician, but he is best remembered for his children's books.
4. Kennedy said, "Ask not what your country can do for you. Ask what you can do for your country."
5. "We have nothing to fear but fear itself," said Franklin D. Roosevelt.
6. Night fell over the lake, and the loons began their crazy calling in the distance.
7. Tell me, Marti, about your journey.
8. Correct

9. The divers took flashlights with them, yet they still could not see through the plankton-filled water.
10. "I want you, Matt, to walk the dog while we are gone," said Dad.

Exercise 4

1. Whatever happens, happens.
2. The stock market crash on October 29, 1929, began the Great Depression.
3. Dear Jill,; Your friend, Tom
4. The bombing of Pearl Harbor on December 7, 1941, marked the beginning of World War II for the United States.
5. Because my parents work for the government, I have lived in Fairbanks, Alaska, and Madrid, Spain.

9. The divers took flashlights with them yet they still could not see through the plankton-filled water.
10. "I want you Matt to walk the dog while we are gone" said Dad.

In dates use a comma between the day of the month and the year.

July 4, 1776   December 7, 1787

In a sentence a comma follows the year.

On July 4, 1776, the delegates signed the Declaration of Independence.

Use a comma between the name of a city or town and the name of its state or country.

Tucson, Arizona   Munich, Germany

In a sentence a comma follows the state or country.
In writing an address as part of a sentence, use a comma after each item.

Forward our mail to 651 Sentinel Drive, Milwaukee, Wisconsin 53203, where we shall be moving next month.

Note that you do not place a comma between the state and the ZIP Code.

Use a comma after the salutation of a friendly letter and after the complimentary close of a friendly letter or a business letter.

Dear Tim,   Yours sincerely,

Use a comma when no specific rule applies but there is danger of misreading or confusion if a comma is not used.

Who she is, is a mystery. Inside, it was warm and cozy.

Exercise 4 Commas Rewrite the following items, adding commas where necessary.

1. Whatever happens happens.
2. The stock market crash on October 29 1929 began the Great Depression.
3. Dear Jill
   Would you please send me the Harrisons' new address? I'd appreciate it.
   Your friend
   Tom
4. The bombing of Pearl Harbor on December 7 1941 marked the beginning of World War II for the United States.
5. Because my parents work for the government, I have lived in Fairbanks Alaska and Madrid Spain.

6. Whatever you do do it well.
7. We ordered our uniforms from the J. C. Wood Company P.O. Box 5835 Richmond Virginia 23220.
8. The Great Chicago Fire of 1871 supposedly started in Mrs. O'Leary's barn at 558 DeKoven Street Chicago Illinois.
9. Whatever it is it is a strange-looking creature.
10. The first transcontinental railroad was completed on May 10 1869 in Promontory Utah.

Exercise 5 End Mark and Comma Review Rewrite the following items, adding periods, question marks, exclamation points, and commas as necessary. If the punctuation is correct, write *Correct.*

1. Robert please make my appointment with Dr Stern at 3:00 PM
2. How right you are
3. When was Justice Sandra D O'Connor appointed to the US Supreme Court
4. Mt Vesuvius erupted and buried Pompeii in AD 79
5. **I** Heroes of the civil rights movement
   A Rev Martin Luther King Jr
   B Ms Rosa Parks
6. Lily Tomlin Carol Burnett and Paula Poundstone are comedians
7. Juanita rolled the car window down stuck her head out and asked for directions
8. First she learned to operate the telegraph; second she memorized the secret code; and third she parachuted behind enemy lines
9. Soft sweet breezes were blowing across the meadow
10. The long brutal winter hurt farmers ranchers truckers and builders
11. In addition Susan has a terrific sense of humor
12. No there is no mail for you but there is a notice from the post office
13. If you hear a strange whoop that will be the cranes
14. "Small incidents cause big conflicts and the result is sometimes war" our history teacher explained
15. Rachel did you say that you had to leave early
16. "It's time" said the captain "to bail out"
17. On Monday April 15 1912 the *Titanic* sank
18. Beyond Steve could see the ocean
19. Write to the National Baseball Hall of Fame Main Street Cooperstown New York 13326 for the information
20. Dear Julia
    We'll see you in Portland Oregon on June 14
    Affectionately
    Lorraine

6. Whatever you do, do it well.
7. We ordered our uniforms from the J.C. Wood Company, P.O. Box 5835, Richmond, Virginia 23220.
8. The Great Chicago Fire of 1871 supposedly started in Mrs. O'Leary's barn at 558 DeKoven Street, Chicago, Illinois.
9. Whatever it is, it is a strange-looking creature.
10. The first transcontinental railroad was completed on May 10, 1869, in Promontory, Utah.

Exercise 5

1. Robert, please make my appointment with Dr. Stern at 3:00 P.M.
2. How right you are!
3. When was Justice Sandra D. O'Connor appointed to the U.S. Supreme Court?
4. Mt. Vesuvius erupted and buried Pompeii in A.D. 79.
5. I. Heroes of the civil rights movement
A. Rev. Martin Luther King Jr.
B. Ms. Rosa Parks
6. Lily Tomlin, Carol Burnett, and Paula Poundstone are comedians.
7. Juanita rolled the car window down, stuck her head out, and asked for directions.
8. First, she learned to operate the telegraph; second, she memorized the secret code; and third, she parachuted behind enemy lines.
9. Soft, sweet breezes were blowing across the meadow.
10. The long, brutal winter hurt farmers, ranchers, truckers, and builders.
11. In addition, Susan has a terrific sense of humor.
12. No, there is no mail for you, but there is a notice from the post office.
13. If you hear a strange whoop, that will be the cranes.
14. "Small incidents cause big conflicts and the result is sometimes war," our history teacher explained.
15. Rachel, did you say that you had to leave early?
16. "It's time," said the captain, "to bail out."
17. On Monday, April 15, 1912, the *Titanic* sank.
18. Beyond, Steve could see the ocean.
19. Write to the National Baseball Hall of Fame, Main Street, Cooperstown, New York 13326, for the information.
20. Dear Julia,
We'll see you in Portland, Oregon on June 14.
Affectionately,
Lorraine

Semicolons

A **semicolon** separates sentence elements. It indicates a more definite break than a comma does but a less abrupt break than a period does.

Use a semicolon to join the two parts of a compound sentence if no coordinating conjunction is used. Remember that a semicolon may be used only if the clauses are closely related.

Julia has finished reading the assignment; Ben has not yet begun.

Conjunctive Adverbs

Here are some common conjunctive adverbs:
- therefore
- however
- otherwise
- consequently
- besides
- nevertheless
- moreover

Sometimes phrases serve similar purposes:
- as a result
- for example
- for instance
- in a similar way

Use a semicolon before a conjunctive adverb that joins the clauses of a compound sentence. A conjunctive adverb is a word such as *therefore* or *however* that shows a relationship between two clauses.

The race was long and difficult; however, everyone in our group managed to finish without difficulty.

Use a semicolon to separate the items of a series if one or more of these items contain commas.

I have lived in these places: New York, New York; Bristol, Maine; Athens, Greece; and Dallas, Texas.

Colons

Use a colon to introduce a list of items. A word or phrase such as *these* or *the following* is often followed by a **colon.** A colon must be preceded by an independent clause; a colon never follows a verb.

You will need the following items when you arrive at camp: a sleeping bag, a flashlight, and a tennis racket.

Use a colon to introduce a long or formal quotation.

Actress Greta Garbo once said: There are many things in your heart you can never tell to another person. They are you, your private joys and sorrows, and you can never tell them. You cheapen yourself, the inside of yourself, when you tell them.

Use a colon between two independent clauses when the second clause explains the first. The first word following a colon is not capitalized unless it is a proper noun or the start of a quotation.

Martinez knows the state of Florida: he used to be its governor.

Use a colon after the greeting in a formal letter.

Dear Sir or Madam: Dear Senator Rudman:

Use a colon between numbers showing hours and minutes.

7:30 P.M. 12:00 A.M.

Hyphens

Use a hyphen between syllables divided at the end of a line.

Have you read the Articles of Confed-
eration?

Use a hyphen in compound numbers from twenty-one to ninety-nine.

ninety-nine forty-five

Use a hyphen in fractions.

one-fifth eight-thirds

Use a hyphen in certain compound nouns.

sister-in-law self-respect

Use a hyphen between the words that make up a compound adjective when the modifier is used before a noun.

self-conscious people well-known commentator

Exercise 6 Semicolons, Colons, and Hyphens Rewrite each item, correcting all errors in the use of semicolons, colons, and hyphens.

1. Allen, fold the laundry Jenny, clean up the yard and Joan, take the dog for a walk.
2. New animals in the collection include a cheetah, an okapi, and a harpy eagle from Africa a tiger, two peacocks, and a rhinoceros from India a snow leopard from Tibet and two caribou, a kodiak bear, and an arctic fox from Alaska.
3. It was a clear day moreover, it was perfect for swimming.
4. John prepared dinner Brian set the table.
5. San Francisco, Los Angeles, and Oakland, California Dallas and Houston, Texas and New York and Buffalo, New York, have professional teams.
6. Jack was born at 645 P.M. his twin sister was born at 703 P.M.
7. The military is divided into the following branches the Air Force the Army the Navy and the Marine Corps.

HYPHENATING AT THE END OF A LINE

Follow these rules:

1. Divide a word only between syllables.
2. Hyphenate only words of two or more syllables.
3. Make sure that at least two letters of the word fall on each line.

WHEN TO HYPHENATE

To determine whether a compound needs a hyphen, look it up in a dictionary.

Exercise 6

1. Allen, fold the laundry; Jenny, clean up the yard; and Joan, take the dog for a walk.
2. New animals in the collection include a cheetah, an okapi, and a harpy eagle from Africa; a tiger, two peacocks, and a rhinoceros from India; a snow leopard from Tibet; and two caribou, a kodiak bear, and an arctic fox from Alaska.
3. It was a clear day; moreover, it was perfect for swimming.
4. John prepared dinner; Brian set the table.
5. San Francisco, Los Angeles, and Oakland, California; Dallas and Houston Texas; and New York and Buffalo, New York, have professional teams.
6. Jack was born at 6:45 P.M.; his twin sister was born at 7:03 P.M.
7. The military is divided into the following branches: the Air Force, the Army, the Navy, and the Marine Corps.

8. In the Federalist papers James Madison wrote these words: "If men were angels, no government would be necessary. If angels were to govern men, neither external nor internal controls on government would be necessary."
9. Dear Senator Kerry:
I am writing to urge you to support the new Clean Air Act.
10. I know why you are excited: your sister and brother-in-law are adopting a baby.
11. More than fifty-one percent of the runners finishing the Boston Marathon were over forty years old.
12. Chester A. Arthur was the twenty-first President.
13. When were your great-grandparents born?
14. St. Martin is a well-known tourist spot in the Caribbean.
15. We shall meet you at 4:30 P.M. at the drive-in.

8. In the Federalist papers James Madison wrote these words "If men were angels, no government would be necessary. If angels were to govern men, neither external nor internal controls on government would be necessary."
9. Dear Senator Kerry
I am writing to urge you to support the new Clean Air Act.
10. I know why you are excited your sister and brother in law are adopting a baby
11. More than fifty one percent of the runners finishing the Boston Marathon were over forty years old.
12. Chester A. Arthur was the twenty first President.
13. When were your great grandparents born?
14. St. Martin is a well known tourist spot in the Caribbean.
15. We shall meet you at 430 P.M. at the drive in.

Apostrophes

Use an apostrophe to form the possessive of singular and plural nouns.
To form the possessive of a singular noun, add an apostrophe and *-s,* even if the noun ends in *-s.*

Carlos's book   bank's automatic teller machine

To form the possessive of a plural noun that ends in *-s,* add an apostrophe only. To form the possessive of a plural noun that does not end in *-s,* add both an apostrophe and *-s.*

the boys' bicycles   the men's stories   mice's tails

To form the possessive of an indefinite pronoun, add an apostrophe and *-s.*

no one's   everybody's

Use an apostrophe in a contraction to show where one or more letters have been left out. Contractions are usually avoided in formal writing.

can't = *cannot*   he'll = *he will* or *he shall*
Mick's = *Mick is* or *Mick has*

Use an apostrophe to show the omission of figures in a date.

the winter of '75   the class of '96

Use an apostrophe to show the plurals of letters, numbers, signs, and words referred to as words.

OTHER USES OF APOSTROPHES

Apostrophes are also used to show omitted letters in dialect, old-fashioned speech, or poetry.

'Twas the night before Christmas.

'Tis we own t'ing, man.

There are two *r*'s and two *s*'s in the word *embarrassment.*
There are too many *and*'s in that sentence.

Exercise 7 Apostrophes Rewrite the following sentences, correcting any errors in the use of apostrophes.

1. All the teachers meetings are held in the library.
2. Babe Didrikson Zahariass autobiography reveals her intense love for athletics and her zest for life.
3. Her writings are well known to readers of childrens literature.
4. Jims father drove us to their familys cottage in Iowa.
5. Wasnt that Rosss original plan?
6. Soichiro Hondas company has been producing motorcycles and cars in Japan for about fifty years.
7. Ive always liked the silent movies of Mary Pickford and Charlie Chaplin.
8. Weve heard that there wont be an assembly until next week.
9. Beatrix Potters most famous work is *Peter Rabbit.*
10. The three ships masts were all broken during the storm.

Quotation Marks and Underlining

Use quotation marks to begin and end a direct quotation.

Sarah said, "My feelings were hurt."

Do not use quotation marks to set off an indirect quotation. Indirect quotations are often signaled by the word *that.*

Sarah said that her feelings were hurt.

To punctuate a direct quotation, enclose the exact words used by a speaker or writer in quotation marks. The first word of the quotation is capitalized. Commas are always placed inside the quotation marks. When the end of the quotation falls at the end of the sentence, the period is placed inside the quotation marks.

The Chief of Staff said, "The senator is here is see you."

Put question marks and exclamation marks inside the quotation marks if they are part of the quotation.

"How deep is the mid-Atlantic trench?" asked Maria.
"Help!" cried the shepherd. "There's a wolf circling my flock!"

Put question marks and exclamation marks outside the quotation marks if they are not part of the quotation.

Exercise 7

1. All the teachers' meetings are held in the library.
2. Babe Didrikson Zaharias's autobiography reveals her intense love for athletics and her zest for life.
3. Her writings are well known to readers of children's literature.
4. Jim's father drove us to their family's cottage in Iowa.
5. Wasn't that Ross's original plan?
6. Soichiro Honda's company has been producing motorcycles and cars in Japan for about fifty years.
7. I've always liked the silent movies of Mary Pickford and Charlie Chaplin.
8. We've heard that there won't be an assembly until next week.
9. Beatrix Potter's most famous work is *Peter Rabbit.*
10. The three ships' masts were all broken during the storm.

Did Lincoln say, "malice toward none" or "malice toward one"?

Always put commas and periods inside the quotation marks.

The president of the World Bank said, "We now understand the importance of preserving the rain forest."

"We now understand the importance of preserving the rain forest," the president of the World Bank said.

Enclose the parts of a divided quotation in quotation marks. Do not capitalize the first word of the second part unless it begins a new sentence.

"I'd rather play chamber music," said Linda Hecker, "than go to a party or a movie."

"Our standard of living is increasing," said the foreign minister of Zimbabwe. "However, we are now facing an ecological crisis."

In punctuating dialogue, begin a new paragraph to indicate a new speaker.

"Lavinia," whispered Helen.
"What?"
"As we came in, a man in a dark suit, across the street, crossed over. He just walked down the aisle and is sitting in the row behind us."
"Oh, Helen!"

—*Dandelion Wine,* Ray Bradbury

When quoting passages longer than one paragraph, use quotation marks at the beginning of each paragraph and at the end of only the last paragraph.

Here's what Annie Dillard said about how very young children view their elders:

"Our parents and grandparents, and all their friends, seemed insensible to their own prominent defect, their limp, coarse skin.

"We children had, for instance, proper hands; our fluid, pliant fingers joined their skin. Adults had misshapen, knuckley hands loose in their skin like bones in bags; it was a wonder they could open jars. They were loose in their skins all over, except at the wrists and ankles, like rabbits."

Use quotation marks to enclose the titles of short stories, poems, essays, magazine and newspaper articles, chapters, television episodes, and songs.

Short Story	"The Most Dangerous Game"
Poem	"The Road Not Taken"
Essay	"Montgomery Boycott"
Magazine or Newspaper Article	"The Suspected Shopper"
Chapter	"The Whiteness of the Whale"
Television Episode	"The Giant Panda"
Song	"This Land Is Your Land"

The titles of books, newspapers, magazines, movies, television series, plays, works of art, and long musical compositions are underlined in writing and italicized in print.

Book	*Dandelion Wine*
Newspaper	*The Peterborough Transcript*
Magazine	*Natural History*
Movie	*Dances with Wolves*
Television Series	*Nova*
Play	*Visit to a Small Planet*
Work of Art	Michelangelo's *David*
Long Musical Composition	Wagner's *The Ring*

Exercise 8 Quotation Marks and Underlining Rewrite the following sentences, adding quotation marks or underlining as necessary.

1. Meryl Streep hosted a T.V. series called Race to Save the Planet.
2. Bradbury's story The Veldt appeared in his book The Illustrated Man.
3. A little rebellion now and then is a good thing, wrote Thomas Jefferson.
4. The tree of liberty, wrote Jefferson, must be refreshed from time to time with the blood of patriots and tyrants.
5. Each employee tends to rise to his level of incompetence, wrote Tom Peters. Thus, every post tends to be filled by an incompetent employee.
6. One of the most powerful songs of the civil rights movement was We Shall Overcome.
7. Chapter 1 of Annie Dillard's book Pilgrim at Tinker Creek is called Heaven and Earth in Jest.
8. The New York Times and The Washington Post carry the names of particular cities but are actually national newspapers.
9. Did you see the episode of Nature called Super Senses?
10. Have you heard Puccini's opera La Bohème? asked Marc.
11. You don't really like opera, said Inez. Do you?
12. But I do! said Marc. I've been listening to it for years at home.

Exercise 8

1. Meryl Streep hosted a television series called Race to Save the Planet.

2. Bradbury's story "The Veldt" appeared in his book The Illustrated Man.

3. "A little rebellion now and then is a good thing," wrote Thomas Jefferson.

4. "The tree of liberty," wrote Jefferson, "must be refreshed from time to time with the blood of patriots and tyrants."

5. "Each employee tends to rise to his level of incompetence," wrote Tom Peters. "Thus, every post tends to be filled by an incompetent employee."

6. One of the most powerful songs of the civil rights movement was "We Shall Overcome."

7. Chapter 1 of Annie Dillard's book Pilgrim at Tinker Creek is called "Heaven and Earth in Jest."

8. The New York Times and The Washington Post carry the names of particular cities but are actually national newspapers.

9. Did you see the episode of Nature called "Super Senses"?

10. "Have you heard Puccini's opera La Boheme?" asked Marc.

11. "You don't really like opera," said Inez. "Do you?"

12. "But I do!" said Marc. "I've been listening to it for years at home."

Index of Fine Art

Index of Skills

Literary Terms

Reading and Critical Thinking Skills

All Responding to Reading *questions draw upon a variety of critical thinking skills.*

Grammar, Usage, and Mechanics

Writing Skills, Modes, and Formats

Language and Vocabulary Skills

Research and Study Skills

Opportunities for developing research and study skills also appear in the Options for Learning *activities that follow many selections.*

Speaking, Listening, and Viewing Skills

Index of Titles and Authors

Page numbers that appear in italics refer to biographical information.

Acknowledgments

(continued from copyright page)
Earthworks Press: "Don't Can Your Aluminum," from *50 Simple Things You Can Do to Save the Earth.* By permission of Earthworks Press.
Farrar, Straus & Giroux, Inc.: Excerpt from *Coming into the Country* by John McPhee. Copyright © 1976, 1977 by John McPhee. Reprinted by permission of Farrar, Straus & Giroux, Inc. "After You, My Dear Alphonse," from *The Lottery* by Shirley Jackson. Copyright © 1948, 1949 by Shirley Jackson, renewal copyright © 1976, 1977 by Laurence Hyman, Barry Hyman, Mrs. Sarah Webster, and Mrs. Joanne Schnurer. Reprinted by permission of Farrar, Straus & Giroux, Inc.
Angel Flores: "A Letter to God" by Gregorio López y Fuentes, from *Classic Tales From Spanish America,* translated by Angel Flores. By permission of the translator.
GRM Associates, Inc.: "Incident," from *On These I Stand* by Countee Cullen. Copyright 1925 by Harper & Brothers, renewed 1953 by Ida M. Cullen. By permission of GRM Associates, Inc., agents for the Estate of Ida M. Cullen.
Harcourt Brace Jovanovich, Inc.: "Improved Farm Land," from *Slabs of the Sunburnt West* by Carl Sandburg. Copyright 1922 by Harcourt Brace Jovanovich, Inc., renewed 1950 by Carl Sandburg. "Love Is Not Concerned," from *Horses Make a Landscape Look More Beautiful* by Alice Walker. Copyright © 1984 by Alice Walker. Reprinted by permission of the publisher.
Harper & Row, Publishers, Inc.: "Tsali of the Cherokees," from *American Indian Mythology* by Alice Marriott and Carol K. Rachlin. Copyright © 1968 by Alice Marriott and Carol K. Rachlin. "The Street," from *Black Boy* by Richard Wright. Copyright 1937, 1942, 1944, 1945 by Richard Wright. Reprinted by permission of Harper & Row, Publishers, Inc.
Margaret J. Hoddinott: "Look at Me. Please, See Me" by Margaret J. Hoddinott, from *Finding Yourself, Finding Others* by Clark E. Moustakas. By permission of the author.
Andrew Holleman: "David Meets Goliath at City Hall" by Andrew Holleman, from *Mother Earth News,* March-April 1990 issue. By permission of the author.
Henry Holt and Company, Inc.: "A Start in Life," from *Iowa Interiors* by Ruth Suckow. Copyright 1926 by Alfred A. Knopf, Inc., 1954 by Ruth Suckow Nuhn. "Montgomery Boycott" (pp. 111–119), from *My Life With Martin Luther King, Jr.* by Coretta Scott King. Copyright © 1969 by Coretta Scott King. "The Road Not Taken," from *The Poetry of Robert Frost,* edited by Edward Connery Lathem. Copyright 1916, © 1969 by Holt, Rinehart and Winston. Copyright 1944 by Robert Frost. Reprinted by permission of Henry Holt and Company, Inc.
Houghton Mifflin Company: "Courage," from *The Awful Rowing Toward God* by Anne Sexton. Copyright © 1975 by Loring Conant, Jr., Executor of the Estate of Anne Sexton. Reprinted by permission of Houghton Mifflin Company.
International Creative Management, Inc.: *Twelve Angry Men* by Reginald Rose, from *Six Television Plays.* Copyright © 1956 by Reginald Rose. Reprinted by permission of International Creative Management, Inc.
John Johnson (Authors' Agent) Limited: "Warning," from *Rose in the Afternoon* by Jenny Joseph. Copyright © Jenny Joseph, J. M. Dent, London 1974. By permission of the author's agent.
Johnson Publishing Co. for Eugenia W. Collier: "Marigolds" by Eugenia W. Collier. Reprinted by permission of Eugenia Collier and *Negro Digest,* © 1969 Johnson Publishing Company, Inc.
Louisiana State University Press: "Love Poem," from *Women Whose Lives Are Food, Men Whose Lives Are Money* by Joyce Carol Oates. Copyright © 1978 by Joyce Carol Oates. Reprinted by permission of Louisiana State University Press.
Rona Maynard: "The Fan Club" by Rona Maynard. By permission of the author.

Scott Meredith Literary Agency: "The Weapon," from *Mad Scientists* by Fredric Brown. Reprinted by permission of the author and author's agent, Scott Meredith Literary Agency, Inc., 845 Third Avenue, New York, NY 10022.

Estate of Norma Millay Ellis: "Travel" by Edna St. Vincent Millay, from *Collected Poems*, Harper & Row. Copyright 1921, 1948 by Edna St. Vincent Millay. Reprinted by permission of Elizabeth Barnett, Literary Executor.

William Morrow & Company, Inc.: "Choices," from *Cotton Candy on a Rainy Day* by Nikki Giovanni. Copyright © 1978 by Nikki Giovanni. By permission of William Morrow & Co.

Walter Dean Myers: "The Treasure of Lemon Brown" by Walter Dean Myers, from *Boys' Life*, March 1983. By permission of the author.

New Directions Publishing Corp.: "Building Boom," from *By the Waters of Manhattan* by Charles Reznikoff. Copyright © 1972 by Charles Reznikoff. Reprinted by permission of New Directions Publishing Corp.

The New York Times: "Darkness at Noon" by Harold Krents, *The New York Times*, May 26, 1976 (Op-Ed). Copyright © 1976 by The New York Times Company. Reprinted by permission.

Harold Ober Associates, Inc.: "Love Is a Gimmick," from *Further Confessions of a Story Writer* by Paul Gallico. Copyright © 1955 by The Curtis Pub. Co. Reprinted by permission of Harold Ober Associates, Inc.

Dwight Okita: "In Response to Executive Order 9066: All Americans of Japanese Descent Must Report to Relocation Centers" by Dwight Okita, Greenfield Review Press. By permission of the author.

Organization of American States: "Lather and Nothing Else" by Hernando Téllez, from *Americas*, bimonthly magazine published by the General Secretariat of the Organization of American States in English and Spanish.

Penguin USA: Excerpt from *Wilma* by Wilma Rudolph. Copyright © 1977 by Bud Greenspan. "Day Work," from *Maggie's American Dream* by James P. Comer, M.D. Copyright © 1988 by James P. Comer, M.D. Reprinted by permission of New American Library, a division of Penguin Books USA, Inc.

Phil Petrie: "It Happened in Montgomery" by Phil Petrie. By permission of the author.

Prentice-Hall, Inc.: "My Shirt Is for Church," from *Journey to Washington* by Senator Daniel K. Inouye with Lawrence Elliott. Copyright © 1967. Used by permission of Prentice-Hall, Inc., Englewood Cliffs, N.J.

The Putnam Publishing Group: "Diablo Country," from *While Reagan Slept* by Art Buchwald. Copyright © 1983 by Art Buchwald. "Rules of the Game," from *The Joy Luck Club* by Amy Tan. Copyright © 1989 by Amy Tan. Reprinted by permission of The Putnam Publishing Group. "The Third Floor Flat," from *Three Blind Mice and Other Stories* by Agatha Christie. Copyright 1928 by Agatha Christie. Reprinted by permission of Harold Ober Associates Incorporated and The Putnam Publishing Group.

Random House, Inc.: "Miss Rosie," from *Good Times* by Lucille Clifton. Copyright © 1969 by Lucille Clifton. By permission of Random House, Inc. Specified excerpts from *All I Really Need to Know I Learned in Kindergarten* by Robert Fulghum. Copyright © 1986 by Robert Fulghum. By permission of Villard Books, a Division of Random House, Inc. "Fast Break," from *Wild Gratitude* by Edward Hirsch. Copyright © 1985 by Edward Hirsch. "Ex-Basketball Player," from *The Carpentered Hen and Other Tame Creatures* by John Updike. Copyright © 1957, 1982 by John Updike. "Mother to Son," from *Selected Poems of Langston Hughes*. Copyright 1926 by Alfred A. Knopf, Inc., and renewed 1954 by Langston Hughes. By permission of Alfred A. Knopf, Inc.

Reader's Digest: "Stowaway!" by Armando Socarras Ramírez as told to Denis Fodor and John Reddy (*Reader's Digest*, January 1970). Copyright © 1969 by The Reader's Digest Assn., Inc. Reprinted with permission from the January 1970 *Reader's Digest*.

Martin Secker & Warburg Ltd.: "The Letter A," from *My Left Foot* by Christy Brown. Copyright © 1954 by Christy Brown. Reprinted by permission of Martin Secker & Warburg Ltd.

Simon & Schuster, Inc.: "The Suspected Shopper," from *Keeping in Touch* by Ellen Goodman. Copyright © 1985 by The Washington Post Company. Reprinted by permission of Summit Books, a division of Simon & Schuster, Inc.
Theodore L. Thomas: "Test" by Theodore L. Thomas, from the *Magazine of Fantasy and Science Fiction*. Copyright © 1962 by Mercury Press. By permission of the author.
Tribune Media Services: "A Couple of Really Neat Guys" by Dave Barry and illustration by Jeff MacNelly, from *Chicago Tribune*, March 18, 1990. Reprinted by permission of Tribune Media Services.
The University of North Carolina Press: "The Street of the Cañon," from *Mexican Village* by Josephina Niggli. Copyright 1945 by The University of North Carolina Press. Reprinted by permission.
University of Pittsburgh Press: "The Bass, the River, and Sheila Mant," from *The Man Who Loved Levittown* by W. D. Wetherell. Copyright © 1985 by W. D.Wetherell. By permission of the University of Pittsburgh Press.
University of Washington Press: "Tanforan: A Horse Stall for Four" by Yoshiko Uchida, from *Desert Exile*. Copyright © 1982 by Yoshiko Uchida. By permission of University of Washington Press.
Gore Vidal: *Visit to a Small Planet* by Gore Vidal. Copyright © 1956 by Gore Vidal. By permission of the author.
Tino Villanueva: "Not Knowing, in Aztlan" by Tino Villanueva. Originally appeared in *Tejidos*, University of Texas-Austin (Vol.I, No. 2, March 1974). Copyright © 1974 by Tino Villanueva. Reprinted by permission of the author.
The Wilderness Society: "Hard Questions" by Margaret Tsuda, from *The Living Wilderness*, Autumn 1970. By permission of The Wilderness Society.

The authors and editors have made every effort to trace the ownership of all copyrighted selections found in this book and to make full acknowledgment for their use.

Illustrations

Robert Borja, 657; Rebecca D. Brown, 105; David Cunningham, 286; Kurt Fischer, 661; Barbara Laing, 63, 290; Mary MacDonald, 175, 345; Michele Mitchell, 525; Richard Nichols, 392, 662. MAPS: Keith Kraus and Linda Gephardt, 94, 136, 178, 268, 327.

Author Photographs

AP/Wide World Photos, Inc., New York: Isaac Asimov 656, Dave Barry 865, Art Buchwald 689, Borden Deal 200, Horton Foote 315, Paul Gallico 866, Daniel Inouye 113, Reginald Rose 591, Wilma Rudolph 868, Anne Sexton 357, Kurt Vonnegut, Jr. 258; The Bettmann Archive, New York: William Shakespeare 836; Jane Bown: Gore Vidal 717; Carol Bruchac: Joseph Bruchac 865; Henri Cartier-Bresson/Magnum Photos, Inc., New York: Langston Hughes 867; Nancy Crampton: Nikki Giovanni 53; Culver Pictures, New York: Edna St. Vincent Millay 187; *El Tiempo*, Bogotá, Colombia: Hernando Téllez 129; Robert Foothorap: Amy Tan 379; Globe Photos, New York: Ray Bradbury 80, Robert Frost 53, Coretta Scott King 519, Rudyard Kipling 357, Carl Sandburg 868, Richard Wright 443; The Granger Collection, New York: W.W. Jacobs 163, William Saroyan 868; Iowa State Historical Society: Ruth Suckow 475; J. William Johnson: Hugh Pentecost 46; Dan Lamont: Robert Fulghum 866; Angus McBean/Globe Photos, New York: Agatha Christie 865; *Milwaukee Journal:* Fredric Brown 865; Museum of the City of New York: Walt Whitman 187; Schlesinger Library, Radcliffe College, Cambridge, Massachusetts: Richard Connell 431; Hy Sim/Globe Photos, New York: John Updike 385; Deborah Storms: Yoshiko Uchida 507; Erik Weber: Richard Brautigan 665; Carolyn Wright: Tino Villanueva 869.

Miscellaneous Art Credits

viii VISTA II 1987 Hughie Lee-Smith Courtesy of June Kelly Gallery, New York; x A WORLD WITHIN #44 1988 Humberto Calzada By permission of the artist; xii FOOTBALL PAINTING #2 1956 William Theophilus Brown Collection of the Santa Barbara Museum of Art Gift of Paul Wonner; xiv THE FLAG IS BLEEDING 1967 Faith Ringgold Bernice Steinbaum Gallery, New York; xvi DOLPHIN PARADISE Bill Wyland Wyland Galleries, Oahu, Hawaii; xvii THE TRIUMPH OF CAESAR c. 1430 Andrea Mantegna © Reserved to Her Majesty Queen Elizabeth II; 4 (above) STONE CITY, IOWA (detail) 1930 Grant Wood Joslyn Art Museum, Omaha, Nebraska; 4 (below) COMPUTER SCULPTING ITS OWN KEYBOARD 1987 Barry Blackman From *Special Effects for Print Art Directors, Designers, and Photographers* by Barry Blackman, Van Nostrand Reinhold Publishing Company; 6 SUBJECT/OBJECT 1989 David Furman Elaine Horwitch Galleries, Scottsdale, Arizona; 7 © Richard Hutchins/Photo Researchers, New York; 16 PEARBLOSSOM HWY., 11–18TH APRIL 1986 #2 (detail) David Hockney Photographic collage 78″ × 111″ © 1986 David Hockney; 30 SANDIA/WATERMELON (detail) 1986 Carmen Lomas Garza By permission of the artist; 62 PLANTING (detail) 1943 Rex Gorleigh Smithsonian Institution, Washington, D.C.; 81 WORKERS ON A LUNCH BREAK Walker Evans Walker Evans Estate, Bethany, Connecticut; 121 FAITHFUL (detail) Charles Edward Perugini National Museums and Galleries on Merseyside, Walker Art Gallery, Liverpool, England; 174 CHALK VINES (detail) 1988 Robert Vickrey Kennedy Galleries, New York; 183 © 1990 Luis D'Eca/FPG, International, New York; 188 HERCULES AND ANTAEUS (detail) Vase Louvre, Paris/Art Resource, New York; 215 PAS DE DEUX (detail) 1983 Alex Katz Collection of Paul J. Schupf, courtesy of Marlborough Gallery, New York; 216 © The Secretary to Sherlock Holmes, London; 232 © 1990 Joseph Giannetti/Third Coast Stock Source, Milwaukee, Wisconsin; 243 © John Cancalosi/Peter Arnold, Inc., New York; 267 THE VISITOR (detail) 1953 Richard Lindner © 1990 ARS, New York/ADAGP; 278, 351, 494 The Bettmann Archive, New York; 326 (detail) Everett Collection, Miramax; 337 Rod Tuach/Globe Photos, New York; 365 Jeff Reed/Stock Shop, New York; 366 Steve Elmore/Tom Stack and Associates, Colorado Springs, Colorado; 380 Dennis Dzielak/The Image Bank, New York; 409 RAIN FOREST, JAMAICA, WEST INDIES (detail) 1865 Frederic E. Church Cooper-Hewitt Museum, Smithsonian Institution/Art Resource, New York; 410 © 1987 Comstock, New York; 454 By Suzanne Anderson From *Song of the Earth Spirit* by Suzanne Anderson, McGraw-Hill Publishing Company; 455 San Francisco Academy of Comic Art; 460 STONE CITY, IOWA (detail) 1930 Grant Wood Joslyn Art Museum, Omaha, Nebraska; 476 Aztec Quexalott Head Museum of Mankind, London/The Bridgeman Art Library, London; 481 © Willie L. Hill/Stock Boston; 495 *The Seattle Post-Intelligencer*, Washington; 548, 674, 737, 740, 759, 789, 800, 807, 819 Photofest, New York; 549 The Granger Collection, New York; 602 WET WOODLAND (detail) Carl Schwartz By permission of the artist; 619 © Peter Arnold, New York; 623 S. Feld/H. Armstrong Roberts, Chicago; 638, 644 COMPUTER SCULPTING ITS OWN KEYBOARD 1987 Barry Blackman From *Special Effects for Print Art Directors, Designers, and Photographers* by Barry Blackman, Van Nostrand Reinhold Publishing Company; 690 *Close Encounters of the Third Kind* movie still, Columbia Pictures © 1977, Kobal Collection, Superstock, International, New York; 782, 821 Kobal Collection, Superstock, International, New York; 728 Engraving from a Roman medal in F. du Chaul's *Discovers de la Religion des Anciens Romains,* 1567; 729 The British Museum, London; 731 Illustration by George Strickland From *Illustrators XXX;* 792 Shooting Star, Hollywood, California; 832 Culver Pictures, New York.

McDougal, Littell and Company has made every effort to locate the copyright holders for the images used in this book and to make full acknowledgment for their use.

Scope and Sequence Charts

The charts that follow show the literature, writing and language skills presented in McDougal Littell's *Literature and Language* series.

Literary Terms and Techniques	Grade 9	Grade 10	American Literature	English and World Literature
Act	26, 90-91, 659, 808, 864	142-43, 855	937	944
Allegory			193, 937	
Alliteration	60, 470, 864	47, 855	226, 276, 937	450, 535, 802, 944
Allusion	719, 864	628, 731, 855	150, 316, 489, 581, 806, 937	711, 944
Anecdote	384, 864		166, 937	
Antagonist/Villain	174	288, 575, 834, 855		103, 944
Aphorism/Epigram			117, 118, 270, 351, 937	
Aside	90, 864	855		281, 293, 944
Assonance/Consonance	60, 864	47, 855, 856	417, 937	802, 944, 945
Autobiography	37, 40, 48, 51, 224, 342, 464, 570-79, 864	28, 111, 343, 386, 436, 855	118, 765, 937	451, 458, 489, 835, 944
Ballad				90, 95, 686, 944
Biography	40, 417, 443, 446-49, 864	28, 275, 343, 855	411, 937	390, 944
Blank Verse	719, 864	730, 753, 855	456-57, 937	271, 944
Catastrophe	843, 865	856		367, 945
Character	17-18, 80, 90-91, 92, 102, 151-54, 194-95, 281, 285, 286, 287, 349, 443, 556, 567, 609, 632, 659, 684, 730, 760, 771, 823, 843, 864-65	17-18, 102, 120, 130, 230-31, 278, 290, 313, 335, 486, 539, 564, 575, 603, 611, 709, 716, 729, 752, 785, 834, 856	193, 531, 563, 583, 630, 684, 774, 775, 872, 938	47, 103, 401, 410, 435, 488, 695, 810, 944, 945, 950
Characterization	295, 301, 443, 483, 512, 533, 595, 598, 738, 865	44, 366, 591, 603, 611, 715, 752, 856	352, 481, 531, 755, 775, 938	212, 479, 945
Climax/Turning Point	17-18, 37, 482, 493, 684, 807, 865	17, 163, 198, 441, 589, 797	645, 674, 938	245, 330, 398, 444, 945
Colloquialism	419, 865	120, 619, 856	648, 829, 938	945
Comedy	717		574	863, 915, 945
Comic Relief	824, 865	808, 856	898	310, 945
Conflict	69, 91, 140, 184, 222, 251, 311, 339, 377, 430, 454, 466, 567, 569, 595, 609, 659, 683, 702, 749, 865	17, 139, 181, 275, 399, 517, 816, 856	311, 392, 507, 571, 675, 844, 872, 898, 911, 938	44, 258, 577, 751, 757, 835, 897, 945
Couplet				227
Dialogue	38, 62, 78, 90-91, 109-10, 132, 133, 135, 231, 235, 311, 313, 340, 360, 391, 494, 512, 579, 866	92, 127, 142-43, 201, 214, 207, 261, 315, 730-31, 828, 835, 857	178, 218, 219, 393, 445, 481, 775, 938	90, 95, 120, 835, 946
Drama	26, 90-91, 92, 102, 104, 231, 253, 283, 284, 285-87, 303, 313, 349, 360, 579, 597, 632-33, 658-59, 683, 684, 702, 704, 716, 717, 718-19, 730, 743, 749, 760, 771, 797, 804, 807, 808, 823, 843, 844, 864, 866, 871	142-43, 163, 290, 550-51, 564, 589, 591, 690, 728, 729-32, 753, 764, 771, 785, 797, 817, 828, 834-35	356, 459, 898, 937, 938, 945, 946	106, 120, 269-71, 410, 602, 604, 902, 915, 944, 946, 952

Dynamic and Static Characters				810, 945
End Rhyme	66-67		221, 831, 944	950
Epic Hero	151-152, 194, 195, 866			31
Epic Poetry	151-54, 175, 194-96, 285-86, 866			31, 59, 946
Epic Simile	174, 195, 866			58, 946
Essay	40, 384, 866	28, 481-85, 619, 657-60, 684-88, 857-59	258, 939	458, 918, 944, 946
Eulogy	192, 302, 866			45
Exposition (in plot)	17-18, 609, 807, 867	17, 858	645, 939	245, 751, 947
Fable	513, 598, 867			746
Falling Action	17-18, 482, 523, 807, 843	17, 198, 858	939	245
Fantasy	130, 588, 867		734, 939	743, 947
Farce				915
Fiction	17-18, 27, 29, 37, 69, 89, 104, 122, 124, 132, 195, 222, 229, 230, 266, 281, 283, 312, 313, 314, 482, 523, 566, 567, 609, 867	17-18, 26, 44, 91, 94, 102, 130, 198, 216, 230-31, 242, 256, 278, 392, 404, 539, 589, 603, 611, 858	177, 228, 549, 633, 734, 940, 942, 945	743, 821, 853, 947, 949, 950, 951, 952
Figures of Speech	61, 577, 584-85, 620, 719, 867	344, 731, 817, 858	108, 249-50, 269, 278, 284, 561, 693, 788, 835, 940	
Flashback	281, 332, 609, 658, 867	257-58, 858	382, 531, 940	444, 846, 947
Folk Tale	598, 867			552, 574, 577, 947
Foreshadowing	360, 609, 621, 777, 867	161, 429, 858	207, 940	293, 778, 853
Form (in poetry)	60, 133, 867	47, 183, 356, 858	940	947
Frame Story				398, 947
Free Verse	60, 867	47, 186, 858	272, 276, 788, 940	622, 901, 947
Genre	17-18, 40-41, 60-61, 90-91, 598, 602, 868	858	940	948
Hero/Protagonist	151, 194, 195, 556, 868	571, 865	42, 242, 914, 915	20, 21, 31, 34, 47, 103, 330, 435, 946, 948, 950, 952
Historical Fiction	130, 281, 866		177, 940	
Horror Story/Supernatural Tale	349, 361		210	853, 952
Humor	92, 102, 213, 339, 342, 348, 384, 717, 719, 868	619, 622, 688, 709, 729, 730, 858	898, 940	161, 391, 652, 663, 769, 901, 915, 948, 951
Hyperbole/Exaggeration	339, 348, 377, 384, 867	859	574, 741, 779, 940	948
Iamb/Iambic Pentameter		730, 753, 859		572, 948
Idiom	554, 621, 868	859	940	948
Imagery/Sensory Details	60-61, 194, 224, 311, 319, 320, 323, 360, 395, 470, 719, 868, 871	47, 239, 241-42, 377, 432, 480, 662, 795, 859, 863	71, 284, 334, 451, 818, 941, 945	200, 204, 447, 461, 510, 527, 660, 948
Irony	77, 868	102, 505, 616, 654, 683, 859	133, 218, 311, 352, 417, 699, 506-07, 574, 941	161, 652, 769, 901, 948
Journalism/Journalistic Style	608	45, 314, 518, 590, 789, 837-40	289, 609	590
Lyric			779, 941	948-49

Metaphor	61, 577, 584-85, 620, 868-69	48, 230, 335, 344, 360, 683, 731, 817, 859-60	33, 107, 108, 250, 764, 833, 835, 941-42	224, 228, 282, 311, 947, 949
Meter	323, 869	730, 753, 860	942	572, 949
Middle English				949
Monologue	89, 687	207	763	602, 604, 946
Mood	311, 312, 360, 609, 869	91, 242, 356, 505, 835, 860	218, 631, 769, 815, 898, 942	349, 499, 949
Moral		639, 860	917, 942	949
Morality Tale				132
Motif				349, 949
Motivation	27, 48, 130, 159, 174, 323, 337, 376, 377, 430, 595, 608, 620, 683	19, 377, 860	524, 563, 588, 942	120, 141, 183, 285, 481, 488, 719, 769, 896, 949
Mystery		216, 230-31	633, 942	
Myth/Legend/Creation Story	113, 717, 869	188, 198, 628, 731, 860	23, 48, 941, 942	
Narrative	40, 241, 284-87, 304, 869	28, 111, 175, 860	425, 616, 942	949
Narrative Poetry	62		23, 942	21, 946
Narrator	27, 196, 295, 301, 303, 304, 567, 568, 609, 622, 869	35, 92, 103, 175, 207, 266, 289, 392, 860	521, 942	949
Nonfiction	37, 40-41, 48, 51, 55, 223, 224, 231, 304, 342, 384, 417, 443, 464, 512, 570-79, 864, 866, 869	28-29, 111, 175-80, 268-77, 343, 386, 436, 441, 623-27	118, 258, 289, 609, 765, 937, 939, 941, 942	385, 390, 451, 458, 489, 660, 835, 944, 946, 949
Novel	17-18, 869	17, 860	943	949
Objective/Subjective Writing	407, 418, 443		63, 943	
Parable			677, 943	181, 949
Paradox			258, 560, 943	
Parody				663
Personification	61, 62, 66-67, 584-85, 869	48, 335, 356, 384, 441-42, 480, 861	250, 284, 728, 792, 835, 943	530, 949
Plot	17, 37, 62, 69, 90-91, 92, 104, 151-52, 175, 195, 196, 231, 266, 283, 284, 285-87, 349, 658, 717, 807, 843, 844, 869-70	17-18, 142-43, 163, 198, 216, 230, 392, 399, 441, 589, 603, 611, 797	382, 480, 483, 531, 645, 674, 938, 939, 940, 944	245, 330, 398, 444, 552, 945, 947, 950, 951
Poetry	60-61, 62, 66-67, 133, 135, 151-52, 195, 320, 391, 393, 395, 467, 470, 719, 870	47-48, 183, 186, 353, 356, 360, 476, 478-79, 614, 618, 664, 730, 753, 861	23, 278, 452, 788, 779, 940, 943	21, 31, 59, 224, 227, 228, 271, 527, 572, 622, 947-52
Point of View	27, 29, 48, 51, 55, 88, 105, 185, 222, 443, 464, 493, 512, 534, 554, 567	28, 35, 92, 103, 111, 175, 198, 207, 289, 392, 450, 484, 858, 864	489, 490, 521, 572, 943	127, 153, 212, 615, 652, 810, 950
Pun		731, 861-62		
Quatrain				227
Realism		862	445	435, 950
Realistic Fiction	130, 556, 870	17, 862	944	435, 950
Refrain			535, 944	
Repetition	66, 470	664, 862	23, 105, 226, 324, 535, 788, 944	35, 744, 800, 950

Writing Skills, Modes, and Formats	Grade 9	Grade 10	American Literature	English and World Literature
The Writing Process				
Prewriting	51-52, 105-107, 141-42, 199-200, 232-33, 284-86, 324-26, 363-64, 397-98, 446-48, 497-98, 536-38, 581-83, 624, 706-08, 846-49, 878	54-47, 61, 114-17, 164-67, 209-11, 213, 259-62, 316-19, 358-60, 401-03, 444-47, 486-89, 541-43, 592-93, 595, 630-33, 666-68, 718-21, 837-41, 870, 872-74	51-52, 136-37, 180-81, 245-47, 290-91, 335-36, 394-95, 433-34, 491-92, 536-38, 595-96, 653-55, 700-01, 746-47, 781-82, 834-35, 918-19, 921, 952-53	66-67, 123-25, 167-69, 216-17, 261-63, 370-72, 413-15, 462-63, 513-15, 561-62, 593-95, 628-29, 668-70, 722-24, 780-81, 838-39, 880-82, 926-27, 929, 958, 959-60
Drafting	52-53, 107, 142-43, 200, 234-35, 286-87, 326, 364-65, 398-99, 448-49, 452, 498-99, 538, 582, 624-25, 708-09, 846-49, 878, 883-84	55, 116-17, 166, 210, 260-61, 318-19, 360, 403, 488-89, 542, 594, 632, 667-68, 719-20, 839, 841, 870, 875-76	52-53, 137-38, 181-82, 247, 292, 336-37, 435, 493-94, 538, 596, 655, 702-03, 747-49, 782-83, 835-36, 919-20, 921, 952, 954	67-68, 125-26, 169, 218, 263-64, 372-73, 415-16, 463, 515-16, 562-63, 595-96, 629-30, 670-71, 724-25, 781-82, 839-41, 882-83, 927-28, 929, 958
Revising and Editing (Proofreading)	53-54, 55, 108, 109, 110, 143, 145, 200-01, 232, 234-35, 287, 327, 328, 366, 399, 449, 451, 499, 538-39, 583, 626, 627, 709, 710, 712, 846-49, 878, 893, 895-96, 898-900, 901, 905, 912, 933, 939, 962, 964, 965	56-57, 60, 117, 119, 166, 170, 211, 261-62, 265, 319, 360, 364, 403-04, 407, 446-47, 489, 543-44, 594-95, 636, 668, 671, 720-21, 840, 870, 883	54, 138-39, 142, 182-83, 247-48, 292-93, 297, 337-38, 396-97, 435-36, 494, 539, 597, 655, 703, 749, 783, 836, 920, 952, 954, 963-64	68-69, 126, 169-70, 218, 264, 373, 416, 464, 516, 563, 596, 630-31, 671, 725, 782, 841, 883, 928, 929, 960
Presenting and Publishing	54, 108, 143, 201, 235, 327, 366, 399, 449, 499, 539, 583, 626, 709, 878, 882	57, 117, 167, 211, 262, 319, 360, 404, 447, 489, 595, 633, 668, 721, 840, 870, 874	54, 139, 183, 246, 293, 338, 397, 436, 494, 539, 597, 656, 703, 749, 783, 837, 920, 952, 955	69, 126, 170, 218, 264, 373, 416, 464, 516, 563, 596, 631, 782, 841, 883, 928, 958
Elements of Writing Style				
Audience	51, 105, 141, 198, 205, 232, 284, 324, 363, 397, 446, 496, 536, 580, 623, 706, 846, 879	54, 114, 118-19, 164, 208, 259, 316, 319, 358, 401, 444, 486, 592, 630, 666, 837, 871	51, 55, 86, 101, 136, 180, 245, 290, 335, 394, 433, 491, 536, 594, 653, 700, 746, 780, 834, 918, 953	66, 123, 167, 216, 261, 370, 413, 560, 593, 628, 668, 722, 779, 838, 880, 882, 926, 959
Conclusions	53, 449, 499, 625	210, 360, 403, 446, 488-89, 543, 594, 668, 720, 841	181, 292, 396, 538, 596, 655, 703, 748, 749, 920	126, 264, 416, 463, 516, 563, 596, 630, 671, 724, 725, 782, 840, 927
Introductions	52, 286, 326, 364, 398, 448, 498, 624, 708	210, 318, 360, 404, 445, 488, 543, 594, 667-68, 719-20, 839, 841	181, 292, 337, 396, 596, 655, 702, 748, 919-20	67, 125, 169, 171-72, 216, 217-18, 263, 415, 463, 515-16, 562, 596, 629-30, 670-71, 724, 725, 781-82, 839, 927
Journals	19, 87, 133, 254, 263, 314, 372, 376, 384, 420, 454, 504, 526, 533, 547, 556, 577, 608, 730, 878	30, 49, 81, 118, 216, 327, 351, 392, 603, 619, 690, 773, 870	107, 118, 166, 168, 221, 254, 441, 459, 500, 509, 563, 648, 662, 677, 740, 755, 765, 806, 818, 831, 914	34, 96, 156, 205, 451, 536, 611, 618, 653, 800
Manuscript Form	890-92	883	964	970
Organization	52, 325, 448, 498, 538, 582, 708, 846, 879	55, 115-16, 165-67, 175, 209-11, 277, 289, 345, 384, 403, 431, 445-46, 488-89, 519, 527, 543, 593, 613, 667-68, 798, 838-41, 871, 880-81	39, 53, 137, 181, 246, 292, 336-37, 434-35, 655, 748, 953, 961	124, 168, 217, 263, 415, 463, 594-95, 629, 669-70, 724
Outlining	106, 285, 888	260, 318, 613, 623, 629, 880-81	434-35, 748, 961	595-96
Parallelism			158, 272, 316, 788, 943	632-34
Peer Interaction	51-52, 58, 79, 89, 104, 124, 132, 195, 223, 253, 283, 303, 362, 378, 466, 484, 495, 514, 525, 535, 555, 632, 880, 882	56, 61, 114-15, 116, 167, 213, 259, 261, 262, 319, 360, 361, 403-04, 447, 489, 544, 595, 632-33, 668, 840, 872, 873-74	54, 138, 182, 247, 291, 337-38, 396-97, 435, 494, 539, 597, 655, 703, 749, 836, 920, 954	68, 126, 169, 218, 416, 464, 516, 596, 630-31, 671, 725, 782, 841, 960

Purpose	51, 105, 141, 198, 205, 232, 284, 324, 363, 397, 446, 496, 536, 580, 623, 706, 846, 879	54, 114, 164, 208, 259, 316, 358, 401, 444, 486, 592, 630, 666, 718, 837	51, 56, 86, 136, 180, 245, 290, 335, 394, 433, 491, 536, 594, 653, 700, 746, 780, 834, 918, 953	66, 123, 167, 216, 261, 370, 413, 560, 593, 628, 668, 722, 779, 838, 880, 926, 959
Self-Assessment/ Portfolios	108, 144, 201, 235, 287, 327, 366, 449, 499, 539, 583, 626, 709, 849, 880-81	57, 60, 117, 167, 170, 211, 213, 265, 319, 322, 360, 364, 404, 447, 450, 492, 544, 595, 633, 668-69, 671, 724, 840-41, 872, 873-74	54, 139, 142, 248, 251, 338, 340, 400, 436, 497, 539, 542, 656, 703, 706, 752, 783, 840, 921, 924, 954	69, 72, 126, 129, 169, 170, 264, 266, 416, 419, 464, 467, 516, 518, 596, 631, 634, 671, 728, 784, 841, 883, 886, 928, 929, 939, 960
Sentence Combining	288-90, 328-29, 500-01, 627-29, 898-900	320-22, 842-44, 892-94	398-400, 971-72	465-67, 597-99, 977-78
Sentence Variety	710-12	670-71, 892-94, 945-48	838-40	726-28, 977
Transitions	450-51	545-46	292, 751	517-18, 885
Word Choice	145, 205, 584-85	47, 168-70, 213, 265, 364, 407, 446, 493, 633, 671, 871, 876, 909	249, 272, 704, 775, 957	222, 963

Writing Modes ***(Numbers listed represent the types of activities presented.)***

Expressive and Personal Writing	19, 39, 51-52, 87, 136, 230, 252, 342, 377, 384, 454, 494, 553, 554, 578, 580-83, 596, 598, 658, 683, 776, 846	49, 52, 93-94, 103, 118, 144, 278, 345, 358-61, 432, 508, 520, 575, 590, 612-14, 639, 660, 716, 798, 889	51-54, 85, 167, 178, 208, 270, 312, 334, 398, 426, 432, 451, 490, 515, 652, 693, 720, 769, 779, 816, 833, 918-20	34, 96, 104, 123-26, 156, 204, 205, 213, 227, 231, 246, 411, 445, 450, 451, 459, 578, 583, 698, 800
Observation and Description	28, 103, 124, 141-44, 195, 198-201, 222, 230, 231, 252, 329, 362, 554, 578, 608, 808, 846	49, 164-67, 207, 243, 377, 430, 459, 591, 612	40, 51-54, 70, 84, 108, 151, 178, 313, 325, 334, 335-38, 412, 417, 457, 481, 561, 631, 693, 816, 834-37, 873	32, 45, 104, 166, 311, 399, 411, 445, 461-64, 479, 591, 810, 854, 897
Narrative and Imaginative Writing	28, 38, 51-54, 78, 105-108, 135, 175, 195, 223, 252, 265, 319, 418, 431, 444, 483, 513, 524, 536-39, 555, 580-83, 623-26, 846, 847	27, 45-46, 103, 140, 119, 242, 289, 336, 391, 459, 480, 540, 590, 612-13, 643, 690, 753, 798, 817, 889	49, 64, 85, 119, 178, 208, 219, 245-48, 259, 312, 353, 393, 417, 444, 481, 522, 532, 536-39, 631, 675, 775, 780-83, 805, 917	88, 89, 95, 104, 105, 123-26, 142, 154, 166, 213, 259, 261-64, 294, 331, 368, 370-73, 411, 459, 511, 661, 778, 803, 916, 917
Informative (Expository) Writing: Analysis	49, 67, 105, 123, 136, 230, 264, 282, 302, 312, 324-27, 363-66, 377, 397-400, 431, 494, 547, 578, 596, 847	29, 92, 170, 201, 265, 315, 364, 378-79, 401-04, 410, 430, 443, 474, 518, 593, 603, 628, 689, 724, 773	71, 120, 227, 259, 290-93, 393, 426, 451, 457, 491-94, 507, 515, 535, 561, 646, 653-56, 699, 700-03, 816, 830, 917	59, 88, 238, 294, 350, 399, 450, 459, 489, 511, 513-16, 628-31, 720, 770, 779-82, 836, 854, 864, 901
Informative (Expository) Writing: Classification	30, 49, 67, 78, 80, 89, 214, 282, 314, 348, 391, 444, 534, 568, 569, 578, 622, 659, 703, 704	19, 92, 94, 112-13, 122, 127, 129-30, 140, 241, 268, 315, 474, 519, 527, 545, 575, 592-95, 684, 689	29, 30, 65, 66, 84, 145, 160, 161, 193, 209, 393, 432, 444, 508, 582, 610, 675, 683, 775, 816, 899	88, 161, 199, 331, 350, 436, 552, 593-96, 622, 652, 685, 711, 750, 758, 822, 836, 916, 925
Informative (Expository) Writing: Synthesis	175, 222, 264, 282, 284-87, 340, 467, 621, 622, 623-26, 847	260, 316-19, 401-03, 446, 485, 488-89, 543, 575, 594, 630-33, 643, 667, 716, 720-21, 753, 845	49, 65, 108, 109, 119, 136-39, 178, 208, 260, 329, 412, 426, 451, 481, 508, 523, 610, 683, 720, 873	32, 155, 161, 183, 192, 204, 331, 350, 399, 500, 591, 604, 610, 616, 667, 744, 758, 802, 879, 926-29
Persuasion	29, 38, 104, 198-201, 232-35, 364-67, 418, 465, 469-99, 630, 847	45, 114-17, 128, 140, 208-11, 276, 278, 289, 444-47, 485-89, 541-44, 564, 655, 660, 666-69, 753, 773, 798, 817	108, 180-87, 227, 260, 312, 313, 325, 444, 457, 481, 490, 507, 508, 610, 646, 745, 746-49, 753, 764, 899, 912	32, 66-69, 121, 215-18, 222, 436, 530, 711, 722-25, 729, 744, 798, 838-41, 922
Writing About Literature	38, 103, 175, 185, 221, 232-35, 282, 303, 323, 348, 361, 363-66, 395, 397-99, 444, 447-49, 453, 568, 608, 621, 706-09, 777, 843	35, 92, 103, 128, 140, 162, 165, 175, 207, 256, 345, 378, 401-04, 442, 518, 526-27, 549, 590, 603, 612, 716-17, 752-53, 798, 817	159, 179, 284, 290-93, 353, 532, 561, 588, 594-97, 610, 646, 652, 653-56, 693, 699, 755, 769, 779, 792, 816, 914, 917	32, 45, 59, 88, 104, 121, 166, 213, 294, 331, 368, 411, 445, 459, 500, 513-16, 559, 604, 667, 720, 770, 864

Reports	223, 445, 446-49, 569, 622, 847, 885-90	103, 141, 182, 391, 404, 475, 507, 689, 753, 773, 798, 817, 835, 877-83	179, 244, 325, 335-38, 426, 433-36, 458, 646, 700-03, 776, 805, 873, 899, 913, 958-64	167-70, 593-96, 745, 778

Writing Formats and Structures

Advertisement	29, 104, 135	613, 655	70, 209, 393, 522, 873	166, 259
Advice	776, 825, 848	474	109, 136-39, 227, 334, 393, 412, 481, 507, 522, 610	155, 192, 331, 500, 610, 802
Alternative Endings	28, 361, 483, 596, 808, 844	27, 45, 103, 128, 400, 442, 459, 474, 655, 773, 835	444, 588, 631, 675, 741	104, 697, 758
Applications/Forms	502, 702, 853	637		468
Argumentation	159, 223, 465, 602, 751, 825	112, 208-11, 289, 441-47, 541-44, 688	40, 227, 312, 325, 444, 457, 481, 507, 741, 746-49, 745, 746-49, 764, 899, 912	32, 66-69, 121, 215-18, 222, 390, 436, 500, 530, 661, 711, 722-25, 729, 798, 838-41, 922
Autobiographical Incident/Personal Narrative	51-54, 230, 465, 471, 494, 504, 536-39, 846	54, 186, 207, 242, 290, 366, 392, 432, 435, 442, 460, 485, 520	119, 334, 343, 393, 426, 459, 490, 500, 515, 582, 765, 769, 806, 818, 830	34, 96, 123-26, 192, 227, 231, 445, 451, 578, 583, 611, 653, 698, 874
Biography/Biographical Sketch	141-43, 446-49	316-18	151, 417, 805	167-70
Brochure/Pamphlet	198-201, 253, 313, 341		631	
Business Letter	891-92	208-11, 630-33	610, 965-66	838-41, 971-72
Cause/Effect	363-66, 847	837-40	561, 653-56	500, 514-15, 668-71, 770, 864, 873
Character Sketch	78, 103, 195, 222, 230, 377, 554, 705	164-67, 243, 430	40, 151, 481, 610	399
Comparison/Contrast	19, 78, 88, 103, 282, 323, 340, 348, 361, 391, 395, 444, 513, 534, 568, 621, 659, 703, 706-09, 776, 844	19, 52, 112, 130, 356, 384, 474, 480, 540, 545-46, 592-95, 618, 664	66, 86-89, 119, 151, 167, 260, 290-93, 313, 329, 412, 457, 522, 532, 561, 582, 588, 593, 652, 675, 683, 775, 792	32, 45, 65, 142, 213, 246, 294, 311, 350, 445, 559, 593-96, 652, 685, 711, 750, 758, 836, 879, 925
Criticism	569, 824		914	368, 916, 926-29
Definition	19, 377, 526	19, 639	394-97, 830	194, 413-16
Dialogue	38, 123, 131, 159, 175, 340, 431, 494, 750	27, 92, 127, 182, 199, 207, 231, 242, 257, 260-62, 315, 336, 442, 628, 835, 889	41, 65, 178, 219, 259, 393, 457, 481, 675	213, 259, 489, 511, 661, 864, 897
Diary Entry	391, 568, 751	45, 315, 391	49, 178, 780-83, 873	445
Directions/Instructions	395	46, 379	481, 508, 720, 830	260
Drama (Stage, TV, Radio)	39, 223, 313	258, 259-62	244	105, 880-83
Editorial	222, 418, 496-99	289, 688		500, 661, 744
Epic Simile	195			59
Epitaph			417, 490	59, 204
Essay	38, 67, 135, 282, 444, 578	485, 541-44, 656	51-54, 70, 208, 259, 290-93, 312, 393, 481, 507, 536-39, 561, 653-56, 693, 764, 779, 816, 918-20	560-63, 674
Eulogy	195, 302	79		45
Evaluation	38, 569, 596, 847	603	259, 426, 594-97, 660, 700-03, 707	66-69, 926-29, 933, 961

Eyewitness Account	418		75, 84, 178	
Interview	444, 495, 704	507, 656, 689	109, 329, 515, 522, 523, 805	32, 142
Journal/Learning Log	19, 133, 136, 252, 254, 314, 342, 372, 420, 454, 471, 504, 515, 547, 556, 570, 878	30, 49, 81, 118, 216, 327, 351, 392, 603, 619, 690, 773	23, 30, 107, 118, 168, 254, 261, 382, 441, 500, 524, 648, 677, 755, 777, 806, 818, 831, 914, 952	34, 96, 156, 536, 653, 800, 958
Literary Analysis	103, 123, 195, 282, 302, 312, 362, 397-99, 470, 535, 578, 596, 621, 659, 703, 705, 706-09, 777	92, 112, 162, 199, 207, 378, 526, 540, 603, 717, 752, 817	290-93, 393, 532, 561, 582, 588, 593, 594-97, 615, 631, 646, 652, 653-56, 693, 699, 732, 741, 764, 755, 775, 792, 805	294, 489, 513-16, 572, 577, 720, 770
Magazine Article		666-69	700-03, 912	
Memo	131, 524		594-97	
Memoir		54-57		
Monologue	303, 312, 568, 579, 684	207, 276	763, 764	294
Newspaper Article	444, 623-26, 750, 846-47	314, 518, 590, 798, 837-40	49, 64, 335-38, 353, 380, 631, 646, 720, 727, 912	95, 142, 154, 368, 511, 552, 661, 668-71
Obituary		430		368, 810
Opinion	49, 123, 213, 222, 252, 282, 340, 377, 384, 483, 513, 524, 554, 596, 843	564, 575, 590, 660, 716, 798	49, 227, 243, 426, 441, 481, 515, 532, 535, 572, 588, 699, 727, 873, 899, 912	411, 445, 578, 583, 647
Oral History				261-64
Parody				610, 667
Personal Letter	28, 135, 252, 264, 302, 340, 444, 808, 843, 848	92, 128, 182, 276, 459, 618, 643, 683, 817	40, 49, 70, 108, 167, 178, 227, 270, 284, 312, 316, 329, 353, 393, 412, 432, 444, 593, 775, 769	104, 192, 204, 213, 227, 231, 479, 591, 897
Poem	39, 135, 175, 185, 395, 418, 513, 580-83, 602	52, 93, 358-61	178, 227, 276, 284, 457, 582, 720, 769, 775, 779, 792, 830, 833, 834-37	89, 104, 246, 459, 559
Predictions	49, 88, 222, 282, 312, 348, 349, 431, 578	103, 232, 242, 257, 474, 575, 612, 655, 678, 718-21	312, 481, 507, 532, 615, 648, 662, 675, 775	411, 744
Problems/Solutions	131, 175, 223, 312, 470, 824	94, 436, 630-33	593, 491-94, 873	
Process	123, 324-27		952	
Profile	28, 377, 431, 578		481	779-82
Proposal	284-87, 847	630-33	646	
Recommendation	232-35, 377, 494, 847		108	879
Research Report	419, 704, 885-90	475, 507, 689, 753, 773, 798, 817, 835	244, 260, 433-36, 458, 573, 700-03, 958-64, 960-63	60, 167-70, 247, 593-96, 712, 898
Resumé			543, 610	785
Retelling	175, 185, 323, 465	27, 45, 79, 128, 199, 207, 378, 400, 430, 655, 678	522, 582, 764	88, 104, 166, 246, 370-73, 459, 696, 697, 758
Satire				479
Self Evaluation	108, 144, 201, 235, 287, 327, 366, 449, 499, 539, 583, 626, 709, 849	57, 60, 117, 119, 167, 170, 211, 213, 265, 319, 322, 364, 404, 407, 450, 489, 671, 724, 872	54, 120, 139, 183, 240, 293, 338, 397, 436, 494, 539, 597, 656, 703, 749, 783, 836, 921, 954	69, 72, 126, 170, 172, 416, 419, 464, 467, 516, 596, 631, 634, 728, 784, 841, 883, 886, 929
Song Lyric	39, 196, 844	46, 443	33, 85, 167, 535, 720, 775, 833	227, 685

Speech	131, 140, 159, 432, 808	336, 344, 485, 629, 753, 835	50, 151, 180-83, 276, 313, 816	121, 798
Story	67, 78, 105-08, 195, 304, 513, 578, 596	79, 232, 277, 289, 443	42, 208, 210, 245-48, 312, 334, 353, 451, 532, 631, 683, 917	105, 123-26, 142, 552, 577, 697, 759, 803, 880-83, 917
Summary	38, 252, 291, 569, 621, 703, 808	260, 401-02, 403, 446, 485, 488, 489, 543, 575, 594, 643, 667, 716, 720, 721, 753, 845	49, 59, 108, 134, 178, 228, 254, 270, 439, 481, 573, 615, 616, 646, 775, 960-61	45, 46, 59, 350, 459, 667, 758

Grammar, Usage, and Mechanics	Grade 9	Grade 10	American Literature	English and World Literature
Writing Complete Sentences				
Parts of Speech	893, 901-42	320-21, 888	928, 967	973
Subjects	401-02, 894, 906-07, 945-48	263-65, 406-07, 448, 490, 888, 892-94, 939-41, 942, 946-47	140, 398-99, 968, 972, 979, 980-81, 982, 1016-22, 1023	70, 128, 418, 973, 974, 977, 1018-24
Predicates	710, 894, 899	888, 893-94, 959	140, 398-99, 968, 972, 978-79, 980, 982, 1023	70, 128, 973, 974, 978, 985, 986-87, 994, 996, 1024
Objects	894, 909-10	449-50, 888, 901, 904-05	784, 968, 972, 979, 980-81, 982, 1023	128, 842, 974, 985
Compound parts	710, 899, 947-48	59-60, 945-49, 959, 962, 963-64		
Sentence Fragments	202-03, 895-96, 900	490-91, 889-90, 891-92, 894	184-85, 969	70-72, 975, 976-77
Run-on Sentences	203-04, 896-98, 900	491-92, 890-92, 894	184, 186, 970	70-72, 976
Nouns				
Classes of Nouns	901	895	973	979
Plurals	902-03	634-36, 895-98, 922-24	973-75, 976, 1042	979-81
Possessives	903-04	59-60, 897-98, 964-65	975-76, 1042	981-82, 1043
Pronouns				
Classes of Pronouns	905	899	977	983
Personal Pronouns	55-57, 905, 906-13	899-906	977, 978-81	983, 984-89
Interrogative Pronouns (who/whom)	905, 911-12	899, 904	977, 982	983, 988
Reflexive/Intensive Pronouns	905, 913-14	905-06	784-85, 977, 983	842-43, 983, 989-90
Indefinite Pronouns	400-02, 905, 914-15, 945-47	263-65, 899, 906-08, 939-41, 964-65	495-97, 977, 984, 1018-19, 1042	983, 990-91, 1020, 1043
Pronoun Problems		908-10	980-82	992-93
Modifiers				
Adjectives	145-46, 917, 918-19	168-70, 887, 911-13, 921-22, 944	294-96, 967, 988-91, 1029, 1041	973, 994
Adverbs	145-46, 917, 918-20	168-70, 887, 911-14, 922, 962, 963-64	140, 294-96, 967, 972, 988-91, 1005, 1024, 1040	973, 994-95
Prepositional Phrases as Modifiers	920-22	915-16	991-93	997-99

Comparisons	236-38, 922-27	597, 916-21, 25	294-96, 993-96	999-1003
Special Problems with Modifiers	927-31	634-36, 921-25	704-06, 998-99	1003-1005

Verbs

Action/Linking	932	913-14, 926	1003	1007
Transitive/Intransitive		926	1003	1007
Auxiliary	932	926-27	968, 1003	974, 1007
Principle Parts of Verbs	933-37	927-33	1004-07	1008-12
Tenses	540-42, 938-40	722-24, 933-36	1009-12	1012-15
Progressive Emphatic Forms			1009-10	1013
Tense Shifts	540-42, 939-40		1009-12	1014-15
Active/Passive Voice			1013-15	375, 672-73, 1015-17
Commonly Confused Verbs	850-52, 941-42	935-36	922-94, 1014	374-76, 1016-17

Subject and Verb Agreement

Agreement in Number	367, 943-44	937-38	1016	417-19, 1018-23
Phrases Between Subject and Verb	367-68, 944-45	405-07, 938-39	1017	417-18
Agreement with Indefinite Pronouns	401-2, 945-47	263-65, 939-41	495-97, 984-85, 1018-19	1020-21
Agreement with Compound Subjects	368-69, 947-48	406-07, 942	1020	418-19, 1002
Agreement with doesn't/don't	948	942-43	1021	1022-23

Sentence Structure

Simple Sentences	710-12, 950-52	944-45	140, 398-99, 838, 1023	726-28, 1024
Compound Sentences	710-12, 950-52, 966-71	58, 60, 892, 903-04, 945-46	140, 398, 838, 1023-24, 1037, 1040	726-28, 1024-25, 1027, 1039, 1041
Complex Sentences	710-12, 952-55	946-47	438, 1024-25	727-28, 1025-27
Clauses	628-29, 710-12, 953-54, 970-71	59-60, 761, 844, 946-47, 959, 962-64	437-38, 599, 838, 969, 1024-25, 1038, 1040	564-66, 597-99, 726, 975, 988-89, 1025-27

Capitalization

	956-60	890-92, 948-53	1029-34	1028-34

Punctuation

End Marks	109, 962-64, 965-66, 968-69	890-92, 954-57, 965	1033-35	71, 1035-37
Commas	109, 964-69	59-60, 954, 957-61	1035-39	265-66, 466, 564, 565, 599, 976, 977, 978, 1037-41, 1044, 1045
Semicolons	969, 970-71	59-60, 954, 962, 963-64	1040	726, 976, 978, 1041
Colons	969-70	59-60, 954, 962, 963-64	1040-41	1042
Hyphens	970-71	59-60, 954, 963-64	1041	1042
Apostrophes	971-72	59-60, 954, 964-65	1042	981-82, 1043-44
Quotation Marks	109, 972-75, 974-75	954-57, 965-67	1043-45	265-66, 1044-46
Underlining	974-75	954, 965, 967	1044	1046

Professional Reading

Teaching At-Risk Students

■ Bloom, Benjamin S. *Human character-characteristics and school learning.* New York: McGraw-Hill Book Company. 1976.

■ Brophy, J. *Synthesis of research on strategies for motivating students to learn.* Educational Leadership 45, 2: 40-49. 1987.

■ Brophy, J., & Good, T. *Teacher behavior and student achievement.* In Handbook of Research on Teaching, edited by Merlin Wittrock. New York: Macmillan. 1986.

■ Carnegie Foundation for the Advancement of Teaching. *The imperiled generation.* New York: Carnegie Foundation for the Advancement of Teaching. 1988.

■ Catterall, James S. *On the social costs of dropping out of school.* The High School Journal. 19-30. October/November, 1987.

■ Committee for Economic Development. *Children in need: Investment strategies for the educationally disadvantaged.* New York: Committee for Economic Development. 1987.

■ Corcoran, T.; Walker, L., & White, L. *Working in urban schools.* Washington, DC: Institute for Educational Leadership. 1988.

■ Dworkin, A. G. *Teacher burnout in the public schools: Structural causes and consequences for children.* Albany, NY: SUNY Press. 1986.

■ Ekstrom, R. B.; Goertz, M. E.; Pollack, & Rock, D. A. *Who drops out of high school and why. Findings from a National Study.* Teachers College Record 87, 3: 356-375. 1986.

■ Erickson, F. A. *Transformation and school success: The politics and culture of educational achievement.* Anthropology and Education Quarterly 18, 3: 335-356. 1987.

■ Firestone, W. A.; Rosenblum, S., & Webb, A. *Building commitment among students and teachers: An exploratory study of 10 urban high schools.* Philadelphia: Research for Better Schools. 1987.

■ Ford Foundation. *The forgotten half: Non-college youth in America.* New York: Ford Foundation. 1987.

■ Hess, G. Alfred, Jr., & Greer, James L. *Educational triage and dropout rates.* In Dropouts, Pushouts, and Other Casualties, William T. Denton (Ed.). Bloomington, IN: Phi Delta Kappa Center on Evaluation, Development, and Research. March, 1987.

■ Kennedy, M.; Jung, R., & Orland, M. *Poverty, achievement and the distribution of compensatory education services.* Washington, DC: U.S. Department of Education. 1986.

■ Lehr, J. B., & Harris, H. W. *At-risk low-achieving students in the classroom.* Washington, DC: National Education Association Professional Library. 1988.

■ Leinhardt, G., & Bickel, W. *Instruction's the thing wherein to catch the mind that falls behind.* Educational Psychologist 22: 177-207. 1987.

■ McMillan, Samuel H., & Behrman, Carolyn A. *Our troubled teens.* Pittsburgh: The Public Television Outreach Alliance. 1986.

■ Parnell, Dale. *The neglected majority.* Washington, DC: The Community College Press. 1985.

■ Purkey, William Watson, & Novak, John M. *Inviting school success: A self-concept approach to teaching and learning* (2nd ed.). Belmont, CA: Wadsworth Publishing Co. 1984.

■ Wehlage, G. *Effective programs for the marginal high school student.* Bloomington, IN: Phi Delta Kappa Educational Foundation. 1983.

Assessment Options

■ Costa, A. L. *Re-assessing assessment.* Educational Leadership. April, 1989.

■ Gardner, Howard. *Assessment in con-text: The alternative to standardized testing.* Paper prepared for the National Commission on Testing and Public Policy, Berkeley, CA. 1988.

■ Haney, Walter, & Madaus, George. *Searching for alternatives to standardized tests: whys, whats, and whithers. Phi Delta Kappan. May, 1989.*

■ Hoge, Robert D., & Coladarci, Theodore. *Teacher-based judgments of academic achievement: A review of the literature.* Review of Educational Research, AERA. Fall, 1989.

■ Liftig, R. A. *Feeling good about student writing: Validation in peer evaluation.* English Journal. February, 1990.

■ Valencia, Sheila. *Alternative assessment: Separating the wheat from the chaff.* The Reading Teacher. 1990.

■ Wasserman, Selma. *Reflections on measuring thinking, while listening to Mozart's Jupiter Symphony.* Phi Delta Kappan. January, 1990.

Cooperative/Collaborative Learning

■ Cohen, E. *Designing Groupwork.* New York: Teacher's College, Columbia University. 1987.

■ Graves, N., & Graves, T. *Creating a cooperative learning environment: An ecological approach.* In Learning to Cooperate, Cooperating to Learn, R. Slavin, et al (Eds.). New York: Plenum Publishing Corp. 1985.

■ Hertz-Lazarowitz; Bejarano, Y.; Raviv, A., & Sharan, Y. *Cooperative learning in the classroom: Research in desegrated schools.* Hillsdale, NJ: Erlbaum. 1984.

■ Johnson, D. *Student teacher interaction: The neglected variable in education.* Educational Researcher, 10 (1), 5-24.

■ Johnson, D. W., & Johnson, R. T. *Learning together and alone* (2nd ed.). Englewood Cliffs, NJ: Prentice-Hall. 1986.

■ Johnson, R., & Johnson, D. W. *Warm-ups, grouping strategies, and group activities.* New Brighton, MN: Interaction Book Company, 1985.

■ Kagan, S.; Sharan, S., & Kussell, P. R. *Cooperative learning resources for teachers.* Riverside, CA: University of California Department of Psychology. 1985.

■ Slavin, R. E. *Cooperative learning.* New York: Longman. 1983a.

■ Slavin, R. E. *When does cooperative learning increase student achievement?* Psychological Bulletin 94: 429-445. 1983b.

■ Slavin, R. E. *Team assisted individualization: Cooperative learning and individualized instruction in the mainstreamed classroom.* Remedial and Special Education 5, 6: 33-42. 1984.

■ Slavin, R. E. *Using student team learning* (3rd ed.) Baltimore, MD: Center for Research on Elementary and Middle Schools, Johns Hopkins University. 1986.

■ Slavin, R.; Sharan, S.; Lazarowitz, R.; Webb, C., & Schmuck, R. (Eds.). *Learning to cooperate, cooperating to learn.* New York: Plenum Publishing Corp.

■ Stevens, R. J.; Madden, N. A.; Slavin, R. E., & Farnish, A. M. *Cooperative integrated reading and composition: Two field experiments.* Reading Research Quarterly, 22 (4), 433-454. 1987.

Integrated Studies

■ Atkins, G. Douglas, & Johnson, Michael. *Writing and reading differently: Deconstruction and the teaching of composition and reading.* Lawrence: University of Kansas Press. 1985.

■ Atwell, Nancie. *In the middle: Writing, reading, and learning with adolescents.* Portsmouth, NH: Heinemann. 1987.

■ Barnes, Douglas; Britton, James, & Rosen, Harold. *Language, the learner, and the school.* New York: Penguin. 1969.

■ Goodman, K. S.; Goodman, Y. M., & Hood, W. J. *The whole language evaluation book.* Portsmouth, NH: Heinemann. 1988.

■ Horner, Winifred B. (Ed.). *Composition and literature: Bridging the gap.* Chicago: University of Chicago Press. 1983.

■ Jensen, Julie, (Ed.). *Composing and comprehending.* Urbana, IL: National Council of Teachers of English. 1984.

■ Johnson, Terry, & Louis, Daphne. *Literacy through literature.* Portsmouth, NH: Heinemann. 1988.

■ Matthews, Dorothy. *Writing assignments based on literary works.* Urbana, IL: National Council of Teachers of English. 1985.

■ McCormick, Kathleen; Waller, Gary, & Flower, Linda. *Reading texts: Reading, responding, writing.* Lexington, MA: D. C. Heath. 1987.

■ Moffett, James, & Wagner, Betty Jane. *Student-centered language arts and reading, K-13* (3rd ed.). Boston: Houghton Mifflin, n.d.

■ Newman, J. M. *Whole language: Theory in use.* Portsmouth, NH: Heinemann Educational Books. 1985.

■ Peterson, Bruce, (Ed.). *Convergences: Transactions in reading and writing.* Urbana, IL: National Council of Teachers of English. 1986.

■ Purves, Alan. *Reading and literature.* Urbana, IL: National Council of Teachers of English. 1981.

■ Purves, Alan, & Rippere, Victoria. *Elements of writing about a literary work: A study of response to literature.* Urbana, IL: National Council of Teachers of English. 1968.

Multimodal Learning

■ Dunn, R. *Research on instructional environments: Implications for student achievement and attitudes.* Professional School Psychology 11, 2: 43-52. 1987.

■ Dunn, R. Commentary: *Teaching students through their perceptual strengths or preferences.* Journal of Reading 31, 4: 304-309. 1988.

■ Dunn, R.; DellaValle, J.; Dunn, K.; Geisert, G.; Sinatra, R., & Zenjausern, R. *The effects of matching and mismatching students' mobility preferences on recognition and memory tasks.* Journal of Educational Research 79, 5: 267-272. 1986.

■ Dunn, R.; Dunn, K., & Price, G. E. *Learning style inventory.* Price Systems, Box 1818, Lawrence, KS 66044-0067. 1975, 1979, 1981, 1985.

■ Dunn, R., & Griggs, S. A. *Learning style: Quiet revolution in American secondary schools.* Reston, VA: National Association of Secondary School Principals. 1988.

■ Dunn, R.; Krimsky, J.; Murray, J., & Quinn, P. *Light up their lives: A review of research on the effects of lighting on children's achievement.* The Reading Teacher 38, 9: 863-869 (The International Reading Association, Newark, DE). 1985.

■ Griggs, S. A., & Dunn, R. *High school dropouts: Do they learn differently from those who remain in school?* The Principal 35, 1: 1-8 (Board of Jewish Education of Greater New York). September/October, 1988.

■ Kirby, Patricia. *Cognitive style, learning style and transfer skill acquisition.* Columbus, OH: The National Center for Research in Vocational Education, Ohio State University. 1979.

■ Kolb, David A. *Experiential learning: Experience as the source of learning and development.* Englewood Cliffs, NJ: PrenticeHall. 1983.

■ Lawrence, Gordon. *People types and tiger stripes: A practical guide to learning styles* (2nd ed.). Gainesville, FL: Center for Applications of Psychological Types, Inc. 1982.

■ *Learning Styles Network Newsletter.* New York: National Association of Secondary School Principals and St. John's University. Winter 1980-Autumn 1988.

■ Macmurray, John. *Reason and emotion.* London: Faber and Faber Ltd. 1962.

■ Maslow, Abraham H. *Toward a psychology of being* (2nd ed.) New York: Van Nostrand Reinhold Company. 1968.

■ May, Rollo. *The courage to create.* New York: Norton and Company. 1975.

■ McCarthy, Bernice, & Leflar, Susan (Ed.). *4MAT in action.* Barrington, IL: Excel, Inc. 1983.

■ McKim, R. *Experiences in visual thinking.* Monterey, CA: Brooks/Cole Publishing. 1972.

■ Merril, David W., & Reid, Roger H. *Personal styles and effective performance.* Radnor, PA: Chilton Book Company. 1981.

■ Moustakas, Clark. *Creativity and conformity.* New York: D. Van Nostrand Company. 1967.

■ Myers, Isabel. *Gifts differing.* Gainesville, FL: Center for Applications of Psychological Types. 1981.

■ NASSP National Task Force. *National task force defines learning style operationally and conceptually.* Learning Styles Network Newsletter 4, 2: 1 (National Association of Secondary School Principals and St. John's University). Summer, 1983.

■ Nebes, R. D. *Direct examination of cognitive function in the right and left hemispheres.* In Asymmetrical Function of the Brain, M. Kinsbourne (Ed.). Cambridge, MA: Cambridge University Press. 1978.

■ Piaget, Jean, & Inhelder, B. *The language and thought of a child.* New York: Meridian. 1955.

■ Ramiriz, M., & Castaneda, A. *Cultural democracy, bicognitive development, and education.* New York: Academic Press. 1974.

■ Rico, Gabriele Lusser. *Writing the natural way: Using right-brain techniques to release your expressive powers.* Los Angeles, CA: J. P. Tarcher, Inc. 1983.

■ Samples, Bob. *The metaphoric mind: A celebration of creative consciousness.* Reading, MA: Addison-Wesley Publishing. 1976.

■ Samples, Bob. *Openmind, wholemind: Parenting and teaching tomorrow's children, today.* Rolling Hills Estates, CA: Jaimar Press. 1987.

■ Simon, Anita, & Byram, Claudia. *You've got to reach 'em to teach 'em.* Dallas, TX: T. A. Press. 1977.

■ Springer, Sally, & Deutsch, George. *Left brain, Right brain.* San Francisco, CA: W. H. Freeman and Company. 1980.

■ Suzuki, Shinichi. *Nurtured by love: A new approach to education.* New York: Exposition Press. 1969.

■ Torrance, E. Paul. *The Search for Satori and creativity.* Buffalo, NY: Creative Education Foundation, Inc. 1979.

■ Torrance, E. Paul & Sato, Saburo. *Differences in Japanese and United States styles of thinking.* Creative Child and Adult Quarterly 4. 1979.

■ Whitaker, M. A. & Ojemann, G. A. *Lateralization of higher cortical functions: A critique.* Annals of the New York Academy of Sciences, pp. 299 and 459-473. 1977.

■ Witelson, Sandra, F. *The feminine situation.* E. Sullerot (Ed.). New York: Doubleday. 1979.

Teaching the Limited English Proficient Student

■ Arias, M. B. *The context of education for Hispanics: An overview.* American Journal of Education 95, 1. 1986.

■ Bermúdez, A. B. *Analyzing the impact of home learning on problem-solving styles.* Journal of Educational Equity and Leadership, 6 (3), 248-250. 1986.

■ Bermúdez, A. B. *Developing writing skills in LEP learners.* A paper presented to the Greater Houston Area Writing Project, Houston, TX. June, 1989.

■ Bermúdez, A. B. & Padron, Y. N. *Teachers' perception of errors in second language learning and acquisition.* In L. Malavé Theory, research and applications: Selected Papers (pp. 113-124). Fall River, MA: National Dissemination Center. 1988.

■ Bermúdez, A. B. & Prater, D. L. *Using brainstorming and clustering to develop elaboration skills.* TESOL Quarterly, 24 (3). 1990.

■ Casas, J., & Furlong, M. *In search of an understanding and a responsible resolution to the Mexican-American educational dropout problem.* California Public Schools Forum 1: 45-63. 1986.

■ Chamot, A. U. & O'Malley, J. M. *The cognitive academic language learning approach: A bridge to the mainstream.* TESOL Quarterly, 21 (2), 227-249. 1987.

■ Ford Foundation. *Hispanics: challenges and opportunities.* New York: Ford Foundation. 1984.

■ Freeman, Y. S. *Do Spanish methods and materials reflect current understanding of the reading process?* Reading Teacher, 7, 654-662. 1988.

■ Kaplan, R. B. *Cultural thought patterns in intercultural education.* In K. Croft (Ed.), Readings in English as a second language: For teachers and teacher trainees (pp. 399-418). Cambridge, MA: Winthrop. 1980.

■ National Commission on Secondary Schooling for Hispanics. *Make something happen: Hispanics and urban high school reform*, Vol. 1. Washington, DC: Hispanic Policy Development Project. 1984.

■ Orum, L. *The education of Hispanics, selected statistics.* Washington, DC: Council of La Raza. 1985.

■ Padron, Y. N., & Bermúdez, A. B. *Promoting effective writing strategies for ESL students.* Southwest Journal of Educational Research Into Practice, 2, 19-26. 1988.

■ Parker, D. *How to support LEP students' English language development and academic success in spite of a lack of primary language resources.* Sacramento: California State Department of Education. 1987.

■ Raimes, A. *Composition: Controlled by the teacher, free for the student.* In K. Croft (Ed.), Readings on English as a second language: For teachers and teacher trainees (pp. 386-398), Cambridge, MA: Winthrop. 1980.

Teaching Literature

■ Andrasick, Kathleen D. *Opening texts: Using writing to teach literature.* Portsmouth, NH: Heinemann. 1990.

■ Applebee, A. N., & Purves, A. C. *Literature and the English language arts.* In P. Jackson (Ed.), Handbook of Curriculum Research. NY: Macmillan. In press.

■ Atkins, G. Douglas, & Morrow, Laura (Eds.). *Contemporary literary theory.* Amherst, MA: University of Massachusetts Press. 1989.

■ Bleich, David. *Subjective criticism.* Baltimore: Johns Hopkins University Press. 1978.

■ Bloom, B. S. *The thought process of students in discussion.* In S. J. French (Ed.), Accent on teaching (p. 83). New York, NY: Harper. 1984.

■ Britton, J. *Language and learning.* London: Penguin. 1970.

■ Britton, J. *Writing and the story world.* In B. Kroll & G. Wells (Eds.), Explorations in the Development of Writing. New York: Wiley. 1983.

■ Bruner, J. S. *Actual minds, possible worlds.* Cambridge, MA: Harvard University Press. 1986.

■ Cazden, Courtney. *Classroom discourse.* Portsmouth, NH: Heinemann. 1988.

■ Cooper, Charles. *Researching response to literature and the teaching of literature.* Norwood, NJ: Ablex. 1985.

■ Eagleton, Terry. *Literary theory.* Minneapolis: University of Minnesota. 1983.

■ Freund, Elizabeth. *The return of the reader: Reader-response criticism.* London: Methuen. 1987.

■ Graff, Gerald. *Professing literature.* Chicago: University of Chicago Press. 1987.

■ Langer, J. A. *Children reading and writing: Structures and strategies.* Norwood, NJ: Ablex. 1986.

■ Langer, J. A. *How readers construct meaning: An analysis of reader performance on standardized test items.* In R. Freedle (Ed.), Cognitive and Linguistic Analyses of Standardized Test Performance. Norwood, NJ: Ablex. 1987.

■ Langer, J. A. *Levels of questioning: An alternative view.* Reading Research Quarterly 20, 586-602. 1985.

■ Langer, J. A. *The process of understanding literature.* Albany, NY: Center for the Learning and Teaching of Literature, SUNY, Albany. 1989.

■ Langer, J. A. *The process of understanding: Reading for literary and informative purposes*, Research in the Teaching of English, 24, 220-256. 1990.

■ Langer, J. A. *Reading, thinking, writing...and teaching.* Language Arts, 59, 336-341. 1982.

■ Langer, J. A. *Speaking of knowing: Conceptions of knowing in the academic disciplines.* In A. Herrington & C. Moran (Eds.), Research and Scholarship in Writing Across the Disciplines. NY: Modern Language Association. In press.

■ Langer, J. A., & Allington, R. *Curriculum research in writing and reading.* In P. Jackson (Ed.), Handbook of Curriculum Research. NY: Macmillan. In press.

■ Langer, J. A., & Applebee, A. N. *Reading and writing instruction: Toward a theory of teaching and learning.* In E. Rothkopf (Ed.), Review of Research in Education. Washington, DC: American Educational Research Association. 1986.

■ Mallioux, Steven. *Interpretive conventions: The reader in the study of American fiction.* Ithaca: Cornell University Press. 1982.

■ Marshall, James. *The effects of writing on students' understanding of literary texts.* Research in the Teaching of English, 21: 30-63. 1987.

■ Miller, Bruce. *Teaching the art of literature.* Urbana, IL: National Council of Teachers of English. 1980.

■ Miller, James. *Eccentric propositions: Essays on literature and the curriculum.* London: Routledge and Kegan Paul. 1984.

■ Minot, Stephen. *Reading fiction.* Englewood Cliffs, NJ: Prentice. 1985.

■ Muldoon, P. A. *Challenging students to think: Shaping questions, building community*. In Education Journal. April, 1990.

■ Nelms, Ben F. (Ed.). *Literature in the classroom: readers, texts, and contexts*. Urbana: NCTE. 1988.

■ Odell, Lee & Cooper, Charles. Describing responses to works of fiction. *Research in the Teaching of English*, 10: 203-225. 1976.

■ Probst, Robert. *Response and analysis*. Portsmouth, NH: Heinemann. 1988.

■ Probst, Robert E. *Response and analysis: Teaching literature in junior and senior high school*. Portsmouth, NH: Boynton-Cook. 1988.

■ Purcell-Gates, V. *On the outside looking in: A study of remedial readers' meaning-making while reading literature*. Journal of Reading Behavior. In press.

■ Purves, Alan, & Beach, Richard. *Literature and the reader: Research on response to literature, reading interests, and teaching of literature*. Urbana, IL: National Council of Teachers of English. 1972.

■ Ravitch, D. & Finn, C. *What do our 17 year olds know? A report of the first national assessment of history and literature*. NY: Harper and Row. 1987.

■ Rockas, Leo. *Ways in: Analyzing and responding to literature*. Portsmouth, NH: Boynton-Cook. 1984.

■ Rosenblatt, L. *The reader, the text, and the poem*. Cambridge, MA: Harvard University Press. 1978.

■ Rosenblatt, Louise. *Literature as exploration* (3rd ed.). New York: Noble and Noble. 1968.

■ Rosenblatt, Louise. *The reader, the text, the poem*. Carbondale: Southern Illinois University Press, 1978.

■ Scholes, Robert. *Textual power*. New Haven: Yale University Press. 1985.

■ Schwartz, Sheila. *Teaching adolescent literature: A humanistic approach*. Rochelle Park, NJ: Hayden. 1979.

■ Smagorinsky, Peter, & Gevinson, Steven. *Fostering the reader's response*. Palo Alto: Dale Seymour. 1989.

■ Spear, Karen. *Sharing writing: Peer response groups in English classes*. Portsmouth, NH: Boynton-Cook. 1988.

■ Tompkins, Jane. *Reader-response criticism: From formalism to post-structuralism*. Baltimore: Johns Kopkins University Press. 1980.

■ Wells, Gordan. *The meaning makers*. Portsmouth, NH: Heinemann. 1986.

Multicultural Literature

■ Allen, Paula Gunn (Ed.). *Studies in American-Indian Literature*. New York: Modern Language Association. 1983.

■ Baker, Houston. *The American literatures: Essays in Chicago, Native American and Asian-American literature*. New York: Modern Language Association. 1982.

■ Baker, Houston, Jr. (Ed.). *Reading Black: Essays in the criticism of African, Caribbean, and Black American literature*. Ithaca: Cornell University Press. 1976.

■ Bennett, Christine. *Comprehensive multicultural education: Theory and practice*. Boston: Allyn and Bacon. 1986.

■ Bruce-Novoa, Juan. *Chicano authors: Inquiry by interview*. Austin: University of Texas. 1980.

■ Brumble, H. David. *An annotated bibliography of American-Indian and Eskimo autobiographies*. Lincoln: University of Nebraska Press. 1981.

■ Chapman, Abraham (Ed.). *Literature of the American Indians: Views and interpretations*. New York: New American Library. 1975.

■ Cheung, King-Kok, & Yogi, Stan (Eds.). *Asian-American literature: An annotated bibliography*. New York: MLA. 1988.

■ Curry, Ann. *Teaching about the other Americans: Minorities in United States history*. Saratoga: Century Twenty-One Publishing. 1981.

■ Dabydeen, David. *The Black presence in English literature*. Manchester: Manchester University Press. 1985.

■ Fisher, Dexter (Ed.). *The third woman: Minority women writers in the United States*. Boston: Houghton Mifflin. 1980.

■ Foster, David William (Ed.). *Sourcebook of Hispanic culture in the United States*. Chicago: American Library Association. 1982.

■ Gates, Louis, Jr. *Black literature and literary theory*. London: Methuen. 1984.

■ Gilbert, Sandra, & Guber, Susan (Eds.). *The Norton anthology of literature by women*. New York: Norton. 1985.

■ Hawkins, John N. *Teacher's resource handbook for Latin-American studies: An annotated bibliography of curriculum materials*. Los Angeles: UCLA Latin-American Center Publications. 1975.

■ Kim, Elaine. *Asian-American literature: An introduction to the writings and their social context*. Philadelphia: Temple University Press. 1982.

■ Martinez, Julio, & Lemoli, Erunico. *Chicago literature: A reference guide*. Westport, CT: Greenwood Press. 1985.

■ Perry, Margaret. *Silence to the drum: A survey of the literature of the Harlem renaissance*. Westport, CT: Greenwood. 1976.

■ Sims, Rudine. Shadow and substance: *Afro-American experience in contemporary children's fiction*. Urbana, IL: National Council of Teachers of English. 1982.

■ Stanford, Barbara, & Amin, Karima. *Black literature for high school students.* Urbana, IL: National Council of Teachers of English. 1978.

■ Stensland, Anna. *Literature by and about the American Indian.* Urbana, IL: National Council of Teachers of English. 1979.

■ Wiget, Gordan. *The meaning makers.* Portsmouth, NH: Heinemann. 1986.

■ Wu, William. *The yellow peril: Chinese-Americans in American fiction.* 1850-1940. Hamden, CT: Shoe String Press. 1982.

■ Wurzel, Jaime. *Toward multi-culturalism: Readings in multicultural education.* Yarmouth, ME: Intercultural Press. 1989.

The Teaching of Writing

■ Applebee, A. N. *A study of writing in the secondary school.* Research Report No. 21. Urbana, IL: National Council of Teachers of English. 1981.

■ Applebee, A. N.; Langer, J., & Mullis, I. *The writing report card: Writing achievement in American schools.* National Assessment of Educational Progress. Princeton, NJ: Educational Testing Service. 1986.

■ Atwell, Nancie. *In the middle: Writing, reading, and learning with adolescents.* Portsmouth, NH: Boynton-Cook. 1987.

■ Calkins, L. M. *The art of teaching writing.* Portsmouth, NH: Heinemann. 1986.

■ Elbow, Peter. *Writing with power.* New York: Oxford University Press. 1981.

■ Elbow, Peter, & Belanoff, Pat. *Sharing and responding.* New York: Random House. 1989.

■ Freedman, S. W. *Response to student writing.* Research Report No. 23. Urbana, IL: National Council of Teachers of English. 1987.

■ Freedman, S. W., & McLeod, A. *National survey of successful teachers of writing and their students.* Technical Report No. 14. Berkeley, CA: Center for the Study of Writing. 1987.

■ Fulwiler, Toby. *The journal book.* Portsmouth, NH: Boynton-Cook. 1987.

■ Graves, D. *Writing: Teachers and children at work.* Portsmouth, NH: Heinemann. 1983.

■ Hillocks, G. *Research on written composition.* Urbana, IL: ERIC Clearinghouse on Reading and Communication Skills and National Conference on Research in English. 1986.

■ Kahn, Elizabeth; Walters, Carolyn, & Johannesen. *Writing about literature.* Urbana, IL: National Council of Teachers of English. 1984.

■ McManus, Ginger, & Kirby, Dan. *Using peer group instruction to teach writing.* English Journal. March, 1988.

■ Parsons, Les. *Response journals.* Portsmouth, NJ: Heinemann. 1990.

■ Perl, Sandra, & Wilson, Nancy. *Through teachers' eyes: Portraits of writing teachers at work.* Portsmouth, NH: Boynton-Cook. 1986.

■ Vavrus, Linda. *Put portfolios to the test.* Instructor, 48-53. August, 1990.

■ Wolf, Dennie P. *Opening up assessment.* Educational Leadership, 24-29. December, 1987/January, 1988.

■ Wolf, Dennie P. *Portfolio assessment: Sampling student work.* Educational Leadership, 35-39. April, 1989.